also from visible ink press

VideoHound's® Golden Movie Retriever®

VideoHound's Independent Film Guide

VideoHound's Video Premieres:
The Only Guide to Video Originals and Limited Releases

VideoHound's Vampires on Video

VideoHound's Sci-Fi Experience:
Your Quantum Guide to the Video Universe

VideoHound's Family Video Guide, 2nd Edition

VideoHound's Complete Guide to Cult Flicks and Trash Pics

The VideoHound and All-Movie Guide StarGazer

Toxic Fame: Celebrities Speak on Stardom

● ● ● ● ●

MusicHound™ Rock: The Essential Album Guide

MusicHound Country: The Essential Album Guide

MusicHound R&B: The Essential Album Guide

MusicHound Blues: The Essential Album Guide

MusicHound Jazz: The Essential Album Guide

VideoHound's
soundtracks

Music from the movies, broadway and television

Edited by DIDIER C. DEUTSCH

Foreword by LUKAS KENDALL

DETROIT • NEW YORK • TORONTO • LONDON

VideoHound's **soundtracks**
Music from the Movies, Broadway and Television

Copyright© 1998 Visible Ink Press®
Visible Ink Press, VideoHound, and the VideoHound logo are trademarks of Gale Research
A Cunning Canine Production™

Published by Visible Ink Press®
a division of Gale Research
835 Penobscot Building
Detroit, MI 48226-4094

Most Visible Ink Press books are available at special quantity discounts when purchased in bulk by corporations, organizations, or groups. Customized printing, special imprints, messages, and excerpts can be produced to meet your needs. For more information, contact Special Markets Manager, Gale Research, 835 Penobscot Building, Detroit, MI 48826. Or call 1-800-776-6265.

Library of Congress Cataloging-in-Publication Data

Deutsch, Didier, 1937-
    VideoHound's soundtracks: music from the movies, broadway, and television / by Didier Deutsch.
       p. Cm. — (VideoHound)
    Includes indexes.
    ISBN 1-57859-025-6 (alk. Paper)
    1. Sound recordings—Reviews. 2. Musicals—Discography. 3. Musical Films—Discography. 4. Motion picture music—Discography. 5. Television music—Discography. I. Title. II. Series: VideoHound (Series)
ML156.9.D48 1997
781.5'4—dc21

MN

97-36767
CIP

ISBN 1-57859-025-6
Printed in the United States of America
All Rights Reserved
10 9 8 7 6 5 4 3 2 1

● contents

"Ever since I was a kid, I always had in mind to come to this country," says Grammy Award-nominated record producer Didier C. Deutsch. "My initial goal was to become a movie director. Instead, I became a record producer and musicologist. Makes sense: music was always an integral part of my life."

Deutsch, who cites Paris-based American deejay Sim Copans as being a major influence on his musical development, was nominated for a Grammy in 1994 for his production of the 12-CD set, "Frank Sinatra: The Columbia Years (1943-1952) — The Complete Recordings," the most ambitious project ever initiated by Columbia Records until then.

While putting the finishing touches to that set, the producer also worked on a four-CD career retrospective of Johnny Mathis for the label, "The Music of Johnny Mathis: A Personal Collection," which was released at the same time.

"Altogether, in my years with Legacy, the Sony label that was created to mine the Columbia and the Epic catalogues, I have produced about 450 reissue albums and compilations in various fields of music, including pop, jazz, soundtracks, Broadway shows, big bands, you name it."

Born in Arcachon, France, in 1937, Deutsch lived the war years in hiding, barely escaping being arrested by the German authorities. After the war, while pursuing his studies, he began writing articles about American music for a number of French publications, and lectured at the United States Information Services in Bordeaux and at the American Cultural Center in Paris.

Shortly after his arrival in New York in 1962, he began a career in journalism, writing for a wide range of magazines and newspapers about the arts, with a special emphasis on the theatre, movies, and music. As a reviewer, he has been covering the Broadway musical scene for more than 30 years.

In 1973, after spending some time in public relations in the private sector, Deutsch became publicity director at CTI Records, the jazz label created by producer Creed Taylor, working with artists like George Benson, Bob James, Grover Washington, Jr., Freddie Hubbard, Paul Desmond, and Chet Baker, among many others.

In a career that has since entirely focused on the music side of the business, Deutsch held various publicity and managerial positions at Tappan Zee, RCA, WEA International, and Atlantic. While at that label, he produced the boxed set "MJQ 40," marking the Modern Jazz Quartet's 40 years in the music business.

In 1986, he began working as a reissue producer for Legacy Records. As part of his activities with that label, he supervised the reissue on compact disc of many of the titles initially released on CTI, as well as some of the soundtracks and Broadway cast albums recorded for Columbia.

Among his most notable achievements, in addition to the Frank Sinatra and Johnny Mathis boxed sets, he also produced a four-CD boxed set of Tony Bennett, marking the singer's 40 years in the industry, as well as numerous recordings by the many artists signed to both Columbia and Epic. On many of those, he also authored the liner notes that put the recordings into their proper historical perspective.

Currently, Deutsch is preparing the CD reissues of the Broadway cast albums of "A Chorus Line," "A Little Night Music" and "Threepenny Opera," as well as an expanded version of Jerry Goldsmith's score for *Star Trek — The Motion Picture*.

Film music today is where jazz was maybe 30-40 years ago, that is to say, as an art form only beginning to be recognized. It's pretty interesting, or at least that's what I tell myself to get through another issue of *Film Score Monthly*. Consider the following:

The music has made the movies. Films like *Lawrence of Arabia* and *The Magnificent Seven* would be successful no matter what, but their respective scores by Maurice Jarre and Elmer Bernstein have made them that much more memorable. It's hard to pin down exactly what the music is doing in a movie like Sam Peckinpah's masterpiece, *The Wild Bunch*, but trust me that it would be a much lesser experience without Jerry Fielding's score. Federico Fellini without music would still be great, but who can forget Nino Rota's unmistakable circus-like atmospheres?

There's been some darn fine music. Many of the classically influenced film composers, like Erich Wolfgang Korngold, Franz Waxman and Aaron Copland, wrote music for cinema that stands on equal footing with their concert music. Bernard Herrmann, the single most influential dramatic film composer of all time, developed a unique style of repeating orchestral cells and colors that predates minimalism by a good two decades. Jerry Goldsmith, in his amazing four decades as a first-rate film composer, has explored and juxtaposed a variety of genres to stunning dramatic effect. Many of John Williams' film themes have become veritable pop hits, and some of the most beautiful music I've ever heard was written for movies by Georges Delerue.

Film music is a legitimate form of post-modern art. Without taking the time to define post-modernism, film music is one of those things that has crept up in the present-day technological world. There have been countless thousands of hours of visual programming over the past 50 years for television, 70 years for sound film, and 100 years for film overall. A good percentage of that has had music — pre-recorded music, original music, whatever the case. The juxtaposition of music and image has ranged from banal to utilitarian to brilliant. We

are only beginning to catalog all of this film music — its origins, influences and impact.

Consider these cool facts: bone-crunching, atonal music of the style of Schoenberg, Berg and Webern has been around for three-quarters of a century, but it has been only through movies that the general public has embraced it, or even heard of it. They would run screaming from a concert of 12-tone music, but find it perfectly acceptable and even likeable in movies scored by composers like Leonard Rosenman, Alex North and Jerry Goldsmith — like *Planet of the Apes*. Also, listen to any urban thriller Lalo Schifrin score from the 1970s (they all rock, by the way) and it immediately engenders the reaction, "Oh, '70s music." And yet, you'd have to look long and hard to find this particular style of orchestra, pop, funk and drama in anything but *movies* from that era.

See, the thing I love about film music is that it is not a single "type" of music. It's this weird subset that affects movies in fascinating and profound ways, and often stands on its own as a unique listening experience. *The Third Man* was scored with a zither. Martin Scorsese "scored" *Mean Streets* with his record collection. Composers like John Barry, the irreplaceable Ennio Morricone, and the sadly missed Henry Mancini have fused symphonic literature with pop trends to form their own, highly personal respective styles. Their work was cutting-edge at the time and has become standards of pop culture ever since — or maybe you can't remember the James Bond theme, the sound of Clint Eastwood/Sergio Leone spaghetti westerns, and the Pink Panther theme?

And finally, you could scour the world over and never find a piece of orchestral literature that is as crazy, as post-modern, prescient and beautiful as a Carl Stalling score for a Warner Bros. cartoon of the 1930s, '40s or '50s.

Enjoy this book, folks.

Lukas Kendall

As anyone who's been in a record store lately will attest, soundtracks are "in." It depends, of course, what we call soundtracks, but that's a point we'll deal with in a short while. Bins overflow with new titles. Film music sections, that once seemed relegated to a darkened corner area next to classical, have expanded dramatically. More significantly, many labels, independents as well as majors, seem intent on cashing in on the trend, and actively release new albums of current scores as well as reconstructions and reissues of past glories.

Which brings us back to the definition of soundtrack albums. To some, it means music from a score that was specifically written for a motion picture. To others, it is a compilation of pop songs, some of which served as source material in a scene from the film, usually in abbreviated form, or which have been "inspired" by a film when the concept is stretched to its utmost limits, as is frequently the case nowadays.

Dispensing rapidly with the latter, purists will tell you that pop compilations are not soundtrack albums but pop compilations, and that labels—usually the majors which have ready access to the vast pop catalogue in their vaults—use this euphemism to peddle the same golden oldies they have recycled in a number of other ways in the past. There are, of course, notable exceptions to the concept. Sometimes the songs are new and specifically created for the film, which was the case, for instance, of the songs for the original *Batman*, written by Prince, or those for *Dick Tracy*, penned by Stephen Sondheim. And sometimes, the pop compilations are indeed an important part of the film (i.e. *Forrest Gump*, in which the many songs were used to give the time period a specific authenticity). But unless a film is a musical, a song compilation is *not* really a soundtrack album. Which brings us back to the other kind of soundtrack albums, the instrumental ones.

Again, as collectors and fans will point out, soundtracks existed long before song compilations—a phenomenon that

started in the 1960s—came into being. Soundtrack albums can be traced back to 1943 and composer Miklos Rozsa who was the first to record a musical suite from his score for the Alexander Korda production of *The Jungle Book*, with Sabu, who had starred in the film, as narrator. It marked the first time a major film score received an accompanying record release and its success paved the way to soundtrack albums as we know them today.

For those interested in a little history, while film music existed almost from the moment a locomotive entered (silently) into the station of La Ciotat, in France, in the first film made by the brothers Lumiere, most of the "scores" performed in the days of the silents consisted of classical themes used for stock situations. If there was a scene of action, Rossini's *William Tell* Overture was promptly dusted off. A tearjerker immediately invoked Tchaikovsky's *Pathetique* Symphony; and what marriage scene could have existed without Mendelssohn's triumphant nuptial march.

When movies began to talk, the studio heads brought to Hollywood the most respected composers from Europe to serve as advisors and orchestrators, since the longer classical themes needed to be pruned down for the screen time during which they were actually needed. The first to break with tradition was Max Steiner, then a young composer in charge of the music department at RKO Studios, who convinced David O. Selznick to let him write an original series of cues for a single reel of *Symphony of Six Million*. The effect on audiences was electrifying, something that didn't get lost on Selznick who agreed to let Steiner score an entire film, *Bird of Paradise*, in 1932. Soon, every movie studio had to have its own music department, with its own contingent of composers.

All along, however, the studio heads kept music in an artistic netherland of sorts. To them, it seemed like a necessary evil, something they realized the audiences expected, but something for which they themselves had little taste and certainly no respect. In their opinion, composers were hacks who could (and sometimes were asked to) replace an original theme with a classical piece if a producer demanded it, even if the piece didn't fit the format of the film itself.

Miklos Rozsa recounts how upset he was when scoring *Ben-Hur*, after he was asked to include "Adeste Fideles" for the Nativity scene, with total disregard for the fact that it was a medieval Latin hymn which had been composed several centuries later. Only when he threatened to leave the picture was the idea dropped.

The advent of long-playing in the 1950s didn't provoke an intense interest in film music, but a western did. When the first previews of Fred Zinneman's *High Noon* proved catastrophic, composer Dimitri Tiomkin felt that if the song he had written with Ned Washington, "Do Not Forsake Me, Oh, My Darling," sung in the film by Tex Ritter, were heard more frequently on the radio it might actually help publicize the film. Capitol Records, which had Ritter under contract, refused to let him cut a single for airplay. Tiomkin then approached Columbia Records, which had just signed Frankie Laine, and a deal was made. The song from *High Noon* became a million-seller and, as a result, the film became a huge box office hit. Suddenly, every major motion picture had to have a title song, whether or not it was really called for.

Throughout the 1950s, however, soundtrack albums remained scant and the works of some of the best composers in Hollywood went unrecorded, except for an occasional title that was immediately snatched by fans of film music. There were collectors at the time who already thought that film music should be considered the modern equivalent of classical music, but they were a minority and their silent plea for a particular soundtrack album often went unanswered. Classical fans, for their part, often felt that film music was nothing more than rubbish, and frequently dismissed it as such.

During these lean years, when a soundtrack album was released by the majors, usually it seemed as an afterthought. They seldom received the kind of promotional push and attention usually afforded their pop counterparts. Some of them remained in the catalogues (*Bridge on the River Kwai* and *The Alamo* at Columbia, or *Giant* at Capitol, for instance), but many were deleted almost as quickly as they had been released, leaving some lucky fans with obscure titles whose value steadily increased in the collectors' market, and others paying tantalizingly stiff prices for albums that could have been bought at one time for a few dollars.

Then came 1967 and *The Graduate*, which rang the death toll for film music. The immense success of the songs written for that film by Simon and Garfunkel, which translated itself into a million-selling album, convinced every producer in Hollywood that ancillary benefits could help their film, *any* film. All at once, every movie that came out of the Hollywood studios began to feature rock scores and pop songs, to such extent that legitimate composers found themselves out of work. Some, like Bernard Herrmann and Miklos Rozsa, went to Europe where their works, at least, were treated with greater respect. Others, like Elmer Bernstein, chose to remain until things got better by contributing inane little scores for insipid films in which the basic musical element did not intrude on the pop songs that now prevailed on the soundtracks.

This was also the era of mega-selling albums like *Saturday Night Fever*, *Grease*, *Thank God It's Friday*, and *Footloose*, all of them consisting of pop songs created for or heard in the films that spawned them.

The 1970s brought another change, a beneficial one this time. In 1972, record producer George Korngold, son of the film composer, teamed with conductor Charles Gerhardt, who had quietly championed film music for many years, and together they created a tribute album to the music of Erich-Wolfgang Korngold. *The Sea Hawk*, the first title in the now celebrated Classic Film Scores series, released by RCA Victor, became a huge instrumental success that spawned many additional volumes throughout the 1970s, documenting the works of Hollywood Golden Age composers like Rozsa, Steiner, Tiomkin, Herrmann, Franz Waxman, and Alfred Newman.

Then, in 1977 came *Star Wars*. The epic film by George Lucas would have sounded ridiculous with a pop score. What it needed was a huge, explosive symphonic score like the ones Korngold, Newman and Rozsa wrote so well. John Williams understood it perfectly well and the score he created for the film borrowed every musical trick from the books laid out by his predecessors. The success of the film led to that of the soundtrack album, an unusual two-LP set which sold millions of copies, taking everyone by surprise, including the executives at 20th Century-Fox Records who had not foreseen its tremendous appeal. Instrumental albums were back in grand style.

The trend subsisted until the CD revolution in 1986 which enabled many collectors to finally hear the instrumental scores in state-of-the-art digital sound, grander-than-life, the way they had always wanted to hear them. The digital era also saw the start or expansion of several independent labels (Varese-Sarabande, Intrada, Silva Screen, Rhino), all of them catering specifically to the collectors, and all of them digging back into the history of film music to reissue long-deleted soundtrack albums or release new recordings of classic scores.

Today, the situation has amplified with many other labels, including the majors, suddenly aware of the appeal of film music, joining the fray and, perhaps for the first time, treating it the way classical music is treated. It may only be a passing fancy, but when Sony Classical records an album of music by Bernard Herrmann conducted by Esa-Pekka Salonen, or when Angel Records and Philips release soundtrack albums by James Horner or Philippe Sarde, you know that something new is happening.

In another significant development, this renewal of interest in instrumental film music has also facilitated the arrival of a new generation of composers, nurtured on the precepts left by their predecessors, but ready to innovate and to create their own musical language—James Horner, Alan Silvestri, Danny Elfman, Randy Edelman, Rachel Portman, Marc Shaiman, Basil Poledouris, Joel McNeely, all of them superb exponents of an art some thought was dying or even dead.

To be sure, film music continues to attract a lot of less gifted people, but the composers who actually thrive on it and rewrite the books can easily be singled out, leaving the others behind.

Film music, past and present, has also brought together a motley group of young writers who enjoy it, recognize its virtues, and help publicize it. In preparing this volume, I was fortunate to work with some of these talented young people — Lukas Kendall, editor and publisher of *Film Score Monthly*, a publication dedicated to film music, who also introduced me to some of his regular contributors, Jeff Bond, Andy Dursin and Paul MacLean; and David Hirsch and Randall Larson, recommended to me by my friend, record producer Ford A. Thaxton.

All of them have their own specialty, all of them view music in a different, personal optic, and all of them have very strong likes and dislikes. But even when they express conflicting opinions, their intentions are solidly honest, and what ties them all is their abiding love of film music. They made this book much more interesting and lively and I am indebted to all of them for their impeccable contributions.

Finally, there is you, the buyers and readers, attracted by the topics raised in this book, and no doubt interested to some degree in what we all have to say about some of your favorite film soundtracks. You may not always share our conclusions and that's your unalienable right. But ultimately you are also part of our community, because if you bought this book in the first place, it's certainly because you are interested in film music as a whole. So welcome to our world, welcome to your world.

Didier C. Deutsch

Special thanks to: Gary Graff of *MusicHound* and Pete Howard of *Ice* magazine who were the first instigators of this volume; Julie d'Angelo, and her assistant, Jayne Blume, at Rhino Records; Andy McKaie, at MCA Records; Adam Block, at Legacy Records; Jenni Glenn, at Milan Records; Marilyn Egol, at RCA Victor; Susan Schiffer, at Sony Classical; Laurence Vittes, at Marco Polo Records; Christina Carrillo, at Silva America; Lukas Kendall, for his suggestions; and Ford A. Thaxton, for *his* suggestions.

● using VideoHound's soundtracks

Videohound's Soundtracks has got to be the most comprehensive source on soundtracks out there, and even better, it's easy to use. The book is divided into four sections covering motion picture soundtracks, Broadway and screen musicals, television soundtracks, and compilation soundtracks.

Though the first three sections are pretty self-explanatory, the last section is a little more tricky. The compilation section lists those CDs that encompass the works of a certain composer, or the works of a genre, or the works included in an actor's films. For instance, here you can find not only *The Best of John Barry*, but you can also find the Elvis soundtracks from *Blue Hawaii* to *Viva Las Vegas*. You can also find *Great Epic Film Scores* and *The Best of James Bond*. So this section covers everything else that didn't fit in the first three.

Here's what you'll find in the entries and how each part can be helpful in selecting the best music for your collection:

The information following the title and bone rating (we'll talk about that later) contains many important pieces of information which may include the CD release year, the label, the source of the music (i.e. the film title or Broadway play), the film production studio and the film release year or year the Broadway play was performed.

The **Album Notes** contain the credits. This may include the music composer, editor, conductor, orchestrator, album or CD producer, song producers, engineers and any other credits you would find on the CD cover. And in Broadway shows, it may even list the cast.

Selections lists the tracks on the CD. Here you will find track numbers, track titles, running time, writers and performers if not performed by the orchestra.

The **Review** is the meat of the entry. Here you'll read fun and informative expert advice on the soundtracks listed in this volume. As with any opinions, all of what you'll read is subjective and personal. Of course, we think the Hound will ultimately point you in the right direction. However, if you have a bone to pick, we'd like to hear about it, because after all, this book is for you, the fans.

A byline will appear if the entry was reviewed by anyone except our trusty leader Didier C. Deutsch. So, if you don't see one, you know who wrote it, too.

As for the bone rating—it's not too tough to figure out. ♪♪♪♪♪ CDs are the cat's meow, er, um, I mean, the top dog and a **Woof** is dog chow. So, enjoy the book and be sure to let us know what you think. Really—it's important to us!

Editor
Didier C. Deutsch, Grammy Award-nominated record producer, says music has always been an integral part of his life. His love for music spawned his love for film and Broadway music and nurtured his career as a producer and Broadway critic.

Managing Editor
Devra M. Sladics

Soundtracks Staff
Beth Fhaner, Amber E. Foulkrod, Holly A. Monacelli, Christine Tomassini

Technology Wizard
Jeffrey Muhr

Art Direction
Tracey Rowens

Production
Mary Beth Trimper, Dorothy Maki, Evi Seoud, Shanna Heilveil

Typesetting
GGS Information Services

Marketing & Promotion
Kim Intindola, Cyndi Naughton, Betsy Rovegno, Susan Stefani, Lauri Taylor

Soundtracks Development
Martin Connors, Julia Furtaw, Terri Schell

Contributors
Jeff Bond owes his knowledge of film music to years of watching television reruns and movies in the '60s and '70s, when he could often be found holding the microphone of his cassette recorder up to the speaker of his TV set to record the themes from "Star Trek," "The Undersea World of Jacques Cousteau" and "The Man from U.N.C.L.E." In 1992, he began writing reviews for *Film Score Monthly* and has been regularly featured in that magazine ever since. He has also contributed regular features and reviews to *SciFi Universe* magazine, and has written articles on music in the "Star Trek" television series and feature films for *Star Trek Communicator* magazine. He and his wife, Brooke, currently reside in Los Angeles.

Andy Dursin has profiled film composers and filmmakers for *Film Score Monthly, Home Movies* and *Movie Collector* magazines, where he has also written extensively about films, soundtrack albums and laserdiscs. A recent graduate of Boston College, Andy is a proud native Rhode Islander, who you'll find at the beach if he's not at the local movie theatre.

Gary Graff is an award-winning journalist and supervising editor of Visible Ink Press' *MusicHound* series. His work appears regularly in *Replay, Guitar World, ICE, San Francisco Chronicle, Detroit Sunday Journal/Detroit Journal* and other publications.

Chuck Granata, record producer, is an authority on Frank Sinatra, whose work can be seen on a variety of CD titles released by Sony/Legacy, Capitol and Reprise. He is also very knowledgeable about and a fan of Broadway and film music, and often writes about both.

David Hirsch, an avid soundtrack collector for the past 30 years, learned to appreciate film music when, before video tape, the only way to relive one's favorite film or TV show was through its soundtrack album. Formerly an associate editor of *Starlog* magazine, David has co-authored eight books, including the *Space: 1999 Official Alpha Moonbase Technical Manual* and *TV Episode Guides, Volumes 1 & 2.* Currently, he is a music columnist for both *Starlog* and *Soundtrack!* magazines, and has either written liner, consulted on or produced over 50 soundtrack albums, including *Supergirl* (Silva Screen), *Flight* *of the Navigator* (Super Tracks) and *Star Trek: Volume Two* (GNP Crescendo).

Lukas Kendall is the editor and publisher of *Film Score Monthly*, the magazine of motion picture and television music (www.filmscoremonthly.com). He has produced soundtrack CDs on his Retrograde Records label (such as *The Taking of Pelham One Two Three* and *Deadfall*), and contributed liner notes for such releases as *Star Wars Trilogy: The Original Soundtrack Anthology* and *Raiders of the Lost Ark*. Lukas is building a soundtrack fighting force of extraordinary magnitude.

Marc Kirkeby, a former editor of *Rolling Stone*, writes frequently about music, theater and film. His essays have appeared in *The New Yorker*, *The New York Times*, *The Village Voice* and *American Film*.

Randall D. Larson is the former editor and publisher of *CinemaScore: The Film Music Journal* (1981-1987), and a long-time contributing editor to *Soundtrack!* A frequent film music writer for *Cinefantastique*, Larson is also the author of *Musique Fantastique: A Survey of Film Music in the Fantastic Cinema* (Scarecrow, 1984), and *Music for the House of Hammer* (Scarecrow, 1986).

Paul Andrew MacLean contributes reviews and interviews to *Film Score Monthly, Soundtrack!, Music from the Movies* and also serves as film reviewer for *Renaissance* magazine.

Jerry Thomas, a collector and fan of Broadway and screen musicals, writes frequently about both, and has also contributed liner notes for a number of Broadway cast album and film soundtrack reissues.

Many of the albums listed in this volume can be found at record stores around the country, or can be ordered from the following specialized shops and dealers:

Footlight Records
113 East 12th Street
New York, NY 10003
phone: (212) 533-1572
fax: (212) 673-1496

Screen Archives Entertainment
P.O. Box 5636
Washington, D.C. 20016-1236
phone: (202) 364-4333
fax: (202) 364-4343

Sound Track Album Retailers
P.O. Box 487
New Holland, PA 17557-0487
phone/fax: (717) 656-0121

The following specialized magazines carry information relating to newly released soundtrack and/or cast albums and reissues and are essential reading:

Film Score Monthly
5967 Chula Vista Way #7
Los Angeles, CA 90068
phone: (213) 464-7919
fax: (213) 464-5916

Soundtrack!
Astridlaan 171
2800 Mechelen
Belgium

Show Music
P.O. Box 466
East Haddam, CT 06423-0466
phone: (800) 873-8664

VideoHound's soundtracks

Absolute Power ♪♪♭

1997, Varese-Sarabande Records; from the movie *Absolute Power*, Castle Rock Entertainment, 1997.

Album Notes: *Music*: Lennie Niehaus; *Music Editor*: Donald K. Harris; Orchestra conducted by Lennie Niehaus; *Album Producer*: Lennie Niehaus; *Engineer*: Bobby Fernandez.

Selections: 1 Kate's Theme (C. Eastwood)(2:05); 2 The Mansion (1:31); 3 Christy Dies (2:27); 4 The Mansion Chase (4:33); 5 Christy's Dance (3:40); 6 Waiting For Luther/Wait For My Signal (6:56); 7 Dr. Kevorkian I Presume (1:43); 8 Sullivan's Revenge (2:16); 9 Kate's Theme (C. Eastwood)/End Credits (4:43).

Review: The dour, oppressive themes developed by Lennie Niehaus for this contemporary political drama are frequently too derivative and too unmelodic to satisfy a casual listener. The story is about a retired detective investigating a covered-up murder possibly involving the President of the United States. Meandering musical lines, occasionally punctuated by synthesized pulses, may work very well on the screen behind the action, but don't make much of an impact when isolated from their primary function. Exceptions include a jazz-tinged "Christy's Dance," and the lovely, melodic "Kate's Theme," played in concertante style with the "End Credits."

The Abyss ♪♪♪

1989, Varese-Sarabande; from the movie *The Abyss*, 20th Century-Fox, 1989

Album Notes: *Music*: Alan Silvestri; *Orchestrations*: James B. Campbell; Orchestra conducted by Alan Silvestri; *Album Producer*: Alan Silvestri; *Engineer*: Dennis Sands.

Selections: 1 Main Title (1:31); 2 Search The Montana (1:56); 3 The Crane (2:01); 4 The Manta Ship (6:24); 5 The Pseudopod (5:37); 6 The Fight (1:46); 7 Sub Battle (3:19); 8 Lindsey Drowns (4:43); 9 Resurrection (1:59); 10 Bud's Big Dive (6:10); 11 Bud On The Ledge (3:14); 12 Back On The Air (1:41); 13 Finale (6:47).

Review: This score for director James Cameron's underwater epic is as eclectic as the film itself. Composer Alan Silvestri deftly mixes three distinct styles, each to represent the film's three protagonists. Standard scoring techniques, in particular the composer's own trademarked bombastic horn punches, are used to represent the human element of the film. As the protagonists penetrate deeper into the undersea trench, a New Age-style electronic theme is used to express the overall mystery that builds throughout the film. Finally, a choir personifies the delicate translucent alien life form hiding below. As the film builds to its climax, all three motifs merge into one chorus, a hymn for an uncertain future. The music tells us there's still a mystery, but perhaps a better world will come of it all.

David Hirsch

The Accidental Tourist ♪♪♪♪

1989, Warner Bros. Records; from the movie *The Accidental Tourist*, Warner Bros., 1989.

Album Notes: *Music*: John Williams; *Orchestrations*: Ken Wannberg; Orchestra conducted by John Williams; *Album Producer*: John Williams; *Engineer*: Dan Wallin; *Assistant Engineers*: Sue McLean, John Rotundi.

Selections: 1 Main Title (2:31); 2 Macon Alone (4:41); 3 Trip To London (1:53); 4 The Healing Process (5:09); 5 Fixing The Plumbing On A Rainy Afternoon (3:13); 6 A Second Chance (3:10); 7 Wedding Scene (2:49); 8 Back With Sara (4:03); 9 Bedroom Conversation (4:36); 10 Rose And Julian (2:08); 11 A New Beginning (3:26); 12 End Credits (A Second Chance)(3:10).

Review: For this contemporary story of a man's slow emotional rebirth following the breakup of a long-term relationship, John Williams wrote an unabashedly romantic and gorgeously understated score, in which the piano, the oboe and the clarinet play an important solo role to create the appropriate reflective moods. The recurring main theme binds the various cues together, in a display of thoughtful music that holds its own on a purely listening basis. The faster-paced "A Second Chance" contrasts happily with the more sullen expression in the other tracks, and exudes a warm, glorious feeling.

Ace Ventura: When Nature Calls 🦴🦴🦴

1995, MCA Records; from the movie *Ace Ventura: When Nature Calls*, Warner Bros., 1995.

Album Notes: *Album Producers*: Danny Bramson, Kathy Nelson.

Selections: 1 Spirits In The Material World (Sting)(4:40) *Pato Banton, Sting*; 2 Secret Agent Man (P.F. Sloan/S. Barri)(2:16) *Blues Traveler*; 3 Don't Change (INXS)(3:41) *The Goo Goo Dolls*; 4 Burnin' Rubber (Mr. Mirainga) (3:18) *Mr. Mirainga*; 5 Boll Weevil (C. Ballew)(3:16) *The Presidents of the United States of America*; 6 Blur The Technicolor (W. Zombie/ R. Zombie)(4:09) *White Zombie*; 7 Watusi Rodeo (Attaway/Walls/ Kordecki)(2:34) *Reverend Horton Heat*; 8 Here Comes The Night (B. Burns) (3:27) *Native*; 9 Jungle Groove (M. Jordan)(5:13) *Montell Jordan*; 10 Ife (A. Kidjo/J. Hebrail)(4:23) *Angelique Kidjo*; 11 My Pet (M. Sweet)(2:46) *Matthew Sweet*; 12 It's Alright (E. Sloan/J. Pence/Emosia)(4:54) *Blessid Union of Souls*; 12 Ace In Africa (R. Folk)(2:39) *Robert Folk*.

Review: It's hard to come up with a soundtrack that adequately conveys the energy Jim Carrey brings to the screen. This one does in spots—on the Goo Goo Dolls' firey cover of Inxs' "Don't Change," on the Presidents of the United States of America's "Boll Weevil," and on Reverend Horton Heat's "Watusi Rodeo." Sting teams up with Pato Banton for a fluid rendition of the Police's "Spirits in the Material World," while White Zombie's "Blur the Technicolor" is appropriately frenetic. The breakthrough from this album was almost Mr. Mirainga, whose "Burnin' Rubber" was a minor radio hit, but the band never came through on its own.

Gary Graff

Aces: Iron Eagle III 🦴🦴🦴

1991, Intrada Records; from the movie *Aces: Iron Eagle III*, Carolco Pictures, 1991.

Album Notes: *Music*: Harry Manfredini; *Orchestrations*: Bobby Muzingo; *Music Editor*: Jack Tillar; Orchestra conducted by

Harry Manfredini; *Album Producer*: Harry Manfredini; *Engineers*: Ron Capone, Jerry Lambert.

Selections: 1 The Aces Theme (1:53); 2 Escape From Peru (4:36); 3 Chappy's Surprise (2:39); 4 Trouble In Brownsville (1:53); 5 Chappy Survives (1:47); 6 Anna's Theme (2:03); 7 The Aces Agree (1:35); 8 Horikoshi Confesses (1:41); 9 Anna In Action (5:38); 10 Aces In Action (3:13); 11 Getting The Message (:32); 12 Too Much Seasoning (3:12); 13 Action In The Andes (4:21); 14 Tee-Vee Does The Right Thing (2:43); 15 The Messerschmidt 163/Hero In A Zero (1:29); 16 Chappy Saves The Day (3:34); 17 Kleiss Is Diced; 18 Final Credits (4:47).

Review: Harry Manfredini has come up with a heroic score built around a trio of themes for this aerial adventure film. The dominant motif is the "Aces Theme," an old-fashioned militaristic march that carries the heroism of the vintage fighter pilots throughout the score. A secondary theme, associated with the heroine, is played by French horns and strings counterpointed by piping trumpets and winds; the counterpointed measures lend a forceful drive to the slow-moving theme. The third major motif is that of the Nazi drug lord—a fast-paced polyrhythmic riff for percussion and electric bass counterpointed against marimba and flute that captures the cold, relentless violence of the villain. Manfredini has concocted a cohesive score which works well in the film and on the CD, although the orchestra occasionally sounds a little thin. The 50-minute disc is nicely sequenced and packaged, including detailed notes by the composer who describes each cue and his use of the various themes.

Randall D. Larson

Across the Sea of Time 🦴🦴🦴

1995, Epic Soundtrax; from the movie *Across the Sea of Time*, Columbia Pictures, 1995.

Album Notes: *Music*: John Barry; The English Chamber Orchestra, conducted by John Barry; *Album Producer*: John Barry; *Engineer*: Shawn Murphy.

Selections: 1 The Wonder Of America (1:36); 2 Into New York (3:14); 3 Ellis Island (2:21); 4 Never Have I Felt So Free (2:12); 5 The Lower East Side (1:17); 6 The Automobile, The Telephone, The Skyscraper (3:15); 7 The Subway (1:00); 8 The Subway Ride (:59); 9 Coney Island (2:47); 10 Up To The Sky (1:26); 11 Flight Over New York (5:40); 12 Central Park (1:49); 13 Times Square and Broadway (1:56); 14 Scary Night In The Park (1:07); 15 A New Day Will Come (1:57); 16 Searching (1:36); 17 Welcome To America, Welcome To New York (3:31); 18 Across The Sea Of Time (5:20).

Review: The American experience (or more pointedly the New York experience) elicited this unusual score from composer John Barry for a documentary made in cooperation with Sony New Technologies to promote the IMAX system. Typical of Barry's scores of late, it is a lyrical effort, marked by long lovely melodic lines in which the music effortlessly soars and captures the imagination. The catchy recurring main theme "The Wonder Of America" binds together the various selections, often in a dialogue between a solitary reed and the string section. An occasional pulsating tune ("The Subway Ride," or the blues-tinged "Times Square and Broadway") adds an extra dimension to the score, and keeps reminding the listener that John Barry, who was a master at it, used to write more frequently in that vein earlier in his career.

Act of Piracy/ The Great White ♪♪♪

1991, Prometheus Records/Belgium; from the movies *Act of Piracy* and *The Great White*, Laurelwood Productions, 1991.

Album Notes: *Music*: Morton Stevens; Orchestra conducted by Ken Thorne; *Album Producer*: Ford A. Thaxton.

Selections: *ACT OF PIRACY*: 1 Main Title/The Barracuda At Sea (2:20); 2 Wartime Memories (2:27); 3 Attack On The Barracuda (2:55); 4 Ted Survives (:44); 5 Ted Takes The Blame (2:27); 6 O'Connor's Escapade (1:00); 7 Railroad Yard (2:30); 8 Arrival At Skiathos (5:28); 9 Alto Sax Blues (1:34); 10 Sally Seduces Stevens (2:08); 11 Ted Runs Into Trouble (3:05); 12 Ted Unties The Family (1:25); 13 The Ramming (1:41); 14 In The Water (1:26); 15 The End Of Wilcox/Ted Swims To The Boat/End Title (6:42);

THE GREAT WHITE: 16 Main Title (2:37); 17 Shark Scare (2:40); 18 Teen Folly No. 1 (2:10); 19 Dazed Trauma (1:04); 20 Divers Trapped (2:10); 21 Shark Attack (2:06); 22 Coma (2:27); 23 Divers Set Trap (1:24); 24 Teen Folly No. 2 (:58); 25 The Final Shark Attack (2:52); 26 Aftermath (1:08).

Review: Pleasant enough music is mostly notable as Morton Stevens' last score before his untimely passing in 1988. Conducted by Ken Thorne, this is a more melodic work than the average action film score (the main title theme is particularly indelible) and the influence of Jerry Goldsmith is certainly evident. Stevens worked with Goldsmith for many years, both as an orchestrator and co-composer (he did the final two installments of the mini-series *Masada* and the finale fight cue for *Outland*). Since much of his music has gone unreleased, one can forgive the desire to include the flatter sounding recording of *The Great White*, a 1982 *Jaws* wannabe also in-

cluded on this CD. Oddly, track titles on the package are laid out in LP fashion with numbering restarting at "1" after track "13."

David Hirsch

The Addams Family ♪♪♪

1991, Capitol Records; from the movie *The Addams Family*, Paramount Pictures, 1991.

Album Notes: *Music*: Marc Shaiman; *Orchestrations*: Mark McKenzie, Steve Bartek, Ralph Burns, Dennis Dreith, Jack Eskew, Thom Sharp; *Music Editor*: George Martin; Orchestra conducted by Hummie Mann; *Album Producers*: Marc Shaiman, Hummie Mann; *Engineer*: Tim Boyle.

Selections: 1 Deck The Halls/Main Title (2:19); 2 Morning (2:54); 3 Seances And Swordfights (1:38); 4 Playmates (S. Dowell)(:25) *The Kipper Kids*; 5 Family Plotz (3:54); 6 The Mooche (D. Ellington/I. Mills)(3:31); 7 Evening (3:12); 8 A Party... For Me? (5:21); 9 Mamushka (M. Shaiman/B. Comden/ A. Green)(3:30) *Raul Julia, Christopher Lloyd*; 10 Thing Gets Work (:56); 11 Fester Exposed (2:05); 12 The Rescue (8:04); 13 Finale (2:59).

Review: This broadly comedic score by Marc Shaiman is partly inspired by Vic Mizzy's oddball music for the 1960s TV series and Danny Elfman's "Beetlejuice," but owes much to the classic 1930s Universal horror films which both movie and underscore occasionally parody. Surprisingly romantic in places, the ample orchestral endeavor exhibits a delightful lunatic charm. Several tunes by Duke Ellington and Eddie Cantor are interpolated into the score, which includes the song "Mamushka," co-written by Shaiman with legendary Broadway lyricists Betty Comden and Adolph Green.

David Hirsch

Addams Family Values ♪♪♪

1993, Varese-Sarabande; from the movie *Addams Family Values*, Paramount Pictures, 1993.

Album Notes: *Music*: Marc Shaiman; *Orchestrations*: Hummie Mann, Jeff Atmajian, Brad Dechter, Michael Starobin; *Music Editors*: Nancy Fogarty, Scott Stambler; Orchestra conducted by Artie Kane; *Featured Musicians*: Bruce Dukov, Ralph Morrison (violin); *Album Producer*: Marc Shaiman; *Engineer*: Tim Boyle.

Selections: 1 It's An Addams (2:06); 2 Sibling Rivalry (3:01); 3 Love On A Tombstone (1:02); 4 Debbie Meets The Family (2:17); 5 Camp Chippewa/Camp Chippewa Song (M. Shaiman/ P. Rudnick/S. Wittman)(1:37); 6 Fester's In Love (:33); 7 The

Big Date (2:28); 8 The Tango (2:45); 9 Fester And Debbie's Courtship (2:43); 10 Wednesday And Joel's Courtship (1:18); 11 The Honeymoon Is Over (1:27); 12 Escape From Debbie (3:27); 13 Eat Us (M. Shaiman/P. Rudnick)(1:02); 14 Wednesday's Revolt (2:27); 15 Debbie's Big Scene (6:59); 16 Some Time Later (3:10).

Review: With the same flamboyant style with which he scored the original *Addams Family* feature, Marc Shaiman brings a similar mix of *Beetlejuice* and *Frankenstein* to the podium and lets it fly in all directions. The score is rampantly farcical— quotations from various sources abound—to keep up with the film's hysterical visuals. From riotous bombast to compelling violin virtuosities and moody tangos, everything from Stravinsky to Hans Salter to Astor Piazzola is fair brew in Shaiman's musical stew. With plenty of borrowings from Vic Mizzy's original *Addams Family* TV theme, the score is firmly tongue-in-cheek, but is held together by a straight-faced main theme for the Addams family, which stands powerful and proud, albeit encrusted with a few moldering skeletons in the closet. The orchestral movement on the CD is interrupted by a couple of songs (one of which wasn't used in the film) which are better off programmed out, but the sequel score is a likable mix of musical mayhem. Not quite as fresh or as dynamic as the original score, but likable enough.

Randall D. Larson

Addicted to Love 𝄢𝄢𝄢𝄢ᵛ

1997, TVT Records; from the movie *Addicted to Love*, Warner Bros., 1997.

Album Notes: *Music*: Rachel Portman; *Orchestrations*: Rachel Portman; Orchestra conducted by David Snell; *Engineer*: Chris Dibble.

Selections: 1 Walk Away Renee (M. Lookofsky/B. Calilli/T. Sansone)(2:42) *The Left Banke*; 2 Ma fiancee, elle est partie (D. Brillant)(2:15) *Dany Brillant*; 3 Zoom (MC Solaar/Zdar)(4:00) *MC Solaar*; 4 Je t'aime, moi non plus (S. Gainsbourg)(4:27) *Serge Gainsbourh, Jane Birkin*; 5 Comme toujours (I. Mellino/ M. Crespin)(3:53) *Les Negresses Vertes*; 6 So tinha de ser com voce (A.C. Jobim/L. Oliviera)(3:48) *Elis & Tom*; 7 Soukora (A. Farka Toure)(6:02) *Ali Farka Toure, Ry Cooder*; 8 Autumn Leaves (J. Kosma/J. Prevert)(5:31) *Stephane Grappelli*; 9 Observatory (2:24); 10 Water Pistol Attack (2:31); 11 Sam's Chart (2:31); 12 Painting The Wall (2:39); 13 Maggie Enters Loft (1:34); 14 Rotten Strawberries (1:46); 15 Sam And Maggie Make Love (2:10); 16 Back To The Plan (:58); 17 Cockroaches (2:28); 18 Back From Hospital (1:44); 19 Common Interests

(1:19); 20 Fight (1:44); 21 We're Even (2:30); 22 Walk Across The Street (1:49); 23 Sam Comes Home (3:15).

Review: The folks at TVT can be forgiven for overloading this soundtrack album with selections that apparently were not even in the film (but who can complain when those selections include the classic "Walk Away Renee," Serge Gainsbourg and Jane Birkin whispering the sensuous "Je t'aime, moi non plus," and Stephane Grappelli fiddling his way through "Autumn Leaves"). They also had the good sense of presenting a dozen cues composed by Rachel Portman for the romantic comedy starring Matthew Broderick and Meg Ryan. Portman, one of the best new film composers today, reveals a quirky, whimsical style that's very engaging. She displays an uncanny feel for catchy, melodic material that has an unusual quality to it, and finds a life of its own outside of its primary function. The jaunty theme and variations that find their way in the various cues, occasionally interrupted by more romantic moments ("Sam and Maggie Make Love," "Painting the Wall") make this soundtrack album a real joy to listen to. Don't miss it!

The Adventures of Baron Munchausen 𝄢𝄢𝄢𝄢

1988, Warner Bros. Records; from the movie *The Adventures of Baron Munchausen*, Columbia Pictures, 1988.

Album Notes: *Music*: Michael Kamen; *Kurzwiel, Oboes and Orchestrations*: Michael Kamen; *Additional Orchestrations*: Fiachra Trench, Rick Wentowrth, Alan Arnold, Ed Shearmer, John Fiddy; *Music Editor*: Chris Brooks; The Graunke Orchestra of Munich and The National Philharmonic Orchestra of London, conducted by Michael Kamen; *Album Producers*: Michael Kamen, Stephen P. McLaughlin; *Engineer*: Eric Tomlinson.

Selections: 1 The Town: The Statue In The Square, The Land Of Cheese, What Will Become Of The Baron?, Beautiful Ladies (3:30); 2 The Sultan: The Torturer's Apprentice, A Eunuch's Life Is Hard, Play Up And Win The Game (M. Kamen/E. Idle)(4:29); 3 The War Begins: The Gang Gets The Treasure, The Baron Starts The War, Sally Runs (5:56); 4 Wednesday: Cannonball Ride, Twinkling Of An Eye (2:37); 5 The Balloon: Escape In The Balloon/ Tattletale, Ascending On Bloomers, On The Way To The Moon, Storm (7:35); 6 On The Moon: The Sea Of Tranquility, Moon King Chase, Leaving The Moon (7:33); 7 Vulcan And Venus: A Little Fodder?, Venus Rising, The Munchausen Waltz (7:58); 8 In The Belly Of The Whale (The Gang Together Again): What Will Become Of The Baron?, Death And Bucephalus (3:39); 9 The Final Battle: To The Sultan's Tent, The Battle Begins/Gustavus Blows, The Rt. Ordinary Horatio Jackson Takes Tail, Berthold Chases The Bullet, Albrecht And The

Boats, Elephants (4:26); 10 The Baron Dies And Lives Again: The Baron Shot, Requiem (3:16); 11 Victory: Forward The Players, Open The Gates, Baron Rides Off Into The Sunset (2:55).

Review: Terry Gilliam's epic film of the legendary European liar is blessed with a lavish and innovative orchestral score by Michael Kamen. The opportunity is here to cover just about every kind of mood from dire peril to pompous farce, and Kamen handles it all with an amazing dexterity. From the adventurous flight of "The Balloon" suite, to the choral requiem "What Will Become of the Baron," and finally to the balmy songs for "The Sultan" suite (co-written with ex-"Monty Python" member Eric Idle), the score transcends each diverse level as if they truly belonged together. Kamen even manages to musically capture comedian Robin Williams' inspired zaniness in "On the Moon," a deft mix of orchestral instruments, electronics and natural sounds.

David Hirsch

The Adventures of Huck Finn ♪♪♪ᵇ

1993, Varese-Sarabande Records; from the movie *The Adventures of Huck Finn*, Walt Disney Films, 1993.

Album Notes: *Music*: Bill Conti; *Orchestrations*: Jack Eskew; *Music Editor*: Steve Livingston; Orchestra conducted by Bill Conti; *Album Producer*: Bill Conti; *Engineer*: Lee DeCarlo.

Selections: 1 Main Title (4:43); 2 Missy Finn Goes Shoppin' (2:42); 3 Next Of Kin (2:01); 4 Do The Right Thang (2:48); 5 Once A Slave... (3:26); 6 We're Still Friends (2:43); 7 Billy Gets Killed (2:19); 8 The Barge (2:43); 9 Huck Springs Jim (3:15); 10 All's Well (4:25).

Review: Bill Conti wrote an uplifting, jubilant score for this 1993 Disney adaptation of Mark Twain's classic novel. While the film took some liberties with Twain's text, Conti's score perfectly captures the innocence of childhood with a lyrical soundtrack dominated by strong melodic, often boisterous themes. Not surprisingly, this down-home score has been used as underscore on countless televised sports programs since, most notably the Kentucky Derby. Since *Rocky*, Conti has often had the rotten luck of writing music for either bad movies or films that never had soundtrack albums. *Huck Finn* is not only one of the best albums to originate from the composer since his success with that 1976 Sylvester Stallone milestone, but is also one of his more enjoyable efforts to date.

Andy Dursin

The Adventures of Pinocchio ♪♪♪♪

1996, London Records; from the movie *The Adventures of Pinocchio*, New Line Cinema, 1996.

Album Notes: *Music*: Rachel Portman; *Orchestrations*: Jeff Atmajian, Lawrence Ashmore; *Music Editor*: Graham Sutton; *Producer*: Rachel Portman; *Engineer*: Chris Dibble; *Songs*: Brian May; *Orchestral Arranger*: Lee Holdridge; *Producers*: Brian May, Spencer Proffer; *Songs*: Stevie Wonder; *Orchestral Arrangers*: Lee Holdridge, Spencer Proffer, Steve Cross; *Producers*: Stevie Wonder, Spencer Proffer; *Engineer*: Francis Buckley; *Album Producer*: Spencer Proffer.

Selections: 1 Il Colosso (B. May/L. Holdridge)(7:37) *Just William, Sissel, Jerry Hadley, Gary Martin, Brian May, Jim Beach, Julie Glower, Peter Locke, Robert Lee, Suzanne DuBarry*; 2 Luigi's Welcome (adapted from "Funiculi Funicula")(S. Proffer/ D. Goldsmith/L. Holdridge)(2:34) *Jerry Hadley*; 3 All For One (C. Taubman)(2:29) *The Morling School Ensemble, Jonathan Shell*; 4 Kiss Lonely Goodbye (S. Wonder)(4:38) *Stevie Wonder*; 5 Hold On To Your Dream (S. Wonder)(4:23) *Stevie Wonder*; 6 Theme From Pinocchio (7:19); 7 Lorenzini (3:23); 8 Terra Magica (3:57); 9 Pinocchio Becomes A Real Boy (5:08); 10 Kiss Lonely Good-Bye (instrumnetal version) (S. Wonder)(4:39) *Stevie Wonder (harmonica)*; 11 Pinocchio's Evolution (S. Wonder)(3:47) *Gepetto's Workshop*; 12 What Are We Made Of (B. May)(3:45) *Brian May, Sissel*; 13 Hold On To Your Dream (S. Wonder)(5:57) *Stevie Wonder*; 14 Kiss Lonely Good-Bye (S. Wonder)(5:03) *Stevie Wonder*.

Review: Rachel Portman's lovely score for this retelling of the Pinocchio story is almost dwarfed by the pseudo operatic selections created by Lee Holdridge, Brian May, David Goldsmith and album producer Spencer Proffer, among others, which are heard at the beginning of the set, and shamelessly call the listener's attention to them. At times recalling the manic style in Danny Elfman's music, Portman's score is wonderfully imaginative, diversified, and eclectic, moving effortlessly from wild displays of fiery orchestral outbursts to evocative chamber-like expressions, sometimes all within the same cue, as in "Lorenzini". In fact, it's almost a shame the CD didn't give her music more playing time. Unfortunately, the only tracks that don't fit within the context here are the vocals by Stevie Wonder, who also contributed some exquisite instrumentals in "Kiss Lonely Goodbye" and "Pinocchio's Evolution," simply because his style of singing does not match the "period" moods established in the other numbers, and the derivative "What We Are Made Of," performed by Brian May and Sissel, which also sounds too contemporary.

The Adventures of Priscilla, Queen of the Desert 🎵🎵🎵🎵

1994, Mother Records; from the movie *The Adventures of Priscilla, Queen of the Desert*, Gramercy Pictures, 1994.

Album Notes: *Song Producers*: Ron Miller, Jacques Morali, Steve Buckingham, Dino Fekaris, Freddie Perren, Ettore Stratta, Felipe Delgado, Benny Anderson, Bjorn Ulvaeus, Keith Thomas.

Selections: 1 I've Never Been To Me (K. Kirsch/R. Miller) (3:53) *Charlene*; 2 Go West (J. Morali/H. Belolo/V. Willis) (3:33) *The Village People*; 3 Billy Don't Be A Hero (M. Murray/P. Callander) (3:43) *Paper Lace*; 4 My Baby Loves Lovin' (R. Cook/R. Greenaway) (2:44) *White Plains*; 5 I Love The Nightlife (S. Hutcheson/A. Bridges) (3:25) *Alicia Bridges*; 6 Can't Help Lovin' That Man (J. Kern/O. Hammerstein II) (2:39) *Trudy Richards*; 7 I Will Survive (D. Fekaris/ F. Perren) (3:18) *Gloria Gaynor*; 8 A Fine Romance (J. Kern/D. Fields) (3:12) *Lena Horne*; 9 Shake Your Groove Thing (D. Fekaris/F. Perren) (5:32) *Peaches & Herb*; 10 I Don't Care If The Sun Don't Shine (M. David) (2:42) *Patti Page*; 11 Finally (R.K. Jackson/ C.C. Peniston/F. Delgado/E.L. Limear) (4:08) *Ce Ce Peniston*; 12 Take A Letter Maria (R.B. Greaves) (2:43) *R.B. Greaves*; 13 Mamma Mia (B. Anderson/B. Ulvaeus/S. Anderson) (3:32) *ABBA*; 14 Save The Best For Last (W. Waldman/J. Lind/P. Galdston) (3:38) *Vanessa Williams*; 15 I Love The Nightlife (S. Hutcheson/A. Bridges) (3:34) *Alicia Bridges*; 16 Go West (J. Morali/H. Belolo/V. Willis) (6:34) *The Village People*; 17 I Will Survive (D. Fekaris/F. Perren) (4:51) *Gloria Gaynor*; 18 Shake Your Groove Thing (D. Fekaris/F. Perren) (6:38) *Peaches & Herb*; 19 I Love The Nightlife (S. Hutcheson/A. Bridges) (6:20) *Alicia Bridges*.

Review: The misadventures of three transvestites on a car trip across Australia became the occasion for this soundtrack album in which some of disco's greatest hits have been compiled together in a festive, joyous display. Oddly enough, the lone track that seems utterly out of place in this unbridled dance party is Lena Horne's rendition of the classic "A Fine Romance," which sounds, er... too polite! But don't let that misstep keep you away from this delightful album, honey: you'll love it.

The Adventures of Robin Hood 🎵🎵🎵🎵

1983, Varese-Sarabande; from the movie *The Adventures of Robin Hood*, Warner Bros., 1938.

Album Notes: *Music*: Erich-Wolfgang Korngold; The Utah Symphony Orchestra, conducted by Varujan Kojian; *Album Producer*: George Korngold; *Engineer*: Bruce Leek.

Selections: 1 Prologue (Main Title)(1:34); 2 Banquet at Nottingham Castle (1:52); 3 Robin Enters The Great Hall (:56); 4 Escape From The Castle (5:09); 5 Robin Meets Little John (1:38); 6 The Oath and The Black Arrow (1:54); 7 Robin And Friar Tuck (1:24); 8 Ambush In Sherwood (3:01); 9 Feast In The Forest (2:52); 10 Robin And Marian (3:09); 11 The Archery Tournament (3:04); 12 Escape From The Gallows (2:13); 13 Love Scene (5:40); 14 Dagger Fight: King Richard In Sherwood (2:07); 15 Coronation Procession (3:05); 16 Duel, Victory and Epilogue (3:22).

Review: Over the years, there have been tantalizing snippets of Korngold's thrilling score for *The Adventures of Robin Hood* in various compilations, but none as complete or as exciting as this brilliant recording produced by George Korngold, son of the composer. Here is all the pageantry, color and gorgeous melodies from the original, faithfully reproduced in spacious stereo, in a recording that has long been a trendsetter in its field, and is an essential title in any collection.

Excerpts from the score can also be found in *Music by Erich Wolfgang Korngold*, conducted by Lionel Newman, a recording initially released by Warner Bros. in the early '60s, and for many years a much sought-after collector's item; and in *Captain Blood: Classic Film Scores for Errol Flynn* and *The Sea Hawk: Classic Film Scores of Erich-Wolfgang Korngold*, both conducted by Charles Gerhardt.

See also: The Sea Hawk and Anthony Adverse

The Adventures of the Great Mouse Detective 🎵🎵🎵🎵▷

1992, Varese-Sarabande Records; from the animated feature *The Adventures of the Great Mouse Detective*, The Walt Disney Company, 1992.

Album Notes: *Music*: Henry Mancini; *Orchestrations*: Henry Mancini, Jack Hayes; Orchestra conducted by Henry Mancini; *Album Producer*: Henry Mancini; *Engineer*: John Richards.

Selections: 1 Main Title (1:38); 2 Dawson Finds Olivia (1:19); 3 Enter Basil (2:11); 4 Enter Ratigan (2:17); 5 Crushed Box (1:31); 6 The World's Greatest Criminal Mind (H. Mancini/L. Grosman/ E. Fitzhugh)(5:08) *Vincent Price*; 7 Unusual Foot Prints (1:41); 8 Here's Toby! (3:52); 9 Check Mate (2:40); 10 Reunion (2:37); 11 Let Me Be Good To You (M. Manchester)(3:01) *Melissa Manchester*; 12 Ratigan's Plan (2:00); 13 Goodbye So Soon (H. Mancini/ L. Grossman/E. Fitzhugh)(2:55) *Vincent Price*; 14 Cat Nip (1:44); 15 Big Ben Chase (5:34); 16 Wrap-Up (3:08); 17 End Title/Goodbye So Soon (1:50) *Chorus*.

Review: There often is a cartoon-like quality to Henry Mancini's most inspired musical scores, and it evidently all came together in this delightful series of cues for an animated feature distributed by the Disney company. Without going into too many details about how a mouse becomes the equal of the great Sherlock Holmes, suffice it to say that the villain here, a nasty rat, is none other than Vincent Price, doing a sensational job in two songs (including the revealing "The World's Greatest Criminal," delivered with the right amount of sneers and nasty posturing), and that Mancini's music is constantly amusing and thoroughly entertaining. For added pleasure, Melissa Manchester contributes "Let Me Be Good To You," which she wrote for the occasion. Delicious through and through.

An Affair to Remember ♫♫♫♪

1993, Epic Soundtrax; from the movie *An Affair to Remember*, 20th Century-Fox, 1957.

Album Notes: *Music*: Hugo Friedhofer; The 20th Century-Fox Orchestra and Chorus, conducted by Lionel Newman; *Featured Soloist*: Marnie Nixon; *Engineer CD Reissue*: Kevin Boutote.

Selections: 1 Main Title—An Affair To Remember ("Our Love Affair")(H. Warren/H. Adamson/L. McCarey)(1:52) *Vic Damone*; 2 Continue (3:02); 3 Villefranche and In The Chapel (3:35); 4 Tomorrowland (2:18) *Marni Nixon*; 5 Pink Champagne (1:52); 6 Revelation (3:13); 7 You Make It Easy To Be True (1:11); 8 Proposal (2:34); 9 Continue (1:42) *Marni Nixon*; 10 Night Club Affair (2:17) *Marni Nixon*; 11 Empire State Montage (2:51); 12 Return To Villefranche (3:57) *Marni Nixon*; 13 The Tiny Scout (He Knows You Inside Out)(3:21) *Children's Chorus*; 14 Ballet (1:03); 15 End Title—An Affair To Remember ("Our Love Affair")(3:54).

Review: This stylish 1957 soap opera starring Cary Grant, as an eligible bachelor engaged to a socialite, and Deborah Kerr, as the painter he meets during a trans-Atlantic voyage and with whom he falls in love only to lose track of her after she has a car accident, is best remembered today for the fact that it played an important role in the recent *Sleepless in Seattle*. The score, composed by Hugo Friedhofer, imaginatively played its role behind the scenes, but stands out on its own as a pleasant listening experience. Several vocals by Marni Nixon, and Vic Damone's rendition of the title tune add an extra touch of their own to the enjoyment. The only drawback here is the EQ that gives the recording a slightly unpleasant nasal sound.

See also: Sleepless in Seattle

After Dark My Sweet ♫♫♫♪

1990, Varese-Sarabande Records; from the movie *After Dark My Sweet*, Avenue Pictures, 1990.

Album Notes: *Music*: Maurice Jarre; *Performers*: Michael Boddicker, Ralph Grierson, Michael Fisher; *Album Producer*: Maurice Jarre; *Engineers*: Shawn Murphy.

Selections: 1-3 Suite I: After Dark, My Sweet (1:56/1:35/1:18); 4-7 Suite II: Collie And Fay (4:11/1:10/2:05/:48); 8-12 Suite III: Uncle Bud (3:59/ 1:22/2:53/2:27/:55); 13-16 Suite IV: The Kidnapping (1:09/:52/2:40/3:25).

Review: Written just prior to his popular score for *Ghost*, *After Dark My Sweet* is one of the last completely electronic scores Maurice Jarre composed. An excellent film noir about a vagrant ex-prizefighter seduced by an older women into a kidnapping scheme, the film benefits greatly from its moody, atmospheric score. A mournful solo EVI opens the album with a lonely theme for the protagonist. A pleasant, airy love theme also figures into the score, set most memorably in track 4, with clever electronic percussion writing. The album also features much music which was not included in the film and is among Jarre's most engaging electronic work. Some of the suspense cues are perhaps a bit programmatic-sounding on disc and dominate the last half of the album. *After Dark My Sweet* nevertheless holds some of Jarre's most inviting melodic invention, ranging from pleasant nostalgia to chilling terror.

Paul Andrew MacLean

The Age of Innocence ♫♫♫♫

1993, Epic Soundtrax/Sony Music; from the movie *The Age of Innocence*, Columbia Pictures, 1993.

Album Notes: *Music*: Elmer Bernstein; *Orchestrations*: Emilie A. Bernstein; Orchestra conducted by Elmer Bernstein; *Album Producer*: Elmer Bernstein.

Selections: 1 The Age Of Innocence (4:38); 2 At The Opera ("Faust" Opera)(3:11); 3 Radetzky March (J. Strauss)(2:16) *the Berlin Radio Symphony Orchestra*; 4 Emperor Waltz, op. 437/ Tales From The Vienna Woods (excerpts) (2:27) *the London Philharmonic*; 5 Mrs. Mingott (1:43); 6 Dangerous Conversation (2:14); 7 Slighted (:58); 8 Van der Luydens (2:17); 9 First Visit (2:29); 10 Roses Montage (1:20); 11 Ellen's Letter (2:05); 12 Archer's Book (2:08); 13 Mrs. Mingott's Help (3:50); 14 Archer Pleads (1:49); 15 Passage Of Time (2:44); 16 Archery (1:28); 17 Ellen At The Shore (2:15); 18 Blenker Farm (2:38); 19 Boston Common (:54); 20 Parker House (1:17); 21 Pick Up Ellen

(2:12); 22 Conversation With Letterblair (2:33); 23 Archer Leaves (1:04); 24 Farewell Dinner (2:05); 25 Ellen Leaves (2:43); 26 In Paris (1:12); 27 Ellen's House (:48); 28 Madame Olenska (2:18); 29 End Credits (5:04).

Review: This is a surprisingly different effort from Elmer Bernstein, an unexpectedly delightful symphonic waltz that captures the flavor of director Martin Scorsese's period romance where a man had to marry the right kind of woman, not his true love, the one with a past. The album is marvelously sequenced, playing like a rich melodic concert. You can close your eyes and allow the music to effortlessly transport you back a century. Although it will probably never rank with *The Magnificent Seven* as a pillar of his career, this score is nonetheless one of the finest works by Bernstein. Several classical pieces, excerpted in the film, lead off the album, preceding the main theme which serves as the album's overture.

David Hirsch

Agnes of God 🦴🦴🦴ᵛ

1992, Varese-Sarabande Records; from the movie *Agnes of God*, Columbia Pictures, 1985.

Album Notes: *Music*: Georges Delerue; The Toronto Symphony Orchestra, conducted by Georges Delerue; *Featured Soloists*: The Elmer Isler Singers; *Album Producer*: Georges Delerue; *CD Producer*: Robert Townson.

Selections: Agnes of God: Symphonic Suite for Chorus and Orchestra: 1 Part 1 (1:47); 2 Part 2 (3:29); 3 Part 3 (1:53); 4 Part 4 (2:54); 5 Part 5 (3:40); 6 Part 6 (:33); 7 Part 7 (2:25); 8 Part 8 (1:38); 9 Part 9 (1:15); 10 Part 10 (1:45); 11 Part 11 (5:57); 12 Part 12 (3:30).

Review: A dramatic film with a religious background provided Georges Delerue with the opportunity to write a deeply moving score in which his natural flair for long romantic lines effectively combined with the mystical moods suggested by the locale, an isolated convent where a naive nun, Agnes, apparently gave birth to a baby whom she subsequently murdered, a mystery investigated by a psychiatrist (Jane Fonda) assigned to the case. Throughout, the moods are quietly evoked in a captivating series of cues (unfortunately untitled) that subtly underscore the more poignant moments in the story and also make for an intelligent, if at times eerie, audio experience.

The Agony and the Ecstasy/ The Pride and the Passion
🦴🦴ᵛ

1991, Cloud Nine Records; from the movies *The Agony and the Ecstasy*, 20th Century-Fox, 1965, and *The Pride and the Passion*, United Artists, 1957.

Album Notes: *The Pride and the Passion*: *Music*: George Antheil; Orchestra conducted by Ernest Gold; *The Agony and the Ecstasy*: *Music*: Alex North; Orchestra conducted by Alex North.

Selections: *THE PRIDE AND THE PASSION:* 1 Main Title (2:30); 2 Juana's Flamenco (2:18); 3 The British Captain (2:28); 4 Windmill Camp At Night (2:20); 5 The Knife Fight (2:42); 6 Juana's Love Theme (4:04); 7 Rescue Of The Gun (4:06); 8 Juana's Choice (3:49); 9 The Pride And The Passion (bolero) (5:59); 10 Miguel's Theme (2:41); 11 The Procession (3:53); 12 Fulfillment and End Title (2:47);

THE AGONY AND THE ECSTASY: 13 Prelude/The Mountains of Carrara (2:57); 14 The Warrior Pope (2:43); 15 The Medici (2:35); 16 The Sketch Of The Apostles (3:13); 17 Genesis (3:36); 18 The Sistine Chapel (3:04); 19 The Contessina (2:50); 20 The Agony (4:01); 21 Michelangelo's Recovery (2:13); 22 Festivity In St. Peter's Square (2:07); 23 The War (2:06); 24 Michelangelo's Magnificent Achievement and Finale (2:41).

Review: While best remembered as one of Frank Sinatra's colossal film flops, *The Pride and the Passion* merits attention primarily because of Sinatra's pairing with his celebrated co-stars, Cary Grant and Sophia Loren. Despite the fairly thin story line, composer George Antheil's score survives as a thoughtful work of art, and magnificent staging aside, the film's single appealing quality.

Antheil effectively captures the spirit of the Spanish setting, beginning with a bold, rhythmic "Main Title" that is rooted in the elements of Latin American music, particularly the bolero. What follows is an array of romantic and dramatic themes, based on authentic Hispanic motifs, and Iberian folk music. The CD issue utilizes the original 1957 Capitol Records masters, and other than a bit of analog tape hiss, the monophonic sound is enjoyable.

The Agony and the Ecstasy tells the story of the intense artistic and personal conflict between artist Michaelangelo and Pope Julius II, after the Papal command for the artist to paint the ceiling of the Sistine Chapel. Utilizing both modern and ancient instrumental voicings, composer Alex North stunningly paints a portrait that is at once majestic, religious, and reflective of the tension of the relationship between the artist, his work, and the Pope.

With the original masters culled from the film's soundstage recordings, the stereo recording displays its age, and could use a dose of modern sonic restoration. Nonetheless, this is a splendid score, and a most enjoyable recording.

Charles L. Granata

Air America ♫♫♫♫

1990, MCA Records; from the movie *Air America*, Carolco Pictures, 1990.

Album Notes: *Song Producers*: Bruce Fairbairn, Don Was, Don Smith & Charlie Sexton, Gary Katz, Edgar Winter & Rick Derringer, Lou Adler, Brian Holland & Lamont Dozier, William "Smokey" Robinson, Billy Davis, Sky Saxon & Marcus Tybalt; *Soundtrack Executive Producers*: Becky Mancuso & Tim Sexton; *Album Producer*: John Boylan; *Engineer*: John Boylan.

Selections: 1 Love Me Two Times (J. Densmore/R. Kreiger/R. Manzarek/J. Morrison)(3:22) *Aerosmith*; 2 Right Place Wrong Time (M. Rebennack)(3:37) *B.B. King, Bonnie Raiit*; 3 Long Cool Woman In A Black Dress (R. Crook/ A. Clarke/R. Greenaway)(4:15) *Charlie Sexton*; 4 Do It Again (D. Fagen/W. Becker)(5:01) *Steely Dan*; 5 Free Ride (D. Hartman)(3:23) *Edgar Winter, Rick Derringer*; 6 California Dreamin' (J. Phillips/M. Gilliam)(2:38) *The Mamas & The Papas*; 7 Baby, I Need Your Lovin' (E. Holland/L. Dozier/B. Holland)(2:44) *The Four Tops*; 8 Get Ready (W. Robinson)(2:38) *The Temptations*; 9 Rescue Me (C.W. Smith/R. Miner)(2:53) *Fontella Bass*; 10 Pushin' Too Hard (S. Saxon)(2:35) *The Seeds*.

Review: A bright, intelligent pop collection, this compilation represents the soundtrack for the film based on Christopher Robbins' 1979 book, about two pilots flying the CIA's "dope airline," the agency's privately owned Air America, which was used to deal in drugs in order to finance the war effort in Southeast Asia. The songs, representative of the era, contain several interesting selections, and unlike some compilations that become quite redundant when they are tagged as "soundtrack" albums, this one makes sense and is quite enjoyable.

Airport ♫♫♫♫♪

1993, Varese-Sarabande; from the movie *Airport*, Universal Pictures, 1970.

Album Notes: *Music*: Alfred Newman; *Orchestra conducted by* Alfred Newman; *Album Producers*: Ken Darby, Stanley Wilson.

Selections: 1 Airport (Main Title)(3:11); 2 Airport Love Theme (3:30); 3 Inez' Theme (1:29); 4 (Guerreo's Goodbye (2:37); 5 Ada Quonsett Stowaway (1:26); 6 Mel And Tanya (2:27); 7 Airport Love Theme #2 (2:40); 8 Joe Patroni Plane Or Plows?

(2:22); 9 Triangle! (3:50); 10 Inez — Lost Forever (1:45); 11 Emergency Landing! (1:38); 12 Airport (End Title).

Review: Alfred Newman received a posthumous Oscar nomination for this score, in which he deftly created a set of contemporary cues to evoke the passion and drama on board a jet taken over by a terrorist who wants the plane to land at an airport during a snow blizzard. To say that they don't write scores like this anymore is an understatement. Melodic to a fault, and thoroughly attractive, the various cues stand out on their own, making this CD as enjoyable a listening experience as it is a memento of the film itself. The popular "Love Theme" ranks high among the best selections here, along with tracks like "Inez' Theme," "Ada Quonsett Stowaway," "Triangle!," or the action-packed "Emergency Landing!."

The Alamo ♫♫♫♫♫

1995, Sony Legacy; from the movie *The Alamo*, Batjac/M-G-M, 1960.

Album Notes: *Music*: Dimitri Tiomkin; *Orchestra conducted by* Dimitri Tiomkin; *CD Producer*: Didier C. Deutsch; *Engineer*: Chris Herles.

Selections: 1 Overture (3:06); 2 (a) Main Title (2:09), (b) Legend Of The Alamo (R. Mellin/B. Russell/D. Johnston)(:38), (c) Sam Houston (:28); 3 Davy Crockett And The Tenesseans (:57); 4 Cantina Music (2:10); 5 Davy Crockett's Speech (2:10) *John Wayne*; 6 Love Scene (6:32); 7 Crockette And The Tennesseans Enter The Alamo (2:34); 8 The Mexicans Arrive (2:37); 9 Intermission (1:01); 10 Entr'acte (3:44); 11 Tennessee Babe (D. Tiomkin/ P.F. Webster)(2:30); 12 Here's To The Ladies (D. Tiomkin/P.F. Webster) (1:10); 13 Raid For Cattle (4:36); 14 Santa Anna (1:09); 15 Crossing The Line (2:49); 16 The Green Leaves Of Summer (D. Tiomkin/P.F. Webster)(3:19); 17 Charge Of Santa Anna/Death Of Davy Crockett/The Final Assault (7:00); 18 Finale (1:50); 19 Exit Music (1:09); 20 Davy Crockett And Flaca (3:46) *John Wayne*; 21 Alternate Ending: The Eyes Of Texas Are Upon You (1:10); 22 Ballad Of The Alamo (D. Tiomkin/ P.F. Webster)(3:38) *Marty Robbins*; 23 The Green Leaves Of Summer (D. Tiomkin/P.F. Webster)(2:54) *The Brothers Four*.

Review: Christopher Palmer, in his book *The Composer in Hollywood*, cites *The Alamo* as "the best of the great Tiomkin westerns." Few would dispute this, despite the fact that some might argue in favor of some of the composer's other classic film scores, including *High Noon*, *Gunfight at O.K. Corral*, *The Guns of Navarone* and *Rio Bravo*.

Opinions aside, one thing is certain: *The Alamo* is an absolute treasure! Bursting with color and drama, Tiomkin's score contributes mightily to the successful realization of the story, as envisioned by producer, director and star John Wayne. All of the excitement that sparked the magic of the film and its music are vividly preserved in this newly remastered edition, which restores eight musical cues that were left off the original Columbia soundtrack LP.

Charles L. Granata

Albino Alligator ♪♪♪

1997, 4.A.D. Records; from the movie *Albino Alligator*, Miramax Pictures, 1997.

Album Notes: *Music*: Michael Brook; *Featured Musicians*: Michael Brook (guitar, keyboards), Anton Schwartz (saxophone), Bob Adams (string bass, organ), Jason Lewis (drums), James Pinker (percussion), Hafez Modirzaden (ney, saxophone); *Album Producer*: Michael Brook; *Engineer*: Michael Brook, Tuti, James Pinker.

Selections: 1 Arrival (5:02); 2 Doggie Dog (1:52); 3 Slow Town (2:35); 4 Preparation (3:18); 5 Miscalculation (1:45); 6 Aftermath (4:40); 7 Tunnel (5:01); 8 Albo Gator (4:18); 9 The Promise (4:37); 10 The City (5:46); 11 The Kicker (1:29); 12 Exit (4:16); 13 Ill Wind (You're Blowing Me No Good (H. Arlen/T. Koehler)(3:34) *Jimmy Scott, Michael Stipe.*

Review: Newcomer Michael Brook fashioned a satisfying moody score for this story, set in New Orleans, about a trio of misfits involved in a robbery, who seek refuge in an old bar below street level with no windows and no backdoor exit, where they are soon trapped by police and federal agents (the title of the film apparently refers to a pool-playing ruse in which a player misses a shot on purpose in order to better defeat his opponent later). The jazz, in turns jazzy and disquieting, is particularly effective at enhancing the claustrophobic atmosphere that permeates much of the film, an impression further reinforced in the gloomy rendition of the Harold Arlen-Ted Koehler song, "Ill Wind."

Alexander the Great/ Barabbas ♪♪♪

1996, DRG Records; from the movies *Alexander the Great*, United Artists, 1956, and *Barabbas*, Columbia Pictures, 1962.

Album Notes: *Music*: Mario Nascimbene; *Orchestrations*: Mario Nascimbene; Orchestra conducted by Mario Nascimbene; *Album Producers*: Mario Nascimbene, Claudio Fuiano; *Engineer*: Gianni Mazzarini.

Selections: *ALEXANDER THE GREAT:* 1 Main Titles (1:53); 2 Philip's Return (1:27); 3 Olympia's Party/Burning Of Alexandropolis (1:20); 4 Eurydice And Alexander (3:37); 5 The

Battle Of Cheronea (2:59); 6 Barsina And Alexander (:51); 7 Battle Of Granicus (2:34); 8 Hemnon's Death and Storming Of Mileto (1:24); 9 Battle Of Gaugamela (5:58); 10 Chase and Death Of Darius (1:25); 11 Alexander's Death (:55);

BARABBAS: 12 Main Titles (2:03); 13 Oriental Dance (2:36); 14 Eclipse (3:18); 15 The Empty Tomb (2:45); 16 The Mines (4:10); 17 Intermezzo (1:52); 18 Arrival In Rome (1:46); 19 Rome Afire (3:28); 20 The Death Of Barabbas (2:39).

Review: Following the success of his score for *The Barefoot Contessa* (q.v.), Mario Nascimbene wrote the music for *Alexander the Great*, a big screen epic starring Richard Burton as the famed conqueror and military genius. In it, he essentially developed two sets of cues, one played by a large brass ensemble to evoke Alexander's armies on the move, the other using acoustic Oriental instruments for the more intimate scenes. Both play off each other in this recording to create a vivid musical tapestry befitting the subject matter.

Equally original and impressive is the composer's score for *Barabbas*, a retelling of the Crucifixion, starring Anthony Quinn as the thief and murderer whose life was traded for Jesus Christ. Using a sound-mixing console to create a wide range of unusual sonorities, Nascimbene wrote a score which is evocative and strangely attractive.

The only drawback here is the overall sound quality of the recording, very dry in both scores, with some notable distortion and poor editing in *Alexander*, and a generally muffled tone in *Barabbas*, made all the more striking in these digital transfers.

Alfie ♪♪♪♪♪

1997, MCA Records; from the movie *Alfie*, Paramount Pictures, 1966.

Album Notes: *Music*: Sonny Rollins; *Orchestrations*: Oliver Nelson; conducted by Olivier Nelson; *Featured Musicians*: Sonny Rollins, Oliver Nelson, Bob Ashton (tenor sax), Jimmy Cleveland, J.J. Johnson (trombone), Phil Woods (alto sax), Danny Bank (baritone sax), Kenny Burrell (guitar), Roger Kellaway (piano), Walter Booker (bass), Frankie Dunlop (drums); *Album Producer*: Bob Thiele; *Engineer*: Rudy Van Gelder.

Selections: 1 Alfie's Theme (9:41); 2 He's Younger Than You Are (5:09); 3 Street Runner With Child (3:59); 4 Transition Theme For Minor Blues or Little Malcolm Loves His Dad (5:49); 5 On Impulse (4:28); 6 Alfie's Theme Differently (3:44).

Review: Everybody, it seems, remembers the song "What's it all about, Alfie?," warbled by Dionne Warwick, so this soundtrack album, which does not even include it, may come as a refreshing surprise. Actually, the song itself, by Burt Bacharach and Hal David, never made it into the final version of the film, but the jazzy score, written and performed by Sonny Rollins, is an essential element that contributes enormously to the success of this modern-day story of a charming, if somewhat glib and at times cynical Cockney romeo, whose sole pursuit in life is to bed down any woman crossing his path. The album, long a favorite among jazz collectors, finds the tenor saxophonist at the top of his creativity, surrounded by many familiar jazz aces, including J.J. Johnson, Phil Woods, Kenny Burrell, Roger Kellaway, and arranger Oliver Nelson. The long selections enable everyone to "stretch" and make some excellent music in the process.

Alien

Alien ♪♪♪♪

1988, Silva Screen; from the movie *Alien*, 20th Century-Fox, 1979.

Album Notes: *Music:* Jerry Goldsmith; *Orchestrations:* Arthur Morton; Orchestra conducted by Jerry Goldsmith; *Album Producer:* Jerry Goldsmith; *Engineer:* Eric Tomlinson.

Selections: 1 Main Title (3:30); 2 Face Hugger (2:32); 3 Breakaway (3:00); 4 Acid Test (4:35); 5 The Landing (4:29); 6 The Droid (4:40); 7 The Recovery (2:44); 8 The Alien Planet (2:28); 9 The Shaft (3:57); 10 End Title (3:02).

Review: Jerry Goldsmith not only set the tone for the series with his dark melodies, but he once again developed a style that would be often mimicked throughout the genre. Brooding, sometimes romantically melodic, the score for the first film is peppered with various shrill and innovative percussion effects that set the heart racing. The monster, vaguely seen through most of the film, is represented both on and offscreen through Goldsmith's music. What is most surprising about the soundtrack album is that it reflects the composer's original intent for the film, the final score having been alerted with "tracked" cues by director Ridley Scott who used Howard Hanson's Symphony #2 "Romantic" as the finale and end title, and cues from Goldsmith's own score to *Freud*.

David Hirsch

Alien 3 ♪♪♪♪

1992, MCA Records; from the movie *Alien 3*, 20th Century-Fox, 1992.

Album Notes: *Music:* Elliot Goldenthal; *Orchestrations:* Elliot Goldenthal, Robert Elthai; Orchestra conducted by Jonathan Sheffer; *Synthesizer Programming:* Richard Martinez; *Album Producer:* Matthias Gohl; *Engineers:* Tim Boyle, Joel Iwataki.

Selections: 1 Agnus Dei (4:30) *Nick Nackley*; 2 Bait And Chase (4:42); 3 The Beast Within (3:09); 4 Lento (5:49); 5 Candles In The Wind (3:21); 6 Wreckage And Rape (2:44); 7 The First Attack (4:20); 8 Lullaby Elegy (3:41); 9 Death Dance (2:18); 10 Visit To The Wreckage (2:05); 11 Explosion And Aftermath (2:21); 12 The Dragon (3:08); 13 The Entrapment (3:42); 14 Adagio (4:15).

Review: For the third film in the series, Elliot Goldenthal created an intricately orchestrated symphony that is overwhelmingly sad, sometimes frightening but not without beauty, and curiously closer in tone to another Goldsmith score, *The Omen*, particularly in its use of a boy soprano soloist on "Agnus Dei." This motif not only reflects the religious zeal of the prison inmates, but also prefaces Ripley's own pseudo-crucifixion at the end of the film. Goldenthal is most effective when he represents the spider-like Face Hugger with rattling sounds, in the track "Bait and Chase," in which he breaks from his usual style in an innovative technique that shocks the listener. This is also the case in the attempted rape of Ripley ("Wreckage and Rape"), in which a violent flurry of percussion and screaming vocal effect is used to reflect the vileness of the attack. A score far superior to the film.

David Hirsch

Aliens ♪♪♪

1986, Varese-Sarabande; from the movie *Aliens*, 20th Century-Fox, 1986.

Album Notes: *Music:* James Horner; *Orchestrations:* Greig McRitchie; *Music Editors:* Robin Clark, Michael Clifford; The London Symphony Orchestra, conducted by James Horner; *CD Producer:* James Horner; *Engineer:* Eric Tomlinson.

Selections: 1 Main Title (5:10); 2 Going After Newt (3:08); 3 Sub-Level 3 (6:11); 4 Ripley's Rescue (3:13); 5 Atmosphere Station (3:05); 6 Futile Escape (8:13); 7 Dark Discovery (2:00); 8 Bishop's Countdown (2:47); 9 Resolution and Hyperspace (6:10).

Review: Although James Horner created a military motif and a bolder sound to represent director James Cameron's tale of U.S. Space Marines versus an entire horde of creatures, the basis of his score, particularly the plodding "creeping" figure, is derived from Goldsmith's work. Where Horner deviates the most is on bold action cues such as "Going After Newt" or "Resolution" (a cue tracked into the finale of *Die Hard* and countless film trailers). Standard percussion effects are used to establish tension while electronics represent the aliens. Aram Khachaturian's adagio from his "Gayne Ballet Suite" is incorporated into the main and closing titles, the first of several adaptations of this piece. In all, an average effort for Horner not without its moments.

David Hirsch

Alive 🎵🎵🎵🎵

1993, Hollywood Records; from the movie *Alive*, Touchstone Pictures, 1993.

Album Notes: *Music*: James Newton Howard; *Orchestrations*: James Newton Howard, Brad Dechter, Mark McKenzie, Chris Boardman; Orchestra conducted by Marty Paich; *Album Producer*: James Newton Howard; *Engineer*: Shawn Murphy.

Selections: 1 The First Night (4:10); 2 Home (:58); 3 Nando Awakes (2:18); 4 Finding The Tail (3:27); 5 Alberto (1:48); 6 Eating (5:00); 7 Are You Ready? (1:13); 8 Frozen Climbers (1:51); 9 It's God (2:40); 10 The Final Climb (3:28); 11 End Title (3:04).

Review: A gruesome tale of survival in the subfreezing Andes following a plane crash (resulting in cannibalism, no less!), *Alive*, based on a true story, received an atmospheric score from James Newton Howard, who wrote appropriately sullen (one might be tempted to say frigid) cues reflective of the intense action and its desolate locale. The evocation of other situations ("Home"), enhanced by the current situation of the survivors, is hinted at in an attractive fashion, but the *piece de resistance*, so to speak, is the five-minute "Eating," in which the composer turns the ultimate act of survival into... an almost palatable morsel. The film's topic might not have been to everyone's taste, but this score should.

All Dogs Go to Heaven

All Dogs Go to Heaven 🎵🎵🎵🎵

1989, Curb Records; from the animated feature *All Dogs Go to Heaven*, United Artists, 1989.

Album Notes: *Music*: Ralph Burns; *Songs*: Al Kasha, Joel Hirschhorn, Michael Lloyd, Charles Strouse, T.J. Kuenster; *Album Producer*: Ralph Burns; *Engineer*: Keith Grant.

Selections: 1 Love Survives (A. Kasha/J. Hirschhorn/M. Lloyd)(3:25) *Irene Cara, Freddie Jackson*; 2 Mardi Gras (1:17); 3 You Can't Keep A Good Dog Down (C. Strouse)(2:30) *Burt Reynolds, Dom De Luise*; 4 Hell Hound (2:09); 5 What's Mine Is Yours (C. Strouse)(1:48) *Burt Reynolds*; 6 At The Race Track (1:49); 7 Let Me Be Surprised (C. Strouse)(4:54) *Melba Moore, Burt Reynolds*; 8 Soon You'll Come Home (T.J. Kuenster)(2:38) *Lana Beeson*; 9 Money Montage (3:43); 10 Dogs To The Rescue (3:10); 11 Let's Make Music Together (C. Strouse)(2:24) *Ken Page, Burt Reynolds*; 12 Goodbye Anne-Marie (2:10); 13 Hallelujah (T.J. Kuenster)(1:21) *Candy Devine*.

Review: See entry below.

All Dogs Go to Heaven 2 🎵🎵🎵

1996, Angel Records; from the animated feature *All Dogs Go to Heaven 2*, M-G-M, 1996.

Album Notes: *Music*: Mark Watters; *Songs*: Barry Mann, Cynthia Weil; *Orchestrations*: Bruce Fowler, Larry Blank, Mark Watters, Ira Hearshen, Chris Klatman; *Arrangers*: Barry Mann, Guy Moon, Mark Watters, Mike Tavera, Kevin Bassinson; *Music Editor*: Dominick Certo; *Album Producers*: Mark Watters, Barry Mann, Kelly Ward, Mark Young; *Engineers*: Rick Winquest, Steve Price.

Selections: 1 Main Title/Heavenly Ceremony (2:52); 2 It's Too Heavenly Here (3:26) *Jesse Corti*; 3 Count Me Out (2:40) *Sheena Easton*; 4 My Afghan Hairless (2:00) *Jim Cummings*; 5 It Feels So Good To Be Bad (3:31) *George Hearn, Ernest Borgnine*; 6 On Easy Street (3:18) *Adam Wiley, Jesse Corti, Dom De Luise*; 7 I Will Always Be With You (2:22) *Sheena Easton, Jesse Corti*; 8 Gabriel's Horn/New Arrivals (2:22); 9 Carface Steals The Horn/Charlie Volunteers (5:26); 10 Police Chase (3:34); 11 Red's Transformation (1:39); 12 We Meet David (4:07); 13 Battle For Gabriel's Horn (5:47); 14 Family Reunion/It's Too Heavenly Here (reprise) (1:28); 15 I Will Always Be With You (End Title)(3:17) *Danny Frazier, Helen Darling*.

Review: The incredible success of the Disney animated features was bound to compel other animators to try and tap the same market of youngsters and their captive parents, while providing songwriters with another opportunity to create catchy songs to beef up the inevitable soundtrack albums. Created by Don Bluth, the two *All Dogs Go to Heaven* movies rank among the best efforts in the genre, though the two CDs here differ wildly in impact and appeal. The first, with a lively score by Ralph Burns, and diversified songs by Charles Strouse (of *Bye Bye Birdie* and *Annie* fame) and Al Kasha and Joel Hirschhorn, has a definite Caribbean flair (check out the infectious calypso instrumental, "Mardi Gras," or the colorful "What's Mine Is Yours"), and is a melodic, bouncy affair, superbly pulled off by some of the performers who lent their talents—Burt Reynolds, Dom DeLuise, Melba Moore, Irene Cara, and Freddie Jackson, among them.

The sequel, *All Dogs Go to Heaven 2*, has equally catchy songs by Barry Mann and Cynthia Weil, and a portentous score by Mark Watters that dwarfs the simplicity of Burns' contribution. Sheena Easton heads the cast of singers who perform the songs here, including Jesse Corti and Jim Cummings, and Broadway veteran George Hearn teams up with Ernest Borgnine for a devastating "It Feels So Good To Be Bad," the CD's highlight. But somehow the element of fun that made the first album so enjoyable seems to be sorely missing here.

All the Brothers Were Valiant 𝄞𝄞𝄞𝄞

1991, Prometheus Records/Belgium; from the movie *All the Brothers Were Valiant*, M-G-M, 1953.

Album Notes: *Music*: Miklos Rozsa; The M-G-M Studio Orchestra, conducted by Miklos Rozsa; *Album Producer*: Mordecai Jacobs; *Engineer*: R. Earl Day.

Selections: 1 Main Title (1:39); 2 The House Of Shore (2:32); 3 Proposal (2:31); 4 The Boat (2:33); 5 Full Sail (1:19); 6 High Sea (1:05); 7 Love And Pride (1:32); 8 Fighting/Pursuit/Capsized (6:58); 9 The Girl (1:15); 10 The Island (1:41); 11 Abduction (1:32); 12 Fright (1:04); 13 Murder/The Pearls (5:45); 14 Disillusion (:58); 15 Ashamed (2:48); 16 Showdown/Mutiny/ Fight (10:34); 17 Finale (2:45).

Review: A seafaring adventure film starring Robert Taylor, Stewart Granger and Ann Blyth, *All the Brothers Were Valiant* received a commanding, rousing Miklos Rozsa score, which ended up in shambles in the final version of the film. This recording restores it the way the composer created it, and it is a fitting companion to the many titles currently on CD under his

name. For this story of two brothers with contrasting characters aboard a New England whaler, their love for the same woman, and their search for an elusive treasure, Rozsa wrote a series of cues that captures the drama and action in this colorful production. Sonically, the recording could have used a little reverb, but the stereo imaging and the close miking belie the age of the original session tapes.

Almost an Angel 𝄞𝄞𝄞𝄞𝄞

1990, Varese-Sarabande Records; from the movie *Almost an Angel*, Paramount Pictures, 1990.

Album Notes: *Music*: Maurice Jarre; Orchestra conducted by Maurice Jarre; *Album Producer*: Maurice Jarre; *Engineer*: Shawn Murphy.

Selections: 1 Some Wings (M. Jarre/R. Underwood)(3:08) *Vanessa Williams*; 2 Almost An Angel (4:06); 3 Fly (5:41); 4 Rose And Terry (3:29); 5 The Mafia Bluff (3:40); 6 Steve's Run (3:12); 7 Let There Be Light (10:04).

Review: Spearheaded by the song "Some Wings," attractively performed by Vanessa Williams, the score for this romantic fantasy unfolds in atypical fashion, with exquisite melodies lining this story of a con man and electronics expert who has a revelation following an accident and dedicates the rest of his life doing some good around himself. The mixture of bold orchestral chords, synth counterpoints, heavenly choir and organ obbligato (for the out-of-body experience by the con man who "dreams" he meets with God) provides a diversified texture that enhances the appeal of this concoction, presented without a break, as a continuous suite. The 10-minute-plus "Let There Be Light" brings all these elements into sharp focus for a last musical exploration that reveals the fluidity in Jarre's style and his knack for striking melodic concepts.

Altered States 𝄞𝄞𝄞𝄞𝄞

1981, RCA Victor; from the movie *Altered States*, Warner Bros., 1981.

Album Notes: *Music*: John Corigliano; Orchestra conducted by Christopher Keene; *Album Producer*: John Corigliano; *Engineer*: Larry Franke.

Selections: 1 Main Title and First Hallucination (Ritual Sacrifice and Religious Memories)(4:40); 2 Love Theme (3:37); 3 Second Hallucination (Hinchi Mushroom Rite and Love Theme Trio)(5:14); 4 First Transformation (Primordial Regression)(3:40); 5 Primeval Landscape (In The Isolation Chamber)(2:15); 6 Second Transformation (The Ape Man Sequence)(Escape From The Laboratory, Stalking The Dogs and The Fight, The Zoo and Final Hunt) (8:02); 7 Religious Memories and Father's Death (2:08); 8 The Laboratory Experiment: Jessup's Transformation, Collapse Of The Laboratory, The Whirlpool and Journey To Another Dimension, Return To Reality (6:12); 9 The Final Transformation (4:17).

Review: Looking back from the jaundiced perspective of the '90s it's hard to believe that a single year, 1981, could produce three scores as memorable as John Williams' *Raiders of the Lost Ark*, Alex North's *Dragonslayer*, and *Alteretered States,* concert hall composer John Corigliano's mind-blowing score for director Ken Russell's trippy sci-fi tale of one man's exploration of racial memory and its terrible consequences. Corigliano wrote a primarily acoustic work that is powerful, frightening, disorienting and as mind-expanding as the peyote that William Hurt's obsessed anthropologist ingests in order to facilitate his archetypal, hallucinogenic sense memories in the film. The composer produced wild, colorful passages to underscore the film's spectacular hallucination sequences and coiling, rumbling low string and brass clusters to illustrate Dick Smith's remarkable makeup transformations as Hurt's body is physically altered by his experiences. There are also stunning evocations of primitivism as Hurt experiences memories of ancient rituals and is himself transformed into a loping man-beast late in the film. But Corigliano is just as adept at characterizing the film's dramatic and psychological elements: there's a deeply disturbing distortion of a religious chorale associated with Hurt's father in the film, as well as a rich and moving love theme that resolves this score's incredibly agitated final passage. It's a wild, virtuoso effort that won't be to everyone's taste, but a must for anyone interested in late 20th-century composition.

Jeff Bond

Always 🐾🐾🐾🐾

1990, MCA Records; from the movie *Always*, Universal Pictures, 1990.

Album Notes: *Music*: John Williams; *Music Editor*: Ken Wannberg; Orchestra conducted by John Williams; *Featured Soloist*: Jim Thatcher (French horn); *Album Producer*: John Williams; *Engineer*: Shawn Murphy.

Selections: 1 Smoke Gets In Your Eyes (J. Kern/O. Hammerstein II)(2:51) *J.D. Souther*; 2 Boomerang Love (5:19) *Jimmy Buffett*; 3 Cowboy Man (2:51) *Lyle Lovett*; 4 Give Me Your Heart (3:54) *Denette Hoover, Sherwood Ball*; 5 A Fool In Love (4:09) *Michael Smotherman*; 6 Smoke Gets In Your Eyes (J. Kern/O. Hammerstein II)(2:38) *The Platters*; 7 Among The Clouds (8:34); 8 Follow Me (1:14); 9 Pete In Heaven (6:41); 10 Saying Goodbye (3:13); 11 Pete And Dorinda (3:18); 12 The Return (2:29); 13 The Rescue Operation (5:14); 14 Seeing Dorinda (3:33); 15 Intimate Conver-

sation (1:26); 16 Promise To Hap (2:29); 17 The Old Timer's Shack (4:52); 18 Dorinda Solo Flight (3:16).

Review: Although the main characters in the film fight forest fires from the air, this is really an intimate story of three people. Pete, a pilot who has been killed, has unfinished business keeping him earthbound and he must guide his love, Dorinda, and old friend Hap through the pain. Despite the fact that Steven Spielberg's camera work captures the scope of the wide American vistas, this John Williams' score is remarkably restrained, delicate, as if it all existed on glass. Even the action cue "The Rescue Operation" is overwhelmed with a gentleness that contrasts with the action. An appropriately dreamy New Age style cue "Pete in Heaven," is used in a scene set in a fire ravaged forest where Pete talks to an angel. The album features 47 minutes of instrumental music with five country/ western tunes heard in the bar hangout, and two versions of the film's apropos signature song, "Smoke Gets in Your Eyes."

David Hirsch

Amadeus 🐾🐾🐾🐾

1984, Fantasy Records; from the movie *Amadeus*, Orion Pictures, 1984.

Album Notes: *Music*: Wolfgang-Amadeus Mozart; The Academy of St. Martin-in-the-Fields, conducted by Neville Marriner; *Album Producer*: John Strauss; *Engineers*: Eric Tomlinson, George Horn.

Selections: CD 1: 1 Symphony No. 25 in g, K.183 (1st movement)(7:46); 2 Stabat Mater (G. Pergolesi)(4:13) *Choir of Westminster Abbey, Simon Preston* ; 3 Early XVIIIth Century Bohemian Music: Bubak and Hungaricus (1:17); 4 Serenade For Wind Instruments, K.361 (6:09); 5 The Abduction From The Seraglio (Turkish Finale)(1:23) *The Ambrosian Singers, John McCarthy*; 6 Symphony No. 29 in A, K.201 (1st movement)(5:39); 7 Concerto No. 10 in E flat for 2 Pianos, K.365 (7:11) *Imogen Cooper, Anne Queffeleck*; 8 Kyrie from the Mass in c, K.427 (6:27) *Felicy Lott, The Academy of St. Martin-in-the-Fields Chorus, Laszlo Heltay*; 9 Sinfonia Concertante in E flat for Violin and Viola, K.364 (1st movement)(13:31) *Levon Chilingirian, Csaba Erdelyi*.

CD 2: 1 Concerto for Piano and Orchestra No. 22 in E flat, K.482 (3rd movement)(11:04) *Ivan Moravec*; 2 "Ecco la marcia," from *The Marriage of Figaro*, Act III (2:26) *Samuel Ramey, Richard Stilwell, Felicy Lott, Isabel Buchanan, Willard White*; 3 "Ah, tutti contenti," from *The Marriage of Figaro*, Act IV (2:33) *Samuel Ramey, Richard Stilwell, Felicy Lott, Anne Howells, Deborah Rees, Patricia Payne, Alexander Oliver, Robin Leggate, John Tomlinson, Willard White*; 4 Il Commendatore from

Don Juan, Act II (6:57) *John Tomlinson, Richard Stilwell, Willard White*; 5 Ruhe Sanft, from *Zaide*, K.344 (6:23) *Felicy Lott*; Requiem, K.626: 6 Introitus (:58); 7 Dies Irae (1:51); 8 Rex tremendae majestatis (2:03); 9 Confutatis (2:17); 10 Lacrymosa (3:44) *The Academy of St. Martin-in-the-Fields Chorus, Laszlo Heltay*; 12 Concerto for Piano and Orchestra No. 20 in d, K.466 (2nd movement)(9:51) *Imogen Cooper*.

Review: From beginning to end, this album is a real treat! One of the most outstanding elements in this outrageous film is the use of music. As a result, each track brings to mind a specific dramatic moment in the film in which it is heard. Of course, there is more music on this album than in the film because only fragments were utilized at key moments by the director. However, the longer excerpts give the listener the joy of hearing more of this wonderful music. The performances are all excellent and fully up to the standards expected by the classical crowd. While the selections include many familiar works, there are also enough unfamiliar or unusual excerpts to interest and challenge even the most reticent connoisseur. For those who are knowledgeable about Mozart and classical music, and for those who aren't but are interested, this album is a must.

Jerry J. Thomas

Amarcord ♪♪♪♪

1991, CAM Records/Italy; from the movie *Amarcord*, Warner Bros., 1973.

Album Notes: *Music*: Nino Rota; Orchestra conducted by Carlo Savina.

Selections: 1 Amarcord (2:02); 2 La "Fogaraccia" (2:11); 3 Le "manine" di primavera (3:07); 4 Lo "Struscio" (3:52); 5 L'emiro e le sue odalische (2:26); 6 Gary Cooper (1:18); 7 La gradisca e il principe (2:25); 8 Ti ricordi di "Siboney" (2:04); 9 Danzando nella nebia (1:46); 10 Tutti a vedere il Rex (2:24); 11 Quanto mi piace la gradisca (3:05); 12 La gradisca si sposa e se ne va (2:14).

Review: Nino Rota's vibrant musical cues are forever linked to the best films made by Federico Fellini, but this "recollection" from the director's youth evidently inspired the composer to write a score that teems with bouncy, zestful selections. Whether illustrating some of the wild denizens in Fellini's memories (a saucy hairdresser, a crazy man called Giudizio, the fascists who take over the town), or the myriad incidents that provided fodder in their everyday lives and contributed to the film's disjointed narrative, Rota's score is beautifully illustrative and melodically striking. Released on the Italian CAM label (distributed in this country), it is well worth hunting down even if you have never seen the film.

Amazing Grace and Chuck
♪♪♪♪ ▷

1987, Varese-Sarabande; from the movie *Amazing Grace and Chuck*, Tri-Star Pictures, 1987.

Album Notes: *Music*: Elmer Bernstein; *Orchestrations*: Christopher Palmer; Orchestra conducted by Elmer Bernstein; *Featured Musicians*: Klaus Koenig (oboe), Cynthia Millar (Ondes Martenot); *Album Producer*: Elmer Bernstein.

Selections: 1 Home Town (5:15); 2 Nukes (5:20); 3 Amazing (2:33); 4 Fun And Games (2:33); 5 The Movement (3:02); 6 Chuck And Dad (1:15); 7 Good And Bad Guys (2:30); 8 Decisions (2:05); 9 Remembering Amazing (2:20); 10 Dad And Sis (2:55); 11 Steamroom (2:50); 12 Final Victory (4:30); 13 End Credits (2:33).

Review: The anti-nuclear message in the film, about a Little League pitcher, Chuck, whose refusal to play after he is shown a missile under the field where he is practicing and eventually provokes the near cancellation of the baseball season when the pro athletes join in his protest, may be hokey, but it prompted Elmer Bernstein to write a delightful score, oozing with emotion and lyricism. Contrasting the innocence and simple-life pleasures of Chuck, expressed by the oboe, the ominous tone of the low strings and the Ondes Martenot and the composer's signature syncopations signal the threat posed by the "other side," those who endanger civilization with their nuclear arsenal. The conflict between the two, and the more personal relationship that develops between the kid and Amazing Grace Smith, star of the Boston Celtics and Chuck's first supporter, eventually lead to the rousing "Final Victory," a track that resolves everything, at least where the film is concerned. A brilliant score you shouldn't miss.

American Buffalo/
Threesome ♪♪♪

1996, Varese-Sarabande Records; from the movies *American Buffalo*, Samuel Goldwyn, 1996; and *Threesome*, TriStar Pictures, 1994.

Album Notes: *Music*: Thomas Newman; *Orchestrations*: Thomas Pasatieri; *Music Editor*: Bill Bernstein; *Featured Musicians*: George Doering (guitars, harmonica), Chas Smith (steel guitar), Rick Cox (saxophone), George Budd (phonograph), Michael Fisher (toys, trump), Jon Clarke (saxophones), Bill Bernstein (acoustic guitar), Harvey Mason (drums), Randy Kerber (piano), Thomas Newman (baritone ukulele); *Album Producers*: Thomas Newman, Bill Bernstein; *Engineer*: Dennis Sands.

Selections: *AMERICAN BUFFALO*: 1 Buffalo Head (2:43); 2 Classical Money (1:33); 3 Bobby (:54); 4 What Kind Of This (2:10); 5

Jaw (1:11); 6 Bobby Bobby Bobby Bobby (1:22); 7 King High Flush (1:01); 8 Nothing Out There (T. Newman/R. Cox)(1:25); 9 Chump Change (1:17); 10 The Guy (1:20); 11 Tails You Lose (2:43);

THREESOME: 12 Different Species (:33); 13 Stranded (B. Bernstein)(1:08); 14 Threesome (2:24); 15 Post-Modern Eve (:46); 16 Doomed Relationships (1:29); 17 Sacred Vows (1:36); 18 Concupiscence (:49); 19 Leprechaun (2:03); 20 Drive Away (1:09).

Review: Two scores by the vastly talented Thomas Newman, the first for a claustrophobic character study based on David Mamet's play about an attempted robbery which never happens; the second for a smart coming-of-age comedy with all the trappings the genre itself invokes. The contrasting moods in both films are fully explored, with *American Buffalo* conjuring up several tracks that are dominated by heavy percussive effects, and booming bass guitar lines, reflective of the confined, one-set environment in which the mostly psychological action takes place. On a purely audio basis, it has its moments, but it is not the kind of music one might want to listen to on a bad day. Conversely, *Threesome* features some light and airy cues, pleasant to the ear and quite attractive, with repetitive lines building up in layers to create a melodic texture.

American Graffiti ♪♪♪♪

1973, MCA Records; from the movie *American Graffiti*, Universal Pictures, 1983.

Album Notes: *Engineers:* Bill Inglot, Dan Hersch.

Selections: CD 1: 1 (We're Gonna) Rock Around The Clock (J. DeKnight/M. Freedman)(2:10) *Bill Haley & The Comets*; 2 Sixteen Candles (L. Dixon/A. Khent)(2:50) *The Crests*; 3 Runaway (C. Westover/M. Crook)(2:18) *Del Shannon*; 4 Why Do Fools Fall In Love (F. Lymon/M. Levy)(2:17) *Frankie Lymon & The Teenagers*; 5 That'll Be The Day (J. Allison/N. Petty/B. Holly)(2:15) *Buddy Holly*; 6 Fanny Mae (C. Lewis/M. Levy/W. Glasco)(2:55) *Buster Brown*; 7 At The Hop (A. Singer/J. Medora/D. White)(2:26) *Flash Cadillac & The Continental Kids*; 8 She's So Fine (K. Moe/L. Phillips)(2:21) *Flash Cadillac & The Continental Kids*; 9 The Stroll (N. Lee/C. Otis) (2:26) *The Diamonds*; 10 See You In September (S. Wayne/S. Edwards)(2:08) *The Tempos*; 11 Surfin' Safari (B. Wilson/M. Love)(2:05) *The Beach Boys*; 12 He's The Great Imposter (J. DeShannon/M. Sheeley)(2:10) *The Fleetwoods*; 13 Almost Grown (C. Berry)(2:19) *Chuck Berry*; 14 Smoke Gets In Your Eyes (J. Kern/O. Harbach)(2:37) *The Platters*; 15 Little Darlin' (M. Williams)(2:07) *The Diamonds*; 16 Peppermint Twist (J. Henry/D. Glover)(2:02) *Joey Dee & The Starlighters*; 17 Barbara Anne (F.

Fassert) (2:12) *The Regents*; 18 Book Of Love (Davis/ Patrick/ Malone)(2:18) *The Monotones*; 19 Maybe Baby (N. Petty/B. Holly)(2:01) *Buddy Holly*; 20 Ya Ya (C. Lewis/M. Levy)(2:25) *Lee Dorsey*; 21 The Great Pretender (B. Ram) (2:39) *The Platters.*

CD 2: 1 Ain't That A Shame A. Domino/D. Bartholomew(2:25) *Fats Domino*; 2 Johnny B. Goode (C. Berry)(2:39) *Chuck Berry*; 3 I Only Have Eyes For You (H. Warren/A. Dubin)(3:31) *The Flamingos*; 4 Get A Job (The Silhouettes) (2:45) *The Silhouettes*; 5 To The Aisle (S. Wiener/B. Smith)(2:44) *The Five Satins*; 6 Do You Wanna Dance (B. Freeman)(2:33) *Bobby Freeman*; 7 Party Doll (J. Bowen/B. Knox)(2:12) *Buddy Knox*; 8 Come Go With Me (C.E. Quick)(2:40) *The Del-Vikings*; 9 You're Sixteen, You're Beautiful (And You're Mine)(B. Sherman/D. Sherman)(1:56) *Johnny Burnette*; 10 Love Potion No. 9 (J. Leiber/M. Stoller)(1:51) *The Clovers*; 11 Since I Don't Have You (J. Beaumont/J. Vogel/ J. Verscharen/W. Lester/J. Taylor/J. Rock/L. Martin) (2:37) *The Skyliners*; 12 Chantilly Lace (J.P. Richardson)(2:20) *The Big Bopper*; 13 Teen Angel (J. Surry)(2:40) *Mark Dinning*; 14 Crying In The Chapel (A. Glenn) (3:01) *Sonny Till & The Orioles*; 15 A Thousand Miles Away (T. Sheppard/M. Miller)(2:24) *The Heartbeats*; 16 Heart And Soul (H. Carmichael/F. Loesser) (1:51) *The Cleftones*; 17 Green Onions (B. Jones/S. Cropper/A. Jackson/L. Steinberg)(2:27) *Booker T. & The M.G.'s*; 18 Only You (And You Alone)(B. Ram/ A. Rand)(2:40) *The Platters*; 19 Goodnight, Well It's Time To Go (J. Carter/W. Hudson)(2:43) *The Spaniels*; 20 All Summer Long (B. Wilson)(2:06) *The Beach Boys.*

Review: The first, and by far the best, rock'n'roll compilation you're likely to find anywhere, this soundtrack album to this film by George Lucas sums up everything that was and still is so exciting about the early years of pop-rock music. Even if Elvis is sorely missing from this double CD of oldies/goodies, there is enough here to satisfy the most demanding customer, including all the glorious hits you might ever want to hear from these exciting years when rock songs didn't last more than two minutes, performed by the stars who made them famous, Bill Haley & The Comets, Buddy Holly, The Beach Boys, Chuck Berry, The Platters, Fats Domino, The Big Bopper, and on and on. An eye-popping, ear-blasting collection that'll keep you bopping for days on end.

The American President ♪♪♪

1995, MCA Records; from the movie *The American President*, Castle Rock Entertainment, 1995.

Album Notes: *Music:* Marc Shaiman; *Orchestrations:* Jeff Atmajian; *Music Editor:* Scott Stambler; Orchestra conducted by Artie Kane; *Album Producer*: Marc Shaiman; *Engineer*: Dennis Sands.

Selections: 1 Main Titles (2:23); 2 Call Me Andy (1:36); 3 I Like Her (1:48); 4 It's Meatloaf Night (:40); 5 The First Kiss (2:21); 6 The Slow Down Plan (1:13); 7 The Morning After/Meet The Press (2:11); 8 Politics As Usual (:57); 9 Never Have An Airline Strike At Christmas (:35); 10 "I Have Dreamed" (The State Dinner)(R. Rodgers/O. Hammerstein II)(2:57); 11 Camp David (1:30); 12 Gathering Votes (2:36); 13 Make The Deal (3:42); 14 Decisions (1:45); 15 President Shepherd (7:28); 16 End Titles (5:05).

Review: It's a tribute to composer Marc Shaiman that his music for *The American President* is every bit as romantic, sweeping, and yes, even perhaps as sappy as you would imagine this score to be, yet it's nevertheless memorable and works well—both as an album and as an underscore to Rob Reiner's formulaic film. Shaiman, who's had the fortune (or misfortune, in the case of the director's more recent movies) to score all of Reiner's films since *Misery*, utilizes his usual orchestral approach for *The American President*, which is ideal since the film requires a specific, straightforward musical statement, namely an uplifting, "feel-good" score to back-up the on-screen romance of Michael Douglas and Annette Bening. And, just as he did on *City Slickers*, Shaiman has risen to the occasion by creating a pleasant, distinguished score that once again highlights his penchant for composing distinct, well-developed themes, the likes of which should bring listeners, particularly those who enjoy sugary scores with heavy dramatic passages, back for more on repeat listenings.

Andy Dursin

An American Tail

An American Tail ♪♪♪♪

1986, MCA Records; from the animated feature *An American Tail*, Universal Pictures, 1986.

Album Notes: *Music*: James Horner; *Orchestrations*: Greig McRitchie; *Music Editor*: Michael Clifford; The London Symphony Orchestra, conducted by James Horner; *Album Producer*: James Horner; *Engineer*: Eric Tomlinson.

Selections: 1 Main Title (5:07); 2 The Cossack Cats (2:15); 3 There Are No Cats In America (J. Horner/B. Mann/C. Weil) (3:00) *Nehemiah Persoff, John Guarnieri, Warren Hays*; 4 The Storm (3:59); 5 Give Me Your Tired, Your Poor (2:44); 6 Never Say Never (J. Horner/B. Mann/C. Weil)(2:25) *Christopher Plummer, Phillip Glasser*; 7 The Market Place (3:02); 8 Some-

where Out There (J. Horner/B. Mann/C. Weil)(2:40) *Phillip Glasser, Betsy Cathcart*; 9 Somewhere Out There (J. Horner/B. Mann/C. Weil)(3:59) *Linda Ronstadt, James Ingram*; 10 Releasing The Secret Weapon (3:38); 11 A Duo (J. Horner/B. Mann/C. Weil)(2:38) *Dom DeLuise, Phillip Glasser*; 12 The Great Fire (2:54); 13 Reunited (4:44); 15 Flying Away and End Credits (5:59).

An American Tail: Fievel Goes West ♪♪♪♪

1991, MCA Records; from the animated feature *An American Tail: Fievel Goes West*, Universal Pictures, 1991.

Album Notes: *Music*: James Horner; *Orchestrations*: John Neufeld, Greig McRitchie; *Music Editor*: Jim Henrikson; Orchestra conducted by James Horner; *Song Producer*: David Foster; *Engineer*: Dave Reitzas; *Album Producer*: James Horner; *Engineer*: Shawn Murphy.

Selections: 1 Dreams To Dream (Finale Version)(J. Horner/W. Jennings) (4:43) *Linda Ronstadt*; 2 American Tail Overture (Main Title) (7:09); 3 Cat Rumble (7:29); 4 Headin' Out West (2:37); 5 Way Out West (J. Horner/W. Jennings) (1:48); 6 Green River/Trek Through The Desert (5:44); 7 Dreams To Dream (Tanya's Version) (J. Horner/W. Jennings) (2:34) *Cathy Cavadini*; 8 Building A New Town (2:44); 9 Sacred Mountain (2:22); 10 Reminiscing (2:13); 11 The Girl You Left Behind (J. Horner/W. Jennings) (1:42) *Cathy Cavadini*; 12 In Training (1:50); 13 The Shoot-Out (5:29); 14 A New Land/The Future (8:17).

Review: James Horner struck a particularly rich vein with these two scores for Steven Spielberg's animated features about a cute little Russian mouse, Fievel, seeking personal safety and a chance to live in peace away from the Cossack cats, and finding instead adventure and emotion galore first in New York City and, in an even more imaginative sequel, in the American wild West. The instrumental cues, both action and romantic, emphasize Horner's particular gift for melodic material, with the songs adding an extra shade to his creativity. Highlights in the first set include the rollicking "There Are No Cats in America," performed by Nehemiah Persoff, John Guarnieri and Warren Hays, which gives Horner an opportunity to deal successfully with various ethnic styles; "A Duo," shared by Dom DeLuise and Phillip Glasser (the voice of Fievel); and the exhilarating "Flying Away and End Credits," which neatly sums up the pains and joys of the film's charming hero and his friends.

In the second CD, mostly instrumental, Horner's musical brogue goes wild with western type cues ("Headin' Out West," "Green River/Trek Through the Desert," "Building A

New Town," "The Shoot-Out") that deftly recall some of the best scores in the genre while retaining a winning edge of originality.

In both, Linda Ronstadt contributes a vocal which neither adds to nor detracts from the general happy moods in the other tracks.

Anaconda 🎵🎵🎵

1997, edel America Records; from the movie *Anaconda,* **Columbia Pictures, 1997.**

Album Notes: *Music:* Randy Edelman; *Orchestrations:* Ralph Ferraro; *Music Editor:* Joanie Diener; Orchestra conducted by Randy Edelman; *Engineers:* Elton Ahi, Dennis Sands.

Selections: 1 Anaconda (Main Title)(4:46); 2 Watching And Waiting (4:44); 3 Night Attack (2:47); 4 This Must Be Heaven (1:39); 5 Down River (2:44); 6 Seduction (3:28); 7 Travelogue (2:45); 8 Baiting The Line (2:47); 9 My Beautiful Anna... (conda)(2:54); 10 The Totem's Sacred Ground (2:27); 11 Sarone's Last Stand (3:00).

Review: Randy Edelman was supposed to write a score at least partially integrating Brazilian jungle music for this sleeper hit, but what ended up in the finished product sounded an awful lot like the typical Edelman soundtrack — that distinct combination of synthesizers and orchestra with a strong percussive sound. In Louis Llosa's film, Edelman's music is all over the action, often undermining the suspense and tension of the situations at hand. As a soundtrack album, the score is much easier to digest, with the composer's penchant for composing easily accessible melodic ideas on full display. Given Edelman's musical capabilities, *Anaconda,* then, is not the great, interesting ethnic score it might have been, but it's still a step up from the traditionally cliched horror soundtrack.

Andy Dursin

Anastasia 🎵🎵🎵🎵

1993, Varese-Sarabande; from the movie *Anastasia,* **20th Century-Fox, 1956.**

Album Notes: *Music:* Alfred Newman; The 20th Century-Fox Studio Orchestra, conducted by Alfred Newman; *Choral Director:* Ken Darby; *CD Producer:* George Korngold; *Engineer:* Len Engel.

Selections: 1 Fox Fanfare: Anastasia/Paris/Russian Easter (5:27); 2 Valese (3:51); 3 Self-Destruction (2:43); 4 Who Am I/ The Troika (2:12); 5 The Beginning (1:53); 6 The Tivoli/The Sleeping Princess (3:32); 7 Anastasia Waltz (4:11); 8 The Meeting (3:39); 9 The Wildfeuer Polka (2:04); 10 Recognition (2:54);

11 Riberhaus Marsch/Marche de bataille (2:23); 12 Frustration (2:31); 13 End Title/Anastasia (2:13); 14 Anastasia (1:41) *Alfred Newman.*

Review: Typical of Alfred Newman, the music for this passionate drama about a destitute woman who may be the sole heir to the Romanoff throne and fortune, spearheaded by the familiar main theme, teems with broadly romantic and expansive themes. The various European settings of the action suggested to the composer a series of colorful images that evoke these locales ("Paris," "Russian Easter," "The Tivoli"); but it is in the underscoring to some of the film's more powerful scenes that Newman let his lyricism take over, delivering cues that match in intensity Anna's search for her own identity and recognition from those around her ("Who Am I," "The Meeting," "Recognition"). Adding a different color to the Oscar-nominated score, some brilliant setpieces ("Valse," "Anastasia Waltz," "Marche de bataille") reveal yet another side to Newman's creativity and composing genius. As a bonus, a previously unreleased track finds the composer playing the main theme on the piano.

Anatomy of a Murder 🎵🎵🎵🎵🎵

1987, Rykodisc; from the movie *Anatomy of a Murder,* **1959.**

Album Notes: *Music:* Edward Kennedy "Duke" Ellington; The Duke Ellington Orchestra, conducted by Duke Ellington; *Featured Soloists:* Clark Terry, Cat Anderson, Shorty Baker, Ray Nance (trumpet), Paul Gonsalves, Jimmy Hamilton, Russell Procope, Johnny Hodges, Harry Carney (saxophone); *Album Producer:* Duke Ellington.

Selections: 1 Main Title/Anatomy of a Murder (3:53); 2 Flirtbird (2:11); 3 Way Early Subtone (3:59); 4 Hero To Zero (2:12); 5 Low Key Lightly (3:38); 6 Happy Anatomy (2:29); 7 Midnight Indigo (2:42); 8 Almost Cried (2:26); 9 Sunswept Sunday (1:53); 10 Grace Valse (2:30); 11 Happy Anatomy (1:27); 12 Haupe (2:38); 13 Upper And Outest (2:22).

Review: During his lifetime, Duke Ellington wrote for almost every possible media, including the stage and the screen. Even though his forays in the latter were somewhat limited, he left two outstanding film scores, *Paris Blues,* which has yet to be reissued on compact disc, and *Anatomy of a Murder,* written for a film directed by Otto Preminger. A gripping murder mystery, involving an Army officer, his wife, and the tenacious lawyer who defends them, the film called for a score with contemporary overtones that would give the action a solid musical support, yet would also achieve a life of its own. Ellington delivered just the right thing — setpieces that add a necessary dramatic flair to the action, but that can also provide great listening pleasure. With many long-time members of his band taking solo turns, the soundtrack album is a great, festive Ellington party, sometimes gently low-keyed, sometimes brilliantly effervescent.

And the Band Played On
♪♪♪♪

1993, Varese-Sarabande; from the movie *And the Band Played On*, HBO Pictures, 1993.

Album Notes: *Music*: Carter Burwell; *Orchestrations*: Carter Burwell; *Music Editor*: Adam Smalley; Orchestra conducted by Carter Burwell; *Featured Musician*: John Moses (clarinet); *Album Producer*: Carter Burwell; *Engineer*: Gary Chester.

Selections: 1 Africa (2:17); 2 Burning Bodies (1:34); 3 Dead Doctors (:50); 4 The Party's Over (1:06); 5 Lymph (2:22); 6 Three Sixes (2:01); 7 They're Scared (:51); 8 The French Fail (1:00); 9 His Other Life (1:41); 10 One Of Your Donors (3:02); 11 The French Succeed (3:30); 12 How Long To Sink In (2:00); 13 Tell That To Gallo (1:30); 14 Gallo Press Conference (1:45); 15 Rain (1:28); 16 Krause Collapses (1:41); 17 Blood Meeting (1:12); 18 He's Gone Too Far (2:08); 19 Tongues (4:22); 20 Sexual Transmission (:37); 21 Paris Meeting (:55); 22 And The Band Played On (4:34).

Review: This is a dark and brooding effort by Carter Burwell which deftly captures the pathos of the incipient advance of one of the most terrible diseases of our time. The film recounts the story of how early detection and investigation into AIDS is hindered not only by a clash of egos within the medical community, but a serious lack of general concern (especially since the affliction was initially thought to be restricted only to homosexuals). Burwell's music, perhaps one of his most inspired mainstream efforts, best personifies the advance of the disorder with slow string and woeful brass motifs, connecting with discomforting clarity the image of souls slowly wasting away from the effects. He counterpoints with a a demented waltz motif, played by plucking the string instruments, representing scientists as they dance around each other. Surely anyone who has grieved for the loss of a loved one can connect with the bleak atmosphere Burwell conjures up.

David Hirsch

Andre ♪♪♪♭

1994, Milan Records; from the movie *Andre*, Paramount Pictures, 1994.

Album Notes: *Music*: Bruce Rowland; *Arrangements*: Bruce Rowland; The Victorian Philharmonic Orchestra, conducted by

Bruce Rowland; *Album Producers*: Bruce Rowland, Spencer Proffer; *Engineer*: Robin Gray.

Selections: 1 Sea Ballet (Opening Montage)(2:47); 2 An Orphan Pup (2:01); 3 Toni Meets Andre (2:40); 4 Let's Call Him Andre (2:17); 5 Andre's First Swim (1:09); 6 The Coat Button/Thanks To You (2:33); 7 Winter In The Barn (2:12); 8 The Storm (6:19); 9 Off To The Aquarium (1:41); 10 T.N.T. (1:19); 11 Halloween (1:13); 12 Let Nature Take Its Course (1:37); 13 Robinson's Rock (2:18); 14 Butterflies Are Free (:54); 15 Back To The Wild (1:08); 16 "16, Dad, 16" (1:24); 17 Frogman Dad (:22); 18 How Can I Make It Up To You? (1:22); 19 An Attempt On Andre's Life (1:25); 20 He's On His Way (2:40); 21 Welcome Home (:53); 22 Thanks To You (3:20).

Review: For this *Free Willy*-clone, about the friendship between a young girl and a seal, Bruce Rowland plays the sentimental chords with cues that tug at all the right heart strings. But this highly charged score is also chockful of delightful little moments that make it much more important and interesting than it would appear to be in the first place. At its most inspired, string instruments (harp, guitar) and wind instruments combine to create an amalgam of vivid little vignettes that are endearing and quite attractive. At other times, a lovely piano melody is strikingly set off by a lute or a harp to evoke images that may work very well within the context of the screen action but that also have a magic of their own as music. Many of the tracks, however, could have taken a longer exposition, and while several manage to grab one's attention, only the six minute-plus "The Storm" succeeds in creating a strong momentum.

Angel ♪♪

1993, Intrada Records; from the movie *Angel*, New World Pictures, 1993.

Album Notes: *Music*: Craig Safan; *Orchestrations*: Craig Safan; Orchestra conducted by Craig Safan; *Album Producer*: Craig Safan; *Engineer*: Dennis Sands.

Selections: 1 Angel (2:45); 2 Hollywood Boulevard (3:31); 3 He Kills (3:11); 4 Drag Fight (3:50); 5 Yo-Yo Man (1:29); 6 Killer's Haircut (1:48); 7 Reflecting Angel (2:07); 8 Back On The Street (4:00); 9 Angel's Triump (6:09); 10 Honor Student (3:54).

Review: This modest little score by Craig Safan is, regretfully, very much like the film in that it really should have been more fun than it turned out to be. Despite some pleasant themes ("Angel," "Yo-Yo Man"), the bulk of the score comes across as a surprisingly uninspired effort when compared to his other work, like the sensational *The Last Starfighter,* for example. The orchestra is dressed with some tired, standard electronic overlays that inspire very little as musical entertainment. This film score most likely suffers because Safan admittedly was only given a week in which to compose it. That's a ridiculously short period of time. *Angel* is certainly not a poor album, but Safan deserves to be judged by other works that better reflect his talents.

David Hirsch

Angels in the Outfield ♪♪♪♪

1994, Hollywood Records; from the movie *Angels in the Outfield*, Walt Disney Pictures, 1994.

Album Notes: *Music*: Randy Edelman; *Orchestrations*: Ralph Ferraro; *Music Editor*: Joanie Diener; Orchestra conducted by Randy Edelman; *Album Producer*: Randy Edelman; *Engineers*: Elton Ahi, Dennis Sands.

Selections: 1 Opening (2:42); 2 The Wave (2:36); 3 Torn Apart (2:23); 4 Skyburst (2:20); 5 Rock And Roll Angels (1:18); 6 Nighttime (2:05); 7 Al Pops Up (1:31); 8 A Warm Conversation (1:55); 9 Sandlot Shuffle (2:40); 10 Press Conference (2:19); 11 A Place For Mel (1:59); 12 Magical Moments (1:56); 13 Man Of The Hour (3:52); 14 Black Clouds (2:14); 15 Finale (1:55).

Review: The opening of this score recalls the stately grace of Edelman's magnificent score for *Gettysburg*, recorded the previous year; at least until a pop beat is added. The beat gives the score a catchy, up-tempo feel, associated with the contemporary milieu and the kids around whom the story revolves, while the initial theme returns to capture the mysterious glory of the angelic sportsmen who offer invisible aid to a failing baseball team. Between the two styles of music is an engaging score. It's mostly lighthearted and breezy, but with enough passion to make it genuinely moving in spots. Edelman's theme for the angels becomes just as much a theme for the boy who can see them, whose story becomes the focus of the picture.

Another baseball fantasy with angelic overtones, *Angels In The Outfield* must have particularly inspired Randy Edelman. His score is wonderfully whimsical ("Al Pops Up"), exhilaratingly melodic ("Magical Moments"), and just plain beautiful. The themes, lightly sketched but attractive, convey the moods in the film, from the despair felt by the players whose team has not had a win in many moons in "Torn Apart" to the sudden arrival of saviours from above in "Rock and Roll Angels," and on to the final inning. It helps, of course, that this is a Disney film, and that the players get some encouragement from two kids who truly believe in their eventual victory, but Edelman knows how to write melodic material that sticks in the ear and demonstrates it effortlessly in this totally engaging score.

Randall Larson/Didier C. Deutsch

Angie ♪♪

1994, Varese-Sarabande Records; from the movie *Angie*, Hollywood Pictures, 1994.

Album Notes: *Music*: Jerry Goldsmith; *Orchestrations*: Arthur Morton; *Music Editor*: Ken Hall; Orchestra conducted by Jerry Goldsmith; *Album Producer*: Jerry Goldsmith; *Engineer*: Bruce Botnick.

Selections: 1 Angie's Theme (3:32); 2 Shopping (1:21); 3 Family Life (1:20); 4 The Museum (2:32); 5 Two Bells (2:34); 6 Thais (J. Massenet) (4:21); 7 We're Having A Baby (1:07); 8 The Prognosis (3:28); 9 The Journey Begins (2:27); 10 Something Better (3:52); 11 It Ain't Easy (3:02); 12 He's Alive (3:07); 13 Angie's Theme (reprise) (1:22).

Review: Jerry Goldsmith's status as a legendary film composer just about guarantees that any film he scores will have a soundtrack album released. Case in point: this slight effort for the Geena Davis "dramedy" *Angie*, which Goldsmith scored with a low-key, subtly pop-influenced approach that's like a very subdued version of some of his tender dramatic scores of the '60s like *Patch of Blue* and *The Trouble with Angels*. Unfortunately audience intolerance for the kind of rhythmic and orchestrational development Goldsmith brought to his '60s scores makes *Angie* so subtle you'll barely notice you're listening to it. It's pleasant but rarely interesting, with one traveling cue that's similar to chase material from Goldsmith's *Basic Instinct* and a piece of classical source music that eats up a large chunk of this album's brief running time.

Jeff Bond

Animal House ♪♪

1978, MCA Records; from the movie *National Lampoon's Animal House*, Universal Pictures, 1978.

Album Notes: *Music*: Elmer Bernstein; Orchestra conducted by Elmer Bernstein; *Album Producers*: Kenny Vance, Mark Davis; *Engineers*: Joe Feria, Mike Moran, Jim Reeves.

Selections: 1 Faber College Theme (E. Bernstein) (:24); 2 Louie, Louie (R. Berry) (2:55) *John Belushi*; 3 Twistin' The Night Away (S. Cooke) (2:38) *Sam Cooke*; 4 Tossin' And Turnin' (R. Adams/M. Rene) (2:15) *Bobby Lewis*; 5 Shama Lama Ding Dong (M. Davis) (2:55) *Lloyd Williams*; 6 Hey Paula (R. Hildebrand) (2:37) *Paul & Paula*; 7 Animal House (S. Bishop) (4:05) *Stephen Bishop*; 8 Intro (E. Bernstein) (:48); 9 Money (That's What I Want) (2:28) *John Belushi*; 10 Let's Dance (J. Lee) (2:15) *Chris Montez*; 11 Dream Girl (S. Bishop) (4:39) *Stephen Bishop*; 12 (What) A Wonderful World (S. Cooke/H. Alpert/L. Adler) (2:06)

Sam Cooke; 13 Shout (R. Isley/R. Isley/O. Isley)(4:23) *Lloyd Williams*; 14 Faber College Theme (E. Bernstein)(1:55).

Review: At a time when most Hollywood composers were looking for an instrumental gig anywhere, this film and its soundtrack album gave veteran Elmer Bernstein a reputation as the best man in town to score comedies in the *Saturday Night Live* vein. Unfortunately the album shortchanges the composer, sadly represented by only a couple of tracks, the "Faber College Theme" used at the top of the set and again as the closing number, and the "Intro" strangely positioned somewhere in the middle. However, that theme captures the zany moods of the film starring John Belushi better than the many vocal selections assembled here, with the possible exception of Belushi singing "Louie, Louie," which also qualifies as a genuine film track.

Another Dawn ✍✍✍✍

1996, Marco Polo; from the movie *Another Dawn*, Warner Bros., 1937.

Album Notes: *Music*: Erich-Wolfgang Korngold; *Orchestrations*: John Morgan; The Moscow Symphony Orchestra, conducted by William T. Stromberg; *Engineers*: Edvard Shakhnazarian, Vitaly Ivanov.

Selections: 1 Escape Me Never (ballet fantasy)(7:41); 2 Main Title/The Outpost (3:45); 3 On The Ocean Liner (3:36); 4 The Golf Course (1:36); 5 Evening Scene (2:29); 6 Afternoon Tea (1:33); 7 The Cable (2:24); 8 The Arrival/The Meeting (2:47); 9 Talk In The Bedroom (2:00); 10 The Ride-Out (3:19); 11 The Stars (1:35); 12 The Arabian Love Song (2:50); 13 The Cricket Game/The Bow Tie (1:02); 14 Garden Love Scene (3:24); 15 The Ride-Out (continued)(:50); 16 The Desert/The Battle/Radio Station (4:39); 17 The Battlefield (2:42); 18 The Sandstorm Starts (2:23); 19 The Kiss (2:23); 20 The Next Morning/The Order (4:38); 21 Another Dawn Finale (3:43).

Review: Known more for his "swashbuckler" scores, this CD showcases the tender side of Erich Wolfgang Korngold with the score to yet another Errol Flynn film, the 1937 soap opera *Another Dawn*. There's plenty of action, to be sure, but the film was intended to be a romantic endeavor for its two stars. Efforts by the producers to save the poorly plotted film resulted in some heavy editing of Korngold's score, but John Morgan has wisely chosen to go back and lovingly reconstruct what Korngold originally wrote, including the initial finale, changed when an alternate ending was used so that Flynn's character would survive. Another unusual selection, the "Ballet/Fantasy" from *Escape Me Never*, leads off the album.

David Hirsch

Another 48 Hrs. ✍

1990, Scotti Bros.; from the movie *Another 48 Hrs.*, Paramount Pictures, 1990

Album Notes: *Music*: James Horner.

Selections: 1 (The Boys Are) Back In Town (B. O'Neal)(4:02) *Jesse Johnson*; 2 Give It All You Got (M. Williams)(4:38) *Curio*; 3 I Just Can't Let It End (L. Dozier)(3:52) *Curio*; 4 I've Got My Eye On You (L. Dozier) (3:42) *Curio*; 5 The Courthouse (3:18); 6 Main Title From "Another 48 Hrs." (4:12); 7 King Mei Shootout (7:36); 8 Birdcage Battle (4:44); 9 I'll Never Get You Out Of This World Alive (H. Williams/F. Rose)(2:24) *Michael Stanton*.

Review: Listeners may want to dispense with the vocal selections that are totally interchangeable (In addition to getting strictly one-dimensional performances by Curio, "Give It All You Got," "I Just Can't Let It End" and "I've Got My Eye on You" evidence the same one-two rhythmic beat and trite lyrics.) and concentrate instead on the four instrumental cues composed and conducted by James Horner, but chances are you will also be disappointed. Writing in a contemporary vein, the composer relies on synth accents to play off a wailing clarinet that at times evokes Kenny G, with pulse-pounding effects to suggest that this is an action film. It may be quite effective behind the scenes, but taken on its own musical terms, it is ultimately less than endearing.

Anthony Adverse ✍✍✍✍

1991, Varese-Sarabande, from the movie *Anthony Adverse*, Warner Bros., 1936.

Album Notes: *Music*: Erich-Wolfgang Korngold; The Berlin Radio Symphony Orchestra, conducted by John Scott; *Album Producer*: George Korngold; *Engineer*: Hansjorg Saladin; *Assistant Engineer*: Oliver Reinhardt.

Selections: 1 The Lovers (11:01); 2 Anthony Is Born (10:30); 3 Casa Da Bonnyfeather (8:38); 4 Anthony and Angela (7:47); 5 From Leghorn To Cuba (7:09); 6 Adventures In Africa (11:18); 7 Anthony Returns To Europe (16:44).

Review: In comparison to his most flamboyant efforts (*The Adventures of Robin Hood* and *Sea Hawk*, for instance), the music Korngold wrote for this screen adaptation of the Harvey Allen bestseller sounds more pleasant than epic. But his lyricism is present everywhere in these seven long suites that regroup together all the principal themes and settings heard in the film as shorter cues. Though the script provided plenty of action scenes and unexpected developments in this romantic tale set during the Napoleonic era, the composer seemed to have been primarily attracted to the challenge presented by the varying moods in the main characters, and set out to write

Antony and Cleopatra

"Even as a child, I found myself paying attention to the music in movies. I didn't really have an interest in doing it; I was really terrified of it."

James Newton Howard
on film composing (The Hollywood Reporter, 1-16-96)

what is essentially an operatic score without the words. As a result, the leitmotifs that recur throughout may not have the immediacy and vibrancy of pure action cues, but the thematic material unfolds in breathtaking fashion to create a score that has great impact and strength.

Possibly also as a result, The Berlin Radio Symphony Orchestra, conducted by John Scott, does not display the flashy style exhibited by the Utah Symphony in both *Robin Hood* and *Sea Hawk* for the same label. The production values, though, are still first-rate.

Antony and Cleopatra ♪♪♪♪

1992, JOS Records; from the movie *Antony and Cleopatra*, Rank Films, 1972.

Album Notes: *Music*: John Scott; *Music Editor*: John Strother; The Berlin Radio Symphony Orchestra and Choir conducted by John Scott; *Album Producer*: John Scott; *Engineer*: Robert Vosgien.

Selections: 1 Overture (9:17); 2 Main Titles (3:36); 3 Undying Love (3:38); 4 Give Me To Drink Mandragora (2:02); 5 Pompey (1:58); 6 Cleopatra Deserted (1:38); 7 Rome And Octavia (1:47); 8 The Barge She Sat In (4:19); 9 Battle Of Actium (6:16); 10 Anthony's Army Deserts (1:44); 11 Whither Hast Thou Led Me Egypt (2:26); 12 Death Of Enobarbus (2:05); 13 One Last Night Of Love (3:02); 14 He Goes Forth Gallantly (3:52); 15 Sometimes We See A Cloud That's Dragonish (2:42); 16 Death Of Antony (3:57); 17 Pretty Worm Of Nilus (1:50); 18 Epilogue: Eternal Rest (2:10).

Review: This 1972 filmed adaptation of Shakespeare's play (not to be confused with another 1963 extravaganza with a somewhat similar title) was directed by and starred Charlton Heston in one of his most felicitous screen portrayals as Antony, opposite Hildegard Neil as Cleopatra. Deftly using the

medium's wide possibilities, Heston opened up the stage play and beefed it up with often impressive panoramic battle scenes shot on location in Spain. Matching his vision almost frame for frame, John Scott provides a score that shares its best moments between sweeping romantic themes ("Undying Love," "One Last Night Of Love") and throbbing action cues ("Battle of Actium"). The Berlin Radio Symphony Orchestra, conducted by the composer, plays it with all the fire and passion necessary, making this CD a highly desirable addition to any collection, though, like the hard-to-get film, you probably will have to do some digging to find it.

Apocalypse Now ♪♪

1979, Elektra Records; from the movie *Apocalypse Now*, United Artists, 1979.

Album Notes: *Music*: Carmine Coppola, Francis Coppola; *Album Producer*: David Rubinson.

Selections: CD 1: 1 The End (The Doors)(4:15) *The Doors*; 2 Saigon (narration and dialogue)(1:38); 3 The End, Part 2 (1:37) *The Doors*; 4 Terminate (narration and dialogue)(5:44); 5 The Delta (2:38); 6 P.B.R. (narration and dialogue)(2:02); 7 Dossier #1 (1:51); 8 Colonel Kilgore (narration and dialogue)(5:43); 9 Orange Light (2:15); 10 The Ride Of The Valkyries (R. Wagner)(2:00) *The Vienna Philharmonic, Sir Georg Solti*; 11 Napalm In The Morning (dialogue)(:55); 12 Pre-Tiger (4:50); 13 Dossier #2 (3:30); 14 Susie Q (D. Hawkins/S. Lewis/E. Broadwater)(4:26); 15 Dossier #3 (3:09); 16 75 Klicks (dialogue)(1:09); 17 The Nung River (3:10).

CD 2: 1 Do Lung Bridge (9:37); 2 Letters From Home (2:39); 3 Clean's Death (3:10); 4 Chief's Death/Strange Voyage (6:47); 5 Strange Voyage (4:16); 6 Kurtz' Compound (dialogue)(2:18); 7 Willard's Capture (1:18); 8 Errand Boy (dialogue)(2:04); 9 Chef's Head (2:04); 10 The Hollow Men (T.S. Eliot) (1:09); 11 Horror (dialogue)(5:42) 12 Even The Jungle Wanted Him Dead (dialogue)(1:01); 13 The End (3:14) *The Doors*.

Review: This is really a two-disc, abridged, audio presentation of the film that mixes music and dialogue. When it was first released in 1979, it may have been something unique, but today it has become something of a relic. After all, since you can now buy the film on video for less money and with better sound, why not just watch it? The set pretty much covers all the best sequences and features The Doors title track. As with most albums of this kind, the dialogue is mixed much lower than the music, creating a jarring parade of sound levels.

David Hirsch

Apollo 13 ♫♫♫

1995, MCA Records; from the movie *Apollo 13*, **Universal Pictures, 1995.**

Album Notes: *Music*: James Horner; *Orchestrations*: James Horner, Steve Bramson; *Music Editor*: Tom Drescher; *Featured Artists*: Annie Lenox (vocals), Tim Morrison (trumpet solos); Orchestra conducted by James Horner; *Album Producer*: James Horner; *Engineer*: Shawn Murphy; *Assistant Engineers*: Dave Marquette, Jay Selvester, Andy Bass.

Selections: 1 Main Title/One Small Step (2:29), dialogue spoken by Walter Cronkite, Neil Armstrong; 2 Night Train (J. Forrest/ L. Simpkins/ O. Washington)(3:27) *James Brown*; 3 Groovin' (F. Cavaliere/E. Brigati) (2:26) *The Young Rascals*; 4 Somebody To Love (G. Slick)(2:55) *Jefferson Airplane*; 5 I Can See For Miles (P. Townshend)(4:09) *The Who*; 6 Purple Haze (J. Hendrix)/Launch Control(2:46) *Jimi Hendrix*; 7 All Systems Go/The Launch/ Welcome To Apollo 13 (10:04), dialogue spoken by Tom Hanks; 8 Spirit In The Sky (N. Greenbaum)/House Cleaning/Houston, We Have A Problem (3:50), dialogue spoken by Kevin Bacon, Tom Hanks, Gary Sinise, and Brett Cullen, *Norman Greenbaum*; 9 Master Alarm/What's Going On? (3:36), dialogue spoken by Tom Hanks and Gary Sinise; 10 Into The Lem/Out Of Time (4:18), dialogue spoken by Tom Hanks, Ed Harris and Kevin Bacon; 11 Darkside Of The Moon/Failure Is Not An Option (4:49), dialogue spoken by Ed Harris; 12 Honky Tonkin' (H. Williams) (2:42) *Hank Williams*; 13 Blue Moon (R. Rodgers/L. Hart)/Waiting For Disaster/A Privilege (4:01), dialogue spoken by Ed Harris and Gary Sinise/dialogue spoken by Tom Hanks, *The Mavericks*; 14 Re-Entry And Splashdown (8:53); 15 End Titles (6:59).

Review: One of James Horner's most effective works is marred by a hodgepodge album presentation that, for all intents and purposes, is nothing more than an audio dramatization of the film. Eight pop songs of the period, dialogue sequences and sound effects weave in and out of the score. One might as well just watch the film on home video for all the enjoyment it gives. The fact that portions of the music are obviously lifted verbatim from Horner's own score for *Sneakers* doesn't help either. Add a rating point if none of this matters to you. The soundtrack album is also available in a Dolby Surround 24k gold CD with additional dialogue.

David Hirsch

Arabian Knight ♫♫♫

1995, Milan Records; from the animated feature *Arabian Knight*, **Miramax Films, 1995.**

Album Notes: *Music*: Robert Folk; *Orchestrations*: Robert Folk, Peter Tomashek, John Kull, Randy Miller; *Music Editor*: Doug Lackey; The London Symphony Orchestra, conducted by Robert Folk; *Songs*: Norman Gimbel, Robert Folk; *Album Producer*: David Franco; *Engineer*: Eric Tomlinson.

Selections: 1 Am I Feeling Love? (2:12) *Bobby Page, Steve Lively*; 2 Opening Title (2:29); 3 Tack And Thief (2:18); 4 Polo Game (1:46); 5 She Is More (2:28) *Bobby Page*; 6 The Courtroom (4:09); 7 The Brigands (2:21); 8 Pole Vault (2:44); 9 Club Sahara (2:50); 10 So Incredible (3:29); 11 Bom, Bom, Bom, Beem, Bom (2:18) *The Beem Bom Singers*; 12 Thief Gets The Ball (2:59); 13 One Eyes Advance (2:06); 14 It's So Amazing (3:25) *Andrea Robinson, Arnold McCuller*; 15 Climactic End (2:12); 16 Witch Riddle (1:22); 17 Thief After The Balls (3:09).

Review: Not to be confused with Disney's *Aladdin*, Robert Folk's large orchestral music for *Arabian Knight* makes for an exciting soundtrack album whose style is reminiscent of a typical James Horner fantasy score (think *Willow* or *Krull*). The film, originally titled *The Thief and the Cobbler* and released on video under that name, was an ambitious effort from Oscar-winning animator Richard Williams that sat on the shelf for nearly two decades before it was taken out of his hands and completed by other filmmakers. Some of the new elements added to the director's original vision include songs written by Folk and lyricist Norman Gimbel in a pseudo-Alan Menken style, but what should be of interest to most listeners ought to be the score, which is derivative but entertaining, marked by lush themes performed to perfection by the London Symphony Orchestra. It has fun toiling around in the vein of Korngold and Williams, and sounds just as much of a homage to those sources as the Aladdin-"inspired" songs appear modeled right after their superior Disney counterparts.

Andy Dursin

Arachnophobia ♫♫♫

1990, Hollywood Records; from the movie *Arachnophobia*, **Hollywood Pictures, 1990.**

Album Notes: *Music*: Trevor Jones; *Orchestrations*: Lawrence Ashmore, Shirley Walker, Guy Dagul; *Music Editor*: Thomas A. Carlson; Orchestra conducted by Shirley Walker; *Featured Soloists*: Michael Boddicker (synthesizers), Phil Todd (wind synthesizers), Tom Scott (saxophone), Tommy Morgan (harmonica), Mike Lang (piano); *Song Producers*: Gred Ladanyi, Ray Bardani, Brent Hutchins, Julian Raymond, Steve Jones, John Boylan, Elliott Scheiner, Michael Utley; *Engineers*: Frank Roszak, Ray Bardani, Carmen Rizzo, Gary Platt, Tom Fletcher, Joe Borja, Paul Grupp, Elliot Scheiner; *Producer*: Trevor Jones; *Engineer*: John Richards.

Selections: 1 Blue Eyes Are Sensitive To The Light (B. Steinberg/T. Kelly/Martika)(5:11) *Sara Hickman*; 2 Atherton's Terrarium (:21); 3 Arachnophobia (B. Hutchins)(4:53) *Brent Hutchins*; 4 Miller's Demise (:37); 5 Spiders And Snakes (J. Stafford/D. Bellamy)(3:40) *The Party*; 6 Offspring (:51); 7 Boris The Spider (J. Entwistle)(2:59) *Pleasure Thieves*; 8 Delbert Squishes The Spider (:49); 9 The Spider And The Fly (M. Jagger/K. Richards) (2:52) *The Poorboys*; 10 Web Photo (:26); 11 Caught In Your Web (Swear To Your Heart)(D. Warren)(4:28) *Russell Hitchcock*; 12 Main Title (5:36); 13 Don't Bug Me (J. Buffett/M. Utley/J. Oliver)(3:27) *Jimmy Buffett*; 14 The Casket Arrives (1:55); 15 Delbert's Theme (2:04); 16 Canaima Nightmare (6:21); 17 Along Came A Spider (2:37); 18 Cellar Theme (1:20); 19 End Title (3:54); 20 I Left My Heart In San Francisco (G.C. Cory, Jr./D. Cross)(3:02) *Tony Bennett*.

Review: A quirky combination of often goofy songs and a fun score by Trevor Jones comprise this soundtrack album for one of 1990s surprise box-office hits. With the album's running time split virtually halfway between Jones' music and the pop songs, there ought to be something here for every listener. Sara Hickman's catchy "Blue Eyes are Sensitive to the Light" and Jimmy Buffett's silly "Don't Bug Me" are indicative of the tongue-in-cheek tone of the songs, which also include forgettable rock tracks by Brent Hutchins, The Party, Pleasure Thieves and The Poorboys, along with an alternate version of Russell Hitchcock's ballad "Swear to Your Heart" called "Caught in Your Web." Jones' music fares better, with a terrific main title theme supporting itself quite well through a number of theme and variations. Purists may object to the inclusion of dialogue on some tracks (a hard-to-find German import of the soundtrack features more score, less songs, and no dialogue by comparison), but given the tone of this album, they seem to fit right in.

Andy Dursin

Around the World in 80 Days 🎵🎵🎵🎵

1989, MCA Records; from the movie *Around the World in 80 Days*, Universal Pictures, 1956.

Album Notes: *Music*: Victor Young; The Universal-International Orchestra, conducted by Victor Young.

Selections: 1 Around The World, Part 1 (3:01); 2 Passepartout (3:21); 3 Paris Arrival (2:47); 4 Sky Symphony (4:30); 5 (a) Invitation To A Bull Fight, (b) Entrance Of The Bull March (2:34); 6 India Country Side (3:53); 7 Around The World, Part 2 (4:00); 8 The Pagoda Of Pillagi (4:00); 9 Temple Of Dawn (2:15); 10 Prairie Sail Car (1:47); 11 Land Ho (6:56); 12 Epilogue (6:22).

Review: At a time when big screen all-star superproductions were still something relatively new, Michael Todd's treatment of Jules Verne's *Around the World in 80 Days* was as big as they came. Wasting little time for character studies, it relies on a breathless pace to recount in three hours the many adventures of round-the-world travellers Phineas Fogg (David Niven) and his astute manservant Passepartout (Cantinflas), from their English homebase to such exotic locales as Spain, India, Japan, and America. Along the way, they encounter and match wits with a literal who's who of 1950s filmdom, including John Carradine, Frank Sinatra, Marlene Dietrich, George Raft, Red Skelton, Charles Boyer, Noel Coward, Buster Keaton, Peter Lorre, Cesar Romero, and, as a lovely Indian princess they rescue from a funeral pyre, Shirley MacLaine.

Superbly filmed using the Todd-AO Process, the film also benefits from a sensational Academy Award-winning score composed by Victor Young, spearheaded by the evocative "Main Title," a tune that has since become a particular favorite. While the soundtrack album only contains about 45 minutes from that score, the selections cover enough to provide a fair sampling of Young's contribution, including such memorable cues as "Passepartout," the jaunty "Paris Arrival," the Spanish-flavored "Invitation to a Bull Fight" and "Entrance of the Bull March," the exotic "India Country Side" and "The Pagoda of Pillagi," and the western-inspired "Prairie Sail Car."

On a purely technical basis, the CD was evidently mastered using the original 1958 two-track stereo tapes, and its overall sound quality no longer meets the stringent requirements of the digital era. The recording evidences a somewhat brittle sound, some distortion, and a lot of noticeable hiss on the tracks. This is one clear instance when an important score deserves to be completely redone from the multi-track session tapes.

The Arrival 🎵🎵🎵

1996, Silva Screen; from the movie *The Arrival*, Orion Pictures, 1996.

Album Notes: *Music*: Arthur Kempel; *Music Editor*: Chris Ledesma; The Northwest Sinfonia, conducted by Arthur Kempel; *Album Producers*: Arthur Kempel, Ford A. Thaxton; *Engineer*: Rick Winquest.

Selections: 1 Main Title (2:34); 2 Day Of The Dead (2:13); 3 The Elevator (2:52); 4 The Clone (1:41); 5 Mexico (2:14); 6 Satellite

Man (1:32); 7 Planting The Imploder (2:10); 8 Perhaps They're Talking? (2:25); 9 Zane Sneaks In (2:32); 10 Gordian's Arrival (3:55); 11 Stranger Than You Can Imagine (:40); 12 The Conspiracy (2:33); 13 The Underground World (4:06); 14 Finale (5:06); 15 The Arrival (2:34).

Review: Atypical sci-fi action score makes good use of synthesized effects to create an air of unease as radio astronomer Charlie Sheen investigates alien infestation. To further suggest the gulf between the invaders' covert operation and humanity's ignorance, composer Arthur Kempel paints each world with distinct musical colors, juxtaposing the idyllic "New Age" sounds of Sheen's lackadaisical life against the back street percussion of a hostile south of the border town.

David Hirsch

Arthur 2 ♫♫ᵛ

1988, A&M Records; from the movie *Arthur 2: On the Rocks*, Warner Bros, Pictures, 1988.

Album Notes: *Music*: Burt Bacharach; *Song Producers*: Burt Bacharach, Carol Bayer Sager, Stanley Clarke, Brenda Russell, Stephen Hague, Trevor Veitch, Emilio Castillo, Stock Aitken Waterman, Hal Willner, Steve Miller; *Album Executive Producers*: David Anderle, Gary LeMel; *Engineer*: Mick Guzauski.

Selections: 1 Love Is My Decision (B. Bacharach/C. Bayer Sager/C. De Burgh) (4:06) *Chris De Burgh*; 2 Gravity (B. Russell/G. Cole)(3:32) *Brenda Russell*; 3 Secret (OMD)(3:56) *Orchestral Manoeuvres in the Dark*; 4 Speed Of Light (D. Gibson)(3:49) *Reimy*; 5 Boys Night Out (E. Hall)(4:46) *Tower of Power*; 6 The Best Of Times (B. Bacharach)(4:21) *Burt Bacharach*; 7 The Loco-motion (G. Goffin/C. King)(3:13) *Kylie Minogue*; 8 Reflections (T. Monk) (6:21) *Steve Khan, Donald Fagen*; 9 Devotion (L. Story)(3:02) *Liz Story*; 10 Love Theme From Arthur (B. Bacharach)(4:46) *Burt Bacharach*.

Review: You know how the saying goes: if you liked the original, you'll love the sequel... Well, not in this case! While the soundtrack of the first *Arthur* still awaits a first release on compact disc, this sorry hodgepodge only hints at the elements that made the original so enjoyable. The pop selections, while relatively pleasant, seem more manufactured than in the first album, and even Burt Bacharach's themes ("The Best of Times," and "Love Theme") don't have the freshness that characterized his earlier contributions. The film, too, was not on the same comedic level as the original, so that might also explain why its soundtrack sounds less inspired.

Article 99 ♫♫ᵛ

1992, Varese-Sarabande Records; from the movie *Article 99*, Orion Pictures, 1992.

Album Notes: *Music*: Danny Elfman; *Orchestrations*: Steve Bartek; *Music Editor*: Bob Badami; Orchestra conducted by Shirley Walker; *Album Producer*: Danny Elfman; *Engineer*: Shawn Murphy.

Selections: 1 Main Title (4:00); 2 Death (4:23); 3 Mayday (2:47); 4 Montage (1:35); 5 Shooter (2:57); 6 Revelation (1:11); 7 Rebellion (3:10); 8 Salute (1:29); 9 Love Theme (1:00); 10 Confrontation (5:01); 11 End Credits (6:46).

Review: Danny Elfman nearly buries his traditional, dark-tinged self in an uplifting, noble musical score for an earnest but fatally flawed comedy-drama about Veterans' Administration hospital abuses by the U.S. government. Elfman's score is atypical for the composer in a number of ways, from the lack of dark, dissonant sections of music to the stable, soaring main theme, which represents the heart of the score. It's interesting to see how the composer, along with his usual collaborators (orchestrator Steve Bartek and conductor Shirley Walker), treats the music for this well-intentioned movie. The tone is inspiring, it's nice to listen to, but it all tends to evaporate right after you hear it, a fact further compounded by the scant running time and notable lack of thematic development (the love theme, for example, barely runs a minute). Best recommended for Elfman completists.

Andy Dursin

The Associate ♫♫♫♫

1997, Super Tracks; from the movie *The Associate*, Hollywood Pictures, 1997.

Album Notes: *Music*: Christopher Tyng; *Orchestrations*: Tim Simonec; *Music Editor*: Daryl Kell; The Seattle Symphony Orchestra and the Tri-City Singers Gospel Choir, conducted by Christopher Tyng; *Synths/Percussion/ Programming*: Christopher Tyng; *Featured Musician*: Michael Now (guitar); *Album Producers*: Christopher Tyng, Ford A. Thaxton; *Engineer*: Tim Boyle.

Selections: 1 Main Titles (2:39); 2 Meet Laurel And Sally (2:07); 3 The Big Whammy (1:18); 4 Creating Cutty (1:50); 5 Laurel's Woes (3:00); 6 The Glass Ceiling (1:52); 7 The "Other" Partner (2:03); 8 Sally "Meets" Cutty (1:59); 9 The New Man In The City (2:09); 10 The Look Of Cutty (1:16); 11 Laurel's Theme (2:19); 12 Aesop's Secret (1:40); 13 Frank Gets His/Laurel (3:07); 14 Plaza Chase/Sunk Cutty (2:59); 15 Laurel Has Her Day/ATI (4:27); 16 Finale (3:33).

Review: Freshman Christopher Tyng just flies in the face of modern (i.e. nondescript) film scoring to create a delightfully bright and energetic score for this Whoopi Goldberg comedy in which she plays a financial analyst facing the legendary glass ceiling. Blatantly comedic, Tyng's music is primary like that for an animated film, highlighting (a.k.a. "Mickey Mousing") each moment. Although it's nothing original, Tyng's use of gospel singers, doing everything from excerpts from "Joy to the World" to scats, keeps the energy level constantly up. You'll never know, however, where the music is going to go next, into a pleasant theme or a flurry of brass. Superb performances by both the Seattle Symphony Orchestra and the Tri-City Singers Gospel Choir.

David Hirsch

At Play in the Fields of the Lord 🎵🎵🎵

1992, Fantasy Records; from the movie *At Play in the Fields of the Lord*, 1992.

Album Notes: *Music:* Zbigniew Preisner; The Polish Radio Grand Symphony Orchestra, conducted by Antoni Wit; *Featured Soloists:* Mariusz Pedzialek (oboe), Jacek Ostaszewski (sopranino recorder); *Album Producer:* Robert Randles; *Engineers:* Zbigniew Maleki, Aleksander Dowsilas, David Luke, Tom Size, Michael Semanick, Eric Thompson, Richard Duarte.

Selections: 1 Main Title Themes (3:07); 2 Sirimbo (Pinduca)(3:50); 3 Mac de Deus (Z. Preisner/R. Randles)(:55); 4 Sem Voce Eu Nao Sou Gente (A. Lelo) (1:57); 5 Cachoeira dos Anjos (Z. Preisner/M. Miranda/R. Randles/M. Adler) (6:09) *Marlui Miranda*; 6 Paz e Amor (G. Santos)(3:40); 7 Revelations (3:02); 8 Encontro Fatal (Bezerra/Coulo)(1:50); 9 Amazon Beginnings (Z. Preisner/M. Miranda/M. Adler/R. Randles)(3:49); 10 Bringing The Light (Z. Preisner/R. Randles)(4:43); 11 Just An Echo In The Valley (Z. Preisner/R. Randles)(3:16); 12 Niaruna (Z. Preisner/R. Randles/M. Miranda) (3:17); 13 Legends (Z. Preisner/R. Randles)(3:38); 14 Andy And Moon's Theme (3:10); 15 Nao Tem Jeito Que De Jeito (R. Soldado)(2:57); 16 Times Of Tears (Z. Preisner/R. Randles) (8:54); 17 Finale (Z. Preisner/R. Randles/M. Adler/ M. Miranda)(9:40).

Review: Three composers were used to incorporate indigenous tribal music into Zbigniew Preisner's orchestral score. This mixing of diverse styles works brilliantly on film and probably would have on the CD, but unfortunately, the album fails to allow the haunting underscore to fully develop the mood it tries so very hard to create. While the score cues move effortlessly between the sustained harmonics of its orchestral themes and the powerful rhythms of the Niaruna tribe, the haphazard placement of several "Jukebox" recordings completely sabotage what could have been a mystical musical journey.

David Hirsch

Atlantic City 🎵🎵🎵

1981, DRG Records; from the movie *Atlantic City*, Paramount Pictures, 1981.

Album Notes: *Music:* Michel Legrand; Orchestra conducted by Michel Legrand.

Selections: 1 Costa Diva (from Norma)(V. Bellini)(6:45) *Elizabeth Harwood, The London Philharmonic Orchestra*; 2 Slot Machine Baby (3:37); 3 Bellini Rock (2:45); 4 Atlantic City, My Old Friend (P. Anka) (2:35) *Robert Goulet*; 5 Balcon (1:25); 6 Piano Blackjack (4:33); 7 Steel Pier (2:32); 8 Song Of India (N. Rimsky-Korsakov)(2:50); 9 Road Map For A Free Jazz Group (5:14); 10 No Gambling Allowed (1:05); 11 AC/DC (1:59); 12 Trio Jazz (5:18).

Review: Burt Lancaster portrayed a small-time mafioso in this film by Louis Malle, set in the New Jersey gambling mecca, for which Michel Legrand provides a gritty, diversified score far removed from his most recognizable screen contributions. At its liveliest and most genuinely interesting, the score offers jazz selections ("Piano Blackjack," "Road Map for a Free Jazz Group," "Trio Jazz") in which the composer plays the piano, surrounded by an assortment of uncredited sidemen (including, probably, Ron Carter on bass). On the other side of the scale, a strident "Bellini Rock" proves a real turn-off, while the meandering "No Gambling Allowed" and "Slot Machine Baby" are not sufficiently developed to really attract. Somewhere in-between, Robert Goulet is remarkably bland but okay in the Paul Anka song, "Atlantic City, My Old Friend," making this album a little bit of undefined everything for everybody.

Austin Powers 🎵🎵🎵

1997, Hollywood Records; from the movie *Austin Powers*, New Line Cinema, 1997.

Album Notes: *Music:* George S. Clinton; *Executive Soundtrack Album Producers:* Mitchell Leib, Mike Myers, Demi Moore, Suzanne Todd, Jennifer Todd.

Selections: 1 The Magic Piper (Of Love)(E. Collins)(3:51) *Edwyn Collins*; 2 BBC (M. Myers/M. Sweet/S. Hoffs/S. Johnson/C. Ward)(2:07) *Ming Tea*; 3 Incense And Peppermints (J. Carter/T. Gilbert)(2:49) *Strawberry Alarm Clock*; 4 Carnival (P. Svensson/M. Svensson/N. Persson)(3:38) *The Cardigans*; 5 Mas Que Nada (J. Ben)(2:41) *Sergio Mendes, Brasil '66*; 6 Female Of The Species (T. Scott/J. Edwards/F. Griffiths/A.

Pearle)(3:09) *Space*; 7 You Showed Me (R. McGuinn/G. Clark)(4:07) *The Lightning Seeds*; 8 Soul Bossa Nova (Q. Jones)(2:46) *Quincy Jones and His Orchestra*; 9 These Days (T. Orme/A. Miller/G. Hufflemann)(3:13) *Luxury*; 10 Austin's Theme (G.S. Clinton)(3:39) *The James Taylor Quartet*; 11 I Touch Myself (B. Steinberg/T. Kelly/C. Amphlett/M. McEntee)(3:47) *The Divinyls*; 12 Call Me (T. Hatch)(2:52) *The Mike Flowers Pops*; 13 The Look Of Love (B. Bacharach/H. David)(3:46) *Susanna Hoffs*; 14 What The World Needs Now Is Love (B. Bacharach/H. David)(3:58) *Burt Bacharach & The Posies*; 15 The Book Lovers (J. Cargill/P.A. Keenan/R.B. Stevens)(3:34) *Broadcast*; 16 Austin Powers (D. Sahanaja)(2:46) *Wondermints*; 17 The "Shag-adelic" Austin Powers Score Medley (G.S. Clinton) (4:50).

Review: The soundtrack to this amiable send-up of the spy thrillers of the 1960s will no doubt bring a smile to anyone listening to it. The film, about a nerd who imagines he is the world's greatest spy, is rife with references to that benign period when our man Flint was cool as a cucumber and even smarter and when the funniest flick of its kind was another spoof, *Casino Royale*. There is more than a passing reference to that last film, as a matter of fact, with Susanna Hoffs singing "The Book of Love" (too bad they couldn't get the actual recording by Dusty Springfield!), and composer Burt Bacharach (who scored it), contributing a new version of "What the World Needs Now" to this mildly zany album. There are also other genuinely engaging tracks, including Sergio Mendes' "Mas Que Nada," and Quincy Jones' "Soul Bossa Nova," but the palm must go to George S. Clinton's whimsical "Shag-adelic" medley, filled with amusing quotes from the James Bond and other spy films of the period. Not a great album, but quite delightful.

Avalon 🎵🎵🎵🎵

1990, Reprise Records; from the movie *Avalon*, Tri-Star Pictures, 1990.

Album Notes: *Music:* Randy Newman; *Orchestrations:* Jack Hayes; *Featured Musicians:* Stuart Canin (violin), Michael Lang (piano), Malcolm McNab (trumpet), Randy Newman (piano); *Album Producers:* James Flamberg, Frank Wolf; *Engineer:* Frank Wolf.

Selections: 1 1914 (3:42); 2 Weekend Musicians (1:35); 3 Avalon/Moving Day (2:35); 4 Jules and Michael (2:39); 5 Television, Television, Television (:46); 6 Circus (3:44); 7 Wedding (1:53); 8 The Family (5:00); 9 The Fire (3:36); 10 No More Television (:45); 11 Funeral (3:21); 12 End Titles (7:19).

Review: This delightful score by Randy Newman is tinged with melancholy. Director Barry Levinson's critically acclaimed story tells of the loss of faith felt by an immigrant as he watches his family grow up not with the values of his homeland, but those of America. Newman's music takes us along through the years of hopes and shattered dreams in a moving symphony.

David Hirsch

Awakenings 🎵🎵🎵🎵

1991, Reprise Records; from the movie *Awakenings*, Columbia Pictures, 1991.

Album Notes: *Music:* Randy Newman; *Orchestrations:* Jack Hayes; *Featured Musicians:* Dan Higgins (soprano sax), Ralph Grierson (piano), Louise Ditullio (flute); *Album Producers:* Jim Flamberg, Randy Newman; *Engineer:* Shawn Murphy.

Selections: 1 Leonard (4:32); 2 Dr. Sayer (1:40); 3 Lucy (3:11); 4 Catch (1:11); 5 Rilke's Panther (3:11); 6 L Dopa (3:10); 7 Awakenings (5:42); 8 Time Of The Season (3:14) *The Zombies*; 9 Outside (1:06); 10 Escape Attempt (:50); 11 Ward Five (3:29); 12 Dexter's Tune (2:40) *Randy Newman*; 13 The Reality Of Miracles (2:30); 14 End Title (6:01).

Review: This moving Randy Newman score captures very well the parallels in the two existences that are at the core of this film—a shy doctor who avoids dealing with his own life, and that of a former comatose patient, awakened to find he has to deal with being a middle-aged adult. Though it starts off on a very poignant note, as the two men learn from each other how to cope with their lives, the score evolves to become brighter and more optimistic. The album also includes the song "Time of the Season" by The Zombies.

David Hirsch

Babe 🎵🎵🎵

1995, Varese-Sarabande; from the movie *Babe*, Universal Pictures, 1995.

Album Notes: *Music:* Nigel Westlake; The Victorian Philhamonic Orchestra, conducted by David Stanhope, Carl Vine; *Album Producers:* George Miller, Doug Mitchell, Bill Miller; *Engineer:* Robin Gray.

Selections: 1 If I Had Words (2:50); 2 This Is A Tale... (1:48); 3 Fairground (2:05); 4 I Want My Mum (1:08); 5 The Way Things Are (2:14); 6 Crime And Punishment (1:28); 7 Anorexic Duck Pizzicati (1:24); 8 Repercussions (1:43); 9 Toreador/Mother and Son (2:28); 10 Pork Is A Nice Sweet Meat/Away In A Manger (2:47); 11 Christmas Morning (1:43); 12 Blue Moon (:37); 13 Round Up (2:04); 14 Babe's Round Up (1:39); 15 The

Sheep Pig (1:28); 16 Dog Tragedy (1:34); 17 Hoggett Shows Babe (1:00); 18 Maa's Death (1:00); 19 Cantique de Jean Racine/The Cat (2:22); 20 If I Had Words (1:52); 21 Baa Ram Ewe (:46); 22 The Gauntlet/Moment Of Truth (1:42); 23 That'll Do Pig, That'll Do (1:26).

Review: Delightful concept album that mixes music and dialogue from the hit fantasy film about a farm populated by talking animals. Though live-action, composer Nigel Westlake chose well to paint this film with a broad cartoon-like score. While most soundtrack purists find the notion detestable, the dialogue sound bites are well interpolated here with the film's underscore, which is based primarily on various classical and contemporary compositions. Most notable is the adaption of Saint-Saens *Symphony No. 3* which, with lyrics by Johnathon Hodge, became the signature tune for the film's singing mice trio. The result is just plain fun and a good way to introduce the classics to young children.

David Hirsch

The Babe ♫♫♫♪

1991, MCA Records; from the movie *The Babe*, Universal, 1991.

Album Notes: *Music:* Elmer Bernstein; *Orchestrations:* Emilie A. Bernstein; Orchestra conducted by Elmer Bernstein; *Musician:* Malcolm McNab (trumpet solos); *Album Producer:* Emilie A. Bernstein.

Selections: 1 Yankee Stadium (Main Title)(3:46); 2 Orphanage 1902-1914 (1:09); 3 Baseball & Freedom (2:16); 4 Here Come The Bostons (J. Liles) (1:13) *The Chiefs of Staff*; 5 Kids Ride (1:26); 6 Courting Helen (2:40); 7 Proposal (2:36); 8 Ruth Is Sold (:42); 9 Claire & The Dream (1:11); 10 Diga Diga Doo (D. Fields/J. McHugh)(2:28) *Orbert Davis & The Speakeasys*; 11 Baby (2:09); 12 Helen Leaves (:57); 13 N.Y. Yankees (newsreel)(:43); 14 Crying & Friends (4:27); 15 New Life, 1927 (newsreel)(:46); 16 End Of The Road (2:17); 17 End Credits (3:18); 18 The Hero (1:23).

Review: The Babe, of course, was Babe Ruth, whose picturesque life story is the basis for this screen biography starring John Goodman. An important part of the film's flair is due to Elmer Bernstein's broad score, whose more rambunctious cues echo the exuberant lifestyle of one of baseball's most colorful folk heroes. Obviously sharing director Arthur Hiller's evident fondness for the character, Bernstein wrote one of his most rewarding middle-of-the-road efforts here, drawing his inspiration from the period (the 1920s and '30s), the locales where the action unfolds, and the natural vitality in the sport itself. Among the many remarkable highlights, "Kids Ride," the in-

ventive "Proposal," "Claire and the Dream," and "Helen Leaves" strike a more felicitous note, but the whole score is unusually lively and enjoyable.

The Baby-Sitters Club ♫♫♫

1995, Sony Wonder; from the movie *The Baby-Sitters Club,* Columbia Pictures, 1995.

Album Notes: *Song Producers:* Richard Gottehrer, Jeffrey Lesser, Paul McKercher, Kevin Moloney, Jermaine Dupri, David Russo, Brad Wood, Mike Denneen, James McVay, Michael Frank, Todd Smallwood; *Album Producer:* G. Marq Roswell.

Selections: 1 Summertime (G. Salgado/E. Encarnacion/T. DePala/K. Ward Encarnacion)(2:51) *Moonpools*; 2 Say It (P. Young/D. Easton/J. Phillips/R. Whittingham)(2:11) *Clouds*; 3 Hannah, I Locked You Out (J. Faye)(3:13) *The Caulfields*; 4 Let Me Know (J. Dupri/M. Seal/M. Bell)(3:43) *Xscape*; 5 Hold On (J. Jones/D. Russo)(4:40) *Sun 60*; 6 Everything Changes (M. Sweet) (3:51) *Matthew Sweet*; 7 Don't Leave (B. Lee)(2:00) *Ben Lee*; 8 Step Back (G. McKenna/K. Hanley)(2:34) *Letters To Cleo*; 9 Daddy's Girl (L. Stark) (3:55) *Lisa Harlow Stark*; 10 Girl-Girlfriend (D. Frank/T. Smallwood/K. Krakower) (3:57).

Review: An endearing, charmingly offbeat big screen take on the familiar book and cable series by Ann M. Martin, *The Baby-Sitters Club* is the occasion for a group of seven young girls to create a pool so that someone would always be available should the sitter be otherwise engaged (usually with a boyfriend). Modest and somewhat untheatrical, the film boasts a soundtrack consisting of nicely scrubbed pop songs without a single offensive lyric (which may explain, in a way, why it was issued on Sony Wonder, Sony's kiddie label. The performances are also appropriately harmless.

Baby the Rain Must Fall/ The Caretakers ♫♫♪

1991, Mainstream Records; from the movies *Baby the Rain Must Fall,* Columbia Pictures, 1965; and *The Caretakers,* United Artists, 1963.

Album Notes: *Music:* Elmer Bernstein; *Baby The Rain Must Fall: Arrangements:* Shorty Rogers; *Album Producer:* Jackie Mills; *Engineer:* Lanky Listrot; *CD Producer:* Jackie Mills.

Selections: *BABY THE RAIN MUST FALL:* 1 Main Title (E. Bernstein/E. Sheldon) (2:36); 2 Henry's Heap (2:51); 3 Shine For Me (E. Bernstein/E. Sheldon)(2:31) *The We Three Trio*; 4 Highway #2 (Travelin' Lady)(2:44); 5 Gospel Time (2:35); 6 Pecan Grove Rock (2:45); 7 Baby The Rain Must Fall (E. Bernstein/E. Sheldon)(2:27) *The We Three Trio*; 8 Highway #1 (Wagon Wheel Watusi)(1:52); 9 Main Title (reprise)(2:42);

THE CARETAKERS: 10 Black Straight Jacket (2:03); 11 Blues For A Four String Guitar (2:37); 12 Take Care (2:00); 13 Birdito (2:19); 14 Party In The Ward (1:58); 15 Main Title (2:15); 16 The Cage (1:59); 17 Electrotherapy (2:01); 18 Day Hospital (1:39); 19 Seclusion (1:40); 20 Finale (2:14).

Review: Two early Elmer Bernstein scores, unfortunately marred by poor mastering and heavy reverb which harkens back to the 1960s. Starring Steve McQueen as a rockabilly singer who takes a walk on the wild side, *Baby the Rain Must Fall* elicited a rock-based score from Bernstein, with folk vocals by The We Three Trio that also reflect the film's time period. Shorty Rogers' explosive arrangements are a big plus.

Robert Stack and Joan Crawford share billing in *The Caretakers*, a shallow drama set in a West Coast mental institution. Belying the serious subject matter, Bernstein's score turns out to be for the most part a bouncy, jazzy affair, with only two tracks ("The Cage" and "Electrotherapy") making direct references to the film's background.

Sonically, the CD sounds very hissy, with distortion on some of the tracks, and particularly noticeable hum in *The Caretakers*.

Back to School

1986, Varese-Sarabande Records; from the movie *Back to School*, Orion Pictures, 1986.

See: Pee-Wee's Big Adventure.

Back to the Future

Back to the Future 🎵🎵🎵▽

1985, MCA Records; from the movie *Back to the Future*, Universal Pictures, 1985.

Album Notes: *Music*: Alan Silvestri; The Outatime Orchestra, conducted by Alan Silvestri; *Song Producers*: Huey Lewis & The News, Lindsey Buckingham & Richard Dashut, Phil Collins, Maxwell Davis, Bones Howe; *Album Supervisor*: Bones Howe; *Engineer*: Steve Hall.

Selections: 1 The Power Of Love (3:43) *Huey Lewis & The News*; 2 Time Bomb Town (2:45) *Lindsey Buckingham*; 3 Back To The Future (A. Silvestri) (3:17); 4 Heaven Is One Step Away (E. Clapton)(4:08) *Eric Clapton*; 5 Back In Time (4:17) *Huey Lewis & The News*; 6 Back To The Future Overture (A. Silvestri) (8:16); 7 The Wallflower (Dance With Me Henry)(E. James)(2:41) *Etta James*; 8 Night Train (J. Forrest/O. Washington/L. Simpkins)(2:15) *Marvin Berry & The Starlighters*; 9 Earth Angel (Will You Be Mine)(C. Williams)(2:59) *Marvin Berry &*

The Starlighters; 10 Johnny B. Goode (3:05) *Marty McFly & The Starlighters*.

Review: See *Back to the Future, Part III* for combined review.

Back to the Future, Part II
🎵🎵🎵

1989, MCA Records; from the movie *Back to the Future, Part II*, Universal Pictures, 1989.

Album Notes: *Music*: Alan Silvestri; *Orchestrations*: James B. Campbell; Orchestra conducted by Alan Silvestri; *Album Producer*: Alan Silvestri; *Engineer*: Dennis Sands.

Selections: 1 Main Title (2:17); 2 The Future (5:20); 3 Hoverboard Chase (2:46); 4 A Flying Delorean? (4:27); 5 My Father (2:01); 6 "Alternate 1985" (3:02); 7 If They Ever Did (3:53); 8 Pair O' Docs (1:24); 9 The Book (4:45); 10 Tunnel Chase (5:17); 11 Burn The Book (2:22); 12 Western Union (1:49); 13 End Title (4:34).

Review: See *Back to the Future, Part III* for combined review.

Back to the Future, Part III
🎵🎵🎵🎵

1990, Varese-Sarabande; from the movie *Back to the Future, Part III*, 1990.

Album Notes: *Music*: Alan Silvestri; *Orchestrations*: James B. Campbell; Orchestra conducted by Alan Silvestri; *Album Producer*: Alan Silvestri; *Engineer*: Dennis Sands.

Selections: 1 Main Title (3:05); 2 It's Clara (The Train, Part II)(4:33); 3 Hill Valley (2:20); 4 The Hanging (1:40); 5 At First Sight (3:12); 6 Indians (1:10); 7 Goodbye Clara (2:57); 8 Doc Returns (2:50); 9 Point Of No Return (The Train, Part III)(3:45); 10 The Future Isn't Written (3:35); 11 The Showdown (1:28); 12 Doc To The Rescue (:51); 13 The Kiss (1:51); 14 We're Out Of Gas (1:15); 15 Wake Up Juice (1:11); 16 A Science Experiment? (The Train, Part I)(3:05); 17 Doubleback (Z.Z. Top)(1:30); 18 End Credits (4:34).

Review: The time travel paradox format of this trilogy has allowed series composer Alan Silvestri to rework his themes in several ways. The first album is nothing more than a song compilation, though all the songs actually are heard in the film, especially during the big dance sequence. The theme is included as well as a nine minute suite of the finale credited as the "Back to the Future Overture."

The second album is all underscore, but because of the darker aspects of the film, Silvestri does tend to paint a gloomy picture by stretching things out a bit. The themes crawl along before they are resolved, and while the need exists to make the danger more severe, the comedic aspect of the series is only sporadically present.

For the third chapter, Silvestri backtracks even further away from the naivete of the 1950s to adopt a whimsical tone for this child-like, innocent adventure and romance of the old, wild West. He even successfully spoofs the genre by interpolating classic (if not cliched) western motifs like the harmonica. He also develops a delightfully romantic new theme presented here for Doc Brown's love interest, Clara, the schoolmarm. Some film series tend to abandon the overuse of thematic material to keep things from getting boring (i.e. the James Bond films), but the need was never so vital to keep audiences clued in as in this trilogy's vast plate of reoccurring time travel gags.

David Hirsch

Backdraft ♪♪♪♪

1991, Milan Records; from the movie *Backdraft*, Universal Pictures, 1991.

Album Notes: *Music*: Hans Zimmer; *Orchestrations*: Shirley Walker, Bruce Fowler, Larry Rench; *Music Editor*: Laura Perlman; Orchestra and choir conducted by Shirley Walker; *Album Producers*: Hans Zimmer, Jay Rifkin; *Engineer*: Jay Rifkin.

Selections: 1 Set Me In Motion (B. Hornsby/J. Hornsby)(5:20) *Bruce Hornsby & The Range*; 2 Fighting 17th (4:26); 3 Brothers (3:32); 4 The Arsonist's Waltz (1:58); 5 335 (3:02); 6 Burn It All (5:19); 7 You Go, We Go (5:11); 8 Fahrenheit 451 (2:59); 9 Show Me Your Firetruck (3:31); 10 The Show Goes On (B. Hornsby)(7:32) *Bruce Hornsby & The Range*.

Review: A memorable and powerful score by Hans Zimmer, *Backdraft* represents one of the composer's earliest but most successful cinematic endeavors, one which continues to be used in countless movie trailers and television spots. With his trademark collection of heavy percussion, pounding synthesizers and blaring orchestra, Zimmer uses strong melodic themes to underscore Ron Howard's entertaining firefighting melodrama, and it fits this particular film like a glove; from the bombastic and triumphant opening fanfare to its dissonant sections with chorus, *Backdraft* is a larger-than-life dramatic score that makes for an ideal listening experience, and certainly remains one of Zimmer's most satisfying efforts to date. The album also contains a pair of good songs by Bruce Hornsby & the Range, one of which ("Set Me in Motion") was written specifically for the movie.

Andy Dursin

The Bad and the Beautiful
♪♪♪♪

1996, Rhino Records; from the movie *The Bad and the Beautiful*, M-G-M, 1952.

Album Notes: *Music*: David Raksin; *Orchestrations*: David Raksin; The M-G-M Studio Orchestra, conducted by David Raksin; *CD Producer*: Merilee Bradford; *Engineer*: Doug Schwartz.

Selections: 1 Introduction (Main Title)(1:24); 2 Jonathan Calling (2:07); 3 Jonathan Calling, Part 2 (1:24); 4 Fred (1:19); 5 The House (:35); 6 Eighteen Years Ago (1:40); 7 Don't Blame Me (J. McHugh/D. Fields)(2:05) *Peggy King*; 8 Came The Dawn (:49); 9 Oh Yes, He Is! (1:05); 10 Busy As A B (:31); 11 The Dark (:41); 12 Hurry and Keep Hurrying (1:16); 13 Cat People — Main and End Titles (:14); 14 Newsreel March (:17); 15 The Letdown (2:11); 16 The Far Away Mountain (:37); 17 Roland In Babylon (:39); 18 Temptation (N.H. Brown/A. Freed)(2:04) *Hadda Brooks, Milt Raskin*; 19 Brief Holiday (:21); 20 The Betrayal (1:56); 21 The Witch Goddess (:17); 22 Where Credit Is Due (:38); 23 Georgia (1:28); 24 Two Very Early Hours (:23); 25 The Defeat (:35); 26 Almost Time, Parts 1 & 2 (3:16); 27 Lonely Girl (1:49); 28 Fall From Grace (1:28); 29 Ilyich All Over/More Of Same (2:37); 30 Fourteen Wonderful Weeks (:59); 31 Smoke That Cigarette (:29); 32 Phrygian Wedding (:30); 33 The Premeer (:55); 34 Where You Are/We Are Not Alone (:46); 35 Katharsis Indicated (:23); 36 Katharsis Achieved (:38); 37 James Lee's Narrative (2:17); 38 California (:30); 39 I Started To Work/How Well Is Enough (1:10); 40 I Started To Work/How Well Is Enough (reprise)(1:58); 41 Let's Get To Work (:27); 42 The Proud Land (:40); 43 She Wasted You (:35); 44 The Spellbinder (End Title) (2:18); 45 Introduction (Main Title)(unused version #1)(1:53); 46 Introduction (Main Title)(unused version #2)(1:55); 47 The Spellbinder (End Title)(unused version)(2:24).

Review: It is always preferable to listen to a recording of a piece of music that has been orchestrated and conducted by the composer himself, because theoretically, the listener is guaranteed that every musical texture, dynamic and nuance that the composer had in mind when creating the music will survive through their own, personal interpretation for the recording. Such is the case with Rhino's comprehensive release of David Raksin's score for *The Bad and the Beautiful*, which is a long-awaited, eagerly anticipated CD issue.

In creating this complete soundtrack recording, the producer has included 44 musical cues (some far greater in length than those edited for the final cut of the film), and three supplemental versions of the main and end titles, which were revised by the composer for the edited film. Such completeness and the inclusion of the bonus tracks allows film music buffs and historians alike to analyze the creative process and understand exactly how the scoring and editing process works. In this case, this enjoyable task is made even easier, because of the wonderfully personal recollections of Raksin himself, who has penned a concise history of the film and his music for the accompanying 28 page booklet. While the original stereo master recordings were destroyed in the 1960s, 1/4 mono tape copies survived and are the primary source for this release, which has very pleasing sonic characteristics.

Charles L. Granata

See also: Composers' section

Bad Girls ♫♫♫

1994, Fox Records; from the movie *Bad Girls*, **20th Century-Fox, 1994.**

Album Notes: *Music*: Jerry Goldsmith; *Orchestrations*: Alexander Courage; *Music Editor*: Ken Hall; Orchestra conducted by Jerry Goldsmith; *Album Producer*: Jerry Goldsmith; *Engineer*: Bruce Botnick.

Selections: 1 The John (2:18); 2 The Hanging (3:17); 3 Bank Job (4:54); 4 Jail Break (3:36); 5 No Money (2:08); 6 Ambush (5:45); 7 I Shot Him (2:35); 8 Josh's Death (3:42); 9 No Bullets (3:51); 10 My Land (6:50).

Review: Although the film itself was wretched, Goldsmith wrote a rousing action score for this all-female western that's one of the composers best works of the '90s. After a pastoral opening of keyboard and guitar, the score takes off with some breakneck cues for chases, a bank robbery, and an ambush, as well as a good-natured, bucolic "Jail Break," all done in the composer's indelible western style of the '60s and '70s. It's percussive and highly inventive rhythmically, with a big, broad John Wayne-style brass theme blasting over many of the action highlights; the "Ambush" cue is a particularly exciting and sustained piece featuring a thrilling brass fugue.

Jeff Bond

Bad Moon ♫♫♫

1996, Silva America; from the movie *Bad Moon*, **Morgan Creek Production, 1996.**

Album Notes: *Music*: Daniel Licht; *Orchestrations*: Daniel Licht, Pete Anthony, Jon Kull; The Northwest Sinfonia, conducted by Pete Anthony; *Album Producer*: Daniel Licht; *Engineer*: Rick Winquest.

> "There are boundaries, but it's such a great opportunity to invent music, then stand in front of a fabulous orchestra and hear it played back. I have to pinch myself every time."
>
> **Michael Kamen**
> *(USA Today, 2-12-96)*

Selections: 1 Flying (Main Title)(1:58); 2 Nepal (2:05); 3 Man Of The House (1:42); 4 Don't Look Up (1:47); 5 On The Road (1:14); 6 Lore Of The Werewolf (2:16); 7 Ted Phones Home (:58); 8 Handcuffed (3:110; 9 The Diary (3:01); 10 Demise Of A Salesman (1:11); 11 Piss Off/Claw To Claw (5:57); 12 Goodbye Thor (3:37); 13 Brett And Janet (3:26); 14 The Transformation (3:00); 15 Confrontation (4:05); 16 Ted's Last Trail (1:48); 17 End Credits (4:07).

Review: Still too young to be jaded, composer Daniel Licht seems to have ignored the quality of this film and put his best foot forward. He shows real potential by pulling off this surprisingly well-composed and entertaining orchestral score. It manages to inject a surprising amount of emotional drama into a strictly cliched "Lassie vs. The Werewolf" horror film that really didn't deserve this much effort. He's definitely a promising talent.

David Hirsch

The Ballad of Little Jo ♫♫♫♫

1993, Intrada Records; from the movie *The Ballad of Little Jo*, **Fine Line Features, 1993.**

Album Notes: *Music*: David Mansfield; *Album Producer*: David Mansfield; *Engineers*: Dan Gellert, Daegal Bennett, David Mansfield, Mike Krowiak.

Selections: 1 Prologue (:48); 2 Parasol Road (1:28); 3 The Chase (1:52); 4 Rub City (4:58); 5 Hoping For Gold (1:17); 6 Think About Your Future (:29); 7 Miner's Dance (3:09); 8 Homestead (1:59); 9 Line Camp (3:04); 10 Jo's New Coat (:24); 11 Sheep Shearing (:42); 12 Returning The Doll (:53); 13 Mary's Wedding (1:50); 14 Tin Man (5:20); 15 Slaughter (1:47); 16 Sewing A Dress (:38); 17 Jo Makes A Deal (1:27); 18 Run Little Lady (1:34); 19 Ruth's Cure (1:59); 20 A Sister's Letter (:57); 21 Change Of Heart (3:03); 22 Jo Dies (1:18); 23 The Secret's Out

(:25); 24 Frank Reads A Letter (1:00); 25 Ballad For Little Jo (End Title)(D. Mansfield/N. O'Byrne)(3:12) *Kate & Anna McGarrigle.*

Review: Some films (and some soundtracks) are like rare wines—they need to be tasted to be fully appreciated, but the rewards are enormous. Such is the case with this delightful score by David Mansfield, who also created the music for the revisionist western *Heaven's Gate.* The film's setting, the post-Civil War American West, inspired the composer to write a series of charmingly expressive cues that find their roots in the traditional music of the frontier. The film, which starred Bo Hopkins, Ian McKellen and Carrie Snodgress, was not a tremendous success and quickly disappeared. Its soundtrack album is well worth hunting for.

Balto ♪♪♪♪'

1995, MCA Records; from the animated feature *Balto,* Universal Pictures, 1995.

Album Notes: *Music*: James Horner; *Orchestrations*: Steve Bramson, Don Davis; *Music Editor*: Jim Henrikson; The London Symphony Orchestra, conducted by James Horner; *Album Producer*: James Horner; *Engineer*: Shawn Murphy.

Selections: 1 Reach For The Light (J. Horner/B. Mann/C. Weil)(4:25) *Steve Winwood*; 2 Main Title/Balto's Story Unfolds (4:41); 3 The Dogsled Race (1:41); 4 Rosy Goes To The Doctor (4:06); 5 Boris And Balto (1:30); 6 The Journey Begins (5:07); 7 Grizzly Bear (5:23); 8 Jenna/Telegraphing The News (2:23); 9 Steele's Treachery (4:38); 10 The Epidemic's Toll (3:30); 11 Heritage Of The Wolf (5:54); 12 Balto Brings The Medicine (4:54); 13 Reach For The Light (long version)(J. Horner/B. Mann/C. Weil)(5:27) *Steve Winwood*.

Review: Another animated feature from Steven Spielberg's Amblin Entertainment, sporting another winning score by James Horner. Who could complain about it! Avoiding the obvious cute approach the medium might have suggested, the composer decided instead to write a set of epic cues to accompany this inspiring story of a stray half-dog, half-wolf on a rescue mission to a remote Alaskan outpost filled with sick kids. In the course of the action, Balto gets to win the heart of an attractive female, Jenna, whose owner, Rosy, is one of the sick children, and shares some light-hearted moments in the company of his friends, Boris, a Russian goose, and Muk and Luk, two polar bears. Most of Horner's cues are often more exciting than the action would seem to require, but the bombast is offset by a couple of introspective selections, like "Rosy Goes To The Doctor," that give the whole score greater scope and impact.

Bandolero! ♪♪♪♪

1990, Cinema Show/edel Records; from the movie *Bandolero!,* 20th Century-Fox, 1968.

Album Notes: *Music*: Jerry Goldsmith; The 20th Century-Fox Orchestra conducted by Lionel Newman.

Selections: 1 Main Title (1:56); 2 The Trap (2:23); 3 El Jefe (:50); 4 The Bait (2:08); 5 Ambushed (3:57); 6 Sabinas (2:51); 7 Dee's Proposal (5:29); 8 Across The River (1:01); 9 A Bad Day For Hanging (3:02); 10 A Better Way (3:34).

Review: Jerry Goldsmith's picaresque score for this 1968 Jimmy Stewart western features a classically direct, folksy title theme that's whistled over shots of Stewart riding the range. The rest of the score offers a fascinating contrast between the traditional elements of the title music and the kind of hard-edged, experimental writing Goldsmith produced for his legendary *Planet of the Apes* score released the same year. There are several exciting action cues marked by powerful staccato rhythms and striking use of a grinding bass harmonica, as well as a moody love theme for marimba. It's an unusual score very much recommended to fans of Goldsmith's '60s style, its comic elements working almost as a satire of the standard western sound.

Jeff Bond

BAPS ♪♪'

1997, Milan Records; from the movie *BAPS,* New Line Cinema, 1997.

Album Notes: *Music*: Stanley Clarke; *Orchestrations*: Ira Hearshen, Kennard Ramsey, Ron Hess; Orchestra conducted by William Kidd; *Song Producers*: Danny Mano, Eric Quinones, Howie Tee, Eumir Deodato, Michael Angelo Saulsberry, Danny D, The 88/X Unit, Chris Bolden, Billy Griffin, Steve Appel; *Album Producer*: Stanley Clarke; *Engineers*: John Richards, Ralph Sutton.

Selections: 1 No One But You (Veronica/S. Aiken/D. Mano)(5:07) *Veronica, Craig Mack*; 2 Move On (S. Ford-Payne/ H. Tee/A. Spanador Mosely) (4:26) *Sheree Ford-Payne*; 3 Get Down On It (Kool & The Gang/Bell/ Taylor) (4:54) *Kool & The Gang*; 4 Get Your Groove On (L. Smith/J. Hutchins/J. Fletcher/ M. Saulsberry/P. White)(3:32) *Gyrl*; 5 Giddy Up Let's Ride (Kinsui) (3:28) *Kinsui*; 6 A Fifth Of Beethoven (L. Van Beethoven/W. Murphy)(1:26) *The 88/X Unit*; 7 I'm So Glad (C. Bolden/ B. Griffen/S. Appel)(4:43) *Alex Brown*; 8 The Will (1:22); 9 Let's Meet Isaac (1:59); 10 Nisi At Peace (3:41); 11 Welcome To L.A. (2:26); 12 Variation On "Forever" (2:23); 13 Problem With Mr. B. (1:42); 14 Mr. B. Dies (2:02); 15 Dreams (1:10).

Review: Once you get past those seven mediocre rap and pop music tunes intended to appeal to the kids, you'll be pleasantly surprised to find an impressively well-written orchestral score. Hidden at the end, Stanley Clarke's music is filled with a lot of emotion, supported by a charming main theme. It's quite a contrast from the tone set by the album's first half and certainly more practical entertainment. That may not be enough of a reason, for Clarke's music only amounts to about 17 minutes on this album. That translates to spending $1.00 per minute on it. Considering this score was written for a mediocre comedy film, who would go out of their way to purchase this album? Perhaps only Stanley Clarke fans, for few others might feel the investment worthwhile.

David Hirsch

Barabbas

1996, DRG Records; from the movie *Barabbas*, Columbia Pictures, 1962.

See: Alexander the Great

Baraka ♫♫♭

1992, Milan Records; from the movie *Baraka*, Samuel Goldwyn, 1992.

Album Notes: *Music:* Michael Stearns; *Album Producer:* David Franco; *Engineer:* Joe Gatswirt.

Selections: 1 Mantra (S. Satoh)(1:18)/Organics (3:24); 2 Wipala (G. Vargas) (5:04) *Inkuyo*; 3 The Host Of Seraphim (6:18) *Dead Can Dance*; 4 Village Dance (2:55); 5 Wandering Saint (L. Subramaniam)(6:41); 6 African Journey (Anugama/Sebastiano)(3:34) *Anugama & Sebastiano*; 7 Rainbow Voice (D. Hykes) (2:57) *David Hykes & The Harmonic Choir*; 8 Monk With Bell (2:33); 9 Broken Vows/A Prayer Of Kala Rupa/An Daorach Bheag (4:39) *The Monks of the Dip Tse Chok Ling Monastery*; 10 Finale (4:34); 11 End Credits (3:26).

Review: Quoting the liner notes, "Baraka is an ancient Sufi word [...] simply translated as a blessing, or the breath or essence of life from which the evolutionary process unfolds." Taking a cue from this concept, director Ron Fricke took his cameras to such diverse locations as Brazil, Nepal, Cambodia, Kuwait, India, Tanzania and Iran, to create a "non-verbal" film that tells the story of our planet's evolution, man's diversity and the impact we have had on the environment. To illustrate musically this "journey of rediscovery that plunges into nature, history, the human spirit, and finally into the realm of the infinite," the soundtrack gathers together performances recorded around the world, with composer Michael Stearns contributing the instrumental cues that link these selections into a seamless entity. Call this the ultimate world music soundtrack.

The Barbarians ♫♫

1990, Intrada Records; from the movie *The Barbarians*, Cannon International, 1987.

Album Notes: *Music:* Pino Donaggio; *Synthesizer Sequencing:* Maurizio Guarini, Paolo Steffan; The Unione Musicisti di Roma, conducted by Natale Massara; *Album Producer:* Pino Donaggio; *Engineer:* Gaetano Ria; *Digital Engineer:* Bob Stone.

Selections: 1 Main Titles (4:38); 2 Attack To Ragnick Caravan (6:00); 3 Canary's Promise (1:39); 4 Kara And The Twins In Talchet/China's Magic (2:22); 5 Encounter Twins And Canary (2:37); 6 Kadar In Harem (1:42); 7 Crown Room (1:00); 8 Surrounding Of The Caravan (2:52); 9 Casual Encounter With Ibar (1:27); 10 China's Arrival At Harem (1:50); 11 Sepulcre (2:17); 12 Kara And The Twins In The Forest (:51); 13 China Takes Ruby (2:16); 14 Kadar And Canary At Morass (4:15); 15 Duel Between Kadar And The Twins (4:12); 16 Ruby Dawn (P. Donaggio/P. Steffan)(3:45) *Ronnie Jackson*.

Review: This big score by Pino Donaggio with spectacular ambient sound is a blend of heavily pulsating synth sounds framed by the orchestral support provided by Rome's Unione Musicisti, one of Italy's grandest film orchestras. The film, a pseudo epic starring two beefy musclemen, David and Peter Paul, is more cartoonish in approach than *Conan* or *Xena*, and, for that matter, so is Donaggio's music. However, in the midst of the pounding "action" cues, the composer reveals a tender side with lovely melodic tunes like "Encounter Twins And Canary," or "Kadar in Harem," which soften the music and make it sound more attractive than it really is. One serious drawback in the gorgeously layered sound is the fact that some cues don't seem to be totally realized and end up in a quick fade without actually making much of an impact. "Ruby Dawn," a vocal tune with an anachronistic Eurobeat, closes the set.

The Barefoot Contessa/ The Quiet American/ Room at the Top ♫♫♫

1996, DRG Records; from the movies *The Barefoot Contessa*, United Artists, 1954; *The Quiet American*, Warner Bros., 1958; and *Room at the Top*, Continental Film Distribution, 1959.

Album Notes: *Music:* Mario Nascimbene; *Orchestrations:* Mario Nascimbene; Orchestras conducted by Franco Ferrara (The Barefoot Contessa), Mario Nascimbene (The Quiet American), Lambert Williamson (Room At The Top); *Album Producers:* Mario Nascimbene, Claudio Fuiano; *Engineer:* Gianni Mazzrini.

Selections: *THE BAREFOOT CONTESSA:* 1 Main Titles (1:48); 2 Recalling At The Graveyard (1:52); 3 Harry Meets Maria Vargas

(4:45); 4 Gypsy Bolero (2:46); 5 A Guitar For Maria (3:40); 6 Nocturne Bolero (2:58); 7 Death Of Maria and Finale (4:59);

ROOM AT THE TOP: 8 Main Titles (3:10); 9 Alice And Joe At The Pub (:51); 10 Alice's Beguine (2:43); 11 Alice And Joe At Home (3:03); 12 Alice And Joe (1:54); 13 Alice Alone (1:03); 14 Joe, Alice Is Dead (2:26); 15 Joe And The Prostitute (3:27); 16 Joe After The Fight (1:15); 17 Finale (:34);

THE QUIET AMERICAN: 18 Main Titles (1:22); 19 City Streets (2:14); 20 The Cathedral (1:30); 21 The Morgue (3:40); 22 Psychological And Passionate (1:58); 23 The Search For Tuong (2:25); 24 Finale (:47).

Review: Italian film composer Mario Nascimbene made quite an impression with his score for *The Barefoot Contessa*, which gave Ava Gardner one of her most sensual screen roles as a cabaret dancer whose rise to international fame and subsequent marriage to an Italian count ends after he murders her in a jealous fit. Writing in a remarkably subdued and melodic vein, Nascimbene delivered a series of eloquent cues that set off the film's most important scenes.

As a result of the film's success, the composer was asked to work on such illustrious projects as *Alexander the Great* and David O. Selznick's *A Farewell to Arms* (q.v.), before scoring *The Quiet American,* a pre-Vietnam War old-fashioned thriller set in Saigon, starring Audie Murphy, for which he used a blend of ethnic instruments to give his music the right tonal color.

For the British working-class drama, *Room at the Top,* created a year after *The Quiet American,* Nascimbene again devised a score that set off the screen action and enhanced it with a series of musical cues that drew much of their dramatic strength from the judicious use of brass instruments over the orchestral texture.

All three scores, presented here in a recording supervised by the composer, show their age, with the CD containing many technical flaws (image shifting, hiss, distortion, bad editing) that do little to enhance their presentation.

Barton Fink

1996, TVT Records; from the movie *Barton Fink,* 20th Century-Fox, 1991.

See: Fargo

Basic Instinct ♪♪♪

1992, Varese Sarabande; from the movie *Basic Instinct,* Tri-Star Pictures, 1992.

Album Notes: *Music:* Jerry Goldsmith; *Orchestrations:* Alexander Courage; *Music Editor:* Ken Hall; The National Philhar-

monic Orchestra, conducted by Jerry Goldsmith; *Album Producer:* Jerry Goldsmith; *Engineer:* Bruce Botnick.

Selections: 1 Main Title (Theme From Basic Instinct)(2:15); 2 Crossed Legs (4:50); 3 Night Life (6:03); 4 Kitchen Help (3:59); 5 Pillow Talk (5:00); 6 Morning After (2:29); 7 The Games Are Over (5:36); 8 Catherine's Sorrow (2:41); 9 Roxy Loses (3:17); 10 An Unending Story (7:56).

Review: Goldsmith's most recent Oscar-nominated score for director Paul Verhoven's erotic thriller has become a staple of movie previews with its insinuating, atmospheric title music and hammering, ostinato-driven chase cues. Goldsmith achieves some evocative "sex music" with an undulating string figure and a minor mode woodwind melody that functions as a moody siren song beckoning Michael Douglas' detective character to his ruin; his scoring of the movie's graphic sex scenes employs a moaning wind instrument effect similar to his use of the medieval serpent in *Alien*. The pulsating car chase cues "Night Life" and "Roxy Loses" are vintage Goldsmith action pieces that the composer honed to perfection here and in Verhoven's earlier *Total Recall*. The brooding low-key piano theme that emerges out of the center of the score sometimes recalls John Barry's work on *Body Heat*, but Goldsmith carves out his own territory here for a consistently involving album.

Jeff Bond

Bat 21 ♪♪♪♪

1988, Varese-Sarabande; from the movie *Bat 21,* Tri-Star Pictures, 1988.

Album Notes: *Music:* Christopher Young; *Music Editor:* Jim Weidman; *Featured Musician:* Masa Yoshizawa (Shakuhachi); *Album Producer:* Christopher Young; *Engineers:* Jeff Vaughn, Daniel Hersch.

Selections: 1 Bat-21 (3:03); 2 Bonding (2:59); 3 Big Sky (5:05); 4 The Lesson (2:38); 5 A North Passage (5:06); 6 Birddog (4:33); 7 I Killed A Man Today (4:51); 8 Zulu Zulu 5, Lima Hotel 7 (5:06); 9 Nobody's Home (3:07); 10 Cobra Leader (4:47); 11 Fly Boy Ross (5:11); 12 First Light (3:25); 13 Positive Contact (2:53); 14 No More Killing (4:06); 15 The Swanee (2:14).

Review: Early mainstream breakout score for Christopher Young that is driven by the intensity of his passion to create unusual sound clusters. In fact, Young set a whole new standard, that was repeatedly copied thereafter, for scoring Vietnam era war films. By utilizing Far Eastern instruments, like the shakuhachi, for solo performances, as opposed to relegating them for mere effects, this formula effectively brings an intense anxiety to the film's isolated jungle settings. A simple, but highly charged, emotional theme (something Young is reluctant to admit he does exceptionally well) counterpoints the action cues. This theme represents the growing bond between the downed officer and his would-be rescuer, circling above.

David Hirsch

Batman

Batman ♫♫♫♫

1989, Warner Bros. Records; from the movie *Batman*, Warner Bros., 1989.

Album Notes: *Music*: Danny Elfman; *Orchestrations*: Steve Bartek, Shirley Walker, Steven Scott Smalley; *Music Editors*: Bob Badami, Robin Clarke; The Sinfonia of London, conducted by Shirley Walker; *Album Producers*: Danny Elfman, Steve Bartek; *Engineers*: Eric Tomlinson, Shawn Murphy.

Selections: 1 The Batman Theme (2:38); 2 Roof Fight (3:20); 3 First Confrontation (4:43); 4 Kitchen, Surgery, Face-Off (3:07); 5 Flowers (3:51); 6 Clown Attack (1:45); 7 Batman To The Rescue (3:56); 8 Roasted Dude (1:01); 9 Photos/Beautiful Dreamer (S. Foster)(2:27); 10 Descent Into Mystery (1:31); 11 The Bat Cave (2:35); 12 The Joker's Poem (:56); 13 Childhood Remembered (2:43); 14 Love Theme (1:30); 15 Charge Of The Batmobile (1:41); 16 Attack Of The Batwing (4:44); 17 Up The Cathedral (5:04); 18 Waltz To The Death (3:55); 19 The Final Confrontation (3:47); 20 Finale (1:45); 21 Batman Theme (reprise)(1:28).

Review: See *Batman Forever* for combined review.

Batman ♫♫♫

1989, Warner Bros. Records; from the movie *Batman*, Warner Bros., 1989.

Album Notes: *Music*: Prince; *Songs arranged and performed*: Prince; *Performers*: The Sounds of Blackness Choir, Eric Leeds and Atlanta Bliss, The Clare Fischer Orchestra; *Album Producer*: Prince; *Engineers*: Prince, Femi Jiya, Chris Lord; *Assistant Engineers*: David Friedlander, Heidi Hanschu, Chuck Zwicky, Eddie Miller.

Selections: 1 The Future (4:07); 2 Electric Chair (4:09); 3 The Arms Of Orion (Prince/S. Easton)(5:03) *Prince, Sheena Easton*; 4 Partyman (3:12); 5 Vicki Waiting (4:52); 6 Trust (4:24); 7 Lemon Crush (4:15); 8 Scandalous (Prince/J.L. Nelson)(6:16); 9 Batdance (6:14).

Review: See *Batman Forever* for combined review.

Batman Returns ♫♫♫♫

1992, Warner Bros. Records; from the movie *Batman Returns*, Warner Bros., 1992

Album Notes: *Music*: Danny Elfman; *Orchestrations*: Steve Bartek, Mark McKenzie; *Music Editors*: Bob Badami, Bill Bernstein; Orchestra conducted by Jonathan Sheffer; *Album Producers*: Danny Elfman, Steve Bartek; *Engineers*: Shawn Murphy.

Selections: 1/2 Birth Of A Penguin (5:37); 3/4 The Lair (5:46); 5/6 Selina Transforms (5:27); 7 The Cemetery (2:55); 8 Cat Suite (5:42); 9 Batman vs. The Circus (2:35); 10/11 The Rise And Fall From Grace (5:49); 12 Sore Spots (2:16); 13/14 Rooftops/Wild Ride (7:55); 15 The Children's Hour (1:47); 16/17 The Final Confrontation (10:07); 18/19 The Finale (5:00); 20 End Credits (4:42); 21 Face To Face (4:17) *Siouxsie and the Banshees*.

Review: See *Batman Forever* for combined review.

Batman Forever ♫♫♫

1995, Atlantic Records; from the movie *Batman Forever*, Warner Bros., 1995.

Album Notes: *Music*: Elliot Goldenthal; *Orchestrations*: Robert Elhai, Elliot Goldenthal; *Music Editors*: Christopher Brooks, Joey Rand; Orchestra conducted by Jonathan Shaeffer; *Featured Soloists*: Bruce Dukov (violin), Paul Shure (theremin), Elliot Goldenthal and Harmonic Voices (vocals); *Album Producer*: Matthias Gohl; *Engineer*: Steve McLaughlin.

Selections: 1 Main Titles and Fanfares (1:50); 2 Perpetuum Mobile (:54); 3 The Perils Of Gotham (3:01); 4 Chase Noir (1:45); 5 Fledermausmarschmusik (1:15); 6 Nygma Variations (An Ode To Science)(6:02); 7 Victory (2:32); 8 Descent (1:07); 9 The Pull Of Regret (2:50); 10 Mouth To Mouth Nocturne (2:14); 11 Gotham City Boogie (2:02); 12 Under The Top (5:42); 13 Mr. E's Dance Card (Rhumba, Foxtrot, Waltz and Tango)(3:21); 14 Two-Face Three Step (2:20); 15 Chase Blanc (1:21); 16 Spank Me Overture (2:46); 17 Holy Rusted Metal (1:51); 18 Batterdammerung (1:21).

Review: See *Batman Forever* below for combined review.

Batman Forever ♫♭

1995, Atlantic Records; from the movie *Batman Forever*, Warner Bros., 1995.

Album Notes: *Song Producers*: Nellee Hooper, Bono, The Edge, Flood, Polly Jean Harvey, John Parish, Lenny Kravitz, Trevor Horn, Massive Attack, David Roback, Thom Wilson, Prince Rakeem, Tim Simenon, The Devlins, Rick Nowels, Billy Stenberg, Gary Hughes, Brad Wood, The Flaming Lips; *Engineers*: Robbie Adams, Flood, Terry Manning, David Domanich,

Steve Fitzmaurice, Oliver Jones, Lee Shephard, Tim Weidner, Thom Wilson, Prince Rakeem, Tim Simenon, Willie Mannion, Scott Benson; *Album Executive Producers*: Jolene Cherry, Joel Schumacher, Gary LeMel.

Selections: 1 Hold Me, Thrill Me, Kiss Me, Kill Me (Bono/U2)(4:47) *U2*; 2 One Time Too Many (PJ Harvey)(2:53) *PJ Harvey*; 3 Where Are You Now? (L. Kravitz)(3:57) *Brandy*; 4 Kiss From A Rose (SEAL)(3:39) *SEAL*; 5 The Hunter Gets Captured By The Game (W. Robinson)(4:06) *Massive Attack, Tracey Thorn*; 6 Nobody Lives Without Love (Tonio K./L. Klein)(5:05) *Eddi Reader*; 7 Tell Me Now (Sandoval/D. Roback)(4:18) *Mazzy Star*; 8 Smash It Up (Rat Scabies/Captain Sensible/D. Vanian/A. Ward)(3:27) *The Offspring*; 9 There Is A Light (T. Friese-Greene)(4:23) *Nick Cave*; 10 The Riddler (C. Smith/R. Diggs/N. Hefti)(3:31) *Method Man*; 11 The Passenger (J. Osterberg/R. Gardiner)(4:38) *Michael Hutchence*; 12 Crossing The River (B. Steinberg/R. Nowels/C. Devlin)(4:45) *The Devlins*; 13 8 (Sunny Day Real Estate)(5:27) *Sunny Day Real Estate*; 14 Bad Days (Coyne/Ivins/Drozd/Jones)(4:40) *The Flaming Lips*.

Review: Danny Elfman's music for the first two *Batman* films proves a splendid complement to director Tim Burton's vision of the world of Gotham City. Much of the flavor harkens back to the film-noir genre of the 1940s, set in large, dark metropolitan vistas where evil grows and the good must fight back in any way possible. Costumed superheroes are only believable if the worlds they inhabit are realistic and in the first one, Elfman used his lush palette to develop this nightmarish vision. He musically portrayed the constant struggle of good versus evil and beauty against ugliness by twisting an alluring lullaby into something uncomfortable, thus representing the duality of Batman/Bruce Wayne and the Joker's twisted psyche.

For the second film *Batman Returns*, Elfman centered his score around the two new villains, the Penguin and Catwoman. Since the former is initially represented on screen only by his deformed hands, Elfman musically painted the Penguin with a darker version of his *Edward Scissorhands* score, with sweeping strings and chorus. Less subtle, perhaps, are the screeching string passages used as Catwoman goes on the prowl. Although *Batman* set the standard for the series, it is with the second film that Elfman really created his most entertaining and intriguing work.

With *Batman Forever*, came a new look as director Joel Schumacher abandoned Burton's ghostly lighting for the bright colors of the Sunday comics. Elliot Goldenthal, already having scored *Alien* and *Demolition Man* with his unique orchestrations, was set to reveal a whole new music voice for the world of the Caped Crusader. Once again, the film's schizo-

phrenia is reflected in the music's ever changing style. Though suited perfectly for the screen action, Goldenthal's score is less enjoyable on CD. Very few themes ever complete themselves before they become overwhelmed with something newer and busier. Even the new theme for Batman (really just a fanfare) never reaches a satisfying climax. The listener is sadly left wanting. Points do go to the most clever cues titles ever, though.

Prince's contributions to the first film, a series of percolating vocal and instrumental numbers, are exactly what you might expect from the artist-with-the-most-complicated-identifying-logo-in-the-whole-history-of-the-music-industry (why didn't he call himself the Artist-With-No-Name, instead?). This is certainly not meant as a put-down, but your overall acceptance of the set will hinge entirely on how you feel about Prince himself, whose brilliance and creativity is not always to everyone's taste.

Such is not the case with the pop song compilation for the third film which brings together various performers, in selections that have a much more limited appeal. In the film, these songs were mercifully heard as snippets in the background and did not interfere with the action, but brought upfront in the CD, they reveal their apparent lack of creativity, and do not stand well under close scrutiny.

David Hirsch/Didier C. Deutsch

Batman And Robin ♪♪♪▷

1997, Warner Bros. Records; from the movie *Batman And Robin*, Warner Bros. Pictures, 1997.

Album Notes: *Music*: Elliot Goldenthal; *Song Producers*: Nellee Hooper & Billy Corgan, D.J. U-Neek, R. Kelly, Arkarna, Scott Litt & R.E.M., Peter Collins, Sean Slade, Gary Clark, Soul Coughing, Roisin Murphy & Mark Brydon, David Gamson, Eric Benet, George Nash, Jr., & Demonte, Matthais Gohl, Rick Smith; *Album Executive Producers*: Danny Bramson, Gary LeMel; *Engineers*: Chris Shepard, R. Kelly & Stephen George, Ollie, John Holbrook, Tom Lord-Alge, Gary Clark, Bil Emmons, Goh Hotoda, Mike Nielsen.

Selections: 1 The End Is The Beginning Is The End (B. Corgan)(5:09) *The Smashing Pumpkins*; 2 Look Into My Eyes (Bone/D.J. U-Neek)(4:27) *Bone Thugs-n-Harmony*; 3 Gotham City (R. Kelly)(4:56) *R. Kelly*; 4 House On Fire (Arkarna)(3:25) *Arkarna*; 5 Revolution (Berry/Buck/Mills/Stipe)(3:05) *R.E.M.*; 6 Foolish Games (J. Kilcher)(4:00) *Jewel*; 7 Lazy Eye (J. Rzeznik) (3:47) *The Goo Goo Dolls*; 8 Breed (L. Christy/G. Clark)(3:05) *Lauren Christy*; 9 The Bug (M. Doughty/Soul Coughing)(3:09) *Soul Coughing*; 10 Fun For Me (R. Murphy/M. Brydon)(5:08) *Moloko*;

11 Poison Ivy (J. Leiber/M. Stoller)(3:33) *Me' Shell NedgeOcello*; 12 True To Myself (E. Benet/G. Nash, Jr.)(4:41) *Eric Benet*; 13 A Batman Overture (E. Goldenthal)(3:36); 14 Moaner (Underworld) (10:17) *Moaner*; 15 The Beginning Is The End Is The Beginning (B. Corgan) (5:01) *The Smashing Pumpkins.*

Review: The jukebox approach of "Batman Forever" worked so well that there was no question what approach would be taken for the fourth edition of the caped crusader's series. Like its predecessor, this aims squarely at pop radio, bringing together top artists from the modern rock and R&B worlds. Smashing Pumpkins bookend the set with the same song performed two different ways—"The End is the Beginning is the End" and "The Beginning is the End is the Beginning." R. Kelly's gospel-tinged "Gotham City" is gentle ear candy, while Me'shell Ndegeocello offers a clever re-invention of the classic "Poison Ivy."

Gary Graff

Batman: Mask of the Phantasm ♪♪♪♪

1993, Reprise Records; from the animated feature *Batman: Mask of the Phantasm,* Warner Bros., 1993.

Album Notes: *Music*: Shirley Walker; *Orchestrations*: Ian Walker, Lolita Ritmanis, Peter Tomashek, Harvey R. Cohen, Michael McCuistion, Larry Rench; *Music Editor*: Thomas Milano; *Featured Musician*: Hans Zimmer (synthesizer); *Album Producer*: Shirley Walker; *Engineer*: Robert Fernandez.

Selections: 1 Main Title (1:35); 2 The Promise (:43); 3 Ski Mask Vigilante (3:00); 4 Phantasm's Graveyard Murder (3:35); 5 First Love (1:32); 6 The Big Chase (5:28); 7 A Plea For Help (1:51); 8 The Birth Of Batman (4:15); 9 Phantasm And Joker Fight (4:03); 10 Batman's Destiny (3:42); 11 I Never Even Told You (S. Garrett/G. Ballard)(4:21) *Tia Carrere.*

Review: Shirley Walker, who developed quite a following through her work on some of Hans Zimmer's most intelligent soundtracks, began striking out on her own, notably with this score, written for an animated feature based on the Batman comic strip, which evidences her solid qualities as a film composer. In contrast to the bombastic action cues one might expect to find in a film of this kind, "First Love" reveals a romantic side that's most endearing, with chimes mingling around a melodic line to create an attractive cue; and "A Plea For Help" evolves around another lovely melody, played on the organ with orchestral backing, and limned by the soft accompaniment of a choir (a recurring device in Walker's score). An obligatory vocal by Tia Carrere, however, proves jarring amid

all the great orchestral sounds devised by the composer, while it fails to add anything to the recording itself.

*batteries not included ♪♪♪♪°

1987, MCA Records; from the movie *batteries not included*, Universal Pictures, **1987**.

Album Notes: *Music*: James Horner; *Orchestrations*: Greig McRitchie, Billy May; *Music Editors*: Jim Flamberg, Else Blangsted; Orchestra conducted by James Horner; *Album Producer*: James Horner; *Engineer*: Shawn Murphy.

Selections: 1 Main Title (4:55); 2 Night Visitors (8:47); 3 Hamburger Rhumba (3:39); 4 New Babies (3:45); 5 Cafe Swing (3:32); 6 Times Square and Farewell (6:06); 7 Arson (6:08); 8 A New Family/End Credits (8:28).

Review: The "Main Title," a great big band number, sets the tone for this attractive soundtrack album. Horner's score, for this "space"-related story about alien visitors presented under the aegis of Steven Spielberg, is a deft mixture of ominous-sounding instrumental chords and thoroughly enjoyable 1940s dance numbers. Two exhilarating selections stand out in the mix, "Hamburger Rhumba" and "Cafe Swing," both of which evoke specific corresponding scenes in the film.

Creating a different, though equally attractive aura of their own, the long cues marked "Night Visitors," "Time Square and Farewell," "Arson," and "A New Family/End Credits" enable the composer to fully develop his musical ideas and present them in ways that emphasize the intricacies and the solidity in the writing.

Battle of Neretva ♪♪♪♪°

1987, Southern Cross Records; from the movie *Battle of Neretva*, American International Pictures, **1970**.

Album Notes: *Music*: Bernard Herrmann; The London Philharmonic Orchestra, conducted by Bernard Herrmann; *Album Producer*: John Lasher; *Engineers*: Bob Auger, Bill Giolando, Fred Mitchell.

Selections: 1 Prelude (2:33); 2 The Retreat (3:41); 3 Separation (4:01); 4 From Italy (3:16); 5 Chetnik's March (1:46); 6 Farewell (1:50); 7 Partisan March (1:29); 8 Pastorale (1:58); 9 The Turning Point (5:15); 10 The Death Of Danica (2:12); 11 Victory! (Finale)(2:33).

Review: Even though it boasts an international cast that includes Yul Brynner, Curt Jurgens, Franco Nero, Hardy Kruger, Silva Koscina, and Orson Welles, portraying an unlikely royalist senator, the epic *Battle of Neretva,* made in 1971, is not particularly remembered, nor is, for that matter, Bernard Herrmann's score mentioned among his best known achievements. One of the many decisive battles fought during World War II, Neretva was the scene of an intense, brutal confrontation between Tito's ragged, small partisan army and Hitler's well-appointed Panzer divisions. Though he had only scored one war film before that, *The Naked and the Dead,* in 1958, Herrmann proved his skills in this score, drawing descriptive motifs from Ukrainian folk-type melodies, brass figures, and string ostinato to portray the scene of the action and the unequal forces at play. Characteristically flavorful, it is an unusual score, with strongly evocative themes, which deserves to be discovered, though the recording itself would gain at sounding a bit warmer than it does.

Beaches 🎵🎵🎵♭

1988, Atlantic Records; from the movie *Beaches,* Touchstone Pictures, 1988.

Album Notes: *Arrangers:* Marc Shaiman, Arif Mardin, Robbie Buchanan, Robbie Kondor; *Featured Vocalists:* Bette Midler, David Pack, David Lasley, Marcy Levy, Arnold McCuller, Rachele Cappelli, Angela Cappelli, Ula Hedwig, Gene Merlino, Gail Farrell, Angie Jaree, Melissa MacKay, Robert Tibow, Joe Pazulo; *Album Producer:* Arif Mardin; *Engineers:* Jack Joseph Puig, Joey Wolpert.

Selections: 1 Under The Boardwalk (A. Resnick/K. Young)(4:19); 2 Wind Beneath My Wings (L. Henley/J. Silbar)(4:53); 3 I've Still Got My Health (C. Porter)(1:29); 4 I Think It's Going To Rain Today (R. Newman)(3:30); 5 Otto Titsling (B. Midler/J. Blatt/C. Seger/M. Shaiman)(3:12); 6 I Know You By Heart (D. Pitchford/G. Merrill/S. Rubicam)(4:39); 7 The Glory Of Love (B. Hill)(3:14); 8 Baby Mine (N. Washington/F. Churchill)(2:06); 9 Oh Industry (B. Midler/W. Waldman)(4:05); 10 The Friendship Theme (G. Delerue) (1:58).

Review: This is nothing more than a clever Bette Midler showcase, with solid renditions of songs she wrote ("Otto Titsling," "Oh Industry"), some standards ("Under the Boardwalk"), some unusual choices ("Baby Mine," from the Disney film *Dumbo,* and Cole Porter's "I've Still Got My Health"), the whole thing capped by a short instrumental theme penned by Georges Delerue. It may be strictly for fans, but don't deny yourself the enjoyments of which there are quite a few!

The Beast 🎵🎵🎵

1988, A&M Records; from the movie *The Beast,* Columbia Pictures, 1988.

Album Notes: *Music:* Mark Isham; *Arrangements:* Mark Isham; *Album Producer:* Mark Isham; *Engineer:* Stephen Krause.

Selections: 1 Badal (27:18); 2 Nanawatai (23:31).

Review: A powerful war drama set in 1981, based on *Nanawatai,* a play by William Mastrosimone, *The Beast* recounts a fictional incident during the Russian occupation of Afghanistan, about a tank, the "beast" of the title, and its occupants, who are trapped in a valley following the destruction of a village. There is a confrontational situation elicited between the Russian soldiers and their commander, a fanatic not above killing his own men, and the Afghan partisans. But while Mark Isham's atmospheric synth score might have well served the tense screen action, it proves less than compelling on its own terms, with electronic lines and an occasional horn sound, colliding with percussive effects in the two stretched-out tracks that recombine the cues composed for the occasion.

Beastmaster 2: Through the Portal of Time 🎵🎵🎵🎵♭

1991, Intrada Records; from the movie *Beastmaster 2: Through the Portal of Time,* New Line Cinema, 1991.

Album Notes: *Music:* Robert Folk; *Orchestrations:* Robert Folk, Peter Tomashek, Richard Bronskill; *Music Editor:* Doug Lackey; The Berlin Radio Concert Orchestra, conducted by Robert Folk; *Album Producer:* Robert Folk; *Engineer:* Brian Masterson.

Selections: 1 Main Title (1:52); 2 Dar The Hero (9:49); 3 Creature's Story (2:22); 4 Through The Portal (5:09); 5 Jackie Alone On Desert (1:29); 6 Swamp Creature Attacks (2:35); 7 Travel Montage (3:08); 8 Mind Suck (2:05); 9 Police Escape (1:06); 10 Jackie Gets Some Sleep (:51); 11 I.D. Badges (4:25); 12 Get Arklon (1:47); 13 The Great Escape (4:26); 14 Sharawk Leads The Way (3:32); 15 Neutron Detonator (5:40); 16 Key To The Heart (5:32).

Review: Robert Folk succeeded Lee Holdridge for this sequel to the epic *The Beastmaster,* featuring another sword-wielding muscled Adonis whose peculiar talent is that he can communicate with animals and travel through time. As he explains in his notes to the album, Folk seized upon the opportunity *Beastmaster 2: Through the Portal of Time* offered him to write a score firmly rooted in the epic genre, yet laid out in contemporary terms since portions of the story take place in modern-day San Francisco. In every respect, he fulfilled his obligation, creating a set of musical cues that evoke the primitive world from which the hero comes, and the modern setting in which he suddenly finds himself.

But beyond the mere logistics that were imposed on him by the storyline, Folk wrote an outstanding score, beautifully delineated and lyrically expressive, that must count among the best efforts in the genre. Cue after cue, the music, superbly performed by the Berlin Radio Concert Orchestra, unveils its many layers of gorgeous sounds and satisfying melodies to create a musical programming that stands out on its own merits. There are many highlights in the set, but for starters you may want to try "Dar the Hero," "Through the Portal," "The Great Escape" and "Key to the Heart." Now, about that unbelievable story about a muscleman from the past who...

The Beautician and the Beast 🎵🎵🎵▷

1997, Milan Records; from the movie *The Beautician and the Beast*, Paramount Pictures, 1997.

Album Notes: *Music*: Cliff Eidelman; *Orchestrations*: Patrick Russ, Pete Anthony, Geoff Alexander, Greg Knowles; *Music Editor*: Jay Richardson; The London Metropolitan Orchestra, conducted by Cliff Eidelman; *Album Producer*: Cliff Eidelman; *Engineers*: Chris Dibble, Bruce Botnick.

Selections: 1 Prelude (1:13); 2 Joy Falls On A Cloud (1:19); 3 The Castle (1:37); 4 Party Preparations (1:41); 5 Walking On The Edge (1:29); 6 Falling For The President (2:35); 7 Pochenko Meets The Peasants (2:07); 8 L'Internationale (E. Pottier/P. Degeyter)(1:46); 9 Kleist Blackmails Joy (2:02); 10 His Excellency (:35); 11 Cinderella's Confession (1:52); 12 The Chicken (1:10); 13 Ballroom Waltz (1:32); 14 The J Waltz (J. Graff)(2:44); 15 Boris' Proud Speech (1:11); 16 You Are A Beast (2:11); 17 Going Away (2:20); 18 The Prince And The Princess (1:35).

Review: This album boasts a charmingly old fashioned romantic score by Cliff Eidelman, which certainly adds some big screen feel to *The Nanny* Fran Drescher's uninspired feature film variation on her TV persona. Much of Eidelman's score is appropriately built on a waltz motif, an attempt to create an atmosphere similar to the one established in Hollywood films of the 1940s, the ones with European locales. Romance is certainly an emotion that Eidelman writes from the heart. Includes the standard "L'Internationale," sung with a full chorus.

David Hirsch

Beavis and Butt-Head Do America 🎵🎵🎵

1996, Milan Records; from the movie *Beavis and Butt-Head Do America*, 1996.

Album Notes: *Music*: John Frizzell; *Orchestrations*: Frank Bennett, Emilie A. Bernstein; *Music Editor*: Abby Treloggen; The

London Metropolitan Orchestra, conducted by Allan Wilson; *Album Producer*: John Frizzell; *Engineer*: Chris Dibble.

Selections: 1 Buttkong (2:57); 2 The Flood (2:05); 3 The Unit In Beavis' Pants (2:07); 4 Dying In The Desert (3:33); 5 The ATF (1:21); 6 Dallas And Muddy (1:47); 7 Searching For The T.V. (:51); 8 Beavis The Sperm (1:45); 9 The Freeway Incident (1:36); 10 DEFCON 4 (1:46); 11 Judgorian Chant (:37); 12 Mr. President, We're Gonna Score (1:50); 13 The Walk Into The Sunset (1:04); 14 The Standoff (3:31); 15 Aunque La Mona (:54); 16 Mucha Muchacha (J. Garcia Esquivel)(2:18) *Juan Garcia Esquivel.*

Review: John Frizzell's unbelievably large scale orchestral score sounds nothing like what you'd expect for the feature film spin-off of this MTV animated series. The composer wisely chose to play against type by not writing a comedic score, and somehow it works remarkably well. Pieces like "Beavis the Sperm" are so honestly sincere in their intent that they just can't fail in making the film even funnier by taking it all so seriously. We're sure the real words in "Judgorian Chant" say nothing good, but who can tell?

David Hirsch

Bed & Breakfast 🎵🎵🎵▷

1992, Varese-Sarabande Records; from the movie *Bed & Breakfast*, Hemdale Films, 1992.

Album Notes: *Music*: David Shire; *Orchestrations*: David Shire; *Music Editor*: Lori Slomka; The Irish Film Orchestra, conducted by David Shire; *Featured Musicians*: Audrey Collins (violin), Jay Rosen (electronic violin); *Album Producer*: David Shire; *Engineer*: Joe Gastwirt.

Selections: 1 Main Title/Cassie's Toccata (3:20); 2 Claire Remembers Blake (2:30); 3 After Dinner Concert/Amos, Roth And Lobsters (2:25); 4 Renovations Montage (2:25); 5 What Cassie Knows/Renovation Montage II (2:35); 6 Chalk Talk/Beach Walk (2:45); 7 Summer Solstice (3:30); 8 Rowboat Scene (2:35); 9 Heart To Heart (2:00); 10 Where's Adam/Attic Scene/Decision Montage (4:20); 11 Claire Sailing (3:10); 12 End Credits (2:40).

Review: *Bed and Breakfast* is a 1991 film nobody saw, beautifully photographed on the Maine coast, about a charming rogue (Roger Moore) who comes to stay with a household of women from three generations. One of them is a violinist, which inspires a large portion of David Shire's gem of a score, a lost piece of melodic *joie de vivre* put out on Varèse Sarabande's short-lived composer-vanity label (i.e. a few albums Varèse released, but not through their regular distributor). Shire comes from a background of both Broadway and film (he

"I heard *The Simpson's* theme was voted the most obnoxious theme of the '90s. I rejoiced! To me that's a great compliment."

Danny Elfman
(Entertainment@Home, 4-97)

did such '70s masterpieces as *The Taking of Pelham One Two Three, The Conversation* and *All the President's Men)* and the two genres merge for a score that features several completely realized pieces, but is dramatically understated and flowing throughout. Solo lines dominate, brimming with melody, making the score like another character in the film—at times dancing, reflecting, singing, or speaking a soft lullaby. The size of the orchestra would almost seem too much for the story, but with his chamber/minimalist-like arpeggios Shire makes it honest, gentle and poignant. It's not as large as the Maine coast, or as small as an individual, but rather as big as life by the sea can make you feel.

Lukas Kendall

Bed of Roses ♫♫♫

1996, Milan Records; from the movie *Bed of Roses*, New Line Cinema, 1996.

Album Notes: *Music*: Michael Convertino; *Orchestrations*: John Neufeld, Conrad Pope, Bobby Muzingo; *Music Editor*: Kenn Wannberg; Orchestra conducted by Artie Kane; *Album Producer*: Michael Convertino; *Engineer*: Shawn Murphy.

Selections: 1 Boom (3:56); 2 Tuesday (3:02); 3 Dream (2:39); 4 Independent Love Song (C. Parker/J. Youle)(3:50) *Scarlet*; 5 Too Much Perfection (1:44); 6 I Looked Up (2:56); 7 Ice Cream (S. McLachlan)(2:42) *Sarah McLachlan*; 8 In Winter (1:51); 9 Amelia And The King Of Plants (3:07); 10 Family (2:13); 11 Wait (1:56); 12 Killing Time (T. Harris/D. O'Brien)(3:32) *Daniel O'Brien*; 13 Nervous Heart (M. Addison/J. Zimmerman) (3:22) *The Borrowers*; 14 Snow Fell On Walter (2:29).

Review: Michael Convertino is one of those composers who writes distinct and consistently fine music for films, but always seems to get overlooked. *Bed of Roses*, the watchable but almost fatally low-key romance with Christian Slater and Mary Stuart Masterson, features a Convertino score that provides a musical atmosphere that's melodic and earthy, characterized

by an almost new-age feel that provides ambiance at the same time it works to accentuate the relationship of the two characters. Convertino's music often lacks numerous "themes" in the traditional sense, but rather contains recurring motives that come and go within the musical "space" that the composer creates in his scores. The result here is an emotional but tranquil effort that is different enough from traditional film scores to grab your attention, and good enough to keep you listening intently.

Andy Dursin

Beethoven

Beethoven ♫♫♫

1991, MCA Records; from the movie *Beethoven*, Universal Pictures, 1991.

Album Notes: *Music*: Randy Edelman; *Orchestrations*: Greig McRitchie; *Music Editor*: Tom Carlin; *Album Producer*: Randy Edelman; *Engineer*: Robert Fernandez.

Selections: 1 Opening (4:21); 2 Discovering The Neighborhood (2:24); 3 Ciao, Baby (:40); 4 Ted And The Bullies (2:36); 5 Beethoven To The Rescue (2:11); 6 A Stroll Through Town (1:41); 7 Puppy Snatchers (3:01); 8 The Dog Has To Go (2:04); 9 Table Spin (:49); 10 Sparkie's Chase (1:53); 11 George Gets Turned On (1:29); 12 Family In Pursuit (1:39); 13 The Break-In (1:51); 14 Our Heroes (2:20); 15 The Dogs Let Loose (1:25); 16 A Sad Return (2:19); 17 Ryce's Theme (1:31); 18 Roll Over Beethoven (C. Berry)(4:42) *Paul Shaffer and the World's Most Dangerous Band*.

Review: See entry below.

Beethoven's 2nd ♫♫♫

1993, Columbia Records; from the movie *Beethoven's 2nd*, Universal Pictures, 1993.

Album Notes: *Music*: Randy Edelman; *Orchestrations*: Greig McRitchie, Ralph Ferraro, Mark McKenzie; *Music Editor*: Kathy Durning; *Album Producer*: Randy Edelman; *Engineer*: Elton Ashi.

Selections: 1 The Day I Fall In Love (C. Bayer Sager-J. Ingram-C. Magness) (4:09) *Dolly Parton, James Ingram*; 2 Opening (Snoozing With Beethoven) (3:31); 3 Chance Meeting At The Park (3:48); 4 Burger Binge (1:53); 5 First Kiss (1:48); 6 Feeding Time (3:15); 7 Discovering The Pups (3:00); 8 Two-Dog Walk (2:44); 9 The Facts Of Life (3:38); 10 A New Day (1:56); 11 Rhyce And Seth (1:13); 12 Finding Missy (1:14); 13 Over The Cliff

(2:54); 14 In The Moonlight (2:28); 15 Going Up The Mountain (2:08); 16 Raging Water/Home Again (1:22); 17 Finale (1:13).

Review: Were it not for the jaunty main theme, you might think that Randy Edelman's grander-than-life music for *Beethoven* had been composed for an epic. Actually, it may be one of the score's greatest flaws. While quite attractive and ultimately fun to listen to, it is much too lush to convince anyone that the film was nothing more than a minor comedy. In fact, in cue after cue, it sounds as if Edelman had been trying to outclass Danny Elfman or James Horner. This said, there are many delightful moments amid the bombast for one to enjoy on a pleasant Sunday afternoon, or any other day for that matter.

And since it worked so well the first time, Edelman encored for the sequel, in which his cues sound equally lovely and overly orchestrated. Now let's be realistic — the film may be called *Beethoven's 2nd*, but it really has nothing to do with Ludwig van, and a little restraint might have worked just as well.

Beetlejuice *🎵🎵🎵🎵*

1988, Geffen Records; from the movie *Beetlejuice*, Warner Bros., 1988.

Album Notes: *Music*: Danny Elfman; *Orchestrations*: Steve Bartek; *Music Editors*: Bob Badami, Nancy Fogarty; Orchestra conducted by Bill Ross; *Album Producers*: Danny Elfman, Steve Bartek; *Engineer*: Bob Fernandez.

Selections: 1 Main Titles (2:27); 2 Travel Music (1:07); 3 The Book/ Obituaries (1:30); 4 Enter… "The Family"/Sand Worm Planet (2:50); 5 The Fly (:50); 6 Lydia Discovers? (:59); 7 In The Model (1:35); 8 Juno's Theme (:48); 9 Beetle-Snake (2:08); 10 "Sold" (:35); 11 The Flier/Lydia's Pep Talk (1:25); 12 Day-O (E. Darling/B. Carey/A. Arkin)(3:05) *Harry Belafonte*; 13 The Incantation (3:11); 14 Lydia Strikes A Bargain… (:52); 15 Showtime! (1:05); 16 "Laughs" (2:33); 17 The Wedding (2:02); 18 The Aftermath (1:21); 19 End Credits (2:47); 20 Jump In Line (Shake, Shake Senora)(3:08) *Harry Belafonte*.

Review: This delightfully manic Danny Elfman score actually proves that carnival-style music can be used to make a bona fide film score! Bright and bouncy, it crosses effortlessly between the equally bizarre world of the undead and a country home possessed by the ghosts of its former owners. With the dark and twisted textures of director Tim Burton's production design, the score turns it all into a twisted live action cartoon. Heavy influences are drawn from Harry Belafonte's Caribbean songs, two of which are featured on the album, for some very bizarre musical numbers.

David Hirsch

Before and After *🎵🎵🎵🎵*

1996, Hollywood Records; from the movie *Before and After*, Hollywood Pictures, 1996.

Album Notes: *Music*: Howard Shore; *Orchestrations*: Jeff Atmajian; *Music Editor*: Suzana Peric; The London Philharmonic Orchestra, conducted by Howard Shore; *Album Producer*: Howard Shore; *Engineer*: John Kurlander.

Selections: 1 Main Title (4:03); 2 Searching For Clues (1:54); 3 Destroying Evidence (3:03); 4 Looking For Jacob (2:07); 5 First Postcard (1:48); 6 Dr. Ryan (:51); 7 Apprehended (3:12); 8 Preliminary Hearing (1:05); 9 Ben And Carolyn (1:27); 10 Treehouse (2:55); 11 The Confession (4:49); 12 The Grand Jury (1:46); 13 Carolyn (2:11); 14 It's Your Fault (1:54); 15 The Truth (1:41); 16 Jacob's Gone (2:00); 17 Before And After (4:14).

Review: A criminal case with romantic undertones, starring Meryl Streep and Liam Neeson, *Before and After* elicited a dramatic score from Howard Shore, demonstrating particularly emotive skills in writing themes that are attractive, despite the deliberately slow and ominous tone adopted. The relentless somber moods might not be to everyone's liking, but the music is quite striking with the recording by the London Philharmonic Orchestra extracting all the flavor in a very effective reading.

Ben-Hur

Ben-Hur *🎵🎵🎵🎵*

1989, Silva Screen Records; from the movie *Ben-Hur*, M-G-M/ Turner, 1925.

Album Notes: *Music*: Carl Davis; *Orchestrations*: Colin Matthews, David Matthews; The Royal Liverpool Philharmonic Orchestra, conducted by Carl Davis; *Album Producer*: Paul Wing; *Engineer*: Mike Hatch.

Selections: 1 Opening Titles (3:29); 2 The Nativity: The Cave Of David/ Star Of Bethlehem/The Adoration Of The Magi (5:21); 3 Esther And The Young Prince (3:56); 4 Roman March and Disaster: Gratus' Entry Into Jerusalem/ Storming The Palace and Arrest (6:00); 5 Galley Slave (4:55); 6 Pirate Battle (5:58); 7 Iras The Egyptian (7:40); 8 The Chariot Race: The Gathering Of The Chariots/The Race (13:57); 9 Ben-Hur's Return: The Palace Of Hur/Lepers (11:03); 10 Via Dolorosa: The Way Of The Cross/Miracle (5:06); 11 Earthquake And New Dawn: Collapse Of The Senate/The Resurrection (3:46).

Review: Anyone familiar with Miklos Rozsa's massive score for the 1959 *Ben-Hur* (see below) will be doubly interested in listening to this soundtrack album. First because Carl Davis was differently inspired than Rozsa by the basic storyline,

motion picture soundtracks

second because Davis writing a new score for the silent film of 1925 was not under the same constraints and limitations imposed to Rozsa, and may have been more at liberty to let his imagination run free.

The basic concepts of religious reverence and epic outbursts are very much in evidence in his score, as they were in Rozsa's, and his treatment of "The Chariot Race," for instance, has nothing to envy the music for the 1959 version. If anything Davis' thunderous "Gathering of the Chariots," with its heavy reliance on drums, contrasts with Rozsa's clarion-clear trumpet calls. But while Davis' overall approach may sound more traditionally symphonic in a Wagnerian sense, the end result is a score that is equally stirring. Playing by the Royal Liverpool is consistently solid and exciting.

Ben-Hur 🎵🎵🎵🎵🎵

1996, Rhino Records; from the movie *Ben-Hur*, M-G-M, 1959.

Album Notes: *Music*: Miklos Rozsa; *Orchestrations*: Miklos Rozsa, Eugene Zador; The M-G-M Studio Orchestra and Chorus, conducted by Miklos Rozsa; *Album Producer*: Marilee Bradford; *Engineer*: Douglas Schwartz.

Selections: CD 1: 1 Overture (6:32); 2 Anno Domini (1:32); 3 Star of Bethlehem (1:33); 4 Adorations Of The Magi (2:04); 5 Shofar Call (:11); 6 Prelude (Main Title)(2:10); 7 Marcia Romana (1:56); 8 Spirit And Sword (:51); 9 Friendship (4:23); 10 The House Of Hur (1:41); 11 The Conflict (1:42); 12 Esther (2:35); 13 The Unknown Future (:43); 14 Love Theme (2:11); 15 Ring For Freedom (2:39); 16 Salute For Gratus (:33); 17 Gratus' Entry To Jerusalem (1:57); 18 The Arrest (1:18); 19 Reminiscences (1:47); 20 Revenge (1:21); 21 Condemned (:55); 22 Escape (2:06); 23 Vengeance (:45); 24 The Prison (:39); 25 The Desert (2:14); 26 Exhaustion (2:08); 27 The Prince Of Peace, Part 1 (3:07); 28 The Prince Of Peace, Part 2 (1:49); 29 Roman Galley (:57); 30 Salute For Arrius (:20); 31 Quintus Arrives (:40); 32 Roman Fleet (1:05); 33 The Galley (Rowing Of The Galley Slaves), Part 1-4 (3:14); 34 Rest (1:19); 35 Battle Preparations, Parts 1 & 2 (1:59); 36 The Pirate Fleet (1:06); 37 Attack! (1:27); 38 Ramming Speed! (:18); 39 The Battle, Parts 1 & 2 (3:05); 40 Rescue (1:53); 41 Roman Sails (:48); 42 The Rowers (:25); 43 Victory Parade, Parts 1 & 2 (2:50).

CD 2: 1 Fertility Dance (:59); 2 Arrius' Party, Parts 1 & 2 (1:30); 3 Nostalgia (:35); 4 Farewell To Rome (1:39); 5 Judea, Part 1 (2:55); 6 Judea, Part 2 (:24); 7 A Barren Coast (:27); 8 Balthasar (2:00); 9 Balthasar's World (1:56); 10 Homecoming (1:22); 11 Memories (2:48); 12 Hatred (1:34); 13 Lepers (1:00); 14 Return (2:51); 15 Promise (2:29); 16 Sorrow and Intermission (1:24); 17 Entr'acte (3:47); 18 Panem et Circenses (Bread And Circus) March (:52); 19 Circus Fanfares (:42); 20 Panem et Circenses March (1st reprise) (:52); 21 Fanfare For Circus Parade (:14); 22 Circus Parade (Parade Of The Charioteers)(2:13); 23 Fanfare For Start Of Race (:11); 24 Panem et Circenses March (2nd reprise) (:56); 25 Victory March (:17); 26 Bitter Triumph (:46); 27 Aftermath, No. 1 (2:06); 28 Valley Of Lepers (1:11); 29 The Search (2:19); 30 The Uncleans (2:28); 31 Road Of Sorrow (2:48); 32 The Mount (:39); 33 The Sermon (:39); 34 Frustration (1:15); 35 Valley Of The Dead (2:35); 36 Tirzah Saved (2:22); 37 The Procession To Calvary (2:54); 38 The Bearing Of The Cross (2:46); 39 Recognition (1:27); 40 Aftermath, No. 2 (2:22); 41 Golgotha (:52); 42 Shadow Of A Storm (1:00); 43 The Miracle (1:46); 44 Finale (3:07); 45 Star Of Bethlehem (alternate take) (1:33).

Review: See entry below.

Ben-Hur 🎵🎵🎵🎵

1985, London Records; from the movie *Ben-Hur*, M-G-M, 1959.

Album Notes: *Music*: Miklos Rozsa; The National Philharmonic Orchestra and Chorus, conducted by Miklos Rozsa.

Selections: 1 Fanfare To Prelude (3:59); 2 Star Of Bethlehem and Adoration Of The Magi (4:03); 3 Friendship (3:55); 4 The Burning Desert (5:24); 5 Arrius' Party (1:46); 6 Rowing Of The Galley Slaves (2:39); 7 Parade Of The Charioteers (3:34); 8 The Mother's Love (2:54); 9 Return To Judea (2:33); 10 Ring For Freedom (2:50); 11 Lepers' Search For The Christ (3:14); 12 Procession To Calvary (4:46); 13 Mirace and Finale (5:32).

Review: A hugely popular soundtrack, the music from *Ben-Hur* was initially released on one LP by M-G-M Records to coincide with the film's first run. The success of that album soon prompted the label to issue a second volume on the subsidiary label, Leo Records, though that album was deleted soon after.

With the advent of CDs, *Ben-Hur* was then reissued several times, but the Rhino set finally presents the colossal score in all its grandeur, with each cue properly sequenced, plus many outtakes and selections that were initially composed but discarded before the final cut.

Though Rozsa created many outstanding scores during his long and prolific career as a film composer, *Ben-Hur* must be considered his crowning achievement. The 2-CD set does it full justice.

For those less inclined to purchase the Rhino set, the National Philharmonic Orchestra and Chorus, under the direction of the composer, give a sumptuous reading of highlights from the score, in what might be a recording of choice.

Benny & Joon ♫♫♫♫

1993, Milan Records; from the movie *Benny & Joon*, M-G-M, 1993.

Album Notes: *Music*: Rachel Portman; *Orchestrations*: Rachel Portman; *Music Editor*: Bill Abbott; Orchestra conducted by J.A.C. Redford; *Album Producer*: David Franco; *Engineer*: John Richards.

Selections: 1 I'm Gonna Be (500 Miles)(3:34) *The Proclaimers*; 2 Benny And Joon (2:45); 3 Snorkel's Mask (1:03); 4 Joon's Medicine (1:41); 5 Hubcaps (:31); 6 Sam's New Home/Raisins (2:39); 7 Balloon (1:49); 8 In The Park (5:09); 9 Love Theme (3:08); 10 Sam Is Kicked Out (3:36); 11 On The Bus (4:10); 12 Swinging (2:59); 13 Sam And Joon (1:39); 14 Benny And Joon (reprise)(2:44).

Review: In recent years, women composers have succeeded in making themselves heard in a field that had essentially been a man's world. High on that list of relative newcomers is Rachel Portman, who made quite an impression with this quirky score for a film starring Johnny Depp, in which the influence of Danny Elfman is occasionally apparent. Writing for a handful of solo instruments within the larger framework provided by the orchestra, Portman developed a series of attractive cues anchored by the main theme, with the clarinet and the flute playing an essential role in the mix ("Balloon," "In the Park," "Love Theme").

The Benny Goodman Story
♫♫♫♫♫

1972, MCA Records; from the movie *The Benny Goodman Story*, Universal Pictures, 1955.

Album Notes: *Featured Musicians*: Benny Goodman and His Orchestra, The Benny Goodman Quartet, The Benny Goodman Trio.

Selections: 1 Let's Dance (F. Baldridge/J. Bonine/G. Stone)(2:17); 2 Down South Camp Meetin' (3:03); 3 King Porter Stomp (F. Morton)(2:40); 4 It's Been So Long (H. Adamson/W. Donaldson)(3:17); 5 Roll 'Em (3:13); 6 Bugle Call Rag (E. Blake/ C. Morgan)(2:57); 7 Don't Be That Way (M. Parish/B. Goodman/E. Sampson)(3:52); 8 You Turned The Tables On Me (S. Mitchell/L. Alter)(2:54) *Martha Tilton*; 9 Goody Goody (M. Malneck/J. Mercer)(2:17); 10 Slipped Disc (B. Goodman)(4:13) *The Benny Goodman Octet*; 11 Stompin' At The Savoy (A. Razaf/ B. Goodman/E. Sampson/C. Webb)(2:32); 12 One O'Clock Jump (W. Basie/H. James) (3:07); 13 Memories Of You (E. Blake/A. Razaf) (2:48) *The Benny Goodman Trio*; 14 China Boy (D. Winfree/P. Boutelje) (3:32) *The Benny Goodman Trio*; 15 Moonglow (E. DeLange/W. Hudson/I. Mills)(6:49) *The Benny Goodman Quartet*; 16 Avalon (A. Jolson/B.G. DeSylva/V.

Rose)(6:05) *The Benny Goodman Quartet*; 17 And The Angels Sing (Z. Elman/J. Mercer)(2:59) *Martha Tilton*; 18 Jersey Bounce (B. Feyne/R. Wright/B. Plater/T. Bradshaw/E. Johnson)(3:00); 19 Shine (C. Mack/L. Brown/ F. Dabney)(:58) *Harry James*; 20 Sing Sing Sing (With A Swing) (L. Prima)/Christopher Columbus (L. Berry/A. Razaf)(7:59).

Review: Even if the story of the legendary Benny Goodman is highly romanticized in the film *The Benny Goodman Story* and hardly reflected the reality of his life, one thing that is truly authentic in the film is the music, performed by the great man himself, and many of the sidemen who had made the journey to fame with him back in the '30s, including Harry James, Gene Krupa, Lionel Hampton, Teddy Wilson and Martha Tilton, among many others. The selections, heard in this soundtrack album, are actual recreations of the band's most famous hits, including Goodman's signature songs, "Let's Dance," "One O'Clock Jump" and "Stompin' at the Savoy," as well as "Moonglow," "Avalon," "And the Angels Sing," "Don't Be That Way," and the always thrilling "Sing Sing Sing" with its "Christopher Columbus" interpolation, which was one of the highlights at the celebrated Carnegie Hall concert in 1938. If you like jazz, and if you like big bands, and even if you hate the saccharine film, you owe it to yourself to have this album.

The Best Years of Our Lives
♫♫♫♫♫

1988, Preamble Records; from the movie *The Best Years of Our Lives*, Samuel Goldwyn Productions, 1946.

Album Notes: *Music*: Hugo Friedhofer; *Orchestrations*: Jerome Moross, Edward B. Powell, Leo Shuken, Sidney Cutner; *Orchestrations reconstructed*: Tony Bremner; The London Philharmonic Orchestra, conducted by Franco Collura; *Featured Soloist*: Bob Burns (alto sax); *Album Producer*: John Lasher; *Engineer*: Bob Auger.

Selections: 1 Main Title (1:26); 2 Homecoming (6:17); 3 The Elevator/ Boone City/Peggy (4:12); 4 Fred And Peggy (2:22); 5 The Nightmare (6:12); 6 Fred Asleep (2:19); 7 Neighbors/ Wilma/ Homer's Anger (7:31); 8 Homer Goes Upstairs (5:49); 9 The Citation/Graveyard And Bombers (4:21); 10 End Title and End Cast (Wilma)(1:58); 11 Exit Music (1:54).

Review: This classic Academy Award-winning score by Hugo Friedhofer was created to illustrate the lives of three veterans coming back to their hometown at the end of World War II, and the problems they encounter trying to adjust to the changes that have occurred within themselves and around them. Beautifully lyrical, but eschewing a maudlin sentimentality that could have seemed unnecessary in less experienced hands, Friedhofer wrote a score that confronted and underlined the powerful, emotionally charged story in which the full range of human feelings found an expression, from wrenching torment to liberating love, from tears to laughter.

The recording, one of the earliest reconstructions of a classic film score, does full justice to the many beauties contained in the music, with the London Philharmonic Orchestra, conducted by Franco Collura, giving a top-notch performance, further enhanced by the superlative ambient sound.

Betrayed 🎜🎜🎜

1988, Varese-Sarabande Records; from the movie *Betrayed*, United Artists, 1988.

Album Notes: *Music*: Bill Conti; *Orchestrations*: Jack Eskew; Orchestra conducted by Bill Conti; *Featured Musicians*: John Goux (guitar), Tommy Morgan (harmonica), Bill Conti (piano); *Album Producers*: Bill Conti, Lee DeCarlo; *Engineer*: Lee DeCarlo.

Selections: 1 Main Title (2:15); 2 The Stalk (1:33); 3 To The Bank (1:13); 4 The Way (2:11); 5 Riding To Work (1:18); 6 Shoot The Horse (1:30); 7 Guns (1:36); 8 The Bank Robbery (:44); 9 I'm Back (1:38); 10 There Ain't No Going Back (1:12); 11 Another Way (2:16); 12 Trip To Chicago (:53); 13 Passing Time (:57); 14 The Contract (1:35); 15 Rock Country (1:18); 16 My F.B.I. (1:01); 17 Marry Me (:50); 18 Kill Me Kathy (1:14); 19 End Title (3:58).

Review: Bill Conti fashioned a very engaging, country-styled score for this political thriller, set in the Midwest, about an attractive undercover FBI operative (Debra Winger), who infiltrates a radical group suspected of having murdered a controversial radio talk show host. With a predominance of motifs for guitar and harmonica, the flavorful cues set the scene of the action and give specific moments in it a vibrant musical support ("The Way," "Riding to Work," "Another Way," "Rock Country"), making this an album that's quite pleasant to listen to.

Betty Blue 🎜🎜🎜🎜

1986, Virgin Records; from the movie *Betty Blue*, Alive Films, 1986.

Album Notes: *Music*: Gabriel Yared.

Selections: 1 Betty and Zorg (2:24); 2 Storms Over Night (3:13); 3 Cargo Voyage (1:13); 4 Garbage Cooking (1:47); 5 To Humidify The Mount (1:45); 6 Little Nicolas (3:35); 7 Gyneco Zebra (1:40); 8 Like Two Fingers In The Hand (1:06); 9 Zorg and Betty (2:15); 10 Chili con carne (3:10); 11 It's The Wind, Betty (4:11); 12 Sunset Hanging On A Tree (1:04); 13 Lisa Rock (1:15); 14 The Heart In A Purple Skai (1:12); 15 Bungalow Zen (1:30); 16 37.2 In The Morning (2:54); 17 Damned Fair Rides (2:24).

Review: For this gritty drama by *Diva* director Jean-Jacques Beineix, Gabriel Yared wrote a convincing score that blends elements of romance and pathos. The story of two youngsters, steady Zorg and batty Betty, on a free-wheeling romp in the country, the film is noticeably distinguished by Beineix's colorful approach to filmmaking, and by Beatrice Dalle's sensual portrayal as Betty. Yared's music captures the poetic focus that contrasted and enhanced the character's slow descent into madness.

The Beverly Hillbillies 🎜🎜🎜🎜

1993, Fox Records; from the movie *The Beverly Hillbillies*, 20th Century-Fox, 1993.

Album Notes: *Song Producers*: Johnny Slate, Joe Diffie, Richard Landis, Buddy Cannon, Norro Wilson, Scott Hendricks, Garth Fundis, Joe Walsh, Steve Earle, Chris Lord-Alge, Steve Buckingham, Bill Halverson, Dolly Parton, Bela Fleck; *Engineers*: Mike Bradley, Chuck Ainlay, Billy Sherrill, Chris Lord-Alge, Gary Paczosa, Bill Halverson, Csaba Petocz, Charlie Brocca; *Album Executive Producers*: Ron Fair, Elliot Lurie.

Selections: 1 White Lightnin' (J.P. Richardson)(3:12) *Joe Diffie*; 2 I Ain't Never (M. Tillis/W. Pierce)(2:25) *The Oak Ridge Boys*; 3 Crying Time (B. Owens)(3:08) *Lorrie Morgan*; 4 I'm Movin' On (H. Snow)(2:55) *Danny Kershaw*; 5 I'm So Lonesome I Could Cry (H. Williams)(4:03) *Aaron Tippin*; 6 Hot Rod Lincoln (C. Ryan/W.S. Stevenson)(2:47) *Jim Varney, Ricky Skaggs*; 7 Honey Don't (C. Perkins)(3:31) *Joe Walsh, Steve Earle*; 8 Together Again (B. Owens)(2:36) *Doug Supernaw*; 9 If You've Got The Money I've Got The Time (L. Frizzell/J. Beck)(2:01) *Ricky Van Shelton*; 10 Wasted Days And Wasted Nights (F. Fender/W. Duncan)(3:03) *Freddy Fender & The Texas Tornadoes*; 11 If You Ain't Got Love (D. Parton)(2:51) *Dolly Parton*; 12 The Ballad Of Jed Clampett (P. Henning)(1:20) *Jerry Scoggins*.

Review: This big screen remake of the television series yielded this exuberant soundtrack album, graced by the presence of a great lineup of country performers, including Dolly Parton, The Oak Ridge Boys, Ricky Van Shelton, The Texas Tornadoes, and Lorrie Morgan who does a great rendition of "Crying Time." About a compilation such as this, there is really very little to say. The songs are good natured and pleasant and very enjoyable, and your reaction to the album will largely depend on how you feel about the artists and their stylings. For the record, though, it should be noted that Jerry Scoggins does a cover version of "The Ballad of Jed Clampett." They probably should have used the original!

See also: The TV soundtrack section

Beverly Hills Cop

Beverly Hills Cop ♫♫♫♭

1984, MCA Records; from the movie *Beverly Hills Cop*, Paramount Pictures, 1984.

Album Notes: *Music:* Harold Faltermeyer; *Song Producers:* Howie Rice, Peter Bunetta, Rick Chudacoff, Hawk, Howard Hewett, Nigel Martinez, Richard Perry, Keith Forsey, Harold Faltermeyer, Steve Bartek, Danny Elfman, Paul Ratajczak, Mic Murphy, David Frank; *Album Executive Producers:* Don Simpson, Jerry Bruckheimer, Martin Brest.

Selections: 1 New Attitude (S. Robinson/J. Gilutin/B. Hull)(4:36) *Patti LaBelle*; 2 Don't Get Stopped In Beverly Hills (Hawk/H. Hewett/M. Free) (4:20) *Shalamar*; 3 Do You Really (Want My Love?)(Junior/G. Nightingale)(3:44) *Junior*; 4 Emergency (H. Rice/S. Sheridan)(3:28) *Rockie Robbins*; 5 Neutron Dance (A. Wills/D. Sembello)(4:12) *Pointer Sisters*; 6 The Heat Is On (K. Forsey/H. Faltermeyer)(3:45) *Glenn Frey*; 7 Gratitude (D. Elfman)(5:04) *Danny Elfman*; 8 Stir It Up (A. Willis/D. Sembello)(3:35) *Patti LaBelle*; 9 Rock'n'Roll Me Again (M. Bennon/R. Theiner)(3:14) *The System*; 10 Axel F (H. Faltermeyer)(3:00) *Harold Faltermeyer*.

Review: One of the more popular song compilation albums still in print years after the release of the film, it owes much of its success to an excellent selection of artists. Many of the songs are prominently featured in the film, particularly some fine work by Patti LaBelle ("New Attitude," "Stir It Up"), Glen Frey ("The Heat is On") and The Pointer Sisters ("Neutron Dance"). The album also features "Gratitude," a vocal performance by Danny Elfman who would breakout the following year with *Pee Wee's Big Adventure*. A few other songs that were not used in the movie still capture the energy and mood of this fast-paced Eddie Murphy comedy/adventure vehicle. Of course there's also the original version of Harold Faltermeyer's "Axel F" theme, the only piece that could possibly be considered underscore since it was used so often throughout the film.

David Hirsch

Beverly Hills Cop III ♫♭

1994, MCA Records; from the movie *Beverly Hills Cop III*, Paramount Pictures, 1994.

Album Notes: *Song Producers:* Carl "Groove" Martin, Daniell Van Rensauer, Marc Gay, Garfield Bright, Ian Lewis, Touter Harvey, Doctor Jam, Jimmy Jam, Terry Lewis, Keith Forsey, Raphael Wiggins, Nile Rodgers, Brian Holland, Lamont Dozier;

Album Executive Producers: John Landis, Leslie Belzberg; *Engineer:* Tom Baker.

Selections: 1 The Place Where You Belong (C. Martin/T. Lorenz/D. Van Bensauer/M. Gay/G. Bright)(4:22) *Shai*; 2 Summer Jamming (I. Levis)(4:03) *Inner Circle*; 3 Luv 4 Dem Gangsta'z (K. Carter/Doctor Jam)(4:33) *Eazy-E*; 4 Mood (J. Harris III/T. Lewis/C. Moore)(4:10) *Chante Moore*; 5 The Right Kinda Lover (J. Harris III/T. Lewis/A. Bennett-Nesby/J. Wright)(4:52) *Patti LaBelle*; 6 Keep The Peace (K. Forsey/M. Younger-Smith/A. Farriss/ M. Hutchance)(4:29) *INXS*; 7 Right Thing, Wrong Way (J. Harris III/T. Lewis/T. Trent D'Arby)(5:13) *Terence Trent D'Arby*; 8 Leavin' (R. Wiggins/ J.L. Smith) (4:06) *Tony Toni Tone*; 9 Axel F ((H. Faltermeyer)(2:57) *Nile Rodgers, Richard Hilton*; 10 Come See About Me (B. Holland/E. Holland/ L. Dozier)(2:37) *The Supremes*.

Review: Like the film series, the "Beverly Hills Cop" musical franchise ran out of steam by its third time out. One can never speak ill of a Supremes classic like "Come See About Me," and there are reasonably good selections from Tony! Toni! Tone! ("Leavin'") and Terence Trent D'Arby ("Right Thing, Wrong Way"). But there's certainly nothing as memorable as any of the hits from the original "Beverly Hills Cop" soundtrack.

Gary Graff

Beverly Hills Ninja ♫♫♫♫

1997, EMI Records; from the movie *Beverly Hills Ninja*, TriStar Pictures, 1997.

Album Notes: *Music:* George S. Clinton; *Song Producers:* Little Dave Greenberg, Tony Shimkin, The Patti Rothberg Band, Mike Chapman, Ulfuls, Jerry Goldstein, Maurizio Bassi, Frank Acersa, Biddu, Tommy D., Mike Denneen, George S. Clinton; *Album Producer:* Pete Ganbarg.

Selections: 1 "You're a Ninja?" (:16); 2 Kung Fu Fighting (C. Douglas)(3:14) *Patti Rothberg*; 3 One Way Or Another (D. Harry/N. Harrison)(3:36) *Blondie*; 4 "We are in danger..." (:13); 5 Tsugihagi Boogie Woogie (T. Matsumoto)(3:13) *Ulfuls*; 6 Low Rider (S. Allen/H.R. Brown/M. Dickerson/L. Jordan/C. Miller/ L. Oskar/H. Scott/J. Goldstein)(3:11) *War*; 7 "The blackness of my belt..." (:20); 8 Tarzan Boy (M. Bassi/N. Hackett)(3:51) *Baltimora*; 9 "My identity must remain mysterious..." (:19); 10 Turning Japanese (D.V. Fenton) (3:24) *The Hazies*; 11 "You're the big, fat Ninja, aren't you?" (:17); 12 Kung Fu Fighting (C. Douglas)(3:14) *Carl Douglas*; 13 I'm Too Sexy (F. Fairbrass/R. Fairbrass/R. Manzoli)(2:50) *Right Said Fred*; 14 "...close to the temple, not inside." (:24); 15 I Think We're Alone Now (Japanese version) (R. Cordell)(2:46) *Lene Lovich*; 16 Finally

Got It (S. Freeman)(3:36) *Little John*; 17 "...Yes, I guess I did" (:32); 18 The End (G.S. Clinton)(1:19).

Review: Introduced by a funny bit of dialogue, "You're a Ninja?..." that sets the scene for the album, this compilation presents several songs that are part of the soundtrack for this frequently hilarious film about a karate expert who became a Ninja when it would seem he should have been a sumo wrestler instead. But don't let the silliness of the premise drive you crazy—watching the film will suffice. Or try this album, informed by several other moments of nonsense from the soundtrack ("My identity must remain mysterious...," "You're the big, fat Ninja, aren't you," "Close to the temple, not inside..."), and featuring some songs guaranteed to entertain you, even if they don't always delight you, like "Tsugihagi Boogie Woogie," "Tarzan Boy," "Turning Japanese," and Lene Lovich's perversely humorous rendition of "I Think We're Alone Now (Japanese Version)."

The Big Chill ♫♫♫♫

1983, Motown Records; from the movie *The Big Chill*, Columbia Pictures, 1983.

Album Notes: *Album Producer*: Roger Nichols; *Engineer*: John Matousak.

Selections: 1 I Heard It Through The Grapevine (N. Whitfield/B. Strong) (5:04) *Marvin Gaye*; 2 My Girl (W. Robinson, Jr./R. White)(2:55) *The Temptations*; 3 Good Lovin' (R. Clark/A. Resnick)(2:28) *The Rascals*; 4 The Tracks Of My Tears (W. Robinson, Jr./W. Moore/M. Tarplin)(2:53) *Smokey Robinson & The Miracles*; 5 Joy To The World (H. Axton)(3:24) *Three Dog Night*; 6 Ain't Too Proud To Beg (N. Whitfield/E. Holland, Jr.)(2:31) *The Temptations*; 7 (You Make Me Feel Like A) Natural Woman (G. Goffin/C. King/J. Wexler)(2:41) *Aretha Franklin*; 8 I Second That Emotion (W. Robinson, Jr./A. Cleveland)(2:46) *Smokey Robinson & The Miracles*; 9 A Whiter Shade Of Pale (K. Reid/G. Brooker)(4:03) *Procol Harum*; 10 Tell Him (B. Russell)(2:29) *The Exciters*.

Review: A solid collection of golden oldies that marked a generation and actually rekindled the fortunes of Motown Records when they were used in the soundtrack of this film. Nothing but the best here, and each song chockful of fond memories. Okay, the album is kind of short with ten tracks adding up to 31 minutes of playing time, but for once you still might want to pick up a copy and listen to it, just for the fun of it.

The Big Country ♫♫♫♫

1988/1995, Silva America; from the movie *The Big Country*, United Artists, 1958

Album Notes: *Music*: Jerome Moross; *Orchestrations*: B. Mayers, George Grau, Conrad Salinger, Alexander Courage; *Music*

Editor: Lloyd Young; The Philharmonia Orchestra, conducted by Tony Bremner; *Album Producer*: Christopher Palmer; *Engineer*: Mike Ross-Trevor.

Selections: 1 Main Title (3:13); 2 Julie's House (1:57); 3 The Welcoming (3:19); 4 Courtin' Time (1:23); 5 Old Thunder (1:46); 6 The Raid and Capture (4:55); 7-10 Major Terrill's Party (dance suite): (a) dance 1 (1:47), (b) dance 2 (1:03), (c) waltz (2:47), (d) polka (1:00); 11 McKay's Ride/McKay Is Missing/The Old House (5:30); 12 Waiting (1:55); 13 The Big Muddy (3:02); 14 McKay Alone/Night At Ladder Ranch/The Fight (4:30); 15 Cattle At The River (2:18); 16 Attempted Rape (1:45); 17 The War Party Gathers/McKay In Blanco Canyon/The Major Alone (7:16); 18 The Duel/The Death Of Buck Hannassey/End Title (5:33).

Review: One of the great western scores, the music for *The Big Country* was, for many years, available only on a United Artists mono or rechanneled stereo LP of dubious sonic quality. The score deserved a reevaluation, and this superior recording fills the gap. With The Philharmonia, conducted by Tony Bremner, giving an outstanding performance, Jerome Moross' music emerges full force as the extraordinary effort it always was. Everything in this recording works to emphasize the positive aspects of the score, including the splendid, wide-open sonics, as well as the packaging, with an informative booklet providing behind-the-score glances that will delight any fan of film music.

The Big Easy ♫♫♫♫

1987, Antilles Records; from the movie *The Big Easy*, Columbia Pictures, 1987.

Album Notes: *Album Compiler*: Danny Holloway; *Engineers*: Ken Perry, Bill Inglot.

Selections: 1 Iko Iko (S. Jones/J. Jones/M. Jones/J. Thomas/B. Hawkins/R. Hwakins/J. Johnson)(2:03) *The Dixie Cups*; 2 Tipitina (H.R. Byrd)(3:37) *Professor Longhair*; 3 Ma 'Tit Fille (S. Dural)(6:51) *Buckwheat Zydeco*; 4 Colinda (p.d.)(3:05) *Zachary Richard*; 5 Tell It Like It Is (G. Davis/L. Diamond)(4:18) *Aaron Neville & The Neville Brothers*; 6 Zydeco Gris Gris (M. Doucet)(4:08) *Beausoleil*; 7 Oh Yeh Yai (T. Simien)(3:13) *Terrance Simien & The Mallet Playboys*; 8 Hey Hey (Indians Comin')(C. Neville/G. Landry)(4:00) *The Wild Tchoupitoulas*; 9 Closer To You (D. Quaid/T. Simien)(4:58) *Dennis Quaid*; 10 Saviour, Pass Me Not (C. Jeter)(5:06) *The Swan Silvertones*; 11 Buck's Nouvelle Jole Blon (C. Breaux)(4:42) *Buckwheat Zydeco & Ils Sont Partis Band*; 12 Pine Grove Blues (N. Abshire) (1:03) *Dewey Balfa*.

Review: The New Orleans setting of this offbeat police drama suggests a score that would make use of the specific sounds heard in that city, with The Dixie Cups, Professor Longhair,

Buckwheat Zydeco, and Aaron Neville & The Neville Brothers among the local artists represented. Dennis Quaid, who plays in the film an extrovert homicidal detective, hot after Ellen Barkin, a transfer from another city, the moment she shows up in his office, also wrote and performs a number, "Closer to You," which does not seem so out of place in the context. A flavorful, frequently exhilarating album.

Big Jake

1986, Varese-Sarabande Records; from the movie *Big Jake,* 20th Century-Fox, 1971.

See: The Shootist

Big Time 🎵🎵

1988, Island Records; from the movie *Big Time,* Island Visual Arts, 1988.

Album Notes: *Music:* Tom Waits; *Featured Musicians:* Michael Blair (drums, percussion, bongos), Ralph Carney (saxes, clarinets, horn), Greg Cohen (electric bass, alto horn), Marc Ribot (guitars, banjo, trumpet), Willie Schwarz (accordion, Hammond organ, sitar, conga), Fred Tackett (guitar), Richie Hayward (drums), Larry Taylor (upright bass), Tom Waits (organ, vocals); *Album Producers:* Tom Waits, Kathleen Brennan; *Engineer:* John Oster.

Selections: 1 16 Shells From A Thirty-Ought-Six (4:10); 2 Red Shoes (4:06); 3 Underground (2:20); 4 Cold Cold Ground (3:18); 5 Straight To The Top (T. Waits/G. Cohen)(2:45); 6 Yesterday Is Here (T. Waits/K. Brennan)(2:57); 7 Way Down In The Hole (4:26); 8 Falling Down (4:12); 9 Strange Weather (T. Waits/K. Brennan)(3:20); 10 Big Black Mariah (2:41); 11 Rain Dogs (3:52); 12 Train Song (2:54); 13 Johnsburg, Illinois (1:32); 14 Ruby's Arms (4:44); 15 Telephone Call From Istanbul (4:15); 16 Clap Hands (4:43); 17 Gun Street Girl (4:00); 18 Time (4:00).

Review: An account of live performances by Tom Waits and his band, recorded in Los Angeles, San Francisco, Dublin, Stockholm, and Berlin, this album is largely a showcase for the songwriter and presents songs that his fans will identify with. As is frequently the case in films such as this, the scope and impact are limited, with Waits' raucous vocals unlikely to attract anyone other than hardcore followers.

Big Top Pee-Wee 🎵🎵🎵

1988, Arista Records; from the movie *Big Top Pee-Wee,* Paramount Pictures, 1988.

Album Notes: *Music:* Danny Elfman; *Orchestrations:* Steve Bartek, William Ross; *Music Editor:* Dick Bernstein; Orchestra

conducted by William Ross; *Album Producer:* Danny Elfman; *Engineer:* Dan Wallin; *Assistant Engineer:* Susan McLean.

Selections: 1 Main Title (1:23); 2 The Girl On The Flying Trapeze (2:01) *Pee-Wee Herman;* 3 Pee-Wee Flies (:52); 4 Happy House/Pee-Wee Herman Had A Farm (1:16) *Pee-Wee Herman and Vance the Pig;* 5 Rise 'n Shine (2:52); 6 The Greenhouse (1:00); 7 Sneaky Walk (:48); 8 Race To School (:29); 9 The Big Storm (2:18); 10 Pee-Wee To The Rescue/Lion Problems (1:23); 11 Where's Midge? (:28); 12 Circus Parade (1:03); 13 Sad Drive Home (1:23); 14 Circus In The House (1:23); 15 Happy Circus (1:39); 16 Zsa Zsa's Delight (1:13); 17 Elephant Ride (2:36); 18 The Big Kiss (:53); 19 Rejection (1:41); 20 Mace's Speech (1:13); 21 Man To Man (:27); 22 Psycho Winnie (1:09); 23 Rimprovero (trad.) (:44) *Pee-Wee Herman;* 24 I Love You (3:09); 25 Pee-Wee Tries/Town Spies (1:30); 26 Pee-Wee's Love Theme (2:45); 27 Angry Mob (:30); 28 Transformations (1:16); 29 Big Top Finale (3:31) *Pee-Wee Herman and The Big Top Company;* 30 Pee-Wee's Big Surprise (2:26); 31 End Credits (3:02).

Review: This 1988 follow-up to the 1985 cult classic *Pee-Wee's Big Adventure* didn't bring Tim Burton back behind the camera, but did, at least, reunite Danny Elfman with its daffy protagonist, who here gets involved with a traveling carnival. This setting affords Elfman the opportunity at writing some irresistibly goofy circus music and fanfares, interspersed with more charming, Rota-esque Pee-Wee motifs, newly composed for this sequel (the result of the picture being produced by another studio). There's even a song Pee-Wee croons in his best Sinatra style ("The Girl on the Flying Trapeze"), along with a duet between Pee-Wee and his farm animal sidekicks. The result is an enthusiastic score filled with all the quirky instrumentations associated with Elfman's most offbeat works; dialogue is incorporated in several of the tracks, but they do less to detract from the music than they do to cement the charm of the material. One of Elfman's early scores, the Arista album is now hard-to-find but worth the effort to seek out.

Andy Dursin

Billy Bathgate 🎵🎵🎵♭

1991, Milan Records; from the movie *Billy Bathgate,* Touchstone Pictures, 1991.

Album Notes: *Music:* Mark Isham; *Orchestrations:* Tom Pasatieri; *Music Editor:* Todd Kasow; Orchestra conducted by J.A.C. Redford, Enrico DiCecco; *Album Producer:* Mark Isham; *Engineers:* James Nichols, Marian Conaty.

Selections: 1 The Dutchman (2:52); 2 A Capable Boy (1:34); 3 A Model Citizen (1:19); 4 Bye Bye Blackbird (M. Dixon/R. Henderson)(3:21) *Rachel York*; 5 Rebecca (1:23); 6 A Girl Whos Not Named Lola (:48); 7 Oyfn Pripetshok (On The Hearth)(M. Warshawsky)(1:56) Children Chorus; 8 Manhattan (:40); 9 Bathgate Avenue (:49); 10 I'm In The Mood For Love (J. McHugh/D. Fields) (2:16); 11 Killer Of Dreams (2:10); 12 To The Fields Of Onondaga (1:49); 13 Latest Development (1:43); 14 I Get A Kick Out Of You (C. Porter)(1:29); 15 Miss Lola Miss Drew (1:29); 16 A Country Town (:42); 17 Irving And Otto (1:27); 18 My Romance (R. Rodgers/L. Hart)(1:57); 19 A Chase At The Races (3:15); 20 Drew Preston (3:35); 21 Billy Bathgate (4:06).

Review: Excessively somber orchestral score by Mark Isham. I actually appreciated the welcome breaks afforded by the selection of period music, pieces such as Cole Porter's "I Get a Kick Out of You." These songs are the only bright spots in a composition that captures the ill-fated life of a young man who joins up with gangster Dutch Schultz (Dustin Hoffman). Isham's work interacts very well with songs, flowing easily and providing some stable emotional support to the film. However, by "A Chase at the Races," it all becomes extremely dark and ominous. Actress Rachel York's vocal version of "Bye Bye Blackbird" is included on the album, as is "Oyfn Pripetshok (On the Heath)," a children's choir theme used for the *Schindler's List* trailers.

David Hirsch

The Birdcage **Woof**

1996, edel America Records; from the movie *The Birdcage,* United Artists, 1996.

Album Notes: *Song Producers*: Steven Goldstein, Michael O'Martian, Andy Garcia, John Lurie, Emilio Esteban; *Album Editor*: Charles Martin Inouye.

Selections: 1 We Are Family (B. Edwards/N. Rodgers)(3:35) *The Goldman Girls*; 2 William Tell Overture (G. Rossini)(1:28); 3 She Works Hard For The Money (D. Summer/M. O'Martian)(3:54) *Donna Summer*; 4 Can That Boy Fox Trot (S. Sondheim)(2:37) *Nathan Lane*; 5 Mi Guajira (I. Lopez)(3:53) *Cachao*; 6 Little Dream (S. Sondheim)(3:26) *Nathan Lane*; 7 No Pain For Cakes (J. Lurie)(3:57) *The Lounge Lizards*; 8 Love Is In The Air (S. Sondheim)(3:08) *Christine Baranski, Robin Williams*; 9 I Could Have Danced All Night (A.J. Lerner/F. Loewe)(1:10) *Hank Azaria, Gene Hackman, Nathan Lane, Dianne Wiest, Robin Williams*; 10 We Are Family (reprise)(B. Edwards/N. Rodgers)(2:59) *The Goldman Girls*; 11 Family Salsa (B. Edwards/N. Rodgers)(2:14); 12 Conga (E. Garcia)(3:57) *Gloria Estefan & Miami Sound Machine.*

Review: This is a clear example of Hollywood at its most commercially crass. Take a funny foreign movie, *La cage aux folles* (a.k.a. *Birds of a Feather*), and remake it with an American cast, but make sure to revamp it so that it sounds as if it had originated here. Where the original had a marvelous, whimsical score by Ennio Morricone, replace it now with nondescript songs from various sources (including, God forgive them!, a couple of numbers written by Stephen Sondheim, Broadway's emeritus composer/lyricist and wunderkind, performed in screeching style by the film's stars). Put together a "soundtrack" album, and the poor suckers who saw the film will shell out their $16 gladly to get it. Sorry, but the album truly doesn't deserve it.

The Black Cauldron ♫♫♫♫

1985, Varese-Sarabande; from the animated feature *The Black Cauldron*, Walt Disney Pictures, 1985.

Album Notes: *Music*: Elmer Bernstein; The Utah Symphony Orchestra, conducted by Elmer Bernstein; *Musician*: Cynthia Millar (Ondes Martinot); *Album Producer*: Elmer Bernstein.

Selections: 1 Escape From The Castle (2:29); 2 Taran (4:01); 3 The Witches (2:16); 4 Gurgi (3:24); 5 The Horned King (2:55); 6 The Fair Folk (3:08); 7 Hen Wen's Vision (3:44); 8 Eilonwy (5:05); 9 Finale (4:35).

Review: Based on Lloyd Alexander's sword-and-sorcery "Chronicles of Prydain," *The Black Cauldron* may have seemed too serious and adult an animated feature to entice its target audience of tykes, despite the fact that it involved a stock assortment of daring youngsters and their cuddly animal characters in their fight-to-save-the-world against a group of evil monsters. But it prompted composer Elmer Bernstein to write one of his most interesting scores, a subtle brew of epic and romance, well-designed to play under the screen action and give it more impact while making for an enjoyable listening experience when appreciated on its own terms. The Utah Symphony, conducted by the composer, delivers the goods in this spacious-sounding CD, with the right gusto and usual flourishes.

Black Orpheus ♫♫♫♫

1989, Verve Records; from the movie *Black Orpheus*, 1960.

Album Notes: *Music*: Luis Bonfa, Antonio Carlos Jobim; *CD Producers*: Cees Schrama, Richard Seidel, Seth Rothstein.

Selections: 1 Main Title (1:09); 2 A Felicidade (A.C. Jobim/V. De Moraes) (2:34); 3 Frevo (A.C. Jobim)(4:27); 4 O nosso amor (A.C. Jobim) (1:10); 5 O nosso amor (A.C. Jobim)(accordion and tambourine)(4:16); 6 Manha de carnaval (L. Bonfa)(3:04); 7 Sunrise (A.C. Jobim)(:47); 8 Manha de carnaval (1:32); 9 Macumba Scenes (trad.)(3:11); 10 O nosso amor (A.C. Jobim)(7:36); 11 Manha de carnaval (L. Bonfa)(2:57); 12 Samba de Orfeo (L. Bonfa/A. Maria)(1:58); 13 Drum Schools (trad.)(4:45); 14 Bola Sete Medley: Manha de carnaval (L. Bonfa)/ A Felicidade (A.C. Jobim)/Samba de Orfeo (L. Bonfa)(13:35).

Review: Two of Brazil's most important composers, Antonio Carlos Jobim and Luis Bonfa, teamed to create the explosive musical score for this colorful retelling of the Orpheus legend set in Rio during the Carnival. The film was the Grand Prize Winner at the Cannes Film Festival in 1959. The song "Manha de carnaval" (Morning of the Carnival), performed by Breno Mello, the film's Orfeo to Marpessa Dawn's Eurydice, is an early expression of the bossa nova movement that swept this country in the mid-1960s.

Black Rain ♫♫

1989, Virgin Movie Music; from the movie *Black Rain*, Paramount Pictures, 1989.

Album Notes: *Music*: Hans Zimmer; *Orchestrations*: Shirley Walker; *Featured Artists*: Iggy Pop, UB40, Soul II Soul, Ryuichi Sakamoto, Les Rita Mitsouko and Sparks, Gregg Allman.

Selections: 1 Livin' On The Edge Of The Night (J. Rifkin/E. Rackin)(3:38) *Iggy Pop*; 2 The Way You Do The Things You Do (R. Rogers/W. Robinson) (3:16) *UB40*; 3 Back To Life (Jam On The Groove Mix)(B. Romeo/S. Law/P. Hooper) (5:07) *Soul II Soul, Caron Wheeler*; 4 Laserman (R. Sakamoto)(4:48) *Ryuichi Sakamoto*; 5 Singing In The Shower (R. Mael/R. Mael)(4:23) *Les Rita Mitsouko and Sparks*; 6 I'll Be Holding On (D. Paich)(5:39) *Gregg Allman*; Black Rain Suite (H. Zimmer): 7 Sato (4:45); 8 Charlie Loses His Head (7:04); 9 Sugai (6:52); 10 Nick And Masa (2:55).

Review: Hans Zimmer's volatile percussive mix of orchestral and synthesized performances is a perfect mate for Ridley Scott's breakneck paced action film. The composer keeps the instrumentation at the high end, avoiding bass instruments, and interpolates familiar Far Eastern motifs to create an ethnic flavor for the Japanese locale of the story. Unfortunately, without Scott's visuals, the music loses a lot of the dramatic power it has in the film. The result is a surprising, but disappointingly ordinary synth score. The 20 minutes presented here as the "Black Rain Suite" is a forerunner to the assembled concert style presentations Zimmer would adopt on later albums like *Crimson Tide*. Among the six songs that lead off the CD is

"Laserman," a composition by fellow film composer Ryuichi Sakamoto.

David Hirsch

Black Robe ♫♫♫♫

1991, Varese-Sarabande Records; from the movie *Black Robe*, Alliance Communications/Samuel Goldwyn, 1991.

Album Notes: *Music*: Georges Delerue; *Music Editor*: Dan Carlin; The String Plus and The Sydney Philharmonia Choir, conducted by Georges Delerue; *Featured Soloist*: Christopher Taplin (soprano); *Album Producer*: Georges Delerue; *Engineer*: Michael Spavrou.

Selections: 1 Black Robe Main Title (1:52); 2 Daniel And Annuka (1:47); 3 The Journey Begins (1:11); 4 Daniel Rescues La Forgue (:56); 5 First Kiss (1:35); 6 Flashback (1:21); 7 Conspiracy (1:25); 8 Lost In Forest (3:18); 9 Flagellation (1:41); 10 The Journey Continues (:44); 11 Traveling (:29); 12 Hostile Country (1:21); 13 The Iroquois Attack (1:45); 14 The Natives Abandon La Forgue (2:17); 15 Chomina Decides To Go Back (:50); 16 The Escape (2:36); 17 Chomina Prepares To Die (3:59); 18 The Final Canoe Trip (1:21); 19 La Forgue's Farewell To Daniel And Annuka (1:06); 20 Taretendi And La Forgue (:38); 21 Libera Me (5:02).

Review: In one of his last efforts shortly before his death, Georges Delerue wrote a highly emotionally-charged score for Bruce Beresford's epic adventure of a young, idealistic Jesuit priest who embarks on a perilous journey through the rugged 17th-century Canadian wilderness to convert the Huron Indians. Both story and locale provided the composer with the essential ingredients he needed. The deep mysticism of the film's hero, the romantic aspects of his quest, the culture clash between his own upbringing and the lifestyle of the Indians he seeks to convert, and the majestic beauty of the Canadian wilderness all found their way into his musical expression. As a result, his score is intensely reflective and deeply exciting, an attractive mixture that reflects both aspects of the screen action.

Black Sunday/Baron Blood ♫♫♫♫

1992, Bay Cities Records; from the movies *Black Sunday*, 1960; and *Baron Blood*, 1972.

Album Notes: *Music*: Les Baxter; Orchestras conducted by Les Baxter; *Album Producer*: Nick Redman; *Engineer*: Daniel Hersch.

Selections: *BLACK SUNDAY*: 1 Suite (33:59);

BARON BLOOD: 2 Suite (25:34).

"I got into some choppy waters being a director who also composes music. You expect a certain resistance but I've always done it in parallel."

Mike Figgis
(The Hollywood Reporter, 1-16-96)

Review: Two horror films scored by Les Baxter, better known today as a kitschy band arranger-conductor and pop orchestrator. Made in 1960 in Italy, *Black Sunday* was a stylish adaptation of a ghost story by Gogol, starring Barbara Steele in a dual role as a charming innocent and as her sexually irresistible ancestor who returns from the undead to haunt her. Baxter's score, uncommonly dark, with bizarre effects and instrumentations, seemed the perfect complement to the film, and though in mono sound in this recording (in which the cues are presented together in one long suite) it is still profoundly affecting and scary.

Another Italian-made film, *Baron Blood,* released in 1972, dealt with the impoverished owner of an estate in Europe whose evil ancestor, in an all-too familiar twist, returns from the undead to haunt him. Once again, Baxter provided a perfectly spooky score, even more chilling and pervasive than the one for *Black Sunday,* in which light, airy melodies contrast and inform the more malevolent accents in the music. And he did it all without any synthesizer! Makes you wonder...

Blade Runner

Blade Runner ♫♫♭

1982, Warner Bros. Records; from the movie *Blade Runner,* Warner Bros., 1982.

Album Notes: *Music*: Vangelis; *Orchestrations*: Patrick Williams, Eddie Karam, Angela Morley; The New American Orchestra, conducted by Jack Elliott; *Featured Musicians*: Tom Scott (alto sax), Ian Underwood (synthesizers), Bill Watrous (trombone), Tommy Tedesco, Dan Ferguson (guitar), Michael Lang (Fender Rhodes, piano), Richard Tee (piano), Chuck Findley (flugelhorn), Steve Schaeffer (drums), Neil Stubenhaus (bass); *Album Producer*: Jack Elliott; *Engineer*: Hank Cicalo.

Selections: 1 Love Theme (4:12); 2 Main Title (5:01); 3 One More Kiss, Dear (4:00); 4 Memories Of Green (4:50); 5 End Title (4:17); 6 Blade Runner Blues (4:38); 7 Farewell (3:10); 8 End Title (reprise)(3:08).

Review: See entry below.

Blade Runner ♫♫♫♭

1994, Atlantic Records; from the movie *Blade Runner,* Warner Bros., 1982.

Album Notes: *Music*: Vangelis; *Arranged and Performed*: Vangelis; *Featured Musician*: Dick Morrisey (saxophone); *Album Producer*: Vangelis; *Engineers*: Raine Shine, Frederick Rousseau, Philippe Colonna.

Selections: 1 Main Titles (3:42); 2 Blush Response (5:47); 3 Wait For Me (5:27); 4 Rachel's Song (4:46) *Mary Hopkins*; 5 Love Theme (4:56); 6 One More Kiss, Dear (Vangelis/P. Skellern) (3:58) *Don Percival*; 7 Blade Runner Blues (8:53); 8 Memories Of Green (5:05); 9 Tales Of The Future (4:46) *Demis Roussos*; 10 Damask Rose (2:32); 11 Blade Runner (End Titles) (4:40); 12 Tears In Rain (3:00).

Review: Vangelis' original score has long been unavailable (despite mention of a soundtrack release in the film's on-screen credits), although a rerecorded version done by the New American Orchestra was produced shortly after the release of the film. Vangelis' score is almost completely electronic and the well-intentioned attempts (some arranged by Patrick Williams) to recreate the music orchestrally fail miserably. But the jazzier tracks (notably "Memories of Green" and "Bladerunner Blues") actually benefit from the elimination of some of the bleating electronic textures employed by Vangelis in the film.

Vangelis finally released his original score in 1995, but it too is a compromise for those interested in hearing the unadulterated score. Vangelis interpolates dialogue and sound effects, as well as a few rather more pop-flavored compositions ostensibly composed for but not used in the final cut of the film. Some of these are actually enjoyable listening ("Rachel's Song" for example, is hauntingly beautiful), but are markedly different from the primarily atmospheric, dreamy textures Vangelis created for the rest of the film's music. Most of the high points are here, however, including the rapturous scoring of an early Spinner car flight, the wailing, quasi-oriental "Legends of Future Past,", Vangelis' touching, saxophone solo love music and his hammering, cheesy disco-era end titles. Fans of New Age "space" music will find this album fits right into their collection.

Jeff Bond

Blind Date ♪

1987, Rhino Records; from the movie *Blind Date*, Tri-Star Pictures, 1987.

Album Notes: *Music*: Henry Mancini; Orchestra conducted by Henry Mancini; *Song Producers*: Peter Bunetta, Rick Chudacoff, Larry Brown; *Engineers*: Daren Klein, John Richards; *Album Producers*: Al Bunetta, Tom Bocci; *Engineer*: Ken Perry.

Selections: 1 Simply Meant To Be (H. Mancini/G. Merrill/S. Rubicam)(4:14) *Gary Morris, Jennifer Warnes*; 2 Let You Get Away (B. Vera)(4:47) *Billy Vera & The Beaters*; 3 Oh, What A Nite (B. Vera)(3:19) *Billy Vera & The Beaters*; 4 Anybody Seen Her? (L.R. Brown/B. Vera)(3:32) *Billy Vera & The Beaters*; 5 Talked About Lover (K. L'Neire/L. Brown)(4:10) *Keith L' Neire*; 6 Crash, Bang, Boom (P. Bunetta/J. Ericksen)(3:39) *Gubert Tubbs*; 7 Something For Nash (H. Mancini)(3:31); 8 Treasures (S. Jordan)(2:27) *Stanley Jordan*; 9 Simply Meant To Be (H. Mancini)(3:46).

Review: Another sorry example of a favorite composer undone by the commercial considerations that often preside over the creation of a film soundtrack and its related album. The unfortunate victim in this instance is Henry Mancini, only represented here by two cues he created for this otherwise hilarious Blake Edwards romp about a serious-minded financial analyst on a date with a dizzy girl who can't hold her champagne, and the mayhem that ensues at a function after she's had two glasses. Billy Vera and The Beaters and the other performers here are doing what they have been asked to do, but their vocal contributions mean very little while Mancini's cues only whet one's desire to hear more of his music for this film.

Blink ♪♪

1994, Milan Records; from the movie *Blink*, New Line Cinema, 1994.

Album Notes: *Music*: Brad Fiedel; *Music Editor*: Allan K. Rosen; *Featured Musicians*: Ross Levinson (electric violin), Doug Norwine (saxophones); *Featured Vocalists*: The Drovers: Sean Cleland (violin, mandolin, viola), Michael Kirkpatrick (guitar, mandolin, vocals), David Callahan (bass, vocals), Jackie Moran (drums, percussion, vocals), Winston Damon (percussion, trombone, vocals); *Song Producers*: Michael Kirkpatrick, David Blocker; *Engineer*: John Ray Castellanos; *Score Producer*: Brad Fiedel; *Engineer*: Tim Boyle.

Selections: 1 The Boys And The Babies (M. Kirkpatrick/D. Callahan/J. Moran/ K. Keane)/Is Craig Here? (M. Kirkpatrick)(4:08) *The Drovers*; 2 Emma's Eyes (3:51); 3 Bumps in the Night (3:31); 4 What Is Beautiful? (1:18); 5 When Fortune Turns Her Wheel (M. Kirkpatrick)(3:56) *The Drovers*; 6 Witness On The Run (3:22); 7 On The Floor (1:24); 8 Open Your Eyes (3:29);

9 Escape From Illusion (3:19); 10 Clean Hands (1:33); 11 The Blinds Come Down (2:26); 12 The Eyes You Stole (7:33); 13 John And Emma's Theme (1:36); 14 Insulated Man (M. Kirkpatrick)(4:42) *The Drovers, Chantal Wentworth*.

Review: Known more for his industrial strength synthesized scores for *The Terminator* films, Brad Fiedel created a serene, and somewhat enjoyable low-key score, thanks in part to the use of piano solos to represent the central character, the visually impaired Emma. Her sight only recently restored, but not quite perfect, she may or may not have witnessed a murder. For that aspect of the film, Fiedel relied on his old musical bag of tricks. The alternative Irish/American band, The Drovers, appear as themselves in the film (Emma is purported to be their fiddler) and they are featured in four songs on the soundtrack.

David Hirsch

Bliss ♪♪♪♪

1997, Varese-Sarabande Records; from the movie *Bliss*, Triumph Films, 1997.

Album Notes: *Music*: Jan A.P. Kaczmarek; *Orchestrations*: Krzesimir Debski; The Sinfonia Varsovia, conducted by Krzesimir Debski; *Featured Musicians*: Pawel Losakiewicz, Krzesimir Debski (violin), Andrzej Jagodzinski (piano), Jacek Urbaniak (recorder); *Featured Vocalist*: Marta Boberska (soprano); *Album Producer*: Jan A.P. Kaczmarek; *Engineer*: Rafal Paczkowski.

Selections: 1 Overture (2:21); 2 Wedding (4:14); 3 If You Love Me (3:19); 4 I Want A Good Marriage (1:57); 5 Discovery and Confrontation (1:09); 6 Blue Bedroom (3:12); 7 The Dance (1:14); 8 Joseph And Maria (2:44); 9 Baltazar's Teachings (1:34); 10 Bliss Carezza (1:35); 11 Tears and The Night Swimming (2:48); 12 Bondage (2:47); 13 Love Making (2:57); 14 It Was My Father (2:40); 15 Separation With Hope (2:50); 16 Waltz Again (2:04); 17 First Touch (2:56); 18 Maria's Confession (2:29); 19 Reunion (3:04); 20 Rushing Waltz (1:27); 21 Finale (3:01).

Review: If the movie itself, about a young couple and their sexual problems, were not so banal and only worthy of a quick fadeout at the box office, this soundtrack might possibly attract more people than it will, and it should. Lushly romantic, with attractive melodies to sustain one's attention, it has at least some redeeming values. But don't let the track titles throw you off course. While they apply to the narrative and follow poor Joseph and Maria on their path to marital bliss, they are simply meant here as an indication of the intent actually pursued by the composer to conform with the storyline. You won't need them to enjoy the album.

The Blood of Heroes 🦴🦴🦴

1989, Intrada Records; from the movie *The Blood of Heroes*, New Line Cinema, 1989.

Album Notes: *Music*: Todd Boekelheide; *Orchestrations*: Mark Adler, Todd Boekelheide; Orchestra conducted by Mark Adler; *Album Producer*: Todd Boekelheide; *Engineers*: Dave Luke, Danny Koppelson.

Selections: 1 Juggers Coming! (1:50); 2 Main Title (3:06); 3 A Game At Samchin (3:23); 4 Party, Party, Party! (2:26); 5 Dog Boy's Pain (:54); 6 Leaving Home (:48); 7 Enforcement (2:11); 8 Watching, Waiting (1:14); 9 Kidda Stabds Up (1:20); 10 Tested (1:27); 11 A Struggle, A Triumph (4:38); 12 One Eye From Blind (1:49); 13 Fear Of The Red City (2:43); 14 The First Sixty Stones (3:22); 15 Hang On (4:55); 16 The Juggers Of Doom (7:51).

Review: Not a score that will be appreciated by every ear, but nonetheless a fascinatingly creative work to experience, Todd Boekelheide abandons most conventional forms of musical composition to portray the barbaric world of a decaying future. He does this, not only by interpolating usual instruments into his orchestra, but by sampling sounds created by throwing odd pieces of junk around his basement! Every so often, he breaks away with some standard fare, like the harmonic solo on "Watching, Waiting," or the offbeat "Party, Party, Party," which sounds more like it would at home in the bar on "The Drew Carey Show." Played frequently in 12/8 time, a rhythm favored in African music, Boekelheide's score is both powerful and refreshingly original.
David Hirsch

Blown Away 🦴🦴🦴

1994, Epic Soundtrax; from the movie *Blown Away*, M-G-M, 1994.

Album Notes: *Music*: Alan Silvestri; *Orchestrations*: William Ross; *Music Editor*: Ken Karman; Orchestra conducted by Alan Silvestri; *Featured Performers*: Big Head Todd and the Monsters, October Project, U2, Aretha Franklin, The Pogues, The Sundays, The Jayhawks, Joe Cocker & Bekka Bramlett; *Album Producers*: Richard B. Lewis, John Watson; *Engineer*: Joe Gastwirt.

Selections: 1 In The Morning (T. Park Mohr) (3:55) *Big Head Todd And The Monsters*; 2 Return To Me (E. Adler/J. Flanders) (4:16) *October Project*; 3 With Or Without You (P. Hewson/D. Evans/A. Clayton/L. Mullen) (4:55) *U2*; 4 All Night Long (C.R. Lewis) (3:05) *Aretha Franklin*; 5 Tuesday Morning (P. Stacey) (3:29) *The Pogues*; 6 Here's Where The Story Ends (D. Gavurin/ H. Wheeler) (3:52) *The Sundays*; 7 Darling Today (Olson/Louris)

(2:58) *The Jayhawks*; 8 You'll Lose A Good Thing (B.L. Ozen) (2:38) *Aretha Franklin*; 9 Take Me Home (J. Capek/S. Kipner/M. Jordan) (4:21) *Joe Cocker, Bekka Bramlett*; 10 Main Title — Prince's Day (A. Silvestri) (2:26).

Review: A modest but pleasant listen that mixes big names with fresh talent. It's hard to go too wrong when there are *two* Aretha Franklin cuts to listen to, and U2's "With or Without You" sounds good in most any contest. Meanwhile, the hipness impaired will be well-educated by sampling songs by Big Head Todd, the Sundays, the Jayhawks and Big Head Todd & the Monsters.
Gary Graff

Blue Chips 🦴🦴🦴

1994, MCA Records; from the movie *Blue Chips*, Paramount Pictures, 1994.

Album Notes: *Song Producers*: John Mellencamp, Jimi Hendrix, John Fogerty, J.D. Miller, Willie Mitchell, Al Green, Nile Rodgers, Jed Leiber, Dick Rowe; *Album Executive Producer*: William Friedkin; *Engineer*: Tom Baker.

Selections: 1 Baby, Please Don't Go (J. Williams) (3:14) *John Mellencamp*; 2 All Along The Watchtower (B. Dylan) (3:59) *Jimi Hendrix*; 3 Lookin' Out My Back Door (J. Fogerty) (2:31) *Creedence Clearwater Revival*; 4 Money (That's What I Want) (B. Gordy/J. Bradford) (2:26) *John Lee Hooker*; 5 Shake Your Hips (J. Moore) (2:29) *Slim Harpo*; 6 Let's Stay Together (A. Green/W. Mitchell/A. Jackson) (3:13) *Al Green*; 7 Western U Medley: Dolphin Fight Song (J. Leiber)/ End Game/Game #1 (N. Rodgers)/Dolphin Fight Song (reprise) (J. Leiber)/Land Of A Thousand Dances (C. Kenner) (7:47) *Nile Rodgers*; 8 The Practice (N. Rodgers) (2:10) *Nile Rodgers*; 9 The Drills Medley: 3 On 3/Campus Tour (N. Rodgers)/ Dolphin Fight Song (J. Leiber)/ Shake Your Hips (J. Moore) (4:10) *Nile Rodgers*; 10 Butch's Chicago Blues (N. Rodgers) (2:53) *Nile Rodgers*; 11 Baby, Please Don't Go (J. Williams) (2:41) *Them*.

Review: A sports film without Queen's "We Will Rock You" — now *there's* a concept. Bookended by versions of Joe Williams' "Baby, Please Don't Go" — one by John Mellencamp, the other by Them — *Blue Chips* mixes oldies with score pieces by Chic's Nile Rodgers. Having fairly obscure stuff like John Lee Hooker doing "Money (That's What I Want)" and Slim Harpo's "Shake Your Hips" puts *Blue Chips* in the bonus. And at least there's no rapping from hoops sensation and film co-star Shaquille O'Neal.
Gary Graff

Blue Hawaii

1991, RCA Records; from the movie *Blue Hawaii*, M-G-M, 1961.

See: Elvis Presley in Compilations

Blue in the Face 🎵🎵🎵🎵

1995, Luaka Bop/Warner Bros. Records; from the movie *Blue in the Face*, Miramax Films, 1995.

Album Notes: *Songs Producers*: Arto Lindsay, Susan Rogers, David Byrne, Angel Fernandez, Brian Hardgroove, Soul Coughing, Paula Cole, Michael Franti, Salaam Remi, Michael Ivey, Greggy Tah, John Lurie, Kip Hanrahan; *Engineers*: Susan Rogers, Richard Clarke, Hugo Dwyer, Mark Hutchins, Gary Noble, Michael Ivey, Marco Delmar, Joe Feria, Don Hunerberg, Steve Rosenthal; *Album Executive Producers*: David Byrne, Yale Evelev; *Mastering Engineer*: Scott Hull.

Selections: 1 Danny Hoch as Caribbean Tiger (:35); 2 God's Child (D. Byrne) (4:14) *David Byrne, Selena*; 3 Danny Hoch as Andy (:42); 4 The Brooklynites (Soul Coughing)(3:36) *Soul Coughing*; 5 Mi Barrio (L. Diaz/A. Fernandez/D. Byrne)(4:18) *La Casa*; 6 Suwannee Jo (P. Cole)(3:42) *Paula Cole*; 7 To My Ba-bay! (M. Franti/C. Young/M. Daulne/S. Nyolo)(5:23) *Spearhead and Zap Mama*; 8 Brooklyn Movements (J. Hanna/A. Dillon/H. Lee/S. Remi)(4:03) *Da Bush Babees*; 9 Danny Hoch with Basehead as Flex (:57); 10 Why Can't We Be Friends? (Allen/Brown/Dickerson/Jordan/Miller/Oskar/Scott/ Goldstein)(3:23) *Geggy Tah*; 11 Let's Get Ready To Rhumba (J. Lurie)(1:14) *John Lurie National Orchestra*; 12 Tango Apasionado (A. Piazzolla)(3:30) *Astor Piazzolla*; 13 Danny Hoch as Shaddjeh (:43); 14 Happy Suicide (D. Byrne/ V. Anad)(9:42) *David Byrne, Vijaya Anand*; 15 Egg Cream (L. Reed) (3:57) *Lou Reed*; 16 The Return of Flex (:44) *Danny Hoch*.

Review: David Byrne's somewhat iconoclastic approach is evident all over this soundtrack album in which Danny Hoch, assuming various personalities, introduces some of the selections, performed by a motley group of recording stars, from Soul Coughing to Astor Piazzolla, from Paula Cole to Lou Reed, from Selena (and David Byrne) to Vijaya Anand (and David Byrne). Some good, exotic tracks, too, with La Casa's "Mi Barrio," Spearhead and Zap Mama's "To My Ba-bay!," and John Lurie National Orchestra's "Let's Get Ready to Rhumba," among the best. Spicy hot, and tasty!

The Blue Lagoon 🎵🎵🎵🎵♭

1987, Southern Cross Records; from the movie *The Blue Lagoon*, Columbia Pictures, 1987.

Album Notes: *Music*: Basil Poledouris; *Orchestrations*: Greig McRitchie; The Australian Symphony Orchestra, conducted by Basil Poledouris; *Album Producer*: Basil Poledouris; *Engineer*: Roger Savage; *CD Engineer*: Danny Hersch.

Selections: 1 Love Theme (Emmeline)(2:31); 2 Main Title (2:35); 3 Fire (1:17); 4 The Island (1:43); 5 The Sands Of Time (2:24); 6 Paddy's Death (1:18); 7 The Children Grow (4:09); 8 Lord Of The Lagoon (1:04); 9 Love Theme (reprise)(1:10); 10 Underwater Courtship (1:58); 11 The Kiss (2:33); 12 Richard Sees Paddy (2:20); 13 The Birth (1:13); 14 Bad People/Baby Swim (2:59); 15 The Memories (1:18); 13 3 Points To Port/End Titles (3:20).

Review: Many viewers have tried to forget this tepid 1980 remake about a boy and a girl stranded on a desert isle, allowing only the images of Brooke Shields, Nestor Almendros' sumptuous cinematography, and the lovely music by Basil Poledouris to linger in their memories. Poledouris, coming off his fine score for John Milius' *Big Wednesday* (which remains sadly unavailable), scored the movie with a lyrical passage for a piano solo that gradually integrates the full orchestra, setting the stage for an evocative collection of romantic cues that never feels overtly saccharine in its most melodramatic moments. A contrasting music-box motif evokes the innocence of the stranded teens without pounding you over the head with its importance to the narrative, and this relatively low-key approach fills the entire score. The Australian Symphony Orchestra's performance is competent and the soundtrack remains one of Poledouris's most interesting scores for its subject matter, which is as far removed from his work on the Milius and Paul Verhoeven films as one could imagine.

Andy Dursin

The Blue Max 🎵🎵🎵🎵

1995, Legacy Records/Sony Music; from the movie *The Blue Max*, 20th Century-Fox, 1966.

Album Notes: *Music*: Jerry Goldsmith; Orchestra conducted by Jerry Goldsmith; *CD Producer*: Didier C. Deutsch; *Engineer*: Chris Herles.

Selections: 1 The Blue Max (Main Title)(2:24); 2 The New Arrival (1:23); 3 A Toast To Bruno (1:41); 4 First Blood (2:23); 5 First Victory (:41); 6 The Captive (1:45); 7 The Victim (2:33); 8 The Cobra (1:39); 9 The Attack (6:30); 10 A Small Favor (:56); 11 Love Theme (1:16); 12 The Rivals (:26).

Review: While Jerry Goldsmith's dramatic score for the World War I epic *The Blue Max* has been reissued several times, this Columbia/ Legacy CD issue offers its most complete presentation to date. Assembled from the original elements (including nine reels of previously lost music, located in a vault at the Fox Studios), this gorgeous restoration effectively captures the occasionally dark, yet always strong spirit of the film's plot, the aerial confrontation of two skilled pilots, on opposite sides of the conflict, and Goldsmith's poignant musical themes. While it is generally considered one of the composer's lesser known works, it is highly recommended as one of his finest, as this outstanding reissue definitely demonstrates.

Charles L. Granata

Blue Velvet ♫♫♫

1986, Varese-Sarabande Records; from the movie *Blue Velvet*, Dino De Laurentiis Entertainment, 1986.

Album Notes: *Music*: Angelo Badalamenti; The Film Symphony of Prague, conducted by Angelo Badalamenti; *Album Producer*: David Lynch; *Engineer*: Jiri Sobac.

Selections: 1 Main Title (1:27); 2 Night Streets/Sandy And Jeffrey (3:42); 3 Frank (3:34); 4 Jeffrey's Dark Side (1:48); 5 Mysteries Of Love (French horn solo)(D. Lynch/A. Badalamenti)(2:10); 6 Frank Returns (4:39); 7 Mysteries Of Love (instrumental)(D. Lynch/A. Badalamenti)(4:41); 8 Blue Velvet (B. Wayne/L. Morris)(1:19)/Blue Star (D. Lynch/A. Badalamenti) (1:55); 9 Lumberton U.S.A. (D. Lynch/A. Badalamenti)(:30)/Going Down To Lincoln (1:43); 10 Akron Meets The Blues (2:40); 11 Honky Tonk Part I (B. Doggett/C. Scott/S. Sheppard/B. Butler/H. Glover)(3:09) *Bill Doggett*; 12 In Dreams (R. Orbison)(2:48) *Roy Orbison*; 13 Love Letters (V. Young/E. Heyman)(2:36) *Ketty Lester*; 14 Mysteries Of Love (D. Lynch/A. Badalamenti)(4:22) *Julee Cruise*.

Review: Angelo Badalamenti's score for David Lynch's stylish mystery thriller is darkly romantic. His melodies are pretty but somber, a beautiful gown worn by a corpse. The omnipresent darkness and deviation that is the film's undercurrent is reflected in Badalamenti's musical style. His main theme, violins playing against violins in almost kaleidoscopic spirals, creates a somewhat Hitchcockian mood of hidden menace. Another theme, heard vocally as well as in two instrumentals, is a sorrowful love song, resolutely unhappy — is also appropriate to the film's depiction of romance gone askew. There's only about 20 minutes of score on the CD, the balance filled out by moody songs, source music, even a strange sound effects suite.

Randall Larson

Bodies, Rest & Motion ♫♫♫⬥

1993, Big Screen Records; from the movie *Bodies, Rest & Motion*, Fine Line Features, 1993.

Album Notes: *Music*: Michael Convertino; *Orchestrations*: Marc Falcone; *Music Editor*: Kenn Wannberg; Orchestra conducted by Marc Falcone, Artie Kane; *Featured Vocalists*: Marva Hicks, Lynne Fiddmont-Linsey, Debra Parsons, Katrina Perkins, Mindy Stein, Susan Beaubian, Kiki Ebsen, Michael Convertino;

Album Producer: Michael Convertino; *Engineers*: Paul Brown, Dennis Sands.

Selections: 1 Main Title (2:39); 2 The Desert (1:07); 3 Going (1:04); 4 Pray (2:23); 5 Cactus (1:37); 6 Transcendence And Appliance (:53); 7 Everything Must Ride (:58); 8 Your Whole Life (:47); 9 Where Luck Can Find You (:54); 10 To The August House (1:31); 11 I'm Happy (1:15); 12 Soul Station (:46); 13 Here And There And Now (1:40); 14 Beautiful Young Girl (1:25); 15 It's A Big Planet (2:15); 16 End Title (2:29); 17 Postlude (1:29); 18 Love Making (1:35); 19 This Rain (3:31); 20 Sid Invisible (1:37).

Review: Set in the Arizona desert, this odd tale of youngsters who meet, make love, and go on their merry way elicited from Michael Convertino a New Age score permeated with Native American sounds and chanting. Strangely atmospheric and unusual, it is greatly evocative and quite attractive, though it probably gains at being heard in connection with the screen action. Some selections like "To the August House" or "It's a Big Planet" are particularly pretty.

Body Bags ♫

1993, Varese-Sarabande Records; from the movie *Body Bags*, Showtime, 1993.

Album Notes: *Music*: John Carpenter, Jim Lang; *Album Producers*: John Carpenter, Jim Lang; *Engineer*: Jim Lang.

Selections: 1 The Coroner's Theme (6:28); 2 The Picture On The Wall (1:14); 3 Alone (3:46); 4 Cornered (1:41); 5 Locked Out (3:11); 6 The Corpse In The Cab (3:00); 7 Body Bag #1 (2:16); 8 Brain Trouble (4:50); 9 Long Beautiful Hair (5:40); 10 Broken Glass (1:05); 11 Dr. Lang (2:44); 12 The Operation (1:15); 13 I Can See (1:05); 14 Vision (:54); 15 Vision And Voices (4:34); 16 Put Them In The Ground (1:22); 17 Vision And Rape (2:21); 18 John Randle (4:20); 19 ...Pluck It Out (3:47).

Review: Listening to this soundtrack album, one almost feels tempted to say, like Shakespeare, that it is "much ado about nothing." John Carpenter, who has occasionally shown bits of brilliance in his scores, seems to have taken the easy way out here. The musical ideas are trite, the expression vapid, the execution uninspired. Here and there, one can hear flashes of interesting ideas trying to develop ("Long Beautiful Hair," "I Can See"), but generally speaking the score is one long, unsubstantial exercise.

Body Heat ♫♫♫♫

1989, SCSE Records; from the movie *Body Heat*, The Ladd Company, 1981.

Album Notes: *Music*: John Barry; *Album Producer*: Al Woodbury; *Engineers*: Dan Wallin, Colin Derek.

Selections: 1 Ladd Company Logo (J. Williams)/Main Title (3:39); 2 I'm Weak (3:15); 3 Chapeau Gratis (1:12); 4 Heather (1:58); 5 I'm Frightened (2:33); 6 Kill For Pussy (2:48); 7 Us And Oscar (1:18); 8 Surprise/Explosion (2:30); 9 Heather And Roz (1:36); 10 Glasses (:46); 11 Better Get Him (6:05); 12 Matty Was Mary Ann (4:16).

Review: The quintessential John Barry mystery score. You can just feel all the sweat of a hot and humid summer night in South Florida. The principal theme, played by an alto sax, has since been covered on many jazz albums and has often been copied in other films. Barry's score is surprisingly limited thematically and very often repetitious. Nothing unusual for this composer, whose music is still dramatically powerful. It captures not just the sexual tension between lovers William Hurt and Kathleen Turner ("Kill for Pussy"), but the anxiety of their plot to murder Turner's husband. The buildup to the explosion of the house ("Better Get Him") is a real nail biter, one of Barry's most suspenseful moments. The album includes John Williams' music for the Ladd Company logo and detailed notes by Royal S. Brown. It is rumored to have been mastered from an audio cassette, which may account for the minor tape hiss and some high end audio breakup that can be heard, but none of that has kept this score from becoming a highly prized album. Originally released as a limited edition, first as a 45 rpm vinyl 12" disc in 1983, and then on CD six years later, *Body Heat* became a top collectible fetching upwards of $150 for either format.

David Hirsch

Body of Evidence ♪♪♪▷

1993, Milan Records; from the movie *Body of Evidence,* Dino de Laurentiis/M-G-M Pictures, 1993.

Album Notes: *Music:* Graeme Revell; *Orchestrations:* Graeme Revell, Tim Simonec; *Music Editor:* Dick Bernstein; *Synthesizers and Programming:* Graeme Revell; Members of the Munich Philharmonic Orchestra, conducted by Tim Simonec; *Featured Musician:* Eberhard Weber (bass); *Album Producer:* Graeme Revell; *Engineer:* Dan Wallin.

Selections: 1 Main Title (3:12); 2 The Passion Theme (G. Revell/J. Silbar/ W. Hill)(4:49) *Warren Hill;* 3 The Funeral (3:30); 4 The House Boat (4:34); 5 Hot Wax And Champagne (5:38); 6 The Fight (3:05); 7 The Handcuffs (4:21) *Darlene Koldenhoven, Donna Davidson, Bobby Page, Linda Harmon, John Laird, Gene Merlino;* 8 The Parking Garage (2:57); 9 Waiting For The Jury (3:19); 10 Confrontation (1:39); 11 Karma/End Credits (4:06).

Review: The actual, very real merits of *Body of Evidence,* a crime drama of a different kind, may have been obscured by the fact that it stars Madonna as a sex-starved woman, accused of having inflicted too much of a good thing on her now defunct husband, and willing to demonstrate *in situ* to the district attorney what it is she did. Among the elements that are somewhat ignored in the process is Graeme Revell's contemporary score, a mix of synth effects and orchestral lines that seem to be there more for atmosphere than for musical support, though a couple of strong selections (notably "The Passion Theme," performed by Warren Hill, and "The Handcuffs") are particularly memorable.

Body Parts ♪♪♪

1991, Varese-Sarabande Records; from the movie *Body Parts,* Paramount Pictures, 1991.

Album Notes: *Music:* Loek Dikker; *Orchestrations:* Loek Dikker; *Music Editor:* Carl Zittrer; The Munich Symphony Orchestra, conducted by Allan Wilson; *Album Producer:* Loek Dikker; *Engineer:* Chris Dibble.

Selections: 1 Main Titles (4:27); 2 Life Imprisonment (1:33); 3 The Freeway Wreck (1:57); 4 Organ Transplant (2:59); 5 Full Recovery (2:36); 6 Family Life (2:39); 7 Learning To Walk (2:16); 8 Nightmare (2:47); 9 The Doctor Won't Do It (1:56); 10 Charlie Comes Calling (2:20); 11 Draper Pays His Debt (2:35); 12 Death Of Lacey (1:18); 13 The Chase (2:32); 14 Charlie's Escape (2:31); 15 Final Confrontation (2:35); 16 Death Of Evil (2:33); 17 End Credits (4:10).

Review: Ever heard a "singing saw" before? If not, then here's your chance—Loek Dikker's soundtrack for this modestly entertaining 1991 horror movie with Jeff Fahey and Kim Delaney features, yes, a singing saw that creates an appropriately eerie sound. Director Eric Red clearly wanted a large orchestral score for his "dangers of body transplants" thriller, and the composer has responded with a low-key, almost subtle (at times) music score that has some rather odd sounding string arrangements to nicely compliment the singing saw. The tone is dissonant and rather unembracing, but hey, it's a horror movie out of the Dr. Frankenstein school, so why carp? Body Parts is a better movie, and music score, than many of its genre peers.

Andy Dursin

The Bodyguard ♪♪♪▷

1992, Arista Records; from the movie *The Bodyguard,* Warner Bros., 1992.

Album Notes: *Songs Producers and Arrangers:* David Foster, Narada Michael Walden, Jud Friedman, Bebe Winans, Whitney

Houston, Cedric J. Caldwell, Walter Afanasieff, Ian Devaney, Andy Morris, Robert Clivilles, David Cole, Danny Kotchmar, Charlie Midnight; *Engineers*: Dave Reitzas, Matt Rohr, Marc Reyburn, Mick Guzauski, Barney Perkins, Milton Chan, Mike McCarthy, Victor Caldwell, Bobby Boughton, Acar S. Key, Marc DeSisto, Dennis Sands, John Rollo; *Album Executive Producers*: Clive Davis, Whitney Houston.

Selections: 1 I Will Always Love You (D. Parton)(4:31) *Whitney Houston*; 2 I Have Nothing (D. Foster/L. Thompson)(4:50) *Whitney Houston*; 3 I'm Every Woman (N. Ashford/V. Simpson)(4:47) *Whitney Houston*; 4 Run To Me (A. Rich/J. Friedman)(4:24) *Whitney Houston*; 5 Queen Of The Night (W. Houston/L.A. Reid/Babyface/D. Simmons)(3:09) *Whitney Houston*; 6 Jesus Loves Me (A. Warner/W. Bradbury)(5:12) *Whitney Houston*; 7 Even If My Heart Would Break (F. Golde/A. Gurvitz)(4:58) *Kenny G, Aaron Neville*; 8 Someday (I'm Coming Back)(L. Stansfield/A. Morris/I. Devaney)(4:59) *Lisa Stansfield*; 9 It's Gonna Be A Lovely Day (B. Withers/S. Scarborough/R. Clivilles/D. Cole/T. Never/M. Visage)(4:51) *The S.O.U.L. S.Y.S.T.E.M.*; 10 (What's So Funny 'Bout Peace) Love And Understanding (N. Lowe)(4:06) *Curtis Stigers*; 11 Theme From The Bodyguard (A. Silvestri)(2:43) 12 Trust In Me (C. Midnight/M. Swersky/F. Beghe)(4:14) *Joe Cocker, Sass Jordan*.

Review: Whitney Houston's film debut made musical history. Her broad, melodramatic rendition of Dolly Parton's "I Will Always Love You" set a record for consecutive weeks at No. 1 on the Billboard charts (14) before being upended by Boyz II Men. This is actually half a Houston album, but she certainly made the most of it, putting two more singles ("I Have Nothing" and "I'm Every Woman") into the Top 5, though her best performances comes on the gospel showcase "Jesus Loves Me." The album was also good news for British rocker Nick Lowe. Curtis Stiger covered his "Peace, Love and Undertstanding," snaring Lowe a well-deserved $1 million royalty check.

Gary Graff

Bolero 🎜🎜🎜♭

1984, Prometheus Records/Belgium; from the movie *Bolero*, Cannon Films, 1984.

Album Notes: *Music*: Peter Bernstein; *Orchestrations*: Christopher Palmer; *Music Editor*: Kathy Durning; The Rome Studio Symphony Orchestra, conducted by Elmer Bernstein; *Featured Musician*: Cynthia Millar (Ondes Martenot); *Album Producer*: Alan E. Smith.

Selections: 1 Bullero (2:06); 2 The Sleepless Night (2:42); 3 Moroccan Holiday (3:12); 4 "What, Me Worry?" (1:44); 5 Welcome To The Casbah (1:47); 6 The Bolero Bolero (2:45); 7 Chase To The Beach (1:04); 8 Ride On The Beach (1:35); 9 Opium Den (2:15); 10 Belly Dance (1:13); 11 Take Off (1:40); 12 Ecstasy (E. Bernstein)(4:47); 13 Dinner Music (4:44); 14 Foreplay/The Sheik (4:02); 15 Tango For Rudy (1:27); 16 The Bull Ring (2:02); 17 Cotton And Mac Talk/Graduation Present (3:11); 18 Angel/Gypsy Dance (2:43); 19 Gored (:54); 20 Cry (1:37); 21 Kidnapping (2:10); 22 First Lesson/Eureka (E. Bernstein) (5:04); 23 March Of The Bull Fighters (1:25).

Review: Evidently, Peter Bernstein has learned his music lessons well, and the score he wrote for *Bolero*, Bo Derek's unending search for the man who will ravish her and make her a woman, is greatly satisfying. Happily mixing genres (as in tauromachy and Spanish dancing for the cleverly-titled "Bullero"), Bernstein's cues denote a sure hand and an even surer ear for attractive film music. It helps, of course, that Papa Elmer is at the helm conducting the Rome Studio Symphony, and that he contributed a couple of selections, but the bulk of the score is Peter's and many of his compositions ("The Sleepless Night," "Ride on the Beach," "Foreplay/The Sheik") are appropriately descriptive. In the midst of the heavily-scented evocations, he also threw in some fiery moments, including a languorous "Bolero Bolero," a throbbing "Tango for Rudy," and an impassioned "Gypsy Dance."

The Bonfire of the Vanities
🎜🎜🎜♭

1991, Atlantic Records; from the movie *The Bonfire of the Vanities*, Warner Bros., 1991.

Album Notes: *Music*: Dave Grusin; Orchestra conducted by Dave Grusin; *Album Producer*: Brooks Arthur.

Selections: 1 Prologue (1:44); 2 Bonfire Of The Vanities Theme (4:34); 3 Master Of The Universe (:53); 4 Concorde (:59); 5 Bronx Exit (3:00); 6 Yo! (1:32); 7 Get-Away (1:41); 8 Love Drums, part 1 (:47); 9 Love Drums, Part 2 (:46); 10 Coma (:48); 11 End Of The Road (:39); 12 Hang-Out (3:19); 13 Jackals, Part 1 & 2 (2:37); 14 Subway Breakdown (Prelude)(1:36); 15 Blues For Caroline (3:34); 16 Thinking Of Caroline (1:35); 17 Out Of My Life (:41); 18 Blues (reprise)(1:02); 19 Bugged (1:23); 20 Father/Son (:58); 21 Decency (1:41); 22 Speechless/Case Dismissed (1:09); 23 Sword Of Justice (3:44); 24 Epilog-Peter's Theme (1:17); 25 End Credit Theme (3:42).

Review: This standard jazz fusion fare from Dave Grusin sounds more like any one of his own GRP albums than a film score. While his bouncy music suggests that he seemed to find the film funnier than most audiences and critics did, on CD it makes a pleasant diversion. The music maintains its attitude all the way through, apparently never taking things too seriously. Inexplicably, Grusin's name appears nowhere on the cover of this Atlantic Records' release, except in the small print on the movie credit block. Odd considering his popularity as a jazz artist.

David Hirsch

Bopha! 🦴🦴

1993, Big Screen Records; from the movie *Bopha!*, Paramount Pictures, 1993.

Album Notes: *Music:* James Horner; *Music Editor:* Jim Henrikson; *Performers:* James Horner, Mike Fisher, Ralph Grierson, Warren Luening, Jr., Kazu Matsui, Ian Underwood; *Album Producer:* James Horner; *Engineer:* Shawn Murphy.

Selections: 1 Amandla! (3:36); 2 Main Title (3:23); 3 Pride Of The S.A.P. (1:28); 4 The Depot (5:35); 5 "Necklaced" Effigy/Micah Moves To The Compound (3:51); 6 Micah And Rosie/Indefinite Detention (6:49); 7 Nightfall (3:05); 8 "Arrest The Children" (4:43); 9 Estrangement (1:32); 10 Uprising (3:54); 11 Torching Micah's House (3:55); 12 A Shattered World (2:37); 13 Naledi Saves Zweli (1:46); 14 Theme From Bopha!/Amandla! (6:02).

Review: James Horner abandoned much of the compositional techniques for which he's become known to take a fresh approach for this film. Perhaps the score owes much of its inspiration to the African motifs that are incorporated, particularly the Zulu tribal marches which are interpolated with electronic effects. This medley yields a tense and dark otherworldly effect that is most likely effective as a film score. However, what it gains for creativity, it lacks in pure entertainment value making this one of Horner's less interesting albums.

David Hirsch

Born on the Fourth of July 🦴🦴🦴🦴🦴

1989, MCA Records; from the movie *Born on the Fourth of July*, Universal Pictures, 1989.

Album Notes: *Music:* John Williams; *Music Editor:* Ken Wannberg; Orchestra conducted by John Williams; *Featured Soloist:* Tim Morrison (principal trumpet, The Boston Pops Orchestra); *Album Producer:* John Williams; *Engineer:* Armin Steiner.

"The most beautiful American score ever written. As a foreigner, this score is what I see America as."

Hans Zimmer
on Randy Newman's Avalon
(Entertainment Weekly Online, 2-3-95)

Selections: 1 A Hard Rain's A Gonna Fall (B. Dylan)(4:58) *Edie Brickell & New Bohemians;* 2 Born On The Bayou (J. Fogerty)(4:54) *The Broken Homes;* 3 Brown Eyed Girl (V. Morrison)(3:07) *Van Morrison;* 4 American Pie (D. McLean)(8:32) *Don McLean;* 5 My Girl (W. Robinson/R. White)(2:43) *The Temptations;* 6 Soldier Boy (L. Dixon/F. Green)(2:39) *The Shirelles;* 7 Venus (E. Marshall)(2:21) *Frankie Avalon;* 8 Moon River (H. Mancini/J. Mercer)(2:41) *Henry Mancini and his Orchestra;* 9 Prologue (1:22); 10 The Early Days, Massapequa, 1957 (4:57); 11 The Shooting Of Wilson (5:07); 12 Cua Viet River, Vietnam, 1968 (5:02); 13 Homecoming (2:38); 14 Born On The Fourth Of July (5:44).

Review: An outstanding score by John Williams is the centerpiece of the soundtrack album for Oliver Stone's cluttered 1989 biopic of Vietnam vet Ron Kovic. So masterful in conveying all the dramatic requirements of Kovic's decades-spanning story is Williams' score, in fact, that you forget his music actually takes up less than half of the album's running time, the remainder of which contains Edie Brickell & New Bohemians' "A Hard Rain's a Gonna Fall" along with a number of period songs strictly generic in their selection (Don McLean's "American Pie," Van Morrison's "Brown Eyed Girl," Henry Mancini's "Moon River," etc.). But Williams' score, featuring a downbeat trumpet fanfare performed by Tim Morrison, is one of his most powerful and potent efforts, offering both moments of tragedy and uplift, culminating in a knockout finale. It's just one more jewel in Williams' crown, and certainly one of the best film scores to come out of the last half of the 1980s.

Andy Dursin

Born to Be Wild 🦴🦴🦴

1995, Milan Records; from the movie *Born to Be Wild*, Warner Bros., 1995.

Album Notes: *Music:* Mark Snow; *Music Editor:* Jeff Charbonneau; Orchestra conducted by Mark Snow; *Album Producer:*

David Franco; *Engineers*: Joe Gastwirt, Ramon Breton.

Selections: 1 Plucked From The Jungle (4:01); 2 Water Paint (3:18); 3 Bobo's Dream/Sweeping (2:06); 4 Surf And Rescue (2:00); 5 River Celebration/ The Verdict (1:40); 6 Hats On The Rolling Van (3:14); 7 Campfire (2:42); 8 Train Chase/Right And Wrong (3:39); 9 Stealing Katie (2:17); 10 Statues (1:10); 11 Cornfield Chase (1:20); 12 Goodbye (3:34); 13 Back To The Species (M. Snow/Lebo M)(2:41) *Lebo M*; 14 Born To Be Wild (M. Bonfire)(3:45) *Green Jelly*.

Review: Known primarily these days for his brilliant nonthematic work on the "X-Files" TV series, Mark Snow gets to strut his melodic stuff here for one of the several *Free Willy* knock-offs produced around the time, with a domesticated gorilla replacing in this case the seagoing beastie. Backed with a full symphonic orchestra, Snow has created a bright score, featuring some charming, albeit sugar-coated themes ("Goodbye") with several tracks interpolated with African inspired rhythms ("Plucked from the Jungle"). Artist Lebo M, who also worked with Jerry Goldsmith on *Congo*, co-composed the song "Back to the Species" with Snow and performs on the album. The rock group Green Jelly also brings Steppenwolf's "Born to Be Wild" into the '90s.

David Hirsch

Boy on a Dolphin ♪♪♪♪

1992, MCA Records/Japan; from the movie *Boy on a Dolphin*, 20th Century-Fox, 1957.

Album Notes: *Music*: Hugo Friedhofer; *Orchestrations*: Edward Powell; *Lyrics*: Paul Francis Webster, Takis Morakis; The 20th Century-Fox Orchestra and Chorus, conducted by Lionel Newman.

Selections: 1 Main Title: Boy On A Dolphin (4:09) *Mary Kaye*; 2 Phaedra Finds The Boy On A Dolphin (4:00) *Marni Nixon*; 3 The Acropolis (2:06); 4 The Cafe (3:01); 5 Montage: The Road To Meteora: (a) The Harbor, (b) The Mountains, (c) The Monastery, (d) Street Music (5:57); 6 The Dive (2:06); 7 The Search (2:27) *Mary Kaye*; 8 Nocturnal Sea (6:15) *Marni Nixon*; 9 Mondraki Bay (2:38); 10 Love Scene (2:58); 11 The Captive (2:53); 12 End Title: Boy On A Dolphin (3:14).

Review: Alan Ladd and Sophia Loren, looking for an antique Greek sculpture buried at the bottom of the Aegean Sea, discovered more than they bargained for in this pleasantly innocuous film shot on location and sporting a serenely evocative Academy Award-nominated score by Hugo Friedhofer. Using the basic components at his disposal—a romantic love story, an exotic setting, and a rich musical culture—the com-

poser created a stylishly impressionistic series of cues, effectively mixing into them elements of Mediterranean folk music to give them the right tonal colors. Mary Kaye delivers the nostalgic title tune, while Marni Nixon vocalizes on a couple of tracks. The CD, issued in Japan only, can be found in this country at specialty stores.

The Boy Who Could Fly
♪♪♪♪♪

1986, Varese-Sarabande; from the movie *The Boy Who Could Fly*, Lorimar Motion Pictures, 1986.

Album Notes: *Music*: Bruce Broughton; *Album Producer*: Bruce Broughton; *Engineers*: Keith Grant, Daniel Hersch.

Selections: 1 Main Title (2:36); 2 New Starts (3:51); 3 Millie's Science Project (3:09); 4 Family (2:57); 5 Flying (4:29); 6 Eric On The Roof (2:23); 7 Eric Agitated/Louis Defeated (3:55); 8 Millie And Eric Flee (3:45); 9 In The Air (4:31); 10 The Boy Who Could Fly (2:41).

Review: This gentle, monothematic score by Bruce Broughton tells of the blooming friendship between a young girl who moves next door to an autistic boy. Millie has a younger brother who has been tormented by the local bullies and dreams simply of just getting safely around the block. The mysterious Eric, however, believes he can really fly and before long, Millie begins to suspect it might be true. By altering his one theme, Broughton was able to create a symphonic poem for the three youngsters that grows from its light, innocent beginning ("Main Title") to a full-flourished orchestral movement that tells that real life can be even more amazing than one's fantasies ("In The Air").

David Hirsch

Boys on the Side ♪♪♪♪▿

1995, Arista Records; from the movie *Boys on the Side*, Warner Bros., 1995.

Album Notes: *Songs Producers*: Don Was, James Stroud, Stephen "Scooter" Weintraub, Peter Collins, Chris Thomas, Ian Stanley, Stephen Street, Stephen Lipson, Pierre Marchand, Glyns Johns; *Engineers*: Rik Pekkonen, Chuck Ainlay, David Streeby, David Leonard, David "Chipper" Nicholas, Steve Williams, Stephen Street, Heff Moraes, Pierre Marchand, Glyns Johns, Jim Webb.

Selections: 1 You Got It (R. Orbison/T. Petty/J. Lynne)(3:25) *Bonnie Raitt*; 2 I Take You With Me (M. Etheridge)(4:48) *Melissa Etheridge*; 3 Keep On Growing (E. Clapton/B. Whitlock)(5:24) *Sheryl Crow*; 4 Power Of Two (E. Saliers)(5:22)

Indigo Girls; 5 Somebody Stand By Me (S. Crow/T. Wolf) (5:05) *Stevie Nicks*; 6 Everyday Is Like Sunday (Morrisey/S. Street) (3:41) *Pretenders*; 7 Dreams (N. Hogan/D. O'Riordan)(4:30) *The Cranberries*; 8 Why (A. Lennox)(4:53) *Annie Lennox*; 9 Ol' 55 (T. Waits) (4:11) *Sarah McLachlan*; 10 Willow (J. Armatrading)(4:01) *Joan Armatrading*; 11 Crossroads (R. Johnson)(2:49) *Jonell Mosser*; 12 You Got It (R. Orbison/T. Petty/J. Lynne)(3:08) *Whoopi Goldberg*; 13 You Got It (R. Orbison/T. Petty/J. Lynne) (3:25) *Bonnie Raitt.*

Review: Whoopi Goldberg, Mary-Louise Parker and Drew Barrymore star in this comedy romp as a trio of cross country travelers heading for San Diego and much more than they had bargained for when they started off. Making the trip a great deal more enjoyable are the songs heard on the soundtrack, performed by some of the top female singers today, including Bonnie Raitt, Melissa Etheridge, Sheryl Crow, Stevie Nicks, Annie Lennox, and Whoopi herself. The album brings the performers and their songs center stage for what amounts to a sensational all-star showcase. When pop compilation soundtracks are that good, one only has to listen and enjoy.

The Brady Bunch Movie 🎵♭

1995, Milan Records; from the movie *The Brady Bunch Movie*, Paramount Pictures, 1995.

Album Notes: *Featured Artists*: Mudd Pagoda, Generation Why, The Original Brady Bunch Kids; *Album Producer*: Steve Tyrell.

Selections: 1 The Brady Bunch (Grunge version)(S. Schwartz/ F. DeVol) (1:02); 2 It's A Sunshine Day (S. McCarthy)(2:38) *The Original Brady Bunch Kids*; 3 I'm Feeling Nothing (DADA)(2:26) *DADA*; 4 "Marsha, I have to tell you something" (:13); 5 Venus (R. Van Leeuwen) (3:00) *Shocking Blue*; 6 Girl (C. Fox/N. Gimbel)(3:48) *Davy Jones*; 7 "You're all a part of me" (:08); 8 Whatever (S. Tyrell/M. Landau/S. Tyrell)(3:44) *Zak*; 9 Supermodel (You Better Work) (R. Charles/J. Harry/L. Tee)(3:43) *RuPaul*; 10 "You kids have no idea what it takes to impress a chick" (:08); 11 Till I Met You (S. Schwartz/L. Schwartz/B. Williams)(1:45) *Mudd Pagoda*; 12 The Beast Is Out Of Hand (S. Tyrell/K. Savigar/S. Tyrell)(2:55) *Mudd Pagoda*; 13 Have A Nice Day (S. Tyrell/B. Coffing/S. Tyrell/M. Landau)(3:01) *Barry Coffing, Zachary Throne*; 14 I'm Looking Around (S. Tyrell/B. Coffing/S. Tyrell/M. Landau) (3:11) *Generation Why*; 15 "Marsha did it again..." (:04); 16 I Wish I Could Be Like You (S. Tyrell/K. Savigar/S. Tyrell)(3:28) *Mudd Pagoda*; 17 "I think Peter's a babe..." (:07); 18 Keep On (T. Jenkins/J. Mills) (2:50) *The Original Brady Bunch Kids*; 19 "And as a wise man once said..." (:08); 20 The Brady Bunch (S. Schwartz/F. DeVol) (:58)

Lauren Tyrell, Megan Joyce, Christina Tyrell, Kristina Oloffson, Zachary Throne.

Review: Stop laughing! Not only did they make the movie — it was a hit! The same can't be said for the companion album, though, whose only chart hits are prior smashes by Venus ("Shocking Blue") and RuPaul ("Supermodel (You Better Work)"). For kitsch lovers, this set includes the original Brady cast's "It's a Sunshine Day" as well as cute Monkee Davy Jones serenading Marcia with "Girl." And, of course, there's the Brady Bunch theme, which you can hear at least three times a day on cable TV.

Gary Graff

Brainstorm 🎵🎵🎵🎵

1983, Varese-Sarabande Records; from the movie *Brainstorm*, M-G-M/UA, 1983.

Album Notes: *Music*: James Horner; The London Symphony Orchestra, The Ambrosian Singers and The Boys Choir Of New College, Oxford, conducted by James Horner; *Album Producer*: James Horner; *Engineer*: Eric Tomlinson.

Selections: 1 Main Title (2:15); 2 Lillian's Heart Attack (3:18); 3 Gaining Access To The Tapes (2:49); 4 Michael's Gift To Karen (6:54); 5 First Playback (3:21); 6 Race For Time (4:53); 7 Final Playback/End Titles (6:50).

Review: This is a strikingly powerful early effort in James Horner's career, one of the scores that made a lot of people sit up and take notice of his ability to convey the emotions reflected on-screen. As a team of scientists seek to perfect a virtual reality device that records from and plays back images directly to the brain, Horner conceived symphonic battle between the light and the dark, with a screeching army of voices to speak for the unknown. The seven tracks form individual movements of a concerto, bouncing from the fear of death with heavy handled percussion effects ("Lillian's Heart Attack") to the wonder of a living man's peak at heaven with the use of a mixed boys and adult choir ("Final Playback"). Horner uses a passionate, classically inspired love theme ("Michael's Gift to Karen") when researcher Christopher Walken attempts to rekindle the lost passion with his estranged wife by showing her a VR recording of how he really perceives her. This is an immensely entertaining effort, despite the fact that several themes have since been reused on other Horner scores. "Race for Time," for example, was recycled into *Clear and Present Danger* for virtually the same sequence! This early digital recording has a superb dynamic range.

David Hirsch

Brassed Off! 🎵🎵🎵🎵

1997, RCA Victor Records; from the movie *Brassed Off!*, Miramax Films, 1997.

Album Notes: *Music:* Trevor Jones; *Orchestrations:* Trevor Jones, Geoff Alexander; Orchestra conducted by Trevor Jones; *Featured Soloist:* Maurice Murphy (trumpet, flugelhorn); The Grimethorpe Colliery Band, conducted by John Anderson; *Featured Soloists:* Paul Hughes (flugelhorn), Shaun Randall (cornet); *Album Producer:* Trevor Jones; *Engineers:* Mike Sheady, Simon Rhodes.

Selections: 1 Death Or Glory (R.B. Hall)(2:49); 2 A Sad Old Day (:48); 3 Floral Dance (K. Moss)(2:59); 4 Aforementioned Essential Items (:32); 5 En Aranjuez con tu amor (J. Rodrigo)(4:04); 6 Years Of Coal (:35); 7 March Of The Cobblers (R. Barrett/E. Siebert)(3:09); 8 There's More Important Things In Life (1:47); 9 Cross Of Honour (W. Rimmer)(2:14); 10 Jerusalem (Parry/Blake, arr.: V. Herbert)(2:23); 11 Florentiner March (Fucik, arr.: Barsotti); 12 Danny Boy (Londonderry Air)(trad., arr.: P. Grainger)(3:07); 13 We'll Find A Way (3:25); 14 Clog Dance (Marcangelo)(2:40); 15 Colonel Bogey (K. Alford) (3:15); 16 All Things Bright And Beautiful (Monk/Alexander, arr.: D. Rimmer) (2:04); 17 William Tell Overture (G. Rossini, arr.: G.J. Grant)(3:23); 18 Honest Decent Human Beings (1:37); 19 Pomp And Circumstance (E. Elgar, arr.: O. Hume)(3:19).

Review: This roaring, brassy album, with incidental music by Trevor Jones, is so ingratiating it's almost too good to miss. The film, about a fictional Yorkshire mining town (slyly named Grimley, in reference to Grimethorpe) faced with the closure of its pit, and threatening to retaliate with the disbanding of its champion brass band, called for a soundtrack that features brass numbers. Among the selections heard in the film and on this CD, several (Rodrigo's "Concerto de Aranjuez," Alford's "Colonel Bogey," and Elgar's "Pomp and Circumstance," among them) will be well known, even if the arrangements for brass give them a new luster. Other lesser known tunes provide pleasant discoveries. In the mix, Trevor Jones' touching, haunting cues seem swallowed, but are equally enjoyable and on the button.

Braveheart 🎵🎵🎵🎵

1995, London Records; from the movie *Braveheart*, Paramount Pictures, 1995.

Album Notes: *Music:* James Horner; *Orchestrations:* James Horner; *Music Editor:* Jim Henrikson; *Assistant Music Editors:* Christine Cholvin, Joe E. Rand; The London Symphony Orchestra, conducted by James Horner; *Instrumental Soloists:* Tony Hinnegan (kena and whistle), James Horner (keyboards), Eric Rigler (Uilleann pipes), Mike Taylor (Bodhran drum and whis-

tle), Ian Underwood (synth programming), Choristers of Westminster Abbey, Martin Neary, director; *Album Producer:* James Horner; *Engineer:* Shawn Murphy; *Assistant Engineer:* Jonathan Allen.

Selections: 1 Main Title (2:51); 2 A Gift Of A Thistle (1:37); 3 Wallace Courts Murron (4:25); 4 The Secret Wedding (6:33); 5 Attack On Murron (3:00); 6 Revenge (6:23); 7 Murron's Burial (2:13); 8 Making Plans/ Gathering The Clans (2:05); 9 "Sons of Scotland" (6:19); 10 The Battle Of Stirling (6:07); 11 For The Love Of A Princess (4:07); 12 Falkirk (4:04); 13 Betrayal and Desolation (7:48); 14 Mornay's Dream (1:18); 15 The Legend Spreads (1:09); 16 The Princess Pleads For Wallace's Life (3:38); 17 "Freedom"/The Execution/ Bannockburn (7:24); 18 End Credits (7:12).

Review: In Mel Gibson's marvelous historical drama, the character of William Wallace is that of a man who rises from despair and loss to lead a nation in gaining their independence, becoming a larger-than-life, mythic figure along the way. In James Horner's equally brilliant film score, the composer captures the intimacy of Wallace with his allies and loved ones, just as he adeptly echoes the stirring, impassioned cries for freedom that Wallace represents. For all of its 70-plus minutes, then, Horner's *Braveheart* takes you on a rich sonic journey with changing emotions and varied dramatic situations, and virtually all of it works—the battle music is propulsive and dynamic, the main theme moving, tragic and triumphant all at the same time, while the ethnic instrumentation works perfectly with the London Symphony Orchestra in building a lyrical musical landscape that's undoubtedly one of Horner's most complex and satisfying works yet.

Andy Dursin

Brazil 🎵🎵🎵🎵

1992, Milan Records; from the movie *Brazil*, Universal Pictures, 1992.

Album Notes: *Music:* Michael Kamen; *Orchestrations:* Michael Kamen; The National Philharmonic Orchestra of London, conducted by Michael Kamen; *Featured Soloists:* Mel Colins (saxophone), Derick Collins (clarinet), Sid Sax (violin); *Album Producer:* Michael Kamen; *Engineers:* Eric Tomlinson, Andy Jackson.

Selections: 1 Central Services/The Office (1:41); 2 Sam Lowry's First Dream/Brazil (2:10) *Kate Bush*; 3 Ducts (:42); 4 Waiting For Daddy/Sam Lowry's Wetter Dream ("The Monoliths Erupt") (3:00); 5 Truck Drive (1:15); 6 The Restaurant (You've Got To Say The Number) (1:34); 7 Mr. Helpmann (1:14); 8 The Elevator (:45); 9 Jill Brazil/Power Station (2:07); 10 The Party (Part 1)/Plastic Surgery (1:03); 11 Ducting Dream (1:53); 12 Brazil/Geoff Muldaur

(3:26); 13 Days And Nights In Kyoto/The Party (Part 2) (1:18); 14 The Morning After (1:46); 15 Escape? (1:03); 16 The Battle (4:30); 17 Harry Tuttle, "A Man Consumed By Paperwork" (1:50); 18 Mother's Funeral/Forces Of Darkness (1:44); 19 Escape! No Escape! (2:26); 20 Bachianas Brazil Samba (2:51).

Review: Michael Kamen's music provides a superb backdrop to Terry Gilliam's multi-faceted drama of dreams and disillusionment in the near future. Central to the score is the 1930 Ary Borroso tune "Brazil," which refers both to the character of revolutionary Jill Brazil, and to a place better than the dismal bureaucratic world in which Sam Lowry exists. The Borroso tune runs throughout, but Kamen's own romantic theme, a sweeping, soaring Korngold-esque melody, captures all of Lowry's hopeful longing and accompanies his visions of heroism and love. Scattered amongst these two cornerstone motifs is a great variety of music, from comic "Central Services" pseudo-TV advertisements (seen in the film on video monitors), to pop tunes used as background fillers, and plenty of adventurous symphonic cues.

Randall D. Larson

Breakfast at Tiffany's 🎵🎵

1990, RCA Records; from the movie *Breakfast at Tiffany's*, Paramount Pictures, 1961.

Album Notes: *Music:* Henry Mancini; Orchestra conducted by Henry Mancini; *CD Producer:* Chick Crumpacker; *CD Engineer:* Dick Baxter.

Selections: 1 Moon River (H. Mancini/J. Mercer)(2:41); 2 Something For Cat (3:07); 3 Sally's Tomato (3:05); 4 Mr. Yunioshi (2:29); 5 The Big Blow Out (2:26); 6 Hub Caps And Tail Lights (2:24); 7 Breakfast At Tiffany's (2:45); 8 Latin Golightly (2:57); 9 Holly (3:18); 10 Loose Caboose (3:08); 11 The Big Heist (3:07); 12 Moon River Cha Cha (H. Mancini/J. Mercer) (2:35).

Review: Someone with some clout at BMG, the controlling agent for RCA Victor Records, should take the bull by the horns, make the executive decision to begin a thoughtful, realistic assessment of their immense, historically vital catalog, and create CD reissues that reflect the importance of the music. Is anybody out there listening?

A perfect case to argue this point is the label's so-called budget series that contains many of RCA Victor's legendary albums, including Henry Mancini's pivotal soundtracks for the television series "Peter Gunn," and films such as *The Pink Panther* and *Breakfast at Tiffany's.*

The last one is an important film, and next to the two other aforementioned Mancini works, the composer's most

celebrated effort, including the most gorgeous version of "Moon River" ever. It is sad that the powers-that-be at RCA don't believe the soundtrack is deserving of better treatment.

This low-end, early CD issue will have to do for now, with no liner notes or historical information, no extra musical selections or up-to-date digital restoration. It's a shame! (The rating doesn't reflect the quality of the music, but its shabby presentation).

Charles L. Granata

Breaking the Waves 🎵🎵🎵

1996, Hollywood Records; from the movie *Breaking the Waves*, 1996.

Album Notes: *Album Producers:* Ray Williams, Mark Warrick; *Engineer:* Crispin Metropolis.

Selections: 1 In A Broken Dream (D. Bentley)(3:40) *Python Lee Jackson*; 2 Hot Love (M. Bolan)(4:56) *T-Rex*; 3 Child In Time (Lord/Blackmore/ Gillan/Glover/Paice)(10:18) *Deep Purple*; 4 Suzanne (L. Cohen)(3:49) *Leonard Cohen*; 5 Virginia Plain (B. Ferry)(2:56) *Roxy Music*; 6 All The Way To Memphis (I. Hunter)(4:55) *Mott the Hoople*; 7 He's Gonna Step On You Again (J. Kongos/C. Demetriou)(4:19) *John Kongos*; 8 Whisky In The Jar (Lynott/Bell/Downey)(5:43) *Thin Lizzy*; 9 A Whiter Shade Of Pale (K. Reid/ G. Brooker)(4:05) *Procol Harum*; 10 Goodbye Yellow Brick Road (E. John/B. Taupin)(3:13) *Elton John*; 11 Cross-Eyed Mary (I. Anderson)(4:09) *Jethro Tull*; 12 Siciliana from Sonata No. 2 for Flute and Harpsichord, BWV 1031 (2nd Movement)(J.S. Bach)(4:30) *Christian Steenstrup, Carl-Ulrik Much Andersen*.

Review: There is something perversely endearing about an album that brings together selections by T-Rex ("Hot Love"), Deep Purple ("Child in Time"), Leonard Cohen (the classic "Suzanne"), Procol Harum ("A Whiter Shade of Pale"), Elton John ("Goodbye Yellow Brick Road"), and... Johann-Sebastian Bach (the "Siciliana" movement from the Sonata BWV 1031)!

How these relate to the film written and directed by Lars von Trier is quite another question, but the fact is the disparities in the musical programming actually work very nicely.

The Bride of Frankenstein
🎵🎵🎵🎵

1993, Silva Screen; from the movie *The Bride of Frankenstein*, Universal Pictures, 1935.

Album Notes: *Music:* Franz Waxman; *Orchestrations:* Clifford Vaughan; *Re-orchestrations:* Tony Bremner, Soren Hyldgaard; The Westminster Philharmonic Orchestra, conducted by Kenneth Alwyn; *Album Producer*: Soren Hyldgaard; *Engineer*: Mike Ross-Trevor.

Selections: 1 The Bride Of Frankenstein — Main Title (1:24); 2 Prologue — Minuetto and Storm (3:52); 3 Monster Entrance (2:14); 4 Processional March (2:16); 5 A Strange Apparition/ Pretorius' Entrance/You Will Need A Coat (2:55); 6 Bottle Sequence (2:13); 7 Female Monster Music/Pastorale/Village/ Chase (4:30); 8 Crucifixion/Monster Breaks Out (3:11); 9 Fire In The Hut/ Graveyard (2:07); 10 Danse macabre (2:09); 11 The Creation (10:14); 12 The Tower Explodes and Finale (3:10); 13 The Invisible Ray Suite (F. Waxman) (5:54).

Review: Franz Waxman's monumental score for the 1935 *The Bride of Frankenstein* was one of the earliest fully-developed film scores in a day when most films had very sparse musical accompaniment. With its blend of romantic motifs and a variety of inventive horrific passages — the most notable being the "Creation" music, wherein the composer musically depicted the chilling noises of the laboratory equipment to create an impressionistic and unique musical sequence — it was a milestone in film music. This recreation of the score is superbly performed and very nicely packaged, including a 20-page booklet which analyzes the music one cue at a time. The CD is also notable for including, for the first time, a six-minute suite from Waxman's *The Invisible Ray*, another very early and very good Universal horror score.

Randall D. Larson

The Bridge on the River Kwai 🦴

1995, Legacy Records/Sony Music Entertainment; from the movie *The Bridge on the River Kwai*, Columbia Pictures, 1957.

Album Notes: *Music*: Malcolm Arnold; The Royal Philharmonic Orchestra, conducted by Malcolm Arnold; *Album Producer*: Didier C. Deutsch; *Engineer*: Chris Herles.

Selections: 1 Overture (4:24); 2 Colonel Bogey March (2:52); 3 Shear's Escape (3:58); 4 Nicholson's Victory (4:45); 5 Sunset (3:54); 6 Working On The Bridge (2:58); 7 Trek To The Bridge (8:28); 8 Camp Concert Dance (2:36); 9 Finale (2:12); 10 River Kwai March (2:58); 11 (I Give My Heart (To No One But You)(3:16); 12 Dance Music (4:54); 13 The River Kwai March/ Colonel Bogey March (2:28) *Mitch Miller & His Orchestra*.

Review: When Columbia Records released the soundtrack to *The Bridge on the River Kwai* in late 1957, no one anticipated the immense popularity it would enjoy. While the score by British classical composer Malcolm Arnold would go on to win an Academy Award, the Columbia soundtrack LP would remain

a "hit" in its own right, despite some technical flaws that affected its sonics. Probably the greatest boost for the evocative, dramatic score was the waxing of the film's most memorable themes, "The River Kwai March" and "Colonel Bogey March" by Mitch Miller. Issued as a single and included on the soundtrack LP, this million selling hit drew heaps of attention to the film, and its captivating music.

Freshly restored from the original mono session tapes, the CD offers pitch/speed corrected masters (a problem inherent in the original LP issues), and while not quite perfect, markedly improved sound. As a bonus, three newly discovered session tracks are included.

Charles L. Granata

The Bridges of Madison County 🦴

1995, Malpaso Records; from the movie *The Bridges of Madison County*, Warner Bros. Pictures, 1995.

Album Notes: *Music*: Lennie Niehaus, Clint Eastwood; Orchestra conducted by Lennie Niehaus; *Album Producer*: Clint Eastwood.

Selections: 1 Doe Eyes (Love Theme)(C. Eastwood)(1:06); 2 I'll Close My Eyes (B. Kaye/B. Reid)(2:50) *Dinah Washington*; 3 Easy Living (L. Robin/R. Rainger)(6:26) *Johnny Hartman*; 4 Blue Gardenia (B. Russell/L. Lee)(5:18) *Dinah Washington*; 5 I See Your Face Before Me (H. Dietz/A. Schwartz) (5:04) *Johnny Hartman*; 6 Soft Winds (F. Henderson/F. Royal)(3:02) *Dinah Washington, Hal Mooney and His Orchestra*; 7 Baby, I'm Yours (V. McCoy) (2:33) *Barbara Lewis*; 8 It's A Wonderful World (J. Watson/H. Adamson/J. Savitt) (2:32) *Irene Kral, The Junior Mance Trio*; 9 It Was Almost Like A Song (H. David/A. Jordan)(2:49) *Johnny Hartman*; 10 This Is Always (H. Warren/M. Gordon)(3:22) *Irene Kral, The Junior Mance Trio*; 11 For All We Know (S. Lewis/J.F. Coots)(5:31) *Johnny Hartman*; 12 Doe Eyes (reprise)(5:00).

Review: The movie might have been slow and monotonous, but at least the soundtrack album is a bit easier to take, being comprised of Lennie Niehaus instrumentals and a selection of jazz standards. Included are several tracks each from Dinah Washington, including "I'll Close My Eyes" and "Blue Gardenia," and Johnny Hartman's "For All We Know" and "It Was Almost Like a Song," in addition to songs from Barbara Lewis and Irene Kral. Niehaus' score is represented on the album by two cuts — a brief opening cut and a full rendition of the theme "Doe Eyes," composed by Niehaus and Eastwood, heard in the end credits of the picture and on the end of the album. Like

Eastwood's theme for *Unforgiven*, "Doe Eyes" is a lovely, lyrical tune that is minimally performed at first (here by solo piano) before being developed gradually into a full-fledged orchestral arrangement. It all makes for pleasant listening, though still recommended most strongly for fans of the film.

Andy Dursin

Bright Angel ♫♫♫♫

1991, Intrada Records; from the movie *Bright Angel*, **Hemdale Film Corporation, 1991.**

Album Notes: *Music*: Christopher Young; *Orchestrations*: Christopher Young; *Music Editors*: John Lasalandra, Virginia Ellsworth; *Featured Musicians*: Mark Zimoski (synthesizers, electronic percussion), Daniel Licht (synthesizers, extended guitar techniques); *Album Producer*: Christopher Young; *Engineers*: Jeff Vaughn, Michael Aarvold.

Selections: 1 Bright Angel (3:30); 2 Wasteland White Light (3:39); 3 Sweetgrass Hills (2:41); 4 Milk River Runaway (2:24); 5 Lost Lullaby (2:44); 6 Nothing Worth Hiding (2:12); 7 Fish Feel Pain (3:58); 8 Sunburst (3:23); 9 Things Pass Too Fast (3:45); 10 Red Rover, Red Rover (3:49); 11 Just Another Casper Night (6:20); 12 Too Morose? (2:00); 13 Wheatstraw Blind (4:29); 14 Gateway (5:23); 15 Trails End Where They Should (2:34).

Review: Christopher Young masterfully captured the emotional disposition of this Middle American character play about a troubled teenage boy as he travels cross country with an equally distressed young girl. His main themes are a collection of anxious, blue-grass style tunes, all lacking in any tranquility and overburdened with brooding anguish. The real creativity, however, comes with cues like "Wasteland White Light," a jumble of dissonant melodies that reflect the confusion in the lives of the young protagonists. Real life endings aren't always happy, and Young accomplished what he set out to do for the film—instill a real sense that there would ever be one for these two.

David Hirsch

Broken Arrow ♫♫♫♫

1995, Milan Records; from the movie *Broken Arrow*, **20th Century-Fox, 1995.**

Album Notes: *Music*: Hans Zimmer; *Music Editor*: Adam Smalley; Music conducted by Bruce Fowler, D. Harper; *Featured Musicians*: Hans Zimmer (synthesizers), Duane Eddy (baritone guitar), Bob Daspit (guitars), Emil Richards (percussion), Walt Fowler (trumpet), Bruce Fowler (one-note trombone), Ryeland Allison (weird noises), Lisbeth Scott (vocals); *Album Producers*: Hans Zimmer, Jay Rifkin; *Engineer*: Slamm Andrews.

Selections: 1 Brothers (7:05); 2 Secure (4:47); 3 Stealth (7:35); 4 Mine (5:42); 5 Nuke (10:48); 6 Greed (11:00); 7 Hammerhead (4:40); 8 Broken (7:37).

Review: Hans Zimmer's score for *Broken Arrow* makes the most out of its musical palette. A few faint melodies trickle throughout, but the music's main attribute is its ambient texture. Typical of the composer's approach, the 10:47 "Nuke" carries on this resolute disposition with a dispassionate female choir, intoning slowly over eerie shards of electronic sound, broken for a momentary segue into a rhythmic action melody. The cue develops into a cyclone of ambient sound whirling around a relentless rhythm of percussiveness which builds in speed and force through its culmination with choir and high-end synths. Another, "Greed," carries the form into further regions, creating a compelling rhythm of slow-moving synth tones over fast-moving percussive taps—and of course altering the shape, size, and speed of the rhythm throughout the cue. Zimmer's orchestration swirls in layers, waves of sound overlapping each other, each wave conveying with it another new sound on a storm-tossed musical tide. It's to Zimmer's credit that the CD's hour's-worth of music is consistently varied, fresh, and audibly interesting, not always the case with action scores.

Randall D. Larson

A Bronx Tale ♫♫♫♫

1993, Epic Soundtrax; from the movie *A Bronx Tale*, **Tribeca/Savoy Pictures, 1993.**

Album Notes: *Featured Performers*: Cool Change, Dion & The Belmonts, Della Reese, The Cleftones, Jerry Butler, Dean Martin, The Rascals, Aaron Neville, Bobby Watson, The Gerry Niewood Quartet, Wilson Pickett, The Moonglows, The Flamingos, The Complexions, The Moody Blues, The Four Tops, Butch Barbella, The Jimi Hendrix Experience, The Impressions, James Brown, Donald Byrd; *Album Producers*: Philip Sandhaus, Chandra Beard; *Engineer*: Vlado Meller.

Selections: 1 Streets Of The Bronx (B. Barbella)(2:55) *Cool Change*; 2 I Wonder Why (R. Weeks/A. Olayinka)(2:18) *Dion & The Belmonths*; 3 Little Girl Of Mine (M. Levy/H. Cox)(3:11) *The Cleftones*; 4 Don't You Know? (B. Worth) (2:31) *Della Reese*; 5 For Your Precious Love (J. Butler/A. Brooks/ R. Brooks)(2:44) *Jerry Butler*; 6 Ain't That A Kick In The Head (S. Cahn/J. Van Heusen)(2:30) *Dean Martin*; 7 Father And Son (B. Barbella)(:49) *Cool Change*; 8 A Beautiful Morning (F. Cavaliere/E. Brigati, Jr.)(2:32) *The Rascals*; 9 Tell It Like It Is (G. Davis/L. Diamond)(2:38) *Aaron Neville*; 10 Bustalk (R. Watson)(1:30) *Bobby Watson*; 11 I Only Have Eyes For You (H. Warren/A.

Dubin)(2:40) *The Gerry Niewood Quartet*; 12 Ninety-Nine And A Half (Won't Do)(S. Cropper/E. Floyd/W. Pickett)(2:36) *Wilson Pickett*; 13 Ten Commandments Of Love (M. Paul)(4:02) *The Moonglows*; 14 I Only Have Eyes For You (H. Warren/A. Dubin)(3:50) *The Flamingos & The Complexions*; 15 Nights In White Satin (J. Hayward)(4:26) *The Moody Blues*; 16 Baby I Need Your Loving (B. Holland/L. Dozier/E. Holland)(2:43) *The Four Tops*; 17 Regrets (B. Barbella)(:50) *Butch Barbella*; 18 All Along The Watchtower (B. Dylan)(3:58) *The Jimi Hendrix Experience*; 19 I'm So Proud (C. Mayfield)(2:47) *The Impressions*; 20 It's A Man's Man's Man's World (J. Brown/B. Newsome)(2:46) *James Brown*; 21 Cristo Redentor (D. Pearson) (5:38) *Donald Byrd*; 22 Streets Of The Bronx (B. Barbella)(4:46) *Bells and String Orchestra*.

Review: The diversified collection of pop vocals heard in this album reflects the choices made by executive producer Robert De Niro to serve as the soundtrack to this film which bears his creative imprint. The story of a young boy torn between his streetwise, working class father, played by De Niro, and a charismatic neighborhood crime boss (Chazz Palminteri), whom the boy worships, *A Bronx Tale* finds a natural musical mine in the songs that dominated the radio air waves in the 1960s, the period of the film. The mix of doo-wop songs and classic rock tunes is strongly evocative of the era, extending as it does from golden oldies by Dion and the Belmonts, The Cleftones, and The Moon Glows, to hits by Dean Martin, Della Reese, Aaron Neville, The Moody Blues, and Jimi Hendrix. A trip down Memory Lane if ever there was one...

Brother's Keeper ♪♪♪♪

1993, Angel Records; from the documentary *Brother's Keeper*, American Playhouse Theatrical Films, 1993.

Album Notes: *Music:* Jay Ungar, Molly Mason; *Featured Musicians:* Jay Ungar (violin, viola, mandolin, guitar), Molly Mason (guitar, bass), Guy "Fooch" Fischetti (pedal steel guitar), Peter O'Brien (drums); *Album Producers:* Jay Ungar, Molly Mason; *Engineer:* Chris Andersen.

Selections: 1 Brother's Keeper (3:17); 2 Lyman's Walk (:58); 3 The Streets Of Munnsville (2:13); 4 The Golden Eagle Two-Step (3:06); 5 I'm Just a-Fiddlin' (2:15); 6 Waltzing With You (2:37) *Jay Ungar, Molly Mason*; 7 Fog Scene (1:06); 8 Roscoe's Waterfall (2:35); 9 Fiddler Elbow (4:18); 10 Johnson Road (2:46); 11 The Auction (1:45); 12 Fall To Winter (:48); 13 Delbert's Tear (2:32); 14 The Tractor Breakdown (2:47); 15 Gobblers (1:56); 16 Cows On The Hill (3:45); 17 The Trial (3:25); 18 Waltzing With You (2:33); 19 Brother's Keeper (1:59).

Review: For this award-winning documentary about four New York State dairy farming brothers whose lives are shattered when one is accused of murder, Jay Ungar and Molly Mason wrote a score that draws its inspiration from its strong rural American roots. Eloquent in its simplicity, it makes no concessions to current trends, and succeeds in being both profoundly compelling and unusually attractive.

The Buccaneer ♪♪♪♪

1988, Varese-Sarabande; from the movie *The Buccaneer*, Paramount Pictures, 1958.

Album Notes: *Music:* Elmer Bernstein; Orchestra conducted by Elmer Bernstein.

Selections: 1 Prelude (3:35); 2 Honest Dominique/The Lady And The Pirate (5:00); 3 Barataria (4:30); 4 Mutiny (1:58); 5 Ravens Pursuit And Hanging (2:40); 6 Back To Barataria (2:55); 7 The Knife (1:51); 8 Lovers United (1:33); 9 Treachery At Barataria (4:01); 10 Battle At New Orleans (4:12); 11 Polka (1:32); 12 Valse Tragique (3:41); 13 Out To Sea (3:25).

Review: One of the last great swashbucklers, *The Buccaneer* starred Yul Brynner as buccaneer Jean Lafitte, and Charlton Heston as Andrew Jackson, who wins the 1812 Battle of New Orleans against the British, only after he strikes a deal with Lafitte who provides him with much-needed men and guns. Not always historically accurate, but rife with action scenes, the colorful production, supervised by Cecil B. De Mille and directed by Anthony Quinn, received a brilliant score created by Elmer Bernstein. In a vibrant display of all the tones at his disposal on his musical palette, the composer wrote a series of cues that cover the gamut of emotions in the action, from the derring-do of the high seas adventures to the romantic interludes between Lafitte and his tempestuous mistress (portrayed by Claire Bloom), from the courtly living in the Jackson ranks to the ultimate devastating battle that sealed the fate of the British forces. The 1958 recording, in aggressive stereo, is in need of good mastering.

Bugsy ♪♪♪♪

1991, Epic Soundtrax; from the movie *Bugsy*, Tri-Star Pictures, 1991.

Album Notes: *Music:* Ennio Morricone; *Orchestrations:* Ennio Morricone; *Music Editor:* James Flamberg; Unione musicisti di Roma, conducted by Ennio Morricone; *Featured Musicians:* Francesco Santucci (flugelhorn), Paolo Zampini (flutes), Rosario Giuliani (alto sax); *Album Producer:* Ennio Morricone; *Engineer:* Franco Patrignani.

Selections: 1 Ac-cent-tchu-ate The Positive (J. Mercer/H. Arlen)(2:49) *Johnny Mercer*; 2 For Her, For Him (4:52); 3 Act Of Faith (3:20); 4 The Die Is Cast (3:25); 5 That Night In Last vegas (2:01); 6 Humiliated (1:35); 7 United (3:31); 8 Bugsy's Arrest (3:48); 9 In Cuba (1:44); 10 Why Don't You Do Right? (J. McCoy)(2:26) *Peggy Lee*; 11 Candy (A. Kramer/M. David/J. Whitney)(3:13) *Johnny Mercer, Jo Stafford*; 12 Fly Away (4:26); 13 On Sale (1:38); 14 Act Of Faith (3:15); 15 Desert Mirage (1:30); 16 On A Street At Night (2:08); 17 More Money (1:57); 18 At Great Expense (2:40); 19 Bugsy's Death (4:25); 20 Virginia Waits (2:18); 21 Neurotic Love (2:15); 22 Long Ago And Far Away (J. Kern/I. Gershwin)(2:54) *Jo Stafford*.

Review: A frequently compelling romantic drama about the man who "created" Las Vegas, *Bugsy* found in Ennio Morricone a composer with a special understanding for psychological studies mixed with gangster overtones. Based on the true, grander-than-life story of Bugsy Siegel, a childhood friend of George Raft and Meyer Lansky, the film retraces his arrival in Hollywood, his involvement with a charming but empty-headed would-be actress, his friendship with Lucky Luciano, his high society connections, and his ignominious death by the hands of his former friends and protectors. With typical flair, Morricone details various salient moments in the action, outlining them with themes that are ingeniously sketched and interestingly written. While the overall tone of the cues is in the slow mode characteristic of his writing style for the thriller genre, the score contains some signature effects, like a pesky buzzing over an ominous string line ("Humiliated"), or a lovely theme for oboe against a full orchestral texture ("Act of Faith"). Augmenting the score and providing a different mood, four standards by Johnny Mercer, Peggy Lee and Jo Stafford situate the action and its musical accompaniment squarely into its 1940s time period.

Bull Durham ♫♫♫♪

1988, Capitol Records; from the movie *Bull Durham*, Orion Pictures, 1988.

Album Notes: *Featured Artists*: Joe Cocker, The Fabulous Thunderbirds, Los Lobos, George Thorogood & The Destroyers, The Blasters, House Of Shock, John Fogerty, Pat McLaughlin, Bennie Wallace & Dr. John, Stevie Ray Vaughan, Bonnie Raitt; *Producers*: Charlie Midnight, Denny Bruce, T-Bone Burnett, Steve Berlin, Terry Manning, Richard Gottehrer, John Fogerty, Mitchell Froom, Bennie Wallace; *Album Producers*: Danny Bramson, Tim Devine.

Selections: 1 A Woman Loves A Man (D. Hartman/C. Midnight)(4:09) *Joe Cocker*; 2 Can't Tear It Up Enuff (K. Wilson)(2:45) *The Fabulous Thunderbirds*; 3 I Got Loaded (C.

Bob)(3:23) *Los Lobos*; 4 Born To Be Bad (G. Thorogood)(3:33) *George Thorogood & The Destroyers*; 5 So Long Baby, Goodbye (D. Alvin)(2:23) *The Blasters*; 6 Middle Of Nowhere (G. Schock/V. DeGeneres) (3:36) *House Of Shock*; 7 Centerfield (J.C. Fogerty)(3:53) *John Fogerty*; 8 You Done Me Wrong (P. McLaughlin)(3:31) *Pat McLaughlin*; 9 Try A Little Tenderness (Woods/Campbell/Connelly)(3:15) *Bennie Wallace & Dr. John*; 10 All Night Dance (B. Wallace)(5:47) *Bennie Wallace & Dr. John, Stevie Ray Vaughan*; 11 Love Ain't No Triple Play (B. Wallace/M. Rebennack)(3:27) *Bennie Wallace & Dr. John, Bonnie Raitt*.

Review: A hodgepode, sure enough, but it's a good hodgepodge. A double, if not quite a home run. John Fogerty's "Centerfield" is appropriate. George Thorogood's "Bad to the Bone" seems a bit heavy duty for a film about minor league baseball, but juke joint stuff like the Fabulous Thunderbirds' "Can't Tear It Up Enuff" and Los Lobos' "I Got Loaded" fits the bill perfectly. Dr. John is the real all-star here, though, working out on three songs, including duets with Stevie Ray Vaughan and Bonnie Raitt. A cracker jack collection, fer sure.

Gary Graff

Bulletproof ♫♫♪

1996, Varese-Sarabande; from the movie *Bulletproof*, 1996

Album Notes: *Music*: Elmer Bernstein; *Orchestrations*: Emilie A. Bernstein, Patrick Russ; Orchestra conducted by Elmer Bernstein; *Album Producer*: Emilie A. Bernstein; *Engineer*: Keith Grant.

Selections: 1 Buddies (:59); 2 The Bust (3:17); 3 Shots (1:05); 4 Gurney (:37); 5 Flying (2:56); 6 In The Desert (2:18); 7 Cliff (2:02); 8 Phone (4:25); 9 Darryl's Rescue (3:13); 10 Fighting (1:06); 11 Thugs And Hugs (1:22); 12 Mistakes (3:36).

Review: It seems kind of odd that Elmer Bernstein would come back to a genre he obviously abandoned a decade earlier. There is a lot to be said of the fun in listening to any score reminiscent of his many comedy/adventure scores and, in fact, portions of "Flying" frequently quotes a motif he used in *Ghostbusters*. Overall, though, this score seems to be somewhat nondescript, with no real character. It leaves you feeling as if you walked into the second act of something, perhaps an episode of a 1960s TV cop show. Maybe Adam Sandler's antics just don't motivate Bernstein, or maybe he's truly tired of this genre.

David Hirsch

Buster 🦴🦴🦴🦴

1988, Atlantic Records; from the movie *Buster*, Vestron Pictures, 1988.

Album Notes: *Music:* Anne Dudley; The London Film Orchestra, conducted by Anne Dudley; *Album Producers:* Anne Dudley, Phil Collins, Lamont Dozier.

Selections: 1 Two Hearts (P. Collins/L. Dozier)/Gardening By The Book (3:23) *Phil Collins*; 2 Just One Look (D. Payne/G. Carroll)/...And I Love Her (2:28) *The Hollies*; 3 Big Noise (L. Dozier/P. Collins) (3:54) *Phil Collins*; 4 The Robbery (7:31); 5 I Got You Babe (S. Bono) (3:09) *Sonny & Cher*; 6 Keep On Running (J. Edwards)/Alone In Acapulco(2:44) *Spencer Davis Group*; 7 Loco In Acapulco (P. Collins/L. Dozier) (4:11) *The Four Tops*; 8 How Do You Do It? (M. Murray)/Thoughts Of Home (1:53) *Gerry & The Peacemakers*; 9 I Just Don't Know What To Do With Myself (H. David/B. Bacharach)/The Good Life (3:02) *Dusty Springfield*; 10 Sweets For My Sweet (D. Pomus/M. Shuman) (2:26) *The Searchers*; 11 Will You Still Be Waiting? (1:54); 12 A Groovy Kind Of Love (T. Wine/C. Bayer Bacharach) (3:30) *Phil Collins*.

Review: Phil Collins stars as the title happy-go-lucky small-time thief, who hits the big time when he robs a trainload of used banknotes with the help of a gang led by a friend. On the run from the law, he moves to Mexico, only to find out that once the money is gone life in the sun is not as rosy as he had anticipated. Punctuating this bittersweet comedy are several classic rock tracks by Gerry & The Pacemakers, Dusty Springfield, Sonny and Cher, and The Hollies, among others, as well as a couple of new original songs by Collins. Tying in all these elements together is the incidental music, composed by Anne Dudley, in one of her early efforts, and already demonstrating some of the qualities that have made her a top scorer in more recent years. A bright, breezy album that's quite enjoyable.

Butch Cassidy and the Sundance Kid 🦴🦴🦴🦴

1987, A&M Records; from the movie *Butch Cassidy and the Sundance Kid*, 20th Century-Fox, 1969.

Album Notes: *Music:* Burt Bacharach; *Lyrics:* Hal David; Orchestra conducted by Burt Bacharach.

Selections: 1 The Sundance Kid (2:10); 2 Raindrops Keep Fallin' On My Head (2:57) *B.J. Thomas*; 3 Not Goin' Home Anymore (3:27); 4 South American Getaway (5:14); 5 Raindrops Keep Fallin' On My Head (2:31); 6 On A Bicycle Built For Joy (3:07) *B.J. Thomas*; 7 Come Touch The Sun (2:27); 8 The Old Fun City (N.Y. Sequence) (3:59); 9 Not Goin' Home Anymore (reprise) (1:04).

Review: Burt Bacharach wrote one of his most endearing scores for this amusing western loosely based on the exploits of the so-called Hole-in-the-Wall band of outlaws, led by the quick-witted Butch Cassidy and his quiet cohort, the Sundance Kid (portrayed by Paul Newman and Robert Redford, respectively). While their screen exploits, glossier no doubt than the pair's real-life petty crimes, and the two stars' obvious chemistry helped make the film a tremendous box-office hit, that success was also due in large part to Bacharach's whimsical and jaunty score, in which the song "Raindrops Keep Fallin' on My Head" played an important role. The recording's only drawback is that its playing time is so short (under 28 minutes). When the going is that good and that enjoyable, you wish it would last a bit longer.

Butterfly 🦴🦴🦴

1991, Prometheus Records/Belgium; from the movie *Butterfly*, Par-Par Productions, 1991.

Album Notes: *Music:* Ennio Morricone; Orchestra conducted by Ennio Morricone; *Album Engineer:* Michel Van Achter.

Selections: 1 Main Title (4:17); 2 Hot Tin Tub (2:42); 3 Discipline (1:57); 4 Moke Shot (2:37); 5 Pokin' Moke (1:22); 6 Girl On My Porch (3:06); 7 It's Belle (1:35); 8 I'm Your Daughter (2:55); 9 Silver Mine (1:10); 10 Daddy Agrees (1:41); 11 Here For The Wedding (1:54); 12 She's Not Your Kid (2:23); 13 Chippings (2:04); 14 The Trial (2:13); 15 A Son-In-Law (1:06); 16 Suburst (1:36); 17 Kady (2:49); 18 Main Title (alternate version)(3:52); 19 It's Wrong For Me To Love You (3:51) *Pia Zadora*.

Review: This is a somewhat pedestrian romantic score, and quite an unexpected effort from Ennio Morricone. Perhaps he couldn't keep a straight face while watching this Pia Zadora vanity effort financed by her ex-husband, in which she plays a young waif claiming to be miner Stacy Keach's long-lost daughter, and then seduces him! Morricone plays everything with a very minimalist approach and that does keep with the film's claustrophobic nature, but it doesn't make for a too thoroughly entertaining listen. The CD is twice as long as the original LP release and features eleven tracks (approximately 21 minutes) previously unreleased. Surprisingly, these are some of Morricone's more interesting cues. Zadora performs the song "It's Wrong for Me to Love You," proving she's a far better singer than actress.

David Hirsch

Bye Bye, Love 🦴🦴🦴

1995, Giant Records; from the movie *Bye Bye, Love*, 20th Century-Fox, 1995.

Album Notes: *Music:* J.A.C. Redford; *Orchestrations:* J.A.C. Redford; *Music Editor:* Michael T. Ryan; Orchestra conducted by J.A.C. Redford; *Song Producers*: John Boylan, Frak Filipetti, James Taylor, The Everly Brothers, Pete Wingfield, John Jennings, Mary Chapin Carpenter, Graham Nash, Don Everly, Dave Edmunds, Peter Asher; *Engineer*: Bernie Grundman.

Selections: 1 Let It Be Me (M. Curtis/P. Delanoe/G. Becaud) (3:11) *Jackson Browne, Timothy B. Schmit*; 2 I Will (J. Lennon/ P. McCartney) (3:09) *Ben Taylor*; 3 Don't Worry Baby (B. Wilson/R. Christian)(3:23) *The Everly Brothers, The Beach Boys*; 4 Bye Bye, Love (B. Bryant/ F. Bryant)(2:49) *The Proclaimers*; 5 Stones In The Road (M. Chapin Carpenter)(4:34) *Mary Chapin Carpenter*; 6 Our House (G. Nash)(3:03) *Crosby, Stills, Nash & Young*; 7 So Sad (To Watch Good Love Go Bad)(D. Everly)(2:37) *The Everly Brothers*; 8 This Little Girl Of Mine (R. Charles)(2:23) *Dave Edmunds*; 9 Falling In Love Again (F. Hollander/S. Lerner)(2:40) *Linda Ronstadt*; 10 The Main Thing (Original Score Ballad) (J.A.C. Redford)(2:27).

Review: O.K., let's get this straight. The Everly Brothers *don't* perform their classic rendition of the title track. That one's done by the Proclaimers. But the Everlys turn up twice, singing "So Sad (To Watch Good Love Go Bad)" and joining the Beach Boys on an harmony-drenched version of "Don't Worry Baby." Jackson Browne and Eagles bassist Timothy B. Schmit are also duet partners ("Let It Be Me"), while Ben Taylor — son of James Taylor and Carly Simon — contributes "I Will." But so-so performances and already available songs make this a tepid collection.

Gary Graff

Cahill, United States Marshall

1986, Varese-Sarabande Records; from the movie *Cahill, United States Marshall*, Columbia Pictures, 1973.

See: The Shootist

Cal 🎵🎵🎵🎵♪

1984, Vertigo/PolyGram; from the movie *Cal*, 1984.

Album Notes: *Music*: Mark Knopfler; *Featured Musicians*: Mark Knopfler (guitars), Paul Brady (mandolin, tin whistle), Liam O'Flynn (Uillean pipes), Guy Fletcher (keyboards), John Illsley (bass), Terry Williams (drums); *Album Producer*: Mark Knopfler; *Engineer*: Neil Dorfsman.

Selections: 1 Irish Boy (3:55); 2 The Road (2:08); 3 Waiting For Her (:38); 4 Irish Love (2:24); 5 A Secret Place/Where Will You Go (1:45); 6 Father And Son (7:41); 7 Meeting Under The Trees (:48); 8 Potato Picking (2:06); 9 In A Secret Place (1:08); 10

ENNIO MORRICONE

As one of the most eclectic and prolific composers of the twentieth century, Ennio Morricone has created soundtracks for over 350 films and television productions released in English, Italian, and French. Although he established his "name" by composing scores for Italian westerns (often called "spaghetti westerns"), Morricone has composed mystery thrillers, romantic dramas, comedies, and epics, including *The Untouchables, City of Joy, In the Line of Fire, Wolf,* and *Disclosure*.

Morricone's work with director Sergio Leone on the classic 1960s "man with no name" trilogy vaulted both Morricone and actor Clint Eastwood to instant cult stardom. In scores for *A Fistful of Dollars, For a Few Dollars More,* and *The Good, the Bad, and the Ugly,* Morricone mirrored the violence, irony, and campy humor pervading the classic Eastwood western. Besides his work with Leone, Morricone has worked with major directors such as Franco Zefferelli, Federico Fellini, Roman Polanski, and Roland Joffe.

Born in Rome, Italy, in 1928, Morricone started writing music at the age of six. He holds diplomas in composition, trombone, and orchestra direction from the Santa Cecilia Conservatory in Rome, and he still plays trombone with a local music group called Nuova Consonaza. Along with his classical compositions, he has composed a ballet (Requiem for Destiny) but little other non-film music.

Nominated for five Academy Awards for best score, Morricone is perhaps best known for his work on the 1968 film *Once Upon a Time in the West.*

Fear And Hatred (2:18); 11 Love And Guilt (3:04); 12 The Long Road (7:13).

Review: The nice thing about Mark Knopfler is that when he writes film scores they tend to be gracefully attractive, sometimes sentimental, but usually very expressive. For *Cal*, a romantic drama with political overtones set in Ireland, he fashioned a wonderful score in which the Uillean pipes and tin whistle help create the proper atmosphere, while the guitars, mandolin and keyboards state the various melodies with great restraint and much feeling. Two long cues ("Father and Son" and "The Long Road") are particularly representative of the score itself, with gorgeous melodies that capture the tender moods in the story and bring them forward in a compelling display that transcends the medium for which they were originally designed.

California Suite ♫♫♫

1980, CBS Records; from the movie *California Suite,* Columbia Pictures, 1978.

Album Notes: *Music:* Claude Bolling; *Featured Musicians:* Hubert Laws (flute), Claude Bolling (piano), Chuck Damonico (bass), Shelly Manne (drums), Bud Shank (flute/soprano sax), Tommy Tedesco (guitar), Ralph Grierson (piano); *Album Producer:* Claude Bolling; *Engineer:* Dan Wallin.

Selections: 1 California (5:04); 2 Love Theme from California Suite (7:02); 3 Black Battle (3:38); 4 Hanna's Daughter (1:16); 5 Black Folks (4:19); 6 Hanna's Theme (4:25); 7 Academy Awards (4:03); 8 Beverly Hills (5:10); 9 California (2:28).

Review: This bouncy, easy-going, jazzy soundtrack did much to establish the popularity of Claude Bolling in America, and provided a pleasantly innocuous musical setting to the screen comedy, based on a stage play by Neil Simon. The catchy themes, developed by the composer at the piano with master flutist Hubert Laws, presage Bolling's future pop-classical collaborations with Jean-Pierre Rampal, Yo-Yo Ma, Pinchas Zukerman, and other great soloists.

Cape Fear ♫♫♫

1991, MCA Records; from the movie *Cape Fear,* Universal Pictures, 1991.

Album Notes: *Music:* Bernard Herrmann; *Orchestrations:* Emilie A. Bernstein; *Music Consultant:* Christopher Palmer; Adapter, Arranger and Orchestra conducted by Elmer Bernstein; *Album Producer:* Emilie A. Bernstein; *Engineer:* Shawn Murphy.

Selections: 1 Max (5:39); 2 Sam's Story (1:47); 3 Love? (1:59); 4 Strip Search (3:38); 5 Rape and Hospital (3:56); 6 Frightened Sam (2:14); 7 Cady Meets The Girls (2:07); 8 Sam Hides (2:20); 9 Drive (1:11); 10 Teddy Bear Wired (2:46); 11 Kersek Killed (3:37); 12 Houseboat (1:48); 13 The Fight (1:55); 14 Destruction (2:36); 15 The End (5:36).

Review: The original soundtrack recording from Martin Scorsese's 1991 remake of the 1962 classic, *Cape Fear* is the perfect vehicle for the collaboration of two of the most celebrated modern-day film composers—Bernard Herrmann and Elmer Bernstein. Working from the late Herrmann's original score, Bernstein has deftly adapted and re-orchestrated the original's eerie, chilling theme music, and in doing so, has filled a (hitherto) noticeable void in the Herrmann catalog. Notes director Scorsese, "[Herrmann's] music is noted for its unique instrumentation, and the manner in which it underlines the psychology of the characters, often creating a trance-like state." In this instance, Herrmann's exquisite use of the orchestra (mostly strings, but including other elements as well) imbues just the right essence of terrifying fear and drama—reminiscent of, yet different in texture and orchestral voicing, from his work for the great Hitchcock film thrillers. With this newly revised score, Bernstein has hit the mark dead-on, bringing us a first-rate, high-fidelity documentation of one of Herrmann's most important compositions.

Charles L. Granata

Captain Kronos, Vampire Hunter

1982, Varese-Sarabande; from the movie *Captain Kronos, Vampire Hunter,* 1972.

See: Laurie Johnson in Composers' section

Car Wash/Best of Rose Royce from Car Wash ♫♫♫♪

1996/1988, MCA Records; from the movie *Car Wash,* Universal Pictures, 1976.

Album Notes: *Music:* Norman Whitfield; Orchestra conducted by Paul Riser; *Featured Performers:* Rose Royce, The Pointer Sisters, Richard Pryor; *Album Producer:* Norman Whitfield; *CD Producer:* Andy McKaie; *Engineer:* Paul Elmore

Selections: *CAR WASH:* 1 Car Wash (5:06) *Rose Royce;* 2 6 O'Clock DJ (Let's Rock)(1:09); 3 I Wanna Get Next To You (3:58) *Rose Royce;* 4 Put Your Money Where Your Mouth Is (3:25) *Rose Royce;* 5 Zig Zag (Rose Royce) (2:30); 6 You're On My Mind (L. Jobe/H. Garner, Jr.)(3:27); 7 Mid Day DJ Theme (1:43); 8 Born To Love You (Rose Royce)(3:06) *Rose Royce;* 9 Daddy Rich (3:24) *Rose Royce;* 10 Richard Pryor Dialogue/Rich Reprise (5:05) *Richard Pryor;* 11 You Gotta Believe (2:51) *The Pointer Sisters;* 12 I'm Going Down (3:36) *Rose Royce;* 13 Yo Yo (Rose Royce)(4:17) *Rose Royce;* 14 Sunrise (10:46); 15 Righteous Rhythm (2:30); 16 Water (3:31); 17 Crying (2:57) *Rose Royce;* 18 Doin' What Comes Naturally (3:10) *Rose Royce;* 19 Keep On Keepin' On (6:39) *Rose Royce.*

BEST OF ROSE ROYCE: 1 Car Wash (5:06); 2 I Wanna Get Next To You (4:00); 3 I'm Going Down (3:38); 4 Put Your Money Where Your Mouth Is (3:26); 5 Born To Love You (3:07); 6 Yo Yo (4:17); 7 Daddy Rich (3:16); 8 Keep On Keepin' On (6:39); 9 Doin' What Comes Naturally (3:10); 10 Crying (2:58).

Review: In a rare synergy between pop music and the movies, the songs are an important element to the dramatic/comedic action in *Car Wash*, a film which took place, as its title indicates, in a downtown Los Angeles gas station where a loud speaker continually blares the latest hits. The songs, created by Norman Whitfield and performed for the most part by Rose Royce, are woven into the screen action which involved such colorful characters as Franklyn Ajaye, George Carlin, Irwin Corey, Ivan Dixon, and, as a fancy preacher, Richard Pryor, followed by his retinue of attractive females, The Pointer Sisters. The soundtrack album offers all the original songs heard in the film (there were quite a few others that probably were not licensed to the label), while the "Best of Rose Royce" features only the tracks recorded by that group.

The Cardinal 🎜🎜🎜ᵇ

1987, Preamble Records; from the movie *The Cardinal*, 1963.

Album Notes: *Music:* Jerome Moross; *Music Editor:* Leon Birnbaum; Orchestra conducted by Jerome Moross; *Album Producers:* Jerome Moross, Clyde Allen; *Engineers:* Harold Lewis, Ernie Oelrich; *CD Producer:* John Lasher; *Engineer:* Fred Mitchell.

Selections: 1 Main Title (4:02); 2 Stonebury (1:55); 3 Dixieland/Tango (2:50); 4 The Cardinal's Faith (4:51); 5 They Haven't Got The Girls In The U.S.A. (J. Moross/A. Stillman)(2:50) *Bobby Morse and His Adora-Belles*; 6 The Cardinal In Vienna (6:07); 7 Annemarie (2:55); 8 The Cardinal's Decision (3:35); 9 Way Down South (1:55); 10 The Cardinal Themes (4:59).

Review: Composer Jerome Moross' rich Americana style is unmistakable, whether it's in the service of a western like *The Big Country*, a medieval epic like *The War Lord*, or a soaper like Otto Preminger's *The Cardinal*. In this last effort, Moross' opening theme, set against the bells of a cathedral, is a warm, sentimental brass-and-string anthem alternating against a wavering brass figure that winds majestically heavenward and forms the graceful spine of much of the later material. There's a rather mocking waltz setting for "Vienna" and a dance-like melody that's an ingenious take on the opening phrase of the Shaker melody Aaron Copland adapted for his *Appalachian Spring* ballet. Even in this sometimes glitzy setting Moross' melodic progressions are sublime, and although this score

doesn't match the power of some of his better-known works, it makes a welcome addition to the Moross canon.
Jeff Bond

The Caretakers

1991, Mainstream Records; from the movie *The Caretakers*, United Artists, 1965.

See: Baby The Rain Must Fall

Carlito's Way 🎜🎜ᵇ

1993, Varèse-Sarabande; from the movie *Carlito's Way*, 1993.

Album Notes: *Music:* Patrick Doyle; *Orchestrations:* Lawrence Ashmore; *Music Editor:* Roy Prendergast; Orchestra conducted by William Kraft; *Album Producers:* Patrick Doyle, Maggie Rodford; *Engineers:* John Richards, Carl Glanville.

Selections: CD 1: (score) 1 Carlito's Way (5:17); 2 Carlito And Gail (4:05); 3 The Cafe (1:59); 4 Laline (2:36); 5 You're Over, Man (2:09); 6 Where's My Cheesecake? (2:12); 7 The Buoy (4:04); 8 The Elevator (1:45); 9 There's An Angle Here (2:18); 10 Grand Central (10:08); 11 Remember Me (4:52).

CD 2: (songs) 1 I Love Music (K. Gamble/L. Huff)(4:50) *Rozalla*; 2 Rock The Boat (W. Holmes)(3:06) *The Hues Corporation*; 3 That's The Way I Like It (H. Casey/R. Finch)(3:03) *KC And The Sunshine Band*; 4 Rock Your Baby (H. Casey/ R. Finch)(3:40) *Ed Terry*; 5 Parece Mentira (P. Flores)(5:24) *Marc Anthony*; 6 Backstabbers (L. Huff/G. McFadden/J. Whitehead)(3:07) *The O'Jays*; 7 TSOP — The Sound Of Philadelphia (K. Gamble/L. Huff)(3:35) *MFSB, The Three Degrees*; 8 Get To Be Real (C. Lynn/D. Paich/D. Foster) (5:05) *Cheryl Lynn*; 9 Lady Marmalade (K. Nolan/B. Crewe)(3:55) *LaBelle*; 10 Pillow Talk (S. Robinson/M. Burton)(3:46) *Sinoa*; 11 El Watusi (R. Barretto)(2:38) *Ray Barretto*; 12 Oye como va (T. Puente)(4:14) *Santana*; 13 You Are So Beautiful (B. Preston/B. Fisher)(4:49) *Billy Preston*.

Review: A disco-era gangster film gives us, well, plenty of disco. And once you've had "Saturday Night Fever," everything else seems superfluous. "Carlito's Way" has a few of the genre's greatest hits — K.C. & the Sunshine Band's "That's the Way I Like It," LaBelle's "Lady Marmalade," the Hues Corporation's "Rock the Boat." And Carlos Santana is probably alarmed at how comfortably his "Oye Coma Va" fits into the proceedings. But Billy Preston's "You Are So Beautiful" doesn't hold a candle to Joe Cocker's.
Gary Graff

Carried Away ♫♫♫

1996, Intrada Records; from the movie *Carried Away*, Fine Line Features, 1996.

Album Notes: *Music*: Bruce Broughton; *Orchestrations*: Bruce Broughton; Orchestra conducted by Bruce Broughton; *Album Producer*: Bruce Broughton; *Engineer*: Armin Steiner.

Selections: 1 Main Title (1:33); 2 At School (3:01); 3 Joe Meets Catherine (2:18); 4 Time To Marry Me (1:30); 5 The Coyote (2:17); 6 Momma (3:20); 7 The Funeral (8:01); 8 Joe Waits For The Major (3:23); 9 The Barn Fire (1:49); 10 Joe Returns To Rose (2:00); 11 At The Ocean (2:17); 12 End Credits (3:29).

Review: An acclaimed "small" picture from director Bruno Rubeo, *Carried Away* boasts an intimate score by Bruce Broughton. Performed by a small ensemble orchestra that's ideally suited for this character-driven drama starring Dennis Hopper and the director's wife, Amy Irving, Broughton grounds his score in a theme for solo piano that reflects the inner emotions of the film's characters, with the orchestra used sparingly, thereby reducing overly melodramatic moments. The cumulative effect is that of an extremely subdued but amiable and poignant work nicely illustrating the composer's quieter side, though anyone expecting *Silverado* or even *The Boy Who Could Fly* will most likely be disappointed.

Andy Dursin

Carrington ♫♫♫♫

1995, Argo Records; from the movie *Carrington*, Gramercy Pictures, 1995.

Album Notes: *Music*: Michael Nyman; *Featured Musicians*: The Michael Nyman Band: Michael Nyman (piano), Beverly Davison, Ann Morfee, Claire Thompson, Nicholas Ward, Boguslow Kosteki, Harriet Davies (violin), Catherine Musker, Bruce White, Philip D'Arcy, Jim Sleigh (viola), Anthony Hinnigan, Justin Pearson, Tony Lewis (cello), Martin Elliott (bass guitar), David Roach (soprano/alto sax), Jamie Talbot (alto/tenor sax), Richard Clews (horn); *Album Producer*: Michael Nyman; *Engineer*: Michael J. Dutton.

Selections: 1 Outside Looking In (9:14); 2 Opening Titles (1:21); 3 Fly Drive (1:40); 4 Cliffs Of Fall (2:00); 5 Every Curl Of Your Beard (2:24); 6 Virgin On The Roof (1:40); 7 Gertler (3:15); 8 Leaving Gertler (1:27); 9 Painting The Garden Of Eden (1:59); 10 Partridge (1:54); 11 Floating The Honeymoon (2:45); 12 Brenan (6:53); 13 Beacus (2:58); 14 Leaving Brenan (1:59); 15 Ham Spray House (1:39); 16 The Infinite Complexities Of Christmas (4:18); 17 Something Rather Impulsive (1:48); 18 If This Is Dying (1:46); 19 Adagio from String Quintet in C (F. Schubert)(15:11) *Amadeus Quartet, Robert Cohen*.

Review: Christopher Hampton's biographical drama about the relationship between painter Dora Carrington and writer Lytton Strachey sports a beautiful score by Michael Nyman that blends the sort of formalized chamber orchestra approach you might expect from this sort of period movie with the composer's own minimalist leanings. The repeated phrases, primarily played by strings, manage to evoke all sorts of things: the uncontainable energy of sex, the creative drive as expressed through Carrington's paintings, and especially Carrington's obsessive feelings for Strachey, which eventually lead to her suicide after Strachey's death (a sequence effectively treated with a lengthy and morose Schubert adagio). There's a Coplandesque, syncopated cue for a carriage ride, and Nyman's thematic material for the love relationship between the two artists is gorgeous. On the whole this is one of the composer's most accessible and effective works for film.

Jeff Bond

Casino ♫♫♫♫♪

1995, MCA Records; from the movie *Casino*, Universal Pictures, 1995.

Album Notes: *Album Producer*: Robbie Robertson; *Engineer*: Tom Baker.

Selections: CD 1: 1 Contempt/Theme de Camille (G. Delerue) (2:31) *Georges Delerue*; 2 Angelina/Zooma, Zooma (medley) (A. Roberts/Doris Fisher/ P. Citarella/L. Prima) (4:16) *Louis Prima*; 3 Hoochie Coochie Man (W. Dixon) (2:50) *Muddy Waters*; 4 I'll Take You There (A. Isbell) (4:29) *The Staple Singers*; 5 Nights In White Satin (J. Hayward) (4:27) *The Moody Blues*; 6 How High The Moon (N. Hamilton/M. Lewis) (2:06) *Les Paul, Mary Ford*; 7 Hurt (J. Crane/A. Jacobs) (2:26) *Timi Yuro*; 8 Ain't Got No Home (C. Henry) (2:20) *Clarence ''Frogman'' Henry*; 9 Without You (W. Ham/T. Evans) (3:20) *Nilsson*; 10 Love Is The Drug (B. Ferry/A. MacKay) (4:07) *Roxy Music*; 11 I'm Sorry (R. Self/D. Albritten) (2:36) *Brenda Lee*; 12 Go Your Own Way (L. Buckingham) (3:37) *Fleetwood Mac*; 13 The Thrill Is Gone (R. Hawkins/R. Darnell) (5:26) *B.B. King*; 14 Love Is Strange (S. Robinson/ M. Baker) (2:53) *Mickey and Sylvia*; 15 The "In" Crowd (B. Page) (5:50) *Ramsey Lewis*; 16 Stardust (H. Carmichael/M. Parish) (3:46) *Hoagy Carmichael*.

CD 2: 1 Walk On The Wild Side (E. Bernstein/M. David) (5:53) *Jimmy Smith*; 2 Fa-Fa-Fa-Fa-Fa (Sad Song) (O. Redding/S. Cropper) (2:40) *Otis Redding*; 3 I Ain't Superstitious (W. Dixon) (4:52) *Jeff Beck, Rod Stewart*; 4 The Glory Of Love (B. Hill) (2:51) *The Velvetones*; 5 (I Can't Get No) Satisfaction (M. Jagger/K. Richards) (2:38) *Devo*; 6 What A Difference A Day Makes (S. Adams/M. Grever) (2:28) *Dinah Washington*; 7 Working In A Coalmine

(A. Toussaint) (2:43) *Lee Dorsey*; 8 House Of The Rising Sun (A. Price) (4:38) *Eric Burdon*; 9 Those Were The Days (P. Baker/M. Taylor) (2:53) *Cream*; 10 Who Can I Turn To (When Nobody Needs Me) (L. Bricusse/A. Newley) (2:55) *Tony Bennett*; 11 Slippin' And Slidin' (R. Penniman/A. Collins/J. Smith/E. Bocage) (2:41) *Little Richard*; 12 You're Nobody Till Somebody Loves You (R. Morgan/L. Stock) (2:12) *Dean Martin*; 13 Compared To What (G. McDaniels) (8:34) *Les McCann, Eddie Harris*; 14 Basin Street Blues/When It's Sleepy Time Down South (medley) (C. Music/L. Rene/O. Rene) (4:12) *Louis Prima*; 15 Matthaus Passion (J.S. Bach) (6:26) *The Chicago Symphony Orchestra*.

Review: The Band's Robbie Robertson produced this gem, a collection of bluesy '60s and '70s rock spiced by a few left turns—Dean Martin's "You're Nobody Till Somebody Loves You," for instance, or "Flight of the Bumble Bee." The rest of the set blends Britain (the Rolling Stones, the Moody Blues, Jeff Beck, Eric Burdon), Memphis (B.B. King, the Staple Singers, Otis Redding) and New York (Lou Reed) into a hot stew of consistently good tunes.

Gary Graff

Casino Royale *♫♫♫*

1990, Varese-Sarabande; from the movie *Casino Royale*, Columbia Pictures, 1967.

Album Notes: *Music*: Burt Bacharach; *Lyrics*: Hal David; Orchestra conducted by Burt Bacharach; *Album Producer*: Phil Ramone; *Engineer*: Jack Clegg; *CD Producers*: Tom Null, Robert Townson; *Engineer*: Neil Devine.

Selections: 1 Casino Royale Theme (Main Title)(2:34) *Herb Alpert and The Tijuana Brass*; 2 The Look Of Love (4:00) *Dusty Springfield*; 3 Money Penny Goes For Broke (2:30); 4 Le Chiffre's Torture Of The Mind (2:08); 5 Home James, Don't Spare The Horses (1:28); 6 Sir James' Trip To Find Mata (3:46); 7 The Look Of Love (2:40); 8 Hi There Miss Goodthighs (1:12); 9 Little French Boy (2:22); 10 Flying Saucer—First Stop Berlin (2:52); 11 The Venerable Sir James Bond (2:50); 12 Dream On James, You're Winning (1:15); 13 The Big Cowboys And Indians Fight At Casino Royale/Casino Royale Theme (reprise)(4:50) *Herb Alpert and The Tijuana Brass*.

Review: As soundtracks go, this is really a piece of fluff, but at the time it was created, it beautifully captured the lightweight zany atmosphere of the late 1960s, and of the film itself, an amusing spoof of the James Bond spy thrillers. Some selections ("The Look of Love," and "Casino Royale") have since become hits in their own right, and it is a renewed pleasure to find them again here. The instrumental cues, while not as well-known, pretty much define the best comedic aspects of the film, and make for a very entertaining listening experience.

Casper *♫♫♫▽*

1995, MCA Records; from the movie *Casper*, Universal Pictures, 1995.

Album Notes: *Music*: James Horner; *Orchestrations*: Greig McRitchie, Art Kempel, Dan Davis, James Horner; *Music Editors*: Jim Henrikson, Joe E. Rand; Orchestra conducted by James Horner; *Album Producers*: James Horner, Shawn Murphy; *Engineer*: Shawn Murphy; *Assistant Engineers*: Andy Bass, Dave Marquette, Jay Selvester.

Selections: 1 "No Signs Of Ghosts" (7:31); 2 Carrigan And Dibs (2:40); 3 Strangers In The House (2:36); 4 First Haunting/The Swordfight (5:01); 5 March Of The Exorcists (2:45); 6 The Lighthouse/Casper And Kat (4:57); 7 Casper Makes Breakfast (3:42); 8 Fond Memories (3:39); 9 "Dying" To Be A Ghost (7:02); 10 Casper's Lullaby (5:40); 11 Descent To Lazarus (10:20); 12 One Last Wish (4:19); 13 "Remember Me This Way" (D. Foster/L. Thompson) (4:28) *Jordan Hill*; 14 "Casper The Friendly Ghost" (M. David/J. Livingston)(2:11) *Little Richard*; 15 The Uncles Swing/End Credits (6:21).

Review: Considering this is a film geared toward young children, James Horner had the unenviable task of reminding the audience that Casper is the ghost of a dead child. To be sure, there are funny elements to the story, but the pathos of Casper's unearthly existence is an essential plot point. A gentle lullaby for orchestra and chorus captures the soul of the friendly ghost perfectly, despite the all too obvious comparisons to Danny Elfman's *BeetleJuice* on the comedy bits. That said, this is a marvelously pleasant listen, marred only by Little Richard's screeching rendition of the old cartoon theme, better adapted by Horner for the main title (though it is regrettably absent from the CD).

David Hirsch

The Cassandra Crossing *♫♫♫*

1990, RCA/BMG Ariola (Italy); from the movie *The Cassandra Crossing*, 1977.

Album Notes: *Music*: Jerry Goldsmith; The Symphonic Orchestra Unione musicisti di Roma, conducted by Jerry Goldsmith; *Album Producer*: Jerry Goldsmith; *Engineer*: Federico Savina.

Selections: 1 Main Title (3:21); 2 Break-In (2:20); 3 Safe Living (4:08); 4 I Can't Go (4:35); 5 Helicopter Rescue (3:34); 6 It's All A Game (J. Goldsmith/H. Shaper)(3:00); 7 I'm Still On My Way (D. Jordan)(2:30) *Ann Turkel*; 8 The Climber (2:29); 9 It's God Will (3:03); 10 Kaplan's Death (3:31); 11 End Titles (1:48).

Review: Goldsmith's music to this peculiar disaster/conspiracy thriller is a watershed '70s action score with a distinctly European sound set up in its moody, romantic title theme (later adapted into a song, "It's All a Game"). The agitated string writing of action cues like "Break In" and "I Can't Go" bring to mind Goldsmith's work on *Logan's Run*, but the score's set piece, "Helicopter Rescue" is in a class by itself. It's a spectacular cue built around some wildly unpredictable, jazz-influenced rhythms that you could probably dance to if you were double-jointed. Almost as good is the propulsive "The Climber," with its more literal use of locomotive-like rhythms and sounds from the orchestra. Other cues emphasize harpsichord and bongos, a melancholy woodwind theme and a reverberating metallic sound to underscore scenes of the Cassandra Crossing itself, a gigantic, rickety metal bridge. This Italian release adds another song, "I'm Still on My Way" warbled by actress Ann Turkel, but the star is Goldsmith's score, despite a less-than-stellar orchestral performance.

Jeff Bond

Castle Freak ♪♪�

1995, Intrada Records; from the movie *Castle Freak,* Full Moon Entertainment, 1995.

Album Notes: *Music:* Richard Band; *Orchestrations:* Richard Band; Orchestra conducted by Richard Band; *Album Producer:* Richard Band; *Engineer:* Joe Tarantino.

Selections: 1 Prologue (6:30); 2 The Toy Room (1:28); 3 The Castle (3:19); 4 Giorgio Unleashed (3:08); 5 The Family Tomb (3:02); 6 John's Despair (1:35); 7 Giorgio Snaps (4:32); 8 Il castelli di giove (2:08); 9 Giorgio Abducts Becky (7:50); 10 The Final Battle (8:07).

Review: Richard Band has always managed to squeeze every last dollar out of his meager scoring budgets to yield the maximum effect. By combining his home studio battery of state-of-the-art synthesizers with as many acoustic players as he can afford (in this case a battery of strings for the theme for the title freak), he can avoid many of the shapeless, and mindless, sound clusters that have become standard fare for the horror film genre. Typical of much of Band's other genre work, this score is no less effective.

David Hirsch

Casualties of War ♪♪♪♪▯

1989, Columbia Records; from the movie *Casualties of War*, Columbia Pictures, 1989.

Album Notes: *Music:* Ennio Morricone; *Orchestrations:* Ennio Morricone; Orchestra and Chorus Unione Musicisti di Roma, conducted by Ennio Morricone; *Featured Soloist:* Trencito De Los Andes (Pan flutes); *Album Producer:* Ennio Morricone; *Engineer:* Sergio Marcotulli.

Selections: 1 Casualties Of War (9:25); 2 Trapped In A Tunnel (4:37); 3 No Escape (7:02); 4 The Abduction (4:47); 5 No Hope (2:31); 6 The Rape (4:00); 7 The Death Of Oahn (2:32); 8 The Healing (2:14); 9 The Fragging (1:19); 10 Waste Her (3:40); 11 Elegy For A Dead Cherry (1:16); 12 Elegy For Brown (3:44).

Review: This grim portrayal of war and the terrible toll it takes on soldiers and civilians alike elicited a moving score from Morricone, in which the haunting Pan flute creates a nostalgic aura. Brian de Palma's film, the story of four American GIs who rape and kill a Vietnamese woman, became the basis for a broad indictment of this country's role in Vietnam in the 1960s. It prompted Morricone to write a profoundly reflective score, in which the horrors of war and the sorrow brought by the crime itself are subtly intermingled. The nine minute-plus title track, a dirge-like elegy for chorus and orchestra, punctuated by the Pan flute, sets the tone for the entire album, with its long melodic lines suggestive of an eerie civilized world where such "casualties" can happen. The other selections pretty much follow the thread of the story, from the woman's abduction, her rape, and her death over the objections of one of the men, a "cherry" private played by Michael J. Fox. Recalling in some ways his music for *The Mission* (q.v.), Morricone's score is a powerful statement, all at once disturbing and compellingly attractive.

Cat People ♪♪♪▯

1982, MCA Records; from the movie *Cat People*, RKO-Universal Picture, 1982.

Album Notes: *Music:* Giorgio Moroder; *Orchestrations:* Sylvester Levai; *Music Editor:* Bob Badam; *Album Producer:* Giorgio Moroder; *Engineer:* Carla Ridge.

Selections: 1 Cat People (G. Moroder/D. Bowie)(6:43) *David Bowie*; 2 The Autopsy (1:31); 3 Irena's Theme (4:20); 4 Night Rabbit (1:58); 5 Leopard Tree Dream (4:01); 6 Paul's Theme (Jogging Chase)(3:51); 7 The Myth (5:11); 8 To The Bridge (2:50); 9 Transformation Seduction (2:44); 10 Bring The Prod (1:57).

Review: This stylish remake of the 1942 thriller, which takes as its premise that a race of cat people, resulting from the ancient mating of women with big cats, roams the Earth and, under certain conditions, reverts to the predators' killer instinct before turning human again, may be best remembered today for the fact that Nastassia Kinski, who stars in it, is such a lovely cat woman. Giving the film an extra aura of mystery and fright,

Giorgio Moroder's electronic/instrumental score has its ominous moments, and generally speaking holds its own. At times melodic, but most often exploring sound effects that are more effective on the screen, the album is a mixed bag. David Bowie's hypnotic performance of the main theme, "Putting Out Fire," is a definite plus.

The Cemetery Club 🎵🎵🎵🎵

1993, Varese-Sarabande Records; from the movie *The Cemetery Club*, Touchstone Pictures, 1993.

Album Notes: *Music*: Elmer Bernstein; Orchestra conducted by Elmer Bernstein; *Featured Soloist*: Cynthia Millar (piano); *Album Producer*: Elmer Bernstein; *Engineer*: Brian Masterson.

Selections: 1 Esther, Doris And Lucille (2:32); 2 First Date (1:00); 3 Friends (1:19); 4 Alone (1:59); 5 Cemetery (2:30); 6 Ben (2:11); 7 Walk (2:21); 8 Doris (2:32); 9 Fight (2:38); 10 New Life (1:12); 11 Kiss (1:10); 12 Weekend (:38); 13 Funerals (1:30); 14 Search (1:21); 15 Endings (1:29); 16 The Club (3:06); 17 For Sentimental Reasons (D. Watson/W. Best)(2:50) *Cle Thompson*; 18 There Will Never Be Another You (H. Warren/M. Gordon) (2:13) *Etta Cox*; 19 Kiss Of Fire (L. Allen/R. Hill)(2:47) *Diane Ladd*.

Review: Ignoring the sadder aspects of the story, Elmer Bernstein concentrated on the feel-good side of this sly, bittersweet comedy about three widows, whose bereavement brings them together, and who band to face the outside world with more serenity before launching themselves again on the dating scene. While the score has its moments of melancholy, most of the moods projected in the cues are lovely expressions of romanticism that are quite endearing, when not outright charming, with a recurring motif for "Esther, Doris and Lucille" tying everything together, and reaching a climax in a spirited little waltz ("The Club"). Three pop selections are welcome additions and complement the feelings expressed in the score.

Chain Reaction 🎵🎵🎵

1996, Varese-Sarabande Records; from the movie *Chain Reaction*, 20th Century-Fox Film, 1996.

Album Notes: *Music*: Jerry Goldsmith; *Orchestrations*: Arthur Morton, Alexander Courage; *Music Editor*: Ken Hall; Orchestra conducted by Jerry Goldsmith; *Album Producers*: Jerry Goldsmith, Bruce Botnick; *Engineer*: Bruce Botnick.

Selections: 1 Meet Eddie (4:52); 2 Assassins (5:16); 3 Open Minds (2:46); 4 Ice Chase (5:49); 5 No Solution (2:41); 6 System Down (2:27); 7 Open Door (3:12); 8 Out Of The Hole (3:31).

Review: Regretfully, this is simply an uninspired assemblage of cues from Jerry Goldsmith's score that repeatedly teases you with the prospect that it's going to go somewhere, but never quite manages to make the effort. The same three-note motif (the main theme?) is aimlessly repeated over and over. Hopelessly dull and unentertaining overall, it's only with the final cue, "Out of the Hole" that any true sign of the master is revealed, but by then it's just too late for you to care.

Goldsmith's score for one of the more idiotic action films of the '90s marked a return to the heavy, elaborate orchestral stylings of late '70s/early '80s efforts like *Outland* and *The Swarm* in several large-scale action cues, notably the five minute "Ice Chase" and the percussive "Closed Door". The staccato, heavily rhythmic action material stands rather uncomfortably alongside less textured (and less interesting) quasi-romantic cues like "Open Minds" and "Out of the Hole" that are more in keeping with Goldsmith's current, subdued style, while the chase cues hint at the glories of the past. The score also features a wailing electric guitar as a motif for paunchy hero Keanu Reeves, an effect that rarely achieves organic unison with the modernistic film score sound of the rest of the music.

David Hirsch/Jeff Bond

The Chamber 🎵🎵

1996, Varese-Sarabande; from the movie *The Chamber*, Universal Pictures, 1996.

Album Notes: *Music*: Carter Burwell; *Orchestrations*: Carter Burwell, Sonny Kompanek; *Music Editor*: Adam Smalley; Orchestra conducted by Carter Burwell; *Album Producer*: Carter Burwell; *Engineer*: Michael Farrow.

Selections: 1 We Leapfrog To Our Death (2:08); 2 Two Small Bodies (1:48); 3 Dark Roots Of The Tree (1:42); 4 Parchman Farm, By Car (1:35); 5 Teddy Meeks' Execution (2:45); 6 Hall Of Records (3:23); 7 Cowards (1:36); 8 Tale Of The Laurel Tree (5:43); 9 Mitigating Circumstances (3:10); 10 Klan Teaching (4:02); 11 Ripples (2:36); 12 Lady Justice (4:27); 13 The Goodbye (3:42); 14 The Walk (2:48); 15 The Chamber (1:10); 16 The End (2:33).

Review: This is a fairly straightforward Carter Burwell effort that is well-composed and orchestrated, but just never quite seems to stick in your mind. It is surprisingly unmemorable for such an established composer, probably because Burwell seems to do his best work for the quirky films created by the Coen Brothers, like *Raising Arizona* and *The Hudsucker Proxy*.

David Hirsch

Change of Habit

1995, RCA Records; from the movie *Change of Habit,* Universal Pictures, 1969.

See: Elvis Presley in Compilations

Chaplin ♫♫

1992, Epic Soundtrax; from the movie *Chaplin,* Tri-Star Pictures, 1992.

Album Notes: *Music:* John Barry; The English Chamber Orchestra, conducted by John Barry; *Album Producer:* John Barry; *Engineer:* Shawn Murphy.

Selections: 1 Chaplin: Main Theme (3:06); 2 Early Days In London (4:17); 3 Charlie Proposes (3:01); 4 To California/The Cutting Room (3:45); 5 Discovering The Tramp/The Wedding Chase (4:01); 6 Chaplin's Studio Opening (1:58); 7 Salt Lake City Episode (2:11); 8 The Roll Dance (2:34); 9 News Of Hetty's Death/Smile (3:42); 10 From London To L.A. (3:20); 11 Joan Barry Trouble/Oona Arrives (2:15); 12 Remembering Hetty (2:57); 13 Smile (2:05); 14 The Roll Dance (1:47); 15 Chaplin: Main Theme/Smile (3:38); 16 Smile (3:38) *Robert Downey, Jr.*

Review: While the music from *Chaplin* is fine accompaniment to the film, it doesn't stand quite as well on its own as a general "listening" CD. Composer John Barry has created a quietly beautiful score, but without the visuals, it often sounds heavy and plodding—perhaps because it lacks any real, melodic "theme." While it has a number of interesting moments ("Salt Lake City Episode" and "The Roll Dance" among them), fans of the film will probably enjoy it more than casual listeners. A vocal version of Chaplin's own composition, "Smile," performed by Robert Downey Jr., is included. The sonics are, as expected, excellent.

Charles L. Granata

Charade ♫♫♫♫

1988, RCA Records; from the movie *Charade,* Universal Pictures, 1963.

Album Notes: *Music:* Henry Mancini; Orchestra conducted by Henry Mancini; *CD Producer:* Chick Crumpacker; *Engineer:* Dick Baxter.

Selections: 1 Charade (Main Title)(2:07); 2 Bistro (1:48); 3 Bateau Mouche (2:52); 4 Megeve (2:58); 5 Bye Bye Charlie (3:05); 6 The Happy Carousel (1:28); 7 Charade (H. Mancini/J. Mercer)(2:34) Chorus; 8 Orange Tamoure (1:52); 9 Latin Snowfall (2:31); 10 The Drip-Dry Waltz (1:49); 11 Mambo Parisienne (2:30); 12 Punch And Judy (1:49); 13 Charade (Carousel) (1:37).

Review: A romantic comedy thriller set in France, *Charade* received the right musical touch from maestro Mancini, whose amiable and diverting score seems a perfect companion to the screen action. The story involves Audrey Hepburn, a widow in distress pursued by a trio of thugs trying to recover the money her late husband may have swindled from them, and Cary Grant, as the dashing knight in suit and tie who comes to her rescue. Like many Mancini scores, the tone in the cues is lightweight and attractive, with the pleasantly catchy title tune, with lyrics by Johnny Mercer, adding a melodically memorable element to the proceedings. One drawback, however, characteristic of RCA at that time, is that the recording is aggressively close-miked and dry, resulting in a brittle, unflattering sound, with a significant amount of hiss at the top.

Chariots of Fire ♫♫♫♫♫

1981, Polydor Records; from the movie *Chariots of Fire,* 20th Century-Fox, 1981.

Album Notes: *Music:* Vangelis; *Album Producer:* Vangelis; *Engineers:* Raphael Preston, John Walker, Raine Shine.

Selections: 1 Titles (3:33); 2 Five Circles (5:20); 3 Abraham's Theme (3:20); 4 Eric's Theme (4:18); 5 100 Meters (2:04); 6 Jerusalem (H. Parker) (2:47) *The Ambrosian Singers;* 7 Chariots Of Fire (20:41).

Review: A daring effort by director Hugh Hudson that could have backfired as brilliantly as it paid off. Imagine the idea of completely scoring a film about two runners at the 1924 Olympics with electronics, composed by a musician known for making the music up as he watches the film instead of writing it in advance. The concept seems like something destined for failure, but under the brilliant instincts of Vangelis, the music created garnered both a best-selling soundtrack album and a 1981 Academy Award for Best Original Score. An early music video, showing slow-motion runners moving in time to the theme, made the music synonymous with the sport in the public's mind. The 21-minute "Chariots of Fire" track is most likely a suite of the original underscore cues, while the five initial tracks appear to be fleshed out cover versions of the primary themes.

David Hirsch

Charro!

1995, RCA Records; from the movie *Charro!,* National General Pictures, 1969.

See: Elvis Presley in Compilations

The Chase ♪♪♪♪▷

1989, Varese-Sarabande Records; from the movie *The Chase,* Columbia Pictures, 1966.

Album Notes: *Music*: John Barry; Orchestra conducted by John Barry; *Album Producer*: John Barry; *CD Producers*: Tom Null, Richard Kraft.

Selections: 1 Main Title: The Chase (2:44); 2 The Chase Is On (4:41); 3 Saturday Night Philosopher (4:44); 4 What Did I Do Wrong? (2:38); 5 Call That Dancin'? (3:37); 6 Stop Talking Foolish, Stop Talking Anything (3:34); 7 Look Around (2:00); 8 The Beating (3:23); 9 And You've Got One! (2:41); 10 I Came To The End Of Me! (2:51); 11 Blues For Bubber (4:05); 12 The Junkyard (5:27); 13 I'll Drink To That (2:45); 14 The Killing/Next Morning (5:19).

Review: John Barry wrote a taut score for this pulse-pounding story of an escaped convict (Robert Redford) who returns to his hometown, a small Texas community, to try and clear himself from what might have been a false charge, only to be hunted down by the town's high-minded citizens. The film, a study of a close-knit society where alcoholism, adultery and fanatical evangelism are the prevailing ills, prompted Barry to write a score in which the dominant note is a pervading sense of drama about to erupt at any moment. The ominous tone in most of the tracks is temporarily relieved by an occasional blues number, in what is essentially a richly expressive and rewarding score.

Cheyenne Autumn ♪♪♪♪▷

1987, Label X; from the movie *Cheyenne Autumn,* Warner Bros. Pictures, 1964.

Album Notes: *Music*: Alex North; *Orchestrations*: Gil Grau, Henry Brandt; Orchestra conducted by Alex North; *Engineer*: Federico Savino; *CD Producer*: John Lasher.

Selections: 1 Overture (3:10); 2 Main Title (2:17); 3 Indians Arrive (1:27); 4 Friend Deborah/Waiting For Supplies (2:25); 5 The School House (1:16); 6 Archer (1:51); 7 Rejection (4:15); 8 Truth (:52); 9 Entr'acte (1:17); 10 River Crossing (2:24); 11 Sick Girl (3:26); 12 The Battle (3:40); 13 Dodge City (2:14); 14 Cattle Drive (1:46); 15 Old Chief (1:37); 16 Lead Our People Home (3:09); 17 Death (2:35); 18 The People (1:10); 19 Spring/Soldiers/ Alarm (3:18); 20 Hope (1:10); 21 End Title and End Cast (:52).

Review: Alex North produced this rich, thoughtful western score at the tail end of his epic period (shortly after composing *Spartacus* and *Cleopatra*), and *Cheyenne Autumn* works as a kind of warmer response to those occasionally brutal works, shot through with Americana and the ceremonial dignity of the Native American people John Ford's film concerned itself with. The score mixes sharp-edged martial fanfares with somber, reflective passages marking the hardship of the Cheyenne tribe struggling to maintain their identity as they're relegated to reservation life in the late 1800s. There are deeply percussive battle cues, a melancholy Americana love theme, even a Samuel Barber-like satirical use of the "Camptown Races" melody for a revisionist sequence involving Wyatt Earp (Jimmy Stewart). Ford evidently hated this score, but it's by far the best music ever associated with one of his features, and no film composer ever captured the emotion of anguish better than North.

Jeff Bond

Children of a Lesser God ♪♪♪

1986, GNP Crescendo; from the movie *Children of a Lesser God,* Paramount Pictures, 1986.

Album Notes: *Music*: Michael Convertino; *Orchestrations*: Michael Convertino, Shirley Walker, Chris Boardman; Orchestra conducted by Shirley Walker; *Album Producer*: Michael Convertino; *Engineers*: Dan Wallin, Bruce Botnick.

Selections: 1 Main Title (3:03); 2 Silence And Sound (3:26); 3 Sarah Sleeping (1:42); 4 Rain-Pool (1:09); 5 Underwater Love (1:23); 6 On The Ferry (1:45); 7 James And Sarah (1:08); 8 Goodnight (1:21); 9 Boomerang (3:26); 10 Forgiveness/Winter Into Spring (4:05); 11 Double Concerto in D Minor for Violins, 2nd Movement (J.S. Bach)(2:27); 12 Searching For Sarah (1:14); 13 Love On The Couch (1:25); 14 James Alone On The Pier (:53); 15 Joined (2:11); 16 End Title (3:02).

Review: This early new age style score by Michael Convertino is hauntingly romantic and, with its simple, catchy main theme, is one of the key reasons for the film's success. Played primarily by string instruments and a synclavier, the score captures the unblemished innocence of a young, introverted deaf woman (Marlee Matlin in her Academy Award-winning performance) brought out of self-imposed isolation by teacher William Hurt. Originally released as an LP, the inclusion of the song "Boomerang" on track nine devastates the score's dreamy pacing. Packaging, a holdover from the LP version as well, fails to list any track numbers (but does have the bizarre legends "Side One" and "Side Two").

David Hirsch

Children of the Corn II ♪♪▷

1992, Bay Cities Records; from the movie *Children of the Corn II,* Fifth Avenue Entertainment, 1992.

Album Notes: *Music*: Daniel Licht; *Orchestrations*: Pete Anthony, Daniel Licht; Orchestra conducted by Tim Simonec; *Al-*

> "There's a total sense of popcorn fun. It's a fountainhead score—the beginning of something new."
>
> **Thomas Newman**
> on Max Steiner's King Kong
> (Entertainment Weekly Online, 2-3-95)

bum Producer: Daniel Licht; *Engineers*: Rick Winquest, Daniel Hersch.

Selections: 1 Main Title (Red Bear's Theme)(2:28); 2 The Waterfall/Micah's Transformation (3:22); 3 Love In The Corn (2:08); 4 Nosebleed (2:23); 5 On The Porch, At The Table, In The Circle (3:50); 6 Doc Appleby (3:24); 7 A Combine And A House (6:12); 8 Stalking The Newsvan (3:05); 9 Danny And Lacy Kiss (2:33); 10 Hallfire Suite (6:18); 11 Ring Sacrifice/ Finale (4:29); 12 Children Of The Children (End Credits)(2:55).

Review: This early effort by Daniel Licht (*Bad Moon*) shows he was always able to rise above this type of trash. Licht does manage to squeeze quite a lot energy out of his meager budget, even finding a way to combine a modest sized choir with his orchestra. The voices chant out pseudo-American Indian verses to represent "He Who Walks Between the Rows," the evil spirit that has possessed the young. "Nose-bleed" is the cue that perhaps best represents the composer's intent for the dark nature of the children. He also manages to inject some pleasant alternative direction with the romantic start to "A Combine and a House," while imbuing some genuine oddness with the use of some Far Eastern motifs. Licht endows this film, the second chapter in a laughingly bad trilogy adapted from a single Stephen King short story, with some credence of seriousness. He deserves better opportunities than these.

David Hirsch

Children of the Night 🦴🦴🦴🦴

1990, Bay Cities Records; from the movie *Children of the Night*, Fangoria Films, 1990.

Album Notes: *Music*: Daniel Licht; *Music Editor*: John LaSalandra; Orchestra conducted by Tim Simonec; *Album Producer*: Daniel Licht; *Engineer*: Jeff Vaughn.

Selections: 1 Main Titles (1:40); 2 The Girl's Theme (1:13); 3 The Girls Go To Chuch (2:43); 4 Mark Meets Karen (3:00); 5 Matty's Story (1:46); 6 Bloodsucker's Ball (3:37); 7 Billy's Theme/Karen Loves Frank (2:11); 8 Grandma Attack/Cocoon Love (3:34); 9 Dance Of Karen's Lights (1:43); 10 Cindy Dies (2:10); 11 Old Friends' Reunion (2:20); 12 Young Blood/Meet Zakir (1:44); 13 Morning Music (1:15); 14 Drive Montage (1:24); 15 Zakir Goes To Church (2:19); 16 Ride To Old Mill/A Milkman's Revenge (2:14); 17 Endgame (3:21); 18 End Credits (2:08).

Review: Though written for a horror film, this melodic score shows Daniel Licht in a very positive light, with themes that are for the most part attractive and catchy, and seem to belie the darker aspects of the story itself. The score opens on a series of cues that presage the arrival of a vampire in the small middle-American town where the action takes place, and where various light incidents are the occasion for spirited musical moments that are quite engaging. But as the action progresses, the moods evolve into a darker, more percussive mode, though without losing their melodic content, and become increasingly more ominous and darker. Using the full forces of the orchestra, Licht then unleashes the final strokes with themes that signal the end of the nightmare. It's all very effective, and enjoyably easy on the ear.

Chinatown 🦴🦴🦴🦴

1995, Varese-Sarabande; from the movie *Chinatown*, Paramount Pictures, 1974.

Album Notes: *Music*: Jerry Goldsmith; *Orchestrations*: Arthur Morton; *Featured Artist*: Uan Rasey (trumpet); Orchestra conducted by Jerry Goldsmith; *Album Producer*: Tom Mack; *Engineers*: John Norman, Thorne Nogar.

Selections: 1 Love Theme From Chinatown (Main Title)(1:59); 2 Noah Cross (2:27); 3 Easy Living (L. Robin/R. Rainger)(1:49); 4 Jake And Evelyn (2:41); 5 I Can't Get Started (I. Gershwin/V. Duke)(3:35) *Bunny Berigan and His Orchestra*; 6 The Last Of Ida (2:59); 7 The Captive (3:05); 8 The Boy On A Horse (2:05); 9 The Way You Look Tonight (J. Kern/D. Fields)(2:16); 10 The Wrong Clue (2:32); 11 J.J. Gittis (3:05); 12 Love Theme From Chinatown (End Title)(2:03).

Review: This moody and incredibly atmospheric work was a replacement score written and recorded by Goldsmith in an astonishing 11 days. The richly nostalgic solo trumpet theme is justly famous and lends tremendous emotional weight to cues like "Jake and Evelyn" and "The Wrong Clue," while the rest of the score creates a memorably dark feeling almost entirely with piano, from hand-stopped low end notes to an almost tide-like effect created by brushing the piano strings themselves. There's also a brutally violent staccato piano solo and some disturbing, atonal avant garde string effects that stretch the tension and masterfully hint at the terrible psychological wounds hidden within the characters of Roman Polanski's brilliant gumshoe film. This long-overdue release from Varese boasts superb sound that immerses the listener in the score's percussive sonic world, and its few pieces of period source music blend seamlessly with Goldsmith's music. A must-have.

Jeff Bond

Christopher Columbus: The Discovery 🎵🎵🎵🎵

1992, Varese-Sarabande Records; from the movie *Christopher Columbus: The Discovery*, Warner Bros. Pictures, 1992.

Album Notes: *Music*: Cliff Eidelman; *Orchestrations*: Mark McKenzie, William Kidd; *Music Editor*: Robin Eidelman; The Seattle Symphony Orchestra, conducted by Cliff Eidelman; *Album Producer*: Cliff Eidelman; *Engineer*: Joe Gastwirt.

Selections: Act 1: Spain: 1 The Great Sea (1:35); 2 Come O Come Emanuel (2:23); 3 The Broken Cloud (3:39); 4 Never Forget (2:00); 5 Spain Defeats The Moors (3:09); 6 Houses Of Gold (1:07); Act 2: The Sea: 7 The Voyage (1:29); 8 Mutiny On The Bounty (3:17); 9 Remembering Home (1:31); 10 Saint Elmo's Fire (4:07); 11 The Discovery (Gloria)(3:03); Act 3: The West Indies: 12 The New World (3:22); 13 Alvarao's Fatal Act (2:17); Act 4: The Sea: 14 Storm (1:02); Act 4 Part II: Spain: 15 The Return (:41); 16 A Hero's Welcome (dialogue) (7:27).

Review: Once in a while you come across music written for a bad movie that is far better than it has any right to be, and even surpasses the picture itself in terms of its popularity. That's certainly the case with *Christopher Columbus: The Discovery*, the first of two big-budget 1992 flops depicting the discovery of the New World. This film, produced by Alexander Salkind, features a grand, old-fashioned orchestral score by Cliff Eidelman, who seized the opportunity to write music in the great swashbuckling tradition of Korngold and latter-day composers like John Williams. It's stirring, robust and downright glorious in its best portions, illustrating young Eidelman's adept handling of both chorus and orchestra, and resulting in what is really a sensational album. The movie might be a dud, but just as Vangelis wrote a great score for the equally disastrous Ridley Scott bomb *1492*, Eidelman has come up with a terrific stand-alone work that has already outlasted the unintentionally funny inadequacies of its source.

Andy Dursin

See also: 1492: Conquest of Paradise

Cinema Paradiso 🎵🎵🎵🎵

1990, DRG Records; from the movie *Cinema Paradiso*, 1989.

Album Notes: *Music*: Ennio Morricone; *Orchestrations*: Ennio Morricone; Orchestra Unione Musicisti di Roma, conducted by Ennio Morricone; *Featured Soloists*: Franco Tamponi (violin), Baldo Maestri (saxophone, clarinet), Marianne Eckstein (flute), Enrico Pierannunzi, Alberto Pomeranz (piano), Francesco Romano (guitar); *Album Producer*: Ennio Morricone; *Engineer*: Franco Finetti, Sergio Marcotulli.

Selections: 1 Cinema Paradiso (2:57); 2 Maturity (2:18); 3 Thinking Of Her (1:15); 4 Childhood And Maturity (2:13); 5 Movie Theatre Ablaze (2:45); 6 Love Theme (2:45); 7 After The Destruction (2:00); 8 First Youth (2:15); 9 Love Theme For Nata (4:07); 10 Visit To The Movie Theatre (2:20); 11 Four Interludes (1:55); 12 Fugue, Search And Return (2:05); 13 Projection For Two (2:05); 14 From American Sex-Appeal To The First Fellini (3:25); 15 Toto And Alfredo (1:16); 16 For Elena (1:48).

Review: Ennio Morricone struck a particularly emotional chord in this Academy Award-winning score for the film of Giuseppe Tornatore, permeated with a deep sense of melancholy and nostalgia. Heard behind the screen action, the score subtly underlines the feelings of a successful filmmaker who goes back to his little hometown only to be confronted by the ghosts of his past, and particularly the memory of an old projectionist who became his first mentor and sparked his interest in the movies. But beyond being a mere recollection of a youngster slowly coming of age, the film is a paean to a time when the cinema was something special and unique in the lives of everyone, and when going to the movies meant an unforgettable magic adventure in a land that only existed on celluloid. In his score, Morricone was able to capture the deep emotional moods evoked by the film, and turned in one of the most eloquent soundtracks of his long and distinguished career.

Circle of Friends 🎵🎵◗

1995, Warner Bros. Records; from the movie *Circle of Friends*, Savoy Pictures, 1995.

Album Notes: *Music*: Michael Kamen; *Orchestrations*: Michael Kamen; *Music Editor*: Chris Brooks; The London Metropolitan Orchestra, conducted by Michael Kamen; *Album Producer*: Michael Kamen; *Engineer*: Stephen P. McLaughlin.

Selections: 1 You're The One (M. Kamen/S. MacGowan)(4:00) *Shane MacGowan, Maire Brennan*; 2 Ireland 1949 (2:29); 3 The Cottage (3:02); 4 Dublin (2:53) *The Chieftains*; 5 Knock Glen (1:06); 6 Air—You're The One (3:57) *The Chieftains*; 7 Bo Weevil (A. Domino/D. Bartholomew)(1:53) *Fats Domino*; 8

Sean (2:20); 9 Benny And Jack (2:00); 10 Father's Death (3:54); 11 Love Is A Many Splendored Thing (S. Fain/P.F. Webster)(4:04) *The Long John Jump Band.*

Review: Soundtrack listeners tend to dislike dialogue mixed in with their music, and with *Circle of Friends*, you can see why — the dialogue disrupts any momentum that Michael Kamen's score attempts to build up during the course of its abbreviated running time. What you end up with, then, are very brief, mostly unexceptional snippets of music interspersed with dialogue that will only appeal to die-hard fans of the movie. This comes in spite of the fact that Kamen's music is pleasant enough (with the Chieftains onboard, it comes off as an agreeable distant cousin to *Far and Away*), and the Shane McGowan-Maire Brennan duet, "You're the One," written by Kamen and McGowan, is actually quite good, even with a pair of vocalists whose styles are seemingly at odds with each other. But what more can you say about an under-30 minute album where dialogue is seemingly used to pad the running time?

Andy Dursin

Citizen Kane 🐾🐾🐾🐾

1991, Preamble Records; from the movie *Citizen Kane*, RKO Radio Pictures, 1941.

Album Notes: *Music*: Bernard Herrmann; The Australian Philharmonic Orchestra, conducted by Tony Bremner; *Album Producers*: Riccardo Formosa, John Lasher; *Engineer*: Robin Gray.

Selections: 1 Prelude (2:19); 2 Susan In Night Club (Rain Sequence) (:52); 3 Thatcher Library (Litany): Ms. Reading & Snow Picture/Mother's Sacrifice/ Charlie Meets Thatcher (3:23); 4 Galop (:57); 5 Dissolve To Thatcher/Second Ms./ Bernstein's Narration (1:40); 6 Kane's New Office/Carter's Exit/ Chronicle Scherzo (2:57); 7 Bernstein's Presto (:39); 8 Kane's Return/Valse Presentation (1:39); 9 Sunset Narrative (2:17); 10 Theme and Variations (Breakfast Montage) (3:18); 11 Kane Meets Susan/Susan's Room/Mother Memory (3:07); 12 The Trip To Susan's/Getty's Departure/Kane Marries (2:08); 13 Salaambo's Aria (4:21) *Rosamund Illing*; 14 Leland's Dismissal (:57); 15 Susan In Night Club (New Dawn Sequence) (:52); 16 Opera Montage (:46) *Rosamund Illing*; 17 Xanadu/Jigsaw Puzzle (Perpetual Motion)/Second Xanadu (3:49); 18 Kane's Picnic/Susan Leaves (:38); 19 El Rancho (Second Dawn Sequence) (:38); 20 The Glass Ball (1:21); 21 Finale (2:21).

Review: This sensational recreation of Bernard Herrmann's music for Orson Welles' *Citizen Kane* must rank among the most successful attempts at bringing into the digital era a score from the early days of Hollywood. Herrmann himself recorded at vari-

ous times some cues from his score, and others, notably Charles Gerhardt in his *Classic Film Scores* series, have made sure to include excerpts from the momentous score, but this recording is its only complete representation, with Tony Bremner conducting the Australian Philharmonic Orchestra in a flawless performance. A trend-setter in every way *Citizen Kane* is probably the most famous film ever made in Hollywood, an icon of moviemaking which launched the screen careers of many of its creators, including writer/director Welles, and co-star Joseph Cotten.

For Herrmann, by his own admission, it was a dream come true. Unlike the prevailing practice that gives a composer two to three weeks to write his music once the film is shot, he began scoring it almost from the first day of shooting, with his cues not only reflecting the unfolding screen action, but becoming part of it when Welles decided to match some scenes to the music Herrmann had written. The cues presented here follow the drama about press tycoon Charles Kane, from his youth to his two marriages and the last word ("Rosebud") he whispers on his deathbed. At times deeply introspective, at times vibrant and descriptive, the score immediately established Herrmann as a vigorous, somewhat iconoclastic composer who worked by his own rules, a reputation he nurtured throughout the rest of his career. Like some books in a personal library, some recordings are essential in any basic collection. *Citizen Kane* is one of them!

City Hall 🐾🐾🐾

1996, Varese-Sarabande; from the movie *City Hall*, Castle Rock Films, 1996.

Album Notes: *Music*: Jerry Goldsmith; *Orchestrations*: Arthur Morton; Orchestra conducted by Jerry Goldsmith; *Album Producer*: Jerry Goldsmith; *Engineer*: Bruce Botnick.

Selections: 1 The Bridge (2:05); 2 The Meet (2:57); 3 The Hospital (2:17); 4 When I Was A Kid (2:21); 5 The Cabin (1:06); 6 The King Maker (2:22); 7 Old Friends (2:49); 8 Swartz Is Dead (2:45); 9 Think About It (1:22); 10 The Report (1:37); 11 Take A Vacation (3:31); 12 Count On It (4:50).

Review: Jerry Goldsmith brought some echoes of *On the Waterfront* to this story of New York political intrigue, one of the few intelligent dramas scored by the composer in the '90s. There's a relentless pulse of timpani moving through virtually every cue of this score that functions as a kind of heartbeat for the Big Apple, moving from the gritty romanticism of the opening blues theme through hammering, violent street crime encounters, and finally surging under the film's subtle dramatic underscoring, which ranges from a swaggering blues theme for a political "kingpin" to more lyrical, introspective moments filling out the back end of the album. There's a real regression from the percusive, agitated first half of the CD to the more measured tones on which it ends, but the rumble of low percussion makes for an unusually cohesive listening experience.

Jeff Bond

City of Joy ✍✍✍✍ʼ

1992, Epic Soundtrax; from the movie *City of Joy*, TriStar Pictures, 1992.

Album Notes: *Music*: Ennio Morricone; *Orchestrations*: Ennio Morricone; *Music Editor*: Richard Blackford; The Unione musicisti di Roma, conducted by Ennio Morricone; *Featured Musicians*: Laura Pontecorvo (recorder), Paolo Zampini (flutes), Stefano Novelli (piccolo clarinet), Felice and Raffaele Clemente (Pan pipes), Amedeo Tommasi, Gianluca Podio (synthesizers), The London Studio Orchestra and The Stephen Hills Singers, conducted by Ennio Morricone; *Featured Musicians*: Mike Taylor (Indian flute), Levine Andrade (viola), Sirish Manji (tabla), Manti Aswin (tampura), Chandra Ramesh (sitar), Erwin Keiles (scinai) Glen Keiles, Richard Blackford (synthesizers); *Album Producer*: Ennio Morricone; *Engineers*: Franco Patrignani, Dick Lewzey.

Selections: 1 City Of Joy (2:12); 2 The Family Of The Poor (2:41); 3 One Night By Chance (3:33); 4 Crack Down (3:21); 5 Hope (2:19); 6 In The Labyrinth (1:43); 7 The Family Of The Poor (2:09); 8 A Surgeon In Despair (2:23); 9 One Night, By Chance (1:47); 10 For A Daughter's Dowry (3:59); 11 Godfather Of The Bustee (2:27); 12 Monsoon (2:10); 13 Calcutta (4:19); 14 Bustee Day (1:39); 15 The Birth (2:16); 16 The Worm Turns (3:51); 17 The Labyrinth (5:39); 18 To Calcutta (6:50); 19 The Family Of The Poor (1:37); 20 To Roland (1:52).

Review: In a style not unlike the one that served him so well for *The Mission*, Ennio Morricone conceived for *City of Joy* a score that exudes vibrancy and excitement, with an impressive array of musicians and vocalists lending their help. The film, about an American doctor in Calcutta and the struggle he wages against local thugs trying to control the slums, motivated Morricone to write a deeply emotive and lyrical score, in which the Indian instruments often play a dominant role. It is a very stylized, attractive effort with many qualitative themes that paint vivid, colorful pictures.

City Slickers

City Slickers ✍✍✍✍

1991, Varese-Sarabande; from the movie *City Slickers*, Castle Rock Entertainment, 1991.

Album Notes: *Music*: Marc Shaiman; *Orchestrations*: Mark McKenzie, Hummie Mann; *Music Editor*: Scott Stambler; Or-

chestra conducted by Hummie Mann, Mark McKenzie; *Album Producer*: Marc Shaiman; *Engineer*: Joel Moss.

Selections: 1 Main Title (2:42); 2 Career End (2:11); 3 Find Your Smile (6:07); 4 Walking Funny (1:25); 5 Cowabunga (2:29); 6 Young At Heart (J. Richards/C. Leigh)(2:48) *Jimmy Durante*; 7 Birth Of A Norman (5:23); 8 The River (5:48); 9 Mitchy The Kid (4:19); 10 Where Did My Heart Go? (3:52) *James Ingram*.

Review: See entry below.

City Slickers II: The Legend of Curly's Gold ✍✍✍✍

1994, Chaos Records; from the movie *City Slickers II: The Legend of Curly's Gold*, 1994.

Album Notes: *Music*: Marc Shaiman; *Orchestrations*: Jeff Atmajian, Frank Bennett, Larry Blank, Brad Dechter, Jerry Hey; *Music Editor*: Michael Linn; Orchestra conducted by Artie Kane; *Album Producer*: Marc Shaiman; *Engineer*: Shawn Murphy; *Assistant Engineers*: Andy Bass, Jay Selvester, David Marquette, Fred Vogler, Leslie Ann Jones, Sue McLean, Greg Dennen, Mark Eshelman, Bill Talbott, Tom Hardisty.

Selections: 1 Mitch's Dream (2:35); 2 Main Title (2:50); 3 Found: One Smile (1:14); 4 Discovering The Map (1:53); 5 Oh! Brother (1:26); 6 Gold Diggers Of 1994 (:46); 7 The Map Is Real... And On Fire (1:31); 8 On The Trail (:48); 9 Real Men (:48); 10 Let's Get That Gold! (1:51); 11 Duke Saves The Day (2:46); 12 Come And Get Me! (2:21); 13 The Stampede (7:23); 14 Look Who's Bonding Too (1:57); 15 Over The Buffalo's Back, Under The Frozen People (2:28); 16 To The Bat Cave! (2:48); 17 There's Gold In Them Thar Hills (4:58); 18 A Box Full Of Lead (5:38); 19 Jackpot! (3:39).

Review: With *City Slickers*, and its sequel *The Legend of Curly's Gold*, Marc Shaiman wrote a music that takes its inspiration in the western genre, while gently poking fun at it, in much the same way Elmer Bernstein devised his score for *The Hallelujah Trail*, which *City Slickers* sometimes evokes.

The rambunctious, rollicking adventures of three urban cowboy wannabes on a two-week vacation at a dude ranch, driving cattle across the west under the guidance of a surly cowboy named Curly (Jack Palance), the first film became a festive occasion to oppose two totally different lifestyles, with many humorous situations evolving from the confrontation. Shaiman's score, taking a cue from the script, keeps its musical tongue firmly in cheek and makes several amusing turns that will delight fans of film music as well as first listeners. A performance of the classic song "Young At Heart," by Jimmy Durante, seems oddly out of place in the context.

The Legend of Curly's Gold finds the three city slickers (Billy Crystal, Daniel Stern and Bruno Kirby) back in the west, looking for a treasure their late trail boss might have hidden somewhere. Helping along in the search is Curly's brother (also played by Palance). The film may tread over familiar grounds, but once again the moods are kept lightweight and entertaining, with Shaiman's score, much more expansive in this longer-playing recording, revisiting his previous effort and adding several new themes for another enjoyable musical romp.

The Clan of the Cave Bear
♫♫♫

1986, Varese-Sarabande Records; from the movie *The Clan of the Cave Bear*, Warner Bros., 1986.

Album Notes: *Music*: Alan Silvestri; *Performed by*: Alan Silvestri; *Album Producer*: Alan Silvestri; *Engineer*: Dennis Sands.

Selections: 1 Main Title (3:13); 2 The Bear Skull (1:32); 3 Ayla Finds The Cave (1:36); 4 Ayla Alone (2:10); 5 The Glacier Trek (2:26); 6 The Clan Finds Ayla (3:25); 7 Kreb On The Mountain (1:42); 8 The Counting (2:40); 9 Kreb Gives Ayla Totem (3:20); 10 Wolf Attack (1:27); 11 The Vision (3:36); 12 Iza's Death (2:08); 13 Caught (4:08); 14 The Clan (1:55); 15 Ayla Hugs Kreb (2:10); 16 The Rape (1:35); 17 End Title (6:30).

Review: Like Raquel Welch before her, Darryl Hannah is an eye-popping prehistoric siren in *The Clan of the Cave Bear,* but very little else in this unimaginative adaptation of Jean Auel's novel matched her physical charms or the rugged beauty of the Canadian scenery. One exception however is Alan Silvestri's compelling score, a deft blend of orchestral and synthesized sounds, some devised to resemble the grunts that passed for language at that remote time, others to evoke moods and feelings in a society with minimal forms of expression. Not every track works in the context, and while some ("Ayla Alone") are particularly effective, others ("The Glacier Trek") sound repetitive and dry. But one might excuse the flaws in this score, as the overall impression it leaves is positive.

Class Action ♫♫♫♫

1991, Varese-Sarabande Records; from the movie *Class Action*, 20th Century-Fox, 1991.

Album Notes: *Music*: James Horner; *Music Editor*: Jim Hendrickson; *Synthesizer Programming*: Ian Underwood, Ralph Grierson; *Performed by*: James Horner, Ralph Grierson; *Album Producer*: James Horner; *Engineer*: Shawn Murphy.

Selections: 1 Main Title (2:57); 2 Memories Of Mom (4:13); 3 Do You Like Me (1:44); 4 The Deposition (2:41); 5 The More I See You (H. Warren/M. Gordon) (1:57); 6 Depth Charge (1:52); 7 Michael Revealed (1:22); 8 Iron Mountain (:47); 9 Paper Blizzard (2:46); 10 Stolen Files (1:14); 11 The Trial (2:48); 12 Healing The Rift (5:23); 13 End Title (2:37).

Review: A taut courtroom drama opposing a veteran lawyer against his own daughter in a class action suit, *Class Action* was an ideal vehicle for Gene Hackman and Mary Elizabeth Mastrantonio, both stimulatingly effective in a face-to-face confrontation that pulled no punches but wound up sounding realistic and emotionally charged. In a very uncharacteristic, low-key style, James Horner wrote a series of cues that subtly underlined the action while avoiding to call too much attention to them. Taken on their own musical merits, however, they emerge as attractive pieces of music, beautifully realized and captivating. A piano solo performance of the old chestnut "The More I See You," by Ralph Grierson, adds the right poetic touch to the score itself.

Clear and Present Danger
♫♫♫

1994, Milan Records; from the movie *Clear and Present Danger*, Paramount Pictures, 1994.

Album Notes: *Music*: James Horner; *Orchestrations*: Don Davis; *Music Editors*: Jim Henrikson, Joe E. Rand; *Assistant Music Editor*: Helena Lea; Orchestra conducted by James Horner; *Featured Musicians*: Michael Fisher, Ralph Grierson, Tony Hinnigan, James Horner, Randy Kerber, Mike Taylor, Ian Underwood; *Album Producers*: James Horner, Shawn Murphy; *Engineer*: Shawn Murphy; *Assistant Engineers*: Andy Bass, Dave Marquette, Jay Selvester.

Selections: 1 Main Title/A Clear And Present Danger (5:24); 2 Operation Reciprocity (3:25); 3 The Ambush (9:50); 4 The Laser-Guided Missile (3:51); 5 Looking For Clues (3:32); 6 Deleting The Evidence (4:41); 7 Greer's Funeral/ Betrayal (6:21); 8 Escobedo's New Friend (5:28); 9 Second Hand Copter (2:15); 10 Truth Needs A Soldier/End Title (5:48).

Review: Except for the occasional use of South American flutes to suggest the Colombian scenes, *Clear and Present Danger* is rooted in dramatic Americana. Opening with a heraldic trumpet fanfare, a graceful melody for strings over low brass tones creates an elegant, dignified feel. The feeling doesn't last long, though, as most of the score consists of suspense and action motifs. There are plenty of rhythmic, surging cues for brass and percussion, some vaguely pretty but more often furtive violin melodies, dissimulated by dark, brooding string chords, plenty of suspenseful woodwinds and percussion figures, and some neat textural synth-percussion effects. Horner develops the score's minor two-note motif from minimalist winds and drums to a fever pitch of frenzied swirling strings, pounding drums, eerily rising brasses and scattering piano notes. It's a good score, its listenability reduced somewhat due to an overabundance of the action/suspense motifs, but on the whole it is effectively presented and well orchestrated.

Randall D. Larson

Clerks *♫♫♫*

1994, Chaos/Columbia Records; from the movie *Clerks*, Miramax Films, 1994.

Album Notes: *Song Producers*: Love Among Freaks, Ted Nicely, Alice In Chains, Rick Parasher, Matt Hyde, Bash & Pop, Cliff Shrimper, Critter & The Jesus Lizard, Paul Pacific, Andy Wallace, Bad Religion, John Fryer, John Custer, Clint Werner, Seaweed, Soul Asylum, Toby Wright; *Song Engineers*: Steve De Acutis, Ted Nicely, Eli Janney, Scott, Matt Hyde, Virgil Gentile, Critter, Sir James Bunchberry, Andy Wallace, Stabbing Westward, Richard Mouser, Clint Werner, Seaweed, Toby Wright; *Executive Music Producers*: Bob Weinstein, Harvey Weinstein, Scott Greenstein; *Engineer*: Wally Traugott.

Selections: 1 Dante's Lament (:05); 2 Clerks (S. Smyth/S. Angley) (3:41) *Love Among Freaks*; 3 Kill The Sex Player (Girls Against Boys) (3:18) *Girls Against Boys*; 4 No Time For Love, Dr. Jones (:10); 5 Got Me Wrong (J. Cantrell) (4:11) *Alice in Chains*; 6 Randall And Dante On Sex (:20); 7 Making Me Sick (T. Stinson/G. Gershunoff/R. Bradbury) (3:01) *Bash & Pop*; 8 A Bunch Of Muppets (:24); 9 Chewbacca (Art/Hank/Dave) (1:26) *Supernova*; 10 Panic In Cicero (The Jesus Lizard) (3:29) *The Jesus Lizard*; 11 Shooting Star (P. Rodgers) (4:42) *Golden Smog*; 12 Leaders And Followers (G. Graffin) (2:41) *Bad Religion*; 13 I Like To Expand My Horizons (:15); 14 Violent Mood Swings (W. Flakus/C. Hall/J. Sellers/D. Suycott/S. Zechman) (5:34) *Stabbing Westward*; 15 Berserker (S. Smyth/S. Angley/K. Smith) (2:09) *Love Among Freaks*; 16 Big Problems (R. Mullin/W. Weatherman) (2:15) *Corrosion of Conformity*; 17 Go Your Own Way (L. Buckingham) (3:51) *Seaweed*; 18 Social Event Of The Season (:28); 19 Can't Even Tell (D. Pirner) (3:14) *Soul Asylum*; 20 Jay's Chant (:11).

Review: Life in a convenience store, and the odd assortment of people it seems to attract on a regular basis, *Clerks*, an independent black-and-white film that made a splash at the Sundance Festival, has its moments of humor and pathos, but amounts to little else than a splash-dash effort of unconnected scenes, all aiming to chronicle the problems faced on his first day by a new clerk, Dante. Punctuating the action, and giving it an extra dimension, is the soundtrack, a collection of grunge songs by such groups as Girls Against Boys, Alice In Chains, Supernova, Love Among Freaks, and others. Bits of dialogue (some actually quite funny) are interspersed from time to time, the better to situate the songs in the development of the action.

The Client *♫♫♫*

1994, Elektra Records; from the movie *The Client*, Warner Bros., 1994.

Album Notes: *Music*: Howard Shore; *Orchestrations*: Howard Shore; *Music Editor*: Ellen Segal; Orchestra conducted by Howard Shore; *Featured Musicians*: Steve Jordan, Danny Kotchmar, Michael Lang, Rim May, Simon Franglen; *Album Producer*: Howard Shore; *Engineer*: John Richards.

Selections: 1 The Client (1:35); 2 Romey's Suicide (8:32); 3 Have You Told Me Everything? (2:23); 4 Reggie's Theme (1:57); 5 Barry The Blade (3:50); 6 I'll Take The Fifth (2:04); 7 Unfit (2:25); 8 Kill Them All (1:33); 9 Jailbird (1:23); 10 The Morgue (4:53); 11 I Know Where The Body's Buried (3:37); 12 The Boathouse (8:52); 13 Leaving Memphis (:53); 14 Bye Reggie (1:27); 15 The Flight To Phoenix (1:47); 16 The End (3:39).

Review: A fairly intense dramatic score by Howard Shore for the 1994 adaptation of John Grisham's best seller. The album is extremely dark in its overall tone, taking seriously the concept of its central figure, a child whose life is in jeopardy from the Mob. In the use of a "Southern Twang" motif to reinforce the setting ("Reggie's Theme"), the apprehension is extremely prevalent, and even at the end, when the good guys win, Shore doesn't let us off too easily.

David Hirsch

Cliffhanger *♫♫*

1993, Scotti Bros.; from the movie *Cliffhanger*, Tri-Star Pictures, 1993.

Album Notes: *Music*: Trevor Jones; *Orchestrations*: Brad Dechter, Jeff Atmajian, Larry Ashmore, Guy Dagul, Geoffrey Alexander, Trevor Jones; The London Philharmonic Orchestra, conducted by David Snell; *Album Producer*: Trevor Jones; *Engineer*: John Richards; *Assistant Engineer*: Andrew Taylor.

Selections: 1 Cliffhanger Theme (3:52); 2 Sarah's Farewell (2:14); 3 Sarah Falls (3:53); 4 Gabe Returns (3:11); 5 I Understand (1:40); 6 Sunset Searching (1:19); 7 Tolerated Help (2:55); 8 Base Jump (4:10); 9 Bats (2:25); 10 Two Man Job (2:08); 11 Kynette Is Impaled (4:00); 12 Fireside Chat (:33); 13 Frank's Demise (2:37); 14 Rabbit Hole (1:33); 15 Icy Stream

(1:39); 16 Jessie's Release (3:42); 17 Helicopter Fight (1:30); 18 End Credits (7:23).

Review: This Trevor Jones score opens well with the unabashedly romantic "Cliffhanger Theme." Never before has dangling over a sheer drop seemed so adventurous. At that moment, you really think you're about to hear a sweeping score. Wrong. From that point on, everything slows down to a crawl and whatever momentum the main theme has generated is quickly lost. The album plods through the next five tracks before evidencing some signs of life on "Tolerated Help." Most of the album's gusto seems to have been saved for the final five or six tracks, particularly the seven and a half minute "End Credits."

David Hirsch

Clockers

Clockers 🎵🎵🎵

1995, Columbia Records; from the movie *Clockers*, Universal Pictures, 1995.

Album Notes: *Music*: Terence Blanchard; *Featured Musicians*: Terence Blanchard (trumpet), Edward Simon (piano), Troy Davis (percussion); Orchestra conducted by Terence Blanchard; *Album Producers*: Robin Burgess, Alex Steyermark; *Engineer*: James P. Nichols.

Selections: 1 Strike Rides With Rodney (3:09); 2 Strike Packs Up (3:03); 3 Tyrone/Brothers (1:55); 4 Jail Visit/Strike Teaches Tyrone (5:27); 5 Errol/ Family (1:45); 6 Drive With Andre (2:09); 7 Rodney's Plan/Rocco (3:02); 8 In The Joint/Rocco Grills Strike (5:29); 9 Trains And Crack (1:59); 10 Brothers' Photos (2:21); 11 Something Personal/Evil Rodney (3:54); 12 Iris Wants To Know (2:50); 13 Rough Ride With Rodney (3:00); 14 Tyrone's Story (4:11); 15 Self-Defense (1:51); 16 Strike Leaves Town/Finale (7:24).

Review: Terence Blanchard's music to this Spike Lee "joint" is the last thing you'd expect for a gritty urban crime procedural—a heartfelt, richly emotional orchestral score that's almost suggestive of Aaron Copland in its opening moments of plaintive woodwind playing. Relentlessly downbeat, with a steady, deliberate rhythmic tread that suggests the inevitability of the film's tragic storyline, the score has some of the same emotional directness and sense of anguish that made Howard Shore's *Silence of the Lambs* so effective. There are some very low key suggestions of a blues sensibility at work in the score, but for most of this album Blanchard just works away at an ebbing, regretful melody with his small group of strings, piano and woodwinds.

Jeff Bond

Clockers 🎵🎵🎵

1995, MCA Records; from the movie *Clockers*, Universal Pictures, 1995.

Album Notes: *Song Producers*: Raymond Jones, David Gamson & Chaka Khan, Tim Atack, Prince Sampson & Des'ree, DJ Premier, Salaam Remi, Branford Marsalis, Ski-Original Flavor, DJ Ali & DJ Trouble, Uneek, Gordon Chambers & Ike Lee III; *Executive Soundtrack Producers*: Spike Lee, Bill Stephney; *Engineer*: Tom Baker.

Selections: 1 People In Search of a Life (R. Jones)(6:11) *Marc Dorsey*; 2 Love Me Still (C. Khan/B. Hornsby)(3:25) *Chaka Khan*; 3 Silent Hero (Des'ree/ P. Sampson)(5:01) *Des'ree*; 4 Bird Of Freedom (Seal)(5:13) *Seal*; 5 Return Of The Crooklyn Dodgers (C. Rock/O.C./Jeru The Damaja/DJ Premier)(5:03) *Crooklyn Dodgers*; 6 Bad Boy No Go A Jail (M. Higgins/G. Williams)(4:21) *Mega Banton*; 7 Blast Of The Iron (Rebelz of Authority/S.R. Gibbs)(4:10)*Rebelz of Authority*; 8 Reality Check (B. Marsalis/R. DaCosta)(2:51) *Buckshot LeFonque*; 9 Illa Killa (R. Brown)(4:29) *Strictly Difficult*; 10 Sex Soldier (G. Kahni/M. Henningham)(3:32) *Rebelz of Authority*; 11 Reality (D. Edwards/S. McFadden)(3:22) *BrooklyNytes*; 12 Changes (G. Chambers/Ike Lee/J. Alexander) (4:10) *Marc Dorsey*.

Review: Bringing a different, streetwise sensitivity to the film by Spike Lee, this collection of songs illuminate this tale of an innercity kid, involved in a crime, to which his brother confesses. Marc Dorsey's "People in Search of a Life" serves as an effective introduction to the lineup of songs, with its implied references to the story itself, with Chaka Khan's "Love Me Still," Seal's "Bird of Freedom," and Des'ree's "Silent Hero" among the highlights. "Return of the Crooklyn Dodgers" provides a bridge to another Spike Lee film, and the reggae-like "Bad Boy No Go a Jail," by Mega Banton, is also flavorful, but the other tracks do not provide the same levels of enjoyment.

A Clockwork Orange 🎵🎵🎵🎵

1972, Warner Bros. Records; from the movie *A Clockwork Orange*, Warner Bros., 1971.

Album Notes: *Music*: Wendy Carlos, Rachel Elkind; *Producer*: Rachel Elkind.

Selections: 1 Title Music from Music For The Funeral Of Queen Mary (H. Purcell/W. Carlos/R. Elkind) (2:21) "*Walter*" *Carlos*; 2 The Thieving Magpie (G. Rossini) (5:57); 3 Beethoviana (Theme From A Clockwork Orange) (W. Carlos/R. Elkind) (1:44) "*Walter*" *Carlos*; 4 Ninth Symphony: 2nd Movement (abridged) (L. Van Beethoven) (3:48); 5 March From A Clockwork Orange (from Ninth Symphony: 4th Movement) (L. Van Beethoven/W. Carlos) (7:00) "*Walter*" *Carlos*; 6 William Tell

Overture (abridged) (G. Rossini) (1:17) *"Walter" Carlos*; 7 Pomp And Circumstance March No. 1 (E. Elgar) (4:28); 8 Pomp And Circumstance March No. 4 (abridged) (E. Elgar) (1:33); 9 Timsteps (W. Carlos) (4:13) *"Walter" Carlos*; 10 Overture To The Sun (T. Tucker) (1:40); 11 I Want To Marry A Lighthouse Keeper (E. Eigen) (1:00) *Erika Eigen*; 12 William Tell Overture (abridged) (G. Rossini) (2:58); 13 Suicide Scherzo (Ninth Symphony: 2nd movement) (L. Van Beethoven/W. Carlos) (3:07) *"Walter" Carlos*; 14 Ninth Symphony: 4th movement (abridged) (L. Van Beethoven) (1:34); 15 Singin' In The Rain (A. Freed/N.H. Brown) (2:36) *Gene Kelly*.

Review: Composer and early synthesizer player Wendy Carlos (working under the pseudonym Walter Carlos, deemed more acceptable in some music quarters at the time), contributed atmospheric electronic variations to classical selections, plus her own compositions for this extraordinary study by Stanley Kubrick of violence and depravation in British youth. Even though synthesizers have long since become an integral part of many horror films, this chilling score remains one of the most powerfully expressive of its kind, and plainly justifies its Academy Award nomination.

Close Encounters of the Third Kind ♫♫♫♫♫

1990, Varese-Sarabande; from the movie *Close Encounters of the Third Kind*, Columbia Pictures, 1977.

Album Notes: *Music*: John Williams; *Music Editor*: Ken Wannberg; Orchestra conducted by John Williams; *Album Producer*: John Williams; *Engineer*: John Neal.

Selections: 1 Main Title and Mountain Visions (3:17); 2 Nocturnal Pursuit (2:34); 3 The Abduction Of Barry (4:33); 4 I Can't Believe It's Real (6:33); 5 Climbing Devil's Tower (2:29); 6 The Arrival At Sky Harbor (4:31); 7 Night Siege (6:22); 8 The Conversation (3:06); 9 The Appearance Of The Visitors/When You Wish Upon A Star (L. Harline/N. Washington)/ Resolution/ End Title (14:58).

Review: It's amazing how sheer simplicity can often be the ideal approach for a film score. John Williams' well-known, five-note motif that represents the musical communication between the human scientists and extraterrestrial ships in Steven Spielberg's sci-fi classic is deceptive in its seemingly humble musical origins. Yet with Williams' superlative themes and variations, the motif becomes lyrical, emotional and dramatic, perfectly capturing how music can play such a crucial role in a film's narrative. The rest of the score is likewise outstanding, with chorus and orchestra creating a seamless musical fabric

simultaneously representing the otherworldly visitors and the decidedly human conflict of protagonist Roy Neary (Richard Dreyfuss). In short, it's a masterpiece. Listeners should be aware that the initial, out-of-print Arista release retains the original album packaging, including notes by Spielberg. The newer Varese issue features different liner notes, along with a disco version of the main theme and a forthcoming remastered Sony re-issue will feature previously unreleased tracks.

Andy Dursin

Cobb ♫♫♫♪

1994, Sony Classical; from the movie *Cobb*, Warner Bros., 1994.

Album Notes: *Music*: Elliot Goldenthal; *Orchestrations*: Robert Elhai, Elliot Goldenthal; *Music Editor*: Dan Carlin; Orchestra conducted by Jonathan Sheffer; *Featured Musicians*: Phil Smith (trumpet), Billy Drewes (saxophone), Bill Mays (piano), John Beal (bass), Jamie Haddad (drums), Elliot Goldenthal (vocals, piano rags); *Album Producer*: Matthias Gohl; *Engineer*: Joel Iwataki.

Selections: 1 Variations On An Old Baptist Hymn (3:05); 2 Stump Meets Cobb (1:50); 3 Cooperstown Aria, part 1 (1:43); 4 Nevada Nightlight (2:28); 5 Reno Ho', part 1 (2:37); 6 Newsreel Mirror (3:26); 7 Meant Monk (2:17); 8 Cooperstown Aria, part 2 (2:00); 9 Winter Walk (1:11); 10 Hart And Hunter (1:16); 11 Georgia Peach Rag (2:29); 12 The Baptism (1:30); 13 Reno Ho', part 2 (2:35); 14 The Homecoming (6:18); 15 Sour Mash Scherzo (1:09); 16 Cobb Dies (1:49); 17 The Beast Within (2:24); 18 The Ball Game (W. Carr) (3:05) *Sister Wynona Carr*.

Review: Powerful orchestral score by Elliot Goldenthal that weaves Gospel and classical music to create an edgy Americana motif worthy of one of baseball's most volatile figures. The overall mood is oppressive and dark, completely overwhelming, much like Ty Cobb himself. This even holds true for the somewhat romantic "Cooperstown Aria," which never quite seems to climb into the light. Interestingly, the cue "The Beast Within" was tracked in from Goldenthal's own *Alien* score and included on this album, so it's easy to draw parallels between the two scores about the nature of the beast. The composer performs some of the vocals and the piano rags on the album.

David Hirsch

Cocktail ♫♫♫♪

1988, Elektra Records; from the movie *Cocktail*, Touchstone Pictures, 1988.

Album Notes: *Song Producers*: Phil Galdston, Starship, Terry Manning, Robbie Nevil, Tom Lord-Alge, Linda Goldstein, The

Georgia Satellites, Brenda O'Brien, Terry Melcher, John Cougar Mellencamp, Ry Cooder, Preston Smith, Art Rupe; *Album Executive Producer*: Brad Neufeld; *Engineer*: Stephen Marcussen.

Selections: 1 Wild Again (J. Bettis/M. Clark)(4:43) *Starship*; 2 Powerful Stuff (W. Wilson/M. Henderson/R. Field)(4:48) *The Fabulous Thunderbirds*; 3 Since When (R. Nevil/B. Walsh)(4:02) *Robbie Nevil*; 4 Don't Worry, Be Happy (B. McFerrin)(4:48) *Bobby McFerrin*; 5 Hippy Hippy Shake (C. Romero)(1:45) *The Georgia Satellites*; 6 Kokomo (M. Love/T. Melcher/J. Phillips/S. Mackenzie) (3:34) *The Beach Boys*; 7 Rave On (S. West/N. Petty/B. Tilghman)(3:13) *John Cougar Mellencamp*; 8 All Shook Up (E. Presley/O. Blackwell)(3:29) *Ry Cooder*; 9 Oh, I Love You So (P. Smith) (2:42) *Preston Smith*; 10 Tutti Frutti (R. Penneman/D. LaBostrie/J. Lubin) (2:23) *Little Richard*.

Review: *Cocktail*, a *Saturday Night Fever* in a bar, is marked by an exhilarating performance from Tom Cruise, as a handsome young man, fresh from the Army, who takes New York and the hip crowd by storm as an eclectic bartender in a chic, well-appointed room. Contributing a contemporary flavor to the film is its clever assortment of pop songs, featuring performances by frontline artists such as The Beach Boys, John Cougar Mellencamp, Ry Cooder, The Fabulous Thunderbirds, and Starship. On its own terms, the album proves a powerful reminder of the screen action, as well as a pleasantly programmed compilation. Bobby McFerrin's cheery "Don't Worry, Be Happy" is a highlight.

Cocoon

Cocoon ♫♫♫♪

1985, Polydor; from the movie *Cocoon*, 20th Century-Fox, 1985.

Album Notes: *Music*: James Horner; *Orchestrations*: Herbert Spencer, Billy May; *Music Editor*: Ken Wannberg; Orchestra conducted by James Horner; *Album Producer*: James Horner; *Engineer*: Armin Steiner.

Selections: 1 Through The Window (3:00); 2 The Lovemaking (4:28); 3 The Chase (4:32); 4 Rose's Death (2:15); 5 The Boys Are Out (2:41); 6 Returning To The Sea (4:19); 7 Gravity (C. Sembello)(4:04) *Michael Sembello*; 8 Discovered In The Poolhouse! (2:51); 9 First Tears (1:55); 10 Sad Goodbyes (2:17); 11 The Ascension (6:01); 12 Theme From "Cocoon" (6:05).

Review: See entry below.

Cocoon: The Return ♫♫♫♫

1988, Varese-Sarabande; from the movie *Cocoon: The Return*, 20th Century-Fox, 1988.

Album Notes: *Music*: James Horner; *Orchestrations*: Greig McRitchie; *Music Editor*: Jim Henrikson; Orchestra conducted by James Horner; *Album Producer*: James Horner; *Engineer*: Shawn Murphy.

Selections: 1 Returning Home (6:05); 2 Taking Bernie To The Beach (4:31); 3 Joe's Gift (8:06); 4 Remembrances/The Break-In (8:24); 5 Basketball Swing (6:58); 6 Jack's Future (2:44); 7 Growing Old (1:55); 8 Good Friend (3:16); 9 Rescue/The Ascension (11:29).

Review: In some of his early scores (see also *batteries not included*), James Horner often indulged his love for the big bands. In both *Cocoon* and *Cocoon: The Return*, he included some tracks ("The Boys are Out," in the former, "Taking Bernie to the Beach" and "Basketball Swing," in the latter) that reflect his fondness for the genre and his particular talent at writing exciting cues in that vein. By far, those are the most engaging moments in both scores. The rest of the time, the music, sometimes grandiloquent, sometimes understated, is confined to reflecting the moods of some senior citizens in a Florida retirement home who become young again after they discover a miraculous spring, with their further adventures being the focus of the sequel. Both films, in combining the Peter Pan syndrome with pseudo-galactical fantasies, succeeded in tapping into humanity's age-old dream of remaining forever young and healthy. Except for the exuberant numbers singled out earlier, Horner's scores echoed these feelings with great restraint and subtle understatement, achieving in the process a cohesive musical presentation which, in these recordings, comes across quite effectively. A pop vocal by Michael Sembello ("Gravity") in the first album, proves totally unnecessary and, in fact, breaks the overall unity of the score.

The Collector ♫♫♫♪

1991, Mainstream Records; from the movie *The Collector*, Columbia Pictures, 1965.

Album Notes: *Music*: Maurice Jarre; Orchestra conducted by Maurice Jarre; *CD Producer*: Jackie Mills; *Engineer*: Jackie Mills.

Selections: 1 The Collector (3:38); 2 The Catch (2:23); 3 Trapped (2:22); 4 Captive (4:31); 5 The Garden (2:09); 6 The Bargain (1:39); 7 Temptation (4:20); 8 Last Day (3:12); 9 Seduction (4:39); 10 Death (5:12); 11 Theme from "David And Lisa" (M. Lawrence)(2:16); 12 Somewhere My Love (from "Doctor Zhivago")(M. Jarre/P.F. Webster)(4:04); 13 I Will Wait For

You (from "Umbrellas Of Cherbourg")(M. Legrand/N. Gimbel/ J. Demy)(2:58); 14 The Sweetheart Tree (from "The Great Race")(J. Mercer/H. Mancini)(2:09).

Review: Leave it to Maurice Jarre to take a chilling film of abduction, and score it 180-degrees different from the psychological thrillers of Hitchcock and Herrmann only a few years earlier. *The Collector* is a 1966 picture directed by the legendary William Wyler, starring Terence Stamp as a nut who kidnaps his true love, an art student played by Samantha Eggar. The bulk of the film is the struggle between captor and captive, but Jarre's score is practically upbeat, featuring a pleasant, if a bit hyperactive waltz that is disturbing due to its sheer obliviousness towards the on-screen action. It's like this little fantasy running through the abductor's head, a serene and infectious tune laced with harpsichord, as if it was "playing house" throughout, or scoring the idyllic setting in a rural English home. The score is nicely listenable on its own, a ballet of sweetness amidst a gripping, tragic tale of an "I'll *make* her love me" wacko gone unchecked.

Lukas Kendall

Coma 🎜🎜🎜

1990, Bay Cities Records; from the movie *Coma*, M-G-M, 1978.

Album Notes: *Music*: Jerry Goldsmith; *Orchestrations*: Arthur Morton; Orchestra conducted by Jerry Goldsmith; *Album Producer*: Harry V. Lojewski; *CD Producer*: Nick Redman.

Selections: 1 Jefferson Institute (1:59); 2 Study In Anatomy (3:13); 3 A Chance Encounter (5:01); 4 Love Theme From "Coma" (2:38); 5 A Free Ride (2:58); 6 O.R. 8 (4:53); 7 The Long View (3:42); 8 A Lucky Patient (5:06); 9 Love Theme From "Coma" (disco version)(4:29); 10 Disco Strut (D. Peake) (2:33).

Review: A superior thriller score that blends the Goldsmith trademarks of staccato piano playing and unnerving string effects with an eerie, dangling metallic clang that foreshadows the film's set piece of a roomful of comatose living organ donors hanging from the ceiling. Michael Crichton's film had no music at all until it was halfway over, so without a piece of title music the album is a jumble of nonchronological cues and some regrettable source pieces from the disco era. But the score's highlights are well worth searching for, from the Bartok-influenced creepiness and fluttering, unsettling piano runs of "The Jefferson Institute" to the clanking, malevolent "O.R. 8" and the climactic, heart-pounding piano chase, "A Lucky Patient," this is a textbook example of Goldsmith's command of the genre.

Jeff Bond

The Comancheros/True Grit
🎜🎜🎜🎜

1985, Varese-Sarabande; from the movies *The Comancheros*, 20th Century-Fox, 1961, and *True Grit*, Paramount Pictures, 1969.

Album Notes: *Music*: Elmer Bernstein; *Orchestrations*: Leo Shuken, Jack Hayes (*The Comancheros*); The Utah Symphony Orchestra, conducted by Elmer Bernstein; *Featured Soloists*: Edmund Cord (trumpet), Leonard Braus (violin); *Album Producer*: George Korngold; *Engineers*: Bruce Leek, Fred Mitchell.

Selections: THE COMANCHEROS: 1 Main Title (1:39); 2 Escort (3:21); 3 McBaine And The Prairie (2:35); 4 Jake Surveys The Camp (3:45); 5 Pursuit (2:03); 6 Mexican Dance (2:15); 7 Indian Attack (3:08); 8 Finale (1:03);

TRUE GRIT: 9 Main Title (1:42); 10 Rooster And Runaway (2:54); 11 Bald Mountain (4:29); 12 Pony Mine And Papa's Things (2:09); 13 The Dying Moon (3:09); 14 Big Trail (1:52); 15 Sad Departure/The Pace That Kills (3:00); 16 Warm Wrap-Up (1:55).

Review: Through their many contributions in the genre, some composers defined the western score and gave its most recognizable musical expressions (one would almost be tempted to say "cliches"), but none as eloquently and exhilaratingly as Elmer Bernstein. Whether writing for a serious film (*The Magnificent Seven*, of course, but also *The Comancheros* or *True Grit*, both represented here), or spoofing himself (as he did so effectively in *The Hallelujah Trail*), Bernstein never lost sight of what made his western movie music so characteristic. It always was, in a nutshell, as it should always sound, bold, spacious, and spectacular. Between the pulse-racing motifs suggesting the wide open spaces, or the Mexican-tinged accents descriptive of south of the border action, his music is always thrilling, colorful, exciting. These two scores are fine examples of his approach to the genre, and both evidence the very qualities that make his music so uniquely lively. This is the first time *The Comancheros* is available in an album, and while there is an original soundtrack album to *True Grit* (q.v.), this rerecording is far superior to it sonically, and introduces several cues not found elsewhere. The Utah Symphony, conducted by the composer, plays these scores with the right amount of dynamism and gusto.

See also: The Shootist

Come See the Paradise 🎜🎜🎜

1990, Varese-Sarabande; from the movie *Come See the Paradise*, 20th Century-Fox, 1990.

Album Notes: *Music*: Randy Edelman; *Orchestrations*: Greig McRitchie; Orchestra conducted by Randy Edelman; *Album*

"He was the first minimalist. The score was played at a volume where it wouldn't compete with the movie's sound effects."

Elliot Goldenthal
on Bernard Herrmann's Cape Fear
*(Entertainment Weekly Online,
2-3-95)*

Producers: Randy Edelman, Alan Parker; *Engineers*: Elton Ahi, Armin Steiner.

Selections: 1 Love Theme (4:45); 2 Fire In A Brooklyn Theatre (1:20); 3 Shikataganai (:26); 4 Love Is The Sweetest Thing (R. Noble) (3:14) *Mark Earley*; 5 Lily And Mini (:49); 6 Flowers That Bloom In The Rain (F. Ikeda-Takashi) (2:21) *Mariko Seki*; 7 Kawamura Family Theme (A. Parker/J. Parker) (2:50); 8 Jack And Lily (1:25); 9 Nevertheless (B. Kalmar/H. Ruby) (1:48); 10 You Can't Spit At Heaven (:50); 11 Forget Me Not (Y. Hosoda/H. Mogami) (3:27) *Sanae Hosaka*; 12 Little Tokyo (:56); 13 Terminal Island (:40); 14 Santa Anita (A. Parker/J. Parker) (:39); 15 Don't Sit Under The Apple Tree (L. Brown/S. Stept/C. Tobias) (2:28) *Teri Eiko Koide, Jumi Emizawa, Cynthia Lawren*; 16 Bad Days (:30); 17 Love Birds (M. Kume/Harano) (2:20) *Syoji*; 18 Nine Tiny Seconds (A. Parker/J. Parker) (:48); 19 A Little Bag Of Magic (2:08).

Review: This charming, emotionally moving score by Randy Edelman suffers greatly on CD from poor sequencing. Period songs, most sung in Japanese (and one with record surface noise!), frequently break in between the cues. They were probably inserted in this fashion because the actual underscore cues take up very little total time. The music, a blend of electronics and acoustics, would have probably flowed better had the underscore been edited into a suite. Three tracks were written by Alex and Jake Parker. Edelman's dramatically charged "Fire in a Brooklyn Theatre" is used frequently in film trailers.

David Hirsch

The Commitments 🎵🎵🎵

1991/1992, MCA Records; from the movie *The Commitments*, 20th Century-Fox, 1991.

Album Notes: *Featured Musicians*: Conor Brady (guitar), Fran Beehan (drums), Paul Bushnell (bass), Ronan Dooney (trumpet), Eamann Flynn (keyboards), Carl Geraghty (tenor/baritone sax), Felim Gormley (alto sax), Alex Acuna (percussion), Mitchell Froome (keyboards), Dean Parks (guitar); *Albums Producers*: Paul Bushnell, Kevin Killen, Alan Parker; *Engineers*: Kevin Killen, Tim Martin; *Assistant Engineers*: Eric Rudd, Robbie Adams.

Selections: VOLUME 1: 1 Mustang Sally (B. Rice) (4:02) *Andrew Strong*; 2 Take Me To The River (A. Green/M. Hodges) (3:36) *Andrew Strong*; 3 Chain Of Fools (D. Covay) (2:58) *Angeline Ball, Maria Doyle*; 4 The Dark End Of The Street (D. Penn/C. Moman) (2:34) *Andrew Strong*; 5 Destination Anywhere (N. Ashford/V. Simpson) (3:08) *Niamh Kavanagh*; 6 I Can't Stand The Rain (D. Bryant/A. Peebles/B. Miller) (3:12) *Angelina Ball*; 7 Try A Little Tenderness (H. Woods/J. Campbell/R. Connelly) (4:31) *Andrew Strong*; 8 Treat Her Right (G. Kurtz/R. Head) (3:35) *Robert Arkins*; 9 Do Right Woman Do Right Man (D. Penn/C. Moman) (3:15) *Niamh Kavanagh*; 10 Mr. Pitiful (O. Redding/S. Cropper) (2:07) *Andrew Strong*; 11 I Never Loved A Man (R. Shannon) (3:09) *Maria Doyle*; 12 In The Midnight Hour (W. Pickett/S. Cropper) (3:09) *Andrew Strong*; 13 Bye Bye Baby (M. Wells) (3:21) *Maria Doyle*; 14 Slip Away (W. Terrell/M. Daniels/W. Armstrong) (4:27) *Robert Arkins*.

VOLUME 2: 1 Hard To Handle (A. Jones/A. Isbell/O. Redding) (2:23) *Andrew Strong*; 2 Grits Ain't Groceries (T. Turner) (3:45) *Andrew Strong*; 3 I Thank You (I. Hayes/D. Porter) (3:40) *Robert Arkins*; 4 That's The Way Love Is (N. Whitfield/B. Strong) (4:08) *Angeline Ball*; 5 Show Me (J. Tex) (2:57) *Andrew Strong*; 6 Saved (J. Leiber/M. Stoller) (2:55) *Andrew Strong*; 7 Too Many Fish In The Sea (N. Whitfield/E. Holland, Jr.) (2:45) *Angeline Ball*; 8 Fa-Fa-Fa-Fa-Fa (Sad Song) (O. Redding/S. Cropper) (2:52) *Robert Arkins*; 9 Land Of A Thousand Dances (C. Kenner/A. Domino) (3:16) *Andrew Strong*; 10 Nowhere To Run (B. Holland/L. Dozier/E. Holland) (3:40) *Niamh Kavanagh*; 11 Bring It On Home To Me (S. Cooke) (3:41) *Robert Arkins, Angeline Ball*.

Review: Not the original, but an incredible simulation. This ensemble of Irish musicians is charming in the movie and they play these old rhythm 'n' blues favorites with convincing spirit, and the best vocalists—Maria Doyle and Andrew Strong—often make the Commitments sound even better than a top-shelf bar band. Seven of the songs on "Vol. 2" weren't performed in the film, but it really doesn't matter; like *The Big Chill*, this is feel-good stuff that doubles as terrific party music.
Gary Graff

Company Business 🎵🎵

1991, Intrada Records; from the movie *Company Business*, M-G-M, 1991.

Album Notes: *Music*: Michael Kamen; *Orchestrations*: Michael Kamen; Orchestra conducted by Michael Kamen; *Album Produ-*

cers: Michael Kamen, Stephen McLaughlin; *Engineer*: Stephen McLaughlin.

Selections: 1 Journey To Alexanderplatz (10:55); 2 Faisal's Escape (14:51); 3 Natasha (1:28); 4 Cafe Jatte (5:11); 5 Eiffel Tower (7:27); 6 The Island (4:09).

Review: This is one of those soundtracks which reminds the listener that film music, while it sometimes makes for a listenable recording, is nevertheless not written with that purpose in mind. Michael Kamen is of course an immensely gifted composer, but the programmatic requirements of this spy thriller, for whatever reason, needed music which does not work on a record album. The first track, "Journey to Alexanderplatz" is a surging suspense cue, nicely orchestrated (by Kamen himself). However, removed from the film, it simply meanders on disc (that this track is also 11 minutes long does not increase its allure). The second track, "Faisal's Escape" is similarly meandering, but more subdued and even less interesting (and this track lasts fifteen minutes!). The only listenable cue is "Cafe Jatte", a jazzy pastiche/source cue for saxophone, piano and rhythm section, which unfortunately segues into more meandering suspense music after three minutes. The sax theme returns however in the closing track, "The Island." The score for *Company Business* is not bad. It is just programmatic to the extent that there is no shape, architecture or melody for the listener to grab hold of. As such, listening to this CD is ultimately a maddening experience.

Paul Andrew MacLean

Con Air ♪

1997, Hollywood Records; from the movie *Con Air*, Touchstone Pictures, 1997.

Album Notes: *Music*: Mark Mancina, Trevor Rabin; *Orchestrations*: Gordon Goodwin, Nick Glennie-Smith, Bruce Fowler, Trevor Rabin, Mark Mancina; Orchestra conducted by Gordon Goodwin, Nick Glennie-Smith; *Featured Musician*: Lou Molino III (drums); *Album Producers*: Trevor Rabin, Mark Mancina, Paul Linford; *Engineers*: Steve Kempster, Paul Linford, Christopher Ward.

Selections: 1 Con Air Theme (1:31); 2 Trisha (1:04); 3 Carson City (3:04); 4 Lear Crash (4:44); 5 Lerner Landing (3:28); 6 Romantic Chaos (1:22); 7 The Takeover (3:52); 8 The Discharge (1:09); 9 Jailbirds (:59); 10 Cons Check Out Lerner (1:55); 11 Poe Saves Cops (2:25); 12 The Fight (:22); 13 Battle In The Boneyard (7:41); 14 Poe Meets Larkin (1:14); 15 Bedlam Larkin (:49); 16 Fire Truck Chase (4:22); 17 Overture (4:18).

Review: An action-driven score, it took not one but two composers to come up with this electronic-cum-orchestra mishmash

which probably makes a lot of appropriate noises in connection with the various scenes on-screen, but which elicits a yawn otherwise. Making a prominent place for the drumming of Lou Molino III, who carries the majority of the tunes, the selections unfold one after the other, sounding exactly alike, with soft moments leading to big surges that mean very little, at least in musical terms. In the mush, one track, "Trisha," actually comes out for a hot minute as being genuinely attractive.

Conan

Conan the Barbarian ♪♪♪♪♪

1989, Varese-Sarabande; from the movie *Conan the Barbarian*, Universal Pictures, 1982.

Album Notes: *Music*: Basil Poledouris; *Text*: Basil Poledouris; *Orchestrations*: Greig McRitchie; *Text Translation*: Beth Lawson, Teresa Cortey; Members of the Orchestra and Chorus of Santa Cecila and the Radio Symphony of Rome, conducted by Basil Poledouris; *Album Producer*: Basil Poledouris; *Engineers*: Pedegro Savina (Rome), Frank Jones (Burbank).

Selections: 1 Anvil Of Crom (2:34); 2 Riddle Of Steel/Riders Of Doom (5:36); 3 Gift Of Fury (3:50); 4 Wheel Of Pain (4:09); 5 Atlantean Sword (3:50); 6 Theology/Civilization (3:13); 7 Wifeing (Love Theme from Conan The Barbarian)(2:10); 8 The Leaving/The Search (5:59); 9 Mountain Of Power Procession (3:21); 10 The Tree Of Woe (3:31); 11 Recovery (2:11); 12 The Kitchen/The Orgy (B. Poledouris/Z. Poledouris)(6:30); 13 Funeral Pyre (4:29); 14 Battle Of The Mount (4:52); 15 Death Of Rexor (5:34); 16 Orphans Of Doom/The Awakening (5:31).

Review: See entry below.

Conan the Destroyer ♪♪♪

1989, Varese-Sarabande; from the movie *Conan the Destroyer*, Universal Pictures, 1984.

Album Notes: *Music*: Basil Poledouris; *Orchestrations*: Greig McRitchie, Jack Smalley, Scott Smalley; The Unione Musicisti di Roma Orchestra, conducted by Basil Poledouris; *Album Producer*: Basil Poledouris; *Engineers*: Antonio Rampotti.

Selections: 1 Main Title/Riders Of Taramis (3:31); 2 Valeria Remembers (3:02); 3 The Horn Of Dagoth (2:17); 4 Elite Guard Attacks (2:23); 5 Crystal Palace (6:00); 6 The Katta (1:05); 7 Dream Quest (1:30); 8 Night Bird (2:21); 9 Approach To Shadizaar (2:40); 10 The Scrolls Of Skelos (2:26); 11 Dueling Wizards (1:25); 12 Illusion's Lake (1:27); 13 Conan And Bombaata Battle (1:16).

Review: Basil Poledouris' music for these two movies, a poetic tribute to the romantic notions of Robert E. Howard's pulp fiction tales set in a bloody, uncivilized age, established him as a premier composer for epic action films. During the opening 20 minutes of the first film, director John Milius kept dialogue to a minimum, using Poledouris' music to literally tell the story of Conan's early life (tracks 1 through 4 on the CD). All of the cues are not epic, however, and some, like "Wifeing," provide a counterpoint to the bombast with remarkable gentleness. Various choral verses, drawn from Latin and Gregorian chants, are also interpolated to great effect to reflect the religious fervor of villain Thulsa Doom's dreaded Snake Cult.

In comparison, the music for the second film pales because of the paltry budget that was set aside for the creation of its score. Saddled with an orchestra that was just a shadow of the powerhouse he had on the first film, Poledouris wrote a score that works best in its softer moments, the action cues suffering from a notable lack of percussion. Still, this album has a lot of fine music to offer (i.e. "The Horn of Dagoth"), but it simply cannot compete with its predecessor's intensity.

David Hirsch

Coneheads 🦴🦴🦴

1993, Warner Bros. Records; from the movie *Coneheads*, Paramount Pictures, 1993.

Album Notes: *Song Producers*: Mike Clink, Slash, Mike Thorne, Stephen Hague, Paul Simon, Scott Litt, R.E.M., Rick Rubin, Michael Phillip Wojewoda, T. Bailey, Peter Aykroyd, Bruce Gowdy; *Executive Album Producers*: Michael Ostin, Peter Afterman; *Engineer*: Stephen Marcussen.

Selections: 1 Magic Carpet Ride (J. Kay/R. Moreve)(3:41) *Slash, Michael Monroe*; 2 Tainted Love (E.C. Cobb)(2:43) *Soft Cell*; 3 No More Tears (Enough Is Enough)(P. Jabara/B. Roberts)(3:52) *k.d. lang, Andy Bell*; 4 Kodachrome (P. Simon)(3:30) *Paul Simon*; 5 Can't Take My Eyes Off You (B. Gaudio/B. Crewe)(3:44) *Morten Harket*; 6 It's A Free World Baby (J.M. Stipe/W. Berry/P. Buck/M. Milles)(5:13) *R.E.M.*; 7 Soul To Squeeze (A. Kiedis/Flea/J. Frusciante/C. Smith)(4:52) *Red Hot Chili Peppers*; 8 Fight The Power (C. Ridenhour/H. Shocklee/E. Sadler/K. Shocklee)(4:06) *Barenaked Ladies* ; 9 Little Renee (Digable Planets)(3:22) *Digable Planets*; 10 Chale Jao (T. Bailey)(4:11) *Babble*; 11 Conehead Love (P. Aykroyd/B. Gowdy)(4:16).

Review: This one's aimed hard at the modern rock market, with new offerings from the Red Hot Chili Peppers ("Soul to Squeeze," a hit) and R.E.M. ("It's a Free World Baby," a dud). Remakes are the order of the day on the rest of the album,

including hilarious takes on "Fight the Power" by Barenaked Ladies and a show-stopping duet on "No More Tears (Enough is Enough)" by k.d. lang and Erasure's Andy Bell. The latter is as much fun as a potent cone ring.

Gary Graff

Congo 🦴🦴

1995, Epic Soundtrax; from the movie *Congo*, Paramount Pictures, 1995.

Album Notes: *Music*: Jerry Goldsmith; *Orchestrations*: Arthur Morton, Alexander Courage; *Lyrics*: Lebo M; *Vocal Arrangements*: Lebo M; *Music Editors*: Ken Hall, Darrell Hall; Orchestra conducted by Jerry Goldsmith; *Album Producers*: Jerry Goldsmith, Lebo M; *Engineer*: Bruce Botnick; *Assistant Engineers*: Paul Wertheimer, Dominic Gonzales, Norm Dlugatch.

Selections: 1 Spirit Of Africa (2:43) *Lebo M*; 2 Bail Out (2:59); 3 No Customs (1:50); 4 Deep Jungle (2:35); 5 Hippo Attack (2:27); 6 Crash Site (2:01); 7 Gates Of Zinj (4:04); 8 Amy's Nightmare (2:12); 9 Kahega (2:19); 10 Amy's Farewell/Spirit Of Africa (10:29) *Lebo M*.

Review: Give Jerry Goldsmith a creative challenge and he can usually create something better than any film as silly as this ever deserved. The score's strength comes from "Spirit of Africa," a beautiful theme song co-written by Goldsmith with singer/songwriter Lebo M, that's sung first in an African dialect, then later in English. This is the high point of the album and, unfortunately, the film doesn't inspire much else. Goldsmith interjects various African rhythms throughout, but uses his standard electronic jiggery-pokery to spice up the rather ordinary action cues. Adding to the irritation, the correct order of the CD tracks can only be found on the disc itself, not on the packaging!

David Hirsch

Cookie 🐾

1989, UNI Records; from the movie *Cookie*, Warner Bros., 1989.

Album Notes: *Music*: Thomas Newman; *Song Producers*: Steve Lovell, Andy Richards, Duncan Bridgeman, Tony Brown, Nanci Griffth, CCP, Arthur Baker, Fred Zarr; *Engineers*: Tony Phillips, Zeus B. Held, John Vigran.

Selections: 1 Americanos (H. Johnson)(3:36) *Holly Johnson*; 2 Revolution Baby (N.C. Sayer)(4:52) *Transvision Vamp*; 3 Jingle Bell Rock (J. Beal/J. Boothe)(2:08) *Bobby Helms*; 4 Never Mind (H. Howard)(3:42) *Nanci Griffith*; 5 Slammer (T. Newman)(1:52); 6 Hard Work (D. Palmer/C. Hubert/P. Chapman) (3:56) *CCP*; 7 Save Your Love (M. Duigan/R. Sainte-Rose)(4:45)

Jet Vegas; 8 Love Is A Many Splendored Thing (S. Fain/P.F. Webster)(2:58) *The Four Aces*; 9 Never Had It So Good (T. Paige/A. Forbes)(3:20) *Tommy Page*.

Review: Unless you listen attentively or you read the fine print on the label copy, you probably wouldn't guess that Thomas Newman wrote the score for this dispensable comedy about a mafia boss, back home after some years spent behind bars, and the independent teenage daughter with whom he must now contend. The people lending their talents to this soundtrack album probably deserve better; so did Newman, represented here by the "Cookie Theme"; so do you.

Cool Hand Luke *♪♪♪♪*

1996, MCA Records/Japan; from the movie *Cool Hand Luke*, Warner Bros., 1967.

Album Notes: *Music:* Lalo Schifrin; Orchestra conducted by Lalo Schifrin; *Album Producer:* Tom Mack; *Engineers:* Thorne Nogar, Andy Richardson.

Selections: 1 Main Title (2:05); 2 Just A Closer Walk With Thee (2:55); 3 Tar Sequence (3:13); 4 Lucille (2:46); 5 Egg Eating Contest (2:58); 6 Plastic Jesus (E. Rusk/G. Cromarty)(1:58); 7 Bean Time (1:12); 8 Ballad Of Cool Hand Luke (2:36); 9 Arletta Blues (2:55); 10 The First Morning (1:51); 11 The Chase (3:18); 12 Road Gang (1:49); 13 End Title (2:13).

Review: In one of his better screen roles, Paul Newman portrays in *Cool Hand Luke* a convicted felon doing time on a chain gang in a Southern prison, a loner ("What we have here is a failure to communicate") whose only salvation comes when he is gunned down by prison guards after he tries to escape. As memorable as Newman's tour-de-force portrayal is Lalo Schifrin's biting Academy Award-nominated score, in which the use of various solo instruments (notably the harmonica and the banjo) adds a distinctive Southern rural touch. Schifrin's signature staccato orchestral outbursts permeate some of the most powerful moments in the score (particularly the "Tar Sequence," which New Yorkers should recognize as the theme used by a local news station, and "The Chase"), while the tense moods are occasionally relieved by lighter tracks like "Egg-Beating Contest" or the lilting "Ballad of Cool Hand Luke." This CD, released in Japan only, can be found in specialty stores.

Cool World *♪♪♪▷*

1992, Varese-Sarabande; from the movie *Cool World*, Paramount Pictures, 1992.

Album Notes: *Music:* Mark Isham; *Music Editors:* Scott Grusin, Christopher Kennedy; The Munich Symphony Orchestra, conducted by Allan Wilson; *Featured Musicians:* Terry Bozzio

(drums), Nigel Hitchcock (saxophone), Dave Hartley (piano), Greg Knowles (percussion), Claus Reichstaller (trumpet), Mark Isham (trumpet), Rick Keller (saxophone), Roy Babbington (double bass), Felici Civitareale (lead trumpet); *Album Producer:* Mark Isham; *Engineer:* Chris Dibble; *Assistant Engineers:* Peter Fuchs, Mark Tucker, Paul Golding, Declan McGovern.

Selections: 1 The Cool World Stomp (1:33); 2 The Desert Gamble (2:08); 3 Lonette (3:10); 4 A Cool New World (3:54); 5 Nails (1:00); 6 The Slash Club (5:53); 7 I'm No Dream (2:22); 8 Miss Holli Would (4:08); 9 A Pen Job! (1:55); 10 The Death Of Nails (1:00); 11 The Bunny And The Poppers (1:03); 12 Harris And Lonette (3:08); 13 The Legend Of Vegas Vinnie (2:00); 14 A Trip Through The Past (1:12); 15 A Night Out In Cool World (3:05); 16 She Would If She Could (5:25); 17 The Spike Of Power (7:15); 18 He's A Doodle! (2:26); 19 The Cool World Stomp (reprise) (4:37).

Review: One of those instances where the soundtrack is far more interesting than the film it was composed for. Mark Isham here gets the chance at writing a score that's right up his alley — an eclectic mixture of swinging Big Band, jazz, techno, and orchestral passages that zips right along for nearly the entire duration of the album. A small jazz ensemble, including Isham himself on the trumpet, leads the way through the score's liveliest passages, like "The Cool World Stomp", while the composer also includes a lush love theme for saxophone and orchestra to go along with the fast-tempo of the majority of the score. Simply put, there is something here to please both traditional soundtrack listeners and fans of Isham's solo albums, even though many tracks were either buried under sound effects or entirely taken out of the movie itself (and are designated as such here). Regardless, this is an energetic, often dynamic effort that functions perfectly as an album.

Andy Dursin

Copycat *♪♪♪▷*

1995, Milan Records; from the movie *Copycat*, Warner Bros., 1995.

Album Notes: *Music:* Christopher Young; *Orchestrations:* Pete Anthony, Christopher Young; *Music Editor:* Thomas Milano; Orchestra conducted by Thomas Milano; *Synthesizer Programmers:* Daniel Licht, Mark Zimoski; *Featured Soloist:* Gary Nesteruk (piano); *Album Producer:* David Franco; *Engineer:* Robert Fernandez.

Selections: 1 Get Up To This (3:54) *New World Beat*; 2 Carabu Party (2:55) *Steven Ray*; 3 Techno Boy (3:21) *Silkski*; 4 Main Title (3:00); 5 Stick Him Or Shoot Him (6:02); 6 Housebound (2:05); 7 Silent Screams; 8 Murder's An Art (5:57); 9 In Darkness (2:14); 10 Take A Life (2:09); 11 Next To The Devil (1:30);

12 Pastoral Horror (4:17); 13 Silhouette (2:36); 14 Gallows (2:01); 15 Butchers And Bakers (2:31); 16 Panic (1:09); 17 Who's Afraid (3:35); 18 Lay Me Down (4:51); 19 Largo al factotum (G. Rossini)(4:32) *Roberto Servile, Failoni Chamber Orchestra, Will Humburg*; 20 Vissi d'arte (G. Puccini)(3:20) *Gabriela Benackova, Czech Philharmonic Orchestra, Bohumil Gregor.*

Review: Playing against the film's storyline, Chris Young's symphonic score paints a dark psychological portrait of the serial murderer who copies infamous crimes of past serial killers. Offsetting this evil poignancy is Young's deliciously frightening suspense and terror music. In one outstanding cue after another, he keeps reminding us that the terror is still there, even if offscreen. "Pastoral Horror" is a prime example of the music's duality, alternately horrifying and elegant, yet thoroughly captivating. "Lay Me Down," which concludes the score with a graceful dynamic, has slowly-swaying violins over a writhing sea of rustling strings in a powerful resolve to the music that's gone before. The cue—melodic yet ambient, compelling yet frightening—is penetrating, and recalls previous horrors while acknowledging the price of survival.

Randall D. Larson

Corrina, Corrina 🎵🎵🎵

1994, RCA Records; from the movie *Corrina, Corrina*, New Line Cinema, 1994.

Album Notes: *Music:* Thomas Newman; *Songs Producers:* Aaron Zigman, Ron Fair, Tony Berg, Bob Shad, Ancient Future, Ahmet Ertegun, Jerry Wexler, Bones Howe, Dick Jacobs, Henry Glover, J.D. Steele; *Engineers:* Michael C. Ross, John Paterno, Chris Papastephanou, Robert M. Biles, Tom Winslow, Tom Garneau, Tom Tucker, Jr., Shane Keller; *Album Executive Producers:* Ron Fair, Bonnie Greenberg, Paula Mazur, Jessie Nelson.

Selections: 1 We Will Find A Way (S. Diamond/S. Sheridan) (4:42) *Oleta Adams, Brenda Russell*; 2 Corrina, Corrina (M. Parish/B. Chapman/J. Williams) (3:39) *Ted Hawkins*; 3 Little Bitty Pretty One (R. Byrd) (2:23) *Thurston Harris*; 4 They Can't Take That Away From Me (G. & I. Gershwin) (2:41) *Sarah Vaughan*; 5 You Go To My Head (F. Coots/H. Gillespie) (6:24) *Louis Armstrong, Oscar Peterson*; 6 What A Difference A Day Makes (M. Grever/S. Adams) (2:29) *Dinah Washington*; 7 I Only Have Eyes For You (H. Warren/A. Dubin) (5:31) *Niki Haris, Peter Cox*; 8 Corrina, Corrina (M. Parish/B. Chapman/J. Williams) (2:53) *Big Joe Turner*; 9 It Don't Mean A Thing If It Ain't Got That Swing (E.K. Ellington/I. Mills) (3:10) *Ivie Anderson, Duke Ellington and His Orchestra*; 10 Over The Rainbow (H. Arlen/E.Y. Harburg) (4:46) *Jevetta Steele*; 11 'Reet Petite (T. Carlo/B. Gordy) (2:41) *Jackie Wilson*; 12 Pennies From Heaven (J. Burke/A. Johnson) (3:18)

Billie Holiday; 13 Finger Poppin' Time (H. Ballrd) (1:51) *Hank Ballard, The Midnighters*; 14 Home Movies (T. Newman) (2:03); 15 This Little Light Of Mine (trad.) (4:35) *The Steeles.*

Review: An interracial love affair between a black housekeeper and her white employer, father of a motherless little girl, is the interesting premise of this enjoyable comedy, which yielded this equally delightful soundtrack compilation. The 1950s setting of the film pretty much dictated what the music would be, with songs from the period performed by Sarah Vaughan, Dinah Washington, Billie Holiday, and Louis Armstrong and Oscar Peterson forming the core of this compilation. New songs, also in the style of the era, complement the soundtrack album, with the title tune, a jaunty little tune, making a particularly favorable impression in Big Joe Turner's rendition. Thomas Newman's single incidental music cue, "Home Movies," would suggest that he wrote more in this vein, though it never made it to the album.

The Cotton Club 🎵🎵🎵🎵

1984, Geffen Records; from the movie *The Cotton Club*, Orion Picture, 1984.

Album Notes: *Music:* John Barry; *Music Re-creation:* Bob Wilber; *Orchestrations:* Al Woodbury, John Barry; *Vocal and Dance Arrangements:* Joyce Brown; Orchestra conducted by John Barry; *Featured Musicians:* Dave Brown, Marky Markowitz, Randy Sandke, Lew Soloff (trumpet), Bob Wilber, Lawrence Feldman, Joe Temperley, Frank Wess, Chuck Wilson (reeds), Dan Barrett, Joel Helleny, Britt Woodman (trombone), John Goldsby (bass), Mike Peters (guitar, banjo), Chuck Riggs (drums), Mark Shane (piano); *Album Producer:* John Barry; *Engineer:* Tom Jung, Rebecca Everett, Fred Bova.

Selections: 1 The Mooche (E.K. Ellington/I. Mills) (3:29); 2 Cotton Club Stomp #2 (M. Parish/I. Mills/E.K. Ellington) (2:40); 3 Drop Me Off In Harlem (N. Kenny/E.K. Ellington) (3:03); 4 Creole Love Call (E.K. Ellington) (3:01) *Priscilla Baskerville*; 5 Ring Dem Bells (E.K. Ellington/I. Mills) (2:46); 6 East St. Louis Toodle-O (E.K. Ellington/B. Miley) (3:20); 7 Truckin' (T. Koehler/R. Bloom) (2:00); 8 Ill Wind (T. Koehler/H. Arlen) (2:17) *Lonette McKee*; 9 Cotton Club Stomp #1 (J. Hodges/H. Carney/E.K. Ellington) (2:49); 10 Mood Indigo (E.K. Ellington) (3:34); 11 Minnie The Moocher (C. Calloway/ I. Mills) (3:07) *Larry Marshall*; 12 Copper Colored Gal (B. Davis/J.F. Coote) (1:15) *Gregory Hines*; 13 Dixie Kidnaps Vera (J. Barry) (2:37); 14 The Depression Hits/Best Beats Sandman (J. Barry) (2:42); 15 Daybreak Express Medley (E.K. Ellington) (3:43).

Review: Music by Duke Ellington, and acceptable facsimiles by John Barry, make up this rousing soundtrack to a gangster movie set in Harlem in the 1930s. The big band recreations, in full digital sound, are tremendously exciting, and played to the hilt by a group of seasoned musicians for whom this kind of music no longer has any secret. An occasional vocal sparks the proceedings, with film star Gregory Hines contributing an excellent version of the classic "Copper Colored Gal." The cues by John Barry fit nicely within this program of standards, and add an element of originality to the soundtrack.

Courage Under Fire ♪♪♪

1996, Angel Records; from the movie *Courage Under Fire*, 20th Century-Fox, 1996.

Album Notes: *Music*: James Horner; *Orchestrations*: James Horner; *Music Editor*: Jim Henrikson; Orchestra conducted by James Horner; *Album Producers*: James Horner; *Engineer*: Shawn Murphy; *Assistant Engineers*: Andy Bass, Marc Gebauer, Dave Marquette, Jay Selvester, Kirsten Smith.

Selections: 1 Hymn (3:39); 2 Al Bathra/Main Title (10:12); 3 Friendly Fire/Ilario's Story (3:07); 4 The Elegy (3:46); 5 Courage Under Fire (6:38); 6 Monfriez's Suicide (3:21); 7 Night Mutiny (2:58); 8 The Betrayal (3:10); 9 Playing Back The Tape (2:55); 10 The Medal Of Honor/A Final Resting Place (14:39).

Review: When you're presented with track titles like "Hymn" and "The Elegy" on a soundtrack album for a film that isn't a biblical drama, you can't help but wonder if somebody isn't taking things a little too seriously. James Horner's *Courage Under Fire* score has a tendency to drown the listener in its good intentions, canonizing the fictional character Meg Ryan plays in the film, when the point of the narrative is that Ryan's character is all too human, neither superhero, coward or saint. The score is most convincing when it deals with the adrenaline-charged rhythms of the battlefield, from an ascending two-note motif in low brass (similar to an effect often employed by composer Jerry Goldsmith in scores like *Capricorn One*) to some fierce orchestral heroics that presage some of the exciting effects Horner achieved in his *Apollo 13* score. The above-mentioned "Hymn" and "Elegy" offer some moving, lyrical melodies that function quite beautifully on their own but pad out the album's lengthy denouement unmercifully.

Jeff Bond

Cousins ♪♪♪♪

1989, Warner Bros. Records; from the movie *Cousins*, Paramount Pictures, 1989.

Album Notes: *Music*: Angelo Badalamenti; *Orchestrations*: Angelo Badalamenti, Charles Samek, Ronnie Lawson; *Featured*

Musicians: Mike Lang (piano), Kirk Whalum (saxophone); Orchestra conducted by Angelo Badalamenti, Nick Perrito; *Album Producer*: Angelo Badalamenti; *Engineer*: Joel Moss; *Assistant Engineer*: Ethan Chase.

Selections: 1 Overture (3:27); 2 Maria's Theme (2:19); 3 Adulterer's Blues (2:08) *Kirk Whalum*; 4 Love Theme (3:20); 5 Adulterer's Blues Two (1:50) *Kirk Whalum*; 6 Cousins Waltz (2:46); 7 Montage (Maria's Theme) (2:41); 8 Love Theme (piano solo) (1:58); 9 Adulterer's Blues (jazz quintet) (2:20); 10 Classicval restaurant (3:34); 11 I Love You For Today (2:46); 12 Love Theme (Finale) (2:36); 13 Cousins Waltz (Credits) (3:10).

Review: There's something about the often avant-garde musical sensibilities of Angelo Badalamenti that lend itself easily to the creepy dreamscapes of David Lynch, but people tend to forget that the composer has penned some other, equally successful film scores for genres that are as far removed from *Twin Peaks* as you could imagine. *Cousins* is the enjoyable 1989 remake of the French farce *Cousin, Cousine*, and it contains a romantic score by Badalamenti that can be best described as infectious — the elegant piano solo which comprises the love theme, the daffy chase music that sounds like it's out of some Henry Mancini score from the '60s, and the lyrical "Cousins Waltz" all help to make this an easy-going, charming score, illustrating that Badalamenti can work quite well outside of atmospheric mood pieces and horror shows, if he's ever given the chance.

Andy Dursin

The Cowboys ♪♪♪♪♪

1994, Varese-Sarabande; from the movie *The Cowboys*, Warner Bros., 1974.

Album Notes: *Music*: John Williams; *Music Editor*: Donald Harris; The Warner Bros. Studio Orchestra, conducted by John Williams; *Album Producer*: John Williams.

Selections: 1 Main Title (2:18); 2 Schoolboys Or Cowboys? (1:09); 3 Learning The Ropes (1:28); 4 Wild Horses (1:40); 5 Deserted (1:40); 6 Crazy Alice (1:58); 7 Alternate Main Title (1:27); 8 The Ranch (2:31); 9 Overture (2:30); 10 Bedtime Story (1:44); 11 Rustlers (1:16); 12 Stealing Back The Herd (1:22); 13 Nightfall (1:53); 14 A Sad Day (1:33); 15 Into The Trap (2:12); 16 The Drive (1:42); 17 Summer's Over (1:29).

Review: It took 20 years for this soundtrack to get a commercial release, but it was well worth the wait. John Williams, who has often expressed himself in the adventure and epic genres, only wrote occasionally in the western idiom (unless you consider all the *Indiana Jones* films to be westerns of a different kind) but one happy exception was the score he wrote for *The*

Cowboys. Starring John Wayne as an aging, leather-tough trail master who takes along with him a band of inexperienced youngsters to drive a herd of cattle across 400 miles of the West's most treacherous territory after his regular hands desert him, the film elicited from the composer a rambunctious, Americana-flavored music, which at times evokes *The Reivers,* also directed by Mark Rydell, but most often creates its own poetic imagery. For several years, the only selection from the score that was available was the brilliant overture Williams recorded with The Boston Pops. Much shorter, and with different instrumentations, it is found here as the "Main Title," with the other tracks pretty much following the storyline from "Learning the Ropes," to "The Drive," which finds the young cowboys delivering the herd after successfully completing their journey. In an awkward bit of sequencing, however, an alternate version of the "Main Title" and the "Overture" have been inserted in the middle of the program, while both the "Entr'acte" and "End Credits," which are available on the laserdisc, are missing.

The Craft

The Craft 🎵🎵🎵

1996, Columbia Records; from the movie *The Craft,* Columbia Pictures, 1996.

Album Notes: *Music:* Graeme Revell; *Album Producer:* Ralph Sall; *Engineers:* Larry Ferguson, Ralph Sall.

Selections: 1 Tomorrow Never Knows (J. Lennon/P. McCartney) (4:14) *Our Lady Peace;* 2 I Have The Touch (P. Gabriel) (4:17) *Heather Nova;* 3 All This And Nothing (V. Dombroski) (4:19) *Sponge;* 4 Dangerous Type (R. Ocasek) (3:40) *Letters to Cleo;* 5 How Soon Is Now? (S. Morrissey/J. Marr) (4:27) *Love Spit Love;* 6 Dark Secret (M. Sweet) (4:03) *Matthew Sweet;* 7 Witches Song (M. Faithfull/J. Mavety/B. Reynolds/T. Stannard/S. York) (4:36) *Juliana Hatfield;* 8 Jump Into The Fire (H. Nilsson) (5:45) *Tripping Daisy;* 9 Under The Water (J. Kilcher/R. Sall) (4:59) *Jewel;* 10 Warning (R. Sall/T. DeLaughter) (4:45) *All Too Much;* 11 Spastica (J. Frischmann) (2:30) *Elastica;* 12 The Horror (R. Langdon) (4:50) *Spacehog;* 13 Bells, Books And Candles (G. Revell) (3:48).

Review: A supernatural thriller about four high school girls who discover their inner power through witchcraft, *The Craft* yielded this song compilation album which features an eclectic mix of cutting-edge bands and artists introducing new songs or doing covers of songs created by others, like The Beatles' "Tomorrow Never Knows," The Cars' "Dangerous Type," The Smiths' "How Soon Is Now," Peter Gabriel's "I Have The Touch," and Harry Nilsson's "Jump Into the Fire." This witches' brew works most of the time, with "All This and Nothing" by Sponge, "Witches Song" by Juliana Hatfield, and "Under the Water" by Jewel, among the tunes best remembered from the film, in which they make a perfect counterpoint to the screen action. Both Elastica and Spacehog present previously unreleased material ("Spastica" and "The Horror," respectively), with Graeme Revell contributing "Bells, Books and Candles," from his original score.

The Craft 🎵🎵🎵

1996, Varese-Sarabande Records; from the movie *The Craft,* Columbia Pictures, 19956.

Album Notes: *Music:* Graeme Revell; *Orchestrations:* Tim Simonec; *Music Editor:* Josh Winget; *Keyboards, Programming and Arrangements:* Roger Mason; *Album Producer:* Graeme Revell; *Engineer:* Mark Curry.

Selections: 1 Ours Is The Power (1:07); 2 Bitches Of Eastwick (3:18); 3 A Natural Witch (1:27); 4 Calling The Corners (1:31); 5 The Magic Store (2:19); 6 Bonnie (2:23); 7 Invocation (4:24); 8 The Glamour (1:58); 9 The Nightmare (1:47); 10 Behind The Curtain (2:16); 11 By The Power Of 3x3 (4:27); 12 Sarah's Revenge (1:37); 13 Trouble With Snakes And Insects (1:53); 14 I Bind You, Nancy (2:30); 15 Lightning Strikes (2:04).

Review: Graeme Revell has conjured up another inventive fantasy film score. Very similar to *The Crow* in its approach, he combines various opposing musical styles once again to create an unsettling mood. Indian chants are principally used ("The Magic Store") to separate "normal" reality from the supernatural world into which four young girls will cross once they begin dabbling in witchcraft. As the girls start using their powers, Revell mates the chanting with a rock track to signify these are '90s "Bitches of Eastwick."

David Hirsch

Crash 🎵🎵🎵

1996, Milan Records; from the movie *Crash,* Fine Line Features, 1996.

Album Notes: *Music:* Howard Shore; *Orchestrations:* Howard Shore; *Music Editor:* Suzana Peric; *Electronic Music Preparation:* Simon Franglen; Orchestra conducted by Howard Shore; *Featured Musicians:* Robert Piltch, Mike Francis, Edward Quinlan, James Tait, Rick Whitelaw, Tony Zory (electronic guitars), Erica Goodman, Marie Boisvert, Janice Lindskoog (harps), Joseph Orlowski, Melvin Berman, Douglas Stewart (woodwinds), Robin Engelman, Brian Leonard (percussion); *Album Producer:* Howard Shore; *Engineers:* Gary Gray.

Selections: 1 Crash (3:36); 2 CineTerra (1:04); 3 Mechanism Of Occupant Ejection (2:05); 4 Mirror Image (3:24); 5 Where's The Car? (2:39); 6 Sexual Logic (4:07); 7 Road Research Laboratory (2:12); 8 Mansfield Crash (3:37); 9 Chromium Bower (3:38); 10 A Benevolent Psychopathology (2:23); 11 Two Semi-Metallic Human Beings (2:22); 12 Triton (2:45); 13 Accident... Accident... (2:59); 14 A Crushed Convertible (1:55); 15 Prophecy Is Dirty And Ragged (5:48).

Review: *Crash*, David Cronenberg's latest examination of sexual aberration, features an unusual score, performed by a small group consisting of six electric guitars, three harps, three woodwinds and two percussionists, with the unusual ensemble creating a uniquely effective miasmic ambiance which emphasizes the contemporary sensuality of the picture. Created by Cronenberg's long-time collaborator Howard Shore, its highly modernistic, somewhat decadently erogenous accents are very suitable to the obsessive, carnal darkness of the filmmaker's cinematic vision. There are no real melodies, but the guitars and harps, which double one another, succeed in evoking an almost unbearable claustrophobic sensitivity. Remixing and resynthesizing the tracks also added to this chaotic ambiance. Though the overall discordant sound suffers somewhat on its own, Shore's inventiveness translates into an interesting and sensually charged score.

Randall D. Larson

Crimes of the Heart ♪♪♪♪♪

1986, Varese-Sarabande Records; from the movie *Crimes of the Heart*, Dino De Laurentiis Entertainment, 1986.

Album Notes: *Music*: Georges Delerue; Orchestra conducted by Georges Delerue; *Featured Soloists*: Roy Willox (alto sax), Ronnie Price (keyboard); *Album Producers*: Georges Delerue, Freddie Fields; *Engineer*: Eric Tomlinson.

Selections: 1 Introduction (2:40); 2 Crimes Of The Heart (4:30); 3 Meg (2:45); 4 Ice Cream (2:43); 5 Doc Porter (3:26); 6 Babe (1:00); 7 Night To Day (2:06); 8 Broom Chase (1:41); 9 Lonely Hearts Club (:55); 10 Meg And Babe (1:42); 11 Study (1:46); 12 Flirtation (1:37); 13 Willy Jay (2:46); 14 Toes (1:50); 15 Bus Ride (:30); 16 Old Granddaddy (2:50); 17 Sunset (1:32); 18 Main Theme (1:00); 19 Willy Jay Away (1:32); 20 Dusk For Night (1:39); 21 Crimes (:30); 22 End Title (4:30).

Review: Based on Beth Henley's 1980 eponymous stage play, *Crimes of the Heart* became a wonderful screen vehicle for Jessica Lange, Diane Keaton and Sissy Spacek, portraying three sisters who get back together momentarily in their North Carolina home and reflect about their past, the world around them and their relationship with one another, in a riveting display of superb acting and gripping melodramatic comedy. Enhancing the many moods of the film, and giving the action an extra boost of its own, Georges Delerue wrote a strongly appealing score, in which the main motif, a soulful saxophone romance leading to an exuberant waltz, developed in "Crimes of the Heart," sets the tone. Drawing upon his many resources as a master melodist, he detailed the sisters and other characters with whom they interrelate in individual cues that are among the choicest moments in this beautiful score, and imaginatively described in striking musical terms some of the action's most important scenes.

Criminal Law ♪♪♪½

1988, Varese-Sarabande; from the movie *Criminal Law*, Hemdale Film Corp., 1988

Album Notes: *Music*: Jerry Goldsmith; *Music Editor*: Kenneth Hall; Orchestra conducted by Jerry Goldsmith; *Album Producer*: Jerry Goldsmith; *Engineer*: Bruce Botnick.

Selections: 1 The Victim (2:29); 2 The Body (3:21); 3 Start Remembering (1:30); 4 About Last Night (1:24); 5 The Closet (2:29); 6 The Garden Pavillion (3:15); 7 The Drive (1:13); 8 Avenger (1:13); 9 The Game (1:58); 10 The Clinic (2:12); 11 Poor Ben (4:37); 12 Hostage (:46); 13 Burnout (1:13); 14 End Title (2:44).

Review: This second all-electronic score by Jerry Goldsmith, after the abrasive *Runaway*, is far more textural, moving from a fluttering, echoed pan flute effect to a delicately lyrical piano theme (the only acoustic sounds in the score) and some throbbing, ostinato-driven suspense cues for Martin Campbell's entry in the briefly-popular "lawyers-in-distress" film cycle of the late '80s. Unlike the obvious electronic sounds of *Runaway, Criminal Law* is often indistinguishable from acoustically-created music and it's an extremely listenable (albeit brief) album, although essentially ambient in nature. Like Goldsmith's earlier work on films like *Freud* and his *Twilight Zone* television scores, *Criminal Law* doesn't so much grab you by the throat as slowly hypnotize you.

Jeff Bond

Crimson Tide ♪♪

1995, Hollywood Records; from the movie *Crimson Tide*, Hollywood Pictures, 1995.

Album Notes: *Music*: Hans Zimmer; *Orchestrations*: Nick Glennie-Smith, Bruce Fowler, Ladd McIntosh, Suzette Moriarty; *Music Editor*: Bob Badami; Orchestra conducted by Nick Glennie-Smith; The London Choir conducted by Harry Gregson-Williams; *Featured Musician*: Malcolm McNab (trumpet); *Album Producers*: Hans Zimmer, Jay Rifkin; *Engineers*: Jay Rifkin, Alan Meyerson.

Selections: 1 Mutiny (8:58); 2 Alabama (23:50); 3 Little Ducks (2:03); 4 1SQ (18:04); 5 Roll Tide (7:34) *The London Choir*.

Review: This album of Hans Zimmer's score was heavily edited into five suites to create a lavish 67-minute symphonic presentation. Unfortunately, the downside of this overlong album (one track, "Alabama," is almost 24 minutes long!) is that the music spends too much time languishing on low-key "tension" music. The score is filled with seemingly wild electronic effects, and one can't help but grow tired of it all very quickly. As a result, there's quite often the feeling that you've heard the same passage before. Worse still, every so often Zimmer quotes a string passage that he used earlier in *Backdraft*. Perhaps this flurry of action music serves just to keep you awake.

David Hirsch

Criss Cross 🎵🎵ᵛ

1992, Intrada Records; from the movie *Criss Cross*, M-G-M, 1992.

Album Notes: *Music*: Trevor Jones; *Orchestrations*: Trevor Jones, Guy Dagul; Orchestra conducted by Guy Dagul; *Featured Musicians*: Trevor Jones, Guy Dagul, Roger King (synthesizers), Andy Sheppard (saxophone), Mike Moran (synthesizer programmer), Gerry Leonard (electric guitar); *Album Producer*: Trevor Jones; *Engineer*: Roger King.

Selections: 1 Opening Titles (2:02); 2 Chris Hitches A Ride (3:30); 3 Tracy Cries (5:19); 4 Summer In The Keys (1:43); 5 Drug Revelation (2:39); 6 Chris At Transent (1:27); 7 Fine mi lassa (V. Bellini)(1:41); 8 Moon To Pool (1:44); 9 The Bust (3:40); 10 Chris And Mum Move (3:07); 11 End Credits (3:11).

Review: Trevor Jones monothematic score for this quiet relationship drama is suitably small and poignant. Drawn around an acoustic guitar melody embellished by massed strings, the music lends a voice to the inner hearts of the working mother and teenage son whose broken relationship becomes the focus of the story. Aside from the guitar theme, Jones provides a variety of ambient material to support activities, while the guitar theme always speaks for the heart. As pretty as the main theme is, it's rather simple and as a result it grows rather repetitive. The synth motifs are effective but don't make for entirely enjoyable listening. *Criss Cross* is a pretty score but in the end it may be too reliant upon its one melodic theme to sustain the entire score. Likeable but not a big repeat player.

Randall D. Larson

Critters 🎵🎵🎵

1993, Intrada Records; from the movie *Critters*, New Line Cinema, 1993.

Album Notes: *Music*: David Newman; Orchestra conducted by David Newman; *Album Producer*: Douglass Fake; *Engineer*: Tim Boyle.

Selections: 1 Main Title (6:46); 2 Charlie's Accident (:43); 3 Jay And Brad Look For The Critters (2:38); 4 Jeff Is Dinner (:59); 5 Looking In The Cellar (4:25); 6 The Bounty Hunters/Critters Get Steve (3:51); 7 Critters Hunt For Lunch (3:56); 8 Brad Burns A Critter (3:13); 9 They're Growing (2:09); 10 Meanwhile Back At The House (2:08); 11 Looking For Chewy (1:41); 12 Brad Goes After April (2:17); 13 The Critters Are Destroyed (3:50); 14 The House Returns (5:06); 15 Critter Skitter (D. Newman/J. Vigran) (3:27).

Review: A minor, long-forgotten classic horror film, *Critters* gave David Newman an unusual opportunity to write a score which effectively blends electronics and a full orchestra in a slow build-up that forcefully reaches a climax and dissipates until the unavoidable sequel. In an unusual display of craftmanship, Newman only uses the electronics at the very start of the "Main Title," during the pre-title segment set in outer space (where the critters of the title are growing and multiplying before they invade Earth), but as soon as the action switches to the farm where most of the action next takes place, the orchestra takes over. From then on, most of the cues rely on the orchestra and individual solo instruments, adding layers of frightful sounds that paint the horror pictured in the film as the voracious man-eating critters wreak havoc in middle America.

Only once the critters have been destroyed does the music relax and end on a peaceful note. At the same time, in another compositional tour-de-force, Newman has devised many soft-sounding, elegiac cues that belie and contrast the tension in the film. It is a clever device that forces the listener's attention, while it effectively conveys the power of the drama unfolding on the screen. Taken as a listening experience, the score offers many inspiring moments, though ultimately it probably will appeal mostly to those who have seen the film and have enjoyed it thoroughly.

Crooklyn

Crooklyn 🎵🎵🎵ᵛ

1994, MCA Records; from the movie *Crooklyn*, Universal Pictures, 1994.

Album Notes: *Song Producers*: Al Bell, Sly Stone, Robert Poindexter, Richard Poindexter, Poncho Cristal, Eugene Record, Thom Bell, Wandell Quezerque, Stan Vincent, James Brown,

David Rubinson, Narada Michael Walden; *Album Executive Producer*: Spike Lee; *Engineer*: Herb Powers.

Selections: 1 Crooklyn (E.K. Archer/K. Blake/D. Clear/J. Davis/A. Muhammad) (4:32) *The Crooklyn Dodgers*; 2 Respect Yourself (M. Rice/L. Ingram) (4:53) *The Staple Singers*; 3 Everyday People (S. Stewart) (2:19) *Sly And The Family Stone*; 4 Pusher Man (C. Mayfield) (5:02) *Curtis Mayfield*; 5 Thin Line Between Love And Hate (R. Poindexter/R. Poindexter/J. Members) (3:24) *The Persuaders*; 6 El Pito (I'll Never Go Back To Georgia) (J. Sabater/J. Cuba) (5:32) *Joe Cuba*; 7 ABC (A. Mizell/F. Perren/D. Richards/B. Gordy) (2:57) *The Jackson Five*; 8 Oh Girl (E. Record) (3:47) *The Chi-Lites*; 9 Mighty Love (J. Jefferson/B. Hawes/C. Simmons) (4:57) *The Spinners*; 10 Mr. Big Stuff (J. Broussard/R. Williams/C. Washington) (2:46) *Jean Knight*; 11 Ooh Child (S. Vincent) (3:17) *The Five Stairsteps*; 12 Pass The Peas (J. Brown/C.F. Bobbit/ J. Starks) (3:11) *The JB's*; 13 Time Has Come Today (J. Chambers/W. Chambers) (4:54) *The Chambers Brothers*; 14 People Make The World Go Round (T. Bell/L. Creed) (5:05) *Marc Dorsey*.

Review: Shamelessly old school, this soundtrack reaches back for vintage Jackson 5 ("ABC"), Sly & the Family Stone ("Everyday People"), JB's ("Pass the Peas"), Staple Singers ("Respect Yourself"), Chambers Brothers ("Time Has Come Today") and too many more to mention. The Crooklyn Dodgers' hip-hopping "Crooklyn," however, pales before such vaunted company.

Gary Graff

Crooklyn: volume II   *♪♪♪*

1994, MCA Records; from the movie *Crooklyn*, Universal Pictures, 1994.

Album Notes: *Song Producers*: John Schroeder, Thom Bell, Sly Stone, Hal Davis, James Brown, Manu Dibango, Stan Watson, Al Bell, Harvey Aveme, Isaac Hayes, Henry Cosby & Smokey Robinson, Johnny Nash; *Album Executive Producer*: Spike Lee; *Engineer*: Herb Powers.

Selections: 1 People Make The World Go Round (T. Bell/L. Creed) (6:22) *The Stylistics*; 2 Signed, Sealed, Delivered, I'm Yours (S. Wright/S. Wright/L. Garrett/L.M. Hardaway) (2:38) *Stevie Wonder*; 3 Bra (P. Patterson/S. Scipion) (5:02) *Cymande*; 4 I'm Stone In Love With You (A. Bell/T. Bell/L. Creed) (3:17) *The Stylistics*; 5 Everybody Is A Star (S. Stewart) (3:00) *Sly & The Family Stone*; 6 Never Can Say Goodbye (C. Davis) (2:56) *The Jackson Five*; 7 Soul Power (J. Brown) (4:23) *James Brown*; 8 Soul Makossa (M. Dibango) (4:25) *Manu Dibango*; 9 La La (Means I Love You) (W. Hart/T. Bell) (3:19) *The Delfonics*; 10 I'll Take You There (A. Isbell) (4:31) *The Staple Singers*; 11 Puerto Rico (E. Palmieri/I. Quintana) (6:57) *Eddie Palmieri*; 12 Theme From Shaft (I. Hayes/J. Allen) (3:19) *Isaac Hayes*; 13 Tears Of A Clown (S. Wonder/ H. Cosby/W.

Robinson) (3:03) *Smokey Robinson & The Miracles*; 14 I Can See Clearly Now (J. Nash) (2:41) *Johnny Nash*.

Review: Continuing along the same lines as volume one, this second anthology of wonderful 1960s black pop tunes delivers the goods, with tunes by The Stylistics, Stevie Wonder, The Jackson Five, Smokey Robinson, Isaac Hayes, Johnny Nash, and several others. Uncomplicated, direct, enjoyable, it may be a throwback to happier (?) times, but it's also something that you can put on your CD player, and play many times over, just for the fun of it.

Crossing the Line   *♪♪♪*

1991, Varese-Sarabande Records; from the movie *Crossing the Line*, Miramax Films, 1991.

Album Notes: *Music*: Ennio Morricone; The Unione musicisti di Roma, conducted by Ennio Morricone; *Album Producer*: Ennio Morricone.

Selections: 1 Running In The Park (:53); 2 Main Titles (3:26); 3 Beth Says No (2:47); 4 Road Training 1 (2:18); 5 Road Training 3 (1:34); 6 Rain In Gobi Desert (1:18); 7 Journey To Fight (3:19); 8 Round Four (1:03); 9 Road Training 2 (1:09); 10 The Wasteland (2:38); 11 Round One (2:14); 12 Round Two (1:40); 13 Round Six (3:37); 14 There's Blood On That Money (2:53); 15 Danny Runs Home (1:18); 16 End Titles (3:24).

Review: Ennio Morricone's darkly-hued score for orchestra and chorus powerfully underlines the drama and the tension in this film set in Scotland about a miner, a man of ideals, down on his luck and in search of his own self. Many of the cues in the score are on the down side, with moody expressions reflecting both the rural environment in which the action unfolds and the feelings of the film's main character, played by Liam Neeson. Following his slow ascent to personal salvation, the music builds up to a climax which sums up his experience, and points the way to a gradual acceptance of the fate he's inherited. In the profusely descriptive score, some cues emerge for their lyricism, notably "Road Training 2," or "The Wasteland," in which the main theme, played by a saxophone against a floating string line, is inexplicably marred by a sudden glitch in the recording.

Crossroads   *♪♪♪♪*

1986, Warner Bros. Records; from the movie *Crossroads*, Warner Bros., 1986.

Album Notes: *Music*: Ry Cooder; *Featured Musicians*: Ry Cooder, Otis Taylor (guitar), Jim Keltner, John Price (drums), Jim Dickinson, Van Dyke Parks, William Smith (piano, organ), Alan Pasqua (synthesizer), Nathan East, Jorge Calderon, Rich-

> "The industry pushed them away for years, but distinctive themes for (television) shows are coming back. Themes are great hooks. When you hear them, they set up for something good to come."
>
> **Joe LoDuca**
> *(Detroit Free Press, 4-27-97)*

ard Holmes (bass), Sonny Terry, Frank Frost, John Logan (harmonica), George Bohannon (baritone horn), Walt Sereth (saxophone), Miguel Cruz (percussion); *Album Producer*: Ry Cooder; *Engineer*: Mark Ettel.

Selections: 1 Crossroads (R. Johnson) (4:23) *Ry Cooder*; 2 Down In Mississippi (J.B. Lenoir) (4:26) *Terry Evans, Bobby King, Willie Green, Jr.*; 3 Cotton Needs Pickin' (F. Frost/R. Holmes/O. Taylor/J. Price) (2:58); 4 Viola Lee Blues (N. Lewis) (3:11) *Ry Cooder*; 5 See You In Hell, Blind Boy (R. Cooder) (2:12); 6 Nitty Gritty Mississippi (F. Burch/D. Hill) (2:57) *Jim Dickinson*; 7 He Made A Woman Out Of Me (F. Burch/D. Hill) (4:12) *Amy Madigan*; 8 Feelin' Bad Blues (R. Cooder) (4:17); 9 Somebody's Callin' My Name (trad.) (1:45) *Bobby King, Sam King, Arnold McCuller, Willie Green, Jr.*; 10 Willie Brown Blues (R. Cooder/J. Seneca) (3:46) *Joe Seneca*; 11 Walkin' Away Blues (S. Terry/R. Cooder) (3:40).

Review: Rooted in the music of the South, this excellent soundtrack album will mostly appeal to anyone interested in the blues, but it should also find a broader audience among those who have enjoyed this saga of a young Juilliard scholar who embarks on a tour of the Mississippi Delta, allegedly to discover Robert Johnson's "unknown 30th song." Deftly performing the works of local songwriters, including Johnson's title tune, as well as his own compositions, Cooder and cohorts deliver a potent brew of foot-stompers and gut-wrenchers, both vocal and instrumental, that are difficult to resist, let alone ignore.

The Crow

The Crow 🎵🎵🎵🎵

1994, Varese-Sarabande; from the movie *The Crow*, Miramax/ Dimension Pictures, 1994.

Album Notes: *Music*: Graeme Revell; *Orchestrations*: Tim Simonec, Graeme Revell; *Music Editor*: Dick Bernstein; Orches-

tra conducted by Tim Simonec; *Featured Musicians*: Djivan Gasparyan (Armenian duduk), Kazu Matsui (shakuhachi), Oscar Brashear (trumpet), M.B. Gordy (percussion), Karl Verheyen, Philip Tallman (guitars), Graeme Revell (keyboards), Bobbie Page, Darlene Koldenhoven, Chris Snyder (voices); *Album Producer*: Graeme Revell; *Engineer*: Dan Wallin.

Selections: 1 Birth Of The Legend (6:16); 2 Resurrection (2:10); 3 The Crow Descends (2:30); 4 Remembrance (2:54); 5 Rain Forever (2:32); 6 Her Eyes... So Innocent (2:45); 7 Tracking The Prey (3:35); 8 Pain And Retribution (2:34); 9 Believe In Angels (3:31); 10 Captive Child (2:32); 11 Devil's Night (2:30); 12 On Hallowed Ground (2:42); 13 Inferno (5:02); 14 Return To The Grave (3:45); 15 Last Rites (3:55).

Review: Gritty urban score that successfully mixes diverse elements of jazz and rock music with European, Eastern and Island elements. Electric guitars unconventionally share the spotlight with an Armenian duduk and a Japanese shakuhachi. There's even two remarkably tender love themes, a complete contrast from everything else, one for the back-from-the-dead rock musician who seeks vengeance on the punks who murdered both him and his fiancee, and one for the child who loved them both. Dark, deeply moving, at times disturbing, but boldly creative.

David Hirsch

The Crow: City of Angels
🎵🎵🎵▿

1996, Miramax Records; from the movie *The Crow: City of Angels*, Miramax/ Dimension Films, 1996.

Album Notes: *Song Producers*: Ric Ocasek, Terry Dale, Ulrich White, Polly Jean Harvey, John Parish, Flood, Tricky, Dobie, The Gravediggaz, Jason Ross, Jason Pollock, Tom Morris, Bill Bottell, Paul Leary, Julian Raymond, Phil Kaffel, Ross Robinson, Matt Wallace, Thorn Wilson, Iggy Pop, Eric Ross, Pet, Tony G, Julio G; *Engineers*: Pat McCarthy, Terry Date, Flood, Ali Staton, Tom Morris, Blair Lamb, Mark Cross, Stuart Sullivan, Phil Kaffel, Chuck Johnson, Matt Wallace, Robert Carranza, Tony Gonzalez.

Selections: 1 Gold Dust Woman (S. Nicks) (5:07) *Hole*; 2 I'm Your Boogieman (H.W. Casey/R. Finch) (4:27) *White Zombie*; 3 Jurassitol (Filter) (5:13) *Filter*; 4 Naked Cousin (PJ Harvey) (3:56) *PJ Harvey*; 5 In A Lonely Place (I. Curtis/P. Hook/S. Morris/B. Summer) (5:58) *Bush*; 6 Tonite Is A Special Nite (Tricky/A. Campbell/R. Diggs) (4:41) *Tricky vs. The Gravediggaz*; 7 Shelf Life (J. Ross/J. Pollock) (4:30) *Seven Mary Three*; 8 Knock Me Out (L. Perry/M. Wilson-Piper/G. Slick) (6:48) *Linda Perry, Grace*

Slick; 9 Paper Dress (V.T. Lewis/D. Herbert) (4:44) *Toadies*; 10 Spit (B. West) (5:52) *NY Loose*; 11 Sean Olson (B. Welch/J. Davis/ D. Silveria/J. Staffer/R. Arizu) (4:46) *Korn*; 12 Teething (S. Carpenter/C. Cheng/A. Cunningham/C. Moreno) (3:33) *Deftones*; 13 I Wanna Be Your Dog (J. Osteberg/D. Alexander/R. Asteton/S. Asteton) (4:40) *Iggy Pop*; 14 Li'l Boots (L. Papineau/ T. Bates) (4:08) *Pet*; 15 City Of Angels (Frost/G. RueDaFlores/J. Gonzalez/K. Gully) (4:52) *Above The Law, Frost*.

Review: Following a predecessor that hit No. 1 is an unenviable task — especially since *The Crow* also established a foothold for modern (aka alternative) rock in Hollywood. *City of Angels* didn't hit the same heights, but it's nearly as good, with Hole's steroid-fueled version of Fleetwood Mac's "Gold Dust Woman," White Zombie's "I'm Your Boogieman" and an inspired duet by Linda Perry and Jefferson Airplane/Starship matron Grace Slick on "Knock Me Out." Tricky and The Gravediggaz team up on the head-bobbing "Tonite is a Special Nite," and Iggy Pop's "I Wanna Be Your Dog" is a welcome inclusion on any rock collection.

Gary Graff

The Crow: City of Angels
♫♫♫♭

1996, Miramax/Hollywood Records; from the movie *The Crow: City of Angels*, Miramax/ Dimension Pictures, 1996.

Album Notes: *Music*: Graeme Revell; *Orchestrations*: Tim Simonec, Graeme Revell; *Music Editor*: Josh Winget; *Keyboard and Programming*: Graeme Revell; Orchestra conducted by Tim Simonec; *Featured Musicians*: Masakazu Yoshizawa (shakuhachi), M.B. Gordy (drums, percussion), Karl Verheyen (guitars); *Album Producer*: Graeme Revell; *Engineer*: Wolfgang Aichholz.

Selections: 1 City Of Angels (3:19); 2 Camera Obscura (2:27); 3 The Crow Rises (3:14); 4 Santa Muerte (1:17); 5 "...A Dream On The Way To Death" (2:13); 6 Temple Of Pain (2:46); 7 A Murder Of Crows (1:59); 8 Mirangula: Sign Of The Crow (2:03); 9 Lament For A Lost Son (3:30); 10 "Hush Little Baby..." (3:03); 11 Dias de las murtes (3:31); 12 The Campanile (4:11); 13 La Masquera (5:09); 14 "I'll Wait For You" (1:49); 15 Believe In Angels (G. Revell/H. Nova) (5:43) *Graeme Revell, Heather Nova*.

Review: Graeme Revell's score for this sequel is decidedly darker than his work for the original, if that's even possible. It's a true mark of talent that he can form something fresh from what was simply a poor retread of the original film. Once again, Revell combines an eclectic mix of instrumentation and vocals,

from the almost ordinary chant "Santa Muerte" to the gloomy and twisted "Temple of Pain." The original theme from *The Crow* is quoted on several tracks and Revell co-wrote the song "Believe in Angels" with singer Heather Nova.

David Hirsch

The Crucible ♫♫♫♭

1996, RCA Victor; from the movie *The Crucible*, 20th Century-Fox, 1996.

Album Notes: *Music*: George Fenton; *Orchestrations*: Jeff Atmajian; *Music Pre-Production and Synthesizers*: Adrian Thomas; Orchestra conducted by George Fenton; *Album Producers*: George Fenton, Eliza Thompson; *Engineer*: Paul Hulme.

Selections: 1 Front Titles: Dancing In The Forest (5:18); 2 John Proctor (3:55); 3 The Village (2:06); 4 Reverend Hale (2:56); 5 Meeting At The Inn (1:25); 6 Tituba's Confession (3:34); 7 Judge Danforth Arrives (1:12); 8 Vengeance (4:44); 9 Elizabeth Accused (2:24); 10 Hale Leaves The Village (2:45); 11 Taking Elizabeth (3:02); 12 Interrogation (5:44); 13 The Hanging (2:12); 14 Abigail Disappears; 15 The Beach (2:10); 16 Proctor Confesses (6:52); 17 Forgive Us (End Credits) (3:18).

Review: This depressing tale about sexual hysteria and religious persecution in 17th-century Salem, Mass. translated itself into a striking score for George Fenton, who wrote a series of cues well-designed to subliminally enhance the screen action. Based on Arthur Miller's wrenching play, a thinly disguised indictment written at the height of the McCarthy witch hunt of the 1950s, the film depicted the religious repression that follows accusations by some sexually exacerbated Puritan girls that a local farmer is an agent of the Devil. The main motifs devised by Fenton to underscore the story strictly evoke the drama in a very subdued way, more threatening than any violent outburst. Occasionally, a simple melody suggests the innocence of the victims ("Elizabeth Accused"), but much of the music is bathed in the undefined ominous moods that permeate it. A heady score it may be, but a magnificent one nonetheless.

Cry Freedom ♫♫♫♭

1987, MCA Records; from the movie *Cry Freedom*, Universal Pictures, 1987.

Album Notes: *Music*: George Fenton, Jonas Gwangwa; *Orchestrations*: George Fenton, Peter Whitehouse; Orchestra conducted by George Fenton; *Vocal Director*: Jonas Gwangwa; *Featured Musicians*: Torera (Mbira), Thebe Lipere (Berembau, percussion); *"Shebeen" Band*: Lucky Ranku (guitar), Ernest Mothle (bass), Fats Mogoboya (congas), Churchill Jolobe (drums), Mervin Africa (piano), Dudu Pukwana, Teddy Osei, Bheki Mseleku (saxophone), David De Fries (trumpet); *Album Producers*: George Fenton, Keith Grant; *Engineer*: Keith Grant.

Selections: 1 Crossroads—A Dawn Raid (2:16); 2 Gumboots (1:46); 3 Black Township (2:32); 4 Shebeen Queen (2:58); 5 Asking For Trouble (2:23); 6 Dangerous Country (1:38); 7 Detention (2:00); 8 The Mortuary (2:27); 9 The Funeral (September 25, 1987) (4:40); 10 At The Beach (3:25); 11 The Getaway (3:23); 12 The Frontier (2:59); 13 Last Thoughts (1:35); 14 Deadline (2:15); 15 The Phone Call (2:01); 16 Telle Bridge (2:47); 17 Soweto—and vocal reprise (1:08); 18 Cry Freedom (4:41).

Review: For Richard Attenborough's moving depiction of apartheid as experienced by newspaperman Donald Woods and South African activist Stephen Biko, George Fenton has delved deeply into African musical traditions to create a score which is rich in rhythm, song and soft melody. Its combination of orchestral and vocal music, African and European, sorrowful and triumphant, gives it a unique quality. There are four primary themes, two African and two European in style. The first half of the film tells Biko's story, and the music consequently is predominantly African. After his death, the film focuses on Woods' efforts to publicize Biko's martyrdom, and the European music dominates amid faint echoes of the African sounds.

The closing song, "Cry Freedom" (sung by Fenton and Gwangwa, backed by a large choir), reflects the pain and suffering of what Biko and too many others have gone through in the cause of freedom; yet the music remains filled with pride, hope, and confidence. Despite the suffering, it suggests that the cause is not lost.

Randall D. Larson

Cry, the Beloved Country
♪♪♪

1995, Epic Soundtrax; from the movie *Cry, the Beloved Country*, Miramax Films, 1995.

Album Notes: *Music*: John Barry; The English Chamber Orchestra, conducted by John Barry; *Album Producer*: John Barry; *Engineer*: Shawn Murphy.

Selections: 1 Main Title/The Letter (3:36); 2 The Beginning Of The Journey (2:10); 3 The Train To Johannesburg (2:48); 4 You've Been Robbed (1:28); 5 Emaxambeni (E. Nomvete)(2:29) *The Havana Swingsters*; 6 I've Been A Bad Woman (2:31); 7 Is It My Son? (2:32); 8 He Was Our Only Child (1:42); 9 What Sort Of Life Did They Lead (1:25); 10 Hamba Notsokolo (D. Masuka)(2:37) *Dorothy Masuka*; 11 Bastards, Bloody Bastards (1:03); 12 Did It Seem Heavy? (:48); 13 Cry, Cry The Beloved

Country (1:45); 14 Christ, Forsake Me Not (3:19); 15 The Boys Club (1:36); 16 We Taught Him Nothing (2:05); 17 Amazing Grace (trad.) (3:33) *Ladysmith Black Mambazo*; 18 Go Well Umfundisi (1:09); 19 Do Not Spoil My Pleasure (2:38); 20 It Is My Son—That Killed Your Son (3:53); 21 The Marriage (2:55); 22 The Shadow Of Death (2:53); 23 The Fifteenth Day (3:17).

Review: Set in South Africa at the height of apartheid, this second film adaptation of Alan Paton's striking novel about two men, a white patriarch and a black minister brought together by a murder, prompted John Barry to write a fluid score that strangely contrasts with the racial tension in the action. His various cues, long on melodic orchestral lines but relatively short on real emotion, seem a far cry from the more-to-the-point music he wrote for *Born Free* in 1966, in which his use of African drums and sonorities at least had the merits of suggesting in strong evocative terms the rugged environment and some of the rapid-pace action in that film. Here, the music is at best serviceable, though, true to the composer's reputation as a master melodist, it is also very attractive. Tracks by South African recording stars (The Havana Swingsters, Ladysmith Black Mambazo, et al.) are awkwardly interspersed.

The Cure ♪♪♪⌐

1995, GRP Records; from the movie *The Cure*, Universal Pictures, 1995.

Album Notes: *Music*: Dave Grusin; *Featured Musicians*: Dean Parks, George Doering (guitars), Jimmy Johnson (electric bass), Harvey Mason (drums), Mike Fisher (percussion), Jim Walker (recorder, penny-whistle, alto flute), Tommy Morgan (hamonica, blues harp), Dave Grusin (piano), Ralph Grierson (orchestral piano); conducted by Dave Grusin; *Album Producers*: Dave Grusin, Scott Grusin; *Engineers*: John Richards, Michael Landy, Scott Grusin.

Selections: 1 First Visit (1:52); 2 Battleship (1:20); 3 Shopping Cart Ride (1:20); 4 "Soon as they find a cure..." (1:52); 5 Candy Montage (1:33); 6 Gathering Leaves (2:12); 7 Bedtime/Big Changes (2:54); 8 Mississippi Montage (2:07); 9 "Make mine a T-bone" (1:34); 10 A Million Light Years (3:17); 11 Found Money (2:13); 12 Chase And Confrontation (2:46); 13 Going Home (2:59); 14 "We call it a miracle" (1:56); 15 Rain/ Realization (1:41); 16 Requiem (3:25); 17 Last Visit (2:17); 18 Down The River/End Credits (5:30).

Review: A lyrical, touching score by Dave Grusin accompanied this 1995 drama of two young boys learning to cope with terminal illness. Much like his score for *On Golden Pond* and equally reminiscent of *The Heart Is a Lonely Hunter*, Grusin utilizes his roots in orchestral film scoring and jazz recording in combining both poignant, emotional cues and strong, bouncy country/R&B tracks, giving the film an atmospheric, rural musical accompaniment. As with many Grusin albums (and soundtracks), most of the selections here are performed by the composer on piano with solid backing from fellow jazz artists, including Jim Walker, Dean Parks, George Doering, and Jimmy Johnson. If you enjoy Grusin's jazz albums and want a taste of his film scoring, *The Cure* works as a perfect introductory album, just as it comes highly recommended for listeners already accustomed to his fine work for movies and television.

Andy Dursin

Curly Sue ♫♫♭

1991, Giant Records; from the movie *Curly Sue,* Warner Bros., 1991.

Album Notes: *Music*: Georges Delerue; Orchestra conducted by Georges Delerue; *Album Producer*: Georges Delerue; *Engineer*: Bobby Fernandez.

Selections: 1 Main Title (3:05); 2 Thirty-Five-Thirty (P. Williams) (3:34); 3 Two Shades Of Grey (2:26); 4 Innocent Believer (J. Hughes III/M. Deakin) (4:34) *2YZ, Terry Wood*; 5 A Hot Bath And A Pizza, Aah! (1:01); 6 They Cut My Hair (2:15); 7 Big Girls Go To School (1:41); 8 Grey Was A Girl Once, Too (3:45); 9 Yacht Club Swing (J.C. Johnson/T. Waller/H. Autrey)(3:10); 10 Git Down (J. Hughes III/M. Deakin)(4:53) *2YZ, Andrea Salazar, Kenyatta Vaughn*; 11 Every Girl Needs A Mom (4:50); 12 Someone's Always Hitting Bill (1:40); 13 Bill Can Be Cool/Shop N' Bop (G. Delerue/J. Smalley)(2:55); 14 The Train Calls To Bill (2:30); 15 You Never Know (S. Dorff/J. Betts)(4:03) *Ringo Starr*; 16 Separation And Reunion (3:48).

Review: John Hughes has worked with virtually every major composer in Hollywood, talents ranging from John Williams, Michael Kamen, Alan Silvestri, Bruce Broughton, Jerry Goldsmith and Maurice Jarre, and his 1991 comedy *Curly Sue*, Hughes' most recent directorial effort, sported an adequate score by the late Georges Delerue. The music is lyrical with long, flowing melodic lines, the trademark of Delerue, who came from a background in France where he scored numerous films for Francois Truffaut and other esteemed directors. This score is forgettable, genteel, and harmless, working to convey a fairy tale quality in Hughes' film, though, like a lot of Delerue's Hollywood work from this time, doesn't quite have the freshness or spontaneity of some of his earlier works. The album also includes several source music tracks, along with a catchy Ringo Starr ballad, "You Never Know," written by Steve Dorff.

Andy Dursin

D3: The Mighty Ducks ♫♭

1996, Hollywood Records; from the movie *D3: The Mighty Ducks*, Walt Disney Pictures, 1996.

Album Notes: *Music*: J.A.C. Redford; *Orchestrations*: J.A.C. Redford, Carl Johnson, Greg Smith, Marty Jabara, Thomas Pasatieri; Orchestra conducted by J.A.C. Redford; *Song Producers*: Michael Phillip-Wojewoda, The Stone Coyotes, Mark Alan Miller, Andy Wallace, Little Steven, Donnie Wahlberg, Tommy LiPuma, Queen, John Spinks; *Album Producer*: J.A.C. Redford; *Engineer*: Geoff Foster.

Selections: 1 Grade 9 (A. Creeggan/J. Creeggan/S. Paige/E. Robertson/T. Stewart)(2:54) *Barenaked Ladies*; 2 Changing Of The Guard (B. Keith)(4:13) *The Stone Coyotes*; 3 Hey Man (D. Hill/A. Bonter)(2:58) *The Poorboys*; 4 Shake 'Em Down (S. Van Zandt)(3:13) *Southside Johnny*; 5 Good Vibrations (D. Wahlberg/M. Wahlberg/Spice)(4:31) *Marky Mark & The Funky Bunch*; 6 Ac-Cent-Tchu-Ate The Positive (H. Arlen/J. Mercer)(3:54) *Dr. John*; 7 We Will Rock You (B. May)(2:02) *Queen*; 8 Winning It All (J. Spinks)(3:22) *The Outfield*; 9 D3: The Might Ducks Main Title (3:29); 10 Mr. Goldberg's Wild Ride (2:21); 11 Morning Showdown (4:48); 12 Victory Over The Varsity (4:54).

Review: The weakest of the "Ducks" films actually has one of the series' more interesting soundtracks, though it's nothing particularly special. Barenaked Ladies' "Grade 9" is a good showcase of the Canadian band's wit, while Dr. John's "Accent-tchu-ate the Positive" and Southside Johnny's "Shake 'em Down" are classy inclusions. Most of the set belongs to J.A.C. Redford's score, which is better off in the penalty box than on your CD player.

Gary Graff

Damage ♫♫♫

1992, Varese-Sarabande; from the movie *Damage*, 1992.

Album Notes: *Music*: Zbigniew Preisner; The Symphonic Orchestra of Warsaw, conducted by Wojciech Michniewski; *Featured Soloists*: Lapinski Zdzislaw (cello), Konrad Mastylo (piano), the Tomasz Stonko Jazz Group; *Album Producer*: Zbigniew Preisner; *Engineers*: Rafal Paczkowski, Leszek Kaminski.

Selections: 1 Introduction (1:45); 2 The Last Time (3:01); 3 Stephen I (:45); 4 Anna I (1:12); 5 At The Beginning (1:34); 6 Cafe Royal (1:46); 7 Anna II (1:36); 8 Intimacy (1:28); 9 Brussels-Paris (1:22); 10 Lutecia Hotel (1:22); 11 Memories (2:03); 12 In The Country (2:20); 13 The Night (2:30); 14 Dramatic Departure (3:19); 15 Late Thought (1:18); 16 Stephen II (:52); 17

The Last Time II (3:01); 18 Fatal Exit (1:04); 19 Memories Are Made For This (2:05); 20 Damage (1:43); 21 End Title (1:44).

Review: Zbigniew Preisner follows British politician Jeremy Irons down the road to ruin in an affair with his son's girlfriend, Juliette Binoche. One might expect a score of hot sexual tension, ala *Body Heat*, but Preisner mainly uses a classical air to express the stuffiness of the English family and make the affair seem that much more "dirty." Even the occasional use of a jazz motif (particularly on "The Last Time") only further acts to degrade the conduct of Irons and Binoche.

David Hirsch

Damien: Omen II ♫♫♫♫

1988, Silva Screen; from the movie *Damien: Omen II*, 20th Century-Fox, 1978.

Album Notes: *Music*: Jerry Goldsmith; *Orchestrations*: Arthur Morton; Orchestra conducted by Lionel Newman; *Choral Director*: John McCarthy; *Album Producer*: Jerry Goldsmith; *Engineer*: Eric Tomlinson.

Selections: 1 Main Title (5:01); 2 Runaway Train (2:39); 3 Claws (3:15); 4 Thoughtful Night (3:08); 5 Broken Ice (2:21); 6 Fallen Temple (2:54); 7 I Love You, Mark (4:39); 8 Shafted (3:00); 9 The Knife (3:21); 10 End Title (3:25).

Review: Jerry Goldsmith adapted much of his music for the original *Omen* thriller for this sequel, expanding his orchestrations for a rich, lush-sounding album. The opening title music features a driving, epic-style rendition of his "Ave Satani" music from *The Omen*, while other cues emphasize heavy, driving rhythms to create the effect of a kind of "machine of evil" that cranks up as devil boy Damien's satanic cohorts deal death and destruction to all who oppose him. Most of the cues explode with spectacular violence, and Goldsmith and his choir leader conjure up some unnerving vocal effects as choir members hiss, growl and wail their way through the composer's "black mass." Goldsmith serves up some spectral, spine-chilling moments of tonal beauty along with the mayhem in cues like "Sleepless Night."

Jeff Bond

See also: The Final Conflict and The Omen

Dances with Wolves ♫♫♫♫♫

1990, Epic Records/CBS Records; from the movie *Dances with Wolves*, Orion Pictures, 1990.

Album Notes: *Music*: John Barry; Orchestra conducted by John Barry; *Album Producer*: John Barry; *Engineer*: Shawn Murphy.

Selections: 1 Main Title — Looks Like A Suicide (3:57); 2 The John Dunbar Theme (2:15); 3 Journey To Fort Sedgewick (3:22); 4 Ride To Fort Hays (2:00); 5 The Death Of Timmons (2:25); 6 Two Socks: The Wolf Theme (1:28); 7 Pawnee Attack (3:45); 8 Kicking Bird's Gift (2:08); 9 Journey To The Buffalo Killing Ground (3:39); 10 The Buffalo Hunt (2:41); 11 Stands With A Fist Remembers (2:07); 12 The Love Theme (3:52); 13 The John Dunbar Theme (2:05); 14 Two Socks At Play (1:57); 15 The Death Of Cisco (2:42); 16 Rescue Of Dances With Wolves (2:07); 17 The Loss Of The Journal and The Return To Winter Camp (2:07); 18 Farewell and End Title (8:40).

Review: Rarely do cinematic beauty and musical splendor marry as sympathetically as in Kevin Costner's epic tale, *Dances with Wolves*. John Barry's Academy Award-winning score is simply breathtaking, hauntingly majestic, and melancholy in an almost imperceptible way. The themes have unique melodic qualities — the Main Title ("Looks Like a Suicide") is stark and foreboding; "The John Dunbar Theme" and "Journey to Fort Sedgewick" deceptively simple, yet rich with complex harmonies that resonate grandly with the exquisite orchestrations of Greig McRitchie. Each selection is, in its own right, a musical gem. The recordings, made at Columbia Studios in Los Angeles, are superb. The strings shimmer, the horns and woodwinds shine, and the percussion rumbles with heart-stopping, earth-shaking depth.

Charles L. Granata

Dangerous Liaisons ♫♫♫♫

1989, Virgin Movie Music; from the movie *Dangerous Liaisons*, Warner Bros., 1989.

Album Notes: *Music*: George Fenton; Orchestra conducted by George Fenton; Baroque Orchestra, conducted by David Woodcock; *Featured Musicians*: Maurice Cochrane (harpsichords, fortepiano, baroque organ), Elizabeth Wallfisch & Alison Bury (solo violins); *Album Producer*: George Fenton.

Selections: 1 Dangerous Liaisons Main Title/Dressing (G. Fenton/A. Vivaldi) (4:20); 2 Madame de Tourvel (2:16); 3 The Challenge (2:06); 4 O Malheureuse Iphigenie! (C. Gluck) (4:28) *Catherine Bott*; 5 Going Hunting (extract from Organ Concerto No. 13 in F, "The Cuckoo and the Nightingale," by G.F. Handel) (1:21); 6 Valmont's First Move/The Staircase (G. Fenton/A. Vivaldi) (2:16); 7 Beneath The Surface (2:12); 8 The Set-Up (G. Fenton/J.S. Bach) (2:13) *Leslie Pearsons, Roderick Elms, Guy Dagul, John Toll*; 9 The Key (J.S. Bach) (2:44); 10 Her Eyes Are Closing (3:40); 11 Ombra Mai Fu (G.F. Handel) (2:41) *Paulo Abel do Nascimento*; 12 Tourvel's Flight (2:10); 13 Success (2:36); 14 Emilie (2:30); 15 Beyond My Control (4:25); 16 A Final Request

(3:13); 17 Ombra Mai Fu (reprise)/The Mirror (G.F. Handel/G. Fenton) (2:33); 18 Dangerous Liaisons End Credits (2:59); 19 Concerto in A minor for four harpsichords (J.S. Bach) (4:12).

Review: Happily mixing original cues with works by some of the best Baroque composers, George Fenton's music for *Dangerous Liaisons* is a rare treat, a score that brims with great taste and intelligence, and a delightful audio experience from beginning to end. If you really like film music and don't mind being a bit adventurous, don't let the above description deter you. Classical music, when well adapted to the needs of screen action, can be as effective as any score you are likely to hear. One of our most sophisticated composers, Fenton knows and understands the qualities that make classical selections so perfectly suited to a specific screen action, and even when he adapts the works by other composers or he writes his own music, he succeeds in creating cues that sound true to the period, yet have an edge of modernity that is appropriate to the cinematic medium itself. Typically, his score for *Dangerous Liaisons* shows great elegance and appeal. In the film, it perfectly matched the tone of the action; on its own, it makes for an attractive recording which will provide many hours of listening pleasure.

Dangerous Minds 🎵🎵🎵

1995, MCA Records; from the movie *Dangerous Minds*, Hollywood Pictures, 1995.

Album Notes: *Song Producers*: Doug Rasheed, Mr. Dalvin, Pimp C, Frank Hudson, Cyrus Esteban, Michael J. Powell, The Bass Mechanics, Chris Stokes, Claudio Cuenti, Evil Dee, Trevor Horn; *Album Executive Producers*: Don Simpson, Jerry Bruckheimer, DeVante; *Engineer*: Herb Powers.

Selections: 1 Gansta's Paradise A.Ivey, Jr./L. Sanders/D. Rasheed)(4:01) *Coolio, L.V.*; 2 Curiosity (M. Dalvin/M. Elliott)(4:03) *Aaron Hall*; 3 Havin Thangs (M. Barnett/W. Barnett)(4:45) *Big Mike*; 4 Problems (A. Forte/ F. Hudson)(3:31) *Rappin' 4-Tay*; 5 True O.G. (M. Dalvin/S. Garrett/T. Mosely) (3:41) *Mr. Dalvin & Static*; 6 Put Ya Back Into It (T. Black/M. Powell)(5:42) *Tre Black*; 7 Don't Go There (Da S.W.A.T. Team) (3:32) *24-K*; 8 Feel The Funk (C. Stokes/S. Scarborough)(4:44) *Immature*; 9 It's Alright (M. Elliott/ C. Mack/E. Dee)(5:13) *Sista, Craig Mack*; 10 A Message For Your Mind (F. Perren/A. Mizell/ B. Gordy/D. Richards/ A. Forte)(5:00) *Rappin' 4-Tay*; 11 Gin And Juice (DeVante)(5:09) *DeVante*; 12 This Is The Life (W. Melvoin/L. Coleman/K. Bell)(4:38) *Wendy & Lisa*.

Review: This was a career launcher for rapper Coolio. It vaulted his "Gangsta's Paradise" to No. 1 on the Billboard charts, which in turn carried the album to No. 1 as well, with

sales in excess of four million copies. No other song on the album is as successful, but it remains a decent sampler of mid-'90s urban styles, including the teenybop of Immature's "Feel the Funk" and the potent street swagger of selections by Rappin' 4-Tay, DeVante and Aaron Hall.
Gary Graff

Dante's Peak 🎵🎵🎵

1997, Varese-Sarabande; from the movie *Dante's Peak*, Universal Pictures, 1997.

Album Notes: *Music*: John Frizzell; *Orchestrations*: Jeff Atmajian, Frank Bennett, Brad Dechter, Robert Elhai, Andrew Kinney, Bruce Fowler; Orchestra conducted by Artie Kane; *Music Editors*: Abby Thelogen, Jim Weidman; *Album Producer*: John Frizzell; *Engineer*: Dennis Sands.

Selections: 1 Main Titles (J. Newton Howard)(5:30); 2 The Close Call (1:43); 3 Trapped In The Crater (5:03); 4 On The Porch (2:31); 5 The Evacuation Begins (4:12); 6 The Helicopter Crash (1:28); 7 Escaping The Burning House (2:32); 8 Sinking On Acid Lake (2:37); 9 Stuck In The Lava (1:44); 10 The Rescue (3:05).

Review: Built around an effectively apocalyptic James Newton Howard theme, John Frizzell's score overflows with hyper-dramatic action. Frizzell orchestrates this energetic material effectively and creates plenty of sonic suspense through a cohesive orchestral dissonance. Heavy on brass and percussion, the score is sufficiently cataclysmic, though it seems at its best when grounded solidly upon the Howard theme. Frizzell does incorporate his own love theme in "On the Porch," accompanying a tender dialog between Pierce Brosnan and Linda Hamilton, then recapitulates it as a triumphant finale in "The Rescue." But it's Howard's ominous horn theme that's linked to the malevolent mountain; all other musical material remains subordinate to the volcanic fury of the mountain's music. It's this material which will, ultimately, remain the most memorable on the CD. At 30:27 minutes, though, it's quite a short one, and the fury of much of the music makes it go by all that much quickly.
Randall D. Larson

The Dark Half 🎵🎵

1993, Varese-Sarabande; from the movie *The Dark Half*, Orion Pictures, 1993.

Album Notes: *Music*: Christopher Young; *Orchestrations*: Christopher Young, Jeff Atmajian; *Music Editors*: John La Salandra, E. Gedney Webb; The Munich Symphony Orchestra, conducted by Allan Wilson; *Album Producer*: Christopher Young; *Engineer*: Eric Tomlinson.

Selections: 1 Prologue and Tumor (6:14); 2 Twin Ghosts (2:42); 3 Mind Snatcher (1:54); 4 Green To Green (2:02); 5 Dano (2:41); 6 Mr. Machine (4:02); 7 Omnibus Death (10:23); 8 Catechize (1:19); 9 Berol Black Beauty (2:25); 10 Half Divided One (2:01); 11 Fool's Stuffing (3:38); 12 Sparrows (2:48); 13 The Dark Half (4:39).

Review: Despite a pleasantly melodic opening, the underscore for this film doesn't quite yield an entertaining CD. Then again, Christopher Young's primary goal is always to support the film, not make records. If the filmmakers' ultimate intent was that they needed a dreary, sullen score, then he certainly succeeded in delivering the goods. Once down in its pit of despair, it rarely rises up. One has to wonder, however, if Young was simply prohibited from devising another one of his creative orchestrations for fear that it might outshine the film, which was critically lambasted and disowned by Stephen King, and which could have used all the help it could get. If so, then Young's talent was certainly wasted.

David Hirsch

Darkman ♫♫♫

1990, MCA Records; from the movie *Darkman*, Universal Pictures, 1990.

Album Notes: *Music:* Danny Elfman; *Orchestrations:* Steve Bartek; *Music Editor:* Bob Badami; Orchestra conducted by Shirley Walker; *Album Producer:* Danny Elfman; *Engineers:* Bob Fernandez, Dennis Sands, Shawn Murphy.

Selections: 1 Main Titles (1:37); 2 Woe, The Darkman... Woe (6:09); 3 Rebuilding/Failure (3:16); 4 Love Theme (:56); 5 Julie Transforms (1:11); 6 Rage/Peppy Science (1:37); 7 Creating Pauley (3:19); 8 Double Durante (1:50); 9 The Plot Unfolds (Dance Freak)(7:01); 10 Carnival From Hell (3:16); 11 Julie Discovers Darkman (1:59); 12 High Steel (4:19); 13 Finale/End Credits (3:39).

Review: Danny Elfman wrote a lot of "dark" scores during the late 1980s—*Batman*, *Beetlejuice* and *Nightbreed* among them—but *Darkman* may just be the most representative score of the composer's work from this period. The music is popular enough to be copied in subsequent genre films in addition to being used in numerous movie trailers, so listeners may be familiar with the score even if they don't instantly know where the music comes from. With his trademark frantic, jumpy, unstable strings, an ominous, foreboding tone, and colorful orchestrations (courtesy of collaborator Steve Bartek), Elfman has written a score that's always interesting to listen to, very much in the style of *Batman* and his other efforts around this time, though its intense tone may wear some listeners down in album format.

Andy Dursin

Dave ♫♫♫♫

1993, Big Screen Records; from the movie *Dave*, Warner Bros., 1993.

Album Notes: *Music:* James Newton Howard; *Orchestrations:* James Newton Howard, Brad Dechter, Chris Boardman; *Music Editor:* Jim Weidman; Orchestra conducted by Marty Paich; *Album Producer:* James Newton Howard; *Engineer:* Shawn Murphy.

Selections: 1 Main Titles (2:56); 2 The Picnic (4:13); 3 To The White House (3:04); 4 You're On (2:02); 5 Are You Threatening Me? (3:25); 6 She Hates me (3:12); 7 The Teaching Montage (1:07); 8 Do You Like Magic? (2:24); 9 Dave Passes Out (1:11); 10 The Tunnel (1:49); 11 How'd You Get Started? (2:01); 12 Into The Fog (3:40); 13 End Titles (4:13).

Review: James Newton Howard's score for this romantic comedy is a delightful series of cues that are well adapted to the screen action but also exude strong musical characteristics that make this soundtrack album a particularly enjoyable one to listen to. At times elegiac ("The Picnic"), at times amusingly delineated ("She Hates Me"), it overflows with attractive ideas, compactly expressed yet totally convincing and strongly suggestive. In a rare display of Newton Howard's best qualities as a film composer, *Dave* is a real charming effort.

Dawn of the Dead ♫♫

1979, Varese-Sarabande; from the movie *Dawn of the Dead*, United Film Distribution, 1979.

Album Notes: *Music:* Goblin; *Featured Musicians:* Massimo Morante (guitars, bass, mandolin), Claudio Simonetti (keyboards, synthesizers, organ, violin), Fabio Pignatelli (guitar, bass), Agostino Marangolo (piano, percussion), Maurizio Guarini (synthesizer, violin); *Album Producers:* Goblin.

Selections: 1 Dawn Of The Dead (6:05); 2 Zombie (4:24); 3 Safari (2:11); 4 Pie In The Face (1:54); 5 Edge Of Madness (1:31); 6 Shriek (3:35); 7 The Hunt (3:39); 8 Target Shooting (2:51); 9 Oblivion (5:12); 10 The Awakening (1:04).

Review: For George Romero's visceral horror show, the Italian group Goblin was brought in by executive producer Dario Argento, who had worked with them before and insisted they replace many of the library cues originally patched together by Romero. Goblin provides an effective counterpart to Romero's vivid scenes of flesh-eating zombies invading an abandoned shopping mall, eager for the surviving humans trapped inside. Their music is desolate and brutal, but often satirical, and built around pulsating rock rhythms and textures, both electric and acoustic. Dominated by guitar and drums, the music leads the assault of the zombies, evoking a claustrophobic mood of impending and inescapable terror. It worked very well in the film, but it's less interesting on CD where it tends to drone away rather aimlessly. Unless you're into the throbbing zombie beat, the CD may not be a frequent flyer on your home stereo.

Randall D. Larson

The Day the Earth Stood Still ♫♫♫♫

1993, Fox Records; from the movie *The Day the Earth Stood Still*, 20th Century-Fox, 1951.

Album Notes: *Music:* Bernard Herrmann; The 20th Century-Fox Orchestra, conducted by Bernard Herrmann, Lionel Newman, Alfred Newman; *Featured Artist:* Sam Hoffman (theremin); *CD Producer:* Nick Redman; *Digital Mastering:* Dan Hersch.

Selections: 1 20th Century-Fox Fanfare (A. Newman)(:12); 2 Prelude/Outer Space/Radar (3:45); 3 Danger (:22); 4 Klaatu (2:15); 5 Gort/The Visor/The Telescope (2:23); 6 Escape (:52); 7 Solar Diamonds (1:04); 8 Arlington (1:08); 9 Lincoln Memorial (1:27); 10 Nocturne/The Flashlight/The Robot/ Space Control (5:58); 11 The Elevator/Magnetic Pull/The Study/The Conference/The Jewelry Store (4:31); 12 Panic (:42); 13 The Glowing/ Alone/Gort's Rage/Nikto/The Captive/Terror (5:11); 14 The Prison (1:42); 15 Rebirth (1:38); 16 Departure (:52); 17 Farewell (:32); 18 Finale (:30).

Review: Herrmann's music for the 1951 Robert Wise film about a wise extraterrestrial ambassador's visit to Earth is the quintessential '50s sci-fi score, most often remembered for its wailing, eerie theremin effects. The score was unavailable apart from some brief rerecorded suites prior to this 1993 release, which assembles the entire original score, including a few moments not used in the film. The portentous title music gives way to Herrmann's nervous "Radar" cue of low piano and vibraphone, but the highlight of the album involves the arrival of the alien Klaatu (Michael Rennie) and his immense robot Gort, characterized by Herrmann with an unforgettable series of crushing, ascending brass chords and hair-raising theremin glissandos as the robot lays waste to a phalanx of soldiers in Washington, D.C. No fan of Herrmann or science fiction film scores should be without this classic release.

Jeff Bond

Daylight ♫♫♫

1996, Universal Records; from the movie *Daylight*, Universal Pictures, 1996.

Album Notes: *Music:* Randy Edelman; *Orchestrations:* Ralph Ferraro; Orchestra conducted by Randy Edelman; *Album Producer:* Randy Edelman; *Engineer:* Elton Ahi.

Selections: 1 Daylight (3:34); 2 Laura's Theme (3:07); 3 Searching For A Miracle (1:58); 4 Survival (2:30); 5 Kit's Plan (3:30); 6 A Community Is Formed (2:46); 7 Leaving George (3:13); 8 Rats (1:54); 9 The Tunnel Claims Its Own (2:13); 10 Power! (2:30); 11 A Short Swim Under Water (2:11); 12 The Sandhog's Chapel (2:17); 13 Light At The End (5:28); 14 Madelyne's Fate (3:27); 15 Whenever There Is Love (B. Roberts/S. Roman)(4:35) *Bruce Roberts, Donna Summer*; 16 Don't Go Out With Your Friends Tonite (L. Bryan/ R. Bryan/ D. Hoffpauir/K. Kerby)(2:53) *Ho-Hum.*

Review: An unusual, relatively subtle action score from Randy Edelman, *Daylight* coasts right along with some exciting action cues that fortunately never overwhelm the claustrophobic suspense of Sylvester Stallone's entertaining disaster movie. Edelman utilizes his standard bag of tricks here (synths combined with full orchestra), but the percussive beat of many of his scores is notably missing, and it results in a solid outing that ought to appeal to action fans and aficionados of the composer. The album also includes "Wherever There is Love," a power ballad performed by Bruce Roberts and Donna Summer, which—thanks to its catchy chorus and typically lush David Foster production sheen—is one of the more enjoyable songs to come out of a disaster movie since, well, "The Morning After" from *The Poseidon Adventure*, anyway.

Andy Dursin

Days of Thunder ♫♫♫

1990, DGC Records; from the movie *Days of Thunder*, Paramount Pictures, 1990.

Album Notes: *Song Producers:* Richie Sambora, Bill Champlin, Dennis Matkosky, Trevor Horn, Mike Clink, Kenny Laguna, Don Was, Peter Asher, Andre Cymone, Martin Page, Ron Nevison; *Album Executive Producers:* Don Simpson, Jerry Bruckheimer; *Engineer:* Dan Hersch.

Selections: 1 The Last Note Of Freedom (H. Zimmer/B. Idol)(5:44) *David Coverdale*; 2 Deal For Life (M. Page/B. Taupin)(4:36) *John Waite*; 3 Break Through The Barrier (A. Cymone/G. Cole)(4:47) *Tina Turner*; 4 Hearts In Trouble (B. Champlin/D. Matkosky/K. Dukes)(5:14) *Chicago*; 5 Trail Of Broken Hearts (R. Sambora/T. Marolda/B. Foster)(4:32) *Cher*; 6 Knockin' On Heaven's Door (B. Dylan)(5:36) *Guns N' Roses*; 7 You Gotta Love Someone (E. John/B. Taupin)(4:59) *Elton John*; 8 Show Me Heaven (J. Rifkin/E. Rackin/M. McKee) (3:48) *Maria McKee*; 9 Thunder Box (A. Smile)(3:49) *Apollo Smile*; 10 Long Live The Night (J. Jett/R. Cantor/M. Caruso)(3:57) *Joan Jett & The Blackhearts*; 11 Gimme Some Lovin' (S. Winwood/M. Winwood/S. Davis)(5:01) *Terry Reid*.

Review: Ever since *Risky Business*, Tom Cruise star vehicles have been good for high-profile soundtracks. And this one doesn't disappoint, with a jukebox chock full o' biggies — Elton John, Tina Turner, Chicago, Cher. Hard rockers Guns 'N Roses stuck their previously unavailable cover of Bob Dylan's "Knockin' on Heaven's Door" here to lure the rock crowd, and ambitious listeners could find some real gems, like Terry Reid's version of "Gimme Some Lovin'" and Maria McKee's "Show Me Heaven" amidst a load of luke-warm castaways from the more established names.

Gary Graff

The Dead/Journey Into Fear
🦴🦴🦴🦴

1987, Varese-Sarabande Records; from the movies *The Dead*, Vestron Pictures, 1987; and *Journey Into Fear*, Stirling Gold, 1975.

Album Notes: *Music:* Alex North; *The Dead:* *Featured Musicians:* Ann Stockton (Irish harp), Paul Shure, Bonnie Douglas, Sheldon Sanov, Arnold Belnick, Bruce Dukov, Israel Baker (violin), Milton Thomas, David Schwartz (viola), Frederick Seykora, Dennis Karmazyn (cello), Milton Kastenbaum (bass), Sheridon Stokes (flute), Tom Boyd (oboe), Dominick Fera (clarinet), John Berkman (keyboard); *Journey Into Fear:* *Orchestrations:* Richard E. Bronskill; *Music Editor:* Kenn Wannberg; The Graunke Symphony Orchestra, conducted by Alex North; *Album Producer:* Alex North.

Selections: THE DEAD: 1 Main Title (2:05); 2 The Story Of Michael Furey (3:01); 3 Gretta's Young Romance (1:49); 4 Gabriel's Mournful Reflections (5:12); 5 Aunt Kate Recalls Parkinson (:52); 6 Gretta's Fond Memory (1:45); 7 Grim Gabriel (1:09); 8 The Lass Of Aughrim (3:05) *Frank Patterson;*

JOURNEY INTO FEAR: 9 Main Title (1:47); 10 Dead Agent (1:34); 11 Loneliness (2:55); 12 The Weapon (1:29); 13 The Search (1:50); 14 Deadly Quest (2:44); 15 Troubled Romance (3:18); 16 Pursuit (3:15); 17 Despair (1:23); 18 Desperate Straits (2:18); 19 It's Over (End Title)(2:42).

Review: Belying its apparently downbeat subject, a dramatic screen rendition of the Joyce story set at the turn of the century, the score for *The Dead*, a film directed by John Huston, is an attractive series of little musical miniatures for chamber orchestra and solo instruments, among them the flute, the oboe and the clarinet. Introduced by the "Main Title," a piece for solo harp, it segues into a collection of themes that underline the screen action, notably about Gretta, married to Gabriel, who, on the occasion of a family reunion at their aunts'

home in Dublin, reveals to her husband that she loved another when she was younger.

In contrast to the romantic simplicity and loveliness of *The Dead*, *Journey Into Fear*, a contemporary murder mystery, elicited a score that sometimes verges on the atonal, with bursts of orchestral violence to portray the "aggressiveness inherent in this propulsive story," as the composer himself described it. Occasionally, a melodic interlude ("Loneliness," "Troubled Romance") provides some relief to the musical tension, but the title of the film appropriately describes the overall tones of the score, played with great energy by the Graunke Symphony Orchestra.

Dead Again 🦴🦴🦴

1991, Varese-Sarabande; from the movie *Dead Again*, Paramount Pictures, 1991.

Album Notes: *Music:* Patrick Doyle; *Orchestrations:* Lawrence Ashmore; *Music Editor:* Roy Prendergast; Orchestra conducted by William Kraft; *Album Producer:* Patrick Doyle; *Engineer:* John Richards.

Selections: 1 The Headlines (3:26); 2 Final Request (2:30); 3 A Walk Down Death Row (:59); 4 The Woman With No Name (3:34); 5 Winter 1948 (2:56); 6 Two Halves Of The Same Person (2:19); 7 It Never Rains In LA (1:40); 8 I'm Not Roman (1:29); 9 Inga's Secrets (1:04); 10 Hightower House (2:52); 11 Fate Happens/Death Of A Mad Son (4:38); 12 The Door Is Closed (1:11); 13 Dead Again (3:03).

Review: The second collaboration between director-actor Kenneth Branagh and composer Patrick Doyle results in a bombastic, often over-the-top but nevertheless enjoyable score similar to the composer's most pulsating works (think *Mary Shelley's Frankenstein*). To fit the Hitchcock-esque tone of Branagh's entertaining "film noir," Doyle ventures into some elegiac string territory worthy of Bernard Herrmann, while still retaining his own voice through the propulsive action music accompanying the film's opening titles or the poignant love theme, with echoes of tragedy, that brings the picture to a close. Minor quibble: some of the music is written in strict accordance to the action on-screen, meaning some tracks don't translate well to album form, though the brief running time at least means that the music never wears out its welcome. A worthy effort into the Branagh-Doyle series, though it is far from the best — or the worst — score to result from their collaborative relationship.

Andy Dursin

Dead Man Walking

Dead Man Walking ♫♫♫

1995, Columbia Records; from the movie *Dead Man Walking*, Gramercy Pictures, 1995.

Album Notes: *Song Producers*: Bruce Springsteen & Chuck Plotkin, Ry Cooder, Mitchell Froom & Suzanne Vega, Lyle Lovett & Billy Williams, Tom Waits & Kathleen Brennan, David Rubinson, John Jennings & Mary Chapin Carpenter, Steve Earle & Ray Kennedy, David Robbins; *Song Engineers*: Toby Scott, Allen Sides, Tchad Blake, Nate Cunkel, Biff Dawes, Leslie Ann Jones, Bob Dawson, Ray Kennedy; *Album Executive Producers*: Tim Robbins, David Robbins.

Selections: 1 Dead Man Walkin' (B. Springsteen)(2:43) *Bruce Springsteen*; 2 In Your Mind (J. Cash)(4:14) *Johnny Cash*; 3 Woman On The Tier (I'll See You Through)(S. Vega)(2:25) *Suzanne Vega*; 4 Promises (L. Lovett)(3:03) *Lyle Lovett*; 5 The Face Of Love (D. Robbins/T. Robbins/N. Khan)(5:39) *Nusrat Fateh Ali Khan, Eddie Vedder*; 6 The Fall Of Troy (T. Waits/K. Brennan)(2:59) *Tom Waits*; 7 Quality Of Mercy (M. Shocked)(3:38) *Michelle Shocked*; 8 Dead Man Walking (A Dream Like This)(M. Chapin Carpenter)(3:34) *Mary Chapin Carpenter*; 9 Walk Away (T. Waits/K. Brennan) (2:43) *Tom Waits*; 10 Ellis Unit One (S. Earle)(4:39) *Steve Earle*; 11 Walking Blind (O. Ray)(4:39) *Patti Smith*; 12 The Long Road (E. Vedder)(5:31) *Eddie Vedder, Nusrat Fateh Ali Khan*.

Review: See entry below.

Dead Man Walking ♫♫♫♫

1995, Columbia Records; from the movie *Dead Man Walking*, Gramercy Pictures, 1995.

Album Notes: *Music*: David Robbins, Eddie Vedder, Nusrat Fateh Ali Khan, Ry Cooder, V.M. Bhatt; *Orchestrations*: David Campbell; *Producers*: Ry Cooder, Michael Brook, Kavichandran Alexander; *Featured Musicians*: Ry Cooder, David Robbins, David Spinozza (guitar), Frank Centeno (bass guitar), Brian Dobbs, Joel Diamond (organ), Joachim Cooder (dumbek), David Ratajczak (drums), Mino Cinelu (percussion), John Vartan (tambour), Joel Diamond (organ); *Featured Vocalists*: The Dusing Singers; *Engineer*: Gary Chester.

Selections: 1 The Face Of Love (R. Robbins/T. Robbins/N. Khan)(10:02) *Nusrat Fateh Ali Khan, Eddie Vedder*; 2 Helen Visits Angola Prison (D. Robbins/ N. Khan)(2:50) *Nusrat Fateh Ali Khan, Amina Annabi, David Robbins*; 3 Dudouk Melody (A Cool Wind Is Blowing)(trad.)(1:47); 4 This Is The Day The Lord Has Made (trad.)(4:02) *Rev. Donald R. Smith, The Golden Voices Gospel Choir of St. Francois de Salles Catholic Church*; 5 The Possum (D. Robbins/N. Khan) (1:21) *David Robbins, Nusrat Fateh Ali Khan*; 6 Shadow (N. Khan)(3:03) *Nusrat Fateh Ali Khan*; 7 Helen Faints/Helen's Nightmare (D. Robbins)(1:30) *David Robbins, Nusrat Fateh Ali Khan, Amina Annabi*; 8 Dudouk Melody (I Will Not Be Sad In This World)(trad.)(2:39); 9 Sacred Love (G. Sviridov)(3:14) *The Dusing Singers*; 10 The Execution (D. Robbins/N. Khan)(4:21) *David Robbins, Nusrat Fateh Ali Khan*; 11 The Long Road (E. Vedder/N. Khan)(16:41) *Eddie Vedder, Nusrat Fateh Ali Khan*; 12 Isa Lei (A.W. Caten)(7:38) *Ry Cooder, Vishwa Mohan Bhatt*.

Review: A complex psychological film, set in New Orleans, *Dead Man Walking* told the unique story of a nun and a convicted killer awaiting execution, and the unusual emotional ties that eventually bind their existences. Adding a pertinent fold to the absorbing drama, the soundtrack relied on the powerful combination of contemporary songs and rare instrumental cues written by a wide range of composers. A cornucopia of top frontline performers provide the enjoyment in the first album which brings together the talents of Bruce Springsteen, Johnny Cash, Suzanne Vega, Lyle Lovett, Mary Chapin Carpenter, Tom Waits and Patti Smith, to name a few. Unless you have seen the film (and even if you have), it is sometimes difficult to assess how each song fits within the dramatic texture of the screen action, but taken on its own musical merits this compilation album is certainly better than most.

In a total genre departure, the second album presents various selections, many of them in the Pakistani Sufi idiom, a devotional style rich with tradition, used to express the transcendental moods that permeate some of the scenes in the film. By combining those with the songs of a gospel choir, film composer David Robbins was able to create a highly unusual, strikingly powerful soundtrack which does not seek any compromise and will probably regrettably attract only a limited audience. But if you like the first album, try to find the second for a broader, richer musical experience.

Dead Presidents ♫♫♫♫

1995, Capitol Records; from the movie *Dead Presidents*, Hollywood Pictures, 1995.

Album Notes: *Music*: Danny Elfman; *Featured Artists*: Sly & The Family Stone, Isaac Hayes, James Brown, The Spinners, Barry White, Harold Melvin & The Blue Notes, The Dramatics, Curtis Mayfield, Aretha Franklin, Jesse & Trina, Al Green, The O'Jays; *Album Producers*: Albert Hughes, Allen Hughes, Darryl Porter; *Engineer*: Wally Traugott.

"In two episodes last season, we used a Nick Cave song, 'Red Right Hand.' It was a song I'd heard on an alternative radio station and thought was amazing, very 'X-Files'-ish. People started thinking I had some secret source for cool music..."

Chris Carter
*"X-Files" executive producer
(People, 4-29-96)*

Selections: 1 If You Want Me To Stay (S. Stewart)(2:58) *Sly & The Family Stone*; 2 Walk On By (B. Bacharach/H. David)(4:34) *Isaac Hayes*; 3 The Payback (J. Brown/F. Wesley/J. Starks)(7:41) *James Brown*; 4 I'll Be Around (T. Bell/P. Hurtt)(3:11) *The Spinners*; 5 Never Gonna Give You Up (B. White) (7:59) *Barry White*; 6 I Miss You (K. Gamble/L. Huff)(8:29) *Harold Melvin & The Blue Notes*; 7 Get Up And Get Down (T. Hester)(3:11) *The Dramatics*; 8 If There's Hell Below (C. Mayfield)(7:44) *Curtis Mayfield*; 9 Do Right Woman, Do Right Man (D. Penn/C. Moman)(3:16) *Aretha Franklin*; 10 Where Is The Love (R. MacDonald/W. Salter)(4:12) *Jesse & Trina*; 11 Tired Of Being Alone (A. Green) (2:48) *Al Green*; 12 Love Train (K. Gamble/L. Huff)(2:59) *The O'Jays*; 13 The Look Of Love (B. Bacharach/ H. David)(11:13) *Isaac Hayes*; 14 Dead Presidents Theme (D. Elfman)(4:22).

Review: If this sounds like something the Dead Kennedys should be part of, think again. This soundtrack comprises soul classics from front to back, a hall of fame assemblage that includes Aretha Franklin, Curtis Mayfield, Sly & the Family Stone, Harold Melvin & the Blue Notes, the Spinners, Isaac Hayes, James Brown, Al Green and the inimitable rumble of Barry White. You'll feel good, like you knew that you would.
Gary Graff

Dead Solid Perfect ♪♪♪

1990, Silva Screen Records; from the movie *Dead Solid Perfect,* HBO Pictures, 1989.

Album Notes: *Music*: Tangerine Dream; *Music Editor*: Allen K. Rosen; *Album Producers*: David Stoner, James Fitzpatrick; *Engineer*: Alan Howarth.

Selections: 1 Theme From Dead Solid Perfect (3:20); 2 In The Pond (1:16); 3 Beverly Leaves (:59); 4 Of Cads And Caddies (2:13); 5 Tournament Montage (2:38); 6 A Whore In One (2:14); 7 Sand Trap (1:22); 8 In The Rough (:42); 9 Nine Iron (1:39); 10 U.S. Open (1:41); 11 My Name Is Bad Hair (2:32); 12 In The Hospital Room (:36); 13 Welcome To Bushwood/Golfus Interruptus (1:33); 14 Deja Vu (I've Heard This Before!)(1:32); 15 Birdie (1:20); 16 Divot (1:19); 17 Kenny And Donny Montage (1:40); 18 Off To See Beverly (:33); 19 Phone To Beverly (1:19); 20 Nice Shots (2:43); 21 Sinking Putts (2:05); 22 Kenny's Winning Shot (1:07).

Review: Unlike most Tangerine Dream albums, this score for a lighthearted pre-*Tin Cup* look at the world of professional golf was assembled not from the full-length themes composed by the group, but from the cues edited down to create the film underscore. Until I was asked to assist engineer Alan Howarth and producer Ford A. Thaxton in creating a listenable album, I had not fully appreciate the group's ability to capture the nature of a film. I soon found we could assemble the wealth of short pieces into one big coherent symphonic suite. Having been most familiar with the film, and its quirky ambience, I discovered much to my amazement that Tangerine Dream's musical instincts were pretty much on target. I could hear pro-golfer Randy Quaid struggling with both his personal and professional life, with the music effectively capturing both the tension of the tournaments and Quaid's more lighthearted off-the-green antics ("A Whore in One").
David Hirsch

The Dead Zone ♪♪♪

1994, Milan Records; from the movie *Dead Zone*, Paramount Pictures, 1983.

Album Notes: *Music*: Michael Kamen; *Orchestrations*: Michael Kamen; The National Philharmonic Orchestra of London, conducted by Michael Kamen; *Featured Soloist*: Sid Sax (violin); *Album Producer*: Michael Kamen; *Engineers*: Eric Tomlinson, John McLure.

Selections: 1 Opening Titles (4:20); 2 Coma (4:24); 3 Hospital Visit (1:09); 4 First Vision—Second Sight (1:33); 5 Lost Love (1:23); 6 Drowning Vision—Through The Ice (2:46); 7 School Days (2:14); 8 In The Snow—Hope (2:22); 9 Alone (3:57); 10 Political Death (2:27); 11 Rally—Meet Your Local Candidate (3:52); 12 Realisation—Destiny (2:15); 13 Death Of A Visionary (2:12); 14 Civic Duty And Sacrifice (1:48); 15 The Dead Zone (2:39); 16 Coda To A Coma—The Balcony (2:25).

Review: This long overdue release of Michael Kamen's score to director David Cronenberg's successful adaption of the

Stephen King story will be welcomed by all fans of the composer. Dreamy in pacing, subdued in nature, Kamen centers it all around Johnny, a man who has awakened from a coma to find he now has "second sight." It's not a gift, but a curse and Johnny, no matter how good his deed, will not be rewarded with happiness. He foreshadows the inevitable conclusion by drawing out as much pathos as he can muster, and even the theme "Lost Love" reeks with agony. As Johnny descends ineluctably into madness, Kamen makes sure we know that.

David Hirsch

Deadfall

1997, Retrograde Records; from the movie *Deadfall*, 20th Century-Fox, 1968.

Album Notes: *Music*: John Barry; *Orchestrations*: John Barry; The London Philharmonic Orchestra, conducted by John Barry; *Featured Soloist*: Renata Tarrago (guitar); *CD Producer*: Lukas Kendall; *Engineer*: Daniel Hirsch.

Selections: 1 My Love Has Two Faces (J. Barry/J. Lawrence)(3:52) *Shirley Bassey*; 2 The Meeting (2:45); 3 Statue Dance (2:44); 4 The Last Deadfall (6:13); 5 My Love Has Two Faces (3:16); 6 Romance For Guitar And Orchestra (14:12); 7 My Love Has Two Faces (male vocal version)(3:32); 8 My Love Has Two Faces (alt. instrumental)(3:18).

Review: For many years, this soundtrack album (released on LP by 20th Century-Fox Records, at a time when such a label existed) was every collector's prized possession or most-wanted title. There is, of course, a very simple reason for that. Written by John Barry for a thriller directed by Bryan Forbes, it featured among its choicest moments a sensational romance for guitar and orchestra which is considered one of the composer's most complete, most comprehensive creations, as well as one of his most attractive. Superbly performed by Renata Tarrago, it is the centerpiece of this new CD release, and impresses once again as a work of striking beauty and imagination (it is heard during one of the film's crucial sequences, a robbery that takes place during a concert, and lasts precisely as long as the performance of the piece itself). Characteristic of Barry's highly charged style, it is a work of striking originality, with strong romantic leanings, played for all its worth. The rest of the score, announced by Shirley Bassey's vocal on the song "My Love Has Two Faces," is an amalgam of flavorful cues that delineate specific moments in the action, with this CD edition adding two previously unreleased tracks, both featuring the main song title in an alternate instrumental, and in a male vocal version.

The Deadly Affair

1996, Verve Records; from the movie *The Deadly Affair*, Columbia Pictures, 1967.

See: The Pawnbroker

Deadly Care ♫♫♪

1992, Silva America Records; from the movie *Deadly Care*, Universal Pictures, 1987.

Album Notes: *Music*: Tangerine Dream; *Album Producers*: Tangerine Dream, Ford A. Thaxton; *Engineer*: John Goodmanson.

Selections: 1 Deadly Care (Main Title)(4:56); 2 Paddles/Stolen Pills (2:54); 3 A Strong Drink/A Bad Morning (2:00); 4 Wasted And Sick (1:22); 5 Hope For The Future (4:01); 6 The Hospital (5:42); 7 In Bed (1:52); 8 Annie And Father (1:25); 9 More Pills (1:26); 10 In The Head Nurse's Office/At The Father's Grave (1:26); 11 Clean And Sober (4:02).

Review: This score is one of Christopher Franke's last collaborations with the group Tangerine Dream before he left in 1987 to launch his own career as a film composer. It is a dark representation of a nurse's descent into drug and alcohol abuse, told with somber melodies and minimal orchestrations. It is an interesting change of pace for the group, known more for somewhat brighter harmonies (though not as bleak as *The Keep*). The CD was assembled from the group's original studio recordings as opposed to the edited down versions adapted for use as the underscore.

David Hirsch

Death Becomes Her ♫♫

1992, Varese-Sarabande; from the movie *Death Becomes Her*, Universal Pictures, 1992.

Album Notes: *Music*: Alan Silvestri; *Orchestrations*: William Ross; *Music Editor*: Kenneth Karman; Orchestra conducted by Alan Silvestri; *Featured Soloist*: Stuart Canin (violin); *Album Producer*: Alan Silvestri; *Engineer*: Dennis Sands; *Assistant Engineers*: Tom Hardisty, Sue McLean.

Selections: 1 Main Title (1:32); 2 "Me" (G. Aymar/M. Donovan/D. Koepp) (2:18) *Meryl Streep*; 3 Woman On The Verge (1:30); 4 Lisle (1:05); 5 A Touch Of Magic (2:32); 6 Now, A Warning (:52); 7 Sempre Viva (1:49); 8 Another Drunk Driver (1:47); 9 Hurry Up, You Wimp (1:57); 10 It's Alive (3:00); 11 Helen Spies (2:00); 12 Another Miracle (2:31); 13 I'll Be Upstairs (:38); 14 Loving You (2:30); 15 I'd Rather Die (2:59); 16 End Credits (5:45).

Review: If you took the most frantic, frenzied string sections of *Who Framed Roger Rabbit?* and *Back to the Future*, then wrote an entire score around them without composing a substantial theme to tie it all together, what you'd come up with would undoubtedly resemble *Death Becomes Her*. An often engaging, macabre fantasy from Robert Zemeckis (made after the *Future* sequels and prior to *Forrest Gump*) that never quite hits the bull's-eye, this rather tedious score from his long-time collaborator Alan Silvestri frequently grates on the listener for almost the length of its entire album, offering little variation or musical surprises outside of its dark, dissonant nature and thumping percussion section. It's an atmosphere score to be certain, working just fine as musical wallpaper in the movie, but it doesn't function at all outside of the film context it was intended to accompany. Recommended only for Silvestri completists.

Andy Dursin

The Deceivers 🎵🎵🎵

1988, RCA Victor; from the movie *The Deceivers,* Merchant Ivory Productions, 1988.

Album Notes: *Music*: John Scott; The Graunke Symphony Orchestra, conducted by John Scott; *Album Producer*: John Scott; *Engineer*: Peter Kramper.

Selections: 1 In The Beginning (2:46); 2 The Deceivers (Main Title) (2:12); 3 Massacre Of The Nawab's Company (3:05); 4 Journey To Madya (2:00); 5 Forest Murders (1:41); 6 Purge (2:51); 7 Deceivers Waltz (2:14); 8 Madya Quadrille (1:09); 9 Tiger Hunt (1:47); 10 A Killing Grove (:58); 11 William And Sarah (2:49); 12 The House Of Feringeea (1:34); 13 Invocation To Kali (2:18); 14 The Rumal Strikes (1:39); 15 William Kills (2:39); 16 The Consecrated Goor (1:40); 17 Dance To Kali (1:57); 18 Beloved Of Kali (3:52); 19 The Widow's Warning (2:48); 20 River Massacre (2:09); 21 Defeat Of The Deceivers (4:07); 22 End Credits (2:41).

Review: John Scott, another highly literate composer, provided the attractive score for this Merchant Ivory production, starring Pierce Brosnan, set in India at the turn of the century. Though the instrumentations occasionally call for an "ethinic" drum or rhythm, sometimes mixed with the more traditional orchestral figures, much of the music is written in broad, colorful epic and romantic tones that have little to do with the setting but that describe in bold terms the dramatic action on the screen.

Many cues are particularly attractive in the overall mix, but some stand out noticeably, among them the descriptive "Purge," a stately lovely "Deceivers Waltz," a jaunty "Madya Quadrille," and the bold "Defeat of the Deceivers." Performance by the Graunke Symphony Orchestra is right on target, though sonics are somewhat unfocused due to distant miking which flatters individual solo instruments but results in less definition when the full orchestra is heard.

The Deer Hunter 🎵🎵

1989, Capitol Records; from the movie *The Deer Hunter,* Universal Pictures, 1979.

Album Notes: *Music*: Stanley Myers; Orchestra conducted by Stanley Myers; *Featured Artist*: John Williams (guitar); *Soundtrack Recording Engineer*: Aaron Rochim; *Album Producers*: David Cavanaugh, Rupert Perry; *Engineer*: Hugh Davies.

Selections: 1 Cavatina (3:32) *John Williams*; 2 Praise The Name Of The Lord (trad., arr. K. Kovach)(1:44); 3 Troika (trad., arr. S. Myers)(2:20); 4 Katyusha (trad., arr. K. Kovach)(1:38); 5 Struggling Ahead (3:04); 6 Sarabande (2:54) *John Williams*; 7 Waiting His Turn (1:27); 8 Memory Eternal (trad., arr. K. Kovach)(1:13); 9 God Bless America (I. Berlin) (1:45); 10 Cavatina (reprise)(3:54) *John Williams*.

Review: A stirring, sprawling saga, *The Deer Hunter* is an epic film in every sense of the word. Laced with literary allusions, it follows a group of friends from a small town in Pennsylvania whose coming-of-age includes a Russian orthodox marriage, a hunt, and a stint in Vietnam, where they are captured by the Vietcong and forced to submit to a game of Russian roulette. While symbols and references abound in the film directed by Michael Cimino, a contributing element to its success is its soundtrack, which incorporates Stanley Myers' informed music, traditional songs, and sound effects. This short (24 minutes) CD can hardly be said to effectively represent the film, but it contains Myers' lovely "Cavatina," performed by guitarist John Williams. Certainly, a film of this importance (it won five Oscars, including Best Picture and Best Direction) would justify a soundtrack album more representative than this...

Def-Con 4 🎵🎵🎵

1990, Intrada Records; from the movie *Def-Con 4: Defense Condition 4,* New World Pictures, 1990.

Album Notes: *Music*: Christopher Young; *Orchestrations*: Christopher Young; Orchestra conducted by Paul Francis Witt; *Featured Musicians*: John Fitzgerald (metallic sound sculptures/drums), Ara Tokatlian (South American woodwinds), Gary Nesteruk (piano), Larry Giannecchini (electric guitar), Mike Nelson (sax), Gregg Nestor (classical guitar), Karl Vincent (bass), David McKelvy (harmonica); *Album Producer*: Christopher Young; *Engineer*: Jeff Vaughn.

Selections: 1 Def-Con 4 (Main Title)(1:39); 2 Forced Landing (2:21); 3 The Liberation Of Fort Liswell (2:36); 4 Armageddon (2:14); 5 Ghost Planet (2:02); 6 Gideon's Law (1:41); 7 The Terminals (1:05); 8 A New Man's Destiny (2:33); 9 Defense Condition 1 (2:18); 10 The Juggernaut (1:32); 11 Electronic Ocean (2:20); 12 A Message From Home (2:00); 13 I Can't Go On (2:12); 14 The New Dark Age (2:11);

AVENGING ANGEL: 15 Kit Carson (3:26); 16 Overdrive (2:16); 17 Molly Mey (2:23); 18 Ratamacue (2:42); 19 Dark Angel (4:22); 20 Never (1:04); 21 Bughouse Bust (2:07); 22 Good Golly Solley (2:39);

TORMENT: 23 Thanatos (10:25);

THE TELEPHONE: 24 Vashti Blue (3:22); 25 Definitely Not Manhattan (3:20); 26 Pantomime (3:24); 27 Christmas In July (2:30).

Review: This excellent overview anthology of Christopher Young's early career starts off with 14 selections from his score to the 1985 post-apocalypse film *Def-Con 4*, notable because this was where he first created what he refers to as "Metallic Sound Sculptures." This tact is allowed to flourish even further on "Thantos," a track from the score for *Torment*, which, despite its electronic sounding demeanor, is strictly an acoustic creation. For fans of his more tonal work, Young has nicely contrasted these with selections from *Avenging Angel*, featuring a fine mix of broadly comical music and street jazz, and *The Telephone*. For the latter, he composed some excellent jazz tunes, but these cues were abandoned by the filmmakers in favor of previously tracked material. Some of the music from *Def-Con 4*, particularly "Armageddon," was tracked into the U.S. version of *Godzilla 1985*.

David Hirsch

Demolition Man 🎵🎵🎵♭

1993, Varese-Sarabande Records; from the movie *Demolition Man*, 1993.

Album Notes: *Music*: Elliot Goldenthal; *Orchestrations*: Bob Elhai, Elliot Goldenthal, David John Olsen, Lolita Ritmanis; *Music Editors*: J.J. Geroge, Eric Reasoner; Orchestra conducted by Jonathan Sheffer; *Album Producer*: Matthias Gohl; *Engineers*: Steve McLaughlin, Bobby Fernandez.

Selections: 1 Dies Irae (1:51); 2 Fire Fight (1:35); 3 Fuilty As Charged (3:58); 4 Action, Guns, Fun (1:26); 5 Machine Waltz (1:56); 6 Defrosting (1:43); 7 Confronting The Chief (:32); 8 Museum Dis Duel (1:56); 9 Subterranean Slugfest (1:44); 10 Meeting Cocteau (1:42); 11 Tracking Simon Phoenix (3:03); 12 Obligatory Car Chase (3:06); 13 Flawless Pearl (1:15); 14 Final Confrontation (1:55); 15 Code 187 (:41); 16 Silver Screen Kiss (1:30).

Review: Here's the '90s in a bottle: *Demolition Man* (1993) is a futuristic story with Sylvester Stallone and ditzy sidekick Sandra Bullock hunting down evil Wesley Snipes in new agey "San Angeles." It is completely over the top in mean-spirited noise and violence, but does not take itself seriously and is halfway entertaining, if you don't mind the aesthetic and moral values being sucked right out of you. Elliot Goldenthal turned in a loud, technically ambitious score that is also a '90s signpost. Screaming Wagnerian brass, electronics, percussion loops and minimalist keyboards blend into an earful of stylized mainstream cinema. However, unlike some of its techno-orchestra progeny, *Demolition Man* is actually good and seems to make a statement in its complete collision of genres, from orchestra to Philip Glass to new age. At the least, it has cool track titles like "Obligatory Car Chase." For New York-based composer Goldenthal—who really does know what he's doing—it was obviously another quarter-million dollar orchestration lesson paid for by the Brothers Warner.

Lukas Kendall

Dennis the Menace 🎵🎵♭

1993, Big Screen Records; from the movie *Dennis the Menace*, Warner Bros., 1993.

Album Notes: *Music*: Jerry Goldsmith; *Orchestrations*: Arthur Morton, Alexander Courage; *Music Editor*: Ken Hall; Orchestra conducted by Jerry Goldsmith; *Featured Musicians*: Jim Self (tuba), Tommy Morgan (harmonica); *Album Producers*: Jerry Goldsmith, Bruce Botnick; *Engineer*: Bruce Botnick.

Selections: 1 Dennis The Menace (Main Title)(2:52); 2 Baby Sitting (3:50); 3 Fun With False Teeth (1:54); 4 Bed Time (5:10); 5 The Shaggy Dog (4:02); 6 The Heist (4:14); 7 Wanna See My Sling Shot (1:21); 8 Tied Up (2:08); 9 Beans (4:09); 10 Real Love (1:29); 11 Hung Up (1:29); 12 He's Back (2:18); 13 Forgetful Sam (1:28); 14 Toasted Marshmallow (4:22).

Review: Jerry Goldsmith's entry in the *Home Alone* sweepstakes captures the spirit of its adorable tike star a bit too well. It's brimming with energy and good feeling, but also awfully annoying. The title theme is positively exuberant, charging along with the title character in a manner enjoyably reminiscent of the composer's propulsive theme to *The Great Train Robbery*, but most of the remainder of the album descends into Mickey Mousing hell as Goldsmith is forced to score the film's numerous pratfalls and kindergarten-level sight gags. Everything comes together for the obligatory heart-tugging finale, but by then you might be tempted to leave this CD with the sitter.

Jeff Bond

Desperado

Desperado ♫♫▹

1995, Epic Soundtrax; from the movie *Desperado*, Columbia Pictures, 1995.

Album Notes: *Music*: Los Lobos; *Songs*: Los Lobos; *Album Producers*: Los Lobos.

Selections: 1 Cancion del Mariachi (Morena de mi corazon)(C. Rosas)(2:07) *Los Lobos, Antonio Banderas*; 2 Six Blade Knife (M. Knopfler)(4:34) *Dire Straits*; 3 Jack The Ripper (M. Grant/L. Wray)(2:31) *Link Wray & His Ray Men*; 4 Manifold De Amour (D. Hidalgo/L. Perez)(2:03) *Latin Playboys*; 5 Forever Night Shade Mary (D. Hidalgo/L. Perez)(3:01) *Latin Playboys*; 6 Pass The Hatchet (R. Theriot/R. Leon, Jr./E.S. Oropeza)(3:01) *Roger & The Gypsies*; 7 Bar Fight (Los Lobos)(1:55) *Los Lobos*; 8 Strange Face Of Love (T. Larriva)(5:52) *Tito & Tarantula*; 9 Bucho's Gracias/Navajas Attacks (Los Lobos)(3:57) *Los Lobos*; 10 Bulletproof (Los Lobos)(1:43) *Los Lobos*; 11 Bella (C. Santana)(4:29) *Carlos Santana*; 12 Quedate aqui (M. Villafane) (2:06) *Salma Hayek*; 13 Rooftop Action (Los Lobos)(1:37) *Los Lobos*; 14 Phone Call (Los Lobos)(2:17) *Los Lobos*; 15 White Train (Showdown)(T. Larriva)(5:58) *Tito & Tarantula*; 16 Back To The House That Love Built (T. Larriva/T. Marsico/V. Marsico/C. Midnight)(4:41) *Tito & Tarantula*; 17 Let Love Reign (Los Lobos)(3:22) *Los Lobos*; 18 Mariachi Suite (Los Lobos)(4:24) *Los Lobos*.

Review: If you had picked up this soundtrack, you might not have been surprised when Antonio Banderas landed the Che role in "Evita" — although his warble-along with Los Lobos on "Cancion Del Mariachi (Morena De Mi Corazon)" hardly establishes his singing prowess. The rest of the album flaunts a cooly consistent Latin flavor, though it seems more restrained than it should be. Carlos Santana plays some beautiful solos on "Bella," and Link Wray & His Ray Men get a welcome resurrection on "Jack the Ripper."

Gary Graff

Desperately Seeking Susan/ Making Mr. Right ♫♫

1987, Varese-Sarabande Records; from the movies *Desperately Seeking Susan*, Orion Pictures, 1987; and *Making Mr. Right*, Orion Pictures, 1985.

Album Notes: *Music*: Thomas Newman (*Desperately Seeking Susan*), Chaz Jankel (*Making Mr. Right*); *Album Producers*: Thomas Newman, John Vigran; *Engineer*: John Vigran.

Selections: *DESPERATELY SEEKING SUSAN:* 1 Leave Atlantic City! (2:33); 2 Port Authority By Night (1:14); 3 New York City By Day (1:07); 4 Through The Viewscope (:40); 5 St. Mark's Place (1:30); 6 A Key And A Picture Of (1:22); 7 Battery Park/Amnesia (1:06); 8 Jail/Port Authority (2:23); 9 Rain (:51); 10 Running With Birds In Cages (1:12); 11 Trouble Almost (:43);

MAKING MR. RIGHT: 12 Chemtech Promo Video (1:52); 13 Ulysses' Escape (3:00); 14 Night Visit (1:00); 15 Frankie's Drive (1:05); 16 Ulysses (1:41); 17 In The Lab (1:15); 18 Sondra And Jeff (:57); 19 Mr. Right (1:28); 20 Wedding Reception (1:56); 21 Parting Glance (1:09).

Review: Under the guise of presenting two soundtracks to two films directed by Susan Seidelman, this CD compiles together the works of two composers who couldn't be farther apart, Thomas Newman and Chaz Jankel. Newman wrote the superior score for the film *Desperately Seeking Susan,* which had the distinction of being Madonna's first film, in which she played a free-spirit and occasional jewel thief who trades her lifestyle with that of Rosanna Arquette, a suburban housewife with a bad case of amnesia. Matching the action's quirky turns, Newman, in one of his earliest efforts, created an inventive little score that borrows from various styles to underline the various moods in the film.

Conversely, the charms in *Desperately* didn't wind up in *Making Mr. Right*, made two years later, which starred Ann Magnuson as a Florida woman who gets involved with an android. Saddled with a subject matter that might have been less than inspiring, Chaz Jankel concocted a series of cues that are, at best, serviceable, but rely too much on rhythm and not enough on melodic substance ("Frankie's Drive"). As a result, his score is generally dry and not very interesting, something which devalues the whole album.

Destination Moon ♫♫♫♫

1994, Citadel Records; from the movie *Destination Moon*, Eagle-Lion Films, 1950.

Album Notes: *Music*: Leith Stevens; The Vienna Concert Orchestra, conducted by Heinz Sandauer; *Album Producer*: Tom Null; *Engineer*: Bruce Leek.

Selections: 1 Earth (2:59); 2 In Outer Space (19:28); 3 On The Surface Of The Moon (4:14); 4 Escape From The Moon(3:02); 5 Finale (13:01).

Review: A trend-setter and pioneering effort in space exploration, *Destination Moon* may seem laughable today, particularly in view of the tremendous technical advances made by the movies since it was produced almost half a century ago. But in its time, it was a tremendous cinematographic achievement that owed a large part of its success to George Pal's extraordinary special effects, and to Leith Stevens' bold score, a perfect musical illustration of the engrossing screen adventure. Presented in five sections, including two long cues, the score essentially follows the film's action, with "In Outer Space" attempting to describe in sheer musical terms the effects of weightlessness, and with the "Finale" erupting in joyous accents as the daring space explorers make their trip back to Earth. The score may be closer in spirit to the musical techniques used at the time than the selections that eventually made it into the much more advanced *2001: A Space Odyssey* (q.v.). But it is very effective in capturing the moods of this early odyssey, at a time when going to the moon was still a dream, and stands out well as a pure piece of film music.

Devil in a Blue Dress ♫♫♫ᵛ

1995, Columbia Records; from the movie *Devil in a Blue Dress*, TriStar Pictures, 1995.

Album Notes: *Music*: Elmer Bernstein; *Orchestrations*: Emilie A. Bernstein; Orchestra conducted by Elmer Bernstein; *Soundtrack Executive Producers*: Carl Franklin, Gary Goetzman; *Engineer*: Dan Wallin.

Selections: 1 West Side Baby (J. Cameron/D. Bartley)(2:46) *T-Bone Walker*; 2 Ain't Nobody's Business (P. Grainger/J. Witherspoon/R. Prince/C. Williams) (2:54) *Jimmy Witherspoon*; 3 Hy-Ah Su (D. Ellington) *Duke Ellington*; 4 Hop, Skip And Jump (R. Milton)(2:34) *Roy Milton*; 5 Good Rockin' Tonight (R. Brown)(2:47) *Wynonie Harris*; 6 Blues After Hours (P. Crayton/J. Taub)(2:29) *Pee Wee Crayton*; 7 I Can't Go On Without You (S. Nix/H. Glover)(3:00) *Bull Moose Jackson*; 8 'Round Midnight (B. Hanighen/ C. Williams/T. Monk)(3:10) *Thelonious Moon*; 9 Chicken Shack Boogie (L. Callum/A. Milburn)(2:51) *Amos Milburn*; 10 Messin' Around (F. Hunt)(3:04) *Memphis Slim*; 11 Chica Boo (L. Glenn)(2:22) *Lloyd Glenn*; 12 Theme From Devil In A Blue Dress (2:32); 13 Malibu Chase (1:29); 14 End Credits (3:02).

Review: Anyone buying this soundtrack album on the assumption that the music was composed by Elmer Bernstein may be confronted with a serious case of mistaken identity. Bernstein indeed wrote the score for this film, a murder mystery set in Los Angeles in the days following World War II that mixes races and politics, but his contribution is only represented here by three selections, including the film's "Theme" and "End Credits." In this case, however, the rest of the music is solidly rooted into some of the period's classic recordings, with rare and exciting sides by T-Bone Walker, Jimmy Witherspoon, Duke Ellington, Thelonious Monk, and Memphis Slim, among others, that define better than any other the rich background of the film itself. Contrasting with these mono recordings, Bernstein's cues may sound oddly out of place, but since they

are relatively short and come completely at the end the effect is not too jarring. Also, it must be said that, though stylistically different, they are quite attractive, whetting one's appetite for a more comprehensive "score" album.

The Devil's Own ♫♫♫♫♫

1997, Beyond Music; from the movie *The Devil's Own*, Columbia Pictures, 1997.

Album Notes: *Music*: James Horner; *Orchestrations*: James Horner; *Music Editor*: Jim Henrikson; Orchestra conducted by James Horner; *Featured Musicians*: Sara Clancy, Tony Hinnigan, Tommy Hayes, Randy Kerber, Eric Rigler, Ian Underwood; *Album Producer*: James Horner; *Engineer*: Shawn Murphy.

Selections: 1 Main Title (4:35); 2 God Be With You (D. O'Riordan)(3:32) *Dolores O' Riordan*; 3 Ambush (2:30); 4 The Irish Republican Navy (1:20); 5 The New World (4:31); 6 Launching The Boat (3:03); 7 Secrets Untold (5:02); 8 The Pool Hall (2:30); 9 Rory's Arrest/Diaz Is Killed (4:21); 10 Quiet Goodbyes (1:02); 11 Rooftop Escape (1:45); 12 The Mortal Blow (5:10); 13 Going Home (J. Horner/W. Jennings)(7:10).

Review: The Gaelic folk song "There Are Flowers Growing Upon the Hill," which bookends this album and contrasts its most searing moments, seems a perfect complement to this engrossing story of a member of the IRA who avoids arrest and prosecution by going into hiding in America and moving into the house of a New York Irish cop. Between the action cues that detail his flight from justice and involvement in additional revolutionary activities from his American base, and the more lyrical accents that underscore the Irish soul of the story, James Horner's music, unusually low key and emotionally affecting, unfolds with great majesty and power. Some cues ("The New World," or "Secrets Untold," with its distant evocation of Ralph Vaughan Williams) are particularly attractive and denote a new level of maturity in the composer. Similarly, cues like "Launching the Boat" draw their strength from the deft use of Irish-inspired melodies and instruments (notably the Uilleann flute and hornpipe) that confer them greater intensity and poetry. It all adds up to a very attractive and enjoyable soundtrack album.

Diabolique ♫♫♫

1996, edel America Records; from the movie *Diabolique*, 1996.

Album Notes: *Music*: Randy Edelman; *Orchestrations*: Ralph Ferraro; *Music Editor*: John LaSalandra; Orchestra conducted by Randy Edelman; *Featured Soloist*: Randy Edelman (piano); *Album Producer*: Randy Edelman; *Engineers*: Robert Fernandez, Elton Ahi.

Selections: 1 Main Title (3:41); 2 Desperation (4:09); 3 Scene Of The Crime (2:48); 4 Missing Persons (2:15); 5 A Stimulating Bath (6:18); 6 Empty Pool (2:35); 7 Suburban Pittsburgh (3:09); 8 Searching Through Drawers (4:12); 9 Mia (3:00); 10 Getting Dizzy (2:19); 11 Darkened Hallway (2:54); 12 Two Females And A Guy (5:52); 13 Finale (3:37); 14 In The Arms Of Love (M. Marinangeli/F. Maddlone)(2:26) *Sherry Williams*.

Review: Though lacking some of the suspense in Henri-Georges Clouzot's 1955 thriller upon which this remake was based, *Diabolique* offers its share of throat-tightening moments in this exploration of the murder of an authoritarian schoolmaster in the hands of his sickly wife and strong-headed mistress, played by Isabelle Adjani and Sharon Stone respectively. Informing the chiller and some of its most visually frightful moments, Randy Edelman's score at times evokes Bernard Herrmann's urgently feverish music for some of Alfred Hitchcock's best dramas. Most often, however, there is little tension in the cues and none of the hallucinatory effects that would have taken the score to a higher level of effective illustration, as if the composer had been afraid to be too extrovert. "A Stimulating Bath," "Empty Pool" and "Darkened Hallway," however, are appropriately somber and ominous sounding.

Diamonds are Forever ♫♫♫⁵

1995, Capitol-EMI Music; from the movie *Diamonds are Forever*, United Artists, 1971.

Album Notes: *Music*: John Barry; Orchestra conducted by John Barry; *Album Producer*: John Barry.

Selections: 1 Diamonds Are Forever (Main Title)(2:40) *Shirley Bassey*; 2 Bond Meets Bambi And Thumper (2:16); 3 Moon Buggy Ride (3:12); 4 Circus, Circus (2:57); 5 Death At The Whyte House (3:43); 6 Diamonds Are Forever (3:45); 7 Diamonds Are Forever (2:32); 8 Bond Smells A Rat (1:51); 9 Tiffany Case (3:44); 10 007 And Counting (3:30); 11 Q's Trick (2:24); 12 To Hell With Blofeld (1:28).

Review: John Barry was at the peak of his creativity when he scored the James Bond films. Though he derisively characterized his contributions to the screen exploits of Agent 007 as "million-dollar Mickey Mouse music," the fact is that no one else (and there have been others) managed to match the sense of fun and sheer merriment Barry brought to his scores. Fans of Bond and Barry (the two names have become almost inseparable) often argue over which of Barry's scores stand out among those he wrote, but *Diamonds are Forever* is often mentioned as one of the best, which doesn't mean that this recorded representation is necessarily as good as it should be. As a

matter of fact, among the Bond score recordings, this is probably the one that most closely resembles a near-miss: the best cues in the film have been left out of the soundtrack album, and those that have been included sound in dire need of a good remixing and mastering. Still, there are some memorable moments in the album, notably the quirky "Moon Buggy Ride," with its fun extrapolations on xylophone and flute; "Tiffany Case," a seductive kitschy lounge cue; the jazzy "Q's Trick," with its enjoyable big band riff; and of course Shirley Bassey's rendition of the title tune, which was perhaps not as pungent as "Goldfinger," but again nothing could have possibly matched that song and Bassey's treatment of it.

Dick Tracy

Dick Tracy ♫♫♫

1990, Sire Records; from the movie *Dick Tracy*, Warner Bros., 1990.

Album Notes: *Music*: Danny Elfman; *Orchestrations*: Steve Bartek, Shirley Walker, Jack Hayes; *Music Editor*: Bob Badami; Orchestra conducted by Shirley Walker; *Album Producer*: Danny Elfman, Steve Bartek, Bob Badami; *Engineers*: Dennis Sands, Shawn Murphy; *Assistant Engineers*: Sue McLean, Sharon Rice.

Selections: 1 Main Titles (3:36); 2 After The "Kid" (1:45); 3 Crime Spree (1:54); 4 Breathless' Theme (2:13); 5 Big Boy/Bad Boys (2:10); 6 Tess' Theme (1:09); 7 Slimy D.A. (1:41); 8 Breathless Comes On (2:54); 9 Meet The Blank (1:43); 10 The Story Unfolds (1:59); 11 Blank Gets The Goods (2:25); 12 Rooftops (2:01); 13 Tess' Theme (reprise)(1:17); 14 The Chase (2:57); 15 Showdown/Reunited (4:07); 16 Finale (1:00).

Review: It only seemed natural that after *Batman*, Danny Elfman would become the top composer of the comic strip hero, a position he quickly tired of. In his music for *Dick Tracy*, however, the novelty had not yet worn out, and his whimsical approach is less rooted in the dark detective film-noir, and more in the gangster epics of Elliot Ness and *The Untouchables*, and the music of Gershwin. Making it even more seductive, there's some nice "Big Band" influences to portray bad girl torch singer Breathless Mahoney, and an innocent love theme for Tracy's girl, Tess Trueheart.

David Hirsch

Dick Tracy ♫⁵

1990, Sire Records; from the movie *Dick Tracy*, Warner Bros., 1990.

Album Notes: *Album Producer*: Andy Paley; *Engineers*: Mark Linett, Roger Wake, Brian Malouf.

Selections: 1 Ridin' The Rails (N. Claflin/A. Paley)(2:17) *k.d. lang, Take 6*; 2 Pep, Vim And Verve (B. Elliot/N. Claflin/A. Paley)(3:21) *Jeff Vincent, Andy Paley*; 3 It Was The Whiskey Talkin' (Not Me)(3:39)(A. Paley/N. Claflin/J. Paley/M. Kernan)(3:39) *Jerry Lee Lewis*; 4 You're In The Doghouse Now (J. Lass/A. Paley/M. Kernan/N. Claflin)(1:58) *Brenda Lee*; 5 Some Lucky Day (M. Kernan/A. Paley)(2:33) *Andy Paley*; 6 Blue Nights (A. Paley/J. Lass/J. Paley)(2:44) *Tommy Page*; 7 Wicked Woman, Foolish Man (J. Paley/J. Lassa/A. Paley/N. Claflin)(2:12) *August Darnell*; 8 The Confidence Man (N. Claflin/J. Lass/A. Paley)(2:23) *Patti Austin*; 9 Looking Glass Sea (A. Bell/V. Clarke)(2:45) *Erasure*; 10 Dick Tracy (A. Paley/J. Lass)(2:37) *Ice-T*; 11 Slow Rollin' Mama (D. Pomus/B. Marshall/A. Paley)(2:24) *LaVern Baker*; 12 Rompin' And Stompin' (J. Vincent/N. Claflin)(2:05) *Al Jarreau*; 13 Mr. Fix-It (1930's version)(A. Paley/J. Lass)(2:50) *Darlene Love*; 14 Mr. Fix-It (A. Paley)(3:15) *Darlene Love*; 15 It Was The Whiskey Talkin' (Not Me) (rock'n'roll version)(A. Paley/N. Claflin/J. Paley/M. Kernan)(2:55) *Jerry Lee Lewis*; 16 Dick Tracy (90's mix)(A. Paley/J. Lass)(5:28) *Ice-T*.

Review: See entry below.

Madonna: I'm Breathless ♫♫♫

1990, Sire Records; from the movie *Dick Tracy*, Warner Bros., 1990.

Album Notes: *Album Producers*: Madonna, Patrick Leonard, Kevin Gilbert, Shep Pettibone, Bill Bottrell; *Engineers*: Brian Malouf, Shep Pettibone.

Selections: 1 He's A Man (Madonna/P. Leonard)(4:42); 2 Sooner Or Later (S. Sondheim)(3:18); 3 Hanky Panky (Madonna/P. Leonard)(3:57); 4 I'm Going Bananas (M. Kernan/A. Baley)(1:41); 5 Cry Baby (Madonna/P. Leonard)(4:04); 6 Something To Remember (Madonna/P. Leonard)(5:03); 7 Back In Business (Madonna/P. Leonard)(5:10); 8 More (S. Sondheim)(4:56); 9 What Can You Lose (S. Sondheim)(2:08); 10 Now I'm Following You, Part 1 (1:35); 11 Now I'm Following You, Part 2 (3:18); 12 Vogue (4:50).

Review: If Andy Paley, whose name is all over the first album as producer, writer or co-writer of most of the songs, and occasional artist/performer, were slightly more talented, this *Dick Tracy* CD could actually be enjoyable. But the pop songs he wrote for the occasion border on the banal, and only the performances by an all-star cast (which includes k.d. lang, Jerry Lee Lewis, Darlene Love, Patti Austin, Al Jarreau, August Darnell, Ice-T and LaVern Baker, among its most recognizable names) make this album more interesting than it actually is.

Also, notably missing from that collection are the songs written by Stephen Sondheim, and performed by Madonna as Breathless Mahoney, which can be found on the second CD. In this case, the combination of the gifted songwriter and the talented performer proves explosive, and turns the album into a totally delirious burst of enjoyment. Madonna demonstrates another side of her creativity by co-writing some of the other songs on the album, which are not at all bad.

Die Hard

Die Hard 2: Die Harder ♫♫

1990, Varese-Sarabande; from the movie *Die Hard 2: Die Harder*, 20th Century-Fox, 1990.

Album Notes: *Music*: Michael Kamen; *Orchestrations*: Michael Kamen, Chris Boardman, Bruce Babcock, William Ross, Don Davis, Mark Koval, Phil Giffin, Ron Gorow; The Los Angeles Motion Picture All-Stars Orchestra, conducted by Michael Kamen; *Featured Soloists*: Mel Colins (saxophone), Derick Collins (clarinet), Sid Sax (violin); *Album Producers*: Michael Kamen, Stephen P. McLaughlin, Christopher S. Brooks; *Engineer*: Armin Steiner.

Selections: 1 Colonel Stuart (1:29); 2 Baggage Handling (3:49); 3 General Esperanza (2:13); 4 The Annexe Skywalk (3:11); 5 The Church (1:15); 6 The Doll (3:50); 7 The Runway (3:57); 8 In The Plane (1:37); 9 Icicle (2:54); 10 Snowmobiles (2:40); 11 The Terminal (6:13); 12 Finlandia (J. Sibelius) (7:29).

Review: See entry below.

Die Hard with a Vengeance ♫

1995, RCA Victor; from the movie *Die Hard with a Vengeance*, 20th Century-Fox, 1995.

Album Notes: *Music*: Michael Kamen; *Orchestrations*: Michael Kamen; *Music Editor*: Christopher S. Brooks; The Symphony Seattle, conducted by Michael Kamen; *Album Producers*: Michael Kamen, Stephen P. McLaughlin, Christopher S. Brooks; *Engineer*: Stephen P. McLaughlin.

Selections: 1 Summer In The City (J. Sebastian/S. Boone/M. Sebastian) (2:45) *The Lovin' Spoonful*; 2 Goodbye Bonwits (6:28); 3 Got It Covered (R. Roachford/L. Maturine/R. Kirkpatrick) (4:14) *Fu-Schnickens*; 4 John And Zeus (3:19); 5 In Front Of The Kids (D. Lee) (2:45) *Extra Prolific*; 6 Papaya King (5:20); 7 Take A-nother Train (2:55); 8 The Iron Foundry (A. Mosolov) (3:09); 9 Waltz Of The Bankers (4:14); 10 Gold Vault (3:46); 11

Surfing In The Aquaduct (2:31); 12 Symphony No. 1 (excerpt, 4th movement) (J. Brahms) (15:00); 13 Symphony No. 9 (excerpt, 4th movement) (L. van Beethoven) (9:48).

Review: These lackluster follow-ups to the original film score (still unreleased at press time) fail to capture the energy Michael Kamen established with his first effort. Instead, both albums wander aimlessly, "mickey mousing" the action with nary a memorable theme present. This all may be partly due to poor sequencing, especially on *Die Hard with a Vengeance*, since that score was unfinished when the CD was pressed to meet its release date (which also explains the lack of track titles on the packaging). Pop songs and classical cues were added on the latter to fill time.

David Hirsch

Diggstown ♪

1992, Varese-Sarabande; from the movie *Diggstown*, M-G-M, 1992.

Album Notes: *Music*: James Newton Howard; *Orchestrations*: James Newton Howard; Orchestra conducted by James Newton Howard; *Featured Musicians*: Marc Bonilla (guitars), John Robinson (drums), Neil Stubenhaus (bass guitar), Tommy Morgan (harmonica), Michael Finnigan (Hammond organ), Bob Zimmitti (percussion); *Album Producers*: James Newton Howard, Michael Mason; *Engineer*: Robert Schaper; *Assistant Engineers*: Charlie Paakkari, Tom Hardisty.

Selections: 1 Main Title (3:19); 2 Do I Have It Or Not (:55); 3 Training Montage (1:58); 4 Emily (1:26); 5 Lane Sees Emily (1:35); 6 Tank (1:33); 7 Digg's House (1:49); 8 Slim's Fight (1:28); 9 Billy's Fight (1:11); 10 Hambone (4:23); 11 Hammerhead (3:40); 12 Torres Fight (1:59); 13 The Mock Ending (1:05); 14 End Credits (3:32).

Review: The lack of musical focus in this score may be its most characteristic aspect. Literally speaking, the music is all over the place, not knowing whether to call it rock, soundtrack, folk or quits. For the most part, the cues tend to be dominated by electric guitar riffs over long synth lines that go nowhere, and an obligatory booming drum beat. Unfortunately, it sounds very dry, not very inspired and in bad need of a central thematic idea. Even semi-interesting concepts like "Tank," with its blues ending, are not sufficiently developed to catch one's interest. James Newton Howard has done much better things before and since.

Diner ♪♪♪♪

1982, Elektra/Asylum Records; from the movie *Diner*, M-G-M, 1982.

Album Notes: *Album Producers*: Carol Thompson, Roger Mayer.

Selections: 1 Whole Lotta Shakin' Going On (D. Williams) (2:51) *Jerry Lee Lewis*; 2 A Teenager In Love (D. Pomus/M. Shuman) (2:27) *Dion & The Belmonts*; 3 A Thousand Miles Away (J. Sheppard/W. Miller) (2:25) *The Heartbeats*; 4 Somethin' Else (S. Sheeley/B. Cochran) (2:06) *Eddie Cochran*; 5 I Wonder Why (M. Fair/R. Weeks) (2:16) *Dion & The Belmonts*; 6 Honey Don't (C. Perkins) (2:47) *Carl Perkins*; 7 Mr. Blue (D. Blackwell) (2:22) *The Fleetwoods*; 8 Reconsider Baby (L. Fulson) (3:08) *Lowell Fulson*; 9 Ain't Got No Home (C. Henry) (2:19) *Clarence Henry*; 10 Come Go With Me (C. Quick) (2:38) *The Del Vikings*; 11 Beyond The Sea (C. Trenet/J. Lawrence) (2:09) *Bobby Darin*; 12 Theme From A Summer Place (M. Steiner) (2:08); 13 Fascination (F. Marchetti) (2:20) *Jane Morgan*; 14 Where Or When (R. Rodgers/L. Hart) (2:48) *Dick Haymes*; 15 It's All In The Game (C. Sigman/C. Dawes) (2:37) *Tommy Edwards*; 16 Whole Lot Of Loving (A. Domino/D. Bartholomew) (1:38) *Fats Domino*; 17 Take Out Some Insurance (J. Reed) (2:21) *Jimmy Reed*; 18 Dream Lover (B. Darin) (2:29) *Bobby Darin*; 19 Don't Be Cruel (O. Blackwell/E. Presley) (2:02) *Elvis Presley*; 20 Goodbye Baby (J. Scott) (2:07) *Jack Scott*.

Review: Great movie, great soundtrack — in fact, maybe the best collection of '50s music in any movie this side of *American Graffiti*. It doesn't have everybody (no Chuck Berry, for instance), but the names that are here — Elvis Presley, Jerry Lee Lewis, Fats Domino, Jimmy Reed, Dion & the Belmonts, Jack Scott and more — are all hall-of-fame choices.

Gary Graff

Dingo ♪♪♪♪♪

1991, Warner Bros. Records; from the movie *Dingo*, Greycat Films, 1991.

Album Notes: *Music*: Miles Davis, Michel Legrand; *Orchestrations*: Michel Legrand; *Featured Musicians*: Miles Davis, Chuck Findley, Nolan Smith, Ray Brown, George Graham, Oscar Brashear (trumpet), Kei Akagi, Alan Oldfield, Michel Legrand (piano), Mark Rivett (guitar), John Bigham, Ricky Wellman, Harvey Mason, Alphonse Mouzon (drums, percussion), Benny Rietveld, "Foley," Abe Laboriel (bass), Kenny Garrett (saxophone); *Album Producers*: Rolf de Heer, Michel Legrand; *Engineer*: Peter D. Smith.

Selections: 1 Kimberley Trumpet (2:15) *Chuck Findley*; 2 The Arrival (2:05) *Miles Davis*; 3 Concert On The Runway (3:50) *Miles Davis*; 4 The Departure (1:05) *Miles Davis*; 5 Dingo Howl (:08) *Chuck Findley*; 6 Letter As Hero (1:22) *Chuck Findley*; 7 Trumpet Cleaning (3:56) *Miles Davis*; 8 The Dream (3:45) *Miles Davis*; 9 Paris Walking I (1:58) *Chuck Findley*; 10 Paris Walking II (3:17) *Miles Davis*; 11 Kimberley Trumpet In Paris (2:05)

Chuck Findley; 12 The Music Room (2:50); 13 Club Entrance (4:12) *Chuck Findley*; 14 The Jam Session (6:00) *Miles Davis, Chuck Findley*; 15 Going Home (2:05) *Miles Davis*; 16 Surprise! (4:52) *Chuck Findley*.

Review: Early in their respective careers, Miles Davis and French composer Michel Legrand worked together on a trend-setting jazz album, so this soundtrack may, in a sense, be considered a reunion of sorts. The score, for a film made in Australia, is mostly noteworthy for Legrand's sometimes explosive cues ("Concert on the Runway," "Letter as Hero," "Paris Walking II," "The Jam Session"), and for Davis' unmistakable style. Chuck Findley, who takes the spotlight on several tracks, brings to the proceedings a different flair, with both trumpeters receiving solid support from an impressive array of seasoned performers, including Abe Laboriel on bass, Harvey Mason and Alphonse Mouzon on drums, and Legrand himself on piano. An occasional bit of dialogue places some of the tracks into the film's context.

Disclosure *♫♫♫ᵛ*

1995, Virgin Movie Music; from the movie *Disclosure*, Warner Bros., 1995.

Album Notes: *Music*: Ennio Morricone; *Orchestrations*: Ennio Morricone; Orchestra Unione Musicisti di Roma, conducted by Ennio Morricone; *Album Producer*: Ennio Morricone; *Engineers*: Franco and Fabio Patrignani; *Assistant Engineer*: Andrea Morricone.

Selections: 1 Serene Family (4:11); 2 An Unusual Approach (7:07); 3 With Energy And Decision (2:07); 4 Virtual Reality (6:24); 5 Preparation And Victory (4:04); 6 Disclosure (:49); 7 Sad Family (1:29); 8 Unemployed! (1:10); 9 Sex And Computers (2:50); 10 Computers And Work (2:00); 11 Sex And Power (2:33); 12 First Passacaglia (4:21); 13 Second Passacaglia (1:41); 14 Third Passacaglia (4:33); 15 Sex, Power And Computers (4:23).

Review: The lovely "Serene Family" which introduces this score soon gives way to more ominous sounds, as if to indicate that not everything is quite right in this complex story of a computer analyst whose new boss turns out to be an old flame, and who finds himself accused of sexual harassment when he refuses to rekindle their love affair. With his usual crafty sense of drama and tension, Morricone conjures up the best and worst in the screen action, with cues that subtly underscore it while creating an aura of their own that is difficult to dismiss. Most fascinating in this set of musical images are the three similarly-themed "Passacaglias," in which the composer uses

all the orchestral resources at his disposal to create cues that are particularly evocative.

The Distinguished Gentleman *♫♫♫*

1992, Varese-Sarabande; from the movie *The Distinguished Gentleman*, Hollywood Pictures, 1992.

Album Notes: *Music*: Randy Edelman; *Orchestrations*: Randy Edelman, Greig McRitchie; *Music Editor*: Tom Carlson; Orchestra conducted by Randy Edelman; *Album Producer*: Randy Edelman; *Engineer*: Elton Ahi.

Selections: 1 Where The Money Is (2:50); 2 The Distinguished Gentleman (2:07); 3 A Kiss By The Potomac (1:50); 4 Wrong Place, Wrong Time (1:45); 5 Mr. Johnson Finds A Cause (1:13); 6 Girls Of Many Nations In D.C. (1:37); 7 Lucrative Luncheon (1:27); 8 Trouble (1:20); 9 Perks (1:16); 10 A Quick Getaway (:34); 11 Soft Rebellion (1:21); 12 Three Ring Hearing Room (:59); 13 Taking Sides On The Issue (1:14); 14 You, Me And A Martini (2:56); 15 Art Of The Con (1:43); 16 On The Campaign Trail (2:06); 17 The Distinguished Gentleman (reprise)/Finale (2:23).

Review: An exuberant calypso, "Where the Money Is," sets the extravagant tone to this colorful comedy starring Eddie Murphy as a small-time con man from Miami who is transported into the world of politics after he is mistaken for a deceased congressman. Contrasting the happy tones of this telling tune, Randy Edelman created a series of grander-than-life cues to depict the general atmosphere that pervades the new surroundings in which the con-man, and his associates, suddenly find themselves. It is an amusing juxtaposition that gives the score its greatest strength, and turns it into a joyous musical affair. In the process, the composer reveals a quirky mind in tunes like the pleasantly lilting "Lucrative Luncheon," and a flair for the grandiloquent in selections like "The Distinguished Gentleman March" or "Taking Sides on the Issue." It would be significantly more exciting, however, had the cues been further developed than they are (many of them hover between a minute and a minute-and-a-half of playing time, not enough to truly make a lasting impression).

Diva *♫♫♫*

1986, Rykodisc/DRG Records; from the movie *Diva*, Galaxie Films & Greenwich Film Productions, 1981.

Album Notes: *Music*: Vladimir Cosma; The London Symphony Orchestra, conducted by Vladimir Cosma; *Featured Soloists*: Hubert Varron (cello), Raymond Allesandri (piano), Vladimir

"He was very anxious that the music should follow the on-screen progress of the two women, Marianne and Kate. I had to find a balance between melancholy and optimism, a delicate balance."

Patrick Doyle
on working with Sense and Sensibility *director Ang Lee (The Hollywood Reporter, 1-16-96)*

Cosma (piano); *Featured Artist*: Wilhelmenia Wiggins Fernandez; *Album Producer*: Vladimir Cosma.

Selections: 1 Aria from "La Wally" (A. Catalani) (3:30) *Wilhelmenia Wiggins Fernandez*; 2 Sentimental Walk (2:38); 3 Dead End (3:04); 4 Gorodish (3:00); 5 The Zen In The Art Of Bread And Butter (2:04); 6 La Wally (instrumental version) (A. Catalani) (3:09); 7 Sentimental Walk (piano solo) (3:20); 8 Ground Swell (4:21); 9 Metro Police (2:35); 10 The Priest And The West Indian (1:30); 11 Abandoned Factory (3:10); 12 Aria from "La Wally" (reprise) (3:22) *Wilhelmenia Wiggins Fernandez*.

Review: Vladimir Cosma, one of France's most popular film composers but a relative unknown in this country, delivered one of his best scores for this film, directed by Jean-Jacques Beineix, about the young admirer of a celebrated soprano, and a recording he made of one of her performances, which bootleggers want to acquire. The film did much to popularize Alfredo Catalini's aria from the obscure opera "La Wally," but it also attracted attention to Cosma for the wonderful qualities in his score, particularly the evocative "Sentimental Walk," heard in a scene in which the soprano and her young fan are seen walking in the rain in the desolated Jardin des Tuileries in Paris. Unlike some of Cosma's more quirky efforts, however, the other selections here are less defined and not as powerfully imaginative.

Divine Madness ♪♪♪♪

1980, Atlantic Records; from the movie *Divine Madness*, Warner Bros., 1980.

Album Notes: *Music Arrangers*: Tony Berg, Randy Kerber; *Album Producer*: Dennis Kirk; *Engineer*: Dennis Kirk.

Selections: 1 Big Noise From Winnetka (G. Rodin/B. Crosby/B. Haggart/R. Bauduc)(3:52); 2 Paradise (H. Nilsson/G. Garfield/

P. Botkin, Jr.)(4:09); 3 Shiver Me Timbers (T. Waits)(3:56); 4 Fire Down Below (B. Seger)(3:05); 5 Stay With Me (J. Ragovoy/G. Weiss)(6:24); 6 My Mother's Eyes (T. Jans) (2:29); 7 Chapel Of Love (J. Barry/E. Greenwich/P. Spector)/Boogie Woogie Bugle Boy (D. Raye/H. Prince)(4:02); 8 E Street Shuffle (B. Springsteen)/ Summer (The First Time)(B. Goldsboro)/Leader Of The Pack (G. Morton/J. Barry/E. Greenwich) (9:42); 9 You Can't Always Get What You Want (M. Jagger/ K. Richards)/I Shall Be Released (B. Dylan)(5:56).

Review: This recording of standards and new tunes performed by the exhilarating Bette Midler will no doubt appeal to all her fans, if they don't already own the CD. Others will react to it according to their own tolerance for the tongue-in-cheek style of the star, and her often outrageous stage antics. Recording during a concert performance, the selections have the spontaneity and energetic drive that usually characterize the singer's free-wheeling approach when she finds herself in front of an audience totally attuned to her. Sonically, the recording is not all that it should be, with the large hall blurring some of the sound qualities, particularly in the big up-tempo numbers, but don't let that deter you from enjoying it.

Doc Hollywood ♪♪♪▷

1991, Varese-Sarabande; from the movie *Doc Hollywood*, Warner Bros., 1991.

Album Notes: *Music*: Carter Burwell; *Orchestrations*: Sonny Kompanek; *Music Editor*: Adam Smalley; Orchestra conducted by Sonny Kompanek; *Album Producer*: Carter Burwell; *Engineer*: Michael Farrow.

Selections: 1 The Lady In The Lake (:42); 2 Speedster (3:35); 3 Stones Rounds (2:22); 4 Kije's Wedding (S. Prokofiev)(1:27); 5 Meat Is Murder (:35); 6 Down Ten Dollars (:21); 7 Jasmine Strut (:54); 8 Chant (2:22); 9 Slow Squash Love (:36); 10 Pee Zydeco (:24); 11 Voices Cross A Lake (2:10); 12 The Millwood Stomp (:58); 13 Crazy (W. Nelson)(2:43) *Patsy Cline*; 14 Polegnala e Todora (P. Kouter)(2:48); 15 Fireflies And Night Shade (2:30); 16 Stone Walks Alone (:49); 17 Escape From Grady (1:11); 18 Breech Birth (:37); 19 Remembrance Of Things Past (:57); 20 A Shooting Star (:51); 21 Back To The Interstate, Ben Stone (2:52); 22 Life Sentence (4:24).

Review: Ths delightfully off-base score by Carter Burwell does well contrasting the high-powered dreams of a big city doctor (Michael J. Fox) sentenced to perform community service in a small Southern town. The use of zydeco music, previously established in the "Northern Exposure" TV series, adds the right amount of absurdity, especially in an hilarious sequence called "Pee Zydeco" (see the movie to find out). However, it's

Burwell's moving variations on a romantic, ambient vocal theme, particularly "Voices Across the Lake," that really stick in the mind.

David Hirsch

Doctor Faustus

1997, DRG Records; from the movie *Doctor Faustus*, Columbia Pictures, 1968.

See: Francis of Assisi

Dr. Giggles ♫♫▹

1992, Intrada Records; from the movie *Dr. Giggles*, Largo Entertainment/Universal Pictures, 1992.

Album Notes: *Music*: Brian May; *Music Editor*: Bill Abbott; Orchestra conducted by Brian May; *Album Producers*: Brian May, Michael Linn; *Engineers*: Robin Gray, Joe Tarantino.

Selections: 1 Dr. Giggles (5:19); 2 Tivoli Street (3:01); 3 Re-Opening Case (2:37); 4 The Doctor's In (1:52); 5 The Gentle Blue Pill (4:07); 6 The Cops Search (2:17); 7 Jenny Talks To Max (:46); 8 We Are What We Eat (1:42); 9 A Heart Problem (1:48); 10 Mirror Maze (4:31); 11 Magruder's Flashback (4:03); 12 Doctor Heal Thy Self (4:35); 13 Have A Heart (3:54); 14 The Rescue (3:01); 15 Fight And Flight (5:39); 16 He's Not Dead (4:36).

Review: Brian May scored the first two *Mad Max* films for director George Miller, and even though the film brought great success to Miller and star Mel Gibson, the Australian May never quite broke into the Hollywood studio system, despite having a great deal of talent that never seemed to realize its full potential on this side of the Atlantic. One of May's rare late excursions into U.S. films came when he scored *Dr.Giggles*, Manny Coto's tired horror-parody with *L.A. Law* star Larry Drake. With a full-blooded orchestra behind him, May wrote a decent score for a movie that didn't deserve as much, marked by a motif for the title protagonist that's dark and menacing, but more like an old-time Universal horror movie than Danny Elfman. The music is well-done but offers few surprises, so genre addicts might want to check it out, though others are advised to head elsewhere.

Andy Dursin

Dr. Jekyll and Ms. Hyde ♫♫♫♫

1995, Intrada Records; from the movie *Dr. Jekyll and Ms. Hyde*, Savoy Pictures, 1995.

Album Notes: *Music*: Mark McKenzie; *Orchestrations*: Mark McKenzie, Patrick Russ; *Music Editors*: Dick Bernstein, John Finklea, Jim Young; Orchestra conducted by Randy Thornton; *Featured Vocalist*: Patricia Swanson (soprano); *Album Producer*: Mark McKenzie; *Engineer*: Andy Waterman.

Selections: 1 Overture (6:08); 2 Old Movie Music (2:20); 3 Off To Work (2:20); 4 Great Grandfather's Books (2:37); 5 Something Electrical (2:18); 6 A Little Surprise (1:47); 7 Breakfast Transformation (2:35); 8 Charades (2:20); 9 Irresistible Helen (1:41); 10 Helen Deflates (2:02); 11 The Unstable Gene (2:12); 12 Taking Back My Chromosomes (1:57); 13 Narrow Escape (2:19); 14 Footsy (based on "Habanera" from Carmen)(G. Bizet)(1:55); 15 Final Transformation (2:46); 16 Acid Love Potion (2:46).

Review: A spin off the old chestnut horror story about Dr. Jekyll and his nefarious alter ego Mr. Hyde (in this case a feminine incarnation for added fun), *Dr. Jekyll and Ms. Hyde* gave Mark McKenzie an opportunity to write an expansive, lyrical score, in which broad swathes of musical humor add an unexpected and welcome touch. The recurring main theme, a deft confrontation of two musical elements (one for each of the main character's dual personalities), amusingly pervades the score, in which an occasional Gothic accent is brought by the cliched contribution of an organ. Throughout, in keeping with the film's tongue-in-cheek approach to its subject, McKenzie displays his thorough musical flair, with some delightful moments ("Off to Work," "A Little Surprise," "Helen Deflates") emerging as a result. Even the inclusion of the "Habanera," from Bizet's opera *Carmen,* does not seem so out of place in the overall outrageous score.

Dr. No ♫♫

1995, EMI Records; from the movie *Dr. No*, United Artists, 1962.

Album Notes: *Music*: Monty Norman; Orchestra conducted by Monty Norman.

Selections: 1 James Bond Theme (1:45); 2 Kingston Calypso (2:42); 3 Jamaican Rock (2:03); 4 Jump-Up (2:08); 5 Audio Bongo (1:30); 6 Under The Mango Tree (2:20); 7 Twisting With James (3:08); 8 Jamaica Jazz (1:04); 9 Under The Mango Tree (2:40); 10 Jump Up (1:25); 11 Dr. No's Fantasy (1:40); 12 Kingston Calypso (2:30); 13 The Island Speaks (3:18); 14 Under The Mango Tree (2:37); 15 The Boy's Chase (1:30); 16 Dr. No's Theme (1:57); 17 The James Bond Theme (2:20); 18 Love At Last (1:49).

Review: Forget the credits, this album automatically raises the question who did actually write the famous "James Bond Theme"? Is it Monty Norman, whose only other screen credits include the obscure *House of Fright* and *Dickens of London*? Or is it, as he all along contended, John Barry, whose impeccable credentials include, in addition to a dozen other James Bond scores, a flurry of Academy Award-nominated and -winning contributions? Whatever the case, this soundtrack to the first James Bond film teems with some good moments, mostly those relating to the exotic Caribbean locale of the action, like "Kingston Calypso," "Jump-Up," "Under the Mango Tree," and some painfully dispensable ones, like "Audio Bongo," for instance, which offers very little, musically speaking, or the dated "Twisting With James." This, however, is not the only problem with this generally charmless album. The fact that the tracks are improperly sequenced notwithstanding, this is probably the worst sounding CD you are likely to find, with a lot of hiss on the tracks, some distortion, and a shrillness that makes the best tracks difficult to listen to. Chalk this one up as yet another soundtrack album that needs to be properly EQ'd before it is deemed acceptable by digital standards.

Dr. Strangelove: Or How I Learned to Stop Worrying and Love the Bomb

1982, Varese-Sarabande; from the movie *Dr. Strangelove: Or How I Learned to Stop Worrying and Love the Bomb*, Columbia Pictures, 1964.

See: Laurie Johnson in Compilations' section

Doctor Zhivago ♪♪♪♪▷

1995, Rhino Records; from the movie *Doctor Zhivago*, M-G-M, 1965.

Album Notes: *Music*: Maurice Jarre; *Orchestrations*: Maurice Jarre, Leo Arnaud; The M-G-M Studio Orchestra, conducted by Maurice Jarre; *Album Producers*: Marilee Bradford, Bradley Flanagan.

Selections: 1 Overture (4:22); 2 Main Title (2:38); 3 Kontakion/Funeral Song (3:15); 4 Lara Is Charming (1:16); 5 The Internationale (1:12); 6 Lara And Komarovsky Dancing Up A Storm (:40); 7 Komarovsky With Lara In The Hotel (3:51); 8 Interior Student Cafe (1:34); 9 Sventitsky's Waltz/After The Shooting (2:17); 10 Military Parade (2:11); 11 They Began To Go Home (2:06); 12 After Deserters Killed The Colonel (1:05); 13 At The Hospital (1:00); 14 Lara Says Goodbye To Yuri (1:27); 15 Tonya Greets Yuri (:46); 16 The Stove's Out (1:30); 17 Yevgraf Snaps His Fingers (3:09); 18 Evening Bells/Moscow Station (1:03); 19 Flags Flying Over The Train (1:04); 20 Yuri Gazing Through A Tiny Open Hatch (:37); 21 The Door Is Banged Opened (1:48); 22 Intermission (:43); 23 Yuri Follows The Sound Of The Waterfall (:44); 24 Tonya And Yuri Arrive At Varykino (2:56); 25 They Didn't Lock The Cottage (1:33); 26 Varykino Cottage, Winter Snow (:57); 27 Yuri And The Daffodils (1:17); 28 On A Yuriatin Street (1:36); 29 In Lara's Bedroom (:34); 30 Yuri Rides To Yuriatin (:22); 31 Yuri Is Taken Prisoner By The Red Partisans (:49); 32 For As Long As We Need You (:40); 33 Yuri Is Escaping (2:17); 34 Yuri Approaches Lara's Apartment (:50); 35 Yuri Looks Into The Mirror (:30); 36 Lara And Yuri Arriving At Varykino (1:39); 37 Yuri Is Trying To Write (1:19); 38 Yuri Frightens The Wolves Away, Part 1 (:49); 39 Lara Reads Her Poem (:40); 40 Yuri Frightens The Wolves Away, part 2 (1:55); 41 Yuri Works On (:52); 42 Then It's A Gift (End Title) (1:43); 43 Lara's Theme (jazz version) (1:57); 44 Lara's Theme (rock'n'roll version) (2:39); 45 Lara's Theme (swing version) (1:15).

Review: This new reissue of Maurice Jarre's score for *Dr. Zhivago* is another brilliant example of what can be accomplished with vision, diligence, and creative fortitude. For that's what the Rhino editions of the MGM classic soundtracks are all about — dedication. If you love *Dr. Zhivago*, this disc is for you! Every snippet of Jarre's music for the tremendously successful film can be found here, in its original, unedited form. Of course, "Lara's Theme" (the leitmotif for the entire film) is included, and as a bonus, the producers have added three alternate versions that were made as impromptu "tension breakers" at the original scoring sessions. It's a treat to hear this group of veteran Hollywood musicians interpret the theme as a jazz, rock and swing tune! There are also a number of outtakes and the accompanying booklet contains commentary by Jarre, and in-depth examinations of the story and score. The sound, as is often the case with these Rhino reissues, is excellent.

Charles L. Granata

Dolores Claiborne ♪♪♪♪

1995, Varese-Sarabande Records; from the movie *Dolores Claiborne*, Columbia Pictures, 1995.

Album Notes: *Music*: Danny Elfman; *Orchestrations*: Danny Elfman, Edgardo Simone; *Music Editor*: Curt Sobel; Orchestra conducted by Richard Stone; *Album Producers*: Danny Elfman, Curt Sobel; *Engineers*: Bobby Fernandez, Shawn Murphy.

Selections: 1 Main Titles (2:46); 2 Vera's World (3:42); 3 Flashback (1:54); 4 Getting Even (1:48); 5 Ferry Ride (:55); 6 Sad Room (:53); 7 Eclipse (7:16); 8 Finale (5:35); 9 End Credits (5:16).

Review: This is a superb, poetic score from Danny Elfman, who here downplays his brooding "dark" tone (from *Batman*, *Nightbreed*, et al) in favor of equally somber but more restrained cues that reflect the distinct personalities of the two female protagonists at the heart of Stephen King's novel, outstandingly adapted here for the screen by Taylor Hackford.

Elfman's string-laden score is effective throughout, whether it frantically underscores the revelation of the title character's dark secret, or the growing bond between the hardened Dolores Claiborne and her troubled journalist daughter. Elfman teamed with his usual film-music collaborators here (including Steve Bartek, who receives no credit on the album for some strange reason), and the result is one of his best. Alas, Varese's album runs a scant 30 minutes, and would have benefited from some additional cues that could have fleshed out the album to a more satisfying length.

Andy Dursin

Dominick & Eugene 🎜🎜♭

1988, Varese-Sarabande Records; from the movie *Dominick & Eugene*, Orion Pictures, 1988.

Album Notes: *Music:* Trevor Jones; Orchestra conducted by Trevor Jones; *Album Producer:* Trevor Jones; *Engineer:* Rico Goldomon.

Selections: 1 Main Theme (Opening Titles)(4:42); 2 Nicky Runs To Hospital (4:15); 3 Fred Is Killed (1:18); 4 Dominck & Eugene (2:30); 5 Chernax Dismisses Nicky (:54); 6 Nicky Rescues Joey (2:38); 7 Nicky's Problem (2:05); 8 Gino And Nicky In Warehouse (1:59); 9 Fred/Chernax's Reprise (1:53); 10 Nicky Interrupts Kiss (1:09); 11 Hospital Reprise (2:50); 12 Nicky Is Contrite (2:41); 13 Rescue (Part 2)(1:21); 14 Departure (3:57).

Review: This film about the relationship of two brothers, one of them retarded, furnished Trevor Jones with one of the few "people" stories in a list of credits which otherwise encompasses mostly thrillers or epics. Jones has always had a particular gift for memorable and engaging themes and does not disappoint here. The main theme is a beautiful lament for small orchestra and solo guitar, performed by an uncredited John Williams. Much as in Jones' *Last of the Mohicans* however, this is a case of a wonderful theme stretched a little too thin. Lovely as it is, this theme appears several times with little variation and by the fourth appearance becomes rather redundant. The other cues are mostly synthesized "atmosphere" or suspense cues, which, while effective in the film, are not really very listenable. Still, the main theme remains wonderful, and this alone makes this CD worth owning.

Paul Andrew MacLean

Don Juan DeMarco 🎜🎜🎜♭

1995, A&M Records; from the movie *Don Juan DeMarco*, New Line Cinema, 1995.

Album Notes: *Music:* Michael Kamen; *Orchestrations:* Michael Kamen, Robert Elhai, Nick Ingman, Ed Shearmur; *Music Editor:*

Zigmund Gron; The London Metropolitan Orchestra, conducted by Michael Kamen; *Featured Musicians:* Julian Bream, Paul Kamen, Paco de Lucia, Juan Martin, John Themis, Chucko Merchan, Orlando Rincon, Sol de Mexico, Anna Maria Velez (guitar), Christopher Warren-Green (violin), Caroline Dale (cello); Luis Jardim (percussion); *Album Producers:* Michael Kamen, Stephen McLaughlin, Christopher Brooks; *Engineers:* Andy Warwick, Bob Ludwig.

Selections: 1 Have You Ever Really Loved A Woman? (B. Adams/R.J. Lange/M. Kamen)(4:51) *Bryan Adams*; 2 Habanera (2:08); 3 Don Juan (4:08); 4 I Was Born In Mexico (2:25); 5 Has amado una mujer de veras? (B. Adams/R.J. Lange/M. Kamen)(2:45) *Michael Kamen, Jose Hernandez, Nydia*; 6 Dona Julia (4:58); 7 Don Alfonso (6:47); 8 Arabia (7:53); 9 Don Octavio del Flores (1:46); 10 Dona Ana (7:31).

Review: You may dispense with Bryan Adams' "Have You Ever Really Loved a Woman?" which sounds hopelessly wrong for this modern retelling of Lord Byron's *Don Juan*. The film finds Johnny Depp as the latest incarnation of the fabled great lover, now apparently distraught over the loss of the one woman he actually loved, and Marlon Brando the psychiatrist who gives him new hopes and to whom Don Juan tells about his more than 1,000 conquests. The great strength of this album is Michael Kamen's gorgeous Mexican-flavored score, complete with guitar calls, castanets, and the full array of south of the border colorful tonalities one hopes to find (but seldom does) in a music of this kind. The composer's own rendition of the title song, with Spanish vocals by Jose Hernandez and Nydia, is everything Bryan Adams' version is not, and one of the pleasurable highlights in the album. Other tracks that attract and make a lasting impression include the delicate "Dona Julia," the habanera-like "Arabia," and "Dona Ana," another beautiful selection.

Donnie Brasco 🎜🎜♭

1997, Hollywood Records; from the movie *Donnie Brasco*, Mandalay Entertainment, 1997.

Album Notes: *Music:* Patrick Doyle; *Album Producers:* Mike Newell, Mark Johnson, Gail Mutrux; *Engineer:* John Polito.

Selections: 1 A Stranger On Earth (S. Feller/R. Ward)(2:58) *Dinah Washington*; 2 (The Gang That Sang) Heart Of My Heart (B. Ryan)(2:32) *Lou Monte*; 3 Happiness (A. Toussaint)(3:58) *The Pointer Sisters*; 4 What You Won't Do For Love (B. Caldwell/A. Kettner)(4:44) *Bobby Caldwell*; 5 Heart Of Glass (D. Harry/C. Stein)(4:34) *Blondie*; 6 Love Machine, Pt. 1 (W. Moore/W. Griffin)(3:01) *The Miracles*; 7 Don't Bring Me Down

(J. Lynne) (4:02) *Electric Light Orchestra*; 8 Disco Inferno (L. Green/R. Kersey) (10:55) *The Trammps*; 9 Brooklyn Girls (R. Freeland/B. Labounty)(3:24) *Robbie Dupree*; 10 Return To Me (D. Di Minno/C. Lombardo)(2:24) *Dean Martin*; 11 The Latin One (R. Espinosa/A. Baeza/M. Lespron/E. Rodriguez/J. Salas/ B. Magness)(4:40) *El Chicano*; 12 Just Around The Corner (H. Hancock/M. Ragin)(7:35) *Herbie Hancock*; 13 Donnie And Lefty (4:25).

Review: The true soundtrack to this true-life mob infiltration film is gunfire, but that doesn't play well on a CD. Instead, this is a hodgepodge of mostly danceable songs from the era of the Donnie Brasco investigation, with a few well-worn hits— Electric Light Orchestra's "Don't Bring Me Down," Blondie's "Heart of Glass," the Trammps' *Saturday Night Fever* hit "Disco Inferno"—and some less familiar fare, such as the Miracles' "Love Machine, Pt. 1," the Pointer Sisters' "Happiness" and Herbie Hancock's "Just Around the Corner." Ultimately, this is the kind of random collection you're better off *fahgeddin'* about.

Gary Graff

Don't Be a Menace to South Central While Drinking Your Juice in the Hood ♪♭

1996, Island Records; from the movie *Don't Be a Menace to South Central While Drinking Your Juice in the Hood*, Miramax Films, 1996.

Album Notes: *Song Producers*: The Rza, Mr. Sex & Buttnaked TimDawg, Tizone, Mr. Dalvin, D.J. Clark Kent, Erick Sermon, D-Flow Production Squad, R. Kelly, Joe, Lord Jamar, Mobb Deep, Frankie Cutlass, T-Mor, Sean Greene, Geary J. McDowell, Stanley Brown; *Album Executive Producer*: Hiriam Hicks.

Selections: 1 Winter Warz (D. Coles/E. Turner/L. Hawkins/D. Hill/C. Woods/ R. Diggs)(5:10) *Ghostface Killer, Masta Killa, U-God, Raekwon & Cappadonna*; 2 Renee (T. Kelly)(5:00) *Lost Boyz*; 3 Funky Sounds (Tizone) (4:00) *Lil Bud & Tizone*; 4 Give It Up (D. Degrate/C. Halley/J. Halley) (3:53) *Jodeci*; 5 Can't Be Wasting My Time (A. Antoine/A. Evans/J. Austin/ T. Patterson/ G. Duncan/Lost Boyz)(4:33) *Mona Lisa, Lost Boyz*; 6 Time To Shine (R. Franklin/K. Jones/T. Patterson)(4:40) *Junior Mafia's Lil Kim, Mona Lisa*; 7 Maintain (E. Sermon)(3:14) *Erick Sermon*; 8 We Got More (G. Jacobs/G. Husbands/J. Ellis)(3:05) *Shock G, The Luniz*; 9 Let's Lay Together (R. Kelly)(4:42) *The Isley Brothers*; 10 All The Things (Your Man Won't Do) (J. Thomas/J. Thompson/M. Williams)(6:20) *Joe*; 11 Tempo Slow (R. Kelly) (4:28) *R. Kelly*; 12 Live Wires Connect (Pimp C/Bun B/K. Murray/L. Jamar/C. Budda)(6:03) *UGK, Keith Murray & Lord Jamar*;

13 Up North Trip (A. Johnson/K. Muchita)(5:02) *Mobb Deep*; 14 Freak It Out! (D. Davis/B. Moody/L. Campbell/F. Malaze)(3:13) *Doug E. Fresh*; 15 Suga Daddy (T. Stevens/T. Mor) (3:28) *Suga-T*; 16 It's Time (J. Thompson/S. Greene/G.J. McDowell/C. Thomas) (5:25) *Blue Raspeberry*; 17 Don't Give Up (S. Brown/ D. Lawrence)(3:57) *The Island Inspirational All-Stars, Kirk Franklin & The Family, Hezekiah Walker & The Fellowship Choir, Donald Lawrence & The Tri-City Singers, Karen Clark-Sheard*.

Review: A good assemblage of contemporary R&B talent, mostly of the hip-hop variety, keeps all of its best songs bottled up here. Joe's "All the Things (Your Man Won't Do)" is a worthy hit, but the other top names— R. Kelly, Jodeci, Doug E. Fresh and Lost Boyz—come in with mediocre fare that may add some flavor to the film but doesn't make for much of a listening experience.

Gary Graff

Double Dragon ♪

1994, Milan Records; from the movie *Double Dragon*, Universal Pictures, 1994.

Album Notes: *Music*: Jay Ferguson; *Song Producers*: Dobbs The Wino, Basement Boys, Michael Lattanzi, George Morel, Tolga Katas & Stevie B., Paul Scott & Sank Thompson, Graham McPherson, Kevin O.; *Album Producer*: David Franco; *Engineer*: Jeff Faustman.

Selections: 1 I Remember (A. Ivey, Jr.)(4:48) *Coolio*; 2 What I Need (R. Payton/D. Smith/C. Waters)(4:43) *Crystal Waters*; 3 Love Will Shine On Me (M. Lattanzi)(4:11) *Michael Lattanzi, Crystal Tallefero*; 4 I Know (M. Lattanzi/N. Kalliongis)(7:12) *George Morel, Lillias White*; 5 Dream About You (M. D'Allesandro/T. Katas)(4:04) *Stevie B.*; 6 You Bring Me Joy (P. Scott/S. Thompson)(6:02) *Rhythm Factor*; 7 All Together Now (P. Hooten/S. Grimes)(5:40) *The Farm*; 8 Say You're Gonna Stay (J. Labrit/L. Labrit/K. Oliphant/D. D'Bonneau)(4:14) *Darryl D' Bonneau*; 9 Starting Over (T. Swider/D. Freebairn/A. Shore/T. Lane)(5:21) *D.F.M.*; 10 Main Title (2:42); 11 The Tournament (2:30); 12 Huey And Lewis (1:55); 13 Monster Truck (3:35); 14 Welcome (2:43); 15 Junk Rumble (2:19); 16 The Chief Readies His Troops (2:08).

Review: Everybody has been through this scenario before: you walk into a record store's cut-out bin hoping to find a buried treasure for a cheap price. After thumbing through hundreds of titles, all you can find are some Vanilla Ice albums and several copies of *Double Dragon*, the lousy soundtrack to the 1994 adaptation of the popular video-game that came and went from theaters in a matter of days. Jay Ferguson composed the primarily-electronic score, which is surrounded by bubblegum tracks by the likes of Crystal Waters, Stevie B. and rapper Coolio, who performs "I Remember." To put it mildly, the music to *Mortal Kombat* is a bit more effective.

Andy Dursin

Dracula *♪♪♪♪*

1990, Varese-Sarabande; from the movie *Dracula*, Universal Pictures, 1979.

Album Notes: *Music*: John Williams; The London Symphony Orchestra, conducted by John Williams; *Album Producer*: John Williams.

Selections: 1 Main Title and Storm Sequence (5:08); 2 The Night Visitor (2:12); 3 To Scarborough (2:42); 4 The Abduction Of Lucy (3:34); 5 Night Journeys (5:12); 6 The Love Scene (2:04); 7 Meeting In The Cave (3:29); 8 The Bat Attack (2:46); 9 For Mina (2:15); 10 Dracula's Death (2:57); 11 End Titles (3:58).

Review: John Williams' *Dracula* music is highly romantic, emphasizing, as did John Badman's filmic style in this 1979 variation, the exotic sensuality of the vampire. Opening with a swelling, fully symphonic love theme, the music grasps us into its harmonic power much the way Count Dracula seduces the hapless heroine in his own hypnotic power. Eschewing the throbbing, pulse-pounding, gut-wrenching dissonances of previous *Dracula* scores, Williams invests into the film a sense of poignancy and lyricism that embodies the power, passion, and horror of the Dracula figure, while at the same time lending a noble sympathy to his adversaries.

Randall D. Larson

Dragon: The Bruce Lee Story *♪♪♪♪*

1993, MCA Records; from the movie *Dragon: The Bruce Lee Story*, Universal Pictures, 1993.

Album Notes: *Music*: Randy Edelman; *Orchestrations*: Randy Edelman, Greig McRitchie; Orchestra conducted by Randy Edelman; *Album Producer*: Randy Edelman; *Engineer*: Elton Ahi.

Selections: 1 Dragon Theme/A Father's Nightmare (3:33); 2 Yip Man's Kwoon (2:27); 3 Lee Hoi Chuen's Love (2:09); 4 Bruce And Linda (2:44); 5 The Challenge Fight Warm-Up (2:14); 6 Sailing On The South China Sea (2:12); 7 Fists Of Fury (1:17); 8 The Tao Of Jeet Kune Do (2:15); 9 Victory At Ed Parker's (1:32); 10 Chopsaki (1:11); 11 Brandon (2:04); 12 The Mountain Of Gold (:44); 13 The Premiere Of "The Big Boss" (1:45); 14 Fighting Demons (2:36); 15 The Dragon's Heartbeat (5:09); 16

First Date (2:16); 17 The Hong Kong Cha-Cha (R. Cohen-R. Randles)(3:43) *Lynn Ray, Xiao Fen Min.*

Review: *Dragon: The Bruce Lee Story* inspired Randy Edelman to write a florid score in which the throbbing action cues (with dominant synth effects) mix with more reflective selections (played by the orchestra) intended to underscore the scenes in which Lee is seen not as an indomitable screen hero and karate expert but as the vulnerable human being he was offscreen. These last cues ("Lee Hoi Chuen's Love," "Bruce and Linda," "Sailing on the South China Sea") are by far the most revealing, as they enable the composer to show his sentimental side and come up with melodies that are quite attractive. A splendid anthem, "The Dragon's Heartbeat," first played on the piano and reprised by the full orchestra, that eventually dissolves into a pulsating rocker, sums up the general moods projected by the score. A blues ("First Date," with its faint echo of "Moonglow and Theme from Picnic") and an exotic number ("The Hong Kong Cha Cha") round up the selections.

See also: John Barry's Game of Death

Dragonheart *♪♪♪♪♭*

1996, MCA Records; from the movie *Dragonheart*, Universal Pictures, 1996.

Album Notes: *Music*: Randy Edelman; *Orchestrations*: Ralph Ferraro; *Music Editor*: Joanie Diener; Orchestra conducted by Randy Edelman; *Album Producer*: Randy Edelman; *Engineers*: Elton Ahi, Dennis Sands.

Selections: 1 The World Of The Heart/Main Title (3:17); 2 To The Stars (3:11); 3 Wonders Of An Ancient Glory (2:21); 4 Einon (3:53); 5 The Last Dragon Slayer (4:00); 6 Bowen's Ride (2:33); 7 Mexican Standoff (2:20); 8 Draco (1:13); 9 A Refreshing Swim (1:25); 10 Re-Baptism (2:47); 11 Bowen's Decoy (3:22); 12 Kyle, The Wheat Boy (4:24); 13 The Connection (2:25); 14 Flight To Avalon (2:54); 15 Finale (5:28).

Review: The delightful epic fantasy score by Randy Edelman exploits the whimsical notion of a dragon slayer teaming with the last dragon to scam villagers of "protection money." At the core of the score is the bond that forms between two former mortal enemies who now must depend on each other to survive in a world that has outgrown them. Although he touches briefly on instrumentation appropriate for the era, Edelman scored the picture more as a contemporary "buddy" adventure that could be set in any era. In so doing, he breathed a dignified life into the mythical creature.

David Hirsch

Dragonslayer 🎵🎵🎵🎵

1990, SCSE Records; from the movie *Dragonslayer*, **Paramount Pictures, 1981.**

Album Notes: *Music*: Alex North; *Orchestrations*: Henry Brandt; Orchestra conducted by Alex North; *Album Producers*: Alex North, Len Engel; *Engineer*: Len Engel.

Selections: 1 Urlander's Mission (Main Titles)(2:44); 2 "No Sorcerers, No Dragons" (1:45); 3 Hodge's Death (2:15); 4 Forest Romp (1:29); 5 The Lair (1:46); 6 Valerian And Galen's Romance (1:54); 7 Tyrian And Valen Fight (2:11); 8 Jacopus Blasted (2:21); 9 Galen Jailed/Galen's Escape (1:16); 10 Ulrich's Death/Mourning (5:49); 11 Galen's Search For The Amulet (3:11); 12 Maiden Sacrifice (6:57); 13 Elspeth's Destiny/ Dragon's Scales (2:29); 14 Vermithrax's Lair/Landslide (4:29); 15 Dragon's Flight/Burning Villages (2:14); 16 The Lottery (3:14); 17 Elspeth At The Stake/Vermithrax's Triumph/ Galen's Encounter (5:46); 18 Galen's Desperation And Spirit Revitalized (1:50); 19 Eclipse/Love And Hope (2:38); 20 Resurrection Of Ulrich (2:29); 21 "Destroy That Amulet!"/Ulrich Explodes/ Vermithrax's Plunge (6:38); 22 The White Horse/Into The Sunset (End Credits)(4:30).

Review: Alex North's final entry in the epic genre is this stunningly complex, modernistic masterwork for Hal Barwood's fascinatingly cynical tale of a dragon, sorcery, and medieval corruption. I can't imagine anything more portentous than North's title music, a crushing blast of low horns, grinding, dissonant string chords and nervous piccolo exclamations, leading into a cowed, mournful low string melody for the medieval villagers struggling under the threat of the dragon Vermithrax Pejorative. North wrote a glistening series of piccolo and celeste effects for the death and resurrection of a sorcerer, two scenes that bookend the film's action, and there are disturbing, percussive passages for the dragon attacks, a religious chorale for the death of an arrogant monk, a brutal, lengthy battle cue for the hero's first confrontation with the monster, a subdued love theme, and a remarkable introduction to the film's final showdown between sorcerer and dragon, full of spine-tingling sense-of-wonder orchestrations. North adapted music from his rejected score to Stanley Kubrick's *2001* for several sequences and the overall tone and approach of both scores is quite similar. The music for the final battle with the dragon (an unusually lyrical approach to the action) went unused in the film along with a couple of other cues, but the album presents the score as composed by North. Highly recommended to fans of this composer, but North's hardedged, tonally uncentered style may be tough to digest for the uninitiated.

Jeff Bond

The Draughtsman's Contract 🎵🎵

1993, DRG Records; from the movie *The Draughtsman's Contract*, **1993.**

Album Notes: *Music*: Michael Nyman; *Featured Musicians*: The Michael Nyman Band: Michael Nyman (harpsichord, piano), Alexander Balanescu, Elizabeth Perry (violin), Malcolm Bennett (bass guitar), Andrew Findon, John Harle, Ian Mitchell, Keith Thompson (saxophones, clarinets), Stave Saunders (bass trombone, euphonium), Barry Guy (double bass); *Album Producer*: Michael Nyman; *Engineers*: J. Martin Rex, Brad Grisdale, Dave Hunt, Steve Smith, Robert Zimbler.

Selections: 1 Queen Of The Night (6:11); 2 (Drawing 3) The Disposition Of The Linen (4:50); 3 Return Of Neville/Death Of Herbert/A Watery Death (3:35); 4 (Drawing 6) The Garden Is Becoming A Robe Room (6:07); 5 (Drawing 1) Chasing Sheep Is Best Left To Shepherds (2:36); 6 (Drawing 5) An Eye For Optical Theory (5:13); 7 (Death Of Neville) Bravura In The Face Of Grief (12:17).

Review: Michael Nyman's music may not be to everyone's liking, but it won't leave you indifferent. And whether you respond to it favorably or not will depend in large part on how you react to his minimalist approach to film scoring. The music, performed here by a small chamber ensemble, played an important role in this odd story about an architect working for a British lady who trades his landscaping designs for her favors. But taken on its own merits, it tends to sound dry and unattaching after a while. And when it takes, as in the last track, endless variations on the same theme, it may turn off even the most lenient listener. Not helping either is the grating sound quality of the recording.

Dream Lover 🎵🎵🎵🎵

1994, Koch Screen; from the movie *Dream Lover*, **Gramercy Pictures, 1994.**

Album Notes: *Music*: Christopher Young; *Orchestrations*: Pete Anthony, Christopher Young; *Music Editor*: John La Salandra; Orchestra conducted by Pete Anthony; *Synthesizers and Percussions*: Mark Zimoski; *Album Producer*: Christopher Young; *Engineer*: Rick Winquest.

Selections: 1 Dream Lover (2:40); 2 Moreland's Galloper Waltz (2:51); 3 Just For You (4:07); 4 One Last Dance (2:31); 5 Seen Before (2:09); 6 The Green Palace (1:44); 7 False Face (1:47); 8 Lena Lai (3:55); 9 Forget Me Not (3:36); 10 Black Widow (3:15); 11 Flying (4:36); 12 Dead Of Night (3:16); 13 Dream Lover's Waltz (1:34); 14 Sweet Dreams (3:34).

Review: Tubular bells over an attractive orchestral melody supported by ethereal vocalists, a quirky waltz performed by a carousel organ, and an exuberant ragtime are some of the many delights that await the listener in this soundtrack signed by Christopher Young for an erotic drama about a young architect and the emotionally unbalanced sexy woman who becomes his wife. The broad range and wide diversity of the musical cues, which also include a pseudo-oriental composition and a Parisian-styled waltz, combine to create a score which is both challenging and consistently satisfying.

Dressed to Kill ♫♫♫

1980, Varese-Sarabande Records; from the movie *Dressed to Kill*, Filmways Pictures, 1980.

Album Notes: *Music*: Pino Donaggio; Orchestra conducted by Natale Massara; *Album Producer*: Pino Donaggio; *Engineer*: Paul Brown.

Selections: 1 The Shower (Theme from Dressed To Kill)(4:09); 2 The Museum (6:19); 3 The Note (3:18); 4 Flight From Bobbi (2:18); 5 Death In The Elevator (2:15); 6 Liz And Peter: A Romantic Interlude (1:48); 7 The Erotic Story (2:42); 8 The Transformation/The Storm/The Revelation (3:57); 9 Kate's Confession (:41); 10 The Forgotten Ring/The Murder (3:24); 11 The Cab (1:56); 12 The Asylum/The Nightmare (4:14); 13 Finale (2:30).

Review: Brian de Palma took more than a single cue from suspense master Alfred Hitchcock when he directed this stylish essay about an attractive woman with a particularly sexy disposition, who meets with a rather nasty killer in an elevator, and the high-class prostitute who finds herself accused of the murder. And while Pino Donaggio is not Bernard Herrmann, his score for the film was the perfect musical complement to De Palma's erotic visions ("The Shower," "The Erotic Story," "The Cab"). Even if "Death in the Elevator" lacks the subtle, terrifying impact of Herrmann's famous shower scene in *Psycho*, Donaggio's elegant and classy musical cues set this score aside and qualify it as a real winner.

Driving Miss Daisy ♫♫♫♫♭

1989, Varese-Sarabande Records; from the movie *Driving Miss Daisy*, Warner Bros. Pictures, 1989.

Album Notes: *Music*: Hanz Zimmer; *Arrangements*: Hans Zimmer; *Engineer*: Jay Rifkin.

Selections: 1 Kiss Of Fire (L. Allen/R. Hill)(3:04) *Louis Armstrong*; 2 Santa Baby (T. Springer/P. Spring/J. Javitz)(3:23) *Eartha Kitt*; 3 Driving (6:50); 4 Home (3:23); 5 Georgia (7:55); 6

End Titles (4:51); 7 Song To The Moon (A. Dvorak)(6:05) *Gabriela Benachova, Czech Philharmonic, Vaclav Neumann*.

Review: The soundtrack to this Academy Award-winning film is an odd lot. First you have pop standards, Louis Armstrong doing the tango "Kiss of Fire," and Eartha Kitt singing her signature Yule song, "Santa Baby." On the other side of the spectrum, there is a long excerpt from Antonin Dvorak's "Song to the Moon," performed by the soprano Gabriela Benachova with the Czech Philharmonic. Somewhere in between are four cues from the score composed by Hans Zimmer, an effervescent synthesizer music that helps evoke this affectionate story about an elderly Southern lady and the black chauffeur who has been in her employ for years and the warm relationship that has settled between them. Surprisingly, the combination of all these elements works wonders, with the album eliciting a positive response despite its disparate components.

Drop Zone ♫♫♫♫

1994, Varese-Sarabande Records; from the movie *Drop Zone*, Paramount Pictures, 1994.

Album Notes: *Music*: Hans Zimmer, Nick Glennie-Smith, Ryeland Allison; *Orchestrations*: Hans Zimmer, Nick Glennie-Smith, Ryeland Allison; *Featured Vocalists*: Rose Stone, Randelle K. Stainback; *Album Producers*: Hans Zimmer, Jay Rifkin; *Engineer*: Alan Meyerson.

Selections: 1 Drop Zone (1:45); 2 Hyphopera (R. Allison)(1:41) *Randelle K. Stainback*; 3 Hi Jack (4:35); 4 Terry's Dropped Out (1:01); 5 Flashback And Fries (N. Glennie-Smith)(4:21); 6 Miami Jump (5:14); 7 Too Many Notes, Not Enough Rests (10:39); 8 After The Dub (8:07).

Review: With this energetic mix of rockin' synthesizers and orchestra, Hans Zimmer triumphs with this highly charged score for the John Badham-directed Wesley Snipes action film. There's never a dull moment. The music shifts effortlessly from the movie's thrilling guitar-driven skydiving cues ("Hi Jack") to the more poignant emotional sequences ("Terry Dropped Out"). Kudos especially to Zimmer's wonderful and humorously well-titled "Too Many Notes—Not Enough Rests," the bane of any action movie composer's existence! One of Zimmer's best works for this genre.
David Hirsch

Dune ♫♫♫♫♭

1984, Polydor Records; from the movie *Dune*, Universal Picture, 1984.

Album Notes: *Music*: Toto; *Adaptation and Additional Music*: Marty Paich; *Additional Orchestrations*: Allyn Ferguson; The Vienna Symphony Orchestra and The Vienna Volkoper Choir, conducted by Marty Paich, Allyn Ferguson; *Featured Musicians*: David Paich (keyboards), Jeff Porcaro (drums, percussion), Steve Porcaro (keyboards), Mike Porcaro (bass, percussion), Steve Lukather (guitars); *Album Producer*: Toto; *Engineers*: Tom Knox, Shep Lonsdale, Al Schmitt, Tom Fletcher, Geoff Workman.

Selections: 1 Prologue (1:47); 2 Main Title (1:15); 3 Robot Fight (1:18); 4 Leto's Theme (1:43); 5 The Box (2:37); 6 The Floating Fat Man (The Baron) (1:24); 7 Trip To Arrakis (2:35); 8 First Attack (2:43); 9 Prophecy Theme (B. Eno/D. Lanois/R. Eno)(4:19); 10 Dune (Desert Theme)(5:30); 11 Paul Meets Chani (3:04); 12 Prelude (Take My Hand)(:59); 13 Paul Takes The Water Of Life (2:48); 14 Big Battle (3:06); 15 Paul Kills Feyd (1:51); 16 Final Dream (1:25); 17 Take My Hand (2:35).

Review: This is a surprisingly well-written score by the pop group Toto for the David Lynch adaptation of Frank Herbert's best-seller. Even more remarkable is the fact that this has been their only film effort. The group appears to have a real sense of what is needed in this film, though the level of their contribution against those by orchestrators/conductors Marty Paich (credited with additional music) and Allyn Ferguson, remains a mystery. As an album, *Dune* is a glorious blend of electronics, orchestral and choral motifs. Notable cues include the thrilling "First Attack," the mystical "Paul Meets Chani" and the finale "Take My Hand." New age artist Brian Eno contributes the "Prophecy Theme" and the two dialogue sequences don't detract from the experience.

David Hirsch

Dying Young 🎵🎵🎵🎵

1991, Arista Records; from the movie *Dying Young*, 20th Century-Fox, 1991.

Album Notes: *Music*: James Newton Howard; *Orchestrations*: Brad Dechter; Orchestra conducted by Marty Paich; *Featured Musicians*: Kenny G, Michael Lang (piano), Dean Parks (guitar), Jeffrey Porcaro (drums), Michael Fisher (percussion), Neil Stubbenhaus (bass), Gayle Levant (harp); *Album Producer*: James Newton Howard; *Engineer*: Shawn Murphy.

Selections: 1 Theme from *Dying Young* (4:00) *Kenny G*; 2 Driving North/ Moving In (4:15) *Kenny G, James Newton Howard*; 3 The Clock (1:23); 4 Love Montage (2:56); 5 The Maze (2:38); 6 All The Way (S. Cahn/J. Van Heusen) (3:30) *Jeffrey Osborne*; 7 Hillary's Theme (3:08) *Kenny G, James Newton Howard*; 8 Victor Teaches Art (1:22); 9 The Bluff (:59); 10 San Francisco (2:03); 11 Victor (1:39); 12 All The Way (S. Cahn/J. Van Heusen)(5:29) *King Curtis*; 13 I'll Never Leave You (Love Theme)(2:55) *Kenny G, James Newton Howard*.

Review: For once, Kenny G's detractors will have to admit that his contribution to this film score actually enhances it. Playing in the romantic style that has insured his enormous success, *Dying Young*, a soap opera if there ever was one, provides the instrumentalist with the right emotional moods to express his own romanticism in a way that's extremely attractive and welcome. Much of the credit must also go to James Newton Howard, obviously inspired by this maudlin story of a doomed love affair, for which he wrote a lush series of cues, in which the dominant note is also strongly evocative of the film's main theme. The old standard, "All the Way," performed as a vocal by Jeffrey Osborne and as an instrumental by King Curtis, contributes an inspired note to this standout soundtrack album.

The Eagle Has Landed

1987, Label X Records; from the movie *The Eagle Has Landed*, 1977.

See: The Four Musketeers

Earthquake 🎵🎵🎵

1990, Varese-Sarabande; from the movie *Earthquake*, Universal Pictures, 1974.

Album Notes: *Music*: John Williams; Orchestra conducted by John Williams; *Album Producer*: Sonny Burke; *Engineer*: Mickey Crofford.

Selections: 1 Main Title (2:52); 2 Miles On Wheels (2:36); 3 City Theme (2:53); 4 Something For Rosa (2:30); 5 Love Scene (2:26); 6 The City Sleeps (2:24); 7 Love Theme (2:26); 8 Cory In Jeopardy (2:23); 9 Medley: (a) Watching and Waiting, (b) Miles' Pool Hall, (c) Sam's Rescue (3:40); 10 Something For Remy (3:47); 11 Finale/End Title (1:47); 12 Earthquake: Special Effects (2:42); 13 Aftershock (:24).

Review: Before he became the uncontested champion of big orchestral scores with *Star Wars* in 1977, John Williams carved himself a special niche as the composer best qualified to write the music for the many disaster films which flourished in the early 1970s, including *Jaws*, *The Towering Inferno* and *The Poseidon Adventure*. Add to those the score he created for *Earthquake*, the film that saw Los Angeles disappear long before it was toast in *Volcano*... (or was it *Dante's Peak?*). In this particularly remarkable effort, Williams wrote a broad range of cues, from a tender love scene to a chase to the actual disaster. In addition, there are many other moments to enjoy in his diversified music, from a bluesy "City Theme," to a lightly jazzy "Something For Rosa," to a lusty "Love Theme." A word of warning: the last two tracks are low-rumbling recordings of an earthquake that will rattle and destroy your speakers if you play the CD too loud.

Easy Come, Easy Go

1995, RCA Victor; from the movie *Easy Come, Easy Go*, Paramount Picture, 1967.

See: Elvis Presley in Compilations

Eat Drink Man Woman 🎵🎵🎵▷

1994, Varese-Sarabande; from the movie *Eat Drink Man Woman*, Samuel Goldwyn, 1994.

Album Notes: *Music*: Mader; *Arrangers*: Mader, Hector Martignon, Sarah Plant; *Featured Musicians*: Wu Man (pipa, ruan), Wang Tien Jou (erhu), Cao Ying Ying (sanxian), Sarah Plant (flute), Steve Elson (saxophone, clarinet), Hector Martignon (piano), Thomas Ulrich (cello), Mario Rodriguez (bass), Armando Sanchez, Louis F. Bouzo, Joe Gonzales (percussion), Mader (marimba, keyboard), Dina Emerson (vocals); *Album Producer*: Mader; *Engineer*: Eric Liljestrand.

Selections: 1 Awake (2:32); 2 Good Morning, My Life! (1:12); 3 Mambo City (10:53); 4 The Daughter's Heart 1 (4:08); 5 Night Moon (2:41); 6 Destiny (1:54); 7 Pa's Kitchen 1 (1:09); 8 Emptiness (:58); 9 Up Or Down (:24); 10 Pa's Kitchen 2 (1:40); 11 Loneliness (:34); 12 The Banquet (1:54); 13 Pa's Secret (:46); 14 Who's With Me (3:33); 15 Kitchen Impro (1:33); 16 Darkroom (:40); 17 Revelation (:47); 18 The Daughter's Heart 2 (4:08).

Review: Absolutely nothing like what you'd expect for a film about a collision of generations in a Chinese/American household. Composer Mader has created a brilliant montage of musical styles that complement each other in a refreshing way few scores do. The album moves with a surprising ease between an authentic Chinese motif to a contemporary film cue and finally to mambo! Mader, in an act of sheer gall, composed a blues piece, "The Daughter's Heart 1," that suddenly shifts into a passage played by Chinese instruments! This is a true melting pot of world music and a delightful change of pace.

David Hirsch

Ed Wood 🎵🎵🎵

1994, Hollywood Records; from the movie *Ed Wood*, Touchstone Pictures, 1994.

Album Notes: *Music*: Howard Shore; The London Philharmonic Orchestra, conducted by Howard Shore; *Featured Musicians*: Lydia Kavina (theremin), Cynthia Millar (Ondes Martenot); *Album Producer*: Howard Shore; *Engineers*: John Kurlander, Keith Grant, Gary Chester.

Selections: 1 Main Title (5:04); 2 Backlot (1:06); 3 Mr. Lugosi/ Hypno Theme (1:56); 4 Beware (:56); 5 Glen Or Glenda (1:18); 6 Eddie, Help Me (1:56); 7 Elmogambo (3:20); 8 Bride Of The Monster (1:17); 9 I Have No Home (1:20); 10 Kuba Mambo

> "**B**ecause *Batman Forever* had a new director (Joel Schumacher), it made it mandatory to not look at the earlier pictures. I made believe it was just a movie about 'Batman.'"
>
> **Elliot Goldenthal**
> *(The Hollywood Reporter, 1-16-96)*

(1:53); 11 Nautch Dance (1:27); 12 Angora (1:23); 13 Sanitarium (3:42); 14 Ed, Kathy (1:28); 15 Elysium (2:16); 16 "Grave Robbers" Begin (1:16); 17 Lurk Him (1:04); 18 Ed Takes Control (4:06); 19 Eddie Takes A Bow (1:00); 20 This Is The One (1:58); 21 Ed Wood (video) (3:22).

Review: Dedicated to the memory of Henry Mancini, Howard Shore's fine score for *Ed Wood* brims with nostalgia. Shore perfectly captures the sonic nuances of low-budget 1950s sci-fi/ monster film music, including the use of the icon of science fiction instruments, the theremin and the Ondes Martenot. His music lends an appropriate backdrop to the film's production scenes — recreations of such classic bargain-basement sci-fi as *Bride of the Monsters* and *Plan 9 From Outer Space*, the stereotypical '50s horror music — and also quotes from Tchaikovsky's 'Swan Lake' and the main title music from the original *Dracula* and *Mummy* films. In contrast a number of beat-generation jazz cues provide a contemporary mid-'50s sound, suitably thin and carrying their own sense of nostalgia and slight weirdness. More than an exercise in nostalgia, though, it's a finely crafted composition which works effectively as film music while also conveying a sort of homage to these corny yet beloved film music clichés.

Randall D. Larson

The Eddy Duchin Story 🎵🎵🎵

1990, MCA Records; from the movie *The Eddy Duchin Story*, Columbia Pictures, 1956.

Album Notes: The Columbia Picture Studio Orchestra, conducted by Morris Stoloff; *Featured Artist*: Carmen Cavallaro (piano).

Selections: 1 To Love Again (Main Title)(based on F. Chopin's E Flat Nocturne)(M. Stoloff/N. Washington)(3:02); 2 Manhattan (R. Rodgers/L. Hart)(3:01); 3 Shine On Harvest Moon (N. Bayes/J. Norworth)(2:48); 4 It Must Be True (You Are Mine, All

Mine)(G. Arnheim/G. Clifford/H. Barris) (2:26); 5 Whispering (M. Schonberger/R. Coburn/J. Schonberger)(2:57); 6 Dizzy Fingers (Z. Confrey)(2:00); 7 You're My Everything (H. Warren/J. Young/M. Dixon) (3:06); 8 Chopsticks (trad.)(2:28); 9 On The Sunny Side Of The Street (D. Fields/J. McHugh)(2:07); 10 Brazil (Aquarela do Brasil)(A. Barroso)(3:34); 11 La vie en rose (E. Piaf/Louiguy)(3:28); 12 To Love Again (Finale)((based on F. Chopin's E Flat Nocturne)(M. Stoloff/N. Washington) (3:34).

Review: The life story of sweet band pianist and conductor Eddy Duchin, portrayed by Tyrone Power, provides for a remarkably effective musical film in which the highlights are the many standards from the 1920s and '30s that Duchin performed to the great delight of high society people. Carmen Cavallaro, himself an accomplished pianist, plays these selections on the soundtrack and in this album which is consistently enjoyable, even when all that's required is background music.

Edward Scissorhands ♫♫♫♫

1990, MCA Records; from the movie *Edward Scissorhands*, 20th Century-Fox, 1990.

Album Notes: *Music*: Danny Elfman; *Orchestrations*: Steve Bartek; *Music Editor*: Bob Badami; Orchestra conducted by Shirley Walker; *Album Producer*: Danny Elfman; *Engineers*: Shawn Murphy, Dennis Sands, Bill Jackson; *Assistant Engineers*: Sue McLean, Sharon Rice.

Selections: Part One: Edward Meets The World... 1 Introduction (Titles) (2:36); 2 Storytime (2:35); 3 Castle On The Hill (6:25); 4 Beautiful New World/Home Sweet Home (2:05); 5 The Cookie Factory (2:14); 6 Ballet de Surburbia (suite)(1:17); 7 Ice Dance (1:45); 8 Etiquette Lesson (1:38); 9 Edward The Barber (3:19); Part Two: ...Poor Edward! 10 Esmeralda (:27); 11 Death! (3:29); 12 The Tide Turns (suite)(5:31); 13 The Final Confrontation (2:17); 14 Farewell (2:46); 15 The Grand Finale (3:26); 16 The End (4:47); 17 With These Hands (A. Silver/B. Davis)(2:43) *Tom Jones.*

Review: The always inventive Danny Elfman surpassed himself when he wrote this brilliant score for Tim Burton's strange and poetic fantasy about a youth whose hands are scissors, and who, because of it, discovers himself a unique talent as a landscape artist. The childlike qualities in the main character, the creation of a mad scientist who dies before he has a chance to finish his work, as well as the fable-like aspects of the screenplay inspired Elfman to write cues in which the main accents evoke a wonderland where anything and everything can happen, and often does. "Storytime," in fact, sets the right musical atmosphere from the start, with the other selections

detailing the strange and wonderful tale of Edward, and the problems he encounters when he attempts to enter the real world. Throughout the soft-hued score, an evanescent chorus and tinkling bells add an imaginative lilt to the cues. In this creative canvas, the only discordant note is Tom Jones' abrasive performance of "With These Hands," mercifully heard at the end, which breaks the moods established by the score.

The Egyptian ♫♫♫♫♫

1990, Varese-Sarabande; from the movie *The Egyptian*, 20th Century-Fox, 1954.

Album Notes: *Music*: Alfred Newman, Bernard Herrmann; The Hollywood Symphony Orchestra and Chorus, conducted by Alfred Newman; *Featured Soloist*: Doreen Tryden; *CD Producers*: Tom Null, Robert Townson; *Engineer*: Michele Stone.

Selections: 1 Prelude/The Ruins/The Red Sea and Childhood/The Nile and The Temple (6:37); 2 Her Name Was Merit (3:03); 3 The Pharaoh Akhnaton (3:51); 4 Nefer, Nefer, Nefer (7:17); 5 The Lotus Pool (3:53); 6 The Valley Of The King (5:33); 7 At The Tomb Of Amenhotep (The Great Pharaoh)(5:02); 8 The Martyrdom Of Merit (4:20); 9 The Death Of Akhnaton (4:57); 10 Horemheb, The New Pharaoh (2:21); 11 Exile And Death (1:41).

Review: In a collaborative effort almost unique in the annals of film music, two of Hollywood's greatest composers, Alfred Newman and Bernard Herrmann, wrote the glorious score for this offbeat epic drama, set 33 centuries ago, about a monotheist Pharaoh, and the physician (the "Egyptian" of the title) he befriends, a humanist with a unique vision about his own role on earth. Actually, the two composers didn't work together as each took a certain number of scenes and wrote his cues independently, but the general texture of the score belies its varied origins, and its overall excellence testifies to the professionalism of both composers who viewed the film itself as a limitless forum for musical expression. In his comprehensive liner notes, Kevin Mulhall details which tracks were composed by Herrmann and which by Newman, as well as the unusual situation that brought the two men to write this score. The recording, while appropriately spacious and grandiose, is in mono. Presumably the multi-tracks still exist at 20th Century-Fox and the day when we might hear a full stereophonic version of this great score may not be far away. In the meantime, this CD is the next best thing.

The Eiger Sanction ♫♫♫♫

1990, Varese-Sarabande; from the movie *The Eiger Sanction*, Universal Pictures, 1975.

Album Notes: *Music*: John Williams; Orchestra conducted by John Williams; *Album Producer*: John Williams.

Selections: 1 Main Title (2:24); 2 Theme From "The Eiger Sanction" (2:53); 3 Fifty Miles Of Desert (2:50); 4 The Icy Ascent (3:41); 5 Friends And Enemies (3:01); 6 The Top Of The World (3:05); 7 Theme From "The Eiger Sanction" (2:09); 8 Training With George (2:13); 9 Theme From "The Eiger Sanction" (2:07); 10 George Sets The Pace (2:39); 11 The Microfilm Killing (2:04); 12 Up The Drainpipe (3:18); 13 The Eiger (2:14).

Review: This suspense film starring Clint Eastwood, as a former secret agent and avid mountain climber who comes out of retirement to handle a delicate assignment, elicited another flavorful pre-*Star Wars* score from John Williams. Characteristic of the composer's style at the time, the main theme from the film is a jazzy tune that swings lightly over a melodic orchestral line, and is reprised twice in stylistically different versions. The other cues detail the action in terms that embody it and at the same time provide an appealling musical program. The sound quality in this CD is not as good as it should be, with a semi-monochromatic sound and an EQ that generally lacks brightness.

8 Heads in a Duffel Bag **Woof**

1997, Varese-Sarabande Records; from the movie *8 Heads in a Duffel Bag*, Orion Pictures, 1997.

Album Notes: *Music*: Andrew Gross; *Music Editor*: Lee Scott; The Northwest Sinfonia, conducted by Andrew Gross; *Album Producer*: Andrew Gross; *Engineer*: John Kurlander.

Selections: 1 Orion Logo (:23); 2 Main Titles Part One (:59); 3 Main Titles Part Two/Boarding The Plane (2:43); 4 Wrong Bag (:53); 5 Arrival In Mexico (:25); 6 Rico's Threat (1:02); 7 I Didn't Really Invite You (:46); 8 Annette's Lost It (1:25); 9 Tommy Enters Fraternity (1:24); 10 Taking Out The Trash (:49); 11 Hiding The Heads (1:20); 12 Annette Looks For Heads (:41); 13 Charlie Looks For Heads (:58); 14 Laundry Room (:56); 15 Meet The Banditos (1:17); 16 Airport Security (1:12); 17 Charlie Packs Heads (1:02); 18 We've Gotta Move (1:11); 19 Laurie Bonks Annette (:44); 20 Return Of The Banditos (1:30); 21 Desert Music (2:16); 22 Tommy Counts Heads (1:58); 23 Charlie Takes Control (1:38); 24 Ska Cha Chase (2:21); 25 Tango To The End (2:05).

Review: Granted, action in comedies must be swift, and so it derives must be the music that underscores it. But this is ridiculous. Out of 25 tracks in this soundtrack album, fully 10 are under one minute of playing time, and another 11 are under two minutes. Talk about swiftness! The cues by Andrew Gross, a newcomer on the scene, don't even have the time to make any kind of impact.

8 Seconds ♪♪♪♪

1994, MCA Records; from the movie *8 Seconds,* New Line Cinema, 1994.

Album Notes: *Music*: Bill Conti; *Song Producers*: James Stroud, Pam Tillis, Josh Leo, Keith Thomas, Ronnie Dunn, Tony Brown, Andrew Gold and Kenny Edwards, Reba McEntire, Mark Wright, Don Was; *Executive Producers*: Tony Brown, Kathy Nelson.

Selections: 1 Burnin' Up The Road (T. McBride/B. Carter/R. Ellsworth)(3:41) *John Anderson*; 2 Pull Your Hat Down Tight (L. Storey)(2:31) *Pam Tillis*; 3 No More Cryin' (T. McBride/J. Leo)(3:02) *McBride & The Ride*; 4 Standing Right Next To Me (K. Bonoff/W. Waldman)(3:47) *Karla Bonoff*; 5 Ride 'Em High, Ride 'Em Low (R. Dunn)(3:23) *Brooks & Dunn*; 6 Just Once (D.L. Muprhy/K. Tribble)(3:00) *David Lee Murphy*; 7 When Will I Be Loved (P. Everly)(2:04) *Vince Gill, Karla Bonoff*; 8 If I Had Only Known (J. Stanfield/C. Morris)(4:01) *Reba McEntire*; 9 Texas Is Bigger Than It Used To Be (R. Rogers/M. Wright/J. Johnston)(4:08) *Mark Chestnutt*; 10 You Hung The Moon (P. Smyth/K. Savigar)(3:59) *Patty Smyth*; 11 Once In A While (S. Dorff/J. Bettis) (3:59) *Billy Dean*; 12 Lane's Theme (3:36).

Review: Some soundtrack compilations have an engaging quality that seems to come through even as you read the credits. Such is the case with this collection of country tracks, featuring some well-known and respected artists from this side of the border, which is as pleasant and entertaining as can be and which help illustrate the saga of a young and avid bronco rider, whose goal in life is to stay on the eight seconds it takes to qualify at the rodeo. Nothing fancy, just some good clean fun, and a feeling that sometimes soundtrack albums can be as uncomplicated and enjoyable as, well... riding a wild beast? In all this country charm, Bill Conti's "Lane's Theme" almost sounds like an odd intruder.

El Cid

El Cid ♪♪♪♪⁵

1996, Koch Int'l; from the movie *El Cid*, M-G-M, 1961.

Album Notes: *Music*: Miklos Rozsa; *Music Editor*: Edna Bulluck; The New Zealand Symphony Orchestra, conducted by James Sedares; *Featured Artists*: Tamra Saylor Fine (organ), The New Zealand Youth Choir, Karen Grylis, director; *Album Producer*: Michael Fine; *Engineer*: Keith Warren; *Assistant Engineer*: David Merrill.

Selections: 1 Overture (3:19); 2 Prelude (3:15); 3 Courage And Honor (8:14); 4 Fight For Calahorra (4:18); 5 Palace Music #1

(1:36); 6 Palace Music #2 (1:52); 7 Palace Music #3 (1:21); 8 Road To Asturias (2:41); 9 Wedding Night (5:35); 10 Coronation (2:18); 11 Love Scene (8:37); 12 El Cid March (3:45); 13 Battle Of Valencia (6:48); 14 Death Of El Cid (5:02); 15 Legend And Epilogue (5:58).

Review: See entry below.

El Cid 🎵🎵🎵🎵

1991, Sony Music Special Products; from the movie *El Cid*, M-G-M, 1961.

Album Notes: *Music*: Miklos Rozsa; The Graunke Symphony Orchestra of Munich, conducted by Miklos Rozsa; *Album Producer*: Miklos Rozsa; *Engineer*: Debra Parkinson.

Selections: 1 Overture (3:15); 2 Prelude (3:31); 3 Palace Music (:59); 4 Fight For Calahorra (3:37); 5 Thirteen Knights (2:33); 6 Farewell (6:27); 7 Intermezzo: El Cid March (4:04); 8 The Twins (2:25); 9 Battle Of Valencia (7:30); 10 The Cid's Death (3:09); 11 Legend And Epilogue (5:06).

Review: The superlative Koch recording, a superb recreation of the score with several previously unrecorded cues, is the current best representation of the epic music Rozsa wrote for the Samuel Bronston extravaganza, recounting the medieval tale of the Spanish hero (Charlton Heston at his dashing best) and how he defeated several centuries of dominance by the Moors. The handsome package (the booklet features profuse liner notes, including an introduction by Martin Scorsese, and many pictures from the production) is a magnificent complement to the music, delivered with the right amount of zest and enthusiasm by the New Zealand Symphony in sonics that are detailed and spacious, if at times a trifle fuzzy.

　　The Sony set is the actual soundtrack recording, with the composer conducting the Graunke Symphony in a spirited performance, made even more exciting thanks to the brilliant sound quality of the CD. However, while this album contains a few tracks that are not on the Koch album ("Thirteen Knights," "The Twins") it also misses quite a few others. Hopefully, Rhino, current holder of the rights to this M-G-M soundtrack, will eventually reissue it in a complete format.

The Electric Horseman 🎵🎵🎵▿

1987, Columbia Records; from the movie *The Electric Horseman*, Columbia Pictures, 1979.

Album Notes: *Music*: Dave Grusin; *Orchestrations*: Dave Grusin; Orchestra conducted by Dave Grusin; *Album Producers*: Dave Grusin, Larry Rosen; *Engineers*: Dan Wallin, Larry Rosen; *Assistant Engineer*: Ollie Cotton.

Selections: 1 Midnight Rider (G. Allman) (2:41) *Willie Nelson*; 2 My Heroes Have Always Been Cowboys (S. Vaughan) (3:03) *Willie Nelson*; 3 Mammas Don't Let Your Babies Grow Up To Be Cowboys (E. Bruce/P. Bruce) (3:27) *Willie Nelson*; 4 So You Think You're A Cowboy (W. Nelson/H. Cochran) (2:16) *Willie Nelson*; 5 Hands On The Wheel (B. Callery) (2:48) *Willie Nelson*; 6 Electro-Phantasma (5:00); 7 Rising Star (Love Theme) (2:32); 8 The Electric Horseman (3:42); 9 Interlude: Tumbleweed Morning (:27); 10 Disco Magic (5:00); 11 Freedom Epilogue (2:11).

Review: Grusin wrote the score, but Willie Nelson (with five songs on this album and a co-starring role in the film) gets all the credit. Actually, who should complain when the songs include "My Heroes Have Always Been Cowboys" and "Mammas Don't Let Your Babies Grow Up To Be Cowboys," two of Nelson's most popular hits. As for Dave Grusin, writing in an idiom that is closer to his own roots, he does well for himself with cues that are attractively designed and strongly evocative of the specific atmosphere of the film, a romantic comedy starring Robert Redford as an ex-rodeo champion seeking a richer and more rewarding life, and Jane Fonda as the TV reporter who comes to share his views. "Electro-Phantasma," a bouncy, jazzy tune, and "Disco Magic," Grusin's concession to the omnipresent fad at the time, are quite enjoyable. "Love Theme," in a more subtle vein, proves equally fetching.

The Elephant Man 🎵🎵🎵▿

1994, Milan Records; from the movie *The Elephant Man*, Paramount Pictures, 1980.

Album Notes: *Music*: John Morris; *Orchestrations*: Jack Hayes; The National Philharmonic Orchestra, conducted by John Morris; *Album Producer*: John Morris; *Engineer*: John Richards.

Selections: 1 The Elephant Man Theme (3:44); 2 Dr. Treves Visits The Freak Show And Elephant Man (4:08); 3 John Merrick And Psalm (1:16); 4 John Merrick And Mrs. Kendal (2:02); 5 The Nightmare (4:38); 6 Mrs. Kendal's Theater And Poetry Reading (1:57); 7 The Belgian Circus Episode (2:59); 8 Train Station (1:54); 9 Pantomime (2:19); 10 Adagio For Strings (S. Barber) (9:28) *The London Symphony Orchestra, Andre Previn*; 11 Recapitulation (5:35).

Review: A gruesome story about a man's deformity and the strange fascination he exerted on his contemporaries in Victorian England, *The Elephant Man* inspired John Morris to write a generally somber score, well in keeping with the nature of the drama. The horror provoked by John Merrick's appearance, his inner thoughts and his dream about having a more normal existence, are fully explored in cues in which the main theme, a wistful melody initially heard as a delicately attractive waltz, returns as an adagio filled with morose undertones. In contrast, other cues announce in a gritty, almost unbearably harsh way, the plastic carnival exuberance that marks his exhibition at various fairgrounds, the only way he could make a living. A sardonic "The Nightmare" blends both elements in a grotesque display that is both vivid and frightening. Adding a somewhat unnecessary touch to this score, strong enough to exist on its own terms, is yet another version of Samuel Barber's "Adagio For Strings," performed by the LSO and Andre Previn.

Elizabeth and Essex 🎜🎜🎜🎜

1992, Bay Cities Records; from the movie *The Private Lives of Elizabeth and Essex*, Warner Bros., 1939.

Album Notes: *Music:* Erich-Wolfgang Korngold; The Munich Symphony Orchestra, conducted by Carl Davis; *Album Producer:* Paul Wing; *Engineer:* Mike Ross-Trevor.

Selections: 1 Elizabeth And Essex (suite): Main Title/Narrative/ March/ Shadow And Parade/The Throne Room/After Elizabeth Slaps Essex/Elizabeth And Essex (8:14); 2 The Queen (suite): The Courier/The Chess Game/Mirror Scene/ The Queen/Messenger/Poor Child (13:11); 3 Reconciliation (suite): The Hunting/ Raleigh And Essex/Silver Armor/Lady Penelope/Darling/Card Game/Love Scene (11:55); 4 Ireland (suite): Council Dismissed/ Love And The Ring/ Ireland/Shadow Of Penelope/Elizabeth Weeps/The Battle/The Truce (9:37); 5 Essex Returns (suite): The Palace/Queen Elizabeth/Essex Returns/Love Scene/ Arrest (10:13); 6 The Tower Of London (suite): The Tower/Cecil/Essex/ Love Scene/Executioner/End Cast (12:25).

Review: Carl Davis and the Munich Symphony Orchestra conjure up all the drama and passion in Korngold's score for *The Private Lives of Elizabeth and Essex* in a recording marked by its brilliant sonics and the excellence of its performance. Instead of presenting the score as a disjointed series of short cues, the recording regroups the main themes in six long suites that follow the unfolding historical drama starring Errol Flynn as the ambitious Lord Essex, a hero in his own country after he defeated the Spaniards at Cadiz, and Bette Davis as the Queen of England, with whom Essex has an affair before she has him beheaded when she senses his real ambition is to overthrow her and seize power. Much in the line of his other swashbucklers, like *Sea Hawk* or *Captain Blood,* Korngold wrote a score that teems with gorgeous romantic melodies and rambunctious action cues. The whole brew is served with the right dose of pageantry and pathos by the orchestra, wonderfully together behind its conductor.

Emma 🎜🎜🎜🎜

1996, Miramax-Hollywood Records; from the movie *Emma,* Miramax Pictures, 1996.

Album Notes: *Music:* Rachel Portman; *Orchestrations:* Rachel Portman; Orchestra conducted by David Snell; *Featured Musicians:* Hugh Webb (harp), Nick Bucknall (clarinet), Linda Coffin (flute); *Album Producer:* Rachel Portman; *Engineer:* Keith Grant.

Selections: 1 Main Titles (4:26); 2 Harriet's Portrait (1:11); 3 Sewing And Archery (3:07); 4 Frank Churchill Arrives (2:30); 5 Celery Root (2:55); 6 Mr. Elton's Rejection (1:59); 7 Emma Tells Harriet About Mr. Elton (1:06); 8 The Coles Party (3:10); 9 Mrs. Elton's Visit (1:32); 10 Emma Dreams Of Frank Churchill (:50); 11 The Dance (1:17); 12 Gypsies (:47); 13 The Picnic (2:29); 14 Emma Insults Miss Bates (2:00); 15 Emma Writes Her Diary (2:53); 16 Mr. Knightley Returns (1:58); 17 Proposal (4:22); 18 End Titles (4:21).

Review: With its deft use of classical-sounding themes, many of them crafted for a chamber ensemble in which delicate instruments like the harp, clarinet and flute play a predominant role, this magnificent score must rank among some of the best film music written last year. Composed for yet another adaptation of a Jane Austen novel (Hollywood's greatest screenwriter of late), this discriminating score is achingly beautiful, superbly nuanced, and gorgeously melodic. Heard behind the scenes on the screen, it subtly underscores the action, adding its own commentary without overstressing its presence. Isolated from the film, it stands out as a marvelous example of solid music composition, at times joyously expressive, at times compassionately poignant, but always pleasantly listenable, and constantly inventive. In other words, it's everything good film music should always be.

Empire of the Sun 🎜🎜🎜🎜

1987, Warner Bros. Records; from the movie *Empire of the Sun,* Warner Bros., 1987.

Album Notes: *Music:* John Williams; *Music Editor:* Ken Wannberg; Orchestra conducted by John Williams; *Album Producer:* John Williams; *Engineers:* Shawn Murphy, Armin Steiner (remix).

Selections: 1 Suo Gan (p.d., arr. by John McCathy)(2:19) *The Ambrosian Junior Choir, John McCarthy, James Rainbird;* 2 Cadillac Of The Skies (3:48); 3 Jim's New Life (2:33); 4 Lost In The Crowd (5:39); 5 Imaginary Air Battle (2:35); 6 The Return To The City (7:45); 7 Liberation: Exsultate Justi (1:46); 8 The British Grenadiers (trad.)(2:25); 9 Toy Planes, Home and

Hearth (Chopin Mazurka, op. 17, No. 4)(4:37); 10 The Streets Of Shanghai (5:11); 11 The Pheasant Hunt (4:24); 12 No Road Home/Seeing The Bomb (6:10); 13 Exsultate Justi (4:59).

Review: Considered by many one of John Williams' best efforts, this striking score yielded at least two recognizable hits in the composer's canon, if not on the charts, "Cadillac of the Skies" and the anthem "Exsultate Justi." But this brilliantly colorful film by Steven Spielberg, about a young boy caught in World War II China by the Japanese invasion, inspired the composer to write a rich series of cues, highlighted by some unforgettable moments like "Jim's New Life," "Imaginary Air Battle," or the actively exotic "The Streets of Shanghai." Typical of Williams' florid style, the cues overflow with great melodic themes, excitingly expressive and wonderfully stated. One exception, however, is "The Pheasant Hunt," for percussion and ethnic instruments, which might have been very effective on the screen behind the action, but which makes no real musical statement of its own and seems a bit of a waste in the current context.

The Empire Strikes Back
♫♫♫♫♫

1997, RCA Victor Records; from the movie *The Empire Strikes Back*, 20th Century-Fox, 1980/1997.

Album Notes: *Music*: John Williams; *Orchestrations*: Herbert W. Spencer; The London Symphony Orchestra conducted by John Williams; *Album Producer*: John Williams; *Engineer*: Eric Tomlinson; *CD Producer*: Nick Redman; *Engineers*: Michael Matessino, Brian Risner, Dan Hersch.

Selections: CD 1: 1 20th Century-Fox Fanfare (A. Newman)(:22); 2 Main Title/The Ice Planet Hoth (8:09); 3 The Wampa's Lair/Vision Of Obi-Wan/ Snowspeeders Take Flight (8:44); 4 The Imperial Proble/Aboard The Executor (4:24); 5 The Battle Of Hoth: Ion Cannon/Imperial Walkers/Beneath The At-At/Escape In The Millenium Falcon (14:48); 6 The Asteroid Field (4:15); 7 Arrival On Dagobah (4:54); 8 Luke's Nocturnal Visitor (2:35); 9 Han Solo And The Princess (3:26); 10 Jedi Master Revealed/Mynock Cave (5:44); 11 The Training Of A Jedi Knight/The Magic Tree (5:16)

CD 2: 1 The Imperial March (Darth Vader's Theme)(3:02); 2 Yoda's Theme (3:30); 3 Attacking A Star Destroyer (3:04); 4 Yoda And The Force (4:02); 5 Imperial Starfleet Deployed/City In The Clouds (6:04); 6 Lando's Palace (3:53); 7 Betrayal At Bespin (3:46); 8 Deal With The Dark Lord (2:37); 9 Carbon Freeze/Darth Vader's Trap/Departure Of Boba Fett (11:50); 10 The Clash Of Lightsabers (4:18); 11 Rescue From Cloud City/ Hyperspace (9:10); 12 The Rebel Fleet/End Title (6:28).

Review: John Williams reached the culmination of his block-buster style with this first *Star Wars* sequel, which features a dizzying array of memorable themes as it underscores the dark middle section of George Lucas's space epic trilogy. Williams originally scored almost every moment of *Empire*, and this deluxe 2-CD set presents the entire score for the first time with amazing fidelity and showmanship. Included is a great deal of music Williams wrote for early sections of the film as action ensues on the ice planet of Hoth, and album producer Nick Redman and sequencer Mark Mattesino have ingeniously organized this music to reflect both the familiar movie editing of the music and the score as it might have been, with plenty of music that's never been released in any form. The throbbing early passages involving Luke Skywalker and Han Solo exploring on their two-legged Taun-Tauns and Williams's thrillingly sustained, agitated battle sequences dominate the first third of the album, while his delicate, exquisitely lyrical material for Yoda lends a reflective quality to the score's midsection. The heavy, percussive sounds of Bespin's carbon freeze chamber and a throbbing, dirge-like melody raise the stakes for the film's climactic sequences, with the composer at his swash-buckling best in "The Duel" and whipping up amazing drama and suspense with Luke "Losing a Hand" and barely escaping Darth Vader during the propulsive jump to "Hyperspace." You might be exhausted by the umpteenth take on "Darth Vader's Theme" by the time this is over, but *Empire* remains a magnificent, unforgettable epic score.

Jeff Bond

See also: Star Wars and Return of the Jedi

Enemies, A Love Story ♫♫♫♫

1989, Varese-Sarabande Records; from the movie *Enemies, A Love Story*, 20th Century-Fox, 1989.

Album Notes: *Music*: Maurice Jarre; Orchestra conducted by Maurice Jarre; *Featured Soloist*: Giora Feidman (clarinet); *Album Producer*: Maurice Jarre; *Engineer*: Bobby Fernandez.

Selections: 1 Herman (5:24); 2 A Third Wife (5:08); 3 Tamara (4:03); 4 Kretchmar Country Club (2:43); 5 In The Wood (2:17); 6 The Rumba (2:22); 7 Masha (4:40); 8 Baby Masha (4:55).

Review: Maurice Jarre returned to a seldom explored side of his vast creative talent with this score written for Paul Mazursky's biting satire about a man, a survivor of the Holocaust, living in New York and married to three women, with all the complications this deliciously unusual situation created. As he already had demonstrated a year before in the director's *Moon Over Parador*, Jarre can easily handle the most spurious aspects of broad comedy, even going as far as spoofing his own style to add extra pep to his concoctions. Here, the situation enabled him to add to the mix some Jewish accents, with Giora Feidman handling the obligatory clarinet solos. Posing ever so slightly to reflect on the individual charms of the three women, as does the hero of the film, the music moves merrily into its own territory, with a "kretchmar" and a rumba among its most enjoyable side trips.

Enemy Mine ♫♫♫♫▷

1985, Varese-Sarabande; from the movie *Enemy Mine*, 20th Century-Fox, 1985.

Album Notes: *Music*: Maurice Jarre; The Studioorchester of Munich, conducted by Maurice Jarre; *Electronic Ensemble*: Michael Boddicker, Maurice Jarre, Martin Levy, Michel Mention, Kristian Schultze, Nyle Steiner; *Album Producer*: Maurice Jarre; *Engineers*: Ulrich Ullmann (electronic), Peter Kramper (orchestral).

Selections: 1 Fyrine IV (5:02); 2 The Relationship (3:55); 3 The Small Drac (2:45); 4 The Crater (2:15); 5 The Birth Of Zammis (6:14); 6 Spring (1:27); 7 The Scavengers (4:48); 8 Davidges Lineage (3:33); 9 Football Game (:44); 10 Before The Drac Holy Council (9:54).

Review: This wonderful thematic score by Maurice Jarre is cleverly sequenced like a symphonic suite so that the music evolves from a focus on electronics to acoustics. In fact, early cues in the film are also more electronic and the finale almost all orchestral. This shifting of orchestrational style allowed Jarre to play up the sci-fi aspects of the film against the emotional core of the story. Even with all the film's futuristic trappings, it still all boils down to a basic story of friendship and parental love between two who were once mortal enemies. Chiefly, Jarre used his electronics to play the alien aspects of the planet locale and the hostility between the lizard-like Draconian marooned with a human fighter pilot. The theme for the mystical Draconian religion is brought into full bloom during the finale, "Before the Drac Holy Council," through the use of an electronically augmented chorus.

David Hirsch

The English Patient ♫♫♫♫

1996, Fantasy Records; from the movie *The English Patient*, Miramax Films, 1996.

Album Notes: *Music*: Gabriel Yared; *Music Editor*: Robert Randles; The Academy of St. Martin-in-the-Fields, conducted by Harry Rabinowitz; *Featured Musician*: John Constable (piano); *Featured Vocalist*: Marta Sebestyen; *Album Producer*: Robert Randles; *Engineer*: Keith Grant.

Selections: 1 The English Patient (3:30); 2 A Retreat (1:21); 3 Rupert Bear (1:22); 4 What Else Do You Love? (1:00); 5 Why Picton? (1:04); 6 Cheek To Cheek (I. Berlin) (3:15) *Fred Astaire*; 7 Kip's Lights (1:24); 8 Hana's Curse (2:06); 9 I'll Always Go Back To That Church (1:48); 10 Black Nights (1:53); 11 Swoon, I'll Catch You (1:47); 12 Am I K. In Your Book? (:55); 13 Let Me Come In! (2:35); 14 Wang Wang Blues (G. Mueller/H. Busse/B. Johnson) (2:47) *Benny Goodman*; 15 Convento di Sant'Anna (9:09); 16 Herodotus (1:04); 17 Szerelem, Szerelem (trad.) (4:32) *Muszikas, Marta Sebestyen*; 18 Ask Your Saint Who He's Killed (1:04); 19 One O'clock Jump (C. Basie) (3:10) *Benny Goodman*; 20 I'll Be Back (4:00); 21 Let Me Tell You About Winds (:55); 22 Read Me To Sleep (4:56); 23 The Cave Of Swimmers (1:55); 24 Where Or When (R. Rodgers/L. Hart) (2:14) *Shepheard's Hotel Jazz Orchestra*; 25 Aria from The Goldberg Variations (J.S. Bach) (2:57) *Julie Steinberg*; 26 Cheek To Cheek (I. Berlin) (3:42) *Ella Fitzgerald*; 27 As Far As Florence (5:16); 28 En Csak Azt Csodalom (Lullaby For Katharine) (trad) (1:07).

Review: Dismissing the several pop songs included in this album, which neither add nor detract from the music itself and certainly provide a period flavor, portions of this Oscar-winning score by Gabriel Yared may actually have been more effective on the screen than in this soundtrack album. One basic reason is that many of the cues, short as they are, are not sufficiently developed to really attract, and often sound unfinished. There are, of course, some happy exceptions, including a lovely "Kip's Lights," played by a romantic piano against an attractively evanescent orchestral background; "I'll Always Go Back To That Church," with its faint evocation of Italy; "Convento di Sant'Anna," a piano sonata, staid yet poetic in its subtle simplicity; and "Read Me To Sleep," another piece for piano solo that is starkly eloquent. These, and some of the other selections succeed in recreating the atmosphere that permeates this romantic drama about an amnesiac aviator and the Canadian nurse who tends to him in an old monastery in Tuscany, in the last days of World War II.

The Englishman Who Went Up a Hill But Came Down a Mountain ♫♫♫♫▷

1995, Epic Soundtrax; from the movie *The Englishman Who Went Up a Hill But Came Down a Mountain*, Miramax Films, 1995.

Album Notes: *Music*: Stephen Endelman; *Orchestrations*: Stephen Endelman; Orchestra conducted by Stephen Endelman; *Featured Performers*: Sian James (vocals), Gwalia Male Voice Choir, Giles Lewin (bagpipe, flute, pennywhistle); *Album Producer*: Jeffrey Kimball; *Engineer*: James P. Nichols.

Selections: 1 Opening Credits/English Drive (1:28); 2 Johnny's Triumph (1:51); 3 Hustle And Bustle (2:40); 4 Johnny's Barrow (1:20); 5 Never Ending Rain (:44); 6 The Brothers Tup (2:02); 7 Lovers On The Mountain (2:11); 8 Reverend Jones' Death (2:00); 9 It's A Hill (:44); 10 Villagers Begin Building (2:59); 11 The Sermon (1:50); 12 The Rain (3:37); 13 Anson And Betty (4:28); 14 Tommy Two Strokes (1:13); 15 Men Of Harlegh (1:51); 16 Ffynnon Garw (2:11); 17 Magnificent Peak (3:59).

Review: The beautifully exotic score for this film starring Hugh Grant was composed by Stephen Endelman, who is not to be confused with either Cliff Eidelman or Randy Edelman. Not that you will, once you have heard this extraordinary profuse orchestral score, subtly relying on the flute and the pennywhistle to create its own poetic atmosphere. Rooted in the English folk tradition, the themes evolve out of the orchestral texture to reveal the uncanny talent of the composer who succeeds in accenting the stronger aspects of the story, as well as evoking the raw beauty of the countryside in which it takes place. Some cues ("Never Ending Rain," "Lovers on the Mountain," "Magnificent Peak") are particularly striking, but the score as a whole is remarkably attractive.

Eraser ♫♫

1996, Atlantic Records; from the movie *Eraser*, Warner Bros., 1996.

Album Notes: *Music*: Alan Silvestri; *Orchestrations*: Williams Ross, Mark McKenzie, Conrad Pope; *Music Editors*: Kenneth Karman, William Kaplan; Orchestra conducted by Alan Silvestri; *Album Producer*: Alan Silvestri; *Engineer*: Dennis Sands; *Assistant Engineers*: Tom Hardisty, Sue McLean, Dave Marquette, Andy Bass.

Selections: 1 Eraser Original Maintitle (2:38); 2 "She's In" (6:11); 3 Kruger's Story (1:56); 4 Cabin Raid (4:41); 5 Kruger Escapes (4:23); 6 "Your Luggage" (3:18); 7 "When I Have Proof" (3:15); 8 Cyrez Break In (6:52); 9 Union Trouble (3:21); 10 Dock Fight (3:13); 11 Reunion (1:39); 12 "The Eraser" (1:45).

Review: A lackluster action film score, especially by Alan Silvestri standards. There's a sense of boredom all around here as the music just plods along. It takes until track 5, "Kruger Escapes," before there's any sign of life. The screeching guitar passages seem more necessary to keep the listener awake than serve any dramatic purpose. The main theme seems to be going somewhere, but exactly where is never clear.

David Hirsch

Escape from L.A. ♫♫

1996, Milan Records; from the movie *Escape from L.A.*, Paramount Pictures, 1996.

Album Notes: *Music*: Shirley Walker, John Carpenter; *Orchestrations*: Lolita Ritmanis, Michael McCuistion; *Music Editor*: Thomas Milano; Orchestra conducted by Shirley Walker; *Featured Musicians*: Nyle Steiner (electronic valve instrument), Jamie Muhoberac (sample synthesist), Mike Watts, Shirley Walker (keyboard synthesists), Mike Fisher (electronic percussion), Tommy Morgan (harmonica), Daniel Greco (hammer dulcimer), John Goux (guitar), Nathan East (bass guitar), John Rosinson (rock drums), Tom Raney, Greg Goodall (timpani), Robert Zimmitti (Daiko drum), Endre Granat (violin), Jon Clarke (soprano oboe); *Album Producer*: Shirley Walker; *Engineers*: Robert Fernandez, Doug Botnick.

Selections: 1 Escape From New York Main Title (J. Carpenter/ A. Howarth) (2:07); 2 History Of Los Angeles (J. Carpenter/S. Walker)(2:09); 3 Snake's Uniform (J. Carpenter)(:58); 4 Submarine Launch (S. Walker)(2:36); 5 Sunset Boulevard Bazaar (S. Walker)(2:03); 6 Motorcycle Chase (S. Walker) (2:23); 7 Showdown (J. Carpenter)(1:27); 8 Beverly Hills Surgeon General (J. Carpenter/ S. Walker)(4:10); 9 The Future Is Right Now (S. Walker) (2:00); 10 Hang Glider Attack (S. Walker)(2:30); 11 The Black Box (S. Walker)(1:14); 12 Escape From Coliseum (S. Walker)(1:53); 13 Helicopter Arrival (S. Walker)(2:05); 14 Fire Fight (S. Walker)(2:49); 15 Escape From Happy Kingdom (S. Walker)(1:30); 16 Crash Landing (S. Walker)(1:38).

Review: Somewhat disappointing follow up to the delightfully minimalist score to *Escape from New York*. Original composer John Carpenter contributed to this effort, most notably the new Morricone-inspired theme for anti-hero Snake Plisskin. The bulk of the work was created by Shirley Walker, who scored Carpenter's also disappointing *Memoirs of an Invisible Man*, and uses contemporary action film orchestral and synthesizer techniques here, without making any attempt to blend her compositional style with Carpenter's (compare her "Fire Fight" with his "Showdown"). What made the first film's score so popular was that it captured Plisskin's dark, brooding personality so well. He was a bad ass with no love for a world that didn't care about him. This time, Walker and Carpenter seem hell bent on spoofing not only the entire genre of post apocalyptic films, but their own as well. They're even making fun of Kurt Russell's less than subtle Clint Eastwood-like performance of Plisskin by clearly defining the connection musically.

David Hirsch

E.T. The Extra-Terrestrial

E.T. The Extra-Terrestrial
♪♪♪♪♪

1982, MCA Records; from the movie *E.T. The Extra-Terrestrial*, Universal Pictures, 1982.

Album Notes: *Music*: John Williams; *Orchestrations*: Ken Wannberg; *Music Editor*: Ken Hall; Orchestra conducted by John Williams; *Album Producers*: John Williams, Bruce Botnick; *Engineers*: Lyle Burbridge.

Selections: 1 Three Million Light Years From Home (2:57); 2 Abandoned And Pursued (2:58); 3 E.T. And Me (4:49); 4 E.T.'s Halloween (4:07); 5 Flying (3:20); 6 E.T. Phone Home (4:18); 7 Over The Moon (2:06); 8 Adventure On Earth (15:06).

Review: See entry below.

E.T.: The Extra-Terrestrial
♪♪♪♪♪

1996, MCA Records; from the movie *E.T.: The Extra-Terrestrial*, Universal Pictures, 1982.

Album Notes: *Music*: John Williams; *Orchestrations*: Ken Wannberg; *Music Editor*: Ken Hall; Orchestra conducted by John Williams; *Album Producers*: John Williams, Bruce Botnick; *Engineers*: Lyle Burbridge, Bruce Botnick; *CD Reissue Producer*: Shawn Murphy; *Engineer*: Shawn Murphy.

Selections: 1 Far From Home/E.T. Alone (6:49); 2 Bait For E.T. (1:43); 3 The Beginning Of A Friendship (2:50); 4 Toys (3:11); 5 "I'm Keeping Him" (2:19); 6 E.T.'s Powers (2:42); 7 E.T. And Elliott Get Drunk (2:53); 8 Frogs (2:10); 9 At Home (5:37); 10 The Magic Of Halloween (2:53); 11 Sending The Signal (3:57); 12 Searching For E.T. (4:16); 13 Invading Elliott's House (2:22); 14 E.T. Is Dying (2:17); 15 Losing E.T. (2:00); 16 E.T. Is Alive! (4:18); 17 Escape/Chase/Saying Goodbye (15:04); 18 End Credits (3:51).

Review: Call it the lighter side of *Close Encounters of the Third Kind,* if you will, but having to deal once again with alien visitors under the aegis of film magician Steven Spielberg, John Williams wrote a score that is as exhilarating and florid as his previous score was brooding and somber. Of course, the story itself suggested as much. Instead of government agents trying to make contact with people from another planet, not knowing what their ultimate intentions might be, this time around the extra-terrestrial, stranded on Earth following a landing accident, is trying to elude government agents intent on capturing him. With the help of a little guy who captures his confidence, E.T. eventually succeeds in going back home, but not before living some rousing, unforgettable moments. Williams' score, exquisitely shaded and warmly effusive, helps give the tale an extra element of verisimilitude, with a cohesive combination of musical themes all designed to enhance the screen action.

When the film was initially released, Williams went to the studio, and rerecorded several of the themes for an album which has been in the MCA catalogue ever since, first as an LP and, since the late 1980s, as a CD. The music, focusing on the lighter cues in the score, has made many converts, with one selection in particular, "Flying," achieving the status of a popular hit.

Recently, without saying much about it, MCA has added to its catalogue a vastly expanded version of the soundtrack, which is remarkably different from the previous album. Instead of using the studio rerecording, these are the actual soundtrack cues, which have different tempi, somewhat altered orchestrations, and a greater abundance of the darker cues from the score. More profuse, and certainly truer to the music one can hear in the film itself, this album makes fewer concessions to the popular aspects of the score and gives a broader scope of Williams' actual work, a startling combination of dark and light moments, all coming together in a mesmerizing display of his creative bent. Which of the two should you get? Both, of course, as they seem to complement each other while offering slightly different takes on the same score.

Europa Europa

1992, DRG Records; from the movie *Europa Europa*, Orion Pictures, 1991.

See: Olivier Olivier

Even Cowgirls Get the Blues
♪♪♪♩

1993, Sire Records; from the movie *Even Cowgirls Get the Blues*, Fine Line Features, 1993.

Album Notes: *Music*: k.d. lang, Ben Mink; *Album Producers*: k.d. lang, Ben Mink; *Engineer*: Marc Ramaer.

Selections: 1 Just Keep Me Moving (4:42); 2 Much Finer Place (:51); 3 Or Was I (3:07); 4 Hush Sweet Lover (4:05); 5 Myth (4:08); 6 Apogee (:37); 7 Virtual Vortex (:44); 8 Lifted By Love (3:02); 9 Overture (2:03); 10 Kundalini Yoga Waltz (1:07); 11 In Perfect Dreams (3:07); 12 Curious Soul Astray (3:40); 13 Ride Of Bonanza Jellybean (1:47); 14 Don't Be A Lemming Polka (2:17); 15 Sweet Little Cherokee (2:48); 16 Cowgirl Pride (1:47).

NINO ROTA

Italian composer Nino Rota, best known for his prolific composition of filmscores, was also an esteemed music teacher and classical composer who worked on operas, ballets, masses, and orchestral and chamber pieces. Although he worked with several directors, he attained prominence by providing the musical scores for the most memorable films of Federico Fellini and Francis Ford Coppola.

Rota's distinctive soundtracks set the dramatic tone of more than 40 films, starting with *His Young Wife* in 1945. In the United States, the films that brought Rota the most exposure were Coppola's *The Godfather* and *The Godfather, Part II.* However, Fellini film enthusiasts throughout the world lauded the composer's scores for 1954's *La Strada,* 1960's *La Dolce Vita,* 1965's *Juliet of the Spirits,* and 1974's *Amarcord.*

Rota was born and raised in Milan, Italy, and was the grandson of pianist/composer Giovanni Rinaldi. At the age of eight, he began studying the piano and composing. When he was 12, he entered the Milan Conservatory and studied under Italy's most distinguished musical teachers, including Casella and Pizzetti. He later attended the Curtis Institute in Philadelphia on a special musical scholarship and studied composition with Rosario Scalero while in the United States. Upon returning to Italy, Rota resumed his studies and received an arts degree in literature from Milan University.

In 1974, Rota shared a best original dramatic score Oscar for his work with Carmine Coppola on the music to *The Godfather, Part II.* He continued composing soundtracks until shortly before is death in 1979.

Review: k.d. lang's songs and score (written in collaboration with Ben Mink) enhance this fantasy based on Tom Robbins' 1973 quirky cult novel, in which a virgin hippie girl with abnormally developed thumbs (ideal for hitchhiking) ends up on an Oregon ranch where the cowboys are actually cowgirls. When the dispirited girls take over the ranch, and feed some peyote to a flock of cranes, resulting in an ecological disaster, the Army decides to intervene, in a painful echo to some of the political upheavals of the late 1960s. In this bizarre topsy-turvy set-up, the score explores various styles, with some uplifting rockers among its most endearing moments. While one could dispense with the strange-sounding "Much Finer Place," "Virtual Vortex," and "Apogee," (which is mercifully short) which tie some of the selections together, the other tracks (particularly "Lifted By Love," the old-fashioned "In Perfect Dreams," or the exuberant "Don't Be a Lemming Polka") are quite enjoyable.

Everyone Says I Love You 🎵🎵

1997, RCA Victor; from the movie *Everyone Says I Love You,* Miramax Pictures, 1997.

Album Notes: *Music:* Dick Hyman; *Vocal Arranger:* Dick Hyman; The New York Studio Players and The Helen Miles Singers conducted by Dick Hyman; *Album Producer:* Dick Hyman; *Engineer:* Roy B. Yokelson

Selections: 1 Just You, Just Me (R. Klages/J. Greer)(3:09) *Ed Norton, Vivian Cherry, Paul Evans, Deva Gray, Olivia Hayman, Arlene Martell, Helen Miles;* 2 My Baby Just Cares For Me (W. Donaldson/G. Kahn)(4:04) *Ed Norton, Natasha Lyonne;* 3 Recurrence (D. Hyman)/I'm A Dreamer (Aren't We All?)(B.G. DeSylva/L. Brown/R. Henderson)(2:59) *Olivia Hayman;* 4 Makin' Whoopee (W. Donaldson/G. Kahn)(2:56) *Timothy Jerome, Emily Bindiger, Michael Mark, Arlene Martell, Helen Miles, Daisy Prince, Lenny Roberts;* 5 Venetian Scenes (D. Hyman)/I'm Through With Love (G. Kahn/M. Malneck/J. Livingston)(2:42) *Woody Allen, John Frosk, Derek Smith;* 6 All My Life (S. Stept/S. Mitchell)(6:08) *Julia Roberts, John Frosk, Joe Wilder, Derek Smith;* 7 Just You, Just Me (salsa version)(R. Klages/J. Greer)(3:12) *Jon Gordon, Byron Stripling, Jim Pugh, Dick Hyman, James Saporito;* 8 Cuddle Up A Little Closer (K. Hoschna/O. Harbach) (1:46) *Billy Crudup, Sanjeev Ramabhadran;* 9 Looking At You (C. Porter)(1:35) *Alan Alda, Dick Hyman;* 10 Recurrence (D. Hyman)/If I Had You (T. Shapiro/J. Campbell/R. Connelly)(2:41) *Tim Roth, Dick Hyman;* 11 Enjoy Yourself (It's Later Than You Think)(H. Magidson/C. Sigman)(3:25) *Patrick Cranshaw, Frank Wess, Paul Evans, Arlene Martell, Ashley H. Wilkinson;* 12 Chiquita Banana (L. MacKenzie/G. Montgomery/W. Wirges)(:49) *Christy Romano;* 13 Hooray For Captain Spaulding (B. Kalmar/H. Ruby)(2:00) *The Helen Miles Singers;* 14 I'm Through With Love (G. Kahn/M. Malneck/J. Livingston)(3:36) *Goldie Hawn, John Frosk,*

Derek Smith; 15 Everyone Says I Love You (B. Kalmar/H. Ruby)(3:03) *The Helen Miles Singers.*

Review: It did make sense, of course, that Woody Allen would eventually attempt to make a film musical, and that he would call upon the services of his favorite composer, Dick Hyman, to create the original score and write the orchestrations for some of the standards heard in it. But like the "tap dancing" in "My Baby Just Cares For Me," this soundtrack album, delightful as it may be, sounds strangely out of step and out of focus. Whether it is the recording itself, oddly without much sonic definition, or the performances that fail to ignite, the result is an album that seems to promise a lot but never quite delivers. The selections include many standards from the '30s, performed by the stars of the film (including Goldie Hawn, Alan Alda and Julia Roberts), and some nifty instrumentals with Dick Hyman on piano and Woody Allen himself on clarinet.

Executive Decision ♪♪♪

1996, Varese-Sarabande; from the movie *Executive Decision*, Warner Bros., 1996.

Album Notes: *Music*: Jerry Goldsmith; *Orchestrations*: Alexander Courage; *Music Editor*: Ken Hall; Orchestra conducted by Jerry Goldsmith; *Album Producer*: Jerry Goldsmith; *Engineer*: Bruce Botnick.

Selections: 1 The Map (1:30); 2 All Aboard (5:40); 3 Drill Team (5:39); 4 Do It (2:33); 5 Pick It Up (2:31); 6 Starting Over (2:55); 7 The Sleeper (3:28); 8 The Ramora (2:19); 9 Hold It (1:58).

Review: Jerry Goldsmith's spare, militaristic score for this excellent airborne nail-biter harkens back to the sound of '70s works like *Twilight's Last Gleaming* and *The Cassandra Crossing*, although the film's claustrophobic setting never really allows much opportunity to open the music up. Most of the score consists of statements of the straightforward military theme that opens the film, and there's at least one hard-charging, pulsating action cue ("All Aboard") that's similar to the composer's driving *Total Recall* title music. Much of the rest of the score consists of some percussive, low-key sneaking-around music as commandos infiltrate a hijacked 747 in midair. A simple, sitar-like electronic motif somewhat jingoistically portrays the Middle Eastern hijackers. The climactic action slugfest is "The Sleeper," with some harsh brass textures and a full-on attack theme as the commandos finally storm the hijackers. It's not exactly *Capricorn One*, but it does mark a welcome return to a grittier orchestral style for the composer.

Jeff Bond

Exit to Eden ♪♪♪

1994, Varese-Sarabande Records; from the movie *Exit to Eden*, Savoy Pictures, 1994.

Album Notes: *Music*: Patrick Doyle; *Orchestrations*: Lawrence Ashmore; *Music Editor*: Roy Prendergast, John Bell, Gavin Greenaway; Orchestra conducted by David Snell; *Album Producers*: Patrick Doyle, Maggie Redford; *Engineer*: Paul Hulme.

Selections: 1 Nina (3:05); 2 Shoot Out (:53); 3 Follow That Cab (1:22); 4 Goodbye Dad (:52); 5 The Arrival (1:55); 6 Eyes Straight (2:24); 7 The Temptation (2:13); 8 Fair Day (1:13); 9 Sheila In The Mirror (1:16); 10 Get With The Programme (4:11); 11 Streetscene (1:31); 12 The Bedroom (:47); 13 Elliot And Lisa (1:34); 14 Excuse Me (3:05); 15 Tommy And Sheila (1:02); 16 Careless Love (3:08); 17 Dixie Time (1:27).

Review: A kinky comedy about, of all things, sexual deviations, *Exit to Eden* received an amusingly provocative score from Patrick Doyle, who must have had a field day concocting this one. Driven by a central theme, "Nina," a jaunty little tune that recurs at various points, the score explores many grounds and develops in the process attractive ideas, from a wistful "The Temptation," to a mock anthem ("The Arrival"), to a delightfully well etched selection titled "Get with the Programme." The jazzy "Sheila in the Mirror" and a ragtime, "Streetscene," add a different and ultimately satisfying touch to the whole thing.

Exodus ♪♪♪♪

1988, RCA Records; from the movie *Exodus*, United Artists, 1960.

Album Notes: *Music*: Ernest Gold; The Sinfonia of London Orchestra, conducted by Ernest Gold; *CD Producer*: John Snyder; *Engineer*: Joe Lopes.

Selections: 1 Theme Of Exodus (2:27); 2 Summer In Cyprus (2:14); 3 Escape (1:20); 4 Ari (2:56); 5 Karen (2:00); 6 Valley Of Jezreel (4:38); 7 Flight For Survival (1:31); 8 In Jerusalem (3:38); 9 The Brothers (1:12); 10 Conspiracy (3:00); 11 Prison Break (3:24); 12 Dawn (4:04); 13 Flight For Peace (1:25).

Review: The fervently grandiose theme Ernest Gold wrote for this recounting of the events that led to the creation of the state of Israel somehow captures the breadth and scope of the historical facts, but dwarfs in the process his other cues for the film. It must be said that the huge popularity of the theme, which was "covered" by every instrumental group and soloist around the world when it was first created, also turned it into a musical saw that overstayed its welcome. The score received the Oscar in 1960, besting such heavy contenders as Dimitri Tiomkin's *The Alamo*, Elmer Bernstein's *The Magnificent*

Seven, and Alex North's *Spartacus,* which probably were more worthy. Certainly, one cannot deny the raw power behind the bombastic cues written by Gold, though the score as a whole seems most effective in its quietest moments ("Karen," "In Jerusalem," "Dawn"). The recording, sloppily remastered, evidences some hiss, a huge amount of reverb, and a rather harsh sound that is not very conducive for repeated listening.

Exotica ♪

1994, Varese-Sarabande; from the movie *Exotica,* Alliance Films, 1994.

Album Notes: *Music:* Mychael Danna; *Featured Musicians:* Amenee Shishakly (clarinet), Ron Korn (flute), Hovhaness Tarpinian (tar), Aruna Narayan Kalle (sarangi), Nabil Saab (oud), Kamel Saab (darabukha), Adel Saab (tambourine), Paul Intson (bass guitar), Rakesh Kumar, Annie Szamosi, Garo Tchaliguian, Harrison Kennedy (voices); *Album Producer:* Mychael Danna; *Engineers:* Gaurav Chopra (Bombay), Paul Intson.

Selections: 1 Exotica (3:43); 2 Something Hidden (2:46); 3 Dilko Tamay Huay (b. Swaroop Rahi)(5:26); 4 Field 1, Field 2 (2:28); 5 Pagan Song (3:43); 6 The Kiss (1:33); 7 Inside Me (4:31); 8 My Angel (1:33); 9 A Little Touch (3:23); 10 Field 3 (3:14); 11 Snake Dance (6:04); 12 Field 4 (2:15); 13 Mujay Yaad (5:07); 14 The Ride Home (3:54).

Review: Winner of the International Critics' Prize at Cannes, this minor essay from Canadian filmmaker Atom Egoyan explores the lower depths of human sentiments in a drama that is set for the most part in a seedy strip joint, and ultimately doesn't prove very interesting. The chilling, depraved atmosphere that pervades the film got a boost from Mychael Danna's score, in which exotic Middle-Eastern instruments add a rather mysterious touch. Still, when it comes to listening to this CD on its own terms, the music sounds rather tepid and fails to attract, in a clear demonstration that not all film scores lend themselves to the soundtrack album treatment.

Explorers ♪♪♪♪

1990, Varese-Sarabande; from the movie *Explorers,* Paramount Pictures, 1985.

Album Notes: *Music:* Jerry Goldsmith; *Orchestrations:* Arthur Morton; Orchestra conducted by Jerry Goldsmith; *Album Producer:* Jerry Goldsmith; *Engineer:* Bruce Botnick.

Selections: 1 The Construction (2:25); 2 Sticks And Stones (2:03); 3 No Air (2:24); 4 The Bubble (1:43); 5 First Flight (2:45); 6 Free Ride (3:33); 7 Fast Getaway (4:47); 8 She Likes Me (2:28); 9 Have A Nice Trip (7:54); 10 All Around The World

(2:18) *Robert Palmer;* 11 Less Than Perfect (4:06) *Red 7;* 12 This Boy Needs To Rock (3:57) *Night Rider.*

Review: Jerry Goldsmith's score for this underrated Joe Dante fantasy is perfect, surging with boyish optimism as its pulsing chords and infectiously good-natured melodies underscore the efforts of three socially-misfit young boys to construct their own spaceship (with the help of a little alien technology). Although not as audacious as Dante's *Gremlins, Explorers* is more heartfelt, juggling the director's satiric sensibilities (mainly expressed by a bizarre rockabilly theme for some pop culture-obsessed extraterrestrials) with an honest and moving sense of youthful excitement at the wonders of the universe and the thrill of staying up past your bedtime. The cues involving the building and flight of the spacecraft ("Construction," "First Flight" and "No Air") pump as much adrenaline as Goldsmith has ever pumped, particularly as the latter cue launches with a spine-tingling synthesized choir and no-nonsense brass over busily churning strings and woodwinds. Goldsmith developed most of the score from a five note motif for the alien technology, including a lovely romantic motif for the film's wonderfully optimistic denouement of the boys flying through a dream-like nocturnal cloudscape.

Jeff Bond

Extreme Measures ♪♪♪♪

1996, Varese-Sarabande; from the movie *Extreme Measures,* Castle Rock Entertainment, 1996.

Album Notes: *Music:* Danny Elfman; *Orchestrations:* Steve Bartek, Edgardo Simone, Mark McKenzie; *Music Editor:* Ellen Segal; Orchestra conducted by Artie Kane; *Album Producers:* Danny Elfman, Ellen Segal; *Engineers:* Andy Bass, Patricia Sullivan.

Selections: 1 Main Title (2:29); 2 Hard Guys (2:40); 3 Cokie (2:24); 4 Dumped (1:17); 5 The Descent (6:38); 6 Tough News (2:40); 7 Hope?/Fey (4:24); 8 Elevator Madness (2:29); 9 Epilogue/End Credits (4:32).

Review: This score is both a surprising and refreshing change of pace for Danny Elfman. As the first bars of the "Main Title" play, you'd never guess this is the work of the same man who composed *Batman* or *Beetlejuice.* The film, a murder mystery dealing with the subject of human experimentation by a prominent physician, motivated Elfman to paint on a more mature musical canvas. Although he still uses a chorus of voices similar to those in *Edward Scissorhands,* the effect here is anything but whimsical. They sing a litany for the souls losing their lives in the name of medical progress. The rest of the score is deliciously dark, a concoction of somber motifs filled with a woeful marriage of strings, piano, rolling drums, and a smattering of creative percussion. Elfman has definitely become more proficient as a film composer.

David Hirsch

Extreme Prejudice ♫♫▷

1992, Intrada; from the movie *Extreme Prejudice*, Tri-Star Films, 1987.

Album Notes: *Music*: Jerry Goldsmith; *Orchestrations*: Arthur Morton, Alexander Courage; The Hungarian State Opera Orchestra, conducted by Jerry Goldsmith; *Album Producer*: Jerry Goldsmith; *Engineer*: Bruce Botnick.

Selections: 1 Arrivals (5:19); 2 Cash (7:28); 3 The Set-Up (3:21); 4 Dust (4:16); 5 Identities (1:48); 6 Extreme Prejudice (2:13); 7 The Plan (9:22); 8 To Mexico (3:05); 9 No Friendlies (2:40); 10 They Didn't Care (3:39); 11 The Funeral (2:07); 12 A Deal (4:41).

Review: This unusual techno-western score is a strange mix of Goldsmith's brassy *Capricorn One*-style atmosphere, some of the electronicized South American feel of *Under Fire*, and a whole lot of drum machines. There are some extended action sequences that are developed in almost lyrical fashion, and the back end of the album boasts a pretty over-the-top synthesized take-off of Ennio Morricone's familiar spaghetti western motif from *The Good, the Bad and the Ugly*. More effective is an atmospheric, vaguely militaristic solo trumpet effect echoing over the proceedings. This is a transitional score that marks Goldsmith's early foray into electronics, and thus may be less appealing to those weaned on his grittier orchestral efforts of the '60s and '70s. Fans of the composers later works might find it more appealing.

Jeff Bond

Eye of the Panther/ Not Since Casanova ♫♫♫

1996, Prometheus Records; from the movies *Eye of the Panther*, and *Not Since Casanova*.

Album Notes: *Music*: John Debney; Orchestras conducted by John Debney; *Album Producer*: Ford A. Thaxton; *Engineer*: James Nelson.

Selections: *EYE OF THE PANTHER:* 1 In The Fields/Hunter (3:32); 2 Children In The Wilderness (1:36); 3 A Panther Watches (1:07); 4 The Candle Expires/The Ravaging (3:03); 5 Escape (1:06); 6 The Meeting (1:27) 7 Love Grows (1:01); 8 Strange Yearning (2:19); 9 Love Theme (2:12); 10 Transformation (1:32); 11 A Wolf In Her Clothes (1:02); 12 A Love Beyond Words (2:03); 13 Beware, She Bites (2:15); 14 A Panther Strikes/Resurrection (2:10);

NOT SINCE CASANOVA: 15 Overture (4:50); 16 Dreams (1:16); 17 First Kiss (1:27); 18 Gina, The Dream Girl (1:24); 19 How To Put It Into Words (2:04); 20 At Sunset (1:08); 21 Will You Walk With Me? (3:17); 22 Irish Wedding (1:05); 23 Dreams Fulfilled (1:27); 24 The Carousel Of Life (2:15).

Review: Two soundtracks could not be more different, yet both reveal facets of a composer who has recently made himself more and more visible in a crowded field. *Eye of the Panther*, Dabney's first full "horror score," was created for a television film about a young woman who turns into a panther at night. It was written for a large chamber orchestra, an unusual style in itself. *Not Since Casanova*, composed for a little-seen independent film, elicited a gentle, romantic score with baroque overtones. In both cases, Dabney asserts himself as an interesting composer, whose talent is undeniable but who has done much better since these early efforts.

The Fabulous Baker Boys ♫♫♫

1989, GRP Records; from the movie *The Fabulous Baker Boys*, 20th Century-Fox, 1989.

Album Notes: *Music*: Dave Grusin; Orchestra conducted by Dave Grusin; *Featured Musicians*: Ernie Watts (saxophones), Sal Marquez (trumpet), Lee Ritenour (guitar), Brian Bromberg (bass), Harvey Mason (drums); The Duke Ellington Orchestra, conducted by Mercer Ellington; *The Benny Goodman Quartet*: Benny Goodman (clarinet), Teddy Wilson (piano), Lionel Hampton (vibraphone), Gene Krupa (drums); *The Earl Palmer Trio*: Karen Hernandez (piano), Ernie McDaniels (bass), Earl Palmer (drums); *Album Producers*: Dave Grusin, Joel Sill; *Engineer*: Don Murray; *Assistant Engineers*: Mike Kloster, Tom Nellen, Rick Winquest.

Selections: 1 Main Title (Jack's Theme) (6:39); 2 Welcome To The Road (5:32); 3 Makin' Whoopee (W. Donaldson/G. Kahn) (3:08) *Michelle Pfeiffer*; 4 Suzie And Jack (4:58); 5 Shop Till You Bop (4:44); 6 Soft On Me (2:29); 7 Do Nothin' Till You Hear From Me (E.K. Ellington/B. Russell) (3:25) *The Duke Ellington Orchestra*; 8 The Moment Of Truth (3:54); 9 Moonglow (W. Hudson/E. DeLange/I. Mills) (3:25) *The Benny Goodman Quartet*; 10 Lullaby Of Birdland (G. Shearing) (2:29) *The Earl Palmer Trio*; 11 My Funny Valentine (R. Rodgers/L. Hart) (3:01) *Michelle Pfeiffer*.

Review: Michelle Pfeiffer slinking her way across the top of a grand piano, while warbling a sexy rendition of the old chestnut "Makin' Whoopee," is the image most filmgoers remember from this mildly entertaining romantic comedy. Otherwise, this rather conventional story, about two brothers who hire an attractive vocalist to give more pep to their lackluster lounge act, had its moments of fun but ended up being relatively tame in the end. Echoing the moods in the film, Dave Grusin wrote a score that had its moments, though his contribution fell somewhat short of his usual best. The choice cuts here, as in the film, are the vocals by Pfeiffer, deliciously wanton, and source music by Duke Ellington and Benny Goodman.

Face/Off ♪♪♪

1997, Hollywood Records; from the movie *Face/Off*, Paramount Pictures, 1997.

Album Notes: *Music*: John Powell; *Orchestrations*: Bruce Fowler, Suzette Moriarty, Ladd McIntosh, Walt Fowler, Lucas Richman, Steve Fowler; *Music Editor*: Sally Boldt; Orchestra conducted by Lucas Richman; *Featured Musicians*: Michael Fisher (live percussion), Bob Daspit, Geoff Zanelli (guitars), Craig Hara (trumpet), Martin Tillmann (electric cello); *Featured Performers*: Boston Baroque Orchestra & Chorus; *Album Producer*: Hans Zimmer; *Engineer*: Alan Meyerson.

Selections: 1 Face On (4:58); 2 80 Proof Rock (4:29); 3 Furniture (7:12); 4 The Golden Section Derma Lift (3:15); 5 This Ridiculous Chin (6:52); 6 No More Drugs For that Man (7:28); 7 Han's Loft (3:37); 8 Ready For The Big Ride, Bubba (3:54).

Review: John Powell, scoring his first major film under the aegis of Hans Zimmer, created an unusual series of cues for this thriller starring John Cage as a crime-driven maniac, and John Travolta as a FBI agent trying to nab him. When he finally does, the movie is only halfway through, because Cage's demented brother now threatens to blow up the entire city of Los Angeles, and Travolta, in order to prevent the disaster, takes on Cage's persona, physical as well as psychological, while Cage becomes Travolta. Adding his support to the unusual story, Powell has devised textures that emphasize its various aspects, with heavy emphasis on electronic and live percussion to create a greater sense of urgency. It works terrifically well in the movie, but not, unfortunately, as just film music. Occasionally, when the melodic content in the cues is allowed to develop and be heard, then the soundtrack album becomes lyrical and most effective. Those moments, however, are rare and infrequent.

The Falcon and the Snowman ♪♪♪♪

1985, EMI Manhattan; from the movie *The Falcon and the Snowman*, Orion Pictures, 1985.

Album Notes: *Music*: Pat Metheny, Lyle Mays; *Orchestrations*: Pat Metheny, Lyle Mays; *Featured Performers*: The Pat Metheny Group; *Album Producers*: Pat Metheny, Lyle Mays; *Engineer*: Marcellus Frank.

Selections: 1 Psalm 121/Flight Of The Falcon (4:08); 2 Daulton Lee (5:56); 3 Chris (3:16); 4 "The Falcon" (4:59); 5 This Is Not America (P. Metheny/L. Mays/D. Bowie)(3:53) *David Bowie*; 6 Extent Of The Lie (4:15); 7 The Level Of Deception (5:45); 8 Capture (3:57); 9 Epilogue (Psalm 121)(2:14).

Review: It is, in a sense, unfortunate that Pat Metheny has not written more frequently for the screen. This fine effort for a real-life Cold War thriller set in the world of computers and drugs, gave him the impetus to create with Lyle Mays a score that is genuinely affecting and exciting. True to their jazz roots, there is plenty of great music, performed by the Pat Metheny Group, in tracks that do not necessarily try to match the screen action, but that constitute the substance for an intelligent, highly enjoyable album. A vocal by David Bowie, "This Is Not America," adds an extra dimension, consistent with the tone of the rest of the music.

The Fall of the Roman Empire

The Fall of the Roman Empire ♪♪♪♪♭

1989, Varese-Sarabande; from the movie *The Fall of the Roman Empire*, PC Films, 1964.

Album Notes: *Music*: Dimitri Tiomkin; *Lyrics*: Paul-Francis Webster; *Music Editor*: George Korngold; Orchestra conducted by Dimitri Tiomkin; *Album Producer*: Irving Townsend; *Engineer*: Robert Jones; *CD Producers*: Tom Null, Richard Kraft.

Selections: 1 Overture (2:40); 2 The Fall Of Love (2:33); 3 Lucilla's Sorrow (1:45); 4 Ballomar's Barbarian Attack (1:37); 5 Morning (1:03); 6 Profundo (2:32); 7 Notturno (1:58); 8 Pax Romana (bolero) (5:15); 9 The Prophecy (1:05); 10 Persian Battle (2:01); 11 Dawn Of Love (2:20); 12 The Roman Forum (4:35); 13 Addio (1:55); 14 Tarantella (2:15); 15 Resurrection (2:53); 16 The Fall Of Rome (2:08).

Review: See entry below.

The Fall of the Roman Empire ♪♪♪♪♭

1991, Cloud Nine Records; from the movie *The Fall of the Roman Empire*, PC Films, 1964.

Album Notes: *Music*: Dimitri Tiomkin; *Lyrics*: Paul-Francis Webster; *Music Editor*: George Korngold; Orchestra conducted by Dimitri Tiomkin; *Album Producer*: Irving Townsend; *Engineer*: Robert Jones; *CD Producers*: Tom Null, David Wishart.

Selections: 1 Fanfares and Flourishes (:51); 2 Prelude (2:42); 3 Dawn On The Northern Frontier (2:17); 4 Livius' Arrival (1:02); 5 Old Acquaintances (4:31); 6 Pax Romana (5:12); 7 The Dawn Of Love (2:19); 8 Decoy Patrol (:57); 9 The Battle In The Forest/Reinforcements (3:49); 10 The Funeral Of Marcus Aurelius (2:32); 11 The Roman Forum/By Jove and Intermission Title (5:24); 12 Intermezzo: Livius and Lucilla (2:17); 13 Conflict In The Caverns (1:45); 14 Aftermath and Journey To Rome (2:27); 15 The Army Enters Rome/The New God/The Challenge (4:03); 16 Finale (2:08).

Review: Dimitri Tiomkin, delving into an area that seemed exclusive to Miklos Rozsa, came up with a sensational epic score for this Samuel Bronston monumental screen extravaganza about the glory that once was Rome. With its spectacular scenes of red-capped legions parading or going to war, its grander-than-life sets, and the majestic sweep of its three-hour story of greed and the abuse of power in ancient Rome, the film needed a score that matched its scope. Tiomkin obliged, writing one of his most memorable efforts. At the time of its release, a somewhat simplified soundtrack album was issued by Columbia Records, consisting of some of the most important cues from the film that had been rearranged for the album. This is the album that was eventually reissued on compact disc by Varese-Sarabande.

The Cloud Nine album, on the other hand, contains the actual film tracks (some unfortunately in mono only), which supplement Tiomkin's rerecording and add to it many cues that had been omitted. Put together, both albums provide a broad picture of the composer's intents, notably revealing that, unlike the scholarly research done for such films as *Quo Vadis* or *Ben-Hur* by Rozsa, who included many reconstructed Roman instruments to give his musical cues the sound of authenticity, Tiomkin was more interested in writing a music that matched the sweep of the screen action, regardless of the period feel (the organ which broadly announces the "Overture," for instance, is a modern creation). Just the same, his score is a splendid effort, one that can sustain repeated playings and provide many hours of listening enjoyment.

The Fan ♪

1996, TVT Records; from the movie *The Fan*, 1996.

Album Notes: *Music*: Hans Zimmer; *Orchestrations*: Bruce Fowler; *Music Editor*: Adam Smalley; Orchestra conducted by Harry Gregson-Williams; *Featured Musicians*: Steve Erdody

(cello), Bob Daspit (guitars), Martin Tillman (electric cello); *Score Producers*: Hans Zimmer, Adam Smalley, Ryeland Allison; *Engineer*: Alan Meyerson.

Selections: 1 Did You Mean What You Said (Sovory/M. Antoine/M. Mishaw) (3:49) *Sovory*; 2 Letting Go (T. Trent D'Arby/H. Zimmer)(5:35) *Terence Trent D'Arby*; 3 Unstoppable (M. McDermon/P. Phillips)(3:47) *Mic Geronimo*; 4 Hymn Of The Big Wheel (R. Del Naja/G. Marshall/A. Vowles/N. Cherry/H. Andy) (6:35) *Massive Attack*; 5 (Let Me Up) I've Had Enough (K.W. Shepherd/M. Selby/J. Nadeau)(2:44) *Kenny Way Shepherd*; 6 Little Bob (S. Ryder/D. Saber/ P. Leveridge)(5:36) *Black Grape*; 7 Border Song (Holy Moses)(E. John/B. Taupin)(3:37) *Raymond Myles*; 8 What's Goin' Down (M. Elliss/S. Wright/I. Dury/C. Jankel)(4:19) *Honky*; 9 Deliver Me (M. Brooks/D. Blanes)(3:58)*Foreskin 500*; 10 Forever Ballin' (J. Jackson/T. Himes)(4:25)*Johnny "J"*, *Big Syke*; 11 I'm da Man (Jeune/Shiro)(5:24) *Jeune*; 12 Sacrifice (H. Zimmer) (19:09).

Review: An unmemorable baseball film starring Robert De Niro and Wesley Snipes, *The Fan* yielded a "soundtrack" album in which undistinguishable selections by Sovory, Mic Geronimo, Honky, and Jeune (some of which actually were not even heard in the film, but are added here in a deceptive ploy to beef up the album) vie for the listener's attention with songs by Terence Trent D'Arby ("Letting Go"), Massive Attack ("Hymn of the Big Wheel"), and a 19 minute-plus instrumental ("Sacrifice"), composed by Hans Zimmer. Not enough to satisfy one's appetite, particularly at today's rates.

Fantasia ♪♪♪♪

1990, Disney Records; from the animated feature *Fantasia*, Walt Disney Films, 1940.

Album Notes: Orchestra conducted by Leopold Stokowski; *Album Producer*: Ted Kryczko; *Sound Restoration*: Terry Porter; *Engineer*: Mel Metcalfe.

Selections: CD 1: 1 Toccata and Fugue In D Minor, BMV 565 (J.S. Bach) (9:22); The Nutcracker Suite, Op. 71A (P.I. Tchaikovsky): 2 Dance Of The Sugar Plum Fairy (2:41); 3 Chinese Dance (1:02); 4 Dance Of The Reed Flutes (1:48); 5 Arabian Dance (3:18); 6 Russian Dance (1:04); 7 Waltz Of The Flowers (4:25); 8 The Sorcerer's Apprentice (P. Dukas)(9:17); 9 The Rite Of Spring (I. Stravinsky)(22:28).

CD 2: Symphony No. 6 ("Pastoral"), Op. 68 (L. Van Beethoven): 1 Allegro ma non troppo (4:40); 2 Andante molto mosso (6:23); 3 Allegro/Allegro/ Allegretto (10:57); 4 Dance Of The Hours (from "La Gioconda")(A. Ponchielli)(12:13); 5 A Night On Bald

Mountain (M. Mussorgsky)(7:25); 8 Ave Maria, Op. 52 No. 6 (F. Schubert)(6:27).

Review: Classical music as the ultimate film score, and for an animated feature no less! But when Leopold Stokowski, ever the pioneer, and Walt Disney teamed to create *Fantasia*, with scenes based on the classical repertoire, this meeting of minds resulted in a breakthrough film which, even today, stands as the most perfect of its kind, even though it met with less than enthusiastic response when it was initially released. The choice of selections, drawing from the compositions most likely to elicit a nod of recognition even from the uninitiated, can hardly be faulted. And even if Stokowski's playing is not to everyone's taste, his flamboyant style comes excitingly through in the most memorable moments from the film, particularly Paul Dukas' *The Sorcerer's Apprentice*, Modeste Mussorgsky's *Night On Bald Mountain,* and everyone's favorite, Amilcare Ponchielli's *Dance Of The Hours,* which proved that even hippopotami could make gracile ballerinas. The soundtrack, available here in primitive-sounding stereo, was re-recorded in full digital sound in 1982 with Irwin Kostal conducting the orchestra, but since the new recording attempted to match Stokowski's tempo, it often sounds stilted and unexciting. The original, warts and all, is the one to have.

Far and Away ♪♪♪

1992, MCA Records; from the movie *Far and Away*, Universal Pictures, 1992.

Album Notes: *Music:* John Williams; *Music Editor:* Ken Wannberg; Orchestra conducted by John Williams; *Featured Soloists:* Paddy Moloney (penny whistle), Jerry O'Sullivan (Uilleann pipes), Tony Hinnigan, Michael Taylor (pan flutes); *Album Producer:* John Williams; *Engineer:* Shawn Murphy; *Assistant Engineer:* Susan McLean.

Selections: 1 County Galway, June 1892 (1:55); 2 The Fighting Donellys (2:18) *The Chieftains*; 3 Joe Sr.'s Passing/The Duel Scene (4:41); 4 Leaving Home (1:55); 5 Burning The Manor House (2:43); 6 Blowing Off Steam (1:31); 7 Fighting For Dough (2:02) *The Chieftains*; 8 Am I Beautiful? (3:38); 9 The Big Match (5:56); 10 Inside The Mainsion (4:24); 11 Shannon Is Shot (4:06); 12 Joseph's Dream (3:08); 13 The Reunion (3:50); 14 Oklahoma Territory (2:12); 15 The Land Race (4:56); 16 Settling With Steven/The Race To The River (4:08); 17 Joseph And Shannon (3:14); 18 Book Of Days (Enya/R. Ryan)(2:53) *Enya*; 19 End Credits (6:35) *The Chieftains*.

Review: For this grand and glorious story of love and life from Ireland to Oklahoma, John Williams has provided a rich, tender yet often thunderous score drawn from Irish folk styles. The

Main Theme evokes the plaintive, Irish countryside as much as the boundless Oklahoma plains. It also embodies the proud, resistant spirit of Joseph (Tom Cruise) and of Shannon (Nicole Kidman), as well as eloquently evoking the love the two of them share. It's a grand, sweeping theme that mirrors the intensity of the human spirit depicted in the film. Williams superbly captures both the large scope of the picture as well as the characters' innermost feelings and brings them both to life with this excellent score.

Randall D. Larson

A Far Off Place ♪♪♪♪

1993, Intrada Records; from the movie *A Far Off Place*, Walt Disney/Amblin Entertainment, 1993.

Album Notes: *Music:* James Horner; *Orchestrations:* Frank Bennett, Brad Dechter, Tom Pasatieri, Joel Rosenbaum; *Music Editor:* Jim Henrikson; *Album Producer:* James Horner; *Engineer:* Shawn Murphy.

Selections: 1 Main Title (5:17); 2 The Slaughter (4:35); 3 The Elephant (5:06); 4 Attacked From The Air (3:43); 5 Gemsbock Gift (2:14); 6 The Swamp (3:46); 7 Sandstorm! (6:58); 8 Death In The Mine (2:48); 9 Epilogue/End Credits (5:40).

Review: A Walt Disney family adventure set in Africa, about two orphaned teens and their Bushman guide making their way back to civilization, *A Far Off Place* received a broad, symphonic score from James Horner, evidently inspired by the subject matter. The cues overflow with colorful, dynamic accents, sometimes subtly underscored by a variety of exotic-sounding percussive instruments, sometimes framing the contribution of a lonely reed. The lengthy playing time of some of the cues enables them to make more than a passing impression, in effect forcing the listener to become involved and enjoy the music for its own sake. There is a lot to like in this score, which incidentally eschews the facile ethnic effects in favor of a more complex but ultimately more rewarding orchestral approach, with selections like "The Elephants," "Sandstorm," or "Death in the Mine," inviting repeated playing.

Faraway, So Close ♪♪♪♪♪

1994, SBK Records; from the movie *Faraway, So Close*, Sony Pictures Classics, 1994.

Album Notes: *Music:* Laurent Pettigrand; Orchestra conducted by Sherry Bertram; *Featured Soloists:* David Darling (cello), Irene Maas (soprano); *Album Producer:* Gareth Jones; *Engineer:* Gareth Jones.

Selections: 1 Faraway, So Close (3:56) *Nick Cave*; 2 Stay (Faraway, So Close!)(6:06) *U2*; 3 Why Can't I Be Good (4:22) *Lou Reed*; 4 Chaos (4:51) *Herbert Groenemeyer*; 5 Travelin' On (3:49) *Simon Bonney*; 6 The Wanderer (5:16) *U2, Johnny Cash*; 7 Cassiel's Song (3:36) *Nick Cave*; 8 Slow Tango (3:29) *Jane Siberry*; 9 Call Me (4:08) *The House of Love*; 10 All God's Children (4:42) *Simon Bonney*; 11 Tightrope (3:18) *Laurie Anderson*; 12 Speak My Language (3:36) *Laurie Anderson*; 13 Victory (4:06); 14 Gorbi (2:51); 15 Konrad 1st Part (1:56); 16 Konrad 2nd Part (3:41); 17 Firedream (3:01); 18 Allegro (3:27); 19 Engel (4:44); 20 Mensch (1:38).

Review: Wim Wenders is a filmmaker who uses music to both amplify and to inspire his visuals. This time he weaves Celtic and mostly moody selections into the mix, leaning on artists such as U2, Nick Cave, Simon Bonney and Laurie Anderson, each of whom contribute two selections. U2's pair—"Stay (Faraway, So Close)" and "The Wanderer" with Johnny Cash— also appear on the group's own "Zooropa" album, but sound fine in this context. First-rate contributions from Lou Reed and House of Love are valuable additions to an exceptional effort. *Gary Graff*

A Farewell to Arms/ Sons and Lovers ♫♫♫

1996, DRG Records; from the movies *A Farewell to Arms*, David O. Selznick/ 20th Century-Fox, 1957; and *Sons and Lovers*, 1960.

Album Notes: *Music:* Mario Nascimbene; *Orchestrations:* Mario Nascimbene; Orchestras conducted by Franco Ferrara, Mario Nascimbene; *Album Producers:* Mario Nascimbene, Claudio Fuiano; *Engineer:* Gianni Mazzarini.

Selections: *A FAREWELL TO ARMS:* 1 Main Titles (2:35); 2 March Of The Alpini (2:13); 3 At The Front: Death Of Sgt. Passini (1:15); 4 First Encounter Of Henry And Catherine (3:20); 5 Feast At The Village For The Departure (1:35); 6 Love Encounter At Piccolo Hotel (10:14); 7 Retreat At Caporetto (9:26); 8 Henry's Escape (3:42); 9 Escape To The Lake and Arrival In Switzerland (4:38); 10 Peaceful Life (2:13); 11 Waiting For Little Catherine (3:33); 12 Foreboding (1:34); 13 Catherine's Death and Finale (2:52);

SONS AND LOVERS: 14 Main Titles (1:34); 15 Encounter With Myriam (2:57); 16 The Mine's Tragedy (2:16); 17 Love Scene (1:08); 18 Night Of Love and Finale (4:07).

Review: If you can live with the degraded sonics in this recording with flutters, distortions, and a harsh, grating sound apparent on most of the tracks, there is a lot to be enjoyed in these two scores from the fertile pen of Italian master Mario Nascimbene. For David O. Selznick's brilliant treatment of the

Hemingway novel, starring Rock Hudson and Jennifer Jones as the star-crossed lovers caught on the Italian war front in the last brutal days of World War I, Nascimbene wrote a score that mixes both aspects of the drama—the war effort and the lovers' passion—in cues that teem with romantic themes and heroic echoes. The lovely tune, a waltz, that marks the lovers' first encounter and follows them through their idyll and unhappy ending, has justifiably become a favorite theme among fans of film music, and is heard here in several variations. *Sons and Lovers,* a drama set in the bleak north countryside of England, elicited from Nascimbene a score that contrasts the grim aspects of the story and the environment with cues that sometimes affect a jaunty lilt. Sound quality here is also a problem, with heavy hiss on the tracks, some distortion, and an occasional dropout.

Fargo/Barton Fink ♫♫♫♫

1996, TVT Records; from the movies *Fargo*, Gramercy Pictures, 1996; and *Barton Fink*, 20th Century-Fox, 1991.

Album Notes: *Music:* Carter Burwell; *Orchestrations:* Carter Burwell, Sonny Kompanek, Larry Wilcox; *Music Editor:* Todd Kasow; *Featured Soloists:* Paul Peabody (violin), Carter Burwell (piano); Orchestras conducted by Carter Burwell, Sonny Kompanek, Larry Wilcox; *Album Producer:* Carter Burwell; *Engineer:* Michael Farrow.

Selections: *FARGO:* 1 Fargo, North Dakota (2:49); 2 Moose Lake (:41); 3 A Lot Of Woe (:54); 4 Forced Entry (1:23); 5 The Ozone (:58); 6 The Trooper's End (1:04); 7 Chewing On It (:54); 8 Rubbernecking (2:06); 9 Dance Of The Sierra (1:25); 10 The Mallard (1:02); 11 Delivery (4:48); 12 Bismark, North Dakota (1:05); 13 Paul Bunyon (:34); 14 The Eager Beaver (3:14); 15 Brainerd, Minnesota (2:41); 16 Safe Keeping (1:45);

BARTON FINK: 17 Fade In (1:08); 18 Big Shoes (1:33); 19 Love Theme (1:21); 20 Barton In Shock (1:58); 21 Typing Montage (2:12); 22 The Box (3:06); 23 Barton In Flames (:58); 24 Fade Out/The End (3:37).

Review: The nostalgic accents of a fiddle permeate the soundtrack to *Fargo*, a rural crime drama in which a car salesman, over his head in debts, hires two inept ex-cons to kidnap his wife, hoping to extract the ransom money from his father-in-law. However, the well laid plan unravels hopelessly after one of the cons kills a state trooper who had stopped the pair on a minor infraction. While most of the cues Burwell wrote for the film capture the drama-in-the-making, the moods struck are very sullen and grave, and fail to actually communicate the dark humor in the story itself, which made the film so disarmingly funny despite the seriousness of the storyline. *Barton Fink,* also produced by Joel and Ethan Coen, makers of *Fargo,* elicited a score that seems more in keeping with the light, eccentric moods in this story of a Broadway playwright whose success takes him to Hollywood, despite his hatred for the medium. Soon, however, Fink (played in tortured fashion by John Turturro) has become implicated in a series of murders, and that's only the beginning... The few cues assembled here give an excellent impression of Burwell's surrealist music for the film, with the composer adding his pianistic touch to the proceedings. Enjoyable through and through.

Fahrenheit 451

1995, Varese-Sarabande Records; from the movie *Fahrenheit 451,* 1967.

See: Bernard Herrmann in Compilations

Fatal Attraction ✍

1987, GNP Crescendo Records; from the movie *Fatal Attraction,* Paramount Pictures, 1987.

Album Notes: *Music:* Maurice Jarre; *Electronic Ensemble:* Michael Boddicker, Ralph Grierson, Rick Marvin, Judd Miller, Alan Pasqua, Emil Richards, Nyle Steiner, John Van Tongeren; *Album Producer:* Maurice Jarre; *Engineer:* Joel Moss.

Selections: 1 Fatal Attraction; 2 Following Dan; 3 Madness; 4 Where Is Ellen; 5 Beth; 6 Confrontation.

Review: Electronic score by Maurice Jarre starts off well enough with its pleasant main theme, but it quickly degrades by track two into a collection of uninteresting effects and several tumults of noise. Much of the electronic instrumentation sounds dated just ten years later, making it hard to believe it's not a score for a direct-to-video independent film instead of one of Paramount Pictures' biggest box office hits. Poorly packaged CD uses art from initial LP release and lists only six tracks on the back cover while player counts off 14!

David Hirsch

Father of the Bride

Father of the Bride ♫♫♫

1991, Varese-Sarabande; from the movie *Father of the Bride,* Touchstone Pictures, 1991.

Album Notes: *Music:* Alan Silvestri; *Music Editor:* Katherine Quittner; Orchestra conducted by Alan Silvestri; *Album Producer:* Alan Silvestri; *Engineers:* Dennis Sands, Bob Fernandez, Bruce Botnick.

Selections: 1 Main Title (2:36); 2 Annie's Theme (:48); 3 Drive To Brunch (1:40); 4 Snooping Around (:46); 5 Pool Cue (1:00); 6 $250 A Head (:22); 7 Annie Asleep (:48); 8 Basketball Kiss (:51); 9 The Wedding (1:10); 10 Snow Scene (1:21); 11 Nina At The Stairs (:33); 12 The Big Day (1:00); 13 Annie At The Mirror (1:05); 14 Pachelbel Canon (4:46) *The Baroque Chamber Orchestra, Ettore Stratta;* 15 The Way You Look Tonight (J. Kern/ D. Fields) (3:05) *Steve Tyrell;* 16 My Annie's Gone (:45); 17 The Way You Look Tonight (reprise) (2:00); 18 End Credits (3:10).

Review: Alan Silvestri's sugar-coated score for this 1991 Steve Martin remake of the classic Spencer Tracy film is good fun, thanks to a memorable main theme and a brief collection of tracks that range from introspective and touching to downright jazzy and off the wall. Varese's album also contains Pachelbel's "Canon" and a cover of "The Way You Look Tonight" by Steve Tyrell, which is also interpolated quite nicely with Silvestri's score as the music comes to a close. Many of the tracks are short and the thematic development of the musical material is, subsequently, fairly limited, but this is a pleasant album as far as it goes, and if you've seen and enjoyed the movie, you'll probably want the soundtrack as well.

Andy Dursin

Father of the Bride, Part II ♫♫♫ ▹

1995, Hollywood Records; from the movie *Father of the Bride, Part II,* Touchstone Pictures, 1995.

Album Notes: *Music:* Alan Silvestri; *Orchestrations:* William Ross; *Music Editor:* Andrew Silver; *Album Producer:* Alan Silvestri; *Engineer:* William Ross.

Selections: 1 Give Me The Simple Life (R. Bloom/H. Ruby) (3:16) *Steve Tyrell;* 2 Annie Returns (:47); 3 Jubilant George (3:56); 4 The Way You Look Tonight (J. Kern/D. Fields) (4:32) *Steve Tyrell;* 5 New Baby Suite (1:19); 6 At Last (H. Warren/M. Gordon) (2:59) *Etta James;* 7 When The Saints Go Marching In (trad.) (2:25) *Fats Domino;* 8 Summer Montage (1:41); 9 George Walks (3:14); 10 Remembering Annie (Basketball Montage) (:47) *Randy Waldman, Phillip Ingram (vocal);* 11 We're Having A Baby (1:45); 12 Rush Down Corridor (1:30); 13 George Tells A Story (5:26); 14 On The Sunny Side Of The Street (D. Fields/J. McHugh) (2:53) *Steve Tyrell;* 15 End Credits Suite (2:58).

Review: As uncomplicated as the first score, yet equally melodic and occasionally jazzy, *Father of the Bride, Part II* does not break any new grounds, but is enjoyable in its own right. Steve Tyrell is back on board for another round of classic standards ("Give Me the Simple Life," "The Way You Look Tonight," "On the Sunny Side of the Street"), with Etta James and Fats Domino also on hand for a couple of tunes, including the always rousing "When the Saints Go Marching In." If any real criticism can be leveled against it, it would have to be about the short playing time of some of the cues (:47 for "Annie Returns," not long enough for any theme to make any kind of impression), but the overall balance tips toward the positive. So, play it and have a good time.

Fearless Woof

1993, Elektra Records; from the movie *Fearless*, Warner Bros., 1993.

Album Notes: *Music*: Maurice Jarre; *Featured Artists*: Kronos Quartet, Dumisani Maraire (ngoma/hosho), Dawn Upshaw (soprano).

Selections: 1 Max (M. Jarre)(:53); 2 Mai Nozipo (Mother Nozipo)(D. Maraire)(6:56) *Kronos Quartet*; 3 Polymorphia (K. Penderecki)(11:46) *National Philharmonic Orchestra, Leonard Slatkin*; 4 Sin Ella (Gipsy Kings)(3:57) *Gipsy Kings*; 5 Fearless (M. Jarre)(3:33); 6 Symphony No. 3 (H. Gorecki)(26:26) *Dawn Upshaw, London Sinfonietta, David Zinman.*

Review: Multiple Oscar-winning film composer Maurice Jarre is credited with writing the score for this film starring Jeff Bridges. You wouldn't know it from listening to this "soundtrack album" which features two of his cues for a total playing time of four minutes, in addition to long selections from other recordings of modern classical music already available elsewhere on the Elektra label. Unfortunately, this is as misleading as can be, with fans of Jarre and of film music the losers in this dishonest, mindless exploitation.

Feast of July ♪♪♪♪▷

1995, Angel Records; from the movie *Feast of July*, Touchstone Pictures, 1995.

Album Notes: *Music*: Zbigniew Preisner; Orchestra conducted by Zdzislaw Szostak; *Album Producer*: Geoffrey Alexander; *Engineer*: Kirsty Whalley; *Assistant Engineer*: Toby Wood.

Selections: 1 Winter: Burial/Flashback (4:24); 2 Spring: The Present/ Bella And Con (5:24); 3 Summer: The Harvest/Arch Wilson (4:34); 4 Will You Marry Me? (2:01); 5 The Murder (4:12); 6 Autumn: Con's Vision (1:48); 7 Con's Death (3:45); 8 End Credits: Departure For Ireland (7:41); Harvest Dances (R. Portman): 9 Corn Riggs (1:21); 10 Harvest Waltz (1:28); 11 Haste Of Wedding (1:29).

Review: Characteristic of the Merchant Ivory productions, this slick late 19th-century period drama about a young woman,

seduced and abandoned by a married man, and rescued in her hour of need by a kindly couple and their three sons, elicited a flavorful, very restrained score by Zbigniew Preisner, dominated by solo passages for a variety of instruments like the harp, guitar, flute and piano. While the cues are presented in a haphazard order and do not entirely follow the progression of the screen action, they have also been assembled in four distinctive parts, each part representing a season, a satisfying device that strengthens the overall musical picture and gives it a sharper focus. There are many lovely moments in the score, further enhanced by the addition of three short folk-themed "Harvest Dances," composed by Rachel Portman. A rich, satisfying score.

Fedora ♪♪♪

1989, Varese-Sarabande Records; from the movie *Fedora*, United Artists, 1979.

Album Notes: *Music*: Miklos Rozsa; The Graunke Symphony Orchestra, conducted by Miklos Rozsa; *Album Producer*: George Korngold; *Engineer*: Hans Endrulat.

Selections: *FEDORA:* 1 Prelude and Fedora Appears (1:14); 2 The Island (2:48); 3 Dejected (1:05); 4 Rain (4:37); 5 Souvenir de Corfu (1:25); 6 Always The Actress (4:18); 7 Discovered (1:29); 8 Disappointed (1:00); 9 No Escape (1:52); 10 The Oscar (4:00); 11 Search In The Villa (7:04); 12 Fedora's Daughter (1:18); 13 Butcher! (3:05); 14 Star Mother (1:06); 15 Metamorphosis (:50); 16 Deception (3:00); 17 Escape (2:27); 18 Finale (1:31);

CRISIS: 19 Introduction (1:12); 20 March Of The Revolution (1:01); 21 Village Square (3:42); 22 Fandango (1:20); 23 La carta de Rehen (1:18); 24 Finale (1:06).

Review: This limited edition CD offers the last score composed by Miklos Rozsa, for a film by Billy Wilder starring William Holden, Marthe Keller and Henry Fonda, in which the basic themes are the evanescence of youth, the destructive power of beauty, and the romance of a bygone era — the golden days of Hollywood. These moods suggested to the composer a score in which his own romantic leanings and sensitive writing share the scene in a kaleidoscopic display. This is a rare and beautiful example of the composer's creativity, further enhanced with the addition of his guitar suite for *Crisis.*

Feds ♪♪♪

1988, GNP Crescendo Records; from the movie *Feds*, Warner Bros., 1988.

Album Notes: *Music*: Randy Edelman; *Orchestrations*: Ralph Ferraro; *Album Producer*: Randy Edelman; *Engineers*: Elton Ahi, Tim Boyle.

"Whitney Houston's title song entered the charts at No. 1. It's the first time ever that a song from a film has done that."

Robert Kraft
Fox music chief on Kenny "Babyface" Edmonds Waiting to Exhale *(The Hollywood Reporter, 1-16-96)*

Selections: 1 On To Washington (2:45); 2 Ellie's Theme (1:30); 3 The Bank (2:19); 4 You Have The Right To Remain Silent (:45); 5 Main Goal (J.L. Walker) (3:43) *Joe Louis Walker*; 6 Exam Cram (:26); 7 Let's Kick Butt (2:48); 8 All Lips 'n Hips (C. Blomquist)(4:05) *Electric Boys*; 9 Lights Are On But Nobody's Home (G. Collins)(4:32) *Albert Collins*; 10 Good Plan (1:36); 11 The Date (1:27); 12 Bilecki's Scam (1:25); 13 I Met A Sailor (:33); 14 Special Kinda Lovin' (B. Goldberg)(3:12) *Roy Gaines, Barry Goldberg*; 15 Ain't No Piece Of Cake (1:33); 16 Flunking Out (:50); 17 On The Move (1:30); 18 Final Assault (1:25); 19 Graduation (1:20).

Review: Randy Edelman, in one of his early efforts, made a good impression with this colorfully inventive score for a low-key comedy about female agents of the FBI, and the havoc they create when they take over a case. The themes, many in an attractive contemporary mold, make little demands on the intellect but are listenable and quite enjoyable in their own right. Some vocal selections alter the focus of the recording at various points, and prove less addictive than the instrumental score.

Ferngully... The Last Rain Forest

Ferngully... The Last Rain Forest ♪♪♪♪

1992, MCA Records; from the animated feature *Ferngully... The Last Rain Forest,* 20th Century-Fox, 1992.

Album Notes: *Music:* Alan Silvestri; *Orchestrations:* William Ross; *Music Editor:* Jacqueline Tager; *Synclavier Programming:* Simon Franglen; *Album Producer:* Alan Silvestri; *Engineer:* Dennis Sands.

Selections: 1 Main Title (2:28); 2 Skylarking (2:28); 3 Magi Lune's Cave (2:44); 4 Xanthoreas (1:28); 5 Crysta's Journey: Mt. Warning/Blue Light/ Darwin's Grab Bag (3:00); 6 Rainforest Suite (1:14); 7 The Leveller (1:38); 8 Going To Ferngully: Pickpockets/Sail Away/Another Perfect Landing (6:58); 9 The Grotto Song (A. Silvestri/J. Webb)(4:57); 10 I'm Back: Humans Did It/The Holocaust/Gather Everyone In The Circle (4:27); 11 The Battle For Old Highrise (3:30); 12 Remember Everything (3:03); 13 Spirit Of The Trees (3:42); 14 Genesis (2:28).

Review: See entry below.

Ferngully... The Last Rain Forest ♪♪♪♪

1992, MCA Records; from the animated feature *Ferngully... The Last Rain Forest,* 20th Century-Fox, 1992.

Album Notes: *Songs:* Thomas Dolby, Jimmy Buffett & Michael Utley, Jimmy Webb & Alan Silvestri, Chris Kenner, Raffi, Bruce Roberts & Elton John; *Song Producers:* Hilton Rosenthal, Thomas Dolby, David Foster, Teddy Riley, Chris Porter & Bruce Roberts; *Engineers:* Thomas Dolby, Mick Guzauski, Chris Porter, Dave Reitzas, Al Schmitt, Brian Schueble, Bobby Summerfield, Dave Way.

Selections: 1 Life Is A Magic Thing (T. Dolby)(4:31) *Johnny Clegg*; 2 Batty Rap (T. Dolby)(2:52) *Robin Williams*; 3 If I'm Goanna Eat Somebody (It Might As Well Be You)(J. Buffett/M. Utley)(4:02) *Tone-Loc*; 4 Toxic Love (T. Dolby)(4:40) *Tim Curry*; 5 A Dream Worth Keeping (J. Webb/A. Silvestri)(3:18) *Sheena Easton*; 6 Land Of A Thousand Dances (C. Kenner) (2:59) *Guy*; 7 Raining Like Magic (Raffi)(4:19) *Raffi*; 8 Some Other World (B. Roberts/E. John)(4:42) *Elton John.*

Review: Characteristic of some recent soundtracks, *Ferngully... The Last Rain Forest* (an animated feature with a message—the protection of the rainforests) elicited two different releases, one for the score by Alan Silvestri, the other compiling some of the pop songs heard during the course of the action, sometimes in much abbreviated form. The good news here is that the song album is a first-class compilation, bringing together several frontline performers for some decidedly enjoyable results, including Robin Williams, who does a hilarious "Batty Rap," Johnny Clegg, Tone-Loc, Sheena Easton, and Elton John, particularly effective in the inspirational "Some Other World."

The score album, featuring the music of Alan Silvestri over the varied sounds of a rain forest (birds chirping, a rainfall, thunderstorm), is appropriately atmospheric, with many dynamic elements ("Skylarking," "Crysta's Journey,"

"The Grotto Song") that enliven it and provide the musical enjoyment. With its careful dosage of big orchestral riffs and effective synthesized sounds, it stands out as a very attractive effort.

A Few Good Men 𝄢𝄢𝄢♭

1992, Columbia Records; from the movie *A Few Good Men*, Columbia Pictures, 1992.

Album Notes: *Music*: Marc Shaiman; *Orchestrations*: Mark McKenzie, Hummie Mann; *Music Editor*: Curtis Roush; Orchestra conducted by Artie Kane; *Album Producers*: Marc Shaiman, Hummie Mann; *Engineer*: Joel Moss.

Selections: 1 Code Red/Semper Fidelis (J.P. Sousa)(2:13); 2 Kaffe (2:17); 3 Facts And Figures (1:56); 4 Guantanamo Bay (2:48); 5 Hound Dog (J. Leiber/M. Stoller)(2:51) *Willie Mae ''Big Mama'' Thornton*; 6 Plea Bargain (2:19); 7 Trial And Error (3:33); 8 Pep Talk (3:18); 9 Honor (3:49); 10 Stars And Stripes Forever (J.P. Sousa)(2:07).

Review: A striking murder trial set in a military compound, *A Few Good Men* is a provocative film starring Tom Cruise and Demi Moore charged with the prosecution of two marines accused of killing a cadet, only to discover that a high-ranking officer, played by Jack Nicholson, might have been actually responsible. Contrasting the potent elements in this courtroom drama, Marc Shaiman created a score that is surprisingly melodic and low-key. While some ominous undertones announce the trial itself, and the potential dangers in probing too deeply into the killing, the lovely floating chords used by Shaiman seem to contradict, yet reinforce the moods in the film itself. A performance of "Hound Dog" by Big Mama Thornton, while a part of the soundtrack, seems totally unnecessary to the dramatic development of the score itself.

The Field 𝄢𝄢𝄢𝄢

1991, Varese-Sarabande; from the movie *The Field*, Avenue Pictures, 1991.

Album Notes: *Music*: Elmer Bernstein; The Irish Film Orchestra, conducted by Elmer Bernstein; *Musician*: Liam O'Flynn (Uilleann pipes); *Album Producer*: Cynthia Miller; *Engineer*: Brian Masterson.

Selections: 1 The Land (5:43); 2 The Bird (2:19); 3 To The Field (4:58); 4 Stranger (3:46); 5 Auction (2:11); 6 Revelation (5:08); 7 Killing (2:59); 8 The Widow And The Dance (1:51); 9 Questions (2:33); 10 Caravan (1:31); 11 The Church (1:55); 12 Discovery (2:59); 13 The Cliffs And The Sea (3:16); 14 Credits (3:33).

Review: A film which took as its background the difficult existence of poor Irish farmers in the 1920s and '30s, *The Field* presented an artistic challenge to composer Elmer Bernstein about what he calls in his notes to this album "the necessity of making a decision about the degree to which the 'language' of the music should contain ethnic elements." To this end, he judiciously chose to use the evocative Uilleann pipes to convey the moods and feelings characteristic to the film's setting, and added to them subtle electronic effects and the specific sound of the Ondes Martenot, on which he has been increasingly relying in recent years, to delineate the brooding drama about an Irish farmer who obstinately attempts to keep a sterile piece of land from the American developer who wants to buy it. The end result is a generally brooding score occasionally marked by some lovely melodies ("To the Field") and haunting effects ("Auction"), a deft blend that ultimately proves most endearing.

Field of Dreams 𝄢𝄢𝄢𝄢

1989, RCA/Novus Records; from the movie *Field of Dreams*, Universal Pictures, 1989.

Album Notes: *Music*: James Horner; *Orchestrations*: Greig McRitchie, James Horner, Billy May; *Music Editors*: Jim Henrikson; Orchestra conducted by James Horner; *Featured Musicians*: Tommy Tedesco, Ian Underwood, Ralph Grierson, Tim May, Steve Schaeffer, Neil Stubenhaus, Jim Thatcher, Mike Taylor, Tony Hennigan; *Album Producer*: James Horner; *Engineer*: Shawn Murphy.

Selections: 1 The Cornfield (5:34); 2 Deciding To Build The Field (5:51); 3 Shoeless Joe (2:14); 4 The Timeless Street (2:38); 5 Old Ball Players (2:44); 6 The Drive Home (2:13); 7 Field Of Dreams (3:30); 8 The Library (2:29); 9 "Moonlight" Graham (2:03); 10 Night Mists (4:19); 11 Doc's Memories (3:17); 12 The Place Where Dreams Come True (9:06); 13 End Credits (4:07).

Review: One of James Horner's most poignant, lyrical and haunting compositions to date, *Field of Dreams* is one of those soundtracks that you'll find in even the libraries of the most casual "pop music" collector. Everybody who hears it just seems to like it. In this score, Horner works his magic through the mystical tones of the film's nostalgic piano beginning and Big Band section (arranged by Billy May, who worked with Horner a number of times during this period), never overplaying his hand before the film's climax, which culminates in a fugue for the brass section and orchestra that signals the cyclical nature of the film's theme of father and son, of one family generation crossing over into the next. It's a lovely section of music that is alluded to only briefly in the music before, and also one of Horner's best—its usage in numerous televised sports programs and news features since then is clearly a testament to the score's continued popularity with listeners of all musical persuasions.

Andy Dursin

Fierce Creatures 🦴🦴🦴🦴

1997, Varese-Sarabande; from the movie *Fierce Creatures*, Universal Pictures, 1997

Album Notes: *Music*: Jerry Goldsmith; *Music Editor*: Ken Hall; Orchestra conducted by Jerry Goldsmith; *Album Producer*: Jerry Goldsmith; *Engineer*: Mike Ross-Trevor.

Selections: 1 Willa's Theme (2:10); 2 First Day (1:17); 3 Chores (2:17); 4 To The Zoo (2:07); 5 The Funeral (2:33); 6 Trained Seals (1:55); 7 Under Control (2:30); 8 Contact (1:27); 9 A Good Idea (2:13); 10 The Grave (2:04); 11 A Long Story (2:25); 12 You're Fired (2:07); 13 End Credits (3:34).

Review: For this low-key comedy effort (a sequel to the much more effective and enjoyable *A Fish Called Wanda*) Goldsmith wrote one of his better comedy scores, a blend of amiable, low-key jazz elements and some surprisingly affecting romanticism that thankfully avoids over-emphasizing the comic aspects of the story. There's a bouncy, light quality to many of the cues that's quite infectious, and some surprisingly lyrical moments as Goldsmith underscores some outlandish animal acts. It all adds up to a score that, while not one of Goldsmith's more memorable efforts, still makes for a very enjoyable listening experience on its own.

Jeff Bond

55 Days at Peking 🦴🦴🦴🦴🦴

1989, Varese-Sarabande; from the movie *55 Days at Peking*, 1963.

Album Notes: *Music*: Dimitri Tiomkin; The Sinfonia Of London, conducted by Dimitri Tiomkin; *CD Producers*: Tom Null, Richard Kraft; *Engineer*: Michele Stone.

Selections: 1 Overture (2:53); 2 Main Title (3:02); 3 Welcome Marines (1:54); 4 Hotel Blanc (2:23); 5 Explosion Of The Arsenal (2:40); 6 Natasha's Waltz (2:18); 7 The Peking Theme (So Little Time)(D. Tiomkin/P.F. Webster) (2:27); 8 The Peking Theme (So Little Time)(D. Tiomkin/P.F. Webster)(2:45) *Andy Williams*; 9 Children's Corner (1:37); 10 Moon Fire (5:45); 11 Attack On The French Legation (3:17); 12 Death Of Natasha (2:48); 13 Help Arrives (2:49); 14 End Title (1:35).

Review: A spectacular epic adventure, recounting the 1900 Boxer Rebellion against the major powers established in China at the time (England, France, Germany, and the United States among them), accused of crass commercialism and of exploiting the Chinese, *55 Days at Peking* elicited a vibrant score from Dimitri Tiomkin in which heroic accents and romantic themes vie to draw the listener into their attractive musical web. In typical Tiomkin fashion, the cues that are strongly evocative of the screen action ("Explosion of the Arsenal," "Attack on the French Legation") come off best, with layers upon layers of orchestral riffs building up to a climax. However, the tension in those tracks is pleasantly relieved by some exquisite romantic cues ("Natasha's Waltzes," "Children's Corner") that are equally evocative. Andy Williams' perfunctory rendition of "The Peking Theme" is a dispensable filler. The recording, incidentally, is extremely noisy—a problem that exists on the original tapes, and not exclusively on this CD.

Final Analysis 🦴🦴🦴🦴

1992, Varese-Sarabande Records; from the movie *Final Analysis*, Warner Bros., 1992.

Album Notes: *Music*: George Fenton; *Orchestrations*: Jeff Atmajian; *Music Editor*: Sally Boldt; Orchestra conducted by George Fenton; *Album Producers*: George Fenton, Eliza Thompson; *Engineer*: John Richards.

Selections: 1 Final Analysis Front Titles (2:38); 2 I Had The Dream Again (:38); 3 The Rain's Stopped (3:34); 4 Do It (1:51); 5 The Day Lighthouse (3:07); 6 The Murder (2:07); 7 The Courtroom (2:46); 8 The Tea Room (2:35); 9 The Switch (2:24); 10 The Bay Marina (2:09); 11 The Kidnap (1:05); 12 The Night Lighthouse (5:48).

Review: A surprisingly effective old-fashioned thriller, *Final Analysis* brought together Richard Gere, as a San Francisco psychiatrist, and Kim Basinger, as the married sister of one of his patients with whom he has an affair, and who eventually disposes of her husband in order to marry him. The film, which at times evokes such classic thrillers as *The Maltese Falcon* and *Vertigo*, not surprisingly inspired George Fenton to write a vivid score neither Miklos Rozsa nor Bernard Herrmann would have disavowed. Boldly affirmative and muscular for the most part, it follows the narrative with pungent cues that set the tone for much of the screen action, underscoring it or subtly reinforcing it when the need arises. Among its many convincing moments, "The Rain's Stopped," "The Tea Room," "The Bay Marina," and the chilling "The Murder," particularly stand out.

The Final Conflict ♪♪♪♪▷

1990, Varese-Sarabande; from the movie *The Final Conflict* (The Last Chapter in The Omen Trilogy), 20th Century-Fox, 1981.

Album Notes: *Music*: Jerry Goldsmith; The National Philharmonic Orchestra, conducted by Lionel Newman; *Album Producer*: Jerry Goldsmith; *Engineer*: Len Engel.

Selections: 1 Main Title (3:22); 2 The Ambassador (4:45); 3 Trial Run (2:10); 4 The Monastery (3:13); 5 A TV First (2:45); 6 The Second Coming (3:16); 7 Electric Storm (5:17); 8 The Hunt (3:58); 9 The Blooding Reel (3:32); 10 Lost Children (3:40); 11 Parted Hair (6:30); 12 The Iron (2:18); 13 The Final Conflict (3:40).

Review: Jerry Goldsmith wrapped up his *Omen* trilogy with this spectacular work, his equivalent of a biblical epic. Although it continues the Latin chants and evocative choral effects of the first two Omen scores, *The Final Conflict* develops entirely new melodic material, from an imposing horn theme for the adult Damien Thorn (based on a motif from Prokofiev's *Alexander Nevsky*) to a beautiful pastoral melody for the forces of good as they gather to battle Damien's hordes for the fate of mankind. If only the movie had been as spectacular and gripping as the score. The sheer scale of this work easily ranks it as one of the landmarks in Goldsmith's career. Check out the climactic cue, which underscores nothing less than the second coming of Christ! There are also amazingly powerful cues written for a fox hunt and a mystical conjunction of stars. It's the ultimate soundtrack guilty pleasure, a score that evokes the final conflict between good and evil far more convincingly than the film for which it was written.

Jeff Bond

See also: Damien: Omen II and The Omen

Firestarter ♪♪♪▷

1984, Varese-Sarabande; from the movie *Firestarter*, Universal Pictures, 1984.

Album Notes: *Music*: Tangerine Dream; *Album Producers*: Tangerine Dream.

Selections: 1 Crystal Voice (3:07); 2 The Run (4:50); 3 Testlab (4:00); 4 Charly The Kid (3:51); 5 Escaping Point (5:10); 6 Rainbirds Move (2:31); 7 Burning Force (4:17); 8 Between Realities (2:26); 9 Shop Territory (3:15); 10 Flash Final (5:15); 11 Out Of The Heat (2:30).

Review: Typical of Tangerine Dream, the score for *Firestarter*, a film about a little girl with pyrokinetic powers, is an amalgam of attractively designed synth figures, laid over a rhythm track, that are fairly evocative. Unlike some of their most adventurous works, however, their music here is accessible, with me-

lodic themes that develop along conventional lines, adding layers upon layers of ideas that prove enjoyable in a purely musical context.

The Firm ♪♪♪▷

1993, GRP Records; from the movie *The Firm*, Paramount Pictures, 1993.

Album Notes: *Music*: Dave Grusin; Orchestra conducted by Dave Grusin; *Album Producers*: Dave Grusin, Joel Sill; *Engineer*: Don Murray; *Assistant Engineer*: Michael Kloster.

Selections: 1 The Firm Main Title (3:48); 2 Stars On The Water (R. Crowell) (3:15) *Jimmy Buffett*; 3 Mitch And Abby (2:22); 4 M-O-N-E-Y (L. Lovett) (3:15) *Lyle Lovett*; 5 Memphis Stomp (3:36); 6 Never Mind (H. Howard) (3:42) *Nanci Griffith*; 7 Ray's Blues (4:33); 8 Dance Class (A. Narell) (5:46) *Dave Samuels*; 9 The Plan (4:43); 10 Blues: The Death Of Love And Trust (3:11); 11 Start It Up (R. Ford) (3:43) *Robben Ford, The Blue Line*; 12 Mud Island Chase (3:53); 13 How Could You Lose Me?/End Title (3:39).

Review: Dave Grusin wrote one of his most unusual scores for this contemporary drama starring Tom Cruise, with Jimmy Buffett, Lyle Lovett and Dave Samuels among the performers who also contributed their talent to the soundtrack. While he expresses himself in the jazz style that has been his mainstay for many years, Grusin does so here in unadorned piano solos that are particularly affecting and create a definitely unique atmosphere.

First Blood ♪♪♪♪▷

1990, Intrada; from the movie *First Blood*, Carolco Pictures, 1988.

Album Notes: *Music*: Jerry Goldsmith; *Orchestrations*: Arthur Morton; Orchestra conducted by Jerry Goldsmith; *Album Producer*: Jerry Goldsmith; *Engineer*: Allan Snelling.

Selections: 1 Home Coming (2:21); 2 Escape Route (2:39); 3 First Blood (4:36); 4 The Tunnel (4:02); 5 Hanging On (3:29); 6 Mountain Hunt (6:06); 7 My Town (1:55); 8 The Razor (3:08); 9 No Power (2:51); 10 Over The Cliff (2:03); 11 It's A Long Road (2:51); 12 It's A Long Road (J. Goldsmith/H. Shaper) (3:19) *Dan Hill*.

Review: Birthplace of all the main themes for Jerry Goldsmith's mainstream megahit was *Rambo: First Blood Part II*, but with a more human element present than the bombastic superhero-style score of the sequel. There's also a distinct sense of sadness in *First Blood*, personified by the principle theme song, "It's a Long Road." The lyrics are an analogy for the difficulties Vietnam veterans faced while they tried to reassimilate back into society. Although Rambo seeks peace, he is a trained fighter who can explode when pushed too far. Goldsmith's music, likewise, can launch from a pleasant refrain into a flurry of brass. His trademark use of electronic textures serves him well as a means of heightening the tension. The album also includes Dan Hill's vocal version of "It's a Long Road."

David Hirsch

See also: Rambo and Rambo III

First Knight 🦴🦴🦴ᵛ

1995, Epic Sountrax/Sony Music; from the movie *First Knight*, Columbia Pictures, 1995.

Album Notes: *Music*: Jerry Goldsmith; *Orchestrations*: Alexander Courage; *Music Editor*: Ken Hall; Orchestra conducted by Jerry Goldsmith; *Album Producer*: Jerry Goldsmith; *Engineer*: Bruce Botnick; *Assistant Engineer*: Sue McLean.

Selections: 1 Arthur's Fanfare (:46); 2 Promise Me (4:06); 3 Camelot (2:20); 4 Raid On Leonesse (4:28); 5 A New Life (4:56); 6 To Leonesse (3:27); 7 Night Battle (5:40); 8 Village Ruins (3:21); 9 Arthur's Farewell (5:27); 10 Camelot Lives (5:42).

Review: If you can accept Richard Gere as Sir Lancelot you'll be more than willing to take Goldsmith's lush, glitteringly romantic take on the Camelot legend, brimming with large-scale, old-fashioned action cues and fulsome pomp-and-circumstance involving Sean Connery's King Arthur and the glory of Camelot itself. There's a ringing fanfare for Arthur and a Tristam-and-Isolde-style romantic theme that's drenched in hopeless longing. Everything climaxes in a furious choral cue that should bring back fond memories of Goldsmith's *Omen* scores as the forces of good and evil battle for the future of Camelot, and Goldsmith's epic eulogy for the dying Arthur is one of the most moving pieces of music the composer has produced in a long time. Overall *First Knight* stands as a slightly more intelligent take on his earlier approach to the medieval adventure *Lionheart*, and while it may strike some as too traditional in its approach, it will probably be exactly what fans of the composer's recent work are looking for.

Jeff Bond

First Men in the Moon 🦴🦴🦴🦴

1991, Cloud Nine Records; from the movie *First Men in the Moon*, Columbia Pictures, 1964.

Album Notes: *Music*: Laurie Johnson; Orchestra conducted by Laurie Johnson; *Album Producer*: David Wishart.

Selections: 1 Prelude (1:59); 2 Modern Moon Landing (1:53); 3 Newscasters/ Union Jack/Journey To Dymchurch (2:02); 4 Cherry Cottage/Kate And Bedford (3:08); 5 Arguments (1:25); 6 Cavor's Experiments (4:45); 7 The Sphere (1:14); 8 Love Theme (2:41); 9 To The Moon (2:22); 10 Lunar Landing/ Moonscape/ Weightlessness/Planting The Union Jack (1:33); 11 Lens Pit/ Shadows (1:56); 12 Battle With The Selenites (2:15); 13 Search For The Sphere/Kate In Peril (3:52); 14 The Moon Beast (4:20); 15 Lens Complex/ Dismantling The Sphere/ Cocooning Selenites/The Eclipse (3:05); 16 End Of The Eclipse/The Grand Lunar (3:41); 17 Bedford Shoots At The Grand Lunar (1:28); 18 Pursuit And Escape From The Moon/End Title (2:06).

Review: Though thoroughly outdated by the time it was released in 1964, a few years ahead of Neil Armstrong's first walk on the lunar surface, *First Men in the Moon,* based on H.G. Wells' 1901 novel, is an engrossing space adventure, featuring the wonders of Ray Harryhausen's dynamation skills. The story, slyly brought to the mid-century with the first moon exploration, circa 1964, finding evidence that a previous, unheralded expedition took place at the turn of the century, required a score that would all at once have elements of thrill and romance, something Laurie Johnson provided with accomplished skill. The romantic aspects of the story are detailed in the cues that evoke the turn-of-the-century escapade, with themes that are wonderfully explicit and descriptive. Conversely, for the Moon sequences, the composer devised cues that are more monothematic, using woodwind and brass instruments playing in their nethermost registers, to the exclusion of strings. The combination of both makes for a very unusual, comprehensive score that remains pleasantly attractive when removed from its primary function. Unfortunately, this thin-sounding, mono recording doesn't give a flattering image of the composer's achievements, and proves at times less endearing than it could have been.

The First Wives Club 🦴🦴🦴🦴

1996, Varese-Sarabande Records; from the movie *The First Wives Club*, Paramount Pictures, 1996.

Album Notes: *Music*: Marc Shaiman; *Orchestrations*: Jeff Atmajian, Frank Bennett, Pat Russ, Brad Dechter, Jon Kull; *Music Editors*: Nic Ratner, Nicholas Meyers; Orchestra conducted by Artie Kane, Edward Karam; *Album Producer*: Marc Shaiman; *Engineer*: Dennis Sands.

Selections: 1 Cynthia (2:14); 2 Annie (:46); 3 Elise (:48); 4 Brenda (:45); 5 Bad News (:51); 6 Wham, Bam, Divorce Me Ma'am (1:23); 7 Letter To Three Wives (1:55); 8 The First Wives Club (1:48); 9 Gathering Information (1:54); 10 Setting Up Shop (1:10); 11 Tea Time With Gunilla (2:51); 12 Duarto Makes His Entrance (:40); 13 The Big Break In (5:18); 14 Phone Tag (1:00);

15 The Auction (1:58); 16 Operation Hell Hath No Fury (4:45); 17 The Unveiling (:56).

Review: A stinging social comedy about three married women jilted by their respective husbands who organize a "club" and seek revenge, *The First Wives Club* was scored by Marc Shaiman who developed a series of cues which match the biting tone of the story and display fun touches of their own. First drawing a portrait of the three heroines — Elise (played by Goldie Hawn), Brenda (Bette Midler), and Annie (Diane Keaton) — Shaiman let the storyline dictate where his music would interfere most effectively, and his cues, as a result, are representative of the unfolding screen action. It is not very difficult to follow the progression as the three abandoned wives agree to create the club, and go into action in order to repay in kind the men who have treated them so badly. All along, Shaiman keeps his score with tongue firmly in cheek with cues that provoke the listener while they recall the film's best scenes. Amusingly entertaining, the music is a total delight.

A Fish Called Wanda ♪♪♪♭

1988, Soundscreen; from the movie *A Fish Called Wanda*, M-G-M, 1988.

Album Notes: *Music:* John Du Prez; Orchestra conducted by John Du Prez; *Featured Soloists:* John Williams (guitar), Paul Robinson (drums), Ray Russell (guitar), Luis Jardin (bass, percussion), Kevin Powell (bass), John Du Prez (keyboards); *Album Producer:* Andre Jacquemin; *Engineer:* Andre Jacquemin.

Selections: 1 End Titles (3:16); 2 Main Title (2:33); 3 First Encounter With Otto (:27); 4 Robbery (2:25); 5 George Arrested (1:12); 6 Empty Safe (:46); 7 Wanda Meets Archie (:36); 8 Otto Jealousy (:40); 9 Sword Ballet (:50); 10 Humping (2:07); 11 Wanda Visits Archie At Home (2:14); 12 Assassination 1 (:20); 13 Choir Boys (:24); 14 Wanda Meets Archie At Flat 1 (1:12); 15 Assassination 2 (:40); 16 Wanda Meets Archie At Flat 2 (1:40); 17 Assassination 3 (:53); 18 Ken's Sadness (:44); 19 Chase 1 (1:32); 20 Chase 2 (2:36); 21 A Fish Called Wanda Suite (14:55).

Review: It matters little if this album is rather oddly sequenced (where else but in a Monty Python album would you find the "End Titles" as the first track?), what counts here is the music. John Du Prez, who has written the scores for several Python films, has created a quirky series of cues, propelled by an omnipresent electronic beat in which guitarist John Williams brings a definitely different flavor. Some tracks ("First Encounter with Otto," "Wanda Meets Archie," "Otto's Jealousy") are meant to underscore specific moments in the film, and as such make less of an impression as pure musical statements. But

the longer selections, capped by a long suite, reflect the specific flavor of the zany comedy with the suite essentially reprising the main themes into a long orchestral elaboration. The suite, incidentally, is in effect track 23 (and not 21 as indicated on the backtray information) and lasts 16:55 minutes (not 14:55). Bet you anything that these Python guys were again responsible for that snafu!

The Fisher King ♪♪♪

1991, MCA Records; from the movie *The Fisher King*, Tri-Star Pictures, 1991.

Album Notes: *Music:* George Fenton; *Orchestrations:* George Fenton, Jeff Atmajian; Orchestra conducted by George Fenton; *Album Producer:* George Fenton; *Engineers:* Keith Grant, Gerry O'Riordan, Simon Smart.

Selections: 1 Intro: The Jack Lucas Radio Show (:11); 2 Chill Out Jack (C. Samrai/R. Williams/P. Harvey/J. Templeton)(2:45) *Trip*; 3 Pet Peeves (:31); 4 I'm Sorry (R. Self/D. Allbritten)(2:24) *Brenda Lee*; 5 Sunrise Confession (1:24); 6 The Power (B. Benitez/J. Garrett III/Toni C./R. Frazier/M. James)/ Sign Off (5:53) *Chill Rob G*; 7 I Wish I Knew (H. Warren/M. Gordon)(4:53) *John Coltrane*; 8 How About You (B. Lane/R. Freed)(4:18) *Harry Nilsson*; 9 The Grand Central Waltz (2:15); 10 The Story Of The Fisher King (2:49); 11 Jack Meets Perry (4:19); 12 Everything's Coming Up Videos ("Some People/ Rose's Turn")(J. Styne/S. Sondheim)(1:21) *Michael Jeter*; 13 An Evening Out/Lydia, The Tattooed Lady (H. Arlen/E.Y. Harburg)(4:52) *Robin Williams*; 14 Quest For The Grail (3:02); 15 The Red Knight Suite (6:48); 16 How About You (B. Lane/R. Freed)(2:47).

Review: Despite a preponderance of pop songs on this typically song-oriented soundtrack, we are given a good 20 minutes of George Fenton's contemporary mix of classical music and moody jazz to convey the varied personalities housed within Terry Gilliam's unusual exploration of the thin line between reality and fantasy. The score's standout cue, at almost seven minutes, is the introspective "Red Knight Suite," which offers a contrast to the bristling action cues heard previously. A jazzy trumpet over electric guitar speaks quietly while suggesting a contemporary, urban milieu, while a Morricone-esque harmonica lends an effective counterpoint. The cue moves quickly into the fantastic with the entry of a choir overdriving string and horn figures. The choir supports the film's Grail-like sense of Quest, and the cue builds to a ferocious climax before dissolving, leaving only a stately, classical string motif which heralds a return to normalcy, to sophistication, after our dalliance with fantasy. The assembly of the CD, its first half an attempt to mimic the style of a live radio broadcast with shock-jock introductory patter, may not appeal to those interested only in Fenton's score, but the ability-to program the CD allows Fenton's music to be heard without interruption.

Randall D. Larson

Flaming Star

1995, RCA Victor; from the movie *Flaming Star,* 20th Century-Fox, 1960.

See: Elvis Presley in Compilations

The Flintstones ♫♫♫◡

1994, MCA Records; from the movie *The Flintstones,* Universal Pictures, 1994.

Album Notes: *Music:* David Newman; *Orchestrations:* David Newman, Randy Miller, Bruce Fowler; *Song Producers:* Don Was, Stereo Mcs, Buzz McCoy, David A. Stewart, Arthur Baker, Mick Jones, Andre Shapps, Mel Simpson, Geoff Wilkinson, Nile Rodgers, Vic Malle, Jerry Harrison, Sylvia Massy, C.J. Buscaglia, David Was, Al Yankovic; *Album Executive Producers:* Kathy Nelson, Burt Berman; *Engineer:* Tom Baker.

Selections: 1 (Meet) The Flintstones (W. Hanna/J. Barbera/H. Curtin) (2:24) *The BC-52's;* 2 Human Being (Bedrock Steady)(R. Birch/N. Hallam) (3:54) *Stereo MC's;* 3 Hit And Run Holiday (B. McCoy/G. Mann)(2:57) *My Life With The Thrill Kill Kult;* 4 Prehistoric Daze (D. Stewart/S. Fahey) (5:01) *Shakespears Sister, The Holy Ghost;* 5 Rock With The Caveman (T. Steele/L. Bart/M. Pratt)(2:29) *Big Audio Dynamite;* 6 I Showed A Caveman How To Rock (M. Simpson/G. Wilkinson/Fortson)(5:19) *Us3 Featuring Dee Jef;* 7 The Bedrock Twitch (W. Hanna/J. Barbera/H. Curtin)(4:31) *The BC-52's;* 8 I Wanna Be A Flintstone (Carter/Moon)(2:29) *The Screaming Blue Messiahs;* 9 In The Days Of The Caveman (B. Roberts)(3:43) *Crash Test Dummies;* 10 Anarchy In The U.K. (J. Lydon/S. Jones/G. Matlock/P. Cook) (3:28) *Green Jelly;* 11 Walk The Dinosaur (D. Was/D. Was/R. Jacobs)(4:22) *Was Not Was;* 12 Bedrock Anthem (A. Kledis/Flea/J. Frusciante/C. Smith) (3:41) *"Weird Al" Yankovic;* 13 Mesozoic Music (D. Newman)(5:49).

Review: Good concept, good bands and some awfully fun songs. As one might expect, the B-52's—excuse us, the BC-52's—crank up the grins with "Bedrock Twitch" and their version of "(Meet) The Flintstones." Some blasts from the past include Was (Not Was)' "Walk the Dinosaur" and Screaming Blue Messiahs' "I Wanna Be a Flintstone," while "I Showed a Caveman How to Rock" by US3 and Def Jef brings the prehistoric set into the hip-hop age. We're still not sure what Green Jelly's "Anarchy in the U.K." is doing here, but it's just as funny as everthing else. Yabba dabba doo!

Gary Graff

Flipper ♫♫♫◡

1996, The Track Factory; from the movie *Flipper,* Universal Pictures, 1996.

Album Notes: *Music:* Joel McNeely; *Orchestrations:* David Slonaker; *Music Editor:* Craig Pettigrew; The London Symphony Orchestra, conducted by Joel McNeely; *Featured Artists:* Crosby, Stills and Nash; *Album Producer:* Tim Sexton; *Engineer:* Shawn Murphy.

Selections: 1 In The Summertime ('96 version) (R. Dorset) (3:59) *Shaggy, Rayvon;* 2 Do It Again (B. Wilson/M. Love) (2:25) *The Beach Boys;* 3 It's Not Unusual (G. Mills/L. Reed)(1:59) *Tom Jones;* 4 Tipitina (R. Byrd) (3:35) *Professor Longhair;* 5 Flipper (H. Vars/B. Dunham)(2:07) *Matthew Sweet;* 6 Main Title for Flipper(3:47) *Crosby Stills & Nash;* 7 Abandoned And Alone (1:46); 8 Sandy Meets Flipper (2:09); 9 Flipper Ballet (3:09); 10 He Belongs At Sea (2:59); 11 Marv Meets Flipper (1:57); 12 The Secret Weapon (2:59); 13 Sandy Searches (3:56); 14 Attack Of The Hammerhead (2:51); 15 Flipper Goes Home (3:34).

Review: If the formula works, why not try it again... and again... so, after Willy and Andre, here comes Flipper, another docile marine mammal who develops a friendship with a rebellious boy. You get the picture! In this case, though, the film has serious antecedents in the guise of a popular television series in the 1960s and a couple of previous features. It is also the occasion for some attractive underwater and abovewave scenes, and for a pertinent score by Joel McNeely. With the formidable London Symphony Orchestra playing the score for all it's worth, there are some lovely moments to be enjoyed. The "Main Title" (featuring Crosby, Stills and Nash) is a fluid lyrical anthem, faintly evocative of Simon and Garfunkel or The Mamas and The Papas. The other cues are flavorful musical statements with a pervading poetic imagery that are compelling and frequently attractive, like in "Marv Meets Flipper". The "enhanced CD" also contains various pop vocals by The Beach Boys, Professor Longhair and Tom Jones (who cares to hear "It's Not Unusual" once more) that can be programmed out.

The Fly ♫♫♫◡

1986, Varese-Sarabande; from the movie *The Fly,* Brooksfilms Ltd., 1986.

Album Notes: *Music:* Howard Shore; *Orchestrations:* Homer Denison; The London Philharmonic Orchestra, conducted by Howard Shore; *Album Producer:* Howard Shore; *Engineer:* Keith Grant.

Selections: 1 Main Title (1:52); 2 Plasma Pool (1:51); 3 The Last Visit (2:22); 4 Stathis Enters (2:17); 5 The Phone Call (2:03); 6

Seth Goes Through (2:02); 7 Ronnie Comes Back (:52); 8 The Jump (1:19); 9 Seth And The Fly (1:41); 10 Particle Magazine (:58); 11 The Armwrestle (:57); 12 Brundlefly (1:41); 13 Ronnie's Visit (:33); 14 The Street (:43); 15 The Stairs (1:24); 16 The Fingernails (2:31); 17 Baboon Teleportation (:55); 18 The Creature (2:05); 19 Steak Montage (:55); 20 The Maggot/Fly Graphic (1:32); 21 Success With Baboon (:55); 22 The Ultimate Family (1:55); 23 The Finale (2:45).

Review: Howard Shore's score for this remake of the 1958 classic is a real nail-biting horror score, featuring a poignant three-note main theme with forlorn horns calling out in ever building motifs. What the album lacks, however, is a break from all the tension. Anything that could remotely be called a light moment ("Success with Baboon," "Particle Magazine") simply foreshadows the coming nightmare. One of Shore's more thematic scores for director David Cronenberg may not be considered entertainment by everybody, but it's an excellently written, hauntingly dark piece of work. The CD contains three additional tracks that went unused in the final film. *David Hirsch*

Follow That Dream

1995, RCA Records; from the movie *Follow That Dream*, United Artists, 1962.

See: Elvis Presley in Compilations

Footloose ♫♫♫

1984, Columbia Records; from the movie *Footloose*, Paramount Pictures, 1983.

Album Notes: *Song Producers*: Kenny Loggins & Lee DeCarlo, George Duke, Keith Olsen, Jim Steinman, Bill Wolfer, David Foster, John Boylan, Sammy Hagar; *Soundtrack Executive Producers*: Becky Shargo, Dean Pitchford; *Soundtrack Associate Producer*: Craig Zadan; *Engineers*: Wally Traugott.

Selections: 1 Footloose (K. Loggins/D. Pitchford) (3:47) *Kenny Loggins*; 2 Let's Hear It For The Boy (T. Snow/D. Pitchford) (4:21) *Deniece Williams*; 3 Almost Paradise (Love Theme) (E. Carmen/D. Pitchford) (3:51) *Ann Wilson, Mike Reno*; 4 Holding Out For A Hero (J. Steinman/D. Pitchford) (5:50) *Bonnie Tyler*; 5 Dancing In The Sheets (B. Wolfer/D. Pitchford) (4:03) *Shalimar*; 6 I'm Free (Heaven Helps The Man) (K. Loggins/D. Pitchford) (3:46) *Kenny Loggins*; 7 Somebody's Eyes (T. Snow/D. Pitchford) (3:34) *Karla Bonoff*; 8 The Girl Gets Around (S. Hagar/D. Pitchford) (3:23) *Sammy Hagar*; 9 Never (M. Gore/D. Pitchford) (3:48) *Moving Pictures*.

Review: This monster album, which sold several million copies at the time of its release, was literally put together for the film,

about a group of young people, led by rebellious Kevin Bacon, anxious to have a dancehall but prevented from doing so by straight-laced local authorities. Today, the film may seem quaintly old-fashioned and dated, but the album still throbs with its great collection of dance numbers, spearheaded by the uncontested hits "Let's Hear It for the Boy," "Dancing in the Sheets," and "Footloose." A better-than-average pop-rock compilation.

For Love or Money ♫♫♫♫♭

1992, Big Screen Records; from the movie *For Love or Money*, Universal-International, 1992.

Album Notes: *Music*: Bruce Broughton; *Orchestrations*: Donald Nemitz; *Musicians*: "Rev." Dave Boruff (alto sax), Bill Broughton (trombone); *Music Editor*: Patricia Carlin; Orchestra conducted by Bruce Broughton; *Album Producer*: Bruce Broughton; *Engineer*: Larry Walsh.

Selections: 1 Main Title (2:52); 2 Mr. Ireland (2:22); 3 Barneys (2:37); 4 Doug Goes Home (1:06); 5 Ticket Exchange (1:15); 6 I Owe You One (1:21); 7 Fat Belly Dancer (:45); 8 Wochenend und Sonnenschein (M. Ager/J. Yellen) (1:15); 9 The Doug (4:41); 10 Chopper To The Hamptons (2:16); 11 Done Deal (7:09); 12 For Love Or Money (4:04); 13 In Your Eyes (M. Shaiman/R. McLean) (3:05) *Bobby Short*; 14 (Your Love Has Lifted Me) Higher And Higher (C. Smith/G. Jackson/R. Miner) (3:07) *Jimmy Barnes*.

Review: The underscoring for this lightweight comedy starring Michael J. Fox features prominently two solo instruments, an alto sax and a trombone, both of which confer to the music a specific flavor that is at once endearing. If that were not sufficient, however, Broughton's muscular cues revel in exploring musical lines that can be in turn strongly delineated ("Mr. Ireland"), strikingly sentimental ("Doug Goes Home"), bouncy ("Ticket Exchange"), or simply exhilarating ("Done Deal"). An amusing German rendition of "Happy Days are Here Again" adds a different touch to this enjoyable album.

For the Boys ♫♫♫♫

1991, Atlantic Records; from the movie *For the Boys*, 20th Century-Fox, 1991.

Album Notes: *Arrangers*: Marc Shaiman, Billy May, Dave Grusin, Marty Paich, Ralph Burns, Robbie Buchanan, Arif Mardin, Joe Mardin; *Album Producers*: Arif Mardin, Marc Shaiman; *Engineers*: Jack Joseph Puig, Michael O'Reilly, Don Murray, Bob Schaper, Joey Wolpert.

Selections: 1 Billy-A-Dick (H. Carmichael/P.F. Webster(1:35) *Bette Midler*; 2 Stuff Like That There (J. Livingston/R. Evans)(2:51) *Bette Midler*; 3 P.S. I Love You (J. Mercer/G. Jenkins)(3:34) *Bette Midler*; 4 The Girl Friend Of The Whirling Dervish (A. Dubin/J. Mercer/H. Warren) (1:17); 5 I Remember You (J. Mercer/V. Schertzinger)/Dixie's Dream (M. Shaiman)(2:21) *Bette Midler, James Caan*; 6 Baby It's Cold Outside (F. Loesser)(1:30) *Bette Midler, James Caan*; 7 Dreamland (D. Grusin/A. & M. Bergman)(3:16) *Bette Midler*; 8 Vickie And Mr. Valves (L. LaCroix)(2:29); 9 For All We Know (J.F. Coots/S. Lewis)(4:01) *Bette Midler*; 10 Come Rain Or Come Shine (H. Arlen/J. Mercer)(3:30) *Bette Midler*; 11 In My Life (J. Lennon/P. McCartney)(3:26) *Bette Midler*; 12 I Remember You (J. Mercer/V. Schertzinger)(3:35) *Bette Midler*; 13 Every Road Leads Back To You (D. Warren)(3:48) *Bette Midler*.

Review: The Divine Ms. M. struck a particularly felicitous note in this heart-warming story about a singer entertaining the troops over a fifty-year period, and her relationship with another performer, James Caan, married to someone else. In her stage shows, Midler's great gift as a vocalist sometimes takes second place to her broad antics, but she is quite fetching in her treatment of the chestnuts that comprise the program in this delightful CD, with sensational charts by veterans Billy May, Ralph Burns and Marty Paich, among others. A brilliant showcase for this particular side of her talent, Midler shares the spotlight with Caan (whom she easily outshines) on a couple of selections and introduces a previously unrecorded song by Hoagy Carmichael and Paul Francis Webster, as well as a lovely ballad penned by Dave Grusin and Alan and Marilyn Bergman.

For Whom the Bell Tolls
♪♪♪♪♪

1991, Stanyan Records; from the movie *For Whom the Bell Tolls*, Warner Bros., 1943.

Album Notes: *Music*: Victor Young; *Orchestrations*: Leo Shuken, George Parrish; The Warner Bros. Studio Orchestra, conducted by Ray Heindorf; *CD Producer*: Rod McKuen; *Engineers*: Michael M. Arick, Steve Hoffman.

Selections: 1 Main Title/Roberto And Kashin Blow Up A Train/ Kashin Falls (3:40); 2 Roberto And Anselmo Climb To The Cave/Pablo/Rafael, The Gypsy/ Pablo's Jealousy/Roberto And Maria (5:29); 3 Pilar/Pilar Sees Death In Roberto's Palm (4:25); 4 Politics In The Cave/Roberto Explains His Cause/ Maria Warns Roberto About Pablo (3:17); 5 Maria's Confession/ Roberto's Kiss/"I Don't Know How To Kiss" (3:10); 6 Maria (3:00); 7 El Sordo Retreats/ "What Use Is Courage?" (2:20); 8 Maria And Roberto: Their Night Alone (3:45); 9 The Sun Rises/ Maria Alone/The Bridge Is Blown (4:13); 10 Roberto Returns To

Maria/Roberto Awaits Death/Roberto Sends Maria Away/ End Title (5:45); 11 Main Title From *America, America* (M. Hadjidakis) (3:03); 12 Barbarossa (R. McKuen) (3:36); 13 Kiev (R. McKuen)(4:03).

Review: Victor Young's percussive Oscar-nominated score for this Spanish Civil War drama, based on the novel by Ernest Hemingway, received a loving treatment in a rerecording made in the late 1950s by Ray Heindorf and the Warner Bros. Studio Orchestra. When he wrote it, Young essentially focused on two basic elements, the tragedy of a country and its people split into two warring factions, and the tender feelings that slowly develop between Roberto, an American dynamite expert on the side of the guerrillas, and Maria, an orphan girl. Propelled by a breathtaking "Love Theme," lushly played by the strings, and with the constant support of an acoustic guitar to give the music its flavor, the music unfolds with great passion and strength. The recording itself has the closeness and immediacy usually associated with recordings from the era, with excellent stereo definition. The CD also features a cue from Manos Hadjidakis' score for the 1963 *America, America* and two selections composed by Rod McKuen for the 1978 *The Unknown War* which are totally out of place in the context.

Forbidden Planet ♪♪♪♪ᵛ

1989, Small Planet/GNP Crescendo; from the movie *Forbidden Planet*, M-G-M, 1956.

Album Notes: *Electronic Music*: Louis and Bebe Barron; *Album Producers*: Louis and Bebe Barron; *Engineers*: Louis Barron, Mary Ellen Kabat, Bob Hata.

Selections: 1 Main Titles/Overture (2:20); 2 Deceleration (:50); 3 Once Around Altair (1:09); 4 The Landing (:40); 5 Flurry Of Dust/A Robot Approaches (1:09); 6 A Shangri-La In The Desert/Garden With Cuddly Tiger (1:32); 7 Graveyard/A Night With Two Moons (1:15); 8 Robby, Make Me A Gown (1:16); 9 An Invisible Monster Approaches (:46); 10 Robby Arranges Flowers, Zaps Monkey (1:17); 11 Love At The Swimming Hole (3:11); 12 Morbius' Study (:37); 13 Ancient Krell Music (1:47); 14 The Mind Booster/Creation Of Matter (:56); 15 Krell Shuttle Ride and Power Station (2:31); 16 Giant Footprints In The Sand (:45); 17 Nothing Like This Claw Found In Nature! (1:23); 18 Robby, The Cook, And 60 Gallons Of Booze (:56); 19 Battle With Invisible Monster (2:50); 20 Come Back To Earth With Me (1:17); 21 The Monster Pursues/Morbius Is Overcome (5:45); 22 The Homecoming (1:56); 23 Overture (reprise)(2:13).

Review: The Barrons' seminal all-electronic score for this classic 1950s space opera is a true test of the open-mindedness of the listener as this soundtrack stakes out a territory that exists somewhere between music, sound effects, and something altogether indefinable. Created long before the invention of the synthesizer, this "score" was produced by the Barrons by building specially-designed circuits to generate the required sounds and then recording them, but the result is astonishingly organic and atmospheric. Despite the abstract nature of the sounds produced, there are recognizable motifs, such as the percolating theme for Robby the Robot and a frightening "footstep" effect for the movie's invisible Id monster. Some of the cues will set your teeth on edge, particularly the hair-raising "Deceleration," while many create hypnotic, undulating textures that might actually lower your blood pressure. You can argue about whether this is actually music or not, but it's still fascinating listening.

Jeff Bond

Forbidden Zone ♫♫♫♪

1990, Varese-Sarabande Records; from the movie *Forbidden Zone*, 1990.

Album Notes: *Music:* Danny Elfman; *Orchestrations:* Steve Bartek; *Featured Artists:* Danny Elfman and The Mystic Knights of the Oingo Boingo; *Album Producers:* Richard Elfman, Michael Boshears, Loren Paul Caplin; *Engineers:* Michael Boshears, Brad Kay.

Selections: 1 Forbidden Zone (2:45) *Danny Elfman;* 2 "Hercules" Family Theme (1:37); 3 Some Of These Days (S. Brooks)(2:50) *Cab Calloway, The Kipper Kids;* 4 Journey Through The Intestines (:55); 5 Squeezeit's Vision Of His "Sister" (:30); 6 Queen's Revenge (2:40) *Danny Elfman, Susan Tyrrell, Marie-Pascale Elfman;* 7 Factory (:58); 8 Love Theme — Squeezeit And The Chickens (:42); 9 Flash And Gramps (:56); 10 Squeezeit The Moocher (Minnie The Moocher)(C. Calloway)(4:48) *Danny Elfman, Toshiro Baloney;* 11 Alphabet Song (1:58); 12 Cell 63 (1:20); 13 Witch's Egg (G. Mishalsky/S. Tyrrell)(2:22) *Susan Tyrrell;* 14 Yiddishe Charleston (B. Rose/B. Fischer) (1:33) *Susan Tyrrell, R. Yossele Elfman;* 15 Bim Bam Boom (N. Morales/J. Comacho)(1:53) *Miguelito Valdez;* 16 Chamber Music (1:58); 17 Pleure (J. Savary)(:37) *Marie-Pascale Elfman;* 18 Battle Of The Queens (3:04); 19 Love Theme: King And Queen (1:08); 20 Finale (3:20).

Review: Anyone who has enjoyed Danny Elfman's outstanding contributions to film music over the past 6-7 years will have a blast listening (or, as the case may be, discovering for the first time) this delirious score (or "musical schizophrenia," as Elfman himself describes it) for a film, starring Herve Villechaize and Susan Tyrrell, as rulers of an underground kingdom called

the "Sixth Dimension," made by Richard Elfman, that has mercifully left relatively no trace. Many of the composer's quirky musical ideas can be tracked down to this early effort, in which he gets support from The Mystic Knights of the Oingo Boingo, built around period songs (most notably Cab Calloway's "Some of These Days" and "Minnie the Moocher," the last one thoroughly, but enjoyably destroyed by Elfman and Toshiro Baloney). As Danny Elfman writes in his short commentary, the score, which is guaranteed to bring a broad smile to your face, is "a great chance to stretch out and go nuts." He succeeded beyond all expectations!

Forever Young ♫♫♫

1992, Big Screen Records; from the movie *Forever Young*, Warner Bros., 1992

Album Notes: *Music:* Jerry Goldsmith; *Orchestrations:* Arthur Morton, Alexander Courage; *Music Editor:* Ken Hall; *Featured Artists:* Mike Lang (piano solo), Joel Peskin (soprano sax solo); Orchestra conducted by Jerry Goldsmith; *Album Producer:* Jerry Goldsmith; *Engineer:* Bruce Botnick.

Selections: 1 Love Theme From Forever Young (4:02); 2 Test Flight (3:40); 3 The Experiment (3:12); 4 Tree House (3:04); 5 Kitchen Aid (2:41); 6 The Diner (1:57); 7 The Air Show (2:29); 8 She's Alive (3:28); 9 Let Go (3:01); 10 Reunited (7:42); 11 The Very Thought Of You (R. Noble)(2:44) *Billie Holiday.*

Review: Jerry Goldsmith goes for the romance in this glossy but forgettable blend of star-crossed love, Rip Van Winkle and childhood antics. For chase and flight cues involving Mel Gibson's pilot character Goldsmith brought in some heavy-duty rhythmic orchestral material, similar to some of the pounding, percussive chases in the earlier *Total Recall,* while electronic passages mark suspense in other passages. The centerpiece of the score is a rhapsodic Hollywood-style love theme that Goldsmith developed into its own separate presentation for this album. Unfortunately the theme itself is less effective than some of the less-calculated incidental material that precedes it. That leaves *Forever Young* as a well-crafted and recorded album that just doesn't represent Goldsmith at his most interesting.

Jeff Bond

Forget Paris ♫♫♫♪

1995, Elektra Records; from the movie *Forget Paris*, Columbia Pictures, 1995.

Album Notes: *Music*: Marc Shaiman; *Orchestrations*: Jeff Atmajian, Larry Blank, Harvey Cohen; *Music Editor*: Scott Stambler; Orchestra conducted by Artie Kane; *Album Producer*: Marc Shaiman; *Engineer*: Dennis Sands; *Assistant Engineers*: Paul Wertheimer, Dominic Gonzales, Norm Dlugatch, Tom Hardisty.

Selections: 1 When You Love Someone (C. Bayer Sager/M. Shaiman/A. Baker) (4:10) *Anita Baker, James Ingram*; 2 Love Is Here To Stay (G. Gershwin/I. Gershwin) (3:42) *Billie Holiday*; 3 April In Paris (V. Duke/E.Y. Harburg) (1:57); 4 For All We Know (J.F. Coots/S. Lewis) (2:53) *Billie Holiday*; 5 Lazy River (S. Arodin/H. Carmichael) (3:28) *Louis Prima*; 6 Come Rain Or Come Shine (J. Mercer/H. Arlen)(4:37) *David Sanborn*; 7 April In Paris (V. Duke/ E.Y. Harburg)(6:35) *Ella Fitzgerald, Louis Armstrong*; 8 Paris Suite (6:13); 9 Swish (2:34); 10 Craig And Lucy (1:48); 11 Tea For Two (V. Youmans/ I. Caesar)/It Don't Mean A Thing (If It Ain't Got That Swing)(E.K. Ellington/ I. Mills)(3:01); 12 Nice Work If You Can Get It (G. Gershwin/I. Gershwin) (2:00); 13 My Melancholy Baby (E. Burnette/G. Norton)(3:00); 14 When You Love Someone (C. Bayer Sager/M. Shaiman/A. Baker)(4:26); 15 To Marriage (1:03).

Review: The combination of some great songs, great vocal performances, and Marc Shaiman's flavorful jazzy score makes for a particularly strong soundtrack album that has undeniable charm. The film, a romantic comedy starring Billy Crystal and Debra Winger, already had a good flair of its own, but the musical contributions here add significant touches that enhance the screen proceedings. In the context "When You Love Someone," a duet with typical sliding inflections by Anita Baker and James Ingram, may strike as being out of style, but the tracks by Louis Armstrong, Billie Holiday, Louis Prima and Duke Ellington are wonderful. "April in Paris," played big band style, and "Come Rain or Come Shine," with David Sanborn blowing a mean sax, also rank among the rewarding selections here, along with the cues by Shaiman, which cover the gamut from a Gallic-flavored "Paris Suite," to several tracks with a pleasant jazz feel ("Craig and Lucy," "To Marriage"), to explo-

sive big band treatments of classic hits ("Nice Work If You Can Get It," "My Melancholy Baby"). A rich and satisfying album.

Forrest Gump

Forrest Gump ♫♫♫♪

1995, Epic Records/Sony Music; from the movie *Forrest Gump*, Paramount Pictures, 1995.

Album Notes: *Music*: Alan Silvestri; *Orchestrations*: William Ross; *Music Editor*: Kenneth Karman; Orchestra conducted by Alan Silvestri; *Album Producer*: Alan Silvestri; *Engineer*: Dennis Sands; *Assistant Engineers*: Sue McLean, Greg Dennen, Bill Talbott, Mark Eshelman, Bill Smith.

Selections: 1 I'm Forrest... Forrest Gump (2:41); 2 You're No Different (1:00); 3 You Can't Sit Here (2:27); 4 Run Forrest Run (2:14); 5 Pray With Me (:57); 6 The Crimson Gump (1:08); 7 They're Sending Me To Vietnam (2:24); 8 I Ran And Ran (1:43); 9 I Had A Destiny (1:20); 10 Washington Reunion (:45); 11 Jesus On The Main Line (2:01); 12 That's My Boat (1:17); 13 I Never Thanked You (:48); 14 Jenny Returns (2:43); 15 The Crusade (2:01); 16 Forrest Meets Forrest (1:42); 17 The Wedding Guest (1:48); 18 Where Heaven Ends (1:34); 19 Jenny's Grave (1:26); 20 I'll Be Right Here (:50); 21 Suite From Forrest Gump (6:34).

Review: See entry below.

Forrest Gump ♫♫♫♫

1995, Epic Records/Sony Music; from the movie *Forrest Gump*, Paramount Pictures, 1995.

Album Notes: *Music*: Alan Silvestri; *Orchestrations*: William Ross; *Music Editor*: Kenneth Karman; Orchestra conducted by Alan Silvestri; *Album Producer*: Alan Silvestri; *Engineer*: Dennis Sands; *Assistant Engineers*: Sue McLean, Greg Dennen, Bill Talbott, Mark Eshelman, Bill Smith.

Selections: CD 1: 1 Hound Dog (J. Leiber/M. Stoller) (2:19) *Elvis Presley*; 2 Rebel Rouser (D. Eddy/L. Hazlewood)(2:25) *Duane Eddy*; 3 (I Don't Know Why) But I Do (P. Gayten/R. Guidry)(2:22) *Clarence ''Frogman'' Henry*; 4 Walk Right In (H. Woods/G. Cannon/B. Svanoe/E. Darling) (2:36) *The Rooftop Singers*; 5 Land Of 1000 Dances (C. Kenner)(2:26) *Wilson Pickett*; 6 Blowin' In The Wind (B. Dylan)(2:38) *Joan Baez*; 7 Fortunate Son (J. Fogerty)(2:22) *Creedence Clearwater Revival*; 8 I Can't Help Myself (Sugar Pie Honey Bunch)(E. Holland/L. Dozier/B. Holland)(2:44) *The Four Tops*; 9 Respect (O. Redding)(2:29) *Aretha Franklin*; 10 Rainy Day Women #12 & 35 (B. Dylan)(4:38) *Bob Dylan*; 11 Sloop John B (B. Wilson)(2:58) *The Beach Boys*; 12 California Dreamin' (J. Phillips/M. Phillips)(2:42) *The Mamas And The Papas*; 13 For What It's Worth (S. Stills)(2:41) *Buffalo Springfield*; 14 What The World Needs Now Is Love (B. Bacharach/H. David)(3:14) *Jackie De Shannon*; 15 Break On Through (To The Other Side)(The Doors)(2:30) *The Doors*; 16 Mrs. Robinson (P. Simon) (3:51) *Simon & Garfunkel*.

CD 2: 1 Volunteers (M. Balin/P. Kantner)(2:09) *Jefferson Airplane*; 2 Let's Get Together (C. Powers)(4:39) *The Youngbloods*; 3 San Francisco (Be Sure To Wear Some Flowers In Your Hair)(J. Phillips)(3:01) *Scott McKenzie*; 4 Turn! Turn! Turn! (To Everything There Is A Season)(P. Seeger)(3:58) *The Byrds*; 5 Medley: Aquarius/Let The Sunshine In (G. McDermot/J. Rado/G. Ragni)(4:50) *The Fifth Dimension*; 6 Everybody's Talkin' (F. Neil)(2:46) *Harry Nilsson*; 7 Joy To The World (H. Axton) (3:19) *Three Dog Night*; 8 Stoned Love (F.E. Wilson/Y. Samoht)(3:02) *The Supremes*; 9 Raindrops Keep Falling On My Head (B. Bacharach/H. David)(3:03) *B.J. Thomas*; 10 Mr. President (Have Pity On The Working Man)(R. Newman) (2:48) *Randy Newman*; 11 Sweet Home Alabama (R. Van Zant/E. King/ G. Rossington)(4:46) *Lynyrd Skynyrd*; 12 It Keeps You Runnin' (M. McDonald) (4:22) *The Doobie Brothers*; 13 I've Got To Use My Imagination (G. Goffin/ B. Goldberg)(3:32) *Gladys Knight & The Pips*; 14 On The Road Again (W. Nelson)(2:33) *Willie Nelson*; 15 Against The Wind (B. Seger)(5:36) *Bob Seger & The Silver Bullet Band*; 16 Forrest Gump Suite (A. Silvestri)(8:50).

Review: The phenomenal success of the 2-CD set illustrates better than most the incredible synergy that exists at times between the movies and the recording industry. One of the most creative compilations of pop songs used in a film, the set includes many of the tunes that marked the period from the late '50s through the '70s. Among its highlights are Elvis Presley's "Hound Dog," The Four Tops' "I Can't Help Myself," Aretha Franklin's "Respect," Bob Dylan's "Rainy Day Women #12 & 35," The Mamas and The Papas' "California Dreamin'," Simon & Garfunkel's "Mrs. Robinson," Harry Nilsson's "Everybody's Talkin'," Willie Nelson's "On The Road Again" — all of them songs that can be found elsewhere but which, combined together, make for a most attractive and enjoyable package.

The score by Alan Silvestri serves as a perfect counterpoint to these classic pop hits, and emphasizes the more romantic aspects of this docu-fable about the slow-witted innocent (played by Tom Hanks) who finds himself unwillingly involved in some of the most remarkable events of the past 30 years.

Four in the Morning

See: Elizabeth Taylor in London, in Television soundtracks

The Four Musketeers/ The Eagle Has Landed/ Voyage of the Damned ♫♫♫

1987, Label X; from the movies *The Four Musketeers*, 1975; *The Eagle Has Landed*, 1977; and *Voyage of the Damned*, 1976.

Album Notes: *Music:* Lalo Schifrin; Orchestras conducted by Lalo Schifrin; *Album Producer:* Lalo Schifrin; *Engineers:* Richard Lewzey, Peter Wandless.

Selections: THE FOUR MUSKETEERS: 1 Overture (3:40); 2 Athos' Story (2:20); 3 Chase To The Convent (2:39); 4 The Musketeers Rescue Constance (1:51); 5 Breakfast At The Bastion (2:46); 6 A Lovely Adventure (1:08); 7 Chased From The Louvre (1:50); 8 Frozen Pond Fight (4:52); 9 Milady's Theme (2:59); 10 End Credits (1:50);

THE EAGLE HAS LANDED: 11 Main Title (2:25); 12 The Eagle Grows, Pt. 1 (2:56); 13 The Eagle Grows, Pt. 2 (2:36); 14 Flight Of The Eagles (3:07); 15 Eagles vs. Fox (4:34); 16 End Credits (March) (2:22);

VOYAGE OF THE DAMNED: 17 Main Title (2:21); 18 House Painter March (1:49); 19 Hotel Nacionale (2:18); 20 Lament (2:30); 21 Tragedy/Time Pulse (3:59); 22 Our Prayers Have Been Answered (2:16); 23 End Credits (Foxtrot) (2:30).

Review: Lalo Schifrin strangely unaffecting score for *The Four Musketeers* is a serious letdown in this sequel to the original film made by Richard Lester, which had been scored by Michel Legrand. But whereas Legrand had approached the first film with great personal empathy for it subject matter, Schifrin's totally detached and by-the-book cues completely miss the flavor of the period and end up sounding as a purely routine job. He fared somewhat better with *The Eagle Has Landed,* a World War II adventure centered around an improbable German plot to kidnap Winston Churchill, in which the cymbalom provides an interesting colorful motif that recurs throughout the score. He also did better with his cues for *The Voyage of the Damned,* a sensitive drama about the plight of Jewish refugees from war-torn Europe on board a ship no country wants to accepts. Further marring one's appreciation of these scores, the recording contains various sonic glitches, including poorly focused sound, some analog dropouts, and tape noises that could have been easily eliminated.

See also: The Three Musketeers

Four Weddings and a Funeral ♫♫♫♪

1994, London Records; from the movie *Four Weddings and a Funeral*, Gramercy Pictures, 1994.

Album Notes: *Song Producers:* Wet Wet Wet, Graeme Duffin, Stephen Lindsey, Nicky Brown, Lawrence Johnson, Dino

Fekaris, Freddie Perren, Gus Dungeon, Swing Out Sister, Pete Smith, Squeeze, Neil Dorfsman, Sting; *Engineers*: Bob Clearmountain, Pete Smith.

Selections: 1 Love Is All Around (R. Presley)(3:59) *Wet Wet Wet*; 2 But Not For Me (G. & I. Gershwin)(3:01) *Elton John*; 3 The Right Time (E. Van De Horst/E. Smidt)(3:29) *I To I*; 4 Smoke Gets In Your Eyes (J. Kern/O. Harbach) (4:26) *Nu Colours*; 5 I Will Survive (F. Perren/D. Ferakis)(3:53) *Gloria Gaynor*; 6 Crocodile Rock (E. John/B. Taupin)(3:55) *Elton John*; 7 La La La (Means I Love You)(T. Bell/W. Hart)(5:06) *Swing Out Sister*; 8 Loving You Tonight (C. Difford/G. Tilbrook)(4:49) *Squeeze*; 9 The Secret Marriage (Sting/H. Eisler)(2:09) *Sting*; 10 Chapel Of Love (P. Spector/E. Greenwich/J. Barry)(3:42) *Elton John*; 11 Four Weddings And A Funeral: After The Funeral (R.R. Bennett)(1:52) *John Hannah*.

Review: A cheery collection of British pop, with occasional diversions for wedding reception fare such as Gloria Gaynor's "I Will Survive." The covers are coolest, though — Wet Wet Wet's exuberant "Love is All Around," Swing Out Sister's sumptuous "La La La (Means I Love You)" and Elton John's "Chapel of Love," which is as reckless as he's sounded in years.

Gary Graff

1492: Conquest of Paradise
🎵🎵🎵🎵

1992, Atlantic Records; from the movie *1492: Conquest of Paradise*, Paramount Pictures, 1992.

Album Notes: *Music*: Vangelis; *Featured Musicians*: Bruno Manjares, Pepe Martinez (Spanish guitars, voices), Francis Darizcuren (mandolin, violin), Didier Malherbe (flutes), Guy Protheroe (vocals); The English Chamber Choir, conducted by Guy Protheroe; *Album Producer*: Vangelis; *Engineer*: Philippe Colonna.

Selections: 1 Opening (1:21); 2 Conquest Of Paradise (4:48); 3 Monastery Of La Rabida (3:39); 4 City Of Isabel (2:16); 5 Light And Shadow (3:47); 6 Deliverance (3:29); 7 West Across The Ocean Sea (2:53); 8 Eternity (2:00); 9 Hispanola (4:57); 10 Moxica And The Horse (7:06); 11 Twenty Eighth Parallel (5:14); 12 Pinta, Nina, Santa Maria (Into Eternity)(13:20).

Review: Despite the fact that Vangelis uses guitars and mandolins to give his score the necessary Spanish flavor, there is something definitely odd about the sounds of a synthesizer in the context of an epic that takes place in the 15th century. Not that one should necessarily be a stickler for authenticity, but the effect here is somewhat jarring. This said, the score for

1492: Conquest of Paradise has its share of great musical moments, with sweeping melodies that are appropriately overblown, in keeping with its subject matter. The title tune, a spacey selection with rhythm and choral work, is quite effective. Adding to the impression of a vast musical canvas on display, many of the cues fade into one another, making for a somewhat continuous program of impressive scope and dimension.

See also: Christopher Columbus: The Discovery

Francis of Assisi/
Doctor Faustus 🎵🎵🎵

1997, DRG Records; from the movies *Francis of Assisi*, 20th Century-Fox, 1961; and *Doctor Faustus*, Columbia Pictures, 1968.

Album Notes: *Music*: Mario Nascimbene; *Orchestrations*: Mario Nascimbene; Orchestras conducted by Franco Ferrara, Mario Nascimbene; *Featured Musician*: Severino Gazzelloni (flute); *Featured Artists*: Lucia Vinardi (soprano); Vocal Sextet "Luca Marenzio" conducted by Piero Cavalli; Concentus antiqui conducted by Carlo Quaranta; *Album Producers*: Mario Nascimbene, Claudio Fuiano; *Engineer*: Gianni Mazzarini. Nascimbene, Mario,

Selections: FRANCIS OF ASSISI: 1 Main Titles (3:14); 2 First Meeting With God (1:20); 3 Chamber Music (2:24); 4 Second Meeting With God (2:38); 5 Building The Church (2:31); 6 Clare's Theme (3:23); 7 Stigmata (2:27); 8 Death Of Francis (1:49); 9 Finale (2:59);

DOCTOR FAUSTUS: 10 Introductory Theme (2:10); 11 Invocation Of Faustus To Mephistopheles: Apparition Appears/The Angel Of Good And The Angel Of Evil Contend For The Soul Of Faustus (10:34) *Richard Burton*; 12 Catacombs: Supernatural Visions And Voices (2:58) *Richard Burton*; 13 Apparition Of Helen (1:26); 14 The Garden Of Delight (1:47); 15 Music At The Court (2:40); 16 Helen's Theme (1:26); 17 Ballet (1:32); 18 Another Ballet (2:26); 19 Faustus Appeals To Mephistopheles For Helen's Love: Faustus And Helen Love Scene (5:16) *Richard Burton*; 20 Eleven O'Clock Sounds: Monologue Of Faustus/ Twelve O'Clock Sounds/Helen Drags Faustus Into The Abyss/ Finale (9:37) *Richard Burton*.

Review: An epic religious drama, *Francis of Assisi* stars Bradford Dillman as the young 13th-century Italian nobleman who swears off a dissolute existence to spend the rest of his life in poverty and contemplation. For this inspirational tale, composer Mario Nascimbene created a series of cues that mix broad orchestral accents and heavenly choirs in a score that sounds at times dry and cliched, but is occasionally redeemed by some lovely themes ("Chamber Music," "Building The Church," "Clare's Theme"). The mono recording evidences serious tape damage, with flutter, distortion and dropouts on some of the tracks.

Doctor Faustus, starring Richard Burton delivering his lines with the ardor that characterized some of his most theatrical performances, is another variation on the Faust legend in which the good doctor sells his soul to the Devil in exchange for youth and eternal life. Nascimbene's music, heard here in another technically deficient recording with oddly uneven stereo separation, often sounds appropriately ominous, though he did create a lovely theme for Helen that is reprised a couple of times, and also wrote a very attractive series of cues marked "Ballet," "Another Ballet," and "Music at the Court."

Frank and Jesse 🎵🎵🎵⯈

1994, Intrada Records; from the movie *Frank and Jesse,* Trimark Pictures, 1994.

Album Notes: *Music:* Mark McKenzie; *Orchestrations:* Mark McKenzie; *Music Editor:* Jim Young; Orchestra conducted by Mark McKenzie; *Album Producer:* Mark McKenzie; *Engineer:* Andy Waterman.

Selections: 1 Frank And Jesse Suite (5:27); 2 Main Title (3:55); 3 Family Moments (2:28); 4 Gentle Spirits (1:06); 5 Tragedy At Home (3:07); 6 Meet The James Gang (2:07); 7 Marauding (1:52); 8 Daring Escape (1:28); 9 Frank's Despair (1:03); 10 The Peace Ranch (1:18); 11 Mountain Top Dance (1:19); 12 The Lord Is Callin' Youn (3:06); 13 Northfield Battle (2:15); 14 I Play Not Marches... (2:24); 15 Goodbye Jesse (2:12); 16 Justice Will Be Served (3:16).

Review: In recent times, westerns have fallen into disfavor, and even though there have been attempts at rekindling the genre these have been few and far between. Made in 1994, *Frank and Jesse,* yet another variation on the lives of the famous James brothers, didn't meet with great success at the box office, but it enabled Mark McKenzie, scoring his third feature, to write a bold, impassioned series of cues in which the epic grandeur of the film and its most intimate moments are fully explored. Using a quintet of authentic 19th-century instruments, he created some lovely themes ("Family Moments," "The Peace Ranch") to underscore the close feelings between the siblings, relying on the fuller orchestral textures to depict the moments of action ("Marauding," "Daring Escape," "Northfield Battle"). It may not be *The Magnificent Seven* or *The Alamo,* but the score has a sweep of its own that is ultimately quite engaging.

Frankenstein 🎵🎵🎵

1994, Epic Soundtrax/Sony Music; from the movie *Mary Shelley's Frankenstein,* Tri-Star Pictures, 1994.

Album Notes: *Music:* Patrick Doyle; *Orchestrations:* Lawrence Ashmore; *Music Editor:* Roy Prendergast; Orchestra conducted by David Snell; *Album Producers:* Patrick Doyle, Maggie Rodford; *Engineer:* Paul Hulme; *Assistant Engineers:* Geoff Foster, Bernard O'Reilly, Neil Mason, Andy Strange.

Selections: 1 To Think Of A Story (3:28); 2 What's Out There (2:52); 3 There's An Answer (4:37); 4 I Won't If You Won't (1:58); 5 A Perilous Direction (3:20); 6 A Risk Worth Taking (3:18); 7 Victor Begins (:54); 8 Even If You Die (2:16); 9 The Creation (2:00); 10 Evil Stitched To Evil (4:43); 11 The Escape (1:47); 12 The Reunion (:45); 13 The Journal (1:04); 14 Friendless (2:09); 15 William! (2:44); 16 Death Of Justine/Sea Of Ice (3:54); 17 Yes I Speak (5:37); 18 God Forgive Me (:57); 19 Please Wait (3:21); 20 The Honeymoon (1:16); 21 The Wedding Night (2:05); 22 Elizabeth (4:11); 23 She's Beautiful (3:36); 24 He Was My Father (6:10).

Review: A chilling, provocative orchestral score, Patrick Doyle's music for *Mary Shelley's Frankenstein* conjures up images of a monster creation let loose in an unsuspecting world, all the more frightening that it is underplayed, as a threat that looms without speaking its name. In bold, colorful strokes, the music paints these visions, first as an idea born in the mind of a deranged scientist, then as a solid plan that eventually yields a real creature, articulate and even more dangerous as a result. A love theme, heard in fragments throughout but eventually fully developed in "The Wedding Night," brings a romantic counterpoint to the subliminal horror. It may be far from the Gothic accents invented by Franz Waxman or Hans Salter in earlier times, but the music created by Doyle is strangely, almost eerily beautiful and elegant, which is part of the fascination it exerts.

Frankie Starlight 🎵🎵🎵🎵⯈

1993, Varese-Sarabande Records; from the movie *Frankie Starlight,* Fine Line Features, 1993.

Album Notes: *Music:* Elmer Bernstein; *Orchestrations:* Emilie A. Bernstein; *Music Editor:* Kathy Durning; Orchestra conducted by Elmer Bernstein; *Featured Soloist:* Cynthia Millar (ondes Martenot); *Album Producer:* Emilie A. Bernstein; *Engineer:* Andrew Boland.

Selections: 1 From My Window (E. Bernstein/E.A. Bernstein)(3:36) *Belinda Pigeon;* 2 Moon (Main Title)(2:25); 3 Windows And Memories (1:39); 4 Flashback (1:43); 5 Visions

(2:33); 6 A New Life (1:01); 7 Jack And Bernadette (3:46); 8 Emma's Revenge (2:41); 9 At Play (1:09); 10 Wild Ride (1:35); 11 Rooftops And Starlight (2:00); 12 Release (2:18); 13 In Paris (1:36); 14 Farewells (1:39); 15 Proposal (2:42); 16 Roofdance (End Credits)(4:03).

Review: "From My Window," performed by Belinda Pigeon, which recalls some of Sondheim's best moments, effectively introduces this gorgeous soundtrack recording which finds Elmer Bernstein in a very lyrical frame of musical mind. The wistful romantic moods, explored in the main theme, "Moon," are sustained almost throughout the entire score, with gentle extrapolations that are fetching and intelligently expressive. Only occasionally does the score indulge in some more animated releases ("At Play," and "Wild Ride," with its bouncy syncopated rhythms reminiscent of some cues from *The Magnificent Seven),* which provide surprising relief and enjoyment.

Frantic 🎵🎵🎵🎵

1988, Elektra Records; from the movie *Frantic,* Warner Bros., 1988.

Album Notes: *Music:* Ennio Morricone; *Orchestrations:* Ennio Morricone; Orchestra conducted by Ennio Morricone.

Selections: 1 I'm Gonna Lose You (M. Hucknall)(4:04) *Simply Red;* 2 Frantic (4:05); 3 On The Roofs Of Paris (6:00); 4 One Flugel Horn (3:16); 5 Six Short Interludes (4:31); 6 Nocturne For Michel (3:16); 7 In The Garage (4:12); 8 The Paris Project (3:16); 9 Sadly Nostalgic (1:47); 10 Frantic (6:03).

Review: Ennio Morricone wrote a particularly effective score for this taut thriller, starring Harrison Ford, about an American doctor unwillingly drawn into a web of political intrigues while attending a convention in Paris. Underscoring the suspense in the film, the cues detail the main character's search for a truth that eludes him, with Morricone's signature rhythmic syncopations subtly conveying the tension that permeates the action. The eerie moods (strangely contrasted in "On the Roofs of Paris" by the lilt of an accordion waltz) build up to a climax that is powerfully stated in a reprise of the main theme. This soundtrack album, enhanced by the forlorn "I'm Gonna Lose You," performed by Simply Red, is both surprising and remarkably enjoyable.

Free Willy

Free Willy 🎵🎵

1993, Epic Soundtrax; from the movie *Free Willy,* Warner Bros., 1993.

Album Notes: *Music:* Basil Poledouris; *Orchestrations:* Greig McRitchie; *Music Editor:* Tom Milano; *Synthesizers:* Michael

Boddicker; Orchestra conducted by Basil Poledouris; *Album Producers:* Joel Sill, Gary LeMel, Jerry Greenberg, Basil Poledouris; *Engineer:* Tim Boyle.

Selections: 1 Will You Be There (Theme From Free Willy)(M. Jackson) (5:54) *Michael Jackson;* 2 Keep On Smilin' (N.M. Walden/S. Jackson/S.Jo Dakota)(4:36) *NKOTB;* 3 Didn't Mean To Hurt You (T. Jackson/T. Jackson/ T.J. Jackson)(5:48) *3T;* 4 Right Here (B.A. Morgan/J. Bettis/S. Porcaro) (3:50) *SWV-Sisters With Voices;* 5 How Can You Leave Me Now (P. Frazier) (5:44) *Funky Poets;* 6 Main Title (5:07); 7 Connection (1:44); 8 The Gifts (5:20); 9 Friends Montage (3:41); 10 Audition (2:05); 11 Farewell Suite: (a) Jessie Says Goodbye, (b) Let's Free Willy!, (c) Return To Freedom (12:02); 12 Will You Be There (reprise)(M. Jackson)(3:40) *Michael Jackson.*

Review: This set mixes yawn-inducing instrumental music with yawn-inducing, but far more successful, vocal music. SWV's "Right Here/Human Nature" medley charted higher, but Michael Jackson's emotive "Will You Be There" is the film's theme and its most recognizable track. It could be worse; New Kids on the Block have a song on here, too.

Gary Graff

Free Willy 2 🎵🎵

1995, Epic Soundtrax; from the movie *Free Willy 2,* Warner Bros., 1995.

Album Notes: *Music:* Basil Poledouris; *Orchestrations:* Greig McRitchie; *Music Editor:* J.J. George; Orchestra conducted by Shirley Walker, Basil Poledouris; *Featured Artist:* Michael Boddicker (synthesizers); *Producers:* Tim Boyle, Basil Poledouris; *Engineer:* Sue McLean; *Song Producers:* Michael Jackson, Steve Lindsey, Soulshock & Karlin, Guy Roche, Ian Stanley, Michael Vail Blum; *Song Engineers:* Bruce Swedien, Richard Browne, David Cole, Gabe Veltri, Thom Russo, Mario Luccy; *Album Producers:* Gary LeMel, Joel Still.

Selections: 1 Childhood (M. Jackson)(4:27) *Michael Jackson;* 2 Forever Young (B. Dylan)(4:25) *Rebbie Jackson;* 3 Sometimes Dancin' (featuring Spragga Benz)(N. Gilbert/J. O'Brien/Jonah/ Soulshock/Karlin/L. James)(5:10) *Brownstone;* 4 What Will It Take (T. Jackson)(5:17) *3T;* 5 I'll Say Goodbye For The Two Of Us (D. Warren)(4:35) *Expose;* 6 Forever Young (B. Dylan)(5:00) *Pretenders;* 7 Lou's Blues (N. Cavaleri)(3:14) *Nathan Cavaleri Band;* 8 Main Titles (3:28); 9 Whale Swim (3:15); 10 Reunion (3:38); 11 Childhood (instrumental)(M. Jackson)(4:27) *Michael Jackson.*

Review: The sappy "Childhood" ("Have you seen my childhood?") crooned by Peter Pan (sorry, Michael Jackson!), introduces this sequel to the story of a child who befriends an orca, with the soundtrack album consisting mostly of similarly youth-oriented pop songs, including two not in the film, that are unlikely to get an R-rating or even an adult warning. In the mush, Basil Poledouris' score is virtually lost with only three selections that add up to ten minutes of playing time. As usual, his music is flavorful and aggressively romantic, with great orchestral textures, but in this context who cares!

The French Lieutenant's Woman ♪♪♪ᵛ

1981, DRG Records; from the movie *The French Lieutenant's Woman*, Juniper Films, 1981.

Album Notes: *Music*: Carl Davis; *Orchestrations*: Carl Davis, Brian Gascoigne; Orchestra conducted by Carl Davis; *Featured Soloists*: Erich Gruenber (violin), Kenneth Essex (viola), Keith Harvey (cello), John Lill (piano); *Album Producer*: Carl Davis; *Engineer*: John Richards.

Selections: 1 Sarah's Walk (1:30); 2 A Proposal (2:06); 3 Period Research (1:36); 4 Her Story (3:53); 5 Decision Taken (1:38); 6 Towards Love (2:17); 7 Location Lunch (2:23); 8 Together (3:53); 9 Domestic Scene (2:12); 10 Resurrection (2:12); 11 A House In Windmere (from Adagio of Sonata in D, K.576)(W.A. Mozart)(6:17) *John Lill*; 12 End Of Shoot Party (3:35); 13 The Happy Ending (6:25).

Review: A complex film with a story-within-a-story, this adaptation by Harold Pinter of John Fowles' romantic novel strongly benefitted from Meryl Streep's extraordinary performance as a mysterious woman who befriends a French soldier in 1867 England, only to be ostracized as a result, and as the modern actress who portrays her and who has an affair with the actor (Jeremy Irons) playing an English gentleman attracted to the "French Lieutenant's woman." The screen action, teetering between the contemporary and the period love affairs, received a strong musical support from Carl Davis' effective score, with some of the cues ("Sarah's Walk," "Her Story," "Towards Love") reflecting the romantic surge in the period story, while others ("Location Lunch," "Domestic Scene," "End of Shoot Party") stressed the contemporary aspects of the film in progress.

Fried Green Tomatoes

Fried Green Tomatoes ♪♪♪ᵛ

1991, MCA Records; from the movie *Fried Green Tomatoes*, Universal Pictures, 1991.

Album Notes: *Music*: Thomas Newman; *Song Producers*: Arthur Baker, Hal Willner, Anthony Heilbut, Thomas Newman,

John Vigran; *Album Executive Producers*: Jon Avnet, Jordan Kerner; *Engineer*: Howie Weinberg.

Selections: 1 I'll Remember You (B. Dylan) (5:09) *Grayson Hugh*; 2 What Becomes Of The Brokenhearted (J. Dean/P. Riser/W. Weatherspoon)(4:34) *Paul Young*; 3 Cherish (Hip Hop version)(T. Kirkman)(3:59) *Jodeci*; 4 Danger Heartbreak Dead Ahead (C. Paul/I.J. Hunter/W. Stevenson)(3:20) *Taylor Dayne*; 5 Rooster Blues (J. West)(3:15) *Peter Wolf, Ronnie Earl and The Broadcasters*; 6 Barbeque Bess (B. Jackson)(2:55) *Patti LaBelle*; 7 If I Can Help Somebody (A. Androzzo)(3:50) *Aaron Hall*; 8 Cool Down Yonder (I. Tucker) (3:11) *Marion Williams*; 9 Cherish (movie version) (T. Kirkman)(2:30) *Jodeci*; 10 Ghost Train (Main Title)(3:11); 11 Visiting Ruth (1:47); 12 A Charge To Keep I Have (trad.)(1:50) *Marion Williams*.

Review: See entry below.

Fried Green Tomatoes ♪♪♪ᵛ

1991, MCA Records; from the movie *Fried Green Tomatoes*, Universal Pictures, 1991.

Album Notes: *Music*: Thomas Newman; *Orchestrations*: Thomas Pasatieri; *Music Editor*: Bill Bernstein; Orchestra conducted by Thomas Newman; *Featured Musicians*: John Beasley (piano), Michael Fisher (percussion), Jeff Elmassian (clarinet), John C. Clarke (double reeds), George Doering (guitars, mandolin); *Album Producers*: Thomas Newman, John Vigran, Bill Bernstein; *Engineer*: John Vigran.

Selections: 1 Ghost Train (Main Title) (3:10) *Marion Williams*; 2 Whistle Stop, Ala. (1:17); 3 A Charge To Keep I Have (trad.) (2:34) *Marion Williams*; 4 Xmas In Hooverville (1:51); 5 The Treehouse (1:12); 6 Night Baseball (:58) *Marion Williams*; 7 Wither Thou Goest I Will Go (1:53); 8 Buddy Threadgoode (1:19); 9 Didn't It Rain (trad.)(2:53) *Marion Williams*; 10 The Bee Charmer (2:00); 11 Wallpaper (1:31); 12 The Smell Of Coffee (1:13); 13 Visiting Ruth (1:46); 14 Miss Otis Died (1:27); 15 The Town Follies (R. Grierson)(:46) *Ralph Grierson*; 16 Klansmen (2:04); 17 Smokey Lonesome (1:22); 18 Big George (1:51) *Marion Williams*; 19 Night Baseball (mandolin reprise)(1:01); 20 The Whistle Stop Cafe (2:28).

Review: This affecting story of life in a Southern town, and of an unsolved murder that took place years before, got much of its flavor from Thomas Newman's beautifully stated score and from the many pop songs heard on the soundtrack that both defined the locale and the given time period of the screen action. Thankfully, both are available on individual CDs, with the score detailing some of the most memorable scenes from the film, in cues that have an incredible energy and lyrical expression.

The songs, with performances by a wide range of seasoned performers (Jodeci, Paul Young, Patti LaBelle, Taylor Dayne), capture the essence of the action, and give it a palpable and recognizable frame of reference. Common to both are Marion Williams' spirited numbers which, better than most, provide an appropriate Southern flavor to the albums.

The Frighteners ♫♫♫

1996, MCA Records; from the movie *The Frighteners*, Universal Pictures, 1996.

Album Notes: *Music*: Danny Elfman; *Orchestrations*: Steve Bartek, Mark McKenzie, Edgardo Simone; *Music Editor*: Ellen Segal; Orchestra conducted by Artie Kane; *Album Producer*: Danny Elfman; *Engineer*: Shawn Murphy.

Selections: 1 Intro/Titles (5:43); 2 The "Lads" (2:00); 3 Poltergeists (2:05); 4 Victim #38 (1:52); 5 Who's Next? (1:39); 6 The Garden (3:08); 7 Chilly (1:29); 8 Time (4:41); 9 Patty's Place (2:12); 10 Flashbacks (1:07); 11 Patty Attack (3:04); 12 Frank's Wife (:50); 13 Doom (3:08); 14 Heaven (1:46); 15 Don't Fear The Reaper (5:46) *The Mutton Birds*.

Review: This score can best be described as *Beetlejuice* gone bad. Portions of Elfman's early work can be heard here in the more humorous use of harpsichord and string arrangements, but because the film wasn't a comedy (though it had been promoted as such), the score was required to be much darker. Unfortunately, the result is that it isn't as fun as *Beetlejuice*, though it's still a cut or two above what anyone else might have done for a similar film. Elfman has a good sense of the absurd, something that is always obvious in much of his other genre work, but this score can boast some genuinely creepy passages, too. The album includes "Don't Fear the Reaper" performed by The Mutton Birds.

David Hirsch

From Dusk Till Dawn ♫♫♫♩

1996, Epic Soundtrax; from the movie *From Dusk Till Dawn*, Miramax Films, 1996.

Album Notes: *Music*: Graeme Revell; *Song Producers*: Jeff Eyrich, David Vaught, Don Cook & Raul Malo, Jimmie Vaughan, Tito Larriva, Robert Rodriguez & Mark Goldenberg, Bill Ham & Billy F. Gibbons, Stevie Ray Vaughan & Double Trouble; *Soundtrack Executive Producers*: Robert Rodriguez, Quentin Tarantino, Lawrence Bender; *Engineer*: Chris Bellman.

Selections: 1 Everybody Be Cool (:05); 2 Dark Night (D. Alvin) (3:49) *The Blasters*; 3 Mexican Blackbird (B. Gibbons/D. Hill/F. Beard) (3:04) *ZZ Top*; 4 Texas Funeral (D. Vaught) (2:32) *Jon Wayne*; 5 Foolish Heart (R. Malo/E. York) (3:33) *The Mavericks*; 6 Would You Do Me A Favor? (:12); 7 Dengue Woman Blues (J. Vaughan) (6:24) *Jimmie Vaughan*; 8 Torquay (G. Tomsco) (2:42) *The Leftovers*; 9 She's Just Killing Me (B. Gibbons/D. Hill/F. Beard) (4:56) *ZZ Top*; 10 Chet's Speech (:42); 11 Angry Cockroaches (Cucarachas enojadas) (T. Larriva/P. Atanasoff) (5:15) *Tito & Tarantula*; 12 Mary Had A Little Lamb (B. Guy) (4:15) *Stevie Ray Vaughan, Double Trouble*; 13 After Dark (T. Larriva/S. Huffsteder) (4:11) *Tito & Tarantula*; 14 Willie The Wimp (And His Cadillac Coffin) (B. Carter/R.E. Ellsworth) (4:35) *Stevie Ray Vaughan, Double Trouble*; 15 Kill The Band (:05); 16 Mexican Standoff (G. Revell) (:50); 17 Sex Machine Attacks (G. Revell) (1:23).

Review: If truth be told, you never know what to expect when you listen to a soundtrack album. For example, this compilation put together for a martial arts and vampire film rolled into one, includes headliners like The Blasters, ZZ Top, Stevie Ray Vaughan, and The Mavericks, among others. Not bad, except that the tunes they perform aren't necessarily big hits for them, just run-of-the-mill numbers that have their genuine moments of flash. Throughout, sound bites prove intriguing, if nothing else. And how about a song called "Texas Funeral" performed (spoken ?) by Jon Wayne (no! not the actor, even though many of the tracks here border on the country genre, but check the spelling of the name...). It all adds up to a definitely strange but compelling album.

From Russia with Love ♫♫♫♫♫

1995, EMI-America; from the movie *From Russia with Love*, United Artists, 1963.

Album Notes: *Music*: John Barry; *Lyrics*: Lionel Bart; Orchestra conducted by John Barry; *Album Producer*: John Barry.

Selections: 1 Opening Titles/James Bond Is Back/From Russia With Love/James Bond Theme (2:24); 2 Tania Meets Klebb (1:27); 3 Meeting In St. Sophia (1:06); 4 The Golden Horn (2:28); 5 Girl Trouble (2:25); 6 Bond Meets Tania (1:18); 7 007 (2:40); 8 Gypsy Camp (1:15); 9 Death Of Grant (2:00); 10 From Russia With Love (2:35) *Matt Monro*; 11 Spectre Island (1:15); 12 Guitar Lament (1:09); 13 Man Overboard/Smersh In Action 2:18); 14 James Bond With Bongos (2:29); 15 Stalking (2:01); 16 Leila Dances (1:57); 17 Death Of Kerim (2:29); 18 007 Takes The Lektor (3:00).

Review: Another monster James Bond score signed by John Barry, and probably his most effective effort in the genre. The score, powered by the almost exclusive use of brass and percussion instruments, has an urgency and drive that seldom lessens and wonderfully captures the excitement in the film. A mandatory vocal, performed with great gusto by Matt Monro (a pleasant change from Shirley Bassey's over-the-top performances of "Goldfinger" and "Diamonds are Forever"), adds an extra zing to the album.

The Fugitive 🎵🎵🎵🎵

1993, Elektra Records; from the movie *The Fugitive*, Warner Bros., 1993.

Album Notes: *Music:* James Newton Howard; *Orchestrations:* James Newton Howard, Chris Boardman, Brad Dechter; Orchestra conducted by Marty Paich; *Featured Musicians:* Wayne Shorter (soprano sax), Chuck Domanico (acoustic bass), James Newton Howard (piano); *Album Producers:* James Newton Howard, Michael Mason; *Engineer:* Robert Schaper; *Assistant Engineers:* Sue MacLean, Tom Hardisty, Greg Dennan.

Selections: 1 Main Titles (3:52); 2 The Storm Drain (4:25); 3 Kimble Dyes His Hair (4:23); 4 Helicopter Chase (4:50); 5 "The Fugitive" Theme (3:06); 6 Subway Fight (2:27); 7 Kimble Returns (3:08); 8 No Press (4:56); 9 Stairway Chase (2:32); 10 Sykes' Apt. (4:19); 11 It's Over (3:40).

Review: Harrison Ford, playing another victim of circumstances on the run from justice, has one of his better screen roles in this big screen remake of the eponymous early 1960s television series. Adding a specific flavor of its own to the action, James Newton Howard wrote a series of cues that spell it out while providing an extra dramatic anchor to it. The tension in the drama comes out particularly effectively in the cues marked "Helicopter Chase," "Subway Fight" and "Stairway Chase," in which the taut orchestral textures echo the gripping screen visuals. The more subliminal accents in some of the other selections, notably "Kimble Dyes His Hair" and "Sykes' Apartment," with their faint ominous tones presaging some forthcoming dangers to the hero, are equally effective. The main theme, a delicate duet between a piano and a soprano sax (James Newton Howard and Wayne Shorter), is yet another expressive track.

Full Metal Jacket 🎵🎵◐

1987, Warner Bros. Records; from the movie *Full Metal Jacket*, Warner Bros., 1987.

Album Notes: *Music:* Abigail Mead; *Programmer:* Abigail Mead; *Engineer:* Tim Pennington.

Selections: 1 Full Metal Jacket (5:01) *Abigail Mead, Nigel Goulding*; 2 Hello Vietnam (T. Hall)(3:04) *Johnny Wright*; 3 Chapel Of Love (J. Barry/ E. Greenwich/P. Spector)(2:46) *The Dixie Cups*; 4 Wooly Bully (D. Samudio) (2:19) *Sam The Sham & The Pharaohs*; 5 I Like It Like That (C. Kenner) (1:56) *Chris Kenner*; 6 These Boots Are Made For Walking (L. Hazelwood) (2:00) *Nancy Sinatra*; 7 Surfin' Bird (A. Frazier/C. White/T. Wilson, Jr./ J. Harris) (2:15) *The Trashmen*; 8 The Marines' Hymn (2:06) *The Goldman Band*; 9 Transition (:32); 10 Parris Island (4:28); 11 Ruins (2:09); 12 Leonard (5:56); 13 Attack (2:02); 14 Time Suspended (1:03); 15 Sniper (3:15).

Review: A somewhat random collection of '60s classics and instrumental pieces composed for the film. At least the songs — "Surfin' Bird," "I Like it Like That," "These Boots Are Made for Walking" — aren't titles that usually show up in films. The original score is pretty blah, however.

Gary Graff

Fun in Acapulco

1993, RCA Records; from the movie *Fun in Acapulco*, Paramount Pictures, 1963.

See: Elvis Presley in Compilations

The Funeral 🎵🎵🎵

1996, Critique Records; from the movie *The Funeral*, October Films, 1996.

Album Notes: *Album Producer:* Brian Interland.

Selections: 1 Il primo amore (C. Buti)(3:45) *Carlo Buti*; 2 Body And Soul (E. Heyman/R. Sour/F. Eyton/J. Green)(3:03) *Coleman Hawkins*; 3 I Can't Get Started (V. Duke/I. Gershwin)(4:48) *Bunny Berigan*; 4 Moonglow (E. DeLange/W. Hudson/I. Mills)(3:25) *Benny Goodman*; 5 Pontiac Blues (S. Williamson)(2:42) *Sonny Boy Williamson*; 6 Take The "A" Train (B. Strayhorn)(2:58) *Duke Ellington*; 7 Tippin In (M. Symes/C. Smith)(3:20) *Erskine Hawkins*; 8 Gloomy Sunday (R. Seress/L. Javor/S. Lewis)(6:04) *Mystic*; 9 Back Bay Shuffle (A. Shaw/D. Macrea)(3:15) *Artie Shaw*; 10 Mr. Downchild (S. Williamson)(2:31) *Sonny Boy Williamson*; 11 I'm Dying To Love (L. Verna/M. Alloco)(2:18) *Concetta Gordon*.

Review: When a mafia boss is gunned down, his death brings together his brothers, who are determined to find his killer and avenge him. This Prohibition period crime drama, filmed by Abel Ferrara, received a smart soundtrack album, thanks to the selection of recordings from the era that have been compiled for the occasion. Opening up the proceedings is Carlo Buti's "Il primo amore," which is the only reference to the Italian background of the story. The other tracks include performances by

"My job was to artistically do a 12th century score but one that was accessible to mainstream audiences."

James Horner
on Braveheart (The Hollywood Reporter, 1-16-96)

Coleman Hawkins, Bunny Berigan, Benny Goodman, Duke Ellington, Erskine Hawkins and Artie Shaw, among others. Surprisingly, however, the Billie Holiday song that anchored the film and situated its time period more strongly than any other is noticeably absent from this otherwise flavorful compilation.

The Fury ✒✒✒✒

1989, Varese-Sarabande; from the movie The Fury, 20th Century-Fox, 1978.

Album Notes: Music: John Williams; The London Symphony Orchestra, conducted by John Williams; CD Producers: Robert Townson, Tom Null; Engineer: Michael Stone.

Selections: 1 Main Title (3:13); 2 For Gillian (2:42); 3 Vision On The Stairs (4:10); 4 Hester's Theme and The House (4:36); 5 Gillian's Escape (6:15); 6 The Search For Robin (2:43); 7 Death On The Carousel (2:52); 8 Gillian's Vision (4:03); 9 Death On The Carousel and End Titles (8:28); 10 Epilogue (4:38).

Review: The Fury is a dark score, underlining the psychic horror of Brian de Palma's telekinetic terror film with a haunting orchestration. Built around a slow, waltz-like main theme, using the same kind of ascending/descending triads that characterized Bernard Herrmann's score for Vertigo, Williams' music develops into a stunning, powerful work, dominated by brass, which emphasizes and embellishes de Palma's omnipresent mood of surreal gloom and terrifying apprehension. Interestingly, the CD (like its previous LP incarnation) isn't the original soundtrack but a much-improved rerecording done by Williams and the London Symphony, which includes a 4 and a half minute epilogue which reconstructs all the score's themes into a thunderous and profound final statement. The CD also includes an additional cue not on the original LP, an alternate version of "Death on the Carousel."

Randall D. Larson

Game of Death/ Night Games ✒✒✒✒▷

1993, Silva Screen Records; from the movies Game of Death, 1973; and Night Games, Next Decade Entertainment, 1979.

Album Notes: Music: John Barry; Orchestra conducted by John Barry; Album Producers: John Barry, Ford A. Thaxton; Engineer: John Goodmanson.

Selections: GAME OF DEATH: 1 Main Title/Set Fight With Chuck Norris (3:42); 2 Will This Be The Song I'll Be Singing Tomorrow (2:22); 3 Three Motorcycles/ Stick Fight With Santo (3:59); 4 Billy's Funeral Dirge (2:59); 5 Garden Fight (2:48); 6 Billy And Ann's Love Theme (2:37); 7 The Big Motorcycle Fight (5:45); 8 Goodbye Dr. Land (1:57); 9 Will This Be The Song I'll Be Singing Tomorrow (2:21) Colleen Camp; 10 Game Of Death: End Title (2:45); 11 Stick Fight (with sound effects)/Main Title (reprise)(6:14);

NIGHT GAMES: 12 Descent Into Decadence (5:59); 13 The Lesbian Tango (2:56); 14 The Wet Spot (3:34); 15 Water Sports/The Dominatrix's Waltz (7:40); 16 Phantom Of The Orgasm (8:24); 17 Afterplay (1:11).

Review: John Barry delivers the punches (make that the chops and the kicks) in the first score, which starred Bruce Lee shortly before his untimely death, and strikes a diffidently erotic note in the second, a sex fantasy directed by Roger Vadim. Bruce Lee's Game of Death actually found the composer in great verve, exploring the possibilities of scoring a martial arts film with all the colorful musical resources at his disposal. That he largely succeeded is a credit to his creativity as a film composer with few peers in the business. The tracks, which sometimes evoke some of Barry's best efforts in the thriller genre in the late 1960s, blend percussive action cues and lovingly detailed romantic expressions, in a score that has great strength and vitality. Best are "Garden Fight" and "The Big Motorcycle Fight," among the former, and "Billy's Funeral Dirge" and "Billy and Ann's Love Theme," among the latter. A "Stick Fight" (with sound effects) provides additional fun.

Though Night Games is, by all critical accounts, a total disaster and an "insult to adult minds," to quote one reviewer, Barry's music easily soars above the most pedestrian aspects of the film to create an elegant and erotic evocation. Three longer cues ("Descent into Decadence," "Water Sports/The Dominatrix's Waltz" and "Phantom of the Orgasm") are particularly striking with their deft blend of long, melodic lines, occasionally supported by a wordless choir. "The Lesbian Tango," with its slow, exotically syncopated rhythms, is a lot of fun.

See also: Dragon: The Bruce Lee Story

Genocide ♪♪♪

1993, Intrada Records; from the movie *Genocide*, MCEG Sterling, 1981.

Album Notes: *Music*: Elmer Bernstein; The Royal Philharmonic Orchestra, conducted by Elmer Bernstein; *Album Producer*: Elmer Bernstein; *Engineers*: John Arrias, Joe Tarantino, Douglass Fake.

Selections: 1 Main Title (3:09); 2 My Brother's Keeper (1:23); 3 A Convenient Enemy (1:51); 4 Herr Hitler (1:33); 5 Dachau (6:12); 6 We Shall Outlive Them (2:03); 7 The Nazi Trap (5:28); 8 Slaughter (3:44); 9 The Butterfly (1:05); 10 Kremer's Diary (5:39); 11 Farewell To Mother (1:41); 12 Be Strong And Brave (3:20); 13 Liberation (1:58); 14 The Legend Of Chaya (:36); 15 The Flag (2:45); 16 End Title (3:34).

Review: An Academy Award-winner as Best Documentary Feature, *Genocide*, narrated by Elizabeth Taylor and introduced by Simon Wiesenthal, was one more attempt at illustrating and trying to explain the extermination of Jews during World War II. For this moving account, Elmer Bernstein wrote an appropriately somber score, with some cues, like "A Convenient Enemy," "Dachau," "Slaughter," exploring in musical terms the unexplainable. Even the more exuberant last tracks fail to shake the dark moods that linger long after the music has stopped.

Gentlemen Don't Eat Poets ♪♪♪♪

1997, Pangea Records; from the movie *Gentlemen Don't Eat Poets*, Live Entertainment, 1997.

Album Notes: *Music*: Anne Dudley; *Orchestrations*: Anne Dudley; Orchestra conducted by Anne Dudley; *Featured Musician*: Phil Todd (saxophone); *Album Producer*: Anne Dudley; *Engineers*: Steve Price, Paul Hulme.

Selections: 1 This Was Never Meant To Be (Sting/A. Dudley)(4:04)*Sting*; 2 Theme From Gentlemen Don't Eat Poets (1:28); 3 Opening Titles: The Fledges Arrive (3:18); 4 Sir Hugo, The Dinosaur... And The Toad (2:08); 5 Meet George Leckie (1:28); 6 Dreaming Of Doris... And Fledge (3:33); 7 The Game Room (2:07); 8 Fledge's Den And Sydney's Disappearance (2:52); 9 Cleo Looks For Clues (1:49); 10 Jiving And Jamming (3:28); 11 Trying It On For Size (2:35); 12 An Apparition... And The Marshes (4:36); 13 Inspector Limp Gives Chase (3:19); 14 Fledge Begins His Conquest (1:43); 15 George's Story (1:29); 16 This Was Never Meant To Be (shellac mix)(1:44); 17 An Innocent Man/Hugo Loses His Mind (3:05); 18 Cleo Plots Her Revenge (2:43); 19 The Last Dance (1:42).

Review: This clever period piece about a poet, with whom an uppercrust English girl falls in love and the effects this dalliance has on the family, serves as the departing point for Anne Dudley's stylish score, in which bits of dialogue set up some of the cue, providing the extra dramatic touch that makes them all the more enjoyable. In the middle of all the expansive romantic cues the composer created, a bouncy "Jiving and Jamming" brings a different, albeit welcome, switch in genres that proves surprising and delightful at the same time. A breathy vocal by Sting, who also appears in the film, is quite satisfying in its own right.

Geronimo ♪♪♪♪

1993, Columbia; from the movie *Geronimo: An American Legend*, Columbia Pictures, 1993.

Album Notes: *Music*: Ry Cooder; *Orchestrations*: George S. Clinton, Van Dyke Parks; Orchestra conducted by George S. Clinton; *Music Editor*: Bunny Andrews; *Album Producer*: Ry Cooder; *Engineer*: Allen Sides.

Selections: 1 Geronimo: Main Title (R. Cooder/Hoon-Hoortoo/ J. Benally/ R.C. Nakai/G. Clinton)(5:09); 2 Restoration (R. Cooder/G. Clinton)(6:19); 3 Goyakla Is Coming (R. Cooder/ Hoon-Hoortoo/R.C. Nakai)(1:11); 4 Bound For Canaan (The 6th Cavalry)(R. Cooder/G. Clinton)(1:37); 5 Cibecue (R. Cooder/ R. Carlos Nakai/J. Benally)(2:03); 6 The Governor's Ball: Get Off The Track/Danza/Battle Cry Of Freedom (V.D. Parks)(9:43); 7 Wayfaring Stranger (R. Cooder/G. Clinton) (3:09); 8 Judgment Day (R. Cooder/G. Clinton)(2:12); 9 Bound For Canaan (Sieber And Davis)(1:31); 10 Embudos (R.C. Nakai)(1:56); 11 Sand Fight (R. Cooder/R.C. Nakai/Hoon-Hoortoo)(1:13); 12 Army Brass Band: The Young Recruit/ The Girl I Left Behind Me/Come Come Away (L. Schwartz)(2:58) *Americus Brass Band*; 13 Yaqui Village (R. Cooder/R.C. Nakai/J. Benally/Hoon-Hootoor)(3:17); 14 I Have Seen My Power (R. Cooder/ R.C. Nakai/J. Benally/ Hoon-Hootoor) (2:16); 15 La visita (R. Cooder)(3:11); 16 Davis (R. Cooder) (2:52); 17 Train To Florida (Hoon-Hootoor/R.C. Nakai/J. Benally)(9:27).

Review: Ry Cooder's appropriately authentic score, with the considerable support of Indian music and chants, serves as a colorful backdrop for this account of the life story of the great Apache warrior. With Cooder's usual contingent of sidemen and associates (among them David Lindley, prominently featured on mandolin and bouzouki, and Van Dyke Parks, who provided some of the orchestrations) contributing their talent, the music establishes its own standards and creates in relatively short time the moods which pervade the whole score. The clash between two cultures and two different sets of forces is fully explored in cues in which the Native American music is contrasted with the martial fife and drum accents of the federal armies. A rich and unusual score, which requires closer attention than most to endear itself, *Geronimo: An American Legend* may well be one of Cooder's best efforts to date.

Get Yourself a College Girl
♫♫ᵇ

1992, Sony Music Special Products; from the movie *Get Yourself a College Girl*, M-G-M, 1964.

Album Notes: none available.

Selections: 1 Whenever You're Around (D. Clark/M. Smith)(2:54) *The Dave Clark Five*; 2 The Girl From Ipanema (A.C. Jobim/N. Gimbel)(2:53) *Stan Getz, Astrud Gilberto*; 3 Around And Around (C. Berry)(2:42) *The Animals*; 4 The Sermon (J. Smith)(2:59) *Jimmy Smith*; 5 Get Yourself A College Girl (F. Karger/S. Miller)(2:38) *Mary Ann Mobley*; 6 Bony Moronie (L. Williams) (2:38) *The Standells*; 7 Thinking Of You Baby (D. Clark/M. Smith) (2:33) *The Dave Clark Five*; 8 Sweet Rain (M. Gibbs)(3:26) *Stan Getz*; 9 Blue Feeling (J. Henshaw)(2:30) *The Animals*; 10 Comin' Home Johnny (trad.) (3:12) *The Jimmy Smith Trio*; 11 Talkin' About Love (F. Bell/R. Linn) (2:22) *Freddie Bell, Roberta Linn & The Bell Boys*; 12 The Swim (L. Tamblyn)(2:31) *Standells*.

Review: Sad to say, but M-G-M, which for many years had dominated the screen musical genre with productions that set the standards for the entire industry, found itself releasing films like *Get Yourself a College Girl* in the 1960s, in imitation of works produced (the term is a generous one) by other studios. An inane campus comedy, *Get Yourself...* concerned a college student, Mary Ann Mobley (Miss America of 1959), who gets into trouble for writing "sophisticated" songs and spends the ensuing 80 minutes trying to get out of the mess, in a film that also stars Nancy Sinatra. One of the film's redeeming values is its soundtrack, sprinkled with "in" songs, performed by an interesting line-up of talent, including The Dave Clark Five, The Animals, Freddie Bell & The Bell Boys, for the bubblegum trade, and Stan Getz, the Jimmy Smith Trio, and Astrud Gilberto, for their elders. The title tune, delivered in a clear-sounding vocal by Mary Ann Mobley herself, unfortunately sets the intellectual tone for much of the album.

Getting Even with Dad ♫♫♫ᵇ

1994, Private Music; from the movie *Getting Even with Dad*, M-G-M, 1994.

Album Notes: *Music*: Miles Goodman; *Orchestrations*: Oscar Gastro-Neves; *Music Editor*: Nancy Fogarty; Orchestra conducted by Miles Goodman; *Album Producers*: Miles Goodman, Joel Moss; *Engineer*: Joel Moss.

Selections: 1 Money (That's What I Want)(B. Gordy/J. Bradford)(2:33) *Barrett Strong*; 2 Do You Love Me (B. Gordy)(2:52) *The Contours*; 3 Ball The Wall (H. Roeland Byrd)(3:17) *Professor Longhair*; 4 I Need Money (Keep Your Alibis)(J. Moore)(2:21) *Slim Harpo*; 5 Blues Ain't Nothin' (T. Mahal) (4:12) *Taj Mahal*; 6 You Can't Get There From Here (A. Croce)(2:37) *A.J. Croce*; 7 I Found Faith (A. Croce)(2:44) *A.J. Croce*; 8 Weight Of The World (B. O'Doherty/F. Velez)(3:53) *Ringo Starr*; 9 Getting Even (3:08); 10 The Coin Heist (4:40); 11 Natural Selection (2:17); 12 The Aquarium (2:12); 13 Getting Closer To Dad (2:17); 14 Theresa (2:19); 15 Comin' Home Baby (B. Dorough/B. Tucker)(3:15); 16 Hide And Seek (4:41); 17 Goodbye For Now (1:58); 18 The Bus To Redding (3:27); 19 Money (New Orleans version)(B. Gordy/J. Bradford)(2:46) *A.J. Croce*.

Review: The many early rock and blues songs heard on the first tracks of this soundtrack album exude a raucous flavor that seems to be missing in Miles Goodman's musical cues. Some of the selections ("The Coin Heist," "The Aquarium," "Getting Closer to Dad") are perhaps more reflective of some of the sentiments expressed in this comedy, about a kid who tries to steer his father, a small-time con artist, in the right direction, but, as is often the case in the genre, music and screen action are sometimes so intimately integrated that once they are separated, the music makes much less sense. But the pop selections are terrific!

Gettysburg ♫♫♫ᵇ

1993, Milan Records; from the movie, *Gettysburg*, New Line Cinema, 1993.

Album Notes: *Music*: Randy Edelman; *Orchestrations*: Ralph Ferraro, Randy Edelman; *Music Editor*: Joanie Diener; Orchestra conducted by Randy Edelman; *Album Producers*: Randy Edelman, David Franco; *Engineers*: Dennis Sands, Elton Ahi.

Selections: 1 Main Title (4:32); 2 Men Of Honor (2:55); 3 Battle Of Little Round Top (3:56); 4 Fife And Gun (3:01); 5 General Lee At Twilight (1:25); 6 The First Battle (2:41); 7 Dawn (1:57); 8 From History To Legend (2:56); 9 Over The Fence (4:09); 10 We Are The Flank (2:14); 11 Charging Up The Hill (2:24); 12 Dixie (2:25)(R.Edelman); 13 General Lee's Solitude (3:39); 14 Battle At Devil's Den (1:45); 15 Killer Angel (4:41); 16 March To Mortality (Pickett's Charge)(3:13); 17 Kathleen Mavourneen (3:15)(R.Edelman); 18 Reunion and Finale (5:44).

Review: Randy Edelman's broad score for this epic Civil War adventure is a vast tribute to the drama and tragedy of the battle that inspired Abraham Lincoln's ageless memorial address.

While a couple of traditional cues appear, the score is derived primarily from Edelman's heroic main theme, which gives the score a hugeness befitting the historical battle and its wide-screen depiction. Thunderous orchestrations, rendered intimate by acoustic guitar, speak eloquently for the soldiers who fought on both sides. Synths merged with symphs lend the main theme a timeless grace as well as a tone of extreme despondence. Even though the story depicts the savagery of warfare, its primary focus remains the people involved in those battles. The score nobly follows suit. "Battle of Little Round Top," for example, is given a slow, surging undercurrent that runs throughout the scene. Rather then matching the action, Edelman attempts to reflect the feeling of the scene. Even within the dissonance of "The First Battle," with its rousing conflagration of rhythmic strings and synths and rapid strokes of drum and violin, the main theme sounds solid amid the fury of activity—capturing the spirit and heart of those so viciously engaged. And, after the fury is spent, Edelman's theme sounds tender on acoustic guitar, a splendidly intimate paean to the heroes fallen.

Randall D. Larson

Ghost ♫♫

1995, Milan Records; from the movie *Ghost*, **Paramount Pictures, 1990.**

Album Notes: *Music*: Maurice Jarre; Orchestra conducted by Maurice Jarre; *Album Producer*: Maurice Jarre; *Engineer*: Shawn Murphy; *Assistant Engineer*: Sharon Rice.

Selections: 1 Unchained Melody (A. North/H. Zaret)(3:36) *The Righteous Brothers*; 2 Ghost (7:24); 3 Sam (5:33); 4 Ditto (3:19); 5 Carl (4:06); 6 Molly (6:17); 7 Unchained Melody (A. North/H. Zaret)(4:01); 8 End Credits (4:16); 9 Fire Escape (3:12); 10 Oda Mae & Carl (3:55).

Review: Maurice Jarre created a love theme that balances between two emotional extremes, the intense love of a young couple and the sense of sadness felt when Sam (Patrick Swayze) is murdered. The intense bond of the lovers keeps Sam's spirit earthbound until he can find a way to save Molly (Demi Moore) from the same fate. This theme is, however, completely overshadowed by the use of The Righteous Brothers' recording of "Unchained Melody" (composed by Alex North) which, for the film-going public, became *Ghost's* signature tune. Jarre's instrumental version of "Unchained Melody" is surprisingly busy with studio noise, perhaps because he realized the uphill battle he was saddled with and resented having to record the theme. His own love theme is also played orchestrally to contrast with the flurry of electronic effects that represent the darkness of the "other side." This gloomy mood

unfortunately makes up the bulk of the album, so it's disappointing that *Ghost* is not as overly romantic in nature as one would expect. The 1995 reissue of the album contains two additional, but unremarkable electronic underscore tracks.

David Hirsch

The Ghost and Mrs. Muir
♫♫♫♫

1985, Varese-Sarabande; from the movie *The Ghost and Mrs. Muir*, **20th Century-Fox, 1947.**

Album Notes: *Music*: Bernard Herrmann; *Orchestrations*: Bernard Herrmann; Orchestra conducted by Elmer Bernstein; *Engineer*: Richard Lewzey.

Selections: 1 Prelude/Local Train/The Sea (3:59); 2 The Ghost/The Storm/ The Apparition (4:43); 3 The Lights/Bedtime (2:51); 4 Poetry (2:19); 5 Lucia/Dictation/Boyhood's End/ Pastoral (3:54); 6 Nocturne (2:25); 7 London/ The Reading/ Local Train (2:34); 8 The Spring Sea (4:51); 9 Romance/Love/ Farewell (5:14); 10 The Home/Sorrow (3:18); 11 The Passing Years/The Late Sea (2:53); 12 Forever (2:43).

Review: In the 1970s, composer Elmer Bernstein created a club for fans of film music, and at their behest began to record significant scores from the past that had not been available or that were in serious danger of totally disappearing. While many of these recordings are still awaiting reissue on compact disc, this rendition of Bernard Herrmann's wonderfully lovely statement for Joseph L. Mankiewicz' 1947 light fantasy fortunately was released by Varese-Sarabande, and should be sought by anyone with a strong interest in good film music or, more generally speaking, in anything Herrmann ever composed. The most striking character of Herrmann's score is that he avoided any otherwordly effect that might have seemed too obvious. Instead, he concentrated on creating a musical canvas that relied on attractive orchestral textures, sometimes pared down to only a few instruments, at other times using the full contingent of players. Making his music even more accessible, many of the shorter cues have been brought together, making the selections more comprehensive and musically more pungent.

The Ghost and the Darkness
♫♫♫

1996, Hollywood Records; from the movie *The Ghost and the Darkness*, **Paramount Pictures, 1996.**

Album Notes: *Music*: Jerry Goldsmith; *Orchestrations*: Alexander Courage; *Music Editor*: Ken Hall; The National Philharmonic Orchestra of London, conducted by Jerry Goldsmith;

Album Producer: Jerry Goldsmith; *Engineer*: Bruce Botnick; *Producer and Arranger, Hindi and Swahili*: George Acogny; *Engineers*: Richard Mitchell, Alan Myerson.

Selections: 1 Theme From "The Ghost and the Darkness" (2:12); 2 The Bridge (4:10); 3 Catch A Train (2:02); 4 Lions Attack (5:18); 5 First Time (2:01); 6 Starling's Death (5:57); 7 Lions Reign (2:41); 8 Preparations (2:47); 9 Remington's Death (2:32); 10 Prepare For Battle (2:01); 11 Final Attack (2:53); 12 Welcome To Tsavo (5:00); 13 Hamara Haath ("Our Hands Unite") (G. Acogny)(3:06) *The Worldbeaters, Nusrat Fateh Ali Khan*; 14 Dueling Chants, part 1: "Jungal Bahar" (G. Acogny)(3:21) *The Worldbeaters, Nusrat Fateh Ali Khan*; 15 Safari Ya Bamba ("Journey To Bamba")(G. Acogny)(2:33) *The Worldbeaters*; 16 Terere Obande (G. Acogny)(2:42) *The Worldbeaters*; 17 Iye Oyeha (G. Acogny)(2:14) *The Worldbeaters*.

Review: Although Goldsmith's mix of Irish, African and British Colonial elements in his opening theme is disappointingly literal, the bulk of *The Ghost and the Darkness* makes for one of the composer's best works of the '90s: a beautiful, flowing score with some amazingly powerful moments, especially when the composer brings in a vivid Hindu chant over his orchestra. Goldsmith's fluid, evocative electronic effects include a repeated breathing effect for the film's man-eating lions, some striking synthesized choral effects, and slashing mixes of vocal effects and animal sounds for the lion attacks. The style of orchestral writing sometimes recalls John Barry in its use of brass, but Goldsmith brings his unmistakable experimentation to the process and the result is probably the composer's most enjoyable album of the '90s.

Jeff Bond

Ghost Story 🎬🎬🎬🎬

1990, Varese-Sarabande Records; from the movie *Ghost Story*, Universal Picture, 1981.

Album Notes: *Music*: Philippe Sarde; *Music Editor*: John Caper, Jr.; *Album Producer*: Philippe Sarde; *Engineer*: Mickey Crofford.

Selections: 1 Ghost Story (3:30); 2 Accidents (4:05); 3 Mansion (2:55); 4 Love Suite (4:18); 5 Dementia (2:05); 6 Fright (2:55); 7 Regression (2:30); 8 Picnic (2:10); 9 Demise (4:08); 10 Finale (5:28).

Review: Just about the only memorable element of John Irwin's 1981 supernatural thriller is Phillipe Sarde's deliciously creepy score, a delirious Halloween treat from its opening, spidery double bass chords to the wailing solo soprano "ghost" melody interspersed throughout its cues. There are pounding,

percussive chase cues, Grand Guignol-style horror underscoring that includes blasting brass exclamations and pipe organ chords, and a wonderful "danse macabre" ("The House") of scratchy, Stravinskyesque fiddle, piano, spinet and celeste. The score leads inevitably from sunny treatments of its gentle love theme down the primrose path to mournful regret and horror, mixing moments of lovely sincerity with a traditional horror movie approach that's so lovably purple you won't know whether to scream or laugh.

Jeff Bond

Ghostbusters II 🎬🎬🎬

1989, MCA Records; from the movie *Ghostbusters II*, Columbia Pictures, 1989.

Album Notes: *Song Producers*: L.A., Babyface, Jellybean Johnson, Eumir Deodato, James Taylor, Bobby Brown, Doug E. Fresh, RUN-D.M.C., Oingo Boingo, Chris Thomas, Glenn Frey, A.Z. Groove, Cornelius Mims; *Album Executive Producers*: Peter Afterman, Kathy Nelson; *Engineer*: Steve Hall.

Selections: 1 On Our Own (L.A. Reid/Babyface/D. Simmons)(4:53) *Bobby Brown*; 2 Supernatural (J. Johnson/T. Lewis/J. Harris)(4:35) *New Edition*; 3 The Promised Land (B. Caldwell/P. Gordon)(4:17) *James "J.T." Taylor*; 4 We're Back (B. Brown/D. Austin)(5:08) *Bobby Brown*; 5 Spirit (D.E. Fresh/ B. Wright) (4:14) *Doug E. Fresh & The Get Fresh Crew*; 6 Ghostbusters (R. Parker, Jr.) (4:09) *RUN-D.M.C.*; 7 Flesh 'n Blood (D. Elfman)(4:16) *Oingo Boingo*; 8 Love Is A Cannibal (E. John/B. Taupin)(3:53) *Elton John*; 9 Flip City (G. Frey/H. Wolinski)(5:12) *Glenn Frey*; 10 Higher And Higher (G. Jackson/C. Smith/R. Miner)(4:08) *Howard Huntsberry*.

Review: This sequel set has the distinction of reuniting Bobby Brown and New Edition — on the same album at least. Brown's "On Our Own" is a keeper and is one of the better singles from the summer of '89, when it resided near the top of the charts. Run-D.M.C.'s "Ghostbusters" is big, hip-hoppin' fun, but the rest is much B-matter by Elton John, Oingo Boingo and the Eagles' Glenn Frey.

Gary Graff

Ghosts of Mississippi 🎬🎬🎬🎬

1997, Columbia Records; from the movie *Ghosts of Mississippi*, Castle Rock Entertainment/Columbia Pictures, 1997.

Album Notes: *Music*: Marc Shaiman; *Orchestrations*: Jeff Atmajian, Patrick Russ; *Music Editor*: Scott Stambler; *Orchestra conducted by* Eddie Karem, Artie Kane; *Album Producer*: Marc Shaiman; *Engineer*: Dennis Sands.

Selections: 1 I Wish I Knew How It Would Feel To Be Free (B. Taylor/D. Dallas) (4:41) *Dionne Farris*; 2 Prologue (6:14); 3 Myrlie Plants The Seed (1:33); 4 Bobby Gets Hooked (3:16); 5 On The Delta (:58); 6 Friday Phone Call (2:09); 7 I Will Live My Life For You (H. Salvador/M. Stellman) (2:28) *Tony Bennett*; 8 The Smoking Gun (1:29); 9 Klandestine Meeting (1:29); 10 Mannish Boy (M. Morganfield/E. McDaniel/M. London) (2:58) *Muddy Waters*; 11 Walking Blues (R. Johnson) (2:32) *Robert Johnson*; 12 The Thrill Is Gone (R. Hawkins/ R. Darnell) (4:37) *B.B. King*; 13 Busted (5:42); 14 Building The Case (1:33); 15 Bomb Scare (1:17); 16 Finding Strength (2:02); 17 Witness For The Prosecution (3:44); 18 DeLay Speaks (2:10); 19 Waiting For The Verdict (1:43); 20 Myrlie Victorious (2:41); 21 I Wish I Knew How It Would Feel To Be Free (B. Taylor/D. Dallas) (4:16) *Nina Simone*.

Review: This account of the life and death of civil rights activist Medgar Evers, and the events spanning 30 years that eventually led to the arrest and conviction of his killer, was powerfully enhanced by Marc Shaiman's appropriately low-key score, in which many of the cues aim to create a quiet rather than a rambunctious atmosphere. Occasionally, a vocal track sets the album on a slightly different course, with B.B. King, Muddy Waters and the ubiquitous Tony Bennett contributing their talents. Nina Simone's intense performance in "I Wish I Knew How It Would Feel to Be Free," which closes the film and the soundtrack album, is worth alone the price of admission.

Giant ♫♫♫♫

1989, Capitol Records; from the movie *Giant*, Warner Bros., 1956.

Album Notes: *Music:* Dimitri Tiomkin; The Warner Bros. Orchestra, conducted by Dimitri Tiomkin, Ray Heindorf.

Selections: 1 Main Title (Giant Theme) (2:11); 2 Hunt Scene (2:59); 3 Love Theme (There's Never Been Anyone Else But You) (1:46); 4 First Love (3:25); 5 Road To Reata (5:08); 6 Jett Rink Theme (6:50); 7 Toy Trumpet March/ Christmas Morning/ Angel's Return (3:47); 8 Romantic Interludes (Love Theme) (4:38); 9 Jett Rink, Oil Baron (5:29); 10 Fight Scene (The Yellow Rose Of Texas) (D. George) (2:20) (R. Heindorf); 11 Home In Reata (4:02); 12 End Title (The Eyes Of Texas Are Upon You) (trad., arr. R. Heindorf) (:40) (R. Heindorf).

Review: The sprawling saga in Edna Ferber's novel received a sensational screen treatment in which Rock Hudson, Elizabeth Taylor and James Dean gave vivid portrayals as the characters whose lives were ultimately dwarfed by the significant social and economical changes that altered the Texan landscape between World War II and the mid-1950s. Contributing significantly to the overall impact of the film was Dimitri Tiomkin's great score, unfortunately abbreviated for its soundtrack album release and available only in mono.

Contrasting the gentle idyll between Bick Benedict, the cattle owner, and Leslie, the Maryland girl he marries and brings to Reata, his Texas home lost in the middle of an immense desolated territory ("There's Never Been Anyone Else But You"), Tiomkin created a pungent theme for Jett Rink, the envious handyman who inherits a small piece of land and becomes immensely wealthy when he discovers a huge oil field underneath his plot, first expressing his dreams and aspirations ("Jett Rink Theme"), then his unbearable selfishness and superiority ("Jett Rink, Oil Baron").

On a broader scale, the film also explored the moral and social changes in Texas, from the pervasive influence oil exerted on the society, when the cattle owners gradually lost their power to a disdainful upstart aristocracy, to the greater role racial relations began to play in this new society, all themes that received equally strong evocations in Tiomkin's profuse score.

Central to the latter was a memorable fistfight between Bick and a burly diner owner who refuses to serve Bick's stepdaughter because she is Mexican, the entire brawl set to the Mitch Miller's thrilling rendition of "The Yellow Rose of Texas," a #1 hit on the charts the year before. The new laserdisc release of the film will contain additional music from that impressive score which will complement, not duplicate, the existing CD.

The Giant of Thunder Mountain ♫♫♫♫

1994, Citadel Records; from the movie *The Giant of Thunder Mountain*, American Happenings, 1994.

Album Notes: *Music:* Lee Holdridge; *Orchestrations:* Ira Hearshen; Symphony Orchestra conducted by Lee Holdridge; *Album Producers:* Lee Holdridge, Tom Null; *Engineer:* John Richards.

Selections: 1 Prologue (Main Theme) (1:07); 2 The Giant (1:43); 3 In The Giant's Cabin (1:53); 4 Up The Mountain (1:21); 5 Taunting The Giant (1:35); 6 Return To The Cabin (1:27); 7 Amy/ The Bear (4:15); 8 In The Forest (:49); 9 Amy And The Giant (1:28); 10 Burning The Cabin (2:00); 11 The Villain (2:43); 12 Hunting The Giant (4:36); 13 Stalking The Villain (3:39); 14 Meadow Walk (1:22); 15 Members Of The Club (1:50); 16 Wood Carving (2:46); 17 Unease (3:23); 18 Pursuit (:57); 19 Villainy (1:12); 20 Finale (2:30).

Review: A folk tale that did not make much of an impression at the box office, *The Giant of Thunder Mountain* inspired Lee

Holdridge to write an appropriately evocative score, rooted in folk themes and instrumentations, with some broad orchestral effects to evoke the drama itself. Lovely melodies detail the poetic aspects of the story, while stronger accents underscore moments of action, sometimes, as in "Amy/The Bear," within the same cue. It all adds up to a remarkably effective score, lyrical to a fault and very entertaining for the most part.

G.I. Blues

1988, RCA Records; from the movie *G.I. Blues,* Paramount Pictures, 1960.

See: Elvis Presley in Compilations

Girl Happy

1993, RCA Records; from the movie *Girl Happy,* M-G-M, 1965.

See: Elvis Presley in Compilations

Girl 6 ♪♪♪▷

1996, Warner Bros. Records; from the movie *Girl 6,* 20th Century-Fox Pictures, 1996.

Album Notes: *Music:* Prince; *Songs:* Prince; *Arrangers/Producers:* Prince, The New Power Generation, David Z. and the Family, The Starr Company.

Selections: 1 She Spoke 2 Me (Prince) (4:19) *Prince;* 2 Pink Cashmere (Prince) (6:15) *Prince;* 3 Count The Days (3:26) *The New Power Generation;* 4 Girls & Boys (Prince) (5:31) *Prince;* 5 The Screams Of Passion (St. Paul/ Susannah) (5:27) *The Family;* 6 Nasty Girl (Vanity) (5:14) *Vanity 6;* 7 Erotic City (Prince) (3:55) *Prince And The Revolution;* 8 Hot Thing (Prince) (5:41) *Prince;* 9 Adore (Prince) (6:31) *Prince;* 10 The Cross (Prince) (4:46) *Prince;* 11 How Come U Don't Call Me Anymore (Prince) (3:53) *Prince;* 12 Don't Talk 2 Strangers (Prince) (3:11) *Prince;* 13 Girl 6 (Prince/T. Barbarella) (4:04) *The New Power Generation.*

Review: Prince is the master of this particular Spike Lee joint, whose soundtrack features a collection of his work plus that of long-gone spin-offs such as The Family and Vanity 6. There are a couple of new songs from his New Power Generation ("Count the Days," "Girl 6"), but it's almost unfair to ask them to hold their own alongside proven past favorites such as "Erotic City" and "The Cross."

Gary Graff

Girls! Girls! Girls!

1993, RCA Records; from the movie *Girls! Girls! Girls!,* Paramount Pictures, 1962.

See: Elvis Presley in Compilations

Give My Regards to Broad Street ♪♪▷

1984, Columbia Records; from the movie *Give My Regards to Broad Street,* 1984.

Album Notes: *Music:* Paul McCartney; *Arrangers:* Paul McCartney, George Martin; *Album Producer:* George Martin; *Engineers:* Geoff Emerick, John Kelly; *Assistant Engineers:* Jon Jacobs, Stuart Breed.

Selections: 1 No More Lonely Nights (4:50); 2 Good Day Sunshine (J. Lennon/P. McCartney)(1:43); 3 Corridor Music (:17); 4 Yesterday (J. Lennon/ P. McCartney)(1:43); 5 Here, There And Everywhere (J. Lennon/P. McCartney) (1:44); 6 Wanderlust (2:48); 7 Ballroom Dancing (4:36); 8 Silly Love Songs (4:29); 9 Silly Love Songs (reprise)(:36); 10 Not Such A Bad Boy (3:19); 11 So Bad (3:12); 12 No Values (4:06); 13 No More Lonely Nights (reprise) (:13); 14 For No One (J. Lennon/P. McCartney)(1:56); 15 Eleanor Rigby (J. Lennon/P. McCartney)/ Eleanor's Dream (1:01); 16 The Long And Winding Road (J. Lennon/P. McCartney)(3:47); 17 No More Lonely Nights (playout version) (4:17); 18 Goodnight Lonely Princess (3:53).

Review: To damn with faint praise, the album is better than the movie. By a little. When an artist starts covering his old hits, as Paul McCartney does on this effort, you know that can't be a good thing. And it isn't. The best thing that came out of the *Broad Street* project was a brief working relationship with former 10cc member Eric Stewart, who collaborated with McCartney on some decent new tunes for the film and worked with the ex-Beatle even more fruitfully on the underappreciated "Press to Play" album.

Gary Graff

The Glass Menagerie ♪♪♪♪▷

1987, MCA Records; from the movie *The Glass Menagerie,* Cineplex Odeon Films, 1987.

Album Notes: *Music:* Henry Mancini; Orchestra conducted by Henry Mancini; *Featured Musicians:* Walt Livinsky (soprano sax), Phil Bodner (clarinet/tenor sax), Mel Davis (trumpet), Dave Bargeron (trombone), Grady Tate (drums), Derek Smith (piano), Bucky Pizzarelli (guitar), Brian Torff (bass); *Album Producer:* Henry Mancini; *Engineer:* Ed Rak.

Selections: 1 Main Title (Tom's Theme)(2:11); 2 Gentlemen Callers (The Glass Menagerie Theme)(P. Bowles)(1:26); 3 Blue Roses (Laura's Theme)(2:05); 4 Laura's Private World (2:11); 5 Jonquils (The Glass Menagerie Theme)(P. Bowles)(2:58); 6 My Sister Laura (3:30); 7 The Magic Scarf (1:26); 8 Make A Wish (2:39); 9 Tom's Theme (End Credits)(2:19); 10 The Blues In

Three (3:06); 11 Easy Ride (2:50); 12 Where Is Dear Old Dad? (2:57); 13 The Rumba You Saved For Me (2:36); 14 Slow And Sassy (6:00); 15 Tango Paradiso (3:34); 16 Paradise Dance Hall Blues (3:20).

Review: A sensitive adaptation of Tennessee Williams 1954 stage play, directed by Paul Newman and starring Joanne Woodward (Newman's wife), *The Glass Menagerie* provided Henry Mancini with a rare opportunity to compose an unusually wistful score in which the dark poetic accents evoke strong emotions and unrealized dreams. Central to the score is the theme for Laura, "Blue Roses," the pathetic crippled waif, forever hoping that a gentleman will call for her and whose life is shattered as a result. Also strongly suggestive is the film's main theme, "Jonquils," which gives the score a solid romantic anchor. In the midst of the dreamy moods suggested by the action, Mancini also created some effective dance numbers that enliven his music, including "The Blues in Three," "The Rumba You Saved for Me," "Slow and Sassy," "Tango Paradiso," and "Paradise Dance Hall Blues," among others, all of which have been placed at the end of the recording in a rather uninspired bit of sequencing.

The Glenn Miller Story ♪♪♪♪

1985, MCA; from the movie *The Glenn Miller Story,* **Universal Pictures, 1954.**

Album Notes: The Universal-International Orchestra, conducted by Joseph Gershenson; *Featured Artists:* Louis Armstrong and the All-Stars: Louis Armstrong (trumpet), Trummie Young (trombone), Barney Bigard (clarinet), Billy Kyle (piano), Bud Freeman (tenor sax), Kenny John (drums), Arvell Shaw (bass).

Selections: 1 Moonlight Serenade (M. Parish/I. Mills)(2:28); 2 Tuxedo Junction (B. Feyne/W. Johnson/E. Hawkins/J. Dash)(2:32); 3 Little Brown Jug (G. Miller/J. Winner)(3:04); 4 St. Louis Blues (W.C. Handy)(3:32); 5 Basin Street Blues (S. Williams)(7:16); 6 In The Mood (A. Razaf/J. Garland)(3:10); 7 A String Of Pearls (E. DeLange/J. Gray)(2:30); 8 Pennsylvania 6-5000 (J. Gray/C. Sigman)(3:10); 9 American Patrol (F.W. Meacham)(3:24); 10 Otchi-Tchor-Ni-Ya (trad.)(7:24).

Review: James Stewart is quite believable as Glenn Miller in the otherwise highly romanticized screen biopic based on the life of the big band leader and Air Force pilot. The music, too, plays with great dynamic drive, sounds authentic, with the U-I Studio Orchestra, conducted by Joseph Gershenson, revisiting the hits from the Miller band, including "Moonlight Serenade," "Tuxedo Junction," "In the Mood," and "Pennsylvania 6-5000," among others. But the true highlight in this sound-

> "I'm lucky to have worked with directors from almost every country in the world. What was missing on my curriculum vitae was a Mexican director, so I was happy to meet (Alfonso) Arau."
>
> **Maurice Jarre**
> on A Walk in the Clouds *(The Hollywood Reporter, 1-16-96)*

track album, as it is in the film, is a scorching version of "Basin Street Blues" by Louis Armstrong and his All-Stars, whose performance is the real thing. No... bones about it!

Glory ♪♪♪♪

1994, Virgin Movie Music; from the movie *Glory,* **Tri-Star Pictures, 1994.**

Album Notes: *Music:* James Horner; *Orchestrations:* Greig McRitchie; *Music Editors:* Jim Henrikson; Orchestra conducted by James Horner; *Featured Artists:* The Boys Choir Of Harlem, Dr. Walter J. Turnbull, director; *Album Producers:* James Horner, Shawn Murphy; *Engineer:* Shawn Murphy.

Selections: 1 A Call To Arms (3:07); 2 After Antietam (2:39); 3 Lonely Christmas (1:54); 4 Forming The Regiment (5:26); 5 The Whipping (2:09); 6 Burning The Town Of Darien (2:30); 7 Brave Words, Braver Deeds (3:09); 8 The Year Of Jubilee (2:25); 9 Preparations For Battle (7:32); 10 Charging Fort Wagner (2:51); 11 An Epitaph To War (2:32); 12 Closing Credits (6:51).

Review: James Horner's music for this impassioned Civil War drama reveals a powerful depth of feeling and a profound sense of honor for the black soldiers of the 54th Regiment. Horner's poignant theme for the boys' choir and orchestra runs throughout the motif-filled variations and historical music that form the score's musical canvas. His single theme maintains the music's focus on its heroes, the soldiers of the 54th. Though war assaults them on every side and ultimately overcomes them, their glorious theme sounds solemnly and nobly through it all. With superb orchestration and outstanding sound—the low end drums and percussion sound through brilliantly on the CD—the music is grand yet intimate, intensely dramatic yet incredibly poignant. The full choir intones purposefully during the climactic battle scenes, chanting like resolute angels joining the 54th in their final, hopeless charge against Fort Baxter. The score is fully emotive and vastly memorable. The music, as with the film's images, lingers long and is presented in one of Horner's finest compositions.

Randall D. Larson

The Godfather

The Godfather 🎵🎵🎵🎵

1988, MCA Records; from the movie *The Godfather*, Paramount Pictures, 1972.

Album Notes: *Music:* Nino Rota; *Engineer:* Don MacDougall; *Re-recording Engineer:* Thorne Nogar.

Selections: 1 Main Title (The Godfather Waltz)(3:04); 2 I Have But One Heart (J. Farrow/M. Symes)(2:57); 3 The Pickup (2:56); 4 Connie's Wedding (C. Coppola)(1:33); 5 The Halls Of Fear (2:12); 6 Sicilian Pastorale (3:01); 7 Love Theme From The Godfather (2:41); 8 The Godfather Waltz (3:38); 9 Appollonia (1:21); 10 The New Godfather (1:58); 11 The Baptism (1:49); 12 The Godfather Finale (3:50).

Review: See entry below.

The Godfather Part II 🎵🎵🎵🎵

1988, MCA Records; from the movie *The Godfather Part II*, Paramount Pictures, 1974.

Album Notes: *Music:* Nino Rota, Carmine Coppola; *Orchestra conducted by* Carmine Coppola; *Album Producer:* Tom Mack; *Engineer:* John Norman; *Re-recording Engineer:* Thorne Nogar.

Selections: 1 Main Title/The Immigrant (3:25); 2 A New Carpet (1:58); 3 Kay (2:58); 4 Ev'ry Time I Look In Your Eyes/After The Party (2:33); 5 Vito And Abbandando (2:36); 6 Senza Mama/ Ciuri-Ciuri/Napule ve salute (2:34) *Livio Giorgio*; 7 The Godfathers At Home (2:33); 8 Remember Vito Andolini (2:59); 9 Michael Comes Home (2:18); 10 March Italian Style (2:00); 11 Lullaby For Michele (2:18) *Nino Palermo*; 12 The Brothers Mourn (3:18); 13 Murder Of Don Fanucci (2:48); 14 End Title (3:51).

Review: See entry below.

The Godfather Part III 🎵🎵🎵🎵

1990, Columbia Records; from the movie *The Godfather Part III*, Paramount Pictures, 1990.

Album Notes: *Music:* Carmine Coppola, Nino Rota; *Orchestrations:* Carmine Coppola; *Orchestra conducted by* Carmine Coppola; *Album Producers:* Francis Ford Coppola, Stephan R. Goldman; *Engineer:* Joel W. Moss.

Selections: 1 Main Title (:43); 2 The Godfather Waltz (1:10); 3 Marcia Religioso (2:51); 4 Michael's Letter (1:09); 5 The Immigrant/Love Theme From The Godfather III (2:37); 6 The Godfather Waltz (1:25); 7 To Each His Own (J. Livingston/R. Evans) (3:21) *Al Martino*; 8 Vincent's Theme (1:50); 9 Altobello (2:09); 10 The Godfather Intermezzo (3:23); 11 Sicilian Medley: Va Pensiero/ Mazurka (Alla Siciliana)/Danza Tarantella (G. Verdi, arr.: C. Coppola) (2:11); 12 Promise Me You'll Remember (Love Theme From The Godfather Part III) (C. Coppola/J. Bettis) (5:12) *Harry Connick Jr.*; 13 Preludio And Siciliana (from "Cavalleria Rusticana") (P. Mascagni/G. Targioni-Tozzetti/G. Menasci) (8:15) *Franco D'Ambrosio*; 14 A Casa Amiche (from "Cavalleria Rusticana") (P. Mascagni/ G. Targioni-Tozzetti/G. Menasci) (2:00) *Franco D'Ambrosio*; 15 Preghiera (from "Cavalleria Rusticana") (P. Mascagni/G. Targioni-Tozzetti/G. Menasci) (5:30) *Chorus*; 16 Finale (from "Cavalleria Rusticana") (P. Mascagni/ G. Targioni-Tozzetti/G. Menasci) (8:13); 17 Coda: The Godfather Finale (2:28).

Review: Francis Ford Coppola's impressive treatment of Mario Puzo's novel about the ups and downs of a Mafia family has long been one of the screen's most successful trilogies. Matching colorful characters and narrative intensity with sensational portrayals and effective cinematography, Coppola created a fresco of incredible scope, vitality and beauty, its sympathetic views of some rather shady people notwithstanding.

As important to the success of the original 1972 film as all its other ingredients is Nino Rota's exceptional score, which beautifully captures the flavor and the essence of the screen drama, and helps take it to a higher level of importance and recognition. Both the "Main Theme," a mournful waltz heard in various guises at different times throughout the action, and the equally popular "Love Theme," achieved hit status in countless cover versions and vocal/instrumental renditions.

Unfortunately, the powerful atmosphere suggested by Rota's original score is considerably diluted by Carmine Coppola's contributions in the following two films. In both, the best musical moments belong to Rota who easily outshines Coppola, whose flair for musical underscoring is mediocre at best. In all three recordings, pop vocals provide an extra dimension to the scores, with an uncredited singer warbling "I Have But One Heart," which should have been performed by Frank Sinatra or Jerry Vale for best results, in the first album; and Al Martino effectively handling "To Each His Own" in the third volume. In the last album, a performance of "Promise Me You'll Remember" by Harry Connick, Jr. is easily dispensable. Overall sound quality in the three albums varies considerably, with a great amount of distortion noticeable in the first.

Gold Diggers: The Secret of Bear Mountain ♫♫♫♫

1995, Varese-Sarabande Records; from the movie *Gold Diggers: The Secret of Bear Mountain*, Universal Pictures, 1995.

Album Notes: *Music*: Joel McNeely; *Orchestrations*: David Slonaker, Art Kempel, Joel McNeely; *Music Editor*: Michael Ryan; Orchestra conducted by Joel McNeely; *Album Producer*: Joel McNeely; *Engineer*: Geoff Foster.

Selections: 1 Bear Mountain (3:39); 2 Exploring The Cave (1:25); 3 The Legend Of Molly Morgan (1:50); 4 Summer Adventures (5:10); 5 A Terrible Tale (2:25); 6 The Great Rescue (5:04); 7 Into The Lake (2:10; 8 Crystal Cavern (3:41); 9 Glow Worms! (4:32); 10 Back From The Dead (2:09); 11 Molly Morgan's Gold (4:32); 12 The Flying Song (C. Hay/C. Fischer)(5:00) *Colin Hay*.

Review: The story of two adventurous young girls, Beth and Jody (played by Christina Ricci and Anna Chlumsky), one the savvy street-wise urbanite, the other the rebellious country pumpkin (and bumpkin), who set out to discover a legendary cache of gold in the wilds of the Pacific Northwest, *Gold Diggers: The Secret of Bear Mountain* elicited a strong, flavorful score from Joel McNeely, whose only major fault is that too often it telegraphed the screen action. On its own, however, it reveals several themes that are quite attractive, including the folk-oriented "Legend of Molly Morgan," laid out in broad, colorful terms. "The Flying Song," performed by Colin Hay, in a style that sometimes evokes Phil Collins, is a fine coda to the recording.

Golden Gate ♫♫♫♪

1993, Varese-Sarabande; from the movie *Golden Gate*, Samuel Goldwyn, 1993.

Album Notes: *Music*: Elliot Goldenthal; *Orchestrations*: Elliot Goldenthal, Robert Elhai; The Pro Arte Orchestra, conducted by Jonathan Sheffer; *Featured Musicians*: Billy Drewes (saxophone), Elliot Goldenthal (keyboards, vocals), Richard Martinez (keyboards), James Haddad (percussion), Steve Gorn (bamboo flute), Matthias Gohl (keyboards, Scott Lee (bass); *Album Producer*: Matthias Gohl; *Engineers*: Steve McLaughlin, Bill Emmons.

Selections: 1 Golden Gate (3:36); 2 The Woman Cries (3:34); 3 Between Bridge And Water (1:55); 4 Tender Deception (3:33); 5 Bopathonix Hex (2:48); 6 The Woman Warrior (2:30); 7 The Softest Heat (3:45); 8 The Moon Watches (1:43); 9 Whisper Dance (1:52); 10 Kwan Ying (2:46); 11 Motel Street Meltdown (1:24); 12 Judgment On Mason Street (2:02); 13 Write It As Time (:28); 14 Between Bridge And Sky (2:51).

Review: Elliot Goldenthal created a fascinating eclectic mix of musical styles that includes jazz, blues and Chinese motifs for this story of an FBI agent who becomes involved with the Chinese community in San Francisco during the McCarthy witch hunt of the 1950s. The score has a dark, brooding quality which does well to capture the mood of the era. Goldenthal himself performs on "Motel Street Meltdown," a piece reminiscent of the bizarre vocal arrangements featured in the TV series "Twin Peaks."

David Hirsch

Goldeneye ♫♪

1995, Virgin Movie Music; from the movie *Goldeneye*, United Artists, 1995.

Album Notes: *Music*: Eric Serra; *Orchestrations*: Eric Serra, John Altman; The London Studio Session Orchestra, conducted by John Altman; *Featured Musicians*: Gavyn Wright (violin), George Robertson (viola), Tony Pleeth (cello), Mike Brittain (bass), Andy Findon (flute), Mike Thompson (Frenh horn), Fiona Hibbert (harp); *Album Producer*: Eric Serra; *Engineer*: Steve Price.

Selections: 1 Goldeneye (Bono/The Edge)(4:46) *Tina Turner*; 2 The Goldeneye Overture (4:24); 3 Ladies First (2:44); 4 We Share The Same Passions (4:46); 5 A Little Surprise For You (2:02); 6 The Severnaya Suite (2:07); 7 Our Lady Of Smolensk (1:01); 8 Whispering Statues (3:26); 9 Run, Shoot And Jump (1:05); 10 A Pleasant Drive In St. Petersburg (4:28); 11 Fatal Weakness (4:43); 12 That's What Keeps You Alone (3:17); 13 Dish Out Of Water (3:57); 14 The Scale To Hell (3:43); 15 For Ever, James (2:01); 16 The Experience Of Love (E. Serra/R. Hine)(5:57) *Eric Serra*.

Review: Whenever someone other than John Barry comes in to score a James Bond movie, you shouldn't hold your breath hoping the results will come close to being a Barry-caliber outing. In fact, the best you can often hope for is that the score won't be an outright dud like Eric Serra's music for *Goldeneye*, Pierce Brosnan's first outing as 007. At times an embarrassing collection of techno/industrial tracks with static orchestral lines, Serra's *Goldeneye* gets off on the wrong foot with what can be best described as "Bond on Bongos" before heading off in other confused directions. His music for the film's tank chase, "A Pleasant Drive in St.Petersburg," included here but thrown out of the film itself, is about as laughable and headache-inducing as the rest of his ill-considered score. The serviceable main theme, performed by Tina Turner and written by U2 members Bono and The Edge, fares much better, but it, too, remains far removed from its more successful predecessors.

Andy Dursin

Goldfinger 🎬🎬🎬🎬

1995, EMI-America; from the movie *Goldfinger*, United Artists, 1964.

Album Notes: *Music*: John Barry; *Lyrics*: Leslie Bricusse, Anthony Newley; Orchestra conducted by John Barry.

Selections: 1 Goldfinger/Into Miami (2:47) *Shirley Bassey*; 2 Alpine Drive/Auric's Factory (5:24); 3 Oddjob's Pressing Engagement (3:05); 4 Bond Back In Action Again (2:29); 5 Teasing The Korean (2:12); 6 Gassing The Gangsters (1:03); 7 Goldfinger (2:08); 8 Dawn Raid On Fort Knox (5:43); 9 The Arrival Of The Bomb and Count Down (3:25); 10 The Death Of Goldfinger/End Titles (2:34).

Review: The best, and probably most effective, contribution by John Barry to the James Bond films, *Goldfinger* is the score to which all others have to measure up. With its strong array of thematic material, powerful melodies, suggestive cues and varied instrumentations, the score managed to musically excite as much as the screen action itself. Even Shirley Bassey's over-the-top performance of the title tune, which is badly distorted in the recording itself, contains more energy than any vocal in the other films, including Ms. Bassey's rendition of "Diamonds are Forever" or Tom Jones' vibrant interpretation of "Thunderball".

More to the point, Barry's use of electric guitar, brass instruments, and percussive devices to underscore the most stirring moments in the action, defined a style that has been imitated (including by Barry himself) but never equalled in terms of raw vitality. In cue after cue, the composer challenges the listener with muscular musical ideas, electrifying sounds, and pervasive concepts that are sustained throughout the score.

In derisive comments he often made about his contributions to the series, Barry was creating "Mickey Mouse" film music, but it is in fact everything film music should be about — bold, assertive, enthusiastic, a total complement to the screen action, and something one might feel compelled to listen to frequently, just because it provides such pleasure.

The CD, incidentally, repeats the flaws in the original LP, and fails to include the four tracks "Golden Girl," "Death of Tilley," "The Laser Beam," and "Pussy Galore's Flying Circus" initially available only in a British pressing, but subsequently released in this country in the 2-CD "30th Anniversary" package (q.v.).

Gone Fishin' 🎬🎬🎬

1997, Hollywood Records; from the movie *Gone Fishin'*, Hollywood Pictures, 1997.

Album Notes: *Music*: Randy Edelman; *Orchestrations*: Ralph Ferraro; *Music Editor*: John La Salandra; Orchestra conducted by Randy Edelman; *Album Producer*: Randy Edelman; *Engineer*: Elton Ahi.

Selections: 1 Down In The Everglades (T. Brown) (2:35) *Willie Nelson*; 2 Gone Fishin' (1:48); 3 Speed Boat Race (2:14); 4 Fisherman's Heaven (1:59); 5 Swamp Music (1:26); 6 Discovering The Map (1:05); 7 Airboats (3:23); 8 Catch's Advice (1:06); 9 Alligators (1:42); 10 The Early Days (Opening) (2:16); 11 Unhitched (2:43); 12 Out Of Gas (2:04); 13 Life Is Good (1:03); 14 A Stolen Vehicle (:41); 15 Sleepwalking (3:32); 16 Closing (1:57); 17 What Went Wrong (A. Kury/R. Cain/P. Love/S. Kromos/M. Lord) (3:40) *The Love Junkies*; 18 Best Friend (A. Kury/R. Cain/P. Love/S. Kromos/M. Lord) (3:02) *The Love Junkies*.

Review: A strongly colloquial score, with folk undertones, Randy Edelman tapped into a new creative vein for this amiable comedy about two long-time fishing friends who win a grand prize vacation to the Florida Everglades, only to be confronted with all kinds of misfires and adventures they had hardly expected along with their winning. At times humorous, at times wistfully reflective, the overall tone of the score is cleverly rollicking in keeping with the action itself, with the most eventful moments receiving appropriate musical comments that suggestively underline them, while making for an entertaining soundtrack album. "Down in the Everglades," by Willie Nelson, and two vocals by The Love Junkies add a welcome touch to the music.

Gone with the Wind

Gone with the Wind 🎬🎬🎬🎬

1996, Rhino Records; from the movie *Gone with the Wind*, Selznick International/M-G-M Pictures, 1939.

Album Notes: *Music*: Max Steiner; *Orchestrations*: Max Steiner; The Warner Bros. Orchestra, conducted by Max Steiner; *Album Producers*: George Feltenstein, Bradley Flanagan; *Engineer*: Doug Schwartz.

Selections: CD 1: 1 Main Title (4:06); 2 Tara (2:13); 3 The O'Hara Family (6:17); 4 Scarlett Prepares For The Barbecue (2:20); 5 Twelve Oaks (1:17); 6 The Barbecue (5:23); 7 Afternoon Nap (1:58); 8 Charles Hamilton Challenges Rhett (1:07); 9 In The Library (2:31); 10 War Is Declared/The Death Of Charles (4:03); 11 At The Bazaar (1:03); 12 Maryland, My Maryland (1:42); 13 Dances (1:51); 14 Gettysburg (:55); 15 Outside The *Examiner* Newspaper Office (2:12); 16 At The Depot (1:06); 17 Christmas At Aunt Pitty's (4:56); 18 Melanie And Scarlett Tend The Wounded (1:21); 19 Scarlett's Promise (3:37); 20 Train Depot (2:08); 21 Melanie In Labor (:35); 22 Rhett Returns (2:59); 23 Escape From Atlanta

(2:46); 24 Soldiers In Retreat (1:22); 25 Rhett And Scarlett On McDonough Road (3:13); 26 Twelve Oaks In Ruin/Scarlett Comes Home (4:40); 27 I'll Never Be Hungry Again (6:06).

CD 2: 1 Alternate Entr'acte (1:48); 2 Battle Montage (2:55); 3 The Deserter (1:33); 4 Melanie And Scarlett (3:14); 5 It's Over (3:04); 6 Frank Kennedy Asks For Suellen's Hand (3:07); 7 Paddock Scene (5:26); 8 Gerald's Death (2:26); 9 Old Folks At Home (Swanee River) (:17); 10 The New Store (:52); 11 Scarlett In Shantytown (2:30); 12 Ashley And Dr. Meade/Frank's Death (1:57); 13 Belle Watling And Melanie (2:42); 14 Scarlett Gets Tipsy (:45); 15 New Orleans Honeymoon (:30); 16 Can-Can (:34); 17 Scarlett's New Wardrobe (:47); 18 Scarlett's Nightmare (2:24); 19 Bonnie's Birth (1:20); 20 Twenty Inches! (4:43); 21 The Lumber Mill (2:11); 22 After The Party (2:52); 23 London (2:35); 24 Rhett And Scarlett's Fight (3:31); 25 The Death Of Bonnie (2:27); 26 Melanie And Mammy (3:49); 27 The Death Of Melanie (5:19); 28 Scarlett In The Mist/Rhett Leaves (5:54); 29 Flashback/Finale (1:20).

Review: See entry below.

Gone with the Wind ♫♫♫♫♫

1989, RCA Victor; from the movie *Gone with the Wind*, Selznick International/ M-G-M Pictures, 1939.

Album Notes: *Music*: Max Steiner; The National Philharmonic Orchestra, conducted by Charles Gerhardt; *Album Producer*: George Korngold; *Engineer*: K.E. Wilkinson.

Selections: 1 Selznick International Trademark (A. Newman)/ Main Title: Dixie/Mammy/Tara/Rhett (3:04); 2 Opening Sequence: The Twins/Katie Bell/ Ashley/Mammy (2:13); 3 Driving Home/Gerald O'Hara/Scarlett/Tara (2:48); 4 Dance Montage: Charleston Heel And Toe Polka/Southern Belle Waltz/Can Can (3:26); 5 Grazioso: Mammy/Ashley/Ashley And Scarlett/Scarlett/Ashley And Melanie Love Theme (5:00); 6 Civil War: Fall Of The South/Scarlett Walks Among The Wounded (5:19); 7 True Love/Ashley Returns To Tara From The War/ Tara In Ruins (3:15); 8 Belle Watling (2:24); 9 Reconstruction: The Nightmare/Tara Rebuilt/Bonnie/The Accident (7:05); 10 Mammy And Melanie On The Staircase/Rhett's Sorrow (2:29); 11 Apotheosis: Melanie's Death/ Scarlett And Rhett/Tara (6:24).

Review: See entry below.

Gone with the Wind ♫♫▷

1988, Stanyan Records; from the movie *Gone with the Wind*, Selznick International/M-G-M Pictures, 1939.

Album Notes: *Music*: Max Steiner; The London Sinfonia, conducted by Muir Mathieson; *CD Producer*: Rod McKuen; *Engineer*: Steve Hoffman.

Selections: 1 Tara's Theme/Invitation To The Dance/Melanie's Theme/ Ashley/ The Prayer/Bonnie Blue Flag/Scarlett O'Hara/ Scarlett's Agony/War (16:52); 2 Belle Watling/Bonnie's Death/ Rhett Butler/Bonnie's Theme/Ashley And Melanie (Love Theme)/The Oath/Return To Tara (20:50); bonus tracks: 3 *America, America:* Farewell Son/The Voyage (M. Hadjidakis) (5:39); 4 *For Whom The Bell Tolls:* The Bridge (V. Young) (4:16); 5 *Spellbound:* Main Theme (M. Rozsa) (4:44); 6 *America, America:* Frustration, Dreams And Loneliness (M. Hadjidakis) (4:14); 7 *The Cardinal:* Theme (Stay With Me) (J. Moross) (2:48); 8 *The Prime Of Miss Jean Brodie:* Overture (R. McKuen) (5:46).

Review: The lavish 2-CD set from Rhino, replete with profuse liner notes and illustrations, documents one of the all-time great film scores, and includes one of the most celebrated tunes from the movies, "Tara's Theme." It is also the most complete and, true to Rhino's usual standards of excellence, its presentation is nothing short of superb.

The variable sonics are the main drawback here, but it's the original music as recorded in 1939, when prevailing techniques were a far cry from today's norms. Despite its technical shortcomings the score largely holds its own, and emerges as a grandiose achievement.

The 1973 RCA Victor rerecording, with the National Philharmonic Orchestra conducted by Charles Gerhardt, while not as comprehensive, boasts superb stereo sound, and playing that is faithful to the spirit of the original.

The only interest in the Stanyan set, conducted by Muir Mathieson, also in stereo, is the fact that it was the first "authentic recording of the complete score authorized by the composer," a claim that is now superseded by the Rhino release. In addition, the bonus selections can only be viewed as unnecessary padding, with some (*America, America* and *The Prime of Miss Jean Brodie*) oddly chosen in this context.

See also: Max Steiner Conducts Gone with the Wind and Other Themes in Compilations

Good Morning, Vietnam ♫♫♫♫▷

1988, A&M Records; from the movie *Good Morning, Vietnam*, Touchstone Pictures, 1987.

Album Notes: *Album Producer*: David Anderle; *Engineer*: Arnie Acosta.

Selections: 1 Adrian Cronauer (2:09); 2 Nowhere To Run (B. Holland/L. Dozier/E. Holland)(2:56) *Martha Reeves & The Vandellas*; 3 I Get Around (B. Wilson)(2:09) *The Beach Boys*; 4

Game Of Love (C. Ballard, Jr.)(2:04) *Wayne Fontana & The Mindbenders*; 5 Adrian Cronauer (:15); 6 Sugar And Spice (F. Nightingale)(2:13) *The Searchers*; 7 Adrian Cronauer (:47); 8 Liar, Liar (J. Donna)(1:51) *The Castaways*; 9 The Warmth Of The Sun (B. Wilson/M. Love) (2:48) *The Beach Boys*; 10 Adrian Cronauer (:34); 11 I Got You (I Feel Good)(J. Brown)(2:44) *James Brown*; 12 Adrian Cronauer (:08); 13 Baby Please Don't Go (J. Williams)2:40) *Them*; 14 Adrian Cronauer (:33); 15 Danger Heartbreak Dead Ahead (W. Stevenson/C. Paul/I.J. Hunter)(2:28) *The Marvelettes*; 16 Five O'Clock World (A. Reynolds)(2:18) *The Vogues*; 17 California Sun (H. Glover/M. Levy)(2:22) *The Rivieras*; 18 Adrian Cronauer (1:21); 19 What A Wonderful World (G. Weiss/B. Thiele)(2:48) *Louis Armstrong*.

Review: Credit this album with establishing Louis Armstrong's "What a Wonderful World", deftly deployed over harsh images of warfare, as a cultural standard, a blessing or a curse depending on how many commercials you've heard it in. Robin Williams' monologues are a joy to have, though the excerpts are often too short. And there's a wealth of tremendous '60s tunes, some of which—such as the Marvelettes' "Danger Heartbreak Dead Ahead," the Searchers' "Sugar and Spice" and the Vogues "Five O'Clock World"—are refreshing choices.
Gary Graff

The Good Son ♫♫♫

1993, Fox Records; from the movie *The Good Son*, 20th Century-Fox, 1993.

Album Notes: *Music*: Elmer Bernstein; *Orchestrations*: Emilie A. Bernstein, Patrick Russ; Orchestra conducted by Elmer Bernstein; *Featured Musician*: Cynthia Millar (Ondes Martenot); *Album Producer*: Elmer Bernstein; *Engineer*: Dan Wallin.

Selections: 1 The Good Son (2:22); 2 Hospital (:51); 3 Mark Arrives (2:49); 4 Evil (2:20); 5 Goodbye (1:41); 6 Treehouse (2:00); 7 Rocks And Rails (1:34); 8 Dog Chase (2:43); 9 Mom (1:47); 10 Killing The Dog (1:55); 11 Mr. Highway (2:13); 12 Dark (2:56); 13 Skating And Drowning (3:26); 14 Funeral (1:48); 15 Susan (2:28); 16 Richard's Duck (1:18); 17 Threat (1:16); 18 The Cliff (4:26); 19 End Credits (4:35).

Review: Elmer Bernstein, a master at evoking a wide range of different moods, came up with one of his most attractive efforts for this film starring Macaulay Culkin, about an orphan boy, and his younger cousin, a psychopath with murderous instincts. Relying on the power of strong, romantic themes, at times gloriously expressed on the piano or Cynthia Millar's oddly atmospheric Ondes Martenot, the music unfolds with often striking beauty, creating an aura that is most fetching. Even the tracks less likely to elicit a positive reaction because of the downbeat moods they evoke ("Killing the Dog," "Skating and Drowning," "Funeral") come out strongly, thanks to the composer's skill at writing particularly exquisite melodies. An unusual, though remarkably sensitive score, only marred by the short playing time of some of the cues.

The Good, the Bad and the Ugly ♫♫♫♫

1985, EMI-Manhattan; from the movie *The Good, the Bad and the Ugly*, United Artists, 1968.

Album Notes: *Music*: Ennio Morricone; *Orchestrations*: Ennio Morricone; Orchestra Unione Musicisti di Roma, conducted by Ennio Morricone.

Selections: 1 The Good, The Bad and The Ugly (Main Title)(2:38); 2 The Sundown (1:12); 3 The Strong (2:20); 4 The Desert (5:11); 5 The Carriage Of The Spirits (2:06); 6 March (2:49); 7 The Story Of A Soldier (3:50); 8 March Without Hope (1:40); 9 The Death Of A Soldier (3:05); 10 The Ecstasy Of Gold (3:22); 11 The Trio (5:00).

Review: Ennio Morricone had one of his most memorable spaghetti western scores with this film by Sergio Leone, a sprawling saga in which Clint Eastwood, in one of his best film performances, and Eli Wallach, in a delightful portrayal as Eastwood's snarling partner and foe, are the main protagonists. The effective set of cues created by the composer (and included in this sadly incomplete soundtrack album) provides the appropriate musical setting for some of the most relevant scenes in this overblown story about two bounty hunters who become unwilling soldiers of fortune while on their way to finding a hidden cache of gold. Among the tracks that stand out, "March," "The Story of a Soldier," "March without Hope" and "The Ecstasy of Gold" have justifiably become popular among fans of the stunning film. But the whole score, even in its abbreviated presentation, is quite successful at evoking the stirring climate that pervades this engrossing, and grandly over-the-top, western epic.

GoodFellas ♫♫♫♪

1990, Atlantic Records; from the movie *GoodFellas*, Warner Bros., 1990.

Album Notes: *Song Producers*: Gielan Berniker, Leonard Chess, Phil Chess, Billy Ward, Richard Barrett, Hy Weiss, Shadow Morton, Jerry Wexler, Ahmet Ertegun, Nesuhi Ertegun, Felix Pappalardi, Johnny Winter, Tom Dowd; *Album Executive Producers*: Martin Scorsese, Barbara Defina.

Selections: 1 Rags To Riches (J. Ross/R. Adler)(2:49) *Tony Bennett*; 2 Sincerely (H. Fuqua/A. Freed)(3:04) *The Moonglows*; 3 Speedo (E. Navarro) (2:19) *The Cadillacs*; 4 Stardust (H. Carmichael/M. Parish)(3:12) *Billy Ward & The Dominoes*; 5 Look In My Eyes (R. Barrett)(2:18) *The Chantels*; 6 Life Is But A Dream (R. Cita/H. Weiss)(2:34) *The Harptones*; 7 Remember (Walkin' In The Sand)(G. Morton)(2:20) *The Shangri-Las*; 8 Baby I Love You (R. Shannon)(2:36) *Aretha Franklin*; 9 Beyond The Sea (C. Trenet/J. Lawrence) (2:52) *Bobby Darin*; 10 Sunshine Of Your Love (J. Bruce/P. Brown/E. Clapton) (4:10) *Cream*; 11 Mannish Boy (M. Morganfield/M. London/E. McDaniel)(5:17) *Muddy Waters*; 12 Layla (piano exit)(E. Clapton/J. Gordon)(3:52) *Derek & The Dominos*.

Review: A brief '50s and '60s set that starts in the ballroom, with Tony Bennett singing "Rags to Riches," moves to the street corner for the doo-wop heaven of the Moonglows, Cadillacs and others, then winds its way through girl group pop before ending up at Muddy Waters' gritty "Mannish Boy" and Cream's power rock classic "Sunshine of Your Love." Not a bad ride, but it's docked a full bone for including only the piano outro to Derek & the Dominos' "Layla."

Gary Graff

A Goofy Movie ♫♫♫♪

1995, Walt Disney Records; from the animated feature *A Goofy Movie*, Walt Disney Pictures, 1995.

Album Notes: *Music*: Carter Burwell, Don Davis; *Orchestrations*: Shirley Walker, Don Davis, Lolita Ritmanis, Bruce Fowler; *Music Editors*: Adam Smalley, Tom Carlson; Orchestra conducted by Shirley Walker, Don Davis; *Album Producers*: Carter Burwell, Don Davis; *Engineers*: Michael Becker, Joe Gastwirt.

Selections: 1 I2I (P. DeRemer/R. Freeland)(4:02) *Tevin Campbell, Rosie Gaines*; 2 After Today (T. Snow/J. Feldman)(2:21) *Aaron Lohr*; 3 Stand Out (P. DeRemer/R. Freeland)(3:00) *Tevin Campbell*; 4 On The Open Road (T. Snow/J. Feldman)(3:01) *Bill Farmer, Aaron Lohr*; 5 Lester's Possum Park (R. Petersen/K. Quinn)(1:25) *Kevin Quinn*; 6 Nobody Else But You (T. Snow/J. Feldman)(2:35) *Bill Farmer, Aaron Lohr*; 7 Opening Fanfare/ Max's Dream (1:50); 8 Deep Sludge (2:04); 9 Bigfoot (2:14); 10 Hi Dad Soup (1:32); 11 Runaway Car (2:17); 12 Junction (:45); 13 The Waterfall!/The Truth (3:10).

Review: The urban contemporary stylings in some of the vocals on this Disney soundtrack album have a flavor that contrasts with the characters originally developed by the master animator, and show how removed from its lily white image the studio has become in recent years. The fact that the songs probably will not appeal to the film's core audience of underage tykes, or that their elders are unlikely to find anything remotely redeeming in a cartoon about Goofy leaves open the question about who will eventually be attracted to this album. The question also raises a doubt about the score created by Carter Burwell which will have a hard time finding an audience. Smart film music fans, always eager to discover some of their favorite composers' latest creations, will be a happy exception and will be amply rewarded with a series of short compact cues that are attractively laid out and cohesively creative. Within the limits set by the animated feature, Burwell and Don Davis have invented some nifty musical moments that are effective and enjoyable, with "Bigfoot" and "Runaway Car" particularly noticeable among them.

Gorillas in the Mist ♫♫♫♫♫

1988, MCA Records; from the movie *Gorillas in the Mist*, Warner Bros., 1988.

Album Notes: *Music*: Maurice Jarre; *The Maurice Jarre Electronic Ensemble*: Michael Boddicker, Ralph Grierson, Judd Miller, Michael Fisher, Dan Greco, Rick Marvin, Nyle Steiner, Emil Richards, Alex Acuna; *Featured Musicians*: Dennis Karmazan, Ron Leonard (cellos); *Album Producer*: Maurice Jarre; *Engineer*: Joel Moss; *Assistant Engineers*: Nick "Beemer" Basich, Phil Jamtaas, Jim Mitchell, George Smith, Bill Talbott.

Selections: 1 African Wonderment (14:22); 2 Black Magic (3:13); 3 Making Contact (5:53); 4 Tenderness and Turmoil (9:40); 5 The Death Of The Digit (5:49); 6 Gorillas In The Mist (5:07).

Review: On various occasions, Maurice Jarre has indulged in creating scores that made a pervasive use of synthesizers, unfortunately not always creatively or interestingly. There have been some happy exceptions, and his score for *Gorillas in the Mist* happens to be one of them. Somehow, the African background for this film about anthropologist Dian Fossey, its exotic sounds, and Jarre's own electronic inventions, supplemented by colorful orchestral textures, seem to blend very well to create a score of great scope and creative importance. Essential to the appreciation of it are two lengthy extrapolations, "African Wonderment," which describes in pure musical terms the landscape and its rich fauna, and "Tenderness and Turmoil," in which Fossey's mind sets find a melodic expression. The other selections are more directly linked to the action, about Fossey's attempts to survey and study the life of gorillas, and the primates' response to her presence in their midst. The score received an Oscar nomination and one can easily understand why.

Gorky Park 🎵🎵🎵♪

1983, Varese-Sarabande Records; from the movie *Gorky Park*, Orion Pictures, 1983.

Album Notes: *Music*: James Horner; *Orchestrations*: Greg Mc-Ritchie; *Music Editor*: George Brand; Orchestra conducted by James Horner; *Album Producer*: James Horner; *Engineers*: Dan Vallen, Danny Hersch.

Selections: 1 Main Title (2:44); 2 Following Girwill (2:59); 3 Irina's Theme (2:34); 4 Following KGB (2:04); 5 Chase Through The Park (1:56); 6 Arkady And Irina (2:40); 7 Faceless Bodies (1:54); 8 Irina's Chase (3:44); 9 The Sable Shed (6:42); 10 Airport Farewell (3:50); 11 Releasing The Sables/End Titles (4:18).

Review: A rather odd East-West crime story about a Russian detective (William Hurt) investigating the murder of three men whose bodies were discovered in Moscow's Gorky Park, and the American sable trader (Lee Marvin) he eventually links with the deed, *Gorky Park* prompted James Horner to write a suitable score, in which the Russian references are swiftly borrowed from Tchaikovsky, enabling him to concentrate on an old-fashioned set of cues that could have been composed for any drama, whatever the setting. With Joanna Pacula providing an extra element to the mix, the score reveals many contrasting moods, all beautifully developed, from the romantic accents in "Irina's Theme" and "Arkady and Irina," to the throbbing riffs in "Chase Through the Park" and "The Sable Shed." While an early effort by Horner, this is also an interesting album well worth looking for.

The Graduate 🎵🎵🎵

1987, Columbia Records; from the movie *The Graduate*, Embassy Pictures, 1967.

Album Notes: *Music*: Dave Grusin; Orchestra conducted by Dave Grusin; *Songs*: Paul Simon, Art Garfunkel; *Album Producer*: Teo Macero.

Selections: 1 The Sound Of Silence (P. Simon)(3:07) *Simon & Garfunkel*; 2 The Singleman Party Foxtrot (2:54); 3 Mrs. Robinson (P. Simon)(1:16) *Simon & Garfunkel*; 4 Sunporch Cha-Cha-Cha (2:55); 5 Scarborough Fair/ Canticle (Interlude)(P. Simon/A. Garfunkel)(1:43); 6 On The Strip (2:01); 7 April Come She Will (P. Simon)(1:51); 8 The Folks (2:28); 9 Scarborough Fair/Canticle (P. Simon/A. Garfunkel)(6:23) *Paul Simon, Art Garfunkel*; 10 A Great Effect (4:08); 11 The Big Bright Green Pleasure Machine (P. Simon)(1:47); 12 Whew (2:12); 13 Mrs. Robinson (P. Simon)(1:14) *Paul Simon, Art Garfunkel*; 14 The Sound Of Silence (P. Simon)(3:08) *Paul Simon, Art Garfunkel*.

Review: Not that it set out to be this way, but *The Graduate* should probably be remembered today as the film that, in effect, signalled the start of a 10-year period during which instrumental music almost totally disappeared from the screens. The tremendous success of this album, fueled in large part by the songs written by Simon and Garfunkel, attracted Hollywood producers to the incredible profits that could be generated for them when a soundtrack album went gold and beyond. And the best way to achieve this, it seemed, was to replace instrumental scores by rock songs that could attract a younger, wider audience. As a result, many of the most respected film composers in town suddenly found themselves unemployed. Some, like Bernard Herrmann, Miklos Rozsa and Dimitri Tiomkin, chose to seek a new career in Europe, where their talents were still admired and widely appreciated. Others, like Elmer Bernstein, "crossed over" and began writing innocuous music scores that could fit neatly between the various songs on the soundtracks while being unobtrusive and totally unmemorable. It would take John Williams and *Star Wars*, in 1977, to bring back film music to its former glory, and enable a new generation of composers like James Horner, Danny Elfman and Alan Silvestri, to draw on their predecessors' contributions to the screen and make a name for themselves with broad-scale instrumental scores.

Meanwhile, *The Graduate* has its moments, notably its evocative pop songs, and no doubt deserves to be in every collection.

Graffiti Bridge 🎵🎵🎵

1990, Paisley Park Records; from the movie *Graffiti Bridge*, 1990.

Album Notes: *Songs*: Prince; *Orchestral Arrangements*: Clare Fischer; *Featured Performers*: Morris Day, Sheila E. (drums), Boni Soyer (organ), Candy Dulfer, Eric Leeds (saxophone), Atlanta Bliss (trumpet), Joseph Fiddler (keyboards); *Album Producer*: Prince; *Engineers*: Michael Koppelman, Dave Friedlander, Tom Garneau, Remi Jiya, Keith Cohen.

Selections: 1 Can't Stop This Feeling I Got (4:24); 2 New Power Generation (3:39); 3 Release It (Prince/L. Seacer, Jr.) (3:54) *The Time*; 4 The Question Of U (4:00); 5 Elephants And Flowers (3:54); 6 Round And Round (3:55) *Tevin Campbell*; 7 We Can Funk (Prince/G. Clinton) (5:28) *George Clinton, Prince*; 8 Joy In Repetition (4:53); 9 Love Machine (Prince/L. Seacer, Jr./M. Day) (3:34) *Morris Day, Elisa, The Time*; 10 Tick... Tick... Bang (3:30); 11 Shake! (4:01) *The Time*; 12 Thieves In The Temple (3:20); 13 The Latest Fashion (4:02) *The Time, Prince*; 14 Melody Cool (3:39) *Mavis Staples*; 15 Still Would Stand All Time (5:23); 16 Graffiti Bridge (3:51) *Mavis Staples, Tevin Campbell*;

17 New Power Generation, Part II (2:57) *Mavis Staples, Tevin Campbell, T.C. Ellis, Robin Power.*

Review: With the film career of the artist formerly known as Prince now taking a well-deserved vacation, we can acknowledge that the best way to enjoy his movies is to play the soundtrack recordings instead. Case in point: this filmed "sequel" to *Purple Rain* comes within a couple of lively production numbers of being wholly forgettable, and yet the soundtrack CD finds the Prince "Ur-groove" in the very first track and never lets it go. The result is a party album hot enough to help you forget the money you spent on the movie ticket. Prince regulars Morris Day and The Time pitch in, as do guest vocalists including Mavis Staples and George Clinton.

Marc Kirkeby

Grand Canyon 🎵🎵🎵🎵

1991, RCA Records; from the movie *Grand Canyon*, 20th Century-Fox, 1991.

Album Notes: *Music:* James Newton Howard; *Orchestrations:* James Newton Howard, Brad Dechter, Chris Boardman; Orchestra conducted by Marty Paloh; *Featured Musicians:* Dean Parks, Davey Johnstone, Michael Landau, Jude Cole (guitars), John Robinson (drums), Michael Fisher (percussion), Gayle Levant (harp), James Newton Howard, Michael Lang (piano), Chuck Domanico (acoustic bass), Michael Boddicker, James Newton Howard (synth programming), Kirk Whalum, Larry Williams (saxophone); *Album Producers:* James Newton Howard, Michael Mason; *Engineer:* John Richards, Brian Reeves; *Assistant Engineers:* Sue MacLean, Charlie Paakkari, Tom Hardisty, Brandon Harris, John Chamberlin.

Selections: 1 Main Titles (3:36); 2 Claire Returns The Baby (1:11); 3 My Sister Lives Around Here/Those Rocks (1:59); 4 Bloodstain (2:05); 5 The Baby (2:48); 6 Don't Work Late (:52); 7 Mack's Flashback (1:22); 8 Don't Want Out (6:44); 9 Searching For A Heart (W. Zevon) (4:16) *Warren Zevon;* 10 Mack And Claire's Dream (5:23); 11 Dee In Brentwood (:48); 12 Otis Runs (3:53); 13 You White? (1:27); 14 Keep The Baby (1:34); 15 Doesn't Matter (:45); 16 Grand Canyon Fanfare/End Titles (4:10).

Review: An emotionally moving, superior effort by James Newton Howard that balances the perceptions of life in modern day Los Angeles, capturing the fears and hopes of those who struggle to survive in the sometimes oppressive, sometimes cold world of the inner city. Although an orchestra is used over the entire score, Howard often primarily utilizes guitars, percussion and/or synthesizers to keep the scope small and personal. The people are the core of this story, the city only the locale. At times, a chorus passes through, personifying our daydreams of a brighter future. The music deftly alternates through several changes in musical

style. Each represents the personal stories of the film's main characters, the privileged upper middle class couple who find themselves growing apart, and those trapped at the bottom in East L.A., struggling to hold onto their dignity and self respect. As their lives converge, each group becomes a source of strength for the other, and Howard melds their themes together, ultimately culminating with the exuberant "Grand Canyon Fanfare," the score's only large scale orchestral cue. Warren Zevon's song "Searching for a Heart," completely appropriate to the mood, is well placed within the album, breaking the score into two suites.

David Hirsch

Grand Slam 🎵

1989, Grudge Records; from the movie *Grand Slam*, 1989.

Album Notes: *Music:* Bill Conti; Orchestra conducted by Bill Conti; *Album Producer:* Bill Conti.

Selections: 1 Grand Slam (B. Conti/M. Mueller) (3:16) *Little Richard;* 2 Home Run Jam (2:49); 3 Dreams (B. Conti/B. Henry) (3:42) *Roberta Flack;* 4 New Born Child (B. Conti/B. Henry) (4:11) *Ashford & Simpson;* 5 Beverly Glen Cop (4:28); 6 You Don't Scare Me (N. Diamond/P. Cook) (3:07) *Linda Williams;* 7 Rockabilly Baseball (3:00); 8 We're Winning (I. Hayes) (5:15) *Isaac Hayes;* 9 Dreams (3:59).

Review: Yet another baseball film, in which Bill Conti's contribution is reduced to a scant four cues. In this case, it really doesn't matter, because Conti, a composer whose career started on a high note but who has not sustained the hopes he nurtured at the time, uses his score to develop dry ideas that go nowhere. Driven by an electronic drum that sounds too dry and too robotic, his cues have all the excitement of a wet rag, with the music in search of an attractive melodic hook that never materializes. The rest of the selections consists of very conventional vocals, with Roberta Flack faring the best with her sensitive performance on "Dreams," and Little Richard the worse with his abrasive reading of the line "Ain't nothin' like a grand slam to make you feel like a real man..." Forget it!

The Great Caruso 🎵🎵

1989, RCA Victor; from the movie *The Great Caruso*, M-G-M, 1951.

Album Notes: *tracks 1-8:* The RCA Victor Orchestra, conducted by Constantine Callinicos; *tracks 9-20:* Orchestra conducted by Paul Baron; *Album Producer:* Nathaniel S. Johnson; *Engineer:* David Satz.

Selections: *RIGOLETTO (G. VERDI):* 1 Questa o quella (1:45); 2 La donna e mobile (2:02); 3 Parmi veder le lagrime (4:37);

TOSCA (G. PUCCINI): 4 Recondita armonia (2:41); 5 E lucevan le stelle (3:03);

L'ELISIR D'AMORE (G. DONIZETTI): 6 Una furtiva lagrima (4:12);

LA GIOCONDA (A. PONCHIELLI): 7 Cielo e mar (3:59);

PAGLIACCI (R. LEONCAVALLO): 8 Vesti la giunna (3:34); 9 Vieni sul mar (anon.) (2:26); 10 Senza nisciuno (DeCurtis/Barbieri) (2:47); 11 Musica proibita (Gastaldon) (3:16); 12 Vaghissima sembianza (Donaudy) (2:54); 13 Serenata (Caruso/Bracco) (3:49); 14 Lolita (Buzzi/Peccia) (3:19); 15 Luna d'estate (Tosti) (2:18); 16 L'alba separa dalla luce l'ombra (D'Annunzio/Tosti) (3:04); 17 Pour un baiser (Doncieux/Tosti) (2:15); 18 La mia canzone (Cimmino/ Tosti) (3:12); 19 Ideale (Errico/Tosti) (3:09); 20 Santa Lucia (Palardi) (2:40).

Review: At the height of his career, Mario Lanza starred as Enrico Caruso in a highly fictional account of the great singer's life made in Hollywood. In the film, Lanza sang several operatic tunes popularized by Caruso, including the eight selections that were eventually released as the film's "soundtrack" album. Eight years later, he recorded additional songs Caruso had either created or covered in his time, all of them from a more popular source. Film fans will notice that three of these were orchestrated by a young arranger named Ennio Morricone. Otherwise, this set is strictly for devotes.

The Great Escape 🎬🎬🎬🎬
1992, Intrada Records; from the movie *The Great Escape*, United Artists, 1964.

Album Notes: *Music:* Elmer Bernstein; *Orchestrations:* Leo Shuken, Jack Hayes; *Music Editor:* Leo Carruth; Orchestra conducted by Elmer Bernstein; *Album Producer:* Douglass Fake; *Engineer:* Joe Tarantino.

Selections: 1 Main Title (2:10); 2 Premature Plans (2:07); 3 Cooler And Mole (2:26); 4 Blythe (2:11); 5 Discovery (2:54); 6 Various Troubles (2:40); 7 On The Road (2:54); 8 Betrayal (2:05); 9 Hendley's Risk (2:24); 10 Road's End (2:00); 11 More Action (1:57); 12 The Chase (2:48); 13 Finale (3:15).

Review: Taken from the original 1963 master tapes, the CD version contains admirable sound quality with minimal and barely noticeable hiss and distortion. The music itself is outstanding, built around a variety of themes representing the various characters who people this ultimate World War II POW film. The main theme, a catchy march for wind instruments over trombones and tuba, sustained by a counter melody for violins over militaristic percussion, evokes the Concentration Camp prisoners and their spirit of resistance against their captors. A generic cue, "On the Road," marked by eerie wood-

wind tones over gentle harp plucks and quietly rising brass chords, represents the mystery and danger beyond the camp's barbed-wire fences. The final theme for freedom is developed into a grand and glorious melody evoking a sense of quiet victory while retaining a sense of sorrow for those lost and left behind. Brassy punches bridge this and the main theme, which closes out the score. An excellent military score and one of Bernstein's best which is very well preserved on CD.
Randall D. Larson

The Great Muppet Caper
🎬🎬🎬▷
1995, Jim Henson Records; from the animated feature *The Great Muppet Caper*, Jim Henson Film, 1995.

Album Notes: *Music:* Joe Raposo; *Orchestrations:* Joe Raposo, Jim Tyler, Richard Lieb; *Music Editor:* Mike Clifford; Orchestra conducted by Joe Raposo, Marcus Dods; *Cast:* Jim Henson (Kermit The Frog, Dr. Teeth, Rowlf, Swedish Chef, Waldorf), Frank Oz (Fozzie Bear, Miss Piggy, Animal, Sam The Eagle), Jerry Nelson (Floyd, Pops, Robin The Frog), Richard Hunt (Scooter, Sweetums, Statler, Janice, Beaker), Dave Goelz (The Great Gonzo, Zoot, Dr. Bunsen Honeydew), Steve Whitmire (Rizzo The Rat, Lips); *Album Producer:* Joe Raposo; *Engineer:* John Richards.

Selections: 1 The Main Title (2:49); 2 Hey, A Movie! (2:42) *Jim Henson, Frank Oz, Dave Goelz;* 3 The Big Red Bus (1:26); 4 Happiness Hotel (3:05) Cast; 5 Lady Holiday (1:12); 6 Steppin' Out With A Star (2:31) *Jim Henson, Frank Oz, Dave Goelz;* 7 The Apartment (:53); 8 Night Life (2:57) *Jim Henson;* 9 The First Time It Happens (4:12) *Jim Henson, Frank Oz;* 10 Couldn't We Ride (3:07) *Jim Henson, Frank Oz;* 11 Piggy's Fantasy (3:58) Cast; 12 The Great Muppet Caper: The Heist/The Muppet Fight Song/ Muppets To The Rescue (3:48) Cast; 13 Homeward Bound (:52); 14 Finale: Hey A Movie! (1:30) Cast; 15 The First Time It Happens (reprise)(1:37) *Jim Henson, Frank Oz.*

Review: Okay, The Muppets are cute! And Joe Rapposo, for many years their musical director, knew better than any other composer how to express in his songs their different personalities and translate the flavor of their antics. But nowhere was this more apparent than in this, their first big screen effort, which saw the whole gang—Kermit, Fozzie, Miss Piggy, Dr. Teeth and the Electric Mayhem—do what they do best, entertain us. Along the way, they performed some entertaining numbers, all found on this sparkling album, most notably "Rainbow Connection," the bouncy "Movin' Right Along," or "I Hope That Somethin' Better Comes Along," Kermit and Rowlf's sad realization that they can't live without a mate. A short (32 minutes) but entertaining album.

The Great White Hype ♫♫♭

1996, Epic Soundtrax; from the movie *The Great White Hype*, 20th Century-Fox, 1996.

Album Notes: *Song Producers:* D.J. U-Neek, Studio Tone, 4th Disciple, Rza, Jocko & Ski, P.M. Dawn, Doug Rasheed, Denzil Foster & Thomas McElroy, Marcus Miller, Mike E. Clark & ICP; *Soundtrack Executive Producer:* Reginald Hudlin.

Selections: 1 Movin' On (A. Lennox/D. Stewart/D.J. U-Neek/NYT Owl)(4:12) *D.J. U-Neek, NYT Owl*; 2 Baller's Lady (P. Broussard/K. Irving/M. Whitman/E. Stevens/V. Webb)(3:42) *Passion, E-40*; 3 Shoot 'Em Up (D.J. U-Neek/Bone Thugs-n-Harmony)(5:18) *Bone Thugs-N-Harmony*; 4 It's Alright With You (D. Hill, L. Hawkins)(3:35) *Cappadonna*; 5 Who's The Champion (R. Diggs, Jr./D. Coles)(3:43) *Ghostface Killer, Rza*; 6 Coolie High (A. Roberts/A. Willis/S. Wallace/S. Wilds)(4:00) *Camp Lo*; 7 Running Song (A. Smith/A. Cordes/C. McIntosh/J. Eugene/S. Nichol)(4:25) *Ambersunshower*; 8 Knocked Nekked (From The Waits Down)(D. Rasheed/J. Foxx/R.R. Moore)(4:36) *Jamie Foxx & Dolemite*; 9 We Got It (T. McElroy/D. Foster)(3:58) *Premier*; 10 I've Got You Under My Skin (C. Porter)(3:58) *Lou Rawls, Biz Markie*; 11 Bring The Pain (C. Smith/R. Diggs, Jr.)(3:18) *Method Man*; 12 And I Love You (M. Miller/D. Ward)(4:39) *Marcus Miller*; 13 Chicken Huntin' (Slaughterhouse No Blood Radio Mix)(ICP/M. Clark/D. Greenburg/H. Dodd/M. Niles)(3:43) *Insane Clown Posse*.

Review: The dichotomy between the film and the soundtrack album is that one is a spoof of urban, innercity life and the world of boxing, while the other almost begs to be taken at face value. Combining performances by East Coast and West Coast hip hop artists, the album only begins to echo the film's irreverent style when Lou Rawls and Biz Markie team for a version of "I've Got You Under My Skin" Cole Porter would never have dreamed of, or when Jamie Foxx shares the spotlight with Dolemite on "Knocked Nekked (From the Waist Down)." But other than those, the tracks in the album don't seem to have the right flair.

Green Card ♫♫♫♫

1991, Varese-Sarabande Records; from the movie *Green Card*, Touchstone Pictures, 1991.

Album Notes: *Music:* Hans Zimmer; *Featured Musicians:* Hans Zimmer (synthesizers), Ian Lees (bass); *Album Producer:* Hans Zimmer; *Engineers:* Brendan Morley, Paul Grant.

Selections: 1 Subway Drums (L. Wright)(1:29) *Larry Wright*; 2 Instinct (3:33); 3 Restless Elephants (2:55); 4 Cafe Afrika (2:59); 5 Greenhouse (3:15); 6 Moonlight (1:24); 7 9 a.m. Central Park (1:48); 8 Adagio from the Clarinet Concerto in A Major (W.A. Mozart)(8:38) *Richard Stolzman, The English Chamber Orchestra*; 9 Silence (4:38); 10 Instinct II (3:10);— 11 Asking You (1:45); 12 Pour Bronte (6:19); 13 Eyes On The Prize (H. Stewart)(3:04) *The Emmaus Group Singers*.

Review: Hans Zimmer has scored this urban romance as if it were a jungle picture. And appropriately so. Emerging out of an urban-percussion composition by Larry Wright, Zimmer's score for *Green Card* is alternately exotic, toe-tapping, and highly romantic. His opening cue is an evocative blend of voice, synth, and percussion, suggesting the urban jungle and its primitive roots, as multi-layered and compelling as any of Zimmer's thickly-orchestrated compositions. His main theme is a catchy, rhythmic motif for reedy synth and heavy percussion. Synth-woodwind and percussion, including what sounds like synth-steel drum, abound in the instrumentation—an unusual style for a romantic comedy (the musical style is as much director Peter Weir's as it is Zimmer's, according to the composer), but one that adds an engaging quality to the music on film as well as on CD. A romantic piano theme rises above the urban jungle music, signifying the awakening love of the main characters that similarly rises above events they are wrapped up in. Also included on the disc is a Mozart Clarinet Concerto, heard in the film, and a closing pop song.

Randall Larson

Gremlins

Gremlins ♫♫♫♫

1993, Geffen Records; from the movie *Gremlins*, Warner Bros., 1984.

Album Notes: *Music:* Jerry Goldsmith; Orchestra conducted by Jerry Goldsmith; *Album Producer:* Jerry Goldsmith; *Engineer:* Bruce Botnick.

Selections: 1 Gremlins... Mega Madness (M. Sembello/M. Hudson/D. Freeman)(3:50) *Michael Sembello*; 2 Make It Shine (M. Ross)(4:10) *Quarterflash*; 3 Out Out (P. Gabriel)(7:00) *Peter Gabriel*; 4 The Gift (4:51); 5 Gizmo (4:09); 6 Mrs. Deagle (2:50); 7 The Gremlin Rad (4:03).

Review: Considering how wonderful Jerry Goldsmith's score for the film is, it seems a real shame that the powers-that-be at Geffen Records chose to include only 15 minutes of his music in this album, on which the playing time is already inordinately short by usual standards. The cues, all four of them, placed at

"Jazz was my first true love in terms of a music I had discovered on my own. I wanted to learn it, study it and do it."

Mark Isham
(The Mark Isham Web Site)

the end of the album, denote the wonderfully whimsical tones adopted by the composer to depict the invasion of an entire city by a colony of furry little things that have an uncanny ability to reproduce once they are exposed to water or any sort of food past the witching midnight hour. "The Gremlin Rag," alone, is an outstanding piece of music, delightful and totally enjoyable. While these selections give an idea of the score Goldsmith created for the film, the album leaves one wanting for more. As for the pop selections, they do seem like a lot of padding.

Gremlins 2: The New Batch 𝄢𝄢ᵛ

1990, Varese-Sarabande; from the movie *Gremlins 2: The New Batch*, Warner Bros., 1990.

Album Notes: *Music*: Jerry Goldsmith; *Orchestrations*: Arthur Morton; *Music Editor*: Ken Hall; Orchestra conducted by Jerry Goldsmith; *Album Producer*: Jerry Goldsmith; *Engineer*: Bruce Botnick.

Selections: 1 Just You Wait (2:11); 2 Gizmo Escapes (3:43); 3 Leaky Faucet (3:45); 4 Cute... (1:58); 5 Pot Luck (3:00); 6 The Visitors (3:31); 7 Teenage Mutant Gremlins (3:23); 8 Keep It Quiet (3:10); 9 No Rats (2:23); 10 Gremlin Pudding (2:13); 11 New Trends (3:39); 12 Gremlin Credits (4:52).

Review: Goldsmith returned to Gremlins territory for this warm-hearted sequel that jettisoned the horror elements in favor of gentle satire, with his score following director Joe Dante's lead with an eclectic brew of electronic tomfoolery, low-key jazz and noble-sounding underscoring for the aspirations of the benevolent Donald Trump-like entrepreneur John Glover. The result is some amusing moments and a particularly lovely denouement, but overall this one falls into a group of pretty unmemorable comedy scores Goldsmith produced in the early '90s.

Jeff Bond

The Grifters 𝄢𝄢𝄢𝄢

1990, Varese-Sarabande; from the movie *The Grifters*, Miramax Pictures, 1990

Album Notes: *Music*: Elmer Bernstein; Orchestra conducted by Elmer Bernstein; *Album Producer*: Cynthia Millar; *Engineer*: Dick Lewzey.

Selections: 1 The City (3:32); 2 The Racetrack (1:46); 3 Roy In Trouble (1:23); 4 School For Grifters (2:48); 5 To The Hospital (3:56); 6 Troubadour Race (2:24); 7 Lilly's Argument (1:45); 8 Bobo (5:01); 9 Carhumba (2:22); 10 Roy Gambles (C. Millar)(1:54); 11 Madness (2:11); 12 Myra's Blues (1:08); 13 Roy And Lilly (C. Millar)(2:20); 14 Chase (2:27); 15 Fright And Flight (4:04); 16 Endings (4:42); 17 Credits (3:30); 18 Do Ya, Do Ya Love Me? (E.A. Bernstein/P. Theodore)(3:17) *Dream World*.

Review: Including a jaunty little tune which pervades the whole score, *The Grifters* ranks among Elmer Bernstein's top efforts and one of his best scores in recent years. Based on a novel by Jim Thompson about a group of small-time con artists and how everyone in the small group cheats on everyone else, the film was permeated with a blend of mordant humor and brooding darkness that gives the narrative a teasing, elusive quality and stands out as one of the most telling themes developed by the composer. These elements found an echo in the score, essentially written for a small chamber ensemble of woodwinds and brass, with electronic sounds designed by Cynthia Millar. In turns humorously eccentric, darkly original, and solidly anchored around the five-note motif in its main theme, the score comes across as an enticing piece of music, with amusing elements and thoughtful interpolations.

Grosse Pointe Blank 𝄢𝄢𝄢𝄢

1997, London Records; from the *Grosse Pointe Blank*, Hollywood Pictures, 1997.

Album Notes: *Song Producers*: Brian Ritchie, Gordon Gano, Tom Grimley, Guy Stevens, Bob Sargeant, Queen, David Bowie, Johnny Nash, Mike Clink & Guns 'N Roses, Steve Berlin, Matt Wallace, Faith No More, Neville Staple, Tom Lowry, Pete Wilson, The Jam, The Clash, K.C. Porter, Chris Thomas, Brian Ritchie; *Executive Producers*: Kathy Nelson, Bill Green.

Selections: 1 Blister In The Sun (G. Gano) (2:07) *Violent Femmes*; 2 Rudie Can't Fail (J. Strummer/M. Jones) (3:29) *The Clash*; 3 Mirror In The Bathroom (The English Beat) (3:06) *The English Beat*; 4 Under Pressure (D. Bowie/F. Mercury/R. Taylor/J. Deacon/B. May) (4:02) *David Bowie, Queen*; 5 I Can See Clearly Now (J. Nash) (2:44) *Johnny Nash*; 6 Live And Let Die (P. McCartney) (3:02) *Guns 'N Roses*; 7 We Care A Lot (Faith No More) (4:02) *Faith No More*; 8 Pressure Drop (T. Hibbert) (4:18) *The Specials*; 9 Absolute Beginners (P. Weller) (2:49) *The Jam*;

10 Armagideon Time (C. Dodd/W. Williams) (3:50) *The Clash*;
11 El Matador (F. Ciancianulo) (4:33) *Los Fabulosos Cadillacs*;
12 Let My Love Open The Door (P. Townshend) (4:56) *Pete Townshend*; 13 Blister 2000 (G. Gano) (2:57) *Violent Femmes*.

Review: A good combination of oldies and new stuff, this soundtrack album serves up a refreshing line-up of great rockers who aren't often found together on the same album. Bookended by two selections by Violent Femmes, the album's best moments include The Clash's "Rudie Can't Fail" and "Armagideon Time," Guns 'N Roses's cover version of Paul McCartney's "Live and Let Die," and The Jam's take on "Absolute Beginners." David Bowie and Queen's collaboration on "Under Pressure" is always nice to have around, as is Pete Townshend's "Let My Love Open The Door." A pleasant surprise is Los Fabulosos Cadillacs, a rarely heard (at least in this country) Argentinian group whose energetic "El Matador" is alone worth a visit.

Groundhog Day ♫♫♫▷

1993, Epic Soundtrax; from the movie *Groundhog Day*, Columbia Pictures, 1993.

Album Notes: *Music*: George Fenton; *Orchestrations*: Jeff Atmajian; *Music Editor*: Sally Boldt; Orchestra conducted by George Fenton; *Featured Musician*: Dan Higgins (saxophone); *Album Producer*: George Fenton; *Engineer*: John Richards.

Selections: 1 Weatherman (G. Fenton/H. Ramis) (4:18) *Delbert McClinton*; 2 Clouds (1:10); 3 I Got You Babe (S. Bono) (3:12) *Sonny & Cher*; 4 Quartet No. 1 in D: The Groundhog (2:08) *Sheldon Sanov, Pam Goldsmith, Bruce Dukov, Dennis Karmayzn*; 5 Take Me Round Again (3:06) *Susie Stevens*; 6 Drunks (2:17); 7 Pennsylvania Polka (L. Lee/Z. Manners) (2:24) *Frankie Yankovic*; 8 You Like Boats But Not The Ocean (1:41); 9 Phil Getz The Girl (3:31) *Dan Higgins*; 10 Phil Steals The Money (1:21); 11 You Don't Know Me (E. Arnold/C. Walker) (4:12) *Ottmar Liebert, Luna Negra*; 12 The Kidnap And The Quarry (2:50); 13 Sometimes People Just Die (1:39); 14 Eighteenth Variation from Rapsodie On A Theme Of Paganini (S. Rachmaninoff) (3:34) *Elizabeth Buccheri*; 15 Medley: Phil's Piano Solo (T. Fryer)/Eighteenth Variation from Rapsodie On A Theme Of Paganini (S. Rachmaninoff) (1:49) *Terry Fryer*; 16 The Ice Sculpture (2:05); 17 A New Day (1:26); 18 Almost Like Being In Love (F. Loewe/A.J. Lerner) (1:52) *Nat King Cole*.

Review: The soundtrack to this zany picture starring Bill Murray is itself deliciously insane, with its blend of a pseudo baroque quartet piece named for the film title next to Sonny and Cher warbling their hit "I Got You Babe." The story of an egotistical weatherman who has keeps living the same day over and over and over, the film's inspired lunacy translated itself into an album that also includes several pop tunes including "Almost Like Being in Love," by Nat King Cole, and "Pennsylvania Polka," played by Frankie Yankovic in another odd pairing. George Fenton contributes some eclectic themes like "Clouds," "Drunks," "The Kidnap and the Quarry," among other, equally welcome moments. Delightfully entertaining is the word.

Grumpier Old Men ♫♫

1995, TVT Records; from the movie *Grumpier Old Men*, Warner Bros., 1995.

Album Notes: *Music*: Alan Silvestri; *Orchestrations*: William Ross; *Music Editors*: Bob Badami, Kenneth Karman, Jacqueline Tager; Orchestra conducted by Alan Silvestri; *Engineer*: Dennis Sands.

Selections: 1 (I'll Be Glad When You're Dead) You Rascal You (S. Theard) (3:05) *Louis Armstrong, Louis Jordan*; 2 Hit The Road Jack (P. Mayfield) (3:15) *Buster Poindexter*; 3 That's Amore (J. Brooks/H. Warren)(3:07) *Dean Martin*; 4 Understand Your Man (J. Cash)(2:42) *Johnny Cash*; 5 Venus (R. Leeuwen)(3:00) *Shocking Blue*; 6 Jump In The Line (Shake Senora)(H. Belafonte/R. DeLeon/G. Oller/S. Samuel)(3:42) *Harry Belafonte*; 7 Stayin' Alive (B. Gibb/R. Gibb/M. Gibb)(4:43) *The Bee Gees*; 8 The Chicken Dance (T. Rendell/W. Thomas)(1:06) *Wally Olson Band*; 9 'S Wonderful (G. & I. Gershwin) (1:32) *Les Brown and His Orchestra, Doris Day*; 10 Almost Like Being In Love (F. Loewe/A.J. Lerner)(1:54) *Nat King Cole*; 11 I Hear Bells (Wedding Bells) (T. Love/B. Strong)(2:27) *Del Vikings*; 12 What The Heck (1:01); 13 End Title (3:44).

Review: The constant one-upmanship between two grumpy old friends (Jack Lemmon and Walter Matthau returning to the roles they created in *Grumpy Old Men*) finds its best musical expression in the lively "(I'll Be Glad When You're Dead) You Rascal You," performed by Louis Armstrong and Louis Jordan, the first selection on the album. Unfortunately, the moods in the film are not sustained in this collection of pop tracks, which include Buster Poindexter's derivative rendition of Ray Charles' hit "Hit the Road Jack," Dean Martin's "That's Amore," and Harry Belafonte's exuberant "Jump in the Line (Shake Senora)," already a highlight in the film *Beetlejuice*. Alan Silvestri's score, reduced here to two cues ("What the Heck" and "End Title"), sounds lovely, but who can tell?

Guarding Tess ♫♫♫

1994, Tristar Music; from the movie *Guarding Tess*, Tristar Pictures, 1994.

Album Notes: *Music*: Michael Convertino; *Orchestrations*: John Neufeld, Conrad Pope; *Music Editor*: Ken Wannberg; Orchestra conducted by Richard Kaufman; *Album Engineer*: Dennis Sands.

Selections: 1 Overture (3:13); 2 Patriots (7:53); 3 Golf (3:26); 4 Outsiders (5:22); 5 A Picnic In Winter (2:24); 6 The President Is Arriving (3:45); 7 "Ich gehe, doch rate ich dir" (from Die Entfuehrung aus dem Serail)(W.A. Mozart)(3:46) *Elzbieta Szmyrka, Gunther Missenhardt, Wiener Symphoniker, Bruno Weil;* 8 With You Alone (1:56); 9 Guarding Tess (2:23).

Review: Charming score by Michael Convertino for this comedy film about the war of wills between a former First Lady and her Secret Service bodyguard. As they snipe at each other, the composer hints at their growing bond with a bold arrangement of strings in "Patriots". Conversely, Convertino relies on classical music-inspired arrangements to play up the absurdity of the government's stuffy sense of self importance.

David Hirsch

Guns for San Sebastian

1991, Sony Music Special Products; from the movie *Guns for San Sebastian*, M-G-M, 1968.

See: Hang 'Em High

The Guns of Navarone 🎵🎵🎵🎵

1989, Varese-Sarabande; from the movie *The Guns of Navarone*, Columbia Pictures, 1961.

Album Notes: *Music:* Dimitri Tiomkin; *Lyrics:* Paul Francis Webster; The Sinfonia of London Orchestra, conducted by Dimitri Tiomkin; *CD Producers:* Robert Townson, Tom Null; *Engineer:* Michele Stone.

Selections: 1 Prologue (3:00), narration by James Robertson Justice; 2 The Guns Of Navarone (D. Tiomkin/P.F. Webster)(3:59) *Mitch Miller and the Sing Along Chorus;* 3 Sea Scene / Odyssey Begins (8:48); 4 Climbing The South Cliff (1:43); 5 Anna (1:31); 6 Death Of Young Pappadimos (1:14); 7 Legend Of Navarone(2:21); 8 Yassu (3:41); 9 Preparation For Guns (1:58); 10 Wedding Music (2:15); 11 Mission Accomplished (7:23); 12 The Guns Of Navarone (3:11).

Review: Another blockbuster score by Dimitri Tiomkin, filled with great energy and heroic accents to underline this World War II drama in which Gregory Peck, David Niven and Anthony Quinn single-handedly defeat the entire German army when they destroy huge guns on the island of Navarone, off the coast of Greece, guarding the open sea. The "legend," introduced in a prologue narrated by James Robertson Justice, sets the tone and provides the background to the tale itself, musically illustrated by the composer, in a stirring display of his florid style. Three themes evoke the action, a martial one to convey the war effort, another with a Greek flavor to stress the locale, and a third, a

lyrical theme, to express the beauty and deep emotional impact of the adventure itself. While the score itself is very attractive and makes for an entertaining listening session, you might want to ignore Mitch Miller and the gang's earnest rendition of the inane title song, in which lyrics try to rhyme such unlikely poetic words as "nitroglycerine" and "saboteurs."

Halloween

Halloween 🎵🎵🎵🎵

1985, Varese-Sarabande; from the movie *Halloween*, Compass International, 1985.

Album Notes: *Music:* John Carpenter; *Album Producer:* Tom Null; *Engineers:* Peter Bergren, Alan Howarth.

Selections: 1 Halloween Theme: Main Title (2:55); 2 Laurie's Theme (2:05); 3 Shape Escapes (1:43); 4 Meyer's House (5:35); 5 Michael Kills Judith (3:11); 6 Loomis And Shape's Car (3:32); 7 The Haunted House (3:33); 8 The Shape Lurks (1:35); 9 Laurie Knows (3:02); 10 Better Check The Kids (3:27); 11 The Shape Stalks (3:10).

Review: See *Halloween: The Curse of Michael Myers* entry below.

Halloween: The Curse of Michael Myers 🎵🎵🎵

1995, Varese-Sarabande; from the movie *Halloween: The Curse of Michael Myers*, Miramax Films, 1995.

Album Notes: *Music:* Alan Howarth, John Carpenter; *Album Producer:* Alan Howarth.

Selections: 1 Jamie's Escape (4:04); 2 Birth Ceremony (2:50); 3 You Can't Have The Baby (3:37); 4 Empty Stomach (2:58); 5 Watching Mom (4:23); 6 Kara Returns (3:38); 7 Thorn (4:08); 8 Carnival Festival (4:07); 9 It's Raining Red (2:59); 10 Look Upstairs (6:25); 11 It's His Game (5:56); 12 Maximum Security (3:40); 13 Operating Room (7:56).

Review: While most synthesized horror film scores tend to sound as if they were made up as the performer went along, director John Carpenter uses the limitations of his early synthesizer work to great advantage in *Halloween*. The resulting work is a minimalist creation as relentless as the film's unstoppable killer. Carpenter based his score on three principal themes, the main title with its infectious mix of repetitive piano, rattle, and stomping, the more subtle "creeping" motif, and a desperate, repetitive "stalking" theme. His wise exploitation of the simplicity of the arrangements created both an effective score and entertaining soundtrack album. By avoiding the use of conventional electronic effects, Carpenter's score shows very little dating 20 years later.

Alan Howarth, who worked closely with Carpenter for several years on a variety of scores, took on the *Halloween* series solo in 1988 with the fourth film, *The Return of Michael Myers*. His latest score in the series, 1995's *The Curse of Michael Myers*, still makes good use of the minimalist style established on the first film, but with the use of a battery of state of the art synthesizers, Howarth can now create a score that sounds positively lavish in comparison to Carpenter's. The *Halloween* theme is brought into the '90s with guitars replacing the piano track and Carpenter's old "creeping" motif returns once again. Howarth puts in a good effort with several interesting moments and some synth passages are so well designed that they sound almost acoustical. It can't, however, equal the first film score simply because of sheer nostalgic value.

David Hirsch

Halloween 2 ♪♪♪

1981, Varese-Sarabande Records; from the movie *Halloween 2: The Nightmare Isn't Over!*, Dino de Laurentiis Corp., 1981.

Album Notes: *Music*: John Carpenter, Alan Howarth; *Recording, editing, sequencing, synthesizer programming*: Alan Howarth; *Album Producer*: Alan Howarth; *Engineer*: John Acoca.

Selections: 1 Halloween Theme (4:27); 2 Laurie's Theme (2:50); 3 He Knows Where She Is! (1:07); 4 Laurie And Jimmy (3:03); 5 Still He Kills (Murder Montage)(4:35); 6 The Shape Enters Laurie's Room (1:33); 7 Mrs. Alves (1:43); 8 Flats In The Parking Lot (1:25); 9 Michael's Sister (3:00); 10 The Shape Stalks Again (3:03); 11 In The Operating Room (1:48); 12 Mr. Sandman (P. Ballard)(2:20) *The Chordettes*.

Review: See *Halloween 5* entry below.

Halloween 3: Season of the Witch ♪♪♪

1982, Varese-Sarabande Records; from the movie *Halloween 3: Season of the Witch*, 1982.

Album Notes: *Music*: John Carpenter, Alan Howarth; *Recording, editing, mixing, sequencing, synthesizing programming*: Alan Howarth; *Album Producer*: Alan Howarth.

Selections: 1 Main Title (2:55); 2 Chariots Of Pumpkins (3:24); 3 Drive To Santa Mira (2:29); 4 Starker And Marge (1:53); 5 First Chase (3:09); 6 Robots At The Factory (2:00); 7 Halloween Montage (1:38) *Tommy Lee Wallace*; 8 Hello Grandma (4:53); 9

The Rock (3:25); 10 Challis Escapes (3:25); 11 South Corridor (2:58); 12 Goodbye Ellie (4:09).

Review: See *Halloween 5* entry below.

Halloween 4: The Return of Michael Myers ♪♪♪♪

1988, Varese-Sarabande Records; from the movie *Halloween 4: The Return of Michael Myers*, Trancas International Films, 1988.

Album Notes: *Music*: Alan Howarth; *Album Producer*: Alan Howarth; *Engineer*: Daniel Hersch.

Selections: 1 Halloween 4: The Return (3:17); 2 Jamie's Nightmare (3:14); 3 Garage (2:39); 4 Be Back By 9:30 (1:57); 5 Return Of The Shape (6:50); 6 Schoolhouse (2:34); 7 Power Company (2:52); 8 Police Station (3:15); 9 Downstairs Alone (3:07); 10 Myers' Finale (5:32); 11 Halloween 4 (reprise) (3:16).

Review: See *Halloween 5* entry below.

Halloween 5: The Revenge of Michael Myers ♪♪♪♪

1989, Varese-Sarabande Records; from the movie *Halloween 5: The Revenge of Michael Myers*, Galaxy International, 1989.

Album Notes: *Music*: Alan Howarth; *Song Producers*: Mike Hennessy, Paul Wood, Greg Townley, Pam Neil, Jay Baumgardner, Diggy Mark Chosak; *Album Producer*: Alan Howarth.

Selections: 1 Romeo, Romeo (M. Hennessy/P. Wood) (3:52) *Becca*; 2 Anything For Money (J. Robert) (4:08) *DV8*; 3 Dancin' On Midnight (R. Chadock/D. Churchill Dries) (4:13) *Churchill*; 4 Second Time Around (T. Guzman Sanchez/P. Guzman Sanchez) (3:34) *Rhythm Tribe*; 5 Sporting Woman (Diggy) (2:46) *Diggy Mark Chosak, Eileen Clark*; 6 Halloween 5/The Revenge (4:32); 7 The Shape Also Rises (2:49); 8 The Evil Child Must Die (2:22); 9 First Victim (2:24); 10 A Stranger In The House (3:39); 11 Tower Farm (4:22); 12 Stop The Rage (4:27); 13 Trapped (3:19); 14 The Attic (5:26); 15 Jail Break (2:24); 16 Halloween Finale (3:20).

Review: The saga of Michael Myers has proven a very fruitful and rewarding franchise for John Carpenter, who initiated it, before leaving to others the fun of completing it (or, as it were, adding to it), and who initially scored it (see above), before turning over this task to Alan Howarth. Though Carpenter's original intentions and not-so-subtle effects eventually were diluted with overuse, one must admit that his successors have skillfully adapted his ideas for maximum results.

A tired, uninspired sequel to the 1985 original, *Halloween 2* began where the previous film ended, providing Carpenter with a nifty reprise of "Laurie's Theme," with Myers (now identi-

motion picture soundtracks

fied as The Shape) on the loose, stalking again, and slashing his way through 92 minutes of a tedious horror film. Still, Carpenter's music, complemented by Howarth's contributions, has an edgy, dangerous tone to it ("Still He Kills," "The Shape Stalks Again") that comes across effectively in this minimalist-sounding soundtrack album. The addition of The Chordettes' "Mr. Sandman," at the end, is a refreshing change of pace.

Carpenter and Howarth returned to the same grounds once more with *Halloween 3: Season of the Witch,* using the same precision and creativity to come up with a score that's inventive in its own way, even though it increasingly seems to rely on ideas that might have been rejects from the previous two scores. Some tracks emerge, however, as particularly well conceived ("Drive to Santa Mira," "The Rock," and the crushingly exhilarating "Halloween Montage").

Halloween 4: The Return of Michael Myers marked a significant change of pace in the series, with Myers resuming his initial identity, Donald Pleasence returning as Dr. Loomis, and the script consciously ignoring the events that had occurred in the previous two sequels. New also was the fact that Alan Howarth assumed responsibilities as the sole composer, bringing to the score a flair somewhat different from John Carpenter's, better realized, less minimalist, and more melody-driven, despite the abundance of synthesized sounds. Though built around Carpenter's original theme for the series, Howarth's score proves more lush overall, and more listenable than Carpenter's, if only because of the greater variety it exhibits.

The fifth installment in the series, *The Revenge of Michael Myers* found Howarth taking some more distance from the previous efforts, and building his score around a tingling descending little motif introduced as the main theme to "The Revenge," that recurs at intervals in the electronic texture. Darker than *Halloween 4* ("The Shape Also Rises," a combination of distorted grunts, drum beat and low-toned electronic riffs, also heard in "The Attic," in particularly frightening), but equally effective, the score also marked a progression for Howarth, who introduced some acoustic instruments in the mix. Some pop/rock vocals at the beginning of the album also give a different tone to the recording.

Hamlet

Hamlet ♫♫

1990, Virgin Movie Music; from the movie *Hamlet,* Warner Bros., 1990.

Album Notes: *Music:* Ennio Morricone; *Orchestrations:* Ennio Morricone; Orchestra Unione Musicisti di Roma, conducted by Ennio Morricone; *Featured Soloists:* Fausto Anzelmo (viola),

Carlo Romano (oboe); *Album Producer:* Ennio Morricone; *Engineer:* Sergio Marcotulli; *Assistant Engineer:* Fabio Venturi.

Selections: 1 Hamlet (Version 1)(3:40); 2 The King Is Dead (4:40); 3 Ophelia (Version 1)(3:45); 4 What A Piece Of Work Is Man (1:36); 5 The Prayer (2:02); 6 The Ghost (5:50); 7 The Play (2:02); 8 The Banquet (1:38); 9 Dance For The Queen (2:12); 10 Ophelia (Version 2)(3:00); 11 Hamlet's Madness (3:17); 12 Hamlet (Version 2)(3:00); 13 Simulated Madness (3:06); 14 The Closet (3:24); 15 Second Madness (1:54); 16 To Be Or Not To Be (3:54); 17 Solid Flesh (1:58); 18 The Vaults (1:40)

Review: This oddly focused film version of Shakespeare's great play, with Mel Gibson playing the melancholy Dane to Glenn Close's semi-detached Gertrude and Franco Zeffirelli handling the directorial chores, compelled Ennio Morricone to write a dark, often sullen score which may seem apt for a Shakespearean drama but not for a listening experience. While recognizing the inherent power of the music itself, most of the cues, introduced by a strong, brooding orchestral chord, convey the somberness in the action, with an organ occasionally reinforcing the generally gloomy moods. "The Banquet," a lively tune, is the only exception, while "Dance for the Queen," which would suggest a lilt in the action, translates itself into something even more mournful than Ravel's "Pavane for a Dead Princess."

Hamlet ♫♫♫

1996, Sony Classical; from the movie *Hamlet,* Castle Rock/Columbia Pictures, 1996.

Album Notes: *Music:* Patrick Doyle; *Orchestrations:* Lawrence Ashmore, John Bell; *Music Editor:* Roy Prendergast; Orchestra conducted by Robert Ziegler; *Album Producers:* Patrick Doyle, Maggie Rodford; *Engineer:* Paul Hulme; *Assistant Engineer:* Ben Georgiades.

Selections: 1 In Pace (3:07) *Placido Domingo;* 2 Fanfare (:48); 3 "All that lives must die" (2:40); 4 "To thine own self be true" (3:04); 5 The Ghost (9:55); 6 "Give me the truth" (1:05); 7 "What a piece of work is a man" (1:50); 8 "What players are they" (1:33); 9 "Out out thou strumpet fortune" (3:11); 10 "To be or not to be" (1:53); 11 "I loved you once" (3:27); 12 "Oh, what a noble mind" (2:41); 13 "If once a widow" (3:36); 14 "Now could I drink hot blood" (6:57); 15 "A foolish prating nave" (1:05); 16 "Oh heavy deed" (:56); 17 "Oh here they come" (4:39); 18 "My thoughts be bloody" (2:53); 19 "The doors are broke" (1:20); 20 "And will 'a not come again?" (1:59); 21 "Alas poor Yorick!" (2:49); 22 "Sweets to the sweet, farewell" (4:39); 23 "Give me your pardon, Sir" (1:24); 24

"Part them they are incensed" (1:47); 25 "Goodnight, sweet prince" (3:36); 26 "Go bid the soldiers shoot" (2:52).

Review: The melancholy Dane gets a perky reworking with this energetic, busy score that settles into more of a chamber mode after its broad orchestral opening. It's percussive, occasionally fiery, coiling along under Kenneth Branaugh's impassioned Hamlet... but despite some involving melodies and Doyle's usual dramatic skills this lengthy score never dwells in the memory the way his groundbreaking *Henry V* or even his sumptuous *Much Ado About Nothing* overture still does. This is much more of an incidental score than the through-composed effort of *Henry V,* dependent on the counter-rhythms of dialogue for many of its effects. Only in lengthier cues like "The Ghost" and "Sweets to the sweet — farewell" does Doyle get the opportunity to sustain and build on the melodies he creates, although the brief sword-fight cue ("Part them they are incensed!") offers some agile, taut string writing. The most noticeable misstep is the surprise appearance by Placido Domingo belting out an opening song, "In Pace," which seems to have little relationship to the score or the film.

Jeff Bond

The Hand that Rocks the Cradle ♪♪♪◦

1993, Hollywood Records; from the movie *The Hand that Rocks the Cradle,* Hollywood Pictures, 1993.

Album Notes: *Music*: Graeme Revell; *Orchestrations*: Graeme Revell, Tim Simonec; *Music Editor*: Dick Bernstein; Orchestra conducted by Tim Simonec; *Album Producer*: Graeme Revell; *Engineers*: Dennis Sands, Dan Wallin.

Selections: 1 Main Title (The Home)(2:52); 2 Poor Wand'ring One (W. Gilbert/A. Sullivan)(2:55) *The D'Oyly Carte Opera Company*; 3 The Miscarriage (2:19); 4 Peyton And Baby Joey (1:30); 5 Solomon (3:15); 6 Oh Dry The Glist'ning Tear (W. Gilbert/A. Sullivan)(3:10) *The D'Oyly Carte Opera Company*; 7 Marlene's Discovery (3:21); 8 The Greenhouse Effect (2:55); 9 Claire Investigates (3:53); 10 You're Not My Mommy (4:55); 11 Solomon's Baby (2:17); 12 End Credit Medley (2:20); 13 One Family Again (2:52).

Review: Graeme Revell's oddly compelling score belies the subtly horrifying moods in this thriller, about a babysitter whose increasingly threatening presence brings havoc in the life of a Seattle family. Progressing with the action, the cues take on a darker edge, though without losing their overall melodic appeal ("Marlene's Discovery," "Claire Investigates"), in a skillfull display of beautifully understated musical

ideas to create a subliminal effect that subtly underlines the tension in the film itself. Even without the impact of the screen images, the music retains its flavor, and in fact acquires a sheen that's most revelatory and endearing.

A Handful of Dust ♪♪♪◦

1988, DRG Records; from the movie *A Handful of Dust,* Stagescreen Productions, 1988.

Album Notes: *Music*: George Fenton; *Orchestrations*: George Fenton, John Warren; Orchestra conducted by George Fenton; *Featured Musicians*: Mike Taylor, Tony Hinnigan (Pan pipes/kenas), Forbes Henderson (charango); *Album Producer*: George Fenton; *Engineers*: Keith Grant, Michael Jarratt.

Selections: 1 A Handful Of Dust Main Title (3:45); 2 Meeting Mr. Beaver (2:45); 3 Cafe de Paris (1:10); 4 Learning To Be Nicer (1:50); 5 Moving Away, Part 1 (2:40); 6 A Course In Economics? (3:35); 7 Weekend Episodes (3:45); 8 Talking Pipes (1:20); 9 A New Outlook (2:05); 10 Moving Away, Part 2 (Adagio) (3:30); 11 The Falls (2:15); 12 Trying To Please (1:55); 13 Pivari Party/A Time Of Waiting (2:45); 14 Memorial (End Credits)(6:35).

Review: Based on a novel by Evelyn Waugh, *A Handful of Dust* translates into a somewhat slight story about some British aristocrats with little care on their mind other than to live the idle, golden existence to which they feel entitled. As befits this kind of screenplay, the moods were kept light, and even if such unspeakable things as an accidental killing and a divorce spiced it up, it was all jolly good and perfectly swell, an overall feeling which George Fenton's score wrapped with elegant orchestral swirls. The 1930s provided the composer with another definite time period to anchor some of his cues, though the overall tone of his score is kept charmingly low-key and lightly melodic. Listen to the woop-dee-doo tone of "Cafe de Paris," or the equally innocuous "Learning to be Nicer," both of which denote in musical terms an attitude that we have come to accept from the wealthy but slight-headed gentry.

The Handmaid's Tale ♪

1990, GNP Crescendo; from the movie *The Handmaid's Tale,* Cinecom, 1990.

Album Notes: *Music*: Ryuichi Sakamoto; *Music Editors*: Robin Clarke, Chris Brooks, Jim Harrison; *Album Producer*: Ryuichi Sakamoto; *Engineer*: Fernando Kral.

Selections: 1 Overture/Snow/Prison Camp/On The Bus/Old Hundredth (Praise God From Whom All Blessings Flow)(L. Bourgeois)/Nocturno/Moira's Hand/Red Veil/Kate/Rape And Rage/The Kiss/Pollution In City/Moira Escapes/ Rape/Shall We Gather By The River (R. Lowry)(20:51); 2 Love In Nick's

motion picture soundtracks

Room/ Amazing Grace (J. Newton) My Daughter Is Alive/Car Bomb/ Travesty/Kate And Moira/Hanging/Particicution/Finding The Knife/Waiting For Murder/Killing Commander/Mayday/Old Hundredth (Praise God From Whom All Blessings Flow)(L. Bourgeois)(20:28).

Review: It is without a doubt a pretty bad idea to amass 27, mostly short, cues into just two overlong 20 minute tracks. The resulting "orchestral suite" approach fails to create any natural sounding flow and yields a rather spotty, unfulfilling mix of musical styles from the Ryuichi Sakamoto score. The lack of indexing especially makes it impossible to follow which of the individual cues listed in mass on the inlay card you are listening to. The album is not without some good points, though they are few and far between. Some of the more poignant moments convey a hint that they might have splendid melodies ("Love in Nick's Room"), but they suffer greatly from some heavy-handed synthesizer work. Generally, there are an awful lot of simplistic musical effects filling up most of the time, from drum tracks to primitive tone build-ups. More often it's vaguely reminiscent of a low budget horror film score.

David Hirsch

Hang 'Em High/Guns for San Sebastian 🦴🦴🦴🦴

1991, Sony Music Special Products; from the movies *Hang 'Em High*, United Artists, 1968; and *Guns for San Sebastian*, M-G-M, 1968.

Album Notes: *Hang ' Em High: Music:* Dominic Frontiere; Orchestra conducted by Dominic Frontiere; *Guns for San Sebastian: Music:* Ennio Morricone; Orchestra conducted by Ennio Morricone; *CD Producer:* Dan Rivard; *CD Engineer:* Debra Parkinson.

Selections: *HANG 'EM HIGH:* 1 Hang 'Em High (2:57); 2 Rachel (Love Theme) (3:02); 3 Tumbleweed Wagon (4:13); 4 Bordello (1:40); 5 I'll Get 'Em Myself (3:00); 6 Rachel (reprise)(2:37); 7 Hang 'Em High (reprise)(2:04); 8 It's No Deal (3:26); 9 They Took Me (3:01); 10 Hang 'Em High (2:58);

KELLY'S HEROES (L. SCHIFRIN): 11 Quick Draw Kelly (3:12);

GUNS FOR SAN SEBASTIAN: 12 The Overture (3:43); 13 The Chase (1:53); 14 The Long Trek (5:10); 15 Love Theme (2:54); 16 Music At The Governor's Dinner (1:51); 17 The White Stallion (1:33); 18 Love Theme (reprise)(2:52); 19 Building The Dam (1:30); 20 The Attack (1:57); 21 The Burning Village (2:35); 22 The Villagers Prepare To Blow Up The Dam (1:28); 23 Teclo's Death (1:23); 24 End Title (4:01).

Review: Perhaps because *Hang ' Em High* starred Clint Eastwood in a role that recalled his portrayal as the Man-With-No-

Name in several spaghetti westerns scored by Ennio Morricone, and *Guns for San Sebastian* had a score by Morricone, it might have seemed like a judicious idea to pair these soundtracks together on one CD. Wrong. Not only are Dominic Frontiere and Morricone miles apart as composers, but the former's derivative contribution, which aims to faintly evoke the latter's, simply doesn't begin to make the sort of impression Morricone's music for Sergio Leone achieved.

If you really are curious to hear a score which Morricone could have written much more eloquently, spend some time with *Hang ' Em High,* then move on to the real thing with *Guns for San Sebastian,* another terrific effort by the master himself. The film, made in Mexico, is a standard story about the legendary mid-18th century rebel Leon Alastray (Anthony Quinn), and his fight against marauding Yaqui Indians, led by Charles Bronson. There is no mistaking the accents or the style in this score, with choral vocals and guitar motifs adding their voice to the relentless orchestral textures created by the composer. Several cues attract particularly here, notably "The Chase," with its percolating riff, the "Love Theme," appropriately lyrical, "Building The Dam," with its evocative guitar lines, and the taut "The Burning Village," which starts on a percussive orchestral line that dissolves into a romantic guitar theme.

Indicative of the total lack of understanding for the music or general insensitivity that presided over the sequencing of this album, a track from *Kelly's Heroes,* composed by Lalo Schifrin, has been inserted for no apparent reason between *Hang ' Em High* and *The Guns for San Sebastian.* The rating, incidentally, applies only to the Morricone score.

Hannah and Her Sisters 🦴🦴🦴▷

1987, MCA Records; from the movie *Hannah and Her Sisters*, Orion Pictures, 1987.

Album Notes: *Album assembled by:* Gene Wooley.

Selections: 1 You Made Me Love You (J. McCarthy/J. Monaco)(3:25) *Harry James and His Orchestra*; 2 I've Heard That Song Before (S. Cahn/J. Styne) (2:50) *Harry James and His Orchestra*; 3 Bewitched (R. Rodgers/L. Hart)(1:20) *Lloyd Noland, Maureen O' Sullivan*; 4 Piano medley: It Could Happen To You (J. Burke/J. Van Heusen)/Polka Dots And Moonbeams (J. Burke/J. Van Heusen)/ Avalon (V. Rose/A. Jolson/B.G. DeSylva)/Just You, Just Me (R. Klages/J. Greer) (5:04) *Dick Hyman*; 5 Concerto For Harpsichord in F Minor, 2nd Movement (J.S. Bach)(3:12) *George Malcolm, Simon Preston, Menuhin Festival Orchestra, Yehudi Menuhin*; 6 Back To The Apple (F. Foster/W. Basie)(4:42) *Count Basie and His Orchestra*; 7 I'm In

Love Again (C. Porter)(2:12) *Bobby Short*; 8 You Are Too Beautiful (R. Rodgers/L. Hart)(3:34) *Derek Smith*; 9 If I Had You (J. Campbell/R. Connelly/ T. Shapiro)(3:32) *Roy Eldridge*; 10 Isn't It Romantic (R. Rodgers/L. Hart) (4:10) *Derek Smith*.

Review: In his films, Woody Allen is very careful to use songs or instrumentals that evocatively complement the stories he develops. His taste runs primarily toward the great recordings of the 1940s and early '50s, with the soundtrack albums compiling these recordings together in a suggestive way. Often, his music director, the excellent Dick Hyman, adds his pianistic touch to the tracks, in a further musical expression that matches the moods of the source material. Both are on display in this album, which includes sides by Harry James ("You Made Me Love You" and "I've Heard That Song Before," both with heavy reverb that totally denatures their original sound) and Count Basie ("Back to the Apple"), a great piano medley by Hyman, as well as standards by Cole Porter and Rodgers and Hart sung by Bobby Short and Derek Smith. Adding a totally different, and slightly surprising, note is a performance of Bach's "Concerto in F Minor," which has the unfortunate effect of breaking the mood established by the other selections.

Hard Target 🎵🎵🎵

1993, Varese-Sarabande Records; from the movie *Hard Target*, Universal Pictures, 1993.

Album Notes: *Music*: Graeme Revell; *Orchestrations*: Graeme Revell, Tim Simonec, Larry Kenton, Ken Kugler; *Music Editor*: Dick Bernstein; Orchestra conducted by Tim Simonec; *Featured Musicians*: John Goux, George Doering (guitars), John Yoakum, Jon Clarke (saxophones, flutes), Mike Fisher (percussion), Tom Ranier, Mike Lang (keyboards), Rick Marotta (drums); *Album Producer*: Graeme Revell; *Engineer*: Dan Wallin.

Selections: 1 Hunting Season Opens (4:50); 2 Natasha (1:32); 3 Chance And Carmen (1:48); 4 Streetfighting Van Damme (1:51); 5 Friends (1:27); 6 The Lark Descending (2:29); 7 Won't You Let Me Go? (S. Dural, Jr.)(4:28) *Buckwheat Zydeco*; 8 The Dove And The Garotte (2:29); 9 Motorcycle Chase (2:46); 10 New Orleans Mission (1:31); 11 On The Docks (1:25); 12 Mardi Gras Graveyard (2:26); 13 Miles To Go (2:50); 14 Fouchon's Death (4:27); 15 Epilogue (1:55).

Review: This is a smart mix, combining the Japanese group Kodo with Graeme Revell's hard hitting orchestral stylings. It yields an exciting action film score that is quite entertaining on its own. Key parts of Revell's work is a delightful blend of musical styles, including some colorful downhome bayou

strains on cues like "Chance and Carmen" and the poignant "Miles to Go." But it is Kodo's creative percussion work that really kicks the action score into high gear ("Hunting Season Begins").

David Hirsch

The Hard Way 🎵🎵🎵

1991, Varese-Sarabande; from the movie *The Hard Way*, Universal Pictures, 1991.

Album Notes: *Music*: Arthur B. Rubinstein; *Featured Musicians*: Joel Peskin (tenor sax), Warren Luning, Rick Baptiste (trumpet), Charlie Loper (trombone), Chuck Domanico (bass), Steve Schaeffer (drums); *Album Producer*: Arthur B. Rubinstein.

Selections: 1 The Big Apple Juice (1:54); 2 Cirque Du Parte Crasher (1:45); 3 Manhattan Tow-Truck (2:46); 4 Ghetto a la Hollyweird (1:30); 5 He Dead/She Dead (1:29); 6 Big Girls Don't Cry (B. Gaudio/B. Crewe)(2:23) *Frankie Vallie & The Four Seasons*; 7 Where Have You Gone, L. Ron? (3:06); 8 Transit Authority (2:12); 9 Gas Attack (2:08); 10 Killer Lang (1:48); 11 Smoking Gun II (3:29); 12 Top Of The World (4:33); 13 The Good, The Badge And The Ugly (1:55); 14 Run Around Sue (E. Maresca/D. DiMucci)(2:43) *Dion*.

Review: This terrific Arthur B. Rubinstein effort starts off with a cue reminiscent of all those jazz scores for the TV cop shows of the 1950s and 60s ("The Big Apple Juice," "Where Have You Gone, L. Ron?"), but it soon shifts into something with a harder edge. Michael J. Fox plays a spoiled actor who bullies his way into the life of harried NYC police detective James Woods to learn how to act like a real cop. Rubinstein juxtaposes the Hollywood created world of cops (the jazz themes) with reality by infusing their exploits with more street-wise motifs, a creative fusion of various urban styles (including, for example, Jamaican steel drums). The film songs "Big Girls Don't Cry" and "Run Around Sue" also appear on the album.

David Hirsch

The Harder They Come 🎵🎵🎵

1973, Mango Records; from the movie *The Harder They Come*, 1972.

Album Notes: *Song Producers*: Jimmy Cliff, Derrick Harriot, Leslie Kong, Byron Lee.

Selections: 1 You Can Get It If You Really Want (J. Cliff)(2:46) *Jimmy Cliff*; 2 Draw Your Brakes (D. Harriot/D. Scott)(3:00) *Scotty*; 3 Rivers Of Babylon (B. Dowe/F. McNaughton)(4:19) *The Melodians*; 4 Many Rivers To Cross (J. Cliff)(3:02) *Jimmy*

Cliff; 5 Sweet And Dandy (F. Hibbert)(3:02) *The Maytals*; 6 The Harder They Come (J. Cliff)(3:43) *Jimmy Cliff*; 7 Johnny Too Bad (Beckford/Crooks/Bailey)(3:06) *The Slickers*; 8 Shanty Town (D. Dekker) (2:47) *Desmond Dekker*; 9 Pressure Drop (F. Hibbert)(3:45) *The Maytals*; 10 Sitting In Limbo (J. Cliff)(4:57) *Jimmy Cliff*; 11 You Can Get It If You Really Want (J. Cliff)(2:45) *Jimmy Cliff*; 12 The Harder They Come (J. Cliff)(3:08) *Jimmy Cliff*.

Review: This soundtrack album is mostly interesting for its mix of great reggae songs ("Rivers of Babylon," "Many Rivers to Cross," "Shanty Town"), performed by Jimmy Cliff, whose hit "You Can Get It If You Really Want" is included twice, The Maytals, and other Jamaican stars. The film, shot in the slums of West Kingston, presented an uncompromising look at the raw world of reggae and Jamaican ganja, and is one of the first to portray the power of drugs and music with such unique vision. Today, others have delved largely into this subculture phenomena, but the songs in *The Harder They Come* have lost none of their original impact and still impress in this coherent, powerful compilation.

Harum Scarum

1993, RCA Records; from the movie *Harum Scarum*, M-G-M, 1965.

See: Elvis Presley in Compilations

Hatari! ♫♫♫

1987, RCA Records; from the movie *Hatari!*, Paramount Pictures, 1962.

Album Notes: *Music*: Henry Mancini; Orchestra conducted by Henry Mancini; *CD Producer*: John Snyder; *Engineer*: Joe Lopes.

Selections: 1 Theme From "Hatari!" (2:56); 2 Baby Elephant Walk (2:42); 3 Just For Tonight (2:02); 4 Your Father's Feathers (3:31); 5 Night Side (3:24); 6 Big Band Bwana (3:03); 7 The Sound Of Hatari (6:42); 8 The Soft Touch (2:43); 9 Crocodile, Go Home! (2:56).

Review: Even the aggressive stereo separation in this soundtrack recording cannot affect the music written by Henry Mancini, in which the sprightly "Baby Elephant Walk" has emerged as one of the composer's most inspired creations. Like most of his scores, treated in a very lackadaisical way by the label to which he was signed for many years, the playing time is kept relatively short and just slightly over 30 minutes, with only one cue ("The Sounds of Hatari," dramatically steeped into a florid bongo drum line) venturing beyond six minutes. Still, it is another example of how great a melodist Mancini was, with themes that are consistently catchy and entertaining.

Haunted Summer ♫♫♫♫

1989, Silva Screen Records; from the movie *Haunted Summer*, Cannon Films, 1989.

Album Notes: *Music*: Christopher Young; *Orchestrations*: Christopher Young; *Music Editors*: Virginia Ellsworth, Lisa Kauppi; *Synthesizers*: Mark Zimoski, Tom Calderaro; *Album Producers*: David Stoner, James Fitzpatrick; *Engineer*: Jeff Vaughn.

Selections: 1 Haunted Summer (2:45); 2 Menage (4:40); 3 Villa Diodati (3:38); 4 The Night Was Made For Loving (7:03); 5 Polidori's Potions (4:13); 6 Ariel (2:03); 7 Confreres (2:04); 8 Geneva (1:29); 9 Alby (2:38); 10 An Unquiet Dream (5:30); 11 Hauntings: Hotel d'Angleterre/In The Caves Of Chillon/Incubus/Mont Blanc (18:00).

Review: Superb effort by Christopher Young that fabricates its own unique world of idyllic beauty and melancholy through a brilliant orchestration of synthesizers and a small selection of acoustical instruments. "The Night Was Made for Loving" is the centerpiece, presenting the composer at his melodic best in a seven-minute romantic concerto that's gently framed by elegant secondary motifs. Of course, one must remember that this is the story of the summer when Mary Shelley conceived of *Frankenstein*, so there's nightmares forthcoming for Young to gnaw his creative teeth upon. Though the foreboding "Polidori's Potions" breaks up the two suites of "bright" music, it is only a taste of things to come. It is still somewhat melodic for what Young saves for dessert. He turns his muse of the macabre loose on the creation of the 18-minute "Hauntings" suite, an edit of four impressively unsettling cues. It all starts off melodically enough with a classical inspired motif, but soon begins to degrade into a twisted witches' brew of dissonant sounds that crawls up your back. The perfect score for the morally challenged.

David Hirsch

Havana ♫♫♫▵

1990, GRP Records; from the movie *Havana*, Universal Pictures, 1990.

Album Notes: *Music*: Dave Grusin; *Orchestrations*: Dave Grusin, Greg MacRitchie, George Hernandez; Orchestra conducted by Dave Grusin; *Featured Musicians*: Alex Acuna, Harvey Mason, Mike Fisher, Ephraim Torres (drums, percussions), Abe Laboriel, Brian Bromberg (bass), Clare Fisher, Dave Grusin (piano), Lee Ritenour, Ramon Stagnaro (guitars), Dave Valentin (flute), Sal Marquez, Arturo Sandoval (trumpet), Don Menza (saxophone); *Album Producer*: Dave Grusin; *Engineers*: Don Murray, John Richards.

Selections: 1 Main Title (3:04); 2 Night Walk (3:26); 3 Cuba Libre ("Se fue")(3:31); 4 Santa Clara Suite: (a) Vayase (1:20), (b) Milicia y refugios (1:55), (c) Fuego peligroso (:54), (d) Epilogue (:53); 5 A los Rumberos de Belen (3:53); 6 Love Theme (3:07); 7 Hurricane Country (4:58); 8 Lost In A Sweet Place (2:27); 9 Mambo Lido (3:53); 10 El Conuco (3:12); 11 Adios Habana (3:05); 12 La Academia (2:48).

Review: There are very few surprises in this highly competent score by Dave Grusin, whose jazz roots occasionally show up in some selections, both as composer and performer. The themes have a pleasant lilt to them, and conjure up the right kind of atmosphere, within and without their original relationship to the film itself, about an American gambler in Havana in the last days of the Batista regime. The Cuban background is evoked by means of a strumming acoustic guitar, as well as by what could be construed as South-of-the-border rhythms and sonorities ("Cuba Libre," "Santa Clara Suite," "Mambo Lido," "El Conuco"). It's all very pretty, and it essentially fulfills its function.

Heart and Souls ♪♪♪♪

1993, MCA Records; from the movie *Heart and Souls*, Universal Picture, 1993.

Album Notes: *Music:* Marc Shaiman; *Orchestrations:* Mark McKenzie, Jeff Atmajian, Dennis Dreith; *Music Editor:* Scott Stambler; Orchestra conducted by Artie Kane, J.A.C. Redford; *Album Producer:* Marc Shaiman; *Engineer:* Joel Moss.

Selections: 1 Main Title (3:04); 2 Julia And John (1:46); 3 Soul Mates (4:42); 4 Goodbye Thomas (5:22); 5 Heart And Soul (H. Carmichael/F. Loesser) (3:00) *Dave Koz*; 6 Souled Out (3:45); 7 Goodbye Milo (3:43); 8 Mr. Hug-A-Bug (3:25); 9 Goodbye Penny (2:04); 10 Julia's Farewell/The End (6:21); 11 Walk Like A Man (B. Crewe/B. Gaudio)(2:17) *Frankie Valli & The Four Seasons*; 12 (You'll Always Be) My Heart And Soul (M. Shaiman)(4:07) *Stephen Bishop*; 13 What'd I Say (R. Charles)(5:05) *Ray Charles*; 14 The Thrill Is Gone (R. Hawkins/ R. Darnell)(4:15) *B.B. King*; 15 The Star-Spangled Banner (F.S. Key/ J.S. Smith)(2:29) *Robert Downey Jr., B.B. King*.

Review: Marc Shaiman delivered a beautifully lyrical score, built around the Hoagy Carmichael-Frank Loesser standard, also heard in an instrumental version by Dave Koz, which subtly recurs throughout and anchors the music and the film, a delightful comedy starring Robert Downey Jr. as a young man in whom four victims of a bus accident have reincarnated. While the overtones of the score are deftly romantic, the music takes frequent, short sidesteps into big band jazz ("Goodbye Thomas," "Souled Out"), the better to offset its more thought-

"Mark Isham is one of the great film composers of today, but in the jazz tradition that almost got lost after Alex North."

Robbie Robertson
*musician (The Mark Isham
Web Site)*

ful moments. Five vocal selections, including "Walk Like a Man," performed by Frankie Valli & The Four Seasons, "What'd I Say," by Ray Charles, and "The Thrill Is Gone," by B.B. King add a different, albeit equally enjoyable flavor to the proceedings.

Heart of Midnight ♪

1992, Silva Screen Records; from the movie *Heart of Midnight*, Samuel Goldwyn, 1989.

Album Notes: *Music:* Yanni; *Album Producer:* Yanni; *Engineer:* Yanni.

Selections: 1 Overture/Carol's Theme (4:03); 2 Welcome To "Midnight" (:48); 3 Carol Through The Rooms (3:15); 4 "Oh, Daddy"/Carol Sees Fletcher/Rathead On Ice (2:35); 5 Carol's Theme/Soft Interlude (1:03); 6 The Rape (Parts 1 & 2) (3:59); 7 Aftermath (1:15); 8 Carol Talks To Maria (1:18); 9 Sharpe #2 Dies/ Carol's Nightmare (2:10); 10 Carol's Theme/Sadness Of The Heart (1:31); 11 The Library Of Porn (3:31); 12 The Cabinet Falls/Carol Out In The Street/Attic/ Dinner And Downstairs In The Club (4:55); 13 The S&M Room (4:36); 14 End Sequence: The Final Confrontation/Carol's Theme/SWisters In Pain/ Sonny's Death (5:55); 15 Finale/Carol's Theme (2:30).

Review: If you're expecting the dulcet New Age tones Yanni has become famous for on public TV, forget it. Despite the pleasing "Carol's Theme," this is just another dated synthesized horror score. The sharp electronic effects serve more of a purpose in keeping the listener awake during long passages that sound as if they were made up on the spur of the moment instead of being thought out. This remarkably poor sounding recording is not one of Yanni's better efforts.

David Hirsch

Heartbreaker ♫♫♭

1995, Silva America; from the movie *Heartbreaker*, **Orion Pictures, 1984.**

Album Notes: *Music:* Tangerine Dream, Christopher Franke, Edgar Froese, Johannes Schmoelling; *Album Producer:* Ford A. Thaxton; *Engineer:* Joe Giannola.

Selections: 1 Heartbreakers (2:30); 2 Footbridge To Heaven (2:56); 3 Twilight Painter (4:15); 4 Gemini (3:38); 5 Rain In N.Y. City (3:23); 6 Pastime (2:57); 7 The Loser (3:19); 8 Breathing The Night Away (2:27); 9 Desire (5:35); 10 Thorny Affair (3:10); 11 Daybreak (4:07).

Review: A bright and bouncy early 1980s Tangerine Dream score from the days of Christopher Franke's association. It holds the attention really well, while capturing all the quirky aspects of the film's story of two lifelong friends and their relationships with women. Where the album works best are on the more gentle cues like "Rain in the City" or "Breathing the Night Away." However, most of the cues, like the aggressive "Twilight Painter," regretfully betray their age with their somewhat dated synthesizer sounds. Add an extra bone if you really do miss the '80s. I don't.

David Hirsch

Heartbreak Hotel ♫♭

1988, RCA Records; from the movie *Heartbreak Hotel*, **Touchstone Pictures, 1988.**

Album Notes: *Featured Musicians:* The Zulu Time Band featuring Dave Davies (guitars, vocals), Michael Moyer (bass, vocals), Cole Hanson (guitar, vocals), Kevin Pearson (drums); *The T. Graham Brown Band:* Michael Thomas (guitar), Joe Mc-Glohon (saxophone, guitar), Garland (keyboards), Greg Watzel (keyboards), Larry Marrs (bass guitar), Gary Kubal (drums).

Selections: 1 Heartbreak Hotel (M. Boren Axton/T. Durden/E. Presley)(2:06) *Elvis Presley;* 2 One Night (D. Bartholomew/P. King)(2:30) *Elvis Presley;* 3 Drift Away (M. Williams)(3:51) *Dobie Gray;* 4 Can't Help Falling In Love (G. Weiss/H. Peretti/L. Creatore)(2:34) *David Keith, T. Graham Brown Band;* 5 Bruning Love (D. Linde)(2:51) *Elvis Presley;* 6 Love Me (M. Stoller/J. Leiber)(1:52) *David Keith;* 7 Ready Teddy (J. Marascalo/R. Blackwell)(2:03) *Elvis Presley;* 8 I'm Eighteen (A. Cooper/M. Bruce/G. Buxton/D. Dunaway/N. Smith)(2:56) *Alice Cooper;* 9 Soul On Fire (F. Carillo/ R. Byrd/R. Kraft)(3:12) *Charlie Schlatter, Zulu Time;* 10 If I Can Dream (W.E. Brown)(3:07) *Elvis Presley;* 11 Heartbreak Hotel (M. Boren Axton/T. Durden/E. Presley)(2:25) *David Keith, Charlie Schlatter, Zulu Time.*

Review: You can hear The King sing the title track, then you can hear actors David Keith and Charlie Schlatter take their stab at it. Need we say more? Keith and Schlatter sing far too much here, and while it's nice to have some more tunes from Elvis, as well as Dobie Gray's "Drift Away" and Alice Cooper's "Eighteen," there are far better ways to get them.

Gary Graff

Heat ♫♫♭

1995, Warner Bros. Records; from the movie *Heat*, **Warner Bros., 1995.**

Album Notes: *Music:* Elliot Goldenthal; *Orchestrations:* Robert Elhai, Elliot Goldenthal; *Music Editors:* Christopher Brooks, Michael Connell, Bill Abbott; Orchestra conducted by Jonathan Sheffer, Stephen Mercurio; *Featured Artists:* Kronos Quartet, "Deaf Elk" *Guitar Orchestra:* Page Hamilton, Andrew Hawkins, David Reid, Eric Hubel; *Album Producer:* Matthias Gohl; *Engineer:* Stephen McLaughlin, Joel Iwataki.

Selections: 1 Heat (7:41) *Kronos Quartet;* 2 Always Forever (B. Eno/U2) (6:55) *Passengers (Brian Eno/U2);* 3 Condensers (2:35); 4 Refinery Surveillance (1:45) *Kronos Quartet;* 5 Last Nite (T. Rypdal)(3:30) *Terje Rypdal;* 6 Ultramarine (M. Brook)(4:35) *Michael Brook;* 7 Armenia (E. Neubauten)(4:58) *Einsturzende Neubauten;* 8 Of Helplessness (2:39); 9 Steel Cello Lament (1:43); 10 Mystery Man (T. Rypdal)(4:40) *Terje Rypdal;* 11 New Dawn Fades (J. Division) (2:55) *Moby;* 12 Entrada and Shootout (1:45); 13 Force Marker (B. Eno)(3:37) *Brian Eno;* 14 Coffee Shop (1:37); 15 Fate Scrapes (1:35); 16 La Bas (L. Gerrard)(3:11) *Lisa Gerrard;* 17 Gloradin (L. Gerrard)(3:56) *Lisa Gerrard;* 18 Run Uphill (2:52); 19 Predator Diorama (2:40) *Kronos Quartet;* 20 Of Separation (2:21); 21 God Moving Over The Face Of The Waters (R. Hall)(6:58) *Moby.*

Review: "Miami Vice" showed that director Michael Mann had a flair for marrying arresting music and visuals. But shorn of the latter, the songs on "Heat" seem dispirate and random — Kronos Quartet's avant chamber music here, Moby's ambient dance fare there. The collection is notable for "Always Forever Now," a track by the Passengers (aka U2 and Brian Eno), but it's hard to spend time with this as a cohesive listening experience.

Gary Graff

Heathers ♫♫♫♭

1989, Varese-Sarabande Records; from the movie *Heathers*, **New World Pictures, 1989.**

Album Notes: *Music:* David Newman; *Music Editor:* Scott Grusin; *Album Producer:* David Newman; *Engineer:* Tim Boyle.

Selections: 1 Strip Croquet (1:56); 2 Suicide Note (2:09); 3 J.D. Blows Up (2:12); 4 The Forest (2:00); 5 You're Beautiful (2:12); 6 Martha Dumptruck (1:13); 7 Third Funeral (1:51); 8 Veronica And J.D. (1:11); 9 First Funeral (1:55); 10 The Dorm (1:01); 11 Back To School (1:11); 12 Forest Chase (1:29); 13 Heather's Locker (1:09); 14 Veronica's Shower (:44); 15 Into The Cafeteria (:50); 16 Veronica's Dream (1:56); 17 J.D.'s Final Stand (2:59); 18 Dorm Party (3:32); 19 Croquet (1:31); 20 Second Funeral (1:28); 21 Poor Little Heather (:56); 22 J.D.'s Bomb (3:53); 23 Petition Montage (2:30).

Review: This sharp (and sharply funny) black comedy about a quartet of stuck-up damsels known as the Heathers, so called because it happens to be the first name of three of them, was the occasion for David Newman to write a serious tongue-in-cheek opus, with dark overtones, that smartly complements the moods of the film. Unlike the large orchestral works for which he has become quite famous in film music circles, Newman chose to go the electronic route this time around, and created a synthesized score in which the only occasional acoustic note is injected by an harmonica. Throughout, there are clever, humorous little touches that make the music even more enjoyable, as in "You're Beautiful," "The Dorm," "Into the Cafeteria".

Heavy Metal ♫♫♫

1981, Full Moon/Elektra Records; from the animated feature *Heavy Metal*, Columbia Pictures, 1981.

Album Notes: *Album Executive Producer*: Irving Azoff; *Album Compilers*: Irving Azoff, Howard Kaufman, Bob Destocki.

Selections: 1 Heavy Metal (S. Hagar/J. Peterik)(3:50) *Sammy Hagar*; 2 Heartbeat (J. Riggs)(4:20) *Jerry Riggs*; 3 Working In The Coal Mine (A. Toussaint)(2:48) *Devo*; 4 Veteran Of The Psychic War (E. Bloom/M. Moorcock) (4:48) *Blue Oyster Cult*; 5 Reach Out (R. James/P. Comita)(3:35) *Cheap Trick*; 6 Heavy Metal (Takin' A Ride)(D. Felder)(5:00) *Don Felder*; 7 True Companion (D. Fagen)(5:02) *Donald Fagen*; 8 Crazy (A Suitable Case For Treatment)(M. Charlton/P. Agnew/D. McCafferty/D. Sweet)(3:24) *Nazareth*; 9 Radar Rider (J. Riggs)(2:40) *Jerry Riggs*; 10 Open Arms (S. Perry/J. Cain) (3:20) *Journey*; 11 Queen Bee (M. Farmer)(3:11) *Grand Funk Railroad*; 12 I Must Be Dreaming (R. Nielsen)(5:37) *Cheap Trick*; 13 The Mob Rules (T. Butler/A. Iommi/R.J. Dio)(2:43) *Black Sabbath*; 14 All Of You (D. Felder) (4:18) *Don Felder*; 15 Prefabricated (B. Bonvoisin/N. Krief/J. Pursey)(2:59) *Trust*; 16 Blue Lamp (S. Nicks)(3:48) *Stevie Nicks*.

Review: One of the great animated features of the 1980s, *Heavy Metal* owed little to the genre dominated for so long by Walt Disney. In fact, the raw energy of the various segments in the film, designed by some of the best illustrators of the day, was in sharp contrast with the saccharine images usually created by the House of the Mouse or even, for that matter, with the slyly sarcastic cartoon shorts made by Warner Bros. So was, for that matter, the explosive soundtrack which brought together some of the greatest names in rock'n'roll — Blue Oyster Cult, Cheap Trick, Devo, Nazareth, Journey, Grand Funk Railroad, Cheap Trick and Black Sabbath, among them — names one would not normally associate with a cartoon feature. But the tremendous volatile power of the score and the extraordinary visual images on the screen combined to create a film unlike anything usually seen in movie houses.

The CD returns to the catalogue a long sought-after soundtrack album which deserves to be in every collection. Missing, however, is the instrumental score, composed by Elmer Bernstein, which was available on a separate LP and has never been reissued on compact disc.

Hello Again ♫♫

1987, Cinedisc Records; from the movie *Hello Again,* Touchstone Pictures, 1987.

Album Notes: *Music*: William Goldstein; *Featured Musician*: Dave Boruff (saxophone); *Album Producer*: William Goldstein; *Engineer*: William Goldstein.

Selections: 1 Hello Again: Main Theme (4:12); 2 Lucy's Reflection (2:30); 3 Kevin And Lucy (3:55); 4 In The Beginning (4:00); 5 Zelda Visits The Beyond (3:57); 6 The Dinner Party/Lucy's Death (3:33); 7 Transfiguration (Resurrection)(2:46); 8 Jason's Remorse/Zelda Clues In Scanlon (3:34); 9 Lucy And Kevin Montage (2:21); 10 Hello Again: Main Theme (reprise)(4:20); 11 Second Thoughts/Lucy And Kevin (3:26); 12 Lucy Despairs/"Kimmy Pie" (4:30); 13 The Grand Finale (3:49).

Review: This synthesized comedy score, written and performed by William Goldstein, has an infectious, innocent charm about it. The main theme is bright and bouncy, but its overuse tends to wear out its welcome. Goldstein's arrangements for the most part work well within the limitations of his electronics, and Dave Boruff's occasional sax solos add some welcome life. However, the synthesized instrumentation sounds awfully primitive just ten years later and, at times, distracts from Goldstein's compositions.

David Hirsch

Hellraiser III: Hell on Earth
🦴🦴🦴

1996, GNP Crescendo; from the movie *Hellraiser III: Hell on Earth*, New World Pictures, 1992.

Album Notes: *Music:* Randy Miller.

Selections: 1 Hellraiser III: Hell On Earth (2:12); 2 Back To Hell (4:39); 3 Cenobites' Death Dance (2:31); 4 Pinhead's Proteges/ The Devil's Mass (12:50); 5 Come To Daddy (2:43); 6 Gothic Rebirth (1:05); 7 Emergency Room (6:32); 8 Mind Invasion (2:42); 9 The Pillar (4:10); 10 Elliot's Story (5:14); 11 Shall We Begin (2:04).

Review: Although Randy Miller quotes from Chris Young's original *Hellraiser* several times in this third outing, his own main theme is a strong contender to Young's, carrying on the cosmic drama of the former films while giving this story a musical sensibility of his own. Like the Cenobite torturers of the film, it quickly overcomes the minor musical motifs set before it—such as the heavy and doom-filled theme heard in "Mind Invasion." In "Elliot's Story," Miller accentuates the interplay between the main theme and the "Mind Invasion" motif, one cue playing softly on the violin, and humanizing the horrific sounds heard earlier. The use of the choir adds drama and power to the score. Low, echoing percussion and slow, shimmering cymbals open the music up to cavernous depths. The main theme sounds strident and omnipresent throughout the score.

Randall D. Larson

Henry and June 🦴🦴🦴🦴

1990, Varese-Sarabande Records; from the movie *Henry and June*, Universal Pictures, 1990.

Album Notes: *Album Producer:* Robert Townson.

Selections: 1 Parlez-moi d'amour (J. Lenoir/B. Slevier)(3:00) *Lucienne Boyer*; 2 Pour l'Egyptienne (C. Debussy)(3:22) *Ensemble Musical de Paris*; 3 Les chemins de l'amour (F. Poulenc)(3:57) *Ransom Wilson, Christopher O'Riley*; 4 Petite Suite (Ballet)(C. Debussy)(3:04) *Alfons Kontarsky, Aloys Kontarsky*; 5 I Found A Million Dollar Baby (H. Warren/M. Dixon/B. Rose)(3:04) *Bing Crosby*; 6 Gnossienne #3 (E. Satie)(3:10) *Pascal Roge*; 7 Je te veux (E. Satie)(4:46) *Jean-Pierre Armengaud*; 8 Sonata For Violin And Piano (First Movement)(C. Debussy)(4:45) *Kyung-Wha Chung, Radu Lupu*; 9 Nocturne No. 1 in C Major (F. Poulenc)(3:57) *Paul Crossley*; 10 Sous les toits de Paris (R. Moretti/R. Nazles)(2:15); 11 Le doux caboulot (J. Larmanjat/F. Carcos)(1:04) *Annie Fratellini*; 12 La plus que lente (C. Debussy)(4:17) *Josef Suk*; 13 Je m'ennuie (W. Berg/C. Francois)(2:18); 14 Coralia (trad.)(4:35); 15 St. James Infirmary (J. Primrose)(2:01); 16 Gran Vals (F. Tarrega)(:43); 17 Basque Song (J. Nin-Culmell)(2:49) *Joaquin Nin-Culmell*; 18 J'ai deux amours (V. Scotto/ H. Varna)(2:12) *Josephine Baker*.

Review: Philip Kaufman's brilliant film, *Henry and June,* centered around the erotic life of two Americans living in Paris who became 20th-century literary giants, Henry Miller and Anais Nin. Set in 1931, the film boldly explores their first encounter and their passionate relationship, further pushed to the limits by Miller's enigmatic and hauntingly sensual wife, June. To musically illustrate this first-rate film, Kaufman assembled various recordings that to him symbolized the period, from both its French and its American perspectives, and gave it its unique cachet. With a few exceptions (Bing Crosby's "I Found a Million Dollar Baby," Lucienne Boyer's "Parlez-moi d'amour" and Josephine Baker's "J'ai deux amours," which bookend the soundtrack album), most of the selections are modern recordings of works from the 1930s, which are strongly evocative of the era, yet are sonically modern in concept and interpretation. Like *The Moderns,* also set in Paris in the 1930s, *Henry and June* is a splendid evocation of a period long gone which had a unique flavor to it. The terrific soundtrack album exudes the same irresistible flair.

Henry V 🦴🦴🦴🦴▸

1989, EMI Angel; from the movie *Henry V,* 1989.

Album Notes: *Music:* Patrick Doyle; *Orchestrations:* Lawrence Ashmore; The City of Birmingham Orchestra, conducted by Simon Rattle; *Album Producers:* Simon Woods, Patrick Doyle, Lawrence Ashmore; *Engineer:* Christopher Dibble.

Selections: 1 Opening Title: "O! For a Muse of Fire" (3:34); 2 Henry V Theme/The Boar's Head (2:46); 3 The Three Traitors (2:03); 4 "Now, Lords, for France!" (2:40); 5 The Death Of Falstaff (1:54); 6 "Once more unto the breach" (3:45); 7 The Threat To The Governor Of Harfleur/Katherine Of France/The March To Calais (5:51); 8 The Death Of Bardolph (2:22); 9 "Upon the King" (4:50); 10 St. Crispin's Day/The Battle Of Agincourt (14:13); 11 "The day is yours" (2:34); 12 "Non nobis, Domine" (4:09) *Patrick Doyle, Stephen Hill Singers, Renaissance Theatre Company*; 13 The Wooing Of Katherine (2:24); 14 "Let this acceptance take" (2:50); 15 End Title (2:35).

Review: There has rarely been as impressive a film scoring debut as Patrick Doyle's score for Kenneth Branaugh's first-time film directing effort, a gritty and inspiring adaptation of Shakespeare's tale of the British king who overcame incredible odds at the Battle of Agincourt. Opening with a rich low string dirge of great, tragic nobility, Doyle's beautiful music accelerates into an exclamation of pure triumph simply to introduce Shakespeare's tale. It's one of the most active underscoring of dialogue in recent memory, pulsing through scenes, erupting in martial fury or in beautiful elegiac lyricism (as in the "Requiem for Falstaff"). Doyle's scoring of Henry's troop-rallying speech before the Agincourt battle is one of the most moving, gorgeous and inspiring musical cues written for a film in the past couple of decades, and his music for the battle proper is a balletic marvel of percussive, rhythmic drive. The entire score compares quite well with William Walton's legendary effort for the Laurence Olivier *Henry V* of 1944. It's a rare soundtrack album that will appeal to lovers of film scores as well as good music in general.

Jeff Bond

Her Majesty Mrs. Brown
♪♪♪♪▷

1997, Milan Records; from the movie *Her Majesty Mrs. Brown*, Miramax Pictures, 1997.

Album Notes: *Music*: Stephen Warbeck; Orchestra conducted by Nick Ingman; *Featured Musicians*: Martin Robertson, Tim Holmes (tarogato), Sarah Horner (whistles), Dermot Crehan (fiddle), Pipe Major Willie Cochrane (bagpipes); *Album Producer*: Stephen Warbeck; *Engineers*: Chris Dibble, Mark Tucker.

Selections: 1 The Walk On The Moors (2:43); 2 The Swim (2:09); 3 Queen Victoria And John Brown (8:16); 4 The Loch (2:57); 5 The Fight (2:34); 6 The First Ride (2:46); 7 The Assassination Attempt (2:29); 8 Typhoid Fever (2:30); 9 The End Of The Loch (:48); 10 Brown And The Pony (3:29); 11 The Pipes: All The Blue Bonnets Are O'er The Border/Atholl Highlanders/Cock O' The North (4:05); 12 Loch Nagar (1:52); 13 After The Dance (3:36); 14 Political Intrigue (2:09); 15 The Promise (2:06); 16 No Toast For Brown (3:04); 17 The Closing (2:43).

Review: A quaint but apparently true story, *Her Majesty Mrs. Brown* centers on a little known fact about England's Queen Victoria (played by Judi Dench), in the years following the death of her beloved husband, Prince Albert, and the warm friendship that established itself between her and a loyal servant and stableman by the name of John Brown (portrayed by Billy Connolly). Stephen Warbeck wrote a beautifully poignant and emotionally rousing score, developed around a solemn, stately theme for the Queen, and a blend of Celtic melodic fragments (played on a tarogato, a Hungarian wood instru-

ment), for Brown, in an odd, yet compelling musical marriage. Both themes dominate the score, either played singly or intermingled, while other cues explore the landscapes, natural and political, that serve as a backdrop to the unusual relationship between the Queen and her stableman, often in terms that are quietly stated and attractive. Lush and stirring, it is an unusual score that deserves to be heard.

Hero ♪♪♪

1992, Epic Soundtrax; from the movie *Hero*, Columbia Pictures, 1992.

Album Notes: *Music*: George Fenton; *Orchestrations*: Jeff Atmajian; *Music Editor*: Michael Connell; Orchestra conducted by George Fenton; *Featured Musicians*: Nat Adderley, Jr. (piano/keyboards), Harvey Mason (drums), William "Doc" Powell (guitar), Byron Miller (bass), Paulinho da Costa (percussion), Wayne Linsey (synthesizer programming/keyboards/cymbals); *Album Producer*: George Fenton; *Engineer*: John Richards.

Selections: 1 Heart Of A Hero (L. Vandross)(3:29) *Luther Vandross, Los Angeles Children's Chorus*; 2 Hero Front Titles (2:01); 3 Keep A Low Profile (2:14); 4 Gale Gayley For Channel 4 News (1:28); 5 Looking For The Truth (2:18); 6 The Plane Crash (9:13); 7 He Said, I'll Save Your Father (2:03); 8 Out Of The Darkness (The Battle Hymn Of The Republic)(2:25); 9 Million Dollar Reward (2:00); 10 The Man I Love (G. & I. Gershwin)(1:57); 11 Dinner For Two (3:18); 12 The Hotel Lobby (2:12); 13 Reunion (1:34); 14 The Angel Of Flight 104 (:51); 15 The Man I Love (reprise)(G. & I. Gershwin) (2:10); 16 The Ledge (Parts 1, 2, 3)(3:33); 17 Lady, I Ain't The Type (2:40); 18 A Pair Of Shoes (1:33); 19 Heart Of A Hero (L. Vandross)(3:24).

Review: Comedy scores do not often make for interesting albums (since they tend to be quirky by nature), and *Hero* is no exception. George Fenton is of course one of the finest composers of our time (with scores like *Cry Freedom*, *Dangerous Liaisons* and *The Fisher King* to his credit, among many others), but this particular score, while dramatically (and comedically) effective, is not really one which comes together to form a cohesive album. The CD opens with Luther Vandross' song, "Heart of a Hero," which is a typically forgettable pop tune. Fenton's ensuing score is a varied amalgam of styles. The main title opens with an arrangement of "Auld Lang Syne," which segues into a Sousa-like march. Much of the music is light pop or programmatic suspense music, but there are a few listenable moments. Track 5, "Looking for the Truth" has a nice Americana flavor to it, and is typical of Fenton's more noble side and his gift for writing music of depth which flows effortlessly. *Hero* is certainly a fine score, but one which is better experienced in the film, where it was meant, rather than on disc.

Announced by Luther Vandross' anthem, "Heart of a Hero," this sarcastic comment on modern society and the role television plays in it, takes off with a soaring score, penned by George Fenton, which happily mixes cues for a large orchestra and themes for a jazz combo that includes many well-known participants. It is all the more surprising because Fenton had not often accustomed us for this muscular type of writing in a contemporary idiom, but he pulls it off with gusto and manages to create a music that has great appeal on its own. The film, about a bum who saves several people after a plane crash, and the "friend" who takes credit for his action because no one believes a bum would do it, is a biting satire about television and the 15-minute heroes it creates. The subject obviously motivated Fenton to write one of his most inspiring scores.

Paul Andrew MacLean/Didier C. Deutsch

Hero and the Terror ♪♪♪

1988, Cinedisc Records; from the movie *Hero and the Terror*, Cannon Films, 1988.

Album Notes: *Music*: David Michael Frank; *Synthesizer Programmer*: Jeff Rona; *Album Producer*: David Michael Frank; *Engineers*: Avi Kipper, Keith Stein.

Selections: 1 Two Can Be One (R. Jason/D. Osso)(3:47) *Joe Pizzulo, Stephanie Reach*; 2 Obsession (2:40); 3 Workout (1:23); 4 The Terror (3:39); 5 Hero's Seduction (:42); 6 San Pedro Bust (3:49); 7 The Ladies Room (1:47); 8 Breakout (2:23); 9 Birthday Wishes (1:56); 10 Discovery (1:49); 11 Showtime! (2:36); 12 Angela (2:15); 13 Subterranean Terror (2:30); 14 Simon's Lair (2:58); 15 The Search (1:23); 16 Living Nightmare (2:42); 17 Love And Obsession (1:40).

Review: Announced by the relatively tepid "Two Can Be One," warbled in contemporary fashion by Joe Pizzulo and Stephanie Reach, *Hero and the Terror* is a combination of orchestral and synthesizer cues, some attractive, some effective, many of them routine. When he stays within an acoustic or orchestral context, David Michael Frank comes up with some lovely tunes ("Hero's Seduction," "Birthday Wishes," "Angela," "Love and Obsession"), but these are defeated by the obvious, and much less creative approach to the electronic cues that constitute the remainder of the score.

Hideaway ♪♪♪

1995, TVT Records; from the movie *Hideaway*, Tri-Star Pictures, 1995.

Album Notes: *Music*: Trevor Jones; *Orchestrations*: Trevor Jones, Geoffrey Alexander, Lawrence Ashmore, Julian Kershaw; *Song Producers*: KMFDM, Phil Parfitt & J.C. Concato, Hacke, Die Warzau, Randall, Warhen & Levy, Colin Richardson, Bill Leeb & Rhys Fulber, Nick Hell, J.K. Broadrick & G.C. Green; *Album Producers*: Carol Sue Baker, William Ewart; *Engineer*: Kevin Hodge.

Selections: 1 Go To Hell (S. Konietzko/E. Esch/S. Am)(5:45) *KMFDM*; 2 She Believes In Me (P. Parlitt)(5:29) *Oedipussy*; 3 Peep Show (M.S. Garden/K. Blake)(3:53) *Miranda Sex Garden*; 4 All Good Girls (V. Christie/J. Marcus) (5:00) *Die Warzau*; 5 Lung (bronchitis mix)(C. Randall/J. Marcus)(3:08) *Sister Machine Gun*; 6 Scumgrief (deep dub trauma mix)(D. Cazares/B. Bell) (6:18) *Fear Factory*; 7 Surface Patterns (B. Leeb/R. Fulber)(5:36) *Front Line Assembly*; 8 Reverberation Nation (J. Thastrom/S. Terrarie)(5:36) *Peace Love & Pitbulls*; 9 Nihil (J.K. Broadrick/G.C. Green)(5:56) *Godflesh*; 10 Cut (M.S. Garden/K. Blake)(4:59) *Miranda Sex Garden*; 11 Main Titles "Nunc Dimitus" (3:48); 12 Into The Light (6:57); 13 Beyond The Shadow Of Death (10:26).

Review: *Hideaway* appears at first glance no more than just another rock and roll collection, trowelled indiscriminately into the film (and the CD) for commercial purposes. However, the three tracks allotted to Trevor Jones' score (placed at the end of this disc) are highly recommended. At roughly 20 minutes, Jones' score is the kind of full orchestral music which highlighted his early work, in scores like *The Dark Crystal* and *The Last Place on Earth*. *Hideaway* is a film dealing with mysticism and the afterlife, and Jones' score reflects these fantastical-religious elements with soaring choral music, which evokes a spiritual etheria. A brooding statement of the "Dies Irae" opens the final track, "Beyond the Shadow of Death" which culminates in a powerful setting of the main theme, though the heavy rock and roll drums which come-in near the end unfortunately compromise its effect. Overall, *Hideaway* represents some of Trevor Jones' better large-orchestral writing. While the rock songs in this release are a forgettable cacophony, Jones' score is a very good one and ultimately makes for rewarding listening.

Paul Andrew MacLean

High Heels ♪♪♪▷

1992, Antilles Records; from the movie *High Heels*, Miramax Films, 1992.

Album Notes: *Music*: Ryuichi Sakamoto; Orchestra conducted by Ryuichi Sakamoto; *Featured Soloist*: Basilio Georges (guitar); *Album Producer*: Ryuichi Sakamoto; *Engineers*: Lolly Crodner, Ryuichi Sakamoto; *Assistant Engineers*: Brian Pollack, Trish McCabe, Jim Viviano, Angelo Lo Coco.

Selections: 1 Main Theme (3:05); 2 Tacones lojanos (1:56); 3 Trauma (3:02); 4 Becky's Guitar (1:02); 5 Plaza (1:12); 6 Kisses

(1:09); 7 Un ano de amor (N. Ferrer/G. Verlor)(3:20) *Luz Casal*; 8 El Cucu #1 (4:28); 9 El Cucu #2 (4:16); 10 Murder (:35); 11 Interrogation (4:23); 12 Driving To Confess (1:07); 13 Tele 7 (:10); 14 Rebecca's Arrest (1:05); 15 Piensa en mi (A. Lare)(4:27) *Luz Casal*; 16 Autumn Sonata (:50); 17 Released Rebecca (1:58); 18 Lethal's Secret (:56); 19 Ambulance Ride (:21); 20 End Title (3:05).

Review: This typically flavorful score by Ryuichi Sakamoto was composed for a Spanish film starring Victoria Abril, which partly explains the inclusion of a couple of vocals in that language, as well as several cues with Spanish titles. Though relying on the sounds of a flamenco guitar to provide an occasional exotic color, Sakamoto wrote a score that is not specifically rooted in either the time or place of the action, about a young woman who finds out that her new husband once had an affair with her own mother, but is more universal in appeal. A diversified mix, the music is an interesting blend of romantic themes and pop/rock tunes, of synthesizer cues and orchestral sounds, all of which combines to give a definitely unusual style to the album.

High Spirits ♫♫♫♪

1988, GNP Crescendo; from the movie *High Spirits*, TriStar Pictures, 1988.

Album Notes: *Music:* George Fenton; *Orchestrations:* Christopher Palmer, George Fenton; The Graunke Symphony Orchestra, conducted by George Fenton; *Featured Musicians:* Dermot Crehan (Irish fiddle), Paul Brennan (Uillean pipes), Catherine Bott (vocals); *Album Producer:* Ford A. Thaxton; *Engineer:* Keith Grant.

Selections: 1 High Spirits Overture (4:37); 2 Prologue and Main Title/ Castle Plunkett (5:00); 3 Plunkett's Lament/Prayers For Freedom (2:16); 4 Ghost Bus Tours (3:36); 5 Ghostly Reflections (1:04); 6 She Is Far From The Land (1:39); 7 Bumps In The Knight (3:42); 8 Mary Appears/Windstorm/A Night For Lovers (5:27); 9 I Could Love You Sir Jack/Shower Surprise (2:37); 10 Knight Time At Castle Plunkett (3:27); 11 The Wedding Night/Jack Saves Mary (2:34); 12 Restless Spirits/The Seastorm (6:12); 13 Madness On All Hallows Eve (4:41); 14 Falling In Love (4:22); 15 The Lovers Dance (Finale)(1:32).

Review: George Fenton's diverse music for *High Spirits* is as varied as its composer's own repertoire. Varying broadly from mysterious female vocals to farcical symphonics, from riotous electronic/ orchestral effects to full-blooded symphonic overtures, the music draws much of its style from Irish folk songs. Yet the score also bristles with the effective moody atmospheres and quaint orchestrations that made Fenton's *A Com-*

pany of Wolves so remarkable. The Irish fiddle runs throughout many of the cues, driving the orchestra into a rhythmic frenzy of tunefulness, and Fenton ably intersperses the traditional Irish material with his own adventurous music to create a score that is both exhilarating and dreamlike.

Randall D. Larson

Higher Learning ♫♫♫

1994, Epic Soundtrax; from the movie *Higher Learning*, Columbia Pictures, 1994.

Album Notes: *Song Producers:* Sir Jinx & Goonz Skwad, David Gamson & Me'Shell NdegeOcello, Chase, Raphael Saadiq, Eric Rosse, Organized Noise, Brendan O'Brien, Brad Wood & Liz Phair, The Brand New Heavies, Ted Niceley, Stanley Clarke; *Song Engineers:* Sir Jinx & Chris Purman, David Gamson & Jason Goldstein, Bob Wartinbee, Darrin Harris & Jerry Brown, John Beverly Jones, Carlos Glover & Alvin Speights, Jim Ebden, Brad Wood, Paul Logus, Andy Baker, Steve Sykes; *Album Producer:* Danny Bramson; *Engineer:* Eddie Schreyer.

Selections: 1 Higher (Ice Cube)(4:32) *Ice Cube*; 2 Something To Think About (:10) *Ice Cube*; 3 Soul Searchin' (I Wanna Know If It's Mine)(M. NdegeOcello)(6:23) *Me' Shell NdegeOcello*; 4 Situation: Grimm (R. Tramwick/E. Clark/C.S. Kenol)(3:54) *Mista Grimm*; 5 Ask Of You (R. Saadiq)(6:02) *Raphael Saadiq*; 6 Losing My Religion (B. Berry/P. Buck/M. Mills/M. Stipe) (5:00) *Tori Amos*; 7 Phobia (P. Wade/P. Murra/P. Brown/A. Benjamin/A. Patton/R. Bailey)(5:57) *OutKast*; 8 My New Friend (:27) *Cole Hauser, Michael Rapaport*; 9 Year Of The Boomerang (Z. De la Rocha)(4:05) *Rage Against The Machine*; 10 Higher Learning/Time For Change (S. Bartholomew/A. Levy/N. Lavenport/J. Kincaid)(4:52) *The Brand New Heavies*; 11 Don't Have Time (L. Phair)(3:14) *Liz Phair*; 12 Butterfly (T. Amos)(3:07) *Tori Amos*; 13 By Your Side (Zhane)(4:52) *Zhane*; 14 Eye (M. Kotch/G. Fitzpatrick)(3:51) *Eve's Plum*; 15 The Learning Curve (S. Clarke)(3:30) *Stanley Clarke*.

Review: A contemporary drama, set in a modern college campus, *Higher Learning* charts a semester in the lives of a handful of students confronting issues of identity, diversity, sexism and escalating racial tension, all of which found an echo in the songs chosen to musically illustrate the film. Featuring recordings from the worlds of R&B, hip hop, rap, and alternative music, the diversified soundtrack brought together performers who also appeared in the film like Ice Cube, Eve's Plum, and others whose contributions were part of the behind-the-action musical make-up, notably Tori Amos, Me'shell NdegeOcello, Liz Phair, and Raphael Saadiq from Tony! Toni! Tone!. Adding a different touch to the proceedings, "Deja," composed by Stan-

motion picture soundtracks

ley Clarke, rounds up the performances on the album, along with two scenes from the film, "Something to Think About" and "My New Friend," with dialogue written by John Singleton, who directed it.

Highlander: The Original Scores ♫♫♫

1995, edel Records; from the movies *Highlander*, Republic Pictures, 1985; *Highlander II: The Quickening*, Columbia Pictures, 1990; and *Highlander: The Final Dimension*, Columbia Pictures, 1994.

Album Notes: *Highlander*: *Music*: Michael Kamen; *Orchestrations*: Michael Kamen; *Music Editors*: Lee Trong Weinrich, Jacky Garston; The National Philharmonic Orchestra, conducted by Michael Kamen; *Featured Musicians*: Bob Murphy (pipes), Ben Murdock (mandora); *Featured Vocalist*: Alexandra Thompson; *Producer*: Michael Kamen; *Engineer*: Eric Tomlinson; *Highlander II The Quickening*: *Music*: Stewart Copeland; *Orchestrations*: Johnathan Sheffer; *Featured Musicians*: Rusty Anderson (guitars); The Seattle Symphony Orchestra, conducted by Johnathan Sheffer; *Producer*: Stewart Copeland; *Engineers*: David Roberts, Andrew Warwick, Joel Moss; *Highlander The Final Dimension*: *Music*: J. Peter Robinson; *Orchestrations*: Michael McCuistion, Larry Rench; The Munich Symphony Orchestra, conducted by J. Peter Robinson; *Producers*: J. Peter Robinson, Michael Hoenig; *Engineer*: Robert Fernandez.

Selections: *HIGHLANDER:* 1 The Highlander Theme (5:19); 2 Rachel's Surprise/ Who Wants To Live Forever (Queen/M. Kamen/B. May)(4:08); 3 The Quickening (3:14); 4 Swordfight At 34th Street (2:24); 5 Under The Garden/The Prize (4:04);

HIGHLANDER II THE QUICKENING: 6 Finger Dip (2:00); 7 Rebel Troops (2:09); 8 Dam Raid (1:22); 9 White Cloud (1:44); 10 Mac Absorbs Reno (2:51); 11 Shield Shatters/Alan Dies (3:52);

HIGHLANDER THE FINAL DIMENSION: 12 Love Theme/Shrine Fight (5:30); 13 Massacre (The Beginning)(5:45); 14 Laundry Room/ Quickening 2 (3:30); 15 Revolution (5:30); 16 Final Battle/ Quickening 3/Epilogue (7:01).

Review: One of the best fantasy scores of the '80s, Michael Kamen's *Highlander* is represented in a 20-minute suite. A colorful blend of orchestra and synthesizers, with a Gaelic flavor, Kamen's score is adventurous, mythic and triumphant, and probably the best he's written. There is a rush of enthusiasm here, which sounds like Kamen was having fun writing it (a feeling that does not come across in his later Hollywood blockbuster scores). The effect of opening the album with Kamen's grand original proves anti-climactic however. Neither of the other scores can compare.

Stewart Copeland's *Highlander II* is a nonsensical cacophony that mixes coarse synth-rock with orchestra. Jonathan Sheffer's orchestrations are impressive, but working from such ignoble source material he is unable to make it anything special.

J. Peter Robinson allots 27 minutes to his music for *Highlander: The Final Dimension*. His music is superior to Copeland's, with a nice romantic theme for MacLeod's 19th-century love affair. However, the meandering "atmosphere" cues, awkward rock and roll passages and bloated climax are disconcerting on disc.

Though only 20 minutes, Michael Kamen's *Highlander* is nevertheless magnificent, and the showpiece of the album. It is this score which ultimately makes the CD recommended.

Paul Andrew MacLean

The Hitcher ♫♫♫

1991, Silva Screen Records; from the movie *The Hitcher*, Cannon Films, 1986.

Album Notes: *Music*: Mark Isham; *Orchestrations*: Mark Isham; *Featured Musicians*: Kurt Wortman, Bongo Bob Smith (percussion), Bill Douglass (bass), Mark Isham (electronics/ flugelhorn); *Album Producer*: Mark Isham; *Engineers*: Gary Clayton, Sam Lehmer.

Selections: 1 Headlights: Main Title (4:02); 2 The Chosen (2:24); 3 Keys (4:13); 4 Dust And Gasoline (3:01); 5 Dream (1:24); 6 Dogs (3:31); 7 Suicide (1:21); 8 Gun (1:44); 9 Cars And Helicopters (5:35); 10 Motel (2:47); 11 Transfer (1:45); 12 Endgame (2:49); 13 Guards And Cards (3:45); 14 The Hitcher: End Credits (4:12).

Review: Mark Isham's atmospheric score underlines the action in this terror-filled drama, a confrontation between good and evil, about a youth on a cross-country trip and the hitchiker he picks up on a deserted road. Using weird and seemingly disparate extremes, Isham created a flavorful synthesized score that captures the personalities of the characters as well as the tension in the action. It's all very effective and works well within the limits imposed by the subject matter and its treatment.

Hoffa ♫♫♫♫

1993, Fox Records; from the movie *Hoffa*, 20th Century-Fox, 1993.

Album Notes: *Music*: David Newman; *Orchestrations*: David Newman; *Music Editor*: Tom Villano; *Synth Programming*: Marty Frasu; Orchestra conducted by David Newman; *Album Producer*: David Newman; *Engineer*: Tim Boyle; *Assistant Engineer*: Sue McLean.

Selections: 1 Hoffa End Credits (7:58); 2 RTA Riot & Wake (6:56); 3 Truck Talk (3:07); 4 Trucker Salute (1:10); 5 Ride To The RTA (3:19); 6 This Man's Going To Be President (1:32); 7 Hoffa Trailer (2:15); 8 First Transition (1:05); 9 Billy Flynn (4:05); 10 Jimmy Goes To Jail (2:43); 11 Meeting The Mafia (1:17); 12 Loading Dock Riot (:48); 13 Going To Jail (1:07); 14 Bobby's Cell (1:43); 15 Ants At A Picnic (1:10); 16 Mob Negotiations (:54); 17 Jimmy's Last Ride (:59)

Review: Director Danny DeVito seeks to tell the story of union organizer Jimmy Hoffa with the larger than life scope afforded to any big screen heroic tale. To establish the appropriate musical accompaniment, DeVito turned to his longtime associate David Newman to create an epic symphonic score that gives Hoffa's battles a major life or death ambience. Cues, such as "RTA Riot & Wake," could have easily been composed for a bloody World War II invasion sequence, rather than a struggle outside an inner city loading dock. Even the small moments, like "Truck Talk," are saturated with Hoffa's noble ambitions for "the cause" and his urgent need to break "big labor" before they break him. Newman's original music for the *Hoffa* advance trailer is also included.

David Hirsch

Hollow Reed ♪♪♪

1997, RCA Victor; from the movie *Hollow Reed*, Scala Productions, 1997.

Album Notes: *Music*: Anne Dudley; *Orchestrations*: Anne Dudley; Orchestra conducted by Anne Dudley; *Featured Musicians*: Michala Petri (recorder), Anne Dudley (piano); *Album Producer*: Anne Dudley; *Engineers*: Roger Dudley, Steve Price.

Selections: 1 Hollow Reed Main Title (1:43); 2 Oliver's Theme (1:53); 3 Upside Down World (2:13); 4 Family Life (2:25); 5 Questioning (1:19); 6 Mother And Son (1:43); 7 Silent Witness (1:44); 8 Waking Nightmare (3:00); 9 A Resolution (2:46); 10 It Will Never Happen Again (1:50); 11 Seeds Of Doubt (1:36); 12 Unnatural Practices (1:31); 13 White Lies (1:35); 14 The Decision (1:41); 15 No Hiding Place (4:02); 16 In A Child's Mind (1:52); 17 Meditations (11:01); 18 I Shall Be Released (B. Dylan)(3:03) *Paul Weller*.

Review: Anne Dudley's score for *Hollow Reed* is generally attractive, with cues that are not always fully realized (many end up too abruptly or trail off without a satisfying conclusion), but develop musical ideas that are essentially compelling. The score, a series of long orchestral lines framing the delicate themes played on a variety of wind instruments, is quite evocative and establishes sustained moods that are striking. The overall effect is one of peace and quietness, which

strongly supports the screen action. Judged on its own merits, the score also makes an excellent impression that obliterates its more basic flaws.

Home Alone

Home Alone ♪♪♪

1990, CBS Records; from the movie *Home Alone*, 20th Century-Fox, 1990.

Album Notes: *Music*: John Williams; *Lyrics*: Leslie Bricusse; *Music Editor*: Ken Wannberg; Orchestra conducted by John Williams; *Album Producer*: John Williams; *Engineer*: Armin Steiner; *Assistant Engineers*: John Bruno, Chuck Carsha, Terry Brown.

Selections: 1 Home Alone (Main Title) ("Somewhere In My Memory") (4:53); 2 Holiday Flight (:59); 3 The House (2:27); 4 Star Of Bethlehem (2:51); 5 Man Of The House (4:33); 6 White Christmas (I. Berlin) *The Drifters*; 7 Scammed By A Kindergartner (3:55); 8 Please Come Home For Christmas (C. Brown/ G. Redd) (2:41) *Southside Johnny Lyon*; 9 Follow That Kid! (2:03); 10 Making The Plane (:52); 11 O Holy Night (A. Adam) (2:48); 12 Carol Of The Bells (P. Wilhousky) (1:25); 13 Star Of Bethlehem (2:59) *Children's Chorus*; 14 Setting The Trap (2:16); 15 Somewhere In My Memory (1:04); 16 The Attack On The House (6:53); 17 Mom Returns and Finale (4:19); 18 Have Yourself A Merry Little Christmas (H. Martin/R. Blane) (3:05) *Mel Torme*; 19 We Wish You A Merry Christmas (trad.)/End Title (4:15).

Review: At a time when most current films seem to eschew the idea of a thoughtful, original score in favor of unremarkable underscoring and commercial-pop style "hook" songs, the soundtrack for *Home Alone* emerges as a warm, fresh and thoroughly appealing disc that lends itself well to repeated playing.

John Williams' compositions, both spirited and sensitive, perfectly capture the essence of the Christmas season, with all its wonderment and fun, as viewed through the innocent (well, almost!) eyes of a child, the film's pint-sized star, Macauley Culkin. The lush orchestral score is enriched with a few carefully chosen pop vocal recordings, like The Drifters' classic version of "White Christmas," a searing "Please Come Home for Christmas" sung by rocker Southside Johnny Lyon, and an exquisite rendition of "Have Yourself A Merry Little Christmas," (perhaps the most perfect recording ever) by Mel Torme. Definitely a keeper for Christmas, or any time!

Charles L. Granata

Home Alone 2: Lost in New York 🎵🎵

1992, Fox Records; from the movie *Home Alone 2: Lost in New York*, 20th Century-Fox, 1992.

Album Notes: *Music:* John Williams; *Lyrics:* Leslie Bricusse; *Music Editor:* Ken Wannberg; Orchestra conducted by John Williams; *Album Producer:* John Williams; *Engineer:* Shawn Murphy; *Assistant Engineer:* Sue McLean.

Selections: 1 Somewhere In My Memory (3:49); 2 Home Alone (2:01); 3 We Overslept Again (2:46); 4 Christmas Star (3:18); 5 Arrival In New York (1:41); 6 Plaza Hotel and Duncan's Toy Store (3:45); 7 Concierge and Race To The Room (2:04); 8 Star Of Bethlehem (3:28); 9 The Thieves Return (4:35); 10 Appearance Of Pigeon Lady (3:19); 11 Christmas At Carnegie Hall: (a) O Come All Ye Faithful, (b) O Little Town Of Bethlehem, (c) Silent Night (5:02); 12 Into The Park (3:49); 13 Haunted Brownstone (3:01); 14 Christmas Star and Preparing The Trap (4:17); 15 To The Plaza Presto (3:22); 16 Reunion At Rockefeller Center (2:36); 17 Kevin's Booby Traps (3:41); 18 Finale (3:55); 19 Merry Christmas, Merry Christmas (2:51).

Review: Like most film sequels, *Home Alone 2* lacks much of the magic that made the original so endearing, and in many respects, this soundtrack follows suit. What's missing is more of the original John Williams music that enhanced the charm of the original. That said, it is a nice collection of holiday songs, performed by a wide variety of artists, including TLC's rap interpretation of "Sleigh Ride," Alan Jackson performing a country rendition of "A Holly Jolly Christmas," and "My Christmas Tree" sung by the Home Alone Children's Choir. Most interesting are Bette Midler's version of the film's theme, "Somewhere In My Memory," and two Williams compositions, "Merry Christmas, Merry Christmas" and "Christmas Star."

Charles L. Granata

Homeboy 🎵🎵🎵🎵⸴

1988, Virgin Records; from the movie *Homeboy*, 1988.

Album Notes: *Music:* Eric Clapton, Michael Kamen; *Featured Musicians:* Eric Clapton (guitar), Michael Kamen (keyboards), Steve Ferrone (drums), Nathan East (bass); *Album Executive Producer:* Fraser Kennedy; *Engineers:* Steve Chase, Jeremy Wheatley, Ben Kape, Lorraine Francis.

Selections: 1 Travelling East (E. Clapton/M. Kamen) (2:50) *Eric Clapton*; 2 Johnny (E. Clapton) (1:29) *Eric Clapton*; 3 Call Me If You Need Me (J.D. Harris) (3:03) *Magic Sam*; 4 Bridge (E. Clapton) (2:25) *Eric Clapton*; 5 Pretty Baby (H. Parker) (4:35) *J.B. Hutto & The New Hawks*; 6 Dixie (trad.) (3:42) *Eric Clapton, Nathan East*; 7 Ruby's Loft (E. Clapton) (2:33) *Eric Clapton*; 8 Country Bikin' (E. Clapton) (1:47) *Eric Clapton*; 9 I Want To Love You Baby (D. Hill) (2:35) *Peggy Scott, Jo Jo Benson*; 10 Bike Ride (E. Clapton) (1:37) *Eric Clapton*; 11 Ruby (E. Clapton) (3:53) *Eric Clapton*; 12 Party (E. Clapton) (1:42) *Eric Clapton*; 13 Living In The Real World (R. Argent) (3:33) *The Brakes*; 14 Training (E. Clapton) (3:58) *Eric Clapton*; 15 Final Fight (E. Clapton) (3:43) *Eric Clapton*; 16 Chase (E. Clapton) (3:33) *Eric Clapton*; 17 Dixie (trad.) (2:34) *Eric Clapton*; 18 Homeboy (E. Clapton/M. Kamen) (4:14) *Eric Clapton*.

Review: Eric Clapton's presence (his guitar playing, his writing) dominates the entire album, providing the score for this film about a washed-out former boxer trying to make a comeback, with much of its drive and energy. While some cues don't work as well as others ("Bridge," for instance, which is much too dry and uninspiring), most of the selections are beautifully reflective of the downbeat, bluesy moods in the film, and make a musical statement of their own, with Michael Kamen, Steve Ferrone and Nathan East providing solid backup to the leader-composer. Occasionally, as in "Training," the rock'n'roll legend shows his mettle in hard-driving tunes, but these moments are rare and far between and the overall tone of the score is more low-key and subdued. Some vocal numbers not by Clapton, add to the flavor of the album.

Homeward Bound

Homeward Bound: The Incredible Journey 🎵🎵🎵🎵

1993, Intrada Records; from the movie *Homeward Bound: The Incredible Journey*, Walt Disney Films, 1993.

Album Notes: *Music:* Bruce Broughton; *Orchestrations:* Don Nemitz; *Music Editor:* Patricia Carlin; Orchestra conducted by Bruce Broughton; *Album Producer:* Bruce Broughton; *Engineer:* Armin Steiner.

Selections: 1 My Name Is Chance (4:23); 2 The Journey Begins (2:52); 3 Fording The Stream (1:14); 4 The Cougar (3:54); 5 Just Over That Next Hill (2:22); 6 Breakfasting With Bears (1:11); 7 The Little Lost Girl (2:50); 8 Escape From The Pound (2:20); 9 Reunited (4:22); 10 End Credits (5:02).

Review: See entry below.

Homeward Bound II: Lost in San Francisco ♫♫♫♫

1996, Walt Disney Records; from the movie *Homeward Bound II: Lost in San Francisco,* Walt Disney Films, 1996.

Album Notes: *Music:* Bruce Broughton; *Orchestrations:* Bruce Broughton; *Music Editor:* Patricia Carlin; Orchestra conducted by Bruce Broughton; *Album Producer:* Bruce Broughton; *Engineer:* Armin Steiner.

Selections: 1 A Homeward Bound Overture (5:06); 2 Sassy And Chance (2:07); 3 Airport Escape (1:20); 4 Dog On A Date (1:49); 5 Chasing Chance (3:03); 6 In The Park (3:22); 7 Bungled Ambush (1:42); 8 The Fire (3:35); 9 Attacking The Red Van (6:08); 10 A Thing Of Beauty (2:39); 11 Delilah Returns (5:02).

Review: Bruce Broughton captured the striking beauty of the outdoor environment and the frantic pace of the action in his scores for the *Homeward Bound* films, about three animals, two dogs and a cat, first in their incredible journey across the Pacific Northwest, then in a sequel that finds the four-legged stars (voiced by Michael J. Fox, Sally Field, Don Ameche and Ralph Waite) lost in the San Francisco wild. It may seem a bit of an overkill to have this lush music used in such a context, but the fact remains that Broughton, one of today's top composers, found the proper voice needed to bring these adventures to musical life. In descriptive terms, he managed to write cues that are frequently picturesque and vivid ("The Cougar," in the first film, "Airport Escape," in the sequel) or simply remarkably attractive ("Just Over That Next Hill," "Dog on a Date"). The main theme that links both scores (developed as "A Homeward Bound" in the second volume) is a catchy, robust piece of business that recalls some of the best western themes heard on the screen.

Honey, I Blew Up the Kid ♫♫♫

1992, Intrada Records; from the movie *Honey, I Blew Up the Kid,* Walt Disney Pictures, 1992.

Album Notes: *Music:* Bruce Broughton; *Orchestrations:* Don Nemitz, David Slonaker; *Music Editor:* Patricia Carlin; Orchestra conducted by Bruce Broughton; *Album Producer:* Bruce Broughton; *Engineer:* Armin Steiner.

Selections: 1 Main Title (3:03); 2 To The Lab (1:53); 3 Adam Gets Zapped (:35); 4 Putting On Weight? (1:19); 5 Macrowaved (3:15); 6 How'd She Take It? (3:11); 7 Sneaking Out (1:12); 8 Don't Touch That Switch! (:26); 9 The Bunny Trick (2:41); 10 Get Big Bunny (4:11); 11 Clear The Streets! (3:00); 12 Car Flight (4:38); 13 Ice Cream! (3:47); 14 Look At That Mother! (2:26); 15 That's All Folks! (4:20).

Review: Broughton's larger-than-life score for the second *Honey...* film is a non-stop comedic score, half cartoon music and half emotive drama. The main theme—associated with Rick Moranis and the colossal results of his experiments—is a jaunty scherzo for saxophone and woodwind which propels the score with the unrelenting force of an animated hurricane. Like Ernest Gold's *It's a Mad, Mad, Mad, Mad World,* Broughton's riotous score throws every piece of its musical pie into the face of its listeners, yet takes time out to soothe them with gentle lyricism when it's called for. Comedy scores often don't hold up well on disc because they either are comprised of tiny, unrelated comic cues or are so full of wall-to-wall Mickey Mouse-isms that they make no sense apart from the visual antics. Broughton's score is a happy exception.

Randall D. Larson

Honeymoon in Vegas ♫♫♫

1992, Epic Soundtrax; from the movie *Honeymoon in Vegas,* Castle Rock Entertainment, 1992.

Album Notes: *Featured Performers:* Billy Joel, Ricky Van Shelton, Amy Grant, Travis Tritt, Bryan Ferry, Dwight Yoakam, Trisha Yearwood, Jeff Beck, Vince Gill, John Mellencamp, Willie Nelson, Bono; *Album Producers:* Peter Afterman, Glen Brunman.

Selections: 1 All Shook Up (O. Blackwell/E. Presley) (2:10) *Billy Joel;* 2 Wear My Ring Around Your Neck (R. Moody/B. Carroll) (2:14) *Ricky Van Shelton;* 3 Love Me Tender (E. Presley/V. Matson) (3:53) *Amy Grant;* 4 Burning Love (D. Linde) (3:35) *Travis Tritt;* 5 Heartbreak Hotel (M. Boren Axton/T. Durden/E. Presley) (3:22) *Billy Joel;* 6 Are You Lonesome Tonight? (R. Turk/L. Handman) (5:00) *Bryan Ferry;* 7 Suspicious Minds (M. James) (3:52) *Dwight Yoakam;* 8 (You're The) Devil In Disguise (B. Giant/B. Baum/F. Kaye) (2:38) *Trisha Yearwood;* 9 Hound Dog (J. Leiber/M. Stoller) (2:14) *Jeff Beck, Jed Leiber;* 10 That's All Right (A. Crudup) (2:44) *Vince Gill;* 11 Jailhouse Rock (J. Leiber/M. Stoller) (3:37) *John Mellencamp;* 12 Blue Hawaii (R. Rainger/L. Robin) (2:37) *Willie Nelson;* 13 Can't Help Falling In Love (G. Weiss/H. Peretti/L. Creatore) (2:05) *Bono.*

Review: An amusing idea (based on the concept that Elvis is alive and well, and performing in Las Vegas) makes for a delightful soundtrack album, with a baker's dozen of the King's hit tunes "covered" by various chartmakers. Not only is this an inspired selection, but anyone who loves Elvis will enjoy discovering these songs performed by others, like Billy Joel, Jeff Beck, Amy Grant, and Willie Nelson, to name a few.

motion picture soundtracks

STEWART COPELAND

Perhaps best known as the percussionist for the enormously successful 1980s pop supergroup the Police, Stewart Copeland has also scored numerous films and operas.

Copeland got his first real break in 1974 as a drummer for the band Curved Air. The demise of Curved Air came in 1977 and Copeland hooked up with Sting and Andy Summers and began to perform as the Police. The group accumulated four platinum albums and nine singles in the Top 40, but eventually the Police disbanded, and the band's members pursued solo careers.

In 1983 the multitalented Copeland composed the soundtrack for Francis Ford Coppola's film *Rumblefish,* which earned him a Golden Globe nomination. Copeland also ventured into the realm of television, penning the themes for George Lucas' "Droids" and "Ewoks" Saturday morning cartoons and composing the music for "The Equalizer," an Emmy Award-winning TV show.

Copeland's earlier success with the film score *Rumblefish* earned him the attention of Hollywood, and he was asked to compose music for a string of motion pictures, including Oliver Stone's *Wall Street* and *Talk Radio* and John Hughes' *She's Having a Baby.* In 1994 he wrote the blues-influenced score for the critically acclaimed film *Fresh.*

Venturing back into the world of popular music, Copeland formed the group Animal Logic in 1989, ultimately releasing two self-titled albums. In 1994 he launched an innovative tour with a sampling of percussion groups from around the world, including Zaire, Spain, and West Africa.

Hook 🎵🎵🎵🎵"

1991, Epic Sountrax; from the movie *Hook*, Tri-Star Pictures, 1991.

Album Notes: *Music:* John Williams; *Lyrics:* Leslie Bricusse; *Music Editor:* Ken Wannberg; Orchestra conducted by John Williams; *Featured Soloist:* Mike Lang (piano); *Album Producer:* John Williams; *Engineer:* Shawn Murphy; *Assistant Engineers:* Sue McLean.

Selections: 1 Prologue (1:31); 2 We Don't Wanna Grow Up (1:50); 3 Banning Back Home (2:22); 4 Granny Wendy (2:57); 5 Hook-Napped (3:56); 6 The Arrival Of Tink and The Flight To Neverland (5:56); 7 Presenting The Hook (2:58); 8 From Mermaids To Lost Boys (4:24); 9 The Lost Boy Chase (3:32); 10 Smee's Plan (1:45); 11 The Banquet (3:08); 12 The Never-Feast (4:40); 13 Remembering Childhood (11:02); 14 You Are The Pan (4:00); 15 When You're Alone (3:14); 16 The Ultimate War (7:53); 17 Farewell Neverland (10:17).

Review: Williams' frequently over-the-top swashbuckling score almost makes one wish the film, a big screen treatment of the story of Peter Pan, had been better than this sometimes messy, often spirited movie actually is. The fact is while the music served its purpose on the screen, it can be best appreciated in this CD in which it makes a different, albeit most enjoyable statement. Williams always excels at creating this type of score, regardless of the merits of the films themselves, and he seldom fails. Here, the score often ends up being quite evocative and exciting, with several cues, like "The Flight to Wonderland," and "The Ultimate War," reaching levels of dynamic enthusiasm that are exhilarating, while others, like "Presenting the Hook," seem to have great fun with the characters and situations they are illustrating. In the process, the composer also takes time to pause and create some lovely melodies, like "Remembering Childhood" for the more reflective moments in the action that add a very good counterpoint to the more active cues. Permeating the whole is the fantasy mood that prevails, making this score one of the composer's most satisfying.

Hoosiers 🎵🎵🎵🎵

1986, Polydor Records; from the movie *Hoosiers*, Orion Pictures, 1986.

Album Notes: *Music:* Jerry Goldsmith; *Orchestrations:* Arthur Morton; Orchestra conducted by Jerry Goldsmith; *Album Producer:* Jerry Goldsmith, Bruce Botnick; *Engineer:* Mike Ross.

Selections: 1 Theme From Hoosiers (4:22); 2 You Did Good (6:59); 3 The Coach Stays (2:40); 4 The Pivot (3:26); 5 Get The Ball (1:46); 6 Town Meeting (4:44); 7 The Finals (15:16).

Review: An inspirational film about basketball and the difficult road to final victory of a high school team from a small Indiana town in 1951, *Hoosiers* (aka *Best Shots*) benefited from a rousing *Chariots of Fire*-like score by Jerry Goldsmith. Propelled by a solid synthesizer theme developed over a pounding rhythm, the cues illustrate the various hurdles, professional and personal, the members of the team must overcome under the guidance of their coach, splendid performed by Gene Hackman. Along the way, Goldsmith finds some striking musical ideas in "The Coach Stays," "Get the Ball," and "The Finals" that more than anything else enhance the sometimes plodding action as it moves to its logical conclusion.

Hot Shots!

Hot Shots! ♫♫♫

1991, Varese-Sarabande; from the movie *Hot Shots!*, 20th Century-Fox, 1991.

Album Notes: *Music:* Sylvester Levay; *Arrangements:* Sylvester Levay; Orchestra conducted by Sylvester Levay; *Featured Musician:* Duane Sciacqua (guitars); *Album Producers:* Sylvester Levay, Jim Abrahams; *Engineer:* Brian Reeves.

Selections: 1 Hot Shots!: Main Title (2:38); 2 Sea Maneuvers (1:50); 3 Flash Back (1:45); 4 This Is For You Dad (1:37); 5 Saboteurs (:33); 6 Enemy Planes (1:00); 7 Topper Returns (1:23); 8 Love Theme (The Fruit Seduction (2:12); 9 The Take-Off (1:43); 10 Rescue/Drive To The Hospital (1:03); 11 Father's Theme (:53); 12 Training Flight (1:38); 13 The Man I Love (G. & I. Gershwin)(2:49) *Valeria Golino*; 14 Aerial Combat (1:56); 15 The Man I Love (reprise)(:35); 16 The Kiss (:46); 17 Dream Lover (B. Darin)(2:40) *Dion*.

Review: See entry below.

Hot Shots! Part Deux ♫♫♫

1993, Varese-Sarabande; from the movie *Hot Shots! Part Deux*, 20th Century-Fox, 1993.

Album Notes: *Music:* Basil Poledouris; *Orchestrations:* Greig McRitchie; *Music Editor:* Curtis Roush; Orchestra conducted by Basil Poledouris; *Album Producer:* Basil Poledouris; *Engineer:* Tim Boyle.

Selections: 1 Main Title (1:29); 2 Dipsong Fight (3:35); 3 The 3 Bears/ Flurvian Sea (3:03); 4 Reel 5 (3:17); 5 Colonel Torture (3:20); 6 Gotta Light? (6:06); 7 Compound Escape (4:03); 8 Saddam Battles/Freedom Fighters (4:59).

Review: The difference between both scores is what separates a laborious effort from a truly imaginative one. While Sylvester Levay is quite an acceptable composer, whose ideas are for the most part interesting but a trifle hackneyed, Poledouris brings to the task a flair that is truly unmistakable. Thus, if there only was Levay's score to listen to, it probably would pass muster and be judged quite favorably. But *Hot Shots! Part Deux*, with its broadly humoristic evocations stands so far above that the music devised by Levay doesn't quite make the grade in comparison. This, by the way, is also in keeping with the general tone in both films, with the first an amiable comedy with some goofy moments in it, while the second is completely over-the-top with hilarious results.

The Hot Spot ♫♫♫♫

1990, Antilles Records; from the movie *The Hot Spot*, Orion Films, 1990.

Album Notes: *Music:* Jack Nitzsche; *Featured Musicians:* Miles Davis (trumpet), Earl Palmer (drums), Tim Drummond (bass), Roy Rogers (slide guitar), Taj Mahal (acoustic guitar), John Lee Hooker (guitar); *Album Producers:* Jack Nitzsche, Michael Hoenig; *Engineer:* Pamela Neal.

Selections: 1 Coming To Town (3:06) *John Lee Hooker*; 2 Empty Bank (2:19) *Taj Mahal*; 3 Harry's Philosophy (2:46) *John Lee Hooker*; 4 Dolly's Arrival (1:17); 5 Harry And Dolly (2:49) *John Lee Hooker*; 6 Sawmill (3:03) *John Lee Hooker*; 7 Bank Robbery (4:31) *Taj Mahal*; 8 Moanin' (3:20) *John Lee Hooker*; 9 Gloria's Story (3:24); 10 Harry Sets Up Sutton (1:41) *John Lee Hooker*; 11 Murder (4:08) *John Lee Hooker*; 12 Blackmail (2:09); 13 End Credits (5:19).

Review: This soundtrack album is almost as interesting for Jack Nitzsche's flavorful score as it is for the musicians who play it, including Miles Davis, John Lee Hooker and Taj Mahal, among them. But the specific atmosphere that permeates Dennis Hopper's *film noir*, about a drifter whose arrival in a small Texas town sets off a chain of events that ends in a fracas in which the various characters reveal their darker leanings, seems to lend itself to this kind of musical treatment. Once the events are set in motion, the course to the unavoidable conclusion is taken at a slow, deliberate pace, an impression further enhanced by the bluesy tone of Jack Nitzsche's evocative music, with John Lee Hooker dominating the tracks with his gritty vocals and Miles Davis delivering a subdued, but quite effective counterpoint. "Dolly's Arrival," a slow sexy tune, played by Roy Rogers on slide guitar, is a highlight, along with "Bank Robbery," in which Miles Davis trades riffs with Taj Mahal on guitar and vocal.

Hour of the Gun 🎜🎜🎜🎜

1991, Intrada Records; from the movie *Hour of the Gun*, United Artists, 1967.

Album Notes: *Music*: Jerry Goldsmith; *Orchestrations*: David Tamkin; Orchestra conducted by Jerry Goldsmith; *Album Producer*: Ray Horricks; *CD Producer*: Douglass Fake.

Selections: 1 The Hour Of The Gun (2:41); 2 Main Title (4:54); 3 New Marshall (1:06); 4 Ballot Box (3:41); 5 Ambush (2:14); 6 Whose Cattle (2:47); 7 The Painted Desert (1:33); 8 The Search (2:48); 9 Doc's Message (4:40); 10 A Friendly Lie (4:23).

Review: In yet another retelling of the events that led to the celebrated gunfight at the O.K. Corral, the one that saw Doc Holliday and Wyatt Earp defeat the Clanton gang, *Hour of the Gun* goes one step further and chronicles the slow descent of the lawman into a maelstrom of personal vindication and revenge, following the showdown. One of various psychological westerns that came from that period, *Hour of the Gun* was as much interested in its characters' motivations and inner thoughts as it was in big action scenes. As a result, action, gritty and violent when it happened, took a back seat to drama, thereby spoiling the film itself from one of its most important elements and an essential ingredient in the genre itself. Responding to the demands of the screenplay, Jerry Goldsmith wrote a score that reflected some of the most intense moments in the film, while also subtly underscoring its more cerebral aspects. Altogether, it was a strong score from a composer who had already found a personal voice in the western and who obviously enjoyed writing for it. The CD reissue simply replicates the original LP, issued on the United Artists label, but with the extra advantage of clean, spacious sound.

See also: Tombstone and Wyatt Earp

House of Frankenstein 🎜🎜🎜🎜♭

1995, Marco Polo Records; from the movie *House of Frankenstein*, Universal-International, 1944.

Album Notes: *Music*: Hans J. Salter, Paul Dessau; *Reconstruction and Orchestrations*: John Morgan, William T. Stromberg; The Moscow Symphony Orchestra, conducted by William T. Stromberg; *Album Producer*: Betta International; *Engineers*: Edvard Shakhnazarian, Vitaly Ivanov.

Selections: 1 Universal Signature (J. McHugh)(:16); 2 Main Title (2:17); 3 Lightning Strikes (1:47); 4 Gruesome Twosome Escape (1:50); 5 Strangulation (:30); 6 Off To Vasaria (1:18); 7 Chamber Of Horrors (:40); 8 Dracula Restored (1:30); 9 Dracula's Ring (1:28); 10 The Burgomaster Murdered (2:06); 11 Rendezvous With Dracula (2:34); 12 The World Beyond (1:29); 13 Dracula Pursued (1:44); 14 Dracula Destroyed (1:09); 15 Gypsy Tantrums (1:47); 16 Ilonka Whipped (1:07); 17 Dan's Love (3:23); 18 The Ruins (1:37); 19 The Monstrosities (2:02); 20 Wolf Man Revived (2:13); 21 Show Me The Records (2:22); 22 Travels (:35); 23 Hunchback's Jealousy (1:51); 24 Niemann's Laboratory (1:30); 25 Liquefying Brains (1:12); 26 Niemann's Revenge (1:07); 27 The Pentagram (1:37); 28 Full Moon (1:15); 29 Silver Bullet (3:33); 30 Dr. Niemann Successful (1:24); 31 The Moon Is Full (1:18); 32 Larry At Peace (1:36); 33 Dr. Niemann Attacked (1:36); 34 Death Of The Unholy Two (1:14); 35 End Cast (:28).

Review: This CD features the complete score for *House of Frankenstein*, composed by Salter and German avant-garde composer Paul Dessau (along with Charles Previn, another Universal staff composer who is co-credited on a few cues). The *House* score is thrilling, vigorous music, a *Symphonie Fantastique* in its own right, broken by the occasional light tune such as a pleasing travelogue romp in "Off to Vasaria" and the delightfully manic carnival cacophony of "Chamber of Horrors." The digital recording really lets Morgan's orchestration shine in this cue. Otherwise, the music is dark and terrible, malevolent music for monstrous mayhem. Motifs spring forth for Dracula (somnambulant winds, a 4-note ascending figure, erupting into furious strings, brass, and snare for his final dawn pursuit), the Hunchback (a sorrowful violin melody), the Wolf-Man (passionate strings and winds, the 3-note descending phrase from *The Wolf-Man*, still mourning Larry Talbot's tragic curse), and the Frankenstein Monster (the dynamic, growling brass motif that makes up the film's primary theme). Spooky sounds for sordid souls.

"A virtual Hollywood camp *Symphony Fantastique*," to quote Bill Whitaker's informative notes, House of Frankenstein is one of many scores Hans J. Salter wrote during his tenure at Universal International, in which his quirky imagination was severely tasked by the requirements of the job. With great support from Paul Dessau, like him another emigre from Nazi Germany, Salter wrote a score that transcends its subject matter, and rightfully takes its place with this sumptuous rerecording among the great compositions from the screen that came out of the era. Unlike the other monster movies that were churned out by the studio at the time, *House of Frankenstein* has a truly all-star cast that included such ungodly characters as Dracula, the Wolfman, the Hunchback, the Mad Doctor, and of course the Monster, all of whom needed appropriate themes. As a result, the score teems with melodies and cues, all aimed at explaining the action while giving the weirdos a proper musical image. Lovingly reconstructed by John Morgan and played with relish by the Moscow Symphony Orchestra conducted by William Stromberg, the score at long last gets its proper due in this digital world premiere recording you won't want to miss.

Randall Larson/Didier C. Deutsch

The House of the Spirits
♪♪♪♪⁷

1993, Virgin Records; from the movie *The House of the Spirits,* **Miramax Films, 1993.**

Album Notes: *Music*: Hans Zimmer; *Orchestrations*: Fiachra Trench, Nick Glennie-Smith; *Arrangements*: Hans Zimmer, Nick Glennie-Smith; Orchestra conducted by Fiachra Trench; *Featured Soloists*: Jurgen Musser (clarinet), Martin Spanner (oboe, cor Anglais), Richard Stuart, Douglas Myers (trumpet), Michael Stevens (guitar), Nick Glennie-Smith (piano); *Album Producers*: Hans Zimmer, Bille August; *Engineer*: Malcolm Luker.

Selections: 1 The House Of The Spirits (10:02); 2 Clara (6:31); 3 Coup (9:34); 4 Pedro And Blanca (9:50); 5 Clara's Ghost/La Paloma (S. De Yradier)/ Closing Titles (7:24).

Review: Hans Zimmer's gorgeous score is one of the winning ingredients in this story, spanning more than 45 years, of an aristocratic Chilean family, dominated by an authoritarian paterfamilias, which also includes his clairvoyant wife, his staunchly severe sister, and his daughter. Some of the more disturbing aspects of the story find an echo in the composer's score, though most of the cues are solidly rooted in romantic themes that seem to belie the turmoil in the screen action. Rearranged for this release into five long selections, the cues gain more interpretive force in this presentation, which also enables the music to make a greater impression.

Housekeeping ♪♪♪⁷

1987, Varese-Sarabande Records; from the movie *Housekeeping,* **Columbia Pictures, 1987.**

Album Notes: *Music*: Michael Gibbs; *Album Producer*: Michael Gibbs.

Selections: 1 Journey To Grandma's (2:20); 2 Ruth And Lucille In Fingerbone (1:35); 3 Hole In The Ice (1:44); 4 Getting To Know Sylvie (3:17); 5 Sylvie (1:39); 6 Life With Sylvie (5:25); 7 Lucille And Ruth Drift (4:10); 8 A Day Out (1:02); 9 On The Lake (1:31); 10 Magic Island (1:49); 11 Waiting And Reminiscing (2:27); 12 Freightcar Ride (1:11); 13 Cleaning House (1:09); 14 Leaving Home (2:48); 15 End Credits (2:43).

Review: Michael Gibbs' folk-tinged score reflects the odd, warm aura of this quirky story about two girls in a small Washington State community, whose lives revolve around the various relatives (all women) who drift in and out of their house, including their mother, grandmother, grand aunts, and aunt. Though solidly suggestive of the moods in the film, the almost chamber-like score, often performed by a couple of solo instruments, sometimes over a sparse orchestral section, appears relatively dry when heard on its own merits, possibly because the musical themes are not sufficiently fleshed out. Only occasionally does the music becomes vibrant ("Freightcar Ride"), exhibiting the very qualities that could have sustained the whole score had they been in display throughout.

How Green Was My Valley
♪♪♪♪♪

1993, Fox Records; from the movie *How Green Was My Valley,* **20th Century-Fox, 1941.**

Album Notes: *Music*: Alfred Newman; The 20th Century-Fox Orchestra, conducted by Alfred Newman; *CD Producer*: Nick Redman; *Engineer*: Dan Hersch.

Selections: 1 20th Century-Fox Fanfare (:12); 2 Main Title/ Huw's Theme (2:50); 3 The Family And Bronwen (6:30); 4 The Strike/Mother And Huw In Broken Ice (4:42); 5 Treasure Island/The Spring Birds (3:51); 6 Angharad And Mister Gruffydd (2:08); 7 Command From The Queen (1:50); 8 Huw Walks Among The Daffodils (3:29); 9 Angharad With The Minister (1:06); 10 Love Denied (4:11); 11 School (1:36); 12 Huw's Lesson/The Mine Tragedy (3:06); 13 Two More Brothers Leave (1:52); 14 The House On The Hill/Gossip (6:57); 15 Goodbyes (1:31); 16 Huw Finds His Father (:53); 17 Finale/End Title (1:42).

Review: One of the great scores to come out of Alfred Newman's fertile pen, *How Green Was My Valley* makes a belated and rousing recording debut in this CD released a few years ago. Set against the stark background of life in the Welsh coal mines, this deeply moving story of a family runs the whole gamut of human emotions, from romance to anger, from unrequited love to personal ambition, from the warmth of friendship to the greed of the ruling class. Making its own comments on the unfolding story, Newman's score echoes these sentiments with themes that are lovingly detailed and beautifully catchy. This is nowhere more evident than in the striking cue marked "The Family and Bronwen," in which the composer found warm accents to describe Huw, the film's narrator looking back at his youth and the feelings he had for his family of struggling miners. Presented in stereo, in a sound quality that is not always up to the exacting demands of the digital era, with noticeable hiss and some distortion on many of the tracks, the CD nonetheless is an important contribution to the ever increasing library of classic film scores from the past.

203

How the West Was Won ♫♫♫

1996, Rhino Records; from the movie *How the West Was Won*, M-G-M, 1962.

Album Notes: *Music*: Alfred Newman; *Lyrics*: Johnny Mercer, Sammy Cahn; *Orchestrations*: Leo Shukin, Jack Hayes, Ken Darby; The M-G-M Studio Orchestra and Chorus, conducted by Alfred Newman, Ken Darby, Robert E. Dolan, Joseph Lilley; *CD Producer*: Didier C. Deutsch; *Engineers*: Darcy M. Proper, Ellen Fitton.

Selections: CD 1: 1 Overture (5:50); 2 Main Title (3:08); 3 This Is The West (3:19); 4 Miss Bailey's Ghost (:26); 5 A Home In The Meadow (2:59); 6 The Erie Canal (:35) *The Whiskeyhill Quartet, The Ken Darby Singers*; 7 Two Hearts On A Tree (2:03); 8 Shenandoah (:29) *The Ken Darby Singers*; 9 First Meeting (2:24); 10 When I Was Single (:41); 11 First Kiss (2:27); 12 The Morning After (:24); 13 The River Pirates (9:02); 14 Godspeed Eve (2:24); 15 The Burial (3:45) *Debbie Reynolds, Carroll Baker*; 16 Wagon Train Forward (2:00); 17 Sit Down Sister (1:36); 18 Wanderin' (1:41) *The Whiskeyhill Quartet*; 19 The Jump Off Point (:22); 20 Cleve Van Valen (5:20); 21 Poor Wayfarin' Stranger (2:02) *The Whiskeyhill Quartet*; 22 Raise A Ruckus Tonight (J. Mercer)(2:25) *Debbie Reynolds, The Whiskeyhill Quartet, The Ken Darby Singers*; 23 Come Share My Life (2:17); 24 Cheyennes (4:47); 25 Careless Love (:26) *Judy Henske, The Whiskeyhill Quartet*; 26 Gold Claim (1:40); 27 What Was Your Name In The States? (J. Mercer)(2:03) *Debbie Reynolds*; 28 He's Gone Away (3:17); 29 Home In The Meadow (S. Cahn)(1:56) *Debbie Reynolds*; 30 Marriage Proposal (1:44).

CD 2: 1 Entr'acte (4:36); 2 Mr. Lincoln (1:09); 3 He's Linus' Boy (3:01); 4 I'm Sad And I'm Lonely (3:02); 5 When Johnny Comes Marching Home (:57) *The Ken Darby Singers*; 6 Zeb's Return (4:03); 7 The Pony Express (1:52); 8 A Railroader's Bride I'll Be (1:18); 9 Workin' (1:04); 10 The Jugglers (:19); 11 No Goodbye (1:48); 12 Zeb And Jethro (3:03); 13 Buffalo Stampede (1:40); 14 Climb A Higher Hill (4:17); 15 The Van Valen Auction (3:59); 16 Gant—Desperado (1:54); 17 No Goodbye (2:35); 18 Celebration (1:49); 19 Finale (:21); 20 Finale Ultimo; 21 Exit Music (2:46); 22 Miss Bailey's Ghost (playback version) (:26) *Imogene Clark, Carl Fortina*; 23 A Home In The Meadow (playback Version)(2:59); 24 When I Was Single (playback Version)(:41) *Imogene Clark, Carl Fortina*; 25 Shenandoah (2:26); 26 Rock Of Ages (1:32); 27 The Erie Canal (1:08); 28 Wait For The Hoedown (J. Mercer)(2:47); 29 First Meeting (alternate version)(2:22); 30 No Goodbye (vocal version)(1:49); 31 Home In The Meadow (alternate version) (2:32) *Debbie Reynolds*.

Review: The blockbuster western that almost ended all westerns now finally has a soundtrack CD on a similarly grand scale, with Rhino's ambitious restoration of more than two hours of Alfred Newman's score. Like the film itself, the soundtrack aims for a comprehensive portrait of more than half a century of Americana, from folk songs to ballads to music hall fare. Newman's main theme, booming out of an 86-piece band, still has its power to stir, and much of the restored orchestration is lovely and evocative, although the frequent appearances of the Ken Darby Singers now seem to belong to a faraway time when a men's chorus lurked behind every cactus. In "Raise a Ruckus Tonight" and "Wait for the Hoedown," Debbie Reynolds scholars will find an early incarnation of the "unsinkable" character that she has been playing ever since.

Marc Kirkeby

How to Make an American Quilt ♫♫♫♫♭

1995, MCA Records; from the movie *How to Make an American Quilt*, Universal Pictures, 1995.

Album Notes: *Music*: Thomas Newman; *Orchestrations*: Thomas Pasatieri; *Music Editor*: Bill Bernstein; Orchestra conducted by Thomas Newman; *Album Producers*: Thomas Newman, Bill Bernstein; *Engineer*: Dennis Sands.

Selections: 1 Quilting Theme (1:43); 2 "The Life Before" (2:23); 3 Swinging On A Star (J. Van Heusen/J. Burke)(2:29) *Bing Crosby*; 4 Hyacinth & Gladiola (1:41); 5 Night Orchard (1:56); 6 He Never Came Back (1:47); 7 Cherry, Cherry (N. Diamond)(2:43) *Neil Diamond*; 8 You Belong To Me (P.W. King/C. Price/R. Stewart)(3:03) *Patsy Cline*; 9 Sophia (2:10); 10 The Sensation Of Falling (:36); 11 Foolish Things (:53); 12 Riffin' At The Ritz (B. Goodman/W. Miller) (3:27) *Benny Goodman*; 13 At Last (H. Warren/M. Gordon) (3:00) *Etta James*; 14 Anna Loves/Leaves (1:37); 15 Crow (1:16); 16 An American Quilt (3:36); 17 I Don't Want To Set The World On Fire (E. Seiler/E. Durham/S. Marcus/B. Benjamin)(2:59) *The Inkspots*; 18 Portraits/Pond (2:00); 19 "Where Love Resides" (1:01); 20 The Diver (2:43).

Review: An excellent score, with a great Americana flair to it, this soundtrack album further benefits from some excellent pop vocal selections, including Bing Crosby's "Swinging on a Star," Patsy Cline's "You Belong to Me," and The Inkspots' "I Don't Want to Set the World on Fire." But the palm here goes to Thomas Newman whose charming, warm series of cues evokes a time and a place that no longer seems to exist, except perhaps in the movies. With cues that seductively explore the myriad variations offered by the central "Quilting Theme," heard as the opening track, the score sets its own moods and reveals a lyrical side that is most engaging. There are many highlights here, outside of the pop selections that give the narrative a strong time period, but a first choice would definitely include "The Life Before," "An American Quilt," "Portraits/Pond," and "The Diver."

Howards End 🎵🎵🎵🎵

1992, Nimbus Records; from the movie *Howards End*, Orion Classics & Merchant Ivory Productions, 1992.

Album Notes: *Music*: Richard Robbins; *Orchestrations*: Robert Stewart; Orchestra conducted by Harry Rabinowitz; *Featured Soloist*: Martin Jones (piano); *Engineer*: Keith Grant.

Selections: 1 Main Title: Howards End (Percy Grainger's Bridal Lullaby) (3:48); 2 Helen And Paul Call It Off (2:53); 3 Music And Meaning (3:04); 4 The Basts/Spring Landscape (7:54); 5 Tango At Simpson's-In-The-Strand (3:17) *Teddy Peiro's Tango Group*; 6 An Unexpected Proposal (4:10); 7 Margaret's Arrival At Howards End (Percy Grainger's Bridal Lullaby)(2:37); 8 At A Castle In Shropshire (4:40); 9 Moving In (2:05); 10 On The River (3:14); 11 The Sisters' Reconciliation (2:08); 12 Leonard's Death (5:30); 13 Return To Howards End (4:22); 14 End Credits (Percy Grainger's Mock Morris)(3:19).

Review: Richard Robbins' approach to film scoring is often very dramatic, with robust romantic themes that sweep the listener into their highly-charged melodic elements, and very effective. *Howards End* is no exception. Anchored around Percy Grainger's "Bridal Lullaby," the title tune creates an atmosphere of its own, elegant and slightly understated. These moods are developed more fully with the first original cue, "Helen and Paul Call It Off," in which the early 20th-century atmosphere of the film elicits an echo in Robbins' music. The other selections fully explore the dramatic possibilities born out of this story about an impoverished young widower, now married to a richer friend of his late wife, in which class prejudice and Edwardian snobbery frequently clash with dramatic results. Bringing a total change of pace, "Tango at Simpson's-in-the-Strand" shows another facet of Robbins' creativity and his knack for more exotic types of music.

The Hudsucker Proxy 🎵🎵🎵🎵

1994, Varese-Sarabande; from the movie *The Hudsucker Proxy*, Warner Bros., 1994.

Album Notes: *Music*: Carter Burwell; *Orchestrations*: Sonny Kompanek; *Arrangements*: Carter Burwell, Todd Kasow; *Music Editor*: Todd Kasow; Orchestra conducted by Sonny Kompanek; *Album Engineer*: Michael Farrow.

Selections: 1 Prologue (A. Khachaturian)(3:20); 2 Norville Suite (3:53); 3 Waring's Descent (:27); 4 The Hud Sleeps (2:13); 5 Light Lunch (A. Khachaturian)(1:38); 6 The Wheel Turns (:52); 7 The Hula Hoop (A. Khachaturian)(4:10); 8 Useful (:40); 9 Walk Of Shame (1:22); 10 Blue Letter (:43); 11 A Long Way Down (1:46); 12 The Chase (1:02); 13 Norville's End (3:52); 14 Epilogue (A. Khachaturian)(2:08); 15 Norville's Reprise (1:22).

Review: A goofball spoof of big business by the Coen brothers (*Fargo*), *The Hudsucker Proxy* has an equally appropriate Carter Burwell score. The composer counterpoints the on-screen antics by playing up the bizarre visual designs and characters "earnest" motives. Two Khachaturian pieces (one is the celebrated "Sabre Dance" from the *Gayane Suite*) are well adapted into the score to add a further air of pomposity to the internal politics at Hudsucker Industries.

David Hirsch

Hundra 🎵🎵🎵🎵🎵

1991, Prometheus Records/Belgium; from the movie *Hundra*, 1991.

Album Notes: *Music*: Ennio Morricone; Orchestra conducted by Ennio Morricone; *Album Producer*: Morris J. Diamond; *Engineers*: Smitty Price, Michel Van Achter.

Selections: 1 Chase (2:19); 2 Love Theme (3:17); 3 Hundra's War Theme (2:02); 4 The Magical Change (1:38); 5 Slaughter In The Village (6:58); 6 Chrysula, The Wise One (1:14); 7 By The Sea (1:00); 8 The Wild Bunch (:46); 9 You're Free (1:29); 10 The Love Temple (:55); 11 Bow To The Bull (:51); 12 Hundra's Return (2:34); 13 The Defeat (1:25); 14 A Funny Man (2:59); 15 Hundra's Revenge (5:14).

Review: It may be somewhat of a surprise to find Ennio Morricone scoring a sword-and-sorcery epic in which the central character is a female Conan, but don't let that deter you from enjoying this tremendously exciting score which teems with great, overblown themes in which heroic accents are the predominant note. When he is inspired to write an action score, Morricone often creates themes that are melodically quite powerful and engaging. Such is the case here with "Hundra's War Theme," "Slaughter in the Village," and "Hundra's Revenge," that are as epic and descriptive as one could wish an action theme to be. Central to their effectiveness are strongly delineated melodies that capture the motion in the screen action and translate it in evocative ways that grab the listener's ear and force his attention. In sharp contrast, the composer also includes in the mix a series of cues that are marked by the attractive musical lines in them, notably "Love

Theme," which is particularly fetching, or "Chrysula, The Wise One," in which an oboe details the melody over the full orchestral texture. A great score that may be overlooked but is well worth discovering.

The Hunger 🎵🎵🎵

1983, Varese-Sarabande; from the movie *The Hunger*, M-G-M/UA, 1983.

Album Notes: *Music*: Michel Rubini, Denny Jaeger; *Album Producers*: Michel Rubini, Denny Jaeger; *Engineer*: Daniel Hersch.

Selections: 1 Trio in E-Flat, op. 100 (excerpt)(F. Schubert)(3:10); 2 Beach House (3:04) *Stefany Spruill*; 3 Suite No. 1 for Solo Cello in G Major, Preludium, 1st movement (excerpt)(J.S. Bach)(2:14); 4 Waiting Room/Flashbacks (1:50); 5 Sarah's Panic (1:50); 6 The Arisen (5:31); 7 Partita No. 3 in E Major, Gavotte en Rondeau (excerpt)(J.S. Bach)(3:09); 8 Lakme (excerpt)(L. Delibes) (6:05); 9 Sarah's Transformation (1:03); 10 The Final Death (2:12); 11 Trio in E Flat, op. 100 (excerpt)(F. Schubert)(4:54).

Review: A classy contemporary vampire story, *The Hunger* recalls through some of its aspects Roger Vadim's *Blood and Roses,* with some twists that even the Gallic director wouldn't have thought about. Starring David Bowie, in a Dorian Gray role, and Catherine Deneuve, the steamy thriller also stars Susan Sarandon, with whom Deneuve has a memorable seduction scene after she has disposed of Bowie in a most ungentlewomanly fashion. Adding a touch of class of its own, the soundtrack collects many works from the classical repertoire, with Michel Rubini providing some cues that also seem quite appropriate. Maybe not to everyone's taste, but interestingly challenging nonetheless.

The Hunt for Red October 🎵🎵🎵🎵

1990, MCA Records; from the movie *The Hunt for Red October,* Paramount Pictures, 1990.

Album Notes: *Music*: Basil Poledouris; *Orchestrations*: Greig McRitchie; *Music Editors*: Tom Villano, Thomas Milano; *Synthesizer*: Michael Boddicker; Orchestra and Chorus conducted by Basil Poledouris; *Album Producer*: Basil Poledouris; *Engineer*: Tim Boyle.

Selections: 1 Hymn To Red October (Main Title)(5:04); 2 Nuclear Scam (7:17); 3 Putin's Demise (:54); 4 Course Two-Five-Zero (:21); 5 Ancestral Aid (2:10); 6 Chopper (2:52); 7 Two Wives (2:41); 8 Red Route I (3:28); 9 Plane Crash (1:46); 10 Kaboom!!! (3:15).

Review: A fresh spin on the old East-West cold war cliches, *The Hunt for Red October* turned out to be a particularly gripping drama, thanks largely to Sean Connery's understated performance as the commander of a Russian nuclear submarine who wants to defect to the West, and who is chased by his own bent on stopping him and the Americans who don't trust his motivations. The taut narrative calls for a powerful score that evokes the drama, its roots, the background of its various participants, and a bit of patriotic accents to limn the whole thing. Basil Poledouris delivered all of these and then some in his outstanding contribution, in which a Russian chorus brings an appropriately Slavic flavor to the "Main Title," and in which the course of the action is charted in vivid musical details that have great descriptive force and persuasion.

I Love Trouble 🎵🎵🎵🎵

1994, Varese-Sarabande Records; from the movie *I Love Trouble,* Touchstone Pictures, 1994.

Album Notes: *Music*: David Newman; *Orchestrations*: Scott Smalley, Chris Boardman; *Music Editors*: Dan Carlin, Jr., Tom Kramer, George Martin, Tom Villano; *Synthesizer Programmer*: Martin Frasu; Orchestra conducted by David Newman; *Album Producer*: David Newman; *Engineers*: Bruce Botnick, Robert Fernandez.

Selections: 1 Here's Peter (5:10); 2 Here's Sabrina (1:55); 3 Calling All Boggs (1:16); 4 Honeymoon Night (4:55); 5 Two Scoop Snoops (3:39); 6 Everybody Buys The Globe (:47); 7 Scoop De Jour (3:16); 8 Sabrina's Hip (1:04); 9 Wild Goose Chase (1:17); 10 The Beekman Agreement (2:02); 11 Keyhole Foreplay (1:21); 12 Happily Ever After (2:22); 13 I Love Trouble (3:43); 14 You've Really Got A Hold On Me (W. Robinson)(3:38) *Robbyn Kirmsse*.

Review: The delicately hewn themes David Newman created for the two protagonists in this heart-warming romantic comedy help conjure up the pleasant atmosphere that pervades it. A story about two rival reporters assigned to cover the same case who reluctantly join forces to crack it and the mutual appreciation that comes out of this cooperation, the screenplay enticed the composer to write a strongly evocative score, strong on romantic echoes, with an occasional soft jazz touch ("Honeymoon Night") to add a spark to it, and generally melodic cues that aim to soothe without making too much of a noise. The goal is achieved with themes that have great appeal ("Two Scoop Snoops," "Scoop De Jour"), adding up to an enjoyably lightweight effort.

I Shot Andy Warhol *♪♪♪*

1996, Tag Recordings; from the movie *I Shot Andy Warhol*, Orion Pictures, 1996.

Album Notes: *CD Producer*: Randall Poster; *Engineer*: Stephen Marcussen.

Selections: 1 Season Of The Witch (D. Leitch)(5:20) *Luna*; 2 Do You Believe In Magic (J. Sebastian)(2:06) *The Lovin' Spoonful*; 3 Love Is All Around (R. Presley)(3:05) *R.E.M.*; 4 Burned (N. Young)(2:35) *Wilco*; 5 Itchycoo Park (R. Lane/S. Marriott)(3:5) *Ben Lee*; 6 Sunshine Superman (D. Leitch)(5:01) *Jewel*; 7 Mais Que Nada (J. Ben)(2:39) *Sergio Mendes, Brasil '66*; 8 Gimi A Little Break (A. Lee)(2:03) *Love*; 9 Sensitive Euro Man (Pavement)(3:16) *Pavement*; 10 Kick Out The Jams (F. Smith/W. Kramer/D. Tomich/R. Derminer/M. Davis)(2:55) *MC5*; 11 I'll Keep It With Mine (B. Dylan)(4:09) *Bettie Serveert*; 12 Demons (I. Kaplan/G. Hubley)(3:37) *Yo La Tenga*; 13 I Shot Andy Warhol Suite (J. Cale)(3:27) *Dave Soldier, Sara Parkins, Regina Carter, Matt Donner, Todd Reynolds, Judith Insell, Martha Mooke, Mark Deffenbaugh, Mark Stewart, Maya Biser, Mark Dressen, Kermit Driscoll.*

Review: Modern rockers doing '60s songs isn't a new idea, but it works well here. Donovan's biggest hits get creditable covers from Jewel ("Sunshine Superman") and Luna ("Season of the Witch"). R.E.M.'s version of the Troggs' "Love is All Around" has been, well, around for awhile, and teen troubadour Ben Lee turns in a refreshingly snotty rendition of the Small Faces' "Itchykoo Park." And the original versions of the MC5's "Kick Out the Jams," Love's "Gimi a Little Break" and the Lovin' Spoonful's "Do You Believe in Magic" bring a little balance to the proceedings.

Gary Graff

Ice Station Zebra *♪♪*

1997, PEG Records; from the movie *Ice Station Zebra*, M-G-M, 1968.

Album Notes: *Music*: Michel Legrand; Orchestra conducted by Michel Legrand.

Selections: 1 Overture (2:45); 2 The Satellite Falls (2:25); 3 The Russian Trawler (3:30); 4 Tigerfish (1:43); 5 The Crevasse (4:08); 6 Entr'acte (1:57); 7 The Lab (4:45); 8 Through The Ice (3:00); 9 The Fight (3:15); 10 Mission Completed (1:43).

Review: A cold War actioner adapted from a novel by Alistair MacLean and starring Rock Hudson, Patrick McGoohan, Ernest Borgnine and Jim Brown, *Ice Station Zebra* elicited an appropriately taut score from French composer Michel Legrand. A race against time between Russians and Americans rushing to a solitary Arctic outpost to recover a fallen satellite which holds the key to victory in an all-too-possible (at the time!) nuclear war between the two countries might appear today a bit far-fetched, but it makes for a fine, suspenseful drama, which Legrand's music emphasizes with all the expected "sturm und drang." The one drawback here is the fact that all the tracks combined amount to just 30 minutes of playing time, which seems just a bit short for anyone's money.

Iceman *♪♪*

1992, Southern Cross Records; from the movie *Iceman*, Universal Pictures, 1984.

Album Notes: *Music*: Bruce Smeaton; *Orchestrations*: Bruce Smeaton; *Music Editor*: Jim Henrikson; Orchestra conducted by Bruce Smeaton; *Album Producer*: Bruce Smeaton; *Engineer*: Dan Wallin.

Selections: 1 Ice Cave (1:17); 2 Main Title (3:28); 3 Discovery/ Charlie/ Defrost (1:43); 4 Monitoring/Relics/It's Alive (2:07); 5 Vivarium (2:21); 6 Wild Pig (1:19); 7 Suicide?/Memories (1:22); 8 Messenger/The Bird (2:04); 9 Breakout (2:31); 10 Maynard Surprised/Freedom (2:28); 11 Dreamwalk (1:26); 12 Charlie's Flight/End Title (5:58).

Review: Composer Bruce Smeaton wrote a particularly effective score for this striking science fiction film about a Neanderthal man found in an Arctic cave where he has been frozen for thousands of years, and his slow awakening in a new world totally alien to him. Using as his primary means of expression a Japanese shakuhachi against the context of a symphonic orchestra, Smeaton created a score that emphasizes the apparent dichotomy between the past, represented by the Iceman, and the present, the modern society in which he is "reborn." While his music can hardly be faulted and in fact proves quite challenging in many ways, the short playing time of the CD (less than 29 minutes) is something that leaves a lot to be desired, particularly at the premium price usually demanded for soundtrack albums.

Il bidone *♪♪♪♪*

1991, CAM Records/Italy; from the movie *Il bidone*, Titanus Films, 1955.

Album Notes: *Music*: Nino Rota; Orchestra conducted by Carl Savina.

Selections: 1 Il bidone (3:16); 2 La moglie del bidonista (2:24); 3 Il tesoro nascosto (:58); 4 Coimbra (5:42); 5 In viaggio per un bidone (1:53); 6 Al cinema (1:30); 7 Cara bambina (2:03); 8 Ballerina Night (3:51); 9 L'ultimo bidone (2:54).

Review: One of Federico Fellini and Nino Rota's early collaborations, *Il bidone* (known in this country as *The Swindle)* is interesting in that it presents in embryo all the musical elements Rota would use, reuse and recycle in his subsequent films for Fellini—rambunctious, malicious themes, jaunty, brassy tunes, romantic motifs, with a touch of jazz thrown in for good measure — all of them colliding in a festive display of the composer's incredibly colorful palette and expressive instrumentations. The film, starring Broderick Crawford, Richard Basehart, Franco Fabrizi and Giulietta Masina, deals with a trio of con artists in Rome, each with ideas of striking it rich, in a sly comedy that provided Rota with the right tones to write a diversified score. Some of the themes he developed for the film showed up in other films, sometimes as main motifs, sometimes as secondary ones, but always recognizable, and always thoroughly enjoyable.

Il Casanova (Fellini's Casanova) 🦴🦴🦴🦴

1991, CAM Records/Italy; from the movie, *Fellini's Casanova*, Titanus Films, 1976.

Album Notes: *Music:* Nino Rota; Orchestra conducted by Carlo Savina.

Selections: 1 O Venezia, Venaga, Venusia (3:41); 2 The Magic Bird (2:07); 3 A pranzo dalla Marchesa Durfe (1:48); 4 The Great Mouna (2:00); 5 Canto della buranella (1:23); 6 The Magic Bird In Paris (1:35); 7 "Intermezzo" Of The Praying Mantis (3:40); 8 Pin Penin (3:03); 9 The Magic Bird In Dresden (1:24); 10 Memories Of Henriette (2:01); 11 The Magic Bird In Rome (1:50); 12 The Duke Of Wuttenberg (4:25); 13 The Automated Doll (1:48).

Review: In his music, Nino Rota pretty much tried to capture and reflect the dreamy-like visions and fancy concoctions of Federico Fellini. Often recycling some of the themes he had used in the director's previous films, he created a body of work which, taken as a whole, constitutes an impressive musical tapestry that matches and echoes Fellini's own creative world. *Il Casanova*, Fellini's tribute to the great 18th-century Venetian lover and adventurer, inspired Rota to write a series of cues around a single motif, "The Magic Bird" (L'uccello magico). The quirky cues, with period instruments occasionally playing strange-sounding melodies, give the music a modern edge mixed with an aura of authenticity, while they evoke Casanova's travels and his many adventures in Paris, in Dresden, and in Rome. The CD, imported from Italy and released by CAM, belongs to that category of hard-to-find titles that will challenge the listener and take him on an unexpected, but rewarding, musical journey.

Il gattopardo (The Leopard) 🦴🦴🦴🦴

1991, CAM Records/Italy; from the movie *The Leopard*, Titanus Films, 1980.

Album Notes: *Music:* Nino Rota; Orchestra conducted by Franco Ferrara.

Selections: 1 Main Title/A Trip To Donnafugata (8:14); 2 Angelica And Tancrede (4:37); 3 A Prince's Dreams (10:35); 4 Mazurka (1:44); 5 Contradance (3:31); 6 Valse brilliante (G. Verdi)(2:30); 7 Polka (1:35); 8 Quadrille (2:32); 9 Galop (1:36); 10 Departure Waltz (3:57).

Review: A brilliant period drama, directed by Luchino Visconti, *The Leopard,* set in late 19th-century Sicily, recounted in bold, colorful strokes the story of an Italian aristocrat and his family troubles, even as the world he had known crumbled around him under the onslaught of widespread social changes. Adding a pervasive melancholy touch to the story, Nino Rota provided a lush, expansive score, eons away from the usually jaunty style that had characterized his scores for the films of Federico Fellini. Also central to the music he devised were several dance numbers, notably "Mazurka," "Polka," "Quadrille" and "Galop," which enliven this excellent recording.

I'll Do Anything 🦴🦴🦴🦴

1994, Varese-Sarabande Records; from the movie *I'll Do Anything,* Columbia Pictures, 1994.

Album Notes: *Music:* Hans Zimmer; *Orchestrations:* Bruce Fowler, Nick Glennie-Smith, Ladd McIntosh, Suzette Moriarty; *Featured Musicians:* Nick Glennie-Smith, Hans Zimmer (synthsizers), Kurt McGettrick (baritone sax), Gary Foster, Jonathan Crosse, Dan Higgins (soprano sax), Steve Fowler (alto sax), Walter Fowler (trumpet), Gary Gray, Jim Kanter, Marty Kristall (clarinet), Phil Ayling, Jon Clarke (oboe), Rose Corrigan, Ken Munday (bassoon), David Duke (French horn), Charlie Loper, Philip Teele (trombone), Mike Lang, Ralph Grierson (piano), Michael Thompson (guitar), Jimmy Johnson (fretless bass), Dale Anderson, Larry Bunker, Alan Estes, Thomas Raney, Wallace Snow (marimbas), Katie Kirkpatrick (harp), Mervyn Warren, Phillip Ingram, Dorian Holley, Rodney Saulsberry, Arnold McCuller (vocals); *Album Producers:* Hans Zimmer, Jay Rifkin; *Engineer:* Jay Rifkin.

Selections: 1 Matt (7:21); 2 Burke (10:03); 3 Cathy (8:07); 4 Jeannie (14:09); 5 You Are The Best (C. King)(2:56) *Whittni Wright.*

Review: This immensely appealing score evokes better than most the charming, oddball comedy for which it was written, about an unemployed actor who takes care of his little girl, only to find himself upstaged by her own career when she lands major parts in films. Initially intended to be a musical, the film suggested many themes which have been arranged here in selections that give them greater overall playing time, with the cues assembled to specifically create portraits of the main characters portrayed by Nick Nolte, Albert Brooks, Joely Richardson, and Julie Kavner. Whittni Wright, who plays the gifted moppet, also takes the spotlight in the album, via a rendition of the jaunty "You Are the Best" she performed in the film.

Immortal Beloved ♪♪♪♪ᵇ

1994, Sony Classical; from the movie *Immortal Beloved*, Columbia Pictures, 1994.

Album Notes: *Music*: Ludwig van Beethoven; The London Symphony Orchestra, conducted by Sir Georg Solti; *Featured Musicians*: Emanuel Ax, Pamela Frank, Gidon Kremer, Yo-Yo Ma, Murray Perahia; *Album Producers*: Michael Haas, Andreas Neubronner, Steven Epstein; *Engineers*: Pauline Heister, Richard King.

Selections: 1 Napoleon Shells Vienna: Allegro con brio (from Symphony No. 5 in C minor, Op.67) (5:48); 2 Childhood Dreams: Fur Elise (2:53) *Murray Perahia*; 3 Ludwig And Julia At Schoenbrunn Palace Gardens: Allegro con brio (from Symphony No 3 in E-flat Major, Op. 55, "Eroica") (5:00); 4 Julia And Her Father Secretly Watch: Piano Sonata No. 14 in C-sharp minor, Op. 27, No. 2 "Moonlight") (4:29) *Murray Perahia*; 5 Ludwig And Caspar Fight: Allegro. Thunderstorm (from Symphony No. 6 in F Major, Op. 68, "Pastoral") (4:08); 6 Ludwig Consoles Anna Marie: Largo assai ed espressivo (from Piano Trio No. 4 in D Major, Op. 70, No. 1, "Ghost") (4:34) *Emanuel Ax, Pamela Frank, Yo-Yo Ma*; 7 The Beethoven Brothers In Baden: Allegro ma non troppo (from Violin Concerto in D Major, Op. 61) (2:58) *Gidon Kremer*; 8 A Concert For Lichnowsky: Adagio cantabile (from Piano Sonata No. 8 in C minor, Op. 13, "Pathetique") (5:21) *Murray Perahia*; 9 The Letter: Rondo. Allegro (from Piano Concerto No. 5 in E-flat Major, Op. 73, "Emperor") (11:26) *Murray Perahia*; 10 The Funeral: Kyrie (from Missa Solemnis in D Major, Op. 123) (6:03) *Renee Fleming, Ann Murray, Vincon Cole, Bryn Terfel, London Voices*; 11 Karl At The Ruins: Allegretto (from Symphony No. 7 in A Major, Op. 92) (2:57); 12 The Carriage Stuck In The Mud: Adagio sostenuto-Presto (from Violin Sonata in A Major, Op. 47, "Kreutzer") (3:27) *Pamela Frank, Emanuel Ax*; 13 The Night Of The Premiere: Ode To Joy (from Symphony No. 9 in D minor, Op. 125) (12:56) *Vinson Cole, London Voices*.

Review: How could anyone resist this impressive "soundtrack" album, when the music was written by none other than

Beethoven? Cleverly packaged to feature some of the composer's best known works, this is in every way a greatest hits compilation, running the gamut from orchestral excerpts (five of the monumental symphonies) to a movement from the brilliant "Emperor" concerto, to chamber music and piano sonatas (both the "Pathetique" and "Moonlight," as well as "Fur Elise"). The music is played with passion by a veritable who's who of longhair performers, including Perahia, Emanuel Ax, Yo-Yo Ma and the LSO, conducted by Sir Georg Solti. Schroeder would love it—so will you!

In Love and War ♪♪♪♪ᵇ

1997, RCA Victor; from the movie *In Love and War*, New Line Cinema, 1997.

Album Notes: *Music*: George Fenton; *Orchestrations*: Simon Chamberlain, Geoffrey Alexander; *Music Editor*: Kevin Lane; Orchestra conducted by George Fenton; *Featured Musicians*: Andy Findon (flute), Michael Jeans (oboe/cor anglais), Nick Bucknall (clarinet), Derek Watkins and Andy Crowley (cornet, trumpet), Edward Hessian (accordion), David Arch (piano); *Album Producers*: George Fenton, Eliza Thompson; *Engineer*: Keith Grant.

Selections: 1 Leaving For The Front (3:57); 2 Private Hemingway Reporting For Duty (1:38); 3 Rescuing Roberto (3:51); 4 The Bullet (3:10); 5 The Drive With Domenico (2:29); 6 Agnes' Theme (1:48); 7 Play The Hand You're Dealt (3:16); 8 Small Talk (1:32); 9 The Medal Ceremony (1:51); 10 La Piave (trad.)(1:55) *Mickey Binelli*; 11 The Lake (1:00); 12 The Cloisters (1:58); 13 Jimmy's Letter (3:33); 14 The Brothel (3:56); 15 POWs (:38); 16 The Trip To Venice (5:19); 17 "Dear Kid" (2:16); 18 The Waltz/Brothel (reprise)(2:28); 19 End Credits (4:00).

Review: Reflective of the moods in this film set during World War I, George Fenton struck a particularly rich vein with themes that underscore the passionate love affair between writer Ernest Hemingway, then a young soldier on the Italian front, and a nurse, eight years older, in a real-life drama that was the spark from which eventually came *A Farewell to Arms*. Largely ignoring the wartime backdrop of the screenplay, Fenton's music focuses on the most romantic aspects of the story, from its timid beginnings while Hemingway recovers from a serious wound in a hospital, to the break-up forced upon the two lovers by forces outside their control. In its often staid expression, the score finds new accents to speak of love and its wonderful and devastating effects, in terms that tug at the right heartstrings. In it, the composer demonstrates once again his uncanny ability to write music that is simply glorious and profoundly affecting.

In the Army Now ♪♪♪♪

1994, Intrada Records; from the movie *In the Army Now*, Hollywood Pictures, 1994.

Album Notes: *Music*: Robert Folk; *Music Editor*: Tom Villano; The Sinfonia of London, conducted by Robert Folk; *Album Producer*: Robert Folk; *Engineer*: Eric Tomlinson.

Selections: 1 Video Game (1:25); 2 Boot Camp (4:48); 3 Grenede Bunker (1:02); 4 Pugal Sticks (1:29); 5 Purified Water (2:04); 6 Ranger Attack (1:30); 7 The Mission (2:33); 8 Lost In The Desert (5:05); 9 New Transportation (1:06); 10 The Cobra (1:41); 11 Camel Traders (:46); 12 Finding The F.A.V.s (:40); 13 Bones (2:01); 14 The Raid Begins (1:06); 15 Last Chance (8:04).

Review: Call it a "guilty pleasure," but Robert Folk has composed an infectiously melodic score for one of the umpteenth brainless Pauly Shore comedies which, presumably, will be as dated one day as disco, bell-bottoms, and the music of Giorgio Moroder are now. Not so for Folk's music, though, which is a large orchestral work performed with appropriate panache by the Sinfonia of London, grounded in a 1941-style military march that culminates in a thrilling, eight-minute long final track that includes some of the best music the composer has written yet. The album is just long enough to sustain repeated visits and Folk's thematic material is strong enough to hold up to them. Unlike the movie, the composer kept a straight face and wrote a seriously good score here, one that might look surprising to someone who spots it upon browsing through your CD rack, but certainly not to anyone who has actually heard it.

Andy Dursin

In the Line of Fire ♪♪♪♪

1993, Epic Soundtrax; from the movie *In the Line of Fire*, Columbia Pictures, 1993.

Album Notes: *Music*: Ennio Morricone; *Orchestrations*: Ennio Morricone; Orchestra Unione Musicisti di Roma, conducted by Ennio Morricone; *Album Producer*: Ennio Morricone; *Engineers*: Franco Patrignani, Fabio Venturi; *Engineer Assistant*: Andrea Morricone.

Selections: 1 In The Line Of Fire (2:22); 2 Lilly And Frank (4:01); 3 "Aim High" (4:21); 4 The Boat (2:10); 5 Leary's Shrine (2:06); 6 On The Rooftops (4:28); 7 Discovery In Phoenix (3:00); 8 Lilly And Frank (2:30); 9 Frank Is Depressed (2:40); 10 Arriving In L.A. (2:39); 11 Lilly And Frank (1:49); 12 Telephone Call (3:32); 13 Dinner Date (2:01); 14 Frank (1:35); 15 Solving The Puzzle (1:46); 16 Another Telephone Call (4:05); 17 Dallas Recalled (3:09); 18 In The Park (2:09); 19 Taking The Bullet (2:39); 20 Arriving In L.A. (1:56); 21 Lilly And Frank (1:33); 22 Collage (5:19); 23 On The Trail (1:51).

Review: In a virtual return to some of the orchestral effects he used in some of his most successful spaghetti westerns, notably *The Good, the Bad and the Ugly*, Morricone wrote a substantial score for this engrossing drama starring Clint Eastwood as a Secret Service agent assigned to protecting the President of the United States, who puts his own life on the line. Many of the cues provide the musical background for the action scenes, with the agent discovering the existence of a plot to kill the President, his efforts to capture the assassin before it's too late, and his ultimate victory over adversity. Setting off the action scenes, which gradually sound more dour and ominous as the drama unfolds, a love theme ("Lilly and Frank"), played in different styles, recurs throughout, as an indication of the isolation in which the Secret Service man finds himself.

In the Mood ♪♪♪♪

1987, Atlantic Records; from the movie *In the Mood*, Lorimar Pictures, 1987.

Album Notes: *Music*: Ralph Burns; *Orchestrations*: Harvey R. Cohen, Eric Boardman, Ralph Burns; *Featured Musicians*: Abe Most (clarinet), Joel Preskin (tenor sax), Bill Watrous (trombone), Gene Estes (vibes), Tom Ranier (piano), Warren Luening (flugelhorn), Bob Cooper (tenor sax), Oscar Brashears (trumpet), Marshal Royal (alto sax), Larry Bunker (vibes); *Featured Vocalists*: Jennifer Holliday, Beverly D'Angelo; *Album Producer*: Ralph Burns; *Engineer*: Dennis Sands.

Selections: 1 In The Mood (A. Razaf/J. Garland/B. Midler/B. Manilow) (3:36) *Jennifer Holliday*; 2 Sonny's Theme (1:42); 3 On

The Road (3:23); 4 Dream (J. Mercer) (3:20) *Beverly D'Angelo*; 5 Champagne Music (2:40); 6 High School Shuffle (2:55); 7 The Escape Of The Woo Woo Kid (1:25); 8 Baby Blues (Sonny's Theme) (R. Burns/P. Robinson) (3:25) *Beverly D'Angelo*; 9 Take The "A" Train (B. Strayhorn) (3:00); 10 Blues For Francine (2:41); 11 Don't Be That Way (B. Goodman/E. Sampson/M. Parish) (3:00); 12 A Place Called Paradise (2:40); 13 Jack The Wonder Dog (3:10); 14 In The Mood (A. Razaf/J. Garland) (3:35).

Review: The setting of this pleasantly innocuous comedy about the coming of age of a young man in the early 1940s led veteran composer and arranger Ralph Burns to create a vibrantly wonderful score. With solid assist from a handful of seasoned musicians, and the vocal support of Jennifer Holliday and Beverly D'Angelo (one of the film's stars), the soundtrack pays homage to the big band era, with powerful renditions of the standards "In the Mood," "Take the 'A' Train," "Dream," and "Don't Be That Way," plus original cues devised in the style of the period by Burns. The film didn't make much of an impression at the box office, but this soundtrack album is one of the best of its kind ever released.

In the Name of the Father ♫♫

1994, Island Records; from the movie *In the Name of the Father*, Universal Pictures, 1994.

Album Notes: *Music*: Trevor Jones; *Orchestrations*: Jeff Atmajian, Trevor Jones; *Music Editor*: Bill Abbott; The London Philharmonic Orchestra, conducted by David Snell; *Album Producer*: Trevor Jones; *Engineer*: Roger King; *Assistant Engineers*: Rupert Coulson, Andy Strange.

Selections: 1 In The Name Of The Father (Bono/G. Friday/M. Seezer)(5:42) *Bono, Gavin Friday*; 2 Voodoo Child (Slight Return)(J. Hendrix)(5:09) *The Jimi Hendrix Experience*; 3 Billy Boola (Bono/G. Friday/M. Seezer)(3:45) *Gavin Friday, Bono*; 4 Dedicated Follower Of Fashion (R. Davies)(3:00) *The Kinks*; 5 Interrogation (7:11); 6 Is This Love (B. Marley)(3:51) *Bob Marley and The Wailers*; 7 Walking The Circle (4:42); 8 Whiskey In The Jar (P. Lymott/ E. Bell/B. Downey)(5:44) *Thin Lizzy*; 9 Passage Of Time (5:52); 10 You Made Me The Thief Of Your Heart (Bono/G. Friday/M. Seezer)(6:21) *Sinead O'Connor*.

Review: The energized mixture of songs and Trevor Jones' underscore accurately captures the mood and period of this story about a young man innocently accused of an IRA bombing. Jones' score, presented in three suites totaling only 18 minutes, is appropriately dark and, on occasion, has an even harder percussive beat than the surrounding songs. Its overall dark ambience may not be for all tastes, though bouncy songs

like The Kinks' "Dedicated Follower of Fashion" and Bob Marley's "Is This Love" actually offer a surprisingly welcome ray of sunshine in all the bleakness.

David Hirsch

Inchon ♫♫♫▷

1988, Intrada Records; from the movie *Inchon*, M-G-M/UA, 1982.

Album Notes: *Music*: Jerry Goldsmith; *Orchestrations*: Arthur Morton; Orchestra conducted by Jerry Goldsmith; *Album Producer*: Douglass Fake; *Engineers*: Len Engel, Bernie Grundman.

Selections: 1 Prologue and Main Title (3:48); 2 Resignation (2:10); 3 The Children (:44); 4 The Bridge (3:30); 5 The Apology (2:36); 6 The Church (4:41); 7 The Mines (5:07); 8 The Landing (1:18); 9 The 38th Parallel (1:15); 10 Corpses (1:44); 11 Task Force (3:07); 12 Medley (2:13); 13 Inchon Harbor (1:12); 14 Love Theme (2:49); 15 The Lighthouse (3:13); 16 The Tanks (3:53); 17 MacArthur's Arrival (:50); 18 Lim's Death (3:12); 19 The Trucks (3:02); 20 Inchon Theme (3:21).

Review: Goldsmith returned to the same material he'd covered in 1975's *MacArthur* with this old-fashioned war epic produced by the Reverend Sun-Yung Moon, but even the middling *MacArthur* seemed like *Patton* compared to this goofy, overblown bomb. The Oriental influences in the score are as atmospheric and interesting as many of the composer's earlier works in this style, particularly the fascinatingly percussive opening of Chinese blocks and col legno effects, but the score stumbles in its overly-effusive patriotic material, particularly a strangely overblown march theme for Douglas MacArthur. There are more than enough pulsating action cues and sympathetic moments of epic tragedy in the score to make up for the bombastic moments, however, particularly in this expanded CD from Intrada, which improved on the original LP's pinched sound. The orchestral performance is still below par in some cues, however.

Jeff Bond

The Incredibly True Adventure of 2 Girls in Love ♫♫♫

1995, Milan Records; from the movie *The Incredibly True Adventure of 2 Girls in Love*, Fine Line Features, 1995.

Album Notes: *Music*: Terry Dame; *Arrangements*: Terry Dame; *Music Editor*: Steve Borne; *Featured Musicians*: Terry Dame (soprano saxophone), Tom Judson (piano), Christine Kuhn (cello), Marie Breyer (percussion); *Album Producer*: Mark Kaufman; *Engineer*: Wally Traugott.

Selections: 1 Gas Pump Blues (1:38); 2 Instrumental No. 1 (:26); 3 Two Girls In Love (1:40); 4 A Typical Love (E. Ziff/A. Palmer/A. Ziff)(3:44) *Betty*; 5 Trouble's Tango/There Is That In Me (4:09); 6 Randy's Theme (2:10); 7 The Clock Song (Scrawl)(3:07) *Scrawl*; 8 Kitchen Mayhem (1:52); 9 Instrumental No. 2 (1:37); 10 Evie's Theme (:42); 11 Dies Irae (from *Requiem* K.626) (W.A. Mozart)(1:54)*Academy Chamber Choir, The Vienna Symphony Orchestra, Jascha Horenstein*; 12 Instrumental No. 3 (1:37); 13 Page Two (Lois) (2:01)*Lois*; 14 Arm Game (4:09); 15 I'm Not That Kind Of Guy (T. Judson) (1:30) *Tom Judson*; 16 Mom!! (1:32); 17 Trouble's Tango (3:26).

Review: A story of first love between two girls in their senior year in high school—Randy, a tomboy, and Evie, an African-American princess—the film received a whimsical score from Terry Dame, a composer and multi-instrumentalist, heard here on soprano sax, in a chamber music format. The instrumental cues have a charm that is easily communicative and winning. The pop songs that interrupt the musical flow, on the other hand, are not very interesting and can be edited out.

Indecent Proposal 🎵🎵🎵

1993, MCA Records; from the movie *Indecent Proposal*, Paramount Pictures, 1993.

Album Notes: *Music:* John Barry; *Song Producers:* Trevor Horn, Tony Brown, Scott Sheriff, Bryan Ferry, Robin Trower, Patrice Rushen, Ian Devaney, Jeff Lynne, Roy Orbison; *Engineers:* Tim Weidner, Elliot Scheiner, Scott Sheriff, Carmen Rizzo, Jr., Sean Chenery, Humberto Gracia, Richard Dodd, Phil McDonald, Don Smith; *Album Producer:* Adrian Lyne; *Engineer:* Steve Hall.

Selections: 1 I'm Not In Love (G. Gouldman/E. Stewart) (3:50) *The Pretenders*; 2 What Do You Want The Girl To Do (A. Toussaint) (5:07) *Vince Gill*; 3 If I'm Not In Love With You (D. Thomas) (3:38) *Dawn Thomas*; 4 Out Of The Window (S. Samuel) (5:55) *Seal*; 5 Will You Love Me Tomorrow (C. King/G. Griffin) (4:15) *Bryan Ferry*; 6 The Nearness Of You (N. Washington/H. Carmichael) (3:16) *Sheena Easton*; 7 In All The Right Places (J. Barry/L. Stansfield/I. Devaney/A. Morris) (5:46) *Lisa Stansfield*; 8 Instrumental Suite from Indecent Proposal (J. Barry) (25:20); 9 A Love So Beautiful (R. Orbison/J. Lynne) (3:31) *Roy Orbison*.

Review: Even with its laughable plot and perfume-commercial caliber direction, *Indecent Proposal* was a box-office smash upon its original release, so there's no question that its music helped play a part in putting it over the top. John Barry composed one of his lush, delicate romantic scores for the film, with solo piano and orchestra gently underscoring the entan-

glements of a young couple with a Donald Trump-type mogul (Robert Redford). The music is expectedly soothing, but even as Barry scores of this ilk go, it's not anywhere near as memorable as *Somewhere in Time* or even *The Scarlet Letter*, and it comprises only a 25-minute suite on the album. The rest of the soundtrack contains various songs by Seal, Bryan Ferry, The Pretenders, Vince Gill and Sheena Easton, and it's all sort of a ho-hum collection of covers with a few new songs that never attained the level of popularity that the film shockingly did with viewers.

Andy Dursin

Independence Day 🎵🎵🎵🎵

1996, RCA Victor; from the movie *Independence Day*, 20th Century-Fox, 1996.

Album Notes: *Music:* David Arnold; *Orchestrations:* Nicholas Dodd; *Music Editor:* Laurie Higgins; Orchestra conducted by Nicholas Dodd; *Album Producer:* David Arnold; *Engineer:* Dennis Sands.

Selections: 1 1969: We Came In Peace (2:04); 2 S.E.T.I.: Radio Signal (1:52); 3 The Darkest Day (4:13); 4 Canceled Leave (1:45); 5 Evacuation (5:47); 6 Fire Storm (1:23); 7 Aftermath (3:35); 8 Base Attack (6:11); 9 El Toro Destroyed (1:30); 10 International Code (1:32); 11 The President's Speech (3:10); 12 The Day We Fight Back (4:58); 13 Jolly Roger (3:15); 14 End Titles (9:08).

Review: Writing in a style that echoes some of the best efforts by others like Jerry Goldsmith, James Horner and John Williams, British composer David Arnold gave extraordinary musical life to this sensational sci-fi thriller about evil aliens who invade Earth. The broad, expansive orchestral cues provide the counterpoint to some of the most exciting action cues in the film, with two longer ones ("Evacuation" and "Base Attack") showing the composer at his most proficient with fully developed themes, filled with lush orchestral strokes and eerie choral sounds. The personal, human side of the story is also explored in sensitive cues, like"Canceled Leave," that illuminate and offset its darkest aspects. A thrilling score by a relative newcomer on the scene, whose career is clearly on the rise.

The Indian in the Cupboard 🎵🎵🎵🎵

1995, Sony Classical; from the movie *The Indian in the Cupboard*, Paramount Pictures, 1995.

Album Notes: *Music:* Randy Edelman; *Orchestrations:* Ralph Ferraro; *Music Editor:* Richard Bernstein; Orchestra conducted by Randy Edelman; *Album Producer*: Randy Edelman; *Engineer*: Dennis Sands.

Selections: 1 Main Title (2:57); 2 Meeting Little Bear (3:47); 3 Omri's Newfound Magic (5:50); 4 Building A New Home (4:39); 5 Brotherly Intrigue (4:10); 6 Cowboys And Indians (2:50); 7 Reconciliation (6:28); 8 Shootout (1:21); 9 Just Another School Day (3:06); 10 Cupboard Disappearance (2:55); 11 Lament For Boone (1:51); 12 Ratattack (6:10); 13 Important Decisions (2:48); 14 Bonded For Life/Closing (5:16).

Review: Based on an award-winning children's novel by Lynne Reid Banks, *The Indian in the Cupboard* is a whimsical fantasy tale about a boy who discovers that, with the turn of a key, he can magically bring to life the three-inch-high toy Indian he placed in the old cupboard in his room. The story prompted Randy Edelman to write a huge, expansive score rife with florid orchestral accents. While the broadness of Edelman's writing might have seemed like overkill on the screen for what is, after all, only a charming little fantasy, the score reveals its many winsome qualities on this soundtrack album recording, with the colorful themes conceived by the composer creating a vibrant tapestry that weaves its own magic. The longer cues help create the overall impression of sheer fun and excitement that pervades the whole effort.

The Indian Runner ♪♪♪♪

1991, Capitol Records; from the movie *The Indian Runner*, The Mount Film Group, 1991.

Album Notes: *Music*: Jack Nitzsche; *Featured Musicians*: David Lindley (guitars), Tim Drummond (bass), James Cruce (drums), John Hammond (harmonica), Tom Margan (harmonica), Bradford Ellis (piano and keyboards), Jerry Hey (trumpet); *Album Producers*: Danny Bramson, Tim Devine, Sean Penn, Jack Nitzsche, Michael Hoenig; *Engineers*: Rik Pekkonen, Pam Neal, Michael Hoenig.

Selections: 1 Feelin' Alright (D. Mason)(4:20) *Traffic*; 2 Comin' Back To Me (M. Balin)(5:24) *Jefferson Airplane*; 3 Fresh Air (J.O. Farrow) (5:18) *Quicksilver Messenger Service*; 4 Green River (J. Fogerty)(2:36) *Creedence Clearwater Revival*; 5 Brothers For Good (E. Haller)(4:12) *Eric & Bret Haller*; 6 Summertime (G. Gershwin/I. Gershwin/D. Heyward)(3:59) *Janis Joplin, Big Brother And The Holding Company*; 7 I Shall Be Released (B. Dylan)(3:14) *The Band*; 8 Cold Day In Omaha (2:29); 9 Flop House (2:45); 10 Goin' To Columbus (3:19); 11 Brothers (2:39); 12 "Bye Mommy" (2:17); 13 The Indian Runner (2:20); 14 Bad News (2:49); 15 Criminal Blood (2:59); 16 My Brother Frank (4:27).

Review: A solid '60s rock compilation that pulls no punches or surprises, but is quite enjoyable most of the time. Some of the greatest bands are brought together here, with Jefferson Airplane, Traffic, Fresh Air, Quicksilver Messenger Service, and Creedence Clearwater Revival, among the most prominent. Janis Joplin's take on "Summertime" is always refreshing. The score selections by Jack Nitzsche fulfill their function, but they can't really compete with the great line-up that precedes them.

Indiana Jones

Indiana Jones and the Last Crusade ♪♪♪

1989, Warner Bros. Records; from the movie *Indiana Jones and the Last Crusade*, Paramount Pictures, 1989.

Album Notes: *Music*: John Williams; *Music Editor*: Ken Wannberg; Orchestra conducted by John Williams; *Album Producer*: John Williams; *Engineer*: Dan Wallin; *Assistant Engineers*: Sue McLean.

Selections: 1 Indy's Very First Adventure (8:11); 2 X Marks The Spot (3:07); 3 Scherzo For Motorcycle And Orchestra (3:49); 4 Ah, Rats!!! (3:36); 5 Escape From Venice (4:21); 6 No Ticket (2:42); 7 The Keeper Of The Grail (3:21); 8 Keeping Up With The Joneses (3:35); 9 Brother Of The Cruciform Sword (1:53); 10 Belly Of The Steel Beast (5:26); 11 The Canyon Of The Crescent Moon (4:16); 12 The Penitent Man Will Pass (3:23); 13 End Credits (Raiders March)(10:36).

Review: Williams' third Indiana Jones score can't hold a candle to the two previous efforts on a technical level, but it's probably a smoother overall listening experience than the overbearing *Indiana Jones and the Temple of Doom*. Williams adopts a slightly more subdued, flowing style here that results in a number of lengthy cues that don't quite have the show-stopping power of anything in *Raiders* or *The Temple of Doom*. There's a sprightly comic chase for an early flashback sequence involving the young Indiana Jones, an engaging syncopated fugue for a motorcycle chase and the lurching, climactic "In the Belly of the Steel Beast" which works as an effective counterpart to *Raiders*' famous truck chase cue. There are plenty of good-natured melodies, including themes for Sean Connery's Professor Jones character and a benevolent guardian of the Holy Grail seen late in the film, but there's really nothing here that lingers in the memory very long.

Jeff Bond

213

Indiana Jones and the Temple of Doom ♫♫♫♫

1984, Polydor Records; from the movie *Indiana Jones and the Temple of Doom*, **Paramount Pictures, 1984.**

Album Notes: *Music*: John Williams; *Music Editor*: Ken Wannberg; Orchestra conducted by John Williams; *Album Producers*: John Williams, Bruce Botnick; *Engineer*: Bruce Botnick.

Selections: 1 Anything Goes (C. Porter)(2:49); 2 Fast Streets Of Shanghai (3:38); 3 Nocturnal Activities (5:53); 4 Shortround's Theme (2:27); 5 Children In Chains (2:42); 6 Slalom On Mt. Humol (2:22); 7 The Temple Of Doom (2:57); 8 Bug Tunnel and Death Trap (3:29); 9 Slave Children's Crusade (3:22); 10 The Mine Car Chase (3:38); 11 Finale and End Credits (6:16).

Review: John Williams' relentless score, a superior effort despite the somber echoes that pervade it, matches the generally downbeat moods in this second installment in the Indiana Jones saga, with an occasional action cue ("Fast Streets Of Shanghai," "The Mine Car Chase") or a swift reprise of the "Raiders' March" reminding the listener that this is still the soundtrack album to an adventure film. On the whole, however, the general tone of the score is more oblique than the composer's previous or subsequent efforts, with often strident orchestral lines underscoring the gloomiest aspects of the film itself, a frightening tale about children being enslaved by an occult sect celebrating Kali, the goddess of death. As if to offset this dark atmosphere, one track, Cole Porter's "Anything Goes" sung in... Chinese, is a real standout, a rib-tickling, grandly overblown performance as exhilarating as it is unexpected.

See also: Raiders of the Lost Ark

Indochine ♫♫♫♫♪

1992, Varese-Sarabande Records; from the movie *Indochine*, **Sony Classics, 1992.**

Album Notes: *Music*: Patrick Doyle; *Orchestrations*: Lawrence Ashmore; Orchestra conducted by William Craft; *Album Producer*: Patrick Doyle; *Engineers*: Chris Dibble, Steve Price.

Selections: 1 The Adoption (3:50); 2 Boat On Fire (1:19); 3 First Date (1:22); 4 We Are Two Persons (3:06); 5 Thunderstorm (3:46); 6 Island Of The Dragon (1:39); 7 The Exodus (1:21); 8 Camille's Journey (2:28); 9 End Of The Journey (5:16); 10 Adrift (4:18); 11 The Decision (2:18); 12 On The Way To China (:55); 13 Birth And Revolution (1:53); 14 The Milk Of Viet-Nam (1:00); 15 The Casket (1:11); 16 Eliane Finds Camille (2:57); 17 I No Longer Have A Past (2:31); 18 Main Title (4:28); 19 Tango (3:40); 20 Yvette's Waltz (1:28); 21 The Last Rhumba (1:26).

Review: A riveting romantic tale of lust and passion set against the rising communist movement that eventually forced French natives to leave Indochina, the Asian country they had once colonized, *Indochine* received a provocative, flavorful score from Patrick Doyle at the top of his creative verve. Matching closely the action in the film, Doyle provided many memorable orchestral cues for this story about a classy, no-nonsense rubber plantation owner (Catherine Deneuve), her adopted Indochinese daughter (Linh Dan Pham), and the handsome young Navy officer (Vincent Perez) who makes both women swoon. Adding dramatic impulse to the story, the silent evolution that opposed traditional attitudes and new ideas within the Indochinese society and the increasing resentment to French colonialist values became further pegs on which Doyle anchors the score, a broadly romantic effort that makes few concessions to an ethnic feel and chooses instead to confine itself to more familiar European grounds. While sequencing of the album seems a bit erratic and does not follow the order in which the story itself unfolds, the cues are attractively assembled and quite enjoyable as a whole.

Infinity ♫♫♫♪

1996, Intrada Records; from the movie *Infinity*, **First Look Pictures, 1996.**

Album Notes: *Music*: Bruce Broughton; *Orchestrations*: Bruce Broughton; Orchestra conducted by Bruce Broughton; *Album Producer*: Bruce Broughton; *Engineers*: Armin Steiner, Joe Tarantino.

Selections: 1 Prologue (3:11); 2 Arline And The Red Dress (2:11); 3 1939 (1:03); 4 A Swelling (:56); 5 Typhoid? (2:38); 6 1941 (1:22); 7 Imaginary Roommate(1:27); 8 Moving To Albuquerque (1:44); 9 Richard And Arline (2:34); 10 Indian Dwellings (2:18); 11 A Nightmare Diagram (3:21); 12 Arline's Death (2:29); 13 The Trip Home (1:27); 14 Exploding The Bomb (2:11); 15 The Dress (Epilogue)(1:30).

Review: Bruce Broughton sensitively handles this pre-World War II love story about A-bomb scientist Richard Feynman and his dying wife, Arlene. Period pieces, such as big band-style tunes, occasionally intrude, but don't break the mood of the score, which concentrates on various moments in the couple's short-lived relationship. Arlene's intensity is first represented with a gentle waltz, while the contrast of her fatal illness plays, first, through a gentle arrangement of strings and woodwinds, before becoming more desolate in tempo as she deteriorates.
David Hirsch

Inner Space 𝄞𝄞𝄞

1987, Geffen Records; from the movie *Inner Space,* Warner Bros., 1986.

Album Notes: *Music*: Jerry Goldsmith; Orchestra conducted by Jerry Goldsmith; *Engineer*: Bruce Botnick; *Song Producers*: Rod Stewart, Peter Wolf, Narada Michael Walden, Bob Ezrin; *Album Executive Producers*: John David Kalodner, Gary LeMel; *Engineer*: Greg Fulginiti.

Selections: 1 Twistin' The Night Away (S. Cooke)(4:10) *Rod Stewart*; 2 Hypnotize Me (Wang Chung)(4:44) *Wang Chung*; 3 Is It Really Love? (N.M. Walden)(4:40) *Narada Michael Walden*; 4 Will I Ever Understand You (J. Crawford)(4:40) *Berlin*; 5 Cupid (S. Cooke)(2:30) *Sam Cooke*; 6 Let's Get Small (5:57); 7 Environmental Adjust (3:57); 8 Space Is A Flop (3:02); 9 Gut Reaction (9:57); 10 Air Supply (2:39).

Review: Goldsmith's third film for director Joe Dante was a comic remake of *Fantastic Voyage*, with a microscopic Dennis Quaid injected into the body of Martin Short. Goldsmith's score emphasized the action and heroism of the storyline for an adventurous effort somewhat in the style of his earlier Explorers work for Dante. The album features around 20 minutes of Goldsmith's score for a satisfying suite, opening with "Let's Get Small," a surprisingly heartfelt heroic anthem. It then continues with some kinetic action cues that balance the undulating sense-of-wonder textures that marked the composer's *Star Trek: The Motion Picture* music against some mechanistic figures that build into a terrific, percolating action climax in "Gut Reaction." The rest of the album is devoted to pop standards, including some Wang Chung and Rod Stewart's take on "Twistin' the Night Away."

Jeff Bond

Intersection 𝄞𝄞

1993, Milan Records; from the movie *Intersection,* Paramount Pictures, 1993.

Album Notes: *Music*: James Newton Howard; *Orchestrations*: Brad Dechter, James Newton Howard; *Music Editor*: Jim Weidman; Orchestra conducted by Marty Paich; The Los Angeles Master Chorale, directed by Paul Salamunovich; *Featured Soloist*: Toots Thielemans (harmonica); *Featured Musicians*: Dean Parks (acoustic guitar), Neil Stubenhaus (electric bass), John Robinson (drums), Michael Fisher (percussion); *Album Producer*: James Newton Howard; *Engineer*: Shawn Murphy.

Selections: 1 Main Titles (2:19); 2 Home (4:05); 3 She Needs Her Father (1:35); 4 What's A Girl Gotta Do? (2:54); 5 The Auction (2:48); 6 First Date (3:43); 7 Letter To Olivia (3:24); 8 The Last Ride (3:19); 9 The Accident (1:39); 10 Vincent's Mes-

sage (2:43); 11 He's Going Flat (2:01); 12 Personal Effects (4:21); 13 End Titles (4:11).

Review: For this mid-life crisis drama, James Newton Howard has sculpted an effective, rhythmic score which accentuates the Richard Gere character's headlong flight back and forth between family fidelity and the allure of infidelity. The score is brooding and subtle, cues linger slowly, indecisively, while a Toots Thielemans harmonic riff plays dreamy jazz over a softly rolling sea of violins. A slow motif for violins and piano also lingers irresolutely, mirroring the conflicts coiling within Gere's character. There are no real melodies. Instead Howard carves a lingering impression through these quiet, reflective cues, which retain a notable sense of vitality even as they are quietly introspective.

Randall D. Larson

Interview with the Vampire 𝄞𝄞𝄞𝄞

1994, Geffen Records; from the movie *Interview with the Vampire*, Geffen Pictures/Warner Bros., 1994.

Album Notes: *Music*: Elliot Goldenthal; *Orchestrations*: Robert Elhai, Elliot Goldenthal; *Music Editors*: Michael Connell, Christopher Brooks; Orchestra conducted by Jonathan Sheffer; *Album Producer*: Matthias Gohl; *Engineers*: Steve McLaughlin, Joel Iwataki.

Selections: 1 Libera Me (2:47) *The American Boychoir*; 2 Born To Darkness, part 1 (3:04); 3 Lestat's Tarantella (:46); 4 Madeleine's Lament (3:06); 5 Claudia's Allegro Agitato (4:46); 6 Escape To Paris (3:09); 7 Marche funebre (1:50); 8 Lestat's Recitative (3:39); 9 Santiago's Waltz (:37); 10 Theatre des Vampires (1:18); 11 Armand's Seduction (1:51); 12 Plantation Pyre (1:59); 13 Forgotten Lore (:31); 14 Scent Of Death (1:40); 15 Abduction and Absolution (4:42); 16 Armand Rescues Louis (2:07); 17 Louis' Revenge (2:36); 18 Born To Darkness, part 2 (1:11); 19 Sympathy For The Devil (M. Jagger/K. Richards) (7:35) *Guns N' Roses*.

Review: A chilling, superlative effort, Elliot Goldenthal's score for *Interview with the Vampire* is in turns sophisticated, broadly expansive, colorful, and consistently inventive. Introduced by the eerie "Libera Me," performed by an evanescent boy soprano, the music plumbs the depths of the main character's darker aspects and quickly settles on his otherwordly features, a strange mixture of fascination and repulsion that finds a vibrant echo in the orchestral sonorities provided by the composer. No stone is left unturned in this literate effort, in which some of the most elegant tracks include a tarantella, a waltz, a funeral march and a cue, "Born to Darkness," where all these elements coalesce into a striking conclusion. The Rolling Stones' "Sympathy for the Devil," in a strident performance by Guns N' Roses, while probably appropriate in the film, seems an odd choice here and breaks the moods established by Goldenthal's music.

Into the West 🎵🎵🎵🎵

1993, SBK Records; from the movie *Into the West*, Miramax Films, 1993.

Album Notes: *Music*: Patrick Doyle; *Orchestrations*: Fiachra Trench; *Music Editor*: Roy Prendergast; Orchestra conducted by Fiachra Trench; *Featured Vocalist*: Margaret Doyle; *Engineer*: Paul Hulme; *Song Producers*: Rick Jude, Chad Irschick, Malcolm Burn, Larry Kirwan, Steve Nye, Nick Martinelli, Peter Van Hooke & Rod Argent; *Engineers*: Steven Hallmark & Francis Buckley, Chad Irschick, Dave Bottrill & Ian Bryan, Jon Goldberger, Bruce Weeden, Simon Smart, John "X" Volaitis & Francis Buckley.

Selections: 1 Eyes Of A Child (R. Jude/M. Garey)(5:33) *Garden Of Joy*; 2 Fare Thee Well Love (J. Rankin)(4:29) *The Rankin Family*; 3 Someone To Talk To (C. Devlin)(4:10) *The Devlins*; 4 Into The West (L. Kirwan)(3:57) *Black 47*; 5 In A Lifetime (C. Brennan/P. Brennan)(2:08) *Clannad*; 6 How 'Bout Us (D. Walden)(4:51) *Lulu*; 7 Mama's Arms (J. Kadison)(3:00) *Joshua Kadison*; 8 Garden Of Joy (R. Jude)(3:03) *Garden Of Joy*; 9 The Blue Sea And The White Horse (3:38); 10 He Turned Into Dust (1:19); 11 Horse In The Lift (1:59); 12 Failed Escape (1:03); 13 Higher (1:28); 14 Boys Remember Mama (1:31); 15 Papa And The Ashes (1:05); 16 Memories Of Mary (1:09); 17 It's The Posse (:51); 18 Let's Go Back (:42); 19 Mary's Grave (2:08); 20 The Devil On Their Side (:54); 21 Boy Under Sea (1:53); 22 Ossie Is Saved (1:33); 23 Ossie Lives (1:09); 24 Peaceful People (1:01); 25 Let Her Go (1:14).

Review: The winsome tale of two orphan boys and the magic white stallion that takes them on a wild ride across the Irish countryside in search of their mother's grave, *Into the West* resulted in a wonderful score from Patrick Doyle, who took a cue from the story's background (the action takes place among the gypsies) to effectively use elements that give his music great depth and poetic impact. Introduced by the various pop selections smartly programmed at the top, and among which "In a Lifetime" by Clannad is a real standout, the instrumental score quickly sets the moods, unfolding in short, attractive bursts that follow the course of the action. Steeped in Celtic music, with melismatic vocalizations adding an original poetic note to some of the cues ("The Blue Sea and the White Horse," "Memories of Mary," "Boy Under Sea"), the score is a bril-

liantly evocative effort, which invites repeated listening in order to reveal its many hidden beauties.

Intolerance 🎵🎵🎵🎵

1990, Prometheus Records/Belgium; from the movie *Intolerance*, 1916.

Album Notes: *Music*: Carl Davis; *Orchestrations*: David Mathews, Colin Mathews; The Luxembourg Radio Symphony Orchestra, conducted by Carl Davis; *Album Producer*: Paul Wing; *Engineer*: Richard Bradford.

Selections: 1 Out Of The Cradle (2:17); 2 The "Dear One" (1:12); 3 Old Paris: The Court Of Catherine de Medici (2:41); 4 Brown Eyes (:56); 5 Strike (4:38); 6 Babylon: The Love Temple (2:32); 7 Uplifters (2:34); 8 The Siege Of Babylon (8:36); 9 Fire Machine and Defeat Of Cyrus (2:15); 10 The Boy's Return and Victory Celebration (3:55); 11 Sacred Dance (2:56); 12 Seduction, Murder and Trial (10:20); 13 Last Dawn (2:40); 14 St. Bartholomew's Day Massacre (3:52); 15 Last Sacrament (4:52); 16 Prospers Rescue Attempt and Via Dolorosa (1:42); 17 Babylon's Last Bacchanale (1:13); 18 The Death Of Brown Eyes (2:14); 19 Cyrus At The Gates (1:25); 20 The Fall Of Babylon (6:31); 21 The Walk To The Scaffold (3:33); 22 Apotheosis (2:28).

Review: D.W. Griffith's mammoth study of social abuses in the capitalistic system, as seen through four episodes—the fall of Babylon (539 B.C.), the Passion of Christ (30 A.D.), the St. Bartholomew's massacre in French Renaissance (1572), and modern days—is a fertile ground for musical expression, particularly given the fact that no known score from the 1916 film exists. Carl Davis tackled the project with evident bravura, finding a new voice for each episode, yet devising a continuous link that ties all four of them, in a "soundtrack" recording that no doubt would have delighted the pioneering filmmaker.

Inventing the Abbotts 🎵🎵🎵🎵

1997, Unforscene Music; from the movie *Inventing the Abbotts*, Fox 2000 Pictures, 1997.

Album Notes: *Music*: Michael Kamen; *Orchestrations*: Michael Kamen, Jesse Levy, Ed Schearmur, Sacha Putnam, D.J. Olson; *Music Editors*: Graham Sutton, Michael Connell, Steve Lotwis; The London Metropolitan Orchestra, conducted by Michael Kamen; *Featured Musicians*: Jeff "Skunk" Baxter (guitars), Lee Rocker (bass), Slim Jim Phantom (drums); *Album Producers*: Michael Kamen, Stephen McLaughlin, Christopher Brooks; *Engineer*: Stephen McLaughlin.

Selections: 1 On Springfield Mountain (trad., arr.: M. Kamen)(3:33) *Tara MacLean*; 2 Inventing The Abbotts (1:46); 3

Little Star (A. Venosa/ V. Picone)(2:44) *The Elegants*; 4 Thunder And Lightning (3:44); 5 Jacey And Eleanor (In The Garage)(1:31); 6 Goodnight, Irene (H. Ledbetter/J. Lomax) (1:55)*Leadbelly*; 7 Picnic (2:01); 8 The Barn (2:47); 9 Eleanor Leaves (1:38); 10 Falling Out Of The Tree (:56); 11 Boathouse (2:35); 12 Re-Inventing The Abbotts (7:03); 13 Toasted Pam (2:16); 14 Mom's Death (1:42); 15 Doug And Pam (5:38); 16 Undecided (C. Shavers/S. Robin)(3:09) *The Ray Gelato Giants, Claire Martin.*

Review: The old-fashioned flavor of this coming-of-age story set in 1957 is beautifully evoked in the Michael Kamen score, and in the songs (doo-wop and early rock) that are part of the soundtrack. *Inventing the Abbotts*, set in a small Illinois town, concerned itself with the Abbott girls (Alice, Eleanor and Pamela, respectively played by Joanna Going, Jennifer Connelly, and Liv Tyler), born in a wealthy family, and their relationship with Doug and Jacey Holt (Joaquin Phoenix and Billy Crudup), their less fortunate friends and occasional flirts. Reflecting the romantic interplay between the five principal characters, the score itself remains firmly rooted in a somewhat melancholy mood that eventually proves most endearing. Echoing the period in which the action is set, some rock numbers ("Inventing the Abbotts," "Thunder and Lightning," "Jacey and Eleanor (In the Garage)," and "Falling Out of the Tree") add a different energy to this striking, suggestive soundtrack album.

Iron Will 🎵🎵🎵

1994, Varese-Sarabande Records; from the movie *Iron Will,* Walt Disney Films, 1994.

Album Notes: *Music*: Joel McNeely; *Orchestrations*: David Slonaker; *Music Editor*: Curtis Roush; Orchestra conducted by Joel McNeely; *Album Producer*: Joel McNeely; *Engineer*: Dan Wallin.

Selections: 1 Main Title (2:57); 2 Jack's Death (3:44); 3 Leaving Birch Ridge (2:29); 4 The Race Begins (2:09); 5 Pushing Onward (1:47); 6 Gus Rescues Will (2:53); 7 Devil's Slide (2:23); 8 The Final Day (3:43); 9 Race To The Finish (2:22); 10 Crossing The Line (3:14); 11 End Credits (3:05).

Review: In another effective replay of the awe-inspiring race between a pack of dogs and a steam engine set in the frozen northern Minnesota landscape, *Iron Will* introduced composer Joel McNeely, scoring his first major feature in a striking display of his nascent talent. Broadly colorful and romantic, and a perfect match to the action, the cues explore the thrill of the race, the hardships it created for men and beasts, and the exhilaration felt by all. McNeely, who has since amply con-

firmed the promises held in this excellent first effort, constantly finds the right voice to perfectly illustrate the tale and attract the listener not familiar with the film itself. Tracks like "The Race Begins" and "Crossing the Line" are fine examples of his writing at its most descriptive.

Is Paris Burning? 🎵🎵🎵🎵🎵

1989, Varese-Sarabande; from the movie *Is Paris Burning?*, Paramount Pictures, 1966.

Album Notes: *Music*: Maurice Jarre; Orchestra conducted by Maurice Jarre.

Selections: 1 Overture (4:00); 2 The Resistance (13:48); 3 The Paris Waltz (2:24); 4 The Liberation (16:15).

Review: The "Paris Waltz," a lovely *valse musette,* first heard as a doleful, plaintive tune, then as an exuberant expression of freedom recovered, probably stands as one of Maurice Jarre's most attractive themes. But this awesome film about the liberation of the French capital from the German occupant in 1944 was also the occasion for the composer to write one of his most emotionally-charged scores. Everything, in the themes developed and in the unusual orchestrations, like Jarre's use of 12 pianos instead of brass instruments to depict the German army parading in the streets of Paris, is combined to create a music that had the right atmosphere and the melodic bent necessary to emphasize the various aspects of the story, from its historic importance to the human element brought to it by the various participants on both sides of the action. For the soundtrack album, Jarre also chose to recombine his various cues into two long suites, the first one to depict the German presence in the city and the occult resistance that slowly undermines the occupants' effectiveness, the second to paint the bloody uprising that eventually led to the liberation of Paris and its inhabitants. As a result, the music emerges as a long tone poem that proves most effective at conjuring up the moods in the film even as it calls attention to its very qualities.

The Island of Dr. Moreau 🎵

1996, Milan Records; from the movie *The Island of Dr. Moreau,* New Line Cinema, 1996.

Album Notes: *Music*: Gary Chang; *Orchestrations*: Todd Hayen; *Music Editors*: Richard Whitfield, Sherry Weintraub; *Electronic Score*: Gary Chang; *Album Producer*: Gary Chang; *Engineers*: Gary Gray, Doug Botnick, Brian Reeves.

Selections: 1 Interimsliebenden-Rausch Remix (5:01) *Einsturzende Neubauten*; 2 Three Thoughts (4:40) *Einsturzende Neubauten*; 3 Main Title (2:24); 4 Dr. Moreau

> "When you establish a collaboration with a director—Neil Jordan and I worked together on *Interview With the Vampire*—a lot more artistic canals are built between two artists and it's easier to communicate."
>
> **Elliot Goldenthal**
> on Michael Collins *(The Hollywood Reporter, 1-15-97)*

(1:54); 5 The Colony (5:13); 6 Moreau's Demise (2:45); 7 The Serum (2:39); 8 The Island (2:23); 9 The Button (1:28); 10 The Stranded (2:41); 11 Aissa's Death (2:44); 12 Epilogue (1:09); 13 The Funeral (2:06); 14 Brandenburg Concerto #2 in F Major, Second Movement (J.S. Bach)(3:40); 15 Concerto For 2 Violins in D Minor, Second Movement (J.S. Bach)(7:16); 16 Trout (5:29)*Monk & Canatella Band*.

Review: *The Island of Dr. Moreau* may best be remembered as the film that teamed Marlon Brando and Val Kilmer, though it is unlikely it will be remembered as a major contribution to film lore. Nor will Gary Chang's appropriately atmospheric electronic score make much of am impression among the thousands of soundtrack albums available these days. Strictly for hardcore fans, and even they might find it tiresome after a while.

Islands in the Stream ♫♫♫♪

1986, Intrada Records; from the movie *Islands in the Stream*, 1977.

Album Notes: *Music:* Jerry Goldsmith; *Orchestrations:* Arthur Morton; The Hungarian State Symphony Orchestra, conducted by Jerry Goldsmith; *Album Producer:* Jerry Goldsmith; *Engineer:* Mike Ross.

Selections: 1 The Island (3:07); 2 The Boys Arrive (3:51); 3 Pillow Fight (1:16); 4 Is Ten Too Old (2:51); 5 Night Attack (2:46); 6 Marlin (12:02); 7 The Boys Leave (2:52); 8 The Letter (3:24); 9 How Long Can You Stay (3:15); 10 I Can't Have Him (2:46); 11 The Refugees (4:23); 12 Eddie's Death (3:09); 13 It Is All True (5:07).

Review: Jerry Goldsmith has often mentioned this was his favorite score and one can see why. It is beautifully understated, elegiac, and filled with gorgeous musical ideas and makes a particularly convincing case for film music as a supportive medium while having a life of its own when appreciated on its own

merits. The film, about a man living on an island, removed from the onset of World War II, might have been too introspective to attract a large public, but the sensitive story compelled Goldsmith to write a score that teems with wonderful themes, and quickly establishes an aura of its own that is most attractive. The lilting "Is Ten Too Old" alone turns out to be a real delight.

It Could Happen to You ♪

1994, Columbia Records; from the movie *It Could Happen to You*, TriStar Pictures, 1994.

Album Notes: *Music:* Carter Burwell; Orchestra conducted by Carter Burwell; *Featured Performers:* Tony Bennett, Shawn Colvin, Billie Holiday, Wynton Marsalis, Lyle Lovett, Mary-Chapin Carpenter, Frank Sinatra; *Album Engineer:* David Mitson.

Selections: 1 Young At Heart (C. Leigh/J. Richards) (2:58) *Tony Bennett, Shawn Colvin;* 2 They Can't Take That Away From Me (G. & I. Gershwin) (4:12) *Billie Holiday;* 3 Now It Can Be Told (I. Berlin) (2:26) *Tony Bennett;* 4 Swingdown, Swingdown (W. Marsalis) (4:19) *Wynton Marsalis;* 5 She's No Lady (L. Lovett) (3:15) *Lyle Lovett;* 6 Always (I. Berlin) (3:53) *Tony Bennett;* 7 Overture (C. Burwell) (2:19); 8 I Fell Lucky (M.C. Carpenter/D. Schlitz) (3:33) *Mary-Chapin Carpenter;* 9 Round Of Blues (S. Colvin/L. Klein) (4:45) *Shawn Colvin;* 10 The Search (C. Burwell) (2:57); 11 Young At Heart (C. Leigh/J. Richards) (2:48) *Frank Sinatra*.

Review: Neatly framed between two different versions of the classic "Young at Heart," in which Sinatra easily wins over Bennett, this set offers a hodgepodge of tunes that may have had some meaning on the screen when heard behind the action, but that fail to make a similar impact when taken on their own individual merits. It's all the more regrettable that some talented people are represented here. Even Carter Burwell's short "Overture" seems hopelessly wasted.

It Happened at the World's Fair

1993, RCA Records; from the movie *It Happened at the World's Fair*, M-G-M, 1963.

See: Elvis Presley in Compilations

It's Alive 2 ♫♫♫♪

1990, Silva Screen Records; from the movie *It's Alive 2*, Warner Bros., 1978.

Album Notes: *Music:* Bernard Herrmann, Laurie Johnson; *Orchestrations:* Laurie Johnson; Orchestra conducted by Laurie Johnson; *Album Producer:* Kerry O'Quinn; *CD Producers:* Ford A. Thaxton, David Stoner, James Fitzpatrick.

Selections: 1 Main Title (2:32); 2 Birth Traumas (2:36); 3 Evil Evolving (3:18); 4 Savage Trilogy (3:20); 5 Nightmares (2:58); 6 Beautiful And Bizarre (2:49); 7 Revulsion (4:10); 8 Basement Nursey (2:01); 9 Lamentation (3:07); 10 Living With Fear (3:10); 11 Stalking The Infants (3:02); 12 Climax (2:37).

Review: When Larry Cohen decided to film a sequel to his hugely popular horror film *It's Alive,* in which Bernard Herrmann's music had played such an integral part, it only seemed normal he would attempt to recombine some of the composer's themes with the new film. To do so, he enlisted the help of famed British composer Laurie Johnson who rescored the cues Herrmann composed for the first film and expanded on them to create a new, bold and consistent score. Like its predecessor, *It's Alive 2* took the horror genre into the nucleus of sacrosanct family life with its horrendous story about homicidal mutant babies and efforts by government agents to destroy them. The tones of the film are laid bare from the beginning, with the "Main Title" setting a disquieting mood with its figures for brass and woodwind mixing with eerie synthesizer lines. In taking the themes created by Herrmann, Johnson managed to give them renewed life and make them as foreboding and threatening as in the original film, no minor feat indeed. Bleak and uncompromising, the score is quite unnerving and particularly striking.

It's My Party ♪♪♪♪

1996, Varese-Sarabande; from the movie *It's My Party,* United Artists, 1996.

Album Notes: *Music:* Basil Poledouris; *Orchestrations:* Greig McRitchie; Orchestra conducted by Basil Poledouris; *Album Producers:* Basil Poledouris, Tim Boyle; *Engineer:* Tim Boyle.

Selections: 1 It's My Party (3:19); 2 Drifting Apart (3:12); 3 Skiing (:55); 4 Reflections (2:00); 5 It's Not My Fault/Setting Sun (2:59); 6 This Is My Home (2:10); 7 Can I Stay? (:50); 8 Be Strong For Me (3:02); 9 The Kiss Goodbye (5:08); 10 I Love Art (2:15); 11 Ski With Me (2:19); 12 Don't Cut Me Down (O. Newton-John)(4:13) *Olivia Newton-John.*

Review: Known more for his testosterone-powered action scores, this work by Basil Poledouris comes as a complete and wondrously pleasant surprise. Poledouris created for this film a gentle concerto embodying the soul of a dying man who wishes to throw one last party with his friends before the imminent end. Performed entirely by one solo piano (a rare achievement), the composer reduces the focus, thus making the entire story very personal. Perhaps, what really makes *It's My Party* Poledouris' most powerful score to date is that its emotional power owes much to the fact that Poledouris him-

self is performing his own work. Rarely has there been a finer example of the passion that flows from the mind of a talented composer into his music when it is not diluted by the interpretation of others. The intensity here just sweeps you up, shoots through your body like a bolt of lightning, and reaches into your very soul in a way an entire orchestra could never do. A vitally important addition to any music lover's collection.
David Hirsch

Ivanhoe ♪♪♪♪

1994, Intrada Records; from the movie *Ivanhoe,* M-G-M, 1952

Album Notes: *Music:* Miklos Rozsa; *Orchestral Reconstruction:* Daniel Robbins; The Sinfonia of London, conducted by Bruce Broughton; *Album Producer:* Douglass Fake; *Engineer:* Mike Ross-Trevor; *Assistant Engineer:* Guy Massey.

Selections: 1 Prelude (2:15); 2 Ransom (3:12); 3 Rotherwood (1:09); 4 Lady Rowena (2:15); 5 Sir Cedric (:30); 6 Squire Wamba (4:38); 7 Rebecca (1:00); 8 The Intruder (3:43); 9 The Rivals (4:55); 10 Sheffield (:38); 11 Rebecca's Love (5:13); 12 Search (1:23); 13 Torquilstone Castle (3:16); 14 Bois-Guilbert's Bargain (3:31); 15 The Battlement (7:15); 16 Saxon Victory (7:53); 17 Farewell (2:36); 18 Challenge and Finale (5:58).

Review: Another vibrant re-creation of a great score, with Bruce Broughton leading The Sinfonia of London in a spirited performance that never lessens, *Ivanhoe* is a sumptuous effort by Miklos Rozsa that long deserved a recording of this caliber. Of all the swashbucklers he scored, this is probably the one that has the best combination of romantic tunes and thrilling action cues, all elements that come clearly to the forefront in this exciting album. With little time wasted on unnecessary asides, Rozsa quickly set the stage for this medieval tale of chivalry and treachery and for its main characters, including Lady Rowena, (Joan Fontaine), Rebecca (Elizabeth Taylor), Bois-Guilbert (George Sanders), and of course Ivanhoe (Robert Taylor, in one of his best screen roles). The spectacular aspects of the tale, the colorful jousts, the exciting battles, also receive their due with cues that aim to broaden the visuals with thrilling musical accents. It all comes excitingly together in this sensational recording, performed with the right dash and recorded in spacious sound.

Jack ♪♪♪♪

1996, Hollywood Records; from the movie *Jack,* Hollywood Pictures, 1996.

Album Notes: *Music:* Michael Kamen; *Orchestrations:* Michael Kamen, Bob Elhai, Lolita Ritmanis, Brad Warnaar, John Sacks; *Music Editor:* David Slusser; The L.A. All-Star Orchestra, conducted by Michael Kamen; *Featured Musicians:* Mario

Grigorov, Michael Kamen (piano), The San Francisco Saxophone Quartet, Frank Marocco (accordion), Rick Baptist, Morty Okin (trumpet), Pete Escovedo (percussion), Paula Hochhalter, Dennis Karmazyn (cello), Fred Tinsley (bass), Bruce Dukov (violin), Marty Kristall (clarinet), Paul Fried (flute), Vince De Rosa (French horn), Buell Neidlinger (double bass); *Album Producers*: Michael Kamen, Stephen McLaughlin, Christopher Brooks; *Engineers*: Stephen McLaughlin, Andy Warwick.

Selections: 1 Jack Conga (3:11); 2 Jack Scherzo (3:17); 3 Sky (1:07); 4 Butterfly (1:36); 5 The Basketball Game (2:24); 6 Cello Jack (3:58); 7 Louie's Mom (A Great School Day)(2:35); 8 Treehouse Collapse (2:34); 9 Jack's Collapse (Butterfly Death)(4:06); 10 Time To Grow Up (:42); 11 The Children's Crusade (Can Jack Come Out And Play)(4:24); 12 Back To School (What Do I Want To Be When I Grow Up? Alive!)(3:03); 13 Valedictorian (Life Is Fleeting)(4:22).

Review: The whimsical accents of this delightful comedy find an echo in Michael Kamen's exhilarating score, which, most appropriately, opens here with an exuberant conga that sets the tone for the rest of the album. To illustrate this story of a 10-year-old boy who evidences the mental and emotional reactions of his age, even though, through a quirk of nature, he actually looks 40, Kamen devised cues that amusingly stress the child-like qualities of the main character, played by Robin Williams, in terms that constantly challenge the listener. Written for a slew of individual instruments taking solos against the broader texture of the orchestra, the music adds an exponential element to the screen action, outlining selected scenes in the life of Jack, his schoolmates, and the adults with whom he comes in contact. Summing up the overall lesson of the film that life is fleeting, "Valedictorian" finds Jack, now 17 but in reality a ripe old 68-year-old, reflecting on the meaning of his brief existence.

Jacob's Ladder ♫♫

1990, Varese-Sarabande Records; from the movie *Jacob's Ladder*, **Carolco Pictures, 1990.**

Album Notes: *Music*: Maurice Jarre; *Orchestra conducted by* Maurice Jarre; *Electronic Ensemble*: Michael Boddicker, Michael Fisher, Ralph Grierson, Rick Marvin, Judd Miller, Nyle Stiner; *Featured Soloists*: Gloria Cheng (piano), Kazu Mitsui (shakuhachi), Shankar (double violin/vocal); *Featured Vocalists*: Jubilant Sykes, Kari Windingstad, The Kitka Eastern European Women's Choir (Bon Brown, vocal director); *Album Producer*: Maurice Jarre; *Engineer*: Shawn Murphy.

Selections: 1 Jacob's Ladder (4:18); 2 High Fever (7:43); 3 Descent To Inferno (8:19); 4 Sarah (7:18); 5 The Ladder (7:14);

6 Sonny Boy (B.G. DeSylva/L. Brown/R. Henderson/A. Jolson)(3:07) *Al Jolson*.

Review: A horror story about a Vietnam vet exposed to chemicals during the war, and who, as a result, experiences frightful visions, *Jacob's Ladder* elicited an effectively eerie score from Maurice Jarre, which might have been more impressive as a subtle suggestion of the screen action than it is as a purely aural experiment. Primarily written for an electronic ensemble, it consists of long synthesizer chords, occasionally contrasted by a simple melody on the piano, over which evocative wordless vocals doubling the sound of the shakuhachi combine to create a strange musical atmosphere. Ultimately, though, the lack of a real hook prevents the cues from being more than a background support for an unseen action, depriving the music from its secondary, strictly audio purpose. The addition of "Sonny Boy," performed by Al Jolson, does little to attract the listener.

James and the Giant Peach
♫♫♫♪

1996, Walt Disney Records; from the movie *James and the Giant Peach*, **Walt Disney Films, 1996.**

Album Notes: *Music*: Randy Newman; *Orchestrations*: Steve Bramson, Don Davis, Chris Boardman, Randy Newman; *Music Editor*: Bob Badami; *Album Producers*: Randy Newman, Frank Wolf, Michael Skloff; *Engineer*: Frank Wolf; *Assistant Engineer*: Sue McLean.

Selections: 1 My Name Is James (2:39); 2 That's The Life (1:59); 3 Eating The Peach (R. Dahl)(2:54); 4 Family (2:44); 5 Main Title (:37); 6 Clouds (1:40); 7 Spiker, Sponge, And A Rhino (3:25); 8 Magic Man (4:15); 9 Giant Peach (1:54); 10 Into The Peach (2:05); 11 James Makes Some Friends (1:08); 12 The Peach Rolls (2:37); 13 All At Sea/That's The Life (reprise) (2:13); 14 100 Seagulls And One Shark (1:58); 15 Lullaby (1:57); 16 James' Dream (1:03); 17 Way Off Course (1:48); 18 The Rhino Attacks (2:51); 19 Empire State Building (2:17); 20 New York City (2:53); 21 Spiker And Sponge Come To America (2:15); 22 A Place Where Dreams Come True (3:58); 23 Good News (4:20) *Randy Newman*.

Review: Based on a story by Roald Dahl, this live-action/stop-motion animation film follows the adventures of James, an orphan raised by two spinster aunts, one fat, one skinny, and both mean. After a mysterious old man assures him that everything will be all right, James discovers in the backyard a giant peach and the six bugs who live in it, setting off the fairy tale that ensues. While the tone of the film itself was more gritty and caustic than the outline suggests, it prompted Randy Newman to write a lightweight score in a display of emotions unusual for him. Amusingly salient scenes in the action, the score features many highlights that elevate it way above the norm and is enhanced by several songs, including two "That's the Life" and "My Name Is James," that are absolutely terrific.

Jane Eyre

Jane Eyre

1993, Fox Records; from the movie *Jane Eyre*, 20th Century-Fox, 1943.

See: Laura

Jane Eyre ♪♪♪♪

1988, Silva Screen; from the movie *Jane Eyre*, Omnibus Films, 1971.

Album Notes: *Music*: John Williams; *Music Editor*: Ken Wannberg; Orchestra conducted by John Williams; *Featured Musicians*: Pat Halling (violin), Bob Docker (piano), Les Pearson (harpsichord), Derek Wiggins (oboe), Peter Lloyd (flute); *Album Producer*: John Williams; *Engineer*: Eric Tomlinson.

Selections: 1 Jane Eye Theme (3:13); 2 Overture (Main Title)(3:53); 3 Lowood (2:23); 4 To Thornfield (1:50); 5 String Quartet—Festivity At Thornfield (2:07); 6 Grace Poole and Mason's Arrival (2:59); 7 Trio—The Meeting (3:06); 8 Thwarted Wedding (2:37); 9 Across The Moors (2:36); 10 Restoration (3:55); 11 Reunion (4:22).

Review: Bringing his own musical sensitivity to Charlotte Bronte's celebrated novel, John Williams scored this 1971 version starring George C. Scott and Susannah York, in a dramatic display of all the elements that single him out as a composer—his brilliant feel for melodic material, his lyrical expression, and above all his unusual combination of varied instruments to create the proper atmosphere. All of these elements are brought to the fore here in cues that enhance this story of passion, longing, madness, and mystery. Particularly effective in this context is the contrast between "To Thornfield," a light gallop, and "The Meeting," for a trio, with its morose accents beneath the lilting melody suggesting the oppressive aura of the place and the mysterious foreboding that hangs over it. It shows Williams in a particularly inventive mood, obviously inspired by the broad romantic aspects of the story, and always in search of new, uncommon ways to express his creativity.

Jane Eyre ♪♪♪♪♪

1994, Marco Polo Records; from the movie *Jane Eyre*, 20th Century-Fox, 1943.

Album Notes: *Music*: Bernard Herrmann; The Slovak Radio Symphony Orchestra of Bratislava, conducted by Adriano;

Album Producer: Emil Nizmansky; *Engineer*: Hubert Geschwandtner.

Selections: 1 Prelude (2:46); 2 Jane's Departure (3:17); 3 Jane Alone (2:16); 4 Dreaming/Vanity (2:04); 5 Elegy/Jane's Sorrow (2:26); 6 Time Passage/The Letter (1:17); 7 Thornfield Hall/Valse Bluette (3:55); 8 Rochester (2:26); 9 The Piano/Promenade (4:07); 10 Rochester's Past/The Fire (5:04); 11 Duo/The Door (3:11); 12 Springtime (2:30); 13 Mr. Mason (3:34); 14 The Room/The Rattle (3:02); 15 The Garden (3:37); 16 Farewell (2:32); 17 Song (Jane's Confession)/The Storm (4:47); 18 The Wedding/The Wife; 19 Jane's Farewell (Rochester's Confession); 20 Jane's Return (3:41); 21 Finale (2:58).

Review: Bernard Herrmann's striking score for this memorable screen adaptation of Charlotte Bronte's Victorian novel receives a wonderful reading in a recording as sumptuous as it is evocative. A riveting drama, starring Joan Fontaine as the orphan waif who becomes governess at Thornfield, a manor house, and falls in love with its owner, played by Orson Welles, the film elicited from Herrmann what may well have been his most romantic, and certainly most profuse work, a score clearly dominated by three essential motifs, one for the two principal characters, and the third for the love they feel for one another. In addition to its abundance of impassioned cues, and belying the darker tones they sometimes project, the score also contains musical themes that are poetic and inspiring, like "Valse Bluette," which contrasts the ominous moods in "Thornfield Hall," the lilting "Springtime," or the lovely "The Garden," beautifully expressive. As is so frequently the case with these recordings featuring the Slovak Radio Symphony Orchestra, conducted by Adriano, all the technical aspects deserve warm plaudits.

Jason and the Argonauts

1988, Cloud Nine Records; from the movie *Jason and the Argonauts*, Columbia Pictures, 1963.

See: Bernard Herrmann in Compilations

Jaws

Jaws ♪♪♪♪♪

1990, MCA Records; from the movie *Jaws*, Universal Pictures, 1975.

Album Notes: *Music*: John Williams; *Music Editor*: Ken Wannberg; Orchestra conducted by John Williams; *Album Producer*: John Williams; *Engineer*: John Neal.

Selections: 1 Main Title (Theme From Jaws)(2:16); 2 Chrissie's Death (1:40); 3 Promenade (Tourists On The Menu)(2:46); 4 Out To Sea (2:27); 5 The Indianapolis Story (2:25); 6 Sea Attack Number One (5:24); 7 One Barrel Chase (3:04); 8 Preparing The Cage (3:24); 9 Night Search (3:29); 10 The Underwater Siege (2:31); 11 Hand To Hand Combat (2:32); 12 End Title (Theme From Jaws)(2:18).

Review: John Williams' classic suspense music was unavailable on CD for years until MCA finally relented and produced this crisp-sounding disk that resurrects Williams' original album arrangement of the score. The chopping, Stravinskyesque shark motif is justly famous, but just as enjoyable is the composer's mock-baroque stylings for "Tourists on the Menu," the bracing sea shanty tune developed for "Out to Sea" and "Two Barrel Chase," and the thrilling classical-styled fugue expanded on for "Building the Cage." Williams' supercharged "Sea Attack Number One" is one of the most exciting, sustained action cues ever heard in a movie, brilliantly playing the shark material off the adventuresome "counterattack" fugue to create a bold, modern pirate movie sound that hyped the thrills in Spielberg's brilliant movie to previously unheard-of proportions. *Jaws* is ultimately a kind of monster movie, but Williams' score is almost all adventure, and his tinkering with the original music for album presentation makes for one of the most thoroughly enjoyable soundtrack albums ever released.

Jeff Bond

Jaws 2 𝄞𝄞𝄞𝄞

1990, Varese-Sarabande; from the movie *Jaws 2*, Universal Pictures, 1978.

Album Notes: *Music:* John Williams; *Music Editor:* Ken Wannberg; Orchestra conducted by John Williams; *Album Producer:* John Williams.

Selections: 1 Finding The "Orca" (Main Title)(3:15); 2 The Menu (1:49); 3 Ballet For Divers (2:56); 4 The Water Kite Sequence (2:52); 5 Brody Misunderstood (2:49); 6 The Catamaran Race (2:08); 7 Toward Cable Junction (3:45); 8 Attack On The Helicopter (1:58); 9 The Open Sea (2:03); 10 Fire Aboard and Eddie's Death (3:25); 11 Sean's Rescue (2:55); 12 Attack On The Water Skier (2:40); 13 The Big Jolt! (4:39); 14 End Title, End Cast (3:21).

Review: Following the huge success of the first film, *Jaws 2* reunited John Williams with the story about the dangerous shark, prompting him to devise new music for this sequel that sounded as compelling and ominous as the first. In truth, Williams surpassed himself, writing a score that had the effective-

ness of the first, and then some. Its cues develop and expand on the shark theme, but take it to new heights of creativity. Among the most interesting moments in the new score, "Ballet for Divers" is a splendid highlight; "Attack on the Helicopter" and "Attack on the Water Skier," both exemplify the composer's strong commitment to descriptive music that draws the listener into its melodic web; and "The Open Sea" stands out as an anthem to the sheer beauty of the spectacle it evokes. All in all, an important score in the composer's canon.

Jefferson in Paris 𝄞𝄞𝄞𝄞

1995, Angel Records; from the movie *Jefferson in Paris*, Touchstone Pictures and Merchant Ivory Productions, 1995.

Album Notes: *Music:* Richard Robbins; *Orchestrations:* Geoff Alexander; *Music Editor:* Gerard McCann; *Featured Performers:* Les Arts Florissants, William Christie, director.

Selections: 1 Pantograph: Opening Titles (3:14); 2 Violin Sonata Op. 5 (A. Corelli) *Hiro Kurosaki, Emmanuel Balsa, William Christie*; 3 Hall Of Mirrors (2:39); Dardanus (A. Sacchini): 4 Overture (4:47); 5 Aria d'Iphise: "Cesse, cruel amour" (2:58); 6 Andantino (1:46); 7 Passe Pied (1:09); 8 Aria: "Jour heureux" (3:03); 9 Finale Ballet (1:41); 10 Balloon (2:02); 11 The Walk (2:24); 12 In Hoc Festo (M.A. Charpentier)(1:28) *Sophie Daneman, Sandrine Piau, Jory Vinikour*; 13 Lucy's Death and Sally (5:09); 14 Mormora (instrumental prelude)(M. Cosway)(1:23) *Simon Heyerick, Bernadette Charbonnier, David Bahanovich, Jory Vinikour*; 15 Mormora (for voice and harp)(M. Cosway)(1:25) *Mary Nichols, Jan Walters*; 16 The Locket And The Third Estate (6:35); 17 Courante In C Minor For Harpsichord (J. Duphly)(2:42) *Jory Vinikour*; 18 End Credits (5:52).

Review: In a brilliant display of elegance and sophistication, the score for *Jefferson in Paris* combines together Richard Robbins' cues and music from the period to give the film a vivid musical illustration that is ultimately most winning. With a superb performance by Les Arts Florissants, the late 18th-century music of the French court sounds quite lovely with Corelli's "Violin Sonata," Charpentier's "In hoc festo," and Duphly's "Courante for Harpsichord" among the choice moments found here. In contrast, Robbins' score sounds more florid, more contemporary in a sense, though no less effective in conjuring up images that are both solidly evocative and musically attractive. In the notes he wrote about the score, the composer explains the role he saw between the musical play and the close relationship he tried to establish between the development of his cues and Jefferson's use of a pantograph (a machine which the American statesman used to make duplicate copies of his letters as he wrote them), a recurring theme throughout the film. The continuity and tension that result make the score an ideal companion to the story on the screen.

Jeffrey 🎵🎵ᵛ

1995, Varese-Sarabande; from the movie *Jeffrey*, MVM Films, 1995.

Album Notes: *Music*: Stephen Endelman; *Album Executive Producers*: Michael Caprio, Bruce Kimmel, Bill Meade; *Engineer*: Joe Gastwirt.

Selections: 1 "Jeffrey States His Case": On The Way To Your Heart (1:00); 2 "Jeffrey Rents An Apartment": Someone Who's Looking For Me (1:49); 3 "Sharon's Confession": The Gym (3:51); 4 "Jeffrey Sees Mother Theresa": Cocktails At Sterling's (1:10); 5 Stay Till Morning (S. Endelman/B. Russell)(4:49) *Connie Petruk*; 6 "Who's Who?": The Game Show (:49); 7 Helpless (I Don't Know What To Do Without You)(L. Springsteen)(4:33) *Urbanized, Silvano*; 8 "Dave's Confession": Shopping For Answers (1:14); 9 Someone Whos Looking For Me (S. Endelman/B. Russell)(1:07) *Nancy Ticotin*; 10 "Tim's Confession": On The Way To Your Heart (1:10); 11 "Jeffrey Phones Home" (1:22); 12 We're Livin' It Up (The Gay Pride Parade)(S. Endelman/C. Petruk)(1:27) *Connie Petruk*; 13 The Assault (:50); 14 "Jeffrey's Confession": On The Way To Your Heart (S. Endelman/B. Russell)(1:47) *Nancy Lamott*; 15 "Jeffrey Learns A Lesson": Someone Who's Looking For Me (S. Endelman/B. Russell)(3:21) *Karen Mason*; 16 Helpless (I Don't Know What To Do Without You)(dance mix)(8:07) *Urbanized, Silvano*.

Review: Cleverly edited concept album where each musical cue is led off with an hilarious snippet of dialogue from this comedy about a gay man so afraid of contracting AIDS that he avoids any prospect of happiness. Much of Stephen Edelman's score ranges from an atypical workout piece for "The Gym" to transitional cues as performed by a small jazz combo. The music and the songs are pleasant enough, but the dialogue is so outrageous, particularly "Jeffrey Phones Home" where he discusses sex with his parents, it makes the score seem positively impotent in comparison.

David Hirsch

Jerry Maguire 🎵🎵🎵🎵

1996, Epic Soundtrax; from the movie *Jerry Maguire*, TriStar Pictures, 1996.

Album Notes: *Song Producers*: The Who, Walter Becker, Bruce Springsteen, Jon Astley, Paul McCartney, Michael Penn, Nancy Wilson, David Briggs & Neil Young; *Album Producers*: Danny Bramson, Cameron Crowe; *Engineer*: Chris Bellman.

Selections: 1 The Magic Bus (P. Townshend)(7:35) *The Who*; 2 Sitting Still Moving Still Staring Outlooking (W. Defever)(3:21) *His Name Is Alive*; 3 Gettin' In Tune (P. Townshend)(4:47) *The Who*; 4 Pocketful Of Rainbows (F. Wise/B. Weisman)(3:16) *Elvis Presley*; 5 World On A String (N. Young)(2:25) *Neil Young*; 6 We Meet Again (Theme from Jerry Maguire)(N. Wilson)(3:04) *Nancy Wilson*; 7 The Horses (R.L. Jones/W. Becker)(4:48) *Rickie Lee Jones*; 8 Secret Garden (B. Springsteen)(4:28) *Bruce Springsteen*; 9 Singalong Junk (P. McCartney)(2:36) *Paul McCartney*; 10 Wise Up (A. Mann)(3:28) *Aimee Mann*; 11 Momma Miss America (P. McCartney)(4:05) *Paul McCartney*; 12 Sandy (N. Wilson) (4:40) *Nancy Wilson*; 13 Shelter From The Storm (alternate version)(B. Dylan) (6:00) *Bob Dylan*.

Review: Proof that good, listenable soundtracks can be made from something other than already proven hits. Bruce Springsteen's "Secret Garden" deserves the boost it got from being this movie's love theme (though the radio programmer who came up with the idea of overlaying film dialogue on the song should be shot). Bob Dylan's alternate version of "Shelter from the Storm" adds a verse not heard in the original, while Beatles devotees will make a beeline for Paul McCartney's "Momma Miss America" and the aptly titled "Singalong Junk." Obscure tracks from Neil Young ("World on a String"), Elvis Presley ("Pocketful of Rainbows") and modern rockers His Name is Alive ("Sitting Still Moving Still Staring Outlooking") round out a compelling set.

Gary Graff

The Jewel of the Nile 🎵

1985, Arista/Jive Records; from the movie *The Jewel of the Nile*, 20th Century-Fox, 1985.

Album Notes: *Music*: Jack Nitzsche; *Song Producers*: Wayne Brathwaithe, Barry J. Eastmond, Bryan "Chuck" New, Hugh Masekela, The Willesden Dodgers, Larry Smith, Jon Astrop, Mark Shreeve, Pete Q. Harris, Richard Jon Smith, Michael Hoenig.

Selections: 1 When The Going Gets Tough, The Tough Get Going (W. Brathwaithe/B. Eastmond/R. Lange/B. Ocean)(5:43) *Billy Ocean*; 2 I'm In Love (J. Butler/S. May)(3:30) *Ruby Turner*; 3 African Breeze (J. Butler)(6:00) *Hugh Masekela, Jonathan Butler*; 4 Party (No Sheep Is Safe Tonight)(P. Harris/ N. Green/R. Smith)(5:10) *The Willesden Dodgers*; 5 Freaks Come Out At Night (L. Smith/J. Hutchins)(4:45) *Whodini*; 6 The Jewel Of The Nile (T. Britten/G. Lyle)(4:18) *Precious Wilson*; 7 Legion (Here I Come)(M. Shreeve/P. Harris/R. Smith)(4:49) *Mark Shreeve*; 8 Nubian Dance (P. Harris/R. Smith)(3:35) *The Nubians*; 9 Love Theme (J. Nitzsche)(2:26); 10 The Plot Thickens (J. Nitzsche) (4:15).

Review: On the screen, *The Jewel of the Nile* is a diverting adventure film that recalls some aspects of the Indiana Jones epics, a contemporary swashbuckler that exudes great moments of action and romance, subtly blended together for a nonstop rollercoaster. To pull off this kind of film, a strong score is usually *de rigueur*, and while Jack Nitzsche is not John Williams, the music he wrote on this occasion is serviceable and quite adequate. Although you wouldn't know it from listening to this so-called soundtrack album in which only two of his cues, "Love Theme" and "The Plot Thickens", have been included, for a total playing time of less than seven minutes. The rest of the "action" is taken by non-descript, and frequently boring, pop songs that may play a minor role in the film, but are totally uninspiring in this context.

JFK ♫♫♫♫

1991, Elektra Records; from the movie *JFK*, Warner Bros., 1991.

Album Notes: *Music*: John Williams; *Music Editor*: Ken Wannberg; Orchestra conducted by John Williams; *Featured Musicians*: Tim Morrison (principal trumpet, The Boston Pops Orchestra), James Thatcher (French horn); *Album Producer*: John Williams; *Engineer*: Armin Steiner.

Selections: 1 Prologue (4:00); 2 The Motorcade (5:14); 3 Drummers' Salute (arr. D.G. McCroskie)(2:55) *The Royal Scots Dragoon Guards*; 4 Theme From JFK (2:23); 5 Eternal Father, Strong To Save (For Those In Peril On The Sea)(W. Whiting/J.B. Dykes)(1:19); 6 Garrison's Obsession (2:33); 7 On The Sunny Side Of The Street (D. Fields/J. McHugh)(4:23) *Sidney Bechet*; 8 The Conspirators (4:04); 9 The Death Of David Ferrie (2:47); 10 Maybe September (P. Faith/J. Livingston/R. Evans)(4:03); 11 Garrison Family Theme (2:14); 12 Ode To Buckwheat (B. Lewis)(3:54) *Brent Lewis*; 13 El Watusi (R. Barretto)(2:41) *Ray Barretto*; 14 The Witnesses (2:46); 15 Concerto No. 2 For Horn and Orchestra, K. 417 (Allegro Maestoso)(W.A. Mozart)(6:29) *Dale Clevenger, Franz Liszt Chamber Orchestra, Janos Rolla*; 16 Arlington (6:29); 17 Finale (3:14); 18 Theme From JFK (reprise)(2:23).

Review: John Williams approached his score for Oliver Stone's paranoiac history lesson almost in the manner of Ennio Morricone, seemingly laying down a number of memorable themes and motifs to be placed at the director's whim throughout the movie rather than writing a truly programmatic score. Yet somehow this approach produces an outstandingly listenable album, provided the listener takes full advantage of the miracle of programmability. Williams' dissonant, harsh material involving the Kennedy assassination is pretty tough to sit through, but his JFK theme and variations, as well as melodies for Kevin Costner's

family relationships in the film, are some of Williams' most beautiful and satisfying compositions. "The Conspirators," with its staccato piano line, is quickly gaining prominence as one of the most copied film music cues of all time, although as represented on this CD it's curiously thin-sounding, lacking the driving power and mystery of the film version.

Jeff Bond

See also: Nixon

Johnny Guitar ♫♫♫♫

1993, Varese-Sarabande; from the movie *Johnny Guitar*, Republic Picture, 1954.

Album Notes: *Music*: Victor Young; Orchestra conducted by Victor Young.

Selections: 1 (1:29); 2 Johnny Guitar (V. Young/P. Lee)(2:04) *Peggy Lee*; 3 (3:33); 4 (:46); 5 (:28); 6 (5:54); 7 (1:32); 8 (5:11); 9 (1:32); 10 (3:13); 11 (3:57); 12 (3:12); 13 (2:29); 14 (4:35); 15 (1:43); 16 (2:05); 17 (2:09); 18 (6:01); 19 Johnny Guitar (1:06) *Peggy Lee*.

Review: An unusually bleak western with a neurotic direction by Nicholas Ray, *Johnny Guitar* is a lyrical masterpiece with baroque overtones. Joan Crawford, clad in black denim, gives one of her strongest performances as an aggressive, no-nonsense saloon owner whose only goal in life is to get rich. Mercedes McCambridge is the bitter, sexually frustrated leader of the little community opposing Crawford's plans for expansion. Even though the story itself could have played in any given context, much of the score Victor Young composed for the film is in the standard western idiom, solidly anchored by the title tune, written with and performed onscreen by Peggy Lee. The album, obviously taken from the original acetates (the surface noise on some tracks indicates this much), was initially released on LP in the early 1980s, without identifying the selections. The CD repeats the same mistake, making it difficult to associate a specific cue with a corresponding scene in the film.

Johnny Handsome ♫♫♫♪

1989, Warner Bros. Records; from the movie *Johnny Handsome*, Tri-Star Pictures, 1989.

Album Notes: *Music*: Ry Cooder; *Horns Arranger*: Van Dyke Parks; *Featured Musicians*: Jim Keltner (drums/percussion), Ry Cooder (guitars/keyboards/bass/accordion/fiddle/percussion), Steve Douglas (saxophones); *Horn Band*: George Bohanon (trombone), Harold Battiste (soprano sax), Bobby Bryant (trumpet), John Bolivar, Ernie Fields, Herman Riley (saxophone); *Album Producer*: Ry Cooder; *Engineer*: Larry Hirsch.

Selections: 1 Main Theme (1:52); 2 I Can't Walk This Time/The Prestige (6:49); 3 Angola (2:01); 4 Clip Joint Rhumba (R. Cooder/J. Keltner)(3:18); 5 Sad Story (2:34); 6 Fountain Walk (2:17); 7 Cajun Metal (1:59); 8 First Week At Work (1:04); 9 Greasy Oysters (R. Cooder/J. Keltner)(1:52); 10 Smells Like Money (R. Cooder/J. Keltner)(2:26); 11 Sunny's Tune (2:53); 12 I Like Your Eyes (2:23); 13 Adios Donna (1:32); 14 Cruising With Rafe (3:01); 15 How's My Face (1:48); 16 End Theme (3:20).

Review: A downbeat contemporary drama about a convict whose violent demeanor is not the least bit altered after he undergoes plastic surgery to change his appearance, *Johnny Handsome* receives a flavorful, uplifting score from Ry Cooder, who performed it with splendid musical support from a handful of great jazz players. While the correlation between the music and the film seems less important in this context, the striking feature of the album is the number of cues that create an aura of their own and call for closer scrutiny. Essential to one's appreciation of the score is the expressive "I Can't Walk This Time/The Prestige," which allows the musicians to stretch and fully explore the many positive aspects of the music. Other tracks that also establish themselves include the rousing "Clip Joint Rhumba," with its bouncy zydeco flair, "Sunny's Tune," and "Cruising with Rafe."

Josh and S.A.M. ♫♫▷

1993, Varese-Sarabande Records; from the movie *Josh and S.A.M.*, Castle Rock Entertainment, 1993.

Album Notes: *Music*: Thomas Newman; *Orchestrations*: Thomas Pasatieri; *Music Editors*: Bob Badami, Bill Bernstein; Orchestra conducted by Thomas Newman; *Album Producers*: Thomas Newman, John Vigran, Bill Bernstein; *Engineer*: John Vigran.

Selections: 1 Is You All A Problem (Main Title)(1:39); 2 Night Drive (1:44); 3 Ouagadougou (1:49); 4 In Her Care (1:39); 5 Utah Proper (1:18); 6 Saltwater Palace (1:31); 7 Trains (2:42); 8 Same Wish, Same Weather (1:05); 9 Toward The Settin' Sun (B. Bernstein/B. Badami)(1:12) *The Drunks*; 10 Bus To Canada (2:38); 11 Orchard (1:06); 12 Targhee Pass (1:00); 13 Shuttle (:46); 14 Brothers (2:44); 15 Cold Corner (1:43); 16 Nowhere (:58); 17 Food And Gas (1:19); 18 End Title (2:51).

Review: There are some winning moments in this otherwise uneven score by Thomas Newman for a touching story about two brothers (one of them thinks he is a robot) who steal a car and take a wild ride across the country. However, the overall impression is less than satisfying. Some cues seem to wander off into a netherland in which they fail to find a resolution, others trail off after having built some momentum that never

really materializes. It may be that the score plays better with the film itself. Judged on its own merits, it is not so convincing.

The Joy Luck Club ♫♫♫♫▷

1993, Hollywood Records; from the movie *The Joy Luck Club*, Hollywood Pictures, 1993.

Album Notes: *Music*: Rachel Portman; *Orchestrations*: Rachel Portman, John Neufeld; *Music Editor*: Bill Abbott; Orchestra conducted by J.A.C. Redford; *Featured Musicians*: Masakazu Yoshizawa, Chris Fu, Shufeng He (Chinese instruments), Karen Hua-Qi Han (Chinese violin), Jim Walker (concert and bamboo flutes); *Album Producer*: Rachel Portman; *Engineer*: John Richards.

Selections: 1 The Story Of The Swan (2:30); 2 Escape From Guilin (5:35); 3 Lindo's Story (1:50); 4 Best Quality Heart (2:27); 5 Upturned Chairs (1:58); 6 June Meets Her Twin Sisters (2:58); 7 His Little Spirit Had Flown Away (4:33); 8 An-Mei's Mother Returns (1:50); 9 Most Important Sacrifice (2:44); 10 Tiger In The Trees (3:23); 11 Lindo's Last Night (3:32); 12 The Babies (3:57); 13 An-Mei's New Home (2:38); 14 Swan Feather (:51); 15 End Titles (3:15).

Review: Not what you might think this is, *The Joy Luck Club*, about four sets of Chinese-American mothers and daughters and their diverse reactions to the different sets of values that define the world in which they live, prompted Rachel Portman to write a truly exquisite score. It is filled with great melodies, many in a very romantic vein, in which an occasional Chinese instrument provides the ethnic touch required by the story. Slowly unfolding and in the process setting the tone of the film, the cues explore the many dramatic possibilities suggested by the screenplay, with some great moments of expression finding a voice along the way. Strong romantic elements clearly dominate in the music, with the composer reaching new heights of lyricism in selections like "Best Quality Heart," "June Meets Her Twin Sisters," or "An-Mei's New Home." A lovely, prolific score, in which a deliberately slow pace may leave some listeners unfazed, but which should satisfy many fans of instrumental music.

Judge Dredd ♫♫♫▷

1995, Epic Soundtrax; from the movie *Judge Dredd*, Hollywood Pictures, 1995.

Album Notes: *Music*: Alan Silvestri; *Orchestrations*: William Ross; *Music Editor*: Kenneth Karman; The Sinfonia of London, conducted by Alan Silvestri; *Album Producer*: Alan Silvestri; *Engineer*: Dennis Sands; *Assistant Engineers*: Toby Wood, Charlie Paakkari.

Selections: 1 Dredd Song (Smith/Gallup/Bamonte/Cooper/ O'Donnell) (4:16) *The Cure*; 2 Darkness Falls (M. Johnson) (3:43) *The The*; 3 Super-Charger Heaven (W. Zombie/R. Zombie) (3:36) *White Zombie*; 4 Need-Fire (Cocteau Twins) (4:14) *Cocteau Twins*; 5 Release The Pressure (N.Barnes/P. Daley/E. Daley) (7:39) *Leftfield*; 6 Judge Dredd Main Theme (4:56); 7 Judgement Day (5:53); 8 Block War (4:39); 9 We Created You (3:46); 10 Council Chaos (5:43); 11 Angel Family (5:36); 12 New World (9:13).

Review: If you haven't gone deaf after listening to the five mindless songs that lead off this soundtrack (only "Dredd Song" appears in the film), you'll realize that Alan Silvestri's "Judge Dredd Main Theme" is making good use of CD sonics with its quiet one-minute buildup of synth and chorus. Once it gets going, Silvestri's score is a powerful, addictive mix of driving percussion. This is particularly notable in "Block War." Dredd's own theme is a focused march, embodying the judge's own narrow view that says only the letter of the law matters. Silvestri seems to be having real fun recreating a twisted version of his *Predator 2* theme for the cannibalistic, mutated "Angel Family." He uses several odd synth effects, including some warped whale songs. Jerry Goldsmith was originally scheduled to score this film and created the trailer music. It was recorded on the *Hollywood '95* (q.v.) album and it's interesting to compare the approaches of these two composers to the same subject.

David Hirsch

Judicial Consent 🎵🎵🎵🎵

1995, Intrada Records; from the movie *Judicial Consent*, Rysher Entertainment, 1995.

Album Notes: *Music*: Christopher Young; *Orchestrations*: Pete Anthony, Christopher Young; *Music Editor*: Doug Lackey; Orchestra conducted by Lex de Azevedo; *Synthesizers and Electronic Programming*: Mark Zimoski; *Album Producer*: Christopher Young; *Engineer*: Mark Siddoway.

Selections: 1 Judicial Consent (2:09); 2 Black Thorn (2:50); 3 Hot Mustard Leadpipe (4:40); 4 Double Sin (2:38); 5 The Horizontal Man (1:36); 6 Clue Glue (4:54); 7 Themus (5:29); 8 Gavel On (6:35); 9 Silence (3:23).

Review: This score is brimming with rhythmic mysteriousness: winds over piano, keyboard fingering tentative, a soft flurry of notes, pausing a few beats, to return in a new flurry, with string chords surging in, high register. Low, moaning Herrmannesque chords play off of high-end piano notes with reverbed harp, and always the sustained strings. Young maintains an orches-

tral sensibility—very little electronics make their presence known—but his instrumentation is wicked. Stabs of percussion echoed by a downward violin shriek punctuate a tonal ambiance of whispering strings, low moaning winds, shimmering bells and moody timpani. A harsh strum of chain-like drums slams down amid low pianistic echoes, sinewy string groans, and an incessantly chattering percussion rapping. In the end, Young's pretty main theme survives the horrors and closes the score on a note of melancholy. He captivates the listener, as he does the viewer, with a dominating musical permeation that creates an inescapable atmosphere of foreboding, excitement, suspense, horror and ultimate relief. Few modern composers do it as well.

Randall Larson

Julia and Julia 🎵🎵

1988, Varese-Sarabande Records; from the movie *Julia and Julia*, Cinecom Entertainment, 1988.

Album Notes: *Music*: Maurice Jarre; *Featured Musicians*: Rick Marvin (keyboards), Judd Miller (E.V.I.); *Album Producer*: Maurice Jarre; *Engineer*: Joel Moss.

Selections: 1 Julia (4:44); 2 The Old Lady (1:48); 3 Happy Days (8:35); 4 The Tunnel (3:31); 5 The Penthouse (3:30); 6 Daniel (3:08); 7 With Paolo, Forever (6:27).

Review: For this film about a woman who experiences a time-warp situation, one in which her husband is dead and she has a lover, the other in which her husband is still alive, Maurice Jarre wrote a score that attempts to match in musical terms the odd, dual situation in which the main character finds herself. That he doesn't entirely succeed is indicative of the problems that face the film itself. In his multi-layered electronic score, Jarre tries to convey the strange events that shape up the screen action. He partly succeeds in the long cue, "Happy Days," in which the moods projected manage to convey the sense of insecurity and disorientation Julia must feel when confronted with a perplexing situation she cannot explain. But the other cues, much less elaborated and thinly constructed, fail to convey the same impressions and dissolve into a noisy form of expression that has no fixed goal.

Julius Caesar 🎵🎵🎵🎵

1995, Intrada Records; from the movie *Julius Caesar*, M-G-M, 1953.

Album Notes: *Music*: Miklos Rozsa; *Orchestral Reconstruction*: Daniel Robbins; The Sinfonia of London, conducted by Bruce Broughton; *Featured Artists*: Jane Emanuel (soprano), the Sinfonia Chorus, Jenny O'Grady, director; *Album Producer*:

Douglass Fake; *Engineer*: Mike Ross-Trevor; *Assistant Engineer*: Steve Orchard.

Selections: 1 Julius Caesar Overture (3:15); 2 Praeludium (3:38); 3 Caesar's Procession (2:45); 4 Flavius Arrested (:18); 5 Feast Of Lupercal (:44); 6 Caesar And His Train (:51); 7 The Scolding Winds (2:42); 8 Brutus' Soliloquy (6:34); 9 Brutus' Secret (2:11); 10 They Murder Caesar (1:08); 11 The Ides Of March (4:36); 12 Black Sentence (3:55); 13 Brutus' Camp (1:31); 14 Heavy Eyes (1:47); 15 Gentle Knave (2:07); 16 Ghost Of Caesar (1:42); 17 Most Noble Brutus (1:10); 18 Battle At Philippi (1:28); 19 Titinius Enclosed (:40); 20 Caesar Now Be Still (8:54); 21 Finale (1:10).

Review: Of all the Golden Age masters, Miklós Rózsa was the one who paid the least attention to catching on-screen action. His music has more of a through-composed quality which has survived the decades well. *Julius Caesar*, starring Marlon Brando, is one of his first "historical epic" scores, and one of his darkest, blending smaller period-type cues with the symphonic foreboding of his film noir period. For most of it, the string section simply seems to be playing lower than in his later, sunnier biblical epics, with cello soliloquies accompanying the Shakespearean portent on screen. It's not really "period" music—what did music in the 1st century B.C. really sound like?—but Rózsa's Eastern European romanticism conveys a certain *Roman*-ness which is appropriate. Between the shorter, distinctly Rózsa motifs, with their evocative intervalic leaps, and the longer lines which expand into entire pieces, it's one of his most absorbing historical scores. (Many of the cues were cut or abridged in the actual film.) Intrada's album, which goes on forever, is a new recording done in 1995, with Bruce Broughton conducting the Sinfonia of London and Sinfonia Chorus.

Lukas Kendall

Jumanji ♫♫♫♫

1995, Epic Soundtrax; from the movie *Jumanji*, Tri-Star Pictures, 1995.

Album Notes: *Music*: James Horner; *Orchestrations*: Steve Bramson; *Music Editors*: Jim Henrikson; *Assistant Music Editors*: Christine Cholvin, Joe E. Rand; Orchestra conducted by James Horner; *Featured Instrumental Soloists*: Michael Fisher, Ralph Grierson, Tony Hinnegan, James Horner, Randy Kerber, Qu-Chao Liu, Kazu Matsui, Mike Taylor, Ian Underwood; *Album Producers*: James Horner; *Engineer*: Shawn Murphy; *Assistant Engineers*: Andy Bass, Marc Gebauer, Dave Marquette, Jay Selvester, Kirsten Smith.

Selections: 1 Prologue and Main Title (3:42); 2 First Move (2:20); 3 Monkey Mayhem (4:42); 4 A New World (2:40); 5 "It's Sarah's Move" (2:36); 6 The Hunter (1:56); 7 Rampage Through Town (2:28); 8 Alan Parrish (4:18); 9 Stampede! (2:12); 10 A Pelican Steals The Game (1:40); 11 The Monsoon (4:48); 12 "Jumanji" (11:47); 13 End Titles (5:55)

Review: A thriller with grim overtones, *Jumanji* induced James Horner to write an unusual score filled with ominous sounds, midway between fantasy and horror. The name of the film refers to a very unusual board game with supernatural powers, whose surreal and potentially lethal aspects compel the player to enter into a world totally controlled by the game. As each roll of the dice brings out new elements that prove frightening as well as dangerously beautiful, Horner matches the action with musical themes well-studied to enhance it. "Monkey Mayhem," for instance, is a rollicking cue that underscores a scene in which an unruly group of apes disrupts the suburban New England home of the two youngsters who play the game. Similarly, "Rampage Through Town" evokes a herd of elephants suddenly creating havoc in the little town, smashing everything that happens to be in their path. Each incident in the film calls for (and gets) an inventive musical cue, with Horner conjuring up some chaotic fun along the way. Ultimately, not a very substantial score, but an entertaining one nonetheless.

The Jungle Book

The Jungle Book

1983, Varese-Sarabande Records; from the movie *The Jungle Book*, United Artists, 1940.

See: The Thief of Bagdad

The Jungle Book ♫♫♫♫

1994, Milan Records; from the movie *The Jungle Book*, Buena Vista Pictures, 1994.

Album Notes: *Music*: Basil Poledouris; *Orchestrations*: Greig McRitchie, Larry Ashmore, John Bell, Nick Ingman, Conrad Pope; *Music Editor*: Tom Villano; Orchestra conducted by David Snell; *Engineer*: Tim Boyle.

Selections: 1 Main Titles/The Caravan (4:23); 2 Shere Kahn Attacks (4:48); 3 Mowgli (3:40); 4 Monkey City (4:39); 5 Kitty (5:22); 6 Treasure Room (4:11); 7 Civilization (5:33); 8 Baloo (2:51); 9 Spoils (9:11); 10 Finale (3:29).

Review: For this umpteenth screen treatment of the Rudyard Kipling story about a boy raised by a pack of wolves in the Indian jungle, Basil Poledouris created a score that is rife with lush, colorful orchestral accents, in a way that takes it miles

"We overhauled that score many, many times to get it right.... there were quite a few very tricky cues that played around dialog."

Rachel Portman
on the Academy-award winning score to Emma (The Hollywood Reporter, 1-15-97)

away from the music Miklos Rozsa wrote about the same subject (see above). In many ways, Poledouris' set of cues is very evocative of the screen action, with the selections devoted to the main characters ("Mowgli," "Baloo," "Shere Khan Attacks") striking a bold, sometimes overly rich vein. But this is also music that breathes and needs to express itself in broad terms, something the composer understood perfectly when he wrote the score. As a result, the sweep in the music is incredibly exciting and overpowering.

The Jungle Book

1990, Walt Disney Records; from the animated feature *The Jungle Book*, Walt Disney Pictures, 1967.

See: Broadway and Screen Musicals

Jungle Fever ♪♪♪°

1991, Motown Records; from the movie *Jungle Fever*, Universal Pictures, 1991.

Album Notes: *Music & Lyrics*: Stevie Wonder; *Album Producer*: Stevie Wonder; *Engineers*: Steve Van Arden, R.R. Harlan.

Selections: 1 Fun Day (4:40); 2 Queen In The Black (4:46); 3 These Three Words (4:54); 4 Each Other's Throat (4:17); 5 If She Breaks Your Heart (5:03); 6 Gotta Have You (6:26); 7 Make Sure You're Sure (3:31); 8 Jungle Fever (4:56); 9 I Go Sailing (3:58); 10 Chemical Love (4:26); 11 Lighting Up The Candles (4:09).

Review: Your reaction to this soundtrack album will largely depend on how you feel about Stevie Wonder, who wrote the songs heard in the film directed by Spike Lee and performs them. Generally speaking, the Wonder-man comes across most effectively in ballads ("These Three Words," "Make Sure You're Sure," "I Go Sailing"), possibly because the uptempo numbers seem too grating and abrasive, without much feeling.

Junior ♪♪♪°

1994, Varese-Sarabande Records; from the movie *Junior*, Universal Picture, 1994.

Album Notes: *Music*: James Newton Howard; *Orchestrations*: Brad Dechter, James Newton Howard, Chris Boardman; *Music Editor*: Jim Weidman; Orchestra conducted by Artie Kane; *Album Producers*: James Newton Howard, Michael Mason; *Engineer*: Shawn Murphy.

Selections: 1 Is There A Mother? (2:28); 2 Diana Moves In (1:14); 3 Main Titles (2:39); 4 The Lab (4:16); 5 Thunder And Lightning (2:33); 6 My Body, My Choice (2:08); 7 Natural Born Mother (1:34); 8 Labor (4:06); 9 First Pregnant Man (3:11); 10 It's A Girl (2:41); 11 Junior (2:57); 12 I've Got You Under My Skin (C. Porter)(3:06) *Cassandra Wilson*; 13 Are You In The Mood? (S. Grappelli/D. Reinhardt)(3:28) *Stephane Grappelli*.

Review: A minor (very minor!) comedy about a man who is pregnant (Arnold Schwarzenegger, if you can believe it), *Junior* received a much better score than it actually merited from the always inventive and interesting James Newton Howard. Though the action may not have deserved the attention it got, the composer wrote several cues that are quite enjoyable, musically speaking, with broad sonorous accents that compel the listener to pay close attention ("Main Titles," "First Pregnant Man," "Junior"). Adding a whimsical touch to the score, two source selections, "I've Got You Under My Skin," sung by Cassandra Wilson, and "Are You in the Mood?," exhilaratingly played by Stephane Grappelli, give a slightly different spin to this eloquent album.

Jurassic Park ♪♪♪♪♪

1993, MCA Records; from the movie *Jurassic Park*, Universal Pictures, 1992.

Album Notes: *Music*: John Williams; *Music Editor*: Ken Wannberg; Orchestra conducted by John Williams; *Album Producer*: John Williams; *Engineer*: Shawn Murphy; *Assistant Engineer*: Sue McLean.

Selections: 1 Opening Titles (:34); 2 Theme From Jurassic Park (3:28); 3 Incident At Isla Nublar (5:20); 4 Journey To The Island (8:53); 5 The Raptor Attack (2:49); 6 Hatching Baby Raptor (3:20); 7 Welcome To Jurassic Park (7:55); 8 My Friend, The Brachiosaurus (4:17); 9 Dennis Steals The Embryo (4:56); 10 A Tree For My Bed (2:12); 11 High-Wire Stunts (4:09); 12 Remembering Petticoat Lane (2:48); 13 Jurassic Park Gate (2:04); 14 Eye To Eye (6:32); 15 T-Rex Rescue and Finale (7:40); 16 End Credits (3:26).

Review: How do you musically spell "blockbuster"? The answer may well be in this sensational soundtrack, in which John

Williams makes no bones — prehistoric or otherwise — about his intentions from the first bars of the "Opening Titles." The lovely theme he develops, with oozing arpeggios and strong lyrical accents, belies the threat posed by the various monsters that eventually inhabit the film, something the composer clearly enjoys to define when he approaches such crucial scenes as "The Raptor Attack," "My Friend, The Brachiosaurus," or "Eye to Eye."

Also characteristic of his approach is the melodically strong themes Williams created for the occasion. Once again, we are in the presence of a composer who understands that film music must have a momentum of its own, and that the only way to provide it is to create themes that are essentially catchy. Even when the screen action demands a cue which may not call as much attention to itself, Williams succeeds in fulfilling his obligations while attracting the casual listener by the sheer power of the melody he has conceived for the moment. In every way, this is an outstanding score.

See also: The Lost World

Just Cause ♫♫♫

1995, Varese-Sarabande Records; from the movie *Just Cause*, Warner Bros., 1995.

Album Notes: *Music*: James Newton Howard; *Orchestrations*: Brad Dechter, Jeff Atmajian, Chris Boardman, James Newton Howard; *Music Editor*: Tom Dresher; Orchestra conducted by Artie Kane; *Album Producer*: James Newton Howard; *Engineer*: Shawn Murphy.

Selections: 1 Main Titles (1:37); 2 Searching For Clues (1:54); 3 Bobby Earl In The Elevator (1:20); 4 That's Laurie's Car (2:22); 5 Finding The Scimitar (2:26); 6 Bobby's Confession (3:02); 7 Ida Remembers (3:05); 8 Read The Signs (2:49); 9 Sullivan Phones (2:10); 10 The Execution (3:44); 11 Conviction Overturned (1:40); 12 Phony Message (1:58); 13 Case Closed (2:48).

Review: The confrontation between a law professor (Sean Connery), researching a case about a young man he believes has been falsely accused of a crime, and the small-town Florida cop (Laurence Fishburne) who obtained the confession, possibly through torture and coercion, *Just Cause* is a suspense-filled drama with plenty of twists to keep the audience on the edge of its seats. Contributing an element of strength to the whole brew is the score by James Newton Howard, whose cues slyly accent and modify the action on the screen, sometimes in bold, exciting terms. For once, however, the short playing time of the CD, which is slightly above 30 minutes, seems sufficient

to have the music make its impression without overstaying its welcome.

Kafka ♫♫♫

1992, Virgin Movie Music; from the movie *Kafka*, Miramax Films, 1992.

Album Notes: *Music*: Cliff Martinez; *Album Producers*: Cliff Martinez, Jeff Rona; *Engineer*: Leanne Ungar.

Selections: 1 Eddie's Dead (Main Title)(3:26); 2 Romanian Leave It To Beaver Music, Part 1 (:52); 3 Prelude To A Sneeze (4:22); 4 Walk With The Anarchists (2:00); 5 Romanian Leave It To Beaver Music, Part 2 (:52); 6 Goodnight Mr. Bizzlebek (1:17); 7 Bum Attack (1:52); 8 Hore Hronom, Dolu Hronom (trad.)(3:23) *Josef Balaz Gypsy Band*; 9 Snez (trad.)(3:13) *Josef Balaz Gypsy Band*; 10 The Abduction (1:15); 11 Allegiance To Something Other Than The Truth (1:21); 12 Burgel Goes To The Toilet (1:43); 13 He Came In Through The Bathroom Window (2:43); 14 Miller Time (4:40); 15 Son Of Balloon (1:15); 16 Wrong End Of The Microscope (7:35); 17 Meanwhile, Back At The Ranch (1:06); 18 Why Should Today Be Different? (2:27); 19 Let's Hit The Wall (End Title)(3:28).

Review: No doubt inspired by its subject matter and the defiant personality of the title character, Cliff Martinez wrote a greatly atmospheric score for *Kafka*, in which the cues are separated into two distinct categories, those that apply to the writer's real life, and those that underscore the arcane world in which his imagination often takes him. In the first, the cymbalom plays a vitally important role, suggestive of the Bohemian locale of the action, Prague shortly after the end of World War I, and the apparently impersonal but orderly existence of Kafka. In the second, however, Martinez chose to use an electronic underscoring that would have seemed out of place in 1919 but has a modern resonance that suits Kafka's moods of alienation in the presence of the unknowable ("Bum Attack," "Allegiance to Something Other Than the Truth," "Wrong End of the Microscope"). The combination of both reflects the narrative in its complex duality and provides the anchors upon which the story unfolds.

Kansas City ♫♫♫°

1996, Verve Records; from the movie *Kansas City*, Sandcastle 5/Ciby 2000, 1996.

Album Notes: *Music Arrangers*: Steven Bernstein, Craig Handy, Geri Allen, Don Byron; *Featured Musicians*: Kevin Mahogany (vocal), Olu Dara (cornet), Nicholas Payton, James Zollar (trumpet), Curtis Fowlkes, Clark Gayton (trombones), Don Byron (clarinet), Don Byron, James Carter, Jesse Davis,

David "Fathead" Newman, Craig Handy, David Murray, Joshua Redman (saxophones), Russell Malone, Mark Whitfield (guitars), Geri Allen, Cyrus Chestnut (piano), Ron Carter, Tyrone Clark, Christian McBride (bass), Victor Lewis (drums); *Album Producer*: Hal Willner; *Engineer*: Eric Liljestrand.

Selections: 1 Blues In The Dark (W. Basie/J. Rushing)(4:53) *James Carter, Joshua Redman*; 2 Moten Swing (B. Moten/B. Moten)(3:42) *Jesse Davis, James Carter*; 3 I Surrender Dear (H. Barris/G. Clifford)(6:01) *James Carter, Nicholas Payton, Cyrus Chestnut*; 4 Queer Notions (C. Hawkins)(5:39) *David Murray, Russell Malone, Cyrus Chestnut*; 5 Lullaby Of The Leaves (J. Young/B. Petkere)(4:26) *Jesse Davis, Clark Gayton, Geri Allen*; 6 I Left My Baby (W. Basie/A. Gibson/J. Rushing)(7:24) *Mark Whitfield, David "Fathead" Newman, Craig Handy, Curtis Fowlkes*; 7 Yeah, Man (J. Russell Robinson/N. Sissle)(4:59) *Craig Handy, Joshua Redman*; 8 Froggy Bottom (J. Williams)(6:21) *Geri Allen, David "Fathead" Newman, Mark Whitfield*; 9 Solitude (E. DeLange/E.K. Ellington/I. Mills)(6:00) *Joshua Redman*; 10 Pagin' The Devil (W. Page/M. Gabler)(5:27) *Don Byron, Olu Dara, Clark Gayton*; 11 Lafayette (W. Basie/E. Durham)(4:04) *Nicholas Payton, James Zollar, Olu Dara*.

Review: Robert Altman's often muddled story of crime, race and politics in the 1930s is only temporarily relieved by some great jazz played in the background. Fortunately, the soundtrack album focuses on the music, and succeeds in evoking the era and the locale of the film, without the tedious action that makes it so painful to watch. There is indeed some great playing here, with several veterans (Joshua Redman, David "Fathead" Newman, Ron Carter, Curtis Fowlkes, Don Byron, James Carter, to name a few) displaying the essence of their unique talent in settings that obviously inspire them. Too bad the film could not reach the high quality levels of its soundtrack!

Kazaam *♫♫*

1997, Super Tracks Records; from the movie *Kazaam*, Touchstone Pictures, 1997.

Album Notes: *Music*: Christopher Tyng; *Orchestrations*: Tim Simonec, Steve Zuckerman, Larry Kenton; *Music Editor*: Daryl Kell; *Synths/Percussion/Programming*: Christopher Tyng; *Featured Musician*: Bob Daspit (guitar); The London Film Symphony Orchestra, conducted by Tim Simonec; *Album Producers*: Christopher Tyng, Ford A. Thaxton; *Engineer*: Tim Boyle.

Selections: 1 Interscope Logo/Main Title (2:53); 2 First Wish Backfires (:43); 3 Junk Food From Here To The Sky (1:23); 4 Bike Chase (2:00); 5 DiJinn Explained (1:12); 6 Maljk's Way (1:40); 7 Max And Alice (1:43); 8 Lose The Pointy Shoes (2:20); 9 The Father/Stepfather Conflict (2:21); 10 Never Challenge A Genie (2:14); 11 Tape Theft (2:14); 12 Genie Groove (2:05); 13 Flying French Toast (:46); 14 Maljk Gets His (3:32); 15 The Transformation (4:53); 16 End Titles (3:17).

Review: Basketball star Shaquille O'Neal is the congenial genie who grants three wishes to a 12-year-old, setting the stage for this modern fairy tale unlikely set against a typically violent urban background. Before the relationship between the benevolent 3,000-year-old genie and his reluctantly cynical master finally yields an upbeat solution, much will have happened to both, and all of it is set to the score created by Christopher Tyng, a fresh voice on the film music scene. While the selections clearly indicate the potential of the composer, writing in a variety of styles, most of his cues sound incomplete, some stopping abruptly in the middle of a melodic phrase, others trailing off before they have a chance to reach a logical conclusion. This is all the more regrettable because Tyng is evidently gifted and comes up with attractive melodies whenever necessary, like "Max And Alice." On the screen, this shortcoming might not make much difference; on the album, however, it is too noticeable.

Keeper of the City *♫♫♫*

1991, Intrada Records; from the movie *Keeper of the City*, Viacom Pictures, 1991.

Album Notes: *Music*: Leonard Rosenman; *Orchestrations*: Ralph Ferraro; *Music Editor*: John Caper; The Utah Symphony Orchestra, conducted by Leonard Rosenman; *Album Producer*: Leonard Rosenman; *Engineer*: Mickey Crawford.

Selections: 1 Church (3:58); 2 The Keeper (1:41); 3 Cityscape (1:13); 4 Closet Shrine (4:28); 5 Reflections (:56); 6 Donetti Dies (:54); 7 Vince And Scotty (2:12); 8 Freeway Killing (3:59); 9 Kidnapped (1:27); 10 Vince And Dela (:59); 11 Frank Walks (2:53); 12 Closeted (3:24); 13 Endwrap (4:07).

Review: The "keeper of the city" in this contemporary drama set in a big city is a detective with definite notions about how to deal with criminals. Leonard Rosenman created a vibrant score, centered around two main themes — one to give an aural identity to the environment in which the hero of the film operates, the second to portray a criminal with pseudo-religious fanaticism who challenges the detective and the authority he represents. Heard throughout the score, the two themes collide with each other, complement each other, and eventually blend into one another in a climactic finale. Rosenman, an old hand at creating this type of music, is quite eclectic in his choice of themes and harmonies, and powerfully evokes the scene of the crime and the participants in it. The recording, oddly off-balanced in many cues with most of the musicians apparently regrouped on the right side, is otherwise clearly defined and appropriately dry.

Kid Galahad

1993, RCA Records; from the movie *Kid Galahad*, United Artists, 1962.

See: Elvis Presley in Compilations

A Kid in King Arthur's Court ♫♫♫♪

1995, Walt Disney Records; from the movie *A Kid in King Arthur's Court*, Walt Disney Films, 1995.

Album Notes: *Music*: J.A.C. Redford; *Orchestrations*: Eric Schmidt, Carl Johnson, Larry Kenton, Christopher Guardino, Michael Harriton, Mark Gasbarro, Tim Kelly; *Music Editors*: Mark Green, David Cates; The City Of Prague Philharmonic Orchestra, conducted by J.A.C. Redford; *Featured Musician*: Liona Boyd (classical guitar); *Album Producer*: J.A.C. Redford; *Engineer*: Eric Tomlinson.

Selections: 1 A Kid In King Arthur's Court (Main Title)(2:46); 2 Strike Out/Earthquake (2:57); 3 Captured In Camelot (3:11); 4 Combat Rock 2:26); 5 Now Let Us Eat! (2:04); 6 Merlin's Lair (2:30); 7 Two Modest Proposals (2:36); 8 Successful Swording (1:24); 9 The Law Of The Land (1:55); 10 Calvin And Katie (2:54); 11 The Plot Thickens (4:30); 12 Between You And Me/Under Arrest (2:34); 13 You *Do* Care (1:32); 14 Horses To Water (1:33); 15 Rescuing Katie (4:07); 16 The Fight In The Castle/Sir Calvin Of Reseda (3:37); 17 The Tournament (4:34); 18 Black Magic (1:59); 19 In Shining Armor (2:23); 20 Warm Goodbyes/Home Run (4:16); 21 A Kid In King Arthur's Court (End Title)(3:04); 22 The Conscience Of The King (4:34).

Review: In a fresh, inventive variation on Mark Twain's classic "Connecticut Yankee" story, a kid with little mettle travels back in time to the days of Camelot, where his unusual appearance and bagful of odd contrivances (a portable CD player, rollerblades, a Swiss Army knife) immediately single him out as some sort of magician. Providing the musical peg on which the emotional balance of the action finds its fodder, J.A.C. Redford wrote a score that harkens back to the days of yore, when swashbucklers spoke of deadly deeds and courtly manners, but with a modern twist in keeping with the contemporary elements of the fantasy. Along the way, there are some nifty moments, including the abrasive "Combat Rock," the medieval-sounding "Now Let Us Eat!," the rousing "Successful Swording," and the love romance "Calvin and Katie." At times

sounding a mite too profuse and lush for such a slight amusement, the score nonetheless delights and proves quite enjoyable. A theme for classical guitar ("The Conscience of the King") is particularly attractive.

The Killing Fields ♫♫♫

1984, Virgin Records; from the movie *The Killing Fields*, 1984.

Album Notes: *Music*: Mike Oldfield; *Choral and Orchestral Arrangements*: David Bedford; The Orchestra of the Bavarian State Opera and The Tolzer Boys Choir, conducted by Eberhard Schoener; *Featured Musicians*: Mike Oldfield (guitars, synthesizers), Preston Heyman (Oriental percussion), Morris Pert (percussion); *Album Producer*: Mike Oldfield; *Engineers*: Mike Oldfield, Geoff Young.

Selections: 1 Pran's Theme (:49); 2 Requiem For A City (2:11); 3 Evacuation (5:14); 4 Pran's Theme 2 (1:41); 5 Capture (2:24); 6 Execution (4:47); 7 Bad News (1:13); 8 Pran's Departure (2:08); 9 Worksite (1:16); 10 The Year Zero (:28); 11 Blood Sucking (1:22); 12 The Year Zero 2 (:34); 13 Pran's Escape/The Killing Fields (3:17); 14 The Trek (2:03); 15 The Boy's Burial/Pran Sees The Red Cross (2:43); 16 Good News (1:46); 17 Etude (4:41).

Review: Classic rock instrumentalist Mike Oldfield, whose "Tubular Bells" had played such an important function in the film *The Exorcist,* contributed an effective score to this Oscar-nominated film about Cambodia and the war-related horrors that have plagued the country over the past 20 years. The story of the friendship that binds an American journalist and the educated native who serves as his guide, the film focuses on the two men's journey through Khmer Rouge territory, their eventual arrest, and escape from a re-education camp in the Year Zero. Oldfield's score, an eerie mixture of electronic sounds (and tubular bells) augmented by a boys choir over an orchestral texture, seems like a necessary embellishment on the soundtrack. Away from the screen drama, it still conjure up images that may not all be related to the film itself but that are quite effective.

Kindergarten Cop ♫♫♫♫

1990, Varese-Sarabande; from the movie *Kindergarten Cop*, Universal Pictures, 1990.

Album Notes: *Music*: Randy Edelman; *Orchestrations*: Greig McRitchie, Mark McKenzie; *Music Editor*: Kathy Durning; *Orchestra* conducted by Randy Edelman; *Album Producer*: Randy Edelman; *Engineer*: Shawn Murphy, Elton Ahi.

Selections: 1 Astoria School Theme (1:07); 2 Children's Montage (3:22); 3 Love Theme (Joyce)(2:31); 4 Stalking Crisp

motion picture soundtracks

(3:40); 5 Dominic's Theme/A Rough Day (1:55); 6 The Line-Up/Fireside Chat (2:57); 7 Rain Ride (1:56); 8 The Kindergarten Cop (1:27); 9 Poor Cindy/Gettysburg Address (2:07); 10 A Dinner Invitation (:48); 11 Love Theme Reprise (1:26); 12 A Magic Place (2:54); 13 Kimball Reveals The Truth (1:45); 14 The Tower/Everything Is OK (2:30); 15 Fire At The School (5:40); 16 Closing (2:15).

Review: What a selling job Randy Edelman had—Schwarzenegger teaching kindergarten! But one listen to the sweet and gentle "Astoria School Theme" and you know he's succeeded in transforming "The Terminator" into a cream puff. The film does have its share of action music when Arnold acts like a cop ("Stalking Crisp," "Fire at the School"), but mostly breezes effectively through the upbeat comedic moments when he must perform his duties undercover as a teacher. Edelman performs the piano on the "Love Theme".

David Hirsch

King Creole

1988, RCA Records; from the movie *King Creole*, Paramount Pictures, 1958.

See: Elvis Presley in Compilations

King Kong ♪♪♪♪

1984, Southern Cross Records; from the movie *King Kong*, RKO Radio Pictures, 1933.

Album Notes: *Music*: Max Steiner; *Orchestrations*: Bernard Kaun, Christopher Palmer; The National Philharmonic Orchestra, conducted by Fred Steiner; *Album Producer*: John Lasher; *Engineers*: Bob Auger, Joe Gastwirt.

Selections: 1 Main Title/A Boat In The Fog (3:37); 2 Forgotten Island/Jungle Dance (4:50); 3 Sea At Night (2:23); 4 Aboriginal Sacrifice Dance (4:00); 5 Entrance Of Kong (4:18); 6 The Bronte/Log Sequence (4:34); 7 Cryptic Shadows (1:49); 8 Kong!/The Cave (9:30); 9 Sailors Waiting (1:33); 10 Return Of Kong (4:10); 11 King Kong Theatre March (1:30); 12 Kong Escapes/Aeroplanes/ Finale (4:40).

Review: The music for *King Kong*, is, in the words of Oscar Levant, "a Max Steiner concert illustrated by pictures," evidently an apt description of the importance of the score, the first of its kind ever written for a motion picture. An impressive achievement at the time, it continues to mesmerize by the sheer force of its musical power, particularly in this recording made in 1976, in which Fred Steiner (no relation to the composer) conducted the National Philharmonic Orchestra in a spirited reading of the score. Broadly dramatic and colorfully exotic, the music evokes the first and one of the best monster

pictures ever made, with weird, dissonant chords contrasting pretty melodies for a multi-layered, effective score that endures.

King of Kings ♪♪♪♪

1992, Sony Music; from the movie *King of Kings*, M-G-M, 1961.

Album Notes: *Music*: Miklos Rozsa; The M-G-M Studio Orchestra, conducted by Miklos Rozsa; *CD Producer*: Dan Rivard.

Selections: 1 Overture (3:45); 2 Prelude (3:24); 3 Roman Legions (1:29); 4 Road To Bethlehem/Nativity (4:13); 5 Slaughter Of The Innocents (1:40); 6 Pilate's Arrival (2:42); 7 John The Baptist (1:26); 8 Revolt (2:39); 9 Temptation (4:40); 10 Herod's Feast (2:26); 11 Miracles (2:50); 12 Jugglers And Tumblers/Herod's Desire (2:57); 13 Salome's Dance (1:45); 14 Mount Galilee/Sermon On The Mount (4:55); 15 The Lord's Prayer (2:38); 16 Entr'acte (4:20); 17 Jesus Enters Jerusalem (1:45); 18 Tempest In Judea/ Defeat/Phalanx (5:05); 19 The Feast Of Passover (2:53); 20 Gethsemane/ Agony In The Garden (3:44); 21 Scourging Of Christ/Crown Of Thorns (2:16); 22 Via Dolorosa (2:57); 23 Last Words Of Christ (1:28); 24 Pieta (2:49); 25 Resurrection (2:06); 26 Epilogue (2:08).

Review: Following *Ben-Hur*, Miklos Rozsa became known as the Hollywood composer best qualified to score Biblical films, a notion he could not dispel, despite the fact that he wrote *King of Kings* and *El Cid* almost back to back. Like *Ben-Hur*, however, *King of Kings* enabled the composer to write in an idiom in which he was by now thoroughly familiar, and in which he had pioneered the use of ancient instruments to give his music the authenticity he felt it needed. A dramatic retelling of the story of Christ, the film provided Rozsa with an extra difficulty, in that it covered essentially the same grounds the composer had already explored in *Ben-Hur*. Undaunted, Rozsa rose to the challenge and wrote a score which may not be up to the standards set by the previous film, but which exhibits nonetheless the same feelings of pious adoration and epic accents. This time, however, he relies on new Jewish themes to augment the Roman themes he had previously created for both *Ben-Hur* and *Quo Vadis*. In another significant departure, Rozsa also created a piece of 12-tone music to describe the temptation of Christ in the desert, the only time he wrote atonal music.

With its sweeping romantic themes and thrilling epic accents, the score is truly awe-inspiring, a splendid effort which ranks among Rozsa's most important contributions to the screen. As befits a score of this importance, the CD reissue includes many cues that were previously unreleased. The sound, however, leaves a lot to be desired. Frequently harsh and without the warmth usually associated with a good mastering job, it presents occasional distortion on some tracks, and overall uneven sonic qualities, and despite the claim that it is in stereo for the first time, some tracks are evidently in mono. These technical questions set aside, the CD is still a very important addition to any serious collection of film music.

King of the Wind ♪♪♪♪ ▷

1990, JOS Records; from the movie *King of the Wind*, HTV International, 1990.

Album Notes: *Music*: John Scott; The Munich Studio Orchestra, conducted by John Scott; *Album Producer*: John Scott; *Engineer*: Bob Auger.

Selections: 1 The Birth Of Sham (2:51); 2 King Of The Wind (2:52); 3 The Royal Court At Tunis (2:48); 4 Race With Wild Horses (2:16); 5 Set Sail For France (2:40); 6 Death Of Ahmed (2:20); 7 Arrival In France (1:50); 8 Monsieur Richard: Chef Royale (1:08); 9 Agba And Sham At Versailles (1:08); 10 The Abduction Of Sham (4:44); 11 A New Life In England (2:00); 12 Sham Shows His Metal (1:20); 13 Death Of Coke (2:57); 14 Newgate Prison (3:18); 15 The Earl Of Godolphin (1:42); 16 Lord Granville (1:02); 17 Sham Fights For Roxanna (1:33); 18 Banishment To Hangman's Noose (3:16); 19 A Letter From Hannah (2:08); 20 The Newmarket Races (2:40); 21 Winning The King's Plate (3:07); 22 The Godolphin Arabian (End Titles)(3:16).

Review: The story of a mute Arab boy called Agba and a horse called Sham, and their adventures as they journey from Tunis to England in the early 18th century, *King of the Wind* gave John Scott a colorful tale and diversified background to write a score that is quite unusual. As exotic as the story itself and as complex as the many elements that constitute it, the cues follow the saga of the two friends through North Africa, across the Mediterranean Sea, and to the court of Louis XV. Further misadventures occur in England where Agba is imprisoned and Lath, the son of Sham, wins the King's Cup at Newmarket and becomes the forebear of the English racing thoroughbreds.

Strikingly evocative of the many territories covered, and the events that occur, the music is in turn Arabic and baroque, romantic and epic, with some pulse-racing moments in-between. The various cues explore all these elements in depth, in a brilliant musical tapestry that weaves its own tale. Among the striking cues assembled in this album, "Race with Wild Horses," "The Abduction of Sham," "The Earl of Godolphin," "The Newmarket Races," and "Winning the King's Plate" are notably effective, but the entire score is melodically outstanding.

King Rat ♪♪♪ ▷

1995, Legacy Records/Sony Music Entertainment; from the movie *King Rat*, Columbia Pictures, 1965.

Album Notes: *Music*: John Barry; Orchestra conducted by John Barry; *CD Producer*: Didier C. Deutsch; *Engineer*: Chris Herles

Selections: 1 King Rat March (3:03); 2 Main Title (4:05); 3 Tuned In At Changi (1:58); 4 Just As You Were (3:13); 5 There Is A Radio In This Hut (3:29); 6 Just As You Were (2:43); 7 Touch And Go (2:57); 8 Grey's Day (3:57); 9 Just As You Were (2:14); 10 The Recovery Of Marlowe (3:17); 11 The End Is At Hand (1:44); 12 King Rat March (2:03).

Review: For director Bryan Forbes' dark film about prisoners of war confined in the notorious Japanese Changi Prison on Singapore Island, John Barry created a unique score which utilized unusual instrumentation and orchestration—techniques that effectively convey the images of humans involved in a struggle for survival in a completely oppressive, horrendous environment. The sparseness of the musical theme and the texture Barry achieves through careful use of exotic percussion instruments painfully underscores the glum tenseness of the plot, and serve to make this one of his most unusual and intriguing film works. The recording, newly remastered, is excellent.

Charles L. Granata

King Solomon's Mines ♪♪♪♪

1991, Intrada Records; from the movie *King Solomon's Mines*, Cannon Films, 1985.

Album Notes: *Music*: Jerry Goldsmith; *Orchestrations*: Arthur Morton; The Hungarian State Opera Orchestra, conducted by Jerry Goldsmith; *Album Producer*: Jerry Goldsmith; *Engineer*: Mike Ross.

Selections: 1 Main Title (3:26); 2 Welcoming Committee (:48); 3 No Sale (3:22); 4 The Mummy (1:10); 5 Have A Cigar (3:24); 6 Good Morning (2:23); 7 Under The Train (2:57); 8 Dancing Shots (3:25); 9 Pain (2:54); 10 Forced Flight (5:05); 11 The Chieftain (:58); 12 Pot Luck (3:30); 13 Upside Down People (4:44); 14 The Crocodiles (2:56); 15 The Mines (1:20); 16 The Ritual: Low Bridge (9:02); 17 Falling Rocks (4:05); 18 No Diamonds (4:07).

Review: Jerry Goldsmith's broad and elaborate satire of *Raiders of the Lost Ark* will test your tolerance for large-scale action cues and hyperkinetic heroic fanfares as it clatters along with over an hour of hammering, non-stop adventure music. It will drive some listeners crazy, but if you're a fan of Goldsmith's action material you won't want to miss this effort, which was the composer's last completely orchestral score until 1996's *First Knight*. Goldsmith's bracingly old-fashioned opening cue makes brilliant use of African rhythmic effects, while the rest of the score mixes a broad take-off of Wagner's "Ride of the Valkyries" with some of the most spectacular over-the-top, brassy action writing the composer has ever produced. It's not to be taken seriously but it's certainly a far more enjoyable romp than the film itself.

Jeff Bond

Kings Go Forth/
Some Came Running ♫♫♫

1992, Cloud Nine Records, from the movies *Kings Go Forth*, United Artists, 1958, and *Some Came Running*, M-G-M, 1959

Album Notes: *Music:* Elmer Bernstein; Orchestras conducted by Elmer Bernstein.

Selections: KINGS GO FORTH: 1 Kings Go Forth (2:11); 2 The Riviera (4:01); 3 Monique's Theme (1:27); 4 The Bunker (2:07); 5 Sam's Theme (1:40); 6 Sam And Monique (4:43); 7 Sam's Return (4:25); 8 Monique's Theme (1:27); 9 Le Chat Noir (2:55); 10 Quiet Drive (1:10); 11 Britt's Kiss (3:19); 12 Monique's Despair (3:18); 13 Displaced (4:15); 14 Finale (2:55);

SOME CAME RUNNING: 15 Prelude To Some Came Running (1:17); 16 To Love And Be Loved (2:30); 17 Dave's Double Life (2:01); 18 Dave And Gwen (1:52); 19 Fight (1:26); 20 Gwen's Theme (2:35); 21 Ginny (3:18); 22 Short Noise (1:49); 23 Live It Up (1:30); 24 Tryst (2:36); 25 Seduction (2:39); 26 Smitty's Place (2:32); 27 Rejection (2:44); 28 Pursuit (4:42); 29 Finale (2:24).

Review: While neither the scores for *Kings Go Forth* or *Some Came Running* ever had the commercial success of many other film compositions by Elmer Bernstein, they remain an important part of the composer's canon, and are of particular interest within the realm of the work of the films' star, Frank Sinatra.

With *Kings Go Forth* (set in war-torn Italy, circa 1944), Bernstein's task was to musically portray a love triangle between a sensuous femme (Natalie Wood), and two American soldiers enjoying a well-deserved furlough on the French Riviera (Frank Sinatra and Tony Curtis). As always, his music hits the mark, bringing a combination of dramatic themes and romantic interludes together to effectively depict the tensions of battle, and the relationship between the three main characters. The sound on this portion of the disc is monophonic.

The plot of *Some Came Running* is also cursed by a love triangle, however in this instance the setting is a small home town, instead of the European battlefront. The themes demand a dark, tragic overtone (Sinatra's character is a cynical, brooding type), and, once again, Bernstein deftly achieves this

through the careful use of strings, sax, piano and percussion to create a bluesy, dissonant atmosphere that perfectly heightens the sense of gloom and despair. The score, which contains jazz-tinged pieces reminiscent of Bernstein's work for another Sinatra film, *The Man with the Golden Arm* and some utterly dramatic selections, is certainly one of the composer's most underrated efforts. It is heard here in full stereo.

It is interesting to note that both films yielded themes that went unsung by Sinatra on the screen, yet enjoyed commercial vocal recordings by the singer—"Monique" from *Kings Go Forth*, and "To Love and be Loved" from *Some Came Running*.

Charles L. Granata

Kings Row ♫♫♫♫♫

1980, Varese-Sarabande Records; from the movie *Kings Row*, Warner Bros. Pictures, 1942.

Album Notes: *Music:* Erich Wolfgang Korngold; The National Philharmonic Orchestra, conducted by Charles Gerhardt; *Album Producer:* George Korngold; *Engineer:* Robert Auger; *CD Producers:* Tom Null, Chris Kuchler; *Engineer:* Danny Hersch.

Selections: 1 Main Title/The Children (Parris and Cassie)/ Parris And Grandmother/Cassie's Party/Icehouse Operation/ Cassie's Farewell/Parris Goes To Dr. Tower/Winter/Grandmother's Last Will/Seduction/All Is Quiet/Grandmother Dies/ Sunset (23:38); 2 Parris Leaves Kings Row/Flirtation/Vienna And Happy New Year 1900/Dandy And Drake/Financial Ruin/ Accident And Amputation/Drake Awakens/Vienna/Cable/ Randy And Drake/Letters Across The Ocean/Parris Come Back/Kings Row/Elise/Parris' Decision/Finale (24:31).

Review: Even though he only composed 19 scores during the time he spent in Hollywood between 1935 and 1947, Erich Wolfgang Korngold made a profoundly indelible impression on film music which can still be felt on the scores created today. But while he is best remembered for the swashbucklers like *The Adventures of Robin Hood* or *The Sea Hawk*, for which he became justifiably famous, some of his other efforts, notably his music for *Kings Row*, are equally noteworthy.

Based on a popular novel by Henry Bellamann about life in a small town at the turn of the century, the film, starring Ronald Reagan, Robert Cummings and Ann Sheridan, is an engrossing drama covering several years in the life of his main protagonists, from childhood to adulthood, and the many changes they go through as their world is being transformed around them. Taking a cue from the story, Korngold delivers one of his most serene and affecting scores, in a superb display of his craft, with many leitmotifs detailing the various characters in the film and their interactions.

While not as flamboyant as some of his other creations, *Kings Row* is best remembered today for its main theme, a striking epic tune which Korngold composed before he had a chance to read the script, mistakenly thinking that the "King" in the title referred to another cape-and-dagger yarn. The recording, produced by the composer's son, and lovingly detailed by the National Philharmonic Orchestra conducted by Charles Gerhardt, is essential.

Knight Moves Woof

1992, Milan Records; from the movie *Knight Moves*, Republic Pictures, 1992.

Album Notes: *Music:* Anne Dudley; *Orchestrations:* Anne Dudley; The Pro Arte Orchestra of London, conducted by Anne Dudley; *Featured Musicians:* Phil Todd (saxophone), Anne Dudley (keyboards), Andy Pask (bass), Harold Fisher (drums), Luis Jardim (percussion); *Album Producer:* Anne Dudley; *Engineer:* Roger Dudley.

Selections: 1 I Put A Spell On You (3:25) *Carol Kenyon*; 2 1972 Washington State Chess Tournament (7:09); 3 Looking For Connections (1:52); 4 I Used A Variation (1:38); 5 The Shadow Of The Castle (2:19); 6 If You Met Him Could You Tell? (:58); 7 The Game Continues (1:47); 8 They Found The Third Girl (2:29); 9 The Prince Of Darkness (1:47); 10 The Tarakoss Opening (2:11); 11 You're Starting To Make Mistakes (:51); 12 You Like To Play Games Don't You (:51); 13 He'll Kill Again (3:51); 14 You Have No Idea What I Am (2:15); 15 Remember/Eventually Revenge (:56); 16 The Game's Over (3:50); 17 Fool That I Am (3:50) *Carol Kenyon*.

Review: Mindless collection of synthesized noises (including ambient sound effects) with no distinct melody or musical direction. Anne Dudley has the nerve to claim she composed, orchestrated and conducted this repetitive mess. Not nearly as exciting as watching paint dry. Best used by the F.B.I. to force militiamen out of their compounds by repetitive performance.

David Hirsch

Knights of the Round Table ♫♫♫♪

1983, Varese-Sarabande; from the movie *Knights Of The Round Table*, M-G-M, 1953.

Album Notes: *Music:* Miklos Rozsa; The M-G-M Studio Orchestra, conducted by Muir Mathieson; *Album Producers:* Harry Lojewski, Tony Thomas; *CD Producers:* Tom Null, Richard Kraft; *Engineer:* Daniel Hersch.

Selections: 1 Prelude — Mordred's Plot/Lancelot Meets Elaine, Lancelot Meets Arthur/Chivalry, First Battle, Sanctus/Cortege/Alleluia, Hawking (20:31); 2 Departure/Pict Battle/Return, Distant Thoughts And Dreams, The Death Of Arthur/Resignation, To The Death/Finale and End Title (19:57); Lydia (piano suite): 3 Love Theme (1:59); 4 Bubbling Stars (1:25); 5 Sleighride (1:49); 6 Waltz (2:59); 7 The Sea (2:14); 8 Farewell (3:18); 9 Concerto (Four Hands)(2:28) *Albert Dominguez*.

Review: *Knights of the Round Table* reunited composer Miklos Rozsa with the star, Robert Taylor, and the creative staff, director Richard Thorpe and producer Pandro S. Berman, who had presided over the success of *Ivanhoe*, two years before. But while this big screen epic retelling of the legend of King Arthur, based on Sir Thomas Mallory's *Le Morte d' Arthur*, seems to have everything going for it, its characters don't exhibit the spirit and dash of those in the previous film. There is quite a few scenes of battles and jousts to delight fans of the medieval epic genre, spectacularly filmed in CinemaScope, but the pageantry seems to lose some of its shine next to this story about the alleged infidelities of Queen Guinevere, smitten by the handsome Lancelot du Lac, and the web of deceit and villainy which her enemies, the malevolent Sir Mordred and the baleful Morgan Le Fay, spin around her.

True to form, Rozsa nonetheless delivered a score that has all the elements of bravura needed for this handsome spectacle, creating cues that cover every ground in the story, from the exciting battle scenes to the romantic sweep of the love scenes to the religious overtones that permeate some of the most inspirational moments in the medieval tale. The recording, an early transfer from the 1953 stereo master tapes, generally lacks warmth and would benefit from a better EQ to correct its harsh, hollow sound. The CD also contains a piano suite from *Lydia*, a 1941 drama starring Merle Oberon as an older woman reunited after 35 years with the inconsistent lover who deserted her.

Krull ♫♫♫♫♪

1992, SCSE Records; from the movie *Krull*, Columbia Pictures, 1983.

Album Notes: *Music:* James Horner; *Orchestrations:* James Horner, Greig McRitchie; The London Symphony Orchestra and The Ambrosian Singers, conducted by James Horner; *Album Producer:* James Horner; *Engineer:* John Richards; *CD Producer:* Douglass Fake; *CD Engineer:* Robert Vosgien.

Selections: 1 Main Title/Colwyn's Arrival (7:34); 2 Slayer's Attack (9:17); 3 Quest For The Glaive (7:22); 4 The Seer's Vision (2:17); 5 The Battle In The Swamp (2:40); 6 Quicksand (3:37); 7

Leaving The Swamp (1:59); 8 The Widow's Web (6:17); 9 Colwyn And Lyssa (Love Theme)(2:34); 10 The Widow's Lullaby (5:01); 11 Ynyr's Death (1:39); 12 Riding The Fire Mares (5:21); 13 Battle On The Parapets (2:52); 14 Inside The Black Fortress (6:14); 15 Death Of The Beast/Destruction Of The Black Fortress (8:33); 16 Epilogue And End Credits (4:52).

Review: A fantasy tale of epic proportions about a young prince and the maiden-in-distress he has to rescue from a malevolent Beast and its dark forces before the closing titles, *Krull* exhibits all the swashbuckling ingredients dear to fans of the genre, including an impressive score composed for the occasion by James Horner, in one of his earliest efforts in this field. Using the huge forces at his disposal, the London Symphony Orchestra, one of the best orchestras in the world for this type of music, the Ambrosian Singers, another respected group, and the discrete contribution of synthesizers to add extra texture to his score, Horner created cues that underline the sweep of this sword-and-sorcery saga, in bold, exciting strokes. Many moments in this recording, an expanded version containing many selections that were previously unavailable, reveal the composer's genuine feel for the genre, an impression he confirmed in later years, with grand themes that unfold with all the power and majesty usually associated with this kind of musical expression.

La Bamba 🎵🎵🎵🎵

1987, Slash/Warner Bros. Records; from the movie *La Bamba*, Columbia Pictures, 1987.

Album Notes: *Song Producers*: Steve Berlin, Mitchell Froom, Don Davis, Garry Talent, Marshall Crenshaw, Don Gehman, Willie Dixon; *Album Executive Producers*: Taylor Hackford, Joel Sill.

Selections: 1 La Bamba (2:54) *Los Lobos*; 2 Come On, Let's Go (1:58) *Los Lobos*; 3 Ooh! My Head (1:43) *Los Lobos*; 4 We Belong Together (1:58) *Los Lobos*; 5 Framed (2:33) *Los Lobos*; 6 Donna (2:19) *Los Lobos*; 7 Lonely Teardrops (3:27) *Howard Huntsberry*; 8 Crying, Waiting, Hoping (2:20) *Marshall Crenshaw*; 9 Summertime Blues (2:40) *Brian Setzer*; 10 Who Do You Love (3:00) *Bo Diddley*; 11 Charlena (2:45) *Los Lobos*; 12 Goodnight My Love (3:16) *Los Lobos*

Review: O.K., so it's a little weird that this soundtrack from a film about the late Richie Valens doesn't include a single performance by him, nor is there a single songwriting credit for him in the booklet. That's legalities, for you. But if anyone is going to fill his spot, it should be Los Lobos, who do a masterful job on all of his hits and scored a smash of their own with the title track. But don't overlook ace performances by Marshall Crenshaw on

Buddy Holly's "Crying, Waiting, Hoping," Brian Setzer on Eddie Cochran's "Summertime Blues," and Howard Huntsberry on Jackie Wilson's "Lonely Teardrops."
Gary Graff

La belle et la bete 🎵🎵🎵🎵🎵

1996, Marco Polo Records; from the movie *La belle et la bete*, Gaumont Films, 1946.

Album Notes: *Music*: Georges Auric; The Moscow Symphony Orchestra and the Axios Chorus, conducted by Adriano; *Album Producer*: Betta International; *Engineers*: Edvard Shakhnazarian, Vitaly Ivanonv.

Selections: 1 Main Title (2:04); 2 Beauty And Avenant (1:26); 3 In The Forest (3:16); 4 The Banquet Hall (3:36); 5 The Theft Of A Rose (1:49); 6 The Merchant's Return (1:00); 7 Beauty's Departure (1:38); 8 Mysterious Corridors (3:38); 9 Appearance Of The Beast (1:39); 10 In The Bedroom (1:19); 11 The Dinner (3:40); 12 Frightful Moments (4:14); 13 The Draper's Prank (2:52); 14 Conversations In The Park (4:01); 15 The Promise (2:07); 16 Beast's Jealousy (1:30); 17 Love's Despair (1:39); 18 The Five Secrets (4:04); 19 The Waiting (2:08); 20 Avenant's Proposal (1:26); 21 The Mirror And The Glove (3:30); 22 Diana's Pavilion (4:17); 23 Prince Charming (2:51); 24 Flying Upwards (2:23).

Review: French composer Georges Auric's music for Jean Cocteau's 1946 French version of *Beauty and the Beast* is sumptuously classical. In the early scenes in the haunted forest and in the Beast's castle, the music takes on a darker tonality. But much of the score, quiet and static, is delicate—non-moving figures and chords emphasizing the unusualness of the setting and the events, which contrast nicely with those moments when Auric lets loose with audible energy. At times, the music takes on an almost balletic quality, equally as impressionistic as Cocteau's direction and the marvelous sets designed by Christian Berard. Throughout, a choir is used to emphasize the monstrous nature of the Beast, echoing emotions he is unable to verbalize. The CD contains the complete score, including those cues deleted from either or both the American and French prints of the film. A 16-page booklet is included with plenty of black-and-white photos and notes on the film, the music, and the composer.
Randall D. Larson

La dolce vita 🎵🎵🎵🎵

1991, CAM Records; from the movie *La dolce vita*, Cineriz Films, 1959.
Album Notes: *Music*: Nino Rota; Orchestra conducted by Carlo Savina.

Selections: 1 Main Title (5:08); 2 La dolce vita (a) Arrivederci Roma (R. Rascel/G. Garinei/G. Giovannini), (b) Caracolla's/La Bersagliera (5:41); 3 La dolce vita: Via Veneto (1:35); 4 Patricia (P. Prado)/Canzonetta/ Entrance Of The Gladiators/Waltz (3:45); 5 Lola/Yes Sir, That's My Baby (W. Donaldson)/ Waltz/ Stormy Weather (H. Arlen/T. Koehler)(4:22); 6 Via Veneto And The Nobles (1:23); 7 Blues (The "dolce vita" Of The Nobles) (5:42); 8 Nocturne Or Early Morning (1:30); 9 La dolce vita (3:01); 10 La dolce vita At The Villa di Fregene: Can Can/Jingle Bells/Blues/La dolce vita (6:21); 11 Why Wait (2:58).

Review: While they worked together before and subsequently, *La dolce vita* is the closest Federico Fellini and Nino Rota ever came to creating a film in which the images and the music are so intimately interwoven. In fact, it now seems difficult to separate one from the other, as the cues devised by the composer matched so beautifully the suggestive power of the film's best remembered scenes, from the dissonant three-note motif in "Via Veneto," to the wistful trumpet solo in "Lola," to the bluesy "La dolce vita dei nobili," with its organ counterpoint, to its wild Latin take on the Christmas standard "Jingle Bells." Truly a momentous film steeped in its own time period but as exciting today as it was at the time, *La dolce vita* yielded one of the most memorable soundtracks in Rota's extraordinarily active and prolific career. One word of warning: even though this CD claims that it was remastered in Dolby Surround, it is obviously a transfer from LP source, a fact confirmed by the apparent surface noise on some of the quieter selections.

La Femme Nikita 🎵🎵

1990, Varese Sarabande; from the movie *La Femme Nikita*, Gaumont Films, 1990.

Album Notes: *Music*: Eric Serra; *Arrangements*: Eric Serra; *Featured Musicians*: Gilbert Dall'Anese (saxophone); *Album Producer*: Eric Serra; *Engineers*: Dominik Borde, Isabelle Martin, Sophie Masson, Alex Firla.

Selections: 1 Rico's Gang Suicide (3:12); 2 Playing On Saucepans (1:28); 3 As Cold As Ice (:43); 4 The Sentence (1:24); 5 Paradise? (1:10); 6 Failed Escape (3:37); 7 Learning Time (4:08); 8 A Smile (1:18); 9 Fancy Face (1:47); 10 First Night Out (4:00); 11 NPOKMOP (4:01); 12 The Last Time I Kiss You (:58); 13 The Free Side (3:41); 14 I Am On Duty! (2:25); 15 Josephine And The Big Dealer (:48); 16 Mission In Venice (5:56); 17 Fall (2:41); 18 Let's Welcome Victor (1:10); 19 Last Mission (2:14); 20 We Will Miss You (2:56); 21 The Dark Side Of Time (E. Serra/ L. Besson)(4:23) *Eric Serra*.

Review: Today, Eric Serra is perhaps better known in this country for his scores for *GoldenEye* and *The Fifth Element,* two efforts that called attention to his talent as a composer. In France, where his music for Luc Besson's *Le grand bleu* and *La Femme Nikita* have made him a household name, he is considered one of the most important film composers of the new generation. His artistic merits notwithstanding (his score for *GoldenEye* was roundly panned), there is no denying the feel that emanates from his contributions, in which the extensive use of synthesizers give a definite accent to his music. Nowhere is this more evident than in *La Femme Nikita,* a techno-pop effort with heavy-layered synthesizer melodies, set against various percussive effects that range from electronic drumming to finger-snapping. The music itself is meant to create an atmosphere that echoes the moods of this cloak-and-dagger story about a strikingly attractive criminal recruited by a secret government agency to carry off dangerous missions, including the elimination of enemies from the "other" side. Characteristic of Serra's contributions, the cues often match the screen action, but turn out to be dry and austere in a musical environment. They fail to really grab one's interest when taken on their own terms, though "The Last Time I Kiss You," an all-too-brief simple melody on the piano, makes a different and much more attractive statement.

Labyrinth 🎵🎵

1986, EMI America; from the movie *Labyrinth*, 1986.

Album Notes: *Music*: Trevor Jones; *Orchestrations*: Trevor Jones; Orchestra conducted by Trevor Jones; *Featured Performer*: David Bowie; *Featured Musicians*: Ray Russell, Nicky Moroch, Albert Collins (lead guitar), Dan Huff, Jeff Mironov, Kevin Armstrong (guitar), Paul Westwood (bass guitar), Will Lee, Matthew Seligman (bass), Harold Fisher, Neil Conti, Steve Ferrone (drums), Nick Plytas, Robbie Buchanan, David Lanson, Brian Gascoigne, Trevor Jones (keyboards), Richard Tee (acoustic piano, Hammond B-3 organ), Ray Warleigh, Bob Gay (saxophone), Maurice Murphy (trumpet); *Album Producer*: Trevor Jones; *Engineer*: Marcellus Frank; *Assistant Engineers*: Chips, Martin O'Donnell.

Selections: 1 Opening Titles (D. Bowie/T. Jones)(3:18) *David Bowie*; 2 Into The Labyrinth (2:10); 3 Magic Dance (D. Bowie) (5:11) *David Bowie*; 4 Sarah (3:10); 5 Chilly Down (D. Bowie) (3:44) *David Bowie*; 6 Hallucination (3:00); 7 As The World Falls Down (D. Bowie)(4:49) *David Bowie*; 8 The Goblin Battle (3:29); 9 Within You (D. Bowie)(3:29) *David Bowie*; 10 Thirteen O'Clock (3:06); 11 Home At Last (1:46); 12 Underground (D. Bowie) (5:57) *David Bowie*.

Review: Five new David Bowie songs are the selling point for this album, and none of them have popped up on any of his various career retrospectives—an indication of how crucial they are, even though Bowie was in the midst of a major commercial renaissance at the time. It's worth noting that he collaborated on these with lush popmaster Arif Mardin, and Bowie has always done better work with edgier, more adventurous cohorts.

Gary Graff

Lady Sings the Blues 🎵🎵🎵ᵛ

1972, Motown Records; from the movie *Lady Sings the Blues*, Paramount Pictures, 1972.

Album Notes: *Music*: Michel Legrand; *Arrangers*: Gil Askey, Benny Golson, Oliver Nelson; Orchestra conducted by Gil Askey; *Album Producers*: Suzanne de Passe, Iris Gordy; *Engineers*: Larry Miles, Cal Harris, Bill MacMeekin, Dave Ramsey, Art Stewart, Russ Terrana, Gordon Day, Dave Docendorf, John Norman.

Selections: 1 The Arrest (:15); 2 Lady Sings The Blues (B. Holiday/H. Nicholas)(1:03) *Diana Ross*; 3 Baltimore Brothel (:25); 4 Billie Sneaks Into Dean & Dean's/Swingin' Uptown (G. Askey)(:49); 5 T'ain't Nobody's Bizness If I Do (P. Grainger/E. Robbins)(1:06) *Blinky Williams*; 6 Big Ben (2:31) *C.C. Rider*; 7 All Of Me (S. Simons/G. Marks)(2:19) *Diana Ross*; 8 The Man I Love (G. & I. Gershwin)(2:27) *Diana Ross*; 9 Them There Eyes (M. Pinkard/W. Tracey/D. Tauber)(1:03) *Diana Ross*; 10 Gardenias From Louis (2:03); 11 Cafe Manhattan/Have You Been Around (R. Miller/B. Yuffy/R. Jacques/A. Vanderberg) (3:33) *Michele Aller*; 12 Any Happy Home (G. Askey)(:37); 13 I Cried For You (Now It's Your Turn To Cry Over Me)(A. Lyman/G. Arnheim/A. Freed)(:37) *Diana Ross*; 14 Billie And Harry/Don't Explain (B. Holiday/A. Herzog, Jr.)(2:12) *Diana Ross*; 15 Mean To Me (R. Turk/F. Ahlert)(1:18) *Diana Ross*; 16 Fine And Mellow (B. Holiday)(:45) *Diana Ross*; 17 What A Little Moonlight Can Do (H. Woods)(2:09)

Diana Ross; 18 Louis Visits Billie On Tour/Love Theme (3:48); 19 Cafe Manhattan Party (1:37); 20 Persuasion/T'ain't Nobody's Bizness If I Do (P. Grainger/E. Robbins)(3:06) *Diana Ross*; 21 Agent's Office (1:09); 22 Love Is Here To Stay (G. & I. Gershwin)(2:01) *Diana Ross*; 23 Fine And Mellow (B. Holiday)(2:54) *Diana Ross*; 24 Lover Man (Oh, Where Can You Be?)(J. Davis/J. Sherman/R. Ramirez)(3:22) *Diana Ross*; 25 You've Changed (B. Carey/C. Fisher) (2:34) *Diana Ross*; 26 Gimme A Pigfoot (And A Bottle Of Beer)(W. Wilson) (2:06) *Diana Ross*; 27 Good Morning Heartache (I. Higgenbotham/E. Drake/D. Fisher)(2:21) *Diana Ross*; 28 All Of Me (S. Simon/G. Marks)(2:04) *Diana Ross*; 29 Love Theme (2:53); 30 My Man (Mon Homme)(M. Yvain/A. Willemetz/J. Charles/C. Pollock)(2:26) *Diana Ross*; 31 Don't Explain (B. Holiday/A. Herzog, Jr.)(2:10) *Diana Ross*; 32 I Cried For You (Now It's Your Turn To Cry Over Me)(A. Lyman/G. Arnheim/A. Freed)(2:13) *Diana Ross*; 33 Strange Fruit (L. Allan)(3:35) *Diana Ross*; 34 God Bless The Child (B. Holiday/A. Herzog, Jr.)(2:42) *Diana Ross*; 35 Closing Theme (1:08).

Review: While this soundtrack album is probably best thought of as a Diana Ross album, the singer, portraying the great Billie Holiday in her screen debut, is only heard in about half the selections, arguably the best tracks here and the hits associated with her screen persona. Whether Ross was actually suited to impersonate Holiday is a matter better left to others, who may debate if the film should have emphasized Ross interpreting Holiday, rather than Ross as Holiday. The fact remains that Diana Ross did a most commendable job as an actress, and actually performed the songs created by Holiday with the passion and gusto that seemed required. Of course the styles of both singers are quite different, and where Holiday was more conversant in jazz, Ross' forte is pop and soul, a nuance that will more or less dictate where the listener's own reaction to the album may be.

The rest of the album, with a few exceptions, consists of instrumental selections written by Michel Legrand, often reduced to their simplest expression and masked by chunks of dialogue taken from the soundtrack, something of a disservice to a composer with an impressive track record. As a result, the rating here refers to Ross and her performance, and not to Legrand's contribution.

Ladyhawke 🎵🎵🎵🎵

1995, GNP Crescendo; from the movie *Ladyhawke*, Warner Bros./20th Century-Fox, 1985.

Album Notes: *Music*: Andrew Powell; *Orchestrations*: Andrew Powell; Orchestra conducted by Andrew Powell; *Album Producer/Engineer*: Alan Parsons.

Selections: 1 Main Title (2:59); 2 Phillippe's Escape (1:40); 3 The Search For Phillippe (3:25); 4 Tavern Fight (Phillippe) (2:08); 5 Tavern Fight (Navarre) (2:38); 6 Pitou's Woods (4:04); 7 Phillippe Describes Isabeau (1:11); 8 Bishop Procession (2:50); 9 Wedding Music (1:41); 10 Navarre's Ambush (4:53); 11 Imperius Removes Arrow (1:33); 12 Chase/Fall/ Transformation (2:06); 13 Cesar's Woods (5:29); 14 She Was Sad At First (2:06); 15 Navarre Returns To Aquila (1:36); 16 Turret Chase/ The Fall (Film Version) (2:46); 17 Wolf Trapped In Ice (2:34); 18 Navarre And Isabeau's Dual Transformation (3:23); 19 Navarre And Marquet Duel (4:22); 20 Marquet's Death (1:59); 21 Bishop's Death (2:26); 22 Final Reunion/End Title (8:14); 23 Ladyhawke Theme (Single Version)(3:35).

Review: Andrew Powell's robust and energetic soundtrack for Richard Donner's romantic medieval adventure might sound dated to some with its very '80s synths, but most listeners aren't going to care. A powerful outing with memorable themes and enough passion to fill up several ordinary soundtracks, *Ladyhawke* is a stirring effort marked by potent orchestral passages, many of which are being heard on this expanded soundtrack CD for the first time. In fact, the music's then-contemporary roots are much less evident when listening to the entire score now than from the most egregiously "pop" sections memory instantly recalls. Producer Alan Parsons assisted Powell on the music's production, resulting in a score that's unabashedly romantic and melodramatic, a listener favorite that has weathered the years better than one might expect.

Andy Dursin

Land and Freedom ♪♪♪

1995, DRG Records; from the movie *Land and Freedom*, Gramercy Pictures, 1995.

Album Notes: *Music*: George Fenton; *Orchestrations*: George Fenton; Orchestra conducted by George Fenton; *Featured Musician*: Anthony Pleeth (cello); *Album Producers*: George Fenton, Eliza Thompson; *Engineer*: Paul Hulme.

Selections: 1 Opening Credits: Land And Freedom (3:02); 2 No pasaran (2:24); 3 Journey To The Front (2:21); 4 Blanca's Theme (1:51); 5 The Common Cause (2:06); 6 Coogan's Funeral (1:21); 7 Taking The Village (5:43); 8 Divided (2:36); 9 Execution (2:16); 10 Consolation (2:10); 11 Leaving Barcelona (1:51); 12 The Attack (3:47); 13 Between The Bullet And The Lie (2:36); 14 Going Home (3:10); 15 The Price Of Freedom (1:25); 16 The Fight Goes On (:42); 17 Land And Freedom Main Title, Parts 1 & 2 (2:32).

Review: A sweeping contemporary drama set in the early days of the Spanish Civil War, *Land and Freedom* follows the personal saga of a young factory worker from Liverpool who goes to Spain in 1936 to fight fascism, only to find the Republicans bitterly divided into rival groups. Once he gets involved, he find himself torn between his loyalty to the Communist Party and the militia whom he has joined, with tragic consequences that result when he has to take sides. Adding strength to this personal struggle and the broader conflict in the background, George Fenton's music is at once eloquent and evocative. In contrast to the turmoil in the narrative, the score is mostly lyrical in its expression and seems at first understated, but eventually emerges as greatly powerful as a result. Songs from the period in Spanish add the right ethnic color to the soundtrack.

The Land Before Time ♪♪♪♪♪

1988, MCA Records; from the animated feature *The Land Before Time*, Universal Picture, 1988.

Album Notes: *Music*: James Horner; *Orchestrations*: Greig McRitchie; *Music Editor*: Jim Henrickson; The London Symphony Orchestra and The King's College Choir, conducted by James Horner; *Album Producer*: James Horner; *Engineer*: Shawn Murphy.

Selections: 1 The Great Migration (7:49); 2 Sharptooth And The Earthquake (10:33); 3 Whispering Winds (9:00); 4 If We Hold On Together (J. Horner/W. Jennings)(4:07) *Diana Ross*; 5 Foraging For Food (7:15); 6 The Rescue/ Discovery Of The Great Valley (12:43); 7 End Credits (6:22).

Review: Though the recording only contains six tracks of instrumental cues, the long playing time of these selections enables the music to evolve and gradually make its impact, providing the listener with better parameters to enjoy it and formulate an opinion than if the cues were shorter. The result is a score which, though written for an animated feature and possibly deemed a minor exercise because of it, is wonderful. It's filled with inventive melodic themes that involve the participation of various solo instruments, a large choir, and the vivid orchestral colors of the London Symphony. Horner, a master at this type of music, seems to know intuitively how to use each element in this broad canvas to come up with a music that is solidly attractive and consistently fun to listen to. In this context, it matters little if the music fits the narrative, or how it serves it. Judged on its own merits it does what any good score should do — provide hours of listening delight and invite repeat performances.

Larger Than Life 🎵🎵🎵

1996, Milan Records; from the movie *Larger Than Life*, United Artists, 1996.

Album Notes: *Music*: Miles Goodman; *Orchestrations*: Oscar Castro-Neves; *Music Editor*: Nancy Fogarty; Orchestra conducted by Miles Goodman; *Album Producers*: Miles Goodman, Joel Moss; *Engineer*: Joel Moss.

Selections: 1 Life Is A Carnival (R. Robertson/L. Helm/R. Danko) (3:56) *The Band*; 2 Psycho (L. Payne) (3:32) *Jack Kittel*; 3 Main Title (2:28); 4 Salad Bar (1:47); 5 Dad's Trunk (2:18); 6 Flying Elephant (3:31); 7 An Elephant Miracle (2:03); 8 Airport Chase (2:58); 9 Swimming (2:19); 10 The Magnificent Seven Theme (E. Bernstein) (2:46); 11 The Blue Danube (J. Strauss)(3:05).

Review: Sadly, this outrageous Bill Murray comedy about a man and the elephant he takes on a cross-country trip, was the last film composer Miles Goodman scored before he passed away at the age of 47. Goodman, an accomplished film composer and record producer, left a scant recorded legacy even though he wrote the scores for more than 35 films. Stylistically, his music is enjoyably lightweight and makes few demands on the intellect, though it proves suitably charming and melodious. The seven selections found here under his name denote a flair for broad comedy underscoring, with "Salad Bar," a rousing rag, "Flying Elephant," a brassy anthem, and "Airport Chase," a fast-paced ditty, among the most inspired moments.

Lassie 🎵🎵🎵

1994, Sony Wonder; from the movie *Lassie*, Paramount Pictures, 1994.

Album Notes: *Music*: Basil Poledouris; *Music Editor*: Curtis Roush; The London Metropolitan Orchestra, conducted by Allan Wilson; *Featured Soloist*: Sally Haeth (piano); *Album Producer*: Basil Poledouris; *Engineer*: Tim Boyle.

Selections: 1 Lassie: Main Title (1:55); 2 Accident (3:14); 3 Morning Glory (2:27); 4 The Diary/Wolf Attack (4:58); 5 New Beginnings (2:51); 6 Commitment (2:40); 7 Lassie Protects The Herd (2:53); 8 Rustling (3:05); 9 Lassie Saves Matt (10:25); 10 Return/Reunion (3:20).

Review: The exploits of Lassie over the years have provided ample fodder for a stream of countless films and television series. Even though this new big screen incarnation didn't break any new grounds, with the notorious collie facing new challenges in the Virginia wild and overcoming them with its usual resolve,it enabled Basil Poledouris to write a score that sounds at times more important than its subject matter deserved. An old hand at this type of music, the composer essentially let the narrative dictate the direction his music would take. Low key, romantic themes line some of the story's quieter moments, while broad, dramatic cues accompany the action scenes, as an occasional theme for piano and orchestra make a different statement. Put together, it's quite effective and pleasantly attractive.

Last Action Hero 🎵🎵🎵🎵

1993, Columbia Records; from the movie *Last Action Hero*, Columbia Pictures, 1993.

Album Notes: *Music*: Michael Kamen; *Orchestrations*: William Ross, Jack Hayes, Brad Warnaar, Randy Kerber, Lolita Ritmanis, Danny Troob, Michael McCuistion, Jonathan Sacks; *Music Editor*: Eric Reasoner; The Los Angeles All-Stars Orchestra and The Los Angeles Rock and Roll Ensemble, conducted by Michael Kamen; *Featured Musicians*: Michael Kamen (oboe/keyboards), Buckethead, Chris DeGarmo, John Goux, Frank Simes, Rick Nielsen, John Shanks, Jerry Cantrell (guitar), Guy Pratt, Mike Inez, Mike Baird, Tom Petersson (bass), Scott Rockenfield (drums); *Album Producers*: Michael Kamen, Stephen McLaughlin, Christopher Brooks; *Engineers*: Bobby Fernandez, Andrew Warwick, Sue McLean.

Selections: 1 Jack And The Ripper (3:48); 2 Danny (4:24); 3 Jack Hamlet (1:14); 4 River Chase (2:49); 5 Benedict (2:46); 6 Practice (4:18); 7 Leo The Fart (4:33); 8 Benedict Gets The Ticket (3:20); 9 The Real World (3:44); 10 Premiere (3:20); 11 Saving Danny (1:39); 12 Big Mistake (4:51).

Review: The generally unfavorable reaction to this big screen adventure film starring Arnold Schwatzenegger, might have cast an unfair pall over the various ingredients in the movie, including Michael Kamen's original score. In keeping with the modern tones of this wild fantasy, about a kid who joins his favorite film hero and shares his on-screen adventures, Kamen wrote a series of themes that are solidly embedded in the contemporary rock tradition which are performed on the soundtrack and the album by various rock musicians, like Rick Neilson and Tom Petersson of Cheap Trick, Mike Inez and Jerry Cantrell of Alice in Chains, Chris DeGarmo of Queensryche, and Buckethead. Played against the structural canvas provided by a large orchestra, the selections throb with great energy and skill, some like "River Chase" and "Saving Danny," making a particularly strong impression.

The Last Butterfly 🎵🎵🎵

1990, Varese-Sarabande Records; from the movie *The Last Butterfly*, HTV Films, 1990.

Album Notes: *Music*: Alex North, Milan Svoboda; The Prague Film Symphony Orchestra, conducted by Mario Klemens,

Stepan Konicek; *Musicians*: The Prague Jazzfonic Orchestra: Milan Svoboda (piano), Vaclav Sykora (bass recorder), Ivan Zeaty (violin), Vida Skalska, Hana Hegerova (vocals); *Album Producers*: Robert Townson, Steven North; *Engineer*: Jiri Kriz.

Selections: 1 Main Title (A. North) (2:01); 2 Antoine's New Digs (A. North) (:27); 3 Foxtrot In Cabaret (M. Svoboda) (1:33); 4 Mr. Grondin Pantomime (M. Svoboda) (1:07); 5 Antoine's Playoff Music (M. Svoboda) (1:10); 6 Michelle's Demise (A. North) (:37); 7 The Flashback (A. North) (:19); 8 The Nightmare Begins (A. North) (1:23); 9 The Gordian Knot (H. Purcell) (1:22); 10 Afternoon Coffee (M. Svoboda) (3:19); 11 Things Don't, People Do (A. North) (:21); 12 Avinu Malkenu (Yiddish Song) (3:28); 13 Snow White Ballet (M. Svoboda) (3:23); 14 Signs Of Spring (A. North/M. Princi) (1:41); 15 The Hit (M. Svoboda) (2:44); 16 Butterfly (A. North) (2:51); 17 The Red Umbrella (A. North) (:24); 18 Ocarina Yiddish Dance (M. Svoboda) (:49); 19 Save Stella (A. North) (:42); 20 The Last Performance (A. North) (1:15); 21 Hansel And Gretel Ballet (M. Svoboda) (6:02); 22 Lulinka (Yiddish Song) (2:18); 23 End Title (A. North) (4:24).

Review: One of the grand masters of film music, Alex North wrote one of his last scores for this quirky European production, starring Tom Courtney in one of his most unusual screen roles. At times poignantly dramatic, at times exuberantly elegiac, the cues created by North reveal that the composer, aged 80 at the time he composed this score, had lost none of his verve or his creative energy. While songs like "Michelle's Demise," "The Flashback," and "The Red Umbrella," too short to make more than a passing impact, might be considered charming musical miniatures at best, others like "Main Title," "Butterfly," "The Last Performance," and "End Title" are sufficiently expanded to make a stronger impression and show the composer at his best. North's selections are supplemented by original compositions written and performed by Milan Svoboda in a standard jazz style that will seem old-fashioned but which has its attractive merits.

Last Dance ♪♪♪

1996, Hollywood Records; from the movie *Last Dance*, Touchstone Pictures, 1996.

Album Notes: *Music*: Mark Isham; *Orchestrations*: Ken Kugler; *Music Editor*: Craig Pettigrew; The London Metropolitan Orchestra, conducted by Ken Kugler; *Featured Musicians*: David Goldblatt (piano), Sally Dworsky (voice), Mark Isham (electronics); *Album Producer*: Mark Isham; *Engineer*: Stephen Krause.

Selections: 1 Last Dance (2:42); 2 Twenty-three And One Half Hours A Day (2:48); 3 What Do You Have To Lose? (2:40); 4

Keep Your Distance (1:32); 5 Last Dance (reprise)(2:34); 6 Nothing Except Justice (2:02); 7 The Killing Machine (3:18); 8 Almost The Girl Next Door (1:52); 9 Death Warrant (2:01); 10 We'll Always Be Brother And Sister (3:50); 11 On My Terms (1:37); 12 His Sole Power (1:09); 13 Taj Mahal (5:59).

Review: A crime drama, starring Sharon Stone as a murderess on death row who gets an eleventh hour reprieve after a young lawyer on the review board detects a flaw in her conviction, *Last Dance* got a provocative and appropriately somber score from Mark Isham, who delves into a contemporary field in which he is totally confident and comfortable. The attractive main theme ("Last Dance") with its broad orchestral lines, over which a piano and a wordless vocalist trade occasional riffs, is quite catchy and satisfyingly anchors the whole score. "On My Terms," a self-assertive comment made by Sharon Stone who demands to die when she wants to, "because that's all I've left," is also a poignant statement, admirably expressed in Isham's underscoring.

The Last Emperor ♪♪♪♭

1987, Virgin Movie Music; from the movie *The Last Emperor*, 1987.

Album Notes: *Music*: Ryuichi Sakamoto, David Byrne, Cong Su; *Album Producer*: Ryuichi Sakamoto; *Mixing Engineer*: Steve Nye; *Engineers*: Shigeru Takise, Shinichi Tanaka, Mike Jarrat, Haydn Bendall; *Album Producer*: David Byrne; *Engineer*: Clive Martin.

Selections: *THE LAST EMPEROR (R. SAKAMOTO):* 1 First Coronation (1:47); 2 Open The Door (2:54); 3 Where Is Armo? (2:26); 4 Picking Up Brides (2:40); 5 The Last Emperor—Theme Variation 1 (2:19); 6 Rain (I Want A Divorce) (1:49); 7 The Baby (Was Born Dead)(:56); 8 The Last Emperor—Theme Variation 2 (4:29); 9 The Last Emperor—Theme (5:54);

THE LAST EMPEROR (D. BYRNE): 10 Main Title Theme (4:01); 11 Picking A Bride (2:00); 12 Bed (5:01); 13 Wind, Rain And Water (2:19); 14 Paper Emperor (1:48); 15 Lunch (C. Su)(4:54) *Cong Su*; 16 Red Guard (trad.)(1:21) *The Red Guard Accordion Band*; 17 The Emperor's Waltz (J. Strauss)(3:07) *The Ball Orchestra of Vienne, Leopold Schnell*; 18 The Red Guard Dance (trad.)(:39) *The Girls Red Guard Dancers*.

Review: *The Last Emperor* musically is a strange bird. Bernardo Bertolucci's film chronicled the life of China's last emperor—from ascending the Imperial throne at the age of three in the Forbidden City, through revolution and war and his eventual life as a gardener—and it's pretty enchanting. Japanese composer Ryuichi Sakamoto (also an actor in the film), occasional film contributor David Byrne, and the mysterious

Cong Su won an Oscar for their efforts, but hardly seem to have worked together. The lion's share of the music is by Sakamoto, whose style blends Chinese gestures with accessible melodies. His themes are deeply romantic, sometimes melodramatic, characterizing the opulence, mystery and ultimate sadness of the emperor's life. They also brim with a very western symphonic flavor, casting an epic scope upon the story, and recalling a time when western culture was admired around the world for its luxury and inventiveness.

David Byrne's five tracks on the album include the insidiously catchy "Main Title," which is probably what won the score its Oscar, and more intimate synth-and-Chinese-instruments cues for life inside the Forbidden City. There is one track from Cong Su—who now has the same number of Oscars as Bernard Herrmann and Jerry Goldsmith—a bit of traditional Chinese plinking and plunking. Two communist sing-alongs and a Strauss waltz round out this unusual but memorable soundtrack.

Lukas Kendall

Last Exit to Brooklyn 🦴🦴🦴🦴

1989, Warner Bros. Records; from the movie *Last Exit to Brooklyn*, Neue Constantin Film, 1989.

Album Notes: *Music*: Mark Knopfler; *Performed by*: Guy Fletcher; *Featured Musicians*: David Nolan, Irvine Arditti (violin), Chris White (saxophone), Mark Knopfler (guitar); *Album Producer*: Mark Knopfler; *Engineer*: Bill Schnee.

Selections: 1 Last Exit To Brooklyn (4:59); 2 Victims (3:30); 3 Think Fast (2:46); 4 A Love Idea (3:04); 5 Tralala (5:28); 6 Riot (6:20); 7 The Reckoning (7:12); 8 As Low As It Gets (1:28); 9 Finale: Last Exit To Brooklyn (6:18).

Review: Based on Hubert Selby's 1964 novel, *Last Exit to Brooklyn* takes a close look at life in one of New York's least attractive boroughs in a rundown working class neighborhood near the navy yards, plagued by an ungoing strike against a local factory. To give meaning to this gritty tale, Mark Knopfler wrote a diversified score in which striking melodies ("Last Exit to Brooklyn," "A Love Idea") contrast with tunes in which the desperate atmosphere that pervades the film find a remarkable echo. One cue, "Victims," starts with what resembles the sound of machinery interrupted by the horn of a ship, strongly evocative of the background against which the story unfolds. The film's centerpiece, a sensational action scene that opposes the strikers against police forces, gives way here to a spectacular cue called "Riot", boldly expressive and superbly realistic. There are, along the way, many other musical moments that evoke specific scenes in the film, notably "Tralala" and "As Low as It Gets," but the whole recording is one outstanding track after another.

Last of the Dogmen 🦴🦴🦴🦴▷

1995, Atlantic Records; from the movie *Last of the Dogman*, Savoy Pictures, 1995.

Album Notes: *Music*: David Arnold; *Orchestrations*: Nicholas Dodd; *Music Editor*: Laurie Higgins; *Synthesizer Programming*: Mike Barnes, David Arnold; The London Symphony Orchestra, conducted by Nicholas Dodd; *Album Producer*: David Arnold; *Engineer*: Goeff Foster.

Selections: 1 Last Of The Dogmen (3:17); 2 The Wilderness (1:50); 3 Somebody's Out There (2:46); 4 The First Arrow (1:50); 5 The Story Of Jacko (1:43); 6 War Party (3:04); 7 Medicine Run (2:51); 8 Cheyenne Valley (2:46); 9 The County Line (1:59); 10 The Truth (2:12); 11 Go In A Good Way (1:57); 12 Leaving Forever (3:58); 13 Faith And Courage (3:55); 14 The Last Arrow (1:55).

Review: Immediately after completing *Stargate*, David Arnold took on this epic story of the discovery of a lost tribe of Cheyenne. Although the story begins with tracker Tom Berringer searching for a group of escaped convicts, at the core of the film, and the score, is an aura of romance. Director Tab Murphy treats his North American wilderness setting, the last unspoiled, untamed land, with reverence and awe. While Berringer's character finds love with Native American expert Barbara Hershey, she in turn finds it in the culmination of her life's dream with the discovery of the simple lifestyle of the Cheyenne, who have remained unexposed to modern civilization for centuries. There are gentle hints of western motifs with Arnold's score, but only enough to reinforce the notions of an earlier age. The film is, after all, about the clash of cultures. Arnold remarkably captures all this in a score that deftly shifts through the film's ever-changing moods, providing a solid foundation that makes even the tiniest emotion an epic experience. While his work on *Stargate*, and later *Independence Day*, are also of epic quality, it is the smaller, personal moments in *Last of the Dogmen* that sets it above the rest. It is a score that truly comes from his heart.

David Hirsch

The Last of the Mohicans 🦴🦴🦴▷

1992, Morgan Creek Records; from the movie *The Last of the Mohicans*, 20th Century-Fox, 1992.

Album Notes: *(tracks 1-9) Music*: Trevor Jones; *Orchestrations*: Brad Dechter, Jack Smalley, Bobby Muzingo, Guy Dagul; orchestra conducted by Daniel A. Carlin; *Producer*: Trevor Jones; *Engineer*: John Richards John Whynot, Dennis Sands; *(tracks*

10-15) Music: Randy Edelman; *Orchestrations*: Greig Mc-Ritchie; orchestra conducted by Randy Edelman; *Producer*: Randy Edelman; *Engineer*: Elton Ahi.

Selections: 1 Main Title (1:44); 2 Elk Hunt (1:49); 3 The Kiss (2:47); 4 The Glade, Part II (2:34); 5 Fort Battle (4:20); 6 Promontory (6:13); 7 Munro's Office/Stockade (2:30); 8 Massacre/Canoes (6:52); 9 Top Of The World (2:44); 10 The Courier (2:27); 11 Cora (2:30); 12 River Walk and Discovery (5:30); 13 Parlay (3:46); 14 The British Arrival (2:00); 15 Pieces Of A Story (4:58); 16 I Will Find You (C. Brennan)(1:42)*Clannad*.

Review: With *The Last of the Mohicans*, we are given a poignant sense of orchestral drama from two notable composers. The first nine cues on the CD are by Jones, the remaining six by Edelman. Though their styles are different and thematically unrelated, they complement each other. Jones' theme sounds solid and steadfast amid the myriad of orchestral figures he sets against it in the battle scenes. Edelman's music is less exhilarating but equally effective, built around a very pretty melody for synth and accordion over acoustic guitar and strings, growing in force and tone. Where Jones uses electronics as a minor member of the orchestra for textural purposes, Edelman relies on synths more dominantly as lead instruments. Trevor Jones introduces his main theme out of native drums, a grandly sweeping music for brass, strings and timpani, counterpointed in "Elk Hunt" by perpendicular strokes of strings and rapidly-toned synth. It's an immensely powerful opening. Edelman is an accomplished synthesist and his score is strident and evocative. This is forceful and compelling music, lofty and earthy and at the same time gloriously romantic, brimful of the romance of adventure as well as the romance of love.

Randall D. Larson

The Last Picture Show &

1971, Columbia Records; from the movie *The Last Picture Show*, Columbia Pictures, 1971.

Album Notes: *Featured Performers*: Tony Bennett, Eddie Fisher, Lefty Frizzell, Pee Wee King, Frankie Laine, Johnnie Ray, Hank Snow, Jo Stafford; *Album Producer*: Thomas Z. Shepard; *Engineer*: John Guerriere.

Selections: 1 Cold Cold Heart (H. Williams)(2:41) *Tony Bennett*; 2 Give Me More, More, More Of Your Kisses (L. Frizzell/R. Price/J. Beck)(2:18) *Lefty Frizzell*; 3 Wish You Were Here (H. Rome)(2:57) *Eddie Fisher*; 4 Slow Poke (P. King/R. Stewart/C. Price)(3:02) *Pee Wee King*; 5 Blue Velvet (B. Wayne/L. Morris)(3:02) *Tony Bennett*; 6 Rose, Rose, I Love You (W. Thomas/

C. Langdon) (2:35) *Frankie Laine*; 7 You Belong To Me (P. King/ R. Stewart/ C. Price) (3:05) *Jo Stafford*; 8 A Fool Such As I (B. Trader)(2:32) *Hank Snow*; 9 Please, Mr. Sun (S. Frank/R. Getzov)(3:01) *Johnnie Ray*; 10 Solitaire (R. Borek/C. Nutter/K. Guion)(3:18) *Tony Bennett*.

Review: A nostalgic trip to the '50s via a collection of hits from that period, performed by the stars who made them famous, this soundtrack album to the film directed by Peter Bogdanovich has one serious drawback. For the money, the playing time is quite short and its sound quality is seriously deficient. Since the same selections can often be found in many other remastered compilations, this collection seems a bit redundant.

The Last Starfighter &&&&

1995, Intrada Records; from the movie *The Last Starfighter*, Universal Pictures, 1983.

Album Notes: *Music*: Craig Safan; *Orchestrations*: Al Clausen, Joel Rosenbaum, Craig Safan; Orchestra conducted by Craig Safan; *Album Producer*: Craig Safan; *Engineers*: Lyle Burbridge (orchestra), Rick Riccio (electronics).

Selections: 1 Main Title (2:31); 2 Alex Dreams (1:44); 3 Centauri Into Space (5:59); 4 Rylos (2:01); 5 Centauri Dies (6:51); 6 Target Practice (2:17); 7 Alex's First Test (2:51); 8 Beta's Sacrifice (6:07); 9 Death Blossom/Ultimate Weapon (4:44); 10 Big Victory March/Alex Returns (5:44); 11 Into The Starscape (7:21).

Review: One of the few post-*Star Wars* blockbuster scores to approach the heights of John Williams' Korngoldesque space opera scores is this spectacular effort from Craig Safan for the agreeable Nick Castle space shoot-em-up that's primarily remembered now for its early, ground-breaking CGI effects. Although there is scope and bombastic action material galore in this incredibly brassy, sharply-performed score, Safan's greatest achievement is the emotional accessibility of this score. It's actually quite touching for a space opera, dealing movingly with its hero's Luke Skywalker-like wanderlust as he stumbles onto a video game that's designed to train real star warriors for an interstellar conflict. Safan's opening theme, while bearing comparison to Williams' in its martial brassiness, achieves its own distinctive power through a couple of thrilling repeating horn figures and a primary melody that is just as effective generating feelings of compassion and tenderness in its more intimate settings as it is whipping up a frenzy of rah-rah excitement here. This Intrada release showcases the entire score, expanding the music heard on an old Southern Cross CD and providing improved sound for what was already a barnstorming recording.

Jeff Bond

The Last Unicorn ♪♪♪

1982, Virgin Records; from the animated feature, *The Last Unicorn*, 1982.

Album Notes: *Music*: Jimmy Webb; The London Symphony Orchestra conducted by Jimmy Webb; *Featured Performers*: America (Dan Peek, Gerry Beckley, Dewey Bunnell).

Selections: 1 The Last Unicorn (3:07); 2 Man's Road (3:23); 3 In The Sea (3:15); 4 Now That I'm A Woman (2:36); 5 That's All I've Got To Say (2:42); 6 The Last Unicorn, Part 2 (3:07); 7 The Forest Awakens: The Unicorn/The Forest/ The Hunters (2:09); 8 Red Soup (:30); 9 The Red Bull Attacks (3:36); 10 The Cat (1:39); 11 The Tree (1:19); 12 Haggard's Unicorns (2:10); 13 Bull/Unicorn/ Woman (2:46); 14 Unicorns In The Sea (1:50); 15 Unicorn And Lear (3:28).

Review: The rock group America is prominently featured in this soundtrack album to an animated film, with a score by Jimmy Webb. The songs, an attractive lot with good melodic lines and pleasant lyrics, were quite effective on the soundtrack and also make a favorable impression on a pure audio level. The combination of the rock band with a large orchestra usually works very well and makes this a most enjoyable album.

The Last Waltz ♪♪♪♪

1978, Warner Bros. Records; from the movie *The Last Waltz*, Filmways, 1978.

Album Notes: *Featured Musicians*: The Band featuring Rick Danko (bass, violins, vocals), Levon Helm (drums, mandolin, vocals), Garth Hudson (organ, accordion, saxophone, synthesizers), Richard Manuel (piano, keyboards, drums, vocals), Robbie Robertson (guitar, piano, vocals); *Guest Artists*: Paul Butterfield, Eric Clapton, Neil Diamond, Bob Dylan, Emmylou Harris, Ronnie Hawkins, Dr. John, Joni Mitchell, Van Morrison, The Staples, Ringo Starr, Muddy Waters, Ron Wood, Neil Young; *Album Producer*: Robbie Robertson; *Engineers*: Terry Becker, Tim Kramer, Elliot Mazer, Wayne Neuendorf, Ed Anderson, Neil Brody.

Selections: CD 1: 1 Theme from The Last Waltz (R. Robertson)(3:28); 2 Up On Cripple Creek (R. Robertson)(4:44); 3 Who Do You Love (E. McDaniels)(4:16); 4 Helpless (N. Young)(5:47) *Neil Young, Joni Mitchell*,; 5 Stagefright (R. Robertson)(4:25); 6 Coyote (J. Mitchell)(5:50) *Joni Mitchell, Dr. John*; 7 Dry Your Eyes (N. Diamond)(3:57) *Neil Diamond*; 8 It Makes No Difference (R. Robertson)(6:48); 9 Such A Night (M. Reben-

nack)(4:00) *Dr. John*; 10 The Night They Drove Old Dixie Down (R. Robertson)(4:34); 11 Mystery Train ((H. Parker, Jr./S. Phillips)(4:59) *Paul Butterfield*; 12 Mannish Boy (M. London/M. Morganfield/E. McDaniels)(6:54) *Muddy Waters, Paul Butterfield*; 13 Further On Up The Road (J. Medwick Veasey/D.B. Robey)(5:08) *Eric Clapton*.

CD 2: 1 Shape I'm In (R. Robertson)(4:06); 2 Down South In New Orleans (J. Anglin/J. Wright/J. Anglin)(3:06) *Dr. John*; 3 Ophelia (R. Robertson)(3:53); 4 Tura Lura Lural (That's An Irish Lullaby)(J.R. Shannon)(4:15) *Van Morrison*; 5 Caravan (V. Morrison) *Van Morrison*; 6 Life Is A Carnival (R. Danko/L. Helm/R. Robertson)(4:32); 7 Baby Let Me Follow You Down (Rev. G. Davis)(3:00) *Bob Dylan*; 8 I Don't Believe You (She Acts Like We Never Had Met)(B. Dylan)(3:23) *Bob Dylan*; 9 Forever Young (B. Dylan)(4:42) *Bob Dylan*; 10 Baby Let Me Follow You Down (reprise)(2:46) *Bob Dylan*; 11 I Shall Be Released (B. Dylan)(3:53) *Bob Dylan, Neil Young, Joni Mitchell, Ronnie Hawkins, Dr. John, Neil Diamond, Paul Butterfield, Bobby Charles, Eric Clapton, Van Morrison*; The Last Waltz Suite: 12 The Well (R. Robertson)(3:27); 13 Evangeline (R. Robertson)(3:17) *Emmylou Harris*; 14 Out Of The Blue (R. Robertson)(3:08); 15 The Weight (R. Robertson)(4:38) *The Staples*; 16 The Last Waltz Refrain (R. Robertson)(1:28); 17 Theme from The Last Waltz (with orchestra)(R. Robertson)(3:22).

Review: The farewell concert by the Band, Bob Dylan's onetime backup group, brought together as fine an assortment of rock stars as we are ever likely to see on one stage, and the Martin Scorsese documentary that resulted ranks among the best concert films. The two-CD soundtrack compilation boasts performances cut from the movie, most notably a Van Morrison-Richard Manuel duet on "Tura-Lura-Lural." Other highlights come from Neil Young, Muddy Waters, Eric Clapton, and Dylan. The Band itself had better nights. Singer Levon Helm lost his voice during the show, which may explain why several of the group's favorites were re-recorded on a soundstage after the fact, then stitched into a less-than-stellar dream sequence.

Marc Kirkeby

Laura/Jane Eyre ♪♪♪▷

1993, Fox Records; from the movies *Laura*, 20th Century-Fox, 1944; and *Jane Eyre*, 20th Century-Fox, 1943.

Album Notes: *Music*: David Raksin, Bernard Herrmann; The 20th Century-Fox Orchestra, conducted by Alfred Newman, Bernard Herrmann; *CD Producer*: Nick Redman.

Selections: 1 20th Century-Fox Fanfare (A. Newman)(:13); 2 *Laura:* Theme and Variations (27:16); 3 *Jane Eyre:* Main Title

(2:38); 4 Jane's Departure (2:32); 5 Elegy and Jane's Sorrow (2:26); 6 Thornfield Hall (1:42); 7 The Piano 2:12); 8 Rochester's Past (2:04); 9 The Fire (2:54); 10 Mr. Mason (3:26); 11 The Garden (3:43); 12 The Storm (2:28); 13 The Wedding (1:24); 14 Jane's Farewell (4:14); 15 Jane's Return (2:42); 16 The Finale (2:39).

Review: Of all the romantic murder mysteries born of the 1940s, *Laura* reigns supreme as the regal Queen—elegant, romantic, suspenseful, sad. Director Otto Preminger's classic is one of a handful of films of this genre that hold up remarkably well today, over 50 years after its initial release in 1944. Resilient, too, has been David Raksin's original score, the one that transformed a simple musical theme into a vocal pop standard and made the composer's name a household word.

Originally, Preminger had planned to use Duke Ellington's "Sophisticated Lady" as the main theme for the picture whose story turns a murder victim into the prime suspect. However, with Raksin's intervention and personal struggle over a long weekend, a new theme was developed. "Laura" emerged as one of the most mysterious, intriguing melodies of all-time. Once lyricist Johnny Mercer added the lyrics, it became an instant sensation and one of the most recorded tunes in history.

That hauntingly romantic theme, dressed in a variety of disguises, is what underscores and creates the atmosphere for this wonderful film. A 1975 recording featuring the New Philharmonia Orchestra, conducted by David Raksin, is available on RCA Victor. This reissue has been newly remixed by the composer himself and contains a six-minute segment titled "Laura." While it is nice to hear the theme in glorious, modern stereo, this small sampling leaves you aching for more.

For this, nothing surpasses the original 1944 soundtrack (20th Century Fox Film Scores), which is comprised of a 28-minute composition titled "Suite for Laura: Theme and Variations." It is here that you can really appreciate the subtle textures and nuances in Raksin's score. The monophonic film track sound is very good, with a remarkable amount of detail noted among the individual instruments, and the recording has a nice, warm 1940s sound and feel to it.

Charles L. Granata

Lawnmower Man 2: Beyond Cyberspace ♪♪♪

1996, Varese-Sarabande Records; from the movie *Lawnmower Man 2: Beyond Cyberspace*, Allied Film Productions, 1996.

Album Notes: *Music*: Robert Folk; *Orchestrations*: Robert Folk, Peter Tomashek, Jon Krull; The London Sinfonia, conducted by Robert Folk; *Album Producer*: Robert Folk.

Selections: 1 Main Title (4:14); 2 The City (2:48); 3 Kids In Cyberspace (3:35); 4 Virtual Light Tour (3:02); 5 Jobe's Memory (1:40); 6 Jobe's Realization (1:57); 7 The Train (5:52); 8 Jobe's Theme (2:03); 9 Institute Recon (5:04); 10 Stealing The Kicon Chip (6:34); 11 The Alarm (4:54); 12 Inspecting The Kiron Chip (2:10); 13 The President (2:58); 14 Jobe's War (4:00); 15 Streets Of Anarchy (3:46); 16 Virtual Reality Battleground (4:56); 17 The Kiron Explosion (2:18); 18 Finale (2:41).

Review: For this high-tech cyberthriller, Robert Folk has based his score around a romantic melody for full orchestra. That theme brackets the ferocious action music that makes up the bulk of this score. This is a heavy action score, but it's all very tonal and under control. Folk uses straightforward orchestration, synths mixed with symphonics, to color this world of cyberspace and virtual reality. By doing so—and avoiding the complete plunge into computerized music that the story might have suggested—Folk humanizes the film and its characters, linking them to the real world even in the midst of their virtual adventures, even in the midst of his furious action music. And in the end, Folk's main theme returns, glorious and magnificent, wrapping up the frantic activity of the middle section with a purposeful resolve, shutting the doors on cyberspace and enfolding the characters in the warm embrace of the real world.

Randall Larson

Lawrence of Arabia

Lawrence of Arabia ♪♪♪♪

1990, Varese-Sarabande; from the movie *Lawrence of Arabia*, Columbia Pictures, 1962.

Album Notes: *Music*: Maurice Jarre; *Orchestrations*: Gerard Schurmann; The London Philharmonic Orchestra, conducted by Sir Adrian Boult.

Selections: 1 Overture (4:17); 2 Main Title (1:57); 3 Miracle (3:09); 4 Nefud Mirage (2:24); 5 Rescue Of Gasim (2:13); 6 Bringing Gasim Into Camp (3:36); 7 Arrival At Auda's Camp (2:03); 8 The Voice Of The Guns (K. Alford)(2:01); 9 In Whose Name Do You Ride? (1:25); 10 Continuation Of The Miracle (2:18); 11 Sun's Anvil (3:12); 12 Lawrence And Body Guard (2:08); 13 That Is The Desert (2:54); 14 End Title (3:42).

Review: Has there ever been an orchestrated film soundtrack more beautiful, more evocative? Here begins Maurice Jarre's string of Oscars and his memorable collaboration with the British director David Lean. Thirty-five years on, this landmark work stands in the company of the best "classical music" ever written for Hollywood. Lean's film, perhaps the greatest of the bigger-than-big movie epics of the late '50s and early '60s, is unimaginable without this music, particularly in its first half, and especially in those sweeping long shots of the desert. A fan can only wish for more, and in the CD era, there should be. At 37 minutes, this soundtrack recording offers nothing more than the original LP. Monsieur Jarre, where are those master tapes?

Marc Kirkeby

Lawrence of Arabia ♫♫♫ᵈ

1989, Silva Screen Records; from the movie *Lawrence of Arabia*, Columbia Pictures, 1962.

Album Notes: *Music*: Maurice Jarre; The Philharmonia Orchestra, conducted by Tony Bremner; *Album Producer*: Geoffrey Alexander; *Engineer*: Dick Lewzey.

Selections: 1 Overture (4:22); 2 Main Titles (2:13); 3 First Entrance To The Desert/Night And Stars/Lawrence And Tafas (9:37); 4 Miracle (2:27); 5 That Is The Desert (2:51); 6 Nefud Mirage/The Sun's Anvil (5:24); 7 Rescue Of Gasim/Bringing Gasim Into Camp (4:07); 8 Arrival At Auda's Camp (2:09); 9 On To Akaba/The Beach At Night (4:40); 10 Sinai Desert (1:06); 11 The Voice Of The Guns (K. Alford)(2:01); 12 Horse Stampede/Ali Rescues Lawrence/Lawrence And His Bodyguard (5:15); 13 The End/Playoff Music (4:34).

Review: Besides restoring the cues in the order in which the plot unfolded on the screen, this re-recording introduces several selections not available on the soundtrack album. This would be everything fans have been waiting for were it not for the fact that when all is said and done, the performance by The Philharmonia, while sonically spectacular, doesn't match in excitement and fire the London Philharmonic in the original. To actually pinpoint the differences is a subtle exercise that requires a sensitivity few won't care about, but the playing often sounds stilted, studied, and at times a bit too reverential. Casual listeners, more interested in the sweep of the music than in academic disputes over the way it should be performed, will no doubt enjoy the recording in all its splendor.

A League of Their Own ♫♫♫

1992, Columbia Records; from the movie *A League of Their Own*, Columbia Pictures, 1992.

Album Notes: *Music*: Hans Zimmer; *Orchestrations*: Bruce Fowler; *Music Editor*: Laura Perlman; Orchestra conducted by Shirley Walker; *Producers*: Hans Zimmer, Jay Rifkin; *Engineers*: Armin Steiner, Jay Rifkin; *Assistant Engineer*: Michael Stevens; *Featured Soloists*: Jim Kanter (clarinet), Rick Baptist (trumpet),

Mike Lane (piano), Kurt McGettrick (baritone sax), Kathy Lenski (violin), Phil Ayling (cor anglais); *Featured Performers*: Carole King, The Manhattan Transfer, James Taylor, Billy Joel, Art Garfunkel, Doc's Rhythm Cats, The Rockford Peaches; *Album Producer*: Jay Landers; *Engineer*: Bernie Grundman.

Selections: 1 Now And Forever (C. King)(3:17) *Carole King*; 2 Choo Choo Ch'Boogie (V. Harton/D. Darling/M. Gabler)(2:58) *The Manhattan Transfer*; 3 It's Only A Paper Moon (B. Rose/E.Y. Harburg/H. Arlen)(2:51) *James Taylor*; 4 In A Sentimental Mood (E.K. Ellington/E. Kurtz/I. Mills)(4:04) *Billy Joel*; 5 Two Sleepy People (H. Carmichael/F. Loesser)(3:39) *Art Garfunkel*; 6 I Didn't Know What Time It Was (R. Rodgers/L. Hart)(3:38) *James Taylor*; 7 On The Sunny Side Of The Street (D. Fields/J. McHugh)(3:19) *The Manhattan Transfer*; 8 Flying Home (B. Goodman/L. Hampton)(2:58) *Doc's Rhythm Cats*; 9 Life Goes On (H. Zimmer)(6:10); 10 The Final Game (H. Zimmer)(9:31); 11 The All American Girls Professional Baseball League Song (L.P. Davis)(1:24) *The Rockford Peaches*.

Review: As compilations of this kind go, this is quite an enchanting one. Some of today's most recognizable frontline performers deliver a handful of classic tunes in a program that is as beguiling as it is familiar. Hans Zimmer's two longer selections add a zest of instrumental class that tops off this soundtrack album with a delicious touch.

Leap of Faith Woof

1992, MCA Records; from the movie *Leap of Faith*, Paramount Pictures, 1992.

Album Notes: *Song Producers*: Don Henley, George Duke, Tony Brown, Brian Tankersley, Lyle Lovett, Todd Rundgren; *Album Producer*: Kathy Nelson; *Engineer*: David Collins.

Selections: 1 Sit Down You're Rockin' The Boat (F. Loesser)(4:34) *Don Henley*; 2 Ready For A Miracle (A. Reynolds/B. Hull)(3:38) *Patti LaBelle*; 3 Change In My Life (B. Straits)(3:16) *John Pagano*; 4 Stones Throw From Hurtin' (E. John/B. Taupin)(4:33) *Wynonna*; 5 King Of Sin Medley: Lord Will Make A Way (Somehow)(T. Dorsey)/God Said He Would See You Through (Rev. M. Biggham)/God Will Take Care Of You (E. Hawkins)/Psalm 27 (arr.: W. Whitman) (5:19) *The Angels Of Mercy, YaDonna Wise, Lizz Lee, Lynette Hawkins Stephens, Lawrence Matthews*; 6 Pass Me Not (F. Crosby/W. Doane)(5:01) *Lyle Lovette, George Duke*; 7 Rain Celebration Medley: Jesus On The Mainline (arr.: E. Hawkins/G. Duke)/Ready For A Miracle (A. Reynolds/B. Hull)/ It's A Highway To Heaven (M. Gardner/T. Dorsey)(5:03) *The Angels Of Mercy, Lizz Lee, Delores Hall, Leon P. Turner, Patti LaBelle, Gheri LeGree-McDonald*; 8 Blessed Assurance (F. Crosby/J.

Knapp)(2:38) *Albertina Walker*; 9 Paradise By The Dashboard Light (J. Steinman)(8:24) *Meat Loaf*.

Review: Whoever thought it would be a great idea to have Don Henley sing "Sit Down You're Rocking the Boat," from *Guys and Dolls* should have his/her head examined. Not only is the singer out of his league with this song, but his delivery is totally wrong for it. That's not the only thing wrong with this soundtrack album in which there is too much of too many things to please even the least discriminating listener. The moods in this album move from rock to gospel to blues to country without much rhyme or reason. Of course, there might have been a reason in the film, about one of those evangelists who proliferate in the South, but sad to say not here.

Legend

Legend ♫♫♫♫

1992, Silva Screen; from the movie *Legend*, 20th Century-Fox, 1985.

Album Notes: *Music*: Jerry Goldsmith; *Lyrics*: John Bettis; The National Philharmonic Orchestra, conducted by Jerry Goldsmith.

Selections: 1 Main Title/The Goblins (5:45); 2 My True Love's Eyes/The Cottage (5:04); 3 The Unicorn (7:53); 4 Living River/Bumps & Hollow/The Freeze (7:21); 5 The Faeries/The Riddle (4:52); 6 Sing The Wee (1:07); 7 Forgive Me (5:13); 8 Fearie Dance (1:51); 9 The Armour (2:16); 10 Oona/The Jewels (6:40); 11 The Dress Waltz (2:47); 12 Darkness Fails (7:27); 13 The Ring (6:28); 14 Re-United (5:18).

Review: Ridley Scott's striking fairy tale didn't fare too well at the box office in the U.S., nor did Jerry Goldsmith's superb score which was dropped in favor of a selection of pop tunes by Tangerine Dream. The substitution did not help the film, but it deprived American filmgoers from enjoying one of the great scores written for the screen. In it, Goldsmith eloquently captured the cinematic vision of the director and transposed it in strikingly beautiful musical terms. The recording does it full justice.

Legend ♫♫♫

1995, Varese-Sarabande; from the movie *Legend*, 20th Century-Fox, 1985.

Album Notes: *Music*: Tangerine Dream; *Album Producers*: Tangerine Dream; *Engineers*: Tangerine Dream.

Selections: 1 Our Love Strong Enough (5:10) *Bryan Ferry*; 2 Opening (2:53); 3 Cottage (3:19); 4 Unicorn Theme (3:27); 5 Goblins (3:00); 6 Fairies (2:55); 7 Loved By The Sun (5:56) *Jon*

> "(D)irector) Michael (Hoffman) and I have done four pictures together now.... He's probably the only director I work with who is actually in the room for a good portion of the time while I'm actually writing the score."
>
> **James Newton Howard**
> *on scoring* One Fine Day *(The Hollywood Reporter, 1-15-97)*

Anderson; 8 Blue Room (3:22); 9 The Dance (2:22); 10 Darkness (3:03); 11 The Kitchen/Unicorn Theme (reprise) (4:53).

Review: This pleasant synthesized alternate score by the German pop group replaced Jerry Goldsmith's work composed for the film in the U.S. when studio heads thought they needed music that "the kids could relate to better." The film suffered more from their decision to edit 20 minutes from the original Ridley Scott's cut, than the replacement of Goldsmith's inventive composition. Tangerine Dream's work is certainly effective, to a lesser degree, but also gives the film a more claustrophobic feel, as synthesized scores often do. It holds up much better on the album as an independent musical piece than as movie music.

David Hirsch

Legends of the Fall ♫♫♫♫♫

1994, Epic Soundtrax/Sony Classical; from the movie *Legends of the Fall*, Tri-Star Pictures, 1994.

Album Notes: *Music*: James Horner; *Orchestrations*: Thomas Pasatieri, Don Davis; *Music Editor*: Jim Henrikson; *Assistant Music Editor*: Joe E. Rand; The London Symphony Orchestra, conducted by James Horner; *Featured Musicians*: Jay Ungar, Kazu Matsui, Tony Hinnegan, Mike Taylor, Maggie Boyle, Dermot Crehan; *Album Producers*: James Horner, Shawn Murphy; *Engineer*: Shawn Murphy; *Assistant Engineers*: Andy Bass, Geoff Foster, Matt Howe, Leslie Ann Jones.

Selections: 1 Legends Of The Fall (4:17); 2 The Ludlows (6:40); 3 Off To War (5:55); 4 To The Boys... (2:49); 5 Samuel's Death (8:24); 6 Alfred Moves To Helena (3:01); 7 Farewell/Descent Into Madness (8:13); 8 The Changing Seasons/Wild Horses/Tristan's Return (5:11); 9 The Wedding (3:06); 10 Isabel's Murder/Recollections Of Samuel (3:58); 11 Revenge (6:20); 12 Goodbyes (3:12); 13 Alfred, Tristan, The Colonel, The Legend... (15:09).

Review: For this poignant romantic drama set during World War I and in the years following about two brothers, their father, and the beautiful, compelling young woman who irrevocably changes each of their lives, James Horner wrote a superb score. "At once brooding and lush, redolent of both love and loss," in director Ed Zwick's own comments. In it, the composer evoked the wilds of Montana, where the action takes place, its native rhythms and its wilderness, and Cornwall, where the main protagonists came from initially. As a result, his composition is filled with sweeping melodies, made even more striking with the use of a fiddle and a shakuhachi that give it its unusual colors and flavor. As is often the case in Horner's expansive scores, the last track, "Alfred, Tristan, The Colonel, The Legend..." is an expressive piece of orchestral music that slowly evolves and builds into a magnificent tone poem of impressive magnitude and character.

The Leopard Son 🎬🎬🎬🎬

1996, Ark 21 Records; from the movie *The Leopard Son*, Discovery Pictures, 1996.

Album Notes: *Music*: Stewart Copeland; *Orchestrations*: Michael T. Andreas; The Los Angeles Symphony Orchestra conducted by Michael T. Andreas; *Featured Musicians*: Stewart Copeland (piano, drums & percussion), Stanley Clarke (acoustic bass), Judd Miller (ethnic wind instruments), Michael Thompson (guitars); *Album Producers*: Stewart Copeland, Jeff Seitz; *Engineers*: Joseph Magee, Jeff Seitz.

Selections: 1 Baboon Gang (3:30); 2 Cub Explores (2:17); 3 Changing Skies (1:41); 4 Hyena Family (2:27); 5 The Lion Bitches (2:30); 6 The Mud Lions (2:11); 7 Cheetah Gang (2:37); 8 Familiar World (1:15); 9 Childhood Friends (1:42); 10 Eagle Flies (2:11); 11 Leopard Twins (3:34); 12 Mother Is Dead (5:16); 13 Cub Riff (1:40); 14 Leopard Love (3:06).

Review: A compelling documentary about a cub growing up on the Seregenti Plain, *The Leopard Son* strongly benefitted from Stewart Copeland's eclectic score, solidly anchored by Stanley Clarke's lively bass work. Since much of the screen action is reduced to scenes involving the cub, his environment, and other animals (a family of hyenas, some lions, a gang of cheetahs) Copeland's engaging score, which frequently mixes sounds effects, remains purely naturalistic with cues that help detail what happens in simple, easy to appreciate terms. As a result, the music is constantly enjoyable and includes many delightful mo-

ments such as "Cub Explores," "Changing Skies," a muscular "The Lion Bitches" (in which the animal's roar gives added strength to the music) or even the mournful "Mother Is Dead," a touching moment in the film and in this recording.

Leprechaun 🎬🎬🎬

1992, Intrada Records; from the movie *Leprechaun*, Trimark Pictures, 1992.

Album Notes: *Music*: Kevin Kiner; *Orchestrations*: Kevin Kiner; *Album Producer*: Kevin Kiner; *Engineer*: Mark Evans.

Selections: 1 Main Title (2:37); 2 O'Grady (3:24); 3 The Crate (2:29); 4 Ozzie Attacked (4:06); 5 Rainbow (1:04); 6 Ozzie And Alex (:53); 7 The Cat (2:46); 8 Endless Chase (7:46); 9 Bear Trap (4:34); 10 The Truck (3:30); 11 Rambo (4:51); 12 The Gold (2:04); 13 The Fence (3:16); 14 Hospital Chase (3:37); 15 Clover's End (7:39); 16 Leprechaun (2:13).

Review: With just a hint of Irish through prominent featuring of piccolo as a lead instrument throughout the score, Kevin Kiner's music for this malevolent movie of minuscule mayhem is full of chilling charm. A fluidly orchestral composition, *Leprechaun* counterpoints a very pleasant, almost American theme for its main characters (Ozzie and Alex) against the dark music signifying the evil leprechaun. The score is almost entirely orchestral, and its many layers belie its reliance upon the two motifs for its thematic base. Kiner's suspenseful sonorities and aggressive arpeggios give the score most of its energy and keep its orchestration and tonality interesting. His chase music races along, driven by frantic string pulses and keyboard, the ever present piccolo signifying the dangerously playful menace of the leprechaun. A workable score on film, Kiner's music is an enjoyable suspenseful-dramatic score on CD.

Randall Larson

Les Miserables 🎬🎬🎬🎬

1989, Marco Polo Records; from the movie *Les Miserables*, 1934.

Album Notes: *Music*: Arthur Honegger; The Slovak Radio Symphony Orchestra of Bratislava, conducted by Adriano; *Album Producer*: Martin Sauer.

Selections: 1 Main Title (3:41); 2 Jean Valjean On The Road (3:47); 3 Evocation Of The Chain Gang (1:55); 4 Storm Inside A Brain (6:43); 5 Fantine (4:11); 6 Jean Valjean Escapes (1:01); 7 Cosette And Marius (2:09); 8 Fair At Montfermeil (7:39); 9 The Luxembourg (2:32); 10 The Garden Of Rue Plumet/The Night Convoy (5:12); 11 The Riot (2:46); 12 Death Of Eponine (2:18); 13 The Assault (2:15); 14 In The Sewers (5:39); 15 Music At

Gillenormand (1:55); 16 Solitude (1:39); 17 Death Of Jean Valjean (2:47).

Review: The dramatic breadth and scope in Victor Hugo's classic tale of revenge and passion, *Les Miserables,* has been translated into numerous stage or screen adaptations (including, of course, the current musical hit still playing on Broadway, in London and elsewhere around the world). In addition to the various plays built around the descriptive story of Jean Valjean, his flight from justice, and his eventual redemption in the 1848 street riots in Paris, the drama inspired more than half a dozen screen versions, with some of the most polished actors of their generation essaying the role of Valjean, the former escaped convict forever one step ahead of the relentless police officer Javert.

One of the most successful films is a French version made by Raymond Bernard in 1934, with Harry Baur, unforgettable as Valjean, a powerful drama heightened by Arthur Honegger's remarkably evocative score. Painstakingly reconstructed by Swiss musicologist and conductor Adriano and solidly performed by the Slovak Radio Symphony Orchestra of Bratislava, Honegger's music underlines all the passion and drama in Hugo's tale, and reveals itself a striking composition with great appeal when taken on its own terms. A revelation, as well as a reminder that film music can often reach the loftiest heights in the hands of creative composers.

See also: Napoleon in Motion Pictures and Honegger in Compilations.

Lethal Weapon

Lethal Weapon 2 ♫♫♫♫♭

1989, Warner Bros. Records; from the movie *Lethal Weapon 2,* Warner Bros., 1989.

Album Notes: *Music:* Michael Kamen, Eric Clapton; Orchestra conducted by Michael Kamen; *Featured Soloists:* Eric Clapton (guitar), David Sanborn (alto sax), Michael Kamen (Kurzweil), Gregory Phillinganes (keyboards), Tom Barney (bass), Sonny Emory (drums), Lew Soloff (trumpet); *Album Producers:* Michael Kamen, Stephen P. McLaughlin, Christopher S. Brooks; *Engineer:* Stephen P. McLaughlin, Bobby Fernandez.

Selections: 1 Cheer Down (G. Harrison/T. Petty) (4:07) *George Harrison*; 2 Still Cruisin' (After All These Years) (M. Love/T. Melcher) (3:36) *The Beach Boys*; 3 Knockin' On Heaven's Door (B. Dylan) (4:58) *Randy Crawford*; 4 Riggs (5:16); 5 The Embassy (5:38); 6 Riggs And Roger (M. Kamen/E. Clapton/D. Sanborn) (5:53); 7 Leo (M. Kamen) (3:43); 8 Goodnight Rika (4:05); 9 The

Stilt House (4:21); 10 Medley: The Shipyard (M. Kamen/E. Clapton/D. Sanborn)/Knockin' On Heaven's Door (B. Dylan) (4:45).

Review: See entry below

Lethal Weapon 3 ♫♫♫♫♭

1992, Warner Bros. Records; from the movie *Lethal Weapon 3,* Warner Bros. 1992.

Album Notes: *Music:* Michael Kamen, Eric Clapton; *Orchestrations:* Michael Kamen, Jonathan Sacks, William Ross, Brad Warnaar; The Greater Los Angeles Orchestra and The Greater New York Alumni Orchestra, conducted by Michael Kamen; *Album Producers:* Michael Kamen, Stephen P. McLaughlin, Christopher S. Brooks; *Engineer:* Stephen P. McLaughlin, Bobby Fernandez.

Selections: 1 It's Probably Me (M. Kamen/E. Clapton/Sting) (6:22) *Sting*; 2 Runaway Train (E. John/B. Taupin/O. Romo) (5:25) *Elton John, Eric Clapton*; 3 Grab The Cat (M. Kamen/E. Clapton/D. Sanborn) (1:35); 4 Leo Getz Goes To The Hockey Game (M. Kamen) (2:57); 5 Darryl Dies (M. Kamen) (4:54); 6 Riggs And Rog (2:55); 7 Roger's Boat (M. Kamen/E. Clapton/D. Sanborn) (5:00); 8 Armour Piercing Bullets (4:33); 9 God Judges Us By Our Scars (1:57); 10 Lorna — A Quiet Evening By The Fire (3:34).

Review: One of the most interesting elements in the *Lethal Weapon* films has been the scores devised by Michael Kamen, with assist and support from Eric Clapton and David Sanborn. Writing in a style that reflects the films' urban contemporary setting and the volatile action in them, Kamen's scores are particularly strong and imaginatively descriptive. The point is made in these two albums (the soundtrack album of the first film has never been released on compact disc) in which Sanborn's soulful saxophone and Clapton's doleful guitar work set off the melodies written by the composer. Augmenting the impression made by the instrumental cues, all are more or less reflective of the fast-paced action on the screen and the feuding friendship that binds the two cops portrayed by Mel Gibson and Danny Glover, but equally effective in a purely aural setup. Both CDs contain performances by well-known vocalists, George Harrison, The Beach Boys and Randy Crawford in the first, Sting and Elton John in the second. First class all the way!

Leviathan ♫♫

1989, Varese-Sarabande; from the movie *Leviathan,* M-G-M, 1989.

Album Notes: *Music:* Jerry Goldsmith; *Orchestrations:* Arthur Morton, Nancy Beach; The Orchestra di Santa Cecilia di Roma, conducted by Jerry Goldsmith; *Album Producer*: Jerry Goldsmith; *Engineer*: Alan Snelling.

Selections: 1 Underwater Camp (3:23); 2 Decompression (3:16); 3 Discovery (5:24); 4 One Of Us (1:41); 5 The Body Within (4:33); 6 Escape Bubbles (5:37); 7 Can We Fix It (3:25); 8 Situation Under Control (1:49); 9 It's Growing (3:10); 10 Too Hot (3:27); 11 A Lot Better (3:31).

Review: This rotten 1986 film is a cross between *Alien* and the 1981 Sean Connery space film *Outland*, and unfortunately, so is Goldsmith's rather simplistic score. The opening, with its distorted whale calls and melancholy woodwind theme, works well enough, as do later cues like "Situation Under Control" and "Escape Bubbles" which make good use of the main theme. But the film's action cues ("Decompression," "Discovery," "Too Hot") rely on a maddening two note rhythmic device that just repeats and repeats without any of Goldsmith's usual complex development and ornamentation, making the album's slight 30-minute running time seem like an eternity. And Goldsmith's upbeat, heroic finale, although listenable on its own, was completely at odds with the mood of the film.

Jeff Bond

Liar Liar 🎵🎵

1997, MCA Records; from the movie *Liar, Liar*, Universal Pictures, 1997.

Album Notes: *Music*: John Debney; *Orchestrations*: Brad Dechter, Frank Bennett, Don Nemitz; *Music Editor*: Mark Ryan; Orchestra conducted by John Debney; *Album Producers*: John Debney, Mick Stern; *Engineer*: Shawn Murphy.

Selections: 1 My Dad's A Liar (2:40); 2 To Court (1:04); 3 The Pen Is Blue (3:02); 4 I'm A Bad Father (1:46); 5 Pulled Over (1:16); 6 The Unwish (1:41); 7 Bathroom Folly (1:47); 8 I Love My Son (2:36); 9 Airport Chase (1:45); 10 It's Fletcher (1:30); 11 Together (2:25); 12 The Claw Returns (1:39); 13 End Credits (3:36); 14 Outtake Montage (2:34).

Review: A very funny comedy, starring Jim Carrey as a chronic liar who is forced to tell the truth in spite of himself for 24 hours, *Liar Liar* elicited a score from John Debney, which proved right on the money when heard along with the screen action, but fails to make the grade in one's living room. The reason is simple. The cues were written for a fast-paced action, with all the quirks and turns usually found in a comedy, with the music matching the moves with similar sharp turns and oddball thrusts. On their own, however, the cues often sound too disjointed, as if the composer had chosen to write down one idea, only to abandon it the second after for another, totally different. As a result, the music is all too often jumpy, all over the place, without real focus. This is too bad,

because Debney, an excellent scorer, has written some themes that are vibrant and exciting, when they are given a chance to be developed. A clear case of a score which needed to be rethought and reconstructed for its soundtrack album.

License to Kill 🎵🎵🎵▵

1989, MCA Records; from the movie *License to Kill*, United Artists, 1989.

Album Notes: *Music*: Michael Kamen; The National Philharmonic Orchestra, conducted by Michael Kamen; *Album Producer*: Michael Kamen.

Selections: 1 Licence To Kill (5:13) *Gladys Knight*; 2 Wedding Party (3:53) *Ivory*; 3 Dirty Love (3:45) *Tim Feehan*; 4 Pam (3:50); 5 If You Asked Me To (3:58) *Patti LaBelle*; 6 James And Felix On Their Way To Church (3:53); 7 His Funny Valentine (3:26); 8 Sanchez Is In The Bahamas/Shark Fishing (2:06); 9 Ninja (6:03); 10 Licence Revoked (9:11).

Review: Once again, the point is clearly made that John Barry is the only composer whose music perfectly captures and matches the moods and slyly ridiculous situations in which agent 007 usually finds himself. Without taking anything away from Michael Kamen's own artistic bend, magnificently evident in other soundtrack recordings, his score for *License to Kill* in which the dashing James Bond was portrayed by Timothy Dalton, simply doesn't have the characteristic flair one can find in Barry's own scores. This said, Kamen's music has its moments of panache and glory, with cues that are evocative and can stand against any other music written for a motion picture. But even though he quotes from Barry's "Bond Theme" and provides a new, fresh approach to the musical concept of a James Bond film, his score ultimately sounds anything but. Because of that, the rating reflects the quality of the music itself, not the fact that this is a James Bond score, which would automatically lower the rating.

Life and Nothing But 🎵🎵🎵🎵

1989, DRG Records; from the movie *Life and Nothing But*, Orion Classics, 1989.

Album Notes: *Music*: Oswald d'Andrea.

Selections: 1 Horseriders On The Beach (Main Title)(3:24); 2 The Grezaucourt Suite (12:17); 3 Bliss (1:42); 4 Irene And Dellaplane (2:15); 5 Meandering (2:13); 6 The Shell (2:16); 7 The Cart (1:54); 8 The Two Fighters (2:33); 9 God, Do You Believe? (3:04); 10 Blackboat (1:38); 11 The Letter (End Credits)(7:02).

Review: A sobering, unglorified look at the devastating effects of war in general, Bertrand Tavernier's scathing film follows the efforts by the French military command to find at the end of

World War I, a suitable "unknown soldier" worthy of receiving the nation's undying respect and admiration. The score, by Oswald d'Andrea, equally stern and unfussy, italicized the unfolding drama, justifiably earning a Cesar, France's equivalent to the Oscar, for "Best Musical Score" in 1990. Two selections in particular, "The Grezaucourt Suite" and "The Letter" clearly explain the reasons for its success.

Lifeforce ♪♪♪♪♭

1989, Milan Records; from the movie *Lifeforce,* Cannon Films, 1989.

Album Notes: *Music:* Henry Mancini; The London Symphony Orchestra, conducted by Henry Mancini; *Album Producer:* Emmanuel Chamboredon.

Selections: 1 The Lifeforce Theme (3:32); 2 The Discovery (4:43); 3 Space Walk (3:06); 4 Into The Alien Craft (2:48); 5 Exploration (2:58); 6 Sleeping Vampires (2:21); 7 Evil Visitation (4:12); 8 Carlson's Story (3:28); 9 The Girl In The Raincoat (2:54); 10 The Web Of Destiny (2:53); 11 End Titles (4:11).

Review: *Lifeforce* is Henry Mancini's *Star Wars,* a symphonic sci-fi epic. Actually that's not entirely true. *Star Wars* is a good and popular film, and *Lifeforce* is a laughably awful 1985 Tobe Hooper space-vampire flick. Furthermore, John Williams' score for *Star Wars* emphasizes leitmotives, whereas Mancini's *Lifeforce* is through-composed, a tone-poem of symphonic moods. But they are both incredibly good. *Lifeforce* brought Mancini, best known for catchy pop hits, back to the science fiction and horror genres, where he started as a staff composer for Universal in the 1950s. The score is romantic and huge, a sweeping epic bristling with the orchestrational know-how and chord structures that Mancini carried inside his amazing brain. The most flashy piece is the end title, an unusual march in 3/4, but the rest of the score has a moody richness as haunting in the subtle sequences as it is propulsive in the climactic ones. There are few themes per se; rather, the whole thing has a unified feeling, whereby certain gestures and contrapuntal blends become associated with the story. One of the best sequences is the film's opening "Discovery" suite running 14-minutes, in which a space shuttle discovers a vampire ship inside a comet — the film is largely a showcase for Mancini's music. Alas, this was cut from the final print, as were certain other scenes, Mancini's music abridged and selectively replaced with synthesizer music by Michael Kamen. (There is a restored version available on laserdisc.) It is unfortunate that Mancini rarely revisited the "John Williams" genres for the latter portion of his career, because *Lifeforce* is a knockout.

Lukas Kendall

Lightning Jack ♪♪♪♪

1994, Festival Records/Australia; from the movie *Lightning Jack,* Village Roadshow Pictures, 1994.

Album Notes: *Music:* Bruce Rowland; *Orchestrations:* Bruce Rowland, Nerida Tyson-Chew; Orchestra conducted by Bruce Rowland; *Featured Musicians:* Peter Harper (harmonica), Tony Naylor, Doug DeVries, Simon Paterson, Don Stevenson (guitars), Roger McLaughlin, Mike Grabowski (electric bass), Ron Sandilands (drums); *Album Producer:* Bruce Rowland; *Engineer:* Robin Grey.

Selections: 1 Opening (:25); 2 The Bad Guys (2:18); 3 Meet Lightning Jack Kane (2:11); 4 Kane's Escape (1:28); 5 Jack Takes A Hostage (2:56); 6 Kane Rides Away (1:35); 7 A Snake Bite Bonding (1:42); 8 Ben's First Job (1:38); 9 Kane — Alive Or Dead (2:04); 10 It's Been A Long Time Jack (1:07); 11 Teaching Ben To Shoot (1:04); 12 Arizona Chicken (2:00); 13 On The Lookout For Kane (2:19); 14 A Greenhorn Like You/Monument Montage (2:44); 15 They're Comanches (3:38); 16 Who's There (1:38); 17 The Fire (2:31); 18 Lightning Rag (1:28); 19 Ben's First Poke (1:27); 20 I'm Scared (1:33); 21 John T Coles/Two Riders (5:33); 22 Ben's Betrayal (1:05); 23 $10,000 Reward (1:45); 24 Closing Credits (2:12).

Review: An exhilarating Australian western, *Lightning Jack* takes its subject humorously, providing star Paul Hogan with a vehicle that has the wacky appeal of his *Crocodile Dundee* films, while taking him to a new environment, the American West. Indicative of the tone adopted in this frequently diverting film, Hogan's Jack, quick on the draw but slightly nearsighted about his own possibilities, teams with a riding partner, a taciturn character whose laconism is only due to the fact that he is a mute. As for the slightly inconsequential story itself, it gives the star enough rope to enable him to display another facet of his congenial personality, in a plot with enough twists and turns to delight his fans. Making sly comments of its own, Bruce Rowland's music at times evoked his own *Man from Snowy River* scores, with a tongue-in-cheek discordant note that echoed the antics on the screen. Heard in this flavorful soundtrack album, some expository cues, like "A Snake Bite Bonding" and "They're Comanches," not so subtly enhanced by the harmonica in yet another concession to a tried-and-true formula, display the right thematic approach and make this score a thoroughly enjoyable effort.

Lilies of the Field ♪♪♪♪

1997, P.E.G. Recordings; from the movie *Lilies of the Field,* United Artists, 1963.

Album Notes: *Music:* Jerry Goldsmith; Orchestra conducted by Jerry Goldsmith; *Featured Vocalist:* Jester Hairston.

Selections: 1 Main Title (1:49); 2 Homer Returns (1:32); 3 The Roof (1:15); 4 Homer Awakes/Breakfast (3:09); 5 Feed The Slaves/Drive To Mass (1:35); 6 Amen/Sunday Morning/Amen (3:56); 7 The Contractor (2:26); 8 Out Of Bricks (1:05); 9 No Hammer/Return Of The Prodigal (4:18); 10 Lots Of Bricks/Aid Given/Aid Rejected (6:51); 11 Amen (2:15); 12 End Title/End Cast (1:25).

Review: Anchored by the main theme, a variation on the choral "Amen," also heard, this wonderful Americana-bathed score by Jerry Goldsmith resonates with joyous accents, punctuated by various acoustic instruments (a harmonica, a guitar, a banjo, an accordion) often playing over a jaunty string section. Written for a minor comedy, about a former G.I. on the loose, who comes upon and helps five nuns, refugees from behind the Iron Curtain, in building a chapel in the middle of the Arizona desert, the score captures the funny, warm-hearted moods of the story, giving it an extra, most winning dimension. Available for the first time since its release in 1963, the album suffers from an almost intolerable hiss, all the more noticeable because the sparse instrumentation cannot hide it.

The Linguini Incident ♫♫♫♫ ⌐

1992, Varese-Sarabande; from the movie *The Linguini Incident*, Academy Entertainment, 1992.

Album Notes: *Music*: Thomas Newman; *Music Editors*: Bill Bernstein, Virginia Ellsworth, Paul O'Bryan; Orchestra conducted by Thomas Newman; *Featured Musicians*: John Beasley (piano), Chuck Domanico (string bass), Harvey Mason (drums), Sal Marquez (trumpet), George Thatcher (trombone), Jim Self (tuba), Bill Bernstein (flute), Jeff Elmassion (single reeds), Michael Fisher (percussion), Thomas Newman (ukulele, piano); *Album Producers*: Thomas Newman, John Vigran, Bill Bernstein.

Selections: 1 Cruel, Cruel World (1:57); 2 El Gran Pescado (Pray For Rain) (3:49) *Dan Wool, Jim Woody, Gary Brown, Jeff Beal, Karl Parazzo, Tom Yoder*; 3 Houdini's Bimbo (1:13); 4 Habanera (3:13); 5 Lethal Cleavage (1:30); 6 Lucy The Ethereal (1:44); 7 Piano Sobre Mi Pia (Pray For Rain)(3:49) *Dan Wool, Jim Woody, Gary Brown, Jeff Beal, Karl Parazzo, Tom Yoder*; 8 Trigger Man (1:09); 9 Platinum Bezel (1:32); 10 Perdida en Arabia (3:24) (Pray For Rain)(3:49) *Dan Wool, Jim Woody, Gary Brown, Jeff Beal, Karl Parazzo, Tom Yoder*; 11 Shut Up Pedro (2:04); 12 Coney Island (2:41); 13 Bad Acid (R. Cox/J. Elmassion/T. Newman) (2:07); 14 Drip Goes The Clock (1:02); 15 The Linguini Incident (1:45); 16 Mas O Menos Salsa (2:52) (Pray For Rain)(3:49) *Dan Wool, Jim Woody, Gary Brown, Jeff Beal, Karl Parazzo, Tom Yoder*; 17 Aquarium Escape (2:11); 18 Straight Jacket (2:24); 19 Many Happy Returns (2:04).

Review: The explosive contemporary jazz accents in Thomas Newman's diversified score underline the ferocious aspects of this biting satire starring David Bowie, Julian Lennon, Rosanna Arquette and Buck Henry as wacky characters in a swanky restaurant whose conversation turns to the meaning of life. Performed by many excellent musicians and developed along varied rhythmic lines, the music is consistently surprising, sometimes corrosive, and sometimes plain entertaining. There are many changes that will delight adventurous listeners unwilling to settle for the ordinary. With a predominance of Latin tunes, but not exclusively limited to this type of expression, the score is totally enjoyable, with Newman pulling all stops in a dazzling display of his creative streak and talent as an instrumentalist.

Link ♫♫ ⌐

1986, Varese-Sarabande Records; from the movie *Link*, Cannon Screen Entertainment, 1986.

Album Notes: *Music*: Jerry Goldsmith; *Orchestrations*: Arthur Morton; The National Philharmonic Orchestra, conducted by Jerry Goldsmith; *Album Producer*: Jerry Goldsmith; *Engineer*: Mike Ross.

Selections: 1 Main Link (1:35); 2 Welcome Link (3:04); 3 Helpful Link (4:56); 4 Bravo Link (4:38); 5 Swinging Link (6:19); 6 Missing Link (4:43); 7 Peeping Link (3:02); 8 Mighty Link (2:39); 9 Angry Link (2:06); 10 Flaming Link (3:19); 11 End Link (3:01).

Review: Jerry Goldsmith's approach to this odd suspense film about a trained orangutan is one of the composer's strangest—a goofball, circus-like approach featuring a quasi-calliope tune and heavy use of synthesized rhythms, stacked against the composer's usual modernistic action writing. It's a wildly uneven listen, mixing cringe-inducing slapstick comedy with powerful orchestral treatments of suspense and action, and a beautiful, lyrical melody of strings and electronic effects. For every moment of vintage Goldsmith there's something that will have you clutching for the "skip" button on your CD player, but you have to give Goldsmith some points for audaciousness here. The biggest problem with the score is the drum machines, which just drown out too much of the orchestra. *Jeff Bond*

The Lion in Winter ♫♫♫♫

1995, Legacy Records/Sony Music Entertainment; from the movie *The Lion in Winter*, Avco Embassy, 1968.

Album Notes: *Music*: John Barry; *CD Producer*: Didier C. Deutsch; *Engineer*: Chris Herles.

Selections: 1 Main Title/The Lion In Winter (2:39); 2 Chinon/ Eleanor's Arrival (3:28); 3 Allons Gai Gai Gai (1:50); 4 To The Chapel (1:48); 5 The Christmas Wine (2:44); 6 God Damn You (4:15); 7 To Rome (4:06); 8 The Herb Garden (4:40); 9 Eya, Eya, Nova Gaudia (2:11); 10 How Beautiful You Make Me (3:01); 11 Media vita in morte sumus (In The Midst Of Life We Are In Death)(2:15); 12 We're Jungle Creatures (2:46).

Review: John Barry's quasi-medieval Academy Award winning score for *The Lion in Winter*, starring Katharine Hepburn and Peter O'Toole, truly demonstrates the composer's incredibly versatile perspective. With a daunting task at hand (creating an original musical score for a historical drama that occurs in the year 1183), Barry devised with "great trepidations" (his own words) a beautiful, harmonically complex set of compositions which are rich with texture and substance, and still hold up remarkably well nearly 30 years later. The themes depicting the Catholic church are particularly powerful, and two original "period" songs (composed by Barry and James Goldman) stand out as brilliant examples of the composer's willingness to integrate new forms into his repertoire of musical stylings. With the current, renewed interest in Gregorian chant, this disc becomes a fascinating example of the power found in this type of liturgical expression, used to such gratifying results in this score. The meticulous stereo remastering allows the full breadth of the rich original recording (made at Cine Tele Studios in London) to shine through with unequaled brilliance.

Charles L. Granata

Lionheart

Lionheart ♪♪♪♪

1987, Varese-Sarabande Records; from the movie *Lionheart*, Orion Pictures, 1987.

Album Notes: *Music*: Jerry Goldsmith; *Orchestrations*: Arthur Morton, Alexander Courage; Orchestra conducted by Jerry Goldsmith; *Album Producer*: Jerry Goldsmith; *Engineer*: Bruce Botnick.

Selections: 1 The Ceremony (2:42); 2 Failed Knight (3:18); 3 Robert And Blanche (3:49); 4 Children In Bondage (5:02); 5 The Banner (5:58); 6 The Lake (3:37); 7 Mathilda (5:57); 8 The Wrong Flag (3:16); 9 King Richard (8:34).

Review: See entry below.

Lionheart: Volume 2 ♪♪♪♪

1987, Varese-Sarabande Records; from the movie *Lionheart*, Orion Pictures, 1987.

Album Notes: *Music*: Jerry Goldsmith; *Orchestrations*: Arthur Morton, Alexander Courage; Orchestra conducted by Jerry Goldsmith; *Album Producer*: Jerry Goldsmith; *Engineer*: Bruce Botnick.

Selections: 1 The Castle (1:26); 2 The Circus (3:07); 3 Gates Of Paris (2:09); 4 The Plague (5:33); 5 Final Fight (3:13); 6 The Road From Paris (2:04); 7 The Dress (2:23); 8 Forest Hunt (7:45); 9 Paris Underground (4:09); 10 Bring Him Back (2:39); 11 The Future (5:45).

Review: See entry below.

Lionheart ♪♪♪♪

1987, Varese-Sarabande Records; from the movie *Lionheart*, Orion Pictures, 1987.

Album Notes: *Music*: Jerry Goldsmith; *Orchestrations*: Arthur Morton, Alexander Courage; Orchestra conducted by Jerry Goldsmith; *Album Producer*: Jerry Goldsmith; *Engineer*: Bruce Botnick.

Selections: 1 The Ceremony (2:42); 2 Failed Knight (3:18); 3 The Circus (3:07); 4 Robert And Blanche (3:49); 5 Children In Bondage (5:02); 6 The Road From Paris (2:04); 7 The Lake (3:37); 8 The Banner (5:58); 9 The Castle (1:26); 10 Mathilda (5:57); 11 The Wrong Flag (3:16); 12 The Dress (2:23); 13 Forest Hunt (7:45); 14 Final Fight (3:13); 15 King Richard (8:34).

Review: A film of epic proportions, *Lionheart,* directed by Franklin J. Schaffner, is a big screen retelling of the 12th century Children's Crusade, a dark episode in medieval times which saw youngsters organize an expedition in search of Richard the Lion-hearted, whose adventures, real or imaginary, became the grist for so many swashbucklers set in Sherwood Forest. Richard, who set out to reclaim the Holy Land invaded by the Moors, was subsequently taken prisoner. The screenplay, taking some liberties with historical facts, focuses on a young knight and two circus performers he has befriended, and their efforts to thwart the threat of a malevolent Black Knight whose henchmen have received instructions to round up the children and sell them as slaves.

The most interesting thing about the film, which received theatrical release in Canada only but has been available on video and laserdisc, is the fact that its profuse score was composed by Jerry Goldsmith, whose working relationship with Schaffner had already extended over six previous films.

Goldsmith found in this film an occasion to express himself in an idiom in which he has seldom found a voice. In fact, so extensive was Goldsmith's contribution that the score had to be spread over two albums, with the third volume listed here combining together the most significant highlights from the other two.

With a central three-note motif recurring throughout, and binding the cues together, the score comes across as a cohesive, wonderfully vivid effort with a full contingent of big epic moments, romantic themes, exciting battles and pulse-racing action scenes. It is all neatly wrapped up in a broad, colorful orchestral canvas fleshed out by the subtle use of electronics, dramatically played by the Hungarian State Opera Orchestra. The recording, broad and spacious, enhances all the positive aspects of the score and makes them even more impressive and grander-than-life.

Lionheart 𝄞𝄞𝄞ᵛ

1990, Intrada Records; from the movie *Lionheart*, Universal Pictures, 1990.

Album Notes: *Music:* John Scott; The Munich Symphony Orchestra, conducted by John Scott; *Album Producer:* John Scott; *Engineer:* Keith Grant.

Selections: 1 North Africa: The Burn/North Africa (7:20); 2 The Voyage (3:11); 3 New York Streets (2:53); 4 Meet The Lady (3:55); 5 Joshua And Lyon (1:45); 6 The Wrong Hood (1:31); 7 The Big Orange (:57); 8 Lyon's Grief (2:37); 9 Partners (:47); 10 The Lady's Apartment (3:29); 11 Dating The Lady (3:31); 12 Fighting The Scot (4:14); 13 Helping Hand (1:27); 14 Nicole (2:38); 15 Fighting The Brazilian (3:06); 16 The Foreign Legion (3:14); 17 Attila The Killa (1:04); 18 The Wrong Bet (9:06); 19 Farewell (2:07); 20 Freedom For Lyon (:54); 21 Lionheart (4:12).

Review: For this contemporary adventure film (not to be confused with Schaffner's medieval epic), John Scott develops a series of cues that reflected the various locales in which the action took place — North Africa, Los Angeles, New York City — as well as the character of the story's main protagonist, a kickboxing soldier of fortune named Lyon (Jean-Claude Van Damme), bent on avenging his brother killed by drug dealers. As is often the case in films of this nature, the score is much better than the film itself, with the symphony orchestra giving a distinct and powerful color to the cues. An occasional jazz track, performed by a quintet, provides a different perspective on Scott's creativity, while it also fits the sometimes explosive action scenes in the film.

Little Buddha 𝄞𝄞

1993, Milan Records; from the movie *Little Buddha*, 1993.

Album Notes: *Music:* Ryuichi Sakamoto; *Orchestrations:* David Arch, Kevin Townend, Gil Goldstein; *Music Editor:* Michael Connell; Orchestra conducted by Ryuichi Sakamoto; *Featured Soloists:* The Ambrosian Singers, John McCarthy, dir., Catherine Bott (soprano), L. Subramaniam, Zakir Hussain, Nishat Khan, Shahee Samad, Kanika; *Album Producer:* Ryuichi Sakamoto; *Engineers:* Steve Price; *Assistant Engineers:* Niall Acott, Jamie Cullum, Brian Tibberts.

Selections: 1 Main Theme (2:50); 2 Opening Titles (1:47); 3 The First Meeting (1:50); 4 Raga Kirvani (1:28) *L. Subramaniam*; 5 Nepalese Caravan (3:01); 6 Victory (1:43); 7 Faraway Song (3:17); 8 Red Dust (4:38); 9 River Ashes (2:24); 10 Exodus (2:31); 11 Evan's Funeral (4:28); 12 The Middle Way (1:50); 13 Raga Naiki Kanhra/The Trial (5:24) *Shruti Sadolikar*; 14 Enlightenment (4:28); 15 The Reincarnation (1:51); 16 Gompa-Heart Sutra (2:38); 17 Acceptance — End Credits (8:58).

Review: For this story that combines the tales of a Tibetan monk who believes an American born child is the reincarnation of his mentor and the life of Prince Siddhartha, Ryuichi Sakamoto integrates a standard Hollywood-style film underscore with several Indian motifs. The result is disappointing if you don't enjoy the somewhat abrasive contrast of cultures.
David Hirsch

Little Man Tate 𝄞𝄞𝄞𝄞ᵛ

1991, Varese-Sarabande Records; from the movie *Little Man Tate*, Orion Pictures, 1991.

Album Notes: *Music:* Mark Isham; *Arrangements:* Ken Kugler, Mark Isham; *Featured Musicians:* Bob Sheppard (tenor sax), David Goldblatt (piano), Tom Warrington (bass), Mark Isham (trumpet), Sid Page (violin), Kurt Wortman (drums), Ken Kugler (trombone); *Engineer:* Stephen Krause.

Selections: 1 Little Man Swing (2:13); 2 Little Man Lost (6:37); 3 With And Without Science (2:17); 4 A Walk On The Cool Side (3:12); 5 Fred And Dede (4:32); 6 Shadowplay (2:01); 7 Missing You Too (1:10); 8 Clipper Ships (2:04); 9 White Iris (1:42); 10 Kids And Grownups (2:33); 11 The Combustion Bounce (1:01); 12 Books, Dreams And Shadows (3:05); 13 Home And Not Alone (1:23); 14 The Little Man Swing (reprise)(2:44).

Review: This soundtrack album engagingly begins on a finely sketched swing track that augurs well for the overall feel of the score. The promises held in that first track are confirmed in the others with Mark Isham's upbeat score for this heart-tugging story about a 7-year-old little genius evidencing all the elements that contribute to turn a modest effort into an enjoyable listening experience. The moods set forth are strictly in a jazz mode, something that might deter potential listeners. But when the music is that good and that gratifying, one only has to turn on the volume, relax and savor.

A Little Princess ♫♫♫

1995, Varese-Sarabande Records; from the movie *A Little Princess*, Warner Bros., 1995.

Album Notes: *Music*: Patrick Doyle; *Orchestrations*: Lawrence Ashmore; *Music Editor*: Roy Prendergast; Orchestra conducted by David Snell; *Featured Musicians*: Frank Ricotti, Gary Kettel, William Lockhart, Glyn Mathews, Paul Clarvis, Kuljit Bhamra (percussion), Craig Pruess (sitar/percussion), The New London Children's Choir; *Album Producers*: Patrick Doyle, Maggie Rodford; *Engineer*: Paul Hulme.

Selections: 1 Ramayana: A Morning Raga (2:02); 2 Children Running (:53); 3 Cristina Elisa Waltz (3:02); 4 The Miss Minchin School For Girls (1:38); 5 Knowing You By Heart (2:33); 6 Breakfast (:56); 7 Letter To Papa (1:38); 8 Angel Wings (1:06); 9 False Hope (1:57); 10 The Trenches (Adagio from Quintet in C Major, Op. 88)(M. Haydn)(1:02); 11 Crewe And The Soldier (1:22); 12 Alone (1:20); 13 The Attic (2:00); 14 On Another's Sorrow (1:16); 15 The Shawl (:55); 16 Tyger Tyger (:32); 17 Compassion (:36); 18 For The Princess (1:36); 19 Kindle My Heart (3:00); 20 The Locket Hunt (3:00); 21 Midnight Tiptoe (1:11); 22 I Am A Princess (1:13); 23 Just Make Believe (1:33); 24 Touched By An Angel (1:41); 25 Emilia Elopes (1:36); 26 The Escape (2:59); 27 Papa! (2:29); 28 The Goodbye (4:18).

Review: Recalling in a way some of the incidents in *The Secret Garden*, by the same author, Frances Hodgson Burnett's *A Little Princess* is a touching story about a little girl sent to a strict boarding school during World War I, who is forced to become a maid to the austere headmistress when her father is reported missing in action. Subtly limning this heartwarming tale in its screen transfer, Patrick Doyle contributed a score that oozes charm and loveliness in every track. Following the little heroine from India, where she shares a life of wonder to the boarding school in New York to the fantasyland in which she takes refuge in order to escape the hardships that come her way, the score reflects with imagination the diverse situations that shape the story, providing sounds that recall these different backgrounds and also evoke the various states of mind of the "little Princess" herself. Despite the disparate elements that contribute to its final makeup, it comes across as an inventive, often inspired score, quite exquisite and enjoyable.

A Little Romance ♫♫♫♫

1992, Varese-Sarabande Records; from the movie *A Little Romance*, Orion Pictures, 1979.

Album Notes: *Music*: Georges Delerue; Orchestra conducted by Georges Delerue; *Album Producers*: Tom Null, Robert Townson; *Engineer*: Richard Simpson.

Selections: 1 Main Title (3:10); 2 Love's Not Like That (1:00); 3 Paris Montage (2:32); 4 Julius Edmond Santorin (3:45); 5 The Young Lovers (1:49); 6 Off To Italy (2:15); 7 Birthday Party (2:40); 8 Outdoor Cafe/Moving On (3:10); 9 A Little Romance (1:25); 10 The Bicycle Race (4:30); 11 The Lovers' Decision (1:00); 12 Venice (1:25); 13 Hiding In The Movies (2:21); 14 No Turning Back (1:07); 15 The Gondola (2:00); 16 Farewell... For Now/End Titles (5:29).

Review: Directed by George Roy Hill, *A Little Romance* recounts the adventures of a young French boy and his American girlfriend who decide, at the behest of a mysterious old man whom they follow, to relive the legend of two Venetian youths who swore their love to each other in a gondola. In one of his most spirited efforts, Georges Delerue took a cue from the many lighthearted moods in the story and wrote a score that teems with a multitude of diversified cues, in turn exuberant ("Paris Montage," "The Bicycle Race"), and romantic ("A Little Romance," "The Gondola"), with a little touch of jazz along the way ("Birthday Party"). The whole thing is imaginatively laid out and performed for all its worth. Signature themes, like "The Young Lovers" and "Off to Italy," are also found in abundance in this richly entertaining score, which won a well deserved Academy Award in 1979.

Little Women ♫♫♫♪

1995, Sony Classical; from the movie *Little Women*, Columbia Pictures, 1995.

Album Notes: *Music*: Thomas Newman; *Orchestrations*: Thomas Pasatieri; *Music Editor*: Bill Bernstein; The London Symphony Orchestra, conducted by Thomas Newman; *Album Producers*: Thomas Newman, Bill Bernstein; *Engineer*: Shawn Murphy; *Assistant Engineer*: Jonathan Allen.

Selections: 1 Orchard House (Main Title)(3:29); 2 Meg's Hair (:45); 3 Snowplay (:48); 4 Scarlet Fever (1:10); 5 Ashes (:43); 6 Spring (:57); 7 La Fayette's Welcome (F. Johnson)(1:01); 8 A Telegram (:45); 9 Two Couples (1:32); 10 Burdens (1:57); 11 New York (2:15); 12 Harvest Time (1:25); 13 Maria Redowa (G. Donizetti)(1:22); 14 Letter From Jo (1:17); 15 Amy Abroad (1:04); 16 Limes (:35); 17 Beth's Secret (2:08); 18 For The Beauty Of The Earth (C. Kocher/F. Pierpoint)(:26) *Trini Alvarado, Kirsten Dunst, Claire Danes*; 19 Little Women (1:19); 20 Learning To

"I very definitely tried to pay homage to Ravel and Debussy, who are my favorite French impressionistic composers. I had fun using a certain early 20th-century style and melding that with the tension that has to be used in a thriller."

Randy Edelman
on Diabolique *(The Hollywood Reporter, 1-15-97)*

Forget (2:20); 21 Valley Of The Shadow (2:09); 22 Port Royal Gallop (C. Grafulla)(:55); 23 Domestic Experiences (:51); 24 The Laurence Boy (:37); 25 Lovelornity (1:21); 26 Under The Umbrella (End Title)(3:41).

Review: Based on the classic 1868 novel by Louisa May Alcott about love, family and becoming a woman, this retelling of *Little Women* received its fair share of accolades for its splendid treatment of the romantic dramas and adventures of Mrs. March and her four "little women" — spirited Jo, beautiful Meg, fragile Beth, and romantic Amy. Among the technical elements that contributed to the success of the film was Thomas Newman's score, which masterfully italicizes some of the most striking moments in the narrative, giving them an extra perspective through the illuminating support of his sensitively detailed music. The cues assembled in this soundtrack album give a general idea of the real beauty of the score, but its strengths are somewhat undermined by the fact that many of the cues are much too short, and probably would have gained at being presented in longer suites.

Live a Little, Love a Little

1995, RCA Records; from the movie *Live a Little, Love a Little*, M-G-M, 1968.

See: Elvis Presley in Compilations

Live and Let Die 🎵🎵🎵

1988, EMI Manhattan Records; from the movie *Live and Let Die*, United Artists, 1973.

Album Notes: *Music*: George Martin.

Selections: 1 Live And Let Die (Main Title)(P. & L. Mc-Cartney)(3:10) *Paul McCartney, Wings*; 2 Just A Closer Walk

With Thee (trad.)/New Second Line (M. Batiste)(2:13) *Harold A. "Duke" Dejan & The Olympia Brass Band*; 3 Bond Meets Solitaire (2:15); 4 Whisper Who Dares (1:42); 5 Snakes Alive (2:24); 6 Baron Samedi's Dance Of Death (1:15); 7 San Monique (1:57); 8 Fillet Of Soul/New Orleans/Live And Let Die (P. & L. McCartney)/Fillet Of Soul (3:17) *BJ Arnau*; 9 Bond Drops In (3:28); 10 If He Finds It, Kill Him (1:21); 11 Trespassers Will Be Eaten (2:45); 12 Solitaire Gets Her Cards (1:49); 13 Sacrifice (2:30); 14 James Bond Theme (M. Norman)(1:28).

Review: Listening to the soundtracks to *Live and Let Die* and *The Living Daylights* one after the other, one gets a clearer perspective about the reasons why John Barry's scores for the James Bond pictures work so well where other composers' do not. George Martin's music for *Live and Let Die,* propelled by Paul and Linda McCartney's terrific title tune (the first time a rock number was used in the series), is serviceable at best but not terribly memorable. The tracks actually worked much better behind the action than they do on a purely audio level, with their strongly accented guitar riffs reminiscent of other scores from the same period, notably *Shaft.*

The Living Daylights 🎵🎵🎵

1987, Warner Bros. Records; from the movie *The Living Daylights*, United Artists, 1987.

Album Notes: *Music*: John Barry; *Orchestrations*: John Barry; Orchestra conducted by John Barry; *Album Producer*: John Barry; *Engineer*: Dick Lewzey.

Selections: 1 The Living Daylights (4:14) *a-ha*; 2 Necros Attacks (2:00); 3 The Sniper Was A Woman (2:27); 4 Ice Chase (4:00); 5 Kara Meets Bond (2:43); 6 Koskov Escapes (2:20); 7 Where Has Every Body Gone (3:33) *The Pretenders*; 8 Into Vienna (2:44); 9 Hercules Takes Off (2:12); 10 Mujahadin And Opium (3:09); 11 Inflight Fight (3:08); 12 If There Was A Man (2:44) *The Pretenders.*

Review: Conversely, even though it was Barry's eleventh James Bond score, *The Living Daylights* displays the same inventiveness and fresh approach to its subject matter that had marked the composer's previous efforts. Without repeating himself, but displaying the signature accents that tie together all his contributions to the series, the score is another dazzling effort in which Barry explores the myriad possibilities offered by the action and finds new ways to tread over old grounds. While acknowledging some of the changes that occurred in music since he first began to score these films (the new electronic beat in "Ice Chase," for instance), Barry remains true to the spirit of excitement that permeates the series, and true to himself by reinventing and renovating the themes that singled him out as the composer of choice for the films. The pop selections by a-ha and The Pretenders are also quite effective within the context.

Local Hero ♫♫♫♫

1983, Vertigo Records; from the movie *Local Hero*, 1983.

Album Notes: *Music*: Mark Knopfler; *Featured Musicians*: Mark Knopfler (guitars, synthesizers, percussion), Alan Clark (piano, synthesizers, Hammond organ), Hal Lindes (rhythm guitar), Mike Brecker (saxophone), Mike Mainieri (vibes), Gerry Rafferty (vocals), Neil Jason, Tony Levin, John Illsley, Eddie Gomez (bass), Steve Jordan, Terry Williams (drums); *Album Producer*: Mark Knopfler; *Engineer*: Neil Dorfsman.

Selections: 1 The Rocks And The Water (3:30); 2 Wild Theme (3:40); 3 Freeway Flyer (1:50); 4 Boomtown (Louis' Favourite) (4:10); 5 The Way It Always Starts (4:08); 6 The Rocks And The Thunder (:40); 7 The Ceilidh And The Northern Lights (4:07); 8 The Mist-Covered Mountains (5:13); 9 The Ceilidh: Louis' Favourite/Billy's Tune (3:42); 10 Whistle Theme (:53); 11 Smooching (5:05); 12 Stargazer (1:31); 13 The Rocks And The Thunder (:40); 14 Going Home: Theme Of The Local Hero (5:01).

Review: A quirky collection of tunes masterfully captures the odd nature of a tiny seaside Scottish village in this film that was the acknowledged inspiration for the *Northern Exposure* TV series. An early film score for Dire Straits guitarist Mark Knopfler, it is filled with wonderful moments, particularly the infectious "Theme of the Local Hero." But the oddly sequenced album, with several tracks split into three suites, was most likely done to combine all the music related to the town party, though the opening suite seems a bit disjointed. Sounds of waves crashing against the shore are incorporated into several tracks. It adds a melancholy touch, but also serves to represent how utterly isolated the village is from the rest of the world.

David Hirsch

Logan's Run ♫♫♫♫▷

1990, Bay Cities; from the movie *Logan's Run*, M-G-M, 1976.

Album Notes: *Music*: Jerry Goldsmith; *Orchestrations*: Arthur Morton; Orchestra conducted by Jerry Goldsmith; *Album Producer*: Harry V. Lojewski; *Engineer*: Aaron Rochin; *CD Producer*: Nick Redman.

Selections: 1 The Dome (2:08); 2 On The Circuit (3:45); 3 The Sun (2:11); 4 Flameout (3:26); 5 The Monument (8:13); 6 You're Renewed (2:50); 7 Ice Sculpture (3:36); 8 Love Shop (3:45); 9

The Truth (2:08); 10 Intensive Care (4:00); 11 End Of The City (2:25); 12 Love Theme From "Logan's Run" (2:27).

Review: Jerry Goldsmith produced a seminal science fiction effort for Michael Anderson's watered-down adaptation of the pop sci-fi novel about a future society where no one is allowed to live past the age of 30. Opening with a pulsating electronic figure that symbolized the omnipresent threat of "Lastday" termination, Goldsmith wrote a richly evocative harmonic brass piece for the movie's futuristic, domed city, while the rest of the score features some of Goldsmith's most supercharged and idiosyncratic action music, kind of a mix of Bartok and Leonard Bernstein for the film's numerous fights and chases. "The Sun" is an incredibly vivid, melodically brilliant characterization of the protagonist's first sight of the outside world after escaping from the dome, while "The Monument" mixes aspects of Stravinsky and Copland in an unforgettably atmospheric sketch of both the mystery and beauty of nature, as well as the haunted echoes of patriotism that hang over the ruined city of Washington, D.C. Somewhat less effective are some purely electronic passages inside the city that date what is otherwise a timeless, vivid work that's among Goldsmith's finest scores.

Jeff Bond

Lone Wolf McQuade ♫♫♫♫

1983, Varese-Sarabande Records; from the movie *Lone Wolf McQuade*, Orion Pictures, 1983.

Album Notes: *Music*: Francesco de Masi; *Orchestrations*: Francesco de Masi; Orchestra conducted by Francesco de Masi; *Featured Soloist*: Alessandro Alessandroni (whistler).

Selections: 1 Main Title (2:42); 2 Observation Of Jefe (4:32); 3 Jefe Loses Teeth (3:25); 4 Cuban Connection (1:46); 5 Nice Wolf (:26); 6 Guns And Super Chargers (2:32); 7 Lola's Theme (2:47); 8 Party Brawl (:43); 9 Highway Hijack (2:20); 10 Sally Bedside (:32); 11 Snow's Place (:48); 12 A Meeting With Snow (3:02); 13 Lola And McQuade (1:28); 14 The Deadly Hand (1:01); 15 It's OK, Kid (1:27); 16 Lola Comforts McQuade (4:27); 17 I'm Going To Miss You, Honey (:36); 18 Rawley's Arsenal (3:05); 19 McQuade's Short Burial (5:27); 20 Mountain Climbing (1:15); 21 Quiet Arrival At Fort (1:05); 22 The Big Fight (3:30); 23 The Final Conflict (4:37); 24 Lone Wolf End Credits (3:27).

Review: A superior action adventure score by Francesco de Masi, *Lone Wolf McQuade* harkens back to the days when Italian westerns were at the peak of their popularity, with scores that were at once representative of the screen action and had a life of their own when removed from it. Though solidly anchored in today's world, but obviously inspired by the westerns of Sergio Leone, *Lone Wolf McQuade* stars Chuck Norris as a kickboxing Texas Ranger, engaging in a fight to the death with some arms smugglers on the wrong side of the law. To give this 1983 modern western the proper feel, de Masi revisited the type of music he and others, like Ennio Morricone, had pioneered in the early days of the spaghetti westerns, complete with a mournful harmonica wailing in the distance, solid steel guitar riffs, and lonely whistling to add an extra forlorn feel to the proceedings. It may sound like a throwback to the days of yore, but it is still quite effective and it makes its point, with the only concession to the modern setting of the story being the use of some electronic instruments in the mix. This profuse score, with many exciting cues to detail the rough screen action, is totally enjoyable.

The Long Riders ♫♫♫♫

1980, Warner Bros. Records; from the movie *The Long Riders*, United Artists, 1980.

Album Notes: *Music*: Ry Cooder; *Featured Musicians*: Curt Bouterese (dulcimer), Jim Dickinson (harmonium/piano), Billy Bryson (bass), David Lindley (banjo/mandolin/fiddle/electric guitar), Tom Sauber (banjo/guitar), Milt Holland, Baboo Pierre (percussion), Jim Keltner (drums), Ry Cooder, Mitch Greenhill (guitar); *Album Producer*: Ry Cooder; *Engineer*: Les Herschberg.

Selections: 1 The Long Riders (3:13); 2 I'm A Good Old Rebel (2:18) *Mitch Greenhill*; 3 Seneca Square Dance (1:58); 4 Archie's Funeral (Hold To God's Unchanging Hand)(2:40); 5 I Always Knew That You Were The One (3:04); 6 Rally 'Round The Flag (4:20) *Pico Payne, Joe Chambers, Lester Chambers, Ry Cooder*; 7 Wildwood Boys (4:10) *Jim Keach*; 8 Better Things To Think About (1:24); 9 Jesse James (2:33); 10 Cole Younger Polka (2:22); 11 Escape From Northfield (1:14); 12 Leaving Missouri (:57); 13 Jesse James (5:04).

Review: An inventive retelling of the notorious James gang's ride to fame, *The Lone Riders* is special in many ways, not the least being the casting of real-life brothers David and Keith Carradine and Stacy and James Keach to portray the screen outlaws and their gang. Another is the use of Ry Cooder's flavorful score to enhance the screen action and give it its period flavor. Cooder, an exponent of early American music, brought together several musicians with similar likings (notably David Lindley, a frequent collaborator), and provided them with themes ("Seneca Square Dance," "I Always Knew That You Were the One," "Cole Younger Polka") that strongly evoke the frontier at the turn of the century. The screen action itself

suggests other tunes that also make a striking comment ("Escape From Northfield," "Jesse James") for what amounts to a most engaging soundtrack album.

The Long Walk Home ♫♫♫▷

1991, Varese-Sarabande Records; from the movie *The Long Walk Home*, Miramax Films, 1991.

Album Notes: *Music*: George Fenton; *Orchestrations*: George Fenton, Simon Chamberlain; *Music Editor*: Chuck Martin; Orchestra conducted by George Fenton; *Featured Musicians*: Gary Foster (alto sax), Michael Lang (piano), Michael Melvoin (Hammond organ), Tim May (guitar), Neil Stubenhaus (bass guitar), Gary Coleman, Bob Zimmitti (percussion); The Long Walk Home Gospel Choir, conducted by Dr. Clifford Bibb; *Album Producer*: George Fenton; *Engineer*: John Richards.

Selections: 1 Jordan River (trad.)(2:57) *The Long Walk Home Gospel Choir*; 2 The Long Walk Home Main Title (2:35); 3 The First Empty Bus (3:00); 4 Leaning On The Everlasting Arms (trad.)(1:15) *The Long Walk Home Gospel Choir*; 5 Mary Catherine And Odessa's Theme (2:58); 6 Selma Breaks The Boycott (4:36); 7 No Not One (trad.)(3:13) *The Long Walk Home Gospel Choir*; 8 Don't Pass Montgomery By (2:50); 9 Happy To Walk (1:46); 10 Do Not Pass Me By (trad.)(2:42) *The Long Walk Home Gospel Choir*; 11 A Deeper Divide (2:52); 12 Norman Joins The Citizens' Council (3:02); 13 The Carpool (1:18); 14 I Stretch My Hands To Thee (Pugh)/The Posey Parking Lot (7:25) *The Long Walk Home Gospel Choir*; 15 I'm Going Through (trad.)(2:22) *Dorothy Love Coates*; 16 The Long Walk Home End Credits (Marching To Zion)(trad.)(4:38) *The Long Walk Home Gospel Choir*.

Review: The 1955 setting of this drama about two Southern families, one white, one black, caught in the social turmoil of the civil rights movement resulted in a profoundly affecting score from composer George Fenton. With several gospel songs adding a definite flavor to the soundtrack, Fenton wrote a series of cues in which the sparse instrumentation helps to create a specific aura. Echoing the moods in the film, which avoid the maudlin sentimentality the subject might have suggested, the composer settles for a no-nonsense approach, all the more effective because it is controlled and straightforward.

Looking for Richard ♫♫♫♫

1996, Angel Records; from the movie *Looking for Richard*, 20th Century-Fox, 1996.

Album Notes: *Music*: Howard Shore; *Orchestrations*: Jeff Atmajian; *Music Editor*: Suzana Peric; *Latin Text*: Elizabeth

Cotnoir; The London Philharmonic Orchestra and The London Voices, conducted by Howard Shore; *Album Producer*: Howard Shore; *Engineer*: John Kurlander.

Selections: 1 Richard, Duke Of York (4:09); 2 Queen Margaret (3:13); 3 Lady Anne Neville (10:29); 4 George, Duke Of Clarence (11:42); 5 William, Lord Hastings (5:22); 6 Ghosts (4:05); 7 Henry, Earl Of Richmond (6:02).

Review: Al Pacino's revisionist "Richard III," a combination of lectures about the play and performances of some of the most important scenes in full costume regalia, is an offbeat, unusual way to approach one of the Bard's most powerful dramas. Adding support and great vitality to the project is the score Pacino commissioned from composer Howard Shore. Freed from the usual constraints of action-related cues, the composer created a medieval-sounding music that seems totally appropriate for the somber aspects in Shakespeare's play, while adding to it a more modern sound for the documentary scenes in the film. The result is a music that is at once reminiscent of the dual screen action and particularly suggestive when appreciated on its own terms.

The Lord of the Rings 🎵🎵🎵🎵

1991, Intrada Records; from the animated feature *The Lord of the Rings*, Fantasy Films, 1978.

Album Notes: *Music*: Leonard Rosenman; *Orchestrations*: Ralph Ferraro; *Music Editor*: Jim Henrikson; Orchestra conducted by Leonard Rosenman; *Engineer*: Grover Helsley.

Selections: 1 History Of The Ring (6:31); 2 Gandalf Throws Ring (3:55); 3 The Journey Begins: Encounter With The Ringwraiths (4:28); 4 Trying To Kill Hobbits (3:03); 5 Escape To Rivendell (6:22); 6 Company Of The Ring (1:39); 7 Mines Of Moria (6:10); 8 The Battle In The Mines/The Balrog (5:08); 9 Mithrandir (3:17); 10 Frodo Disappears (2:38); 11 Following The Orcs (3:16); 12 Fleeing Orcs (2:31); 13 Attack Of The Orcs (4:04); 14 Gandalf Remembers (2:19); 15 Riders Of Rohan (3:43); 16 Helm's Deep (7:02); 17 The Dawn Battle: Theoden's Victory (5:34); 18 The Voyage To Mordor: Theme From The Lord Of The Rings (4:43).

Review: This opulent orchestral score for an animated feature by Ralph Bakshi, based on J.R.R. Tolkien's fantasy novels "The Fellowship of the Ring" and "The Two Towers," gave composer Leonard Rosenman a rare opportunity to prepare a work that blended many varied elements, "violence, eerie marches, chases, and wild battle scenes." Combining together traditional triadic harmonies with dissonant and serial lines, he created for the early scenes an almost surrealistic mood, representative of

the other-worldly nature of the film's story. He contrasted them, as the script suggested, with lyrical passages that set them off and gave them added power. As a result, his score magnificently underlines the specific dark moods in the narrative, and illuminates the story's lighter aspects, making his contribution a superb complement to Bakshi's designs. It is little wonder then that his score, released on LP by Fantasy but not available after that for many years, should have become a prized collector's item. Its reissue on compact disc, with enhanced sonics that properly detail its many assets, again emphasizes its importance in the film music canon. Clearly, it is not a score that will attract everybody—the ominous tones in some of the tracks like "Escape to Rivendell" may deter some listeners to pursue any further. Those who do, however, will be amply rewarded by the riches the score contains and will find further exhilaration in the final pages, with rousing moments coming out of "Helm's Deep" and "Lord of the Rings."

The Lost Boys 🎵🎵🎵

1987, Atlantic Records; from the movie *The Lost Boys*, Warner Bros., 1987.

Album Notes: *Song Producers*: Mark Opitz, Pat Moran, Lou Gramm, Beau Hill, Ray Manzarek, Michael Mainieri, B.A. Robertson, Richie Zito, Hugh Padgham; *Album Producer*: Joel Schumacher; *Engineer*: Dennis King.

Selections: 1 Good Times (G. Young/H. Vanda)(3:49) *INXS, Jimmy Barnes*; 2 Lost In The Shadows (The Lost Boys)(P. Moran/L. Gramm)(6:17) *Lou Gramm*; 3 Don't Let The Sun Go Down On Me (E. John/B. Taupin)(6:09) *Roger Daltrey*; 4 Laying Down The Law (M. Hutchence/A. Farris/J. Farris/K. Pengilly/G. Beers/J. Barnes)(4:24) *INXS, Jimmy Barnes*; 5 People Are Strange (The Doors)(3:36) *Echo & The Bunnymen*; 6 Cry Little Sister (Theme From The Lost Boys)(G. McMann/ M. Mainieri)(4:03) *Gerard McMann*; 7 Power Play (B. Robertson/P. Pickett) (3:57) *Eddie & The Tide*; 8 I Still Believe (M. Been/J. Goodwin)(3:42) *Tim Cappello*; 9 Beauty Has Her Way (D. Banks/P. Brook)(3:56) *Mummy Calls*; 10 To The Shock Of Miss Louise (T. Newman)(1:21) *Thomas Newman*.

Review: This pop compilation, put together for a modern-day vampire film set in a West coast community, is actually better than most if only because it features performances by rock groups that are interesting: INXS, Roger Daltrey, Lou Gramm, and Echo & The Bunnymen among them. The recording will appeal primarily to fans of the respective individuals and groups represented, but they will find many rewards in the songs performed. Thomas Newman, incidentally, scored the film, and is represented here by one track with a relatively modest playing time that can hardly do justice to his contribution.

Lost Highway 🎵🎵

1996, Interscope Records; from the movie *Lost Highway*, October Films, 1996.

Album Notes: *Music*: Angelo Badalamenti; The City Of Prague Philharmonic, conducted by Angelo Badalamenti; *Featured Musicians*: Bob Sheppard (saxophone), Ernest Hamilton (bass), Ralph Penland (drums), Ronald Brown, Henry Kranen (baritone sax); *Album Producer*: Trent Reznor; *Album Engineers*: Charlie Clouser, Trent Reznor.

Selections: 1 I'm Deranged (D. Bowie/B. Eno)(2:38) *David Bowie*; 2 Videodrones, Questions (T. Reznor/P. Christopherson)(:44) *Trent Reznor*; 3 The Perfect Drug (Nine Inch Nails)(5:16) *Nine Inch Nails*; 4 Red Bats With Teeth (2:57); 5 Haunting And Heartbreaking (2:09); 6 Eye (B. Corgan)(4:51) *The Smashing Pumpkins*; 7 Dub Driving (3:43); 8 Mr. Eddy's Theme 1 (B. Adamson) (3:32) *Barry Adamson*; 9 This Magic Moment (D. Pomus/M. Shuman)(3:23) *Lou Reed*; 10 Mr. Eddy's Theme 2 (B. Adamson)(2:14) *Barry Adamson*; 11 Fred And Renee Make Love (2:05); 12 Apple Of Sodom (M. Manson)(4:27)*Marilyn Manson*; 13 Insensatez (A.C. Jobim/V. De Moraes)(2:53) *Antonio Carlos Jobim*; 14 Something Wicked This Way Comes (B. Adamson)(2:55) *Barry Adamson*; 15 I Put A Spell On You (J. Hawkins)(3:31) *Marilyn Manson*; 16 Fats Revisited (2:32); 17 Fred's World (3:01); 18 Rammstein (Kruspe/Lindermann/Lenders/Lorenz/Schneider/ Riedel)(3:26) *Rammstein*; 19 Hollywood Sunset (B. Adamson)(2:01) *Barry Adamson*; 20 Hierate Mich (Kruspe/Lindermann/Lenders/Lorenz/Schneider/Riedel) (3:03) *Rammstein*; 21 Police (1:40); 22 Driver Down (T. Reznor)(5:18) *Trent Reznor*; 23 I'm Deranged (reprise)(D. Bowie/B. Eno)(3:48) *David Bowie*.

Review: David Bowie's strange, erratic "I'm Deranged" bookends this uneven score, in which hard-rock performers (Nine Inch Nails, The Smashing Pumpkins, Lou Reed) vie for the listener's attention with Antonio Carlos Jobim's "Insensatez," or Angelo Badalamenti's weird-sounding and not-too-terribly-engaging instrumental cues, and Barry Adamson's evocations of Henry Mancini's "Peter Gunn." It's too much of a hodgepodge without focus to really satisfy anyone. Perhaps the David Lynch film justified this type of music combination, but programmed on an album it makes very little sense.

Lost in Yonkers 🎵🎵🎵▷

1993, Varese-Sarabande; from the movie *Lost in Yonkers*, Columbia Pictures, 1993

Album Notes: *Music*: Elmer Bernstein; *Orchestrations*: Emilie A. Bernstein; Orchestra conducted by Elmer Bernstein; *Album Producer*: Emilie A. Bernstein.

Selections: 1 Beginnings (3:19); 2 The Candy Store (1:25); 3 Street Walk (1:18); 4 Meeting Grandma (1:20); 5 Train (1:36); 6 Harry (2:00); 7 The Boys (3:04); 8 Campfire (1:07); 9 Bad Day (2:05); 10 Bella Speaks (2:53); 11 Communications (4:16); 12 Leaving Yonkers (1:43); 13 Endings (5:57).

Review: Like the films of Woody Allen, the plays of Neil Simon have an aura that places them squarely within a definite time and place. Because of that, scoring any of them proves a challenge to any composer, and a strong reward as the moods explored have to reflect the specificity of their locale. While perhaps not exactly "right," the score Elmer Bernstein created for *Lost in Yonkers* successfully evokes the 1920s-1930s feel of the film based on the play, about two boys sent to live with their grandmother when their father goes away on business, and suggests images that capture the moods of the period. Some of the cues devised by the composer are actually quite delightful ("The Candy Store," "Leaving Yonkers"), but others may seem a little too dark for what is essentially a light romantic comedy. Though he may be amiss, Bernstein remains intelligently challenging, however, and his cues are still quite enjoyable where music is concerned.

The Lost World 🎵🎵🎵🎵

1997, MCA Records; from the movie *The Lost World*, Universal Pictures, 1997.

Album Notes: *Music*: John Williams; *Orchestrations*: Kenn Wannberg; Orchestra conducted by John Williams; *Album Producer*: John Williams; *Engineer*: Shawn Murphy.

Selections: 1 The Lost World (3:34); 2 The Island Prologue (5:03); 3 Malcolm's Journey (5:44); 4 The Hunt (3:30); 5 The Trek (5:24); 6 Finding Camp Jurassic (3:03); 7 Rescuing Sarah (4:01); 8 Hammond's Plan (4:31); 9 The Raptors Appear (3:43); 10 The Compys Dine (5:07); 11 The Stegosaurus (5:20); 12 Ludlow's Demise (4:27); 13 Visitor In San Diego (7:38); 14 Finale and Jurassic Park Theme (7:54).

Review: Guaranteed to keep you on the edge of your seat, or at least intensely rapt, the score John Williams wrote for this second installment in the Jurassic Park saga teems with exciting new themes and motifs, broadly announced by thundering thumping in "The Lost World." The first selections serve as a preamble to the action that will materialize later on, with the various cues detailing plans for a visit to Site B, another part of Jurassic Park, also inhabited by giant predators, who soon turn the intruders into their prey. With an abundance of drums and percussion instruments (maracas and the like) punctuating the appearance of the Raptors, and weird, shrieking noises supposed to imitate their cries, the feast starts off with great orchestral sounds that seldom lessen after that. With skill, Williams creates ominous moods, interrupted by pulsing flashes, somewhat reminiscent of the famous theme he devised for "Jaws," but dealing here with animals that are even bigger, more ferocious, and thankfully extinct. The score's moments of bravura, "Visitor in San Diego" and the long "Finale," are alone worth the price of admission, and are terrific in every sense of the word.

Love Affair ♫♫♫♪

1994, Reprise Records; from the movie *Love Affair*, Warner Bros., 1994.

Album Notes: *Music:* Ennio Morricone; *Orchestrations:* Ennio Morricone; The Unione musicisti di Roma, conducted by Ennio Morricone; *Featured Soloists:* Gilda Butti (piano), Vincenzina Capona (harp), Paolo Zampini (flute), Stefano Novelli (clarinet), Luciano Giuliani (horn); *Featured Vocalist:* Edda Dell'Orso; *Album Producer:* Ennio Morricone; *Engineer:* Franco Patrignani.

Selections: 1 Never Let Your Left Hand Know What Your Right Hand's Doin' (T. Delaney)(2:40) *Louis Jordan*; 2 Changes (W. Donaldson)(3:06) *Bobby Short*; 3 Life Is So Peculiar (J. Burke/J. Van Heusen)(3:23) *Louis Jordan, Louis Armstrong*; 4 The Christmas Song (Chestnuts Roasting On An Open Fire)(M. Torme/R. Wells)(4:32) *Ray Charles*; 5 For Annette And Warren (3:03); 6 A Promise In The Air (4:53); 7 Waiting For That Day (1:54); 8 Anxiety And Joy (2:41); 9 Piano Solo (2:14); 10 Sentimental Walk (2:27); 11 Journey Of Love (1:47); 12 Return (1:48); 13 Finding Each Other Again (5:10); 14 Love Affair (End Credit)(4:13).

Review: Louis Jordan's whimsical "Never Let Your Left Hand Know What Your Right Hand's Doin'" is a great opener for this soundtrack album, but it would have been largely sufficient to set the necessary moods before moving on to the Morricone selections. Instead, we are treated to Bobby Short's rendition of "Changes," Jordan and Louis Armstrong's duet in "Life is So Peculiar," and (why not!) Ray Charles singing "The Christmas Song." Someone with little A&R imagination put those together and figured out it would be alright. The point is, when you have a composer of Morricone's caliber, you don't treat his music like second-rate stuff.

Fortunately, the score, true to the composer's usual impeccable standards, easily overcomes this shabby treatment and makes itself heard powerfully. The film starring Warren Beatty as a fading sports figure and Annette Bening as a performer who find themselves stranded on an island and discover they're made for each other, despite their engagement to others, inspired Morricone to write some low-key themes that perfectly match the moods of this weepy tearjerker. Beautifully sketched, with lush romantic touches sparkling throughout, it is a gorgeous and supremely eloquent score, evidencing many Morricone characteristics, like a three-note motif repeated on the piano behind elongated orchestral lines. As its title suggests, "Piano Solo" is a track that is superb in its simplicity, with a singer humming the theme played by the piano. "Sentimental Walk" is another selection for piano and orchestra that's really beautiful and the lovely "For Annette and Warren" catches the overall moods in this score in a single tune that's exquisitely detailed.

Love at Large ♫♫♫♪

1990, Virgin Records; from the movie *Love at Large*, Orion Pictures, 1990.

Album Notes: *Music:* Mark Isham; *Featured Musicians:* Mark Isham (saxophone/electronics/trumpet), Peter Maunu, David Torn (guitar), Dorothy Remsen (harp), Kurt Wortman (drums); *Album Producer:* Mark Isham; *Engineer:* Steve Krause.

Selections: 1 Let's Begin (:43); 2 Ain't No Cure For Love (L. Cohen)(4:48) *Leonard Cohen, Anjani*; 3 The Principal Piece In A Game Of Chess (1:46); 4 Looking For A Sign (2:40); 5 You Don't Know What Love Is (G. DePaul/D. Raye)(2:28) *Anne Archer*; 6 Variation On A Popular Theme (#3) For Solo Harp (2:51); 7 But We Never Talk (1:58); 8 Don't Cry For Me (G. & G. Walker)(2:34) *Grady Walker*; 9 What If I Said I Loved You (2:36); 10 Here Comes Rick! (1:20); 11 Love At Large (2:16); 12 You Don't Know What Love Is (G. DePaul/D. Raye)(1:52) *Warren Zevon*; 13 And Love Is My Value (1:14); 14 Variation On A Popular Theme (#87) For Solo Guitar(3:59); 15 Out On A Limb (Where The Fruit Is)(1:26); 16 Moves On A Board (2:17); 17 Searching For A Heart (W. Zevon)(4:09) *Warren Zevon*.

Review: A humorous sendup of the detective films of the 1940s, *Love at Large* slyly makes fun of the Raymond Chandler thrillers, while adding some tongue-in-cheek comments of its own about the whole genre. Taking a hint from the story, about a gumshoe hired by a beautiful blonde to find her missing lover and the wrong trail he follows that leads to a totally different case with amusing complications, Mark Isham developed several cues that are pleasantly catchy and amusingly entertaining. Warren Zevon and Anne Archer have fun with the standard "You Don't Know What Love Is," while Leonard Cohen gleefully adds his two cents with "Ain't No Cure for Love," a real delight.

Love Field 🎵🎵🎵

1993, Varese-Sarabande Records; from the movie *Love Field*, Orion Pictures, 1993.

Album Notes: *Music*: Jerry Goldsmith; *Orchestrations*: Alexander Courage; *Music Editor*: Ken Hall; Orchestra conducted by Jerry Goldsmith; *Album Producer*: Jerry Goldsmith; *Engineer*: Bruce Bostnick.

Selections: 1 Family Album (1:48); 2 The Posters (1:37); 3 The Assassination (2:25); 4 Lost Luggage (3:22); 5 Roadside Incident (2:43); 6 Pretending (2:06); 7 We're Not Alone (2:31); 8 The Motel (6:23); 9 Together Again (5:36).

Review: Jerry Goldsmith's score to this all-but-forgotten Michelle Pfeiffer period vehicle benefits from a blues influence that gives what might otherwise be an entirely bland romantic drama score a needed stylistic edge. Like his *Not Without My Daughter* music, *Love Field* suffers from a simple melody of flute, piano and strings that's just too ordinary. But an early cue, "The Posters" is a welcome return to the kind of busy, bucolic writing Goldsmith excelled in during the '60s in scores like *A Patch of Blue*. There's an anguished string elegy for the death of President Kennedy, and a tough, throbbing chase climax that comes out of nowhere but does illustrate why Goldsmith has long been sought out for this kind of music. It all resolves itself in a beautiful finale reminiscent of *The Secret of NIMH*. This still reflects a weak period for Goldsmith, but it's an enjoyable listen.

Jeff Bond

Love Jones 🎵🎵🎵ᵛ

1997, Columbia Records; from the movie *Love Jones*, New Line Cinema, 1997.

Album Notes: *Song Producers*: Randy Jackson, Dionne Farris, Van Hunt, Lauryn Hill & Wyclef, Darryl Pearson, Musze, Brice P. Wilson, Jermaine Dupri, Samuel J. Sapp, Cassandra Wilson, Marcus Miller, The Brand New Heavies, Cassie, Kenny Lattimore, Bob Thiele; *Soundtrack Executive Producers*: Theodore Witcher, Nick Wechsler.

Selections: 1 Brother To The Night (A Blues For Nina) (R. Gibson) (3:18) *Larenz Tate*; 2 Hopeless (V. Hunt/D. Farris) (3:53) *Dionne Farris*; 3 The Sweetest Thing (L. Hill) (4:49) *Refugee Camp All-Stars, Lauryn Hill*; 4 I Got A Love Jones For You (3:38) (M. Sedeck/D. Pearson/Pras/Wyclef/R. Murph/C. Johnson/R. Eskridge) (3:38) *Melky And Day*; 5 Sumthin' Sumthin' (Musze/Ware) (4:12) *Maxwell*; 6 Never Enough (A. Larrieux/B. Wilson) (4:24) *Groove Theory*; 7 Inside My Love (M. Ripperton/L. Ware/R. Rudolph) (4:13) *Trina Broussard*; 8 In The Rain (T. Hester) (5:14) *Xscape*; 9 You Move Me (C. Wilson)

(4:17) *Cassandra Wilson*; 10 Rush Over (M. Miller/M. NdegeOcello) (5:19) *Marcus Miller, Me' Shell NdegeOcello*; 11 I Like It (S. Bartholomew/S. Garrett/ J. Kincaid/A. Levy) (3:34) *The Brand New Heavies*; 12 Girl (Cassie) (3:56) *Cassie*; 13 Can't Get Enough (C. Haggins/K. Lattimore/K. Lerum) (3:59) *Kenny Lattimore*; 14 Jelly, Jelly (E. Hines/B. Eckstine) (5:46) *The Lincoln Center Jazz Orchestra*; 15 In A Sentimental Mood (E.K. Ellington) (4:14) *Duke Ellington, John Coltrane*; 16 I Am Looking At Music (P.G. Lane) (2:29) *Nia Long*.

Review: A breezy, sexy romantic comedy set among the overeducated and underemployed in downtown Chicago, *Love Jones* deftly captured the rhythms of modern courtship, while asking the age-old question—is love forever? Reflecting the smart urban sounds heard among today's better educated youths, this soundtrack album compilation places the spotlight on various frontline performers, including Dionne Farris, Maxwell, Xscape, Cassandra Wilson, Kenny Lattimore, and Me'Shell NdegeOcello. A slightly more sophisticated touch is provided by the addition of "Jelly, Jelly," performed by the Lincoln Center Jazz Orchestra, an organization presided over by Wynton Marsalis, and of "In a Sentimental Mood," featuring John Coltrane and Duke Ellington. The film's two stars, Larenz Tate and Nia Long, also appear framing the album, Tate with a reading of the poem his character, Darius, has written in celebration of Long's character, Nina; and Long in another piece, written about Tate, with both being read in front of the audience at the Sanctuary, the night spot where the two initially met and fell in love.

Loving You

1988, RCA Records; from the movie *Loving You*, Paramount Pictures, 1957.

See: Elvis Presley in Compilations

Lust for Life 🎵🎵🎵🎵

1993, Varese-Sarabande; from the movie *Lust for Life*, 1956.

Album Notes: *Music*: Miklos Rozsa; The Frankenland State Symphony Orchestra conducted by Miklos Rozsa; *Album Producers*: Robert Townson, Dub Taylor.

Selections: *LUST FOR LIFE SUITE:* 1 Prelude (3:06); 2 Summer (Pastorale) (4:18); 3 Brotherly Love (3:03); 4 Sunflowers (4:57); 5 Postman Roulin (1:40); 6 Madness (2:30); 7 Finale (2:32);

BACKGROUND TO VIOLENCE SUITE: 8 Prelude To Murder (from *Brute Force*)(4:49); 9 Nocturno (from *Brute Force*)(5:12); 10 Scherzo (from *Brute Force*)(2:07); 11 Despair (from *The Killers*)(3:16); 12

Pursuit (from *The Naked City*)(2:28); 13 Epilogue: The Song Of A City (from *The Naked City*)(3:10).

Review: The story of Vincent Van Gogh (portrayed by Kirk Douglas), *Lust for Life* is a big Hollywood biography that elicits a splendid score from Miklos Rozsa, taking a break from the swashbucklers and Roman epics he had scored recently. The music, robust and lyrical, is strikingly evocative and colorful, as befits a film about a painter. The manic sonorities in "Madness" further enhance the composer's naturalistic approach to this subject.

Consisting of selections from Rozsa's score for *The Killers* (1946), *Brute Force* (1947), and *Naked City* (1948), all three realistic urban dramas and prime examples of films noir, the "Background to Violence Suite" presents another facet of Rozsa's talent, one that has often been celebrated and admired. In stark melodic themes that contrast with the more florid style he used in the period dramas and adventure films he scored, Rozsa detailed with admirable sensitivity the darker aspects of life in the big cities, and the violence that often resulted from the confined environment in which people live. Using pulsating rhythms, brutal brass chords, dramatic accents that all reflect the contained violence in these films, Rozsa conceived powerful scores which reflect the screen action as much as they expand on it. This suite presents an overview of his concepts in a searing, dramatic display of his writing at its most eloquent.

M Butterfly ♫♫♫♪

1993, Varese-Sarabande; from the movie *M Butterfly*, Geffen Pictures, 1993.

Album Notes: *Music*: Howard Shore; *Orchestrations*: Howard Shore; *Music Editor*: Suzana Peric; The London Philharmonic Orchestra, conducted by Howard Shore; *Album Producers*: Howard Shore, Suzana Peric; *Engineer*: John Kurlander.

Selections: 1 M Butterfly (2:03); 2 Concubine (4:10); 3 Entrance Of Butterfly (G. Puccini)/Drunken Beauty (3:03) *Michelle Couture, John Lone*; 4 Dragonfly (3:18); 5 The Great Wall (1:49); 6 Even The Softest Skin (4:39); 7 Sha Jia Bang (trad.)(2:10); 8 Bonfire Of The Vanities/Cultural Revolution (3:27); 9 He Was The Perfect Father (:54); 10 Are You My Butterfly? (2:19); 11 The Only Time I Ever Really Existed (4:08); 12 What I Loved Was The Lie (1:04); 13 Everything Has Been Destroyed (1:45); 14 Un bel di (G. Puccini) (4:15) *Maria Tereza Uribe*; 15 My Name Is Rene Gallimard (3:35).

Review: The somewhat incredible true story of a French diplomat in China and the long-lasting love affair he enjoyed with a diva from the Beijing opera, unaware of the fact that she was in fact a man, *M Butterfly* found in Howard Shore a composer whose talent and creative sensitivity compelled him to write a score which overflows with striking romantic themes, played by the harp and backed by an ensemble of strings and wind instruments. Adding a different color, arias from some well-known operas and traditional Chinese songs provide the background for a tale that straddles different worlds and different cultures, in an album that is frequently challenging and musically surprising.

MacArthur ♫♫♪

1990, Varese-Sarabande; from the movie *MacArthur*, Universal Pictures, 1977.

Album Notes: *Music*: Jerry Goldsmith; *Orchestrations*: Arthur Morton; Orchestra conducted by Jerry Goldsmith; *Album Producer*: Sonny Burke; *Engineer*: John Neal; *CD Producers*: Robert Townson, Tom Null.

Selections: 1 MacArthur March (Main Title)(2:48); 2 I Shall Return (3:57); 3 The Treaty (2:34); 4 The Tunnel (2:35); 5 Statistics (3:03); 6 Stand By (2:04); 7 A Last Gift (2:22); 8 New Era (3:25); 9 The Landing (3:40); 10 The Minefield (2:30); 11 I Bid You Farewell/MacArthur March (4:20).

Review: Jerry Goldsmith's second military biography after *Patton* suffers from comparisons to his earlier, classic work for director Franklin Schaffner. The opening theme makes some interesting use of low-end pedal piano notes as a rhythmic device, but Goldsmith's brassy, strident theme for MacArthur sounds too much like a standard John Philips Sousa march to make for pleasant listening. There is one exciting battle sequence, but the film's real strength is in its surprisingly lyrical and quieter moving passages and in a rich arrangement of the traditional Japanese melody "Cherry Blossoms" for low strings and the harp. The underscoring of MacArthur's final farewell speech is quite beautiful as well. Unfortunately, it leads back into that overbearing march again!

Jeff Bond

Mad Dog and Glory ♫♪

1992, Varese-Sarabande; from the movie *Mad Dog and Glory*, Universal-International, 1992.

Album Notes: *Music*: Elmer Bernstein; *Orchestrations*: Emilie A. Bernstein; *Music Editor*: Joe Debeasi; Orchestra conducted by Elmer Bernstein; *Musician*: Lawrence Feldman (alto sax solos); *Album Producer*: Emilie A. Bernstein

Selections: 1 Cops And Robbers (6:44); 2 The Lonely Guy Theme (2:43); 3 Frank And Wayne (3:08); 4 Mad Dog And Glory (3:53); 5 Window Magic (4:07); 6 Just A Gigolo (I Ain't Got

Mad Max Beyond Thunderdome

Nobody))(I. Caesar/L.N. Casucci/S. Williams/R. Graham)(4:42) *Louis Prima*; 7 That Old Black Magic (H. Arlen/J. Mercer)(2:55) *Louis Prima, Keely Smith*.

Review: When the best selections in a soundtrack album happen to be the pop tunes, you know something is definitely wrong. Sad to say, but the most enjoyable moments in this album are the two vocals by Louis Prima and Keely Smith. Evidently, this tired comedy starring Bill Murray as a police photographer, Robert De Niro as a gangster, and Uma Thurman as the gangster's moll, did not inspire Elmer Bernstein much. With the exception of a few moments within the tracks "Frank and Wayne" and "Window Magic," his music is rather forgettable, a series of riffs that go nowhere and mean even less. The listener is not inspired, either.

Mad Max Beyond Thunderdome ♪♪♪♪

1985, EMI Records; from the movie *Mad Max Beyond Thunderdome*, 1985.

Album Notes: *Music:* Maurice Jarre; The Royal Philharmonic Orchestra, conducted by Maurice Jarre; *Album Producer:* Maurice Jarre.

Selections: 1 We Don't Need Another Hero (Thunderdome)(T. Britten/G. Lyle) (6:07) *Tina Turner*; 2 One Of The Living (H. Knight) (5:58) *Tina Turner*; 3 We Don't Need Another Hero (Thunderdome)(T. Britten/G. Lyle)(instrumental) (6:30) *Tina Turner*; 4 Bartertown (8:27); 5 The Children (2:12); 6 Coming Home (15:12).

Review: For the third and final Mad Max installment, styled as a *Lawrence of Arabia* desert adventure, director George Miller turned to none other than the composer of *Lawrence*, Maurice Jarre. The resultant score is large, sweeping and distinctly Jarre, featuring orchestra, choir, an Ondes Martenot (an early electronic instrument), Australian didgeridoo, a few pop elements, and a variety of percussion. Fortunately, Jarre is the kind of composer whose style is distinct enough to focus this kind of kitchen-sink scale, and *Mad Max Beyond Thunderdome* is one of the most exciting scores of the past two decades. Jarre eschews the machinery-and-gasoline grit of Brian May's sound world, and follows Max's turn as a leader of lost children to their promised land with symphonic grandeur. With *Tai-Pan* and *Enemy Mine*, this soundtrack forms a triptych of somewhat clunky but exciting mid-'80s Jarre scores, orchestrated to the brim by the late Christopher Palmer. The album includes three pop songs along with the 25 minutes of score, including the Tina Turner hit "We Don't Need Another Hero" (she's

also the villain in the film), but unfortunately leaves off Jarre's pumped-up and slightly deranged "two men enter, one man leaves" fanfare and battle music for the Thunderdome duel itself.

Lukas Kendall

The Madness of King George ♪♪♪♪♭

1994, Epic Soundtrax; from the movie *The Madness of King George*, Samuel Goldwyn Pictures, 1994.

Album Notes: *Music:* Georg-Friedrich Handel; Arranged and adapted by George Fenton; *Orchestrations:* George Fenton; Baroque Orchestra, conducted by Nicholas Kraemer; *Album Producer:* George Fenton, Eliza Thompson; *Engineers:* Keith Grant, Peter Mew.

Selections: 1 Opening The Houses Of Parliament (4:11); 2 Prelude (1:25); 3 The Madness Of King George Front Titles (3:09); 4 Smile, It's What You're Paid For (1:00); 5 The King Goes Riding (2:23); 6 A Family Matter (2:25); 7 The Cricket Match (1:35); 8 The King Wakes Up Early/Do It, England (3:38); 9 The Concert (2:51); 10 We Have No Time (1:48); 11 He Will Be Restrained (2:20); 12 London Is Flooded (3:56); 13 Going To Kew (1:47); 14 Starting To Recover (2:52); 15 The Chancellor Drives To London (2:07); 16 The Prince Regent (1:37); 17 Mr. And Mrs. King (3:04); 18 The Madness Of King George End Credits (4:48).

Review: When he made this historic drama about the court of George III of England and the King's slow descent into obsession and madness, director Nicholas Hytner felt intuitively that only the music of Handel would seem appropriate for his film. But in order to give the music a cinematic edge, he asked George Fenton to select the various pieces that eventually were shaped into the score, and to adapt and arrange them. Fenton, who deliberately took a back seat to his illustrious predecessor, succeeded in giving Handel's compositions a slightly modern sound and made them more appropriately cinematographic. As such, they remain sufficiently close to their origins to please classicists and dramatic enough to attract fans of film music. Lovers of baroque music, in particular, will appreciate what Fenton has done with the well-known extracts from "Music for the Royal Fireworks" and "Water Music." In only one case, "A Family Matter," did Fenton write his own cue, using themes by Handel, in a way that doesn't betray the style of the score, but in fact enhances it. The only reservation one can formulate about the album is that the playing sometimes lacks excitement.

Magdalene ♪♪♪♪▷

1992, Intrada Records; from the movie *Magdalene*, **Tat Films, 1988.**

Album Notes: *Music:* Cliff Eidelman; *Orchestrations:* Mark Watters; The Munich Symphony Orchestra, conducted by Cliff Eidelman; *Album Producer:* Cliff Eidelman; *Engineer:* Alan Snelling.

Selections: 1 The Revolution (2:22); 2 The Death Of Hans (4:07); 3 Magdalene In Love (1:06); 4 Father Mohr (3:45); 5 Going To Heaven (2:32); 6 The Archbishop's Entertainment (1:52); 7 The Aftermath Of War (4:45); 8 Christmas Time (1:59); 9 Absolve Me Of My Sins (4:01); 10 Temptation (4:42); 11 Silent Night (:48); 12 Freedom In Salzburg (1:56); 13 Magdalene's Prayer (5:11); 14 Kyrie Eleison (1:31); 15 Will You Forget Me (1:10); 16 Mohr's Farewell (4:32).

Review: Cliff Eidelman's first score is a magnificent example of his understanding about what makes film music fulfill its function on the screen and as an audio-only experience. The story of an 18th-century prostitute willing to change her ways after she meets a dedicated priest, the story prompted Eidelman to write a strongly inspirational score, permeated with the music of the Church, "the all empowered force in the lives of all the characters," but also reflective of the young composer's beautiful melodic sense. Several cues attract particularly, "Magdalene in Love," a short but expressive piece, and "Father Mohr," in which Eidelman paints the serene portrait of a man of the cloth suddenly caught in a very human love dilemma; also "The Archbishop's Entertainment," written in the style of the period, around a theme that's pleasantly understated but quite effective, and the mournful "Mohr's Farewell," passionately romantic and florid. Quite impressive for a 22-year-old.

Magic in the Water ♪

1995, Varese-Sarabande; from the movie *Magic in the Water*, **Tri-Star Pictures, 1995.**

Album Notes: *Music:* David Schwartz; *Orchestrations:* William T. Stromberg, Lennie Moore; *Music Editor:* Sharon H. Smith; Orchestra conducted by William T. Stromberg; *Album Producer:* David Schwartz; *Engineer:* Jeff Vaughn, Glen Neibaur.

Selections: 1 Clouds/Frank Gets Orked (4:04); 2 Ride To Glenorky (1:00); 3 Uncle Kipper (1:36); 4 Oreos For Orky (2:02); 5 Ashley Gets A Grip (5:09); 6 Grow Up (2:47); 7 Come, Must Hurry (3:57); 8 Sand Castles/The Lake (2:16); 9 Damn Monster Huggers (2:24); 10 Joe Pickletrout (1:06); 11 The Kids Chase Orky/Dorky Sinks (5:10); 12 Orky's Cave (3:50); 13 Ashley And Jack/ Transformation (4:58).

Review: Disappointing effort by David Schwartz, who has done much more creative things on the TV series "Northern Exposure." Pretty and pleasant enough to service this minor kiddie feature, this score is so average that little of it remains after you've listened to it. Uninspiring.

David Hirsch

The Magnificent Ambersons ♪♪♪♪♪

1990, Preamble Records; from the movie *The Magnificent Ambersons*, **RKO Radio Pictures, 1942.**

Album Notes: *Music:* Bernard Herrmann; The Australian Philharmonic Orchestra, conducted by Tony Bremner; *Featured Musicians:* Neville Taweel (violin), Henry Wenig (cello), Janet Perkins (organ); *Album Producer:* Maria Vandamme; *Engineer:* Robin Gray; *Assistant Engineer:* Adam Rowland.

Selections: 1 Theme & Variations/George's Homecoming (7:14); 2 Snow Ride (3:00); 3 The Door/Death & Youth (1:01); 4 Toccata (1:07); 5 Pleasure Trip (1:01); 6 Prelude (1:25); 7 First Nocturne (4:03); 8 Garden Scene (1:09); 9 Fantasia (2:05); 10 Scene Pathetique (2:14); 11 Waiting 1 and 2 (1:27); 12 Ostinato (1:47); 13 First Letter Scene (3:20); 14 Second Letter Scene/ Romanza (2:07); 15 Second Nocturne (3:17); 16 Departure/ Isabel's Death (1:43); 17 First Reverie/Second Reverie (2:35); 18 The Walk Home (2:44); 19 Garden Music (2:54); 20 Elegy (1:18); 21 End Title (2:19).

Review: A companion volume to the complete *Citizen Kane* (q.v.), this magnificent recording brings together the same team—producer John Lasher, conductor Tony Bremner, and the players of the Australian Philharmonic Orchestra—in a reading of another early score by Bernard Herrmann, skillfully reconstructed for this occasion. As would be expected, the results are nothing less than splendid. Next to *Citizen Kane*, *The Magnificent Ambersons*, also directed by Orson Welles, was probably one of Herrmann's most impressive achievements, even though, like the film itself, the composer's original music was treated with total disregard by studio executives who discarded many of the cues as the film was being recut to fit their own concept of it.

Compared with the brooding aura that pervaded his earlier score, however, the music for *Magnificent Ambersons* reveals Herrmann in a somewhat lighter mood, with the chamber music approach resulting in a texture that strikes for its sheer simplicity. Throughout individual instruments are called upon to provide an anchor for themes that are catchy and melodic, with the whole score emerging at once as a brilliant

HENRY MANCINI

Henry Mancini was a composer, songwriter, and recording artist who became one of the most prolific composers of film scores of the 1960s and 1970s. He was a staff composer for Universal in the early 1950s, working on the jazz-oriented movies *The Glenn Miller Story* (for which he received his first Oscar nomination in 1954) and *The Benny Goodman Story* (1956). But it was his work in television, with theme songs for the series "Peter Gunn" and "Mr. Lucky" that first brought him fame. Those series marked the beginning of an association with director Blake Edwards that was to be very productive for both men.

Mancini's work on Edwards' *Breakfast at Tiffany's* (1961) earned him his first two Academy Awards, one for the score and one for Best Song, "Moon River," with lyrics by Johnny Mercer. Mercer and Mancini teamed up the following year for another Academy Award-winning song, the title tune from Edward's *Days of Wine and Roses.*

Mancini's most famous film theme was the score for Blake Edwards' *The Pink Panther* (1964). Like "Inspector Clouseau," the bumbling hero of the series, the animated animal (complete with theme song) had a long and prosperous life in six films, a cartoon series, and advertisements. The theme won 1964 Grammy awards for Best Instrumental Arrangement, Best Instrumental Composition, and Best Instrumental Performance in the non-jazz categories. Among his other Edward's collaborations have been the backstage musicals *Darling Lili* and *Victor-Victoria.*

Born in Cleveland, Ohio, on April 16, 1924, Mancini studied flute and taught himself piano as a child. He continued composing film scores up until a few years before his death in 1994.

and thoroughly compelling effort. The recording itself is for the most part superb, with just a slight distortion on the left channel in a couple of tracks and studio noises to make it slightly less than perfect.

The Magnificent Seven ♪♪♪♪

1996, Koch International; from the movie *The Magnificent Seven*, United Artists, 1962.

Album Notes: *Music*: Elmer Bernstein; *Orchestrations*: Elmer Bernstein, Christopher Palmer; The Phoenix Symphony Orchestra, conducted by James Sedares; *Album Producer*: Michael Fine; *Engineer*: Michael Fine.

Selections: 1 Main Titles and Calvera's Visit (4:01); 2 Council Of War (3:40); 3 Strange Funeral (4:46); 4 After The Brawl (2:28); 5 The Journey (3:51); 6 Toreador (2:15); 7 Training (1:34); 8 Fiesta and Celebration (1:59); 9 Calvera's Return (2:11); 10 Calvera Routed and Petra's Declaration (3:49); 11 Ambush (3:06); 12 Surprise and Crossroads (7:27); 13 Enemy Camp and Nightmare (1:50); 14 Defeat (3:41); 15 Showdown and Finale (10:31); 16 The Hallelujah Trail: Overture for Chorus and Orchestra (6:54) *Arizona State University Concert Choir*.

Review: Amazingly, this popular western never actually yielded a soundtrack album. When it originally came out, United Artists included the main theme in a compilation album. Later on, the label did release the soundtrack from *Return of the Seven*, also composed by Bernstein, which reprised the main theme from the first film. Neither of these has been reissued on compact disc at this writing.

The 1993 Koch recording, reconstructed and edited by the composer with musicologist Christopher Palmer, includes many cues from the original score new to the recorded medium, played in breathtaking fashion by the Phoenix Symphony, a recent comer on the film music scene. It is everything a western score should be, fiery, exciting, and open-spaced, a superb demonstration of everything that makes this kind of film music so vibrant and entertaining. This CD is another essential addition to any collection.

The Main Event ♪♪♪♪

1989, Columbia Records; from the movie *The Main Event*, Warner Bros., 1979.

Album Notes: *Music*: Michael Melvoin; Orchestra conducted by Michael Melvoin; *Album Producer*: Barwood Films Ltd.; *Engineer*: John Arrias.

Selections: 1 The Main Event (P. Jabara/B. Roberts)/Fight (P. Jabara/B. Esty)(11:40) *Barbra Streisand*; 2 The Body Shop (G. Michalski/N. Ooversteen) (5:15) *Michalski & Ooversteen*; 3 The

Main Event (P. Jabara/B. Roberts)/Fight (P. Jabara/B. Esty)(short version)(4:55) *Barbra Streisand*; 4 Copeland Meets The Coasters/ Get A Job (:57); 5 Big Girls Don't Cry (B. Crewe/B. Gaudio)(2:28) *Frankie Valli, The Four Seasons*; 6 It's Your Foot Again (3:09); 7 Angry Eyes (K. Loggins/J. Messina)(2:26) *Loggins & Messina*; 8 I'd Clean A Fish For You (1:03); 9 The Main Event (P. Jabara/B. Roberts)(ballad)(4:17) *Barbra Streisand*.

Review: Barbra Streisand is always good for a moment, even when she wants to spar with beau hunk Ryan O'Neal, as is the case in this 1979 film in which Streisand tries to recover the money she'd lost on boxer O'Neal by getting him back in shape for a championship match. Lucky for her fans, she also had Paul Jabara to write a knockout of a song ("The Main Event") for her, even though she overstated it by recording it three times, in case the loooong first version was not enough. Loggins & Messina and Frankie Valli & The Four Seasons also contributed shorter songs for an album that's relatively pleasant, all things considered.

Malcolm X

Malcolm X ♫♫♫♫

1992, Qwest Records; from the movie *Malcolm X*, Warner Bros., 1992.

Album Notes: *Album Executive Producers*: Quincy Jones, Spike Lee; *Engineer*: Lee Herschberg.

Selections: 1 Revolution (T. Thomas/T. Aerle Jones)(4:49) *Arrested Development*; 2 Roll 'Em Pete (P. Johnson/J. Turner)(3:45) *Joe Turner*; 3 Flying Home (B. Goodman/L. Hampton)(3:15) *Lionel Hampton*; 4 My Prayer (J. Kennedy/G. Boulanger)(3:16) *The Ink Spots*; 5 Big Stuff (L. Bernstein)(2:29) *Billie Holiday*; 6 Don't Cry Baby (J. Johnson/S. Unger/S. Bernie)(3:21) *Erskine Hawkins*; 7 Brass And Cornbread (F. Clark/E. Moore)(2:51) *Louis Jordan*; 8 Azure (E.K. Ellington)(2:22) *Ella Fitzgerald*; 9 Alabama (J. Coltrane)(2:26) *John Coltrane*; 10 That Lucky Old Sun (Just Rolls Around Heaven)(D. Gillespie/B. Smith)(4:23) *Dizzy Gillespie*; 11 Arabesque Cookie (E.K. Ellington/B. Strayhorn)(5:47) *Duke Ellington*; 12 Shotgun (A. DeWalt) (3:03) *Jr. Walker & The All-Stars*; 13 Someday We'll All Be Free (D. Hathaway/E. Howard)(8:21) *Aretha Franklin*.

Review: See *The Malcolm X Jazz Suite* entry below.

Malcolm X ♫♫♫♫

1992, Columbia Records; from the movie *Malcolm X*, Warner Bros., 1992.

Album Notes: *Music*: Terence Blanchard; *Orchestra conducted by* Terence Blanchard; *Featured Musicians*: Terence Blanchard,

James Hynes, John Longo (trumpet), Mike Davis, Britt Woodman, Timothy Williams (trombones), Jerry Dodgion, Jerome Richardson, Branford Marsalis (saxophone), Sir Roland Hanna, Bruce Barth (piano), Tarus Mateen, Nedra Wheeler (bass), Eugene Jackson, Jr. (drums); *Album Producer*: Terence Blanchard; *Engineer*: James P. Nichols.

Selections: 1 Opening Credits (2:15) *The Boys Choir Of Harlem*; 2 Young Malcolm (2:16) *The Boys Choir Of Harlem*; 3 Cops And Robbers (:45); 4 Earl's Death (:38); 5 Flashback (4:19); 6 Numbers (1:12); 7 Fire (1:43); 8 Back To Boston (1:00); 9 Malcolm Meets Baines (3:05); 10 Black And White (3:56); 11 Little Lamb Vision (3:47); 12 Malcolm's Letter (1:40); 13 Malcolm Meets Elijah (1:55); 14 The Old Days (4:00); 15 Betty's Theme (1:03); 16 Fruit Of Islam (3:51); 17 First Minister (2:28) *The Boys Choir Of Harlem*; 18 Betty's Conflict (3:33); 19 Malcolm Speaks To Secretaries (1:42); 20 Malcolm Confronts Baines (2:16); 21 Chickens Come Home (1:03); 22 Going To Mecca (1:51); 23 Firebomb (2:51); 24 Assassins (:48); 25 Assassination (:46); 26 Eulogy (3:51) *The Boys Choir Of Harlem*.

Review: See *The Malcolm X Jazz Suite* entry below.

The Malcolm X Jazz Suite ♫♫♫♫

1992, Columbia Records; from the movie *Malcolm X*, Warner Bros., 1992.

Album Notes: *Music*: Terence Blanchard; *Featured Musicians*: Terence Blanchard (trumpet), Sam Newsom (tenor saxophone), Bruce Bath (piano), Troy Davis (drums), Tarus Mateen (bass); *Album Producer*: Terence Blanchard; *Engineer*: James P. Nichols.

Selections: 1 The Opening (8:30); 2 Melody For Laura (6:26); 3 Theme For Elijah (5:24); 4 Blues For Malcolm (12:06); 5 The Nation (4:54); 6 Malcolm's Theme (6:07); 7 Betty's Theme (7:39); 8 Malcolm Makes Hajj (4:37); 9 Malcolm At Peace (11:22); 10 Perpetuity (4:30); 11 Malcolm's Theme (1:47).

Review: Musically, Spike Lee's impressive cinematographic portrait of Malcolm X is solidly rooted in the sights and sounds of the 1960s, and in the flavorful jazz themes Terence Blanchard created for the film.

The first aspect of this musical background can be found in the compilation released by Quincy Jones' Qwest label. Dismissing the first track, "Revolution," which is too contemporary to even suggest the period when Malcolm X thrived (a better, and more historically appropriate choice would have been a recording by The Last Poets), the rest of the album presents various gratifying performances by some of the top black entertainers from the 1940s through the 1960s, including

Lionel Hampton, The Ink Spots, Billie Holiday, Ella Fitzgerald, John Coltrane, Ray Charles, Duke Ellington, and Aretha Franklin, in a compilation that astutely combines rhythm and blues and jazz. It's an excellent cross-section of both genres, and it effectively reflects the historic background of the film itself.

The two recordings from Columbia, on the other hand, present Terence Blanchard's underscoring for the film, the first volume as it was in the original score, the second volume in a more jazz-flavored rearrangement that brings together many of the cues into a consistent programming concept. Featuring several vocals by the Boys Choir Of Harlem, the score is a strong, evocative affair. Instrumental cues played by a symphonic orchestra are sometimes augmented by soloists Branford Marsalis or Blanchard himself, and interspersed with more jazz-oriented numbers in which Blanchard leads a group of seasoned musicians, which includes Marsalis, Sir Roland Hanna, Jerome Richardson, and Jerry Dodgion, among others. Those various elements combine to create a music that is diversified, strongly eloquent, and a fitting complement to the screen action.

The "Malcolm X Jazz Suite" presents a more coherent and unified picture of the music Blanchard wrote, with the cues reorganized into a seamless series of themes, performed by a jazz combo. It's another innovative approach to what is a profuse score to begin with, with many undertones that truly deserve to be fully exploited and expressed in as many modes as possible. Listeners who may not be inclined to sit through the score album itself, might delight in this musical extrapolation which fills a gap and adds new textures to the original music.

Malice ♫♫

1993, Varese-Sarabande; from the movie *Malice*, Castle Rock Entertainment, 1993.

Album Notes: *Music:* Jerry Goldsmith; *Orchestrations:* Arthur Morton, Alexander Courage; *Music Editor:* Ken Hall; Orchestra conducted by Jerry Goldsmith; *Album Producer:* Jerry Goldsmith; *Engineer:* Bruce Botnick.

Selections: 1 Main Title (3:31); 2 A Lift Home (1:45); 3 No Friends (1:33); 4 With Malice (2:54); 5 The Handyman (2:45); 6 Clues (7:15); 7 No Choice (2:39); 8 The Body (10:43).

Review: Made in the wake of *Basic Instinct*, *Malice* co-opted the earlier film's mix of eroticism and moral confusion and Goldsmith's score for it ranges from extensions of *Basic Instinct*'s pulsing chase music to some climactic brass chords that might have been more at home in a science fiction movie. The best thing about the album is the opening theme, built off a hesitant, simple keyboard melody with a tense, building string chord that gives way to a haunting female chorus sing-

ing a beautiful title melody; it's the flip side of Goldsmith's lullaby-like *Poltergeist* title theme. Unfortunately much of the later suspense cues give in to the current "less-is-more" school of droning, textureless monotony that just doesn't make for very interesting listening.

Jeff Bond

The Mambo Kings ♫♫♫♫▷

1991, Elektra Records; from the movie *The Mambo Kings*, Warner Bros., 1991.

Album Notes: *Song Producers:* Robert Kraft, Johnny Pacheco, Peter Asher; *Album Producer:* Robert Kraft; *Engineers:* Michael Golub, Michael Farrow, Frank Wolf.

Selections: 1 La dicha mia (J. Pacheco)(3:20) *Celia Cruz;* 2 Ran Kan Kan (T. Puente)(2:59) *Tito Puente;* 3 Cuban Pete (J. Norman)(2:25) *Tito Puente;* 4 Mambo Caliente (A. Sandoval)(3:26) *Arturo Sandoval;* 5 Quiereme mucho (G. Roig/A. Rodriguez)(3:20) *Linda Ronstadt;* 6 Sunny Ray (R. Santos)(2:35) *Mambo All-Stars;* 7 Melao de cana (Moo la lah)(M. Pedroso)(2:51) *Celia Cruz;* 8 Beautiful Maria Of My Soul (R. Kraft/A. Glimcher)(4:10) *Antonio Banderas, Mambo All-Stars;* 9 Para los rumberos (T. Puente)(1:51) *Tito Puente;* 10 Perfidia (A. Dominguez/M. Leeds)(3:41) *Linda Ronstadt;* 11 Guantanamera (F. Diaz)(3:05) *Celia Cruz;* 12 Tea For Two (V. Youmans/I. Caesar)(2:31) *Mambo All-Stars;* 13 Accidental Mambo (C. Franzelli)(1:23) *Mambo All-Stars;* 14 Como fue (E.D. Brito)(2:54) *Beny More;* 15 Tanga, Rumba Afro-Cubana (M. Bauza)(3:31) *Mambo All-Stars;* 16 Beautiful Maria Of My Soul (R. Kraft/A. Glimcher)(4:26) *Los Lobos.*

Review: Percolating Caribbean polyrhythms are the order of the day here, played by some of the finest progenitors of the form. You may not recognize a single name in the Mambo All-Stars, but you won't be thinking about that as you soak in the group's crisp performances. Tito Puente's rendition of "Cuban Pete" will make you forget about Jim Carrey's campy hit version from *The Mask*, while Linda Ronstadt, Arturo Sandoval, Celia Cruz and Los Lobs make valuable contributions to this mambo music primer.

Gary Graff

A Man and a Woman/ Live for Life ♫♫♫♫

1996, DRG Records; from the movies *A Man and a Woman*, Allied Artists, 1965, and *Live for Life*, United Artists, 1967.

Album Notes: *Music:* Francis Lai, Baden Powell, Vinicius de Moraes.

Selections: *A MAN AND A WOMAN:* 1 A Man And A Woman (2:39); 2 Samba Saravah (B. Powell/V. De Moraes/P. Barouh)(4:33) *Pierre Barouh, with Baden Powell and Orchestra;* 3 Aujourd'hui c'est toi (F. Lai/P. Barouh)(2:07) *Nicole Croisille;* 4 Un homme et une femme (F. Lai/P. Barouh)(2:36) *Nicole Croisille, Pierre Barouh;* 5 Stronger Than Us (3:16); 6 Today It's You (2:31); 7 A l'ombre de nous (F. Lai/P. Barouh)(4:54) *Pierre Barouh;* 8 Plus fort que nous (F. Lai/P. Barouh)(3:43) *Nicole Croisille, Pierre Barouh;* 9 124 Miles An Hour (2:28);

LIVE FOR LIFE: 10 Live For Life (3:05); 11 Theme To Catherine (2:53); 12 Theme To Candice (1:44); 13 Live For Life (3:07); 14 Des ronds dans l'eau (R. Le Senechal/P. Barouh/S. Miller)(3:14) *Nicole Croisille, Annie Girardot;* 15 Theme To Catherine (2:00); 16 Theme To Robert (3:18); 17 Live For Life (2:26); 18 Aujourd'hui c'est toi (F. Lai/P. Barouh/J. Keller)(2:39) *Louis Aldebert;* 19 Zoom (2:12); 20 Live For Life (2:49).

Review: Francis Lai achieved international fame for the first score, driven by the theme that permeates Claude Lelouch's sensitive study of a widow with a child (Anouk Aimee), and the car racer (Jean-Louis Trintignant), who meet, fall in love, separate and eventually get back together. The Oscar-winning film launched the career of Lelouch, and helped establish Lai as another French composer (after Michel Legrand and Maurice Jarre) whose music struck a responsive note worldwide. *Live for Life,* Lelouch's follow-up failed to get the same recognition, though Lai again delivered another fine, compelling score. In both, the songs performed in both French and English contribute enormously to the overall appreciation of the music.

The Man from Snowy River
𝄞𝄞𝄞𝄞ᵛ

1982, Varese-Sarabande Records; from the movie *The Man from Snowy River,* 20th Century-Fox, 1982.

Album Notes: *Music:* Bruce Rowland; *Orchestrations:* Bruce Rowland; Orchestra conducted by Bruce Rowland; *Album Producers:* Tom Null, Chris Kuchler; *Engineers:* Roger Savage, Ian McKenzie.

Selections: 1 Main Theme (1:23); 2 Jim's Ride (1:28); 3 The Chase (4:59); 4 Jessica's Theme (Breaking In The Colt)(3:18); 5 Henry Dies/Farewell To Frew (1:45); 6 Rosemary Recalls (1:22); 7 Mountain Theme (1:51); 8 Jessica's Sonata (:47); 9 Jim Brings In The Brumbies (1:58); 10 Clancy's Theme (trad.)(2:06); 11 The Brumbies (2:09); 12 Harrison Homestead/Jim Gets His Horse (2:28); 13 Searching For Jessica (3:58); 14 End Titles (3:54).

Review: A western made down under, *The Man from Snowy River,* based on a well-known poem, found Kirk Douglas in a dual role as two brothers, one a respected landowner, the other a gruff prospector, engaged in a fratricidal struggle on the wild Australian range. The spectacular film sports a sensational score by Bruce Rowland, evidently tailored after the scores written by Hollywood composers for this type of film, but with a definite touch of originality and themes that are stimulating to the extreme. Amid the pulse-racing, throbbing action cues developed by the composer, magnificently performed in a recording that has a booming, resonant sound to it well-suited for this kind of music, Rowland strikes a more romantic note in cues like the gorgeous "Jessica's Theme (Breaking in the Colt)," or the equally lovely "Rosemary Recalls," which gave his score greater depth and sentimental appeal.

See also: Return to Snowy River

The Man in the Moon 𝄞𝄞𝄞ᵛ

1991, Reprise Records; from the movie *The Man in the Moon,* M-G-M, 1991.

Album Notes: *Music:* James Newton Howard; *Orchestrations:* Brad Dechter; Orchestra conducted by Marty Paich; *Featured Musicians:* Dean Parks (guitar), David Grisman (mandolin), Michael Fisher (percussion), James Newton Howard (piano), Jay Rosen (violin); *Album Producers:* James Newton Howard, Michael Mason; *Engineer:* Robert Schaper, Shawn Murphy; *Assistant Engineers:* Sue MacLean, Sharon Rice, Charlie Paakkari.

Selections: 1 Dani Brings Court Water (3:36); 2 Back Door (1:18); 3 First Kiss (1:48); 4 Lovemaking (1:02); 5 My Goodness (1:14); 6 The Walk (1:13); 7 The Pond (:56); 8 Dani Remembers (1:31); 9 The Funeral (2:54); 10 Daydreaming (1:20); 11 Court's Accident (3:00); 12 End Titles (2:32); 13 Go Home (1:09); 14 Girls In Hallway (:30); 15 Dani And Dad (:27); 16 Swimming Hole (1:23); 17 Dani Sees Court (1:20); 18 Graveyard (3:10).

Review: A lovely score by James Newton Howard accompanies Robert Mulligan's beautiful examination of the trials and tribulations of a young girl growing up in 1957 Louisiana farm country. Howard interpolates some atmospheric guitar riffs into his score, giving the music a "down home" feel while at the same time it uses the orchestra poignantly to accentuate the drama of the story. The music feels small and intimate in nature, a perfect score for a character-driven piece, and also an ideal listening experience for anyone searching for strong themes that aren't overwhelmingly melodramatic or saccharine in emotional quality. At times the music has a wistful, melancholic edge to it, but perhaps that's unsurprising given Mulligan's previous cinematic portrayals of growing up—classics which include *Summer of '42* and *To Kill a Mockingbird.* Both of those pictures have outstanding scores, and

Howard's music for *The Man in the Moon* is not at all out of place in their company.

Andy Dursin

Man on Fire 🎵🎵🎵

1987, Varese-Sarabande Records; from the movie *Man on Fire*, Tri-Star Pictures, 1987.

Album Notes: *Music*: John Scott; The Graunke Symphony Orchestra, conducted by John Scott; *Album Producer*: John Scott; *Engineer*: Peter Kramper.

Selections: 1 Man On Fire (4:43); 2 The Bomb (2:50); 3 Snake's First Victim (2:03); 4 Sam Wins The Race (2:00); 5 The Villa At Night (1:40); 6 The Ransom Drop (1:47); 7 Start Of The Search (2:38); 8 Death Of Creasy (2:52); 9 Becoming Friends (1:49); 10 The Kidnapping (1:09); 11 We've Got Each Other (1:56); 12 Rabbia Must Die (3:07); 13 Sam Runs Into Danger (1:11); 14 Reconciliation (1:44); 15 Premature Death (1:45); 16 Reunited (3:14).

Review: John Scott fashions some of his more memorable romantic themes and terrifying suspense cues in this score. Dealing with the relationship between a bodyguard and the young girl he is assigned to protect, the film has been forgotten, but John Scott's music remains effective and highly listenable. Most suspense scores during the '80s are little more than dreary electronic noise, but Scott went against the grain of the time by scoring *Man of Fire* with a surging, powerful orchestral score. Even the subdued passages grab the listener. The first track, "Man of Fire" opens with tremolo violins beneath a tender flute melody, which at once evokes delicacy and trepidation. This opens up into the main theme, a beautiful, lushly romantic piece. Some of the score's other highlights include "Start of the Search" with its snarling rock and roll drums and marimba, and the surging and triumphant "Sam Wins the Race". Scott's skillful and adroit gift for orchestration pervades the score. The music works beautifully on disc, cues often flowing together seamlessly. Track changes are often not noticed. So effective was this score that some of it was actually later used in *Die Hard*.

Paul Andrew MacLean

Man Trouble 🎵🎵🎵🎵

1992, Varese-Sarabande Records; from the movie *Man Trouble*, 20th Century-Fox, 1992.

Album Notes: *Music*: Georges Delerue; *Music Editor*: Curtis Roush; Orchestra conducted by Georges Delerue; *Album Producer*: Georges Delerue; *Engineer*: Robert Fernandez.

Selections: 1 Main Title (2:48); 2 Duking It Out With The Duke (1:04); 3 Love Theme (2:13); 4 Joan Throws A Fit (3:00); 5 Introducing June (:51); 6 Making Love (1:55); 7 Nocturne in E-Flat, Op. 9, No. 2 (F. Chopin) (4:40); 8 Romance And Garage Assault (4:37); 9 The Red Negligee (2:38); 10 Hospital Scam (5:41); 11 Harry Searches For The Book (1:50); 12 It's Over (1:38); 13 Through The Hospital (1:44); 14 Harry And Eddie Fight (1:11); 15 The Helicopter (1:36); 16 Man Trouble End Titles (2:45).

Review: Throughout his life, Georges Delerue particularly excelled at catching the varied moods in romantic comedies, all at once exhibiting the drama and passion usually needed for this type of screen fare, and informing the audience without being necessarily obvious about the general intent. *Man Trouble*, about a well-known musician pursued by an admirer who decides to acquire a guard dog and gets involved with its trainer, elicited a score that reflects both aspects, in a rich display of melodic themes in "Love Theme" and "Making Love" and pleasantly lilting cues in "Joan Throws a Fit" and "Harry and Eddie Fight." A fitting coda to his career, Delerue died shortly after completing this score.

The Man Who Would Be King 🎵🎵🎵🎵🎵

1990, Bay Cities; from the film *The Man Who Would Be King*, Allied Artists, 1975.

Album Notes: *Music*: Maurice Jarre; The National Philharmonic Orchestra, conducted by Maurice Jarre; *Album Producer*: Carl Prager; *Engineer*: Eric Tomlinson.

Selections: 1 The Man Who Would be King (3:08); 2 Sikandergul (2:36); 3 Journey To Kafiristan (5:20); 4 The King's March (1:58); 5 Bashkai's (2:08); 6 Pushtukan (3:14); 7 The Dream (2:36); 8 Roxanne (3:15); 9 Dravor's Farewell (trad.)(3:40) *Sean Connery, Michael Caine*; 10 End Title (2:31).

Review: Maurice Jarre always seems at his best when he scores epic films, and this was again clearly the case when he wrote the music for John Huston's hearty account of Rudyard Kipling's story about two English con men in late 18th-century India who journey to distant Kafiristan, a remote Himalyan kingdom, where they become *de facto* rulers after they take control of the country's warring tribes. Happily mixing Hindu sounds with swashbuckling accents, Jarre wrote a score that, like the film, never takes itself too seriously, while it details the action on the screen with its broad, grander-than-life posturing. The whimsical main theme, heard throughout, further enhances the frequently rollicking aspects of this entertaining rags-to-riches tale of friendship and adventure.

The Man with the Golden Gun ♫♫♫

1988, EMI-Manhattan Records; from the movie *The Man with the Golden Gun*, United Artists, 1974.

Album Notes: *Music*: John Barry; *Lyrics*: Don Black; Orchestra conducted by John Barry; *Album Producer*: John Barry.

Selections: 1 Main Title: The Man With The Golden Gun (2:38) *Lulu*; 2 Scaramanga's Fun House (4:40); 3 Chew Me In Crisly Land (4:02); 4 The Man With The Golden Gun (2:33); 5 Getting The Bullet (2:46); 6 Goodnight Goodnight (5:25); 7 Let's Go Get 'Em (3:45); 8 Hip's Trip (3:22); 9 Kung Fu Fight (1:58); 10 In Search Of Scaramanga's Island (2:32); 11 Return To Scaramanga's Fun House (6:30); 12 End Title: The Man With The Golden Gun (3:06) *Lulu*.

Review: Despite more than ten years scoring the James Bond series, John Barry never fell prey to creative staleness. Of all his Bond scores, *The Man with the Golden Gun* is his most fun and tongue-in-cheek. The score is colorful and broad, encompassing a wide array of styles. The album kicks off with a wildly nutty title song, sung by Lulu, with typically hokey lyrics by Don Black. The ensuing score has beautifully exotic passages evoking the Hong Kong setting of the film, invested with ethnic instrumental color. "Kung Fu Fight" is a giddy romp and something of an homage to Albert Kettelby's "In a Chinese Temple." Also fun is Barry's dixieland arrangement of the main theme.

The score is of course not without the more dangerous moments, which mark it as a 007 score. Barry pulls out the James Bond theme in "Lets Go Get 'Em", and furnishes a suspenseful, almost chilling climax in "Return to Scaramanga's Fun House." The album closes with a reprise of the title song, this time with even sillier lyrics. Anyone expecting the hard edge of *Goldfinger* will be disappointed, but *The Man With The Golden Gun* score is a highly entertaining and fun soundtrack.

After skipping out on the first Roger Moore 007 epic, *Live and Let Die*, John Barry returned to the series for this sub-par outing that suffers from a too-eclectic mix of musical styles. Barry's rich, majestic main theme, often played by low strings, is a melodically beautiful yet manly Orientalism that functions well in both broad orchestral statements, to color the film's lush tropical settings, and during some staccato chase sequences. Unfortunately it's a washout as belted out by British pop crooner Lulu in the film's title song, an incredibly cheesy pop/rock anthem that doesn't exactly conjure up memories of Shirley Bassey in her prime. Elsewhere the chase and suspense cues are often compromised by the tongue-in-cheek intrusion of off-kilter comic and atmospheric effects, like a hideous slide whistle in the middle of an otherwise exciting car chase cue and excruciating honky-tonk piano and jazz band sections during Bond's final showdown with the villain Scaramanga.

Paul Andrew MacLean/Jeff Bond

The Man Without a Face ♫♫♫♫

1992, Philips Records; from the film *The Man Without a Face*, Warner Bros., 1992.

Album Notes: *Music*: James Horner; *Orchestrations*: Tom Pasatieri; *Music Editors*: Jim Henrikson; The London Symphony Orchestra conducted by James Horner; *Album Producer*: James Horner; *Engineer*: Shawn Murphy.

Selections: 1 A Father's Legacy (6:14); 2 Chuck's First Lesson (2:49); 3 Flying (3:49); 4 McLeod's Secret Life (1:58); 5 Nightmares and Revelations (4:22); 6 McLeod's Last Letter (2:58); 7 Lost Books (1:57); 8 The Merchant Of Venice (2:55); 9 The Tutor (3:21); 10 No Compromise (4:56); 11 "Ch'ella mi creda" (G. Puccini) (2:26) *Jussi Bjoerling*; 12 Lookout Point/End Credits (7:57).

Review: The compelling story of a man whose scarred face and taciturn behavior have made him an outcast in a small Maine community and the fatherless 12-year-old who befriends him, *The Man Without a Face* prompted James Horner, writing in an uncharacteriscally low-key mode, to create a very sensitive, admirably nuanced score. Quickly establishing the moods that pervade the film, "A Father's Legacy" is a romantic theme, with the piano playing a quiet melody against soft orchestral textures, a device repeated in various cues, most effectively in "Chuck's First Lesson," "The Merchant of Venice," and "Lookout Point."

Mandela: Son of Africa, Father of a Nation ♫♫♫♫

1996, Mango Records; from the documentary *Mandela: Son of Africa, Father of a Nation*, Island Pictures, 1996.

Album Notes: *Music*: Cedric Gradus Samson.

Selections: 1 Robben Island Ambiance (:30); 2 Father Of Our Nation (3:30) *Jennifer Jones, Hugh Masekela*; 3 Childhood (1:36); 4 Sign n' Fly (N.Piliso) (4:11) *The African Jazz Pioneers*; 5 In The Queue (T. Matshikizo/P. Williams) (2:15) *Original Cast of the All-African Jazz Opera ''King Kong''*; 6 Yiyole (E. Nomvete) (2:37) *The Havana Swingers*; 7 Oula Kgosi Seretse (M. Makeba) (2:53) *The Skylarks*; 8 Ndenzeni Na? (What Have I Done?) (G. Makhene) (2:16) *Father Huddleston Band*; 9 Vuka Vuka (N. Mdledle/J. Magotsi/R. Khoas/R. Schume) (2:30) *Manhattan Brothers*; 10 De Makeba (M. Davashe) (2:46) *The*

Jazz Dazzlers; 11 Lalelani (M. Makeba) (2:50) *The Skylarks*; 12 Mandela—Madiba (:57); 13 Toyi Toyi Mix (trad.) (2:30) *The African National Congress Choir*; 14 Heavyweight (W. Swinney/ L. Rampolokeng) (2:56) *The Kalahari Surfers, Lesego Rampolokeng*; 15 Wars Of Old (:56); 16 Asimbonanga (Mandela) (J. Clegg) (4:47) *Johnny Clegg, Savuka*; 17 Family Theme (1:16); 18 Nelson Mandela (J. Dammers) (4:29) *The Specials*; 19 Rest In Peace (:34); 20 When You Come Back (V. Mahlasela) (4:05) *Vusi Mahlasela*; 21 Transkei (1:01); 22 Guns And Pangas (W. Swinney/S. Naidoo) (4:11) *The Kalahari Surfers, Shaun Naidoo*; 23 Sad Song (:42); 24 Phansi Ngodlame (B. Mlangeni) (4:13) *Babsy Mlangeni*; 25 Mmalo-we (J. Khanyile/T. Khomo) (6:19) *Bayete and Jobu Khanyile*; 26 Black President (B. Fassie/S. Chicco Twala) (4:28) *Brenda Fassie*.

Review: A documentary that lionizes Nelson Mandela while chronicling his life struggle and eventual victory against apartheid (but at what cost!), *Mandela, Son of Africa, Father of a Nation* offers an uncompromising portrait of the South African leader. Making the film even more vibrant is its soundtrack, in which a large number of South African performers add their voices to create an exciting musical portrait of the man and his time. There are many remarkable moments in this recording, some a little too brief, that all add up to a vivid description of a moment in humanity's long-winded history.

The Marrying Man ♫♫♫°

1991, Hollywood Records; from *The Marrying Man*, Hollywood Pictures, 1991.

Album Notes: *Music*: David Newman; *Music Editor*: Tom Villano; *Scoring Engineer & Mixing*: Tim Boyle; *Featured Artists*: Stan Getz (tenor sax), Don Menza (tenor sax), Jack Sheldon (trumpet), Chuck Findley (trumpet); *Album Producer*: Tim Hauser; *Engineer*: Gary Lux.

Selections: 1 Main Title (1:50); 2 Let's Do It (C. Porter)(3:33) *Kim Basinger*; 3 L.D.'s Bounce (T. Hauser)(2:05); 4 "Murder" He Says (J. McHugh/F. Loesser)(2:33) *Kim Basinger*; 5 Honeysuckle Rose (T. Waller/A. Razaf)(3:12) *Kim Basinger*; 6 You're Driving Me Crazy (What Did I Do?)(W. Donaldson)(2:00) *Alan Paul*; 7 Backstage Beat-Up (3:30); 8 Why Can't You Behave (C. Porter) (3:37) *Kim Basinger*; 9 Satisfy My Soul (B. Johnson)(2:57) *Kim Basinger*; 10 Let's Do It (reprise)(C. Porter)(2:29) *Kim Basinger*; 11 Run, Charley, Run (4:48); 12 Mama Look A Boo Boo (L. Melody)(2:49) *Tim Hauser*; 13 Love Is The Thing (V. Young/N. Washington)(4:45) *Kim Basinger*.

Review: Though an inconsequential little comedy set in 1948 Las Vegas, *The Marrying Man* resulted in a great jazz album. With stalwarts Stan Getz, Don Menza, Jack Sheldon and Chuck Findley

providing the solos, and Manhattan Transfer's Tim Hauser producing the album and contributing a fancy rendition of "Mama Look A Boo Boo," the flavor of the album is unmistakable and a total gas. Even Kim Basinger, not known previously as a singer, reveals a new side of her talent as a vocalist in several standards in which her delivery is quite acceptable, though her version of "Honeysuckle Rose" seems a trifle lifeless. David Newman, writing in a style also unusual for him, turns in some terrific big band cues with "Backstage Beat-Up," "Run, Charley, Run," and the "Main Title."

Mars Attacks! ♫♫♫♫

1996, Atlantic Classics Records; from the movie *Mars Attacks!*, Warner Bros., 1996.

Album Notes: *Music*: Danny Elfman; *Orchestrations*: Steve Bartek, Edgardo Simon, Mark McKenzie; *Music Editors*: Ellen Segal, Bob Badami; Orchestra conducted by Artie Kane; *Album Producers*: Danny Elfman, Steve Bartek, Ellen Segal; *Engineer*: Shawn Murphy.

Selections: 1 Introduction (1:40); 2 Main Titles (2:22); 3 First Sighting (1:26); 4 The Landing (6:01); 5 Ungodly Experiments (:53); 6 State Address (3:06); 7 Martian Madame (3:02); 8 Martian Lounge (2:54); 9 Return Message (2:17); 10 Destructo X (1:17); 11 Loving Heads (1:20); 12 Pursuit (2:55); 13 The War Room (1:31); 14 Airfield Dilemma (2:05); 15 New World (1:45); 16 Ritchie's Speech (3:09); 17 End Credits (3:53); 18 Indian Love Call (R. Friml/O. Harbach/O. Hammerstein II)(3:08) *Slim Whitman*; 19 It's Not Unusual (G. Mills/L. Reed)(2:00) *Tom Jones*.

Review: Danny Elfman has composed a suitably over-the-top score for Tim Burton's broad science fiction comedy, *Mars Attacks!* From the eerily furtive moments preceding the stampede of burning cattle to the raucous battle music against the Martian invaders, Elfman captures the film's manic sense of nostalgic '50s sci-fi, best summed up in the relentless, brassy main theme, driven by the soaring strains of the omnipresent theremin and frequent use of choir. The score, full of bizarre and nostalgic orchestrations and plenty of musical tongue-in-cheek, is pure fun and excitement in an emerald cranium. It supports Burton's bizarre visions on-screen and splashes like a crimson death ray across home speaker systems.

Randall D. Larson

Marvin's Room ♫♫♫♫

1996, Miramax/Hollywood Records; from the movie *Marvin's Room*, Miramax Films, 1996.

Album Notes: *Music*: Rachel Portman; *Orchestrations*: Rachel Portman, Jeff Atmajian; *Music Editor*: Dan Lieberstein; *Orches-*

tra conducted by Michael Kosarin; *Featured Musicians*: Ken Bichel (piano), Jesse Levy (cello); *Album Producers*: Rachel Portman, Scott Rudin; *Engineer*: John Richards.

Selections: 1 Two Little Sisters (C. Simon)(3:25) *Carly Simon*; 2 Main Titles (3:03); 3 The Wig (3:33); 4 Burning Down The House (3:36); 5 Reflections (1:11); 6 The Loony Bin (1:55); 7 Florida (2:56); 8 The Toolbox (2:16); 9 I've Been So Lucky (2:30); 10 End Title (3:48); 11 The Toolbox II (1:13); 12 The Beach (2:24); 13 Tall Tales (3:03); 14 Clarence James (1:49); 15 Someplace Else (1:24); 16 Marvin's Room (3:37).

Review: In a narrative that sometimes finds deep, emotional accents to convey its story about two estranged sisters who are brought together after 20 years when one is diagnosed with having leukemia that can only be controlled with a bone marrow transplant from a close relative, *Marvin's Room* is an engaging, serious film with funny overtones. It avoids the usual pitfalls of melodrama or overbearing sentimentality to spin its tale in rich, down-to-earth details that make it both spirited and heartwarming. Adding the right colors to the story is Rachel Portman's excellent score, a delightful collection of cues, both serious and exhilarating, with catchy themes that perfectly match the tones of the story itself. Though presented here in a sequencing that doesn't follow the storyline, it easily makes its point, and proves essentially attractive and compelling. Carly Simon's "Two Little Sisters" is another nice touch in a thoroughly winning album.

Mary Reilly 🎵🎵🎵

1996, Sony Classical; from the movie *Mary Reilly*, TriStar Pictures, 1996.

Album Notes: *Music*: George Fenton; *Orchestrations*: Jeff Atmajian, Geoffrey Alexander; The London Symphony Orchestra, conducted by George Fenton; *Featured Musicians*: Lucia Lin, Janice Graham (violin); *Album Producers*: George Fenton, Eliza Thompson; *Engineer*: Keith Grant.

Selections: 1 The House Of Henry Jekyll (Opening Credits)(5:16); 2 The Birth Of Hyde (2:11); 3 The Announcement (1:43); 4 The Story Of The Scars (3:54); 5 Mary's Errand (2:16); 6 Mrs. Farraday's (2:35); 7 It Comes In Like The Tide (3:37); 8 Mary Meets Hyde (3:55); 9 The Shopping Trip (2:44); 10 Butler's Night Off (1:58); 11 Haffinger's (5:31); 12 The Transformation (6:45); 13 Mary Reilly (End Credits)(3:05).

Review: An interesting spin-off on the Gothic story about staid Dr. Jekyll and his murderous alter ego, Mr. Hyde, as seen from the point of view of Mary Reilly, a housemaid working for Dr. Jekyll with a secret as murky as her employer's, the film was mostly distinguished by the dark tones that pervaded it, something reflected in George Fenton's relentlessly somber score.

With a few exceptions ("Mrs. Farraday"), most of the cues are densely lugubrious, and fail to really attract in a strictly listening program, because very little in them contains the spark that would ignite one's interest.

M*A*S*H 🎵🎵

1995, Sony Legacy; from the movie *M*A*S*H*, 20th Century-Fox, 1970.

Album Notes: *Music*: Johnny Mandel; "Moments and minutes of music, madness and melodrama" featuring Hawkeye, Trapper, Duke, Lt. Dish, Hot Lips, Henry, Radar O'Reilly, Dago Red, Painless, Spearchucker and Radio Tokyo; *CD Producer*: Didier C. Deutsch; *Engineer*: Chris Herles.

Selections: 1 Suicide Is Painless (2:52) *The MASH*; 2 Duke And Hawkeye Arrive At M*A*S*H (10:38); 3 The Operating Theater (1:07); 4 Major Houlihan And Major Burns (6:35); 5 Painless' Suicide, Funeral And Resurrection (7:56); 6 "Hot Lips" Shows Her True Colors (3:46); 7 Moments To Remember (1:12); 8 The Football Game (7:59); 9 Going Home (3:31); 10 M*A*S*H Theme (2:48) *Ahmad Jamal*; 11 Dedication Scroll/Jeep Ride (1:04); 12 The Jig's Up (:56); 13 To Japan (:54); 14 Japanese Children's Hospital (1:51); 15 Tent Scene (1:56); 16 Kill 'Em Galop (3:25).

Review: Most die-hard fans of the film (starring Donald Sutherland and Elliott Gould, among others) will thoroughly enjoy this CD reissue of the original soundtrack, complete with bits of dialog, underscored and joined together by instrumental themes. Others may find the whole thing tedious after one listening—if they even listen to the whole disc!

Whatever your feeling, the soundtrack from *M*A*S*H* fairly drips with the madcap comedic highjinks that make the film such a delight. However, it may not be nearly as effective, or enjoyable, without the benefit of the full story and its accompanying visuals. As a record, it's more a curiosity than an experience you'll want to relive again and again. On the positive side, in addition to the theme song "Suicide is Painless," sung by The MASH and performed as a jazz instrumental by Ahmad Jamal, the disc also includes six instrumental cues, *sans* dialogue.

Charles L. Granata

The Mask

The Mask 🎵🎵🎵

1994, Tri-Star Records/Sony Music; from the movie *The Mask*, New Line Cinema, 1994.

Album Notes: *Music*: Randy Edelman; *Orchestrations*: Ralph Ferraro; *Music Editor*: John La Salandra; The Irish Film Orchestra, conducted by Randy Edelman; *Album Producer*: Randy Edelman; *Engineer*: Elto Ahi.

Selections: 1 Opening/The Origin Of The Mask (3:20); 2 Tina (2:00); 3 Carnival (2:19); 4 Transformation (2:18); 5 Tango In The Park (2:10); 6 Lovebirds (2:43); 7 Out Of The Line Of fire (2:09); 8 A Dark Night (2:18); 9 The Man Behind The Mask (2:01); 10 Dorian Gets A New Face (3:05); 11 Looking For A Way Out (1:37); 12 The Search (1:09); 13 Forked Tongue (1:49); 14 Milo To The Rescue (2:43); 15 The Mask Is Back (2:19); 16 Finale (1:47).

Review: See entry below.

The Mask 🎵🎵🎵

1994, Chaos/Sony Music; from the movie *The Mask*, New Line Cinema, 1994.

Album Notes: *Featured Performers*: Jim Carrey, Xscape, Domino, Tony Toni Tone, Harry Connick Jr., Vanessa Williams, K7, Fishbone, The Brian Setzer Orchestra, Royal Crown Revue, Susan Boyd. *Album Producer*: Maureen Crowe.

Selections: 1 Cuban Pete (C & C Pop Radio Edit)(J. Norman)(3:34) *Jim Carrey*; 2 Who's That Man (J. Dupri/M. Seal/L. Scott/T. Scott)(3:23) *Xscape*; 3 This Business Of Love (P. Roy/N. Klein/H. Hersh)(3:28) *Domino*; 4 Bounce Around (D. Wiggins/P. Wiggins/T. Riley)(4:33) *Tony Toni Tone*; 5 (I Could Only) Whisper Your Name (H. Connick, Jr./R. McLean)(3:55) *Harry Connick Jr.*; 6 You Would Be My Baby (K. Thomas/P. Galdston)(3:55) *Vanessa Williams*; 7 Hi De Ho (C. Calloway/C. Gaskill/I. Mills/H. White/L. Sharpe/T. Moran)(4:35) *K7*; 8 Let The Good Times Roll (S. Theard/F. Moore)(3:29) *Fishbone*; 9 Straight Up (Merritt/Lambert/B. Setzer)(3:12) *The Brian Setzer Orchestra*; 10 Hey Pachuco (E. Nichols)(3:06) *Royal Crown Revue*; 11 Gee Baby, Ain't I Good To You (D. Redman/A. Razaf)(2:48) *Susan Boyd*; 12 Cuban Pete (Arkin Movie Mix)(J. Norman)(2:10) *Jim Carrey*.

Review: Rare instance where both the song and score albums work well in concert with each other. Both capture the manic pace of the film, but the song compilation more so. It starts off strong with the radio version of "Cuban Pete," Jim Carrey's show-stopping musical number in the film which contains dialogue snippets. The film version concludes the album. Other songs that follow all have the characteristics of escapees from some 1940s Tex Avery cartoon (the film's effects were inspired by Avery's style). Bouncy '90s versions of Cab Calloway's 'Hi De Ho" share the spotlight with Vanessa Williams' steamy and romantic "Would You Be My Baby."

Randy Edelman's orchestral score alternates mainly between the calmer and darker moments of the film. However, when the Mask is on screen, Edelman's music becomes just as off the wall as Carrey's green goblin ("Out of the Line of Fire"). Warning! Both CDs feature the same cover art. The song album has a black border, while purple is the color for the score. *David Hirsch*

Masters of the Universe 🎵🎵🎵🎵

1992, Silva Screen Records; from the movie *Masters of the Universe*, Cannon Films, 1987.

Album Notes: *Music*: Bill Conti; *Orchestrations*: Bill Conti, Ralph Ferraro, Joel Rosenbaum; *Music Editor*: Steve Hope; The Graunke Orchestra of Munich, conducted by Harry Rabinowitz; *Album Producer*: Bill Conti; *Engineer*: Mike Ross.

Selections: 1 Main Title/Eternia Besieged (7:25); 2 Gwildor's Quadrille (1:51); 3 Quiet Escape (2:39); 4 Earthly Encounter (4:23); 5 Battle At The Gym (6:29); 6 Procession Of The Mercenaries (2:50); 7 Evilyn's Deception (2:43); 8 Centurion Attack (5:52); 9 Skeletor The Destroyer (3:11); 10 He-Man Enslaved (4:42); 11 Transformation Of Skeletor (2:30); 12 Kevin's Plight/After Them (9:13); 13 Julie's Muzak (1:47); 14 The Power Of Greyskull (3:33); 15 Good Journey (4:40); 16 He-Man Victorious/End Titles (5:13).

Review: A sword-and-sorcery film, opposing an impossibly handsome he-man and a fiendish looking ghoul, named Skeletor, in a fight to the death for control of the Universe, *Masters of the Universe* received an appropriately epic score from Bill Conti. The composer gleefully uses all the tenets of the genre to write cues that are all at once amusingly exhilarating and grandly representative of the screen action. Very few surprises here, just a rock solid score that delivers the goods, with the Graunke Orchestra doing a bang-up job in this spirited recording.

Matinee 🎵🎵🎵

1993, Varese-Sarabande Records; from the movie *Matinee*, Universal Pictures, 1993.

Album Notes: *Music*: Jerry Goldsmith; *Orchestrations*: Alexander Courage; *Music Editor*: Ken Hall; Orchestra conducted by Jerry Goldsmith; *Album Producer*: Jerry Goldsmith; *Engineer*: Bruce Botnick.

Selections: 1 Coming Attraction (2:09); 2 Hold On (3:08); 3 Brother To Brother (2:27); 4 Real People (2:13); 5 The Scam (4:08); 6 Halfway Home (3:45); 7 Showtime (4:33); 8 The Wrong Business (3:39); 9 This Is It (3:51); 10 The Next Attraction (7:56).

Review: This warm, nostalgic score for one of Joe Dante's best—and least-known—movies effectively captures the film's '50s setting and offers a couple of amusing send-ups of the horror film scores of the period. Unfortunately it's all so low-key and repetitive, particularly in its parody of the old prom standard "Theme to a Summer Place," that it just can't stand on its own as a listening experience, even though Goldsmith's rambunctious theme for John Goodman's William Castle-like character is perfect.

Jeff Bond

Maurice ♪♪♪♪

1987, RCA Victor; from the movie *Maurice*, Cinecom and Merchant Ivory Productions, 1989.

Album Notes: *Music:* Richard Robbins; Orchestra conducted by Harry Rabinowitz; *Recording Engineer:* Brian Masterson; *Remix Engineer:* Keith Grant.

Selections: 1 Prologue: The Lesson (5:05); 2 At The Pianola (1:33); 3 Two Letters (1:30); 4 In Greece/The Wedding (2:39); 5 Miserere (G. Allegri)(7:10) *King's College Choir of Cambridge, David Willcocks;* 6 Pendersleigh In Gloom (:59); 7 The Cafe Royale (1:30); 8 Miss Edna Mae's Surprise/The Train (4:38); 9 The Moonlit Night (3:46); 10 In The Renault (1:12); 11 Alec's Farewell (1:13); 12 The Boathouse (2:26); 13 Clive And Anne (1:59); 14 End Titles (3:28).

Review: A surprisingly sensitive screen treatment of E.M. Foster's Edwardian novel, *Maurice* details a young man's awakening to his own homosexuality when he finds himself attracted and responding to the attentions of another student at Cambridge. As is frequently the case with Merchant Ivory, the production company specializing in magnificently reconstructed period films, the delicately chiseled score crafted by Richard Robbins gives *Maurice* its proper atmosphere and evokes a period which overflows with romantic accents. The music, incredibly rich and versatile, features transpositions of themes by Tchaikovsky, "At the Pianola" and "In the Renault," a superb period waltz, "The Cafe Royale," and a bouncy piano rag, "Miss Edna Mae's Surprise," among its many highlights. It all adds up to a catchy, enjoyable album that compels the listener to return to it frequently.

Maverick

Maverick ♪♪♪♪

1994, Reprise Records; from the movie *Maverick*, Warner Bros., 1994.

Album Notes: *Music:* Randy Newman; *Orchestrations:* Jack Hayes, Don Davis; *Music Editor:* James Flamberg; Orchestra

"It was one of those films where I could be anthemic without being pretentious, because the scale of the film supports that genre of music."

David Arnold
on Independence Day *(The Hollywood Reporter, 1-15-97)*

conducted by Randy Newman; *Featured Musician:* Malcolm McNab; *Album Producer:* Frank Wolf; *Engineer:* Frank Wolf; *Assistant Engineer:* Sue McLean.

Selections: 1 Opening (5:37); 2 Annabelle (2:28); 3 Fight (2:06); 4 Coop (:41); 5 Money In The Bank (1:07); 6 In And Out Of Trouble (1:27); 7 Magic Cards, Maybe/Lucky Shirt (1:32); 8 Headed For The Game (1:31); 9 Runaway Stage (4:49); 10 Sneakin' Around (:47); 11 Maverick (:56); 12 Joseph And The Russian (1:08); 13 Oh Bret (2:06); 14 A Noble Aims (:49); 15 Trap (1:51); 16 The Hanging (2:01); 17 Bret Escapes (1:26); 18 Bret's Card/Sore Loser (1:28); 19 Coop Sails Away (1:33); 20 Annabelle Toodleoo (1:56); 21 The Commodore (1:24); 22 Pappy Shuffle (1:11); 23 Bath House (:40); 24 Tartine De Merde (1:34).

Review: Randy Newman's western score is grandly expansive and as jaunty and spry as the film's easygoing charm. Newman frequently switches gears from heavy dramatics to amusing pomp and bombast, to high Coplandesque adventure. His main theme takes its cue from the high-spirited, fast-moving Maverick character. The theme is pure Americana and steeped in Hollywood tradition. In contrast is a slightly deceptive theme for Annabelle, a lilting, old-fashioned cue for violins. These primary themes are central to the score, which remains cleverly playful in orchestration and tone. Newman's baton is planted firmly in his cheek as he concocts a spirited and likable exercise in Hollywood western musicology. As obvious and occasionally over-the-top the themes and their interplay may be, the score remains contagiously likable.

Randall D. Larson

Maverick ♪♪♪♪

1994, Atlantic Records; from the movie *Maverick*, Warner Bros., 1994.

Album Notes: *Song Producers:* Tracy Lawrence, Clint Black, James Stroud, Josh Leo, Michael Omartian, Vince Gill, Carlene

Carter, Doug Johnson, Barry Beckett, Allen Reynolds, Jim Rooney, Emory Gordy, Jr., Don Was, James Newton Howard; *Album Executive Producers*: Mark Hartley, Larry Fitzgerald; *Engineer*: Denny Purcell.

Selections: 1 Renegades, Rebels And Rogues (P. Nelson/L. Boone/E. Clark) (2:36) *Tracy Lawrence*; 2 A Good Run Of Bad Luck (C. Black/H. Nicholas) (2:43) *Clint Black*; 3 Maverick (D. Buttolph/P.F. Webster) (2:40) *Restless Heart*; 4 Ophelia (R. Robertson) (3:38) *Vince Gill*; 5 Something Already Gone (C. Carter/A. Anderson) (3:34) *Carlene Carter*; 6 Dream On Texas Ladies (S. Mills) (3:08) *John Michael Montgomery*; 7 Ladies Love Outlaws (L. Clayton) (3:39) *Confederate Railroad*; 8 Solitary Travelers (H. Ketchum) (4:26) *Hal Ketchum*; 9 The Rainbow Down The Road (E. Gordy, Jr./R. Foster) (2:57) *Patty Loveless, Radney Foster*; 10 You Don't Mess Around With Me (W. Jennings) (4:26) *Waylon Jennings*; 11 Ride Gambler Ride (R. Newman) (3:52) *Randy Newman*; 12 Amazing Grace (trad.) (3:14) *The Maverick Choir*

Review: Country music soundtracks have generally come up short (and if you think *Urban Cowboy* is country, you're wrong). This does a better job than most, with a group of established veterans and fresh up-and-comers performing new songs written for or old songs chosen for this film. "Dream on Texas Ladies" proves that John Michael Montgomery is a gifted singer, even when presented with so-so material. Patty Loveless and Radney Foster do a nice duet turn on "Rainbow Down the Road," but it's three old hats, Waylon Jennings, Clint Black and Randy Newman, who are responsible for "Maverick's" best tracks.

Gary Graff

Max and Helen 🎵🎵🎵🎵

1991, Bay Cities Records; from the movie *Max and Helen*, Turner Pictures, 1990.

Album Notes: *Music*: Christopher Young; *Orchestrations*: Jeff Atmajian, Christopher Young; *Featured Musicians (in **Black Dragon**)*: Christopher Young (pianos/deowas), Masa Yoshizawa (hichiriki/nokan/shakuhachi/voice), Hiromi Hashibe (featured voice/bass koto), Tateo Takahashi (shamisen), Suenobu Togi (sho), Daniel Licht (bass suling/bansuri flute/genggong), Bob Fernandez, John Fitzgerald, David Johnson, Mark Zimoski (Japanese percussion); *Album Producer*: Nick Redman; *Engineers*: Jeff Vaughn, Mark Zimoski.

Selections: *MAX AND HELEN:* 1 In Memory (1:45); 2 Piano Etude No. 3 in E (excerpt) (F. Chopin) (1:36); 3 Stories Must Be Told (3:33); 4 Heart Lost (4:30); 5 Zloczow Square (1:39); 6 Zalesie (4:50); 7 Must Continue (3:01); 8 Forgiveness (2:39); 9 Masses (32:52);

BLACK DRAGON: 10 Koku-ryu (Black Dragon)(18:05).

Review: Though presented under the title of *Max and Helen*, from a 1990 film starring Treat Williams and Alice Krige, about a pair of lovers separated by World War II and brought back together fortuitously several years later, the CD actually gives an inordinately long playing time to two other, non-film related works, the 33-minute *Masses*, and the 18-minute *Koku-ryu (Black Dragon)*, an avant-garde composition that may prove off-putting to some listeners. A riveting combination of solo voices, sonic manipulations, and ethnic folk music, *Max and Helen* aims to create a multi-layered tapestry which reinforces the screen action and gives it a stronger emotional tug.

Maximum Risk 🎵

1996, Varese-Sarabande Records; from the movie *Maximum Risk*, Columbia Pictures, 1996.

Album Notes: *Music*: Robert Folk; *Orchestrations*: Robert Folk, Peter Tomashek, Jon Kull; *Music Editor*: Jay Richardson; *Album Producer*: Robert Folk; *Engineer*: Hal Sachs.

Selections: 1 Tour de Nice (4:42); 2 Mikhail's Diary (3:33); 3 Maximum Conflagration (3:21); 4 Brighton Beach Mob Wars (2:35); 5 Maximum Erotica (1:45); 6 Cirque du Cernivore (2:40); 7 Extreme Reaction (4:40); 8 Terminal Betrayal (4:31); 9 Unchained Heart (2:02); 10 Without You (R. Folk/T. Wood/G. Wells)(3:18) *Terry Wood*.

Review: An otherwise solid actioner starring Jean-Claude Van Damme, about the strong spiritual connection that exists between twins, set against the backdrop of violent life in a big city, *Maximum Risk* inspired Robert Folk to write a constantly driven score that may have been quite effective on-screen to illustrate and underline the action in the scenes, but fails to make much of a statement when heard in one's living room. A collision of synthesizer chords and percussive effects that lead nowhere, the cues often tend to sound limited and dry, with incredible energy being wasted on very little. Or, as someone else would have said in other times, much ado about nothing.

Medicine Man 🎵🎵🎵

1992, Varese-Sarabande; from the movie *Medicine Man*, Cinergi Productions, 1992.

Album Notes: *Music*: Jerry Goldsmith; *Orchestrations*: Arthur Morton; *Music Editor*: Ken Hall; The National Philharmonic Orchestra, conducted by Jerry Goldsmith; *Album Producer*: Jerry Goldsmith; *Engineer*: Mike Ross.

Selections: 1 Rae's Arrival (5:06); 2 First Morning (3:46); 3 Campbell And The Children (1:57); 4 The Trees (6:01); 5 The Harvest (3:11); 6 Mocara (3:36); 7 Mountain High (2:41); 8

Without A Net (4:19); 9 Finger Painting (2:30); 10 What's Wrong (1:52); 11 The Injection (2:09); 12 The Sugar (2:08); 13 The Fire (2:10); 14 A Meal And A Bath (8:03).

Review: Jerry Goldsmith's music for *Medicine Man* is an evocative tapestry of orchestral color, vibrantly splashed with expert strokes and subtle undercurrents onto his musical canvas. The scene is set with a bouncy, Latin American-styled motif with flutes, marimba, and percussion embellished by synth. The real theme emerges half-way through, altering the jaunty tempo and texture with a dark, evocative ambiance of rustling electronics and harsh, primitive percussion. Violins foreshadow the film's main theme, a graceful melody which captures all the majesty, mystery and tragedy of the tropical rain forest in which the action takes place. That theme reappears frequently, through quotations or variations, in several succeeding cues, associated with both the rain forest and the noble cancer research undertaken therein.

Throughout, Goldsmith superbly captures the alternating moods in the storyline — exhilaration to despair — through a moment's orchestral counterpoint. The frequent use of water-droplet synth sounds as a rhythmic measure is an effective and clever device to suggest the humid wetness of the rain forest.

Randall D. Larson

Memoirs of an Invisible Man 𝄞𝄞𝄞♭

1992, Varese-Sarabande; from the movie *Memoirs of an Invisible Man,* Warner Bros., 1992.

Album Notes: *Music*: Shirley Walker; *Orchestrations*: Shirley Walker, Larry Rench, Lisa Bloom, Bruce Fowler; *Synthesizer Programmer*: Hans Zimmer; Orchestra conducted by Shirley Walker; *Album Producer*: Shirley Walker; *Engineers*: Robert Fernandez, Doug Bostnick.

Selections: 1 Theme Medley (3:22); 2 In A State Of Molecular Flux (4:00); 3 Fear Creeps In (3:09); 4 Love In The Rain (1:38); 5 Nick Escapes The Apartment Siege (3:31); 6 The Final Chase (3:14); 7 Nick And Alice In Love (2:28); 8 Jenkins Closes In (4:37); 9 The Invisible Man Reveals Himself (1:40); 10 You're Not Alone Anymore (2:11).

Review: Shirley Walker's first feature film score is one of the best elements of this John Carpenter/Chevy Chase misfire. The album opens with a "suite" (actually the film's end credit music) that blends the score's primary material with great showmanship, from a heartbreakingly beautiful love theme to the foreboding, crashing sounds of science gone awry and some pulse-pounding, rapid-fire pursuit music. Walker's skill

at writing portentous, complex and heavily-textured action music is unquestioned (what is questionable is why she doesn't get more high-profile assignments like this), but what's really surprising is that someone so adept at underscoring the testosterone-pumped world of action movies can also produce such wonderfully touching romantic melodies.

Jeff Bond

Memphis Belle 𝄞𝄞𝄞𝄞

1990, Varese-Sarabande Records; from the movie *Memphis Belle,* Warner Bros., 1990.

Album Notes: *Music*: George Fenton; *Orchestrations*: George Fenton, Jeff Atmajian; Orchestra conducted by George Fenton; *Album Producers*: George Fenton, Eliza Thompson; *Engineers*: Keith Grant, Geoff Young.

Selections: 1 The Londonderry Air/Front Titles Memphis Belle (3:50); 2 Green Eyes (N. Mendez/E. Rivera/E. Wood)(3:25); 3 Flying Home (B. Goodman/L. Hampton)(2:57); 4 The Steel Lady (1:44); 5 Prepare To Take Off (Amazing Grace)(trad.)(2:39); 6 The Final Mission (3:51); 7 With Deep Regret (2:02); 8 I Know Why (And So Do You)(M. Gordon/H. Warren)(2:55) *Glenn Miller and His Orchestra*; 9 The Bomb Run (1:30); 10 Limping Home (2:25); 11 Crippled Belle: The Landing (3:26); 12 Resolution (1:06); 13 Memphis Belle End Title Suite (7:37); 14 Danny Boy (trad.)(3:20) *Mark Williamson*.

Review: Set during World War II, amid the gallant pilots who flew the US Air Force B-17 bombers, the film chronicles the 25th and last mission of the Memphis Belle and its crew, in a final flight over Germany for a bombing that was to decide the conclusion of the war. In the cues he wrote for the film, George Fenton deftly evokes the moods of suspense and drama, fun and exhilaration, heroism and glory that marked the mission. Setting the score into its time period, rerecordings of standards, like "Green Eyes," "Flying Home," and "I Know Why," provide an occasional bow to the musical trends of the era, resulting in a strongly suggestive score. The long "Memphis Belle End Title Suite" regroups the most important themes into a striking cohesive musical coda.

Meridian 𝄞

1991, Moonstone Records; from the movie *Meridian,* Full Moon Entertainment, 1991.

Album Notes: *Music*: Pino Donaggio; *Synthesizers Programming*: Paolo Steffan; The Sinfonica di Milano, conducted by Natale Massara; *Album Producer*: Pino Donaggio; *Engineer*: Paolo Bocchi.

Selections: 1 Meridian Overture (3:14); 2 Unholy Seduction (4:05); 3 You Are The One (1:06); 4 Forbidden Love (5:05); 5 Dangerous Dimensions (4:19); 6 Blood Brothers (3:26); 7 Confessional (2:17); 8 Beast To The Rescue (4:40); 9 Life Into Stone (1:12); 10 Animal Passion (3:58); 11 Catherine's Theme (:47); 12 Revelations (2:55); 13 Circus From The Past (3:09); 14 Trip To The Castle (:49); 15 It's Just A Dream (1:12); 16 Kill This Beast (6:19).

Review: This dark version of the classic "Beauty and the Beast" tale got an equally gloomy score from acknowledged horror music master Pino Donaggio. Unfortunately, the score's pace is just as pedestrian as the film and therein lies the problem. Despite lovely melodies like "Catherine's Theme" (too short!) or "Beast to the Rescue," there are just too many others that crawl along. "Unholy Seduction," a synthesized cue whose primary melody was cleverly created by sampled voices, ends up being too repetitive. And why was "Circus from the Past" played by synthesizers when they had an orchestra that could have made it not sound so embarrassingly primitive? Although it works effectively on film, this score is just too bland and lacking in anything substantial to support the soundtrack's almost 50-minute running time.

David Hirsch

Mermaids 𝄞𝄞𝄞▷

1990, Geffen Records; from the movie *Mermaids*, Orion Pictures, 1990.

Album Notes: *Album Producer*: John David Kalodner; *Engineer*: Dan Hersch.

Selections: 1 The Shoop Shoop Song (It's In His Kiss)(R. Clark)(2:51) *Cher*; 2 Big Girls Don't Cry (B. Crewe/B. Gaudio)(2:23) *Frankie Valli & The Four Seasons*; 3 You've Really Got A Hold On Me (W. Robinson)(2:57) *Smokey Robinson & The Miracles*; 4 It's My Party (H. Wiener/J. Gluck/W. Gold)(2:21) *Lesley Gore*; 5 Johnny Angel (L. Pockriss/L. Duddy)(2:22) *Shelley Fabares*; 6 Baby I'm Yours (V. McCoy)(3:19) *Cher*; 7 Just One Look (G. Carroll/D. Payne) (2:26) *Doris Troy*; 8 Love Is Strange (S. Robinson/M. Baker/E. McDaniel) (2:55) *Mickey & Sylvia*; 9 Sleepwalk (S. Farina/J. Farina/A. Farina)(2:21) *Santo & Johnny*; 10 If You Wanna Be Happy (C. Guida/F. Guida/J. Royster)(2:11) *Jimmy Soul*.

Review: A quirky little comedy, about an ever so slightly eccentric woman and her two equally unconventional daughters, *Mermaids* is considerably brightened up by its cheerful soundtrack, which includes many songs from the early 1960s, time period of the action. While offering little that's new in terms of music (with the possible exception of "The Shoop Shoop Song," and a surprisingly laid-back version of "Baby, I'm Yours," performed by Cher, who also stars), the album compiles together various songs that are bound to evoke many pleasant memories of a time when things seemed much less complicated and easier to enjoy, with performances by Frankie Valli and The Four Seasons, Smokey Robinson and The Miracles, Lesley Gore, Mickey and Sylvia, and Shelley Fabares, among its better moments. Nothing earthshaking, just a nifty combination of a few memorable tunes that goes a long way in creating the right atmosphere.

Merry Christmas Mr. Lawrence 𝄞𝄞𝄞

1985, London Records; from the movie *Merry Christmas Mr. Lawrence*, 1985.

Album Notes: *Music*: Ryuichi Sakamoto; *Album Producer*: Ryuichi Sakamoto; *Engineers*: Shinichi Tanaka, Seigen Ono, Ryuichi Sakamoto.

Selections: 1 Merry Christmas Mr. Lawrence (4:37); 2 Batavia (1:19); 3 Germination (1:49); 4 A Hearty Breakfast (1:24); 5 Before The War (2:15); 6 The Seed And The Sower (5:03); 7 A Brief Encounter (2:23); 8 Ride Ride Ride (Celliers' Brother's Song)(1:04); 9 The Fight (1:33); 10 Father Christmas (2:09); 11 Dismissed! (:10); 12 Assembly (2:18); 13 Beyond Reason (2:01); 14 Sowing The Seed (1:55); 15 23rd Psalm (2:00); 16 Last Regrets (1:47); 17 Ride Ride Ride (reprise)(1:06); 18 The Seed (1:05); 19 Forbidden Colours (4:46) *David Sylvan*.

Review: Composer Ryuichi Sakamoto stars along with David Bowie in this film set during World War II in a Japanese prison camp. Two years earlier, Vangelis had shown that modern synthesized music could work in context with the period setting of *Chariots of Fire*. Sakamoto follows his lead, but creatively infuses some of his work here with sound effects in "Ride, Ride, Ride" and unusual musical colors in "A Brief Encounter." He also relies on traditional orchestral music for one standout cue called "Germination."

David Hirsch

Michael 𝄞𝄞𝄞▷

1996, Revolution Records; from the movie *Michael*, Turner Pictures, 1996.

Album Notes: *Album Supervisors*: Jolene Cherry, Jeff Aldrich, Daniella Capretta; *Music Supervisor*: Nicholas Meyers; Mastered by Bob Ludwig.

Selections: 1 Through Your Hands (J. Hiatt)(4:18) *Don Henley*; 2 I Don't Care If You Love Me Anymore (R. Malo)(3:07) *The Mavericks*; 3 Chain Of Fools (D. Covey)(2:46) *Aretha Franklin*; 4

Bright Side Of The Road (V. Morrison) (3:45) *Van Morrison*; 5 Heaven Is My Home (R. Newman)(3:07) *Randy Newman, Valerie Carter*; 6 The Spider And The Fly (M. Jagger/K. Richards)(3:50) *Kenny Wayne Shepherd, James Cotton*; 7 Feels Like Home (R. Newman) (4:36) *Bonnie Raitt*; 8 What A Wonderful World (G. Weiss/R. Thiele)(2:14) *Willie Nelson*; 9 Love God (And Everyone Else) (Tonio K./J. Keller)(4:16) *Al Green*; 10 Sittin' By The Side Of The Road (T. James/T. Wilson)(2:18) *Andie MacDowell*; 11 Spirit In The Sky (N. Greenbaum)(3:59) *Norman Greenbaum.*

Review: A romantic fable about a photogenic mutt, an angel (John Travolta, in another winning screen performance), and the journalists who are after him for a scoop, *Michael* is the occasion for a festive music celebration with several songs, heard on the soundtrack, that deal with love, happiness, elation, or just simply good feelings. This compilation brings it all back home, with performances by many enjoyable singers, like Van Morrison, Bonnie Raitt, Willie Nelson, Aretha Franklin, and Don Henley. An ingratiating collection that makes few demands on the intellect but is guaranteed to provide a good time.

Michael Collins ♪♪♪♪♪

1996, Atlantic Records; from the movie *Michael Collins*, Geffen Pictures, 1996.

Album Notes: *Music*: Elliot Goldenthal; *Orchestrations*: Robert Elhai, Elliot Goldenthal; *Additional Orchestrations*: Sonny Kompanek, Deniz Hughes, Ned Ginsberg, Richard Lee, Matthias Gohl; *Choir conductor*: Rick Cordova; Orchestra conducted by Jonathan Sheffer; *Electronic Music Producer*: Richard Martinez; *Album Producer*: Matthias Gohl; *Engineers*: Joel Iwataki, Steve McLaughlin.

Selections: 1 Easter Rebellion (3:15) *Sinead O' Connor*; 2 Fire And Arms (1:42); 3 Train Station Farewell (1:56); 4 Winter Raid (2:39); 5 Elegy For A Sunday (3:08); 6 Football Match (1:50); 7 On Cats Feet (4:29); 8 Defiance And Arrest (1:50); 9 Train To Granard (1:31); 10 Boland Returns (Kitty's Waltz) (1:19); 11 His Majesty's Finest (2:12); 12 Boland's Death (1:40); 13 Home To Cork (1:19); 14 Civil War (2:11) *Sinead O' Connor*; 15 Collins' Proposal (1:26); 16 An Anthem Deferred (1:45); 17 She Moved Through The Air (4:57) *Sinead O' Connor*; 18 Funeral/Coda (4:34); 19 Macushla (D. MacMurrough/J. Rowe) (3:30) *The Cafe Orchestra.*

Review: A film that exudes tremendous energy and transcends its bleak subject of political activism in Ireland, *Michael Collins* owes a lot of its impact on the screen to director Neil Jordan's deft handling of the struggle for independence from the British

and his understanding that the topic needed an uplifting cinematic approach to reach a broad audience. He achieved his goal by staging this account of the campaign waged in 1916 by Michael Collins, an early pioneer in the fight against Britain, with all the ingredients usually found in contemporary dramas—fast-paced action scenes and rousing dramatic performances. Adding a specific comment of its own to the story, Elliot Goldenthal wrote a robust, compelling score, rife with great themes that unfold with force and persuasion, with an occasional Irish sonority to anchor the music into its specific ethnic background, something further complemented through the addition of various vocals by Sinead O'Connor. From the first track, "Fire and Arms," the tone is readily apparent that this is going to be a vibrant essay, filled with great orchestral sounds and strong melodic ideas. Goldenthal doesn't disappoint. The score throbs with excitement, occasionally pausing for a softer, reflective theme, but keeping the listener on edge most of the time.

Midas Run/The Night Visitor
♪♪♪ ⁷

1995, Citadel Records; from the movies *Midas Run*, 1969; and *The Night Visitor*.

Album Notes: *Music*: Elmer Bernstein, Henry Mancini; The Rome Cinema Orchestra, conducted by Elmer Bernstein; Orchestra conducted by Henry Mancini; *Featured Performers*: Elmer Bernstein (piano), Dorothy Remsen (harp), Martin Ruderman (flute), Armand Kaproff (cello); *Album Producer*: Tony Thomas, Tom Null; *Engineer*: Bruce Leek.

Selections: MIDAS RUN: 1 Main Theme (2:25); 2 Love Affair (1:01); 3 The Foreign Office (1:07); 4 Police Chase (:48); 5 Mr. Pedley At The Palace (2:07); 6 Memories (1:24); 7 Love In The Country (3:54); 8 Morning Dew (2:55); 9 The Palace Guards (1:52); 10 Disco (2:20); 11 The Caper (1:03); 12 Change Of Heart (1:19); 13 The End (1:29);

HOUSE AFTER 5 YEARS OF LIVING: 14 Prologue and Elements (:52); 15 Setting (1:58); 16 Living Room (2:07); 17 Upstairs (1:44); 18 Studio (1:43); 19 Conclusion (1:58); 20 Reflections (:44);

THE NIGHT VISITOR: 21 Suite (18:00).

Review: Written for a film starring Fred Astaire as a charming British agent who steals a large shipment of government gold on its way to Tanzania from Zurich and Italy, *Midas Run* was a total disaster at the box office, though it enabled Elmer Bernstein to write a straightforward little score that was immensely appealing, the sort Henry Mancini was quite famous for. Shot on locations in London, Milan, Venice and Rome, the locales of the action provided the composer with the proper scenic colors, while the action itself suggested some of the most virile accents in the score. As Tony Thomas points out in his liner notes, it is a clear example of "film music being better than the picture for which it was designed."

House: After 5 Years of Living was an assignment of another kind which came in 1955 from furniture designers Charles and Ray Eames, who asked Bernstein to score an art film about the house they had designed. As for *The Night Visitor*, starring Max Von Sydow as a farmer wrongly accused of murder by his sister and her husband, and subsequently committed to an asylum, it also is an obscure film that failed to find an audience. It elicited a taut, hypnotic score from Henry Mancini, writing for a synthesizer and 17 instruments, in a style that seems miles away from the comedies he was mostly scoring at this stage in his career. It is also in sharp contrast to what precedes it and as a result seems a rather odd choice in this context.

Midnight Cowboy 🦴🦴🦴🦴✎

1985, EMI-Manhattan Records; from the movie *Midnight Cowboy*, United Artists, 1969.

Album Notes: *Music*: John Barry; *Orchestrations*: John Barry; Orchestra conducted by John Barry.

Selections: 1 Everybody's Talkin' (F. Neil)(2:30) *Nilsson*; 2 Joe Buck Rides Again (3:46); 3 A Famous Myth (J. Comanor)(3:22) *The Groop*; 4 Fun City (3:52); 5 He Quit Me (W. Zevon)(2:46) *Leslie Miller*; 6 Jungle Gym At The Zoo (R. Sussman/R. Frank/S. Bronstein) (2:15) *Elephants Memory*; 7 Midnight Cowboy (2:34); 8 Old Man Willow (R. Sussman/M. Shapiro/M. Yules/S. Bronstein)(7:03) *Elephants Memory*; 9 Florida Fantasy (2:08); 10 Tears And Joy (J. Comanor)(2:29) *The Groop*; 11 Science Fiction (1:57); 12 Everybody's Talkin' (F. Neil)(1:54) *Nilsson*.

Review: While Nilsson's evocative rendition of "Everybody's Talkin'" might have clouded John Barry's own achievements, the soundtrack of *Midnight Cowboy* has always been a deft combination of both, the song and Barry's cues, and that's what ultimately subsists after one has listened to the album. Certainly, the instrumental selections, particularly "Joe Buck Rides Again" and "Fun City," do much to capture the squalid moods in John Schlesinger's film about a young hustler from Texas who becomes a boy prostitute in New York City and befriends a seedy, tuberculous-stricken street character with whom he moves to Florida. The pop songs, notably "A Famous Myth" by The Groop (sounding like a clone of The Mamas and The Papas) and "Jungle Gym at the Zoo" by Elephants Memory, are also very much a part of this memorable film, even though they sound dated by now.

Midnight Run 🦴🦴🦴🦴✎

1988, MCA Records; from the movie *Midnight Run*, Universal Pictures, 1988.

Album Notes: *Music*: Danny Elfman; *Orchestrations*: Danny Elfman, Steve Bartek, Mark Coniglio; *Music Editor*: Bob Badimi, Julie Hall; *Musicians*: Ira Engber, Paul Jackson, Jr. (guitars), Neal Stubenhaus (electric bass), Chuck Domanico (acoustic bass), John "Vatos" Hernandez (drums), Mike Fisher (percussion), Ralph Grierson (keyboards), Frank Morocco (accordion), John "Juke" Logan (harmonica), John Goux (additional guitar); *Album Producer*: Steve Bartek, Danny Elfman; *Engineer*: Bill Jackson

Selections: 1 Walsh Gets The Duke (1:47); 2 Main Titles (2:21); 3 Stairway Chase (:54); 4 J.W. Gets A Plan (1:41); 5 Gears Spin I (:54); 6 Dorfler's Theme (1:24); 7 F.B.I. (1:16); 8 Package Deal (1:07); 9 Mobocopter (2:42); 10 Freight Train Hop (1:18); 11 Drive To Red's (1:04); 12 In The Next Life (1:06); 13 The River (1:19); 14 The Wild Ride (1:31); 15 Amarillo Dawn (:26); 16 Potato Walk (1:09); 17 Desert Run (4:45); 18 Diner Blues (1:19); 19 Dorfler's Problem (1:01); 20 Gear's Spin II (1:30); 21 The Confrontation (2:30); 22 The Longest Walk (1:32); 23 Walsh Frees The Duke (2:44); 24 End Credits: "Try To Believe" (4:16) *Mosley & The B-Men*.

Review: In one of his earliest scoring efforts, Danny Elfman hit the right note with his music for *Midnight Run*, an iconoclastic comedy starring Robert De Niro as a gruff bounty hunter ready to throw in the towel, but accepts for his last job the task of bringing back to a Las Vegas mobster an accountant who has embezzled millions of dollars. Elfman, who was still recording with his group Oingo Boingo at the time, wrote a fast-paced, rock score that reflects his intentions of moving away from the kind of music that had made him famous, while keeping a foot firmly planted in a genre that was familiar to him. With bouncy, cheerful little themes—some combining the harmonica and the accordion for an unusual, slightly unorthodox sound—the score is a constant delight, its effectiveness only slightly defeated by the short playing time of some of the selections.

Mighty Morphin Power Rangers: The Movie

Mighty Morphin Power Rangers: The Movie 🦴🦴🦴✎

1995, Varese-Sarabande; from the movie *Mighty Morphin Power Rangers: The Movie*, 20th Century-Fox, 1995.

Album Notes: *Music*: Graeme Revell; *Orchestrations*: Tim Simonec, Ken Kugler, Larry Kenton, Mark Gasbarro; *Music*

Editor: Josh Winget; The West Australian Symphony Orchestra, conducted by Tim Simonec; *Album Producer*: Graeme Revell; *Engineer*: Dan Wallin.

Selections: 1 Prologue (:58); 2 Ivan Ooze (2:07); 3 The Great Power (2:15); 4 The Tengu's Attack (1:34); 5 Zordon Is Dying (1:49); 6 The Rangers On Phaedros (1:17); 7 Dolcea To The Rescue (:57); 8 Journey To The Plateau (1:23); 9 Summoning The Ninjetti (3:26); 10 Jurassic Ride (2:55); 11 The Monolith (1:26); 12 Battle With The Gatekeepers (3:43); 13 Metamorphicons Confront The Rangers (2:22); 14 The Megazord Battle (2:12); 15 Leap To Our Doom (1:46); 16 Power Rangers Triumph (1:26); 17 Freddy To The Rescue (:57); 18 Zordon Is Saved (2:35).

Review: "Balls to the wall" orchestral score by Graeme Revell unexpectedly provides more fun and excitement than this silly film ever could muster. Certainly, Revell manages to give the story a more mystical air (the use of a chorus in "Summoning the Ninjetti" for example) and the desperation of the Rangers' plight is endowed with a real sense of urgency in "Zordon is Dying." Even the bombastic brass arrangements of the battle cues, like "The Megazord Battle," give the film a spectacular scope it could not achieve on its own. Revell has a real flair at creating dramatic scores for these types of effects-laden action films.

David Hirsch

Mighty Morphin Power Rangers: The Movie 🎜🎜

1995, Atlantic/Fox Records; from the movie *Mighty Morphin Power Rangers: The Movie*, 20th Century-Fox, 1995.

Album Notes: *Song Producers*: Ron Nevison, Michael Beinhorn, Con, Devo, Snap, Fun Tomas, Kid Capelli, Van Halen, Mick Jones, Donn Landee, Neil Dorfsman, Dan Hartman, Rick Parker, Power Jet, Graeme Revell, Ron Wasserman, Ron Kenan; *Engineers*: Ron Nevison, Robert Casale, Snap, Jeo, Neil Dorfsman, Michael Barbiero, Rick Parker, Ron Wasserman, Mark Ettel; *Album Executive Producers*: Happy Walters, Pilar McCurry; *Engineer*: Dave Collins.

Selections: 1 Go Go Power Rangers (S. Levy/K. Mahchi)(5:04) *The Power Rangers Orchestra*; 2 Higher Ground (S. Wonder)(3:22) *Red Hot Chili Peppers*; 3 Trouble (J. Blake/C. Askew/C. Fitzpatrick)(3:20) *Shampoo*; 4 Are You Ready? (M. Mothersbaugh/G. Casale)(3:01) *Devo*; 5 The Power (B. Benitez/J. Garrett/ Toni C.)(5:44) *Snap*; 6 Kung Fu Dancing (F. Tomas/K. Cappelli/C. Douglas) (3:46) *Fun Tomas, Carl*

Douglas; 7 Dreams (E. Van Halen/S. Hagar/M. Anthony/A. Van Halen)(4:51) *Van Halen*; 8 Free Ride (D. Hartman)(7:03) *Dan Hartman*; 9 SenSurround (J. Flansburgh/J. Linnell)(3:05) *They Might Be Giants*; 10 Ayeyaiyai (Alpha Song)(L. Tierney/T. Cullen)(3:48) *Power Jet*; 11 Firebird (G. Revell)(3:40) *Graeme Revell*; 12 Cross My Line (R. Wasserman/R. Kenan)(3:10) *Aaron Waters (The Mighty Raw)*.

Review: Hard to believe, but these teen superheroes were once hotter than Beanie Babies, and they're destined to become favorites at '90s dress-up parties. The music for their first feature film is fairly mundane, making use of some proven hits, like Red Hot Chili Peppers' funky take on "Higher Ground" and Van Halen's Teflon-smooth "Dreams," and oddball adaptations, such as Carl Douglas joining Fun Tomas for something called "Kung Fu Dancing." But, never fear, it does have the "Go Go Power Rangers" theme, if it isn't already plastered in your memory.

Gary Graff

The Mighty Quinn 🎜🎜🎜

1989, A&M Records; from the movie *The Mighty Quinn*, M-G-M, 1989.

Album Notes: *Song Producers*: UB40, Ray "Pablo" Falconer, Alphonsus Cassell, Tyrone Downie, Michael Rose, Yello, Daniel Lanois, Lloyd James, Cecil Forbes; *Album Producer*: David Anderle; *Engineer*: Arnie Acosta.

Selections: 1 I Gotta Keep Moving On (C. Mayfield)(4:36) *UB40*; 2 Groove Master (A. Cassell)(6:02) *Arrow*; 3 Guess Who's Coming To Dinner (M. Rose) (3:39) *Michael Rose*; 4 (I'm) Hurting Inside (B. Marley)(4:43) *Sheryl Lee Ralph, Cedella Marley, Sharon Marley Prendergast*; 5 Giving/Sharing (L. Roberts)(3:30) *Half Pint*; 6 La Habanera (B. Blank/D. Meier)(5:11) *Yello*; 7 Yellow Moon (A. Neville/J. Neville)(4:04) *The Neville Brothers*; 8 Send Fi Spanish Fly (L. James)(3:18) *Little Twitch*; 9 Mary Jane (J. Engerman/J. Engerman/F. Gumbs)(6:14) *Seventeen Plus*; 10 The Mighty Quinn (B. Dylan) (2:39) *Sheryl Lee Ralph, Cedella Marley, Sharon Marley Prendergast*.

Review: An odd compilation for a murder mystery set in the Caribbean, with some happy rhythms (UB 40's "I Gotta Keep Moving On," Michael Rose's "Guess Who's Coming to Dinner," Neville Brothers' "Yellow Moon"), some okay tracks (Arrow's "Groove Master," Half Pint's "Giving/Sharing," Yello's "La Habanera"), and some dispensable (Little Twitch's "Send Fi Spanish Fly"). Bob Dylan's "The Mighty Quinn" gets an abrasively funny reading by Sheryl Lee Ralph, Cedella Marley and Sharon Marley Prendergast.

Miller's Crossing ♪

1990, Varese-Sarabande; from the movie *Miller's Crossing*, 20th Century-Fox, 1990.

Album Notes: *Music*: Carter Burwell; *Orchestrations*: Sonny Kompanek; *Album Producer*: Carter Burwell; *Engineer*: Michael Farrow.

Selections: 1 Opening Titles (1:54); 2 Caspar Laid Out (1:57); 3 A Man And His Hat (:56); 4 King Porter Stomp (F. Morton/S. Burke/S. Robin)(2:10); 5 The Long Way Around (1:39); 6 Miller's Crossing (2:36); 7 After Miller's Crossing (:42); 8 Running Wild (J. Grey/L. Wood/A. Gibbs)(3:06); 9 Rage Of The Dane (:06); 10 All A You Whores (sic)(:24); 11 Nightmare In The Trophy Room (1:37); 12 He Didn't Like His Friends (:22); 13 Danny Boy (p.d.)(4:07) *Frank Patterson*; 14 What Heart? (:50); 15 End Titles (4:44); 16 Goodnight Sweetheart (R. Vallee/R. Noble/J. Campbell/R. Connelly)(:55) *Frank Patterson*.

Review: Some soundtrack albums aren't helping the cause of their composers or film music in general. Take, for instance, this album, which, even though it has 16 tracks, clocks in at 28 minutes, with four totally dispensable pop selections taking up more than 10 minutes of playing time. Carter Burwell's score gets literally lost in the process and certainly deserved better than the shoddy treatment it gets here.

Miracle on 34th Street ♪

1994, Fox Records; from the movie *Miracle on 34th Street*, 20th Century-Fox, 1994.

Album Notes: *Music*: Bruce Broughton; *Orchestrations*: Bruce Broughton; *Music Editor*: Patricia Carlin; Orchestra conducted by Bruce Broughton; *Score Producer*: Bruce Broughton; *Engineer*: Armin Steiner; *Song Producers*: Tommy LiPuma, Jeremy Lubbock & Elliot Lurie, Kenny G, Randy Nicklaus & Steve Barri, Pierre Marchand; *Arrangers*: John Clayton, Jr., Jeremy Lubbock, Kenny G & Walter Afanasieff, John Schreiner, Sarah McLachlan.

Selections: 1 Overture (2:40); 2 Jingle Bells (J. Pierpont)(3:32) *Natalie Cole*; 3 It's Beginning To Look A Lot Like Christmas (M. Willson)(2:21) *Dionne Warwick*; 4 Have Yourself A Merry Little Christmas (H. Martin/R. Blane) (3:54) *Kenny G*; 5 Santa Claus Is Comin' To Town (H. Gillespie/J.F. Coots) (3:02) *Ray Charles*; 6 Joy To The World (I. Watts/G.F. Handel)(3:01) *Aretha Franklin & Members Of The Fame Freedom Choir*; 7 Santa Claus Is Back In Town (J. Leiber/M. Stoller)(2:03) *Elvis Presley*; 8 Signing (2:03); 9 Bellevue Carol (2:13); 10 Song For A Winter's Night (G. Lightfoot)(3:46) *Sarah McLachlan*.

Review: Instead of trusting his composer, Bruce Broughton, and give him an opportunity to write Christmas music for this remake of *Miracle on 34th Street* in the manner in which he had let John Williams write an instant classic score for *Home Alone*, John Hughes chose instead to stuff his soundtrack with covers of some well-known Christmas songs by Natalie Cole, Dionne Warwick, Ray Charles, Elvis Presley, Aretha Franklin and (eeech!) Kenny G.

Broughton's contribution is reduced in this CD to three little cues that denote a wonderful feel for the action in progress, but can only whet one's appetite for a longer expression. Another missed opportunity for lovers of film music.

The Mirror Has Two Faces ♪♪♪

1996, Columbia Records; from the movie *The Mirror Has Two Faces*, Tri-Star Pictures, 1996.

Album Notes: *Music*: Marvin Hamlisch; *Orchestrations*: Jack Hayes, Torrie Zitto, Brad Dechter; *Music Editor*: Charles Martin Inouye; Orchestra conducted by Marvin Hamlisch; *Album Producer*: Barbra Streisand; *Engineer*: Shawn Murphy; *Assistant Engineer*: Sue McLean.

Selections: 1 Main Title/In Questa Reggia (G. Puccini) (3:44); 2 Got Any Scotch? (B. Streisand/M. Hamlisch) (2:31); 3 An Ad? (:43); 4 In A Sentimental Mood (E.K. Ellington) (2:37); 5 Rose Sees Greg (B. Streisand/M. Hamlisch) (:43); 6 Alex Hurts Rose (B. Streisand/M. Hamlisch) (1:14); 7 The Dating Montage (B. Streisand/M. Hamlisch) (1:51); 8 My Intentions? (B. Streisand) (1:07); 9 You Picked Me! (:31); 10 A Funny Kind Of Proposal (B. Streisand/M. Hamlisch) (1:10); 11 Picnic In The Park (1:33); 12 Greg Falls For Rose (B. Streisand/M. Hamlisch) (3:23); 13 Try A Little Tenderness (H. Woods/J. Campbell/R. Connelly) (3:11) *David Sanborn*; 14 The Mirror (B. Streisand/M. Hamlisch) (1:02); 15 Going Back To Mom (B. Streisand/M. Hamlisch) (1:09); 16 Rocking In The Chair (B. Streisand) (:49); 17 The Power Inside Of Me (K. Thomas/R. Marx) (3:06) *Richard Marx*; 18 Rose Leaves Greg (B. Streisand/M. Hamlisch) (1:47); 19 Ruby (M. Parish/H. Roemheld) (3:14); 20 Rose Dumps Alex (B. Streisand) (:57); 21 Greg Claims Rose (1:29); 22 The Apology/Nessun Dorma (G. Puccini) (3:17) *Luciano Pavarotti*; 23 I Finally Found Someone (B. Streisand/ M. Hamlisch/R.J. Lange/B. Adams) (3:42) *Barbra Streisand, Bryan Adams*; 24 All Of My Life (B. Streisand/M. Hamlisch/A. & M. Bergman) (3:34) *Barbra Streisand*.

Review: This romantic comedy was produced and directed by Barbra Streisand, who also starred, as an exploration of "the modern myths of beauty and sex and how they complicate relationships," with beau-hunk Jeff Bridges as the object of Ms. Streisand's lust. If this doesn't sound too convincing, try the soundtrack album, in which Streisand shares composing credits with Marvin Hamlisch, a lightweight but nonetheless interesting writer, and performs a couple of songs (noblesse oblige!). It is difficult in a case like this to properly assess the amount of work done by one or the other in the collaboration. For the sake of argument, the score is mindlessly pleasant, somewhat reminiscent of the type of music Henry Mancini did so much better, with lilting melodies receiving the piano-cum-orchestra treatment. To what extent did Streisand contribute musical ideas is a question only she and Hamlisch can answer, though the "Love Theme" for which she takes full credit is virtually undistinguishable stylistically from the tracks composed by Hamlisch himself. David Sanborn and Luciano Pavarotti are the star's other odd partners in this minor effort.

Misery ♪♪♪

1990, Bay Cities Records; from the movie *Misery*, Columbia Pictures, 1990.

Album Notes: *Music:* Marc Shaiman; *Orchestrations:* Dennis Dreith, Hummie Mann, Bruce Fowler; *Music Editor:* Scott Stambler; Orchestra conducted by Dennis Dreith; *Album Producer:* Marc Shaiman; *Engineer:* Armin Steiner.

Selections: 1 Number One Fan (6:40); 2 She Can't Be Dead (6:16); 3 Open House (4:17); 4 Go To Your Room (2:28); 5 Buster's Last Stand (4:14); 6 Misery's Return (6:04).

Review: Interestingly, *Misery* is the first score Marc Shaiman ever wrote for a full-length feature, an impressive debut that marked the start of a great career which has since seen the creation of many important scores, including *Addams Family*, *City Slickers*, *Ghosts of Mississippi*. It was an even greater achievement, considering the fact that this claustrophobic two-character film—based on a Stephen King novel about a famous writer, the victim of a car accident, who finds himself immobilized and tended to by his "number one fan," a nurse with murderous instincts—called for a score that enhanced a study in psychological terror. Shaiman conceived a carefully constructed full-scale dramatic score as a series of ominous-sounding themes, in which the low strings create the oppressive atmosphere reflective of the action and the locale, a secluded house further isolated from the outside world by a raging snowstorm. Bold, assertive outbursts mark the writer's rebellion and the end of his ordeal. A strong, highly competent first effort.

The Mission ♪♪♪♪

1986, Virgin Movie Music; from the movie *The Mission*, 1986.

Album Notes: *Music:* Ennio Morricone; *Orchestrations:* Ennio Morricone; The London Philharmonic Orchestra, conducted by Ennio Morricone; *Indian instrumentation:* Incantation; *Album Producer:* Ennio Morricone; *Engineer:* Dick Lewzey; *Assistant Engineer:* Steve Price.

Selections: 1 On Earth As It Is In Heaven (3:48); 2 Falls (1:53); 3 Gabriel's Oboe (2:12); 4 Ave Maria Guarani (2:48); 5 Brothers (1:30); 6 Carlotta (1:19); 7 Vita Nostra (1:52); 8 Climb (1:35); 9 Remorse (2:46); 10 Penance (4:00); 11 The Mission (2:47); 12 River (1:57); 13 Gabriel's Oboe (2:38); 14 Te Deum Guarani (:46); 15 Refusal (3:28); 16 Asuncion (1:25); 17 Alone (4:18); 18 Guarani (3:54); 19 The Sword (1:58); 20 Miserere (:59).

Review: Themes from this Academy Award-winning score have been so widely quoted and imitated that it almost seems redundant to introduce it again. Certainly, Ennio Morricone surpassed himself when he wrote this score for the powerful epic starring Robert De Niro as a man of the sword and Jeremy Irons as a man of the cloth in 18th-century South America, who team to protect an Indian tribe from being wiped out by invading colonialists. Visually resplendent, breathtakingly beautiful, the film is further enhanced by its haunting music in which "Gabriel's Oboe" and "On Earth as It Is in Heaven" soon emerged as unlikely, given the solemnity of the writing, popular hits. With its inspired blend of instrumental themes, liturgical anthems, Indian chanting, drumming and flute playing, the soundtrack album is a wonderful musical treat from beginning to end.

Mission: Impossible

Mission: Impossible ♪♪♪♪

1996, Point Records; from the movie *Mission: Impossible*, Paramount Pictures, 1996.

Album Notes: *Music:* Danny Elfman; *Orchestrations:* Steve Bartek, Mark McKenzie, Steven Scott Smalley; *Music Editor:* Ellen Segal; Orchestra conducted by Artie Kane; *Album Producers:* Danny Elfman, Ellen Segal, Shawn Murphy; *Engineer:* Shawn Murphy; *Assistant Engineers:* Sue McLean, Patrick Weber, Greg Dennen, Mark Eshelman.

Selections: 1 Sleeping Beauty (2:29); 2 Mission: Impossible Theme (L. Schifrin) (1:03); 3 Red Handed (4:21); 4 Big Trouble (5:33); 5 Love Theme? (2:22); 6 Mole Hunt (3:02); 7 The Disc (1:54); 8 Max Found (1:03); 9 Looking For "Job" (4:38); 10 Betrayal (2:56); 11 The Heist (5:47); 12 Uh-Oh! (1:29); 13 Biblical Revelation (1:33); 14 Phone Home (2:25); 15 Train Time (4:12); 16 Menage a trois (2:55); 17 Zoom A (1:53); 18 Zoom B (2:54).

Review: Danny Elfman's *Mission: Impossible* is one of the best "event movie" scores of the '90s. The completely incoherent film, a virtual Tom Cruise rape of the original TV series, did sport interesting Brian de Palma direction, and Elfman, replacing a more traditional Alan Silvestri score at the last minute, found a perfect blend of contemporary suspense and retro grooves. The '60s Lalo Schifrin theme is there in the beginning and end — a little more bombastic than before — and Elfman weaves fragments of it into his own, prickly motives and colors. Technically, it's one of Elfman's most accomplished works, taking the Schifrin tradition of woodwinds and percussion, and updating it with modern samples — a constant *tiki tiki tiki* in the background that lends forward motion to it all. If you want style, this has it by the buckets, but the quirks are shaped with impressive subtlety. One of the film's most suspenseful setpieces, an infiltration of a top-secret CIA computer room, not only features no music, but virtually no sound! When the action finally breaks out in the climactic helicopter-and-train chase, it builds and builds, until it finally explodes into the classic Schifrin theme.

Lukas Kendall

Mission: Impossible ♫♫

1996, Mother Records; from the movie *Mission: Impossible*, Paramount Pictures, 1996.

Album Notes: *Music*: Danny Elfman; *Orchestrations*: Steve Bartek, Mark McKenzie, Steven Scott Smalley; *Music Editor*: Ellen Segal; Orchestra conducted by Artie Kane; *Album Producers*: Danny Elfman, Ellen Segal, Shawn Murphy; *Engineer*: Shawn Murphy; *Assistant Engineers*: Sue McLean, Patrick Weber, Greg Dennen, Mark Eshelman.

Selections: 1 Theme From Mission: Impossible (L. Schifrin) (3:27) *Larry Mullen, Adam Clayton*; 2 Spying Glass (Vowles/ Del Naja/Marshall/N. Hooper/H. Hinds) (5:20) *Massive Attack*; 3 I Spy (N. Banks/J. Cocker/C. Doyle/ S. Mackey/R. Senior/M. Webber) (5:56) *Pulp*; 4 Impossible Mission (D. Elfman) (5:35) *Danny Elfman*; 5 Headphones (B. Gudmundsdottir/ Tricky) (5:40) *Bjork*; 6 Weak (Skin/Ace/Cass/France) (3:31) *Skunk Ansansie*; 7 On And On (Hunt) (4:11) *Longpigs*; 8 Claire (D. Elfman) (2:55) *Danny Elfman*; 9 Dreams (D. O'Riordan/N. Hogan) (4:13) *The Cranberries*; 10 You, Me And World War III ("Big" Single Remix) (G. Friday/M. Seezer) (4:28) *Gavin Friday*; 11 So (Salt) (3:33) *Salt*; 12 Trouble (D. Elfman) (3:32) *Danny Elfman*; 13 No Government (Nicolette) (5:31) *Nicolette*; 14 Alright (J. Power) (3:35) *Cast*; 15 Mission: Impossible Theme (Mission Accomplished) (L. Schifrin) (3:05) *Adam Clayton, Larry Mullen*.

Review: Interestingly, the song album adds another 12 minutes from Elfman's score, with the rest being turned over to various pop selections. These include two versions of Lalo Schifrin's theme for *Mission: Impossible* updated by Adam Clayton and Larry Mullen, who probably couldn't leave well enough alone,

but who contributed nothing really novel to the tune and various pop/rock tunes by Massive Attack, Bjork, The Cranberries, Salt, and Nicolette. Even though most of these were not in the film, they succeed in conveying the tense atmosphere in some of the action-driven scenes ("Spying Glass," "I Spy"), or evoking the specific moods in it. But even though the album claims that it contains "music from and inspired" by the film, there is something quite amoral and deceptive in peddling ten selections that have no relation whatsoever with the film advertised, and try to make it pass as a soundtrack album.

Mississippi Burning ♫♫♫▹

1989, Antilles Records; from the movie *Mississippi Burning*, Orion Pictures, 1989.

Album Notes: *Music*: Trevor Jones; *Orchestrations*: Trevor Jones; *Album Producer*: Trevor Jones; *Engineer*: Paul Hulme.

Selections: 1 Take My Hand Precious Lord (T. Dorsey) (2:40) *Mahalia Jackson*; 2 Murder In Mississippi, Part 1 (3:08); 3 Some Things Are Worth Dying For (2:11); 4 Murder In Mississippi, Part 2 (1:06); 5 Anderson And Mrs. Pell (3:04); 6 When We All Get To Heaven (E. Wilson/E. Hewitt) (2:13) Choral; 7 Try Jesus (R. Martin) (2:17) *Vesta Williams*; 8 Abduction (2:40); 9 You Live It, You Breathe It, You Marry It (3:03); 10 Murder In Mississippi, Part 3 (:57); 11 Requiem For Three Young Men (3:49); 12 Burning Cross (1:32); 13 Justice In Mississippi (4:20); 14 Walk On By Faith (vocal) (J. Cleveland) (2:43) *Lannie McBride*; 15 Walk On By Faith (J. Cleveland) (5:70) *Lannie McBride*.

Review: A striking, provocative drama about the civil rights movement, and the hidden demons thriving in our society, *Mississippi Burning* evoked in stark, uncompromising terms the investigation into the outright murder of three civil rights workers by a local Mississippi sheriff, portrayed by Gene Hackman. The somber tones in the story receive additional support from the score written by Trevor Jones, a powerful set of cues in which the obsessive "Murder in Mississippi" mixes sound effects and lines from the dialogue with a relentless beat over percolating synth lines. Often poignant in its stark expression, the music never attempts to explain or underline a scene, but aims instead to create an "effect," an atmosphere that won't let go. Ultimately, it is disturbing, but musically very compelling, though this is the kind of cerebral score that demands a lot from any listener.

Mrs. Doubtfire ♫♫♫

1993, Fox Records; from the movie *Mrs. Doubtfire*, 20th Century-Fox, 1993.

Album Notes: *Music*: Howard Shore; *Orchestrations*: Howard Shore; *Music Editor*: Ellen Segal; Orchestra, conducted by Howard Shore; *Album Producer*: Howard Shore; *Engineer*: Dan Wallin.

Selections: 1 Mrs. Doubtfire (2:58); 2 Divorce (2:56); 3 My Name Is Elma Immelman (2:55); 4 Meeting Mrs. Doubtfire (2:14); 5 Tea Time With Mrs. Sellner (3:58); 6 Dinner Is Served (2:18); 7 Daniel And The Kids (2:29); 8 Cable Cars (4:56); 9 Bridges Restaurant (6:13); 10 The Show's Over (3:26); 11 The Kids Need You (3:21); 12 Figaro (G. Rossini)/Papa's Got A Brand New Bag (J. Brown) (3:23).

Review: Robin Williams has a field day in this comedy in which he portrays a divorced man who turns himself into the matronly Mrs. Doubtfire, an indispensable housekeeper, in order to stay close to his kids. But while the film thrived on the comedian's broad antics as the irrepressible title character, it elicited a surprisingly low-key score from Howard Shore who chose to ignore the farcical side of the story and concentrate instead on its more romantic aspects. As a result, the cues, with a few exceptions which essentially repeat the same theme ("Tea Time with Mrs. Sellner," "Bridges Restaurant"), are very lovely but seem to miss an important point made by the film. On a pure audio level, however, they add up to a generously pleasant album.

Mrs. Winterbourne 🎵🎵🎵

1996, Varese-Sarabande; from the movie *Mrs. Winterbourne*, Tri-Star Pictures, 1996

Album Notes: *Music*: Patrick Doyle; *Orchestrations*: Lawrence Ashmore; *Music Editor*: Roy Prendergast; *Musicians*: Bruce Dukov (violin solo), Randy Kerber (piano); Orchestra conducted by Mark Watters; *Album Producers*: Patrick Doyle, Maggie Rodford; *Engineer*: John Richards.

Selections: 1 Connie's Story (1:07); 2 Connie And Steve's Life (1:27); 3 Homeless Blues (1:12); 4 Train To Boston (1:59); 5 Where's My Baby (2:26); 6 Ride To The Mansion (1:53); 7 Bill's Tour Of Boston (3:50); 8 You're A Winterbourne (4:01); 9 Wedding Prep Montage (:40); 10 Steve's Back (1:59); 11 (It's De Different (1:14); 12 Dead Steve (2:20); 13 Bill And Connie Come Clean (1:35); 14 Remembering New York (1:33); 15 Connie Tells Grace (3:23); 16 Connie's Song (2:19).

Review: Based on a novel by Cornell Woolrich, about a pregnant single woman mistaken for the widow of the heir to the Winterbourne family fortune, this romantic comedy succeeded primarily because of Shirley MacLaine's superb performance as an old dowager, and Ricki Lake's winsome appeal as the young woman whose unconventional behavior clashed with

> "The fact that this film will be listened to for the next 40 years, I took very seriously.... The music spoke for the animals, similar to 'Peter and the Wolf,' a story told by music."
>
> **Michael Kamen**
> on 101 Dalmatians
> *(The Hollywood Reporter, 1-15-97)*

the stultified old-fashioned family clan forced to accept her. Trying to match in the score the basic moods projected in the picture, Patrick Doyle provided a competent effort that is at times a bit too schmaltzy for its own good, but in which some cues like "Connie and Steve's Life" bring a different, welcome change. Interesting, but the composer has been known to do better.

Mr. & Mrs. Bridge 🎵🎵

1990, Novus Vision/BMG; from the movie *Mr. & Mrs. Bridge*, Cineplex Odeon Films and Merchant Ivory Productions, 1990.

Album Notes: *Music*: Richard Robbins; *Orchestrations*: Robert Stuart; *Album Producer*: John Snyder; *Engineers*: Sue Fisher, Mike Farrow.

Selections: 1 Opening Titles (2:51); 2 Boogie Woogie (C. Smith)(3:08) *Tommy Dorsey and His Orchestra*; 3 The Painting Class (1:13); 4 String Of Pearls (J. Gray)(3:13) *Glenn Miller and His Orchestra*; 5 Little Brown Jug (J. Wilnner)(2:52) *Glenn Miller and His Orchestra*; 6 The Rhumba Jumps (H. Carmichael/J. Mercer)(2:48) *Glenn Miller and His Orchestra, Marion Hutton & Tex Beneke*; 7 Ruth's Journey (2:12); 8 Jeepers Creepers (J. Mercer/ H. Warren)(2:47) *Ethel Waters, Edward Mallory and His Orchestra*; 9 Blues In The Night (H. Arlen/J. Mercer)(3:08) *Dinah Shore*; 10 Stormy Weather (H. Arlen/T. Koehler)(3:46) *Lena Horne, Lou Bring and His Orchestra*; 11 She Was My Best Friend (1:41); 12 Take Me, I'm Yours (1:38) *Allison Sneegas*; 13 Choo Choo Conga (1:46); 14 Down On The Farm (trad.)(4:22) *Charles Perkins, Richard Ross, Allen K. Monroe, Milt Abel*; 15 Locking Up (1:54); 16 Closing Credits (3:00).

Review: The story of a stiff American couple living in Kansas during the great depression, *Mr. & Mrs. Bridge* brought the occasion for Richard Robbins to write a sensitive score suffused with sadness and joy, reflecting the varied moods of the film itself, and the drab existence of the film's central characters. His contribution, however, is limited here to about half the tracks, with themes that seem attractive but don't have much of a chance to make any kind of impact given their short playing time. Several standard selections ("String of Pearls," "Little Brown Jug," "The Rhumba Jumps," all performed by Glenn Miller; "Blues in the Night," by Dinah Shore; "Stormy Weather," by Lena Horne) add a period touch to the recording, though it should be noted that no effort has been made to clean these sides and make them sonically acceptable, something particularly noticeable in Tommy Dorsey's "Boogie Woogie," which has a lot of surface noise, distortion, image shifts, and dropouts, among its detrimental ills.

Mr. Baseball ♪♪♪♪

1992, Varese-Sarabande Records; from the movie *Mr. Baseball*, Universal Pictures, 1992.

Album Notes: *Music*: Jerry Goldsmith; *Orchestrations*: Alexander Courage, Arthur Morton; *Music Editor*: Ken Hall; Orchestra conducted by Jerry Goldsmith; *Album Producer*: Jerry Goldsmith; *Engineer*: Bruce Botnick.

Selections: 1 Mr. Baseball (2:33); 2 First Night Out (1:54); 3 Acceptance (1:54); 4 New Apartment (:45); 5 The Dragons (1:04); 6 Call Me Jack/A Wise Brain (2:45); 7 Winning Streak/ The Locker Room (1:06); 8 The Bath (3:07); 9 Training (2:31); 10 Go Get 'Em/He's Still Got It (1:25); 11 Team Effort (2:50); 12 Swing Away (1:46); 13 Final Score (5:04); 14 Shabondama Boogie (You/S. Toda)(4:23) *Fairchild*.

Review: Jerry Goldsmith must have enjoyed writing this score for a comedy starring Tom Selleck as the American coach of a Japanese baseball team, if one is to believe the rollicking accents he found for the rambunctious title tune. Expressing himself in a style in which he excels but he seems to seldom approach these days, Goldsmith delivered a flavorful set of cues, in which jazz touches, like "First Night Out" and "Team Effort," mix with electronic rock, like "Training" and "Final Score," and some romantic interludes to create a delicious souffle, light as the film itself, and devilishly enjoyable. It's nothing like the composer's most noteworthy efforts, but something to listen to when the moods need to be slightly buoyant and easy on the mind. "Shabondama Boogie," performed by Fairchild, is a hilarious rock number, the kind only the Japanese can write when they try to imitate their American counterparts.

Mr. Destiny ♪♪♪

1990 , Varese-Sarabande Records; from the movie *Mr. Destiny*, Touchstone Pictures, 1990.

Album Notes: *Music*: David Newman; Orchestra conducted by David Newman; *Album Producers*: David Newman, Tim Boyle; *Engineer*: Tim Boyle.

Selections: 1 Mr. Destiny (5:05); 2 Main Title (1:45); 3 Larry's Life Is Changed (3:43); 4 Cindy Joe's Present (1:14); 5 Larry Sees His Office (:50); 6 Larry Sees The House (1:56); 7 Leo Sneaks Around (:30); 8 Larry Meets Jerry (4:17); 9 Larry Looks For Ellen (3:53); 10 Larry Punches Out Niles (1:07); 11 Going Back Home (:48); 12 Larry Is Home (5:07).

Review: A light comedy evoking *Angels in the Outfield* and *Field of Dreams*, among other inspirational romantic comedies about baseball and angels, *Mr. Destiny* dealt with yet another misfit whose guardian angel helped him rebuild his life and win the big game, in a formula that never fails to elicit strong emotional reactions in the audience. David Newman scored the whole thing with obvious empathy for the subject, developing broad instrumental themes that capture the moods in the film, soaring to a climax when the action required it, playing it soft and low when necessary. The contrasted effort is pleasantly listenable, generally attractive, but altogether not too terribly memorable, the type of music that may play in any given situation as long as it doesn't require too much attention.

Mr. Holland's Opus

Mr. Holland's Opus ♪♪♪♪

1995, London Records; from the movie *Mr. Holland's Opus*, Hollywood Pictures, 1995.

Album Notes: *Music*: Michael Kamen; *Orchestrations*: Michael Kamen, Stephen McLaughlin, Christopher Brooks; *Music Editors*: Michael Ryan, David Olson; The Seattle Symphony Orchestra and The London Metropolitan Orchestra, conducted by Michael Kamen; *Featured Soloists*: Jonathan Snowden (flute), Dominic Miller (guitar), Pino Paladino (bass), Jim Keltner (drums); *Album Producers*: Michael Kamen, Stephen McLaughlin, Christopher Brooks; *Engineer*: Stephen McLaughlin.

Selections: 1 Mr. Holland Begins (2:56); 2 Iris And Glen (2:28); 3 Practice, Practice, Practice (3:51); 4 New Baby/Coltrane/ Children Should Listen To Mozart (3:17); 5 Rush To Hospital (3:17); 6 Symphony No. 7 (Allegretto) (L. Van Beethoven) (11:06); 7 Cole's Tune (4:18); 8 Vietnam (4:30); 9 Rowena (6:11); 10 Concerto For Three Harpsichords in C (1st movement) (J.S. Bach) (7:50) *George Shangrow, Jillon Stoppels Dupree,*

Robert Kechley; 11 Thank You, Mr. Holland (5:08); 12 An American Symphony (Mr. Holland's Opus) (8:27); 13 Cole's Song (M. Kamen/ J. Lennon/ J. Clayton) (3:49) *Julian Lennon.*

Review: A joyous score by Michael Kamen was the perfect complement to this highly entertaining Richard Dreyfuss picture about a high school music instructor who offered more than a little inspiration to the students he taught. Centering his score around an "Opus" that is never fully revealed until its concert performance at the very end, Kamen has written a melodic score that makes for an ideal soundtrack album, thanks to a fine mixture of cues ranging from poignant orchestral accompaniment to bold themes that reflect the many special moments in Mr. Holland's life. Kamen further grounds his score in an emotional vein with an elegy to "Vietnam" that gives the music an extra dimension before concluding with the rousing, Grammy-winning "An American Symphony," heard in its entirety only on the score album. Like the film, Kamen's music could have been merely simplistic and sappy, yet the composer is able to walk that thin line between emotion and sentimentality perfectly. And kudos to the producers for including Julian Lennon's vocal performance of "Cole's Tune" on the London CD, making this album fully representative of Kamen's complete work on the film.

Andy Dursin

Mr. Holland's Opus ♪♪♪

1995, Polydor Records; from the movie *Mr. Holland's Opus,* Hollywood Pictures, **1995.**

Selections: 1 Visions Of A Sunset (S. Stockman)(4:31) *Shawn Stockman*; 2 One, Two, Three (B. Holland/E. Holland/L. Dozier/J. Madara/D. White/L. Broisoff)(2:25) *Len Barry*; 3 A Lover's Concerto (S. Linzer/D. Randell)(2:38) *The Toys*; 4 Keep On Running (J. Edwards)(2:42) *Spencer Davis Group*; 5 Uptight (Everything's Alright)(H. Cosby/S. Moy/S. Wonder)(2:53) *Stevie Wonder*; 6 Imagine (J. Lennon)(3:01) *John Lennon & The Plastic Ono Band*; 7 The Pretender (J. Browne)(5:52) *Jackson Browne*; 8 Someone To Watch Over Me (G. & I. Gershwin)(3:32) *Julia Fordham*; 9 I Got A Woman (R. Charles) (2:50) *Ray Charles*; 10 Beautiful Boy (Darling Boy)(J. Lennon)(4:00) *John Lennon, Yoko Ono*; 11 Cole's Song (J. Lennon/J. Clayton/M. Kamen)(3:48) *Julian Lennon*; 12 An American Symphony (Mr. Holland's Opus)(M. Kamen)(3:14) *The London Metropolitan Orchestra, Michael Kamen.*

Review: A time travelogue not unlike *Forrest Gump, Mr. Holland's Opus* takes pieces of assorted eras for a pleasant if not entirely cohesive package. The individual selections are good, though, if a little tame — a couple of pieces by John Lennon

("Imagine," "Beautiful Boy (Darling Boy)"), Ray Charles' "I Got a Woman," Jackson Browne's "The Pretender." What it cries for is some tougher-edged music, the kind of stuff high school kids really listened to.

Gary Graff

Mr. Saturday Night ♪♪♪♪

1992, Giant Records; from the movie *Mr. Saturday Night,* Columbia Pictures, **1992.**

Album Notes: *Music*: Marc Shaiman; *Orchestrations*: Mark McKenzie, Brad Dechter, Tom Sharp; *Music Editors*: Hummie Mann, Scott Stambler; Orchestra conducted by Artie Kane; *Featured Musicians*: Jack Sheldon, Bruce Dukov, Jerry Goodman, Abe Most, Dan Higgins, Randy Kerber, Steve Schaeffer; *Featured Vocalists*: Randy Crenshaw, Geoff Koch, Steve Lively, Rick Logan; *Album Producers*: Marc Shaiman, Hummie Mann; *Engineer*: Joel Moss.

Selections: 1 The Coleman Comedy Hour: Buddy, Buddy (M. Shaiman/B. Crystal/ L. Ganz/B. Mandel)/My Buddy (G. Kahn/ W. Donaldson (3:32) *The Big Chief Dancers*; 2 Main Title: My Buddy (G. Kahn/W. Donalson)(2:37); 3 Amateur Night (1:38); 4 Elaine (1:39); 5 See What I Did/Roumania, Roumania (A. Lebedeff) (2:12) *Aaron Lebedeff, Billy Crystal*; 6 Table Eight, Polka Dot Dress (2:11); 7 Fantastic, That's You (B. Thiele/M. Greene/G. Cates)(2:55) *Louis Armstrong*; 8 Mama (2:30); 9 Buddy's Blue (1:55); 10 It Should Have Been You (3:12); 11 Susan, Where's That Doubletake (3:36); 12 Brothers (2:57); 13 When You're Smiling (The Whole World Smiles With You)(M. Fisher/J. Goodwin/L. Shay)(3:11) *Louis Prima.*

Review: Billy Crystal had one of his most pleasant screen roles in this film in which he played a congenial entertainer, raised in New York's Jewish East Side, who got his start in vaudeville, and ended as a television host, a cigar-chomping character he created early in his nightclub act and which he polished up for this big screen debut. If the film, an affectionate tribute to an era long gone, is a romp from beginning to end, with Crystal absolutely devilish as the ebullient old-timer with a tart tongue and a sharp sense of humor, it finds an equally inspired echo in composer Marc Shaiman's vibrant score, a special blend of subtle ethnic elements, not-so-subtle showbiz chutzpah, and just great themes to enjoy and delight in. Several well-chosen vocals, including Louis Armstrong's "Fantastic, That's You," and Louis Prima's "When You're Smiling," add the right element of nostalgia to the musical background, evoking an era when vaudeville was king and borscht belt comedians were at the peak of their popularity.

Mr. Wrong ♫♫♫♪

1996, Hollywood Records; from the movie *Mr. Wrong*, Touchstone Pictures, 1996.

Album Notes: *Music:* Craig Safan; *Song Producers:* Wayne Kirkpatrick, John Leventhal, Steve Addabbo, Scott Hendricks, Joan Osborne, Eric Jacobson, Kenny Laguna, Thom Panunzio, Joe Bashuron, Ben Folds, Tony Berg, Arturo Sandoval, Richard Eddy.

Selections: 1 The Things We Do For Love (E. Stewart/G. Gouldman) (3:22) *Amy Grant*; 2 Nothin' On Me (S. Colvin/J. Leventhal) (3:58) *Shawn Colvin*; 3 Kisses Good (J. Freeman) (3:19) *Once Blue*; 4 Since I Laid Eyes On You (E. Shipley/B. Steinberg/S. Stewart) (4:11) *Faith Hill*; 5 Strenuous Acquaintances (J. Osborne) (5:23) *Joan Osborne*; 6 I'm So Lonesome I Could Cry (H. Williams) (2:36) *Chris Isaak*; 7 Crazy Little Thing Called Love (F. Mercury) (2:45) *Queen*; 8 Love Stinks (P. Wolf/S. Justman) (3:32) *Joan Jett and The Blakhearts*; 9 I Gotcha (J. Tex) (3:42) *Sophie B. Hawkins*; 10 Song For The Dumped (B. Folds/D. Jessee) (3:32) *Ben Folds Five*; 11 It's Not Unusual (L. Reed/G. Mills) (5:15) *The Wild Colonials*; 12 Suavito (M.A. Gomez) (3:38) *Arturo Sandoval*; 13 Mr. Wrong Main Title (C. Safan) (2:21).

Review: The soundtrack for Ellen DeGeneres' pre-coming out star vehicle hit a few right notes, with a modest collection of modern rock focused on a falling-in-love theme. Amy Grant's remake of 10cc's "The Things We Do For Love" is perky, while Joan Osborne and Sophie B. Hawkins bring a bit of sultriness via "Strenuous Acquaintances" and "I Gotcha," respectively. Men have their say, too, with contributions such as Ben Folds Five's hilarious "Songs for the Dumped"), Chris Isaak's cover of Hank Williams' "I'm So Lonesome I Could Cry" and Arturo Sandoval's "Suavito."

Gary Graff

Mo' Better Blues ♫♫♫♫

1990, Columbia Records; from the movie *Mo' Better Blues*, Universal Pictures, 1990.

Album Notes: *Strings Arranger:* Clare Fisher; Orchestra conducted by Clare Fisher; *Featured Musicians:* Branford Marsalis (tenor/ soprano sax), Kenny Kirkland (piano), Robert Hurst (bass), Jeff "Tain" Watts (drums), Terence Blanchard (trumpet); *Album Producers:* Bill Lee, Delfeayo Marsalis, Raymond Jones; *Engineers:* Larry DeCarmine, Patrick Smith, Rob Hunter.

Selections: 1 Harlem Blues (W.C. Handy)(4:51) *Cynda Williams*; 2 Say Hey (B. Marsalis)(3:19); 3 Knocked Out The Box (B. Marsalis)(1:35); 4 Again Never (B. Lee)(3:55); 5 Mo' Better Blues (B. Lee)(3:40); 6 Pop Top 40 (S. Lee/B. Marsalis)(5:40) *Denzel Washington, Wesley Snipes*; 7 Beneath The Underdog (B. Marsalis)(5:07); 8 Jazz Thing (L.E. Elie/B. Marsalis/C. Martin/K. Elam) (4:50) *Gangstarr*; 9 Harlem Blues (Acapulco version)(W.C. Handy)(4:48) *Cynda Williams*.

Review: A film about the New York jazz scene, starring Denzel Washington as a self-centered trumpet player, *Mo' Better Blues* already had a striking musical expression that eventually resulted in this highly satisfying soundtrack album, featuring Terence Blanchard, Branford Marsalis and Kenny Kirkland, among its better known performers. Cynda Williams, who also appeared in the film as one of the central character's "main squeezes," does a standout rendition of W.C. Handy's "Harlem Blues," and Washington and Wesley Snipes read a somewhat dispensable "Pop Top 40" against musical accompaniment. The album will please jazz fans and those interested in adventurous musical fares.

Mobsters ♫♫♫♪

1991, Varese-Sarabande Records; from the movie *Mobsters*, Universal Pictures, 1991.

Album Notes: *Music:* Michael Small; *Orchestrations:* Jack Hayes, Christopher Dedrick; *Featured Musicians:* Ralph Grierson (piano solos/keyboards), Ian Underwood, Mike Lang (keyboards), Gary Foster (soprano sax solos), Warren Leuning, Jr. (trumpet), Mike Fisher (electronic percussion); *Album Producer:* Michael Small; *Engineer:* Armin Steiner.

Selections: 1 Main Titles (2:00); 2 Charlie's New York (4:12); 3 Confrontations (5:03); 4 Theme For Mare (4:40); 5 Whiskey Business (1:19); 6 Ice Pick Love (1:09); 7 Doublecross (3:50); 8 Mara's Murder (3:43); 9 The Don Is Dead (1:23); 10 Finale (2:28).

Review: Lucky Luciano, Meyer Lansky, Bugsy Siegel and Frank Costello are glorified once again on the big screen in *Mobsters*, a film that's interesting for its clear-eyed view of the reasons why these men succeeded so well in their life of crime. Viewing the gangsters as they began to assert themselves and take control of their specific territories, the film, with a solid dramatic screenplay by Michael Mahern and Nicholas Kazan, detailed the rise and fall of the four men in terms that made few concessions to romantic attitudes. An interesting side aspect of the film is its score, written by Michael Small, an attractive mixture of stark-sounding orchestral riffs, occasionally interrupted by big band outbursts like "Whiskey Business," suggestive of the days of Prohibition. With the "Theme for Mara," a lovely, expansive cue for piano, clarinet and orchestra, one of the highlights, much of the music gives the action on the screen a dramatic, sometimes explosive expression, that translates very well in this soundtrack album.

The Moderns ♪♪♪♪♪

1988, Virgin Movie Music Records; from the movie *The Moderns*, Nelson Films, 1988.

Album Notes: *Music*: Mark Isham; *Arrangements*: Mark Isham, Ken Kugler, Rick Ruttenberg; *L' Orchestre Moderne*: Mark Isham (trumpet, electronics), Peter Maunu (violin, mandolin, electric guitar), Ed Mann (vibraphone, marimba, snare drum), Dave Stone (acoustic bass), CharlElie Couture (vocals, piano), Rick Ruttenberg (piano), Patrick O'Hearn (acoustic and electric bass), Michael Barsimanto (drum machine), Suzie Katayama (cello); *Album Producer*: Mark Isham; *Engineer*: Stephen Krause.

Selections: 1 Les Modernes (6:00); 2 Cafe Selavy (4:25); 3 Paris La Nuit/ Selavy (3:32); 4 Really The Blues (3:37); 5 Madame Valentin (5:50); 6 Dada Je Suis (1:10); 7 Parlez-moi d'amour (retro)(2:55); 8 La Valse Moderne (2:49); 9 Les Peintres (2:24); 10 Death Of Irving Fagelman (1:53); 11 Je ne veux pas de tes chocolats (2:14); 12 Parlez-moi d'amour (moderne)(8:28).

Review: A tale of betrayal and deceit, set against the backdrop of late 1920s art world in Paris, *The Moderns* stars Keith Carradine as an American painter with enough talent to forge a convincing Cezanne, Linda Fiorentino as a beautiful brunette who motivated him, and John Lone as her ruthless, art collecting husband. Beautifully matching the tones of this triangular comedy and capturing the moods of the period itself, Mark Isham devised a score that is at once vibrant and evocative, a sensational music that speaks volumes. Essential to the feel of the score is its unusual instrumentation, with the violin, vibraphone and marimba creating a sound that evokes the period itself and gives its cachet to the whole album. The vocal contribution of CharlElie Couture, a French composer and performer, whose occasional interventions "Paris la nuit/Selavy" and "Parlez-moi d'amour (moderne)" give the score a specific Parisian flavor. It all adds up to a sensational album, and one of the best scores devised by Isham.

Moll Flanders ♪♪♪♪½

1996, London Records; from the movie *Moll Flanders*, M-G-M, 1996.

Album Notes: *Music*: Mark Mancina; *Orchestrations*: Mark Mancina, John Van Tongeren, Don Harper; Orchestra conducted by Don Harper; *Album Producer*: Don Harper; *Engineer*: Scott Hull.

Selections: 1 Moll Flanders (4:18); 2 Moll's Jig (2:11); 3 Flesh And Blood (3:31); 4 A New World (3:25); 5 Devil Woman (4:48); 6 We Were One (1:26); 7 Voyage (1:52); 8 Hibble's Tale (1:48); 9 Life Begins (3:31); 10 Sparrows (3:24); 11 Flora's Choice (1:35); 12 Full Of Grace (S. McLachlan)(3:38) *Sarah McLachlan*; 13 Belle nuit, o nuit d'amour (from The Tales Of Hoffman)(J. Offenbach)(4:08) *L' orchestre de la Suisse Romande, Richard Bonynge*; 14 Air (from Suite No. 3 in D Major, BWV 1068) (J.S. Bach)(5:11) *Academy of St. Martin-in-the-Fields, Neville Marriner*; 15/16 Allegro/Largo (from Concerto in C, RV 425)(A. Vivaldi)(2:33/3:32) *Pepe Romero*; 17 Allegro (from Brandenburg Concerto No. 3 in G Major, BWV 1048)(6:48) *English Chamber Orchestra, Benjamin Britten, cond.*; 18 Hornpipe and Andante (from Water Music Suite No. 1 in F Major (G.F. Handel)(8:02) *Academy of St. Martin-in-the-Fields, Neville Marriner*; 19 Moll Reprise (3:05).

Review: The notorious 18th-century English wench, already the subject of a 1965 romp starring Kim Novak, is on a rampage again in this loose screen adaptation of Daniel Defoe's 1722 novel, a picaresque tale about an attractive, fiercely independent woman, aware of her powers and ready to use them to elevate herself above her menial condition. Giving the tale a lift of its own, Mark Mancina provided a vibrant and lively score that chronicles the myriad incidents in Moll's rise from rags to riches, while detailing some of the many characters she encounters on the way – Mrs. Allworthy, owner of a classy bordello where Moll starts her "career" in earnest; a mysterious character only identified as The Artist, who rescues Moll when she is at her lowest, and makes her a model; Hibble, Mrs. Allworthy's servant, and Moll's only loyal friend; and Flora, Moll's daughter. Interestingly, the soundtrack album regroups Mancina's various cues in such a way that those pertaining to a given character are presented together, while more or less following the film's narrative. It is an acceptable device that gives greater strength and credibility to the score as a listening device.

The score itself is enriched with the addition of several selections from the classical repertoire, including an anachronistic aria from Offenbach's "The Tales of Hoffman," which had not been composed (and would not be for many moons) at the time when the story takes place.

The Molly Maguires ♪♪♪♪½

1990, Bay Cities Records; from the movie *The Molly Maguires*, Paramount Pictures, 1970.

Album Notes: *Music*: Henry Mancini; *Orchestrations*: Henry Mancini; Orchestra conducted by Henry Mancini; *Album Producer*: Tom Mack.

Selections: 1 Theme From *The Molly Maguires* (Pennsylvania, 1876)(4:18); 2 The Mollys Strike (2:45); 3 Main Title (1:44); 4 Fiddle And Fife (1:53); 5 Work Montage (2:13); 6 Jamie And Mary (The Hills Of Yesterday)(2:42); 7 Room And Board (Theme From The Molly Maguires)(1:54); 8 The Hills Of Yesterday (1:40); 9 Pennywhistle Jig (1:00); 10 Sandwiches And Tea (Theme From The Molly Maguires)(2:08); 11 Trip To Town (1:45); 12 The Mollys Strike Again (2:09); 13 A Brew With The Boys (1:38); 14 A Suit For Grandpa (2:09); 15 The End (Theme From *The Molly Maguires*)(:43).

Review: Based on a true story, and set in the Pennsylvania coal mining country in 1876, *The Molly Maguires* finds Henry Mancini writing in a dramatic vein, and relying on a variety of unusual instruments, such as the Irish harp, a button accordion, a pennywhistle and an ocarina, to convey the proper moods. To depict the drama and the screenplay's side elements about a rebellion of the miners, mostly Irish immigrants, led by Sean Connery, against the mine owners, Mancini essentially developed three themes—the main title, which sets the action and the bleak landscape where it happens; another, with specific Irish tonalities, to portray the Molly Maguires, an underground militant group whose only effective mean of fighting the abusive mine owners was through violent raids; and a third, a love theme describing the tender relationship between an Irish girl, Mary, played by Samantha Eggar, and a detective hired by the owners to infiltrate the workers' ranks, portrayed by Richard Harris.

All three themes provide the gist for the score, sometimes played independently, sometimes collapsing together, always attracting for their striking beauty and effectiveness. Mancini was particularly fond of this score and listening to it one can understand his reaction. The album, released on the now defunct Bay Cities label, may be hard to find, but is well worth looking for.

Mom and Dad Save the World 🎵🎵🎵🎵♭

1992, Varese-Sarabande Records; from the movie *Mom and Dad Save the World*, Warner Bros., 1992.

Album Notes: *Music:* Jerry Goldsmith; *Orchestrations:* Alexander Courage; *Music Editor:* Ken Hall; The National Philharmonic Orchestra, conducted by Jerry Goldsmith; *Album Producer:* Jerry Goldsmith; *Engineer:* Mike Ross.

Selections: 1 Meet Spengo (2:42); 2 The Death Ray Laser (2:28); 3 Morning Paper/The Abduction (4:17); 4 Photo Session (1:46); 5 Family Talk (1:21); 6 Tod, The Destroyer (:41); 7 The Lub-lubs (2:47); 8 True Power (2:23); 9 The Needle (3:18); 10 Target Practice (1:59); 11 Rebel Dance (1:08); 12 I Love My Wife (1:38); 13 Gathering Forces (5:46); 14 Misunderstood (4:44); 15 The Flight Home (2:10); 16 On The Roof (:56).

Review: A minor little comedy, about an urban American family suddenly responsible for saving the Earth from the somber designs of a galactic villain, *Mom and Dad Save The World* would be easily dismissed were it not for the fact that its composer happened to be Jerry Goldsmith, not one to ignore no matter what project he finds himself involved with. Indeed, his score for this fantasy is a real musical romp, rife with grandiose themes that don't seem to take themselves too seriously, and that are played with the right sense of humor by no less a formidable group than the National Philharmonic Orchestra. Talk about class! Flash Gordon never had it so good. Particularly delightful in the context is the anthem "Tod, The Destroyer," amusingly sung by a chorus, and brief enough to make its point while not stretching it and a lively "Rebel Dance," silly enough to evoke more than its simple tune might suggest. When Jerry Goldsmith has fun scoring a film, everyone has a ball. Such is the case here.

Money Train 🎵♭

1995, 550 Music/Epic Soundtrax; from the movie *Money Train*, Columbia Pictures, 1995.

Album Notes: *Music:* Mark Mancina; *Song Producers:* Robert Livingston & Shaun Pizzonia, Walter Kahn & Skee-Lo, Sean Combs, Teddy Riley, Dave Hall, Tim Kelley & Bob Robinson, Jimmy Jam & Terry Lewis, Mark C. Rooney & Nark Morales, Heavy D & Poke, Alexander Richbourg, Mike Smoov & B Laidback, Larry Hanby, Mark Mancina; *Soundtrack Executive Producers:* Jon Peters, Tracy Barone, Joe Ruben, Ron Sweeney, Michael Dilbeck; *Engineer:* Herb Powers.

Selections: 1 The Train Is Coming (K. Boothe/O. Burrell) (4:06) *Shaggy, Ken Boothe*; 2 Top Of The Stairs (Skee-Lo) (4:31) *Skee-Lo*; 3 Do You Know (T. Robinson) (3:24) *Total*; 4 Show You The Way To Go (K. Gamble/L. Huff) (5:29) *Men Of Vizion*; 5 Hiding Place (D. Hall/G. Chambers/Patra) (4:32) *Assorted Phlavors, Patra*; 6 Making Love (T. Kelley/B. Robinson/K. Wales/M. Keith/D. Jones/M. Scandrick/Q. Parker) (5:44) *112*; 7 The Thrill I'm In (J. Harris/T. Lewis) (4:12) *Luther Vandross*; 8 Still Not Over You (T. Lorenz/M. Rooney/M. Morales) (4:50) *Trey Lorenz*; 9 It's Alright (J. Oliver/ Heavy D/T. Robinson) (4:32) *Terri & Monica*; 10 Oh Baby (A. Richbourg/M. Horton/T. Hightower/S. Crumbley/J. Sylvain/R. Jackson) (3:58) *4.0*; 11 Merry Go Round (M. Bell/B. Edwards/R. Finks/F. Thomas/L. Troutman/R. Troutman) (4:06) *Ubu*; 12 Hold On I'm Coming (I. Hayes/D. Porter) (3:37) *The Neville Brothers*; 13 Money Train Suite (M. Mancina) (4:50).

Review: Another case of a composer whose contribution to a film receives an all too short selection. Mark Mancina, whose considerable talent has enlightened many excellent films in recent years, (*Moll Flanders, Speed, Twister,*) is represented here by the short "Money Train Suite," an expressive cue that might have gained at being presented as part of a more comprehensive instrumental album. The other selections in the album, all pop vocals, range from the okay in songs like "The Thrill I'm In," "Hold On I'm Coming," and "Merry Go Round" to the so-what in "Hiding Place," "Do You Know," and "Oh, Baby." Is it what a film soundtrack is really all about?

Monterey Pop ✐✐✐✐

1992, Rhino Records; from the documentary *The Monterey International Pop Festival*, 1967.

Selections: CD 1: 1 Festival Introduction (:52) *John Phillips*; 2 Along Comes Mary (2:47) *The Association*; 3 Windy (3:00) *The Association*; 4 Love Is A Hurtin' Thing (3:29) *Lou Rawls*; 5 Dead End Street (4:27) *Lou Rawls*; 6 Tobacco Road (6:20) *Lou Rawls*; 7 San Franciscan Nights (4:17) *Eric Burdon & The Animals*; 8 Hey Gyp (7:11) *Eric Burdon & The Animals*; 9 Rollin' And Tumblin' (4:19) *Canned Heat*; 10 Dust My Broom (5:02) *Canned Heat*; 11 Bullfrog Blues (3:01) *Canned Heat*; 12 Not So Sweet Martha Lorraine (5:38) *Country Joe & The Fish*; 13 Down On Me (3:26) *Big Brother & The Holding Company*; 14 Combination Of The Two (5:23) *Big Brother & The Holding Company*; 15 Harry (:37) *Big Brother & The Holding Company*; 16 Road Block (6:18) *Big Brother & The Holding Company*; 17 Ball And Chain (8:15) *Big Brother & The Holding Company*.

CD 2: 1 Look Over Yonders Wall (2:50) *The Butterfield Blues Band*; 2 Mystery Train (4:17) *The Butterfield Blues Band*; 3 Born In Chicago (4:05) *The Butterfield Blues Band*; 4 Double Trouble (4:45) *The Butterfield Blues Band*; 5 Mary Ann (3:11) *The Butterfield Blues Band*; 6 Mercury Blues (4:28) *The Steve Miller Band*; 7 Groovin' Is Easy (3:58) *The Electrical Flag*; 8 Wine (2:48) *The Electric Flag*; 9 Bajabula Bonke (Healing Song) (3:44) *Hugh Masekela*; 10 Renaissance Fair (3:16) *The Byrds*; 11 Have You Seen Her Face (2:44) *The Byrds*; 12 Hey Joe (Where You Gonna Go) (2:53) *The Byrds*; 13 He Was A Friend Of Mine (3:11) *The Byrds*; 14 Lady Friend (2:46) *The Byrds*; 15 Chimes Of Freedom (4:42) *The Byrds*; 16 So You Want To Be A Rock 'n' Roll Star (2:25) *The Byrds*; 17 Dhun: Fast Teental (excerpts) (6:05) *Ravi Shankar*; 18 Wake Me, Shake Me (11:49) *The Blues Project*.

Review: The summer of love, and much else, truly began with this pioneering pop/rock festival. It was put together around The Mamas and the Papas (!), who were on their way out, but it wound up enshrining Jefferson Airplane, Otis Redding, Janis Joplin, The Who, and Jimi Hendrix on their way in, as folk-rock gave way to something darker and, you bet, louder. Rhino's four-CD boxed set goes far beyond the performances preserved in the movie—which created the "rockumentary" form—and makes it clear that, song for song, artist for artist, raindrop for raindrop, this was better than Woodstock.
Marc Kirkeby

Monty Python and the Holy Grail ✐✐✐✐

1997, Arista Records; from the movie *Monty Python and the Holy Grail*, Tristar Pictures, 1975.

Album Notes: *Music:* De Wolfe; *Songs:* Neil Innes; *Album Producers:* Andre Jacquemin, Dave Howman, Michael Palin, Terry Jones, Terry Gilliam; *Engineers:* Garth Marshall, Terry Gilliam; *CD Producer:* Didier C. Deutsch; *Engineer:* Kevin Hodge.

Selections: 1 Introduction To The Executive CD Edition (1:08); 2 Tour Of The Classic Silbury Hill Theatre (:12); 3 Live Broadcast From London/Premier Of The Film (3:57); 4 Narration From The Silbury Hill Gentlemen's Room/"You're Using Cocoanuts" (2:56); 5 "Bring Out Your Dead" (1:03); 6 King Arthur And The "Old Woman"/A Lesson In Anarcho-Syndicated Commune Living (2:57); 7 "A Witch" (2:47); 8 A Lesson In Logic (2:51); 9 "Camelot" (1:35); 10 "The Quest For The Holy Grail" (1:11); 11 Live From The Parking Lot At The Silbury Hill Theatre (1:02); 12 The Castle Of Louis de Lombard/"A Strange Person" (2:25); 13 Bomb Scare (:44); 14 Executive CD Edition Announcement (:17); 15 Another Executive CD Edition Announcement (:30); 16 The Story Of The Film So Far (2:12); 17 The Tale Of Sir Robin (1:54); 18 The Knights Who Say "Ni!" (2:35); 19 Interview With Filmmaker Carl French (2:38); 20 The Tale Of Sir Lancelot: At Swamp Castle (4:08); 21 Tim, The Enchanter/A Shakespearean Critique (3:30); 22 "A Foul-Tempered Rabbit" (2:33); 23 The Bridge Of Death (3:59); 24 Executive CD Edition Addendum (:55); 25 The Castle Aaargh/The End (2:47).

Review: The saga of Arthur and his valiant Knights of the Round Table will probably never survive this delirious send-up in which the Monty Python comedians thoroughly destroyed the legend to create a film (and soundtrack recording) that has long since become a cult favorite. Many scenes, like "You're Using Cocoanuts," "Old Woman," "A Strange Person," or "The Knights Who Say 'Ni!,'" are oft-quoted classics in their own right and rib-ticklers that never fail to elicit a smile from the cognizant. The CD version incorporates additional moments of zany outbursts that were not on the LP.

Moon 44 🎵🎵🎵♪

1990, Silva Screen Records; from the movie *Moon 44*, Spectrum Entertainment, 1989.

Album Notes: *Music*: Joel Goldsmith; *Orchestrations*: Christopher L. Stone, Jack Smalley; The Graunke Symphony Orchestra conducted by Christopher L. Stone; *Featured Vocalist*: Heather Forsyth; *Album Producer*: Joel Goldsmith; *Engineer*: Keith Grant; *Assistant Engineers*: Gerry O'Riordan, Peter Fuchs.

Selections: 1 Main Title/Felix The Cop (3:05); 2 First Training Flight (5:14); 3 So Long Felix (4:08); 4 Navigator's Hang Up (1:28); 5 Armed And Dangerous No. 1 (3:30); 6 Drones, Drones (But Not A Drop To Drink)(2:53); 7 Sykes Gets Caught (2:10); 8 Armed And Dangerous No. 2 (4:28); 9 So You Like It Fast (Hard And Rough)(1:47); 10 Jake To The Rescue/Joel's Outlandish Adventure (2:25); 11 Lee Bombs Out (3:02); 12 Welcome To Moon 44 (:50); 13 Taxi Driver ("You Talkin' To Me")(2:49); 14 The Cookie Crumbles/Bumpy Taxi Ride/The End Of Moon 44 (8:08); 15 Aferthmath (1:15); 16 Heading For Earth (:59); 17 Terry On The Moon/Finale (1:13); 18 Shut Out (1:34).

Review: This dynamic and exciting film score from Jerry Goldsmith's son is Joel Goldsmith's first large orchestral recording after many years of low-budget film and TV music. The music for this futuristic science fiction thriller is heavy on action, with no real melodies. Goldsmith keeps firm control over the orchestra even in the most furious of orchestral moments. His dissonances remain tonal and fluid and they continue to drive the action ahead. Naturally, some of these action cues are reminiscent of his father's, especially in the low horn phrases over snare drum and counterpointed strings melodies, but for the most part Joel Goldsmith is developing into a talented filmscorer in his own right. The CD is well-produced with an informative 8-page booklet. The only real drawback is the inclusion of the loud, raucous punk rock vocal, which is quite out of sync with the rest of the music — and quite a jolt after all the dynamic symphonics.

Randall D. Larson

Moon over Parador 🎵🎵🎵🎵

1988, MCA Records; from the movie *Moon over Parador*, Universal Pictures, 1988.

Album Notes: *Music*: Maurice Jarre; Orchestra conducted by Maurice Jarre; *Album Producer*: Maurice Jarre; *Engineer*: Joel Moss; *Assistant Engineer*: Scott MacPherson.

Selections: 1 Parador (2:00); 2 Madonna's Tango (3:08); 3 History Lesson (6:36); 4 Momma's Back (3:32); 5 Carnival (2:43); 6 Dictator's Workout (2:56); 7 The Part Of A Lifetime (2:43); 8 Flyaway (6:38).

Review: Maurice Jarre provided a wholly symphonic and wholly delightful score for this Paul Mazursky comedy about an actor masquerading as the dictator of an obscure Latin American country. The score is lively, often comic and often romantic, always vibrant. It captures Jarre's strongest symphonic capabilities and allows them to breathe. *Moon over Parador* lets its themes shine, giving both a Latin flavor through acoustic guitars, solo trumpets, tambourines, and Latin rhythms to its broad musical landscape, embellished with full orchestrations. The "Parador" theme is one of Jarre's most likable themes, a tuneful, inescapable rhythm that captures all of the film's many moods in a single melody. This is an invigorating score and among Jarre's best cinematic endeavors.

Randall D. Larson

Moonraker 🎵🎵🎵🎵

1988, EMI-Manhattan; from the movie *Moonraker*, United Artists, 1979.

Album Notes: *Music*: John Barry; *Lyrics*: Hal David; Orchestra conducted by John Barry; *Album Producer*: John Barry.

Selections: 1 Main Title: Moonraker (3:12) *Shirley Bassey*; 2 Space Lazer Battle (2:50); 3 Miss Goodhead Meets Bond (2:49); 4 Cable Car and Snake Fight (3:10); 5 Bond Lured To Pyramid (2:06); 6 Flight Into Space (6:33); 7 Bond Arrives In Rio and Boat Chase (2:39); 8 Centrifuge and Corrine Put Down (2:38); 9 Bond Smells A Rat (2:26); 10 End Title: Moonraker (2:30) *Shirley Bassey*.

Review: One of the best Bond films starring Roger Moore, *Moonraker* also got a great boost from John Barry, evidently in much better form than in the previous *Man with the Golden Gun,* and determined to have fun with it. The cues, more clearly detailed and using instrumentations that seem better suited, sound a bit more sedate than the throbbing cues in the Sean Connery films. The new addition of a distant choir confers to several of the cues an aura that is most attractive. The best moments here, as in the film, are the vibrant action scenes, with cues including "Cable Car and Snake Fight" and "Bond Arrives in Rio and Boat Chase," but a magnificent highlight is the poetic "Flight into Space," as effective in the album as it is in the film. Shirley Bassey's vocals seem almost as essential as Barry's score.

Moonstruck 🎵🎵🎵♪

1987, Capitol Records; from the movie *Moonstruck*, Metro-Goldwyn-Mayer, 1987.

Album Notes: *Music*: Dick Hyman; *Orchestrations and Arrangements*: Dick Hyman; Orchestra conducted by Dick Hyman; Orchestra and Chorus of the Academy of Santa Cecilia of Rome, conducted by Tullio Serafin; *Featured Performers*: Jack Zaza (mandolin), Dominic Cortese (accordion), Ed Bickert (guitar), Moe Koffman (alto sax), Nora Shulman (flute), Dick Hyman (piano); *Album Producers*: Dick Hyman, Patrick Palmer, Norman Jewison; *Engineer*: Andrew S. Hermant.

Selections: 1 That's Amore (H. Warren/J. Brooks)(3:09) *Dean Martin*; 2 Canzone per Loretta/Addio, Mulberry Street (2:57); 3 Mr. Moon (1:01); 4 It Must Be Him (G. Becaud/M. Vidalin/M. David)(2:52) *Vikki Carr*; 5 Old Man Mazurka (2:29); 6 Lament For Johnny's Mama (1:14); 7 Che gelida manina (G. Puccini)(1:47); 8 Donde lieta usci (G. Puccini)(3:32) *Renata Tebaldi*; 9 Canzone per Loretta (:58); 10 O soave fanciulla (G. Puccini)(4:01) *Carlo Bergonzi, Renata Tebaldi*; 11 Musetta's Waltz (G. Puccini)(4:29); 12 Musetta's Entrance (G. Puccini)(1:20); 13 Instrumental Excerpts From La Boheme (G. Puccini)(3:32); 14 Gettin' Ready (1:47); 15 Brooklyn Heights Stroll (3:16); 16 Beautiful Signorina (3:17); 17 Moonglow (W. Hudson/E. DeLange/I. Mills)(2:54); 18 Canzone per Loretta/Gioventu mia, tu non sei morta (G. Puccini)(2:16) *Gianna D'Angelo, Renata Tebaldi, Carlo Bergonzi, Fernando Corena, Ettore Bastiani, Renato Cesari, Cesare Siepi*.

Review: Talk about a film that started modestly enough and ended up a surprise hit among both audiences and critics. Cher stars in a fetching Oscar-winning performance as a widow re-signed to a life of mediocrity suddenly torn between two suitors, a bland neighbor, Johnny (Danny Aiello), and his beguiling brother, Ronny (Nicholas Cage). Much of the film's atmosphere came from the judicious choice of musical selections put together for the occasion, from the various vocal and instrumental opera tunes, to the pop songs, to the light jazzy touch provided by Dick Hyman. These apparently disparate elements blend together to create an aura that reflects the Italian background of the Brooklyn neighborhood where the action took place and of the characters who peopled the film. The soundtrack album reflects the same aura in a way that does not come across as cohesively here as it did in the film, though it provides a musical programming that has more ups than downs.

More ♫♫♫♫

1989, Capitol Records; from the movie *More*, 1969.

Album Notes: *Music*: Pink Floyd (Roger Waters/David Gilmour/Nick Mason/Rick Wright).

Selections: 1 Cirrus Minor (5:15); 2 The Nile Song (3:26); 3 Crying Song (3:34); 4 Up The Khyber (2:13); 5 Green Is The Colour (2:59); 6 Cymbaline (4:50); 7 Party Sequence (1:10); 8 Main Theme (5:32); 9 Ibiza Bar (3:17); 10 More Blues (2:12); 11

Quicksilver (7:11); 12 A Spanish Piece (1:05); 13 Dramatic Theme (2:16).

Review: The touching love story of a German youth and an American girl, set against the psychedelic culture of the late 1960s, much of the actual flavor in *More* is due to Pink Floyd's trend-setting, atmospheric score. A cult favorite since its initial release, this soundtrack album continues to exert its spell-binding attraction, evoking not only an era that seems, in retrospect, simpler and more poetic, but making a musical statement which, decades later, has lost none of its immediacy and importance.

Mortal Kombat

Mortal Kombat ♫♫♫

1995, TVT Records; from the movie *Mortal Kombat*, New Line Cinema, 1995.

Album Notes: *Music*: George S. Clinton; *Orchestrations*: George S. Clinton; Orchestra conducted by George S. Clinton; *Featured Musician*: Buckethead (guitar).

Selections: 1 A Taste Of Things To Come (:47); 2 Demon Warriors/Final Kombat (3:49); 3 Goro vs. Art (3:00); 4 Goodbye (Gravity Kills)(3:10) *Gravity Kills*; 5 Juke-Joint Jezebel (E. Esch/S. Konietzko/G. Schulz/R. Watts) (5:17) *KMFDM*; 6 Unlearn (D. Lenz/P. Sebastien)(7:29) *Psykosonik*; 7 Control (Juno Reactor Instrumental)(T. Lords/B. Watkins)(6:28) *Traci Lords*; 8 Halcyon+On+On (P. Hartnoll/P. Hartnoll/E. Barton)(9:28) *Orbital*; 9 Utah Saints Take On The Theme From Mortal Kombat (The Utah Saints/O. Adams)(3:00) *Utah Saints*; 10 The Invisible (G. Butler)(4:30) *GZR*; 11 Zero Signals (D. Cazares/R. Herrera/B. Bell)(5:58) *Fear Factory*; 12 Burn (Sister Machine Gun)(4:40) *Sister Machine Gun*; 13 Blood & Fire (Out Of The Ashes Mix) (Steele)(4:35) *Type O Negative*; 14 I Reject (C. Liggio)(2:57) *Bile*; 15 Twist The Knife (Slowly)(M. Harris/S. Embury)(2:53) *Napalm Death*; 16 What U See/We All Bleed Red (M. Moore/L. Branstetter)(4:09) *Mutha's Day Out*; 17 Techno-Syndrome 7;dp Mix (O. Adams)(3:22) *The Immortals*.

Review: What kind of music do you program for the film version of one the most popular video game bloodlettings of all time? Check out the song titles: "Blood & Fire," "Burn," "Demon Warriors," "Twist the Knife Slowly." Check out the band names: Type O Negative, Napalm Death, Fear Factory, Sister Machine Gun. Sounds like a match to us. And it should be noted that *Kombat* used techno, Orbital's "Halcyon + On + On," a couple of years before it became the hip thing to do. *Gary Graff*

Mortal Kombat ♫♫⌐

1995, TVT Records; from the movie *Mortal Kombat*, New Line Cinema, 1995.

Album Notes: *Music*: George S. Clinton; *Orchestrations*: George S. Clinton; *Music Editor*: Joanie Diner; The Testosterone Orchestra conducted by George S. Clinton; *Featured Musicians*: Buckethead (guitar), Brain (drums), Scott Breadman, Scott Higgins (percussion), Brice Martin (shakuhachi), Arjuna (resonator), George S. Clinton (keyboards); *Engineer*: John Whynot.

Selections: 1 A Taste Of Things To Come (1:19); 2 Liu vs. Sub-Zero (2:13); 3 It Has Begun; 4 The Garden (1:16); 5 Goro vs. Art (3:10); 6 Banquet (1:11); 7 Liu vs. Katana (1:35); 8 Liu's Dream (1:24); 9 Liu vs. Reptile (1:40); 10 Stairway (:43); 11 Goro Goro (:41); 12 Kidnapped (1:21); 13 Zooom (:17); 14 Johnny vs. Scorpion (1:20); 15 Hand And Shadow (2:40); 16 Scorpion And Sub-Zero (:50); 17 Soul Snatchin' (:37); 18 On The Beach (1:24); 19 Johnny Cage (1:06); 20 Goro Chase (1:27); 21 Evening Bells (:55); 22 Monks (:56); 23 Friends (1:51); 24 Flawless Victory (6:23); 25 Farewell (1:10); 26 Kids (1:18).

Review: Relentlessly energetic action score by George S. Clinton just erupts with its hard and heavy percussion, pounding like a primitive war dance. This was never going to be a quiet soundtrack as the film gave Clinton little opportunity to do anything else. He makes inventive use of his synthesizers and ethnic instruments, giving his orchestra several layers of dark and eerie musical textures. The album's one failing is that many tracks are under two minutes (one only 17 seconds!) and this makes the album prone to start and stop fits, giving little time to develop an overall feeling for the score.

David Hirsch

The Mosquito Coast ♫♫♫

1986, Fantasy Records; from the movie *The Mosquito Coast,* Fantasy Films, 1986.

Album Notes: *Music*: Maurice Jarre; *Electronic Ensemble*: Michael Boddicker, Michael Fisher, Ralph Grierson, Judd Miller, Nyle Steiner, Ian Underwood; conducted by Maurice Jarre; *Album Producer*: Maurice Jarre; *Engineer*: Joel Moss.

Selections: 1 The Mosquito Coast (5:44); 2 Goodbye America (And Have A Nice Day)(9:04); 3 Gimme Soca (A. Carter)(1:46) *Byron Lee & The Dragonaires*; 4 Up The River (1:43); 5 Jeronimo (4:35); 6 Fat Boy (7:30); 7 Destruction (5:23); 8 The Storm (1:37); 9 Allie's Theme (8:09).

Review: Maurice Jarre, writing for an electronic ensemble, delivered a superbly atmospheric score for this film by Peter Weir, starring Harrison Ford as a man with a utopian vision, who decides to leave modern civilization and moves with his wife and four kids to the jungle of a remote Caribbean island. The music, generally very attractive and poetic, benefits from the synthesizer sound up to a point, but the overall effect tends to be overpowering after a while. The exuberant "Gimme Soca," short as it may be, relieves the sullen moods and confirms one's impression that the score would have been stronger with the addition of another tune or two with that kind of drive and energy.

Mother ♫♫♫♫

1996, Hollywood Records; from the movie *Mother*, Paramount Pictures, 1996.

Album Notes: *Music*: Marc Shaiman; *Orchestrations*: Jeff Atmajian; *Music Editor*: Scott Stambler; Orchestra conducted by Artie Kane; *Album Producer*: Marc Shaiman; *Engineer*: Dennis Sands.

Selections: 1 Mrs. Robinson (P. Simon)(3:51) *Steve Lively, Jess Harnell*; 2 Main Title (3:22); 3 Such A Surprise (1:06); 4 In My Room (B. Wilson/G. Usher)(2:14) *The Beach Boys*; 5 Circling The Market (2:00); 6 Berate Me Tomorrow/The Blank Screen (1:42); 7 Trip To The Mall (4:23); 8 Land Of A Thousand Dances (C. Kenner)(2:26) *Wilson Pickett*; 9 At The Zoo (2:34); 10 The Hat Box (3:05); 11 Understanding Mother (4:48); 12 Look Who's Writing (1:14); 13 Across The Line (R. Cray/R. Cousins/P. Boe/D. Olson/D. Amy/J.L. Walker/H. Oden)(4:07) *The Robert Cray Band*; 14 Keep On Movin' (Jazzie B) (6:00) *Soul II Soul*.

Review: The delightful spoof of Paul Simon's "Mrs. Robinson," retitled here "Mrs. Henderson," to fit the character portrayed by Debbie Reynolds, augurs well for this soundtrack album to a charming comedy about a grownup man (Albert Brooks) who moves back in with "Mother" when his marriage ends up in divorce... again! The same whimsical moods pervade the cues written by Marc Shaiman, gently amusing and catchy, culminating in an exuberant "Understanding Mother," that sums up everything in the score that's so endearing. Selected pop tunes, wisely chosen, add a definite flair to the whole album.

Mother Night ♫♫♫♫

1997, Varese-Sarabande Records; from the movie *Mother Night*, Fine Line Features, 1996.

Album Notes: Michael Convertino; *Orchestrations*: John Neufeld, Bobby Muzingo, Michael Convertino; *Music Editor*: Ken Wannberg; Orchestra conducted by Artie Kane; *Album Producer*: Michael Convertino; *Engineers*: Shawn Murphy, Dave Marquette.

Selections: 1 Spiegel I'm Spiegal/A Nation Of Two (5:17); 2 The Jews Are Eating The Future (2:15); 3 You Are What You Pretend To Be (4:15); 4 A New No-Life (3:38); 5 The Hanging Man (3:50); 6 Cantus In Memoriam (B. Britten) (6:06); 7 Allegro (from The Four Seasons: Autumn)(A. Vivaldi)(5:08) *The Bournemouth Sinfonietta, Richard Studt*; 8 Fratres (A. Part)(11:13); 9 Love Raises The Dead (1:36); 10 Leichentrager zur Wache (2:34); 10 Spiegel I'm Spiegal/War (4:48).

Review: A complex character study, *Mother Night*, based on a novel by Kurt Vonnegut, touches upon questions that transcend its subject matter even as it delves into different cinematographic genres. It is all reflective of the widespread screen action that takes its main protagonist, an American radio announcer (Nick Nolte) caught in the maelstrom of Nazi Germany, whose sympathies for the regime eventually owe him to be hunted after the war, and brought to Israel to be tried as a criminal. In turns a gritty black comedy, a political thriller, and a romantic drama, one of the film's unifying threads is Michael Convertino's low-key score, a collection of long orchestral themes that aim to underscore specific scenes while providing a musical atmosphere common to all of them. Two classical selections, Britten's "Cantus in Memoriam," and an excerpt from Vivaldi's *The Four Seasons*, add an extra element of beauty that's welcome. Missing, however, is Bing Crosby's rendition of "White Christmas" which was essential to the opening sequence in the film.

Mountains of the Moon ♫♫♫◦

1990, Polydor Records; from the movie *Mountains of the Moon*, Carolco Pictures, 1990.

Album Notes: *Music:* Michael Small; *Orchestrations:* Christopher Dedrick; The Graunke Symphony Orchestra, conducted by Allan Wilson; *Featured Musicians:* Foday Muso Suso (Karinya, Tama, Nyanyeri, percussion), Gordon Gottlieb (percussion), "Crusher" Bennett (percussion), Tony Hajar (Arabic flute), Bill Ochs (Uillean pipes); *Album Producer:* Michael Small; *Engineer:* Shawn Murphy.

Selections: 1 Main Title (1:41); 2 Journey (1:15); 3 Sandy Camp (1:36); 4 The Market (2:03); 5 Escape To England (2:31); 6 Isabelle (2:38); 7 Return To Africa (2:14); 8 Mabruki And The Lion Shoot (3:54); 9 The Long Walk (1:37); 10 Burton Sings (The Lone Rock)(1:51) *Patrick Bergin*; 11 Desert Trek (4:12); 12 It's The Lake (:50); 13 Poison Water (1:41); 14 Dark Caravan (3:12); 15 Ambush (:45); 16 Ngola's Court (1:44); 17 Speke And The Great Lake (4:03); 18 Farewell To Mabruki (1:42); 19 Journey Home (2:06); 20 The Wedding (Isabelle's Theme)(1:26); 21

"A funny thing happens when you're a film composer. You actually take on the role of director when it comes to the music because you know the director is very much in charge."

Hans Zimmer
(The Hollywood Reporter, 1-15-97)

The Decision (2:11); 22 Burton's Theme (2:02); 23 Journey Finale (2:22).

Review: Composer Michael Small is primarily known for his adept scoring of some classic "paranoia" thrillers of the '70s like *The Parallax View, Klute, The Stepford Wives* and *Marathon Man*, but here he showcases an unexpected talent for the broader canvas of this historical adventure film about the explorer Sir Richard Burton. Small strays from his psychological approach of his earlier scores, here adopting a style more in keeping with John Williams or Georges Delerue, but what he lacks in originality he more than makes up for in melodic inventiveness. Several sweeping, gorgeous tunes fill out the epic scope of the story, from a noble, adventuresome theme for Burton to a beautiful waltz-like melody for Burton's romance with an English noblewoman. It makes for great listening, although the 18th-century romanticism often stands uncomfortably next to native African songs and percussion lines, with no attempt to integrate the two disparate styles. The score's immensely satisfying emotional qualities squash any other quibbles.

Jeff Bond

Much Ado about Nothing ♫♫♫♫♫

1993, Epic Soundtrax/Sony Music; from the movie *Much Ado about Nothing*, Samuel Goldwyn Pictures, 1993.

Album Notes: *Music:* Patrick Doyle; *Orchestrations:* Lawrence Ashmore, John Bell; *Music Editor:* Roy Prendergast; Orchestra conducted by David Snell; *Album Producers:* Patrick Doyle, Maggie Rodford; *Engineer:* Chris Dibble; *Assistant Engineer:* James Collins.

Selections: 1 The Picnic (2:58); 2 Overture (4:22); 3 The Sweetest Lady (2:07); 4 The Conspirators (2:43); 5 The Masked

Ball (1:57); 6 The Prince Woos Hero (1:20); 7 A Star Danced (2:47); 8 Rich She Shall Be (1:44); 9 Sigh No More Ladies (1:59); 10 The Gulling Of Benedick (3:13); 11 It Must Be Requited (2:01); 12 The Gulling Of Beatrice (1:41); 13 Contempt Farewell (1:38); 14 The Lady Is Disloyal (2:18); 15 Hero's Wedding (:48); 16 Take Her Back Again (3:12); 17 Die To Live (4:45); 18 You Have Killed A Sweet Lady (3:04); 19 Choose Your Revenge (1:51); 20 Pardon Goddess Of The Night (4:35); 21 Did I Not Tell You (1:42); 22 Hero Revealed (1:28); 23 Benedick The Married Man (2:09); 24 Strike Up Pipers (2:42).

Review: A grand, glorious score by Patrick Doyle, *Much Ado about Nothing* is one of those magical soundtracks whose popularity seems to grow as time goes on. You can't turn on any Olympic competition without hearing the majestic "Overture" at least once or twice, nor can one easily forget the soaring chorus of "Sigh No More Ladies," a track which gives this second Kenneth Branagh adaptation of Shakespeare its musical soul. Unlike his superb though sometimes over-the-top *Henry V* or the context-heavy score for *Hamlet*, Doyle's *Much Ado* is pretty much a stand-alone classic, and is certainly the most accessible score of the three Branagh-Doyle Shakespeare efforts. In fact, it is very hard to find fault with any of Doyle's compositions, or their sequencing as an album. The music flows splendidly from one track to the next, offering sweeping, memorable themes that linger in the mind long after they have finished. The cumulative effect is that of a superior listening experience that is rare at the cinema now. Indeed, when looking at how derivative and vapid most movie music currently is, *Much Ado* truly stands out as one of the finest film scores composed in the last decade.

Andy Dursin

Mulholland Falls 🎬🎬

1996, edel America Records; from the movie *Mulholland Falls*, M-G-M, 1996.

Album Notes: *Music*: Dave Grusin; *Orchestrations*: Brad Dechter; Orchestra conducted by Dave Grusin; *Album Producer*: Dave Grusin; *Engineer*: Shawn Murphy.

Selections: 1 Mulholland Falls (4:33); 2 Just A Girl... (2:46); 3 Hurting For Allison (3:31); 4 Flashback And Revelation (3:03); 5 Kate's Theme/The End Of Jimmy (3:04); 6 Nuclear Madness/ Hats In The Desert (4:14); 7 Home Movies (1:41); 8 It's Over/ Flashback (2:59); 9 Separation (1:32); 10 To The Base/ Fallout For Timms (3:24); 11 Finale: Hats Off (2:55); 12 No Common Ground/End Credits (6:49); 13 Harbor Lights (J. Kennedy/H. Williams)(3:23) *Aaron Neville.*

Review: The true story of four LAPD detectives whose taste for expensive clothes and rough handling of criminals earned them the name of the "Hat Squad" in the early '50s, and the personal involvement of one of them with a young woman and crime victim, *Mulholland Falls* is a drama that never really attains the lofty heights to which it aspired. Possibly reflective of the uncertainties about the narrative itself, which, despite strong performances by Nick Nolte, Melanie Griffith, Chris Penn and John Malkovich, never gets off the ground and turns introspective instead of focusing on action, Dave Grusin's score, as heard in this soundtrack album, remains grounded in banalities. With little of the urgency or drive evidently needed for a film of this nature, it wanders aimlessly from one cue to another, with only "Kate's Theme" attracting for its melodic content.

The Muppet Movie 🎬🎬🎬🎬

1993, Jim Henson Records; from the animated feature *The Muppet Movie*, Jim Henson Productions, 1993.

Album Notes: *Music*: Paul Williams; *Songs*: Paul Williams & Kenny Ascher; *Orchestrations*: Ian Freebairn-Smith; Orchestra conducted by Ian Freebairn-Smith; *Cast*: Jim Henson (Kermit The Frog, Dr. Teeth, Rowlf, Swedish Chef, Waldorf), Frank Oz (Fozzie Bear, Miss Piggy, Animal), Jerry Nelson (Floyd, Robin The Frog, Crazy Harry), Richard Hunt (Scooter, Sweetums, Statler, Janice, Beaker), Dave Goelz (The Great Gonzo, Zoot, Dr. Bunsen Honeydew); *Album Producer*: Paul Williams; *Engineers*: Garry Ulmer, Danny Wallen.

Selections: 1 Rainbow Connection (3:16) *Jim Henson*; 2 Movin' Right Along (2:58) *Jim Henson, Frank Oz*; 3 Never Before, Never Again (2:30) *Frank Oz*; 4 Never Before, Never Again (3:53); 5 I Hope That Somethin' Better Comes Along (3:58) *Jim Henson*; 6 Can You Picture That? (2:31) *Jim Henson*; 7 I Hope That Somethin' Better Comes Along (2:30); 8 I'm Going To Go Back There Someday (2:52) *Dave Goelz*; 9 America (:53) *Frank Oz*; 10 Animal... Come Back Animal (1:31); 11 Finale: The Magic Store (5:17)*Cast*.

Review: The first, and to many, the best Muppet film, *The Muppet Movie* brings to the big screen the lovable gang in a story that doesn't make too much sense, but gives equal time to all the familiar characters, and proves thoroughly enjoyable from beginning to end. This is also due, to a large extent, to the wonderful score and songs created by Paul Williams, which includes the Grammy Award-winning "Rainbow Connection." In a case like this, little can be said: all you have to do is sit down, take the scene, and revel in the silly nonsense.

Muppet Treasure Island 🎵🎵🎵🎵

1996, Angel Records; from the animated feature *Muppet Treasure Island*, Walt Disney Pictures, 1996.

Album Notes: *Music*: Hans Zimmer; *Songs*: Barry Mann, Cynthia Weil; *Orchestrations*: Bruce Fowler, Suzette Moriarty, Ladd McIntosh, Walt Fowler, Steve Fowler, Conrad Pope, Elizabeth Finch; *Music Editor*: Adam Smalley; Orchestra conducted by Harry Gregson-Williams; *Album Producers*: Hans Zimmer, Adam Smalley; *Engineer*: Paul Hulme; *Assistant Engineers*: Gregg Silk, Slamm Anders.

Selections: 1 Treasure Island (1:08); 2 Shiver My Timbers (2:25) *Dave Goelz, Steve Whitmire, Jerry Nelson, Kevin Clash, Bill Barretta, Barry Mann, Frank Oz*; 3 Something Better (3:00) *Dave Goelz, Steve Whitmire, Kevin Bishop*; 4 Sailing For Adventure (2:59) *Tim Curry, Dave Goelz, Steve Whitmire, Jerry Nelson, Kevin Clash, Bill Barretta, Mak Wilson, Barry Mann, Kevin Bishop, Frank Oz*; 5 Cabin Fever (2:18) *Dave Goelz, Steve Whitmire, Jerry Nelson, Kevin Clash, Bill Barretta, Barry Mann, Frank Oz*; 6 A Professional Pirate (3:15); 7 Boom Shakalaka (1:22); 8 Love Led Us Here (2:23) *Steve Whitmire, Frank Oz*; 9 The Map (4:35); 10 Captain Smollet (2:04); 11 Land Ho (2:39); 12 Compass (1:07); 13 Long John (3:57); 14 Rescue (7:01); 15 Honest Brave And True (3:55); 16 Love Power (3:42) *Ziggy Marley and The Melody Makers*; 17 Love Led Us Here (3:45) *John Berry, Helen Darling*.

Review: A retelling of Robert Louis Stevenson's classic story, but with many liberties taken during the course of the action with the original, *Muppet Treasure Island* gives the Muppets an opportunity to interact with human actors, sail the high seas in search of a treasure, and throw in a couple of song-and-dance numbers even Stevenson with his wild imagination couldn't have dreamed up. The sum total is an entertaining lark, spiced up with some good musical moments, and the antics of the always engaging furry characters. If the kids will enjoy it for what it is, adults will also be amply rewarded, as long as they are not looking for *Traviata* or *The Pirates of Penzance*. Tim Curry, among the humans involved in this swinging swashbuckler, is outstanding as a singing Long John Silver.

Muriel's Wedding 🎵🎵🎵

1995, Polydor Records; from the movie *Muriel's Wedding*, Miramax Pictures, 1995.

Album Notes: *Music*: Peter Best; *Album Executive Producer*: Chris Gough; *Engineer*: David Hemming.

Selections: 1 Bridal Dancing Queen (B. Anderson/S. Anderson/B. Ulvaeus) (1:10) *The Wedding Band, Blazey Best*; 2 Sugar Baby Love (W. Bickerton/T. Waddington)(3:28) *The Rubettes*; 3 We've Only Just Begun (P. Williams/R. Nichols)(3:03) *The Carpenters*; 4 Lonely Hearts (P. Best)(1:02) *The Wedding Band*; 5 The Tide Is High (J. Holt/T. Evans/H. Barrett)(4:34) *Blondie*; 6 Waterloo (B. Anderson/S. Anderson/B. Ulvaeus)(2:42) *ABBA*; 7 I Go To Rio (P. Allen/A. Anderson)(3:16) *Peter Allen*; 8 Bean Bag (P. Best)(2:09) *The Wedding Band, John Barrett*; 9 T-Shirt And Jeans (G. McLean/J. Thorpe/K. Djalkovsky)(4:08) *Razorbrain*; 10 I Just Don't Know What To Do With Myself (B. Bacharach/H. David)(3:00) *Dusty Springfield*; 11 Bridal Dancing Queen (B. Anderson/S. Anderson/B. Ulvaeus)(3:05) *The Wedding Band, Blazey Best*; 12 I Do, I Do, I Do, I Do, I Do (B. Anderson/S. Anderson/B. Ulvaeus)(3:16) *ABBA*; 13 Happy Together (G. Bonner/A. Gordon)(2:53) *The Turtles*; 14 Muriel's Wedding (P. Best)(3:31) *The Wedding Band*; 15 Dancing Queen (B. Anderson/S. Anderson/B. Ulvaeus)(3:49) *ABBA*.

Review: How you'll feel about this soundtrack depends on your taste for Abba, who account for three songs, and cheesey wedding band music, which accounts for four songs. It's another hodgepodge collection, loosely based around reception ditties such as the Carpenters' syrupy "We've Only Just Begun," the Turtles' "Happy Together" and Peter Allen's limbo-provoking "I Go to Rio." But without "Proud Mary" or "Celebrate," there's no way this can claim to be authentic.
Gary Graff

Music Box 🎵🎵🎵

1989, Varese-Sarabande Records; from the movie *Music Box*, Carolco Pictures, 1989.

Album Notes: *Music*: Philippe Sarde; *Orchestrations*: Bill Byers, Hubert Bougis; The Hungarian State Symphony Orchestra and The Muzsikas, conducted by Harry Rabinowitz; *Album Producer*: Philippe Sarde; *Engineer*: William Flageollet.

Selections: 1 Ann's Theme (2:30); 2 Blood Red Danube (1:42); 3 Federal Building (3:19); 4 Departure From Court (:56); 5 Ann Studies Documents (2:09); 6 Journey To Budapest (4:27); 7 The Scar (1:11); 8 Ann And Georgina In Talbot's Library (2:27); 9 The Mirror (1:43); 10 Cemetery (2:19); 11 Candor (The Gendarmes)(3:45); 12 Remembering Of Ann's Mother (3:11); 13 Music Box (3:41); 14 The Newspaper (:55); 15 Finale (1:02).

Review: A powerful drama, enhanced by Jessica Lange's sensitive portrayal as a successful Chicago lawyer forced to defend her own father, facing deportation to Hungary for crimes he allegedly committed during World War II, *Music Box* could have benefitted from a stronger score than the one created here by Philippe Sarde. Not that the composer failed director Costa-Gavras, but saddled with little physical screen action and a poorly developed screenplay, all Sarde could do was provide cues that try to make a point when there is none to make. The only times the score comes alive is when the vivacious accents of a Hungarian csardas kick in as in "Departure from Court" and "Journey to Budapest," in a bit of local color that's particularly welcome.

My Best Friend's Wedding
♫♫♫♫

1997, Work Records; from the movie *My Best Friend's Wedding*, TriStar Pictures, 1997.

Album Notes: *Music:* James Newton Howard; *Orchestrations:* Brad Dechter, James Newton Howard; Orchestra conducted by Artie Kane; *Song Producers:* Andy Marvel, Ani DiFranco, Jann Arden & Ed Cherney, Jimmy Bralower & Jeff Bova, Marc Tanner, Danny Bennett, Mary Chapin Carpenter, Lars Halapi, Eddie Arkin; *Album Executive Producers:* Glen Brunman, Bonnie Greenberg; *Engineer:* Bernie Grundman.

Selections: 1 I Say A Little Prayer (B. Bacharach/H. David)(3:38) *Diana King*; 2 Wishin' And Hopin' (B. Bacharach/H. David)(3:18) *Ani DiFranco*; 3 You Don't Know Me (C. Walker/E. Arnold)(3:27) *Jann Arden*; 4 Tell Him (B.R. Berris)(2:37) *The Exciters*; 5 I Just Don't Know What To Do With Myself (B. Bacharach/H. David)(4:21) *Nicky Holland*; 6 I'll Be Okay (T. Clark/G. Wells) (4:59) *Amanda Marshall*; 7 The Way You Look Tonight (D. Fields/J. Kern) (3:26) *Tony Bennett*; 8 What The World Needs Now (B. Bacharach/H. David) (3:15) *Jackie DeShannon*; 9 I'll Never Fall In Love Again (B. Bacharach/H. David)(3:53) *Mary-Chapin Carpenter*; 10 Always You (S. Zelmani/Q. Starkie) (2:52) *Sophie Zelmani*; 11 If You Wanna Be Happy (C. Guida/F. Guida/J. Royster)(2:23) *Jimmy Soul*; 12 I Say A Little Prayer (B. Bacharach/H. David) (2:31) The Cast Of "My Best Friend's Wedding"; 13 Suite From "My Best Friend's Wedding"(J. Newton Howard)(6:12).

Review: What a bright, cheerful little album! Featuring many songs written by Burt Bacharach and Hal David, and performances by a host of pop performers, including Jackie DeShannon, Mary Chapin Carpenter, and the ubiquitous Tony Bennett, the album plays like a wonderful, joyous celebration to the best of pop music in the 1960s. Even the cast of the film, including Julia Roberts, Dermot Muroney and Cameron Diaz, join in the fun, with James Newton Howard providing six

minutes (not much, but enough to appreciate his contribution) of instrumental merriment.

My Cousin Vinny ♫♫♫

1992, Varese-Sarabande Records; from the movie *My Cousin Vinny*, 20th Century-Fox, 1992.

Album Notes: *Music:* Randy Edelman; *Orchestrations:* Ralph Ferraro; *Music Editor:* Kathy Durning; Orchestra conducted by Randy Edelman; *Album Producer:* Randy Edelman; *Engineers:* Elton Ahi, Dennis Sands.

Selections: 1 Something's Wrong (2:43); 2 Meeting The Judge (1:07); 3 Booked For Murder (1:03); 4 Life On The Open Road (1:03); 5 Brooklyn Reflections (:29); 6 Pig Squawk And Prison Talks (1:27); 7 Sworn Testimony (2:25); 8 Stiffled (1:13); 9 Lisa's Theme (1:31); 10 Shakey Vinny Takes The Case (2:16); 11 Trotter Unfolds The Tale (1:52); 12 Kicking J.T.'s Butt (1:44); 13 Wazoo Junction (2:08); 14 The Tide Turns (1:20); 15 Hot Wheels (1:58); 16 Mud Slide Vin (1:00); 17 Norton Gets Nuked (2:05); 18 Brainstorm (1:41); 19 Victory (1:24); 20 Closing and Reprise Of Wazoo Junction (3:09).

Review: Randy Edelman has teamed with director Jonathan Lynn a number of times over the years, but their most fruitful collaboration turned out to be *My Cousin Vinny*, the Joe Pesci comedy that earned Marisa Tomei an Oscar for her hilarious comedic performance. Edelman's score is typical of the composer, interspersing synths with orchestra and a small acoustic ensemble that simultaneously echoes both the street-savvy New Yorker who heads down to Alabama to handle a court case and the down home, decidedly Southern lifestyle that he runs into. The score is frequently bouncy and always energetic, though it's hard to believe that listeners who haven't seen the film will find the music of great interest, thus leaving the album recommended most strongly for fans of the movie. By the way, anyone looking for the two Travis Tritt songs that open and close the film will have to look elsewhere, as the record label opted not to include them here.

Andy Dursin

My Fellow Americans ♫♫♫♪

1996, TVT Records; from the movie *My Fellow Americans*, Warner Bros., 1996.

Album Notes: *Music:* William Ross; *Orchestrations:* Scott Smalley, Conrad Pope, Chris Boardman; *Engineer:* Robert Fernandez; *Featured Artists:* Lipps, Inc., Stevie Wonder, Wilson Pickett, Elvis Presley, Creedence Clearwater Revival, ZZ Hill, The Tweezers & Jen, Louis Jordan with Louis Armstrong, Ella Fitzgerald, Dorothy Norwood, Peter Segal, Mihoko Toro; *Album*

Producers: Jon Peters, Tracy Barone, Peter Segal, Michael Dilbeck; *Engineer*: Kevin Hodge.

Selections: 1 Funkytown (S. Greenberg)(4:05) *Lipps Inc.*; 2 Superstition (S. Wonder)(4:27) *Stevie Wonder*; 3 In The Midnight Hour (W. Pickett/S. Cropper)(2:33) *Wilson Pickett*; 4 Treat Me Nice (J. Leiber/M. Stoller)(2:13) *Elvis Presley*; 5 Bad Moon Rising (J. Fogerty)(2:20) *Creedence Clearwater Revival*; 6 Down Home Blues (G. Jackson)(5:14) *ZZ Hill*; 7 Macarena (A. Romero/R. Ruiz/C.A. de Yarza/M. Triay)(3:53) *The Tweezers & Jen*; 8 Life Is So Peculiar (J. Burke/J. Van Heusen)(3:23) *Louis Jordan, Louis Armstrong*; 9 Don't Be That Way (M. Parrish/B. Goodman/E. Sampson)(4:06) *Ella Fitzgerald*; 10 Brick House (L. Richie/W. Orange/T. McClary)(3:34) *Dorothy Norwood*; 11 Presidential Booty (aka White Men Can't Rap)(C. Magness/P. Segal) (1:55) *Peter Segal*; 12 We're In The Money (H. Warren/A. Dubin)(1:02) *Mihoko Toro*; 13 Main Title/Country Club Stomp/ Trouble At The White House/ Finale (10:39).

Review: An odd mixture of genres—techno-pop with "Funkytown," R&B with "Superstition," country-rock with "Down Home Blues," pop-jazz with "Don't Be That Way," standard with "Life Is So Peculiar," rock with "Treat Me Nice"—this soundtrack album sounds as if it were trying to be too many things to too many people, at least creatively speaking. After a while, it sounds as if it were on overdrive, something that might reflect the tone of this frantic comedy, starring Jack Lemmon, James Garner, Dan Aykroyd and Lauren Bacall. William Ross' "original motion picture score" (sic), reduced to a 10-minute suite put together by splicing four cues with no connective thread, is not bad and reminiscent of the type of music Elmer Bernstein might write on an off-day. If you don't mind jumping from one style to another in the space of a few minutes, you might actually take a shine to this unorthodox album.

My Girl

My Girl ♫♫♫♫

1991, Epic Soundtrax; from the movie *My Girl*, Columbia Pictures, 1991.

Album Notes: *Music:* James Newton Howard; *Featured Performers*: The Temptations, Spiral Starecase, Sly and The Family Stone, The Fifth Dimension, Manfred Mann, Todd Rundgren, The Rascals, Creedence Clearwater Revival, Harold Melvin and The Blue Notes, The Flamingos, Chicago; *Album Producers*: Brian Grazer, David T. Friendly.

Selections: 1 My Girl (R. White/W. Robinson, Jr.)(2:43) *The Temptations*; 2 More Than Yesterday (P. Upton)(2:55) *Spiral Starecase*; 3 Hot Fun In The Summertime (S. Stewart)(2:37) *Sly*

and The Family Stone; 4 Wedding Bell Blues (L. Nyro)(2:42) *The Fifth Dimension*; 5 Do Wah Diddy Diddy (J. Barry/E. Greenwich)(2:22) *Manfred Mann*; 6 I Saw The Light (T. Rundgren)(2:59) *Todd Rundgren*; 7 Good Lovin' (A. Resnick/R. Clark)(2:29) *The Rascals*; 8 Bad Moon Rising (J. Fogerty)(2:18) *Creedence Clearwater Revival*; 9 If You Don't Know Me By Now (K. Gamble/L. Huff)(3:25) *Harold Melvin and The Blue Notes*; 10 I Only Have Eyes For You (H. Warren/A. Dubin)(3:21) *The Flamingos*; 11 Saturday In The Park (R. Lamm)(3:53) *Chicago*; 12 Theme From My Girl (J. Newton Howard)(3:35).

Review: The film is about pre-pubescents in the early '60s, and the songs on the soundtrack follow that lead. They're all Top 20 hits and all love songs, from Sly & the Family Stone's "Hot Fun in the Summertime" to Manfred Man's "Do Wah Diddy Diddy" to the Young Rascals' "Good Lovin'" and Spiral Starecase's "More Today Than Yesterday." Oops, almost forgot— and the Temptations' "My Girl." Duh.

Gary Graff

My Girl 2 ♫♫♫♭

1994, Epic Soundtrax; from the movie *My Girl 2*, Columbia Pictures, 1994.

Album Notes: *Music:* Cliff Eidelman; Orchestra conducted by Cliff Eidelman; *Featured Performers*: Crosby, Stills, Nash & Young, Johnny Rivers, The Supremes, Jackson Browne, Steve Miller Band, Elton John, Rick Price, Rod Stewart, The Beach Boys, The Temptations; *Album Producers*: Brian Grazer, David T. Friendly.

Selections: 1 Our House (G. Nash)(2:58) *Crosby Stills Nash & Young*; 2 Rockin' Pneumonia & The Boogie Woogie Flu (H.P. Smith)(3:11) *Johnny Rivers*; 3 Baby Love (B. Holland/L. Dozier/ E. Holland)(2:35) *The Supremes*; 4 Doctor My Eyes (J. Browne)(3:13) *Jackson Browne*; 5 Swingtown (S. Miller/C. McCarty) (3:27) *Steve Miller Band*; 6 Bennie And The Jets (E. John/ B. Taupin)(5:22) *Elton John*; 7 Tiny Dancer (E. John/B. Taupin)(6:14) *Elton John*; 8 Walk Away Renee (M. Lookofski/A. Sansone/R. Calilli)(4:25) *Rick Price*; 9 Reason To Believe (T. Hardin)(4:06) *Rod Stewart*; 10 Don't Worry Baby (B. Wilson/R. Christian)(2:45) *The Beach Boys*; 11 My Girl (R. White/W. Robinson, Jr.) (2:41) *The Temptations*; 12 Orchestral Suite From My Girl 2 (C. Eidelman) (6:36).

Review: The sequel begins in the '60s—Crosby Stills, Nash & Young's "Our House," the Supremes' "Baby Love," a repeat of the Temptations' title song—but moves into the early and mid-'70s to follow the characters. It makes its musical point with some of the biggest artists of the era, including Jackson Browne ("Doctor My Eyes"), the Steve Miller Band ("Swingtown"), Rod Stewart ("Reason to Believe") and Elton John ("Tiny Dancer," "Bennie and the Jets"). But what this lacks is the forgotten gem or surprise cut. Johnny Rivers' rendition of "Rockin' Pneumonia & the Boogie Woogie Flu" comes close, but we'd rather have Professor Longhair, anyway.

Gary Graff

My Left Foot/Da 🎵🎵🎵🎵

1989, Varese-Sarabande; from the movies *My Left Foot*, Miramax Films, 1989, and *Da*, 1988.

Album Notes: *Music*: Elmer Bernstein; Orchestra conducted by Elmer Bernstein; *Featured Musician*: Cynthia Millar (Ondes Martenot solos); *Album Producer*: Cynthia Millar; *Engineer*: Brian Masterson.

Selections: MY LEFT FOOT: 1 Mother (3:40); 2 Unspoken Fear (4:23); 3 Therapy (2:55); 4 Church And Witches (2:52); 5 Study For Christy (3:05); 6 Happy Moment (2:33); 7 Gift For Mother/Cold (2:54); 8 Struggle And Frustration (3:52); 9 Love Spoken (4:49);

DA: 10 Da And Memories (2:35); 11 Temptress (2:00); 12 Drown The Dog! (2:52); 13 Secrets (1:28); 14 Old Matters (2:15); 15 Goodbyes (1:00); 16 Resolution (3:58).

Review: Two scores by the always reliable Elmer Bernstein combined together on one CD have two somewhat similar moods of personal struggle and emotional recovery and both are included for the price of one. Who could complain? Taking things sequentially, *My Left Foot* is a warm, affectionate look at the lifestory of Christy Brown (played by Daniel Day-Lewis), an Irish artist born with cerebral palsy, a debilitating disease, into a poor family, who overcame all odds to become a writer and painter. Eschewing the sappy sentimentality that could have destroyed its fragile dramatic balance, the film states its case with little embellishments, relying instead on the fabric of the story itself to make its impact. The moods are beautifully sustained by the score, in which Cynthia Millar's Ondes Martenot provides a specific atmosphere in "Mother," the first word the handicapped Christy wrote with a piece of chalk in his left foot to the amazement of his relatives.

Based on the book and eponymous play by Hugh Leonard, *Da* recounts the emotional journey of an Irish playwright (Martin Sheen) living in New York who attends the funeral of his father in Ireland and goes through a regenerative self-discovery trip. Once again, Bernstein's score finds new accents to underline the spiritual adventure of the film's hero, with the Ondes Martenot adding their unusual nostalgic sonorities to this wonderfully delineated music.

My Life 🎵🎵🎵🎵🎵

1993, Epic Soundtrax; from the movie *My Life*, Columbia Pictures, 1993.

Album Notes: *Music*: John Barry; *Music Editor*: Clif Kohlweck; Orchestra conducted by John Barry; *Featured Soloist*: Michael Lang (piano); *Album Producer*: John Barry; *Engineer*: Shawn Murphy.

Selections: 1 Main Title (1:37); 2 A Childhood Wish (2:40); 3 Pictures From The Past (1:26); 4 I'm Still In The Game (3:12); 5 My Life: Love Theme (1:35); 6 The Old Neighborhood (1:51); 7 I Used To Hide In There (2:02); 8 You're A Believer (1:42); 9 My Last Trip Home (1:53); 10 Moments (2:58); 11 D-Day (1:53); 12 Child's Play (2:57); 13 The Circus (2:15); 14 Nice To Meet You Brian (2:19); 15 The Roller Coaster (2:04); 16 End Title (3:20).

Review: John Barry's propensity for long, romantic orchestral lines is particularly suited for this story of a man who finds out he is dying of cancer, and decides to make a video that will explain to his unborn child who he was and where he came from. The topic must have hit a particularly sentimental chord with the composer who wrote a gorgeous, low-key score, filled with emotional and beautifully tender moments. Subtly shaded, the music unfolds with striking grace, revealing themes that are stated with warmth and played for all their worth. This one must have come from the heart.

Mysterious Island 🎵🎵🎵🎵

1993, Cloud Nine Records; from the movie *Mysterious Island*, Columbia Pictures, 1961.

Album Notes: *Music*: Bernard Herrmann; Orchestra conducted by Bernard Herrmann; *CD Supervision*: David Wishart; *Digital Editing*: Gus Shaw.

Selections: 1 Fanfare (:39); 2 Prelude (1:26); 3 Civil War (1:05); 4 Escape To The Clouds (7:58); 5 The Island (5:13); 6 The Giant Crab (2:49); 7 The Granite House (4:19); 8 The Phorarhacos (3:20); 9 Pirates! (3:13); 10 Nemo/The Grotto (1:53); 11 The Cephalopod (4:13); 12 Escape From The Island (5:48).

Review: Bernard Herrmann struck a particularly pleasant note in his relationship with Ray Harryhausen, writing wonderfully animated scores for the filmmaker's flights of cinematographic fantasy, *The Three Worlds of Gulliver, Jason and the Argonauts, The Seventh Voyage of Sinbad,* and *Mysterious Island.* Of these, *Mysterious Island* may be the most interesting, because of the colorful orchestral textures and brilliant themes that add musical life to Harryhausen's wonderful dynamation creatures ("The Giant Crab," "The Phorarhacos," "The Cephalopod"). As was true of Herrmann's previous contributions to these fantasy films, the music for *Mysterious Island* is a vibrant testimony to his unbridled imagination and his sense of action and movement, splendidly illustrated in this recording, available for the first time in stereo. Even though the CD evidences some audio problems, inherent, we are told, to the original recording itself, the effect achieved is often unique and sensational, making the album an essential addition to any collection.

See also: Bernard Herrmann in Compilations

The Mystery of Rampo 🎵🎵🎵▷

1995, Discovery Records; from the movie *The Mystery of Rampo,* **Samuel Goldwyn, 1995.**

Album Notes: *Music:* Akira Senju; The Czech Philharmonic Orchestra, conducted by Vaclav Neumann, Mario Klemens; *Album Producers:* Kazuyoshi Okuyama, Hiroshi Hirai; *Engineers:* Michal Petarek, Lubomir Novacek, Tomoyoshi Ezaki.

Selections: 1 Love Theme For Rampo (4:19); 2 Fantasy (3:07); 3 Main Title (2:19); 4 Love Theme For Rampo (music box version)(1:35); 5 Silent Stream (1:43); 6 The Castle (2:03); 7 Love Theme For Rampo I (2:23); 8 Epilogue (3:17); 9 Introduction (2:31); 10 Illusion I (1:24); 11 The Shade Of The Tree (:23); 12 Making Love In The Foggy (1:56); 13 The Back Of The Mirror (3:01); 14 Love Theme For Rampo II (2:57); 15 Illusion II (2:03); 16 Theme Of Akechi (2:49); 17 Theme Of Marquis (5:13); 18 Amazing (1:35); 19 Showdown (:56); 20 Love Theme For Rampo (4:20).

Review: The musical setting for a film dealing with a Japanese novelist whose fictional characters find a strange echo in real life, *The Mystery of Rampo* elicited a strikingly beautiful Westernized score from composer Akira Senju, which at times recalls some of the most inspired moments from Ennio Morricone. Romantic elements pervade this elegant music, dominated by the nominal cue "Love Theme for Rampo," played in a variety of forms throughout, with the Czech Philharmonic Orchestra, conducted by Vaclav Neumann (no less!) and by Mario Klemens, bringing its own sensitivity to the flawless performance. A surprising recording well worth a detour.

Mystery Train 🎵🎵🎵

1989, RCA Victor Records; from the movie *Mystery Train,* **Orion Classics, 1989.**

Album Notes: *Music:* John Lurie; *Featured Musicians:* John Lurie (guitar, harmonica), Marc Ribot (guitar, banjo), Tony Garnier (bass), Douglas Browne (drums); *Album Producer:* Emmanuel Chamboredon; *Engineer:* Tom Lazarus.

Selections: 1 Mystery Train (S. Phillips)(2:23) *Elvis Presley*; 2 Mystery Train (S. Phillips)(2:22) *Junior Parker*; 3 Blue Moon (R. Rodgers/L. Hart) (2:38) *Elvis Presley*; 4 Pain In My Heart (N. Neville)(2:22) *Otis Redding*; 5 Domino (S. Phillips)(2:15) *Roy Orbison*; 6 The Memphis Train (M. Rice/R. Thomas/W. Sparks)(2:30) *Rufus Thomas*; 7 Get Your Money Where You Spend Your Time (T. Tate/J. Palmer)(3:47) *Bobby Blue Bland*; 8 Soul Finger (J. King/J. Alexander/T. Jones/R. Cauley/R. Caldwell/C. Cunningham)(2:19) *The Bar-Kays*; 9 Mystery Train (suite): Long Spell Of Cold Day/Banjo Blues/Chaucer Street (2:07); 10 Tuesday Night In Memphis/To Be Alive And In A Truck (3:20); 11 Girls/Random Screamin' Jay (1:21); 12 Italian Walk (:55); 13 A Lawyer Can't Take You To Another Planet (suite): Groove Truck/Drunk Blues/Big Harmonica Escape (4:27); 14 Dream Sun King (:13); 15 Chaucer Street (3:44); 16 Tuesday Night In Memphis (2:29).

Review: Two versions of the title song, one by Elvis Presley and one by Junior Parker, plus a "Mystery Train Suite," just in case you forgot the film's title are included. Memphis is dutifully represented on this soundtrack with the likes of Otis Redding, Roy Orbison, Rufus Thomas, Bobby Blue Bland and the Bar-Kays, and it would be nice to have more of that and less of John Lurie's Memphis via Hollywood score.

Gary Graff

The Naked Gun 2½: The Smell of Fear 🎵🎵🎵▷

1991, Varese-Sarabande; from the movie *The Naked Gun 2½: The Smell of Fear,* **Paramount Pictures, 1991.**

Album Notes: *Music:* Ira Newborn; *Orchestrations:* Alf Clausen, Don Nemitz; *Music Editor:* Jeff Carson; Orchestra conducted by Ira Newborn; *Album Producer:* Ira Newborn; *Engineer:* Gary Ladinsky.

Selections: 1 Beirut Vacation (:57); 2 Drebin—Hero! (1:04); 3 Main Title (2:01); 4 Meat Miss Spencer (5:28); 5 There's Been A Bombing (:48); 6 The Exciting Chase (2:44); 7 Bad Boys And Meinheimers (2:45); 8 Miss Spencer (1:01); 9 Hey Look At These (:45); 10 On The Ledge (1:37); 11 Thinking Of... Him! (2:33); 12 The Date (:57); 13 Roof, Roof!! (4:14); 14 I Must Kill Frank (3:11); 15 I Want A World (1:48); 16 End Credits (4:33).

Review: It was only natural that Ira Newborn would adapt his effective "Police Squad!" TV scores to the *Naked Gun* films. A lampoon of the 1950s cop shows, particularly *M-Squad,* the short-lived TV series enabled Newborn to borrow from the jazz style of that era and to create a memorable body of work. The main theme for "Police Squad!" is a boisterous big band style tune inspired by *M-Squad'*s main title, while bumbling cop Frank Drebin's theme is a shameless march. The CD successfully mixes up cues from both the sequel and the first film, *The Naked Gun: From the Files of Police Squad!* into a surprisingly cohesive presentation.

David Hirsch

Naked in New York 🎵🎵🎵ᵛ

1994, Sire Records; from the movie *Naked in New York*, Fine Line Features, 1994.

Album Notes: *Song Producers*: Tony Bongiovi, Thomas Erdelyl, Michael Phillip-Wojewoda, Scott Billington, Mike Mc-Mackin, Kevin Maloney, Joe R. Brown, Andy Paley, Acid Test, Lenny DeRose, D-Ream, Tom Frederikse, Ted Ottaviano, Trevor Horn, Gary Wilkinson; *Album Producer*: Andy Paley.

Selections: 1 Rockaway Beach (J. Hyman/J. Cummings/D. Calvin/T. Erdelyl) (2:07) *The Ramones*; 2 Palomar (D. Bidini/M. Tielli/T. Vesley/D. Clark) (4:20) *Rheostatics*; 3 Feel Like Going Home (C. Rich) (4:48) *Charlie Rich*; 4 Present Tense (W. Haas/C. Bernat/M. Reyhons/J. Toal) (3:13) *Tripmaster Monkey*; 5 Listen, It's Gone (D. Schelzel) (3:46) *The Ocean Blue*; 6 One Love (W. Bailey) (4:04) *David Rudder*; 7 Simple Brain (J. Plumb/A. Paley) (5:46) *The Waltons*; 8 Shake (L. DiSanto) () *Acid Test*; 9 U R The Best Things (P. Cunnah) (4:45) *D:Ream*; 10 Ugly On The Outside (J. Heiskell/J. Sughrue/D. Jenkins/E. Winters/P. Noe) (3:48) *The JudyBats*; 11 Conga Te (T. Ottaviano/B. Lucas) (3:36) *Doubleplusgood*; 12 Enchanted (S. Ottaviano/T. Ottaviano) (3:58) *Book Of Love*; 13 Crazy (S. Samuel/G. Sigsworth) (4:31) *Seal*; 14 Crash (D. Schelzel) (3:29) *The Ocean Blue*; 15 Comfort (P. Hooton/K. Mullin/C. Hunter) (4:51) *The Farm*; 16 Too Good To Be True (A. Paley) (3:10) *The Greenberry Woods*.

Review: Anything that starts with the Ramones' "Rockaway Beach" is bound to be at least interesting and this set is better than that. Mostly it's a modern rock sampler, self-serving in that it's loaded with Sire/Reprise artists, but at least they deliver the goods. Rheostatics' "Palomar" is good fun, while the Farm and Greenberry Woods kick it on "Comfort" and "Too Good to Be True," respectively. Judybats' "Ugly on the Outside" is an under-appreciated gem, and Seal's "Crazy" is always nice to have around.

Gary Graff

Naked Lunch 🎵🎵

1992, Milan Records; from the movie *Naked Lunch*, 20th Century-Fox, 1992.

Album Notes: *Music*: Howard Shore; *Orchestrations*: Homer Denison; *Music Editor*: Suzana Peric; The London Philharmonic Orchestra, conducted by Howard Shore; *Featured Musicians*: Ornette Coleman (saxophone); Denardo Coleman (drums), Barre Phillips (bass), J.J. Edwards (Sintir), Aziz Bin Salem (Nai), David Hartley (piano); *Album Producer*: Howard Shore; *Engineer*: Alan Snelling.

Selections: 1 Naked Lunch (2:27); 2 Hauser And O'Brien/Bugpoweder (O. Coleman)(2:39); 3 Mugwumps (2:54); 4 Centipede (2:03); 5 The Black Meat (1:24); 6 Simpatico/Misterioso (T. Monk)(1:34); 7 Fadela's Coven (3:31); 8 Interzone Suite (5:11); 9 William Tell (1:43); 10 Mujahaddin (1:54); 11 Intersong (O. Coleman)(3:45); 12 Dr. Benway (3:11); 13 Clark Nova Dies (2:03); 14 Ballad: Joan (O. Coleman)(2:37); 15 Cloquet's Parrots/Midnight Sunrise (O. Coleman)(1:43); 16 Nothing Is True, Everything Is Permitted (1:55); 17 Welcome To Annexia (3:33); 18 Writeman (O. Coleman)(3:53).

Review: Based on the sci-fi cult novel by William S. Burroughs, and mixing elements of his personal life, like the accidental death of his wife during a wild party, *The Naked Lunch* is distinguished by an abrasive Howard Shore score, performed by Ornette Coleman. Quoting Coleman, "the voicings of the woodwinds, brass, strings, percussion, non-tempered instruments and the uses of the alto soloist work so that one can hear these instruments creating harmonies, melodies, rhythms, modulations and dynamics mirroring each other categorically." Ultimately, acceptance of the album will largely depend on the reaction to Coleman's grating, iconoclastic playing, deemed awful by some, genial by others. The fact is that this soundtrack album is bound to find as many admirers as it will find detractors. On a purely listening basis, it may be uncompromising musically but difficult at times to really appreciate, Ornette Coleman's playing notwithstanding.

The Name of the Rose 🎵🎵🎵🎵

1986, Teldec; from the movie *The Name of the Rose*, 20th Century-Fox, 1986.

Album Notes: *Music*: James Horner; Orchestra conducted by James Horner; *Featured Artists*: Charles Brett, Counter Tenor and The Choir of the Choir School, Maria Schulz, Kurt Rieth, director; *Album Producer*: James Horner.

Selections: 1 Main Titles (3:00); 2 Beata viscera (trad.)(2:19) *Charles Brett*; 3 First Recognition (2:27); 4 The Lesson (4:20); 5 Kyrie (trad.)(2:23) *Choir of The Choir School Maria Schulz*; 6 The Scriptorium (3:52); 7 Veni Sancte Spiritus (trad.)(3:13) *Choir of The Choir School Maria Schulz*; 8 The Confession (3:10); 9 Flashbacks (2:04); 10 The Discovery (2:28); 11 Betrayed (2:56); 12 Epilogue (6:05); 13 End Titles (3:12).

Review: An odd murder mystery, set in an isolated Italian monastery in medieval time, *The Name of the Rose* received scant distribution at the time of its release and little publicity, despite superb portrayals by Sean Connery, as a sly monk with a detective instinct, and F. Murray Abraham, as a ruthless inquisitor. Providing an extra ounce of symbolism to the occult drama is James Horner's cleverly enigmatic score, in which tintinnabulating bells ominously announce the next victim. Mixing strange sonorities and Gothic plainchant to create an oppressive atmosphere with mysterious undertones, the score is wonderfully imaginative and well-suited for this story based on a novel by Umberto Eco. Unfortunately, the soundtrack album was only released in Germany, on the Teldec label, and may prove difficult to find. But it's well worth the effort.

Napoleon

Napoleon ♫♫♫

1994, Erato Records; from the movie *Napoleon*, 1926-27.

Album Notes: *Music*: Arthur Honegger, Marius Constant; The Orchestra Philharmonique de Monte Carlo, conducted by Marius Constant; *Album Producer*: Michel Garcin; *Engineers*: Jacques Doll, Jean-Marie Golaz.

Selections: 1 Opening Credits (M. Constant)(3:23); 2 The Night Of August 10th (M. Constant)(1:39); 3 The Storm (A. Honegger)(4:21); 4 Calm (A. Honegger)(3:56); 5 The Siege Of Toulon (M. Constant)(3:22); 6 Admiral Hood (M. Constant)(:58); 7 The English Army (M. Constant)(2:58); 8 The Attack (M. Constant)(4:34); 9 After The Battle (M. Constant)(2:58); 10 Violine (A. Honegger)(2:09); 11 The Terror (M. Constant)(2:23); 12 The Shadows (A. Honegger)(2:49); 13 The Empress' Chaconne (A. Honegger)(4:14); 14 Massena (A. Honegger)(1:29); 15 The Beggars Of Glory (3:34); 16 The Army Of Italy (M. Constant)(2:46); 17 The Eagle (1:12); 18 End Credits (3:41).

Review: See entry below.

Napoleon ♫♫♫♫

1983, Silva Screen Records; from the movie *Napoleon*, 1926-27.

Album Notes: *Music*: Carl Davis; The Wren Orchestra, conducted by Carl Davis; *Album Producer*: John Boyden; *Engineer*: Tony Faulkner.

Selections: 1 Eagle Of Destiny (3:36); 2 Teaching The Marseillaise (5:49); 3 Reunion In Corsica (4:06); 4 Pursued (3:47); 5 Double Storm (8:51); 6 Drums Of The 6th Regiment (2:25); 7 Victor Of Toulon (3:54); Bal des victimes: 8 Gigue (2:24); 9 The Fan (1:05); 10 Tambourine (1:12); 11 Acting Lesson (4:37); 12

Ghosts (3:29); 13 Peroration (3:53); 14 Strange Conductor In The Sky (3:24).

Review: See entry below.

Napoleon ♫♫

1981, CBS Records; from the movie *Napoleon*, Images Film Archive, 1927.

Album Notes: *Music*: Carmine Coppola; The Milan Philharmonic Orchestra, conducted by Carmine Coppola; *Album Producers*: Mike Berniker, Carmine Coppola; *Engineer*: Paolo Bocchi.

Selections: 1 Napoleon's March (2:03); 2 Officers Waiting and Love Theme (3:51); 3 Snow Fight (3:59); 4 Fort Carre Prison (3:39); 5 Pozzo Theme (Enemy Theme)(3:45); 6 Cafe Scene (General Carteaux)(4:31); 7 Exit Music (2:21); 8 Carriage Ride and Love Theme (2:28); 9 Family Theme (2:40); 10 The Wedding (4:23); 11 Les Victimes Ball (4:46); 12 Victorious In Italy and Finale (6:04).

Review: Abel Gance's sweeping *Napoleon* continues to inspire awe and admiration more than 70 years after it was made. A five-hour drama of epic proportions, this silent film "speaks" volumes, both in terms of dramatic performances (Albert Dieudonne as young Bonaparte is unforgettable), and as a visual spectacle in which Gance pioneered many modern techniques, including multiple-screen projection (30 years before Cinerama), and camera movements to follow the action.

Throughout the years, various composers have attempted to capture in musical terms the visual excitement of this extraordinary film. Arthur Honegger was the first to do so for the film's initial presentation, in a score that only exists today in fragmented sketches. When a restored version of the film was shown in Paris in 1979, Marius Constant contributed new cues which, together with the selections from the Honegger score, can be heard on the excellent recording he subsequently made for Erato.

For a gala performance at the Empire in London in 1980, British composer Carl Davis also created a new set of cues said to closely match the director's intentions. His score, another impressive achievement, finds the composer conducting the Wren Orchestra, in a reissue from Silva Screen Records. (see also Compilations)

Finally, Carmine Coppola introduced his own variations on the theme for another roadshow presentation in 1981, in what is ultimately a downright tedious and derivative score, lacking real dramatic substance.

The point between all three scores, of course, is how the same subject matter inspired four different composers, and how they each approached the same epic film with varying ideas.

The Natural 🎞🎞🎞🎞

1986, Warner Bros. Records; from the movie *The Natural*, Tri-Star Pictures, 1984.

Album Notes: *Music*: Randy Newman; *Orchestrations*: Jack Hayes; *Music Editor*: Joe Tuley; Orchestra conducted by Randy Newman; *Album Producer*: Lenny Waronker; *Engineers*: Lyle Burbridge, Lee Herschberg.

Selections: 1 Prologue 1915-1923 (5:20); 2 The Whammer Strikes Out (1:56); 3 The Old Farm 1939 (1:07); 4 The Majors: The Mind Is A Stranger Thing (2:14); 5 "Knock The Cover Off The Ball" (2:17); 6 Memo (2:02); 7 The Natural (3:33); 8 Wrigley Field (2:13); 9 Iris And Roy (:58); 10 Winning (1:00); 11 A Father Makes A Difference (1:53); 12 Penthouse Party (1:10); 13 The Final Game (4:37); 14 The End Title (3:22).

Review: Writing in a style that irresistibly evokes some of the best pages by Aaron Copland, Randy Newman created a wonderful Americana-tinged score for this film, starring Robert Redford as a baseball player finally making the big time in his last season, after having shown great promises that never materialized throughout his career. One of Newman's earliest scores, the music flows with grace and charm, all bathed in a faint echo of nostalgia, in what was and still remains a very endearing effort. Subsequently, Newman continued in the same vein and scored other films with equal success, but this one is a real gem.

Near Dark 🎞🎞🎞

1987, Varese-Sarabande Records; from the movie *Near Dark*, DeLaurentiis Entertainment, 1987.

Album Notes: *Music*: Tangerine Dream; *Arrangements*: Tangerine Dream; *Album Producers*: Tangerine Dream; *Engineers*: Tangerine Dream.

Selections: 1 Caleb's Blues (3:10); 2 Pick Up At High Noon (4:56); 3 Rain In The Third House (2:56); 4 Bus Station (includes Mae's Theme)(8:38); 5 Good Times (2:35); 6 She's My Sister (Resurrection I)(7:20); 7 Mae Comes Back (2:00); 8 Father And Son (Resurrection II)(2:55); 9 Severin Dies (2:45); 10 Fight At Dawn (4:40); 11 Mae's Transformation (4:20).

Review: Propelled by an exciting score by Tangerine Dream, *Near Dark* is a vampire film of another sort, about a group of nasty-looking bikers with a mean streak in them that compels them to roam the countryside in a rural community and kill for fun once the sun has set. Punctuating the action and giving it an extra edge of vibrancy whenever needed, Tangerine Dream's score, an electronic concoction with emphasis on the beat, succeeded in enhancing the terror in the visuals. Taken on its own terms, it proves somewhat less ingratiating, though "Caleb's Blues" and "Good Times" are great rocking numbers.

Needful Things 🎞🎞🎞🎞

1993, Varese-Sarabande Records; from the movie *Needful Things*, Castle Rock Entertainment, 1993.

Album Notes: *Music*: Patrick Doyle; *Orchestrations*: Lawrence Ashmore, John Bell; *Music Editor*: Roy Prendergast; Orchestra and Choir conducted by David Snell; *Featured Vocalist*: Nicole Tibbels; *Album Producers*: Patrick Doyle, Maggie Rodford; *Engineer*: Paul Hulme.

Selections: 1 The Arrival (2:56); 2 To My Good Friend Brian (5:29); 3 Needful Things (2:37); 4 Brian's Deed (1:38); 5 More Deeds (2:23); 6 Art And The Minister (1:43); 7 Gaunt's Web (2:51); 8 Racing Towards Apple Throwing Time (4:43); 9 Nettie Finds Her Dog (1:49); 10 Ave Maria (F. Schubert)(3:51); 11 Peer Gynt: Hall Of The Mountain King (E. Grieg)(2:14); 12 Go Upstairs (2:58); 13 The Turning Point (12:08); 14 They Broke The Law (1:56); 15 The Devil's Here (4:31); 16 Just Blow Them Away (2:46); 17 End Titles (3:53).

Review: Even when he writes a horror film score, Patrick Doyle can't avoid being more elegant and sophisticated than most. His music for this scary concoction about an olde shoppe in Maine that may harbor some evil force, if one is to believe that people who shop there end up being haunted by the objects they purchase, is as malevolent as it is delicious. Broadly announced by a choir in what sounds like an ominous pronouncement of things to come, the music, at first gracious and quite lovely, but becoming increasingly dark and brooding, unfolds with great charm, before exploding in a climactic cue ("Just Blow Them Away") that marks all at once the end of the spell, of the shop, and of the movie. In-between, some elements create strong images, like the use of a music box theme that recurs at intervals throughout the score and belies some of the subjacent horror in the story, or the choral writing that evokes both good and evil pitted in an endless struggle, something that the two classical selections included here also denote.

Nemesis 🎞

1992, High Tide Recordings; from the movie *Nemesis*, Imperial Entertainment, 1992.

Album Notes: *Music*: Michel Rubini; *Orchestrations*: Michel Rubini, Kevin Maloney; The Los Angeles Symphony Orchestra, conducted by Michel Rubini; *Album Producer*: Michel Rubini; *Engineer*: Brian Vessa.

Selections: 1 Jared's Theme (4:04); 2 Main Titles (1:20); 3 On The Hunt (3:33); 4 Big Rocket (3:44); 5 Down The Slide (1:00); 6 Desert Run (3:42); 7 Shang Loo (2:11); 8 Blue Julian (2:41); 9 Hammerheads (3:04); 10 Robotomaniac (2:28); 11 Exit Anji (3:01); 12 Cable Ride (3:19); 13 Marion Face (2:20); 14 Jared's Theme (Blue Alex)(2:30); 15 Volcano Run (3:14); 16 Time To Go (:42); 17 End Credits (3:23).

Review: A futuristic film that had a short existence in movie theatres and didn't make much of a dent afterwards, *Nemesis* is somewhat enlivened by the score Michel Rubini wrote for the occasion. With an abundance of electronic sounds and effects attempting to evoke the moods in the film, only those tracks that feature acoustic instruments over orchestral themes actually succeed in creating some enjoyment when judged on their own merits. "Jared's Theme" is a case in point, with its flavorful images strikingly painted by a heavily-echoed guitar, but the rest of the "score" is nothing more than electronic mush that means little outside of its screen context.

The Net ♪♪♭

1995, Varese-Sarabande Records; from the movie *The Net,* Columbia Pictures, 1995.

Album Notes: *Music:* Mark Isham; *Orchestrations:* Ken Kugler, Kim Scharnberg, Dell Hake, Larry Blank; *Programming:* Jeff Rona; conducted by Ken Kugler; *Featured Musicians:* David Goldblatt, Rich Ruttenberg (piano solos); *Album Producer:* Mark Isham; *Engineer:* Stephen Krause.

Selections: 1 Act I (3:42); 2 Act II (11:53); 3 Act III (3:20); 4 Act IV (10:34).

Review: A powerful suspense thriller starring Sandra Bullock as a lonely Internet surfer and her involvement in murky government dealings, *The Net* reveals some dark Hitchcockian undertones in its standard story about an apparently innocent victim of circumstances being sucked into a maelstrom of criminal activities and almost losing her life as a result. While Mark Isham is a reliable composer, whose scores always keep the listener interested, he is not Bernard Herrmann, something that is plainly evidenced here. The selections, broken down in four parts, follow the story, gradually becoming more threatening as the Bullock character finds herself more and more in serious danger, with increasingly somber orchestral textures occasionally interrupted by percussion elements, synthesized sounds, and weirdly ominous sonorities. It may work very well on the screen, as a complement to the action, but as pure audio programming, it often leaves a lot to be desired. The CD is unusually short (29:30 minutes of music!) but given the low impact of the music, it seems largely sufficient.

> "(Director) Tim (Burton) and I both grew up on the same kind of movies, and it was fun to do like a pure science-fiction old-fashioned score like this, with big brass and all these inspirations from those cheesy old movies, blurting out these dissonant chords."
>
> **Danny Elfman**
> *on* Mars Attacks!
> *(The Hollywood Reporter, 1-15-97)*

Netherworld ♪♪♪

1991, Moonstone Records; from the movie *Netherworld,* Paramount Pictures, 1991.

Album Notes: *Music:* David Bryan, Larry Fast; *Music Editor:* Carl Zittrer; *Song Performers:* Edgar Winter, John Duva, Bernie Pershey, Bobby Gianetti, Tonk's House Band: Edgar Winter (vocals/sax), David Bryan (piano/backing vocals), Troy Turner (guitar), Harold Scott (bass), Stanley Watson (drums), Nancy Buchan (violin); *Album Producers:* David Bryan, Larry Fast; *Engineers:* John Bogosian, Michael Polopolus.

Selections: 1 Stranger To Love (D. Palotta)(4:41) *Edgar Winter*; 2 Tonk's Place (2:31); 3 Birds Of A Feather (2:50); 4 Black Magic River (2:38); 5 Open Door Policy (J. Adams)(3:41); 6 My Father's Sins 3:10); 7 The Ceremony (5:05); 8 Into The Netherworld (3:38); 9 If I Didn't Love You (J. Turnbow/J. Wachbrit) (4:55) *Edgar Winter*; 10 Inherit The Dead (2:50); 11 Mirror Image (3:39); 12 What's Your Plesure? (4:45); 13 100 Reasons (J. Adams); 14 Netherworld Waltz (5:25).

Review: Full Moon movies often feature obnoxious musical scores by the likes of Richard Band, but here's one that's refreshingly different. For *Netherworld,* rock artist Edgar Winter croons a number of his original songs and offers a similarly rock/R&B tinged score for a typically unappealing Charles Band-produced direct-to-video genre feature (one that's still a bit better than most efforts from this studio!). Winter is well-known in pop music circles and his music here certainly gives more to the movie than the film does for him — the solo piano that performs the final track is elegant and graceful, probably working better on its own than it does in the laughable movie. Unlike most Full Moon projects, the music surprisingly doesn't

motion picture soundtracks

sound like a video-game underscore. Winter fans especially should definitely give this one a listen.

Andy Dursin

Never Say Never Again 🎵🎵🎵🎵

1993, Silva America; from the movie *Never Say Never Again*, Taliafilm, 1983.

Album Notes: *Music*: Michel Legrand; Orchestra conducted by Michel Legrand; *Album Producer*: Michel Legrand; *Engineer*: Keith Grant.

Selections: 1 Bond Back In Action (:50); 2 Main Title: Never Say Never Again (M. Legrand/A. & M. Bergman)(3:10) *Lani Hall, Herb Alpert*; 3 Prologue/Enter 007 (:27); 4 Fatima Blush/A Very Bad Lady (3:46); 5 Dinner With 007 (1:08); 6 Bahama Island (2:49); 7 Bond Smells A Rat/Nurse Blush? (1:27); 8 Plunder On A Nuclear Missile (1:55); 9 The Big Band Death Of Jack Petachi (1:43); 10 Bond And Domino (2:03); 11 Fight To The Death With The Tiger Sharks (4:50); 12 Une chanson d'amour (M. Legrand/S. Della/J. Drejac)(4:24) *Sophie Della*; 13 Video Duel/Victory (1:41); 14 Nuclear Nightmare (1:06); 15 Tango To The Death (2:21); 16 Bond Returns Home (:25); 17 The Death Of Nicole/Chase Her (1:20); 18 Felix And James Exit (:36); 19 Jealousy (3:15); 20 Largo's Waltz (1:26); 21 Bond To The Rescue (4:42); 22 The Big Escape (1:19); 23 Tears Of Allah (2:21); 24 The Underwater Cave (4:37); 25 Fight To The Death (2:21); 26 Bond In Retirement/End Title: Never Say Never Again (M. Legrand/A. & M. Bergman)(4:53) *Lani Hall*.

Review: After having sworn off his James Bond screen persona for the second time following *Diamonds are Forever* (he already had left the series once before, after filming *You Only Live Twice*), Sean Connery relented one last time and agreed to portray the apparently invincible 007 in *Never Say Never Again*, a thinly disguised remake of *Thunderball*. That film, however, was significantly different from the other James Bond films. It was not produced by Albert R. Broccoli and Harry Saltzman, who had succeeded in cornering the market by purchasing the rights to all the stories written by Ian Fleming save two (the other was *Casino Royale*), and the film producers Jack Schwartzman and Kevin McClory could not secure the services of the James Bond composer-in-residence, John Barry.

Instead, they turned to Michel Legrand who wrote a strongly evocative score, even though it failed to evoke James Bond in the way John Barry managed so effectively in the many outings he scored. Comparisons with Barry's *Thunderball* in fact are unavoidable, with Legrand's music suffering as a result. Taken on its own terms, however, it is a series of action cues that match the pace of the film itself, with some excellent locale-suggestive moments ("Bahama Island," "Big Band Death of Jack Petachi," "Tango to the Death," Tears of Allah"), and strongly-flavored cues ("Bond and Domino," "Bond Returns Home," "Felix and James Exit," "Largo's Waltz"). Two vocal tracks, the main title performed by Lani Hall with Herb Alpert, and "Une chanson d'amour," by Sophie Della, add a different touch.

The NeverEnding Story

The NeverEnding Story 🎵🎵🎵

1984, EMI Records; from the movie *The NeverEnding Story*, Neue Constantin Films, 1984.

Album Notes: *Music*: Giorgio Moroder, Klaus Doldinger.

Selections: 1 NeverEnding Story (3:33) *Limahl*; 2 Swamps Of Madness (1:57); 3 Ivory Tower (3:10); 4 Ruined Landscapes (3:04); 5 Sleepy Dragon (3:58)(G. Moroder); 6 Bastian's Happy Flight (3:16); 7 Fantasia (:56); 8 Atreju's Quest (2:52); 9 Theme Of Sadness (2:43); 10 Atreju Meets Falkor (2:31); 11 Miprorgate/Southern Oracle (3:10); 12 Gmork (:29); 13 Moonchild (1:24); 14 The Auryn (2:20); 15 Happy Flight (1:21) (K. Doldinger).

Review: Originally, this German-made fantasy film was entirely scored by Klaus Doldinger (*Das Boot*) and released in that country with only his music. However, when the film was acquired by Warner Brothers for the U.S., the studio brought in music pop producer Giorgio Moroder to create a "hip" main title song, sung by pop artist Limahl. Moroder eventually went on further to write four additional synthesized underscore themes that are interpolated with Doldinger's orchestral work. Surprisingly, this mix holds up in part because Moroder doesn't ignore the ambience set by Doldinger. Both artists draw on the film's wonderful sense of childhood adventure and the things they fear. Moroder's new theme for the "Swamp of Sadness" isn't all that different from Doldinger's "Theme of Sadness," though the former draws on a less than original classical motif to accomplish his task. The only real distinction between each composer's style is the lack of acoustical instruments on Moroder's cues. Both have their music collected into two suites on the U.S. soundtrack album, though I still prefer listening to the German album with Doldinger's entire original score. It has a somewhat more mature quality that appeals to my aging sensibilities.

David Hirsch

The NeverEnding Story II: The Next Chapter 🎵🎵🎵🎵

1990, Warner Bros.; from the movie *The NeverEnding Story II: The Next Chapter*, Neue Medien und Elektronikvertrieb, 1990.

Album Notes: *Music*: Robert Folk; *Songs*: Giorgio Moroder; *Orchestrations*: Robert Folk, Randy Miller; *Music Editor*: Doug Lackey; Members of the Symphony Orchestra of the Bavarian Broadcasting Corporation, Bavarian State Orchestra, Orchestra of the Bavarian State Opera, Choir of the Bavarian State Opera, and Grosses Rundfunkorchester Berlin, conduted by Robert Folk; *Album Producer*: Giorgio Moroder; *Engineers*: Alan Snelling, Brian Masterson.

Selections: 1 Searching For Fantasia (2:19); 2 Dreams We Dream (G. Moroder/ T. Whitlock)(4:23) *Joe Milner*; 3 Heaven's Just A Heartbeat (G. Moroder/T. Whitlock)(4:10) *Joe Milner*; 4 The NeverEnding Story (G. Moroder/K. Forsey) (3:29) *Joe Milner*; 5 Dreams We Dream (G. Moroder/T. Whitlock)(4:27); 6 Bastian's Dream (2:05); 7 Falkor's Quest (2:33); 8 Flight Of The Dragon (3:32); 9 Silver Mountains (1:29); 10 Morning In Fantasia (1:08); 11 The Childlike Empress (2:15); 12 The Giants' Attack (2:11); 13 Silver Lake (2:54); 14 Xayide's Castle (1:26); 15 Atreyu's Return To The Great Plains (3:10); 16 Bastian's Lost Memories (1:03); 17 Silver City (2:05); 18 The NeverEnding Story (G. Moroder/K. Forsey)(reprise)(:54).

Review: Robert Folk has created a grand, sweeping orchestral and choral score for the second installment in this series that manages to match the tone set by Klaus Doldinger on the first film ("Searching for Fantasia"). He also manages to show a musical side he was rarely able to express during the years he scored comedy films like the *Police Academy* series. "Morning in Fantasia" is a particularly exciting cue with its intense brass orchestration, while "The Childlike Empress" shows Folk's tender side. As with the first film, the album also features songs by Georgio Moroder.

David Hirsch

New Jersey Drive 🎵🎵🎵🎵

1995, Tommy Boy Records; from the movie *New Jersey Drive*, Gramercy Pictures, 1995.

Album Notes: *Volume 2 Song Producers*: Roc Raida & Knobody, Evil Dee & Mr. Walt, Naughty By Nature & Al Mal, DJ Premier, KRS-One, Organized Konfusion, Funkmaster Flex; *Album Executive Producers*: Nick Gomez, Monica Lynch.

Selections: 1 Funky Piano (W. Brown)(5:14) *E. Bros*; 2 Headz Ain't Ready (B. Powell/J. McNair/S. Price/J. Bush/D. Yates/T. Williams/K. Blake/G. Evans)(5:19) *Black Moon, Smif 'n'*

Wessun; 3 Connections (K. Gist/A. Criss/V. Brown)(3:11) *Naughty By Nature*; 4 Nobody Beats The Biz (B. Markie)(5:05) *Biz Markie*; 5 Invasion (K.J. Davis/C. Martin)(3:11) *Jeru The Damaja*; 6 Own Destiny (M. Lion/K. Parker/N.Pigford/E. Paris)(4:37) *Mad Lion*; 7 You Won't Go Far (O. Credle/T. Jamerson/L. Baskerville)(3:43) *O.C., Organized Konfusion*; 8 Flip Squad's In Da House (B. Collins/G. Clinton/W. Morrison/G. Jacobs)(4:08) *Flip Squad Allstars, Flex, Big Kap*.

Review: An album and an EP filled with funk-influenced hip-hop. Both East and West coast are represented here, with top names, like Biz Markie and Naughty By Nature and cutting edgers such as Flip Squad Allstars, Flex, and Big Kap. Volume one, also available, includes producer Sean "Puffy" Combs' group Total, whose "Can't You See" samples James Brown's "The Payback" and features a guest shot by the late Notorious B.I.G.

Gary Graff

Night and the City 🎵🎵

1992, Hollywood Records; from the movie *Night and the City*, 20th Century-Fox, 1992.

Album Notes: *Music*: James Newton Howard; *Song Producers*: Freddie Mercury, Mike Moran, David Richards, Gardner Cole, James Newton Howard, Dennis Matkosky; *Engineers*: Brian Malouf, Robert Schaper, Michael Mason.

Selections: 1 The Great Pretender (B. Ram)(3:26) *Freddie Mercury*; 2 Cool Jerk (D. Storball)(2:32) *The Capitols*; 3 Money (That's What I Want)(B. Gordy/J. Bradford)(4:12) *Jr. Walker and The All Stars*; 4 You Really Got A Hold On Me (W. Robinson)(2:43) *Smokey Robinson and The Miracles*; 5 Wooly Bully (S. Samudio)(2:14) *Sam The Sham and The Pharaohs*; 6 Love Doesn't Matter (G. Cole/J. Newton Howard)(4:02) *Rodney Saulsberry*; 7 Deep Water (D. Brown/D. Matkosky)(3:47) *Bill Champlin*; 8 Forgiveness (D. Matkosky)(3:43) *Lynn Davis*; 9 Never Gonna Stop (G. Cole/J. Newton Howard)(3:42) *Gardner Cole*; 10 The Boxing Gym (1:31).

Review: At 33 minutes, this is a pretty chintzy outing, though a blast of '60s frat party smashes—the Capitols' "Cool Jerk," Smokey Robinson & the Miracles' "You Really Got a Hold on Me," Sam the Sham & the Pharaohs "Wooly Bully" and Jr. Walker & the All-Star's version of "Money (That's What I Want)"—is hard to beat. However, Bill Champlin warbles "Deep Water" to bring us back to reality.

Gary Graff

Night Breed 🎬🎬🎬🎬

1990, MCA Records; from the movie *Night Breed,* 20th Century-Fox, 1990.

Album Notes: *Music:* Danny Elfman; *Orchestrations:* Steve Bartek, Shirley Walker; *Music Editors:* Sally Boldt, Bob Badami; Orchestra conducted by Shirley Walker; *Featured Vocalists:* Members of the L.A. Master Chorale; *Album Producers:* Danny Elfman, Steve Bartek; *Engineers:* Shawn Murphy, Bobby Fernandez.

Selections: 1 Main Titles (2:40); 2 Dream (1:03); 3 Carnival Underground (3:23); 4 Into Midian (2:31); 5 Meat For The Beast (2:10); 6 Resurrection Suite (3:37); 7 Boone Transforms (:56); 8 The Initiation (2:50); 9 Scalping Time (1:54); 10 Rachel's Oratory (1:04); 11 Party In The Past (:51); 12 Poor Babette (1:41); 13 Uh-Oh... Decker! (1:39); 14 Then Don't Say It! (1:28); 15 Boone Gets A Taste (2:44); 16 Breed Love (1:02); 17 Mayhem In Midian (1:43); 18 Baphomet's Chamber (2:01); 19 Farewell (:59); 20 Second Chance (1:34); 21 End Credits (4:33); 22 Country Skin (4:15) *Michael Stanton.*

Review: One of the scores written during the time when Danny Elfman took on *Batman* and a number of other similarly-themed projects (*Darkman, Dick Tracy,* et al), *Nightbreed* offers a traditionally dissonant, percussive score that is distinctly Elfman. The composer, working again with orchestrator Steve Bartek and conductor Shirley Walker, employs a large chorus to go along with a primal-sounding percussion section and symphony orchestra, and the results are in keeping with Elfman's eclectic, offbeat musical sensibilities, though, for some reason, this score holds up better as a cohesive soundtrack album than many of his other efforts from the same period. The music is frequently expansive in scope, with some soaring, lyrical passages offering hope to the proceedings—a contrast that is further illustrated by its surprisingly poignant final notes. If you don't own many Elfman scores and want a good representation of his early film music, *Nightbreed* is as solid and satisfying as you can get.

Andy Dursin

Night Crossing 🎬🎬🎬🎬

1987, Intrada Records; from the movie *Night Crossing,* Buena Vista Pictures, 1982.

Album Notes: *Music:* Jerry Goldsmith; *Orchestrations:* Arthur Morton; The National Philharmonic Orchestra, conducted by Jerry Goldsmith; *Album Producer:* Jerry Goldsmith; *Engineer:* Eric Tomlinson.

Selections: 1 Main Title (1:48); 2 All In Vain (3:24); 3 The Picnic (4:04); 4 Plans (5:06); 5 Success (3:43); 6 First Flight (9:45); 7 The Patches (2:50); 8 Tomorrow We Go (1:03); 9 No Time To Wait (5:36); 10 Final Flight (6:16); 11 In The West (3:34).

Review: Goldsmith wrote a thunderous score for this early Disney effort at live-action drama, about a family that escapes from behind the Iron Curtain in a balloon. The opening theme recalls *Capricorn One* with its pounding, jagged percussion lines and wailing brass motif to represent the threat of the Wall and its East German troops, while a soaring, lyrical melody underscores the bonding of the family and their attempts to escape, climaxing in an exultant, celebrational climactic cue. It's almost too large-scale an effort for this rather personal story, but it does make for a spectacular album with a heavy, almost gothic sound and a constant undercurrent of rumbling percussion.

Jeff Bond

Night Digger 🎬🎬🎬🎬

1994, Label X; from the movie *The Night Digger,* 1971.

Album Notes: *Music:* Bernard Herrmann; Orchestra conducted by Bernard Herrmann; *Recording Engineer:* Bob Auger; *CD Producer:* John Steven Lasher; *CD Engineer:* Don Bartley.

Selections: 1 Scene One (6:04); 2 Scene Two (3:42); 3 Scene Three (6:40); 4 Scene Four (4:20); 5 Scene Five (2:46); 6 Scene Six (8:17); 7 Scene Seven (6:32).

Review: One of Bernard Herrmann's last scores is also one of his most tender and haunting. The 1971 film was directed by Alastair Reid and written for the screen by Roald Dahl, a curious psychological thriller about a handyman (who murders in his off-hours) who comes to stay with two country women. The score is largely for strings, with solo instruments of a viola d'amore and harmonica representing the two main characters (the handyman plays harmonica on-screen as well). Between Herrmann's usual, idiosyncratic mastery of unresolved sequences, here fragile and reflective a la the "Walking Distance" episode of *The Twilight Zone,* and the timbres of the solo instruments, it's stunningly evocative and nostalgic. Even the more frenetic passages lack the shock violence of *Psycho,* instead resonating with sadness and disquiet. The album is arranged into a seven-scene "Scenario Macabre for Orchestra."

Lukas Kendall

The Night of the Generals 🎬🎬🎬🎬🎬

1990, Intrada Records; from the movie *The Night of the Generals,* Columbia Pictures, 1966.

Album Notes: *Music:* Maurice Jarre; The New Philharmonia Orchestra, conducted by Maurice Jarre; *Album Producer:* Neely Plumb; *CD Producer:* Douglass Fake.

Selections: 1 March From The Night Of The Generals (2:22); 2 Love Theme From The Night Of The Generals (2:25); 3 In The Museum (2:10); 4 On The Terrace At Versailles (2:26); 5 On The Bridge (1:52); 6 Exit Maxim's (2:04); 7 Tanz At The Tavern (1:55); 8 Lieutenant General Tanz (1:23); 9 Love Theme (reprise)(2:25); 10 War And Madness (1:55); 11 Drive Around Paris (2:16); 12 Tanz Comes Back (2:05); 13 Arrest (2:04); 14 The Night Of The Generals (12:46).

Review: In the 1960s, Maurice Jarre scored several films with a World War II theme, notably *Is Paris Burning?*, perhaps his greatest achievement in this vein, *The Damned, Behold a Pale Horse, The Train,* and this attractively designed score for a film directed by Anatole Litvak. Based on a best-selling novel by Hans Helmut Kirst, *The Night of the Generals* started as a standard murder mystery, involving the death of a prostitute, and led to an inquiry into the depraved mores of a trio of Nazi generals in occupied Warsaw. Characteristic of the style he used at the time, broadly florid and musically inventive, Jarre essentially devised two sets of cues. The first, a series of dark marches, played by the brass and percussion instruments, depict the sturm-und-drang of the German army, in often savage and bitter tones that have nothing glorious in them. The second, a very attractive, recognizable "Love Theme," returns frequently throughout the recording to portray the moods and feelings of some of the actors in this drama of passion, though the lilt in it often belies the sadness that permeates it. The CD, marred by a significant amount of hiss on some of the tracks, includes an extended suite of the principal themes, making this release one of the most important in the Jarre canon.

Night of the Running Man
♪♪♪

1995, Super Tracks Music Group; from the movie *Night of the Running Man*, Trimark Pictures, 1995.

Album Notes: *Music:* Christopher Franke; The Berlin Symphonic Orchestra, conducted by Alan Wagner; *Album Producer:* Richard E. Roth; *Engineer:* Richard E. Roth.

Selections: 1 American World Pictures Logo (:16); 2 Opening Credits (3:25); 3 Taxi Ride (2:59); 4 Killer Love (2:07); 5 Neck Break/Total Cash (1:44); 6 Trailer Break In (3:19); 7 Train Chase/Hoover Dam (3:15); 8 Couple Argument (2:03); 9 Airport Escape (4:34); 10 Mills House (1:39); 11 Torture (4:15); 12 Hospital Escape (2:22); 13 Continental Chase, parts 1 & 2 (3:55); 14 Love Scene (1:48); 15 Killer In The House (2:16); 16 Back To Vegas (3:02); 17 Surprise/Girl Beating/End Fight (7:28); 18 Explosion/The End (3:14); 19 Natasha's Theme (2:08).

Review: *Night of the Running Man* is a well-written and performed film score by Christopher Franke. It plays at times very much like his work on the "Babylon 5" TV series and could almost be interchangeable were it not for the occasional use of contemporary guitar and percussion. Franke once more combines his own synth work with the Berlin Symphonic Film Orchestra, though the acoustical instruments are heavily overshadowed by the electronics. The finale cue, "Natasha's Theme," is a lovely piano solo.

David Hirsch

The Nightmare Before Christmas ♪♪♪⁄

1993, Walt Disney Records; from the movie *The Nightmare Before Christmas*, Touchstone Pictures, 1993.

Album Notes: *Music:* Danny Elfman; *Lyrics:* Danny Elfman; *Orchestrations:* Steve Bartek, Mark McKenzie; *Music Editor:* Bob Badami; Orchestra conducted by Chris Boardman, J.A.C. Redford; *Album Producers:* Danny Elfman, Bob Badami, Richard Kraft; *Engineers:* Bill Jackson (vocals), Bobby Fernandez and Shawn Murphy (songs), Shawn Murphy (score); *Assistant Engineers:* Sharon Rice, Bill Easytone, Mike Piersante, Andy Bass.

Selections: 1 Overture (1:47); 2 Opening (:58); 3 This Is Halloween (3:16) *Citizens of Halloween;* 4 Jack's Lament (3:14) *Danny Elfman;* 5 Doctor Finklestein/In The Forest (2:37); 6 What's This? (3:05) *Danny Elfman;* 7 Town Meeting Song (2:57) *Danny Elfman;* 8 Jack And Sally Montage (5:17); 9 Jack's Obsession (2:46) *Danny Elfman;* 10 Kidnap The Sandy Claws (3:03) *Paul Reubens, Catherine O'Hara, Danny Elfman;* 11 Making Christmas (3:58) *Danny Elfman, Citizens of Halloween;* 12 Nabbed (3:04); 13 Oogie Boogie's Song (3:17) *Ken Page, Ed Ivory;* 14 Sally's Song (1:48) *Catherine O'Hara;* 15 Christmas Eve Montage (4:44); 16 Poor Jack (2:31) *Danny Elfman;* 17 To The Rescue (3:38); 18 Finale/Reprise (2:45) *Danny Elfman, Catherine O'Hara, Citizens of Halloween;* 19 Closing (1:26); 20 End Title (1:13).

Review: Though Danny Elfman is known mostly for his instrumental scores, he deftly brought vocals into the mix for Tim Burton's bent musical about Halloween hijacking Christmas. Elfman, the former lead singer of Oingo Boingo, does some of the singing himself but also gets wonderful performances from Paul Reubens (aka Pee Wee Herman) and Catherine O'Hara. The ensemble pieces, such as "Town Hall Meeting," are a hoot, and the instrumental selections, orchestrated by Boingo guitarist Steve Bartek, retain Elfman's playfully skewed approach to mood pieces.

Gary Graff

A Nightmare on Elm Street 3 ♫♫

1987, Varese-Sarabande; from the movie *A Nightmare on Elm Street 3: Dream Warriors*, New Line Cinema, 1987.

Album Notes: *Music*: Angelo Badalamenti; *Orchestrations*: Angelo Badalamenti, Joe Turrin, Glen Daum; *Album Producer*: Angelo Badalamenti; *Engineers*: John Mahoney, Ray Niznik.

Selections: 1 Opening (1:50); 2 Puppet Walk (3:18); 3 Save The Children (1:25); 4 Taryn's Deepest Fear (3:05); 5 Deceptive Romance (1:45); 6 Snake Attack (1:56); 7 Magic Butterfly (1:20); 8 The Embrace (:42); 9 Quiet Room/Wheelchair/Icy Bones (2:41); 10 Rumbling Room (1:15); 11 Dreamspace (:46); 12 The Dreame House (1:50); 13 Is Freddy Gone?/Trouble Starting/Prime Time TV/Icy Window (4:32); 14 Grave Walk (1:11); 15 Nursery Theme (1:55); 16 Light's Out (1:00).

Review: Taking on the *Nightmare on Elm Street* franchise, Angelo Badalamenti served up a score that is appropriately ominous and scary, for this third foray into the unspeakable activities of Freddy Krueger. Starring Heather Langenkamp, reprising the role she created in the first film in the series, *Dream Warriors* (as this third installment is subtitled) exhibits its usual share of scary moments and hoots (depending on one's state of mind), with Badalamenti dutifully adding his own musical comments to the screen proceedings. As is often the case in films such as this, the score is so intimately integrated in and reflective of the action that it proves largely uninteresting once it is removed from the visuals. Despite Badalamenti's valiant efforts, his cues, with a few rare exceptions, mean very little when programmed for one's listening enjoyment.

Nine Months ♫♫♫

1995, Milan Records; from the movie *Nine Months*, 20th Century-Fox, 1995.

Album Notes: *Music*: Hans Zimmer, Nick Glennie-Smith; *Orchestrations*: Bruce Fowler, Ladd McIntosh, Suzette Moriarty; *Music Editor*: Adam Smalley; Orchestra conducted by Nick Glennie-Smith; *Featured Performer*: Jim Kanter (clarinet); *Album Producers*: Hans Zimmer, Jay Rifkin; *Engineers*: Jay Rifkin, Alan Meyerson.

Selections: 1 The Time Of Your Life (S. Van Zandt)(5:56) *Little Steven*; 2 Let's Get It On (M. Gaye/E. Townsend)(3:58) *Marvin Gaye*; 3 Turn Back The Hands Of Time (B. Thompson/J. Daniels)(2:38) *Tyrone Davis*; 4 Baby, Baby (4:00); 5 It's A Boy (9:17); 6 Voodoo Woman (3:54); 7 Baby's Room (4:13); 8 From Russia... (N. Glennie-Smith)(:59); 9 We Can Work It Out (5:04); 10 Open Your Eyes (4:32).

Review: With his boyish grin and cute looks, Hugh Grant seems the perfect match for a frantic father-to-be in this mildly amusing comedy in which he portrays a child psychiatrist and confirmed bachelor whose girlfriend becomes pregnant. Starting off with a pretty little tune well in keeping with the light moods in the film ("Baby, Baby"), Hans Zimmer built an attractive score that transcends its modest origins and actually makes a very positive impression. The cues stay firmly on the romantic side of this comedy, with melodies that catch one's attention and keep it. The tired-sounding pop vocals at the beginning of the album seem to have been selected for something altogether different and detract from more than they complement Zimmer's score. Fortunately, they can be programmed out.

1941 ♫♫♫♫°

1990, Bay Cities; from the movie *1941*, Columbia Pictures, 1979.

Album Notes: *Music*: John Williams; *Music Editor*: Ken Wannberg; Orchestra conducted by John Williams; *Album Producer*: John Williams; *Engineer*: John Neal; *CD Producer*: Nick Redman; *Engineer*: Daniel Hersch .

Selections: 1 The March From 1941 (4:06); 2 The Invasion (8:17); 3 The Sentries (3:28); 4 Riot At The U.S.O. (1:16); 5 To Hollywood And Glory (3:12); 6 Swing, Swing, Swing (4:03); 7 The Battle Of Hollywood (5:37); 8 The Ferris Wheel Sequence (1:28); 9 Finale (6:14).

Review: John Williams' rollicking score echoes the frequently amusing antics of a group of World War II misfits, led by John Belushi, attempting to ward off a suspected invasion of California by the Japanese in this unlikely story concocted by Steven Spielberg. With much of the broad action involving an odd assortment of manic soldiers, overpatriotic homeowners, nostalgic officers, and some Hollywood characters with more than screen glory on their mind, Williams had a wide spectrum to explore, and he did so in a spirited fashion, in a grandiloquent score spearheaded by a "March" worth alone the price of admission. Two major cues, "The Invasion" and "The Battle of Hollywood," expand on the main theme, and enable the composer to write some ear-catching motifs that make for great listening. Also adding an exhilarating uplift is "Swing, Swing, Swing," that captures the period of the big band era, while providing a cue that's wonderfully foot-stomping. A great score, unfortunately truncated for this release which replicates the original LP but fails to include a great deal more composed for the occasion.

Nixon ♫♫♫♫

1995, Hollywood Records; from the movie *Nixon*, Hollywood Pictures, 1995.

Album Notes: *Music*: John Williams; *Orchestrations*: John Neufeld; *Music Editor*: Ken Wannberg; Orchestra conducted by John Williams; *Featured Musician*: Tim Morisson (first trumpet, The Boston Pops Orchestra); *Album Producer*: John Williams; *Engineer*: Shawn Murphy; *Assistant Engineer*: Sue McLean.

Selections: 1 The 1960s: The Turbulent Years (5:04); 2 Main Title... The White House Gate (4:17); 3 Growing Up In Whittier (2:42); 4 The Ellsberg Break-In and Watergate (2:43); 5 Love Field: Dallas, November 1963 (4:51); 6 Losing A Brother (3:18); 7 The Battle Hymn Of The Republic (W. Steffe/J. Ward Howe)(1:03); 8 Making A Comeback (2:20); 9 Track 2 and The Bay Of Pigs (4:47); 10 The Miami Convention, 1968 (3:19); 11 The Meeting With Mao (3:09); 12 "I Am That Sacrifice" (4:49); 13 The Farewell Scene (5:01).

Review: This account of the life and times of Richard M. Nixon, strikingly portrayed by Anthony Hopkins, and the scandal that eventually brought him down benefitted tremendously from the serious score created for the occasion by John Williams. Having to deal here with a much more serious subject than all the grander-than-life epic sagas that are his mainstay, Williams thoughtfully concentrated on writing themes that have great dramatic impact, reasonably commenting on the story itself and its many political and personal implications. This does not mean that his score is dry or uninspiring, far from it—in fact, it is a solidly written piece of instrumental music, profoundly affecting and frequently compelling. There is a certain grandeur to the themes developed, in which the main characteristics are the absence of real urgency and pervading dark tones, even in the most strident moments. This, incidentally, was touted at the time of its release as the first interactive CD soundtrack, though the results leave a lot to be desired. Williams' score, however, strikes a totally positive note.

See also: JFK

No Escape ♫♫♫♪

1994, Varese-Sarabande; from the movie *No Escape*, 1994.

Album Notes: *Music*: Graeme Revell; *Orchestrations*: Tim Simonec, Graeme Revell; *Music Editors*: Dick Bernstein, Philip Tallman; Orchestra conducted by Tim Simonec; *Featured Musician*: Philip Tallman (12-string guitar); *Album Producer*: Graeme Revell; *Engineer*: Keith Grant.

Selections: 1 No Escape: Main Titles (1:58); 2 Helicopter To Absolom (2:13); 3 Robbins Captured By The Outsiders (1:52); 4 Ralph: Director Of Aquatic Activities (:48); 5 The Father (1:55); 6

The Insider Camp (1:34); 7 Wet Dreams (2:05); 8 I Love Those Boots (1:47); 9 Banishment (1:32); 10 On The Ramparts/Outsiders Attack (3:24); 11 Battle With Marek (1:26); 12 The Funeral Pyre (1:31); 13 Robbins Returns To The Outsiders' Camp (1:30); 14 Casey Tortured (3:35); 15 Robbins Kills Casey (1:19); 16 Redemption And New Hope (2:16); 17 Marek's Death (1:39); 18 The Traitor Unmasked (1:38); 19 The Trap Is Set and Freedom (3:46).

Review: Lavishly orchestrated Graeme Revell score makes dazzling use of the ambient sounds and ethnic music he recorded during several expeditions to out-of-the-way places like Papua-New Guinea. In the film, Ray Liotta is sent to prison on an island where criminals have divided into two groups. The civilized ones live inside a protected camp, safe from the homicidal "Outsiders" who live in the forest. Revell uses his odd sampled sounds to make these "Outsiders" more barbaric, like unthinking animals ("Robbins Captured By the Outsiders"). Other highlights include Philip Tallman's terrific blue grass 12-string guitar solo on "I Love Those Boots."

David Hirsch

No Man's Land ♪

1987, Varese-Sarabande Records; from the movie *No Man's Land*, Orion Pictures, 1987.

Album Notes: *Music*: Basil Poledouris; *Orchestrations*: Steven Scott Smalley; *Album Producer*: Basil Poledouris; *Engineers*: Joel Moss, Garth Richardson.

Selections: 1 Main Title (3:00); 2 P.C.H. (1:02); 3 First Score (2:16); 4 Lone Score (1:21); 5 Love Theme (1:39); 6 Chase (5:29); 7 Porsche Power (:38); 8 Drive My Car? (2:13); 9 Ann Buttons (1:15); 10 Payoff (3:28); 11 Showtime (4:19); 12 End Credits (3:02).

Review: Basil Poledouris' loud and uninspired score for this modern thriller about an undercover cop (Charlie Sheen), the thief he is trying to bring in, and his involvement with the thief's sister, is not very worthy of the man who scored the *RoboCop* films or, better yet, the exhilarating *Conan* epics. To be totally effective, synthesizer music must exhibit some signs of intelligent life, but when it means so very little as it does here ("First Score," "Payoff"), one can only dismiss it and move on to the next CD.

No Sun in Venice ♫♫♫♫

1975, Atlantic Records; from the movie *No Sun in Venice*, Kingsley International Pictures, 1957.

Album Notes: *Music*: John Lewis; *Featured Musicians*: The Modern Jazz Quartet: John Lewis (piano), Milt Jackson (vibraharp), Percy Heath (bass), Connie Kay (drums); *Album Producer*: Nesuhi Ertegun.

Selections: 1 The Golden Striker (3:39); 2 One Never Knows (9:20); 3 The Rose Truc (4:55); 4 Cortege (7:24); 5 Venice (4:26); 6 Three Windows (6:43).

Review: The elegant, soigne music of John Lewis, as performed by the Modern Jazz Quartet, is a key ingredient in Vadim's flavorful 1957 film set in present-day Venice, about three young people and an older Baron whose influence dominates their lives during the short period they spend in the fabled Italian city. The cool, classicist lines in Lewis' compositions, set off by the striking contribution of vibraharpist Milt Jackson, supported by Connie Kay on drums and Percy Heath on bass, have long been admired by jazz fans everywhere, and this score, a rare foray by the MJQ in film music, seems the perfect complement to the story. Since the creation of the score, one theme, "The Golden Striker," has become a standard in the MJQ canon, and two others, "One Never Knows" (the actual translation of the French film title *Sait-on jamais)* and "Three Windows" are regular staples in the group's repertoire. A classy effort, if there ever was one.

No Way Out 𝄞𝄞𝄞

1987, Varese-Sarabande Records; from the movie *No Way Out*, Orion Pictures, 1987.

Album Notes: *Music*: Maurice Jarre; *Featured Musicians*: Michael Boddicker, Ian Underwood, Ralph Grierson (keyboards), Nyle Steiner, Judd Miller (E.V.I.), Michael Fisher (percussion); *Album Producer*: Maurice Jarre; *Engineer*: Joel Moss.

Selections: 1 No Way Out (5:46); 2 National Security (2:47); 3 Cover-Up (5:38); 4 In The Pentagon (3:24); 5 We Can Interface (5:40); 6 Susan (6:06).

Review: A pertinent modern-day remake of the classic 1948 film noir *The Big Clock*, *No Way Out* stars Kevin Costner as a liaison officer at the Pentagon, reporting to Gene Hackman, who witnesses his boss in the act of killing a girl with whom he had a love affair. Reflecting the taut atmosphere of this crime drama, Maurice Jarre wrote a synthesized score that's intelligently crafted and listenable, even as it effectively supports the screen action. Relying on the solid instrumental techniques of a trio of seasoned musicians (Michael Boddicker, Ian Underwood and Ralph Grierson, with whom Jarre has also worked on other scores), and the percussion effects of Michael Fisher, Jarre has devised cues that create an atmosphere of relentless tension, presented here in six long selections that support and develop the many twists in the film (in which Costner is instructed by Hackman, who knows there

was a witness to his crime, to find out the identity of that witness). Even the reprogramming does not make for an always compelling listening experience, but individual reactions to this type of music can vary wildly, and Jarre, at least, is a composer who remains always more interesting than most.

Noble House 𝄞𝄞𝄞▹

1988, Varese-Sarabande Records; from the movie *Noble House,* De Laurentiis Entertainment Group, 1988.

Album Notes: *Music*: Paul Chihara; The London Symphony Orchestra, conducted by Paul Chihara; *Featured Musician*: Ray Warleigh (saxophone); *Album Producers*: Paul Chihara, Brian Gascoigne; *Engineer*: Richard Lewzey.

Selections: 1 Main Title (Noble House Theme)(1:58); 2 Stormy Night (2:30); 3 Taipan In Love (3:53); 4 Jon Chen's Plot (1:56); 5 Love Boat To Macao (3:04); 6 Four-Finger Wu (2:01); 7 Dunross (1:30); 8 The Curse (2:19); 9 The Day After (4:00); 10 Opium Drop (2:05); 11 Linc's Death (1:50); 12 Coin Joined (2:25); 13 Finale (4:14).

Review: Appropriately epic and grandiose, the "Main Title" seems to signal the start of what may be an important score. But even though Paul Chihara does not always sustain the character he so effectively projected in this opening cue, much of his music is eminently entertaining and atmospheric. The broad romantic themes are developed by the strings in a style that recalls Victor Young or Percy Faith, occasionally enshrining the bluesy playing of a lone saxophone, or contrasting selections that give a prominent role to synthesizers. The story itself, based on the novel by James Clavell and set in Southeast Asia, might have suggested some cues with a more ethnic approach, but the tone here is squarely on sweeping conventional tunes that are attractively shaped and played.

Nobody's Fool 𝄞𝄞𝄞𝄞

1994, Milan Records; from the movie *Nobody's Fool*, Paramount Pictures, 1994.

Album Notes: *Music*: Howard Shore; *Orchestrations*: Howard Shore; *Music Editor*: Suzana Peric; The London Philharmonic Orchestra and The London Metropolitan Orchestra, conducted by Howard Shore; *Album Producer*: Howard Shore; *Engineer*: John Kurlander.

Selections: 1 Main Title (2:47); 2 Fool's Triple (1:10); 3 You Are A Man Mong Men (:54); 4 Will (1:33); 5 Bowdin Street (1:30); 6 We'd Be Like Bonnie And Clyde (1:18); 7 Hattie Escapes (1:47); 8 Tip Top Construction (1:37); 9 Will At The Wheel (1:14); 10 Sully (3:01); 11 The Stopwatch (1:29); 12 Thanksgiving (3:18); 13 Miss Beryl (1:28); 14 Rub Quits (2:23); 15 The Ultimate

Escape, Escapes (3:16); 16 You Are My Best Friend (2:46); 17 Toby's Theme (3:11); 18 The Wooden Leg (1:23); 19 Trifecta Ticket (:58); 20 Would You Like A Cup Of Tea? (2:56).

Review: A sensitive portrayal by Paul Newman, as a man alone approaching the twilight of his years, sets the tone for this bittersweet on-the-edge screen story, that resulted in an effectively low-key and lovely score from Howard Shore. With a keen ear for melodic material that makes a musical statement while reflecting the moods of the film itself, Shore built a series of strikingly beautiful cues, with various solo instruments — a harp, a clarinet, a flute — riding over gorgeous, long orchestral lines to paint a canvas that's very attractive and unusually pleasant to the ear.

Norma Jean and Marilyn
♪♪♪♪

1996, Intrada Records; from the movie *Norma Jean and Marilyn*, HBO Pictures, 1996.

Album Notes: *Music:* Christopher Young; *Orchestrations:* Pete Anthony, Christopher Young; *Music Editors:* Carl Zittrer, Eduardo Ponsdomenech; Orchestra conducted by Pete Anthony; *Album Producer:* Christopher Young; *Engineer:* Tim Boyle.

Selections: 1 Norma Jean And Marilyn (2:08); 2 Blond Akk Over (2:36); 3 Multiple Parents (3:17); 4 My Best Friends (2:44); 5 The Public Eye (3:50); 6 The Seven Year Itch (2:00); 7 Nude Confessions (2:15); 8 Rescue Me (2:23); 9 Gladys (3:11); 10 Our Angel (2:01); 11 Too Young (3:14); 12 Marilyn (3:13).

Review: The idea of having two different actresses portray Norman Jean Baker and Marilyn Monroe, one the obverse image of the other, is only one of several interesting things about this film Christopher Young tried to express in his effusive score. The challenges were many. Behind the glamour in the life of Marilyn is her darker private side and the demons that haunted her, two opposite aspects of her personality which the composer translated into a single motif with a simultaneously ascending and descending figure, played by the piano, harp, and vibes. In addition, the musical moods needed to conform with a 1950s reality, an evocation Young captured in a theme for soprano sax and trumpet over string harmonies. It all adds up to a very compelling score, warm and nostalgic, melodic with an occasional sharp edge to it, and above all profoundly attractive.

North ♪♪♪♪

1994, Epic Soundtrax; from the movie *North*, Columbia Pictures, 1994.

Album Notes: *Music:* Marc Shaiman; *Arrangements:* Marc Shaiman; *Orchestrations:* Jeff Atmajian, Larry Blank, Brad

Dechter, Mark McKenzie; *Music Editor:* Scott Stambler; Orchestra conducted by Artie Kane; *Album Producers:* Marc Shaiman, Nick Vidar; *Engineer:* Shawn Murphy.

Selections: 1 Main Title: If I Were A Rich Man (J. Bock/S. Harnick)(2:59); 2 A Very Successful Life (1:23) *Elijah Wood;* 3 The Secret Spot (2:43); 4 North Goes To Court (3:10); 5 Let's Get Crackin' (:40); 6 Texas (Theme from Dallas)(J. Immel)(:48); 7 Bonanza (J. Livingston/R. Evans/R. Reiner/M. Shaiman/A. Zweibel)(1:03) *Reba McIntyre, Dan Aykroyd;* 8 North Looks West (2:17); 9 Hawaii: Hawaiian War Chant (J. Noble/Leleiohaku)/Tiny Bubbles (L. Pober)/My Little Grass Shack (J. Noble/B. Cogswell/T. Harrison)/Vlue Hawaii (R. Rainger/L. Robin)/Aloha Oe (Queen Liliuokalani)(3:21); 10 North Heads North (1:02); 11 Alaska: Winter Wonderland (F. Bernard/D. Smith)(2:00); 12 Winchell's Master Plan (1:07); 13 The World Traveler: Amazing Grace (J. Newton)/Can-Can (J. Offenbach)(1:35); 14 Bedford: Father Knows Best (D. Ferris/I. Friedman)(1:53); 15 Homesick (1:13); 16 Winchell, Lies And Videotape (1:52); 17 New York City: Sobre las olas (Rosas)(5:29); 18 North Figures It Out (2:28); 19 Race To The Finish (2:17); 20 Reunion (3:41).

Review: The whimsical tale of an 11-year-old whose search for the ideal parents has international repercussions, this pleasantly diverting comedy directed by Rob Reiner translated itself into an eclectic soundtrack album in which Marc Shaiman's music looks into different cultures and ethnic forms of expression to emphasize some of the broader aspects of the story. Freely borrowing themes from various well-known sources, like "Dallas," "Bonanza," and "Father Knows Best" or familiar standards, like "Winter Wonderland" and "Amazing Grace," the cues are pleasant without being maudlin, and reflect in a positive way the film's light and entertaining moods.

North By Northwest

North By Northwest ♪♪♪♪

1996, Rhino Records; from the movie *North By Northwest*, M-G-M, 1959.

Album Notes: *Music:* Bernard Herrmann; *Orchestrations:* Bernard Herrmann; *Arrangements:* Bernard Herrmann; The M-G-M Studio Orchestra, conducted by Bernard Herrmann; *CD Producers:* Marilee Bradford, Bradley Flanagan; *Engineer:* Ted Hall.

Selections: 1 Overture (2:14); 2 The Streets (1:03); 3 It's A Most Unusual Day (J. McHugh/H. Adamson)(1:08); 4 Kidnapped (2:15); 5 The Door (:42); 6 Cheers (:41); 7 The Wild Ride (2:49); 8 Car Crash (:21); 9 The Return (:25); 10 Two Dollars (:47); 11 Rosalie (C. Porter)(1:32); 12 In The Still Of The Night

"In the academic world, writing in Hollywood still has a little stigma to it. But the fact that you can't take film music out on the concert stage and stand on its own is not derogatory. It speaks to its function, which is to be part of a tapestry."

John Williams
(Time Magazine, 9-11-95)

(C. Porter)(2:23); 13 The Elevator (:45); 14 The U.N. (1:01); 15 Information Desk (:50); 16 The Knife (:48); 17 Fashion Show (A. Previn)(5:19); 18 Interlude (1:15); 19 Detectives (:28); 20 Conversation Piece (3:03); 21 Duo (1:09); 22 The Station (:53); 23 The Phone Booth (1:14); 24 Farewell (:45); 25 The Crash (:53); 26 Hotel Lobby (1:21); 27 The Reunion (:51); 28 Goodbye (:54); 29 The Question (:46); 30 The Pad and Pencil (1:03); 31 The Auction (1:06); 32 The Police (:26); 33 The Airport (:58); 34 The Cafeteria (1:14); 35 The Shooting (1:06); 36 The Forest (1:22); 37 Flight (:19); 38 The Ledge (1:09); 39 The House (3:11); 40 The Balcony (:44); 41 The Match Box (1:59); 42 (The Message (:21); 43 The TV (:40); 44 The Airplane (:58); 45 The Gates (:47); 46 The Stone Faces (1:31); 47 The Ridge (2:00); 48 On The Rocks (2:23); 49 The Cliff (1:37); 50 Finale (:46).

Review: Rhino's expanded edition of Bernard Herrmann's score for Alfred Hitchcock's *North By Northwest* (among the composers most intriguing and romantic for a Hitchcock film) is a shining example of everything a well-restored CD soundtrack should be. It's all here, including original music, expanded cues, outtakes, detailed and informative liner notes. Having the ability to listen to this music as Herrmann originally scored it, for the uncut, unedited film, is an absolute thrill, and a glimpse into history itself.

Although the film itself was released with a monophonic soundtrack, the original scoring sessions were recorded in stereo, and are presented as such here. While the music tracks were left virtually untouched in storage since 1959, some deterioration of the original tapes have occurred, and the listener may note some minor flaws during the program. Overall, however, the sonics are excellent.

A pared down "Suite for North By Northwest" (18 minutes) is also available on a Milan CD, *Alfred Hitchcock Film Music*, which features Herrmann conducting the National Philharmonic Orchestra. While excellent as a "taste," the complete soundtrack is preferable by far.

A London CD, *Psycho: Great Hitchcock Movie Thrillers* contains only a three-minute cue from the score, and hardly bears mention.

Charles L. Granata

North By Northwest ♪♪♪▿

1980, Varese-Sarabande Records; from the movie *North By Northwest*, M-G-M, 1959.

Album Notes: *Music*: Bernard Herrmann; *Orchestrations and Arrangements*: Bernard Herrmann; The London Studio Orchestra, conducted by Laurie Johnson; *Album Producer*: Laurie Johnson; *Engineers*: John Goldsmith, Geoffrey Barton.

Selections: 1 Main Title (3:11); 2 Abducting George Kaplan (1:56); 3 The Elevator (1:23); 4 Murder At The U.N. (3:14); 5 Romance On The Train (4:21); 6 Crash Of The Cropduster (2:04); 7 The Auction and The Airport (2:08); 8 Duo (Love Theme)(reprise)(1:26); 9 Cafeteria Shooting (2:11); 10 Stalking Vandamm's House (4:21); 11 The Match Box (1:48); 12 Mount Rushmore/Finale (8:31).

Review: This re-recording, conducted by Laurie Johnson, for many years the only one available of Herrmann's score, features better sonics and some cues that apparently didn't make it on the original. However, it also has much less music, and altogether can only be considered as a complement to the Rhino definitive album.

Nostradamus ♪♪♪♪▿

1994, London Records; from the movie *Nostradamus*, Orion Classics, 1994.

Album Notes: *Music*: Barrington Pheloung; *Orchestrations*: Barrington Pheloung; The London Metropolitan Orchestra, conducted by Barrington Pheloung; *Featured Musician*: Tom Finucane (lute); *Featured Vocalists*: Sarah Eaton (soprano), Andrew Gant (tenor), Katherine Willis (soprano), Edward Caswell (bass), Guy Protheroe (tenor); The New London Consort, Philip Pickett, director; The English Chamber Choir, Guy Protheroe, director; The Choir Of Selwyn College, Cambridge, Andrew Gant, director; *Engineers*: Dave Hunt, John Taylor; *Assistant Engineers*: Andrew Taylor, Toby Wood.

Selections: 1 The World Is Breaking (2:55); 2 Love Theme (4:21) *Sarah Eaton, Andrew Gant*; 3 Kyrie I (1:07); 4 Christe (1:40); 5 Kyrie II (from Missa Pange Lingua)(J. Des Prez)(1:06); 6 The Inquisition (2:23); 7 The Family History (1:41); 8 Et quand je suis couche (anon.)(:31); 9 Vray Dieu d'amour (A. Brumel)(1:09); 10 Black Rain (1:29); 11 Agnus Dei I (1:42); 12 Agnus Dei II (2:19); 13 Agnus Dei III (from Missa Pange Lingua)(J. des Prez)(3:24); 14 Love Theme (reprise)(1:17); 15 I Have Seen Paradise (4:33); 16 Basse Danse (T. Susato)(1:54); 17 Gaillarde (T. Susato)(:51); 18 The Plague (2:38); 19 L'amour de moy (anon.)(2:12) *Katherine Willis, Andrew Gant, Edward Caswell*; 20 The Passion (3:05); 21 Danse du Roy (T. Susato)(1:07); 22 Saltarello (:39); 23 Mille regrets (J. des Prez/T. Susato)(1:50); 24 The Monastery (2:10) *Guy Protheroe*; 25 Allegez moy (J. des Prez)(2:10); 26 A New Trust (:57); 27 Mille regretz (J. des Prez/L. de Narvaes)(2:51); 28 Love/The Showering Of Christ (1:46); 29 The Wedding/The Burning Of The Books (5:20); 30 Absalon fili mi (J. des Prez)(4:42); 31 Danger/Inspiration/Paradise (1:55); 32 Sed quando sub movenda erit ignorantia/Main Theme (7:07).

Review: The mysterious personality of Nostradamus, the Renaissance philosopher and scientist (1503-1566) whose deliberately nonconformist attitude irritated the religious and medical authorities of his time and whose prophecies have haunted mankind for their alleged accuracy and relevance to modern history, may have seemed a fascinating yet unusual subject for a screen epic. But the broader canvas of 16th-century life in Europe, with its ills, medical as well as political and religious (the devastating plagues, the Inquisition), provides the solid background against which the known facts in his life found an illustration. Holding it all together is Barrington Phenoung's diligently scholarly score, extensively quoting from Josquin des Prez, in which musical instruments from the period conferred the proper tone and colors, and effectively blended with modern orchestral textures. This soundtrack album manages to evoke the film and its central character, and makes for a rather unusual but ultimately eloquent and satisfying listening experience.

Not Without My Daughter
♫♫♭

1991, Intrada Records; from the movie *Not Without My Daughter*, M-G-M/UA, 1991.

Album Notes: *Music*: Jerry Goldsmith; *Orchestrations*: Arthur Morton; *Music Editor*: Ken Hall; The National Philharmonic Orchestra, conducted by Jerry Goldsmith; *Album Producer*: Jerry Goldsmith; *Engineer*: Alan Snelling.

Selections: 1 The Lake (2:37); 2 No Job (3:15); 3 Threats (1:30); 4 Trapped (2:46); 5 School's Out (1:09); 6 Night Stories (1:59); 7 Don't Leave (3:30); 8 Dry Spell (5:52); 9 The Promise (1:59); 10 First Break (4:37); 11 Home Again (5:44).

Review: For this intimate and rather jingoistic study of an American woman's escape from an abusive marriage in Iran, Jerry Goldsmith wrote a surprisingly low-key score. Like the film, the score somewhat predictably and manipulatively balances a tender Americana theme of strings and solo piano against increasingly oppressive and violent Middle Eastern effects. Its highlight is a lengthy sequence illustrating the woman's escape through desert territory at night. Atmospheric, blending both electronic and acoustic textures in a minimalistic technique, the cue works as an update of Goldsmith's experimental work on *Planet of the Apes*, but it belongs in a better score and film. Even Goldsmith has admitted this score didn't warrant an album release.

Jeff Bond

Nothing But Trouble Woof

1991, Warner Bros. Records; from the movie *Nothing But Trouble*, Warner Bros., 1990.

Album Notes: *Music*: Michael Kamen; Orchestra conducted by Michael Kamen; *Song Producers*: Marty Paich, Greg Jacobs, Madonna & Shep Pettibone, Bob Crewe, Ron Nevison, Bruce Gowdi & Peter Aykroyd, Barry Beckett; *Album Executive Producers*: Michael Ostin, Gary LeMel.

Selections: 1 The Good Life (J. Readon/S. Distel)(3:13) *Ray Charles*; 2 Same Song (G. Jacobs/R. Brooks/T. Shakur)(6:32) *Digital Underground*; 3 Get Over (Madonna/S. Bray)(5:06) *Nick Scotti*; 4 Big Girls Don't Cry (B. Crewe/B. Gaudio)(2:25) *Frankie Valli & The Four Seasons*; 5 Tie The Knot (G. Jacobs) (3:17) *Digital Underground*; 6 Bonestripper (J. Blades/T. Shaw/T. Nugent) (4:35) *Damn Yankees*; 7 Atlantic City (Is A Party Town)(P. Aykroyd)(3:40) *Elwood Blues Revue*; 8 La Chanka (P. Aykroyd/J.P. Beledo)(3:19) *Bertila Damas*; 9 I Mean I Love You (H. Williams, Jr.)(2:59) *Hank Williams Jr.*; 10 Valkenvania Suite (M. Kamen)(4:21).

Review: The music in this film may have been attributed to Michael Kamen, but like the comedy tag affixed to this sordidly mindless effort, it proves a misnomer, at least in this soundtrack album where the composer is represented by one selection, "Valkenvania Suite." The bulk of the album, as is so often the case, consists of pop selections that can be found in various other compilations and that have been hastily put together here, simply because brief snippets of these songs could be heard behind the screen action. If that's what you're after, by all means go and buy this album. Otherwise, forget about it.

Now and Then

Now and Then ♫♫♫

1995, Columbia Records; from the movie *Now and Then*, New Line Cinema, 1995.

Album Notes: *Soundtrack Album Coordinator*: Michelle Belcher; *Engineer*: David Mitson.

Selections: 1 Sugar, Sugar (J. Barry/A. Kim)(2:45) *The Archies*; 2 Knock Three Times (I. Levine/L. Brown)(2:54) *Tony Orlando & Dawn*; 3 I Want You Back (F. Perren/A. Mizell/B. Gordy/D. Lussier)(2:53) *Jackson 5*; 4 Signed, Sealed, Delivered I'm Yours (S. Wright/L. Garrett/L. Hardaway/S. Wonder)(2:39) *Stevie Wonder*; 5 Band Of Gold (E. Wayne/R. Dunbar)(2:53) *Freda Payne*; 6 Daydream Believer (J. Stewart)(2:49) *The Monkees*; 7 No Matter What (P. Ham) (2:59) *Badfinger*; 8 Hitchin' A Ride (M. Murray/P. Callander)(2:55) *Vanity Fare*; 9 All Right Now (A. Fraser/P. Rodgers)(5:29) *Free*; 10 I'm Gonna Make You Love Me (J. Ross/K. Gamble/J. Williams)(3:06) *Diana Ross & The Supremes, The Temptations*; 11 I'll Be There (H. Davis/B. Gordy/B. West/W. Hutch) (3:56) *Jackson 5*; 12 Now And Then (S. Hoffs/C. Caffey/J. Wiedlin)(5:34) *Susanna Hoffs*.

Review: See entry below.

Now and Then ♫♫♫♫

1995, Varese-Sarabande; from the movie *Now and Then*, New Line Cinema, 1995.

Album Notes: *Music*: Cliff Eidelman; *Orchestrations*: Cliff Eidelman, Gregory Smith; *Music Editor*: Bill Abbott; Orchestra conducted by Cliff Eidelman; *Album Producer*: Cliff Eidelman; *Engineer*: Armin Steiner.

Selections: 1 Main Title (3:05); 2 Remembrance (1:57); 3 Secret Meeting (2:11); 4 On The Swing (1:26); 5 It's My Mom (2:32); 6 Spirits Are Here (2:17); 7 Sam's Dad Leaves (1:56); 8 It's A Girl (1:48); 9 Roberta Fakes Death (1:26); 10 Best Friends For Life (3:07); 11 Pete Saves Sam (2:29); 12 The Pact (3:10); 13 No More Seances (1:44); 14 Rest In Peace Johnny (4:22).

Review: The affecting story of four 12-year-olds, their joys, their disappointments, and the adventures they shared over a summer in 1970, *Now and Then* exudes warmth and pathos, and most of all paints the image of a friendship that transcends everyday problems to give its four main characters the memories they'd recall with fondness in later years.

Anchoring the film in its specific time period, several '70s pop tunes by the Monkees, Diana Ross and the Supremes, Jackson Five, and other performers provide the appropriate musical background. The first album brings these songs together in a compilation that seems better than most, even if the same selections can be found elsewhere.

The second album focuses on the fine instrumental themes developed by Cliff Eidelman that seem omnipresent, yet subtly understated. Conjuring up moods that are bathed in rose-tinted nostalgia similar to those in the film narrative, Eidelman's score comes to the forefront with great sensitivity and charm in this wonderful album. Some selections ("Remembrance," "It's a Girl," "Best Friends for Life") particularly tug at the right heartstrings, but the whole effort is quite memorable and enjoyable.

The Nun's Story ♫♫♫♫♭

1991, Stanyan Records; from the movie *The Nun's Story*, Warner Bros., 1959.

Album Notes: *Music*: Franz Waxman; Orchestra conducted by Franz Waxman; *CD Producer*: Rod McKuen; *Engineer*: Steve Hoffman; *Assistant Engineer*: Kevin Gray.

Selections: 1 Main Title/Gaby And Her Father (4:45); 2 Leaving (1:23); 3 Gaby Enters The Convent (3:00); 4 Goodbye (4:09); 5 New Home (1:34); 6 First Day/Mother Superior (2:42); 7 Sister Luke (1:15); 8 I Accuse Myself (1:08); 9 Haircutting/Gran Coro (3:47); 10 Penance (1:42); 11 Angel Gabriel (2:53); 12 Departure and The Congo (2:58); 13 European Hospital (3:34); 14 Bad Accident (1:56); 15 Killing Of Aurelie (1:44); 16 Sister Luke Bids Farewell (1:20); 17 Return To Belgium (:56); 18 Letter From Dr. Fortunati/ Convent Life/War (4:12); 19 The Underground (1:07); 20 News Of Father's Death (2:54); 21 Leaving The Convent (:51); 22 Finale (3:13).

Review: In one of her finest portrayals, Audrey Hepburn gave a luminous performance in this unconventional story, based on the book by Kathryn C. Hulme, of a young Belgian woman who decides to abandon the comforts and pleasures of her privileged world for a life of austerity and contemplation as a nun, only to discover that life in a convent is no less challenging and confusing. For composer Franz Waxman, the story meant dealing with various sets of musical themes, from ecclesiastical ones to reflect the apparent calm and serenity of the religious life, to Congolese rhythms evocative of the African setting of some of the scenes, to 12-tone composition to illustrate a scene that takes place in an insane asylum. Superbly evocative and compelling, the score earned the composer an Oscar nomination, though he lost to Miklos Rozsa's *Ben-Hur*. This first reissue on CD returns to the catalogue an album that was for many years a prized collectors' item, with selections that were previously unavailable. The transfer from the three-channel 35mm optical film reveals some dryness, a significant amount of hiss, and some distortion that could have been easily corrected, despite a disclaimer to the contrary.

Obsession ♫♫♫♫

1989, Masters Film Music; from the movie *Obsession,* Columbia Pictures, 1976.

Album Notes: *Music*: Bernard Herrmann; The National Philahrmonic Orchestra, conducted by Bernard Herrmann; *CD Producer*: Robert Townson.

Selections: 1 Main Title/Valse Lente/Kidnap (5:55); 2 Newsboy/The Tape/The Ferry (4:55); 3 The Tomb/Sandra (8:03); 4 The Church/Court's Confession/Bryn Mawr (9:25); 5 New Orleans Wedding/Court: The Morning After (4:27); 6 The Plane/Court And LaSalle's Struggle/Airport (5:56).

Review: Bernard Herrmann returned to familiar grounds to the suspense film in which he had illustrated himself so vividly, with this stylish score for the film directed by Brian de Palma, a thinly disguised remake and tribute to Alfred Hitchcock's *Vertigo*. Like that film, *Obsession* deals with the anguish of a man (Cliff Robertson), still haunted by the kidnapping and apparent death of his wife 16 years before, who encounters a woman (Genevieve Bujold) who bears an uncanny resemblance to her during a trip abroad. Elaborating on musical devices he had already utilized in *Vertigo*, Herrmann wrote a sensational score, filled with powerful themes, ominously underlined by an organ, or a harp, sometimes with abrupt choral flourishes, in eerie evocations of a mystery that refuses to reveal itself. Shortly before his death, the composer assembled for this album the various cues in six mini-suites that present a stronger and more coherent vision of his music. The score marked another important milestone in the career of the composer. This recording, a limited edition release well worth looking for, eloquently shows why.

Octopussy ♫♫♫

1983, A&M Records; from the movie *Octopussy*, MGM/UA, 1983.

Album Notes: *Music*: John Barry; *Lyrics*: Tim Rice; Orchestra conducted by John Barry; *Album Producer*: John Barry.

Selections: 1 Main Title: All Time High (3:04) *Rita Coolidge*; 2 Bond Look-Alike (2:59); 3 009 Gets The Knife and Gobinda Attacks (3:06); 4 That's My Little Octopussy (3:14); 5 Arrival At The Island Of Octopussy (3:23); 6 Bond At The Monsoon Palace (3:03); 7 Bond Meets Octopussy (3:37); 8 Yo-Yo Fight and Death Of Vijay (3:45); 9 The Chase Bomb Theme (1:56); 10 End Title: The Palace Fight (4:33); 11 All Time High (3:05) *Rita Coolidge*.

Review: While this soundtrack occasionally fails to rise to the high levels John Barry reached in some of his best efforts for the James Bond films, it is still a most attractive one, with the composer's signature themes used to best effect to illustrate yet another highly implausible story in which Bond confronts his usual share of villains (a suave trader in art forgeries, played by Louis Jourdan, a Russian general bent on exploding an atomic device, some murderous circus performers) and beauties (including Maud Adams, the "Octopussy" of the title). Spearheaded by the vaguely nostalgic "All Time High," performed by Rita Coolidge, and reprised as an instrumental "That's My Little Octopussy," the cues unfold as predictably as the story itself, with more highs than lows, as befit an action film that relies on the charisma and personal charm of its main character. It's an indispensable addition to any Barry or Bond collection, and besides it's most enjoyable.

Odds Against Tomorrow

Odds Against Tomorrow ♫♫♫♫♫

1991, Sony Music Special Products; from the movie *Odds Against Tomorrow,* United Artists, 1959.

Album Notes: *Music*: John Lewis; *Featured Musicians*: The Modern Jazz Quartet: John Lewis (piano), Milt Jackson (vibraharp), Percy Heath (bass), Connie Kay (drums); *Album Producer*: John Lewis; *CD Engineer*: Ken Robertson.

Selections: 1 Prelude To Odds Against Tomorrow (1:44); 2 A Cool Wind Is Blowing (1:20); 3 Five Figure People Crossing Paths (1:40); 4 How To Frame Pigeons (1:04); 5 Morning Trip To Melton (3:09); 6 Looking At The Caper (2:01); 7 Johnny Ingram's Possessions (1:08); 8 The Carousel Incident (1:44); 9 Skating In Central Park (3:29); 10 No Happiness For Slater (3:56); 11 Main Theme: Odds Against Tomorrow (3:24); 12 Games (2:17); 13 Social Call (3:53); 14 The Impractical Man (3:00); 15 Advance On Melton (1:58); 16 Waiting Around The River (3:51); 17 Distractions (1:25); 18 The Caper Failure (1:23); 19 Postlude (:45).

Review: See entry below.

Odds Against Tomorrow ♫♫♫♫♫

1990, Blue Note Records; from the movie *Odds Against Tomorrow*, United Artists, 1959.

Album Notes: *Music*: John Lewis; *Featured Musicians*: The Modern Jazz Quartet: John Lewis (piano), Milt Jackson (vibraharp), Percy Heath (bass), Connie Kay (drums); *Album Producer*: Jack Lewis; *Engineer*: Dick Olmsted; *CD Producer*: Michael Cuscuna; *Engineer*: Malcolm Addey.

Selections: 1 Skating In Central Park (6:07); 2 No Happiness For Slater (5:18); 3 A Social Call (4:45); 4 Cue #9 (5:00); 5 A Cold Wind Is Blowing (7:29); 6 Odds Against Tomorrow (3:33).

Review: In another unusual foray into film music, John Lewis scored this taut crime drama in which Harry Belafonte, Robert Ryan and Ed Begley are unlikely partners in a bank robbery, with the unusual casting eliciting added comments about racist attitudes. Characteristic of Lewis' subtly understated music, performed on screen as in these albums by The Modern Jazz Quartet, the moods are squarely on jazz, with the fanciful interplay between Lewis on piano and Milt Jackson on vibra-harp at the center of the group's tight performance, with Connie Kay and Percy Heath providing the essential rhythm foundation and occasional inspired solos. The first album is the actual soundtrack to the film, with the selections reflecting the shorter playing time usually asked for by a given scene, but with a greater abundance of themes not found elsewhere.

The second album is a rerecording of some of the most important themes from the score (including the acowledged highlights, "Skating in Central Park," "No Happiness for Slater" and "A Cold Wind is Blowing"), considerably expanded and with a greater amount of improvisation in the playing. A richer sound quality is also a prime consideration here, as opposed to the thinner-sounding soundtrack album. Both, however, are deserving of the highest consideration.

Of Mice and Men ♫♫♫♫

1992, Varese-Sarabande Records; from the movie *Of Mice and Men*, M-G-M, 1992.

Album Notes: *Music*: Mark Isham; *Orchestrations*: Ken Kugler; *Music Editor*: Tom Carlson; Orchestra conducted by Ken Kugler; *Featured Soloists*: Rich Ruttenburg (piano), Peter Manau (guitar); *Album Producer*: Mark Isham; *Engineer*: Stephen Krause.

Selections: 1 The Train (1:38); 2 Red Dress (2:59); 3 Soledad (1:15); 4 Guys Like Us (2:01); 5 The Bunkhouse (:56); 6 After Supper (:44); 7 The Puppy (:46); 8 Buckin' Barley (2:20); 9 Candy's Loss (:57); 10 Flight (1:06); 11 The Dream (1:29); 12 The Hope (1:09); 13 The Fight (2:14); 14 Comfort (:53); 15 The Ranch (:48); 16 Sundown (:38); 17 Curly's Wife (1:19); 18 Pigeons (:38); 19 Discovery (1:21); 20 River Run (3:13); 21 George And Lennie (2:03); 22 Of Mice And Men (End Titles)(3:33).

Review: Based on John Steinbeck's story about two itinerant workers, George, a quiet optimist with great sensitivity, and Lennie, endowed with unusual strength and the simple mind of a child, who roam the California countryside in search of job

opportunities, this remake of the classic 1939 film elicited a score with folk-like simplicity from Mark Isham, writing in a remarkably low-key style. With an abundance of cues for strings and woodwinds, the music is often appropriately reflective and atmospheric, only occasionally departing from its quiet, lyrical moods to underline a specific situation ("The Bunkhouse," "Buckin' Barley," "Comfort," "The Ranch").

Ultimately, the blend of both elements in the writing combine to create music that is hauntingly striking, and evocative of the drama on the screen and its multifaceted aspects. For the record, the original film was scored by Aaron Copland, and while Mark Isham's music may not achieve the kind of perennial appeal Copland's score has exerted since it was written, it is still a pretty eloquent statement from this very talented composer.

Off Limits ♫♫

1988, Varese-Sarabande Records; from the movie *Off Limits*, 20th Century-Fox, 1988.

Album Notes: *Music*: James Newton Howard; *Featured Musicians*: James Newton Howard (keyboards/synth), Jeff Porcaro, Joe Porcaro, Emil Richards, Michael Mason (percussion), Michael Landau, Basil Fung (guitar), Robby Weaver (synclavier programming); *Album Producer*: James Newton Howard; *Engineer*: John Vigran.

Selections: 1 Questioning Maurice (1:05); 2 The War Zone (2:11); 3 Nicole's Theme (2:15); 4 Chase (:59); 5 Following Col. Armstrong (2:45); 6 Spotting Nicole (1:06); 7 Love Theme (1:37); 8 Body Bombing (1:44); 9 Final Chase (3:24); 10 Getting A Look (1:12); 11 Arrest (:57); 12 Car Bombing (2:24); 13 Nam Is Dead (:52); 14 Bombing (2:45); 15 Sgt. Flowers (1:37); 16 Sapper Chase (2:08); 17 The Viet Cong Post (2:58); 18 Killer (1:39); 19 Love Theme (reprise)(1:37).

Review: James Newton Howard's atmospheric synthesizer score for this suspense thriller starring Willem Dafoe and Gregory Hines, has its moments, but might have proved more effective on the screen than in the living room. While there is diversity in some of the cues, the grist of the music often gets lost in cues that fail to catch one's interest or end up sounding too repetitious after a while.

An Officer and a Gentleman ♫♫♫♪

1982, Island Records; from the movie *An Officer and a Gentleman*, Paramount Pictures, 1982.

Album Notes: *Music*: Jack Nitzsche, Buffy Sainte-Marie; *Song Producers*: Stewart Levine, Van Morrison, Bill Ham, Keith

Olsen, Jerry Kennedy, Lee Ritenour, Jimmy Iovine, Mark Knopfler.

Selections: 1 Main Title (J. Nitzsche/B. Sainte-Marie)(1:41); 2 Up Where We Belong (W. Jennings/J. Nitzsche/B. Sainte-Marie)(3:55) *Joe Cocker, Jennifer Warnes*; 3 Hungry For Your Love (V. Morrison)(3:40) *Van Morrison*; 4 Tush (B. Gibbons/D. Hill/F. Beard)(2:15) *ZZ Top*; 5 Treat Me Right (P. Benatar/D. Lubahn)(3:15) *Pat Benatar*; 6 Be Real (D. Sahm)(2:35) *The Sir Douglas Quintet*; 7 Up Where We Belong (W. Jennings/J. Nitzsche/B. Sainte-Marie)(3:55) *Joe Cocker, Jennifer Warnes*; 8 Love Theme (J. Nitzsche/B. Sainte-Marie/L. Ritenour)(5:19) *Lee Ritenour*; 9 Tunnel Of Love (M. Knopfler)(8:13) *Dire Straits*; 10 The Morning After Love Theme (J. Nitzsche/B. Sainte-Marie)(3:09).

Review: This one launched a monster hit with the Joe Cocker/Jennifer Warnes' duet "Up Where We Belong"—soft, lush, schmaltzy, ech. That song was elevator music *before* it was released. Some decent rockers help redeem the set, though, such as ZZ Top's "Tush," Dire Straits' epic "Tunnel of Love" and the Sir Douglas Quintet's "Be Real." But unless you need to hear more aural wall paper from the likes of Jack Nitzsche and Lee Ritenour, you can find all those on far better albums.

An early pop soundtrack, this collection of songs is notable for the stars who perform them, a factor which explains its popularity. Of course, the success of this album was no doubt also tied to that of the film, about the agonizing training period candidates to the Naval Aviation Officer School must undergo in the hands of a relentless drill instructor. However, the songs selected and the caliber of the performers had something to do with it, as did the fact that "Up Where We Belong," written by Waylon Jennings, Buffy Sainte-Marie and Jack Nitzsche, won the Oscar for Best Original Song. More than 15 years later, it still holds its own, and in fact shows how far superior it is to some of the drivel that was created in its wake.

Gary Graff/Didier C. Deutsch

Old Gringo 🎵🎵🎵🎵♭

1989, GNP Crescendo Records; from the movie *Old Gringo*, Columbia Pictures, 1989.

Album Notes: *Music*: Lee Holdridge; *Orchestrations*: Ira Hearshen; *Music Editor*: Tom Carlson; Orchestra conducted by Lee Holdridge; *Featured Musicians*: Ray Kramer (cello), Malcolm McNab (trumpet), Louise Ditullio, Earle Dunler, Gary Gray, Tom Boyd, Barbara Northcutt, Michael O'Donovan (woodwind), Dennis Budimir, George Doering, Marcos Loya (guitars); *Album Producers*: Lee Holdridge, Ford A. Thaxton; *Engineer*: Bobby Fernandez.

Selections: 1 Prologue (Main Title)(2:33); 2 Ride To The Hacienda (4:08); 3 The Battle (Conflict)(3:12); 4 Harriet's Theme (5:45); 5 Bitter's Last Ride (2:51); 6 The Mirrors (3:02); 7 Nighttime (2:49); 8 The Bell Tower (1:17); 9 The Sigh (5:42); 10 The Battle (Resolution)(2:09); 11 Bitter's Destiny (3:18); 12 Finale (4:58).

Review: *Old Gringo*, starring Gregory Peck, Jane Fonda and Jimmy Smits, is an old-fashioned epic tale of passion and power that elicited an old-fashioned score from composer Lee Holdridge. Set against the backdrop of the Mexican Revolution, the narrative details the complex love story between a 40-something American spinster (Fonda), and a dashing Mexican general in Pancho Villa's army (Smits), with Gregory Peck, portraying Ambrose Bierce, the cynical, brilliant 71-year-old journalist on a quest for adventure. With a meaty storyline and colorful landscapes to ignite his creative expression, Holdridge wrote a score for large orchestra that brims with excitement, solidly anchored by three major themes for the three main characters. The glorious theme he created for Harriet, notably, is simply magnificent.

The Old Man and the Sea
🎵🎵🎵🎵

1989, Varese-Sarabande; from the movie *The Old Man and the Sea*, Warner Bros., 1958.

Album Notes: *Music*: Dimitri Tiomkin; Orchestra conducted by Dimitri Tiomkin; *CD Producers*: Tom Null, Richard Kraft; *Engineer*: Michele Stone.

Selections: 1 The Old Man And The Sea (2:39); 2 Cojimar Harbor And The Old Man (3:24); 3 The Boy (1:15); 4 Fisherman's Cantina (2:42); 5 The Old Man Loved The Boy (1:58); 6 The Fisherman's Lament (1:57); 7 And The Old Man Rowed Out To The Ocean (1:40); 8 The Old Man Catches His Bait (2:34); 9 Sunset And Red Clouds (2:17); 10 I Am Your Dream (2:42); 11 A Small Bird Came Toward The Skiff (3:20); 12 In The Tavern At Casa Blanca (2:17); 13 Just Before It Was Dark (2:41); 14 The Duel With The Fish (4:44); 15 The Shark Fight (1:53); 16 The Lost Fight (1:50); 17 Cubana (1:09); 18 Finale (1:46).

Review: Dimitri Tiomkin left behind the bombast of his western and epic music when he created this Academy Award-winning score for the film, based on the novel by Ernest Hemingway, about an old fisherman, portrayed by Spencer Tracy in a splendidly low-key performance, whose sole ambition in life is to catch a big fish. With the exception of a couple of cues, with a strong tropical flavor ("Fisherman's Cantina," "In The Tavern At Casa Blanca"), the score centers on the fisherman's determination to succeed, his lonely fight with the huge fish he finally nabs, and with the predator shark attracted by his prey. Subtly expressive and magnificently sketched (the lovely "I Am Your Dream" is probably one of the most attractive tunes ever composed by Tiomkin), the score won an Academy Award.

Olivier Olivier/ Europa Europa 𝄞𝄞𝄞𝄞

1992, DRG Records; from the movies *Olivier Olivier*, Sony Pictures Classics, 1992; and *Europa Europa*, Orion Pictures, 1991.

Album Notes: *Music*: Zbigniew Preisner.

Selections: *OLIVIER OLIVIER:* 1 Main Title (1:47); 2 Main Title (Version 2)(2:41); 3 Affection And Love (:48); 4 At The Cafe (:55); 5 Elizabeth Faints (1:15); 6 Policemen In The Hallway (2:10); 7 Main Credits (3:13); 8 Olivier (1:27); 9 After The Chimney (1:38); 10 Olivier Chases Nadine (1:21); 11 Main Title (Version 3)(2:29); 12 Olivier With His Sister (1:23); 13 After The Party (1:36); 14 After The Kiss (1:22); 15 Main Title (Version 4)(2:29); 16 Marcel's Trumpet (:54); 17 End Credits (2:29);

EUROPA EUROPA: 18 Exodus (:39); 19 Attack From The Air (:39); 20 Battle (1:36); 21 The Truck Leaves (:48); 22 Checking The I.D. Papers (:54); 23 The Germans (:37); 24 In The Woods (:39); 25 Near The Fire (1:50); 26 Intensity (:40); 27 The Youngsters Leave (1:20); 28 The Boats Leave (:32); 29 Bombing The Factory (:27); 30 Intensity (:53); 31 Troubles (:35); 32 Hitler Stalin (1:16).

Review: Two films, one set in contemporary France, the other in war-torn Poland, both directed by Agnieszka Holland, received vibrant scores from Zbigniew Preisner. In the first, filled with ambiguities and innuendos that belie the simplicity of its storyline, a provincial French couple welcomes a young Parisian street prostitute whom they believe to be their long-lost son. In the second, based on a a true story, a young Jewish boy tries to convince the German soldiers who have arrested him that he is a gentile. Using a determinatedly low-key approach to both stories, Preisner crafted scores that are eloquently flavorful and sparse, with only a hint of predictability—faint accordion in the first, a little Jewish theme in the second—to underline the film's respective backgrounds.

The Omen 𝄞𝄞𝄞𝄞

1990, Varese-Sarabande; from the movie *The Omen*, 20th Century-Fox, 1976.

Album Notes: *Music*: Jerry Goldsmith; *Orchestrations*: Arthur Morton; The National Philharmonic Orchestra, conducted by

Lionel Newman; *Album Producer*: Jerry Goldsmith; *Engineer*: John Richards.

Selections: 1 Ave Satani (2:32); 2 The New Ambassador (2:33); 3 Killer Storm (2:52); 4 A Sad Message (1:42); 5 The Demise Of Mrs. Baylock (2:52); 6 Don't Let Him (2:48); 7 The Piper Dreams (J. Goldsmith/C. Bayer Sager) (2:39) *Carol Heather*; 8 The Fall (3:42); 9 Safari Park (2:04); 10 The Dog's Attack (5:50); 11 The Homecoming (2:43); 12 The Altar (2:00).

Review: Goldsmith's only Oscar-winning score has become one of the most influential works in the film music canon and probably started the trend for using Carl Orff's "O Fortuna" in every movie trailer with its spine-chilling use of a Latin-chanting chorus and Stravinsky-like, aggressive string passages to underscore the exploitative 1976 Richard Donner film about an evil little tike who's the son of Satan. Although Goldsmith scored later sequels with a fuller, more expansive sound, the original effort is almost a chamber score that lends an intimate, personal feel to the devilish proceedings. The dirge-like opening and chaotic frenzy of cues like "Killer Storm" and "Mrs. Blalock" are undeniably frightening, but just as disturbing is the low-key choral murmuring that opens the "Dogs Attack" piece, one of the grimmest horror cues Goldsmith ever produced. There's also a surprisingly lyrical, piano-voiced love theme that threads through many of the quieter pieces.

Jeff Bond

See also: Damien: Omen II and The Final Conflict

On Deadly Ground 𝄞𝄞𝄞𝄞

1994, Varese-Sarabande Records; from the movie *On Deadly Ground*, Warner Bros., 1994.

Album Notes: *Music*: Basil Poledouris; *Orchestrations*: Greig McRitchie; *Music Editor*: Curtis Roush; Orchestra conducted by Basil Poledouris; *Featured Vocalists*: Qaunaq Mikkigak, Timangiak Petaulassie (Inuit throat singing); *Album Producer*: Basil Poledouris; *Engineer*: Tim Boyle.

Selections: 1 Main Titles (2:20); 2 Aegis Flameout (1:44); 3 Forrest Found (1:36); 4 The Journey (7:57); 5 Forrest Decides/ Horse Chase (3:55); 6 Jennings Goes Down (4:47); 7 The Warning/End Credits (7:19).

Review: Steven Seagal, an unlikely martial arts expert with a mission, roams the Alaskan range in this environmentally-minded saga in which he confronts an oil prospector unmoved by the pristine beauty of the landscape but moved by the huge profits he might make with his rigs. Far-fetched as the story might have been, it prompted Basil Poledouris to write a superb score in which big orchestral textures and synthesizer sounds, in a rare happy confluence of two styles that seldom agree, effectively blend to paint a broad musical panorama. Adding a touch of authenticity to the musical proceedings, Inuit throat singers provide a suggestive local color.

On Her Majesty's Secret Service ♪♪♪♪♪

1988, EMI-Manhattan Records; from the movie *On Her Majesty's Secret Service,* United Artists, 1969.

Album Notes: *Music:* John Barry; *Lyrics:* Hal David; Orchestra conducted by John Barry; *Album Producer:* Phil Ramone; *Engineer:* Phil Ramone.

Selections: 1 We Have All The Time In The World (3:16) *Louis Armstrong;* 2 This Never Happened To The Other Fella (4:28); 3 Try (3:28); 4 Ski Chase (2:55); 5 Do You Know How Christmas Trees Are Grown? (3:22) *Nina;* 6 Main Theme: On Her Majesty's Secret Service (2:37); 7 Journey To Blofeld's Hideaway (3:29); 8 We Have All The Time In The World (3:00); 9 Over And Out (2:42); 10 Battle At Piz Gloria (4:04); 11 We Have All The Time In The World/James Bond Theme (4:34).

Review: Even though Secret Agent 007 is portrayed by a newcomer (George Lazenby, who hardly made the grade when compared with Sean Connery, despite his own personal charm), very little else is changed in this by-the-numbers exciting tale of derring-do, primarily set in the Swiss Alps. John Barry's score, also one of his best for the series, matches the break-neck pace of the action, and pauses long enough to also indulge in a significant love theme and in a tongue-in-cheek comment about the previous owner of the title role. One jarring note in the otherwise excellent album is the dispensable "Do You Know How Christmas Trees Are Grown?," but Louis Armstrong's rendition of the nostalgia-tinged "We Have All the Time in the World" is a great classic.

Once Around ♪♪♪

1990, Varese-Sarabande Records; from the movie *Once Around,* Universal Pictures, 1990.

Album Notes: *Music:* James Horner; *Orchestrations:* Billy May, John Neufeld; *Music Editor:* Jim Henrikson; Orchestra conducted by James Horner; *Album Producer:* James Horner; *Engineer:* Shawn Murphy.

Selections: 1 Big Band On Ice (4:38); 2 The Apology (4:16); 3 Fly Me To The Moon (B. Howard)(2:29) *Danny Aiello;* 4 Emperor Waltz (J. Strauss)(5:32) *The Vienna Opera Orchestra;* 5 The Arrival (2:08); 6 Sulu Kule (Karsllama)(G. Abdo)(3:35)

George Abdo & The Flames Of Araby Orchestra; 7 Fly Me To The Moon (instrumental version)(B. Howard)(1:16); 8 Glory Of Love (B. Hill)(1:34) *Danny Aiello;* 9 A Passage Of Time (8:42).

Review: James Horner, who has always shown a particular fondness for big bands, was right in his element for this score in which he worked with the great Billy May, writing a number, "Big Band on Ice," that brightens up the whole album. The film, a romantic comedy-drama about the family problems facing a 30-something spinster when she meets an unrefined condo salesman and makes plans to get married, results in cues that are appropriately evocative. Since much of the action centered around the woman's life with her family and the usual rituals involved, many of the selections in this soundtrack album are source music ranging from the stately "The Emperor Waltz" to an oriental fantasy. Danny Aiello, who also appears in the film as the *pater familias,* effectively handles two vocals, including "Fly Me to the Moon," reprised as an instrumental.

Once Upon a Forest ♪♪♪♪

1993, Fox Records; from the animated feature *Once Upon a Forest,* 20th Century-Fox, 1993.

Album Notes: *Music:* James Horner; *Orchestrations:* John Neufeld; *Music Editor:* Jim Henrikson; The London Symphony Orchestra and The New London Children's Choir, conducted by James Horner; *Featured Soloists:* Mike Taylor, Tony Herrigan, The Andrae Crouch Singers; *Album Producer:* James Horner; *Engineer:* Shawn Murphy.

Selections: 1 Once Upon A Time With Me (W. Jennings/J. Horner)(5:56) *Florence Warner Jones, The New London Children's Choir;* 2 The Forest (9:11); 3 Cornelius' Nature Lesson (3:41); 4 The Accident (4:24); 5 Bedside Vigil (2:15); 6 Please Wake Up (W. Jennings/M. Tavera/K. Ward/M. Young/J. Horner) (2:36) *Michael Crawford;* 7 The Journey Begins (8:08); 8 He's Back (A. Crouch/S. Crouch/J. Horner)(2:00) *Ben Vereen & The Andrae Crouch Singers;* 9 Flying (4:49); 10 Escaping From The Yellow Dragons/The Meadow (6:36); 11 Flying Home To Michelle (6:32); 12 The Children/Maybe One Day..., Maybe One Day (4:41); 13 Once Upon A Time With Me/End Credits (W. Jennings/J. Horner) (5:56) *Florence Warner Jones, The New London Children's Choir.*

Review: Interestingly this soundtrack album invites comparisons with *Ferngully... The Last Rain Forest,* if only because it is also an animated feature with an ecological message to it. But where Alan Silvestri scored the first with an abundance of synthesized sounds, James Horner brings to his music the superlative expression of the London Symphony Orchestra, and themes that are grandly sweeping and profusely florid. As is often the case with his cues, often reconstructed for the soundtrack album, there is a huge amount of music here, notably "The Forest," "The Journey Begins," "Escaping from the Yellow Dragons/The Meadow," and "Flying Home to Michelle," which all have plenty of time to make a strong impression.

Also as usual with Horner, the themes are truly beautiful, romantic and melodic, and always broad to the extreme. They match the animated action in which the usual contingent of cuddly characters — Abigail, a mouse, Edgar, a mole, Russell, a hedgehog, and Michelle, a badger — are exposed to the dangers of life outside the forest. When Michelle gets sick, her wise old uncle, Cornelius, directs the other three to go find a rare herb, which they eventually do after having met a gospel group led by a perky preacher, and barely escaped the "yellow dragons," the bulldozers at a construction site. It may be conventional stuff, but Horner pulls all the stops and delivers a score that underlines these events in the story with much delight.

Once Upon a Time in America 🎵🎵🎵🎵

1985, Mercury Records; from the movie *Once Upon a Time in America*, Hapax Int'l Pictures, 1984.

Album Notes: *Music*: Ennio Morricone; *Orchestrations*: Ennio Morricone; Orchestra conducted by Ennio Morricone; *Featured Artists*: Gheorghe Zamfir (Pan flute), Edda Dell'Orso (vocals); *Album Producer*: Ennio Morricone; *Engineer*: Sergio Marcotulli; *Assistant Engineer*: Alessandro Marcotulli.

Selections: 1 Once Upon A Time In America (2:14); 2 Poverty (3:38); 3 Deborah's Theme (4:25) *Edda Dell' Orso*; 4 Childhood Memories (3:24); 5 Amapola (5:22); 6 Friends (1:36); 7 Prohibition Dirge (4:21); 8 Cockey's Song (4:21) *Edda Dell' Orso*; 9 Amapola, part 2 (3:09); 10 Childhood Poverty (1:45); 11 Photographic Memories (1:03); 12 Friends (1:24); 13 Friendship And Love (4:16) *Edda Dell' Orso*; 14 Speakeasy (2:23); 15 Deborah's Theme/Amapola (6:13).

Review: A story of the world of gangsters in the United States spread over several decades, *Once Upon a Time in America* may be viewed as Sergio Leone's companion film to his *Once Upon a Time in the West*. Whereas the popular "spaghetti western" explores a time and place that are significant in this country's development the conquest of the West, Once Upon a Time in America is equally relevant in its exploration of another time and place, life in the Eastern big cities during the Prohibition and after, that also shaped the country as we know it today. In it,

Leone used the rivalries that existed between various criminal groups over their claim to certain territories, to focus on an aging New York Mafia boss (Robert De Niro), eager to avenge the death of his girlfriend 35 years earlier, during the Prohibition era, at the hands of members of a rival gang.

Once again bringing his own sensitivity to illustrate Leone's vision, Ennio Morricone wrote a vibrant score, marked by themes that are in turns romantic and exuberant, in a display of unusually strong musical ideas that match in invention and impact the ones he had conceived for the earlier *Once Upon a Time in the West*. From early jazz tunes to evocative nostalgia-limned songs, he painted a broad, colorful canvas that is irresistibly alive and convincing.

Once Upon a Time in the West 🎵🎵🎵🎵

1988, RCA Records; from the movie *Once Upon a Time in the West*, Paramount Pictures, 1972.

Album Notes: *Music*: Ennio Morricone; *Orchestrations*: Ennio Morricone; Orchestra Unione Musicisti di Roma, conducted by Ennio Morricone; *Featured Soloist*: Franco De Gemini (harmonica), Alessandro Alessandroni (whistler), I Cantori Moderni di Alessandroni (chorus), Edda Dell'Orso (vocal); *Album Producer*: Ennio Morricone; *CD Producer*: Chick Crumpacker; *Engineer*: Dick Baxter.

Selections: 1 Once Upon A Time In The West (3:43); 2 As A Judgement (3:05); 3 Farewell To Cheyenne (2:37); 4 The Transgression (4:40); 5 The First Tavern (1:38); 6 The Second Tavern (1:31); 7 Man With A Harmonica (3:28); 8 A Dimly Lit Room (5:06); 9 Bad Orchestra (2:22); 10 The Man (1:00); 11 Jill's America (2:45); 12 Death Rattle (1:42); 13 Finale (4:10).

Review: Even though he had already scored several magnificent westerns that called attention to his unique brand of creativity (*The Good, the Bad and the Ugly* comes to mind), Ennio Morricone reached the pinnacle of his art with this sensational effort for the sprawling saga filmed by Sergio Leone. Central to the popularity of the score is the haunting "Man with a Harmonica," which is heard throughout the film as a theme for a lonely avenger portrayed by Charles Bronson. The poignancy in the theme captures the moods of the narrative, a tale of greed and revenge, in which Bronson's "man-with-no-name" confronts Henry Fonda and Jason Robards, two heavies intent on taking control of a small community in a deserted area of the wild West, in anticipation of the windfall that will come their way once the railroad comes through the town. Also making a strong comment on the action, "Farewell to Cheyenne" and "Jill's America" stand out in the rich and flavorful score.

One Against the Wind ♫♫♫♫

1993, Intrada Records; from the movie *One Against the Wind,* Republic Pictures, 1993.

Album Notes: *Music:* Lee Holdridge; *Orchestrations:* Lee Holdridge, Ira Hearshen; Orchestra conducted by Lee Holdridge; *Album Producer:* Lee Holdridge; *Engineer:* Rick Riccio.

Selections: 1 Wartime (Prologue and Main Theme)(2:56); 2 Mary Helps James (5:01); 3 Escape (2:37); 4 Simple Acts Of Courage (5:33); 5 Mary's Trial (2:03); 6 Captured And Wounded (4:38); 7 Mary In Danger (2:01); 8 Leaving Mary Behind (3:19); 9 Reunion and Finale (2:22); 10 End Credits (Main Theme)(1:14).

Review: Based on the real life story of a British countess living in Paris during World War II and her heroic efforts to help downed Allied fliers escape arrest, *One Against the Wind* suggested to composer Lee Holdridge a score that swells up with broad romantic moods, reflective of the countess' character, and martial cues to dangers presented by the German occupant. As he explains it in his notes, the score is pretty much presented as "a tone poem spread across the events and moments of the film," with the two colliding motives, a tense descending "wartime" action theme played by the brass section, and a rising hymn-like theme, played by the strings, outlining the various elements in the narrative. An unusually strong and descriptive score.

One Fine Day ♫♫

1996, Columbia Records; from the movie *One Fine Day,* 20th Century-Fox, 1996.

Album Notes: *Music:* James Newton Howard; *Orchestrations:* Brad Dechter, James Newton Howard; Orchestra conducted by Artie Kane; *Song Producers:* David Sancious, Peter Asher, Marc Tanner, Shawn Colvin, Matthew Wilder, Van Morrison, John Porter, Danny Bennett, Tracey Freeman; *Album Executive Producers:* Michael Hoffman, Peter Afterman, Glen Brunman.

Selections: 1 One Fine Day (G. Goffin/C. King)(2:45) *Natalie Merchant;* 2 The Boy From New York City (J. Taylor/G. Davis)(3:01) *The Ad Libs;* 3 For The First Time (J. Newton Howard/A.D. Rich/J. Friedman)(4:29) *Kenny Loggins;* 4 Mama Said (L. Dixon/W. Denson)(2:09) *The Shirelles;* 5 Someone Like You (V. Morrison)(4:11) *Shawn Colvin;* 6 Love's Funny That Way (T. Arena/D. Tyson/D. McTaggart)(4:37) *Tina Arena;* 7 Have I Told You Lately? (V. Morrison)(4:20) *Van Morrison;* 8

The Glory Of Love (W. Hill)(2:59) *Keb' Mo';* 9 What A Diff'rence A Day Made (M. Grever/S. Adams)(2:28) *Tony Bennett;* 10 Isn't It Romantic (R. Rodgers/L. Hart)(3:02) *Ella Fitzgerald;* 11 This Guy's In Love With You (B. Bacharach/H. David)(3:48) *Harry Connick Jr.;* 12 Just Like You (K. Moore/J.L. Parker)(3:27) *Keb' Mo';* 13 One Fine Day (G. Goffin/C. King) (2:10) *The Chiffons;* 14 Suite from One Fine Day (8:55).

Review: The Chiffons' original rendition of the title track is near-perfection, so it didn't need anyone messing around with it. Unfortunately, Natalie Merchant tries her hand and delivers something that misses its predecessors' vigor and innocence. A bunch of other tepid love songs—new and old—by Kenny Loggins, Tina Arena and Harry Connick, Jr., round out the set, though the rootsy Keb' Mo' acquits himself well on two selections.

Nine minutes of James Newton Howard's music is all you get in this "soundtrack" album, in which the remainder is spent on an odd assortment of song performances ranging from excellent ("For the First Time," "Have I Told You Lately," "What a Diff'rence a Day Made," "Isn't It Romantic") to mediocre ("Love's Funny That Way," "The Glory of Love," "This Guy's in Love with You," "Just Like You"). It's your money...
Gary Graff/Didier C. Deutsch

101 Dalmatians ♫♫♫♫♪

1996, Walt Disney Records; from the movie *101 Dalmatians,* Walt Disney Pictures, 1996.

Album Notes: *Music:* Michael Kamen; *Orchestrations:* Micahel Kamen, Robert Elhaj, Brad Warnaar; *Music Editor:* Michael T. Ryan; The L.A. All-Star Orchestra, conducted by Michael Kamen; *Album Producers:* Michael Kamen, Stephen P. McLaughlin, Christopher S. Brooks; *Engineer:* Stephen P. McLaughlin.

Selections: 1 Cruella De Vil (M. Levin)(4:07) *Dr. John;* 2 One Hundred And One Dalmatians (Main Title)/Good Morning, Pongo/Walking The Dogs (3:56); 3 The House Of De Vil (Cruella's Catwalk)/Love At First Sight/ Roger Goes Swimming (6:55); 4 Daisy, Daisy (Anita Goes Swimming)(2:03); 5 The Wedding (Cup Of Marriage)/Horace And Jasper/Skinner (7:04); 6 Going To Have A Puppy/I Adore Puppies (2:40); 7 Birth (15 Puppies)/The Heist (7:18); 8 Kipper The Die Hard Dog (1:27); 9 Woof On The Roof (3:26); 10 Rescue (2:09); 11 Kipper Finds The Puppies (5:18); 12 Pup, Pup, Pup, Pup, Puppies (4:17); 13 Reunion In The Barn (5:19); 14 Puppies In The Mist (1:59); 15 Home—One Big Happy Family (3:45).

Review: Dr. John's delightfully wicked rendition of the song "Cruella De Vil" sets the tone for this inspired live-action

> "We all look up to him. He invigorated the idea that the orchestra is the way to go when making film scores. He emphasizes the tonal possibilities, the excitement of a hundred people playing music."
>
> **Michael Kamen**
> *on John Williams*
> *(Time Magazine, 9-11-95)*

remake of the Disney animated feature, with Michael Kamen taking his cue from the storyline to deliver a score that's right on the button. While one might have wondered whatever prompted the powers-that-be at Disney to remake one of their most successful films, one can't dispute the fact that they were right in hiring Kamen to write the score. His music is constantly innovative and amusing, appropriately matching the grander-than-life elements in the film, while adding the right touch to its more down-to-earth aspects. Particularly welcome here is the sentimental "Going to Have A Puppy" with its sarcastic downside "I Adore Puppies," and the heroic "Rescue," brimming with great action tonalities. The entire score is a total joy.

Only the Lonely 🦴🦴🦴🦴

1991, Varese-Sarabande Records; from the movie *Only the Lonely*, 20th Century-Fox, 1991.

Album Notes: *Music*: Maurice Jarre; Orchestra conducted by Maurice Jarre; *Album Producer*: Maurice Jarre; *Engineer*: Shawn Murphy.

Selections: 1 Only The Lonely (R. Orbison/J. Melson)(2:27) *Roy Orbison*; 2 Rose (6:12); 3 Guilt (2:57); 4 Teresa (3:20); 5 Ladder Proposal (11:15); 6 It Couldn't Be Better (4:25); 7 Someone Like You (V. Morrison)(4:05) *Van Morrison*.

Review: An amusing romantic comedy, *Only the Lonely* paints the picture of a bachelor cop, essentially a portly nice guy, still living with his domineering Irish mother in an unassuming working-class neighborhood in Chicago. Acutely observed and frequently transcending the limited parameters of the genre, the film provided Maurice Jarre with a broad range of characters and situations to write a pleasantly colorful score. In one long, expansive moment ("Ladder Proposal"), the composer was able to pack all the best elements in the film to write a piece that echoes the feelings of the main character, played by John Candy, after he meets and falls in love with a timid funeral parlor cosmetician. The two pop vocals, Roy Orbison's "Only the Lonely," and Van Morrison's "Someone Like You," neatly bookend the score for what amounts to a flavorful musical package.

Only You 🦴🦴🦴🦴

1994, Columbia Records; from the movie *Only You*, TriStar Pictures, 1994.

Album Notes: *Music*: Rachel Portman; *Orchestrations*: Rachel Portman; *Music Editor*: Bill Abbott; Orchestra conducted by David Snell; *Featured Soloist*: Christopher Warren Green (violin); *Album Producer*: Rachel Portman; *Engineer*: Dick Lewzey.

Selections: 1 Only You (And You Alone) (B. Ram/A. Rand) (3:13) *Louis Armstrong*; 2 Written In The Stars (1:16); 3 Some Enchanted Evening (R. Rodgers/O. Hammerstein II) (3:02) *Ezio Pinza*; 4 I'm Coming With You (2:22); 5 Venice (1:51); 6 O Sole Mio (E. Di Capua/G. Capurro/A. Mazzucchi) (3:10) *Quartetto Gelato, Peter De Sotto*; 7 Libiamo ne' lieti calici (G. Verdi) (2:58) *Agnes Baltsa, Jose Carreras*; 8 Lost In Tuscany (2:29); 9 Arriving At Damon's Restaurant (1:40); 10 Running After Damon (:58); 11 Gypsy Blessing (3:21); 12 Positano (1:46); 13 Quartet In B Flat Major, Rondo (J.S. Bach) (4:54) *Quartetto Gelato*; 14 Do You Love Him? (3:16); 15 Theme From "Only You" (3:35); 16 Once In A Lifetime (M. Bolton/D. Warren/W. Afanasieff) (5:56) *Michael Bolton*.

Review: Rachel Portman's cues are often lost in this soundtrack album in which the top pop selections often seem to command more attention. But as usual, the composer eventually impresses with the high quality levels of her compositions, though many of the selections are shamefully too short. One of the most interesting film composers to hit her stride in recent years, Portman often writes in a romantic, expansive style that seems particularly suited to this well-heeled romantic comedy about a couple (Marisa Tomei and Robert Downey Jr.) who meet and eventually fall in love against the exotic background provided by Venice, Rome, the fields of Tuscany and the Amalfi coast. Particularly enjoyable here are the cues marked "I'm Coming with You," "Arriving at Damon's Restaurant," and the short but expressive "Running After Damon," which pretty much define what the score is all about.

Operation Dumbo Drop 🦴🦴🦴🦴

1995, Hollywood Records; from the movie *Operation Dumbo Drop*, Walt Disney Films, 1995.

Album Notes: *Music*: David Newman; *Orchestrations*: David Newman, Xandy Janko, Randy Miller, Scott Smalley, William

Ross; *Music Editor*: Tom Villano; The Sinfonia Of London, conducted by David Newman; *Featured Instrumentalists*: Marty Frasu (synthesizers), Dr. Devious, Arthur McGillycuddy (ethnic flutes); *Album Producer*: David Newman; *Engineer*: Robert Fernandez.

Selections: 1 Opening (1:55); 2 (Your Love Keeps Lifting Me) Higher And Higher (C. Smith/G. Jackson/R. Miner)(2:57) *Jackie Wilson*; 3 Botat And Lihn (2:57); 4 You'se A Son Of A Gun (A. Story/L. Brown/G. Gordy)(2:28) *Marvin Gaye*; 5 Elephant Temple/Lihn's Flashback (6:00); 6 Hang On Sloopy (W. Ferrell/ B. Russell)(3:53) *The McCoys*; 7 Operation Dumbo Drop (8:23); 8 Think (T. White/A. Franklin)(2:15) *Aretha Franklin*; 9 Farewell (3:40); 10 When I See An Elephant Fly (N. Washington/O. Wallace)(1:54) *Cliff Edwards, Jim Carmichael, The Hall-Johnson Choir*.

Review: Here is another case where the pop selections seem to intrude on the development of the original score, written by none other than the excellent David Newman. Apparently based on a real-life incident involving American Green Berets in Vietnam, some local mountain villagers with an exacting ritual, a pachyderm which must be hauled over 200 miles of enemy jungle territory, and a cute 12-year-old orphan boy in need of some love and understanding, the film makes extensive use of period pop tunes, faithfully compiled here to the detriment of Newman's score. The composer's cues, using some anachronistic synthesizer sounds, appropriate ethnic flutes, and the orchestral textures of the Sinfonia of London, create an atmosphere that also seems quite remote from the tone of the film itself, with long, expansive romantic themes that are exquisite but hardly the kind you might expect to hear in a comedy.

Orchestra Wives

1986, Polygram Records; from the movie *Orchestra Wives*, 20th Century-Fox, 1942.

See: Sun Valley Serenade

Oscar ♫♫♫♫

1991, Varese-Sarabande; from the movie *Oscar*, Touchstone Pictures, 1991.

Album Notes: *Music*: Elmer Bernstein; *Orchestrations*: Patrick Russ, Emilie A. Bernstein; Orchestra conducted by Elmer Bernstein; *Album Producer*: Elmer Bernstein.

Selections: 1 Largo al Factotum (G. Rossini)(from *The Barber of Seville*) (4:42) *Earle Patriarco*; 2 Grifting (5:43); 3 Lisa Dreams (3:46); 4 Tea And Romance (4:29); 5 Revelations (5:27); 6 Cops And Real Crooks (concluding with Finucci Piano Boogie)(5:45)

Ralph Grierson; 7 Sweet Georgia Brown (B. Bernie/ K. Casey/ M. Pinkard) (2:54) *Bing Crosby*; 8 Rockin' In Rhythm (E.K. Ellington/I. Mills/H. Carney)(3:21) *Duke Ellington and his Orchestra*; 9 Tea For Two (V. Youmans/I. Caesar)(3:21) *Fred Waring and His Pennsylvanians*; 10 Plain Dirt (C. Stanton)(2:38) *McKinney's Cotton Pickers*.

Review: Sylvester Stallone seems an unlikely foil for a comedy set in 1931, though he played a former hitman intent on reforming and setting a good example for his children. Using as a basic source of inspiration Rossini's "Barber of Seville," Elmer Bernstein crafted an amusing score that has many merits even if it is not exactly earth-shaking. In longer-than-usual cues, in which his ideas have time to find an expression, he delivers music that remains frequently innovative and catchy ("Lisa Dreams"), and representative of the screen action ("Cops and Real Crooks"). Providing a different spin of their own, several pop selections give the album an early '30s feel.

Othello

Othello ♫♫♫♫▿

1993, Varese-Sarabande Records; from the movie *Othello*, Castle Hill, 1952.

Album Notes: *Music*: Angelo-Francesco Lavagnino, Alberto Bargeris; *Music Reconstruction*: Michael Pendowski; Members of The Chicago Symphony Orchestra; The Chicago Lyric Opera Chorus, conducted by Bob Bowker; *Album Producers*: Michael Pendowski, Michael Dawson; *Engineer*: Bob Bennett.

Selections: 1 Main Title/Chant (4:06); 2 There Was Once In Venice A Moor (1:06); 3 The Wrath Of Brabantio/Iago's Theme/ "An Hour To Spend With Thee" (4:12); 4 The Turks Retreat (1:52); 5 The Proclamation/Deceiving Rodrigo (3:39); 6 The Celebration and Antagonism Of Cassio (3:23); 7 "My Reputation, Iago, My Reputation" (1:59); 8 The Seed Of Doubt (3:03); 9 The Handkerchief (1:37); 10 Othello Eavesdrops (5:41); 11 "Let Me See Your Eyes" (:55); 12 "Who Is Thy Lord" (2:04); 13 The Murder Of Rodrigo (The Public Thermae)(5:56); 14 "Put Out The Light, Then Put Out The Light" (2:18); 15 The Deceiver Is Revealed/The Death Of Othello (2:27).

Review: See entry below.

Othello ♫♫♫♫

1995, Varese-Sarabande Records; from the movie *Othello*, Columbia Pictures, 1995.

Album Notes: *Music*: Charlie Mole; *Orchestrations*: Nick Ingman, John Bell; Orchestra conducted by Nick Ingman; *Featured*

Soloists: John Themis (oud, guitar, flutes, solo voice), Paul Clarvis (African percussion), Keith Thomson (ethnic flutes, oboes, shawm), Nick Curtis (Moorish wailing); *Album Producer*: Charlie Mole; *Engineer*: Mike Ross-Trevor.

Selections: 1 Main Title (3:12); 2 The Garden (1:22); 3 The Arrival (3:37); 4 Torch Dance (2:39); 5 Revelry (4:16); 6 The Fight (4:24); 7 Divinity Of Hell (3:37); 8 Flashback (3:08); 9 The Beach (1:01); 10 The Fit (2:14); 11 Behind Bars (2:06); 12 The Turret (2:03); 13 Go! (2:16); 14 The Prayer (1:52); 15 The Well (1:11); 16 The Willow Song (2:05); 17 It Is The Cause (3:30); 18 Desdemona's Death (3:39); 19 Iago's Stabbing (1:35); 20 Burial (3:44); 21 End Credits (4:33).

Review: One subject, two versions, two very different scores. The first, for the 1952 film directed and starring Orson Welles, was written by Francesco-Angelo Lavagnino, one of the most respected and proficient Italian composers of the 1950s. Dark and frequently disturbing, but also a very adventurous score in its expression, it involves a wide range of musical effects (North African sonorities, Elizabethan melodies, brass flourishes, medieval tunes, dissonant choral accents) that combine together, collide and mix to paint a brooding, multi-faceted diorama, representative of the action and the background against which it happens. Painstakingly restored, it is performed here in a new recording by members of the Chicago Symphony Orchestra and the Chicago Lyric Opera, in a magnificent display that reveals its many telling aspects.

Surprisingly written along more traditional lines, Charlie Mole's music, heard in the version starring Laurence Fishburn and Kenneth Branagh, also makes use of ethnic instruments, primarily North African, for a score which is equally somber but eventually more one-dimensional in its expression. Unlike the cues written by Lavagnino, Mole's score also seems to be less melodically inclined, with floating lines weaving in and out of rhythmic patterns that may prove more effective on screen than on a strictly audio basis.

Out of Africa 🎜🎜🎜🎜

1986, MCA Records; from the movie *Out of Africa*, Universal Pictures, 1985.

Album Notes: *Music*: John Barry; Orchestra conducted by John Barry; *Album Producer*: John Barry; *Engineers*: Nicholas Basich, Mike Novitch.

Selections: 1 Main Title (I Had A Farm In Africa)(3:07); 2 I'm Better At Hello (Karen's Theme I)(1:15); 3 Have You Got A Story For Me? (1:12); 4 Concerto For Clarinet And Orchestra In A (K. 622)(W.A. Mozart)(2:46) *Jack Brymer, The Academy of St. Martin-in-the-Fields, Neville Marriner*; 5 Safari (2:40); 6 Karen's

Journey/ Siyawe (African Traditional)(4:46); 7 Flying Over Africa (3:22); 8 I Had A Compass From Denys (Karen's Theme II)(2:27); 9 Alone In The Farm (1:55); 10 Let The Rest Of The World Go By (E.R. Ball/J. Keirn Brennan)(3:12); 11 If I Know A Song Of Africa (Karen's Theme III)(2:11); 12 End Title (You Are Karen)(4:03).

Review: John Barry won a well-deserved Academy Award for this remarkable score, which gave its specific romantic flavor to this tale based on the true-life experiences of writer Isak Dinesen in Kenya in the days before World War I. Though married at the time, Dinesen got involved with a charming, boyish aviator, in a relationship that did not last, even though she became available, because of his independent nature. Sometimes more a travelogue than a romantic drama, the film is marked by its many breathtaking views of unspoiled African landscapes, lovingly captured in gorgeous scenes, in which Barry's music serves as a necessary complement to the image. "Flying over Africa" is one of the score's choicest moments. For the most part eschewing the ethnic rhythms that had marked his other African epic *Born Free*, Barry delivered a series of strikingly original romantic themes that masterfully capture the moods and feels of the film. A Japanese release of this soundtrack album, incidentally, contains an extra selection not in the American release.

Out To Sea 🎜🎜🎜

1997, Milan Records; from the movie *Out To Sea*, 20th Century-Fox, 1997.

Album Notes: *Music*: David Newman; *Orchestrations*: David Newman, Xandy Janko, Daniel Hamuy, Brad Dechter; *Synthesizer Programming*: Marty Frasu; Orchestra conducted by David Newman; *Ballroom Music Arrangements*: Chris Boardman; Ballroom Music conducted by Chris Boardman; *Ballroom Music Producer*: Chris Boardman; *Engineers*: Bones Howe, Bobby Fernandez, Bruce Botnick, Marty Frasu.

Selections: 1 Main Titles (D. Newman)(1:08); 2 You're Our Guest (C. Boardman/R.N. Jacobs)(:44) *Brent Spiner*; 3 Cheek To Cheek (I. Berlin)(2:44) *Brent Spiner*; 4 Celebration (R. Bell/C. Smith/G. Brown/J. Taylor/R. Mickens/E. Toon/D. Thomas/R. Bell/E. Deodato)(3:10); 5 First Kiss/Charlie And Liz (D. Newman)(2:23); 6 Canadian Sunset (N. Gimbel/E. Heywood)(3:00); 7 Oye Como Va (T. Puente)(3:22) *Brent Spiner*; 8 Mambo #5 (D.P. Prado)(2:05); 9 Proposal (D. Newman)(1:54); 10 Jumpin' At The Woodside (C. Basie)(4:17); 11 Sway (P.B. Ruiz/N. Gimbel)(2:36) *Brent Spiner*; 12 Nurse Collins (D. Newman) (1:34); 13 Sea Cruise (H.P. Smith)(1:50); 14 More (R. Ortolani/N. Oliviero/M. Ciocciolini/N. Newell)(2:27) *Bobby Darin*; 15 Finale (D. Newman)(7:04).

Review: If you've ever felt like taking a cruise in the Caribbean, but couldn't afford to get seasick, then this album might do the trick and help you dream that you're actually on one of those luxury liners. Several of the tracks ("Cheek to Cheek," "Celebration," "Canadian Sunset," "Mambo #5," "Jumpin' at the Woodside," "Sea Cruise," etc.) are performed in sophisticated lounge/cruise ship style, with Brent Spiner providing an occasional vocal that's right on target—unobtrusive, upfront and handsomely bland. For added pleasure, they've dusted off Bobby Darin's rendition of "More," from the film *Mondo Cane*. And David Newman has thrown in some cues from his instrumental score, creating a different set of moods, equally welcome. The film, by the way, stars grumpy old actors Jack Lemmon and Walter Matthau, in yet another innocuous comedy-by-the-numbers, as mismatched brothers-in-law who wind up aboard a luxury ship as... dance hosts, who think nothing of meeting (and fleecing) the wealthy women on the cruise. As long as they keep that music playing, welcome aboard!

Outbreak 𝄞𝄞

1995, Varese-Sarabande; from the movie *Outbreak*, Warner Bros., 1995.

Album Notes: *Music*: James Newton Howard; *Orchestrations*: Robert Elhai, Brad Dechter, Chris Boardman, James Newton Howard; *Music Editor*: Jim Weidman; Orchestra conducted by Artie Kane; *Featured Musicians*: Dean Parks (guitar), Emil Richards, Joe Porcaro, Michael Fisher, Lenny Castro (percussion), Steve Porcaro, Bob Daspit (synth programming), L.A. Master Chorale, Paul Salamunovich, director; *Album Producers*: James Newton Howard, Michael Mason; *Engineer*: Shawn Murphy.

Selections: 1 Main Titles (3:19); 2 Motaba River Valley (1:00); 3 Final Authorization (2:34); 4 White Flags (1:44); 5 Casey Rips His Suit (2:20); 6 Finding The Ship (1:42); 7 Casey Goes Down (2:04); 8 Robbie's Bedside (2:38); 9 Jimbo Gets Sick (1:43); 10 Cedar Creek Exodus (1:07); 11 A Little Resistance (2:48); 12 They're Coming (7:14).

Review: A suitably dramatic orchestral score with electronic effects, James Newton Howard's music for *Outbreak* sounds fittingly ominous and ballsy at the right places, though it eventually seems dry-bone and wrenching despite the many flourishes meant to embellish this tale about a rare disease imported from Africa and running rampant in a middle-American town. The impression is that the score, eloquent as it may be (and it is, just listen to "They're Coming"!), takes too long to build some kind of momentum.

Outland/Capricorn One
𝄞𝄞𝄞𝄞

1993, GNP/Crescendo; from the movies *Outland*, Warner Bros., 1978; and *Capricorn One*, Warner Bros., 1981.

Album Notes: *Music*: Jerry Goldsmith; *Orchestrations*: Arthur Morton; The National Philharmonic Orchestra of London, conducted by Jerry Goldsmith; *Album Producer*: Jerry Goldsmith.

Selections: *OUTLAND:* 1 The Mine (3:52); 2 Early Arrival (4:09); 3 The Message (2:07); 4 The Air Lock (4:42); 5 Hot Water (4:49); 6 The Hunted (5:14); 7 Spiders (2:29); 8 The Rec Room (3:23); 9 The Hostage (4:18); 10 Final Message (3:27);

CAPRICORN ONE: 11 Main Title (2:47); 12 Bedtime Story (3:01); 13 Docking (2:55); 14 No Water (2:26); 15 The Message (4:33); 16 Break Out (3:13); 17 Kay's Theme (3:17); 18 The Station (3:30); 19 The Snake (3:37); 20 The Long Climb (3:53); 21 The Letter (2:52); 22 The Celebration (3:04).

Review: Two of Goldsmith's finest action scores are well represented on this lengthy album, which showcases the percussive, elaborately-developed style of writing that dominated the composer's work until the mid-'80s. The 1981 *Outland* is a gritty and extremely dark outer space effort featuring a throbbing suspense motif of woodwinds and low strings, some delicately-textured electronics and crushing, monolithic action cues that hammer home the horror of dying in the emptiness of space. There's a spectacular cue for a foot chase in "Hot Water" and a surprisingly lyrical, romantic finale. *Capricorn One* is a landmark action score sporting a remarkably driving, jagged title march emphasizing harsh, militaristic brass and percussion. Insidiously subtle suspense cues alternate with arid desert portraits featuring a lonely solo trumpet figure and several spectacular action cues, notably the virtuoso "Breakout" which climaxes in a wild section of whirling horn and trumpet glissandos. They don't write 'em like this anymore.

Jeff Bond

Pacific Heights 𝄞𝄞𝄞𝄞

1990, Varese-Sarabande Records; from the movie *Pacific Heights*, Morgan Creek Films, 1990.

Album Notes: *Music*: Hans Zimmer; *Orchestrations*: Shirley Walker, Bruce Fowler, Steve Bartek; Orchestra conducted by Shirley Walker; *Featured Soloists*: Chuck Domanico (bass), Mike Lang (piano), Walt Fowler (trumpet), Gene Cipriano (saxophone), Carmen Twilley (voice); *Album Producers*: Hans Zimmer, Jay Rifkin; *Engineer*: Jay Rifkin.

Selections: 1 Part I (12:14); 2 Part II (7:26); 3 Part III (9:24); 4 Part IV (8:05).

Review: Presented on CD in four long suites, Zimmer's textural music for this psychological thriller is comprised not so much of melodies or themes but of motifs and recurring figures and phrases. Zimmer creates a complex and compelling musical world comprised of orchestra, synthesizer, and voice. Instrumentally, the score is quite varied, yet it captures a consistent mood of apprehension, of danger, of working evil. A solo saxophone evokes a somewhat sensuous eloquence to the score's apprehensiveness, while a brief melody for female voice adds a tonality of ominous jeopardy. Zimmer provides a number of warm musical moments, the pretty piano theme heard every so often brings a sense of intimacy and compassion to the otherwise suspenseful or frightening moments, but it's always the stronger, nonmelodic musical figures that predominate, just as the strange circumstances of the film constantly overwhelm the calmer moments. Zimmer's score likewise mirrors this counterpoint with notable style and flavor. The music is so varied and the orchestrations so interesting that the music is constantly listenable, always turning something new that wasn't heard before.

Randall Larson

The Pagemaster ♫♫♫♪

1994, Fox Records; from the movie *The Pagemaster*, 20th Century-Fox, 1994.

Album Notes: *Music*: James Horner; *Orchestrations*: Don Davis, Thomas Pasatieri; *Music Editor*: Jim Henrikson; Orchestra conducted by James Horner; *Song Producers*: Keith Thomas, David Fosterl; *Engineers*: Bill Whittington, Dave Reitzas & Felipe Elgueta; *Album Producer*: James Horner; *Engineer*: Shawn Murphy.

Selections: 1 Dream Away (D. Warren)(4:38) *Babyface, Lisa Stansfield*; 2 Whatever You Imagine (C. Weil/B. Mann/J. Horner) (3:27) *Wendy Moten*; 3 Main Title (2:27); 4 A Stormy Ride To The Library (2:52); 5 The Library... The Pagemaster... (4:41); 6 Meeting Adventure And Fantasy (5:12); 7 Horror (3:20); 8 Dr. Jekyll And Mr. Hyde (5:05); 9 A Narrow Escape (2:01); 10 Towards The Open Sea... (7:01); 11 Pirates! (4:07); 12 Loneliness (3:11); 13 The Flying Dragon (3:10); 14 Swallowed Alive!/The Wonder In Books (7:56); 15 New Courage/The Magic Of Imagination (4:03).

Review: James Horner, who seems to have made a career out of scoring animated features (just kidding!), delivered another outstanding score for this fanciful tale about a kid whose love of video games compels him to enter a fantasy world in which he finds himself surrounded by a host of eccentric characters who teach him an invaluable lesson. Solidly crafted, and thoroughly epic in its expression, the recording benefits from the longer playing time of some of the cues, which gives the music an opportunity to make itself heard and appreciated. In another display of his talent, and feel for this type of action cues, Horner relies on the wide range of colors in the orchestral palette to paint images that are wonderfully evocative and strikingly imaginative. Even if "The Library... The Pagemaster" irresistibly evokes Paul Dukas' "The Sorcerer's Apprentice," there is a genuine feel for excitement in Horner's virile accents, a notion further confirmed in other cues like "Towards the Open Sea..." or "The Flying Dragon." In the context, the two mandatory pop vocals at the beginning seem superfluous and can easily be edited out.

The Pallbearer ♫♫

1996, Miramax Records; from the movie *The Pallbearer*, Miramax Pictures, 1996.

Album Notes: *Soundtrack Producers*: Peter Afterman, Mitchell Leib, Jeffrey Kimball.

Selections: 1 Love Is A Beautiful Thing (S. Swinsky)(5:27) *Al Green*; 2 You Got It In Your Soulness (L. McCann)(7:35) *Les McCann, Eddie Harris*; 3 Sambolero (L. Bonfa)(2:09) *Stan Getz, Luis Bonfa*; 4 Papa Loves Mambo (A. Hoffman/D. Manning/B. Reichner)(2:41) *Perry Como*; 5 Cantaloupe Island (H. Hancock)(5:28) *Herbie Hancock*; 6 Move On Up (C. Mayfield)(8:53) *Curtis Mayfield*; 7 Super Freak (R. James/A. Miller)(3:26) *Rick James*; 8 Listen Here (E. Harris)(7:39) *Eddie Harris*; 9 Viva Tirado, Part 1 (G. Wilson)(4:44) *El Chicano*; 10 Bill's Dead/Milk Montage (S. Copeland)(4:00) *Stewart Copeland*; 11 I Surrender Dear (H. Barris/G. Clifford)(3:42) *Django Reinhardt*; 12 Ruth Shows Up (S. Copeland)(1:42) *Stewart Copeland*; 13 Follow (J. Merrick)(6:20) *Richie Havens*.

Review: Barely six minutes of Stewart Copeland's underscore for this comedy made it onto the album, packed instead with an eclectic collection of party songs by artists such as Al Green ("Love Is a Beautiful Thing"), Perry Como ("Papa Loves Mambo") and Rick James ("Super Freak"). The score samples are fairly undistinguished synth cues with little impact, as is the song selection.

David Hirsch

The Paper ♫♫♫

1994, Reprise Records; from the movie *The Paper*, Universal Pictures, 1994.

Album Notes: *Music*: Randy Newman; *Orchestrations*: Jack Hayes; *Music Editors*: Tom Kramer, James Flamberg; Orchestra conducted by Randy Newman; *Featured Musicians*: Malcolm McNab (trumpet), Ralph Grierson (piano); *Album Producer*: Frank Wolf; *Engineer*: Frank Wolf.

Selections: 1 Opening (1:14); 2 Clocks (3:11); 3 Henry Goes To Work (1:55); 4 The Sun (:47); 5 Bernie Calls Deanne (2:11); 6 Busting The Guys (1:14); 7 Marty And Henry (1:15); 8 The Newsroom: 7:00 p.m. (2:51); 9 More Clocks (1:45); 10 Henry Leaves With McDougal (1:10); 11 Bernie Finds Deanne (1:07); 12 Bernie (1:55); 13 Stop The Presses (:55); 14 Henry's Fired (1:01); 15 Marty (:42); 16 Marty's In Trouble (1:55); 17 To The Hospital (:41); 18 Little Polenta Is Born (2:27); 19 A New Day: 7:00 a.m. (5:01); 20 Make Up Your Mind (3:14) *Randy Newman*.

Review: Life in a big city daily paper and the various conflicting personalities that animate it, exacerbated in this story by the fate of two black kids unjustly accused of a crime they have not committed, is the main focus in this affectionate look at the press. Tension as well as the dreaded deadline finds its expression in Randy Newman's score in cues with a tick-tocking feel, while the personal relations between the various members of the staff elicit themes with a more romantic approach. Though at times compelling, the score ultimately doesn't appeal as much as it should, the result of some selections being much too short and seemingly unfulfilled. Newman's vocal on "Make Up Your Mind" is a throwaway at best.

Papillon 🎵🎵🎵🎵♭

1988, Silva Screen/U.K.; from the movie *Papillon*, Allied Artists, 1974.

Album Notes: *Music*: Jerry Goldsmith; Orchestra conducted by Jerry Goldsmith; *Album Producer*: Jerry Goldsmith.

Selections: 1 Theme From "Papillon" (2:15); 2 The Camp (2:57); 3 Reunion (4:33); 4 New Friend (2:02); 5 Freedom (3:53); 6 Gift From The Sea (6:42); 7 Antonio's Death (2:25); 8 Cruel Sea (1:26); 9 Hospital (3:46); 10 Survival (5:20).

Review: Containing one of Goldsmith's best themes, for accordion over harpsichord and orchestra, *Papillon* is a compelling score. Lushly orchestrated, Goldsmith musically depicts the cruelty of the Devil's Island penitentiary and its tangled jungles in such a way that much of his score might be considered a tone poem—a rather brutal one, at that—for the monstrously savage island prison. There is a brutal theme for the island itself. In a more symbolic sense, it's actually a theme for imprisonment, an echoed series of nine notes for reeds, ascending and then dropping off, which in its unresolved melody perfectly captures the claustrophobic sense of entrapment felt by Henri Charriere, the hero of the film, played by Dustin Hoffman. Rising above it, though, is the brilliant main

theme, a beautiful melodic rhythm embodying Charriere's courage and spirit in his relentless pursuit of freedom. Arthur Morton's orchestrations are brilliant, taking the score into ever-new environments, keeping it fresh and constantly interesting, even in its dissonant moments. The score also contains one of Goldsmith's best love themes ("Gift from the Sea").
Randall D. Larson

Paradise Road 🎵🎵🎵🎵

1997, Sony Classical; from the movie *Paradise Road*, For Searchlight Pictures, 1997.

Album Notes: *Music*: Ross Edwards; The Tall Poppies Orchestra, conducted by David Stanhope; *Featured Performers*: Vrouwenkoor Malle Babbe Women's Choir of Haarlem, Holland, Leny van Schaik, conductor; *Vocal Arrangements*: Margaret Dryburgh, Norah Chambers; *Album Producers*: The Malle Babbe Choir; *Engineers*: Christo Curtis (score), Lex van Diepen (choir).

Selections: 1 Guard Falls (bamboo flute)(:21); 2 Largo from Symphony No. 9, "New World" (A. Dvorak)(5:24) *Malle Babbe Women's Choir*; 3 Andante Cantabile from String Quartet (P.I. Tchaikovsky)(6:40) *Malle Babbe Women's Choir*; 4 Minuet in G (L. Van Beethoven)(2:54) *Malle Babbe Women's Choir*; 5 Snake Brings List (:35); 6 Prelude No. 20, "Funeral March" (F. Chopin)(1:36) *Malle Babbe Women's Choir*; 7 Miss Drummond Dies (1:40); 8 Jesu, Joy Of Man's Desiring (J.S. Bach)(2:23) *Malle Babbe Women's Choir*; 9 Handkerchief Dance, Country Gardens (P. Grainger)(2:59) *Malle Babbe Women's Choir*; 10 Wings Choral (:37); 11 Faery Song, from The Immortal Hour (R. Boughton)(2:52) *Malle Babbe Women's Choir*; 12 Auld Lang Syne (trad.)(3:39) *Malle Babbe Women's Choir*; 13 Mrs. O'Riordan Dies (1:09); 14 To A Wild Rose (E. MacDowell) (1:48) *Malle Babbe Women's Choir*; 15 The Captives' Hymn (M. Dryburgh)(4:51) *Malle Babbe Women's Choir*; 16 Wing's Death (1:48); 17 Bolero (M. Ravel) (2:46) *Malle Babbe Women's Choir*; 18 Londonderry Air ("Danny Boy")(trad.) (4:45) *Malle Babbe Women's Choir*.

Review: This has to be one of the loveliest and most unusual soundtrack albums available. Surprisingly, however, it is not Ross Edwards' somewhat perfunctory cues (reduced to a minimum here) that appeal the most, but the Malle Babbe Women's Choir's ethereal performances of classical selections, all the more effective for the calm and peaceful impression they exude. Standouts in this collection include the largo from Dvorak's "New World" Symphony, better known as the spiritual "Going Home"; the traditional Londonderry Air, also known as "Danny Boy"; and Bach's breathtakingly beautiful "Jesu, Joy of Man's

Desiring." But the whole album is a priceless gem that you'll want to hear over and over again, particularly when a moment of rest is what you need most in the world.

Parenthood 🎵🎵🎵

1989, Reprise Records; from the movie *Parenthood*, Universal Pictures, 1989.

Album Notes: *Music*: Randy Newman; *Orchestrations*: Jack Hayes; *Music Editor*: Dan Carlin, Sr.; *Album Producers*: Lenny Waronker, Randy Newman; *Engineer*: Shawn Murphy.

Selections: 1 Introduction/I Love To See You Smile (3:24); 2 Kevin's Graduation (2:37); 3 Helen And Julie (:56); 4 Kevin's Party (Cowboy Gil)(3:22); 5 Gary's In Trouble (2:50); 6 Father And Son (2:30); 7 Drag Race/Todd And Julie (2:30); 8 Kevin Comes Through (1:32); 9 Karen And Gil/Montage (4:51); 10 End Title (I Love To See You Smile)(3:39).

Review: Spearheaded by the Academy Award-nominated song "I Love to See You Smile," this affectionate look at the foibles and trials of parenthood finds a winning musical expression in Randy Newman's score, in which even the short-lived "Helen and Julie" seems appropriately sentimental and relevant. Other delightful moments in the score include the south-of-the-border/hoedown feel in "Kevin's Party," and the lilt in "Drag Race/Todd and Julie." In fact, everything about this soundtrack album would be just right, were it not for the fact that its total playing time is less than 29 minutes. The rating reflects one's utter disgust and disappointment.

Paris, Texas 🎵🎵🎵

1985, Warner Bros. Records; from the movie *Paris, Texas*, 20th Century-Fox, 1985.

Album Notes: *Music*: Ry Cooder; *Featured Musicians*: Ry Cooder, Jim Dickinson, David Lindley; *Album Producer*: Ry Cooder; *Engineers*: Allen Sides, Mark Ettel.

Selections: 1 Paris, Texas (2:56); 2 Brothers (2:06); 3 Nothing Out There (1:30); 4 Cancion Mixteca (trad.)(4:17) *Harry Dean Stanton*; 5 No Safety Zone (1:55); 6 Houston In Two Seconds (2:00); 7 She's Leaving The Bank (R. Cooder/ J. Dickinson)(5:56); 8 On The Couch (1:28); 9 I Knew These People (8:38) *Harry Dean Stanton, Nastassja Kinski*; 10 Dark Was The Night (W. Johnson) (2:50).

Review: A wrenching contemporary drama, about a drifter looking for his ex-wife and finding her working in a strip joint, *Paris, Texas* elicited an evocative Tex-Mex score from Ry Cooder, writing in an idiom in which he feels most comfortable and creative. Essentially a series of cues for acoustic guitars

(played by Cooder, Jim Dickinson and David Lindley), the score is striking in its simplicity, effectively conveying the moods of the characters in the story. A long 8:38 minute segment, "I Knew These People," finds stars Harry Dean Stanton and Nastassja Kinski in a reading of the most poignant scene, with Cooder's music playing underneath, with the track itself, unfortunately marred by heavy hiss, evoking the stark atmosphere that permeates the whole film.

Pascali's Island 🎵🎵🎵🎵

1988, Virgin Records; from the movie *Pascali's Island*, Avenue Pictures, 1988.

Album Notes: *Music*: Loek Dikker; The Royal Philharmonic Orchestra of Flanders, conducted by Huub Kerstens; *Featured Soloists*: Koen de Gans (kaval), Marten Scheffer (bouzouki); *Album Producer*: Loek Dikker; *Engineer*: Ernest Scheerder.

Selections: 1 Pascali's Theme (Pritouritze Planinata) (trad.) (4:38); 2 The Pasha's Castle (1:46); 3 Nisi By Night (1:38); 4 Jealous Pursuit (3:04); 5 Izzet Effendi (2:18); 6 Pascali's Passion (2:52); 7 Nightmares (3:15); 8 The Sultan's Spy (3:00); 9 Fear Of Greeks (2:22); 10 The Deal Complete (:45); 11 Mysterious Englishman (:34); 12 Discovery (2:42); 13 Growing Despair (2:16); 14 Under Cover Of Night (3:53); 15 Lydia's Death (1:08); 16 Pascali's Grief (6:33).

Review: Loek Dikker's score for *Pascali's Island*, a film set on the Aegean, oozes with sounds that evoke the sunny Mediterranean islands and some of the tension in this story of a small-time secret agent, forever lost on a Greek island occupied by the Turks, whose universe is shattered by the arrival of a handsome archeologist and antique-plunderer. With the support of a bouzouki and a kaval, the composer fashioned a score that all at once captures the moods in the narrative and gives them a voice of their own, with a restraint that speaks eloquently for his creativity, while conjuring up images of the setting in which the action takes place. It's a low-key effort, nicely shaded, and handsomely executed.

A Passage to India 🎵🎵🎵🎵🎵

1989, Capitol Records; from the movie *A Passage to India*, Columbia Pictures, 1984.

Album Notes: *Music*: Maurice Jarre; The Royal Philharmonic Orchestra, conducted by Maurice Jarre.

Selections: 1 A Passage To India (1:52); 2 The Marabar Caves (3:06); 3 Bombay March (2:34); 4 The Temple (5:20); 5 Frangipani (3:00); 6 Chandrapore (4:46); 7 Adela (4:25); 8 Expectations (3:07); 9 Bicycle Ride (3:27); 10 Climbing To The Caves (3:59); 11 Kashmir (2:19); 12 Back To England (2:30).

Review: The strong creative relationship between filmmaker David Lean and composer Maurice Jarre, which had already manifested itself in *Lawrence of Arabia* and *Ryan's Daughter,* reached a new high with this film, set in India in the late 1920s, about a well-heeled young British woman, who cannot abide by the haughty attitudes of her compatriots, and who pays dearly for her spirit of independence. Jarre, at his florid best, came up with many memorable themes that capture the gist of the action and the specific time and place in which it occurred, with this effort rewarded by an Academy Award. Standout among the many selections is the jaunty "Bicycle Ride," another exhilarating tune in the Jarre canon.

Passenger 57 ♫♫♫

1992, Epic Soundtrax; from the movie *Passenger 57,* Warner Bros., 1992.

Album Notes: *Music:* Stanley Clarke; *Arranger:* Stanley Clarke; *Featured Musicians:* Stanley Clarke (tenor bass guitar, electric bass guitar, piccolo bass guitar, acoustic bass, synthesizers), George Duke, Bobby Lyle (keyboards), Paul Jackson, Jr. (guitar), John Robinson, Gerry Brown (drums), Gerald Albright (soprano sax, alto sax), Reggie Hamilton, Neil Stubenhauser (electric bass guitar); *Album Producer:* Stanley Clarke; *Engineers:* Dan Humann, Steve Sykes, Robert Fernandez.

Selections: 1 Looking Good (Cutter's Theme)(3:49); 2 Lisa (5:55) *Alexis England;* 3 Cruisin' (5:31); 4 Rane To Plane (2:06); 5 Fight (1:27); 6 Skyjack (5:41); 7 What Is The Plan? (1:36); 8 Just Lookin' Good (Cutter's Theme) (1:30); 9 Big Fall (2:36); 10 Motorcycles (:54); 11 Have A Nice Flight (1:42); 12 Just Cruisin' (2:34); 13 Ferris Wheel (2:30); 14 Let Me Tell Him (2:57); 15 Tracking Rane (1:12); 16 Chaos On The Tarmac (4:37); 17 Anything Wet (1:37); 18 Flight Fight (4:00).

Review: A taut, gripping airborne drama, about a terrorist hijacking a plane and the cop who succeeds in overcoming him, *Passenger 57* is notable for the fact that its score was written by jazz artist Stanley Clarke, who called upon many of his peers in the business—George Duke, Bobby Lyle, Paul Jackson, Jr., and Gerald Albright, among them—to come and share in the fun. There is little that's surprising or innovative about the music, just some jazz fusion themes that are pleasantly attractive, combined with standard action cues ("Skyjack," "Big Fall," "Chaos on the Tarmac") that mean less musically but fill a function.

Pastime ♫♫♫♫

1991, Bay Cities Records; from the movie *Pastime,* Miramax Films, 1991.

Album Notes: *Music:* Lee Holdridge; *Orchestrations:* Ira Hearshen, Lee Holdridge; Orchestra conducted by Lee Holdridge; *Featured Musicians:* Randy Waldman (piano), George Doering (guitar), Earl Dumier (oboe, English horn), Sheridon Strokes (flute), Charles Boito, Gary Herbig (clarinet), Jack Sheldon (trumpet); *Album Producers:* Lee Holdridge, Robin B. Armstrong; *Engineer:* Jim Bailey.

Selections: 1 Main Title: Swing Low Sweet Chariot/Main Theme (2:46) *Jubilant Sykes;* 2 The Game Of His Life (2:10); 3 Roy Dean's Solitude (1:48); 4 Kansas City (J. Lieber/M. Stoller)(3:00) *Wilbert Harrison;* 5 Roy Dean Misses The Pitch (3:03); 6 Teaching Tyrone (:59); 7 Sleepwalk (A. Farina/D. Wolf/J. Santo)(2:22) *George Doering;* 8 Montage Of Moments: Good Gum/Stan Musial Story/After The Fight (2:17); 9 Late Night Radio (1:34); 10 Roy Dean's Finale Decision (1:38); 11 Tyrone's Farewell (4:23); 12 Inez Says Goodbye (1:48); 13 Tyrone's Great Game/This One's For Roy Dean (2:28); 14 End Title: Swing Low Sweet Chariot/Main Theme (reprise)(3:45).

Review: The story of "a major miracle in the minor league," *Pastime* is set in central California in 1957, and deals with two outcasts, a 41-year-old reliever on a minor league club whose only title to glory is that he played ever so briefly in the big league, and a vastly talented young black pitcher with few opportunities to be noticed. For this little, unheralded masterpiece, Holdridge wrote a score that echoes the sentiments flowing between the two main characters and those around them, and, on a much broader scope, the strong emotions and aspirations the game elicits. Deeply felt and lyrical, it is diversified and eloquent, a strongly etched piece of music with many attractive facets.

Pat Garrett & Billy the Kid ♫♫♫♪

1973, Columbia Records; from the movie *Pat Garrett & Billy the Kid,* M-G-M, 1973.

Album Notes: *Music:* Bob Dylan; *Songs:* Bob Dylan; *Featured Musicians:* Bob Dylan (guitar), Booker T. (Bass), Bruce Langhorn (guitar), Roger McGuinn (guitar), Terry Paul (bass), Carl Fortina (harmonium), Jim Keltner (drums), Gary Foster (recorder, flute), Carol Hunter (guitar), Byron Berline (fiddle), Jolly Roger (banjo); Donna Weiss, Priscilla Jones, Byron Berline, Terry Paul, Brenda Patterson (voices); *Album Producer:* Gordon Carroll; *Engineer:* Dan Wallin.

Selections: 1 Main Title Theme (Billy)(6:06); 2 Cantina Theme (Workin' For The Law)(2:57); 3 Billy 1 (3:55); 4 Bunkhouse Theme (2:16); 5 River Theme (1:29); 6 Turkey Chase (3:34); 7 Knockin' On Heaven's Door (2:33); 8 Final Theme (5:23); 9 Billy 4 (5:03); 10 Billy 7 (2:08).

Review: Bob Dylan, who gave a very uneven performance in the film, turned in an unexpectedly proficient score for this retelling of the struggle between former saddle buddies, sheriff Pat Garrett (James Coburn) and outlaw Billy The Kid (Kris Kristofferson), directed by Sam Peckinpah, who publicly disowned the initial version. While unlikely to give nightmares to composers better versed in the genre than he is, Dylan manages to evoke the folksy feel of the western, and contributes at least one memorable theme in "Knockin' on Heaven's Door."

Patriot Games ♪♪♪♪

1992, RCA Records; from the movie *Patriot Games*, Paramount Pictures, 1992.

Album Notes: *Music*: James Horner; *Orchestrations*: John Neufeld, Conrad Pope; *Music Editor*: Jim Henrikson; Orchestra conducted by James Horner; *Album Producer*: James Horner; *Engineer*: Shawn Murphy.

Selections: 1 Main Title (2:58); 2 Attempt On The Royals (3:45); 3 Harry's Game (P. Brennan)(2:31) *Clannad*; 4 The Hit (8:08); 5 Putting The Pieces Together (2:14); 6 Highland's Execution (2:26); 7 Assault On Ryan's House (11:00); 8 Electronic Battlefield (3:21); 9 Boat Chase (4:30); 10 Closing Credits (4:11).

Review: Harrison Ford stars in this explosive, action-packed thriller, based on Tom Clancy's best-seller, as a former CIA analyst vacationing in England, who becomes the target of an Irish killer when he unwillingly gets caught in the middle of a terrorist attack and saves a member of the royal family. With a preponderance of synthesizer sounds and Irish sonorities limning his score, James Horner sketches potent musical images that help underline the action on the screen, often in dark, somber tones that sound threatening and ominous, and are punctuated by heavy drumming as if to signal the inevitability of the most dramatic aspects in the story. Clannad's evocative performance in "Harry's Game" is a bit of a relief, even as it anchors the score more deeply in its Irish background.

The Pawnbroker/ The Deadly Affair ♪♪♪♪

1996, Verve Records; from the movies *The Pawnbroker*, 1965, and *The Deadly Affair*, Columbia Pictures, 1966.

Album Notes: *Music*: Quincy Jones; *Featured Musicians*: Freddie Hubbard (trumpet), J.J. Johnson (trombone), Anthony Ortega (soprano sax), Oliver Nelson (alto sax, tenor sax), Jerry Dodgion (alto sax), Don Elliot (vibraphone), Bobby Scott (piano), Kenny Burrell (guitar), Tommy Williams (bass), Elvin Jones (drums), Ed Shaughnessy (percussion); *Album Producers*: Quincy Jones, Creed Taylor; *Engineer*: Rudy Van Gelder; *CD Producer*: Michael Lang; *Engineer*: Gary N. Mayo.

Selections: THE PAWNBROKER: 1 Theme From The Pawnbroker (Q. Jones/J. Lawrence)(3:09) *Marc Allen*; 2 Main Title (3:43); 3 Harlem Drive (1:56); 4 The Naked Truth (4:10); 5 Otez's Night Off (5:01); 6 Theme From The Pawnbroker (4:07); 7 How Come You People (2:50); 8 Rack 'Em Up (2:40); 9 Death Scene (5:01); 10 End Title (3:07); 11 Theme From The Pawnbroker (2:34) *Sarah Vaughan*;

THE DEADLY AFFAIR: 12 Who Needs Forever? (Q. Jones/H. Greenfield) (3:07) *Astrud Gilberto*; 13 Dieter's First Mistake (4:53); 14 Main Theme (2:11); 15 Postcard Signed "S"/Mendel Tails Elsa/Tickets To "S" (5:40); 16 Main Theme (version No. 2)(3:06); 17 Don't Fly It's Foggy (1:13); 18 Blondie Tails (1:18); 19 Main Theme (version No. 3)(2:07); 20 Ridiculous Scene (1:49); 21 Body On Elevator (:58); 22 Bobb's At Gunpoint (:56); 23 End Title (1:45).

Review: In the early days of his career, when he was more interested in writing solid "mood music" and big band jazz themes than the vapid rap songs in which he so often indulges these days, Quincy Jones scored several films that were particularly memorable. Both *The Pawnbroker* and *The Deadly Affair* belong to that category. With its blend of urgent string melodies and effective jazz tracks, the score for *The Pawnbroker* seems the adequate musical comment for this study of a Jewish man, portrayed by Rod Steiger, who survived the indignities of Nazi camps, only to find another form of discrimination in Harlem where he operates a pawnshop. Featuring such stalwarts as Freddie Hubbard, J.J. Johnson, Oliver Nelson, Kenny Burrell, and Elvin Jones, the music is strongly anchored in the modern jazz sounds that prevailed at the time the film was made. The moods in the film receive an additional boost with the inclusion of the track "How Come You People," that mixes excerpts of dialogue with Jones' music.

Based on a novel by John Le Carre, *The Deadly Affair* deals with a British intelligence officer, played by James Mason in one of his most compelling screen portrayals, trying to solve the mystery surrounding the suicide of a diplomat. The cues Quincy Jones wrote for the film denote the influence of the bossa nova sounds that were heard at the time. But even when he gives in to fleeting trends, Jones always writes material that is far superior to what others do, a point made again with this exquisitely flavored score, reminiscent in some ways of the music Michel Legrand used to write during the same period.

Pee-Wee's Big Adventure/ Back to School *♫♫♫♫*

1988, Varese-Sarabande; from the movies *Pee-Wee's Big Adventure*, Warner Bros., 1985; and *Back to School*, Orion Pictures, 1988.

Album Notes: *Music*: Danny Elfman; *Orchestrations*: Steve Bartek; The National Philharmonic Orchestra, conducted by John Coleman; *Album Producer*: Tom Null; *Engineer*: Mike Ross; *Second Engineer*: Dave Knight.

Selections: *PEE-WEE'S BIG ADVENTURE:* 1 Overture/The Big Race (3:08); 2 Breakfast Machine (2:37); 3 Park Ride (1:15); 4 Stolen Bike (1:44); 5 Hitchhike (:57); 6 Dinosaur Dream (:49); 7 Simone's Theme (1:36); 8 Clown Dream (1:59); 9 Studio Chase (1:25); 10 The Drive-In (2:02); 11 Finale (3:13);

BACK TO SCHOOL: 12 Overture (2:13); 13 "Do Not Go Gently..." (1:08); 14 The Brawl (:52); 15 Action Medley (1:30); 16 Classroom Secretary (1:01); 17 Triple Lindy (2:04); 18 Love Suite (2:29); 19 Study Montage (2:01).

Review: Whether it was Paul Reubens' quirky personality as the childlike Pee-Wee Herman, or the subject of the film itself, Danny Elfman hit a particularly fertile vein when he scored *Pee-Wee's Big Adventure*. In a style that is at once jaunty and mischieviously impish, with broad echoes of Kurt Weill's sardonic tones to round it off, the music is a brilliant display of Elfman's creativity and his inventive, always surprising way with melodic lines and odd instrumentations. It matters little that the film is also a showcase for Pee-Wee's fantasies about his bicycle, stolen by a heavy who gets his comeuppance at the right time. Both the music and the image melded into a whole that is descriptive and totally enjoyable. Without the image, the music is even more vibrant and mesmerizing.

Back to School is another inane little comedy, starring moon-faced Rodney Dangerfield as the father of a college-age kid who decides to go back to school and finish his studies, the attempt resulting in utter chaos. Once again, Elfman's bright inventions match the tone of the broad antics, in a more muscular style than in *Pee-Wee's Big Adventure*, but with equally satisfying results. The often manic, eccentric cues assembled in this album are completely exhilarating.

Peggy Sue Got Married *♫♫*

1986, Varese-Sarabande Records; from the movie *Peggy Sue Got Married*, Tri-Star Pictures, 1986.

Album Notes: *Music*: John Barry; Orchestra conducted by John Barry; *Album Producer*: Paul R. Gurian; *Engineer*: Daniel Hersch.

DANNY ELFMAN

Composer Danny Elfman has scored over fifteen films, created numerous television themes, and until 1990 was writing songs and performing with the rock band Oingo Boingo. Elfman composed his first score in 1980 for his brother Richard's cult film *Forbidden Zone*. Actor Paul Reubens (a.k.a. Pee-wee Herman) saw the film and was interested in acquiring a non-traditional composer for his project *Pee-wee's Big Adventure*, which was released in 1985. This became Elfman's first full orchestral score.

Pee-wee's Big Adventure marked Elfman's first collaboration with director Tim Burton, with whom he has enjoyed a strong partnership. Their second film together was 1988's *Beetlejuice*, which is often cited as Elfman's best work. In 1989, Elfman and Burton collaborated on *Batman*, one of the most commercially successful movies of all time. The score earned the composer a Grammy nomination for best score and the prized statuette, for best instrumental, in 1990. The composer's next film with Burton, 1990's *Edward Scissorhands*, produced a score that deftly evoked Burton's fairy-tale imagery.

Besides his ventures with Burton, Elfman has composed for a wide range of directors and genres. Some of his other projects have been scoring the soundtracks for the 1988 box-office hit comedy *Midnight Run* and the 1990 film *Dick Tracy*. Elfman also composed the scores for two horror films, Clive Barker's *Nightbreed* and Sam Raimi's *Darkman*, which brought him back to the genre he loves the most. In addition to soundtracks, Elfman has composed several television themes for successful shows like Fox-TV's extremely popular animated "The Simpsons" and HBO's highly acclaimed "Tales from the Crypt." And it's been reported that the prolific Elfman is branching out again, this time into screenwriting and directing.

Selections: 1 Peggy Sue's Homecoming (3:28); 2 Charlie's Unplayed Guitar (2:24); 3 Did We Break Up? (2:39); 4 Charlie, I Had The Strangest Experience (5:48); 5 Peggy Sue Got Married (B. Holly)(1:50) *Buddy Holly*; 6 I Wonder Why (R. Weeks/A. Anderson)(2:22) *Dion & The Belmonts*; 7 He Don't Love You (C. Mayfield/C. Carter/J. Butler)(3:12) *Nicolas Cage, Pride & Joy*; 8 Teenager In Love (D. Pomus/M. Shuman)(2:37) *Dion & The Belmonts*; 9 You Belong To Me (C. Price/P.W. King/R. Stewart)(2:36) *The Marshall Crenshaw Band*.

Review: An unfortunately very short 26:56 minute album, that adds insult to injury by presenting four instrumental cues clocking in at a scant 14 minutes, *Peggy Sue Got Married* found composer John Barry in one of his expansive moods, and writing music that was beautifully stated and melodically attractive. The film, a time warp fantasy that enables a forlorn housewife to return to her teenage years and attempt to correct the mistakes she had made at the time, is nothing more than a charming little tale, but Barry's cues find rich, evocative accents ("Charlie's Unplayed Guitar") to make it seem much more important than it is. The pop selections that complement the album also play a role in setting the tone of the period (the 1950s) which Peggy Sue revisits, but it is sad to realize that even they are being treated in a rather shabby way in this album.

The Pelican Brief 🎵🎵🎵

1993, Giant Records; from the movie *The Pelican Brief*, Warner Bros., 1993.

Album Notes: *Music*: James Horner; *Orchestrations*: Don Davis, Tom Pasatieri; *Music Editor*: Jim Henrikson; Orchestra conducted by James Horner; *Featured Musicians*: Michael Fisher, Ralph Grierson, James Horner, Randy Kerber, Ian Underwood; *Album Producer*: James Horner; *Engineer*: Shawn Murphy.

Selections: 1 Main Title (2:33); 2 The Pelican Brief (3:50); 3 Researching The Brief (1:32); 4 Hotel Chase (4:00); 5 The Killing (3:16); 6 Bourbon Street (4:05); 7 Planting The Bomb (4:16); 8 Chasing Gray (3:15); 9 Darby's Emotions (3:37); 10 Darby's Theme (3:55); 11 Morgan's Final Testament (1:48); 12 Garage Chase (5:01); 13 Airport Goodbye (11:08).

Review: Opening with a truly haunting motif, James Horner's suspense score for this Julia Roberts-Denzel Washington thriller is perhaps the most satisfying music yet composed for a John Grisham big-screen potboiler. While Horner's dramatic underscore is fairly predictable, with big piano and orchestra crescendos comprising the tension in the music (along with a recurring percussion motif ripped off from John Williams's *JFK*), the most substantial and satisfying material comes from Horner's swelling romantic theme for Roberts' heroine, heard most clearly in an arrangement written expressly for the album. The composer finishes off the score with a lengthy, eloquent, horn-laden finale ("Airport Goodbye") that's in keeping with some of the more impassioned music to come from him in recent times (think *Apollo 13* and *Field of Dreams*). The end result is a thriller score that's clearly a step above most generic genre efforts, with enough lyrical passages to bring listeners back for subsequent listenings.

Andy Dursin

The People Under the Stairs 🎵

1991, Bay Cities Records; from the movie *The People Under the Stairs*, Universal Pictures, 1991.

Album Notes: *Music*: Graeme Revell, Don Peake; *Music Editor*: Dick Bernstein; Orchestra conducted by Tim Simonec; *Score Producers*: Graeme Revell, Don Peake; *Album Producer*: Nick Redman; *Engineer*: Daniel Hersch.

Selections: 1 Suite Part One (G. Revell)(13:41); 2 Suite Part Two (G. Revell)(15:14); 3 The People Under The Stairs Suite (D. Peake)(25:05).

Review: Considering two composers worked on this score, the album is surprisingly bland. Don Peake (who composed the majority of the "Knight Rider" TV scores) received main credit while Graeme Revell (an early effort) received additional music credit at the film's end. Equal time is given to each composer, though their music has been massed together into overlong suites. Revell utilizes an orchestra and vainly attempts to create several unusual, though unremarkable, sound clusters. On the other hand, Peake tries to establish a darker tone through the use of synthesizers, but ultimately, the entire presentation has a less than musical feel. It's almost a collection of sound effects that spends so much time on attempting to create minimalistic motifs that it never truly defines itself. A pretty forgettable experience that leaves you feeling as if 50 minutes of your life has just disappeared.

David Hirsch

The People vs. Larry Flynt 🎵🎵◗

1996, Angel Records; from the movie *The People vs. Larry Flynt*, Columbia Pictures, 1996.

Album Notes: *Music*: Thomas Newman; *Orchestrations*: Thomas Pasatieri; *Music Editor*: Bill Bernstein; Orchestra conducted by Thomas Newman; *Album Producers*: Thomas Newman, Bill Bernstein; *Engineers*: Dennis Sands, Tom Winslow.

Selections: 1 Eggsplat (:13); 2 Kentucky, 1952 (2:47); 3 Hello Walls (W. Nelson)(2:26) *Faron Young*; 4 Hang On Sloopy (B. Russell/W. Farrell)(3:55) *The McCoys*; 5 Tick Tick Tick (1:50); 6 Jail Bait (1:09); 7 Lewd And Shameful Manner (:55); 8 Cold Turkey Pervert (1:14); 9 Battle Hymn Of The Republic (trad.)(1:08) *Ruby Wilson, Kurt Clayton*; 10 My Soul Doth Magnifiy The Lord (O. Draper) (1:48) *The Collins Chapel Youth Choir, John Reddick, Jacquelyn Reddick*; 11 Shooting (Georgia, 1978)(2:42); 12 Porn Again (1:17); 13 Polonaise From "Rusalka" (L. Pesek)(:58) *The Czech Philharmonic Orchestra*; 14 Triple Dose (:57); 15 Surgery (North Carolina, 1983)(:32); 16 Fanfare And March From "Dalibor" (L. Pesek)(2:18) *The Czech Philharmonic Orchestra*; 17 The Half With The Brain (1:57); 18 Psycho Ward (:35); 19 Althea (1:17); 20 I'm Your Boogie Man (H. Casey/R. Finch)(4:05) *KC & The Sunshine Band*; 21 Twenty-One (:56); 22 Scumbag Like Me (1:51); 23 Deep Depravity (:41); 24 Falwell Verdict (Virginia, 1984)(:59); 25 Happy You And Merry Me (V. Lawnhurst/T. Seymour)(:42) *Mae Questil*; 26 Los Angeles, 1987 (1:20); 27 Stabat Mater Dolorosa (ending)(L. Pesek)(1:10) *The Czech Philharmonic Orchestra*; 28 Rosefall (:41); 29 Stabat Mater Dolorosa (beginning)(L. Pesek)(7:35) *The Czech Philharmonic Orchestra*; 30 Dream Weaver (G. Wright)(4:18) *Gary Wright*.

Review: Never known for creating anything that could be confused with an "average" film score, Thomas Newman mixes his odd musical compositions this go around with a variety of bluegrass tunes (the 12-second "Eggsplat" fades into the more standard "Kentucky, 1952" for example). However, most of the album is taken up with a variety of songs to depict the passage of 35 years from the film's start to finish. These songs include the McCoys' "Hang on Sloopy," "I'm You're Boogy Man" by K.C. and the Sunshine Band, and there are even several excerpts from classical compositions by Antonin Dvorak. All of these are interpolated throughout the album, which does well to capture the manic air of Flynt's life. If you find Newman's avant-garde style of film scoring more palatable in small doses (many of the cues are extremely short, too), then this presentation will work for you.

David Hirsch

A Perfect World ♪♪♪▷

1993, Reprise Records; from the movie *A Perfect World*, Warner Bros., 1993.

Album Notes: *Music*: Clint Eastwood, Lennie Niehaus; Orchestra conducted by Lennie Niehaus; *Album Executive Producers*:

Steven Baker, Gregg Geller, Michael Ostin, Lenny Waronker; *Engineer*: Lee Herschberg.

Selections: 1 Ida Red (B. Wills)(2:52) *Bob Wills And His Texas Playboys*; 2 Blue Blue Day (D. Gibson)(1:54) *Don Gibson*; 3 Guess Things Happen That Way (J. Clement)(1:50) *Johnny Cash*; 4 Sea Of Heartbreak (H. David/P. Hampton) (2:32) *Don Gibson*; 5 Don't Worry (M. Robbins)(3:10) *Marty Robbins*; 6 Abilene (J. Loudermilk/L. Brown/B. Gibson)(2:12) *George Hamilton IV*; 7 Please Help Me, I'm Falling (In Love With You)(D. Robertson/H. Blair)(2:22) *Hank Locklin*; 8 Dark Moon (N. Miller)(2:31) *Chris Isaak*; 9 Catch A Falling Star (P. Vance/L. Pockriss)(2:30) *Perry Como*; 10 The Little White Cloud That Cried (J. Ray)(2:20) *Chris Isaak*; 11 Night Life (W. Nelson/W. Breeland/P. Buskirk)(2:27) *Rusty Draper*; 12 Big Fran's Baby (C. Eastwood)(2:28) *Clint Eastwood*; 13 End Credits: Big Fran's Baby (C. Eastwood)/Butch's Theme/Phillip's Theme (L. Niehaus)(5:19).

Review: Country soundtracks can be tough. Too often they're watered down by producers afraid that the real thing won't win over the masses. But with favorites from Bob Wills & His Texas Playboys and Don Gibson, *A Perfect World* thumbs its nose at the idea of playing it safe. Johnny Cash, Marty Robbins and Hank Locklin are also represented here, while country-influenced rocker Chris Isaak provides a modern touch with his "Dark Moon."

Gary Graff

Pet Sematary ♪♪♪

1989, Varese-Sarabande Records; from the movie *Pet Sematary*, Paramount Pictures, 1989.

Album Notes: *Music*: Elliot Goldenthal; The Orchestra of St. Luke's, conducted by Steven Mercurio; *Synthesizer Programming*: Matthias Gohl; *Featured Soloists*: Elliot Goldenthal, Matthias Gohl (piano); *Featured Vocalists*: The Zarathustra Boys Chorus; *Album Producer*: Elliot Goldenthal; *Engineer*: Phil Bulla.

Selections: 1 The Pet Sematary (3:02) *The Zarathustra Boys Chorus*; 2 Dead Recollection (1:20); 3 Hope And Ordeal (1:23); 4 Adieu Gage (1:22); 5 Rachel Against Time (:51); 6 The Return Game (Jud And Gage) (3:43); 7 Moving Day Waltz (:31); 8 The Warning Tour (1:42); 9 Death Do Us Part (Rachel Hugs Louis) (:54); 10 Nine Lives Minus Seven (:15); 11 Up In Flames (Flashback) (1:39) *The Zarathustra Boys Chorus*; 12 Bitter Loss (Flashback) (1:51) *The Zarathustra Boys Chorus*; 13 Rachel's Dirty Secret (:23); 14 Return Game Attack (1:55); 15 Rachel's Blow Out (:22); 16 I Brought You Something Mommie (:35); 17 The Return Game II (Louis And Gage) (2:53); 18 Gentle Exhuming (1:03); 19 To The

Micmac Grounds (2:46); 20 Chorale (:30); 21 Kite And Truck (1:22); 22 Immolation (1:38) *The Zarathustra Boys Chorus*.

Review: Elliot Goldenthal, who has since graduated to bigger and better projects, made quite an impression with his score for this horror movie based on a novel by Stephen King. While some cues ("Dead Recollection") were evidently written as underscoring for some of the screen action and fail to attract on their own merits, most of the score is cleverly constructed and is quite evocative. Several selections feature the Zarathustra Boys Chorus, a group that lives up to its appealing name and limns the themes with its otherwordly vocal contribution. Pointing the way to Goldenthal's future in the film music world, "Moving Day Waltz," "Rachel's Dirty Secret," "Kite and Truck," while somewhat too short, reveal the composer's talent for attractive, catchy melodies.

The Phantom ♫♫♫

1996, Milan Records; from the movie *The Phantom*, Paramount Pictures, 1996.

Album Notes: *Music*: David Newman; *Orchestrations*: David Newman, Xandy Janko, Steven Scott Smalley, Randy Miller, Conrad Pope, Jeff Atmajian, Brad Dechter; *Music Editors*: Tom Villano, George A. Martin; The London Metropolitan Orchestra, conducted by David Newman; *Featured Artists*: Tony Hinnigan, Mike Taylor (Pan pipes); *Album Producer*: David Newman; *Engineer*: Robert Fernandez; *Assistant Engineers*: Toby Wood, Caroline Daniel, Don Mack.

Selections: 1 For Those Who Came In Late (1:21); 2 The Tomb (2:57); 3 The Phantom (5:40); 4 Anything's Possible (1:33); 5 The Rescue (4:33); 6 The Escape (5:45); 7 Must Be The Humidity (2:06); 8 Diana Must Leave/New York (1:00); 9 Ray Gets The Point (1:23); 10 The Museum (2:40); 11 Flying To The Island (6:09); 12 Quill Is Destroyed (2:28); 13 Escaping The Island (8:48).

Review: Composer David Newman weaves an effective blend of current scoring trends (marked by extensive, rapid-fire percussion and smooth romanticism) and the heyday of action serials with this nicely flowing work that will probably stand the test of time better than the middling movie for which it was written. Newman's five-note motif for "The Phantom" is ingeniously malleable, functioning both as an imposing fanfare, a crisp action motif and a warm melody for the benevolent qualities of Billy Zane's bemused hero. There's also a beautiful love theme for piano and orchestra, and both themes collude fluidly in the movingly ambivalent finale. The heroic material tends to saw away a bit too much, but overall this is an enjoyable, if not exactly indelible, adventure score.

Jeff Bond

Phenomenon ♫♫♫▷

1996, Reprise Records; from the movie *Phenomenon*, Touchstone Pictures, 1996.

Album Notes: *Music*: Thomas Newman; *Song Producers*: Babyface, Trevor Horn, Don Was, Taj Mahal, Peter Gabriel, David Lord, Gloria Jones, Pamela Sawyer, Justin Niebank, Tommy Couch, James Stroud, Wolf Stephenson, Audie Ashworth, J.J. Cale; *Engineers*: Brad Gilderman, Stephen Fitzmaurice, Rik Pekkonen, Robbie Robertson, Tom Winslow.

Selections: 1 Change The World (T. Sims)(3:57) *Eric Clapton*; 2 Dance With Life (The Brilliant Light)(B. Taupin/M. Page)(6:15) *Bryan Ferry*; 3 Crazy Love (V. Morrison)(4:31) *Aaron Neville, Robbie Robertson*; 4 Corinna (T. Mahal/J. Davis)(3:01) *Taj Mahal*; 5 Have A Little Faith In Me (J. Hinn)(4:25) *Jewel*; 6 I Have The Touch (P. Gabriel)(5:28) *Peter Gabriel*; 7 Piece Of Clay (P. Sawyer/G. Jones)(5:11) *Marvin Gaye*; 8 Para Donde Vas (J. Cabral/R. Hodges)(3:18) *The Iguanas*; 9 Misty Blue (B. Montgomery)(3:40) *Dorothy Moore*; 10 A Thing Going On (J.J. Cale)(2:38) *J.J. Cale*; 11 The Orchard (T. Newman)(2:33).

Review: "Change the World," the unlikely collaboration between rock icon Eric Clapton and r&b hitmaker Babyface, is a Grammy winning smash and a stick-to-your-ears tune even if you tried hard not to like it. The rest of the soundtrack is a bit more interesting, with Taj Mahal's "Corrina," Aaron Neville's gorgeous rendition of "Crazy Love" and refreshingly obscure selections from Bryan Ferry ("Dance With Life (The Brilliant Light)"), Peter Gabriel ("I Have the Touch") and Marvin Gaye ("Piece of Clay"). A sleeper that deserves thorough investigation.

Gary Graff

Philadelphia ♫♫♫♫▷

1993, Epic Soundtrax; from the movie *Philadelphia*, Tri-Star Pictures, 1993.

Album Notes: *Music*: Howard Shore; *Orchestrations*: Howard Shore; *Music Editor*: Suzana Peric; Orchestra conducted by Howard Shore; *Album Producer*: Howard Shore; *Engineer*: John Kurlander.

Selections: 1 Senior Associate Andrew Beckett (1:30); 2 Minor Catastrophe (3:14); 3 Birth (2:20); 4 Non temer amato bene (from "Idomeneo")(W.A. Mozart)(4:05) *Lucia Popp*; 5 I Have A Case (4:02); 6 The Missing Document (4:42); 7 The Essence Of Discrimination (4:58); 8 Going Home (3:30); 9 The Trial (3:27); 10 Ebben? Ne andro lontana (from "La Wally") (A. Catalani) (4:48) *Maria Callas*; 11 Trying To Survive (5:54); 12 La mamma morta (from "Andrea Chenier")(U. Giordano) (4:48) *Maria*

Callas); 13 An Excellent Lawyer (2:43); 14 Calculated Risks (2:31); 15 The Verdict (2:46); 16 I'm Ready (1:20).

Review: An extraordinary movie like *Philadelphia* needed a brilliant score, and Howard Shore rose to the challenge with great flair. His cues capture the intensity and emotion in the movie with thorough accuracy, enhancing the action, and at the same time setting aside enough flavor to provide attractive listening with this soundtrack album. Oftentimes understated and not overly dramatic, the music retains a great deal of expression, and proves extremely compelling. Operatic excerpts add a certain luster to the recording, though they are by no means essential to one's enjoyment of Shore's music.

The Philadelphia Experiment/Mother Lode
♪♪♪♪

1991, Prometheus Records/Belgium; from the movies *The Philadelphia Experiment,* New World Pictures, 1984; and *Mother Lode,* Agamemnon Films, 1982.

Album Notes: *Music:* Ken Wannberg; *The Philadelphia Experiment: Orchestrations:* Albert Woodbury; The National Philharmonic Orchestra, conducted by Ken Wannberg; *Engineer:* Eric Tomlinson; *Album Producer:* Alan E. Smith.

Selections: *THE PHILADELPHIA EXPERIMENT:* 1 Main Theme (3:06); 2 The Experiment Begins/Time Slip (5:49); 3 The "Eldridge" Remains (2:04); 4 David Confronts His Past (2:04); 5 The Vortex Sucks/David's Escape (4:38); 6 A Tender Moment (1:29); 7 The Doctor Reflects (2:29); 8 The Chase (1:32); 9 Fugitives In Love (2:31); 10 Storming The Compound (2:00); 11 David's Father (2:18); 12 David's Decision/Fate Of The Vortex (6:53); 13 David's Choice/End Title (5:32);

MOTHER LODE: 14 Magee's Theme (2:20); 15 The Plane Crash (2:10); 16 Underwater Search (4:00); 17 The Flight (5:06); 18 The Mine (3:05); 19 Magee's Cabin/The Trap (2:36); 20 The Lovers Argue (1:43); 21 Goodmanson's Gold (1:09); 22 The Price Of Greed (6:14); 23 Magee's Lament (:58); 24 Finale and End Title (3:16).

Review: *The Philadelphia Experiment* has always been one of my favorite films, especially because of its score by Ken Wannberg. Two Navy sailors, participating in a World War II experiment to make ships radar invisible, are hurled into the future (1984) where the same scientists are now attempting to recreate the experiment, which will threaten the survival of the entire world. A modest budgeted film, Wannberg gave the story an ambience of epic scope, while keeping it all personal by focusing on the main character, David (Michael Pare), through a simple 2-note motif. This is accomplished by keep-

ing the score mainly acoustical, only employing minimal electronic effects to represent the experiment, not a central element to the story, just its catalyst. Wannberg doesn't even overplay the romantic element. "Fugitives in Love" finds David, and his present day companion Allison, desperately longing for each other, but haunted by their uncertain future. That skepticism permeates the entire score, adding a tense desperation to the proceedings. The CD also features music from *Mother Lode,* a 1982 gold rush adventure starring Charlton Heston and Kim Basinger. Surprisingly, the best cue in that film, the wistfully romantic "The Flight," was cut from the final version! When I interviewed Ken Wannberg for *Soundtrack!* magazine several years ago, I was surprised to discover that he never wanted to actively pursue a career in film scoring. He has been extremely content juggling his work as Hollywood's preeminent music editor, occasionally taking a compositional assignment that interested him. How many other films could have benefited from his talent and instincts?

David Hirsch

The Piano ♪♪⌐

1993, Virgin Records; from the movie *The Piano,* CIBY 2000, 1993.

Album Notes: *Music:* Michael Nyman; *Orchestrations:* Michael Nyman; Members of the Philharmonic Orchestra of Munich, conducted by Michael Nyman; *Featured Musicians:* John Harle, David Roach (soprano/alto sax), Andrew Findon (tenor/baritone sax, flute), Michael Nyman (piano); *Album Producer:* Michael Nyman; *Engineers:* Michael J. Dutton, Malcolm Luker.

Selections: 1 To The Edge Of The Earth (4:06); 2 Big My Secret (2:51); 3 A Wild And Distant Shore (5:50); 4 The Heart Asks Pleasure First (1:33); 5 Here To There (1:02); 6 The Promise (4:14); 7 A Bed Of Ferns (:46); 8 The Fling (1:28); 9 The Scent Of Love (4:16); 10 Deep Into The Forest (2:58); 11 The Mood That Passes Through You (1:13); 12 Lost And Found (2:24); 13 The Embrace (2:36); 14 Little Impulse (2:11); 15 The Sacrifice (2:46); 16 I Clipped Your Wing (4:34); 17 The Wounded (2:26); 18 All Imperfect Things (4:03); 19 Dreams Of A Journey (5:30).

Review: Michael Nyman rose to fame with his New Age-style score for the Jane Campion drama starring Holly Hunter, Sam Neill and Harvey Keitel. As an album, though, one can hear the deficiencies in Nyman's score, which basically shifts between delicate piano solos (think Yanni or John Tesh) and less assured, almost static orchestral writing, making you want to see the sumptuous visuals in Campion's movie to understand just how the score works in the film. Nyman's orchestral music, on the other hand, just doesn't offer enough substance or diversity to work on its own terms, though fervent admirers of the picture will be quick to point out how memorable some of the piano themes are in relation to much of today's typical film music. They may have a point, though that still doesn't mean that the album is an essential one to have in your library.

Andy Dursin

Picnic 🎵🎵🎵▸

1988, MCA Records; from the movie *Picnic*, Columbia Pictures, 1958.

Album Notes: *Music*: George Duning; The Columbia Pictures Orchestra, conducted by Morris Stoloff.

Selections: 1 Love Theme (2:34); 2 Hal's Theme (1:54); 3 The Owens Family (4:11); 4 Flo And Madge (4:25); 5 Hal's Boots (2:13); 6 Moonglow (W. Hudson/E. De Lange/I. Mills) And Love Theme (G. Duning)(3:45); 7 It's A Blue World (B. Wright/C. Forrest)/Torn Shirt, part 1 (4:58); 8 Torn Shirt, part 2/Hal's Turmoil (6:32); 9 Rosemary Pleads/Rosemary Alone (2:10); 10 Culmination/Hal's Escape (5:52); 11 That Owens Girl/Millie (1:31); 12 You Love Me/Madge Decides (5:40).

Review: Duning's score is essentially a series of cues that are serviceable and work particularly well within the dramatic context of the film. As a listening experience, however, the sometimes atonal music (faithful to the adventurous nature of film music in the mid- to late-1950s), doesn't always make a favorable impression, and is not always easy to listen to. The soundtrack, however, features an extraordinary classic in "Moonglow and Love Theme," which illustrates one of the crucial scenes in the film and which remains the highlight of this album.

Picture Bride 🎵🎵🎵🎵▸

1995, Virgin Movie Music; from the movie *Picture Bride*, Miramax Films, 1995.

Album Notes: *Music*: Mark Adler; *Orchestrations*: Mark Adler; Orchestra conducted by Mark Adler; *Music Editor*: Joanie Diener; *Featured Musicians*: Jim Walker (bamboo flutes), Peter Maunu (guitars); *Album Producer*: Mark Adler; *Engineers*: Dennis Sands; *Assistant Engineer*: Tom Hardisty.

Selections: 1 Haiku (1:24); 2 Picture Bride (1:51); 3 Carriage Ride (1:18); 4 A New Home (1:20); 5 Field Work (1:58); 6 The Bath (1:39); 7 Older Than My Father (:43); 8 Kana And Riyo (2:15); 9 Riyo's Resolve (1:59); 10 Miss Peiper (2:05); 11 Kana And The Wind (:47); 12 Riyo's Disappointment (:49); 13 Yayoi's Farewell (1:30) *Tamlyn Tomita*; 14 Matsuji's Valentino (3:42); 15 The Fire (4:22); 16 Banana Leaves (:54); 17 Cane Fields (1:15); 18 Riyo Runs (1:39); 19 Riyo's Vision And Return (2:46);

20 Riyo And Matsuji (1:42); 21 Ceremony (2:05); 22 Only The Wind (:37).

Review: The story of a 16-year-old Japanese girl, Riyo, who leaves behind a troubled past and ventures to Hawaii as a picture bride in 1918, *Picture Bride* elicited a strikingly beautiful score from Mark Adler, who succeeded in conveying the hardships, sorrow and unexpected joys in the lives of Japanese laborers caught in a daily struggle for survival, respect and their eventual independence. With the bamboo flutes creating haunting images that often transcend the ethnicity in the action, Adler wrote a score that teems with gorgeous melodies, as precious and lovely as a porcelain doll, soothing and striking in their calm beauty. The unassuming "Miss Peiper" is a case in point, but almost everyone of the 22 selections in this CD is an illuminating joy, one's enduring pleasure throughout being only marred by the briefness of some of the tracks.

Pink Cadillac 🎵🎵🎵🎵

1988, Warner Bros.; from the movie *Pink Cadillac*, Warner Bros., 1988.

Album Notes: *Song Producers*: Steve Gibson, Hank Williams, Barry Beckett, Jim Ed Norman, Robby Adcock, Kyle Lehning, Southern Pacific, Josh Leo, Larry Michael, Billy Hill, Bryan Adams, Scott Ferguson, Robben Ford; *Album Producer*: Jim Ed Norman; *Engineer*: Denny Purcell.

Selections: 1 Never Givin' Up On Love (M. Smotherman)(3:48) *Michael Martin Murphy*; 2 There's A Tear In My Beer (H. Williams)(2:48) *Hank Williams Jr., Hank Williams Sr.*; 3 If It Wasn't For The Heartache (C. Waters/K. Brooks)(2:38) *Jill Hollier*; 4 Card Carryin' Fool (B. Hill/T. Bays) (2:24) *Randy Travis*; 5 Any Way The Wind Blows (J. McFee/A. Pessis)(3:36) *Southern Pacific*; 6 Reno Bound (J. McFee/A. Pessis)(3:07) *Southern Pacific*; 7 Beneath The Texas Moon (J.C. Crowley/J.W. Routh)(3:45) *J.C. Crowley*; 8 Rollin' Dice (D. Robbins/J. Scott Sherrill/B. DiPiero)(3:24) *Billy Hill*; 9 Drive All Night (B. Adams)(3:00) *Dion*; 10 Born Under A Bad Sign (B.T. Jones/W. Bell)(3:41) *Robben Ford*.

Review: A solid country-flavored soundtrack compilation, for a film starring Clint Eastwood as a bounty hunter, chasing bill dodgers in his pink Cadillac, with Bernadette Peters, wife of one of his preys, as his travelling companion. Some excellent frontliners are on board, including Michael Martin Murphey, Randy Travis, J.C. Crowley, Billy Hill, and Dion, whose rockin' "Drive All Night" is a joy. Hank Williams, Jr. even duets with his father on "There's a Tear in My Beer," in another display of technical fancy.

The Pink Panther ♪♪♪♪

1989, RCA Records; from the film *The Pink Panther*, United Artists, 1963.

Album Notes: *Music:* Henry Mancini; Orchestra conducted by Henry Mancini; *Album Producer:* Joe Reisman; *Engineer:* Jim Malloy; *CD Producer:* Chick Crumpacker; *Engineer:* Dick Baxter.

Selections: 1 The Pink Panther Theme (2:37); 2 It Had Better Be Tonight (1:46); 3 Royal Blue (3:11); 4 Champagne And Quail (2:45); 5 The Village Inn (2:36); 6 The Tiber Twist (2:50); 7 It Had Better Be Tonight (H. Mancini/J. Mercer)(1:57); 8 Cortina (1:55); 9 The Lonely Princess (2:28); 10 Something For Sellers (2:49); 11 Piano And Strings (2:38); 12 Shades Of Sennett (1:26).

Review: Even if he only had written one score, for this romp in which, for the first time, bumbling Inspector Jacques Clouseau of the French Surete gained full-fledged status as a film celebrity, Henry Mancini would rightfully belong in the pantheon of great screen composers. Though he was frequently dismissed as too lightweight, compared to some of his most prestigious peers, Mancini was a master at defining the parameters of comedy music and exploiting the themes for all their delicious worth. Brightly introduced by the celebrated theme, the score evidences all the positive assets usually found in Mancini's scores — tunes with a catchy lilt, themes with a pop sensibility that immediately set a scene or situation, memorable musical moments that invite repeated listening and never overstay their welcome. All of these and more can be found here in a score that brims with delightful little quirks, amusing tidbits that prove charming, and at least one other great pop tune in "It Had Better Be Tonight."

See also: Revenge of the Pink Panther, Son of the Pink Panther and The Trail of the Pink Panther

Pirates ♪♪♪♭

1986, Varese-Sarabande Records; from the movie *Pirates*, Cannon Films, 1986.

Album Notes: *Music:* Philippe Sarde; The Orchestre de Paris, conducted by Bill Byers; *Album Producers:* Philippe Sarde, Bill Byers; *Engineer:* William Flageollet.

Selections: 1 Pirates! (2:49); 2 Dead Man's Nag (3:34); 3 Pirates Aboard! (3:26); 4 Pirates Sneak Into Maracaibo (1:20); 5 Captain Red — Galleon Master (3:51); 6 Death Of A Captain (2:25); 7 Captain Red Gains The Throne While The Frog Loses Dolores (6:06); 8 Two Hungry Pirates, Adrift (3:16); 9 Spanish Recapture The Neptune (2:19); 10 Captain Red's Jailbreak (2:34); 11 Red, The Frog, And The Throne/Boomako And The Snake (2:19); 12 Mutiny (3:43); 13 Pirates Pursue The Neptune (2:07); 14 Captain Red, The Frog, And The Shark (1:08); 15 Dolores (Love Theme)(6:30); 16 Setting Sail For New Adventures (2:36); 17 Don Alfonso Escapes (4:30); 18 Rescued-Yet-Captured (4:47).

Review: This opulent score is actually much better than the film directed by Roman Polanski, which could not be saved by all of Walter Matthau's snarling and posturing as a dangerous high sea shark in the days when piracy was at its height. Sarde's score, magnificently played by the venerable Orchestre de Paris, cannot compare, of course, with Korngold's *The Sea Hawk*, probably the best of its kind, but on its own terms, it exudes an appeal in which romance and bravura happily mix to create a most colorful sonic imagery.

Planes, Trains and Automobiles ♪♪♪♭

1987, MCA Records; from the movie *Planes, Trains and Automobiles*, Paramount Pictures, 1987.

Album Notes: *Song Producers:* Stephen Hague, Mark Ferda, Steve Brown, Ivan Ivan, Hugh Padgham, Nick Laird-Clowes, Steve Earle, Tony Brown, Dave Edmunds, Jimmy Bowen, Larry Least, Paul Barrett; *Album Producers:* John Hughes, Tarquin Gotch; *Engineer:* Greg Fulginiti.

Selections: 1 I Can Take Anything (Love Theme)(3:46) *E.T.A., Steve Martin, John Candy*; 2 Ba-Na-Na-Bam-Boo (2:58) *Westworld*; 3 I'll Show You Something Special (3:28) *Balaam & The Angel*; 4 Modigliani (Lost In Your Eyes)(3:53) *Book Of Love*; 5 Power To Believe (5:13) *The Dream Academy*; 6 Six Days On The Road (3:06) *Steve Earle & The Dukes*; 7 Gonna Move (3:32) *Dave Edmunds*; 8 Back In Baby's Arms (2:02) *Emmylou Harris*; 9 Red River Rock (3:26) *Silicon Teens*; 10 Wheels (3:08) *Stars Of Heaven*.

Review: Reflecting the contrasting aspects of this film, about a businessman trying to go home for the Thanksgiving holidays, and forced to travel across the country with a salesman who has wrecked his rental car and destroyed his bags, this soundtrack album is divided into two parts, a "town" compilation and a "country" one. In the first, rockers Westworld and Balaam and the Angel try to keep up with Book of Love and The Dream Academy, whose contributions are engaging. On the country side, there is no mistaking the immediate appeal of Dave Edmunds and Emmylou Harris, though Silicon Teens and Stars of Heaven trail behind. "I Can Take Anything," the so-called "Love Theme" from the film, features Steve Martin and John Candy, who star in it.

Planet of the Apes ♫♫♫♫

1992, Intrada Records; from the movie *Planet of the Apes*, 20th Century-Fox, 1968.

Album Notes: *Music*: Jerry Goldsmith; *Orchestrations*: Arthur Morton; Orchestra conducted by Jerry Goldsmith; *Album Producer*: Jerry Goldsmith; *Engineer*: Vinnie Vernon.

Selections: 1 Main Title (2:13); 2 The Revelation (1:34); 3 The Clothes Snatchers (2:38); 4 The Hunt (5:10); 5 New Identity (2:04); 6 The Forbidden Zone (3:06); 7 The Search (4:56); 8 The Cave (1:19); 9 A Bid For Freedom (1:21); 10 A New Mate (1:05); 11 No Escape (5:17).

Review: Goldsmith's classic landmark science fiction score is a masterpiece of avant garde modernism that still hasn't been properly presented on CD, although this Intrada release offers improved sound and remedies at least one inexcusable omission of the original Project 3 album by adding the stupendous action cue "The Hunt," which to this day probably stands as the finest marriage of film imagery and music the composer ever produced. It's four minutes of relentless, Stravinskyesque orchestral assault dominated by the unforgettable use of a ram's horn to herald the film's first shot of intelligent apes on horseback. The rest of the score is primarily atmospheric, creating a strange alien world with echoed percussion effects, the unearthly moan of a bass slide whistle and a tide-like, metallic rush of air. The album's sequencing is non-chronological, climaxing with the brilliant staccato piano playing of "No Escape." This is as far from current film scoring sensibilities as you're likely to get, but no self-respecting fan of the medium should be without it.

Jeff Bond

The Player ♫♫♫♫

1992, Varese-Sarabande; from the movie *The Player*, New Line Cinema, 1992.

Album Notes: *Music*: Thomas Newman; *Orchestrations*: Thomas Pasatieri; *Music Editor*: Bill Bernstein; Orchestra conducted by Thomas Newman; *Featured Musicians*: Thomas Newman (piano, electronics), Rick Cox (also sax, prepared guitar), George Budd (sample electronics), Jeff Elmassian (winds), Michael Fisher (percussion, Harvey Mason (drums), Ralph Grierson (piano, electronics), Buell Neidlinger (upright bass); *Album Producers*: Thomas Newman, John Vigran, Bill Bernstein; *Engineer*: John Vigran.

Selections: 1 Funeral Shark (1:02); 2 St. James (1:02); 3 Six Inches Of Dirty Water (1:41); 4 Main Title (1:45); 5 Rose's Cafe (A. Nicholls) (1:39) *Akio Ushikubo*; 6 Icy Theme (2:30); 7 That's All He Wrote (2:48); 8 Schechter Bros. (1:23); 9 Sex (3:16); 10 Desert Drive (1:15); 11 Tema para Jobim (G. Mulligan/J. Nascimento) (1:23) *Joyce and Milton Nascimento*; 12 The Graduate Pt. 2

(2:20); 13 Lineup (1:16); 14 Good Dog's Water (2:39); 15 Detective DeLongpre (1:11); 16 Silent Night (trad.) (:28) *Jack Lemmon*; 17 Opening 3 (1:05); 18 Griffin's Plan/ Let's Begin Again (R. Altman/R. Ecton) (:51) *Brian Tochi*; 19 The Player (3:06).

Review: It's rare today that a composer gets a chance to define the sound of a genre. Thomas Newman did it on Robert Altman's *The Player*, musically codifying the quirky-Hollywood-insider-murder-mystery (note the similarities with the later *Get Shorty*, scored by John Lurie). Tim Robbins stars as a cold-hearted, smug studio executive stalked by a disgruntled writer. He kills the wrong writer, then falls for the murdered wrong writer's mysterious artist girlfriend (Greta Scacchi), until finally Altman brings it together in a sarcastic, anti-twist ending. Newman's score features modal piano loops and unusually bright themes set on a background of minimalist repetition and simplicity — as well as countless, strange samples, from chainsaws to bass harmonics to improvised saxophones.

On album the score pushes its fragmented, strange-upon-noir approach even further by seguing in and out of several disparate cocktail-lounge source cues, to give a sense of the different, superficial worlds within the picture. It also includes one of the most original approaches to a sex scene — all percussion. Newman's music is as distinct as a rich cup of coffee, set in a form interwoven with the film (see it!) — a minor masterpiece of irony.

Lukas Kendall

Poetic Justice ♫♫

1993, Epic Soundtrax; from the movie *Poetic Justice*, Columbia Pictures, 1993.

Album Notes: *Song Producers*: Dallas Austin, Tim & Bob, Warren G., Babyface, L.A. Reid, Daryl Simmons, Tim Thomas & Ted Bishop, Raphael Wiggins & Derek Allen, Pete Phillips, Darryl Swann, Naughty By Nature, Kevin Dean, Dr. Dre, 2Pac Shakur & Warren Griffin III, Sly Dunbar & Robbie Shakespeare, Nice & Smooth, Henry Crosby, Stanley Clarke; *Soundtrack Executive Producer*: John Singleton; *Engineer*: Carlton Batts.

Selections: 1 Get It Up (Prince) (4:26) *TLC*; 2 Indo Smoke (R. Trawick/W. Griffin III) (5:24) *Mista Grimm*; 3 Well Alright (Babyface) (4:00) *Babyface*; 4 Camm Me A Mack (T. Thomas/T. Bishop/U. Raymond) (4:07) *Usher Raymond*; 5 Waiting For You (D. Allen) (5:15) *Tony! Toni! Tone!*; 6 One In A Million (C. Penn/P. Phillips/J. McDuff) (4:05) *Pete Rock, C.L. Smooth*; 7 Nite And Day (D. Swann/P. LaSean Williams/C. Walker) (5:04) *Cultural Revolution*; 8 Poor Mann's Poetry (A. Chriss/V. Brown/K. Gist) (3:00) *Naughty By Nature*; 9 I've Been Waiting (T. Robinson/T. Geter/K. Dean) (4:21) *Terri & Monica*; 10 Niggas Don't

Give A Fuck (C. Broadus/D. Arnaud/R. Brown)(4:41) *Dogg Pound*; 11 Definition Of A Thug Nigga (T. Shakur/W. Griffin III)(4:11) *2Pac*; 12 I Wanna Be Your Man (J. Tayler/E. Bonner/S. Dunbar/R. Shakespeare/L. Willis)(3:55) *Chaka Demus*, *Pliers*; 13 Cash In My Hands (D. Barnes/G. Mays)(3:53) *Nice & Smooth*; 14 Never Dreamed You'd Leave In Summer (S. Wonder/S. Wright)(2:55) *Stevie Wonder*; 15 Justice's Groove (S. Clarke)(4:35) *Stanley Clarke.*

Review: There is something for everyone in this compilation album, it seems, some good, and some bad. Dealing with the negatives first, only those with a strong tolerance for rap and its dry expressions will enjoy the selections by Pete Rock & C.L. Smooth, Nice & Smooth, Dogg Pound, and 2Pac, among others, whose contributions here echo the intense urban street sounds in this film set in South Central, which involves a young black woman (Janet Jackson), growing up with nothing but disappointments, but finding solace in the poetry she writes, and the hardworking young man (Tupac Shakur), a struggling musician, who enters her life. On the positive side, however, are "listenable" songs by Stevie Wonder, Babyface, Tony! Toni! Tone!, and Terri & Monica, which make a different kind of statement, and prove much more endearing. One track from Stanley Clarke's instrumental score, makes one wish more of his music had been included.

Point of No Return ♪♭

1993, Milan Records; from the movie *Point of No Return*, Warner Bros., 1993.

Album Notes: *Music:* Hans Zimmer, Nick Glennie-Smith; *Arrangements:* Hans Zimmer; *Featured Musician:* Bob Daspit (guitar); *Album Producers:* Hans Zimmer, Jay Rifkin; *Engineer:* Jay Rifkin.

Selections: 1 Hate (7:26); 2 Happy Birthday, Maggie (5:36); 3 Wedding Bells (8:06); 4 Hells Kitchen (5:08); 5 Here Comes The Sun (G. Harrison)(3:35) *Nina Simone*; 6 I Want A Little Sugar In My Bowl (N. Simone)(2:31) *Nina Simone*; 7 Feeling Good (L. Bricusse/A. Newley)(2:53) *Nina Simone*; 8 Wild Is The Wind (D. Tiomkin/N. Washington)(6:57) *Nina Simone*; 9 Black Is The Color Of My True Love's Hair (trad.)(3:26) *Nina Simone.*

Review: An almost interminable bombardment of overdone musical tracks composed by Hans Zimmer, *Point of No Return* is one of those way over-the-top scores that hits you over the head with its melodramatic indulgences. Here, Zimmer offers us his usual bag of tricks — gigantic-sounding synths, blaring orchestra, sampled electronic sounds — and it's simply too much to take, being obnoxious, excessive, and grating all at the same time. So much so, in fact, that Zimmer's music tends to overwhelm the action in

John Badham's tedious remake of *La Femme Nikita*, with Bridget Fonda in the lead role. Milan's album also includes a number of Nina Simone songs, prominently featured in the movie and a lot easier to take than any second of Zimmer's score.

Andy Dursin

Poltergeist

Poltergeist ♪♪♪♪♪

1997, Rhino Records; from the movie *Poltergeist*, M-G-M, 1982.

Album Notes: *Music:* Jerry Goldsmith; *Orchestrations:* Arthur Morton; Orchestra conducted by Jerry Goldsmith; *Album Producer:* Jerry Goldsmith; *CD Producer:* Nick Redman; *Engineer:* Dan Hersch.

Selections: 1 The Star Spangled Banner (F. Scott Key) (1:30); 2 The Calling/ The Neighborhood (Main Title) (4:07); 3 The Tree (outtake) (2:26); 4 The Clown/ They're Here/Broken Glass (outtake)/The Hole (outtake)/TV People (5:12); 5 Twisted Abduction (6:56); 6 Contacting The Other Side (5:10); 7 The Light (2:05); 8 Night Visitor/No Complaints (9:07); 9 It Knows What Scares You (7:37); 10 Rebirth (8:23); 11 Night Of The Beast (3:51); 12 Escape From Suburbia (7:10); 13 Carol Anne's Theme (End Title) (4:19).

Review: Jerry Goldsmith's superlative ghost story music is captured in its entirety in this beautifully-produced CD which features the complete score sequenced in chronological order, from the opening source music of "The Star-Spangled Banner" to the nightmarish orchestral violence of the "Escape from Suburbia" finale. The original LP featured only the highlights of the score, but this release put together by film music archeologist Nick Redman restores some of Goldsmith's most fascinating compositions, including the malevolent woodwind motif for a frightening toy clown and the disturbing, rumbling underscoring that musically characterizes the unseen concepts of "The Other Side" and "The Beast," which Goldsmith almost single-handedly brings to life in the film. The blend of rhapsodic impressionism, elaborate dissonance, and spine-tingling beauty makes this one of Goldsmith's most varied and spectacular works, a marvel of complexity and effectiveness.

Jeff Bond

Poltergeist 2 ♪♪♪♭

1993, Intrada Records; from the movie *Poltergeist 2: The Other Side*, M-G-M, 1986.

Album Notes: *Music:* Jerry Goldsmith; Orchestra conducted by Jerry Goldsmith; *Album Producer:* Jerry Goldsmith.

Selections: 1 The Power (7:48); 2 The Gift (1:58); 3 Where Are You? (2:10); 4 Late Call (3:28); 5 They're Back (3:39); 6 The Butterflies (:51); 7 Dental Problems (2:19); 8 The Plan (3:17); 9 The Smoke (4:45); 10 The Worm/Vomit Creature (8:07); 11 Back To Cuesta Verde (3:16); 12 Reaching Out (8:31); 13 Carol Anne's Theme (3:05).

Review: Goldsmith's follow-up to his Oscar-nominated score, *Poltergeist 2* can't measure up to the original, although the composer's approach is laudably innovative, discarding all but a few motifs and themes from his original score and composing an entirely new work that plays off the film's opposing forces of Native American mysticism (illustrated in an unusual title theme based on an electronic melody representing a Native American Shaman and a Coplandesque horn motif for the man's supernatural disciplines) and mis-applied Christian values (depicted by a hauntingly distorted hymnal tune). Where the original score is almost completely acoustic, *Poltergeist 2* revels in its sizzling electronic effects which sometimes threaten to overwhelm the orchestra. There are also abundant choral effects, from the moaning cries of the damned that accompany the twisted hymn to the guttural, devilish chants that greet the apparitions that return to torment the child Carol Anne.

Jeff Bond

Portrait of a Lady 🦴🦴🦴🦴ᵛ

1996, London Records; from the movie *Portrait of a Lady*, Propaganda Films, 1996.

Album Notes: *Music*: Wojciech Kilar; *Orchestrations*: Wojciech Kilar; Orchestra conducted by Stepan Konicek, Nic Raine; *Featured Soloists*: Jean-Yves Thibaudet (piano), The Brindisi Quartet; *Album Producer*: Mike Woolcock, Brian Lock; *Engineers*: John Timperley, Jonathan Stokes, Graham Meek; *Assistant Engineers*: Martin Astle, Michael Hradisky, Jan Holzner.

Selections: 1 Prologue: My Life Before Me (4:08); 2 The Portrait Of A Lady (5:49); 3 Flowers Of Firenze (4:00); 4 Twilight Cellos (3:05); 5 A Certain Light (6:48); 6 Cypresses (2:06); 7 Impromptu in G Flat (F. Schubert)(6:47) *Jean-Yves Thibaudet*; 8 Impromptu in A Flat (F. Schubert) (7:05)*Jean-Yves Thibaudet*; 9 String Quartet in D minor "Death And The Maiden" (F. Schubert)(8:22) *Brindisi Quartet*; 10 Epilogue: The Portait Of A Lady (5:12); 11 Phantasms Of Love (4:00); 12 The Kiss (2:05); 13 Love Remains (3:06); 14 End Credits (5:05).

Review: This incredibly beautiful score, quietly mesmerizing and strikingly evocative, paints a vivid picture that combines colorful musical strokes with concentrated artistry. The score,

written for Jane Campion's much-anticipated follow-up to her Academy Award-winning *The Piano*, summons the atmosphere that permeates the film, a rousing period melodrama, based on Henry James' 1881 novel set in England and Italy, about a headstrong young American woman who challenges the confines of her would-be sheltered destiny. Echoing the moods in the film, in which moments of darkness and light, wisdom and innocence are deftly contrasted, Wojciech Kilar's music is laid out in specific romantic terms that are expressive and extremely attractive. Two selections by Franz Schubert add the right period touch to the music, even though Kilar's score is strong enough to evoke the late 1800s without them.

The Postman/Il Postino
🦴🦴🦴🦴ᵛ

1994, Hollywood Records; from the movie *The Postman (Il postino)*, Miramax Pictures, 1994.

Album Notes: *Music*: Luis Bacalov; *Orchestrations*: Luis Bacalov; Orchestra Sinfonietta di Roma, conducted by Luis Bacalov; *Featured Musicians*: Luis Bacalov (piano), Hector Ulises Passarella (bandoneon), Riccardo Pellegrino (violin, mandolin); *Poems*: Pablo Neruda; *Album Producer*: Jeffrey Kimball; *Engineer*: Joseph Magee.

Selections: *POETRY & MUSIC SUITE:* 1 Theme (1:53); 2 Morning (Love Sonnet XXVII)(:53) *Sting*; 3 Poetry (1:40) *Miranda Richardson*; 4 Leaning Into The Afternoons (1:36) *Wesley Snipes*; 5 Poor Fellows (1:29) *Julia Roberts*; 6 Ode To The Sea (1:36) *Ralph Fiennes*; 7 Fable Of The Mermaid And The Drunk (2:09) *Ethan Hawke*; 8 Ode To A Beautiful Nude (2:30) *Rufus Sewell*; 9 I Like For You To Be Still (1:33) *Glenn Close*; 10 Walking Around (3:08) *Samuel L. Jackson*; 11 Tonight I Can Write (2:45) *Andy Garcia*; 12 Adonic Angela (1:21) *Willem Dafoe*; 13 If You Forget Me (2:01) *Madonna*; 14 Integrations (1:33) *Vincent Perez*; 15 And Now You're Mine (Love Sonnet LXXXI)(3:05) *Andy Garcia, Julia Roberts*;

MUSIC: 16 The Postman (Titles) (2:40); 17 Bicycle (2:25); 18 Madreselva (3:13) *Carlos Gardel*; 19 The Postman Lullaby (:49); 20 Beatrice (4:04); 21 Metaphors (2:02); 22 Loved By Women (3:27); 23 The Postman (Trio version)(2:33); 24 Sounds Of The Island (2:28); 25 The Postman's Dreams (3:19); 26 Pablito (:41); 27 Milonga Del Poeta (1:13); 28 Madreselva (instrumental)(2:17); 29 The Postman Poet (3:20); 30 The Postman (harpsichord and string version)(:44); 31 The Postman (guitar and bandoneon version)(3:09).

Review: Evidencing a lyrical sensitivity seldom found in contemporary scores, Luis Bacalov's Academy Award-winning score for *Il postino* is agreeably infectious and flavorful, and draws much of its appeal from the inclusion of some unusual, yet typically expected instruments like the bandoneon and mandolins. The music displays a definite Mediterranean attitude that matches the moods in this memorable little tale about a postman on an isolated island who finds new reasons to like his job when he befriends the exiled poet Pablo Neruda, who introduces him to the wonderfully imaginative world of poesy. The various cues composed by Bacalov subtly underline the moods and situations in the film, with catchy motifs that are endearing and attractively drawn. Dressing up the music and giving it a slightly different spin, an occasional jazzy tune ("Loved by Women") and a pop recording ("Madreselva," performed by the great tango performer Carlos Gardel) provide a pleasant change of pace. The main theme, reprised on several occasions in different musical formats, proves noticeably catchy.

Because of its success, and Oscar win no doubt, the American release of this soundtrack also features several poems by Neruda, read by a wide—and odd—assortment of well-known performers, including Sting, Wesley Snipes, Julia Roberts, Ralph Fiennes, Glenn Close, Willem Dafoe and Madonna. The first time around, it is interesting to hear these texts, but unless one feels otherwise inclined, repeated playing tends to become somewhat tiresome. The Italian soundtrack album, on the CAM label, only contains the score.

Powder *✍✍*

1995, Hollywood Records; from the movie *Powder*, Hollywood Pictures, 1995.

Album Notes: *Music*: Jerry Goldsmith; *Orchestrations*: Alexander Courage; *Music Editor*: Ken Hall; The National Philharmonic Orchestra, conducted by Jerry Goldsmith; *Album Producer*: Jerry Goldsmith; *Engineer*: Bruce Botnick.

Selections: 1 Theme From Powder (4:32); 2 Spoon Trick And The Trestle (2:17); 3 Nightmare In The Forest (5:10); 4 First Kiss (2:25); 5 Steven And The Snow (8:26); 6 Freakshow (4:42); 7 Wanna See A Trick? (4:01); 8 Everywhere (3:54).

Review: The Disney Studio had a firestorm of controversy on its hands when *Powder* writer-director Victor Salva's past history of child molestation filtered into the news media, resulting in an outcry from enraged protesters about how the company could let such an individual make a movie. Well, he did, and regardless of his personal background, *Powder* is an unwatchable mess, a syrupy concoction about individuality and "being true to yourself" that makes for unbearable, heavy-handed viewing—a fact further accentuated by a thoroughly pedes-

trian, equally by-the-numbers score from Jerry Goldsmith that's all too indicative of the composer's lifeless film scores of the '90s. The music is routine, slow, and offers no surprises, with a main title theme meant to illicit emotion that instead reminds you of other, more memorable works written by both other composers and Goldsmith himself, who has done a far better job elsewhere.

Andy Dursin

Predator 2 *✍✍✍✍*

1990, Varese-Sarabande; from the movie *Predator 2*, 20th Century-Fox, 1990.

Album Notes: *Music*: Alan Silvestri; *Orchestrations*: James B. Campbell; *Music Editor*: Kenneth Karman; The Skywalker Symphony Orchestra conducted by Alan Silvestri; *Album Producer*: Alan Silvestri; *Engineer*: Dennis Sands; *Assistant Engineers*: M.T. Silvia, Tony Eckert.

Selections: 1 Main Title (2:42); 2 First Carnage (2:35); 3 Tunnel Chase (5:10); 4 Truly Dead (4:58); 5 Danny Gets It (3:19); 6 Rest In Pieces (1:33); 7 El Scorpio (2:41); 8 This Is History (6:26); 9 Swinging Rude Boys (2:38); 10 Dem Bones (4:27); 11 End Title (8:45).

Review: From the jungles of South America to the jungles of 21st century East L.A., Alan Silvestri powers up the themes from his earlier score and energizes them with his interpretation of a futuristic urban beat. The roller coaster nature of Silvestri's orchestrations are done justice here by the wide sonic range of digital technology. Besides the mesmerizing percussion, he also incorporates a variety of unusual sounds, including voices in "Rest in Pieces." Most notable is the nine-minute "End Title," an exhilarating update of the original main title that kicks into high gear just three minutes in and doesn't let up.

David Hirsch

Prefontaine *✍✍✍✍*

1997, Hollywood Records; from the movie *Prefontaine*, Hollywood Pictures, 1997.

Album Notes: *Music*: Mason Daring; *Song Producers*: John Fogerty, Jimi Hendrix, The Who, Stephen Stills, Joe Vitale, Mason Daring, Al Kooper, Du Kane, Luke Baldry, Pely, Bob Monaco, John Simon, Julian Raymond, Phil Kaffel, The Pistoleros; *Album Executive Producers*: Peter Gilbert, Steve James.

Selections: 1 Fortunate Son (J. Fogerty)(2:20) *Creedence Clearwater Revival*; 2 Crosstown Traffic (J. Hendrix)(2:27) *Jimi*

Presumed Innocent

"Ideally the music shouldn't be noticed at all."

James Horner
(Time Magazine, 9-11-95)

Hendrix; 3 Baba O'Riley (P. Townshend)(5:09) *The Who*; 4 Love The One You're With (S. Stills)(3:05) *Stephen Stills*; 5 Yvonne (M. Daring)(1:37); 6 Tuesday's Gone (A. Collins/R. Van Zandt)(7:30) *Lynyrd Skynyrd*; 7 Munich Race (M. Daring)(4:43); 8 If 60's Were 90's (J. Hendrix)(6:11) *Beautiful People*; 9 Once You Get Started (G. Christopher)(4:28) *Rufus, Chaka Khan*; 10 I Shall Be Released (B. Dylan)(3:13) *The Band*; 11 Forever Young (B. Dylan)(4:07) *The Pistoleros*.

Review: Steve Prefontaine's runs to glory during the late '60s and early '70s provide the parameters for this soundtrack, which features a handful of classic tracks from the era. Some of it is stuff you don't readily hear on soundtracks, too—Jimi Hendrix' "Crosstown Traffic," for instance, or Rufus' "Once You Get Started" and Lynyrd Skynyrd's "Tuesday's Gone." Of particular note is "If 60's Were 90's" by Beautiful People, a British instrumental group that builds its intriguing compositions around samples of Hendrix music.

Gary Graff

Presumed Innocent 🎜🎜🎜

1990, Varese-Sarabande; from the movie *Presumed Innocent*, Warner Bros., 1990.

Album Notes: *Music:* John Williams; *Music Editor:* Ken Wannberg; Orchestra conducted by John Williams; *Album Producer:* John Williams; *Engineer:* Armin Steiner.

Selections: 1 Presumed Innocent (4:10); 2 Remembering Carolyn (2:17); 3 Family Life (1:30); 4 Love Scene (4:06); 5 The B File (3:28); 6 The Bedroom Scene (4:20); 7 Carolyn's Office (3:24); 8 "Leon Talks" (1:59); 9 Rusty Accused (2:07); 10 Case Dismissed (1:53); 11 The Boat Scene (2:15); 12 The Basement Scene (2:55); 13 Barbara's Confession (5:17); 14 End Credits (4:03).

Review: In the world of suspense-genre scores, *Presumed Innocent* is competent and certainly above-average. In terms of its place in the John Williams canon of movie music, however, it ranks fairly low on the ladder. For this Alan J. Pakula adaptation

of Scott Turow's bestselling novel, Williams composed a haunting theme for piano and orchestra, with unsettling strings building to a memorable crescendo. The theme is memorable in itself, but the rest of the score involves a lot of somber, low-key underscore cues that more or less work strictly in accordance with the action on-screen. While that doesn't mean that Williams didn't do his job admirably here, it does mean that, unlike a lot of the composer's works, there isn't much here to grab onto by itself, leaving the album recommended mostly for Williams aficionados, who will most likely be disappointed by the rather ordinary tone of much of the music.

Andy Dursin

Pret-A-Porter 🎜🎜🎜🎜

1994, Columbia Records; from the movie *Pret-A-Porter*, Miramax Films, 1994.

Album Notes: *Song Producers:* Salaam Remi, Sly Dunbar, Cheryl James, M People, Jimmy Jam & Terry Lewis, Don Was & The Glimmer Twins, T Bone Burnett, Stephen Street, Eric Mouquet & Michel Sanchez, The Brand New Heavies, Dave Morales, T.T.D., Flood, Brian Eno & The Edge; *Album Music Superviror:* Allan Nicholls.

Selections: 1 Here Comes The Hotstepper (Heartical Mix)(I. Kamoze/S. Gibbs/ J. Kenner/A. Domino/A. Konley/K. Nix)(4:08) *Ini Kamoze*; 2 My Girl Josephine (A. Domino/D, Bartholomew)(3:40) *Supercat*; 3 Here We Come (C. James/R. Evans/M. Scott)(4:05) *Salt-N-Pepa*; 4 Natural Thing (M. Pickering/P. Heard) (5:03) *M People*; 5 70's Love Groove (J. Jackson/J. Harris III/T. Lewis) (5:45) *Janet Jackson*; 6 Jump On Top Of Me (M. Jagger/K. Richards)(4:26) *The Rolling Stones*; 7 These Boots Are Made For Walkin' (L. Hazlewood)(2:57) *Sam Phillips*; 8 Pretty (remix)(D. O'Riordan/N. Hogan)(3:39) *The Cranberries*; 9 Martha (E. Mouquet/M. Sanchez)(4:01) *Eric Mouquet, Michel Sanchez, Deep Forest*; 10 Close To You (A. Levy/J. Kincaid/N. Davenport/S. Bartholomew)(4:04) *The Brand New Heavies*; 11 Keep Givin' Me Your Love (West End mix)(S. Nicholas/B. Sibley/C. Shock/K. Karlin)(5:55) *Cece Peniston*; 12 Get Wild (The New Power Generation)(5:58) *The New Power Generation*; 13 Supermodel Sandwich (T.T. D'Arby)(3:42) *Terence Trent D'Arby*; 14 Lemon (Perfecto mix)(Bono/U2)(8:56) *U2*.

Review: This set does a nice job of catching the aural end of the fashion show industry well—high energy with big, thumping and phat bass lines to drive the models down the runway. Ina Kamoze's "Here Comes the Hotstepper" provides a nice kick-off to a propulsive batch of songs, highlighted by Terence

Trent D'Arby's "Supermodel Sandwich," a "perfecto mix" of U2's "Lemon," Sam Phillips' cheeky remake of "These Boots are Made for Walkin'" and M People's "Natural Thing." In this context, however, rockers such as the Rolling Stones ("Jump on Top of Me") and the Cranberries ("Pretty") seem to be included only for name value.

Gary Graff

Pretty Woman ♪

1990, EMI Records; from the movie *Pretty Woman*, Touchstone Pictures, 1990.

Album Notes: *Featured Artists*: Natalie Cole, David Bowie, Go West, Jane Wiedlin, Roxette, Robert Palmer, Peter Cetera, Christopher Otcasek, Lauren Wood, Roy Orbison, Red Hot Chili Peppers; *Producers*: Andre Fischer, David Bowie, Harry Maslin, Peter Wolf, Peter Collins, Clarence Ofwerman, Robert Palmer, David Foster, Ron Fair, Peter Bunetta, Rick Chudacoff, Fred Foster, Norwood Fisher; *Album Producer*: Ron Fair; *Engineer*: George Marino.

Selections: 1 Wild Women (G. Prestopino/S. Lorber/M. Wilder)(4:06) *Natalie Cole*; 2 Fame 90 (D. Bowie/J. Lennon/C. Alomar)(3:36) *David Bowie*; 3 King Of Wishful Thinking (P. Cox/R. Drummie/M. Page)(4:00) *Go West*; 4 Tangled (J. Wiedlin/S. Cutler)(4:18) *Jane Wiedlin*; 5 It Must Have Been Love (P. Gessle)(4:17) *Roxette*; 6 Life In Detail (R. Palmer/A. Powell)(4:07) *Robert Palmer*; 7 No Explanation (D. Foster/L. Thompson-Jenner/B. LaBounty/B. Foster)(4:19) *Peter Cetera*; 8 Real Wild Child (Wild One)(J. O'Keefe/J. Greenan/D. Owen)(3:39) *Christopher Otcasek*; 9 Fallen (L. Wood)(3:59) *Lauren Wood*; 10 Oh Pretty Woman (R. Orbison/W. Dees)(2:55) *Roy Orbison*; 11 Show Me Your Soul (A. Kiedis/Flea/C. Smith/J. Frusciante)(4:20) *Red Hot Chili Peppers*.

Review: So '80s—even if it was released at the turn of the decade. Selling more than three million copies, this is a power-house pop singles vehicle, shooting Roxette's "It Must Have Been Love," Go West's "King of Wishful Thinking" and the Roy Orbison title track into the upper reaches of the charts. But with the exception of the latter, already a classic by the time the film came out, when was the last time you heard these songs on the radio. And shame on David Bowie for his absolutely unnecessary "Fame 90."

Gary Graff

The Pride and the Passion

1991, Cloud Nine Records; from the movie *The Pride and the Passion*, United Artists, 1957.

See: The Agony and the Ecstasy

Primal Fear ♪♪

1996, Milan Records; from the movie *Primal Fear*, Paramount Pictures, 1996.

Album Notes: *Music*: James Newton Howard; *Orchestrations*: Brad Dechter, James Newton Howard; *Music Editor*: Jim Weidman; Orchestra conducted by Artie Kane; *Featured Soloists*: Terence Blanchard (horn), Barbara Northcutt (English horn); *Album Producer*: James Newton Howard; *Engineer*: Shawn Murphy.

Selections: 1 Introitus: Cibavit eos (W. Byrd)(3:35) *The Christ Church Cathedral Choir, Stephen Darlington*; 2 Martin Meets Aaron (1:17); 3 Molly's Interview (1:02); 4 The Murder Scene (2:39); 5 Courtroom Montage (2:15); 6 Chasing Alex (2:38); 7 Got An Aspirin? (1:05); 8 Cancao do mar (F. De Brito/F. Trindale)(5:15) *Dulce Pontes*; 9 Aaron On Stand (1:11); 10 Roy Appears (1:35); 11 Under The Tracks (1:10); 12 Janet Finds Video (1:05); 13 Don't Deceive Me (Please Don't Go)(C. Willis)(4:16) *Johnny Otis*; 14 Dinner With Shaughnessy (1:04); 15 Don't Smile (1:21); 16 I'm Arrogant (1:24); 17 Martin Reviews Crime Scene (1:51); 18 Switching Videos (2:17); 19 What Did You Say? (2:54); 20 Roy's Freeze Frame (1:01); 21 Love Hurts (1:33); 22 Lacrimosa (from Requiem)(W.A. Mozart)(3:16) *Wiener Sangerknaben*.

Review: Once in a while you hear a film score that just isn't crying out to be a soundtrack album. *Primal Fear*, which has a capable but unmemorable score by James Newton Howard, is clearly one of those cases. Thriller scores are typically a tough genre for composers, since the music is usually restrained, building up mystery and suspense to climaxes that will then (generally) contain a great deal of music. But even then, the story is supposed to be the star, not the composer or sound editor. In *Primal Fear*, Howard tries his best by underscoring the picture in one of three manners—quiet, brooding orchestral accompaniment, more powerful dramatic cues, and pulsating, synth-accompanied tracks modeled after the composer's own score for *The Fugitive*. That said, however, Howard is more or less restricted by the confines of the genre here, and is never able to open up any new avenues in his music for listeners to take hold of. The music works perfectly in the film, but it just isn't fit for soundtrack album consumption.

Andy Dursin

Prince of Darkness ♪♪

1987, Varese-Sarabande; from the movie *Prince of Darkness*, Universal Pictures, 1987.

Album Notes: *Music*: John Carpenter; *Album Producer*: Alan Howarth.

Selections: 1 Opening Titles (4:14); 2 Team Assembly (4:33); 3 Darkness Begins (2:54); 4 A Message From The Future (5:30); 5 Hell Breaks Loose (4:53); 6 Mirror Image (6:46); 7 The Devil Awakens (8:57); 8 Through The Mirror (5:50).

Review: With *Prince of Darkness,* a horror film which attempted to prove that the Evil One is nothing more than a green, slimy slug, John Carpenter struck a particularly malevolent note. Though hardly the terrifying picture he might have envisioned, it is made more frightening by the director's unique electronic concoction, an amalgam of ominous, low sounds that presaged the horror soon to materialize itself. With a chorus of disembodied voices adding an otherwordly touch, the score did enhance the moods on the screen, but loses some of its effectiveness and proves somewhat less appealing or enjoyable when heard in one's home environment.

The Prince of Tides 🎵🎵🎵◗

1991, Columbia Records; from the movie *The Prince of Tides*, Columbia Pictures, 1991.

Album Notes: *Music*: James Newton Howard; *Orchestrations*: Brad Dechter, Marty Paich, Hummie Mann; *Music Editor*: Jim Weidman; Orchestra conducted by Marty Paich; *Album Producers*: James Newton Howard, Barbra Streisand; *Engineer*: Shawn Murphy; *Assistant Engineers*: Sue MacLean, Sharon Rice, Gil Morales, Charlie Paakkari, Marnie Riley, Koji Egawa, Chris Rich.

Selections: 1 Main Title (4:28); 2 Teddy Bears (:55); 3 To New York (1:28); 4 The Bloodstain (1:19); 5 The Fishmarket (:59); 6 The New York Willies (2:43); 7 The Village Walk (2:59); 8 Lila's Theme (3:10); 9 Home Movies (1:36); 10 Daddy's Home (1:37); 11 The Hallway (Love Theme)(2:44); 12 They Love You Dad (:43); 13 So Cruel (1:34); 14 Savannah Awakes (1:03); 15 Love Montage (4:00); 16 Tom Comes Home (1:13); 17 The Outdoors (1:17); 18 Tom's Breakdown (1:05); 19 The Street (3:11); 20 For All We Know (J.F. Coots/S. Lewis)(2:17) *Kirk Whalum, Bobby Lyle, Leroy Hyter, Lionel Cordew, Tom Barney*; 21 The Reunion (2:21); 22 End Credits (3:45); 23 For All We Know (J.F. Coots/S. Lewis)(4:14) *Barbra Streisand, Kirk Whalum, Johnny Mandel*; 24 Places That Belong To You (J. Newton Howard/A. & M. Bergman)(3:39) *Barbra Streisand*.

Review: Listeners who enjoy romantic, melodic film scores ought to eat up James Newton Howard's lovely music for the 1991 Barbra Streisand adaptation of Pat Conroy's bestselling novel. Howard grounds his score in a pleasing main theme for piano and strings that's richly evocative of the main characters, a theme that is later used for "Places That Belong to You," a Streisand vocal with lyrics by Alan and Marilyn Bergman. The

song was not used in the movie but rather recorded expressly for the album, which also features a Streisand performance of the standard "For All We Know." The majority of the album, though, belongs to Howard's score, which is able to walk over musical ground previously traveled by composers like Marvin Hamlisch, but without becoming overly sentimental or melodramatic. The music is highly enjoyable by itself and even non-Streisand fans should appreciate Howard's superb score.

Andy Dursin

The Princess Bride 🎵🎵

1987, Warner Bros.; from the movie *The Princess Bride*, 20th Century-Fox, 1987.

Album Notes: *Music*: Mark Knopfler; *Arrangements*: Mark Knopfler; Performed by Mark Knopfler and Guy Fletcher; *Album Producer*: Mark Knopfler; *Engineers*: Bill Schnee, Marc De Sisto.

Selections: 1 Once Upon A Time... Storybook Love (4:00); 2 I Will Never Love Again (3:05); 3 Florin Dance (1:33); 4 Morning Ride (1:37); 5 The Friends' Song (3:03); 6 The Cliffs Of Insanity (3:18); 7 The Swordfight (2:44); 8 Guide My Sword (5:12); 9 The Fireswamp And The Rodents Of Unusual Size (4:47); 10 Revenge (3:51); 11 A Happy Ending (1:53); 12 Storybook Love (W. DeVlle)(4:24) *Willy DeVille*.

Review: Here's a strange example of a composer with a rock music background (Mark Knopfler is a member of the band Dire Straits) being hired for a fantasy film on the strength of his pop music and then being asked to produce something akin to a straight adventure score. Knopfler's delicate love theme of guitar and strings (also nicely performed by the composer as a song) works perfectly in the film and makes for enjoyable, mellow listening in album form. Unfortunately, the movie also called for mock-serious action and suspense music of a more conventional nature, and Knopfler provided a mostly electronic, percussive low-key underscore. It serves the film well because its ramshackle, bleating textures fit right in with the deliberately low-tech feel of Rob Reiner's movie, but it bears no relationship to the love theme and doesn't function well enough on its own as music to make the rest of the album much fun to hear.

Jeff Bond

Princess Caraboo 🎵🎵🎵◗

1994, Varese-Sarabande; from the movie *Princess Caraboo*, Tri-Star Pictures, 1994.

Album Notes: *Music*: Richard Hartley; *Orchestrations*: John Bell, Richard Hartley; *Music Editor*: Jupiter Sen; The Munich

Symphony Orchestra, conducted by Richard Hartley; *Album Producer*: Richard Hartley; *Engineer*: Keith Grant.

Selections: 1 Destiny (2:36); 2 Girl From Javasu (1:40); 3 Farewell Princess (1:03); 4 On The Cupola (1:03); 5 One Of Our Finest Frocks (1:37); 6 Portrait Of A Princess (2:07); 7 Minuet in D (L. Boccherini)(1:31); 8 Sweet, Green Land (2:42); 9 The Dress Maker (1:36); 10 A Good Story (1:54); 11 Sweet Dreams, My Dear (1:16); 12 Black Teeth In The Family (2:03); 13 Caraboo Buku (1:02); 14 Love Dance At Knole (2:03); 15 A Princess From Far Away (3:03); 16 End Credits (3:22).

Review: An endearing score by Richard Hartley is the foundation for this comic satire about 19th-century English aristocracy, in which a well-meaning family takes in a mysterious young girl, believing her to be a Princess from some exotic country. In keeping with the tone of the film, Hartley created a score that has a dream-like, fairy tale quality. There are pompous English waltzes to be sure, but it's the magical influence the "Princess" has over the family that drives the music.

David Hirsch

The Professional 𝄞𝄞𝄞ᵛ

1994, TriStar Records; from the movie *The Professional*, Columbia Pictures, 1994.

Album Notes: *Music*: Eric Serra; *Orchestrations*: Eric Serra; Orchestra conducted by John Altman; *Featured Musicians*: Andy Findon (Chinese bamboo flutes), Keith Thompson (Indian shawm, soprano schalmei, soprano dulcian), Juan Jose Mosalini Jr. (Bandoneon), Rene Marc Bini (piano), Eric Serra (guitar, bass, keyboards, timpani, percussion, computer programming); *Album Producer*: Eric Serra; *Engineers*: Isabelle Martin, Serge Devesvre.

Selections: 1 Noon (4:02); 2 Cute Name (3:29); 3 Ballad For Mathilda (2:15); 4 What's Happening Out There? (3:05); 5 A Bird In New York (1:21); 6 She Is Dead (1:32); 7 Fatman (5:16); 8 Leon The Cleaner (1:50); 9 Can I Have A Word With You? (1:14); 10 The Game Is Over (1:37); 11 Feel The Breath (3:18); 12 Room 4602 (1:18); 13 Very Special Delivery (2:41); 14 When Leon Does His Best (2:11); 15 Back On The Crime Scene (2:34); 16 Birds Of Storm (1:37); 17 Tony The IBM (1:57); 18 How Do You Know It's Love? (1:29); 19 The Fight (Part 1: The Swat Squad)(2:30); 20 The Fight (Part 2: Bring Me Everyone)(4:34); 21 The Fight (Part 3: The Big Weapon)(3:03); 22 The Fight (Part 4: One Is Alive)(3:15); 23 Two Ways Out (3:11).

Review: Luc Besson's first English language film is this sentimental tale of a hitman (Jean Reno) who befriends an orphaned girl (Natalie "Jailbait" Portman) in her run from a crooked cop (Gary "Over the Top" Oldman). Lolita-ish sexual tension, underworld suspense and bloodshed ensue, but thanks to Eric Serra, with a moody eeriness and melody. Serra, a French rock star who scores all of Besson's films, comes from a textural, keyboard-and-live-overdubs school, like Vangelis. Much of his music is created in the electronic domain, performed by the composer himself. The resulting *Professional* score incorporates slow pop loops, distinctly Serra samples, an ethnically Arabic cast for New York (its buildings reminded the composer of the Egyptian pyramids), sensitive guitar and violin solos, and larger orchestral forces than usual for Serra. In the movie, it's pretty good; on the album, its wallpaper aesthetic slows it down, and it goes on too long. It also suffers for the same reason the film does. It's at once full of low-key, isn't-this-subtle portent, but is practically screaming, *isn't the relationship between the hit man and little girl oddly sexual?* Still, Serra's score is to be admired for its progressive (for film) blend of genres and point of view.

Lukas Kendall

The Professionals 𝄞𝄞𝄞𝄞ᵛ

1992, Silva Treasury; from the movie *The Professionals*, Columbia Pictures, 1967.

Album Notes: *Music*: Maurice Jarre; *Orchestrations*: Leo Arnaud; Orchestra conducted by Maurice Jarre; *Album Producers*: Neely Plumb, Carol Rice; *Engineer*: John Norman; *CD Producers*: James Fitzpatrick, Ford A. Thaxton, David Stoner.

Selections: 1 Proposition For The Professionals/Main Title (3:43); 2 Start Of The Quest (1:56); 3 Dolworth's Word (2:29); 4 Hacienda Intrigue (3:28); 5 Rigging The Pass (2:20); 6 Train And Raza (2:37); 7 Hacienda Happenings (2:25); 8 Chiquita's Dance (1:58); 9 Hacienda Ole (2:09); 10 The Escape and Storm (3:05); 11 Maria and Intrepid Dolworth (3:49); 12 Desert Sun and Ehrengard's Collapse (2:41); 13 Chiquita's Demise (2:25); 14 The Road Back/End Title (2:49).

Review: A flavorful western set in Mexico in 1917, *The Professionals* elicited a vibrantly exciting score from Maurice Jarre, filled with dynamic cues reflective of the fast-paced action and warm south-of-the-border accents evocative of the various locales in which it takes place. The story of four soldiers of fortune who are recruited by an American oil tycoon to rescue his beautiful wife, held for ransom by a notorious Mexican bandito, the film found in Jarre a sympathetic composer whose music helps set the various moods of adventure, heroism, violence and lust in the narrative. There is plenty of good, solid music to be heard here, with repeated listening helping discover previously unnoticed little details that make the whole experience all the more enjoyable. Even though the CD was assembled from vinyl source transfers, the result of the original master tapes having been lost, there is little noticeable loss in the sound quality and no surface noise to speak of.

Promised Land 𝄢𝄢𝄢𝄢ᵛ

1987, Private Music Records; from the movie *Promised Land*, Vestron Pictures, 1987.

Album Notes: *Music*: James Newton Howard; *Featured Musicians*: James Newton Howard (keyboards and synthesizer programming), Robby Weaver (synclavier programming), Dean Parks (guitar), David Grisman (mandolin), Michael Fisher (percussion), Neil Stubenhaus (bass); *Album Producer*: James Newton Howard; *Engineer*: Ross Pallone.

Selections: 1 Plymouth Waltz (4:07); 2 Winter Scene (4:16); 3 Promised Land Suite (6:13); 4 O Magnum Mysterium (6:25) *The King's College Choir, Philip Ledger*; 5 Main Titles (1:54); 6 Danny And His Dad (2:03); 7 The Hot Springs (1:44); 8 Circle K Shooting (4:06); 9 Ice Skating (1:44); 10 Telephone Call (1:14); 11 Bev Cuts Danny's Hair (1:35); 12 Leaving Knolls (1:19); 13¾ #1 (1:19); 13 Dreams And Promises (J. Street)(5:03).

Review: The wonderful folk accents in James Newton Howard add the right touch to this acoustic-and-synthesizer elegiac score for a contemporary drama set in a small Western community, about two former high-school friends who get back together several years later, only to realize that the plans they had made way back then didn't materialize. The delightful "Plymouth Waltz," which opens the album, sets the tone for the rest of the score, in which the many highlights include the gorgeous "Winter Scene," "The Hot Springs," "Ice Skating," and the quietly eloquent "Bev Cuts Danny's Hair." Contributing a different, albeit equally enjoyable note to the music, "O Magnum Mysterium," in a performance by the King's College Choir, and "Dreams and Promises," written by Janey Street, are also evocative of the film's moods.

The Proprietor 𝄢𝄢𝄢𝄢

1996, Epic Soundtrax; from the movie *The Proprietor*, Merchant Ivory/Warner Bros. Pictures, 1996.

Album Notes: *Music*: Richard Robbins; *Orchestrations*: Geoffrey Alexander; Orchestra conducted by Harry Rabinowitz; *Album Producer*: Geoffrey Alexander; *Engineers*: Bill Sommerville-Large, Kirsty Whalley.

Selections: 1 Opening Titles (2:12); 2 The Art Gallery (3:56); 3 Je m'appelle France (2:39); 4 Adrienne's Dream (4:34); 5 Memories Of Maxim's (3:33); 6 To Leave? To Stay? (1:57); 7 Father

And Son (2:29); 8 Coming Home (5:36); 9 Patrice And Virginia At The Chateau (2:56); 10 Ostrogoth's Tango (2:04); 11 If I Didn't Care (J. Lawrence)(2:44); 12 Call Me French (1:40); 13 The Auction (2:44); 14 What Did He Say? (2:26); 15 The Ghost Of Fan Fan (3:06); 16 The Letter (2:14); 17 End Credits (3:09); 18 Will The Circle Be Unbroken (C. Gabriel)(4:49).

Review: A sensitive study of an aging woman whose childhood memories are rekindled when the apartment where she spent her youth is put up for sale, *The Proprietor* found composer Richard Robbins striking a very emotional chord in a score with great pathos. Robbins, whose eclecticism has manifested itself in many films with varied exotic locales, pulls no surprises here, grounding his music in themes that are pleasantly evocative and lightly romantic. The story, about a French writer who cannot reconcile the fact that her mother was sent to a concentration camp during the war, translates itself into a series of cues in which the strong flavor of nostalgia is a predominant motif, even when the moods tend to be light and elegant, as in "Memories of Maxim's" and "Ostrogoth's Tango." Throughout, there is an abundance of lovely themes — "Patrice and Virginia at the Chateau," "The Ghost of Fan Fan" — which contribute to making this a very attractive and pleasant soundtrack album. On a purely technical note, a puzzling thing about this recording is the fact that it is in mono.

Prospero's Books 𝄢𝄢𝄢𝄢ᵛ

1991, London Records; from the movie *Prospero's Books*, 1991.

Album Notes: *Music*: Michael Nyman; The Michael Nyman Band, conducted by Michael Nyman; *Musicians*: Michael Nyman (piano), Alexander Balanescu, Jonathan Carney, Elisabeth Perry, Clare Connors (violin), Kate Musker (viola), Tony Hinnigan, Justin Pearson (cello), Paul Morgan, Tim Amhurst, Lynda Houghton (double bass), Martin Elliott (bass guitar), David Rix (clarinets), John Harle, David Roach, Jamie Talbot (soprano/alto sax), Andrew Findon (tenor/baritone sax, flute), Graham Ashton (trumpet), Richard Clews, Marjorie Dunn (horn), Nigel Barr, Steve Saunders (trombone); *Featured Vocalists*: Sarah Leonard, Marie Angel, Ute Lemper, Deborah Conway; *Album Producer*: David Cunningham; *Engineer*: Michael J. Dutton.

Selections: PROSPERO'S BOOKS: 1 Full Fathom Five(1:58); 2 Prospero's Curse (2:38); 3 While You Here Do Snoring Lie (1:06); 4 Prospero's Magic (5:11); 5 Miranda (3:54); 6 Twelve Years Since (2:45); 7 Come Unto These Yellow Sands (3:44); 8 History Of Sycorax (3:25); 9 Come And Go (1:16); 10 Cornfield (6:26); 11 Where The Bee Sucks (4:48); 12 Caliban's Pit (2:56); 13 Reconciliation (2:31); 14 The Masque (12:12).

Review: An intellectually challenging and erotically charged screen adaptation of Shakespeare's "The Tempest," *Prospero's Books* elicited a vigorous score from Michael Nyman, with brassy accents, eerie vocals for "boy soprano voice" (performed by Sarah Leonard), and an abundance of melodic themes that underline some of the most telling moments in the film. While retaining the minimalist approach that is part of his stylistic invention, the cues are diversified enough to attract the attention. Undaunted by the task of writing a florid score for a play set on an "isle full of noises," Nyman devised several tricks that challenge the listener, while helping propel the action on the screen, like speeding up the music of "Miranda," to give it a calliope sound, or suddenly throwing in a call of trumpet, like in "Come Unto These Yellow Sands," to enhance a theme. It is an intelligent, rewarding effort that will constantly surprise and keep the listener off balance.

An extrapolation, *The Masque* is a richly elaborated composition, central to the concept of *Prospero's Books,* but different from it, that brings together three vocalists with a different tradition, Marie Angel, Ute Lemper, and Deborah Conway. Once again, Nyman's work is full of unexpected details that prove compelling and thoroughly effective in a purely musical context, though, because of the demands it imposes on the listener, the recording will not be to everyone's taste.

Providence ♫♫♫♫

1980, DRG Records; from the movie *Providence,* 1980.

Album Notes: *Music:* Miklos Rozsa; *CD Producer:* Van John Sfiridis.

Selections: 1 Twilight Waltz (3:43); 2 Main Title (2:04); 3 Leaves (2:23); 4 Chase (2:45); 5 Arrival At The House (1:53); 6 Sonia And The Holy Shroud (:57); 7 Twilight Waltz (piano)(3:43); 8 Providence (2:03); 9 Disenchantment (2:40); 10 Kevin And Sonia (1:36); 11 The Dead City (2:58); 12 Helen (2:54); 13 The Public Garden (1:54); 14 The Street (:59); 15 Finale (2:01).

Review: French director Alain Resnais' stylish story, about an imaginative novelist who may or may not be dying, his rapports with other members in his family, and his rambling dissertations about his new book, made *Providence* a vivid picture, tremendously enhanced by John Gielgud's sensational portrayal as the writer. Resnais, whose admiration for American filmmakers of the 1940s was enormous, enlisted Miklos Rozsa to write the score, with the composer creating a profoundly compelling series of cues which give the film extra dimension and energy. Anchored by a central theme ("Twilight Waltz,"

heard in two versions, one instrumental, the other in a piano solo), the score contains several moments that are solidly etched, with striking string embellishments that recall some of Rozsa's most powerful efforts. Unfortunately, the recording itself is not all that it should be, with noticeable studio noises, which could not be corrected, bad splicing and some hiss, which could have.

Psycho

Psycho ♫♫♫♫

1989, Unicorn-Kanchana Records; from the movie *Psycho,* Universal Pictures, 1960.

Album Notes: *Music:* Bernard Herrmann; The National Philharmonic Orchestra, conducted by Bernard Herrmann; *Album Producer:* Christopher Palmer; *Engineer:* Bob Auger.

Selections: 1 Prelude (2:07); 2 The City/Marion/Marion and Sam (4:36); 3 Temptation (3:08); 4 Flight/The Patrol Car/The Car Lot/The Package/The Rainstorm (8:47); 5 Hotel Room/The Window/The Parlour (4:04); 6 The Madhouse (2:13); 7 The Peephole (3:10); 8 The Bathroom/The Murder/The Body (2:03); 9 The Office/The Curtain/The Water/The Car/The Swamp (6:40); 10 The Search/The Shadow/Phone Booth (2:25); 11 The Porch/The Stairs/The Knife (4:34); 12 The Search/The First Floor/Cabin 10/Cabin 1 (6:09); 13 The Hill/The Bedroom/The Toys/The Cellar/Discovery (5:25); 14 Finale (1:49).

Review: The familiar, shrieking cello strains of "The Murder," from the shower scene in Alfred Hitchcock's *Psycho,* comprise what is probably the single most famous theme from any thriller. Carefully orchestrated by Herrmann, *Psycho* marked a rather radical technical departure for the composer, who opted to use only strings for this score, feeling this best complemented the stark, black and white image of the film. Critics initially scoffed at Herrmann's rationale, but a study of the music reveals the genius of his approach. While a certain amount of tonal color is lost with the elimination of woodwinds, brass and percussion, the composer was forced to utilize the entire breadth of the strings, and develop a completely new palette of hues and gradations derived from the single "color" within the section. The resulting music, mostly individual "motifs" suited for particular scenes, is all at once subtle, terrifying, and completely effective at drawing the listener into the film, to experience the disturbing mix of sensitivity and tension that Hitchcock so masterfully created.

While no true soundtrack of the music recorded for the film exists, the most complete recording of *Psycho* is available on a Unicorn CD, simply titled *Music for Psycho*. This superior recording features Herrmann conducting the National Philharmonic Orchestra, and contains 39 musical cues—nearly one hour of music. Who could argue with the perspective of the composer interpreting his own music? The playing is beautiful, and the recording fine.

Charles L. Granata

Psycho II 𝄞𝄞𝄞𝄞

1990, Varese-Sarabande; from the movie *Psycho II*, Universal Pictures, 1983.

Album Notes: *Music*: Jerry Goldsmith; Orchestra conducted by Jerry Goldsmith; *Album Producer*: Jerry Goldsmith.

Selections: 1 The Murder (B. Herrmann)(:57); 2 Main Title (1:37); 3 Don't Take Me (4:48); 4 Mother's Room (4:01); 5 It's Not Your Mother (5:11); 6 New Furniture (2:04); 7 The Cellar (4:02); 8 Blood Bath (3:37); 9 End Title (4:13).

Review: Goldsmith took on the thankless task of following up Bernard Herrmann's classic *Psycho* score for this sequel, but he wisely produced an entirely original work that bears no comparison to Herrmann's unforgettable efforts. Goldsmith's eerie title music of keyboard, piano, strings and woodwinds emphasize the haunted innocence of Norman Bates, while later suspense cues create tension with dissonant string chords, unusual synthesized effects and percussion as Goldsmith depicts the gradual breakdown of Norman's mind. Slashing, knife-like wind effects and howling horns and strings underscore most of the violent sequences, climaxing in the lengthy "It's Not Your Mother" cue with its characteristic low-end piano performance.

Jeff Bond

The Public Eye 𝄞𝄞

1992, Varese-Sarabande Records; from the movie *The Public Eye*, Universal Pictures, 1992.

Album Notes: *Music*: Mark Isham; *Orchestrations*: Ken Kugler; *Music Editor*: Tom Carlson; Orchestra conducted by Ken Kugler; *Featured Musicians*: Jim Walker (flutes), Chuck Domanico (bass), Kurt Wortman (snare drum), Rich Ruttenberg (piano), Mark Isham (electronics); *Album Producer*: Mark Isham; *Engineer*: Stephen Krause.

Selections: 1 The Public Eye (3:24); 2 Nightime Developments (1:09); 3 The Meat Market (1:26); 4 Flying Home (S. Robin/B. Goodman/L. Hampton)(3:01) *Oren Waters*; 5 An Artist Once (1:27); 6 The Bureau At Night (1:55); 7 Pictures In The Dark (3:44); 8 Topsy (E. Durham/E. Battle)(2:21); 9 The Great

Bernzini (1:18); 10 Many Questions? (3:27); 11 Cafe Society Blues (S. Rogers)(3:54); 12 Portrait Of An Artist (2:32); 13 Waiting, Then Calling (3:25); 14 Undecided (S. Robin/C. Shavers)(4:35); 15 Waiting, Then Hiding (1:57); 16 You Would Have Been Surprised (1:22); 17 The Massacre (1:29); 18 The Kiss (1:22); 19 The Public Eye (End Credits)(5:21).

Review: Mark Isham replaced an original score by Jerry Goldsmith for this rather unusual 1940s melodrama starring Joe Pesci and Barbara Hershey. Isham, who has dabbled in both acclaimed jazz and new age albums off the screen, chose not to concentrate on the obvious musical preferences of the period (though there are new vocal performances of standards like "Undecided"), and instead wrote a heavy atmospheric, electronic-laden score that basically serves strictly as a musical undercurrent to the dramatic proceedings in Howard Franklin's film. What all this means is that the music is not that interesting apart from its source, and might have been more melodic, and dramatic, had Isham scored the picture from more of a jazz or swing standpoint. As it is, there's not much here to listen to.

Andy Dursin

Pulp Fiction 𝄞𝄞𝄞𝄞⌐

1994, MCA Records; from the movie *Pulp Fiction*, Miramax Films, 1994.

Album Notes: *Song Producers*: Jim Monsour, Kool & The Gang, Willie Mitchell, Bob Irwin, Ricky Nelson, Ozzie Nelson & Jimmy Haskell, Jerry Wexler, Tom Dowd & Arif Mardin, Bob Keene, Urge Overkill & Kramer, Bruce Brody & Maria McKee, Bill Wenzell, Jerry Kennedy; *Album Executive Producers*: Quentin Tarantino, Lawrence Bender, Karyn Rachtman.

Selections: 1 Pumpkin And Honey Bunny/Misirlou (F. Wise/M. Leeds/S.K. Russell/N. Roubanis) (2:27) *Dick Dale & His Del-Tones*; 2 Royale With Cheese (1:42); 3 Jungle Boogie (R. Bell/C. Smith/G. Brown/R. Mickens/D. Boyce/R. Westfield) (3:05) *Kool & The Gang*; 4 Let's Stay Together (A. Green/A. Jackson, Jr./W. Mitchell) (3:15) *Al Green*; 5 Bustin' Surfboards (G. Sanders/ J. Sanders/N. Sanders) (2:26) *The Tornadoes*; 6 Lonesome Town (B. Knight) (2:13) *Ricky Nelson*; 7 Son Of A Preacherman (J. Hurley/R. Wilkins) (2:25) *Dusty Springfield*; 8 Zed's Dead, Baby/ Bullwinkle Part II (D. Rose/E. Furrow) (2:39) *The Centurions*; 9 Jack Rabbit Slims Twist Contest/You Never Can Tell (C. Berry) (3:12) *Chuck Berry*; 10 Girl, You'll Be A Woman Soon (N. Diamond) (3:09) *Urge Overkill*; 11 If Love Is A Red Dress (Hang Me In Drags) (M. McKee) (4:55) *Maria McKee*; 12 Bring Out The Gimp/ Comanche (The Revels) (2:10) *The Revels*; 13 Flowers On The Wall (L. DeWitt) (2:23) *The Statler Brothers*; 14 Personality Goes

A Long Way (1:00); 15 Surf Rider (B. Bogle/N. Edwards/D. Wilson) (3:18) *The Lively Ones*; 16 Ezekiel 25:17 (:51).

Review: Quentin Tarantino's attention to detail always includes the music for his films, and this is his crowning achievement. Dick Dale's firey surf classic "Misirlou" is as responsible for the movie's flavor as any aspect of Tarantino's script, while Urge Overkill's remake of Neil Diamond's "Girl, You'll Be a Woman Soon" is brilliantly reverent. There are plenty of satisfying oldies—Chuck Berry's "You Never Can Tell," Al Green's "Let's Stay Together," Dusty Springfield's "Son of a Preacher Man"—all laced between snippets of dialogue from the film. Masterful.

Gary Graff

A Pure Formality 🎵🎵🎵

1994, Sony Classical; from the movie *A Pure Formality*, 1994.

Album Notes: *Music*: Ennio Morricone; *Orchestrations*: Ennio Morricone; Orchestra Unione Musicisti di Roma, conducted by Ennio Morricone; *Featured Soloist*: Franco Tamponi (violin); *Album Producer*: Ennio Morricone; *Engineer*: Franco Patrignani; *Assistant Engineer*: Donato Salone.

Selections: 1 Breathlessly (2:59); 2 Remembering (E. & A. Morricone/G. Tornatore/P. Quignard)(4:09) *Gerard Depardieu*; 3 The Palace Of Nine Frontiers (3:25); 4 The Bum (3:38); 5 A Troublesome Clue (2:10); 6 Waiting For The Police Inspector (1:07); 7 In Search Of Onoff (2:42); 8 An Old Diary (2:51); 9 Photos (1:17); 10 Mosaic (1:06); 11 Leonardo da Vinci (3:09); 12 Contradictions (2:17); 13 The Trap and The Mouse (1:24); 14 Escape From Onoff (1:33); 15 Bloodstains (2:36); 16 After The Nightmare (1:02); 17 A Mere Memory Lapse (1:58); 18 Repressed Memories (1:55); 19 Revelation (1:42); 20 A Night In February (2:11); 21 To Obliterate The Past (E. & A. Morricone/G. Tornatore/P. Quignard)(4:10) *Gerard Depardieu*.

Review: In a style that's frequently more abstract than some of his most popular works, Ennio Morricone fashioned a fascinating, dense score for this drama, directed by Giuseppe Tornatore, essentially an intellectual two-character tour-de-force about a crime suspect, who says he is a famous author currently suffering from a writer's block, and the calm, insinuating police inspector who interrogates him, and seems to know by heart everything the author has written. Matching the various mood shifts on the screen, as well as creating an increasingly disturbing atmosphere of its own, Morricone's score brings together a variety of slow cues, some featuring persistently enervating little noises, others shrieking strings and bells, that prove quite unsettling, yet frighteningly compelling. Gerard Depardieu (sounding like Marcello

Mastroianni) performs two songs, "Ricordare" and "Effacer le passe," that add nothing to nor detract anything from his talent as an actor. Hardly the kind of CD you'll put on at any given moment, but one that will play well under the right circumstances for the right audience.

Purple Rain 🎵🎵🎵🎵

1984, Warner Bros. Records; from the movie *Purple Rain*, Warner Bros. Pictures, 1984.

Album Notes: *Music*: Prince; *Album Producers*: Prince & The Revolution; *Engineers*: Peggy Mac, David Leonard.

Selections: 1 Let's Go Crazy (4:39); 2 Take Me With U (3:54) *Prince & Apollonia*; 3 The Beautiful Ones (5:15); 4 Computer Blue (3:59); 5 Darling Nikki (4:15); 6 When Doves Cry (5:52); 7 I Would Die 4 U (2:51); 8 Baby I'm A Star (4:20); 9 Purple Rain (8:45).

Review: Prince (later to be known as the "artist-formerly-known-as-Prince") revealed another, unsuspected side of his vast talent when he wrote and appeared in the semi-autobiographical *Purple Rain*, in which he portrays a misunderstood youngster who finds solace in his music. Surrounded by members of his "rock family," and co-starring Apollonia Kotero, his girlfriend at the time, the film is essentially a showcase for Prince's songs, a blend of striking and sensuous numbers, many of them propelled by a percolating rhythm that is in marked contrast with the central character's gloomy existence. The songs, assembled in this album, offer little that Prince fans don't already know and like about him. Others, who may be discovering it for the first time, will enjoy the joy and exuberance that pervade many of the selections, and will revel in the film's unquestionable hits, "Let's Go Crazy," "Darling Nikki," "When Doves Cry," and "Purple Rain."

Quartet 🎵🎵🎵🎵

1994, Angel Records; from the movie *Quartet*, Merchant Ivory Productions, 1994.

Album Notes: *Music*: Richard Robbins; *Orchestrations*: Luther Henderson; *Featured Musicians*: Allen Jackson (bass), Rudy Collins (drums), Benny Powell (trombone), Jerome Richardson (tenor sax, clarinet), Marshall Royal (alto sax, clarinet), J. Leonard Oxley (pianist, conductor), Al Arons (trumpet).

Selections: 1 Opening Title Music (2:59); 2 Five-O-Nine (2:51) *Armelia McQueen*; 3 Blues For H.J. (2:47); 4 Black King Foxtrot (3:01); 5 Full Time Lover (3:07) *Armelia McQueen*; 6 In The Country/Arabesque Valsante (M. Levitsky)(2:17); 7 Pars (1:08) *Isabelle Adjani*; 8 Au bal musette (2:31); 9 Five-O-Nine (2:43); 10

Full Time Lover (2:59); 11 Maggie's Trot (2:46); 12 Quartet Tango (1:57); 13 End Title Music/Arabesque Valsante (M. Levitsky) (1:59).

Review: Set in Paris in the 1920s, *Quartet* evokes a time and place where artists, particularly American ones, had found a second home, in a world Ernest Hemingway described as "a moveable feast." The moods were light, active, stimulating, marked by the new syncopated accents of jazz which, already, struck a more responsive note there than it did at home. The period, brilliantly recreated in the film, inspired Richard Robbins to create a score with a strong jazz flavor, performed by a distinguished group of instrumentalists — Allen Jackson, Benny Powell, Jerome Richardson, Marshall Royal — in Luther Henderson's feel-right arrangements. Tremendously exhilarating, the album needs no pre-sequencing to be enjoyed and lends itself to excellent straight programming. Armelia McQueen adds some flavorful vocals to the mix, as does Isabelle Adjani as a woman stranded in Paris when her husband, an art dealer, is sent to prison. She becomes a passive participant in a *menage a trois*, when she accepts a couple's invitation to stay with them.

The Quest 🎵🎵▵

1996, Varese-Sarabande; from the movie *The Quest*, Universal Pictures, 1996.

Album Notes: *Music*: Randy Edelman; *Orchestrations*: Ralph Ferraro; *Music Editor*: David Bondelevitch; Orchestra conducted by Randy Edelman; *Album Producer*: Randy Edelman; *Engineer*: Elton Ahi.

Selections: 1 Opening/The Dream (1:52); 2 Chris Beats Germany (3:27); 3 Old New York (1:20); 4 Invitation (2:34); 5 Khan Kills Phang (3:47); 6 Flashback (1:49); 7 To The City Of Battle (3:46); 8 Drums On The Beach (3:12); 9 Smile Please (1:28); 10 The Greatest Fighters (3:11); 11 Sentenced to Death (3:53); 12 Brazil Accompaniment (2:52); 13 Monkey Boy And Snake Eyes (1:09); 14 The Wire (1:05); 15 American Theme (2:18); 16 Finale/Fulfillment Of The Quest (2:50).

Review: Randy Edelman's always friendly fusion of acoustic and electronic instruments brings an epic quality to Jean-Claude Van Damme's directorial debut. Set during the early part of this century, Van Damme plays a pickpocket on the run from the law who becomes a contestant in a world-class fighting tournament in Asia. The score alternates between lavish orchestrations for the period ("Old New York"), some humorous string passages ("Smile Please"), and the kind of hard hitting percussion Edelman first established in *Dragon: The Bruce Lee Story* for the fight sequences ("Chris Beats Germany").

David Hirsch

Quest for Fire 🎵🎵🎵🎵

1982, RCA Records; from the movie *Quest for Fire*, 20th Century-Fox, 1981.

Album Notes: *Music*: Philippe Sarde; The London Symphony Orchestra, The London Philharmonic Orchestra, The Ambrosian Singers, The Percussion Ensemble of Strasbourg, conducted by Philippe Sarde; *Featured Musicians*: Syrinx (pan flute), Michel Sanvoisin (bass flute); *Album Producers*: Philippe Sarde, Michel Larmand; *Engineer*: William Flageollet.

Selections: 1 Creation Of Fire (1:46); 2 Wagabous (1:56); 3 Cave Attack (4:14); 4 The Last Ander (3:05); 5 Saber-Teeth Lions (6:30); 6 The Small Blue Female (1:15); 7 Kzamns (3:36); 8 Quest For Fire (Love Theme)(5:00); 9 The Village Of Painted People (2:50); 10 Mammoths (2:17); 11 Naoh's Distress (2:09); 12 The Birth Of Love (3:39); 13 The Bear Fight (4:50); 14 The Beginning Of Future (1:32).

Review: One of the most unique films of the '80s, Jean-Jacques Annaud's *Quest for Fire* took on the daunting task of trying to realistically depict the prehistoric world, and succeeded brilliantly. One reason for the film's success is the excellent score by Philippe Sarde. Given that the film has no dialogue whatsoever, it fell to Sarde's music to serve as one of the film's primary communicative tools. As a result of its assertive role, Sarde's music is highly listenable on disc. There are some derivative moments ("Creation of Fire" owes heavily to Penderecki), but overall this is an impressive work of much originality. Expansive and brooding, it evokes the primitive, austere and brutal world of pre-history. The orchestration is large and full, and the performance superb, featuring the London Symphony, London Philharmonic, Ambrosian Singers and Les Percussions de Strasbourg, conducted by Peter Knight (who also orchestrated). "Village of the Painted People" is scored exclusively for percussion and one of the most interesting tracks, while Sarde's love theme is rapturous and full. Recorded at Abbey Road Studios, the sound quality is particularly excellent. A wonderfully epic and other-worldly score, *Quest for Fire* is one of Philippe Sarde's most brilliant efforts.

Paul Andrew MacLean

The Quick and the Dead 🎵🎵🎵

1995, Varese-Sarabande; from the movie *The Quick and the Dead*, Tri-Star Films, 1995.

Album Notes: *Music*: Alan Silvestri; *Orchestrations*: William Ross; *Music Editor*: Kenneth Karman; Orchestra conducted by Alan Silvestri; *Album Producer*: Alan Silvestri; *Engineer*: Dennis Sands.

Selections: 1 Redemption (3:25); 2 Gunfight Montage (1:41); 3 Couldn't Tell Us Apart (1:17); 4 John Herod (1:22); 5 Ellen's First Round (1:10); 6 Lady's The Winner (:47); 7 Dinner Tonight (2:11); 8 Cort's Story (1:02); 9 Ellen vs. Dred (1:10); 10 Kid vs. Herod (4:17); 11 I Don't Wanna Die (2:00); 12 The Big Day (2:27); 13 Ellen Returns (3:54); 14 The Law's Come Back To Town (:49); 15 The Quick And The Dead (End Credits)(3:30).

Review: Alan Silvestri goes Ennio Morricone in this amiable enough pastiche of western movie music cliches. Since the movie—the unsuccessful Sam Raimi western with Sharon Stone—is somewhat of a take-off on the classic Eastwood pictures (with Stone as "The Woman with No Name"), it figures that Silvestri's score would be modeled on the Leone sound-tracks to a point. After hearing the high-pitched, *The Good, the Bad and the Ugly*-based motif, we know that's exactly what we're going to get, as Silvestri has written an enjoyable con-glomeration that represents both his often percussive-driven style and the obvious influence from Italian westerns. While the music isn't original or inventive enough to work on its own terms, on the level of parody, the score succeeds admirably.

Andy Dursin

The Quiet American

1996, DRG Records; from the movie *The Quiet American*, United Artists, 1958.

See: The Barefoot Contessa

The Quiet Man

1994, Varese-Sarabande Records; from the movie *The Quiet Man*, Republic Pictures, 1952.

See: Samson and Delilah

The Quiet Man 𝄞𝄞𝄞𝄞𝄞

1995, Scannan Film Classics; from the movie *The Quiet Man*, Republic Pictures, 1952.

Album Notes: *Music*: Victor Young; *Orchestrations*: Victor Young, Leo Shuken; The Dublin Screen Orchestra, conducted by Kenneth Alwyn; *Featured Artists*: Gerard Farrelly (key-boards), Anne Buckley (vocal), The Dublin Pub Singers; *Album Producer*: Philip Lane; *Engineer*: Vinnie Kilcullen.

Selections: 1 Main Title/Castletown Opening (2:00); 2 This Way!/Journey To Innisfree/Humble Cottage (2:25); 3 Sean Sees Mary Kate For The First Time (Sheep Grazing)/Arrival In Innisfree (2:33); 4 The Wild Colonial Boy/River Cottage (2:22); 5 The Race (3:11); 6 The Courting/Bicycle Made For Two (Vil-lage Street)(3:43); 7 Love Scene (The Stream/The Grave-

"The orchestra has a limited sound palette, synthesizers a vast one. But a synthesizer score sounds old very rapidly. Orchestral scoring is what you use for a long shelf life."

Trevor Jones
(Time Magazine, 9-11-95)

yard)(4:21); 8 Trooper Thorn (The Fight Bell)(1:19); 9 The Isle Of Innisfree (R. Farrelly) (3:20) *Anne Buckley*; 10 I'll Take You Home Again Kathleen (T. Westendorf) (3:45); 11 Cottage Fireside (Forlorn)(2:39); 12 Galway Bay (2:24) *The Dublin Pub Singers*; 13 Prelude To The Big Fight (2:51); 14 The Fight (2:26); 15 Finale/End Title (2:06); 16 The Isle Of Innisfree (reprise)(R. Farrelly) (4:08).

Review: One of John Ford's most memorable films, *The Quiet Man* stars John Wayne as an unlikely romantic leading man (after years of playing a rugged cowboy or a no-nonsense GI), an Irish American who returns to the land of his ancestors, buys the country home where he was born, and takes an immediate shine to a local girl, who is not insensitive either (Maureen O'Hara, resplendent in a role that seemed tailor-made), immediately irk-ing her brother, a bully landowner who also wanted to buy the cottage. Told in a slow, affecting style that is part of its endearing charm, the film ends in a sensational showdown between the two men, a brawl to end all brawls. The score for the film was com-posed by Victor Young, who, at Ford's request, made use of many Irish folk tunes to give his music the right coloring. At the time the film came out, excerpts from his score were released on an LP on the Decca label, and they can be found coupled with *Samson and Delilah* (q.v.), another score by Young, on a primitive-sounding mono CD from Varese-Sarabande.

This new CD, recorded by the Dublin Screen Orchestra conducted by Kenneth Alwyn, brings Young's music into the digital era in a recording that brims with excitement and in-cludes many cues previously unavailable. An uncommonly flor-id score, *The Quiet Man* enabled Young to tap into a rich lode of folk material, including "The Isle of Innisfree" and "I'll Take You Home Again Kathleen," and develop these tunes into breathtaking themes that are strongly evocative and beautiful. The resulting album is a joy from beginning to end, and strongly recommended.

Quigley Down Under 🎵🎵🎵▷

1990, Intrada Records; from the movie *Quigley Down Under*, M-G-M, 1990.

Album Notes: *Music*: Basil Poledouris; *Orchestrations*: Greig McRitchie, Mark McKenzie; *Music Editor*: Tom Villano; Orchestra conducted by Basil Poledouris; *Album Producer*: Basil Poledouris; *Engineer*: Tim Boyle.

Selections: 1 Main Title (3:17); 2 The Fight (4:57); 3 Native Montage (2:11); 4 Marston's Murderers (3:31); 5 Cora's Story (3:18); 6 The Fire (2:57); 7 The Gift (5:25); 8 The Attack (2:49); 9 The Capture (2:44); 10 Freedom (3:34); 11 Matthew Quigley (5:22).

Review: Basil Poledouris, of *Conan* fame, brought his rich sense of barbarian melody to this Simon Wincer film about a sharpshooter (Tom Selleck) who travels to Australia in the 1860s to work for a wealthy, evil land baron (Alan Rickman), and soon joins the side of the aborigines. Poledouris tips his hat to the western genre and American lead with an expansive and rhythmic, symphonic scope, characterizing the Australian setting not with any specific folk elements (no didgeridoos), but as a wide-open place of adventure and danger. Quigley's theme is a lilting, energetic piece with a mostly pentatonic clarinet melody over enthusiastic orchestra and banjo — think of Selleck's ear-to-ear, mustached smile — and this whimsical tune seems to characterize both the main character and his not-in-Kansas-anymore location. A love theme brings a tender, reflective contrast. Fans of Poledouris's big themes from *Conan, RoboCop, Flesh + Blood,* and *Lonesome Dove* will find more to love here.

Lukas Kendall

The Quiller Memorandum 🎵🎵🎵🎵

1989, Varese-Sarabande; from the movie *The Quiller Memorandum*, 20th Century-Fox, 1966.

Album Notes: *Music*: John Barry; *Lyrics*: Mack David; *Orchestrations*: John Barry; Orchestra conducted by John Barry; *Album Producer*: John Barry.

Selections: 1 Main Theme: Wednesday's Child (2:10); 2 Quiller Caught/The Fight (2:48); 3 The Barrel Organ (2:39); 4 Oktober/Walk From The River (3:45); 5 Downtown (T. Hatch)(2:20); 6 Main Title Theme (2:03); 7 Wednesday's Child (2:35) *Matt Monroe*; 8 The Love Scene/The Old House (3:49); 9 Autobahn March (2:43); 10 He Knows The Way Out (2:16); 11 Night Walk In Berlin (3:03); 12 Quiller And The Bomb (2:33); 13 Have You Heard Of A Man Called Jones?/End Title (1:53).

Review: In the days when John Barry used to have fun, he scored many films that were distinguished by the imaginative themes he created and in which he smartly captured the exciting pace of the narrative. In one such example, *The Quiller Memorandum*, he wrote a score that has endured, matching the evocative tones in this spy thriller set in contemporary Germany, in which George Segal plays a charmingly engaging undercover British agent sent to West Berlin to infiltrate a group of neo-Nazis. While a saxophone rendition of the pop song "Downtown" sounds somewhat dispensable, the suggestive cues, in which a cymbalum provides an effective, colorful aura, reflect the unfolding action scene and the loneliness of the agent who knows he cannot even rely on his own people to help him if he gets caught. Matt Monro's delivery of "Wednesday's Child," is appropriately atmospheric.

Quiz Show 🎵🎵🎵🎵🎵

1994, Hollywood Records; from the movie *Quiz Show*, Hollywood Pictures, 1994.

Album Notes: *Music*: Mark Isham; *Orchestrations*: Ken Kugler, Dell Hake; *Jazz Arrangements*: Mark Isham, Ken Kugler, Kim Scharmberg; Orchestra conducted by Ken Kugler; *Featured Musicians*: David Goldblatt (piano), John Clayton (bass), Ed Shaughnessy (drums), Dennis Budimir (guitar), Rick Baptiste, Conte Candoli, Charles Davis, Charles Findley, Mark Isham (trumpet), Nicholas Lane, John Lane, Bruce Paulson, Charles Loper (trombone), Marshall Royal, Steven Tavaglione, Peter Christlieb, Bob Sheppard, Jack Nimitz (saxophone), Dale Anderson (marimba), Larry Bunker (vibraphone), Kurt Wortman (percussion); *Album Producer*: Mark Isham; *Engineer*: Stephen Krause.

Selections: 1 Moritat (K. Weill/B. Brecht)(4:44) *Lyle Lovett*; 2 The World's Smartest Man (5:22); 3 The Oversight Blues (10:39); 4 The Underdog (4:24); 5 Your Secret's Safe With Me (3:12); 6 Hunting In Your Underwear (3:52); 7 On The Shoulders Of Life (1:24); 8 Books And Learning (1:24); 9 A Chance Is What I'm Giving You (1:50); 10 The Committee Calls (2:14); 11 The Word Is Bluffing (1:14); 12 Television On Trial (3:06); 13 Everything Has Its Price (4:18).

Review: Lyle Lovett's slow-paced and slyly sardonic rendition of "Moritat," the song of Mack the Knife, seems a perfect way to get into this soundtrack album to the story of the quiz show scandal that rocked television in the late 1950s. The song, however, is the low point in a brilliant jazz score fashioned by Mark Isham, that prominently features some great soloists, including Conte Candoli, the legendary West Coast trumpet player. While some cues in the score are relatively short, two, "The World's Smartest Man" and "The Oversight Blues," are generously long and explicit, and make a powerful contribution to the album itself. The diversity in the score, with some cues written for big band, some for a quartet, and others for solo instruments, makes listening to it all the more enjoyable, with the moods projected occasionally interrupted by flavorful bits of underscoring ("Books and Learning," "Television on Trial") that provide still another different orchestral color to the proceedings.

Quo Vadis 🎵🎵🎵🎵🎵

1985, London Records; from the movie *Quo Vadis*, M-G-M, 1951.

Album Notes: *Music:* Miklos Rozsa; The Royal Philharmonic Orchestra and Chorus, conducted by Miklos Rozsa.

Selections: 1 Prelude (2:12); 2 Marcus And Lygia (3:59); 3 Fertility Hymn (1:24); 4 The Burning Of Rome (3:42); 5 Petronius' Banquet/Meditation and Death (4:30); 6 Ave Caesar (4:50); 7 Chariot Chase (3:06); 8 Assyrian Dance (1:56); 9 Aftermath (Death Of Peter, Death Of Poppaea, Nero's Suicide) (5:07); 10 Hail Galba (1:57); 11 Finale (4:37); 12 Epilogue (2:56).

Review: The first Roman epic scored by Miklos Rozsa, *Quo Vadis* contains in embryo form all the concepts and ideas the composer would expand on in later efforts like *Ben-Hur* and *King of Kings* — heavily ornamented brass flourishes, liturgical hymns, strongly etched love themes, exciting action cues. Combining reconstructed sounds from Greek origin to replace the non-existent Roman music, and early Judaic themes with his own European idiom, Rozsa wrote a remarkably "authentic" set of cues that became a blueprint for films with a similar background. Though played under the action on the screen and necessarily overlooked, the music soars when appreciated on its own terms and mesmerizes the listener with its vibrancy and barely contained excitement. Cues like "The Burning of Rome," "Chariot Chase," and "Hail Galba," among others, stand out in a score that is extraordinarily rich and rewarding. While the original soundtrack album, which consisted of dramatic highlights and was in mono sound in the original LP issue, awaits reissue on compact disc (possibly without the dialogues, but with the full score in stereo if the multitrack tapes still exist), this rerecording, with the composer conducting one of England's two great orchestras, stands as the only authoritative album available.

Radio Days 🎵🎵🎵🎵

1987, Novus/RCA Records; from the movie *Radio Days*, Orion Pictures, 1987.

Album Notes: *Album Producer:* Michael Brooks; *Engineers:* Dennis Ferrante, Edward Rich.

Selections: 1 In The Mood (3:31) *Glenn Miller and His Orchestra*; 2 I Double Dare You (2:42) *Larry Clinton and His Orchestra*; 3 Opus No. 1 (2:55) *Tommy Dorsey and His Orchestra*; 4 Frenesi (3:02) *Artie Shaw and His Orchestra*; 5 The Donkey Serenade (3:20) *Allan Jones*; 6 Body And Soul (3:28) *Benny Goodman Trio*; 7 You And I (2:44) *Tommy Dorsey and His Orchestra*; 8 I Remember Pearl Harbor (2:26) *Swing & Sway With Sammy Kaye*; 9 That Old Feeling (2:42) *Guy Lombardo and His Royal Canadians*; 10 (There'll Be Blue Birds Over) The White Cliffs Of Dover (2:53) *Glenn Miller and His Orchestra*; 11 Goodbye (3:23) *Benny Goodman and His Orchestra*; 12 I'm Getting Sentimental Over You (3:38) *Tommy Dorsey and His Orchestra*; 13 Lullaby Of Broadway (2:27) *Richard Himber and His Ritz-Carlton Orchestra*; 14 American Patrol (3:20) *Glenn Miller and His Orchestra*; 15 Take The "A" Train (2:56) *Duke Ellington and His Orchestra*; 16 One, Two, Three, Kick (3:18) *Xavier Cugat and His Waldorf-Astoria Orchestra*.

Review: A great big band album that beautifully captures the feel and moods that permeate Woody Allen's fond memories of the time when radio reigned supreme, *Radio Days* is a genuine treat for anyone with love for the music or the era. With not a single misstep in the track selection and performances by some of the greatest bands around at the time (Glenn Miller, Tommy Dorsey, Duke Ellington, Benny Goodman, Sammy Kaye, Artie Shaw, among others), this is simply a wonderful recording, only slightly marred by the sound quality which is not always up to par. However, many of these tracks have since been remastered and appear elsewhere in much improved sound.

Radio Flyer 🎵🎵

1992, Giant Records; from the movie *Radio Flyer*, Columbia Pictures, 1992.

Album Notes: *Music:* Hans Zimmer; *Orchestrations:* Shirley Walker, Bruce Fowler; *Music Editor:* Laura Perlman; Orchestra conducted by Shirley Walker; *Featured Musicians:* Richard Harvey (Pan pipes), Nick Glenne-Smith (piano), Tommy Morgan (harmonica), Jim Kanter (clarinet); *Album Producers:* Hans Zimmer, Jay Rifkin; *Engineer:* Jay Rifkin.

Selections: 1 Radio Flyer Part 1: Building The Flyer/On The Road To Geronimo/Lost Secrets and Fascination (9:58); 2 Radio Flyer Part 2: Expeditioning/Mix The Potion/Four Discoveries (7:00); 3 Radio Flyer Part 3: Sampson And Shane/Fisher's Legend/The Big Idea (13:37); 4 The Name Game (L. Chase/S. Elliston) (3:00) *Shirley Ellis*.

Review: If you make a movie about child abuse, you'd best not portray the subject as a glossy children's fantasy — the mistake that Richard Donner made when directing this expensive bomb, one of the biggest money losers of the early 1990s. Hans Zimmer's completely uneven score features all of his usual ingredients (the large symphony orchestra conducted by Shirley Walker, plenty of synthesizers as well as chorus), and can either be irritating to the point where you think your brain is about to explode (as in the sappy kid's chorus sections), or so uplifting and downright melodramatic that you have to admire the score for keeping such a straight face while going absurdly over-the-top. Whatever your opinion of this score, you must admit that the composer tried his hardest to entertain. The out-of-print album has become something of a staple in record store cut-out bins, (mis)leading some to believe that the CD will be valuable one day, even if it is only loosely connected to the movie itself, that's about the only hope for a profit this project will ever make.

Andy Dursin

Radioland Murders ♫♫♫♫

1994, MCA Records; from the movie *Radioland Murders,* **Universal Pictures, 1994.**

Album Notes: *Music:* Joel McNeely; *Orchestrations:* David Slonaker; *Music Preparation:* Vic Fraser; *Song Arrangements:* Joel McNeely, David Slonaker, Michael Patterson, Matt Harris, Steven Bramson; Orchestra conducted by Joel McNeely; *Featured Vocalists:* Randy Crenshaw, Al Dana, Michael Gallup, Jim Gilstrap, Rick Logan, Susan Stevens Logan, Amy London, Melissa Mackay, Susan McBride, Bobbi Page, Jackie Presti, Eugene Ruffolo, Don Shelton, Sally Stevens, Kerry Walsh, Dick Wells, Kim Wertz; *Album Producer:* Joel McNeely; *Engineers:* John Kurlander, Chris Dibble, Malcolm Luker, Dan Wallin, Scott Houle.

Selections: 1 Love Is On The Air Tonight (2:03); 2 Welcome To Radioland (3:43); 3 WBN Logo/Applebaum Shorts (:44); 4 A Guy What Takes His Time (3:08); 5 Back In The Saddle Again (G. Autry/R. Whiteley)(1:54) *Tracy Byrd;* 6 Gene's Pork And Beans (:58); 7 I'll Be Glad When You're Dead (You Rascal You)(C. Davenport)(2:11); 8 Suspect Roundup/Spy Story (3:39); 9 That Old Black Magic (H. Arlen/J. Mercer)(1:36) *Billy Barty;* 10 Crazy People (2:06); 11 Java Jive (1:26); 12 In The Mood (A. Razaf/J. Garland)(3:16); 13 Interrogation Opera: Grand Inquisitor's Aria (from *Don Carlo*)(G. Verdi)/Queen Of The Night's Aria (from *The Magic Flute*)(W.A. Mozart)(2:47); 14 King's Washing Machines/WBN Logo (1:15); 15 That Old Feeling (S. Fain/L. Brown)(3:13) *Rosemary Clooney;* 16 I Miss You So (2:51) *The Voltage Brothers;* 17 Hudson Automobiles/ Darabont's BBQ Sauce (1:25); 18 Tico Tico/Don't Let Your Love Go Wrong/WBN Logo (4:06); 19 What'll I Do (I. Berlin)(2:44) *Joey Lawrence;* 20 Gork, Son Of Fire (2:26); 21 The Killer Is...

(4:36); 22 Death On The Radio Tower (5:05); 23 And The Angels Sing (Z. Elman/J. Mercer)(1:59); 24 End Titles (And The Angels Sing)(4:41).

Review: *Radioland Murders* is another big band era recording with a twist. While it quotes performances by artists from the radio era, this wonderfully evocative album draws its strength from the cues, written in the style of the period by Joel McNeely, including the whimsical, and accurately correct, "WBN logo" heard throughout in different versions. McNeely, making a much noticed contribution with this catchy score to a film that has its eccentric moments, captured the flavor of radio's golden age and provided sly comments of his own to this amusing mystery set in a Chicago radio station where someone is murdering the company employees one by one. The potential suspects (or victims)—an odd sound effects man, a sultry singer, a slick announcer and the station owner— all find their comeuppance, with each turn in the convoluted story eliciting a wry musical expression.

A Rage in Harlem ♫♫ᵖ

1991, Varese-Sarabande; from the movie *A Rage in Harlem,* **Miramax Films, 1991.**

Album Notes: *Music:* Elmer Bernstein; *Orchestrations:* Christopher Palmer; Orchestra conducted by Elmer Bernstein; *Album Producer:* Cynthia Millar; *Engineer:* Brian Masterson.

Selections: 1 A Rage In Harlem (2:05); 2 Imabelle (1:44); 3 Seduction (3:34); 4 Jackson (2:34); 5 New Toy Love (3:39); 6 Easy Money (3:32); 7 Morning At Jackson's (2:35); 8 Jackson And Goldie (3:03); 9 Tender Words (1:43); 10 Major Chase (2:57); 11 Gus (2:37); 12 Big Kathy Killed (4:24); 13 Fight (2:06); 14 Pop Slim (1:33); 15 Aftermath (:28); 16 Happy Train (2:51).

Review: Elmer Bernstein found great success utilizing jazz when composing his scores for films like *The Man with the Golden Arm* and *Love with the Proper Stranger,* and *A Rage in Harlem,* Bill Duke's 1991 adaptation of the Chester Himes novel, represents a return trip to earlier times for the composer. Unfortunately, there's just something rather stagnant about this score, which features cues with appropriate jazz-ensemble focused orchestrations but also the tendency to just coast along with by-the-numbers melodies. There's nothing infectious or particularly buoyant about the music here, and that lack of energy sadly makes this score far inferior to Bernstein's predecessing jazz efforts, and a rather large disappointment overall.

Andy Dursin

Raggedy Man ♪♪♪

1981, Varese-Sarabande Records; from the movie *Raggedy Man,* Universal Pictures, 1981.

Album Notes: *Music:* Jerry Goldsmith; Orchestra conducted by Jerry Goldsmith; *Album Producer:* Jerry Goldsmith.

Selections: 1 Main Title (3:53); 2 Henry And Harry (5:11); 3 Number Please (4:34); 4 The Kite (4:40); 5 Runaways (6:28); 6 Mexican Tune (2:57); 7 End Of Calvin (3:54); 8 End Title (2:09).

Review: One of a handful of "limited edition" releases sold by Varese Sarabande Records in 1991, this is, in actuality, only an average Jerry Goldsmith score. Written in the same vein as scores like Elmer Bernstein's *To Kill a Mockingbird* and other poignant, character-driven works by Goldsmith (i.e. *The Flim-Flam Man*), *Raggedy Man* boasts a deliberately paced score for flute, harmonica and orchestra, creating a pleasant small-town feel that is sustained throughout the album — with the notable exception of some dissonant material thrown in at the end to coincide with the movie's rather odd left turn into climactic melodrama. The score is engaging but ultimately unremarkable, and went unreleased at the time of the film's 1981 theatrical playdates when the movie failed in theaters. While the concept of Varese's "CD Club" was initially mouth-watering to fans of movie music, it's a shame that a number of other scores held in high regard by listeners, like John Williams' *Heartbeeps*, Elmer Bernstein's *Slipstream*, Bill Conti's *Victory*, never received the red-carpet treatment that this serviceable — particularly considering Goldsmith standards — but rather pedestrian score did.

Andy Dursin

The Raggedy Rawney ♪♪

1988, Silva Screen Records; from the movie *The Raggedy Rawney,* Hand Made Films, 1988.

Album Notes: *Music:* Michael Kamen; *Featured Musician:* Michael Kamen (Kurzweil 250, oboe); *Songs:* John Tams; *Album Producer:* Michael Kamen; *Engineer:* Stephen McLaughlin.

Selections: 1 The Tribe (4:21); 2 You Should See Nellie Pass Water (:49) *Bob Hoskins* ; 3 Caravans (4:49); 4 The Horse Race (2:51); 5 Farmyard (:45); 6 Rolling Home (J. Tams)(1:32) *John Tams*; 7 Jessie And Tom (4:35); 8 Daisy Chain (1:46); 9 Wedding Dress (1:19); 10 Bullroarer/Band Of Lace (J. Tams) (2:47); 11 Peanock Polka (Darky's Polka)(J. Tams)(1:25); 12 Simon Drowned (2:55); 13 Funeral Lament (M. Bell)(2:33) *Maggie Bell*; 14 Prayer (2:04); 15 The Officer (1:47); 16 The Children (2:44); 17 The Raggedy Rawney (1:09).

Review: This plaintive score is a far cry from *Die Hard* and *Lethal Weapon,* but it's intriguing in its simplicity. Kamen composed and performed the score primarily on an oboe and a Kurzweil synthesizer, with some Irish music and songs provided by John Tams. This is not a terribly melodic score. The music is primarily atmospheric, full of woodwindish synths, eerie, straining chords, and strident zimbalom notes from the Kurzweil. The score's ambiance is very subdued and slow-moving, its orchestration sparse and plain. As a result, it's a difficult score to grasp at times.

Randall Larson

Raiders of the Lost Ark ♪♪♪♪

1995, DCC Compact Classics; from the movie *Raiders of the Lost Ark,* Paramount Pictures, 1981.

Album Notes: *Music:* John Williams; *Orchestrations:* Herbert W. Spencer; The London Symphony Orchestra conducted by John Williams; *Album Producer:* John Williams; *Engineer:* Eric Tomlinson; *CD Producer:* Nick Redman; *Engineer:* Steve Hoffman.

Selections: 1 The Raiders March (2:50); 2 Main Title: South America, 1936 (4:10); 3 In The Idol's Temple (5:26); 4 Flight From Peru (2:20); 5 Journey To Nepal (2:11); 6 The Medallion (2:55); 7 To Cairo (1:29); 8 The Basket Game (5:04); 9 The Map Room: Dawn (3:52); 10 Reunion and The Dig Begins (4:10); 11 The Well Of The Souls (5:28); 12 Airplane Fight (4:37); 13 Desert Chase (8:15); 14 Marion's Theme (2:08); 15 The German Sub/To The Nazi Hideout (4:32); 16 Ark Trek (1:33); 17 The Miracle Of The Ark (6:05); 18 The Warehouse (:56); 19 End Credits (5:20).

Review: This beautifully-produced restoration of Williams' classic adventure score assembles the lion's share of the score (78 minutes) with superior sound quality. Produced at the height of Williams' epic period (between *Superman* and *The Empire Strikes Back*), *Raiders* is a rip-snorting action ride that begins early on after a moody, low-key opening as intrepid archeologist Indiana Jones enters a booby-trapped cave in the jungles of Peru. Williams' scoring of the escape from the cavern is a showcase of frenzied, virtuoso orchestral effects beautifully capped by the energetic pizzicato of "Escape from Peru" with its engaging introduction of the brassy, infectious Indiana Jones fanfare. There are action highlights to spare, including the film's indelible truck chase (restored from the sliced-and-diced original album presentation) and some furious accompaniment to a deadly fistfight beneath the propellers of a flying wing, as well as the spectral, mysterious underscoring of scenes involving the search for the Ark of the Covenant, including a beautiful Middle Eastern-sounding woodwind theme and the eerie, imposing passages played under the discovery and excavation of the Ark's resting place ("The Map Room: Dawn" and "The Well of Souls"). Like Williams' *Star Wars*, *Raiders* has a freshness that's somewhat lacking in his more calculated efforts on the second and third films in the series.

Jeff Bond

See also: Indiana Jones and the Temple of Doom and Indiana Jones and the Last Crusade

Rain Man ✶✶✶✶

1989, Capitol Records; from the movie *Rain Man*, United Artists Pictures, 1989.

Album Notes: *Music*: Hans Zimmer; *Featured Artists*: The Belle Stars, Johnny Clegg and Savuca, The Delta Rhythm Boys, Etta James, Ian Gilland and Roger Glover, Bananarama, Rob Wasserman with Aaron Neville, Lou Christie; *Producers*: Brian Tench, Hilton Rosenthal, Tony Romeo; *Album Producer*: Allan Mason.

Selections: 1 Iko Iko (Hawkins/Jones/Hawkins/Jones/ Johnson/Jones/Thomas) (2:54) *The Belle Stars*; 2 Scatterlings Of Africa (J. Clegg)(4:06) *Johnny Clegg and Savuca*; 3 Dry Bones (p.d.)(2:55) *The Delta Rhythm Boys*; 4 At Last (H. Warren/M. Gordon)(3:01) *Etta James*; 5 Lonely Avenue (D. Pomus)(3:10) *Ian Gillan, Roger Glover*; 6 Nathan Jones (L.Caston/K. Wakefield)(5:12) *Bananarama*; 7 Leaving Wallbrook/On The Road (H. Zimmer)(2:54); 8 Las Vegas/End Credits (H. Zimmer)(8:22); 9 Stardust (H. Carmichael/M. Parrish)(4:36) *Rob Wasserman, Aaron Neville*; 10 Beyond The Blue Horizon (L. Robin/R. Whiting) (3:45) *Lou Christie*.

Review: If only because of the line-up of performers who appear on it (Johnny Clegg and Savuca, The Delta Rhythm Boys, Bananarama, Lou Christie, Aaron Neville, etc.), this soundtrack album would be worth having. But the musical selections are also quite strong, with several standards sprinkled along the way, and songs that are generally quite enjoyable. In all this display of inventive tunes and interpretations, Hans Zimmer's lonely two cues hardly make a dent, though the composer seems to have perfectly caught the spirit of this story about two brothers with diametrically opposed lifestyles, one an autistic genius, capable of having complex thoughts and being mentally limited all at once, the other a selfish luxury car salesman whose only motivation is to make money fast. The two selections here detail the cross-country trip made by the brothers, Raymond and Charlie, after Charlie discovers that their dead father has left all his money to his sibling, a trip that will result in a better understanding of themselves and the bonds that tie them together. Zimmer's music, in keeping with the tone of the story, is forceful and extremely evocative.

The Rainbow ✶✶✶½

1989, Silva Screen Records; from the movie *The Rainbow*, Vestron Pictures, 1989.

Album Notes: *Music*: Carl Davis; *Orchestrations*: Nic Raine; The Graunke Symphony Orchestra, conducted by Carl Davis; *Featured Musicians*: The Hartford Motors Concert Brass, conducted by Dr. Keith Wilkinson; *Album Producer*: Nic Raine; *Engineer*: Allan Snelling.

Selections: 1 Prelude and Opening Titles (4:13); 2 Walking Home (1:03); 3 The Swingboats (1:37); 4 Ursula And Winifred (2:40); 5 Seduction/The Lettuce Patch (3:17); 6 Exam Results (2:02); 7 School Assembly (Playmates) (I. Hampden) (1:22); 8 Mr. Harby (3:34); 9 The Wedding: The British Grenadiers Fanfare (trad.)/The Lancers(trad.)/Poor Wandering One (A. Sullivan/W. Gilbert) (4:58) *The Hartford Motors Concert Brass*; 10 Moonlight Lovers (2:42); 11 Military Two-Step (1:26); 12 The Waterfall (3:27); 13 Cottage Idyll (2:57); 14 Pursuit Through The Forest (4:14); 15 Ursula's Dream (1:37); 16 The Rainbow End Titles (2:47); 17 Opening Titles (alt. version) (2:43); 18 Moonlight Lovers (alt. version) (2:14); 19 The Rainbow End Titles (alt. version) (2:45).

Review: Thanks to his world tours, where he conducts live his scores to classic silent films like *Napoleon*, *Ben-Hur* and others, Carl Davis seems destined to be less likely remembered as the composer of contemporary film scores. *The Rainbow* is typically bombastic and overtly romantic for its period setting. Davis plays the seduction and sexual education of a young schoolteacher to the hilt with his broad musical strokes. Like most collections of his work, this album has a distinct feel of a classical concert piece, and that makes it a delightful listen, devoid of any experience with the film. The score's flow is carefully divided by Ida Hampton's "School Assembly," and a suite of traditional military and Gilbert & Sullivan music for "The Wedding" sequence. Davis has also included three alternate variations of cues that were changed at the request of director Ken Russell. "Moonlight Loves," for example, was toned down from its original version (track 18) when Russell expressed to the composer that something simpler (track 10) was needed for the film.

David Hirsch

Raintree County ✶✶✶✶½

1989, Preamble Records; from the movie *Raintree County*, M-G-M, 1957.

Album Notes: *Music*: Johnny Green; The M-G-M Studio Symphony Orchestra and Chorus, conducted by Johnny Green; *Album Producers*: Johnny Green, Jesse Kaye; *Engineer*: William Steinkamp; *CD Producer*: John Lasher; Engineer Robert Vosgien.

Selections: CD 1: 1 Overture (3:35); 2 Prologue (Song Of Raintree County) (J. Green/P.F. Webster)(2:46); 3 Nell And Johnny's Graduation Gifts (3:46); 4 Johnny's Search For The Raintree (3:44); 5 Flash Perkins' Theme (2:27); 6 Johnny And Susanna's First Meeting (4:23); 7 July Picnic (6:01); 8 Johnny's Farewell To Nell/River Wedding Night (7:24); 9 Burned-Out Mansion/ Susanna's Obsession/Lament For Henrietta (5:19); 10 Carriage Ride (:51); 11 Return To Raintree County (4:05).

CD 2: 1 Susanna's Madness/War Begins (6:39); 2 Flash Joins Up/Little Jeemie Is Born/Nell Returns (5:03); 3 Susanna's Se-cret/Susanna And Jeemie Disappear/ Johnny Leaves For The Front/Finale, Act One (6:17); 4 Prologue, Act Two (3:00); 5 Battle Montage/Atlanta Destroyed (3:02); 6 Johnny And Flash At Fairweather/Jeemie Is Found/The Ambush/Flash Dies (5:13); 7 Johnny's Escape/ War's End/Reunion With Susanna/ Lincoln's Funeral Train (5:33); 8 Susanna's Tragic Decision and Her Death/Nell, Johnny And Jeemie Together/Finale (8:13).

Review: Though he spent more than 10 years at M-G-M, where he was General Music Director and Executive in Charge of Music, and he scored many important films during that time, Johnny Green is not often thought of as a great composer in the same league with his more visible peers from that era. The one film for which he is best remembered, however, is a lavish Civil War drama, *Raintree County,* based on a novel by Ross Lockridge, which the studio wanted to be a follow-up of sorts to the blockbuster *Gone with the Wind.* Filmed at great expense, using the newly developed 65mm process, and with a brilliant cast that included Elizabeth Taylor, Montgomery Clift and Eva Marie Saint, the film captures the passion and drama in the novel, set against the broad rich canvas of the Lincoln presidency and the turmoil between the North and the South. It may not be *Gone with the Wind* redux, but it is big, epic, and memorable. So is Green's score, which was perfectly adapted to the needs of the story, though it does not mark the film indelibly the way Max Steiner's score marks *Gone with the Wind,* nor does its main theme, the evocative "Song of Raintree County," ever hope to become another "Tara Theme." Still, quite professional in its approach and accurately reflecting the sweep-ing action on-screen, *Raintree County* remains an important score, magnificently serviced by this complete 2-CD release.

Raising Arizona/ Blood Simple 🎵🎵🎵

1985, Varese-Sarabande; from the movies *Raising Arizona* and *Blood Simple,* Circle Films, 1985.

Album Notes: *Music:* Carter Burwell; *Featured Musicians: Rais-ing Arizona:* Carter Burwell (synthesizers, samples), Ben Freed (banjo), John Crowder (yodeling), Mieszyslaw Litwinski (whis-

tling, guitar), Geoffrey Gordon, Skip LaPlante (percussion), Alan Drogin, Steven Swartz, Don Peyton (ukuleles); *Blood Simple:* Carter Burwell (keyboards), Stanley Adler (bass guitar), Stephen Bray, Stanton Miranda (percussion); *Album Producer:* Carter Bur-well; *Engineers:* Sebastian Niessen, Rod Hui.

Selections: *RAISING ARIZONA:* 1 Introduction: A Hole In The Ground (:32); 2 Way Out There (Main Title)(1:18); 3 He Was Horrible (1:24); 4 Just Business (1:13); 5 The Letter (2:24); 6 Hail Lenny (2:12); 7 Raising Ukuleles (3:30); 8 Dream Of The Future (2:25); 9 Shopping Arizona (2:45); 10 Return To The Nursery (:37);

BLOOD SIMPLE: 11 Crash And Burn (2:26); 12 Blood Simple (3:30); 13 Chain Gang (4:50); 14 The March (2:30); 15 Monkey Chant (1:02); 16 The Shooting (3:23); 17 Blood Simpler (1:19).

Review: The schizophrenic score for *Raising Arizona* has a problem deciding just what it wants to be, and that's what creates its charm. From the blue grass banjo opening, it morphs into a strange series of style changes, yodeling in the main title and eerie synth cues that stress danger. One track, "Just Business," is a mix of odd vocals and the rattling, per-haps, of garbage can lids. "Hail Lenny" seems to have been inspired by Ennnio Morricone's "Spaghetti Western" scores and, oh yeah, there's a couple of real melodies, too, like "Dreaming of the Future." Perhaps what makes this score so intriguing is that it never sits in one place long enough to wear out its welcome, just like the Coen Brothers' movie did, chang-ing tone at the most bizarre moments. Also included on the album is Burwell's first score for the Coens, *Blood Simple,* a restrained synth score that contrasts nicely with *Arizona's* dementia, and provides a solid base for the murder mystery's dark *film noir* aura.

David Hirsch

Raising Cain 🎵🎵ᵛ

1992, Milan Records; from the movie *Raising Cain,* Universal Pictures, 1992.

Album Notes: *Music:* Pino Donaggio; *Orchestrations:* Pino Donaggio, Natale Massara; *Electronic Sound Creations/Com-puter Performances:* Paolo Steffan; The Unione Musicisti di Roma, conducted by Natale Massara; *Album Producer:* Pino Donaggio; *Engineer:* Sergio Marcotulli.

Selections: 1 Raising Cain (2:00); 2 Tricking Karen (1:50); 3 Cain Takes Over (4:47); 4 Love Memories (3:12); 5 A Blow On The Head (4:17); 6 Jenny And Carter Talk (1:22); 7 Jenny's Return (2:39); 8 The Clock (2:25); 9 Father Against Cain (2:25); 10 The Sinking (1:36); 11 Dr. Walheim Hypnotizes Carter (5:10); 12 The Gift Giver (2:22); 13 Following Margo (2:00); 14 Shadows Of The Past (2:42); 15 Jenny Tries To Save Amy (1:44); 16 Flying Babies (3:38); 17 Carter's Return (1:21); 18 The Plan (3:15); 19 Love Wins (3:22).

Review: Pino Donaggio reteamed with Brian DePalma for the first time in eight years with this shameless hodge-podge score for one of the director's most unsatisfying ventures into Hitchcock territory. A music-box motive is joined by yearning strings in search of a resolution in Donaggio's score, which sounds like Michel Legrand's *Summer of '42* one moment and Bernard Herrmann's *Psycho* the next. Still, if you're a thriller fan and can get past the stylistic "influences," you'll probably get a kick out of Donaggio's score, which offers up a sexy sax during the film's love theme (is there any other instrument than conveys passion better than the saxophone?) with plenty of energy to spare. There's nothing here you haven't heard before, but that—at least somewhat—seems to be the point.

Andy Dursin

Rambling Rose 🎵🎵🎵🎵

1991, Virgin Movie Music; from the movie *Rambling Rose*, Seven Arts-New Line Cinema, 1991.

Album Notes: *Music*: Elmer Bernstein; Orchestra conducted by Elmer Bernstein; *Album Producer*: Cynthia Millar; *Engineer*: Brian Masterson.

Selections: 1 "Hello, I'm Rose" (5:23); 2 The Family Meets Rose (2:18); 3 Father's "Reverse Insomnia" (:55); 4 Orphans (1:41); 5 Revelation (3:14); 6 Love (1:59); 7 Dixie (Rose On The Town) (:42) *Louis Armstrong and The Dukes of Dixieland*; 8 "That Scruffy Looking Man" (3:06); 9 "Let The Crazy Creature Out" (2:26); 10 Fever (1:36); 11 Safe Home (1:01); 12 "Hired, Mired And Fired" (1:26); 13 Compassion (2:46); 14 Rose And Buddy (4:25); 15 Goodbyes (2:46); 16 "So Long Rose" (2:57); 17 Dixie (3:44) *Louis Armstrong and The Dukes of Dixieland*; 18 If I Could Be With You One Hour Tonight (H. Creamer/J. Johnson) (2:56) *Ruth Etting*.

Review: Throughout his career, Elmer Bernstein has written some seriously attractive scores, but none that have matched the serene beauty of this wonderful effort for a film starring Robert Duvall and Laura Dern. A flavorful story of an oversexed young woman, working as a maid in a small Georgia town in the mid-'30s and the effect she has on her employer and his family, the amusingly provocative tale prompted Bernstein to write a score, beautifully understated and brimming with delightful folksy little touches, which play an important role in giving the film the right atmosphere and makes for a very enjoyable listening experience. In his notes for this album, Bernstein remarks that when he first saw the film as a work in

progress, after he had been asked to write the music for it, "I felt [a] particular sense of excitement." The excitement translated itself into a remarkably distinctive score!

Rambo

Rambo: First Blood Part II
🎵🎵🎵🎵

1987, Varese-Sarabande; from the movie *Rambo: First Blood Part II*, 1985.

Album Notes: *Music*: Jerry Goldsmith; *Orchestrations*: Arthur Morton; The National Philharmonic Orchestra, conducted by Jerry Goldsmith; *Album Producers*: Jerry Goldsmith, Bruce Botnick; *Engineer*: Bruce Botnick.

Selections: 1 Main Title (2:08); 2 Preparation (1:12); 3 The Jump (3:12); 4 The Snake (1:43); 5 Stories (3:23); 6 The Cage (3:48); 7 Betrayed (4:20); 8 Escape From Torture (3:30); 9 Ambush (2:38); 10 Revenge (6:12); 11 Bowed Down (1:02); 12 Pilot Over (1:48); 13 Home Flight (2:56); 14 Day By Day (2:06); 15 Peace In Our Life (F. Stallone/P. Schless/J. Goldsmith) (3:12).

Review: Goldsmith hit his stride with this second *Rambo* film, the epitome of Reagan-era jingoistic action, which he scored with a nimble, adventurous work that is diametrically opposed to the dark, heavy sound of the original *First Blood*. The score launches with a surprisingly beautiful oriental theme that gives way to a new Americana theme for the Rambo character, although Goldsmith's familiar Rambo fanfare punctuates most of the film's triumphant action moments. It's almost non-stop chases and fights, alternating with sneaky suspense cues, but Goldsmith makes this surprisingly emotional, keying in on Sylvester Stallone's wounded characterization of the hypermuscled hero. The mix of strong melodic material and heavy-duty action rhythms makes this a score that should appeal to both longtime Goldsmith fans and younger listeners used to the composer's more romantic scores of the '90s.

Jeff Bond

See also: First Blood

Rambo III 🎵🎵🎵♭

1989, Intrada; from the movie *Rambo III*, Carolco Entertainment, 1988.

Album Notes: *Music*: Jerry Goldsmith; *Orchestrations*: Arthur Morton, Nancy Beach; The Hungarian State Opera Orchestra, conducted by Jerry Goldsmith; *Album Producer*: Jerry Goldsmith; *Engineer*: Mike Rossi; *CD Producer*: Douglass Fake.

Selections: 1 Another Time (3:58); 2 Preparations (6:21); 3 The Money (:52); 4 I'm Not Used To It (1:00); 5 Pesha War (1:12); 6

Afghanistan (2:38); 7 Questions (3:37); 8 Then I'll Die (3:34); 9 The Game (2:25); 10 Flaming Village (4:07); 11 The Aftermath (2:44); 12 Night Entry (3:58); 13 Under And Over (2:55); 14 Night Fight (6:50); 15 First Aid (2:46); 16 The Long Climb (3:25); 17 Going Down (1:52); 18 The Cave (3:31); 19 The Boot (1:53); 20 You Did It John (1:08); 21 The Show Down (1:26); 22 Final Battle (4:50); 23 I'll Stay (9:00).

Review: This Goldsmith trip to the Rambo well is probably the most lyrical score ever written for a film of this type, mixing smooth ethnic and electronic rhythms, coiling, propulsive action cues and some graceful, almost nocturne-like interludes. This lengthy, 70-minute CD features plenty of action highlights, from the ritualistic beat of "The Game" to the elaborate "Fire Fight" with its escalating series of frenzied string variations over pulsing flutes and woodwinds, and "The Boot" which builds a simple rhythmic motif into a monolithic tutti orchestral statement. The opening cue is built almost entirely from percussion, with some rhythm elements that could have come from a Doors song, while more subdued cues like "Then I'll Die" and "Peshawar" create beautifully evocative ethnic rhythms. Since Goldsmith's score was heavily sliced and diced in the film, this is the only way to hear it as he originally intended, including the composer's original end credits, which were replaced with pop songs in the movie.

Jeff Bond

Rampage ♪♪♪♪

1987, Virgin Movie Music; from the movie *Rampage*, DEG Films, 1987.

Album Notes: *Music*: Ennio Morricone; *Orchestrations*: Ennio Morricone; Orchestra Unione Musicisti di Roma, conducted by Ennio Morricone; *Album Producer*: Ennio Morricone; *Engineer*: Sergio Marcotulli.

Selections: 1 Rampage (4:15); 2 Son (:45); 3 Findings (1:21); 4 Over To The Jury (1:35); 5 Run, Run, Run (2:33); 6 Since Childhood (3:20); 7 Magma (2:16); 8 Rampage (3:59); 9 Gruesome Discovery (2:56); 10 Carillon (2:08); 11 District Attorney (1:40); 12 Mother (1:57); 13 Recollections (3:40).

Review: In another step away from the style he used for his most popular efforts, Ennio Morricone created a disturbing score, full of threatening sounds and angular themes, for this crime drama about a serial killer on the loose with a bent for satanic practices. Characteristic of Morricone's approach for this type of film, the cues are profuse elaboration for strings, with layers upon layers of textures creating an ominous sound, occasionally accented by a solo violin, or an otherwordly chorus performing in counterpoint. Breaking with the moods cre-

ated, "Since Childhood" brings a different evocation, with its gentle crystalline bells over an attractive, melancholy-tinged melody, in a theme reprised with more forcefulness in "Carillon" in which it achieves a different, more dangerous effect. A strangely evocative score that will appeal to a limited audience, but is well worth discovering.

Ransom ♪

1996, Hollywood Records; from the movie *Ransom*, Touchstone Pictures, 1996.

Album Notes: *Music*: James Horner; *Orchestrations*: James Horner, Don Davis, David Slonaker; *Music Editor*: Jim Henrikson; Orchestra conducted by James Horner; *Album Producer*: James Horner; *Engineer*: Shawn Murphy; *Assistants Engineers*: Sabdy Bass, Marc Gebauer, David Marquette, Jay Selvester, Kirsten Smith.

Selections: 1 The Kidnapping (4:35); 2 Delivering The Ransom (12:04); 3 The Quarry (4:22); 4 A Two Million Dollar Bounty (4:24); 5 Parallel Stories (2:35); 6 A Fatal Mistake (4:52); 7 A Dark Reunion (3:08); 8 The Payoff/End Credits (12:22); 9 Rats (B. Corgan)(3:07) *Bill Corgan*; 10 Worms (B. Corgan)(4:17) *Bill Corgan*; 11 Spiders (B. Corgan) (3:34) *Bill Corgan*; 12 Lizards (B. Corgan)(3:11) *Bill Corgan*; 13 Worms, Part 2 (B. Corgan)(4:40) *Bill Corgan*; 14 Squirrels With Tails (B. Corgan)(5:20) *Bill Corgan*.

Review: This oft-times subdued effort by James Horner was actually a replacement score for a work by another composer. Since Horner relies on his usual bag of musical tricks (i.e. the beating xylophone, the flurry of percussion), this could easily be mistaken for outtakes from his last effort for director Ron Howard, *Apollo 13*. Sadly, at no point does anything unique or interesting come out and in, the end, there's nothing here that feels as if its worth listening to. Even the "End Title" is just okay. Billy Corgan, a member of the rock group The Smashing Pumpkins, also composed a portion of the score, six mind-numbing tracks of techno-rock music played in the film by the kidnappers. These tracks were obviously created to eliminate any empathy for them by torturing the audience. Corgan definitely shows the potential for a second career scoring horror films.

David Hirsch

Ransom/The Chairman ♪♪♪♭

1991, Silva Screen Records; from the movies *Ransom (The Terrorists)*, British Lion Films, 1975; and *The Chairman*, 20th Century-Fox, 1969.

Album Notes: *Music*: Jerry Goldsmith; *Ransom*:The National Philharmonic Orchestra, conducted by Jerry Goldsmith; *Engineer*: Eric Tomlinson; *The Chairman*: Orchestra conducted by

Jerry Goldsmith; *Engineer*: John Neal; *CD Producers*: Ford A. Thaxton, David Stoner, James Fitzpatrick; *Engineer*: Steve Fisk.

Selections: *RANSOM*: 1 Queen's Messenger (2:38); 2 Mission Aborted (5:04); 3 No Alternative (2:22); 4 Sky Chaser (5:37); 5 Course Of Action (2:36); 6 Peeping Tom (2:36); 7 End Title (2:36);

THE CHAIRMAN: 8 Main Title (2:23); 9 Goodbye For Now (1:45); 10 The Fence (1:45); 11 The Tour (2:37); 12 Soong Chu (2:17); 13 Fire Fight (3:20); 14 The World Only Lovers See (Love Theme)(2:25) *Jerry Goldsmith (piano solo)*; 15 The Red Guard (3:15); 16 Hathaway's Farewell (2:45); 17 A Late Visitor(2:44); 18 Escape (3:02); 19 Finale/End Title (3:13).

Review: Silva Screen rescued two important Jerry Goldsmith scores at once with this lengthy CD, but lack of access to the original studio tapes means that this is essentially a recording of an LP and some commercially-available cassettes, resulting in the kind of sound quality that will make audiophiles cringe. For those who just want to hear the music, however, this is an exciting album, with Goldsmith's bombastic, European-flavored *Ransom* score making heavy use of a declamatory four-note horn theme, which surges through chase and suspense cues over low-end piano and harpsichord. "Sky Chaser" expands a soaring romantic theme through shimmering orchestral textures, even taking it through a jazz-influenced riff. *The Chairman* showcases Goldsmith's striking skill at adapting Oriental melodies and orchestral effects, from its haunting shaikiku theme plays over rice and snare drums until it's eventually taken up by the entire orchestra, to some amazingly nimble, agitated action cues like "The Fence" and "Firefight." The intense suspense and action cues alternate with some gorgeously soothing atmospheric cues.

Jeff Bond

Rapid Fire *♪♪♪♪*

1992, Varese-Sarabande Records; from the movie *Rapid Fire*, 20th Century-Fox, 1992.

Album Notes: *Music*: Christopher Young; *Orchestrations*: Christopher Young; *Music Editor*: Tom Milano; *Synthesizers/Electronic Percussion*: Mark Zimoski, Daniel Licht; *Album Producer*: Christopher Young.

Selections: 1 Rapid Fire (3:04); 2 Da-Daiko (1:28); 3 Be Or Not (1:56); 4 Witness To A Murder (3:37); 5 Together Alone (2:51); 6 Mousetrap (2:54); 7 Good Humor (1:58); 8 Glory Trail (3:10); 9 Fed Funk Muck (3:54); 10 Slim Princess (1:11); 11 Free Fire (4:14); 12 Say (2:58); 13 Kix (1:50); 14 Kaper Kut (5:40); 15 Wish You Wish (1:34).

Review: When a college student, who is also a karate champion, witnesses a mob murder, what do you get? An expert score by Christopher Young! The 1992 movie suggested a deft blend of electronic sounds and percussive effects that emphasize the screen action, while giving it a greater focus. The explicit cues detail the action with great force and consistency, providing an extra dramatic edge that strikes a responsive note in the recording as well. In the midst of all the action, a tender moment ("Together Alone") provides an unexpected change of pace.

The Rapture *♪♪♪*

1991, Polydor Records; from the movie *The Rapture*, New Line Cinema, 1991.

Album Notes: *Music*: Thomas Newman; *Orchestrations*: Thomas Pasatieri; *Music Editor*: Bill Bernstein; Orchestra conducted by Thomas Newman; *Album Producer*: Denis McNamara; *Engineer*: Dennis Drake.

Selections: 1 Hymn No. 27 (Opening Theme)(3:45); 2 Wave (A.C. Jobim)(2:51) *Antonio Carlos Jobim*; 3 Ruler Of My Heart (N. Neville)(2:36) *Irma Thomas*; 4 Now I Lay Down (1:39); 5 Directly From My Heart To You (R. Penniman)(2:44) *Little Richard*; 6 Six Years Later (1:31); 7 Aguas de Marco (A.C. Jobim)(3:04) *Elis Regina*; 8 Writhe And Wither (1:30); 9 Alarm (1:31); 10 Well Enough (S. Wilk/J. Christensen)(3:31) *Julie Christensen*; 11 I'll Be Your Mirror (L. Reed)(2:14) *The Velvet Underground*; 12 Grace Disengaged (1:39); 13 Shallow Grave (2:16); 14 In Jail (3:30); 15 Next Diaspora (2:10); 16 Cheap Sleep (1:31); 17 Astronaut Anthem (M. Monk)(4:57) *Meredith Monk*

Review: *The Rapture* is a downright strange score written for the story of a disillusioned young woman (Mimi Rogers) drawn into a super-Fundamentalist religious cult. Thomas Newman has had a profound influence on dramatic scoring in the 1990s and this early score features many of the techniques that have become the sound of seriousness — eerie wails and dissonant strings over transcendent drones, so that it seems to be flying apart just as it is ground to the earth. Percussion samples prove unsettling, repeating loops of ticks and tacks unnaturally sped up. A piano is introduced, lightly playing two delicate chords of ambiguous harmony. This is music where the timbres and the melodies are intertwined. The whole thing hits with a deeply ambiguous, distorted meaning. Continuing another trend of the '90s, the album includes several songs of varied genres, from Little Richard's "Directly from My Heart to You" to Meredith Monk and Vocal Ensemble's choral hymnal "Astronaut Anthem."

Lukas Kendall

Raw Deal Woof

1986, Varese-Sarabande; from the movie *Raw Deal*, De Laurentiis Entertainment, 1986.

Album Notes: *Music*: Tom Bahler, Albhy Galuten, Chris Boardman, Jerry Hey, Randy Kerber, Steve Lukather, Joel Rosenbaum, Claude Gaudette; *Album Producer*: Richard Kraft; *Engineer*: Allen Sides.

Selections: 1 Brains And Trains (T. Bahler/A. Galuten/C. Boardman)(1:18); 2 Kaminski Stomps (C. Gaudette/C. Boardman/A. Galuten)(3:39); 3 Cemetery Tense (T. Bahler/A. Galuten/C. Boardman)(1:31); 4 Lamanski Chase (C. Boardman/T. Bahler/A. Galuten/R. Kerber/J. Hey/S. Lukather)/Lamanski's Syn (T. Bahler/A. Galuten/C. Boardman)(5:39); 5 In A Squeeze (C. Gaudette/C. Boardman/A. Galuten)(1:32); 6 Ice Cold Bomb (T. Bahler/A. Galuten)(1:04); 7 J.P. Brenner Emerges (1:13); 8 Going To War (C. Gaudette/C. Boardman/A. Galuten)(2:14); 9 Water Heater (T. Bahler/A. Galuten/C. Boardman)(1:14); 10 Hi, Rudy (A. Galuten)(1:06); 11 Petro Camp (C. Gaudette/C. Boardman/A. Galuten) (1:50); 12 I'm Smart (T. Bahler/A. Galuten/C. Boardman)/What's The P? (C. Gaudette/C. Boardman/A. Galuten)/Leak Alley (T. Bahler/A. Galuten/C. Boardman)(2:42); 13 Jogger Cop/Magic Or Magnets (T. Bahler/A. Galuten/C. Boardman)/Your Lights (T. Bahler/A. Galuten/C. Boardman)(2:11); 14 Meet Me (C. Gaudette/C. Boardman/A. Galuten)(:39); 15 Harry Shot (T. Bahler/A. Galuten/C. Boardman)(1:15); 16 Harry Walks (J. Rosenbaum/C. Boardman)(:48).

Review: It took no less than eight composers to create this vapid, vaguely pretentious musical hodgepodge for a film starring Arnold Schwarzenegger. A series of electronic noises, punctuated by a rhythm track, with amplified guitars playing some undistinguished tunes, it might have been effective behind the screen action, where it went by without being noticed, but it doesn't cut it as musical background sans the visuals. It's predictable, it's empty, it's annoying! In short, it's the kind of album that gives film music a bad name.

The Razor's Edge ♫♫♫♫

1992, Preamble Records; from the movie *The Razor's Edge*, Columbia Pictures, 1984.

Album Notes: *Music*: Jack Nitzsche; The London Symphony Orchestra, conducted by Stanley Black; *Featured Musician*: Bruno Hoffman (glass harmonica); *Album Producer*: Jack Nitzsche; *Engineer*: Eric Tomlinson.

Selections: *ORCHESTRAL SUITE*: 1 Main Title (2:25); 2 Night Picnic (1:04); 3 Trenches (2:00); 4 Fireworks/World War I (1:35); 5 Motorcycle/Climbing The Stairs (1:54); 6 Maturin's

> "We composers are at least as significant as the stars who make $14 million or $15 million. We are actors on the screen. You just don't see us."
>
> **Michael Kamen**
> (*Time Magazine*, 9-11-95)

Funeral (1:57); 7 Larry Leaves The Monastery (:46); 8 Opium Den (3:18); 9 Piedmont Hit (1:21); 10 Piedmont's Death (1:00); 11 End Title/End Credits (4:02);

LARRY'S JOURNEY: 12 Arrival In India (2:26); 13 The Monastery (1:20); 14 Larry's Journey (3:25); 15 Can't Stop Dancing (P. Murray) (3:25); 16 A Toda Vela (F. Frank/A. Ladriere)(3:21); 17 Organ Grinder (1:36).

Review: Early in his career, Bill Murray starred in this bizarre remake, based on W. Somerset Maugham's novel, about a "dreamer of beautiful dreams" who delays his marriage to a wealthy and proper society girl, so that he can "find himself" among the Lost Generation in bohemian Paris of the early 1920s. Murray's performance notwithstanding, the film called for and received an eloquent musical score from Jack Nitzsche, whose own sensitivity found ample fodder in its subject matter. Beautifully expressive, with longing romantic cues that expand on the storyline and flesh it out considerably, the score (presented here in the "Orchestral Suite") is particularly striking and one of the best efforts from this often unheralded composer. "Larry's Journey," which consists of source music is also interesting as an adjunct to Nitzsche's score.

The Re-Animator/ Bride of the Re-Animator ♫♫♫ᵖ

1991, Silva Screen Records; from the movies *The Re-Animator*, 1987, and *Bride of the Re-Animator*, 1990.

Album Notes: *Music*: Richard Band; *Orchestrations*: Richard Band; The Rome Philharmonic Orchestra, conducted by Richard Band; *Album Producer*: Richard Band; *Engineer*: Nick Vidar.

Selections: *THE RE-ANIMATOR*: 1 Prologue Parts 1 & 2/Main Title (4:09); 2 Halsey Grabs Meg (1:07); 3 Halsey Alive/First Corpse To Be Reanimated/Corpses Reanimated (5:11); 4 Searching

The Morgue For A Body/Waiting For A Reaction/ Meg And Dr. Hill/Body And Soul/The Cat Experiment/Halsey Lobotomized/ "Where's The Cat?" (11:31); 5 "Parts, Whole Parts"/End Sequence: The Corpses Run Amok! (7:08); 6 Meg Reanimated/ End Title (3:52);

BRIDE OF THE RE-ANIMATOR: 7 Prologue: Hill Head/Main Title (3:44); 8 Building The Bride (3:36); 9 West And Dan In The Furnace Room To Get The Body (2:06); 10 Driving To The House (:42); 11 Dr. Hill Goes Batty/The Bride Lives! (3:50); 12 The Body Parts Room/West Steals The Feet (2:51); 13 The Bat Sequence (1:42); 14 "Well, We Could" (4:11); 15 Sex Scene (1:13); 16 West Cons Dans (3:12); 17 West Cons Dan (Again!)(3:30); 18 End Sequence: West Looks For Hill's Head/ The Bride Revealed/West's Justification/Dan Rejects The Bride/The Dead Heads Attack (9:07); 19 The Freak Show/The End Of Herbert West (Until "Re-Animator 3") (4:06).

Review: Richard Band shamelessly makes a play on Bernard Herrmann's score for *Psycho*, an adaption that adds to the manic quality of this perversely funny horror series. Few critics though failed to make the connection Band was implying between the sexually repressed Norman Bates and the obsessed re-animator, Dr. Herbert West. Much of his music concentrates on showing off the horror element, a move that substantially emphasizes the black humor. For this project, Band was able to go to Italy and score the entire film with The Rome Philharmonic Orchestra, with this portion of the CD affording a rare look at what he can do when the budget allows him to work with a full-scale symphonic orchestra. Remarkably, little seemed lost when Band had to score the sequel with synthesizers five years later. In fact, the playing of the *Psycho*-inspired theme on all synthesizers gives the impression more than ever that West is just a sniveling ratboy. A genuinely funny goof on the whole genre.

David Hirsch

Rebecca ♫♫♫♫

1991, Marco Polo Records; from the movie *Rebecca*, Selznick International, 1940.

Album Notes: *Music:* Franz Waxman; The Czecho-Slovak Radio Symphony Orchestra, conducted by Adriano; *Featured Soloist:* Viktor Simcisko, violin; *Album Producers:* Karol Kopernick, Hubert Geschwandtner.

Selections: 1 Selznick International Trademark (A. Newman)/ Foreword/ Opening Scene (4:30); 2 Hotel Lobby (waltz)(3:44); 3 Terrace Scene/Tennis Montage I/Tennis Montage II (7:51); 4 Proposal Scene/Marriage/Arrival At Manderley (5:14); 5 Entrance Hall/Mrs. Danvers (3:57); 6 Morning Room (2:45); 7 Beatrice (1:04); 8 Bridge Sequence/Walk To The Beach/The Boathouse/Coming Back From The Boathouse (7:14); 9 The New Dress (1:18); 10 Rebecca's Room/The New Mrs. De Winter (8:18); 11 Sketching Scene (2:24); 12 Manderley Ball (3:23); 13 After The Ball/The Rockets/At Dawn (6:57); 14 Confession Scene/Telephone Rings (6:45); 15 Fireplace Tableau/The Fire/ Epilogue (5:25).

Review: In the profuse history of Hollywood film music, which has been marked by so many superlative scores, Franz Waxman's music for *Rebecca* will always stand out as a milestone and one of the best scores ever composed for the screen. Based on the Gothic novel by Daphne du Maurier, the film, starring Joan Fontaine and Laurence Olivier, directed by Alfred Hitchcock, exudes an impenetrable aura of mystery and suspense, coupled with romantic undertones and youthful flights of fancy that soften the drama, yet ultimately give it a sharper edge by contrast. All these elements eventually find their way into the composer's expression, in a score that teems with sweeping themes, richly expressive and sophisticated. This superb new recording, in widespread digital sound, features the Czecho-Slovak Radio Symphony Orchestra conducted by Adriano in a flawless performance that brings out all the nuances in the music and details some of the salient moments in the score. It is a worthy addition to any collection that invites repeated listening.

Red Dawn ♫♫♫♫

1989, Intrada Records; from the movie *Red Dawn*, United Artists, 1985.

Album Notes: *Music:* Basil Poledouris; *Orchestrations:* Greig McRitchie, Jack Smalley, Scott Smalley; Orchestra conducted by Basil Poledouris; *Album Producers:* Basil Poledouris, Douglass Fake; *Engineers:* Aaron Rochin, Hank Cicalo; *Assistant Engineer:* Stanley Carr.

Selections: 1 Main Title (2:38); 2 The Invasion (5:18); 3 The Drive-In (6:20); 4 Let It Turn (1:10); 5 Wolverines (2:05); 6 Flowers (3:04); 7 The Eulogy (2:51); 8 Robert's End (3:50); 9 Death And Freedom/End Title (6:35).

Review: Intrada's debut collector's LP is an excellent choice, preserving Basil Poledouris' confident symphonic adventure score for John Milius' communist invasion movie. The nine cues appearing on the CD are fairly long ones, totaling about 35 minutes of music (short by CD standards, but sufficient). Two themes dominate the score, the "Red Dawn Theme," a deep, throbbing motif which signifies the invasion, and the "Wolverine Theme," a heroic, three-note melody which denotes the teenage guerrillas who struggle against the Communist invaders. These themes are very nicely integrated into Poledouris' rhythmic and tonal action cues, merging Americana and militaristic sensibilities into a cohesive score that bristles with dynamic range and vigor.

Randall D. Larson

Red Heat ♫♫♫

1988, Virgin Records; from the movie *Red Heat,* Carolco International, 1988.

Album Notes: *Music*: James Horner; *Music Editor*: Nany Fogarty; Orchestra conducted by James Horner; *Featured Soloists*: Michael Boddicker, Brandon Fields, James Horner, Kazu Matsui, Tim May, Steven Schaeffer, Neil Stubenhaus, Ian Underwood; *Album Producer*: James Horner; *Engineer*: Shawn Murphy.

Selections: 1 Main Title (3:00); 2 Russian Streets (1:35); 3 Cleanhead Bust (4:16); 4 Victor Escapes (2:53); 5 Tailing Kat/ The Set Up (7:55); 6 Hospital Chase (4:30); 7 The Hotel (6:21); 8 Bus Station (9:34); 10 End Credit (4:04).

Review: James Horner worked with director Walter Hill a number of times over the years, from the raucous comedy of *48 Hrs.* through his rejected score for *Streets of Fire* (which was ultimately replaced with music by Ry Cooder). *Red Heat*, Hill's engaging 1988 action picture, gets a definite boost from the film's twist on the old cop-buddy formula — while we still have a stereotypical, chain-smoking Chicago police officer (Jim Belushi), this time he's paired with a Russian cop (the one and only Arnold Schwarzenegger) tracking a drug dealer from his homeland. This affords Horner the opportunity to write bold Russian chorus music to complement the traditional action film suspense cues, and the combination results in a competent score that seems to have later been part of the inspiration behind Basil Poledouris' similar-sounding approach for *The Hunt for Red October.*

Andy Dursin

Red King, White Knight ♫♫♫ᵛ

1991, Intrada Records; from the movie *Red King, White Knight,* Cital Entertainment/Zenith Productions, 1991.

Album Notes: *Music*: John Scott; *Orchestrations*: John Scott; Orchestra conducted by John Scott; *Album Producer*: John Scott; *Engineer*: Adrian Kerridge.

Selections: 1 The KGB Faction (4:36); 2 The Assassin Is Clancy (4:18); 3 Bad Memories (1:15); 4 Clancy Prepares (1:23); 5 Memories Of A Past Love (1:02); 6 The Cemetery (2:33); 7 Airport Killing (4:19); 8 Music Box (1:54); 9 A Clancy Execution (2:32); 10 Idyll And Nightmare (3:26); 11 Cemetery Preparations (6:48); 12 Killer In A Crowd (2:01); 13 Laying The Wreath (3:29); 14 Clancy Strikes (3:58); 15 Aftermath and Epilogue (3:28).

Review: This nicely old-fashioned spy movie score by John Scott is reminiscent of a lot of those 1960s cold war films in which composers always portrayed the Russians with blatant ethnic motifs. As with all of Scott's work, the arrangements are full-bodied, but the overall tone is surprisingly darker and more forceful ("Airport Killing" for example) than his usual efforts, thanks in part to his uncharacteristic use of shrill brass effects. Scott, for the most part, often writes with that larger-than-life quality typical of 1940s film scoring, but here he attacks the material as never before. While scoring the music for the film, which follows the attempts of an American agent to stop the assassination of Soviet Premier Gorbachev, Scott was recording in Budapest when Hungary opened its boarders to East Germans on the eve of the fall of Communism.

David Hirsch

Red Scorpion ♫♫♫ᵛ

1989, Varese-Sarabande; from the movie *Red Scorpion,* 1989.

Album Notes: *Music*: Jay Chattaway; *Orchestrations*: Joseph Smith; *Music Editor*: Jack Tillar; *Featured Musicians*: Steve Croes, Pete Levin (electronic music), Judd Miller (African flute); *Album Producer*: Jay Chattaway; *Engineer*: Dan Hahn.

Selections: 1 Gift Of Sandals (1:21); 2 Desert Struggle (2:47); 3 Nik's Decision (1:20); 4 The Battle (3:09); 5 Porto Silva (3:37); 6 Attack On Mbaja (3:21); 7 Aftermath (:53); 8 Pins And Needles (2:45); 9 Dewey's Rescue (1:53); 10 Farewell Sundata (2:20); 11 Escape From The Compound (2:33); 12 Torch Song (1:19); 13 Oath Of Allegiance (1:57); 14 Village Of Death (3:47); 15 Farewell To Arms (1:19); 16 Nik Takes Charge (:56); 17 Victory Celebration (:46).

Review: Jay Chattaway produced an entertaining orchestral work for this standard Dolph Ludgren action yarn. Peppered with some intriguing synthesizer overlays and African flute solos, as in "Farewell Sundata," it captures the eerie mood of the desert locale and the battles between the Soviets and local tribes. Chattaway's action cues, like "The Battle" and "Attack on Mbaja," have some notably dynamic percussion work. This was the score that led to his selection as a regular composer on *Star Trek: The Next Generation.*

David Hirsch

The Reivers ♪♪♪

1995, Sony/Legacy; from the movie *The Reivers*, Cinema Center Films, 1969.

Album Notes: *Music*: John Williams; Orchestra conducted by John Williams; *Album Producer*: Thomas Z. Shepard; *CD Producer*: Didier C. Deutsch; *Engineer*: Chris Herles.

Selections: 1 Main Title/First Instruction/The Winton Flyer (5:11); 2 Family Funeral/Lucuius' First Drive (2:30); 3 The Road To Memphis (1:42); 4 Corrie's Entrance/The Picture (2:10); 5 Reflections (1:36); 6 The Sheriff Departs/The Bad News/Ned's Secret (4:09); 7 Memphis (1:21); 8 Ned's Trade (2:02); 9 The People Protest (1:05); 10 Prayers At Bedtime (2:40); 11 Lucius Runs To Corrie/Back Home (3:33); 12 Finale (4:15).

Review: John Williams' original score for *The Reivers* is what attracted Stephen Spielberg's attention to the composer, and one listen to this soundtrack recording will demonstrate exactly what endeared Williams to Spielberg and why their future collaborations worked so well.

This music is fun! In a thoroughly playful and light-hearted way, Williams proves his uncanny ability to set the stage for nearly any film setting — in this case, William Faulkner's novel about a boy's coming of age in turn-of-the-century Mississippi. The music so perfectly complements the complex thematic content of the film, it's as if the book and screenplay were written to accompany the music!

While shades of the future "Williams' sound" make cameo appearances throughout the score, we can also discern the influence of Aaron Copland (arguably the quintessential composer of American music), and orchestrator Robert Russell Bennett on Williams' work.

Charles L. Granata

The Remains of the Day ♪♪♪♪

1993, Angel Records; from the movie *The Remains of the Day*, Columbia Pictures, 1993.

Album Notes: *Music*: Richard Robbins; *Orchestrations*: Robert Stewart; Orchestra conducted by Harry Rabinowitz; *Engineers*: Bill Sommerville-Large, Keith Grant.

Selections: 1 Opening Titles/ Darlington Hall (7:27); 2 The Keyhole And The Chinaman (4:14); 3 Tradition And Order (1:51); 4 The Conference Begins (1:33); 5 Sei Mir Gegrusst (F. Schubert/ F. Ruckert) (4:13) *Ann Murray, Graham Johnson*; 6 The Cooks In The Kitchen (1:34); 7 Sir Geoffrey Wren And Stevens, Sr. (2:41); 8 You Mean A Great Deal To This House (2:21); 9 Loss And Separation (6:19); 10 Blue Moon (R. Rodgers/L. Hart) (4:57); 11 Sentimental Love Story/Appeasement/In The Rain (5:22); 12 A Portrait Returns/Darlington Hall/End Credits (6:54).

Review: The quiet, elegant beauty of Richard Robbins' score is as strongly evocative of this Merchant Ivory production as the calm distinction of its central character, a perfect English butler, whose mistaken sense of duty for the owner of Darlington Hall over many years has cost him the love of an attractive young housekeeper, and any other trace of personal life. Tradition and strict adherence to the rules of propriety are elements that pervade Robbins' score ("Tradition and Order," "The Cooks in the Kitchen"), while the butler's realization, 30 years later, that his life has passed and he has little to show for it, is starkly evoked in "Sentimental Love Story/Appeasement/ In the Rain," in which his emotional journey takes him back to today's realities. Robbins' strongly suggestive score is striking in its sober account, yet profoundly revealing of the deep, emotional currents that motivate the film's central character.

Renaissance Man ♪♪♪♪

1994, Varese-Sarabande Records; from the movie *Renaissance Man*, Touchstone Pictures, 1994.

Album Notes: *Music*: Hans Zimmer; *Additional Music*: Nick Glennie-Smith, John Van Tongeren, Bruce Fowler; *Orchestrations*: Bruce Fowler, Nick Glennie-Smith; *Featured Soloist*: Malcolm McNab (trumpet); *Album Producers*: Hans Zimmer, Jay Rifkin; *Engineer*: Bruce Botnick.

Selections: 1 Welcome To The Army (3:55); 2 Letter From Home (4:25); 3 Serving Your Country (4:11); 4 To Thine Own Self... (4:36); 5 Stay With Me (2:11); 6 Victory Starts Here (7:28); 7 Benitez Does Henry (2:32); 8 Everyone Is A Hero (4:26); 9 Marky Mark — "To Be Or Not To Be" (2:44).

Review: A bittersweet comedy about a civilian unemployed advertising executive who gets a job training new Army recruits, *Renaissance Man* enabled composer Hans Zimmer to tap into two very dissimilar, opposed sources — the no-nonsense, straightforward military background, which translated itself into brassy marches, with occasional flights of fancy; and the laissez-faire of the advertising man, played by Danny DeVito, who has a total disregard for Army regulations, which resulted in leisurely sedate cues. The two combine effectively, sometimes within the same cue, to create a diversified score that often has a sharp edge to it, with some melodic themes mingling with more abrasive tunes.

Rent-A-Cop ♪♪

1987, Intrada Records; from the movie *Rent-A-Cop*, Kings Road Entertainment, 1987.

Album Notes: *Music*: Jerry Goldsmith; *Orchestrations*: Arthur Morton; The Hungarian State Opera Orchestra, conducted by

Jerry Goldsmith; *Album Producers*: Jerry Goldsmith, Douglass Fake; *Engineer*: Alan Snelling.

Selections: 1 Rent-a-Cop (2:20); 2 The Bust (6:00); 3 Lonely Cop (1:35); 4 Russian Roulette (1:39); 5 The Station (2:49); 6 Worth A Lot (2:32); 7 Lights Out (2:15); 8 This Is The Guy (3:53); 9 They Need Me (1:45); 10 The Room (3:12); 11 Lake Forest (2:10); 12 Jump (4:34).

Review: You'd think the pairing of Burt Reynolds and Liza Minnelli would have made for box office dynamite, but this '80s time capsule from the waning moments of Reynolds' career was a disaster for all concerned, and composer Jerry Goldsmith didn't fare much better. His title theme features a bluesy, bittersweet trumpet solo, but the tune quickly escalates into some kind of pop anthem that's as far from *Chinatown* as Goldsmith is likely to get. The trumpet theme actually grows on you, but the rest of the album consists of some distinctly unmemorable, ticking electronic suspense cues that aren't likely to please either fans of the composer's earlier work or devotees of Harold Faltermeyer.

Jeff Bond

The Rescuers Down Under
🎵🎵🎵🎵ᵛ

1990, Walt Disney Records; from the animated feature *The Rescuers Down Under*, Walt Disney Films, 1990.

Album Notes: *Music*: Bruce Broughton; *Orchestrations*: Don Nemitz, Mark McKenzie; *Music Editor*: Kathleen Bennett; Orchestra conducted by Bruce Broughton; *Album Producer*: Bruce Broughton; *Engineers*: Robert Fernandez, Armin Steiner.

Selections: 1 Main Title (1:35); 2 Answering Faloo's Call (1:29); 3 Cody's Flight (6:01); 4 Message Montage (A. Robbins/C. Connors)(2:46); 5 At The Restaurant (3:04); 6 Wilbur Takes Off (1:25); 7 McLeach Threatens Cody (1:17); 8 The Landing (1:59); 9 Bernard Almost Proposes (1:33); 10 Escape Attempt (1:28); 11 Frank's Out! (3:21); 12 Cody Finds The Eggs (1:31); 13 Bernard The Hero (3:35); 14 End Credits (3:36).

Review: The further adventures of Bernard and Bianca and their friend Cody, inspired Bruce Broughton to write a whimsical, inspired score which easily transcends its animated feature origin to provide an entertaining musical concept. Cleverly conceived to match the development of the story—in which Bernard, the world's bravest mouse, and Miss Bianca, answering a request for help from their friend Cody deep in the heart of Australia's vast and unpredictable outback, to save a magnificent eagle from a ruthless poacher, find themselves thrown in more difficulties than they had anticipated—Broughton's music pulls all the stops, from heroic to romantic, from soulful to romantic, in a vivid

display that proves most satisfying. Of course, it's cartoon music, but of the better kind, and even adults will enjoy the tremendously exciting accents the composer conjures up along the way.

Restoration 🎵🎵ᵛ

1995, Milan Records; from the movie *Restoration*, Miramax Films, 1995.

Album Notes: *Music*: James Newton Howard, Henry Purcell; *Orchestrations*: Brad Dechter, Geoff Alexander, Frank Bennett, Don Nemitz, James Newton Howard; *Music Editors*: Jim Weidman, Robin Clarke, Bob Hathaway; Orchestra conducted by Artie Kane, Rick Wentowrth, Robert Zeigler; *Album Producers*: Michael Mason, Shawn Murphy; *Engineers*: Shawn Murphy, Geoff Foster, Paul Hulme.

Selections: 1 If Love's A Sweet Passion (1:31); 2 Main Titles (2:57); 3 Frost Dance in C (1:34); 4 A Night With Lulu (1:21); 5 Minuet in G (:53); 6 Here The Deities Approve (2:28); 7 A Creature Of The New Age (1:09); 8 Overture in D (2:25); 9 The Wedding (1:39); 10 Hornpipe in D Minor (1:26); 11 Arrival In Bidnold (1:08); 12 The Cabinet Of Curiosities (2:54); 13 The Land Of Mar (1:11); 14 The Lie (1:19); 15 A New Ground in E Minor (:52); 16 Merivel Woos Celia (2:26); 17 Katharine Sleeps (3:23); 18 Taking Bidnold Back (1:35); 19 Muzette 1 in A Minor (M. Marais) (2:56) *Laurence Dreyfus, Jakob Lindberg* ; 20 The Right Knowledge (2:06); 21 The Plague (2:09); 22 Katharine's Death (4:37); 23 Night Sweats (3:03); 24 Hospital (2:54); 25 Doctor Merivel (1:50); 26 Listening To Celia's Heart (1:39); 27 The Fire (3:18); 28 Allegro from Sinfonia (Act II) (1:19); 29 Your Child I Believe (1:13); 30 Newcastle (trad.) (:38); 31 2nd Overture in D (1:27).

Review: James Newton Howard has scored all sorts of movies, from sci-fi adventures to romantic comedies, and he's done an admirable job no matter what time frame or galaxy he's working in. *Restoration* is his first "period" score, coming for a movie set in 1600s England, and the results are somewhat hard to gauge—the music works fine in the movie, but it is hard to fully review Howard's original work, which is more or less an adaptation of or modeling on classical works by composers of the period, including Henry Purcell and Marin Marais. The album never really finds its own voice, which leaves it most recommended for fans of the movie, who will be able to recall moments from the film through the music contained herein.

Andy Dursin

Return of the Jedi 🎵🎵🎵ᵛ

1997, RCA Records; from the movie *Return of the Jedi*, 20th Century-Fox, 1983/1997.

Album Notes: *Music*: John Williams; *Orchestrations*: Herbert W. Spencer; The London Symphony Orchestra conducted by

John Williams; *Album Producer*: John Williams; *Engineers*: Eric Tomlinson, Jonathan Allen; *CD Engineer*: Dan Hersch.

Selections: CD 1: 1 20th Century-Fox Fanfare (A. Newman) (:22); 2 Main Title/Approaching The Death Star/Tatooine Rendezvous (9:21); 3 The Droids Are Captured (1:17); 4 Bounty For A Wookie (2:50); 5 Han Solo Returns (4:01); 6 Luke Confronts Jabba/Den Of The Rancor/Sarlacc Sentence (8:51); 7 The Pit Of Carkoon/Sail Barge Assault (6:02); 8 The Emperor Arrives/The Death Of Yoda/ Obi-Wan's Revelation (10:58); 9 Alliance Assembly (2:13); 10 Shuttle Tydirium Approaches Endor (4:09); 11 Speeder Bike Chase/Land Of The Ewoks (9:38); 12 The Levitation/Threepio's Bedtime Story (2:46); 13 Jabba's Baroque Recital (3:09); 14 Jedi Rocks (J. Hey)(2:42); 15 Sail Barge Assault (alternate)(5:04).

CD 2: 1 Parade Of The Ewoks (3:28); 2 Luke And Leia (4:46); 3 Brother And Sister/Father And Son/The Fleet Enters Hyperspace/Heroic Ewok (10:40); 4 Emperor's Throne Room (3:26); 5 The Battle Of Endor I: Into The Trap/Forest Ambush/ Scout Walker Scramble/Prime Weapon Fires (11:50); 6 The Lightsaber/The Ewok Battle (4:31); 7 The Battle Of Endor II: Leia Is Wounded/The Duel Begins/ Overtaking The Bunker/ The Dark Side Beckons/The Emperor's Death (10:03); 8 The Battle Of Endor III: Superstructure Chase/Darth Vader's Death/The Main Reactor (6:04); 9 Leia's News/Light Of The Force (3:24); 10 Victory Celebration/End Title (8:34); 11 Ewok Feast/Part Of The Tribe (4:02); 12 The Forest Battle (concert suite)(4:05).

Review: The score for the final film in the original *Star Wars* trilogy is as redundant and uninspired as the movie itself, resurrecting numerous stretches of scoring from *Star Wars* and *The Empire Strikes Back* while providing little in the way of memorable new themes (unless you have a hankering to hum Jabba the Hutt's rattling tuba melody). However, Nick Redman and Michael Mattesino have done a masterful job of reassembling the knotted original elements of *Jedi*'s score, which was extensively edited in the movie (sometimes tracking actual cues from the earlier films into scenes for which John Williams had written new music). Most of the sequences involving Luke Skywalker's struggle with the evil Galactic Emperor, the gathering forces of the Rebel starfleet and the countdown to the movie's gigantic space battle are genuinely gripping, with an unearthly male choir underscoring the Emperor's scenes (culminating in the hair-raising, spectral "The Dark Side Beckons") and some involving militaristic themes and pulsing, brassy rebel fleet music. But much of the score is weighted down by leaden, meandering dialogue underscoring and the lightweight silliness of the Ewok music that sabotages

the drama of much of the movie's final showdown between the Rebels and the Empire. Williams is too good a composer for *Jedi* to be a complete drag, but it's by far the weakest of the three *Star Wars* scores.

Jeff Bond

See also: Star Wars and The Empire Strikes Back

Return to Snowy River Part II 🎵🎵🎵🎵🎵

1988, Varese-Sarabande Records; from the movie *Return to Snowy River*, Walt Disney Pictures, 1988.

Album Notes: *Music*: Bruce Rowland; *Orchestrations*: Bruce Rowland; Orchestra conducted by Bruce Rowland; *Album Producer*: Bruce Rowland; *Engineer*: Ross Cockle.

Selections: 1 A Long Way From Home (3:02); 2 The Man From Snowy River II (3:20); 3 By The Fireside (2:13); 4 Eureka Creek (1:15); 5 Back To The Mountains (3:05); 6 Skill At Arms (2:29); 7 Jessica's Sonata #2 (2:00); 8 Pageant At Harrison's (1:25); 9 Gathered To The Fray (1:24); 10 Alone In The Mountains (2:29); 11 Farewell To And Old Friend "Now Do We Fight Them!" (10:29); 12 You Should Be Free (1:35); 13 Closing Credits (4:19).

Review: This sequel to *The Man From Snowy River* (q.v.) compelled Bruce Rowland to revisit his earlier score and expand on it in terms that remain attractive and thoroughly enjoyable. With the opening selection, "A Long Way from Home," a lovely theme for flute and two harmonic guitars over a synth texture, setting the tone, the music boldly unfolds with bright, exhilarating cues, smoothly executed, and bluesy themes, representative of more personally intense emotions. A long track, "Farewell to an Old Friend," brings together the heroic and the pathos in an amazing symphonic display that's all western and all fun.

Revenge 🎵🎵

1990, Silva Screen Records; from the movie *Revenge*, Columbia Pictures, 1990.

Album Notes: *Music*: Jack Nitzsche; *Featured Performers*: Bradford Ellis, Tommy Tedesco (acoustic guitar); *Album Producer*: Michael Hoenig; *Engineer*: Pamela Neal.

Selections: 1 Love Theme (4:38); 2 Friendship (1:27); 3 Miryea (3:24); 4 Betrayal (2:01); 5 Jeep Ride (1:24); 6 On The Beach (3:07); 7 Illicit Love (3:21); 8 Tibey's Revenge (3:35); 9 Whorehouse And Healing (4:10); 10 Dead Texan (2:37); 11 Confrontation (3:35); 12 Miryea's Death (5:17).

Review: Jack Nitzsche composed this pleasing synth score for the 1990 Kevin Costner action yarn. It starts off well with a tender "Love Theme" and the acoustic guitar solos by Tommy Tedesco. Some ethnic percussion added to the subsequent tracks give the score a delightful Spanish flavor, representative of the film's Mexican locale.

David Hirsch

Revenge of the Pink Panther
✓✓✓✓✓

1988, EMI-Manhattan; from the film *Revenge of the Pink Panther*, United Artists, 1978.

Album Notes: *Music:* Henry Mancini; Orchestra conducted by Henry Mancini; *Featured Soloists:* Tony Coe (saxophone), Henry Mancini, Leslie Pearson (piano), Sidney Sax (violin); *Album Producer:* Joe Reisman; *Engineer:* John Richards.

Selections: 1 The Pink Panther Theme (Main Title)(4:41); 2 Simone (4:33); 3 Give Me Some Mo'! (3:00); 4 Thar She Blows! (2:55); 5 Balls' Caprice (2:36); 6 Move 'Em Out! (H. Mancini/L. Bricusse)(3:27) *Loni Satton;* 7 A Touch Of Red (5:14); 8 After The Shower (3:43); 9 Hong Kong Fireworks (3:23); 10 Almond Eyes (3:15); 11 The Pink Panther Theme (reprise)(1:02); 12 Thank Heaven For Little Girls (F. Loewe/A.J. Lerner) (2:32) *Inspector Clouseau (Peter Sellers) and the Surete Brass Band.*

Review: Some ten years after the success of *The Pink Panther,* and its sequel *A Shot in the Dark,* director Blake Edwards returned to the rich lode he had mined, and between 1975 and 1978 filmed three more comedies around the central character of Chief Inspector Jacques Clouseau of the French Surete (portrayed in ineffable manner by Peter Sellers), *The Return of the Pink Panther* (1975), *The Pink Panther Strikes Again* (1976), and *The Revenge of the Pink Panther* (1978), all three with an appropriately delirious score by Henry Mancini. While the soundtrack albums to the first two are still awaiting release on compact disc in this country (*Return* came out in Japan), *Revenge* is available and it is every bit as enjoyable as one might remember it was. A murky tale involving Dyan Cannon as the very private secretary to a ship magnate and dope smuggler, who gets ditched by her boss and teams up with Clouseau to bring his downfall, the film is merely an excuse for Peter Sellers to broaden his antics as Clouseau, notably disguised as a would-be Mafia don and as an old tar with a wooden leg lost in the fog. As usual, Mancini was right on the button writing a score that brims with mordantly amusing themes, including "Hong Kong Fireworks," an inspired moment of lunacy in the film. Another gem in the album finds Peter Sellers warbling "Thank Heaven for Little Girls" from *Gigi,* in a send-up to end all send-ups.

Rich in Love ✓✓✓✓✓

1993, Varese-Sarabande Records; from the movie *Rich in Love,* M-G-M, 1993.

Album Notes: *Music:* Georges Delerue; *Music Editor:* Jeff Carson; Orchestra conducted by Georges Delerue; *Album Producer:* Georges Delerue; *Engineer:* Robert Fernandez.

Selections: 1 Main Title (1:25); 2 We Have To Find Her (1:29); 3 Hello Mother (1:44); 4 Put The Best Face On It (1:14); 5 Stop Thinking About Her (3:52); 6 Good To Have You Home (:48); 7 Lulu's Exit/The Kiss (1:14); 8 Warren Waits/Sunset (2:10); 9 Time To Move On (2:19); 10 Of Course You Can (1:30); 11 Lucille And Wayne Make Love (1:01); 12 Let's Take A Walk (2:56); 13 I Got Her Pregnant (2:03); 14 Lucille And Bill (1:24); 15 Escape On Mower (:45); 16 Leaving The House (2:01).

Review: Georges Delerue was at his most romantically eloquent when he wrote this attractive score (his last) in which the graceful moods are expressed by a variety of solo instruments (flute, guitar,clarinet, oboe, violin, etc.). "It is as though Georges was writing a good-bye for each of his friends," notes Robert Townson in the text he prepared for this CD. And, indeed, each cue sounds like a delicate little concerto. Adding poignancy to the proceedings is the fact that the themes Delerue wrote are so exquisite. A dramatic comedy rooted in a Southern background, involving a couple, their two daughters, and the daughters' various boyfriends, the story suggested a series of lovely cues that actually don't need the screen action to attract the listener.

Richard III ✓✓✓✓✓

1996, London Records; from the movie *Richard III,* United Artists, 1996.

Album Notes: *Music:* Trevor Jones; *Orchestrations:* Geoffrey Alexander, Trevor Jones, Julian Kershaw; Orchestra conducted by David Snell; *Featured Soloist:* Phil Todd (sax, flute); *Album Producer:* Trevor Jones; *Engineer:* Kirsty Whalley, Paul Golding; *Assistant Engineers:* Toby Wood, Eric Jordan, James Manning.

Selections: 1 The Invasion (1:37); 2 Come Love With Me (film version)(T. Jones/C. Marlowe)(5:40) *Stacey Kent, The Vile Bodies;* 3 Now Is The Winter Of Our Discontent (1:01) *Ian McKellen;* 4 The Mortuary (1:26) *Kristin Scott Thomas, Ian McKellen;* 5 Bid Me Farewell/I'll Have Her (1:21) *Ian McKellen, Kristin Scott Thomas;* 6 Clarence's Dream (3:04); 7 Crimson (3:13); 8 Clarence's Murder (2:05) *Nigel Hawthorne, Adrian Dunbar, Michael Elphick;* 9 The Tower (2:06); 10 The Blessing (:27) *Ian McKellen, Maggie Smith;* 11 Conspiracy (:35); 12 Toe Tappers (2:14); 13 Let Sorrow Haunt Your Bed (1:29) *Kristin Scott Thomas;* 14 The Reach Of Hell/Long Live The King (1:15) *Roger Hammond,*

Edward Hardwicke, Jim Broadbent; 15 Good Angels Guard You (:28) *Annette Benning*; 16 Coronation Haze (1:11); 17 Prelude From Te Deum (M.A. Charpentier)(1:41); 18 The Golden Dew Of Sleep (:30) *Kristin Scott Thomas*; 19 My Regret (2:46); 20 Pity Dwells Not This Eye (:25) *Ian McKellen*; 21 Westminster (3:14); 22 My Most Grievous Curse (:49) *Maggie Smith*; 23 The Duchess Departs (:52); 24 The Devil's Temptation (:54) *Ian McKellen, Annette Benning*; 25 Richmond (:52); 26 Defend Me Still (2:47) *Roger Hammond, Dominic West*; 27 I Did But Dream (:45) *Ian McKellen*; 28 Elizabeth And Richmond (1:37) *Kate Stevenson-Payne, Dominic West*; 29 My Kingdom For A Horse (:39) *Ian McKellen*; 30 Battle (4:42) *Ian McKellen*; 31 I'm Sitting On Top Of The World (R. Henderson/J. Young/S. Lewis)(1:49) *Al Jolson*; 32 Come Live With Me (location version)(T. Jones/C. Marlowe)(5:18) *Stacey Kent, The Vile Bodies*.

Review: It may seem incongruous to find a recording of Al Jolson's "I'm Sitting on Top of the World" in the soundtrack of a film based on William Shakespeare's *Richard III*, but that's not the only odd thing about this unusual quirky production set in the 1930s, which starts (on the album, at least) in a volley of gunfire, immediately followed by a big band number. Of course, as is sometimes the case in filmizations of well-known stage works, most of the music plays under the action to such extent that isolating it becomes difficult and redundant. Trevor Jones went around the difficulty by creating flavorful big band numbers which make their own statement, and punctuate the action, while anchoring it in the time period in which it is set. Some of the cues are introduced by excerpts from the dialogue, but these are not intrusive, and actually help appreciate the changes that have occurred in the concept of the film and, as a direct result, the flavor Jones chose to give his score. It all comes together as a vibrant display of a celebrated drama, with musical accompaniment that enhances the action and gives it the support it richly deserves.

Richie Rich *????*

1994, Varese-Sarabande Records; from the movie *Richie Rich*, Warner Bros., 1994.

Album Notes: *Music*: Alan Silvestri; *Orchestrations*: William Ross; *Music Editor*: Ken Karman; Orchestra conducted by Alan Silvestri; *Album Producer*: Alan Silvestri; *Engineer*: Dennis S. Sands.

Selections: 1 I Have A Son (5:30); 2 Surprise Guests (1:35); 3 Chief Executive Kid (3:30); 4 Access Terminated (2:10); 5 Something's Missing (1:40); 6 Cliffhangers (4:31); 7 Sandlotters Attack (4:30); 8 Bomb Surprise (2:02); 9 Bean Saves The Team (3:09); 10 Richest Kid In The World (1:23).

Review: Though a mindless little comedy starring Macaulay Culkin and John Larroquette, *Richie Rich* received a major score from Alan Silvestri, whose natural verve and exuberance obviously found a rich source of inspiration in this tired story about an obnoxious rich boy (guess who!), whose idleness leads him to more mischiefs than he has millions in the bank. Unfazed by the tale's obvious trappings, Silvestri served up a score that's quite enjoyable, with funny jerky little cues that spell out the story without spilling the beans. It may not be Beethoven's Ninth, but neither is the film *Gone with the Wind,* and all things considered this joyous score is much better than one might have expected.

The Right Stuff/ North and South *????*

1986, Varese-Sarabande Records; from the movies *The Right Stuff*, Warner Bros., 1983; and *North and South*, Warner Bros., 1985.

Album Notes: *Music*: Bill Conti; The London Symphony Orchestra, conducted by Bill Conti; *Album Producer*: Bill Conti; *Engineer*: Eric Tomlinson.

Selections: *THE RIGHT STUFF:* 1 Breaking The Sound Barrier (4:45); 2 Almost Ready (1:25); 3 The Training (1:16); 4 Glenn's Flight (5:19); 5 Yeager's Triumph (5:09);

NORTH AND SOUTH: 6 Main Title (3:45); 7 Southern Life (1:38); 8 Love In The Chapel (4:04); 9 A Close Call (2:00); 10 Returning Home (2:13); 11 Last Embrace (2:57); 12 Final Meeting (2:28).

Review: Bill Conti won an Oscar for his great score for *The Right Stuff*, the outstanding 1983 Philip Kaufman filming of Tom Wolfe's bestselling book about the early days of Chuck Yeager and NASA, yet his original music was never released as a soundtrack album. Conti was given the opportunity to produce a concert suite with the London Symphony Orchestra in 1985, and the results were released on this tremendously well-recorded album, which couples a 16-minute suite from *The Right Stuff* with a slightly longer suite from the composer's score for *North and South*, the mega-successful TV mini-series. Conti's music is magnificent in each case. For *The Right Stuff*, he wrote a triumphant score that was modeled after "The Planets' at certain points, yet contains enough of his stirring, invigorating style to mark it as distinctly the work of its composer. *North and South*, meanwhile, is a beautifully flowing melodic score, with a gorgeous main theme comprising the heart of the musical material. Together, they make for a fantastic album in which the only flaw is that it doesn't go on longer than it does.

Andy Dursin

Rio Conchos ♫♫♫♪

1989, Intrada Records; from the movie *Rio Conchos*, **1964.**

Album Notes: *Music:* Jerry Goldsmith; The London Symphony Orchestra, conducted by Jerry Goldsmith; *Album Producer:* Jerry Goldsmith; *Engineer:* Bruce Botnick; *Assistant Engineer:* Chris Brown.

Selections: 1 The Agony And The Ecstasy Prologue: Rome/Florence/The Crucifix/The Stone Giants/The Agony Of Creation (12:37); 2 Rio Conchos (2:26); 3 Where's The Water (1:55); 4 Bandit's Ho (6:58); 5 The River (2:04); 6 River Crossing (4:22); 7 The Aftermath (2:06); 8 Wall Of Fire (2:21); 9 Lonely Indian (3:24); 10 Chief Bloodshirt (2:27); 11 The Corral (2:45); 12 The Intruder (6:00); 13 Special Delivery (6:12).

Review: Rerecorded with the London Symphony Orchestra for this revitalization of his landmark 1964 Western score, Jerry Goldsmith's *Rio Conchos* is exciting, stimulating, and highly romantic. The principal theme is a rhythmic violin melody over guitar and tambourine, given a poignant turn by oboe midway through. The guitar, tambourine, and other percussion gives the score an agreeable rhythm and a down-to-earth feel, while the soaring melodies and complex action writing drives the characters and their confrontations. Like Elmer Bernstein in his own Western scores, Goldsmith develops a signature style which would later be recalled in films like *Rio Lobo* and *Bandolero!*. Added to the score's 45 minutes is a 12.5 minute "Prologue" from Goldsmith's triumphant music for the long-lost prelude to *The Agony and the Ecstasy*, which becomes a powerful tone poem about the sculptor Michelangelo, expressive and lofty, emphasizing strings, harp, and French horn. Intrada's fine production qualities abound in this important soundtrack restoration.

Randall D. Larson

Rio Grande ♫♫♫♫

1993, Varese-Sarabande; from the movie *Rio Grande*, **Republic Pictures, 1950.**

Album Notes: *Music:* Victor Young; Orchestra conducted by Victor Young; *CD Producer:* Robert Townson.

Selections: 1 Main Title (2:17); 2 Return From Patrol (1:53); 3 Soldiers Fight (1:46); 4 I'll Take You Home Again, Kathleen (trad.)(2:34) *The Sons Of The Pioneers, Ken Curtis*; 5 Dispossessed (:55); 6 Cattle Call (T. Owens)(1:11) *The Sons Of The Pioneers*; 7 Aha, San Antone (D. Evans)(:45) *Ben Johnson, Harry Carey Jr., Claude Jarman Jr.*; 8 Reunion (2:34); 9 Indian Raid/Escape (5:03); 10 Erie Canal (trad.)(:31) *The Sons Of The Pioneers*; 11 Laundresses' Row (:56); 12 Yellow Stripes (S. Jones)(:54) *The Sons Of The Pioneers*; 13 My Gal Is Purple (S. Jones)(1:32) *The Sons Of The Pioneers*; 14 Down By The Glen Side (trad.)(2:08) *The Sons Of The Pioneers, Ken Curtis*; 15 Footsore Cavalry (S. Jones)(:48) *The Sons Of The Pioneers*; 16 Meeting At The Rio Grande (1:18); 17 Confederate Dollars And Yankee Gold (1:45); 18 Departure For Fort Bliss (The Girl I Left Behind)(:54); 19 Tyree Meets The Wagon Train/Indian Attack (6:34); 20 Call Your Volunteers (:42); 21 Nighttime Approach/Rescuing The Children (6:52); 22 Coming Home (1:34); 23 Dixie (End Title)(1:03).

Review: Even though it was recorded in 1950, and plays in a rather grainy mono sound, there is no denying the immense power and sweep of this excellent western score by Victor Young. While the screenplay provided the composer with a stock contingent of action scenes (solidly expressed in cues like "Indian Raid/ Escape," or "Tyree Meets the Wagon Train/Indian Attack"), it also gave him an unusually broader canvas to work on with its story about two strong-willed and very private souls, Lt. Col. Yorke, and his wife, Kathleen, who have been separated for 16 years, after they found themselves on opposite sides during the Civil War, and are unexpectedly reunited again in an isolated outpost in the West. This situation suggested to Young a richer and more musically diversified score, with many cues built around the traditional folk song "I'll Take You Home, Kathleen," a biting comment on the couple's current relationship, since Yorke destroyed his wife's Southern estate during the war. Adding an extra musical element, several vocals by The Sons of the Pioneers give the score some western authenticity.

Rising Sun ♫♫♪

1993, Fox Records; from the movie *Rising Sun*, **20th Century-Fox, 1993.**

Album Notes: *Music:* Toru Takemitsu; Tokyo Concert Orchestra conducted by Hiroyuki Iwaki; *Album Producer:* Toru Takemitsu; *Engineer:* Shanji Hori.

Selections: 1 Taiko Drum Opening (:44) *Seiichi Tanaka & The San Francisco Taiko Dojo*; 2 Don't Fence Me In (C. Porter)(1:43); 3 Drive To Connor's Loft (1:57); 4 Web Meets Connor (:50); 5 Eddie Revealed On Disc (2:34); 6 Chase (1:04); 7 So Eddie Witnessed The Murder (2:06); 8 Yakuza Pursuit (1:01); 9 Medley (3:04); 10 Single Petal Of A Rose (E.K. Ellington)(2:06); 11 Web's Confession (2:45); 12 Eddie's Showdown (6:10); 13 Mystery Figure Revealed (2:49); 14 Senator Morton Gets Faxed (1:59); 15 Tsunami (S. Tanaka)(8:06) *Seiichi Tanaka & The San Francisco Taiko Dojo*.

Review: *Rising Sun* is a 1993 Philip Kaufman film from the controversial Michael Crichton book. Sean Connery and Wesley Snipes star as detectives investigating a murder at a Japanese firm in Los Angeles and the film mixes suspense and culture—shock characterization with silliness and boredom. The filmmakers did have the conviction to hire famed Japanese modernist Toru Takemitsu for his first and only Hollywood score. Takemitsu, who had composed for numerous Japanese pictures such as *Ran* for Akira Kurosawa, fashioned an intriguing sound world of orchestra and traditional Japanese instruments. The score overall is textural and only fleetingly melodic, but provides a real sense of disquiet and tension to the film's complicated flashback structure and themes of cultural infiltration. One of the most discernible motives, for ascending saxophone, blends dissonant, post-tonal textures with an almost Gershwin-esque Americana theme—western culture swallowed up by the rest of the world and not the other way around. The CD is a fascinating listen for the post-tonally schooled—it also includes a traditional taiko drum performance—but is not for the traditionally minded, and is probably only second-rate Takemitsu. Reportedly the filmmakers made a veritable stir-fry of the cues in the dubbing process and Takemitsu cursed American filmmaking until his untimely death in 1996.

Lukas Kendall

The River 𝄞𝄞𝄞𝄞ᵛ

1984, Varese-Sarabande; from the movie *The River*, Universal Pictures, 1984.

Album Notes: *Music*: John Williams; Orchestra conducted by John Williams; *Featured Musicians*: Jim Walker (flute), Warren Luening (trumpet), Tommy Tedesco (guitar); *Album Producer*: John Williams; *Engineer*: Dan Wallen.

Selections: 1 The River (4:30); 2 Growing Up (2:52); 3 The Pony Ride (3:17); 4 Love Theme (4:54); 5 The Ancestral Home (4:32); 6 Rain Clouds Gather (3:07); 7 From Farm To Factory (2:44); 8 Back From Town (3:40); 9 Tractor Scene (2:18); 10 A Family Meeting (2:39); 11 Young Friends Farewell (2:39).

Review: Tapping a musical vein he has seldom fully explored, John Williams wrote a score rooted in Americana for *The River*, made by Mark Rydell, the director with whom he had previously worked on *The Reivers*. In this story of a couple of farmers (portrayed by Mel Gibson and Sissy Spacek) uncompromisingly attached to their land and determined to stay on it despite a speculator willing to buy it and a disastrous flood that threatens to engulf all they have, Williams found the elements for a thoughtful and rewarding score, nominated for an Academy Award, in which little pleasures ("The Pony Ride"), downhome feelings ("Tractor Scene"), and seemingly insurmountable pains ("Rain Clouds Gather") elicit a lyrical and immensely touching response.

A River Runs Through It 𝄞𝄞𝄞

1992, Milan Records; from the movie *A River Runs Through It*, Columbia Pictures, 1992.

Album Notes: *Music*: Mark Isham; *Orchestrations*: Ken Kugler, Kim Scharnberg, Dell Hake; *Music Editor*: Allan Rosen; Orchestra conducted by Ken Kugler; *Featured Musicians*: Sid Page (violin), Louise Di Tullio (flute), Rich Ruttenberg (piano), Dorothy Remsen (harp), Katie Kirkpatrick (harp), John Isham (Uilleann pipes); *Album Producer*: Mark Isham; *Engineers*: Stephen Krause; *Assistant Engineers*: Sue McLean, Mark Eshelman, Greg Dennen, Robert Loftus, Gil Morales, Bill Talbott.

Selections: 1 A River Runs Through It (2:22); 2 Casting Presbyterian Style (1:29); 3 A Land Filled With Wonder (1:32); 4 Down The Alley (With You) (2:20); 5 A Summer Of Lumber And Fishing (1:44); 6 Shooting The Chutes (1:52); 7 Three Fisherman (1:55); 8 A Trip To The Unknown (2:28); 9 Four-Count Reason (2:27); 10 The Sheik Of Araby (H. Smith/T. Snyder/F. Wheeler) (1:56); 11 Bye Bye Blackbird (M. Dixon/R. Henderson) (1:57) *Prudence Johnson*; 12 Je ne sais quoi (:56); 13 Swing Me High, Swing Me Low (2:29); 14 A Place Remembered (:54); 15 A Remark Was Passed (2:23); 16 Rugged Cross (trad.) (2:50); 17 Muskrat Ramble (R. Gilbert/E. Ory) (1:58); 18 Rawhide (:58); 19 The Wild Ride (2:27); 20 Early Departure (:50); 21 The Splendor In The Grass (1:10); 22 Jessie And Norman (2:59); 23 Lolo's (1:15); 24 The High Road (1:01); 25 Yes, Quite A Day (1:05); 26 A Fine Fisherman And The Big Blackfoot River (1:41); 27 The Moment That Could Not Last (1:23); 28 Too Deep For Tears (:46); 29 Without Complete Understanding (1:21); 30 In The Half-Light Of The Canyon (2:46); 31 Haunted By Waters/A River Runs Through It (reprise) (4:18).

Review: Mark Isham's flowing, low-key, poetic score for Robert Redford's character-driven drama is genteel and relaxing enough. Replacing a score initially composed by Elmer Bernstein, Isham's music does a superlative job not overstating the emotions of Redford's film, working to gently push our heartstrings instead of melodramatically tugging them like so many other Hollywood film scores do. The only problem is that the music may be too subtle for its own good. The score lacks a degree of distinction contained in the best scores for films of this type, with a main theme that is, if anything, a bit too restrained. Nevertheless, the music paints yet another picture

of Isham, whose versatile talents have been utilized in composing often successful film scores for any kind of genre film.
Andy Dursin

The River Wild 🎵🎵🎵

1994, RCA Records; from the movie *The River Wild*, Universal Pictures, 1994.

Album Notes: *Music*: Jerry Goldsmith; *Orchestrations*: Arthur Morton, Alexander Courage; *Music Editor*: Ken Hall; Orchestra conducted by Jerry Goldsmith; *Album Producer*: Jerry Goldsmith; *Engineer*: Bruce Botnick.

Selections: 1 The Water Is Wide (trad.)(3:10) *Cowboy Junkies*; 2 Gale's Theme (Main Title)(2:24); 3 Big Water (2:51); 4 Wade Goes Under (3:18); 5 Tom Hangs On (3:21); 6 Vision Quest (2:57); 7 Little Niagara (2:40); 8 Same Old Story (2:12); 9 Vacation's Over (9:51); 10 Family Reunion (End Title)(5:47).

Review: Goldsmith stepped in to replace Maurice Jarre's work on this Meryl Streep action thriller, utilizing the same folk tune, "The River Is Wide" as an affecting title theme that weaves its way through several exultant, fast-paced river rafting sequences before giving way to a halting, heavy orchestral rhythm that gradually overwhelms the score. Goldsmith effectively characterized the film's raging river currents with swelling, tremuloso chords from the string section and a "splashing" synthetic percussion effect. The final cue, "The Vacation's Over," develops the primary action material in impressive fashion over the course of nine minutes as the entire orchestra chops away at Goldmith's percussive motifs. Is it ingeniously cohesive or just repetitious?

Jeff Bond

The Road to Wellville 🎵🎵🎵🎵

1994, Varese-Sarabande Records; from the movie *The Road to Wellville*, Columbia Pictures, 1994.

Album Notes: *Music*: Rachel Portman; *Orchestrations*: Rachel Portman; Orchestra conducted by David Snell; *Album Producers*: Rachel Portman, Alan Parker; *Engineer*: Dick Lewzey.

Selections: 1 Ladies' Laughing Exercise (:22); 2 Intro (2:44); 3 Treatments (1:36); 4 Life Is Death Postponed (2:23); 5 Where The Spirits Soar (J. Parker) (:52); 6 The Battle Creek San (1:07); 7 Canzonetta (F. Mendelssohn)(1:33); 8 Badger's Picnic (:52); 9 Fire At The San (1:16); 10 Daddy (1:13); 11 A Chewing Song (J. Hayden/T. Metz)(:37); 12 The San Waltz (1:54); 13 Handhabung Therapeutik (1:14); 14 Charles (:39); 15 Waltz Of The Flowers (P.I. Tchaikovsky)(2:01); 16 Der Lindenbaum (F. Schubert)(:17); 17 Eleanor (:49); 18 Stairs (1:01); 19 Where The Spirits Soar (J. Parker)(1:11); 20 Endymion (1:15); 21 History Is About To Be Eaten (:56); 22 Rigoletto (G. Verdi)(1:15); 23 Wellville (3:03); 24 Where The Spirits Soar (J. Parker)(1:16).

Review: One of today's brightest young composers, Rachel Portman took a direct cue from the amusing storyline behind this somewhat eccentric little film and concocted a cheerful score that's a whole lot of fun. Set at the turn of the century, *The Road to Wellville* concerned itself with the evidently odd Kellogg health sanitarium, where "patients" could get rid of all kinds of real or imaginary ailments by following a therapeutic regimen that involved the consumption of strange medicinal remedies and the use of even stranger contraptions. Matching the tone of the film and cleverly blending bits of dialogue to set-off the selections, Portman's score delights in cues that, on the surface, seem quite demure, but are in fact wickedly funny and delicious in their expression. Adding an eccentric note of their own, some classical selections, played in a way their composers would certainly never have imagined, fit very neatly in the whole musical package.

The Road Warrior 🎵🎵🎵

1982, Varese-Sarabande; from the movie *The Road Warrior*, Warner Bros., 1982.

Album Notes: *Music*: Brian May; Orchestra conducted by Brian May; *Album Producer*: Tom Null; *Engineer*: Danny Hersch.

Selections: 1 Montage/Main Title (4:53); 2 Confrontation (2:32); 3 Marauder's Massacre (3:14); 4 Max Enters Compound (4:09); 5 Gyro Saves Max (3:55); 6 Break Out (3:26); 7 Finale And Largo (5:06); 8 End Title (3:20); 9 SFX Suite: (a) Boomerang Attack, (b) Gyro Flight/The Big Rig Starts, (c) Breakout/The Refinery Explodes/Reprise (4:37).

Review: There have been lots of kinetic action films since George Miller's *The Road Warrior*, but this is the masterpiece that kicked them off, a seminal piece of modern post-apocalyptic sci-fi. Brian May's music is the sound of Mad Max, thrashing and sinister — Herrmann on high-octane as the rogue Max scavenges for petrol, bike and car gangs rape and pillage, and a lone community tries to survive. Ultimately it is Max who saves them but ends up even worse off, and the score, unlike its *Mad Max* (1979) predecessor, features a tragic, romantic/symphonic side in addition to its propulsive action base. May invests his music with a considerable personality of orchestration and gestures (too bad the recording, made in Australia, is so muddled) which successfully link the suspenseful moments with the flat-out, 120mph chases. Not far from the disorienting, dissonant textures of the first *Mad Max,* with a hopeful eye on

"In a hundred years we could be dazzled with what is done with electronic sound. Music and film is just starting, but it will be the entertainment medium of the next centuries."

John Williams
(Time Magazine, 9-11-95)

the symphonic sweep of Maurice Jarre's music for the third film, *Beyond Thunderdome*, and left to rot with a tankerful of sand in the Australian wasteland is this, the late Brian May's most famous score.

Lukas Kendall

See: Mad Max Beyond Thunderdome

Rob Roy 🎵🎵🎵

1995, Virgin Movie Music; from the movie *Rob Roy*, M-G-M, 1995.

Album Notes: *Music:* Carter Burwell; *Orchestrations:* Sonny Kompanek; *Music Editor:* Adam Smalley; Orchestra conducted by Carter Burwell, Sonny Kompanek; *Featured Musicians:* Davy Spillane (Uillean pipes and low whistles), Maire Breatnach (fiddle), Tommy Hayes (bodhran), Ronan Brown (penny whistle), Miriam Stockley (voice); *Album Producer:* Carter Burwell; *Engineer:* Michael Farrow; *Assistant Engineers:* Geoff Foster, Rob Kirwan.

Selections: 1 Overture: (a) Rob Roy (2:17), (b) The Rieving Party (2:23); 2 Home From The Hills (2:45); 3 Hard Earth (2:08) *Karen Matheson*; 4 Procession For The Ill-Used (1:38); 5 Blood Sport (1:15); 6 The Gaelic Reels (1:06) *Capercaillie*; 7 Ailein Duinn (2:36) *Karen Matheson*; 8 The Last Peaceful Night (1:50); 9 Troops In The Mist (1:14); 10 Honor Inflamed (3:19); 11 The Dispossessed: (a) The Cave (:56), (b) Hard Home On The Moor (1:06); 12 The Blunt Reels (2:10) *Capercaillie*; 13 Highland Justice: (a) Call Of The Claymore (1:24), (b) Assize Of The Gregorach (1:33); 14 A Standing Stone, A Silk Purse (3:34); 15 Theid mi Dhachaig (I'll Go Home)(1:19); 16 Rannoch Moor Suite: (a) Scorched Earth (1:11), (b) Rannoch Moor Retreat (1:45), (c) The Mists (2:28), (d) Rob Come To Hand (:40); 17 Morag's Lament (:50) *Karen Matheson*; 18 Born By Rapids (2:24); 19 Love And Death Suite: (a) My Beloved (1:59), (b) A Matter Of Honor (1:19), (c) Cunningham's End (:48); 20 Robert And Mary (3:14).

Review: In 1995 we had *Braveheart*, *Dragonheart*, and *Rob Roy*. Who says there isn't enough imitation in Hollywood? Carter Burwell had the opportunity at scoring *Rob Roy*, the first and least successful of the three big-screen Highlands epics, featuring good performances but draggy pacing and indifferent direction. Burwell's music, combined with the sweeping cinematography, is enough to make the movie easy to watch, but on its own, it's all too clear to spot the flaws in the soundtrack album—namely, it's redundant to a fault. The main theme just repeats itself over and over again, and while it's beautiful the first time you hear it, you won't be feeling the same way by the time you reach the end of the soundtrack, which also contains vocals by Karen Matheson and Gaelic group Capercaillie.

Andy Dursin

The Robe 🎵🎵🎵🎵🎵

1993, Fox Records; from the movie *The Robe*, 20th Century-Fox, 1953.

Album Notes: *Music:* Alfred Newman; The 20th Century-Fox Orchestra and Chorus, conducted by Alfred Newman; *CD Producer:* Nick Redman; *Engineers:* Mike McDonald, Dan Hersch.

Selections: 1 20th Century-Fox Fanfare (:13); 2 Prelude/Main Title (1:25); 3 The Slave Market (Diana)(2:34); 4 Caligula's Arrival (1:03); 5 Caligula's Departure (1:06); 6 The Map Of Jerusalem (5:02); 7 Palm Sunday (2:14); 8 The Carriage Of The Cross (2:01); 9 Marcellus Returns To Capri (2:04); 10 Attempted Suicide (1:51); 11 Tiberius' Palace (1:43); 12 The Market Place (4:52); 13 Elegy (4:30); 14 Marcellus' Redemption (chorus only) (2:25); 15 Justus' Death (11:45); 16 Hymn For The Dead (1:06); 17 In His Service (1:46); 18 The Catacombs (5:00); 19 Room In The Catacombs (:36); 20 Hope (1:29); 21 Demetrius' Rescue (parts 1 & 2)(3:16); 22 Gallio's House (2:18); 23 Peter Heals Demetrius (3:03); 24 Marcellus' Farewell (1:22); 25 Interior Dungeon (2:54); 26 Finale/Hallelujah (2:00).

Review: One of the first big screen epics of the 1950s with a Biblical theme, *The Robe* is distinguished by the fact that it is the first film to use the anamorphic CinemaScope process and the first which introduced multi-track stereophonic sound in many roadshow theatres. An inspirational story, based on Lloyd C. Douglas' best-seller, the film recounts the conversion of a Roman tribune (Richard Burton), when he realizes that the Man crucified on the Golgotha, and whose garment he had inherited, might have been the Son of God. Playing a decisive role in this conversion are his Greek slave, Demetrius, played by Victor Mature, already a Christian; his childhood sweetheart, Diana (Jean Simmons), ward of Emperor Tiberius, also an early convert; and crazed Prince Regent Caligula (Jay Robinson in a scene-stealing portrayal), who eventually sent him and Diana to their deaths. Availing themselves of the letterbox gimmick, already a strong attraction in itself, the makers of the film spared no expense to turn *The Robe* into a spectacular presentation. Huge crowds involving thousands of extras competed with impressive circus scenes, gigantic sets and breathtaking races (charging directly at the cameras) to mesmerize audiences who had seldom been treated to such a display on such a large screen scale.

Enhancing the performance is Alfred Newman's superlative score, a deeply felt assortment of grandeur and bravura mixed with more intimate expressions of love and religious respect. Interestingly, even though it had been recorded in stereo, the score was initially released on record in mono only (the recording industry catching up with the innovations in film sound techniques some four years later). This release on compact disc marks the first time the score, which includes many cues available for the first time, is heard in stereo, the way it was initially recorded, and it sounds mighty impressive, particularly to those who have grown up with the original mono version. In later years, Newman's achievements would be somewhat overshadowed by his own contributions to other films, and by Miklos Rozsa's compositions for similar Roman spectacles like *Ben-Hur* or *King of Kings*. The fact remains that *The Robe* is an exceptional score.

Robin Hood ♪♪♪

1991, Silva Screen Records; from the movie *Robin Hood,* 20th Century-Fox, 1990.

Album Notes: *Music*: Geoffrey Burgon; *Orchestrations*: Geoffrey Burgon; Orchestra conducted by Geoffrey Burgon; *Album Producer*: Geoffrey Burgon; *Engineer*: Alan Snelling.

Selections: 1 Main Titles/Hunting The Poacher (5:16); 2 Robin Meets Marian/ Fight On The Battlements (6:59); 3 Robin Traps Folcanet (3:11); 4 The Outlaw's Band (3:13); 5 Rob And Will/ Robbing The Taxes (5:32); 6 Marian To The Rescue (3:45); 7 Robin And Marian Reach Safety (1:11); 8 Prince John (3:13); 9 Attack On The Castle/The Death Of Folcanet (3:12); 10 The Wedding/End Titles (2:32).

Review: The story — real or imaginary — of Robin Hood and His Merry Men has inspired many screen adaptations, starting with an early silent film starring Douglas Fairbanks, all the way to a (eeech!) politically-correct television series currently underway as these lines are being written. Likewise, each version resulted in new musical takes from composers inspired by the tale, and perhaps secretly hoping to emulate Erich-Wolfgang Korngold's trend-setting score for the Errol Flynn version, *The Adventures of Robin Hood,* the definite model against which all others have to measure up.

Starring Patrick Bergin as the legendary outlaw and Uma Thurman as Maid Marian, this remake offers little that is new and is steadfast in its conventional narrative. Equally safe in its expression is Geoffrey Burgon's score, appropriately heroic and romantic, as the multi-tiered action dictated, but ultimately more descriptive than melodic, with a lot of kettle drumming punctuating the themes spelled out by the woodwind and brass instruments. It sounds grand and epic, but a trifle dull.

Robin Hood: Men in Tights
♪♪♪♪

1993, Milan Records; from the movie *Robin Hood: Men in Tights,* TriStar Films, 1993.

Album Notes: *Music*: Hummie Mann; *Orchestrations*: Brad Dechter, Frank Bennett, Don Nemitz; *Music Editor*: Chris Ledesma; *Album Producer*: David Franco; *Engineer*: Joe Gaswirt.

Selections: 1 Marian (H. Mann/M. Brooks)(3:36) *Cathy Dennis, Lance Ellington*; 2 Main Title (3:04); 3 Sherwood Forest Rap #1 (H. Mann/M. Brooks) (1:10) *Kevin Dorsey, The Merry Men Singers*; 4 Escape From Kahlil Prison (:58); 5 Robin's Pledge/ The Great Voyage (1:05); 6 Stick Fight With Little John (1:47); 7 Prince John's Party/Robin's Entrance (1:29); 8 The Great Hall Fight (3:14); 9 Men In Tights (M. Brooks)(1:24) *The Merry Men Singers*; 10 The Witch In The Tower (1:39); 11 Villager's Training Sequence (1:32); 12 The Night Is Young (B. Rose/I. Kahal/D. Suesse)(1:48) *Arthur Rubin, The Merry Men Singers*; 13 Romantic Marian (:49); 14 Royal Country Fayre/The Abbott's March (1:31); 15 Villagers To The Rescue (2:19); 16 The Wedding (:39); 17 Marian (M. Boorks/H. Mann)(1:37) *Debbie James*; 18 Sherwood Forest Rap #2 (M. Brooks/H. Mann)(:23) *Kevin Dorsey, The Merry Men.*

Review: There is no way one could mistake this often hilarious sendup of the Robin Hood legend with the real thing. After having merrily mistreated westerns, horror films, and space epics, it somehow made sense than funny man Mel Brooks would set his sight on swashbucklers. And which story better to spoof than Robin Hood, the swashbuckler *par excellence.* Naysayers might frown at the mere idea that the hero of so many medieval deeds might be reduced to a cartoon character, but as Brooks not so subtly hints, "the legend had it coming..." Matching the verve in the film, Hummie Mann wrote a score with its tongue firmly in cheek that brims with good melodic material. If at times, the music sounds appropriately medieval, with occasional forays into bombastic posturing or romantic sidesteps, funny ideas (like using an epic version of "Row, row the boat" in "Escape from Kahlil Prison," or indulging in not one but two rap songs, performed by Robin's Merry Men Singers) leave little doubt about Mel Brooks' intentions. Ultimately, the film might not have been as successful as some of the director's earlier sendups. But this score is a gas.

Robin Hood: Prince of Thieves ♪♪♪

1991, Morgan Creek Records; from the movie *Robin Hood: Prince of Thieves*, Warner Bros., **1991**.

Album Notes: *Music*: Michael Kamen; *Orchestrations*: Michael Kamen, Jack Hayes, William Ross, Don Davis, Bruce Babcock, Albert Olson, Pat Russ, Brad Warnaar, Lolita Ritmanis, Mark Watters, Elliot Kaplin, Jonathan Sacks, Richard Davis, Harvey Cohen, Beth Lee, Chris Boardman; *Music Editors*: Christopher Brooks, Eric Reasoner; The Greater Los Angeles Orchestra, conducted by Michael Kamen; *Album Producers*: Michael Kamen, Stephen P. McLaughlin, Christopher S. Brooks; *Engineer*: Bobby Fernandez.

Selections: 1 Overture and A Prisoner Of The Crusades (8:28); 2 Sir Guy Of Gisborn and The Escape To Sherwood (7:28); 3 Little John And The Band In The Forest (4:53); 4 The Sheriff And His Witch (6:03); 5 Maid Marian (2:58); 6 Training — Robin Hood, Prince Of Thieves (5:15); 7 Marian At The Waterfall (5:34); 8 The Abduction and The Final Battle At The Gallows (9:54); 9 (Everything I Do) I Do It For You (B. Adams/R.J. Lange/M. Kamen)(6:38) *Bryan Adams*; 10 Wild Times (M. Kamen/J. Lynne)(3:13) *Jeff Lynne*.

Review: Pretty much all anybody remembers about this movie and soundtrack album is the Bryan Adams ballad "Anything I Do (I'd Do It For You)," which has certainly transcended the bloated Kevin Costner version of the Robin Hood myth it originates from. Adams wrote the mega-successful song with R.J. "Mutt" Lange and Michael Kamen, who also composed — with a number of orchestrators due to a massive shortage of time — the film's original score. Unfortunately, despite a magnificent opening theme and a rousing climax, Kamen's score rarely comes close to Korngoldian heights. Too much of the score listlessly punctuates the action on-screen, never really finding any central focus aside from the main fanfare, and certainly underwhelms during the romantic passages, with a low-key tinkering of the song motive barely qualifying as being anything more than functional to the proceedings. Kamen delivered a far more effective score in a similar vein for *The Three Musketeers* remake just a short time later.

Andy Dursin

RoboCop

RoboCop ♪♪♪♪

1987, Varese-Sarabande; from the movie *RoboCop*, Orion Pictures, **1987**.

Album Notes: *Music*: Basil Poledouris; *Orchestrations*: Steven Scott Smalley; *Music Editor*: Tom Villano; The Sinfonia of London Orchestra, conducted by Howard Blake, Tony Britton; *Synthesizers*: Derek Austin; *Album Producer*: Basil Poledouris; *Engineers*: Eric Tomlinson.

Selections: 1 Main Title (:32); 2 Van Chase (4:50); 3 Murphy's Death (2:30); 4 Rock Shop (3:38); 5 Home (4:05); 6 Robo vs. ED-209 (2:00); 7 The Dream (3:00); 8 Across The Board (2:28); 9 Betrayal (2:12); 10 Clarance Frags Bob (1:40); 11 Drive To Jones' Office (1:40); 12 We Killed You (1:30); 13 Directive IV (1:00); 14 Robo Tips His Hat (2:00); 15 Showdown (5:00).

Review: See *Robocop 3* entry below.

RoboCop 2 ♪♪♪♪

1990, Varese-Sarabande, from the movie *RoboCop 2*, Orion Pictures, **1990**.

Album Notes: *Music*: Leonard Rosenman; *Orchestrations*: Ralph Ferraro; Orchestra conducted by Leonard Rosenman; *Album Producer*: Leonard Rosenman; *Engineer*: Dan Wallin; *Assistant Engineer*: Sue McLean.

Selections: 1 Overture: RoboCop (6:02); 2 City Mayhem (3:37); 3 Happier Days (1:28); 4 Robo Cruiser (4:40); 5 Robo Memories (2:07); 6 Robo And Nuke (2:22); 7 Robo Fanfare (:32); 8 Robo And Cain Chase (2:41); 9 Creating The Monster (2:47); 10 Robo I vs. Robo II (3:41).

Review: See *Robocop 3* entry below.

RoboCop 3 ♪♪♪

1993, Varese-Sarabande; from the movie *RoboCop 3*, Orion Pictures, **1993**.

Album Notes: *Music*: Basil Poledouris; *Orchestrations*: Greig McRitchie; *Music Editor*: Tom Villano; Orchestra conducted by Basil Poledouris; *Synthesizers*: Michael Boddicker; *Album Producer*: Basil Poledouris; *Engineers*: Tim Boyle.

Selections: 1 Main Title/The Resistance (2:35); 2 Robo Saves Lewis (3:56); 3 Resistance Base (1:36); 4 Otomo Underground (1:49); 5 Murphy's Memories (4:36); 6 Robo Fights Otomo (4:27); 7 Nikko And Murphy (1:53); 8 Death Of Lewis (3:46); 9 Sayonara, McDaggit (3:38).

Review: Like Spielberg's *Jaws*, Paul Verhoven's excellent, original *Robocop* has been sullied by two gratuitous sequels that diluted the brilliant high concept of the first film. Basil

Poledouris' original *Robocop* score features a bombastic, near-satirical heroic theme for the Robocop character that only needs some booming lyrics to push it right over the top. But the rest of his score perfectly captures the affecting, emotional resonance that is at the heart of the film's stealth appeal. Despite, or perhaps because of his eviscerated humanity, Robocop is a rare action hero you could actually care about. Poledouris movingly scored the character's death and his haunting attempts to rediscover his identity, and rousingly underscored action scenes in which the character, wittingly or unwittingly, lashed out at the villains who'd robbed him of his humanity, in cues like "Rock Shop" and "Showdown."

Leonard Rosenman's score to the Irvin Kirshner-directed follow-up is marked by the composer's unmistakable modernistic style, but while Rosenman's score is far more intellectually sophisticated it doesn't capture the emotional punch of Poledouris' original.

By the time *Robocop 3* rolled around the character had been completely juvenilized (as well as portrayed by another, less-effective actor), and Poledouris' score is a by-the-numbers affair that resurrects the material, but not the passion of the original.

Jeff Bond

The Rock ♫♫▹

1996, Hollywood Records; from the movie *The Rock*, Hollywood Pictures, 1996.

Album Notes: *Music*: Nick Glennie-Smith, Hans Zimmer, Harry Gregson-Williams; *Orchestrations*: Bruce Fowler, Suzette Moriarty, Ladd McIntosh, Walt Fowler, Dennis Dreith; *Music Editors*: Bob Badami, John Finklea; Orchestra conducted by Nick Glennie-Smith, Bruce Fowler, Don Harper; *Featured Musicians*: Bob Daspit, Michael Thomson, Michael Stevens (guitars); *Album Producers*: Nick Glennie-Smith, Hans Zimmer, Harry Gregson-Williams; *Engineers*: Alan Meyerson, Bruce Botnick.

Selections: 1 Hummell Gets The Rockets (6:25); 2 Rock House Jail (10:12); 3 Jade (2:01); 4 In The Tunnels (8:40); 5 Mason's Walk/First Launch (9:34); 6 Rocket Away (14:25); 7 Fort Walton/Kansas (1:37); 8 The Chase (7:35).

Review: The music for Michael Bay's hyperventilating team-up of Nicholas Cage and Sean Connery typifies the action film scoring sensibility cultivated by mega-producer Jerry Bruckheimer: tons of percussion, both acoustic and synthesized, streaming bursts of synthetic chords, pulsating rhythms, and wailing electric guitars, all custom-designed not so much to engage the viewers within the movie's storyline as to convince them that they're watching the "coolest" piece of cinematic merchandise currently available and are thus incredibly cool themselves. Some of the rhythms are infectious, but the overall approach here is indistinguishable from that obtained in most beer commercials of the '80s. It's all part of the headache-inducing overkill that values adrenaline (if not pure testosterone) above anything else, and while scores like this may provide the same thrill ride as the films to which they're attached, the thrill is a transitory one that is going to date these efforts brutally.

Jeff Bond

Rockers ♫♫♫♫

1979, Mango Records; from the movie *Rockers*, Island Pictures, 1979.

Album Notes: Album Compiled by Chris Blackwell; *Executive Producers*: Theodore Bafakoulos, Avrom Robin; *Engineers*: Godwin Logie & Groucho.

Selections: 1 We 'A' Rockers (T. Lewis/B. Harvey) (3:24) *Inner Circle*; 2 Money Worries (H. Wilson) (3:22) *The Maytones*; 3 Police And Thieves (J. Murvin/L. Perry) (3:53) *Junior Murvin*; 4 Book Of Rules (B. Llewellyn/H. Johnson) (3:28) *The Heptones*; 5 Stepping Razor (P. Tosh) (3:16) *Peter Tosh*; 6 Tenement Yard (J. Miller/R. Lewis) (2:35) *Jacob Miller*; 7 Fade Away (E. Smith) (3:05) *Junior Byles*; 8 Rockers (N. Livingstone) (5:37) *Bunny Wailer*; 9 Slave Master (G. Isaacs) (2:28) *Gregory Isaacs*; 10 Dread Lion (L. Perry) (3:11) *Scratch & The Upsetters*; 11 Graduation In Zion (F. Dowding) (2:47) *Kiddus I*; 12 Jah No Dead (W. Rodney) (2:12) *Burning Spear*; 13 Satta Masagana (L. Manning/D. Manning/B. Collins) (3:32) *Third World*; 14 Natty Take Over (J. Hines/M. Roper) (3:07) *Justin Hines & The Dominoes*.

Review: The wonderful soundtrack to *The Harder They Come* kind of ruined it for most reggae film music, but this still deserves propers as a fine collection of both artists and tunes. Many of the giants of contemporary reggae are here — Peter Tosh, Bunny Wailer, Burning Spear, Third World. But "Rockers" also provides an opportunity to hear some lesser-known talents such as Inner Circle, Kiddus I and Junior Murvin.

Gary Graff

The Rocketeer ♫♫♫▹

1991, Hollywood Records; from the movie *The Rocketeer*, Walt Disney Pictures, 1991.

Album Notes: *Music*: James Horner; *Orchestrations*: John Neufeld, Elliot Kaplan, Billy May, Conrad Pope; *Music Editor*: Jim Henrikson; Orchestra conducted by James Horner; *Album Producer*: James Horner; *Engineer*: Shawn Murphy.

Selections: 1 Main Title/Takeoff (4:30); 2 The Flying Circus (6:30); 3 Jenny (5:10); 4 Begin The Beguine (C. Porter)(3:36) *Melora Hardin*; 5 Neville Sinclair's House (7:20); 6 Jenny's Rescue (3:20); 7 Rendezvous At Griffith Park Observatory (8:10); 8 When Your Lover Has Gone (E.A. Swan)(3:25) *Melora Hardin*; 9 The Zeppelin (8:00); 10 Rocketeer To The Rescue/ End Title (6:30).

Review: James Horner's enthusiastic score is much better than this tepid actioner about the comic strip hero that inspired it. With the music firmly planted into the film's period, the 1930s, the composer has integrated some original big band numbers to his cues, writing a score that often bounces and throbs, and provides the listener with an enjoyable ride (or flight, as it were). The addition of two vocals (including Cole Porter's nifty *Begin the Beguine*) performed in breathless fashion by Melora Hardin, further conjure up the era and prove equally pleasurable.

Rocky

Rocky ♫♫♫♫♫

1995, EMI-America Records; from the movie *Rocky*, United Artists, 1976.

Album Notes: *Music*: Bill Conti; *Orchestrations*: Bill Conti; Orchestra conducted by Bill Conti; *Album Producer*: Bill Conti; *Engineer*: Ami Hadani.

Selections: 1 Gonna Fly Now (Theme From "Rocky")(B. Conti/ C. Conners/A. Robbins)(2:47) *DeEtta Little, Nelson Pigford*; 2 Philadelphia Morning (2:21); 3 Going The Distance (2:39); 4 Reflections (3:19); 5 Marine's Hymn (anon.)/Yankee Doodle (trad.)(1:44); 6 Take You Back (F. Stallone)(1:47) *Valentine*; 7 First Date (1:52); 8 You Take My Heart Away (B. Conti/C. Conners/A. Robbins)(4:45) *DeEtta Little, Nelson Pigford*; 9 Fanfare For Rocky (2:34); 10 Butkus (2:11); 11 Alone In The Ring (1:09); 12 The Final Bell (1:55); 13 Rocky's Reward (2:04).

Review: See *Rocky III* entry below.

Rocky II ♫♫♫♪

1995, EMI-America Records; from the movie *Rocky II*, United Artists, 1979.

Album Notes: *Music*: Bill Conti; *Orchestrations*: Bill Conti, Pete Myers; Orchestra conducted by Bill Conti; *Featured Musicians*: Mike Lang (keyboards), Steve Schaeffer (drums), Chuck Berghofer (bass), Dennis Budimer (guitar), Bob Zimmitti (percussion); *Album Producer*: Bill Conti; *Engineer*: Dennis Sands.

Selections: 1 Redemption (Theme From "Rocky II")(2:34); 2 Gonna Fly Now (B. Conti/C. Conners/A. Robbins)(2:34); 3 Con-

quest (4:40); 4 Vigil (6:30); 5 All Of My Life (4:00); 6 Overture (8:38); 7 Two Kinds Of Love (2:36); 8 All Of My Life (2:28).

Review: See *Rocky III* entry below.

Rocky III ♫♫♫

1995, EMI-America Records; from the movie *Rocky III*, United Artists, 1982.

Album Notes: *Music*: Bill Conti; *Orchestrations*: Bill Conti; Orchestra conducted by Bill Conti; *Album Producer*: Bill Conti; *Engineers*: Danny Wallin, Tom Steel, Bill Benton, Bill Fresh.

Selections: 1 Eye Of The Tiger (3:54) *Survivor*; 2 Take You Back (Tough Gym)(1:49) *Frank Stallone*; 3 Pushin' (3:12) *Frank Stallone*; 4 Reflections (3:22); 5 Mickey (4:41); 6 Take You Back (3:40) *Frank Stallone*; 7 Decision (2:06); 8 Gonna Fly Now (2:51) *DeEtta Little, Nelson Pigford*; 9 Adrian (1:42); 10 Conquest (4:42).

Review: Few film scores have reached the level of popularity in American culture as Bill Conti's Oscar-winning, instantly recognizable themes for the *Rocky* series. The original 1976 soundtrack contained the chart-topping hit "Gonna Fly Now," which continues to this day to be performed at all sorts of sporting events and other functions as a fanfare for hard work, determination, and fulfilling one's dreams. The vocal, performed by DeEtta Little and Nelson Pigford, was written by the composer, and remains permanently instilled in the minds of anyone who has seen the movie or heard the music. Along with the street-sounding harmonies of Valentine's "Take You Back," the rest of Conti's score is similarly energetic, propulsive, and filled with emotion, a trait that would come to mark many of the composer's works.

For *Rocky II*, the stylistic influence shifts from the often gritty, raw sound of the original film to a more disco-oriented approach, which doesn't benefit a children's chorus version of "Gonna Fly Now" (heard in a different version in the film), though Conti did compose a completely orchestral cue ("Conquest") and other impressive new material that is not as dated, and just as thematically strong as anything in the original film.

In *Rocky III*, the big new addition is another hugely popular song, Survivor's "Eye of the Tiger," which is contained on what's basically a compilation album with three new Conti cues, several Frank Stallone vocals, and tracks taken from the preceding *Rocky* soundtracks. Seeing that there are a number of Rocky compilations available, your best bet is to pick up one of those CDs and either or both of Conti's first two efforts in the series, which contain some of the most memorable film music ever written.

Andy Dursin

Romeo & Juliet

Romeo & Juliet 🎵🎵🎵🎵

1989, Capitol Records; from the movie *Romeo & Juliet*, Paramount Pictures, 1968.

Album Notes: *Music:* Nino Rota; Orchestra conducted by Nino Rota; *Featured Artists:* Leonard Whiting (Romeo), Olivia Hussey (Juliet).

Selections: 1 Prologue (2:50); 2 Romeo's Foreboding and The Feast At The House Of Capulet (a) What Is A Youth (N. Rota/E. Walter) (7:28) *Glen Weston*; 3 The Balcony Scene (9:29); 4 Romeo And Juliet Are Wed (3:05); 5 The Death Of Mercutio And Tybalt (3:34); 6 Farewell Love Scene (4:24); 7 The Likeness Of Death (2:37); 8 In Capulet's Tomb (7:52); 9 All Are Punished (2:09).

Review: See entry below.

Romeo + Juliet 🎵🎵🎵

1996, Capitol Records; from the movie *Romeo + Juliet*, 20th Century-Fox, 1996.

Album Notes: *Soundtrack Producers:* Nellee Hooper, Baz Luhrmann, Karyn Rachtman; *Soundtrack Coordinators:* Jane Chapman, Carol Dunn, Sandy Dworniak; *Engineer:* Wally Traugott.

Selections: 1 Crush (Garbage) (4:47) *Garbage*; 2 Local God (A. Alexakis/ Everclear) (3:56) *Everclear*; 3 Everybody's Free (To Feel Good) (T. Cox/N. Swanston) (4:19) *Quindon Tarver*; 4 To You I Bestow (Mundy) (4:53) *Mundy*; 5 Angel (G. Friday/M. Seezer) (4:58) *Gavin Friday*; 6 Pretty Piece Of Flesh (N. Hooper/ M. De Vries/J. Warfield) (4:09) *One Inch Punch*; 7 Talk Show Host (Radiohead) (3:18) *Radiohead*; 8 Little Star (S. Nordenstam) (4:16) *Stina Nordenstam*; 9 Kissing You (Love Theme From *Romeo + Juliet*) (Des'ree/T. Attack) (1:44) *Des'ree*; 10 Whatever (I Had A Dream) (Butthole Surfers) (3:58) *Butthole Surfers*; 11 You And Me Song (P. Wiksten/F. Schonfeldt/S. Schonfeldt/G. Karlsson/C. Bergmark) (4:17) *The Wannadies*; 12 Lovefool (P. Svensson/N. Persson) (3:40) *The Cardigans*; 13 Young Hearts Run Free (D. Crawford) (2:53) *Kym Mazelle*.

Review: There couldn't be two soundtracks more different than these to illustrate what is essentially the same story. Rota's approach to the Franco Zeffirelli film is pretty much straight forward and academic, with the music used to subtly underscore the emotions in the Shakespearean drama. Adding more impact to the proceedings, the soundtrack also features the dialogues and sound effects for most important scenes, giving an overall sonic impression that pretty much reflects the film itself.

In contrast, *Romeo + Juliet* is a contemporary take-off on the story, a sort of what kind of music would Romeo and Juliet

listen to if they had lived today? Some of it works very well and has a definite appeal; some of the tracks, however, sound redundant and ill-chosen, at least for a straight listening experience.

And in case you might wonder what other treatment the story might have led to, see also *West Side Story*, possibly the most successful adaptation of Shakespeare's drama, set against the background of modern-day New York City.

Romeo Is Bleeding 🎵🎵🎵🎵

1994, Verve Records; from the movie *Romeo Is Bleeding*, Gramercy Pictures, 1994.

Album Notes: *Music:* Mark Isham; *Music Editor:* Tom Carlson; *Synthesizer Programming:* Jeff Rona, Mark Isham; *Featured Musicians:* Mark Isham (trumpet, flugelhorn, electronics), David Goldblatt (piano), Chuck Domanico (acoustic bass), Kurt Wortman (drums); *Album Producer:* Mark Isham; *Engineer:* Stephen Krause.

Selections: 1 Romeo Is Bleeding (6:20); 2 Bird Alone (A. Lincoln) (8:30) *Abbey Lincoln*; 3 Romeo Is Moving (:56); 4 Romeo And Juliette (4:20); 5 Nightmare On Maple Street (3:24); 6 I Know Better Now (A.J. Croce) (3:11) *A.J. Croce*; 7 Romeo Is Searching (3:40); 8 Romeo And Natalie (4:40); 9 Mona (2:06); 10 Take Two Toes (2:04); 11 Back Seat Driving (2:55); 12 Mona Lends A Helping Hand (3:54); 13 Dance Of Death (2:30); 14 Empty Chambers/Romeo Is Dreaming (6:50); 15 Romeo Alone (4:20).

Review: Mark Isham's strongly-accented jazz score comes across full force in this recording in which the cues have time to make their impression, away from the screen action. The film, a comic book account of a tinted New York police officer who gets involved with a Russian mafiosa and pays dearly for it, needed a forceful musical statement to give it the right flavor. Isham created a series of cues that capture the essence of the story, and add to it with great skill, in cues that display the right amount of the type of jazz one usually associates with this kind of drama. As a result, the album is highly enjoyable on its own terms, and is further enhanced by a couple of well chosen vocals, including a sensational rendition of "Bird Alone," performed by Abbey Lincoln.

Romy and Michele's High School Reunion 🎵🎵🎵

1997, Hollywood Records; from the movie *Romy and Michele's High School Reunion*, Touchstone Pictures, 1997.

Album Notes: *Album Producers:* Mitchell Leib, Judy Kemper.

Selections: 1 Our Lips Are Sealed (J. Wiedlin/T. Hall) (2:46) *The Go-Go's*; 2 Venus (R. Van Leeuwen) (3:40) *Bananarama*; 3 (There's) Always Something There To Remind Me (B. Bacharach/H. David) (3:41) *Naked Eyes*; 4 Dance Hall Days (J. Hues/N. Feldman/D. Costin) (3:58) *Wang Chung*; 5 Turning Japanese (D. Fenton) (3:45) *The Vapors*; 6 Blood And Roses (P. Di Nizio) (3:36) *The Smithereens*; 7 Karma Chameleon (G. O'Dowd/J. Moss/M. Craig/R. Hay/P. Pickett) (4:13) *Culture Club*; 8 I Want Candy (B. Feldman/G. Goldstein/R. Gottehrer/B. Berns) (2:47) *Bow Wow Wow*; 9 Everybody Wants To Rule The World (R. Orzabal/I. Stanley/C. Hughes) (4:12) *Tears For Fears*; 10 Heaven Is A Place On Earth (R. Nowels/E. Shipley) (4:12) *Belinda Carlisle*; 11 We Got The Beat (C. Caffey) (2:30) *The Go-Go's*.

Review: A winning, if somewhat insignificant, comedy about two attractive dimwits on their way to a high school reunion, who decide to try and impress their former schoolmates by pretending that they have become rich and successful, *Romy and Michele's High School Reunion* boasts a sparkling soundtrack consisting of popular songs by The Go-Go's, Wang Chung, Culture Club, Bow Wow Wow, and The Smithereens, among others. There is little that's exceptional about this compilation, just a good collection that happens to work well in the context of the film and for one's listening pleasure.

Room at the Top

1996, DRG Records; from the movie *Room at the Top*, Continental Films, 1959.

See: The Barefoot Contessa

A Room with a View ♫♫♫♫ᵛ

1986, DRG Records; from the movie *A Room with a View*, Cinecom and Merchant Ivory Productions, 1986.

Album Notes: *Music*: Richard Robbins; *Orchestrations*: Francis Shaw, Barrie Guard; *Album Producer*: Simon Heyworth.

Selections: 1 O mio babbino caro (G. Puccini)(2:29) *Kiri Te Kanawa*; 2 The Pensione Bertollini (1:22); 3 Lucy, Charlotte And Miss Lavish See The City (1:55); 4 In The Piazza Signoria (3:57); 5 The Embankment (2:24); 6 Phaeton And Persephone (:54); 7 Chi il bel sogno di Doretta (G. Puccini)(3:21) *Kiri Te Kanawa*; 8 The Storm (2:40); 9 Home and The Betrothal (1:38); 10 The Sacred Lake (2:22); 11 The Allan Sisters (1:14); 12 In The National Gallery (1:30); 13 Windy Corner (3:10); 14 Habanera (2:08); 15 The Broken Engagement (1:56); 16 Return To Florence (1:52); 17 End Titles (3:44).

Review: In much the same way that *Elvira Madigan* was defined by Mozart's Piano Concerto in C, Puccini's "O mio babbino caro" gave *A Room with a View* a definite cachet, and permeated this

sensitive romantic comedy of manners, set in 1907 and based on E.M. Forster's classic novel, about a young English couple who meet in Italy and, despite their social differences, and the Victorian convictions of their elders, dare to be true to their feeling and each other. The Italian and English settings, and the turn-of-the-century time frame provided the pegs for Richard Robbins' score, a collection of sprightly musical tunes that depict the various incidents in the screenplay, augmenting the action with their subtle melodic contributions, and making an otherwise arresting statement. Overflowing with great romantic themes, occasionally sprinkled with the witty addition of a mandolin or a lovely call of bells, the score unfolds with magic splendor, revealing its many charms in cues that are programmed to be equally effective on their own.

Roommates ♫♫ᵛ

1995, Hollywood Records; from the movie *Roommates*, Hollywood Pictures, 1995.

Album Notes: *Music*: Elmer Bernstein; *Orchestrations*: Emilie A. Bernstein, Patrick Russ; *Musician*: Cynthia Millar (Ondes Martenot solos); Orchestra conducted by Elmer Bernstein; *Album Producer*: Emilie A. Bernstein; *Engineer*: Andrew Boland.

Selections: 1 Main Title (1:48); 2 Prologue (1:58); 3 Snoring (1:04); 4 Cards (:46); 5 Microscope (1:10); 6 Condemned (1:31); 7 To Columbus (:21); 8 Cards Again (:26); 9 New Snore (1:24); 10 Lost Patient (1:25); 11 Michael's Flat (1:09); 12 Beth Meets Rocky (1:39); 13 Love Music (:24); 14 Proposal (:59); 15 Left (:59); 16 Operation (2:05); 17 Tension (1:54); 18 To Town (:54); 19 Crash (3:27); 20 Bad News (1:44); 21 Takeover (:44); 22 Drunk (:57); 23 Michael Freezes (1:23); 24 Ice Cream (1:32); 25 Kidnapped (1:14); 26 Rebirth (:45); 27 Goodbyes (2:08); 28 End Credits/Beer Barrel Polka (Roll Out The Barrel)(L. Brown/W. Timm/V. Zeman/J. Vejvoda)(4:37).

Review: The first hour of this Peter Yates' film starring Peter Falk and D.B. Sweeney is filled with cliches, playing out very much like a theatrical sitcom. For whatever reason, the movie surprisingly turns itself around in the second half into a genuinely affecting, poignant family drama with terrific performances by the two leads. Elmer Bernstein scored the picture, but despite some fine moments, his music doesn't lend itself easily to working as a soundtrack album. Many of the cues are very short (most are under a minute, in fact), which doesn't allow for the composer to develop thematic material. The music is perfect in the movie, but this is unfortunately one of those cases where the album format doesn't add much to the film score.

Andy Dursin

The Rosary Murders ♪♪♪♭

1986, Cinedisc Records; from the movie *The Rosary Murders*, New Line Cinema, 1986.

Album Notes: *Music*: Bobby Laurel, Don Sebesky; The London Royal Philharmonic Orchestra, conducted by Don Sebesky; *Album Producers*: Bobby Laurel, Don Sebesky; *Engineer*: Pat Sheedy.

Selections: 1 In Your Eyes (Main Theme) (B. Laurel/D. Leahy) (3:10); 2 Jogging (1:52); 3 Phone Company (2:30); 4 The Marble Orchard (3:36); 5 Second Story Priest (2:21); 6 Pull Yourself Together (2:30); 7 Scratch Father Steel (1:13); 8 Sister Blabbermouth(2:26); 9 Confessional Call (1:18); 10 Father Koesler And Pat Take A Walk (:59); 11 Find The Obituary (2:16); 12 Sister Ann's Last Bath(1:54); 13 Jeanette (B. Laurel) (2:34) *Bobby Laurel*; 14 Read The Letter (1:31); 15 Hearing The Good Stuff (2:44); 16 Sister Ann's Death (2:10); 17 Mr. Javison Meets Father Nabors (4:56); 18 I'm The One (2:21); 19 Flowers For Pat (:38).

Review: Nancy Wood's strained rendition of the main title, "In Your Eyes," in a style that desperately tries not to evoke Barbra Streisand, is hardly conducive to open up to this album. Fortunately, Don Sebesky's score is forcefully interesting and compelling, and attracts the attention with its skillfull display of cues outlining some of the most intense moments in this flavorful thriller, about a killer in Detroit, with a grudge against representatives of the Catholic Church, who is hunted down by a priest turned sleuth. As befits the genre, the various cues actually belie the tension, focusing instead on the more subliminous threatening aspects of the murder mystery. A chorus in the background occasionally provides sounds that evoke the more religious aspects of the story.

Rosewood ♪♪♪♪

1997, Sony Classical; from the movie *Rosewood*, Warner Bros., 1997.

Album Notes: *Music*: John Williams; *Music Editor*: Kenn Wannberg; Orchestra conducted by John Williams; *Featured Soloists*: Shirley Caesar (vocals), Dean Parks (guitar), Tommy Morgan (harmonica); *Album Producer*: John Williams; *Engineer*: Dennis Sands; *Assistant Engineer*: Sue McLean.

Selections: 1 Rosewood (3:34); 2 Look Down, Lord (2:13); 3 The Hounds Of Summer (1:50); 4 Healing (4:10); 5 Light My Way (3:43); 6 Trouble In Town (3:16); 7 Aunt Sarah's Death (3:18); 8 After The Fire (3:38); 9 The Town Of Summer (2:37); 10 The Town Burns (4:21) *Shirley Caesar*; 11 Scrappie And Mann Bond (4:14); 12 The Freedom Train (1:53); 13 False Accusation (3:18); 14 Mann At Rosewood (3:15); 15 Look Down, Lord (reprise)/Finale (4:13).

> "Every film is different. It goes to both extremes—from starting before they've even begun a movie to having it drop in your lap when the movie is completely finished, and you have to hit the ground running."
>
> **Danny Elfman**
> *(Entertainment@Home, 4-97)*

Review: Proof that John Williams can write memorable music for virtually any kind of film is fully evident in *Rosewood*, John Singleton's mostly fictitious dramatization of the real-life tragedy that was heavily criticized by some for its traditional western story elements. There's nothing formulaic in any regard, however, about Williams' complex, haunting score, which finds dissonant guitar-and-piano motives combined with elegiac string writing, creating a powerful collection of cues whose contrasting uplift is found in a pair of spirituals ("Look Down, Lord," "Light My Way"), also written by the composer. The country-flavored instrumentation recalls Williams' past successes on *The Missouri Breaks* and even *The Reivers*, though this score has a strong dramatic tone all its own, characterized by standout work from guitarist Dean Parks and harmonica soloist Tommy Morgan. A different kind of score from a composer who continues to surprise us all with his sense of dramatic film scoring, one that consistently translates into great stand-alone music in the process.

Andy Dursin

Roustabout

1993, RCA Records; from the movie *Roustabout,* Paramount Pictures, 1964.

See: Elvis Presley in Compilations

Roxanne ♪♪♪♭

1987, Cinedisc Records; from the movie *Roxanne*, Columbia Pictures, 1987.

Album Notes: *Music*: Bruce Smeaton; *Engineer*: Joel Moss.

Selections: 1 Roxanne (Main Title)(2:03); 2 Starry Sky (3:34); 3 Just Honest/We Did It (3:41); 4 Roxanne's Theme (2:28); 5 Game, Set, Match (2:14); 6 The Panache (P. Melnick)(3:43); 7

Roxanne's Eyes (3:13); 8 The Blue Danube Waltz (J. Strauss)(10:54); 9 Written In The Wind (J. Curiale)(3:23); 10 Roxanne (End Title)(4:07).

Review: It might have made sense to turn Edmond Rostand's stageplay about *Cyrano de Bergerac* into a modern-day fantasy, starring Steve Martin as the long-nosed fellow, hopelessly in love with Roxanne, played by the delightful Daryl Hannah. The problem is that Cyrano's dilemma about his proboscis in this tepid adaptation could have been fixed in no time with plastic surgery, thereby spoiling the film from its much needed novel approach.

But Bruce Smeaton's clever, if at times slightly hackneyed score not only fit the bill handsomely, it also made for pleasant if unobtrusive background musical enjoyment, smartly captured in this soundtrack album.

Ruby 🎵🎵🎵

1992, Intrada Records; from the movie *Ruby*, PolyGram/Triump, 1992.

Album Notes: *Music*: John Scott; *Orchestrations*: John Scott; *Music Editor*: Steve Livingston; Orchestra conducted by John Scott; *Album Producer*: John Scott; *Engineer*: Toby Foster.

Selections: 1 Main Title (2:31); 2 Ruby Meets Candy (3:07); 3 Telephone Trixie (1:47); 4 The Hanging (2:46); 5 Cuba (1:02); 6 The Camera (4:48); 7 Never Go Back (1:15); 8 Later Hank (1:24); 9 Confidence (1:11); 10 JFK Arrival In Vegas (1:40); 11 A Ride With Maxwell (1:09); 12 Just Do Your Duty (2:08); 13 Presidential Suite (1:56); 14 Thanks For Everything (1:05); 15 Some Expert Advice (2:28); 16 Candy's Back (2:07); 17 Pre-Assassination (3:34); 18 Ruby Kills Oswald (3:59); 19 Candy And Ruby (2:35); 20 End Titles (4:48).

Review: For this Jack Ruby docudrama, John Scott contrasts a small jazz ensemble with a lovely symphonic melody which captures a contradictory innocence that belies the message of the film. His main theme is grandly symphonic, almost majestic, its sense of joy and innocence becomes a counterpoint to the darker, conspiratorial tonality of the film. As it develops, the main theme is often overwhelmed by the dark jazz figures, as Scott musically delineated the innocence of Jack Ruby as it is tantalized, tempted and finally overwhelmed by the thrust of irreversible circumstances into which he allows himself to become immersed. With its mixture of jazz and symphonic orchestral colorations, and its brilliant contrast of melody with rhythm, innocence with evil, control with irrevocable destiny, *Ruby* is one of Scott's best scores.

Randall D. Larson

Rudy 🎵🎵🎵▾

1993, Varese-Sarabande Records; from the movie *Rudy*, Tri-Star Pictures, 1993.

Album Notes: *Music*: Jerry Goldsmith; *Orchestrations*: Alexander Courage, Arthur Morton; *Music Editor*: Ken Hall; Orchestra conducted by Jerry Goldsmith; *Album Producer*: Jerry Goldsmith; *Engineer*: Bruce Botnick.

Selections: 1 Main Title (3:35); 2 A Start (2:27); 3 Waiting (2:35); 4 Back On The Field (2:07); 5 To Notre Dame (6:55); 6 Tryouts (4:27); 7 The Key (3:55); 8 Take Us Out (1:51); 9 The Plaque (2:36); 10 The Final Game (6:16).

Review: This extremely popular Goldsmith effort for the true story of a lad who dreams of playing football at Notre Dame works as a more acoustic follow-up to his Oscar-nominated *Hoosiers* score, full of rah-rah inspiration that also conjures up memories of Goldsmith's *Patton*. The score opens with a beautiful, plaintive tune based on an old Irish ballad, richly played by the orchestra, while later cues develop a delicate piano motif until some hard-charging inspirational music heralds Rudy's participation in team practices and eventually in a real game. You can't help but get caught up in the optimism and warmth of this score, but at the same time there's a repetitiveness, a sameness in the tempos and a lack of Goldsmith's complex development that may be off-putting to fans of the composer's earlier, more hard-edged style.

Jeff Bond

Runaway 🎵🎵

1987, Varese-Sarabande; from the movie *Runaway*, Tri-Star Pictures, 1985.

Album Notes: *Music*: Jerry Goldsmith; *Synthesizer Programming*: Joel Goldsmith; *Album Producer*: Jerry Goldsmith; *Engineer*: Bruce Botnick.

Selections: 1 Main Title (1:44); 2 Crazed Robot (3:08); 3 She Went Home (1:37); 4 Alley Flight (2:06); 5 Shootin' Up The Ritz (3:24); 6 The Bullet (3:06); 7 Sushi Switch (3:18); 8 Lockons (4:06); 9 Psychic Reading (1:09); 10 Ground Floor (1:03); 11 40th Floor (1:24); 12 Over The Edge (3:07); 13 Luther Dies (1:12); 14 Resolution (5:32).

Review: Goldsmith's first all-electronic score is an abrasive, metallic effort for Michael Crichton's silly near-future thriller about a kind of SWAT team for malfunctioning robots. Much of the music achieves an almost acoustic quality as Goldsmith, with the assistance of son Joel, blends layers of synthetic textures and repeating electronic figures. Particularly effective is a barbaric moment of solo percussion in the suspenseful (and idiotically named) "Sushi Switch." And Goldsmith brings the same rhythmic intensity to the cacophonous chase cues "Alley Flight" and "Lockons" that he does to his orchestral scores. But the constant presence of pounding drum machines and the harsh overall sound is bound to be off-putting to fans of the composer's earlier works. Still, this difficult-to-find album has some collector's value.

Jeff Bond

Runaway Train ♪♪♪♪

1986, Milan Records; from the movie *Runaway Train*, Cannon Films; 1986.

Album Notes: *Music*: Trevor Jones; *Featured Musicians*: Dave Lawson, Brian Gascoigne, Simon Lloyd (keyboards), Ray Russell (guitar), Harold Fisher (drums), Paul Hirsh (shakuhachi), Catherine Bott (solo vocalist); *Album Producers*: Trevor Jones, Jack Fishman; *Engineer*: Paul Hume.

Selections: 1 Jailbreak! (2:00); 2 Moving On (3:43); 3 Destination Unknown (2:20); 4 Clear The Tracks (4:05); 5 Reflections (2:59); 6 Runaway (4:43); 7 Prison Memories (A. Masters)/The Yellow Rose Of Texas (D. George)(3:03) *The Jamborees*; 8 Collision Course (2:18); 9 Past, Present—Future? (2:23); 10 Red For Danger (3:07); 11 Gloria in D (2nd movement)(A. Vivaldi)(6:48) *The USSR Academic Russian Choir, The Moscow Conservatory Students' Orchestra, Alexsander Sveshnikov*; 12 End Of The Line (3:57).

Review: Andrei Konchalovsky' gripping rail drama, starring Jon Voight, Eric Roberts and Rebecca de Mornay, and based on a screenplay by Akira Kurosawa, elicited a taut score from composer Trevor Jones, solidly rooted in contemporary sounds. Following a prison escape, two convicts find themselves unwilling passengers on board an out-of-control train in the Alaskan wild in this fast-paced film, as exciting as it is well-sketched. Jones's score subtly underlines the action without overstretching the point, in cues that are particularly effective on the screen and are equally well defined on a purely audio level. In a striking counterpoint, Vivaldi's "Gloria in D" provides a welcome change of pace that doesn't detract from the main motifs, yet adds to the overall flavor of the score.

The Running Man ♪♪

1987, Varese-Sarabande; from the movie *The Running Man*, Tri-Star Pictures, 1987.

Album Notes: *Music*: Harold Faltermeyer; *Album Producer*: Harold Faltermeyer; *Engineer*: Brian Reeves.

Selections: 1 Intro/Bakersfield (2:00); 2 Main Title/Fight Escape (3:46); 3 Buzzsaw/Richard's Fight (1:50); 4 Captain Freedom's Workout (2:31); 5 Mick's Broadcast/Attack (5:03); 6 Valkyrie (2:38); 7 Buzzsaw Attack (2:08); 8 Medical Checkup (2:24); 9 Fireball Intro (1:19); 10 Buzzsaw/Dynamo Attack (1:49); 11 Massacre Highlights (1:07); 12 Sub-Zero Intro (2:02); 13 Sub-Zero (4:22); 14 Fireball Chase (2:02); 15 Spare Dynamo (2:20); 16 Weiss Discovers Dish/Amber's Launch (2:26); 17 Revolution/End Credits (1:58).

Review: This likable enough synthesized action score by Harold Faltermeyer has its moments, but suffers mainly from the fact that many of the themes are never fully developed. Several of the more satisfying tracks are the themes for the "Running Man" TV show's gladiators. "Captain Freedom's Workout" is one of the few that rises above the din of squealing guitar rifts and drum machines Faltermeyer relies on and it's great for that step aerobic workout, too! However, when Faltermeyer gets down to one of his more interesting cue, "Mick's Broadcast/Attack," he just leaves us hanging by stopping the music cold after an engaging five-minute buildup. That may work great for the film, but not on an album. The first two cues, "Intro/Bakersfield" and "Main Title/ Fight Escape" do not appear in the final film as heard on the album.

David Hirsch

The Russia House ♪♪♪▹

1990, MCA Records; from the movie *The Russia House*, M-G-M, 1990.

Album Notes: *Music*: Jerry Goldsmith; *Orchestrations*: Arthur Morton; *Featured Artists*: Branford Marsalis (saxophone), Michael Lang (piano), John Patitucci (bass); Orchestra conducted by Jerry Goldsmith; *Album Producer*: Jerry Goldsmith; *Engineer*: Bruce Botnick.

Selections: 1 Katya (3:57); 2 Introductions (3:12); 3 The Conversation (4:13); 4 Training (2:01); 5 Katya And Barley (2:32); 6 First Name, Yakov (2:53); 7 Bon Voyage (2:11); 8 The Meeting (3:59); 9 I'm With You/What Is This Thing Called Love (C. Porter) (2:39) *Branford Marsalis, Billy Childs, Tony Dumas, Ralph Penland*; 10 Alone In The World (J. Goldsmith/A. & M. Bergman) (4:09) *Patti Austin*; 11 The Gift (2:34); 12 Full Marks (2:27); 13 Barley's Love (3:24); 14 My Only Country (4:34); 15 Crossing Over (4:13); 16 The Deal (4:09); 17 The Family Arrives (7:38).

Review: Jerry Goldsmith took the unusual approach of writing a jazz-textured score for this film about espionage filmed in the former Soviet Union, adapting a love theme he originally wrote for the movie *Alien Nation* and building some flowing, low-key bass and piano rhythms to underscore the film's suspense scenes. This is also notable as Goldsmith's lone experiment with long album form, with a generous hour of music from his score. But as Goldsmith himself has noted, there's too much music here, in this case because the style he adopted for the picture emphasizes repetition, with only the improvisation of Wynton Marsalis and some other jazz performers to break up the monotony. Nevertheless, the very congruence of style here makes for an unusually smooth, coherent listening experience, entirely lacking in harsh dissonances or violent moments, each piece flowing seamlessly into the next. This may be more appealing to fans of jazz fusion or new age music than Goldsmith fans.

Jeff Bond

Ryan's Daughter ♪♪♪

1991, Sony Music Special Products; from the movie *Ryan's Daughter's*, M-G-M, 1970.

Album Notes: *Music*: Maurice Jarre; Orchestra conducted by Maurice Jarre.

Selections: 1 Main Title (4:33); 2 Overture (4:01); 3 The Major (2:33); 4 You Don't Want Me Then (2:53); 5 Michael's Theme (3:11); 6 Ride Through The Woods (2:46); 7 Obsession (2:04); 8 The Shakes (based On Michael's Theme) (2:09); 9 Rosy On The Beach (1:41); 10 Song Of The Irish Rebels (2:08); 11 Rosy And The Schoolmaster (2:42); 12 Michael Shows Randolph His Strange Treasure (3:05); 13 Rosy's Theme (2:05);

THE TRAIN (M. JARRE): 14 Main Title (2:05); 15 Papa Boule On The Move (2:43);

GRAND PRIX (M. JARRE): 16 Overture (4:36); 17 Scott & Pat/Sarti & Louise (2:10); 18 The Zan Voort Race (5:20).

Review: The creative relationship between director David Lean and composer Maurice Jarre found another fertile ground in this intimate love story, set in Ireland in 1916, at a time when Europe was ravaged by "the war to end all wars" and Ireland itself was about to know an equally devastating uprising against the British. Starring Sarah Miles, as the young, romantic Rosy Ryan, Robert Mitchum as the stiff schoolmaster she marries, and Christopher Jones as the handsome officer with whom she has an affair, *Ryan's Daughter* gave Maurice Jarre the elements he needed to write an overwhelmingly romantic score, teeming with cues that detail the action and brightly comment on it. Spearheaded by the sweeping main theme that recurs throughout the score, the music also makes allowances for other themes that project different moods, like the brassy march for "The Major," or the liltingly jaunty "Rosy on the Beach." Overflowing with attractive musical ideas, *Ryan's Daughter* is an excellent score that spells its many charms in this CD reissue, augmented with selections from two other Jarre scores, for *The Train* and *Grand Prix*.

Sabrina ♪♪♪

1996, A&M Records; from the movie *Sabrina*, Paramount Pictures, 1996.

Album Notes: *Music*: John Williams; *Music Editor*: Ken Wannberg; Orchestra conducted by John Williams; *Featured Musician*: Dick Nash (trombone); *Album Producer*: John Williams; *Engineer*: Shawn Murphy.

Selections: 1 Theme From Sabrina (4:30); 2 Moonlight (J. Williams/A. & M. Bergman)(5:20) *Sting*; 3 Linus' New Life (2:45); 4 Growing Up In Paris (3:02); 5 (In The) Moonlight (2:59); 6 Sabrina Remembers /La Vie en Rose (Louiguy/E. Piaf)(1:42); 7 Sabrina Comes Home (4:14); 8 Nantucket Visit (2:31); 9 The Party Sequence/When Joanna Loved Me (J. Segal/R. Wells)/The Shadow Of Your Smile (P.F. Webster/J. Mandel)/Call Me Irresponsible (S. Cahn/ J. Van Heusen)/Stella By Starlight (V. Young/N. Washington)(10:53); 10 Sabrina And Linus Date (2:40); 11 How Can I Remember (J. Williams/A. & M. Bergman) (2:50) *Michael Dees*; 12 Sabrina's Return To Paris (2:22); 13 Theme From Sabrina (reprise)(5:23).

Review: This ill-advised remake of the charming 1954 Billy Wilder romantic comedy was a total disaster at the box office, despite the presence of Harrison Ford and Julia Ormond in the roles originally created by Humphrey Bogart and Audrey Hepburn. One of its most positive elements, however, is the delicately overblown score John Williams wrote for it. Introduced by the "Theme From Sabrina," essentially a romantic mini-concerto for piano and orchestra, the score reveals great ingenuity and feel for its subject, with the recurring "Moonlight" motif playing an important role in the cues. In one instance ("Sabrina Remembers/ La vie en rose"), Williams lets a theme meld into a well-known song that sets the decor better than anything he himself might have written, and in a long medley ("The Party Sequence") even takes several standards around which to build his cue. It's an interesting, flavorful way to present source material, and much more effective than having a cover version which might break the moods set by the instrumental cues. The only letdown in this otherwise very attractive score is Sting's vocal rendition of "Moonlight," only because the singer tries too hard to sound romantic.

Sahara ♪♪♪♪

1992, Intrada Records; from the movie *Sahara*, Cannon Films, 1983.

Album Notes: *Music*: Ennio Morricone; Orchestra conducted by Ennio Morricone; *Album Producer*: Douglass Fake; *Engineers*: Douglass Fake, Joe Tarantino.

Selections: 1 Theme From Sahara (4:17); 2 The Party (a) Charleston, (b) Ragtime Dance (5:09) *The Pasadena Roof Orchestra*; 3

Father's Death (1:58); 4 Arabia (3:04); 5 On Your Marks... (1:04); 6 Get Set... Go (1:49); 7 Armour Car (3:31); 8 Oasis (3:20); 9 Desert Music (4:38); 10 Waterfall Kiss (1:52); 11 Panther Chase (3:27); 12 More Desert Music (2:20); 13 Car Trouble (:37); 14 More Car Trouble (:29); 15 Battle I (8:40); 16 Rasoul (2:40); 17 Battle II (3:05); 18 Battle III (4:42); 19 End Titles (4:16); 20 Sahara (3:09) *Cathy Cole, Ennio Morricone and His Orchestra.*

Review: On various occasions, Morricone scored films that had a Saharian motif to them (*Secret of the Sahara, Prince of the Desert,* etc.), something which inspired him to renew himself and find new ways to celebrate the poesy and mystery of the desert. If he did indulge his interest in exotic music when he wrote the music for this film ("Arabia," "Oasis," "Desert Music," "More Desert Music"), the story also gave him many other opportunities to let his imagination run wild. Set in 1928, the film stars Brooke Shields as Dale Packard, determined to win the Sahara International Car Rally, despite the fact that only men are allowed to enter the race. In the course of the action, she faces many dangers ("Panther Chase," "Car Trouble"), and is abducted by a wandering Tuareg leader whom she is forced to marry, but she still wins the race at the end. The various difficulties encountered by the young woman led to vibrantly detailed cues that constitute the bulk of the score. Mining another rich musical vein, Morricone created ceremonial music with a pseudo-British brass flair, for the beginning and end of the race, and he combined a variety of North African instruments and sonoroties to his music to depict the exotic locales in which the story took place. Dominating the whole, he wrote for Dale a lovely romantic theme, which recurs throughout the score and contrasts with the rapid-fire action in the other cues. In the Morricone body of work, *Sahara* may not be as well known as some of his most memorable creations, but it is a very unusual, compelling score that deserves to be discovered.

The Saint

The Saint ♫♫

1997, Virgin Records; from the movie *The Saint,* Paramount Pictures, 1997.

Album Notes: *Song Producers:* Orbital, Line of Flight & Jim Abbiss, Moby, Fluke, Daniel Lanois, Tony Mangurian & Jill Cuniff, The Chemical Brothers, Underworld, TV Mania, Thomas Bangalter & Guy-Manuel de Homen-Christo, David Bowie, Superior, Rupert Hine, Ben Watt; *Album Supervisors:* Nancy Berry, Kaz Utsunomiya, Gemma Corfield, George Maloian.

Selections: 1 The Saint Theme (E. Astley) (4:32) *Orbital*; 2 Underground (Howe/Corner/Pickering/Barry) (3:53) *Sneaker Pimps*; 3 Oil 1 (R. Hall) (5:31) *Moby*; 4 Atom Bomb (Fluke) (3:54) *Fluke*; 5 Roses Fade (J. Cuniff) (2:31) *Luscious Jackson*; 6 Setting Sun (Rowlands/Simons/Gallagher) (7:00) *The Chemical Brothers*; 7 Pearl's Girl (R. Smith/K. Hyde/D. Emerson) (9:32)*Underworld*; 8 Out Of My Mind (S. LeBon/N. Rhodes/W. Cuccurullo) (4:16) *Duran Duran*; 9 Da Funk (T. Bangaller/G.-M de Homem-Christo) (5:28) *Daft Punk*; 10 Dead Man Walking (D. Bowie) (6:50) *David Bowie*; 11 Polaroid Millenium (Superior) (3:21) *Superior*; 12 A Dream Within A Dream (G. Roberts/T. Brian/H. Williams) (6:08) *Dreadzone*; 13 In The Absence Of Sun (D. Sheik) (5:04) *Duncan Sheik*; 14 Before Today (B. Watt) (4:17) *Everything But The Girl.*

Review: Featuring tracks by established performers, and lesser-known acts, this compilation tries desperately to be slick and now. But somehow, the flavor that was so specific to the early films and television series, respectively starring George Sanders and Roger Moore as Leslie Chasteris' title character, seems hopelessly lost in this hodgepodge, which tries to claim some legitimacy by using the familiar motif in "The Saint Theme," updated to satisfy today's musical taste. As pop compilations go, this one — with new songs by David Bowie, Everything But The Girl, and Duran Duran among its better moments — is not all that bad. But what has it got to do with The Saint?

The Saint ♫♫♫

1997, Angel Records; from the movie *The Saint,* Paramount Pictures, 1997.

Album Notes: *Music:* Graeme Revell; *Orchestrations:* John Bell, Nick Ingman, Graeme Revell; *Music Editor:* Joe E. Rand; The London Metropolitan Orchestra, conducted by Allan Wilson, David Snell; *Album Producer:* Graeme Revell; *Engineer:* Chris Dibble.

Selections: 1 Main Title (6:25); 2 Break-In (3:46); 3 Shelley Monument (2:16); 4 Searching Apartment (3:38); 5 Love Theme (2:55); 6 The River Chase (3:16); 7 The Tunnels (2:36); 8 Race To Embassy (2:22); 9 Tempelhof (2:41); 10 Love Theme (2nd version)(2:54); 11 Kremlin Riot/Karpov's Room (4:40); 12 Red Square (3:09); 13 The Fight (5:40); 14 Love Theme Finale (5:27).

Review: Indicative of the increasing respect film music seems to be getting in some circles, this soundtrack album was released on the classical label, Angel Records, which, with Sony Classical and London Records, seems intent on making this kind of music the modern day equivalent of classical music. No one should complain about that. Which doesn't mean that Graeme Revell's music should be confused with the works of the great classic composers. In fact, the score for *The Saint* is too often bathed in cliches to really compel the listener. There are some genuinely attractive moments in it (the "Love Theme," heard in three different versions), but the overall effect seems to be more along the lines of listless synth lines mingled with lush orchestral textures, and an occasional electronic rhythm track added to it, no doubt to signify increased screen action. What is mostly lacking here are genuine melodic themes, as if the music were essentially meant to be a wall of orchestral sounds, a problem all too frequent these days when melodic ideas don't seem to matter as much as noise.

The Saint of Fort Washington 🦴🦴🦴🦴

1993, Varese-Sarabande; from the movie *The Saint of Fort Washington*, Warner Bros., 1993.

Album Notes: *Music:* James Newton Howard; *Orchestrations:* James Newton Howard; *Music Editors:* Jim Weidman, David Olson; Orchestra conducted by Marty Paich; *Featured Musicians:* Chuck Findley (trumpet); *Album Producers:* James Newton Howard, Michael Mason; *Engineer:* Robert Schaper; *Assistant Engineer:* Charlie Paakkari.

Selections: 1 Main Titles (4:42); 2 Sewing Money (4:46); 3 Rosario (4:40); 4 The Rainstorm (3:11); 5 Matthew Takes A Picture (3:21); 6 Back To The Shelter (2:32); 7 Matthew's Casket (2:22); 8 End Titles (4:25).

Review: The moving story of a homeless Vietnam vet and the street kid he takes under his wing, *The Saint of Fort Washington* elicited a soberly eloquent score from James Newton Howard, evidently inspired by its subject. Overall, the moods projected are remarkably low-key and attractive, with a synth melody and an occasional piano theme detailing specific scenes in the narrative, and tugging at the proper heartstrings.

Salvador

1987, Varese-Sarabande Records; from the movie *Salvador*, Cinema '85, 1985.

See: Wall Street

Samson and Delilah/ The Quiet Man 🦴🦴🦴🦴ᵛ

1994, Varese Sarabande; from the movies *Samson and Delilah*, Paramount Pictures, 1949; and *The Quiet Man*, Republic Picture, 1952.

Album Notes: *Music:* Victor Young; The Paramount Symphony Orchestra (*Samson and Delilah*), and The Victor Young Orchestra (*The Quiet Man*), conducted by Victor Young; *CD Producer:* Robert Townson.

Selections: *SAMSON AND DELILAH:* 1 Suite: Samson's Call/ Miriam And The Dance Dragon/The Valley Of Zorah/The Feather Dance/Delilah's Remorse/The Feast Dance/ Bacchanale/Delilah's Harp/Samson And Delilah (23:22);

THE QUIET MAN: 2 Danaher's House (2:19); 3 My Mother (2:45); 4 The Big Fight (2:40); 5 Forlorn (Mary Kate's Lament)(3:05); 6 I'll Take You Home Again Kathleen (T. Westendorf)(2:47); 7 St. Patrick's Day (2:26).

Review: Victor Mature is a beefy Samson and Hedy Lamarr a beguiling Delilah, in Cecil B. DeMille's impressive retelling of the Biblical tale about the strongman and his fall from grace when he succumbs to the siren's charms, and she shears his long hair, source of his strength, in the unkindest cut of all. Spearheaded by a lovely main theme, the score Victor Young wrote for the film displays the appropriate contrasting elements of passion and action, in this oft-told story of love and betrayal. The exotic accents in some of the themes aim to evoke, in typical Hollywood style, the time and locale of the narrative, which means that the effects are predictable but quite suggestive. Presented as a long suite, with the themes evolving in and out of the orchestral texture, the music is all at once reassuring in its conventional approach and very exciting.

Also very attractive in its own depiction of an unusual love story set in Ireland, *The Quiet Man* enabled Young to compose a score that beautifully conveys the various moments in the action with melodies that are serenely fetching and vibrant. A recent rerecording, conducted by Kenneth Alwyn (q.v.), is much more complete and sonically superior to the selections offered here, but these are the original soundtrack cues, conducted by the composer, and as such they have an importance one can hardly ignore.

The Sandpiper 🦴🦴🦴🦴ᵛ

1996, Verve Records; from the movie *The Sandpiper*, M-G-M, 1965.

Album Notes: *Music:* Johnny Mandel; *Orchestrations:* Johnny Mandel; Orchestra conducted by Robert Armbruster; *Album Producer:* Quincy Jones; *CD Producer:* Michael Lang; *Engineer:* Steven Fallone.

Selections: 1 The Shadow Of Your Smile (J. Mandel/P.F. Webster)(1:54); 2 Main Title (4:15); 3 Desire (2:27); 4 Seduction (5:00); 5 San Simeon (4:14); 6 Weekend Montage (4:28); 7 Baby Sandpiper (3:51); 8 Art Gallery (5:35); 9 End Title (2:36); 10 Bird Bath (2:14); 11 Weekend Montage (unedited version) (4:59).

Review: The enormous popular success of "The Shadow of Your Smile," an Academy Award winner in 1966, should not becloud the overall appeal of the score written by Johnny Mandel. The song, performed here by a characterless chorus, is in fact one of the least remarkable tracks in the recording (one recalls the much more vibrant renditions by seasoned vocalists like Tony Bennett, Johnny Mathis, Frank Sinatra or Jerry Vale, among the more than 100 cover versions it elicited). Weaving itself in and out of the cues in this album, the theme permeates the whole score with its deftly nostalgic strains, a haunting refrain that captures the poignancy in this failed love affair between two opposite characters, she (played by Elizabeth Taylor) a free-wheeling spirit, he (portrayed by Richard Burton) a staid Episcopal minister, as well as the loneliness of the Big Sur location where the story unfolds. The familiarity of the tune is one of the most engaging elements in the score, with this album guaranteed to be a real discovery for those unfamiliar with it.

The Santa Clause ♫♫♫♭

1994, Milan Records; from the movie *The Santa Clause*, Walt Disney Pictures, 1994.

Album Notes: *Music*: Michael Convertino; *Orchestrations*: John Neufeld, Conrad Pope, Bobby Muzingo; *Music Editor*: Kenn Wannberg; Orchestra conducted by Artie Kane; *Album Producer*: Michael Convertino; *Engineer*: Dennis Sands.

Selections: 1 Let's Go (1:03); 2 Believing Is Seeing (3:24); 3 The Sash Completes The Ensemble (1:04); 4 Flight (:46); 5 Weightless (1:33); 6 Away To The Window (2:11); 7 The Bells Of Christmas (L. McKennitt)(2:21) *Loreena McKennitt*; 8 Listen (3:05); 9 Goodnight, Goodnight... Don't Forget The Fire Extinguisher (1:08); 10 Visitation (2:19); 11 Rose Suchak Ladder (1:29); 12 The List (1:24); 13 Elves With Attitude (:50); 14 Someone In Wrapping (1:31); 15 Near Capture (:46); 16 Comfort And Joy (2:10); 17 Not Over Any Oceans (1:50); 18 Christmas Will Return (J. Webb)(4:05) *Brenda Russell, Howard Hewett*.

Review: Anyone who enjoys Christmas-themed soundtracks will definitely want to give a listen to Michael Convertino's immensely appealing score from *The Santa Clause*, the Tim Allen blockbuster comedy of 1994. The music can best be described as magical, with a quirky, offbeat approach perfectly suiting this yuletide comedy, which also boasts soaring orchestral passages and strong melodic themes. Convertino worked with a number of John Williams' collaborators here (conductor Artie Kane, orchestrator John Neufeld), and the results are just as warmly inviting as Williams' memorable music from the *Home Alone* pictures. The soundtrack also contains a vocal performance by Canadian singer Loreena McKennitt ("The Bells of Christmas") and an original Jimmy Webb

song, "Christmas Will Return," making the album ideal for perennial holiday listening.
Andy Dursin

Satchmo the Great ♫♫♫♫

1993, Legacy Records; from the movie *Satchmo the Great*, 1955.

Album Notes: *Featured Musicians*: Louis Armstrong (trumpet), Trummy Young (trombone), Edmond Hall (clarinet), Billy Kyle (piano), Arvell Shaw (bass), Barrett Deems (drums); *Album Producer*: George Avakian; *CD Producer*: Didier C. Deutsch; *Engineer*: Kevin Boutote.

Selections: 1 Introduction (:25) Edward R. Murrow; 2 When It's Sleepy Time Down South (L. Rene/O. Rene/C. Muse)(3:44); 3 (Back Home Again) In Indiana (B. MacDonald/J. Hanley)(4:49); 4 Paris Interview (6:22) *Edward R. Murrow*; 5 Flee As A Bird To The Mountain (M.S. Dana/G.F. Root)/Oh, Didn't He Ramble (W.C. Handy/B. Cole/J.R. Johnson)(4:33); 6 Mack The Knife (K. Weill/B. Brecht/M. Blitzstein)(4:11); 7 Mahogany Hall Stomp (S. Williams)(5:02); 8 All For You, Louis (Sly Mongoose)(R. Belasco)(2:51); 9 (What Did I Do To Be So) Black And Blue (A. Razaf/T. Waller/H. Brooks)(4:11); 10 St. Louis Blues (Concerto Grosso)(12:31) *Louis Armstrong, Lewisohn Stadium Symphony Orchestra, Leonard Bernstein*.

Review: "Hannibal crossed the Alps in 218 B.C. with 37 elephants and 12,000 horses. Louis Armstrong crossed the Alps in the mid-20th century with one trumpet and five musicians." So begins fabled CBS newsman Edward R. Murrow's commentary at the opening of this disc, the soundtrack from the first feature film to focus on one individual jazz musician's international tour. Bear in mind that this took place in 1955 and 1956, a time when modern jazz did not necessarily have the widespread appeal and audience that it enjoys today. But *Satchmo the Great* is a unique and important collaboration, especially for its time. Where else could you find the acknowledged Ambassador of Jazz (Armstrong), and the brilliant conductor Leonard Bernstein grooving together? Their 12-minute "St. Louis Blues (Concerto Grosso)" was recorded for the Guggenheim Concert at New York's Lewisohn Stadium, for the CBS News presentation *See It Now*, and is a fitting finale for this album). What about "All For You, Louis (Sly Mongoose)" — recorded with African musicians at the Accra Airport in upon Louis' arrival? Both live and studio performances are interwoven with commentary and interviews of Armstrong by Murrow, and the album as a whole (even without the video images) is a fascinating documentation of the trumpeter completely at ease, in his element, performing for live audiences. Included among the 10 numbers are two Armstrong classics: "When It's Sleepy Time Down South," and "Mack The Knife." Newly remastered, the superior sonics truly belie the age of the original recordings.

Charles L. Granata

Saturday Night Fever 🎵🎵🎵🎵

1995, Polydor Records; from the movie *Saturday Night Fever*, 1977.

Album Notes: *Music*: David Shire; *Songs (unless otherwise indicated)*: Barry Gibb, Maurice Gibb, Robin Gibb; *CD Producer*: Bill Oakes.

Selections: 1 Stayin' Alive (4:44) *Bee Gees*; 2 How Deep Is Your Love (4:03) *Bee Gees*; 3 Night Fever (3:31) *Bee Gees*; 4 More Than A Woman (3:16) *Bee Gees*; 5 If I Can't Have You (2:58) *Yvonne Elliman*; 6 A Fifth Of Beethoven (W. Murphy)(3:02) *Walter Murphy*; 7 More Than A Woman (3:16) *Tavares*; 8 Manhattan Skyline (D. Shire)(4:43); 9 Calypso Breakdown (W. Eaton) (7:49) *Ralph McDonald*; 10 Night On Disco Mountain (D. Shire)(5:12); 11 Open Sesame (R. Bell/R. Bell/G. Brown/D. Thomas/C. Smith)(3:59) *Kool and The Gang*; 12 Jive Talkin' (3:43) *Bee Gees*; 13 You Should Be Dancing (4:13) *Bee Gees*; 14 Boogie Shoes (H. Casey/R. Finch)(2:16) *K.C. & The Sunshine Band*; 15 Salsation (D. Shire)(3:50); 16 K-Jee (C. Hearndon/H. Fuqua)(4:13) *M.F.S.B.*; 17 Disco Inferno (L. Green/R. Kersey)(10:50) *The Trammps*.

Review: More than 25 million copies later, there's almost nothing left to say. If someone wants to know what disco was all about, you just hand them this album, a polyester suit and let them soak in the enduring smashes by the Bee Gees, Yvonne Elliman, the Trammps, K.C. & the Sunshine Band, even Walter Murphy's insipid "A Fifth of Beethoven" is here. But regardless of your feelings about disco, gold chains, mirror balls and falsettos, this package is a trendsetter. Where previous soundtrack albums are usually good for one hit single, *Fever* ushered in the era of the multi-hit collection, and pop soundtracks were never the same after that.

Gary Graff

The Scarlet Letter 🎵🎵🎵

1995, Epic Soundtrax/Sony Music; from the movie *The Scarlet Letter*, Hollywood Pictures, 1995.

Album Notes: *Music*: John Barry; The English Chamber Orchestra, conducted by John Barry; *Album Producer*: John Barry; *Engineer*: John Kurklander.

Selections: 1 Main Title (P. Buffett)/The Arrival/Search For Home (6:17); 2 Hester Rides To Town (1:05); 3 The Bird/The Swimmer (P. Buffett)(3:08); 4 A Very Exhilarating Read (2:11); 5 I'm Not The Man I Seem (2:41); 6 Agnus Dei (based on Samuel Barber's Adagio for Strings)(10:51) *The Robert Shaw Festival Singers*; 7 I Can See What Others Cannot (1:04); 8 Love Scene (6:45); 9 Are You With Child (2:06); 10 A Small Act Of Contrition (2:25); 11 The Birth (2:06); 12 I Baptize This Child/Pearl (2:02); 13 She Will Not Speak (3:24); 14 Dr. Rodger Prynne (1:41); 15 Hester Walks Through Town (1:51); 16 Poor Fatherless Child (2:08); 17 An Attempt At Rape (3:01); 18 The Savages Have Killed Him (1:51); 19 The Round-Up (1:54); 20 I Am The Father Of Her Child (2:16); 21 The Indians Attack (2:48); 22 The Letter Has Served A Purpose (2:36); 23 End Title (4:14).

Review: It might be suicidal to one's critical reputation to say that you actually enjoyed Demi Moore and Roland Joffe's re-working of Hawthorne's *The Scarlet Letter*, so I'm only going to admit that I found the picture not nearly as disastrous as many others did. The movie boasts a number of positive attributes, including Alex Thomson's fine cinematography and a typically lush score by John Barry, who creates a deliberately paced musical sound that's a close relative to *Somewhere in Time* and all those other romantic soundtracks the composer is famous for. Thus, there's nothing here you haven't heard before, but it still works thanks to Barry's soothing orchestrations. Curiously, Barry was the third composer on the project, following Elmer Bernstein and Ennio Morricone. While Bernstein's music was recorded but ultimately rejected, Morricone was thrown off the project after he handed the producers a demo tape that was actually not original music but rather a pastiche of scores he had composed for various Italian projects!

Andy Dursin

Scent of a Woman 🎵🎵🎵🎵

1992, MCA Records; from the movie *Scent of a Woman*, Universal Pictures, 1992.

Album Notes: *Music*: Thomas Newman; *Orchestrations*: Thomas Pasatieri; *Music Editors*: Bob Badami, Bill Bernstein; Orchestra conducted by Thomas Newman; *Album Producers*: Thomas Newman, John Vigran, Bill Bernstein; *Engineer*: John Vigran.

Selections: 1 Main Title (2:59); 2 A Tour Of Pleasures (:50); 3 Tract House Ginch (1:05); 4 45 In 25 (3:24); 5 Balloons (:54); 6 Cigars Part Two (2:31); 7 Por una cabeza (C. Gardel)(2:15) *The Tango Project*; 8 Long Gray Line (1:02); 9 The Oakroom (:35); 10 Park Avenue (4:30); 11 Witnesses (1:21); 12 Beyond Danger (2:45); 13 La Violetera (J. Padilla)(3:35) *The Tango Project*; 14

Other Plans (2:09); 15 Assembly (2:04); 16 Fleurs de rocaille (2:50); 17 End Title (2:36).

Review: A brilliant tour-de-force by Al Pacino, as a blind ex-officer cared for over a Thanksgiving weekend by a college student, is one of the highlights in this modest comedy in which the youngster, deftly played by Chris O'Donnell, accompanies the cane-wielding, cantankerous sightless soldier on a spree to New York City, forging along the way solid affective ties with him. Based on a 1974 Italian film, scored by Armando Trovaioli, which received scant distribution in the U.S., *Scent of a Woman* (the title refers to the blind man's uncanny ability to identify an attractive woman just by sniffling the aura around her) exuded great charm and sensitivity, further enhanced by Thomas Newman's appealingly varied and low-key approach to his music. Two dance numbers, performed by the Tango Project, enliven the proceedings, casting a different, albeit equally enjoyable note into the mix.

Schindler's List ◢◢◢◢

1993, MCA Records; from the movie *Schindler's List*, Universal Pictures, 1993.

Album Notes: *Music*: John Williams; *Music Editor*: Ken Wannberg; Orchestra conducted by John Williams; *Featured Soloist*: Itzhak Perlman (violin), Giora Feidman (clarinet); *Album Producer*: John Williams; *Engineer*: Shawn Murphy; *Assistant Engineers*: Andrew Bass, Greg Denon.

Selections: 1 Theme From Schindler's List (4:14); 2 Jewish Town (Krakow Ghetto, Winter '41)(4:38); 3 Immolation (With Our Lives, We Give Life) (4:43); 4 Remembrance (4:19); 5 Schindler's Workforce (10:36); 6 OYF'N Pripetshok (M. Warschafsky) and Nacht Aktion (3:51) *Li-Ron Herzeliya Children's Choir, Ronit Shapira*; 7 I Could Have Done More (5:52); 8 Auschwitz-Birkenau (3:41); 9 Stolen Memories (4:17); 10 Making The List (5:06); 11 Give Me Your Names (4:56); 12 Yeroushalaim Chel Zahav (Jerusalem Of Gold)(N. Shemer)(2:14) *Ramat Gan Chamber Choir, Hana Tzur*; 13 Remembrances (with Itzhak Perlman)(5:16); 14 Theme From Schindler's List (reprise) (3:57).

Review: John Williams went along with Steven Spielberg's directorial approach on *Schindler's List* and refused to compose overly melodramatic moments in his Oscar-winning score for the 1993 movie. Working with violinist supreme Itzhak Perlman, Williams composed an elegiac, poignant score that is mournful and sad, tragic yet uplifting, perfectly establishing the emotional tone of Spielberg's Holocaust drama and gently underscoring the heroic actions of the title protagonist. The music is surprisingly low-key for a Williams score from a Spiel-

berg picture, lacking the full-blooded orchestral finales of *E.T.* and *Empire of the Sun*, for example, and is—if anything—restrained perhaps a bit too much at the conclusion. Yet it is consistent with the manner in which Williams scored character pieces like *The Accidental Tourist* and *Stanley & Iris*, making for subtle and sublime film music composition.
Andy Dursin

School Ties ◢◢◢◤

1992, Giant Records; from the movie *School Ties*, Paramount Pictures, 1992.

Album Notes: *Music*: Maurice Jarre; *Music Editor*: Dan Carlin, Sr.; Orchestra conducted by Maurice Jarre; *Album Producer*: Maurice Jarre; *Engineer*: Shawn Murphy.

Selections: 1 School Ties (2:06); 2 Smokey Joe's Cafe (J. Leiber/M. Stoller)(2:45) *The Robins*; 3 David (16:03); 4 Ain't That A Shame (D. Bartholomew/A. Domino)(2:32) *Fats Domino*; 5 School Moments (6:26); 6 Let Me Go Lover (J.L. Carson/K.G. Twomey/F. Wise/B. Weisman)(2:21) *Patti Page*; 7 The Last Word (6:38).

Review: Maurice Jarre's pretty and adventurous melody gives a sense of grandness and size to this localized prep school drama. The use of bells characterizes the film's setting, while the main theme suggests the free spirits of the characters. The heart of the score is found in "David," a 16-minute cue (longest of the CD's four score-only cues) that varies greatly in tempo and becomes a compelling tone-poem for the character, occasionally introspective and vulnerable, elsewhere bold and confident. In addition to the CD's 31 minutes of score, there are three source-cue pop songs which don't really need to be here, but they can easily be bypassed to afford maximum attention to Jarre's symphonic work. A good score nicely preserved on disc.
Randall D. Larson

The Sea Hawk ◢◢◢◢◢

1988, Varese-Sarabande; from the movie *The Sea Hawk*, Warner Bros., 1940.

Album Notes: *Music*: Erich-Wolfgang Korngold; The Utah Symphony Orchestra and Chorus, conducted by Varujian Kojian; *Album Producer*: George Korngold; *Engineers*: Jeff Ostler, David Bytheway.

Selections: 1 Main Title (1:55); 2 The Spanish Galleass/Galley Slaves/The "Albatross" (4:00); 3 The Captain's Table (1:44); 4 Dona Maria And Captain Thorpe/Elizabeth Throne Room (6:25); 5 Thorpe's Pet Monkey (7:03); 6 Map Of Panama (1:45); 7 The Chess Game (2:57); 8 Coach To Dover (2:21); 9 Farewell/

389

Panama (1:45); 10 Jungle March and Battle (3:32); 11 Return To The "Albatross" (3:05); 12 Condemned To The Galley/Dona Maria's Song (E.W. Korngold/H. Koch) (1:42) *Carol Wetzel*; 13 Queen Elizabeth/ Maria's Anguish (2:12); 14 Escape From The Galley/Fight On Deck/"Strike For The Shores Of Dover" (E.W. Korngold/ H. Koch/J. Scholl)(4:21); 15 Reunion (3:41); 16 Thorpe Confronts Wolfingham/ The Duel (2:38); 17 Fanfare and Finale (1:26) *Utah Symphony Chorus, Ed Thompson*.

Review: In the absence of an actual soundtrack album, which probably wouldn't sound too great given the recording techniques that prevailed at the time the film was made, this sensational rerecording, supervised by the composer's son, is more than a valid substitute. As was the case with *The Adventures of Robin Hood* (q.v.), the Utah Symphony and Varujian Kojian have approached Korngold's music with fervor and dedication, and a lot of enthusiasm that can easily be felt in the crackling performance. Possibly the only drawbacks might be the vocal and choral sections, which do not have the film's definite aura, but even that should not detract anyone from listening to and enjoying to the hilt this superlative soundtrack recreation.

The Sea Wolf 🎵🎵

1993, Bay Cities Records; from the movie *The Sea Wolf*, Turner Pictures, 1993.

Album Notes: *Music*: Charles Bernstein; *Music Editor*: Bruce Niznik; *Album Producer*: Charles Bernstein; *Engineer*: Daniel Hersch.

Selections: 1 Main Titles: Shipwreck and Rescue (3:33); 2 Man Overboard! (2:23); 3 Flaxen And Hump (1:48); 4 Down The Mast (2:33); 5 Captain Breaks Johnson (3:12); 6 Attempted Rape and Fight (4:15); 7 All Boats Away! (1:04); 8 Murder On Deck (1:50); 9 Who Did It? (1:39); 10 Mutiny (1:01); 11 Hump's Diary (1:30); 12 The Captain's Madness (1:59); 13 Hump's Seasick Discovery (2:40); 14 Life Aboard The Ghost (1:52); 15 The Meaning Of Dignity (1:18); 16 Adrift In The Night (3:42); 17 Hump And Flaxen's Escape (1:50); 18 The Ghost Sinks: Final Confrontation (3:33); 19 Ending Credits (1:41).

Review: A seafaring drama, starring Charles Bronson, as Captain Wolf Larsen, a tortured man bent on loneliness and self-destruction, and Christopher Reeve, as Humphrey Van Weyden, a socialite and involuntary seaman under Larsen's command, *The Sea Wolf* resulted in an often dark score by Charles Bernstein, reflective of the many somber aspects in the story. The relentless, oppressive moods in the music are occasionally relieved by a more romantic theme, describing Flaxen

Brewster (Mary Catherine Stewart), an attractive young woman, whose presence on board "The Ghost," Larsen's ship, triggers some of the conflicts in the narrative. With a predominance of percussive effects and broody synth lines, the music establishes moods and atmosphere that might have been what the action on the screen called for, but otherwise prove banal and not conducive to repeated listening.

Searching for Bobby Fischer 🎵🎵🎵

1993, Big Screen Records; from the movie *Searching for Bobby Fischer*, Paramount Pictures, 1993.

Album Notes: *Music*: James Horner; *Orchestrations*: James Horner, Thomas Pasatieri; *Music Editor*: Jim Henrikson; Orchestra conducted by James Horner; *Featured Musicians*: James Horner, Ralph Grierson, Randy Kerber, Jim Thatcher, Ian Underwood; *Album Producer*: James Horner; *Engineer*: Shawn Murphy.

Selections: 1 Main Title (3:03); 2 Early Victories (3:30); 3 Contempt (2:40); 4 The Castle (2:04); 5 Josh vs. Dad (3:18); 6 Josh's First Lesson (2:38); 7 Trip To Chicago (3:24); 8 Washington Square (2:45); 9 Start Your Clock/Master Class Points (4:06); 10 Josh And Vinnie (3:31); 11 The Nationals (3:25); 12 Final Tournament (7:55); 13 Epilogue/End Credits (7:10).

Review: James Horner is often criticized for quoting both classical works and his own previous soundtracks at times, but despite these often uneven attributes in his compositions, he usually produces soundtracks that are nevertheless entertaining and invite repeated listening. Such is the case once again with his music from *Searching for Bobby Fischer*, the 1993 film by Steven Zaillian about the life of Josh Waitzkin, a real-life chess wiz who shot to fame at the age of seven. Sure, Horner's music sounds like *Field of Dreams*, *Sneakers*, and a few of his other scores, but as a pastiche, it's certainly an enjoyable one, with pleasant melodies and elegant orchestrations making this as easy to listen to as it is to identify the sections you'll recall from other sources.

Andy Dursin

The Secret Garden 🎵🎵

1993, Varèse-Sarabande; from the movie *The Secret Garden*, Warner Bros., 1993.

Album Notes: *Music*: Zbigniew Preisner; *Music Editor*: Curt Sobel; The Sinfonia Varsovia, conducted by Wojciech Michniewski; The Boys Choir of The Cracovian Philharmonic,

Stanislaw Kravceyski, dir.; *Boy Soloist*: Tomasz Borik; *Album Producer*: Zbigniew Preisner; *Engineer*: Rafal Paczkowski.

Selections: 1 Main Title (3:33); 2 Leaving The Docks (1:27); 3 Mary Downstairs (2:05); 4 First Time Outside (1:24); 5 Skipping Rope (:53); 6 Entering The Garden (:59); 7 Walking Through The Garden (1:52); 8 Mary And Robin Together (:49); 9 Shows Dickon Garden (1:05); 10 Awakening Of Spring (1:48); 11 Craven Leaves (2:35); 12 Taking Colin To The Garden (1:10); 13 Colin Opens His Eyes (2:00); 14 Colin Tries Standing (:51); 15 Colin Loves Mary (:55); 16 Craven's Return (2:16); 17 Looking At Photos (:42); 18 Craven To The Garden (:35); 19 Colin Senses Craven (1:32); 20 Happily Ever After (2:25).

Review: Often agreeable, but overall disappointing presentation of Zbigniew Preisner's score. The album starts off in a very scattershot manner with cues frequently averaging a minute and a half, or less. It fails to generate any emotional response early on because the music is over before any emotional mood can develop. That's a real shame because the score does have its moments. "Craven Leaves," "Walking Through the Garden," and "Awakening of Spring" show some real possibilities. The pacing does improve in the later half, but by then it may have lost you.

David Hirsch

The Secret of N.I.M.H. ♫♫♫♫

1982, Varese-Sarabande Records; from the animated feature *The Secret of N.I.M.H.*, United Artists, 1982.

Album Notes: *Music*: Jerry Goldsmith; *Orchestrations*: Arthur Morton; The National Philharmonic Orchestra and The Ambrosian Singers, conducted by Jerry Goldsmith; *Album Producer*: Jerry Goldsmith; *Engineer*: John Richards.

Selections: 1 Main Title (3:14); 2 The Tractor (2:59); 3 The Sentry Reel/Story Of NIMH (6:04); 4 Step Inside My House (4:41); 5 The House Raising (4:33); 6 Moving Day (7:56); 7 No Thanks (2:02); 8 Allergic Reaction/Athletic Type (2:40); 9 Flying Dreams (Lullaby)(J. Goldsmith/P. Williams)(3:17) *Sally Stevens*; 10 Escape From NIMH/In Disguise (4:59); 11 Flying High/End Title (2:41); 12 Flying Dreams (J. Goldsmith/P. Williams)(3:25) *Paul Williams.*

Review: When you think of soundtracks from animated children's films, usually musicals or pop songs are the first things to enter into your mind—music like Alan Menken's mega-successful Disney efforts or songs like "Somewhere Out There" from *An American Tail*. Animated features with serious, classically-themed film scores are few and far between, but Jerry Goldsmith was given the rare chance at making a sub-

stantial contribution to Don Bluth's *The Secret of NIMH*, the 1982 theatrical feature which has since become a kids' staple on video and cable TV. Goldsmith faced the challenges of scoring for often incomplete animation and came up with one of his finest scores of the 1980s, with strongly thematic passages punctuated by thrilling cues that sound more like an action film score than they do befitting a children's soundtrack. Even the movie's original song, "Flying Dreams," co-written and performed by Paul Williams, is memorable and quite lovely, perfectly putting the cap on a superior effort by Goldsmith all around.

Andy Dursin

Selena ♫♫♫♫

1997, Angel Records; from the movie *Selena*, Warner Bros., 1997.

Album Notes: *Music*: Dave Grusin; *Music Editor*: Robert Garrett; Orchestra conducted by Dave Grusin; *Album Producer*: Dave Grusin; *Engineers*: John Richards, Don Murray.

Selections: 1 Main Title: Selena (1:41); 2 Kids And Chickens (2:42); 3 South Texas Jive Cats (2:40); 4 Selena's Dream/Mi corazon (2:25); 5 Theme From "A Summer Place" (M. Steiner/M. Discant)(2:42) *Gary Lemel*; 6 Leaving Our Home (1:32); 7 Selena Theme (4:05) *Dave Grusin*; 8 Cumbia: "La manzana" (R. Vela/S. James/B. Moore)(2:36); 9 "Salinas" y los Low Riders (1:45); 10 Chris And Selena (2:47); 11 Small Talk And Salsa (3:22); 12 Dreams Of The People (1:46); 13 Leap Of Faith (3:42); 14 Don't Quit Music/Betrayal (1:46); 15 Final Dream (2:53); 16 Como la flor... For Selena (A.B. Quintanilla III/P. Astudillo)(4:06) *Dave Grusin*; 17 End Credits (3:10).

Review: This explosive real-life drama about the Tex-Mex performer murdered by one of her fans pretty much dictated Dave Grusin's approach to the music he wrote: with characteristic flair, he devised for many of the cues enjoyably bouncy tunes rooted in the fusion jazz in which he excels ("Kids and Chickens," "South Texas Jive Cats," "Salinas y los Low Riders"), keeping for the more romantic aspects in the story ("Selena's Dream," "Dreams of the People," "Don't Quit Music/Betrayal") a florid instrumental style that proves very ingratiating. The simply-stated "Selena Theme" and "Como la flor... for Selena," two gorgeously expressive piano pieces, also stand out, as do a couple of entertaining numbers denoting south-of-the-border influence ("Cumbia: La Manzana"). The only questionable selection in this otherwise highly entertaining score album is the inclusion of "Theme from 'A Summer Place'," sung by Gary Lemel, which seems an odd choice in the musical context.

motion picture soundtracks

> "I find writing songs for an assignment relatively easy... Compared to scoring a picture, in terms of time, it's one-fiftieth as hard. And that's being conservative."
>
> **Randy Newman**
> *(The Detroit News, 12-22-95)*

Sense and Sensibility ♫♫♫♫

1995, Sony Classical; from the movie *Sense and Sensibility*, Columbia Pictures, 1995.

Album Notes: *Music*: Patrick Doyle; *Orchestrations*: Lawrence Ashmore; *Music Editor*: Roy Prendergast; Orchestra conducted by Robert Ziegler; *Artists*: Jane Eaglen (soprano), Tony Hymas (piano), Jonathan Snowdon (flutes), Richard Morgan (oboes), Robert Hill (clarinet); *Album Producers*: Patrick Doyle, Maggie Rodford; *Engineer*: Paul Hulme; *Assistant Engineers*: Ben Georgiades, John Bailey, Steve Orchard.

Selections: 1 Weep You No More Sad Fountains (3:05); 2 A Particular Sum (1:15); 3 My Father's Favorite (5:27); 4 Preying Penniless Woman (1:32); 5 Devonshire (1:04); 6 Not A Bean For Miles (1:57); 7 All The Better For Her (1:17); 8 Felicity (1:22); 9 Patience (1:42); 10 Grant Me An Interview (1:05); 11 All The Delights Of The Season (1:14); 12 Steam Engine (1:19); 13 Willoughby (1:39); 14 Miss Grey (2:21); 15 Excellent Notion (1:39); 16 Leaving London (2:12); 17 Combe Magna (2:59); 18 To Die For Love (2:55); 19 There Is Nothing Lost (:59); 20 Throw The Coins (3:08); 21 The Dreame (2:30).

Review: Jane Austen's understanding of the dual aspects in anyone's life (so well defined in the title of this film adapted from her first novel) found a remarkable echo in Patrick Doyle's gloriously literate and lovingly understated score. At times properly rambunctious, at other times deliciously gracile, the cues offer a carefully wrought depiction of this classic comedy-drama about three young girls (and their mother) in 18th century England suddenly left destitute by the death of their father, whose considerable estate is inherited by a son from a previous marriage and his insufferable wife. Some selections, like "Willoughby," strike for their charming simplicity, while the profuse style in others ("My Father's Favorite") proves equally endearing. Two vocals by Jane Eaglen bookend this

delightful album, both exuding a lovely lilt mixed with a sense of melancholy, superbly reflective of the film's dual moods.

Serial Mom ♫♫♫♫

1994, MCA Records; from the movie *Serial Mom*, Sony Pictures, 1994.

Album Notes: *Music*: Basil Poledouris; *Featured Performers*: Kathleen Turner, Matthew Lillard, Patricia Dunnock, Mink Stole, Beau James, Patricia Hearst; *Album Producers*: L-7, Brett Gurewitz, Barry Manilow, Ron Dante, Basil Poledouris.

Selections: 1 Gas Chamber (L-7/J. Waters)(4:02) *L-7*; 2 Daybreak (B. Manilow/A. Anderson)(3:08) *Barry Manilow*; 3 Main Title (Mom's Suburban Dream)(4:49); 4 Morning Suite (I'll Get You Pussyface!)(2:06); 5 It's Been A Crazy Day, Hasn't It? (3:24); 6 Flea Market Suite (Stood Up And Skewered) (7:02); 7 The Sterner Payback (5:40); 8 Buckle Up, Scotty! (2:37); 9 Courtroom Suite (In Memory Of A Fashion Victim)(3:02); 10 I'm Coming Home! (3:20).

Review: Kathleen Turner had one of her most enjoyable screen roles as a mother with a killer instinct, in this cheerful comedy by John Waters. Adding spice to this devilishly amusing story about a perfect housewife and mother who reveals another side to her personality when she starts murdering her annoying neighbors, Basil Poledouris wrote a delightfully perverse little score that moves from a serene opening to a series of increasingly frantic cues, all of them detailing with glee the lady's misdeeds, in a style Bernard Herrmann would not have disowned. Some of the cues are set off by brief excerpts from the dialogue, further enhancing their impact. A neglected minor masterpiece, *Serial Mom* is wryly entertaining. This soundtrack album is equally rewarding, though you might want to skip the screechy "Gas Chamber" song, performed (if that is the word) by L-7.

Set It Off ♫♫♫♫♭

1997, Varese-Sarabande Records; from the movie *Set It Off*, New Line Cinema, 1997.

Album Notes: *Music*: Christopher Young; *Orchestrations*: Christopher Young, Pete Anthony; *Music Editor*: Christopher Kennedy; Orchestra conducted by Pete Anthony; *Featured Musicians*: Mike Lang (keyboards), John Goux (nylon string guitar), Brandon Fields, Mike Vacarro (saxophone), Nick Kirgo, George Doering (guitars), Carl Vincent (electric bass), MB Gordy, Steve Schaefer (drums); *Album Producer*: Christopher Young; *Engineers*: Robert Fernandez, Fred Vogler.

Selections: 1 Up Against The Wind (C. Young/D. Goldsmith) (3:28) *Lori Perri*; 2 Set It Off (4:08); 3 Hell Blowin Hard (2:18); 4

Buttercrunch (2:20); 5 Rota Rooter (4:01); 6 Four-One (1:55); 7 Squeezebox (1:39); 8 Balboa Blood (2:14); 9 Toupee Souffle (2:23); 10 Q. For A Day (2:58); 11 Flame On Fire (2:07); 12 Up Against The Wind (reprise) (C. Young/D. Goldsmith) (4:28) *Lori Perri*.

Review: Outstanding black urban score by Christopher Young that shows he's not out of fresh and innovative ideas. He's taken all he's learned from his past efforts and assembled some powerful orchestrations, particularly the use of some imaginative vocal arrangements that incorporate the sound of breathing as well as traditional "scats." The album also includes a lovely ballad, "Up Against the Wind," co-written by Young. Remarkable effort from a white boy from the Jersey shore.

David Hirsch

Se7en ♪♪♪ᵖ

1995, TVT Records; from the movie *Se7en*, New Line Cinema, 1995.

Album Notes: *Music:* Howard Shore; Orchestra conducted by Howard Shore; *Producer:* Howard Shore; *Engineer:* John Kurlander.

Selections: 1 In The Beginning (D. Cochran/K. Twomley/B. Weisman/F. Wise) (2:22) *The Statler Brothers*; 2 Guilty (Gravity Kills)(4:06) *Gravity Kills*; 3 Trouble Man (M. Gaye)(3:50) *Marvin Gaye*; 4 Speaking Of Happiness (J. Radcliffe/B. Scott) (2:33) *Gloria Lynne*; 5 Suite No. 3 in D Major, BWV 1068 (J.S. Bach) (3:40) *Stuttgarter Kammerorchester, Karl Muchinger*; 6 Love Plus One (N. Heyward)(3:37) *Haircut 100*; 7 I Cover The Waterfront (J. Green/E. Heyman)(3:21) *Billie Holiday*; 8 Now's The Time (C. Parker)(4:17) *Charlie Parker*; 9 Straight, No Chaser (T. Monk)(9:38) *Thelonious Monk*; 10 Portrait Of John Doe (4:57); 10 Suite From Seven (14:49).

Review: It opens with the Statler Brothers' "In the Beginning" and slams immediately to Gravity Kills' pulverizing "Guilty" before shifting back to Marvin Gaye's "Trouble Man." An arresting opening salvo that's supported by pieces of Bach and performances by blues queen Billie Holiday and jazz masters Charlie Parker and Thelonious Monk. For listeners who thrive on variety.

Gary Graff

The Seventh Sign ♪♪ᵖ

1988, Cinedisc Records; from the movie *The Seventh Sign*, Tri-Star Pictures, 1988.

Album Notes: *Music:* Jack Nitzsche; *Album Producer:* Michael Hoenig; *Engineer:* Pamela Neal.

Selections: 1 Opening/Fish/Desert/Wrath/First Seal (4:44); 2 The Nightmare (2:01); 3 David's Apartment and The Story Of "The Gulf" (3:15); 4 Abby Follows David To The Synagogue (4:01); 5 A World In Trouble (2:41); 6 Parchment 2/29 (2:48); 7 The Stabbing (2:25); 8 Attempted Suicide And Light (4:07); 9 Lucci Revealed (3:22); 10 The Last Martyr (2:06); 11 The Walk To The Gas Chamber (5:38); 12 Birth (1:11); 13 Abby's Death (3:12); 14 End Credits (3:57).

Review: A horror film with pseudo-Biblical overtones, *The Seventh Sign* stars Demi Moore as a pregnant woman confronted by the possibility that her unborn child might be the final sign announced in the Apocalypse. Using a disembodied chorus and electronic sounds, Jack Nitzsche fashioned a score that's richly evocative and appropriately ominous, though its real importance might have been better appreciated in the theatre, as a support to the screen action.

The 7th Voyage of Sinbad ♪♪♪♪ᵖ

1980, Varese-Sarabande; from the movie *The 7th Voyage of Sinbad*, Columbia Pictures, 1958.

Album Notes: *Music:* Bernard Herrmann; Orchestra conducted by Bernard Herrmann; *CD Producer:* Tom Null; *Engineer:* Danny Hersch.

Selections: 1 Overture/Bagdad (3:50); 2 Sultan's Feast/The Vase/Cobra Dance (2:33); 3 The Cyclops (3:36); 4 Night Magic/ Tiny Princess/Street Music (3:34); 5 The Flight/Battle With The Cyclops (3:16); 6 The Roc/The Nest (4:10); 7 The Dragon (2:13); 8 Transformation (2:01); 9 The Skeleton/ The Duel With The Skeleton/The Sword (2:54); 10 The Death Of The Cyclops/ The Crossbow/The Death of The Dragon (3:20); 11 Finale (2:19).

Review: In the 1950s and '60s, Bernard Herrmann specialized in fantasy films, scoring several for special effects ace Ray Harryhausen, beginning with this rousing adventure which features a sprightly title theme and a number of evocative cues for Harryhausen's parade of animated mythical creatures. Highlights include rumbling, ominous low brass and percussion tones for a Cyclops and a dragon, a dazzling repeated brass fanfare for a gigantic two-headed bird ("The Roc"), and an audacious battle cue for Sinbad's fight with a walking skeleton, scored almost entirely for xylophone. The threatening brass chords for the Cyclops often recall Herrmann's work on *The Day the Earth Stood Still*, while the composer's pastiche Middle Easternisms vividly conjure up the Arabia of childhood stories. This hard-to-find CD features a masterly recording and performance, although this score is so strident and aggressive in its orchestral effects and repeated textures that it may drive crazy anyone but the most ardent Herrmann fans.

Jeff Bond

See also: Bernard Herrmann in Compilations

sex, lies, and videotape ♪

1989, Virgin Movie Music; from the movie *sex, lies, and videotape,* Miramax Films, 1989.

Album Notes: *Music:* Cliff Martinez, Mark Mangini; *Album Producers:* Cliff Martinez, Mark Mangini; *Engineer:* Larry Blake.

Selections: 1 Garbage (M. Mangini)(:37); 2 Look Like A Tablecloth (4:01); 3 Take My Shirt Off (2:06); 4 Are You Comfortable (2:18); 5 Here We Go (2:16); 6 What Other Men...? (2:55); 7 Sniff The Jacket (3:25); 8 You've Got A Problem (7:04); 9 I'm Gonna Drawl (4:37).

Review: Sexy and totally unabashed about its subject, *sex, lies, and videotape* took a close-up look at four people, and what motivates them erotically. If the film is beautifully nuanced and unusually imaginative, the same cannot be said of Cliff Martinez's uneven score which often meanders into vapid synth lines without expression, punctuated at times by an electronic rhythm track, possibly to try and give them more meaning. One cannot but wonder what a more inspired composer (Patrick Doyle or Christopher Young, for instance) might have done with the same subject.

The Shadow ♪♪♪

1994, Arista Records; from the movie *The Shadow,* Universal Pictures, 1994.

Album Notes: *Music:* Jerry Goldsmith; *Orchestrations:* Arthur Morton, Alexander Courage; *Music Editor:* Ken Hall; Orchestra conducted by Jerry Goldsmith; *Album Producer:* Jerry Goldsmith; *Engineer:* Bruce Botnick.

Selections: 1 The Shadow Knows... 1994 (:08) *Alec Baldwin;* 2 Original Sin (Theme From "The Shadow")(J. Steinman)(6:27) *Taylor Dayne;* 3 The Poppy Fields (Main Title)(3:16); 4 Some Kind Of Mystery (D. Warren)(3:48) *Sinoa;* 5 The Sanctum (3:33); 6 Who Are You? (4:02); 7 Chest Pains (3:26); 8 The Knife (3:05); 9 The Hotel (5:53); 10 The Tank (4:08); 11 Frontal Lobotomy (2:28); 12 Original Sin (Theme From "The Shadow")(J. Steinman)(5:02) *Taylor Dayne;* 13 The Shadow Radio Show 1937: Who Knows What Lurks in the Hearts of Men? (:29) *Orson Welles.*

Review: Skip the obligatory dialog and rock tracks (the first four and the last two) and enjoy Goldsmith's splendid heroic

adventure score for this campy pulp-era superhero saga. His main theme is a rhythmic, ascending figure for brass over horns, reeds, and thundering percussion, with a weaving surge of violins underneath; it sounds ominously and resolutely, and lends an effective air of mystery (the strings) and power (the horns) to the shadowy crime-fighter. The various action cues are less effective, a collection of percussion hits, strings mysteriosos, and wind furtiveness, often in need of the powerful main theme to bring the score to life. A great moment is achieved with the appearance of the "invisible" hotel, phrases of the main theme intone upwards with electronic whale-like moans and tangy synth twangs in a very evocative and compelling six-minute cue. With little more than 26 minutes of score on the CD, though, there aren't enough great moments like that, even with such a likable theme at hand.

Randall D. Larson

Shadow Conspiracy ♪♪♪

1996, Intrada Records; from the movie *Shadow Conspiracy,* Hollywood Pictures, 1996.

Album Notes: *Music:* Bruce Broughton; The Sinfonia Of London, conducted by Bruce Broughton; Album Produced by Bruce Broughton; *Engineers:* Paul Hulme, Armin Steiner, Joe Tarantino.

Selections: 1 The Hit (3:50); 2 To The White House (Main Title)(1:38); 3 The Oval Office (2:43); 4 Georgetown Pursuit (6:23); 5 Touched By Evil (3:08); 6 Frank Is Dead (:59); 7 A Secured Line (:43); 8 Hitter On The Roof (5:32); 9 White House Chaos (14:12); 10 Tracking Amanda (2:32); 11 The Conspirators (2:18); 12 Final Details (3:15); 13 Attempted Assassination/End Credits (10:10).

Review: Bruce Broughton first collaborated with filmmaker George P. Cosmatos on the hit western *Tombstone,* and was later reunited with the *Rambo* director for the box-office dud *The Shadow Conspiracy,* which is one of a number of 1997 films revolving around White House conspiracies and/or assassinations (a select group that also included Clint Eastwood's modestly successful *Absolute Power* and the Wesley Snipes' turkey *Murder at 1600*). Broughton's score is a brooding, at-times thundering brassy outing featuring solid work from the Sinfonia of London. In short, if you like large-scale suspense scores, you could do far worse than to give this a listen. The main theme is, in fact, written in the same vein as *Tombstone,* so if you liked that score, it goes without saying that you ought to enjoy this one as well.

Andy Dursin

Shadow of the Wolf 🎵🎵🎵

1993, Milan Records; from the movie *Shadow of the Wolf*, Vision International/Malofilm Distribution, 1993.

Album Notes: *Music*: Maurice Jarre; *Music Editor*: Dan Carlin, Sr.; The Royal Philharmonic Orchestra, conducted by Maurice Jarre; *Featured Musicians*: Maurice Jarre, Ralph Grierson, Rick Marvin (synthesizers), Judd Miller, Nyle Steiner, Mick Fisher (E.V.I.); *Album Producer*: Maurice Jarre; *Engineer*: Shawn Murphy.

Selections: 1 Agaguk (10:55); 2 The White Wolf (5:09); 3 Igiyook (6:03); 4 Henderson (5:19); 5 To The Top Of The World (8:43); 6 The Shaman Hawk (7:33); 7 Always And Forever (M. Jarre/N. Carsen)(English version)(2:33) *Nathalie Carsen*; 8 Always And Forever (L'amour eternel)(M. Jarre/N. Carsen)(French version)(2:55) *Nathalie Carsen*.

Review: I often get the feeling that we should be hearing more film scores composed by Maurice Jarre than we do. This is, after all, the same man who wrote the music for *Lawrence of Arabia* and *Dr. Zhivago*, and whenever he scores a movie these days, the results are impressive and certainly far superior to the generic material that comprises most modern soundtracks. That certainly holds true on *Shadow of the Wolf*, which features an operatic, symphonic score performed by the stellar-sounding Royal Philharmonic Orchestra. The music, written for the rather bland 1993 adaptation of the bestselling Canadian novel "Agaguk," has the same epic feel that marks many of the composer's best works, and its often melodic quality ought to remind listeners that, for evocative orchestral scores with a larger-than-life feel, few do it better than Maurice Jarre.

Andy Dursin

Shadowlands 🎵🎵🎵🎵

1993, EMI/Angel Records; from the film *Shadowlands*, Savoy Pictures, 1993.

Album Notes: *Music*: George Fenton; The London Symphony Orchestra, conducted by George Fenton; The Choir of Magdalen College, Oxford, directed by Grayston Ives; *Album Producer*: George Fenton; *Engineer*: Keith Grant.

Selections: 1 Veni Sancte Spiritus: Front Titles (2:19) *Daniel Cochlin*; 2 The Golden Valley (1:58); 3 Quartet in D "The Randolph" (1:49) *Michael Davis, Janice Graham, Paul Silverthorne, Rod McGrath*; 4 The Wardrobe (2:39); 5 "The Plot Thickens" (2:33); 6 The Lake (3:14); 7 O Little Town Of Bethlehem (trad.)(2:12); 8 Once In Royal David's City (1:37) *Daniel Cochlin*; 9 The Friendship (2:09); 10 The Wedding (2:43); 11 Summer Is Icumen In (13th century anon.)(1:38); 12 The Drive To The Hotel (1:31); 13 The Golden Valley, part two (1:58); 14 Mr. C.S. Lewis (1:42) *Nicholas Rodwell*; 15 Joy Goes Home (2:33); 16 "I'll Be Here Too" (1:56); 17 The Silence (1:54); 18 "As A Boy And As A Man" (3:26) *Daren Geraghty*; 19 Sanctis Solemniis (2:03); 20 Joy And Douglas (1:41); 21 Shadowlands (End Credits)(3:35).

Review: George Fenton proves once again to be one of the finest film composers around, with his graceful and classy music for *Shadowlands*. The film is based on the life of Christian author and professor C.S. Lewis, and his painful attempts to reconcile his wife's protracted death by cancer with his faith. Obviously in such a story the pitfalls for a composer are many, with the risk of becoming melodramatic ever-present. Fenton however delivers a score of impeccable class and refinement, yet accessibility, performed to perfection by the London Symphony Orchestra and the Choir of Magdalen College. The music owes largely to the English tradition, Fenton providing a number of impressive choral cues (evoking the Oxford setting) and a lyrically English pastoral tone for the love story. The result is a beautiful and deeply moving score, with the kind of depth which eludes most other composers these days.

Paul Andrew MacLean

Shag the Movie 🎵🎵🎵

1989, Sire Records; from the movie *Shag the Movie*, Hemdale Film Corp., 1989.

Album Notes: *Song Producers*: Andy Paley, Tommy Page, Sonni Jonzun, Michael Jonzun, Richard Gottehrer, Erik Jacobsen; *Engineers*: Mark Linett, Mark Partis, Mike Dignam, Richard Barraclough, Rob Dimit, Phil Greene, Jeffrey Lesser, Mark Needham.

Selections: 1 The Shag (T. Page/A. Paley)(4:18) *Tommy Page*; 2 I'm In Love Again (A. Domino/D. Bartholomew)(2:03) *Randy Newman*; 3 Our Day Will Come (B. Hilliard/M. Garson)(2:37) *k.d. lang & the reclines, Take 6*; 4 Ready To Go Steady (A. Paley/M. Jonzun)(3:20) *The Charmettes*; 5 Shaggin' On The Grandstand (A. Paley/H. Ballard/L. Stein)(2:50) *Hank Ballard*; 6 Oh What A Night (Junior/Funches)(2:51) *The Moonliters*; 7 Saved (M. Stoller/J. Leiber) (3:01) *LaVern Baker*; 8 I'm Leaving It All Up To You (Harris/Terry)(2:14) *LaVern Baker, Ben E. King*; 9 Surrender (L. Goffin/D. King)(4:11) *Louise Goffin*; 10 Diddley Daddy (G. McDaniel/H. Fuqua)(4:04) *Chris Isaak*.

Review: This often hilarious soundtrack compilation was put together for a zany film purporting to document what happened over a wild weekend in 1963, when a new dance craze, the shag, "started the party that caused the uproar that led to the weekend of the century." The songs, written in imitation of the sounds that could be heard on radio at the time, are amusing for the most part, and beat-driven, but two emerge in particular—"Ready to Go Steady," performed by The Charmettes in a dead-on spoof of The Supremes, complete with bells, "oohs," and saxophone break; and k.d. lang's excellent reading of "Our Day Will Come," worth alone the price of this entertaining album.

The Shawshank Redemption
♫♫♫♪

1994, Epic Soundtrax; from the movie *The Shawshank Redemption*, Columbia Pictures, 1994.

Album Notes: *Music*: Thomas Newman; *Orchestrations*: Thomas Pasatieri; *Music Editor*: Bill Bernstein; Orchestra conducted by Thomas Newman; *Album Producers*: Thomas Newman, Bill Bernstein; *Engineer*: Dennis Sands; *Assistant Engineer*: Tom Winslow.

Selections: 1 May (:33); 2 Shawshank Prison (Stoic Theme)(1:53); 3 New Fish (1:50); 4 Rock Hammer (1:51); 5 An Inch Of His Life (2:48); 6 If I Didn't Care (J. Lawrence)(3:03) *The Inkspots*; 7 Brooks Was Here (5:06); 8 His Judgement Cometh (2:00); 9 Suds On The Roof (1:36); 10 Workfield (1:10); 11 Shawshank Redemption (4:26); 12 Lovesick Blues (C. Friend/I. Mills)(2:42) *Hank Williams*; 13 Elmo Blatch (1:08); 14 Sisters (1:18); 15 Zihuatanejo (4:43); 16 Duettino — Sull 'aria (from The Marriage Of Figaro)(W.A. Mozart)(3:32) *The Deutsche Oper Berlin, Karl Bohn*; 17 Lovely Raquel (1:55); 18 And That Right Soon (1:08); 19 Compass And Guns (3:53); 20 So Was Red (2:44); 21 End Title (4:05).

Review: Thomas Newman has been typecast into scoring movies that are good. One of them is *The Shawshank Redemption*, Frank Darabont's 1994 prison saga based on a story by Stephen King. Tim Robbins and Morgan Freeman share the ennui of a lifetime in jail until their eventual—well, you can guess. It's a somber tale which Newman handles perfectly, with folk-oriented fiddle music, a sensitive theme for piano, and delicate orchestral/metallic samples which express the passage of time. Even the big moments have a restraint—this is a prison movie whose climactic jailbreak is told in flashback—but the subtlety never comes at the expense of musical coherence. Newman taps into different modes and altered scales which gives his melodic writing a lot of zing. He also continues a tradition of Americana in the original spirit of Copland, without sounding like Copland. Overall, it's a triumph of pitch over volume. The album includes a lot of imperceptible plinking (and a few source cues) which does make it less satisfying as separated listening.

Lukas Kendall

She's Out of Control ♫♫♫

1989, MCA Records; from the movie *She's Out of Control*, Weintraub Entertainment, 1989.

Album Notes: *Song Producers*: George E. Tobin, Tommy Faragher, Lotti Golden, Phil Thornalley, David Cole, Michael Verdick, Keith Forsey, Harold Faltermeyer, Jim Ladd, Danny Elfman, Steve Bartek, John Avila, Brian Wilson, Eugene E. Landy, Peter DeAngelis, Robert P. Marcucci, Shel Talmy, Tom Allom; *Album Producer*: John Boylan; *Engineer*: John Boylan.

Selections: 1 Where's The Fire (M. Keefner/D. Green/D. Abravanel) (3:49) *Troy Hinton*; 2 You Should Be Loving Me (L. Golden/T. Faragher) (3:43) *Brenda K. Starr*; 3 Concentration (P. Thornalley) (3:47) *Phil Tornalley*; 4 The Loneliest Heart (M. Jeffries/J. Logan) (3:47) *Boys Club*; 5 Hunger Of Love (H. Faltermeyer/K. Forsey) (4:41) *Harold Faltermeyer*; 6 KHEY-FM Radio Sweeper (J. Ladd) (:12) *Jim Ladd*; 7 Winning Side (D. Elfman) (3:56) *Oingo Boingo*; 8 Daddy's Little Girl (B. Wilson/A. Morgan/E. Landy) (3:13) *Brian Wilson*; 9 Venus (E. Marshall) (2:20) *Frankie Avalon*; 10 You Really Got Me (R. Davies) (2:12) *The Kinks*; 11 Feel The Shake (M. Finn/F. Rod) (4:10) *Jetboy*.

Review: Tony Danza treads on Michael J. Fox territory in this light comedy about the plight of a single father with a teenage daughter who begins to assert her sexuality. Uncertain about what he is supposed to do, he follows her every opportunity he has to ensure that she keeps her virginity. Punctuating the screen action, the soundtrack offers a mixture of rock songs, some oldies and some newies, which make up this strange but enjoyable album. On the new side are songs by Troy Hinton, Brenda K. Starr, Boys Club, and Phil Thornalley. On the old side are selections by Brian Wilson, Frankie Avalon, and The Kinks. Somewhere in between, Oingo Boingo (bless them!) deliver "Winning Side," which is a refreshing change from all the synth drums in the tracks that precede, and paves the way for the golden oldies.

She's the One ♫♫♫♪

1996, Warner Bros. Records; from the movie *She's the One*, 20th Century-Fox, 1996.

Album Notes: *Songs (unless otherwise indicated)*: Tom Petty and The Heartbreakers; *Album Producers*: Rick Rubin, Tom Petty, Mike Campbell; *Engineers*: Jim Scott, Sylvia Massey.

Selections: 1 Walls (Circus)(4:25); 2 Grew Up Fast (5:10); 3 Zero From Outer Space (3:08); 4 Climb That Hill (T. Petty/M. Campbell)(3:58); 5 Change The Locks (L. Williams)(4:57); 6 Angel Dream (No. 4)(2:27); 7 Hope Your Never (3:03); 8 Asshole (B. Campbell)(3:12); 9 Supernatural Radio (5:22); 10 California (2:40); 11 Hope On Board (1:18); 12 Walls (No. 3)(3:04); 13 Angel Dream (No. 2)(2:27); 14 Hung Up And Overdue (5:49); 15 Airport (:58).

Review: Tom Petty and the Heartbreakers deliver a lively set of great rock songs for this fetching romantic comedy that doesn't take the beaten path to seduce its audiences with its story about two brothers, a cab driver and a Wall Street stockbroker, and the women in their life. The songs by Petty, which include the hit "Walls," make few demands on the intellect but beg to be heard again once the album is over. What their relationship with the movie might be is definitely not hinted at in the lyrics, but when the songs are solid and well defined, who's to complain?

The Sheltering Sky ♫♫♫♫

1990, Virgin Movie Music; from the movie *The Sheltering Sky*, Warner Bros., 1990.

Album Notes: *Music:* Ryuichi Sakamoto; *Orchestrations:* John Altman, David Arch; The Royal Philharmonic Orchestra, conducted by John Altman, David Arch; *Music Editor:* Diane Eaton; *Album Producer:* Ryuichi Sakamoto; *Engineer:* Matt Howe; *Assistant Engineers:* Spence May, Jamie Cullum, Chris Ludwinski.

Selections: 1 The Sacred Koran (:40) *Ibrahim Canakkaleli, Fevzi Misir, Yusuf Gebzeli, Aziz Bahriyeli;* 2 The Sheltering Sky Theme (5:19); 3 Belly (1:27); 4 Port's Composition (1:23); 5 On The Bed (Dream)(1:37); 6 Loneliness (1:30); 7 On The Hill (6:10); 8 Kyoto (1:04); 9 Cemetery (1:25); 10 Dying (3:30); 11 Market (1:42); 12 Grand Hotel (2:06); 13 The Sheltering Sky Theme (piano version)(4:16); 14 Je chante (C. Trenet)(2:44) *Charles Trenet;* 15 Midnight Sun (L. Hampton/S. Burke/J. Mercer)(3:14) *Lionel Hampton;* 16 Fever Ride (R. Horowitz)(3:50) *Richard Horowitz;* 17 Chant avec cithare (trad.) (:44); 18 Marnia's Tent (R. Horowitz)(3:02) *Richard Horowitz;* 19 Goulou Limma (5:47) *Chaba Zahouania;* 20 Happy Bus Ride (1:41) *Zarzis;* 21 Night Train (R. Horowitz)(1:57) *Richard Horowitz.*

Review: Based on Paul Bowles' 1949 novel, *The Sheltering Sky* took a clinical look at an American couple, married for 10 years, travelling through Morocco, Algeria, Niger, and other exotic locales in the days following World War II, whose relationship is unraveling. Reflecting the emotional journey of the two characters, and the slow disintegration of their love story, Ryuichi Sakamoto wrote a rich, profusely emotive score, in which some of the pauses seem more revelatory than the musical accents. While a faint vocal in the background sometimes serves as an exotic counterpoint to the main themes ("On the Hill"), the local colors are provided by other selec-

tions, some composed by Richard Horowitz ("Marnia's Tent"), some featuring traditional musical groups from Burundi, Tunisia and other North African countries. The main theme, reprised on the piano, is particularly striking.

Shine ♫♫♫♫

1996, Philips Classics; from the movie *Shine*, Fine Line Features, 1996.

Album Notes: *Music:* David Hirschfelder; *Arrangements:* David Hirschfelder, Ricky Edwards; Orchestra conducted by Ricky Edwards; *Featured Artists:* David Helfgott, Ricky Edwards, David Hirschfelder (piano), Mary Doumany (harp), Geoffrey Payne (trumpet), Jeffrey Crellin (oboe), Geoffrey Lancaster (harpsichord), Gerald Keuneman (cello); *Album Producer:* David Hirschfelder; *Engineers:* Michael Letho, Robin Gray, David Williams, Adam Rhodes.

Selections: 1 With The Help Of God, Shine (3:19); 2 The Polonaise (F. Chopin) (1:20); 3 Did He Win? (:43); 4 Will You Teach Me? (2:33); 5 Scales To America (2:29); 6 Scenes From Childhood: "Almost Too Serious" (R. Schumann) (1:32) *Wilhelm Kempff;* 7 These People Are A Disgrace (1:15); 8 Raindrop Prelude (F. Chopin) (:42); 9 Your Father Your Family (2:34) *Noah Taylor;* 10 Tell Me A Story, Katharine (2:03); 11 Back Stage (1:16); 12 Punished For The Rest Of Your Life (1:02); 13 Moments Of Genius (:46); 14 La Campalesson (F. Liszt) (:49); 15 Letters To Katharine (1:27); 16 1st Movement Cadenza From The Rach. 3 (S. Rachmaninoff) (2:37); 17 Night Practice (S. Rachmaninoff)/Parcel From Katharine (1:19); 18 As If There Was No Tomorrow (1:44); 19 The Rach. 3 (S. Rachmaninoff) (4:17); 20 Complicato In Israel (1:56); 21 Raindrop Reprise (F. Chopin) (1:44); 22 Bath To Daisy Beryl (1:30); 23 Gloria (A. Vivaldi) (2:26); 24 Hungarian Rhapsody No. 2 (F. Liszt) (3:39); 25 Prelude In C # Minor (S. Rachmaninoff) (2:17); 26 Flight Of The Bumble Bee (N. Rimsky-Korsakov) (1:08); 27 Rach. 3 Reborn (S. Rachmaninoff) (1:13); 28 Goodnight Daddy (2:03); 29 A Loud Bit Of Ludwig's 9th (L. Van Beethoven) (:41); 30 Sospiro (F. Liszt) (2:45); 31 What's The Matter, David/Appassionata (L. Van Beethoven) (1:12); 32 La Campanella (F. Liszt) (1:02); 33 Familiar Faces/Rach. 3 Encore (S. Rachmaninoff) (1:35); 34 Nulla In Mundo Pax Sincera (A. Vivaldi) (4:38) *Jane Edwards.*

Review: The true, inspirational story of iconoclastic Australian concert pianist David Helfgott, who overcame severe debilitation and bouts of madness, caused in his youth by his father's total control and eventual rejection, *Shine* chronicles the artist's slow descent into the eccentric behavior that saw him spend 15 years of his life in a psychiatric hospital, unable to communicate except through his brilliant interpretations of complex works by Liszt, Rachmaninoff, and other classical composers. Helfgott himself is heard in this soundtrack album, in which he interprets some of the pieces that helped him regain some control of his life, as well as new works written by David Hirschfelder, who composed the original score, well in keeping with the overall tone of the whole film. Given its classical approach, this soundtrack album will obviously attract primarily listeners with a natural bent for this kind of music. Others, however, should discover in it pieces they might have heard in other situations, as well as instrumental cues that are enjoyably descriptive and reflective of a story that transcends musical genres.

Shining Through ♫♫♭

1992, RCA Records; from the movie *Shining Through,* 20th Century-Fox, 1992.

Album Notes: *Music*: Michael Kamen; *Orchestrations*: Michael Kamen, Jonathan Sacks, Albert Olson, Danny Troob, Sonny Kompanek, Homer Denison, Nick Ingram, Arnold Black; *Music Editor*: Joseph S. DeBeasi; The Alma Mater Symphony Orchestra of New York, conducted by Michael Kamen; *Album Producers*: Michael Kamen, Stephen McLaughlin, Christopher Brooks; *Engineer*: Stephen McLaughlin.

Selections: 1 Main Titles (2:02); 2 My Cousin Sophie (2:50); 3 Airport Goodbyes (1:54); 4 Enter Berlin (3:44); 5 The Boathouse (5:01); 6 Kinderstrasse (4:59); 7 Escape To Margrete (3:44); 8 Gestapo Search (4:11); 9 Exit Berlin (5:25); 10 The Swiss Border (3:26); 11 End Credits (2:18); 12 I'll Be Seeing You (S. Fain/I. Kahal)(3:25) *Deirdre Harrison*.

Review: Michael Douglas and Melanie Griffith star in this unlikely story of a woman with a Jewish background, in World War II Berlin, posing as a governess to a German officer, the better to help American forces fight the Nazis. Listening to Michael Kamen's "Main Titles," in this soundtrack album, one might have a feeling that the score would have some kind of sustained excitement to it. But with a few exceptions ("The Boathouse," "Exit Berlin"), the cues are expressionless orchestral swatches that probably served the narrative very well in the theatre, but don't add up to much in one's living room. The inclusion of "I'll Be Seeing You," performed by Deirdre Harrison, while perfectly pleasant, is equally baffling in the overall musical context.

Shipwrecked ♫♫♫♫

1991, Walt Disney Records; from the movie *Shipwrecked,* Walt Disney Pictures, 1991.

Album Notes: *Music*: Patrick Doyle; *Orchestrations*: Lawrence Ashmore, Fiachra Trench; *Engineer*: Chris Dibble.

Selections: 1 Opening Titles (1:39); 2 Death Of Howell (1:02); 3 Homecoming (:59); 4 The Sheriff's Arrival (1:11); 5 Off To The Sea (2:02); 6 Scrubbing The Deck (2:22); 7 The Flora Departs (:50); 8 Captain Madsen Is Poisoned (1:54); 9 Hakon Finds Mary (1:12); 10 Mary Is Rescued (1:39); 11 Exploring The Island (1:20); 12 Dreaming Of Home (1:06); 13 Hakon Survives A Fall (1:27); 14 Treasure Is Found (1:06); 15 Building The Traps (1:51); 16 Hakon Builds His Boat (1:56); 17 Pirates Discovered (1:34); 18 The Chase (1:59); 19 Home To Norway (3:35); 20 End Titles, Part I (2:39); 21 End Titles, Part II (3:29).

Review: Patrick Doyle, who seldom misses a beat, does a bang-up job in this high seas adventure score for a film released by Disney, the story of a young boy's test of strength and courage at the hands of evil pirates. Portraying in rich details the various events facing Hakon, the young Norwegian boy who, to avoid being sent to a home, embarks on a ship, Doyle used broad swatches of tonal colors to paint the myriad adventures that await him, from exploring a deserted South Pacific island, to discovering a treasure, and befriending a young girl, Mary, like him alone in the world. The cues, muscular and exhilarating, are wonderfully melodic and descriptive, making this joyous soundtrack album a delight to listen to.

Shogun Mayeda ♫♫♫♫

1991, Intrada Records; from the movie *Shogun Mayeda,* 1991.

Album Notes: *Music*: John Scott; *Orchestrations*: John Scott; *Music Editor*: Richard Allen; The Hungarian State Opera Orchestra, conducted by John Scott; *Album Producer*: John Scott; *Engineers*: Keith Grant, John Richards.

Selections: 1 Main Title: Shogun Mayeda (2:34); 2 Battle Of Sekigahara (3:55); 3 Inner Strength (1:33); 4 Yorimune's Court (:57); 5 Attack On Yorimune (2:05); 6 Mayeda's Grief (1:49); 7 Vasco, Servant Of The Devil (2:15); 8 Set Sail: Storm At Sea (8:15); 9 Memories Of The Lost Ones: Arrival (3:27); 10 Courts Of Spain (4:29); 11 Duel With Don Pedro (1:49); 12 The Kings Protector (2:22); 13 Leaving Spain (3:14); 14 Bath-Time On Board (2:08); 15 Pirate Attack (5:07); 16 Prisoners In Morocco (4:24); 17 Checkmate (2:33); 18 Cecilia Declares Her Love (4:12); 19 Fight To The Death (4:12); 20 Leaving Morocco (2:27); 21 On To New Adventures (4:18).

Review: An epic film about Japanese Samurais who journey to Spain to acquire guns, *Shogun Mayeda* proved underwhelming, but John Scott's score makes for an exciting and adventurous soundtrack. Given his vast knowledge of Japanese music and culture, Scott was ideally suited to this assignment. At 66:46 (21 tracks) there is perhaps more music than the album needs, but much of it is very good — large and epic, in which Scott blends the Hungarian State Opera Orchestra with a small group of Japanese instruments. (As is his usual practice, Scott also orchestrated the score himself). The main theme is attractively majestic and brassy, and appears within numerous guises and enough variety that it stays fresh throughout. "Battle of Sekigahara" is a pensive, atmospheric cue, somewhat reminiscent of Scott's *William The Conqueror*, but invested with an exotic Japanese flavor. The various battle scenes, sea journey, and love story elements give Scott much to play-off, and the result is a rich and colorful epic score. One's only dismay is that the music was not written for a more deserving film.

Paul Andrew MacLean

The Shooting Party/ Birds and Planes ♪♪♪♪

1991, JOS Records; from the movie *The Shooting Party*, European Classics, 1984, and the documentary *Birds and Planes*, 1964.

Album Notes: *Music:* John Scott; The Royal Philharmonic Orchestra, conducted by John Scott; *Album Producer:* John Scott; *Engineers:* Richard Lewzey (*The Shooting Party*), Adrian Kerridge (*Birds and Planes*).

Selections: *THE SHOOTING PARTY:* 1 Main Title (3:12); 2 The First Day (1:45); 3 The Letter (1:11); 4 Dinner At Nettleby (2:16); 5 Lionel And Olivia (2:39); 6 Thou Shalt Not Kill (3:06); 7 Luncheon By The Lake (2:08); 8 Ideals (1:51); 9 Signs In The Fire (:43); 10 The Poacher (1:32); 11 In Search Of Elfrida Beetle (1:27); 12 The Philosopher (1:08); 13 Spanish Dance (2:36); 14 Nettleby Polka (1:33); 15 The Finale Day (:56); 16 The Competition (2:08); 17 The Consequences (2:58); 18 Epilogue (4:29);

BIRDS AND PLANES: 19 The Awakening Of The Birds And Planes (3:21); 20 Take Off (1:01); 21 In Flight (5:46); 22 Condor And Glider (2:15); 23 End Of The Day (1:52).

Review: A film dealing with England's rural aristocracy on the eve of World War I, *The Shooting Party* is a beautiful evocation of the English countryside. Performed by the Royal Philharmonic, the score opens with a majestic trumpet fanfare, its bright sound evoking a misty morning sunrise. A pastoral flavor pervades the score, which is some of Scott's most particularly "English" sounding work ever. The "Epilogue" however ends the score in a somber tone, reprising the opening fanfare, counterpointed with a contorted variation on "The Last Outpost" (the British military funeral call), portending the ruin war is soon to bring upon the characters.

A pitfall of soundtrack albums is that film scores can have awkward moments on disc, due to their programmatic requirements. *The Shooting Party* however is somewhat unique in that it plays with a near-perfect fluidity from cue to cue (track changes are in fact rarely noticed). Also included on this CD is Scott's music for a 1964 Hugh Hudson documentary *Birds and Planes*. Featuring piano, string quartet and four basses, the score is largely atonal, yet ethereal, and shows off Scott's inventive gift for scoring for a smaller chamber ensemble.

Paul Andrew MacLean

The Shootist/Big Jake/ Cahill United States Marshall ♪♪♪♪♪

1986, Varese-Sarabande; from the movies *The Shootist*, Paramount Pictures, 1976; *Big Jake*, 20th Century-Fox, 1971; and *Cahill, United States Marshall*, Columbia Pictures, 1973.

Album Notes: *Music:* Elmer Bernstein; The Utah Symphony Orchestra, conducted by Elmer Bernstein; *Album Producer:* George Korngold; *Engineer:* Jeff Ostler.

Selections: *THE SHOOTIST:* 1 Main Title (3:16); 2 Ride (2:36); 3 In The Fire (2:57); 4 Epilogue (3:32);

CAHILL, UNITED STATES MARSHALL: 5 Nectie Party (4:22); 6 Nocturne (4:18);

BIG JAKE: 7 Riders (2:37); 8 Reunion (2:11); 9 All Jake (3:40); 10 Buzzards (3:34); 11 Going Home/Finale (2:15).

Review: Elmer Bernstein, whose western scores rank among the best and most descriptive ever written, conducted the Utah Symphony in this remarkable musical tribute to John Wayne, the quintessential movie cowboy, consisting of selections from the scores he composed for three of Wayne's last films. Neatly balancing the focus of each score between his signature staccato riding themes, and lovely romantic tunes, sometimes flavored with a south-of-the-border flair, Bernstein demonstrates again the reasons that have made him such a master in a genre that has known many exponents: his music throbs with color and excitement, painting vast landscapes against which the broad action can unfold with all the desired fire and passion. The orchestra milks the cues for all their worth, expressing the sweep and movement in them with evident delight.

See also: The Comancheros

A Show of Force 🎵🎵🎵🎵♪

1990, Colossal Records; from the movie *A Show of Force*, Paramount Pictures, 1990.

Album Notes: *Music*: Georges Delerue; *Music Editor*: Daniel Allen Carlin; The Graunke Symphony Orchestra, conducted by Georges Delerue; *Album Producer*: Georges Delerue; *Engineer*: Alan Snelling.

Selections: 1 Prologue (2:37); 2 Main Title (2:32); 3 The Hearing (1:04); 4 Flashback (2:40); 5 Kate To Cerro Marravilla (1:03); 6 Testimony (2:05); 7 Show Of Force (3:38); 8 Final Flashback (2:16); 9 Kate Argues With Dad (1:33); 10 Danse macabre (1:58); 11 Courtroom Photographs (1:38); 12 Remembrance (2:40); 13 The Hearings Begin (1:23); 14 Kate Watches Fireworks (1:20); 15 Forensic Science (1:19); 16 End Title (3:39).

Review: A passionate courtroom drama starring Amy Irving and Robert Duvall on opposite sides of a political murder investigation and trial in Brazil, *A Show of Force* inspired Georges Delerue to write a particularly strong score, in which the strains of samba are among the most ingratiating elements that combine to make it such a delightful audio experience. Delerue, a master melodist, wasted little time in idle textures, preferring instead to rely on solid, attractive tunes that meant something. And while his cues in this album are typically short, they all exude a definite musical flavor that is most endearing. Individual instruments (a harmonica, a guitar, a bandoneon) are used frequently throughout the score to paint vivid pictures that attract for the lovely musical images they evoke. It all adds up to a score that has great flair when appreciated on its own merits.

Showgirls ♪

1995, Interscope Records; from the movie *Showgirls*, United Artists, 1995.

Album Notes: *Song Producers*: Warne Livesey, David Bowie, Brian Eno, Roli Mosiman, Siouxsie & The Banshees, Buzz Mc-Coy, Tim O'Heir, Matthew Wilder, Youth, David A. Stewart, Freaks Of Desire, Toni Halliday, Alan Moulder; *Engineers*: Alan Moulder, Dave Richards, Roli Mosiman, Roger Bechirian, Tim O'Heir, Paul Palmer, Dave Wray, Chris Potter, Olle Romo, Tristin Norwell, Frank Filipetti, Nick Wollange; *Album Producers*: Robin Glenn, Alan Marshall; *Engineer*: Stephen Marcussen.

Selections: 1 Animal (K. McMahon)(4:08) *Prick*; 2 I'm Afraid Of Americans (D. Bowie/B. Eno)(5:12) *David Bowie*; 3 Kissing The Sun (F. Treichler)(4:31) *The Young Gods*; 4 New Skin (S. Sioux)(5:36) *Siouxsie & The Banshees*; 5 Wasted Time (3:56)

My Life With The Thrill Kill Kult; 6 Emergency's About To End (R. Zabrecky)(2:38) *Possum Dixon*; 7 You Can Do It (G. Tefani/E. Stefani/ T. Dumont/T. Kanal)(4:14) *No Doubt*; 8 Purely Sexual (X. Dphrepaulezz)(4:01) *Xavier*; 9 Hollywood Babylon (Killing Joke)(6:44) *Killing Joke*; 10 Beast Inside (Thomas/Campbell/Wilson)(5:43) *Freaks Of Desire*; 11 Helen's Face (T. Halliday/A. Moulder)(4:55) *Scylla*; 12 Somebody New (2:37) *My Life With The Thrill Kill Kult*; 13 Goddess (D.A. Stewart)(3:27) *David A. Stewart*; 14 Walk Into The Wind (D.A. Stewart/T. Hall)(5:37) *Andrew Carver*.

Review: When sex bombs at the box office, you know something's wrong, but that's exactly what happened with *Showgirls*, Paul Verhoeven's semi-nude Las Vegas extravaganza that hardly caused a ripple when it opened (and closed) in a matter of days. Listening to this sorry soundtrack compilation, one is almost tempted to dismiss it as quickly as the critics dismissed the film, if it were not for the fact that a couple of tracks feature some usually reliable favorites, Davie Bowie and Siouxsie & The Banshees. But if you can listen to the first track in its entirety, then welcome to this CD! After all, every kind of taste can be found in nature! That cover design, though, with its sinuous half-nude model, is attractive. That's about the only thing that is.

Shy People 🎵🎵🎵🎵

1987, Varese-Sarabande Records; from the movie *Shy People*, Cannon Films, 1987.

Album Notes: *Music*: Tangerine Dream; *Album Producers*: Edgar Froese, Christoph Franke, Paul Haslinger; *Engineers*: Edgar Froese, Christoph Franke, Paul Haslinger.

Selections: 1 Shy People (lyrics: E. Froese)(8:02) *Jacquie Virgil*; 2 Joe's Place (2:12); 3 The Harbor (lyrics: P. Haslinger/C. Franke)(4:06) *Diamond Ross*; 4 Nightfall (4:09); 5 Dancing On A White Moon (lyrics: E. Froese)(3:06) *Jacquie Virgil*; 6 Civilized Illusions (3:54); 7 Swamp Voices (3:15); 8 Transparent Days (3:05); 9 Shy People (5:04).

Review: *Shy People*, a film about a middle-class New York woman and her teenage daughter and the surprising journey they make to far-away, foreign Louisiana, was flavored by a remarkably effective score by Tangerine Dream with vocals. The inviting moods in the score not only enhance the story but sound downright attractive when heard in a different environment. The lyrical beauty of "Dancing on a White Moon" and "Transparent Days," particularly, demonstrates the electronic trio's unusual diversity.

The Silence of the Lambs ♫♫

1991, MCA Records; from the movie *The Silence of the Lambs*, Orion Pictures, 1990.

Album Notes: *Music:* Howard Shore; *Orchestrations:* Homer Denison; *Music Editor:* Suzana Peric; The Munich Symphony Orchestra, conducted by Howard Shore; *Album Producer:* Howard Shore; *Engineer:* Alan Snelling.

Selections: 1 Main Title (5:04); 2 The Asylum (3:53); 3 Clarice (3:03); 4 Return To The Asylum (2:35); 5 The Abduction (3:01); 6 Quid Pro Quo (4:41); 7 Lecter In Memphis (5:41); 8 Lambs Screaming (5:34); 9 Lecter Escapes (5:06); 10 Belvedere, Ohio (3:32); 11 The Moth (2:20); 12 The Cellar (7:02); 13 Finale (4:50).

Review: By virtue of the nature of the film's plot, the music composed by Howard Shore for *Silence of the Lambs* is dark, brooding, and ominous. While it makes for fine underscoring for the film, it suffers somewhat outside the context of the movie, becoming a bit more tedious with repeated listening. Disturbing to this listener are some very noticeable edits in the first minute or so of the opening track, the "Main Title." Wasn't the producer listening when they edited and mastered the album? As with a number of other recent film scores, this one's better off heard as you view the film.

Charles L. Granata

Silent Fall ♫♫♫♫

1994, Morgan Creek Records; from the movie *Silent Fall*, Warner Bros. Pictures, 1994.

Album Notes: *Music:* Stewart Copeland; *String Arrangements:* Michael Andreas; *Music Editor:* Michael Dittrick; *Producer:* Jeff Seitz; *Engineers:* Jeff Seitz, Joseph Magee.

Selections: 1 The First Clue (:19); 2 Sylvie's Charm (3:23); 3 A Cheerful Moment (3:18); 4 Lunch Madness (:37); 5 Our Parents' House (4:01); 6 Kitchen Cognition (1:55); 7 Bruce's Theme (1:51); 8 Smell Of Ghost (1:57); 9 Drama On Ice (6:19); 10 The Scene Of The Crime (1:49); 11 The Little Boy's Knife (:52); 12 Jake's Office Test (2:01); 13 Roof Top (1:24); 14 You're Quitting Again (2:18); 15 Main Title (5:04); 16 Healing (4:04) *Wynonna & Michael English*.

Review: An interesting thriller involving an autistic child, who witnesses the murder of his parents, and the psychiatrist who attempts to break the incoherent wall of silence that will lead to resolving the crime, *Silent Fall* found in Stewart Copeland a composer with a great deal of empathy for the film and its subject matter. The cues he wrote, many of them performed by an acoustic guitar, coupled with a clarinet or dueting with a piano over an orchestral texture ("Our Parents' House,"

STEPHEN SONDHEIM

Broadway composer and lyricist Stephen Sondheim is known for redefining the concept of American musicals. Considered one of the masterpieces of American theater, *West Side Story* established Sondheim as a prominent Broadway lyricist at the age of twenty-seven. He followed the show with the successful *Gypsy* in 1959. While 1962 marked the success of the burlesque comedy *A Funny Thing Happened on the Way to the Forum,* Sondheim was composer and lyricist for plays with varying degrees of acceptance over the next decades. Offbeat and experimental productions such as *Anyone Can Whistle, Do I Hear a Waltz?, Company, Follies, A Little Night Music,* and *Merrily We Roll Along* brought Sondheim an intellectual cult following.

A lyricist and composer who has been known to find inspiration in unlikely sources, Sondheim based his 1984 musical *Sunday in the Park With George* on pointillist art. Portraying painter George Seurat and the characters from Seurat's neo-impressionist work "A Sunday Afternoon on the Island of La Grand Jatte," the unusual musical was a commercial success as well as a 1985 Pulitzer Prize winner.

Born March 22, 1930, in New York City, Sondheim grew up in the affluent atmosphere of Central Park West in Manhattan. Sondheim found a close friend in a boy his age named Jamie Hammerstein, son of lyricist Oscar Hammerstein II, who became a surrogate father to the adolescent Sondheim, and his musical mentor in the years that followed.

Dubbed "Broadway's brightest hope," Sondheim has won numerous citations, including Grammy awards, Tony awards, and New York Drama Critics awards for best musical. Not always praised, but generally acknowledged for expanding the limits of the American musical, Sondheim alternately irritates and moves his audiences with songs and subject matter.

"Kitchen Cognition"), are very endearing and evocative. Others, using the full complement of the orchestra, also paint vivid images that seem more specifically adapted to the screen action, but still make a favorable impression. "Healing," performed by Wynonna and Michael English, is an appropriately fitting coda to the score.

Silverado 🦴🦴🦴🦴

1992, Intrada Records; from the movie *Silverado*, Columbia Pictures, 1985.

Album Notes: *Music*: Bruce Broughton; *Orchestrations*: Chris Boardman, Don Nemitz; Orchestra conducted by Bruce Broughton; *Album Producer*: Bruce Broughton; *Engineer*: Armin Steiner.

Selections: 1 Main Title (4:47); 2 To Turley (2:43); 3 The Getaway/Riding As One (4:21); 4 Ezra's Death (1:53); 5 The McKendrick Attack (1:38); 6 Augie Is Taken (2:36); 7 On To Silverado (6:26); 8 This Oughta Do (4:51); 9 Augie's Rescue (6:36); 10 Slick, Then McKendrick (4:03); 11 Goodbye, Cobb (2:06); 12 End Credits (We'll Be Back)(4:22).

Review: A big, brassy western score in the tradition laid down by his predecessors in the field is what Bruce Broughton created for this western in which every gesture is grand and exhilaratingly overstated. With good guys (drifters Kevin Kline, Scott Glenn and Kevin Costner) and bad guys (Brian Dennehy, delightful as a corrupt sheriff, and Jeff Goldblum) facing it off in a powerful showdown, everything in the film evokes the grandeur the West never was, with Broughton's score emphasizing every twist in the narrative with surprisingly effective cues that are greatly enjoyable. In his brief comments about the score, the composer talks about "the power, strength and energy" he found in the screenplay and tried to convey in his music. He succeeded admirably.

A Simple Twist of Fate 🦴🦴🦴

1994, Varese-Sarabande; from the movie *A Simple Twist of Fate*, Touchstone Pictures, 1994.

Album Notes: *Music*: Cliff Eidelman; *Orchestrations*: Mark McKenzie, Cliff Eidelman; *Music Editor*: Scott Stambler; Orchestra conducted by Cliff Eidelman; *Album Producer*: Cliff Eidelman; *Engineer*: Armin Steiner.

Selections: 1 A Simple Twist Of Fate (suite)(5:06); 2 Matilda's Fantasy (2:27); 3 The Bracelet (1:24); 4 Prelude To Tanny's Fate (3:03); 5 Floating On Air (1:57); 6 Red Is The Rose (1:38); 7 Okay You're Free (1:50); 8 Into The Light (3:07); 9 A New Life (3:05); 10 Red Is The Rose (reprise)(3:41); 11 Transcending (2:23); 12 Michael's Theme (2:06).

Review: Cliff Eidelman succeeds once again in creating another delightfully gentle, romantic musical fantasy. This time, it's about the bond between a man, who has shut the world out of his life, and the small child who comes into his care, changing everything he knows and believes in. Eidelman personifies this fusion of their souls though the use of a small female choir within the orchestra. The mood is occasionally broken by darker passages, such as the Bernard Herrmann-esque "Prelude to Tanny's Fate," and several variations on "Red Is The Rose." Eidelman performs the piano solo on "Michael's Theme."

David Hirsch

Sirens 🦴🦴🦴

1994, Milan Records; from the movie *Sirens*, Miramax Films, 1994.

Album Notes: *Music*: Rachel Portman; *Orchestrations*: Rachel Portman; Orchestra conducted by David Snell; *Album Producer*: Ian P. Hierons; *Engineer*: Chris Dibble.

Selections: 1 March Past Of The Kitchen Utensils (R. Vaughn Williams)(3:07) *The Queensland Symphony Orchestra, Patrick Thomas*; 2 The Yearning/Sirens Suite (3:27); 3 Sam Sawnoff's Pipe (:35); 4 Allure (4:16); 5 Sam Sawnoff's Horn (:46); 6 Sirens (2:50); 7 Calliope House (D. Richardson/R. Heenan/A. Marr)(3:49) *Boys Of The Lough*; 8 Hylas And The Nymphs/Waves (5:25); 9 Beckoning/Promise And Regret (2:13); 10 The Sprightly Don (2:15); 11 Mysterioso (2:26); 12 Candide (2:20); 13 Terra Australis (2:54); 14 Grey Funnel Line (C. Tawney)(3:02) *Silly Sisters: Maddy Prior & June Tabor*; 15 Ophelia (1:07).

Review: The *Sirens* album opens with Ralph Vaughan Williams's jaunty "March Past of the Kitchen Utensils," and the Rachel Portman score that follows blends the English precision of that piece with the lyricism of Georges Delerue and the quirky rhythms of Elmer Bernstein. Of course this is a crude approximation. Portman, a recent Oscar winner for *Emma,* has a distinct style that has grown out of these worthy influences. *Sirens* is a period piece about Hugh Grant, sensuality and naked supermodels, and the score is charming and buoyant, with dreamy, transparent orchestrations. The handful of different themes are self-contained and memorable—you will especially remember them over the course of the album, as each one is repeated almost verbatim several times.

Lukas Kendall

Sister Act 🦴🦴🦴

1992, Hollywood Records; from the movie *Sister Act*, Touchstone Pictures, 1992.

Album Notes: *Music*: Marc Shaiman; *Orchestrations*: Marc Shaiman, Jimmy Vivino, Tom Malone, Mark McKenzie, Hummie

Mann; *Music Editor*: Curtis Roush; Orchestra conducted by Artie Kane; *Featured Vocalists*: Deloris & The Sisters with Whoopi Goldberg, Maggie Smith, Andrea Robinson, Kathy Najimy, Mary Wickes, Rose Parenti, and Deloris & The Ronelles with Whoopi Goldberg, Jennifer Lewis, Charlotte Crossley; *Album Producer*: Marc Shaiman, Jimmy Vivino, Joel Moss, Maurice Starr; *Engineer*: Joel Moss.

Selections: 1 The Lounge Medley: (Love Is Like A) Heat Wave (B. Holland/L. Dozier/E. Holland)/My Guy (W. Robinson, Jr.)/I Will Follow Him (A. Altman/N. Gimbel/J. Plante/J.W. Stole/D. Roma) (3:39) *Deloris, The Ronelles*; 2 The Murder (2:33); 3 Getting Into The Habit (2:40); 4 Rescue Me (C. Smith/R. Miner) (2:54) *Fontella Bass*; 5 Hail Holy Queen (trad.) (3:29) *Deloris & The Sisters*; 6 Roll With Me Henry (E. James/H. Ballard/J. Otis) (2:56) *Etta James*; 7 Gravy (K. Mann/D. Appell) (2:11) *Dee Dee Sharp*; 8 My Guy (My God) (W. Robinson, Jr.) (2:35) *Deloris & The Sisters*; 9 Just A Touch Of Love (Everyday) (R. Clivilles) (5:38) *C&C Music Factory*; 10 Deloris Is Kidnapped (1:45); 11 Nuns To The Rescue (4:48); 12 Finale: I Will Follow Him (A. Altman/ N. Gimbel/J. Plante/D. Roma) (3:13) *Deloris & The Sisters*; 13 Shout (R. Isley/R. Isley/O. Isley) (4:16) *Deloris & The Sisters, The Ronelles*; 14 If My Sister's In Trouble (D. Barratt/W. Clift) (4:00) *Lady Soul*.

Review: For this amiable Whoopi Goldberg comedy, Marc Shaiman transforms a quartet of gospel hymns into Motown-styled rockers. The majority of the CD is taken up by these, and six straightforward rock tunes. Shaiman is given four cues (about 13 minutes) to present his underscore—mostly rhythm section action music. Adopting the film's initial Las Vegas setting, Shaiman's brassy music captures an appropriate Vegas lounge feel. In one cue, he orchestrally addresses several of the Motown tunes heard from the choir earlier, contrasting them with the Vegas jazzy chase-music as the villains, nuns, and Whoopi all meet up and settle their differences in a Vegas casino. This score may not be for everyone, and in fact it's got little actual film music, However, Shaiman's Motown-hymns are so catchy and his action cues nicely done enough to make the disc quite likable.

Randall D. Larson

Sisters ♫♫♫♫

1985, Southern Cross Records; from the movie *Sisters*, American International, 1973.

Album Notes: *Music*: Bernard Hermann; Orchestra conducted by Bernard Hermann; *Album Producer*: John Lasher; *Engineer*: Eric Tomlinson.

Selections: 1 Main Title (1:20); 2 The Dressing Room (1:13); 3 The Ferry/The Apartment/Breton (3:32); 4 The Scar/The Pills/Duo

(2:49); 5 The Cake/The Car/The Candles (2:19); 6 Phillip's Murder/Window View (2:55); 7 Clean-Up/Split-Screen/The Search (2:49); 8 Plastic Bag/The Dress/Cake Box (2:15); 9 Apartment House/The Windows (2:30); 10 The Couch (1:05); 11 Siamese Twins (2:31); 12 The Solution/The Clinic/Hypnotic Trance (3:47); 13 The Dream/The Syringe (5:07); 14 Separation Nightmare/Breton's Murder/Dirge (4:56); 15 Aftermath/Finale (2:02).

Review: After years of toiling on juvenile fantasy films in the '60s, Bernard Herrmann saw his reputation completely overhauled in the '70s as a new generation of film directors sought him out; chief among them was Brian DePalma, who mirrored the Hitchcock/ Herrmann collaboration by hiring the composer for a series of unusual suspense films. *Sisters*, a bizarre shocker about separated Siamese twins, is the weirdest of the bunch, and Herrmann's score is probably his most frightening and unsettling effort since his classic *Psycho* score. The opening is a terrifying fall through layers of descending string, celeste and xylophone textures and a hair-raising synthesized howl (played over microscopic fetal photography in the film's title sequence). This aggressive horror approach alternates with a delicate, lullabye-like chime melody throughout the score. It's not exactly easy listening, but it's a great example of how Herrmann was still able to push the boundaries of the medium even in the final years of his career.

Jeff Bond

Six Days Six Nights ♫♫♫♪

1994, Virgin Movie Music; from the movie *Six Days Six Nights*, Fine Line Features, 1994.

Album Notes: *Music*: Michael Nyman; The Michael Nyman Band, conducted by Michael Nyman; *Album Producer*: Michael Nyman; *Engineer*: Michael J. Dutton.

Selections: 1 Solitude (1:36); 2 Broken Glass (4:58); 3 Sisters (1:42); 4 The Intruder (2:40); 5 Waltzing The Bird (3:16); 6 A New Beginning (1:22); 7 Stolen Memories (1:09); 8 A la folie... (5:48); 9 The Streets Of Paris (2:39); 10 Love Forever (1:19); 11 Love Theme (2:35); 12 Point Of No Return (2:55); 13 Escape (3:37); 14 Broken Dreams (4:19); 15 Dark Fantasy (2:25); 16 Six Days Six Nights (5:51).

Review: Depending on the type of film he is scoring, Michael Nyman can be painfully austere or brightly illuminating. *Six Days Six Nights*, an intimate, powerful and intense tale of sexual intrigue and all-consuming passion, directed by Diane Kurys, must have inspired him particularly. While still evidencing strains of minimalist writing, one of the composer's characteristic elements of style, his score is exquisitely composed, with cues that exude a florid melodic aura, and themes that, for once, are pleasantly attractive. The Michael Nyman Band, a conglomeration of talented "regulars," involving a string section, a brass ensemble, and a basic rhythm group, plays the selections with evident empathy and delight, something which comes across in specific cues like "Sisters," "Waltzing the Bird," "A la folie...," "Love Forever," and the title track, among the best moments in this recording.

Six Degrees of Separation 🎵🎵

1994, Elektra Records; from the movie *Six Degrees of Separation*, M-G-M, 1994.

Album Notes: *Music*: Jerry Goldsmith; *Orchestrations*: Arthur Morton; *Music Editor*: Ken Hall; The Victorian Philharmonic Orchestra of Melbourne, conducted by Jerry Goldsmith; *Featured Performers*: Stockard Channing (Ouisa), Will Smith (Paul), Donald Sutherland (Flan), Mary Beth Hurt (Kitty), Bruce Davison (Larkin), Jeffrey Abrams (Doug); *Album Producer*: Jerry Goldsmith; *Engineer*: Robin Gray.

Selections: 1 Ouisa And Flan (1:53); 2 Six Degrees Of Separation (1:22) *Stockard Channing*; 3 Just One Of Those Things (C. Porter)(1:06); 4 Sidney Poitier (1:26) *Will Smith*; 5 Give Six (P. Grabowsky)(2:32); 6 Painters (:30) *Donald Sutherland*; 7 There Is A God (1:30); 8 Cats (:51) *Stockard Channing*; 9 The Teacher (1:36); 10 Dream About Painters (1:09) *Donald Sutherland*; 11 The Blade (:43); 12 Imagination (1:55) *Will Smith*; 13 The Kiss (:55); 14 Dream Sequence (:44) *Will Smith*; 15 Safe Trip (:45); 16 Both Sides (:25); 17 Do We Have A Story To Tell You (1:28) *Stockard Channing, Donald Sutherland, Mary Beth Hurt, Bruce Davison*; 18 No Heart (1:05); 19 You're An Idiot (:44) *Jeffrey Abrams*; 20 Not Family (:33); 21 The Truth (:29) *Stockard Channing*; 22 Quartet in G Minor, Op. 10 (C. Debussy)(1:18); 23 Listen To Me (2:04) *Will Smith*; 24 I Read Today (2:21) *Stockard Channing*; 25 No Heart (5:05).

Review: This score for Fred Schiepsi's film adaptation of the Broadway play is one of Jerry Goldsmith's most intelligent and beautifully crafted scores of the '90s... unfortunately it's also one of the few Goldsmith scores that fails to stand on its own very well when listened to apart from the film. Most of the music is based around a tango Goldsmith wrote for the title theme, but it's an extremely brief, low-key effort and the producers of this album have judiciously padded out the CD's running length with generous doses of out-of-context dialogue from the film. This is an approach that has long been rendered obsolete by the availability of the videocassette, and programming out the verbiage to get to the score is probably more effort than most people will want to go through. Goldsmith's music interacts with the onscreen images and ideas brilliantly, but the album is a hard sell.

What is one to make of this "soundtrack" album which, with one single exception (the last track), only offers brief snippets of Jerry Goldsmith's score, laced with excerpts from the film's dialogue. As an audio experience, the first time around it holds one's interest, but repeated listening soon becomes tiresome, and while Goldsmith's music might have proved compelling had it been presented without interruptions, here it becomes simply annoying and an intrusion. Don't blame the composer, however, unless he was the one responsible for putting the album together in this manner.

Jeff Bond/Didier C. Deutsch

The 6th Man 🎵🎵

1997, Hollywood Records; from the movie *The 6th Man,* Touchstone Pictures, 1997.

Album Notes: *Music*: Marcus Miller; *Song Producers*: Emosia, Doug E. Fresh, Vassal Benford, Big Band Theory, Savory, Chad "Dr. Ceuss" Elliott, Guru, Joleen Belle, Trevor Horn, Troy Taylor, Charles Farrar, Johnny Gill, Laytham Armor, Christopher Troy, Zac Harmon, Dominica, Tim Laws.

Selections: 1 Like This And Like That (Emosia/M. Lorello) (4:04) *LaKiesha Berri*; 2 Superstition (S. Wonder/D.E. Fresh) (4:57) *Doug E. Fresh*; 3 Keep On Risin' (V. Benford) (4:47) *JADE, Lil' Rachett, VAZ*; 4 Tasty (R. Robinson/E. Wilcox/T. Hardson) (5:15) *Pharcyde*; 5 Deeper Than Blood (T. Lacy) (4:19) *Savory*; 6 Make Me Say It Again Gil (O. Isley/R. Isley/R. Isley/E. Isley/M. Isley/C. Jasper) (6:36) *Stokley Of Mint Condition*; 7 Illest Man (K. Elam/J. Sims) (3:37) *Guru*; 8 Down And Dirty (J. Belle/K. Jackson) (3:37) *J' Son*; 9 Invisible (C. Sturken/E. Rogers/Public Demand) (4:15) *Public Demand*; 10 All He's Supposed To Be (J. Gill/T. Taylor/C. Farrar/C. Thomas) (4:31) *Johnny Gill*; 11 Bumpin' Coasties (M. Bell/L. Armor) (4:19) *Marquis*; 12 Get Up (Z. Harmon/C. Troy/R. Herrera) (4:28) *Dominica*; 13 Trouble (T. Laws/P. Curran) (4:35) *Ortis*; 14 Anything Can Happen (Theme From The 6th Man) (5:22).

Review: R&B and rap of the new school variety, whether it's New Jack crooning from Johnny Gill ("All He's Supposed to Be") or slamming hip-hop by Doug E. Fresh ("Superstition) and Pharcyde ("Tasty"). There's not a lot of A-matter here, however, making this more of a commercial than a creative exercise.

Gary Graff

Sleepers 🎵🎵🎵

1996, Philips Records; from the movie *Sleepers,* Warner Bros., 1996.

Album Notes: *Music*: John Williams; *Music Editor*: Ken Wannberg; Orchestra conducted by John Williams; *Featured Solo-*

ists: James Thatcher (French horn), Janet Ferguson (flute); *Album Producer*: John Williams; *Engineer*: Shawn Murphy; *Assistant Engineer*: Sue McLean.

Selections: 1 Sleepers At Wilkinson (3:41); 2 Hell's Kitchen (5:23); 3 The Football Game (4:09); 4 Saying The Rosary (6:53); 5 The Trip To Wilkinson (2:35); 6 Time In Solitary (4:23); 7 Revenge (2:46); 8 Michael's Witness (4:09); 9 Learning The Hard Way (5:21); 10 Last Night At Wilkinson (3:51); 11 Father Bobby's Decision (3:56); 12 Reliving The Past (3:40); 13 Reunion and Finale (5:30).

Review: Outstanding is the best word to characterize this masterful, Oscar-nominated score from John Williams, a full-blooded dramatic outing that stands as the composer's finest "serious" score of the 1990s (i.e. music written for a supposedly award-worthy picture). Quite a contrast from the excellent though rather one-dimensional attributes of his scores for Oliver Stone's *JFK* and *Nixon*, Williams here ventures into a challenging musical landscape filled with often dissonant, eclectic combinations of electric guitar, synthesizer and full orchestra, dominated by a central motive that fails to find a resolution until the very end. Along the way, the composer treats us to a veritable "tour de force'" of musical cues that are by turns both poignant and disturbing, seductive yet unsettling, marked by tracks that simply explode with musical energy ("The Football Game"). Williams builds his score perfectly from the start, culminating in a truly lyrical finale that puts an ideal cap on a score that's easily the best of 1996, and further proof that great music can come from films that fail to live up to their potential.

Andy Dursin

Sleeping with the Enemy ♫♫♫

1991, Columbia Records; from the movie *Sleeping with the Enemy*, 20th Century-Fox, 1991.

Album Notes: *Music*: Jerry Goldsmith; *Orchestrations*: Alexander Courage; *Music Editor*: Ken Hall; orchestra conducted by Jerry Goldsmith; *Album Producer*: Jerry Goldsmith; *Engineer*: Bruce Botnick; *Assistant Engineer*: Sue McLean.

Selections: 1 Morning On The Beach (2:34); 2 The Funeral (3:24); 3 Brown-Eyed Girl (V. Morrison)(3:07) *Van Morrison*; 4 Thanks Mom (4:26); 5 Spring Cleaning (2:31); 6 The Ring (2:09); 7 A Brave Girl (3:50); 8 Fears (2:57); 9 What Did He Do (2:28); 10 The Storm (3:13); 11 The Carnival (2:55); 12 Remember This (7:57).

Review: Jerry Goldsmith has provided one of his loveliest romantic scores for this drama of spousal abuse and liberation,

with two contrasting motifs—a very pretty love theme for Julia Roberts and a percussion-and-synth ambiance for her abusive husband. Roberts' theme is arranged for woodwinds over weaving strings which recall the swaying motion of the ocean into which her character fakes her death. The husband's ambient theme, with its synth rustles, sharp drum pounds and rhythmic bell gongs, is associated with the terror Roberts lived under and which she faces when her husband discovers her whereabouts and confronts her again. While "The Funeral" contrasts both motifs sequentially, in "The Ring," Goldsmith meshes them into a single variation—the powerful, frightening ambiance for the husband facing up to Roberts' lovely melody at the moment he discovers he has been deceived. The score ends on a victorious note, with the theme for Roberts' character soaring freely, unshackled at last from the oppressive presence of her husband's violent domination.

Randall D. Larson

Sleepless in Seattle ♫♫♫♫

1993, Epic Soundtrax; from the movie *Sleepless in Seattle*, TriStar Pictures, 1993.

Album Notes: *Featured Performers*: Jimmy Durante, Louis Armstrong, Nat King Cole, Dr. John, Carly Simon, Gene Autry, Joe Cocker, Harry Connick, Jr., Tammy Wynette, Celine Dion & Clive Griffin.

Selections: 1 As Time Goes By (H. Hupfeld)(2:29) *Jimmy Durante*; 2 A Kiss To Build A Dream On (B. Kalmar/H. Ruby/O. Hammerstein II)(3:02) *Louis Armstrong*; 3 Stardust (H. Carmichael/M. Parrish)(3:15) *Nat King Cole*; 4 Makin' Whoopee (W. Donaldson/G. Kahn)(4:09) *Dr. John, Rickie Lee Jones*; 5 In The Wee Small Hours Of The Morning (D. Mann/B. Hilliard)(3:16) *Carly Simon*; 6 Back In The Saddle Again (G. Autry/R. Whitley)(2:35) *Gene Autry*; 7 Bye Bye Blackbird (R. Henderson/M. Dixon)(3:30) *Joe Cocker*; 8 A Wink And A Smile (M. Shaiman/R. McLean)(2:48) *Harry Connick Jr.*; 9 Stand By Your Man (B. Sherrill/T. Wynette)(2:41) *Tammy Wynette*; 10 An Affair To Remember (H. Warren/H. Adamson/L. McCarey)(2:31); 11 Make Someone Happy (J. Styne/B. Comden/A. Green)(1:52) *Jimmy Durante*; 12 When I Fall In Love (E. Hayman/V. Young)(4:21) *Celine Dion, Clive Griffin*.

Review: Without a doubt, this compilation (for it is truly a compilation, as opposed to a recording featuring music originally composed for the film) is one of the finest collections of its nature, which seem to be *de rigueur* for many of Hollywood's most popular films of late. While the centerpiece of the recording is the incredibly successful chart hit "When I Fall In Love" (performed by Celine Dion and Clive Griffin), there are time honored standards that should warm the hearts of every music lover: Jimmy Durante's "As Time Goes By," Nat Cole's "Stardust" and "A Kiss to Build a Dream On" (with Louis Armstrong's distinct imprint) emerging as highlights. As well, a number of contemporary artists offer their unique take on the "classics," with excellent performances of "Bye Bye Blackbird" by Joe Cocker, and "Makin' Whoopee" by Dr. John and Ricki Lee Jones. It's refreshing to see Hollywood's directors utilizing one of our most important cultural treasures, American popular music, to enhance the mood and texture of their films, introducing these essential songs and interpretations to a new, younger generation of filmgoers. If nothing else, this recording serves that purpose—in a romantically delightful manner!

Charles L. Granata

Sliver ♫♫♭

1993, Virgin Movie Music; from the movie *Sliver*, Paramount Pictures, 1993.

Album Notes: *Featured Artists*: UB40, Enigma, Fluke, Massive Attack, Lords Of Acid, Shaggy, Neneh Cherry, Aftershock, Heaven 17, The Young Gods, Verve, Bigod 20; *Producers*: Michael Cretu, Jonny Dollar, Booga Bear, Jade 4 U, Oliver Adams, Praga Khan, Tommy D., Roli Mosimann, John Leckie, Nino Tielmann; *Album Producer*: Tim Sexton; *Engineer*: Dan Hersch.

Selections: 1 Can't Help Falling In Love (G.D. Weiss/H. Peretti/L. Creatore)(3:23) *UB40*; 2 Carly's Song (M. Cretu)(3:46) *Enigma*; 3 Slid (M. Bryant/M. Tournier/J. Fugler)(3:43)*Fluke*; 4 Unfinished Sympathy (G. Marshall/R. Del Naja/A. Vowles/J. Sharp/S. Nelson)(5:07) *Massive Attack*; 5 The Most Wonderful Girl (O. Adams/N. Van Lierop/M. Engelen)(4:45) *Lords Of Acid*; 6 Oh Carolina (3:05) *Shaggy*; 7 Move With Me (N. Cherry/C. McVey)(5:19) *Neneh Cherry*; 8 Slave To The Vibe (J. Smith/P. Lord/G. Routte)(5:44) *Aftershock*; 9 Penthouse And Pavement (I. Marsh/M. Ware/G. Gregory)(3:56) *Heaven 17*; 10 Skinflowers (R. Mosimann/Franz)(5:06) *The Young Gods*; 11 Star Sail (S. Jones/P. Salisbury/N. McCabe/R. Ashcroft)(3:57) *Verve*; 12 Wild At Heart (M. Nikolai/Z. Campisi)(4:13) *Bigod 20*; 13 Carly's Loneliness (M. Cretu)(3:11) *Enigma*.

Review: A very modern-sounding collection of disassociated bands and songs. UB40 had a hit with its reggaefied rendition of Elvis Presley's "Can't Help Falling in Love." Dig deep, and you'll find a goodly number of cutting edge artists—Enigma, Neneh Cherry, Shaggy, Lords of Acid, Massive Attack—though these are not necessarily their shining moments. Not one you'd be ashamed to own, but not something you'll play a lot, either.

Gary Graff

Smilla's Sense of Snow ♫♫♫♫

1997, Teldec Records; from the movie *Smilla's Sense of Snow*, Constantin Films, 1997.

Album Notes: *Music*: Herry Gregson-Williams, Hans Zimmer; *Orchestrations*: Bruce Fowler; *Music Editor*: Adam Smalley; Orchestra conducted by Harry Gregson-Williams; *Album Producer*: Slamm Andrews; *Engineer*: Geoff Foster.

Selections: 1 Greenland: Anno 1859 (4:14); 2 Isaiah's Theme (2:06); 3 Smilla Learns More (4:22); 4 Threatened With Jail (4:47); 5 Who Is The Mechanic? (4:26); 6 Secrets Of The Ship (7:11); 7 Chase At Sea (8:07); 8 Greenland Revisited (10:28); 9 The Truth Revealed (6:41); 10 End Titles (2:23).

Review: A brilliant thriller, based on a novel by Peter Hoeg, *Smilla's Sense of Snow* stars Julia Ormond as a half-Inuit scientist who reveals intuitive powers of investigation when she attempts to solve the murder of a young neighbor. Reflecting the increasing tension in the story, as well as its more metaphysical aspects, Hans Zimmer and Harry Gregson-Williams have devised a score with its share of suspense. In addition to providing specific themes for the murdered boy ("Isaiah's Theme"), and a mysterious man only known as The Mechanic, who helps Smilla uncover the truth though his real motives for doing so are as enigmatic as his personality ("Who Is The Mechanic?"), the two composers have deftly bookended the score with two cues ("Greenland: Anno 1859" and "Greenland Revisited"), in which the recurring motifs evoke another mysterious event 140 years earlier that has a direct bearing on the current action. Though occasionally predictable, and often punctuated by riffs that give it an artificial sense of urgency, the score is nonetheless quite effective in establishing the aura of mystery that pervades the whole film until its satisfying conclusion.

Smoke ♫♫♭

1995, Miramax Records; from the movie *Smoke*, Miramax Pictures, 1995.

Album Notes: *Music*: Rachel Portman; *Album Producer*: Jeffrey Kimball.

Selections: 1 Brooklyn Boogie (L. Prima/E. Bostic) (3:02) *Louis Prima*; 2 Cigarettes And Coffee (J. Butler/E. Thomas/J. Walker) (5:37) *The Jerry Garcia Band*; 3 Downtown Train (T. Waits) (3:51) *Tom Waits*; 4 Augie's Photos (2:28); 5 Baby Wants Kisses (Annabouboula) (4:20) *Annabouboula*; 6 Supa Star (C. Martin/J. Felder/J. Heath) (4:16) *Group Home*; 7 Sexy Dumb Dumb (S. George) (4:00) *Sophia George*; 8 Hong Kong (J. Hawkins/I. Nahan) (2:21) *Screamin' Jay Hawkins*; 9 Prelude And Fugue For Piano No. 1 in C Major, op. 87 (D. Shotakovich) (5:33) *Tatiana Nikolaeva*; 10 Snow Story (2:23); 11 Innovent

When You Dream (Barroom) (T. Waits) (4:16) *Tom Waits*; 12 Smoke Gets In Your Eyes (J. Kern/O. Harbach) (4:25) *The Jerry Garcia Band.*

Review: A weird little outing, with two songs each from the Jerry Garcia Band ("Cigarettes and Coffee" and "Smoke Gets in Your Eyes") and Tom Waits ("Downtown Train" and "Innocent When You Dream"). Cheers for including Louis Prima's "Brooklyn Boogie" and Screaming Jay Hawkins' "Hong Kong," but with a skimpy nine songs, there's not a great deal of heft to this one.
Gary Graff

Sneakers ♫♫♫

1992, Columbia Records; from the movie *Sneakers*, Universal Pictures, 1992.

Album Notes: *Music*: James Horner; *Orchestrations*: Brad Dechter, Frank Bennett; *Music Editor*: Jim Henrikson; Orchestra conducted by James Horner; *Featured Musicians*: Branford Marsalis, Mike Fisher, Ralph Grierson, James Horner, Joel C. Peskin, Ian Underwood; *Album Producer*: James Horner; *Engineer*: Shawn Murphy.

Selections: 1 Main Title (2:59); 2 "Too Many Screts" (6:17); 3 The Sneakers Theme (3:35); 4 Cosmo... Old Friend (7:09); 5 The Hand-Off (3:08); 6 Planning The Sneak (3:22); 7 Playtronics Break-In (10:39); 8 The Escape/ Whistler's Rescue (3:24); 9 Goodbye (3:25); 10 "...And The Blind Shall See" (4:29).

Review: Former "Tonight Show" bandleader Branford Marsalis found great success performing and improvising on Jerry Goldsmith's lovely score for *The Russia House* in 1990, and filmmaker Phil Alden Robinson thought it would be a good idea to unite Marsalis' saxophone with composer James Horner when scoring *Sneakers*, Robinson's 1992 follow-up to *Field of Dreams*. While not as memorable as his *Russia House* stint, Marsalis' collaboration with Horner on the *Sneakers* score is still one of the least forgettable elements in Robinson's cliche-ridden thriller—the music is fast-paced and energetic enough, with a sprightly main theme working hard to offset some of the recycled material in the rest of Horner's work. Thus, when Marsalis is spotlighted, the score is pleasantly diverting, but listeners might want to skip past the tired "suspense" music in Horner's dramatic underscore.
Andy Dursin

Soap Dish ♫♫♫♫♭

1991, Varese-Sarabande Records; from the movie *Soap Dish*, Paramount Pictures, 1991.

Album Notes: *Music*: Alan Silvestri; *Orchestrations*: Alan Silvestri, James Campbell; *Music Editor*: Jim Harrison; *Auricle/*

Synclavier Programming: David Bifano; The Skywalker Symphony Orchestra, conducted by Alan Silvestri; *Album Producer*: Alan Silvestri; *Engineer*: Dennis Sands.

Selections: 1 Mambo Glamoroso (3:51); 2 You're Fired (Just Kidding)(1:38); 3 I Want Celeste To Burn (1:09); 4 On The Machine (:46); 5 Mr. Barne's Cha Cha Cha (2:04); 6 America's Sweetheart (underbelly)(2:11); 7 In The Soup Kitchen (:51); 8 Makeover Mambo (2:29); 9 El sol tambien se pone (L. Felsenstein) (instrumental)(3:08); 10 Mambo Incognito (2:22); 11 Miss Moorehead's Tango (:49); 12 Life Is Soap Is Life Is... (1:58); 13 Mambo Nervoso (:35); 14 Lori Meets The Pres (1:10); 15 Sunset's Showdown (1:48); 16 Brain Surgery (1:44); 17 She's A Boy (2:16); 18 El sol tambien se pone (L. Felsenstein)(3:03) *Ludar.*

Review: Alan Silvestri scored this riotous screwball comedy spoof of daytime TV dramas utilizing variations on the West Indian dance styles of mambo, tango and rumba. As the cast of self important actors plot to ruin each other's career, Silvestri amplifies their machinations into epic proportions of absurdity. He even has a theme for Sally Field's "America's Sweetheart" that's so sugary sweet, listening to it will rot out your teeth. The soundtrack is so bright, bouncy, and entertaining that it's more than likely to be the only underscore you can dance to.
David Hirsch

Solomon and Sheba

1996, DRG Records; from the movie *Solomon and Sheba*, United Artists, 1960.
See: The Vikings

Some Came Running

1992, Cloud Nine Records; from the movie *Some Came Running*, M-G-M, 1959.
See: Kings Go Forth

Some Kind of Wonderful ♫♫♫♭

1987, MCA Records; from the movie *Some Kind of Wonderful*, Paramount Pictures, 1987.

Album Notes: *Album Producer*: Stephen Hague.

Selections: 1 Do Anything (P. Shelley)(3:38) *Pete Shelley*; 2 Brilliant Mind (T. Whelan/J. Irvin/H. Lee/S. Still)(4:10) *Furniture*; 3 Cry Like This (D. Joyner/T. Cook/S. Hague)(4:04) *Blue Room*; 4 I Go Crazy (J. Mitchell/K. Mills/N. Marsh/R. Barker)(3:50) *Flesh For Lulu*; 5 She Loves Me (S. Duffy) (3:40) *Stephen Duffy*; 6 The Hardest Walk (J. Reid/W. Reid)(3:10) *The*

Jesus And Mary Chain; 7 The Shyest Time (P.M. Walsh)(3:31) *The Apartments*; 8 Miss Amanda Jones (M. Jagger/K. Richards)(3:12) *The March Violets*; 9 Can't Help Falling In Love (L. Creatore/H. Peretti/G. Weiss)(3:07) *Lick The Tins*; 10 Turn To The Sky (L. Elliott/T. Ashton/C. Murray)(3:58) *The March Violets*.

Review: A lively contemporary love triangle, starring Eric Stoltz, Mary Stuart Masterson, Craig Sheffer and Lea Thompson, *Some Kind of Wonderful* is a predictably romantic comedy, which elicited a hard-driving rock soundtrack. While all the songs here may not always evidence the same level of quality, some, like "Brilliant Mind," "Cry Like This," "The Shyest Time" and "Turn to the Sky" are better than average. Also interesting in this collection is Lick The Tins' rendition of the classic "Can't Help Falling in Love," with lead vocalist Allison Marr displaying an engaging sense of urgency in her breathy delivery.

Some Mother's Son ♪♪♪⹁

1996, Atlantic Records; from the movie *Some Mother's Son*, Columbia Pictures, 1996.

Album Notes: *Music*: Bill Whelan; *Orchestrations*: Bill Whelan; *Music Editor*: Tom Drescher; The Irish Film Orchestra, conducted by Bill Whelan; *Featured Performers*: Declan Masterson (Uilleann pipes, bouzouki, whistles), Nikola Parov (gadulka, kavals), Kenneth Edge (soprano sax), Eileen Ivers (fiddle), Mairtin O'Connor (accordion), Neil O'Callanain (bouzouki), Desi Reynolds, Noel Eccles (percussion), Jimmy Higgins (bodhran, percussion); *Album Producer*: Bill Whelan; *Engineers*: Andrew Boland, Philip Begley.

Selections: 1 Some Mother's Son (Opening Titles)(2:35); 2 Bridge Attack (2:42); 3 The Seabird (4:55) *Eleanor McEvoy*; 4 Watching Annie's House (:58); 5 Escape And Capture (2:28); 6 At The Police Station (2:17); 7 Meeting Bobby Sands (1:18); 8 No Slop Out (1:54); 9 The Kiss (1:48); 10 Alice's Theme (1:57); 11 Prison Mass (:40); 12 Bobby Calls The Strike (:53); 13 Kathleen Joins Up (1:40); 14 Roisin Dubh (trad.) *Eleanor McEvoy*; 15 The Strikers Stand Firm (2:40); 16 The Seabird (instrumental)(2:35); 17 Kathleen's Decision (2:19); 18 I Had To Do It (1:47); 19 The Seabird (reprise)(1:47) *Eleanor McEvoy*; 20 Some Mother's Son (Oganaigh Oig)(4:24) *Eleanor McEvoy*.

Review: Possibly because this score was written by the composer of *Riverdance*, as soon as you hear the first explosive strains of "Bridge Attack," you might be tempted to look around to see if Michael Flatley, the self-anointed "Lord of the Dance," or any other tap-dancing misfit from these big dance extravaganzas, accompanied by a line-up likely to send the Rockettes at Radio City Music Hall into fits of envy, is not prancing around your living room. Actually, this "celtic" score is not really that bad, with effective cues conveying the sense of suspense and urgency in the screen narrative, yet another story about the struggle of Northern Irish to free themselves from British domination. Seen from the perspective of the mothers of the IRA freedom fighters, the film presents the usual share of violence, anguish, armed rebellion, jail terms, and everything that has fueled other films like this one for decades. Nothing in the rest of the score matches the excitement in "Bridge Attack," though one cue, "The Seabird," is striking in its poetic evocation, and several vocals (including some in Gaelic) enhance the musical proceedings.

Something to Talk About ♪♪♪♪

1995, Varese-Sarabande; from the movie *Something to Talk About*, Warner Bros. Pictures, 1995.

Album Notes: *Music*: Hans Zimmer, Graham Preskett; *Orchestrations*: Bruce Fowler, Ladd McIntosh, Suzette Moriarty, Elizabeth Finch; *Music Editor*: Laura Perlman; *Featured Musicians*: Mike Lang (piano), Jimmy Johnson, Nathan East (bass), John Van Tongeren (Hammond B-3), Carlos Vega, Russ Kunkel (drums), Greg Leisz (dobro), Pete Haycock, Tim Pierce, Bob Duspit, Tim May (guitars), Graham Preskett (violin, harmonica), Bill Knopf, Tim May (banjo), Mike Fisher, Bob Zimmitti (percussion); *Album Producer*: Hans Zimmer, Jay Rifkin; *Engineers*: Jay Rifkin, Alan Meyerson.

Selections: 1 Dysfunctionally Yours (9:36); 2 Kings Of Carolina (1:21); 3 Dinner For Two (10:02); 4 The Witches (2:10); 5 Grace (5:39); 6 Southern Comfort (3:10); 7 Tall Horses (4:50).

Review: A comedy about marital infidelities, with fresh new spins to enliven a tale as old as humanity itself, *Something to Talk About* found composers Hans Zimmer and Graham Preskett in eloquent verve for a score often tartly ingratiating and buoyantly effervescent. Echoing some of the caustic accents in this story of a Southern young woman (Julia Roberts) and her apparently unfaithful husband (Dennis Quaid), the score details the salient moments in the narrative, particularly in two longer cues, "Dysfunctionally Yours," and "Dinner for Two," echoing in the latter some of the emotional depth in a half-baked attempt at reconciliation between the two main characters. Driven by a large number of acoustic instruments (guitars, dobro, violin, harmonica and banjo, all of which evoke the kind of music one might hear in a small Southern community), the album is quite enjoyable on its own terms.

Something Wild ♫♫♫

1986, MCA Records; from the movie *Something Wild*, Orion Pictures, 1986.

Album Notes: *Song Producers*: David Byrne; Jerry Harrison & Fine Young Cannibals; UB-40; Danny Elfman, Steve Bartek; Bob Rose; Sonny Okossun; New Order; Percy Chin, Jah Life, Arthur Baker.

Selections: 1 Loco de amor (Crazy For Love) (3:45) *David y Celia*; 2 Ever Fallen In Love (3:48) *Fine Young Cannibals*; 3 Zero, Zero Seven Charlie (3:48) *UB-40*; 4 Not My Slave (4:23) *Oingo Boingo*; 5 You Don't Have To Cry (3:57) *Jimmy Cliff*; 6 With You Or Without You (4:46) *Steve Jones*; 7 Highlife (3:40) *Sonny Okossun*; 8 Man With A Gun (4:32) *Jerry Harrison*; 9 Temptation (3:28) *New Order*; 10 Wild Thing (4:05) *Sister Carol*.

Review: An unusually clever thriller, starring Jeff Daniels and Melanie Griffith, *Something Wild* adroitly derived some of its strength from the combined musical contributions of performers like Fine Young Cannibals, Oingo Boingo, UB-40, New Order, and Jimmy Cliff, admittedly an odd assortment, whose songs delineated the contemporary feel of the action and helped propel it. "Wild Thing" (not the Jimi Hendrix tune) seems a fitting ending to the story and to the album.

Somewhere in Time ♫♫♫♫

1985, MCA Records; from the movie *Somewhere in Time*, Universal Pictures, 1980.

Album Notes: *Music*: John Barry; *Orchestrations*: John Barry; Orchestra conducted by John Barry; *Album Producer*: John Barry; *Engineer*: Dan Wallin.

Selections: 1 Somewhere In Time (2:58); 2 The Old Woman (2:49); 3 The Journey Back In Time (4:22); 4 A Day Together (6:02); 5 Rhapsody On A Theme Of Paganini (S. Rachmaninoff)(2:57) *Chet Switkowski*; 6 Is He The One (3:10); 7 The Man Of My Dreams (1:35); 8 Return To The Present (4:04); 9 Theme From "Somewhere In Time" (3:20) *Roger Williams*.

Review: There are "classics" and then there are classics. John Barry's score for *Somewhere in Time* is one of those instances where film music completely transcends the movie it originates from, and takes on a life of its own outside of its original context. Not that the movie itself — a 1980 time-travel fantasy with Christopher Reeve and Jane Seymour — hasn't become something of a classic in the years since its initial release, but Barry's music is one of the composer's most beloved scores. The elegant main theme for piano and orchestra (performed by Roger Williams in a beautiful arrangement here) is only part of the listening pleasure to be derived from the soundtrack,

which also includes the gorgeous "Rhapsody on a Theme of Paganini," by Rachmaninoff. It truly is one of the loveliest scores in Barry's long, established career of composing many lyrical, soothing scores, and its continued status as a successful soundtrack album stands as a testament to the music's enduring popularity with listeners.

Andy Dursin

Sommersby ♫♫♫♫

1993, Eletra Records; from the movie *Sommersby*, Warner Bros., 1993.

Album Notes: *Music*: Danny Elfman; *Orchestrations*: Steve Bartek, Thomas Pasatieri, Jack Hayes, Philip Giffin; *Music Editors*: Ellen Segal, Bob Badami; Orchestra conducted by Jonathan Sheffer, Thomas Pasatieri; *Album Producers*: Danny Elfman, Ellen Segal, Richard Kraft; *Engineer*: Shawn Murphy; *Assistant Engineers*: David Marquette, Andy Bass, Jay Silvester, Sharon Rice.

Selections: 1 Main Titles (4:41); 2 The Homecoming (1:58); 3 Welcoming (1:34); 4 First Love (3:54); 5 At Work (2:01); 6 Alone (4:23); 7 Return Montage (5:20); 8 Mortal Sin (4:39); 9 Homer (1:07); 10 Going To Nashville (1:42); 11 Baby (2:14); 12 Tea Cups (1:44); 13 Townsend's Tale (6:09); 14 Death (2:12); 15 Finale (4:05); 16 End Credits (3:16).

Review: He's scored movies with super heroes, stop-motion figures, ghastly monsters and Pee-Wee Herman, but some of Danny Elfman's finest work for the movies comes from a decidedly human angle. His score for *Sommersby*, the 1993 Americanization of *The Return of Martin Guerre*, remains one of the composer's most impressive efforts. With a tone that is alternately unsettled and brooding, a la Bernard Herrmann, or unabashedly romantic, Elfman and orchestrator Steve Bartek have put together a thematically strong score that fulfills all the dramatic requirements of Jon Amiel's film. In addition, the ensemble accompaniment representing the rural Virginia backdrop adds yet another layer to the score, which is quite different from the traditional Elfman sound, but is just as satisfying — if not more so — than anything else the composer has written for the movies yet.

Andy Dursin

Son of the Morning Star ♫♫♫♪

1992, Intrada Records; from the movie *Son of the Morning Star*, Republic Pictures, 1992.

Album Notes: *Music*: Craig Safan; *Featured Soloists*: Ed Gornik (trumpet); Holly Gornik (oboe); Tom Mauchahty-Ware (Native

American flute); *Album Producer*: Craig Safan; *Engineers*: Dennis Sands (orchestra), Gregg Karukas (Native American music).

Selections: 1 Elegy (2:05); 2 Night Ride (2:42); 3 Soldiers And Messages (2:42); 4 Premonitions (1:37); 5 Crazy Horse Dreams (1:54); 6 Westward Expansion (4:07); 7 Washita Massacre (3:17); 8 Libby Worries (4:01); 9 Fields Of The Dead (4:50); 10 Call To Arms (1:50); 11 Last Goodbyes (3:51); 12 Night Mysteries (2:04); 13 Soldiers Prepare (1:23); 14 Gathering Of Tribes (2:35); 15 Moving Armies (3:09); 16 Little Big Horn (17:29).

Review: The under-appreciated Craig Safan is known primarily for writing the theme music to the "Cheers" television show, but he's a talented dramatic composer who wrote one of the most exciting space opera scores of the '80s (*The Last Starfighter*) as well as this sophisticated take on the story of legendary General George Custer and the events that led to his downfall at Little Big Horn. Safan's score builds dramatic weight through the repetition of a dense, rich and bittersweet string melody that views the historical events depicted here as American tragedy rather than adventure. There's a beautiful love theme and an epic sweep to this album that make it a rarity in made-for-television scores, an effort that holds up against some of the better theatrical film scores of the period.

Jeff Bond

Son of the Pink Panther ♪♪♪

1993, Milan/RCA Records; from the movie *Son of the Pink Panther*, United Artists, 1993.

Album Notes: *Music*: Henry Mancini; *Orchestrations*: Henry Mancini, Jack Hayes; *Music Editor*: Steve Hope; The National Philharmonic Orchestra, conducted by Henry Mancini; *Featured Musician*: Phil Todd (tenor sax); *Album Producer*: Henry Mancini; *Engineer*: Alan Snelling.

Selections: 1 The Pink Panther Theme (3:10) *Bobby McFerrin*; 2 Son Of The Pink Panther (1:33); 3 The Snatch (2:22); 4 God Bless Clouseau (H. Mancini/L. Bricusse)(2:01); 5 Samba de Jacques (2:24); 6 The Gambrelli Theme (2:23); 7 The Bike Chase (1:52); 8 The Dreamy Princess (3:58); 9 Riot At Omar's (2:40); 10 Mama And Dreyfus (1:43); 11 Rendez-Vous With Cato (1:53); 12 The King's Palace (1:47); 13 The Showdown (3:31); 14 The Pink Panther Theme (4:18).

Review: Unable to leave well enough alone following the death of Peter Sellers, Blake Edwards devised this tired number in his successful *Pink Panther* series, starring Italian actor Roberto Benigni as Inspector Clouseau's equally inept illegitimate son. Back to confer the ounce of legitimacy needed to make things fly are Herbert Lom as Commissioner Dreyfus and

Burt Kwouk as Clouseau's faithful manservant Cato, as well as Henry Mancini, who provided the score as he had done in all previous *Pink Panther* films. Somehow, despite his natural verve and penchant for this type of comedy, the composer didn't seem much inspired by the antics of yet another Clouseau, and though his thoroughly professional score has its share of enjoyable moments ("Samba de Jacques," "Riot at Omar's"), some of the joy and effervescence that marked his previous efforts seem to be sadly missing here. In fact, the most original note in this album is Bobby McFerrin's impish rendition of "The Pink Panther Theme."

Sons and Lovers

1996, DRG Records; from the movie *Sons and Lovers*, 1960.

See: A Farewell to Arms

Sophie's Choice ♪♪♪

1984, Southern Cross Records; from the movie *Sophie's Choice*, Universal Pictures, 1984.

Album Notes: *Music*: Marvin Hamlisch; *Orchestrations*: Jack Hayes; Orchestra conducted by Marvin Hamlisch; *Album Producer*: John Lasher; *Engineers*: Frank Jones, Colin Derek, Terri Fiyalko, Danny Hirsch.

Selections: 1 Love Theme (1:53); 2 Train Ride To Brooklyn (2:44); 3 Returning The Tray (2:32); 4 Coney Island Fun (1:00); 5 Songs Without Words, Op. 30, No. 1 (F. Mendelssohn)(1:43) *Ralph Grierson*; 6 Emily Dickinson (1:58); 7 Aren't All Women Like You? (1:53); 8 Rite On The Brooklyn Bridge (2:45); 9 Stingo/Polish Lullaby (1:42); 10 Nathan Returns (1:23); 11 Southern Plantation (1:54); 12 I'll Never Leave You (1:23); 13 Stingo And Sophie Together (3:03); 14 Ample Make This Bed (2:09); 15 End Credits (3:04).

Review: Marvin Hamlisch wrote one of his few straight dramatic scores for this Alan Pakula adaptation of the William Styron novel. The elegiac, deeply regretful title music is one of Hamlisch's most beautiful and haunting melodies, but the score itself tends to meander aimlessly until gathering up its forces to restate the theme broadly in some of the movie's hokier sequences. The score is better off when subtly underscoring the drama with an effective chamber orchestra approach. Hamlisch's deliberate, consonant string passages and piano phrases make for pleasant, bittersweet listening, but the darker territory of the story and its characters is rarely explored convincingly.

Jeff Bond

Sorcerer ✎✎✎

1977, MCA Records; from the movie *Sorcerer*, Universal-Paramount, 1977.

Album Notes: *Songs*: Tangerine Dream (Edgar Froese, Peter Baumann, Christoph Franke).

Selections: 1 Main Title (5:29); 2 Search (2:54); 3 The Call (1:58); 4 Creation (5:00); 5 Vengeance (5:34); 6 The Journey (2:00); 7 Grind (2:49); 8 Rain Forest (2:36); 9 Abyss (7:10); 10 The Mountain Road (1:54); 11 Impressions Of Sorcerer (2:53); 12 Betrayal (Sorcerer Theme)(3:41).

Review: A remake of Henri-Georges Clouzot's frighteningly real *Le salaire de la peur (Wages Of Fear)*, this film by William Friedkin elicited a convincingly powerful score by Tangerine Dream, even though the music the group created consisted of impressions they gathered from reading the script, and not from viewing the film as is common practice. While the "Main Title" really fails to attract with its electronic effects devoid of any musical meaning, the other selections make a different impression, with some ("Search," "Impressions of Sorcerer") surprisingly evocative of the screen drama itself. The album may seem strictly for fans of electronic music, but it also offers some rewarding moments for listeners less accustomed to this type of music.

The Sound and the Fury ✎✎✎✎

1990, Varese-Sarabande; from the movie *The Sound and the Fury*, 20th Century-Fox, 1959.

Album Notes: *Music*: Alex North; The 20th Century-Fox Orchestra, conducted by Lionel Newman.

Selections: 1 Main Title: The Sound And The Fury (4:25); 2 Quentin's Theme (1:52); 3 Sex Rears (3:33); 4 Caddie (2:17); 5 What's His Name (3:43); 6 Ben Spies On Lovers (1:58); 7 Southern Breeze (2:45); 8 Hot (2:39); 9 Jason And Quentin (2:59); 10 Sweet Baby (3:51); 11 Do You Love Me, Charlie? (3:53); 12 Ben Departs (2:16); 13 Too Much Woman/End Title (4:31).

Review: Released in 1959, *The Sound and the Fury* is a provocative big screen adaptation of William Faulkner's searing novel about the decline and fall of a once wealthy family in a small Mississippi community. Starring Joanne Woodward, as a young woman who craves the kind of affection she never got at home, and Yul Brynner, as the adopted stepson of the family estate who exerts control over everything and everyone, the film paints the drab portrait of a desperate family, fraying at the seams and on the verge of financial collapse. Underlining the

> "First his film scores convey fantastic levels of humor and emotion that help tell the story. Think about his scores for *The Natural* and *Avalon* and *Awakenings*."
>
> **director John Lasseter**
> on *Randy Newman*
> (The Detroit News, 12-22-95)

moods in the story, as well as adding a comment of its own, Alex North's score derives much of its impact from the use of progressive (one hesitates to use the word avant-garde) jazz that occasionally prevailed in film soundtracks at the time, often in imitation of the trend pioneered by Elmer Bernstein. Without losing sight of the emotional context in some of the scenes ("What's His Name," "Southern Breeze," "Sweet Baby"), some of the cues devised by the composer rely on more contemporary accents to give the music an identity that takes it away from standard instrumental fares. This is particularly evident in the "Main Title" which realizes a symbiosis of the various styles North used in the score, and in the explosive "Sex Rears," in which the syncopated jazz accents effectively convey the steam and the tension in the film.

South Seas Adventure ✎✎✎

1993, Label X Records; from the movie *South Seas Adventure*, Cinerama, 1958.

Album Notes: *Music*: Alex North; The Cinerama Symphony Orchestra and The Norman Luboff Choir, conducted by Alex North.

Selections: 1 Overture (2:37); 2 Journey To Hawaii (4:41); 3 Song Of The Islands (C.E. King)(:51); 4 Ted And Kay (1:25); 5 Surf Riding (1:26); 6 Fire Dance (trad.)(1:15); 7 Hawaiian War Chant (J. Noble)(1:33); 8 Start Of Te Vega's Voyage (2:58); 9 King Neptune (:43); 10 Trip To Tonga (3:09); 11 Ma Ulu Ulu (trad.)(2:07); 12 Behold The Lamb Of God (G.F. Handle)(1:45); 13 Onward Christian Soldiers (A. Sullivan)(1:15); 14 Fiji Chanting (trad.)(:44); 15 Head Diver Sequence (1:35); 16 Entr'acte (2:59); 17 Driving Through New Zealand (3:35); 18 Poi Chant (trad.)(1:09); 19 Welcome (1:41); 20 Sheep Shearing (Click Go The Shears)(trad.)(2:04); 21 Kangaroo Roundup (1:48); 22 Finale (1:28); 23 Credits (1:36); 24 Exit (Click Go The Shears)(2:05).

Review: Before it turned to more commercial fare, Cinerama first made its mark with sensational travelogues that used its three-screen diorama to best effect. Accompanying those were scores which, for the most part, were serviceable but not tremendously exciting or imaginative. One happy exception was this effort by composer Alex North, who took the South Pacific locations as a cue to write broad, colorful music, inspired by and based on traditional themes. While the sonics in this CD sometime leave a lot to be desired (the stereo is rather crude and not very flattering to the ear), there is no denying the charm and solid flair of the music itself.

Space Jam 🎵🎵🎵🎵

1996, Warner Sunset/Atlantic Records; from the movie *Space Jam*, Warner Bros., 1996.

Album Notes: *Music:* James Newton Howard; *Song Producers:* Seal, Brian Dobbs, Jay McGowan, C.C. Lemonhead, R. Kelly, D'Angelo, David Foster, Todd Terry, Lou Adler, Jamey Jaz, Rashad Smith, Armando Colon, Jimmy Jam, Terry Lewis, Danny Kortchmar, Peter Denenberg; *Engineers:* Tim Weidner, Glen Machese, Leonard Jackson, C.C. Lemonhead, Chris Bickley, Rick Behrens, Bill Esses, Russell Elevado, Felipe Elgueta, Tim Lauber, Carl Nappa, Greg Thompson, Steve Hodge, Stephen George, Peter Denenberg; *Album Executive Producers:* Ken Ross, Craig Kallman, Dominique Trenier.

Selections: 1 Fly Like An Eagle (S. Miller) (4:15) *Seal*; 2 The Winner (A. Ivey, Jr./B. Dobbs/C. Mayfield) (4:03) *Coolio*; 3 Space Jam (J. McGowan/N. Orange/V. Bryant) (5:07) *Quad City DJ's*; 4 I Believe I Can Fly (R. Kelly) (5:22) *R. Kelly*; 5 Hit 'Em High (The Monstars' Anthem) (L. Fresse/T. Smith/A. Ivey. Jr./T. Smith/C. Smith/J.C. Olivier/S. Barnes) (4:18) *B Real, Busta Rhymes, Coolio, LL Cool J, Method Man*; 6 I Found My Smile Again (D'Angelo) (6:15) *D'Angelo*; 7 For You I Will (D. Warren) (4:57) *Monica*; 8 Upside Down ('Round-n-'Round) (B. Edwards/N. Rodgers/C. James/S. Denton) (4:17) *Salt-N-Pepa*; 9 Givin' U All That I've Got (Robin S./T. Terry) (4:05) *Robin S.*; 10 Basket Ball Jones (T. Chong/R. Marin) (5:40) *Barry White, Chris Rock*; 11 I Turn To You (D. Warren) (4:54) *All-4-One*; 12 All Of My Days (R. Kelly) (4:01) *R. Kelly, Changing Faces, Jay-Z*; 13 That's The Way (I Like It) (H. Casey/R. Finch) (3:50) *Spin Doctors, Biz Markie*; 14 Buggin' (J. Newton Howard/S. Carter) (4:15) *Bugs Bunny*.

Review: Michael Jordan meets Bugs Bunny — with Tweety Bird thrown in? Alert the kiddies. Actually, there's not much to dislike about this family-friendly collection of tunes. Seal does a lovely take on Steve Miller's "Fly Like an Eagle," R. Kelly's "I Believe I Can Fly" is easy on the ears and "Hit 'em High (The Monstars' Anthem")" is a big-fun collaboration between top-shelf rappers B

Real, Busta Rhymes, Coolio, LL Cool J and Method Man. And Bugs' own "Buggin'" is a cheery way to close the album.
Gary Graff

Spaceballs 🎵🎵

1987, Atlantic Records; from the movie *Spaceballs*, M-G-M, 1987.

Album Notes: *Music:* John Morris; *Orchestrations:* Jack Hayes, Angela Morley; Orchestra conducted by John Morris; *Album Executive Producers:* Jerry Greenberg, Bob Greenberg.

Selections: 1 Spaceballs Main Title Theme (2:30); 2 My Heart Has A Mind Of Its Own (G. Sklerov/L. Macaluso) (3:56) *Kim Carnes, Jeffrey Osborne*; 3 Heartstrings (J. Crawford/T. Nunn/R. Brill/M. Reid) (4:10) *Berlin*; 4 Spaceballs Love Theme Instrumental (2:22); 5 The Winnebago Crashes/The Spaceballs Build Mega-Maid (2:25); 6 Spaceballs (J. Pescetto/C. Lieberman/M. Brooks) (3:43) *The Spinners*; 7 Hot Together (S. Robinson) (4:11) *The Pointer Sisters*; 8 Good Enough (E. Van Halen/S. Hagar/M. Anthony/A. Van Halen) (4:02) *Van Halen*; 9 Wanna Be Loved By You (D. Bauerle) (3:34) *Ladyfire*.

Review: Having already sent up westerns, musicals, horror films, and historical epics, Mel Brooks could have done much worse than turn his attention to the outerspace sagas, and which better one to spoof than the granddaddy of them all, *Star Wars*. There's little one can say about the story of Lone Starr, a second-rate Han Solo, and Princess Vespa, the Jewish American babe he saves from the grips of a would-be Darth Vader (Rick Moranis, coiffed with a helmet ten times too big for his head), except that the satire is often, if not always, right on target. Also right on the button is John Morris' frequently hilarious score, a subtle take-off on John Williams' grandiloquent music for *Star Wars*. Sadly, the instrumental tracks are sacrificed here to meaningless pop songs, which are heard faintly in the background in the film, but which get spotlighted though their importance to the action in the film is close to nil. As a result, Morris' contribution is reduced to three selections, the "Main Title," "Love Theme," and "The Winnebago Crashes/The Spaceballs Build Mega-Maid." Better watch the film, it is more fun. And may the farce be with you!

Spartacus 🎵🎵🎵🎵🎵

1991, MCA Records; from the movie *Spartacus*, Universal Pictures, 1960.

Album Notes: *Music:* Alex North; Orchestra conducted by Alex North.

Selections: 1 Main Title (3:16); 2 Spartacus Love Theme (2:48); 3 Gladiators Fight To The Death (2:17); 4 Blue Shadows And Purple

Hills (3:11); 5 Homeward Bound: (a) On To The Sea, (b) Beside The Pool (6:27); 6 Hopeful Preparations, Vesuvius Camp (1:57); 7 Prelude To Battle: (a) Quiet Interlude, (b) The Final Conflict (5:10); 8 On To Vesuvius: (a) Forward Gladiators, (b) Forest Metting (4:51); 9 Oysters And Snails/Festival (3:22); 10 Headed For Freedom (2:18); 11 Goodbye My Life, My Love/End Title (6:16).

Review: A powerful big screen retelling of the revolt of the slaves against the Romans in the century before Christ, *Spartacus* is a handsome ancient history spectacle, bold and audacious, a film with a single focus, magnificently directed by Stanley Kubrick, then only 32 years of age, and written by Dalton Trumbo, who had been blacklisted since 1947 because of his political beliefs. Playing Spartacus is Kirk Douglas, who also produced, in one of his most memorable screen portrayals as the Thracian slave who led his men, all former slaves like him, against the Roman legions, until he was defeated and killed in 70 b.c. Sharing the spotlight with him are Jean Simmons, Tony Curtis, Laurence Olivier, and many others in this all-star package.

Matching the heroic spirit that pervaded the story, Alex North wrote a sensational score in which the epic accents occasionally gave way to romantic interludes, built around the gorgeously evocative "Spartacus Love Theme." Unfortunately, while the film was only recently completely restored and given the proper care it deserved for its theatrical and video rerelease, this CD, mastered from the original two-track soundtrack album tapes, was not. Forget the fact that it doesn't contain any extra music, as an important reissue of this type would warrant, but it evidences a lot of hiss, a frequently horrendously shrill sound, and occasional analog dropouts, all of which could and should have been corrected. If you still want to try and enjoy this CD, defeat the treble completely, boost the bass, and even then the results will be less than satisfactory, though not as aggravating. The rating is for the music, not for this CD, which gets a very low rating.

The Specialist

The Specialist ♫♫♫♫

1994, Epic Soundtrax/Sony Music; from the movie, *The Specialist* Warner Bros., 1994.

Album Notes: *Music:* John Barry; The Royal Philharmonic Orchestra, conducted by John Barry; *Orchestrations:* John Barry; *Album Producer:* John Barry; *Engineer:* Shawn Murphy.

Selections: 1 Main Title (1:41); 2 Bogota 1984 (2:49); 3 The Specialist In Miami (2:34); 4 May And Ray At The Cemetary

(1:52); 5 May Dances With Tomas/ "Did You Call Me" (2:35); 6 Ray Covers May/"Did You Call Me" (2:38); 7 After Tomas (2:57); 8 The First Bomb/Ray's Place (2:57); 9 Explosive Trent (1:57); 10 The Parking Lot Bomb (2:32); 11 Don't Touch Me Ned/Bomb For Tomas (3:18); 12 The Death Of Tomas (2:07); 13 May's Room/"Did You Call Me" (1:27); 14 Ray Meets May At Her Funeral (2:34); 15 Let's See That Beautiful Face/"Did You Call Me" (2:43); 16 Closing In On Ray (2:57); 17 There Goes The Hotel Room/The Fight (2:20); 18 May Meets Joe/I'm Not A Woman You Can Trust (2:59); 19 You Go In And Get Him/"Did You Call Me" (4:05); 20 The Whole Place Is Wired/She's Hot Ray (3:26); 21 Get To Hell Out Of Here (2:15); 22 You Bastard/ How Do You Feel?/Better!/"Did You Call Me"/End Title (3:09).

Review: Fans have been disappointed that John Barry, the man who defined the James Bond sound back in the 1960s, hasn't scored a 007 outing since 1987s *The Living Daylights*, but anyone wanting to hear the equivalent of new Barry Bond soundtrack — minus the famous title theme, of course — should definitely check out the score album from *The Specialist*. Unlike most action movies filled with explosions in full Dolby Stereo, Barry got a favorable sound mix from producer Jerry Weintraub, and was able to write a steamy, dense atmospheric score with sexy lyrical passages and suspenseful action cues in the classic John Barry mold, but this time with a definite accent on jazz. The score is easily the best of Barry's recent works; rest assured that agent 007 would approve.

Andy Dursin

The Specialist ♫♫♫♪

1994, Epic Soundtrax/Sony Music; from the movie, *The Specialist* Warner Bros., 1994.

Selections: 1 Turn The Beat Around (P. Jackson/G. Jackson) (3:52) *Gloria Estefan*; 2 Jambala (E. Estefan/J.Casas/C. Ostwald) (3:21) *MSM (Miami Sound Machine)*; 3 Real (J. Secada/D. Warren) (3:38) *Donna Allen*; 4 All Because Of You (H. Garrido) (2:54) *MSM (Miami Sound Machine)*; 5 Shower Me With Love (J. Secada/L. Dermer) (4:29) *Lagaylia*; 6 El baile de la vela (J. Marquez) (4:04) *Cheito*; 7 Slip Away (L. Dermer) (5:12) *Lagaylia*; 8 El duro soy yo (D. Tatis) (4:34) *Tony Tatis y su merengue Sound*; 9 Mental Picture (J. Secada/M. Morejon) (4:19) *Jon Secada*; 10 Que manera de quererte (L. Rios) (4:29) *Albita*; 11 Love Is The Thing (L. Dermer) (3:38) *Donna Allen*; 12 El amor (F. Salgado/K. Santander) (4:52) *Azucar Moreno*; 13 Did You Call Me (5:24); 14 The Specialist (5:39).

Review: This showcases the Miami sound, focusing, not surprisingly, on commercial heavyweights such as Gloria Estefan & Miami Sound Machine and Jon Secada. But it also includes acts such as Azucar Moreno, Cheito, Albita and Lagaylia, whose music hasn't been whitewashed quite as much into the pop mainstream. We're not so sure how John Barry and the Royal Philharmonic Orchestra fit into this, though.

Speed ♫♫♫

1994, Fox Records; from the movie *Speed*, 20th Century-Fox, 1994.

Album Notes: *Music*: Mark Mancina; *Orchestrations*: Bruce Fowler, Ladd McIntosh, Y.S. Moriarty, Don Harper, Mark Mancina; Orchestra conducted by Don Harper; *Featured Musicians*: Mike Fisher (percussion), Allan Holdsworth (guitar); *Engineers*: Jay Rifkin, Alan Meyerson.

Selections: 1 Main Title (3:37); 2 The Rescue (4:01); 3 Entering Airport (1:00); 4 Rush Hour (6:04); 5 Helen Dies (2:19); 6 The Gap (2:49); 7 Choppers (1:00); 8 Pershing Square (3:18); 9 Elevator Peril (:28); 10 Fight On Train (1:19); 11 Dangling Feet (:34); 12 City Streets (1:41); 13 Wildcat (1:04); 14 The Dolly (1:28); 15 Move (2:05); 16 Pop Quiz (2:23); 17 Freight Elevator (2:29); 18 Elevator Stall (:50); 19 End Title (1:49).

Review: With this, his first major feature score, Mark Mancina proved a most capable composer. *Speed* is a wildly energetic score, finding its base in its fast-paced rhythm and its main theme, an eight-note motif nicely evocative of danger as well as heroism. With synths accompanied by orchestra, Mancina's main theme stands solidly above the driving acceleration of throbbing synths and percussion that support it. The furiously scurrying synths occasionally part, allowing the main theme to sound assuredly from violins, punctuated by stridently ar-rhythmic drum beats. Strokes of strings pedal the chords faster and faster, while an eerie synth wail suggests unseen danger. There are some static moments but for the most part the score speeds along effectively, benefited by Mancina's superior orchestrations and a winning heroic/romantic theme.

Randall Larson

Speedway

1995, RCA Records; from the movie *Speedway*, M-G-M, 1968.

See: Elvis Presley in Compilations

Spellbound ♫♫♫♫

1988, Stanyan Records; from the movie *Spellbound*, RKO Radio Pictures, 1945.

Album Notes: *Music*: Miklos Rozsa; The Warner Bros. Studio Orchestra, conducted by Ray Heindorf.

Selections: 1 Main Theme (4:43); 2 The Dressing Gown (4:17); 3 Scherzo (3:15); 4 Love Theme (3:10); 5 The Burned Hand

(4:40); 6 Spellbound (3:10); 7 The Razor (4:17); 8 Constance (2:47); 9 The Dream (3:00); 10 Ski Run (2:49); 11 Finale (3:27);

JOANNA (R. MCKUEN): 12 Peter's Theme (I'll Catch The Sun)(3:21); 13 I'm Only Me (Two Girls Bathing)(2:25); 14 Joanna In Paris (Run To Me, Fly To Me)(1:59);

THE BORROWERS (R. MCKUEN): 15 Off On The Great Adventure (2:46);

AROUND THE WORLD IN EIGHTY DAYS (V. YOUNG): 16 Roadshow Overture To Around The World In Eighty Days (4:58).

Review: The innovative use of the theremin (an early synthe-sizer) singles out this soundtrack as a precursor in a field that has become very crowded in recent years. The instrument also conferred to the music composed by Miklos Rozsa its specific-ity in creating an atmosphere of mystery for this film directed by Alfred Hitchcock. Starring Gregory Peck, as an amnesiac trying to recall some events surrounding a murder he is afraid he might have committed, and Ingrid Bergman, as the psychia-trist who attempts to help him, *Spellbound* is a terrific, sus-penseful drama, in which the action is as much psychological as it is physical. Contrasting the uncertain moods evoked by the film's "Main Theme," outlined by the theremin, Rozsa also developed other cues that create a false sense of mirth and security ("Scherzo," "Love Theme"), for what has become one of the most remarkable scores in his career, an achievement that was duly recognized by an Academy Award in 1945.

This recording, made in the late 1950s with Ray Heindorf conducting the Warner Bros. Studio Orchestra, is totally faith-ful to the spirit of the original, and quietly sensational in its expression. The CD also features selections from Rod Mc-Kuen's *Joanna* and *The Borrowers*, and the roadshow overture to Victor Young's *Around the World in 80 Days*, which have been probably added to increase the total playing time, but have no business being here, stylistically.

Spies Like Us ♫♫♫

1985, Varese-Sarabande; from the movie *Spies Like Us*, Warner Bros. Pictures, 1985.

Album Notes: *Music*: Elmer Bernstein; *Orchestrations*: Christo-pher Palmer; *Music Editor*: Kathy Durning; The Graunke Sym-phony Orchestra, Munich, Germany, conducted by Elmer Bern-stein; *Album Producer*: Elmer Bernstein; *Engineer*: Dan Wallin.

Selections: 1 The Ace Tomato Company (5:06); 2 Off To Spy (1:52); 3 Russians In The Desert (2:21); 4 Pass In The Tent (2:58); 5 Escape (3:25); 6 To The Bus (3:14); 7 The Road To Russia (3:39); 8 Rally 'Round (2:39); 9 W.A.M.P. (2:48); 10

Martian Act (3:08); 11 Arrest (2:21); 12 Recall (2:38); 13 Winners (1:16).

Review: Typical Elmer Bernstein comedy score is nonetheless entertaining. As much of the film plays like an old Bob Hope/Bing Croby *Road* picture (Hope even makes an appearance), Bernstein approaches things with the same broad comic feel, playing out obvious and familiar sounding desert motifs that just slap the audience's face and scream, "We're in the desert, stupid! See there's sand!" This, of course, does work to get us over some of the film's dull spots (especially when the uneducated fail to grasp the gag of having famous directors and effects people in bit parts). Particularly funny to music fans is Bernstein's satirization of his own score from *The Magnificent Seven* ("Off to Spy").

David Hirsch

The Spirit of St. Louis ♪♪♪♪♪

1989, Varese-Sarabande; from the movie *The Spirit of St. Louis*, Warner Bros., 1957.

Album Notes: *Music*: Franz Waxman; *Orchestrations*: Lenoid Raab; The Warner Bros. Studio Orchestra, conducted by Franz Waxman; *Album Producers*: John W. Waxman, Tom Null, Richard Kraft; *Engineer*: Daniel Hersch.

Selections: 1 Prelude (Main Title)(1:24); 2 Building The Spirit (4:06); 3 First Test Flight (1:19); 4 Flight To St. Louis (1:13); 5 St. Christopher (:41); 6 New York To Cape Cod (7:04); 7 Nova Scotia (3:03); 8 St. John's (6:52); 9 Barnstorming (2:37); 10 Fishing Boats (2:57); 11 The Old Jenny (1:27); 12 The Spirit Of St. Louis (1:16); 13 Rolling Out (5:24); 14 Asleep (4:07); 15 Ireland (4:08); 16 Plymouth (3:28); 17 Le Bourget/End Title (6:47).

Review: Directed by Billy Wilder, *The Spirit of St. Louis* stars James Stewart in a faithful recreation of Charles Lindbergh's historic solo flight from New York to Paris, in May, 1927. The film cried out for a score that would fulfill a double task: underline the momentous scenes in the script, based on Lindbergh's own autobiography, and provide an extra dramatic impetus to the long stretches of screen time that involved the aviator, alone inside the cockpit of his plane, during his transatlantic flight. In writing it, Franz Waxman acquitted himself superbly of the demands imposed on him. His cues, superbly shaded and sober in their expression, detail the frustrations initially encountered by Lindbergh, when he began building the plane that would eventually take him to his ambitious destination, the problems posed by the first test flights, and finally the long, seemingly endless journey across the unknown, before the final strains in the music signal the success of his undertaking. Like Tiomkin's music for

The Old Man and the Sea, Waxman's score for *The Spirit of St. Louis* became an essential component of the film's dramatic structure. Heard in this recording in its entirety, with many previously unavailable tracks further detailing Lindbergh's pioneering effort, it emerges as a powerful musical statement, with a vibrancy that immediately compels the listener's attention and immerses him into the unfolding story.

The Spitfire Grill ♪♪♪

1996, Sony Classical; from the movie *The Spitfire Grill*, Columbia Pictures, 1996.

Album Notes: *Music*: James Horner; *Orchestrations*: James Horner; *Music Editor*: Jim Henrikson; Orchestra conducted by James Horner; *Album Producer*: James Horner; *Engineer*: Shawn Murphy.

Selections: 1 An Uncertain Future/Main Title (3:38); 2 Shelby And Percy (5:55); 3 Hannah's Fall (1:58); 4 The Mystery Of The Night (1:21); 5 Open For Business (2:25); 6 Remembering Eli (1:54); 7 The Trees (1:39); 8 A Gift From The Forest (4:43); 9 Reading The Letters (2:02); 10 A Healing Balm (5:59); 11 A New Life For Gilead (1:25); 12 Wrongful Blame (2:15); 13 A Desperate Decision (5:07); 14 ...Care Of The Spitfire Grill (9:53).

Review: When Castle Rock snapped up the rights to this audience winner at the Sundance Film Festival, they spruced up a number of the film's aural elements, including the addition of a new music score by James Horner. Fortunately, this jaunty, often country-flavored score doesn't go overboard in Hollywood saccharine, as Horner keeps things on a tuneful, lyric level that's easily accessible for listeners without being overtly simplistic. The main theme of the film is quite nice, and the variations that the composer uses in his score keep it fresh and not nearly as derivative as some of his other works. It's a pleasant album, inoffensive and relaxing.

Andy Dursin

The Spy Who Loved Me ♪♪

1995, EMI Records; from the movie *The Spy Who Loved Me*, United Artists, 1977.

Album Notes: *Music*: Marvin Hamlisch; Orchestra conducted by Marvin Hamlisch; *Featured Musicians*: Barry Desouza (drums), Laurence Juber (guitar), Chris Rae (second electric guitar), Mike Egan (acoustic guitar), Bruce Lynch, Brian Ogdes (bass guitar), Derick Plater (saxophone solo), Marvin Hamlisch (piano), Ron Aspery (flute/soprano sax), Paul Buckmaster (cello synthesizer), Fre Goodyear (bass guitar), Brother James (congas/percussion), Paul Robinson (drums); *Album Producer*: Marvin Hamlisch

Selections: 1 Nobody Does It Better (M. Hamlisch/C. Bayer Sager)(3:33) *Carly Simon*; 2 Bond 77 (James Bond Theme)(4:23); 3 Ride To Atlantis (3:30); 4 Mojave Club (2:16); 5 Nobody Does It Better (4:48); 6 Anya (3:23); 7 The Tanker (4:27); 8 The Pyramids (1:37); 9 Eastern Lights (3:27); 10 Conclusion (1:35); 11 End Titles: Nobody Does It Better (M. Hamlisch/C. Bayer Sager) (3:26) *Carly Simon*.

Review: One of the first James Bond films not scored by John Barry, *The Spy Who Loved Me* offers what is probably the best and the worst in the soundtracks for the series. The best is Carly Simon's superb rendition of the title song, written by Carole Bayer Sager, which bookends this CD. One of the best theme songs in the series, it is as much memorable today as it was when it was first created. The worst is Marvin Hamlisch's ho-hum score, a series of cues with long cascading lines, percolating rhythms, guitar riffs and wah-wah effects that attempt to find an original tone but fail miserably. It really didn't matter much behind the action on the screen, as the cues fulfilled a function that was essentially secondary. But thrown in the spotlight, they reveal the absence of genuine feel for the series and what it is all about, with themes that are routine at best, and altogether not very interesting.

Stand and Deliver 🎜🎜🎜ᵛ

1988, Varese Sarabande; from the movie *Stand and Deliver*, Warner Bros., 1988.

Album Notes: *Music*: Craig Safan; *Album Producer*: Craig Safan.

Selections: 1 Main Title/East L.A. (2:28); 2 Kimo's Theme (2:50); 3 Fight (1:13); 4 Summer Hot School (1:23); 5 Picking On Claudia (1:01); 6 The First Test/Release (1:56); 7 Heart Attack (1:10); 8 Stand And Deliver Suite (7:00); 9 Night Fright (:43); 10 Pancho And Lupe (1:05); 11 Retaking The Test (4:17); 12 The Big News (:58); 13 Success (4:05).

Review: The specific atmosphere of the barrio in East Los Angeles is given credible musical life in the score Craig Safan wrote for this film, about a gang of Latinos who discover the importance of mathematics, thanks to a dedicated high school teacher. Relying on expressive synth melodies and effects, Safan created a score that evidences remarkable flair, even as it evokes some of the events and characters involved in the screen action. Moving with ease from Spanish-accented themes ("Pancho and Lupe"), to a soft Japanese tune ("Kimo's Theme"), to delicately phrased cues built around harp-like arpeggios ("Picking on Claudia," "The First Test/Release"), the music is multi-layered and attractively laid out. The seven-minute "Stand

and Deliver Suite" recaps the overall moods into one long evocation that has moments of fun and depth in it.

Stanley & Iris 🎜🎜🎜🎜

1990, Varese-Sarabande Records; from the movie *Stanley & Iris*, M-G-M, 1990.

Album Notes: *Music*: John Williams; *Music Editor*: Kenn Wannberg; Orchestra conducted by John Williams; *Album Producer*: John Williams; *Engineer*: Dan Wallin.

Selections: 1 Stanley And Iris (3:24); 2 Reading Lessons (2:26); 3 The Bicycle (3:07); 4 Factory Work (1:23); 5 Finding A Family (1:41); 6 Stanley At Work (1:31); 7 Looking After Papa (3:10); 8 Stanley's Invention (1:17); 9 Night Visit (1:58); 10 Letters (3:25); 11 Putting It All Together (1:46); 12 End Credits (3:03).

Review: It might run under half an hour, but this score by John Williams is more developed thematically than many other, far lengthier soundtracks. Williams' score here is relatively simple and reflective in nature, adeptly setting the scene for this 1990 Martin Ritt drama with Jane Fonda and Robert De Niro. But it is the Autumnal warmth flowing out of this score that makes it so memorable. the themes are succinct and lovely, the orchestrations subtle and appropriate for a character drama, and the nature of the music makes repeated listenings not only easily endurable but a genuine pleasure. This is the kind of character-driven score Williams excels at whenever he is given the opportunity at scoring one, and is also one of the most underrated works in the composer's filmography.

Andy Dursin

Star Crash

1990, Silva Screen Records; from the movie *Star Crash*, 1978.

See: Until September

The Star Maker 🎜🎜

1996, Miramax-Hollywood Records; from the movie *The Star Maker*, Miramax Films, 1996.

Album Notes: *Music*: Ennio Morricone; *Orchestrations*: Ennio Morricone; Orchestra Unione Musicisti di Roma, conducted by Ennio Morricone; *Featured Soloists*: Franco Tamponi (violin solos), Laura Pontecorvo (dolce flute), Paolo Zampini (ottavino flute), Stefano Novelli (clarinet), Filippo Rizzuto (guitar); *Album Producer*: Ennio Morricone; *Engineer*: Franco Patrignani; *Assistant Engineer*: Donato Salone.

Selections: 1 The Star Maker (3:02); 2 In The Stars (1:47); 3 Voices (5:27); 4 The Arrest (1:32); 5 Hollywood Of The Poor

(4:45); 6 Joe Morelli Talent Scout (2:37); 7 Beata And Joe (3:41); 8 Ahi Quinto, Ahi Quinto, Ahi Quinto (2:39); 9 Stardust (M. Parish, H. Carmichael) (6:21); 10 Beata (2:22); 11 The Truck (1:32); 12 Talking With The Stars (2:34); 13 Screen Test (3:23); 14 Sicily (4:27); 15 Maciste And His Brothers (1:06); 16 Funeral March (4:11) *Banda Vincenzo Bellini of Monterosso*.

Review: Years ago when he scored *The Thing*, Ennio Morricone remarked on how that score was about "nothing happening." The suspenseful, anticipatory ambiance he sustained in that score hinted at something happening, but "nothing happens." Morricone's score for *The Star Maker* would have been as appropriate a score for *The Thing* because it's one of the most static, nothing-happening scores the maestro has composed recently. The music is plain boring. Peeling back layers of violins, Morricone exposed multiple strains of the same basic chords and notes, with the occasional flute wandering in and out. There's virtually no melody and no rhythm. The ponderous "thematic" material and the few period pop tunes, not to mention the recording's overall low volume, make this score recommended primarily for insomniacs. It's an unfortunate commentary on a score by the composer who really woke me up to film music for the first time, but there's nothing terribly interesting or inventive about this sleepy score.

Randall Larson

Star Trek: The Motion Picture ♪♪♪♪

1997, Legacy Records/Sony Music; from the movie *Star Trek: The Motion Picture*, Paramount Pictures, 1979.

Album Notes: *Music:* Jerry Goldsmith; *Orchestrations:* Arthur Morton; *Music Editor:* Ken Hall; Orchestra conducted by Jerry Goldsmith; *Album Producer:* Jerry Goldsmith; *Engineer:* Bruce Botnick; *CD Producer:* Didier C. Deutsch; *Engineer:* Chris Herles.

Selections: 1 Ilia's Theme (2:59); 2 Main Title/Klingon Battle (6:49); 3 Total Logic (3:46); 4 The Enterprise (5:56); 5 Leaving Drydock (3:27); 6 Spock's Arrival (1:57); 7 The Cloud (4:55); 8 Vejur Flyover (4:54); 9 The Force Field (5:00); 10 Games/Spock Space Walk (7:58); 11 Inner Workings (3:06); 12 Vejur Speaks/The Meld/A Good Start (9:29); 13 End Title (3:15).

Review: Composers often produce outstanding scores under the worst possible conditions. On the hastily-constructed, overbudget sci-fi feature *Star Trek: The Motion Picture*, Jerry Goldsmith had just a handful of days to write a film score that would be evocative, epic, majestic, and mystical, benefiting the massive special effects of this production while refusing to

be an exact clone of *Star Wars*. Even under this time crunch, Goldsmith came through with flying colors, with a magnificent, Oscar-nominated soundtrack containing perhaps his most well-known theme (later utilized for both TV's "Star Trek: The Next Generation" and the Goldsmith-scored theatrical sequels), a wealth of fascinating musical cues for the alien being "Vejur," and, in contrast, an aggressively percussive motif for the Klingons (a la *The Wind and the Lion*). The music works perfectly in the movie and on its own, and stands as one of the crowning achievements in Goldsmith's career.

Andy Dursin

Star Trek II: The Wrath of Khan ♪♪♪♪

1990, GNP Crescendo Records; from the movie *Star Trek II: The Wrath of Khan*, Paramount Pictures, 1982.

Album Notes: *Music:* James Horner; *Orchestrations:* Jack Hayes; *Music Editor:* Bob Badami; Orchestra conducted by James Horner; *Album Producer:* James Horner; *Engineer:* Dan Wallin; *Assistant Engineer:* Tom Steel.

Selections: 1 Main Title (3:03); 2 Surprise Attack (5:06); 3 Spock (1:10); 4 Kirk's Explosive Reply (4:02); 5 Khan's Pets (4:18); 6 Enterprise Clears Moorings (3:32); 7 Battle In The Mutara Nebula (8:08); 8 Genesis Countdown (6:36) 9 Epilogue/End Title (8:40).

Review: Nicholas Meyer's take on the *Star Trek* myths revitalized the film franchise after the moribund *Star Trek: The Motion Picture*. It also launched the career of composer James Horner, who brought a wonderful, windswept nautical quality to his title music, which spins up from a whirling horn figure into sweeping, romantic rapture. If it sometimes seems more appropriate for Sherwood Forest than an outer space epic, it's only appropriate given director Meyer's Prisoner-of-Zenda take on the material. Horner's space attack cues are uproarious, contrasting the pagan fury of a chaotic brass motif for Ricardo Montalban's villainous Khan against the naval heroism of William Shatner's Kirk and a surprisingly lyrical, bittersweet melody for the self-sacrificing Spock. "Battle in the Mutara Nebula" and "Genesis Countdown" are still two of the most exciting and sustained musical cues Horner has ever written, and his setting of Alexander Courage's mysterioso TV show opening as the finale of the film (under Leonard Nimoy's recitation of the famous Trek "to boldly go" manifesto will make the hairs on the back of your neck stand at attention. A highlight of both the *Trek* film series and Horner's career.

Jeff Bond

Star Trek III: The Search for Spock ♫♫◦

1990, GNP Crescendo Records; from the movie *Star Trek III: The Search for Spock*, Paramount Pictures, 1984.

Album Notes: *Music*: James Horner; *Orchestrations*: Greig Mc-Ritchie; *Music Editor*: Bob Badami; Orchestra conducted by James Horner; *Album Producer*: James Horner; *Engineer*: Dan Wallin, Bill Benton.

Selections: 1 Prologue and Main Title (6:27); 2 Klingons (5:55); 3 Stealing The Enterprise (8:33); 4 The Mind Meld (2:30); 5 Bird Of Prey Decloaks (3:37); 6 Returning To Vulcan (4:49); 7 The Katra Ritual (4:29); 8 End Title (6:12); 9 The Search For Spock (3:43).

Review: James Horner's second *Star Trek* score comes off as a pallid retread of much of his stupendous *Wrath of Khan* effort, but it still has its moments, including the sparkling accompaniment to the Enterprise's return to its space dock moorings early in the film and the throbbing suspense licks of "Stealing the Enterprise," which climaxes in one of the more bombastic treatments of Alexander Courage's TV show fanfare ever heard in the film series. Horner's attempt to co-opt the appeal of Jerry Goldsmith's Prokofiev-like Klingon motifs from the original film, as well as his rehash of his own *Brainstorm* finale for the film's climactic mind-meld sequence, is less appealing. If you can't get enough of the composer's *Wrath of Khan* score, here's less of the same.

Jeff Bond

Star Trek IV: The Voyage Home ♫♫♫◦

1986, MCA Records; from the movie *Star Trek IV: The Voyage Home*, Paramount Pictures, 1986.

Album Notes: *Music*: Leonard Rosenman; *Orchestrations*: Ralph Ferraro; *Music Editor*: Else Blangsted; *Album Producer*: Leonard Rosenman; *Engineer*: Dan Wallin.

Selections: 1 Main Title (2:39); 2 The Whaler (2:00); 3 Market Street (4:39) *The Yellowjackets*; 4 Crash-Whale Fugue (8:15); 5 Ballad Of The Whale (5:03) *The Yellowjackets*; 6 Gillian Seeks Kirk (2:42); 7 Chekov's Run (1:19); 8 Time Travel (1:29); 9 Hospital Chase (1:13); 10 The Probe (1:17); 11 Home Again: End Credits (5:40).

Review: After the increasingly soap opera-ish plotlines for *Star Trek II* and *III*, the producers wisely decided to take an entirely different approach for *Star Trek IV: The Voyage Home*, and the results were the most successful Trek film of all—a re-freshingly comic, thoroughly entertaining time-travel yarn that remains the most satisfying big screen adventure of Captain Kirk and friends. To fit the change in tone, Nimoy turned to veteran composer Leonard Rosenman to write the score, and the results were an energetic, Oscar-nominated effort that refuses to take itself too seriously; Rosenman's main theme is a lot of fun, written in the same vein as some of his other genre works (i.e. Lord of the Rings), but his music for the film's aquatic protagonists, the Humpback whales, is more serious and noble in nature. The music by itself is highly enjoyable, with the album including a pair of tracks by the jazz group The Yellowjackets, who worked with Rosenman on the picture's "modern day" music that Kirk, Spock and the rest of the Enterprise crew encounter when they travel back to 1986 San Fransisco.

Andy Dursin

Star Trek V: The Final Frontier ♫♫♫♫

1989, Epic Records; from the movie *Star Trek V: The Final Frontier*, Paramount Pictures, 1989.

Album Notes: *Music*: Jerry Goldsmith; *Orchestrations*: Arthur Morton, Alexander Courage; *Music Editor*: Ken Hall; Orchestra conducted by Jerry Goldsmith; *Album Producer*: Jerry Goldsmith; *Engineer*: Bruce Botnick.

Selections: 1 The Mountain (3:54); 2 The Barrier (2:54); 3 Without Help (4:21); 4 A Busy Man (4:42); 5 Open The Gates (3:03); 6 An Angry God (6:58); 7 Let's Get Out Of Here (5:15); 8 Free Minds (3:20); 9 Life Is A Dream (3:59); 10 The Moon's A Window To Heaven (4:00) *Hiroshima*.

Review: Jerry Goldsmith's second voyage with the crew of the Starship *Enterprise* yields a variety of musical quality, no doubt due to the film's own slapdash continuity. Certainly "The Mountain" is far and away one of the composer's more inspired cues, a marvelous companion to the images of Kirk scaling the sheer mountain El Capitain in Yosemite National Park. The bold re-orchestration of his original theme from *Star Trek: The Motion Picture* is a joy, going a long way in making the film more exciting, but working against it all is his lighthearted variation on the Klingon theme. It only goes to further belittle these characters, who suffer massive indignation from their comedic on-screen antics. Overall, Goldsmith's score actually plays better outside of the film where his wondrously reverent motifs for the "god" entity aren't sabotaged by the limp visual effects. The closing song, "The Moon's A Window To Heaven," performed here by the jazz fusion group Hiroshima, did not appear in the film. However, Nichelle Nichols (Uhura) sung a portion of it during her ludicrous fan dance sequence.

David Hirsch

Star Trek VI: The Undiscovered Country ♫♫♫♫

1991, MCA Records; from the movie *Star Trek VI: The Undiscovered Country*, Paramount Pictures, 1991.

Album Notes: *Music:* Cliff Eidelman; *Orchestrations:* Mark McKenzie, William Kidd; *Music Editor:* Bunny Andrews; Orchestra conducted by Cliff Eidelman; *Album Producer:* Cliff Eidelman; *Engineer:* Armin Steiner.

Selections: 1 Overture (2:57); 2 An Incident (:53); 3 Clear All Moorings (1:39); 4 Assassination (4:45); 5 Surrender For Peace (2:46); 6 Death Of Gorkon (1:10); 7 Rura Penthe (4:22); 8 Revealed (2:38); 9 Escape From Rura Penthe (5:34); 10 Dining On Ashes (1:00); 11 The Battle For Peace (8:03); 12 Sign Off (3:13); 13 Star Trek VI Suite (6:18).

Review: Originally, director Nicholas Meyer wanted composer Cliff Eidelman to write a score based on Gustav Holst's *The Planets* for his film. When Paramount Pictures failed to come to terms with the copyright owners, Eidelman was asked to create a work in a similar vein. As a result, his score is vastly different from any previous in the *Star Trek* series. Dark, bleak, desperate... the Federation is now on the brink of an all out war with their mortal enemies, the Klingons, and events are being controlled by traitors within. Eidelman even uses a chorus to symbolize the menacing Klingon horde. A unique approach was also used in assembling the album: Eidelman perceived the entire score as a grand symphony, and, with occasionally cross-fading the cues together in strict film order, he created a running concerto that starts deliberately and builds in force until the spectacular eight-minute "Battle for Peace" finale.

David Hirsch

Star Trek: First Contact ♫♫♫

1996, GNP Crescendo; from the movie *Star Trek: First Contact*, Paramount Pictures, 1996.

Album Notes: *Music:* Jerry Goldsmith; *Orchestrations:* Arthur Morton, Alexander Courage, Jeff Atmajian; *Music Editor:* Ken Hall, Clifford Kaliweck; Orchestra conducted by Jerry Goldsmith; *Album Producer:* Jerry Goldsmith; *Engineer:* Bruce Botnick.

Selections: 1 Main Title/Locutus (4:17); 2 Red Alert (2:13); 3 Temporal Wake (2:07); 4 Welcome Aboard (2:40); 5 Fully Functional (3:18); 6 Retreat (3:59); 7 Evacuate (2:19); 8 39.1

> "For a non-musician, music is a very intimidating prospect. However, I find that non-musicians—in the capacity of a director—are very successful at telling me in their own way and with their own words, what they like and dislike, what they want it to sound like and what they don't want it to sound like."
>
> **James Newton Howard**
> *(The Hollywood Reporter, 1-16-96)*

Degrees Celsius (4:44); 9 The Dish (7:05); 10 First Contact (5:52); 11 End Credits (5:24); 12 Magic Carpet Ride (J. Kay/R. Moreve)(4:25) *Steppenwolf*; 13 Ooby Dooby (W. Moore/D. Penner)(2:22) *Roy Orbison*.

Review: Jerry Goldsmith has crafted this score with an understated eloquence. His music is embroidered with a sense of grand legendry, his theme seasoned and elegant rather than bombastic and vigorous. The heroism of the *First Contact* score is a quiet, reflective one, and stresses in positive terms the proud camaraderie between Captain and crew, and all they have gone through. The new theme, an affecting recapitulation of all the adventures that have come before in the TREK universe, is also a tribute to the harmonic future envisioned in *First Contact* and the entire Star Trek milieu. Goldsmith's original theme from *Star Trek: The Motion Picture* and the "Next Generations" series brackets this new score during its opening and closing credits, which remain unabashedly heroic and triumphant. And, of course, strains from Alexander Courage's original *Trek* fanfare provide the link with the original series and its various spin-offs. The CD, one of several "enhanced CD soundtracks" released lately, includes a data program, with interviews with Goldsmith and other *First Contact* participants.

Randall D. Larson

Star Trek: Generations ♫♫♫

1995, GNP Crescendo; from the movie *Star Trek: Generations*, Paramount Pictures, 1994.

Album Notes: *Music:* Dennis McCarthy; *Orchestrations:* William Ross, Mark McKenzie, Brad Warnaar; Orchestra conducted by Dennis McCarthy; *Album Producer*: Dennis Mc-Carthy; *Engineers*: Robert Fernandez, Paul Wertheimer, Bob Fisher.

Selections: 1 Star Trek: Generations Overture (4:13); 2 Main Title (A. Courage)(2:52); 3 The Enterprise B/Kirk Saves The Day (3:13); 4 Deck 15 (1:39); 5 Time Is Running Out (1:12); 6 Prisoner Exchange (2:57); 7 Outgunned (3:20); 8 Out Of Control/The Crash (2:05); 9 Coming To Rest (:57); 10 The Nexus/A Christmas Hug (7:07); 11 Jumping The Ravine (1:37); 12 Two Captains (1:32); 13 The Final Fight (6:15); 14 Kirk's Death (2:45); 15 To Live Forever (2:40); Star Trek: Generations Sound Effects: 16 Enterprise B Bridge (3:13); 17 Enterprise B Doors Open (:13); 18 Distress Call Alert (:10); 19 Enterprise B Helm Controls (:18); 20 Neus Energy Ribbon (1:38); 21 Enterprise B Deflector Beam (:08); 22 Enterprise B Warp Pass-By (:14); 23 Enterprise B Transporter (:12); 24 Tricorder (:30); 25 Hypo Injector (:03); 26 Communicator Chirp (:06); 27 Door Chime (:07); 28 Enterprise D Warp Out #1 (:22); 29 Bird Of Prey Bridge/Explosion (2:51); 30 Klingon Sensor Alert (:08); 31 Bird Of Prey Cloaks (:04); 32 Bird Of Prey De-Cloaks (:10); 33 Klingon Transporter (:12); 34 Soran's Gun (:11); 35 Soran's Rocket De-Cloaks (:05); 36 Shuttlecraft Pass-By (:21); 37 Enterprise D Bridge/Crash Sequence (3:21); 38 Enterprise D Warp-Out #2 (:09).

Review: Television composer Dennis McCarthy got the nod to score the first theatrical adventure of the "Next Generation" crew, and even though his score is not quite as interesting as the Goldsmith and Horner outings from the preceding *Trek* films, this is still an enjoyable effort. McCarthy's main theme for the film is rather basic but nevertheless perfectly suited for the picture, with a triumphant, heroic sound defining the valiant intentions of Captains Picard and Kirk, united in a "Nexus" at the far edge of the galaxy. For the otherworldly "Nexus," McCarthy wrote new age-style music that sounds suspiciously close to John Williams' "Fortress of Solitude" material from Superman, though without the melodic invention of that earlier work. Nevertheless, on its own terms, *Generations* is still a satisfying soundtrack that should not disappoint die-hard fans of the series.

Andy Dursin

Star Wars ♪♪♪♪♪

1997, RCA Records; from the movie *Star Wars*, 20th Century-Fox, 1977/1997.

Album Notes: *Music*: John Williams; *Orchestrations*: Herbert W. Spencer; The London Symphony Orchestra conducted by John Williams; *Album Producer*: John Williams; *Recording Engineer*: Eric Tomlinson; *CD Engineer*: Dan Hersch.

Selections: CD 1: 1 20th Century-Fox Fanfare (A. Newman) (:23); 2 Main Title/Rebel Blockade Runner (2:14); 3 Imperial Attack (6:43); 4 The Dune Sea Of Tatooine/Jawa Sandcrawler (5:01); 5 The Moisture Farm (2:25); 6 The Hologram/Binary Sunset (4:10); 7 Landspeeder Search/Attack Of The Sand People (3:20); 8 Tales Of A Jedi Knight/Learn About The Force (4:29); 9 Burning Homestead (2:50); 10 Mos Eisley Spaceport (2:16); 11 Cantina Band (2:47); 12 Cantina Band #2 (3:56); 13 Binary Sunset (alternate) (2:19);

CD 2: 1 Princess Leia's Theme (4:27); 2 The Millenium Falcon/Imperial Cruiser Pursuit (3:51); 3 Destruction Of Alderaan (1:32); 4 The Death Star/The Stormtroopers (3:35); 5 Wookie Prisoner/Detention Block Ambush (4:01); 6 Shootout In The Cell Bay/Dianoga (3:48); 7 The Trash Compactor (3:07); 8 The Tractor Beam/Chasm Crossfire (5:18); 9 Ben Kenobi's Death/The Fighter Attack (3:51); 10 The Battle Of Yavin: Launch From The Fourth Moon/X-Wings Draw Fire/ Use The Force (9:07); 11 The Throne Room/End Title (5:38).

Review: More than twenty years after its initial release, what hasn't been written or said about *Star Wars* that needs to be stated? John Williams' grand, outstanding operatic score—incorporating Korngold-esque swells of emotion as well as Wagnerian motives for the film's various characters—redefined film music, and continues to this day to influence the way movies sound. Just as importantly, it made legions of audiences into film music fans, resurrected interest in classical music, and created a whole new market for movie soundtracks to flourish in. Aside from all of the cultural significance, Williams' score remains a classic all the way, from the opening blast of his fanfare through the "galactic jazz" of the Cantina Band, culminating in the thrilling Death Star climax and triumphant "Throne Room" finale. After a handful of previous releases, RCA Victor's 1997 re-issue (accompanying the film's "Special Edition" release) is now rightfully considered the definitive issue of Williams' work, with expanded tracks and superb, digitally remastered sound creating the ultimate listening experience for one of the movies' all-time great scores.

Williams' original *Star Wars* score marked the beginning of his fruitful "epic" period that lasted from 1977 to 1983's *Return of the Jedi*, and it's still the standard by which epic science fiction adventure scores are measured. It's been argued that this score set the medium back by decades with its retro approach to the material, taking its cue from Korngold and Holst to produce a wholesome, swashbuckling sound that's been copied in countless bad ways since. But Williams found the perfect music for George Lucas' essentially innocent space opera, and *Star Wars* is a vibrant, unforgettable work from its spectacular opening titles (with a blasting, martial fanfare straight out of a Roman epic) and hammering, Holst-inspired underscoring of an attack by a gigantic Imperial star destroyer to its evocative Tatooine desert scoring and brilliant, Benny Goodman-styled cantina music. The outrageously loud and mechanistic "The Fighter Attack" is unlike anything ever heard in a movie up to that time, its shimmering spectral opening, repeated brass hits and declamatory Rebel fanfare melding with Lucas' dizzyingly edited space battle sequence to produce a kind of psychotic, exhilarating filmic video game. Even better is the lengthy and supremely exciting Death Star battle music, presented here in its entirety for the first time, from the suspenseful, pulsating "Launch from the Fourth Moon" to the exhilarating martial fanfares of "X-Wings Draw Fire"—there has rarely been a more thrilling accompaniment to a cinematic combat sequence. The quiet moments are just as engaging, from the haunting "The Princess Appears" to the deeply lyrical, moving statement of Ben Kenobi's theme as Luke Skywalker stares longingly into the "Binary Sunset." Extras include Williams' first take on that sequence, more of an epic, tragic rendition that speaks to young Luke's desolation as he contemplates another year on Tatooine, and a hidden collection of alternate takes of the title music. Beautifully produced and assembled by Nick Redman and Michael Mattesino, this two-CD set belongs in anyone's collection.

Andy Dursin/Jeff Bond

See also: The Empire Strikes Back and Return of the Jedi

Stargate ♪♪♪

1994, Milan Records; from the movie *Stargate*, M-G-M, 1994.

Album Notes: *Music*: David Arnold; *Orchestrations*: Nicholas Dodd; *Music Editor*: Laurie Higgins; The Sinfonia of London and The Chameleon Arts Chorus, conducted by Nicholas Dodd; *Synthesizer Programming*: Mike Barnes; *Album Producer*: David Arnold; *Engineer*: Geoff Foster.

Selections: 1 Stargate Overture (3:01); 2 Giza, 1928 (2:10) *Natacha Atlas*; 3 Unstable (2:07); 4 The Coverstones (:58); 5 Orion (1:29); 6 The Stargate Opens (3:58); 7 You're On The Team (1:55); 8 Entering The Stargate (2:57); 9 The Other Side (1:44); 10 Mastadge Drag (:56); 11 The Mining Pit (1:34); 12 King Of The Slaves (1:15); 13 Caravan To Nagada (2:16) *Natacha Atlas*; 14 Daniel And Shauri (1:53); 15 Symbol Discovery (1:15); 16 Sarcophagus Opens (:55); 17 Daniel's Mastadge (:49); 18 Leaving

Nagada (4:09); 19 Ra—The Sun God (3:22); 20 The Destruction Of Nagada (2:08); 21 Myth, Faith, Belief (2:18); 22 Procession (1:43); 23 Slave Rebellion (1:00); 24 The Seventh Symbol (:57); 25 Quartz Shipment (1:27); 26 Battle At The Pyramid (5:02); 27 We Don't Want To Die (1:57); 28 The Surrender (1:44); 29 Kasuf Returns (3:06); 30 Going Home (3:09).

Review: British composer David Arnold's orchestral background serves him well for this massive, sweeping score which effectively captures the textural nuances of the alien civilization as well as the heroic scope of the story. While incorporating synthesizers and modern instrumentation and recording techniques, Arnold's compositional style is rooted in Hollywood classicism. With his main theme's compelling melody, strikingly orchestrated throughout its many guises, and the rhythmical flurries and furiously energetic figures of the action cues, accentuated by evocative female choir vocalisms, Arnold's *Stargate* is a standout score. The 30 cues on the CD are varied, and Arnold weaves his music carefully, with as many bold strokes as there are quiet interludes.

Randall D. Larson

Starman ♪

1984, Varese Sarabande; from the movie *Starman*, Columbia Pictures, 1984.

Album Notes: *Music*: Jack Nitzsche; *Album Producers*: Tom Null, Chris Kuchler; *Engineer*: Joe Gastwirt.

Selections: 1 Jenny Shot (1:30); 2 Here Come The Helicopters (5:04); 3 Honeymoon (:55); 4 Road Block (1:38); 5 Do You Have Somebody? (1:18); 6 Pickup Truck (3:01); 7 What's It Like Up There? (1:46); 8 All I Have To Do Is Dream (B. Bryant) (3:29) *Jeff Bridges, Karen Allen*; 9 Lifting Ship (1:22); 10 I Gave You A Baby (2:11); 11 Morning Military (1:04); 12 Define Love (1:33); 13 Balls (1:10); 14 Starman Leaves/End Title (7:04).

Review: Jack Nitzsche was one of several composers director John Carpenter used during the period when he worked for the major studios and couldn't score his own pictures. That's a real shame here because this score is a major disappointment. Repetitive and dull, its only major melodic piece is the very limited main theme. Nitzsche constantly plugs it in when something personal is needed. Most of the action cues on the CD have that "made up as they went along" feel, with repetitive layers being added and subtracted in an attempt to vary the tone. The Jeff Bridges/Karen Allen duet of "All I Have to Do is Dream" stands out just because it's so damn thematic compared to the rest of the album.

David Hirsch

The Stars Fell on Henrietta
♫♫♫♫♫

1995, Varese-Sarabande; from the movie *The Stars Fell on Henrietta*, Warner Bros., 1995.

Album Notes: *Music*: David Benoit; *Orchestrations*: David Benoit, Lolita Ritmani, Chris Boardman; *Music Editor*: Steve Hope; *Featured Soloists*: Grant Geissman (banjo), Pat Kelly (guitar), Mike Lang, David Benoit (piano); *Album Producer*: David Benoit; *Engineer*: Bobby Fernandez, Clark Germaine.

Selections: 1 Main Title (1:16); 2 A New Start (2:11); 3 The Hunt Begins (1:59); 4 Divining Matilda (1:32); 5 Festivities Begin (1:58); 6 June 19th (1:37); 7 Off To California (:37); 8 X Marks The Spot (1:52); 9 I'm So Sorry (:34); 10 The Plan Sputters (:44); 11 The Big Boom (3:21); 12 Goodbye Mr. Cox (2:02); 13 End Credits (4:34); 14 Theme And Variation (3:58).

Review: Delightful and hauntingly touching score by David Benoit that captures the very soul of Depression-era Texas. Gentle guitar solos and soft piano phrases conjure up a simpler time when people only sought to survive the day, struggled and persevered through those the hardest of times. The main theme is an intoxicating motif, filled with hope, and dignity. An emotionally moving score that can be appreciated without ever having experienced the film.

David Hirsch

State of Grace ♫♫♫♪

1990, MCA Records; from the movie *State of Grace*, Orion Pictures, 1990.

Album Notes: *Music*: Ennio Morricone; *Orchestrations*: Ennio Morricone; Orchestra Unione Musicisti di Roma, conducted by Ennio Morricone; *Album Producer*: Ennio Morricone; *Engineer*: Sergio Marcotullu.

Selections: 1 Hell's Kitchen (3:02); 2 Park Ave. (2:03); 3 The Shootout (5:53); 4 Hundred Yard Dash (1:21); 5 State Of Grace (2:37); 6 New Jersey (:44); 7 Mott Street (5:02); 8 The Confrontation (3:39); 9 Finn (1:27); 10 Terry Noonan (2:27); 11 St. Patrick's Day (4:01); 12 The Backroom (1:35); 13 Jackie's Death (3:23); 14 Terry And Kate (3:21); 15 The Kitchen (6:40); 16 Bronx Drug Deal (1:37); 17 Murder In Matty's Bar (2:23); 18 The First Date (1:14).

Review: For this tale of Irish gangsters in Hell's Kitchen, Ennio Morricone provides a somber, moody score emphasizing a mournful low flute melody over brass and woodwind chords that hangs over the proceedings like a pall when it's not pulsing with extended suspense cues of bubbling strings and a staccato spinet line. Morricone maintains a consistently dreary tone throughout, although there is one startling burst of brightness and romanticism that ironically underscores the setting of an arson fire ("Hundred Yard Dash"). Like most of this composer's work, *State of Grace* is rich with haunting melodies and textures, and it's a good bet for devotees.

Jeff Bond

Stavisky

1988, RCA Victor; from the movie *Stavisky*, 1974.

See: Follies under Broadway Musicals

Stealing Home ♫♫♪

1988, Atlantic Records; from the movie *Stealing Home,* Warner Bros., 1988.

Album Notes: *Music*: David Foster; *Orchestrations*: David Foster; *String Arrangements*: Jeremy Lubbock, David Foster; *Music Editor*: Dan Carlin, Jr.; *Featured Musicians*: David Foster (keyboards), Rhett Lawrence (Fairlight drums), Rick Bowan, Michael Boddicker, David Foster (synthesizers), Dean Parks (acoustic guitars), Michael Landau (electric guitars), Dave "Rev" Boruff (saxophone); *Album Producer*: David Foster; *Engineer*: Jeffrey "Woody" Woodruff.

Selections: 1 Stealing Home (3:35); 2 Sherry (B. Gaudio)(2:30) *The Four Seasons*; 3 And When She Danced (Love Theme)(D. Foster/L. Thompson-Jenner) (3:50) *Marilyn Martin, David Foster*; 4 Poison Ivy (J. Leiber/M. Stoller) (3:21) *The Nylons*; 5 All I Have To Do Is Dream (B. Bryant)(2:20) *The Everly Brothers*; 6 Home Movie (2:10); 7 Great Balls Of Fire (J. Hammer/O. Blackwell)(1:50) *Jerry Lee Lewis*; 8 Baby, It's You (B. Bacharach/M. David/B. Williams)(2:38) *The Shirelles*; 9 Stealing Home (reprise)(5:08); 10 Bo Diddley (E. McDaniel)(2:19) *Bo Diddley*; 11 Katie's Theme (2:26).

Review: Five of the 11 numbers are performed by uber-slick producer David Foster, guaranteeing a languid affair. The rest are decently chosen oldies, plus vocal group The Nylons' inventive version of "Poison Ivy." But what it lacks is a truly fresh, new composition to really get things off the ground.

Gary Graff

Steel Magnolias ♫♫♫

1989, Polydor Records; from the movie *Steel Magnolias*, Tri-Star Pictures, 1989.

Album Notes: *Music*: Georges Delerue; Orchestra conducted by Georges Delerue; *Engineer*: John Richards.

Selections: 1 Main Title Introduction (4:41); 2 Tree Fireworks (1:17); 3 Good News, Bad News (3:59); 4 The Drive To Aunt

Fern's (5:15); 5 Easter Picnic/Departure (4:18); 6 End Title (3:34); 7 I Got Mine (R. Cooder)(4:25) *Ry Cooder*; 8 Two-Step Mamou (W. Toups/J. Miller/J. Arceneaux)(3:22) *Wayne Toups, Zydecajun*; 9 Jambalaya (On The Bayou)(H. Williams)(2:51) *Hank Williams*; 10 Main Title (reprise)(4:41).

Review: This average tear-jerker about women in a small southern town is elevated to the level of an effective drama by Georges Delerue's sublime music. Unsurprisingly, his music retains its appeal on disc as well. Delerue's score is often light, but never fluffy. His lush string sound is put to good use, the music appealingly evocative of small town life, investing the otherwise ordinary lives of the characters with a kind of poetry. Highlights include the main title, with its folky harmonica, the mournful viola which opens "Drive to Aunt Fern's", and the celeste waltz in "Good News, Bad News." In fact, the only thing which spoils this soundtrack is the inclusion of three tacky country western songs (one of which was not even in the film), which are totally out-of-place among Delerue's music. (Fortunately they are sequenced back to back, and easily skipped.) The original Polydor soundtrack is long out-of-print and hard to find. However, some of the score was rerecorded by the composer on *Georges Delerue: The London Sessions Volume II* (on Varese Sarabande), in a suite which Delerue arranged and conducted with listening more specifically in mind.

Paul Andrew MacLean

The Sting ♫♫♫♭

1987, MCA Records; from the movie *The Sting*, Universal Pictures, 1973.

Album Notes: *Music*: Marvin Hamlisch, Scott Joplin; Orchestra conducted by Marvin Hamlisch; *Featured Soloist*: Marvin Hamlisch (piano); *Album Producer*: Marvin Hamlisch; *Engineer*: Ami Hadami.

Selections: 1 Solace (orchestra)(3:35); 2 The Entertainer (orchestra) (3:03); 3 Easy Winners (2:44); 4 Hooker's Hooker (2:48); 5 Luther (3:08); 6 (a) Pine Apple Rag, (b) Gladiolus Rag (2:32); 7 The Entertainer (piano) (2:22); 8 The Glove (1:46); 9 Little Girl (2:00); 10 Pine Apple Rag (2:35); 11 Merry-Go-Round Music: (a) Listen To The Mocking Bird, (b) Darling Nellie Gray, (c) Turkey In The Straw (2:44); 12 Solace (piano)(3:35); 13 (a) The Entertainer, (b) Rag Time Dancer (3:45).

Review: What could be more appropriate as the background to a story about two con men, set in 1920s Chicago, than the jazz tinged compositions of Scott Joplin? In fact, notwithstanding Robert Redford's association with the film, the most remarkable thing about *The Sting* is the music, for after all is said and done, the film endures as the perfect vehicle for a renewed interest in Joplin's music, and the art of the rag: a jaunty musical style formerly acceptable only in the seedier establishments of life, gin joints, gambling halls and brothels among them! While the early '70s recording (issued early on in the CD era) could benefit from a '90s sonic "makeover," the toe-tapping ragtime music is infectious, and Joplin's ballads ("Solace" and "Luther") have a haunting, compelling quality to them. A fine introduction, this disc will no doubt leave you with a desire to explore more of Joplin's wonderful work.

Charles L. Granata

Stonewall ♫♫♫

1996, Columbia Records; from the movie *Stonewall*, Strand/BBC Films, 1996.

Album Notes: *Album Producer*: Randall Poster; *Engineer*: David Mitson.

Selections: 1 Give Him A Great Big Kiss (G. Morton) (2:15) *The Shangri-Las*; 2 Gee Baby Gee (J. Barry/E. Greenwich) (2:38) *The Butterflies*; 3 Sophisticated Boom (G. Morton) (2:12) *The Shangri-Las*; 4 Ooh Poo Pah Doo (J. Hill) (2:19) *The Shirelles*; 5 Remember (Walkin' In The Sand) (G. Morton) (2:21) *The Shangri-Las*; 6 Boy From New York City (J. Taylor/G. Davis) (3:02) *The Ad Libs*; 7 Zing Went The Strings Of My Heart (J. Hanley) (2:57) *Judy Garland*; 8 Down The Aisle (A. Levinson) (3:34) *Patti LaBelle & The Bluebelles*; 9 Go Now (M. Bennett/L. Banks) (2:43) *Bessie Banks*; 10 Over The Rainbow (H. Arlen/ E.Y. Harburg) (2:50) *Judy Garland*; 11 What A Good Boy (S. Page/E. Robertson) (3:53) *Barenaked Ladies*; 12 Give Him A Great Big Kiss (G. Morton/J. Taylor/ G. Davis) (7:41) *The Shangri-Las*.

Review: An intriguing mix that bridges the generations as it brings together songs performed by Judy Garland, Patti LaBelle and The Bluebelles, The Shangri-Las, The Shirelles, Barenaked Ladies, and other contemporary groups. It is difficult to assess who might actually be interested by this compilation, though in all fairness it actually sounds and plays much better than one might have anticipated.

Straight No Chaser ♫♫♫♫

1989, Columbia Records; from the movie *Straight, No Chaser*, Warner Bros., 1989.

Album Notes: *Music*: Thelonious Monk; *Featured Musicians*: Thelonious Monk (piano), John Coltrane, Charlie Rouse, Johnny Griffin (tenor sax), Wilbur Ware, Larry Gales (bass), Shadow Wilson, Ben Riley (drums), Ray Copeland (trumpet), Jimmy Cleveland (trombone), Phil Woods (alto sax); *Album Producer*: Orrin Keepnews; *Engineer*: Danny Kopelson.

Selections: 1 Straight No Chaser (and Opening Narration) (1:51) *Samuel E. Wright*; 2 Pannonica (5:11); 3 Trinkle, Trinkle (6:38); 4 Ugly Beauty (rehearsal) (2:31); 5 Ugly Beauty (7:18); 6 Epistrophy (T. Monk/K.S. Clarke) (5:38); 7 Evidence (9:01); 8 I Mean You (Stickball) (rehearsal and performance) (T. Monk/C. Hawkins) (4:19); 9 Lulu's Back In Town (H. Warren/A. Dubin) (4:14); 10 Don't Blame Me (J. McHugh/D. Fields) (2:54); 11 Sweetheart Of All My Dreams (A. Fitch/K. Fitch/B. Lowe) (1:43); 12 'Round Midnight (T. Monk/ C. Williams/B. Hanighen) (2:14).

Review: The soundtrack to a documentary portraying the famous jazz pianist and composer, *Straight No Chaser* will primarily appeal to fans of Thelonious Monk and his music, with plenty of selections to satisfy even the most difficult. Some of the tracks feature dialogue, studio talk, and other elements that somewhat distract from the essential, though they are kept to brief moments. The bulk of the recording, of course, consists of Monk's performances, alone or with some of his musicians, including John Coltrane, in tunes that capitalized his career ("Epistrophy," "Ugly Beauty," "'Round Midnight," etc.).

Street Fighter *♪♪♪*

1994, Varese-Sarabande Records; from the movie *Street Fighter*, Universal Pictures, 1994.

Album Notes: *Music*: Graeme Revell; *Orchestrations*: Tim Simonec, Graeme Revell, Larry Kenton, Ken Kugler, Mark Gasbarro; *Music Editor*: John Winget; The London Symphony Orchestra, conducted by Tim Simonec; *Featured Musicians*: Mark Zimoski (percussion), John Yoakum (soprano sax/flute/oboe), Rex Thomas (pedal steel guitar); *Album Producer*: Graeme Revell; *Engineer*: Dan Wallin.

Selections: 1 Showdown In Shadaloo (4:44); 2 Habanera (Vega & Ryu) (G. Bizet) (3:16); 3 Chun-Li Enters The Morgue (2:16); 4 Colonel Guile Addresses The Troops (2:47); 5 The Circus Tent (2:13); 6 General M. Bison (1:20); 7 Honda Is Tortured (:44); 8 Bison Troopers Marching Song (Zangief) (G. Revell/S. De Souza) (:58); 9 Chun-Li's Story (2:07); 10 Dhalsim Reprograms Blanka (1:36); 11 The Stealth Boat Attack (3:07); 12 "Game Over" (1:42); 13 Chun-Li And Bison (2:57); 14 Guile Discovers Blanka (2:10); 15 "Raise The Chamber" (Guile Attacks) (2:26); 16 Clash Of The Titans (Honda And Zangief) (1:51); 17 Guile Faces Bison (2:57); 18 Vega And Sagat vs. Ken And Ryu (3:07); 19 Bison Dies (2:02); 20 The Aftermath (3:17); 21 Attitude Adjuster (G. Acogny/A. Brown/D. De Lory) (4:29) *World Beaters*.

Review: Energetic action score by Graeme Revell, who seems to be excelling in this genre as the new master of the testosterone-powered movie. This film, where warriors from all over the world

are assembled to fight an evil warlord, offers Revell the opportunity to exploit a vast array of musical styles with a variety of ethnic motifs—Chinese ("Chun-Li Enters the Morgue"), Middle Eastern ("The Circus Tent") and a good old fashioned steamy "American" sex theme ("Chun-Li & Bison")—which helps to keep the score fresh. Scriptwriter Steven de Souza contributed the esperanto lyrics to the "Bison Troopers Marching Song."
David Hirsch

A Streetcar Named Desire

A Streetcar Named Desire/ Since You Went Away/Now Voyager/The Informer *♪♪♪*

1992, Capitol Records/Cloud Nine Records; from the movies *A Streetcar Named Desire*, Warner Bros., 1951; *Since You Went Away*, Vanguard Films, 1944; *Now, Voyager*, Warner Bros., 1942; and *The Informer*, RKO Radio Pictures, 1935.

Album Notes: *Music*: Alex North, Max Steiner; The Warner Bros. Studio Orchestra, conducted by Ray Heindorf; Orchestras conducted by Max Steiner.

Selections: *A STREETCAR NAMED DESIRE (A. NORTH)*: 1 Streetcar (2:51); 2 Four Deuces (3:09); 3 Belle Reeve (3:07); 4 Blanche (2:39); 5 Della Robia Blue (2:58); 6 Flores para los muertos (Flowers For The Dead) (4:50); 7 Mania (1:56); 8 Lust (3:18); 9 Soliloquy (2:51); 10 Redemption (1:53);

SINCE YOU WENT AWAY (M. STEINER): 11 Suite (9:44);

NOW, VOYAGER (M. STEINER): 12 Suite (8:55);

THE INFORMER (M. STEINER): 13 Suite (7:34).

Review: Long considered one of Hollywood's groundbreaking film scores, Alex North's compositions for *A Streetcar Named Desire* endure as some of the most exciting, provocative tunes ever written for a dramatic film: in this case, the hot, steamy stage-to-screen adaptation of Tennessee Williams' Pulitzer Prize winning masterpiece. With *Streetcar,* North created a new language for the fine art of film composition, juxtaposing modern jazz, blues and classical elements in a fashion that searingly communicates the lust, greed, passion and deception that accentuate the story's powerful, disturbing emotion.

Two CD issues offer the exact same repertoire, from the exact same masters. The first is on Capitol Records' and must be avoided at all costs: the sound is shrill and distorted, due to poor transfers from the original acetate discs. Far preferable is the Cloud Nine CD (from masters leased from Capitol), which has been carefully remastered, and sports clear, undistorted sonics. Both the Capitol and Cloud Nine CDs also offer three of

Max Steiner's Academy Award winning compositions: *Since You Went Away, Now, Voyager* and *The Informer*—all conducted by the composer.

Charles L. Granata

A Streetcar Named Desire
♫♫♫♫♫

1995, Varese-Sarabande; from the movie *A Streetcar Named Desire*, 1951.

Album Notes: *Music*: Alex North; The National Philharmonic Orchestra, conducted by Jerry Goldsmith; *Featured Musicians*: Sidney Sax (violin), Tony Coe (clarinet), Ronnie Price (piano), Allen Walley (bass), Harold Fisher (drums), John Barclay (trumpet); *Album Producers*: Jerry Goldsmith, Robert Townson; *Engineer*: Mike Ross-Trevor.

Selections: 1 Main Title (1:23); 2 New Orleans Street (1:29); 3 Belle Reve Reflections (2:15); 4 Stan Meets Blanche (3:03); 5 Blanche And Mitch (3:43); 6 Stan And Stella (3:01); 7 Blanche (2:43); 8 Belle Reve (2:50); 9 Birthday Party (3:09); 10 Revelation (5:12); 11 Mania (2:00); 12 Soliloquy (3:50); 13 Seduction (4:31); 14 Della Robia Blue (2:52); 15 The Doctor/Affirmation (4:16).

Review: This rerecording, splendidly recorded by the National Philharmonic Orchestra, conducted by Jerry Goldsmith, is yet another great example of a classic film score receiving the care and attention it merits. With dynamics and tempos that match and often surpass North's own readings (see above), and the splendor of the all-digital sound combining with several new cues to make this the most complete version in the best possible sound available, this recording of *Streetcar* belongs in any collection that aims to be comprehensive.

Streets of Fire ♫♫♫♭

1984, MCA Records; from the movie *Streets of Fire*, Universal Pictures, 1984.

Album Notes: *Song Producers*: Jim Steinman, Jimmy Iovine, Rupert Hine, Richard Perry & Greg Phillinganes, Phil Alvin & Pat Burnette, Tom Petty, Dan Hartman, Ry Cooder.

Selections: 1 Nowhere Fast (J. Steinman)(6:02) *Fire Inc.*; 2 Sorcerer (S. Nicks)(5:06) *Marilyn Martin*; 3 Deeper And Deeper (C. Curbin/J. West/Oram) (3:45) *The Fixx*; 4 Countdown To Love (K. Vance/M. Kupersmith)(3:00) *Greg Phillinganes*; 5 One Bad Stud (J. Leiber/M. Stoller)(2:28) *The Blasters*; 6 Tonight Is What It Means To Be Young (J. Steinman)(6:58) *Fire Inc.*; 7 Never Be You (T. Petty/B. Tench)(4:06) *Maria McKee*; 8 I Can Dream About You (D. Hartman)(4:07) *Dan Hartman*; 9 Hold That Snake (R. Cooder/J.L. Dickinson) (2:36) *Ry Cooder*; 10 Blue Shadows (D. Alvin)(3:17) *The Blasters*.

Review: A better-than-average rock soundtrack compilation, with superior performances by The Blasters, Ry Cooder, Dan Hartman, and The Fixx, among others. The film, about a famous rock star who is held for ransom and the detective who investigates the case, is arguably only a pretext to introduce a percussive rock score that punctuates the action. The tracks included here are all part of that score, and on their own make a great impression.

Striptease ♫♫♭

1996, EMI Records; from the movie *Striptease*, Columbia Pictures, 1996.

Album Notes: *Featured Artists*: Spencer Davis Group, Billy Ocean, Blondie, Soul Survivors, Booker T & The MG's, Laldin, Chynna Phillips, Smokey Robinson & The Miracles, Billy Idol, Prince, Joan Jett & The Blackhearts, Eurythmics, Dean Martin; *Album Producer*: Pete Ganbarg; *Engineer*: Michael Sarsfield.

Selections: 1 Gimme Some Lovin' (S. Davis/M. Winwood/S. Winwood) (2:58) *Spencer Davis Group*; 2 Get Outta My Dreams, Get Into My Car (R.J. Lange/B. Ocean) (5:34) *Billy Ocean*; 3 The Tide Is High (J. Holt/T. Evans/H. Barrett) (4:43) *Blondie*; 4 Expressway To Your Heart (K. Gamble/L. Huff) (2:16) *Soul Survivors*; 5 Green Onions (B.T. Jones/S. Cropper/A. Jackson Jr./L. Steinberg) (2:52) *Booker T & The MG's*; 6 Love Child (Halaila) (P. Sawyer/F. Wilson/D. Richards/D. Taylor) (3:19) *Laladin*; 7 I Live For You (C. Phillips/D. Child) (3:46) *Chynna Phillips*; 8 You've Really Got A Hold On Me (W. Robinson Jr.) (3:00) *Smokey Robinson & The Miracles*; 9 Mony Mony (T. James/R. Cordell/ R. Bloom/B. Gentry) (5:03) *Billy Idol*; 10 If I Was Your Girlfriend (Prince) (3:46) *Prince*; 11 I Hate Myself For Loving You (J. Jett/D. Child) (4:13) *Joan Jett & The Blackhearts*; 12 Sweet Dreams (Are Made Of This) (A. Lennox/D.A. Stewart) (3:36) *Eurythmics*; 13 Return To Me (C. Lombardo/D. DiMinno) (2:24) *Dean Martin*.

Review: One of those soundtracks that you listen to and go...Huh? Imagine Joan Jett next to Dean Martin, the Spencer Davis Group alongside Billy Ocean, Prince not far from Chynna Phillips (as in Wilson Phillips). Someone just went on a song-licensing shopping spree here, scooping up individual songs without giving much thought to how they'd work together.

Gary Graff

Stuart Saves His Family ♫♫

1995, Milan Records; from the movie *Stuart Saves His Family*, Paramount Pictures, 1995.

Album Notes: *Music*: Marc Shaiman; *Orchestrations*: Jeff Atmajian, Frank Bennett, Larry Blank, Jimmy Vivino; *Music Editor*: Charles Martin Inouye; Orchestra conducted by Artie

Kane; *Album Producer*: Marc Shaiman; *Engineer*: Dennis Sands.

Selections: 1 Daily Affirmation Theme (C. Hardwick)(:49) *Cheryl Hardwick*; 2 Stuart Makes "An Amends" To Roz (1:54); 3 Stuart Starts His Journal (1:21); 4 Dad Was Our Hero (1:48); 5 Aunt Paula's Two Funerals (1:53); 6 Everything's Coming Up Roses (J. Styne/S. Sondheim)(3:13) *Ethel Merman, The London Festival Orchestra*; 7 Julia's Family (2:33); 8 Stuart "Borrows" The Videotape (1:27); 9 Stuart Uses The "V" Word (1:23); 10 Stuart Takes The Stand (1:28); 11 Dad Shoots Donnie (:53); 12 Stuart And Donnie Talk (1:41); 13 The Hollywood Incident (2:43); 14 Stuart's Dream (1:06); 15 Bus Station Goodbyes (2:46); 16 Silver Bells (J. Livingston/R. Evans)(3:10) *Rachel Sweet*; 17 Donnie Shows Up (:32); 18 On The Sunny Side Of The Street (D. Fields/J. McHugh)(2:08) *Jack Sheldon*; 19 What Makes A Family (1:33) *Warren Wiebe*; 20 One Final Word (:06) *Phil Hartman*.

Review: This standard comedic effort by Marc Shaiman is likable enough, but offers little new beyond what he's done in the past. Shaiman obviously likes to score comedies much like an animated film with unmistakable standard themes ("A Closer Walk With Thee" is used for a portion of "Aunt Paula's Two Funerals"), hitting the mark and changing tempos as often as possible. The album is by no means of poor quality, and there are some fine moments ("Julia's Family"), but once you've heard a Shaiman comedy score, you've heard them all.

David Hirsch

The Subterraneans 🎝🎝🎝🎝

1991, Sony Music Special Products; from the movie *The Subterraneans*, M-G-M, 1960.

Album Notes: *Music*: Andre Previn; *Featured Musicians*: Andre Previn (piano), Carmen McRae (vocals), Red Mitchell (bass), Dave Bailey (drums), Russ Freeman (piano), Bob Enevoldsen (trombone), Gerry Mulligan (baritone sax), Shelly Manne (drums), Art Farmer (trumpet), Buddy Clark (bass), Art Pepper (alto sax), Bill Perkins (sax), Jack Sheldon (trumpet); *CD Engineer*: Ken Robertson.

Selections: 1 Why Are We Afraid (1:57); 2 Guido's Blackhawk (3:05); 3 Two By Two (4:00); 4 Bread And Wine (4:12); 5 Coffee Time (2:43) *Carmen McRae*; 6 A Rose And The End (3:24); 7 Should I (2:28); 8 Look Ma, No Clothes (1:32); 9 Things Are Looking Down (5:39); 10 Analyst (4:19); 11 Like Blue (1:58); 12 Raising Caen (3:02).

Review: In the days when he was still known as a film and jazz composer, Andre Previn occasionally combined both in scores that were amazingly alive and powerful in their expression. One such occasion is *The Subterraneans*, starring Leslie Caron and Georges Peppard, based on the Jack Kerouac "beat generation" novel, and set amid San Francisco's New Bohemians. While the film itself failed to find grace with critics and audiences, its score, bringing together the talents of West Coast instrumentalists Gerry Mulligan, Shelly Manne, Art Farmer, Art Pepper, Jack Sheldon, and Red Mitchell, and vocalist Carmen McRae, has long been regarded as one of the best examples of the use of jazz in films. Particularly striking is the fact that Previn wrote the cues for his eminent soloists, often performing against an orchestral background in a carefully dosed and effective blend of jazz riffs and symphonic sounds. There are many highlights in this excellent CD, which should attract those interested in solid instrumental soundtrack albums with a modern approach to its music.

Suburbia Woof

1997, Geffen Records; from the movie *Suburbia*, Sony Pictures Classics, 1997.

Album Notes: *Album Executive Producers*: Mark Kates, Richard Linklater, Randall Poster; *Engineer*: Stephen Marcussen.

Selections: 1 Unheard Music (E. Cervenka/J. Doe)(2:51) *Elastica, Stephen Malkmus*; 2 Bee-Bee's Song (Sonic Youth)(4:43) *Sonic Youth*; 3 Bullet Proof Cupid (Girls Against Boys)(4:53) *Girls Against Boys*; 4 Feather In Your Cap (B. Hansen)(3:45) *Beck*; 5 Berry Meditation (J. Lavelle/M. Kudo/T. Goldsworthy/M. Nishita)(7:34) *U.N.K.L.E.*; 6 I'm Not Like Everybody Else (R.D. Davies)(3:31) *Boss Hog*; 7 Cult (D.R. Goettel/E. Key/N. Ogre)(3:04) *Skinny Puppy*; 8 Does Your Hometown Care? (Superchunk)(4:17) *Superchunk*; 9 Sunday (Sonic Youth)(7:56) *Sonic Youth*; 10 Human Canninbal (Butthole Surfers)(3:49) *Butthole Surfers*; 11 Tabla In Suburbia (Sonic Youth)(2:17) *Sonic Youth*; 12 Hot Day (The Flaming Lips)(1:39) *The Flaming Lips*; 13 Psychic Hearts (T. Moore)(3:58) *Thurston Moore*; 14 Town Without Pity (D. Tiomkin/N. Washington)(2:55) *Gene Pitney*.

Review: It's amazing what passes as a soundtrack these days. If at least the songs were interesting, lyrically and melodically, or elicited interesting performances, perhaps one might overlook the obvious lack of talent that permeates most of them. But this sad rock compilation, which has nothing going for it, not even a singer able to hold a tune, is a sad reminder that songs that once constituted the soundtrack to our lives have now been replaced by uninspired noise. For that we don't even have to go to *Suburbia*. We find it in abundance in the streets of our big cities. Bring back the jackhammers: at least they don't have artistic pretensions!

Sudden Death ♫♫

1995, Varese-Sarabande Records; from the movie *Sudden Death*, Universal Pictures, 1995.

Album Notes: *Music*: John Debney; *Orchestrations*: Brad Dechter, Frank Bennett, Don Nemitz; *Music Editor*: Tom Carlson; Orchestra conducted by John Debney; *Album Producer*: John Debney; *Engineers*: John Richards, Dennis Sands.

Selections: 1 Main Title/Kitchen Fight (5:31); 2 Finding The Bombs (2:29); 3 Seeing Tyler (:59); 4 Locker Room Chase (2:28); 5 Choppers/Scaling The Dome (4:01); 6 Race Against The Clock/The Abduction (6:36); 7 Countdown (:44); 8 Rooftop Battle (5:26); 9 Chooper Explodes/Resolution (2:02).

Review: Take a pounding percussion section, a massive symphony orchestra, and musical selections all too obviously modeled after John Williams' *JFK* "Conspirators" cue and action scores too numerous to mention (though *The Fugitive* and *Die Hard* seem to pop up here and there), then combine them all and you get the recipe for a rather hackneyed movie soundtrack. Composer John Debney has done some terrific work in the movies, but his two scores for director Peter Hyams (*Sudden Death* was followed by the unreleased *The Relic*) are clearly not his best efforts. Most likely forced to compose along the strict, thankless guidelines of the action genre, Debney's music is bombastic to an extreme, with few melodic ideas taking charge out of the mayhem. It's hard to imagine anyone other than die-hard Van Damme fans wanting to hear this music outside of the cinematic context it was composed for.

Andy Dursin

A Summer Story ♫♫♫♪

1988, Virgin Records; from the movie *A Summer Story*, Atlantic Entertainment Group, 1988.

Album Notes: *Music*: Georges Delerue; *Orchestrations*: Georges Delerue; Orchestra conducted by Georges Delerue.

Selections: 1 Love In The Loft (1:49); 2 Summer Poem (1:37); 3 We Meet Megan (:59); 4 Sheep Shearing (1:19); 5 Ashton Arrives (3:20); 6 Waiting For Megan (1:56); 7 Falling In Love (1:29); 8 Coming To Town (:32); 9 Abandoned (4:54); 10 Flashback And Rescue (2:09); 11 The Gentle Maiden (1:47); 12 Return To The Hill (3:26); 13 At The Beach (:34); 14 Megan Leaves Forever (1:44); 15 Missed The Train (1:18); 16 Megan At Work (:49); 17 Night Meeting (1:27); 18 Megan In The Field (1:16); 19 Thinking Of Ashton (:33); 20 Ashton's Son (Theme From A Summer Story)(3:23).

Review: Georges Delerue had probably the greatest gift for lyricism and sentiment of any film composer ever. Thus he was perfectly suited to this bittersweet love story about a wealthy young Englishman's romance with a farm girl in 1916. The score evokes a feeling of pastoral England not unlike that in the works of Frederick Delius or Ralph Vaughan Williams, but *A Summer Story* is finally and consummately in the style of Georges Delerue. Throughout, Delerue's inimitable string sound is prominent. His music gushes with honest sentiment and romance, yet never once does it become sappy or cloying. For all its warmth however, there hangs a sense of tragedy over *A Summer Story*, and the score ultimately evokes an intense feeling of nostalgia and loss. Romantic scores of this calibre rarely come along, and since Delerue's passing have been conspicuously more rare, making this CD something of a treasure.

Paul Andrew MacLean

Sun Valley Serenade/ Orchestra Wives ♫♫♫♫

1986, Mercury Records; from the movies *Sun Valley Serenade*, 20th Century-Fox, 1941, and *Orchestra Wives*, 20th Century-Fox, 1942.

Album Notes: The Glenn Miller Orchestra, featuring Johnny Best, Billy May, Ray Anthony, Wade McMickle, Bobby Hackett (trumpet), Glenn Miller, Paul Tanner, Jimmy Priddy, Fran D'Annolfo (trombone), Tex Beneke, Al Klink, Ernie Caceres, Willie Schwartz, Hal McIntyre (saxophone), Chummy McGregor (piano), Jack Lathrop (guitar), Trigger Alpert (bass), Maurice Purtill (drums), Tex Beneke, Ray Eberle, Marion Hutton, Six Hits and A Miss, The Modernaires (vocals); *Album Producer*: Donald Elfman; *Engineers*: Dennis Drake, Gert Van Houyen.

Selections: *SUN VALLEY SERENADE*: 1 In The Mood (J. Garland/A. Razaf)(3:18); 2 I Know Why (And So Do You)(H. Warren/M. Gordon)(3:45) *The Modernaires, John Payne, Lorraine Elliot*; 3 Sun Valley Jump (J. Gray)(2:30); 4 The Spirit Is Willing (J. Gray)(3:25); 5 It Happened In Sun Valley (H. Warren/M. Gordon) (2:15) *The Modernaires, Six Hits and A Miss*; 6 Chattanooga Choo-Choo (H. Warren/M. Gordon)(4:40) *Tex Beneke, The Modernaires*; 7 Measure For Measure (A. May)(2:38);

ORCHESTRA WIVES: 8 Serenade In Blue (H. Warren/M. Gordon) (5:44) *Pat Friday, Ray Eberle, The Modernaires*; 9 Bugle Call Rag (J. Pettis/ B. Myers/E. Schoebel)(2:47); 10 Moonlight Serenade (G. Miller/M. Parish) (1:04); 11 American Patrol (J. Gray)(3:34); 12 At Last (H. Warren/M. Gordon) (4:17) *Pat Friday, Ray Eberle*; 13 Boom Shot (G, Miller/A. May)(2:31); 14 That's Sabotage (H. Warren/M. Gordon)(2:39) *Marion Hutton*; 15 I've Got A Gal In Kalamazoo (H. Warren/M. Gordon)(5:24)

Tex Beneke, Marion Hutton, The Modernaires; 16 Moonlight Sonata (L. Van Beethoven)(4:45); 17 People Like You And Me (H. Warren/M. Gordon)(3:43) *Marion Hutton, Ray Eberle, Tex Beneke, The Modernaires*; 18 You Say The Sweetest Things Baby (H. Warren/M. Gordon) (2:23).

Review: Both films were more or less tailored to feature the Glenn Miller Orchestra in the early days of World War II, when the country had not yet joined the conflict, but public sentiment was already being frayed and people needed some kind of entertainment to forget the dark clouds that amassed across the Atlantic and elsewhere. These light, enjoyable musical films have plots that are not too terribly obtrusive and musical numbers that often are terrific, and they exude the kind of mindless vibrancy most filmgoers hope to find when they go to the movies. The amazing thing about this CD, however, is the fact that the performances by the Glenn Miller Orchestra are in stereo, painstakingly reconstructed from the sound strips that were recorded at the time, long before stereophonic sound existed in the movies, let alone in the recording industry. The sound quality leaves a bit to be desired, to be sure, and the stereo is a trifle primitive, but where else would you hear "In the Mood," "It Happened in Sun Valley," "Chattanooga Choo-Choo," "Moonlight Serenade," "I've Got a Gal in Kalamazoo," and all the other hits made popular by the band in glorious two-channel definition? Besides, the music here is totally exhilarating, and explains why the big band era has left such a wonderful glow in the lives of those who experienced it.

Sundown ✍✍✍ʔ

1990, Silva Screen Records; from the movie *Sundown*, Vestron Pictures, 1989.

Album Notes: *Music*: Richard Stone; *Orchestrations*: Richard Stone, Mark Watters, Philip Griffen, Conrad Pope; *Music Editor*: Allan K. Rosen; The Graunke Symphony Orchestra, conducted by Allan Wilson; *Album Producers*: Ford A. Thaxton, Richard Stone; *Engineers*: Allan Snelling, Jim Scheffler.

Selections: 1 Overture and Shane's Ride (3:56); 2 The Gathering (3:06); 3 Van Helsing Drops In (2:56); 4 Night Flight (2:01); 5 Seduction (2:25); 6 Count Mardulak (2:39); 7 Shane In Pursuit (2:41); 8 Come To Bed (1:23); 9 Mort's Duel In The Sun (1:59); 10 Attack And Retreat (4:16); 11 The Siege (1:52); 12 Mort's Drive Through Purgatory (:43); 13 Sandy Handcuffed (4:58); 14 Anna Und Otto (1:30); 15 Mardulak's Speech (2:03); 16 Hell In Purgatory (3:30); 17 Showdown (2:36); 18 Redemption Of The Damned (Finale)(5:43).

Review: At first, the whole premise seems totally ludicrous—a vampire western film, set in the aptly named Purgatory, a small town lost in the Arizona desert. But drawing from both genres, composer Richard Stone has come up with a score that amusingly spoofs westerns and horror films, while retaining its creative edge. The end result is a soundtrack album one might easily have overlooked, filled with cues that are appealing and original. Well worth hunting for!

Supergirl ✍✍✍✍

1993, Silva Screen Records; from the movie *Supergirl*, Warner Bros., 1984.

Album Notes: *Music*: Jerry Goldsmith; *Orchestrations*: Arthur Morton; *Music Editor*: Ken Hall; The National Philharmonic Orchestra and Chorus, conducted by Jerry Goldsmith; *Album Producer*: Jerry Goldsmith; *Engineer*: Eric Tomlinson.

Selections: 1 Overture (6:07); 2 Main Title and Argo City (3:15); 3 Argo City Mall (:56); 4 The Butterfly (1:36); 5 The Journey Begins (1:12); 6 Arrival On Earth/Flying Ballet (5:36); 7 Chicago Lights/Steel Attack (2:23); 8 The Superman Poster (:52); 9 A New School (2:13); 10 The Map (1:10); 11 Ethan Spellbound (2:13); 12 The Monster Tractor (7:34); 13 Flying Ballet (alternate version)(2:13); 14 The Map (alternate version) (1:13); 15 The Bracelet (1:44); 16 First Kiss/The Monster Storm (4:35); 17 "Where Is She?"/The Monster Bumper Cars (2:57); 18 The Flying Bumper Car (1:28); 19 "Where's Linda?" (1:21); 20 Black Magic (4:08); 21 The Phantom Zone (3:42); 22 The Vortex/The End Of Zaltar (5:49); 23 The Final Showdown & Victory/End Title (short version) (12:10).

Review: While Jerry Goldsmith has often contributed outstanding film music, too many times he has stood in the shadow of John Williams, scoring movies that were either imitative of or were ripoffs of successful pictures scored by Williams (i.e. where Williams scored *Raiders of the Lost Ark*, *Jurassic Park* and *Home Alone*, Goldsmith wrote *King Solomon's Mines*, *Congo* and *Dennis the Menace*). Yet another case is *Supergirl*, the failed but entertainingly campy 1984 spin-off of the *Superman* series from producer Alexander Salkind, featuring a great score from Goldsmith that went overlooked due to the film's dismal critical and box-office performance. The composer did a yeoman's job here, writing a romantic, soaring score that compares favorably to its predecessor, featuring thrilling action cues backed by outstanding performances from the National Philharmonic Orchestra and Chorus. The initial CD release from Varese was superceded by an extended re-issue from Silva Screen in 1993, boasting unreleased and alternate cues, as well as the dumbest credit line in soundtrack album history ["The Superman Poster," "track 8, composed by Jerry Goldsmith (75%) and John Williams (25%)."]

Andy Dursin

Superman The Movie 🎵🎵🎵🎵

1991, Warner Bros. Records; from the movie *Superman The Movie*, Warner Bros., 1978.

Album Notes: *Music:* John Williams; *Music Editor:* Ken Wannberg; The London Symphony Orchestra, conducted by John Williams; *Album Producer:* John Williams; *Engineer:* Eric Tomlinson.

Selections: 1 Theme From Superman (Main Title)(4:24); 2 The Planet Krypton (4:45); 3 Destruction Of Krypton (5:58); 4 The Trip To Earth (2:23); 5 Love Theme From Superman (5:00); 6 Leaving Home (4:48); 7 The Fortress Of Solitude (8:29); 8 The Flying Sequence and Can You Read My Mind (J. Williams/L. Bricusse)(8:08); 9 Super Rescues (3:24); 10 Superfeats (5:00); 11 The March Of The Villains (3:33); 12 Chasing Rockets (7:33); 13 Turning Back The World (2:01); 14 End Title (6:24).

Review: This sadly mistreated soundtrack, one of John Williams' most memorable contributions to the screen, certainly would deserve better than the CD released, after many years of simply ignoring it altogether, by Warner Bros. Records, in a shortened version that eliminates a couple of cues ("Growing Up" and "Lex Luthor's Lair") "to facilitate a single, specially-priced compact disc." In an era where most important scores are being reissued not once but often several times, and always with extra tracks, *Superman The Movie* stands alone as a case in point where a label simply doesn't seem to give a damn about the riches in its vaults.

This said, the score created by John Williams teems with tunes that are outright exciting and wonderfully evocative of the action on the screen. Typically, Williams created a rousingly heroic theme for the superhero, with stirring brassy accents that spell out his invincibility, and a delicately wrought "Love Theme" that brings a delightful softer note to the score. The villains are dealt with in a sardonic anthem that displays glee and glum all at once ("The March of the Villains"), while Superman's deeds are detailed in cues in which the main theme is often used as an anchor to other, evolutive motifs.

Played with the right amount of fire and excitement by the London Symphony Orchestra (that unmistakable brass section is sensational!), the long score follows the screen narrative with expressive details that imaginatively convey its scope and its importance. Margot Kidder's reading of "Can You Read My Mind" is the only apparent weak point in this thrilling score, an otherwise spectacular display of Williams' creativity and beguiling musical invention.

Surrender 🎵♭

1987, Varese-Sarabande Records; from the movie *Surrender*, Warner Bros., 1987.

Album Notes: *Music:* Michel Colombier.

Selections: 1 A Moment Of Doubt (1:00); 2 Space Museum (3:43); 3 She's Different (:53); 4 Sean And Daisy (1:12); 5 Got A Date With An Angel (1:23); 6 Surrender (4:01); 7 200,000 Copies (:34); 8 Hi, Jay (:24); 9 Goodbye, Seanstein (1:30); 10 Paid By The Hour (1:37); 11 Bad Dream (1:16); 12 Deep Into The Night (2:31); 13 The Wolf (:32); 14 The Revenge (1:54); 15 Just An Old Fashion Blues (1:24); 16 I'm Not A Woman (:30); 17 Surrender (reprise) (4:13).

Review: Aah, the 1980s! Movie soundtracks often featured power-rock songs produced by David Foster, and wacky scores sometimes performed entirely on synthesizers. Don't you wish you could go back to those carefree times? Well, perhaps not, but if you ever did, Michel Colombier's synthetic and bland score for this 1987 Cannon Group comedy will fit the bill. The movie stars Michael Caine (who seemingly appeared in more movies in 1987 than were made in 1997), Sally Field and Steve Guttenberg, and if that cast wasn't '80s enough, take a listen to Colombier's score, which feels like it's constantly treading water in trying to create a musical backdrop for the film's laughless shenanigans. The album is long out-of-print, but you still may be able to find it in one of those cut-out bins featuring albums by Debbie Gibson, Tiffany, and all those other artists whose spotlight time expired before the clock turned past 1989.

Andy Dursin

Surviving Picasso 🎵🎵

1996, Epic Soundtrax; from the movie *Surviving Picasso*, Warner Bros., 1996.

Album Notes: *Music:* Richard Robbins; *Orchestrations:* Geoffrey Alexander; Orchestra conducted by Harry Rabinowitz; *Album Producer:* Richard Robbins; *Engineer:* Glen Neibaur.

Selections: 1 Grands Augustins (Main Title)(2:47); 2 Francoise (5:02); 3 Menerbes (4:24); 4 "You'd Be My Woman" (1:14); 5 Marie-Therese (2:31); 6 Cubist Flashback (1:16); 7 Olga (2:07); 8 Grandmother (2:49); 9 Jacqueline (2:34); 10 Circus (1:47); 11 Dora (3:32); 12 La Galloise (3:34); 13 Vallauris Corrida (End Credits)(7:57).

Review: Richard Robbins creates the bleakest of symphonic suites for this film about painter Pablo Picasso and the young girl who seeks his tutelage. Very often monothematic, Robbins colors his score in shades of gray. There is a repetitive motif throughout to represent the myopic ambitions of each of the characters, who remain forever wanting because they can never satisfy themselves enough to realize they can reach their goals. Certainly not the happiest score you'll ever hear.

David Hirsch

"There's such an abundance of brilliant musical talent in Hollywood. Most composers are so versatile they can handle any type of score."

Mace Neufeld
producer
(The Hollywood Reporter, 1-16-96)

Swing Kids 🎵🎵🎵🎵

1993, Hollywood Records; from the movie *Swing Kids*, Hollywood Pictures, 1993.

Album Notes: *Music*: James Horner; *Orchestrations*: Joel Rosenbaum; *Music Editors*: Joe E. Rand, Eric Reasoner; *New Swing Recording Arranger*: Chris Boardman; *Featured Musicians*: Jerry Hey, Gary Grant, Larry Hall, Chuck Findley (trumpet), Bill Reichenbach, Lloyd Ulgate, John Johnson (trombone), Abe Most, Dan Higgins, Robert Tricarico, Gene Cipriano, Curt McGettrick (saxophones, woodwinds), Michael Lang (piano), Dennis Budimir, Dean Parks (guitar), Ben Wild, Chuck Domonico (bass), Ralph Humphrey (drums), Sid Page (violin); *Album Producers*: James Horner, Robert Kraft; *Engineers*: Shawn Murphy, Allen Sides.

Selections: 1 Sing, Sing, Sing (With A Swing)(L. Prima)(4:57); 2 Nothing To Report (1:36); 3 Shout And Feel It (W. Basie)(2:27); 4 It Don't Mean A Thing (If It Ain't Got That Swing)(E.K. Ellington/I. Mills)(2:48); 5 The Letter (4:09); 6 Flat Foot Floogee (S. Gaillard/B. Green/S. Stewart)(3:17); 7 Arvid Beaten (2:10); 8 Swingtime In The Rockies (B. Goodman/J. Mundy)(3:08); 9 Daphne (D. Reinhardt)(1:50); 10 Training For Utopia (3:43); 11 Life Goes To A Party/Jumpin' At The Woodside (B. Goodman/H. James)/(W. Basie)(2:17); 12 Goodnight, My Love (M. Gordon/H. Revel)(3:06); 13 Ashes (4:20); 14 Bei Mir Bist Du Schon (S. Secunda/J. Jacobs/S. Cahn/S. Chaplin)(4:09); 15 The Bismarck (3:04); 16 Swing Heil (5:26).

Review: There may have been something ludicrous about the plot of the film (young Germans defying Hitler's Nazi henchmen with their love for swing music and the American big bands), but there is nothing ludicrous about this soundtrack album, in which great recreations of some well-known standards, and new tracks composed by James Horner, combine to create a vivid musical picture that transcends the medium for which it was initially meant.

Swingers 🎵🎵🎵🎵

1996, Miramax Records; from the movie *Swingers*, Miramax Pictures, 1996.

Album Notes: *Album Producers*: Julianne Kelley, Jeffrey Kimball, Beth Rosenblatt.

Selections: 1 You're Nobody 'Til Somebody Loves You (J. Cavanaugh/R. Morgan/L. Stock)(2:12) *Dean Martin*; 2 Paid For Loving (S. Johnson/B. Daughtrey/J. Palmer)(3:23) *Love Jones*; 3 With Plenty Of Money And You (H. Warren/A. Dubin)(1:33) *Tony Bennett, Count Basie and His Orchestra*; 4 You & Me & The Bottle Makes 3 Tonight (Baby)(S. Morris)(3:32) *Big Bad Voodoo Daddy*; 5 Knock Me A Kiss (M. Jackson/A. Razaf)(2:46) *Louis Jordan*; 6 Wake Up (J. Reinhardt)(:52) *The Jazz Jury*; 7 Groove Me (K. Floyd)(2:59) *King Floyd*; 8 I Wan'na Be Like You (R.M. Sherman/R.B. Sherman)(3:25) *Big Bad Voodoo Daddy*; 9 Mucci's Jag M.K. II (J. Altruda)(5:33) *Joey Altruda*; 10 King Of The Road (R. Miller)(2:27) *Roger Miller*; 11 Pictures (J. Reinhardt) (1:04) *The Jazz Jury*; 12 She Thinks I Still Care (D.L. Lipscomb) (2:33) *George Jones*; 13 Car Train (J. Reinhardt) (1:23) *The Jazz Jury*; 14 Pick Up The Pieces (R. Ball/M. Duncan/O. McIntyre/A. Gorrie/H. Stuart/R. McIntosh) (3:59) *Average White Band*; 15 Go Daddy-O (S. Morris)(3:11) *Big Bad Voodoo Daddy*; 16 I'm Beginning To See The Light (J. Hodges/E.K. Ellington/D. George/ H. James)(2:17) *Bobby Darin*.

Review: Inexplicably, the hip nightlife of the late mid-'90s includes martinis, cigars and swinging jazz music. With a few liberties, the soundtrack to this engaging chronicle of the trend nails the bachelor pad *savoir faire* of the music of choice. Dean Martin, Louis Jordan, King Floyd and an enjoyable workout on "With Plenty of Money and You" by Count Basie and Tony Bennett capture swing years past. Selections by Love Jones and Big Bad Voodoo Daddy give a present-day twist to the music. And familiar hits by Roger Miller ("King of the Road") and the Average White Band ("Pick Up the Pieces") sound surprisingly in sync with the rest of this collection.
Gary Graff

Switch 🎵

1991, Varese-Sarabande Records; from the movie *Switch*, Warner Bros., 1991.

Album Notes: *Music*: Henry Mancini; *Orchestrations*: Henry Mancini; *Featured Musicians*: David Wilson (violin), Ray Pizzi (soprano sax), Brandon Fields (alto sax), Steve Schaeffer (drums), Mike Lang, Jim Cox (keyboards), Abe Laboriel, Chuck Domonico (bass), George Doering (guitar); *Album Producer*: Henry Mancini; *Engineer*: Bobby Fernandez.

Selections: 1 Main Title (Theme From Switch)(2:10); 2 Something For Pizzi (4:00); 3 Amanda And The Devil (2:25); 4

Seduction (3:17); 5 Dukes (3:00); 6 It's All There (3:22); 7 They Marry (3:34); 8 Fashion Show (1:42); 9 End Title (Theme From Switch)(4:30).

Review: The long collaboration between Henry Mancini and filmmaker Blake Edwards produced countless undisputed masterpieces in the annals of movie history—from "Moon River" to *The Pink Panther*, Mancini scored Edwards' pictures with classy, distinguished film scores that continue to influence popular music to this day. Towards the end of his career, Mancini still had that old time panache, as evidenced by his terrific work on Edwards' terrible 1988 comic-western *Sunset* and the successful *Victor/Victoria* musical adaptation. While *Sunset* sadly went unreleased, an original score album was issued for Mancini' music from *Switch*, Edwards' 1991 gender-switching, would-be comedy with Ellen Barkin. In a surprising turn of events, Mancini's original music was largely removed from the finished film, but upon listening to this painful soundtrack, it's all too obvious why—his score is, for lack of a better term, a disaster. The music is heavy on electronics and light on melody, almost straining to be "different" from the composer's usual sound. Different it is, but also grating and thoroughly unappealing. Kudos to anyone who manages to get through the entire length of this thankfully brief album without skipping ahead.

Andy Dursin

Tai-Pan ♪♪♪

1986, Varese-Sarabande Records; from the movie *Tai-Pan*, De Laurentis Entertainment, 1986.

Album Notes: *Music:* Maurice Jarre; The Studioorchester of Munich, conducted by Maurice Jarre; *Album Producer:* Maurice Jarre; *Engineer:* Peter Kramper.

Selections: 1 Suite From Tai-Pan, Part 1: Main Title/Macao/Culum/Brock/May-may (18:16); 2 Suite From Tai-Pan, Part 2: Chinese Fog/Jinqua/Love And Typhoon/It Was A Boy/A New Tai-Pan (18:37).

Review: If you're the guy who wrote the music for *Lawrence of Arabia*, you get a lot of calls. Maurice Jarre would be that guy, and *Tai-Pan*, a silly 19th-century Chinese adventure based on the James Clavell novel, must have been one of those calls. Jarre has scored two Asian epics, this and the 1980 mini-series *Shogun*, but *Tai-Pan* is by far the more western and traditional of the two. It's a sweeping, soaring, somewhat clinky symphonic score with Jarre's unmistakable imprint all over it. Jarre almost always sounds like himself, especially in this genre, and he has a way of taking his melodies in unexpected,

excitingly sing-songy directions. The CD features two 18-minute tracks (side A and B on the original vinyl) and is fairly coherent.

Lukas Kendall

Tales from the Darkside: The Movie Woof

1990, GNP Crescendo; from the movie *Tales from the Dark Side: The Movie*, Paramount Pictures, 1990.

Album Notes: *Music:* John Harrison, Chaz Jankel, Jim Manzie, Pat Regan, Donald A. Rubinstein; *Album Producer:* John Harrison.

Selections: 1 Tales From The Darkside: The Movie: Prologue/Theme/Main Title (D.A. Rubinstein)(2:56); 2 "Lot 249" Suite (J. Manzie/P. Regan)(12:49); 3 "The Way Of All Flesh" (from "Lot 249") (J. Manzie)(3:23); 4 "Cat From Hell" Suite (C. Jankel)(11:27); 5 Lover's Vow" Suite (J. Harrison)(12:22); 6 Desperate Pain (from "Lover's Vow")(J. Harrison)(3:33) *Ron ''Byrd'' Foster*; 7 Bye, Bye, Betty (D.A. Rubinstein)(1:29); 8 Tales From The Darkside: The Movie (reprise) (D.A. Rubinstein)(:30).

Review: Despite input from five composers, this score for this anthology, based on the TV series, is simply a mediocre collection of synthesized music. One would expect stories written by the likes of Stephen King and George Romero to inspire something more creative, but that never happens. Each suite representing the four stories is virtually interchangeable in style and the whole package becomes depressingly dull.

David Hirsch

Talk Radio/Wall Street ♪♪♪

1988, Varese-Sarabande Records; from the movies *Talk Radio*, Cineplex Odeon Films, 1988; and *Wall Street*, 20th Century-Fox, 1987.

Album Notes: *Music:* Stewart Copeland; *Performer:* Stewart Copeland; *Album Producer:* Jeff Seitz; *Engineer:* Jeff Seitz.

Selections: *TALK RADIO:* 1 Kent: Unpredictable (2:17); 2 Dietz: Just Come Right In Here, Denise (3:06); 3 TLKa: We Know Where You Live (3:51); 4 Tick: We Feel Too Much (2:47); 5 Trend: He Has Heart (3:11);

WALL STREET: 6 Bud's Scam (2:52); 7 Are You With Me? (1:15); 8 Trading Begins (2:25); 9 The Tall Weeds (3:05); 10 Break-Up (Darian)(2:03); 11 Anacott Steal (2:55); 12 End Title Theme (1:10).

Review: Both films were directed by Oliver Stone, yet two films couldn't have been more different in scope and in approach.

Inspired by the 1984 murder of radio personality Alan Berg in the hands of radicals, *Talk Radio*, set at a station in Dallas, surveyed the personal life and professional career of a late-night talkshow host (portrayed by Eric Bogosian), whose vitriolic, offensive on-the-air comments spare nothing and no one, and attract a sordid, squalid audience. As its title suggests, *Wall Street* took place in the world of high finance, with Charlie Sheen portraying a young, ruthless tyro, manipulated by the man he wants to emulate, a big time financial shark played by Michael Douglas. Giving each film a style of their own, Stewart Copeland's scores are abrasively energetic and descriptive, relying on synth effects, in themes that detail the specific action in each. Of the two, *Talk Radio* seems more fully realized and interesting, but that may also be because of the fact that some of the cues are set off by short excerpts from the dialogue which gives them a greater dramatic focus. However, in *Wall Street* some frighteningly realistic sounds (including dogs barking, perhaps in a more picturesque description of some of the characters that inhabit the financial districts) provide a physical aura to the score that's also quite striking.

Taxi Driver 🎵🎵◗

1989, Varese-Sarabande Records; from the movie *Taxi Driver*, Columbia Pictures, 1976.

Album Notes: *Music*: Bernard Herrmann; *Arrangements*: Dave Blume; Orchestra conducted by Dave Blume, Bernard Herrmann; *Album Producer*: Neely Plumb; *Engineers*: Kevin Cleary, Mickey Crofford, Don Henderson.

Selections: 1 Theme From Taxi Driver (4:13) *Tom Scott*; 2 I Work The Whole City (2:25); 3 Betsy In A White Dress (2:14); 4 The Days Do Not End (4:05); 5 Reprise: Theme From Taxi Driver (2:24); 6 Diary Of A Taxi Driver (4:31) *Robert De Niro*; 7 Theme From Taxi Driver (3:38); 8 The .44 Magnum Is A Monster (3:21); 9 Sport And Iris (2:17); 10 God's Lonely Man (End Title)(1:51).

Review: Legendary composer Bernard Herrmann ended his remarkable career with this brooding score for Martin Scorsese's brilliant look at the underside of New York City night life. Contrasting a low-key jazz theme against his characteristically heavy, brutal low brass and string chord progressions, Herrmann even ended the score with his famous "Hitchcock chord" from *Psycho*, paralleling the madness of Robert De Niro's bizarre antihero Travis Bickle with that of classic screen psychotic Norman Bates. It was an audacious effort that proved Herrmann capable of working at the forefront of his craft right up to the end of his life (he died shortly after recording the score in 1975). Unfortunately, this soundtrack album (originally released by Arista) compromises Herrmann's

dark vision by padding out his score with some terrible pop-influenced readings of the composer's jazz theme.
Jeff Bond

The Ten Commandments
🎵🎵🎵🎵◗

1989, MCA Records; from the movie *The Ten Commandments*, Paramount Pictures, 1956.

Album Notes: *Music*: Elmer Bernstein; The Paramount Studio Orchestra conducted by Elmer Bernstein.

Selections: 1 Prelude (5:07); 2 In The Bulrushes (4:01); 3 The Bitter Life (2:05); 4 Love And Ambition (4:03); 5 The Hard Bondage (2:03); 6 Egyptian Dance (2:52); 7 The Crucible Of God (3:07); 8 And Moses Watered Jethro's Flock (2:15); 9 Bedouin Dance (1:56); 10 I Am That I Am (3:13); 11 Overture (2:06); 12 Thus Says The Lord (3:39); 13 The Plagues (2:51); 14 The Exodus (6:00); 15 The Pillar Of Fire (2:45); 16 The Red Sea (2:30); 17 The Ten Commandments (5:40); 18 Go, Proclaim Liberty! (3:16).

Review: Oh, Moses, Moses! Veteran composer Elmer Bernstein got his first major credit on Cecil B. DeMille's classic Biblical epic, providing a rousing, vibrant score full of unforgettable leitmotifs, from the portentous six note "God" theme to a proud fanfare for Charlton Heston's Moses and a languid melody for Egyptian queen Nefritiri that's just as smoothly campy as Ann Baxter's outrageous performance in the role. Few composers have been handed assignments with this kind of scope so early in their careers, but Bernstein approached apocryphal moments like Moses' encounter with the Burning Bush, the Hebrews' exodus from Egypt and the parting of the Red Sea with moving piety, infectious energy and an uncanny sense of drama and awe. Originally presented as a two LP set, this 70-minute CD presents the lion's share of Bernstein's score, from the sweeping overture and exotic evocation of the river Nile to Bernstein's incredibly moving finale with its gorgeous recapitulation of the composer's gentle melody for Moses' wife, Sephora. Despite the length here, there's not a dull moment, and this broad, exciting album belongs in anyone's collection.
Jeff Bond

Tequila Sunrise 🎵

1988, Capitol Records; from the movie *Tequila Sunrise*, Warner Bros., 1988.

Album Notes: *Music*: Dave Grusin; Orchestra conducted by Dave Grusin; *Featured Musicians*: Dave Sanborn (saxophone), Lee Ritenour (guitar); *Featured Artists*: Ann Wilson & Robin Zander, Duran Duran, Crowded House, Ziggy Marley & The

Melody Makers, The Everly Brothers & The Beach Boys, Andy Taylor, The Church, Bobby Darin; *Producers*: Richie Zito, Jonathan Elias, Daniel Abraham, Mitchell Froom, Rita Marley, Phil and Don Everly, Andy Taylor, Ahmet Ertegun, Dave Grusin; *Album Producers*: Danny Bramson, Tim Devine.

Selections: 1 Surrender To Me (R. Vanelli/R. Marx) (4:09) *Ann Wilson, Robin Zander*; 2 Do You Believe In Shame? (J. Taylor/N. Rhodes/S. Lebon) (4:25) *Duran Duran*; 3 Recurring Dream (N. Finn) (3:25) *Crowded House*; 4 Give A Little Love (D. Warren/A. Hammond) (4:03) *Ziggy Marley & The Melody Makers*; 5 Don't Worry Baby (B. Wilson/R. Christian) (3:18) *The Everly Brothers, The Beach Boys*; 6 Dead On The Money (S. Diamond/T. Cerney) (4:06) *Andy Taylor*; 7 Unsubstantiated (S. Kilbey/M. Willson-Piper/R. Ploog/P. Koppes) (3:32) *The Church*; 8 Beyond The Sea (C. Trenet/J. Lawrence) (2:55) *Bobby Darin*; 9 Tequila Dreams (D. Grusin) (4:17); 10 Jo Ann's Song (D. Grusin) (4:11).

Review: There are reasons to be very, very scared of this soundtrack. Jazz lite master Dave Grusin teaming with David Sanborn on one number and Lee Ritenour on another. Cheap Trick's Robin Zander teaming with Heart's Ann Wilson. The Everly Brothers and the Beach Boys combining on "Don't Worry Baby"—which would have been exciting in 1969, maybe. And don't forget Duran Duran and a solo track by its former guitarist, Andy Taylor. Kinda makes you want to slap on Mel Gibson's solo spot from "Pocahontas."

Gary Graff

Terminal Velocity ♫♫♫▹

1994, Varese-Sarabande Records; from the movie *Terminal Velocity*, Interscope Communications, 1994.

Album Notes: *Music*: Joel McNeely; *Orchestrations*: David Slonaker, Chris Boardman, Art Kempel; *Music Editor*: Thomas Milano; Orchestra conducted by Joel McNeely; *Album Producer*: Joel McNeely; *Engineer*: Shawn Murphy.

Selections: 1 Desert Landing (2:16); 2 Aerial Ballet (2:45); 3 Airborne (1:02); 4 Ditch's Dive (1:42); 5 Easier Ways To Die (1:42); 6 The Second Plane (3:45); 7 Christa Is Caught (4:14); 8 Desert Nocturne (1:09); 9 Cadillac Freefall (5:43); 10 Russian Gold (3:25); 11 End Credits (4:11).

Review: Writing in a solidly muscular style, with lots of orchestral flourishes over a simple synth rhythm line, Joel McNeely created a surprisingly effective score for this aerial cold war spy thriller involving a loot in gold bullion, a gorgeous sky diving agent, and other mid-air happenstances that propel the action and keep it... well, flying! Occasionally (and abruptly) interrupted by scorching rock accents ("Ditch's Dive"), the

score keeps the moods midway between suspense and contemplation, with throbbing chords and evolutive orchestral lines mingling in unexpected, sudden changes for what amounts to a very lively and effective series of cues. While the music works very well behind the screen action, it is also quite descriptive without it.

Terminator

Terminator ♫♫▹

1984, Cinemaster/DCC Compact Classics; from the movie *Terminator*, Orion Pictures, 1984.

Album Notes: *Music*: Brad Fiedel; *Featured Musician*: Ross Levinson (electric violin); *Song Producers*: Kevin Elson, Jay Ferguson, Michael Verdick, John French, Trevor Courtney; *Album Engineer*: Steve Hoffman.

Selections: 1 The Terminator Theme (4:30); 2 Terminator Arrival (3:00); 3 Tunnel Chase (2:50); 4 Love Scene (1:15); 5 Future Remembered (2:40); 6 Factory Chase (3:50); 7 You Can't Do That (3:25) *Tahnee Cain & Tryanglz*; 8 Burnin's In The Third Degree (3:38) *Tahnee Cain & Tryanglz*; 9 Pictures Of You (3:58) *Jay Ferguson, 16 mm*; 10 Photoplay (3:30) *Tahnee Cain & Tryanglz*; 11 Intimacy (3:40) *Linn Van Hek*.

Review: More mood music than listening music, Brad Fiedel's score for the Arnold Schwarzenegger-starrer proved more effective on the screen, behind the action, than it does when brought upfront. With low rumbling chords, synth percussion, and various other effects creating ominous, somber moods, the only track that actually attracts is "Love Scene," a short, relatively quiet expression that might have gained at being a little longer. Adding a strident, rock-oriented note to the album, five songs may prove more attractive to the average listener, if only because they at least are built on stronger melodic hooks than the score itself, even if they all end up sounding the same.

Terminator 2: Judgment Day ♫♫

1991, Varese-Sarabande; from the movie *Terminator 2: Judgment Day*, Tri-Star Pictures, 1991.

Album Notes: *Music*: Brad Fiedel; *Album Producer*: Brad Fiedel; *Engineers*: Brad Fiedel, Ross Levinson.

Selections: 1 Main Title (Terminator Theme)(1:56); 2 Sarah On The Run (2:31); 3 Escape From The Hospital (And T1000)(4:34); 4 Desert Suite (3:25); 5 Sarah's Dream (Nuclear Nightmare)(1:49); 6 Attack On Dyson (Sarah's Solution) (4:07); 7 Our Gang Goes To Cyberdyne (3:11); 8 Trust Me (1:38); 9 John And Dyson Into Vault (:41); 10 SWAT Team Attacks (3:22); 11 I'll Be Back (3:58); 12 Helicopter Chase (2:27); 13 Tanker Chase (1:42); 14 Hasta la vista, Baby (T1000 Freezes)(3:02); 15 Into The Steel Mill (1:25); 16 Cameron's Inferno (2:37); 17 Terminator Impaled (2:05); 18 Terminator Revives (2:14); 19 T1000 Terminated (1:41); 20 It's Over (Goodbye)(4:36).

Review: This non-thematic score by Brad Fiedel is more sound design than underscore. It works brilliantly in the film, and it does have a certain hypnotic charm at times, with some tracks, like "Desert Suite," having a very ambient feel to them. But it is sure a tough listen on its own if you're not prepared for it. The original *Terminator* main theme, the only melodic piece in the score, is played here with a slower, more deliberate pace.

David Hirsch

The Terminator: The Definite Edition 🦴🦴🦴▷

1996, Cinerama/edel Records; from the movie, *The Terminator*, Orion Pictures, 1984.

Album Notes: *Music*: Brad Fiedel; *Music Editor*: Emile Robertson; *Featured Musician*: Ross Levison (electric violin); *Album Producer*: Brad Fiedel; *CD Producer*: Ford A. Thaxton; *Engineer*: Bill Wolford.

Selections: 1 Theme from The Terminator (4:13); 2 The Terminator Main Title (2:14); 3 The Terminator's Arrival (4:53); 4 Reese Chased (3:47); 5 Sarah On Her Motorbike (:35); 6 Gun Shop/Reese In Alley (1:27); 7 Sarah In The Bar (1:49); 8 Tech Noir/Alley Chase (6:49); 9 Garage Chase (6:49); 10 Arm & Eye Surgery (3:23); 11 Police Station/Escape From Police Station (4:47); 12 Future Flashback/Terminator Infiltration (4:18); 13 Conversation By The Window/Love Scene (3:45); 14 Tunnel Chase (3:54); 15 Death By Fire/Terminator Gets Up (3:11); 16 Factory Chase (3:54); 17 Reese's Death/Terminator Sits Up/ "You're Terminated!" (3:26); 18 Sarah's Destiny/The Coming Storm (3:06); 19 Theme from The Terminator (August 29th, 1997, Judgment Day remix).

Review: This "The Definite Edition" (the "iv" between Definite's last two letters has evidently been terminated) provides for the first time Fiedel's complete score, remastered in stereo (the film's audio track had been mono). *The Terminator* is an effectively mechanical score, suitably punctuating the presence and relentless determination of the cyborg assassin through a pulsing, darkly ambient electronic tonality. Featuring a bold, alternatively heroic/malevolent synth melody

(which retains a slightly disconsolate tone, representing the struggles of the future from which the cyborg comes) over a staccato percussion riff, suggesting the tumbling building blocks of our destructive future, Fiedel captures the ideal musical emotion for the film. Outside of a brief piano and oboe love theme and a lot of percussive and atonal suspense music, *The Terminator* is a monothematic score. The machinelike cyborg is the focus of the music, and Fiedel effectively maintains the character's menace through this approach.

Randall Larson

Thank God It's Friday 🦴🦴🦴🦴

1997, Casablanca Records; from the movie *Thank God It's Friday*, Motown-Casablanca FilmWorks, 1978.

Album Notes: *Song Producers*: Alec R. Costandinos, Simon Soussan, Giorgio Moroder & Pete Bellotte, Bob Esty & Paul Jabara, Larry Blackmon, James Carmichael & The Commodores, Arthur G. Wright, Dick St. Nicklaus, Hal Davis; *Music Coordinator*: Marc Paul Simon; *Engineer*: Gary N. Mayo.

Selections: CD 1: 1 Thank God It's Friday (A. Costandinos) (4:14) *Love And Kisses*; 2 After Dark (S. Soussan/S. Soussan) (7:51) *Pattie Brooks*; 3 With Your Love (D. Summer/G. Moroder/P. Bellotte) (3:59) *Donna Summer*; 4 Last Dance (P. Jabara) (8:08) *Donna Summer*; 5 Disco Queen (P. Jabara) (3:46) *Paul Jabara*; 6 Find My Way (J. Melfi) (4:56) *Cameo*; 7 Too Hot Ta Trot (T. McClary/ M. Williams/W. Orange/L. Richie/R. LaPread/W. King) (3:24) *The Commodores*; 8 Leatherman's Theme (A. Wright) (3:23) *Wright Bros. Flying Machine*; 9 I Wanna Dance (P. Bellotte/T. Baldursson) (5:55) *Marathon*.

CD 2: 1 Take It To The Zoo (D. Summer/B. Sudano/J. Esposito) (7:58) *Sunshine*; 2 Sevilla Nights (N. Skorsky) (6:06) *Santa Esmeralda*; 3 You're The Most Precious Thing In My Life (A. Costandinos) (7:57) *Love And Kisses*; 4 Do You Want The Real Thing (D.C. LaRue/B. Esty) (4:40) *D.C. LaRue*; 5 Trapped In A Stairway (P. Jabara/B. Esty) (3:23) *Paul Jabara*; 6 Floyd's Theme (D. St. Nicklaus) (2:57) *Natural Juices*; 7 Lovin', Livin' And Givin' (K. Stover/P. Davis) (4:39) *Diana Ross*; 8 Love Masterpiece (H. Davis/J. Powell/A. Posey) (4:01) *Thelma Houston*; 9 Last Dance (reprise) (P. Jabara) (3:17) *Donna Summer*; 10 Je t'aime (moi non plus) (S. Gainsbourg) (15:47) *Donna Summer*.

Review: A brilliant marketing concept, *Thank God It's Friday* is essentially a long-form video showcasing the talents of the most important disco performers under contract to Casablanca and Motown in 1978. And what a roster: Donna Summer, of course, the reigning queen of disco at the time; Paul Jabara, who copped an Academy Award for "Last Dance"; Thelma

Houston, Diana Ross, Pattie Brooks, The Commodores, Cameo, D.C. LaRue, some as ephemeral as disco itself, others with longer resiliency. One may berate disco for its simpleminded attitudes, and complain that the songs are all beat and no substance. One thing, however, they are fun, and that's all that was needed. In the years since, the music industry has changed course many times, but the songs in *Thank God It's Friday* have remained as fresh and exciting as they were when they were first created. This album is a vivid reminder of an era that probably came and went too fast.

That Old Feeling ♪♪♪♪♪

1997, MCA Records; from the movie *That Old Feeling*, Universal Pictures, 1997.

Album Notes: *Album Producer*: Tim Sexton; *Engineer*: Larry Walsh.

Selections: 1 Love (B. Kaempfert/M. Gabler)(2:36) *Nat King Cole*; 2 Somewhere Along The Way (S. Gallop/K. Adams)(2:19) *Bette Midler, Tommy Flanagan*; 3 Love Is Here To Stay (G. & I. Gershwin)(3:55) *Ella Fitzgerald*; 4 Call Me Irresponsible (S. Cahn/J. Van Heusen)(2:20) *Dinah Washington*; 5 Anything Goes (C. Porter)(2:21) *Tony Bennett, Count Basie*; 6 Baila conmigo (P. Williams)(4:54) *Patrick Williams*; 7 There Will Never Be Another You (H. Warren/M. Gordon)(2:25) *Keely Smith*; 8 One Shining Moment (B. Walsh)(4:55) *Marc Anthony*; 9 You Took Advantage Of Me (R. Rodgers/L. Hart)(3:13) *Billie Holiday*; 10 At Last (H. Warren/M. Gordon) (3:40) *Lou Rawls, Diana Reeves*; 11 That Old Feeling (S. Fain/L. Brown)(2:42) *Louis Armstrong, Oscar Peterson*.

Review: Wow! What an album! Call it a guilty pleasure, call it old fashioned stuff, it doesn't matter. Next to the drivel we are so often subjected to these days, next to songs without music and with words that are not even intelligent or intelligible, this is the real thing. These songs were crafted with the utmost care by people who knew the value of an interesting lyric combined with a melodic hook, and they are performed by people who know how to sing them and extract every juicy ounce from them—in other words the best of both worlds. So, just put the CD in your player, press the "play" button, sit back, and enjoy! You deserve it!

That Thing You Do ♪♪♪♪♪

1996, Play Tone Records/Epic Soundtrax; from the movie *That Thing You Do*, 20th Century-Fox, 1996.

Album Notes: *Album Producers*: Tom Hanks, Gary Goetzman; *Engineers*: Dave Jahnsen, Rick Pekkonen, Michael C. Ross, Doug Ryder, Mark Wolfson.

Selections: 1 Lovin' You Lots And Lots (T. Hanks) (1:54) *The Norm Wooster Singers*; 2 That Thing You Do! (S. Schlesinger) (2:47) *The Wonders*; 3 Little Wild One (D. Gibbs/S. Hurley/P. Hurley/F. Elrighan) (2:30) *The Wonders*; 4 Dance With Me Tonight (S. Rogness/R. Elias) (2:06) *The Wonders*; 5 All My Only Dreams (S. Rogness/R. Elias) (2:57) *The Wonders*; 6 I Need You (That Thing You Do) (S. Rogness/R. Elias/L. Elias) (2:53) *The Wonders*; 7 She Knows It (S. Rogness/R. Elias) (3:01) *The Heardsmen*; 8 Mr. Downtown (T. Hanks/G. Goetzman/ M. Piccirillo) (2:32) *Freddy Fredrickson*; 9 Hold My Hand, Hold My Heart (T. Hanks/G. Goetzman/M. Piccirillo) (3:12) *The Chantrellines*; 10 Voyage Around The Moon (T. Hanks/G. Goetzman/M. Piccirillo) (3:05) *The Saturn 5*; 11 My World Is Over (M. Piccirillo) (3:01) *Diana Dane*; 12 Drive Faster (S. Rogness/ R. Elias) (2:48) *The Vicksburgs*; 13 Shrimp Shack (M. Piccirillo) (2:22) *Cap'n Geech & The Shrimp Shack Shooters*; 14 Time To Blow (S. Tyrell/ R. Mann) (4:22) *Del Paxton*; 15 That Thing You Do! (Live At The Hollywood Television Showcase) (A. Schlesinger) (2:55) *The Wonders*.

Review: Winning Oscars wasn't enough for Tom Hanks: he had to write songs, too. Hanks shares composing credits on four of the songs here, and the whole collection perfectly apes the innocence and occasional sophomorism of early and mid-'60s American pop. The jangley title track is catchy, however, as are most of the other songs "performed" by The Wonders, the fictional group that's the subject of the movie. *That Thing You Do!* also touches on surf instrumentals ("Voyage Around the Moon"), teen torch songs ("My World is Over"), girl groups ("Hold My Hand, Hold My Heart") and bombastic movie-style themes ("Mr. Downtown"). One you'll come back to repeatedly.

Gary Graff

The Thief of Bagdad/ The Jungle Book ♪♪♪♪♪

1988, Varese-Sarabande; from the movies *The Thief of Bagdad*, Universal-International, 1940; and *The Jungle Book*, United Artists, 1942.

Album Notes: *Music*: Miklos Rozsa; The Nurnberg Symphony Orchestra, conducted by Miklos Rozsa, Klauspeter Seibel; *Album Producer*: Armin Luther; *CD Producer*: Tom Null; *Engineer*: Danny Hersch.

Selections: THE THIEF OF BAGDAD: 1 The King's Fanfare (:31); 2 The Harbor Of Bagdad (2:36); 3 Procession (2:41); 4 Eternal Love (4:44); 5 Gallop Of The Flying Horse (1:41); 6 Dance Of The Silvermaid (3:15); 7 The Marketplace Of Basra (2:59);

THE JUNGLE BOOK (ORCHESTRAL SUITE): 8 The Jungle/The Animals Of The Jungle/ Mowgli/Life In The Jungle/Indian Night/Pursuit/Lullaby/Mowgli's Mother/ Among Men/Song Of The Jungle/Panic Of The Animals/Hunt For Shere Khan/The Python Kaa/Combat/Mowgli's Triumph/Finale (29:31).

Review: Miklos Rozsa's first two popular scores, and the ones that really established him as a major Hollywood composer, brilliantly performed by the Nurnberg Symphony Orchestra in sparkling stereo rerecordings that give these scores new life and greater vibrancy. Drawing as much from the colorful music of his Hungarian background as he did from his own idea of what Arabian and Indian accents should sound like, Rozsa created two scores that are exquisitely evocative of the locales and the actions, and that are indissolubly representative of the films for which they were composed.

The often extravagant accents in *The Thief of Bagdad* detail this thousand-and-one-night Arabian fantasy in broad, vibrant musical tones that compare favorably with Rimsky-Korsakov's tone poem, *Sheherazade*, which they often evoke. The epic tale about the poor beggar (actually the heir to the throne, despoiled by a villainous sorcerer) who falls in love with a princess, and, with the aid of a mischievious street urchin, overcomes all odds, the film was a delightful story that happily mixed epic action with fairy tale accounts in a well-rounded, entertaining oriental saga. Rozsa's music was the perfect complement to the story with wonderfully animated cues that melded with the action and gave it an extra bounce.

Based on Rudyard Kipling's oft-told saga of the baby boy, lost in the luxuriant Indian jungle and raised by a pack of wolves, *The Jungle Book* was another storybook brought to the screen in vivid images that captured the wonders of the tale and made it brilliantly palpable. In terms that at times evoked Saint-Saens' *Carnival of the Animals,* Rozsa created a score that gives all the animals in the jungle a distinct personality, emphasized by the use of specific instruments (trombones and tubas for the elephants, horn glissandi for the wolves, sharp contra-bassoon calls for Baloo the bear, long string lines for Bagheera the panther, woodwinds for the Bandarlogs, alto sax for the hyena, etc.). Tremendously stimulating and beautifully descriptive of the action on-screen, the score, presented here as a long, uninterrupted orchestral suite, spins a magic of its own, making this recording a rare treat for the listener.

The Thin Blue Line ♫♫

1989, Elektra/Nonesuch Records; from the movie *The Thin Blue Line,* Euphorbia, 1989.

Album Notes: *Music:* Philip Glass; Orchestra conducted by Michael Riesman; *Featured Musicians:* Wilmer Wise, Steve Burns (trumpet), Sharoe Moe, Tony Miranda, Ron Sell (French

horn), Michael Parloff, Judith Mendenhall (flute), Sergiu Schwartz, Tim Baker (violin), Karl Bargen (viola), Chris Funckel (cello), Barbara Wilson (double bass), Michael Riesman (keyboards), Gordon Gottlieb (percussion), Brian Koonin (guitar); *Album Producer:* Kurt Munkacsi; *Engineer:* Miles Green.

Selections: 1 Opening Credits (1:31); 2 Prologue (4:43); 3 Interrogation, Part One (2:09); 4 Interrogation, Part Two (:37); 5 Turko, Part One (2:38); 6 Turko, Part Two (2:04); 7 Vidor (1:50); 8 Harris' Story (1:32); 9 Adams' Story (1:48); 10 Comets And Vegas (1:36); 11 The Defense Attorneys, Part One (2:08); 12 Harris' Crimes, Part One (1:42); 13 The Judge (:43); 14 The Trial, Part One (2:38); 15 The Trial, Part Two (3:25); 16 The Mystery Eyewitness, Part One (3:01); 17 The Mystery Eyewitness, Part Two (4:25); 18 Elba Carr (:45); 19 The Mystery Eyewitness, Part Three (2:46); 20 The Thin Blue Line (1:04); 21 Dr. Death (4:42); 22 The Electric Chair (2:54); 23 The Defense Attorneys, Part Two (:59); 24 Harris' Testimony (2:04); 25 The Mystery Eyewitness, Part Four (1:51); 26 The Mystery Eyewitness, Part Five (1:07); 27 Harris' Crimes, Part Two (1:34); 28 Hell On Earth (1:44); 29 Harris' Childhood (2:37); 30 The Confession (2:51); 31 End Credits (3:58).

Review: Errol Morris' chilling documentary about a man framed for murder gets a suitably brooding, ominous Philip Glass score, but this soundtrack CD is less interested in letting you hear the music than in telling Randall Adams' Hitchcockian story. For most of the disc's 69 minutes, the tale unfolds through bits of dialogue from the film, with Glass' underscoring, making for a sort of "Books on Tape" experience. Only the opening and closing themes are presented dialogue-free. (Thanks to Morris' film, Adams ultimately did win his freedom, but you'll hear no jubilation here.)

Marc Kirkeby

The Thing ♫♫♫♪

1990, Varese-Sarabande; from the movie *The Thing,* Universal Picture, 1982.

Album Notes: *Music:* Ennio Morricone; *Orchestrations:* Ennio Morricone; Orchestra conducted by Ennio Morricone; *Album Producer:* Ennio Morricone; *Engineer:* Micky Crofford; *Assistant Engineer:* Neil Jack.

Selections: 1 Humanity (Part 1)(6:50); 2 Shape (3:16); 3 Contamination (1:02); 4 Bestiality (2:56); 5 Solitude (5:58); 6 Eternity (5:35); 7 Wait (6:22); 8 Humanity (part 2)(7:15); 9 Sterilization (5:12); 10 Despair (4:58).

Review: *The Thing* is one of the few instances where John Carpenter turned the scoring duties over to another composer (Carpenter most often prefers to score his own films). While better known for his lyrical scores for *The Mission* and Sergio Leone's westerns, *The Thing* displays Ennio Morricone in a much more contemporary, experimental mode (and is in fact more reflective of the kind of music the composer prefers to write). Some of Carpenter's electronic style shows its influence, but Morricone provides music of much greater imagination than that of which Carpenter is capable. This album also features a great deal of music not used in the film, which consists of some compelling 20th century compositional techniques. Moody, atmospheric music, reminiscent of Bartok features in the first track "Humanity" while spine-chilling aleatoric string pizzicati make-up "Contamination." "Bestiality" is a surging Herrmann-like cue, while Morricone dabbles in minimalism in "Eternity", which features a dizzying downward spiral of electronics and cathedral organ. The acoustical and recording quality is clean and crisp (the work of engineer Mickey Crawford) and suits the score perfectly. Anyone who insists nothing inventive or imaginative is ever written for films will be convinced otherwise by a listen to this soundtrack.

Paul Andrew MacLean

This Earth Is Mine

1993, Varese-Sarabande; from the movie *This Earth Is Mine*, Universal-International Pictures, 1959.

See: The Young Lions

This Is My Life ♫♫♫♪

1992, Qwest Records; from the movie *This Is My Life*, 20th Century-Fox Records, 1992.

Album Notes: *Songs*: Carly Simon; Orchestra arranged and conducted by Teese Gohl; *Featured Musicians*: Carly Simon (vocals/acoustic guitar/Keyboards/whistle), Jimmy Ryan, Ben Taylor (guitars), Teese Gohl, Andy Goldmark (synthesizers/piano), Will Lee, Paul Samwell-Smith (bass), Andy Newmark, Richie Morales, Russ Kunkel (drums), Jamey Haddad (percussion), Toots Thielemans (harmonica), Randy Brecker (trumpet), Jim Pugh (trombone), Charles McCracken (cello); *Album Producers*: Frank Filipetti, Carly Simon; *Engineers*: Frank Filipetti, Tom Lord-Alge, James P. Nichols.

Selections: 1 Love Of My Life (3:35) *Carly Simon*; 2 Back The Way (Dottie's Point Of View)(4:51) *Carly Simon*; 3 Moving Day (1:23); 4 Easy On The Eyes (C. Simon/A. Goldberg)(4:44) *Carly Simon*; 5 Walking And Kissing (1:08); 6 The Show Must Go On (3:46) *Carly Simon*; 7 Love Of My Life (2:18) *Toots Thielemans*; 8 Back The Way (Girls' Point Of View)(2:58) *Carly Simon*; 9 Little Troupers (:37); 10 The Night Before Christmas (3:41)

Carly Simon; 11 This Is My Life Suite: Pleasure And Pain/ Coming Home/Uncle Peter (4:44); 12 Love Of My Life (Drive To The City)(3:45).

Review: Literally a showcase for singer-composer Carly Simon, this album is ingratiating because of the performer's frequently glowing personality and attractive way with a melody and a lyric. A comedy-drama about the "tricky business of raising children and maintaining a solid career, without the benefit of a live-in father," in Simon's own description of the plot, the film evidently inspired the songwriter who wrote the several tunes heard in this soundtrack album, as well as the evocative instrumental cues that complement them. Some songs might attract more than others ("Back the Way," a jaunty, winning little tune, and "The Show Must Go On," an exhilarating anthem, are just wonderful), but the overall effect is ingratiating and strongly reinforced with the instrumental sections in which Toots Thielemans' harmonica creates a poetic spin of its own. A very attractive effort.

3 Days of the Condor ♫♫♫♪

1988, EMI-Manhattan Records; from the movie *3 Days of the Condor*, Paramount Pictures, 1975.

Album Notes: *Music*: Dave Grusin; Orchestra conducted by Dave Grusin; *Album Producer*: Neely Plumb; *Engineers*: John Neal, Jay Ranellucci.

Selections: 1 Condor! (Theme From 3 Days Of The Condor) (3:33); 2 Yellow Panic (2:14); 3 Flight Of The Condor (2:28); 4 We'll Bring You Home (2:22); 5 Out To Lunch (2:00); 6 Goodbye For Kathy (Love Theme From 3 Days Of The Condor)(2:15); 7 I've Got You Where I Want You (3:10) *Jim Gilstrap*; 8 Flashback To Terror (2:22); 9 Sing Along With The C.I.A. (1:31); 10 Spies Of A Feather, Flocking Together (Love Theme From 3 Days Of The Condor)(1:54); 11 Silver Bells (J. Livingston/R. Evans)(2:36) *Marti McCall*; 12 Medley: Condor! (Theme)/I've Got You Where I Want You (1:56) *Jim Gilstrap*.

Review: A typically inventive score by Dave Grusin, *3 Days of the Condor* combines the fusion jazz accents that made his reputation, and strongly flavorful themes that detail this spy thriller about a CIA operative (Robert Redford, in a taut portrayal as a man on the run) whose associates have all been killed, and who eventually discovers that the massacre was ordered by a turncoat inside the agency. The cues devised by Grusin do not specifically attempt to underline the screen action, but provide a strong musical base that works well in and out of it. Two throwaway vocals and a routine version of

"Silver Bells" are the only apparent weak spots in the otherwise solid series of cues.

Three Fugitives ♫♫♫♫

1989, Varese-Sarabande Records; from the movie *Three Fugitives*, Touchstone Pictures, 1989.

Album Notes: *Music:* David McHugh; *Album Producer:* David McHugh; *Engineer:* Daniel Hersch.

Selections: 1 Fugitives (5:06); 2 Meg (1:21); 3 Let's Get Dad (3:01); 4 Hi Copper/Hotel (1:27); 5 S.W.A.T. (1:11); 6 To The Warehouse (1:09); 7 Meg Runs Away/Get In (1:40); 8 My Little Girl (1:07); 9 Don't Go (1:29); 10 Meg (reprise)(1:29); 11 Dr. Horvacks (1:57); 12 Children's Home And Lucas (1:39); 13 Meg's Pick-Up (1:01); 14 Fishnets And Sighs (:58); 15 Meg's Visit (:53); 16 Dad (3:00); 17 (Meg's Rescue/On The Road (2:16); 18 Toward Canada (2:57); 19 End Title (4:11).

Review: David McHugh's score for *Three Fugitives* is full of toe-tapping energy and tender innocence. It's a synthesizer-dominated score based on a single theme which is alternately given pop, rock or jazz renditions. McHugh's synthesizer is clear, taking on orchestral qualities while backed by acoustic instruments like trumpet and piano. This is a score that's fun to listen to. It captures the sense of spirited fun and fellowship embodied in the movie, and carries that over into a soundtrack that is extremely pleasant. It's not as harsh or furious as a lot of rock-oriented soundtracks, nor as saccharine as many pop scores. It's light musical entertainment, and McHugh's score is certain to grow on you with repeated listenings. *Three Fugitives* is often exhilarating, happy, highly suitable for the film and extremely listenable on disk.

Randall D. Larson

Three Men and a Little Lady ♫♫♫▷

1990, Hollywood Pictures; from the movie *Three Men and a Little Lady*, Touchstone Pictures, 1990.

Album Notes: *Music:* James Newton Howard; *Orchestrations:* Brad Dechter, Chris Boardman; Orchestra conducted by Marty Paich; *Song Producers:* Tom Snow, Larry Klein, Arif Mardin, Fareed; *Song Engineers:* Doug Ryder, Steve Churchyard & Dan Marnien, Joey Wolpert, Fareed; *Album Producer:* James Newton Howard, Michael Mason; *Engineer:* John Richards.

Selections: 1 Always Thinking Of You (T. Snow/D. Pitchford)(4:04) *Donna DeLory;* 2 Dance (D. Baerwald/L. Klein)(4:14) *David Baerwald;* 3 Waiting For A Star To Fall (G. Merrill/S. Rubicam)(4:34) *Boy Meets Girl;* 4 The Three Men

Rap (C. Peters/G. Love E.)(1:02) *Tom Selleck, Steve Guttenberg, Ted Danson;* 5 Talkin' (N. Rasheed/M. Pleasure)(5:50) *Najee;* 6 Goodnight Swetheart Goodnight (J. Hudson/C. Carter)(1:03) *Tom Selleck, Steve Guttenberg, Ted Danson;* 7 The Big Goodbye (3:00); 8 The Wharf (:48); 9 Where Will You Live (1:10); 10 To England (:53); 11 Peter And Sylvia In Dressing Room (2:26); 12 Pileforth (:44); 13 Peter's Proposal (1:12); 14 Motorcycle Montage (1:29); 15 He Doesn't Like Me (1:25); 16 The Wedding Tent (:36); 17 Rainmaker (1:21); 18 Sylvia To Theatre (1:07); 19 Peter's Plan (3:36); 20 What About Your Needs? (1:21).

Review: This sequel to the amusing *Three Men and a Baby,* itself a remake of the French comedy *Trois hommes et un couffin,* has overstayed its welcome and lacked the subtle essence that made the first film work so well, even though it is nothing more than the mere wisp of a slight comedy. In some ways, the score by James Newton Howard tries to evoke the winsome atmosphere that should have presided over this story about three bachelor hunks (Tom Selleck, Steve Guttenberg and Ted Danson), all three sharing the same apartment and with their own agenda, suddenly saddled with caring for a little five-year old, the daughter of a friend with a pressing engagement. The cues are, for the most part, engaging and charmingly provocative, making this soundtrack album more interesting than the film that inspired it. The insipid pop selections, all too strident and aggressively obvious, are more annoying than awe-inspiring.

The Three Musketeers

The Three Musketeers ♫♫♫▷

1990, Bay Cities; from the movie *The Three Musketeers*, 1974.

Album Notes: *Music:* Michel Legrand; Orchestra conducted by Michel Legrand; *Album Producer:* Michel Legrand; *CD Producer:* Nick Redman.

Selections: 1 Main Titles (2:34); 2 Sword For Your Supper (2:06); 3 To Love A Queen (2:28); 4 Four Abreast (If You'll Pardon The Expression) (2:21); 5 He Ain't Heavy, He's The Cardinal (1:07); 6 All's Fair In Love And Feet (2:06); 7 Foiled Again (5:26); 8 Dirty Business Amongst The Dirty Laundry (3:05); 9 Don't Put Milady On The Stage (1:12); 10 Hawks vs. Doves (2:04); 11 Bursting Buckingham (1:37); 12 A Round And Around (3:09); 13 Three's Company, But Four Will Cost You Extra (3:47); 14 End Titles (1:37).

Review: Michel Legrand has typically been more at home writing songs and pop/jazz scores like *The Umbrellas of Cher-*

bourg than serious film music, but this score for Richard Lester's sly, revisionist take on the famous Daniel Dumas adventure is an exception. Legrand's throbbing, suspenseful scoring of the film's slow motion sword fight title sequence is striking, his adventuresome theme for the Musketeers a perfect fit, and he approaches the film's numerous, elaborately choreographed battles with great energy and zeal. His approach to the film's comic sequences involves some adept recreations of a kind of baroque/Renaissance style, and there's a glittering, harsh fanfare for Charlton Heston's Cardinal Richelieu. Legrand's Broadway sensibilities sometimes get the better of him. The otherwise thrilling fight cue "Dirty Business Among the Dirty Laundry" climbs to such a giddy, showbiz-style conclusion you expect the combatants to burst into song, and he has an unfortunate tendency to interrupt the flow of action cues like "Bustling Buckingham" and the climactic battle to introduce some awful comedy effects. But if you can ignore those gaffes this is a genuine romp.

Jeff Bond

See also: The Four Musketeers

The Three Musketeers 🎵🎵🎵♭

1993, Hollywood Records; from the movie *The Three Musketeers*, Walt Disney Pictures, 1993.

Album Notes: *Music:* Michael Kamen; *Orchestrations:* Michael Kamen, Robert Elhai, Jack Hayes, William Ross, Lolita Ritmanis, Brad Warnaar, Randy Kerber, Chris Boardman, Larry Rench, Ira Hearshen, Don Nemitz, Mike McCuistion; *Music Editor:* Michael T. Ryan; The Greater Los Angeles All-Star Orchestra, conducted by Michael Kamen; *Featured Soloists:* Vince De Rosa (French horn), Malcolm McNab (trumpet), Tommy Johnson (tuba), Paul Fried (flute), Ralph Grearson (harpsichord), Katie Kirkpatrick (harp), Phil Ayling (recorder), Emil Richards (percussion), Randy Kerber (harpsichord), Dan Greco (hammered dulcimer), Jon Clarke (oboe d'amour), David Riddles (bassoon), Bruce Dukov (violin), Tom Boy (cor Anglais); *Album Producers:* Michael Kamen, Stephen McLaughlin, Christopher Brooks; *Engineer:* Stephen P. McLaughlin.

Selections: 1 All For Love (B. Adams/R.J. Lange/M. Kamen) (4:36) *Bryan Adams, Rod Stewart, Sting*; 2 The Cavern Of Cardinal Richelieu (Overture—Passacaille) (2:55); 3 D'Artagnan (Gaillard and Air) (3:17); 4 Athos, Porthos And Aramis (Courante) (5:21); 5 Sword Fight (Bransle) (3:18); 6 Louis XIII, Queen Anne And Constance/Lady In Waiting (Gavotte) (5:03); 7 The Cardinal's Coach (Estampie) (4:41); 8 Cannonballs (Rigadon) (3:27); 9 M'Lady De Winter (Lament) (4:14); 10 The Fourth Musketeer (Concerts Royaux) (5:20).

Review: A rousing and exciting, old-fashioned symphonic score from Michael Kamen, who successfully pays tribute to Korngold and the Errol Flynn adventures in a more consistent, satisfying fashion than he did with his fun but uneven score for *Robin Hood: Prince of Thieves*. With full support from The Greater Los Angeles All-Star Orchestra, Kamen's music provides plenty of gusto to the action, with thrilling passages for orchestra and chorus punctuated by lyrical themes that translate well outside of the theatrical context for which they're composed. As usual for Kamen, there's also a stab at a pop song, the vacuous "All for Love," written once again with Bryan Adams and R.J. "Mutt" Lange, and performed by the once-in-a-lifetime trio of Adams, Sting and Rod Stewart, who were presumably all compensated quite well for their vocal performance here.

Andy Dursin

Three O'Clock High 🎵🎵🎵

1987, Varese-Sarabande Records; from the movie *Three O'Clock High*, Universal Pictures, 1987.

Album Notes: *Music:* Tangerine Dream; Arranged, Performed, Produced and Engineered by Tangerine Dream.

Selections: 1 It's Jerry's Day Today (:35); 2 46-32-15 (:47); 3 No Detention (:55); 4 Any School Bully Will Do (:25); 5 Go To The Head Of The Class (3:03); 6 Sit (S. Levay) (:50) *Sylvester Levay*; 7 The Fight (S. Levay) (2:40) *Sylvester Levay*; 8 Jerry's Decision (S. Levay) (3:25) *Sylvester Levay*; 9 The Fight Is On (S. Levay) (3:35) *Sylvester Levay*; 10 Paper (S. Levay) (1:18) *Sylvester Levay*; 11 Big, Bright Brass Knuckles (1:50); 12 Buying Paper Like It's Going Out Of Style (1:30); 13 Dangerous Trend (:53); 14 Who's Chasing Who? (:55); 15 Bonding By Candlelight (1:30); 16 You'll Never Believe It (2:10); 17 Starting The Day Off

Right (1:05); 18 Weak At The Knees (1:55); 19 Kill Him (The Football Dummy)(1:00); 20 Not So Quiet In The Library/Get Lost In A Crowd (:40); 21 Something To Remember Me By (J. Walker) (6:00) *Jim Walker*; 22 Arrival (R. Moratta/D. Tickle)(2:00) *Rick Moratta, David Tickle.*

Review: Somehow, one doesn't think of Tangerine Dream and comedies in the same vein, yet this mild, innovative story about a meek high school journalist and the bully he wants to interview, prompted the German trio to write a series of cues that are appealling in tone, with typical synth flourishes and melodic lines expanding on the light screen action. It's a flavorful effort, enhanced with additional cues provided by Sylvester Levay, and two solid rock tracks that make a similar favorable impression.

Three Wishes 🎵🎵

1995, Magnatone Records; from the movie *Three Wishes*, Rysher Entertainment, 1995.

Album Notes: *Music:* Cynthia Millar; *Orchestrations:* Emilie A. Bernstein, Patrick Russ; Orchestra conducted by Cynthia Millar; *Featured Musicians:* Anthony Pleeth (cello), Richard Taylor (recorder); *Album Producer:* Cynthia Millar; *Engineer:* Keith Grant.

Selections: 1 The Magic Begins (3:08); 2 Tom Remembers (1:43); 3 The Magic Comes Closer (1:38); 4 The Highway (1:12); 5 Betty Jane Appears (1:23); 6 Hide And Seek (1:27); 7 Jack (1:44); 8 Left Out (1:11); 9 Journal (1:09); 10 Jack's Life (2:27); 11 Phil (1:02); 12 Explorers (2:33); 13 In The Yard (:35); 14 Monster (1:39); 15 Catch (1:22); 16 Gunny (2:48); 17 Father's Day (2:03); 18 Bad News (1:57); 19 Home Run (1:10); 20 Love (3:28); 21 Light Creature (:53); 22 Jack's Cast Comes Off (1:13); 23 Coach (1:32); 24 Gunny's Wish (1:32); 25 Jack's Wish (1:21); 26 Jack And Jeanne (2:30); 27 Gunny Flies (1:59); 28 Homecoming (1:59); 29 Tom Gets His Wish (2:39); 30 End Credits.

Review: Cynthia Millar has long been known as the virtuoso performer who plays the Ondes Martenot, an odd electronic instrument few have mastered, on many of Elmer Bernstein's scores over the last several years. So it's no wonder that portions of this score reflect Bernstein's influence with obviously similar motifs that can be clearly heard in the later part of "The Highway" and "Betty Jane Appears." Naturally, Millar uses the Ondes Martenot for "magical" effects instead of more contemporary electronic instruments. The score is agreeable, but the sequencing of the CD, which does nothing to hide the fact that it is just a collection of very short cues, yields a dull presentation that doesn't allow the music to create any tangible mood on its own.

David Hirsch

The Three Worlds of Gulliver

1988, Cloud Nine Records; from the movie *The Three Worlds of Gulliver*, Columbia Pictures, 1960.

See: Bernard Herrmann in Compilations

Thunderball 🎵🎵🎵🎵

1988, EMI-Manhattan Records; from the movie *Thunderball*, United Artists, 1965.

Album Notes: *Music:* John Barry; *Lyrics:* Don Black; Orchestra conducted by John Barry.

Selections: 1 Main Title: Thunderball (2:59) *Tom Jones*; 2 Chateau Flight (2:26); 3 The Spa (2:40); 4 Switching The Body (2:45); 5 The Bomb (5:42); 6 Cafe Martinique (3:42); 7 Thunderball (4:16); 8 Death Of Fiona (2:39); 9 Bond Below Disco Volante (4:12); 10 Search For Vulcan (2:32); 11 007 (2:30); 12 Mr. Kiss Kiss Bang Bang (2:48).

Review: By most accounts, one of John Barry's most successful scores for the James Bond films, this is a total gas! The cues are sprightly tongue-in-cheek, even as they suggestively underscore the screen action, plainly justifying Barry's dismissive comment about this type of "Mickey Mouse music," but obviously fulfilling a need that no other composer has been able to match. A cheerful, bang-up job and a greatly entertaining album. The CD, incidentally, omits quite a few cues, allegedly composed by Barry after the album was released, ahead of the film. Some of the missing music can be found in the "30th Anniversary" collection (q.v.), and includes the thrilling finale, worth alone the price of admission.

Thunderheart 🎵🎵

1992, Intrada Records; from the movie *Thunderheart*, Tri-Star Pictures, 1992.

Album Notes: *Music:* James Horner; *Music Editor:* Jim Henrikson; Orchestra conducted by James Horner; *Album Producer:* James Horner; *Engineer:* Shawn Murphy.

Selections: 1 Main Title (2:10); 2 The Oglala Sioux (2:35); 3 Jimmy's Escape (3:33); 4 Proud Nation (1:56); 5 Evidence (1:39); 6 First Visions (1:13); 7 Ghost Dance (3:13); 8 The Goons (2:33); 9 Medicine Man (1:00); 10 My People: Wounded Knee (4:28); 11 Thunder Heart (5:25); 12 Run For The Stronghold (5:20); 13 This Land Is Not For Sale/End Titles (8:14).

Review: This fact-based film tells of a half-Native American FBI agent's search for a killer on an Ogala Sioux reservation. The film, notable for its attention to faithful tribal details, required composer James Horner to interpolate authentic vocals into his electronic score. However, the overall ambient nature of the music has produced an album that, while a curiosity since it's the most original thing Horner has done, is also a plodding collection of tones. Effective as a film score, perhaps, but terribly unsettling to listen to as a form of entertainment.

David Hirsch

Ticks/Fist of the North Star

♪♪♪

1996, Intrada Records; from the movies *Ticks*, Republic Pictures, 1996, and *Fist of the North Star*, First Look Pictures, 1996.

Album Notes: *Music*: Christopher Stone; *Orchestra conducted by* Christopher Stone; *Album Producer*: Christopher Stone; *Engineer*: Rick Ruggerie.

Selections: *FIST OF THE NORTH STAR:* 1 Desert Planet (7:59); 2 Blind Girl/Warrior's Entrance (2:55); 3 Acid Rain/First Fight (4:17); 4 Follow Your Destiny (3:58); 5 Warriors Destroy City (4:05); 6 Lost In The Rain (3:40); 7 The Big Fight (5:06); 8 Reunited (6:41);

TICKS: 9 Main Title (4:50); 10 Bad Guys (2:05); 11 Nest Behind The Wall (:58); 12 Chased By Ticks (1:23); 13 Dead Dog (3:03); 14 Ticked Off (3:50); 15 Ticks Everywhere (12:41); 16 Mother Of All Ticks (10:53).

Review: Two diverse scores by Christopher Stone share this album. The first is *Fist of the North Star*, a stimulating orchestral work for a live action adaption of a popular Japanese animated series. Filled with occasional heavy doses of percussion, the main title, "Desert Planet," sets the bombastic pace, while also conjuring up the deep emotions of the hero and his princess, who both share an ultimate destiny to save the Earth. On the "flip side," metaphorically speaking, is the creepy horror score to *Ticks*. Since the film's setting is an isolated mountain cabin, and the villains are a couple of hillbilly rednecks, Stone drops in a few blue grass guitar motifs here and there. There's still lots of room for percussion as the title buggers scurry on by to chomp a bunch of teenagers.

David Hirsch

Time After Time ♪♪♪▷

1987, Southern Cross Records; from the movie *Time After Time*, Orion Pictures, 1979.

Album Notes: *Music*: Miklos Rozsa; *Music Copyist*: Tony Bremner; *The Royal Philharmonic Orchestra, conducted by* Miklos Rozsa; *Featured Soloist*: Eric Parkin, piano; *Album Producers*: John Lasher, Nicholas Meyer; *Engineer*: Keith Grant.

Selections: 1 Warner Bros. Fanfare (M. Steiner) and Prelude (2:07); 2 Search For The Ripper; 3 Decision (2:04); 4 Vaporising Equalizer/The Time Machine (2:10); 5 Time Travel (1:31); 6 Bank Montage (1:10); 7 Utopia (2:03); 8 The Ripper, Pursuit (3:26); 9 Time Machine Waltz (3:58); 10 Man Before His Time (1:55); 11 Redwoods (2:30); 12 Frightened (1:43); 13 Murder (1:43); 14 The Fifth Victim (1:34); 15 The Last Victim (1:34); 16 Nocturnal Visitor (1:38); 17 Dangerous Drive (3:06); 18 Journey's End and Finale (3:58).

Review: "Score this movie exactly as you would have in 1944" is most likely what director Nicholas Meyer said to Miklós Rózsa about his 1978 time travel adventure, *Time After Time* — or even if he didn't, that's exactly what Rózsa did. It was a novel approach. The old-fashioned symphonic score applied to a contemporary film and served the picture well. H.G. Wells (Malcolm McDowell) follows Jack the Ripper (David Warner) in a time machine to present-day San Francisco and protects a very modern woman (Mary Steenburgen). Rózsa's music cast a darkly romantic sheen over the whole film, an out-of-place, dignified European score for an out-of-place, dignified hero. Of all the Golden Age greats, not only was Rózsa one of the few still alive and working at the time, but he had one of the most distinct styles, one changed very little over the years. *Time After Time*, a fine but peculiar film due to its mixture of genres, was sold by his unmistakable melodies and conviction.

Lukas Kendall

A Time of Destiny ♪♪♪

1988, Virgin Movie Music; from the movie *A Time of Destiny*, Columbia Pictures, 1988.

Album Notes: *Music*: Ennio Morricone; *Orchestrations*: Ennio Morricone; *Orchestra conducted by* Ennio Morricone; *Album Producer*: Ennio Morricone.

Selections: 1 Forgiveness (3:23); 2 The Daughter (2:11); 3 Heroes (1:24); 4 The Storm (2:37); 5 Jorge (3:32); 6 The Letter (1:36); 7 For Josie (3:00); 8 The Night Patrol (2:23); 9 RIFAC/The Storm II (2:05); 10 Lunga/ The Home And The Land (2:10); 11 Brotherhood (1:20); 12 Jack, A Soldier Prayer (3:44); 13 Dies Irae/The Bell Tower (3:28); 14 Martin (1:02); 15 Love And Dreams (2:25); 16 In Life And Death (2:01); 17 Destiny (3:01); 18 Awake (2:04).

Review: Much of Ennio Morricone's output in the late '80s (*Rampage, The Untouchables*) was of a strident, unmelodic strain. *A Time of Destiny* signaled a return to the more romantic sound which brought him popularity in the '60s and '70s. A love story set during World War II, the score features Morricone's fondness for vocal writing and romantic orchestration. It is a gentle and subdued score for the most part, but there are a few violent moments, such as the slashingly atonal "The Storm" and the intense and raging choral writing in "Dies Irae- The Bell Tower", which effectively offset the gentler passages. Morricone's love theme is especially attractive, even rapturous, and displays the composer in his finest romantic mode. In all, this is a soundtrack album which holds together very well. While certainly not in league with Morricone's masterpiece, *The Mission*, *A Time of Destiny* remains a very good album with its share of enjoyable moments.

Paul Andrew MacLean

A Time to Kill ♪♪♪

1996, Atlantic Records; from the movie *A Time to Kill*, Warner Bros., 1996.

Album Notes: *Music*: Elliot Goldenthal; *Orchestrations*: Robert Elhai, Elliot Goldenthal, Deniz Hughes; *Music Editors*: Michael Connell, Denise Murray; Orchestra conducted by Jonathan Sheffer; *Featured Musicians*: Howard Levy (harmonica/penny whistle), Billy Drewes (saxophone), Bill Moersch (hammer dulcimer); *Electronic Music*: Richard Martinez; *Album Producer*: Matthias Gohl; *Engineer*: Joel Iwataki.

Selections: 1 Defile And Lament (2:34); 2 Consolation (2:24); 3 Justice Wheel (:47); 4 Pavane For Solace (2:30); 5 Abduction (2:59); 6 An Asurrendering (1:36); 7 Pavane For Loss (1:09); 8 Take My Hand Precious Lord (T. Dorsey)/Retribution (6:50) *The Jones Girls*; 9 Torch And Hood (2:03); 10 Pressing Judgement (1:30); 11 White Sheet (2:38); 12 Pavane For Solace (piano solo)(2:08); 13 Verdict Fanfare (For Aaron)(4:04); 14 Take My Hand Precious Lord (T. Dorsey)(4:04) *Cissy Houston, The Christ Memorial Church Choir, The Andrae Crouch Singers*.

Review: Elliot Goldenthal has really created an evil southern motif ("Defile and Lament") for this film that really cries out to tell us that we're venturing into the darkest side of life, a world ready to explode like a nuclear bomb from racial tension. Even "Consolation," which starts out with such a heartfelt melody, degenerates into a grim oppressiveness. Goldenthal's harmonicas poignantly wail in utter sadness, his fiddles screech in alarm, and the souls of the dead frequently undulate to a pavane (slow dance) of misery. Two gospel pieces are included on the album to represent the lack of justice suffered by the southern black community. One such piece, "Take My Hand Precious Lord" is interpolated with Goldenthal's "Retribution" cue, yielding a powerfully grim effect. This one's gonna bring you down for sure.

David Hirsch

Timecop ♪♪♭

1994, Varese-Sarabande; from the movie *Timecop*, Universal Pictures, 1994.

Album Notes: *Music*: Mark Isham; *Orchestrations*: Ken Kugler, Ardell Hake; *Music Editor*: Tom Carlson; Orchestra conducted by Ken Kugler; *Featured Musician*: Steve Tavaglione (saxophone solos); *Album Producer*: Mark Isham; *Engineer*: Stephen Krause; *Assistnt Engineer*: Paul Wertheimer.

Selections: 1 Time Cop (2:20); 2 Melissa (2:41); 3 Blow Up (2:12); 4 Lasers And Tasers (4:23); 5 Polaroid (6:10); 6 Rooftop (6:16); 7 C4 (2:37); 8 Rescue and Return (3:22).

Review: Musician-composer Mark Isham has dabbled in numerous genres over the course of his eclectic filmography, some more successfully than others. *Timecop* finds Isham attempting a throbbing action film score, and despite a pleasantly lush love theme for saxophone (seemingly right up the composer's alley), the results are just sort of ho-hum. While the music, conducted and co-orchestrated by frequent Isham collaborator Ken Kugler, isn't as blatantly cobbled together as some pastiche action scores are, it also doesn't offer the kind of fresh twist on the material and ability to surprise that it could have, particularly considering Isham's credentials. The end result is an inoffensive but unremarkable soundtrack that is neither as cliched nor as distinguished as some of its genre counterparts.

Andy Dursin

Tin Cup ♪♪♪♪

1996, Epic Soundtrax; from the movie *Tin Cup*, Warner Bros., 1996.

Album Notes: *Song Producers*: Jim Dickinson, Jimmie Vaughan, John Porter, Bruce Hornsby, John Jennings & Mary Chapin Carpenter, Erik Jacobsen, Marc Tanner & Don Was, Shawn Colvin, Emory Gordy, Jr., James House, Joe Ely, William Ross; *Engineers*: Don Smith, John Hampton, Wayne Pooley, Bob Dawson, Mark Needham, Bill Drescher, Fred Remmert, Russ Martin, Mark Capps, Charles Ray, Dennis Sands; *Soundtrack Executive Producers*: Ron Shelton, Glen Brunman, Kellie Davis, Gary Foster; *Engineer*: Chris Bellman.

Selections: 1 Little Bit Is Better Than Nada (D. Sahm)(3:31) *Texas Tornados*; 2 Cool Lookin' Woman (J. Vaughan/P. Ray)(4:37) *Jimmie Vaughan*; 3 Crapped Out Again (K. Moore/J.L. Parker)(2:31) *Keb' Mo'*; 4 Big Stick (B. Hornsby)(3:14) *Bruce Hornsby*; 5 Nobody There But Me (B. Hornsby/C. Haden/J. Hornsby)(3:49) *Bruce Hornsby*; 6 Let Me Into Your Heart (M. Chapin Carpenter) (2:52) *Mary-Chapin Carpenter*; 7 I Wonder (C. Isaak)(2:56) *Chris Isaak*; 8 This Could Take All Night (S. Dorff/L. Thompson)(3:08) *Amanda Marshall*; 9 Back To Salome

(S. Colvin)(3:07) *Shawn Colvin*; 10 Just One More (G. Jones) (3:03) *George Jones*; 11 Where Are You Boy (R. Fagan/G. Kennedy)(3:27) *Patty Loveless*; 12 Every Minute, Every Hour, Every Day (J. Leap)(4:14) *James House*; 13 Character Flaw (J. Ely/P. Flannery)(2:59) *Joe Ely*; 14 Double Bogey Blues (D. Gillon)(3:31) *Mickey Jones*.

Review: Introduced by the ingratiating strains of Texas Tornados' volatile rendition of "Little Bit Is Better Than Nada," this soundtrack album is particularly enjoyable. One of the most endearing aspects of this minor film about a driving-range pro and golf hustler from West Texas whose legendary ball-striking skills are matched only by his self-destructive nature and lowlife charm (Kevin Costner in a solid tour-de-force performance), the diversified soundtrack offers top pop performances by such artists as Mary Chapin Carpenter, Chris Isaak and George Jones. The album, a Grammy nominee, features these performances in their entirety, focusing on the talents involved, minus the sometimes intrusive screen sound effects and dialogues. A good, solid program of entertaining contemporary songs, with an attractive down-home country flavor.

To Die For ♫♫♫

1995, Varese-Sarabande Records; from the movie *To Die For,* Columbia Pictures, 1995.

Album Notes: *Music:* Danny Elfman; *Orchestrations:* Steve Bartek; *Music Editor:* Ellen Segal; Orchestra conducted by Richard Stone; *Featured Musicians:* John Avila (bass), Warren Fitzgerald (guitar), Brooks Wackerman (drums); *Album Producer:* Danny Elfman; *Engineers:* Bobby Fernandez, Bill Jackson.

Selections: 1 Main Titles (4:09); 2 Suzie's Theme (1:41) *Little Gus & The Suzettes*; 3 Busted (2:00); 4 Weepy Donuts (1:50); 5 Creepy Creepy (:50); 6 Murder! (3:51); 7 Angry Suzie 9:36); 8 Finale (3:47); 9 Wasting Away (M. Cavalera/A. Newport) (3:03) *Nailbomb*; 10 Nothing From Nothing (B. Preston/B. Fisher) (2:34) *Billy Preston*; 11 All By Myself (E. Carmen/S. Rachmaninoff) (4:54) *Eric Carmen*; 12 Sweet Home Alabama (E. King/G. Rossington/R. Van Zant) (3:37) *Lynyrd Skynyrd*; 13 Wings Of Desire (M. Tierney/P. Casserly/F. McDonald) (4:48) *Strawpeople*; 14 Season Of The Witch (D. Leitch) (4:54) *Donovan*.

Review: Though only 19 minutes of Danny Elfman's score appears on this album, it's a solid presentation of the loony fantasy style he's become noted for on his various scores for director Tim Burton. The highlight is a manic vocal on "Suzy's Theme." In general, vocal effects play an important part in this score to create a bizarre ambience for Nicole Kidman's homicidal charac-

ter. The CD is surprisingly top heavy with pop tunes for a Varese Sarabande release and features six songs by artists such as Billy Preston ("Nothing From Nothing"), Eric Carmen ("All By Myself"), and Donovan ("Season of the Witch").
David Hirsch

To Gillian on Her 37th Birthday ♫♫♫⌐

1996, Epic Soundtrax; from the movie *To Gillian on Her 37th Birthday*, Triumph Films, 1996.

Album Notes: *Music:* James Horner; *Orchestrations:* James Horner; *Music Editor:* Jim Henrikson; *Album Producer:* James Horner; *Engineer:* Shawn Murphy.

Selections: 1 A Far Away Time/Main Title (3:52); 2 The Boating Accident (2:15); 3 Gillian (3:58); 4 The Lighthouse (2:18); 5 Fond Hopes... Distant Memories (2:07); 6 Rachel's Dream/ Gillian's Visit (6:18); 7 The Decision To Leave Home (3:11); 8 Saying Goodbye/End Title (12:40).

Review: One of the great pleasures in collecting film scores is coming across a superb soundtrack for a movie that didn't make much noise in theaters, yet works as an album better than many scores for far more popular movies. The movie *To Gillian on Her 37th Birthday*, an adaptation of an off-Broadway play by star Michelle Pfeiffer's husband, David E.Kelley, is not a great movie by any means, but it does offer a superb cast, pleasant Nantucket locations, attractive cinematography, and a poignant James Horner music score, dialed down several notches from the typically overwrought musical work that usually accompanies a movie like this. Horner's score is romantic and genteel, flowing calmly as underscore for the character-driven drama, and yet it still becomes highly emotional at times, with lush strings happily working with the action instead of saccharinely pounding you over the head with sappiness. It's a lovely score that's one of the most restrained and elegant works in Horner's career, along with one of the more underrated.
Andy Dursin

To Kill a Mockingbird ♫♫♫♫⌐

1991, Mainstream Records; from the movie *To Kill a Mockingbird*, 1962.

Album Notes: *Music:* Elmer Bernstein; Orchestra conducted by Elmer Bernstein; *Album Producers:* Jackie Mills, Tommy Wolf; *Engineer:* Bill Putnam.

Selections: 1 Main Title: To Kill A Mockingbird (2:49); 2 Roll The Tire (2:03); 3 The Search For Boo (2:44); 4 Jem's Discovery (3:20); 5 To Kill A Mockingbird (2:01); 6 Tree Treasure (3:50); 7

Lynch Mob (2:42); 8 Footsteps In The Dark (1:58); 9 Children Attacked (2:01); 10 Summer's End (2:49); CD bonus tracks: 11 Follow Me (Love Theme from *Mutiny On The Bounty*)(B. Kaper/P.F. Webster)(2:50); 12 A Second Chance (from *Two For The Seesaw*)(A. Previn)(2:45); 13 A Few Tender Words (M. David/L. Murray)(2:59); 14 Indian Summer (A. Dubin/ V. Herbert)(5:56); 15 New Orleans (A. DeLange/M. Alter) (3:08); 16 So Pretty (H. Pan)(3:00).

Review: Dispensing with the negatives first: sometimes, in their misguided desire to beef up CDs that would have a limited playing time (simply because the original albums didn't have much music to begin with), would-be producers indiscriminately added tracks that had no relation with the rest of the album. Case in point, this reissue CD of one of Elmer Bernstein's most evocative scores, augmented with six selections that are totally alien to the soundtrack itself or to one another. In this case, it is all the more distressing that Bernstein also recorded for Mainstream an album of individual selections from his film scores, some of which could have been effectively added here, without even raising the slightest objection.

Other negative points: the sound quality in this recording leaves a great deal to be desired, with some noticeable hiss on many of the tracks, image shifting, uneven levels, flutter, distortion on some of the tracks, and some analog dropouts. If you're going to spend your money for a product, at least know what it is that you're getting. In this case, a rather shabby product.

This said, Bernstein's score is a marvel of understatement, a series of delicately phrased cues that follow this imaginative tale of two youngsters coming of age, and facing their responsibilities in an adult world, set against the backdrop of a criminal court trial in Alabama against a Black man accused of rape. Pretty much describing the fantasy world of the two kids, "To Kill a Mockingbird" skillfully blends a lovely waltz, accented by a lyricless chorus, while the darker "Lynch Mob" evokes the reality of the trial itself. *To Kill a Mockingbird* won an Academy Award for Best Score in 1963. It deserves better than this shoddy CD.

To the Ends of the Earth
♪♪♪▷

1988, Prometheus Records (Belgium); from the movie *To the Ends of the Earth*, 1984.

Album Notes: *Music:* John Scott; *Orchestra conducted by* John Scott; *Album Producer:* John Scott; *Engineer:* Richard Lewzey.

Selections: 1 Prologue (2:37); 2 Main Titles (:48); 3 Past Pioneers (1:27); 4 Arctic Training (1:02); 5 Start Of The Expedi-

tion (:51); 6 Shackleton (2:44); 7 South Seas (1:41); 8 Reaching Antarctica (2:57); 9 On To The South Pole (4:13); 10 The Scott Tragedy (3:41); 11 To Alaska (2:02); 12 Land Of The Musk Ox (2:46); 13 Journey To Ellsmere Island (2:47); 14 Midnight Sun (4:43); 15 Nightride From Alert (4:05); 16 Ice Cracks (2:17); 17 The North Pole (:53); 18 Reunion With The Benji B. (2:43); 19 Epilogue (1:09); 20 End Credits (:53).

Review: This documentary film tells the story of The Transglobe Expedition—a team which circumnavigated the globe along its polar axis. As such, *To the Ends of the Earth* clearly called for music of epic proportions, which depicted the adventurous spirit of exploration. After years as Jacques Cousteau's composer of choice, John Scott was well-versed in the kind of score needed for this production. His music, a surging, full orchestral score, is epic and soaring, evoking both the grandeur and terror inherent in the journey. Although working with a modest-sized orchestra, Scott nevertheless manages a large sound. Throughout, the music conjures the daunting scale of the expedition, and culminates in a finale of grand triumph. The sound of the recording is particularly fine (recorded at CTS Studios by engineer Dick Lewzey). Handsome packaging and informative notes (including a track-by-track description written by Scott himself) round-out this impressive release, which is typical of Prometheus' high standards.

Paul Andrew MacLean

To Wong Foo, Thanks for Everything, Julie Newmar
♪♪♪▷

1995, MCA Records; from the movie *To Wong Foo, Thanks for Everything, Julie Newmar*, Universal Pictures, 1995.

Album Notes: *Music:* Rachel Portman; *Song Producers:* Cheryl James, Bernadette Cooper; Steve "Silk" Hurley; 3 Shep Pettibone; Crystal Waters, The Basement Boys; Junior Vasquez; James Carmichael, The Commodores; Heavy D; Cyndi Lauper, Jimmy Bralower; Nathaniel "Crockett" Wilkie; Rachel Portman; *Album Producers:* Happy Walters, Pilar McCurry, Kathy Nelson.

Selections: 1 I Am The Body Beautiful (B. Cooper/C. James)(4:52) *Salt-N-Pepa*; 2 Free Yourself (S. McKinney/D. Rich/W. McRae)(4:13) *Chaka Khan*; 3 Turn It Out (S. Pettibone/S. Feldman)(4:54) *Patti LaBelle, Nona Hendryx, Sarah Dash*; 4 Who Taught You How (C. Waters/E. Kupper)(4:56) *Crystal Waters*; 5 She's A Lady (P. Anka)(2:20) *Tom Jones*; 6 Brick House (L. Richie/R. LaPread/W. Orange/M. Williams/T. McClary/W. King)(3:34) *The Commodores*; 7 Nobody's Body (Heavy D)(5:21) *Monifah*; 8 Do What You Wanna Do (S. Hurley/T.

Hurley)(4:33) *Charisse Arrington*; 9 Hey Now (Girls Just Want To Have Fun)(R. Hazard/L. Vegas)(3:41) *Cyndi Lauper*; 10 Over The Rainbow (H. Arlen/E.Y. Harburg)(5:38) *Patti LaBelle*; 11 To Wong Foo Suite (R. Portman): a) When I Get To Hollywood (:46), b) A Day With The Girls (:48), c) Moms Mabley (:50), d) Stand Up (:51).

Review: This soundtrack is anything but a drag, though the individual songs work better when accompanying the visuals of Patrick Swayze, Wesley Snipes and John Leguzamo sashaying around in their finery. Crystal Waters' "Who Taught You How" and Salt-N-Pepa's "I am the Body Beautiful" hold their own, however, and hearing Tom Jones sings "She's a Lady" makes you smile even if you haven't seen the movie.
Gary Graff

Tom And Huck ♪♪♪♪

1995, Walt Disney Records; from the movie *Tom And Huck*, Buena Vista Pictures, 1995.

Album Notes: *Music*: Stephen Endelman; *Orchestrations*: Sonny Kompanek; Orchestra conducted by Stephen Endelman; *Featured Musicians*: Andy Stein (fiddle), Richard Sortomme (synthesizer); *Album Producer*: Stephen Endelman; *Engineer*: James P. Nichols.

Selections: 1 Off To Be Steamboat Men (2:05); 2 Huck's Camp (1:53); 3 Main Title (2:13); 4 Tom And Becky In School (1:38); 5 Fence Painting (1:07); 6 The Raft (1:30); 7 Doc's Murder (3:14); 8 Let's Lynch Muff (1:32); 9 The Oath (1:29); 10 Joe's On The Move (1:29); 11 The Hunt For Murrel's Map (2:52); 12 Tom Proposes To Becky (2:14); 13 Huck's Torment (1:16); 14 Tom's Funeral (1:37); 15 Tom Visits Muff In Jail (1:28); 16 Tom's Nightmare (1:52); 17 Huck Leaves (1:45); 18 Tom Rescues Becky (1:31); 19 The Treasure (2:49); 20 Why'd You Come Back, Huck? (4:06).

Review: Mark Twain's favorite imps rode once again in this new Disney screen adaptation, with Stephen Endelman providing the musical background framing and illustrating their various adventures. Evidently inspired by his subject, the composer delivered a score that blends traditional orchestral textures with bluegrass/folk instruments, the whole thing subtly underlined by synthesizer effects. The cues, many of them unfortunately too short with a playing time under two minutes, outline the most salient incidents in the narrative, and display as required some romantic lyricism, some playfulness, some suspense, some epic feel, and generally speaking a sense of fun. Overly effusive and sketched in broad swaths of musical colors, the score is enormously lively and enjoyable.

Tom and Jerry: The Movie ♪♪♪♪▷

1992, MCA Records; from the animated feature *Tom And Jerry: The Movie*, Turner Entertainment, 1992.

Album Notes: *Music*: Henry Mancini; *Lyrics*: Leslie Bricusse; *Orchestrations*: Henry Mancini, Jack Hayes; *Music Editor*: Stephen A. Hope; Orchestra conducted by Henry Mancini; *Featured Vocalists*: Richard Kind (Tom), Dana Hill (Jerry), Charlotte Rae (Aunt Figg), Tony Jay (Mr. Lickboot), Henry Gibson (Dr. Applecheek), Anndi McAfee (Robyn Starling), Rip Taylor (Captain Kiddie), Howard Morris (Squawk), Edmund Gilbert (Pugsy), David L. Lander (Frankie Da Flea), Raymond McLeod, Mitchel D. Moore, Scott Wojahn (The Alley Cats); *Album Producer*: Henry Mancini; *Engineer*: Allan Snelling.

Selections: 1 All In How Much We Give (3:31) *Stephanie Mills*; 2 Friends To The End (3:59); 3 What Do We Care (The Alley Cats' Song)(2:55); 4 God's Little Creatures (2:51); 5 (Money Is Such) A Beautiful World (2:52); 6 I Miss You (Robyn's Song)(2:18); 7 I've Done It All (2:23); 8 Tom And Jerry Theme (Main Title)(4:10); 9 Homeless (3:13); 10 We Meet Robyn (3:24); 11 Food Fight Polka (2:08); 12 Meet Dr. Applecheek (4:09); 13 Chase (5:22); 14 Escape From The Fire (3:32); 15 Finale—Friends To The End (1:47); 16 Tom And Jerry Theme (pop version)(3:23).

Review: Once you have dealt with Stephanie Mills' inflected vocalizations on "All In How Much We Give," settle for a joy ride with Henry Mancini's mischieviously delightful songs and score for this big screen version involving the feuding animated duo created by Bill Hannah and Joe Barbera. Set off by bits of dialogue, lifted from the soundtrack, the album follows the adventures of Tom, the cat, and Jerry, the mouse, as they momentarily abandon their constant chases and pranks on each other and do the impossible, trying to get along, to save the life of a young girl. Augmenting the many songs (with lyrics by Leslie Bricusse) are several nifty instrumentals ("I've Done It All," "Food Fight Polka," "Chase") which Mancini fans may recognize as clones from previous scores he wrote, but demonstrate that his creative verve (or is it nerve?) always was at its peak, no matter what the situation.

Tom & Viv ♪♪♪▷

1994, Sony Classical; from the movie *Tom & Viv*, Miramax Films, 1994.

Album Notes: *Music*: Debbie Wiseman; Orchestra conducted by Debbie Wiseman; *Featured Artist*: Andrew Bottrill (piano); *Album Producer*: Grace Row; *Engineers*: Dick Lewzey, Bob Wolff.

Selections: 1 End Credits (3:02); 2 Maurice's Farewell (2:03); 3 Hospital Scene (1:52); 4 Tom And Viv's Dance (3:12) *Palm Court Theatre Orchestra*; 5 The Honeymoon (2:59); 6 Tom And Bertie (3:09); 7 Bertie And Viv's Pianola Rag (2:43); 8 The Road To Garsington (:39); 9 Viv And Maurice (4:59) *Debbie Wiseman*; 10 Viv Becomes Ill (3:02); 11 Tom Wants Nothing (1:21); 12 Love Theme (2:09); 13 "Fac, ut ardeat cor meum" (from Stabat Mater)(G. Pergolesi)(2:27) *Czech Philharmonic Chorus, Prague Chamber Orchestra, Massimo Bruni*; 14 The Harvard Letter (3:49) *Debbie Wiseman*; 15 Church Scene (1:07); 16 Viv And Louise (1:27); 17 The Poetry Reading (1:36); 18 The Wibbly Wobbly Walk (J.P. Long/P. Pelham)(4:04); 19 The Print Room (5:28) *Debbie Wiseman*; 20 Opening Titles (3:00); 21 "Beim Schlfengehen" (from Four Last Songs)(R. Strauss)(5:26) *Kiri Te Kanawa, The London Symphony Orchestra, Andrew Davis*; 22 Viv Is Excluded (1:16); 23 Viv Explains (1:19); 24 Viv Is Committed (4:48) *Debbie Wiseman*.

Review: Alternately romantic and poignant, Debbie Wiseman musically chronicles the tragic life of socialite Vivienne Haigh-Wood and her marriage to poet Tom (T.S.) Eliot. The underscore is structured like a lush orchestral symphony, broken on occasion by period-styled pieces composed by Wiseman, and three source cues. Wiseman performs the piano solos on four tracks.

David Hirsch

Tombstone 🦴🦴🦴🦴

1993, Intrada Records; from the movie *Tombstone*, Hollywood Pictures, 1993.

Album Notes: *Music*: Bruce Broughton; *Music Editor*: Patricia Carlin; The Sinfonia of London, conducted by David Snell; *Album Producer*: Bruce Broughton; *Engineer*: Mike Ross.

Selections: 1 The Cowboys (3:50); 2 A Family (2:04); 3 Arrival In Tombstone (2:15); 4 Josephine (1:30); 5 Thespian Overture (:45); 6 Gotta Go To Work (1:10); 7 Fortuitous Encounter (5:17); 8 Street Standoff (7:08); 9 The O.K. Corral (7:34); 10 Aftermath (1:30); 11 Cowboy's Funeral (4:29); 12 Morgan's Death (2:12); 13 Wyatt's Revenge (3:52); 14 The Former Fabian (1:34); 15 Brief Encounters (5:37); 16 Finishing It (3:56); 17 Doc And Wyatt (2:47); 18 Looking At Heaven (8:43).

Review: Bruce Broughton met the challenge of improving on his popular *Silverado* score with this powerful, richly melodic western score that opens with a blasting, percussive action cue that will knock you out of your seat. The primary theme for Kurt Russell's Wyatt Earp isn't introduced until well into the score, but it's worth the wait. Broughton's Earp melody is a classic western theme, elaborate and instantly memorable, which

functions perfectly both as a noble heroic characterization, as Earp makes his way into the town of Tombstone, and as a bristling statement of vigilante rage during the virtuoso, standout explosion of percussion and brass that underscores the film's take on the "Gunfight at the O.K. Corral." Broughton achieves something out of Samuel Barber as he contrasts a romantic melody with a moving Americana theme as an elegy for the death of Earp's brother, while later sections of the score hammer home the brutal violence of Earp's and Doc Holiday's pursuit of justice. This lengthy album is marred by a couple of interminable suspense cues, but overall this is an important, beautifully-crafted effort that deserves its place next to Silverado as one of the best western scores ever written.

Jeff Bond

See also: Hour of the Gun and Wyatt Earp

Torn Curtain 🦴🦴

1990, Varese-Sarabande; from the movie *Torn Curtain*, Universal Pictures, 1966.

Album Notes: *Music*: John Addison; Orchestra conducted by John Addison; *Album Producer*: Charles "Bud" Dant; *CD Producers*: Tom Null, Robert Townson.

Selections: 1 Main Title From Torn Curtain (2:15); 2 Love Theme From Torn Curtain (3:02); 3 Behind The Curtain (2:16); 4 Introduction To B (2:17); 5 Premonitions Of Trouble (3:20); 6 Variations On The Love Theme Of Torn Curtain (1:16); 7 B Bus Theme Variations (1:18); 8 Sarah Alone (1:30); 9 The Murder Of Gromek (2:40); 10 Michael And Sarah—Alone On The Hill (1:21); 11 Escape On The B Bus (4:03); 12 Green Years (End Title)(J. Addison/J. Livingston/R. Evans)(3:57) *Johnny Mann Singers*.

Review: A cold war thriller set in East Germany, *Torn Curtain*, directed by Alfred Hitchcock, involves an American nuclear scientist (Paul Newman), who pretends he is a defector to obtain a secret anti-missile formula. When he is accused of murdering a Soviet agent, he and his assistant and fiancee (Julie Andrews) try to return to the West, succeeding only after many close encounters with disaster. Initially, Hitchcock had asked Bernard Herrmann to write the score for this film, something which probably would have led to a tight cliff-hanger along the lines of *North By Northwest*. Instead, the producers rejected Herrmann's score, and, deciding they needed something more commercial, hired John Addison, one of the most respected British composers. While Addison delivered a score that's competent and professional, its style is completely out of synch with the subject of the film. This is noticably evident in the "Love Theme," in which the lyrical beauty of the beginning stanzas fades into a mock comedic coda that doesn't belong in either a love theme or the score for a thriller. At times too lush, at other times too strident, and occasionally too cute and too cheerful, this is clearly a case of the wrong score ending in a film, strictly for commercial considerations. The film itself was not the success Hitchcock had envisioned. Clumsy and drawn out, the screenplay concocted by Brian Moore obviously didn't inspire him, and he did a routine job in which his usual sense of observation and his sardonic humor were noticeably absent. The score didn't help either.

Total Eclipse 𝄞𝄞𝄞𝄞

1995, Sony Classical; from the movie *Total Eclipse*, Fine Line Features, 1995.

Album Notes: *Music*: Jan A.P. Kaczmarek; *Orchestrations*: Krzesimir Debski, Jan A.P. Kaczmarek; The Warsaw Symphony Orchestra, conducted by Krzesimir Debski, Tadeusz Karolak; *Featured Performers*: The Wilanow String Quartet, Marta Boberska (soprano), Orchestra of the Eighth Day, Bogdan Liszka (oboe); *Music Executive Producer*: Krystyna Wydzga; *Engineer*: Rafal Paczkowski.

Selections: 1 The Opening (1:27); 2 Trip To Paris (2:21); 3 The Sea Quartet (1:43); 4 Arrival (1:12); 5 Cafe Andre (1:08); 6 Hashish Kiss (2:06); 7 Looking For Rimbaud (1:23); 8 Naked On The Roof (:52); 9 Cafe Bobino (1:19); 10 Hashish 2 (3:38); 11 Le dormeur du val (1:57); 12 Coming Home (1:01); 13 Triangle (1:05); 14 Knife (2:02); 15 The Sun (3:05); 16 Mathilde And Verlaine (2:11); 17 Two Trains (2:58); 18 Verlaine Escapes (1:43); 19 Rimbaud Wounded (1:54); 20 Memory (2:11); 21 The Sentence (1:12); 22 Tear (1:51); 23 Cafe Bobino 2 (1:44); 24 The Drunken Boat (1:29); 25 Abyssinian Plateau (3:27); 26 The Death (2:24); 27 Eternity (Finale)(2:54); 28 End Credits (2:36).

Review: Trust Agnieszka Holland to make a film away from standard commercial considerations, and one dealing with the relationship between two of late 19th-century France best known versificators, Arthur Rimbaud and Paul Verlaine, one the self-assured and arrogant young lion of poetry, the other an older married man with doubts about his masculinity as well as his talent. Reflecting the many ambiguities and deep emotional conflicts between the two men, and their eventual falling off after Verlaine shot Rimbaud and spent two years in jail as a result, the score by Jan A.P. Kaczmarek is quite lyrical in spurts ("Naked On The Roof," "The Sun"), offset by disturbing moments after ("Knife," "Rimbaud Wounded"). One of Rimbaud's best known poem, "Le dormeur du val" (Sleeper In The Glen) gets a lovely setting, as does "Le bateau ivre" (The Drunken Boat), by Verlaine. Two different sets of cues that recur ("Hashish" and "Cafe Bobino") specifically detail scenes in the film during which both men smoke and drink themselves into a stupor at one of their favorite Parisian hangouts. An intelligent score, filled with attractive melodies, which demands closer than usual attention from the listener, but proves quite rewarding as a result.

Total Recall 𝄞𝄞𝄞𝄞

1990, Varese-Sarabande; from the movie *Total Recall*, Carolco Pictures, 1990.

Album Notes: *Music*: Jerry Goldsmith; *Orchestrations*: Arthur Morton; *Music Editor*: Ken Hall; The National Philharmonic Orchestra, conducted by Jerry Goldsmith; *Album Producer*: Jerry Goldsmith; *Engineer*: Bruce Botnick.

Selections: 1 The Dream (3:33); 2 The Holograms (5:36); 3 The Big Jump (4:33); 4 The Mutant (3:16); 5 Clever Girl (4:31); 6 First Meeting (1:10); 7 The Treatment (5:30); 8 Where Am I? (3:56); 9 End Of A Dream (5:45); 10 A New Life (2:23).

Review: Jerry Goldsmith reached the pinnacle of his supercharged action style for Paul Verhoven's ingenious science fiction vehicle for Arnold Schwarzenneger. The film's pulsating title music seems like a cross between Basil Pouledaris' *Conan the Barbarian* with its broad horn fanfare and a simplified version of Goldsmith's own *Capricorn One*, but Goldsmith uses the title music as a springboard for a score of amazing complexity and intensity, ranging from hammering, wildly propulsive action cues like "The Big Jump" and "Clever Girl" to dreamy, expansive sections of electronics and orchestra like "The Mutant." Everything climaxes in the lengthy (and largely unused) "The End of a Dream" cue, a relentless, crushing, snare-drum-heavy orchestral charge that bears comparison to Goldsmith's brilliant retreat music from his classic *The Blue Max* score. The only criticism you can level at this album is that at around 40 minutes in length, it's too short — the film is full of even more amazing musical highlights that deserve preservation in album form.

Jeff Bond

A Touch of Class 𝄞𝄞𝄞𝄞

1973, DRG Records; from the movie *A Touch of Class*, Avco Embassy, 1973.

Album Notes: *Music*: John Cameron; *Songs*: Sammy Cahn, George Barrie.

Selections: 1 Overture: All That Love Went To Waste (S. Cahn/ G. Barrie)/ Steve's Theme/Vickie's Theme/Love Theme (2:06); 2 A Touch Of Class (1:38); 3 All That Love Went To Waste (instrumental)(S. Cahn/G. Barrie)(4:42); 4 Amor Mio (S. Cahn/

G. Barrie)(2:50); 5 Mrs. Alessio's Rock And Roll Band/Vickie's Theme (2:37); 6 I Always Knew (Love Theme)(J. Cameron/S. Cahn)(2:28); 7 Overture: Bullfight Theme/Golf Theme/Steve's Theme (2:21); 8 Antonio's Restaurant (2:24); 9 She Told Me So Last Night (M. Frank/M. Frank)(2:05); 10 Nudge Me Every Morning (S. Cahn/G. Barrie)/Steve's Theme (2:56); 11 All That Love Went To Waste (S. Cahn/G. Barrie)(2:31) *Madeline Bell*; 12 Finale: All That Love Went To Waste (S. Cahn/G. Barrie)/A Touch Of Class/I Always Knew (:28).

Review: This deliciously bubbly comedy, nearly forgotten today, belongs to a genre that existed in the 1960s, when the film was made, that was altogether fun and pleasantly enjoyable. A charming love story between two people, George Segal and Glenda Jackson, who accidentally meet in London, have a fling, take their romance to Spain and back to America, all the while trying to avoid his friends, in-laws, and wife, it yielded this Academy Award-nominated score by John Cameron, as heady and sparkling as the film itself, with light, delirious little musical comments that often prove convincingly irresistible. Like the scores for *What's New Pussycat?* and *Promise Her Anything*, which it sometimes evokes, the music for *A Touch of Class* is easy on the ear and on the mind, and is winningly delightful.

Touch of Evil ♫♫♫♫

1993, Varese-Sarabande; from the film *Touch of Evil*, Universal Pictures, 1958.

Album Notes: *Music*: Henry Mancini; Orchestra conducted by Henry Mancini; *CD Producer*: Robert Townson, Tom Null.

Selections: 1 Main Title (3:28); 2 Borderline Montuna (2:00); 3 Strollin' Blues (2:38); 4 Orson Around (2:44); 5 Reflection (2:59); 6 Tana's Theme (2:23); 7 Flashing Nuisance (1:35); 8 The Boss (1:05); 9 Pidgeon Caged (:55); 10 Rock Me To Sleep (2:39); 11 The Big Drag (2:19); 12 Ku Ku (2:41); 13 Susan (2:19); 14 Son Of Raunchy (3:01); 15 Lease Breaker (2:45); 16 Background To Murder (7:20); 17 Bar Room Rock (1:14); 18 Blue Pianola (3:13); 19 Something For Susan (1:38); 20 The Chase (1:00).

Review: Throughout most of his career, Henry Mancini was so clearly identified with light comedies, that one may tend to forget he also dwelled in other genres, notably contemporary crime dramas where he also developed a recognizable signature style of strongly jazz accented themes and tight rhythms. A brilliant, absorbing filmization of Whit Masterson's novel, "Badge of Evil," directed by and starring Orson Welles, *Touch of Evil* gave Mancini the occasion to produce an outstanding score replete with explosive themes and catchy melodies, all of them detailing this sordid south-of-the-border story about a narcotics investigator (a mustachioed Charlton Heston), on his honeymoon in a small Mexican frontier town with his wife (Janet Leigh), and the washed-out local captain of police, played by Orson Welles, who team to nab a band of criminals suspected to be involved in a narcotics racket. If the brooding, at times rambling plot that followed left some viewers somewhat baffled, there was no mistaking the masterful visual appeal of the film itself, with its fluid and impressive photography, subtly enhanced by Mancini's provocative score. Using a wide variety of genres (jazz, rock'n'roll, honky-tonk) rather than a singly driven approach, Mancini devised cues that conferred a unique musical color to the film, in turns evoking the stifling atmosphere of the Mexican little town, the moods in some of the places where the action took place, and some of the characters in the story. The mono recording at times sounds dense and opaque, but the vibrancy and drama in the music still comes through eloquently and convincingly.

Toy Soldiers ♫♫♫

1991, Intrada Records; from the movie *Toy Soldiers*, Tri-Star Pictures, 1991.

Album Notes: *Music*: Robert Folk; *Orchestrations*: Randy Miller, Peter Tomashek; The Dublin Symphony Orchestra, conducted by Robert Folk; *Album Producer*: Robert Folk; *Engineer*: Brian Masterson.

Selections: 1 Regis School (1:51); 2 Escape From Barranquilla (3:43); 3 Closing In (2:28); 4 All's Well (2:00); 5 Billy Escape (1:46); 6 Joey's Death (3:43); 7 Regis Captured (3:51); 8 Reflections (2:19); 9 Demands (3:14); 10 Removing The Chips (3:59); 11 The Cellar (1:34); 12 Jack Gets It (1:38); 13 Uneasy Quiet (2:11); 14 Back To Regis (2:29); 15 Border Killing (4:03); 16 Narrow Escape (2:58); 17 Snap Out Of It (4:06); 18 Mouthwash Incident (1:51); 19 Interrogation (1:45); 20 Regis Surrounded (1:32); 21 The Plan (2:11); 22 The Wrath Of Joey's Father (1:14); 23 The End Of Cali (4:08); 24 Toy Soldiers (4:57).

Review: Even if you haven't seen the movie, this is one of those film scores you've probably heard before a number of times. A coming attraction's staple for its use in countless movie trailers, Robert Folk's pleasing, rousing music from this surprisingly good teen action flick is infectious and highly melodic—something usually lacking in most action genre scores. With a sweeping main theme, Folk establishes a peaceful, tranquil musical background for the forthcoming bursts of sporadic action to surprise us in, yet even through the "busy" suspense cues, the composer maintains his tonal intentions and the result is a score that has become a favorite among soundtrack aficionados. One wishes that more genre scores would take the same symphonic route, though alas, that is usually not the case.

Andy Dursin

Toy Story 🎵🎵🎵

1995, Walt Disney Records; from the movie *Toy Story*, **Walt Disney, 1995.**

Album Notes: *Music:* Randy Newman; *Orchestrations:* Don Davis, Randy Newman; Orchestra conducted by Randy Newman; *Album Producers:* Frank Wolf, Don Davis, Jim Flamberg, Randy Newman.

Selections: 1 You've Got A Friend In Me (2:04) *Randy Newman*; 2 Strange Things (3:17) *Randy Newman*; 3 I Will Go Sailing No More (2:57) *Randy Newman*; 4 Andy's Birthday (5:57); 5 Soldier's Mission (1:29); 6 Presents (1:09); 7 Buzz (1:40); 8 Sid (1:20); 9 Woody And Buzz (4:30); 10 Mutants (6:05); 11 Woody's Gone (2:13); 12 The Big One (2:51); 13 Hang Together (6:02); 14 On The Move (6:18); 15 Infinity And Beyond (3:10); 16 You've Got A Friend (2:41) *Randy Newman, Lyle Lovett.*

Review: A bright and enthusiastic score by Randy Newman captures all the magic in this animated movie about a make-believe world where toys have a life of their own. Terrific songs are marred by the question, "Why do producers always let Randy Newman sing?" And partnered with Lyle Lovett (no less!) the two seem a mismatched couple. There's no doubt Newman's a talented composer, but there are certainly better singers who can do his work justice.

David Hirsch

Toys 🎵🎵🎵

1992, Geffen Records; from the movie *Toys*, **20th Century-Fox, 1992.**

Album Notes: Orchestra conducted by Shirley Walker; *Orchestrations:* Shirley Walker, Bruce Fowler; *Song Producers:* Trevor Horn, Nicky Ryan, Hans Zimmer, Pat Metheny; *Album Producer:* Trevor Horn; *Engineer:* Armin Steiner.

Selections: 1 Winter Reveries (P.I. Tchaikovsky) (2:04); 2 The Closing Of The Year (T. Horn/H. Zimmer) (3:28) *Wendy & Lisa*; 3 Ebudae (Enya/R. Ryan) (1:49) *Enya*; 4 The Happy Worker (T. Horn/B. Woolley) (4:20) *Tori Amos*; 5 Alsatia's Lullaby (H. Zimmer) (4:17) *Julia Migenes, Hans Zimmer*; 6 Workers (T. Horn/B. Woolley) (1:12) The Musical Cast Of Toys; 7 Let Joy And Innocence Prevail (H. Zimmer/T. Horn) (5:00) *Pat Metheny*; 8 The General (H. Zimmer) (2:21) *Michael Gambon, Hans Zimmer*; 9 The Mirror Song (T. Horn/B. Woolley) (4:36) *Thomas Dolby, Robin Williams, Joan Cusack*; 10 Battle Introduction (H. Zimmer) (2:45) *Robin Williams*; 11 Welcome To The Plea-

suredome (Gill/Johnson/Nash/O'Toole) (5:00) *Frankie Goes To Hollywood*; 12 Let Joy And Innocence Prevail (H. Zimmer/T. Jones) (5:02) *Grace Jones*; 13 The Closing Of The Year/Happy Workers (reprise) (5:29) ''*Happy Workers.''*

Review: A mostly instrumental soundtrack with a New Age bent, hammered in by Enya's "Ebudae" and Tori Amos' "Happy Worker." Robin Williams and Joan Cusack join Thomas Dolby for the pleasantly wacky "Mirror Song," while Frankie Goes to Hollywood's "Welcome to the Pleasuredome" is a decent fit. And Robin Williams' "Battle Introduction" certainly gives the album a jolt of slightly bent comic juice.

Gary Graff

Trail of the Pink Panther 🎵

1988, EMI-Manhattan; from the movie *Trail of the Pink Panther*, **1982.**

Album Notes: *Music:* Henry Mancini; Orchestra conducted by Henry Mancini; *Album Producer:* Joe Reisman; *Engineers:* Jim Malloy, John Norman, John Richards, Dick Bogert.

Selections: 1 The Trail Of The Pink Panther (5:05); 2 The Greatest Gift (H. Mancini/H. David) (3:23); 3 Hong Kong Fireworks (3:23); 4 A Shot In The Dark (2:35); 5 Simone (4:35); 6 It Had Better Be Tonight (H. Mancini/J. Mercer/F. Migliacci) (2:01); 7 The Easy Life In Paris (2:55); 8 Come To Me (2:59); 9 Bier Fest Polka (2:47); 10 After The Shower (3:43); 11 The Inspector Clouseau Theme (3:13); 12 The Return Of The Pink Panther (5:10).

Review: The film, a lame attempt at perpetuating the myth of Inspector Clouseau following the death of actor Peter Sellers, was merely a compilation of scenes from the previous "Pink Panther" movies. As a result, the soundtrack is also a compendium of selections from the various scores Mancini composed for the previous movies, with only the title tune, "A Shot in the Dark" and the raucously joyous "Bier Fest Polka" making their first appearance on compact disc.

The Trap 🎵🎵🎵🎵

1993, Label X Records; from the movie *The Trap*, **1966.**

Album Notes: *Music:* Ron Goodwin; Orchestra conducted by Ron Goodwin.

Selections: 1 Main Theme (2:21); 2 Eve's Theme (2:23); 3 Printemps (4:30); 4 Abduction (2:43); 5 The Dark Forest (2:15); 6 The Search (2:21); 7 Wolf Pack (1:24); 8 Snow Trek (4:35); 9 Inspiration (2:15); 10 Raging Torrent (2:30); 11 Variations on Eve's Theme and Main Theme (3:52).

Trapped in Paradise

Review: Broadly epic and elegiac, Ron Goodwin's score for *The Trap* seems at odds with this tale of a rugged fur trapper in 19th-century British Columbia, and the naive, mute girl he takes for his companion against her will, eventually winning her despite his rude manners and violent temper. Displaying strains of a neo-Romantic English folk idiom, Goodwin created cues that describe the majestic beauty of the unspoiled landscapes; the crude, earthy character of the trapper, and the girl's winsome, frightened charm; and their constant struggle to survive in the wild, untamed environment. The composer's florid style at first surprises, as one would probably expect a score with a much starker approach befitting the offbeat story and its harsh setting. But the elegiac, almost pastoral tone of some of the cues evokes the grandeur of the theme as well as the imposing setting against which the story unfolds. Eventually, Goodwin's view proves totally correct and right on target, in a score that provides many attractive melodic moments.

Trapped in Paradise

1994, Varese-Sarabande Records; from the movie *Trapped in Paradise*, 20th Century-Fox, 1994.

Album Notes: *Music*: Robert Folk; *Orchestrations*: Robert Folk, Peter Tomashek, Jon Kull; *Music Editor*: J.J. George; Orchestra conducted by Robert Folk; *Album Producer*: Robert Folk; *Engineer*: Armin Steiner.

Selections: 1 Main Title (3:00); 2 All In A Dash (2:07); 3 Firpo Brothers Blues (3:18); 4 The Getaway (2:18); 5 The River (2:16); 6 Back To The Bank (1:12); 7 The Sled Chase (3:50); 8 Sara At Church (1:39); 9 Heroic Merlin (2:35); 10 Conversations (2:26); 11 Feds And Moms (2:41); 12 Finale (2:54); 13 Do You Hear What I Hear? (G. Shayne/N. Regney)(2:43) *Bing Crosby*; 14

You're Nobody Till Somebody Loves You (J. Cavanaugh/L. Stock/R. Morgan) (2:12) *Dean Martin*.

Review: Nicolas Cage, Dana Carvey and Jon Lovitz star in this 1994 Christmas comedy, a box-office dud despite good intentions all around. Robert Folk wrote one of his typically appealing scores for the picture, a warmhearted, Holiday-themed orchestral effort that sounds cobbled together from various sources—including, but not limited to, Danny Elfman's *The Nightmare Before Christmas* and even John Williams' *JFK*, which sounds like it had some kind of influence on Folk's similar-sounding main theme. Nevertheless, there are some good moments here and there, with lush strings and a few big crescendos commenting on the action in the best old-time Hollywood movie music tradition. The album also includes Bing Crosby's classic interpretation of "Do You Hear What I Hear?" and Dean Martin's crooning of "You're Nobody Till Somebody Loves You."

Andy Dursin

Trespass

1993, Sire Records; from the movie *Trespass*, Universal Pictures, 1992.

Album Notes: *Music*: Ry Cooder; *Featured Musicians*: Ry Cooder (guitars, floor slide, array imbira, keyboards); Jim Keltner (drums, percussion); Jon Hassell (trumpet); Nathan East (bass); David Lindley (fiddle); Van Dyke Parks (piano); Larry Taylor (upright bass); *Music Editor*: Bunny Andrews; *Album Producer*: Ry Cooder; *Engineer*: Allen Sides.

Selections: 1 Video Drive-By (1:54); 2 Trespass (Main Title)(1:36); 3 East St. Louis (2:00); 4 Orgill Bros. (1:40); 5 Goose And Lucky (3:32); 6 You Think It's On Now (1:37); 7 Solid Gold (:54); 8 Heroin (4:08); 9 Totally Boxed In (6:45); 10 Give 'Em Cops (2:03); 11 Lucy In The Trunk (1:23); 12 We're Rich (2:21); 13 King Of The Street (R. Cooder/J. Keltner)(3:58); 14 Party Lights (Jr. Brown)(2:58) *Jr. Brown*.

Review: Unlike many of his scores, which are deeply rooted in Americana or exude an appealling Southern flavor, Ry Cooder created an unsettling series of cues for this urban contemporary drama set in the ghetto of East St. Louis. The unrelenting dark visions it evokes (with distant guitar riffs darting in and out of brooding synth lines) may have been what this story about a hidden treasure and gang warfare called for. But taken on its own musical terms, the score fails to make much of an impression when it no longer serves as a complement to the explosive action, and its sonic effects, devoid of melodic content, soon prove tiring and aimless. The only track that actually makes a difference is "Party Lights," written and performed by

Jr. Brown, a solidly flavored country number. Unfortunately, not enough to recommend this album.

The Trip ♫♫♫

1996, Curb Records; from the movie *The Trip*, American-International Pictures, 1967.

Album Notes: *Songs*: Mike Bloomfield; *Song Performers*: The Electric Flag featuring Mike Bloomfield, Buddy Miles, Harvey Brooks, Barry Goldberg, Nick Gravenites, Mark Doubleday, Peter Strazza, Paul Beaver, Bob Notkoff.

Selections: 1 Peter's Trip (2:35); 2 Psyche Soap (:52); 3 M-23 (1:11); 4 Synesthesia (1:43); 5 Hobbit (1:43); 6 Fewghh (:59); 7 Green And Gold (2:47); 8 Flash, Bam, Pow (1:28); 9 Hotel Room (:50); 10 Practice Music (1:24); 11 Fine Jung Thing (7:22); 12 Senior Citizen (2:57).

Review: In the late 1960s, at the height of psychedelia, *The Trip*, released by American-International, was on every acid-head's must-see list, because it dealt with the taboos of LSD, and featured a sensational soundtrack, with songs by Mike Bloomfield and the Electric Flag, an American Music Band. Today, the film, plagued with erratic lensing trying to visually render the images hallucinogenic drugs create in the mind of those who use them, and a murky script written by Jack Nicholson (no less!), looks more like a relic from another age. It may still be of minor interest if only because it stars Susan Strasberg, Bruce Dern, Dennis Hopper, and Peter Fonda as the man who spaces out. But its music, despite changes in trends, has lost none of its vibrancy, even if it brings out echoes of another era.

Triumph of the Spirit ♫♫♫

1989, Varese-Sarabande; from the movie *Triumph of the Spirit*, Nova International Films, 1989.

Album Notes: *Music*: Cliff Eidelman; *Orchestrations*: Mark McKenzie; *Music Editor*: Kenneth Hall; Unione Musicisti di Roma Orchestra and Choir, conducted by Cliff Eidelman; *Album Producer*: Cliff Eidelman; *Engineer*: Alan Snelling.

Selections: 1 Main Title (2:23); 2 Love In Wedlock (:50); 3 Dark Tunnel To Auschwitz (1:51); 4 There Was A Time (1:46); 5 Answer Us (3:51); 6 Mi Dyo Mi (:49); 7 Avram Refuses To Work (2:20); 8 Longing For Home (1:48); 9 A Hard Felt Rest (1:26); 10 Hell Realization (:33); 11 Elena's False Dreams (1:59); 12 There Was A Memory (4:24); 13 Begging For Bread (1:05); 14 The Mourning (2:13); 15 The Slaughter (2:14); 16 It Was A Month Before We Left (1:30); 17 Hunger (1:18); 18 Mercy On To Us (1:28); 19 Salamo desperately Finds Allegra (3:24); 20 Allegra's Punishment (1:36); 21 A New Assignment; 22 Death March (5:35); 23 Epilogue/End Credits (6:53).

Review: For this moving story of survival in a Nazi Death camp, Cliff Eidelman has composed a sensitive score for orchestra and choir, drawing from both Hebrew and Catholic musical sources to build a powerful and emotive backdrop for this affecting motion picture. Comprised of mostly short pieces (0:33 at shortest to 6:53 at longest), the short cues work together to form an extended suite. The music movingly dramatizes the sorrow and the dignity of its struggling protagonist; while it underlines chaos and injustice, it remains full of hope and mirrors the character's will to survive. The score's mix of broad orchestral passages, delicate solo voice, and full choir (both operating and church music) captures a lot of the various feelings suggested or depicted in the film. On disc, it makes for a compelling and moving musical experience.

Randall D. Larson

Trouble in Mind ♫♫♫♫▿

1986, Antilles Records; from the movie *Trouble in Mind*, Alive Films, 1986.

Album Notes: *Music*: Mark Isham; *Featured Musicians*: The Raincity Industrial Art Ensemble featuring Mark Isham (trumpet, saxophone, electronics), Pee Wee Ellis (saxophone), Peter Maunu (guitar), Kurt Wortman (percussion); *Album Producer*: Mark Isham; *Engineers*: Steven Miller, Mark Isham, Gary Clayton.

Selections: 1 Trouble In Mind (The Return)(R.M. Jones)(4:20) *Marianne Faithfull*; 2 Pleasure In Old Sufferings (1:18); 3 To Forget For A Moment (1:54); 4 Members Only (4:30); 5 Conflict... Beyond Understanding (2:39); 6 The Invitation (3:28); 7 Interests Pursued (2:29); 8 A Matter Of Conflict (1:42); 9 Trouble In Mind (reprise)(R.M. Jones)(1:08); 10 Halves Of A Dream (1:42); 11 Confidence From An Old Friend (:55); 12 Postponement Of Virtue (2:15); 13 Intimacy (1:32); 14 The Arrival (:50); 15 By Way Of Preparation Down The Hill (2:50); 16 A Touch Of Iago (2:18); 17 The Hawk (El Gavilan)(K. Kristofferson)(8:20) *Marianne Faithfull*.

Review: Mixing electronics and acoustic brass instruments, this early score by Mark Isham is a classic of the genre, a thoroughly atmospheric set of cues, often dominated and punctuated by the sounds of a muted trumpet, which evoke the dark passions and oppressive moods in this out-of-time stylish tale of a cop caught between the mob and a love triangle, starring Kris Kristofferson, Keith Carradine and Lori Singer, set in Raincity, a futuristic world with strange contemporary overtones. The hypnotic, sustaining moods in the film are splendidly caught in Isham's quietly understated music, with bluesy melodic themes creating an eerily nostalgic feel that's particularly gripping. Marianne Faithfull's vocals add extra flair to this sensational score.

The Trouble with Girls

1995, RCA Records; from the movie *The Trouble With Girls*, M-G-M, 1969.

See: Elvis Presley in Compilations

True Grit ♪♪

1992, Capitol Records; from the movie *True Grit*, Paramount Pictures, 1969.

Album Notes: *Music*: Elmer Bernstein; *Orchestrations*: Artie Butler; *Lyrics*: Don Black; Vocals Produced, Arranged and conducted by Al de Lory; Orchestra conducted by Elmer Bernstein; *Album Producer*: Neely Plumb; *Engineers*: Jack Hunt, Don Henderson.

Selections: 1 True Grit (2:32) *Glen Campbell*; 2 Rooster (2:04); 3 Mattie And Little Blackie (2:20); 4 A Dastardly Deed (3:00); 5 Papa's Things (2:58); 6 True Grit (2:58); 7 Chen Lee And The General (2:55); 8 Big Trail (3:15); 9 Cogburn Country (2:02); 10 True Grit (2:00) *Glen Campbell*.

Review: It's almost jarring to associate the truly forgettable music from *True Grit* with the brilliant film composer Elmer Bernstein, but it was 1968, and both the Charles Portis novel and the resulting film, starring John Wayne and Kim Darby, about a wily U.S. Marshall who aids a young girl tracking down her father's killer, were hugely successful. Enlisting the hot, young country star Glen Campbell to sing the title song, and make his acting debut in the film, certainly guaranteed the success of the Capitol album of music from the film. Today, however, the soundtrack is a curiosity. While Bernstein's other works survive as precious examples of the lost art of film music composition, this particular score is easily dismissable as an interesting foray into the contemporary scene—to this ear, better left to those less gifted than the immeasurably talented Mr. Bernstein. The reissued CD is purely budget. A single slipsheet insert, with barely readable liner notes reproduced on the back of the jewel case.

Charles L. Granata

See also: The Comancheros

True Lies ♪♪♪

1994, Epic Soundtrax; from the movie *True Lies*, 20th Century-Fox, 1994.

Album Notes: *Music*: Brad Fiedel; *Orchestrations*: Brad Fiedel, Shirley Walker, Richard Bronskill; *Music Editor*: Patty Von Arx;

Orchestra conducted by Shirley Walker; *Album Producer*: Brad Fiedel; *Engineer*: Tim Boyle.

Selections: 1 Sunshine Of Your Love (J. Bruce/P. Brown/E. Clapton)(5:18) *Living Colour*; 2 Darkness Darkness (J.C. Young)(4:08) *Screaming Trees*; 3 Alone In The Dark (J. Hiatt)(4:47) *John Hiatt*; 4 Entity (Mother Tongue) (4:21) *Mother Tongue*; 5 Sunshine Of Your Love (remix)(J. Bruce/P. Brown/E. Clapton)(5:49) *Living Colour*; 6 Main Title/Harry Makes His Entrance (2:40); 7 Escape From The Chateau (2:42); 8 Harry's Sweet Home (1:06); 9 Harry Rides Again (7:06); 10 Spying On Helen (4:16); 11 Juno's Place (1:30); 12 Caught In The Act (1:29); 13 Shadow Lover (1:21); 14 Island Suite (6:55); 15 Causeway/ Helicopter Rescue (7:57); 16 Nuclear Kiss (:52); 17 Harry Saves The Day (8:26).

Review: Director James Cameron seems to have an outsized vision of every aspect of filmmaking except for the music his movies require. Brad Fiedel's electronic score for Cameron's *The Terminator* was necessitated by budgetary restraints and fit in well with the movie's mechanistic theme, but Fiedel's work on the epic-scaled *Terminator 2* seemed hapless, and the application of yet another synthesized effort for this gigantic James Bond-type spoof is really hurtful to the power of the film. Fiedel's bright title music almost seems to suggest something Jerry Goldsmith might have done for Joe Dante's *Gremlins/Explorers* period, and while the opening chase sequence and an even more elaborate pursuit on horseback in New York City receive an exciting, pulsating staccato treatment, more than a little of the effect is derived from Shirley Walker's excellent acoustic orchestrations. Much of the rest of the score fades away into synth pad oblivion. Maybe a takeoff of John Barry was too much to ask for here, but Fiedel's approach just doesn't satisfy.

Jeff Bond

True Romance ♪

1993, Morgan Creek Records; from the movie *True Romance*, Warner Bros., 1993.

Album Notes: *Music*: Hans Zimmer; *Music Editor*: Tom Milano; *Song Producers*: Charlie Sexton, Mark Spiro, John Waite, Josh Deutsch, Denzil Slemming, Nick Name, Brent Maher, Teo Macero, Terry Date, Soundgarden, Erik Jacobsen; *Executive Music Producers*: James G. Robinson, Jim Mazza, Maureen Crowe; *Engineer*: Mark Waldren.

Selections: 1 You're So Cool (H. Zimmer)(3:40); 2 Graceland (C. Sexton/ Tonio K.)(3:26) *Charlie Sexton*; 3 In Dreams (J. Waite/M. Spiro)(3:45) *John Waite*; 4 Wounded Bird (E. Chacon/

C. Pettigrew/J. Deutsch)(5:11) *Charles & Eddie*; 5 I Want Your Body (J. Ewbank/M. Vander Kuy)(4:18) *Nymphomania*; 6 Stars At Dawn (H. Zimmer)(2:04); 7 I Need A Heart To Come Home To (R. Smith/J. Jarvis)(4:21) *Shelby Lynne*; 8 Viens Mallika sous le dome (L. Delibes)(3:56); 9 (Love Is) The Tender Trap (S. Cahn/ J. Van Heusen)(2:37) *Robert Palmer*; 10 Outshined (C. Cornell)(5:12) *Soundgarden*; 11 Amid The Chaos Of The Day (H. Zimmer)(4:55); 12 Two Hearts (C. Isaak)(3:33) *Chris Isaak*

Review: Hans Zimmer's flavorful score (sampled through two very short tracks) is given less than its fair share in this album in which several undistinguished pop songs aim to evoke the fast-paced action in the film, about a couple on the run from the mob after they steal some drug money. Further confusing the listener, the celebrated duo from Leo Delibes' *Lakme* ("Viens Mallika sous le dome"), and a tired, expressionless rendition of "(Love Is) The Tender Trap," by Robert Palmer, suddenly pop up for no apparent (musical) reason. On the front inlay card, the album advertises its content as being "very cool music." Indeed!

Tucker ♪♪♪♪

1988, A&M Records; from the movie *Tucker: The Man and His Dream*, Paramount Pictures, 1988.

Album Notes: *Music*: Joe Jackson; *Arrangements*: Joe Jackson; *Featured Musicians*: Paul Spong (trumpet), Raul D'Oliviera (trumpet), Pete Thomas (saxophones), Dave Bitelli (saxophone, clarinet). Bill Charleson (saxophone, flute), Tony Coe (clarinet), Rick Taylor (trombone), Vinnie Zummo (guitar), Dave Green (bass), Gary Burke (drums), Frank Ricotti (percussion), Ed Roynesdal (synthesizers, violin), Arlette Fibon (Ondes Martenot), Joe Jackson (piano, synthesizers, percussion); *Album Producer*: Joe Jackson.

Selections: 1 Captain Of Industry (Overture) (2:33); 2 The Car Of Tomorrow—Today! (1:34); 3 No Chance Blues (2:31); 4 (He's A) Shape In A Drape (2:59); 5 Factory (1:06); 6 Vera (2:29); 7 It Pays To Advertise (:41); 8 Tiger Rag (H. DaCosta/E. Edwards/D. LaRocca/A. Sbarbaro)(2:09); 9 Showtime In Chicago (2:44); 10 Lone Bank Loan Blues (1:12); 11 Speedway (2:40); 12 Marilee (3:01); 13 Hangin' In Howard Hughes' Hangar (2:37); 14 Toast Of The Town (1:23); 15 Abe's Blues (2:39); 16 The Trial (6:45); 17 Freedom Swing/Tucker Jingle (1:38); 18 Rhythm Delivery (3:24).

Review: Joe Jackson composed an invigorating, jazz-filled uptempo score for this acclaimed but little-seen George Lucas-Francis Ford Coppola production. Jackson dabbles in swing, jazz and pop forms throughout the score, making the album full of

fresh twists on familiar material—from standards like "Tiger Rag" to the jumpin' finale, "Rhythm Delivery," which finds Jackson performing vocals in an infectious, energetic big-band original song. The music was initially released on A&M but has been out-of-print for years, though its occasional re-issue as an import seems to confirm its continued popularity with die-hard listeners. A tremendously entertaining album, the soundtrack also features incidental jingle music composed by Carmine Coppola and boasts a wealth of standout ensemble performers.

Andy Dursin

Twelfth Night

1996, Silva Screen Records; from the movie *Twelfth Night*, Fine Line Features, 1996.

Album Notes: *Music*: Shaun Davey; *Orchestrations*: Fiachra Trench, Shaun Davey, Fergus O'Carroll; The Irish National Film Orchestra, conducted by Fiachra Trench; *Featured Musicians*: Shaun Davey (organ), Linda Byrne (piano), Martin O'Connor (accordion), Des Moore (guitar), Noel Eccles (percussion); *Album Producer*: Shaun Davey; *Engineer*: Brian Masterton; *Assistant Engineers*: Ciarac Cahill, Connell Markey.

Selections: 1 I'll Tell Thee A Tale (:56) *Ben Kingsley*; 2 Shipwreck/ Illyria (3:53); 3 Orsino's Horsemen/The Disguise (4:14); 4 The Rose Window/The Food Of Love (2:17); 5 Cesario's First Walk/Malvolio's Inspection (1:29); 6 Sir Andrew Dances/O Mistress Mine (Cabaret)(1:10) *Rita Connolly, Valerie Armstrong, Peter Beamish*; 7 Take Away The Fool (2:42); 8 Farewell Fair Cruelty/Cesario's Charm (3:32); 9 O Mistress Mine (2:45) *Ben Kingsley, Imelda Staunton*; 10 The Lonely Night/ Malvolio's Fantasy/The Sponge (3:26); 11 Cesario's Second Journey (1:32); 12 Come Away Death/Prelude To Act Three (4:05) *Ben Kingsley*; 13 Antonio's Chase (1:34); 14 Malvolio Rampant (2:24); 15 The Reluctant Duellists (5:22); 16 A Witchcraft (1:41); 17 I Am A Gone Sir (:53) *Ben Kingsley*; 18 The Twin Reunion (4:56); 19 The Wind And The Rain (5:36) *Ben Kingsley*.

Review: This well-crafted orchestral score for Trevor Nunn's 1996 treatment of Shakespeare's play opens portentiously with pulsing low string chords that underscore the film's opening shipwreck and an aggressive motif for "Orsino's Horsemen" before giving way to the lighter, energetic motives and textures of court intrigue, love, and mistaken identity that marks this as a high-spirited comedy. Like Patrick Doyle, Davey's background includes experience scoring for Shakespearean stage productions in Great Britain, and he brings some of the same melodic invention and emotional directness to his approach as Doyle. Some of the songs warbled by cast members (including Ben Kingsley, not in very good voice as a troubadour) break up the flow of the orchestral pieces, but there's plenty of invention to make up for those lapses. The score is at its best in its shimmering, through-composed cues, and at its weakest during some comic mickey-mousing for the film's romantic intrigues.

Jeff Bond

12 Monkeys 🦴

1995, MCA Records; from the movie *12 Monkeys*, Universal Pictures, 1995.

Album Notes: *Music*: Paul Buckmaster; *Orchestrations*: Paul Buckmaster; *Music Editor*: Robin Clarke; *Featured Musicians*: Michael Davis (violin), Jack Emblow (bandoneon); Orchestra conducted by Paul Buckmaster; *Album Producer*: Paul Buckmaster; *Engineer*: Eric Tomlinson.

Selections: 1 Introduccion (from Suite Punta del Este)(A. Piazzolla)(:52); 2 Cole's First Dream/Volunteer Duty/Topside (3:11); 3 Silent Night (trad.) (1:07); 4 Spider Research/Introduccion (We Did It)(A. Piazzolla)/The Proposition(1:58); 5 Time Confusion/To The Mental Ward/Planet Ogo (1:52); 6 Wrong Number/Cole's Second Dream/Dormitory Spider/Introduccion (Twin Moons Tango)(A. Piazzolla)(3:31); 7 Vivisection (C. Olins)(1:20) *Charles Olins*; 8 Sleepwalk (J. Farina/A. Farina/S. Farina)(2:23) *B.J. Cole*; 9 Introduccion (Escape To Nowhere)(A. Piazzolla)/Scanner Room/Capture And Sedation (3:32); 10 Cole's Third Dream (:20); 11 Interrogation/Time Capsule/Cole Kidnaps Railly (4:55); 12 Blueberry Hill (A. Lewis/L. Stock/V. Rose)(2:19) *Fats Domino*; 13 What A Wonderful World (B. Thiele/G.D. Weiss)(2:18) *Louis Armstrong*; 14 Cole's Fourth Dream (:25); 15 Comanche (M. Grant/L. Wray)(2:03) *Link Wray & The Wraymen*; 16 Earth Died Screaming (T. Waits)(3:35) *Tom Waits*; 17 Introduccion (Quest For 12 Monkeys)(A. Piazzolla)(4:32); 18 Fateful Bullet/A Boot From The Trunk/Cole's Longing (3:04); 19 Photo Search/Mission Brief (1:27); 20 Back In '96 (2:05); 21 Fugitives/Fateful Love/Home Dentistry (3:22); 22 Introduccion (12 Monkeys Theme reprise)(A. Piazzolla)/Giraffes And Flamingos (1:03); 23 This Is My Dream/Cole's Call/Louis And Jose (3:13); 24 Peters Does His Worst (3:51); 25 Dreamers Awake (3:33).

Review: The focal point of this score is an adaption of Astor Piazzolla's quirky little accordion track, "Introduccion," from the *Suite Punta Del Este*. It became known as the "12 Monkeys Theme," possibly because it brings to mind the image of an organ grinder and his monkey standing on some European back street. This theme appears about six times, cut into Paul Buckmaster's vague and often spotty underscore. Most of the cues have the feel of transitional pieces, too short to develop into anything substan-

tial and, just when you think you've grasped what he's getting at, in comes "Introduccion." Several songs, including Fats Domino's "Blueberry Hill" and "What a Wonderful World" by Louis Armstrong are intercut throughout the album. It's a Terry Gilliam film, so go figure what they're getting at.

David Hirsch

Twilight's Last Gleaming 🦴🦴🦴

1992, Silva Screen Records; from the movie *Twilight's Last Gleaming*, Lorimar Pictures, 1977.

Album Notes: *Music*: Jerry Goldsmith; *Orchestrations*: Arthur Morton; *Music Editor*: John C. Hammell; The Graunke Symphony Orchestra, conducted by Jerry Goldsmith; *Album Producers*: Jerry Goldsmith, Joel Goldsmith; *Associate Producer*: Ford A. Thaxton.

Selections: 1 Silo 3/The Takeover Begins (3:34); 2 General Mackenzie Arrives (1:11); 3 He Has Launch Control/Special Forces Arrive (3:41); 4 The Bubble (2:57); 5 Nuclear Nightmare (3:15); 6 A Reflective Interlude (1:26); 7 After You, Mr. President/Heading For Home/The President Falls (2:34); 8 The Taking Of Silo 3 (3:27); 9 Operation Gold Begins/Watching And Waiting (3:17); 10 The Tanks (3:40); 11 Down The Elevator Shaft/The Gold Bomb (2:14); 12 Gold Team Enters Silo 3 (4:56); 13 The Final Betrayal (1:56).

Review: This suspenseful tale of political paranoia receives a quintessential '70s action score from Jerry Goldsmith, bristling with sharp-edged, harsh string textures, and militaristic effects for brass and percussion as U.S. armed forces attempt to deal with the takeover of a nuclear missile silo. With its gritty acoustic textures, hollow martial brass fanfares and heavy, jagged action rhythms, *Twilight's Last Gleaming* lies somewhere between the European, quasi-chamber sound of *The Cassandra Crossing* and the driving brass lines of *Capricorn One*. The superb sound mix highlights every bizarre effect Goldsmith coaxes out of the orchestra, and the score's few humanistic moments, played out sensitively by low flutes and strings, make for a sharp contrast to the brutal, violent militaristic material.

Jeff Bond

Twin Peaks: Fire Walk with Me 🦴🦴🦴🦴

1992, Warner Bros. Records; from the movie *Twin Peaks: Fire Walk with Me*, New Line Cinema, 1992.

Album Notes: *Music*: Angelo Badalamenti, David Lynch; *Lyrics*: David Lynch; *Orchestrations*: Angelo Badalamenti, David Lynch,

David Slusser; *Featured Musicians*: Angelo Badalamenti, Kinny Landrum (keyboards, synthesizers), Bill Mays, David Slusser, Andy Armer (keyboards), Ken-Ichi Shimazu (piano), Vinnie Bell, David Jaurequi, Myles Boisen, Bob Rose (guitars), Buster Williams, Ron Carter, Rufus Reid (acoustic bass), Don Falzone, William Fairbanks (bass), Grady Tate, Brian Kirk, Steven Hodges, Donald Bailey (drums), Jim Hynes (trumpet), Al Regni, Alvin Flythe, Jr. (sax), Jay Hoggard, David Cooper (vibes), David Lynch (percussion); *Album Producer*: David Lynch, Angelo Badalamenti; *Engineers*: David Bianco, Michael Semanick.

Selections: 1 Theme from Twin Peaks: Fire Walk With Me (6:40); 2 The Pine Float (3:58); 3 Sycamore Trees (3:52) *Jimmy Scott*; 4 Don't Do Anything (I Wouldn't Do)(7:17); 5 A Real Indication (Thought Gang)(5:31) *Angelo Badalamenti*; 6 Questions In A World Of Blue (4:50); *Julee Cruise*; 7 The Pink Room (4:02); 8 The Black Dog Runs At Night (Thought Gang)(1:45) *Angelo Badalamenti*; 9 Best Friends (2:12); 10 Moving Through Time (6:48); 11 Montage from Twin Peaks: Girl Talk/Birds In Hell/Laura Palmer's Theme/Falling (5:27); 12 The Voice Of Love (3:55).

Review: Without drawing on any of the principal themes he created for the original television series (except "Laura Palmer's Theme" and "Falling"), Angelo Badalamenti concocted another brew of wailing blues and jazz solos, mixed with cutting edge techno-rock rhythms. The difference between the film and TV series is that sexual tension more than an army of quirky suspects in a murder mystery provides the core motivation. The main theme is a somber and lazy trumpet solo, a gust of smoky heat to reintroduce us to Laura Palmer, the "good" girl with a rotting core whose untimely demise will launch the plot of the popular cult series. The album features four songs with really bizarre lyrics by director David Lynch, who also composed "The Pink Room" and "Best Friends" (the latter with David Slusser). Badalamenti performs (not be be confused with singing) the songs, "A Real Indication" and "Black Dog Runs at Night" (they call these lyrics?); and "Questions in a World of Blue" was taken from an album by Julee Cruise, "The Road House" chanteuse in the TV pilot film. Perfectly captures all the oddness of Lynch's film.

David Hirsch

Twister

Twister ♫♫♫

1996, Atlantic Records; from the movie *Twister*, Warner Bros., 1996.

Album Notes: *Music*: Mark Mancina; *Orchestrations*: Bruce Fowler, Y.S. Moriarty, Ladd McCintosh, Don Harper, Mark Mancina; *Arrangements*: Mark Mancina, Don Harper, John Van Tongeren; *Music Editor*: Zigmond Gron; *Featured Musicians*: Trevor Rabin (guitar), Doug Smith (nylon guitar), Mike Fisher (percussion); *Album Producer*: Mark Mancina; *Engineers*: Steve Kempster, Shawn Murphy.

Selections: OKLAHOMA: 1 Wheatfield (1:19); 2 Where's My Truck? (:20); 3 Futility (2:14); 4 Downdraft (1:47);

IT'S COMING: 5 Drive In (2:37); 6 The Big Suck (1:10);

THE HUNT: 7 Going Green (2:48); 8 Sculptures (3:03); 9 Cow (5:38); 10 Ditch (1:28);

THE DAMAGE: 11 Wakita (5:02);

HAILSTORM HILL: 12 Bob's Road (2:10); 13 We're Almost There (2:58);

F5: 14 Dorothy IV (1:48); 15 Mobile Home (4:38); 16 God's Finger (1:46);

WILLIAM TELL: 17 William Tell Overture (G. Rossini)/Oklahoma Medley (1:06) *Todd Field, Wendle Josepher*; 18 End Title/Respect The Wind (E. Van Halen/A. Van Halen)(9:18) *Edward & Alex Van Halen*.

Review: Mark Mancina scored *Speed* for director Jan DeBont, and with a resume that also includes writing the music for the action films *Con-Air* and *Bad Boys*, it doesn't take a genius to figure out that Mancina is skilled in composing vibrant genre music that rarely ever holds back with emotion. The score for *Twister*, his second for DeBont, bursts forth with no-holds barred intensity, thanks to an aggressive main title theme that's one of the few hummable pieces of film music written in the last few years. Unlike his previous work on *Speed*, however, *Twister* is more reliant on the orchestra than it is on synthesizers, with full chorus added to some of the album's most powerful cues. It all makes for a solid and enjoyable soundtrack, though some listeners will want to skip past the horrible cast duet "William Tell Overture/Oklahoma Medley,' which doesn't segue out of Mancina's score nearly as well as Eddie & Alex Van Halen's guitarfest "Respect the Wind," heard here as a lengthy extension to the composer's end credits music.

Andy Dursin

Twister ♫♫♫♫

1996, Warner Bros. Records; from the movie *Twister*, Warner Bros., 1996.

Album Notes: *Song Producers*: Bruce Fairbaian, Rusted Root & Tim Bomba, Tori Amos, Mark Knopfler, Chuck Ainlay, Soul Asylum & Eric Pierson, Paul Q. Kolderie & Belly, Patrick Leonard & Jeremy Lubbock, Juan Patino & Lisa Loeb, Rick Rubin, Lou Giordano, Robert John Lange, Lindsey Buckingham, Edward

Van Halen & Alex Van Halen; *Engineers*: Edwin Musper, Rusted Root & Tim Bomba, Mark Hawley, Marcel Van Limbek, Gary Paczosa, Eric Pierson, Paul Q. Kolderie, Juan Patino, D. Sardy, Tom Lord-Alge, Dan Marnien, Edwin Musper; *Album Executive Producers*: Joel Still, Budd Carr; *Engineer*: Stephen Marcussen.

Selections: 1 Human Being (E. Van Halen/A. Van Halen/S. Hagar/M. Anthony) (5:10) *Van Halen*; 2 Virtual Reality (Rusted Root/M. Glabicki) (3:22) *Rusted Root*; 3 Talula (T. Amos) (3:43) *Tori Amos*; 4 Moments Like This (V. Krauss/M. McDonald) (4:58) *Alison Krauss, Union Station*; 5 Darling Pretty (M. Knopfler) (4:28) *Mark Knopfler*; 6 Miss This (D. Pirner) (3:56) *Soul Asylum*; 7 Broken (T. Donelly) (4:02) *Belly*; 8 Love Affair (E. Morricone/A. & M. Bergman) (4:41) *k.d. lang*; 9 How (L. Loeb) (3:52) *Lisa Loeb & Nine Stories*; 10 Melancholy Mechanics (A. Kiedis/Flea/D. Navarro/C. Smith) (4:31) *Red Hot Chili Peppers*; 11 Long Way Down (J. Reznik) (3:29) *Goo Goo Dolls*; 12 No One Needs To Know (S. Twain/R.J. Lange) (3:05) *Shania Twain*; 13 Twisted (S. Nicks) (4:13) *Stevie Nicks*; 14 Respect The Wind (E. Van Halen/A. Van Halen) (5:49) *Edward & Alex Van Halen.*

Review: Another one of those soundtracks that shoots wide in an effort to bring in the broadest audience. For hard rockers there's two songs from Van Halen, country fans have Shania Twain and Alison Krauss, classic rock fans will find Dire Straits' Mark Knopfler and modern rockers will be swept up by an A-list that includes Soul Asylum, Tori Amos, the Red Hot Chili Peppers, Rusted Root, the Goo Goo Dolls and Belly. Quietly in the midst of all this is a reunion of former Fleetwood Mac partners Stevie Nicks and Lindsey Buckingham on "Twisted."

Gary Graff

Two Moon Junction 🎵🎵🎵

1988, Varese-Sarabande Records; from the movie *Two Moon Junction*, Lorimar Pictures, 1988.

Album Notes: *Music*: Jonathan Elias; *Featured Musicians*: Jonathan Elias, Sherman Foote (keyboards, programming), Mark Egan (fretless bass), Ray Foote (guitar); *Album Producer*: Jonathan Elias; *Engineer*: Sherman Foote.

Selections: 1 Water Dreams (2:20); 2 1,000-Mile Stare (1:58); 3 Hideaway (4:49); 4 Meet Me At The Two Moon (2:35); 5 Folk Durge (3:30); 6 The Hiding (1:16); 7 One Step Closer (2:54); 8 Appearance At The Carnival (1:34); 9 Seduction (2:13); 10 Water Dreams (reprise) (1:42); 11 Before Morning (2:08); 12 Follow Me Home (1:15); 13 Return To Two Moon (4:59); 14 The Runaway (3:51).

Review: A moody and evocative ambient score that mists along, like slowly-rising steam or heavy, sluggish storm clouds, laying a rhythmic backdrop of ambient tonalities and building, interpolating chords that are both relaxing and sometimes invigorating. A recurring synthesized pan-flute motif provides a pleasing texture in the midst of Elias' singing guitars, delicate keyboard notes and electronic tones emerging and merging and evaporating. It's somewhat in the vogue of those "new age" synth/acoustic albums, and like some of them, Elias' music runs the risk of becoming monotonous or redundant through under-development, but Elias develops his rhythms and textures and chord-progressions effectively, they don't submerge into a sluggish mire or uncertain orchestration, but they ride an orchestral sea with purpose, slicing through and around and under and over the tonal waves of richly-swelling electronic formations.

Randall Larson

2001

2001 🎵🎵🎵🎵

1993, Varese-Sarabande; from the movie *2001: A Space Odyssey*, M-G-M, 1968.

Album Notes: *Music*: Alex North; The National Philharmonic Orchestra, conducted by Jerry Goldsmith; *Album Producers*: Jerry Goldsmith, Robert Townson; *Engineer*: Mike Sheedy.

Selections: 1 Main Title (1:37); 2 The Foraging (3:44); 3 Eat Meat And The Kill (3:27); 4 The Bluff (3:01); 5 Night Terrors (2:02); 6 The Dawn Of Man (3:14); 7 Space Station Docking (2:22); 8 Trip To The Moon (3:21); 9 Moon Rocket Bus (5:01); 10 Space Talk (3:30); 11 Interior Orion (1:26); 12 Main Theme (2:31).

Review: Alex North's rejected score for Stanley Kubrick's 1968 space epic has long been one of the great mysteries of film music, a work heard by only a select few until composer Jerry Goldsmith and Varese Sarabande's Robert Townson assembled this remarkable recording, with Goldsmith conducting the National Philharmonic Orchestra and resurrecting North's music from the ashes. It's a powerful work, brimming with mysticism, brutal primitiveness and delicate, ethereal beauty. North wrote his own take on Strauss's "Also Sprach Zarathustra," an expansive orchestral fanfare for Kubrick's opening conjunction of planets. Much of the score is taken up with the grinding, violent dissonance of the "Dawn of Man" sequence, with brass and woodwinds growling in tribalistic fury as primitive apes battle over food and water. The famous "Blue Danube" space station sequence is scored with a brilliant, sprightly scherzando after Mendelssohn, while two other space sequences receive delicate, haunting arrangements for strings, harp and vocal soprano. North's work only went as far as a strident Ent'racte for the film's intermission before he was relieved of his duties, but given the power of the music the composer produced for the first half of this unforgettable film, you have to shiver a little at the thought of what North might have come up with for later scenes on the Discovery spacecraft or for the film's completely abstract Stargate sequence. Clearly Kubrick's vision for the film was less conventional than North's modernistic music, but his original score for *2001* still stands on its own as a masterpiece of film composition.

Jeff Bond

2001: A Space Odyssey ♫♫

1996, Rhino Records; from the movie *2001: A Space Odyssey*, M-G-M, 1968.

Album Notes: *Music:* Johann Strauss, Richard Strauss, Gyogy Ligeti; *Album Producers:* Rick Victor, David McLees; *Engineers:* Dan Hersch, Chris Clarke.

Selections: 1 Overture: Atmospheres (G. Ligeti)(2:49) *The Sudwesfunk Orchestra, Ernest Bour*; 2 Main Title: Also Sprach Zarathustra (R. Strauss)(1:41) *The Vienna Philharmonic, Herbert von Karajan*; 3 Requiem For Soprano, Mezzo Soprano, Two Mixed Choirs And Orchestra (G. Ligeti)(6:33) *The Bavarian Radio Orchestra, Francis Travis*; 4 The Blue Danube (J. Strauss)(5:42) *The Berlin Philharmonic Orchestra, Herbert von Karajan*; 5 Lux Aeterna (G. Ligeti)(2:52) *The Stuttgart Schola Cantorum, Clytus Gottwold*; 6 Gayane Ballet Suite (Adagio)(A. Khachaturian)(5:15) *The Leningrad Philharmonic Orchestra, Gennadi Rezhdestvensky*; 7 Jupiter And Beyond (15:13): (a) Requiem For Soprano, Mezzo Soprano, Two Mixed Choirs And Orchestra (G. Ligeti), (b) Atmospheres (G. Ligeti), (c) Adventures (G. Ligeti); 8 Also Sprach Zarathustra (R. Strauss)(1:41); 9 The Blue Danube (J. Strauss)(8:17); 10 Also Sprach Zarathustra (R. Strauss)(1:39) *The Sudwesfunk Orchestra, Ernest Bour*; 11 Lux Aeterna (G. Ligeti)(5:59) *The Stuttgart Schola Cantorum, Clytus Gottwold*; 12 Adventures (G. Ligeti)(10:51) *Internationale Musikinstitut Darmstardt, Gyorgy Ligeti*; 13 HAL 9000 (9:41)

Review: The ultimate music trip, if not necessarily the ultimate soundtrack. While the choice of crisp, disembodied classical selections (albeit from the Romantic and Modern eras) might have seemed odd at first, it perfectly suited the extraordinary space epic and no doubt attracted a lot of moviegoers (and potheads) to the values of serious instrumental music. However, as a pure audio experience, it sounds relatively arid.

Under Siege

Under Siege ♫♫

1992, Varese-Sarabande Records; from the movie *Under Siege,* Warner Bros., 1992.

Album Notes: *Music:* Gary Chang; *Orchestrations:* Todd Hayen; *Music Editor:* Sally Boldt; Orchestra conducted by Gary Chang; *Featured Musicians:* Billy Ward (drums), Kurt Taylor (guitars); *Album Producer:* Gary Chang; *Engineers:* Armin Steiner, Danny Wallin, Brian Reeves.

Selections: 1 Main Title (4:02); 2 Fanfare (:57); 3 The Takeover (1:30); 4 Casey Gets In Touch (2:56); 5 Casey Saves Jordan (1:29); 6 Reveal Sub (:46); 7 Sub Splits (2:02); 8 They Sink The Sub (3:51); 9 Casey Rescues The Laundry (1:48); 10 Sitting Ducks (2:08); 11 The Broadway Shootout (1:44); 12 Casey Meets Strannix (:45); 13 Casey Saves Hawaii (2:46); 14 Epilogue (2:28).

Review: An action film score for orchestra, synthesizers and percussion, Gary Chang's *Under Siege* is so unexciting that it amounts to little else but window dressing. Many of the cues are dark, ominous efforts that try to evoke an atmosphere of tension, with lots of percussion over vague synthesizer effects that may have been useful in the film, but are not too terribly engaging on the CD. The orchestra occasionally kicks in, but even its contribution is so subdued and low-key that it adds little to the overall texture. Not a very interesting score.

Under Siege 2: Dark Territory ♫♫ᵛ

1995, Varese-Sarabande Records; from the movie *Under Siege 2: Dark Territory;* Warner Bros., 1995.

Album Notes: *Music:* Basil Poledouris; *Orchestrations:* Greig McRitchie, Lolita Ritmanis; *Music Editor:* Curtis Roush; Orchestra conducted by Basil Poledouris; *Synthesizers:* Michael Boddicker; *Specialty Percussion:* Steve Forman; *Album Producers:* Basil Poledouris, Tim Boyle, Curtis Roush; *Engineers:* Tim Boyle.

Selections: 1 Main Titles: Dark Territory (2:37); 2 Casey's Family (2:03); 3 Compound Assault (1:47); 4 Access Codes (1:57); 5 Intruder Discovered (4:38); 6 Dead, Not Dead (1:46); 7 The Gates Of Hell/Penn's Wish (8:53); 8 Casey's Farewell/After The Train Has Gone (S. Seagal/T. Smallwood)(3:53) *Todd Smallwood, Abraham McDonald, Jean McCalin, Steve Seagal.*

Review: A likeable enough Basil Poledouris entry which has its moments ("Intruder Discovered"), but suffers from a lack of strong thematic content. It is also surprisingly derivative at times of his other work. You can clearly hear portions of *RoboCop* in the main title, for example. Poledouris seems to have found it awfully hard to get a handle on this film, but when was a Steven Seagal movie ever deep? Either he thought he was fighting a losing battle against the noise levels of gunfire and explosions, or hearing Seagal's vocal on "After the Train Has Gone" just demoralized him into a catatonic state.

David Hirsch

The Underneath ♫♫♫

1995, Varese-Sarabande; from the movie *The Underneath,* Universal Pictures, 1995.

Album Notes: *Music:* Cliff Martinez; *Album Producer:* Cliff Martinez.

Selections: 1 The Green Head (Main Title)(2:55); 2 The Kiss (1:45); 3 He Saw Us (2:12); 4 I Didn't Get You Anything (1:01); 5 You'll Like It (1:16); 6 Every Monday (1:18); 7 An Ad For Fine Wine (2:07); 8 The White Van (2:18); 9 Wake Up Dead (1:17); 10 Gas (:44); 11 Captive Audience (1:04); 12 Michael, Right? (2:43); 13 Why Ya Wanna Do Me (F. LeBlanc)(2:14) *Cowboy Mouth*; 14 Angel With A Broken Wing (J.T. Griffith)(3:24) *Cowboy Mouth*; 15 Fall From Mine (A. Cox/A. Glascock/S. Judge)(4:48) *Wheel*; 16 Skoliosis Skank (L. Myers/J. Pollet/S. May)(2:52) *Gal's Panic*; 17 Gals Panic (L. Myers/J. Pollet/S. May)(4:01) *Gal's Panic*; 18 The Happy Herman Polka (H. Dietrich) (1:46) *Herman The German & Das Cowboy*.

Review: A hybrid tale about a robbery with deep psychological and philosophical undertones, *The Underneath,* a remake of the 1949 film noir *Criss Cross,* sported a disturbingly hypnotic score, signed by Cliff Martinez, which superbly sustained the moods in Steven Soderbergh's suspense melodrama. The various cues, dense and deliberately taken at a slow pace, manage to evoke the same cerebral moods, austere and uncompromising, yet wonderfully atmospheric, though amateurs of melodic material will have to look elsewhere. Unfortunately, some shrieking rock numbers that are not too terribly enjoyable throw the album in overdrive, though "The Happy Herman Polka," a fast instrumental guitar tune, proves quite ingratiating.

Unforgiven ♫♫♫

1992, Varese-Sarabande; from the movie *Unforgiven,* Warner Bros., 1992.

Album Notes: *Music:* Lennie Niehaus; *Orchestrations:* Lennie Niehaus; *Music Editor:* Donald Harris; Orchestra conducted by Lennie Niehaus; *Featured Musician:* Laurindo Almeida (guitar); *Album Producer:* Lennie Niehaus; *Engineer:* Robert Fernandez.

Selections: 1 Claudia's Theme (C. Eastwood)(1:00); 2 Will Looks Off (:32); 3 Davey Leading Horses (:49); 4 Pony For The Lady (1:30); 5 Bucket Of Water (:41); 6 Claudia's Theme (C. Eastwood)(:41); 7 Bill Clips Bob (2:07); 8 Headstone And Flowers (:41); 9 Claudia's Theme (C. Eastwood)(1:04); 10 Give It To Him (1:11); 11 It's Self Defense (:51); 12 Claudia's Theme (C. Eastwood) (:58); 13 Get Up (1:35); 14 Reload This (1:00); 15 Claudia's Theme (C. Eastwood)(1:02); 16 Shave And A Haircut (1:09); 17 Will Rides In (1:04); 18 Claudia's Theme (C. Eastwood)(1:01); 19 Villainous Friends (1:01); 20 He Oughta Get Shot (2:17); 21 Claudia's Theme (C. Eastwood)(1:07); 22 Ned's Body/ Shotgun Appears (3:41); 23 Burn His House Down (2:09); 24 Claudia's Theme (C. Eastwood)(5:41).

Review: Lennie Niehaus performed double-duty for Clint Eastwood for many years, having orchestrated many of Jerry Fielding's Eastwood scores and ghostwritten (often extensively) cues for the composer during the 1970s. When Niehaus was given the chance to contribute music for Eastwood's pictures himself, the results were low-key scores that often contained themes based on material composed by Eastwood himself. *Unforgiven* is one of those cases, with the poignant "Claudia's Theme" (written by the actor-director) contributing the heart of the music here. Performed on solo guitar before being gently developed into a fully orchestral arrangement, the theme represents a reflective look back at the Old West—like the movie, the music is more meditative and subtle than your typical western score, but is certainly no less effective or enjoyable because of that.

Andy Dursin

Unlawful Entry ♫♫ ♪

1992, Intrada Records; from the movie *Unlawful Entry,* 20th Century-Fox, 1992.

Album Notes: *Music:* James Horner; *Music Editor:* Jim Henrikson; Orchestra conducted by James Horner; *Featured Musicians:* Mike Fisher, Ralph Grierson, James Horner, Judd Miller, Ian Underwood; *Album Producer:* James Horner; *Engineer:* Shawn Murphy.

Selections: 1 Main Title (3:14); 2 Intruder (2:08); 3 Being Watched (5:42); 4 Leon's Death (3:01); 5 Drug Bust (3:06); 6 Bail Denied (2:26); 7 Pete's Passion (11:15); 8 End Credits (4:22).

Review: An uneven James Horner score which starts out with an appealing theme and then quickly descends into harsh and atonal synthesizer dissonance. A sensual saxophone theme is worked into a romantic melody for synthesizer over piano. The music becomes a pleasant theme for the couple while retaining a slight edge of foreboding and discomfort, suggesting the terrors they will encounter. The theme is, by turns, happy and pretty and then frightening, and the cue ends ominously with the heartbeat-like faint percussion beats. The bulk of the CD is comprised of horror music: harsh cacophonies of low end piano and strings, horrifying tonal music and dissonant atonal passages. Machine music, appropriately heartless, yet difficult to listen to apart from its visual counterparts. There are some interesting moments but on the whole the CD is too uneven and too imbedded with atonal electronics and disturbing cacophonies to make for a satisfying listen.

Randall D. Larson

Unstrung Heroes ♪♪♪

1995, Hollywood Records; from the movie *Unstrung Heroes*, Hollywood Pictures, 1995.

Album Notes: *Music*: Thomas Newman; *Orchestrations*: Thomas Pasatieri; *Music Editor*: Bill Bernstein; *Featured Musicians*: Michael Fisher (vibraphone, jaw harp, vibratone), Rock Cox (zither, hurdy gurdy, bowed bass dulcimer), Thomas Newman (picnic, piano, psaltery), George Doering (guitars, strums), Bill Bernstein (zither, Indian banjo, door), Steve Kujala (flutes, recorders), Chas Smith (pedal steel guitars), Randy Kerber (sustains); *Album Producers*: Thomas Newman, Bill Bernstein; *Engineer*: Dennis Sands.

Selections: 1 Outside 2B (1:03); 2 Inside 2B (1:30); 3 Nowhere Near 2B (1:06); 4 Is Unstrung (3:12); 5 Star Machine (1:28); 6 South Pole (:49); 7 Ballsound (:39); 8 Trace Harm (1:46); 9 Main Title (A Load Of Lidz)(2:42); 10 Means What It Means (:38); 11 Influenza (:51); 12 The Beast Is Coming (1:08); 13 Lipstick (1:15); 14 Possible Ideas/Available Materials (2:11); 15 Half Amelia (1:27); 16 A Blind Man Could See It (1:06); 17 79 RPMs (:34); 18 Home Movies (2:53); 19 There Is No Conspiracy (3:35).

Review: A delicate, offbeat tale of a 12-year-old coming of age in 1962 Los Angeles, *Unstrung Heroes*, directed by Diane Keaton, elicited an odd, somewhat out-of-synch score by Thomas Newman, with pseudo-Oriental effects that seemed to clash with the film and its unusual premise. Focusing, as it did, on a kid who leaves his dysfunctional middle-class home to live with two eccentric uncles in a rundown hotel, the story needed a score that matched the conflicting moods in the development, while giving an expression to the kid's frail emotions. Only occasionally does Newman fill the demands imposed on him ("Trace Harm"), relying most often on selections that are admittedly attractive and quite enjoyable on

their own musical terms, but that seem to have been written for another, totally different film.

Untamed Heart ♪♪♪⸰

1993, Varese-Sarabande; from the movie *Untamed Heart*, M-G-M, 1993.

Album Notes: *Music*: Cliff Eidelman; *Orchestrations*: Jeff Atmajian, Cliff Eidelman; *Music Editor*: Ken Karman; Orchestra conducted by Cliff Eidelman; *Album Producer*: Cliff Eidelman; *Engineer*: Armin Steiner.

Selections: 1 Untamed Heart (3:26); 2 I'll Give You My Heart (3:48); 3 Rainfall (1:34); 4 Stabbed (2:38); 5 You Are My Peace (2:54); 6 Opening (1:45); 7 Hockey Game (2:50); 8 Lost (4:12); 9 End Credits (2:59).

Review: Romantic symphonic love poem for two unlikely suitors, a waitress (Marissa Tomei) who can't seem to pick the right man, and a quiet, mysterious busboy (Christian Slater) with a heart ailment. Cliff Eidelman gives this poignant story everything he can muster. The bulk of the album is framed by gentle horns and a soft piano melody, but two pieces, the bouncy "Hockey Game" and the nightmarish "Stabbed," offer some variety. The album includes "End Credits" and another cue that were not used in the final film.

David Hirsch

Until September/Star Crash ♪♪⸰

1990, Silva Screen Records; from the movies *Until September*, M-G-M/Pathe, 1984; and *Star Crash*, Columbia Pictures/AIP, 1978.

Album Notes: *Music*: John Barry; Orchestras conducted by John Barry; *Album Producer*: John Barry; *Engineer*: John Richards.

Selections: *UNTIL SEPTEMBER:* 1 Main Title (1:17); 2 It's Love (:56); 3 Not Again (1:32); 4 Second Spat (1:50); 5 He Catches Her (5:45); 6 Candle Light (2:27); 7 Seine (1:43); 8 Foreplay (2:48); 9 One More Time (2:41); 10 Waiting (1:27); 11 Memories (3:25); 12 The Morning After (2:09); 13 End Title (2:32);

STAR CRASH: 14 Main Title (2:37); 15 Escape Into Hyperspace (1:49); 16 Captured (2:10); 17 Launch Adrift (1:42); 18 Beach Landing (2:10); 19 The Ice Planet/Heading For Zarkon (3:04); 20 The Emperor's Speech (3:18); 21 Strange Planet/The Trogs Attack (2:37); 22 Akton Battles The Robots (2:16); 23 Red Ball Attack (1:00); 24 Space War (4:38); 25 Goodbye Akton (3:32); 26 End Title (2:53).

Review: This was the first of two odd pairings of John Barry scores on Silva Screen (the other was the Bruce Lee action film

"The movie was about a movement, it was about a broad sweep of pop culture in America and it was a very, very effective tool in terms of telling the story and marketing. I think it is a text book case in how to use a soundtrack to market a film...."

producer George Jackson
on the soundtrack to
Saturday Night Fever
(The Hollywood Reporter, 1-16-96)

Game of Death and Roger Vadim's sex romp *Night Games*), kind of a yin and yang experience. *Until September* presents Barry at some of his romantic best. Lush string arrangements abound and, most surprisingly, he doesn't sink the score through his overuse of the main theme (that is by Barry standards). *Star Crash*, however, proves that even Barry can make poor creative choices. Space Opera has never provided him with his best source of inspiration. The score itself is passable enough (considering the god-awful film it was written for), but the decision to use a synthesized drum machine on the main theme was equally bad in 1979 when the music was recorded. By today's standards, it's positively laughable, bordering on self-parody. Luckily, the rest of the score doesn't have this or similar effects, and it boasts some pretty good themes ("Launch Adrift," and the eerie "The Ice Planet" for example).

David Hirsch

The Untouchables ♪♪♪♪

1987, A&M Records; from the movie *The Untouchables*, Paramount Pictures, 1987.

Album Notes: *Music*: Ennio Morricone; *Orchestrations*: Ennio Morricone; *Music Editor*: Thomas Drescher; Orchestra conducted by Ennio Morricone; *Album Producer*: Ennio Morricone; *Engineer*: Mike Farrow.

Selections: 1 The Untouchables (End Title)(3:10); 2 Al Capone (2:55); 3 Waiting At The Border (3:46); 4 Death Theme (2:41); 5 On The Rooftops (2:33); 6 Victorious (2:09); 7 The Man With The Matches (2:46); 8 The Strength Of The Righteous (Main

Title)(2:26); 9 Ness And His Family (2:45); 10 False Alarm (1:12); 11 The Untouchables (3:04); 12 Four Friends (2:51); 13 Machine Gun Lullaby (7:02).

Review: A beautifully lyrical score, nominated for an Oscar, *The Untouchables* found Ennio Morricone at the peak of his creative powers, in a set of cues that evoke the feel of this crime drama about Eliot Ness and his band of "untouchables," and the mobsters they relentlessly pursue at the height of the Prohibition era. Brilliantly directed by Brian De Palma, and starring Kevin Costner as Ness, Robert De Niro as Al Capone, and Sean Connery, in one of his finest screen performances as a cop, whose knowledge of the street proves invaluable to Ness, *The Untouchables* ranks among the top crime dramas ever filmed, and inspired Morricone to write a top-notch, very appealing score, rife with epic accents and lyrical themes that mix and mingle in a gorgeous musical canvas that's often explicit and descriptive of the multi-layered action. Laid out in terms that are frequently strikingly melodic, the score reveals many attractive themes ("Ness and His Family," "Four Friends," "Machine Gun Lullaby," the latter a wonderful tinkerbell melody overpowered by strident, ominous off-key overtones) that strengthen its appeal. In fact, the only drawback here is the fact that the cues are oddly presented out of sequence (with the recording kicking off with the "End Title," and the "Main Title" lost somewhere in the middle), necessitating some reprogramming if you wish to listen to the score as it was initially conceived and heard on the screen.

Up Close and Personal ♪♪

1996, Hollywood Records; from the movie *Up Close and Personal*, Touchstone Pictures, 1996.

Album Notes: *Music*: Thomas Newman; *Orchestrations*: Thomas Pasatieri; *Music Editor*: Bill Bernstein; *Album Producers*: Thomas Newman, Bill Bernstein; *Engineer*: Dennis Sands.

Selections: 1 Miss Sierra Logger (2:56); 2 A Week Eight Days (2:33); 3 Uprise (1:30); 4 Vulgar Innuendo (:58); 5 Hong Kong Mambo (T. Puente)(3:47) *Tito Puente*; 6 Up Close (2:45); 7 Moral High Ground (1:41); 8 So Much Cherry Piecrust (2:31); 9 Cafe (R. Gueits/F. Lopez)(6:37) *Eddie Palmieri*; 10 Sun And Moon (1:11); 11 Los Locos (2:11); 12 Upwind (2:46); 13 Cellblock C (2:38); 14 Philly Rebound (1:21); 15 No Justice (2:03); 16 Bonefish (1:50); 17 She Knows Now (2:23).

Review: Though at times a surprisingly melodic effort for Thomas Newman, it's unfortunately also rather unremarkable. There are a few gentle romantic themes like "A Week Eight Days" for the flowering romance between rising news reporter

Michelle Pfeiffer and her producer Robert Redford. The tense drama of the news stories though still affords Newman with the opportunity to create some of his typical wild arrangements for cues such as "Uprise." But the general mood of the album is so low key with its abundance of minor emotional cues, that it all passes by before you've realized it. The CD, incidentally, does not feature Celine Dion's hit song for the film, "Because You Loved Me," which is a pity because it really could have used the infusion of some energy.

David Hirsch

Urban Cowboy *♫♫♫♭*

1980, Full Moon/Elektra Records; from the movie *Urban Cowboy*, Paramount Pictures, 1980.

Album Notes: *Album Executive Producer*: Irving Azoff; *Album Compilers*: Irving Azoff, Howard Kaufman, Becky Shargo.

Selections: 1 Hello, Texas (B. Collins/R. Campbell)(2:33) *Jimmy Buffett*; 2 All Night Long (J. Walsh)(3:50) *Joe Walsh*; 3 Times Like Thse (D. Fogelberg)(3:02) *Dan Fogelberg*; 4 Nine Tonight (B. Seger)(4:15) *Bob Seger And The Silver Bullet Band*; 5 Stand By Me (B.E. King/J. Leiber/M. Stoller) (3:35) *Mickey Gilley*; 6 Cherokee Fiddle (M. Murphy)(4:06) *Johnny Lee*; 7 Could I Have This Dance (W. Holyfield/B. House)(3:14) *Anne Murray*; 8 Lyin' Eyes (D. Henley/G. Frey)(6:23) *The Eagles*; 9 Lookin' For Love (J. Melson/R. Orbison)(3:41) *Johnny Lee*; 10 Don't It Make Ya Wanna Dance (R. Wier)(3:29) *Bonnie Raitt*; 11 The Devil Went Down To Georgia (C. Daniels)(3:35) *The Charlie Daniels Band*; 12 Here Comes The Hurt Again (J. Foster/B. Rice)(2:41) *Mickey Gilley*; 13 Orange Blossom Special/Hoedown (E. Rouse)(2:06) *Gilley's Urban Cowboy Band*; 14 Love The World Away (B. Torrey)(3:11) *Kenny Rogers*; 15 Falling In Love For The Night (C. Daniels)(3:00) *The Charlie Daniels Band*; 16 Darlin' (O. Blandemer)(2:34) *Bonnie Raitt*; 17 Look What You've Done To Me (B. Scaggs/D. Foster)(5:30) *Boz Scaggs*; 18 Hearts Against The Wind (J.D. Souther)(2:58) *Linda Ronstadt, J.D. Souther*.

Review: The soundtrack that sealed country's portal for nearly a decade, mostly because of its anything goes view of the genre. There are, in fact, some very good tracks by rock artists such as Bob Seger ("Nine Tonight"), Joe Walsh ("All Night Long") and Bonnie Raitt ("Darlin'"). But it also offers a fairly narrow view of country, pushing the Charlie Daniels Band and Mickey Gilley when the film could have taken a much broader survey of the form. After all, you can ride a mechanical bronco to just about anything, can't you?

Gary Graff

Used People *♫♫♫♭*

1992, Giant Records; from the movie *Used People*, 20th Century-Fox, 1992.

Album Notes: *Music*: Rachel Portman; *Orchestrations*: Rachel Portman; *Music Editor*: Bill Abbott; Orchestra conducted by David Snell; *Album Producer*: Rachel Portman; *Engineer*: Dick Lewzey.

Selections: 1 Main Title (2:37); 2 Walk And Talk/First Kiss (4:03); 3 The Third Rail (1:52); 4 Man On The Moon (1:31); 5 The Dinner (1:58); 6 Lucy Horseshoe/Pearl Says Yes (5:43); 7 Bibby Leaves (1:28); 8 Out And About (1:28); 9 The Sky Fell Down (L. Alter/E. Heyman)(3:11) *Frank Sinatra, Tommy Dorsey and His Orchestra*; 10 Three On A Bench/Swee' Pea On The Roof (4:50); 11 The Shiva (1:57); 12 Let Me Cook Your Dinner/Deepdale (3:39); 13 The Grave (2:51); 14 It Happened To Me Too (1:51); 15 Kiss The Bride (1:23); 16 End Titles (2:34).

Review: A tearjerker with a '50s sensibility, *Used People* found in Rachel Portman the apt composer to deliver a score overflowing with broadly effusive romantic motifs, that match this tale, set in New York in 1969, about a widow, romanced by an admirer of 23 years on the day of her husband's funeral, who finds herself responding with renewed eagerness to this suitor she had rejected because of their different ethnic backgrounds. At times jocularly humorous, most frequently touchingly lyrical, Portman's music gives greater weight to the film's moods, with beautifully stated themes that are consistently appealing and enjoyable. The somewhat unnecessary inclusion of "The Sky Fell Down," performed by Frank Sinatra, with Tommy Dorsey and his orchestra, interrupts the unity of the score, and seems like a throwaway track.

Utu *♫♫♫♫*

1993, Label X Records; from the movie *Utu*, 1983.

Album Notes: *Music*: John Charles; The New Zealand Symphony Orchestra, conducted by William Southgate; *Album Producers*: John Charles, John Steven Lasher; *Engineers*: Garry Clark, Robert Hagen.

Selections: 1 Theme From Utu (2:08); 2 Drummers (:44); 3 Patrol (1:52); 4 Destroyed Village (1:08) *Rangi Dewes*; 5 Te Wheke Stalks Emily (2:42); 6 Moko (2:17) *Joe Malcolm*; 7 The Raid/After The Raid (2:12); 8 Williamson Retaliates (2:05); 9 Quadruple Barrelled Shotgun/The Army Approaches Te Puna (S.C. Foster)(3:56); 10 Waiata Tangi/Kura And Henare (3:50) *Jane and Paul Makura*; 11 Night Sentry (:49); 12 Fishing/After The Battle (2:16); 13 Williamson Reflects (:40); 14 Te Wheke's Trek (1:12); 15 Williamson Prepares For Utu (1:05); 16 Death Of Te Wheke (Lament) and Finale (2:34) *Rangi Dewes*.

Review: A striking adventure film, about the struggle opposing the European settlers and native Maoris in late 19-century New Zealand, *Utu* was an exceptional entry at the Cannes Film Festival with audiences warming to this tale of passion and revenge ("utu" in Maori), in many ways reminiscent of an old-fashioned American western. When British soldiers protecting newly-arrived colonialists plunder and ravage his native village, rebel leader Te Wheke, once sympathetic to the white cause, turns guerrilla and, in a spiraling web of violence, retaliates in kind until he is captured and shot. John Charles' informed score gives the action extra impetus, with powerful orchestral accents that define the British presence in alien territory ("Williamson Retaliates"), while the addition of traditional Maori chants provides the proper ethnic coloring.

The Vagrant ✍✍✍⌐

1992, Intrada Records; from the movie *The Vagrant*, M-G-M/Pathe, 1992.

Album Notes: *Music:* Christopher Young; *Orchestrations:* Christopher Young; Orchestra conducted by Christopher Young; *Album Producer:* Christopher Young; *Engineer:* Joe Tarantino.

Selections: 1 The Vagrant (3:39); 2 Lady Fingers (3:38); 3 Trash Dreams (1:31); 4 Rag Skin Blues (3:01); 5 Dipiddy Doo (2:31); 6 Dela Rue (1:53); 7 Mine's Mine Mind (1:29); 8 A Giblet Too Tastey (2:200); 9 Squish-O-Rama (2:46); 10 Change The Meter (1:03); 11 Jumbo Children Splat Fat (1:59); 12 Heebie Jeebies (2:51); 13 Cards On The Table (3:31); 14 Vagrant Rhythms (9:45).

Review: Christopher Young's penchant for musique concrete really goes to town in this bizarre and uncategorical psychological horror score. The music is wacky and strange, quirky yet impossible, kind of a hybrid *Honey, I Blew Up The Kid* meets *Hellraiser*. Young mixes a minor-melodied music box theme with vocal tonalities, jazzy acoustic bass, plenty of percussion and a large array of foreign ethnic instruments. The result is nothing you've ever heard before. Both immediately likeable and inconceivably strange, the music is refreshing in its creativity. Once again, Young experiments with new and strange musical combinations and matches that bizarre sensibility with an unorthodox collection of musical colors. He effectively captures the unique personality of the film—which turns out to be not far distant from his own musical personality. *The Vagrant* may not appeal to all tastes, but it's intriguing, effective and unique enough to warrant a listen.

Randall D. Larson

Valley Girl ✍✍✍✍⌐

1994, Rhino Records; from the movie *Valley Girl*, 1983.

Selections: 1 A Million Miles Away (P. Case/Alkes/Fradkin) (3:34) *The Plimsouls*; 2 Johnny, Are You Queer (B. & L. Paine) (2:47) *Josie Cotton*; 3 Eyes Of A Stranger (Hyde/Rock) (3:34) *Payola$*; 4 Angst In My Pants (R. Mael/ R. Mael) (3:31) *Sparks*; 5 Who Can It Be Now? (C. Hay) (3:23) *Men At Work*; 6 Everywhere At Once (P. Case) (3:20) *The Plimsouls*; 7 I La La La Love You (P. Travers) (3:37) *Pat Travers' Black Pearl*; 8 He Could Be The One (B. & L. Paine) (2:49) *Josie Cotton*; 9 Love My Way (J. Ashton/R. Butler/T. Butler/V. Ely) (3:40) *Psychedelic Furs*; 10 Jukebox (Don't Put Another Dime) (T. Orlando) (3:45) *The Flirts*; 11 The Fanatic (J. Spry/J. Spry/Blea/Sands/Ruiz) (3:36) *Felony*; 12 She Talks In Stereo (G. Myrick) (4:01) *Gary Myrick & The Figures*; 13 Oldest Story In The World (P. Case) (3:23) *The Plimsouls*; 14 School Is In (Anderson/Barge) (2:34) *Josie Cotton*; 15 I Melt With You (Modern English) (3:49) *Modern English*.

Review: Rhino did the world a service by reissuing this original 1983 soundtrack and adding more songs from the movie. This is as good an '80s pop collection as you'll find, filled with songs you'll wish you'd paid more attention to the first time around. Among the highlights: the Plimsouls' wonderful "Million Miles Away" and "Everywhere at Once," Modern English's seminal (if overplayed) "I Melt With You," Josie Cotton's flirty "Johnny, Are You Queer?," Men at Work's "Who Can It Be Now?," Psychedelic Furs' "Love My Way," and Sparks' "Angst in My Pants." Pure retro fun.

Gary Graff

Vertigo

Vertigo ✍✍✍✍

1996, Varese-Sarabande; from the movie *Vertigo*, Paramount Pictures, 1958.

Album Notes: *Music:* Bernard Herrmann; The Sinfonia of London, conducted by Muir Mathieson; *CD Producer:* Robert Townson; *Engineers:* Joe Gastwirt, Ramon Breton.

Selections: 1 Prelude and Rooftop (4:39); 2 Scotty Tails Madeleine (6:15); 3 Carlotta's Portrait (1:56); 4 The Bay (2:56); 5 By The Fireside (2:53); 6 The Streets (2:23); 7 The Forest (3:45); 8 The Beach (3:27); 9 The Dream (2:43); 10 Farewell and The Tower (6:54); 11 The Nightmare and Dawn (3:30); 12 The Past and The Girl (3:11); 13 The Letter (4:13); 14 Goodnight and The Park (3:03); 15 Scene d'amour (5:04); 16 The Necklace, The Return and Finale (7:20).

Review: See entry below.

Vertigo ♫♫♫♪

1996, Varese-Sarabande; from the movie *Vertigo*, Paramount Pictures, 1958.

Album Notes: *Music*: Bernard Herrmann; The Royal Scottish National Orchestra, conducted by Joel McNeely; *Album Producer*: Robert Townson; *Engineers*: Geoff Foster, Graham Kirkby.

Selections: 1 Prelude and Rooftop (4:35); 2 Scotty Trails Madeleine (8:22); 3 Carlotta's Portrait (2:34); 4 The Bay (3:08); 5 By The Fireside (3:39); 6 The Forest (3:25); 7 The Beach (3:27); 8 The Dream (2:42); 9 Farewell and The Tower (6:42); 10 The Nightmare and Dawn (4:10); 11 The Letter (3:53); 12 Goodnight and The Park (3:08); 13 Scene d'amour (5:09); 14 The Necklace, The Return and Finale (7:47).

Review: Alfred Hitchcock, a methodical film director, and Bernard Herrmann, a harmonically inclined film composer, were made for each other. For, however divergent their individual temperaments, each understood and appreciated the other's perspective, and thrived creatively on their symbiotic relationship, which resulted in some of the most poignant, critical work ever created in the history of music, and the cinema.

Most critics agree that Hitchcock's *Vertigo* endures as one of his most complex, intensely powerful films. Certainly, half the credit for the success of the film as an acknowledged masterpiece must be attributed to Herrmann's strikingly beautiful score (his fourth of seven collaborations with the director), for it is Herrmann's music that ties all the complex subtleties of the film together.

The newly restored edition of the original soundtrack recordings provides a crucial piece of the Hitchcock/Herrmann puzzle. It is this release that offers the most complete collection of music from the film, including four cues that have never been available in any form.

As with many vintage soundtrack restorations, the disc is not without inherent problems. Because recording was done in two different cities (London and Vienna), the disc, which has been programmed in the correct running order, alternates at times between mono and stereo. Also, the ravages of time have taken their toll on the original tapes from the sessions, and while painstaking efforts were evidently made to restore as much music as possible, some minor disturbances can be heard on the disc. Also due to extensive damage, one important cue, "The Graveyard," could not be included.

The recording of the score with Joel McNeely and the Royal Scottish National Orchestra features over an hour of the music from *Vertigo*, including the aforementioned cue, "The Graveyard." The re-recording is expertly performed, and sumptuously recorded.

Charles L. Granata

The Vikings/Solomon and Sheba ♫♫♫♫♪

1996, DRG Records; from the movies *The Vikings*, United Artists, 1959, and *Solomon and Sheba*, United Artists, 1960.

Album Notes: *Music*: Mario Nascimbene; Orchestras conducted by Franco Ferrara, Mario Nascimbene; *Album Producers*: Mario Nascimbene, Claudio Fuiano; *Engineer*: Gianni Mazzarini.

Selections: *THE VIKINGS:* 1 Violence and Rapes Of The Vikings (1:34); 2 Viking's Horn/Regnar Returns (2:57); 3 Drunk's Song/Eric Is Rescued By Odin's Daughters (9:04); 4 Dancing The Oars (1:13); 5 Eric And Morgana Escape/Love Scene (3:54); 6 Aella Cuts Off Eric's Hand (2:59); 7 Voyage and Landing In Britain (6:54); 8 The Vikings Attack The Castle/Battle And Death Of Aella (10:10); 9 Duel/Eric Kills Einar (1:45); 10 Funeral/End Titles (3:42);

SOLOMON AND SHEBA: 11 Main Titles (2:00); 12 Death Of David (2:39); 13 Solomon In The Temple (1:52); 14 Orgiastic Dance (4:50); 15 Death Of Abishag (1:42); 16 Battle (2:38); 17 Solomon Lifts Sheba (1:22); 18 Purification and Finale (1:53).

Review: Italian composer Mario Nascimbene, who had already developed quite a following after he scored *The Barefoot Contessa* in 1954, made a strong impression when he composed the startling music for *The Vikings*, in 1959, a sprawling saga of revenge and historic mayhem, starring Kirk Douglas and Tony Curtis as half-brothers feuding over the love of Janet Leigh and control of the Viking empire. Frequently rousing and brightly colorful in its depiction of the savage action, Nascimbene's score emphasized the action on the screen and gave it strong emotive support; a year later, Nascimbene encored when he wrote another sensational score, for the Biblical epic *Solomon and Sheba*, a fanciful big screen retelling of the love affair between the 10th century b.c. king of Israel, and the desert queen who ravished his heart. In both cases, writing in a style that owed little to the style that prevailed in Hollywood at the time, but finding a new expression that enhanced the screen visuals, Nascimbene created scores that were memorably effective and sharply detailed. While both are presented here in a production supervised by the composer, it must be noted that the overall quality of this CD leaves a lot to be desired, with a cramped mono sound, image shifting, some distortion, occasional analog dropouts, bad splicings, and harsh sonics that render listening a less than pleasant experience. The only exception is the previously unreleased "Viking's Horn," which denotes the spaciousness and spread these scores should have received. The rating reflects the importance of the score, not the quality of the recording.

Village of the Damned ♫♫♫♪

1995, Varese-Sarabande; from the movie *Village of the Damned*, Universal Pictures, 1995.

Album Notes: *Music*: John Carpenter, Dave Davies; *Featured Musicians*: John Carpenter (synthesizer, bass guitar), Dave Davies (guitars), Bruce Robb (Hammond B-3); *Album Producers*: The Robb Brothers; *Engineers*: The Robb Brothers.

Selections: 1 March Of The Children (8:03) *Mark Hamill*; 2 Children's Carol (1:40); 3 Angel Of Death (1:37); 4 Daybreak (1:12); 5 The Fair (1:32); 6 The Children's Theme (1:15); 7 Ben's Death (3:17); 8 The Funeral (1:54); 9 Midwich Shuffle (2:05); 10 Baptism (1:04); 11 Burning Desire (4:58); 12 Welcome Home, Ben (1:06); 13 The Brick Wall (3:22).

Review: This is indeed a rarity—a John Carpenter score with an orchestra! Although electronics still represent the principal instrumentation, Carpenter, along with Dave Davies of the pop group The Kinks, uses their modest resources to the fullest advantage. The theme for "The March of the Children" is perhaps Carpenter's strongest composition since his original main theme for *Halloween*. There's a steady advance of evil building in the music for this seemingly invincible army of super children bent on world domination. The sparse use of acoustics works well to remind us that the film has a larger scope, the tiny coastal town is but a microcosm simulation of a threat happening across the entire world. With it, Carpenter has really created one of his most elaborate and satisfying scores in years, featuring some of the most delightfully melodic passages ("The Fair," "The Children's Theme") he has ever written.

David Hirsch

Viva Las Vegas

1993, RCA Records; from the movie *Viva Las Vegas*, M-G-M, 1964.

See: Elvis Presley in Compilations

Volcano ♫♫♫♫

1997, Varese-Sarabande Records; from the movie *Volcano*, 20th Century-Fox, 1997.

Album Notes: *Music*: Alan Silvestri; *Orchestrations*: William Ross, Mark McKenzie, Conrad Pope; *Music Editor*: Kenneth Karmen; Orchestra conducted by Alan Silvestri; *Synclavier Programming*: Simon Franglen; *Auricle Programming*: David

Bifano; *Album Producer*: Alan Silvestri; *Engineer*: Dennis Sands.

Selections: 1 Main Title (2:44); 2 Miracle Mile (3:59); 3 Tarnation (5:54); 4 Team Work (2:41); 5 Build A Wall (5:01); 6 March Of The Lava (3:42); 7 Roark's Missing (2:46); 8 Cleansing Rain (2:30).

Review: Somehow, the idea of using electronic music to score a film about a volcanic eruption works better than in most cases. Alan Silvestri effectively demonstrates how to do it, and how to do it well, in his score for this big box-office disaster. Early on, his cues, eerily ominous, yet melodically attractive, contrast life-as-usual and the impending threat of the eruption about to happen: the sense of danger is suggested by sharp, thrill electronic effects, over a building low-string motif that signals to anyone not yet aware of it that something's afoot. Once nature lashes its fury, the full forces of the orchestra join in, bringing the score to a smashing crescendo. Notably effective in this context is "March of the Lava," which shows the unstoppable progression of the river of fire as it submerges everything. By contrast, the almost peaceful "Cleansing Rain" brings the volatile score to an elegiac conclusion. At under 30 minutes of total playing time, the CD seems a little skimpy, but there is so much tense, expressive music contained that it seems just right.

Voyage of the Damned ♫♫♫

1993, Label X; from the movie *Voyage of the Damned*, 1977.

Album Notes: *Music*: Lalo Schifrin; The London Studio Orchestra, conducted by Lalo Schifrin; *Featured Musicians*: Dorothy Remsen (harp), Ken Watson (percussion); *Album Producer*: John Steven Lasher; *Engineers*: Peter Granet, Dick Lewzey.

Selections: 1 Continuum For Solo Harp (4:27); 2 Journeys For Percussion (22:24); *VOYAGE OF THE DAMNED*: 3 What's Past Is Past/Affirmation Of Love (2:51); 4 Lament (2:31); 5 The Arrival/ Theme Of Hope (3:21); 6 The Captain/Goodbye Aunt Jenny/We Need Help (3:11); 7 So Many Things I Wanted To Say (2:08); 8 To Be A Woman (2:07); 9 Tragedy/Time Pulse (4:00); 10 Our Prayers Have Been Answered (2:17).

Review: Based on an eponymous novel by Gordon Thomas and Max Morgan-Witts, *Voyage of the Damned* recounts in stark details the true-life journey of Jewish refugees from the ravages of war-torn Europe, on board a ship that was denied landing authorization by the governments of several countries. The film elicited a chamber-like score from Schifrin who assigned various instruments to portray the central characters in the story, in a dark, reflective series of cues, built around a haunting central theme, that are powerfully evocative of the screen action. Two other compositions, "Continuum for Solo Harp," and the stretched-out "Journeys for Percussion," prove much too arid for listening enjoyment.

See also: The Four Musketeers

Wagons East! ♫♫

1994, Varese-Sarabande Records; from the movie *Wagons East!*, Tri-Star Pictures, 1994.

Album Notes: *Music*: Michael Small; *Orchestrations*: Christopher Dedrick; *Music Editor*: Bunny Andrews; The Irish Film Orchestra, conducted by Michael Small; *Album Producer*: Michael Small; *Engineer*: Andrew Boland.

Selections: 1 The Trail Heads East (2:25); 2 The Wagonmaster (1:26); 3 The Name's Harlow (1:22); 4 Desert Journey (2:07); 5 Jeremiah's Canteen (1:29); 6 A Town Called Prosperity (1:58); 7 Harlow Leaves (:54); 8 River Crossing (1:54); 9 Memories (1:22); 10 Rock Ambush (1:27); 11 Julian's Gunfight (2:51); 12 Desperado Montage (:53); 13 In Indian Country (1:34); 14 Harlow Returns (:51); 15 Three Ring Fist Fight (3:11); 16 The Wagons Keep Rolling (1:06); 17 Land Rush Stampede (1:01); 18 Harlow's Romance (:48); 19 Finale (2:34); 20 Wagons East (1:32).

Review: This film, the remarkably unfunny tale of a wagon master who leads a bunch of fed-up settlers out of the old West and back to "civilization," got more press than it deserved simply because it was actor John Candy's last film before he died. For it, Michael Small created an agreeable enough western-flavored comedy score that relies too much on established cliches of the genre. Nice, but nothing remarkable or special to be recommended.

David Hirsch

Waiting to Exhale ♫♫♫♫

1996, Arista Records; from the movie *Waiting to Exhale*, 20th Century-Fox, 1996.

Album Notes: *Songs*: Babyface; *String Arrangements*: Jeremy Lubbock, Bill Ross; *Featured Musicians*: Babyface (synthesizers/ keyboards/guitars), Greg Philinganes, Alex Alessandroni (piano), Reggie Griffin, Michael Thompson (guitar), Nathan East (bass), Luis Conte, Paulinho da Costa, Larry Bunker (percussion), Brandon Fields, Reggie Griffin (saxophone), Bruce Dukov, Clayton Haslop (violin), Bob Becker (viola), Larry Corbell (cello); *Album Producer*: Babyface; *Engineers*: Brad Gilderman, Jon Gass.

Selections: 1 Exhale (Shoop Shoop)(3:24) *Whitney Houston*; 2 Why Does It Hurt So Bad (4:37) *Whitney Houston*; 3 Let It Flow (4:27) *Toni Braxton*; 4 It Hurts Like Hell (4:19) *Aretha Franklin*; 5 Sittin' Up In My Room (4:52) *Brandy*; 6 This Is How It Works (Babyface/L. Lopes)(5:00) *TLC*; 7 Not Gon' Cry (4:57) *Mary J. Blige*; 8 My Funny Valentine (R. Rodgers/L. Hart)(4:06) *Chaka Khan*; 9 And I Gave My Love To You (Babyface/S. Marie)(4:48) *Sonja Marie*; 10 All Night Long (4:31) *SWV*; 11 Wey U (4:32) *Chante Moore*; 12 My Love, Sweet Love (4:21) *Patti LaBelle*; 13 Kissing You (3:23) *Faith Evans*; 14 Love Will Be Waiting At Home (5:59) *For Real*; 15 How Could You Call Her Baby (5:09) *Shanna*; 16 Count On Me (Babyface/W. Houston/M. Houston)(4:26) *Whitney Houston, Cece Winans*.

Review: Whitney Houston brightens up the screen in this inspirational story about four women who are friends, and share the difficulties they encounter in their lives. Punctuating the action, and giving it a spin that is refreshingly enjoyable, the soundtrack features several songs, written by the ubiquitous Babyface, performed by some of today's best female performers, including Houston who demonstrates again in this album why she is one of the most interesting vocalists in pop music. A bright, easy listening collection that should enjoy a broad audience.

Walk, Don't Run ♫♫♫♫

1991, Mainstream Records; from the movie *Walk, Don't Run*, Columbia Pictures, 1966.

Album Notes: *Music*: Quincy Jones; *Orchestrations*: Leo Shuken, Jack Hayes; *Vocal Orchestrations*: Dick Hazard; The Columbia Studio Orchestra, conducted by Quincy Jones; *Featured Musicians*: Toots Thielemans (harmonica), Harry "Sweets" Edison (trumpet); *Album Producer*: Jackie Mills; *Engineer*: Jackie Mills.

Selections: *WALK, DON'T RUN:* 1 Happy Feet (2:09); 2 Stay With Me (2:53); 3 Copy Cat (Wack A Doo)(2:55); 4 Happy Feet (Q. Jones/P. Lee)(1:43) *Don Elliot Voices*; 5 Papa San (1:45); 6 Abso-Bleedin'-Lutely (2:45); 7 Stay With Me (Q. Jones/P. Lee)(2:18) *Tony Clementi*; 8 One More Time (2:46); 9 20th Century Drawers (3:06); 10 Locked Out (2:10); 11 Happy Feet (reprise)(1:38); 12 Rabelaisian Rutland (1:55); 13 One More Time (reprise)(:41);

THE ASPHALT JUNGLE: 14 Theme (E.K. Ellington)(2:56);

THE SHIRLEY TEMPLE TV SHOW: 15 Enchanted Melody (4:34); 16 Bus Stop (E. Morton)(3:00); 17 Cain's Hundred (J. Goldsmith)(4:28).

Review: A sleek, romantic comedy, with often brightly hilarious moments, *Walk, Don't Run* stars Cary Grant, as a British tycoon in Japan during the Olympics, who finds himself sharing a small apartment with a fastidious young English girl, Samantha Eggar, and an American athlete, Jim Hutton, much to the chagrin of Eggar's neighbors, puzzled and indignant over what they perceive as a menage-a-trois. Echoing the light moods cast in the film, Quincy Jones provided a delightful, slyly humorous score that perfectly captured the whimsical tone of the story. Rounding up the selections from the soundtrack are random tracks from other sources that are painfully out-of-context here, and disrupt the moods created by Quincy Jones' creations.

A Walk in the Clouds ♫♫♫

1995, Milan Records; from the movie *A Walk in the Clouds*, 20th Century-Fox, 1995.

Album Notes: *Music:* Maurice Jarre; *Music Editor:* Dan Carlin Sr.; *Orchestrations:* Tom Pasatieri; Orchestra conducted by Maurice Jarre; *Featured Musician:* Liona Boyd (classical guitar solo); *Album Producer:* Maurice Jarre; *Engineer:* Shawn Murphy.

Selections: 1 Victoria (7:29); 2 Butterfly Wings (2:54); 3 The Harvest (3:01); 4 Crush In The Grapes (L. Brouwer/A. Arau) (2:17) *Roberto Huerta, Juan Jimenez, Febronio Covarrubias, Ismael Gallegos;* 5 First Kiss (3:15); 6 Mariachi Serenade (L. Brouwer/A. Arau) (2:49) *Roberto Huerta, Juan Jimenez, Febronio Covarrubias, Ismael Gallegos;* 7 Fire And Destruction (10:17); 8 A Walk In The Clouds (3:05).

Review: This romantic, Spanish-flavored orchestral work from Maurice Jarre follows the adventures of a young soldier, just returning from World War II, who agrees to pretend he is the husband of a pregnant woman whose family owns an idyllic Napa Valley winery. The score, which has an epic feel to it, is presented in several long symphonic suites, and is intercut with two songs with lyrics written by the film's director, Alphonse Arau.

David Hirsch

Walk on the Wild Side ♫♫♫♫♪

1991, Mainstream Records; from the movie *Walk on the Wild Side*, Columbia Pictures, 1962.

Album Notes: *Music:* Elmer Bernstein; Orchestra conducted by Elmer Bernstein; *Album Producer:* Jackie Mills; *Engineer:* "Bones" Howe.

Selections: 1 Walk On The Wild Side (2:42); 2 Somewhere In The Used To Be (1:58); 3 Hallie's Jazz (3:30); 4 Rejected (3:43); 5 Doll House (2:35); 6 Teresina (1:52); 7 Night Theme (2:18); 8 Walk On The Wild Side Jazz (2:17); 9 Furnished Room (2:31); 10 Kitty (2:34); 11 Oliver (2:27); 12 Comfort Southern (1:41); 13 Finale (1:35); CD bonus tracks: 14 The Chase (from *The Chase*)(J. Barry)(1:30); 15 Cleopatra's Barge (from *Cleopatra*)(A. North)(2:35); 16 Theme from A *Girl Named Tamiko* (E. Bernstein)(2:21); 17 Theme from *Two Weeks In Another Town* (D. Raksin)(2:15); 18 The Man With The Golden Arm (from *The Man With The Golden Arm*)(E. Bernstein)(2:48).

Review: Nelson Algren's naturalistic novel, *A Walk on the Wild Side,* elicited a turbulent, unpredictable and exciting score from Elmer Bernstein, when it was brought to the screen in 1962. Set in New Orleans in the 1930s, and starring Laurence Harvey, Jane Fonda and Barbara Stanwyck in the principal roles, it involves a young man from Texas, looking for the girl he had left behind, and eventually finding her in a bordello run by a lesbian madam. The jazz-influenced score Bernstein wrote evoked the seamy underside of the film's locale and situations, bringing to mind the powerful score he had written a few years earlier for *The Man with the Golden Arm,* but without the benefit of an equally strong main theme. Still, a strong, flavorful music that has held very well all these years, and displays many ingratiating charms.

Walker ♫♫♫♫♪

1987, Virgin Records; from the movie *Walker,* Universal Pictures, 1987.

Album Notes: *Music:* Joe Strummer; *String and Horn Arrangements:* Joe Strummer, Dick Bright; *Guitar Arrangements:* Zander Schloss; *Featured Musicians:* Zander Schloss (guitar, charanga, vuhela, banjo, guitarron, tambour), Rebecca Mauleon (piano, organ), Michael Spiro (congos, bongos, timbales, percussion), Rich Girard (bass), Richard Zobel (harmonica, mandolin, banjo), Mary Fettig (saxophone, flute), Dick Bright (country fiddle, violin), Michael Hatfield (marimba, vibes, piano organ), David Bendigkiet, John Worley (trumpet), Dean Hubbard (trombone), John Tenney, Dean Franke (violin), Susan Chan (viola), Stephen Mitchell (snare drum), Dan Levin (fast piano), Sam Lehmer (bass drum), Joe Strummer, Richard Zobel (vocals); *Album Producer:* Joe Strummer; *Engineer:* Sam Lehmer.

Selections: 1 Filibustero (3:57); 2 Omotepe (3:46); 3 Sandstorm (1:56); 4 Machete (3:04); 5 Viperland (2:40); 6 Nica Libre (3:15); 7 Latin Romance (3:52); 8 The Unknown Immortal (3:45); 9 Musket Waltz (2:38); 10 The Brooding Side Of Madness (3:02); 11 Tennessee Rain (2:54); 12 Smash Everything (3:21); 13 Tropic Of No Return (3:09); 14 Tropic Of Pico (4:26).

Review: Joe Strummer's exotically limned score for this adventure film set in Nicaragua in the middle of the 19th century relies on its tropical rhythms to evoke the time and the place, and attract the listener. It succeeds beautifully. This story of an American adventurer who, with the financial support of Cornelius Vanderbilt, invaded Nicaragua in 1855 at the head of a band of mercenary and set out to become president of the country, found a deep, resonant echo in Strummer's idealistic score, with each cue elaborating on the storyline and giving it an appropriately epic tone, while the many percussion instruments and rhythmic accents anchor it in its specific locale. Highly enjoyable, with many melodic themes that catch one's interest, it is a rare treat, and though probably difficult to find (it was issued ten years ago and was only briefly available), it is well worth looking for.

Walking Thunder 🎵🎵🎵ᵛ

1996, JOS Records; from the movie *Walking Thunder,* Majestic Entertainment, 1994.

Album Notes: *Music:* John Scott; The Munich Symphony Orchestra, conducted by John Scott; *Album Producer:* John Scott; *Engineer:* Keith Grant.

Selections: 1 Overture (2:45); 2 Main Titles/A Son's Sacrifice (2:46); 3 Summer 1850 (2:08); 4 Stranded (5:40); 5 Dark Wind Recounts The Legend (2:29); 6 Journey To Horsecreek (6:56); 7 Horsecreek Rendezvous: Turkey Strut/Darling Rosalinde/Horsecreek Quadrille (6:16); 8 Trouble In Horsecreek (1:13); 9 The Return Journey (5:45); 10 How To Survive With Nature (2:12); 11 Forest Secrets (4:34); 12 The Bad Bunch (2:48); 13 Utah (1:39); 14 A New Life/The Final Reckoning (10:22); 15 Dark Wind Fulfills His Destiny (1:35); 16 The Legend Of Walking Thunder (2:35).

Review: Although the setting is the old West of 1850, John Scott passes on most conventional genre methods and instead focuses his score on the personal story of one family's decision to start a new life in the Utah wilderness after a bear attacks and disables their covered wagon. They eventually meet and befriend a Native American, Dark Wind, who tells them the legend of Walking Thunder, the giant bear. Scott plays out each of the major factors now in the family's life, the vast expanses of their new home, their budding friendships with the neighbors, and the threat from a roving band of marauders. One of Scott's few concessions to the idiom is the use of a motif for Dark Wind, based on an actual Native American mel-

ody, that the actor playing the character sings in the film. There is also a superb theme for the villains, humorously titled "The Bad Bunch," which is an exuberant tip of the hat to genre masters Ennio Morricone and Jerry Fielding. Oddly, the first part of the six-minute suite "Horsecreek Rendezvous," the "Turkey Strut," includes an overlay of ambient crowd noise.

David Hirsch

Wall Street/Salvador 🎵🎵

1987, Varese-Sarabande Records; from the movies *Wall Street,* 20th Century-Fox, 1987; and *Salvador,* Cinema '85, 1985.

Album Notes: *Wall Street*: *Music:* Stewart Copeland; *Performer*: Stewart Copeland; *Salvador*: *Music:* Georges Delerue; The Vancouver Symphony Orchestra, conducted by Georges Delerue; *Album Producers*: Tom Null, Richard Kraft; *Engineers*: Jeff Seitz, Judd Levinson.

Selections: *WALL STREET:* 1 Bud's Scam (2:46); 2 Are You With Me (1:10); 3 Trading Begins (2:43); 4 The Tall Weeds (2:58); 5 Break-Up (Darian)(1:48); 6 Anacott Steal (2:56); 7 End Title Theme (1:07);

SALVADOR: 8 Main Title (2:16); 9 El Playon (2:20); 10 Siege Of Santa Ana (3:00); 11 Goodbye, Maria (1:26); 12 At The Border (1:01); 13 Road Block (1:13); 16 Love Theme/Finale (4:00).

Review: Two scores from early Oliver Stone films are offered on this CD. Stewart Copeland's *Wall Street* is one of the sorriest excuses for a film score ever. A sufficiently talented rock and roll drummer, Copeland is rather less adept at the musical demands of melody and counterpoint. His "score" for *Wall Street* is not so much music as it is musical sound effects (and even resorts to using sampled dog barking!), and is the work of someone of dubious musical inclination cloaking his deficiencies by using sophisticated synthesizers. Any amateur tinkering with a keyboard could have achieved as good a result.

On the other hand, Georges Delerue's *Salvador* is a work of genius. Delerue was a master of melody and rich orchestration. Like most Oliver Stone films, *Salvador* was an infantile, pretentious rant, but it allowed Delerue a departure from his usual assignments, calling for strident, violent music (he was better known for lyrical scores). Admittedly the more dissonant cues do not work quite so well on an album. But Delerue's tragic end title for strings and chorus is one of the most longingly heartfelt evocations of tragedy ever written for a movie. This track alone makes the CD worth owning.

Paul Andrew MacLean

The War 🎵🎵🎵🎵

1994, MCA Records; from the movie *The War*, Universal Pictures, 1994.

Album Notes: *Music:* Thomas Newman; *Orchestrations:* Thomas Pasatieri; *Music Editor:* Bill Bernstein; Orchestra conducted by Thomas Newman; *Featured Vocalist:* Yvonne Williams; *Album Producers:* Thomas Newman, Bill Bernstein; *Engineer:* Dennis Sands.

Selections: 1 Peace Train (Cat Stevens)(4:09) *Cat Stevens*; 2 Think (A. Franklin/T. White)(2:16) *Aretha Franklin*; 3 Summertime (from *Porgy And Bess*) (G. & I. Gershwin/D. Heyward)(3:58) *Janis Joplin*; 4 Daydream (J. Sebastian) (2:19) *The Lovin' Spoonful*; 5 Sunny (B. Hebb)(2:40) *Bobby Hebb*; 6 Spirit In The Sky (N. Greenbaum)(4:00) *Norman Greenbaum*; 7 Follow (J. Merrick) (6:20) *Richie Havens*; 8 Up On Cripple Creek (R. Robertson)(4:29) *The Band*; 9 Someday We'll Be Together (H. Fuqua/J. Bristol/J. Beavers)(3:29) *Diana Ross & The Supremes*; 10 Juliette (3:10); 11 Trolley (2:02); 12 The War (Main Title)(1:13); 13 Hornets (:52); 14 Resuscitation (1:33); 15 Gone Again (2:39); 16 Life Be A Bowlful (1:26); 17 2nd Vietnam (6:13); 18 Junkyard Billy (1:08); 19 Dare (2:32); 20 Hospital (2:33); 21 Angel Pen (3:35).

Review: Set in Mississippi, this sensitive tale of a Vietnam War veteran, disillusioned about everything that he once held dear, and his teenage boy, provided Thomas Newman with the right motivation to write a score that subtly underlined the moods in the film, while making a deep, emotional comment of its own. The beautifully lyrical "Main Theme" and the lengthy "2nd Vietnam" summarize the basic elements in the score, with the strong orchestral motifs outlining the prevalent feelings of loneliness, abandonment and deception, both the vet (played by Kevin Costner), and his son (Elijah Wood), experience to varying degrees and for obviously totally different reasons. It's a very evocative score, with flashes of orchestral gusto, and themes that are particularly meaningful. A selection of pop tunes help set the drama in its appropriate time period.

War and Peace 🎵🎵🎵🎵

1988, Varese-Sarabande; from the movie *War and Peace*, Paramount Pictures, 1956.

Album Notes: *Music:* Nino Rota; Orchestra conducted by Franco Ferrara; *CD Producers:* Tom Null, Richard Kraft; *Engineer:* Daniel Hersch.

Selections: 1 Prelude (4:43); 2 The Orgy (1:51); 3 Andrei Leaving For The War/Pierre And Natasha (2:33); 4 The Battle Of Austerlitz (3:32); 5 Moment Musical/Andrei And Natasha/The Hunt (5:31); 6 War And Peace (Natasha's Waltz)(1:59); 7 Anatole And Natasha (3:44); 8 Winter And The Remembrance Of Andrei (4:03); 9 The Charge Of The Cavalry And The Wounded (4:11); 10 Exodus From Moscow (3:16); 11 Napoleon's Retreat (3:59); 12 The Homecoming At Moscow (4:15).

Review: Nino Rota, best known in this country for the scores he wrote for the films of Federico Fellini and for *The Godfather*, struck a different, original note early in his career for this Napoleonic era romantic saga based on Leo Tolstoy's familiar novel. With the radiant Audrey Hepburn portraying Natasha, Mel Ferrer the handsome Prince Andrey, and Henry Fonda the bespectacled student Pierre, the King Vidor-directed film splashed across the big screen with scenic grandeur and an epic feel that echoed the passionate scope of the book. Opulent and magnificently mounted, the production also afforded Rota with many set-pieces where his lyrical inspiration took a free flight ("The Battle of Austerlitz," "The Charge of the Cavalry," "Exodus from Moscow," "Napoleon's Retreat"), all of which resulted in cues that are still impressively dramatic and powerfully appealing today. One of the film's most ravishing scenes, a whirling ballroom sequence, inspired him to create a lilting waltz ("War and Peace") as fresh and lovely as anything he wrote for the screen, that beautifully captured the giddy atmosphere of the situation. Despite the fact that the recording is in mono, it has all the sweep and magnificence one associates with this superproduction.

The War Lord 🎵🎵🎵🎵⏵

1994, Varese-Sarabande; from the movie *The War Lord*, Universal Pictures, 1965.

Album Notes: *Music:* Jerome Moross; The Universal Studio Orchestra, conducted by Joseph Gershenson; *CD Producer:* Robert Townson.

Selections: 1 Main Title (3:15); 2 Forsaken Village (1:46); 3 Love Theme (2:22); 4 The Ascent To The Tower and Frustrated Love (3:33); 5 The Druid Wedding (2:50); 6 Nocturnal Procession (2:34); 7 Chrysagon And Bronwyn (2:13); 8 The War Lord In Battle (H.J. Salter)(3:17); 9 Premonitions (2:13); 10 The Death Of Draco (H.J. Salter)(1:48); 11 The Reckoning and End Title (4:05).

Review: An impressive medieval epic, *The War Lord* found in Jerome Moross a sympathetic, inventive composer who evidently thrived on this story set in the 11th century, about a war lord of the Duke Of Normandy, fighting the Vikings around the North Sea coast countryside, and the strong, abiding love he feels for a young woman from the Druid village he is defending against the invading hordes. Instead of writing a swashbuckling score, as most composers would have done, Moross took the opposite approach, focusing first on the love story between the Lord, played by Charlton Heston, and the village maiden, portrayed by Rosemary Forsyth, occasionally interrupting the "wistful translucence" with action cues designed to underline the violent confrontations between the Lord, his men and the marauding Vikings. Two cues, composed by Hans J. Salter on themes provided by Moross, add a somewhat different, though nonetheless effective feel to the overall score.

War of the Buttons ♪♪♪♪♭

1994, Varese-Sarabande Records; from the movie *War of the Buttons*, Warner Bros., 1994.

Album Notes: *Music*: Rachel Portman; *Orchestrations*: Rachel Portman; The Irish Film Orchestra, conducted by David Snell; *Album Producer*: Rachel Portman; *Engineer*: Brian Masterson.

Selections: 1 Front Titles (4:34); 2 Murphy's Dunes Mobilization (1:28); 3 Chasing The Fox (3:30); 4 Night Maneuvers (1:18); 5 Battle Of Murphy's Dunes (1:16); 6 Fergus Is Captured (2:22); 7 Naked Battle (4:11); 8 Fishy's Mushrooms (1:16); 9 Buttons (1:29); 10 Battle Of Bunduff Castle (7:32); 11 Fergus Hides In The Woods (2:09); 12 Helicopter Rescue (4:16); 13 Pillow Fight/ End Titles (3:43).

Review: In an early demonstration of the skills that have since singled her out as a vastly talented film composer, Rachel Portman created the flavorful score for this enjoyable screen adaptation of the French novel by Louis Pergaud, *La guerre des boutons*. Set in Ireland, and opposing two groups of youngsters with a common ideal, *War of the Buttons* suggested to Portman a series of whimsical cues that followed the action on the screen, with a flurry of delightful little details that made her score even more appealing than the slight film would have suggested ("Battle Of Murphy's Dunes"). As usual with her scores, the music takes a life of its own when removed from its original supportive role, and in this case becomes an enchanting program one might like to return to frequently.

Warlock ♪♭

1989, Intrada Records; from the movie *Warlock*, New World Pictures, 1989.

Album Notes: *Music*: Jerry Goldsmith; *Orchestrations*: Arthur Morton; Orchestra conducted by Jerry Goldsmith; *Album Producer*: Jerry Goldsmith; *Engineer*: Robin Gray.

Selections: 1 The Sentence (4:03); 2 Ill Wind (2:06); 3 The Ring (2:16); 4 The Trance (5:31); 5 Old Age (4:10); 6 Growing Pains (5:34); 7 The Weather Vane (5:01); 8 Nails (4:24); 9 The Uninvited (4:54); 10 Salt Water Attack (8:42); 11 The Salt Flats (7:07).

IRVING BERLIN

Although he was born in Russia, Irving Berlin created songs that epitomize American music. During his lifetime, Berlin published more than one thousand songs, some failures and many successes; some have been forgotten, and some, such as "White Christmas" and "God Bless America," will be remembered always. Berlin could not read music, but he is one of the 20th century's most beloved composers.

Berlin's life began in poverty. He was born Israel Baline on May 11, 1888. In 1907 he published his first song, "Marie From Sunny Italy." The artist who drew the cover for the printed music of the song misprinted his name as I. Berlin; thinking the name sounded more American than Israel Baline, the composer renamed himself Irving Berlin.

In 1909 he got his first Tin Pan Alley job, as lyricist for the publishing firm of Waterson & Snyder. In 1911 he published "Alexander's Ragtime Band," which immediately thrust him into songwriting fame; his song was such a hit that he was instantly dubbed the "King of Tin Pan Alley."

In 1914 Berlin wrote his first complete Broadway musical, *Watch Your Step*. When sound came to moving pictures in 1929, Berlin began to write film scores. His first two films, *Puttin' on the Ritz* and *Cocoanuts*, were adaptations of Broadway shows. His next film, *Top Hat* (1935) was written expressly for Hollywood. More films followed including *Holiday Inn*, which contains the song that has sold more recordings than any other, "White Christmas."

When the Second World War broke out in Europe, Berlin needed to make a musical statement. When Kate Smith sang Berlin's "God Bless America" on November 11, 1938, the country gained a new—if unofficial— national anthem. Berlin continued writing until the early '60s. He died on September 22, 1989.

Review: Everybody has a bad day once in awhile, and Jerry Goldsmith must have had a very difficult couple of weeks trying to come up with material to score *Warlock*, the 1989 New World production that was shelved for a couple of years when the studio went bankrupt. Not that the movie — a mixture of horrific fantasy and tongue-in-cheek "fish out of water" comedy — gave the composer much to work with, but for whatever reason, Goldsmith wrote a tremendously dull, synthesizer-laden score with a pokey-sounding main motive offering neither horror, fantasy, nor anything musically interesting to entice listeners or viewers. The bulk of the music is, particularly for Goldsmith, atypically atonal and very blah; needless to say, the composer didn't return for the movie's needless follow-up.

Andy Dursin

Warlock: The Armageddon
🦴🦴🦴🦴

1993, Intrada Records; from the movie *Warlock: The Armageddon*, Trimark Pictures, 1993.

Album Notes: *Music*: Mark McKenzie; *Orchestrations*: Pat Russ, Mark McKenzie; *Music Editor*: Jim Young; The Southwest Symphony Orchestra and Choir, conducted by Mark McKenzie; *Album Producer*: Mark McKenzie; *Engineer*: Elliot Solomon.

Selections: 1 The Battle Has Just Begun (4:57); 2 Swimming (2:09); 3 Birth Of The Warlock (3:16); 4 Ken's Magic (3:13); 5 May I Help You Sir? (3:35); 6 Give Me The Stopnes (2:33); 7 Samantha And Ken's Love (2:10); 8 Party Crasher (2:25); 9 Samantha Becomes A Warrior (2:34); 10 Ken's New Life (4:09); 11 Warlock Gathers The Stones (2:16); 12 Armageddon Averted (3:21); 13 A Warlock Fantasia (4:03).

Review: A Requiem mass for disembodied voices and symphonic orchestra sets the tone for this horrific tale, unrelated to the earlier thriller, in which an evil emissary of Satan in a small Northern California community engages in fierce territorial battle with two descendants of 17th century Druids with the power to destroy him. McKenzie's score, contrasting the horror with more lyrical accents, proves very endearing overall. The themes are for the most part quite melodic ("Ken's Magic," "Samantha and Ken's Love"), and paint a vivid picture of the screen action. Recapping the main themes into a single cue, "A Warlock Fantasia" concludes the CD on a bright, positive note. The only real fault here is with the sound quality which emphasizes the highs and defeats the lows, resulting in thin-sounding strings and very little bottom to what should sometimes be a booming recording.

Warning Sign 𝄞

1985, Southern Cross Records; from the movie *Warning Sign*, 20th Century-Fox, 1985.

Album Notes: *Music*: Craig Safan; *Album Producer*: Craig Safan; *Engineer*: Dennis Sands.

Selections: 1 Main Title: Biotek (1:22); 2 Joanie Forced To Talk (1:24); 3 The Disease Takes Hold (1:16); 4 The Massacre (4:27); 5 Joanie Protects Schmidt (1:31); 6 Fairchild And Morse Break Into Biotek (2:15); 7 Joanie Fights (2:10); 8 Joanie Runs (1:57); 9 Discovery Of Serum (2:43); 10 Loading The Serum Guns (1:06); 11 Fighting And Curing (5:12); 12 All Is Well (2:45); 13 End Title (3:19).

Review: A creepy ambient synthesized score by Craig Safan effectively uses a non-thematic minimalist approach, ala *The Andromeda Strain*, for this tale of a chemical spill in a germ warfare lab. Interesting sound design, with an occasional new age theme, it has its moments, but it sounds very repetitious, and wears out its welcome too soon to hold any interest for long, unless you're really prepared to experience something different.

David Hirsch

Waterworld 🦴🦴🦴

1995, MCA Records; from the movie *Waterworld*, Universal Pictures, 1995.

Album Notes: *Music*: James Newton Howard; *Orchestrations*: Brad Dechter, Jeff Atmajian, Robert Elhai, Chris Boardman, James Newton Howard; *Music Editor*: Jim Weidman; Orchestra conducted by Artie Kane; *Featured Musicians*: Steve Porcaro, James Newton Howard (synth and drum programming), Katrin Kern (vocalist), The L.A. Master Chorale, Paul Salamunovich, director; *Album Producers*: James Newton Howard, Michael Mason; *Engineer*: Bruce Botnick.

Selections: 1 Main Titles (4:43); 2 Escaping The Smokers (3:49); 3 The Atoll (1:42); 4 Prodigal Child (1:54); 5 Smokers Sighted (2:10); 6 Swimming (4:15); 7 The Skyboat (3:54); 8 National Geographics (1:46); 9 Speargun (1:44); 10 The Bubble (3:23); 11 Helen Frees The Mariner (3:27); 12 Helen Sews (:50); 13 Slide For Life (4:51); 14 Half An Hour (4:36); 15 We're Gonna Die (2:02); 16 Arriving At The Deez (4:28); 17 Deacon's Speech (3:52); 18 Haircuts (1:32); 19 Gills (1:59); 20 Why Aren't You Rowing? (2:38); 21 Balloon Flight (:48); 22 Dry Land (1:48); 23 Mariner's Goodbye (3:15); 24 Main Credits (2:18).

Review: James Newton Howard did a yeoman's job coming in at the last minute to replace Mark Isham's original score for *Waterworld*, Kevin Costner's super-troubled 1995 sci-fi adventure that nevertheless boasted a number of bright spots — chief among them being Newton Howard's soundtrack. With a tone that ranges from new age-styled synthesizers to rousing, Korngold-inspired action cues, Newton Howard's score maintains a fine balance between being a musical underscore and a major player in Kevin Reynolds' film, often times helping to define the relationship between the various characters in the story and their fight against the evil Deacon (played with great relish by Dennis Hopper). The music is a lot of fun on its own, and works as an enjoyable soundtrack for listeners who typically enjoy large-scale action scores.

Andy Dursin

Wavelength ♫♫♫▹

1983, Varese-Sarabande Records; from the movie *Wavelength*, New World Pictures, 1983.

Album Notes: *Music:* Chris Franke, Edgar Froese, Johannes Schmoelling; *Album Producers:* Tangerine Dream; *Engineers:* Tangerine Dream.

Selections: 1 Alien Voices (:19); 2 Wavelength Main Title (1:56); 3 Desert Drive (2:05); 4 Mojave End Title (4:03); 5 Healing (2:26); 6 Breakout (1:13); 7 Alien Goodbyes (1:51); 8 Spaceship (2:25); 9 Church Theme (3:46); 10 Sunset Drive (3:27); 11 Airshaft (3:15); 12 Alley Walk (2:57); 13 Cyro Lab (2:20); 14 Running Through The Hills (1:36); 15 Campfire Theme (1:28); 16 Mojave End Title (reprise)(3:56).

Review: Tangerine Dream took a very lyrical approach to score this futuristic film, though the minimalist electronic style of the score might not be to everyone's liking. Occasionally ("Main Title," "Alien Goodbyes"), the themes developed are remarkably effective, with acoustic and electronic instruments forming a melodic texture that's quite attractive. More accessible than many of the group's efforts, the score makes a very convincing case for the use of electronics in certain situations.

Wayne's World

Wayne's World ♫♫♫♫▹

1991, Reprise Records; from the movie *Wayne's World*, Paramount Pictures, 1991.

Album Notes: *Song Producers:* Roy Thomas Baker, Gary Lyons, Tom Keifer, David Garrison, Gary Wright, Ted Templeman, Rick Rubin, Black Sabbath, G.E. Smith, Peter Collins,Lenny Waronker; *Album Executive Producers:* Michael Ostin, Ted Templeman.

Selections: 1 Bohemian Rhapsody (F. Mercury) (5:58) *Queen*; 2 Hot And Bothered (T. Keifer/E. Brillingham) (4:17) *Cinderella*;

3 Rock Candy (R. Montrose/S. Hagar/B. Church/D. Carnassi) (5:04) *BulletBoys*; 4 Dream Weaver (G. Wright) (4:26) *Gary Wright*; 5 Sikamikanico (A. Kiedis/J. Frusciante/C. Smith) (3:25) *Red Hot Chili Peppers*; 6 Time Machine (G. Butler/R. James/T. Iommi) (4:20) *Black Sabbath*; 7 Wayne World's Theme (M. Myers/G.E. Smith) (5:15) *Mike Myers, Dana Carvey*; 8 Ballroom Blitz (M. Chapman/N. Chinn) (3:30) *Tia Carrere*; 9 Foxy Lady (J. Hendrix) (3:19) *Jimi Hendrix*; 10 Feed My Frankenstein (A. Cooper/N. Coler/I. Richardson) (4:46) *Alice Cooper*; 11 Ride With Yourself (G. Fields/G. Dolivo) (3:16) *Rhino Bucket*; 12 Loving Your Lovin' (J. Williams) (3:55) *Eric Clapton*; 13 Why You Wanna Break My Heart (D. Twilley) (3:33) *Tia Carrere*.

Review: This *Saturday Night Live* bit clicked in a big way, and hambone guitar rock is a big part of the schtick. We'll never again be able to listen to Queen's "Bohemian Rhapsody" without remembering the cast's hysterical lip-syncing routine, and the film gave Gary Wright's "Dream Weaver" a new life, too. And, of course, it gives us the "Wayne's World Theme" performed by Mike Myers and Dana Carvey. Party on, dudes.

Gary Graff

Wayne's World 2 ♫♫♫

1993, Reprise Records; from the movie *Wayne World's 2*, Paramount Pictures, 1993.

Album Notes: *Song Producers:* Robert Plant, Gin Blossoms, Bernard Edwards, Kenny Laguna, Ricthcie Cordell, Erik Jacobsen, J. Mascis, 4 Non Blondes, Golden Earring, Edgar Winter, Jacques Morali; *Album Executive Producers:* Peter Afterman, Michael Ostin; *Engineer:* Stephen Marcussen.

Selections: 1 Louie, Louie (R. Berry) (2:54) *Robert Plant*; 2 Dude (Looks Like A Lady) (S. Tyler/J. Perry/D. Child) (5:05) *Aerosmith*; 3 Idiot Summer (Gin Blossoms) (4:13) *Gin Blossoms*; 4 Superstar (L. Russell/B. Bramlett) (3:53) *Superfan*; 5 I Love Rock And Roll (A. Merrill/J. Hooker) (2:56) *Joan Jett & The Blackhearts*; 6 Spirit In The Sky (N. Greenbaum) (4:02) *Norman Greenbaum*; 7 Out There (J. Mascis) (5:55) *Dinosaur Jr.*; 8 Mary's House (L. Perry/S. Hall) (4:04) *4 Non Blondes*; 9 Radar Love (G. Kooymans/B. Hay) (5:05) *Golden Earring*; 10 Can't Get Enough (M. Ralphs) (4:15) *Bad Company*; 11 Frankenstein (E. Winter) (4:44) *Edgar Winter*; 12 Shut Up And Dance (S. Tyler/ J. Perry/J. Blades/T. Shaw) (3:44) *Aerosmith*; 13 Y.M.C.A. (H. Belolo/J. Morali/V. Willis) (4:49) *Village People*.

Review: Not quite as successful as its predecessor, mostly because the film wasn't as big a hit. This is still a good compendium of guitar rock, though, and even artfully makes connections between the crunch of Bad Company's "Can't Get

Enough" from the '70s and the woozy attack of Dinosaur Jr.'s "Out There" from the '90s. Led Zeppelin singer Robert Plant doesn't sound like his heart is into covering "Louie Louie," and a couple of overexposed songs—the Village People's "YMCA" and Norman Greenbaum's "Spirit in the Sky" don't add much to the proceedings, either.

Gary Graff

Weeds 🦴🦴🦴

1987, Varese-Sarabande; from the movie *Weeds*, De Laurentiis Entertainment, 1987.

Album Notes: *Music*: Angelo Badalamenti; *Orchestrations*: Angelo Badalamenti, Joe Turrin, Andy Barrett; The Australian Pops Orchestra, conducted by Angelo Badalamenti; *Album Producer*: Angelo Badalamenti.

Selections: 1 Unity And Harmony (3:48); 2 We're Movin' Together (1:47); 3 From Hell To Freedom To Love (3:54); 4 Navarro Dies (2:53); 5 San Quentin Riot (3:23); 6 Theatre Dreams (:43); 7 Letters From The Outside (2:39); 8 Trilogy For Godot (3:29); 9 Elation Turns To Sorrow (1:57); 10 Irony In The Yard (2:03); 11 Mysteries Of Love (A. Badalamenti/D. Lynch)(3:26); 12 I Wanna Go Home (M. Etheridge)(1:46); 13 Texas Tankard (3:17); 14 Pimp Song (O. Stoeber/ A. Mitchell)(1:19); 15 Lock And Key (R. Peasless/O. Stoeber/A. Mitchell)(1:36); 16 We're Movin' Together (1:36).

Review: Normally known for his unconventional work on *Twin Peaks*, Angelo Badalamenti's score for this Nick Nolte film about a prison acting troupe is the complete contradiction in style and content. Done mostly in a classical style, the music for *Weeds* has a realistic, down-to-earth emotional temperament. Since the major characters in the ensemble are ex-cons, the music romanticizes them as lost souls whose only freedom is found within their enthusiasm for acting. Badalamenti does a fine job in creating this moving mix of passion and pathos. Latter part of the album contains instrumental tracks by other composers, including Melissa Etheridge ("I Wanna Go Home") and *Twin Peaks* director David Lynch ("Mysteries of Love").

David Hirsch

Welcome Home Roxy Carmichael 🦴🦴🦴

1990, Varese-Sarabande Records; from the movie *Welcome Home Roxy Carmichael*, Paramount Pictures, 1990.

Album Notes: *Music*: Thomas Newman; *Orchestrations*: Thomas Pasatieri; *Music Editor*: Bill Bernstein; Orchestra conducted by Thomas Newman; *Album Producer*: Thomas Newman; *Engineer*: John Vigran.

Selections: 1 In A Closet (1:46); 2 Little Black Bird (1:23); 3 Hers Are Nicest (1:10); 4 Refrigerator Shrine (2:37); 5 Missing Bossetti Child (:56); 6 Wake Up (1:27); 7 Clyde (1:45); 8 Her Limousine (1:57); 9 Several Letters (1:13); 10 Choke It (2:18); 11 Arriving By Aeroplane (:57); 12 Cleveland (1:13); 13 Yours Are Nice (:41); 14 Baby Soup (2:57); 15 In A Beauty Parlor (:36); 16 G. On A Bike (1:06); 17 Her Majesty's Dress (1:23); 18 This Was My Intention (2:30); 19 In A Small Town (1:33).

Review: Winona Ryder made a striking impression in this film, in which she portrays a 15-year-old adopted nymphet with a rebellious streak, who lives in a small Ohio town suddenly set abuzz with the impending return of Roxy Carmichael, a local girl who has made good as a Hollywood actress. With a sprinkling of electronics, and a deft complement of acoustic instruments, Newman fashioned a score which is a trifle arid, even as it attempts to give support to the screen action. An occasionally attractive track emerges from the ensemble ("Choke It," "In a Beauty Parlor"), but for the most part it's more atmosphere stuff than melodic programming, something which works against the CD as pure musical entertainment.

We're Back 🦴🦴🦴🦴

1993, MCA Records; from the animated feature *We're Back! A Dinosaur's Story*, Universal Pictures, 1993.

Album Notes: *Music*: James Horner; *Orchestrations*: Don Davis, Arthur Kempel, Tom Pasatieri; *Music Editor*: Jim Henrikson; The London Symphony Orchestra, conducted by James Horner; *Featured Musicians*: Charlie Davis, Doug Sharf (trumpet); Iki Levy (drums/ percussion); Thomas Dolby (keyboards); Jon E. Love, Will Ray (guitars); Pasquale Zicari (sax/flute); William Henn (bass); Skip Edwards (piano); *Album Producers*: James Horner, Thomas Dolby; *Engineer*: Shawn Murphy.

Selections: 1 Main Title/Primeval Times (4:14); 2 Flying Forward In Time (5:48); 3 Welcome To New York (2:26); 4 First Wish, First Flight (3:48); 5 A Hint Of Trouble/The Contract (1:49); 6 Roll Back The Rock (To The Dawn Of Time)(J. Horner/T. Dolby)(2:55) *John Goodman*; 7 Grand Slam Demons (2:05); 8 Hot Pursuit (3:18); 9 Central Park (1:21); 10 Screweyes's Circus/Opening Act (1:12); 11 Circus (2:29); 12 Fright Radio/Rex's Sacrifice (6:39); 13 Grand Demon Parade (7:39); 14 The Kids Wake Up/A New Day (2:57); 15 The Transformation (5:30); 16 Special Visitors To The Museum Of Natural History (2:12); 17 Roll Back The Rock (To The Dawn Of Time)(J. Horner/T. Dolby)(2:56) *Little Richard*.

Review: When four cuddly monsters from the dinosaur age fly forward in time to the 20th century, what do you get but a brightly amusing animated feature, courtesy of Steven Spielberg, and a wonderful score to match, composed by James Horner. Not exactly *Jurassic Park*, but close! Frequently exhilarating and whimsical, the motifs created by the composer follow the story while giving musical life to the animated characters that inhabit it, sometimes in portraits that are vividly sketched and amusingly detailed. As is frequently the case with Horner, some cues are extremely profuse, enabling his creativity to better express itself, while his lush, florid style takes full advantage of the colorful orchestral palette in themes that are always quite attractive and enjoyable. There are many, many delightful moments in this score, beginning with the explicit "Main Title/ Primeval Times," but encompassing such ingenious stops as "Welcome to New York," "Hot Pursuit," "Grand Demon Parade," and the jaunty "Special Visitors to the Museum of Natural History." Little Richard's rollicking performance of "Roll Back the Rock (To the Dawn of Time)" adds a tongue-in-cheek coda to the recording that is not even out of place.

The Whales of August ♫♫♫♫

1987, Varese-Sarabande Records; from the movie *The Whales of August*, Nelson Films/Alive Films, 1987.

Album Notes: *Music*: Alan Price; *Orchestrations*: Derek Wadsworth; Orchestra conducted by Derek Wadsworth; *Album Producer*: Alan Price.

Selections: 1 The Whales Of August (1:31); 2 The Morning Walk (1:12); 3 Sarah And Mr. Maranov (:43); 4 In The Winter, In St. Petersburg (:35); 5 Remembering/Libby And Sarah (3:58); 6 Sisters (1:22); 7 Have You Seen The Whales? (1:48); 8 Mr. Maranov (:44); 9 The Whales Of August (reprise)(1:03); 10 First Date (1:46); 11 We're Not Leaving Home, Philip (1:00); 12 Mr. Maranov's Farewell (1:12); 13 The Whales Should Be Back (1:28); 14 Towards The Point (:44); 15 Libby And Sarah: The Old Stereopticon (:39); 16 Hairbrushing/Tisha's Theme (1:59); 17 Flowers For Sarah (:41); 18 Anniversary (3:02); 19 You Can Never Tell (End Titles)(2:09).

Review: This is a delightful orchestral score composed by Alan Price for the 1987 screen adaption of David Berry's stage play about two aging sisters in a seaside Maine house (Bette Davis and Lillian Gish in her last film). The film is a simple, albeit compelling story of the waning years of life, that inspired Price to emphasize the women's strength and dignity, the things that have served them well all their lives. He fashioned slow, careful melodies for them, but the score gets some energy in

the themes for the whales. The sisters eagerly await the return of these magnificent creatures who appear each August. Price also provides a distraction, an ethnic theme for the elderly Russian emigre, Mr. Maranov (Vincent Price). Unfortunately, because the film was based on a dialogue-driven play, the score is only a mere 28 minutes long. I was left wishing for more, but it's still an engaging delight. Derek Wadsworth, who composed the score for the second season of the *Space: 1999* television series arranged and conducted the score.

David Hirsch

When a Man Loves a Woman ♫♫♫♫

1994, Hollywood Records; from the movie *When a Man Loves a Woman*, Touchstone Pictures, 1994.

Album Notes: *Music*: Zbigniew Preisner; The Sinfonia Varsovia, conducted by Wojciech Michniewski; *Featured Soloists*: Tomasz Stanko (trumpet), Konrad Mastylo (piano); *Album Producer*: Zbigniew Preisner; *Engineers*: Rafal Packowski; *Assistant Engineers*: Leszek Kaminski, Geoff Foster.

Selections: 1 When A Man Loves A Woman (A. Wright/C. Lewis)(2:51) *Percy Sledge*; 2 Crazy Love (V. Morrison)(3:47) *Brian Kennedy*; 3 El gusto (Son Huasteco)(E. Ramirez)(2:56) *Los Lobos*; 4 Main Title (2:00); 5 Garbage Compulsion (1:27); 6 Homecoming (2:23); 7 I Hit Her Hard (3:35); 8 Dressing Casey (1:23); 9 Gary (2:02); 10 Michael Decides (:57); 11 Alice And Michael (1:04).

Review: A solid melodrama starring Meg Ryan as an alcoholic woman and Andy Garcia as the man who stands by her in spite of all the scorn and abuse he has to endure, *When a Man Loves a Woman* elicited a wonderful score from Zbigniew Preisner, who developed his own themes rather than use the well-known pop song performed by Percy Sledge (appropriately heard here as the opening track). A veritable recital of gorgeous love motifs, sensitively written and performed, the mesmerizing cues unfold with great serenity, belying the tension and turmoil in the narrative. "Crazy Love" by Brian Kennedy, and "El gusto" by Los Lobos add a different, though equally welcome note.

When Harry Met Sally... ♫♫♫♫

1989, Columbia Records; from the movie *When Harry Met Sally...*, Castle Rock Entertainment, 1989.

Album Notes: *Orchestrations*: Marc Shaiman; *Featured Performers*: Harry Connick, Jr. (piano, vocals), Benjamin Jonah Wolfe (bass), Jeff "Tain" Watts (drums), Frank Wess (tenor sax), Jay Berliner (acoustic guitar); *Album Producers*: Marc Shaiman, Harry Connick Jr.; *Engineer*: Tim Geelan.

Selections: 1 It Had To Be You (I. Jones/G. Kahn)(with big band and vocals) (2:42); 2 Our Love Is Here To Stay (G. & I. Gershwin)(4:13); 3 Stompin' At The Savoy (B. Goodman/C. Webb/E. Sampson)(4:17); 4 But Not For Me (G. & I. Gershwin)(4:34); 5 Winter Wonderland (F. Bernard/D. Smith)(3:05); 6 Don't Get Around Much Anymore (E.K. Ellington/B. Russell)(4:24); 7 Autumn In New York (V. Duke)(2:50); 8 I Could Write A Book (R. Rodgers/L. Hart)(2:31); 9 Let's Call The Whole Thing Off (G. & I. Gershwin)(4:14); 10 It Had To Be You (I. Jones/G. Kahn)(instrumental trio)(1:44); 11 Where Or When (R. Rodgers/L. Hart)(3:53).

Review: This CD, titled *Music from the Motion Picture When Harry Met Sally,* is a true enigma. While *When Harry Met Sally* launched Harry Connick, Jr.'s impressive commercial career, he did not (as is suggested by the title of the album, and the cover art, cleverly taken from the film) perform all of the songs in the movie. What's missing here are Frank Sinatra's gorgeous rendition of the film's most important song, "It Had to Be You," and a number of other numbers that were performed in the film by Ella Fitzgerald, Louis Armstrong and other top musical talents.

So, in a sense, this CD release is misleading. No matter. *When Harry Met Sally* is a witty, whimsical tale—the quintessential "New York" love story—and Connick's cover version is excellent, replete with some of the very finest standards, pleasingly sung and performed, that perfectly complement the tender, romantic plot that Rob Reiner lovingly brought to the screen.

Charles L. Granata

When We Were Kings 🎞🎞🎞🎞▹

1997, DAS/Mercury Records; from the documentary *When We Were Kings,* Gramercy Pictures, 1997.

Album Notes: *Album Executive Producers*: David Sonenberg, Scot McCracken.

Selections: 1 Rumble In The Jungle (W. Jean/P. Michel/L. Hill/M. Taylor/K. Fareed/T. Smith/J. Forte/B. Andersson/B. Ulvaeus/S. Anderson/C. Taylor)(5:07) *The Fugees, A Tribe Called Quest, Busta Rhymes, Forte*; 2 Drew "Bundini" Brown (:07); 3 Ain't No Sunshine/You (B. Withers)(3:00) *Bill Withers*; 4 Sweet Sixteen (B.B. King/J. Josea)(6:14) *B.B. King*; 5 African Girls Chant (:19); 6 "When I get to Africa" (:06) *Ali*; 7 The Payback (J. Brown/F. Wesley/J. Starks)(3:42) *James Brown*; 8 Mobutu Chant (:18); 9 I'll Be Around (T. Bell/P. Hurtt)(3:03) *The Spinners*; 10 Put It Where You Want It (J. Sample)(4:30) *Jazz Crusaders*; 11 "Wait till I kick Foreman's behind" (:06) *Ali*;

12 I Got Some Help I Don't Need (B.B. King/D. Clark)(5:07) *B.B. King*; 13 Gonna Have A Funky Good Time (J. Brown)(4:40) *James Brown*; 14 "Mr. Tooth Decay" (:24) *Ali*; 15 I'm Coming Home (T. Bell/L. Creed)(4:10) *The Spinners*; 16 When We Were Kings (A. Marvel/A. Powers/A. Roman)(4:40) *Brian McKnight, Diana King*; 17 Drew "Bundini" Brown (:20); 18 I'm Calling (Say It Loud)(Z. Davis/A. Marvel/B. Telson/J. Brown/A.J. Ellis)(5:12) *Zelma Davis*; 19 "You out sucker" (:21) *Ali*; 20 Chant (:36).

Review: What turned into a documentary about Muhammad Ali and "The Rumble in the Jungle" actually started out chronicling the all-star R&B concert that occured during the festival surrounding the famed Ali-George Foreman fight. So it's not surprising that there are some incendiary live performances by James Brown, B.B. King, The Spinners, The Jazz Crusaders and Bill Withers, whose "Ain't No Sunshine/You" medley is a great moment in soul music. Some of Ali's diatribes included here hold their own with modern-day rappers—some of whom, notably Fugees and A Tribe Called Quest, open the album with a song called "Rumble in the Jungle."

Gary Graff

Where Angels Fear To Tread 🎞🎞🎞🎞

1991, Virgin Movie Music; from the movie *Where Angels Fear to Tread,* FineLine Features, 1991.

Album Notes: *Music*: Rachel Portman; *Orchestrations*: Rachel Portman; The Hungarian Film and Television Orchestra, conducted David Snell; *Featured Musicians*: Nicholas Bucknall (clarinet), William Bennett (flute); *Album Producer*: Rachel Portman; *Engineer*: Chris Dibble.

Selections: 1 Where Angels Fear To Tread (4:30); 2 Life And Death (2:08); 3 A Night At The Opera (1:57); 4 Monteriano (1:14); 5 Harriet's Mission (2:10); 6 The Storm (3:43); 7 I Love Him Too (5:02); 8 The Mad Scene (from Lucia di Lamermoor)(G. Donizetti)(12:25) *Jennifer Smith, The London Independent Players*; 9 Santa Deodata (1:46); 10 Philip's Visit (1:28); 11 Caroline And Gino (2:04); 12 Lilia's Panic (1:59); 13 Latte freschissimo (1:03); 14 Sawston (1:22); 15 Finale (2:38).

Review: Rachel Portman's first major feature, *Where Angels Fear to Tread* revealed the depth of the composer's creativity, as well as her uncanny ability to write attractive themes with great cinematic power. All the basic elements that have characterized Portman's efforts since can be found in this superbly confident score—an abundance of solid melodic material, intelligently literate, handsomely orchestrated, overflowing with generously romantic ideas that build up in layers, the whole thing served in a particularly winsome way that invites re-peated listening. The film, a sensitive tearjerker about an Italian man whose British wife died when she gave birth to their son, and who must confront her relatives who want to take the child back to England with them, resulted in a profuse series of cues in which the romantic Impressionistic influences dominate. While coherent in the context of the film, the "Mad Scene" from Donizetti's *Lucia di Lammemoor* seems redundant and unnecessary in this soundtrack album, and actually detracts the listener's attention rather than eliciting a more complete vision of the film.

Where the River Runs Black ♪

1986, Varese-Sarabande Records; from the movie *Where the River Runs Black,* M-G-M/UA, 1986.

Album Notes: *Music*: James Horner; Orchestra conducted by James Horner; *Album Producer*: James Horner; *Engineer*: Shawn Murphy.

Selections: 1 Where The River Runs Black (4:36); 2 Underwater Ballet (3:00); 3 Serra Pelada (2:46); 4 Alone (3:39); 5 The Orphanage (3:19); 6 The Dolphins (2:23); 7 Baptism (4:36); 8 Down River (5:59); 9 Magic Kitchen (2:01); 10 Discovered At The Mine (3:51); 11 The City (1:11); 12 The Assassin (1:49); 13 End Title (4:30).

Review: A film dealing with the clash of civilization and indigenous people in South America, *Where the River Runs Black* would seem to offer fertile ground for a composer. James Horner's score however is one of his weakest, and entirely forgettable. Obviously influenced by the music for *The Emerald Forest* (composed a year earlier), Horner's score is a blend of new-age and "ethnic" styles, realized on a sampling keyboard. There are some pleasantly airy moments, but most of the score consists of droning pre-set rhythms, over which the composer fiddles with various samples (strings, voice and most predominantly panpipe, which comes out sounding more like a circus organ than an authentic South American instrument). In fact most of the score sounds like it was improvised as Horner sat at the keyboard. There is little structure and negligible melodic invention. Track 10, "Discovered at the Mine," is literally no more than a continuous programmed rhythm, with no development or (apparently) even human influence. *Where the River Runs Black* is a sad example of how the ease of synthesizers can induce even a talented composer to press a button and allow electronics to do his work for him.

Paul Andrew MacLean

While You Were Sleeping ♪♪♪♭

1995, Uni Records; from the movie *While You Were Sleeping*, Hollywood Pictures, 1995.

Album Notes: *Music*: Randy Edelman; *Orchestrations*: Ralph Ferraro; *Music Editor*: John Lasalandra; Orchestra conducted by Randy Edelman; *Album Producer*: Randy Edelman; *Engineers*: Elton Ahi, Dennis Sands.

Selections: 1 Opening (2:21); 2 Peter's Family (2:07); 3 Love Theme (1:45); 4 An Untimely Accident (2:40); 5 Phone Tag (1:45); 6 Dreaming Of Florence (3:06); 7 He's Alive (2:30); 8 Riverside Walk (5:21); 9 A Testacular Situation (1:48); 10 Jack And Lucy (2:57); 11 Leave It To Sol (2:06); 12 The Dream Is Over (:48); 13 Sound Advice (1:43); 14 Tear Jerking Tale (1:31); 15 Bumpy Encounter (2:36); 16 A Happy Ending (2:21).

Review: Bouncy, infectious melodies distinguish this upbeat score by Randy Edelman. His dance-like opening theme well suits the pace of this comedy about a pretty subway token clerk (Sandra Bullock) who is mistaken for the fiancee of a comatose man. Desperately lonely, she gets drawn into the warmth of his family circle, aided by Edelman's heart-tugging "Love Theme." A delight, though a bit repetitive.

David Hirsch

White Mischief ♪♪♪♪♭

1988, Varese-Sarabande Records; from the movie *White Mischief,* Columbia Pictures, 1988.

Album Notes: *Music*: George Fenton; *Orchestrations*: George Fenton, John Warren, Simon Chamberlain; *Album Producer*: George Fenton; *Engineer*: Keith Grant.

Selections: 1 White Mischief (Main Title)(1:56); 2 Happy Valley Foxtrot (2:39); 3 The Farm (2:13); 4 Dance Of The Sugar Plum Fairy (P.I. Tchaikovsky) (2:10); 5 Muthaiga Club Quickstep (2:28); 6 The Beach At Malindi (1:28); 7 The Picnic (1:56); 8 Begin The Beguine (C. Porter)(3:33); 9 Suspicion (2:02); 10 The Rains/Jungle Stomp (3:03); 11 News At Dawn (3:29); 12 Roadhouse Rumba (G. Fenton/S. Chamberlain)(3:03); 13 The Djinn Palace (5:26); 14 Cocktails At The Grave (2:26); 15 Alphabet Song and End Credit (3:58) *Sarah Miles*; 16 White Mischief (3:45) *Tim Finn*.

Review: A gorgeously dance band-inspired score by George Fenton illuminated this story of British settlers in Kenya's so-called "Happy Valley," whose life of opulence and debauchery during the early days of World War II contrasted with the hardship of their peers at home as well as that of the natives around them. Essentially, a triangular love affair, *White Mischief*, starring Greta Scacchi, Joss Ackland, and Charles Dance, involved itself with a couple of newlyweds, freshly arrived in Nairobi's golden circle of British colonialists. Their relationship turns sour when she meets another man, whose sudden murder unveils the scandalous lifestyle of the "Happy Valley" residents. Punctuating the various incidents in the story, Fenton devised a score that draws its strength from the several cues tailored after the giddy dance numbers evocative of that period ("Happy Valley Foxtrot," "Muthaiga Club Quickstep," "Jungle Stomp," "Roadhouse Rumba," as well as a cover of Cole Porter's "Begin the Beguine"), all of them sprightly and entertaining. Other moods are established with cues that specifically detail the time and place of the screen action, but that are devoid of any "African" accents, in keeping with the isolationist attitude of the British denizens. Film co-star Sarah Miles has a field day performing the "Alphabet Song," while Tim Finn delivers a wicked vocal version of the title tune.

White Nights 🎵🎵🎵▷

1985, Atlantic Records; from the movie *White Nights*, Columbia Pictures, 1985.

Album Notes: *Song Producers*: Arif Mardin, Phil Collins, Hugh Padgham; David Pack, James Newton Howard; Robert Plant, Benji Lefevre; Eumir Deodato, Roberta Flack; Nile Rodgers; Phil Ramone; Robbie Buchanan; David Foster.

Selections: 1 Separate Lives (Love Theme From White Nights)(S. Bishop) (4:06) *Phil Collins, Marilyn Martin*; 2 Prove Me Wrong (D. Pack/J. Newton Howard)(4:19) *David Pack*; 3 Far Post (R. Plant/R. Blunt/J. Woodroffe)(4:43) *Robert Plant*; 4 People On A String (M. Colombier/K. Wakefield)(4:01) *Roberta Flack*; 5 This Is Your Day (N. Rodgers)(3:46) *Sandy Stewart, Nile Rodgers*; 6 Snake Charmer (J. Hiatt)(3:42) *John Hiatt*; 7 The Other Side Of The World (M. Rutherford/B. Robertson)(3:33) *Chaka Khan*; 8 My Love Is Chemical (W. Aldridge)(4:30) *Lou Reed*; 9 tapDance (D. Foster/T. Keane/J. Hey)(4:45) *David Foster*; 10 People Have Got To Move (N. Rodgers)(4:20) *Jenny Burton*.

Review: Robert Plant's "Far Post" is one of the great lost B-sides of the '80s, so it's nice to have that preserved on an album. Phil Collins and Marilyn Martin hit No. 1 with the love duet "Separate Lives," but meatier material is provided by Lou Reed ("My Love is Chemical") and John Hiatt ("Snake Charmer"). Worthwhile, but not essential.
Gary Graff

White Palace 🎵🎵🎵🎵

1990, Varese-Sarabande Records; from the movie *White Palace*, Universal Pictures, 1990.

Album Notes: *Music*: George Fenton; *Orchestrations*: George Fenton, Jeff Atmajian; *Music Editor*: Sally Boldt; Orchestra conducted by George Fenton; *Featured Musicians*: Mike Lang (keyboards), Dan Higgins (alto/soprano sax), Tim May, John Goux (guitar), Gayle Levant, Dorothy Remsen (harp), Neil Stubenhaus (bass guitar), Robert Zimmitti (percussion), Fred Seykora (cello); *Album Producer*: George Fenton; *Engineer*: John Richards.

Selections: 1 White Palace Main Title (3:08); 2 Lost In Thought (2:03); 3 The Dream and Awakening (6:08); 4 I'm 44/I'm 27 (1:48); 5 You Make Me Feel Beautiful (3:00); 6 Slow Contact (4:15); 7 The Reading (3:59); 8 Nora's Secret (2:56); 9 The Breakup (2:17); 10 St. Louis To New York (3:00); 11 Alone In A Crowd (1:15); 12 The Kiss (2:16); 13 A Line From A Poem (3:57); 14 Younger Men (3:06).

Review: With undertones reminiscent of *The Graduate*, *White Palace* stars James Spader as the younger man and Susan Sarandon as the bolder woman, whose encounter results in a May-to-September love affair, in this romantic drama involving a 27-year-old advertising executive and a 44-year-old waitress in a St. Louis diner. Reminiscent of the film's typically hesitant approach to its unconventional story, the score created by George Fenton moves from ruminative melodies to glorious celebrations of love, with acoustic instruments playing over orchestral textures limning the moods in appealling fashion. Along the way, there are many telling selections, including "The Dream and Awakening," with its clearly defined contrasting emotions, the elegiac "You Make Me Feel Beautiful," and the equally rewarding "The Kiss." Throughout, the themes are strongly etched and evocative, making this another vibrant effort from the composer.

Who Framed Roger Rabbit? 🎵🎵🎵🎵

1988, Disneyland Records; from the movie *Who Framed Roger Rabbit?*, Touchstone Pictures, 1988.

Album Notes: *Music*: Alan Silvestri; *Orchestrations*: James Campbell; *Music Editor*: Kenneth Karman; The London Symphony Orchestra, conducted by Alan Silvestri; *Featured Musicians*: Jerry Hey (trumpet), Tom Scott (saxophone), Randy Waldman, Chet Swiatkowski (piano), Chuck Domanico (bass), Harvey Mason, Steve Schaefer (drums); *Album Producer*: Alan Silvestri; *Engineer*: Dennis Sands.

Selections: 1 Maroon Logo (:17); 2 Maroon Cartoon (3:21); 3 Valiant And Valiant (4:19); 4 The Weasels (2:04); 5 Hungarian Rhapsody (dueling pianos) (1:40); 6 Judge Doom (3:48); 7 Why Don't You Do Right? (J. McCoy)(3:02) *Amy Irving*; 8 No Justice For Toons (2:40); 9 The Merry-Go Round Broke Down (Roger's Song)(C. Friend/D. Franklin)(:45); 10 Jessica's Theme (2:01); 11 Toontown (4:40); 12 Eddie's Theme (5:18); 13 The Gag Factory (3:54); 14 The Will (1:06); 15 Smile Darn Ya Smile (C. O'Flynn/J. Meskill/M. Rice)/That's All Folks! (C. Friend/D. Franklin)(1:15); 16 End Title (4:56).

Review: The goofy, unlikely story of a down-at-the-heel private investigator in Hollywood's 1940s, and his involvement with (pardon the word!) 'toon characters is the mischievous premise upon which the hilarious *Who Framed Roger Rabbit* is based. Starring Bob Hoskins, looking appropriately baffled most of the time, Christopher Lloyd as the nefarious Judge Doom bent on destroying all the cute little characters, and Roger Rabbit, un-able to concentrate on acting ever since he and his wife, the sultry Jessica, have become estranged, the whole silly affair is a hoot from beginning to end, thanks largely to its brilliant inte-gration of live action and animation. Adding a comedic voice of its own, Alan Silvestri's frequently rollicking score keeps things in proper musical focus, with slyly tongue-in-cheek cues that enhanced the screen action and provided it with a strong peg. Heard on their own musical merits, however, some selections in this soundtrack album come across as too one-dimensional without the benefit of the dazzling visuals, in a clear indication of how well the score was intimately integrated in the picture. Exceptions include the uproarious "The Merry-Go-Round Broke Down (Roger's Song)"; Jessica's sexy rendition (with Amy Ir-ving's voice) of the standard "Why Don't You Do Right?"; "Jessica's Theme" and "Eddie's Theme," two flavorful instru-mentals; the frantically manic "Toontown," which, more than any other, captured the spirit of the film itself; and "Smile Darn Ya Smile/That's All, Folks!," which provided an appropriate coda to the film and to this disc.

The Whole Wide World ♪♪♪♪

1996, Mojo Trax Records; from the movie *The Whole Wide World,* Sony Pictures Classics, 1996.

Album Notes: *Music:* Hans Zimmer, Harry Gregson-Williams; *Orchestrations:* Harry Gregson-Williams; *Album Producers:* Harry Gregson-Williams, Slamm Andrews; *Engineer:* Slamm Andrews.

Selections: 1 The Love Theme (5:34); 2 Two Sides Of Bob (2:01); 3 Conan Emerges (5:23); 4 Novalyne Reflects (1:01); 5 The Telegram (3:42); 6 A Yarn Unfolds (4:13); 7 Letters At

Sunset/The Cabin (1:27); 8 Bob's Despair (4:09); 9 ...Let Go Of Your Mother (5:01); 10 Novalyne's Theme (0:00); 11 Sombrero (0:00); 12 End Titles (0:00).

Review: A word of explanation about the strange timings for the tracks listed above. The label copy lists twelve tracks; the CD only shows nine. Somebody, somewhere, goofed. Which, in a sense, is really too bad, because Hans Zimmer and Harry Gregson-Williams have written what is essentially a very lovely score for this unconventional little film based on the true-life three-year friendship between a schoolteacher and would-be novelist, Novalyne Price, and Robert E. Howard, creator of such pulp fiction fantasy characters as *Conan the Barbarian* and *Red Sonja.* Beyond the basic feelings that brought these two fiercely independent souls together (the deep intellectual and literary understanding they shared), other, equally profound elements conspired to keep them apart: Price's approach to writing was naturalistic, something for which Howard, more interested in the fantastic tales that came out of his imagination, had very little interest. The film, exploring what was apparently a platonic relationship, moved Zimmer and Gregson-Williams to write sev-eral cues in which the dominant moods are plainly romantic, sometimes with a solo instrument stating the melody over a synthesizer line. The two characters receive detailed motifs ("Two Sides of Bob," "Novalyne's Theme") written in a similar vein. Only occasionally, as in "Conan Emerges," do the com-posers indulge in a bit of epic writing which dissipates quickly. It all adds up to a generally very satisfying score, highly listenable. If only the tracks were properly listed...

Widow's Peak ♪♪♪

1994, Varese-Sarabande Records; from the movie *Widow's Peak,* Fine Line Features, 1994.

Album Notes: *Music:* Carl Davis; *Orchestrations:* Nic Raine; Orchestra conducted by Carl Davis; *Album Producer:* Carl Davis; *Engineer:* Mike Ross-Trevor.

Selections: 1 Main Titles (1:50); 2 Love Theme and Miss O'Hare (1:35); 3 Godfrey's Theme (2:09); 4 Edwina's Theme (1:33); 5 Grogen (1:05); 6 The Tea Party (1:11); 7 Maddie's Theme (1:21); 8 Lookout Point (1:22); 9 A Gold Ring (:46); 10 The Regatta (3:42); 11 Good Evening Maddie (1:41); 12 Leaving (1:21); 13 Lunch (2:18); 14 Boat Trips And Murder (1:51); 15 End Titles (3:09); 16 Fantasia On A Theme By Thomas Tallis (R. Vaughn Williams)(14:19) *The City Of Birmingham Symphony Orchestra, Norman Del Mar.*

Review: This delightfully laid-back collection of cues by Carl Davis transports us back to the early part of the 20th century, when a free spirited World War I widow stirs up a small Irish town. Though comforting at first, like the opening movement of a symphony, the tone eventually degrades into a murky darkness with the nightmarish cues "The Regatta" and "Boat Trips and Murder." The score is quite satisfying, but regretfully short at only about 24 minutes. Vaughn Williams' 14-minute "Fantasia on a Theme by Thomas Tallis" fills out the running time.

David Hirsch

The Wild Angels 🦴🦴🦴

1996, Curb Records; from the movie *The Wild Angels*, American-International Pictures, 1966.

Album Notes: *Songs*: Mike Curb, Harley Hatcher, Davie Allan; Music Arranged and conducted by Mike Curb; *Album Producer*: Mike Curb.

Selections: 1 Theme From The Wild Angels (1:23) *The Visitors, Barbara*; 2 Lonely In The Chapel (1:51) *The Hands Of Time*; 3 Blues Theme (2:09) *Davie Allan and The Arrows*; 4 Theme From The Wild Angels (instrumental)(1:32) *Davie Allan and The Arrows*; 5 Midnight Rider (1:50) *The Hands Of Time*; 6 Rockin' Angel (2:10) *Davie Allan and The Arrows*; 7 The Lonely Rider (1:03) *Davie Allan and The Arrows*; 8 The Unknown Rider (2:12) *Davie Allan and The Arrows*; 9 The Wild Angels Ballad (Dirge)(2:27) *Davie Allan and The Arrows*; 10 The Losers Burial (1:40) *Davie Allan and The Arrows*; 11 Losers Lament (1:32) *Davie Allan and The Arrows*; 12 The Dark Alley (1:42) *Davie Allan and The Arrows*; 13 Wild Angels Chase (3:41) *David Allan and The Arrows*; 14 The Last Ride (:41) *Davie Allan and The Arrows*.

Review: Though widely criticized at the time of its release for its excess of sex and violence, *The Wild Angels* is best remembered today as one of the first movies to effectively deal with the California motorcycle gangs, and to bring together a sensational cast, including Peter Fonda, Nancy Sinatra, Bruce Dern, Michael J. Pollard, and Diane Ladd. Another aspect of the film is its explosive soundtrack, featuring Davie Allan and The Arrows. In view of the many changes that have occurred in rock and in film music over the years, the songs, written by Mike Curb, Harley Hatcher and Davie Allan, may sound rather primitive today, but they have retained the raw edge that made them so vibrant and so much part of the film's appeal at the time, something this reissue on CD clearly evidences.

Wild in the Country

1995, RCA Records; from the movie *Wild in the Country*, 20th Century-Fox, 1961.

See: Elvis Presley in Compilations

Wild Orchid 🦴🦴🦴▷

1988, Sire Records; from the movie *Wild Orchid*, Vision p.d.g., 1988.

Album Notes: *Song Producers*: Geoff MacCormack, Simon Goldenberg, Andy Paley, Marlon Klein, Ofra Haza, Bezabel Aloni, Gragg Lansford, Wally Brill, Momo, Rick Smith, Jeff Vincent, Paul Pesco, David Rudder; *Album Producer*: Andy Paley; *Engineer*: Mark Linett.

Selections: 1 Main Title (G. MacCormack/S. Goldenberg)(3:13) *Paradise*; 2 Elejibo (R. Zulu/Y.Tropicalia)(4:17) *Margareth Menezes*; 3 Dark Secret (D. Rudder/A. Paley/P. Pesco/J. Vincent)(4:53) *David Rudder*; 4 Shake The Sheikh (Josch/Mullrich/Klein/Spremberg)(4:42) *Dissidenten*; 5 I Want To Fly/Slave Dream (O. Haza/B. Aloni/A. Amram)(7:04) *Ofra Haza*; 6 Bird Boy (N. Vasconcelos)(4:34) *Nana Vasconcelos & The Bushdancers*; 7 Love Song (B. Aloni)(2:28) *Ofra Haza*; 8 Twistin' With Annie (H. Ballard/A. Paley)(1:29) *Hank Ballard*; 9 Magic Jewelled Limousine (Momo)(5:04) *Nasa*; 10 Oxossi (Geronimo)(2:36) *Geronimo*; 11 Children Of Fire (Call Of Xango)(J. Vincent/P. Pesco/D. Rudder/A. Paley)(3:25) *David Rudder*; 12 Promised Land (K. Hyde/R. Smith/A. Thomas)(5:24) *Underworld*; 13 Flor cubana (C. Gogo)(2:50) *Simone Moreno*; 14 Wheeler's Howl (J. Wesley Harding/A. Paley/J. Vincent)(4:24) *The Rhythm Methodists*; 15 Love Theme (G. MacCormack/S. Goldenberg)(4:11) *Paradise*; 16 Just A Carnival (D. Rudder)(5:18) *David Rudder*; 17 Dark Secret (D. Rudder/A. Paley/P. Pesco/J. Vincent)(4:49) *David Rudder, Margareth Menezes*.

Review: A soundtrack album as exotic and vibrant as the Brazilian setting for this film, chronicling the power play between an unscrupulous millionaire with kinky sexual tendencies, a sleazy jetset businesswoman, and a young girl from the Midwest on her way to discovering Rio de Janeiro and her own eroticism. The film itself is not too terribly steamy, but this compilation certainly is, with many great tracks featuring some of the most endearing performers in both hemispheres — Ofra Haza, Nana Vasconcelos & The Bushdancers, Simone Moreno, on one hand; and David Rudder, Hank Ballard, Underworld, and The Rhythm Methodists, on the other.

Willow 🦴🦴🦴🦴

1988, Virgin Movie Music; from the movie *Willow*, LucasFilms, 1988.

Album Notes: *Music*: James Horner; *Orchestrations*: Greig McRitchie; *Music Editor*: Jim Henrikson; The London Symphony Orchestra and The King's College Choir, conducted by James Horner; *Featured Soloists*: Ian Underwood (Fairlight), Kazu Matsui (Sakauhachi), Mike Taylor, Tony Hennigan (Pap pipes,

Kena), Robin Williamson (Celtic harp, bagpipes); *Album Producers*: James Horner, Shawn Murphy; *Engineer*: Shawn Murphy.

Selections: 1 Elora Danan (9:45); 2 Escape From The Tavern (5:04); 3 Willow's Journey Begins (5:26); 4 Canyon Of Mazes (7:52); 5 Tir Asleen (10:47); 6 Willow's Theme (3:54); 7 Bavmorda's Spell Is Cast (18:11); 8 Willow The Sorcerer (11:55).

Review: An extraordinarily profuse score and album (73 minutes of music, and not a weak moment in it), *Willow* signaled James Horner's definite entry in the big time as a film composer. Brilliantly imaginative, opulent and emotionally charged, the music added its voice to this sword-and-sorcery tale about misfit heroes, evil magicians, dangerous animals, angry hordes of medieval knights, and a fragile little baby, protected by a dwarf, whose very existence will fulfill an ancient prophecy. Propelled by an epic main theme, called by resonant trumpets, the music devised by Horner, in turns elegiac and heroic, serves the story by providing a strongly imaginative and appropriately illustrative anchor. With robust themes enhancing the exciting action scenes with rich details, the score captures the pageantry and the thrill in the story in broad, colorful swathes that find an extraordinary resonance in the recording. The long selections, which regroups the cues into a comprehensive musical narrative, make for a sumptuous audio experience, one that compels the listener to return to it frequently, with renewed pleasure.

The Wind and the Lion ♫♫♫♫♫

1990, Intrada Records; from the movie *The Wind and the Lion*, M-G-M, 1975.

Album Notes: *Music*: Jerry Goldsmith; *Orchestrations*: Arthur Morton; Orchestra conducted by Jerry Goldsmith; *Album Producer*: Jerry Goldsmith; *Engineer*: George Horn.

Selections: 1 Main Title (1:30); 2 I Remember (Love Theme)(2:44); 3 The Horsemen (3:11); 4 True Feelings (2:33); 5 The Raisuli (2:12); 6 The True Symbol (2:34); 7 Raisuli Attacks (3:17); 8 Lord Of The Riff (2:43); 9 The Tent (1:49); 10 The Palace (2:29); 11 The Legend (4:01); 12 Morning Camp (3:19); 13 The Letter (2:34); 14 Something Of Value (3:49).

Review: Jerry Goldsmith's finest adventure score was written for this John Milius' historical epic about an Arabian desert chieftain played by Sean Connery who kidnaps an American woman during the presidential term of Teddy Roosevelt. From the thunderous percussion of its sweeping title music Goldsmith creates a score of amazing passion and scope, blending a gorgeous romantic melody with some of the most frenzied and rhythmically inventive action music of the composer's career. "Raisuli Attacks" has to stand as one of the most

insanely satisfying action blow-outs ever composed for film, with a devilishly complicated, Arabesque melody rattling through every section of the orchestra, climaxing in a deliriously powerful trumpet solo. Almost as good is the wild, dervish percussion of "The Horsemen" and the rich, barbaric pageantry of cues like "Lord of the Riff" and "The Palace." It's a score in the grand Hollywood tradition, but sparked by Goldsmith's inspired rhythmic and orchestral experimentation, a classic in every respect.

Jeff Bond

Wings of Desire ♫♫♫♪

1989, Nonesuch Records; from the movie *Wings of Desire*, Orion Films, 1989.

Album Notes: *Music*: Juergen Knieper; *Album Producer*: Emmanuel Chamboredon; *Engineer*: Edouard Meyer.

Selections: 1 Sky Over Berlin (4:48); 2 Song Of Childhood (:43) *Bruno Ganz*; 3 Song Of Childhood (:55) *Bruno Ganz*; 4 The Cathedral Of Books (4:45); 5 The Dying Man On The Bridge (2:31); 6 Potsdamerplatz (1:28); 7 Song Of Childhood (:50) *Bruno Ganz*; 8 The Glacial Valley (4:03); 9 The Old Mercedes (2:31); 10 The Paranoid Angel (:47); 11 Song Of Childhood (1:24) *Bruno Ganz*; 12 Marion's Declaration Of Love (5:45) *Solveig Dommartin*; 13 Final Word (:23) *Curt Bois*; 14 The Carny (N. Cave)(8:00) *Nick Cave & The Bad Seeds*; 15 Circus Music (L. Petitgand) (5:37); 16 Angel Fragments (L. Anderson)(2:24); 17 Six Bells Chime (S. Bonney/ B. Adams/R.S. Howard)(5:39) *Crime & The City Solution*; 18 From Her To Eternity (N. Cave/A. Lane/B. Bargeld/M. Harvey/B. Adamson/H. Race)(4:35) *Nick Cave & The Bad Seeds*; 19 Some Guys (L. Van Lieshout/S. Brown/P. Principal)(4:54) *Tuxedomoon*; 20 Pas Attendre (4:34) *Sprung aus der Wolken*; 21 When I Go (S. Birnback/R. Fortis/M. Franken/B. Sakharo/M. Spigel)(3:14) *Minimal Compact*.

Review: The eerily somber moods in Juergen Knieper's score seem totally appropriate for this offbeat story of a couple of angels coming back to Berlin in the 1980s to win their wings, with one of them falling in love with a trapeze artist and deciding he wants to become a human. But while the music works very well within the context of the film, on record it fails to create the desired effect, and proves eventually less compelling and arresting. Further confounding the listener, various texts in German prove a deterrent for those not familiar with the language. Several selections, composed by others (including Laurie Anderson) and placed after the score, sustain the moods with somewhat strident and abrasive sounds that prove more curious than musically attractive. Definitely not for every taste.

Wired ♫♫

1989, Varese-Sarabande; from the movie *Wired*, Lion Screen Entertainment, 1989.

Album Notes: *Music*: Basil Poledouris; *Featured Musicians*: Michael Ruff (keyboardso, Ralph Humphrey (drums), Jimmy Johnson, Jimmy Haslip (bass), W.G. Snuffy Walden, David Williams (guitar), Richard Elliott (saxophone), Marc Caz Macino (saxophone, harmonica), Lee Thornberg, Ralf Rickert (trumpet), Neil Portnow (percussion), Michael Ruff, Howard Smith (background vocals); *Album Producer*: Robert Townson; *Engineers*: Rick Hart, Tim Boyle.

Selections: 1 I'm A King Bee (J. Moore)(2:54) *Michael Chiklis, The Wired Band*; 2 634-5789 (S. Cropper/E. Floyd)(2:55) *Michael Chiklis, The Wired Band*; 3 I Can't Turn You Loose (O. Redding)(:26) *The Wired Band*; 4 Soul Man (I. Hayes/D. Porter)(2:54) *Michael Chiklis, Gary Groomes, The Wired Band*; 5 You Don't Know Like I Know (I. Hayes/D. Porter)(2:42) *Michael Chiklis, Gary Groomes, The Wired Band*; 6 Ravins Theme (B.F. Neary) (2:17) *Brian Francis Neary*; 7 The Choice (1:36); 8 Two Thousand Pound Bee (M. Taylor/D. Wilson)(2:52) *The Ventures*; 9 Still Looking For A Way To Say Goodbye (J. Tempchin/ L. Angelie)(3:51) *Richie Havens*; 10 Love Kills (J. Strummer)(3:59) *Joe Strummer*; 11 Angel Of Death (3:36); 12 You Are So Beautiful (B. Preston/B. Fisher)(2:12) *Michael Chiklis, Billy Preston*; 13 Eulogy (2:22).

Review: A filmed biography of John Belushi, *Wired*, which only missed Belushi's presence to succeed, retraced the comedian's meteoric career, from his early days on *Saturday Night Live*, to his untimely death. Much of this soundtrack album is devoted to recreations of "Blues Brothers" songs by Michael Chiklis, who portrayed Belushi, and Gary Groomes as Aykroyd, with an occasional assist from Billy Preston lending an aura of veracity. But the real thing ("real" if we don't consider that the Blues Brothers were already an imitation to begin with) being on another label, all we have here is a warmed-up, second-hand product. Basil Poledouris was evidently inspired by the storyline if we are to believe the four cues also included here, but his score, too, is given a short shrift in this sorry album.

Wisdom ♫♫

1988, Varese-Sarabande Records; from the movie *Wisdom*, Gladden Entertainment, 1988.

Album Notes: *Music*: Danny Elfman; *Orchestrations*: Steve Bartek, Danny Elfman; *Album Producers*: Danny Elfman, Steve Bartek; *Engineer*: Bill Jackson.

Selections: 1 Change Of Life (6:02); 2 The Mirror (1:52); 3 The Passion Of Wisdom (2:25); 4 Job Search (1:33); 5 The Big Heist (3:19); 6 Karen Decides (2:06); 7 Close Call In Albuquerque (4:25); 8 The Face Off (1:33); 9 Trouble (1:29); 10 The Shootout (2:25); 11 Wisdom Phone Home (2:39); 12 Heist (Part Two)(2:22); 13 Karen Bites The Bullet (1:44); 14 In The Desert (1:31); 15 Finale (3:44); 16 Main Title (3:26).

Review: A strongly accented synth score composed by Danny Elfman, this effort seems eons away from the more vibrant and interesting music he has created since. While the dry, minimalist sounds might have helped establish the basic atmosphere in this story of an idle youngster who robs a bank to impress his girlfriend, taken on their own melodic merits, they often fail to evoke more than a slight interest. Often arid in their expression, and devoid of any real spark, the cues frequently seem more formulaic than genuinely inspiring.

The Witches of Eastwick ♫♫♫♫

1987, Warner Bros. Records; from the movie *The Witches of Eastwick*, Warner Bros., 1987.

Album Notes: *Music*: John Williams; *Music Editor*: Ken Wannberg; Orchestra conducted by John Williams; *Album Producer*: John Williams; *Engineer*: Armin Steiner.

Selections: 1 The Township Of Eastwick (2:47); 2 The Dance Of The Witches (4:57); 3 Maleficio (3:20); 4 The Seduction Of Alex (2:40); 5 Daryl's Secrets (3:55); 6 The Seduction Of Suki and The Ballroom Scene (7:05); 7 Daryl Arrives (2:35); 8 The Tennis Game (2:52); 9 Have Another Cherry! (3:25); 10 Daryl Rejected (3:03); 11 The Ride Home (3:22); 12 The Destruction Of Daryl (5:39); 13 The Children's Carousel (1:54); 14 End Credits (The Dance Of The Witches Reprise)(4:57).

Review: If John Williams hadn't already enjoyed such a formidable reputation as the most eclectic composers around, this happily gritty, sardonic score would have clearly singled him out as one of the best. Delightfully anchored by the sprightly "Dance of the Witches," a motif that dominates it, the music details this modern tale of sorcery and, well... devil-may-care, about three women living in a quaint New England town full of upright people, who are yearning for Mr. Right... and find him in the guise of a wealthy newcomer who proves himself a smooth-talking, eyebrow-waggling, tantrum-throwing little devil (literally!). Matching the seriously tongue-in-cheek mode of this screen adaptation of John Updike's novel, starring Cher, Susan Sarandon, Michelle Pfeiffer and Jack Nicholson, the music is a constant feast of sparkling melodies and themes, which detail the screen action and add an extra ounce (make that a ton) of whimsy to it. Separated from it, it retains its humor and eclat, and proves totally enjoyable.

Witness ♪♪♪ʾ

1985, Varese-Sarabande Records; from the movie *Witness*, Paramount Pictures, 1985.

Album Notes: *Music:* Maurice Jarre; *Featured Musicians:* Michael Boddicker, Randy Kerber, Stewart Levin, Michel Mention, Chris Page, Pete Robinson, Clark Spangler, Nyle Steiner, Ian Underwood; *Album Producer:* Maurice Jarre; *Engineer:* Humberto Gatica.

Selections: 1 Witness (Main Title)/Journey To Baltimore (6:24); 2 The Murder (1:22); 3 Book's Disappearance (3:29); 4 Futility Of An Inside Job/ Delirious John (3:08); 5 Building The Barn (4:58); 6 Book's Sorrow (2:45); 7 Rachel And Book (Love Theme)/Beginning Of The End (4:40); 8 The Amish Are Coming (3:21).

Review: One of the first scores of Maurice Jarre's "electronic period" of the '80s, during which he turned out a number of impressive and effective synthesizer scores, *Witness* is perhaps the best of these electronic efforts, and one of the few synthesizer soundtracks written at the time which does not sound dated today. One reason is probably because Jarre elected to use synthesizers for artistic rather than budgetary reasons. (The film deals with the Amish society—a society which does not believe in musical instruments. As such Jarre determined an orchestral score would not be true to the ethos being depicted.) Although "new age" might best describe the overall tone of the soundtrack, Jarre's score has an eclectic array of moods, mirroring the film's elements of love story, crime thriller and human drama. Suspense cues in most electronic scores are often no more than noise, but the suspenseful

moments in *Witness* are enthralling and satisfyingly musical. The showpiece of the score however is Jarre's music for the barn-raising sequence, which is a noble, Americana-flavored piece, and certainly one of the finest moments in Jarre's career.

Paul Andrew MacLean

Wolf ♪♪♪♪

1994, Columbia/Sony Classical; from the movie *Wolf*, Columbia Pictures, 1994.

Album Notes: *Music:* Ennio Morricone; *Orchestrations:* Ennio Morricone; Orchestra conducted by Ennio Morricone; *Album Producer:* Ennio Morricone; *Engineer:* Dan Wallin; *Assistant Engineer:* Carl Glanville.

Selections: 1 Wolf And Love (3:33); 2 The Barn (1:59); 3 The Dream And The Deer (9:16); 4 The Moon (5:29); 5 Laura Goes To Join Wolf (2:20); 6 Laura And Wolf United (1:24); 7 First Transition (1:29); 8 The Howl And The City (3:22); 9 Animals And Encounters (4:37); 10 Laura Transformed (3:37); 11 Wolf (2:48); 12 Second Transition (1:18); 13 Will's Final Goodbye (1:31); 14 Chase (5:44); 15 Confirmed Doubts (3:41); 16 The Talisman (3:28); 17 Third Transition (:57); 18 A Shock For Laura (2:43); 19 Laura And Will (2:26); 20 Laura (2:37).

Review: Jack Nicholson had another memorable screen role in this great thriller about a middle-aged Manhattan book editor who is bitten by a wild animal, following a car accident on a dark country road, and begins to change into a werewolf as a result. Adding emotional power to this tale, Morricone wrote a musical subtext that enhances and defines the action, with sharp themes that describe it in uncompromising ways. The centerpiece of his score is a nine minute-plus cue, "The Dream and the Deer," in which some of the composer's signature effects (staccato chords darting in and out of a melodic theme) create an uneasy, foreboding mood. "The Chase," another highlight, is an explosive, fierce statement that leaves an unsettling impression as themes collide and combine to create an uneasy, active atmosphere. In the composer's body of work, *Wolf* definitely ranks as a breathtaking achievement.

Woodstock

Woodstock ♪♪♪♪

1970, Atlantic Records; from the movie *Woodstock*, Warner Bros., 1970.

Album Notes: *Album Producer:* Eric Blackstead; *Recording Engineers:* Edwin H. Kramer, Lee Osborne; *Remix Engineers:* Eric Blackstead, Stan Agol, Jack E. Hunt.

Selections: CD 1: 1 I Had A Dream (J. Sebastian)(2:35) *John B. Sebastian*; 2 Going Up The Country (A. Wilson)(3:20) *Canned Heat*; 3 Freedom (R. Havens) (4:36) *Richie Havens*; 4 Rock And Soul Music (J. McDonald/B. Melton/C. Hirsch/B. Barthol/D. Cohen)(2:08) *Country Joe & The Fish*; 5 Coming Into Los Angeles (A. Guthrie)(2:07) *Arlo Guthrie*; 6 At The Hop (A. Singer/J. Medora/ P. White)(2:00) *Sha-Na-Na*; 7 The "Fish" Cheer/I-Feel-Like-I'm-Fixin-To-Die-Rag (J. McDonald)(3:15) *Country Joe MacDonald*; 8 Drug Store Truck Drivin' Man (R. McGuin/G. Parsons)(2:07) *Joan Baez*; 9 Joe Hill (E. Robinson/A. Hayes)(2:40) *Joan Baez*; 10 Suite: Judy Blue Eyes (S. Sills)(8:11) *Crosby Stills & Nash*; 11 Sea Of Madness (N. Young)(3:24) *Crosby Stills Nash & Young*; 12 Wooden Ships (D. Crosby/S. Sills)(5:27) *Crosby Stills Nash & Young*; 13 We're Not Gonna Take It (P. Townshend)(4:25) *The Who*; 14 With A Little Help From My Friends (J. Lennon/P. McCartney)(7:40) *Joe Cocker*.

CD 2: 1 Crowd Rain Chant/Soul Sacrifice (C. Santana/G. Rolie/J. Areas/M. Carabello/D. Brown/M. Schrive)(8:06) *Santana*; 2 I'm Going Home (A. Lee) (9:20) *Ten Years After*; 3 Volunteers (P. Kantner/M. Balin)(2:44) *Jefferson Airplane*; 4 Medley (S. Stewart): Dance To The Music (2:10)/Music Lover (6:59)/ I Want To Take You Higher (4:07) *Sly & The Family Stone*; 5 Rainbows All Over Your Blues (J. Sebastian)(2:10) *John B. Sebastian*; 6 Love March (G. Dinwiddie/P. Wilson)(7:45) *Butterfield Blues Band*; 7 Star Spangled Banner (trad.)/Purple Haze and Instrumental Solo (J. Hendrix)(12:45) *Jimi Hendrix*.

Review: See entry below.

Woodstock Two 🎞🎞🎞🎞

1970, Atlantic Records; from the movie *Woodstock*, Warner Bros., 1970.

Album Notes: *Album Producer*: Eric Blackstead; *Recording Engineers*: Edwin H. Kramer, Lee Osborne; *Remix Engineers*: Eric Blackstead, Stan Agol, Jack E. Hunt.

Selections: CD 1: 1 Jam Back At The House (J. Hendrix)(6:09) *Jimi Hendrix*; 2 Izabella (J. Hendrix)(3:32) *Jimi Hendrix*; 3 Get My Heart Back Together (J. Hendrix)(8:02) *Jimi Hendrix*; 4 Saturday Afternoon/Won't You Try (P. Kantner)(4:52) *Jefferson Airplane*; 5 Eskimo Blue Day (G. Slick/P. Kantner)(6:00) *Jefferson Airplane*; 6 Everything's Gonna Be Alright (W. Jacobs)(8:36) *Butterfield Blues Band*.

CD 2: 1 Sweet Sir Galahad (J. Baez)(3:27) *Joan Baez*; 2 Guinevere (D. Crosby) (5:04) *Crosby Stills Nash & Young*; 3 4+20 (S. Stills)(2:10) *Crosby Stills Nash & Young*; 4 Marrakesh Express (G. Nash)(2:09) *Crosby Stills Nash & Young*; 5 My Beautiful People (M. Safka)(3:45) *Melanie*; 6 Birthday Of The Sun (M. Safka)(3:21) *Melanie*; 7 Blood Of The Sun (L.

West/F. Pappalardi/ G. Collins)(3:05) *Mountain*; 8 Theme For An Imaginary Western (J. Bruce/P. Brown)(4:44) *Mountain*; 9 Woodstock Boogie (R. Hite, Jr.)(12:55) *Canned Heat*; 10 Let The Sunshine In (G. MacDermot/J. Rado.G. Ragni)(:50) *Audience*.

Review: Looking back, that August weekend in 1969 marked more of an end than a beginning, and, thanks to the Michael Wadleigh film, the legend has now utterly obscured the muddy, can't hear/can't see reality. It still makes a nice legend, though, especially on these audio recordings: the abundant wrong notes you hear in the movie were corrected in a New York studio before the original three-LP set was released. And now, with Atlantic's nicely packaged 4-CD set, the sound is even better, and most of the artists missing from the film or the two previous *Woodstock* soundtrack albums have been brought into the fold. Career-making performances by the likes of Joe Cocker, Santana, The Who, and Sly and the Family Stone have weathered the years; the Band and Janis Joplin are no longer missing in action. "We must be in heaven, man."

Marc Kirkeby

A World Apart 🎞🎞🎞🎞

1988, RCA Victor Records; from the movie *A World Apart*, Atlantic Entertainment Group, 1988.

Album Notes: *Music*: Hans Zimmer, Al Clay, Brian Gulland, Gavin Wright, Chris Menges, Shawn Slovo, Judy Freeman; *Music Producer*: Hans Zimmer; *Engineers*: Al, Hans, with Chris Menges, Judy Freeman, Shawn Slovo.

Selections: 1 Nkosi Sikelela I-Afrika (trad.)(2:17) *The Messias Choir, Henry Mlauzi*; 2 A World Apart Suite (17:48); 3 Zithulele Mama (trad.)(1:55) *The Messias Choir*; 4 Amandla (H. Zimmer/ S. Slovo)(2:40); 5 The Pennywhistle Song (L. Majaivana)(2:49) *Lovemore Majaivana & The Zulu Band*; 6 Let's Twist Again (Kalman)(2:25) *Lovemore Majaivana & The Zulu Band*; 7 Bhayakala (L. Majaivana)(3:38) *Lovemore Majaivana & The Zulu Band*; 8 Molly's Theme (:51); 9 A World Apart End Title (4:59).

Review: Set in South Africa in the early 1960s, *A World Apart* took a sobering look at the apartheid system, and its effects on a family of white settlers who oppose the government policy and become the target of a crackdown from the authorities. A story such as this requested a compelling score, and Hans Zimmer provided it in a series of themes that detail the action, as seen through the eyes of Molly, the settlers' 13-year-old uncomprehending daughter. With solid assist from the Messias Choir, Zimmer's score explores the emotional implications in the story, often reaching deep into the moods to come up with forceful expressions that force the listener's attention. The cues, assembled together into a seamless musical suite, provide a narrative that is most engaging. Augmenting the score, selected traditional songs anchor the soundtrack album into its ethnic locale and bring a different touch of authenticity.

Wrestling Ernest Hemingway
♫♫♫

1994, Mercury Records; from the movie *Wrestling Ernest Hemingway*, Warner Bros., 1994.

Album Notes: *Music*: Michael Convertino; *Orchestrations*: John Neufeld, Conrad Pope; *Music Editor*: Tom Carlson; Orchestra conducted by Artie Kane; *Album Producer*: Michael Convertino; *Engineer*: Shawn Murphy.

Selections: 1 Wrestling Ernest Hemingway (1:57); 2 A Ship Offshore (3:58); 3 Rain (3:14); 4 La mujer de Antonio (M. Matamoros)(2:31); 5 Fireworks (6:54); 6 Time At Sea (5:27); 7 Nena (P. Ballagas)(2:59); 8 1939 (4:20); 9 Farewell Frank (4:09); 10 Lagrimas negras (M. Matamoros)(3:50).

Review: Starring Robert Duvall and Richard Harris as two older men trying to outdo each other in the fancily detailed stories they tell about their real (or imagined) past, *Wrestling Ernest Hemingway* received an eloquent musical support from Michael Convertino, whose enjoyably lyrical score finds a new life of its own in this attractive recording. Augmenting the most descriptive cues ("Fireworks," "Time At Sea," "1939"), a trio of tunes in Spanish add a definitely exotic flavor to the proceedings.

Wyatt Earp ♫♫♫

1994, Warner Bros. Records; from the movie *Wyatt Earp*, Warner Bros. Pictures, 1994.

Album Notes: *Music*: James Newton Howard; *Orchestrations*: Brad Dechter, Chris Boardman, James Newton Howard; *Music Editor*: Jim Weidman; The Hollywood Recording Musicians Orchestra, conducted by Marty Paich; *Featured Musicians*: Dean Park (guitars), Alasdair Fraser (solo violin), Frank Marocco (accordion), Phil Ayling (recorders); *Album Producers*: James Newton Howard, Michael Mason; *Engineer*: Shawn Murphy; *Assistant Engineers*: Sue MacLean, Greg Dennen, Mark Eshelman, Bill Talbott.

Selections: 1 Main Title (4:40); 2 Home From The War (1:59); 3 Going To Town (2:00); 4 The Wagon Chase (2:42); 5 Mattie Wants Children (1:56); 6 Railroad (1:50); 7 Nicholas Springs Wyatt (1:31); 8 Is That Your Hat? (2:07); 9 The Wedding (3:16); 10 Stillwell Makes Bail (2:37); 11 It All Ends Now (1:54); 12 Urilla Dies (4:35); 13 Tell Me About Missouri (2:56); 14 The Night

Before (3:11); 15 O.K. Corral (7:02); 16 Down By The River (2:58); 17 Kill 'Em All (5:02); 18 Dodge City (1:02); 19 Leaving Dodge (1:24); 20 Indian Charlie (1:33); 21 We Stayed Too Long (1:50); 22 Winter To Spring (1:18); 23 It Happened That Way (1:10).

Review: *Tombstone* was a major hit in the winter of 1993, and subsequently seemed to take out the wind from the sails of *Wyatt Earp,* the more ambitious but far less successful 1994 epic from star Kevin Costner and co-writer/director Lawrence Kasdan. Well-acted but pretentious and often downright boring, *Earp* was a financial disaster and critical disappointment, though no fingers will ever be pointed at James Newton Howard's outstanding score, which works as both a reflection on the conventions of the western genre and the heroic nature of Earp himself, capturing the various dimensions of the setting and the characters along the way. The score boasts a number of impressive themes and musical ideas, and has been copied in numerous films and movie trailers since; even if you never see the film, Newton Howard's soundtrack stands as a superior film score and comes highly recommended.

Andy Dursin

See also: Hour of the Gun and Tombstone

The Year of Living Dangerously ♫♫♫◦

1983, Varese-Sarabande Records; from the movie *The Year of Living Dangerously*, M-G-M/UA, 1983.

Album Notes: *Music*: Maurice Jarre; *Electronic Realization*: Spencer Lee, Maurice Jarre; *Album Producer*: Maurice Jarre; *Engineer*: Joe Gastwirt.

Selections: 1 Wayang Kulit (4:37); 2 Poverty And Misery (2:47); 3 The Death Of A Child (4:38); 4 Kwan (3:20); 5 Enchantment At Tuga (4:08); 6 Djakarta (3:44); 7 What Can We Do? (3:13); 8 Kwan's Sacrifice (4:58).

Review: Described by Maurice Jarre as "music like an Asian mist," *The Year of Living Dangerously* was his first foray into predominantly electronic scoring. Jarre's encyclopedic knowledge of ethnic music is also put to good use in this film, which deals with journalists covering political unrest in 1960s Indonesia. Stylistically, the score might superficially be described as "new age," given its airy electronic passages, but Jarre also invests the score with music of the region, and features indigenous instruments. Some tracks (such as "Wayang Kulit") are rather atonal and non-melodic, and do not make for enjoyable listening. However they are counterbalanced by tracks like "Enchantment at Tugu" and "Kwan's Sacrifice" both of which offer beautiful, ethereal evocations of Southeast Asia.

It should perhaps be pointed out that the piano theme heard in the love scenes is not included on this recording, as it is not by Maurice Jarre, but from a Vangelis recording which the director tracked into the film (and is available on the album *Opera Sauvage*, on Polydor). However, Maurice Jarre's score remains a thoroughly mystical and sensuous musical experience, and one of the best examples of syntho-ethnic scoring on disc.

Paul Andrew MacLean

Year of the Comet 🎵🎵🎵⁷

1992, Varese-Sarabande; from the movie *Year of the Comet*, Castle Rock Entertainment, 1992.

Album Notes: *Music*: Hummie Mann; *Orchestrations*: Brad Dechter; *Music Editor*: Scott Grusin; Orchestra conducted by Kurt Bestor; *Album Producers*: Hummie Mann, Rick Riccio; *Engineer*: Rick Riccio.

Selections: 1 Maggie Goes To Scotland (2:08); 2 The Seduction (1:46); 3 Finding The Bottle (3:37); 4 Helicopter Chase (3:31); 5 MacPherson Castle (2:23); 6 In Pursuit Of Jamie (3:32); 7 Fight On The Lake (1:29); 8 Nico Comes On Strong (1:02); 9 Driving Through Scotland (:43); 10 Formula On The Box (:57); 11 Maggie's Dive (:44); 12 Chasing The Greeks (:49); 13 It's Gotta Be Love (2:20); 14 The Injection (3:20); 15 Philippe Flips Out (1:23); 16 End Credits (5:13).

Review: This is an energetic and lovely score by Hummie Mann, best known for his orchestrations on many of Marc Shaiman's soundtracks (including *City Slickers*). Despite having an interesting premise and a good cast, *Year of the Comet* was an underwhelming comedy-adventure from Peter Yates and writer William Goldman. Mann's score makes the most of the film's Irish setting and ultimately becomes far more memorable than the picture itself; the tone is sprightly and fun, and Mann's main theme is nothing short of excellent, the kind of infectious tune you wish other soundtracks were built around. Curiously enough, Mann's music was, in fact, a replacement score for the rejected, original soundtrack written by John Barry, a fact that further mystified viewers when Barry's music was prominently heard in the coming attractions trailer!

Andy Dursin

Year of the Gun 🎵

1991, Milan Records; from the movie *Year of the Gun*, Triumph Release, 1991.

Album Notes: *Music*: Bill Conti; *Orchestrations/Synthesizer Programming*: Jack Eskew; *Music Editor*: Steve Livingston; *Album Producer*: Bill Conti; *Engineer*: Lee DeCarlo.

Selections: 1 Main Title (4:37); 2 The Kidnapping (2:22); 3 Lia Rrives Home (2:00); 4 David And Lia (2:01); 5 The Bank Job (2:40); 6 Party Crashers (4:01); 7 Alison And David Walking (2:25); 8 Bianchi's Guest (1:45); 9 Bianchi Follows (3:44); 10 The First Phone Call (1:49); 11 Moro/Terrorists/Lipstick (4:24); 12 Back Door To Venice (3:07); 13 Sunday Afternoon (1:37); 14 Another Phone Call (4:49); 15 Dave's Apartment Trashed (1:32); 16 The Graveyard (2:29); 17 The Big Chase (3:57); 18 Lia Says Trust Me (2:59); 19 Balcony To Grave (2:29); 20 Not Geraldo (2:28); 21 End Title (3:34).

Review: This Bill Conti effort, performed on synthesizers, starts off well enough, but soon degrades into a lackluster collection of mind-numbing effects cues. Despite a passably curious "Main Title," featuring a chanting male choir, the bulk of the score sounds more as if it was composed by some inexperienced youngster rather than the Academy Award-winning artist responsible for *The Right Stuff* and *Rocky*. The score also has one of the most unromantic love cues ever heard ("Alison and David Walking"). None of the music ever fully projects even the slightest effective emotional response. Track #13, "Sunday Afternoon" is so poorly distorted (was this done intentionally?), it should have been left out of the album. Packaging, with no liner notes and just one blurry cover photo, is equally uninspiring. How the mighty have fallen.

David Hirsch

Yor the Hunter from the Future 🎵🎵🎵🎵

1993, Label X Records; from the movie *Yor the Hunter from the Future*, Columbia Pictures, 1983.

Album Notes: *Music*: John Scott; The Unione Musicisti di Roma, conducted by John Scott; *Album Producer*: John Scott; *Engineer*: Paolo Enditti.

Selections: 1 Ka-Laa Dance (2:27); 2 Death Rules This Land (4:05); 3 Pursued By Pygmies (2:28); 4 Queen Road (1:48); 5 Into The Storm (1:36); 6 Yor's Salon de Refuses (29:43).

Review: It's hard to believe, but the majority of this John Scott orchestral score was replaced by an electronic "disco" effort by Guido and Maurizio De Angelis. Of course, if you see the film, and its slapdash mix of stone age and post-Apocalypse genre concepts, you'll realize that the filmmakers never had any idea what they were aiming for. Despite all this, Scott has produced a wonderful score that, taken out of context, has an unabashed innocence and romantic quality. Instead of concentrating on the sci-fi elements, he focused on elements in Yor's primitive and naive culture. Where he was able to draw on all this inspiration remains a mystery, but Scott has always exhibited a knack to rise far above some of the more poorly realized films he has had the unfortunate luck to have been associated with. In fact, hiring him often seems to be the only genuinely inspired idea some of these filmmakers have. On *Yor*, however, that wasn't true in the end. All the unused cues, almost 30 minutes of music, have been assembled into one suite and released on this CD for the first time. Obviously, no one wanted to go back and look at the film to try and title the music. Three of the four individually numbered and titled tracks (except "Death Rules This Land") appeared on the original LP issue along with twelve cues by the De Angelis brothers. These four were all the music by Scott that miraculously survived the final cut.

David Hirsch

You Only Live Twice ♪♪♪♪▷

1988, EMI-Manhattan; from the movie *You Only Live Twice*, United Artists, 1967.

Album Notes: *Music*: John Barry; *Lyrics*: Leslie Bricusse; *Orchestrations*: John Barry; Orchestra conducted by John Barry.

Selections: 1 Title Song: You Only Live Twice (2:39) *Nancy Sinatra*; 2 Capsule In Space (2:51); 3 Fight At Kobe Dock/Helga (2:51); 4 Tanaka's World (2:04); 5 A Drop In The Ocean (2:15); 6 The Death Of Aki (4:16); 7 Mountains And Sunsets (3:06); 8 The Wedding (2:42); 9 James Bond Astronaut? (3:25); 10 Countdown For Blofeld (2:31); 11 Bond Averts World War Three (2:12); 12 End Title: You Only Live Twice (2:45) *Nancy Sinatra*.

Review: This James Bond score, broadly informed by Nancy Sinatra's title song which bookends it, is another John Barry feast, with cues that cleverly enhance the overblown screen action, this time set in Japan, and introduce many new themes, some of them subtly accented with koto sonorities. The sound on this CD reissue is unpleasantly strident and brash, particularly in the brass figures, but don't let that deter you from enjoying it... until, that is, EMI decides to properly remix and master the whole series, hopefully complementing each title with some of the previously unreleased tracks that are still dormant in the company's vaults.

Young Bess ♪♪♪♪♪

1990, Prometheus/Belgium; from the movie *Young Bess*, M-G-M, 1953.

Album Notes: *Music*: Miklos Rozsa; Orchestra conducted by Miklos Rozsa; *Album Producer*: Adam Hart; *Engineer*: John Dekeersmaeker.

Selections: 1 Prelude/Hatfield/Reminiscing/Exit Anne Boleyn (4:33); 2 Changing Mothers/King Henry/New Stepmother/Hat-field Again (2:35); 3 Tom Seymour's Mission/Whitehall/The Prince Of Wales (3:47); 4 Eavesdropping (1:13); 5 Dies Irae (5:07); 6 Princess Elizabeth/Appointment With Love (2:00); 7 Anne Boleyn's Daughter/Dinner Music (2:40); 8 Dreams/Reality/ Disillusion (3:21); 9 The King's Diary/The King's Finances/ The King's English (3:01); 10 Returning Hero (:19); 11 Royal Tact/Old Harry/Chelsea (5:48); 12 The King's Ballad (3:08); 13 Desperate Love/Crossroads/ Catherine's End (5:51); 14 Bad News/Night Visitor/Farewell (6:43); 15 Inquisition/Alone (3:08); 16 Finale (2:01).

Review: This third volume in the Belgian label Prometheus' series, "The Spectacular Film Music of Miklos Rozsa," presents a rare treat: the score the composer created for a big historical film about the early years of the young woman who was to become the Queen of England, starring Jean Simmons, Stewart Granger, Deborah Kerr, and Charles Laughton, the latter reprising the role of Henry VIII that had brought him fame in 1933 in Alexander Korda's *The Private Life of Henry VIII*. Though largely fictional, the film, based on Margaret Irwin's novel of skullduggery under the Tudors, was a sweeping chronicle of life in the 16th century, told in breathtaking cinematographic details, which inspired Rozsa to write a fine, romantic effort, full to the brim with gorgeously heroic accents, jaunty little tunes, and effusive love themes. Though recorded in mono, and with occasional slight image shifting and hiss, the recording is vibrant and richly evocative.

Young Frankenstein ♪♪♪▷

1997, MCA Special Products; from the movie *Young Frankenstein*, 20th Century-Fox, 1975.

Album Notes: *Music*: John Morris; *Orchestrations*: John Morris; *Album Producer*: Steve Barri; *Engineer*: Gene Cantamessa.

Selections: 1 Main Title (2:53); 2 That's Fron-kon-steen! (3:14); 3 Train Ride To Transylvania/The Doctor Meets Igor (2:19); 4 Frau Blucher (2:25); 5 Grandfather's Private Library (3:19); 6 It's Alive! (3:27); 7 He Was My Boyfriend (3:22); 8 My Name Is Frankenstein! (3:18); 9 Introduction/Puttin' On The Ritz (I. Berlin) (3:33); 10 A Riot Is An Ugly Thing (:54); 11 He's Broken Loose (6:15); 12 The Monster Talks (1:50); 13 Wedding Night/ End Title (1:09); 14 Theme From Young Frankenstein (2:53) *Rhythm Heritage*.

Review: One of Mel Brooks' most successful lampoons, *Young Frankenstein* brought together several of the director's "regulars" in a film that happily spoofed all the tenets of the monster genre, all the way to the black and white lensing and atmospheric settings that echoed the moods of the original and its numerous sequels. The icing on the cake was John Morris' oppressively romantic-with-a-wink score, dominated by the plaintive violin tune played by Frau Blucher (horses braying in the background) first to lure Dr. Fron-kon-steen into his grandfather's private library, then to seduce the monster into submission after he escapes. Large portions of dialogue vividly recall some of the film's most hilarious moments, and the album also contains the ultimate sendup, the Monster singing Irving Berlin's "Puttin' on the Ritz." The only discordant note in the set is Rhythm Heritage's totally unnecessary contempo rendition of the Main Theme.

The Young Lions/ This Earth Is Mine 🦴🦴🦴🦴

1993, Varese-Sarabande; from the movies *The Young Lions*, 20th Century-Fox, 1958; and *This Earth Is Mine*, Universal-International Pictures, 1959.

Album Notes: *Music*: Hugo Friedhofer; *The Young Lions*: The 20th Century-Fox Orchestra, conducted by Lionel Newman; *This Earth Is Mine*: The Universal-International Orchestra, conducted by Joseph Gershenson; *CD Producers*: Robert Townson, Dub Taylor.

Selections: CD 1: *THE YOUNG LIONS*: 1 Main Title/Ski Run (2:03); 2 Christian And Francoise/Michael's Theme (5:38); 3 Hope And Noah (4:49); 4 The Captain's Lady (2:07); 5 North American Episode (5:44); 6 Parisian Interlude (5:09); 7 Berlin Aftermath (3:13); 8 A Letter From Noah (2:13); 9 River Crossing (3:03); 10 Death Of Christian/End Title (5:22).

CD 2: *THIS EARTH IS MINE*: 1 Main Title (S. Cahn/J. Van Heusen)(3:27) *Bob Grabeau*; 2 Martha's Vineyard (1:58); 3 The Kiss (1:50); 4 Wine Caves (2:36); 5 Good Catch (3:21); 6 Amorous Andre (1:31); 7 Confessional (4:40); 8 John And Mother (1:05); 9 Be Honest (3:35); 10 Mountain Vineyard (2:26); 11 Catastrophe (2:49); 12 Hospital (2:19); 13 Back To The Soil (2:55); 14 End Title (3:41).

Review: One of Hollywood's most sadly neglected early composers, Hugo Friedhofer is in dire need of a total reevaluation of his impressive achievements. For a long while considered a brilliant orchestrator rather than a composer in his own right, it was not until he reached his full maturity in the late 1940s-early 1950s that he began to be taken seriously as a film scorer, eventually contributing an impressive catalogue of great works, including *The Best Years of Our Lives, Vera Cruz, An Affair to Remember* and *Boy on a Dolphin,* among the best known. From a 1958 World War II drama came *The Young Lions,* for which Friedhofer received an Oscar nomination. Based on a novel by Irwin Shaw, the film presents strikingly

eloquent views of the war as seen through the eyes of a motley group of GIs on one side, and German officers on the other. In the first group, Montgomery Clift portrays an American Jew, confronted with racial prejudice, and Dean Martin a would-be draft dodger caught in spite of himself by the daunting task ahead of him. Portraying a young German officer is Marlon Brando, a true believer in Hitler's Nazi theories, whose sense of humanity eventually found him at odds with the Fuehrer's tenets about total annihilation of the Jewish people. In scoring the film, Friedhofer provided themes and musical ideas that sustained the action, but stayed behind it rather than helped propel it. As a result, his score was a succession of subdued cues with a relatively passive role, that filled a purpose and were serviceable at best, even though they were powerfully adapted to the film's dramatic atmosphere.

A score of a different color, *This Earth Is Mine,* composed a year later, provided Friedhofer with a romantic subject which inspired him to write a richly melodic series of themes. Introduced by a dispensable title tune, courtesy of Sammy Cahn and James Van Heusen, who must have written more title songs than anyone else (with the possible exception of Jay Livingston and Ray Evans), the score unfolds with great tender feelings to illustrate this story, based on a novel by Alice Tisdale Hobart and set in the 1930s in California's Napa Valley, about an older generation of vintners, eager to preserve the traditions that have been their pride, and younger tyros, more interested in a quick profit. Outlining specific moments in the action, and drawing sharp portraits of the various participants (including Claude Rains, Rock Hudson and Jean Simmons), Friedhofer's music is rich in melodic details, and very attractive.

The presentation of both scores in a 2-CD set was a great idea!

Younger and Younger 🦴🦴▹

1993, Varese-Sarabande Records; from the movie *Younger and Younger*, Vine International Pictures, 1993.

Album Notes: *Music*: Hans Zimmer; *Arrangements*: Hans Zimmer; *Featured Musicians*: Alex Wurman, Bob Telson (Mighty Wurlitzer); *Album Producers*: Hans Zimmer, Percy Adlon, Alex Wurman; *Engineers*: Jay Rifkin, Bret Newman.

Selections: 1 Vorspiel (8:32); 2 My Organ (A. Wurman)(1:48) *Don Jon Vaughn*; 3 Roses (1:41); 4 Lazy Afternoon (3:42); 5 The Morning After (A. Wurman)(1:42) *Don Jon Vaughn*; 6 Ghosts In Love (1:16); 7 Penny From Heaven (2:08); 8 Show Me Your Face (B. Telson/L. Breuer)(8:06) *Donald Sutherland, Lisa Angel*; 9 Rabbits (A. Wurman)(2:15) *Don Jon Vaughn*; 10 Disco (A.

Wurman) (3:47); 11 Show Me Your Face (reprise)(B. Telson/L. Breuer)(4:01).

Review: This is an odd collection of moderately pleasing, but insubstantial synthesizer music realized by Hans Zimmer. Despite the fact that he is the only composer credited on the cover, he only wrote four of the album's ten tracks. Zimmer's score cues are interpolated with additional material by Alex Wurman, performed in most cases on The California Theatre's Mighty Wurlitzer organ. The CD is most notable only because actor Donald Sutherland sings (!) a duet with Lisa Angel on the song "Show Me Your Face" (written by Bob Telson and Lee Breuer). Otherwise, it's generally a vacuous effort, with primitive electronic sounds, that vainly attempts, and fails, to create an intimate romantic fantasy score.

David Hirsch

Zulu ♪♪♪♪

1988, Silva Screen Records; from the movie *Zulu,* **Embassy Pictures, 1964.**

Album Notes: *Music:* John Barry; Orchestra conducted by John Barry; *Album Producers:* David Stoner, James Fitzpatrick.

Selections: *ZULU:* 1 Main Title Theme/Isandhlwana 1879 (2:32) *Richard Burton;* 2 News Of The Massacre/Rorke's Drift Threated (3:00); 3 Wagon's Over (1:38); 4 First Zulu Appearance And Assault (5:22); 5 Durnford's Horses Arrive And Depart/The Third Assault (3:05); 6 Zulu's Final Appearance And Salute (3:10); 7 The V.C. Roll and "Men Of Harlech" (1:00) *Richard Burton;*

ELIZABETH TAYLOR IN LONDON: 8 Elizabeth Theme (3:26);

FROM RUSSIA WITH LOVE: 9 Theme (L. Bart)(1:54);

FOUR IN THE MORNING: 10 Theme (1:58);

FROM RUSSIA WITH LOVE: 11 007 (2:21);

ZULU: 12 Monkey Feathers (2:07); 13 Fancy Dance (1:57);

FOUR IN THE MORNING: 14 Judi Comes Back (2:58);

ELIZABETH TAYLOR IN LONDON: 15 The London Theme (3:16);

ZULU: 16 Tetha Leyanto (D. Bethela)(1:58); 17 High Grass (1:58); 18 Zulu Stamp (3:22); 19 Big Shield (3:06); 20 Ngenzini (B. Knoza)(2:32); 21 Kinky (J. Scott)(2:32); 22 Yesterday's Gone (C. Stuart/J. Kidd)(2:18) *Chad & Jeremy;* 23 No Tears For Johnny (D. Springsfield/J. Hawker)(2:13) *Chad & Jeremy;*

ALIKI, MY LOVE: 24 Aliki (M. Hadjidakis)(2:57); 25 The Loneliness Of Autumn (G. Calvi)(3:25).

Review: An impressive retelling of a little known historic incident—the total annihilation of a squadron of British soldiers at the hands of more than 4,000 Zulu warriors—*Zulu* was a major release, enhanced by the generally high quality of the film in all its aspects, including John Barry's seriously-minded score. For the composer, the production marked the first time when he was given an opportunity to display his talent in films other than light comedies or action spy thrillers, that were often dismissed as being too insignificant. For the film, he fashioned a hard-hitting series of cues, accented by the brass instruments anticipating and signalling the eventual doom of the valiant group of soldiers assigned to defend the garrison at Rorke's Drift against their Zulu foes. Though the film itself lasted over two hours, Barry only composed 16 minutes of dense, dramatic music, sparsely used throughout, and augmented with traditional Zulu dances.

To give the CD longer playing time, other selections have been added, including excerpts from Barry's *Elizabeth Taylor in London* and *Four in the Morning,* two scores that cry out to be reissued in complete form, as well as pop vocals by Chad and Jeremy and other instrumental tracks that were arranged by John Barry at a time when his composing career had not yet taken its full flight. Sonically speaking, the CD is not all that it should be, with some analog drops and hiss particularly noticeable on some of the tracks.

Ain't Misbehavin' ♫♫♫♫♫

1987, RCA Victor; from the Broadway production *Ain't Misbehavin'*, 1978.

Album Notes: *Music*: Thomas "Fats" Waller; *Lyrics*: Andy Razaf, Lester A. Santly, Clarence Williams, Richard Maltby, Jr., Murray Horwitz, Billy Rose, J.C. Johnson, George Marion, Jr., Ed Kirkeby; *Featured Musicians*: Luther Henderson, Hank Jones (piano), Seldon Powell (saxophone), Joe Marshall (drums), Arvell Shaw (bass), John Parran (clarinet), Virgil Jones (trumpet), Janice Robinson (trombone); *Cast*: Nell Carter, Andre De Shields, Armelia McQueen, Ken Page, Charlaine Woodard; *Album Producer*: Thomas Z. Shepard; *Engineer*: Paul Goodman.

Selections: CD 1: 1 Ain't Misbehavin'/Lookin' Good But Feelin' Bad/'T Ain't Nobody Bizness If I Do (P. Grainger/E. Robbins)(6:12) *Andre De Shield*; 2 Honeysuckle Rose (3:58) *Ken Page, Nell Carter*; 3 Squeeze Me (3:37) *Amelia McQueen*; 4 Handful Of Keys (3:18)Company; 5 I've Got A Feeling I'm Falling (3:34) *Nell Carter*; 6 How Ya Baby (3:06) *Andre De Shields, Charlaine Woodard*; 7 The Jitterbug Waltz (5:48) Company; 8 The Ladies Who Sing With The Band (2:34) *Andre De Shields, Ken Page*; 9 Yacht Club Swing (1:59) *Charlaine Woodard*; 10 When The Nylons Bloom Again (3:40) *Amelia McQueen, Charlaine Woodard, Nell Carter*; 11 Cash For Your Trash (2:10) *Nell Carter*; 12 Off-Time (2:46)Company; 13 The Joint Is Jumpin' (2:16)Company.

CD 2: 1 Entr'acte (3:06); 2 Spreadin' Rhythm Around (J. Mc-Hugh/T. Koehler) (2:11)Company; 3 Lounging At The Waldorf (3:41) *Amelia McQueen, Charlaine Woodard, Ken Page, Nell Carter*; 4 The Viper's Drag (5:18) *Andre De Shields*; 5 Mean To Me (R. Turk/F. Ahlert)(3:02) *Nell Carter*; 6 Your Feet's Too Big (A. Benson/F. Fisher)(3:06) *Ken Page*; 7 That Ain't Right (N. Cole)(3:03) *Andre De Shields, Amelia McQueen*; 8 Keepin' Out Of Mischief Now (3:47) *Charlaine Woodard*; 9 Find Out What They Like (3:31) *Amelia McQueen, Nell Carter*; 10 Fat And Greasy (P. Grainger/C. Johnson) (2:49) *Andre De Shields, Ken*

Page; 11 Black And Blue (4:59)Company; 12 Finale: I'm Gonna Sit Right Down And Write Myself A Letter (F. Ahlert/J. Young)/Two Sleepy People (H. Carmichael/F. Loesser)/I've Got My Fingers Crossed (J. McHugh/T. Koehler)/I Can't Give You Anything But Love (J. McHugh/ D. Fields)/It's A Sin To Tell A Lie (B. Mayhew)/Honeysuckle Rose (reprise) (7:12) *Ken Page, Amelia McQueen, Charlaine Woodard, Andre De Shields, Nell Carter*.

Review: The songs of Thomas "Fats" Waller received the Broadway treatment in a great revue that not only created a stir at the time it opened on May 9, 1978, but paved the way for other similar shows, including *Sophisticated Ladies* and *Eubie*. With just five fantastically gifted performers on stage (Nell Carter, Armelia McQueen, Charlaine Woodard, Ken Page and Andre De Shields), a solid band led by Luther Henderson, and a wealth of wonderful numbers, the show became the most talked-about hit on Broadway that season, won several Tony Awards, including the one for Best Musical, and enjoyed an unprecedented run of 1,604 performances.

Aladdin ♫♫♫♭

1992, Walt Disney Records; from the animated feature *Aladdin*, Walt Disney, 1992.

Album Notes: *Music*: Alan Menken; *Lyrics*: Howard Ashman, Tim Rice; *Orchestrations*: Danny Troob; *Vocal Arrangements*: David Friedman; *Musical Direction*: David Friedman; *Cast*: Bruce Adler, Jonathan Freeman, Brad Kane, Lea Salonga, Robin Williams; *Album Producers*: Alan Menken, Tim Rice; *Engineer*: Bruce Botnock.

Selections: 1 Arabian Nights (1:19) *Bruce Adler*; 2 Legend Of The Lamp (1:25); 3 One Jump Ahead (2:23) *Brad Kane*; 4 Street Urchins (1:53); 5 One Jump Ahead (reprise)(1:00) *Brad Kane*; 6 Friend Like Me (2:26) *Robin Williams*; 7 To Be Free (1:39); 8 Prince Ali (2:51) *Robin Williams*; 9 A Whole New World (2:40) *Brad Kane, Lea Salonga*; 10 Jafar's Hour (2:43); 11 Prince Ali (reprise)(1:08) *Jonathan Freeman*; 12 The Ends Of The Earth (1:35); 13 The Kiss (1:51); 14 On A Dark Night (2:55); 15 Jasmine Runs Away (:46); 16 Marketplace (2:36); 17 The Cave Of Wonders (4:57); 18 Aladdin's Word (1:51); 19 The Battle (3:38); 20 Happy End In Agrabah (4:11); 21 A Whole New World (4:07) *Peabo Bryson, Regina Belle*.

Review: Following the success of the *Little Mermaid* and *Beauty and the Beast*, Alan Menken and Howard Ashman turned their talent to creating an animated musical based on the 1001-night tale of Aladdin. A large measure of the film's success was due to Robin Williams' inspired performance as the voice of the Genie (which was drawn after Williams' mimicries). The score itself was true to the formula already set by the previous two films, with a standard share of romantic numbers for Ali and Jasmine (vocals by Brad Kane and Lea Salonga), some exciting instrumentals, a couple of humorous moments for the Genie, and a hit song ("A Whole New World"), which won an Academy Award that year.

An American in Paris ♫♫♫♫

1996, Rhino Records; from the screen musical *An American in Paris*, M-G-M, 1951.

Album Notes: *Music*: George Gershwin; *Lyrics*: Ira Gershwin; *Orchestrations*: Conrad Salinger, Al Sendrey, Skip Martin, Johnny Green, Benny Carter, Robert Franklyn, Wally Heglin; *Arrangements*: Saul Chaplin, Johnny Green, Benny Carter, Conrad Salinger, Skip Martin, Wally Heglin, Al Sendrey; The M-G-M Studio Orchestra and Chorus, conducted by Johnny Green; *Cast*: Gene Kelly (Jerry Mulligan), Leslie Caron (Lise Bouvier), Oscar Levant (Adam Cook), Georges Guetary (Georges Matthieu); *Album Producers*: Michael Feinstein, George Feltenstein, Bradley Flanagan; *Engineer*: Doug Schwartz.

Selections: CD 1: 1 Main Title (An American In Paris/'S Wonderful/I Got Rhythm)(1:35)Orchestra; 2 Paris Narration/Left Bank (3:34)Orchestra; 3 Nice Work If You Can Get It (outtake)(1:05) *Georges Guetary*; 4 Embraceable You (2:48)Orchestra; 5 By Strauss (3:43) *Gene Kelly, Georges Guetary, Mac MacLain, Grace Stark, Pete Roberts*; 6 Street Exhibit (:44)Orchestra; 7 I Got Rhythm (3:43) *Gene Kelly*; 8 But Not For Me (1:21) *Benny Carter and His Orchestra*; 9 Medley: Do, Do, Do/Bidin' My Time/I've Got A Crush On You/Love Is Here To Stay (4:07) *Benny Carter and His Orchestra*; 10 Someone To Watch Over Me (outtake)(1:17) *Benny Carter and His Orchestra*; 11 Medley: My Cousin In Milwaukee/A Foggy Day/The Half-Of-It-Dearie Blues/But Not For Me)(outtake)(3:33) *Oscar Levant*; 12 Tra-La-La (3:44) *Gene Kelly, Oscar Levant*; 13 I'm No Enemy (Love Is Here To Stay)(outtake)(2:24) Orchestra; 14 Love Is Here To Stay (3:46) *Gene Kelly*; 15 Medley: What Time Is It?/

Love Is Here To Stay (reprise)(outtake)(1:15) *Gene Kelly*; 16 (I'll Build A) Stairway To Paradise (G. Gershwin/B.G. DeSylva/A. Francis)(2:42) *Georges Guetary*; 17 I've Got A Crush On You (outtake)(2:45) *Gene Kelly*; 18 Love Walked In (outtake)(2:35) *Georges Guetary, Oscar Levant*; 19 Medley: We Would Get Married (Love Walked In)(outtake)/I Don't Think I'll Fall In Love Today (2:49) *Oscar Levant*; 20 Concerto in F (Third Movement) (4:35) *Oscar Levant, The M-G-M Studio Orchestra*.

CD 2: 1 Painting Montage (Tra-La-La)/Love Is Here To Stay (1:32)Orchestra; 2 Kiss Me (outtake)(:56)Orchestra; 3 'S Wonderful (2:47) *Gene Kelly, Georges Guetary*; 4 Lise I Love You ('S Wonderful/Love Is Here To Stay)(2:12) Orchestra; 5 Strike Up The Band (1:48) Orchestra; 6 Liza (:59) *Oscar Levant*; 7 Medley: Oh, Lady Be Good/'S Wonderful (1:58) Orchestra; 8 Medley: That Certain Feeling/Clap Yo' Hands (1:27) Orchestra; 9 I've Got A Crush On You (outtake)(1:05) Orchestra; 10 I Got Rhythm (1:15) Orchestra; 11 Tra-La-La (outtake)(1:03) Orchestra; 12 But Not For Me (outtake)(1:38) *Georges Guetary*; 13 Utrillo Did It (Love Is Here To Stay/An American In Paris/ Nice Work If You Can Get It)(4:19) Orchestra; 14 An American In Paris Ballet (16:38) Orchestra; 15 Finale (1:17) Orchestra; 16 Painting Montage (1:47) Orchestra; 17 Main Title (alternate version)(3:12) Orchestra; 18 Adam Cook Monologue (How Long Has This Been Going On?)(1:39) *Oscar Levant*; 19 Nice Work If You Can Get It (film version)(:30) *Georges Guetary*; 20 Third Prelude (1:01) *Oscar Levant*; 21 My Cousin In Milwaukee (outtake)(1:08) *Oscar Levant*; 22 A Foggy Day (outtake)(1:46) *Oscar Levant*; 23 The Half-Of-It-Dearie Blues (outtake)(:36) *Oscar Levant*; 24 But Not For Me (outtake)(3:37) *Oscar Levant*; 25 Bidin' My Time (outtake)(1:38) *Oscar Levant, Saul Chaplin*; 26 'S Wonderful (reprise)(outtake)(:56) *Gene Kelly*; 27 Finale (alternate version) (1:34) Orchestra.

Review: When George Gershwin wrote his masterful tone poem *An American in Paris*, he based it upon his experiences in that great city, where he resided for a time in the late '20s. As in his other works, Gershwin composed the piece in a way that encouraged personal visualization on the part of the listener. Apparently, Gershwin's composition left a great impression on famed M-G-M producer Arthur Freed, who deftly created a film plot that used the orchestral suite as the vehicle for a ballet within the picture, and enlisted the services of dancing star Gene Kelly: two moves that practically guaranteed the film's success. Rounding out the musical lot were nearly two dozen George and Ira Gershwin songs that, at the time, were already certifiable standards.

What emerges from this expertly restored edition of the original film soundtrack is just how solid Freed's concept, and his execution of the musical portion of the film, really were. It is a delight to hear not only the title composition (cleverly arranged by the venerable Saul Chaplin), but all of the familiar Gershwin tunes that have become so tightly woven into the fabric of American popular music: "Embraceable You," "But Not For Me," "Love Walked In," "I've Got a Crush on You," "Love Is Here to Stay" ... the list goes on and on!

As with each of the Rhino restorations of the soundtracks from the M-G-M film library, this 2 CD set is replete with historically important "bonus" material, culled from the original session recordings, including alternate and outtakes, and extended versions of songs. Insightful liner notes, and a wonderful interview of Saul Chaplin by Michael Feinstein provide the listener with a complete understanding of the importance of the film, and its music.

Charles L. Granata

Annie

Annie

1977, Columbia Records; from the Broadway production *Annie*, 1977.

Album Notes: *Music:* Charles Strouse; *Lyrics:* Martin Charnin; *Orchestrations:* Philip J. Lang; *Musical direction:* Peter Howard; *Cast:* Andrea McArdle (Annie), Reid Shelton (Daddy Warbucks), Sandy Faison (Grace), Robert Fitch (Rooster), Dorothy Loudon (Miss Hannigan), Raymond Thorne (FDR), Edie Cowan, Penny Worth, Donald Craig (Bert Healy), Laurie Beechman; *Album Producers:* Larry Morton, Charles Strouse; *Engineer:* Bud Graham.

Selections: 1 Overture (3:20); 2 Maybe (2:39) *Andrea McArdle*; 3 It's The Hard-Knock Life (2:20) *Andrea McArdle*; 4 Tomorrow (2:06) *Andrea McArdle*; 5 We'd Like To Thank You (2:25) *Hooverville-ites*; 6 Little Girls (2:42) *Dorothy Loudon*; 7 I Think I'm Gonna Like It Here (2:21) *Sandy Faison, Andrea McArdle*; 8 N.Y.C. (4:49) *Reid Shelton, Sandy Faison, Andrea McArdle*; 9 Easy Street (3:22) *Dorothy Loudon, Robert Fitch, Barbara Erwin*; 10 You Won't Be An Orphan For Long (1:41) *Sandy Faison*; 11 You're Never Fully Dressed Without A Smile (3:03) *Donald Craig, Laurie Beechman, Edie Cowan, Penny Worth*; 12 Tomorrow (reprise)(2:20) *Andrea McArdle, Raymond Thorne, Reid Shelton*; 13 Something Was Missing (3:40) *Reid Shelton*; 14 I Don't Need Anything But You (2:27) *Reid Shelton, Andrea McArdle, Sandy Faison*; 15 Annie (1:32) *Sandy Faison*; 16 A New Deal For Christmas (2:10) *Andrea McArdle, Reid Shelton, Sandy Faison, Raymond Thorne*.

Review: See entry below.

Annie ♫♫♫

1987, Columbia Records; from the screen version *Annie*, Columbia Pictures, 1982.

Album Notes: *Music:* Charles Strouse; *Lyrics:* Martin Charnin; *Orchestrations:* Ralph Burns; *Music Editors:* Shinichi Yamakazi, Jeff Carson; *Musical direction:* Ralph Burns; *Cast:* Aileen Quinn (Annie), Albert Finney (Daddy Warbucks), Ann Reinking (Grace), Carol Burnett (Miss Hannigan), Bernadette Peters (Lily), Tim Curry (Rooster), Geoffrey Holder (Punjab), Edward Herrmann (FDR), Peter Marshall (Bert Healy), Lu Leonard (Mrs. Pugh), Roger Minami (Asp), Toni Ann Gisondi (Molly), Lois de Banzie (Eleanor Roosevelt); *Album Producer:* Ralph Burns; *Engineer:* Dan Wallin.

Selections: 1 Tomorrow (1:36) *Aileen Quinn*; 2 It's The Hard-Knock Life (3:41) *Aileen Quinn, Toni Ann Gisondi*; 3 Maybe (1:58) *Aileen Quinn*; 4 Dumb Dog (:54) *Aileen Quinn*; 5 Sandy (2:01) *Aileen Quinn*; 6 I Think I'm Gonna Like It Here (3:34) *Aileen Quinn, Ann Reinking*; 7 Little Girls (3:11) *Carol Burnett*; 8 We Got Annie (2:21) *Ann Reinking, Lu Leonard, Geoffrey Holder, Roger Minami*; 9 Let's Go To The Movies (4:39) *Aileen Quinn, Ann Reinking, Albert Finney*; 10 Sign (2:49) *Carol Burnett, Albert Finney*; 11 You're Never Fully Dressed Without A Smile (3:00) *Peter Marshall*; 12 Easy Street (3:16) *Carol Burnett, Tim Curry, Bernadette Peters*; 13 Tomorrow (White House version)(2:22) *Aileen Quinn, Albert Finney, Lois de Banzie, Edward Herrmann*; 14 Maybe (reprise) (1:38) *Aileen Quinn, Albert Finney*; 15 Finale: I Don't Need Anything But You/We Got Annie/Tomorrow (4:32) *Aileen Quinn, Albert Finney*.

Review: The sun did come out on Broadway when big-voiced moppet Andrea McArdle stepped on the stage as Little Orphan Annie, and belted the show-stopping "Tomorrow," her triumphant claim to fame. The show, based on the celebrated comic strip, opened on April 21, 1977, won seven Tony Awards (including for its score and for Best Musical), and had an enduring run of 2,377 performances, though the popularity of this one-hit wonder was probably overrated, as a recent revival on Broadway sadly confirmed. Co-starring Reid Shelton as Daddy Warbucks, and Dorothy Loudon (another Tony winner) in an over-the-top performance as the nefarious Miss Hannigan, the musical had its ingratiating moments, wonderfully captured in the original cast album.

In 1982, it was transferred to the screen in a splashy version that starred Carol Burnett (delightfully delirious as Miss Hannigan), Albert Finney as Daddy Warbucks, the cute Aileen Quinn as Annie, and Tim Curry, Bernadette Peters, Geoffrey Holder, and Ann Reinking. Despite all the talent that went into its production, the musical looked like an anomaly on the screen and showed signs of decrepitude.

Annie Get Your Gun

Annie Get Your Gun 🎬🎬🎬

1990, MCA Records; from the Broadway production *Annie Get Your Gun*, **1946.**

Album Notes: *Music*: Irving Berlin; *Lyrics*: Irving Berlin; Orchestra conducted by Jay Blackton; *Cast*: Ethel Merman (Annie Oakley), Ray Middleton (Frank Butler), Robert Lenn, Kathleen Carnes, John Garth III (Trainman), Clyde Turner (Porter), Leon Bibb (Waiter); *Album Producer*: Jack Kapp; *CD Producers*: Mike Berniker, Michael Brooks.

Selections: 1 Doin' What Comes Naturally (3:19) *Ethel Merman*; 2 Moonshine Lullaby (3:09) *Ethel Merman, John Garth, Clyde Turner, Leon Bibb*; 3 You Can't Get A Man With A Gun (3:08) *Ethel Merman*; 4 I'm An Indian Too (2:38) *Ethel Merman*; 5 They Say It's Wonderful (3:01) *Ethel Merman, Ray Middleton*; 6 Anything You Can Do (3:06) *Ethel Merman, Ray Middleton*; 7 I Got Lost In His Arms (2:42) *Ethel Merman*; 8 I Got The Sun In The Morning (2:51) *Ethel Merman*; 9 The Girl That I Marry (3:04) *Ray Middleton*; 10 My Defenses Are Down (3:21) *Ray Middleton*; 11 Who Do You Love I Hope? (2:54) *Robert Lenn, Kathleen Carnes*; 12 There's No Business Like Show Business (3:07)*Chorus*.

Review: See entry below.

Annie Get Your Gun 🎬🎬🎬🎬

1988, RCA Victor; from the Broadway revival *Annie Get Your Gun*, **1966.**

Album Notes: *Music*: Irving Berlin; *Lyrics*: Irving Berlin; *Orchestrations*: Robert Russell Bennett; Orchestra conducted by Franz Allers; *Cast*: Ethel Merman (Annie Oakley), Bruce Yarnell (Frank Butler), Jerry Orbach (Charlie Davenport), Benay Venuta (Dolly Tate), Ronn Carroll (Foster Wilson), Rufus Smith (Col. William F. "Buffalo Bill" Cody); David Manning, Donna Conforti, Jeanne Tanzy, Holly Sherwood (children); *Album Producer*: Andy Wiswell; *Engineer*: Ernie Oelrich; *CD Producer*: Didier C. Deutsch; *Engineer*: Paul Goodman.

Selections: 1 Overture (3:38); 2 Colonel Buffalo Bill (2:04) *Jerry Orbach, Benay Venuta*; 3 I'm A Bad, Bad Man (2:24) *Bruce Yarnell*; 4 Doin' What Comes Natur'lly (3:25) *Ethel Merman, Ronn Carroll*; 5 The Girl That I Marry (1:14) *Bruce Yarnell*; 6 You Can't Get A Man With A Gun (4:27) *Ethel Merman*; 7 There's No Business Like Show Business (3:09) *Ethel Merman, Bruce Yarnell, Rufus Smith, Jerry Orbach*; 8 They Say It's Wonderful (3:36) *Ethel Merman, Bruce Yarnell*; 9 Moonshine Lullaby (3:15) *Ethel Merman*; 10 There's No Business Like Show Business (reprise)(1:19) *Ethel Merman*; 11 My Defenses Are Down (3:40) *Bruce Yarnell*; 12 I'm An Indian Too (2:06) *Ethel Merman*; 13 I Got Lost In His Arms (3:07) *Ethel Merman*; 14 I Got The Sun In The Morning (4:14) *Ethel Merman*; 15 An Old-Fashioned Wedding (3:36) *Ethel Merman, Bruce Yarnell*; 16 Anything You Can Do (3:02) *Ethel Merman, Bruce Yarnell*; 17 Finale: There's No Business Like Show Business/They Say It's Wonderful (1:59)*Entire Company*.

Review: See entry below.

Annie Get Your Gun 🎬🎬🎬🎬

1993, Angel Records; from the NBC-TV production *Annie Get Your Gun*, **1957.**

Album Notes: *Music*: Irving Berlin; *Lyrics*: Irving Berlin; Orchestra conducted by Louis Adrian; *Cast*: Mary Martin (Annie Oakley), John Raitt (Frank Butler).

Selections: 1 Overture (2:40); 2 I'm A Bad Bad Man (1:43) *John Raitt*; 3 Doin' What Comes Natur'lly (2:24) *Mary Martin*; 4 The Girl That I Marry (2:14) *John Raitt*; 5 You Can't Get A Man With A Gun (3:19) *Mary Martin*; 6 Moonshine Lullaby (3:36) *Mary Martin*; 7 They Say It's Wonderful (3:35) *Mary Martin, John Raitt*; 8 My Defenses Are Down (3:23) *Bruce Yarnell*; 9 I'm An Indian Too (2:38) *Mary Martin*; 10 I Got Lost In His Arms (3:13) *Mary Martin*; 11 I Got The Sun In The Morning (3:15) *Mary Martin*; 12 Anything You Can Do (3:04) *Mary Martin, John Raitt*; 13 There's No Business Like Show Business (3:03) *Mary Martin, John Raitt*.

Review: The life story of Wild West sharpshooter Annie Oakley became the central idea for a lively, exuberant musical starring Ethel Merman, for whom the show was written. Irving Berlin, who had initially declined to create the score for a "book" show, eventually agreed to undertake it and wrote an incredible amount of popular songs, many of which have since become standards — "They Say It's Wonderful," "You Can't Get a Man With a Gun," "Doin' What Comes Natur'lly," "I Got the Sun in the Morning," "Anything You Can Do," and the all-time anthem to the entertainment industry, "There's No Business Like Show Business." In the somewhat simplified plot devised by Herbert and Dorothy Fields, Colonel Buffalo Bill discovers Annie Oakley, and makes her part of his famous Wild West Show, in which she shares billing with Frank Butler. Soon, Annie discovers that "You Can't Get A Man With A Gun," though in the end love prevails over the rivalry between the two. *Annie Get Your Gun* opened on May 16, 1946, and had an extended run of 1,147 performances; in 1950, it was made into a rip-roaring movie, starring Betty Hutton and Howard Keel.

Of the recordings listed here, the first is the 1946 original cast album, starring Ethel Merman and Ray Middleton. Though no longer up to standard sonics, it is a valuable document, with la Merman at the top of her vocal powers.

Twenty years later, the actress returned to the role in a much-touted revival, presented by producer Richard Rodgers at the then new Music Theater of Lincoln Center in New York, in which Bruce Yarnell was cast as Frank Butler. The cast album recording, on RCA, stands out as the best representation of the score, in vivid stereo sound, with a new song, "An Old Fashioned Wedding," written for this occasion by Irving Berlin.

The recording on Angel features Mary Martin and John Raitt in a 1957 NBC-TV spectacular, reprising the roles they had played ten years earlier in the original road company of the show, and in a San Francisco Civic Light Opera revival a few months prior to the telecast. Though in mono, it is an excellent alternate presentation of the score.

At this writing, the soundtrack to the film has not yet been reissued on compact disc, though songs from the score, performed by Judy Garland, who was scheduled to star in the film before she withdrew from it, can be heard on a Rhino compilation.

Anyone Can Whistle ♪♪♪♪♪

1988, Columbia Records; from the Broadway production *Anyone Can Whistle*, 1964.

Album Notes: *Music*: Stephen Sondheim; *Lyrics*: Stephen Sondheim; *Orchestrations*: Don Walker; *Vocal arrangements and musical direction*: Herbert Greene; *Cast*: Angela Lansbury (Cora Hoover Hoople), Lee Remick (Fay Apple), Harry Guardino (J. Bowden Hapgood), Gabriel Dell (Comptroller Schub), James Frawley (Chief Magruder), Arnold Soboloff (Treasurer Cooly), Janet Hayes (June), Harvey Evans (John), Peg Murray (Mrs. Schroeder), Larry Roquemore (George), Lester Wilson (Martin); *Album Producer*: Goddard Lieberson; *Engineers*: Fred Plaut, Eddie McCowsky, Murray Zimney, Fred Catero; *CD Producer*: Didier C. Deustch; *Engineer*: Tim Geelan.

Selections: 1 Prelude: Orchestra/Me And My Town (5:25) *Angela Lansbury*; 2 Miracle Song (4:28) *Angela Lansbury, Peg Murray, Arnold Soboloff*; 3 There Won't Be Trumpets (2:37) *Lee Remick*; 4 Simple (12:59) *Angela Lansbury, Harry Guardino, Gabriel Dell, Larry Roquemore, Janet Hayes, Harvey Evans, Lester Wilson, James Frawley, Arnold Soboloff*; 5 Come Play Wiz Me (3:22) *Lee Remick, Harry Guardino*; 6 Anyone Can Whistle (3:38) *Lee Remick*; 7 A Parade In Town (3:09) *Angela Lansbury*; 8 Everybody Says Don't (2:17) *Harry Guardino*; 9 I've Got You To Lean On (1:55) *Angela Lansbury, Gabriel Dell, Arnold Soboloff, James Frawley*; 10 See What It Gets You (2:31) *Lee Remick*; 11 The Cookie Chase (9:02) *Angela Lansbury, Don Doherty, Gabriel Dell, Lee Remick*; 12 With So Little To Be Sure Of (5:03) *Lee Remick, Harry Guardino*.

"**W**hat pushed the soundtracks business over the top has been the acceptance, finally, of the film companies in really appreciating and understanding and using the music as a real marketing tool for a movie."

Kathy Nelson
*director of music at Walt Disney's motion picture group
(Billboard, 4-97)*

Review: A brilliant (and brilliantly flawed) musical by Stephen Sondheim, *Anyone Can Whistle* is one of those fabulous flops the history of the American Musical Theatre occasionally spawns. A sardonic study of political corruption in a small town, the show details the efforts by the city management to capitalize on a fake miraculous spring to revive the town's flagging economy. The plans are derailed when patients from a local mental hospital escape and begin mingling with the tourists, much to the horror and dismay of the town council. Starring Angela Lansbury, Harry Guardino and Lee Remic, three film stars with little or no previous Broadway experience, the show was roundly lambasted and closed after only nine performances. It was, however, recorded by Goddard Lieberson, head of A&R at Columbia Records, who, with incredible foresight, saw in it something quite unique. Posterity proved him right: today, *Anyone Can Whistle* is often mentioned as a precursor to the great shows (*Company, Follies, Sweeney Todd*) Sondheim wrote a decade later, a work way ahead of its time in which one can find in embryo the themes the composer developed subsequently, including man's isolation in the modern world, and the fact that "no one's always what they seem to be."

Anything Goes

Anything Goes ♪♪♪♭

1962, Epic Records; from the off Broadway revival *Anything* Goes, 1962.

Album Notes: *Music*: Cole Porter; *Lyrics*: Cole Porter; *Orchestrations*: Julian Stein; Orchestra conducted by Julian Stein; *Cast*: Eileen Rodgers (Reno Sweeney), Hal Linden (Billy Crocker), Barbara Lang (Hope Harcourt), Kenneth Mars (Sir

Evelyn Oakleigh), Mildred Chandler (Mrs. Harcourt), Warren Wade (Elisha J. Whitney), Mickey Deems (Moonface Martin), Margery Gray (Bonnie); *Album Producer*: James Foglesong.

Selections: 1 Overture/You're The Top (4:53) *Eileen Rodgers, Hal Linden*; 2 Bon Voyage (1:07) *Mickey Deems, Barbara Lang, Hal Linden, Kenneth Mars, Kay Norman*; 3 It's Delovely (3:17) *Hal Linden, Barbara Lang*; 4 Heaven Hop (3:20) *Margery Gray*; 5 Friendship (2:03) *Mickey Deems, Hal Linden, Eileen Rodgers*; 6 I Get A Kick Out Of You (3:15) *Eileen Rodgers*; 7 Anything Goes (3:58) *Eileen Rodgers*; 8 Public Enemy Number One/Let's Step Out (2:43) *Margery Gray*; 9 Let's Misbehave (2:29) *Eileen Rodgers, Kenneth Mars*; 10 Blow, Gabriel, Blow (4:08) *Eileen Rodgers*; 11 All Through The Night (4:14) *Hal Linden, Barbara Lang*; 12 Be Like The Bluebird (2:22) *Mickey Deems*; 13 Take Me Back To Manhattan (3:06) *Eileen Rodgers*.

Review: See entry below.

Anything Goes 🦴🦴🦴🦴

1988, RCA Victor; from the Broadway revival *Anything Goes*, 1988.

Album Notes: *Music*: Cole Porter; *Lyrics*: Cole Porter; *Orchestrations*: Michael Gibson; Orchestra conducted by Edward Strauss; *Cast*: Patti LuPone (Reno Sweeney), Howard McGillin (Billy Crocker), Kathleen Mahony-Bennett (Hope Harcourt), Anthony Heald (Lord Evelyn Oakleigh), Anne Francine (Mrs. Harcourt), Rex Everhart (Elisha Whitney), Bill McCutcheon (Moonface Martin); *Album Producer*: Jay David Saks; *Engineers*: Paul Goodman, Anthony Salvatore.

Selections: 1 Prelude (1:31) *Cole Porter*; 2 I Get A Kick Out Of You (2:10) *Patti LuPone*; 3 There's No Cure Like Travel/Bon Voyage (2:59) *Alec Timerman, Michele Pigliavento*; 4 You're The Top (4:10) *Patti LuPone, Howard McGillin*; 5 Easy To Love (4:03) *Howard McGillin*; 6 I Want To Row On The Crew/Sailor's Chantey (2:12) *Rex Everhart, Chantey Quartet*; 7 Friendship (2:46) *Patti LuPone, Bill McCutcheon*; 8 It's De-Lovely (4:05) *Howard McGillin, Kathleen Mahony-Bennett*; 9 Anything Goes (3:58) *Patti LuPone*; 10 Entr'acte (2:21); 11 Public Enemy Number One (1:39) *Company*; 12 Blow, Gabriel, Blow (4:08) *Patti LuPone*; 13 Goodbye, Little Dream, Goodbye (1:24) *Kathleen Mahony-Bennett*; 14 Be Like The Bluebird (2:07) *Bill McCutcheon*; 15 All Through The Night (3:03) *Howard McGillin, Kathleen Mahony-Bennett*; 16 The Gypsy In Me (2:13) *Anthony Heald*; 17 Buddie, Beware (3:25) *Linda Hart*; 18 I Get A Kick Out Of You/Anything goes (2:09) *Company*.

Review: One of Cole Porter's wittiest shows, and a hoot and a holler, *Anything Goes* introduces Broadway audiences to nightclub performer Reno Sweeney, her friend Billy Crocker, in love with socialite Hope Harcourt, and Public Enemy No. 13 Moonface

Martin, all of them passengers on a cruise ship where, as the title whimsically points out, everything and anything goes (actually a reference to the problems initially encountered when putting together the musical, about a shipwreck, in the face of several disasters, including the unrelated sinking of the "S.S. Morro"). Ethel Merman, William Gaxton and Victor Moore starred in the goofball original, for which Porter had written some of his most memorable tunes, including "All Through the Night," "Blow, Gabriel, Blow," "You're the Top," and the title tune. It opened November 21, 1934, for 420 performances, the fourth longest running production of the decade, and was made into a screen musical two years later with Bing Crosby, Ethel Merman, and Charlie Ruggles in the principal roles. In 1956, Crosby starred with Donald O'Connor, Mitzi Gaynor and Zizi Jeanmaire, in another film version which only retained the title of the original, and a couple of songs by Porter.

In a somewhat pared down revival, *Anything Goes* returned to Off Broadway in 1962, with Hal Linden, Eileen Rodgers and Mickey Deems, with the cast album recording, on Epic, documenting this enjoyable but uneven production.

Then, in 1987, it was again revived in a sensational new production, starring Patti LuPone as Reno Sweeney, which opened at Lincoln Center's Vivian Beaumont Theatre, on October 13, 1987, for a long run of 804 performances. That production yielded the original cast album on RCA, which includes several interpolations and is the best representation of the score available by far.

The Apple Tree 🦴🦴🦴ᵛ

1992, Sony Broadway; from the Broadway production *The Apple Tree*, 1967.

Album Notes: *Music*: Jerry Bock; *Lyrics*: Sheldon Harnick; *Orchestrations*: Eddie Sauter; *Musical direction*: Elliot Lawrence; *Cast*: Barbara Harris (Eve/Barbara/Ella/Passionella), Alan Alda (Adam/Sanjar/Flip/The Prince/Charming); Larry Blyden (The Snake/Balladeer/Narrator); *Album Producer*: Goodard Lieberson; *Engineers*: Fred Plaut, Larry Keyes, Robert Waller; *CD Producer*: Didier C. Deutsch; *Engineer*: Tim Tiedemann.

Selections: *THE DIARY OF ADAM AND EVE:* 1 Eden Prelude (1:16); 2 Here In Eden (2:37) *Barbara Harris*; 3 Feelings (1:22) *Barbara Harris*; 4 Eve (3:10) *Alan Alda*; 5 Friends (2:04) *Barbara Harris*; 6 The Apple Tree (Forbidden Fruit)(2:37) *Larry Blyden*; 7 Beautiful Beautiful World (2:14) *Alan Alda*; 8 It's A Fish (1:46) *Alan Alda*; 9 Go To Sleep, Whatever You Are (1:20) *Barbara Harris*; 10 What Makes Me Love Him?/Eden Postlude (3:29) *Barbara Harris*;

THE LADY OR THE TIGER?: 11 Prelude/I'll Tell You A Truth/Make Way (4:13) *Larry Blyden*; 12 Forbidden Love (In Gaul)(3:26)

Alan Alda, Barbara Harris; 13 The Apple Tree (reprise)(:59) *Larry Blyden*; 14 I've Got What You Want (2:00) *Barbara Harris*; 15 Tiger, Tiger (1:58) *Barbara Harris*; 16 Make Way (reprise)/ Which Door?/I'll Tell You A Truth (reprise) (3:40) *Marc Jordan, David McCorkle, Alan Alda, Barbara Harris, Larry Blyden*;

PASSIONELLA: 17 Prelude (:25); 18 Oh, To Be A Movie Star (4:08) *Barbara Harris*; 19 Gorgeous (1:44) *Barbara Harris*; 20 (Who, Who, Who, Who) Who Is She? (1:22) *Barbara Harris*; 21 I Know (2:29) *Barbara Harris*; 22 Wealth (1:33) *Barbara Harris*; 23 You Are Not Real (2:41) *Alan Alda*; 24 Postlude/Finale (2:12) *Alan Alda, Barbara Harris.*

Review: An innovative three one-act musical production, starring Alan Alda, Larry Blyden and Barbara Harris, *The Apple Tree* was the creation of Jerry Bock and Sheldon Harnick, following their hugely successful *Fiddler On The Roof*. The production took its name from the first work, based on Mark Twain's amusing "The Diary Of Adam And Eve," and also included Frank R. Stockton's "The Lady and the Tiger," and Jules Feiffer's ''Passionella.'' Though hardly on the same level as its glorious predecessor, *The Apple Tree* was warmly received by critics when it opened on October 18, 1966, and enjoyed a run of 463 performances. It won a Tony for Barbara Harris' hilarious performance in the third play as a chimney sweeper who dreams of becoming a mooooovie star.

Babes in Arms 🎵🎵🎵🎵🎵
1990, New World Records; from the studio cast recording *Babes in Arms*, 1990.

Album Notes: *Music:* Richard Rodgers; *Lyrics:* Lorenz Hart; The New Jersey Symphony Orchestra, conducted by Evans Haile; *Cast:* Gregg Edelman (Valentine LaMar), Judy Blazer (Billie Smith), Jason Graae (Gus Fielding), Donna Kane (Dolores Reynolds), Judy Kaye (Baby Rose), Adam Grupper (Peter Jackson), Michael Taranto, Christopher May, David Montgomery, Steven Katz: JQ and The Bandits (Quartet); *Album Producer:* Elizabeth Ostrow; *Engineer:* Henk Kooistra.

Selections: 1 Overture (4:35); 2 Where Or When (4:22) *Judy Blazer, Gregg Edelman*; 3 Babes In Arms (2:56) Company; 4 I Wish I Were In Love Again (4:02) *Jason Graae, Donna Kane*; 5 Way Out West (5:05) *Judy Kaye, JQ and The Bandits*; 6 My Funny Valentine (4:03) *Judy Blazer*; 7 Johnny One-Note (2:12) *Judy Kaye*; 8 Ballet: Johnny One-Note (5:35); 9 Imagine (4:11) *Judy Kaye, JQ and The Bandits, Jason Graae*; 10 All At Once (3:35) *Gregg Edelman, Judy Blazer*; Peter's Journey: 11 Imagine (reprise 1)(1:03) *Adam Grupper, JQ and The Bandits, Jason Graae*; 12 Ballet: Peter's Journey (11:25); 13 Imagine (reprise 2) *Adam Grupper, JQ and The Bandits*; 14 The Lady Is A Tramp

(4:20) *Judy Blazer*; 15 You Are So Fair (5:50) *Jason Graae, Donna Kane*; 16 Finale (1:14) Company.

Review: In a classic let's-put-a-barnyard-show-together, a group of teenagers, all of them children of vaudevillian performers, decide to stage a revue in order to avoid being sent to work school, in this whimsical musical by Richard Rodgers and Lorenz Hart. It opened on April 14, 1937, and yielded such standards as "Where or When," "I Wish I Were in Love Again," "My Funny Valentine," "Johnny One-Note," and "The Lady Is a Tramp."

The studio cast album listed above, the only one currently available in the catalogue, beautifully captures the spirited moods of the musical, and brings them forth in an excellent recording that enhances the impish, youthful exuberance of the score.

Ballroom 🎵🎵🎵◗
1992, Sony Broadway; from the Broadway production *Ballroom*, 1979.

Album Notes: *Music:* Billy Goldenberg; *Lyrics:* Alan & Marilyn Bergman; *Orchestrations:* Jonathan Tunick; Orchestra conducted by Don Jennings; *Cast:* Dorothy Loudon (Bea Asher), Vincent Gardenia (Alfred Rossi), Lynn Roberts (Marlene), Bernie Knee (Nathan Bricker); *Album Producers:* Larry Morton, Kala Productions; *Engineers:* Stan Tonkel, Ted Brosnan; *CD Producer:* Didier C. Deutsch; *Engineer:* Tim Tiedemann.

Selections: 1 Overture: The Stardust Waltz (1:48); 2 A Terrific Band And A Real Nice Crowd (4:20) *Dorothy Loudon*; 3 A Song For Dancing (3:23) *Lynn Roberts, Bernie Knee*; 4 One By One (3:13) *Lynn Roberts, Bernie Knee*; 5 Dance Montage (cha-cha)(2:50); 6 Dreams (3:58) *Lynn Roberts*; 7 Somebody Did All Right For Herself/Dreams (3:46) *Dorothy Loudon, Lynn Roberts*; 8 Tango (4:44); 9 Goodnight Is Not Goodbye (1:28) *Lynn Roberts, Bernie Knee*; 10 I've Been Waiting All My Life (3:10) *Bernie Knee*; 11 I Love To Dance (4:01) *Dorothy Loudon, Vincent Gardenia*; 12 More Of The Same (2:46) *Lynn Roberts, Bernie Knee*; 13 Fifty Percent (3:40) *Dorothy Loudon*; 14 I Wish You A Waltz (3:35) *Dorothy Loudon.*

Review: In what is essentially a two-character show, Dorothy Loudon and Vincent Gardenia starred in *Ballroom*, a big dance musical based on the television musical drama, "Queen of the Stardust Ballroom." The drama had aired four years earlier with Maureen Stapleton and Charles Durning, respectively, as a widow and a middle-age married man who meet on the dance floor and have an affair. Brilliantly staged by Michael Bennett, and a showcase for his unique talent as a choreographer, the musical (with a score by Billy Goldenberg, and Alan and Marilyn Bergman) introduced the show-stopping "Fifty Percent," sung by Dorothy Loudon at the peak of her talent, and presented several big band-styled numbers performed by Lynn Roberts and Bernie Knee. Though it only enjoyed a short run of 116 performances, following its December 14, 1978 opening, it yielded a cast album which is perhaps the best thing it had to offer.

Bambi 🎵🎵🎵🎵

1996, Walt Disney Records; from the animated feature *Bambi*, 1942.

Album Notes: *Music*: Frank Churchill, Edward H. Plumb; *Lyrics*: Larry Morey; *Orchestrations*: Charles Wolcott, Paul J. Smith; *Choral Arrangements*: Charles Henderson; The Disney Studio Orchestra and Chorus, conducted by Alexander Steinert; *CD Producer*: Randy Thornton; *Engineer*: John Polito.

Selections: 1 Main Title (Love Is A Song)(2:55) *Donald Novis*; 2 Sleepy Morning In The Woods/Everybody Awake/The Young Prince/ Learning To Walk (5:13); 3 Exploring/Through The Woods/Say Bird/Flower (6:02); 4 Little April Shower (3:53) Chorus; 5 The Meadow/Bambi Sees Faline/Bambi Gets Annoyed (4:56); 6 Gallop Of The Stags/The Great Prince Of The Forest/Man (4:11); 7 Autumn/The First Snow/Fun On The Ice (4:40); 8 The End Of Winter/New Spring Grass/Tragedy In The Meadow (2:32); 9 Wintery Winds (1:09); 10 Let's Sing A Gay Little Spring Song (1:41) Chorus; 11 It Could Even Happen To Flower (2:00); 12 Bambi Gets Twitterpated/Stag Fight (2:32); 13 Looking For Romance (I Bring You A Song)(2:08) Chorus; 14 Man Returns (2:04); 15 Fire/Reunion/ Finale (Love Is A Song)(5:34) Chorus; 16 Rain Drops (demo)(1:37).

Review: One of Walt Disney's best animated features, and certainly the studio's most visually gracile, *Bambi*, based on Felix Salten's classic story about a little fawn, was a huge critical and commercial success when it was initially released on August 21, 1942. With its charming portrayal of many forest denizens, including Thumper, the mischievious little rabbit, and Flower, the skunk, who befriend Bambi, the film is further enhanced by the great score and songs created for it by Frank Churchill, Ed Plumb and Larry Morey, which include "Love Is A Song" and "Let's Sing a Gay Little Spring Song," among its better moments. Properly remastered, and including many instrumental selections available for the first time, the CD reissue is a great memento from this delightful fable.

The Band Wagon 🎵🎵🎵ᵕ

1996, Rhino Records; from the screen version *The Bandwagon*, M-G-M, 1953.

Album Notes: *Music*: Arthur Schwartz; *Lyrics*: Howard Dietz; *Arrangements and Orchestrations*: Roger Edens, Conrad Salinger, Robert Franklyn, Alexander Courage, Lloyd "Skip" Mar-

tin; The M-G-M Studio Orchestra, conducted by Adolph Deutsch; *Cast*: Fred Astaire (Tony Hunter), Cyd Charisse (Gabrielle "Gaby" Gerard), Oscar Levant (Lester Marton), Nanette Fabray (Lily Marton), Jack Buchanan (Jeffrey Cordova), James Mitchell (Paul Byrd); *CD Producers*: George Feltenstein, Bradley Flanagan; *Engineer*: Doug Schwartz.

Selections: 1 Main Title (New Sun In The Sky/I Love Louisa/High And Low) (1:57); 2 By Myself (1:43) *Fred Astaire*; 3 Penny Arcade (Shine On Your Shoes Intro)(1:56); 4 A Shine On Your Shoes (4:30) *Fred Astaire*; 5 Oedipus Bridge (1:28) *Jack Buchanan*; 6 That's Entertainment (3:27) *Fred Astaire, Jack Buchanan, Nanette Fabray, Oscar Levant*; 7 Is It All A Dream (La Femme Rouge) (2:30); 8 Sweet Music (outtake)(4:26) *Nanette Fabray, Oscar Levant*; 9 You Have Everything (outtake)(3:48); 10 Got A Bran' New Suit (outtake)(2:27) *Nanette Fabray, Fred Astaire, Oscar Levant*; 11 Sweet Music (1:05); 12 Medley: Carriage In The Park (R. Edens/C. Salinger)/High And Low (1:54); 13 Dancing In The Dark (3:28); 14 Two-Faced Woman (outtake)(4:07) *India Adams, Oscar Levant*; 15 You And The Night And The Music (1:23); 16 The Egg (C. Salinger)(1:58) Chorus; 17 Something To Remember You By (1:30)Chorus; 18 I Love Louisa (2:31) *Fred Astaire, Nanette Fabray, Oscar Levant*; 19 New Sun In The Sky (1:09) *India Adams*; 20 I Guess I'll Have To Change My Plan (1:47) *Fred Astaire, Jack Buchanan*; 21 Louisiana Hayride (2:00) *Nanette Fabray*; 22 Triplets (2:31) *Fred Astaire, Nanette Fabray, Jack Buchanan*; 23 The Girl Hunt Ballet (11:43) *Fred Astaire*; 24 By Myself (reprise)(:59) *Fred Astaire*; 25 For He's A Jolly Good Fellow (:26) *The M-G-M Studio Chorus*; 26 That's Entertainment (reprise) (1:15) *Fred Astaire, India Adams, Nanette Fabray, Jack Buchanan, Oscar Levant*; 27 Two-Faced Woman (demo)(2:44) *Roger Edens*; 28 That's Entertainment (demo)(3:36) *Roger Edens, Richard Beavers*.

Review: Another in a long line of producer Arthur Freed's films built around specific composers' song catalogs, *The Band Wagon* centers on the music of Arthur Schwartz and the lyrics of Howard Dietz. Starring Fred Astaire and Cyd Charisse, it includes many of the pair's most celebrated collaborations, including "By Myself," "That's Entertainment," "Dancing in the Dark," "You and the Night and the Music," and "I Guess I'll Have to Change My Plan."

The Band Wagon proved to be one of M-G-M's last brilliant successes, and this newly restored "complete" edition, produced under the auspices of George Feltenstein and Bradley Flanagan, is an important addition to the ever-growing library of M-G-M film recordings being preserved by Rhino Records.

Unfortunately, the sonic quality of this particular release is not up to Rhino's usual standard for the M-G-M line, primarily due to the way that the film company transferred the original stereo tracks. According to Feltenstein, while most of the original 1953 sessions were recorded in stereo on 3-track magnetic tape, the only surviving reels are the monophonic, 1/4" mixdowns done in the 1960s, which were the masters used for this release. The outstanding music makes it easy to overlook the abundance of tape hiss, however. As is customary with these issues, Rhino has dipped into the vault and included a specially produced mix of "The Girl Hunter Ballet," and two demo recordings by associate producer Roger Edens.

Charles L. Granata

Barnum ♫♫♫♪

1980, Columbia Records; from the Broadway production *Barnum*, 1980.

Album Notes: *Music*: Cy Coleman; *Lyrics*: Michael Stewart; *Orchestrations*: Hershy Kay; *Vocal Arrangements*: Cy Coleman, Jeremy Stone; *Music Director*: Peter Howard; *Featured Soloists*: Karen Gustafson, Peter Phillips (pianos); *Cast*: Jim Dale (P.T. Barnum), Glenn Close (Chairy), Marianne Tatum (Jenny Lind), Terri White (Joice Heth), Leonard John Crofoot (Tom Thumb), William C. Witter (Ringmaster); *Album Producers*: Cy Coleman, Mike Berniker.

Selections: 1 Overture Chase (1:04); 2 There Is A Sucker Born Ev'ry Minute (2:25) *Jim Dale*; 3 Humble Beginnings Chase (:30) *William C. Witter*; 4 Thank God I'm Old (2:30) *Terri White*; 5 The Colors Of My Life (Part 1)(2:46) *Jim Dale*; 6 The Colors Of My Life (Part 2)(1:53) *Glenn Close*; 7 One Brick At A Time (3:24) *Glenn Close*; 8 Museum Song (1:50) *Jim Dale*; 9 Female Of The Species Chase (:37) *William C. Ritter*; 10 I Like Your Style (3:19) *Jim Dale, Glenn Close*; 11 Bigger Isn't Better (3:56) *Leonard John Crofoot*; 12 Love Makes Such Fools Of Us All (3:20) *Marianne Tatum*; 13 Midway Chase (:41) *William C. Ritter*; 14 Out There (2:15) *Jim Dale*; 15 Come Follow The Band (3:52) *Jim Dale*; 16 Black And White (5:06) *Glenn Close, Terri White, Jim Dale*; 17 The Colors Of My Life (reprise) (1:38) *Jim Dale, Glenn Close*; 18 The Prince Of Humbug (1:43) *Jim Dale*; 19 Join The Circus (5:51) *William C. Witter, Jim Dale*; 20 Finale Chase (:12) *William C. Witter*; 21 The Final Event/There Is A Sucker Born Ev'ry Minute (reprise)(1:31) *Jim Dale*.

Review: The life of Phineas Taylor (P.T.) Barnum provided Cy Coleman, Michael Stewart and Mark Bramble with the gem of an idea for a brassy Broadway show. Agilely portrayed by Jim Dale, with Glenn Close playing Barnum's long-suffering wife, Chairy, the musical was not, by any stretch of the imagination, a circus tent attraction, but an honest-to-goodness production, with big numbers solidly integrated within the development of a book that retraced Barnum's phenomenal career as a showman. Wittily staged by Joe Layton, it offers stylized side glances at circus life, and concentrates instead on Barnum's humble beginnings, his first successes, his romantic involvement with Jenny Lind, the Swedish Nightingale, and his eventual teaming with James A. Bailey in creating the Greatest Show on Earth. Bright, extraordinarily lively and exciting, the score yielded many hits, including "The Colors of My Life," "Come Follow the Band," and "Join the Circus," all delivered with the right amount of dash and personal glee by the energetic Jim Dale (who won a Tony for his performance), as heard in the original cast album. The show opened on Broadway on April 30, 1980, and had a run of 854 performances.

Beauty and the Beast

Beauty and the Beast ♫♫♫♪

1991, Walt Disney Records; from the animated feature *Beauty and the Beast*, Walt Disney Pictures, 1991.

Album Notes: *Music*: Alan Menken; *Lyrics*: Howard Ashman; *Orchestrations*: Alan Menken, Danny Troob, Michael Starobin; *Music Editor*: Kathy Bennett; *Vocal Arrangements and Musical Direction*: David Friedman; *Cast*: Robby Benson (Beast), Jesse Corti (Lefou), Angela Lansbury (Mrs. Potts), Paige O'Hara (Belle), Jerry Orbach (Lumiere), David Ogden Stiers (Cogsworth), Richard White (Gaston); *Album Producers*: Alan Menken, Howard Ashman; *Engineers*: Michael Farrow, John Richards, Bruce Botnick.

Selections: 1 Prologue (3:12); 2 Belle (5:07) *Paige O' Hara*; 3 Belle (reprise)(1:03) *Paige O' Hara*; 4 Gaston (3:37) *Richard White, Jesse Corti*; 5 Gaston (reprise)(2:01) *Richard White*; 6 Be Our Guest (3:42) *Angela Lansbury, Jerry Orbach, David Ogen Stiers*; 7 Something There (2:16) *Robby Benson, Paige O' Hara*; 8 The Mob Song (3:28) *Ensemble*; 9 Beauty And The Beast (2:44) *Angela Lansbury*; 10 To The Fair (1:55); 11 West Wing (3:39); 12 The Beast Lets Belle Go (2:19); 13 Battle On The Tower (5:27); 14 Transformation (5:45); 15 Beauty And The Beast (4:03) *Celine Dion, Peabo Bryson*.

Review: See entry below.

Beauty and the Beast ♫♫♪

1994, Disney Records; from the Broadway production *Beauty and the Beast*, 1994.

Album Notes: *Music*: Alan Menken; *Lyrics*: Howard Ashman, Tim Rice; *Orchestrations*: Danny Troob; *Vocal Arrangements*: David Friedman; *Music Direction*: Michael Kosarin; *Cast*: Susan

Egan (Belle), Terrence Mann (Beast), Kenny Raskin (Lefou), Burke Moses (Gaston), Tom Bosley (Maurice), Heath Lamberts (Cogsworth), Gary Beach (Lumiere), Beth Fowler (Mrs. Potts), Brian Press (Chip), Stacey Logan (Babette), Barbara Marineau (Madame de la Grande Bouche), Gordon Stanley (Monsieur D'Arque), Wendy Oliver (Enchantress), Paige Price, Sarah Solie Shannon, Linda Talcott (Silly Girls); *Album Producers*: Alan Menken, Bruce Botnick; *Engineer*: Bruce Botnick.

Selections: 1 Prologue (2:38) *Wendy Oliver*; 2 Belle (5:18) *Susan Egan, Burke Moses, Kenny Raskin, Paige Price, Sarah Solie Shannon*; 3 No Matter What (3:07) *Tom Bosley, Susan Egan*; 4 No Matter What (reprise)/Wolf Chase (1:56) *Tom Bosley*; 5 Me (2:49) *Burke Moses, Susan Egan*; 6 Belle (reprise)(1:09) *Susan Egan*; 7 Home (3:51) *Susan Egan*; 8 Home (reprise) (:55) *Beth Fowler*; 9 Gaston (5:02) *Kenny Raskin, Burke Moses, Paige Price, Sarah Solie Shannon, Linda Talcott*; 10 Gaston (reprise)(1:38) *Burke Moses, Kenny Raskin*; 11 How Long Must This Go On? (:56) *Terrence Mann*; 12 Be Our Guest (6:56) *Gary Beach, Beth Fowler, Heath Lamberts, Barbara Marineau, Brian Press, Stacey Logan*; 13 If I Can't Love Her (4:06) *Terrence Mann*; 14 Entr'acte/Wolf Chase (4:30); 15 Something There (5:28) *Susan Egan, Terrence Mann, Gary Beach, Beth Fowler, Heath Lamberts*; 16 Human Again (4:45) *Gary Beach, Beth Fowler, Heath Lamberts, Barbara Marineau, Brian Press, Stacey Logan*; 17 Maison des Lunes (2:25) *Burke Moses, Kenny Raskin, Gordon Stanley*; 18 Beauty and the Beast (3:35) *Beth Fowler*; 19 If I Can't Love Her (reprise)(1:35) *Terrence Mann*; 20 The Mob Song (3:03) *Burke Moses, Kenny Raskin, Gordon Stanley*; 21 The Battle (2:34); 22 Transformation (3:27) *Terrence Mann, Susan Egan*; 23 Beauty and the Beast (reprise)(:43) The Company.

Review: The venerable classic 1757 tale by Mme Leprince de Beaumont, about a beautiful maiden and the horrible beast who becomes her guardian in exchange for her father's life, had been a wonderful magical source for the creativity of French filmmaker Jean Cocteau. It proved equally reliable when Disney decided to adapt it for an animated musical feature released in 1991. Deftly combining standard animation and computer imagery, the studio craftsmen created a work that is technically polished and sophisticated, yet completely delightful as only the Disney films can be. Adding to the impact of the film and its soundtrack, well-known performers loan their vocal talents to the film, including Angela Lansbury as the homebody Mrs. Potts; Robby Benson, as the Beast, who turns out to be a Prince under an evil spell; Paige O'Hara, whose crystalline voice gives Beauty incredible life on the screen; and Jerry Orbach who, as Lumiere, the candelabra-holding genial

host at the Beast's castle, adds a welcome touch of show biz chutzpah. Also particularly welcome is the score by Alan Menken and Howard Tashman, which features some excellent numbers, including "Beauty and the Beast," sensitively rendered by Angela Lansbury, and reprised by Celine Dion and Peabo Bryson in a pop version heard over the end credits; the humorous "Gaston," bellowed by Richard White as the insufferable "lover" of Beauty, and Jesse Corti, as Lefou, Gaston's all-'round yes man and friend; and "Be Our Guest," in which Angela Lansbury, Jerry Orbach, and the other household characters at the Beast's castle celebrate the arrival of Beauty.

Much of the magic and enchantment found in the film had dissipated by the time a live version of the musical opened on Broadway on April 18, 1994. Where the animated feature is clever and whimsical, the stage version is heavy-handed and caricatural. New songs added to the original score only confirm this impression, with the all-too-human characters on stage having a difficult time trying to keep up with the animated screen counterparts, and not succeeding too well. As a result, the cast album, featuring Terrence Mann as the Beast, Susan Egan as Belle, and Burke Moses as Gaston may be of interest to those who have seen the show, still running on Broadway, but if you haven't seen the show or aren't sure which version to get, stick with the original soundtrack from the film.

The Belle of New York 🎵🎵🎵🎵

1991, Sony Music Special Products; from the screen musical *The Belle of New York*, M-G-M, 1952.

Album Notes: *Music*: Harry Warren; *Lyrics*: Johnny Mercer; *Orchestrations*: Conrad Salinger, Maurice de Packh; The M-G-M Studio Chorus and Orchestra, conducted by Adolph Deutsch; *Cast*: Fred Astaire (Charles Hill), Vera-Ellen (Angela Bonfils), Alice Pearce (Elsie Wilkins); *CD Producer*: Dan Rivard; *Engineer*: Ken Robertson.

Selections: 1 Overture (When You're Out With The Belle Of New York)(1:31) Orchestra, Chorus; 2 Bachelor's Dinner Song (3:23) *Fred Astaire*; 3 Let A Little Love Come In (R. Edens)(1:41) *Alice Pearce, Anita Ellis*; 4 Seeing's Believing (3:50) *Fred Astaire*; 5 Baby Doll (4:33) *Fred Astaire*; 6 Oops! (4:59) *Fred Astaire*; 7 A Bride's Wedding Day (Thank You, Mr. Currier, Thank You, Mr. Ives)(7:47) *Anita Ellis*; 8 Naughty But Nice (4:40) *Anita Ellis*; 9 Naughty But Nice (reprise)(2:05) *Alice Pearce*; 10 Baby Doll (reprise)(:36) *Fred Astaire*; 11 I Wanna Be A Dancin' Man (4:10) *Fred Astaire*; 12 Finale: When You're Out With The Belle Of New York (1:00) Orchestra.

Review: Based on a musical created in 1897, but sporting a brand new score by Harry Warren and Johnny Mercer, *The Belle* *of New York* is a classic Arthur Freed production, starring Fred Astaire as a dissolute playboy who finds redemption in the arms of an unlikely Salvation Army-type officer, in what is a sly bow in the direction of *Guys and Dolls,* still a running hit on Broadway at the time. Naturally bright and breezy, the screen musical was the occasion for several song-and-dance numbers, among which the most memorable and successful include a long sequence shot before various backdrops borrowed from the Currier and Ives lithographs; "Baby Doll," which became a standard; and "I Wanna Be a Dancin' Man," which Astaire turned into an exuberant signature song.

Bells Are Ringing

Bells Are Ringing ♪♪♪♪♪

1989, Columbia Records; from the Broadway production *Bells Are Ringing*, 1956.

Album Notes: *Music*: Jule Styne; *Lyrics*: Betty Comden & Adolph Green; *Orchestrations*: Robert Russell Bennett; *Vocal arrangements*: Herbert Greene, Buster Davis; *Incidental scoring*: John Morris; *Musical Director*: Milton Rosenstock; *Cast*: Judy Holliday (Ella Peterson), Sydney Chaplin (Jeff Moss), Jean Stapleton (Sue), Eddie Lawrence (Sandor), Eddie Heim (Telephone Man), Peter Gennaro (Carl); *Album Producer*: Goddard Lieberson; *Engineers*: Fred Plaut, Bud Graham, Murray Zimney; *CD Producer*: Didier C. Deutsch; *Engineer*: Tim Geelan.

Selections: 1 Overture (5:36); 2 Bells Are Ringing (2:19) *Eddie Heim, Jean Stapleton*; 3 It's A Perfect Relationship (3:10) *Judy Holliday, Sydney Chaplin*; 4 On My Own (2:27) *Sydney Chaplin*; 5 It's A Simply Little System (2:53) *Eddie Lawrence*; 6 Is It A Crime? (4:17) *Judy Holliday*; 7 Hello, Hello There! (2:27) *Judy Holliday, Sydney Chaplin*; 8 I Met A Girl (2:34) *Sydney Chaplin*; 9 Long Before I Knew You (3:48) *Judy Holliday, Sydney Chaplin*; 10 Mu-Cha-Cha (1:52) *Judy Holliday, Peter Gennaro*; 11 Just In Time (3:40) *Judy Holliday, Sydney Chaplin*; 12 Drop That Name (2:13) *Judy Holliday*; 13 The Party's Over (2:40) *Judy Holliday*; 14 Salzburg (2:39) *Jean Stapleton, Eddie Lawrence*; 15 The Midas Touch (1:34) *Ensemble*; 16 I'm Going Back (3:26) *Judy Holliday*.

Review: See entry below.

Bells Are Ringing ♪♪♪♪

1989, Capitol Records; from the screen version *Bells Are Ringing*, M-G-M, 1960.

Album Notes: *Music*: Jule Styne; *Lyrics*: Betty Comden & Adolph Green; *Orchestrations*: Alexander Courage, Pete King; The M-G-M Studio Orchestra and Chorus conducted by Andre

Previn; *Cast*: Judy Holliday (Ella Peterson), Dean Martin (Jeff Moss), Jean Stapleton (Sue), Eddie Foy, Jr. (Sandor), Hal Linden; *Album Producers*: Lee Gillette, John Palladino.

Selections: 1 Overture (3:30); 2 It's A Perfect Relationship (3:09) *Judy Holliday*; 3 Do It Yourself (1:54)*P*: Dean Martin; 4 It's A Simply Little System (3:01) *Eddie Foy Jr.*; 5 Better Than A Dream (2:45) *Dean Martin, Judy Holliday*; 6 I Met A Girl (1:58) *Dean Martin*; 7 Just In Time (4:02) *Judy Holliday, Dean Martin*; 8 Drop That Name (2:14) *Judy Holliday*; 9 The Party's Over (3:15) *Judy Holliday*; 10 The Midas Touch (3:10) *Hal Linden*; 11 I'm Going Back (3:31) *Judy Holliday*; 12 Finale (1:49) *Chorus*.

Review: An "original book" musical (as opposed to an adaptation), *Bells Are Ringing*, which opened on November 29, 1956 for a run of 924 performances, was the brainchild of Betty Comden, Adolph Green and composer Jule Styne, who fashioned a breezy, often hilarious show for their star, Judy Holliday. The show, about a lonely operator at an answering phone service who meddles in the lives of her customers and gets involved with a playwright with a temporary creative block, is peopled by a collection of colorful characters (actors, socialites, bookies, policemen and subway riders), and is the occasion for a festival of bright, cheery tunes. Among those, the score introduced the jaunty "Just in Time," and one of Broadway's great show-stopping hits, the mournful "The Party's Over." The cast album, Columbia's first in stereo, ranks among the top recordings ever released by the label.

Judy Holliday reprised her Tony Award-winning performance, and Dean Martin replaced Sydney Chaplin as the playwright, when *Bells Are Ringing* went Hollywood in 1960 for a big screen treatment that remained somewhat faithful to the original. Even though its score is seriously downsized, it includes a couple of new numbers, including "Do It Yourself," performed by Martin, and "Better Than a Dream," a duet shared by the two stars, and yielded a soundtrack album that has some bright moments, even though it is a poor substitute to the original.

Ben Franklin in Paris ♪♪

1993, Angel Records; from the Broadway production, *Ben Franklin in Paris*, 1964.

Album Notes: *Music*: Mark Sandrich Jr.; *Lyrics*: Sidney Michaels; *Orchestrations*: Philip J. Lang; *Vocal Arrangements and Musical Direction*: Donald Pippin; *Cast*: Robert Preston (Benjamin Franklin), Ulla Sallert (Comtesse Diane de Vobrillac), Susan Watson (Janine Nicolet), Franklin Kiser (Temple Franklin), Jerry Schaefer (Benjamin Franklin Bache), Bob Kaliban (Pierre Caron de Beaumarchais), Sam Greene (Captain Wickes); *Album Producer*: Dick Jones.

Selections: 1 Overture (3:01); 2 We Sail The Seas (2:41) Company; 3 I Invented Myself (2:35) *Robert Preston*; 4 Too Charming (2:09) *Robert Preston, Ulla Sallert*; 5 Whatever Became Of Old Temple (1:48) *Franklin Riser*; 6 Half The Battle (3:17) *Robert Preston, Jerry Schaefer, Franklin Kiser, Bob Kaliban*; 7 A Balloon Is Ascending (1:28) The Company; 8 To Be Alone With You (3:15) *Robert Preston, Ulla Sallert*; 9 You're In Paris (3:28) *Susan Watson, Franklin Kiser*; 10 How Laughable It Is (2:06) *Ulla Sallert*; 11 Hic Haec Hoc (1:20) Company; 12 God Bless The Human Elbow (2:34) *Robert Preston, Jack Fletcher, Bob Kaliban*; 13 When I Dance With The Person I Love (3:39) *Susan Watson*; 14 Diane Is (1:15) *Robert Preston*; 15 Look For Small Pleasures (4:35) *Robert Preston, Ulla Sallert*; 16 I Love The Ladies (3:27) *Robert Preston, Sam Greene, Bob Kaliban, Franklin Kiser*; 17 Finale (4:32) *Robert Preston*.

Review: The primary interest in this cast album resides in Robert Preston's portrayal of Benjamin Franklin, his first role on Broadway since *The Music Man*. Saddled with an impossible book recounting Franklin's visit to Versailles and the court of French King Louis XVI, and his alleged involvement with Comtesse Diane de Vobrillac, Preston also had to struggle with a score that lacked fire and imagination, and a co-star with whom he shared little stage chemistry. Despite the beguiling presence of Susan Watson, fresh as a daisy in a secondary role, and a minor hit in the song "Half the Battle," spiritedly delivered by Preston and cohorts, the show floundered and mercifully closed after 215 performances.

Best Foot Forward ♪♪♪

1988, DRG Records; from the off-Broadway revival *Best Foot Forward*, 1963.

Album Notes: *Music*: Hugh Martin, Ralph Blane; *Lyrics*: Hugh Martin, Ralph Blane; *Musical Director*: Buster Davis; *Dance Music Arrangements*: William Goldenberg; *Cast*: Paula Wayne (Gale Joy), Liza Minnelli (Ethel Hofflinger), Karin Wolfe (Helen Schlessinger), Glenn Walken (Bud Hopper), Chritopher Walken (Clayton "Dutch" Miller), Edmund Gaynes (Monroe "Hunk" Hoyt), Grant Walden (Jack Haggerty), Renee Winters (Linda Ferguson), Gene Castle (LeRoy "Goofy" Clarke), Don Slaton (Harrison "Satchel" Moyer), Paul Charles (Fred Jones), Jack Irwin (Old Grad); *CD Producer*: Hugh Fordin.

Selections: 1 Wish I May (2:48)Ensemble; 2 Three Men On A Date (2:48) *Glenn Walken, Christopher Walken, Edmund Gaynes*; 3 Hollywood Story (3:48) *Paula Wayne, Grant Walden*; 4 The Three "B's" (5:29) *Liza Minnelli, Kay Cole, Renee Winters*; 5 Ev'ry Time (4:10) *Karin Wolfe*; 6 Alive And Kicking/The Guy Who Brought Me (2:42) *Paula Wayne, Grant Walden, Edmund Gaynes, Christopher Walken, Glenn Walken*; 7 Shady Lady Bird (2:53) *Karin Wolfe, Edmund Gaynes, Gene Castle, Don Slaton, Paul Charles*; 8 Buckle Down Winsocki (4:07) *Jack Irwin, Edmund Gaynes, Paul Charles*; 9 You're Lucky (2:50) *Paula Wayne*; 10 What Do You Think I Am? (3:08) *Liza Minnelli, Edmund Gaynes, Kay Cole, Christopher Walken*; 11 A Raving Beauty (3:00) *Christopher Walken, Kay Cole*; 12 Just A Little Joint With A Juke Box (2:55) *Liza Minnelli, Gene Castle, Don Slaton, Paul Charles*; 13 You Are For Loving (5:13) *Liza Minnelli*; 14 Finale: Buckle Down Winsocki (reprise)(:33) *Paula Wayne*.

Review: The 1963 revival of *Best Foot Forward*, the self-proclaimed "bright musical comedy hit," is best remembered today for the fact that it introduced Liza Minnelli in her first stage role. Initially produced on Broadway in 1941, where it enjoyed a run of 326 performances, *Best Foot Forward* had been a lightweight but delightful vehicle for a group of talented newcomers, including June Allyson and Nancy Walker, cast as prep school students at Winsocki, Pennsylvania, upset when a Hollywood starlet (Rosemary Lane) steals the spotlight and their boyfriends when she appears as a publicity stunt at the school's annual prom. The show, directed by George Abbott, also launched the careers of Hugh Martin and Ralph Blane. In 1943, it was brought to the screen by Arthur Freed, with Lucille Ball, William Gaxton and Gloria de Haven joining June Allyson and Nancy Walker, the only holdovers from the original stage production.

Presented at the Stage 73 Theatre on April 2, 1963, the revival starred Paula Wayne, Christopher Walken, and Karin Wolfe, and kept the original score in which Martin and Blane had interpolated two new songs, including "You Are For Loving," performed as a second act solo by Liza Minnelli. It had a run of 224 performances. Though an obvious piece of fluff, the recording reveals a score that is fairly uncomplicated and easy on the ear, with some recognizable numbers. It will mostly appeal to completists.

The Best Little Whorehouse in Texas ♪♪♪

1988, MCA Records; from the screen version *The Best Little Whorehouse in Texas*, Universal Pictures, 1982.

Album Notes: *Music*: Carol Hall; Lyrics; Carol Hall; *Additional Songs*: Dolly Parton; *Orchestrations*: Gregg Perry; *Background Music*: Patrick Williams; *Cast*: Dolly Parton, Burt Reynolds, Dom DeLuise, Charles Durning, Jim Nabors; *Album Producer*: Gregg Perry; *Engineers*: Ernie Winfrey, Danny Wallin, Mickey Crofford, Mike Bradley, Arnie Frager.

Selections: 1 20 Fans (4:33) *Jim Nabors*; 2 A Lil' Ole Bitty Pissant Country Place (5:26) *Dolly Parton, Teresa Merritt*; 3 Sneakin' Around (D. Parton)(1:53) *Dolly Parton, Burt Reynolds*; 4 Watchdog Report/Texas Has A Whorehouse In It (3:04) *Dom DeLuise and The Dogettes*; 5 Courtyard Shag (3:29); 6 The Aggie Song (7:43); 7 The Sidestep (3:43) *Charles Durning*; 8 Hard Candy Christmas (3:50) *Dolly Parton*; 9 I Will Always Love You (D. Parton)(3:03) *Dolly Parton*.

Review: Like rock, country music has seldom made a successful foray on Broadway, though a particularly effective exception was *The Best Little Whorehouse in Texas*, which opened in 1978. Created by Carol Hall, the musical deals with the Chicken Ranch, a legendary Texas emporium and the only authorized brothel in the country, and efforts by some self-appointed protectors of morality to close the place, even though (or perhaps because) its customers include several influential politicians and important citizens. Deliberately lewd and raunchy, the show was a hit on Broadway and enjoyed a lengthy run of 1,584 performances. Sadly, its cast album has never been reissued on compact disc.

In 1982, however, it was turned into a screen musical, starring Dolly Parton (who contributed a couple of songs to the score) as Miss Mona, the house owner, and Burt Reynolds as the local sheriff and Mona's former lover. The recording presents what remains of Carol Hall's profuse score, which is very little, but it includes the show-stopper "The Sidestep," in which Charles Durning, a politician and customer at the Chicken Ranch, gives his own version of the tactful art of diplomacy, and "Hard Candy Christmas," a novel Yule anthem.

In 1994, the show spawned a sequel in *The Best Little Whorehouse Goes Public,* staged by Tommy Tune, which flopped, though it yielded a cast album on the Varese-Sarabande label.

Big River ♫♫♫♪

1985, MCA Records; from the Broadway production *Big River*, 1985.

Album Notes: *Music:* Roger Miller; *Lyrics:* Roger Miller; *Orchestrations:* Steven Margoshes, Danny Troob; *Musical Direction and Vocal Arrangements:* Linda Twine; *Dance and Incidental Music:* John Richard Lewis; *Cast:* Daniel Jenkins (Huckleberry Finn), Ron Richardson (Jim), Bob Gunton (The King), Rene Auberjonois (The Duke); *Album Producer:* Jimmy Bowen; *Enginners:* Bob Bullock, Josh Abbey, Steve Tillisch.

Selections: 1 Overture (1:48); 2 Do Ya Wanna Go To Heaven? (2:54); 3 The Boys (1:55); 4 Waitin' For The Light To Shine (1:29); 5 Guv'ment (2:02); 6 Hand For The Hog (1:10); 7 I Huckleberry, Me (1:56); 8 Muddy Water (2:30); 9 The Crossing (1:58); 10 River In The Rain (3:27); 11 When The Sun Goes Down In The South (2:28); 12 Entr'acte (1:20); 13 The Royal Nonesuch (2:07); 14 Worlds Apart (2:54); 15 Arkansas/How Blest We Are (4:01); 16 You Oughta Be Here With me (2:19); 17 Leavin's Not The Only Way To Go (2:31); 18 Waitin' For The Light To Shine (reprise)(1:58); 19 Free At Last (2:44); 20 Muddy Water (reprise) (1:09).

Review: "King of the Road" songwriter Roger Miller enjoyed a long, 1,005-performance run with the multiple Tony Award-winning musical *Big River,* a clever adaptation of the Mark Twain stories about Huck Finn and the runaway slave Jim, as they travel on a raft down the Mississippi, from St. Petersburg, Missouri, to Hillsboro, Arkansas. With Heidi Landesman providing the evocative settings that gave the show its local folk colors, *Big River* was a powerful hit that survives to this day through its flavorful cast recording album.

The Boy Friend ♫♫♫

1989, RCA Victor; from the off Broadway production *The Boy Friend*, 1954.

Album Notes: *Music:* Sandy Wilson; *Lyrics:* Sandy Wilson; *Orchestrations:* Ted Royal, Charles L. Cooke; Paul McGrane and His Bearcats, under the direction of Anton Coppola; *Cast:* Millicent Martin (Nancy), Julie Andrews (Polly), Ann Wakefield (Maisie), Stella Claire (Fay), Dilys Lay (Dulcie), Paulette Girard (Hortense), Bob Scheerer (Bobby Van Husen), Ruth Altman (Madame Dubonnet), Eric Berry (Percival Browne), John Hewer (Tony), Geoffrey Hibbert (Lord Brockhurst); *Album Producer:* Hugo Winterhalter; *CD Producer:* Didier C. Deutsch; *Engineer:* Paul Goodman.

Selections: 1 Overture (3:31) *The Bearcats*; 2 Perfect Young Ladies (1:10) *Paulette Girard, Millicent Martin, Ann Wakefield, Stella Claire, Dilys Lay*; 3 The Boy Friend (2:44) *Julie Andrews*; 4 Won't You Charleston With Me? (3:16) *Ann Wakefield, Bob Scheerer*; 5 Fancy Forgetting (2:22) *Ruth Altman, Eric Berry*; 6 I Could Be Happy With You (3:19) *Julie Andrews, John Hewer*; 7 Sur la plage (1:50); 8 A Room In Bloomsbury (2:43) *John Hewer, Julie Andrews*; 9 The You-Don't-Want-To-Play-With-Me Blues (3:10) *Ruth Altman, Eric Berry, The Perfect Young Ladies*; 10 Safety In Numbers (2:49) *Ann Wakefield, The Boy Friends*; 11 The Riviera (2:53) *Ann Wakefield, Bob Scheerer*; 12 It's Never Too Late To Fall In Love (2:02) *Geoffrey Hibbert, Dilys Lay*; 13 Carnival Tango (2:17) *The Bearcats*; 14 Poor Little Pierrette (3:28) *Ruth Altman, Julie Andrews*; 15 Finale (1:28) *Julie Andrews, John Hewer*.

Review: A lighthearted send-up of the simple musicals of the 1920s, *The Boy Friend*, written by Sandy Wilson, was initially created in London in 1953 as an after-hour entertainment at an intimate private theatre club. Set on the Riviera in 1926, its skimpy storyline deals with a young English heiress at Madame Dubonnet's finishing school, and the young delivery boy (actually a peer in disguise) with whom she falls in love. On September 30, 1954, *The Boy Friend* opened at the Royale Theater under the aegis of producers Cy Feuer and Ernest Martin where it played a total of 485 performances. In its cast was a fresh 19-year-old, Julie Andrews, whose next stop on Broadway two years later would be in the huge hit *My Fair Lady*. The show was revived off-Broadway in 1958, for a run that lasted 763 performances, and again on Broadway in 1970 for 119 performances, with Sandy Duncan and Judy Carne in the cast.

The 1954 cast album listed above, while in mono, presents Julie Andrews and cohorts in the first production, in what turns out to be a delightful recording of Sandy Wilson's whimsical score.

The Boys from Syracuse

The Boys from Syracuse
♪♪♪♪⌐

1993, Sony Broadway; from the studio cast recording *The Boys from Syracuse*, 1953.

Album Notes: *Music*: Richard Rodgers; *Lyrics*: Lorenz Hart; Chorus and orchestra conducted by Lehman Engel; *Cast*: Portia Nelson (Adriana), Jack Cassidy (Antipholus of Syracuse/Antipholus of Ephesus), Bibi Osterwald (Luce/Courtesan), Holly Harris (Luciana), Stanley Prager (Dromio of Syracuse/Dromio of Ephesus), Bob Shaver (Singing Policeman); *Album Producer*: Goddard Lierberson; *CD Producer*: Didier C. Deutsch; *Engineer*: Darcy Proper.

Selections: 1 Overture (5:16); 2 He Had Twins (4:43) *Chorus*; 3 Dear Old Syracuse (2:45) *Jack Cassidy*; 4 What Can You Do With A Man? (3:06) *Bibi Osterwald, Stanley Prager*; 5 Falling In Love With Love (3:54) *Portia Nelson*; 6 The Shortest Day Of The Year (4:09) *Jack Cassidy*; 7 This Can't Be Love (2:18) *Jack Cassidy, Holly Harris*; 8 Ladies Of The Evening (2:28) *Chorus*; 9 He And She (3:35) *Bibi Osterwald, Stanley Prager*; 10 You Have Cast Your Shadow On The Sea (4:00) *Jack Cassidy*; 11 Come With Me (2:38) *Bob Shaver*; 12 The Ballet (3:52); 13 Sing For Your Supper (3:09) *Portia Nelson, Holly Harris, Bibi Osterwald*; 14 Oh, Diogenes (2:07) *Bibi Osterwald*; 15 Finale (4:32) *Bibi Osterwald, Jack Cassidy, Portia Nelson*.

Review: See entry below.

The Boys from Syracuse
♪♪♪♪⌐

1993, Angel Records; from the off Broadway revival *The Boys from Syracuse*, 1963.

Album Notes: *Music*: Richard Rodgers; *Lyrics*: Lorenz Hart; *Orchestrations*: Larry Wilcox; *Musical and Choral Direction*: Rene Wiegert; *Cast*: Ellen Hanley (Adriana), Stuart Damon (Antipholus of Syracuse), Clifford David (Antipholus of Ephesus), Karen Morrow (Luce), Cathryn Damon (Courtesan), Julienne Marie (Luciana), Danny Carroll (Dromio of Syracuse), Rudy Tronto (Dromio of Ephesus), Gary Oakes (Singing Policeman); *CD Engineer*: Robert Norberg.

Selections: 1 Opening/I Had Twins (5:50) *Rudy Tronto, Danny Carroll, Matt Tobin, Gary Oakes, Fred Kimbrough, Richard Nieves*; 2 Dear Old Syracuse (2:39) *Stuart Damon*; 3 What Can You Do With A Man? (3:12) *Karen Morrow, Rudy Tronto*; 4 Falling In Love With Love (3:09) *Ellen Hanley*; 5 The Shortest Day Of The Year (2:26) *Clifford David*; 6 This Can't Be Love (3:17) *Stuart Damon, Julienne Marie*; 7 Ladies Of The Evening (2:48) *Gary Oakes*; 8 He And She (3:43) *Karen Morrow, Danny Carroll*; 9 You Have Cast Your Shadow On The Sea (3:47) *Stuart Damon, Julienne Marie*; 10 Come With Me (2:45) *Clifford David, Gary Oakes, Richard Nieves*; 11 Sing For Your Supper (3:44) *Ellen Hanley, Julienne Marie, Karen Morrow*; 12 Oh, Diogenes! (2:22) *Cathryn Damon*; 13 Finale (:54) *Entire Company*.

Review: "If it's good enough for Shakespeare, it's good enough for us." With these words to the wise, on November 23, 1938, Rodgers and Hart introduced their latest musical, *The Boys from Syracuse*. A wild romp through classic antiquity, the musical is based on the Bard's *Comedy of Errors*, itself borrowed from Plautus' *Menaechmi*, and is about two sets of twins separated at birth, one pair living in Ephesus, in Asia Minor, the other in Syracuse. When the boys from Syracuse, named Antipholus and Dromio, arrive in Ephesus, they are immediately mistaken for their Ephesus twins, also named Antipholus and Dromio. In the end, of course, all's well that ends well, with the reunited twins and their respective spouses and mates ready to enjoy life together.

With its irreverent book by George Abbott and a score brimming with many great tunes ("Falling in Love with Love," "This Can't Be Love"), *The Boys from Syracuse* enjoyed a run of 235 performances. In 1940, it was transferred to the screen in a film version that starred Allan Jones and Martha Raye. On April 15, 1963, it was successfully revived off-Broadway for a 25th anniversary production which had a run of 500 performances. That production is documented in the Angel recording listed above, with Stuart Damon, Cathryn Damon, Clifford David and

Karen Morrow in its cast. It is a lively, spirited recording that echoes the impish moods in this amusing musical.

Though a mono recording, the 1953 studio cast recording, starring Jack Cassidy, Portia Nelson and Bibi Osterwald is of interest because it features a fuller orchestra than the 1963 revival, the original orchestrations, and a vibrant cast that evidently enjoys singing the songs by Rodgers and Hart. As an alternative option, you can't go wrong.

Brigadoon

Brigadoon ♪♪♪♪

1988, RCA Victor; from the Broadway production Brigadoon, 1947.

Album Notes: *Music*: Frederick Loewe; *Lyrics*: Alan Jay Lerner; *Musical Director*: Franz Allers; *Cast*: David Brooks (Tommy Albright), Marion Bell (Fiona MacLaren), Pamela Britton (Meg Brockie), Virginia Bosler (Jean MacLaren), Delbert Anderson (Stuart Dalrymple), Hayes Gordon (Sandy Dean), Earl Redding (MacGregor), Lee Sullivan (Charlie Dalrymple); *Album Producers*: Eli Oberstein, Russ Case; *CD Producer*: Didier C. Deutsch; *Engineer*: Paul Goodman.

Selections: 1 Overture/Once In The Highlands/Brigadoon (3:02) *Delbert Anderson*; 2 Down On MacConnachy Square (3:10) *Hayes Gordon, Earl Redding, Delbert Anderson, Pamela Britton*; 3 Waitin' For My Dearie (3:43) *Marion Bell*; 4 I'll Go Home With Bonnie Jean (3:05) *Lee Sullivan*; 5 The Heather On The Hill (3:37) *David Brooks, Marion Bell*; 6 Come To Me, Bend To Me (3:27) *Lee Sullivan*; 7 Almost Like Being In Love (2:42) *David Brooks, Marion Bell*; 8 There But For You Go I (3:37) *David Brooks*; 9 My Mother's Weddin' Day (2:41) *Pamela Britton,*; 10 From This Day On/Brigadoon (3:17) *David Brooks, Marion Bell*.

Review: See entry below.

Brigadoon ♪♪♪

1996, Rhino Records; from the screen version Brigadoon, M-G-M, 1954.

Album Notes: *Music*: Frederick Loewe; *Lyrics*: Alan Jay Lerner; *Orchestrations*: Bob Franklyn, Albert Sendrey; *Arrangements*: Conrad Salinger, Bobby Tucker, Johnny Green; The M-G-M Studio Orchestra and Chorus conducted by Johnny Green; *Cast*: Gene Kelly (Tommy Albright), Van Johnson (Jeff Douglass), Cyd Charisse (Fiona Campbell), Elaine Stewart (Jane Ashton); *CD Producers*: George Feltenstein, Bradley Flanagan; *Engineers*: Allan Fisch, Ted Hall.

Selections: 1 Main Title (1:30); 2 Once In The Highlands (:52) *Dick Beavers*; 3 Brigadoon (2:06) *The M-G-M-Studio Chorus*; 4 Down On MacConnachy Square (3:13) *Lucille Smith, Eddie Quillan, Bill Reeve, Dick Beavers, Warren Tippie, Faith Kruger, Robert Wacker, Ray Linn, Dorothy Tennant, Richard Peel, Lucille Jean Norman, M. McLain, Pete Roberts, Ernie Newton, The M-G-M Studio Chorus*; 5 Waitin' For My Dearie (5:46) *Carol Richards, Bonnie Murray, Anne Biggs, Betty Allen, The M-G-M Studio Chorus*; 6 I'll Go Home With Bonnie Jean (5:17) *John Gustafsen, Gene Kelly, Van Johnson, Paul Roberts, The M-G-M Studio Chorus*; 7 Come To Me, Bend To Me (outtake)(2:59) *John Gustafsen*; 8 The Heather On The Hill (6:36) *Gene Kelly*; 9 Almost Like Being In Love (4:21) *Gene Kelly*; 10 Talk To Dominic (2:29); 11 Till The End Of Our Days (1:14); 12 There But For You Go I (outtake)(4:13) *Gene Kelly*; 13 Two Hundred Years Later (4:43); 14 The Wedding Dance (4:08); 15 The Chase (3:48) *John Gustafsen, Bill Reeve, Ernie Newton, The M-G-M Studio Chorus*; 16 Fiona's Search (1:01); 17 From This Day On (outtake)(4:17) *Gene Kelly, Carol Richards*; 18 Heather On The Hill (reprise)(2:19) *Carol Richards*; 19 Even Miracles (1:35); 20 Finale/End Credits (1:01) *The M-G-M Studio Chorus*; 21 Dinna Ye Know, Tommy (outtake)(:25) *Carol Richards*; 22 Come To Me, Bend To Me (outtake)(:56) *Carol Richards*; 23 Heather On The Hill (reprise)(3:43).

Review: See entry below.

Brigadoon ♪♪♪♪

1992, Angel Records; from the studio cast recording Brigadoon, 1992.

Album Notes: *Music*: Frederick Loewe; *Lyrics*: Alan Jay Lerner; *Musical Director*: John McGlinn; *Cast*: Brent Barrett (Tommy Albright), Rebecca Luker (Fiona MacLaren), Judy Kaye (Meg Brockie), Jackie Morrison (Jean MacLaren), Ian Caley (Stuart Dalrymple), Leo Andrew (Sandy Dean), Donald Maxwell (MacGregor), John Mark Ainsley (Charlie Dalrymple), Frank Middlemass (Mr. Lundie), Gregory Jbara (Jeff Douglas), Susannah Fellows (Jane Ashton), Mark W. Smith (Frank); *Album Producer*: Simon Woods; *Engineers*: John Kurlander, David Flower, Alex Marcou.

Selections: 1 Overture (:54); 2 Once In The Highlands (1:15) *Vernon Midgley*; 3 Brigadoon (2:19) *Brent Barrett, Gregory Jbara*; 4 Vendors' Calls/Down On MacConnachy Square (4:18) *Leo Andrew, Donald Maxwell, Ian Caley, Judy Kaye*; 5 Waitin' For My Dearie (4:02) *Rebecca Luker*; 6 I'll Go Home With Bonnie Jean (2:21) *John Mark Ainsley*; 7 Dance (5:24); 8 The Heather On The Hill (4:08) *Brent Barrett, Rebecca Luker*; 9 The Love Of My Life (3:27) *Judy Kaye*; 10 Jeannie's Packin' Up (1:38); 11 Come To Me, Bend To Me (2:18) *John Mark Ainsley*;

12 Dance (7:07); 13 Almost Like Being In Love (2:44) *Brent Barrett, Rebecca Luker*; 14 Entrance Of The Clans (1:13); 15 Wedding Ceremony (1:24) *Frank Middlemass, John Mark Ainsley, Jackie Morrison*; 16 The Wedding Dance (1:03) *Ian Caley*; 17 Sword Dance/End Of Act One (4:13) *Jackie Morrison, Colin Forsythe*; 18 The Chase (5:17) *Donald Maxwell, Ian Caley, Brent Barrett, Gregory Jbara*; 19 There But For You Go I (3:50) *Brent Barrett, Rebecca Luker*; 20 Glen Scene Opening/My Mother's Weddin' Day (3:17) *Judy Kaye*; 21 Dance (:42); 22 Funeral Dance (2:55); 23 From This Day On/Farewell Music (4:08) *Rebecca Luker, Brent Barrett*; 24 Change Of Scene/ Reprises/Change Of Scene (6:47) *Mark W. Smith, Brent Barrett, Susannah Fellows, Rebecca Luker, John Mark Ainsley*; 25 Finale (2:11) *Frank Middlemass.*

Review: A musical about a Scottish village which reappears for one day every hundred years and the two American travelers that stumble upon it seems a fairly unlikely proposition for a hit Broadway show. However, Alan Jay Lerner and Frederick Loewe succeeded admirably. While the score is near perfection, it does vacillate a bit between traditional musical comedy and the new style of musical play. Regardless, the tunes and lyrics are easily hummed and remain in the memory long after the album ends. In the 1947 original cast album, Marion Bell is lovely as Fiona, the Highland lass who falls in love with the American Tommy, ardently sung by David Bell. Lee Sullivan is a winning Charlie Dalrymple and Pamela Britton enthusiastically sings only one of Meg Brockie's two numbers. This release gets the highest rating in spite of too many cuts and rather ordinary monaural sound.

While the 1954 film has beautiful settings and costumes and well-seasoned performers, it doesn't measure up to the original Broadway production. Unfortunately, the same can be said for the soundtrack. The orchestrations are beautifully done, the singing is more than acceptable and the sound is in stereo, but the score is cut to shreds and several wonderful songs are not included, although a few outtakes and much dance music previously unavailable are. Gene Kelly, Carol Richards and Van Johnson do their best, but there is a certain blandness that affected many of the era's big MGM musicals taken from the Broadway theater.

For its most recent incarnation, the 1992 studio cast, John McGlinn did a wonderful job recreating a theatrical atmosphere within the sterile confines of the recording studio. In fact, the recording is so spectacular, you can almost feel the mist of the Scottish Highlands drift out from your speakers. Arguably, there are no better performers in the Broadway theater today than the ones chosen for this recording. Rebecca

Luker is a lovely, charming Fiona MacLaren, with Brent Barrett a strong, yet sensitive Tommy Albright. Judy Kaye portrays Meg Brockie as a lusty Highland wench and John Mark Ainsley as Charlie Dalrymple sings his songs from the heart. The Ambrosian Chorus and the London Sinfonietta play as if the music were in their blood, which is a very high compliment from this corner. Don't miss this extraordinary recording in terrific, modern stereo digital sound.

Jerry J. Thomas

Bring in 'Da Noise, Bring in 'Da Funk ♫♫

1996, RCA Victor; from the Broadway production *Bring in 'Da Noise, Bring in 'Da Funk*, 1996.

Album Notes: *Music:* Daryl Waters, Zane Mark, Ann Duquesnay; *Lyrics:* Reg E. Gaines; *Orchestrations:* Daryl Waters; *Vocal Arrangements:* Ann Duquesnay; *Musical Director:* Zane Mark; *Featured Musicians:* Zane Mark (keyboards), Lafayette Harris, Jr. (keybaords), Zane Paul (saxophone/clarinet/ flute), David Rogers (trumpet/flugelhorn/kazoo), Vince Henry (guitar/harmonica/banjo), Luico Hopper (bass), Leroy Clouden (drums/percussion); *Cast:* Savion Glover, Ann Duquesnay, Jeffrey Wright, Vincent Bingham, Duke Hill, Jimmy Tate, Baakari Wilder, Jared Crawford, Raymond King; *Album Producer:* James P. Nichols; *Engineers:* James P. Nichols, David Hewitt, Phil Giromer.

Selections: In 'Da Beginning: 1 Bring In 'Da Noise, Bring In 'Da Funk (3:48) *Company*; 2 The Door To Isle Goree (1:00) *Jeffrey Wright*; 3 Slave Ships (3:19) *Ann Duquesnay, Savion Glover*; 4 Som'thin' From Nuthin'/ Circle Stomp (4:04) *Ann Duquesnay, Jeffrey Wright, Dule Hill, Vincent Bingham, Jimmy Tate, Baakari Wilder*; 5 The Pan Handlers (1:17) *Jared Crawford, Raymond King*; Urbanization: 6 The Lynching Blues (3:01) *Ann Duquesnay, Jeffrey Wright, Baakari Wilder*; 7 Chicago Bound (4:12) *Jared Crawford, Ann Duquesnay, Savion Glover*; 8 Shifting Sounds (1:03) *Jeffrey Wright*; 9 Industrialization (3:44) *Savion Glover, Baakari Wilder, Jimmy Tate, Vincent Bingham, Jared Crawford, Raymond King*; 10 Quittin' Time/The Chicago Riot Rag (6:17) *Jeffrey Wright, Ann Duquesnay, Savion Glover, Baakari Wilder, Jimmy Tate, Vincent Bingham*; 11 I Got The Beat/Dark Tower (3:28) *Ann Duquesnay, Jeffrey Wright*; 12 The Whirling Stomp (1:44) *Ann Duquesnay, Savion Glover, Baakari Wilder, Jimmy Tate, Vincent Bingham*; Where's The Beat: 13 Now That's Tap (3:35) *Jeffrey Wright, Ann Duquesnay, Jimmy Tate, Vincent Bingham*; 14 The Uncle Huck-A-Buck Song (3:03) *Jeffrey Wright, Baakari Wilder, Ann Duquesnay, Savion Glover, Jimmy Tate, Vincent Bingham, Jared Crawford*; 15 Kid Go! (3:43) *Jeffrey*

Wright, Ann Duquesnay, Dule Hill; 16 The Lost Beat Swing (2:14) *Ann Duquesnay, Dule Hill*; 17 Green, Chaney, Buster, Slyde (5:46) *Savion Glover*; Street Corner Symphony: 18 Them Conkheads (2:27) *Ann Duquesnay*; 19 Hot Fun (2:19) *Ann Duquesnay, Jeffrey Wright*; 20 Blackout (2:29) Savion Glover, Baakari Wilder, Jimmy Tate, Vincent Bingham; 21 Gospel/Hip Hop Rant (2:41) *Ann Duquesnay, Jeffrey Wright, Savion Glover*; Noise/Funk: 22 Drummin'/Taxi (4:07) *Jared Crawford, Raymond King, Savion Glover, Jimmy Tate, Baakari Wilder, Vincent Bingham*; 23 Conversations/Tradin' Hits (2:04) *Savion Glover, Baakari Wilder, Vincent Bingham, Jimmy Tate, Raymond King, Dule Hill, Jared Crawford*; 24 Hittin' (1:21) *Jeffrey Wright, Savion Glover, Baakari Wilder, Jimmy Tate, Vincent Bingham, Jared Crawford, Raymond King*; 25 Bring In 'Da Noise, Bring In 'Da Funk (2:08) Company.

Review: Some shows are an effective blend of songs and dances, combined with a solid dramatic texture that gives the whole package an uncompromising theatrical flair. Usually, these shows translate very well to the recording medium, even though a large part of their theatricality is no longer part of the mix. Others just don't fare so well. Such is the case with *Bring in 'Da Noise, Bring in 'Da Funk*, a dramatic retelling of the struggle of African Americans from the days of slavery to the Civil Rights movement, as seen though a show which is essentially a songfest of tap dancing and percussion. On stage, the concept is quite effective, largely because of the drive and energy demonstrated by Savion Glover and the dancers in his company. In fact, "Industrialization," a scene which explores the industrial revolution only in terms of tap and percussion, proves an explosive show-stopper. However, the concept proves much less effective on record, simply because it is primarily visual. For this medium, many numbers have mercifully been abbreviated, with the focus shifted to Ann Dusquesnay's inspiring but eventually limited songs. The cast album (if that's what it is) cannot even convey the fire and excitement displayed on stage, much less the intensity evident in most of the performances.

Bubbling Brown Sugar ♫♫♫ᵇ

1986, Amherst Records; from the Broadway production *Bubbling Brown Sugar*, **1976.**

Album Notes: *Choral Arrangements*: Chapman Roberts; *Musical Arrangements and Direction*: Danny Holgate; *Featured Musicians*: Lloyd Mayers (piano), Arvel Shaw (bass), Rudy Stevenson (guitar/banjo), Joe Marshall, Hershel Dwelling, Frank Derrick (drums/percussion), Ernie Royal, Dick Vance, Hal "Money" Johnson (trumpet), Artie Hamilton, John Gordon (trombone), George Dorsey, Vinnie Ferraro, Zane Zacharoff, Russ Andrews (saxophone), Neal Tate (conductor); *Cast*: Avon Long, Josephine Premice, Vivian Reed, Joseph Attles, Carolyn Byrd, Chip Garnett, Barry Preston, Ethel Beatty; *Album Producer*: Pete Spargo; *Engineer*: Steve Friedman.

Selections: 1 Stompin' At The Savoy (A. Razaf/B. Goodman/E. Sampson/C. Webb)/Take The "A" Train (B. Strayhorn)(2:15)The Band; 2 Bubbling Brown Sugar (D. Holgate/E. Kemp/L. Lopez)(1:30)Company; 3 Nobody (A. Rogers/B. Williams)(3:02) *Avon Long*; 4 His Eye Is On The Sparrow/Swing Low Sweet Chariot (trad.)(5:00) *Carolyn Byrd*; 5 Sophisticated Lady (E.K. Ellington/M. Parish/I. Mills)(2:50) *Chip Garnett*; 6 Stormy Monday Blues (B. Eckstine/B. Crowder/E. Hines)(1:30) *Carolyn Byrd*; 7 In Honeysuckle Time, When Emaline Said She'd Be Mine (N. Sissle/E. Blake)(1:15) *Avon Long, Joseph Attles*; 8 Sweet Georgia Brown (B. Bernie/K. Casey/M. Pinkard)(2:52) *Vivian Reed*; 9 Honeysuckle Rose (A. Razaf/T. Waller)(3:17) *Josephine Premice, Avon Long*; 10 I Got It Bad (E.K. Ellington/P.F. Webster)(3:32) *Ethel Beatty*; 11 Harlem Makes Me Feel! (E. Kemp)(2:12) *Barry Preston*; 12 There'll Be Some Changes Made (W.B. Overstreet/B. Higgins)(3:04) *Josephine Premice*; 13 God Bless The Child (B. Holiday/A. Herzog)(3:20) *Vivian Reed*; 14 It Don't Mean A Thing (E.K. Ellington/I. Mills)(4:55)Company.

Review: At heart a jazz/R&B musical revue, *Bubbling Brown Sugar* took some 40 musical numbers by some of the brightest songwriters of the 1930s, and aimed to bring back an era that was particularly rich and evocative, melodically and theatrically speaking. With a cast that included stage stars Josephine Premice and Avon Long (best remembered from the original *Porgy And Bess)*, expert tap dancer Joseph Attles, and nightclub performer Vivian Reed, the revue presented its cast in various songs. Many of them were familiar numbers like "Stompin' at the Savoy," "Take the 'A' Train," "Sophisticated Lady," "Honeysuckle Rose," "I Got It Bad (And That Ain't Good)," "God Bless the Child," and "It Don't Mean a Thing," that are still available in their original cast albums. Propelled by its star-power and its song roster, the musical enjoyed an excellent run of 768 performances following its Broadway premiere on March 2, 1976.

Bye Bye Birdie

Bye Bye Birdie ♫♫♫♫

1989, Columbia Records; from the Broadway production, *Bye Bye Birdie*, **1960.**

Album Notes: *Music*: Charles Strouse; *Lyrics*: Lee Adams; *Orchestrations*: Robert Ginzler; *Dance Arrangements*: John Morris; *Music Director*: Elliot Lawrence; *Cast*: Dick Van Dyke (Albert

"If you have a song in a movie and millions of people see the film, you've got immediate exposure."

Kathy Nelson
*director of music at Walt Disney's motion picture group
(Billboard, 4-97)*

Peterson), Chita Rivera (Rose Grant), Karin Wolfe (Helen), Marissa Mason (Nancy), Sharon Lerit (Alice), Louise Quick (Margie Ann), Lada Edmund (Penelope Ann), Jessica Albright (Deborah Sue), Susan Watson (Kim MacAfee), Paul Lynde (Mr. MacAfee), Dick Gautier (Conrad Birdie); *Album Producer*: Goddard Lieberson; *Engineers*: Fred Plaut, Murray Zimner, Ed McCowsky; *CD Producer*: Didier C. Deutsch; *Engineer*: Tim Geelan.

Selections: 1 Overture (2:40); 2 An English Teacher (2:52) *Chita Rivera, Dick Van Dyke*; 3 The Telephone Hour (3:03) *Karin Wolfe, Marissa Mason, Sharon Lerit, Louise Quick, Tracy Everitt, Jerry Dodge, Dean Stolber, Lola Edmund, Lynn Bowin*; 4 How Lovely To Be A Woman (2:31) *Susan Watson*; 5 Put On A Happy Face (3:18) *Dick Van Dyke*; 6 Normal American Boy (3:53) *Chita Rivera, Dick Van Dyke*; 7 One Boy (2:45) *Susan Watson, Jessica Albright, Sharon Lerit, Chita Rivera*; 8 Honestly Sincere (3:22) *Dick Gautier, Barbara Doherty*; 9 Hymn For A Sunday Evening (2:01) *Paul Lynde, Marijane Maricle, Susan Watson, Johnny Borden*; 10 One Last Kiss (1:34) *Dick Gautier*; 11 What Did I Ever See In Him? (1:55) *Chita Rivera, Susan Watson*; 12 A Lot Of Livin' To Do (2:54) *Dick Gautier, Susan Watson*; 13 Kids (1:29) *Paul Lynde, Marijane Maricle*; 14 Baby, Talk To Me (2:47) *Dick Van Dyke, George Blackwell*; 15 Kids (reprise) (1:09) *Johnny Borden, Paul Lynde, Marijane Maricle*; 16 Spanish Rose (3:21) *Chita Rivera*; 17 Rosie (3:35) *Dick Van Dyke, Chita Rivera*.

Review: See entry below.

Bye Bye Birdie ♫♫

1988, RCA Records; from the screen version, *Bye Bye Birdie*, Columbia Pictures, 1963.

Album Notes: *Music*: Charles Strouse; *Lyrics*: Lee Adams; *Musical Arrangements*: Johnny Green; The Columbia Studio Orchestra conducted by Johnny Green; *Cast*: Dick Van Dyke (Albert Peterson), Janet Leigh (Rose Grant), Ann-Margret (Kim MacAfee), Paul Lynde (Mr. MacAfee), Jesse Pearson (Conrad Birdie), Maureen Stapleton, Bobby Rydell, Ed Sullivan; *Album Producer*: Neely Plumb; *CD Producer*: John Snyder; *Engineer*: Joe Lopes.

Selections: 1 Overture (4:21) *Ann-Margret*; 2 How Lovely To Be A Woman (2:38) *Ann-Margret*; 3 The Telephone Hour (2:52) *Bobby Rydell, The Sweet Apple Teenagers*; 4 Put On A Happy Face (3:34) *Dick Van Dyke, Janet Leigh*; 5 Honestly Sincere (3:16) *Jesse Pearson*; 6 Hymn For A Sunday Evening (2:11) *Ann-Margret, Paul Lynde, Mary LaRoche, Bryan Russell*; 7 One Last Kiss (2:14) *Jesse Pearson*; 8 One Boy (5:06) *Ann-Margret, Janet Leigh, Bobby Rydell*; 9 Kids (2:32) *Dick Van Dyke, Paul Lynde, Maureen Stapleton, Bryan Russell*; 10 A Lot Of Livin' To Do (6:02) *Jesse Pearson, Ann-Margret, Bobby Rydell*; 11 Rosie/ Bye Bye Birdie (End Title) (3:37) *Ann-Margret, Janet Leigh, Dick Van Dyke, Bobby Rydell*.

Review: Taking a cue from Elvis Presley's much publicized induction in the Army, composer Charles Strouse and lyricist Lee Adams, making their Broadway bow, wrote a joyously exhilarating musical which poked amiable fun at its famous model. The first of the great pop-rock musicals, the show was in truth an old-fashioned affair that relied on the trials and tribulations of Albert Peterson, a former English teacher turned music publisher and manager of Conrad Birdie (the show's Elvis alter ego), and his long-suffering girlfriend and secretary, Rose. The device used here is the hope that with Conrad being drafted, Albert might have more time to spend with Rose and make her dream of getting married a reality.

On a broader scale, the show also takes sharp aim at life in a small American town (where Conrad is going to make his last public appearance in a well orchestrated disappearing act), and at the generational misunderstanding between Conrad's teenage fans, all smitten by the nascent rock'n'roll craze, and their uncomprehending parents.

The musical became a springboard for many of its creators, including choreographer Gower Champion, and stars Dick Van Dyke and Chita Rivera. Several songs soon emerged from the score, including the unqualified hit, "Put on a Happy Face."

In its transfer to the big screen, the show retained most of its winning elements, substituting Janet Leigh for Chita Rivera, and adding Ann-Margret for box-office appeal. The recording, however, leaves a lot to be desired, with some distortion on the vocals and overall strident sonics that make it less than an acceptable representation in this digital age.

Cabaret

Cabaret ♫♫♫♫

1966, Columbia Records; from the Broadway production *Cabaret*, 1966.

Album Notes: *Music*: John Kander; *Lyrics*: Fred Ebb; *Orchestrations*: Don Walker; *Musical Direction*: Harold Hastings; *Cast*: Jill Haworth (Sally Bowles), Lotte Lenya (Fraulein Schneider), Jack Gilford (Herr Schulz), Bert Convy (Cliff Bradshaw), Joel Grey (Master of Ceremonies); *Album Producer*: Goddard Lieberson.

Selections: 1 Willkommen (5:14) *Joel Grey*; 2 So What? (3:23) *Lotte Lenya*; 3 Don't Tell Mama (4:03) *Jill Haworth, Joel Grey*; 4 Telephone Song (2:32) *Bert Convy*; 5 Perfectly Marvelous (3:30) *Bert Convy, Jill Haworth*; 6 Two Ladies (2:25) *Joel Grey, Rita O'Connor, Mary Ehara*; 7 It Couldn't Please Me More (Pineapple)(3:19) *Lotte Lenya, Jack Gilford*; 8 Tomorrow Belongs To Me (2:15) *Robert Sharp, Joel Grey*; 9 Entr'acte (2:25) *Kit Kat Band*; 10 Why Shouldn't I Wake Up? (2:31) *Bert Convy*; 11 The Money Song (1:54) *Joel Grey*; 12 Married (2:43) *Lotte Lenya, Jack Gilford*; 13 Meeskite (3:47) *Jack Gilford*; 14 If You Could See Her (Gorilla Song)(2:54) *Joel Grey*; 15 What Would You Do (3:27) *Lotte Lenya*; 16 Cabaret (4:30) *Jill Haworth*; 17 Finale (3:38) *Bert Convy, Jill Haworth, Lotte Lenya, Jack Gilford, Joel Grey*.

Review: See entry below.

Cabaret ♫♫♫♫

1989, MCA Records; from the screen version *Cabaret*, Allied Artists, 1972.

Album Notes: *Music*: John Kander; *Lyrics*: Fred Ebb; *Musical Direction*: Ralph Burns; *Cast*: Liza Minnelli (Sally Bowles), Marisa Berenson (Fraulein Schneider), Fritz Wepper (Herr Schulz), Michael York (Cliff Bradshaw), Joel Grey (Master of Ceremonies); *Album Producer*: Goddard Lieberson.

Selections: 1 Willkommen (4:29) *Joel Grey*; 2 Mein Herr (3:34) *Liza Minnelli*; 3 Two Ladies (3:11) *Joel Grey*; 4 Maybe This Time (3:09) *Liza Minnelli*; 5 Sitting Pretty (2:26); 6 Tiller Girls (1:40); 7 Money, Money (3:04) *Liza Minnelli, Joel Grey*; 8 Heiraten (Married)(3:33) *Greta Keller*; 9 If You Could See Her (3:53) *Joel Grey*; 10 Tomorrow Belongs To Me (3:05) *Ensemble*; 11 Cabaret (3:33) *Liza Minnelli*; 12 Finale (2:30) *Company*.

Review: In a stunning way, *Cabaret* captures a story set in the late 1920s, when storm clouds were beginning to gather over Germany and subsequently over all of Europe. Joel Grey was terrific as the sleazy Master of Ceremonies of the Kit Kat Klub with its slimy, decadent atmosphere of a Berlin that was going mad. Whatever performance she gave on stage, Jill Haworth, as Sally Bowles, created a strong character which comes charmingly across on the original cast album. Her delivery contains the perfect combination of humor and raucousness needed for the part. Saddled with a nondescript part, Bert Convy made the most of his numbers. Lotte Lenya, who personified these very Berlin years with just a shred of voice, was wonderful as Fraulein Schneider, whether expressing delight, tenderness or bitterness. Jack Gilford, a noted comedian, showed another side of his talent as the very sweet and vulnerable Herr Schultz, who, in spite of the madness around him, just wants to marry Fraulein Schneider. While the stereo recording is quite reverberant, it adds to the theatrical feel.

The film, which was a completely re-thought version of the show, was one of the last hit musical films based on a Broadway musical. Every performer in it is perfect, from the stars to the extras behind them, which is very evident on the recording. Arguably, Liza Minnelli, who won an Oscar for her portrayal as Sally Bowles, gave the greatest performance of her career in this film. Joel Grey, recreating and refining his stunning stage portrayal as the Master of Ceremonies in an Oscar winnning performance, was, if possible, even more sleazy and decadent on film than he was on stage. Both take up most of the soundtrack, together and separately. The plot songs from the stage were cut for the film and a few new songs were added. The punch-in-the-gut quality comes across very well on the album, but be warned that the packaging has no cast list and is very, very stingy with much needed information. However, the stereo sound is fine and adds to the impact of this truly enjoyable recording.

Jerry J. Thomas

Cabin in the Sky

Cabin in the Sky ♫♫♫♫

1993, Angel Records; from the off Broadway revival *Cabin in the Sky*, 1963.

Album Notes: *Music*: Vernon Duke; *Lyrics*: John Latouche; *Orchestrations*: Sy Oliver; *Orchestral Conductor*: Sy Oliver; *Cast*: Helen Ferguson (Lily), Rosetta LeNoire (Petunia Jackson), Tony Middleton ("Little Joe" Jackson), Sam Laws (The Lord's General), Bernard Johnson (Headman), Harold Pierson (1st Henchman), Morton Winston (2nd Henchman), Ketty Lester (Georgia Brown); *CD Engineer*: Robert Norberg.

Selections: 1 Wade In The Water (2:07) *Helen Ferguson*; 2 Cabin In The Sky (3:17) *Rosetta LeNoire, Tony Middleton*; 3 Make Way (1:12) *Helen Ferguson, Sam Laws*; 4 The Man Upstairs (3:05) *Sam Laws*; 5 Taking A Chance On Love (4:13)

Rosetta LeNoire; 6 Do What You Want To Do (2:59) *Bernard Johnson, Harold Pierson, Morton Winston*; 7 We'll Live All Over Again (1:56) *Rosetta LeNoire*; 8 Gospel & Great Day (2:11)Ensemble; 9 Honey In The Honeycomb (2:08) *Ketty Lester*; 10 Love Me Tomorrow (3:04) *Ketty Lester, Tony Middleton*; 11 Not A Care In The World (2:44) *Rosetta LeNoire, Tony Middleton*; 12 Not So Bad To Be Good (2:32) *Sam Laws*; 13 Do What You Want To Do (reprise)(1:54) *Ketty Lester, Harold Pierson, Morton Winston*; 14 Love Turned The Light Out (3:02) *Rosetta LeNoire*; 15 Living It Up (2:40) *Ketty Lester, Tony Middleton*; 16 Savanna (2:43) *Rosetta LeNoire*; 17 Cabin In The Sky (reprise)(1:32) *Rosetta LeNoire*.

Review: See entry below.

Cabin in the Sky 🎧🎧🎧🎧

1995, Rhino Records; from the screen version *Cabin in the Sky*, 1949.

Album Notes: *Music*: Vernon Duke; *Lyrics*: John Latouche; *Orchestrations*: George Bassman, Phil Moore, Robert Van Eps, David Raksin; *Arrangements*: Roger Edens, George Bassman, Phil Moore, Ted Fetter, Duke Ellington; *Vocal Arrangements*: Hall Johnson; The M-G-M Studio Orchestra, conducted by Georgie Stoll; *Cast*: Butterfly McQueen (Lily), Ethel Waters (Petunia Jackson), Eddie "Rochester" Anderson ("Little Joe" Jackson), Rex Ingram (Lucius/Lucifer, Jr.), Ernest Whitman (Jim Henry), Kenneth Spencer (The Lord's General), Lena Horne (Georgia Brown); *CD Producers*: Marilee Bradford, Bradley Flanagan; *Engineer*: Doug Schwartz.

Selections: 1 Main Title (1:45); 2 Foreword (R. Edens) (:25) *The Hall Johnson Choir*; 3 Li'l Black Sheep (H. Arlen/E.Y. Harburg) (3:45) *Ethel Waters, The Hall Johnson Choir*; 4 Old Ship Of Zion (trad.) (3:05) *Kenneth Spencer, The Hall Johnson Choir*; 5 But The Flesh Is Weak (R. Edens) (1:14); 6 The Prayer (R. Edens) (:43); 7 The First Revelation (R. Edens) (3:01); 8 Saint Petunia (R. Edens) (2:44); 9 Happiness Is A Thing Called Joe (H. Arlen/E.Y. Harburg) (3:02) *Ethel Waters*; 10 Dat Suits Me (trad.) (1:07) *Ethel Waters, Butterfly McQueen, The Hall Johnson Choir*; 11 Beside The Still Waters (R. Edens) (2:01); 12 Cabin In The Sky (4:28) *Ethel Waters, Eddie "Rochester" Anderson, The Hall Johnson Choir*; 13 Ain't The Truth (H. Arlen/E.Y. Harburg) (outtake) (:23) *Louis Armstrong*; 14 Ain't It The Truth (H. Arlen/E.Y. Harburg) (reprise) (2:30) *Lena Horne*; 15 Taking A Chance On Love (4:20) *Ethel Waters*; 16 The Meek And The Mild (R. Edens/H. Arlen) (4:35); 17 Life's Full O' Consequences (H. Arlen/E.Y. Harburg) (1:49) *Lena Horne, Eddie "Rochester" Anderson*; 18 Petunia In The Wilderness (R. Edens/H. Arlen) (:38); 19 Happiness Is A Thing Called Joe (reprise) (1:25) *Ethel Waters*; 20 Things Ain't What They Used To Be (M. Ellington) (1:26) *Duke Ellington and His Orchestra*; 21 Going Up (E.K. Ellington) (3:38) *Duke Ellington and His Orchestra*; 22 Down At Jim Henry's ([In] My Old Virginia Home [On The River Nile]) (1:38) *Duke Ellington and His Orchestra*; 23 Shine (F. Dabney/L. Brown/C. Mack) (2:50) *John Bubbles, The Hall Johnson Choir, Duke Ellington and His Orchestra*; 24 Honey In The Honeycomb (1:53) *Lena Horne*; 25 Love Me Tomorrow (3:41); 26 Honey In The Honeycomb (1:23) *Ethel Waters*; 27 Sweet Petunia (1:21); 28 The Third Revelation (R. Edens) (2:15); 29 Little Joe Throws Snake Eyes (R. Edens) (4:07); 30 Amen (R. Edens/H. Arlen) (1:16); 31 Taking A Chance On Love (reprise) (:35) *Ethel Waters, The Hall Johnson Choir*; 32 Taking A Chance On Love (full reprise) (1:10) *Ethel Waters, Roger Edens*.

Review: A black musical fable about the eternal struggle between Good and Evil and a rather unsteady sinner named Little Joe Jackson, *Cabin in the Sky* opened on Broadway on October 25, 1940, and immediately became the hottest show in town. With a great score by Vernon Duke and John Latouche, in which a big hit was "Taking a Chance on Love," and a cast that included Ethel Waters, Todd Duncan, Dooley Wilson, Rex Ingram and Katherine Dunham, the show recounted how Little Joe, seriously wounded in a street brawl, was given a reprieve of six months by the Lawd's General to prove himself or be forever cast in Hell, where Lucifer Jr. gleefully waited for him. In a twist that recalled several other shows with similar storylines (*Liliom, The Green Pastures,* and even *Damn Yankees,* many seasons later), Lucifer Jr. tried to trip Little Joe with the help of a sultry siren named Georgia Brown, but to little avail.

Ethel Waters, as Petunia, Little Joe's trusting wife, and Rex Ingram, as Lucifer Jr., were also the stars of the 1943 film version, which was directed by Vincente Minnelli for M-G-M. The film's cast also included Eddie "Rochester" Anderson, playing Little Joe, Lena Horne as Georgia Brown, Louis Armstrong and Duke Ellington and his orchestra. Unlike the stage musical, the film concluded on a different note, with Little Joe waking up at the end to realize it was all a bad dream. Also undergoing modifications was the score, in which only three songs from the original were retained, supplemented with several numbers written by Harold Arlen and E.Y. Harburg, including "Happiness Is a Thing Called Joe," and "Life's Full of Consequences." The film yielded a sensational soundtrack album, recently given the superlative Rhino treatment.

The original stage show was revived in 1964, with Rosetta LeNoire starring as Petunia, in an off Broadway production that had a limited run of 47 performances. The Angel cast album chronicles that revival and is of interest as the only recording of the production as it was originally presented.

Call Me Madam ♫♫♫♫

1995, DRG Records; from the New York City Center concert presentation *Call Me Madam*, **1995.**

Album Notes: *Music and Lyrics*: Irving Berlin; *Orchestrations*: Don Walker; The Coffee Club Orchestra, conducted by Rob Fisher; *Cast*: Tyne Daly (Mrs. Sally Adams), Walter Charles (Cosmo Constantine), Melissa Errico (Princess Maria), Simon Jones Sebastian Sebastian), Lewis Cleale (Kenneth Gibson), MacIntyre Dixon (Senator Brockbank), Christopher Durang (Congressman Wilkins), Ken Page (Senator Gallagher); *Album Producer*: Hugh Fordin; *Engineer*: Cynthia Daniels.

Selections: 1 Overture (4:44) *The Coffe Club Orchestra*; 2 Mrs. Sally Adams (2:11)Company; 3 The Hostess With The Mostes' On The Ball (3:07) *Tyne Daly*; 4 The Hostess With The Mostes' On The Ball (encore)(1:19) *Tyne Daly*; 5 Washington Square Dance (3:44) *Tyne Daly*; 6 Lichtenburg (3:52) *Walter Charles*; 7 Can You Use Any Money Today? (2:02) *Tyne Daly*; 8 Marrying For Love (3:42) *Tyne Daly, Walter Charles*; 9 (Dance To The Music Of) The Ocarina (4:52) *Melissa Errico, Simon Jones*; 10 It's A Lovely Day Today (2:53) *Lewis Cleale, Melissa Errico*; 11 The Best Of Things For You (3:17) *Tyne Daly, Walter Charles*; 12 Entr'acte (2:12) *The Coffee Club Orchestra*; 13 Something To Dance About (4:54) *Tyne Daly*; 14 Once Upon A Time Today (3:24) *Lewis Cleale*; 15 They Like Ike (3:15) *MacIntyre Dixon, Christopher Durang, Ken Page*; 16 It's A Lovely Day Today (reprise)(:33) *Ensemble*; 17 You're Just In Love (3:03) *Lewis Cleale, Tyne Daly*; 18 Mrs. Sally Adams (reprise) (1:24) *Ensemble*; 19 Finale — You're Just In Love (1:00) *Tyne Daly, Walter Charles*.

Review: Ethel Merman, the actress with the mostes', portrayed a reasonable facsimile of Perle Mesta, the hostess with the mostes' (who had recently been appointed American ambassador to Luxembourg by president Harry Truman), in *Call Me Madam*, an engaging musical by Irving Berlin, which opened on October 12, 1950. The show, a breezy satire dealing with an abrasively direct and definitely not diplomatic woman named ambassador to a tiny duchy (the action is set, according to the program notes, "in two mythical countries, Lichtenburg and the United States"), pokes gentle fun at American-style politics abroad, with Berlin delivering a serviceable and frequently enjoyable score. In 1953, the show reached the big screen, with Merman reprising the role, and George Sanders and Donald O'Connor in the cast.

This recording, starring Tyne Daly, originated at New York City Center's Encore! series, and, in the absence of original cast and soundtrack album recordings, provides a clear vision of the score, which included the popular hits "It's a Lovely Day Today" and "You're Just in Love." As is usually the case with this concert series, the performances are spirited and quite enjoyable.

Camelot

Camelot ♫♫♫♫

1960, Columbia Records; from the Broadway production *Camelot*, **1960.**

Album Notes: *Music*: Frederick Loewe; *Lyrics*: Alan Jay Lerner; *Orchestrations*: Robert Russell Bennett, Philip J. Lang; *Dance and Choral Arrangements*: Trude Rittman; *Musical Direction*: Franz Allers; *Cast*: Richard Burton (Arthur), Julie Andrews (Guenevere), Robert Goulet (Lancelot), Roddy McDowall (Mordred), John Cullum (Sir Dinadan), Bruce Yarnell (Sir Lionel), Michael Kermoyan (Sir Ozanna), Mary Sue Berry; *Album Producer*: Goddard Lieberson.

Selections: 1 Overture/I Wonder What The King Is Doing Tonight (5:08) *Richard Burton*; 2 The Simple Joys Of Maidenhood (2:10) *Julie Andrews*; 3 Camelot (2:29) *Richard Burton*; 4 Follow Me (2:29) *Mary Sue Berry*; 5 The Lusty Month Of May (2:57) *Julie Andrews*; 6 C'est Moi (3:27) *Robert Goulet*; 7 Then You May Take Me To The Fair (4:27) *Julie Andrews*; 8 How To Handle A Woman (2:34) *Richard Burton*; 9 If Ever I Would Leave You (3:09) *Robert Goulet*; 10 Parade (1:25) *Orchestra*; 11 Before I Gaze At You (1:56) *Julie Andrews*; 12 The Seven Deadly Virtues (1:22) *Roddy McDowall*; 13 What Do The Simple Folk Do? (4:59) *Julie Andrews, Richard Burton*; 14 Fie On Goodness! (3:31); 15 I Loved You Once In Silence (3:03) *Julie Andrews*; 16 Guenevere (3:15) *Ensemble*; 17 Camelot (reprise)(1:59) *Richard Burton*.

Review: See entry below.

Camelot ♫

1982, Varese-Sarabande; from the Broadway revival *Camelot*, **1982.**

Album Notes: *Music*: Frederick Loewe; *Lyrics*: Alan Jay Lerner; *Orchestrations*: Robert Russell Bennett, Philip J. Lang; *Dance and Choral Arrangements*: Trude Rittman; *Musical Direction*: Gerry Allison; *Cast*: Richard Harris (Arthur), Fiona Fullerton (Guenevere), Robert Meadmore (Lancelot), Michael Howe (Mordred), Roger Nott (Sir Dinadan), David Bexon (Sir Lionel), Claire Moore (Nimue); *Album Producers*: John Yap, Tom Null, Chris Kuchler; *Engineers*: Joe Gastwirt, Danny Hersh.

Selections: 1 Overture (3:04) *David Bexon*; 2 I Wonder What The King Is Doing Tonight? (2:01) *Richard Harris*; 3 The Simple Joys Of Maidenhood (3:30) *Fiona Fullerton*; 4 Camelot (2:31) *Richard Harris, Fiona Fullerton*; 5 Follow Me (2:55) *Claire Moore*; 6 C'est Moi (3:54) *Robert Meadmore*; 7 The Lusty

Month Of May (3:06) *Fiona Fullerton*; 8 How To Handle A Woman (3:44) *Richard Harris*; 9 The Jousts (3:37) The Company; 10 Before I Gaze At You (2:13) *Fiona Fullerton*; 11 Resolution (3:05) *Richard Harris*; 12 Entr'acte/Madrigal (3:39) *Robert Meadmore*; 13 If Ever I Would Leave You (3:28) *Robert Meadmore*; 14 The Seven Deadly Virtues (1:33) *Michael Howe*; 15 Fie On Goodness! (1:33) *Michael Howe*; 16 What Do The Simple Folk Do? (3:41) *Fiona Fullerton, Richard Harris*; 17 I Loved You Once In Silence (3:35) *Fiona Fullerton*; 18 Guenevere (5:00) *David Bexon*; 19 Finale (3:39) *Richard Harris*.

Review: See entry below.

Camelot ♫♫♫

1967, Warner Bros. Records; from the screen version *Camelot*, Warner Bros. Pictures, 1967.

Album Notes: *Music*: Frederick Loewe; *Lyrics*: Alan Jay Lerner; *Orchestrations*: Robert Russell Bennett, Philip J. Lang; *Choral Arrangements*: Ken Darby; *Musical Direction*: Alfred Newman; *Cast*: Richard Harris (Arthur), Vanessa Redgrave (Guenevere), Franco Nero (Lancelot), David Hemmings (Mordred), Lionel Jeffries (King Pellinore), Laurence Naismith (Merlin); *Album Producer*: Sonny Burke; *Engineers*: Lowell Frank; *CD Producer/Engineer*: Lee Herschberg.

Selections: 1 Prelude/Overture (3:08); 2 I Wonder What The King Is Doing Tonight? (2:03) *Richard Harris*; 3 The Simple Joys Of Maidenhood (2:00) *Vanessa Redgrave*; 4 Camelot/The Wedding Ceremony (4:40) *Richard Harris*; 5 C'est Moi (3:59) *Gene Merlino*; 6 The Lusty Month Of May (2:29) *Vanessa Redgrave*; 7 Follow Me and Children's Chorus (1:37); 8 How To Handle A Woman (4:10) *Richard Harris*; 9 Take Me To The Fair (4:55) *Vanessa Redgrave*; 10 If Ever I Would Leave You/Love Montage (5:48) *Gene Merlino*; 11 What Do The Simple Folk Do? (4:12) *Vanessa Redgrave, Richard Harris*; 12 I Loved You Once In Silence (2:57) *Vanessa Redgrave, Gene Merlino*; 13 Guenevere (2:57) Mixed Chorus; 14 Finale Ultimo (2:37) *Richard Harris*.

Review: The original cast recording on Columbia gets a top rating as it is a sheer delight from the upward sweep of the "Overture" to the haunting reprise of the title song that brings the album to its gentle, rueful close. Richard Burton makes an imposing, regal Arthur. Julie Andrews is, by turns, a shy, alluring, then passionate Guenevere. Robert Goulet is sexy and strong as Lancelot and Roddy McDowall shows a richly malevolent streak as Mordred. There is also a young, assertive John Cullum in a small role. Arguably, Alan Jay Lerner never turned in finer lyrics than in this work. Every word is allied with the music in such a way as to be inevitable. Frederick Loewe

continued to grow and enrich the sound of Broadway music with this musical, writing one of the all-time great Broadway scores. While the original production was plagued with problems and illnesses, listening to this album, one would never know it. It sounds effortless and continually fresh, and is a must in any library of Broadway show music.

While the recording of the London revival (on Varese-Sarabande) is wrong where the album of the 1960 Broadway cast is right, there are a few virtues to be found in it. More of the score has been included on this CD than on the original, and it is fairly well played by the orchestra, if somewhat out of tune here and there. The brilliance of the writing by Lerner and Loewe comes through with top honors. Unfortunately, the performances, with the possible exception of Robert Meadmore, a passionate yet sensitive Lancelot, are mediocre at best. Whatever the quality of his performance on stage, and though he tries hard, Richard Harris is just not good as Arthur on this album. He was much more effective in the film and on its soundtrack. Fiona Fullerton gives a small, whiney performance as Guenevere. The rest of the cast is acceptable. However, as there is no Arthur and Guenevere worth the listen, then there is no point in listening. This album is only for completists.

While visual elements of the film were so stunning that the music and lyrics tended to get lost, on the soundtrack recording (on Warner Bros.), the images don't mean anything and one can focus on the musical performances. Unfortunately, Richard Harris as King Arthur, Vanessa Redgrave as Queen Guenevere and Franco Nero (dubbed by Gene Merlino) as Lancelot do not measure up to the original cast in any way. With the exception of Merlino, the actors are non-singers and can be rather difficult to listen to, especially if one is familiar with the Broadway cast album. That said, there are also things to enjoy here. While her tempos and style of singing are quite different, Redgrave is an excellent Guenevere. Harris' Arthur is also very strong and likable, and the singing of Merlino comes across almost as powerful as the original. My choice will always be the original Broadway cast album as the best and most complete version of this truly magical score. However, the soundtrack album has its own particular joys and is well worth the time spent listening to it.

Jerry J. Thomas

Can-Can

Can-Can

1989, Capitol Records; from the Broadway production, *Can-Can*, 1953.

Album Notes: *Music*: Cole Porter; *Lyrics*: Cole Porter; *Orchestrations*: Philip J. Lang; *Musical Direction*: Milton Rosenstock;

Cast: Lilo (La Mome Pistache), Peter Cookson (Judge Aristide Forestier), Hans Conried (Boris Adzinidzinadze), Gwen Verdon (Claudine), Erik Rhodes (Hilaire Jussac).

Selections: 1 Introduction: Maidens Typical Of France (3:03) *Female Chorus*; 2 Never Give Anything Away (2:01) *Lilo*; 3 Quadrille (2:11); 4 C'est Magnifique (3:24) *Lilo, Peter Cookson*; 5 Come Along With Me (4:36) *Erik Rhodes, Hans Conried*; 6 Live And Let Live (1:56) *Lilo*; 7 I Am In Love (2:40) *Peter Cookson*; 8 If You Loved Me Truly (3:14) *Gwen Verdon, Hans Conried*; 9 Montmart' (1:33) *Peter Cookson*; 10 Allez-Vous En, Go Away (2:16) *Lilo*; 11 Never, Never Be An Artist (2:58) *Hans Conried*; 12 It's All Right With Me (2:01) *Peter Cookson*; 13 Every Man Is A Stupid Man (2:24) *Lilo*; 14 I Love Paris (2:29) *Lilo*; 15 Can-Can (2:58) *Lilo*.

Review: Cole Porter's particular fondness for things French found one of its best expressions in *Can Can*, a lullaby to turn-of-the-century Paris, when the "naughty" new dance at the Moulin-Rouge attracted huge crowds of society revelers... and the police, eager to close the place for these lewd exhibitions. In the show, the clash between Judge Forestier, a bastion of morality, and La Mome Pistache, owner of Bal du Paradis, a night club where the dissolute dance is performed nightly, eventually leads to a compromise when the Judge falls for La Mome, and becomes one of the Can-Can's most ardent defenders. Starring Lilo as Pistache and Peter Cookson as Forestier, the show also introduced Gwen Verdon, whose memorable Tony Award-winning turn in the seductive "Garden of Eden" ballet led to a starring role two years later in *Damn Yankees*. The score, one of Porter's most elegantly achieved, included at least two great songs, "C'est magnifique" and "I Love Paris." *Can Can*, which opened on May 7, 1953, had a run of 892 performances.

Can-Can 🎵

1989, Capitol Records; from the screen version, *Can-Can*, 20th Century-Fox, 1960.

Album Notes: *Music*: Cole Porter; *Lyrics*: Cole Porter; *Orchestrations*: Nelson Riddle; The 20th Century-Fox Orchestra, conducted by Nelson Riddle; *Cast*: Shirley MacLaine (Simone Pistache), Louis Jourdan (Philippe Forestier), Frank Sinatra (Francois Durnais), Maurice Chevalier (Paul Barriere), Juliet Prowse (Claudine); *Album Producer*: Dave Cavanaugh.

Selections: 1 Entr'acte (3:24) *Orchestra*; 2 It's All Right With Me (4:16) *Frank Sinatra*; 3 Come Along With Me (3:07) *Shirley MacLaine*; 4 Live And Let Live (1:52) *Maurice Chevalier, Louis Jourdan*; 5 You Do Something To Me (1:59) *Louis Jourdan*; 6

Let's Do It (2:49) *Frank Sinatra, Shirley MacLaine*; 7 Main Title: a. I Love Paris/b. Montmart' (3:04) *Frank Sinatra, Maurice Chevalier*; 8 C'est Magnifique (2:03) *Frank Sinatra*; 9 Maidens Typical Of France (2:06) *Chorus*; 10 Just One Of Those Things (2:11) *Maurice Chevalier*; 11 I Love Paris (2:24) *Frank Sinatra, Maurice Chevalier*; 12 Can-Can (3:19) *Orchestra*.

Review: What a shame that one of the most endearing of all of Frank Sinatra's film soundtracks has never enjoyed a proper presentation, one befitting the charming Cole Porter score, and its very special performances. Such is the case with *Can-Can*, originally released in 1960 as an LP on Capitol Records. At the time, little attention was paid to either the technical quality of the recording, or the actual sequencing of the songs. Unfortunately, little has changed with the transfer of the LP to compact disc. As in the LP, the "Entr'acte" opens the disc, while the "Main Title" appears in the middle of the program.

Sonically, the recording is dull, and the quality of the sound varies from track to track. Particularly distressing is the muffled, distorted sound on one of Sinatra's finest songs, "It's All Right With Me." Others, like the Sinatra-Maurice Chevalier duet on "I Love Paris," sound plain flat and one-dimensional. Overall, the equalization is poor, and the original transfer engineers liberally used reverb to conceal a myriad of defects.

These unforgivable technical problems aside, the Frank Sinatra, Maurice Chevalier and Shirley MacLaine performances of some of Porter's finest songs are essential, and deserve attention for their artistic value.

Charles L. Granata

Candide

Candide 🎵🎵🎵🎵

1991, Sony Broadway; from the Broadway production *Candide*, 1956.

Album Notes: *Music*: Leonard Bernstein; *Lyrics*: Richard Wilbur; *Additional Lyrics*: John Latouche, Dorothy Parker; *Orchestrations*: Leonard Bernstein, Hershy Kay; *Musical Direction*: Samuel Krachmalnick; *Cast*: Max Adrian (Dr. Pangloss), Barbara Cook (Cunegonde), Robert Rounseville (Candide), Irra Petina (The Old Lady), William Olvis (Governor Of Buenos Aires), William Chapman (Ferone), Norman Roland (Prefect Of Police), Robert Mesrobian (Prince Ivan); *Album Producer*: Goddard Lieberson; *CD Producer*: Thomas Z. Shepard; *Engineer*: Kevin Boutote.

Selections: 1 Overture (4:08); 2 Ensemble: The Best Of All Possible Worlds (3:26) *Max Adrian, Barbara Cook, Robert Rounseville*; 3 Duet: Oh, Happy We (1:51) *Robert Rounseville,*

Barbara Cook; 4 Song: It Must Be So (1:52) *Robert Rounseville*; 5 Paris Waltz Scene (1:38) *Orchestra*; 6 Aria: Glitter And Be Gay (5:44) *Barbara Cook*; 7 Duet: You Were Dead, You Know (2:30) *Robert Rounseville, Barbara Cook*; 8 Serenade: My Love (2:04) *William Olvis, Barbara Cook, Irra Petina*; 9 Tango: I Am Easily Assimilated (3:33) *Irra Petina, Barbara Cook*; 10 Quartet Finale (2:46) *Robert Rounseville, Barbara Cook, William Olvis, Irra Petina*; 11 Trio: Quiet (3:49) *Irra Petina, William Olvis, Barbara Cook*; 12 Ballad: Eldorado (3:14) *Robert Rounseville*; 13 Schottische: Bon Voyage (2:36) *William Olvis,*; 14 Waltz: What's The Use? (3:41) *Irra Petina, William Chapman, Norman Roland, Robert Mesrobian*; 15 Gavotte (3:58) *Irra Petina, Robert Rounseville, Max Adrian, Barbara Cook*; 16 Finale: Make Our Garden Grow (4:20) *Entire Company*.

Review: See entry below.

Candide 🎜🎜🎜🎜▸

1985, New World Records; from the New York City Opera revival *Candide*, **1985.**

Album Notes: *Music*: Leonard Bernstein; *Lyrics*: Richard Wilbur; *Additional Lyrics*: John Latouche, Stephen Sondheim; *Orchestrations*: Leonard Bernstein, Hershy Kay; *Musical Direction*: John Mauceri; *Cast*: John Lankston (Voltaire/Dr. Pangloss/ Governor), Erie Mills (Cunegonde), David Eisler (Candide), Joyce Castle (The Old Lady), Maris Clement (Paquette), Scott Reeve (Maximilian), Don Yule (First Inquisitor), William Ledbetter (Second Inquisitor), Jack Harrold (Prefect); *Album Producer*: Elizabeth Ostrow; *Engineer*: Paul Goodman.

Selections: CD 1: 1 Overture (4:26); 2 Fanfare/Life Is Happiness Indeed (4:52) *John Lankston, Erie Mills, David Eisler, Maris Clement, Scott Reeve*; 3 The Best Of All Possible Worlds (2:47) *John Lankston, Erie Mills, David Eisler, Maris Clement, Scott Reeve*; 4 Happy Instrumental/Oh, Happy We (2:22) *David Eisler, Erie Mills*; 5 Candide Begins His Travels (1:02); 6 It Must Be So (2:00) *David Eisler*; 7 Westphalian Fanfare, Chorale, Battle Music and It Must Be So (reprise)(2:55); 8 Entrance Of The Jew (:40); 9 Glitter And Be Gay (6:29) *Erie Mills*; 10 Earthquake Music/Dear Boy (4:07) *John Lankston*; 11 Auto Da-Fe (What A Day)(7:39) *Don Yule, William Ledbetter*; 12 Candide's Lament (3:38) *David Eisler*; 13 You Were Dead, You Know (2:48) *David Eisler, Erie Mills*; 14 Travel (To The Stables)/I Am Easily Assimilated (4:55)*Joyce Castle*; 15 Quartet Finale (3:00)*David Eisler, Erie Mills, Joyce Castle, John Lankston*.

CD 2: 1 Entr'acte (1:08); 2 Ballad Of The New World (3:27) *David Eisler,*; 3 My Love (2:14) *John Lankston, Scott Reeve*; 4 Barcarolle (3:29); 5 Alleluia (2:40) *Scott Reeve, David Eisler, John Lankston*; 6 Eldorado (1:10); 7 Sheep Song (4:26) *Ivy*

Austin, Rhoda Butler, Robert Brubaker, David Eisler, Maris Clement; 8 Governor's Waltz (3:28); 9 Bon Voyage (2:47) *John Lankston,*; 10 Quiet (4:24) *Joyce Castle, Maris Clement, David Eisler*; 11 Constantinople: What's The Use? (3:43) *Jack Harrold, James Billings, John Lankston*; 12 Finale: Make Our Garden Grow (4:21) *David Eisler, Erie Mills, John Pakston, Joyce Castle, Scott Reeve, Maris Clement*.

Review: Some Broadway shows undergo extensive rewrites before their opening, and occasionally even after they have received their official premiere. But few have been as extensively altered and modified than *Candide*, which initially opened on Broadway on December 1, 1956, only to close 76 performances later, and has since been revived (and revised) several times, both winningly and unsatisfactorily.

The first version, written by Lillian Helman, remained faithful to Voltaire's tale of the two innocent lovers, Candide and Cunegonde, who go through the most incredible misadventures before they can live together, wiser and presumably happier. However, it couldn't reconcile the various elements in the narrative with the tale's often idiosyncratic tone set by Voltaire in his satirical comments that all that happens happens for a good reason "in the best of all possible worlds," the truism uttered by Doctor Pangloss, Candide and Cunegonde's beloved teacher. Sometimes too heavy-handed, sometimes awkward, Helman's book failed to match the light, humoristic tones in Leonard Bernstein's brilliant score, which so effectively echoed the irony in Voltaire's novella.

Despite its failure on Broadway, the show became a cult favorite, thanks largely to its cast album, which remained a constant best seller in the Columbia catalogue, with Barbara Cook radiant as Cunegonde, and Robert Rounseville handsomely fetching as Candide.

Finally, in 1973, producer-director Harold Prince decided to try and revisit the show. Helman's book was discarded, and Hugh Wheeler was brought in to write a new, more theatrical version, with Stephen Sondheim contributing some new lyrics to Bernstein's songs. The revised show, pruned down and more effective, opened on Broadway on March 10, 1974, to ecstatic reviews, and enjoyed a run of 740 performances. A cast album, released at the time by Columbia Records, has never been reissued on compact disc, but with a few additional revisions reflecting Prince's more operatic approach to a new staging for the New York City Opera, the New World recording listed above gives an idea of the extensive work that went into the score.

More recently, on April 29, 1997, *Candide* returned to Broadway in a sparkling new edition, again produced and directed by Prince, with more revisions brought to it, and a sensational cast headed by Jim Dale as Pangloss, Harolyn Blackwell as Cunegonde, Jason Daniely as Candide, and Andrea Martin as The Old Lady. A cast album was expected on RCA Victor at this writing, and will no doubt provide a fresh alternative to the other two listed above. In the final analysis, however, the 1956 recording is probably the one that will endure, if only because it was one of the original show's most satisfactory ingredients, and is not weighted down by the book as was the case with the production itself.

Carnival ♪♪♪♪

1989, Polydor Records; from the Broadway production Carnival, 1961.

Album Notes: *Music:* Bob Merrill; *Lyrics:* Bob Merrill; *Orchestrations:* Philip Howard; *Musical Direction and Vocal Arrangements:* Saul Schechtman; *Cast:* Anna Maria Alberghetti (Lili), Jerry Orbach (Paul Berthalet), James Mitchell (Marco The Magnificent), Kaye Ballard (The Incomparable Rosalie), Pierre Olaf (Jacquot), Henry Lascoe (B.E. Schlegel), George Marcy, Tony Gomez, Johnny Nola, Buff Shurr (Roustabouts); *CD Producer:* Larry L. Lash; *Engineer:* Dennis Drake.

Selections: 1 Opening (1:39); 2 Direct From Vienna (1:58)*Henry Lascoe, Kaye Ballard,*; 3 A Very Nice Man (2:01) *Anna Maria Alberghetti*; 4 I've Got To Find A Reason (1:42) *Jerry Orbach*; 5 Mira (3:03) *Anna Maria Alberghetti*; 6 A Sword And A Rose And A Cape (2:09) *James Mitchell, George Marcy, Tony Gomez, Johnny Nola, Buff Shurr*; 7 Humming (3:59) *Kaye Ballard, Henry Lascoe*; 8 Yes, My Heart (2:51) *Anna Maria Alberghetti, George Marcy, Tony Gomez, Johnny Nola, Buff Shurr*; 9 Everybody Likes You (2:15) *Jerry Orbach*; 10 Love Makes The World Go 'Round (1:49) *Anna Maria Alberghetti, Jerry Orbach*; 11 Yum Ticky (:47) *Anna Maria Alberghetti, Jerry Orbach, Pierre Olaf*; 12 The Rich (1:16) *Anna Maria Alberghetti, Jerry Orbach, Pierre Olaf*; 13 Beautiful Candy (2:34)*Anna Maria Alberghetti, Jerry Orbach, Pierre Olaf*; 14 Her Face (2:10) *Jerry Orbach*; 15 Grand Imperial Cirque de Paris (2:20)*Pierre Olaf*; 16 I Hate Him (1:36) *Anna Maria Alberghetti*; 17 Her Face (reprise)(1:12) *Anna Maria Alberghetti, Jerry Orbach*; 18 Always, Always You (1:22) *James Mitchell, Kaye Ballard*; 19 Always, Always You (reprise)(1:57) *Kaye Ballard*; 20 She's My Love (2:32) *Jerry Orbach*; 21 Finale (1:01) *Jerry Orbach*; 22 A Very Nice Man (3:13) *Bob Merrill*; 23 Mira (2:29) *Bob Merrill*; 24 Yes, My Heart (3:34) *Bob Merrill*; 25 Love Makes The World Go 'Round (1:24) *Bob Merrill*; 26 I Hate Him (1:31) *Bob Merrill*; 27 Mira (3:18) *J.J. Johnson*; 28 Magic, Magic (1:25) *Paul Smith*; 29 Love Makes The World Go 'Round (1:36) *Richard Chamberlain*; 30 Her Face (2:44) *Mel Torme.*

Review: M-G-M's lovely fable, *Lili*, about the little orphan girl who joins a carnival and befriends the puppets who saved her life when she was considering suicide became the basis for a new Broadway musical, *Carnival*. The musical had a book by Michael Stewart and a score by Bob Merrill, and opened on April 13, 1961 for a run of 719 performances. While missing some of the charm and lilt of the film, a pervasive song to match the memorable "Hi-Lili, Hi-Lo," and the ingratiating waif-like presence of Leslie Caron, the stage show had a fetching attitude of its own that was most engaging, a lovely hit in the song "Love Makes the World Go 'Round," and Tony Award-winner Anna-Maria Alberghetti as Lili. In it, Jerry Orbach portrayed Paul, the crippled puppeteer whose crankiness contrasted with the warmth he displayed in his puppets behind the scrim. The musical also features James Mitchell as Marco the Magician, the flashy circus entertainer with whom Lili falls in love, not knowing he is already married to Kaye Ballard. The cast album, one of the first to be reissued on compact disc, provides a pleasant memento of the relatively nondescript score, with various bonus tracks that may be of minor interest to musical theatre fans.

Carousel

Carousel ♪♪♪♪

1990, MCA Records; from the Broadway production Carousel, 1945.

Album Notes: *Music:* Richard Rodgers; *Lyrics:* Oscar Hammerstein II; *Orchestrations:* Don Walker; *Dance Arrangements:* Trude Rittman; *Musical Direction:* Joseph Littau; *Cast:* John Raitt (Billy Bigelow), Jan Clayton (Julie Jordan), Jean Darling (Carrie Pipperidge), Christine Johnson (Nettie Fowler), Eric Mattson (Enoch Snow), Murvyn Vye (Jigger Craigin), Connie Baxter (Arminy); *Album Producer:* Jack Kapp; *CD Producer:* Michael Brooks.

Selections: 1 The Carousel Waltz (Prologue)(4:21); 2 You're A Queer One, Julie Jordan/Mr. Snow (4:23) *Jean Darling, Jan Clayton*; 3 If I Loved You (4:19) *Jan Clayton, John Raitt*; 4 Soliloquy (7:26) *John Raitt*; 5 June Is Bustin' Out All Over (3:46) *Christine Johnson, Jean Darling*; 6 When The Children Are Asleep (4:13) *Eric Mattson, Jean Darling*; 7 Blow High, Blow Low/This Was A Real Nice Clambake (3:46) *Murvyn Vye, Eric Mattson, Jean Darling*; 8 There's Nothin' So Bad For A Woman/ What's The Use Of Wond'rin' (4:19) *Murvyn Vye, Connie Baxter, Jan Clayton*; 9 The Highest Judge Of All/You'll Never Walk Alone (4:28) *John Raitt, Christine Johnson, Jan Clayton.*

Review: See entry below.

Carousel ♫♫♫

1990, Capitol Records; from the screen version *Carousel*, 20th Century-Fox, 1956.

Album Notes: *Music:* Richard Rodgers; *Lyrics:* Oscar Hammerstein II; The 20th Century-Fox Orchestra conducted by Alfred Newman; *Vocal Arrangements:* Ken Darby; *Cast:* Gordon MacRae (Billy Bigelow), Shirley Jones (Julie Jordan), Barbara Ruick (Carrie Pipperidge), Claramae Turner (Nettie Fowler), Robert Rounseville (Enoch Snow), Cameron Mitchell (Jigger Craigin); *CD Engineer:* Larry Walsh.

Selections: 1 The Carousel Waltz (7:14); 2 You're A Queer One, Julie Jordan (1:23) *Barbara Ruick, Shirley Jones;* 3 Mister Snow (3:52) *Barbara Ruick;* 4 If I Loved You (6:21) *Shirley Jones, Gordon MacRae;* 5 When The Children Are Asleep (4:49) *Robert Rounseville, Barbara Ruick;* 6 June Is Bustin' Out All Over (3:52) *Claramae Turner, Barbara Ruick;* 7 Soliloquy (7:51) *Gordon MacRea;* 8 Blow High, Blow Low (1:27) *Cameron Mitchell;* 9 This Was A Real Nice Clambake (2:39) *Barbara Ruick, Claramae Turner, Robert Rounseville, Cameron Mitchell;* 10 Stonecutters Cut It In Stone (2:20) *Cameron Mitchell;* 11 What's The Use Of Wond'rin' (3:29) *Shirley Jones;* 12 You'll Never Walk Alone (1:52) *Claramae Turner;* 13 If I Loved You (reprise)(2:01) *Gordon MacRea;* 14 You'll Never Walk Alone (Finale)(2:00) *Shirley Jones.*

Review: See entry below.

Carousel ♫♫♫

1990, RCA Victor; from the Broadway revival *Carousel*, 1965.

Album Notes: *Music:* Richard Rodgers; *Lyrics:* Oscar Hammerstein II; *Orchestrations:* Don Walker; *Musical Direction:* Franz Allers; *Cast:* John Raitt (Billy Bigelow), Eileen Christy (Julie Jordan), Susan Watson (Carrie Pipperidge), Katherine Hilgenberg (Nettie Fowler), Reid Shelton (Enoch Snow), Jerry Orbach (Jigger Craigin); *Album Producers:* George Marek, Joe Linhart; *Engineer:* Ernie Oelrich; *CD Producer:* Arthur Fierro; *Engineer:* Joaquin Lopes.

Selections: 1 The Carousel Waltz (5:29); 2 You're A Queer One, Julie Jordan/Mister Snow (5:48) *Susan Watson;* 3 If I Loved You (9:42) *Eileen Christy, John Raitt;* 4 June Is Bustin' Out All Over (4:51) *Katherine Hilgenberg, Susan Watson,;* 5 Mister Snow (reprise)(2:51) *Susan Watson, Reid Shelton;* 6 Blow High, Blow Low (1:43) *Jerry Orbach;* 7 When The Children Are Asleep (3:59) *Reid Shelton, Susan Watson;* 8 Soliloquy (7:12) *John Raitt;* 9 A Real Nice Clambake (3:26) *Katherine Hilgenberg, Eileen Christy, Reid Shelton, Susan Watson;* 10 What's The Use Of Wond'rin' (3:39) *Eileen Christy;* 11 You'll Never Walk Alone (1:44) *Katherine Hilgenberg;* 12 The Highest Judge Of All (1:58) *John Raitt;* 13 Finale Ultimo: You'll Never Walk Alone (1:39) Company.

Review: See entry below.

Carousel ♫♫♫♫

1994, Angel Records; from the Broadway revival *Carousel*, 1994.

Album Notes: *Music:* Richard Rodgers; *Lyrics:* Oscar Hammerstein II; *Orchestrations:* William David Brohn, Don Walker, Hans Spialek; *Musical Direction:* Eric Stern; *Cast:* Michael Hayden (Billy Bigelow), Sally Murphy (Julie Jordan), Audra Ann McDonald (Carrie Pipperidge), Shirley Verrett (Nettie Fowler), Eddie Korbich (Enoch Snow), Fisher Stevens (Jigger Craigin); *Album Producers:* Jay Landers, Tony McAnany; *Engineer:* Joel Moss.

Selections: 1 Prologue: The Carousel Waltz (7:48); 2 You're A Queer One, Julie Jordan (1:50) *Audra Ann McDonald;* 3 Mister Snow (3:36) *Audra Ann McDonald;* 4 If I Loved You (introduction)(3:14); 5 If I Loved You (8:22) *Michael Hayden, Sally Murphy;* 6 Give It To 'Em Good, Carrie... (1:24); 7 June Is Bustin' Out All Over (3:50) *Shirley Verrett, Audra Ann McDonald;* 8 Mister Snow (reprise)(2:45) *Audra Ann McDonald, Eddie Korbich;* 9 When The Children Are Asleep (4:46) *Eddie Korbich, Audra Ann McDonald;* 10 Blow High, Blow Low (2:30) *Fisher Stevens;* 11 Soliloquy (7:20) *Michael Hayden;* 12 A Real Nice Clambake (3:38) *Shirley Verrett, Sally Murphy, Eddie Korbich, Audra Ann McDonald;* 13 Geraniums In The Winder (1:46); 14 Stonecutters Cut It On Stone (1:59) *Fisher Stevens;* 15 What's The Use Of Wond'rin'(3:22) *Audra Ann McDonald;* 16 You'll Never Walk Alone (1:44) *Shirley Verrett;* 17 Ballet: Pas de Deux (6:07); 18 If I Loved You (reprise)(1:54) *Michael Hayden;* 19 The Sermon (:27); 20 You'll Never Walk Alone (1:33) Company.

Review: The second Rodgers and Hammerstein musical has, in half a century, aged as well as any of their work, and the CD listener can hear it in a variety of forms. The original cast album, on MCA, presents an edited and rearranged version of the score (in monaural, of course) performed by selected cast members. John Raitt, the template for the Broadway leading man of the era, is a fine, larger-than-life Billy Bigelow, and Jan Clayton makes a feisty Julie Jordan. The supporting roles are all also first-rate. The standards—"If I Loved You," "June Is Bustin' Out All Over," "You'll Never Walk Alone"—stand up against their countless cover versions.

Rodgers and Hammerstein's unfairly "sentimental" reputation stems mostly from the movies, not the Broadway shows, and the film version of *Carousel*—which softened and lightened the original—was one of the chief culprits. But

Alfred Newman's musical direction and Ken Darby's vocal arrangements put a fresh spin on the soundtrack—less operatic, especially, than the various Broadway recordings; Gordon MacRae (replacing Frank Sinatra, who quit) "acted" his songs in a compelling way; and Shirley Jones is this listener's favorite Julie. Capitol's CD puts back a couple of songs cut from the movie, and because the film recording was multi-track, the sound is a sort of before-its-time stereo.

Twenty years on, John Raitt returned to play Billy in one of the first of the grand-scale Broadway revivals at the (then new!) Lincoln Center. RCA took the opportunity to release a stereo version of the score with Eileen Christy, Susan Watson, Katherine Hilgenberg and Jerry Orbach in supporting roles. Raitt's Billy no longer sounds desperate enough to kill himself, but the singing holds up. The recording also includes a couple of reprises omitted from the earlier recording.

Fast forward another three decades, and Lincoln Center again presented a *Carousel*, this one a hugely successful British import remarkably staged by Nicholas Hytner. Minus the memorable set and choreography, this loses a bit of its impact, but nonetheless makes a worthy addition to the recorded legacy. Michael Hayden plays Billy as younger and less formidable than Raitt or MacRae, but if anything this makes the character more believable. Among the supporting roles, Audra Ann McDonald's Carrie stands out. The Angel recording offers more of the score than any of its precursors, including the music for the ballet in Act Two. The booklet provides pages of color photography from the show, and an instructive essay by Ethan Mordden.

Marc Kirkeby

Cats ♪♪♪♪

1983, Geffen Records; from the Broadway production *Cats*, 1983.

Album Notes: *Music*: Andrew Lloyd Webber; *Lyrics*: T.S. Eliot; *Orchestrations*: David Cullen, Andrew Lloyd Webber; *Musical Directors*: Stanley Lebowsky, Rene Wiegert; *Cast*: Betty Buckley (Grizabella), Ken Page (Old Deuteronomy), Christine Langner (Rumpleteazer), Wendy Edmead (Demeter), Rene Clemente (Mungojerrie), Terrence Mann (Rum Tum Tugger), Timothy Scott (Mistoffolees), Anna McNeely (Jennyanydots), Cynthia Onrubia (Victoria); *Album Producers*: Andrew Lloyd Webber, Martin Levan.

Selections: CD 1: 1 Overture (2:47); 2 Prologue: Jellicle Songs For Jellicle Cats (5:17) Company; 3 The Naming Of Cats (3:00) Company; 4 The Invitation To The Jellicle Ball (2:07) *Cynthia Onrubia, Timothy Scott*; 5 The Old Gumbie Cat (3:40) *Anna McNeely, Rene Caballos, Donna King, Bonnie Simmons*; 6 The Rum Tum Tugger (3:40) *Terrence Mann*; 7 Grizabella, The Glamour Cat (3:05) *Betty Buckley, Wendy Edmead,, Donna King*; 8 Bustopher Jones (3:07) *Stephen Hanan, Anna McNeely, Bonnie Simmons, Donna King*; 9 Mungojerrie And Rumpleteazer (4:27) *Timothy Scott, Rene Clemente, Christine Langner*; 10 Old Deuteronomy (3:33) *Harry Groener, Terrence Mann, Ken Page*; 11 The Jellicle Ball (9:34) Company; 12 Grizabella (4:17) *Betty Buckley*.

CD 2: 1 The Moments Of Happiness (3:14) *Ken Page, Janet L. Hubert*; 2 Gus: The Theatre Cat (6:38) *Bonnie Simmons, Stephen Hanan*; 3 Growltiger's Last Stand (11:42) *Stephen Hanan, Bonnie Simmons, Harry Groener, Reed Jones, Terrence Mann, Hector Jaime Mercado, Timothy Scott, Steven Gelfer*; 4 Skimbleshanks The Railway Cat (4:53) *Reed Jones*; 5 Macavity (8:23) *Wendy Edmead, Donna King, Hector Jaime Mercado, Kenneth Ard*; 6 Mr. Mistoffolees (4:24) *Timothy Scott, Terence Mann*; 7 Memory (A.L. Webber/T. Nunn)(5:20) *Cynthia Onrubia, Betty Buckley*; 8 The Journey To The Heaviside Layer (2:43) Company; 9 The Ad-dressing Of Cats (4:17) *Ken Page*.

Review: Who would have thought that T.S. Eliot's "Old Possum's Book of Practical Cats" would one day provide the dramatic texture for a musical, and a successful one at that? Yet, *Cats*, which opened in New York on October 7, 1982, has not only enjoyed more than the proverbial nine lives it was supposed to have, but has now become the longest running show on Broadway, leaving behind such blockbusters as *A Chorus Line*, *Les Miserables*, *Phantom of the Opera*, *42nd Street*, *Grease* and *Fiddler on the Roof*. Much of the success of the show, of course, falls squarely on Andrew Lloyd Webber's score, an amalgam of rock'n'pop songs and big theatrical numbers that work effectively on stage and off. Listening to the cast album, one is constantly reminded how delightful the songs are, and how perfectly the melodies complement and enhance Eliot's words. Simple, unaffected, wonderfully direct and effective, Webber's score is far different from the pompous works he has created since, so much so that *Cats* may be considered his most inspired creation. In truth, he just hit the right note with this one, and it shows.

Chicago

Chicago ♪♪♪♪

1996, Arista Records; from the Broadway production *Chicago*, 1975.

Album Notes: *Music*: John Kander; *Lyrics*: Fred Ebb; *Orchestrations*: Ralph Burns; *Musical Direction*: Stanley Lebowsky; *Cast*: Gwen Verdon (Roxy Hart), Chita Rivera (Velma Kelly), Jerry

Orbach (Billy Flynn), Mary McCarty (Matron), M. O'Haughey (Mary Sunshine), Barney Martin (Amos Hart); *Album Producer*: Phil Ramone; *Engineers*: Richard Blakin, Phil Ramone; *CD Producer*: Didier C. Deutsch; *Engineers*: Leon Zervos, Kevin Hodge.

Selections: 1 Overture (1:32); 2 All That Jazz (3:13) *Chita Rivera*; 3 Funny Honey (3:10) *Gwen Verdon, Richard Korthaze, Barney Martin*; 4 Cell Block Tango (5:13) *Chita Rivera, Cheryl Clark, Michon Peacock, Candy Brown, Graciela Daniele, Pamela Sousa*; 5 When You're Good To Mama (3:13) *Mary McCarty*; 6 All I Care About (3:29) *Jerry Orbach*; 7 A Little Bit Of Good (3:16) *M. O'Haughey*; 8 We Both Reached For The Gun (3:44) *Jerry Orbach, Gwen Verdon, M. O'Haughey*; 9 Roxie (5:29) *Gwen Verdon*; 10 I Can't Do It Alone (2:52) *Chita Rivera*; 11 My Own Best Friend (2:31) *Chita Rivera, Gwen Verdon*; 12 Me And My Baby (1:26) *Gwen Verdon*; 13 Mr. Cellophane (3:38) *Barney Martin*; 14 When Velma Takes The Stand (2:02) *Chita Rivera*; 15 Razzle Dazzle (3:09) *Jerry Orbach*; 16 Class (2:52) *Chita Rivera, Mary McCarty*; 17 Nowadays (3:13) *Gwen Verdon, Chita Rivera*; 18 All That Jazz (reprise)(1:05) *Chita Rivera*.

Review: See entry below.

Chicago ♫♫

1996, RCA Victor; from the Broadway revival *Chicago*, 1996.

Album Notes: *Music*: John Kander; *Lyrics*: Fred Ebb; *Orchestrations*: Ralph Burns; *Musical Direction*: Rob Fisher; *Cast*: Ann Reinking (Roxy Hart), Bebe Neuwirth (Velma Kelly), James Naughton (Billy Flynn), Marcia Lewis (Matron), D. Sabella (Mary Sunshine), Joel Grey (Amos Hart); *Album Producer*: Jay David Saks; *Engineers*: James Nichols; *Assistant Engineers*: Paul Falcone, Mark Johnson, Chris Hilt.

Selections: 1 Overture (1:47); 2 All That Jazz (5:03) *Bebe Newirth*; 3 Funny Honey (3:36) *Ann Reinking, Joel Grey, Michael Kubala*; 4 Cell Block Tango (6:13) *Bebe Neuwirth*; 5 When You're Good To Mama (3:20) *Marcia Lewis*; 6 All I Care About (3:48) *James Naughton*; 7 A Little Bit Of Good (3:14) *D. Sabella*; 8 We Both Reached For The Gun (3:58) *James Naughton, Ann Reinking, D. Sabella*; 9 Roxie (5:10) *Ann Reinking*; 10 I Can't Do It Alone (4:48) *Bebe Neuwirth*; 11 I Can't Do It Alone (reprise)(:39) *Bebe Neuwirth*; 12 My Own Best Friend (2:39) *Ann Reinking, Bebe Neuwirth*; 13 Entr'acte (2:19); 14 I Know A Girl (2:05) *Bebe Neuwirth*; 15 Me And My Baby (3:13) *Ann Reinking*; 16 Mr. Cellophane (3:38) *Joel Grey*; 17 When Velma Takes The Stand (2:12) *Bebe Neuwirth*; 18 Razzle Dazzle (3:09) *James Naughton*; 19 Class (3:08) *Bebe Neuwirth, Marcia Lewis*; 20 Nowadays (4:48) *Ann Reinking, Bebe Neuwirth*; 21 Hot Honey Rag (1:48) *The Band*; 22 Finale (1:04) Company.

Review: Subtitled "A Musical Vaudeville", this groundbreaking musical received, the first time around, an original cast recording that enshrined a score filled with such dramatic truth as to make it nearly indispensable to anyone who values the musical theater. While Gwen Verdon, as Roxie Hart, and Chita Rivera, as Velma Kelly, reveal a certain vocal roughness, they surely give the performances of their career, as two "merry murderesses of the Cook County Jail." Jerry Orbach, as the silver-tongued shyster Billy Flynn, and Mary McCarty, as Matron Mama Morton, show just the right combination of sleaze and greed. Barney Martin and M(ichael) O'Haughey are terrific as the unwary innocents caught in a web of deceit, lust, cynicism and venality. The rest of the small cast is superb, as is the orchestra. Everything seems just about perfect, including the remastered sound. Fred Ebb's lyrics and John Kander's music capture both the spirit of the 1920s as well as the flavor of the 1970s in such a timeless manner that it sounds as if the score had been written yesterday.

Brought back to Broadway 20 years later, the splendid score of this incredible musical is given a better recording than the production deserves. More of the score and book are included here than on the 1975 recording and the sound of this recent digital recording is slightly better. But the cynicism of the original is no longer tempered with subtlety. Every joke and situation is related in the most coarse and obvious manner, with Bebe Neuwirth, James Naughton and the orchestra the standouts in the new cast album. The real problem is Ann Reinking as Roxy Hart. She hits each moment with the impact of a sledgehammer, thereby losing the admittedly few tender and vulnerable moments Roxy was allowed. These moments are important to our understanding of the character and what drives her very callous acts throughout the show. As it is, there is nothing scintillating about this sinner.

Jerry J. Thomas

A Chorus Line

A Chorus Line ♫♫♫♫

1976, Columbia Records; from the Broadway production *A Chorus Line*, 1976.

Album Notes: *Music*: Marvin Hamlisch; *Lyrics*: Edward Kleban; *Orchestrations*: Bill Byers, Hershy Kay, Jonathan Tunick; *Musical Direction and Vocal Arrangements*: Donald Pippin; *Cast*: Wayne Cilento, Carole Bishop, Nancy Lane, Kay Cole, Renee Baughman, Don Percassi, Priscilla Lopez, Donna McKechnie, Pamela Blair; *Album Producer*: Goddard Lieberson.

Selections: 1 I Hope I Get It (4:55) Company; 2 I Can Do That (1:32) *Wayne Cilento*; 3 At The Ballet (5:51) *Carole Bishop, Nancy Lane, Kay Cole*; 4 Sing! (1:51) *Renee Baughman, Don Percassi*; 5 Hello Twelve, Hello Thirteen, Hello Love (6:47) Company; 6 Nothing (4:17) *Priscilla Lopez*; 7 The Music And The Mirror (6:36) *Donna McKechnie*; 8 Dance: Ten, Looks: Three (2:49) *Pamela Blair*; 9 One (4:43) Company; 10 What I Did For Love (3:42) *Priscilla Lopez*; 11 One (reprise)/Finale (5:01) Company.

Review: See entry below.

A Chorus Line Woof

1985, Casablanca Records; from the screen version *A Chorus Line*, Embassy Films/PolyGram Pictures, 1985.

Album Notes: *Music*: Marvin Hamlisch; *Lyrics*: Edward Kleban; *Orchestrations*: Ralph Burns; Orchestra conducted by Ralph Burns; *Cast*: Michael Blevins (Mark), Yamil Borges (Morales), Jan Gan Boyd (Connie), Sharon Brown (Kim), Gregg Burge (Richie), Michael Douglas (Zach), Cameron English (Paul), Tony Field (Al), Nicole Fosse (Kristine), Vicki Frederick (Sheila), Janet Jones (Judy), Michelle Johnston (Bebe), Audrey Landers (Val), Pam Klinger (Maggie), Terrence Mann (Larry), Charles Mc-Gowan (Mike), Alyson Reed (Cassie), Justin Ross (Greg), Blane Savage (Don), Matt West (Bobby); *Album Producer*: Brooks Arthur; *Engineer*: Mike Farrow.

Selections: 1 I Hope I Get It (5:00)Ensemble; 2 Who Am I Anyway? (1:02) *Cameron English*; 3 I Can Do That (1:48) *Charles McGown*; 4 At The Ballet (5:42) *Vicki Frederick, Michelle Johnston, Pam Klinger*; 5 Surprise, Surprise (3:59) *Gregg Burge*; 6 Nothing (4:14) *Yamil Borges*; 7 Let Me Dance For You (4:07) *Alyson Reed*; 8 Dance: Ten, Looks: Three (2:38) *Audrey Landers*; 9 One (rehearsal)(3:41)Ensemble; 10 What I Did For Love (2:21) *Alyson Reed*; 11 One (finale) (3:54) Ensemble.

Review: Essentially a work in progress, *A Chorus Line*, a musical without a book, gave a voice and a face to the gypsies, the often unrehalded boys and girls whose thankless task it is to set off and enhance the performance of a musical's headliner. Thrown in the spotlight for the first time, they were allowed to confront their own demons, reveal the sacrifices they had to make just to be in a show, confess the problems and difficulties they so often encountered in their pursuit of an elusive instant in the limelight, before returning as surely into the obscurity and anonymity which is their usual lot. Devised by Michael Bennett, with the collaboration of the various actors and actresses involved in the show itself, *A Chorus Line*

recounted the grueling audition all the gypsies have to go through when they answer a casting call, this time for an unnamed big Broadway musical in which the star (probably a well-known female performer) is "the one." If at times it sounds a bit confessional and revelatory of secrets buried deep within each member of the cast, it is only because the musical itself eventually was a celebration of the talent they all bring to a show.

The score, with music by Marvin Hamlisch and lyrics by Ed Kleban, was unusually sympathetic to members of the cast, and provided solo turns where all could express their aspirations and anguish, and mesmerize the audience with their individual talents. A multi-Tony Award winner (for Best Musical, Best Score, Best Direction, Best Book, among many others), *A Chorus Line* enjoyed incredible life on Broadway, breaking all records of longevity with its run of 6,137 performances, only recently surpassed by *Cats*. The cast album recording, since 1976 a popular title in the Columbia catalogue, has just been remixed and mastered, giving it an overall vibrancy and sheen that makes it sound even better than it ever did.

Sadly, the same cannot be said about the film, a travesty of the genre if there ever was one, and a total disservice to the gypsies it aimed to celebrate. When Fred Astaire began to dance on the screen in his now legendary films with Ginger Rogers for RKO, he made sure that the dances would show him and his partner from head to toe, unlike what had been done before when dancers in action would often be framed down to the waist. The film version of *A Chorus Line* framed the musical and its performers down to the waist, losing so many great aspects from the show in this sorry transfer to the screen that it emerged as a very pale image of the original, loud, brash, and totally misguided. The same faults apply to the soundtrack album which, when compared to the original recording, is a total disaster. The performers who struggled through this mishmash deserved better.

Cinderella

Cinderella ♪♪♪♪ʳ

1996, Walt Disney Records; from the animated feature *Cinderella*, Walt Disney Pictures, 1948.

Album Notes: *Music*: Mack David, Jerry Livingston, Al Hoffman; *Lyrics*: Mack David, Jerry Livingston, Al Hoffman; *Music (score)*: Oliver Wallace, Paul J. Smith; *Music Editor*: Al Teeter; *Orchestrations*: Joseph Dubin; *Cast*: Ilene Woods (Cinderella), William Phipps (Prince Charming), Eleanor Audley (Stepmother), Rhoda Williams, Lucille Bliss (Stepsisters), Verna Felton (Fairy

Godmother), Luis Van Rooten, King, Grand Duke), James Mac-Donald (Jaq, Gus), and Don Barclay, Claire DuBrey; *Album Producer*: Randy Thornton; *Engineers*: John Polito.

Selections: 1 Main Title/Cinderella (2:51) Chorus; 2 A Dream Is A Wish Your Heart Makes (4:35) *Ilene Woods*; 3 A Visitor/Caught In A Trap/Lucifer/Feed The Chickens/Breakfast Is Served/Time On Our Hands (2:11); 4 The King's Plan (1:22); 5 The Music Lesson: Oh, Sing Sweet Nightingale/Bad Boy Lucifer/A Message From His Majesty (2:07) *Ilene Woods, Rhoda Williams*; 6 Little Dressmakers/The Work Song/Scavenger Hunt/A Dream Is A Wish Your Heart Makes/The Dress/My Beads/Escape To The Garden (9:24) Mice Chorus; 7 Where Did I Put That Thing/Bibbidi-Bobbidi-Boo (The Magic Song)(4:48) *Verna Felton*; 8 Reception At The Palace/So This Is Love (5:45) *Ilene Woods, Mike Douglas*; 9 The Stroke Of Midnight/Thank You Fairy Godmother (2:05); 10 Locked In The Tower/Gus And Jaq To The Rescue/Slipper Fittings/Cinderella's Slipper/ Finale (7:17); 11 I'm In The Middle Of A Muddle (demo)(1:55).

Review: Another wonderful animated transmogrification of a classic fairy tale, *Cinderella*, released on March 4, 1950, was Walt Disney's return to a genre that had proved quite successful for the studio, following several less distinguished "compilations" of mini-cartoons, a challenge the studio faced head-on with extraordinary vitality. Adding a new twist to the worn-out tale of the poor orphan girl mistreated by her stepmother and stepsisters, who discovers an 11th-hour romance with a Prince Charming thanks to her fairy godmother, the film introduced several animal characters who provided comic relief and a dose of enjoyment even the Charles Perrault original had never envisioned. Most particularly, the feature was graced by a sensational score in which songs like "Bibbidi Bobbidi Boo," an Academy Award winner, "So This Is Love," and "A Dream Is a Wish Your Heart Makes" soon emerged as standards. The newly mastered CD, with a lot of extra, previously unavailable material, is a lively reminder that the Disney scores were frequently great sources of entertainment in their own right.

Cinderella ♫♫♫♫

1988, Columbia Records; from the CBS-TV production *Cinderella*, 1957.

Album Notes: *Music*: Richard Rodgers; *Lyrics*: Oscar Hammerstein II; *Orchestrations*: Robert Russell Bennett; *Musical Direction*: Alfredo Antonini; *Cast*: Julie Andrews (Cinderella), Jon Cypher (The Prince), Howard Lindsay (The King), Dorothy Stickney (The Queen), Ilka Chase (The Stepmother), Kaye Ballard (Stepsister Portia), Alice Ghostley (Stepsister Joy), Edith Adams (Fairy Godmother), Robert Penn (Town Crier); *Album Producer*: Goddard Lieberson; *Engineers*: Fred Plaut, Robert

Waller, Anthony Janek; *CD Producer*: Didier C. Deutsch; *Engineer*: Tim Geelan.

Selections: 1 Overture (2:55) Orchestra; 2 In My Own Little Corner (3:43) *Julie Andrews*; 3 The Prince Is Giving A Ball (2:34) *Robert Penn*; 4 Royal Dressing Room Scene (1:43) *Dorothy Stickney, Howard Lindsay, Iggie Wolfington, George Hall*; 5 In My Own Little Corner (reprise) (2:34) *Julie Andrews*; 6 Impossible/It's Possible (4:15) *Julie Andrews, Edith Adams*; 7 Gavotte (3:03) Orchestra; 8 Ten Minutes Ago (2:33) *Julie Andrews, Jon Cypher*; 9 Stepsisters' Lament (1:22) *Kaye Ballard, Alice Ghostley*; 10 Waltz For A Ball (3:44) Orchestra, Ensemble; 11 Do I Love You Because You're Beautiful (2:50) *Julie Andrews, Jon Cypher*; 12 When You're Driving Through The Moonlight/A Lovely Night (5:29) *Julie Andrews, Ilka Chase, Kaye Ballard, Alice Ghostley*; 13 The Search (1:18) Orchestra; 14 The Wedding (3:50) Orchestra, Ensemble.

Review: See entry below.

Cinderella ♫♫♫

1993, Columbia Records; from the CBS-TV production *Cinderella*, 1964.

Album Notes: *Music*: Richard Rodgers; *Lyrics*: Oscar Hammerstein II; *Orchestrations*: Robert Russell Bennett, John Green; *Musical Direction*: John Green; *Cast*: Lesley Ann Warren (Cinderella), Stuart Damon (The Prince), Walter Pidgeon (The King), Ginger Rogers (The Queen), Jo Van Fleet (The Stepmother), Pat Carroll (Stepsister Prunella), Barbara Ruick (Stepsister Esmeralda), Celeste Holm (Fairy Godmother), Don Heitgerd (Herald); *Album Producers*: Irving Townsend, Ed Kleban, Thomas Z. Shepard; *Engineer*: Fred Plaut; *CD Producer*: Didier C. Deutsch; *Engineer*: Darcy Proper.

Selections: 1 Overture (5:21) Orchestra; 2 Loneliness Of Evening (2:30) *Stuart Damon*; 3 Cinderella March (3:02) Orchestra; 4 In My Own Little Corner (3:55) *Lesley Ann Warren*; 5 The Prince Is Giving A Ball (3:06) *Don Heitgerd*; 6 Impossible/It's Possible (6:27) *Lesley Ann Warren, Celeste Holm*; 7 Gavotte (3:11) Orchestra; 8 Ten Minutes Ago (3:50) *Stuart Damon, Lesley Ann Warren*; 9 Stepsisters' Lament (1:43) *Pat Carroll, Barbara Ruick*; 10 Waltz For A Ball (3:59) Orchestra, Chorus; 11 Do I Love You Because You're Beautiful (3:36) *Lesley Ann Warren, Stuart Damon*; 12 When You're Driving Through The Moonlight/A Lovely Night (7:03) *Jo Van Fleet, Lesley Ann Warren, Barbara Ruick, Pat Carroll*; 13 Finale (3:05) Orchestra, Ensemble.

Review: Charles Perrault's popular fairy tale became an attractive television special when Richard Rodgers and Oscar Hammerstein set it to music in 1957, in a production that starred Julie Andrews, fresh from her own success as Eliza Dolittle in *My Fair Lady*. While hardly comparable to their stage works,

Cinderella nonetheless proved particularly endearing, with the pair working their own magic in tunes like "In My Own Little Corner," in which Cinderella laments her unglamorous existence and dreams for better tomorrows, and "Ten Minutes Ago," a glorious waltz in which Cinderella and the Prince discover that their hearts beat to the same 3/4 time.

In 1964, Rodgers returned to the work for a new production, also televised by CBS, which introduced Lesley Ann Warren as Cinderella, and was quite enjoyable, though not as exciting as the original.

City of Angels

City of Angels ♪♪♪♪

1990, Columbia Records; from the Broadway production *City of Angels*, 1989.

Album Notes: *Music:* Cy Coleman; *Lyrics:* David Zippel; *Orchestrations:* Billy Byers; *Vocal Arrangements:* Cy Coleman, Yaron Gershovsky; *Musical Direction:* Gordon Lowry Harrell; *Cast:* James Naughton (Stone), Gregg Edelman (Stine), Kay McClelland (Gabby/Bobbi), Randy Graff (Oolie/Donna), Rene Auberjonois (Buddy/Irwin Irving), Dee Holy (Alaura Kingsley/Carla Haywood), Rachel York (Mallory Kingsley/Avril Raines), Shawn Elliott (Munoz/Pancho Vargas), Scott Waara (Jimmy Powers), Peter Davis, Gary Kahn, Amy Jane London, Jackie Presti (Angel City 4); *Album Producers:* Cy Coleman, Mike Berniker; *Engineer:* Mike Farrow.

Selections: 1 Prologue/Theme From *City Of Angels* (4:07) Orchestra, Angel City 4; 2 Double Talk (1:54) *Gregg Edelman*; 3 What You Don't Know About Women (2:16) *Kay McClelland, Randy Graff*; 4 You Gotta Look Out For Yourself (2:16) *Scott Waara, Angel City 4*; 5 The Buddy System (3:38) *Rene Auberjonois*; 6 With Every Breath I Take (3:58) *Kay McClelland*; 7 The Tennis Song (2:37) *James Naughton, Dee Holy*; 8 Ev'rybody's Gotta Be Somewhere (3:51) *James Naughton, Angel City 4*; 9 Lost And Found (2:56) *Rachel York*; 10 All You Have To Do Is Wait (3:05) *Shawn Elliott*; 11 You're Nothing Without Me (3:23) *James Naughton, Gregg Edelman*; 12 Stay With Me (2:04) *Scott Waara*; 13 You Can Always Count On Me (4:31) *Dee Holy*; 14 Alaura's Theme (1:04) *Lee Musiker*; 15 It Needs Work (3:33) *Kay McClelland*; 16 L.A. Blues (2:04) *Jim Pugh*; 17 With Every Breath I Take (2:28) *James Naughton, Kay McClelland*; 18 Funny (2:10) *Gregg Edelman*; 19 I'm Nothing Without You (2:16) *James Naughton, Gregg Edelman*; 20 Epilogue/Theme From City Of Angels (1:35) *James Naughton*; 21 Double Talk Walk (3:22) *Jim Pugh, Glenn Drewes, Mike Migliori*.

Review: See entry below.

City of Angels ♪♪♪♪

1993, RCA Victor; from the London production *City of Angels*, 1993.

Album Notes: *Music:* Cy Coleman; *Lyrics:* David Zippel; *Orchestrations:* Billy Byers; *Vocal Arrangements:* Cy Coleman, Yaron Gershovsky; *Musical Direction:* Richard Balcombe; *Cast:* Roger Allam (Stone), Martin Smith (Stine), Fiona Hendley (Gabby/Bobbi), Haydn Gwynne (Oolie/Donna), Henry Goodman (Buddy/Irwin Irving), Susannah Fellows (Alaura Kingsley/Carla Haywood), Sarah Jane Hassell (Mallory Kingsley/Avril Raines), David Schofield (Munoz/Pancho Vargas), Maurice Clarke (Jimmy Powers), Ben Parry, Neil Rutherford, Zoe Tyler, Annette Yeo (Angel City 4); *Album Producers:* Cy Coleman, Chris Walker; *Engineer:* Tom Leader.

Selections: 1 Prologue/Theme From City Of Angels (2:46) Orchestra, Angel City 4; 2 Double Talk (2:36) *Roger Allam, Susannah Fellows*; 3 Double Talk (1:42) *Henry Goodman, Martin Smith*; 4 What You Don't Know About Women (2:17) *Fiona Hendley, Haydn Gwynne*; 5 Ya Gotta Look Out For Yourself (2:09) *Maurice Clarke, Angel City 4*; 6 The Buddy System (4:13) *Henry Goodman*; 7 With Every Breath I Take (3:56) *Fiona Hendley*; 8 The Tennis Song (2:56) *Roger Allam, Susannah Fellows*; 9 Ev'rybody's Gotta Be Somewhere (4:10) *Roger Allam, Angel City 4*; 10 Lost And Found (2:58) *Sarah Jane Hassell*; 11 All Ya Have To Do Is Wait (3:25) *David Schofields, Billy J. Mitchell, Matt Zimmerman, Jonathan Avery*; 12 You're Nothing Without Me (3:27) *Roger Allam, Martin Smith*; 13 Entr'acte (2:25) *Roger Allam, Angel City 4*; 14 Stay With Me (1:51) *Maurice Clarke, Angel City 4*; 15 You Can Always Count On Me (4:18) *Haydn Gwynne*; 16 The Party/Alaura's Theme (2:20) *Henry Goodman, Matt Zimmerman*; 17 It Needs Work (3:38) *Fiona Hendley*; 18 L.A. Blues (1:28) *Roger Allam, Jeanette Ranger*; 19 With Every Breath I Take (reprise) (2:50) *Roger Allam, Fiona Hendley*; 20 Funny (2:01) *Martin Smith*; 21 I'm Nothing Without You (1:43) *Roger Allam, Martin Smith, Fiona Hendley*,; 22 Exit Music (3:15) *Angel City Band*.

Review: Broadway maverick composer Cy Coleman had a winning show in *City of Angels*, a whimsical spoof of the 1940s' film noir genre, further made exhilarating by its offbeat approach about a Hollywood scriptwriter with a poor record with women, and his alter ego, a gumshoe with a successful track record. With a book by Larry Gelbart, and lyrics by David Zippel, the show opposed the two men, Stine, whose existence happened in a black and white decor, and Stone, who enjoyed the glitz and color of Hollywood films, in another nifty touch that added zest to the stage proceedings. Along for the musical ride were Stine's long-suffering wife, Gabby, and Stone's secretary, Oolie, as well as a bevy of other attractive characters, some sharing Stine's real-life existence, some stemming from Stone's invented background. The score invented by Coleman matched the various moods in the story, with a zest directly borrowed from the big band sound of the 1940s, and songs that were all extremely enjoyable on stage and off, as can be experienced in the original cast album. *City of Angels* opened on December 11, 1989, and enjoyed a run of 878 performances. Among its awards, it won the Tonys for best musical, book and score.

The London cast album, on RCA Victor, is basically similar to the Broadway cast album, though it seems to lack the crackling energy in evidence in its predecessor.

Company

Company *♫♫♫♫*

1997, Sony/Legacy; from the Broadway production *Company*, 1970.

Album Notes: *Music*: Stephen Sondheim; *Lyrics*: Stephen Sondheim; *Orchestrations*: Jonathan Tunick; *Musical Direction*: Harold Hastings; *Cast*: Dean Jones (Robert), Barbara Barrie (Sarah), Charles Kinbrough (Harry), Merle Louise (Susan), John Cunningham (Peter), Teri Ralston (Jenny), George Coe (David), Beth Howland (Amy), Steve Elmore (Paul), Elaine Stritch (Joanne), Charles Braswell (Larry), Pamela Myers (Marta), Donna McKechnie (Kathy), Susan Browning (April), Cathy Corkill, Carol Gelfand, Marilyn Saunders, Dona D. Vaughn (The Vocal Minority); *Album/CD Producer*: Thomas Z. Shepard; *CD Engineer*: Darcy Proper.

Selections: 1 Company (5:44) *Dean Jones*; 2 The Little Things You Do Together (3:03) *Elaine Stritch, Barbara Barrie, Charles Kimbrough*; 3 Sorry-Grateful (3:27) *Charles Kimbrough, George Coe, Charles Braswell, Dean Jones*; 4 You Could Drive A Person Crazy (2:35) *Donna McKechnie, Susan Browning, Pamela Myers*; 5 Have I Got A Girl For You/Someone Is Waiting (5:27) *Charles Braswell, John Cunningham, Steve Elmore, George Coe, Charles Kimbroug, Dean Jones*; 6 Someone Is Waiting (2:54) *Dean Jones*; 7 Another Hundred People (2:40) *Beth Howland, Steve Elmore, Teri Ralston*; 8 Getting Married Today (4:07) *Beth Howland, Steve Elmore, Teri Ralston*; 9 Side By Side By Side/What Would We Do Without You (8:35) *Dean Jones,*; 10 Poor Baby (arr. D. Shire)(3:04) *Barbara Barrie, Teri Ralston, Merle Louise, Beth Howland, Elaine Stritch, Charles Kimbrough, George Coe*; 11 Tick Tock (arr. D. Shire)(3:55) *Barbara Barrie, Teri Ralston, Merle Louise, Beth Howland, Elaine Stritch, Charles Kimbrough, George Coe*; 12 Barcelona (3:15) *Dean Jones, Susan Browning*; 13 The Ladies Who Lunch

(4:26) *Elaine Stritch*; 14 Being Alive (4:48) *Dean Jones*; 15 Finale (1:35) Company; 16 Being Alive (4:48) *Larry Kert*.

Review: See entry below.

Company *♫♫♫♪*

1996, Angel Records; from the Broadway revival *Company*, 1995.

Album Notes: *Music*: Stephen Sondheim; *Lyrics*: Stephen Sondheim; *Orchestrations*: Jonathan Tunick; *Musical Direction*: David Loud; *Cast*: Boyd Gaines (Robert), Kate Burton (Sarah), Robert Westenberg (Harry), Patricia Ben Peterson (Susan), Jonathan Dokuchitz (Peter), Diana Canova (Jenny), John Hillner (David), Veanne Cox (Amy), Danny Burstein (Paul), Debra Monk (Joanne), Timothy Landfield (Larry), La Chanze (Marta), Charlotte D'Amboise (Kathy), Jane Krakowski (April); *Album Producer*: Phil Ramone; *Engineer*: Frank Filipetti.

Selections: 1 Overture (:46); 2 Company (5:00) *Boyd Gaines*; 3 The Little Things You Do Together (2:39) *Debra Monk*; 4 Sorry-Grateful (3:46) *Robert Westenberg, John Hillner, Timothy Landfield*; 5 You Could Drive A Person Crazy (2:31) *Charlotte D'Amboise, 3 Girls*; 6 Company (Reprise I)(:43) *Diana Canova, Jonathan Dokuchitz, Veanne Cox, Danny Burstein, Patricia Ben Peterson, Kate Burton*; 7 Have I Got A Girl For You (1:50) *Timothy Landfield, Jonathan Dokuchitz, Robert Westenberg, Danny Burstein, John Hillner*; 8 Someone Is Waiting (2:54) *Boyd Gaines*; 9 Another Hundred People (2:38) *La Chanze*; 10 Getting Married Today (4:07) *Patricia Ben Peterson, Danny Burstein, Veanne Cox*; 11 Bobby Baby (introduction)(:14) Company Voices; 12 Marry Me A Little (3:23) *Boyd Gaines*; 13 Bobby Baby (finale)(:28)Couples; 14 Side By Side By Side/What Would We Do Without You (7:26) *Boyd Gaines,*; 15 Poor Baby (2:59) *Kate Burton, Robert Westenberg, Diana Canova, John Hillner,Patricia Ben Peterson, Debra Monk, Veanne Cox*; 16 Tick Tock (3:45) *Boyd Gaines, Jane Krakowski*; 17 Barcelona (3:00) *Boyd Gaines, Jane Krakowski*; 18 The Ladies Who Lunch (4:28) *Debra Monk*; 19 Company (reprise II)(:31) Company; 20 Being Alive (4:31) *Boyd Haynes*; 21 Bows (1:35) Company.

Review: A seminal work, *Company* opened on April 26, 1970, and was the first in a streak of productions written by Stephen Sondheim and directed by Harold Prince that revolutionized the Broadway musical throughout the decade. Unlike the shows that were created at the time, many of which still relied on the tried-and-true formula that had prevailed until then, the new musical by Sondheim, finally hitting his stride, took a sobering, uncompromising look at contemporary life in a brilliant, unstructured display that had theatrical flair and personality. With the 35th birthday of Robert, the central character and link between the vignettes that made up the book by George Furth, providing the anchor for most of the action, *Company* was a critical study of married life in a big city, with its various couples revealed in their less-than-happy existence, often portrayed as neurotic individuals, fighting, smoking pot, boozing, and desperately clinging to each other, all the while wishing their lives would be different. The score yielded at least one showstopper in "The Ladies Who Lunch," delivered in drunken stupor by Elaine Stritch, but also brimmed with many great musical moments that come strikingly alive in the newly remixed and mastered CD reissue, which includes two bonus tracks performed by Larry Kert, who replaced Dean Jones on Broadway and went on to star in the London production. The winner of seven Tony Awards (including best musical, book, music, lyrics, and direction), *Company* had a run of 706 performances.

The 1995 revival, headed by Boyd Gaines, took a slightly diffident new approach by hinting at Robert's possible underlying homosexuality, and by also offering the suggestion of his involvement in an interracial relationship. The cast, however talented they may have been, could not compete with the incandescent original.

Crazy for You

Crazy for You 🎻🎻🎻🎻🎻

1992, Angel Records; from the Broadway production *Crazy for You*, 1992.

Album Notes: *Music:* George Gershwin; *Lyrics:* Ira Gershwin; *Orchestrations:* William D. Brohn; *Dance and Incidental Music Arrangements:* Peter Howard; *Musical Direction:* Paul Gemignani; *Cast:* Harry Groener (Bobby Child), Jodi Benson (Polly Baker), Beth Leavel (Tess), Stacey Logan (Patsy), Tripp Hanson (Mingo), Brian M. Nalepka (Moose), Hal Shane (Sam), Bruce Adler (Bela Zangler), Michele Pawk (Irene Roth), John Hillner (Lank Hawkins), Stephen Temperley (Eugene), Amelia White (Patricia); *Album Producer:* Thomas Z. Shepard; *Engineers:* Paul Goodman, James P. Nichols, Sandy Palmer.

Selections: 1 Overture (3:40) *Deadrock Symphony Orchestra*; 2 K-ra-zy For You (1:02) *Harry Groener*; 3 I Can't Be Bothered Now (5:38) *Harry Groener*; 4 Bidin' My Time (1:29) *Tripp Hanson, Brian M. Nalepka, Hal Shane*; 5 Things Are Looking Up (1:13) *Harry Groener*; 6 Someone To Watch Over Me (3:31) *Jodi Benson*; 7 Could You Use Me? (1:27) *Harry Groener, Jodi Benson*; 8 Shall We Dance (3:57) *Harry Groener, Jodi Benson*; 9 Entrance To Nevada (Stairway To Paradise/Bronco Busters/K-ra-zy For You)(2:55) *The Company*; 10 Slap That Bass (3:43)

Harry Groener, Brian M. Nalepka, Beth Leavel, Stacey Logan; 11 Embraceable You (3:49) *Harry Groener, Jodi Benson*; 12 Tonight's The Night (1:15) *Company*; 13 I Got Rhythm (7:34) *Jodi Benson,*; 14 The Real American Folk Song (Is A Rag)(1:49) *Tripp Hanson, Brian M. Nalepka, Hal Shane*; 15 What Causes That? (3:55) *Harry Groener, Bruce Adler*; 16 Naughty Baby (3:25) *Michele Pawk, John Hillner*; 17 Stiff Upper Lip (2:36) *Harry Groener, Jodi Benson, Stephen Temperley, Amelia White*; 18 They Can't Take That Away From Me (2:34) *Harry Groener*; 19 But Not For Me (3:09) *Jodi Benson*; 20 New York Interlude (Concerto in F)(1:05) *Deadrock Symphony Orchestra*; 21 Nice Work If You Can Get It (4:48) *Harry Groener*; 22 Bidin' My Time (French reprise)(:46) *Tripp Hanson, Brian M. Nalepka, Hal Shane*; 23 Finale (4:11)*Company*.

Review: See entry below.

Crazy for You 🎻🎻🎻🎻

1993, RCA Victor; from the London production *Crazy for You*, 1993.

Album Notes: *Music:* George Gershwin; *Lyrics:* Ira Gershwin; *Orchestrations:* William D. Brohn; *Dance and Incidental Music Arrangements:* Peter Howard; *Musical Direction:* Jae Alexander; *Cast:* Kirby Ward (Bobby Child), Ruthie Hanshall (Polly Baker), Vanessa Leagh-Hicks (Tess), Helen Way (Patsy), Kieran McIlroy (Mingo), Jon Clairmonte (Pete), Jeremy Harrison (Sam), Chris Langham (Bela Zangler), Amanda Prior (Irene Roth), Shaun Scott (Lank Hawkins), Colin John Bell (Moose), Paula Tinker (Patricia); *Album Producer:* Paul Gemignani, Stewart Mackintosh; *Engineer:* Toby Alington.

Selections: 1 Overture (3:40) *Orchestra*; 2 I Can't Be Bothered Now (4:14) *Kirby Ward*; 3 Bidin' My Time (1:46) *Kieran McIlroy, Jon Clairmonte, Jeremy Harrison*; 4 Could You Use Me? (1:25) *Kirby Ward, Ruthie Hanshall*; 5 Shall We Dance (3:46) *Kirby*

Ward; 6 Entrance To Nevada (2:42) The Company; 7 Someone To Watch Over Me (3:47) *Ruthie Hanshall*; 8 Slap That Bass (5:08) *Kirby Ward, Jeremy Harrison, Vanessa Leagh-Hicks, Helen May*; 9 Embraceable You (3:56) *Kirby Wards, Ruthie Hanshhall*; 10 Tonight's The Night (:37) Company; 11 I Got Rhythm (7:46) *Ruthie Hanshall, Kirby Ward*; 12 The Real American Folk Song (Is A Rag) (1:49) *Kieran McIlroy, Jeremy Harrison, Jon Clairmonte*; 13 What Causes That? (3:43) *Kirby Ward, Chris Langham*; 14 Naughty Baby (3:38) *Amanda Prior, Shaun Scott*; 15 Stiff Upper Lip (2:44) *Kirby Ward, Ruthie Hanshall, Robert Austin, Paula Tinker*; 16 They Can't Take That Away From Me (2:37) *Kirby Ward*; 17 But Not For Me (1:58) *Ruthie Hanshall*; 18 New York Interlude (Concerto in F)(:41) Orchestra; 19 Nice Work If You Can Get It (4:34) *Kirby Ward*; 20 Bidin' My Time (French reprise)(:48) *Kieran McIlroy, Jon Clairmonte, Jeremy Harrison*; 21 Finale (4:48) Company.

Review: The Gershwins' 1930 hit *Girl Crazy* got a new lease on life as *Crazy for You,* a heavily revamped and modernized version which took Broadway by storm on February 19, 1992, and racked up 1,622 performances, a great deal more than the 272 accumulated by the original. While the new book, by Ken Ludwig, made few concessions to current trends, and in fact harkened back to the days of yore when inconsequential storylines merely served as a way to introduce new songs by the brilliant tunesmiths of the day, what mattered here was the score featuring many familiar numbers by the Gershwins, including "Shall We Dance," "Embraceable You," "Someone to Watch Over Me," and "They Can't Take That Away from Me," all cleverly threaded into the thin plot, and delivered with the right amount of gusto and fun by the spirited cast.

The London cast album is an apt alternative to the Broadway cast, with equally ingratiating performances.

Dames at Sea ♫♫♫♪

1992, Sony Broadway; from the off Broadway production *Dames at Sea,* 1969.

Album Notes: *Music:* Jim Wise; *Lyrics:* George Haimsohn, Robin Miller; *Orchestrations:* Jonathan Tunick; *Vocal Arrangements and Musical Direction:* Richard J. Leonard; *Cast:* Tamara Long (Mona Kent), Sally Stark (Joan), Steve Elmore (Hennessey/The Captain), Bernadette Peters (Ruby), David Christmas (Dick), Joseph R. Sicari (Lucky); *Album/CD Producer:* Thomas Z. Shepard; *Engineers:* Fred Plaut, Arthur Kendy, Glen Kolotkin; *CD Engineer:* Charles Harbutt.

Selections: 1 Overture (2:52)Orchestra; 2 Wall Street (2:36) *Tamara Long*; 3 It's You (2:10) *David Christmas, Bernadette Peters*; 4 Broadway Baby (2:55) *David Christmas*; 5 That Mister

Man Of Mine (3:57) *Tamara Long*; 6 Choo-Choo Honeymoon (2:09) *Sally Stark, Joseph R. Sicari*; 7 The Sailor Of My Dreams (2:56) *Bernadette Peters*; 8 Good Times Are Here To Stay (4:09) *Sally Stark,*; 9 Dames At Sea (3:38) Company; 10 The Beguine (4:25) *Tamara Long, Steve Elmore*; 11 Raining In My Heart (5:26) *Bernadette Peters*; 12 Singapore Sue (4:59) *Joseph R. Sicari*; 13 There's Something About You (2:09) *David Christmas, Bernadette Peters*; 14 The Echo Waltz (2:18) *Tamara Long, Sally Stark, Bernadette Peters*; 15 Star Tar (2:45) *Bernadette Peters*; 16 Let's Have A Simple Wedding (2:18) Company.

Review: A frequently funny, delightful send-up of the Hollywood musicals of the 1930s, *Dames at Sea* took as its plot a storyline not unlike the one developed for the film *42nd Street,* in which a new chorine gets to replace the star of a Broadway-bound musical when the latter can't go on (in this case because she gets seasick when the show, kicked out of its theatre, opens on board a ship anchored in the harbor). Bernadette Peters made a splash in this production, her first major show, as the new kid on the block, with Tamara Long as the displaced star. The score, while not always as musically memorable as the Harry Warren-Al Dubin works it spoofed, came up with some hilariously campy tunes of its own, like "Choo-Choo Honeymoon," "Singapore Sue," and "The Echo Waltz."

Damn Yankees

Damn Yankees ♫♫♫♪

1988, RCA Victor; from the Broadway production *Damn Yankees,* 1955.

Album Notes: *Music:* Richard Adler, Jerry Ross; *Lyrics:* Richard Adler, Jerry Ross; *Orchestrations:* Don Walker; *Musical Direction:* Hal Hastings; *Cast:* Gwen Verdon (Lola), Stephen Douglass (Joe Hardy), Ray Walston (Mr. Applegate), Robert Shafer (Joe Boyd), Shannon Bolin (Meg), Rae Allen (Gloria Thorpe), Russ Brown (Van Buren), Eddie Phillips (Sohovik), Jimmie Komack, Richard Bishop, Nathaniel Frey, Albert Linville (Baseball Players), Jean Stapleton, Ronn Cummins, Jackie Scholle, Cherry Davis (Baseball Fans); *Album Producer:* Hugo Winterhalter, Joe Carlton, E.O. Welker; *CD Producer:* Didier C. Deutsch; *CD Engineer:* Paul Goodman.

Selections: 1 Overture: Six Months Out Of Every Year (4:42) *Shannon Bolin, Robert Shafer*; 2 Goodbye Old Girl (3:13) *Robert Shafer, Stephen Douglass*; 3 Heart (4:40) *Russ Brown, Jimmie Komack, Nathaniel Frey, Albert Linville*; 4 Shoeless Joe From Hannibal, Mo. (3:40) *Rae Allen*; 5 A Little Brains — A Little Talent (3:37) *Gwen Verdon*; 6 A Man Doesn't Know (3:08)

Stephen Douglass, Shannon Bolin; 7 Whatever Lola Wants (3:10) Gwen Verdon; 8 Heart (reprise)(1:23) Jean Stapleton, Ronn Cummins, Jackie Scholle, Cherry Davis; 9 Who's Got The Pain? (2:51) Gwen Verdon, Eddie Phillips; 10 The Game (4:30) Jimmie Komack, Nathaniel Frey; 11 Near To You (3:28) Stephen Douglass, Shannon Bolin; 12 Those Were The Good Old Days (2:35) Douglas Watson; 13 Two Lost Souls (2:15) Gwen Verdon, Stephen Douglass; 14 A Man Doesn't Know (reprise)(1:25) Shannon Bolin, Robert Shafer; 15 Finale (:54) Company.

Review: See entry below.

Damn Yankees 𝄞𝄞𝄞𝄞ᵛ

1989, RCA Victor; from the screen version *Damn Yankees*, Warner Bros. Pictures, 1958.

Album Notes: *Music*: Richard Adler, Jerry Ross; *Lyrics*: Richard Adler, Jerry Ross; *Orchestrations*: Don Walker; The Warner Bros. Studio Orchestra and Chorus conducted by Ray Heindorf; *Cast*: Gwen Verdon (Lola), Tab Hunter (Joe Hardy), Ray Walston (Mr. Applegate), Robert Shafer (Joe Boyd), Shannon Bolin (Meg), Rae Allen (Gloria Thorpe), Russ Brown (Van Buren), Eddie Phillips (Sohovik), Jimmie Komack, Richard Bishop, Nathaniel Frey, Albert Linville (Baseball Players), Jean Stapleton, Ronn Cummins, Jackie Scholle, Cherry Davis (Baseball Fans), Bob Fosse; *Original Album Coordinator*: Simon Rady; *CD Producer*: Didier C. Deutsch; *CD Engineer*: Paul Goodman.

Selections: 1 Overture (1:43) *The Warner Bros. Studio Orchestra*; 2 Six Months Out Of Every Year (1:59) *Shannon Bolin, Robert Shafer*; 3 Goodbye Old Girl (3:14) *Robert Shafer, Tab Hunter*; 4 Heart (2:51) *Russ Brown, Jimmie Komack, Nathaniel Frey, Albert Linville*; 5 Shoeless Joe From Hannibal, Mo. (3:19) *Rae Allen*; 6 There's Something About An Empty Chair (2:10) *Shannon Bolin*; 7 Whatever Lola Wants (2:47) *The Warner Bros. Studio Orchestra*; 8 A Little Brains — A Little Talent (3:26) *Gwen Verdon*; 9 Whatever Lola Wants (3:49) *Gwen Verdon*; 10 Those Were The Good Old Days (2:35) *Douglas Watson*; 11 Who's Got The Pain? (2:51) *Gwen Verdon, Bob Fosse*; 12 Two Lost Souls (2:15) *Gwen Verdon, Tab Hunter*; 13 There's Something About An Empty Chair (reprise)(1:21) *Shannon Bolin, Robert Shafer*.

Review: See entry below.

Damn Yankees 𝄞𝄞𝄞𝄞

1994, Mercury Records; from the Broadway revival *Damn Yankees*, 1994.

Album Notes: *Music*: Richard Adler, Jerry Ross; *Lyrics*: Richard Adler, Jerry Ross; *Orchestrations*: Douglas Besterman; *Vocal*

Arrangements: James Raitt; *Musical Direction*: David Chase; *Cast*: Bebe Neuwirth (Lola), Jarrod Emick (Joe Hardy), Victor Garber (Mr. Applegate), Dennis Kelly (Joe Boyd), Linda Stephens (Meg), Vicki Lewis (Gloria Thorpe), Dick Latessa (Van Buren), Gregory Jbara, Jeff Blumenkrantz, Scott Wise, John Ganun, Joey Pizzi, Scott Robertson, Michael Winther, Cory English, Bruce Anthony Davis, Michael Berresse (The Senators), Paula Leggett Chase, Nancy Ticotin, Cynthia Onrubia, Amy Rider (Baseball Fans); *Album Producer*: Thomas Z. Shepard; *Engineer*: James Nichols.

Selections: 1 Overture (4:29) Orchestra; 2 Six Months Out Of Every Year (4:08) *Linda Stephens, Dennis Kelly, Vicki Lewis*; 3 Scene: The Boyds' Living Room (:45) *Linda Stephens, Dennis Kelly*; 4 Scene: The Boyds' Front Porch (1:52) *Dennis Kelly, Victor Garber*; 5 Goodbye Old Girl (3:03) *Dennis Kelly, Jarrod Emick, Victor Garber*; 6 Blooper Ballet (:44); 7 Scene: The Ball Field (:38) *Dick Latessa*; 8 Heart (5:06) *Dick Latessa*; 9 Scene: The Locker Room (:23) *Victor Garber, Dick Latessa, Jarrod Emick*; 10 Joe At Bat (1:53) *Vicki Lewis*; 11 Shoeless Joe From Hannibal, Mo. (3:24) *Vicki Lewis*; 12 Shoeless Joe (reprise) (2:19); 13 Scene: The Press Conference (1:03) *Vicki Lewis, Jarrod Emick, Dick Latessa, Victor Garber*; 14 Scene: Applegate's Apartment (1:19) *Victor Garber, Bebe Neuwirth*; 15 A Little Brains — A Little Talent (3:19) *Bebe Neuwirth*; 16 Scene: The Boyds' Kitchen (:47) *Jarrod Emick, Linda Stephens*; 17 A Man Doesn't Know (3:15) *Jarrod Emick, Linda Stephens*; 18 Scene: The Locker Room (2:08) *Jarrod Emick, Victor Garber, Bebe Neuwirth*; 19 Whatever Lola Wants (3:51) *Bebe Neuwirth*; 20 Scene: Act I Finale)(1:27) *Victor Garber, Bebe Neuwirth*; 21 Who's Got The Pain? (2:54) *Bebe Neuwirth*; 22 Scene: The Locker Room (:34) *Bebe Neuwirth*; 23 The Game (4:03) *Bebe Neuwirth*; 24 Scene: The Boyds' House (1:10) *Linda Stephens, Jarrod Emmick*; 25 Near To You (3:41) *Linda Stephens, Jarrod Emick, Dennis Kelly*; 26 Those Were The Good Old Days (4:42) *Victor Garber*; 27 The Trial (3:45) *Vicki Lewis, Jarrod Emick, Dick Latessa, Bebe Neuwirth, Victor Garber*; 28 Scene: Limbo (1:56) *Bebe Neuwirth, Jarrod Emick, Victor Garber*; 29 Two Lost Souls (3:14) *Bebe Neuwirth, Victor Garber*; 30 Scene: The Bottom Of The Ninth (3:39) *Victor Garber, Linda Stephens, Bebe Neuwirth, Jarrod Emick, Dennis Kelly, Mel Allen*; 31 A Man Doesn't Know (reprise)(2:11) *Linda Stephens, Dennis Kelly, Victor Garber, Bebe Neuwirth*.

Review: The old Faustian legend about the man who sells his soul to the Devil in order to regain youth and good looks received a clever updating in this whimsical musical, which took the tale and squarely set it against the background of America's favorite pastime, baseball. As reconceived by Douglas Wallop and George Abbott, *Damn Yankees*, based on

Mr. Wallop's novel "The Year the Yankees Lost the Pennant," transplanted Faust into middle-America and gave him the name Joe Boyd. After he makes a pact with the Devil, a businessman more prosaically named Mr. Applegate, Boyd becomes "Shoeless" Joe Hardy, a hard-hitter, who takes the Washington Senators, his favorite team (and perpetual losers), all the way to the finals of the American League game, where they face those "damn Yankees." But this being a musical, set in America, there is a happy ending to the story: in spite of Mr. Applegate, and his assistant, the sultry Lola, Joe Hardy invokes the "escape clause" he and the Devil had agreed on initially, and at the last minute, just before curtain time, returns to his loving wife as Joe Boyd, serene in the knowledge that it was he who helped the Senators win the Pennant.

A multiple Tony Award-winner (including for Best Musical) in 1956, *Damn Yankees* ran for 1,019 performances (a rarity at the time), and made a star of Gwen Verdon, playing Lola, whose siren song, "Whatever Lola Wants," became a huge popular hit. Virtually intact, and with only one major cast change (Tab Hunter replacing Stephen Douglass as Joe Hardy), the show was transferred to the screen in 1958, in a splashy screen transfer that retained all the flavor and guile of the original.

After extensive revisions, in 1994 it was revived on Broadway, with Bebe Neuwirth as Lola and Victor Garber as Mr. Applegate, where it enjoyed a successful run, before going on the road, with Jerry Lewis, billed above the title, taking over as the Devil.

Of the three recordings available, the first Broadway cast offers the original stars (Gwen Verdon, Stephen Douglass, and Ray Walston as Mr. Applegate) in a spirited rendition which has all the freshness and excitement usually experienced when a show first hits Broadway. Its only drawback (if that's the word!) is that it is in mono sound, since stereo didn't become an industry standard until later that year.

The soundtrack album, available for the first time in stereo in this CD version, is almost identical to the Broadway cast album, but offers, in addition to the cast change noted above, and Ray Heindorf's flavorful orchestrations, longer versions of some of the songs, as well as better polished performances overall.

The 1994 Broadway cast album, with its abundance of new selections, and dynamic renditions of the songs by Bebe Neuwirth, Victor Garber, and the other members of the cast, is as good a recording as can be gotten. It has the vibrancy, the fun, and the excitement one usually expects in that kind of production, and its sound quality is up to the latest standards.

Dear World 🐾🐾🐾

1992, Sony Broadway; from the Broadway production *Dear World*, 1969.

Album Notes: *Music:* Jerry Herman; *Lyrics:* Jerry Herman; *Orchestrations:* Philip J. Lang; *Musical Direction and Vocal Arrangements:* Donald Pippin; *Cast:* Angela Lansbury Countess Aurelia, The Madwoman Of Chaillot), Jane Connell (Gabrielle, The Madwoman Of Montmartre), Carmen Mathews (Constance, The Madwoman Of The Flea Market), Milo O'Shea (Sewerman), Pamela Hall (Nina), Kurt Peterson (Julian), Joe Masiell (Prospector), William Larsen (Chairman Of The Board), Clifford Fearl, Charles Karel, Zale Kessler, Charles Welch (Board Members); *Album/CD Producer:* Thomas Z. Shepard; *Engineer:* Francis X. Pierce.

Selections: 1 Overture (5:30) Orchestra; 2 The Spring Of Next Year (1:50) *Joe Masiell, William Larsen, Clifford Fearl, Charles Karel, Zale Kessler, Charles Welch*; 3 Each Tomorrow Morning (4:39) *Angela Lansbury*; 4 I Don't Want To Know (2:39) *Angela Lansbury*; 5 I've Never Said I Love You (3:38) *Pamela Hall*; 6 Garbage (3:21) *Milo O'Shea, Angela Lansbury, Jane Connell, Carmen Mathews*; 7 Dear World (3:54) *Angela Lansbury*; 8 Ballet (2:27) Orchestra; 9 Kiss Her Now (2:04) *Angela Lansbury*; 10 The Tea Party: Memory, Pearls, Dickie, Voices, Thoughts (7:27) *Carmen Mathews, Angela Lansbury, Jane Connell*; 11 And I Was Beautiful (2:55) *Angela Lansbury*; 12 Each Tomorrow Morning (reprise)(1:27) *Kurt Peterson*; 13 One Person (2:32) *Angela Lansbury*; 14 Finale (2:06) Company.

Review: Jean Giraudoux's play *The Madwoman of Chaillot* was the source for this flawed musical by Jerry Herman, which opened on February 6, 1969 for a meager run of 132 performances. Starring Angela Lansbury, Jane Connell, Carmen Mathews and Milo O'Shea, as sure-footed a cast as any, the musical failed to duplicate the success of *Mame* three years earlier largely because its characters were not as endearing, and audiences did not connect with this story about three holdovers from another era trying to fight big business in their desire to save the Paris environment. Though the title song was repeated as frequently in the score as "Hello, Dolly!" and "Mame" were in their respective shows, it too failed to make an impact.

Do I Hear a Waltz? 🐾🐾🐾

1992, Sony Broadway; from the Broadway production *Do I Hear A Waltz?*, 1965.

Album Notes: *Music:* Richard Rodgers; *Lyrics:* Stephen Sondheim; *Orchestrations:* Ralph Burns; *Musical Direction:* Frederick Dvonch; *Cast:* Elizabeth Allen (Leona Samish), Sergio Franchi (Renato Di Rossi), Carol Bruce (Signora Fioria), Madeleine

Sherwood (Mrs. McIlhenny), Julienne Marie (Jennifer Yaeger), Stuart Damon (Eddie Yaeger), Fleury D'Antonakis (Giovanna), Jack Manning (Mr. McIlhenny), Christopher Votos (Mauro), James Dybas (Vito); *Album Producer*: Goddard Lieberson; *Engineers*: Fred Plaut, Ted Brosnan; *CD Producer*: Didier C. Deutsch; *Engineer*: Tim Tiedemann.

Selections: 1 Someone Woke Up (3:40) *Elizabeth Allen*; 2 This Week Americans (2:30) *Carol Bruce*; 3 What Do We Do? We Fly! (3:24) *Madeleine Sherwood, Jack Manning, Elizabeth Allen, Julienne Marie, Stuart Damon*; 4 Someone Like You (3:33) *Sergio Franchi*; 5 Bargaining (2:25) *Sergio Franchi, Elizabeth Allen*; 6 Here We Are Again (6:34) *Carol Bruce, Madeleine Sherwood, Jack Manning, Elizabeth Allen, Julienne Marie, Stuart Damon*; 7 Thinking (2:47) *Sergio Franchi, Elizabeth Allen*; 8 No Understand (3:33) *Stuart Damon, Fleury D' Antonakis, Carol Bruce*; 9 Take The Moment (3:11) *Sergio Franchi*; 10 Moon In My Window (4:51) *Julienne Marie, Carolo Bruce, Elizabeth Allen*; 11 We're Gonna Be All Right (2:25) *Stuart Damon, Julienne Marie*; 12 Do I Hear A Waltz? (3:42) *Elizabeth Allen*; 13 Stay (2:28) *Sergio Franchi*; 14 Perfectly Lovely Couple (2:50) *Madeleine Sherwood, Jack Manning, Elizabeth Allen, Julienne Marie, Stuart Damon, Sergio Franchi, Carol Bruce, Fleury D' Antonakis*; 15 Thank You So Much (2:35) *Elizabeth Allen, Sergio Franchi.*

Review: Based on Arthur Laurents' *Time of the Cuckoo*, which had already served as the basis for the film *Summertime*, starring Katherine Hepburn and Rossano Brazzi, *Do I Hear a Waltz?* had all the earmarks of a great musical. With a score by Richard Rodgers, his first since *No Strings*, and lyrics by Broadway wunderkind Stephen Sondheim, a protégé of the late Oscar Hammerstein, it was already touted as the next Tony Award winner and a rightful successor to some of the best works bearing Rodgers' name. By the time it finally opened on Broadway, on March 18, 1965, however, things are soured considerably, and despite some positive reviews and glowing comments about the score, it failed to attract an audience and closed after 220 performances. Surprisingly, it was the combination Rodgers-Sondheim that failed to ignite: the composer, a traditionalist at heart, evidently didn't take too kindly some of the lyrics his younger collaborator proposed; conversely, Sondheim, forced to comply with the criteria of a "Rodgers musical," was unable to display some of the wit and sardonic edge he had previously exhibited in his own works, like *A Funny Thing Happened on the Way to the Forum*, and more specifically *Anyone Can Whistle*.

By the time the show reached Broadway, this story of an American spinster visiting Venice and falling in love with a married Italian man had become so edulcorated that it had lost much of its bite and had become quite ordinary, if not actually tepid. Further compounding the problems the show encountered during its tryout period was the evident lack of stage chemistry between Elizabeth Allen as the spinster, and Sergio Franchi obviously ill-at-ease as her Latin lover. Still the cast album recording reveals many attractive moments in the score, particularly the lilting title tune, which is Leona's way to find out that she's in love, and the diaphanous "Moon in My Window," in which Leona and two other women dream about love everlasting while looking at the bright Venetian moon.

Do Re Mi 🎵🎵🎵▷

1994, RCA Victor; from the Broadway production *Do Re Mi*, 1961.

Album Notes: *Music*: Jule Styne; *Lyrics*: Betty Comden & Adolph Green; *Orchestrations*: Luther Henderson; *Vocal Arrangements*: Buster Davis; *Musical Direction*: Lehman Engel; *Cast*: Phil Silvers (Hubert Cram), Nancy Walker (Kay Cram), John Reardon (John Henry Wheeler), Nancy Dussault (Tilda Mullen), George Mathews (Fatso O'Rear), David Burns (Brains Berman), George Givot (Skin Demopoulos); *Album Producers*: Hugo Peretti, Luigi Creatore; *Engineer*: Ernest Oelrich; *CD Producer*: Bill Rosenfield; *Engineer*: Jay Newland.

Selections: 1 Overture (4:06) Orchestra; 2 Waiting, Waiting (2:13) *Nancy Walker*; 3 All You Need Is A Quarter (1:55) Chorus; 4 Take A Job (3:39) *Phil Silvers, Nancy Walker*; 5 It's Legitimate (5:02) *Phil Silvers, George Mathews, David Burns, George Givot*; 6 I Know About Love (1:47) *John Reardon*; 7 Cry Like The Wind (2:00) *Nancy Dussault*; 8 Ambition (3:14) *Phil Silvers, Nancy Dussault*; 9 Fireworks (3:13) *John Reardon, Nancy Dussault*; 10 What's New At The Zoo (2:49) *Nancy Dussault*; 11 Asking For You (1:42) *John Reardon*; 12 The Late, Late Show (3:33) *Phil Silvers*; 13 Adventure (5:46) *Phil Silvers, Nancy Walker*; 14 Make Someone Happy (2:51) *John Reardon*; 15 All Of My Life (4:39) *Phil Silvers*; 16 Finale (1:12) Entire Company.

Review: Television and film comedian Phil Silvers starred as an unflinching wheeler-dealer in this delirious musical with a score by Jule Styne, Betty Comden and Adolph Green. In the book written by Garson Kanin, Silvers portrayed a would-be music tycoon, convinced he can make a big deal if he muscles his way into the then-nascent jukebox business with the help of three of his cronies. While he hardly succeeds, he manages to launch the career of a singer, played by Nancy Dussault. Another beloved clown, Nancy Walker, portrayed Silvers' long-suffering wife, with both ensuring that the show, which opened December 26, 1960, would have a long run of 400 performances. Also contributing to the success of the musical was the strong score, in which "Make Some Happy" soon emerged as a showstopping number, as did "It's Legitimate," with Silvers, and his three mobster friends (David Burns, George Mathews and George Givot), evoking the success they're bound to find as music entrepreneurs.

Doctor Dolittle *♫♫♫*

1997, Philips Records; from the screen musical *Doctor Dolittle*, 20th Century-Fox, 1967.

Album Notes: *Music*: Leslie Bricusse; *Lyrics*: Leslie Bricusse; *Orchestrations and Arrangements*: Alexander Courage; The 20th Century-Fox Orchestra, conducted by Lionel Newman; *Cast*: Rex Harrison (Doctor John Dolittle), Samantha Eggar (Emma Fairfax), Anthony Newley (Matthew Mugg), Richard Attenborough (Albert Blossom), Peter Bull (General Bellowes), William Dix (Tommy Stubbins), Geoffrey Holder (William Shakespeare the Tenth); *CD Producer*: Nick Redman; *CD Engineer*: Daniel Hirsch.

Selections: 1 Overture (1:16); 2 My Friend The Doctor (3:31) *Anthony Newley*; 3 The Vegetarian (4:35) *Rex Harrison, Samantha Eggar, Anthony Newley*; 4 Talk To The Animals (2:51) *Rex Harrison*; 5 At The Crossroads (2:08) *Samantha Eggar*; 6 I've Never Seen Anything Like It (2:28) *Richard Attenborough*; 7 Beautiful Things (4:13) *Anthony Newley, Samantha Eggar*; 8 When I Look In Your Eyes (1:47) *Rex Harrison*; 9 Like Animals (4:09) *Rex Harrison*; 10 After Today (2:19) *Anthony Newley*; 11 Fabulous Places (3:42) *Samantha Eggar, Rex Harrison, Anthony Newley*; 12 Where Are The Words (3:50) *Anthony Newley*; 13 I Think I Like You (2:39) *Rex Harrison, Samantha Eggar*; 14 Doctor Dolittle (2:31) *Anthony Newley, William Dix, Polynesia*; 15 Something In Your Smile (2:23) *Rex Harrison*; 16 My Friend The Doctor (:56) *Chorus*.

Review: A big, sprawling musical, *Doctor Dolittle* aimed to be another *Mary Poppins,* though it lacked that film's undeniable charm and memorable songs. Based on Hugh Lofting's original stories about a 19th Century veterinarian who has learned to talk to the animals (in everything from "Alligatorese" to "Zebran"), it starred Rex Harrison as the benign Doctor, along with Anthony Newley, Samantha Eggar and a large, colorful cast. Sadly, the songs by Leslie Bricusse fail to capture the whimsy of the stories. While they are enjoyable in their own right, they never quite achieved the anticipated popularity, though "Talk To The Animals" received an Academy Award in 1967 for "Best Original Song." The CD reissue, marking the 30th anniversary of the film's release, simply replicates the original LP, and is noticeable for the fact that it is particularly hissy in some passages.

Dreamgirls *♫♫♫*

1982, Geffen Records; from the Broadway production *Dreamgirls*, 1982.

Album Notes: *Music*: Henry Krieger; *Lyrics*: Tom Eyen; *Orchestrations*: Harold Wheeler; *Vocal Arrangements*: Cleavant Derricks; *Musical Direction*: Yolanda Segovia; *Cast*: Deborah Burrell, Vanessa Bell, Tenita Jordan, Brenda Pressley (The Stepp Sisters), Sheryl Lee Ralp (Deena Jones), Loretta Devine (Lorrell Robinson), Jennifer Holliday (Effie Melody White), Vondie Curtis-Hall (Marty), Ben Harney (Curtis Taylor, Jr.), Obba Babatunde (C.C. White), Cleavant Derricks (James Thunder Early), Tony Franklin (Wayne), Paul Binotto, Candy Darling, Stephanie Eley (Dave and The Sweethearts); *Album Producer*: David Foster; *Engineer*: Humberto Gatica; *Assistant Engineer*: Ia Eales.

Selections: 1 Move (You're Steppin' On My Heart)(1:56) *Jennifer Holliday, Loretta Devine, Sheryl Lee Ralph*; 2 Fake You Way To The Top (2:27) *Cleavant Derricks, Loretta Devine, Jennifer Holliday, Sheryl Lee Ralph*; 3 Cadillac Car (3:32) *Ben Harney, Cleavant Derricks, Obba Babatunde, Vondie Curtis-Hall, Loretta Devine, Jennifer Holliday, Sheryl Lee Ralph, Paul Binotto, Candy Darling, Stephanie Eley*; 4 Steppin' To The Bad Side (3:44) *Ben Harney, Cleavant Derricks, Obba Babatunde, Tony Franklin, Loretta Devine, Jennifer Holliday, Sheryl Lee Ralph*; 5 Family (3:19) *Jennifer Holliday, Obba Babatunde, Cleavant Derricks, Loretta Devine, Ben Harney, Sheryl Lee Ralph*; 6 Dreamgirls (3:14) *Sheryl Lee Ralph, Loretta Devine, Jennifer Holliday*; 7 Press Conference (1:40) *Sheryl Lee Ralph, Ben Harney*; 8 And I Am Telling You I'm Not Going (4:05) *Jennifer Holliday*; 9 Ain't No Party (2:08) *Loretta Devine*; 10 When I First Saw You (2:41) *Ben Harney, Sheryl Lee Ralph*; 11 I Am Changing (3:59) *Jennifer Holliday*; 12 I Meant You No Harm (1:05) *Cleavant Derricks*; 13 The Rap (2:52) *Cleavant Derricks*; 14 Firing Of Jimmy (1:39) *Cleavant Derricks, Ben Harney, Loretta Devine*; 15 I Miss You Old Friend (1:33) *Obba Babatunde, Jennifer Holliday*; 16 One Night Only (3:42) *Jennifer Holliday, Sheryl Lee Ralph, Loretta Devine, Deborah Burrell*; 17 Hard To Say Goodbye My Love (3:36) *Sheryl Lee Ralph, Loretta Devine, Deborah Burrell*.

Review: Following the success of *A Chorus Line*, Michael Bennett returned to the world of show business and backstage struggles in *Dreamgirls*, which opened December 20, 1981. The plot follows a trio of black female singers who eventually hit the big time, but only after one of them (considered too heavy and therefore less marketable) is replaced by a more glamorous singer. Not only did the show make a star of Jennifer Holliday (the one who was dumped), its sleek, hard-driving look also ensured its enormous success. In fact, it ran for 1,522 performances. With the exception of "And I Am Telling You I'm Not Going," the plaintive lament of Effie (the character played by Holliday) after she has been told that she is no longer a member of the Dreams, a trio loosely shaped after the Supremes, the action-driven score by Henry Krieger and Tom Eyen sounds much less memorable and exciting in the original cast recording than it did in the theatre. With its careful dose of theatrical, by-the-numbers rhythm-and-blues songs, it is enjoyable to a point, but only hits a high in the occasional glitzy moments when the Dreams actually perform together ("Dreamgirls," "One Night Only"). The rest of the time, it is merely routine and without much zest.

Easter Parade ♪♪♪♪

1995, Rhino Records; from the screen musical *Easter Parade*, M-G-M, 1948.

Album Notes: *Music*: Irving Berlin; *Lyrics*: Irving Berlin; *Orchestrations*: Nathan Van Cleave, Bob Franklyn, Sid Cutner, Leo Shuken, Paul Marquardt, Conrad Salinger, Leo Arnaud; *Arrangements*: Conrad Salinger, Roger Edens; The M-G-M Studio Orchestra and Chorus, conducted by Johnny Green, Georgie Stoll; *Cast*: Fred Astaire (Don Hewes), Judy Garland (Hannah Brown), Peter Lawford (Johnny Harrow), Ann Miller (Nadine Hale), Jules Munshin (Francois), Clinton Sundberg (Mike), Rich Beavers (Singer), Benay Venuta (Bar Patron); *Album Producers*: Marilee Bradford, Bradley Flanagan; *Engineer*: Doug Schwartz.

Selections: 1 Main Title (1:19) Orchestra & Chorus; 2 Happy Easter (2:30) *Fred Astaire, The Mel-Tones*; 3 Drum Crazy (4:00) *Fred Astaire*; 4 It Only Happens When I Dance With You (2:44) *Fred Astaire*; 5 Happy Easter (reprise #1)(outtake)(:39) *The Mel-Tones*; 6 Everybody's Doin' It Now (1:00) Orchestra; 7 I Want To Go Back To Michigan (Down On The Farm)(2:34) *Judy Garland*; 8 Happy Easter (reprise #2)(1:36) Chorus; 9 Making Faces (1:24) Orchestra; 10 Beautiful Faces Need Beautiful Clothes (1:17) Orchestra; 11 This Is The Life (1:07) Orchestra; 12 Along Came Ruth (1:05) Orchestra; 13 Call Me Up Some Rainy Afternoon (1:30) Orchestra; 14 A Fella With An Umbrella (2:31) *Judy Garland, Peter Lawford*; Vaudeville Montage: 15 I Love A Piano; 16 Snookey Ookums; 17 Ragtime Violin; 18 When The Midnight Choo-Choo Leaves For Alabam' (5:44) *Judy Garland, Fred Astaire*; 19 Mixed Greens (3:09) Orchestra; 20 That International Rag (:23) Orchestra; 21 Shakin' The Blues Away (3:17) *Ann Miller, The Mel-Tones, The Lyttle Sisters*; 22 It Only Happens When I Dance With You (reprise)(1:53) *Judy Garland, Roger Edens*; 23 Fanfare and Montage: Globe Theatre (:47) Orchestra; 24 Steppin' Out With My Baby (6:00) *Fred Astaire, The Mel-Tones, The Lyttle Sisters*; 25 Mr. Monotony (out-

take)(3:12) *Judy Garland*; 26 A Couple Of Swells (4:33) *Judy Garland, Fred Astaire*; 27 Roof Garden (Drum Crazy) (reprise)(1:05) Orchestra; 28 The Girl On The Magazine Cover (4:09) *Dick Beavers*; 29 New Amsterdam Roof (It Only Happens When I Dance With You)(reprise)(1:59) Orchestra; 30 Better Luck Next Time (4:09) *Judy Garland*; 31 Easter Parade (End Title)(2:42) *Judy Garland*.

Review: A great musical, splashed all over the screen in brilliant colors, *Easter Parade* had a lot going for it: a pleasant story about a hoofer trying to find a new dance partner and discovering love in the process, an inspired pair of co-stars in Fred Astaire and Judy Garland, and a sprightly score by Irving Berlin. The title tune, originally written in 1933 for the Broadway show *As Thousands Cheer*, became the occasion for a festive musical number. While the storyline seemed at best serviceable, it provided many pegs for various big production numbers that continue to delight and dazzle to this day—"A Fella With an Umbrella," shared by Garland and Peter Lawford; "Shakin' the Blues Away," performed in typical frantic manner by Ann Miller; "Steppin' Out With My Baby," which gave Fred Astaire an opportunity to dance in slow-mo in a remarkably inventive moment; "A Couple Of Swells," in which Astaire and Garland echoed an earlier duet, "Be a Clown," between Garland and Gene Kelly in *The Pirate*; and an exhilarating, long "Vaudeville Montage," built around several songs by Irving Berlin ("I Love a Piano," "Snookey Okums," "Ragtime Violin," and "When the Midnight Choo-Choo Leaves for Alabam'"). The soundtrack recording on Rhino, newly mastered and augmented with several instrumental bridges, outtakes, and other incrementa, brings out all the juicy moments from the film, and then some.

Evita

Evita ♪♪♪♪

1979, MCA Records; from the Broadway production *Evita*, 1979.

Album Notes: *Music*: Andrew Lloyd Webber; *Lyrics*: Tim Rice; *Orchestrations*: Hershy Kay, Andrew Lloyd Webber; *Musical Direction*: Rene Wiegert; *Cast*: Patti LuPone (Eva Peron), Mandy Patinkin (Che), Bob Gunton (Peron), Mark Syers (Magaldi), Jane Ohringer (Mistress); *Album Producers*: Andrew Lloyd Webber, Tim Rice; *Engineer*: David Hamilton Smith.

Selections: CD 1: 1 A Cinema In Buenos Aires, 26 July 1952 (1:00); 2 Requiem For Evita/Oh What A Circus (9:11) *Many Patinkin*; 3 On This Night Of A Thousand Stars/Eva And Magaldi/Eva Beware Of The City (7:35) *Patti LuPone, Mark*

Syers; 4 Buenos Aires (4:50) *Patti LuPone*; 5 Goodnight And Thank You (3:09) *Patti LuPone, Mandy Patinkin*; 6 The Art Of The Possible (2:40) *Bob Gunton*; 7 Charity Concert/I'd Be Surprisingly Good For You (5:57) *Mark Syers, Patti LuPone, Bob Gunton*; 8 Another Suitcase In Another Hall (4:42) *Patti LuPone*; 9 Peron's Latest Flame (4:25) *Patti LuPone, Mandy Patinkin*; 10 A New Argentina (6:57) *Patti LuPone, Bob Gunton, Mandy Patinkin*.

CD 2: 1 On The Balcony Of The Casa Rosada/Don't Cry For Me Argentina (9:32) *Bob Gunton, Patti LuPone*; 2 High Flying, Adored (3:45) *Mandy Patinkin, Patti LuPone*; 3 Rainbow High (2:17) *Patti LuPone*; 4 Rainbow Tour (4:47) *Company*; 5 The Actress Hasn't Learned The Lines (You'd Like To Hear) (2:21) *Patti LuPone, Mandy Patinkin*; 6 And The Money Kept Rolling In (And Out)(4:18) *Mandy Patinkin*; 7 Santa Evita (2:01)*Children*; 8 Waltz For Evita And Che (3:44) *Mandy Patinkin, Patti LuPone*; 9 She Is A Diamond (3:09) *Bob Gunton*; 10 Dice Are Rolling (5:06) *Bob Gunton, Patti LuPone*; 11 Eva's Final Broadcast (3:11) *Patti LuPone*; 12 Montage (2:40); 13 Lament (2:51) *Patti LuPone*.

Review: See entry below.

Evita ♪♪♪♪

1996, Warner Bros. Records; from the screen version *Evita,* **Hollywood Pictures, 1996.**

Album Notes: *Music:* Andrew Lloyd Webber; *Lyrics:* Tim Rice; *Orchestrations:* Andrew Lloyd Webber, David Cullen; *Musical Direction:* John Mauceri, David Caddick, Mike Dixon; *Cast:* Madonna (Eva Peron), Antonio Banderas (Che), Jonathan Pryce (Peron), Jimmy Nail (Magaldi), Andrea Corr (Mistress); *Album Producers:* Nigel Wright, Alan Parker, Andrew Lloyd Webber, David Caddick; *Engineers:* Dick Lewzey, David Reitzas, Robin Sellars, Mark "Spike" Stent.

Selections: CD 1: 1 A Cinema In Buenos Aires, 26 July 1952 (1:19); 2 Requiem For Evita (4:17); 3 Oh What A Circus (5:44) *Antonio Banderas, Madonna*; 4 On This Night Of A Thousand Stars (2:25) *Jimmy Nail*; 5 Eva And Magaldi/Eva Beware Of The City (5:21)*Madonna, Jimmy Nail, Antonio Banderas, Julian Littman*; 6 Buenos Aires (4:09)*Madonna*; 7 Another Suitcase In Another Hall (3:33) *Madonna*; 8 Goodnight And Thank You (4:18) *Madonna, Antonio Banderas*; 9 The Lady's Got Potential (4:25) *Antonio Banderas*; 10 Charity Concert/The Art Of The Possible (2:33) *Jimmy Nail, Jonathan Pryce, Antonio Banderas, Madonna*; 11 I'd Be Surprisingly Good For You (4:19) *Madonna, Jonathan Pryce*; 12 Hello And Goodbye (1:46) *Madonna, Andrea Corr, Jonathan Pryce*; 13 Peron's Latest Flame (5:18) *Antonio*

Banderas, Madonna; 14 A New Argentina (8:13) *Madonna, Jonathan Pryce, Antonio Banderas.*

CD 2: 1 On The Balcony Of The Casa Rosada (1:28) *Jonathan Pryce*; 2 Don't Cry For Me Argentina (5:31) *Madonna*; 3 On The Balcony Of The Casa Rosada (2:00) *Madonna*; 4 High Flying, Adored (3:32) *Antonio Banderas, Madonna*; 5 Rainbow High (2:27) *Madonna*; 6 Rainbow Tour (4:51) *Antonio Banderas, Gary Brooker, Peter Polycarpou, Jonathan Pryce, Madonna, John Gower*; 7 The Actress Hasn't Learned The Lines (You'd Like To Hear)(2:32) *Madonna, Antonio Banderas*; 8 And The Money Kept Rolling In (And Out)(3:53) *Antonio Banderas*; 9 Partido Feminista (1:40) *Madonna*; 10 She Is A Diamond (1:40) *Jonathan Pryce*; 11 Santa Evita (2:31); 12 Waltz For Evita And Che (4:13) *Madonna, Antonio Banderas*; 13 Your Little Body's Slowly Breaking Down (1:24) *Madonna, Jonathan Pryce*; 14 You Must Love Me (2:51)*Madonna*; 15 Eva's Final Broadcast (3:05) *Madonna*; 16 Latin Chant (2:11); 17 Lament (5:14) *Madonna, Antonio Banderas.*

Review: In 1979, Andrew Lloyd Webber and Tim Rice took Broadway by storm with *Evita,* smartly directed by Hal Prince, who certainly deserved to share in the success of the show. A fancy account of the life and times of Eva Peron, wife of the Argentinian dictator and inspiration of her beloved "descamisados," the low-life workers to whom she appealed and who canonized her after her death, *Evita* was also the first sung-through musical to hit Broadway. It was a precursor in many ways of the opera-like works Webber and his followers brought to the stage in subsequent years with varying degrees of success.

With Mandy Patinkin portraying a sympathetic Che Guevarra (who in real life never met Eva Peron), Bob Gunton as Peron, and Patti LuPone crying on cue in her bravura performance of the show's hit tune, "Don't Cry For Me Argentina," *Evita* opened on Broadway on September 25, 1979, to rapturous reviews. It won almost every Tony it could take (for Best Musical, Best Book, Best Score, Best Direction, and for Patti LuPone and Mandy Patinkin, among others), and enjoyed a long run of 1,567 performances. Much of its theatricality dissipates on the original cast album recording, though the undeniable dramatic flair of the score occasionally comes across in great style.

Though the show had to wait more than 15 years to make it to the screen, it was well worth it because it found in Madonna the ideal Evita. An actress with enormous charm and charisma, Madonna evidently studied hard and well to overcome her pop stylings and give her performance a more legit flair. Gorgeously lavish and expressive, the screen version of

Evita is further enhanced with the presence of Antonio Banderas as Che, and Jonathan Pryce as Peron. The recording, while presenting the same basic flaws in style found in the original, has a more vibrant pop vitality that gives the score greater impact. And Madonna is simply wonderful in a role she was obviously destined to perform.

Fanny ♪♪♪⁰

1996, RCA Victor; from the Broadway production *Fanny*, 1954.

Album Notes: *Music*: Harold Rome; *Lyrics*: Harold Rome; *Orchestrations*: Philip J. Lang; *Vocal Arrangements and Musical Direction*: Lehman Engel; *Cast*: Ezio Pinza (Cesar), Walter Slezak (Panisse), Florence Henderson (Fanny), William Tabbert (Marius), Nejla Ates (Arab Dancing Girl), Alan Carney (Escartifigue), Gerald Price (The Admiral), Edna Preston (Honorine), Don McHenry (M. Brun), Mohammed el Bakkar (Arab Rug Seller), Lloyd Reese (Cesario); *Album Producers*: Hugo Winterhalter, Joe Carlton; *CD Producer*: Bill Rosenfield; *Engineer*: Marian Conaty.

Selections: 1 Overture (5:03) *Orchestra*; 2 Octopus Song (1:06) *Gerald Price*; 3 Restless Heart (2:48) *William Tabbert*; 4 Never Too Late For Love (2:13) *Walter Slezak*; 5 Cold Cream Jar Song (:28) *Walter Slezak*; 6 Why Be Afraid To Dance? (3:38) *Ezio Pinza*; 7 Shika, Shika (2:27) *Nejla Ates, Mohammed el Bakkar*; 8 Welcome Home (3:25) *Ezio Pinza*; 9 I Like You (2:35) *Ezio Pinza, William Tabbert*; 10 I Have To Tell You (2:09) *Florence Henderson*; 11 Fanny (1:55) *William Tabbert*; 12 Panisse And Son (2:27) *Walter Slezak*; 13 Wedding Dance (2:07) *Chorus*; 14 Finale Act 1 (:52) *Chorus*; 15 Birthday Song (2:22) *Florence Henderson, Edna Preston*; 16 To My Wife (2:13) *Walter Slezak*; 17 The Thought Of You (2:05) *Florence Henderson, William Tabbert*; 18 Love Is A Very Light Thing (2:10) *Ezio Pinza*; 19 Other Hands, Other Hearts (1:48) *Ezio Pinza, Florence Henderson, William Tabbert*; 20 Montage (2:32) *Chorus*; 21 Be Kind To Your Parents (2:21) *Florence Henderson, Lloyd Reese*.

Review: Marcel Pagnol's flavorful Mediterranean film trilogy—*Marius, Fanny, Cesar*—became an odd, though interesting musical when Harold Rome presented his take on it with *Fanny,* which opened on November 4, 1954. Collapsing the complex drama from the three films into one production, the show lost some of the insightful details that made the films so uniquely remarkable. It compensated for it, however, with a strongly emotive score, sharply defined characters, and superb performances by Ezio Pinza as Cesar, owner of a cafe in Marseilles; William Tabbert as his only son, Marius, who only dreams of being a sailor; Florence Henderson as Fanny, who loves Marius, and with whom she has a baby; and Tony Award-

winner Walter Slezak, as Panisse, a well-to-do local businessman, whom Fanny marries after Marius sails out to sea. The show, the first presented under the aegis of legendary David Merrick, had a run of 888 performances.

The Fantasticks ♪♪♪♪

1979, Polydor Records; from the off Broadway production *The Fantasticks*, 1960.

Album Notes: *Music*: Harvey Schmidt; *Lyrics*: Tom Jones; *Musical Direction*: Julian Stein; *Cast*: Jerry Orbach (El Gallo), Kenneth Nelson (Matt), Rita Gardner (Luisa), William Larsen (Hucklebee), Hugh Thomas (Bellomy).

Selections: 1 Overture (2:03) *Orchestra*; 2 Try To Remember (2:47) *Jerry Orbach*; 3 Much More (2:35) *Rita Gardner*; 4 Metaphor (4:15) *Kenneth Nelson, Rita Gardner*; 5 Never Say No (2:16) *William Larsen, Hugh Tomas*; 6 It Depends On What You Pay (4:20) *Jerry Orbach, William Larsen, Hugh Thomas*; 7 You Wonder How These Things Begin (1:15) *Jerry Orbach*; 8 Soon It's Gonna Rain (4:44) *Kenneth Nelson, Rita Gardner*; 9 The Rape Ballet/Happy Ending (3:15) *Hugh Thomas, William Larsen, Rita Gardner, Kenneth Nelson*; 10 This Plum Is Too Ripe (3:36) *Rita Gardner, Kenneth Nelson, William Larsen, Hugh Thomas*; 11 I Can See It (4:07) *Kenneth Nelson, Jerry Orbach*; 12 Plant A Radish (2:33) *William Larsen, Hugh Thomas*; 13 Round And Round (6:00) *Jerry Orbach, Rita Gardner*; 14 There Is A Curious Paradox (:32) *Jerry Orbach*; 15 They Were You (2:43) *Kenneth Nelson, Rita Gardner*; 16 Try To Remember (reprise) (2:04) *Jerry Orbach*.

Review: Close to 40 years and too-many-performances-to-remember later, how do you describe *The Fantasticks,* other than to say it's… well, fantastic! A small, off Broadway musical, loosely based on Edmond Rostand's 1894 play, *Les Romanesques, The Fantasticks* continues to thrive, despite tepid reviews after it opened on May 3, 1960. It has also suffered various disasters, both man-made (newspaper and transportation strikes) and natural (snow blizzards and torrential rainstorms) that all but threatened its precarious run at one time or another. Now comfortably nestled at the 150-seat Sullivan Street Playhouse, in the heart of Greenwich Village, the musical—which launched the careers of Tom Jones and Harvey Schmidt, who wrote it, Jerry Orbach, who first starred in it, and many other thespians who appeared in it before moving on to greater and meatier roles—has become a fixture in New York City, an icon that is taken for granted like the Empire State Building or the Statue of Liberty.

At regular intervals, the show's press agent routinely provides the media with the many outstanding figures that speak on behalf of the production: since its creation, it has known nine Presidents (Eisenhower was still at the White House when it first opened), has spawned more than 10,000 productions around the world, and has repaid its investors close to 10,000% on their initial cash outlay of $16,500.

A playful variation on the Romeo and Juliet theme of star-crossed lovers who belong to feuding families (though in this case the neighboring fathers are conniving to make believe they are enemies), *The Fantasticks*, lest we forget, introduced one of the musical theatre's most evocative songs, "Try to Remember." The song is performed in the show by The Narrator, who also portrays El Gallo, a bandit brought in by the two pater familias to kidnap their Juliet in a well laid out plan so that Romeo will deliver her and fall in love with her.

Fiddler on the Roof

Fiddler on the Roof 🎻🎻🎻🎻

1986, RCA Victor; from the Broadway production *Fiddler on the Roof*, 1964.

Album Notes: *Music*: Jerry Bock; *Lyrics*: Sheldon Harnick; *Orchestrations*: Don Walker; *Vocal Arrangements and Musical Direction*: Milton Greene; *Cast*: Zero Mostel (Tevye), Julia Migenes (Hodel), Tanya Everett (Chava), Joanna Merlin (Tzeitel), Maria Karnilova (Golde), Austin Pendleton (Motel), Sue Babel (Grandma Tzeitel), Gluck Sandor (Rabbi), Ross Gifford (The Russian), Michael Granger (Lazar), Bert Convy (Perchik), Beatrice Arthur (Yente), Leonard Frey (Mendel), Paul Lipson (Avrahm) Carol Sayer (Fruma-Sarah); *Album Producer*: George Marek; *Engineer*: Ernest Oelrich; *CD Producer*: Thomas Z. Shepard.

Selections: 1 Prologue/Tradition (6:53) *Zero Mostel*; 2 Matchmaker (3:41) *Julia Migenes, Tanya Everett, Joanna Merlin*; 3 If I Were A Rich Man (4:54) *Zero Mostel*; 4 Sabbath Prayer (2:26) *Zero Mostel, Maria Karnilova*; 5 To Life (4:11) *Zero Mostel, Michael Granger, Ross Gifford*; 6 Miracle Of Miracles (2:01) *Austin Pendleton*; 7 The Dream (6:07) *Zero Mostel, Maria Karnilova, Sue Babel, Gluck Sandor, Carol Sawyer*; 8 Sunrise Sunset (3:33) *Zero Mostel, Maria Karnilova, Bert Convy, Julia Migenes*; 9 Wedding Dance (2:11) Orchestra; 10 Now I Have Everything (2:03) *Bert Convy, Julia Migenes*; 11 Do You Love Me? (3:08) *Zero Mostel, Maria Karnilova*; 12 The Rumor (1:52) *Beatrice Arthur, Leonard Frey, Paul Lipson*; 13 Far From The Home I Love (3:29) *Julia Migenes, Zero Mostel*; 14 Anatevka (3:08) *Zero Mostel, Maria Karnilova, Beatrice Arthur, Michael Granger, Leonard Frey, Paul Lipson*.

Review: See entry below.

Fiddler on the Roof 🎻🎻🎻🎻

1986, Columbia Records; from the London production *Fiddler on the Roof*, 1967.

Album Notes: *Music*: Jerry Bock; *Lyrics*: Sheldon Harnick; *Orchestrations*: Don Walker; *Vocal Arrangements*: Milton Greene; *Musical Direction*: Gareth Davies; *Cast*: Topol (Tevye), Linda Gardner (Hodel), Rosemary Nichols (Chava), Caryl Little (Tzeitel), Jonathan Lynn (Motel), Heather Clifton (Grandma Tzeitel), Maurice Lane (The Russian), Paul Whitsun-Jones (Lazar), Sandor Eles (Perchik), and George Little, Tony Simpson, Derek Birch, Terence Soall, and Brian Hewitt-Jones.

Selections: 1 Tradition (7:52) *Topol*; 2 Matchmaker (3:32) *Rosemary Nichols, Linda Gardner, Caryl Little*; 3 If I Were A Rich Man (5:11) *Topol*; 4 Sabbath Prayer (2:38) *Topol, Miriam Karlin*; 5 To Life (4:22) *Topol, Paul Whitsun-Jones, Maurice Lane*; 6 Miracle Of Miracles (1:57) *Jonathan Lynn*; 7 Tevye's Dream (6:20) *Topol, Miriam Karlin, Heather Clifton, Susan Paule*; 8 Sunrise Sunset (3:24) *Topol, Miriam Karlin*; 9 Bottle Dance (3:32) Orchestra; 10 Now I Have Everything (2:00) *Sandor Eles, Linda Gardner*; 11 Do You Love Me? (3:12) *Topol, Miriam Karlin*; 12 Far From The Home I Love (2:51) *Linda Gardner, Topol*; 13 Anatevka (3:35) *Topol, Miriam Karlin, Cynthia Greenville, Paul Whitsun-Jones, Brian Hewitt-Jones, George Little*.

Review: See entry below.

Fiddler on the Roof 🎻🎻🎻

1971, EMI America; from the screen version *Fiddler on the Roof*, United Artists, 1971.

Album Notes: *Music*: Jerry Bock; *Lyrics*: Sheldon Harnick; *Orchestrations*: John Williams; *Musical Direction*: John Williams; *Featured Musician*: Isaac Stern (violin); *Cast*: Topol (Tevye), Michele Marsh (Hodel), Neva Small (Chava), Rosalind Harris (Tzeitel), Norma Crane (Golde), Leonard Frey (Motel), Patience Collier (Grandma Tzeitel), Shimen Ruskin (Mordcha), Paul Mann (Lazar), Michael Glaser (Perchik), Molly Picon (Yente), Ruth Madoc (Fruma-Sarah); *Album Producer*: George Marek; *Engineer*: Ernest Oelrich; *CD Producer*: Thomas Z. Shepard.

Selections: 1 Prologue/Tradition/Main Title (11:20) *Topol*; 2 Matchmaker (3:57) *Michele Marsh, Neva Small, Rosalind Harris*; 3 If I Were A Rich Man (5:25) *Topol*; 4 Sabbath Prayer (2:40) *Topol, Norma Crane*; 5 To Life (6:15) *Topol, Shimen Ruskin*; 6 Miracle Of Miracles (2:05) *Leonard Frey*; 7 Tevye's Dream (6:44) *Topol, Norma Crane, Patience Collier, Ruth Madoc*; 8 Sunrise Sunset (3:51) *Topol, Norma Crane, Michael Glaser, Michele Marsh*; 9 Wedding Celebration and The Bottle Dance (3:54) Company; 10 Do You Love Me? (3:14) *Topol, Norma Crane*; 11 Far From The Home I Love (3:02) *Michele Marsh, Topol*; 12 Chava Ballet Sequence (2:36) Orchestra; 13 Anatevka (3:39) *Topol, Norma Crane, Molly Picon, Paul Mann, Leonard Frey*; 14 Finale (1:48) Orchestra.

Review: Sholom Aleichem's *Tevye and His Daughters* became the basis for one of Broadway's brightest productions of the 1960s, *Fiddler on the Roof,* which opened on September 22, 1964. For a while, it held the record as the longest-running musical with 3,242 performances. A poor milkman in the Russian village of Anatevka, Tevye has five daughters whom he plans to marry off to some of his well-to-do neighbors like the next-door butcher. The girls, however, have different views, and with the tacit support of their mother, the eldest marries a poor tailor, the second sets off for Siberia with a revolutionary student, and the third finds someone who is not even Jewish. By the time the Russian Cossacks come in to destroy the village, forcing the people of Anatevka to move out, Tevye philosophically hangs on to what is left of his family as he prepares to emigrate to America.

In turns profoundly moving and exuberant, *Fiddler on the Roof* owed much of its initial success to Zero Mostel's portrayal as Tevye, one of the legendary characterizations the theatre is often fond of evoking. And indeed, in this all-too-human but grander-than-life role, Mostel was certainly unique: even though many others essayed the part subsequently, including the Israeli star Topol, who played the role in the London production, the movie version and in a celebrated Broadway revival, theatre-goers who were fortunate enough to see Zero Mostel in the original production still recall his star turn in this show.

For those who were not as fortunate, the original cast album on RCA Victor gives a dimension of his portrayal, and still stands out as the best recording available.

Topol can be heard in both the London cast recording on Columbia, and the film soundtrack on EMI. The former is an acceptable facsimile that lacks some of the imaginative fire in the original cast recording, and contains at least one less selection ("The Rumor").

The film soundtrack, bigger, glossier, schmaltzier, loses some of the restrained simplicity in the original, and trades it off for the presence of Isaac Stern as the fiddler of the title, lush orchestrations by John Williams (who won an Oscar), and a generally tepid performance by Topol, Molly Picon, Leonard Frey and the other principals.

Finian's Rainbow

Finian's Rainbow ♫♫♫♫

1986, Columbia Records; from the Broadway production *Finian's Rainbow*, 1947.

Album Notes: *Music:* Burton Lane; *Lyrics:* E.Y. Harburg; *Orchestrations:* Robert Russell Bennett, Don Walker; *Vocal Ar-* *rangements:* Lynn Murray; *Musical Direction:* Max Meth; *Cast:* Ella Logan (Sharon McLonergan), David Wayne (Og), Donald Richards (Woody Mahoney), Dolores Martin (Singer), Alan Gilbert, Maude Simmons (Sharecroppers), Lorenzo Fuller, Jerry Laws, Louis Sharp (Passion Pilgrim Gospelers); *Album Producer:* Mitchell Ayres; *Engineer:* Harold Chapman; *CD Producer:* Michael Brooks; *Engineer:* Larry Keyes.

Selections: 1 Overture (3:15) Orchestra; 2 This Time Of The Year (3:03) *Sonny Terry, Alan Gilbert, Lyn Murray Singers;* 3 How Are Things In Glocca Morra? (3:12) *Ella Logan;* 4 If This Isn't Love (3:13) *Ella Logan, Donald Richards, Lyn Murray Singers;* 5 Look To The Rainbow (3:13) *Ella Logan, Donald Richards, Lyn Murray Singers;* 6 Old Devil Moon (3:23) *Ella Logan, Donald Richards;* 7 Something Sort Of Grandish (2:58) *Ella Logan, David Wayne;* 8 Necessity (3:06) *Dolores Martin, Maude Simmons, Lyn Murray Singers;* 9 When The Idle Poor Become The Idle Rich (3:19) *Ella Logan, Lyn Murray Singers;* 10 The Begat (3:08) *Lorenzo Fuller, Jerry Laws, Louis Sharp;* 11 When I'm Not Near The Girl I Love (3:17) *David Wayne;* 12 That Great Come And Get It Day (3:14) *Ella Logan, Donald Richards, Lyn Murray Singers.*

Review: See entry below.

Finian's Rainbow ♫♫♫♪

1988, RCA Victor; from the Broadway revival *Finian's Rainbow*, 1960.

Album Notes: *Music:* Burton Lane; *Lyrics:* E.Y. Harburg; *Orchestrations:* Robert Russell Bennett, Don Walker; *Musical Direction:* Max Meth; *Cast:* Jeannie Carson (Sharon McLonergan), Howard Morris (Og), Biff McGuire (Woody Mahoney), Bobby Howes (Finian McLonergan), Carol Brice (Maude), Sorrell Brooke (Senator Billboard Rawkins), Jerry Laws, Tiger Haynes, Bill Glover (Passion Pilgrim Gospelers); *Album Producer:* Bob Bollard; *Engineer:* Ernest Oelrich; *CD Producer:* Didier C. Deutsch; *Engineer:* Paul Goodman.

Selections: 1 Overture (4:33) Orchestra; 2 This Time Of The Year (2:20) Chorus; 3 How Are Things In Glocca Morra? (3:01) *Jeannie Carson, Bobby Howes;* 4 Look To The Rainbow (3:51) *Jeannie Carson, Biff McGuire;* 5 Old Devil Moon (3:39) *Jeannie Carson, Biff McGuire;* 6 Something Sort Of Grandish (2:38) *Howard Morris, Jeannie Carson;* 7 If This Isn't Love (2:53) *Jeannie Carson, Biff McGuire, Bobby Howes;* 8 Something Sort Of Grandish (reprise)(1:30) *Howard Morris;* 9 Necessity (3:20) *Carol Brice;* 10 That Great Come-And-Get-It Day (3:37) *Biff McGuire, Jeannie Carson;* 11 When The Idle Poor Become The Idle Rich (3:53) *Jeannie Carson;* 12 The Begat (3:05) *Sorrell Brooke, Jerry Laws, Tiger Haynes, Bill Glover;* 13 When I'm Not

Near The Girl I Love (3:47) *Howard Morris*; 14 How Are Things In Glocca Morra? (reprise)(1:07) *Jeannie Carson*.

Review: A whimsical blend of fantasy and social commentary, *Finian's Rainbow*, which opened on Broadway on January 10, 1947, was the brainchild of playwright-lyricist E.Y. Harburg. Harburg combined together two stories he had tried to develop unsuccessfully, one about a stuffy Southern senator who becomes a black man overnight, the other about a leprechaun whose crock of gold has been stolen and who chases the robber to America. The resulting musical, with a score by Burton Lane, dealt with Finian McLonergan, an Irishman newly arrived with his daughter, Sharon, from his native Ireland, who wants to bury the crock of gold he has stolen near Fort Knox, where it will fructify, unaware of the fact that it has the power to grant three wishes. When they settle in Rainbow Valley, in Missitucky, the place becomes prosperous, attracting the attention of Senator Billboard Rawkins who wants to expropriate the valley's current denizens, including Finian and several black families. When Sharon inadvertently expresses the wish that Senator Rawkins should become a black man, things take a turn to the worse, though everything gets straightened out by the last curtain. Following its opening on Broadway, *Finian's Rainbow* had a run of 725 performances; it was successfully revived several times, notably in 1960, and was given a lavish film treatment, directed by Francis Ford Coppola, in 1968, with Fred Astaire cast as Finian (his last dancing role on screen), Petula Clark as Sharon, and Tommy Steele as Og.

The score, with many familiar tunes, yielded the wistful show-stopping "How Are Things In Glocca Morra?"; a jazz favorite, "Old Devil Moon"; and the Leprechaun's amusingly distorted reflexion, "When I'm Not Near the Girl I Love," among its better moments. The original cast album, on Columbia, the first for the label, sounds a trifle dated by today's digital standards, but boasts terrific performances by Ella Logan as Sharon, and David Wayne as Og, the Leprechaun.

The 1960 Broadway revival cast, on RCA, has the advantage of being in stereo, with several reprises not found on the Columbia album, but performances are less inspired overall, and lack the immediacy in the original.

The soundtrack album, available on a Warner Bros. LP, was never reissued on compact disc.

Fiorello! 🎬🎬🎬🎬🎬

1989, Angel Records; from the Broadway production *Fiorello!*, 1959.

Album Notes: *Music*: Jerry Bock; *Lyrics*: Sheldon Harnick; *Orchestrations*: Irwin Kostal; *Musical Direction*: Hal Hastings; *Cast*: Tom Bosley (Fiorello La Guardia), Bob Holiday (Neil), Nathaniel Frey (Morris), Patricia Wilson (Marie), Howard Da Silva (Ben), Pat Stanley (Dora), Ellen Hanley (Thea), Eileen Rodgers (Mitzi), Del Horstmann (Ed Peterson), Stanley Simmonds, Michael Quinn, Ron Husmann, David London, Julian Patrick (Politicians).

Selections: 1 Overture (3:57) *Orchestra*; 2 On The Side Of The Angels (4:47) *Bob Holiday, Nathaniel Frey, Patricia Wilson*; 3 Politics And Poker (3:59) *Howard Da Silva*; 4 Unfair (2:18) *Tom Bosley*; 5 Marie's Law (3:00) *Patricia Wilson, Nathaniel Frey*; 6 The Name's La Guardia (3:18) *Tom Bosley*; 7 The Bum Won (2:23) *Howard Da Silva*; 8 I Love A Cop (3:00) *Pat Stanley*; 9 'Til Tomorrow (3:35) *Ellen Hanley*; 10 Home Again (1:00) *Company*; 11 When Did I Fall In Love (4:25) *Ellen Hanley*; 12 Gentleman Jimmy (2:23) *Eileen Rodgers*; 13 Little Tin Box (3:39) *Howard Da Silva*; 14 The Very Next Man (3:25) *Patricia Wilson*; 15 Finale (2:01) *Tom Bosley, Patricia Wilson*.

Review: This Pulitzer Prize-winning musical was the first Broadway hit for composer Jerry Bock and lyricist Sheldon Harnick—who went on to write *Fiddler on the Roof*—and its New York wiseguy blend of history, humor and wonderful music make it a classic of the genre. The title character, New York City's crusading mayor in the 1930s and '40s, is ably played by Tom Bosley. However, the best songs go to the supporting cast, especially Howard da Silva as a less-than-idealistic political boos, and Patricia Wilson as the mayor's long-suffering secretary. Up against *The Sound of Music*, the show won or tied for six Tony Awards.

Marc Kirkeby

Flora the Red Menace 🎬🎬🎬

1992, RCA Victor; from the Broadway production *Flora the Red Menace*, 1965.

Album Notes: *Music*: John Kander; *Lyrics*: Fred Ebb; *Orchestrations*: Don Walker; *Musical Direction*: Hal Hastings; *Cast*: Liza Minnelli (Flora), Bob Dishy (Harry Toukarian), Mary Louise Wilson (Comrade Ada), Cathryn Damon (Comrade Charlotte), Robert Kaye (Mr. Stanley), Stephanie Hill (Elsa), James Cresson (Bronco Smallwood), Dortha Duckworth (The Lady), Joe E. Marks (Mr. Weiss), Louis Guss (Comrade Golka), Jamie Donnelly (Lulu), Marie Santell (Katie), Danny Carroll (Joe); *Album Producer*: George Marek; *Engineer*: Ernie Oelrich; *CD Producer*: Bill Rosenfield; *Engineer*: Jay Newland.

Selections: 1 Overture (3:32) *Orchestra*; 2 Prologue/Unafraid (3:58) *Liza Minnelli*; 3 All I Need (Is One Good Break)(3:21) *Liza Minnelli*; 4 Not Every Day Of The Week (3:45) *Liza Minnelli, Bob Dishy*; 5 Sign Here (3:51) *Bob Dishy, Liza Minnelli*; 6 The Flame (3:46) *Mary Louise Wilson, Bob Dishy*; 7 Palomino Pal (1:51)

Dortha Duckworth, James Cresson; 8 A Quiet Thing (4:00) *Liza Minnelli*; 9 Hello, Waves (2:38) *Bob Dishy, Liza Minnelli*; 10 Dear Love (3:58) *Liza Minnelli*; 11 Express Yourself (2:48) *Cathryn Damon, Bob Dishy*; 12 Knock Knock (3:08) *Mary Louise Wilson, James Cresson*; 13 Sing Happy (3:29) *Liza Minnelli*; 14 You Are You (3:21) *Joe E. Marks, Liza Minnelli, Robert Kaye, Stephanie Hill, Jamie Donnelly, Marie Santell, Danny Carroll*.

Review: The first musical by John Kander and Fred Ebb (they had previously worked together on Barbra Streisand's hit "My Coloring Book"), *Flora, the Red Menace* also marked the first time Liza Minnelli starred on Broadway, as well as the start of her creative relationship with the songwriting team. The show had its ingratiating moments, although all the parties concerned would eventually know bigger and better successes. Based on Lester Atwell's novel, "Love Is Just Around The Corner," *Flora* deals with a young art student in New York during the Depression years who becomes involved with another student, a Communist, played by Bob Dishy. Received with lukewarm reviews when it opened on May 11, 1965, it copped a Tony for its young star, but closed shortly after, having played only 87 performances. While the score was relatively undistinguished, it offered a couple of good, theatrical moments in "Palomino Pal" and "Dear Love," but today it is hardly memorable. The original cast album reveals why.

Flower Drum Song ♪♪♪♪

1993, Sony Broadway; from the Broadway production *Flower Drum Song*, 1958.

Album Notes: *Music*: Richard Rodgers; *Lyrics*: Oscar Hammerstein II; *Orchestrations*: Robert Russell Bennett; *Dance Arrangements*: Luther Henderson, Jr.; *Musical Direction*: Salvatore Dell'Isola; *Cast*: Miyoshi Umeki (Mei Li), Larry Blyden (Sammy Fong), Juanita Hall (Madame Liang), Ed Kenney (Wang Ta), Keye Luke (Wang Chi Yang), Arabella Hong (Helen Chao), Pat Suzuki (Linda Low), Conrad Yama (Dr. Li), Rose Quong (Liu Ma), Anita Ellis (Night Club Singer), Jack Soo (Frankie Wing), Linda Ribuca, Yvonne Ribuca, Susan Lynn Kikuchi, Luis Robert Hernandez (Children); *Album Producer*: Goddard Lieberson; *Engineers*: Fred Plaut, Bud Graham; *CD Producer*: Didier C. Deutsch; *Engineer*: Darcy Proper.

Selections: 1 Overture (4:10) Orchestra; 2 You Are Beautiful (4:02) *Juanita Hall, Ed Kenney*; 3 A Hundred Million Miracles (4:23) *Miyoshi Umeki, Conrad Yama, Keye Luke, Juanita Hall, Rose Quong*; 4 I Enjoy Being A Girl (3:35) *Pat Suzuki*; 5 I Am Going To Like It Here (3:50) *Miyoshi Umeki*; 6 Like A God (1:33) *Ed Kenney*; 7 Chop Suey (2:36) *Juanita Hall, Patrick Adiarte*; 8 Don't Marry Me (4:10) *Larry Blyden, Miyoshi Umeki*; 9 Grant Avenue (2:33)*Pat Suzuki*; 10 Love Look Away (3:32) *Arabella Hong*; 11 Fan Tan Fannie/Gliding Through My Memoree/Grant Avenue (reprise)(5:02) *Anita Ellis, Jack Soo, Pat Suzuki*; 12 Entr'acte (1:31) Orchestra; 13 The Other Generation (3:15) *Keye Luke, Juanita Hall*; 14 Sunday (4:20) *Pat Suzuki, Larry Blyden*; 15 The Other Generation (reprise)(2:00) *Linda Ribuca, Yvonne Ribuca, Susan Lynn Kikuchi, Luis Robert Hernandez, Baayork Lee, Cely Carrillo, Patrick Adiarte*; 16 Wedding Parade/A Hundred Million Miracles (reprise)(2:28) *Ed Kenney, Miyoshi Umeki*.

Review: Sometimes mentioned as one of the least interesting collaborations by Richard Rodgers and Oscar Hammerstein, *Flower Drum Song*, which opened on December 1, 1958, is in need of a thorough reevaluation. While it may not be on the same level as the pair's greatest hits (*Oklahoma!, The King and I, South Pacific* or *The Sound of Music)*, it is nonetheless a lovely, ingratiating musical with a deftly written score. It has many wonderful moments in its story about a shy picture bride from China, who arrives in San Francisco to marry her intended, a nightclub operator more interested in the star of his floor show, only to fall in love with the son of the old-fashioned Chinese man who gives her and her father temporary shelter. Briskly directed by Gene Kelly (in his only directorial venture on Broadway), the show, based on Chin Y. Lee's novel of the same name, took its dramatic turns from the generational conflicts between traditional first-generation Chinese immigrants and their children, more adapted to the mores in their adopted country. The contrast was also brought into sharp focus in the score in which softer Chinese-styled numbers ("A Hundred Million Miracles") contrasted with jazzier American-inspired songs ("I Enjoy Being a Girl," "Grant Avenue").

The musical, which yielded several notable hits ("I Enjoy Being a Girl," "Sunday"), was also the occasion for Oscar Hammerstein to show the extent to which he had mastered his craft as a lyricist in the inventive pantoum "I Am Going to Like It Here." A pantoum is a rare and sophisticated form of poetry that originated in Malaya, in which the second and fourth lines in a stanza are repeated in the first and third lines of the following quatrain, in a cyclical musical movement.

Flower Drum Song enjoyed a long run of 600 performances. It was made into a beautiful film production in 1961 that had the enormous merits of retaining most of the songs in the score, as well as Miyoshi Umeki and Juanita Hall from the Broadway original, while cleverly expanding on the show's best assets, its big musical numbers. Nancy Kwan and Jack Soo also starred. The soundtrack album, available at one time on LP from Decca, was never reissued on compact disc, but the Broadway original cast album is a worthy and necessary addition to any collection.

Follies

Follies 𝅘𝅥𝅮𝅘𝅥𝅮𝅘𝅥𝅮𝅘𝅥𝅮

1994, Angel Records; from the Broadway production *Follies*, 1971.

Album Notes: *Music*: Stephen Sondheim; *Lyrics*: Stephen Sondheim; *Orchestrations*: Jonathan Tunick; *Musical Direction*: Harold Hastings; *Cast*: Michael Bartlett (Roscoe), Dorothy Collins (Sally), John McMartin (Ben), Gene Nelson (Buddy), Alexis Smith (Phyllis), Harvey Evans (Young Buddy), Kurt Peterson (Young Ben), Marti Ralph (Young Sally), Virginia Sandifur (Young Phyllis), Fifi D'Orsay (Solange), Ethel Shutta (Hattie), Mary McCarty (Stella), Yvonne de Carlo (Carlotta), Justine Johnston (Heidi), Victoria Mallory (Young Heidi); *Album Producer*: Dick Jones.

Selections: 1 Prologue/Beautiful Girls (4:28) *Michael Bartlett*; 2 Don't Look At Me (1:49) *Dorothy Collins, John McMartin*; 3 Waiting For The Girls Upstairs (5:32) *Gene Nelson, John McMartin, Alexis Smith, Dorothy Collins, Kurt Peterson, Marti Ralph, Harvey Evans, Virginia Sandifur*; 4 Ah, Paris!/Broadway Baby (3:18) *Fifi D' Orsay, Ethel Shutta*; 5 The Road You Didn't Take (2:44) *John McMartin*; 6 In Buddy's Eyes (2:36) *Dorothy Collins*; 7 Who's That Woman? (3:34) *Mary McCarty*; 8 I'm Still Here (4:22) *Yvonne de Carlo*; 9 Too Many Mornings (4:25) *John McMartin, Dorothy Collins*; 10 The Right Girl (4:30) *Gene Nelson*; 11 One More Kiss (2:14) *Justine Johnston, Victoria Mallory*; 12 Could I Leave You? (3:05) *Alexis Smith*; 13 You're Gonna Love Tomorrow/Love Will See Us Through (3:41) *John McMartin, Alexis Smith, Gene Nelson, Dorothy Collins*; 14 The God-Why-Don't-You-Love-Me Blues (3:06) *Gene Nelson*; 15 Losing My Mind (3:43) *Dorothy Collins*; 16 The Story Of Lucy And Jessie (1:53) *Alexis Smith*; 17 Live, Laugh, Love/Finale (3:21) *John McMartin*.

Review: See entry below.

Follies 𝅘𝅥𝅮𝅘𝅥𝅮𝅘𝅥𝅮𝅘𝅥𝅮

1990, First Night Records; from the London production *Follies*, 1990.

Album Notes: *Music*: Stephen Sondheim; *Lyrics*: Stephen Sondheim; *Orchestrations*: Jonathan Tunick; *Musical Direction*: Simon Lowe; *Cast*: Paul Bentley (Roscoe), Julia McKenzie (Sally Plummer), Daniel Massey (Ben Stone), David Healey (Buddy Plummer), Diana Rigg (Phyllis Stone), Evan Pappas (Young Buddy), Simon Green (Young Ben), Deborah Poplett (Young Sally), Gillian Bevan (Young Phyllis), Maria Charles (Solange Lafitte), Margaret Courtenay (Hattie Walker), Lynda Baron (Stella Deems), Dolores Gray (Carlotta Campion), Adele Leigh (Heidi Schiller), Michele Todd (Young Heidi), Pearl Carr (Billie Whitman), Teddy Johnson (Wally Whitman), Leonard Sachs

(Dimitri Weisman), Josephine Gordon (Christine Donovan), Jill Martin (Meredith Lane), Dorothy Vernon (Deedee West), Sally Ann Triplett (Margie); *Album Producer*: Chris Walker.

Selections: CD 1: 1 Beautiful Girls (3:28) *Paul Bentley*; 2 Don't Look At Me (2:05) *Julia McKenzie, Daniel Massey*; 3 Montage: Rain On The Roof/Ah! Paree/Broadway Baby (6:51) *Pearl Carr, Teddy Johnson, Maria Charles, Margaret Courtenay*; 4 Waiting For The Girls Upstairs (5:28) *Diana Rigg, Daniel Massey, David Healey, Julia McKenzie, Evan Pappas, Simon Green, Deborah Poplett, Gillian Bevan*; 5 Who's That Woman? (5:13) *Lynda Baron, Diana Rigg, Julia McKenzie, Josephine Gordon, Jill Martin, Dorothy Vernon, Pearl Carr*; 6 In Buddy's Eyes (3:05) *Julia McKenzie*; 7 Country House (3:32) *Diana Rigg, Daniel Massey*; 8 Too Many Mornings (4:52) *Daniel Massey, Julia McKenzie*.

CD 2: 1 Social Dancing (4:49) The Company; 2 I'm Still Here (5:47) *Dolores Gray*; 3 The Right Girl (4:47) *David Healey*; 4 Could I Leave You? (3:02) *Diana Rigg*; 5 One More Kiss (2:55) *Adele Leigh, Michele Todd*; 6 Loveland (3:19) *Paul Bentley*; 7 Love Will See Us Through (2:02) *Evan Pappas, Deborah Poplett*; 8 Buddy's Blues (3:58) *David Healy, Julia McKenzie, Deborah Poplett, Sally Ann Triplett*; 9 Losing My Mind (3:59) *Julia McKenzie*; 10 You're Gonna Love Tomorrow/Ah! But Underneath (6:27) *Simon Green, Gillian Bevan, Diana Rigg*; 11 Make The Most Of Your Music (4:56) *Daniel Massey*; 12 You're Gonna Love Tomorrow/Love Will See Us Through (reprise)(2:17) *Evan Pappas, Simon Green, Deborah Poplett, Gillian Bevan*; 13 Beautiful Girls/Finale (1:27) Company.

Review: See entry below.

Follies In Concert/Stavisky 𝅘𝅥𝅮𝅘𝅥𝅮𝅘𝅥𝅮𝅘𝅥𝅮𝅘𝅥𝅮

1985, RCA Victor; from the concert performance *Follies*, 1985 and from the movie *Stavisky*, Cerito Films, 1974.

Album Notes: *Music*: Stephen Sondheim; *Lyrics*: Stephen Sondheim; *Orchestrations*: Jonathan Tunick; *Dance Music*: John Berkman; The New York Philharmonic, conducted by Paul Gemignani; *Cast*: Andre Gregory (Dimitri Weismann), Arthur Rubin (Roscoe), Barbara Cook (Sally), George Hearn (Ben), Mandy Patinkin (Buddy), Lee Remick (Phyllis), Jim Walton (Young Buddy), Howard McGillin (Young Ben), Liz Callaway (Young Sally), Daisy Prince (Young Phyllis), Betty Comden (Emily Whitman), Adolph Green (Theodore Whitman), Liliane Montevecchi (Solange), Elaine Stritch (Hattie), Phyllis Newman (Stella), Carol Burnett (Carlotta), Licia Albanese (Heidi), Erie Mills (Young Heidi); *Album Producer*: Thomas Z. Shepard; *Engineer*: Paul Goodman.

Selections: CD 1: 1 Overture (5:02) Orchestra; 2 Beautiful Girls (4:58) *Andre Gregory, Arthur Rubin*; 3 Don't Look At Me (2:04) *Barbara Cook, George Hearn*; 4 Waiting For The Girls Upstairs (5:32) *Jim Walton, Howard McGillin, Mandy Patinkin, George Hearn, Lee Remick, Barbara Cook, Daisy Prince, Liz Callaway*; 5 Rain On The Roof (:51) *Betty Comden, Adolph Green*; 6 Ah, Paree! (2:01) *Liliane Montevecchi*; 7 Broadway Baby (3:56) *Elaine Stritch*; 8 The Road You Didn't Take (2:50) *George Hearn*; 9 In Buddy's Eyes (2:59) *Barbara Cook*; 10 Who's That Woman? (5:23) *Phyllis Newman, Barbara Cook, Lee Remick, Elaine Stritch, Betty Comden, Liliane Montevecchi*; 11 I'm Still Here (5:49) *Carol Burnett*; 12 Too Many Mornings (4:52) *George Hearn, Barbara Cook*; 13 The Right Girl (4:40) *Mandy Patinkin*; 14 One More Kiss (2:45) *Licia Albanese, Erie Mills*; 15 Could I Leave You? (3:03) *Lee Remick*; 16 Loveland (2:48) Company; 17 You're Gonna Love Tomorrow/Love Will See Us Through (4:49) *Howard McGillin, Daisy Prince, Jim Walton, Liz Callaway.*

CD 2: 1 Buddy's Blues (3:59) *Mandy Patinkin*; 2 Losing My Mind (4:17) *Barbara Cook*; 3 The Story Of Lucy And Jessie (2:46) *Lee Remick*; 4 Live, Laugh, Love/Finale (4:45) *George Hearn*; 5 Finale: Waiting For The Girls Upstairs/Beautiful Girls (reprise)(4:06) Company;

STAVISKY: 6 Theme From Stavisky (2:08); 7 Salon At The Claridge #1 (2:31); 8 Arlette By Day (1:57); 9 Auto Show (1:28); 10 Easy Life (1:32); 11 Secret Of Night (2:05); 12 Erna (2:14); 13 Distant Past (1:36); 14 Arlette By Night (3:12); 15 Airport At Biarritz (2:15); 16 Trotsky At Saint-Palais (2:11); 17 Montalvo At Biarritz (:39); 18 Operetta (1:33); 19 Arlette And Stavisky (1:58); 20 Recent Past (1:47); 21 Salon At The Claridge #2 (2:11); 22 Suite At The Claridge (1:08); 23 Old House (3:19); 24 Goodbye Arlette (1:26); 25 Hideout At Chamonix (1:20); 26 Erna Remembered (1:27); 27 The Future (1:03); 28 Women And Death (1:50); 29 Theme From Stavisky (1:58).

Review: For some musical-theater devotees, this Stephen Sondheim-James Goldman show about a reunion of "Weismann" Follies girls is as good as Broadway gets. But the original Broadway production was not a hit; the only major revival to date was in London in 1987; and the listener who wants all of *Follies* must invest in the three CD versions listed here.

The Capitol Records original cast album was cut during production from two LPs to one, and except for one song ("One More Kiss"), the deleted material was either discarded or never recorded, so this CD (now on Angel) represents all that survives. Still, the performances are fine throughout, especially that of Alexis Smith, a former Hollywood ingenue who emerged as a Broadway star here.

The London production, on the other hand, was a smash, powered by megawatt performances from Diana Rigg and Julia McKenzie, and established Sondheim's shows as fixtures of the West End. The recording's also first-rate, but here's the catch: with 16 years' hindsight, Sondheim and Goldman rewrote the book, deleted songs and added new ones, and almost completely reworked the "Loveland" fantasy sequence that consumes the show's last half-hour. For this listener, the changes are positive on balance, and matched song-for-song against the Broadway original, this is a better recording, but... it's a different show.

If you can only afford one version of *Follies*, however, this is the one to buy. Culled from two concert performances at New York's Lincoln Center, the recording was conceived and fought for by producer Thomas Z. Shepard, and it endures not just as the only "complete" recording of the original score, but as one of the finest assemblages of musical theater talent ever put on record. Barbara Cook, Lee Remick, Mandy Patinkin and George Hearn are the four marvelous principals, but the cameos, by the likes of Elaine Stritch, Carol Burnett and Phyllis Newman, bring down the house. As far as this listener is concerned, it could go on forever. (Also available, with some hilarious backstage moments, on video.)
Marc Kirkeby

For Me and My Girl ♪♪♪♪
1996, Rhino Records; from the screen musical *For Me and My Girl*, M-G-M, 1942.

Album Notes: *Music*: George W. Meyer; *Lyrics*: Edgar Leslie, E. Ray Goetz; *Orchestrations*: George Bassman, Leo Arnaud, Roger Edens, Conrad Salinger, Paul Marquardt; The M-G-M Studio Orchestra and Chorus, conducted by Georgie Stoll; *Cast*: Gene Kelly (Harry Palmer), Judy Garland (Jo Hayden), George Murphy (Red Metcalfe), Marta Eggerth (Eve Minard), Ben Blue (Sid Sims), Lucille Norman (Lily Duncan), Richard Quine (Danny Duncan), Keenan Wynn (Eddie Miller), Horace McNally (Bert Waring); *Album Producers*: Marilee Bradford, Bradley Flanagan, John Fricke; *Engineer*: Doug Schwartz.

Selections: 1 Main Title (1:43) Orchestra; 2 Vaudeville Routine/Jimmy K. Metcalfe & Company (1:33) Orchestra; 3 The Doll Shop, part 1 (R. Edens)(:47) *Lucille Norman, George Murphy*; 4 Oh, You Beautiful Doll (N. Ayer/S. Brown) (:36) *George Murphy*; 5 The Doll Shop, part 1 (cont'd)(1:20) *George Murphy, Lucille Norman*; 6 Don't Leave Me, Daddy (J. Verges)(1:00) *Judy Garland*; 7 Oh, You Beautiful Doll (1:02) *George Murphy*; 8 The Doll Shop, part 2 (1:05) Orchestra; 9 By The Beautiful Sea (H. Carroll/H. Atteridge)(1:27) *George Murphy, Judy Garland*; 10 Darktown Strutters Ball (S. Brooks)(:46) Orchestra; 11 For Me

And My Gal (5:07) *Judy Garland, Gene Kelly*; 12 The Confession (R. Edens)(1:07) Orchestra; Vaudeville Montage: 13 When You Wore A Tulip (P. Wenrich/J. Mahoney)(1:43) *Gene Kelly, Judy Garland*; 14 Don't Bite The Hand That's Feeding You (J. Morgan/T. Holer)(1:15) *Judy Garland*; 15 Do I Love You? (H. Christine/E.R. Goetz)(3:03) *Marta Eggerth*; 16 It Started With Eve (R. Edens)(1:12) Orchestra; 17 A Women's Prerogative (R. Edens)(:50) Orchestra; 18 After You've Gone (H. Creamer/T. Layton)(2:18) *Judy Garland*; 19 The Spell Of The Waltz (J. Strauss)(outtake)(5:01) *Marta Eggerth*; 20 Love Song (R. Edens) (4:50) Orchestra; 21 A Dream Crashes(R. Edens)(1:36) Orchestra; 22 I'm Sorry I Made You Cry (:58) *George Murphy*; 23 Tell Me (M. Kortlander/W. Calahan)(:59) *George Murphy, Ben Blue*; 24 Tell Me (reprise)(2:00) *Lucille Norman, The Sportsmen Male Quartet*; 25 Till We Meet Again (R. Whiting/R. Egan)(1:18) *Lucille Norman, The King's Men, Judy Garland*; 26 We Don't Want The Bacon, What We Want Is A Piece Of The Rhine (H. Carr/H. Russell/J. Havens)(2:16) *Ben Lessey*; 27 Ballin' the Jack (2:28) *Gene Kelly, Judy Garland*; 28 The Small Time (R. Edens) (2:53) Orchestra; 29 What Are You Going To Do About The Boys? (E. Van Alstyne/G. Kahn)(1:23) *Ben Blue, The King's Men*; 30 How Ya Gonna Keep 'Em Down On The Farm? (W. Donaldson/S. Lewis/J. Young)(1:39) *Judy Garland*; 31 There's A Long, Long Trail (Z. Elliott/S. King)(2:48) *The King's Men*; 32 Where Do We Go From Here? (P. Wenrich/H. Johnson)(:56) *Judy Garland, The King's Men*; Y.M.C.A. Montage: 33 Part 1: Over There (G.M. Cohan)/It's A Long Way To Tipperary (H. Williams/J. Judge)(:54) *Judy Garland*; 34 Part 2: Goodbye Broadway, Hello France (B. Baskette/C.F. Riesner/ B. Davis)(:23) Chorus; 35 Part 3: Yankee Doodle (R. Shackburg)/ Smiles (L. Roberts/W. Callahan)(:21) *Judy Garland*; 36 Part 4: Hincki Dinky Parlay Voo/Oh, Frenchy (:27) *Gene Kelly, Ben Blue*; 37 Part 5: Pick Up Your Troubles In Your Old Kit Bag And Smile, Smile, Smile (F. Powell/G. Asaf)(:50) *Judy Garland*; 38 When Johnny Comes Marching Home (L. Lambert)(1:07) *Judy Garland*; 39 Finale: For Me And My Gal (1:14) *Judy Garland, Gene Kelly*; 40 Main Title (alternate version)(1:20) Orchestra; 41 Dear Old Pal Of Mine (outtake)(G. Rice/H. Robel)(3:10) *The King's Men*; 42 Smiles (outtake)(:40) *Judy Garland*; 43 Three Cheers For The Yanks (H. Martin/R. Blane)(outtake)(2:29) *Judy Garland, Six Hits And A Miss*; 44 For Me And My Gal (outtake) (2:27) *Judy Garland, George Murphy, Gene Kelly.*

Review: A tuneful Arthur Freed production for M-G-M, *For Me and My Gal* starred Gene Kelly in his first Hollywood film following the big impression he had made on Broadway in *Pal Joey*, and Judy Garland in her first major film sans her usual partner, Mickey Rooney. Neither Kelly nor Garland would have to complain, as both gave ingratiating performances that showed his screen personality in the best light, and revealed greater depth in her own ability to sing and dance. The lame story of two vaudevillians in the years of World War I, *For Me and My Gal* was the occasion for many breezy musical numbers in which Garland, Kelly and George Murphy performed songs from the period like "When You Wore A Tulip," "After You've Gone," "Till We Meet Again," and the title tune with style, ease and a charm that belied the overall corny plot. The recently reissued soundtrack album on Rhino, supplemented with a lot of previously unreleased material, proves irresistible and charmingly dated, with the three principals particularly engaging in these musical moments, individually and together.

42nd Street 🎝🎝🎝🎝

1980, RCA Victor; from the Broadway production *42nd Street*, 1980.

Album Notes: *Music:* Harry Warren; *Lyrics:* Al Dubin, Johnny Mercer, Mort Dixon; *Orchestrations:* Philip J. Lang; *Vocal Arrangements and Musical Direction:* John Lesko; *Cast:* Tammy Grimes (Dorothy Brock), Jerry Orbach (Julian Marsh), Lee Roy Reams (Billy Lawlor), Wanda Richert (Peggy Sawyer), Carole Cook (Maggie Jones), Karen Prunczik (Annie), Danny Carroll (Andy Lee), Ginny King (Lorraine), Jeri Kansas (Phyllis), James Congdon (Pat Denning), Joseph Bova (Bert Barry); *Album Producer:* Thomas Z. Shepard; *Engineer:* Paul Goodman.

Selections: 1 Overture/Audition (4:41) *Danny Carroll*; 2 Shadow Waltz (3:27) *Tammy Grimes*; 3 Young And Healthy (2:15) *Lee Roy Reams, Wanda Richert*; 4 Go Into Your Dance (3:18) *Carole Cook, Wanda Richert, Karen Prunczik, Danny Carroll, Ginny King, Jeri Kansas*; 5 You're Getting To Be A Habit With Me (2:00) *Tammy Grimes, Lee Roy Reams, Wanda Richert*; 6 Getting Out Of Town (1:38) *James Congdon, Joseph Bova, Carole Cook, Karen Prunczik, Tammy Grimes*; 7 We're In The Money (3:05) *Karen Prunczik, Wanda Richert, Ginny King, Jeri Kansas, Lee Roy Reams*; 8 Dames (3:19) *Lee Roy Reams*; 9 Sunny Side To Every Situation (2:13) *Karen Prunczik*; 10 Lullaby Of Broadway (4:59) *Jerry Orbach*; 11 About A Quarter To Nine (2:11) *Tammy Grimes, Wanda Richert*; 12 Shuffle Off To Buffalo (3:45) *Karen Prunczik, Joseph Bova, Carole Cook*; 13 42nd Street (7:15) *Wanda Richert, Lee Roy Reams*; 14 Finale: 42nd Street (reprise)/Bows (3:07) *Jerry Orbach.*

Review: The 1933 backstage screen musical, *42nd Street,* became a major stage hit when David Merrick brought it virtually intact to Broadway on August 25, 1980. Retaining the film's basic plot—chorus girl (Wandy Richert) steps up to the spotlight when big star (Tammy Grimes) can't go on and wins the day—as well as many of the songs written by Harry Warren and Al Dubin, plus many others from other films, the show also benefitted from the incredible creative energy and choreographic drive Gower Champion (who died hours before the premiere) gave it, in a breathtaking display of ensemble dancing seldom seen on Broadway. With Jerry Orbach portraying Julian Marsh, the hard-driving director of the show-within-a-show, and Lee Roy Reams as Billy Lawlor, Peggy's love interest and eventual dancing partner, the musical, a razzling-dazzling paean to show business, walked away with the Tony for Best Musical, and enjoyed a long run of 3,486 performances. The original cast album is a brilliant recreation of the musical numbers as they were heard when the show opened.

Funny Face ♪♪♪♪

1996, Verve Records; from the screen musical *Funny Face*, Paramount Pictures, 1956.

Album Notes: *Music*: George Gershwin; *Lyrics*: Ira Gershwin; *Orchestrations*: Mason Van Cleave, Alexander Courage, Skip Martin, Conrad Salinger; The Paramount Studio Chorus and Orchestra, conducted by Adolph Deutsch; *Cast*: Fred Astaire (Dick Avery), Audrey Hepburn (Jo Stockton), Kay Thompson (Maggie Prescott); *Album Producer*: Norman Granz; *CD Producer*: Michael Lang; *Engineer*: Steven Fallone.

Selections: 1 Overture: a) Funny Face, b) 'S Wonderful, c) Think Pink (R. Edens/L. Gershe)(3:48) *Fred Astaire, Kay Thompson*; 2 How Long Has This Been Going On? (5:05) *Audrey Hepburn*; 3 How Long Has This Been Going On? (reprise)(1:05) Orchestra; 4 Funny Face (3:43) *Fred Astaire*; 5 Bonjour, Paris! (6:04) *Fred Astaire, Audrey Hepburn, Kay Thompson*; 6 Clap Yo Hands (3:32) *Fred Astaire, Kay Thompson*; 7 He Loves And She Loves (5:00) *Fred Astaire*; 8 Bonjour, Paris (1:00) Orchestra; 9 On How To Be Lovely (R. Edens/L. Gershe)(2:41) *Audrey Hepburn, Kay Thompson*; 10 Basal Metabolism (2:54) Orchestra; 11 Let's Kiss And Make Up (4:48) *Fred Astaire*; 12 'S Wonderful (2:06) *Fred Astaire, Audrey Hepburn*.

Review: Utilizing five songs written by the Gershwin brothers for the 1927 stage show of the same name, including the title tune, plus material provided by Roger Edens and Leonard Gershe, on loan from M-G-M, *Funny Face* was a delightful screen musical that owed much of its charm to the presence of Audrey Hepburn. Hepburn is delicious as a Greenwich Village bookstore operator who is spirited away to Paris by a famous fashion photographer and becomes a top model, though her one objective is to meet the guru of Empathicalism, a new philosophical movement. Strikingly lensed in the French capital, and with the action smoothly integrating its various musical numbers, the *film a clef* (in which Astaire's Avery was a

stand-in for Richard Avedon, who worked on the film as visual consultant, and Michel Auclair's Professor Flostre was a thinly disguised screen image of Jean-Paul Sartre) gave Fred Astaire ample opportunities to show his undiminished talents as a dancer and singer. Astaire spends much of the film either wooing Audrey Hepburn or sharing the spotlight with Kay Thompson, hilariously cast as a no-nonsense top magazine editor. Unfortunately, the CD soundtrack is in mono, and only replicates the original album the way it was initially released in 1957, without any extras.

Funny Girl

Funny Girl ♪♪♪♪♪

1994, Angel Records; from the Broadway production *Funny Girl*, 1964.

Album Notes: *Music*: Jule Styne; *Lyrics*: Bob Merrill; *Orchestrations*: Ralph Burns; *Vocal Arrangements*: Buster Davis; *Musical Direction*: Milton Rosenstock; *Cast*: Barbra Streisand (Fanny Brice), Sydney Chaplin (Nick Arnstein), Kay Medford (Mrs. Brice), Jean Stapleton (Mrs. Strakosh), Danny Meehan (Eddie Ryan); *Album Producer*: Dick Jones.

Selections: 1 Overture (4:05) Orchestra; 2 If A Girl Isn't Pretty (2:16) *Jean Stapleton, Kay Medford, Danny Meehan*; 3 I'm The Greatest Star (4:01) *Barbra Streisand*; 4 Cornet Man (3:52) *Barbra Streisand, Dick Perry*; 5 Who Taught Her Everything (3:04) *Kay Medford, Danny Meehan*; 6 His Love Makes Me Beautiful (3:21) *John Lankston, Barbra Streisand*; 7 I Want To Be Seen With You Tonight (1:56) *Sydney Chaplin, Barbra Streisand*; 8 Henry Street (1:57) *Ensemble*; 9 People (3:29) *Barbra Streisand*; 10 You Are Woman (3:49) *Sydney Chaplin, Barbra Streisand*; 11 Don't Rain On My Parade (2:45) *Barbra Streisand*; 12 Sadie, Sadie (3:33) *Barbra Streisand*; 13 Find Yourself A Man (2:01) *Danny Meehan, Kay Medford, Jean Stapleton*; 14 Rat-Tat-Tat-Tat (3:22) *Danny Meehan, Barbra Streisand*; 15 Who Are You Now? (2:49) *Barbra Streisand*; 16 The Music That Makes Me Dance (3:52) *Barbra Streisand*; 17 Don't Rain On My Parade (reprise)(2:07) *Barbra Streisand*.

Review: See entry below.

Funny Girl ♪♪♪♪♩

1968, Columbia Records; from the screen version *Funny Girl*, Columbia Pictures, 1964.

Album Notes: *Music*: Jule Styne; *Lyrics*: Bob Merrill; *Orchestrations*: Ralph Burns; *Vocal Arrangements*: Buster Davis; *Musical Direction*: Walter Scharf; *Cast*: Barbra Streisand (Fanny Brice), Omar Sharif (Nick Arnstein), Kay Medford (Rose Brice), Mae

> "We always try to put more of the unknown or newer artists on a soundtrack, because if a half-million people see the movie or hear the soundtrack, then some might actually get turned on to that artist."
>
> **Andrew Shack**
> *Priority VP of soundtracks*

Questel (Mrs. Strakosh), Lee Allen (Eddie Ryan), Anne Francis (Georgia James), Walter Pidgeon (Florenz Siegfeld), Tommy Rall (Dancer); *Album Producer*: Jack Gold.

Selections: 1 Overture (3:57) Orchestra; 2 I'm The Greatest Star (4:03) *Barbra Streisand*; 3 If A Girl Isn't Pretty (2:23) *Mae Questel, Kay Medford*; 4 Roller Skate Rag (1:59) Chorus; 5 I'd Rather Be Blue Over You (F. Fisher/ B. Rose)(2:35) *Barbra Streisand*; 6 His Love Makes Me Beautiful (5:36) *Barbra Streisand*; 7 People (5:01) *Barbra Streisand*; 8 You Are Woman, I Am Man (4:21) *Omar Sharif, Barbra Streisand*; 9 Don't Rain On My Parade (2:37) *Barbra Streisand*; 10 Sadie, Sadie (4:17) *Barbra Streisand*; 11 The Swan (2:48) *Barbra Streisand*; 12 Funny Girl (2:41) *Barbra Streisand*; 13 My Man (M. Yvain/C. Pollock)(2:17) *Barbra Streisand*; 14 Finale(2:20)Ensemble.

Review: The story of vaudeville comedian Fanny Brice, her rise to stardom in the Ziegfeld Follies, her emotional involvement with gangster Nick Arnstein, and the eventual break-up of their marriage provided the strong dramatic elements for a musical by Isobel Lennart, with a sensational score by Jule Styne and Bob Merrill. More specifically, it also launched the career of Barbra Streisand, as Fanny Brice, in one of the theatre's legendary portrayals. The show, which opened March 26, 1964 to rave reviews, yielded many hit tunes, all performed by the nascent star, including "Don't Rain On My Parade," "The Music That Makes Me Dance," "I'm The Greatest Star," and "People," which, alone, became a standard for an entire generation. Though it failed to receive any Tony Award (*Hello, Dolly!* was the big winner that year), *Funny Girl* enjoyed a long run of 1,348 performances. Streisand went on to star in the film version, which added to the score two songs associated with Fanny Brice, "I'd Rather Be Blue Over You" and "My Man." Both the original cast and the soundtrack albums are worthy additions to any musical collection; the former features Streisand at the peak of her talent, in a portrayal that has not

yet become stilted, with Sydney Chaplin appropriately suave as Nick Arnstein, and Kay Medford and Jean Stapleton in supporting roles.

The soundtrack album, overblown and sounding more elaborate than its stage counterpart, substitutes Omar Sharif as Nick Arnstein, but drops several tunes from the show, adding the two cover songs, as well as "Roller Skate Rag," "The Swan," and "Funny Girl," written specifically for the film. By then, Streisand had become a superstar, and her portrayal, while outstanding, also seemed less fresh and genuine than in the original.

Funny Lady ♫♫♫ °

1990, Bay Cities Records; from the screen musical *Funny Lady*, Columbia Pictures, 1975.

Album Notes: *Orchestrations*: Peter Matz; *Musical Direction*: Peter Matz; *Cast*: Barbra Streisand (Fanny Brice), James Caan (Billy Rose), Ben Vereen (Bert Robbins); *Album Producer*: Peter Matz; *Engineers*: Kevin Cleary, John Neal; *CD Producer*: Nick Redman; *Engineer*: Daniel Hersch.

Selections: 1 How Lucky Can You Get (F. Ebb/J. Kander) (4:49) *Barbra Streisand*; 2 So Long Honey Lamb (F. Ebb/J. Kander) (3:12) *Barbra Streisand, Ben Vereen*; 3 I Found A Million Dollar Baby (In A Five And Ten Cent Store) (H. Warren/B. Rose/M. Dixon) (2:00) *Barbra Streisand*; 4 Isn't This Better (F. Ebb/J. Kander) (3:30) *Barbra Streisand*; 5 Me And My Shadow (B. Rose/A. Jolson/D. Dreyer) (3:04) *James Caan*; 6 If I Love Again (J. Murray/B. Oakland) (2:58) *Barbra Streisand*; 7 I Got A Code In My Doze (B. Rose/A. Fields/F. Hall) (1:10) *Barbra Streisand*; 8 (It's Gonna Be A) Great Day (B. Rose/E. Eliscu/V. Youmans) (5:15) *Barbra Streisand*; 9 Blind Date (F. Ebb/J. Kander) (4:57) *Barbra Streisand*; 10 Am I Blue (G. Clarke/H. Akst) (3:21) *Barbra Streisand*; 11 It's Only A Paper Moon/I Like Him (B. Rose/E.Y. Harburg/H. Arlen/F. Ebb/J. Kander) (1:04) *Barbra Streisand*; 12 It's Only A Paper Moon/I Like Her (2:38) *James Caan*; 13 More Than You Know (B. Rose/E. Eliscu/V. Youmans) (2:28) *Barbra Streisand*; 14 Clap Hands, Here Comes Charley (B. Rose/ B. MacDonald/J. Meyer) (2:14) *Barbra Streisand, Ben Vereen*; 15 Let's Hear It For Me (F. Ebb/J. Kander) (3:13) *Barbra Streisand*.

Review: In this sequel to her stage and screen success *Funny Girl*, Barbra Streisand again portrayed Fanny Brice, singing songs the comedienne had created, and new material written specifically for the film by Kander and Ebb. Though taking many liberties with historical accuracy (Brice, now a big Broadway star, still pines for Nick, but eventually marries producer-songwriter Billy Rose, until she finds him in bed with a rival),

Funny Lady, released in 1975, was a huge box office hit for Streisand. Omar Sharif briefly appeared as Nick Arnstein, and James Caan portrayed Billy Rose. The soundtrack album focuses on the various musical numbers performed by Streisand in the film, with occasional assist from Ben Vereen.

A Funny Thing Happened on the Way to the Forum

A Funny Thing Happened on the Way to the Forum

♫♫♫♫

1993, Angel Records; from the Broadway production *A Funny Thing Happened on the Way to the Forum*, 1962.

Album Notes: *Music:* Stephen Sondheim; *Lyrics:* Stephen Sondheim; *Orchestrations:* Irwin Kostal, Sid Ramin; *Musical Direction:* Harold Hastings; *Cast:* Zero Mostel (Pseudolus), David Burns (Senex), Ruth Kobart (Domina), Brian Davies (Hero), Jack Gilford (Hysterium), John Carradine (Lycus), Ronald Holgate (Miles Gloriosus), Preshy Marker (Philia), Eddie Phillips, George Reeder, David Evans (The Proteans); *Album Producers:* Andy Wiswell, Dick Jones; *CD Engineer:* Bob Norberg.

Selections: 1 Overture (3:12) Orchestra; 2 Comedy Tonight (4:59) *Zero Mostel;* 3 Love, I Hear (2:49) *Brian Davies;* 4 Free (3:34) *Zero Mostel, Brian Davies;* 5 Lovely (3:06) *Brian Davies, Preshy Marker;* 6 Pretty Little Picture (2:52) *Zero Mostel, Brian Davies, Preshy Marker;* 7 Everybody Ought To Have A Maid (3:49) *David Burns, Zero Mostel, Jack Gilford, John Carradine;* 8 I'm Calm (2:50) *Jack Gilford;* 9 Impossible (2:31) *David Burns, Brian Davies;* 10 Bring Me My Bride (3:20) *Ronald Holgate, Zero Mostel;* 11 That Dirty Old Man (2:13) *Ruth Kobart;* 12 That'll Show Him (1:48) *Preshy Marker;* 13 Lovely (reprise) (2:55) *Zero Mostel, Jack Gilford;* 14 Funeral Sequence (2:04) *Zero Mostel, Ronald Holgate;* 15 Finale (1:21) Company.

Review: See entry below.

A Funny Thing Happened on the Way to the Forum

♫♫♫

1996, Angel Records; from the Broadway revival *A Funny Thing Happened on the Way to the Forum*, 1996.

Album Notes: *Music:* Stephen Sondheim; *Lyrics:* Stephen Sondheim; *Orchestrations:* Jonathan Tunick; *Musical Direction:* Edward Strauss; *Cast:* Nathan Lane (Pseudolus), Lewis J. Stadlen (Senex), Mary Testa (Domina), Jim Stanek (Hero), Mark Linn-Baker (Hysterium), Ernie Sabella (Lycus), Cris Groenendaal (Miles Gloriosus), Jessica Boevers (Philia), Brad Aspel, Cory English, Ray Roderick (The Proteans), Pamela Everett, Susan Misner, Lori Werner, Mary Ann Lamb, Stephanie Pope (The Courtesans); *Album Producer:* Phil Ramone; *Engineers:* Frank Filipetti, Al Schmitt.

Selections: 1 Overture (1:52) Orchestra; 2 Comedy Tonight (6:53) *Nathan Lane;* 3 Love, I Hear (2:23) *Jim Stanek;* 4 Free (3:17) *Nathan Lane, Jim Stanek;* 5 The House Of Marcus Lycus (8:33) *Nathan Lane, Ernie Sabella, Pamela Everett, Leigh Zimmerman, Susan Misner, Lori Werner, Mary Ann Lamb, Stephanie Pope;* 6 Lovely (2:38) *Jim Stanek, Jessica Boevers;* 7 Pretty Little Picture (2:56) *Nathan Lane, Jim Stanek;* 8 Everybody Ought To Have A Maid (4:02) *Lewis J. Stadlen, Nathan Lane, Mark Linn-Baker, Ernie Sabella;* 9 I'm Calm (1:32) *Mark Linn-Baker;* 10 Impossible (2:31) *Lewis J. Stadlen, Jim Stanek;* 11 Bring Me My Bride (3:04) *Cris Goenendaal, Nathan Lane;* 12 That Dirty Old Man (2:04) *Mary Testa;* 13 That'll Show Him (1:36) *Jessica Boevers;* 14 Lovely (reprise)(2:47) *Nathan Lane, Mark Linn-Baker;* 15 Funeral Sequence (2:42) *Nathan Lane, Cris Groenendaal;* 16 Finale (1:16) Company.

Review: Something appealing, nothing appalling, something for, well, almost everyone... Stephen Sondheim's first music-and-lyrics Broadway outing endures as well as the jokes in this ancient-Rome-meets-Larry Gelbart farce, a favorite through the years and the show that made Zero Mostel a Broadway star. Mostel "acts" superbly on the original cast album recording, as do co-clowns Jack Gilford, David Burns and John Carradine. Performances of several discarded songs—including the lovely "Love Is in the Air"—can be found on various Sondheim CD collections. (Serious collectors—and British listeners—may also want to seek out EMI/Angel's original London cast recording, also available on CD, starring Frankie Howerd.)

The 1996 revival waited a couple of years for Nathan Lane, and he's fine here, as are fellow jokesters Mark Linn-Baker, Lewis J. Stadlen and Mary Testa, so why does this technically flawless recording lack the impact of the original? At this writing, the show's still packing 'em in on Broadway (now with Whoopi Goldberg); the CD captures valuable bits of dialogue and re-expands several of the songs from the '62 cast album; but here, as in math class, you can't divide by Zero. Unique to this CD is the spoken-and-sung "House of Marcus Lycus," which provides the same strange thrill as hearing someone describe a copy of *Playboy.* The recording producer, Phil Ramone, was also kind enough to restore the essential "Pretty Little Picture," although it was absent from this stage production.

Marc Kirkeby

Gentlemen Prefer Blondes
♫♫♫♫♫

1991, Sony Broadway; from the Broadway production *Gentlemen Prefer Blondes*, 1949.

Album Notes: *Music:* Jule Styne; *Lyrics:* Leo Robin; *Orchestrations:* Don Walker; *Vocal Arrangements:* Hugh Martin; *Musical Direction:* Milton Rosenstock; *Cast:* Carol Channing (Lorelei Lee); Yvonne Adair (Dorothy Shaw), Jack McCauley (Gus Esmond), Eric Brotherson (Henry Spofford), Rex Evans (Sir Francis Beekman), Honi Coles, Cholly Atkins, Alice Pearce (Mrs. Ella Spofford), George S. Irving (Josephus Gage); *Album Producer:* Goddard Lieberson; *CD Producer:* Didier C. Deutsch; *Engineer:* Tim Tiedemann.

Selections: 1 Overture (3:26) Orchestra; 2 It's High Time (2:46) *Yvonne Adair*; 3 Bye Bye Baby (3:14) *Jack McCauley, Carol Channing*; 4 A Little Girl From Little Rock (3:04) *Carol Channing*; 5 I Love What I'm Doing (2:18) *Yvonne Adair*; 6 Just A Kiss Apart (3:00) *Eric Brotherson, Yvonne Adair*; 7 The Practice Scherzo (1:09) Orchestra; 8 It's Delightful Down In Chile (3:20) *Rex Evans, Carol Channing*; 9 Sunshine (3:19) *Yvonne Adair, Eric Brotherson*; 10 I'm A'Tingle, I'm A'Glow (2:27) *George S. Irving*; 11 You Say You Care (3:41) *Eric Brotherson, Yvonne Adair*; 12 Mamie Is Mimi (3:04) *Honi Coles, Cholly Atkins*; 13 Diamonds Are A Girl's Best Friend (2:58) *Carol Channing*; 14 Gentlemen Prefer Blondes (1:04) *Carol Channing, Jack McCauley*; 15 Homesick Blues (3:25) *Carol Channing, Yvonne Adair, Jack McCauley, Eric Brotherson, Alice Pearce, George S. Irving*; 16 Keeping Cool With Coolidge (2:14) *Yvonne Adair*.

Review: Carol Channing, portraying a quintessential 1920s gold-digger, became a star in *Gentlemen Prefer Blondes*, the droll, fictional tale of two dizzy American flappers and their search to nail down the right man, preferably one with a large bank account, based on a short story by Anita Loos. Sporting a brilliant score by Jule Styne and Leo Robin, the musical, which opened on December 8, 1949, had a run of 740 performances, and with many alterations (including the deletion of all but three of the songs from the stage show) became the first starring vehicle for Marilyn Monroe in 1953. In its stage treatment, the song-and-dance extravaganza followed the outline of its original source story, and focused on Lorelei Lee, a "little girl from Little Rock," and her friend from the Follies, Dorothy Shaw, as they embark on a transatlantic trip to Europe, a gift from Lorelei's generous "sugar daddy," a button tycoon. On board the "Ile de France," both Lorelei and Dorothy meet various suitably accomodating gentlemen, with Lorelei the center of interest for several of them. The show gave Carol Channing the right opportunity to display her flair for comedy

in a portrayal that has remained legendary in the annals of the musical theatre. The score, replete with many excellent numbers, yielded the hits "A Little Girl From Little Rock" and "Diamonds Are A Girl's Best Friends."

Gigi

Gigi ♫♫♫♫♫

1996, Rhino Records; from the screen musical *Gigi*, M-G-M, 1958.

Album Notes: *Music:* Frederick Loewe; *Lyrics:* Alan Jay Lerner; *Orchestrations:* Bob Franklyn, Al Woodbury, Alexander Courage, Maurice de Packh; *Arrangements:* Conrad Salinger, Andre Previn, Alexander Courage; The M-G-M Studio Chorus and Orchestra, conducted by Andre Previn; *Cast:* Leslie Caron (Gigi), Louis Jourdan (Gaston Lachailles), Maurice Chevalier (Honore Lachailles), Hermione Gingold (Madame Alvarez); *Album Producer:* Merilee Bradford; *Engineer:* Doug Schwartz.

Selections: 1 Main Title (2:10) Orchestra; 2 Opening (1:53) Orchestra; 3 Interlude/And There Is The Future (1:08) *Maurice Chevalier*; 4 Thank Heaven For Little Girls (2:07) *Maurice Chevalier*; 5 Meet Gigi (:46) Orchestra; 6 Gaston's House (:46) Orchestra; 7 Armenonville/It's A Bore Prelude (1:01) Orchestra; 8 It's A Bore (2:14) *Maurice Chevalier, Louis Jourdan*; 9 After It's A Bore (:29) Orchestra; 10 Aunt Alicia (:29) Orchestra; 11 Parisians Introduction (:17) Orchestra; 12 The Parisians (2:23) *Betty Wand*; 13 Ice Skating Sequence (3:06) Orchestra; 14 Dissolve Maxim's/Gossip (2:53) Chorus; 15 Introduction To Maxim's Waltz/Waltz At Maxim's (She Is Not Thinking Of Me)(2:40) *Louis Jourdan*; 16 It's A Bore (reprise)(:40) *Maurice Chevalier, Louis Jourdan, John Abbott*; 17 To The Inn (:44) Orchestra; 18 Goodbye Madame (:41) Orchestra; 19 Bore Montage (1:43) Orchestra; 20 The Night They Invented Champagne (1:43) *Betty Wand, Hermione Gingold, Louis Jourdan*; 21 Trouville (3:07) Orchestra; 22 I Remember It Well (2:22) *Maurice Chevalier, Hermione Gingold*; 23 Painting Grandmama (:20) Orchestra; 24 Lessons (6:58) Orchestra; 25 Upset (:25) Orchestra; 26 Gaston's Soliloquy (2:35) *Louis Jourdan*; 27 Gigi (3:35) *Louis Jourdan*; 28 Gaston With Flowers (:28) Orchestra; 29 You Never Told Me (1:05) Orchestra; 30 I'm Glad I'm Not Young Anymore (2:50) *Maurice Chevalier*; 31 I'm Glad I'm Not Young Anymore (reprise)(1:41) Orchestra; 32 Aunt Alicia's March (1:09) Orchestra; 33 Bracelet (1:03) Orchestra; 34 Say A Prayer For Me Tonight (1:13) *Betty Wand*; 35 Gigi's Big Moment (1:14) Orchestra; 36 Second Gossip (1:11) Chorus; 37 Waltz At Maxim's (4:50) Orchestra; 38 Gaston's Decision (1:56) Orchestra; 39 Change Of Heart/End Title (1:24) *Maurice Chevalier*; 40 The Parisians (3:24) *Leslie Caron, Andre Previn*; 41 The Night

They Invented Champagne (1:43) *Leslie Caron, Hermione Gingold, Louis Jourdan, Andre Previn*; 42 Say A Prayer For Me Tonight (1:05) *Leslie Caron, Andre Previn*.

Review: See entry below.

Gigi 🎵🎵🎵🎵

1973, RCA Victor Records; from the Broadway production *Gigi*, 1973.

Album Notes: *Music*: Frederick Loewe; *Lyrics*: Alan Jay Lerner; *Orchestrations*: Irwin Kostal; *Dance Arrangements*: Trude Rittman; *Musical Direction*: Ross Reimeuller; *Cast*: Karin Wolfe (Gigi), Daniel Massey (Gaston Lachailles), Alfred Drake (Honore Lachailles), Agnes Moorehead (Aunt Alicia), Maria Karnilova (Inez Alvarez), George Gaynes (Maitre Du Fresne), Howard Chitjian (Maitre Duclos); *Album Producer*: Joe Reisman; *Engineer*: Bob Simpson; *CD Producer*: Bill Rosenfield; *CD Engineer*: Jay Newland.

Selections: 1 Overture (3:04); 2 Thank Heaven For Little Girls (2:45) *Alfred Drake*; 3 It's A Bore (2:25) *Daniel Massey, Alfred Drake*; 4 The Earth And Other Minor Things (3:03) *Karin Wolfe*; 5 Paris Is Paris Again (2:26) *Alfred Drake*; 6 She Is Not Thinking Of me (3:57) *Daniel Massey*; 7 The Night They Invented Champagne (3:34) *Maria Karnilova, Daniel Massey, Karin Wolfe*; 8 I Remember It Well (3:26) *Alfred Drake, Maria Karnilova*; 9 Gigi (5:51) *Daniel Massey*; 10 The Contract (8:57) *Agnes Moorehead, Maria Karnilova, George Gaynes, Howard Chitjian*; 11 I'm Glad I'm Not Young Anymore (4:23) *Alfred Drake*; 12 In This Wide Wide World (3:08) *Karin Wolfe*; 13 Finale/Thank Heaven For Little Girls (2:10) *Alfred Drake*.

Review: We are truly fortunate to be living in this modern (digital) world. Technology and a new-found appreciation of our Broadway and Hollywood musical heritage has unlocked the archives of recording companies and film studios the world over. The new soundtrack album recording of *Gigi*, on Rhino, is a testament to the treat we all have in store as these archives become more and more available. In addition to the basic songs that have been available over the years in several incarnations, LP, CD and cassette, we now have available, for our enjoyment, instrumental interludes, reprises, extended versions and even experimental recordings with Leslie Caron's singing voice. As most film buffs are aware, her singing voice was dubbed, in part, by Betty Wand. This classic recording also includes such stars as Maurice Chevalier, Louis Jourdan and Hermione Gingold. The score of this film again shows the versatile talent of Lerner and Loewe, both of whom can catch a character, a place and a time like no other song writing team. While the story of this film is similar to *My Fair Lady*, in a

superficial way, the music and lyrics do not sound like the previous musical at all. The new transfers are in the best stereo sound they have ever had and will pour gloriously from your speakers every time you play this album.

In 1973, *Gigi* was turned into a big, lavish Broadway musical which, unfortunately for all involved, ran not quite three months. However, fortunately for us, a recording was made during the run of the show and it is wonderfully alive. Though none of the principals equal their counterparts in the film, they do capture the spirit and the fun of the material beautifully. Karin Wolfe, while not quite an unknown, was perceived as new to the scene and she played Gigi as a charming young girl on the brink of womanhood. Daniel Massey really understood the character of Gaston down to his fingertips and he displays more voice on the recording than his film counterpart. If Alfred Drake wasn't Maurice Chevalier, he was, well... Alfred Drake, and he brought a touching self-awareness to the character of Honore. Maria Karnilova and Agnes Moorehead were wonderful as Gigi's two role models. Lerner and Loewe wrote several lovely new songs for the show with "The Contract" being a knockout. The stereo sound on the compact disc is good and it reproduces the many felicities of this score well.

Jerry J. Thomas

Girl Crazy

Girl Crazy 🎵🎵🎵🎵

1990, Elektra Records; from the studio cast recording *Girl Crazy*, 1990.

Album Notes: *Music*: George Gershwin; *Lyrics*: Ira Gershwin; *Orchestrations*: Robert Russell Bennett; *Musical Direction*: John Mauceri; *Cast*: Lorna Luft (Kate Fothergill), David Carroll (Danny Churchill), Judy Blazer (Molly Gray), Frank Gorshin (Gieber Goldfarb), David Garrison (Slick Fothergill), Vicki Lewis (Patsy West), Eddie Korbich (Cowboy), Rex Hays (Sam Mason), Stan Chandler, Guy Stroman, Larry Raben, David Engel (Vocal Quartet); *Album Producers*: Tommy Krasker, Leroy Parkins Jr.; *Engineer*: Paul Goodman.

Selections: 1 Overture (5:14) Orchestra; 2 Bidin' My Time #1 (1:22) *Stan Chandler, Guy Stroman, Larry Raben, David Engel*; 3 The Lonesome Cowboy (2:25) *Eddie Korbich*; 4 Could You See Me? (4:28) *David Carroll, Judy Blazer*; 5 Bidin' My Time #2 (2:54) *Stan Chandler, Guy Stroman, Larry Raben, David Engel*; 6 Bronco Busters (3:26) Chorus; 7 Barbary Coast (4:13) *Vicki Lewis*; 8 Embraceable You (3:53) *David Carroll, Judy Blazer*; 9 Embraceable You (encore)(1:58) *David Carroll, Judy Blazer*; 10

Goldfarb! That's I'm! (:51) *Frank Gorshin, David Garrison*; 11 Bidin' My Time #3 (3:04) *Stan Chandler, Guy Stroman, Larry Raben, David Engel*; 12 Sam And Delilah (5:44) *Lorna Luft*; 13 I Got Rhythm (3:08) *Lorna Luft*; 14 I Got Rhythm (1:27) *Lorna Luft, Stan Chandler, Guy Stroman, Larry Raben, David Engel, Dick Hyman*; 15 Finale Act 1 (3:13) *Rex Hays, Judy Blazer, David Carroll, Lorna Luft*; 16 Entr'acte (4:35) *Stan Chandler, Guy Stroman, Larry Raben, David Engel*; 17 Land Of The Gay Caballero (4:14) *Chorus*; 18 But Not For Me (2:58) *Judy Blazer*; 19 But Not For Me (comic reprise)(2:03) *Frank Gorshin, Judy Blazer*; 20 Treat Me Rough (1:58) *David Garrison*; 21 Boy! What Love Has Done To Me! (5:20) *Lorna Luft*; 22 Cactus Time In Arizona (3:14) *Judy Blazer*; 23 Finale Ultimo (1:09) *Company*.

Review: See entry below.

Girl Crazy 🎞🎞🎞🎞

1996, Rhino Records; from the screen version *Girl Crazy*, 1943.

Album Notes: *Music*: George Gershwin; *Lyrics*: Ira Gershwin; *Musical Adaptation*: Roger Edens; *Arrangements and Orchestrations*: Ted Duncan, Sy Oliver, Axel Stordahl, Conrad Salinger, Sid Cutner, David Raksin; *Vocal Arrangements*: Hugh Martin, Ralph Blane; The M-G-M Studio Chorus and Orchestra, conducted by Georgie Stoll; *Cast*: Judy Garland (Ginger Gray), Mickey Rooney (Danny Churchill, Jr.), and June Allyson, Kathleen Carns, Ruth Clark, Nancy Walker, Henry Kruze, Ernie Newton, Hal Hopper, Trudy Erwin, Bobbie Canvin, The Music Maids, Six Hits and a Miss, and Tommy Dorsey and His Orchestra; *Album Producers*: Marilee Bradford, Bradley Flanagan; *Engineers*: Doug Schwartz, Ted Hall.

Selections: 1 Main Title/Montage (2:23) *Orchestra*; 2 Sam And Delilah (:51) *Tommy Dorsey and His Orchestra*; 3 Treat Me Rough (4:47) *June Allyson, Mickey Rooney, The Music Maids, The Stafford Trio, Kathleen Carns, Ruth Clark, Tommy Dorsey and His Orchestra*; 4 Bidin' My Time (4:58) *Judy Garland, The King's Men*; 5 Could You Use Me? (3:49) *Mickey Rooney, Judy Garland*; 6 Ginger Dear (R. Edens)(outtake)(1:09) *Chorus*; 7 Happy Birthday To You (:36) *Chorus*; 8 Embraceable You (4:56) *Judy Garland, Henry Kruze, P. Hanna, G. Mershon, H. Stanton, Ernie Newton, Tommy Dorsey and His Orchestra*; 9 Walking In The Garden (4:12) *Orchestra*; 10 Barbary Coast (4:13) *Tommy Dorsey and His Orchestra*; 11 Fascinating Rhythm (5:26) *Tommy Dorsey and His Orchestra, Mickey Rooner*; 12 Bronco Busters (outtake)(3:14) *Mickey Rooner, Judy Garland, Nancy Walker*; 13 Boy! What Love Has Done To Me! (3:23) *Tommy Dorsey and His Orchestra*; 14 Embraceable You (reprise) (3:01) *Tommy Dorsey and His Orchestra*; 15 But Not For Me (3:20) *Judy Garland*; 16 I Got Rhythm (8:03) *Judy Garland, Mickey Rooney, Six Hits and A Miss, The Music Maids, Hal Hopper, Trudy Erwin, Bobbie Canvin, Tommy Dorsey and His Orchestra*; 17 End Title (:51) *Mickey Rooney, Judy Garland*.

Review: A radiant little musical with a score by George and Ira Gershwin, *Girl Crazy* made very few pretenses other than amuse and entertain its audiences when it opened on October 14, 1930. Set in Arizona, it dealt with a New York playboy sent to the golden West by his millionaire father to manage a ranch, in the hope that the wastrel will forget his fondness for alcohol and the fair sex in the great open spaces. However, the lad, who arrives in the womanless town of Custerville by taxicab from New York has other ideas, and immediately proceeds to transform the place into a dude ranch, glamorizing it with a girl chorus imported from Broadway. Light as the story might have been, it was the occasion for the wonderful score which contained such gems as "Bidin' My Time," "Embraceable You," "I Got Rhythm," and "But Not For Me," among its better moments. Transferred to the screen in 1943 with its score almost intact and the plot bearing a distant resemblance to the one conceived by Guy Bolton and John McGowan for the original, it became another sprightly vehicle for the popular team of Mickey Rooney and Judy Garland. In true, traditional fashion, they took advantage of the storyline to put on a show, actually a grandiose finale, staged by Busby Berkeley.

The Elektra recording, one of several studio cast recreations of the great Gershwin 1930s musicals, stars Lorna Luft (Judy Garland's daughter), Judy Blazer and David Carroll in a spirited rendition of the score, beautifully directed by John Mauceri.

While sonically inferior, the Rhino set presents the M-G-M 1943 film version, starring Judy Garland (a winner in her playful rendition of "Bidin' My Time") and Mickey Rooney, complete with its interpolations (including "Fascinating Rhythm," performed by Rooney at the piano, with Tommy Dorsey and his orchestra), outtakes, instrumental bridges, and, as is usual for the label, a wealth of written and photographic information that makes this CD the ultimate release for this marvelous soundtrack.

Godspell

Godspell 🎞🎞🎞🎞

1971, Arista Records; from the off Broadway production *Godspell*, 1971.

Album Notes: *Music*: Stephen Schwartz; *Lyrics*: Stephen Schwartz; *Musical Arrangement and Direction*: Stephen Schwartz; *Cast*: Lamar Alford, Peggy Gordon, David Haskell,

Joanne Jonas, Robin Lamont, Sonia Manzano, Gilmer McCormick, Jeffrey Mylett, Stephen Nathan, Herb Braha; *Album Producer*: Stephen Schwartz; *Engineer*: Elvin Campbell; *CD Engineers*: Bill Inglot, Ken Perry.

Selections: 1 Prepare Ye The Way Of The Lord (1:58) *David Haskell*; 2 Save The People (3:15) *Stephen Nathan*; 3 Day By Day (3:07) *Robin Lamont*; 4 Learn Your Lessons Well (1:19) *Gilmer McCormick*; 5 Bless The Lord (2:54) *Joanne Jonas*; 6 All For The Best (2:23) *Stephen Nathan, David Haskell*; 7 All Good Gifts (3:26) *Lamar Alford*; 8 Light Of The World (2:45) *Herb Braha, Peggy Gordon, Jeffrey Mylett, Robin Lamont*; 9 Turn Back, O Man (4:12) *Sonia Manzano*; 10 Alas For You (1:55) *Stephen Nathan*; 11 By My Side (J. Hamburger/P. Gordon) (2:35) *Peggy Gordon, Gilmer McCormick*; 12 We Beseech Thee (3:30) *Jeffrey Mylett*; 13 On The Willows (2:57) *Steven Reinhardt, Richard LaBonte, Jesse Cutler*; 14 Finale (5:32) *Stephen Nathan*; 15 Day By Day (reprise)(1:22) *Company*.

Review: See entry below.

Godspell 𝄞𝄞𝄞𝄞

1973, Arista Records; from the screen version *Godspell*, Columbia Pictures, 1973.

Album Notes: *Music*: Stephen Schwartz; *Lyrics*: Stephen Schwartz; *Musical Arrangement and Direction*: Stephen Schwartz; *Cast*: Victor Garber, Lynne Thigpen, David Haskell, Joanne Jonas, Robin Lamont, Merrell Jackson, Jerry Sroka, Gilmer McCormick. Jeffrey Mylett, Katie Hanley; *Featured Musicians*: Hugh McCracken, Jesse Cutler (guitar), Chayim Tamar (Shofar), Charles Macey (banjo), Paul Shaffer (piano/organ), Jeffrey Mylett (recorder), Michael Kamen (ARP synthesizer), Corky Hale (harp); *Album Producer*: Stephen Schwartz; *Engineer*: Elliot Scheiner; *CD Engineers*: Bill Inglot, Ken Perry.

Selections: 1 Prepare Ye The Way Of The Lord (1:56) *David Haskell*; 2 Save The People (4:00) *Victor Garber*; 3 Day By Day (3:22) *Robin Lamont*; 4 Turn Back, O Man (4:15) *Joanne Jonas*; 5 Bless The Lord (2:54) *Lynne Thigpen*; 6 All For The Best (3:48) *Victor Garber, David Haskell*; 7 All Good Gifts (3:40) *Merrell Jackson*; 8 Light Of The World (2:48) *Jerry Sroka, Gilmer McCormick, Jeffrey Mylett, Robin Lamont*; 9 Alas For You (1:25) *Victor Garber*; 10 By My Side (J. Hamburger/P. Gordon)(3:45) *Katie Hanley*; 11 Beautiful City (3:08) *Company*; 12 On The Willows (3:11) *Stephen Reinhardt, Richard LaBonte, Victor Garber*; 14 Finale (6:58) *Victor Garber*.

Review: A modest musical by normal Broadway standards, *Godspell* found its genesis in the Gospel according to St. Matthew, with Stephen Schwartz chronicling the last seven days

in the life of Christ, portrayed wearing clown make-up and a T-shirt emblazoned with an "S," to the rhythms of a rock'n'roll score. Surprisingly, it not only worked very well, it also was quite fetching and entertaining, and not preachy. Initially presented at the off-Broadway Cherry Lane Theatre, on May 17, 1971, it eventually moved to Broadway on June 22, 1976, for a run of 527 performances. Altogether, it played 2,651 performances in New York alone. In 1973, it also was made into a film musical, which essentially retained all the ingredients from the stage show, merely expanding on them and opening up the stage setting to include outdoors shots against the New York skyline. Both the original cast album and the soundtrack recording are virtually identical, and both are equally enjoyable.

Golden Boy 𝄞𝄞♭

1993, Angel Records; from the Broadway production *Golden Boy*, 1964.

Album Notes: *Music*: Charles Strouse; *Lyrics*: Lee Adams; *Orchestrations*; Ralp Burns; *Musical Direction*: Elliot Lawrence; *Cast*: Sammy Davis, Jr. (Joe Wellington), Paula Wayne (Lorna Moon), Billy Daniels (Eddie Satin), Kenneth Tobey (Tom Moody), Terrin Miles (Terry), Johnny Brown (Ronnie), Jaime Rogers (Lopez); *CD Engineer*: Bob Norberg.

Selections: 1 Workout (1:37) *The Company*; 2 Night Song (4:04) *Sammy Davis Jr.*; 3 Everything's Great (2:07) *Kenneth Tobey, Paula Wayne*; 4 Gimme Some (1:52) *Sammy Davis Jr., Terrin Miles*; 5 Stick Around (1:30) *Sammy Davis Jr.*; 6 Don't Forget 127th Street (5:43) *Sammy Davis Jr., Johnny Brown*; 7 Lorna's Here (2:34) *Paula Wayne*; 8 This Is The Life (3:41) *Billy Daniels, Sammy Davis Jr., Paula Wayne*; 9 Golden Boy (2:39) *Paula Wayne*; 10 While The City Sleeps (3:00) *Billy Daniels*; 11 Colorful (2:39) *Sammy Davis Jr.*; 12 I Want To Be With You (4:34) *Sammy Davis Jr., Paula Wayne*; 13 Can You See It (2:24) *Sammy Davis Jr.*; 14 No More (6:30) *Sammy Davis Jr.*; 15 Finale: The Fight (3:05) *Sammy Davis Jr., Jaime Rogers*.

Review: Despite the presence of Sammy Davis, Jr. in the title role, this musical adaptation of Clifford Odets' play was not a great success. Davis, playing an aspiring young boxer who thinks he's made it after he wins a couple of bouts, only to lose a determining championship fight, worked very hard to win support for the show, something that explains his strained voice in this cast album recorded a few weeks after the opening. But the book, a tame version of the play, and particularly the score, by Charles Strouse and Lee Adams (of *Bye Bye Birdie* fame), let the star down. Ultimately, the show had a run of 569 performances, largely due to the star's box office appeal, and the novelty of an interracial relationship between Joe and Lorna (played by Paula Wayne) which challenged Broadway audiences at a time when such things were still being frowned on (see also *No Strings*). The show received Tony nominations for Best Musical, Best Actor, Best Producer, and Best Choreography. Also appearing in the cast were newcomers Louis Gossett and Lola Falana.

Good News ♫♫♫♪

1991, Sony Music Special Products; from the screen musical *Good News*, M-G-M, 1947.

Album Notes: *Music*: Ray Henderson; *Lyrics*: B.G. DeSylva, Lew Brown; *Vocal Arrangements*: Kay Thompson; The M-G-M Studio Chorus and Orchestra, conducted by Lennie Hayton; *Cast*: June Allyson (Connie Lane), Peter Lawford (Tommy Marlowe), Patricia Marshall (Pat McClellan), Joan McCracken (Babe Doolittle), Ray McDonald (Bobby Turner), Mel Torme (Danny); *Cd Producer*: Dan Rivard; *Engineer*: Ken Robertson.

Selections: 1 Title Music (2:03) Orchestra, Chorus; 2 Good News (Tait College)(2:05) *Joan McCracken*; 3 An Easier Way (R. Edens/B. Comden/ A. Green)(3:11) *June Allyson, Patricia Marshall*; 4 He's A Ladies Man (3:30) *Peter Lawford, Ray McDonald, Mel Torme*; 5 Lucky In Love (5:56) *Patricia Marshall, Joan McCracken, Mel Torme, June Allyson, Peter Lawford*; 6 The French Lesson (R. Edens/B. Comden/A. Green)(2:03) *June Allyson, Peter Lawford*; 7 The Best Things In Life Are Free (2:26) *June Allyson*; 8 Pass That Peace Pipe (R. Edens/H. Martin/R. Blane)(4:32) *Joan McCracken*; 9 The Big Game (1:10) Orchestra; 10 Just Imagine (2:49) *June Allyson*; 11 A Visit To The Dean (1:10) Orchestra; 12 The Best Things In Life Are Free (reprise)(3:39) *Mel Torme, Peter Lawford*; 13 Finale: The Varsity Drag (5:28) *June Allyson, Peter Lawford*.

Review: A pleasantly mindless campus musical, *Good News* is best remembered today for the fact that it introduced June Allyson and Peter Lawford in their first starring roles. It also boasts a rousing score in which the natural highlights are the standard "The Best Things In Life Are Free," reprised almost ad nauseam throughout the film, "Pass That Peace Pipe," and "The French Lesson," in which Allyson teaches Lawford the rudiments of the language (or was it the other way around?). Bright and zippy, the film offers the wisp of a storyline about football star Lawford, a chronic failure in every other discipline, forced to study with Allyson, who is secretly in love with him, if he wants to graduate. The hint of a romantic conflict is introduced when Lawford falls for an attractive, but ultimately empty-headed co-ed, played by Patricia Marshall, while Mel Torme croons his way through a couple of numbers. All of it is innocuous, fun, and eventually enjoyable, with the whole cast joining in a spirited "Varsity Drag" to bring the screen shenanigans to a pleasant conclusion, just as it can be heard on the recording.

Grease

Grease ♫♫♫♪

1972, Polydor Records; from the Broadway production *Grease*, 1972.

Album Notes: *Music*: Jim Jacobs, Warren Casey; *Lyrics*: Jim Jacobs, Warren Casey; *Orchestrations*: Michael Leonard; *Vocal/Dance Arrangements and Musical Direction*: Louis St. Louis; *Cast*: Adrienne Barbeau (Betty Rizzo), Don Billett (Vince Fontaine), Walter Bobbie (Roger), Jim Borrelli (Sonny), Barry Bostwick (Danny Zuko), James Canning (Doody), Daniel Deitch (Burger Palace Boy), Carole Demas (Sandy Dumbrowski), Katie Hanley (Marty), Tom Harris (Eugene Florczyk), Ilene Kristen (Patty Simcox), Dorothy Leon (Miss Lynch), Timothy Meyers (Kenickle), Kathi Moss (Cha-Cha Di Gregorio), Alan Paul (Johnny Casino), Joy Rinaldi (Pink Lady), Marya Small (Frenchy), Gary Stephens (Jan); *Album Producer*: Arnold Maxin; *Engineer*: Fred Christy; *CD Engineer*: Jose Rodriguez.

Selections: 1 Alma Mater/Alma Mater (Parody)(2:46) *Dorothy Leon, Ilene Kristen, Tom Harris, Joy Rinaldi, Garn Stephens, Marya Small, Joy Garrett, Meg Nennett, Daniel Deitch, Don Billett, Walter Bobbie, Jim Borrelli*; 2 Summer Nights (3:42) *Carole Demas, Barry Bostwick, Joy Rinaldi, Garn Stephens, Marya Small, Joy Garrett, Meg Nennett, Daniel Deitch, Don Billett, Walter Bobbie, Jim Borrelli*; 3 Those Magic Changes (2:43) *James Canning, Joy Rinaldi, Garn Stephens, Marya Small, Joy Garrett, Meg Nennett, Daniel Deitch, Don Billett, Walter Bobbie, Jim Borrelli*; 4 Freddy, My Love (3:05) *Katie Hanley, Garn Stephens, Marya Small, Adrienne Barbeau*; 5 Greased Lightnin' (2:32) *Timothy Meyers, Daniel Deitch, Don Billett, Walter Bobbie, Jim Borrelli*; 6 Mooning (2:44) *Walter Bobbie, Garn Stephens*; 7 Look At Me, I'm Sandra Dee (1:59 *Adrienne Barbeau)*; 8 We Go Together (2:25) *Joy Rinaldi, Garn Stephens, Marya Small, Joy Garrett, Meg Nennett, Daniel Deitch, Don Billett, Walter Bobbie, Jim Borrelli*; 9 It's Raining On Prom Night (2:29) *Carole Demas*; 10 Born To Hand-Jive (4:20) *Alan Paul*; 11 Beauty School Dropout (3:12) *Alan Paul, Marya Small*; 12 Alone At A Drive-In Movie (2:52) *Barry Bostwick, Daniel Deitch, Don Billett, Walter Bobbie, Jim Borrelli*; 13 Rock'n'Roll Party Queen (1:37) *James Canning, Walter Bobbie*; 14 There Are Worse Things I Could Do (2:52) *Adrienne Barbeau*; 15 Look At Me, I'm Sandra Dee (reprise) (2:19) *Carole Demas*; 16 All Choked Up (3:24) *Carole Demas, Barry Bostwick*; 17 We Go Together (reprise) (:55) Company.

Review: See entry below.

Grease ♫♫♫

1994, RCA Victor; from the Broadway revival *Grease*, 1994.

Album Notes: *Music*: Jim Jacobs, Warren Casey; *Lyrics*: Jim Jacobs, Warren Casey; *Orchestrations*: Steve Margoshes; *Vocal/Dance Arrangements and Musical Direction*: John Mc-Daniel; *Cast*: Rosie O'Donnell (Betty Rizzo), Brian Bradley (Vince Fontaine), Hunter Foster (Roger), Ricky Paull Goldin (Danny Zuko), Sam Harris (Doody), Susan Wood (Sandy Dumbrowski), Megan Mullally (Marty), Paul Castree (Eugene Florczyk), Michelle Blakely (Patty Simcox), Marcia Lewis (Miss Lynch), Jason Opsahl (Kenickle), Sandra Purpuro (Cha-Cha De Gregorio), Jessica Stone (Frenchy), Heather Stokes (Jan); *Album Producer*: Steve Vining; *Engineer*: Sandy Palmer Grassi.

Selections: 1 Alma Mater (1:52) Company; 2 We Go Together (1:51) *The Pink Ladies, The Burger Palace Boys*; 3 Summer Nights (4:14) *Susan Wood, Ricky Paull Goldin*; 4 Those Magic Changes (4:56) *Sam Harris*; 5 Freddy, My Love (2:40) *Megan Mullaly*; 6 Greased Lightnin' (3:19) *Jason Opsahl*; 7 Greased Lightnin' (reprise)(:57) *Rosie O'Donnell*; 8 Rydell Fight Song (:21) *Michelle Blakely*; 9 Mooning (2:22) *Hunter Foster, Heather Stokes*; 10 Look At Me, I'm Sandra Dee (1:34) *Rosie O'Donnell*; 11 Since I Don't Have You (3:37) *Susan Wood*; 12 We Go Together (reprise)(2:19) *Company*; 13 Shakin' At The High School Hop (1:22) *Paul Castree, Clay Adkins, Denis Jones, Patrick Boyd*; 14 It's Raining On Prom Night (2:46) *Susan Wood, Paul Castree, Clay Adkins, Denis Jones, Patrick Boyd*; 15 Born To Hand-Jive (3:19) *Paul Castree, Marcia Lewis*; 16 Beauty School Dropout (8:02) *Billy Porter, Jessica Stone*; 17 Alone At A Drive-In Movie (1:55) *Ricky Paull Goldin, The Burger Palace Boys*; 18 Rock'n'Roll Party Queen (1:17) *Sam Harris, Jason Opsahl*; 19 There Are Worse Things I Could Do (2:03) *Rosie O'Donnell*; 20 Look At Me, I'm Sandra Dee (reprise) (1:31) *Susan Woods, Rosie O'Donnell*; 21 Finale (7:56) Company.

Review: See entry below.

Grease ♫♫♫♫

1978, Polydor Records; from the screen version *Grease*, Paramount Pictures, 1978.

Album Notes: *Music*: Jim Jacobs, Warren Casey; *Lyrics*: Jim Jacobs, Warren Casey; *Cast*: Stockard Channing (Betty Rizzo), Edd Byrnes (Vince Fontaine), John Travolta (Danny Zuko), Barry Pearl (Doody), Olivia Newton-John (Sandy Dumbrowski), Dinah Manoff (Marty), Eddie Deezen (Eugene Florczyk), Susan Buckner (Patty Simcox), Darrell Zwerling (Mr. Lynch), Jeff Conaway (Kenickle), Annette Charles (Cha-Cha), Didi Conn (Frenchy), Jamie Donnelly (Jan), Fannie Flagg (Nurse Wilkin), Eve Arden (Principal McGee), Joan Blondell (Vi), Sid Caesar (Coach Calhoun), Alice Ghostley (Mrs. Murdock), Dody Goodman (Blanche), Sha-Na-Na (Johnny Casino and The Gamblers), Frankie Avalon (Teen Angel); *Album Supervisor and Compiler*: Bill Oakes.

Selections: 1 Grease (B. Gibb)(3:26) *Frankie Valli*; 2 Summer Nights (3:37) *John Travolta, Olivia Newton-John*; 3 Hopelessly Devoted To You (J. Farrar)(3:05) *Olivia Newton-John*; 4 You're The One That I Want (J. Farrar) (2:50) *John Travolta, Olivia Newton-John*; 5 Sandy (L. St. Louis/S. Simon) (2:35) *John Travolta*; 6 Beauty School Dropout(4:00) *Frankie Avalon*; 7 Look At Me, I'm Sandra Dee (1:41) *Stockard Channing*; 8 Greased Lightnin' (3:14) *John Travolta*; 9 It's Raining On Prom Night (2:53) *Cindy Bullens*; 10 Alone At A Drive-In Movie (2:25) *Orchestra*; 11 Blue Moon (R. Rodgers/L. Hart) (2:24) *Sha-Na-Na*; 12 Rock'n'Roll Is Here To Stay (2:02) *Sha-Na-Na*; 13 Those Magic Changes (2:19) *Sha-Na-Na*; 14 Hound Dog (J. Leiber/M. Stoller) (1:25) *Sha-Na-Na*; 15 Born To Hand-Jive (4:40) *Sha-Na-Na*; 16 Tears On My Pillow (S. Bradford/A. Lewis)(2:04) *Sha-Na-Na*; 17 Mooning (2:15) *Louis St. Louis, Cindy Bullens*; 18 Freddy, My Love (2:49) *Cindy Bullens*; 19 Rock'n'Roll Party Queen (2:12) *Louis St. Louis*; 20 There Are Worse Things I Could Do (2:23) *Stockard Channing*; 21 Look At Me, I'm Sandra Dee (reprise) (1:31) *Olivia Newton-John*; 22 We Go Together (2:59) *John Travolta, Olivia Newton-John*; 23 Love Is A Many-Splendored Thing (S. Fain/P.F. Webster)(1:24) *Orchestra*; 24 Grease (reprise)(3:24) *Frankie Valli*.

Review: A 1950s musical, *Grease* took Broadway pundits off-guard when it premiered on February 14, 1972. With its pungent high school antics, its rivalries between gangs of greasers and pink ladies, and its pervasive rhythmic score, the musical offered a devastating, if slightly amusing look at a fictitious high school group of students in the early days of the rock'n'roll era. Spirited, direct, somewhat satirical, it was a great deal of fun, and even though it probably grated on the more traditional audiences usually flocking in to catch the latest shows, it enjoyed an unprecedented long run of 3,388 performances, quite an achievement. Of note, it introduced various talented youngsters who eventually went on to bigger and better things, including Barry Bostwick, Adrienne Barbeau (for a long while film director John Carpenter's egeria), Treat Williams, and John Travolta, who starred in the film version (see below).

In 1994, the show returned to Broadway in a splashy, plastic presentation, staged by Tommy Tune's protégé Jeff Calhoun, in a production that was all show and little flair. Smartly packaged, however, with various name performers

(Rosie O'Donnell, Jasmine Guy, Brooke Shields, Joe Piscopo) starring in it at one time or another, the musical has succeeded in building an audience, and continues to thrive at this writing, with apparently no end for its current run in sight. RCA Victor released two cast albums that are virtually identical and are only differentiated by the fact that Rosie O'Donnell is in one, and Brooke Shields in the other.

The 1978 film version, starring John Travolta and Olivia Newton-John expanded the concept in the original, and brought in frontline groups and performers to tackle the score, thus making what was essentially a simple stage musical into an all-star rock presentation. Surprisingly, it worked very well, and with the two principals bringing their own vocal and dramatic talents to the roles of Danny, the main greaser, and Sandy, the virtuous newcomer to Rydell High, *Grease* further benefitted from the presence in its cast of Frankie Valli, Frankie Avalon, the rock group Sha-Na-Na, and mostly Stockard Channing, hilarious as Betty Rizzo, the leader of the Pink Ladies. The soundtrack album reflected the improvements, and continues to be one of the most enjoyable representations of this musical.

Guys and Dolls

Guys and Dolls ♪♪♪

1991, MCA Records; from the Broadway production *Guys and Dolls*, 1950.

Album Notes: *Music*: Frank Loesser; *Lyrics*: Frank Loesser; *Orchestrations*: George Bassman, Ted Royal; *Vocal Arrangements*: Herbert Greene; *Musical Direction*: Irving Actman; *Cast*: Robert Alda (Sky Masterson), Vivian Blaine (Adelaide), Sam Levene (Nathan Detroit), Isabel Bigley (Sarah Brown), Pat Rooney, Sr., B.S. Pully, Stubby Kaye (Nicely-Nicely Johnson), Tom Pedi, Johnny Silver, Douglas Deane; *Album Producer*: Jack Kapp; *CD Producer*: Ron O'Brien; *Engineer*: Kevin Hayunga.

Selections: 1 Runyonland Music/Fugue For Tinhorns/Follow The Fold (3:19) *Stubby Kaye, Johnny Silver, Douglas Deane, Isabel Bigley and The Mission Group*; 2 The Oldest Established (2:34) *Sam Levene, Stubby Kaye, Johnny Silver*; 3 I'll Know (3:29) *Robert Alda, Isabel Bigley*; 4 A Bushel And A Peck (1:30) *Vivian Blaine, The Hot Box Girls*; 5 Adelaide's Lament (3:17) *Vivian Blaine*; 6 Guys And Dolls (2:49) *Stubby Kaye, Johnny Silver*; 7 If I Were A Bell (2:52) *Isabel Bigley*; 8 My Time Of Day (1:53) *Robert Alda*; 9 I've Never Been In Love Before (2:37) *Robert Alda, Isabel Bigley*; 10 Take Back Your Mink (2:51) *Vivian Blaine, The Hot Box Girls*; 11 More I Cannot Wish You (2:27) *Pat Rooney Sr.*; 12 Luck Be A Lady (2:58) *Robert Alda*; 13

Sue Me (2:24) *Vivian Blaine, Sam Levene*; 14 Sit Down You're Rockin' The Boat (2:09) *Stubby Kaye*; 15 Marry The Man Today (2:51) *Vivian Blaine, Isabel Bigley*; 16 Guys And Dolls (reprise) (:36) *Vivian Blaine, Isabel Bigley*.

Review: See entry below.

Guys and Dolls ♪♪♪♪

1992, RCA Victor; from the Broadway revival *Guys and Dolls*, 1992.

Album Notes: *Music*: Frank Loesser; *Lyrics*: Frank Loesser; *Orchestrations*: George Bassman, Ted Royal, Michael Starobin, Daniel Troob, Michael Gibson; *Dance Arrangements*: Mark Hummel; *Musical Direction*: Edward Strauss; *Cast*: Peter Gallagher (Sky Masterson), Josie de Guzman (Sarah Brown), Nathan Lane (Nathan Detroit), Faith Prince (Miss Adelaide), Walter Bobbie (Nicely-Nicely Johnson). J.K. Simmons (Benny Southstreet), Timothy Shew (Rusty Charlie), John Carpenter (Arvide Abernathy), Eleanor Glockner (Agatha), Leslie Feagan (Calvin), Victoria Clark (Martha), Tina Marie DeLeone, Denise Faye, JoAnn M. Hunter, Nancy Lemenager, Greta Martin, Pascale Faye (Dolls); *Album Producer*: Jay David Saks; *Engineers*: Paul Goodman, James Nichols.

Selections: 1 Runyonland (2:56) Company; 2 Fugue For Tinhorns (1:27) *Walter Bobbie, J.K. Simmons, Timothy Shew*; 3 Follow The Fold (1:17) *Josie de Guzman, John Carpenter, Eleanor Glockner, Leslie Feagan, Victoria Clark*; 4 The Oldest Established (2:34) *Nathan Lane, Walter Bobbie, J.K. Simmons*; 5 I'll Know (4:56) *Josie de Guzman, Peter Gallagher*; 6 A Bushel And A Peck (3:08) *Faith Prince, Tina Marie DeLeone, Denise Faye, JoAnn M. Hunter, Nancy Lemenager, Greta Martin, Pascale Faye*; 7 Adelaide's Lament (3:40) *Faith Prince*; 8 Guys And Dolls (2:58) *Walter Bobbie, J.K. Simmons*; 9 Havana (4:00)Ensemble; 10 If I Were A Bell (2:31) *Josie de Guzman, Peter Gallagher*; 11 My Time Of Day (2:00) *Peter Gallagher*; 12 I've Never Been In Love Before (2:06) *Josie de Guzman, Peter Gallagher*; 13 Entr'acte: Take Back Your Mink (5:20) *Faith Prince,Tina Marie DeLeone, Denise Faye, JoAnn M. Hunter, Nancy Lemenager, Greta Martin, Pascale Faye*; 14 Adelaide's Lament (reprise)(1:27) *Faith Prince*; 15 More I Cannot Wish You (2:21) *John Carpenter*; 16 The Crapshooters' Dance (3:22) Ensemble; 17 Luck Be A Lady (3:02) *Peter Gallagher*; 18 Sue Me (2:50) *Faith Prince, Nathan Lane*; 19 Sit Down You're Rockin' The Boat (2:57) *Walter Bobbie*; 20 Marry The Man Today (2:35) *Faith Prince, Josie de Guzman*; 21 Guys And Dolls (reprise)(1:10) Company.

Review: See entry below.

Guys and Dolls ♪♪

1992, Reprise Records; from the studio cast recording, *Guys and Dolls*, 1964.

Album Notes: *Music*: Frank Loesser; *Lyrics*: Frank Loesser; *Arrangements*: Billy May, Bill Loose, Skip Martin, Nelson Riddle, Jerry Fielding, Nathan Van Cleave, Warren Barker; *Musical Direction*: Morris Stoloff; *Cast*: Frank Sinatra, Bing Crosby, Dean Martin, Jo Stafford, The McGuire Sisters, Dinah Shore, Debbie Reynolds, Clark Dennis, Allan Sherman, Sammy Davis, Jr.; *Album Producer*: Frank Sinatra; *Engineers*: Ralph Valentin, Jim Malloy, Dave Hassinger, Bill Putnam, Bud Morris, Andy Richardson, Al Bulow.

Selections: 1 Overture (3:34)/Fugue For Tinhorns (1:29) *Frank Sinatra, Bing Crosby, Dean Martin*; 2 I'll Know (3:27) *Jo Stafford*; 3 The Oldest Established (2:30) *Frank Sinatra, Bing Crosby, Dean Martin*; 4 A Bushel And A Peck (2:28) *The McGuire Sisters*; 5 Guys And Dolls (2:48) *Frank Sinatra, Dean Martin*; 6 If I Were A Bell (2:37) *Dinah Shore*; 7 I've Never Been In Love Before (2:55) *Frank Sinatra*; 8 Take Back Your Mink (2:55) *Debbie Reynolds*; 9 More I Cannot Wish You (3:15) *Clark Dennis*; 10 Adelaide's Lament (3:50) *Debbie Reynolds*; 11 Luck Be A Lady (5:14) *Frank Sinatra*; 12 Sue Me (2:29) *Debbie Reynolds, Allan Sherman*; 13 Sit Down You're Rockin' The Boat (3:31) *Sammy Davis Jr.*; 14 Guys And Dolls (reprise) (1:51) *Frank Sinatra, Dean Martin*.

Review: Amid the dazzling array of lights, color and motion that create the spectacular Gotham-esque atmosphere of the staging for this pivotal musical comedy lies one of the most alluring scores of all time: fun-filled, action-packed and, at the same time, beautifully tender and romantic. And while it's rare for every element of a production to marry and form a perfect union, it is rarer still for nearly *every* song from a show to become a bona-fide standard, as is the case with Frank Loesser's magnificent compositions for *Guys and Dolls*.

Fortunately, fans of the theatre can instantly transport themselves back to the glamour and panache of Runyonland, via two superb CD issues: the original 1950 Broadway cast recording, and the unmatched 1992 "new" Broadway cast recording—both highly recommended.

The original 1950 cast recording (starring Robert Alda, Vivian Blaine and Sam Levine) features all of the familiar hit songs from the original production, and remains a warm, cherished historic document of the charm that made *Guys and Dolls* an immediate critical success. The sonic restorations from the original recording elements (lacquer discs) are quite good, but in general, the monophonic sound lacks the presence that a show with the sizzle of *Guys and Dolls* requires.

However, the 1992 Broadway cast recording, featuring Nathan Lane, Faith Prince, and Peter Gallagher, completely makes up for any of the original's shortcomings. Crackling with intense energy and excitement, Michael Starobin's crisp, tight orchestrations immediately set the stage for some of the most polished, seamless performances in Broadway history—so bright and snappy, it almost makes the original show's tempos and performances seem lackluster! As a bonus, the recording offers two essential dance sequences appearing for the first time on record: "Havana," and "The Crapshooter's Dance."

Regrettably, no officially issued recording exists for the 1955 film version of the show, starring Marlon Brando, Frank Sinatra and Vivian Blaine. In addition to being a terrific film adaptation, the movie contains several new songs written by Loesser to assist in the show's transition from stage to screen, and the soundtrack is noticeable by its unforgivable absence on the market. Sinatra fans might enjoy the all-star studio recording released by Reprise, enjoyable for the most part except for Debbie Reynolds' misguided performance as Adelaide.

Charles L. Granata

Gypsy

Gypsy ♪♪♪♪

1959, Columbia Records; from the Broadway production *Gypsy*, 1959.

Album Notes: *Music*: Jule Styne; *Lyrics*: Stephen Sondheim; *Orchestrations*: Sid Ramin, Robert Ginzler; *Dance Arrangements*: John Kander; *Musical Direction*: Milton Rosenstock; *Cast*: Ethel Merman (Rose), Jack Klugman (Herbie), Sandra Church (Louise), Lane Bradbury (June), Jacqueline Mayro (Baby June), Karen Moore (Baby Louise), Paul Wallace (Tulsa), Maria Karnilova (Tessie Tura), Faith Dane (Mazeppa), Chotzi Foley (Electra); *Album Producer*: Goddard Lieberson.

Selections: 1 Overture (4:54) Orchestra; 2 Let Me Entertain You (1:12) *Jacqueline Mayro, Karen Moore, Ethel Merman*; 3 Some People (3:42) *Ethel Merman*; 4 Small World (2:18) *Ethel Merman*; 5 Baby June And Her Newsboys (1:35) *Jacqueline Mayro*; 6 Mr. Goldstone, I Love You (2:23) *Ethel Merman*; 7 Little Lamb (2:37) *Sandra Church*; 8 You'll Never Get Away From Me (2:29) *Ethel Merman, Jack Klugman*; 9 Dainty June And Her Farmboys (2:21) *Lane Bradbury*; 10 If Mamma Was Married (2:50) *Lane Bradbury, Sandra Church*; 11 All I Need Is The Girl (4:37) *Paul Wallace*; 12 Everything's Coming Up Roses (3:09) *Ethel Merman*; 13 Together Wherever We Go (2:48) *Ethel Merman, Jack Klugman, Sandra Church*; 14 You Gotta Have A

Gimmick (3:36) *Maria Karnilova, Faith Dane, Chotzi Foley*; 15 Let Me Entertain You (2:57) *Sandra Church*; 16 Rose's Turn (4:22) *Ethel Merman*.

Review: See entry below.

Gypsy ♫♫♫

1990, Elektra Records; from the Broadway revival *Gypsy*, 1990.

Album Notes: *Music*: Jule Styne; *Lyrics*: Stephen Sondheim; *Orchestrations*: Sid Ramin, Robert Ginzler; *Dance Arrangements*: John Kander; *Musical Direction*: Eric Stern; *Cast*: Tyne Daly (Rose), Jonathan Hadary (Herbie), Crista Moore (Louise), Tracy Venner (June), Christen Tassin (Baby June), Kristen Mahon (Baby Louise), Robert Lambert (Tulsa), Barbara Erwin (Tessie Tura), Jana Robbins (Mazeppa), Anna McNeely (Electra); *Album Producer*: John McClure; *Engineer*: Paul Goodman.

Selections: 1 Overture (4:52) Orchestra; 2 Let Me Entertain You (:49) *Christen Tassin, Kristen Mahon*; 3 Some People (3:41) *Tyne Daly*; 4 Small World (3:19) *Tyne Daly, Jonathan Hadary*; 5 Baby June And Her Newsboys (2:02) *Christen Tassin*; 6 Mr. Goldstone, I Love You (2:26) *Tyne Daly, Jonathan Hadary*; 7 Little Lamb (2:30) *Crista Moore*; 8 You'll Never Get Away From Me (2:55) *Tyne Daly, Jonathan Hadary*; 9 Dainty June And Her Farmboys (3:48) *Tracy Venner*; 10 If Mamma Was Married (2:56) *Crista Moore, Tracy Venner*; 11 All I Need Is The Girl (4:52) *Robert Lambert*; 12 Everything's Coming Up Roses (3:07) *Tyne Daly*; 13 Together Wherever We Go (3:09) *Tyne Daly, Jonathan Hadary, Crista Moore*; 14 You Gotta Have A Gimmick (4:21) *Jana Robbins, Anna McNeely, Barbara Erwin*; 15 The Strip (5:05) *Crista Moore*; 16 Rose's Turn (4:20) *Tyne Daly*.

Review: See entry below.

Gypsy ♫♫♫

1993, Atlantic Records; from the television presentation *Gypsy*, 1993.

Album Notes: *Music*: Jule Styne; *Lyrics*: Stephen Sondheim; *Orchestrations*: Sid Ramin, Robert Ginzler, Michael Rafter; *Dance Arrangements*: John Kander, Betty Walberg; *Musical Direction*: Ken Watson; *Cast*: Bette Midler (Rose), Peter Riegert (Herbie), Cynthia Gibb (Louise), Jennifer Beck (June), Lacey Chabert (Baby June), Elisabeth Moss (Baby Louise), Jeffrey Broadhurst (Tulsa), Christine Ebersole (Tessie Tura), Linda Hart (Mazeppa), Anna McNeely (Electra); *Album Producers*: Arif Mardin, Michael Rafter, Curt Sobel; *Engineers*: Robert Schaper, Jr, David Ronner, Matthew John McFadden, Peggy Names.

Selections: 1 Overture (4:57) Orchestra; 2 Let Me Entertain You (:52) *Lacey Chabert, Elisabeth Moss*; 3 Some People (3:16)

Bette Midler; 4 Small World (3:23) *Bette Kidler, Peter Riegert*; 5 Baby June And Her Newsboys (2:09) *Lacey Chabert, Elisabeth Moss, Joey Cee, Blake Armstrong, Teo Weiner*; 6 Mr. Goldstone, I Love You (2:27) *Bette Midler, Peter Riegert, Jennifer Beck, Jeffrey Broadhurst, Peter Lockyer, Michael Moore, Patrick Boyd*; 7 Little Lamb (2:21) *Cynthia Gibb*; 8 You'll Never Get Away From Me (2:57) *Bette Midler, Peter Riegert*; 9 Dainty June And Her Farmboys (4:37) *Jennifer Beck, Jeffrey Broadhurst, Peter Lockyer, Michael Moore, Patrick Boyd, Terry Lindholm, Gregg Russell, Cynthia Gibb*; 10 If Mamma Was Married (2:56) *Cynthia Gibb, Jennifer Beck*; 11 All I Need Is The Girl (4:37) *Jeffrey Broadhurst*; 12 Everything's Coming Up Roses (2:50) *Bette Midler*; 13 Together Wherever We Go (2:59) *Bette Midler, Peter Riegert, Cynthia Gibb*; 14 You Gotta Have A Gimmick (4:07) *Linda Hart, Christine Ebersole, Anna McNeely*; 15 Let Me Entertain You (2:34) *Cynthia Gibb*; 16 Rose's Turn (4:06) *Bette Midler*; 17 End Credits (3:10) Orchestra.

Review: The old girl from the world of showbiz, Mama Rose, proves both indestructable and a fine vehicle for singing female stars. Originally created by Ethel Merman, for whom it was written, the part has been variously handled by Rosalind Russell in the film version (not available on CD), Angela Lansbury, Tyne Daly, and more recently Bette Midler, among many others.

The quintessential backstage musical, and for many the best ever written, *Gypsy* related the real-life story of stripper Gypsy Rose Lee and her sister June Haver, and how each was shaped into a star of the first magnitude by their monster of a stage mother. With a fine, solid book by Arthur Laurents, and a splendid score by Jule Styne (music) and Stephen Sondheim (lyrics), the show has endured through repeated revivals, losing none of its freshness and its strength, even though by now its plot and tunes have become remarkably familiar.

The three recordings listed here are all superb in their own right, the personality of the actress playing Mama Rose being the main focus. Merman, the belter and originator of the part, is still the best, though the recording itself, an early transfer to CD from the original analog tapes, leaves a bit to be desired sonically.

Tyne Daly, in the 1990 Broadway revival, added her own touch to the role, but without significantly altering it, in a performance that has its moments of excellence.

As for Bette Midler, in the 1993 television treatment, she camps the part a bit, but she is also remarkably true to the spirit of the original in a performance that has been justifiably lauded.

Hair

Hair ♪♪♪♪

1988, RCA Victor; from the Broadway production *Hair*, 1968.

Album Notes: *Music*: Galt MacDermot; *Lyrics*: Gerome Ragni, James Rado; *Musical Direction*: Galt MacDermot; *Featured Musicians*: Galt MacDermot (electric piano), Steve Gillette, Alan Fontaine (guitars), Jimmy Lewis (bass), Zane Paul (woodwinds, reeds), Donald Leight, Eddy Williams (trumpets), Warren Chaisson (percussion), Idris Muhammad (drums); *Cast*: James Rado (Claude), Gerome Ragni (Berger), Ronald Dyson (Ron), Steve Curry (Woof), Lamont Washington (Hud), Lynn Kellogg (Sheila), Sally Eaton (Jeanie), Melba Moore (Dionne), Shelley Plimpton (Crissy), Diane Keaton (Waitress), and Donnie Burks, Lorrie Davis, Leata Galloway, Steve Gamet, Walter Harris, Hiram Keller, Marjorie LiPari, Emmaretta Marks, Natalie Mosco, Suzannah Norstrand, Robert I. Rubinsky; *Album Producer*: Andy Wiswell; *Engineer*: Mike Moran; *CD Producer/Engineer*: Rick Rowe.

Selections: 1 Aquarius (2:53) *Ronald Dyson*; 2 Donna (2:08) *Gerome Ragni*; 3 Hashish (1:03) Company; 4 Sodomy (:52) *Steve Curry*; 5 Colored Spade (1:12) *Lamont Washington*; 6 Manchester England (1:20) *James Rado*; 7 I'm Black (:36) *Lamont Washington, Steve Curry, Gerome Ragni, James Rado*; 8 Ain't Got No (:43) *Steve Curry, Lamont Washington, Melba Moore*; 9 I Believe In Love (1:08) *Melba Moore*; 10 Ain't Got No (reprise)(1:17) Company; 11 Air (1:28) *Sally Eaton, Shelley Plimpton, Melba Moore*; 12 Initials (:55) Company; 13 I Got Life (3:05) *James Rado*; 14 Going Down (2:17) *Gerome Ragni*; 15 Hair (2:58) *James Rado, Gerome Ragni*; 16 My Conviction (1:39) *Jonathan Kramer*; 17 Easy To Be Hard (2:35) *Lynn Kellogg*; 18 Don't Put It Down (2:01) *Gerome Ragni, Steve Curry*; 19 Frank Mills (2:07) *Shelley Plimpton*; 20 Be-In (3:05) Company; 21 Where Do I Go? (2:40) *James Rado*; 22 Electric Blues (2:35) *Paul Jabara*; 23 Manchester England (reprise)(:30) *James Rado*; 24 Black Boys (1:10) *Diane Keaton, Suzannah Norstrand, Natalie Mosco*; 25 White Boys (2:28) *Melba Moore, Lorrie Davis, Emmaretta Marks*; 26 Walking In Space (4:55) Company; 27 Abie Baby (2:45) *Lorrie Davis, Lamont Washington, Ronald Dyson, Donnie Burks*; 28 Three-Five-Zero-Zero (3:09) Company; 29 What A Piece Of Work Is Man (1:36) *Ronald Dyson, Walter Harris*; 30 Good Morning Starshine (2:32) *Lynn Kellogg, Melba Moore, James Rado, Gerome Ragni*; 31 The Bed (2:58) Company; 32 The Flesh Failures (Let The Sunshine In)(3:38) *James Rado, Lynn Kellogg, Melba Moore*

Review: See entry below.

Hair ♪♪♪

1989, RCA Victor; from the screen version *Hair*, United Artists, 1979.

Album Notes: *Music*: Galt MacDermot; *Lyrics*: Gerome Ragni, James Rado; *Vocal Arrangements*: Tom Pierson; *Musical Direction*: Galt MacDermot; *Cast*: John Savage (Claude), Treat Williams (Berger), Don Dacus (Woof), Dorsey Wright (Hud), Beverly D'Angelo (Sheila), Annie Golden (Jeanie), Michael Jeter (Sheldon), Richard Bright (Fenton), and Ren Woods, Nell Carter, Leata Galloway, Laurie Beechman, Melba Moore, Ronnie Dyson, Twyla Tharp, Charlaine Woodard; *Album Producer*: Warren Schatz; *Engineer*: Howie Lindeman; *CD Producer*: Didier C. Deutsch; *Engineer*: Paul Goodman.

Selections: 1 Aquarius (4:44) *Ronnie Dyson*; 2 Sodomy (1:29) Company; 3 Donna/Hashish (4:20) *Treat Williams*; 4 Colored Spade (1:31) *Dorsey Wright*; 5 Manchester England (1:57) *John Savage*; 6 Abie Baby/Fourscore (2:44) *Dorsey Wright, Nell Carter, Charlaine Woodard, Don Dacus*; 7 I'm Black/Ain't Got No (2:23) *Don Dacus, Dorsey Wright*; 8 Air (1:27) *Annie Golden*; 9 I Got Life (2:14) *John Savage*; 10 Frank Mills (2:40) *Beverly D'Angelo*; 11 Hair (2:42) *John Savage, Treat Williams*; 12 L.B.J. (Initials)(1:09) Company; 13 Electric Blues/Old Fashioned Melody (3:50) *Richard Bright*; 14 Hare Krishna (3:16) Company; 15 Where Do I Go? (2:49) *John Savage*; 16 Black Boys (1:12); 17 White Boys (2:36) *Trudy Perkins, Nell Carter, Charlaine Woodard*; 18 Walking In Space (6:12) Company; 19 Easy To Be Hard (3:39) *Melba Moore*; 20 Three-Five-Zero-Zero (3:49) Company; 21 Good Morning Starshine (2:24) *Beverly D'Angelo, Nell Carter, John Savage, Treat Williams*; 22 What A Piece Of Work Is Man (1:38); 23 Somebody To Love (4:10); 24 Don't Put It Down (2:23) Company; 25 The Flesh Failures (Let The Sunshine In)(6:04) *John Savage, Treat Williams.*

Review: A seminal rock'n'roll musical, *Hair* opened on April 29, 1968, amid the brouhaha created by several facets of the production. Firstly, conservative Broadway seemed ill-prepared to accept a show advocating the tenets of the flower power generation of the late 1960s. Secondly, the musical was determinedly anti-militarist at a time when the war in Vietnam, though increasingly unpopular, still arose much patriotic fervor. Lastly, a much-publicized "nude" scene went against the accepted, traditionalist norms (the year before, the dancers in *Les ballets africains* had been allowed to appear bare-breasted because the revue was an "ethnic" show). The Jerry Falwells of the world notwithstanding, *Hair* became an immediate success, not the least because it received an unconditional endorsement from Clive Barnes in "The New York Times," who rhapsodized about its many virtues. A "total experience," the show ushered in a new era on Broadway, though, in retrospect, it appears hopelessly rooted in its own time period and so seriously dated by now that various attempts at reviving it in the late 1970s and early 1980s failed completely.

Propelled by its rhythm-driven score, in which "Aquarius," "Good Morning Starshine," and "Let The Sunshine In" soon became great favorites, and songs which, at the time, enjoyed a *succes de scandale* ("Sodomy," "I Believe In Love," "Hashish," "Colored Spade," "Walking In Space"), the loosely-structured show had a run of 1,750 performances, and launched the careers of several performers who appeared in it at one time or another, including Melba Moore, Ronnie Dyson, Diane Keaton, Paul Jabara, Nell Carter, Ben Vereen, Philip Michael Thomas, and Meatloaf.

In 1979, a screen version, directed by Milos Forman, tried to recapture the hippie moods and feelings of the show in an ill-conceived effort that was only mildly successful.

Of the two recordings listed, the original cast album is the one to have, though be prepared to experience something of a culture shock when you listen to it today and realize that it is no longer what it was touted to be.

Even more of a curiosity, the soundtrack album might be of interest to people who must have every title in their collection.

Hallelujah, Baby! ♪♪♪

1992, Sony Broadway; from the Broadway production *Hallelujah, Baby!*, 1967.

Album Notes: *Music*: Jule Styne; *Lyrics*: Betty Comden, Adolph Green; *Orchestrations*: Peter Matz; *Vocal Arrangements and Musical Direction*: Buster Davis; *Cast*: Leslie Uggams (Georgina), Robert Hooks (Clem), Lillian Hayman (Momma), Allen Case (Harvey), Marilyn Cooper (Ethel), Barbara Sharma (Mary), and Clifford Allen, Garrett Morris, Ken Scott, Alan Weeks, Winston DeWitt Hemsley, Hope Clark, Sandra Lein, Saundra McPherson; *Album Producer*: Edward Kleban; *Engineers*: Fred Plaut, Ed Michalski, Russ Payne; *CD Producer*: Didier C. Deutsch; *Engineer*: Tim Tiedemann.

Selections: 1 Overture (4:12) Orchestra; 2 My Own Morning (4:10) *Leslie Uggams*; 3 The Slice (3:11) *Robert Hooks, Leslie Uggams, Clifford Allen, Garrett Morris, Ken Scott, Alan Weeks*; 4 Feet Do Yo' Stuff (2:07) *Winston DeWitt Hemsley, Alan Weeks, Leslie Uggams, Hope Clark, Sandra Lein, Saundra McPherson*; 5 Watch My Dust (2:01) *Robert Hooks*; 6 Smile, Smile (3:00) *Leslie Uggams, Robert Hooks, Lillian Hayman*; 7 Witches' Brew (2:03) *Marilyn Cooper, Leslie Uggams, Barbara Sharma*; 8 Another Day (2:06) *Allen Case, Barbara Sharma, Leslie Uggams, Robert Hooks*; 9 I Wanted To Change Him (2:20) *Leslie Uggams*; 10 Being Good (3:38) *Leslie Uggams*; 11 Talking To Yourself (4:16) *Leslie Uggams, Robert Hooks, Allen Case*; 12 Hallelujah, Baby! (3:37) *Winston DeWitt Hemsley, Alan Weeks, Leslie Uggams*; 13 Not Mine (3:20) *Allen Case*; 14 I Don't Know Where She Got It (3:40) *Robert Hooks, Lillian Hayman, Allen Case*; 15 Now's The Time (3:41) *Leslie Uggams*.

Review: Radical chic came to Broadway in 1967 with this look at race relations and show business, but the results were less than what had been anticipated. In trying to be topical, the creators of *Hallelujah, Baby!* (Arthur Laurents, Jule Styne, Betty Comden and Adolph Green) failed to remember that what mattered in a musical was the music, not so much the message. In trying to portray the life of an entertainer (Leslie Uggams, in a fetching portrayal), her slow ascension to stardom, and her love affairs with a Black man (Robert Hooks) and a white man (Allen Case), intertwined through sixty years of race stuggles and emancipation, they only succeeded in muddling the stage with a story that was not very convincing (the characters did not age, further confusing the audience), and a score that was not too terribly entertaining. By the time the show won the Tony as Best Musical (by default, it should be mentioned), it already had closed and would have been forgotten were it not for this cast album which actually makes it sound much better than it really was.

Hello, Dolly!

Hello, Dolly! ♪♪♪♪

1989, RCA Victor; from the Broadway production *Hello, Dolly!*, 1964.

Album Notes: *Music*: Jerry Herman; *Lyrics*: Jerry Herman; *Orchestrations*: Philip J. Lang; *Vocal Arrangements and Musical Direction*: Shepard Coleman; *Cast*: Carol Channing (Dolly Gallagher Levi), David Burns (Horace Vandergelder), Eileen Brennan (Irene Molloy), Sondra Lee (Minnie Fay), Charles Nelson Reilly (Cornelius Hackl), Jerry Dodge (Barnaby Tucker), Igors Gavon (Ambrose Kemper); *Album Producer*: Andy Wiswell; *Engineer*: Ernie Oelrich; *CD Producer*: Didier C. Deutsch; *Engineer*: Paul Goodman.

Selections: 1 Prologue (1:15) Orchestra; 2 I Put My Hand In (3:07) *Carol Channing*; 3 It Takes A Woman (2:33) *David Burns*; 4 Put On Your Sunday Clothes (4:16) *Charles Nelson Reilly, Jerry Dodge, Carol Channing, Igors Gavon*; 5 Ribbons Down My Back (2:41) *Eileen Brennan, Sondra Lee*; 6 Motherhood (1:47) *Carol Channing, Eileen Brennan, Sondra Lee*; 7 Dancing (4:27) *Carol Channing, Charles Nelson Reilly, Jerry Dodge, Eileen Brennan*; 8 Before The Parade Passes By (3:18) *Carol Brennan*; 8 Before The Parade Passes By (3:18) *Carol*

Channing; 9 Elegance (2:25) *Eileen Brennan, Charles Nelson Reilly, Sondra Lee, Jerry Dodge*; 10 Hello, Dolly! (5:41) *Carol Channing*; 11 It Only Takes A Moment (3:40) *Charles Nelson Reilly, Eileen Brennan*; 12 So Long Dearie (2:59) *Carol Channing*; 13 Finale (4:12) *David Burns, Carol Channing*.

Review: See entry below.

Hello, Dolly! ♫♫♫▽

1991, RCA Victor; from the Broadway production *Hello, Dolly!*, 1967.

Album Notes: *Music and Lyrics*: Jerry Herman; *Orchestrations*: Philip J. Lang; *Vocal Arrangements*: Peter Howard; *Musical Direction*: Saul Schechtman; *Cast*: Pearl Bailey (Dolly Gallagher Levi), Cab Calloway (Horace Vandergelder), Emily Yancy (Irene Molloy), Chris Calloway (Minnie Fay), Jack Crowder (Cornelius Hackl), Winston DeWitt Hemsley (Barnaby Tucker), Roger Lawson (Ambrose Kemper); *Album Producer*: George R. Marek, Andy Wiswell; *Engineer*: Ernie Oelrich; *CD Producer*: Didier C. Deutsch; *Engineer*: Paul Goodman.

Selections: 1 Overture (4:23) *Orchestra*; 2 I Put My Hand In (2:55) *Pearl Bailey*; 3 It Takes A Woman (2:31) *Cab Calloway*; 4 Put On Your Sunday Clothes (4:02) *Jack Crowder, Winston DeWitt Hemsley, Pearl Bailey, Roger Lawson*; 5 Ribbons Down My Back (2:52) *Emily Yancy*; 6 Motherhood (1:43) *Pearl Bailey, Emily Yancy, Chris Calloway*; 7 Dancing (4:22) *Pearl Bailey, Jack Crowder, Winston DeWitt Hensley, Emily Yancy*; 8 Before The Parade Passes By (3:20) *Pearl Bailey*; 9 Elegance (2:14) *Emily Yancy, Jack Crowder, Chris Calloway, Winston DeWitt Hemsley*; 10 Hello, Dolly! (5:46) *Pearl Bailey*; 11 It Only Takes A Moment (3:01) *Jack Crowder, Emily Yancy*; 12 So Long Dearie (3:00) *Pearl Bailey*; 13 Finale (4:05) *Cab Calloway, Pearl Bailey*.

Review: See entry below.

Hello, Dolly! ♫♫▽

1994, Philips Records; from the screen version *Hello, Dolly!*, 20th Century-Fox, 1969.

Album Notes: *Music and Lyrics*: Jerry Herman; *Orchestrations*: Philip J. Lang; The 20th Century-Fox Chorus and Orchestra conducted by Lennie Hayton and Lionel Newman; *Cast*: Barbra Streisand (Dolly Levi), Walter Matthau (Horace Vandergelder), Marianne McAndrew (Irene Molloy), E.J. Peaker (Minnie Fay), Michael Crawford (Cornelius Hackl), Danny Lockin (Barnaby Tucker), Tommy Tune (Ambrose Kemper), Louis Armstrong; *Original Sound Engineer*: Murray Spivack; *CD Producer*: Nick Redman; *Engineers*: Brian Risner, Dan Hersch.

"The greatest movie score of all time is not going to make a bad picture into a good picture."

Randy Newman
(The Hollywood Reporter, 1-15-97)

Selections: 1 Just Leave Everything To Me (3:22) *Barbra Streisand*; 2 It Takes A Woman (3:03) *Walter Matthau*; 3 It Takes A Woman (reprise)(2:13) *Brabra Streisand*; 4 Put On Your Sunday Clothes (5:27) *Michael Crawford, Barbra Streisand*; 5 Ribbons Down My Back (2:26) *Marianne McAndrew, E.J. Peaker*; 6 Dancing (3:26) *Barbra Streisand, Michael Crawford*; 7 Before The Parade Passes By (4:50) *Barbra Streisand*; 8 Elegance (2:25) *Michael Crawford*; 9 Love Is Only Love (3:07) *Barbra Streisand*; 10 Hello, Dolly! (7:50) *Barbra Streisand, Louis Armstrong*; 11 It Only Takes A Moment (4:07) *Michael Crawford*; 12 So Long Dearie (2:36) *Barbra Streisand*; 13 Finale (4:16) *Walter Matthau, Barbra Streisand, Michael Crawford*.

Review: Like *Gypsy, Hello, Dolly!* is a splendid vehicle for a grander-than-life performance. Many actresses have tried it, with varying degrees of success, but to the many fans of the musical and its spirited score by Jerry Herman, the best among them remains Carol Channing, who created the part on Broadway. A recent revival in which she returned to the scene of her former triumph proved, if needed, that she was Dolly Gallagher Levy, even if the show itself had become a lame carbon copy of the original.

Pearl Bailey, who was brought in as an odd replacement with an all-Black cast to rekindle the show's flagging fortunes at the box office (rumor at the time had it that Liberace had also been considered by producer David Merrick to head an all-male cast), added some of her own idiosyncrasies to a part that already had quite a few them written into it. But the show gave her a rare opportunity to return to Broadway where her absence had been sorely noticed for many years.

Were it not for the presence of Louis Armstrong in the cast, the film version, starring Barbra Streisand, totally miscast in a role written for a much older actress, would be a total disaster. Even then, Armstrong's moment of glory, in the seven-minute long title track, is barely sufficient to recommend this sorry recording, in which future-Phantom Michael Crawford also makes an appearance.

Hercules 🎜🎜🎜🎜◗

1997, Walt Disney Records; from the animated feature *Hercules*, Walt Disney, 1997.

Album Notes: *Music:* Alan Menken; *Lyrics:* David Zippel; *Orchestrations and Arrangements:* Danny Trooh; *Vocal Arrangements:* Michael Kosarin; *Music Editors:* Earl Ghaffari, Kathleen Fogarty-Bennett; *Musical Direction:* Michael Kosarin; *Cast:* Lillias White, Cheryl Freeman, LaChanze, Roz Ryan, Tawatha Agee, Vaneese Thomas (The Muses); Roger Bart (Young Hercules); Danny DeVito (Phil); Susan Egan (Meg); *Album Producer:* Alan Menken; *Engineers:* Frank Wolf, John Richards.

Selections: 1 Long Ago... (:31); 2 The Gospel Truth I/Main Titles (2:24) *Lillias White, Cheryl Freeman, LaChanze, Roz Ryan, Vaneese Thomas*; 3 The Gospel Truth II (:59) *Roz Ryan*; 4 The Gospel Truth III (1:04) *Cheryl Freeman, LaChanze, Vaneese Thomas, Lillias White*; 5 Go The Distance (3:13) *Roger Bart*; 6 Oh, Mighty Zeus (:46); 7 Go The Distance (reprise)(:57) *Roger Bart*; 8 One Last Hope (3:00) *Danny DeVito*; 9 Zero To Hero (2:20) *Lillias White, Tawatha Agee, Cheryl Freeman, LaChanze, Roz Ryan, Vaneese Thomas*; 10 I Won't Say (I'm In Love)(2:20) *Susan Egan, Cheryl Freeman, LaChanze, Vaneese Thomas, Lillias White*; 11 A Star Is Born (2:03) *Lillias White, Cheryl Freeman, LaChanze, Roz Ryan, Vaneese Thomas*; 12 Go The Distance (single)(4:41) *Michael Bolton*; 13 The Big Olive (1:05); 14 The Prophecy (:54); 15 Destruction Of The Agora (2:06); 16 Phil's Island (2:26); 17 Rodeo (:40); 18 Speak Of The Devil (1:29); 19 The Hydra Battle (3:28); 20 Meg's Garden (1:14); 21 Hercules' Villa (:37); 22 All Time Chump (:38); 23 Cutting The Thread (3:23); 24 A True Hero/A Star Is Born (5:34).

Review: The latest, at this writing, of Disney's animated musical blockbusters, *Hercules* focuses on the hero of mythology, son of Zeus, the strongest man in the world, in an up-to-date version film that doesn't take its subject too seriously, as the introduction, "Long Ago...," clearly indicates. With David Zippel contributing the clever lyrics to Alan Menken's vastly hummable music, the film introduces several lovable characters well designed to endear the younger members in the audience, while providing the necessary dose of comic relief usually demanded by this type of entertainment. Spearheaded by its hit single, "Go The Distance," also performed by Michael Bolton, the score has great appeal, and is bound to delight many listeners, though sequencing deprives the album of the same continuity enjoyed in the film.

High Society 🎜🎜

1956, Capitol Records; from the screen musical *High Society*, M-G-M, 1956.

Album Notes: *Music:* Cole Porter; *Lyrics:* Cole Porter; *Orchestrations:* Conrad Salinger, Nelson Riddle; The M-G-M Studio Chorus and Orchestra, conducted by Johnny Green; *Cast:* Bing Crosby (Dexter Haven), Grace Kelly (Tracy Samantha Lord), Frank Sinatra (Mike Connor), Celeste Holm (Liz Imbrie).

Selections: 1 High Society (Overture)(3:29) *Orchestra*; 2 High Society Calypso (2:12) *Louis Armstrong and His Band*; 3 Little One (2:30) *Bing Crosby*; 4 Who Wants To Be A Millionaire (2:05) *Frank Sinatra, Celeste Holm*; 5 True Love (3:05) *Bing Crosby, Grace Kelly*; 6 You're Sensational (3:52) *Frank Sinatra*; 7 I Love You, Samantha (4:27) *Bing Crosby*; 8 Now You Has Jazz (4:16) *Bing Crosby, Louis Armstrong and His Band*; 9 Well Did You Evah? (3:47) *Bing Crosby, Frank Sinatra*; 10 Mind If I Make Love To You (2:22) *Frank Sinatra*.

Review: One of Cole Porter's very last musical efforts, *High Society* is probably also one of his most memorable works—due in large part to the stellar cast that starred in the film: Frank Sinatra, Grace Kelly, Bing Crosby, Louis Armstrong and Celeste Holm. Their effervescent performances, and their fine interpretations of some of Porter's wittiest songs have helped rank *High Society* among the classics. Unfortunately, the beauty of the performances, cushioned by the splendid Johnny Green orchestrations, is lost in this soundtrack recording, a sea of sonic murk as are all of Sinatra's Capitol soundtracks.

Poor production values truly detract from enjoyment of the disc. It is difficult to ascertain whether the original film recordings were poorly recorded and inherently sound "brittle" and muffled (doubtful, since new restorations of the M-G-M soundtracks of the 1940s reveal very pleasing sonics), or if the defects were created later, when the film tracks were transferred by the record company for commercial release.

Either way, the situation should have been corrected when the CD was planned for issue. In time, this (and other important soundtracks) will be restored with the attention and care that they deserve. Until then, this unforgivably inferior CD will have to suffice.

Charles L. Granata

House of Flowers 🎜🎜🎜

1990, Sony Music Special Products; from the Broadway production *House of Flowers*, 1955.

Album Notes: *Music:* Harold Arlen; *Lyrics:* Truman Capote; *Dances and Musical Numbers:* Herbert Ross; *Musical Direction:* Jerry Arlen; *Cast:* Pearl Bailey (Mme. Fleur), Diahann Carroll (Ottilie), Juanita Hall (Mme. Tango), Rawn Spearman (Royal), Ada Moore (Pansy), Enid Mosier (Tulip), Dolores Harper (Gladiola); *Album Producer:* Goddard Lieberson.

Selections: 1 Overture (5:19) Orchestra; 2 Waitin' (1:49) *Dolores Harper, Ada Moore, Enid Mosier*; 3 One Man Ain't Quite Enough (3:10) *Pearl Bailey*; 4 A Sleepin' Bee (5:18) *Diahann Carroll, Dolores Harper, Enid Mosier, Ada Moore*; 5 Bamboo Cage (2:20) *Dolores Harper, Ada Moore, Enid Mosier*; 6 House Of Flowers (3:15) *Diahann Carroll, Rawn Spearman*; 7 Two Ladies In De Shade Of De Banana Tree (5:01) *Ada Moore, Enid Mosier*; 8 What Is A Friend For? (3:22) *Pearl Bailey*; 9 Slide "Boy" Slide (2:22) *Juanita Hall*; 10 I'm Gonna Leave Off Wearing My Shoes (2:19) *Diahann Carroll*; 11 Has I Left You Down (3:24) *Pearl Bailey, Dolores Harper, Ada Moore, Enid Mosier*; 12 I Never Has Seen Snow (4:02) *Diahann Carroll*; 13 Turtle Song (3:22) *Diahann Carroll, Rawn Spearman*; 14 Don't Like Goodbyes (2:29) *Pearl Bailey*; 15 Mardi Gras (5:19) *M. Burton*.

Review: A musical set in the fragrant Caribbean, on an island where voodoo and French culture have settled down in amiable unity, *House of Flowers* opened on December 30, 1954, with a cast that included Pearl Bailey, Juanita Hall, and a fresh newcomer named Diahann Carroll. Carroll dazzled first night audiences with her innocent portrayal of a flowergirl who wants to marry a mountain boy and her crystalline vocal talent. Inspired by a short story written by Truman Capote following a trip he had taken to Haiti, the show involves the struggle between two feuding local madames, Mme Tango and Mme Fleur, for the control of the leisure time of both the island's residents and visitors. Temporarily supplanted in her trade by her rival, Mme Fleur is counting on her new protégé, Ottilie, to rekindle her business, though, as we all know, the best laid plans... Punctuating the action with songs that have the right color and occasional carnival exuberance one associates with life in the West Indies, the score by Harold Arlen teemes with bright moments, among which "A Sleepin' Bee," performed by Diahann Carroll, still attracts the most, while Pearl Bailey revealed her devastating side in the show-stopping numbers, "One Man Ain't Quite Enough," "What's a Friend For?," and "Has I Let You Down." *House of Flowers* had a short run of 165 performances, and won a Tony for Oliver Messel's florid settings.

How to Succeed in Business Without Really Trying

How to Succeed in Business Without Really Trying ♪♪♪♪♪

1961, RCA Victor; from the Broadway production *How to Succeed in Business Without Really Trying*, 1961

Album Notes: *Music*: Frank Loesser; *Lyrics*: Frank Loesser; *Orchestrations*: Robert Ginzler; *Musical Direction*: Elliot Law-

rence; *Cast*: Robert Morse (Finch), Rudy Vallee (J.B. Biggley), Bonnie Scott (Rosemary), Charles Nelson Reilly (Frump), Sammy Smith (Mr. Twimble), Claudette Sutherland (Smitty), Paul Reed (Bratt), Mara Landi (Miss Krumholz), Virginia Martin (Hedy), Ruth Kobart (Miss Jones); *Album Producers*: George Avakian, Joe Linhart; *Engineer*: Ernest Oelrich; *CD Producer*: Bill Rosenfield; *Engineer*: Paul Goodman.

Selections: 1 Overture (2:28) Orchestra; 2 How To (1:15) *Robert Morse*; 3 Happy To Keep His Dinner Warm (2:34) *Bonnie Scott, Claudette Sutherland*; 4 Coffee Break (2:37) *Charles Nelson Reilly, Claudette Sutherland*; 5 The Company Way (2:37) *Robert Morse, Sammy Smith*; 6 The Company Way (reprise)(1:33) *Charles Nelson Reilly*; 7 A Secretary Is Not A Toy (4:00) *Paul Reed*; 8 Been A Long Day (3:03) *Claudette Sutherland, Bonnie Scott, Robert Morse*; 9 Grand Old Ivy (2:14) *Rudy Vallee, Robert Morse*; 10 Paris Original (3:45) *Bonnie Scott, Claudette Sutherland, Mara Landi*; 11 Rosemary (3:44) *Robert Morse, Bonnie Scott*; 12 Finaletto Act One (1:31) *Robert Morse, Bonnie Scott, Charles Nelson Reilly*; 13 Cinderella, Darling (3:47) *Claudette Sutherland, Bonnie Scott*; 14 Love From A Heart Of Gold (2:52) *Rudy Vallee, Virginia Martin*; 15 I Believe In You (4:00) *Robert Morse*; 16 Brotherhood Of Man (4:05) *Robert Morse, Sammy Smith, Ruth Kobart*; 17 Finale (2:03) *Bonnie Scott, Robert Morse*.

Review: See entry below.

How to Succeed in Business Without Really Trying ♪♪♪♪

1995, RCA Victor; from the Broadway revival *How to Succeed in Business Without Really Trying*, 1995.

Album Notes: *Music*: Frank Loesser; *Lyrics*: Frank Loesser; *Orchestrations*: Danny Troob; *Vocal Arrangements and Musical Direction*: Ted Sperling; *Cast*: Matthew Broderick (J. Pierrepont Finch), Ronn Carroll (J.B. Biggley), Megan Mullally (Rosemary Pilkington), Jeff Blumenkrantz (Bud Frump), Gerry Vichi (Twimble), Victoria Clark (Smitty), Jonathan Freeman (Bert Bratt), Kristi Lynes (Miss Krumholtz), Luba Mason (Hedy LaRue), Lillias White (Miss Jones), and Walter Cronkite; *Album Producer*: Jay David Saks; *Engineer*: James P. Nichols; *Assistant Engineers*: Carl Glanville, Glen Marchese.

Selections: 1 Overture (3:56) Orchestra; 2 "Dear Reader..." (:47) *Walter Cronkite*; 3 How To Succeed (1:51) *Matthew Broderick*; 4 Happy To Keep His Dinner Warm (2:52) *Megan Mullally, Victoria Clark*; 5 Coffee Break (3:27) *Jeff Blumenkrantz, Victoria Clark*; 6 "You have alertly seized your opportunities..." (:20) *Walter Cronkite*; 7 The Company Way (3:00) *Gerri Vichi,*

Matthew Broderick; 8 The Company Way (reprise)(1:57) *Jeff Blumenkrantz*; 9 The Entrance Of Hedy LaRue (:38) Orchestra; 10 A Secretary Is Not A Toy (3:15) *Jonathan Freeman*; 11 Been A Long Day (3:04) *Victoria Clark, Megan Mullaly, Matthew Broderick*; 12 Been A Long Day (reprise)(1:01) *Jeff Blumenkrantz, Ronn Carroll, Luba Mason*; 13 Saturday Morning Ballet (1:33) Orchestra; 14 Grand Old Ivy (1:34) *Ronn Carroll, Matthew Broderick*; 15 Paris Original (4:17) *Megan Mullaly, Kristi Lynes, Victoria Clark, Lillias White*; 16 Rosemary (4:55) *Matthew Broderick, Megan Mullaly*; 17 Act One Finale (1:32) *Matthew Broderick, Megan Mullaly, Jeff Blumenkrantz*; 18 Entr'acte (1:23) Orchestra; 19 How To Succeed (reprise)(1:10) *Victoria Clark, Kristi Lynes*; 20 "So you are now a vice-president..." (:25) *Walter Cronkite*; 21 Happy To Keep His Dinner Warm (reprise)(:58) *Megan Mullaly*; 22 Love From A Heart Of Gold (2:54) *Ronn Carroll, Luba Mason*; 23 I Believe In You (3:59) *Matthew Broderick*; 24 The Pirate Dance (1:19) Ensemble; 25 "How to handle a disaster..." (:26) *Walter Cronkite*; 26 I Believe In You (reprise)(2:15) *Megan Mullaly*; 27 "By this time, you are a seasoned executive..." (:15) *Walter Cronkite*; 28 Brotherhood Of Man (5:50) *Matthew Broderick, Gerry Vichi, Lillias White*; 29 Finale (1:09) Company.

Review: A Pulitzer Prize-winning musical, something of a rarity in the theatre, *How to Succeed in Business Without Really Trying* was based on a Shepherd Mead's manual, which Abe Burrows took as its inspiration to trace the rise up the corporate ladder of a window washer who, by the time he has finished applying Mr. Mead's recommendations for quick success, indeed finds himself at the head of the World Wide Wicket Company. In the course of the evening, the young tyro defeats his envious rival, nephew of the company's president, and finds love in the eyes of his secretary, Rosemary.

A delightful satire of big business, the show received a tremendous boost in Frank Loesser's exhilarating score, and in Robert Morse's impish portrayal as J. Pierpont Finch, whose guile allows him to succeed without really trying. With Rudy Vallee making a last stage appearance as J.B. Biggley, president of the company, and Charles Nelson Reilly at his manic best as the grudging nephew, *How to Succeed* opened to rave reviews on October 14, 1961, and settled for a long run of 1,417 performances. It won five Tony Awards, including one for Best Musical, and one for Robert Morse as Best Actor. With Michele Lee playing the female lead, and with its score virtually intact, it transferred to the screen in 1966.

A slightly revised, more politically-correct version, starring Matthew Broderick, opened on March 23, 1995, and closed after 548 performances.

Of the two recordings available, the original cast album, starring Robert Morse and Rudy Vallee, remains as lively and vibrant as the day when it was first recorded.

The 1995 revival cast recording, with Matthew Broderick, contains better sonics, more music, a show-stopping rendition of "Brotherhood of Man" performed by Lillias White, and the voice of Walter Cronkite, as the show's narrator.

The Hunchback of Notre Dame ♪♪♪˒

1996, Walt Disney Records; from the animated feature *The Hunchback of Notre Dame*, Walt Disney Pictures, 1996.

Album Notes: *Music*: Alan Menken; *Lyrics*: Stephen Schwartz; *Orchestrations*: Michael Starobin, Danny Troob; *Music Editor*: Kathleen Fogarty-Bennett; *Vocal Arrangements*: David Friedman; *Musical Direction*: Jack Everly; *Cast*: Tom Hulce (Quasimodo), Heidi Mullenhauer (Esmeralda), Hugo (Jason Alexander), Charles Kimbrough (Victor), Mary Wickes/Mary Stout (Laverne), Paul Kandel (Clopin), David Ogden Stiers (Archdeacon), Tony Jay (Frollo); *Album Producers*: Alan Menken, Stephen Schwartz; *Engineer*: Bruce Botnick.

Selections: 1 The Bells Of Notre Dame (6:14) *Paul Kandel, David Ogden Stiers, Tony Jay*; 2 Out There (4:25) *Tony Jay, Tom Hulce*; 3 Topsy Turvy (5:35) *Paul Kandel*; 4 Humiliation (1:40); 5 God Help The Outcasts (3:42) *Heidi Mullenhauer*; 6 The Bell Tower (3:04); 7 Heaven's Light/Hellfire (5:23) *Tom Hulce, Tony Jay*; 8 A Guy Like You (2:53) *Jason Alexander, Charles Kimbrough, Mary Wickes, Mary Stout*; 9 Paris Burning (1:53); 10 The Court Of Miracles (1:27) *Paul Kandel*; 11 Sanctuary! (6:01); 12 And He Shall Smile The Wicked (3:29); 13 Into The Sunlight (2:09); 14 The Bells Of Notre Dame (reprise)(1:09) *Paul Kandel*; 15 Someday (4:18) *All-4-One*; 16 God Help The Outcasts (3:27) *Bette Midler*.

Review: Alan Menken and Stephen Schwartz teamed to write the score for this animated feature, very loosely based on the well-known story by Victor Hugo. The book's plot centers around a deformed hunchback in medieval Paris, who falls in love with the gorgeous gypsy Esmeralda, in love with another, and who loses his life when he attempts to save her from a righteous archdeacon, eager to burn her at the stake, as was a common practice at the time, in order to atone for his own sins. Being that this was a Disney film, the story was slightly modified: Quasimodo gets encouragement and solace from gargoyles suddenly coming to life, and doesn't die at the end; the tone of the film was uplifted to remove the story from anything that might resemble the dour moods of the original; and the songs, of course, had to reflect the upbeat feelings that prevail. Otherwise, the narrative remains relatively faithful to its model, with splashy, colorful expressions of an easy, carnival-like atmosphere that probably would have baffled Parisians in the Middle Ages. The score echoes the hopeful moods in the story, and though it plays by the numbers, it finds attractive connotations to soothe and attract any audience. The film's essential politically-correct message is that "God Helps The Outcasts," a number heard twice in the recording, notably in a moving rendition by Bette Midler. There is nothing terribly earth-shaking about the rest of the recording, which, like most soundtracks written for the Disney films, is enjoyable, not too demanding, and just a tad this side of being bland.

I Can Get It for You Wholesale ♫♫

1995, Columbia Records; from the Broadway production *I Can Get It for You Wholesale*, 1962.

Album Notes: *Music:* Harold Rome; *Lyrics:* Harold Rome; *Orchestrations:* Sid Ramin; *Vocal Arrangements and Musical Direction:* Lehman Engel; *Cast:* Lillian Roth, Jack Kruschen (Maurice Pulvermacher), Harold Lang (Teddy Asch), Elliott Gould (Harry Bogen), Sheree North (Martha Mills), Barbara Monte (Mitzi), William Reilly (Mario), Edward Verso (Eddie), Marilyn Cooper (Ruthie Rivkin), Bambi Linn (Blanche Bushkin), Ken LeRoy (Meyer Bushkin), Barbra Streisand (Miss Marmelstein), Steve Curry (Sheldon Bushkin), James Hickman (Tootsie Maltz), Luba Lisa (Manette), Wilma Curley (Gail), Pat Turner (Miss Springer); *Album Producer:* Goddard Lieberson; *Engineers:* Fred Plaut, Ed Michalski; *CD Engineers:* John Arrias, Bernie Grundman.

Selections: 1 Overture (1:28) *Orchestra;* 2 I'm Not A Well Man (2:21) *Jack Kruschen, Barbra Streisand;* 3 The Way Things Are (1:42) *Elliott Gould;* 4 When Gemini Meets Capricorn (2:49) *Marilyn Cooper, Elliott Gould;* 5 Momma, Momma, Momma (2:57) *Elliott Gould, Lillian Roth;* 6 The Sound Of Money (4:16) *Sheree North, Elliott Gould, Barbara Monte, William Reilly, Edward Verso;* 7 Too Soon (3:05) *Lillian Roth;* 8 The Family Way (3:09) *Lillian Roth, Elliott Gould, Marilyn Cooper, Harold Lang, Bambi Linn, Ken LeRoy;* 9 Who Knows? (3:42) *Marilyn Cooper;* 10 Ballad Of The Garment Trade (3:25) *Barbra Streisand, Marilyn Cooper, Bambi Linn, Elliott Gould, Harold Lang, Ken LeRoy;* 11 Have I Told You Lately? (3:11) *Ken LeRoy, Bambi Linn;* 12 A Gift Today (3:56) *Elliott Gould, Lillian Roth, Ken LeRoy, Marilyn Cooper;* 13 Miss Marmelstein (3:22) *Barbra Streisand;* 14 A Funny Thing Happened (2:39) *Marilyn Cooper, Elliott Gould;* 15 What's In It For Me? (1:57) *Harold Lang;* 16

East A Little Something (2:10) *Lillian Roth;* 17 What Are They Doing To Us? (7:12) *Barbra Streisand, Kelly Brown, James Hickman, Luba Lisa, William Curley, Pat Turner.*

Review: Today, Harold Rome's *I Can Get It For You Wholesale* is best remembered as the musical which launched the career of Barbra Streisand, whose comical performance as Miss Marmelstein (and performance of the song by that title) literally stopped the show. Adapted by Jerome Weidman from his own novel, with songs by Harold Rome, the musical is set in the 1930s and focuses on New York's garment industry. Gloomy and unnecessarily hard-edged, at least for a musical, it follows the rise and fall of a small-time entrepreneur, played by Elliott Gould, determined to succeed by whatever means necessary but unable to reach his goals, simply because he's not cut out for success. Matching the tones of the book, Harold Rome wrote a somber score in which few brighter moments emerged, one of them being the solo by Barbra Streisand. Following its premiere on March 22, 1962, the show had a run of 300 performances.

I Do! I Do! ♫♫♫♫

1966, RCA Victor; from the Broadway production *I Do! I Do!*, 1966.

Album Notes: *Music:* Harvey Schmidt; *Lyrics:* Tom Jones; *Orchestrations:* Philip J. Lang; *Musical Direction:* John Lesko; *Cast:* Mary Martin (She), Robert Preston (He); *Album Producer:* Andy Wiswell; *Engineer:* Ernie Oelrich; *CD Producer:* Didier C. Deutsch; *Engineer:* Paul Goodman.

Selections: 1 All The Dearly Beloved/Together Forever/I Do! I Do! (5:55) *Mary Martin, Robert Preston;* 2 Goodnight (2:13) *Mary Martin, Robert Preston;* 3 I Love My Wife (2:00) *Robert Preston;* 4 Something Has Happened (1:39) *Mary Martin;* 5 My Cup Runneth Over (2:10) *Mary Mary, Robert Preston;* 6 Love Isn't Everything (3:25) *Mary Martin, Robert Preston;* 7 Nobody's Perfect (5:48) *Mary Martin, Robert Preston;* 8 A Well Known Fact (2:37) *Mary Martin, Robert Preston;* 9 Flaming Agnes (3:42) *Mary Martin;* 10 The Honeymoon Is Over (1:55) *Mary Martin, Robert Preston;* 11 Where Are The Snows? (2:39) *Mary Martin, Robert Preston;* 12 When The Kids Get Married (2:10) *Mary Martin, Robert Preston;* 13 The Father Of The Bride (2:56) *Robert Preston;* 14 What Is A Woman? (3:05) *Mary Martin;* 15 Someone Needs Me (1:49) *Mary Martin;* 16 Roll Up The Ribbons (1:23) *Mary Martin, Robert Preston;* 17 This House (1:53) *Mary Martin, Robert Preston.*

Review: A delightful two-character musical, based on Jan de Hartog's "The Fourposter," *I Do! I Do!* brought together Mary Martin and Robert Preston as a couple whose married life becomes the focus of the show. The show follows them from their honeymoon to their golden old age, in an existence that encompasses 50 years, and the usual problems found in long-term relationships, from occasional infidelities, to raising children, to little difficulties and great joys. What set the show apart from other musicals is the fact that it was a traditional Broadway show played out on a small scale, which, in addition to involving only its two principals, was entirely set in the same room in their apartment. Smartly staged by Gower Champion, and boasting flavorful songs by Tom Jones and Harvey Schmidt (among which "My Cup Runneth Over" became a major hit), *I Do! I Do!* opened on December 5, 1966, and closed after 560 performances. The passing years have not diminished the glow left by the show nor the initial impression gathered from the original cast album of a trifle, but a most engaging one.

Into the Woods ♫♫♫♫

1987, RCA Victor; from the Broadway production *Into the Woods*, 1987.

Album Notes: *Music*: Stephen Sondheim; *Lyrics*: Stephen Sondheim; *Orchestrations*: Jonathan Tunick; *Musical Direction*: Paul Gemignani; *Cast*: Bernadette Peters (Witch), Joanna Gleason (Baker's Wife), Chip Zien (Baker), Tom Aldredge (Narrator), Robert Westenberg (Wolf/Cinderella's Prince), Kim Crosby (Cinderella), Ben Wright (Jack), Kay McClelland (Florinda), Lauren Mitchell (Lucinda), Danielle Ferland (Little Red Riding Hood), Pamela Winslow (Rapunzel), Chuck Wagner (Rapunzel's Prince), Merle Louise (Cinderella's Mother/Giant), Maureen Davis (Sleeping Beauty), Jean Kelly (Snow White); *Album Producer*: Jay David Saks; *Engineers*: Paul Goodman, Anthony Salvatore.

Selections: 1 Prologue: Into The Woods (11:55) *Tom Aldredge*; 2 Cinderella At The Grave (1:14) *Kim Crosby, Merle Louise*; 3 Hello, Little Girl (2:32) *Robert Westenberg, Danielle Ferland*; 4 I Guess This Is Goodbye/ Maybe They're Magic (2:02) *Ben Wright, Joanna Gleason, Chip Zien*; 5 I Know Things Now (1:48) *Danielle Ferland*; 6 A Very Nice Prince/First Midnight/ Giants In The Sky (5:18) *Kim Crosby, Joanna Gleason, Ben Wright*; 7 Agony (2:36) *Robert Westenberg, Chuck Wagner*; 8 It Takes Two (2:47) *Chip Zien, Joanna Gleason*; 9 Stay With Me (2:40) *Bernadette Peters, Pamela Winslow*; 10 On The Steps Of The Palace (2:34) *Kim Crosby*; 11 Ever After (2:19) *Tom Aldredge*; 12 Act II Prologue: So Happy (3:48) *Tom Aldredge*; 13 Agony (2:15) *Robert Westenberg, Chuck Wagner*; 14 Lament (2:03) *Bernadette Peters*; 15 Any Moment/Moments In The Woods (4:56) *Robert Westenberg, Joanna Gleason*; 16 Your Fault/Last Midnight (4:43) *Chip Zien, Ben Wright, Danielle Ferland, Bernadette Peters, Kim Crosby*; 17 No More (4:11) *Chip Zien, Tom Aldredge*; 18 No One Is Alone (3:44) *Kim Crosby, Danielle Ferland, Ben Wright, Chip Zien*; 19 Finale: Children Will Listen (5:09) *Bernadette Peters*.

Review: In one of his most popularly accessible works, Stephen Sondheim, with the help of James Lapine, took several well-known fairy tales (Jack and the Beanstalk, Rapunzel, Cinderella, Little Red Riding Hood) and collapsed them into a genuinely inventive musical, *Into the Woods*, which opened November 5, 1987. In the show he not only gently pokes fun at the tales and their various characters, but uses them to web together a single ending where modern societal values and community responsibilities receive a serious thrashing. Clearly divided into two distinct parts (like his previous offering, *Sunday in the Park with George)*, the show first presents its various characters, spinning their individual tales until they finally mesh into one long narrative in which, for instance, the Princes in "Cinderella" and "Rapunzel" share their own doubts about the outcome of their respective fairy tales ("Agony"). The moral of the story, delivered by The Witch, played by Bernadette Peters, is that "Children Will Listen," and that it is up to their parents to teach them the values by which they should be living. Though occasionally muddled by too much rhetoric, it was a brilliant concept which can be enjoyed today in this original cast album, and in a laserdisc edition of the show.

Irene ♫♫

1992, Sony Broadway; from the Broadway revival *Irene*, 1973.

Album Notes: *Music*: Harry Tierney; *Lyrics*: Joseph McCarthy, Charles Gaynor, Otis Clements; *Orchestrations*: Ralph Burns; *Vocal Arrangements and Musical Direction*: Jack Lee; *Cast*: Debbie Reynolds (Irene O'Dare), Monte Markham (Donald Marshall), George S. Irving (Madame Lucy), Ruth Warrick (Emmeline Marshall), Patsy Kelly (Mrs. O'Dare), Ted Pugh (Ozzie Babson), Carmen Alvarez (Helen McFudd), Janie Sell (Jane Burke), and Jeanne Lehman, Penny Worth, Meg Scanlon; *Album/CD Producer*: Thomas Z. Shepard; *Engineer*: Bud Graham; *CD Engineers*: Richard King, Robert Wolff.

Selections: 1 Overture (5:36) Orchestra, Jeanne Lehman, Penny Worth, Meg Scanlon; 2 The World Must Be Bigger Than An Avenue (2:17) *Debbie Reynolds*; 3 What Do You Want To Make Those Eyes At Me For? (2:12) Chorus; 4 The Family Tree (1:57) *Ruth Warrick*; 5 Alice Blue Gown (3:02) *Debbie Reynolds*; 6 They Go Wild, Simply Wild, Over Me (2:20) *George S. Irving*; 7 An Irish Girl (4:02) *Debbie Reynolds*; 8 Mother, Angel, Darling (3:34) *Debbie Reynolds, Patsy Kelly*; 9 The Riviera Rage (1:55) Orchestra; 10 I'm Always Chasing Rainbows (3:48)

Debbie Reynolds; 11 The Last Part Of Ev'ry Party (2:41) *Chorus*; 12 We're Getting Away With It (1:35) *Carmen Alvarez, Janie Sell, George S. Irving, Ted Pugh*; 13 Irene (4:17) *Monte Markham*; 14 The Great Lover Tango (3:11) *Monte Markham, Carmen Alvarez, Janie Sell*; 15 You Made Me Love You (2:12) *Monte Markham, Debbie Reynolds*; 16 You Made Me Love You (reprise)(1:16) *Patsy Kelly, George S. Irving*; 17 Finale (1:48) *Monte Markham, Debbie Reynolds*.

Review: Despite the presence of Debbie Reynolds, radiant in the title role, the 1974 revival of *Irene* had little to offer, particularly as an old-fashioned, glamorous musical in an era that had turned its back on glories of the past. No doubt inspired by the success of the much better *No No Nanette* a couple of seasons before, *Irene* relied too heavily on the status of its star (eventually replaced by another screen luminary, Jane Powell), and too little on the originality of a revamped book, or on a score which, with the exception of "Alice Blue Gown," "I'm Always Chasing Rainbows" (both showstoppers for Debbie Reynolds) and George S. Irving's delightful rendition of "They Go Wild, Simply Wild, Over Me," had not much else to offer to starving audiences. Further compounding the problems the show experienced, Monte Markham, as Irene's romantic interest, didn't have the necessary chemistry. Nonetheless, the show held on for 605 performances.

Irma La Douce 🎵🎵🎵▷

1991, Sony Broadway; from the Broadway production *Irma La Douce*, 1960.

Album Notes: *Music:* Marguerite Monnot; *Lyrics:* Julian More, David Heneker, Monty Norman; *Orchestrations:* Andre Popp, Robert Ginzler; *Vocal Arrangements:* Bert Waller, Stanley Lebowsky; *Dance Music:* John Kander; *Musical Direction:* Stanley Lebowsky; *Cast:* Elizabeth Seal (Irma-la-Douce), Keith Mitchell (Nestor-le-Fripe), Clive Revill (Bob-le-Hotu), Stuart Damon (Frangipane), Fred Gwynne (Polyte-le-Mou), George S. Irving (Police Inspector), Zack Matalon (Jojo-les-Yeux-Sales), Aric Lavie (Roberto-les-Diams), Osborne Smith (Persil-le-Noir), and Rudy Tronto, George Del Monte; *Album Producer:* Teo Macero; *Engineers:* Fred Plaut, Bud Graham; *CD Producer:* Didier C. Deutsch; *Engineer:* Tim Tiedemann.

Selections: 1 Overture (3:15) *Orchestra*; 2 Valse Milieu (3:26) *Clive Revill, Elizabeth Seal*; 3 Sons Of France (2:09) *Clive Revill, Zack Matalon, Aric Lavie, Osborn Smith, Stuart Damon, Fred Gwynne, George S. Irving*; 4 The Bridge Of Caulaincourt (1:24) *Elizabeth Seal, Keith Mitchell*; 5 Our Language Of Love (2:33) *Elizabeth Seal, Keith Mitchell*; 6 She's Got The Lot (1:44) *George S. Irving*; 7 Dis-donc, Dis-donc (4:37) *Elizabeth Seal*; 8 Le Grisbi Is Le Root Of Le Evil In Man (2:17) *Keith Mitchell, Clive*

Revill, Zack Matalon, Aric Lavie, Osborne Smith, Stuart Damon; 9 The Wreck Of A Meck (2:22) *Keith Mitchell*; 10 That's A Crime (1:58) *Clive Revill*; 11 From A Prison Cell (3:16) *Keith Mitchell, Zack Matalon, Aric Lavie, Osborne Smith, Stuart Damon*; 12 Irma-la-Douce (4:23) *Elizabeth Seal*; 13 There Is Only One Paris For That (6:29) *Keith Mitchell*; 14 But (2:39) *Keith Mitchell, George S. Irving, Rudy Tronto, George del Monte, Fred Gwynne*; 15 Christmas Child (1:44) *Company*.

Review: Based on a charming French musical about a "poule," her "mec" and the various low-life denizens of a "typical" Parisian neighborhood near Pigalle, the red light district in the French capital, *Irma La Douce* transcended its local origins, and became a resounding hit on Broadway, where it opened on September 29, 1960. Elizabeth Seal, Keith Mitchell, and Clive Revill reprised the roles they had initially created in London. Also in the cast were Elliott Gould and Fred Gwynne (who went on to achieve greater popularity on television as Herman Munster). Minus its songs, the story provided the basis for a screen version starring Shirley MacLaine and Jack Lemmon.

It's Always Fair Weather 🎵🎵🎵▷

1991, Sony Music Special Products; from the screen musical *It's Always Fair Weather*, M-G-M, 1955.

Album Notes: *Music:* Andre Previn; *Lyrics:* Betty Comden and Adolph Green; *Orchestrations:* Andre Previn; *Vocal Arrangements:* Robert Tucker, Jeff Alexander; The M-G-M Studio Chorus and Orchestra, conducted by Andre Previn; *Cast:* Gene Kelly (Ted Riley), Dan Dailey (Doug Hallerton), Cyd Charisse (Jackie Leighton), Michael Kidd (Angie Valentine), Dolores Gray (Madeline Bradbille), Lou Lubin (Fight Manager), David Burns (Tim); *CD Producer:* Dan Rivard; *Engineer:* Ken Robertson.

Selections: 1 Overture (1:04) *Orchestra*; 2 March, March (1:21) *Gene Kelly, Dan Dailey, Jud Conlin*; 3 The Binge (5:07) *Orchestra*; 4 The Time For Parting (2:01) *Gene Kelly, Dan Dailey, Jud Conlin*; 5 10-Year Montage (2:18) *Orchestra*; 6 The Blue Danube (Why Are We Here)(2:30) *Gene Kelly, Dan Dailey, Jud Conlin*; 7 Music Is Better Than Words (2:10) *Dolores Gray*; 8 Stillman's Gym (2:10) *Lou Lubin*; 9 Baby You Knock Me Out (2:40) *Carole Richards, Lou Lubin*; 10 The Ad Men (:48) *Dan Dailey, Paul Maxey*; 11 Once Upon A Time (3:33) *Gene Kelly, Dan Dailey, Jud Conlin*; 12 Situation-Wide (2:49) *Dan Dailey*; 13 The Chase (1:04) *Orchestra*; 14 I Like Myself (4:10) *Gene Kelly*; 15 Klenzrite (1:34) *Dolores Gray*; 16 Finale: The Time For Parting (1:46) *David Burns*.

Review: A daring, unconventional musical, *It's Always Fair Weather* tells about three former Army buddies who get back together ten years later, only to realize that they have changed, and that, in fact, the bonds that once united them had dissipated to such extent that they really no longer like each other. Initially meant to be a "sequel" to *On The Town*, the new musical displayed a more cynical edge than its exuberant predecessor, and because of it didn't get the enthusiastic audience response its creators had anticipated. Today, however, in view of the changes that have happened in our society, it reveals itself more pungent and truthful than ever before, and where *On the Town* has remained an old-fashioned musical which belongs to the very era it was created, *It's Always Fair Weather* proves that it may, indeed, have been well ahead of its time.

Jamaica 🎵🎵🎵♭

1957, RCA Victor; from the Broadway production *Jamaica*, 1957.

Album Notes: *Music:* Harold Arlen; *Lyrics:* E.Y. Harburg, Fred Saidy; *Orchestrations:* Philip J. Lang; *Musical Direction:* Lehman Engel, Neal Hefti; *Cast:* Lena Horne (Savannah), Ricardo Montalban (Koli), Josephine Premice (Ginger), Ossie Davis (Cicero), Adelaide Hall (Grandma Obeah), Augustine Rios (Quico); *Album Producer:* Dick Peirce; *CD Producer:* Bill Rosenfield; *Engineer:* Jay Newland.

Selections: 1 Overture (3:47) Orchestra; 2 Savannah (1:41) *Ricardo Montaban*; 3 Savannah's Wedding Day (3:55) *Adelaide Hall, Augustine Rios*; 4 Pretty To Walk With (2:51) *Lena Horne*; 5 Push de Button (3:34) *Lena Horne*; 6 Incompatibility (2:52) *Ricardo Montalban, Augustine Rios*; 7 Little Biscuit (3:01) *Josephine Premice, Ossie Davis*; 8 Cocoanut Sweet (2:27) *Lena Horne*; 9 Pity The Sunset (2:14) *Lena Horne, Ricardo Montalban*; 10 Yankee Dollar (2:27) *Josephine Premice*; 11 What Good Does It Do (2:23) *Josephine Premice, Ricardo Montalban, Ossie Davis, Augustine Rios*; 12 Monkey In The Mango Tree (3:08) *Ricardo Montalban*; 13 Take It Slow, Joe (2:36) *Lena Horne*; 14 Ain't It de Truth (4:03) *Lena Horne*; 15 Leave de Atom Alone (3:32) *Josephine Premice*; 16 For Every Fish (2:00) *Adelaide Hall*; 17 I Don't Think I'll End It All Today (3:15) *Lena Horne, Ricardo Montalban*; 18 Napoleon (3:55) *Lena Horne*; 19 Savannah (finale)(1:08) *Lena Horne, Ricardo Montalban*.

Review: Harold Arlen took another foray into the Caribbean culture when he wrote the songs for *Jamaica*. Despite a weak story, the show enjoyed a run of 558 performances following its opening on October 31, 1957, thanks largely to the radiant presence of Lena Horne in the cast. Set on the mythical Pigeon Island, it deals with a simple fisherman (Ricardo Montalban) who wants nothing more than a quiet and easy life on his island, and the girl he loves, Savannah (Lena Horne), who only

dreams of going to that other paradise, Manhattan. Co-starring Josephine Premice, Ossie Davis, Adelaide Hall, and a young dancer by the name of Alvin Ailey, *Jamaica* provides its star with many flavorful numbers which put her stylish delivery to the test, and which she turned into as many show-stopping moments, including "Push De Button," in which she extolled the merits of living in her mechanized dream world, "Ain't It De Truth," and "Napoleon."

Jekyll & Hyde

Jekyll & Hyde 🎵🎵🎵♭

1990, RCA Victor Records; from the production *Jekyll & Hyde*, 1990.

Album Notes: *Music:* Frank Wildhorn; *Lyrics:* Leslie Bricusse; *Orchestrations:* Kim Scharnberg; *Strings and Rhythm Arrangements:* Jeremy Roberts; *Musical Direction:* Kim Scharnberg; *Cast:* Linda Eder (Lucy/Lisa), Colm Wilkinson (Jekyll/Hyde); *Album Producers:* Frank Wildhorn, Karl Richardson; *Engineers:* Lance Phillips, Jeremy Roberts, John Naslen, Karl Richardson; *Assistant Engineers:* Rupert Coulson, Andy Strange, Michael Colomby, John Rodd, Ben Fowler.

Selections: 1 Once Upon A Dream (2:53) *Linda Eder*; 2 Hospital Board (1:51) *Colm Wilkinson*; 3 Love Has Come Of Age (4:10) *Linda Eder, Colm Wilkinson*; 4 Possessed (1:08) *Colm Wilkinson, Linda Eder*; 5 This Is The Moment (3:39) *Colm Wilkinson*; 6 Transformation (2:40) *Colm Wilkinson*; 7 Seduction (1:24); 8 Someone Like You (3:40) *Linda Eder*; 9 No One Must Ever Know (1:59) *Colm Wilkinson*; 10 Till You Came Into My Life (5:35) *Colm Wilkinson*; 11 No One Knows Who I Am (3:20) *Linda Eder*; 12 Retribution (1:01); 13 Letting Go (4:15) *Colm Wilkinson, Linda Eder*; 14 A New Life (4:16) *Linda Eder*; 15 It's Over Now (1:29) *Colm Wilkinson*; 16 We Still Have Time (4:45) *Colm Wilkinson, Linda Eder*; 17 Once Upon A Dream (2:33) *Colm Wilkinson*.

Review: See entry below.

Jekyll & Hyde 🎵🎵🎵🎵

1994, Atlantic Records; from the Alley Theatre production *Jekyll & Hyde*, 1990.

Album Notes: *Music:* Frank Wildhorn; *Lyrics:* Leslie Bricusse; *Orchestrations:* Kim Scharnberg; *Electronic Music and Rhythm Arrangements:* Jeremy Roberts; *Vocal Arrangements:* James May, Jason Howland; *Musical Direction:* Kim Scharnberg; *Cast:* Linda Eder (Lucy Harris), Carolee Carmello (Lisa Carew), Anthony Warlow (Dr. Henry Jekyll/Mr. Edward Hyde), John Raitt (Sir Danvers Carew), Philip Hoffman (John Utterson), Bill Nolte

(Simon Stride), Dave Clemmons (The Bishop Of Basignstoke), Brenda Russell (Nellie), Christine Pedi (Lady Beaconsfield), Willy Falk (Lord Savage), Amick Byram (Sir Archibald Proops), Ray McLeod (General Glossop); *Album Producers*: Frank Wildhorn, Karl Richardson; *Engineers*: Karl Richardson, Brad Aaron, Joe Privitelli; *Assistant Engineers*: Darren Mora, Robert Reed.

Selections: CD 1: 1 Prologue (:48); 2 I Need To Know (3:41) *Anthony Warlow*; 3 Facade (3:58) Company; 4 Bitch, Bitch, Bitch (1:43) Company; 5 The Engagement Party (1:19) Company; 6 Possessed (1:43) *Anthony Warlow, Carolee Carmello*; 7 Take Me As I Am (3:16) *Anthony Warlow, Carolee Carmello*; 8 Lisa Carew (2:09) *Bill Nolte, Carolee Carmello*; 9 Board Of Governors (1:51) *Anthony Warlow, Bill Nolte, John Raitt, Dave Clemmons, Ray McLeod, Willy Falk, Christine Pedi, Amick Byram*; 10 Bring On The Men (5:08) *Linda Eder, The ''Dregs'' Girls*; 11 Lucy Meets Jekyll (2:41) *Linda Eder, Anthony Warlow*; 12 How Can I Continue On? (1:24) *Anthony Warlow, Philip Hoffman*; 13 This Is The Moment (3:31) *Anthony Warlow*; 14 Transformation (4:46) *Anthony Warlow*; 15 Lucy Meets Hyde (2:14) *Linda Eder, Anthony Warlow*; 16 Alive (4:34) *Anthony Warlow*; 17 Streak Of Madness (3:37) *Anthony Warlow*; 18 His Work And Nothing More (4:21) *Anthony Warlow, Philip Hoffman, Carolee Carmello, John Raitt*; 19 Sympathy-Tenderness (1:42) *Linda Eder*; 20 Someone Like You (4:06) *Linda Eder*.

CD 2: 1 Mass (1:28) Company; 2 Murder, Murder! (6:06) Company; 3 Letting Go (3:23) *Carolee Carmello, John Raitt*; 4 Reflections (2:24) *Anthony Warlow*; 5 In His Eyes (4:13) *Linda Eder, Carolee Carmello*; 6 The World Has Gone Insane (3:07) *Anthony Warlow*; 7 The Girls Of The Night (4:06) *Linda Eder, Brenda Russell*; 8 No One Knows Who I Am (3:28) *Linda Eder*; 9 It's A Dangerous Game (4:16) *Linda Eder, Anthony Warlow*; 10 Once Upon A Dream (2:48) *Carolee Carmello*; 11 No One Must Ever Know (4:30) *Anthony Warlow*; 12 A New Life (4:26) *Linda Eder*; 13 Once Upon A Dream (2:25) *Anthony Warlow*; 14 Confrontation (4:26) *Anthony Warlow*; 15 The Wedding Reception (4:16) *Anthony Warlow, Carolee Carmello, Philip Hoffman, Bill Nolte, John Raitt*.

Review: On its way to becoming a Broadway show, *Jekyll & Hyde* underwent several transformations, documented by the three recordings here. The first, from 1990, was the bare-skin score with Colm Wilkinson and Linda Eder both portraying two characters in the show's first incarnation, an elaborate studio cast recording made in London. While necessarily incomplete, it gives a fair notion of the musical in its embryonic form, and is, in this respect, an interesting complement to the other two.

The second recording, made shortly after the show received its world premiere in Houston, in 1994, despite its apparent completeness, is still a work in progress. Many new songs have been added, and some have shifted from one character to another. Linda Eder's portrayal as the woman of easy virtue with whom Jekyll falls in love and whom Hyde eventually kills, has acquired a better sheen, and the overall impression is that the show is finally getting a much stronger identity than it had initially.

Following two years on the road, during which the musical was further honed and refined, *Jekyll & Hyde* finally opened on Broadway on April 28, 1997, with the third recording, the official cast album, reflecting the alterations and additional changes it went through during this period. More defined than in its previous incarnations, but still lacking the sense of humor and wicked fun (think *Sweeney Todd)* which might have made it more acceptable as a strong vehicle (something more apparent in the previous recording in which a couple of songs, displaying a sharper edge, were subsequently eliminated), it gets an inspiring reading with Robert Cuccioli a sexy, mesmerizing Jekyll (and Hyde), and Eder still the focus of his interest.

Jelly's Last Jam ♪♪♪♪

1992, Mercury Records; from the Broadway production *Jelly's Last Jam*, 1992.

Album Notes: *Music*: Jelly Roll Morton; *Lyrics*: Susan Birkenhead; *Orchestrations*: Luther Henderson; *Musical Direction*: Linda Twine; *Cast*: Gregory Hines (Jelly Roll Morton), Savion Glover (Young Jelly), Stanley Wayne Mathis (Jack The Bear), Tonya Pinkins (Anita), Ann Duquesnay (Gran Mimi), Ruden Santiago Hudson (Bunny Bolden), Mary Bond Davis (Miss Mamie), Keith David (The Chimney Man), Mamie Duncan-Gibbs, Stephanie Pope, Allison Williams (The Hunnies); *Album Producer*: Thomas Z. Shepard; *Engineers*: Joe Lopes, James Nichols, Vince Caro; *Assistant Engineers*: Sandy Palmer, Doug McKean, Major Little.

Selections: 1 Prologue (1:11) *Keith David*; 2 The Jam (3:58) *Mamie Duncan-Gibbs, Stephanie Pope, Allison Williams*; 3 In My Day (3:39) *Gregory Hines, Mamie Duncan-Gibbs, Stephanie Pope, Allison Williams*; 4 The Creole Way (1:39) *Savion Glover*; 5 The Whole World's Waitin' To Sing Your Song (4:30) *Gregory Hines, Savion Glover*; 6 Michigan Water (5:43) *Mary Bond Davis, Ruben Santiago-Hudson*; 7 The Banishment (4:13) *Ann Duquesnay, Savion Glover, Gregory Hines*; 8 Somethin' More (5:00) *Gregory Hines, Stanley Wayne Mathis, Keith David, Mamie Duncan-Gibbs, Stephanie Pope, Allison Williams*; 9 That's How You Jazz (6:47) *Gregory Hines, Stanley Wayne Mathis*; 10 The Chicago Strut (3:24) *Gregory Hines, Keith David, Mamie Duncan-Gibbs, Stephanie Pope, Allison Williams*; 11 Play The Music For Me (3:12) *Tonya Pinkins*; 12

Lovin's Is A Lowdown Blues (6:32) *Mamie Duncan-Gibbs, Stephanie Pope, Allison Williams*; 13 Doctor Jazz (2:40) *Gregory Hines*; 14 Good Ole New York (1:35) *Keith David, Gregory Hines, Mamie Duncan-Gibbs, Stephanie Pope, Allison Williams*; 15 Too Late, Daddy (3:28) *Gregory Hines*; 16 That's The Way We Do Things In New York (3:11) *Gregory Hines, Gordon Joseph Weiss, Don Johansen*; 17 Good Ole New York (reprise)(2:25)*Ensemble*; 18 Last Chance Blues (4:17) *Gregory Hines, Tonya Pinkins*; 19 The Last Chance (2:02) *Keith David, Mamie Duncan-Gibbs, Stephanie Pope, Allison Williams*; 20 The Last Rites (1:45) *Company*; 21 Creole Boy (3:14) *Gregory Hines*; 22 Finale: We Are The Rhythms That Color Your Songs (2:39) *Company*.

Review: A celebration of the music of Jelly Roll Morton, the "inventor" of jazz, *Jelly's Last Jam* owed much of its vitality and success to Gregory Hines's portrayal of Morton, and the flavorful way the show itself is put together. The show is not so much as a straight dramatic presentation of the composer's life, but a sort of parable in which various setpieces provide the impetus and background for the musical numbers. To be sure, much of the show's impact came from its visual flair, so much so in fact that the cast album recording, limited as it is, fails to convey much of the excitement that was on display on stage. Still, it brought together a cohesive group of vastly talented performers around Hines, notably Tonya Pinkins, a revelation in the show, Savion Glover, Anne Duquesnay, and Keith David, who, as a master of ceremony in top hat and tails surrounded by a trio of attractive lovebirds, presided over the proceedings.

Jesus Christ Superstar

Jesus Christ Superstar *♫♫♫♫*

1993, MCA Records; from the studio cast recording *Jesus Christ Superstar*, 1970.

Album Notes: *Music*: Andrew Lloyd Webber; *Lyrics*: Tim Rice; *Orchestrations and Musical Direction*: Andrew Lloyd Webber; *Cast*: Murray Head (Judas Iscariot), Ian Gillan (Jesus Christ), Yvonne Elliman (Mary Magdalene), Paul Raven (Priest), Victor Brox (Caiaphas High Priest), Brian Keith (Annas), John Gustafson (Simon Zealotes), Barry Dennen (Pontius Pilate), Annette Brox (Maid By The Fire), Paul Davis (Peter), Mike D'Abo (King Herod); *Album Producers*: Tim Rice, Andrew Lloyd Webber.

Selections: CD 1: 1 Overture (3:56) Orchestra; 2 Heaven On Their Minds (4:21) *Murray Head*; 3 What's The Buzz/Strange Thing Mystifying (4:13) *Ian Gillan, Yvonne Elliman, Murray Head*; 4 Everything's Alright (5:14) *Yvonne Elliman*; 5 This Jesus Must Die (3:33) *Victor Brox, Brian Keith, Paul Raven*; 6 Hosanna (2:08)

Victor Brox, Ian Gillan; 7 Simon Zealotes/Poor Jerusalem (4:47) *John Gustafson,Ian Gillan*; 8 Pilate's Dream (1:26) *Barry Dennen*; 9 The Temple (4:40) *Ian Gillan*; 10 Everything's Alright (:30) *Yvonne Elliman, Ian Gillan*; 11 I Don't Know How To Love Him (4:07) *Yvonne Elliman*; 12 Damned For All Time/ Blood Money (5:07) *Murray Head, Brian Keith, Victor Brox*.

CD 2: 1 The Last Supper (7:06) *Ian Gillan, Murray Head*; 2 Gethsemane (I Only Want To Say)(5:32) *Ian Gillan*; 3 The Arrest (3:20) *Paul Davis, Ian Gillan, Victor Brox, Brian Keith*; 4 Peter's Denial (1:27) *Annette Brox, Paul Davis, Yvonne Elliman*; 5 Pilate And Christ (2:43) *Barry Dennen, Ian Gillan*; 6 King Herod's Song (Try It And See)(3:00) *Mike D'Abo*; 7 Judas' Death (4:14) *Murray Head*; 8 Trial Before Pilate (5:12) *Barry Dennen, Victor Brox, Ian Gillan*; 9 Superstar (4:15) *Murray Head*; 10 The Crucifixion (4:01) *Ian Gillan*; 11 John Nineteen Forty-One (2:04) Orchestra.

Review: See entry below.

Jesus Christ Superstar *♫♫♫♫*

1993, MCA Records; from the screen version *Jesus Christ Superstar*, Universal Pictures, 1973.

Album Notes: *Music*: Andrew Lloyd Webber; *Lyrics*: Tim Rice; *Orchestrations and Musical Direction*: Andrew Lloyd Webber; *Cast*: Carl Anderson (Judas Iscariot), Ted Neeley (Jesus Christ), Yvonne Elliman (Mary Magdalene), Bob Bingham (Caiaphas High Priest), Kurt Yaghjian (Annas), Larry T. Marshall (Simon Zealotes), Barry Dennen (Pontius Pilate), Joshua Mostel (King Herod); *Album Producers*: Tim Rice, Andrew Lloyd Webber.

Selections: CD 1: 1 Overture (5:26) Orchestra, Choir; 2 Heaven On Their Minds (4:22) *Carl Anderson*; 3 What's The Buzz (2:30) *Ted Neeley, Yvonne Elliman, The Apostles*; 4 Strange Thing Mystifying (1:50) *Ted Neeley, Yvonne Elliman, Carl Anderson, The Apostles*; 5 Then We Are Decided (2:32) *Bob Bingham, Kurt Yaghjian*; 6 Everything's Alright (3:36) *Yvonne Elliman, Ted Neeley, Carl Anderson, The Apostles*; 7 This Jesus Must Die (3:45) *Bob Bingham, Kurt Yaghjian*; 8 Hosanna (2:52) *Bob Bingham, Ted Neeley*; 9 Simon Zealotes (4:28) *Larry T. Marshall*; 10 Poor Jerusalem (1:36) *Ted Neeley*; 11 Pilate's Dream (1:45) *Barry Dennen*; 12 The Temple (5:26) *Ted Neeley*; 13 I Don't Know How To Love Him (3:55) *Yvonne Elliman*; 14 Damned For All Time/Blood Money (4:37) *Carl Anderson, Kurt Yaghjian, Bob Bingham*.

CD 2: 1 The Last Supper (7:12) *Ted Neeley, Carl Anderson*; 2 Gethsemane (I Only Want To Say)(5:39) *Ted Neeley*; 3 The Arrest (3:15) *Ted Neeley, Bob Bingham, Kurt Yaghjian*; 4 Peter's Denial (1:26) *Paul Davis, Yvonne Elliman*; 5 Pilate And

Christ (2:57) *Barry Dennen, Ted Neeley*; 6 King Herod's Song(3:13) *Joshua Mostel*; 7 Could We Start Again, Please? (2:44) *Yvonne Elliman, The Apostles*; 8 Judas' Death (4:38) *Carl Anderson, Bob Bingham, Kurt Yaghjian*; 9 Trial Before Pilate (6:47) *Barry Dennen, Bob Bingham, Ted Neeley*; 10 Superstar (3:56) *Carl Anderson*; 11 The Crucifixion (2:40) *Ted Neeley*; 12 John Nineteen Forty-One (2:20) Orchestra.

Review: It's interesting to note that within the same year, two musicals, *Godspell* and *Jesus Christ Superstar*, both chronicling the last seven days of Christ, opened in New York. Unlike its more modest predecessor, however, *Jesus Christ Superstar* came on the heels of a gold studio recording, made the year before, and a large amount of publicity, mostly created by religious groups who resented the idea of seeing Christ portrayed as a rock'n'roll star, and Herod as a buffoon prancing the stage on mod shoes with platform heels.

The studio cast album, listed here since the original Broadway cast album was never reissued on CD by MCA, presents the score Andrew Lloyd Webber and Tim Rice wrote for this show. In it, one song, "I Don't Know How to Love Him," achieved international status as a major hit, but the score itself is not bereft of other attractive moments.

Since bigger on the screen usually doesn't mean better, it is a pleasant surprise to note that the soundtrack album, also on MCA, and also a 2-CD set, is almost as flavorful and enjoyable as the studio cast album. Only the principals have changed, though Yvonne Elliman, who made a career out of portraying Mary Magdalene, is back to sing her hit song.

Joseph and the Amazing Technicolor Dreamcoat

Joseph and the Amazing Technicolor Dreamcoat ♪♪♪♪

1974, MCA Records; from the studio cast recording *Joseph and the Amazing Technicolor Dreamcoat*, 1973.

Album Notes: *Music*: Andrew Lloyd Webber; *Lyrics*: Tim Rice; *Orchestrations*: Andrew Lloyd Webber; *Musical Direction*: Chris Hamel-Cooke, Andrew Lloyd Webber; *Featured Musicians*: B.J. Cole (steel guitar), Tony Lowe (accordion), John Marson (harp), Geoff Westley (piano), George Comerford, John Gustafson, Olly Halsall, Neil Hubbard, Pete Massey, John Priseman, Bruce Rowland (rhythm section); *Cast*: Gary Bond (Joseph), Peter Reeves (The Narrator), Gordon Waller (Pharaoh), Maynard Williams, Roger Watson, Felicity Balfour, David Ballantine, Barbara Courtney, Tim Rice, Honey Simone, Frances Sinclair, The

Children's Choirs from Islington Green Comprehensive School, St. Clement Dane's School and The Barbara Speke Stage School; *Album Producers*: Andrew Lloyd Webber, Tim Rice; *Engineer*: Alan O'Duffy.

Selections: 1 Jacob And Sons/Joseph's Coat (5:45) *Peter Reeves*; 2 Joseph's Dreams (2:45) *Peter Reeves, Gary Bond*; 3 Poor, Poor Joseph (2:14) *Peter Reeves*; 4 One More Angel In Heaven (4:17)Male Ensemble; 5 Potiphar (4:26) *Peter Reeves*; 6 Close Every Door (3:16) *Gary Bond*; 7 Go, Go, Go Joseph (5:12) *Peter Reeves, Gary Bond*; 8 Pharaoh's Story (2:55) *Peter Reeves*; 9 Poor Poor Pharaoh/Song Of The King (4:10) *Peter Reeves, Gary Bond, Gordon Waller*; 10 Pharaoh's Dreams Explained (1:19) *Gary Bond*; 11 Stone The Crows (2:31) *Peter Reeves, Gordon Waller*; 12 Those Canaan Days (3:11)Male Ensemble; 13 The Brothers Come To Egypt/Grovel, Grovel (4:16) *Peter Reeves, Gary Bond*; 14 Who's The Thief (1:53) *Gary Bond, Peter Reeves*; 15 Benjamin Calypso (1:52) Male Ensemble; 16 Joseph All The Time (:55) *Peter Reeves, Gary Bond*; 17 Jacob In Egypt (1:01) *Peter Reeves*; 18 Any Dream Will Do (2:20) *Gary Bond*.

Review: See entry below.

Joseph and the Amazing Technicolor Dreamcoat ♪♪♪♪⁰

1982, Chrysalis Records; from the Broadway production *Joseph and the Amazing Technicolor Dreamcoat*, 1982.

Album Notes: *Music*: Andrew Lloyd Webber; *Lyrics*: Tim Rice; *Orchestrations*: Andrew Lloyd Webber; *Musical Direction*: Martin Silvestri, Jeremy Stone; *Cast*: Bill Hutton (Joseph), Laurie Beechman (The Narrator), Gordon Stanley (Jacob), Robert Hyman (Reuben), Kenneth Bryan (Simeon), Steve McNaughton (Levi), Charlie Serrano (Napthali), Peter Kapetan (Issachar), David Asher (Asher), Phillip Carruba (Benjamin), Tom Carder (Pharaoh), David Ardao (Potiphar); *Album Producers*: Tim Rice, Roger Watson; *Engineers*: Scott Litt, Bob Ludwig.

Selections: 1 Prologue: You Are What You Feel/Jacob And Sons (3:25) *Laurie Beechman*; 2 Joseph's Coat (3:28) *Gordon Stanley, Laurie Beechman, Bill Hutton, Robert Hyman, Kenneth Bryan, Steve McNaughton, Charlie Serrano, Peter Kapetan, David Asher, Phillip Carruba*; 3 Joseph's Dreams (2:33) *Laurie Beechman, Bill Hutton, Robert Hyman, Kenneth Bryan, Steve McNaughton, Charlie Serrano, Peter Kapetan, David Asher, Phillip Carruba*; 4 Poor, Poor Joseph (2:29) *Laurie Beechman, Robert Hyman, Kenneth Bryan, Steve McNaughton, Charlie Serrano, Peter Kapetan, David Asher, Phillip Carruba*; 5 One More Angel In Heaven (3:29) *Robert Hyman, Kenneth Bryan, Steve McNaughton, Charlie Serrano, Peter Kapetan, David Asher, Phil-*

lip Carruba; 6 Potiphar (3:17) *David Ardao, Bill Hutton, Laurie Beechman*; 7 Close Every Door (3:11) *Bill Hutton*; 8 Go, Go, Go Joseph (3:54) *Laurie Beechman, Bill Hutton, Kenneth Bryan, Barry Tarallo*; 9 Pharaoh's Story (3:21) *Laurie Beechman*; 10 Poor Poor Pharaoh/Song Of The King (3:45) *Laurie Beechman, Bill Hutton, Tom Carder*; 11 Pharaoh's Dreams Explained (1:21) *Bill Hutton*; 12 Stone The Crows (2:19) *Laurie Beechman, Tom Carder*; 13 Those Canaan Days/The Brothers Come To Egypt/ Grovel, Grovel (3:08) *Laurie Beechman, Robert Hyman, Kenneth Bryan, Steve McNaughton, Charlie Serrano, Peter Kapetan, David Asher, Phillip Carruba, Bill Hutton*; 14 Who's The Thief (4:39) *Bill Hutton, Laurie Beechman, Robert Hyman, Kenneth Bryan, Steve McNaughton, Charlie Serrano, Peter Kapetan, David Asher, Phillip Carruba*; 15 Benjamin Calypso/Joseph All The Time (3:37) *Laurie Beechman, Bill Hutton, Robert Hyman, Kenneth Bryan, Steve McNaughton, Charlie Serrano, Peter Kapetan, David Asher, Phillip Carruba*; 16 Jacob In Egypt/Any Dream Will Do (4:25) *Laurie Beechman, Bill Hutton*.

Review: See entry below.

Joseph and the Amazing Technicolor Dreamcoat 🎵🎵🎵🎵

1993, Polydor Records; from the revival production *Joseph and the Amazing Technicolor Dreamcoat*, 1993.

Album Notes: *Music*: Andrew Lloyd Webber; *Lyrics*: Tim Rice; *Orchestrations*: Andrew Lloyd Webber; *Musical Direction*: Michael Dixon; *Cast*: Michael Damian (Joseph), Kelli Rabke (The Narrator), Clifford David (Jacob/Potiphar), Marc Kudish (Reuben), Neal Ben-Ari (Simeon), Robert Torti (Levi/Pharaoh), Danny Bolero Zaldivar (Napthali), Bill Nolte (Issachar/Baker), Willy Falk (Asher), Ty Taylor (Benjamin), Glenn Sneed (Butler), Julie Bond (Mrs. Potiphar), Gerry McIntyre (Judah), Michelle Murlin (Reuben's Wife); *Album Producers*: Andrew Lloyd Webber, Nigel Wright; *Engineers*: Robin Sellars.

Selections: 1 Prologue (1:41) *Kelli Rabke*; 2 Any Dream Will Do (2:38) *Michael Damian*; 3 Jacob And Sons (5:38) *Michael Damian, Kelli Rabke, Clifford David*; 4 Joseph's Dreams (2:56) *Michael Damian, Kelli Rabke*; 5 Poor, Poor Joseph (2:36) *Kelli Rabke*; 6 One More Angel In Heaven (3:02) *Marc Kudish, Clifford David, Michelle Murlin*; 7 Potiphar (4:47) *Michael Damian, Kelli Rabke, Clifford David, Julie Bond*; 8 Close Every Door (3:47) *Michael Damian*; 9 Go, Go, Go Joseph (5:23) *Michael Damian, Kelli Rabke, Glenn Sneed, Bill Nolte*; 10 Pharaoh's Story (3:08) *Kelli Rabke*; 11 Poor Poor Pharaoh (1:53) *Michael Damian, Kelli Rabke, Robert Torti, Glenn Sneed*; 12 Song Of The King (Seven Fat Cows)(2:33) *Robert Torti*; 13 Pharaoh's Dreams Explained (1:20) *Michael Damian*; 14 Stone The Crows (2:37) *Michael Damian, Kelli Rabke,*

Robert Torti; 15 Those Canaan Days (4:45) *Neal Ben-Ari, Clifford David*; 16 The Brothers Come To Egypt/Grovel, Grovel (4:11) *Michael Damian, Kelli Rabke*; 17 Who's The Thief (2:19) *Michael Damian, Kelli Rabke,*; 18 Benjamin Calypso (2:56) *Gerry McIntyre*; 19 Joseph All The Time (:59) *Michael Damian, Kelli Rabke*; 20 Jacob In Egypt (1:06) *Kelli Rabke*; 21 Finale: Any Dream Will Do/ Give Me My Colored Coat (3:31) *Michael Damian, Kelli Rabke*; 22 Joseph Megamix (8:59) *Entire Company*.

Review: A Biblical tale that refuses to take its subject seriously, *Joseph and the Amazing Technicolor Dreamcoat* began as a modest, 15-minute piece for a school boys choir, and told the story of Joseph, sold to slavery by his eleven brothers, who ends up as an adviser to Pharaoh, and saves Egypt from a great famine. Expanded first to a full 90 minutes, then to a two-hour presentation, it first came to Broadway on January 27, 1982, where it settled for a run of 747 performances. It returned more recently, on November 10, 1993, for another run of 223 performances. What makes the musical so totally delightful is the impish, almost sophomoric way it approaches its story: the score, a blend of rock'n'roll, calypso, big band numbers, is a virtual romp from beginning to end. The three recordings listed above document the show at various stages in its development, with the earliest one presenting a slightly expanded version from the original concept, involving a lot of school children, and individual performers (including Tim Rice) in a fun recording of the score.

The Chrysalis recording is the cast album of the 1982 Broadway presentation, with Laurie Beechman, a New York favorite, in the crucial role as the Narrator.

The last recording, on Polydor, is the most recent cast album from the 1993 Broadway revival, with Michael Damian as Joseph and Kelli Rabke as the Narrator. It is by far the most satisfying, ending on a nine-minute megamix which reprises many of the songs in the score, performed by the entire company in what has to be the most exhilarating number of any modern-day Broadway show. The same recording, incidentally, with minor variations, was also released on two different occsions, with Jason Donovan in one cast, and Donny Osmond, star of the Canadian production, in the other. Whichever you pick, you cannot go wrong.

The Jungle Book 🎵🎵🎵♭

1990, Walt Disney Records; from the animated feature *The Jungle Book*, Walt Disney Pictures, 1967.

Album Notes: *Music*: George Bruns; *Songs*: Richard M. Sherman, Robert B. Sherman; *Orchestrations*: Walter Sheets; *Music Editor*: Evelyn Kennedy; *Cast*: Phil Harris (Baloo The Bear),

Sebastian Cabot (Bagheera The Panther), Louis Prima (King Louie Of The Apes), George Sanders (Shere Khan, The Tiger), Sterling Holloway (Kaa, The Snake), J. Pat O'Malley (Colonel Hahti, The Elephant), Bruce Reitherman (Mowgli), Chad Stuart, Lord Tim Hudson (Vultures), John Abbott, Ben Wright (Wolves), Darleen Carr (Girl), Verna Felton, Clint Howard (Elephants); *Album Producers*: Randy Thornton, Ted Kryczko; *Engineer*: Bruce Botnick.

Selections: 1 Overture (2:40); 2 Baby (2:09); 3 Colonel Hahti's March (2:30) *J. Pat O' Malley, Verna Felton, Clint Howard*; 4 The Bare Necessities (T. Gilkyson)(4:50) *Phil Harris*; 5 I Wan'na Be Like You (4:01) *Louis Prima, Phil Harris*; 6 Monkey Chase (1:04); 7 Tell Him (2:13); 8 Colonel Hahti's March (reprise)(1:59) *J. Pat O' Malley, Verna Felton, Clint Howard, Bruce Reitherman*; 9 Jungle Beat (1:20); 10 Trust In Me (2:49) *Sterling Holloway*; 11 Watch'a Wanna Do (3:07); 12 That's What Friends Are For (2:03) *Chad Stuart, Lord Tim Hudson*; 13 Tiger Fight (2:41); 14 Poor Bear (1:05); 15 My Own Home (3:29) *Darleen Carr*; 16 The Bare Necessities (reprise)(:51) *Phil Harris, Sebastian Cabot*; 17 Sherman Brothers Interview (16:54).

Review: Walt Disney's *The Jungle Book* needs little introduction. Who among us hasn't experienced the delight of Disney's animated feature, based upon Rudyard Kipling's "Mowgli" stories?

All 16 songs written for the film are here, including "Colonel Hathi's March," "The Bare Necessities," and "I Wan'na Be Like You," plus a recorded interview with songwriters Robert and Richard Sherman (which includes rare demos, and two musical numbers from the album *More Jungle Book*: "Baloo's Blues" and "It's a Kick"). Particularly fun are Louis Prima's "monkeying" around on "I Wan'na Be Like You," and the infectious spontaneity of the Academy Award nominated song, "The Bare Necessities."

The original stereo film recordings are good, save for a small amount of hiss that accompanies most recordings of this vintage.

Charles L. Granata

The King and I

The King and I ♫♫♫

1990, MCA Records; from the Broadway production *The King and I*, 1951.

Album Notes: *Music*: Richard Rodgers; *Lyrics*: Oscar Hammerstein II; *Orchestrations*: Robert Russell Bennett; *Musical Direction*: Frederick Dvonch; *Cast*: Gertrude Lawrence (Anna Leonowens), Yul Brynner (The King), Doretta Morrow (Tuptim), Larry

Douglas (Lun Tha), Dorothy Sarnoff (Lady Thiang); *Album Producer*: Jack Kapp; *CD Producer*: Michael Brooks.

Selections: 1 Overture (3:22) Orchestra; 2 I Whistle A Happy Tune (2:40) *Gertrude Lawrence*; 3 My Lord And Master (2:06) *Doretta Morrow*; 4 Hello Young Lovers (3:06) *Gertrude Lawrence*; 5 March Of The Siamese Children (3:15) Orchestra; 6 A Puzzlement (3:35) *Yul Brynner*; 7 Getting To Know You (3:25) *Gertrude Lawrence*; 8 We Kiss In A Shadow (3:24) *Doretta Morrow, Larry Douglas*; 9 Shall I Tell You What I Think Of You (3:23) *Gertrude Lawrence*; 10 Something Wonderful (2:36) *Dorothy Sarnoff*; 11 I Have Dreamed (3:25) *Doretta Morrow, Larry Douglas*; 12 Shall We Dance? (2:50) *Gertrude Lawrence, Yul Brynner*.

Review: See entry below.

The King and I ♫♫♫♫

1987, Capitol Records; from the screen version *The King and I*, 20th Century-Fox, 1956.

Album Notes: *Music*: Richard Rodgers; *Lyrics*: Oscar Hammerstein II; *Orchestrations*: Edward B. Powell, Gus Levene, Bernard Mayers, Robert Russell Bennett; *Vocal Arrangements*: Ken Darby; The 20th Century-Fox Chorus and Orchestra, conducted by Alfred Newman; *Cast*: Deborah Kerr (Anna Leonowens), Yul Brynner (The King), Rita Moreno (Tuptim), Carlos Rivas (Lun Tha), Terry Saunders (Lady Thiang), Rex Thompson (Louis); *CD Engineer*: Larry Walsh.

Selections: 1 Overture (6:41) Orchestra; 2 I Whistle A Happy Tune (2:45) *Marni Nixon, Rex Thompson*; 3 My Lord And Master (2:13) *Rita Moreno*; 4 Hello Young Lovers (3:31) *Marni Nixon*; 5 March Of The Siamese Children (3:50) Orchestra; 6 A Puzzlement (3:30) *Yul Brynner*; 7 Getting To Know You (3:06) *Marni Nixon*; 8 We Kiss In A Shadow/I Have Dreamed (5:02) *Rita Moreno, Reuben Fuentes*; 9 Shall I Tell You What I Think Of You (3:39) *Marni Nixon*; 10 Something Wonderful (3:11) *Terry Saunders*; 11 Song Of The King (1:34) *Yul Brynner*; 12 Shall We Dance? (3:21) *Marni Nixon, Yul Brynner*; 13 Something Wonderful (finale)(2:32) Chorus.

Review: See entry below.

The King and I ♫♫♫♫

1977, RCA Victor Records; from the Broadway revival *The King and I*, 1977.

Album Notes: *Music*: Richard Rodgers; *Lyrics*: Oscar Hammerstein II; *Orchestrations*: Robert Russell Bennett; *Musical Direction*: Milton Rosenstock; *Cast*: Yul Brynner (The King), Constance Towers (Anna Leonowens), June Angela (Tuptim),

Martin Vidnovic (Lun Tha), Hye-Young Choi (Lady Thiang), Alan Amick (Louis), Gene Profanato (Prince Chulalongkorn); *Album Producer*: Thomas Z. Shepard; *Engineer*: Paul Goodman.

Selections: 1 Overture (5:04) Orchestra; 2 Arrival At Bangkok/I Whistle A Happy Tune (3:27) *Alan Amick, Constance Towers*; 3 My Lord And Master (2:15) *June Angela*; 4 Hello Young Lovers (3:49) *Constance Towers*; 5 March Of The Siamese Children (3:27) Orchestra; 6 Children Sing, Priests Chant (:47) Men's Chorus, Children's Chorus; 7 A Puzzlement (4:31) *Yul Brynner*; 8 The Royal Bangkok Academy (:44) Children's Chorus; 9 Getting To Know You (4:23) *Constance Towers*; 10 So Big A World (1:04) *Yul Brynner*; 11 We Kiss In A Shadow (4:12) *Martin Vidnovic, June Angela*; 12 A Puzzlement (reprise)(1:51) *Gene Profanato, Alan Amick*; 13 Shall I Tell You What I Think Of You (5:28) *Constance Towers*; 14 Something Wonderful (3:21) *Hye-Young Choi*; 15 Finale To Act I (2:31) Company; 16 Western People Funny (1:35) *Hye-Young Choi*; 17 Dance Of Anna And Sir Edward (1:08); 18 I Have Dreamed (3:46) *Martin Vidnovic, June Angela*; 19 Song Of The King (1:12) *Yul Brynner, Constance Towers*; 20 Shall We Dance? (3:21) *Constance Towers, Yul Brynner*; 21 Finale (6:06) *Constance Towers, Yul Brynner, Gene Profanato*.

Review: See entry below.

The King and I 🎬🎬🎬🎬

1996, Varese-Sarabande; from the Broadway revival *The King and I*, 1996.

Album Notes: *Music*: Richard Rodgers; *Lyrics*: Oscar Hammerstein II; *Orchestrations*: Robert Russell Bennett; *Musical Direction*: Michael Rafter; *Cast*: Donna Murphy (Anna Leonowens), Lou Diamond Phillips (The King), Joohee Choi (Tuptim), Jose Llana (Lun Tha), Taewon Kim (Lady Thiang), Ryan Hopkins (Louis), Randall Duk Kim (The Kralahome), Jimmy Higa (Prince Chulalongkorn); *Album Producer*: Bruce Kimmel; *Engineer*: Vincent Cirilli; *Assistant Engineers*: Glen Marchesi, Paul Falcone.

Selections: 1 Overture (1:31) Orchestra; 2 I Whistle A Happy Tune (2:36) *Donna Murphy, Ryan Hopkins*; 3 Royal Dance Before The King (2:36) Company; 4 My Lord And Master (2:07) *Joohee Choi*; 5 Hello Young Lovers (3:14) *Donna Murphy*; 6 March Of The Siamese Children (3:38) Orchestra; 7 A Puzzlement (4:20) *Lou Diamond Phillips*; 8 Getting To Know You (4:48) *Donna Murphy, Joohee Choi, Taewon Kim, Ryan Hopkins*; 9 We Kiss In A Shadow (4:31) *Joohee Choi, Jose Llana*; 10 Shall I Tell You What I Think Of You (5:30) *Donna Murphy*; 11 Something Wonderful (4:17) *Taewon Kim, Randall Duk Kim*; 12 Finale to Act I (2:42) Company; 13 I Have Dreamed (3:13) *Joohee Choi, Jose Llana*; 14 Hello, Young Lovers (reprise)(2:14)

Donna Murphy; 15 Song Of The King (1:15) *Lou Diamond Phillips, Donna Murphy*; 16 Shall We Dance? (4:53) *Donna Murphy, Lou Diamond Phillips*; 17 Confrontation (:59) *Donna Murphy, Randall Duk Kim*; 18 Procession Of The White Elephant (3:51) Company; 19 The Letter (3:07) *Taewon Kim, Donna Murphy, Ryan Hopkins, Jimmy Higa*; 20 Finale (2:48) *Lou Diamond Phillips, Donna Murphy, Jimmy Higa*.

Review: Following the huge success of *South Pacific* two years before, much was expected from Richard Rodgers and Oscar Hammerstein II. *The King and I* didn't disappoint. Based on the book by Margaret Landon's novel, "Anna and the King of Siam," already the source for a 1946 non-musical film starring Rex Harrison and Irene Dunne, the musical was devised as a vehicle for Gertrude Lawrence, who had first suggested it to Rodgers and Hammerstein. The actress portrayed Anna Leonowens, the English teacher who goes to Siam in the 1860s to tutor the royal children. Contrasting the civilized Occidental values with the less sophisticated traditions of the Asian country, *The King and I* gained greater emotional depth when Oscar Hammerstein introduced a secondary romantic plot between Tuptim, a slave girl offered to the King by the Prince of Burma, and Lun Tha, who has been chosen to escort her to Siam. In a particularly clever parallel, Rodgers and Hammerstein, along with choreographer Jerome Robbins, created a ballet adaptation of Harriet Beecher Stowe's "Uncle Tom's Cabin." This device enabled them to further contrast, in song and dances, the differences between East and West. The show, which opened on March 29, 1951, and enjoyed a run of 1,246 performances, made a star of Yul Brynner, as the King, so much so in fact that focus in subsequent revivals shifted from Anna to the King, a trend eventually reversed in the 1996 Broadway production.

Of the various recordings listed above, the original cast album, made in 1951, suffers the most if only because it offers less selections from the profuse score, and is recorded in mono. However, it has the advantage of starring Gertrude Lawrence, radiant in her last stage role, and the budding Yul Brynner in the role that launched his international career.

The 1956 soundtrack album, besides having an incredibly sumptuous sound, was for many years the best recording available. Boasting a new overture orchestrated by Alfred Newman, it starred Brynner, properly regal as the King, and Deborah Kerr (dubbed by Marni Nixon) as Anna, with Rita Moreno as Tuptim. While the soundtrack focuses on the major musical numbers, it is not as complete as the extended version available with the deluxe laserdisc edition of the film, which includes many instrumentals and reprises.

In 1977, Yul Brynner returned to Broadway in the first of several revivals, in which he reprised the role of the King. The RCA Victor recording documents that revival, with a score that includes a lot of music previously unavailable. Though the revival was clearly dominated by Brynner, on the CD the balance between the various participants is better achieved, with the great sonics providing one of the best recordings of that score available up to that point.

With the focus back on Anna Leonowens, glowingly portrayed by Donna Murphy in the 1996 revival, the most recent cast album is the one to have. It features equally strong performances by Lou Diamond Phillips as the King, Taewon Kim as Lady Thiang, the King's first wife, Jose Llana as Lun Tha, and Joohee Choi as Tuptim, and it restores moments from the score ("Procession of the White Elephant"), not available elsewhere. However, like all other recordings, it fails to include the "Little House Of Uncle Thomas" ballet, which, so far, can only be found on the Broadway cast recording of the revue *Jerome Robbins' Broadway* (q.v.).

Kismet

Kismet ♫♫♫♫

1953, Columbia Records; from the Broadway production *Kismet*, 1953.

Album Notes: *Music*: Alexander Borodin; *Musical Adaptation and Lyrics*: Robert Wright, George Forrest; *Orchestrations*: Arthur Kay; *Musical Direction*: Louis Adrian; *Cast*: Alfred Drake (Hajj), Doretta Morrow (Marsinah), Richard Kiley (The Caliph), Joan Diener (Lalume), Henry Calvin (The Wazir Of Police), Richard Oneto (Bangle Man), Hal Hackett (Hassan-Ben), Lucy Andonian (Ayah To Zubbediah); *Album Producer*: Goddard Lieberson.

Selections: 1 Overture/Sands Of Time/Rhymes Have I (8:03) *Richard Oneto, Alfred Drake, Doretta Morrow*; 2 Fate (2:31) *Alfred Drake*; 3 Bazaar Of The Caravans (1:14) *Chorus*; 4 Not Since Nineveh (3:07) *Joan Diener, Henry Calvin*; 5 Baubles, Bangles And Beads (4:13) *Doretta Morrow, Richard Oneto*; 6 Stranger In Paradise (4:12) *Doretta Morrow, Richard Kiley*; 7 He's In Love (2:27) *Hal Kackett*; 8 Gesticulate (4:23) *Alfred Drake, Joan Diener, Henry Calvin*; 9 Night Of My Nights (3:40) *Richard Kiley*; 10 Was I Wazir? (2:15) *Henry Calvin*; 11 Rahadlakum (4:31) *Alfred Drake, Joan Diener, Lucy Andonian*; 12 And This Is My Beloved (4:44) *Alfred Drake, Doretta Morrow, Richard Kiley, Henry Calvin*; 13 The Olive Tree (2:38) *Alfred Drake*; 14 Zubbediya/Samaris' Dance (2:44) *Lucy Andonian*; 15 Finale: Sands Of Time (2:58) *Alfred Drake, Doretta Morrow, Richard Kiley*.

Review: See entry below.

Kismet ♫♫♫♫♫

1995, Rhino Records; from the screen version *Kismet*, M-G-M, 1955.

Album Notes: *Music*: Alexander Borodin; *Musical Adaptation and Lyrics*: Robert Wright, George Forrest; *Orchestrations*: Robert Franklyn, Conrad Salinger, Alexander Courage, Wally Heglin, Arthur Morton; *Arrangements*: Conrad Salinger, Alexander Courage, Andre Previn, Arthur Morton; *Vocal Supervision*: Jeff Alexander; The M-G-M Studio Orchestra and Chorus, conducted by Andre Previn, Jeff Alexander; *Cast*: Howard Keel (Hajj), Ann Blyth (Marsinah), Vic Damone (The Caliph), Dolores Gray (Lalume), Monty Wooley (Omar), Sebastian Cabot (Wazir), Betty Wand, Barbara Allan; *Album Producers*: George Feltenstein, Bradley Flanagan; *Engineer*: Doug Schwartz.

Selections: 1 Main Title (Not Since Nineveh/Stranger In Paradise) (2:26) Orchestra; 2 Rhymes Have I (3:21) *Howard Keel, Ann Blyth*; 3 Fate (5:00) *Howard Keel*; 4 Bazaar Of The Caravans (:52) Orchestra; 5 Not Since Nineveh (5:32) *Dolores Gray*; 6 Dabba (Stranger In Paradise)(1:04) Orchestra; 7 Baubles, Bangles And Beads (4:19) *Ann Blyth*; 8 I Am A Gardener (3:05) Orchestra; 9 Stranger In Paradise (5:20) *Ann Blyth, Vic Damone*; 10 Gesticulate (4:06) *Howard Keel, Dolores Gray*; 11 Bored (3:43) *Dolores Gray*; 12 Fate (reprise)(2:57) *Howard Keel, Dolores Gray*; 13 Night Of My Nights (2:44) *Vic Damone*; 14 The Olive Tree (2:42) *Howard Keel*; 15 Rahadlakum (4:18) *Dolores Gray, Howard Keel, Betty Wand, Barbara Allan*; 16 Marsinah Arrives At Castle/I'm In Love/Certain Young Women (Baubles, Bangles And Beads/Stranger In Paradise)(2:55) Orchestra; 17 And This Is My Beloved (3:06) *Howard Keel, Ann Blyth, Vic Damone*; 18 Innocent Amusement (And This Is My Beloved/Rahadlakum)(2:23) Orchestra; 19 Diwan Dances, Part One (Rahadlakum)(2:06) Orchestra; 20 Diwan Dances, Part Two (Night Of My Nights)(1:29) Orchestra; 21 Drowning Scene/ Sentence (Fate)(4:40) Orchestra; 22 Sands Of Time/End Title (1:50) *Howard Keel*.

Review: See entry below.

Kismet ♫♫♫♫▽

1965, RCA Records; from the Broadway revival *Kismet*, 1965.

Album Notes: *Music*: Alexander Borodin; *Musical Adaptation and Lyrics*: Robert Wright, George Forrest; *Orchestrations*: Arthur Kay; *Musical Direction*: Franz Allers; *Cast*: Alfred Drake (Hajj), Lee Venora (Marsinah), Richard Banke (The Caliph), Anne Jeffreys (Lalume), Henry Calvin (The Wazir Of Police), Rudy Vejar (Bangle Man), Frank Coleman (Hassan-Ben), Anita Alpert (Ayah To Zubbediah), Albert Toigo (Chief Policeman); *Album Producer*: George Marek; *CD Producer*: Bill Rosenfield; *Engineer*: Jay Newland.

PRINCE

After the enigmatic multi-instrumentalist bandleader and singer-songwriter Prince signed a lucrative record deal in 1993, he promptly announced his retirement and changed his name to an unpronounceable symbol. It later became clear that this "retirement" applied only to the now-defunct Prince and not to the artist reborn as the symbol.

While he was Prince, he was one of the most consistent hitmakers in contemporary music, fusing soul, funk, rock, and power pop into a distinctive, exuberant brew. He displayed an astounding versatility, both in the studio and onstage.

By 1978 Prince had released his debut "For You," which featured the single "Soft and Wet." Working with his band the Revolution, Prince developed his trademark mix of funk workouts, soul balladry, and metallic guitar wailing on the subsequent efforts "Prince," "Dirty Mind," and "Controversy." He made his first huge splash with "1999," an ambitious double-length recording that exploded thanks to the apocalyptic dance music of the title track and the crossover sensation "Little Red Corvette." The album remained on the charts for two years, by which time the film and album *Purple Rain* had established Prince as one of pop's megastars.

Although the movie *Purple Rain*—conceived by and starring Prince—was poorly reviewed, it earned nearly ten times what it cost to make. The soundtrack was a sensation and featured both his most daring and his most commercially successful work to date. Featuring the single "When Doves Cry" and the barnburning "Let's Go Crazy," as well as the shimmering balladry of the tile song, the collection earned Prince an Academy Award for best original song score.

Selections: 1 Overture (5:11); 2 Sands Of Time (2:03) *Rudy Vejar & Muezzins*; 3 Rhymes Have I (2:32) *Alfred Drake, Lee Venora*; 4 Fate (2:09) *Alfred Drake*; 5 Not Since Nineveh (3:08) *Anne Jeffreys, Henry Calvin*; 6 Baubles, Bangles And Beads (2:58) *Lee Venora*; 7 Stranger In Paradise (4:07) *Lee Venora, Richard Banke*; 8 He's In Love (2:25) *Albert Toigo*; 9 Gesticulate (4:20) *Alfred Drake, Anne Jeffreys, Henry Calvin*; 10 Bored (2:53) *Alfred Drake, Anne Jeffreys*; 11 Night Of My Nights (3:16) *Richard Banke*; 12 Was I Wazir? (2:20) *Henry Calvin*; 13 Rahadlakum (3:44) *Alfred Drake, Anne Jeffreys, Anita Alpert*; 14 And This Is My Beloved (4:11) *Alfred Drake, Lee Venora, Richard Banke, Henry Calvin*; 15 The Olive Tree (2:41) *Alfred Drake*; 16 Zubbediya (1:08) *Anita Alpert*; 17 Finale (2:58) *Alfred Drake, Lee Venora, Richard Banke*.

Review:

A "musical Arabian Night" solidly rooted in the traditions of the American theatre, *Kismet,* based on a 1911 play by Edward Knoblock, was also the source for two film versions, including one starring Marlene Dietrich and Ronald Coleman. It exhibited an Oriental lushness that won over critics and audiences when it opened on Broadway on December 3, 1953. Many of the musical delights came from Robert Wright and George Forrest's smart adaptations of themes by Alexander Borodin to create their songs for this story. The musical is about an impertinent poet and beggar in ancient Baghdad, who, through his wile and guile, becomes emir of the city overnight (literally, since the action of the musical occurs over a 24-hour period), while his daughter, the lovely Marsinah, marries the Caliph, who has fallen in love with her.

Besides the settings that evoked the Orient with their heavy brocades and colorful designs, audiences were also treated to a legendary, grander-than-life portrayal by Alfred Drake as Hajj, the poet, prancing around the stage with such panache and gusto that the part became forever identified with him. While the show seemed like a sure-fire winner, its opening during a newspaper strike which prevented New York audiences from knowing what was happening around town threatened its very existence for a while. It was saved by Tony Bennett's rendering of the song "Stranger In Paradise," a huge radio hit at the time, which prompted many listeners to go and see for themselves what the show was all about. This ensured its success in the first crucial weeks, and guaranteed a long run of 583 performances afterwards. While the original cast album, in mono, is not up to today's digital standards, it is a resonant memento of the show as it was heard when it first opened, with Doretta Morrow, Joan Diener and Richard Kiley, excellent as Marsinah, Lalume (the Wazir's sexy wife, who takes a shine to

Hajj), and the Caliph, respectively. Also in the cast was a muscular young man named Steve Reeves. The musical won several Tony Awards that season, including one for Best Musical, and another for Alfred Drake.

In 1955, more luscious and opulent than ever, it exploded on the big screen in a visually stunning film version that starred Howard Keel as Hajj, Ann Blyth as Marsinah, Dolores Gray as Lalume, and Vic Damone as the Caliph. It retained the original score almost intact, including "Baubles, Bangles And Beads," "And This Is My Beloved," and, of course, "Stranger In Paradise." The deluxe Rhino recording, complete with outtakes, instrumental ballets and songs previously unreleased, also presents the soundtrack in full stereo for the first time.

Alfred Drake returned to the role in a great revival in 1965, in which he starred opposite Anne Jeffreys as Lalume, Lee Venora as Marsinah, and Richard Banke as the Caliph, with Henry Calvin reprising the role of the Wazir he had created in 1953. This show, which had a limited run over the summer, is documented in the RCA Victor recording.

On March 1, 1978, the show returned to Broadway in a revival retitled *Timbuktu!*, noted for the fact that it was mostly a grandiose fashion extravaganza designed by Geoffrey Holder. Somewhat incidentally, it starred Eartha Kitt and Melba Moore, and had a run of 243 performances.

Kiss Me, Kate

Kiss Me, Kate ♫♫♫♫♫

1989, Columbia Records; from the Broadway production *Kiss Me, Kate*, 1948.

Album Notes: *Music*: Cole Porter; *Lyrics*: Cole Porter; *Orchestrations*: Robert Russell Bennett; *Vocal Arrangements and Musical Direction*: Pembroke Davenport; *Cast*: Alfred Drake (Fred/Petruchio), Patricia Morison (Lilli/Katherine), Lisa Kirk (Lois/Bianca), Harold Lang (Bill/Lucentio), Annabelle Hill (Hattie), Edwin Clay (Gremio), Charles Wood (Hortensio), Lorenzo Fuller (Paul), Eddie Sledge, Fred Davis, Harry Clark, Jack Diamond; *Album Producer*: Mitchell Ayres; *Engineer*: Harold Chapman; *CD Producer*: Michael Brooks; *Engineer*: Tim Geelan.

Selections: 1 Overture/Another Op'nin', Another Show (4:24) *Anabelle Hill*; 2 Why Can't You Behave? (3:09) *Lisa Kirk, Harold Lang*; 3 Wunderbar (3:37) *Patricia Morison, Alfred Drake*; 4 So In Love (3:36) *Patricia Morison*; 5 We Open In Venice (2:02) *Alfred Drake, Patricia Morison, Lisa Kirk, Harold Lang*; 6 Tom, Dick Or Harry (2:05) *Lisa Kirk, Harold Lang, Edwin Clay, Charles Wood*; 7 I've Come To Wive It Wealthily In Padua (2:12) *Alfred Drake*; 8 I Hate Men (2:13) *Patricia Morison*; 9 Were Thine That Special Face (4:12) *Alfred Drake*; 10 Too Darn Hot (3:36) *Lorenzo Fuller, Eddie Sledge, Fred Davis*; 11 Were Is The Life That Late I Led? (4:24) *Alfred Drake*; 12 Always True To You (In My Fashion)(4:00) *Lisa Kirk*; 13 Bianca (2:07) *Harold Lang*; 14 So In Love (reprise)(2:11) *Alfred Drake*; 15 Brush Up Your Shakespeare (1:40) *Harry Clark, Jack Diamond*; 16 I Am Ashamed That Women Are So Simple/Finale (2:39) *Patricia Morison, Alfred Drake, Patricia Morison*.

Review: See entry below.

Kiss Me, Kate ♫♫♫♫

1993, Angel Records; from the Broadway production *Kiss Me, Kate*, 1948.

Album Notes: *Music*: Cole Porter; *Lyrics*: Cole Porter; *Orchestrations*: Robert Russell Bennett; *Vocal Arrangements and Musical Direction*: Pembroke Davenport; *Cast*: Alfred Drake (Fred/Petruchio), Patricia Morison (Lilli/Katherine), Lisa Kirk (Lois/Bianca), Harold Lang (Bill/Lucentio), Annabelle Hill (Hattie), Lorenzo Fuller (Paul), Aloysius Donovan, Alexis Dubroff (Mobsters), Bob Sands (Gremio), Ray Drakely (Hortensio); *Album Producers*: Simon Rady, Alfred Drake; *CD Engineer*: Bob Norberg.

Selections: 1 Overture (2:25) Orchestra; 2 Another Op'nin', Another Show (1:53) *Lorenzo Fuller*; 3 Why Can't You Behave? (2:46) *Lisa Kirk*; 4 Wunderbar (2:29) *Patricia Morison, Alfred Drake*; 5 So In Love (3:38) *Patricia Morison*; 6 We Open In Venice (1:56) *Alfred Drake, Patricia Morison, Lisa Kirk, Harold Lang*; 7 Tom, Dick Or Harry (2:06) *Lisa Kirk, Harold Lang, Bob Sands, Ray Drakely*; 8 I've Come To Wive It Wealthily In Padua (2:07) *Alfred Drake*; 9 I Hate Men (2:05) *Patricia Morison*; 10 Were Thine That Special Face (4:11) *Alfred Drake*; 11 Too Darn Hot (3:20) *Lorenzo Fuller*; 12 Were Is The Life That Late I Led? (3:52) *Alfred Drake*; 13 Always True To You (In My Fashion)(3:47) *Lisa Kirk*; 14 Bianca (2:06) *Harold Lang*; 15 So In Love (reprise)(2:30) *Alfred Drake*; 16 Brush Up Your Shakespeare (1:41) *Aloysius Donovan, Alexis Dubroff*; 17 I Am Ashamed That Women Are So Simple (1:55) *Patricia Morison*; 18 Finale (:47) *Alfred Drake, Patricia Morison*.

Review: See entry below.

Kiss Me, Kate ♫♫♫♫

1996, Rhino Records; from the screen version *Kiss Me Kate*, M-G-M, 1953.

Album Notes: *Music*: Cole Porter; *Lyrics*: Cole Porter; *Orchestrations*: Conrad Salinger, Wally Heglin, Robert Franklyn, Pete Rugolo, Maurice de Packh, Skip Martin; *Arrangements*: Saul Chaplin, Andre Previn, Conrad Salinger; The M-G-M Studio Chorus and Orchestra, conducted by Andre Previn; *Cast*: Howard Keel (Fred/Petruchio), Kathryn Grayson (Lilli/Katherine), Ann Miller (Lois/Bianca), Tommy Rall (Bill/Lucentio), Bobby Van (Gremio), Bob Fosse (Hortensio), Claud Allister (Paul), Keenan Wynn (Lippy), James Whitmore (Slug); *Album Producers*: George Feltenstein, Bradley Flanagan; *Engineer*: Doug Schwartz.

Selections: 1 Overture: Always True To You In My Fashion/Why Can't You Behave/Another Openin', Another Show/So In Love (2:51) Orchestra; 2 Main Title (So In Love/Wunderbar) (2:01) Orchestra; 3 So In Love (2:19) *Kathryn Grayson, Howard Keel*; 4 Too Darn Hot (3:25) *Ann Miller, Bill Lee, Hal Hopper, Bob Wacker, Gene Lanham, Mac McLain, Hermes Pan, Saul Chaplin*; 5 Why Can't You Behave? (4:01) *Ann Miller*; 6 Electric Sign (Another Openin' Another Show) (:33) Orchestra; 7 Lilli's Cork (1:25) Orchestra; 8 Wunderbar (4:00) *Kathryn Grayson, Howard Keel*; 9 So In Love (reprise) (1:37) *Kathryn Grayson*; 10 We Open In Venice (2:16) *Kathryn Grayson, Howard Keel, Ann Miller, Tommy Rall*; 11 Tom, Dick Or Harry (4:12) *Ann Miller, Bob Fosse, Tommy Rall, Bobby Van*; 12 I've Come To Wive It Wealthily In Padua (2:34) *Howard Keel*; 13 I Hate Men (3:53) *Kathryn Grayson*; 14 Were Thine That Special Face (2:06) *Howard Keel*; 15 Finale Act One (Kiss Me Kate) (:24) *Chorus*; 16 And So To Wed (We Open In Venice/I Hate Men) (1:04) Orchestra; 17 I've Come To Wive It Wealthily In Padua (reprise) (:56) *Howard Keel*; 18 Were Is The Life That Late I Led? (5:05) *Howard Keel*; 19 Bianca (1:33) Orchestra; 20 Why Can't You Behave? (1:36) Orchestra; 21 Were Thine That Special Face (1:11) *Chorus*; 22 Always True To You (In My Fashion) (2:43) *Ann Miller, Tommy Rall*; 23 Brush Up Your Shakespeare (3:30) *James Whitmore, Keenan Wynn*; 24 Bianca's Wedding (We Open In Venice) (:27) Orchestra; 25 From This Moment On (3:47) *Ann Miller, Tommy Rall, Bobby Van, Bob Fosse*; 26 Down On Kate) (1:31) Orchestra; 27 Kiss Me Kate (1:28) *Kathryn Grayson, Howard Keel*.

Review: A brilliant adaptation of William Shakespeare's *The Taming of the Shrew*, with a superb score by Cole Porter, *Kiss Me, Kate* brought the audience to its feet when it opened on December 30, 1948, before settling for a long run of 1,077 performances.

The show starred Alfred Drake as Fred Graham, an egocentric director who portrays Petruchio in a revival of "The Taming of the Shrew," and Patricia Morison as Lili Vanessi, Fred's tempestuous ex-wife, also cast as Katharina in the play-within-the-musical. *Kiss Me, Kate* had been suggested to Bella and Samuel Spewack, authors of the libretto, by the celebrated backstage feuds between real-life husband and wife thespians Alfred Lunt and Lynn Fontanne. With a significant assist from Cole Porter, writing his best score for this occasion, the musical follows the

touring actors, while they play Shakespeare on stage, and continue to battle or make up backstage. Adding spice to the plot, the Spewacks imagine an idyll between Fred and his second leading lady, Lois Lane, who is more interested in another actor, Bill Calhoun.

Commenting on the action, and sometimes punctuating it with clever lyrics, Porter wrote songs that have endured to this day. Many of those songs have passed into the language as colloquialisms, including "Another Op'nin', Another Show," "Tom, Dick or Harry," "Too Darn Hot," "Were Thine That Special Face," "Wunderbar," a mock Tyrolian duet, "I've Come To Wive It Wealthily In Padua," and "Brush Up Your Shakespeare," in which the composer amusingly used malapropisms to spoof those whose ignorance of the English language sometimes leads to confusing expressions.

Kiss Me, Kate won a Tony as Best Musical that season, and also earned awards for its authors and composer, among others. Its cast recording, a consistent best-seller in the Columbia catalogue, is a wonderful memento from that glittering show.

With the advent of stereo in the late fifties, record companies looked for new ways to expand their list of available titles. Because of this, in 1959, Capitol Records was successful in bringing together the four leads—Alfred Drake, Patricia Morison, Lisa Kirk and Harold Lang—from the original Broadway cast of a decade earlier, to re-record the songs from the show under the direction of the original musical director, Pembroke Davenport. The resulting album, recorded in aggressive two-channel sound, with a lot of reverb, is still a lot of fun to listen to, and proves that the four performers were still in marvelous voice.

The Rhino recording, again containing much material which is available here for the first time, documents the screen version made by M-G-M in 1953, with Howard Keel and Kathryn Grayson giving sensational portrayals as Fred and Lili, and Ann Miller incandescent as Lois, whose "Too Darn Hot" was a show-stopper in the film, a big CinemaScope, 3-D production.

Kiss of the Spider Woman: The Musical

Kiss of the Spider Woman: The Musical 🎻🎻🎻🎻

1992, RCA Victor; from the Broadway production *Kiss of the Spider Woman: The Musical*, 1992.

Album Notes: *Music*: John Kander; *Lyrics*: Fred Ebb; *Orchestrations*: Michael Gibson; *Musical Direction*: Jeffrey Huard; *Cast*:

Chita Rivera (Aurora), Brent Carver (Molina), Anthony Crivello (Valentin), Merle Louise (Molina's Mother), Kirsti Carnahan (Marta), Jerry Christakos (Gabriel), Herndon Lackey (Warden); *Album Producer*: Martin Levan; *Engineer*: Martin Levan.

Selections: 1 Prologue (2:46) *Chita Rivera, Herndon Lackey*; 2 Her Name Is Aurora (4:33) *Brent Carver*; 3 Over The Wall I (1:28) Male Ensemble; 4 Bluebloods (:58) *Brent Carver, Anthony Crivello*; 5 Dressing Them Up (2:34) *Brent Carver*; 6 I Draw The Line (1:13) *Brent Carver, Anthony Crivello*; 7 Dear One (3:04) *Merle Louise, Kirsti Carnahan, Brent Carver, Antony Crivello*; 8 Over The Wall II (1:56) *Brent Carver, Anthony Crivello*; 9 Where Are You (5:13) *Chita Rivera*; 10 Marta (2:16) *Anthony Crivello*; 11 I Do Miracles (3:23) *Chita Rivera, Kirsti Carnahan*; 12 Gabriel's Letter/ My First Woman (3:02) *Jerry Christakos, Anthony Crivello*; 13 Morphine Tango (1:48) Male Ensemble; 14 You Could Never Shame Me (2:59) *Merle Louise, Brent Carver*; 15 A Visit/Morphine Tango (3:44) *Chita Rivera, Brent Carver*; 16 She's A Woman (2:41) *Brent Carver*; 17 Gimme Love (4:04) *Chita Rivera, Brent Carver*; 18 Russian Movie/Good Times (6:01) *Chita Rivera, Brent Carver, Anthony Crivello, Herndon Lackey*; 19 The Day After That (4:49) *Anthony Crivello*; 20 Mama, It's Me (2:02) *Brent Carver*; 21 Anything For Him (3:30) *Chita Rivera, Brent Carver, Anthony Crivello*; 22 Kiss Of The Spider Woman (2:32) *Chita Rivera*; 23 Only In The Movies (6:25) *Brent Carver*.

Review: See entry below.

Kiss of the Spider Woman: The Musical 𝄞𝄞𝄞𝄞

1995, Mercury Records; from the Broadway production *Kiss of the Spider Woman: The Musical*, **1992.**

Album Notes: *Music*: John Kander; *Lyrics*: Fred Ebb; *Orchestrations*: Michael Gibson; *Musical Direction*: Gregory Dlugos; *Cast*: Vanessa Williams (Aurora), Howard McGillin (Molina), Brian Mitchell (Valentin), Mimi Turque (Molina's Mother), Kirsti Carnahan (Marta), Jerry Christakos (Gabriel), Herndon Lackey (Warden); *Album Producer*: Thomas Z. Shepard; *Engineer*: James P. Nichols; *Assistant Engineers*: Carl Glanville, Danny Bernini.

Selections: 1 Prologue (2:02) *Vanessa Williams, Herndon Lackey*; 2 Scene: The Prison Cell (:24) *Philip Hernandez, Michael McCormick, Herndon Lackey*; 3 Her Name Is Aurora (4:26) *Howard McGillin, Vanessa Williams*; 4 Scene: The Prison Cell(:26) *Howard McGillin, Herndon Lackey*; 5 Over The Wall I (1:02)Male Ensemble; 6 And The Moon Grows Dimmer (:27) *Vanessa Williams*; 7 Bluebloods (:59) Howard McGillin, Brian Mitchell; 8 Dressing Them Up (2:37) *Howard McGillin*; 9 I Draw

The Line (1:12) *Howard McGillin, Brian Mitchell*; 10 Scene: The Prison Cell (:41) *Howard McGillin, Brian Mitchell*; 11 Dear One (3:28) *Mimi Turque, Kirsti Carnahan, Howard McGillin, Brian Mitchell*; 12 Over The Wall II (2:15) *Howard McGillin, Brian Mitchell, Herndon Lackey*; 13 Scene: The Prison Cell (1:30) *Howard McGillin, Vanessa Williams, John Aller*; 14 Where Are You (4:16)Male Ensemble; 15 Marta (2:55) *Brian Mitchell*; 16 I Do Miracles (3:49) *Vanessa Williams, Kirsti Carnahan, Howard McGillin, Brian Mitchell*; 17 Gabriel's Letter/My First Woman (3:27) *Jerry Christakos, Michael McCormick, Brian Mitchell*; 18 Morphine Tango (1:20)Male Ensemble; 19 You Could Never Shame Me (1:49) *Mimi Turque, Howard McGillin*; 20 A Visit (2:49) *Vanessa Williams, Howard McGillin*; 21 She's A Woman (2:54) *Howard McGillin*; 22 Gimme Love (3:59) *Vanessa Williams, Howard McGillin*; 23 Russian Movie/Good Times (6:43) *Vanessa Williams, Howard McGillin, Brian Mitchell, Herndon Lackey*; 24 The Day After That (5:00) *Brian Mitchell*; 25 Mama, It's Me (2:12) *Howard McGillin, Herndon Lackey*; 26 Anything For Him (3:46) *Vanessa Williams, Howard McGillin, Brian Mitchell*; 27 Kiss Of The Spider Woman (2:46) *Vanessa Williams*; 28 Lucky Molina/Over The Wall (2:59) *Michael McCormick, Herndon Lackey, Howard McGillin, Mimi Turque, Jerry Christakos, Kirsti Carnahan*; 29 Scene: The Warden's Office (1:18) *Herdon Lackey, Howard McGillin, Brian Mitchell*; 30 Only In The Movies (4:59) *Howard McGillin*.

Review: Turning Manuel Puig' unremittingly somber novel, *Kiss of the Spider Woman*, about inmates in a South American prison dreaming about an unsubstantial movie star, into a musical might have seemed at first a rather peculiar idea. However, Terrence McNally, John Kander and Fred Ebb combined their efforts to meet the challenge head-on, and managed to create a show that was vibrantly alive and original, while remaining faithful to the spirit of the original. Having not one but two cast albums of the same Broadway production might prove more than an embarrassment of riches — a bit of an overkill. Yet, each recording in its own way contributes a different aspect of the musical, with Chita Rivera and Vanessa Williams succeeding in creating portrayals that are sometimes at odds with each other, while at other times complement each other.

One's decision about opting to listen to one or the other (or both) will largely depend on what one expects from an original cast album. By focusing only on the musical numbers, the Chita Rivera-starrer provides an accurate vision of the score itself. The Vanessa Williams recording, by incorporating bits of spoken dialogue to introduce the songs, gives a better idea of the role played by the musical numbers within the greater framework of the play. Ultimately, both are equally successful and equally enjoyable.

La Cage Aux Folles 🎵🎵🎵🎵

1983, RCA Victor; from the Broadway production *La Cage Aux Folles*, 1983.

Album Notes: *Music*: Jerry Herman; *Lyrics*: Jerry Herman; *Orchestrations*: Jim Tyler; *Musical Direction and Vocal Arrangements*: Donald Pippin; *Cast*: Gene Barry (Georges), George Hearn (Albin), John Weiner (Jean-Michel), Merle Louise (Mme Dindon), Jay Garner (Edouard Dindon), William Thomas Jr. (Jacob), Elizabeth Parrish (Jacqueline), David Cahn, Dennis Callahan, Frank DiPasquale, John Dolf, David Engel, David Evans, Linda Haberman, Eric Lamp, Dan O'Grady, Deborah Phelan, Sam Singhaus (Les Cagelles); *Album Producer*: Thomas Z. Shepard; *Engineer*: Paul Goodman.

Selections: 1 Prelude (3:00); 2 We Are What We Are (3:53) *Les Cagelles*; 3 A Little More Mascara (4:43) *George Hearn*; 4 With Anne On My Arm (3:35) *John Weiner*; 5 With You On My Arm (2:35) *Gene Barry, George Hearn*; 6 Song On The Sand (La Da Da Da)(3:55) *Gene Barry*; 7 La Cage Aux Folles (6:43) *George Hearn, Les Cagelles*; 8 I Am What I Am (3:02) *George Hearn*; 9 Song On The Sand (reprise)(1:50) *Gene Barry, George Hearn*; 10 Masculinity (2:28) *Gene Barry, George Hearn*; 11 Look Over There (2:52) *Gene Barry*; 12 Cocktail Counterpoint (1:52) *Gene Barry, Merle Louise, John Weiner, Jay Garner, William Thomas Jr.*; 13 The Best Of Times (5:35) *George Hearn, Elizabeth Parrish*; 14 Look Over There (reprise)(1:11) *John Weiner, Gene Barry*; 15 The Finale: With You On My Arm/La Cage Aux Folles/ Song On The Sand/The Best Of Times (5:49).

Review: It probably took daring to bring to the musical stage, particularly on Broadway where traditions run high, a show that centered around the love relationship between two men, Georges, owner of a gay club known as "La Cage aux folles," and Albin, who, as Zaza, headlines the revue presented at the club, in which all the performers are boys dressed as girls. It might have helped that the show is set on the French Riviera, where, as we know, spirits are generally much looser than they are in America, but the fact of the matter is that *La Cage Aux Folles* is an old-fashioned Broadway musical in the best sense of the word, with at its core a perfectly standard love affair. The rest of the plot, loosely based on the French stage play by Jean Poiret (also the source for the film of the same name, and the more recent remake titled *The Birdcage)* involved the various shenanigans to which Georges and Albin were subjected when Georges' son (an accident!) decides he wants to marry the daughter of a champion of morality, who insists on meeting his future son-in-law's relatives. With a brilliant score by Jerry Herman (which included such show-stopping numbers as "Song on the Sand," "The Best of Times," "With Anne on My Arm," and the defiant anthem "I Am What I Am"), the musical

opened to rave reviews on August 21, 1983, for a run of 1,176 performances.

Lady, Be Good! 🎵🎵🎵🎵

1992, Elektra Records; from the studio cast recording *Lady, Be Good!*, 1992.

Album Notes: *Music*: George Gershwin; *Lyrics*: Ira Gershwin; *Orchestrations*: Larry Wilcox, Russell Warner, Robert Russell Bennett, William Daly, Charles Grant, Stephen O. Jones, Paul Lannin, Max Steiner; *Musical Direction*: Eric Stern; *Cast*: Lara Teeter (Dick Trevor), Ann Morrison (Susie Trevor), Jason Alexander (Watty Watkins), Michael Maguire (Jack Robinson), John Pizzarelli (Jeff White), Ivy Austin (Daisy Parke), Michelle Nicastro (Shirley Vernon), Robin Langford (Bertie Bassett), Carol Swarbrick (Josephine Vanderwater); *Album Producers*: John McClure, Tommy Krasker; *Engineer*: Shawn Murphy; *Assistant Engineers*: David Marquette, Jay Selvester, Andy Bass, Robert Hart.

Selections: 1 Overture (5:53) *Orchestra*; 2 Hang On To Me (5:12) *Lara Teeter, Ann Morrison*; 3 A Wonderful Party (3:02)*Ensemble*; 4 End Of A String (3:53)*Ensemble*; 5 We're Here Because (2:12) *Robin Langford, Ivy Austin*; 6 Fascinating Rhythm (7:31) *John Pizzarelli, Lara Teeter, Ann Morrison*; 7 So Am I (3:12) *Michael Maguire, Ann Morrison*; 8 Oh, Lady Be Good! (3:44) *Jason Alexander, Ann Morrison*; 9 Finale Act 1 (4:22) *Carol Swarbrick, Lara Teeter, Robin Langford, Ivy Austin, Ann Morrison, Michelle Nicastro, Jason Alexander*; 10 Linger In The Lobby (2:15)*Ensemble*; 11 The Half Of It Dearie Blues (5:37) *Lara Teeter, Michelle Nicastro*; 12 Juanita (1:59) *Ann Morrison*; 13 I'd Rather Charleston (5:54) *Lara Teeter, Ann Morrison*; 14 Reprises (2:38) *Michael Maguire, Ann Morrison*; 15 Little Jazz Bird (3:29) *John Pizzarelli*; 16 Carnival Time (1:29) *Orchestra*; 17 Swiss Miss (3:08) *Lara Teeter, Ann Morrison*; 18 Finale Ultimo (3:49) *Company*.

Review: George and Ira Gershwin made their first splash on Broadway with *Lady, Be Good!*, a jazzy, tuneful musical which opened on December 1, 1924, and pretty much set the tone for the type of music one would hear in the musical theatre for the rest of the decade. Significantly, the show also introduced the song-and-dance team of Fred and Adele Astaire, who would go on to dominate the stage as the leading Broadway performers until Adele decided to retire to get married, while Fred chose to continue in Hollywood with other partners.

Though its plot was, by modern standards, rather simplistic, the show endured for 330 performances, largely due to the fetching presence of its stars and the great score by the Gershwins. The score introduced such standards as "Fascinating Rhythm," and "Oh, Lady Be Good," among its many memorable numbers.

The studio cast recording on Elektra, part of a series documenting all the musicals by the Gershwins, features a cast of well-trained Broadway performers who extract all the juice and fun from the score.

Les Miserables 🎵🎵🎵🎵

1987, Geffen Records; from the Broadway production *Les Miserables*, 1987.

Album Notes: *Music:* Claude-Michel Schonberg; *Lyrics:* Herbert Kretzmer; *Original French Text:* Alain Boublil, Jean-Marc Natel; *Additional Material:* James Fenton; *Orchestral Score:* John Cameron; *Musical Direction:* Robert Billing; *Cast:* Colm Wilkinson (Jean Valjean), Terrence Mann (Javert), Randy Graff (Fantine), Jennifer Butt (Madame Thenardier), Leo Burmester (Thenardier), Braden Danner (Gavroche), Judy Kuhn (Cosette), David Bryant (Marius), Michael Maguire (Enjolras), Frances Ruffelle (Eponine), Anthony Crivello (Grantaire), Norman Large (Bishop); *Album Producers:* Alain Boublil, Claude-Michel Schonberg; *Engineer:* David Hunt; *Assistant Engineers:* Dave O'Donnell, Roy Hendrickson.

Selections: CD 1: 1 Overture/Work Song (3:33) *Colm Wilkinson, Terrence Mann*; 2 Valjean Arrested/Valjean Forgiven (1:52) *Norman Large*; 3 What Have I Done? (3:21) *Colm Wilkinson*; 4 At The End Of The Day (4:43)*Ensemble*; 5 I Dreamed A Dream (4:13) *Randy Graff*; 6 Lovely Ladies (3:50)*Ensemble*; 7 Who Am I? (2:49) *Colm Wilkinson*; 8 Come To Me (3:46) *Colm Wilkinson, Randy Graff*; 9 Confrontation (2:31) *Terrence Mann, Colm Wilkinson*; 10 Castle On A Cloud (1:40) *Judy Kuhn*; 11 Master Of The House (4:54) *Leo Burmester, Jennifer Butt*; 12 The Thenardier Waltz Of Treachery (2:59) *Leo Burmester, Jennifer Butt, Colm Wilkinson*; 13 Look Down (2:55) *Braden Danner*; 14 Stars (2:58) *Terrence Mann*; 15 Red And Black (4:31) *David Bryant, Michael Maguire*; 16 Do You Hear The People Sing? (2:06) *Michael Maguire*.

CD 2: 1 In My Life (5:15) *Judy Kuhn, Colm Wilkinson, David Bryant, Michael Maguire*; 2 A Heart Full Of Love (2:22) *Judy Kuhn, David Bryant, Frances Ruffelle*; 3 Plumet Attack (1:59) *Frances Ruffelle*; 4 One Day More (3:29) *Company*; 5 Upon These Stones (Building The Barricade)(2:09) *Michael Maguire*; 6 On My Own (4:11) *Frances Ruffelle*; 7 Upon These Stones (At The Barricade)(2:27) *Michael Maguire*; 8 Javert At The Barricade/Little People (1:30) *Terrence Mann, Michael Maguire, Braden Danner*; 9 The First Attack (:39) *Michael Maguire*; 10 A Little Fall Of Rain (3:23) *Frances Ruffelle, David Bryant*; 11 Drink With Me (2:39) *Anthony Crivello*; 12 Bring Him Home (3:16)

Colm Wilkinson; 13 Dog Eats Dog (2:15) *Leo Burmester*; 14 Javert's Suicide (3:30) *Terrence Mann*; 15 Turning (2:04) Female Chorus; 16 Empty Chairs At Empty Tables (3:00) *David Bryant*; 17 Wedding Chorale/Beggars At The Feast (2:14) *Jennifer Butt, Leo Burmester*; 18 Finale (4:50) Company.

Review: Victor Hugo's epic story *Les Miserables,* already the source of numerous stage, screen and TV adaptations, became a monstrous international musical hit with this show, sporting a score by the Claude-Michel Schonberg and Alain Boublil. Their original creation premiered in Paris in 1980, before moving to London in 1985, and to Broadway, where it opened on March 12, 1987. The plot centers around a splendid retelling of the story of Jean Valjean, a former convict, who redeems himself and becomes an honorable citizen, only to be pursued by the implacable police officer, Javert, who wants to arrest him again for breaking his parole. The show redefined the criteria by which Broadway musicals would be judged: spectacular in every way, with sharply drawn colorful characters, and a sweeping score of wall-to-wall songs and instrumental bridges tied together without dialogue. The pop opera raised the standards (and costs) of stage productions by being utterly extravagant and theatrical, while bringing a new seriousness to the medium, midway between the glorious musicals of yesteryear and the standard old-fashioned operas forever in search of new audiences.

The show, which is still running at this writing, won several Tony Awards, including for Best Musical, Best Book, and Best Score.

An incredible epic sweep runs throughout the score, replete with moving romantic moments and impressive crowd numbers. It follows Valjean, always one step ahead of Javert, from 1815 and his adoption of the little orphan Cosette, ward of the Thenardiers, a couple of mean-spirited innkeepers, all the way to the 1832 Paris street uprising where Valjean saves the life of Marius, whom Cosette loves, and finally confronts Javert. The splendid 2-CD Broadway cast album recording (one of several available) brings out all the flavor and passion in this extraordinary production.

Li'l Abner 🎵🎵🎵🎵

1990, Sony Music Special Products; from the Broadway production *Li'l Abner*, 1956.

Album Notes: *Music:* Gene de Paul; *Lyrics:* Johnny Mercer; *Orchestrations:* Philip J. Lang; *Musical Direction:* Lehman Engel; *Cast:* Peter Palmer (Li'l Abner), Edith Adams (Daisy Mae), Stubby Kaye (Marryin' Sam), Stanley Simmonds (Dr. Rasmussen T. Finsdale), Howard St. John (General Bullmoose), Carmen

Alvarez, Pat Creighton, Lillian D'Honau, Bonnie Evans, Hope Holiday, Dee Dee Wood (Wives), Marc Breaux, Ralph Linn, Jack Matthew, Robert McClure, George Reeder (Cronies); *Album Producer*: Goddard Lieberson.

Selections: 1 Overture (5:08) *Orchestra*; 2 A Typical Day (4:37)*Ensemble*; 3 If I Had My Druthers (3:32) *Peter Palmer, Marc Breaux, Ralph Linn, Jack Matthew, Robert McClure, George Reeder*; 4 Jubilation T. Cornpone (4:50) *Stubby Kaye*; 5 Rag Offen The Bush (4:03)*Ensemble*; 6 Namely You (2:59) *Edith Adams, Peter Palmer*; 7 Unnecessary Town (2:42) *Edith Adams, Peter Palmer*; 8 The Country's In The Very Best Of Hands (5:13) *Peter Palmer, Stubby Kaye*; 9 Oh, Happy Day (3:31) *Stanley Simmonds, Marc Breaux, Ralph Linn, George Reeder*; 10 I'm Past My Prime (2:42) *Edith Adams, Stubby Kaye*; 11 Love In A Home (3:14) *Peter Palmer, Edith Adams*; 12 Progress Is The Root Of All Evil (3:01) *Howard St. John*; 13 Put 'Em Back (1:44) *Carmen Alvarez, Pat Creighton, Lillian D' Honau, Bonnie Evans, Hope Holiday, Dee Dee Wood*; 14 The Matrimonial Stomp (2:58) *Stubby Kaye*.

Review: Al Capp's comic strip characters came to stage life when *Li'l Abner*, written by Gene De Paul and Johnny Mercer, opened on November 15, 1956. Taking a cue from the strip itself, in which Li'l Abner and Daisy Mae waited many years, to the great frustration of their fans, before getting married, the show also took a satirical look at politics in the rural Southern setting of Dogpatch, U.S.A. It exulted in the big annual occurrence, the frantic Sadie Hawkins' Day man-chasing race, when every eligible bachelorette can try to catch the man in her life. Starring Peter Palmer, looking for all intents and purposes like his comic strip alter ego, and Edith Adams as Daisy Mae, the musical enjoyed a long run of 693 performances. Its delirious score, marked by many humorous songs, yielded one of the theatre's big show-stopping numbers in "Jubilation T. Cornpone," in which Marryin' Sam (played by Stubby Kaye) extols the merits of Dogpatch's hero, an infamous and unglorious Southern general, better known for his incompetence than for his feats. With its cast virtually intact, the show was filmed in 1959.

The Lion King ♫♫♫▹

1994, Walt Disney Records; from the animated feature *The Lion King*, Walt Disney Pictures, 1994.

Album Notes: *Music*: Hans Zimmer; *Orchestrations*: Bruce Fowler, Nick Glennie-Smith; *Arrangements*: Hans Zimmer; *Music Editor*: Adam Smalley; *Songs*: Elton John, Tim Rice; *Vocal Arrangements*: Hans Zimmer, Lebo M., Andrae Crouch, Mark Mancina, Bobbi Page, Bruce Fowler; *Orchestra Conductor*: Nick Glennie-Smith; *Cast*: Carmen Twillie ("Circle Of Life" Solo Singer), Jason Weaver (Young Simba), Rowan Atkinson (Zazu), Laura Williams (Young Nala), Jeremy Irons (Scar), Whoopi Goldberg (Shenzi), Cheech Marin (Banzai), Jim Cummings (Ed), Nathan Lane (Timon), Ernie Sabella (Pumbaa), Sally Dworsky (Adult Nala), Kristle Edwards, Joseph Williams (Adult Simba); *Album Producers*: Hans Zimmer, Mark Mancina, Jay Rifkin, Chris Thomas; *Engineers*: Brett Newman, Alister Glyn, Tanja Somers.

Selections: 1 Circle Of Life (3:53) *Carmen Twillie*; 2 I Just Can't Wait To Be King (2:49) *Jason Weaver, Rowan Atkinson, Laura Williams*; 3 Be Prepared (3:38) *Jeremy Irons, Whoopi Goldberg, Cheech Marin, Jim Cummings*; 4 Hakuna Matata (3:31) *Nathan Lane, Ernie Sabella, Jason Weaver, Joseph Williams*; 5 Can You Feel The Love Tonight (2:56) *Joseph Williams, Sally Dworsky, Nathan Lane, Ernie Sabella, Kristle Edwards*; 6 This Land (2:53); 7 ...To Die For (4:16); 8 Under The Stars (3:42); 9 King Of Pride Rock (5:56); 10 Circle Of Life (4:49) *Elton John*; 11 I Just Can't Wait To Be King (3:35) *Elton John*; 12 Can You Feel The Love Tonight (End Title)(3:59) *Elton John*.

Review: Fast becoming a contemporary classic, *The Lion King* is steeped in the finest Walt Disney tradition. Great story, gorgeous animation, quality music and songs—*The Lion King* sports all of these hallmarks, and more.

Cleverly incorporating the rhythms and sounds of the African jungle into its score, the film features songs by pop music legend Elton John, and Academy Award winning lyricist Tim Rice. Among the familiar hit songs included on the soundtrack are "Hakuna Matata," "Circle of Life," "I Just Can't Wait to Be King," and "Can You Feel the Love Tonight." Special Elton John vocal versions of the last three songs are also heard here, and actor Nathan Lane is featured on "Hakuna Matata."

Quality is what has made Disney films and soundtracks special, and important. Undoubtedly, generations of film fans of all ages will continue to enjoy the music from *The Lion King* through this wonderful soundtrack recording.

Charles L. Granata

Little Me ♫♫♫▹

1993, RCA Victor; from the Broadway production *Little Me*, 1962.

Album Notes: *Music*: Cy Coleman; *Lyrics*: Carolyn Leigh; *Orchestrations*: Ralph Burns; *Musical Direction*: Charles Sanford; *Cast*: Sid Caesar (Noble Eggleston, Mr. Pinchley, Val du Val, Fred Poitrine, Otto Schnitzler, Prince Cherney), Virginia Martin (Belle), Nancy Andrews (Miss Poitrine), Swen Swenson George Musgrove, Joey Faye (Bernie Buchsbaum), Nancy Cushman (Mrs. Eggleston), Mickey Deems (Pinchley, Jr., Yulnick), Peter Turgeon (Patrick Dennis), Mort Marshall (Bennie Buchsbaum);

Album Producers: Hugo Peretti, Luigi Creatore, Joe Linhart; *Engineer*: Ernie Oelrich; *CD Producer*: Bill Rosenfield; *Engineer*: Jay Newland.

Selections: 1 Overture (2:21) Orchestra; 2 The Truth (2:16) *Nancy Andrews, Peter Turgeon*; 3 The Other Side Of The Tracks (1:30) *Virginia Martin*; 4 I Love You (1:41) *Sid Caesar, Virginia Martin*; 5 The Other Side Of The Tracks (reprise)(1:40) *Virginia Martin*; 6 Deep Down Inside (5:04) *Sid Caesar, Virginia Martin, Mickey Deems*; 7 Be A Performer! (2:02) *Joey Faye, Mort Marshall, Virginia Martin*; 8 Dimples (1:38) *Virginia Martin*; 9 Boom-Boom (2:10) *Sid Caesar*; 10 I've Got Your Number (2:52) *Swen Swenson*; 11 Real Live Girl (1:06) *Sid Caesar*; 12 Real Live Girl (3:49) Soldiers' Chorus; 13 Poor Little Hollywood Star (2:52) *Virginia Martin*; 14 Little Me (2:51) *Nancy Andrews, Virginia Martin*; 15 Goodbye (The Prince's Farewell)(3:15) *Sid Caesar, Mickey Deems*; 16 Here's To Us (2:41) *Nancy Andrews*.

Review: Television comedian Sid Caesar found a new lease on life when he appeared on Broadway in *Little Me*, a musical with a book by Neil Simon, one of his regular writers on the "Show of Shows," and a score by Cy Coleman and Carolyn Leigh. *Little Me* opened on November 17, 1962. Initially based on a novel by Patrick Dennis about the rags-to-riches tale of a voluptuous blonde from the skids of an Illinois town to a glamorous Southampton estate, the book became the occasion for Caesar to play no less than seven roles. All of his characters were involved in one way or another with the unlikely-named Belle Schlumpfert, from a snobbish student to a French soldier, from a movie director to a miserly old banker, and from a down-on-his-luck duke to an aspiring genius who wants to be an engineer and musical composer.

While the score didn't have too many memorable songs (much of the stage action being taken by Caesar's antics, who kept the show running for 257 performances), it had an ingratiating one in "Real Live Girl," a wistful lament performed by the star as a soldier who gives the heroine her full name of Belle Poitrine.

The Little Mermaid 𝄞𝄞𝄞𝄞ᵇ

1988, Walt Disney Records; from the animated feature *The Little Mermaid*, Walt Disney Pictures, 1988.

Album Notes: *Music*: Alan Menken; *Lyrics*: Howard Ashman; *Orchestrations*: Thomas Pasatieri; *Vocal Arrangements*: Robbie Merkin, Alan Menken; *Orchestra Conductor*: J.A.C. Redford; *Cast*: Rene Auberjonois (Louis), Jodi Benson (Ariel), Pat Carroll (Ursula), Patti Edwards (Flotsam, Jetsam), Buddy Hackett (Scuttle), Christopher Daniel Barnes (Eric), Jason Marin (Flounder), Kenneth Mars (Triton), Edie McClurg (Carlotta),

Will Ryan (Seahorse), Ben Wright (Grimsby), Samuel E. Wright (Sebastian); *Album Producers*: Alan Menken, Howard Ashman, Robert Kraft.

Selections: 1 Fathoms Below (1:41); 2 Main Titles (1:26); 3 Fanfare (:27); 4 Daughters Of Triton (:38); 5 Part Of Your World (3:13) *Jodi Benson*; 6 Under The Sea (3:12) *Jason Marin, Samuel E. Wright*; 7 Part Of Your World (reprise)(2:15) *Jodi Benson*; 8 Poor Unfortunate Souls (4:49) *Pat Carroll*; 9 Les Poissons (1:33); 10 Kiss The Girl (2:41) *Samuel E. Wright*; 11 Fireworks (:38) 12 Jig (1:32); 13 The Storm (3:18); 14 Destruction Of The Grotto (1:52); 15 Flotsam And Jetsam (1:22) *Patti Edwards*; 16 Tour Of The Kingdom (1:24); 17 Bedtime (1:20); 18 Wedding Announcement (2:16); 19 Eric To The Rescue (3:40); 20 Happy Ending (3:11).

Review: The sagging fortunes of the Disney studios were revived thanks to this clever animated feature adaptation of Hans-Christian Andersen's lovely tale, about the mermaid who sacrifices her voice to acquire legs instead of her tail in order to be near the prince with whom she has fallen in love. Where Andersen's tale ended tragically, however, the film adopted a more uplifting note, in keeping with the studio image solidly burnished since the days of its founding father, Walt Disney. Providing the score (and songs) were a couple of relative newcomers, Alan Menken and Howard Ashman. Their reggae-inflected "Under the Sea," performed by a singing crab and a shy flounder soon became a worldwide hit, further ensuring the popularity of the film. The CD brings it all back home, fun and all.

A Little Night Music

A Little Night Music 𝄞𝄞𝄞𝄞𝄞

1973, Columbia Records; from the Broadway production *A Little Night Music*, 1973.

Album Notes: *Music*: Stephen Sondheim; *Lyrics*: Stephen Sondheim; *Orchestrations*: Jonathan Tunick; *Musical Direction*: Harold Hastings; *Cast*: Glynis Johns (Desiree), Len Cariou (Fredrik Egerman), Hermione Gingold (Madame Armfeldt), Victoria Mallory (Anne), Mark Lambert (Henrik), D. Jamin-Bartlett (Petra), Laurence Guittard (Carl-Magnus Malcolm), Patricia Elliott (Charlotte), George Lee Andrews (Frid), Benjamin Rayson, Teri Ralston, Barbara Lang, Gene Varrone, Beth Fowler (Quintet); *Album Producer*: Goddard Lieberson.

Selections: 1 Overture and Night Waltz (3:39) *Benjamin Rayson, Teri Ralston, Barbara Lang, Gene Varrone, Beth Fowler*; 2 Now/Later/Soon (10:22) *Len Cariou, Mark Lambert, Victoria Mallory, Mark Lambert, Len Cariou*; 3 The Glamorous Life (3:48) *Judy Kahan, Glynis Johns, Hermione Gingold, Benjamin*

Rayson, *Teri Ralston, Barbara Lang, Gene Varrone, Beth Fowler*; 4 Remember (2:21) *Benjamin Rayson, Teri Ralston, Barbara Lang, Gene Varrone, Beth Fowler*; 5 You Must Meet My Wife (4:04) *Glynis Johns, Len Cariou*; 6 Liaisons (5:56) *Hermione Gingold*; 7 In Praise Of Women (3:19) *Laurence Guittard*; 8 Every Day A Little Death (2:24) *Patricia Elliott, Victoria Mallory*; 9 A Weekend In The Country (6:38) *Company*; 10 The Sun Won't Set (1:46); 11 It Would Have Been Wonderful (4:23) *Len Cariou, Laurence Guittard*; 12 Perpetual Anticipation (:53) *Teri Ralston, Barbara Lang, Beth Fowler*; 13 Send In The Clowns (3:24) *Glynis Johns*; 14 The Miller's Son (4:24) *D. Jamin-Bartlett*; 15 Finale: Send In The Clowns, Night Waltz (reprise)(3:06) *Glynis Johns, Len Cariou*.

Review: See entry below.

A Little Night Music 🎵🎵🎵

1996, Tring Records; from the London revival *A Little Night Music*, 1995.

Album Notes: *Music*: Stephen Sondheim; *Lyrics*: Stephen Sondheim; *Orchestrations*: Jonathan Tunick; *Musical Direction*: Jo Stewart; *Cast*: Judi Dench (Desiree), Laurence Guittard (Fredrik Egerman), Sian Phillips (Madame Armfeldt), Joanna Riding (Anne), Brendan O'Hea (Henrik), Issy Van Randwyck (Petra), Lambert Wilson (Carl-Magnus Malcolm), Patricia Hodge (Charlotte), Paul Kynman (Frid), Stephen Hanley (Mr. Lindquist), Ernestina Quarcoo (Mrs. Nordstrom), Di Botcher (Mrs. Andersen), Tim Goodwin (Mr. Erlanson), Morag McLaren (Mrs. Segstrom); *Album Producer*: Paddy Cunneen.

Selections: 1 Overture (1:22) *Stephen Hanley, Ernestina Quarcoo, Di Botcher, Tim Goodwin, Morag McLaren*; 2 Night Waltz (3:15) *The Company*; 3 Now (3:13) *Laurence Guittard*; 4 Later (2:33) *Brandan O'Hea*; 5 Soon (4:22) *Joanna Riding, Brendan O'Hea, Laurence Guittard*; 6 The Glamorous Life (5:54) *Laurence Guittard, Judi Dench, Sian Phillips, Stephen Hanley, Ernestina Quarcoo, Di Botcher, Tim Goodwin, Morag McLaren*; 7 Remember? (2:21) *Stephen Hanley, Ernestina Quarcoo, Di Botcher, Tim Goodwin, Morag McLaren*; 8 You Must Meet My Wife (4:43) *Laurence Guittard, Judi Dench*; 9 Liaisons (5:39) *Sian Phillips*; 10 In Praise Of Women/My Husband The Pig (4:36) *Lambert Wilson, Patricia Hodge*; 11 Every Day A Little Death (2:45) *Patricia Hodge, Joanna Riding*; 12 A Weekend In The Country (6:58) *Company*; 13 The Sun Won't Set (3:19) *Stephen Hanley, Ernestina Quarcoo, Di Botcher, Tim Goodwin, Morag McLaren*; 14 Night Waltz II (2:09) *Stephen Hanley, Ernestina Quarcoo, Di Botcher, Tim Goodwin, Morag McLaren*; 15 It Would Have Been Wonderful (4:05) *Lambert Wilson, Laurence Guittard*; 16 Perpetual Anticipation (1:25) *Ernestina Quarcoo, Di Botcher, Morag McLaren*; 17 Dinner Table (2:01) *The Company*; 18 Send In The Clowns (4:26) *Judi Dench*; 19

The Miller's Son (4:12) *Issy Van Randwyck*; 20 Send In The Clowns (reprise)(3:13) *Laurence Guittard, Judi Dench*; 21 Last Waltz (1:17).

Review: One of Stephen Sondheim's lightest and loveliest scores, *A Little Night Music* received a splendid recording in its original Broadway cast album. From its nearly unique vocal overture to its touchingly hopeful finale, the album is beautiful and pure pleasure. The score has an underlying rhythmic unity that adds a delightful dimension to the music. The cast is just about perfect and has not been equaled by any other production or on any other recording. Glynis Johns as Desiree Armfeldt, the ageing actress, is amazing. While not a singer, her version of the hit song "Send in the Clowns" is the most moving of any you are likely to hear. Len Cariou, as her former lover Fredrik Egerman, delineates the pride and vulnerability of this emotionally vacillating character with expert charm. Laurence Guittard, as Desiree's current lover Count Carl-Magnus, is manly and arrogant in equal degrees and Patricia Elliott as Charlotte, his wife, is delightful in her cunning and hope. The other actors are stunningly good in their parts and sing the music gloriously.

Though the score has received various readings, the 1995 recording is the first to challenge the 1973 Broadway original, at least as far as some of the performances are concerned. Judi Dench has arguably never given a greater performance of a musical role. While she too is not a singer, as the original star was not, she is as memorable in her way as Glynis Johns was in hers. Laurence Guittard here graduates to the role of Fredrik Egerman and steps into Len Cariou's shoes very effectively. Sian Phillips, as Madame Armfeldt, rivals the original Hermione Gingold with her world weary performance. The rest of the cast is not quite on this level, although everyone gives their very best. There is more music and dialogue on this album than on the Broadway recording, which also includes one song that was cut before the show opened on Broadway in 1973. If you can only afford one recording, try the Broadway version first. However, this album is wonderful and repays your attention. At the very least, get one of these versions of this lyrical, wonderful show.

Jerry J. Thomas

Lost in the Stars

Lost in the Stars 🎵🎵🎵🎵

1991, MCA Records; from the Broadway production *Lost in the Stars*, 1949.

Album Notes: *Music*: Kurt Weill; *Lyrics*: Maxwell Anderson; *Orchestrations*: Kurt Weill; *Musical Direction*: Maurice Levine; *Cast*: Todd Duncan (Rev. Stephen Kumalo), Julian Mayfield

(Absalom), Sheila Guyse (Linda), Inez Matthews (Irina), Herbert Coleman (Alex), Julian Mayfield, Guy Spaull; *Album Producer*: Jack Kapp; *CD Producer*: Ron O'Brien; *Engineer*: Doug Schwartz.

Selections: 1 The Hills Of Ixopo (3:20) *Frank Roane*; 2 Thousands Of Miles (2:54) *Todd Duncan*; 3 The Train To Johannesburg/Thousand Of Miles (reprise)/The Search (3:40) *Todd Duncan, Frank Roane*; 4 The Little Gray House (4:04) *Todd Duncan*; 5 Who'll Buy/Trouble Man (3:59) *Sheila Guyse, Inez Matthews*; 6 Murder In Parkwood/Fear (3:09) *Chorus*; 7 Lost In The Stars (3:32) *Todd Duncan*; 8 O Tixo, Tixo, Help Me (4:21) *Todd Duncan*; 9 Stay Well (3:30) *Inez Matthews*; 10 Cry, The Beloved Country (3:53) *Frank Roane*; 11 Big Mole/Chapel Scene (3:40) *Herbert Coleman*; 12 Bird Of Passage/Thousand Of Miles (reprise)(3:36) *Todd Duncan*.

Review: See entry below.

Lost in the Stars ♫♫♫♫

1993, MusicMasters Records; from the studio cast recording *Lost in the Stars*, 1993.

Album Notes: *Music*: Kurt Weill; *Lyrics*: Maxwell Anderson; *Orchestrations*: Kurt Weill; *Musical Direction*: Julius Rudel; *Cast*: Arthur Woodley (Rev. Stephen Kumalo), Reginald Pindell (Absalom), Carol Woods (Linda), Cynthia Clarey (Irina), Jamal Howard (Alex), Gregory Hopkins (Leader), Richard Vogt; *Album Producer*: John McClure; *Engineer*: Paul Goodman.

Selections: 1 The Hills Of Ixopo (4:16) *Gregory Hopkins*; 2 Thousands Of Miles (3:24) *Arthur Woodley*; 3 The Train To Johannesburg (3:28) *Gregory Hopkins*; 4 Little Tin God (1:29) *Reginald Pindell*; 5 The Search (5:24) *Gregory Hopkins*; 6 Intro: The Little Gray House (1:02); 7 Little Gray House (4:51) *Gregory Hopkins*; 8 Who'll Buy (3:06) *Carol Woods*; 9 Trouble Man (3:48) *Cynthia Clarey*; 10 Murder In Parkwood (1:28) *Chorus*; 11 Fear (2:59) *Chorus*; 12 Lost In The Stars (3:32) *Arthur Woodley*; 13 Entr'acte (3:28); 14 The Wild Justice (4:09) *Gregory Hopkins*; 15 O Tixo, Tixo, Help Me (5:13) *Arthur Woodley*; 16 Stay Well (5:07) *Cynthia Clarey*; 17 The Wild Justice (reprise)(:37) *Chorus*; 18 Cry, The Beloved Country (5:53) *Gregory Hopkins*; 19 Big Mole (2:09) *Jamal Howard*; 20 A Bird Of Passage (2:43) *Gregory Hopkins*; 21 Four O'Clock (2:13) *Gregory Hopkins*; 22 Finale (:57)*Ensemble*.

Review: Unfortunately for the world, *Lost in the Stars* was Kurt Weill's last work for the Broadway theater since he died during its too brief run. It is difficult to describe this amazing work set in South Africa. It tackles the very emotional issues of apartheid, murder, lust, unfulfilled relationships between parent and child and one's fundamental belief in God. Weill caught the various emotions and personal struggles of the characters in a score that combines the various styles of musical comedy, opera, cabaret, jazz and folk song into one heterogeneous style. The original 1949 cast recording catches this wild, uncompromising, glorious work in rather mediocre mono sound with too many cuts. However, the cast has an authority that is nearly unassailable. The wonderful Todd Duncan makes his last appearance in a musical and is terrific as is the rest of the ensemble cast, in a recording which is essential in any library of Broadway theater music.

While the 1993 recording does not equal all aspects of the original, it does surpass it in a few respects and holds its own nicely. To begin, it contains much more music than the original, which is a plus, since the additional material that is available makes it easier to understand the complex and difficult relations between these all-too-human characters. Julius Rudel has always had my respect as a wonderful musician and here his conducting is as fine as he has ever done. He is so good that it makes one long to hear him conduct the entire Kurt Weill canon. He has captured the wild highs and the blackest pits of despair that are built into this score by the composer. Arthur Woodley rivals Todd Duncan in the role of Stephen Kumalo, a peaceful man thrust into an extremely difficult situation. Cynthia Clarey is vivid as Irina and Carol Woods burns up the speakers as Linda. The other roles are cast judiciously and the recording, to make everything more attractive, is in full, clear stereo sound.

Jerry J. Thomas

Louisiana Purchase ♫♫♫♫♪

1996, DRG Records; from the Carnegie Hall concert presentation *Louisiana Purchase*, 1996.

Album Notes: *Music*: Irving Berlin; *Lyrics*: Irving Berlin; *Orchestrations*: Robert Russell Bennett, N. Lang Van Cleve; *Vocal Arrangements*: Hugh Martin, Ralph Blane; *Musical Direction*: Rob Fisher; *Cast*: Judy Blazer (Marina Van Linden), Rick Crom (Capt. Whitfield), Erin Dilly (Secretary), Taina Elg (Madame Yvonne Bordelaise), Merwin Goldsmith (Sam Liebowitz/Dean Joseph Manning), Debbie Gravitte (Beatrice), George S. Irving (Sen. Oliver P. Loganberry), Keith Byron Kirk (Alphonse), James Ludwig (Lee Davis), Michael McGrath (Jim Taylor), Michael Marotta (Col. Davis D. Davis, Jr.), Alet Oury (Emmy-Lou), John Wylie (Col. Davis D. Davis, Sr.), *New York Voices*: Peter Eldridge, Lauren Kinhan, Darmon Meader, Kim Nazarian; *Album Producer*: Hugh Fordin; *Engineer*: Cynthia Daniels.

Selections: 1 Overture (3:20) Orchestra; 2 Apologia (2:08) *Erin Dilly, Jamie Baer, Benjamin Brecher, Keith Byron Kirk, James Ludwig, Alet Oury*; 3 Sex Marches On (3:13) *Michael McGrath, Michael Marotta, John Wylie, Merwin Goldsmith, Rick Crom*; 4 Louisiana Purchase (5:27) *Debbie Gravitte*; 5 It's A Lovely Day Tomorrow (2:48) *Taina Elg*; 6 I'd Love To Be Shot From A Cannon With You (3:22) *Alet Oury*; 7 It'll Come To You (2:31) *Taina Elg, Debbie Gravitte*; 8 Louisiana Purchase (reprise)(1:21) *Debbie Gravitte*; 9 Outside Of That I Love You (3:12) *Michael McGrath, Judy Blazer*; 10 You're Lonely And I'm Lonely (2:07) *George S. Irving, Judy Blazer*; 11 Dance With Me (Tonight At The Mardi Gras)(2:07) New York Voices; 12 Finale Act 1 (1:58) Company; 13 Entr'acte (2:26) Orchestra; 14 Wild About You (3:12) *Debbie Gravitte*; 15 Latins know How (2:54) *Taina Elg*; 16 What Chance Have I With Love? (2:54) *George S. Irving*; 17 The Lord Done Fixed Up My Soul (4:17) *Debbie Gravitte*; 18 Fools Fall In Love/Old Man's Darling, Young Man's Slave? (Ballet)(7:07) *Michael McGrath, Judy Blazer*; 19 You Can't Brush Me Off (3:58) *James Ludwig, Alet Oury*; 20 Finale Ultimo (1:35) Company.

Review: A classic Irving Berlin musical from 1940, *Louisiana Purchase* starred Victor Moore as a naive Senator (he had previously played a Vice President in *Of Thee I Sing*, and an Ambassador in *Leave It To Me!)* who finds himself embroiled with the crooked doings of a big business president he is investigating. The score, brimming with catchy Berlin tunes, yielded one major hit in "It's a Lovely Day Tomorrow."

The cast album on DRG stems from a concert performance at Carnegie Hall. It presents a marvelous recreation of the complete score, with an all-star cast, in a great-sounding recording.

Love Me or Leave Me ♪♪♪♪

1993, Sony Legacy; from the screen musical *Love Me or Leave Me*, M-G-M, 1954.

Album Notes: *Musical Direction*: George Stoll; The M-G-M Studio Orchestra conducted by Percy Faith; *CD Producer*: Didier C. Deutsch; *Engineer*: Mark Wilder.

Selections: 1 Overture (1:34) Orchestra; 2 It All Depends On You (B.G. DeSylva/L. Brown/R. Henderson)(2:02) *Doris Day*; 3 You Made Me Love You (I Didn't Want To Do It)(J. Monaco/J. McCarthy)(2:29) *Doris Day*; 4 Stay On The Right Side, Sister (T. Koehler/R. Bloom)(1:00) *Doris Day*; 5 Everybody Loves My Baby (But My Baby Don't Love Nobody But Me)(J. Palmer/S. Williams)(1:11) *Doris Day*; 6 Mean To Me (R. Turk/F. Ahlert)(2:12) *Doris Day*; 7 Sam, The Old Accordion Man (W. Donaldson)(2:06) *Doris Day*; 8 Shaking The Blues Away (I.

Berlin)(3:30) *Doris Day*; 9 What Can I Say After I Say I'm Sorry (W. Donaldson/A. Lyman)/I Cried For You (A. Freed/G. Arnheim/A. Lyman)/My Blue Heaven (R. Whiting/W. Donaldson)/Ten Cents A Dance (R. Rodgers/ L. Hart)(4:13) *Doris Day*; 10 I'll Never Stop Loving You (S. Cahn/N. Brodszky)(1:55) *Doris Day*; 11 Never Look Back (C. Price)(2:26) *Doris Day*; 12 At Sundown (W. Donaldson)(2:14) *Doris Day*; 13 Love Me Or Leave Me (G. Kahn/W. Donaldson)(2:14) *Doris Day*; 14 Finale (:19) Orchestra; 15 I'll Never Stop Loving You (3:03) *Doris Day*; 16 Ten Cents A Dance (outtake)(1:57) *Doris Day*; 17 Love Me Or Leave Me (outtake)(3:11) *Doris Day*

Review: Doris Day had an uncharacteristically dramatic (singing) role in *Love Me Or Leave Me*, the film biography of 1930's torch singer Ruth Etting. In the film, she starred opposite James Cagney, portraying Marty "The Gimp" Snyder, a limping laundry operator who discovered Etting and became her agent and "protector." Doris Day performed many of the songs created by Etting, and had a hit with the song "I'll Never Stop Loving You," written expressly for her by Sammy Cahn and Nicholas Brodszky. A staple in the Columbia catalog for many years, the CD released in 1993 offers the soundtrack for the first time in stereo, with several bonus tracks, including rare studio pre-recordings.

Lovely to Look At ♪♪♪♪

1991, Sony Music Special Products; from the screen musical *Lovely to Look At*, M-G-M, 1952.

Album Notes: *Music*: Jerome Kern; *Lyrics*: Otto Harbach, Oscar Hammerstein II, Dorothy Fields, Jimmy McHugh, Bernard Dougall; *Orchestrations*: Leo Arnaud; *Vocal Arrangements*: Robert Tucker; The M-G-M Studio Chorus and Orchestra, conducted by Carmen Dragon; *Cast*: Howard Keel (Tony Naylor), Red Skelton (Al Marsh), Kathryn Grayson (Stephanie), Marge Champion (Clarisse), Gower Champion (Jerry Ralby), Ann Miller (Bubbles Cassidy); *CD Producer*: Dan Rivard; *Engineer*: Ken Robertson.

Selections: 1 Title Music (1:24) Orchestra; 2 Opening Night (:38) *Howard Keel, Red Skelton, Gower Champion*; 3 I'll Be Hard To Handle (3:26) *Ann Miller*; 4 LaFayette (2:26) *Howard Keel, Red Skelton, Gower Champion*; 5 Yesterdays (1:41) *Kathryn Grayson*; 6 I Won't Dance (3:39) *Marge & Gower Champion*; 7 You're Devastating (2:14) *Howard Keel, Kathryn Grayson*; 8 Lovely To Look At (2:14) *Howard Keel*; 9 Smoke Gets In Your Eyes (3:50) Orchestra; 10 The Most Exciting Night (1:36) *Howard Keel*; 11 Smoke Gets In Your Eyes (2:46) *Kathryn Grayson*; 12 The Irish Tenor (4:38) *Red Skelton*; 13 Fashion Show Sequence (12:53) *Red Skelton*; 14 The Touch Of Your

Hand (1:54) *Kathryn Grayson, Howard Keel*; 15 Finale: Lovely To Look At (1:12) Chorus.

Review: A remake of the 1933 stage musical *Roberta* (previously filmed in 1935, with Fred Astaire, Irene Dunne and Ginger Rogers in the cast), *Lovely to Look At* was a lame excuse to bring together M-G-M's ideal romantic musical couple, Howard Keel and Kathryn Grayson (they had previously starred in *Show Boat*). It also includes surefire box office comedian Red Skelton, and dancers extraordinaire Ann Miller and Marge and Gower Champion. Several songs from the original were dropped, but a couple of novelty numbers for Skelton were inserted, and of course the Kern/Harbach hits ("The Touch of Your Hand," "I'll Be Hard to Handle," "Yesterdays," and "Smoke Gets in Your Eyes") were retained, becoming the film's highlights. Directed with great savvy by Vincente Minnelli and Mervyn LeRoy, *Lovely to Look At* is a splash-dash of colors and songs that lives again in this soundtrack album recording.

See also: Roberta

Mack and Mabel ♫♫♫♫

1992, MCA Records; from the Broadway production *Mack and Mabel*, 1974.

Album Notes: *Music:* Jerry Herman; *Lyrics:* Jerry Herman; *Orchestrations:* Philip J. Lang; *Vocal Arrangements and Musical Direction:* Donald Pippin; *Cast:* Robert Preston (Mack Sennett), Bernadette Peters (Mabel Normand), Lisa Kirk (Lottie Ames), Stanley Simmonds (Eddie); *Album Producer:* Sid Feller; *CD Producer:* Ron O'Brien; *Engineer:* Erik Labson.

Selections: 1 Overture (4:37) Orchestra; 2 Movies Were Movies (2:42) *Robert Preston*; 3 Look What Happened To Mabel (3:35) *Bernadette Peters*; 4 Big Time (2:54) *Lisa Kirk*; 5 I Won't Send Roses (3:06) *Robert Preston*; 6 I Won't Send Roses (reprise)(2:07) *Bernadette Peters*; 7 I Wanna Make The World Laugh (2:05) *Robert Preston*; 8 Wherever He Ain't (3:01) *Bernadette Peters*; 9 Hundreds Of Girls (3:30) *Robert Preston*; 10 When Mabel Comes In The Room (5:29) *Stanley Simmonds*; 11 My Heart Leaps Up (2:17) *Robert Preston*; 12 Time Heals Everything (3:22) *Bernadette Peters*; 13 Tap Your Troubles Away (2:59) *Lisa Kirk*; 14 I Promise You A Happy Ending (2:50) *Robert Preston*.

Review: A failed musical its first time around (it only played 66 performances, following its opening on October 6, 1974), *Mack and Mabel* has become a cult show of sorts. Though it never was revived on Broadway, it received a concert version in London in 1988, and a full production in 1995, which fueled renewed interest in it.

The tragic love story between film director Mack Sennett and his star Mabel Normand, it was unfortunately saddled with an impossible book by Michael Stewart. The book tried desperately to make sense out of an affair that kept the two lovers apart more frequently than they were together, and ended on a negative note contrary to every tenet in the musical theatre.

On the bright side, however, was the score by Jerry Herman, a bittersweet collection of tunes in which the tone is given by the song "I Won't Send You Roses," in which Sennett lays out the rules by which his relationship with Normand will have to abide. There were, to be sure, lighter moods, notably in the opening number, "Movies Were Movies," in which Sennett extols the merits of movies when he was running the show. If anything, *Mack and Mabel* provided a unique opportunity for Robert Preston and Bernadette Peters to appear together in a show which, despite its shortcomings, magically comes to life in its bright cast recording.

Mame ♫♫♫♫

1966, Columbia Records; from the Broadway production *Mame*, 1966.

Album Notes: *Music:* Jerry Herman; *Lyrics:* Jerry Herman; *Orchestrations:* Philip J. Lang; *Vocal Arrangements and Musical Direction:* Donald Pippin; *Cast:* Angela Lansbury (Mame Dennis), Beatrice Arthur (Vera Charles), Jane Connell (Agnes Gooch), Willard Waterman (Dwight Babcock), Charles Braswell (Beauregard Burnside), Frankie Michaels (Patrick Dennis, age 10), Jerry Lanning (Patrick Dennis, 19 to 29), Sab Shimono (Ito); *Album Producer:* Goddard Lieberson.

Selections: 1 Overture (4:05) Orchestra; 2 St. Bridget (1:56) *Jane Connell, Frankie Michaels*; 3 It's Today (4:38) *Angela Lansbury*; 4 Open A New Window (3:46) *Angela Lansbury*; 5 The Man In The Moon (2:56) *Angela Lansbury, Beatrice Arthur*; 6 My Best Girl (3:26) *Frankie Michaels, Angela Lansbury*; 7 We Need A Little Christmas (3:04) *Angela Lansbury, Frankie Michaels, Jane Connell, Sab Shimono*; 8 Mame (6:17) *Charles Braswell*; 9 The Letter (3:00) *Frankie Michaels, Jerry Lanning*; 10 Bosom Buddies (4:10) *Angela Lansbury, Beatrice Arthur*; 11 Gooch's Song (3:28) *Jane Connell*; 12 That's How Young I Feel (2:14) *Angela Lansbury*; 13 If He Walked Into My Life (3:53) *Angela Lansbury*; 14 Finale (2:41) *Angela Lansbury*.

Review: Patrick Dennis' fond ruminations about the extravagant Auntie Mame, already the source for a 1954 play, became the occasion for another effervescent score by Jerry Herman, following the one he had written two years before for *Hello, Dolly!*. With Angela Lansbury at the peak of her stage career in a portrayal that still resonates with crackling energy in the original cast recording, *Mame* was a bustling, exciting musical which enjoyed tremendous longevity, following its opening of May 24, 1966.

In the book by Jerome Lawrence and Robert E. Lee, Mame, a socialite whose excessive lifestyle seems to be one party after another, becomes the guardian of young Dennis, her nephew, whom she encourages to live in a permissive way to best appreciate what life is all about. When the Depression hits and she finds herself without any means of support, Mame bravely seeks a job. Unfortunately, she fails at every attempt to secure a permanent one until she sweeps a Southern gentleman off his feet, Beauregard Burnside, whom she marries. When Beau dies accidentally, Mame, as indomitable as ever, manages to meddle into Dennis' affair with a scatterbrained, snobbish girl, and sets him up with her own assistant, wondering all along what she would do if Dennis walked into her life again.

Brilliantly directed by Gene Saks, with Bea Arthur regularly trading bitchy comments with Mame, her bosom buddy, the musical was a delight from beginning to end. Jerry Herman's score, which included "Open a New Window," "We Need a Little Christmas," "If He Walked Into My Life," and the exuberant "It's Today" and "That's How Young I Feel," is probably the best he's ever written.

Man of La Mancha 🎻🎻🎻🎻🎻

1965, MCA Records; from the Broadway production *Man of La Mancha*, 1965.

Album Notes: *Music*: Mitch Leigh; *Lyrics*: Joe Darion; *Orchestrations*: Music Makers Inc.; *Musical Direction*: Neil Warner; *Cast*: Richard Kiley (Cervantes/Don Quixote); Irving Jacobson (Sancho), Joan Diener (Aldonza), Ray Middleton (The Innkeeper), Robert Rounseville (The Padre), Mimi Turque (Antonia), Eleanore Knapp (The Housekeeper), Gino Conforti (The Barber), Harry Theyard (Muleteer).

Selections: 1 Overture (3:45) *Orchestra*; 2 Man Of La Mancha (I, Don Quixote)(2:31) *Richard Kiley, Irving Jacobson*; 3 It's All The Same (2:56) *Joan Diener*; 4 Dulcinea (2:44) *Richard Kiley*; 5 I'm Only Thinking Of Him (2:58) *Mimi Turque, Robert Rounseville, Eleanore Knapp*; 6 I Really Like Him (2:18) *Irving Jacobson, Joan Diener*; 7 What Do You Want Of Me? (2:10) *Joan Diener*; 8 The Barber's Song (Golden Helmet)(2:54) *Gino Conforti, Richard Kiley, Irving Jacobson*; 9 To Each His Dulcinea (To Every Man His Dream)(1:48) *Robert Rounseville*; 10 The Impossible Dream (The Quest)(2:20) *Richard Kiley*; 11 Little Bird, Little Bird (11:53) *Harry Theyard*; 12 The Dubbing (Knight Of The Woeful Countenance)(1:57) *Ray Middleton, Richard Kiley, Joan Diener, Irving Jacobson*; 13 The Abduction (1:30) *Harry*

Theyard; 14 Aldonza (3:30) *Joan Diener, Richard Kiley*; 15 A Little Gossip (1:43) *Irving Jacobson*; 16 Dulcinea (reprise)/The Impossible Dream (reprise)/Man Of La Mancha (reprise)/The Psalm/Finale (The Impossible Dream)(7:44) *Joan Diener, Richard Kiley, Irving Jacobson, Robert Rounseville*.

Review: Miguel de Cervantes' Don Quixote became the unlikely singing hero of another sensational 1960s musical when *Man of La Mancha* opened on November 22, 1965. It starred Richard Kiley as the gloomy Don, Irving Jacobson as his faithful manservant, Sancho, and Joan Diener as the servant girl the Don mistakes for a fair lady in distress. In a brilliant theatrical tour-de-force, Kiley first portrayed Cervantes, thrown in jail by the Inquisition for an offense against the Church, offering as his defense a reading of a novel he has recently completed about the exploits of a wandering knight. At the court's request, Cervantes then becomes the Don and enacts the story, with the other prisoners becoming the various characters Don Quixote encounters.

High among the tunes that became hits in the score by Mitch Leigh and Joe Darion is "The Impossible Dream," also known as "The Quest," in which Don Quixote mentions all the things it takes to become an errand knight.

The show, which won the Tony for Best Musical, had a run of 2,328 performances. The cast album is a must in any collection.

Mary Poppins 🎻🎻🎻🎻

1990, Disneyland Records; from the screen musical *Mary Poppins*, Walt Disney Pictures, 1964.

Album Notes: *Music*: Richard M. Sherman, Robert B. Sherman; *Lyrics*: Richard M. Sherman, Robert B. Sherman; *Cast*: Julie Andrews (Mary Poppins), Dick Van Dyke (Bert), Glynis Johns (Winifred Banks), David Tomlinson (George Banks), Karen Dotrice (Jane Banks), Matthew Garber (Michael Banks), Ed Wynn (Uncle Albert), Elsa Lanchester (Katie Nanna), Hermione Baddeley (Ellen), Reta Shaw (Mrs. Brill).

Selections: 1 Main Title (4:11) *Orchestra*; 2 The Perfect Nanny (1:39) *Karen Dotrice, Matthew Garber*; 3 Sister Suffragette (1:47) *Glynis Johns*; 4 The Life I Lead (1:58) *David Tomlinson*; 5 A Spoonful Of Sugar (3:05) *Julie Andrews*; 6 Pavement Artist (1:52) *Dick Van Dyke*; 7 Jolly Holiday (2:14) *Julie Andrews, Dick Van Dyke*; 8 Supercalifragilisticexpialidocious (2:08) *Julie Andrews, Dick Van Dyke, Pearlies*; 9 Stay Awake (1:49) *Julie Andrews*; 10 I Love To Laugh (2:47) *Ed Wynn, Julie Andrews, Dick Van Dyke*; 11 A British Bank (2:02) *David Tomlinson*; 12 Feed The Birds (3:54) *Julie Andrews*; 13 Fidelity Fiduciary Bank (3:52) *Dick Van Dyke, David Tomlinson*; 14 Chim-Chim-Cheree

(2:52) *Julie Andrews, Dick Van Dyke, Karen Dotrice, Matthew Garber*; 15 Step In Time (2:07) *Dick Van Dyke*; 16 A Man Has Dreams (4:25) *David Tomlinson, Dick Van Dyke*; 17 Let's Go Fly A Kite (1:53) *David Tomlinson, Dick Van Dyke*.

Review: Julie Andrews, who had been dismissed in favor of Audrey Hepburn when *My Fair Lady* was made into a movie, had a sweet revenge when she appeared that same year in *Mary Poppins*, a delightful musical fantasy made by Walt Disney. In it, she made her screen debut and won the Oscar for Best Actress. Set in Victorian England at the turn of the century, the film, which combined live action and animated characters, told about Mary Poppins, the perfect nanny, whose impromptu arrival at the house of proper banker George Banks results in utter chaos. The chaos begins when she takes the children, Jane and Michael, on a merry trip to an enchanted land where the denizens are cartoon characters, and everyone seems to know her and her friend Bert, a chimney sweeper. When Jane and Michael report to their father what they have experienced, he immediately denounces the nanny for her wild flights of fancy which are a disservice to the education of his children.

Spearheaded by several enjoyable tunes written by Richard M. Sherman and Robert B. Sherman (including "A Spoonful of Sugar," "Supercalifragilisticexpialidocious," and "Chim-Chim Cheree"), and with Julie Andrews delightfully impish as Mary Poppins, the film became one of the studio's all-time big hits. The soundtrack album recording, while in need of complete remastering, provides total enjoyment.

Meet Me in St. Louis ♪♪♪

1990, DRG Records; from the Broadway production *Meet Me in St. Louis*, 1990.

Album Notes: *Music*: Hugh Martin, Ralph Blane; *Lyrics*: Hugh Martin, Ralph Blane; *Orchestrations*: Michael Gibson; *Vocal Arrangements*: Hugh Martin, Bruce Pomahac; *Musical Direction*: Milton Rosenstock; *Cast*: George Hearn (Alonzo Smith), Milo O'Shea (Grandpa Prophater), Charlotte Moore (Mrs. Smith), Betty Garrett (Katie), Courtney Peldon (Tootie), Donna Kane (Esther), Rachel Graham (Agnes), Juliet Lambert (Rose), Gregg Whitney (Douglas Moore), Michael O'Steen (Lon Smith), Jason Workman (John Truitt); *Album Producers*: Michael Gibson, Louis Burke; *Engineer*: Paul Goodman.

Selections: 1 Overture/Meet Me In St. Louis (3:58) *Milo O'Shea, Courtney Peldon*; 2 The Boy Next Door (3:56) *Donna Kane*; 3 Be Anything But A Girl (2:53) *Milo O'Shea, Courtney Peldon, Rachel Graham*; 4 Skip To My Lou (trad.)(2:11) *Juliet Lambert, Donna Kane, Michael O'Steen, Gregg Whitney, Jason Workman, Peter Reardon*; 5 Under The Bamboo Tree (B. Cole) (1:47) *Donna Kane, Courtney Peldon*; 6 Banjos (4:55) *Michael O'Steen*; 7 Ghosties And Ghoulies And Things That Go Bump In The Night/ Halloween Ballet (5:09) *Betty Garrett, Courtney Peldon*; 8 Wasn't It Fun? (1:46) *George Hearn, Charlotte Moore*; 9 The Trolley Song (3:42) *Donna Kane*; 10 Entr'acte/Ice (3:11) *Juliet Lambert*; 11 Raving Beauty (2:28) *Peter Reardon, Gregg Whitney, Juliet Lambert*; 12 A Touch Of The Irish (3:39) *Betty Garrett, Donna Kane, Juliet Lambert*; 13 You Are For Loving (3:15) *Jason Workman, Donna Kane*; 14 A Day In New York (3:41) *George Hearn*; 15 Irish Jig (The Ball)(3:22) *Milo O'Shea*; 16 Diamonds In The Starlight (2:13) *Jason Workman*; 17 Have Yourself A Merry Little Christmas (2:11) *Donna Kane*; 18 Paging Mr. Sousa (3:34) *George Hearn*; 19 Finale (1:26) Company.

Review: In a rare trend reversal, the M-G-M 1944 filmed musical hit, *Meet Me in St. Louis* became a Broadway stage show when it opened on November 2, 1989. That it took more than 45 years to achieve this feat says something about the problem created by such a decision. Indeed, despite an excellent cast led by George Hearn, Milo O'Shea, Charlotte Moore and Betty Garrett, all reliable performers, the show stayed around for only 253 performances, not a very long run by today's standards.

There were multiple reasons for that, but the one that loomed heavy above the entire production was the fact that a musical so magically captured on film could only appear halfway interesting on the stage. Despite Donna Kane's valiant efforts to give a fetching portrayal as Esther, her performance couldn't erase the memory of Judy Garland in the film. In truth, everything conspired to cast the musical into a negative light, by enhancing the stage limitations compared with the movies, and by drawing the unavoidable parallel with the film's performances.

However, the cast album is still of interest, though a clear second choice after the film soundtrack... when the latter becomes finally available from Rhino in that label's continuing restoration of the great musical scores from the M-G-M films.

Merrily We Roll Along ♪♪♪

1992, RCA Victor; from the Broadway production *Merrily We Roll Along*, 1981.

Album Notes: *Music*: Stephen Sondheim; *Lyrics*: Stephen Sondheim; *Orchestrations*: Jonathan Tunick; *Musical Direction*: Paul Gemignani; *Cast*: Jim Walton (Franklin Shepard), Ann Morrison (Mary Flynn), Lonny Price (Charley Kringas), Jason Alexander (Joe Josephson), Donna Marie Elia (Terry), David Loud (Ted), Sally Klein (Beth), Marianna Allen (Girl Auditioning); *Album/CD Producer*: Thomas Z. Shepard; *Engineer*: Paul Goodman.

Selections: 1 Overture (3:52) Orchestra; 2 The Hills Of Tomorrow/Merrily We Roll Along (1980)/Rich And Happy (10:21) *Jim Walton*; 3 Merrily We Roll Along (1979-75)/Old Friends/Like It Was (3:57) *Ann Morrison, Lonny Price*; 4 Merrily We Roll Along (1974-73)/Franklin Shepard, Inc. (5:32) *Lonny Price*; 5 Old Friends (4:36) *Jim Walton, Ann Morrison, Lonny Price*; 6 Not A Day Goes By (2:20) *Jim Walton*; 7 Now You Know (4:09) *Ann Morrison*; 8 It's A Hit! (4:35) *Jason Alexander, Jim Walton, Ann Morrison, Lonny Price*; 9 Merrily We Roll Along (1964-1962)/Good Thing Going (5:40) *Donna Marie Elio, Lonny Price, Jim Walton*; 10 Merrily We Roll Along (1961-1960)/Bobby And Jackie And Jack (5:09), *Lonny Price, Sally Klein, Jim Walton, David Loud*; 11 Not A Day Goes By (2:19) *Jim Walton, Ann Morrison*; 12 Opening Doors (6:52) *Jim Walton, Ann Morrison, Lonny Price, Jason Alexander, Marianna Allen, Sally Klein*; 13 Our Time (4:20) *Jim Walton, Lonny Price, Ann Morrison*; 14 The Hills Of Tomorrow (2:16) Company.

Review: An ambitious failure on Broadway, this time-runs-backwards musical about 25 years of changing relationships among a group of high-school friends endures in the repertoire because of its Stephen Sondheim score, which seems to grow in stature with every revival. "Not a Day Goes By" is as beautiful a song as Sondheim—or anyone else—has written for Broadway. CD listeners should take Sondheim up on his suggestion and try programming this recording in reverse ("chronological") order, noting the development of his musical ideas. Fans of the "Seinfeld" TV series will also want to note Jason Alexander's Broadway musical debut here, playing a Broadway producer.

Marc Kirkeby

Miss Saigon 🎵🎵♭

1991, Geffen Records; from the Broadway production *Miss Saigon*, 1991.

Album Notes: *Music*: Claude-Michel Schoenberg; *Lyrics*: Richard Maltby, Jr., Alain Boublil; *Orchestrations*: William D. Brohn; *Musical Direction*: Dale Rieling; *Cast*: Lea Salonga (Kim), Jonathan Pryce (The Engineer), Isay Alvarez (Gigi), Monique Wilson (Mimi), Jenine Desiderio (Yvette), Dominique Nobles (Yvonne), Simon Bowman (Chris), Peter Polycarpou (John), Keith Burns (Thuy), Claire Moore (Ellen), Mark Bond (Shultz); *Album Producers*: Alain Boublil, Claude-Michel Schonberg; *Engineer*: David Hunt; *Assistant Engineer*: Jonathan Morton.

Selections: CD 1: 1 Overture (3:09) Orchestra; 2 The Heat Is On In Saigon (4:15) *Jonathan Pryce, Monique Wilson, Isay Alvarez,* Lea Salonga, Dominique Nobles, Jenine Desiderio; 3 The Movie In My Mind (4:42) *Isay Alvarez, Lea Salonga*; 4 The Dance (2:44) *Simon Bowman, Lea Salonga, Jonathan Pryce*; 5 Why God Why? (4:52) *Simon Bowman*; 6 This Money's Yours (3:00) *Simon Bowman, Lea Salonga*; 7 Sun And Moon (2:42) *Lea Salonga, Simon Bowman*; 8 The Telephone Song (1:40) *Simon Bowman, Peter Polycarpou*; 9 The Deal (:57) *Simon Bowman, Jonathan Pryce*; 10 The Ceremony (Dju Vui Vai)(3:08) *Lea Salonga, Simon Bowman*; 11 What's This I Find (2:17) *Keith Burns, Lea Salonga, Simon Bowman*; 12 The Last Night Of The World (4:20) *Lea Salonga, Simon Bowman*; 13 The Morning Of The Dragon (2:15) Male Ensemble; 14 I Still Believe (4:44) *Lea Salonga, Claire Moore*; 15 This Is The Hour (6:49) *Jonathan Pryce, Lea Salonga, Keith Burns*.

CD 2: 1 If You Want To Die In Bed (3:41) *Jonathan Pryce*; 2 Let Me See His Western Nose (3:12) *Jonathan Pryce*; 3 I'd Give My Life For You (5:18) *Lea Salonga*; 4 Bui-Doi (4:05) *Peter Polycarpou*; 5 The Revelation (3:25) *Peter Polycarpou, Simon Bowman, Claire Moore*; 6 What A Waste (4:30) *Jonathan Pryce*; 7 Please (2:48) *Simon Bowman, Lea Salonga*; 8 The Fall Of Saigon (4:54) *Peter Polycarpou, Simon Bowman, Lea Salonga*; 9 Room 317 (3:29) *Lea Salonga, Claire Moore*; 10 Her Or Me (3:24) *Claire Moore*; 11 The Confrontation (4:05) *Claire Moore, Simon Bowman, Peter Polycarpou*; 12 The American Dream (6:02) *Jonathan Pryce*; 13 The Sacred Bird/Finale (5:55) *Lea Salonga, Simon Bowman*.

Review: If Claude-Michel Schonberg and Alain Boublil hoped to repeat with *Miss Saigon* the artistic success they had enjoyed with *Les Miserables*, they failed on at least one count: a tear-jerker set in Vietnam on the eve of the Fall of Saigon, their new show brought theatre-as-spectacle to a new high, while proving itself emotionally very empty.

Wall-to-wall instrumental bridges and tedious recitatives can hardly mask the paucity in melodic ideas in a score that only ignites on rare occasions. When the score is good (as in the unquestionable showstoppers, "The Heat Is On in Saigon," "The Morning of the Dragon," or "The American Dream"), it is very good. However, these moments are unfortunately too rare in a show that needs to rely on gimmicks like a much-touted-about helicopter landing on a roof to spellbind its audiences.

In this original London cast recording, Lea Salonga and Jonathan Pryce, who reprised their respective roles on Broadway, are excellent, she as a modern-day Madame Butterfly, whose love for a G.I. turns sour with the disastrous end of the conflict, he as an enterprising conman who, like Bloody Mary in *South Pacific*, makes himself necessary to the G.I.s lost in a foreign land. As Chris, Simon Bowman is vocally fine, but the limitations in his role do not enable him to be more than a casual presence.

In an early radio commercial for the Broadway edition of the show, a "member" of the audience recalled how he had never cried in real life, yet *Miss Saigon* had brought him to tears. Indeed…

The Most Happy Fella ♫♫♫♫

1991, Sony Broadway; from the Broadway production *The Most Happy Fella*, 1956.

Album Notes: *Music*: Frank Loesser; *Lyrics*: Frank Loesser; *Orchestrations*: Don Walker; *Orchestral and Choral Direction*: Herbert Greene; *Cast*: Robert Weede (Tony), Jo Sullivan (Rosabella/Amy), Art Lund (Joe), Susan Johnson (Cleo), Shorty Long (Herman), Mona Paulee (Marie), Lee Cass (Cashier), Betsy Bridge (Gladys), John Henson (Jake), Alan Gilbert (Clem), Roy Lazarus (Al), Rico Froehlich (Pasquale), Arthur Rubin (Giuseppe); *Album Producer*: Goddard Lieberson; *CD Producer*: Thomas Z. Shepard; *Engineer*: Kevin Boutote.

Selections: CD 1: 1 Overture (2:27) Orchestra; 2 "Thank you, good night" (:54) *Lee Cass*; 3 Ooh! My Feet! (2:02) *Susan Johnson*; 4 Mock Ballet (:49) *Lee Cass, Jo Sullivan, Susan Johnson*; 5 "Cleo, I don't care if he fires me!" (1:51) *Jo Sullivan, Susan Johnson*; 6 "My dear Rosabella" (3:52) *Jo Sullivan, Susan Johnson*; 7 Somebody, Somewhere (2:28) *Jo Sullivan*; 8 "Oh, there's the postman"/The Most Happy Fella (3:21) *Lee Cass, Robert Weede*; 9 "Oh, hello, Marie" (:53) *Robert Weede, Mona Paulee, Betsy Bridge*; 10 "What do you really known about her?" (2:19) *Mona Paulee, Robert Weede*; 11 Standing On The Corner (2:45) *Shorty Long, John Henson, Alan Gilbert, Roy Lazarus*; 12 "All Right. Break it up, you guys" (1:03) *Shorty Long, John Henson, Alan Gilbert, Roy Lazarus*; 13 Joey, Joey, Joey (3:58) *Art Lund*; 14 "Soon you gonna leave me, Joe" (1:34) *Robert Weede, Art Lund*; 15 Rosabella (2:46) *Robert Weede*; 16 Abbondanza (1:43) *Rico Froehlich, Arthur Rubin, John Henson*; 17 "This is Tony's barn" (1:09) *Meri Miller, John Sharpe, Robert Weede*; 18 "Alfonso, Fiorello, Mattilda"/"Plenty bambini" (2:17) *Robert Weede, Russell Goodwin, Robert Weede*; 19 Sposalizio (3:53) *Arthur Rubin, John Henson, Rico Froelich*; 20 "Well, here we are"(1:32) *Lee Cass, Jo Sullivan, Art Lund*; 21 Benvenuta (3:39) *Rico Froehlich, John Henson, Arthur Rubin*; 22 Such Friendly Faces (2:23) *Jo Sullivan*; 23 "Well, thank you very much" (2:03) *Jo Sullivan, Art Lund*; 24 "No Home, No Job" (:36) *Jo Sullivan*; 25 "Step back everybody" (3:15) *Keuth Kaldenberg, Jo Sullivan, Robert Weede, Mona Paulee, Art Lund, Russell Goodwin, Shorty Long*; 26 Don't Cry (3:52) *Art Lund, Jo Sullivan*.

> "I think it would be great if in all the reviews of films and television shows the music had some mention…. The music was great or it wasn't great but there was music there, somebody must have written it, so, hey, let's see a name."
>
> **Jay Chattaway**
> *president of the Society of Composers and Lyricists (The Hollywood Reporter, 1-15-97)*

CD 2: 1 Prelude/Fresno Beauties/Cold And Dead (4:56) *Art Lund, Jo Sullivan*; 2 "Ma che specie di medico e?" (:42) *Robert Weede, Keith Kaldenberg*; 3 "Take medicine" (2:14) *Keith Kaldenberg*; 4 Happy To Make Your Acquaintance (4:56) *Robert Weede, Jo Sullivan, Susan Johnson*; 5 "Oh, Cleo!" (1:56) *Mona Paulee, Susan Johnson*; 6 Big D (4:55) *Short Long, Susan Johnson*; 7 How Beautiful The Days (3:22) *Robert Weede, Jo Sullivan, Mona Paulee, Art Lund*; 8 Young People (3:10) *Mona Paulee, Robert Weede*; 9 Warm All Over (4:35) *Jo Sullivan*; 10 "Hey, Herman" (:32) *Rico Froehlich, Shorty Long, Susan Johnson*; 11 I Like Ev'rybody (1:27) *Susan Johnson, Shorty Long*; 12 The Vineyards In July (1:11) Orchestra; 13 I Love Him/Like A Woman Loves A Man (3:21) *Jo Sullivan, Susan Johnson, Robert Weede*; 14 My Heart Is So Full Of You (2:58) *Robert Weede, Jo Sullivan*; 15 "Hey, paesan"/Hoedown (1:45) *Robert Weede*; 16 "Rosabella! What's-a-matter?" (1:57) *Robert Weede, Susan Johnson, Keith Kaldenberg, Jo Sullivan*; 17 Mamma, Mamma (3:12) *Robert Weede*; 18 Prelude Act III/Abbondanza (reprise)(1:48) *Rico Froehlich, Arthur Rubin, John Henson*; 19 "Hey, what are you doin' fellas?" (:56) *Shorty Long*; 20 I Like Ev'rybody (reprise)(3:39) *Susan Johnson, Shorty Long*; 21 Song Of A Summer Night (2:38) *Keith Kaldenberg*; 22 "Carissima!" (1:45) *Robert Weede, Jo Sullivan*; 23 Please Let Me Tell You (1:54) *Jo Sullivan*; 24 "Ma che c'e?" (1:12) *Rico Froehlich, Robert Weede*; 25 "So you're finally gettin' out of town" (4:24) *Roy Lazarus, Alan Gilbert, John Henson, Art Lund, Susan Johnson, Ralph Farnworth*; 26 She Ain't Got No Place To Go (3:47) *Robert Weede*; 27 "Herman" (1:10) *Susan Johnson, Shorty Long*; 28 Finale (4:29) *Robert Weede, Jo Sullivan*.

Review: Frank Loesser had one of his earliest stage successes with *The Most Happy Fella*, a smart adaptation of the 1924 play

"They Knew What They Wanted," about a mail-order bride deceived into believing that her intended is a handsome young man when in reality he turns out to be an ageing Napa Valley vineyard owner of Italian descent. Starring Robert Weede as Tony, the vintner who is shy around women, Jo Sullivan as Rosabella, who answers Tony's marriage offer, and Art Lund as Joey, Tony's foreman, whose picture Tony has sent to Rosabella instead of his own, *The Most Happy Fella* was more a folk opera than a musical. It contained a profuse score that included more than 30 musical numbers, including arias, duets, and recitatives. The writing style, however, was pure Broadway, with tunes like "Standing on the Corner," "Big D," "My Heart Is So Full of You," "Abbondanza," "Warm All Over," and "Joey, Joey, Joey" harking back to the best musical theatre traditions.

The recording, initially an unusual 3-LP set (the first of its kind for Columbia Records), now on 2 CDs, features the entire score, with vibrant performances by all the principals.

The Music Man

The Music Man ♪♪♪♪

1992, Angel Records; from the Broadway production *The Music Man*, 1958.

Album Notes: *Music*: Meredith Willson; *Lyrics*: Meredith Willson; *Orchestrations*: Don Walker; *Vocal Arrangements and Musical Direction*: Herbert Green; *Cast*: Robert Preston (Harold Hill), Barbara Cook (Marian), Pert Kelton (Mrs. Paroo), Eddie Hodges (Winthrop), Adnia Rice (Alma Hix), Peggy Mondo (Ethel Toffelmier), Elaine Swann (Maud Dunlop), Helen Raymond (Eulalie MacKecknie Shinn), Martha Flynn (Mrs. Squires), Iggie Wolfington (Marcellus Washburn), Al Shea, Wayne Ward, Vern Reedbills, Bill Spangenberg (The Buffalo Bills), Russell Goodwin, Hal Norman, Robert Howard, James Gannon, Robert Lenn, Vernon Lusby, Robert Evans (Travelling Salesmen); *Album Producer*: Dick Jones; *CD Engineer*: Robert Norberg.

Selections: 1 Overture/Rock Island (5:27) *Russell Goodwin, Hal Norman, Robert Howard, James Gannon, Robert Lenn, Vernon Lusby, Robert Evans*; 2 Iowa Stubborn (1:57) Ensemble; 3 Ya Got Trouble (3:46) *Robert Preston*; 4 Piano Lesson (1:56) *Barbara Cook, Pert Kelton*; 5 Goodnight My Someone (2:43) *Barbara Cook*; 6 Seventy-Six Trombones (3:00) *Robert Preston*; 7 Sincere (1:38) *The Buffalo Bills*; 8 The Sadder-But-Wiser Girl For Me (1:40) *Robert Preston*; 9 Pick-A-Little, Talk-A-Little (1:55) *Adnia Rice, Peggy Mondo, Elaine Swann, Helen Raymond, Martha Flynn, Robert Preston*; 10 Goodnight Ladies/ Marian The Librarian (2:42) *Robert Preston, The Buffalo Bills*; 11 My White Knight (3:01) *Barbara Cook*; 12 Wells Fargo Wagon

(2:11) *Eddie Hodges*; 13 It's You (1:23) *The Buffalo Bills*; 14 Shipoopi (2:10) *Iggie Wolfington*; 15 Lida Rose/Will I Ever Tell You? (4:13) *The Buffalo Bills, Barbara Cook*; 16 Gary, Indiana (1:24) *Eddie Hodges*; 17 Till There Was You (2:44) *Barbara Cook, Robert Preston*; 18 Finale (2:16) *Robert Preston, Barbara Cook*.

Review: Is Robert Preston's spellbinding con man the finest male performance in this history of the musical theater? Has a more beautiful female voice than Barbara Cook's ever been heard on a Broadway stage? The evidence is here for your consideration, in Meredith Willson's breakthrough hit about his small-town Iowa childhood just after the turn of the century. What may at first seem to be Broadway's corniest classic also has remarkable sophistication, as Willson's score takes the listener on a tour of American musical styles of the period, moving from lovely melodies to songs based almost entirely on rhythm effects and percussion. Americana at its finest.

Marc Kirkeby

The Music Man ♪♪♪♪

1962, Warner Bros. Records; from the screen version *The Music Man*, Warner Bros., 1962.

Album Notes: *Music*: Meredith Willson; *Lyrics*: Meredith Willson; *Orchestrations*: Ray Heindorf, Frank Comstock; *The Warner Bros. Studio Chorus and Orchestra*: Ray Heindorf; *Cast*: Robert Preston (Harold Hill), Shirley Jones (Marian), Pert Kelton (Mrs. Paroo), Ronnie Howard (Winthrop), Hermione Gingold (Eulalie MacKecknie Shinn), Mary Wickes (Mrs. Squires), Buddy Hackett (Marcellus Washburn), Jacey Squirs, Olin Britt, Ewart Dunlap, Oliver Hix (The Buffalo Bills); *CD Engineer*: Lee Herschberg.

Selections: 1 Overture/Rock Island/Iowa Stubborn (7:08) Orchestra, Ensemble; 2 Ya Got Trouble (3:55) *Robert Preston*; 3 Piano Lesson/ If You Don't Mind My Saying So (1:54) *Shirley Jones, Pert Kelton*; 4 Goodnight My Someone (2:43) *Shirley Jones*; 5 Ya Got Trouble/Seventy-Six Trombones (2:45) *Robert Preston*; 6 Sincere (1:38) *The Buffalo Bills*; 7 The Sadder-But-Wiser Girl For Me (1:58) *Robert Preston*; 8 Pick-A-Little, Talk-A-Little (1:58) *Hermione Gingold, The Biddys*; 9 Marian The Librarian (2:37) *Robert Preston*; 10 Being In Love (3:45) *Shirley Jones*; 11 Gary Indiana (1:12) *Robert Preston*; 12 The Wells Fargo Wagon (2:34) Ensemble; 13 Lida Rose/Will I Ever Tell You (4:11) *Shirley Jones, The Buffalo Bills*; 14 Gary, Indiana (:55) *Ronnie Howard*; 15 Shipoopi (2:19) *Buddy Hackett*; 16 Till There Was You (2:57) *Shirley Jones*; 17 Goodnight My Someone/Seventy-Six Trombones (4:04) *Robert Preston, Barbara Cook*.

Review: With Robert Preston reprising his Broadway role as Harold Hill, and Shirley Jones (a more recognizable box-office name at the time) replacing Barbara Cook, *The Music Man* splashed across the big screen in a relatively faithful adaptation of the stage hit by Meredith Willson. Instead of painted settings, audiences were treated to the great outdoors in a small town (filmed on a studio backlot); and with Hermione Gingold, Paul Ford (as River City's mayor), and Buddy Hackett adding the luster of their performances to the storyline, this screen version provided filmgoers who might not have had a chance to see the Broadway show a great opportunity to enjoy it in all its glory. Adding an extra sheen to the score, Ray Heindorf's orchestrations urned the music into a boisterous, exhilarating sonic experience, faithfully captured in the recording. As in the Broadway cast album, Preston is the show.

My Fair Lady

My Fair Lady ♪♪♪♪

1994, Sony Legacy; from the Broadway production *My Fair Lady*, 1956.

Album Notes: *Music*: Frederick Loewe; *Lyrics*: Alan Jay Lerner; *Orchestrations*: Robert Russell Bennett; *Musical Direction*: Franz Allers; *Cast*: Rex Harrison (Henry Higgins), Julie Andrews (Eliza Dolittle), Stanley Holloway (Alfred P. Doolittle), Robert Coote (Colonel Pickering), Gordon Dilworth, Rod McLennan, Philippa Bevans (Mrs. Pearce), John Michael King (Freddy Eynsford-Hill); *Album Producer*: Goddard Lieberson; *Engineers*: Fred Plaut, Bud Graham; *CD Producer*: Didier C. Deutsch; *Engineer*: Darcy Proper.

Selections: 1 Overture (2:59) Orchestra; 2 Why Can't The English? (2:40) *Rex Harrison*; 3 Wouldn't It Be Loverly (3:57) *Julie Andrews*; 4 With A Little Bit Of Luck (4:07) *Stanley Holloway, Gordon Dilworth, Rod McLennan*; 5 I'm An Ordinary Man (4:38) *Rex Harrison*; 6 Just You Wait (2:42) *Julie Andrews*; 7 The Rain In Spain (2:40) *Rex Harrison, Julie Andrews, Robert Coote*; 8 I Could Have Danced All Night (3:30) *Julie Andrews, Philippa Bevans*; 9 Ascot Gavotte (3:14)Ensemble; 10 On The Street Where You Live (2:57) *John Michael King*; 11 You Did It (4:21) *Rex Harrison, Robert Coote, Philippa Bevans*; 12 Show Me (2:11) *Julie Andrews, John Michael King*; 13 Get Me To The Church On Time (2:42) *Stanley Holloway*; 14 A Hymn To Him (3:29) *Rex Harrison*; 15 Without You (2:02) *Julie Andrews*; 16 I've Grown Accustomed To Her Face (5:16) *Rex Harrison*; 17 A Post-Recording Conversation (4:10) *Goddard Lieberson, Rex Harrison, Julie Andrews, Franz Allers, Alan Jay Lerner*.

Review: See entry below.

My Fair Lady ♪♪♪♪

1994, Sony Classical; from the screen version *My Fair Lady*, Warner Bros., 1964.

Album Notes: *Music*: Frederick Loewe; *Lyrics*: Alan Jay Lerner; *Orchestrations*: Alexander Courage, Robert Franklyn, Al Woodbury; *Vocal Arrangements*: Robert Tucker; The Warner Bros. Studio Chorus and Orchestra, conducted by Andre Previn; *Cast*: Rex Harrison (Henry Higgins), Audrey Hepburn (Eliza Dolittle), Stanley Holloway (Alfred P. Doolittle), Wilfrid Hyde-White (Colonel Pickering), Gordon Dilworth (Harry), Rod McLennan (Jamie), Mona Washbourne (Mrs. Pearce), Jeremy Brett (Freddy Eynsford-Hill); *Album Producer*: Goddard Lieberson; *Engineers*: Fred Plaut, Bud Graham; *CD Producer*: Didier C. Deutsch; *Engineer*: Darcy Proper.

Selections: 1 Overture (3:24) Orchestra; 2 Why Can't The English? (3:02) *Rex Harrison*; 3 Wouldn't It Be Loverly (4:20) *Marni Nixon*; 4 The Flower Market (1:55) Orchestra; 5 I'm An Ordinary Man (4:40) *Rex Harrison*; 6 With A Little Bit Of Luck (3:35) *Stanley Holloway*; 7 Just You Wait (2:57) *Marni Nixon*; 8 Servants' Chorus (1:15)Ensemble; 9 The Rain In Spain (2:13) *Rex Harrison, Marni Nixon, Wilfrid Hyde-White*; 10 I Could Have Danced All Night (3:30) *Marni Nixon, Mona Washbourne*; 11 Ascot Gavotte (3:07)Ensemble; 12 Ascot Gavotte (reprise)(2:10)Ensemble; 13 On The Street Where You Live (1:58) *Bill Shirley*; 14 Intermission (1:01) Orchestra; 15 The Transylvanian March (1:29) Orchestra; 16 The Embassy Waltz (1:57) Orchestra; 17 You Did It (4:30) *Rex Harrison, Wilfrid Hyde-White, Mona Washbourne*; 18 Just You Wait (reprise) (1:30) *Marni Nixon*; 19 On The Street Where You Live (reprise)(1:14) *Bill Shirley*; 20 Show Me (2:10) *Marni Nixon, Bill Shirley*; 21 The Flower Market (2:50) *Marni Nixon*; 22 Get Me To The Church On Time (5:28) *Stanley Holloway*; 23 A Hymn To Him (3:35) *Rex Harrison*; 24 Without You (2:31) *Marni Nixon, Rex Harrison*; 25 I've Grown Accustomed To Her Face (5:55) *Rex Harrison*; 26 End Titles (2:05) Orchestra; 27 Exit Music (1:12) Orchestra.

Review: Considered by many to be one of the perfect Broadway musicals, the original Broadway cast recording might therefore be considered the perfect cast album. Every performer from Rex Harrison, Julie Andrews and Stanley Halloway to the smallest supporting player is superb and right in every detail. This exactness must be credited to the director, Moss Hart, as well as the splendid lyrics and music of Alan Jay Lerner and Frederick Loewe. If any cast album is essential, this is it and it is in bright spanking refurbished monaural sound. As a side note, there is a recording made two years later of the original London cast which includes essentially the same cast as the 1956 version. The performances have become more free and less tight than the original, but not in any way lazy or careless. For those who must have stereo, the London cast is fine and no one will feel cheated. However, the 1956 Broadway recording is just that much fresher and about as definitive a recording of a Broadway show score as an album can get.

The soundtrack of the film version proves that there is still life in the fair lady yet. The various dubious casting and dubbing issues aside, this is a big, bold old-fashioned film of a big Broadway show. With the exception of Audrey Hepburn replacing Julie Andrews, the male principals remain the same as the original 1956 Broadway and 1958 London cast recordings. The passage of eight years has taken its toll on the voices, which are beginning to fray around the edges and the performances are much looser and more studied than either of the previous recordings. Hepburn is dubbed, in part, by Marni Nixon and they both do an admirable job. However, it is easy to tell where one voice ends and the other one begins. Included on this release are previously extended dance music episodes, as well as unreleased tracks. The sound quality has been excellently refurbished and the album sounds better than it ever has. All in all, this is a most enjoyable recording of this legendary score.

Jerry J. Thomas

My One and Only 🎞🎞🎞🎞🎞

1989, Atlantic Records; from the Broadway production *My One and Only*, 1983.

Album Notes: *Music*: George Gerhswin; *Lyrics*: Ira Gershwin; *Orchestrations*: Michael Gibson; *Dance Arrangements*: Wally Harper, Peter Larson; *Vocal Arrangements and Musical Direction*: Jack Lee; *Cast*: Tommy Tune (Capt. Billy Buck Chandler), Twiggy (Edith Herbert), Jill Cook (Reporter), Charles "Honi" Coles (Mr. Magix), Bruce McGill (Prince Nicolai Tchatchavadze), Roscoe Lee Browne (Rev. J.D. Montgomery), Denny Dillon (Mickey), Will Blankenship, Carl Nicholas, Adam Petroski, Casper Roos (Ritz Quartette), David Jackson, Ken Leigh Rogers, Ronald Dennis (The New Rhythm Boys); *Album Producers*: Ahmet Ertegun, Wally Harper; *Engineer*: Fred Miller; *CD Producer*: Didier C. Deutsch; *Engineer*: Stephen Benben.

Selections: 1 Overture: I Can't Be Bothered Now/Blah, Blah, Blah (8:50) *Tommy Tune, David Jackson, Ken Leigh Rogers, Ronald Dennis*; 2 Boy Wanted/Soon (4:42) *Twiggy, Jill Cook, Tommy Tune*; 3 Sweet 'n Low Down (2:35) *Charles "Honi" Coles, Tommy Tune, Twiggy*; 4 He Loves And She Loves (5:00) *Twiggy, Tommy Tune*; 5 'S Wonderful (5:48) *Tommy Tune, Twiggy*; 6 Strike Up The Band (2:28) *Tommy Tune*; 7 Entr'acte/In The Swim (2:50) *Orchestra, Female Chorus*; 8 Nice Work If You Can Get It (3:33) *Twiggy*; 9 My One And Only (3:37) *Tommy Tune, Charles "Honi" Coles*; 10 Little Jazz Bird (3:43) *Twiggy, Tommy Tune*; 11 Funny Face (2:16) *Denny Dillon, Bruce McGill*; 12 My One And Only (reprise)(2:15) *Tommy Tune*; 13 Kickin' The Clouds Away (3:20) *Roscoe Lee Browne*; 14 How Long Has This Been Going On? (4:18) *Tommy Tune, Twiggy*.

Review: Initially intended as a straight revival of *Funny Face*, the 1927 musical by George and Ira Gershwin, *My One and Only* evolved into a significantly different musical with little relationship to its original, except for some of the songs that were retained. The new book, devised by Peter Stone, deals with a young aviator and the aquacade star with whom he falls in love: she is already a success, having crossed the English Channel, and he has ambitions of beating Lindbergh in flying over the Atlantic, which he does of course, after surmounting tremendous odds, winning his girl in the process.

The "blithely charming" show starred Tommy Tune and Twiggy in performances that kept luring audiences to it long after the show premiered on May 1, 1983, closing after 757 performances in a considerably longer run than its model.

While it retained many songs from the *Funny Face* score (including "He Loves and She Loves," "'S Wonderful," "Funny Face," and the title song), it also interpolated many other familiar tunes from the Gershwin body of works, among them "I Can't Be Bothered Now," "Soon," "Strike Up The Band," "Nice Work If You Can Get It," "Little Jazz Bird," and "How Long Has This Been Going On?," all delivered with the appropriate period zest by a pleasantly twangy Twiggy and a charmingly self-effaced Tommy Tune, in performances that make the cast album recording an absolute delight.

Nine 🎞🎞🎞🎞🎞

1982, Columbia Records; from the Broadway production *Nine*, 1982.

Album Notes: *Music*: Maury Yeston; *Lyrics*: Maury Yeston; *Orchestrations*: Jonathan Tunick; *Choral Compositions and Musical Continuity*: Maury Yeston; *Musical Direction*: Wally Harper; *Cast*: Raul Julia (Guido Contini), Karen Akers (Luisa), Anita Morris (Carla), Shelly Burch (Claudia), Taina Elg (Guido's Mother), Liliane Montevecchi (Liliane LaFleur), Kim Criswell (Francesca), Kathi Moss (Saraghina), Camille Saviola (Mama Maddalena), Stephanie Cotsirilos (Stephanie Necrophorus), Cameron Johann (Guido at an early age); *Album Producer*: Mike Berniker; *Engineer*: Mike Moran; *Assistant Engineers*: Joe Lopes, Ronnie Olson.

Selections: 1 Overture delle Donne/Spa Music (3:03)*Orchestra*; 2 Not Since Chaplin (3:03) *Company*; 3 Guido's Song (3:29) *Raul Julia*; 4 The Germans At The Spa (4:23) *Camille Saviola*; 5 My Husband Makes Movies (3:53) *Karen Akers*; 6 A Call From

The Vatican (3:30) *Anita Morris, Raul Julia*; 7 Only With You (3:26) *Raul Julia*; 8 Folies Bergeres (5:39) *Liliane Montevecchi, Stephanie Cotsirilos*; 9 Nine (3:21) *Taina Elg*; 10 Be Italian (Ti voglio bene)(5:06) *Kathi Moss*; 11 The Bells Of St. Sebastian (4:33) *Raul Julia*; 12 Unusual Way (3:31) *Shelly Burch*; 13 The Grand Canal (3:48) *Raul Julia*; 14 Simple (3:13) *Anita Morris*; 15 Be On Your Own (4:01) *Karen Akers*; 16 I Can't Make This Movie (4:01) *Raul Julia*; 17 Waltz From Nine/Getting Tall/ Reprises (6:37) *Cameron Johann, Raul Julia*.

Review: A brilliant musical based on Federico Fellini's *8½*, about a celebrated Italian filmmaker with a creative block, resting at a Venetian spa where he is haunted by memories from his youth, his strict Catholic upbringing, and the many women in his life, *Nine* is a dazzling display of music and songs by newcomer Maury Yeston. One of the last great American musicals (before the proliferation of British works that crowded Broadway in the 1990s), *Nine* is an extraordinary work as vibrant as it is original, as exciting as it is imaginative.

In the course of the evening, Guido Contini, the film director, struggles with his memories, while trying to find a way out of the creative impasse that prevents him from starting his new film. As the action progresses, in reality as much as in his mind, he has to deal with a disintegrating marriage, former lovers and current protégés, and his producer, in a show that features only one adult man in an otherwise all-female cast.

There are many superb touches in the score which ranges from electrifying production numbers ("Folies Bergeres," "The Grand Canal"), to highly charged emotional cries of despair ("Be on Your Own"), to sexy siren songs ("A Call from the Vatican"), to evocations of a past that had a strong influence on the present ("The Bells of St. Sebastian").

The original cast album, while unfortunately incomplete (longer excerpts from "Folies Bergere" and "Grand Canal" can be found in the cassette release), is a sensational reflection of this outstanding musical.

No, No, Nanette ♪♪♪♪

1971, Columbia Records; from the Broadway revival *No, No, Nanette*, 1971.

Album Notes: *Music:* Vincent Youmans; *Lyrics:* Otto Harbach, Irving Caesar; *Orchestrations:* Ralph Burns; *Vocal Arrangements and Musical Direction:* Buster Davis; *Cast:* Ruby Keeler (Sue Smith), Jack Gilford (Jimmy Smith), Bobby Van (Billy Early), Helen Gallagher (Lucille Early), Susan Watson (Nanette), Patsy Kelly (Pauline), Roger Rathburn (Tom Trainer), Loni Zoe Ackerman (Betty from Boston), Pat Lysinger (Winnie from Washington), K.C. Townsend (Flora from Frisco); *Album Producer:* Thomas Z. Shepard.

Selections: 1 Overture (3:55)*Orchestra*; 2 Too Many Rings Around Rosie (4:12) *Helen Gallagher*; 3 I've Confessed To The Breeze (3:13) *Susan Watson, Roger Rathburn*; 4 Call Of The Sea (1:51) *Bobby Van*; 5 I Want To Be Happy (6:46) *Jack Gilford, Susan Watson, Ruby Keeler*; 6 You Can Dance With Any Girl (3:12) *Helen Gallagher, Bobby Van*; 7 No, No, Nanette (4:23) *Susan Watson, Roger Rathburn, Patsy Kelly*; 8 Tea For Two (8:19) *Susan Watson, Roger Rathburn*; 9 I Want To Be Happy (reprise)(1:35) *Jack Gilford, K.C. Townsend, Loni Zoe Ackerman, Pat Lysinger*; 10 Telephone Girlie (1:58) *Bobby Van, Loni Zoe Ackerman, K.C. Townsend, Pat Lysinger*; 11 Finaletto Act II (3:21)*Company*; 12 "Where-Has-My-Hubby-Gone" Blues (5:36) *Helen Gallagher*; 13 Waiting For You (2:10) *Susan Watson, Roger Rathburn*; 14 Take A Little One-Step/Finale (2:45) *Ruby Keeler*.

Review: One of the classic musical comedies of the 1920s, *No, No, Nanette* burst out again on the Broadway scene 46 years after its creation. It is as fresh and exciting as ever, thanks largely to the fact that it was staged by the genial Busby Berkeley, one of the movies' most inventive directors. Starring Berkeley's favorite dancer, Ruby Keeler—as sprightly at sixty something as she was when she pranced on the screen in *42nd Street*—and a cast of seasoned theater and film performers (Bobby Van, Helen Gallagher, Jack Gilford, Susan Watson, Patsy Kelly), the Vincent Youmans original never looked so stunning, so enjoyable, so modern.

In its original presentation, in 1925, *No, No, Nanette* was an enormous success, both here and abroad; its popularity fueled by its two biggest hit songs, "Tea for Two" and "I Want to Be Happy." Undoubtedly, it was the most popular musical of the 1920s, a frothy entertainment with great songs and skimpy story line, the kind so amusingly spoofed by Sandy Wilson in *The Boy Friend*. It spawned two movie versions, in 1930 and 1940, and an offshoot, *Tea for Two*, starring Doris Day and Gordon MacRae in 1950.

Its return to Broadway in 1971, its first since 1925, was preceded by the kind of hoopla that usually accompanies the newest productions, not a revival. But the names of Berkeley and Keeler were the catch, and riding on a sudden wave of nostalgia, it opened to great fanfare and rhapsodic reviews on January 19, 1971.

Based on an obscure 1919 play, the book deals with a Bible publisher and philanderer, Jimmy Smith, who has been entertaining three attractive ladies in three different cities; his long-suffering wife, Sue; their schoolgirl ward, Nanette; their friends, Lucille and Billy; and their overworked housemaid, Pauline. When they all converge to Atlantic City for a weekend of rest in the Smith household, utter comic chaos ensues.

Inconsequential as the story might have been, what ignites the musical is its score by Vincent Youmans, Otto Harbach and Irving Caesar, propelled by Busby Berkeley's show-stopping dance routines (the sight of Ruby Keeler, merrily tapping her time away surrounded by an impressive lineup of handsome chorus boys, alone was worth the cost of a dozen tickets). It proved a winning combination, as *No, No, Nanette* collected four Tony Awards, and enjoyed a run of 861 performances, nearly three times longer than its original run of 321 performances in 1925.

No Strings ♫♫♫

1993, Angel Records; from the Broadway production *No Strings*, 1962.

Album Notes: *Music*: Richard Rodgers; *Lyrics*: Richard Rodgers; *Orchestrations*: Ralph Burns; *Dance Arrangements and Musical Direction*: Peter Matz; *Cast*: Diahann Carroll (Barbara Woodruff), Richard Kiley (David Jordan), Mitchell Gregg (Louis de Pourtal), Noelle Adam (Jeanette Valmy), Polly Rowles (Mollie Plummer), Don Chastain (Mike Robinson), Bernice Massi (Comfort O'Connell), Alvin Epstein (Luc Delbert), Ann Hodges (Gabrielle Bertin); *CD Engineer*: Robert Norberg.

Selections: 1 The Sweetest Sounds (5:00) *Diahann Carroll, Richard Kiley*; 2 How Sad (2:32) *Richard Kiley*; 3 Loads Of Love (3:18) *Diahann Carroll*; 4 The Man Who Has Everything (4:11) *Mitchell Gregg*; 5 Be My Host (2:38) *Richard Kiley, Bernice Massi, Don Chastain, Alvin Epstein, Ann Hodges*; 6 La La La (2:31) *Noelle Adam, Alvin Epstein*; 7 You Don't Tell Me (1:51) *Diahann Carroll*; 8 Love Makes The World Go (2:37) *Polly Rowles, Bernice Massi*; 9 Nobody Told Me (4:00) *Richard Kiley, Diahann Carroll*; 10 Look No Further (3:15) *Richard Kiley, Diahann Carroll*; 11 Maine (3:00) *Richard Kiley, Diahann Carroll*; 12 An Orthodox Fool (3:07) *Diahann Carroll*; 13 Eager Beaver (4:25) *Bernice Massi, Don Chastain*; 14 No Strings (4:24) *Richard Kiley, Don Chastain*; 15 Finale: The Sweetest Sounds (reprise)(1:29) *Richard Kiley, Diahann Carroll*.

Review: For his first effort sans Oscar Hammerstein II (who had died shortly after the opening of *The Sound of Music* two years earlier), Richard Rodgers decided to write both the music and lyrics for *No Strings*. Perhaps not so surprisingly, his words faintly echoed those of his former collaborator, revealing a sensitive side to Rodgers' creativity few had suspected he had.

The show itself, with a book by Samuel Taylor, deals with a topic that was still somewhat taboo at the time—an interracial love affair. Perhaps to deflate any possible criticism, it happens in France, where such things were apparently tolerated, and it involves two sophisticated American expatriates, she a glamorous fashion model (played by Diahann Carroll), he a writer (portrayed by Richard Kiley); also, though it is not stated specifically as such, it does not have a happy ending.

While not a great success along the lines of *South Pacific* or *The Sound of Music*, *No Strings* enjoyed a long run on Broadway thanks in part to the three Tonys it earned for Diahann Carroll, Richard Rodgers and director/choreographer Joe Layton.

Of Thee I Sing ♫♫♫♫

1993, Angel Records; from the Broadway revival *Of Thee I Sing*, 1952.

Album Notes: *Music*: George Gershwin; *Lyrics*: Ira Gershwin; *Orchestrations*: Don Walker; *Musical Direction*: Maurice Levine; *Cast*: Jack Carson (John P. Wintergreen), Paul Hartman (Alexander Throttlebottom), Betty Oakes (Betty Turner), Lenore Lonergan (Diana Devereaux), Jonathan Lucas (Sam Jenkins), Joan Mann (Emily Benson), Florenz Ames (French Ambassador).

Selections: 1 Prelude/Wintergreen For President (1:49) Company; 2 Who Is The Lucky Girl To Be? (:52) *Jack Carson, Paul Hartman*; 3 The Dimple On My Knee (:59)Company; 4 Because Because (1:41)Company; 5 Finaletto: Never Was There A Girl So Fair/Some Girls Can Bake A Pie (4:55)Company; 6 Love Is Sweeping The Country (2:24) *Jack Carson*; 7 Of Thee I Sing (2:03) *Jack Carson*; 8 Finaletto: Supreme Court Judges/Here's A Kiss For Cinderella/I Was The Most Beautiful Blossom/Some Girls Can Bake A Pie (reprise)/Of Thee I Sing (reprise) (6:17) Company; 9 Hello, Good Morning (1:57) *Jonathan Lucas, Joan Mann*; 10 Mine (1:45) *Jack Carson, Betty Oakes*; 11 Who Cares? (1:42) *Jack Carson, Betty Oakes*; 12 Finaletto: Garcon, s'il vous plait/The Illegitimate Daughter/Who Cares? (reprise)/Because, Because (reprise)(6:17)Company; 13 The Senate Roll Call/Impeachment (2:51)Company; 14 Finaletto: Jilted/I'm About To Be A Mother (4:21) *Lenore Lonergan, Betty Oakes*; 15 Trumpeter Blow Your Horn (2:05)Company; 16 Finale (:39) Company.

Review: Political satire is not a genre that succeeds very well in this country, but a happy exception is the 1931 Gershwin musical, *Of Thee I Sing*, which takes sharp aim at the quadri annual spectacle of political conventions, the Presidency, congressional shenanigans, the Supreme Court, motherhood and apple pies, everything in fact that makes life worth living. Not only was the show a huge success at the time (it ran for 441 performances, quite a record), it also won the Pulitzer Prize, the first time ever the prestigious award was bestowed on a musical.

Revived in 1952, however, it failed miserably, and closed after a scant 72 performances. Although, happily again, a cast album recording was made at the time, thereby preserving for posterity some of the most stinging and amusing songs ever created by the Gershwin brothers.

The musical is built around a rather absurd plot — the presidential campaign of one John P. Wintergreen and his running mate Alexander Throttlebottom, who easily win the presidency, only to find themselves assailed from all sides: it seems that, during the campaign, Wintergreen's advisers had staged a beauty contest, promising that the winner would marry the candidate if he were elected. The lucky contestant is Diana Devereaux who, when Wintergreen is elected comes to claim her prize. The new president, however, has already married one of his assistants, Mary Turner, thereby setting the stage for a nasty scandal and an international conflict when it is revealed that Diana Devereaux is "an illegitimate daughter of an illegitimate son of an illegitimate nephew of Napoleon." Needless to say, when the Supreme Court is asked to arbitrate, everything gets resolved.

What made the show so enjoyable was the breezy score fashioned by George and Ira Gershwin, which contains several notable tunes — "Because, Because," "Love Is Sweeping the Country," "Of Thee I Sing," and "Mine," among them. The 1952 cast also featured some personable comedians, including Jack Carson, Paul Hartman, Betty Oakes and Lenore Lonergan in the principal roles. The cast recording always was a classic; its release on CD only confirms its status.

Oh, Kay! ♪♪♪♪

1995, Elektra Records; from the studio cast recording *Oh, Kay!*, 1995.

Album Notes: *Music*: George Gershwin; *Lyrics*: Ira Gershwin; *Orchestrations*: Russell Warner; *Vocal Arrangements*: Kevin Cole; The Orchestra of St. Luke's, conducted by Eric Stern; *Cast*: Robert Westenberg (The Duke), Patrick Cassidy (Larry Potter), Adam Arkin (Shorty McGee), Liz Larsen (Philippa Ruxton), Stacey A. Logan (Dolly Ruxton), Dawn Upshaw (Kay), Kurt Ollmann (Jimmy Winter), Susan Lucci (Constance Appleton), Fritz Weaver (Judge Appleton); *Album Producers*: Tommy Krasker, John McClure; *Engineer*: Tom Lazarus; *Assistant Engineers*: Carl Glanville, Greg Pinto, Richard Clarke.

Selections: 1 Overture (6:45)Orchestra; 2 The Moon Is On The Sea (1:20)Ensemble; 3 When Our Ship Comes Sailing In (2:57) *Patrick Cassidy, Robert Westenberg, Adam Arkin*; 4 Don't Ask (2:20) *Patrick Cassidy, Liz Larsen, Stacey A. Logan*; 5 Someone To Watch Over Me (2:51) *Dawn Upshaw*; 6 The Woman's Touch (2:25)Female Ensemble; 7 Dear Little Girl (2:40) *Kurt Ollmann*;

8 Maybe (3:15) *Dawn Upshaw, Kurt Ollmann*; 9 Clap Yo' Hands (4:16) *Patrick Cassidy*; 10 Do, Do, Do (3:06) *Kurt Ollmann, Dawn Upshaw*; 11 Finale Act 1 (5:14) *Adam Arkin, Liz Larsen, Stacey A. Logan, Dawn Upshaw, Kurt Ollmann, Susan Lucci, Fritz Weaver*; 12 Entr'acte (4:22)Orchestra; 13 Bride And Groom (2:31)Ensemble; 14 Ain't It Romantic? (3:59) *Dawn Upshaw, Adam Arkin, Kurt Ollmann*; 15 Fidgety Feet (3:13) *Patrick Cassidy, Liz Larsen*; 16 Heaven On Earth (2:09) *Kurt Ollmann*; 17 Finaletto Act II, Scene 1 (4:14) *Kurt Ollmann, Liz Larsen, Stacey A. Logan, Fritz Weaver, Dawn Upshaw*; 18 Dance Specialty (1:30)Orchestra; 19 Oh, Kay! (3:06) *Dawn Upshaw*; 20 Finale Ultimo (2:01)Company.

Review: A somewhat inconsequential plot, and a great score, are the hallmarks in *Oh, Kay!*, a 1926 musical by George and Ira Gershwin, which centers around the dilemma faced by a young playboy, Jimmy Winter, whose impending marriage is threatened when he finds out he is in love with another woman, Kay Denham. Kay is the sister of a titled Englishman-turned-bootlegger, who has stashed away his stock of liquor in Winter's Long Island manse. Around this slight suggestion of a story, the Gershwins wrote a collection of tunes that yielded such standards as "Someone To Watch Over Me," "Dear Little Girl," "Do, Do, Do," "Maybe," and "Clap Yo' Hands."

The studio cast recording on Elektra, starring the wonderful Dawn Upshaw, is part of a series of Gershwin musicals, well worth looking into and enjoying to the hilt.

Oklahoma!

Oklahoma! ♪♪♪♪

1993, MCA Records; from the Broadway production *Oklahoma!*, 1943.

Album Notes: *Music*: Richard Rodgers; *Lyrics*: Oscar Hammerstein II; *Orchestrations*: Robert Russell Bennett; *Vocal Arrangements and Musical Direction*: Jay Blackton; *Cast*: Alfred Drake (Curly), Joan Roberts (Laurey), Howard da Silva (Jud Fry), Celeste Holm (Ado Annie Carnes), Lee Dixon (Will Parker), Joseph Buloff (Ali Hakim), Betty Garde (Aunt Eller), Ralph Riggs (Andrew Carnes); *Album Producer*: Jack Kapp; *CD Producer*: Ron O'Brien; *Engineers*: Paul Elmore, Robert Stoughton.

Selections: 1 Overture (3:19)Orchestra; 2 Oh, What A Beautiful Mornin' (2:32) *Alfred Drake*; 3 The Surrey With The Fringe On Top (3:08) *Alfred Drake*; 4 Kansas City (2:48) *Lee Dixon*; 5 I Cain't Say No (3:03) *Celeste Holm*; 6 Many A New Day (3:07) *Joan Roberts*; 7 It's A Scandal! It's A Outrage! (3:16) *Joseph Buloff*; 8 People Will Say We're In Love (3:12) *Alfred Drake, Joan Roberts*; 9 Pore Jud Is Daid (2:51) *Alfred Drake, Howard da*

VideoHound's

Oklahoma!

Silva; 10 Lonely Room (2:37) *Alfred Drake*; 11 Out Of My Dreams (2:47) *Joan Robert*; 12 The Farmer And The Cowman (5:22) *Betty Garde, Ralph Riggs*; 13 All Er Nuthin' (3:10) *Celeste Holm, Lee Dixon*; 14 Oklahoma (2:31) *Alfred Drake*; 15 Finale (3:14) *Alfred Drake, Joan Roberts*; 16 Pore Jud Is Daid (alternate take)(3:47) *Alfred Drake, Howard da Silva.*

Review: See entry below.

Oklahoma! 🎵🎵🎵🎵ᵛ

1987, Angel Records; from the screen musical *Oklahoma!*, Magna Films, 1956.

Album Notes: *Music*: Richard Rodgers; *Lyrics*: Oscar Hammerstein II; *Orchestrations*: Robert Russell Bennett; *Vocal Arrangements and Musical Direction*: Jay Blackton; *Cast*: Gordon MacRae (Curly), Shirley Jones (Laurey), Rod Steiger (Jud Fry), Gloria Grahame (Ado Annie Carnes), Gene Nelson (Will Parker), Charlotte Greenwood (Aunt Eller), J.C. Flippen (Ike Skidmore), James Whitmore (Andrew Carnes); *CD Engineer*: Larry Walsh.

Selections: 1 Overture (3:19)Orchestra; 2 Oh, What A Beautiful Mornin' (2:38) *Gordon MacRae*; 3 The Surrey With The Fringe On Top (4:55) *Gordon MacRae, Shirley Jones, Charlotte Greenwood*; 4 Kansas City (2:38) *Gene Nelson, Charlotte Greenwood*; 5 I Cain't Say No (3:12) *Gloria Grahame*; 6 Many A New Day (3:12) *Shirley Jones*; 7 People Will Say We're In Love (4:22) *Gordon MacRae, Shirley Jones*; 8 Poor Jud Is Daid (2:27) *Gordon MacRae, Rod Steiger*; 9 Out Of My Dreams (2:27) *Shirley Jones*; 10 The Farmer And The Cowman (3:00) *Gordon MacRae, Charlotte Greenwood, Gene Nelson, Jay C. Flippen, James Whitmore, Gloria Grahame*; 11 All Er Nothin' (3:02) *Gloria Grahame, Gene Nelson*; 12 Oklahoma (2:31) *Gordon MacRae, Charlotte Greenwood, James Whitmore, Shirley Jones, J.C. Flippen.*

Review: See entry below.

Oklahoma! 🎵🎵🎵🎵🎵

1980, RCA Victor; from the Broadway revival *Oklahoma!*, 1980.

Album Notes: *Music*: Richard Rodgers; *Lyrics*: Oscar Hammerstein II; *Orchestrations*: Robert Russell Bennett; *Musical Direction*: Jay Blackton; *Cast*: Laurence Guittard (Curly), Christine Andreas (Laurey), Martin Vidnovic (Jud Fry), Christine Ebersole (Ado Annie Carnes), Harry Groener (Will Parker), Bruce Adler (Ali Hakim), Mary Wickes (Aunt Eller), Philip Rash (Andrew Carnes), Nick Jolley (Cord Elam), Robert Ray (Ike Skidmore), Stephen Crain (Slim), Martha Traverse (Gertie Cummings); *Album Producer*: Thomas Z. Shepard; *Engineer*: Paul Goodman.

Selections: 1 Overture (3:58)Orchestra; 2 Oh, What A Beautiful Mornin' (2:52) *Laurence Guittard*; 3 Laurey's Entrance (:19)

Christine Andreas; 4 The Surrey With The Fringe On Top (4:32) *Laurence Guittard, Christine Andreas, Mary Wickes*; 5 Kansas City (1:57) *Harry Groener, Mary Wickes*; 6 I Cain't Say No (3:07) *Christine Ebersole*; 7 Many A New Day (5:10) *Christine Andreas*; 8 It's A Scandal! It's A Outrage! (2:44) *Bruce Adler*; 9 People Will Say We're In Love (4:15) *Christine Andreas, Laurence Guittard*; 10 Pore Jud Is Daid (3:51) *Laurence Guittard, Martin Vidnovic*; 11 Lonely Room (2:29) *Martin Vidnovic*; 12 Out Of My Dreams (4:30) *Christine Andreas*; 13 The Farmer And The Cowman (4:17) *Philip Rash, Mary Wickes, Harry Groener, Laurence Guittard, Nick Jolley, Robert Ray, Stephen Crain, Christine Ebersole*; 14 All Er Nuthin' (3:35) *Christine Ebersole*; 15 People Will Say We're In Love (reprise)(2:20) *Laurence Guittard, Christine Andreas*; 16 Oklahoma/Finale: Oh, What A Beautiful Mornin' (reprise)(3:53)Company.

Review: *Oklahoma!*, the first show by Richard Rodgers and Oscar Hammerstein II, was a pioneering work that changed the course of the American musical, launched one of the most prolific teams in the history of Broadway, and saved the sagging fortunes of the Theatre Guild, which produced it.

For the first time completely integrated in the narrative, instead of being inserted at random in the book, as had been so frequently the case before, the songs in *Oklahoma!* actually help propel the action forward. Adding a further element to the progression of the storyline, the musical also introduced the device of a dream ballet to reflect the state of mind of the principals, a novelty. To be sure, some musicals had previously shown a tighter, cohesive blend of book, songs and dances (certainly *Porgy and Bess* and *Pal Joey*, also trendsetters in their own right, denoted a maturity that often had seemed to be missing in most works at the time), but *Oklahoma!* can be said to be the first modern-day musical that brings all these disparate elements into a comprehensive, seamless whole.

For Rodgers, working for the first time with a new partner, following the death of Lorenz Hart, with whom he had written all his works through the 1930s, teaming with Hammerstein seemed a proposition fraught with many question marks: the famed lyricist of *Show Boat* had not had a hit show in many years, and was already written off by many in theatrical circles. The partnership ignited incredible creative responses in both men, with Rodgers reaching new levels of lyricism he had seldom felt with Hart, while Hammerstein found new means of expression that resulted in sharper, more pungent lyrics and book ideas than he had ever experienced before.

Based on "Green Grow the Lilacs," a 1931 play by Lynn Riggs, *Oklahoma!* concerns itself with the romance between a cowboy and his girl, Curly and Laurey, and the possible threat to their idyll represented by a mean-spirited working hand, Jud Fry. The whole story is set against the natural antagonism between farmers and cowmen, and the greater political framework brought by the impending entry of the territory within the Union.

Strikingly beautiful and simple in its expression, *Oklahoma!* is at heart a celebration of the pioneering American spirit, something that struck a particularly responsive note when it opened on March 31, 1943. Hailed as a landmark production, the show enjoyed an incredible run of 2,212 performances (a record at the time), and made stars of many members in its cast, including Alfred Drake who portrayed Curly, Joan Roberts as Laurey, Howard da Silva as Jud Fry, and Celeste Holm as Ado Annie, Laurey's man-crazed friend.

The show also introduced a large number of songs that have become as many classic standards, including "Oh, What A Beautiful Mornin'," "The Surrey with the Fringe on Top," "Kansas City," "People Will Say We're In Love," "Out of My Dreams," "All Er Nuthin'," and the rousing title tune.

On another level, *Oklahoma!* also marked the first time a Broadway musical received a cast album recording. Previously, when a successful show opened on Broadway, the common practice was to take its stars into a recording studio, provide them with fresh arrangements of the most popular tunes in the show, and record them as pop songs.

When *Oklahoma!* opened, the recording industry was in the midst of a long strike from the Musicians' Union, which prevented record labels from making new recordings with orchestral backing. Jack Kapp, A&R head at Decca Records, settled independently with the Union, and immediately looked for a new source of material to release under his new contract. The resounding success of *Oklahoma!* prompted him to take the entire cast into the studio and cut an album of the songs, as performed by the original members of the company. The move marked Decca's entry in the field of cast albums, in which it was a dominant force until 1950.

The first album listed here is the original 1943 cast, and while it may be sonically insufficient by today's standards, and certainly incomplete compared to more recent recordings, it is in many ways an essential, historical document.

The soundtrack album, on Capitol, for many years the best source for anyone wanting to listen to the score under optimum circumstances, still holds its own, with Gordon MacRae and Shirley Jones co-starring as Curly and Laurey, Rod Steiger appropriately menacing as Jud Fry, and Gloria Graham fetching as Ado Annie. The recording, incidentally, is from the standard 35 mm version, and not from the Todd-AO 65 mm roadshow presentation, which had a different, alternate soundtrack.

Revived many times since its creation, *Oklahoma!* came back to Broadway in a sumptuous stage version which opened on December 13, 1979, and yielded the splendid new cast album on RCA Victor. Starring Laurence Guittard, Christine Andreas, Martin Vidnovic and Christine Ebersole in the principal roles, it is by far the most complete and most satisfying recording of this sensational musical.

Oliver!

Oliver! ♫♫♫♪

1989, RCA Victor; from the Broadway production *Oliver!*, 1962.

Album Notes: *Music*: Lionel Bart; *Lyrics*: Lionel Bart; *Orchestrations*: Eric Rogers; *Musical Direction*: Donald Pippin; *Cast*: Clive Revill (Fagin), Georgia Brown (Nancy), Willoughby Goddard (Mr. Bumble), Hope Jackman (Mrs. Corney), Geoffrey Lumb (Mr. Brownlow), John Call (Dr. Grimwig), Danny Sewell (Bill Sikes), Bruce Prochnik (Oliver Twist), Alice Playten (Bet), Helena Carroll (Mrs. Sowerberry), Barry Humphries (Mr. Sowerberry), Michael Goodman (The Artful Dodger); *Album Producers*: Joe Linhart, Charles Gerhardt, George Marek; *Engineer*: Dave Hassinger; *CD Producer*: Didier C. Deutsch; *Engineer*: Paul Goodman.

Selections: 1 Overture/Food, Glorious Food (4:28)The Boys; 2 Oliver! (1:48) *Willoughby Goddard, Hope Jackman, Bruce Prochnik*; 3 I Shall Scream (2:51) *Hope Jackman, Willoughby Goddard*; 4 Boy For Sale/Where Is Love? (4:25) *Willoughby Goddard, Bruce Prochnik*; 5 Consider Yourself (3:51) *Michael Goodman, Bruce Prochnik*; 6 You've Got To Pick A Pocket Or Two (3:15) *Clive Revill, Bruce Prochnik*; 7 It's A Fine Life (3:32) *Georgia Brown, Alice Playten*; 8 I'd Do Anything (3:09) *Michael Goodman, Georgia Brown, Bruce Prochnik, Alice Playten, Clive Revill*; 9 Be Back Soon (2:38) *Clive Revill, Michael Goodman, Bruce Prochnik*; 10 Oom-Pah-Pah (3:16) *Georgia Brown*; 11 My Name (2:22) *Danny Sewell*; 12 As Long As He Needs Me (4:08) *Georgia Brown*; 13 Who Will Buy? (4:21) *Bruce Prochnik*; 14 Reviewing The Situation (4:49) *Clive Revill*; 15 As Long As He Needs Me (reprise)(2:23) *Georgia Brown*; 16 Reviewing The Situation (reprise)(1:00) *Clive Revill*; 17 Finale (2:42)Company.

Review: See entry below.

Oliver! ♫♫♫♪

1968, RCA Records; from the screen musical *Oliver!*, Columbia Pictures, 1968.

Album Notes: *Music*: Lionel Bart; *Lyrics*: Lionel Bart; *Orchestrations*: Johnny Green; The Columbia Studio Chorus and Orchestra, conducted by Johnny Green; *Cast*: Ron Moody (Fagin), Shami Wallis (Nancy), Harry Secombe (Mr. Bumble), Peggy Mount (Mrs. Corney), Oliver Reed (Bill Sikes), Mark Lester (Oliver Twist), Sheila White (Bet), Leonard Rossiter (Mr. Sowerberry), Jack Wild (The Artful Dodger); *CD Producer*: John Snyder.

Selections: 1 Overture (1:58) Orchestra; 2 Food, Glorious Food/Oliver! (5:42) *Mark Lester, Harry Secombe, Peggy Mount*; 3 Boy For Sale (2:47) *Harry Secombe*; 4 Where Is Love? (3:00) *Mark Lester*; 5 Pick A Pocket Or Two (2:40) *Ron Moody*; 6 Consider Yourself (5:47) *Jack Wild, Mark Lester*; 7 I'd Do Anything (3:47) *Jack Wild, Shani Wallis, Sheila White, Mark Lester, Ron Moody*; 8 Be Back Soon (2:49) *Ron Moody*; 9 As Long As He Needs Me (4:43) *Shani Wallis*; 10 Who Will Buy? (6:51) *Mark Lester*; 11 It's A Fine Life (3:25) *Shani Wallis, Sheila White*; 12 Reviewing The Situation (3:39) *Ron Moody*; 13 Oom-Pah-Pah (2:29) *Shani Wallis*; 14 Finale: Where Is Love?/Consider Yourself (1:16) Ensemble.

Review: Charles Dickens' *Oliver Twist* provided the gist for a magnificent new musical, *Oliver!*, which opened on Broadway on January 6, 1963, following a three-year run in London. "Freely adapted" from the novel, and slightly spruced up to conform with the tenets of the song-and-dance genre, the show, entirely conceived and created by Lionel Bart, tells the story of the orphan boy, who runs away from his life of misery and ends up in the streets of London, where he is eventually adopted by a well-to-do benefactor, who turns out to be his grandfather.

Received with glowing reviews from the Broadway pundits, the show enjoyed a profitable run of 774 performances. It introduced many songs that have since become quite popular, including the rousing "Oom-Pah-Pah," performed by customers in a seedy barroom led by Nancy, a woman of easy virtue who takes Oliver under a protecting wing; "Food, Glorious Food," the anthem of the famished orphans; "Consider Yourself," in which The Artful Dodger and his band of young pickpockets welcome Oliver; and mostly "As Long As He Needs Me," the throbbing love song in which Nancy reveals her passion for Sikes, her "protector."

The musical won a Tony Award for composer Lionel Bart, and in 1968 was made into a glossy screen version which retained much of its flavor and kept the entire score minus two songs. Of the two albums listed above, the 1963 cast album is probably the best, with Clive Revill a splendid Fagin, Georgia Brown resplendent as Nancy, and Bruce Prochnik as Oliver; Ron Moody, Shani Wallis and Mark Lester were equally effective in the film version, though the recording itself leaves a bit to be desired, sonically.

On a Clear Day You Can See Forever

On a Clear Day You Can See Forever ♫♫♫♫

1993, RCA Victor; from the Broadway production *On a Clear Day You Can See Forever*, 1965.

Album Notes: *Music*: Burton Lane; *Lyrics*: Alan Jay Lerner; *Orchestrations*: Robert Russell Bennett; *Musical Continuity*: Trude Rittman; *Musical Direction*: Theodore Saidenberg; *Cast*: John Cullum (Dr. Mark Bruckner), Barbara Harris (Daisy/Melinda), Titos Vandis (Themistocles Kriakos), Barbara Monte (Muriel Bunson), William Reilly (James Preston), Gerald M. Teijelo, Jr. (Student), Clifford David (Edward Moncrief), Byron Webster (Sir Hubert Insdale), William Daniels (Warren Smith); *Album Producers*: Joe Linhart, George Marek; *Engineer*: Ernie Oelrich; *CD Producer*: Bill Rosenfield; *Engineer*: Jay Newland.

Selections: 1 Overture (6:13) Orchestra, Chorus; 2 Hurry! It's Lovely Up Here! (4:05) *Barbara Harris, John Cullum*; 3 Tosy And Cosh (3:01) *Barbara Harris*; 4 On A Clear Day (You Can See Forever) (3:56) *John Cullum*; 5 On The S.S. Bernard Cohn (4:32) *Barbara Harris, Barbara Monte, William Reilly, Gerald Teijelo Jr.*; 6 Don't Tamper With My Sister (2:20) *Clifford David, Byron Webster*; 7 She Wasn't You (3:21) *Clifford David*; 8 Melinda (4:18) *John Cullum*; 9 When I'm Being Born Again (3:08) *Titos Vandis*; 10 What Did I Have That I Don't Have (4:23) *Barbara Harris*; 11 Wait Till We're Sixty-Five (2:42) *William Daniels, Barbara Harris*; 12 Come Back To Me (2:21) *John Cullum*; 13 Finale (2:38) Entire Company.

Review: See entry below.

On a Clear Day You Can See Forever ♫♭

1970, CBS Special Products; from the screen musical *On a Clear Day You Can See Forever*, Paramount Pictures, 1970.

Album Notes: *Music*: Burton Lane; *Lyrics*: Alan Jay Lerner; *Orchestrations*: Nelson Riddle; The Paramount Studio Chorus and Orchestra, conducted by Nelson Riddle; *Cast*: Yves Montand (Dr. Marc Chabot), Barbra Streisand (Daisy/Melinda), Larry Blyden (Warren Smith), Jack Nicholson, Bob Newhart; *Album Producers*: Joe Linhart, George Marek; *Engineer*: Ernie Oelrich; *CD Producer*: Bill Rosenfield; *Engineer*: Jay Newland.

Selections: 1 Hurry! It's Lovely Up Here! (2:56) *Barbra Streisand*; 2 Main Title: On A Clear Day (You Can See Forever) (2:27) *Barbra Streisand*; 3 Love With All The Trimmings

(2:51) *Barbra Streisand*; 4 Melinda (2:18) *Yves Montand*; 5 Go To Sleep (3:00) *Barbra Streisand*; 6 He Isn't You (2:14) *Barbra Streisand*; 8 Come Back To Me (4:34) *Yves Montand*; 9 On A Clear Day (You Can See Forever)(2:42) *Yves Montand*; 10 On A Clear Day (You Can See Forever) (reprise)(2:09) *Barbra Streisand*.

Review: Alan Jay Lerner's particular interest in extra-sensory perceptions, reincarnation, time regression, hypnosis, and other psychic phenomena led to this hopelessly flawed, but ultimately fascinating musical in which the heroine, Daisy, recalls a previous existence when she is placed under hypnosis by Dr. Bruckner, a psychologist. The story, an old-fashioned romance that doesn't need the mind trips to the past to succeed, is helped by the strong score, which help to gloss over some of the inconsistencies in the plot.

Much of the charm in the original disappeared in the blown-out-of-proportion screen version, in which Barbra Streisand and Yves Montand fussed as the two principal characters without sharing much empathy or chemistry between them.

Once Upon a Mattress

Once Upon a Mattress ♪♪♪

1993, MCA Records; from the Broadway production *Once Upon a Mattress*, 1959.

Album Notes: *Music*: Mary Rodgers; *Lyrics*: Marshall Barer; *Orchestrations*: Hershy Kay, Arthur Beck, Carroll Huxley; *Musical Direction*: Harold Hastings; *Cast*: Carol Burnett (Princess Winnifred), Joe Bova (Prince Dauntless), Allen Case (Sir Harry), Anne Jones (Lady Larken), Harry Snow (Minstrel), Jane White (The Queen), Robert Weil (Wizard), Matt Mattox (Jester), Ginny Perlowin (The Nightingale Of Samarkand), Jack Gilford (The King); *CD Producer*: Ron O'Brien.

Selections: 1 Overture (4:03)Orchestra; 2 Many Moons Ago (3:09) *Harry Snow*; 3 An Opening For A Princess (2:21) *Joe Bova*; 4 In A Little While (2:39) *Allen Case, Anne Jones*; 5 Shy (3:47) *Carol Burnett, Joe Bova*; 6 Sensitivity (2:39) *Jane White, Robert Weil*; 7 The Swamps Of Home (3:19) *Carol Burnett, Joe Bova*; 8 Normandy (2:32) *Harry Snow, Matt Mattox, Anne Jones*; 9 Spanish Dance (2:18) *Jane White*; 10 Song Of Love (3:47) *Carol Burnett, Joe Bova*; 11 Quiet (1:32) *Jane White*; 12 Studio Dialogue (:22) *Carol Burnett*; 13 Happily Ever After (4:00) *Carol Burnett*; 14 Man To Man Talk (4:26) *Matt Mattox, Joe Bova*; 15 Very Soft Shoes (2:41) *Matt Mattox*; 16 Yesterday I

Loved You (2:46) *Allen Case, Anne Jones*; 17 Nightingale Lullaby (1:48) *Ginny Perlowin*; 18 Finale (2:02) *Joe Bova, Matt Mattox, Jack Gilford*.

Review: See entry below.

Once Upon a Mattress ♪

1997, RCA Victor Records; from the Broadway revival *Once Upon a Mattress*, 1996.

Album Notes: *Music*: Mary Rodgers; *Lyrics*: Marshall Barer; *Orchestrations*: Bruce Coughlin; *Musical Direction*: Eric Stern; *Cast*: Sarah Jessica Parker (Princess Winnifred), David Aaron Baker (Prince Dauntless), Lewis Cleale (Sir Harry), Jane Krakowski (Lady Larken), Lawrence Clayton (Minstrel), Mary Lou Rosato (Queen Aggravain), David Hibbard (Jester), Ann Brown (The Nightingale Of Samarkand), Heath Lamberts (King Sextimus), Tom Alan Robbins (Master Merton); *CD Producer*: Jay David Saks; *Engineer*: James P. Nichols.

Selections: 1 Overture (4:09)Orchestra; 2 Many Moons Ago (3:39) *Lawrence Clayton,*; 3 An Opening For A Princess (2:36) *David Aaron Baker, Jane Krakowski, Maria Calabrese, Thursday Parrar*; 4 In A Little While (3:12) *Jane Krakowski, Lewis Cleale*; 5 On A Stormy Night (1:04) *Lawrence Clayton*; 6 Shy (4:19) *Sarah Jessica Parker, Mary Lou Rosato, Stephen Reed, Nick Cokas, David Aaron Baker*; 7 The Minstrel, The Jester And I (2:07) *David Hibbard, Lawrence Clayton, Heath Lamberts*; 8 Sensitivity (2:53) *Mary Lou Rosato, Tom Alan Robbins*; 9 The Swamps Of Home (2:59) *Sarah Jessica Parker, David Aaron Baker*; 10 Normandy (3:33) *Jane Krakowski, David Hibbard, Lawrence Clayton, Heath Lamberts*; 11 Spanish Panic (3:27) *Mary Lou Rosato, Sarah Jessica Parker*; 12 Song Of Love (4:01) *Sarah Jessica Parker, David Aaron Baker*; 13 Entr'acte (1:27) Orchestra; 14 Quiet (1:40) *David Hibbard*; 15 Goodnight Sweet Princess (1:30) *David Aaron Baker, Sarah Jessica Parker*; 16 Happily Ever After (4:10) *Sarah Jessica Parker*; 17 Man To Man Talk (4:38) *David Aaron Baker, Heath Lamberts*; 18 Very Soft Shoes (3:38) *David Hibbard, David Jennings*; 19 Yesterday I Loved You (2:35) *Lewis Cleale, Jane Krakowski*; 20 Lullaby (2:48) *Ann Brown, Mary Lou Rosato, Sarah Jessica Parker*; 21 Finale (1:49) Company.

Review: Carol Burnett gains at being seen rather than heard, but hints of the infectious comic genius that made her a theatrical star before she became a household name on television can be experienced in this cast album of her first Broadway show. Loosely based on the fairy tale by Andersen, "The Princess and the Pea," the show enables the comedienne to mug her way through a rather limp and flimsy story line, further limited by the so-so score, the product of Mary (daughter of Richard) Rodgers, and Marshall Barer.

The 1996 revival was even less fortunate in Sarah Jessica Parker, whose sense of comedy was not very evident in this sorry production. The cast album does little to convince that the show was worth bringing back to Broadway, let alone spending the money recording it.

On the Town ♫♫♫♫

1991, Sony Classical; from the studio cast recording *On the Town*, 1963.

Album Notes: *Music:* Leonard Bernstein; *Lyrics:* Betty Comden and Adolph Green; *Orchestrations:* Leonard Bernstein; *Musical Direction:* Leonard Bernstein; *Cast:* John Reardon (Gabey), Cris Alexander (Chip), Adolph Green (Ozzie), Betty Comden (Claire de Loon), Nancy Walker (Hildy), George Gaynes (Pitkin), Randel Striboneen (Coney Island Barker); *Album Producer:* Goddard Lieberson; *Engineers:* Fred Plaut, Edward Graham; *CD Producer:* John McLure; *Engineer:* Charles Harbutt.

Selections: 1 Opening: New York, New York/Dance: Miss Turnstiles' Variations (11:26) *Michael Kermorian, Adolph Green, Cris Alexander, John Reardon*; 2 Taxi Number: Come Up To My Place (2:44) *Nancy Walker, Cris Alexander*; 3 Carried Away (2:58) *Betty Comden, Adolph Green*; 4 Lonely Town/Dance: Lonely Town (6:42) *John Reardon/Orchestra*; 5 Carnegie Hall (Do-Do-Re-Do)(2:35)Chorus; 6 I Can Cook Too (2:27) *Nancy Walker*; 7 Lucky To Be Me (2:53) *John Reardon*; 8 Dance: Times Square (3:59)Orchestra; 9 Night Club Sequence: So Long Baby/I'm Blue/Ya Got Me (4:49) *Nancy Walker, Betty Comden, Adolph Green, Cris Alexander*; 10 I Understand (2:09) *George Gaynes*; 11 Ballet: Imaginary Coney Island: Subway Ride/Dance Of The Great Lover/Pas de Deux (7:47)Orchestra; 12 Some Other Time (4:20) *Betty Comden, Nancy Walker, Adolph Green, Cris Alexander*; 13 Dance: The Real Coney Island/Finale (6:01) *Orchestra/Randel Striboneen*.

Review: Leonard Bernstein's infectious ballet, *Fancy Free*, about three sailors on a 24-hour leave in New York City, was turned into an even more exhilarating musical comedy titled *On The Town*. Created in 1944, the composer's collaborators, Betty Comden and Adolph Green, and comedian Nancy Walker played important roles. Excerpts from the show were recorded at the time, and can be heard on an MCA CD in which they are coupled with a 1945 recording of *Fancy Free*.

In 1960, Bernstein returned to the studio with Comden, Green, Walker, and Cris Alexander, also from the original cast, to record the show all over again. A lively, rambunctious celebration of youth and vitality, the show follows the three sailors as they look (and find) their ideal dates for a day, in a score that brims with energy, irreverence, and jazzy style. The recording captures all these elements into one of the most exciting cast albums to be enjoyed.

In 1949, MGM filmed the story, with Gene Kelly and Frank Sinatra as two of the sailors. But with the exception of a couple of songs, including the rousing opening number, "New York, New York," MGM discarded most of Bernstein's sensational score, and replaced it with new songs by Roger Edens, Comden and Green that did not have the vibrant imagination of the original.

On the Twentieth Century ♫♫♫♫

1991, Sony Broadway; from the Broadway production *On the Twentieth Century*, 1978.

Album Notes: *Music:* Cy Coleman; *Lyrics:* Betty Comden and Adolph Green; *Orchestrations:* Hershy Kay; *Musical Direction:* Paul Gemignani; *Cast:* John Cullum (Oscar Jaffe), Madeline Kahn (Mildred Plotka/Lily Garland), Imogene Coca (Letitia Primrose), George Coe (Owen O'Malley), Dean Dittman (Oliver Webb), Kevin Kline (Bruce Granit), Charles Rule (Bishop), Hal Norman (Actor), Tom Batten (Conductor Flanagan), Stanley Simmonds (Train Secretary Rogers), Keith Davis, Quitman Fludd III, Joseph Wise, Ray Stephens (Porters); *Album Producer:* Cy Coleman; *Engineer:* Frank Laico, Stanley Tonkel; *CD Producer:* Didier C. Deutsch; *Engineer:* Tim Tiedemann.

Selections: 1 Overture (3:38) Orchestra; 2 Stranded Again/Saddle Up The Horse/On The Twentieth Century (4:12) *Charles Rule, Hal Norman, George Coe, Dean Dittman, Tom Batten, Stanley Simmonds*; 3 I Rise Again (3:15) *John Cullum, George Coe, Dean Dittman*; 4 Veronique (3:52) *Madeline Kahn, John Cullum*; 5 I Have Written A Play (:48) *Tom Batten*; 6 Together (2:22) *John Cullum*; 7 Never (2:44) *Madeline Kahn, George Coe, Dean Dittman*; 8 Our Private World (3:25) *John Cullum, Madeline Kahn*; 9 Repent (4:03) *Imogene Coca*; 10 Mine (2:18) *John Cullum, Kevin Kline*; 11 I've Got It All (4:29) *Madeline Kahn, John Cullum*; 12 On The Twentieth Century (:33) Company; 13 Entr'acte: Life Is Like A Train (2:58) *Keith Davis, Quitman Fludd III, Joseph Wise, Ray Stephens*; 14 Five Zeros (3:07) *George Coe, Dean Dittman, Imogene Coca, John Cullum*; 15 Sextet (6:17) *George Coe, Dean Dittman, John Cullum, Imogene Coca, Madeline Kahn, Kevin Kline*; 16 She's A Nut (3:41) Company; 17 Babbette (4:16) *Madeline Kahn*; 18 The Legacy (4:35) *John Cullum*; 19 Lily, Oscar (2:42) *Madeline Kahn, John Cullum, George Coe, Dean Dittman*; 20 On The Twentieth Century (reprise)(:55) Company.

Review: A brash, rambunctious musical based on Ben Hecht and Charles MacArthur's 1932 backstage play, *On the Twentieth Century* gave Cy Coleman, Betty Comden and Adolph Green the vehicle with which to fashion a score (and a musical) that was thoroughly entertaining, and a terrific proposition. The plot concerns the efforts of theatrical producer Oscar Jaffee, on board the New York-bound Twentieth Century to escape his creditors, to convince Lily Garland, his former leading actress and lover and now a celebrated movie star, to appear in his next production, "The Passion of Mary Magdalene." Using every trick in the book, he finally succeeds when he pretends he is dying after having shot himself, compelling Lily to affix her name, Peter Rabbit, at the bottom of the contract.

Breathing incredible life into the characters, John Cullum chews the scenery (a striking Art Deco set by Robin Wagner) as Oscar, while Madeline Kahn demurs as Lili, with Imogene Coca portraying a religious nut who gives Oscar a rubber check for his production, while Kevin Kline portrays Lili's current lover, an actor unlikely named Bruce Granit. The Tony Award winning score adds its own point to the proceedings, with Coleman, Comden and Green providing songs that closely match the humorous action.

On Your Toes

On Your Toes 🎭🎭🎭🎭

1996, MCA Records; from the Broadway production *On Your Toes*, 1954.

Album Notes: *Music:* Richard Rodgers; *Lyrics:* Lorenz Hart; *Orchestrations:* Don Walker; *Musical Direction:* Salvatore Dell'Isola; *Cast:* Vera Zorina (Vera Baronova), Bobby Van (Junior), Elaine Stritch (Peggy Porterfield), Ben Astar (Sergei Alexandrovitch), Nicholas Orloff (Konstantine Morrosine), Kay Coulter (Frankie Frayne), Joshua Shelley (Sidney Cohn), Jack Williams (Phil Dolan II), Eleanor Williams (Lil Dolan), David Winters (Phil Dolan III); *CD Producer:* Ron O'Brien; *Engineer:* Paul Elmore.

Selections: 1 Overture (4:19)Orchestra; 2 Two A Day For Keith (2:48) *Jack Williams, Eleanor Williams, David Winters*; 3 The Three B's (2:40) *Bobby Van*; 4 It's Got To Be Love (2:33) *Bobby Van, Kay Coulter*; 5 Too Good For The Average Man (3:45) *Elaine Stritch, Ben Astar*; 6 There's A Small Hotel (3:37) *Bobby Van, Kay Coulter*; 7 The Heart Is Quicker Than The Eye (5:37) *Elaine Stritch, Bobby Van*; 8 Quiet Night (3:07) *Joshua Shelley*; 9 Glad To Be Unhappy (3:34) *Kay Coulter, Joshua Shelley*; 10 On Your Toes (2:40) *Kay Coulter, Bobby Van, Joshua Shelley*; 11 You Took Advantage Of Me (4:54) *Elaine Stritch*; 12 Slaughter On Tenth Avenue (13:19)Orchestra; 13 Finale (1:27) *Company*.

On Your Toes 🎭🎭🎭🎭🎭

1983, Polydor Records; from the Broadway revival *On Your Toes*, 1983.

Album Notes: *Music:* Richard Rodgers; *Lyrics:* Lorenz Hart; *Orchestrations:* Hans Spialek; *Musical Direction:* John Mauceri; *Cast:* Natalia Makarova (Vera Baronova), Lara Teeter (Junior), Dina Merrill (Peggy Porterfield), George S. Irving (Sergei Alexandrovitch), George de la Pena (Konstantine Morrosine), Christine Andreas (Frankie Frayne); Eugene J. Anthony (Phil Dolan II), Betty Ann Grove (Lil Dolan), Philip Arthur Ross (Phil Dolan III), Michael Vita (Hank J. Smith); *Album Producer:* Norman Newell; *Engineer:* John Kurlander.

Selections: 1 Overture (4:12)Orchestra; 2 Two A Day For Keith (2:13) *Eugene J. Anthony, Betty Ann Grove, Philip Arthur Ross*; 3 Questions And Answers (The Three B's)(2:39) *Lara Teeter*; 4 It's Got To Be Love (4:52) *Christine Andreas, Lara Teeter*; 5 Too Good For The Average Man (3:24) *George S. Irving, Dina Merrill*; 6 There's A Small Hotel (4:24) *Christine Andreas, Lara Teeter*; 7 La Princesse Zenobia Ballet (10:19)Orchestra; 8 The Heart Is Quicker Than The Eye (3:50) *Dina Merrill, Lara Teeter*; 9 Glad To Be Unhappy (3:54) *Christine Andreas*; 10 Quiet Night (2:41) *Michael Vita*; 11 On Your Toes (7:57) *Christine Andreas*; 12 Slaughter On Tenth Avenue (14:23)Orchestra.

Review: Unfortunately, no recording of the original 1936 cast of *On Your Toes* was ever made, and there were only scant excerpts by the 1938 London cast. As a result, the 1954 Broadway revival is the first recording of this amazing score, one of the best by Rodgers and Hart. While the top-billed star of the revival was Vera Zorina, the ex-Mrs. Balanchine, she does not appear on the cast album. However, all of the other performers do and they are stylish and grand. Bobby Van, fresh from his appearances in several Hollywood films, is relaxed and charming as Phil Dolan III, the part originally created by Ray Bolger. Kay Coulter as Frankie Frayne is warm and loving. And Elaine Stritch playing the featured part of Peggy Porterfield, the backer of a Russian ballet company, wipes everyone up with her sensational rendition of a song interpolated especially for her, with this recording about as enjoyable as it gets.

Good as the 1954 recording is, the 1983 revival cast album is even better and properly reflects the sound of the 1936 original. Make no mistake, this is a glorious warm, romantic score and this album is a stunner. Every performer is absolutely right and the 1930s performance style is preserved in this recording right down to the taps of the dancers. Lara Teeter captures the light breeziness of the music and lyrics with just the right amount of throwaway charm that is a constant delight. Christine Andreas turns Frankie into a fully believable character and charms the ear with her singing. Dina

Merrill and George S. Irving are just right in their roles. Both ballets are included, as well as much dance music. John Mauceri has never conducted a finer performance than here and it is captured in glorious stereo, digital sound.

Jerry J. Thomas

Out of This World

Out of This World ♫♫♫♫

1992, Sony Broadway; from the Broadway production *Out of This World*, 1950.

Album Notes: *Music*: Cole Porter; *Lyrics*: Cole Porter; *Orchestrations*: Robert Russell Bennett; *Musical Direction*: Pembroke Davenport; *Cast*: Charlotte Greenwood (Juno), William Eythe (Art O'Malley), Priscilla Gillette (Helen), William Redfield (Mercury), Barbara Ashley (Chloe), George Jongeyans-Gaynes (Jupiter), David Burns (Niki Skolianos); *Album producer*: Goddard Lieberson; *CD Producer*: Didier C. Deutsch; *Engineer*: Tim Tiedemann.

Selections: 1 Overture (3:45)Orchestra; 2 Prologue/I Jupiter Rex (3:16) *William Redfield, George Jongeyans-Gaynes*; 3 Use Your Imagination (2:52) *Priscilla Gillette*; 4 Entrance Of Juno: Hail, Hail, Hail/I Got Beauty (3:57) *Charlotte Greenwood*; 5 Where, Oh, Where? (3:34) *Barbara Ashley*; 6 I Am Loved (3:27) *Priscilla Gillette*; 7 They Couldn't Compare To You (3:48) *William Redfield*; 8 What Do You Think About Men? (2:25) *Charlotte Greenwood, Priscilla Gillette, Barbara Ashley*; 9 I Sleep Easier Now (3:44) *Charlotte Greenwood*; 10 Climb Up The Mountain (3:26) Charlotte Greenwood; 11 No Lover (For Me)(3:17) *Priscilla Gillette*; 12 Cherry Pies Ought To Be You (3:12) *William Redfield, Barbara Ashley, David Burns, Charlotte Greenwood*; 13 Hark To The Song Of The Night (2:33) *George Jongeyans-Gaynes*; 14 Nobody's Chasing Me (3:31) *Charlotte Greenwood*; 15 Finale (1:07)Company.

Review: See entry below.

Out of This World ♫♫♫♫

1995, DRG Records; from the concert performance *Out of This World*, 1995.

Album Notes: *Music*: Cole Porter; *Lyrics*: Cole Porter; *Orchestrations*: Robert Russell Bennett; *Musical Direction*: Rob Fisher; *Cast*: Andrea Martin (Juno), Gregg Edelman (Art O'Malley), Marin Mazzie (Helen), Peter Scolari (Mercury), La Chanze (Chloe), Ken Page (Jupiter), Ernie Sabella (Niki Skolianos); *Album producer*: Hugh Fordin; *Engineer*: Cynthia Daniels.

Selections: 1 Overture (4:56)Orchestra; 2 Prologue (1:15) *Peter Scolari*; 3 I Jupiter Rex (2:07) *Ken Page*; 4 Use Your Imagination (2:30) *Marin Mazzie*; 5 Entrance Of Night (:52)Orchestra; 6 Hail, Hail, Hail (3:05)Ensemble; 7 I Got Beauty (2:24) *Andrea Martin*; 8 Maiden Fair (1:02) *La Chanze*; 9 Where, Oh, Where? (3:50) *La Chanze*; 10 They Couldn't Compare To You (4:12) *Peter Scolari*; 11 From This Moment On (3:12) *Marin Mazzie, Gregg Edelman*; 12 What Do You Think About Men? (2:28) *Andrea Martin, Marin Mazzie, La Chanze*; 13 Dance Of The Long Night (2:33)Orchestra; 14 You Don't Remind Me (1:56) *Ken Page*; 15 I Sleep Easier Now (4:20) *Andrea Martin*; 16 I Am Loved (2:39) *Marin Mazzie*; 17 Climb Up The Mountain (4:40) *Andrea Martin*; 18 The Dawn (1:34)Orchestra; 19 No Lover (2:45) *Marin Mazzie*; 20 Cherry Pies Ought To Be You (3:14) *Peter Scolari, La Chanze, Ernie Sabella, Andrea Martin*; 21 Hark To The Song Of The Night (2:42) *Ken Page*; 22 Nobody's Chasing Me (4:42) *Andrea Martin*; 23 Finale (:37)Company.

Review: Arguably, one of the greatest of all of Cole Porter's later Broadway efforts, *Out Of This World* shows the composer/lyricist at his very peak. Unfortunately, the score is better known for what is missing than what is actually included. Shortly before its Broadway premiere, one of Porter's greatest songs, "From This Moment On", was deleted from the score; later added to the film version of *Kiss Me Kate*, it became a hit. That aside, the original cast recording is sheer unalloyed pleasure from beginning to end. There are love songs to suit every taste, delightful comedy songs and scintillating numbers devoted to man's (and woman's) favorite sport, sex. While Charlotte Greenwood was not the first choice to play Juno, she enters into the spirit of fun required by her character with unabashed fervor. George Jongeyans (Gaynes), who has a flawed voice, is enthusiastic and passionate as her errant husband Jupiter. Priscilla Gillette is a delight as the young American mortal who gives Jupiter ants in his pants. The rest of the super-talented performers cast their spell on this splendid sounding monaural album.

The 1995 recording resulted from a successful concert presentation at New York's City Center, which had show buffs eager with anticipation. Andrea Martin, as Juno, is terrific and proves, once again, that she is a wonderful musical comedy performer. She wrings every ounce of nuance, hedonism and joy out of her songs and is breathtaking in her energy and commitment. Ken Page, as the wandering Jupiter, works hard at his difficult role, but does not always succeed. Peter Scolari as Mercury is a lot of fun. Marin Mazzie and Gregg Edelman, as the modern American mortal couple, perform "From This Moment On," which has been restored in the score. Other songs that were either cut from the original production or not included on the original 1950 Broadway cast recording are also recorded here for the first time, making this album a winner in every way.

Jerry Thomas

594

Pacific Overtures 🎵🎵🎵🎵

1976, RCA Victor; from the Broadway production *Pacific Overtures*, 1976.

Album Notes: *Music:* Stephen Sondheim; *Lyrics:* Stephen Sondheim; *Orchestrations:* Jonathan Tunick; *Musical Direction:* Paul Gemignani; *Featured Musicians:* Fusako Yoshida (voice, shamisen), Genji Ito (shakuhachi); *Cast:* Mako, Soon-Teck Oh, Yuki Shimoda, Sab Shimono, Isao Sato, Jae Woo Lee, Alvin Ing, Ricardo Tobia, Mark Hsu Syers, Timm Fujii, Gedde Watanabe, Patrick Kinser-Lau, Conrad Yama, Ernest Harada, Freda Foh Sen, James Dybas; *Album Producer:* Thomas Z. Shepard; *Associate Producer:* Jay David Saks; *Engineer:* Anthony Salvatore.

Selections: 1 The Advantages Of Floating In The Middle Of The Sea (5:44) *Mako;* 2 There Is No Other Way (5:14) *Alvin Ing, Ricardo Tobia;* 3 Four Black Dragons (4:22) *Jae Woo Lee, Mark Hsu Syers, Mako;* 4 Chrysantemum Tea (7:15) *Alvin Ing, Mako, Mark Hsu Syers, Timm Fujii, Gedde Watanabe, Patrick Kinser-Lau, Conrad Yama, Jae Woo Lee, Ernest Harada, Freda Foh Sen;* 5 Poems (4:05) *Isao Sato, Sab Shimono;* 6 Welcome To Kanagawa (3:44) *Timm Fujii, Gedde Watanabe, Patrick Kinser-Lau, Leslie Watanabe, Mako;* 7 Someone In A Tree (7:19) *James Dybas, Mako, Gedde Watanabe, Mark Hsu Syers;* 8 Please Hello (9:10) *Alvin Ing, Yuki Shimoda, Mark Hsu Syers, Mako, Patrick Kinser-Lau, Ernest Harada, James Dybas;* 9 A Bowler Hat (4:24) *Isao Sato;* 10 Pretty Lady (2:53) *Patrick Kinser-Lau, Timm Fujii, Mark Hsu Syers;* 11 Next (3:39) *Mako.*

Review: The remarkable creative partnership between composer Stephen Sondheim and producer Harold Prince made its most daring foray with this musical treatment of the "opening" of Japan to western trade in 1853—from the Japanese perspective. An all-Asian cast turns the Winter Garden stage into a whirling visual spectacle—which the CD listener can only imagine—and marvelously performs Sondheim's demanding score. The music is beautiful if not especially "hummable"; highlights include "Someone in a Tree" and the fast-forward, present-day finale, "Next".

Marc Kirkeby

Paint Your Wagon

Paint Your Wagon 🎵🎵🎵🎵

1989, RCA Victor; from the Broadway production *Paint Your Wagon*, 1951.

Album Notes: *Music:* Frederick Loewe; *Lyrics:* Alan Jay Lerner; *Orchestrations:* Ted Royal; *Dance Arrangements:* Trude Riuttman; *Musical Direction:* Franz Allers; *Cast:* James Barton (Ben Rumson), Olga San Juan (Jennifer Rumson), Tony Bavaar (Julio Valveras), James Mitchell (Pete Billings), Rufus Smith (Steve Bullnack), Robert Penn (Jake Whippany), Dave Thomas (Doctor Newcomb); *Album Producer:* Charlie Grean, Norman Leyden; *CD Producer:* Didier C. Deutsch; *Engineer:* Paul Goodman.

Selections: 1 I'm On My Way (3:53) *Rufus Smith, Robert Penn, Dave Thomas;* 2 Rumson (:48) *Robert Penn;* 3 What's Goin' On Here? (3:27) *Olga San Juan;* 4 I Talk To The Trees (3:32) *Tony Bavaar;* 5 They Call The Wind Maria (3:18) *Rufus Smith;* 6 I Still See Elisa (3:19) *James Barton;* 7 How Can I Wait? (4:15) *Olga San Juan;* 8 In Between (2:40) *James Barton;* 9 Whoop-Ti-Ay (1:45)Chorus; 10 Carino Mio (2:47) *Olga San Juan, Tony Bavaar;* 11 There's A Coach Comin' In (2:00)Chorus; 12 Hand Me Down That Can O' Beans (1:46) *Robert Penn;* 13 Another Autumn (2:54) *Rufus Smith, Tony Bavaar;* 14 All For Him (2:29) *Olga San Juan;* 15 Wand'rin' Star (2:32) *James Barton.*

Review: See entry below.

Paint Your Wagon 🎵🎵

1989, MCA Records; from the screen musical *Paint Your Wagon*, Paramount Pictures, 1977.

Album Notes: *Music:* Frederick Loewe; *Lyrics:* Alan Jay Lerner; *Orchestrations:* Nelson Riddle; *Choral Arrangements:* Joseph J. Lilley; *Choral Music Conductor:* Roger Wagner; *Dance Arrangements:* Trude Rittman; The Paramount Studio Orchestra, conducted by Nelson Riddle; *Cast:* Lee Marvin (Ben Rumson), Jean Seberg (Elizabeth), Clint Eastwood ("Pardner"), Harve Presnell ("Rotten Luck" Willie), Ray Walston ("Mad Jack" Duncan), Alan Dexter (Parson); *Album Producer:* Tom Mack; *Engineers:* Kevin Cleary, Thorne Nogar.

Selections: 1 Main Title (I'm On My Way)(3:50) Chorus; 2 I Still See Elisa (1:49) *Clint Eastwood;* 3 The First Thing You Know (2:02) *Lee Marvin;* 4 Hand Me Down That Can O' Beans (2:49) *Lee Marvin, The Nitty Gritty Dirt Band;* 5 They Call The Wind Maria (3:38) *Harve Presnell,;* 6 A Million Miles Away Behind The Door (3:23) *Jean Seberg;* 7 There's A Coach Comin' In (4:58) *Harve Presnell;* 8 Whoop-Ti-Ay (Shivaree)(2:02)Chorus; 9 I Talk To The Trees (2:56) *Clint Eastwood;* 10 The Gospel Of No Name City (1:44) *Alan Dexter;* 11 Best Things (3:33) *Lee Marvin, Clint Eastwood;* 12 Wand'rin' Star (4:29) *Lee Marvin;* 13 Gold Fever (3:08) *Clint Eastwood;* 14 Finale (6:15) *Harve Presnell, Jean Seberg.*

Review: With the exception of a very few, musicals of the Old West do not succeed on Broadway. Westerns tend to be a product of Hollywood. Regardless of the quality of the book, which need not concern the listener, *Paint Your Wagon* is a happy exception, which can be savored repeatedly on the 1951 original cast album in clear, up-front monaural sound. The versatility of Lerner and Loewe is certainly amazing when this show is compared to their other works. It is not set in the proper parlors of Edwardian London, the mists of the Scottish Highlands, the elegant salons of Paris or in legendary Camelot. The setting here is the touchstone of Americana, the wild West during the Gold Rush. The elegant Lerner had a talent for creating words that seem to come from within the soul of each character. The music confirms that the very European Loewe was one of the most talented and versatile composers of the Broadway theater. While the vocal casting may not come across on the album as well as it surely did in the theater, all of the songs are sung with an energy and style that is appropriate to the setting of the show. While the 1977 film version has the same title and many of the same songs as the Broadway musical, it has almost an entirely new plot with additional characters. Lovers of the original cast album, be warned: the soundtrack recording will certainly give you a huge jolt. There is none of the subtlety or even charm of the original and the innate elegance of Frederick Loewe's music is gone. In fact, the original orchestral sound has been totally altered and replaced with a tough grittiness that was not apparent in the original. The new songs, written by Alan Jay Lerner with Andre Previn, as Loewe was evidently unwilling to work on the project, are actually quite good and don't sound out of place. However, except for Harve Presnell, an extremely gifted Broadway performer, the singing on this album is very rough. Lee Marvin and Jean Seberg were never considered singers and suffice it to say that this is Clint Eastwood's only musical performance. None of them are truly terrible and there is a sort of harsh reality contained in the performances that makes their characters seem real and earthy. Best that can be said is that, though not an important recording, it has its interesting side.

Jerry J. Thomas

The Pajama Game ♫♫♫♫

1954, Columbia Records; from the Broadway production *The Pajama Game*, 1954.

Album Notes: *Music*: Richard Adler, Jerry Ross; *Lyrics*: Richard Adler, Jerry Ross; *Orchestrations*: Don Walker; *Musical Direction*: Hal Hastings; *Cast*: John Raitt (Sid Sorokin), Janis Paige (Bebe Williams), Eddie Foy, Jr. (Hines), Carol Haney (Gladys), Reta Shaw (Mabel), Stanley Prager (Prez), Buzz Miller (Helper), Peter Gennaro (Worker); *Album Producer*: Goddard Lieberson; *CD Engineer*: Larry Keyes.

Selections: 1 Overture (4:54) Orchestra; 2 The Pajama Game/ Racing With The Clock (3:02) *Eddie Foy Jr.*; 3 A New Town Is A Blue Town (2:52) *John Raitt*; 4 I'm Not At All In Love (3:52) *Janis*

Paige; 5 I'll Never Be Jealous Again (3:14) *Eddie Foy Jr., Reta Shaw*; 6 Hey There (3:32) *John Raitt*; 7 Her Is (2:51) *Stanley Prager, Carol Haney*; 8 Once-A-Year-Day! (3:18) *John Raitt, Janis Paige*; 9 Small Talk (3:51) *John Raitt, Janis Paige*; 10 There Once Was A Man (3:10) *John Raitt, Janis Paige*; 11 Steam Heat (4:28) *Carol Haney, Buzz Miller, Peter Gennaro*; 12 Think Of The Time I Save (2:40) *Eddie Foy Jr.*; 13 Hernando's Hideaway (3:47) *Carol Haney*; 14 Seven-And-A-Half Cents (4:32) *Janis Paige, Stanley Prager*; 15 Finale (:52) Entire Company.

Review: One of the classic Broadway show scores of all time has received a recording that puts its charming, exuberant score in the best possible light. With energetic performances by John Raitt, Janis Paige, Eddie Foy, Jr. and Carol Haney along with the rest of the cast, chorus and orchestra, the score sounds better and more exciting than it actually is. There are several classic, well-known songs, but portions of this score are fairly uninteresting. It evens out to be about half and half. The slightly reverberant mono sound is in no way a deterrent to enjoyment. In fact, it takes one back to a time and a Broadway that no longer exist, perhaps never did. For that alone, it is worth listening to.

Jerry J. Thomas

Pal Joey

Pal Joey ♫♫♫♫

1989, Columbia Records; from the studio recording *Pal Joey*, 1950.

Album Notes: *Music*: Richard Rodgers; *Lyrics*: Lorenz Hart; *Orchestrations*: Ted Royal; *Musical Direction*: Lehman Engel; *Cast*: Harold Lang (Joey Evans), Vivienne Segal (Vera Simpson), Beverly Fite (Linda English), Barbara Ashley (Gladys Bumps), Jo Hurt (Melba Snyder), Kenneth Remo (Ludlow Lowell); *Album Producer*: Goddard Lieberson; *Engineer*: Harold Chapman; *CD Producer*: Michael Brooks; *Engineer*: Larry Keyes.

Selections: 1 Overture (3:36) Orchestra; 2 You Mustn't Kick It Around (2:26) *Harold Lang*; 3 I Could Write A Book (3:45) *Harold Lang, Beverly Fite*; 4 That Terrific Rainbow (3:18) *Barbara Ashley*; 5 What Is A Man? (3:01) *Vivienne Segal*; 6 Happy Hunting Horn (2:48) *Harold Lang*; 7 Bewitched, Bothered And Bewildered (3:09) *Vivienne Segal*; 8 Pal Joey (What Do I Care For A Dame?)/Joey Looks Into The Future (ballet) (3:08) *Harold Lang*; 9 Zip (3:19) *Jo Hurt*; 10 Plant You Now, Dig You Later (2:30) *Kenneth Remo, Barbara Ashley*; 11 Den Of Iniquity (3:27) *Harold Lang, Vivienne Segal*; 12 Do It The Hard Way (2:43) *Kenneth Remo*; 13 Take Him (3:25)

broadway & screen musicals

Vivienne Segal, Beverly Fite; 14 Finale (3:07) *Vivienne Segal, Harold Lang.*

Review: The last effort by Richard Rodgers and Lorenz Hart, *Pal Joey* is a ground-breaking, innovative show that raises the musical genre to an art form (though few in 1940 suspected it), and stands today as an early precursor of the musicals Stephen Sondheim would create some 30 years later. Based on the short stories by John O'Hara, it introduces a charming "heel," a small-time nightclub performer who ditches the innocent girl in love with him for a middle-aged socialite in his desire to climb the ladder of success and open his own club. Though the mature aspects of the story left critics divided over the show's real merits, the score by Rodgers and Hart received unanimous praise, and yielded at least one instantly recognizable hit song in "Bewitched."

In 1950, Goddard Lieberson, head of A&R at Columbia Records, recorded a studio cast album of the score, with Vivienne Segal reprising the role of the socialite Vera Simpson, which she had created in the original, and Harold Lang singing Joey, the role originated by Gene Kelly in 1940. The recording was an immediate success, so much so that it led to a successful revival of the show on Broadway the following year. Though in upfront mono sound, the recording remains the closest document available of the score in its near-to-original presentation.

Pal Joey 🎵🎵

1989, Capitol Records; from the screen musical *Pal Joey*, Columbia Pictures, 1957.

Album Notes: *Music*: Richard Rodgers; *Lyrics*: Lorenz Hart; *Orchestrations*: Arthur Morton; *Arrangements*: Nelson Riddle, George Duning; The Columbia Studio Chorus and Orchestra conducted by Morris Stoloff; *Cast*: Frank Sinatra (Joey Evans), Rita Hayworth (Vera Simpson), Kim Novak (Linda English), Barbara Nichols (Gladys Bumps); *CD Engineer*: Bob Norberg.

Selections: 1 Overture (2:36)Orchestra; 2 That Terrific Rainbow (1:50) *Trudy Erwin*; 3 I Didn't Know What Time It Was (2:51) *Frank Sinatra*; 4 Do It The Hard Way (2:00)Orchestra; 5 Great Big Town (1:11)Girls' Chorus; 6 There's A Small Hotel (2:37) *Frank Sinatra*; 7 Zip (3:07) *Jo Ann Greer*; 8 I Could Write A Book (3:55) *Frank Sinatra*; 9 Bewitched (4:26) *Jo Ann Greer*; 10 The Lady Is A Tramp (3:17) *Frank Sinatra*; 11 Plant You Now, Dig You Later (1:50)Orchestra; 12 My Funny Valentine (2:05) *Trudy Erwin*; 13 You Mustn't Kick It Around (2:26)Orchestra; 14 Bewitched (3:41) *Frank Sinatra*; 15 Strip Number (3:25)Orchestra; 16 Dream Sequence: What Do I Care For A Dame/Bewitched/I Could Write A Book (6:08) *Orchestra/ Frank Sinatra.*

Review: As is the case with Frank Sinatra's film soundtrack recordings on Capitol, the CD release of Rodgers & Hart's *Pal Joey* suffers from an interminable lack of quality.

While the musical numbers survive as some of the most endearing, snappy performances of Sinatra's entire career (this was 1957, after all, and the singer was at the peak of his vocal power), their full impact is marred by the lack of detail or presence in the sound quality—a characteristic that has marked this recording since its first release as an LP. Additionally, the original mastering engineers seem to have used pseudo-stereo processing on some tracks (the classic "Lady Is A Tramp," which originates from a Sinatra-Riddle Capitol Studio session, is here reduced to a blur—the clarity and detail of the original purposely destroyed so it would match the poor balance of the other tracks).

Sonic deficiencies aside, the soundtrack vitally preserves Sinatra's definitive performances of songs that have become almost synonymous with his name: "The Lady Is a Tramp," "Bewitched," "I Didn't Know What Time It Was" and "I Could Write a Book" among them. These are the songs, and the interpretations, that define Sinatra's finest hour!

Charles L. Granata

Pal Joey 🎵🎵🎵🎵

1995, DRG Records; from the concert performance *Pal Joey*, 1995.

Album Notes: *Music*: Richard Rodgers; *Lyrics*: Lorenz Hart; *Orchestrations*: Hans Spialek; *Musical Direction*: Rob Fisher; *Cast*: Peter Gallagher (Joey Evans), Patti LuPone (Vera Simpson), Daisy Prince (Linda English), Vicki Lewis (Gladys Bumps), Bebe Neuwirth (Melba Snyder), Arthur Rubin (Louis) Ned Eisenberg (Ludlow Lowell), Lori Werner, Mamie Duncan-Gibbs, Nora Brennan, Lynn Sterling, Georgina Spelvin, Georgette Spelvin; *Album Producer*: Hugh Fordin; *Engineer*: Cynthia Daniels.

Selections: 1 Overture (4:22)Orchestra; 2 You Mustn't Kick It Around (3:31) *Peter Gallagher, Vicki Lewis*; 3 I Could Write A Book (3:46) *Peter Gallagher, Daisy Prince*; 4 Chicago (A Great Big Town)(:58) *Lori Werner, Mamie Duncan-Gibbs, Nora Brennan, Lynn Sterling, Georgina Spelvin, Georgette Spelvin*; 5 That Terrific Rainbow (4:07) *Vicki Lewis*; 6 What Is A Man? (2:28) *Patti LuPone*; 7 Happy Hunting Horn (2:39) *Peter Gallagher*; 8 Bewitched, Bothered And Bewildered (4:46) *Patti LuPone*; 9 Bewitched, Bothered And Bewildered (encore)(:50) *Patti LuPone*; 10 Pal Joey (What Do I Care For A Dame?)(1:13) *Peter Gallagher*; 11 Joey Looks Into The Future (ballet) (5:38) Orchestra; 12 The Flower Garden Of My Heart (4:17) *Arthur Rubin, Lori Werner, Mamie Duncan-Gibbs, Nora Brennan, Lynn Sterling, Georgina Spelvin, Georgette Spelvin*; 13 Zip (4:01)

"What the filmmaker creates may be very different from the concept on the page.... You have to see Daniel Day-Lewis running through the woods in *Last of the Mohicans* looking a certain way and conveying a certain feeling before you can capture it properly in music."

Randy Edelman
(The Hollywood Reporter, 1-15-97)

Bebe Neuwirth; 14 Plant You Now, Dig You Later (4:46) *Ned Eisenberg, Vicki Lewis*; 15 Den Of Iniquity (3:17) *Patti LuPone, Peter Gallagher*; 16 Do It The Hard Way (2:24) *Ned Eisenberg, Vicki Lewis*; 17 Take Him (3:24) *Daisy Prince, Patti LuPone*; 18 Bewitched, Bothered And Bewildered (reprise)(1:25) *Patti LuPone*; 19 I'm Talkin' To My Pal (2:14) *Peter Gallagher*.

Review: Of the several recordings of the score available, this is by far the best: the sound quality is exceptional, and the crackling performances right on target, with Peter Gallagher appropriately charming as a heel, Patti LuPone grandly superb as Vera, Daisy Prince at her fetching best as the innocent Linda, and Bebe Neuwirth, whose rendition of "Zip" is a highlight, particularly effective as Melba. The recording, a result of a concert presentation in New York City Center's highly-acclaimed "Encore!" series, contains many selections not available elsewhere, and is the one to have if you must have only one.

Passion ♫♫♫

1994, Angel Records; from the Broadway production *Passion*, 1994.

Album Notes: *Music:* Stephen Sondheim; *Lyrics:* Stephen Sondheim; *Orchestrations:* Jonathan Tunick; *Musical Direction:* Paul Gemignani; *Cast:* Donna Murphy (Fosca), Jere Shea (Giorgio), Marin Mazzie (Clara), Gregg Edelman (Col. Ricci), Tom Aldredge (Dr. Tambourri); *Album Producer:* Phil Ramone; *Engineers:* Al Schmitt, Frank Filipetti.

Selections: 1 Happiness (5:12) *Marin Mazzie, Jere Shea*; 2 First Letter (1:11) *Marin Mazzie, Jere Shea, Gregg Edelman, Tom Aldredge*; 3 Second Letter (:34) *Marin Mazzie, Jere Shea*; 4 Third Letter (:49) *Marin Mazzie, Jere Shea*; 5 Fourth Letter (:51) *Marin Mazzie, Jere Shea*; 6 I Read (5:27) *Donna Murphy, Jere*

Shea; 7 Transition (:42) *Jere Shea*; 8 Garden Sequence (5:14) *Tom Aldredge, Gregg Edelman, Donna Murphy, Jere Shea, Marin Mazzie*; 9 Transition (1:08) *Donna Murphy, Jere Shea*; 10 Trio (2:18) *Donna Murphy, Jere Shea, Marin Mazzie*; 11 Transition (:37)*Ensemble*; 12 I Wish I Could Forget You (3:15) *Donna Murphy, Jere Shea*; 13 Soldiers' Gossip (1:10) *Francis Ruivivar, George Dvorsky, Cris Groenendaal, William Parry*; 14 Flashback (6:56) *Tom Aldredge, Donna Murphy, Linda Balgord, John Leslie Wolfe, Matthew Porretta, Jere Shea, Juliet Lambert*; 15 Sunrise Letter (1:43) *Marin Mazzie, Jere Shea*; 16 Is This What You Call Love? (1:34) *Jere Shea*; 17 Soldiers' Gossip (:46) *Francis Ruivivar, George Dvorsky, Cris Groenendaal, William Parry*; 18 Transition (:37) *Cris Groenendaal*; 19 Forty Days (:45) *Marin Mazzie*; 20 Loving You (2:07) *Donna Murphy*; 21 Transition (:34) *Duo*; 22 Soldiers' Gossip (:37) *Francis Ruivivar, George Dvorsky, Cris Groenendaal, William Parry*; 23 Farewell Letters (3:09) *Marin Mazzie, Jere Shea*; 24 No One Has Ever Loved Me (4:26) *Donna Murphy, Jere Shea*; 25 Finale (4:57) *Francis Ruivivar, George Dvorsky, Cris Groenendaal, William Parry, Donna Murphy, Jere Shea*.

Review: Stephen Sondheim and James Lapine's tale of obsessive love in 19th century Italy was a hit on Broadway, winning the 1994 Tony award for Best Musical. It made a star of Donna Murphy as a sickly, unattractive woman who wins her officer purely through the force of her longing. The recording is crystalline, the leads beautifully sung, but this music is ultimately more interesting than compelling, and seems unlikely to stand with the great Sondheim scores.

Marc Kirkeby

Peter Pan ♫♫♫♫

1989, RCA Victor; from the Broadway and television productions *Peter Pan*, 1954.

Album Notes: *Music:* Jule Styne, Mark Charlap, Trude Rittman; *Lyrics:* Betty Comden and Adolph Green, Carolyn Leigh; *Incidental Music:* Trude Rittman, Elmer Bernstein; *Orchestrations:* Albert Sendrey; *Musical Direction:* Louis Adrian; *Cast:* Mary Martin (Peter Pan), Cyril Ritchard (Mr. Darling/Capt. Hook), Kathy Nolan (Wendy), Margalo Gillmore (Mrs. Darling), Robert Harrington (John), Joseph Stafford (Michael), Sondra Lee (Tiger Lily), Heller Halliday (Liza); *Album Producer:* Hugo Winterhalter, Joe Carlton; *CD Producer:* Didier C. Deutsch; *Engineer:* Paul Goodman.

Selections: 1 Overture (3:30)*Orchestra*; 2 Prologue (1:56)*Orchestra*; 3 Tender Shepherd (2:00) *Margalo Gillmore, Kathy Nolan, Robert Harrington, Joseph Stafford*; 4 I've Gotta Crow (3:30) *Mary Martin, Kathy Nolan*; 5 Never Never Land (3:22) *Mary Martin,*

Kathy Nolan; 6 I'm Flying (3:51) *Mary Martin, Kathy Nolan, Robert Harrington, Joseph Stafford*; 7 Pirate Song (:54)Pirates, Lost Boys; 8 Hook's Tango (1:26) *Cyril Ritchard*; 9 Indians (2:35)Indians; 10 Wendy (2:37) *Mary Martin, Robert Harrington, Joseph Stafford*; 11 Tarantella (:56) *Cyril Ritchard*; 12 I Won't Grow Up (3:07) *Mary Martin, Kathy Nolan, Robert Harrington, Joseph Stafford*; 13 Oh, My Mysterious Lady (3:28) *Mary Martin, Cyril Ritchard*; 14 Ugg-A-Wugg (3:25) *Mary Martin, Sondra Lee*; 15 Distant Melody (2:14) *Mary Martin, Kathy Nolan*; 16 Captain Hook's Waltz (2:53) *Cyril Ritchard*; 17 Finale: I've Gotta Crow/ Tender Shepherd/I Won't Grow Up/Never Never Land (reprises)(6:57) *Mary Martin, Cyril Ritchard, Heller Halliday, Kathy Nolan, Robert Harrington, Joseph Stafford, Margalo Gillmore.*

Review: Mary Martin scored a personal, long-lasting triumph as the "boy who refuses to grow up" in this musical presentation which bombed on Broadway the first time it was staged, but then went on to make television history when it became a perennial favorite enjoyed by millions in repeated annual showings. Initially created by Mark "Moose" Charlap and Carolyn Leigh (who wrote "I Gotta Crow," "I Won't Grow Up," and the thrilling "I'm Flying"), the score was beefed up with new songs by Jule Styne, Betty Comden and Adolph Green, while the show was still in tryouts on the West Coast. Its arrival on Broadway on October 20, 1954, in the midst of a particularly busy season, was hardly noticed, and it closed after 154 performances, though both Mary Martin and Cyril Ritchard, as the hilariously evil Captain Hook, won Tony Awards for their performances. Though in glorious mono sound, the cast album does full justice to this enjoyable show, and to the star's winning portrayal.

The Phantom of the Opera
♪♪♪♪

1987, Polydor Records; from the Broadway production *The Phantom of the Opera*, 1987.

Album Notes: *Music*: Andrew Lloyd Webber; *Lyrics*: Charles Hart; *Orchestrations*: David Cullen, Andrew Lloyd Webber; *Musical Direction*: Michael Reed; *Cast*: Michael Crawford (The Phantom), Sarah Brightman (Christine), Steve Barton (Raoul), Rosemary Ashe (Carlotta), Janet Devenish (Meg), Janos Kurucz (Buquet), John Savident (Firmin), David Firth (Andre), Mary Millar (Madame Giry), John Aron (Piangi); *Album Producer*: Andrew Lloyd Webber; *Engineer*: Martin Levan.

Selections: CD 1 (54:08): 1 Think Of Me *Rosemary Ashe, Sarah Brightman, Steve Barton*; 2 Angel Of Music *Sarah Brightman, Janet Devenish*; 3 Little Lotte/The Mirror *Steve Barton, Sarah Brightman, Michael Crawford*; 4 The Phantom Of The Opera *Michael Crawford, Sarah Brightman*; 5 The Music Of The Night *Michael Crawford*; 6 I Remember/Stranger Than You Dreamt It *Sarah Brightman, Michael Crawford*; 7 Magical Lasso *Janos Kurucz, Janet Devenish, Mary Millar*; 8 Notes/Prima Donna *John Savident, David Firth, Steve Barton, Rosemary Ashe, Mary Millar, Janet Devenish, Michael Crawford*; 9 Poor Fool, He Makes Me Laugh *Rosemary Ashe*; 10 Why Have You Brought Me Here/Raoul, I've Been There *Steve Barton, Sarah Brightman*; 11 All I Ask Of You *Steve Barton, Sarah Brightman*; 12 All I Ask Of You (reprise) *Michael Crawford.*

CD 2 (46:23): 1 Masquerade/Why So Silent; 2 Notes/Twisted Every Way *David Firth, John Savident, Rosemary Ashe, John Aron, Steve Barton, Sarah Brightman, Michael Crawford*; 3 Wishing You Were Somehow Here Again *Sarah Brightman*; 4 Wandering Child/Bravo, Monsieur *Michael Crawford, Sarah Brightman, Steve Barton*; 5 The Point Of No Return *Michael Crawford, Sarah Brightman*; 6 Down Once More/Track Down This Murderer.

Review: If crashing chandeliers are your thing, then this recording of Andrew Lloyd Webber's musical treatment of the Gaston Leroux celebrated gothic tale set in Paris at the turn of the century, might be right for you. In all fairness to Webber, his score, a wall-to-wall display of tunes that sometimes recall the stylistic profligacies of Puccini, brims with moments that elicit strong romantic response, and strikes a particularly effective theatrical note in the evening's only highlight, "The Music of the Night," sung in dulcet fashion by Michael Crawford. But the show, still running on Broadway at this writing, some ten years after its premiere on January 26, 1988, owes much of its success to Hal Prince's atmospheric staging of this story about a disfigured mad man hiding in Paris' Opera theater, in love with a soprano, has no qualms eliminating in ghoulish fashion anyone who stands in her way to stardom. Webber's wife at the time, Sarah Brightman, sounding better on record than she did on stage, portrays Christine, the Phantom's love interest.

Pinocchio ♪♪♪♪

1992, Walt Disney Records; from the animated feature *Pinocchio*, Walt Disney Pictures, 1940.

Album Notes: *Music*: Leigh Harline; *Lyrics*: Ned Washington, Paul J. Smith; The Disney Chorus and Orchestra, conducted by Leigh Harline; *Cast*: Dickie Jones (Pinocchio), Christian Rub (Gepetto), Cliff Edwards (Jiminy Cricket), Evelyn Venable (The Blue Fairy), Walter Catlett (J. Worthington Foulfellow), Frankie Darro (Lampwick), Charles Judels (Stromboli/The Coachman), Don Brodie (Barker); *Album Producer*: Michael Leon; *Engineers*: John Polito, Doug Schwartz, Bruce Botnick.

Selections: 1 When You Wish Upon A Star (3:13) *Cliff Edwards*; 2 Little Wooden Head (5:43); 3 Clock Sequence (:53); 4 Kitten Theme (:38); 5 The Blue Fairy (3:26); 6 Give A Little Whistle (1:36) *Cliff Edwards, Dickie Jones*; 7 Old Gepetto (4:42); 8 Off To School (4:17); 9 Hi-Diddle-Dee-Dee (An Actor's Life For Me)(1:39) *Walter Catlett*; 10 So Sorry (1:34); 11 I've Got No Strings (2:21) *Dickie Jones*; 12 Sinister Stromboli (2:26); 13 Sad Reunion (3:20); 14 Lesson In Lies (2:29); 15 Turn On The Old Music Box (:48); 16 Coach To Pleasure Island (4:44); 17 Angry Cricket (1:18); 18 Transformation (3:49); 19 Message From The Blue Fairy (1:28); 20 To The Rescue (:32); 21 Deep Ripples (1:27); 22 Desolation Theme (1:40); 23 Monstro Awakens (2:01); 24 Whale Chase (3:18); 25 A Real Boy (1:42).

Review: Walt Disney had a real winner in this 1940 animated morality fable based on the Italian tale about a puppetmaker, Gepetto, whose wish to have a real son is eventually granted by the "Blue Fairy," though Pinocchio also has to win his wings and does so only after he lives many adventures with various unreliable people, and saves Gepetto from certain death. The score, by Leigh Harline and Ned Washington, yielded the Academy Award-winning "When You Wish Upon a Star," and brims with great musical moments that come vividly to life in this mono recording, recently dusted off and remastered, with a lot of instrumental passages added to the album.

The Pirate ♪♪♪♪

1991, Sony Music Special Products; from the screen musical *The Pirate*, M-G-M, 1948.

Album Notes: *Music*: Cole Porter; *Lyrics*: Cole Porter; *Orchestrations*: Conrad Salinger; The M-G-M Studio Chorus and Orchestra, conducted by Lennie Hayton; *Cast*: Gene Kelly (Serafin), Judy Garland (Manuela); *Album Producer*: Dan Rivard; *Engineer*: Ken Robertson.

Selections: 1 Title Music (1:49) Orchestra; 2 History Of The Pirate (:50) *Judy Garland*; 3 Nina (7:01) *Gene Kelly*; 4 The Sea Wall (4:46) Orchestra; 5 Mack The Black (3:57) *Judy Garland*; 6 Manuela's Sacrifice (1:31) Orchestra; 7 The Pirate Ballet (5:36) Orchestra; 8 You Can Do No Wrong (2:00) *Judy Garland*; 9 Be A Clown (3:20) *Gene Kelly, The Nicholas Brothers*; 10 Love Of My Life (2:14) *Judy Garland*; 11 Be A Clown (Finale)(2:52) *Judy Garland, Gene Kelly*; 12 Voodoo (1:47) *Judy Garland*; 13 Love Of My Life (alternate)(3:07) *Judy Garland*.

Review: A legendary flop, *The Pirate* seemed to have the right pedigree for success: a brilliant score by Cole Porter; two beloved artists, Gene Kelly and Judy Garland, billed above the title; a swashbuckling story, at a time when seafaring adventures still lured audiences; amusing characterizations by Walter Slezak and the Nicholas Brothers; superb direction by Vincente Minnelli; and the technicolor gloss that was a hallmark of the best M-G-M productions.

Circus entertainer Gene Kelly made a dashing figure as an 18th-century pirate, about whom feisty Judy Garland romanticized in her lonely Caribbean abode, until he came in and tried to sweep her off her feet; the stylized ballets and gorgeous technicolor photography took full advantage of the myriad technical possibilities offered by the studio's best craftsmen; and the score brimmed with great tunes, in which "Be a Clown" soon became a favorite. A *succes d' estime*, the screen musical is still very much revered today as one of the most attractive films to come out of the studio. The CD recording offers the score, plus two previously unreleased songs (one of them, "Voodoo," written for the film but discarded before its release).

Play On! ♪♪♪♪

1997, Varese-Sarabande Records; from the Broadway production *Play On!*, 1997.

Album Notes: *Music*: Edward Kennedy ("Duke") Ellington; *Lyrics*: Duke Ellington, Billy Strayhorn, Don George, Harry James, Mack David, Ben Carruthers, Irving Mills, Milt Gable, Nick Kenny, Albany Bigard, Irving Gordon, Eddie DeLange, Henry Nemo, John Redmond, Bob Russell, Paul Francis Webster; *Orchestrations*: Luther Henderson; *Musical Direction*: J. Leonard Oxley; *Cast*: Cheryl Freeman (Vy), Andre De Shields (Jester), Larry Marshall (Sweets), Yvette Cason (Miss Mary), Crystal Allen (C.C.), Carl Anderson (Duke), Lawrence Hamilton (Rev), Tonya Pinkins (Lady Liv); *Album Producer*: Bruce Kimmel; *Engineer*: Vincent Cirilli.

Selections: 1 Take The "A" Train (3:43) *Cheryl Freeman*; 2 Drop Me Off In Harlem (4:38) *Cheryl Freeman, Denizens of Harlem*; 3 I've Got To Be A Rug Cutter (1:28) *Andre De Shields, Cheryl Freeman*; 4 I Let A Song Go Out Of My Heart (3:11) *Carl Anderson*; 5 Mood Indigo (3:41) *Tonya Pinkins*; 6 Don't Get Around Much Anymore (2:13) *Cheryl Freeman, Tonya Pinkins*; 7 Don't You Know I Care (2:26) *Lawrence Hamilton*; 8 It Don't Mean A Thing (3:19) *Andre De Shields, Yvette Cason, Larry Marshall, Lawrence Hamilton*; 9 I Got It Bad And That Ain't Good (4:10) *Carl Anderson, Cheryl Freeman*; 10 Hit Me With A Hot Note And Watch Me Bounce (2:19) *Cheryl Freeman, Carl Anderson*; 11 I'm Just A Lucky So And So (3:24) *Andre De Shields*; 12 Solitude (4:34) *Cheryl Freeman, Carl Anderson, Tonya Pinkins, Lawrence Hamilton*; 13 I Ain't Got Nothin' But The Blues (4:51) *Tonya Pinkins*; 14 I'm Beginning To See The

Light (5:19) *Lawrence Hamilton*; 15 I Didn't Know About You (3:03) *Cheryl Freeman*; 16 Rocks In My Bed (5:59) *Larry Marshall, Andre De Shields*; 17 Love You Madly (1:58) *Yvette Cason, Larry Marshall*; 18 Prelude To A Kiss (4:13) *Cheryl Freeman, Carl Anderson*; 19 In A Mellow Tone (2:41) *Cheryl Freeman, Carl Anderson, Tonya Pinkins, Lawrence Hamilton, Denizens of Harlem.*

Review: Initially, it seemed like a terrific idea—Shakespeare's *Twelfth Night*, slyly updated to Harlem in the 1920s, with a score consisting of the best-known songs by the man who epitomized the period, Duke Ellington. But once the show hit Broadway, on March 20, 1997, it became obvious that something was not entirely right. Yes, all the elements were in perfect order—the story, despite the change of century and locale, held together rather well; the score, well... what can you say when the first number that hits you is "Take The 'A' Train" (naturally!), and also includes such gems as "I Let a Song Go Out of My Heart," "Mood Indigo," "Don't Get Around Much Anymore," "It Don't Mean a Thing," "I Got It Bad and That Ain't Good," "Solitude," "Love You Madly," and "Prelude to a Kiss"; and the cast, made of veteran performers and attractive newcomers, couldn't have been more congenial.

But somehow, the production itself looked stilted, polished but without much of the fire and intensity one might have expected from such a combination. As a result, and in the face of lukewarm reviews that did little to compel theatergoers to come and see for themselves, the show closed after a meager 61 performances.

None of the production's failings mar the cast recording, however, and both the songs and the performers literally shine in the most positive light in this exhilarating CD, the only proof positive that *Play On!* was a terrific idea, indeed.

Pocahontas ♪♪♪♪

1995, Walt Disney Records; from the animated feature *Pocahontas*, Walt Disney Pictures, 1995.

Album Notes: *Music*: Alan Menken; *Lyrics*: Stephen Schwartz; *Orchestrations*: Danny Troob, Michael Starobin, Douglas Besterman; *Vocal Arrangements*: Danny Troob, Martin Erskine; *Music Editor*: Kathleen Fogarty-Bennett; *Score Conductor*: Danny Troob; *Songs Conductor*: David Friedman; *Cast*: Mel Gibson, Judy Kuhn, Jim Cummings, Linda Hunt, Bobbi Page, David Ogden Stiers; *Album Producers*: Alan Menken, Stephen Schwartz; *Engineers*: John Richards, Bruce Botnick.

Selections: 1 The Virginia Company (1:30) Chorus; 2 Ship At Sea (2:34); 3 The Virginia Company (reprise)(:35) Mel Gibson; 4 Steady As The Beating Drum (Main Title)(1:46)Chorus; 5

Steady As The Beating Drum (reprise)(:45) *Jim Cummings*; 6 Just Around The Riverbend (2:28) *Judy Kuhn*; 7 Grandmother Willow (1:27); 8 Listen With Your Heart (1:08) *Linda Hunt, Bobbi Page*; 9 Mine, Mine, Mine (3:05) *David Ogden Stiers, Mel Gibson*; 10 Listen With Your Heart (2:44) *Linda Hunt, Bobbi Page*; 11 Colors Of The Wind (3:33) *Judy Kuhn*; 12 Savages (Part 1)(1:43) *David Ogden Stiers, Jim Cummings*; 13 Savages (Part 2)(2:13) *Judy Kuhn, David Ogden Stiers, Jim Cummings*; 14 I'll Never See Him Again (1:54); 15 Pocahontas (1:23); 16 Council Meeting (1:11); 17 Percy's Bath (:51); 18 River's Edge (1:27); 19 Skirmish (2:02); 20 Getting Acquainted (1:30); 21 Radcliffe'sPlan (1:46); 22 Picking Corn (:54); 23 The Warriors Arrive (1:22); 24 John Smith Sneaks Out (1:14); 25 Execution (1:34); 26 Farewell (4:45); 27 Colors Of The Wind (End Title)(4:18) *Vanessa Williams*; 28 If I Never Knew You (End Title)(4:11) *Jon Secada, Shanice.*

Review: A politically-correct retelling of the love story between the feisty Indian beauty, Pocahontas, and handsome Captain John Smith, leading English settlers to Virginia's lush countryside, this Disney animated feature swept the Academy Awards in 1996, winning Oscars for best original score, and best original song ("Colors of the Wind"). The score, by Alan Menken and Stephen Schwartz, is a generally very lively affair, beautifully serviced by the vocal performers, including Judy Kuhn as Pocahontas, whose rendition of "Just Around the River Bend" is a particularly fetching moment in the album. Vanessa Williams' performance of "Colors of the Wind" is fancy and enjoyable, though it sounds stylistically out of context with the rest of the album, as does Jon Secada and Shanice's rendition of "If I Never Knew You," included no doubt for name (read "commercial") value.

Porgy and Bess

Porgy and Bess ♪♪♪♪

1992, MCA Records; from the Broadway revival *Porgy and Bess*, 1942.

Album Notes: *Music*: George Gershwin; *Lyrics*: Ira Gershwin, DuBose Heyward; *Musical Direction*: Alexander Smallens; *Cast*: Todd Duncan (Porgy), Anne Brown (Bess), Avon Long (Sportin' Life), Edward Matthews (Jake), Harriet Jackson (Clara), Ruby Elzy (Serena), Warren Coleman (Crown); *CD Producer*: Ron O'Brien; *Engineer*: Erik Labson.

Selections: 1 Overture/Summertime (3:40) *Anne Brown*; 2 A Woman Is A Sometime Thing/Introducing Summertime (2:46) *Edward Matthews, Harriet Jackson, Eva Jessye Choir*; 3 My Man's Gone Now (4:05) *Anne Brown, Eva Jessye Choir*; 4 It

broadway & screen musicals

Take A Long Pull To Get There (2:06) *Edward Matthews*; 5 I Got Plenty O' Nuttin' (2:42) *Todd Duncan, Eva Jessye Choir*; 6 Buzzard Song (3:44) *Todd Duncan, Eva Jessye Choir*; 7 Bess, You Is My Woman (4:34) *Todd Duncan, Anne Brown, Eva Jessye Choir*; 8 It Ain't Necessarily So (2:46) *Todd Duncan, Eva Jessye Choir*; 9 What You Want Wid Bess? (3:00) *Anne Brown, Todd Duncan*; 10 Strawberry Woman's Call/Crab Man's Call (3:05) *Helen Dowdy, Gladys Goode, William Woolfolk, Georgette Harvey*; 11 I Loves You, Porgy (3:24) *Todd Duncan, Anne Brown*; 12 The Requiem (3:57) *Eva Jessye Choir*; 13 There's A Boat Dat's Leavin' Soon For New York (3:02) *Avon Long, Anne Brown*; 14 Porgy's Lament/Finale (3:20) *Todd Duncan, Eva Jessye Choir*; 15 I Got Plenty O' Nuttin' (2:32) *Avon Long*.

Review: See entry below.

Porgy and Bess 🎞🎞🎞🎞

1977, RCA Victor; from the Broadway revival *Porgy and Bess*, 1976.

Album Notes: *Music:* George Gershwin; *Lyrics:* Ira Gershwin, DuBose Heyward; *Musical Preparation:* George Darden; *Musical Direction:* John DeMain; *Cast:* Donnie Ray Albert (Porgy), Clamma Dale (Bess), Larry Marshall (Sportin' Life), Alexander B. Smalls (Jake), Betty Lane (Clara), Wilma Shakesnider (Serena), Andrew Smith (Crown), Carol Brice (Maria), Phyllis Bash (Strawberry Woman); Dick Hyman (Jasbo Brown); *CD Producer:* Thomas Z. Shepard; *Associate Producer:* Jay David Saks; *Engineers:* Paul Goodman, Anthony Salvatore.

Selections: CD 1: 1 Introduction/Jasbo Brown Blues (5:07) *Dick Hyman*; 2 Summertime (2:41) *Betty Lane*; 3 "Oh, nobody knows when de Lord is gonna call" (6:16) *Bernard Thacker, Alexander B. Smalls, Larry Marshall, Wilma Shakesnider, Hatwell Mace, Glover Parham*; 4 A Woman Is A Sometime Thing (2:12) *Alexander B. Smalls, Larry Marshall, Betty Lane*; 5 "Here come de honey man"/Porgy's Entrance (4:58) *Myra Merritt, Mervin Wallace, Bernard Thacker, Alexander B. Smalls, Carol Brice, Donnie Rae Albert, Wilma Shakesnider*; 6 "Here comes Big Boy!" (Entrance of Bess and Crown)(6:57) *Bernard Thacker, Alexander B. Smith, Hartwell Mace, Andrew Smith, Donnie Rae Albert, Wilma Shakesnider, Clamma Dale, Larry Marshall*; 7 "Oh, little stars, little stars" (4:12) *Donnie Rae Albert, Bernard Thacker, Hartwell Mace, Andrew Smith, Carol Brice, Wilma Shakesnider*; 8 "Wake up an' hit it out" (4:36) *Clamma Dale, Andrew Smith, Larry Marshall, Carol Brice*; 9 Gone, Gone, Gone (3:32) *Wilma Shakesnider, Carol Brice, Clamma Dale*; 10 Overflow (2:32) *Alexander B. Smalls, Mervin Wallace, Donnie Rae Albert, Betty Lane*; 11 "Well, well, well, a saucer-burying setup" (3:35) *Hansford Rowe, Wilma Shakesnider, Myra Merritt, Mervin Wallace, Donnie Rae Albert,*

William Gammon, Alexander B. Smalls; 12 My Man's Gone Now (4:44) *Wilma Shakesnider*; 13 "How de saucer stan' now, my sister?" (2:06) *Cornel Richie, Wilma Shkesnider, Alexander B. Smalls, Donnie Rae Albert*; 14 Leavin' For The Promise' Lan' (4:33) *Clamma Dale*.

CD 2: 1 It Takes A Long Pull To Get There (3:19) *Alexander B. Smalls*; 2 "Mus'be you mens forgot about de picnic" (:39) *Shirley Baines, Alexander B. Smalls, Betty Lane*; 3 I Got Plenty O' Nuttin' (2:47) *Donnie Rae Albert,*; 4 "Lissen there, what I tells you" (1:12) *Wilma Shakesnider, Carol Brice, Larry Marshall*; 5 I Hates Yo' Struttin' Style (1:08) *Carol Brice*; 6 "Mornin', Lawyer" (4:20) *Carol Brice, Raymond Bazemore, Donnie Rae Albert, Clamma Dale, Myra Merritt*; 7 Dey's a Buckra comin'" (2:23) *Alex Carrington, Shirley Baines, Wilma Shakesnider, Kenneth Barry, Bernard Thacker, Betty Lane, Donnie Rae Albert*; 8 The Buzzard Song (3:21) *Donnie Rae Albert*; 9 "'Lo, Bess, goin' to the picnic?" (3:20) *Larry Marshall, Clamma Dale, Donnie Rae Albert, Alexander B. Smalls*; 10 Bess, You Is My Woman (6:01) *Donnie Rae Albert, Clamma Dale*; 11 Oh, I Can't Sit Down (1:37) *Clamma Dale*; 12 "What's de matter wid you, sister?" (2:34) *Carol Brice, Clamma Dale, Donnie Rae Albert*; 13 I Ain't Got No Shame (2:42) *Clamma Dale*; 14 It Ain't Necessarily So (3:11) *Larry Marshall*; 15 Dance/"Shame on all you sinners" (2:18) *Wilma Shakesnider, Carol Brice*; 16 "Crown!" (4:07) *Clamma Dale, Andrew Smith*; 17 What You Want Wid Bess? (2:30) *Clamma Dale, Andrew Smith*; 18 "Lemme go, hear dat boat"(1:22) *Clamma Dale, Andrew Smith*; 19 "Honey, dat's all de breakfast I got time for" (2:30) *Alexander B. Smalls, Steven Alex-Cole, Hartwell Mace, Carol Brice*; 20 "Take yo' hands off me, I say" (2:32) *Clamma Dale, Wilma Shakesnider, Carol Brice, Mervin Wallace, Donnie Rae Albert*; 21 "Oh, Doctor Jesus" (2:18) *Wilma Shakesnider, Donnie Rae Albert, Myra Merritt, Mervin Wallace*; 22 Strawberry Woman/Honey Man/Crab Man (3:11) *Phyllis Bash, Mervin Wallace, Steven Alex-Cole*; 23 "Now de time, oh, Gawd" (3:26) *Donnie Rae Albert, Clamma Dale*; 24 I Loves You, Porgy (3:46) *Clamma Dale, Donnie Rae Albert*.

CD 3: 1 "Why you been out on that wharf so long, Clara?" (2:24) *Carol Brice, Betty Lane*; 2 "Oh, Doctor Jesus" (Hurricane Scene)/Summertime (reprise) (4:48) *Donnie Rae Albert, Betty Lane, Wilma Shakesnider, Larry Marshall*; 3 "What makes you so still, Bess"/"Oh, dere's somebody knockin'" (1:53) *Donnie Rae Albert, Clamma Dale, Carol Brice, Mervin Wallace, Bernard Thacker*; 4 "You is a nice parcel of Christians" (4:17) *Andrew Smith, Wilma Shakesnider, Clamma Dale, Donnie Rae Albert*; 5 A Red-Headed Woman (1:39) *Andrew Smith*; 6 "Jake's boat in de river" (3:00) *Clamma Dale, Betty Lane, Andrew Smith,*

Donnie Rae Albert; 7 Clara, Clara (3:47); 8 "You low-lived skunk" (1:58) *Carol Brice, Larry Marshall*; 9 Summertime (reprise)/ Death Of Crown (4:26) *Clamma Dale, Donnie Rae Albert*; 10 "Wait for us at the corner, Al" (4:08) *Hansford Rowe, Shirley Baines, Wilma Shakesnider, Myra Merritt, John B. Ross*; 11 What is your name?" (3:46) *John B. Ross, Donnie Rae Albert, Hansford Rowe, Clamma Dale, Larry Marshall, William Gammon*; 12 "Oh, Gawd! They goin' make him look on Crown's face!" (1:55) *Clamma Dale, Larry Marshall*; 13 There's A Boat Dat's Leavin' Soon For New York (4:08) *Larry Marshall, Clamma Dale*; 14 Catfish Row Interlude (3:22)Orchestra; 15 "Good mornin', sistuh! Good mornin', brudder!" (2:21)Ensemble; 16 "It's Porgy comin' home" (6:18) *Bernard Thacker, Donnie Rae Albert, Myra Merritt, Carol Brice*; 17 Oh, Bess, Oh, Where's My Bess (2:28) *Donnie Rae Albert, Carol Brice, Wilma Shakesnider*; 18 "Bess is gone" (1:49) *Myra Merritt, Bernard Thacker, Donnie Rae Albert, Wilma Shakesnider*; 19 Oh, Lawd, I'm On My Way (1:38) *Donnie Rae Albert*.

Review: A landmark in the history of the musical theatre, *Porgy and Bess* is a show that leaves critics and admirers alike totally baffled: though no one today denies the importance of the Gershwins and DuBose Heyward's masterpiece, few can agree about what the show should be called. An opera? A folk opera? A musical comedy? By its scope, and its abundance of musical numbers, arias and recitatives, it recalls an opera, though its story, set in Catfish Row, the glum black ghetto in Charleston, South Carolina, would designate it as a folk opera, a subtle nuance that has its importance. And again, because its authors feared that the tag would damage its chances of success when it premiered on October 10, 1935, it was presented in a Broadway theatre as a standard musical, even though there was really nothing standard about it.

Be that as it may, *Porgy and Bess* stands out today as an incredible theatrical achievement, one of the most colorful, large-scale offerings ever to come from the fertile pens of George and Ira Gershwin, who completed it in little over 20 months, a show that is often mentioned as the best example of the American musical theatre at its most creative and expressive. Though not a success in 1935 (it only played 124 performances), it nonetheless attracted both music and theater critics from all the dailies at the time, who only had praises for its score, in which "It Ain't Necessarily So," "I Loves You Porgy," "I Got Plenty O' Nuttin'," and "Summertime," its most recognizable tune, soon emerged as qualified hits.

Revived in 1942, in a somewhat downsized presentation, with Todd Duncan and Anne Brown reprising the roles they had created in 1935, and with Avon Long portraying Sportin' Life,

the drug dealer who convinces Bess to leave Porgy and move to New York, the show had a successful run of 286 performances. It also yielded a cast album recording, the first listed above, which, though in mono sound, and only presenting the highlights from the score, still stands out as a historical document of prime importance.

Subsequently revived several times, it returned to Broadway in 1976, in a sumptuously theatrical production by the Houston Grand Opera that restored many scenes and musical moments previously discarded, and truly made it the "opera" Gershwin had initially envisioned. With Clamma Dale giving a breathtaking performance as Bess, the show had a run of 122 performances, extended from its original four-week engagement, before touring the country for several years. The complete cast album recording, on RCA, made shortly after the premiere on September 25, 1976, is the best available anywhere, a vibrant, outstanding testimony to Gershwin's musical genius.

Purlie ♫♪

1990, RCA Victor; from the Broadway production *Purlie*, 1970.

Album Notes: *Music*: Gary Geld; *Lyrics*: Peter Udell; *Choral Arrangements and Orchestrations*: Garry Sherman, Luther Henderson; *Musical Direction*: Joyce Brown; *Cast*: Cleavon Little (Purlie), Melba Moore (Lutiebelle), Novella Nelson (Missy), Sherman Hemsley (Gitlow), Linda Hopkins (Church Soloist), C. David Colson (Charlie), Helen Martin (Idella), John Heffernan (Ol' Cap'n); *Album Producer*: Andy Wiswell; *Engineer*: Bob Arnold; *CD Producer*: Bill Rosenfield; *Engineer*: Jay Newland.

Selections: 1 Walk Him Up The Stairs (6:03) *Linda Hopkins*; 2 New Fangled Preacher Man (2:17) *Cleavon Little*; 3 Skinnin' A Cat (1:52) *Sherman Hemsley*; 4 Purlie (3:49) *Melba Moore*; 5 The Harder They Fall (2:46) *Cleavon Little, Melba Moore*; 6 The Barrels Of War/The Unborn Love (:46) *C. David Colson, Helen Martin*; 7 Big Fish, Little Fish (2:23) *John Heffernan, C. David Colson*; 8 God's Alive (:31) *C. David Colson, Helen Martin*; 9 I Got Love (3:17) *Melba Moore*; 10 Great White Father (2:37)Male Ensemble; 11 Down Home (6:00) *Cleavon Little, Novella Nelson*; 12 First Thing Monday Mornin' (4:48)Male Ensemble; 13 He Can Do It (4:11) *Novella Nelson, Melba Moore*; 14 The World Is Comin' To A Start (2:47) *C. David Colson*; 15 Walk Him Up The Stairs/Epilogue (2:19) *Cleavon Little*.

Review: Based on Ossie Davis' "Purlie Victorious," *Purlie* is best remembered today for its cast of great performers, which include Cleavon Little, Melba Moore in her first starring role since *Hair*, Linda Hopkins, Sherman Hemsley (before he found grace on television as the irascible Jefferson), and Novella Nelson, a much underrated vocalist. Besides providing Melba Moore with one of her signature songs ("I Got Love"), the predictable score by Gary Geld and Peter Udell (also responsible for *Shenandoah*), has little to recommend it for, though *Purlie* lasted long enough, in a season marked by the absence of great shows, to cop a Tony as Best Musical, as well as one for its female star.

Ragtime ♫♫♫♫

1996, RCA Records; from the studio cast recording *Ragtime*, 1996.

Album Notes: *Music*: Stephen Flaherty; *Lyrics*: Lynn Ahrens; *Orchestrations*: William David Brohn; *Vocal Arrangements*: Stephen Flaherty; *Musical Direction*: Ted Sperling; *Cast*: Brian Stokes Mitchell (Coalhouse Walker, Jr.), Peter Friedman (Tateh), Marin Mazzie (Mother), Audra McDonald (Sarah), Mark Jacoby (Father), Lynnette Perry (Evelyn Nesbit), Steven Sutcliffe (Mother's Younger Brother), Mary Bond Davis (Sarah's Friend), Jim Corti (Harry Houdini), Michael Fletcher (Henry Ford), Camille Saviola (Emma Goldman), Nicholas Rose (Little Boy), Afton Eddy (Little Girl); *Album Producer*: Jay David Saks; *Engineer*: James P. Nichols.

Selections: 1 Ragtime (3:12) *Nicholas Rose*; 2 Goodbye My Love (2:13) *Marin Mazzie*; 3 Journey On (3:38) *Mark Jacoby, Alan Swann, Afton Eddy, Peter Friedman, Marin Mazzie*; 4 The Crime Of The Century (2:06) *Lynnette Perry*; 5 Gettin' Ready Rag (3:07) *Brian Stokes Mitchell, Mary Bond Davis*; 6 Henry Ford (1:38) *Michael Fletcher, Brian Stokes Mitchell*; 7 Your Daddy's Son (3:43) *Audra McDonald*; 8 New Music (4:04) *Mark Jacoby, Marin Mazzie, Steven Sutcliffe, Brian Stokes Mitchell, Audra McDonald*; 9 Wheels Of A Dream (3:39) *Brian Stokes Mitchell, Audra McDonald*; 10 The Night That Goldman Spoke At Union Square (2:15) *Camille Saviola, Steven Sutcliffe*; 11 Gliding (2:14) *Peter Friedman*; 12 'Till We Reach That Day (4:32) *Mary Bond Davis, Brian Stokes Mitchell, Camille Saviola, Marin Mazzie, Peter Friedman, Steven Sutcliffe, Paula Newsome*; 13 What A Game! (2:34) *Mark Jacoby, Nicholas Rose*; 14 Coalhouse's Soliloquy (1:55) *Brian Stokes Mitchell*; 15 He Wanted To Say (3:52) *Steven Sutcliffe, Brian Stokes Mitchell, Camille Saviola*; 16 Buffalo Nickel Photoplay, Inc. (2:05) *Peter Friedman*; 17 Our Children (2:21) *Marin Mazzie, Peter Friedman*; 18 The Show Biz (3:13) *Jim Corti, Lynnette Perry*; 19 Back To Before (3:47) *Marin Mazzie*; 20 Make Them Hear You (2:46) *Brian Stokes Mitchell*; 21 Wheels Of A Dream (reprise)(2:41) *Nicholas Rose, Brian Stokes Mitchell, Audra McDonald*.

Review: It is not unusual for a Broadway-bound musical to release a cast album in advance of its premiere (many of the shows by Andrew Lloyd Webber, and *Jekyll and Hyde*, in recent memory, have taken that route). But the hoopla that has accompanied the release of this cast album of *Ragtime*, fully two years ahead of its anticipated Broadway premiere, and the excitement it has generated is truly unheard of. Written by Lynn Ahrens and Stephen Flaherty, and based on E.L. Doctorow's best-selling novel and the 1981 film it yielded, *Ragtime* is a dazzling, old-fashioned musical, set at the turn of the century, that chronicles the profound social changes that paved the way for modern-day American culture and intellectual importance. Though admittedly a work-still-in-progress, *Ragtime* is as fully realized as anything one might hear or see on Broadway these days, with Marin Mazzie, Mark Jacoby, Audra McDonald and Brian Stokes Mitchell giving incredible life and energy to some of the main characters in this kaleidoscopic story.

Rent ♫♫♫♫

1996, Dreamworks Records; from the Broadway production *Rent*, 1996.

Album Notes: *Music*: Jonathan Larson; *Lyrics*: Jonathan Larson; *Additional Lyrics*: Billy Aronson; *Musical Arrangements*: Steve Skinner, Tim Well; *Musical Direction*: Tim Well; *Featured Musicians*: Steve Mack (bass), Kenny Brescia (guitar), Jeff Potter (drums, percussion), Daniel A. Weiss (synthesizers, Hammond B-3, guitars); Tim Well (piano, synthesizers); *Cast*: Adam Pascal (Roger Davis), Anthony Rapp (Mark Cohen), Jesse L. Martin (Tom Collins), Taye Diggs (Benjamin Coffin III), Fredi Walker (Joanne Jefferson), Wilson Jermaine Heredia (Angel Schunard), Daphne Rubin-Vega (Mimi Marquez), Idina Menzel (Maureen Johnson), and Kristen Lee Kelly, Byron Utley, Gwen Stewart, Timothy Britten Parker, Gilles Chiasson, Rodney Hicks, Aiko Nakasone; *Album Producers*: Arif Mardin, Steve Skinner; *Engineer*: Michael O'Reilly.

Selections: CD 1: 1 Tune Up #1 (:51) *Anthony Rapp, Adam Pascal*; 2 Voice Mail #1 (:36) *Kristen Lee Kelly* ; 3 Tune Up #2 (1:32) *Adam Pascal, Anthony Rapp, Jesse L. Martin, Taye Diggs*; 4 Rent (4:26) *Adam Pascal, Anthony Rapp, Jesse L. Martin, Fredi Walker*; 5 You Okay Honey? (1:42) *Wilson Jermaine Heredia, Jesse L.Martin*; 6 Tune Up #3 (:25) *Adam Pascal, Anthony Rapp*; 7 One Song Glory (2:44) *Adam Pascal*; 8 Light My Candle (4:05) *Adam Pascal, Daphne Rubin-Vega*; 9 Voice Mail #2 (:47) *Idina Menzel, Byron Utley, Gwen Stewart*; 10 Today 4 U (3:31) *Anthony Rapp, Jesse L. Martin, Adam Pascal, Wilson Jermaine Heredia*; 11 You'll See (2:57) *Taye Diggs, Anthony Rapp, Jesse L.Martin, Wilson Jermaine Heredia*; 12 Tango: Maureen (3:29) *Anthony*

Rapp, Fredi Walker; 13 Life Support (1:58) Gilles Chiasson, Timothy Britten Parker, Kristen Lee Kelly, Wilson Jermaine Heredia, Anthony Rapp, Adam Pascal; 14 Out Tonight (3:49) Daphne Rubin-Vega; 15 Another Day (4:44) Adam Pascal, Daphne Rubin-Vega; 16 Will I? (2:30) Gilles Chiasson; 17 On The Street (1:33) Anthony Rapp, Wilson Jermaine Heredia, Gilles Chiasson; 18 Santa Fe (3:13) Wilson Jermaine Heredia, Anthony Rapp, Jesse L. Martin; 19 I'll Cover You (2:28) Anthony Rapp, Wilson Jermaine Heredia; 20 We're Okay (1:23) Fredi Walker; 21 Christmas Bells (6:05) Wilson Jermaine Heredia, Anthony Rapp, Jesse L. Martin, Adam Pascal, Daphne Rubin-Vega; 22 Over The Moon (5:17) Anthony Rapp, Idina Menzel; 23 La Vie Boheme (8:00) Adam Pascal, Idina Menzel, Anthony Rapp, Jesse L. Martin, Wilson Jermaine Heredia, Fredi Walker; 24 I Should Tell You (3:01) Adam Pascal, Daphne Rubin-Vega; 25 La Vie Boheme B (1:53) Idina Menzel, Fredi Walker, Anthony Rapp.

CD 2: 1 Seasons Of Love (2:52) Company; 2 Happy New Year (3:25) Anthony Rapp, Daphne Rubin-Vega, Idina Menzel, Adam Pascal, Fredi Walker, Wilson Jermaine Heredia, Jesse L. Martin; 3 Voice Mail #3 (:50) Aiko Nakasone, Anthony Rapp; 4 Happy New Year B (3:57) Idina Menzel, Anthony Rapp, Fredi Walker, Taye Diggs, Adam Pascal, Daphne Rubin-Vega; 5 Take Me Or Leave Me (3:43) Anthony Rapp, Idina Menzel, Fredi Walker; 6 Seasons Of Love B (1:07) Company; 7 Without You (4:21) Adam Pascal, Daphne Rubin-Vega; 8 Voice Mail #4 (:33) Adam Pascal, Anthony Rapp, Aiko Nakasone; 9 Contact (2:08) Jesse L. Martin, Idina Menzel, Daphne Rubin-Vega, Wilson Jermaine Heredia; 10 I'll Cover You (reprise)(2:51) Jesse L. Martin, Fredi Walker; 11 Halloween (1:49) Anthony Rapp; 12 Goodbye Love (5:58) Daphne Rubin-Vega, Adam Pascal, Idina Menzel, Adam Pascal, Taye Diggs; 13 What You Own (3:56) Anthony Rapp, Adam Pascal; 14 Voice Mail #5 (:57) Aika Nakasone, Byron Utley, Kristen Lee Kelly; 15 Finale (5:30) Adam Pascal, Anthony Rapp, Jesse L. Martin, Daphne Rubin-Vega, Idina Menzel; 16 Your Eyes (2:21) Adam Pascal; 17 Finale B (3:00) Daphne Rubin-Vega, Adam Pascal, Fredi Walker, Idina Menzel; 18 Seasons Of Love (4:27) Stevie Wonder.

Review: A modern treatment of Puccini's *La Boheme,* the ultimate romantic opera, *Rent,* which opened on Broadway on April 29, 1996, and is still running at this writing, is the work of Jonathan Larson, a promising young playwright-songwriter who died of an aortic aneurysm a few hours after the show's final dress rehearsal. Set in New York's East Village, the show is a joyous and turbulent musical that celebrates a community of young artists as they struggle with the soaring hopes and tough realities of today's life. Propelled by a contemporary rock score that gives it a vitality not unlike that of *Hair* three decades

earlier, *Rent* tells the story of friends living in a rundown apartment in the East Village: Roger, an HIV-infected songwriter, and Mark, a would-be filmmaker, forever chronicling on video the various elements of life around them. Enter Mimi, the proverbial girl next door, a dancer in a nightclub of dubious repute and a chronic drug user, who seduces Roger, only to walk out on him later on. Add to the mix of characters Maureen, who has ditched Mark for Joanne, a lawyer; Tom, a computer-age expert and philosopher, who falls for Angel, a transvestite sculptor; and various other cutting-edge denizens, and voila! Brash, brilliant, occasionally unfocused and messy, *Rent* is a rock opera filled with junkies, bohemian types, artists, prostitutes, lesbians and homosexuals, the kind of stuff one would have thought unlikely to succeed in traditional Broadway. Yet, the show was roundly praised by critics, went on to win the Tony as Best Musical, and a Pulitzer Prize to boot (a rare occurrence in the musical theatre), and has been a hot ticket ever since. Though the score, presented complete on a 2-CD set recorded shortly after the opening, doesn't include a hit song along the lines of *Hair*'s "Good Morning Starshine" or "Let the Sunshine In," it receives a colorful, authoritative reading from Adam Pascal, Anthony Rapp, Jesse L. Martin, Fredi Walker, Wilson Jermaine Heredia, Daphne Rubin-Vega, and Idina Menzel in the principal roles, with the anthem-like "La Vie Boheme" very likely to elicit strong, positive reactions from any listener.

The Rink ♪♪♪♪

1984, Polydor Records; from the Broadway production *The Rink*, 1984.

Album Notes: *Music:* John Kander; *Lyrics:* Fred Ebb; *Orchestrations:* Michael Gibson; *Musical Direction:* Paul Gemignani; *Cast:* Liza Minnelli (Angel), Chita Rivera (Anna), Scott Holmes (Dino), Mel Johnson, Jr. (Hiram), Scott Ellis (Sugar), Frank Mastrocola (Tom), Jason Alexander (Lenny), Ronn Carroll (Dino's Father); *Album Producer:* Norman Newell; *Engineer:* John Kurlander.

Selections: 1 Colored Lights (5:32) *Liza Minnelli*; 2 Chief Cook And Bottle Washer (3:55) *Chita Rivera*; 3 Don't Ah Ma Me (2:33) *Chita Rivera, Liza Minnelli*; 4 Blue Crystal (2:58) *Scott Holmes*; 5 Under The Rollercoaster (2:03) *Liza Minnelli*; 6 Not Enough Magic (4:18) *Liza Minnelli, Chita Rivera, Scott Holmes, Mel Johnson Jr., Scott Ellis, Frank Mastrocola, Jason Alexander, Ronn Carroll*; 7 We Can Make It (3:29) *Chita Rivera*; 8 After All These Years (3:55) *Scott Holmes, Mel Johnson Jr., Scott Ellis, Frank Mastrocola, Jason Alexander, Ronn Carroll*; 9 Angel's Rink And Social Center (3:08) *Liza Minnelli, Scott Holmes, Mel Johnson Jr., Scott Ellis, Frank Mastrocola, Jason Alexander, Ronn Carroll*; 10 What Happened To The Old Days? (3:40) *Chita*

Rivera, Mel Johnson Jr., Ronn Carroll; 11 The Apple Doesn't Fall (4:19) Chita Rivera, Liza Minnelli; 12 Marry Me (3:10) Jason Alexander; 13 Mrs. A (3:50) Chita Rivera, Liza Minnelli, Jason Alexander; 14 The Rink (3:40) Scott Holmes, Mel Johnson Jr., Scott Ellis, Frank Mastrocola, Jason Alexander, Ronn Carroll; 15 Wallflower (2:12) Liza Minnelli, Chita Rivera; 16 All The Children In A Row (5:57) Liza Minnelli, Scott Ellis; 17 Finale (1:56) Liza Minnelli, Chita Rivera.

Review: Chita Rivera and Liza Minnelli share the spotlight in this original Kander and Ebb musical in which they portray a mother and her daughter, long estranged, who get back together to save from destruction a seaside roller rink the mother has been running by herself for years. Though flawed, and hardly a big hit by normal standards (it closed after a mere 204 performances, following its premiere on February 2, 1984), the show has a solidly defined score, announced by the Jacques Brel-like "Colored Lights," and featuring many excellent numbers for the two stars. The cast album brings it all together in one superlative recording.

The Roar of the Greasepaint—The Smell of the Crowd ♫♫♫♪

1965, RCA Victor; from the Broadway production The Roar of the Greasepaint — The Smell of the Crowd, 1965.

Album Notes: *Music*: Leslie Bricusse, Anthony Newley; *Lyrics*: Leslie Bricusse, Anthony Newley; *Orchestrations*: Philip J. Lang; *Vocal and Dance Music Arrangements*: Peter Howard; *Musical Direction*: Herbert Grossman; *Cast*: Anthony Newley (Cocky), Cyril Ritchard (Sir), Sally Smith (The Kid), Joyce Jillson (The Girl), Gilbert Price (The Negro), Murray Tannenbaum (The Bully), Rawley Bates, Lori Browne, Lori Caesar, Jill Choder, Gloria Chu, Kay Cole, Marlene Dell, Boni Enten, Mitzi Feinn, Pamela Gruen, Linda Rae Hager, Cyndi Howard, Laura Michaels, Debbie Palmer, Heather Taylor (The Urchins); *Album Producer*: George Marek; *Associate Producer*: Andy Wiswell; *Engineer*: Ernie Oelrich; *CD Producer*: Bill Rosenfield; *Engineer*: Anthony Salvatore.

Selections: 1 Overture (3:22)Orchestra; 2 The Beautiful Land (1:41)The Urchins; 3 A Wonderful Day Like Today (2:10) *Cyril Ritchard*; 4 It Isn't Enough (2:23) *Anthony Newley*; 5 Things To Remember (2:56) *Cyril Ritchard*; 6 Put It In The Book (1:31) *Sally Smith*; 7 With All Due Respect (2:03) *Anthony Newley*; 8 This Dream (2:32) *Anthony Newley*; 9 Where Would You Be Without Me? (2:48) *Anthony Newley, Cyril Ritchard*; 10 My First Love Song (3:15) *Anthony Newley, Joyce Jillson*; 11 Look At That

Face (2:19) *Cyril Ritchard, Sally Smith*; 12 The Joker (2:29) *Anthony Newley*; 13 Who Can I Turn To (When Nobody Needs Me)(3:49) *Anthony Newley*; 14 That's What It Is To Be Young (1:06)The Urchins; 15 What A Man! (1:47) *Anthony Newley, Cyril Ritchard*; 16 Feeling Good (2:39) *Gilbert Price*; 17 Nothing Can Stop Me Now! (2:55) *Anthony Newley*; 18 Things To Remember (reprise)(1:57) *Cyril Ritchard*; 19 My Way (1:45) *Cyril Ritchard, Anthony Newley*; 20 Who Can I Turn To (reprise)(1:11) *Cyril Ritchard*; 21 The Beautiful Land (reprise)/Sweet Beginning (3:13) *Anthony Newley, Cyril Ritchard*.

Review: The eternal struggle between the haves and the have-nots, those in command and those under them, took an inordinate twist in *The Roar of the Greasepaint — The Smell of the Crowd*, in which Anthony Newley portrays Cocky, the eternal hopeful on the losing end, and Cyril Ritchard as Sir, whose obfuscating control Cocky tries to break, although he later realizes he needs it. The consistently satisfying score, conceived by Newley and Leslie Bricusse, is in turn elegiac, good natured, soulful, but always endearing; it yields two great solo numbers, both performed by Newley, "The Joker" and particularly "Who Can I Turn To," which soon became a favorite of cabaret singers all over the world.

Roberta ♫♫♫♪

1990, CBS Special Products; from the studio cast recording *Roberta*, 1952.

Album Notes: *Music*: Jerome Kern; *Lyrics*: Otto Harbach, Oscar Hammerstein II, Dorothy Fields, Jimmy McHugh; *Musical Direction*: Lehman Engel; *Cast*: Joan Roberts, Jack Cassidy, Kaye Ballard, Portia Nelson, Stephen Douglass, Frank Rogier; *Album Producer*: Goddard Lieberson.

Selections: 1 Overture (3:13)Orchestra; 2 Madrigal (3:26)Male Quartet; 3 You're Devastating (3:55) *Stephen Douglass*; 4 Let's Begin (3:11) *Jack Cassidy, Joan Roberts*; 5 (When Your Heart's On Fire) Smoke Gets In Your Eyes (6:03) *Joan Roberts*; 6 I Won't Dance (3:47) *Kaye Ballard, Jack Cassidy*; 7 The Touch Of Your Hand (3:26) *Joan Roberts, Frank Rogier*; 8 Something Had To Happen (2:12) *Kaye Ballard, Jack Cassidy*; 9 Yesterdays (3:57) *Portia Nelson*; 10 I'll Be Hard To Handle (3:35) *Kaye Ballard*; 11 Lovely To Look At (4:21) *Joan Roberts, Stephen Douglass*; 12 Finale (3:55) *Kaye Ballard*.

Review: A routine story, about an American sports figure who inherits a failing fashion house from his aunt in Paris and saves it from bankruptcy with the help of a friend, *Roberta* was the occasion for Jerome Kern to write a score that teems with great standards, including the classic "Smoke Gets in Your Eyes" and "Yesterdays." Initially created in 1933, it was filmed on two occasions, in 1935, with Fred Astaire, Ginger Rogers, Irene Dunne and Randolph Scott in its cast; and again in 1952, as *Lovely to Look At,* with Red Skelton, Kathryn Grayson, Howard Keel, and Marge and Gower Champion.

The studio cast album, recorded in 1952 with Jack Cassidy, Portia Nelson, Joan Roberts, Stephen Douglass, and Kaye Ballard, is the only one currently available, and while not entirely up to today's exacting digital standards, deserves a particular place in any self-serving collection.

The Rocky Horror Picture Show *♪♪♪*

1975, Ode Records; from the screen musical *The Rocky Horror Picture Show,* 1975.

Album Notes: *Music:* Richard O'Brien; *Lyrics:* Richard O'Brien; *Arrangements:* Richard Hartley; *Musical Direction:* Richard Hartley; *Featured Musicians:* Count Ian Blair (guitars), David Wintour (bass guitar), Phil Kenzie (saxophone), Rabbit (keyboards), Richard Hartley (keyboards); *Cast:* Tim Curry (Frank N Furter), Susan Sarandon (Janet Weiss), Barry Bostwick (Brad Majors), Richard O'Brien (Riff Raff), Patricia Quinn (Magenta), Little Nell (Columbia), Jonathan Adams (Dr. Everett Scott), Peter Hinwood (Rocky), Meatloaf (Eddie), Charles Gray (Narrator); *Album Producer:* Richard Hartley; *Engineers:* Keith Grant, Phil Chapman.

Selections: 1 Science Fiction/Double Feature (4:30) *Richard O'Brien;* 2 Dammit Janet (2:51) *Barry Bostwick, Susan Sarandon;* 3 Over At The Frankenstein Place (2:37) *Barry Bostwick, Susan Sarandon, Richard O'Brien;* 4 The Time Warp (3:15) *Richard O'Brien, Little Nell, Patricia Quinn, Charles Gray;* 5 Sweet Transvestite (3:21) *Tim Curry;* 6 Can I Make You A Man (2:07) *Tim Curry;* 7 Hot Patootie — Bless My Soul (3:00) *Meatloaf;* 8 I Can Make You A Man (reprise)(1:44) *Tim Curry;* 9 Touch-A, Touch-A, Touche Me (2:27) *Susan Sarandon;* 10 Eddie (2:44) *Jonathan Adams;* 11 Rose Tint My World: a) Floor Show (2:46) *Barry Bostwick, Susan Sarandon, Little Nell, Peter Hinwood,* b) Fanfare/Don't Dream It (3:34) *P: Tim Curry,* c) Wild And Untamed Thing (1:53) *P: Tim Curry, Richard O'Brien;* 12 I'm Going Home (2:48) *Tim Curry;* 13 Super Heroes (2:45) *Barry Bostwick, Susan Sarandon;* 14 Science Fiction/Double Feature (reprise)(1:26) *Richard O'Brien.*

Review: A cult favorite, *The Rocky Horror Show* took its cue from the classic horror films of the 1950s, introduced in its story elements of transvestism, spruced up the proceedings with a rock score, and set out to conquer the theatrical world. First performed in London, where it opened in June, 1973, it moved to Los Angeles, where it played various venues, including the Roxy, and made a belated debut on Broadway on March 10, 1975, closing 45 performances later. One might have thought that this would mark the end of the saga, but that same year, the show was made into a film, *The Rocky Horror Picture Show,* which has enjoyed incredible longevity throughout the years, particularly as a camp fixture among aficionados who faithfully attend regular midnight presentations to recite the dialogue along with the actors on screen. Starring Tim Curry as the cross-dressing Frank N Furter, and Barry Bostwick and Susan Sarandon as the lovers, the soundtrack album, released under various guises over the years, including an audience-participation version, is a hoot and a holler. Rocker Meatloaf (of "Bat Out of Hell" fame) also makes an appearance, as he did on stage.

Rover Dangerfield *♪♪♪*

1991, Warner Bros. Records; from the animated feature *Rover Dangerfield,* Warner Bros. Pictures, 1991.

Album Notes: *Music:* David Newman; *Songs:* Rodney Dangerfield, Bill Tragesser; *Cast:* Rodney Dangerfield (Rover).

Selections: 1 Las Vegas (3:01); 2 It's A Dog's Life And I Love It (1:59) *Rodney Dangerfield;* 3 Connie Leaves (2:43); 4 Dog Napping (:51); 5 Country (3:27); 6 Meal Time (1:11); 7 Somewhere There's A Party (1:01) *Rodney Dangerfield;* 8 In The Chicken Coop (:51); 9 I'd Give Up A Bone For You (2:13) *Rodney Dangerfield;* 10 The Sheep (:45); 11 Pep Talk (1:22); 12 Doing Well (1:09); 13 I'd Never Do It On A Christmas Tree (3:31) *Rodney Dangerfield;* 14 I'm In Love With The Dog Next Door (1:17) *Rodney Dangerfield;* 15 Back To Connie (1:50); 16 Rocky's Out (1:40); 17 I Found A Four Leaf Clover When I Met Rover (1:39) *Susan Boyd.*

Review: Comedian Rodney Dangerfield lent his voice and persona to this animated feature about a Las Vegas dog, with his mannerisms and talent for quick quips. While not a singer in the real sense of the word, Rover (pardon! Rodney) acquits himself very well of the musical numbers (notably the funny "I'd Give Up a Bone for You" and "I'm in Love with the Dog Next Door"), while David Newman's febrile score keeps its musical tongue firmly in cheek in a perfect reflection of the film's whimsical attitude about its subject.

Royal Wedding *♪♪♪♪*

1991, Sony Music Special Products; from the screen musical *Royal Wedding,* M-G-M, 1951.

Album Notes: *Music:* Burton Lane; *Lyrics:* Alan Jay Lerner; *Orchestrations:* Conrad Salinger, Skip Martin; The M-G-M Studio Chorus and Orchestra, conducted by Johnny Green; *Cast:*

Fred Astaire (Tom Bowen), Jane Powell (Ellen Bowen); *Album Producer*: Dan Rivard; *Engineer*: Ken Robertson.

Selections: 1 Overture (1:27) Orchestra; 2 Ev'ry Night At Seven (4:22) *Fred Astaire*; 3 Sunday Jumps (3:42) Orchestra; 4 Open Your Eyes (4:47) *Jane Powell*; 5 An Audition (1:39) Piano solo; 6 The Happiest Day Of My Life (2:24) *Jane Powell*; 7 How Could You Believe Me When I Said I Loved You When You Know I've Been A Liar All My Life? (6:21) *Fred Astaire, Jane Powell*; 8 Too Late Now (3:48) *Jane Powell*; 9 You're All The World To Me (4:40) *Fred Astaire*; 10 I Left My Hat In Haiti (6:11) *Fred Astaire*; 11 What A Lovely Day For A Wedding (1:14) Chorus; 12 Finale: The Royal Wedding Day (4:06) Chorus.

Review: The 1947 marriage of Princess Elizabeth and Philip Mountbatten, and the pomp and circumstance that framed the event, suggested to M-G-M producer Arthur Freed the idea for a big screen musical. With Fred Astaire set to star, Alan Jay Lerner provided a script that paralleled Astaire's own life when he and his sister, Adele, broke up their successful Broadway song-and-dance act so that she could marry a British lord. With Burton Lane writing the music to Lerner's playful lyrics, the score added the final touch to what became a regal entertainment. Jane Powell co-starred as Ellen Bowen, who fell in love with Peter Lawford while on a transatlantic trip to London, thereby setting the stage for the end of her professional career with brother Tom, whose own interest was piqued by Sarah Churchill, real-life daughter of Sir Winston. In addition to its delightfully romantic plot, and many great songs, *Royal Wedding* is also remembered today as the film in which Fred Astaire, in a feat of technical fancy, dances exhilaratingly on the walls and ceiling of a room.

St. Louis Woman 🎜🎜🎜🎜

1992, Angel Records; from the Broadway production *St. Louis Woman*, 1946.

Album Notes: *Music*: Harold Arlen; *Lyrics*: Johnny Mercer; *Musical Direction*: Leon Leonardi; *Cast*: Harold Nicholas (Little Augie), Fayard Nicholas (Barney), June Hawkins (Lili), Pearl Bailey (Butterfly), Robert Pope (Badfoot), Ruby Hill (Della Green), Rex Ingram (Biglow Brown), Milton J. Williams (Mississippi); *CD Engineer*: Robert Norberg.

Selections: 1 Li'l Augie Is A Natural Man (1:17) *Robert Pope*; 2 Any Place I Hang My Hat Is Home (2:55) *Ruby Hill*; 3 I Had Myself A True Love (3:13) *June Hawkins*; 4 Legalize My Name (2:48) *Pearl Bailey*; 5 Cakewalk Your Lady (1:39) *Robert Pope, Milton J. Williams*; 6 Come Rain Or Come Shine (2:51) *Ruby Hill, Harold Nicholas*; 7 Lullaby (2:59) *Ruby Hill*; 8 Sleep Peaceful, Mr. Used-To-Be (2:41) *June Hawkins*; 9 Leavin' Time (2:48)Cho-

rus; 10 It's A Woman's Prerogative (2:51) *Pearl Bailey*; 11 Ridin' On The Moon (2:44) *Harold Nicholas*.

Review: Harold Arlen's most memorable Broadway score—a high point of his partnership with Johnny Mercer—nonetheless failed to make a hit of this tale of St. Louis at the turn of the century, chiefly because black audiences objected to its less-than-attractive portrayal of their community. More than 50 years later, it's the songs that linger, especially the now-standard "Come Rain or Come Shine" (sung by the show's leads, Ruby Hill and Harold Nicholas) and two that made a star of the young Pearl Bailey, "Legalize My Name" and "It's a Woman's Prerogative."

Marc Kirkeby

Seven Brides for Seven Brothers 🎜🎜🎜🎜🎜

1996, Rhino Records; from the screen musical, *Seven Brides for Seven Brothers*, M-G-M, 1954.

Album Notes: *Music*: Gene De Paul; *Lyrics*: Johnny Mercer; *Orchestrations*: Alexander Courage, Bob Franklyn, Leo Arnaud, Adolph Deutsch; *Arrangements*: Adolph Deutsch, Conrad Salinger, Leo Arnaud; The M-G-M Studio Chorus and Orchestra, conducted by Adolph Deutsch; *Cast*: Jane Powell (Milly), Howard Keel (Adam Pontipee), Jeff Richards (Benjamin), Russ Tamblyn (Gideon), Tommy Rall (Frank), Marc Platt (Daniel), Matt Mattox (Caleb), Jacques d'Amboise (Ephraim), Betty Carr, Norma Doggett (Martha), Ruta Kilmonis (Ruth), Virginia Gibson (Liza), Nancy Kilgas (Sarah), Julie Newmeyer (Dorcas); *Album Producers*: George Feltenstein, Bradley Flanagan; *Engineer*: Doug Schwartz.

Selections: 1 Main Title (2:10)Orchestra; 2 Bless Yore Beautiful Hide (2:28) *Howard Keel*; 3 Do Unto Udders (1:30)Orchestra; 4 Bless Yore Beautiful Hide (reprise)(:49) *Howard Keel*; 5 Wonderful, Wonderful Day (3:16) *Jane Powell*; 6 Adam In Treetop (1:41)Orchestra; 7 When You're In Love (2:11) *Jane Powell*; 8 Goin' Co'tin' (3:34) *Jane Powell, Tommy Rall, Russ Tamblyn, Marc Platt, Matt Mattox, Jacques d'Amboise, Jeff Richards, Howard Hudson, Gene Lanham, Robert Wacker*; 9 Barn Dance (5:51)Orchestra; 10 Barn Raising (2:56)Orchestra; 11 When You're In Love (reprise)(2:18) *Howard Keel*; 12 Brotherly Advice/Lonesome Winter (:58)Orchestra; 13 Lament (Lonesome Polecat)(3:36) *Matt Mattox*; 14 Lovesick (1:22)Orchestra; 15 Sobbin' Women (2:48) *Howard Keel, Tommy Rall, Russ Tamblyn, Matt Mattox, Alan Davies, C. Parlato, Marc Platt, Robert Wacker, Gene Lanham, M. Spergel*; 16 Kidnapped and Chase (5:03)Orchestra; 17 June Bride (3:18) *Virginia Gibson,*

Barbara Ames, Betty Allan, Betty Noyes, Marie Vernon, Norma Zimmer; 18 June Bride (reprise)(1:43) *Virginia Gibson, Barbara Ames, Betty Allan, Betty Noyes, Marie Vernon, Norma Zimmer, Jane Powell*; 19 Spring, Spring, Spring (2:58) *Howard Keel, Tommy Rall, Russ Tamblyn, Matt Mattox, Alan Davies, C. Parlato, Bill Lee, Robert Wacker, Gene Lanham, M. Spergel, Virginia Gibson, Barbara Ames, Betty Allan, Betty Noyes, Marie Vernon, Norma Zimmer*; 20 When You're In Love (reprise)(outtake)(2:51) *Howard Keel, Jane Powell*; 21 End Title (:57)Orchestra; 22 Bless Yore Beautiful Hide (2:33) *Howard Keel, Saul Chaplin*; 23 Goin' Co'tin' (4:23) *Stanley Donen, Saul Chaplin*; 24 Queen Of The May (outtake)(1:27) *Stanley Donen, Saul Chaplin (piano)*; 25 When You're In Love (2:13) *Stanley Donen, Saul Chaplin*; 26 Spring, Spring, Spring (2:58) *Johnny Mercer, Gene De Paul*; 27 Sobbin' Women (3:39) *Johnny Mercer, Gene De Paul.*

Review: A western musical, something of a rarity in the genre, *Seven Brides for Seven Brothers* is a rousing, rambunctious spectacle, which drew its inspiration from Stephen Vincent Benet's story "The Sobbin' Women," itself loosely based on Plutarch's fabled tale about the abduction of the Sabine women. Transposed to the Oregon frontier in the mid-1800s, the story about the kidnapping of six lovely girls by their backwood suitors, is the occasion for a robustly-flavored series of songs and dances, magnificently staged by Michael Kidd, who gives the brothers (all dancers in their own right) two memorable numbers, "Lonesome Polecat," in which the brothers deplore their loneliness in the wilds, and the celebrated "Barn Raising," a sensational dance routine. Starring Howard Keel and Jane Powell, the film received five Academy Awards nominations, and walked away with the Oscar for best score, written by Gene De Paul and Johnny Mercer.

1776 ♫♫♫♪

1992, Sony Broadway; from the Broadway production *1776*, 1969.

Album Notes: *Music*: Sherman Edwards; *Lyrics*: Sherman Edwards; *Orchestrations*: Eddie Sauter; *Musical Direction*: Peter Howard; *Cast*: William Daniels (John Adams), Paul Hecht (John Dickinson), Roy Poole (Stephen Hopkins), Clifford David (Edward Rutledge), Rex Everhart (Benjamin Franklin), David Ford (John Hancock), Ken Howard (Thomas Jefferson), Virginia Vestoff (Abigail Adams), Ron Holgate (Richard Henry Lee), Betty Buckley (Martha Jefferson), Bruce MacKay (Col. Thomas McKean), Jonathan Moore (Dr. Lyman Hall), Ralston Hill (Charles Thomson), Robert Gaus (Caesar Rodney), Emory Bass (James Wilson), William Duell (Andrew McNair), Henry Le Clair (Robert Livingston); *Album/CD Producer*: Thomas Z. Shepard; *Album*

Engineers: Fred Plaut, Arthur Kendy, Glen Kolotkin; *CD Engineer*: Francis X. Pierce.

Selections: 1 Overture (1:53)Orchestra; 2 Sit Down, John (1:57) *William Daniels*; 3 Piddle, Twiddle And Resolve/Till Then (4:54) *William Daniels, Virginia Vestoff*; 4 The Lees Of Old Virginia (2:35) *Ron Holgate, Rex Everhart, William Daniels*; 5 But Mr. Adams (5:09) *William Daniels, Rex Everhart, David Vosburgh, Henry Le Clair, Ken Howard*; 6 Yours, Yours, Yours (2:10) *William Daniels, Virginia Vestoff*; 7 He Plays The Violin (3:03) *Betty Buckley, Rex Everhart, William Daniels*; 8 Cool, Cool, Considerate Men (4:28) *Paul Hecht, David Ford*; 9 Momma Look Sharp (3:24) *Scott Jarvis, William Duell, B.J. Slater*; 10 The Egg (2:44) *Rex Everhart, William Daniels, Ken Howard*; 11 Molasses To Rum (4:40) *Clifford Davis*; 12 Is Anybody There? (2:46) *William Daniels*; 13 Finale (1:24)Company.

Review: The writing of the Constitution might not seem like a subject for a Broadway musical, yet Sherman Edwards spent some ten years of his life to research and write this compelling Tony Award-winning show which swept Broadway off its feet, when it premiered on March 16, 1969. In broad strokes, befitting its reverent topic, Sherman recounts the struggles, compromises, and backroom deals that eventually led to the document on which the destinies of the new-emerging United States were to be based, using as his main focus John Adams' life and personal miseries in writing the final draft. With its cast almost intact (Howard Da Silva, replaced in this recording by Rex Everhart, returned as Ben Franklin), the show was successfully transferred to the screen in 1972.

She Loves Me ♫♫♫♫

1987, Polydor Records; from the Broadway production *She Loves Me*, 1963.

Album Notes: *Music* Jerry Bock; *Lyrics*: Sheldon Harnick; *Orchestrations*: Don Walker; *Musical Direction*: Hal Hastings; *Orchestra Conductor*: John Berkman; *Cast*: Barbara Cook (Amalia Balash), Daniel Massey (Georg Nowack), Jack Cassidy (Steven Kodaly), Barbara Baxley (Ilona Ritter), Ludwig Donath (Mr. Maraczek), Ralph Williams (Arpad Laszlo), Nathaniel Frey (Ladislas Sipos), and Marion Brash, Peg Murray, Trude Adams, Wood Romoff, Jo Wilder, Joe Ross, Gino Conforti; *Album Producer*: Arnold Maxin; *Engineer*: Val Valentin; *CD Producer*: Larry L. Lash; *Engineer*: Dennis Drake.

Selections: 1 Overture (1:08)Orchestra; 2 Good Morning, Good Day (3:05) *Ralph Williams, Daniel Massey*; 3 Sounds While Selling (2:08) *Daniel Massey, Nathaniel Frey, Jack Cassidy, Marion Brash, Peg Murray, Trude Adams*; 4 Thank You, Madam (:15) *Nathaniel Frey, Daniel Massey, Jack Cassidy, Barbara*

Baxley, Marion Brash, Peg Murray; 5 Days Gone By (2:19) *Daniel Massey, Ludwig Donath*; 6 No More Candy (1:26) *Barbara Cook*; 7 Three Letters (2:35) *Daniel Massey, Barbara Cook*; 8 Tonight At Eight (1:56) *Daniel Massey*; 9 I Don't Know His Name (4:14) *Barbara Baxley, Barbara Cook*; 10 Perspective (3:15) *Daniel Massey, Nathaniel Frey*; 11 Goodbye Georg (1:19) *Daniel Massey, Barbara Baxley, Nathaniel Frey, Jack Cassidy, Ralph Williams, Marion Brash, Peg Murray, Trude Adams*; 12 Will He Like Me? (4:19) *Barbara Cook*; 13 Ilona (3:25) *Jack Cassidy*; 14 I Resolve (2:23) *Barbara Baxley*; 15 Romantic Atmosphere (3:33) *Wood Romoff*; 16 Tango Tragique (3:08) *Daniel Massey, Barbara Cook, Wood Romoff*; 17 Dear Friend (2:58) *Barbara Cook*; 18 Overture Act II (4:20)Orchestra; 19 Try Me (3:23) *Ralph Williams, Ludwig Donath*; 20 Where's My Shoe (2:17) *Barbara Cook, Daniel Massey*; 21 Ice Cream (3:09) *Barbara Cook*; 22 She Loves Me (2:52) *Daniel Massey*; 23 A Trip To The Library (4:44) *Barbara Baxley*; 24 Grand Knowing You (2:46) *Jack Cassidy*; 25 Twelve Days To Christmas (3:36) *Jo Wilder, Gino Conforti, Joe Ross*; 26 Ice Cream (reprise)(1:47) *Daniel Massey, Barbara Cook*; 27 Curtain Call (:28)Company.

Review: A creamy little bonbon based on the Ferenc Molnar story *The Shop Around the Corner* (it already had inspired the film *In The Good Old Summertime*, starring Judy Garland and Van Johnson), *She Loves Me* presents the love affair between two young shy people who fall in love by correspondence, unaware that they are actually co-workers in the same perfume shop. The musical provided another splendid starring vehicle for Barbara Cook, as the young saleslady who loves/hates Daniel Massey, with Jack Cassidy and Barbara Baxley adding the strength of their support in two parts equally well-crafted. The score, by Jerry Bock and Sheldon Harnick, totally delightful, was eventually obscured as too lightweight when they came up, a year later, with their blockbuster, *Fiddler on the Roof*.

Shenandoah 🦴🦴▷

1988, RCA Victor; from the Broadway production *Shenandoah*, 1975.

Album Notes: *Music*: Gary Geld; *Lyrics*: Peter Udell; *Orchestrations*: Don Walker; *Musical Direction*: Lynn Crigler; *Cast*: John Cullum (Charlie Anderson), Nathan (Jordan Suffin), Joel Higgins (James), Robert Rosen (Henry), Ted Agress (Jacob), David Russell (John), Joseph Shapiro (Robert, The Boy), Penelope Milford (Jenny), Donna Theodore (Anne), Chip Ford (Gabriel), Gordon Halliday (Sam), Charles Welch (Rev. Byrd), Gary Harper (Corporal); *Album Producers*: Gary Geld, Peter Udell, Philip Rose; *Engineer*: Frank Laico; *CD Producer*: Didier C. Deutsch; *Engineer*: Paul Goodman.

Selections: 1 Raise The Flag Of Dixie (4:07)Ensemble; 2 I've Heard It All Before (2:40) *John Cullum*; 3 Why Am I Me? (2:34) *Joseph Shapiro, Chip Ford*; 4 Next To Lovin' (I Like Fightin') (3:59) *Jordan Suffin, Joel Higgins, Robert Rosen, Ted Agress, David Russell*; 5 Over The Hill (1:57) *Penelope Milford*; 6 The Pickers Are Comin' (3:44) *John Cullum*; 7 Meditation (5:40) *John Cullum*; 8 We Make A Beautiful Pair (3:26) *Donna Theodore, Penelope Milford*; 9 Violets And Silverbells (3:21) *Penelope Milford, Gordon Halliday, Charles Welch*; 10 It's A Boy! (3:22) *John Cullum*; 11 Freedom (2:21) *Donna Theodore, Chip Ford*; 12 Violets And Silverbells (reprise)(2:02) *Joel Higgins, Donna Theodore*; 13 Papa's Gonna Make It Alright (2:50) *John Cullum*; 14 The Only Home I Know (2:53) *Gary Harger*; 15 Meditation II (3:48) *John Cullum*; 16 Pass The Cross To Me (2:11) Ensemble.

Review: Opening, as it did, during a newspaper strike, *Shenandoah* ran the risk of passing unnoticed. Yet this inspirational tale of a peace-loving widower and his six sons caught in the Civil War (already the subject of a celebrated film starring James Stewart), not only managed to survive but went on to a long and healthy life on Broadway, racking up a total of 1,000 performances, quite a feat in those days. Though the story (and the score by Gary Geld and Peter Udell) adopt a paternalistic attitude toward Blacks (a number, "Freedom," performed by Donna Theodore, as a Southern belle, and Chip Ford, as the son of a slave, might have seemed politically correct at the time and no doubt made for good theatre, but sounded hopelessly naive and downright phony in the context), it has its share of rousing moments, and John Cullum, as the widower, made sure that his solo numbers hit the right chord in the audience's emotions.

Show Boat

Show Boat 🦴🦴🦴▷

1992, RCA Victor; from the Broadway revival *Show Boat*, 1966.

Album Notes: *Music*: Jerome Kern; *Lyrics*: Oscar Hammerstein II; *Orchestrations*: Robert Russell Bennett; *Dance Arrangements*: Richard de Benedictis; *Musical Direction*: Franz Allers; *Cast*: Barbara Cook (Magnolia), Constance Towers (Julie), Stephen Douglass (Gaylord Ravenal), William Warfield (Joe), Rosetta Le Noire (Queenie), Allyn Ann McLerie (Ellie), David Wayne (Captain Andy), Eddie Phillips (Frank); *Album Producers*: George Marked, Andy Wiswell; *Engineer*: Ernie Oelrich; *CD Producer*: Didier C. Deutsch; *Engineer*: Paul Goodman.

Selections: 1 Overture (4:46)Orchestra; 2 Cotton Blossom (1:48)Chorus; 3 Make Believe (4:49) *Barbara Cook, Stephen*

Douglass; 4 Ol' Man River (2:47) *William Warfield*; 5 Can't Help Lovin' Dat Man (4:28) *Constance Towers, Rosetta Le Noire, William Warfield*; 6 Life Upon The Wicked Stage (3:33) *Allyn Ann McLerie*; 7 You Are Love (4:59) *Barbara Cook, Stephen Douglass*; 8 At The Chicago World's Fair (Opening Act II) (1:37) Chorus; 9 Why Do I Love You? (4:15) *Barbara Cook, Stephen Douglass, David Wayne*; 10 Bill (4:27) *Constance Towers*; 11 Good Bye My Lady Love (J. Howard)(2:01) *Allyn Ann McLerie, Eddie Phillips*; 12 After The Ball (C. Harris)(2:22) *Barbara Cook*; 13 Finale: Ol' Man River (2:08) *William Warfield*.

Review: See entry below.

Show Boat 🎵🎵🎵🎵

1994, Quality Records; from the Broadway revival *Show Boat*, 1994.

Album Notes: *Music:* Jerome Kern; *Lyrics:* Oscar Hammerstein II; *Orchestrations:* Robert Russell Bennett, William David Brohn; *Dance Arrangements:* David Krane; *Musical Direction:* Jeffrey Huard; *Cast:* Rebecca Luker (Magnolia), Lonette McKee (Julie), Mark Jacoby (Gaylord Ravenal), Michel Bell (Joe), Gretha Boston (Queenie), Dorothy Stanley (Ellie), Robert Morse (Captain Andy), Joel Blum (Frank), Elaine Stritch (Parthy), David Bryant (Pete), Ralph Williams (Windy), Tammy Amerson (Kim); *Album Producers:* Martin Levan, Garth H. Drabinsky; *Engineers:* Gary Gray, Martin Levan.

Selections: 1 Overture (2:47)Orchestra; 2 Cotton Blossom/Cap'n Andy's Ballyhoo (3:19) *Robert Morse, Elaine Stritch*; 3 Make Believe (4:21) *Rebecca Luker, Mark Jacoby*; 4 Ol' Man River (5:47) *Michel Bell*; 5 Can't Help Lovin' Dat Man (4:32) *Lonette McKee, Gretha Boston, Michel Bell*; 6 Till Good Luck Comes My Way (1:21) *Mark Jacoby, Ralph Williams, David Bryant, Joel Blum*; 7 Mis'ry's Comin' Aroun' (4:12) *Gretha Boston*; 8 I Have The Room Above Her (3:58) *Mark Jacoby, Rebecca Luker*; 9 Life Upon The Wicked Stage (2:55) *Dorothy Stanley, Elaine Stritch*; 10 Queenie's Ballyhoo (1:25) *Gretha Boston*; 11 You Are Love (3:38) *Rebecca Luker, Mark Jacoby*; 12 Act One Finale: The Wedding Celebration (1:50)Company; 13 Entr'acte (1:44)Orchestra; 14 Why Do I Love You?/Montage I: The Sports Of Gay Chicago (5:59) *Elaine Stritch*; 15 Alma Redemptoris Mater (2:31) *Michel Bell*; 16 Bill (J. Kern/P.G. Wodehouse/O. Hammerstein II)(4:05) *Lonette McKee*; 17 Can't Help Lovin' Dat Man (reprise)(1:55) *Rebecca Luker*; 18 Good Bye My Lady Love (J. Howard)(2:18) *Dorothy Stanley, Joel Blum*; 19 After The Ball (C. Harris)(2:37) *Rebecca Luker*; 20 Montage II: Ol' Man River (5:14) *Michel Bell*; 21 Kim's Charleston (4:07) *Tammy Amerson, Elaine Stritch*; 22 Act Two Finale (2:27) *Michel Bell*.

Review: See entry below.

Show Boat 🎵🎵🎵🎵

1996, Rhino Records; from the screen musical *Show Boat*, 1951.

Album Notes: *Music:* Jerome Kern; *Lyrics:* Oscar Hammerstein II; *Orchestrations:* Bob Franklyn, Alexander Courage, Paul Marquart; *Arrangements:* Adolph Deutsch, Conrad Salinger; The M-G-M Studio Chorus and Orchestra, conducted by Adolph Deutsch; *Cast:* Kathryn Grayson (Magnolia), Ava Gardner (Julie), Howard Keel (Gaylord Ravenal), William Warfield (Joe), Joe E. Brown (Captain Andy), Agnes Moorehead (Parthy), Robert Sterling (Steve), Marge Champion (Ellie), Gower Champion (Frank); *Album Producers:* Marilee Bradford, Bradley Flanagan; *Engineers:* Doug Schwartz, Ted Hall.

Selections: 1 Main Title (1:44)Orchestra, Chorus; 2 Cap'n Andy's Calliope (:44)Orchestra; 3 Natchez (1:03)Orchestra; 4 Cap'n Andy's Presentation (2:09)Chorus; 5 Cap'n Andy's Ballyhoo (:54)Orchestra; 6 Encore On Dock (1:21)Orchestra; 7 Where's The Mate For Me? (Gambler's Song) (2:48) *Howard Keel*; 8 Young Romance (1:33) Orchestra; 9 Make Believe (3:59) *Kathryn Grayson, Howard Keel*; 10 Can't Help Lovin' Dat Man (3:19) *Annette Warren*; 11 Can't Help Lovin' Dat Man (reprise #1)(1:22) *Kathryn Grayson, Annette Warren*; 12 I Might Fall Back On You (3:16) *Marge Champion, Gower Champion*; 13 Julie Leaves The Boat (1:23)Chorus; 14 Ol' Man River (3:41) *William Warfield*; 15 Ol' Man River (reprise)(2:14) *William Warfield*; 16 You Are Love (2:33) *Kathryn Grayson, Howard Keel*; 17 Why Do I Love You? (3:28) *Kathryn Grayson, Howard Keel*; 18 Ravenal Is Gone (4:25)Orchestra; 19 Bill (J. Kern/P.G. Wodehouse/O. Hammerstein II)(4:05) *Annette Warren*; 20 Can't Help Lovin' Dat Man (reprise #2) (2:29) *Kathryn Grayson, Roger Edens*; 21 Life Upon The Wicked Stage (5:23) *Marge Champion, Gower Champion*; 22 After The Ball (C. Harris) (3:08) *Kathryn Grayson*; 23 Packet Boat (1:23)Orchestra; 24 Natchez Dock (2:00) Orchestra; 25 Make Believe (reprise) (1:30) *Howard Keel*; 26 Reunion (1:47) Orchestra; 27 Ol' Man River (Finale Ultimo) (2:53) *William Warfield*; 28 Can't Help Lovin' Dat Man (outtake) (3:23) *Ava Gardner*; 29 Bill (outtake) (3:22) *Ava Gardner, Roger Edens*.

Review: One of the great Broadway musicals, *Show Boat* deserves a special place in the annals of the American theatre. It's little wonder that 70 years after its creation, it still rings with the same energy and fervor that stirred audiences in 1928. While its extraordinarily rich score brims with many memorable songs, it spawned one unsurpassed hit in "Ol' Man River," probably the most powerful statements about human life ever written. The first true "American" musical, in the best sense of the word, and a pioneering work of imposing magnitude, *Show Boat* presents a broad diorama about the evolution of this country, from the floating crap games aboard steamers down the Mississippi in the last part of the 19th century, to the industrial revolution that swept the country earlier in the present one. While its book remains hopelessly unbalanced (the first act covers a couple of years, while more than 40 years are collapsed into the second, leading to an uneven spread in the dramatic modus operandi), its diversified score includes romantic duets ("Make Believe," "You Are Love"), torch songs ("Bill"), showbiz anthems ("Life Upon the Wicked Stage"), and rousing choruses ("Cotton Blossom") among its many wonderful highlights.

There are many recordings of that legendary musical available, and collectors might be faced with a real dilemma when trying to decide which one to own. The choice is made even more difficult as there is no definitive recording available.

Among those listed above, the 1966 studio cast album is mentioned here, particularly for Barbara Cook's sensitive portrayal as Magnolia.

The 1994 Broadway revival cast album is also highly recommended, despite the fact that Mark Jacoby sounds a bit too "nice" as the cad Ravenal. But the modern sonics are superb, and the recording also contains many selections not otherwise available.

The soundtrack album is a gorgeous treatment in its own right, with Howard Keel and Kathryn Grayson at the peak of their respective talents as Ravenal and Magnolia, and Ava Gardner (dubbed by Annette Warren) resplendent as Julie. This recording also includes several selections not found elsewhere, and, as is usual with Rhino, it is presented with a lot of extras (both audio and visual) that make it a rare treat.

Side by Side by Sondheim
♫♫♫♫

1976, RCA Victor; from the Broadway production *Side by Side by Sondheim*, 1976.

Album Notes: *Music:* Stephen Sondheim, Leonard Bernstein, Mary Rodgers, Jule Styne, Richard Rodgers; *Lyrics:* Stephen Sondheim; *Pianists/Musical Direction:* Tim Higgs, Stuart Pedlar; *Cast:* Millicent Martin, Julia McKenzie, David Kernan; *CD Producer:* Bill Rosenfield; *Engineer:* Paul Goodman.

Selections: CD 1: 1 Comedy Tonight/Love Is In The Air (4:03) *Millicent Martin, Julia McKenzie, David Kernan*; 2 The Little Things You Do Together (2:41) *Julia McKenzie, David Kernan*; 3 You Must Meet My Wife (3:42) *Millicent Martin, David Kernan*; 4 Getting Married Today (4:00) *Millicent Martin, Julia McKenzie, David Kernan*; 5 I Remember (3:07) *David Kernan*; 6

Can That Boy Foxtrot (2:36) *Millicent Martin, Julia McKenzie*; 7 Too Many Mornings (4:40) *Julia McKenzie, David Kernan*; 8 Company/Another Hundred People (3:10) *Millicent Martin, Julia McKenzie, David Kernan, Julia McKenzie*; 9 Barcelona (2:56) *Julia McKenzie, David Kernan*; 10 Being Alive (2:21) *David Kernan, Millicent Martin, Julia McKenzie*; 11 I Never Do Anything Twice (5:55) *Millicent Martin*; 12 Beautiful Girls/Ah, Paree!/Buddy's Blues (4:06) *David Kernan, Millicent Martin, David Kernan, Millicent Martin, Julia McKenzie*; 13 Broadway Baby (3:26) *Julia McKenzie*; 14 You Could Drive A Person Crazy (2:22) *Millicent Martin, David Kernan, Julia McKenzie*.

CD 2: 1 Everybody Says Don't (2:12) *Millicent Martin, David Kernan, Julia McKenzie*; 2 There Won't Be Trumpets (2:51) *Millicent Martin, David Kernan, Julia McKenzie*; 3 Anyone Can Whistle (2:49) *David Kernan*; 4 Send In The Clowns (3:29) *Millicent Martin*; 5 Pretty Lady (2:57) *Millicent Martin, David Kernan, Julia McKenzie*; 6 We're Gonna Be All Right (R. Rodgers)(4:09) *Millicent Martin, David Kernan*; 7 A Boy Like That (L. Bernstein)(3:56) *Millicent Martin, Julia McKenzie*; 8 The Boy From... (M. Rodgers)(2:41) *Millicent Martin*; 9 If Momma Was Married (J. Styne)(2:43) *Millicent Martin, Julia McKenzie*; 10 Losing My Mind (3:51) *Julia McKenzie*; 11 Could I Leave You? (3:04) *David Kernan*; 12 I'm Still Here (4:57) *Millicent Martin*; 13 Side By Side By Side (1:17) *Millicent Martin, David Kernan, Julia McKenzie, Tim Higgs, Stuard Pedlar, Ned Sherrin*.

Review: A clever revue consisting of songs by Stephen Sondheim, *Side by Side by Sondheim* originated in London, where it opened on May 4, 1976, before moving to Broadway on April 18, 1977, for a run of 390 performances. Since the material is already well-known and accepted, what is important here is the caliber of the performers, with Millicent Martin, one of the bright stars from the British stage, making a remarkable contribution, surrounded by Julia McKenzie and David Kernan, with Ned Sherrin providing the sly comments.

See also: A Stephen Sondheim Evening, Sondheim by Sondheim, The Sondheim Songbook, Sondheim: A Celebration at Carnegie Hall, Sondheim Evening: A Musical Tribute and Putting It Together in Compilations

Silk Stockings ♫♫♫♪

1988, RCA Victor; from the Broadway production *Silk Stockings*, 1955.

Album Notes: *Music:* Cole Porter; *Lyrics:* Cole Porter; *Orchestrations:* Don Walker; *Vocal Arrangements and Musical Direction:* Herbert Greene; *Cast:* Don Ameche (Steve Canfield), Hildegarde Neff (Ninotchka), Gretchen Wyler (Janice Dayton), George Tobias (Commissar Markovitch), Henry Lascoe

(Ivanov), Leon Belasco (Brankov), David Opatoshu (Bibinski); *Album Producers*: Hugo Winterhalter, Joe Carlton; *CD Producer*: Didier C. Deutsch; *Engineer*: Paul Goodman.

Selections: 1 Overture (2:38)Orchestra; 2 Too Bad (1:41) *Henry Lasco, Leon Belasco, David Opatoshu*; 3 Paris Loves Lovers (3:14) *Don Ameche, Hildegarde Neff*; 4 Stereophonic Sound (2:21) *Gretchen Wyler, Edward Becker, Tony Gardell, Arthur Rubin*; 5 It's A Chemical Reaction, That's All/All Of You (4:02) *Hildegarde Neff, Don Ameche*; 6 Satin And Silk (3:38) *Gretchen Wyler*; 7 Without Love (3:05) *Hildegarde Neff*; 8 Hail Bibinski (3:05) *David Optaoshu, Henry Lascoe, Leon Belaso*; 9 As On Through The Seasons We Sail (2:29) *Don Ameche, Hildegarde Neff*; 10 Josephine (4:43) *Gretchen Wyler*; 11 Siberia (2:48) *Henry Lascoe, Leon Belasco, David Opatoshu*; 12 Silk Stockings (2:07) *Don Ameche*; 13 The Red Blues (3:51)Chorus; 14 Finale (:48)Company.

Review: East-West relations took a musical turn in this clever adaptation of Melchior Lengyel's amusing play, *Ninotchka*, with Cole Porter providing the *divertissement*. Don Ameche is in top form as an American in Paris, a talent agent who seduces a stern Russian envoy, played by Hildegarde Neff, sent to investigate three former Russian colleagues, and converts her to the Western way of life. While the show, which opened on February 4, 1955, had a somewhat disappointing run of 478 performances, it provided another great vehicle for Fred Astaire, playing opposite Cyd Charisse, when it transferred to the screen in 1957, with its score almost intact.

Singin' in the Rain ♫♫♫♫♪

1996, Rhino Records; from the screen musical *Singin' in the Rain*, M-G-M, 1952.

Album Notes: *Music*: Nacio Herb Brown; *Lyrics*: Arthur Freed; *Orchestrations*: Bob Franklyn, Wally Heglin, Conrad Salinger, Skip Martin, Maurice de Packh; *Arrangements*: Conrad Salinger, Lennie Hayton, Wally Heglin, Roger Edens, Maurice de Packh; *Vocal Arrangements*: Jeff Alexander; The M-G-M Studio Chorus and Orchestra, conducted by Lennie Hayton; *Cast*: Gene Kelly (Don Lockwood), Donald O'Coonor (Cosmo Brown), Debbie Reynolds (Kathy Selden), Jean Hagen (Lina Lamont); *Album Producers*: Marilee Bradford, Bradley Flanagan; *Engineer*: Doug Schwartz.

Selections: 1 Main Title (1:42) *Gene Kelly, Debbie Reynolds, Donald O'Connor*; 2 Dignity (L. Hayton)(:52) Orchestra; 3 Fit As A Fiddle (And Ready For Love)(A. Hoffman/A. Goodhart/A. Freed)(1:41) *Gene Kelly, Donald O'Connor*; 4 Stunt Montage (L. Hayton) (2:03) Orchestra; 5 First Silent Picture (L. Hayton) (1:23) Orchestra; 6 Tango (Temptation)(L. Hayton)(1:05) Or-

"I focus on the characters, the drive of the music, and it depends on the film what kind of music I write."

Patrick Doyle
*(Film Score Monthly,
March/April 1997)*

chestra; 7 All I Do Is Dream Of You (1:25) *Debbie Reynolds*; 8 Gene Dreams Of Kathy (L. Hayton/C. Salinger) (:58) Orchestra; 9 All I Do Is Dream Of You (outtake)(3:25) *Gene Kelly*; 10 Make 'Em Laugh (3:17) *Donald O'Connor*; 11 Beautiful Girl Montage (:59) *Jimmie Thompson, Norma Zimmer, Betty Allan, Dorothy McCarty, Sue Allen*; 12 Beautiful Girl (3:16) *Jimmie Thompson*; 13 Have Lunch With Me (N.H. Brown/L. Hayton)(2:42) Orchestra; 14 The Stage Is Set (L. Hayton)(1:08) Orchestra; 15 You Were Meant For Me (3:32) *Gene Kelly*; 16 You Are My Lucky Star (outtake)(3:39) *Debbie Reynolds*; 17 Moses (R. Edens/B. Comden/A. Green)(3:05) *Gene Kelly, Donald O'Connor*; 18 Good Morning (4:13) *Gene Kelly, Debbie Reynolds, Donald O'Connor*; 19 Good Night, Kathy (N.H. Brown/L. Hayton)(:37) Orchestra; 20 Singin' In The Rain (4:15) *Gene Kelly*; 21 From Dueling To Dancing (L. Hayton)(1:10) Orchestra; 22 Would You? (1:47) *Betty Noyes*; 23 Broadway Melody Ballet (A. Freed/N.H. Brown/L. Hayton)(13:13) *Gene Kelly*; 24 Would You?/End Title (1:31) *Gene Kelly, Betty Noyes*; 25 Singin' In The Rain (In A-Flat)(1:29) *Debbie Reynolds*; 26 Finale (1:37) *Gene Kelly, Debbie Reynolds*; 27 Main Title (alternate)(2:09) Orchestra; 28 Beautiful Girl (alternate)(3:14) *Jimmie Thompson, Gene Kelly, Lennie Hayton*; 29 Would You? (1:49) *Debbie Reynolds*; 30 Singin' In The Rain (radio broadcast)(2:26) *Arthur Freed*.

Review: Some things in life are so familiar, and our senses so attuned to them, that we can almost "sense" them without actually seeing or hearing them fully. Certainly, one of life's great "comfort" sounds is the enchanting, mesmerizing opening patter of the raindrops, and Gene Kelly's soft "Ooo-da-loo-doo"-ing from *Singin' in the Rain*.

Thankfully, the restoration of the soundtrack recording of *Singin' in the Rain* has been entrusted to the tender, loving care of the folks at Rhino Records, specifically producers Marilee Bradford and Bradley Flanagan, who deserve immeasurable credit for undertaking the preservation of the rich catalog of spectacular M-G-M musicals. Finally, one of the most beloved and important musicals in film history has been given the royal treatment it deserves: this new definitive release brims with extended recordings and previously unreleased outtakes, rare production stills and insightful recollections from the writers of the screenplay, Betty Comden and Adolph Green.

The musical selections are presented in their original order (as they appear in the conductor's score), and wherever possible, have been remixed from the original recording "angles" (tracks recorded with different microphone placements) to create the first true stereo recordings from the score. Although the sound is dated by today's standard (keep in mind the relatively primitive conditions under which film tracks were recorded and mixed, and that they weren't intended for modern "home" hi-fi consumption), it is very enjoyable.

In addition to the extended recordings (notably, Gene Kelly's "All I Do Is Dream of You") and other surprises (the restoration of the instrumental opening to "Singin' in the Rain," and the outtake of "You Are My Lucky Star"), the finishing touch is the inclusion of a 1941 performance of the title song by none other than its lyricist, Arthur Freed!

Charles L. Granata

Snow White and the Seven Dwarfs ♫♫♫♫

1993, Walt Disney Records; from the animated feature *Snow White and the Seven Dwarfs*, RKO Radio Pictures, 1937.

Album Notes: *Music:* Frank Churchill, Leigh Harline, Paul J. Smith; *Lyrics:* Larry Morey,; The Disney Studio Chorus and Orchestra, conducted by Frank Chuchill; *Cast:* Adriana Caselotti (Snow White), Harry Stockwell (The Prince), Lucille LaVerne (The Queen), Scotty Matraw (Bashful), Roy Atwell (Doc), Pinto Colvig (Grumpy/Sleepy), Billy Gilbert (Sneezy), Otis Harlan (Happy), Marion Darlington (Birds), The Fraunfelder Family (yodeling); *Album Producers:* Randy Thornton, Michael Leon; *Engineers:* John Polito.

Selections: 1 Overture (2:10); 2 Magic Mirror (1:25); 3 I'm Wishing/One Song (3:06) *Adriana Caselotti, Harry Stockwell*; 4 Queen Theme (:44); 5 Far Into The Forest (2:25); 6 Animal Friends/With A Smile And A Song (4:23) *Adriana Caselotti*; 7 Just Like A Doll's House (2:46); 8 Whistle While You Work (3:24) *Adriana Caselotti*; 9 Heigh-Ho (2:46) *Scotty Matraw, Roy Atwell, Pinto Colvig, Billy Gilbert, Otis Harlan*; 10 Let's See What's Upstairs (1:15); 11 There's Trouble A-Brewin' (4:19); 12 It's A Girl (4:26); 13 Hooray! She Stays (2:48); 14 Bluddle-Uddle-Um-Dum (The Washing Song)(4:25) *Scotty Matraw, Roy Atwell, Pinto Colvig, Billy Gilbert, Otis Harlan*; 15 I've Been Tricked (4:05); 16

The Silly Song (The Dwarfs' Yodel Song)(4:35) *Scotty Matraw, Roy Atwell, Pinto Colvig, Billy Gilbert, Otis Harlan*; 17 Some Day My Prince Will Come (1:53) *Adriana Caselotti*; 18 Pleasant Dreams (2:28); 19 A Special Sort Of Death (2:02); 20 Why Grumpy, You Do Care (2:06); 21 Makin' Pies (3:02); 22 Have A Bite (1:26); 23 Chorale For Snow White (1:05); 24 Love's First Kiss (Finale)(4:08); 25 Music In Your Soup (2:35) *Scotty Matraw, Roy Atwell, Pinto Colvig, Billy Gilbert, Otis Harlan*; 26 You're Never Too Old To Be Young (3:20) *Scotty Matraw, Roy Atwell, Pinto Colvig, Billy Gilbert, Otis Harlan*.

Review: The first, and by far most memorable full-length animated feature from the Disney Studios, *Snow White and the Seven Dwarfs* may have been superseded technically by many of the films that followed it. But its simple story of a charming little princess saved from the evil deeds of her mother-in-law by a group of seven adorable dwarfs made history when it was first released in December, 1937, and has since become an incomparable screen classic. With its exquisite score by Frank Churchill, Leigh Harline and Paul J. Smith, *Snow White* continues to enchant generations of young viewers and their parents, whose earliest memories are forever tied to "With a Smile and a Song," "Whistle While You Work," "Heigh-Ho," and "Someday My Prince Will Come," among the film's many musical highlights. Today, it still stands out as a perfect example of unsurpassed quality in animated filmmaking, made all the more memorable in this compact disc, which includes a lot of incidental music and reprises, available here for the first time.

Sophisticated Ladies ♫♫♫♫

1981, RCA Victor; from the Broadway production *Sophisticated Ladies*, 1981.

Album Notes: *Music:* Duke Ellington, Mercer Ellington, Irving Mills, Billy Strayhorn, Juan Tizol, Harry Carney, Gerald Wilson, Johnny Hodges, Harry James; *Lyrics:* Duke Ellington, John Guare, Don George, Irving Mills, Sid Kuller, Billy Strayhorn, Eddie De Lange, Henry Nemo, John Redmond, Manny Kurtz, Johnny Mercer, Mack David, Bob Russell, Paul Francis Webster, Mitchell Parish; *Orchestrations:* Al Cohn; *Musical Arrangements:* Lloyd Mayers; *Vocal Arrangements:* Malcolm Dodds, lloyd Mayers; *Musical Direction:* Mercer Ellington; *Cast:* Gregory Hines, Judith Jamison, Phyllis Hyman, P.J. Benjamin, Hinton Battle, Gregg Burge, Mercedes Ellington, Priscilla Baskerville, Terri Klausner; *Album Producer:* Thomas Z. Shepard; *Engineer:* Joaquin J. Lopes.

Selections: 1 Overture: Things Ain't What They Used To Be/Sophisticated Lady/Perdido (3:34)*Orchestra*; 2 I've Got To Be A Rug Cutter (2:12) *Hinton Battle, Gregg Burge, Michael Scott Gregory, Michael Lichtefeld*; 3 Music Is A Woman (1:44) *Gregory Hines, Judith Jamison*; 4 The Mooche (2:46)*Orchestra*;

5 Hit Me With A Hot Note And Watche Me Bounce (2:43) *Terri Klausner*; 6 It Don't Mean A Thing (4:51) *Phyllis Hyman*; 7 Bli-Blip (2:03) *P.J. Benjamin, Terri Klausner*; 8 Cotton Tail (2:42)Orchestra; 9 Take The "A" Train (3:24) *Phyllis Hyman, Gregory Hines*; 10 Solitude (3:19) *Priscilla Baskerville*; 11 Don't Get Around Much Any More/I Let A Song Go Out Of My Heart (1:54) *Gregory Hines, Judith Jamison*; 12 Caravan (2:59) *Gregg Burge*; 13 Something To Live For (3:51) *Gregory Hines*; 14 Rockin' In Rhythm (2:26)Company; 15 In A Sentimental Mood (3:24) *Phyllis Hyman*; 16 I'm Beginning To See The Light (2:58) *Judith Jamison, Gregory Hines*; 17 Satin Doll/Just Squeeze Me (3:17) *P.J. Benjamin, Terri Kalusner*; 18 Echoes Of Harlem (3:37)Orchestra; 19 I'm Just A Lucky So-And-So (2:11) *Gregory Hines*; 20 Imagine My Frustration (2:24) *Terri Klausner*; 21 I'm Checking Out Goombye/Do Nothing 'Til You Hear From Me (1:23) *Phyllis Hyman, Gregory Hines*; 22 I Got It Bad And That Ain't Good/Mood Indigo (5:25) *Phyllis Hyman, Terri Klausner*; 23 Sophisticated Lady (3:07) *Gregory Hines*; 24 It Don't Mean A Thing (reprise)(2:22) *Gregory Hines*.

Review: A celebration of the great Duke Ellington, *Sophisticated Ladies,* which opened on Broadway on March 1, 1981, benefitted from the presence in the cast of such luminaries of dance, stage and cabaret as Gregory Hines, Phyllis Hyman and Judith Jamison, as well as the Duke's own band, led by Mercer Ellington. Together, they provide the sleek entertainment that makes the show such a joy to watch.

The recording gives a measure of how successful they are, though in this instance their performances, minus the visual flash of the stage presentation, enable the listener to focus on and truly enjoy the songs of Ellington. Seldom did a composer have such classy performers to interpret his songs, and seldom did performers of this caliber have such great catalogue to work with. The two together spell pure magic!

The Sound of Music

The Sound of Music ♫♫♫♫♫

1993, Sony Broadway; from the Broadway production *The Sound of Music,* 1959.

Album Notes: *Music*: Richard Rodgers; *Lyrics*: Oscar Hammerstein II; *Orchestrations*: Robert Russell Bennett; *Choral Arrangements*: Trude Rittman; *Musical Direction*: Frederick Dvonch; *Cast*: Mary Martin (Maria Rainer), Theodore Bikel (Captain Georg von Trapp), Patricia Neway (The Mother Abbess), Kurt Kaznar (Max Detweiler), Marion Marlowe (Elsa Schraeder), Lauri Peters (Liesl), William Snowden (Friedrich), Kathy Dunn (Louisa), Joseph Stewart (Kurt), Marilyn Rogers

(Brigitta), Mary Susan Locke (Marta), Evanna Lien (Gretl), Brian Davies (Rolf Gruber); *Album Producer*: Goddard Lieberson; *Engineers*: Fred Plaut, Bud Graham; *CD Producer*: Didier C. Deutsch; *Engineer*: Darcy Proper.

Selections: 1 Preludium (2:15)Nuns; 2 The Sound Of Music (2:46) *Mary Martin*; 3 Maria (3:21) *Elizabeth Howell, Karen Shepard, Muriel O'Malley, Patricia Neway*; 4 My Favorite Things (2:46) *Mary Martin, Patricia Neway*; 5 Do-Re-Mi (5:52) *Mary Martin*; 6 Sixteen Going On Seventeen (3:49) *Brian Davies, Lauri Peters*; 7 The Lonely Goatherd (3:20) *Mary Martin*; 8 How Can Love Survive? (3:01) *Kurt Kaznar, Marion Marlowe*; 9 The Sound Of Music (reprise)(3:12) *Mary Martin, Theodore Bikel*; 10 Laendler (2:23)Orchestra; 11 So Long, Farewell (2:50)Children; 12 Climb Ev'ry Mountain (3:29) *Patricia Neway*; 13 No Way To Stop It (3:04) *Marion Marlowe, Kurt Kaznar, Theodore Bikel*; 14 An Ordinary Couple (3:34) *Mary Martin, Theodore Bikel*; 15 Processional (3:49)Ensemble; 16 Sixteen Going On Seventeen (reprise)(2:16) *Mary Martin, Lauri Peters*; 17 Edelweiss (2:05) *Mary Martin, Theodore Bikel*; 18 Climb Ev'ry Mountain (reprise)(1:37) *Patricia Neway*.

Review: See entry below.

The Sound of Music ♫♫♫♫▷

1995, RCA Victor; from the screen musical *The Sound of Music,* 20th Century-Fox, 1965.

Album Notes: *Music*: Richard Rodgers; *Lyrics*: Oscar Hammerstein II; *Orchestrations*: Irwin Kostal; *Vocal Supervision*: Robert Tucker; The 20th Century-Fox Studio Chorus and Orchestra, conducted by Irwin Kostal; *Cast*: Julie Andrews (Maria Rainer), Christopher Plummer (Captain Georg von Trapp), Peggy Wood (The Mother Abbess), Charmian Carr (Liesl), Nicholas Hammond (Friedrich), Heather Menzies (Louisa), Duane Chase (Kurt), Angela Cartwright (Brigitta), Debbie Turner (Marta), Kym Karath (Gretl), Dan Truhitte (Rolf Gruber); *Album Producer*: Neely Plumb; *Engineers*: Murray Spivak, Douglas Williams, John Norman; *CD Producer*: Paul Williams; *Engineers*: Bill Lacey, James P. Nichols.

Selections: 1 Prelude/The Sound Of Music (2:44) *Julie Andrews*; 2 Overture/Preludium (Dixit Dominus)(3:14)Nuns Chorus; 3 Morning Hymn/ Alleluia (2:01)Nuns Chorus; 4 Maria (3:16)Nuns Chorus; 5 I Have Confidence (3:26) *Julie Andrews*; 6 Sixteen Going On Seventeen (3:18) *Dan Truhitte, Charmian Carr*; 7 My Favorite Things (2:18) *Julie Andrews*; 8 Do-Re-Mi (5:33) *Julie Andrews*; 9 The Sound Of Music (2:10) *Bill Lee*; 10 The Lonely Goatherd (3:10) *Julie Andrews*; 11 So Long, Farewell (2:54)Children; 12 Climb Ev'ry Mountain (2:16) *Peggy Wood*; 13

Something Good (3:16) *Julie Andrews, Bill Lee*; 14 Processional/Maria (2:27)Nuns Chorus; 15 Edelweiss (1:50) *Bill Lee, Julie Andrews*; 16 Climb Ev'ry Mountain (reprise)(1:21)Chorus.

Review: Lovers of Rodgers & Hammerstein's perennial family favorite, *The Sound of Music*, have two wonderful ways to savor the melodic hits from the wholesomest of all the pair's collaborations: both the original Broadway cast recording (Mary Martin and Theodore Bikel, 1959), and the classic film soundtrack (Julie Andrews and Christopher Plummer, 1965).

While the original cast album has long lived in the imposing shadow of the film soundtrack, it offers a clearer picture of what Richard Rodgers and Oscar Hammerstein II must have intended for this, the last of their shows. What is important about the performances on this disc is that they seem simpler and less complex than the film. One of the finest in a long line of successful cast albums produced for Columbia by Goddard Lieberson, the recently remixed version has been remastered in 20-bit "high definition" sound, and reveals the breadth and clarity of the original recording (made at Columbia's fabled 30th Street studio — Lieberson's pride and joy, chosen specifically for such sessions) with amazing fidelity.

The famous RCA Victor album has, of course, been etched in the American subconscious, and is what most people fondly recollect whenever *The Sound of Music* is mentioned. And rightfully so. The film was a huge success (and continues to be a strong ratings grabber for television networks): colorful, lavish, and above all, memorable for its breathtaking opening scenes, overall cinematic beauty, and the intriguing, sensitive storyline. But the real ace-in-the-hole here is the young Julie Andrews' enthusiastic, sensitive approach to the songs. This newly remastered version supplants a dull, distorted and sonically inferior early CD, and rectifies former problems with not only the sound but the original running order as well. While one wishes that the producers of this reissue had sought out additional cues and extra musical material (available in a special CD included with the film's rerelease on laserdisc), this disc is an essential part of the venerable R&H catalog.

Charles L. Granata

South Pacific

South Pacific 🎜🎜🎜🎜🎜

1993, Sony Broadway; from the Broadway production *South Pacific*, 1949.

Album Notes: *Music*: Richard Rodgers; *Lyrics*: Oscar Hammerstein II; *Orchestrations*: Robert Russell Bennett; *Musical Direction*: Salvatore dell'Isola; *Cast*: Mary Martin (Nellie Forbush), Ezio

Pinza (Emile de Becque), William Tabbert (Lt. Cable), Juanita Hall (Bloody Mary), Myron McCormick (Luther Billis), Barbara Luna (Ngana), Betta St. John (Liat); *Album Producer*: Goddard Lieberson; *CD Producer*: Didier C. Deutsch; *Engineer*: Darcy Proper.

Selections: 1 Overture (3:34)Orchestra; 2 Dites-moi (1:23) *Barbara Luna*; 3 A Cockeyed Optimist (1:43) *Mary Martin*; 4 Twin Soliloquies (2:26) *Mary Martin, Ezio Pinza*; 5 Some Enchanted Evening (3:01) *Ezio Pinza*; 6 Bloody Mary (2:15)Men's Chorus; 7 There Is Nothin' Like A Dame (3:36)Men's Chorus; 8 Bali Ha'i (3:26) *Juanita Hall*; 9 I'm Gonna Wash That Man Right Out-A My Hair (3:27) *Mary Martin*; 10 A Wonderful Guy (3:32) *Mary Martin*; 11 Younger Than Springtime (3:26) *William Tabbert*; 12 Happy Talk (3:31) *Juanita Hall*; 13 Honey Bun (2:02) *Mary Martin*; 14 You've Got To Be Carefully Taught (1:17) *William Tabbert*; 15 This Nearly Was Mine (3:28) *Ezio Pinza*; 16 Finale (3:00) *Mary Martin, Barbara Luna, Ezio Pinza*; 17 Loneliness Of Evening (3:21) *Mary Martin*; 18 My Girl Back Home (2:58) *Mary Martin*; 19 Bali Ha'i (3:13) *Ezio Pinza*.

Review: See entry below.

South Pacific 🎜🎜

1958, RCA Records; from the screen musical *South Pacific*, 20th Century-Fox, 1958.

Album Notes: *Music*: Richard Rodgers; *Lyrics*: Oscar Hammerstein II; *Orchestrations*: Robert Russell Bennett, Edward Powell, Pete King, Bernard Mayers; The 20th Century-Fox Studio Chorus and Orchestra, conducted by Alfred Newman; *Cast*: Mitzi Gaynor (Nellie Forbush), Rossano Brazzi (Emile de Becque), John Kerr (Lt. Cable), Juanita Hall (Bloody Mary), David Wayne (Luther Billis), Candace Lee (Ngana), France Nuyen (Liat), Ken Clark (Stewpot); *CD Producer*: John Snyder.

Selections: 1 Overture (3:00)Orchestra; 2 Dites-moi (1:17) *Marie Greene*; 3 A Cockeyed Optimist (1:43) *Mitzi Gaynor*; 4 Twin Soliloquies/Some Enchanted Evening (5:51) *Mitzi Gaynor, Giorgio Tozzi*; 5 Bloody Mary (1:55)Men's Chorus; 6 My Girl Back Home (1:39) *Bill Lee*; 7 There Is Nothin' Like A Dame (3:49)Men's Chorus; 8 Bali Ha'i (3:42) *Muriel Smith*; 9 I'm Gonna Wash That Man Right Out-A My Hair (2:53) *Mitzi Gaynor*; 10 A Wonderful Guy (3:21) *Mitzi Gaynor*; 11 Younger Than Springtime/Bali Ha'i (4:57) *Bill Lee*; 12 Happy Talk (3:43) *Muriel Smith*; 13 Honey Bun (1:46) *Mitzi Gaynor*; 14 You've Got To Be Carefully Taught (1:13) *Bill Lee*; 15 This Nearly Was Mine (3:28) *Giorgio Tozzi*; 16 Finale/ Some Enchanted Evening (3:00) *Mitzi Gaynor, Giorgio Tozzi, Marie Greene, Betty Wand*.

Review: One of the best Rodgers and Hammerstein musicals, *South Pacific* received a gorgeous treatment in its first incarnation, with Mary Martin radiant as Nelly Forbush, the American nurse assigned to a Pacific island during World War II, who falls in love with a French planter, Emile de Becque (Ezio Pinza), only to discover that he has two children from a native, something that conflicts with Nelly's small-town values. In a show that makes no bones where its heart is, race relations also play a crucial role in the secondary plot between Lt. Cable and Liat, the daughter of Bloody Mary, the island's wheeler-dealer. This prompted Oscar Hammerstein to write in "You've Got to Be Carefully Taught", an impassioned plea for equal rights, long before it became fashionable.

The magnificent score yields many other memorable moments, among them "Some Enchanted Evening" and "This Nearly Was Mine," powerfully delivered by Pinza, a former basso from the Met making a career comeback in the show; "Bali Ha'i," in which Bloody Mary evokes a mysterious island; "A Wonderful Man" and "A Cockeyed Optimist," in which Nelly shows the exuberant side of her personality; "Younger Than Springtime," which gives Lt. Cable an opportunity to become lyrical in the midst of his personal conflicts; and "There Is Nothin' Like A Dame" and "Bloody Mary," two rousing choruses for the Army and Navy personnel on the atoll. The second musical to be awarded the Pulitzer Prize, *South Pacific* opened on April 7, 1949, for a long run of 1,925 performances, and won nine Tony Awards, including one each for its principals, one each for its creators, and one for Best Musical.

In its transfer to the screen, however, the show fared less well, with Mitzi Gaynor an apt but ultimately bland substitute for Doris Day, the producers' first choice. Rossano Brazzi (dubbed by Giorgio Tozzi)was somewhat better as Emile, and John Kerr (dubbed by Bill Lee) as Cable. Adding to the negative impression left by the film, shot through monochrome lenses in an ill-advised decision to try and create "an effect," some of the other principals were also dubbed, including of all people Juanita Hall, the only holdover from the Broadway original, whose singing voice was Muriel Smith.

Star! ♫♫♫♫

1993, Fox Records; from the screen musical *Star!*, 20th Century-Fox, 1968.

Album Notes: *Arrangements*: Lennie Hayton; The 20th Century-Fox Orchestra and Chorus conducted by Lennie Hayton; *Cast*: Julie Andrews (Gertrude Lawrence), Daniel Massey (Noel Coward), Bruce Forsyth (Arthur Lawrence), Beryl Reid (Rose), Garrett Lewis (Jack Buchanan), and Jeanette Landis, Dinah Ann Rogers, Ann Hubell, Barbara Sandland, Ellen Plasschaert; *Album Producer*: Nick Redman; *Engineers*: Murray Spivack, Douglas O. Williams; *CD Engineer*: Dan Hersch.

Selections: 1 20th Century-Fox Fanfare with CinemaScope Extension (A. Newman)(:21); 2 Overture (3:06); 3 Star! (S. Cahn/J. Van Heusen)(1:19) *Julie Andrews*; 4 Piccadilly (W. Williams/B. Seiver/P. Morande)(2:03) *Julie Andrews, Bruce Forsyth, Beryl Reid*; 5 Oh, It's A Lovely War (J.P. Long/M. Scott)(1:44) *Julie Andrews, Jeanette Landis, Dinah Ann Rogers, Ann Hubell, Barbara Sandland, Ellen Plasschaert*; 6 In My Garden Of Joy (S. Chaplin) (1:32) *Jeanette Landis, Dinah Ann Rogers, Ann Hubell, Barbara Sandland*; 7 'N' Everything (B.G. DeSylva/G. Kahn/A. Jolson)(1:47) *Garrett Lewis*; 8 Burlington Bertie From Bow (W. Hargreaves)(2:03) *Julie Andrews*; 9 Parisian Pierrot (N. Coward)(2:27) *Julie Andrews*; 10 Limehouse Blues (P. Brahm/D. Furber)(4:20) *Julie Andrews*; 11 Someone To Watch Over (G. & I. Gershwin)(3:15) *Julie Andrews*; 12 Dear Little Boy (Dear Little Girl)(G. & I. Gershwin)(1:58) *Julie Andrews, Daniel Massey*; 13 Someday I'll Find You (N. Coward)(1:40) *Julie Andrews*; 14 The Physician (C. Porter)(3:07) *Julie Andrews*; 15 Do, Do, Do (G. & I. Gershwin)(1:38) *Julie Andrews*; 16 Has Anybody Seen Our Ship? (N. Coward)(1:37) *Julie Andrews, Daniel Massey*; 17 My Ship (K. Weill/I. Gershwin)(2:16) *Julie Andrews*; 18 The Saga Of Jenny (K. Weill/I. Gershwin)(5:35) *Julie Andrews*; 19 Forbidden Fruit (N. Coward)(1:39) *Daniel Massey*; 20 Star! (S. Cahn/J. Van Heusen)(2:16).

Review: Julie Andrews, portraying Gertrude Lawrence, is quite fetching in this glossy biographical musical film, in which she performed some of the great hits created by Lawrence. With an abundance of memorable songs, many of them written by the cream of Broadway and London tunesmiths, a glamorous era in the musical theatre as backdrop, and a flamboyant character as its main focus, the film became a veritable showcase for Andrews, who is dazzling in it. The recently-reissued CD includes a couple of previously unreleased numbers.

A Star Is Born ♫♫♫♫♭

1988, Columbia Records; from the screen musical *A Star Is Born*, Warner Bros. Pictures, 1954.

Album Notes: *Music*: Harold Arlen; *Lyrics*: Ira Gershwin; *Orchestrations*: Skip Martin; *Vocal Arrangements*: Jack Cathcart; The Warner Bros. Studio Chorus and Orchestra, conducted by Ray Heindorf; *Cast*: Judy Garland (Esther Blodgett/Vicki Lester), James Mason (Norman Maine), Tommy Noonan (Danny McGuire); *CD Producer*: Didier C. Deutsch; *Engineer*: Tim Geelan.

Selections: 1 Overture (2:04) *Orchestra*; 2 Gotta Have Me Go With You (3:17) *Judy Garland*; 3 The Man That Got Away (4:37) *Tommy Noonan, Judy Garland*; 4 Born In A Trunk (medley): Swanee (G. Gershwin/I. Gershwin)/I'll Get By (R. Turk/F.

Ahlert)/You Took Advantage Of Me (R. Rodgers/L. Hart)/Black Bottom (B.G. DeSylva/L. Brown/R. Henderson)/The Peanut Vendor (M. Sdunshine/L. Gilbert/M. Simon)/My Melancholy Baby (G. Norton/E. Burnett)/Swanee (reprise)(15:07) *Judy Garland*; 5 Here's What I'm Here For (3:09) *Judy Garland*; 6 It's A New World (2:27) *Judy Garland*; 7 Someone At Last (6:41) *Judy Garland*; 8 Lose That Long Face (3:54) *Judy Garland*.

Review: In 1988, Ronald Haver wrote one of the most interesting books pertaining to film history. That book, *A Star Is Born: The Making of the 1954 Movie and its 1983 Reconstruction* deals with the film *A Star Is Born*, and the trials and tribulations that Judy Garland and then husband Sid Luft created and endured in bringing Moss Hart's bittersweet tale of love and fame to the big screen. The book paints a fascinating picture of all the elements that combine together to create what would become Garland's Hollywood "comeback," and her last true success. One of those elements, the music, is what has propelled this terrific film into the annals of Hollywood history—and what survives as one of the most pleasing and alluring of all film soundtrack recordings.

Until the release of this Columbia CD, there existed no stereo album of these familiar songs, most by Harold Arlen and Ira Gershwin. After an ambitious film restoration made it clear that a true stereo recording existed, a search was conducted, and the result is this disc—the finest release of this soundtrack to date. The sonics, carefully restored, are excellent, despite the limitations of stereo film recording technology in 1954 (and several years before stereo became a standard in recording studios). It is a true revelation to hear Garland classics like "The Man That Got Away," "Gotta Have Me Go With You," and the mammoth "Born in a Trunk" sequence without the sonic murk of the original Columbia/Harmony LPS. The music, and Ray Heindorf's outstanding orchestrations are so appealing, that one wishes there were more musical cues to be heard. (There were, initially, but unfortunately these were removed at the last minute, for contractual reasons). While a complete soundtrack, coinciding with the film restoration, would have made for a spectacular release, this outstanding recording fits a special niche, and leaves us hoping that maybe someday...

Charles L. Granata

State Fair ♫♫♫

1996, DRG Records; from the Broadway production *State Fair*, 1995.

Album Notes: *Music*: Richard Rodgers; *Lyrics*: Oscar Hammerstein II; *Orchestrations*: Bruce Pomahac; *Vocal Arrangements and Musical Direction*: Kay Cameron; *Cast*: John Davidson (Abel Frake), Kathryn Crosby (Melissa Frake), Andrea McArdle (Margy

Frake), Donna McKechnie (Emily Arden), Scott Wise (Pat Gilbert), Ben Wright (Wayne Frake), Tina Johnson (Vivian), Leslie Bell (Jeanne), and J. Lee Flynn, Newton R. Gilchrist, John Wilkerson; *Album Producer*: Hugh Fordin; *Engineer*: Cynthia Daniels.

Selections: 1 Overture (3:00)Orchestra; 2 Opening (2:07) *John Davidson, Charles Goff, Kathryn Crosby, Ben Wright*; 3 It Might As Well Be Spring (3:09) *Andrea McArdle*; 4 Driving At Night/ Our State Fair (2:40) *John Davidson, Kathryn Crosby, Andrea McArdle, Ben Wright*; 5 That's For Me (1:53) *Ben Wright*; 6 More Than Just A Friend (2:45) *John Davidson, J. Lee Flynn, Newton R. Gilchrist, John Wilkerson*; 7 Isn't It Kinda Fun? (4:04) *Scott Wise, Andrea McArdle*; 8 You Never Had It So Good (3:31) *Donna McKechnie, Ian Knauer, James Patterson, Michael Lee Scott, Scott Willis*; 9 It Might As Well Be Spring (reprise)(1:37) *Andrea McArdle, Kathryn Crosby*; 10 When I Go Out Walking With My Baby (2:00) *John Davidson, Kathryn Crosby*; 11 So Far (3:34) *Ben Wright, Donna McKechnie*; 12 It's A Grand Night For Singing (4:53)Company; 13 Entr'acte (2:01) Orchestra; 14 The Man I Used To Be (4:00) *Scott Wise, Tina Johnson, Leslie Bell*; 15 All I Owe Ioway (5:23) *John Davidson*; 16 That's The Way It Happens (5:46) *Andrea McArdle, Donna McKechnie, Ian Knauer, James Patterson, Michael Lee Scott, Scott Willis*; 17 Boys And Girls Like You And Me (3:01) *John Davidson, Kathryn Crosby*; 18 The Next Time It Happens (2:28) *Andrea McArdle*; 19 Finale Ultimo (1:04)Company.

Review: The stage presentation of *State Fair*—a film musical that had previously received two screen versions, in 1946 and 1962—was a rather sad affair which looked like a road company (which it was) out of its league among other Broadway productions. With the exception of Donna McKechnie, thoroughly professional and demure as a singer willing to sacrifice everything on her way to stardom, and Scott Wise, as a smart newspaper reporter who finds love while covering a story, the others in the pedestrian cast were not on the same high quality level in this story of an Iowa farmer and his family attending the State Fair, and their adventures. Mercifully, none of the show's shortcomings are apparent on the cast recording, which focuses on the score by Rodgers and Hammerstein, in which "It's a Grand Night for Singing" and "It Might as Well Be Spring" remain two beautiful highlights.

A Stephen Sondheim Evening ♫♫♫♫

1983, RCA Victor; from the concert presentation *A Stephen Sondheim Evening*, 1983.

Album Notes: *Music*: Stephen Sondheim; *Lyrics*: Stephen Sondheim; *Musical Direction*: Paul Gemignani; *Cast*: Liz Callaway, Cris Groenendaal, Bob Gunton, George Hearn, Steven Jacob, Judy Kaye, Victoria Mallory, Angela Lansbury; *Album Producer*: Thomas Z. Shepard; *CD Producer*: Bill Rosenfield; *Engineer*: Jay Newland.

Selections: 1 Invocation and Instructions To The Audience (5:15) *Bob Gunton*; 2 Saturday Night (4:18)Company; 3 Isn't It (2:19) *Victoria Mallory*; 4 Saturday Night (reprise)(1:11) *Cris Groenendaal, Bob Gunton, George Hearn, Steven Jacob*; 5 Poems (4:11) *George Hearn, Bob Gunton*; 6 What More Do I Need? (3:00) *Liz Callaway*; 7 Another Hundred People (2:35) *Judy Kaye*; 8 With So Little To Be Sure Of (4:17) *Victoria Mallory, George Hearn*; 9 Pretty Little Picture (3:31) *Bob Gunton, Liz Callaway, Steven Jacob*; 10 The House Of Marcus Lycus (5:21) *George Hearn, Bob Gunton*; 11 Echo Song (3:29) *Liz Callaway, Steven Jacob*; 12 There's Something About A War (4:27) *Cris Gronendaal*; 13 Being Alive (4:33) *Judy Kaye*; 14 The Miller's Son (4:23) *Liz Callaway*; 15 Johanna (1:55) *Cris Groenendaal*; 16 Not A Day Goes By (2:47) *Victoria Mallory*; 17 Someone In A Tree (8:57) *Bob Gunton, George Hearn, Steven Jacob, Cris Gronendaal*; 18 Send In The Clowns (3:20) *Angela Lansbury, Stephen Sondheim*; 19 Old Friends (2:42) *Stephen Sondheim, Angela Lansbury*.

Review: The result of a concert presentation of songs by Sondheim, held at the Whitney Museum of American Art, in New York, this collection presents 19 numbers selected from the dozen musicals he had created up to that time. The all-star cast (Liz Callaway, Cris Groenendaal, Bob Gunton, George Hearn, Steven Jacob, Judy Kaye and Victoria Mallory, many of them veterans of Sondheim's Broadway shows), received a curtain call support from Angela Lansbury and Sondheim himself. A rare occasion, thankfully captured on this bright recording.

Stop the World—I Want to Get Off ♫♫♫ᵛ

1962, Polydor Records; from the Broadway production *Stop the World — I Want to Get Off*, 1962.

Album Notes: *Music*: Leslie Bricusse, Anthony Newley; *Lyrics*: Leslie Bricusse, Anthony Newley; *Orchestrations*: Ian Fraser, David Lindup, Burt Rhodes, Gordon Langford; *Musical Direction*: Milton Rosenstock; *Cast*: Anthony Newley (Littlechap), Evie (Anna Quayle), Jennifer Baker, Susan Baker; *CD Engineer*: Dennis Drake.

Selections: 1 Overture/The A.B.C. Song/I Wanna Be Rich (7:30) *Anthony Newley*; 2 Typically English (5:15) *Anna Quayle*; 3 Lumbered (4:22) *Anthony Newley*; 4 Glorious Russian/Meilinki Meilchick (5:35) *Anna Quayle, Anthony Newley*; 5

Gonna Build A Mountain (2:42) *Anthony Newley*; 6 Typische Deutsche (3:15) *Anna Quayle*; 7 Family Fugue/Nag! Nag! Nag! (4:58) *Anthony Newley, Anna Quayle, Jennifer Baker, Susan Baker*; 8 Once In A Lifetime (2:07) *Anthony Newley*; 9 All American (3:40) *Anna Quayle*; 10 Mumbo Jumbo (2:50) *Anthony Newley*; 11 Someone Nice Like You (2:33) *Anthony Newley, Anna Quayle*; 12 What Kind Of Fool Am I? (2:31) *Anthony Newley*.

Review: Anthony Newley made a mesmerizing Broadway debut in *Stop the World — I Want to Get Off*, in which he portrayed Littlechap, a character not unlike Charles Chaplin' Little Tramp or Marcel Marceau's Blip, in love with life and its wonders, and forever victimized by those stronger or more influential than him. The overall ingratiating score yielded at least one major hit in "What Kind of Fool Am I?" which was soon covered by cabaret performers all over the world, and still stands out today as one of the most powerful numbers in the standard catalog.

Stormy Weather ♫♫♫♫♫

1993, Fox Records; from the screen musical *Stormy Weather*, 20th Century-Fox, 1943.

Album Notes: The 20th Century-Fox Studio Chorus and Orchestra, conducted by Emil Newman, Alfred Newman; *Cast*: Lena Horne, Cab Calloway, Bill Robinson, Fats Waller, The Nicholas Brothers; *Album Producer*: Nick Redman; *Engineers*: Vincent Cirilli, Rick Victor, Dan Hersch.

Selections: 1 20th Century-Fox Fanfare (A. Newman)(:12); 2 Overture/Stormy Weather Ballet (H. Arlen/T. Koehler)(3:54); 3 Walkin' The Dog (S. Brooks) (1:27); 4 There's No Two Ways About Love (J.P. Johnson/T. Koehler/I. Mills) (2:42) *Lena Horne*; 5 Cakewalk/Camptown Races/At A Georgia Meeting (S.C. Foster/K. Mills)(2:44); 6 Linda Brown (A. Cowans)(3:38) The Tramp Band; 7 Moppin' And Boppin' (T. Waller/B. Carter/E. Kirkeby)(4:21); 8 That Ain't Right (N. Cole/I. Mills)(2:59) *Fats Waller, Ada Brown*; 9 Ain't Misbehavin' (T. Waller/H. Brooks)(3:57) *Fats Waller*; 10 Diga Diga Doo (J. McHugh/D. Fields) (3:58) *Lena Horne*; 11 I Lost My Sugar In Salt Lake City (L. Rene/J. Lange) (1:50) *Mae Johnson*; 12 Nobody's Sweetheart (G. Kahn/E. Erdman/B. Meyers/E. Schoebel)(:59); 13 I Can't Give You Anything But Love (J. McHugh/D. Fields) (2:57) *Lena Horne, Bill ''Bojangles'' Robinson*; 14 Geechy Joe (C. Calloway/S. Palmer/A. Gibson)(3:17) *Cab Calloway*; 15 Stormy Weather (H. Arlen/T. Koehler)(3:57) *Lena Horne*; 16 There's No Two Ways About Love (reprise)(J.P. Johnson/T. Koehler/I. Mills)(3:01) *Cab Calloway, Bill ''Bojangles'' Robinson, Lena Horne*; 17 My, My, Ain't That Somethin' (P. Tomlin/H. Tobias)

(2:31) *Bill ''Bojangles'' Robinson*; 18 Jumpin' Jive (C. Calloway/S. Palmer)(4:33) *Cab Calloway*; 19 My, My, Ain't That Somethin' (reprise) (P. Tomlin/H. Tobias) (1:12) *Bill ''Bojangles'' Robinson, Cab Calloway, Lena Horne*; 20 Good For Nothin' Joe (R. Bloom/T. Koehler)(3:07) *Lena Horne*; 21 Ain't Misbehavin' (alternate ending)(T. Waller/H. Brooks)(1:01) *Fats Waller*; 22 I Lost My Sugar In Salt Lake City (alternate)(L. Rene/J. Lange)(1:00) *Mae Johnson*; 23 Body And Soul (J. Green/E. Heyman/R. Sour/F. Eyton)(6:47) *Cab Calloway and His Band*; 24 Alfred The Moocher (C. Calloway/I. Mills/C. Gaskill)(2:50) *Cab Calloway*.

Review: The storyline is easily dispensable, but the songs and the performances are the thing, in this entertaining backstage saga in which Lena Horne and Bill Robinson play star-crossed lovers forever separated by their own careers. The sultry Ms. Horne delivers her signature song, "Stormy Weather," and "I Can't Give You Anything But Love," among her better moments, while Bill "Bojangles" Robinson dances up a storm in a couple of show-stopping numbers, and Cab Calloway adds his zany big band sound to some of the musical proceedings; but it is Fats Waller who literally steals the scene, the film and everything else in-between with his rendition of "Ain't Misbehavin'."

Strike Up the Band ♫♫♫♫

1991, Elektra Records; from the studio cast recording *Strike Up the Band*, 1991.

Album Notes: *Music:* George Gershwin; *Lyrics:* Ira Gershwin; *Orchestrations:* Russell Warner, William D. Brohn, Steven D. Bowen, William Daily, Dick Hyman, Donald Johnston, Sid Ramin, Larry Wilcox; *Vocal Direction:* Paul Trueblood; *Musical Direction:* John Mauceri; *Cast:* Brent Barrett (Jim Townsend), Don Chastain (Horace J. Fletcher), Rebecca Luker (Joan Fletcher), Jason Graae (Timothy Harper), Beth Fowler (Mrs. Draper), Charles Goff (Colonel Holmes), Juliet Lambert (Anne Draper), Jeff Lyons (Spelvin/Gideon), Dale Sandish (Soldier), James Rocco (Sloane); *Album Producer:* John McClure, Tommy Krasker; *Engineer:* Paul Goodman; *Assistant Engineers:* Vincent Caro, Sandy Palmer.

Selections: CD 1: *Strike Up The Band (1927):* 1 Overture (5:58) *Orchestra*; 2 Fletcher's American Cheese Choral Society (5:25) *Jason Graae, James Rocco, Don Chastain*; 3 17 And 21 (4:11) *Jason Graae, Juliet Lambert*; 4 Typical Self Made American (3:22) *Don Chastain, Brent Barrett*; 5 Meadow Serenade (3:37) *Rebecca Luker, Brent Barrett*; 6 Unofficial Spokesman (7:05) *Don Chastain, Charles Goff*; 7 Patriotic Rally (2:27) *Chorus*; 8 The Man I Love (6:06) *Rebecca Luker, Brent Barrett*; 9 Yankee Doodle Rhythm (3:18) *Jeff Lyons*; 10 7 And 21 (reprise)(1:28) *Beth Fowler, Don Chastain*; 11 Finaletto Act 1 (7:26) *Don*

Chastain, Brent Barrett, James Rocco, Charles Goff, Rebecca Luker, Jason Graae; 12 Strike Up The Band (3:57) *Jason Graae*.

CD 2: 1 Oh This Is Such A Lovely War (4:11) *Ensemble*; 2 Hoping That Someday You'd Care (2:55) *Brent Barrett, Rebecca Luker*; 3 Come-Look-At-The-War Choral Society (:58) *Female Chorus*; 4 Military Dancing Drill (2:20) *Jason Graae, Juliet Lambert*; 5 How About A Man? (2:24) *Beth Fowler, Charles Goff, Don Chastain*; 6 Finaletto Act 2 (4:49) *Don Chastain, Brent Barrett, James Rocco, Charles Goff, Rebecca Luker, Jeff Lyons*; 7 Homeward Bound/The Girl I Love (reprise)(5:41) *Male Chorus*; 8 The War That Ended War (5:56) *Chorus*; 9 Finale Ultimo (1:38) *Company*; *Strike Up The Band (1930):* 10 Interlude: Strike Up The Band (1:51) *Orchestra*; 11 I Mean To Say (3:50) *Juliet Lambert, Jason Graae*; 12 Soon (2:41) *Brent Barrett, Rebecca Luker*; 13 If I Became The President (3:14) *Beth Fowler, Charles Goff*; 14 Hangin' Around With You (4:32) *Jason Graae, Juliet Lambert*; 15 Mademoiselle In New Rochelle (5:16) *Charles Goff, Jeff Lyons*; 16 I've Got A Crush On You (3:49) *Jason Graae, Juliet Lambert*.

Review: Some theatrical shows undergo so many rewritings that it is difficult to keep track of all the changes that went into their production. Such was the case with *Strike Up the Band*, a 1927 musical by George and Ira Gershwin, with a gloomy book by George S. Kaufman, so rife with anti-militarist ideas that it closed before it even reached Broadway. Revised, updated, and now sporting a lighter libretto—a zany story about the United States and Switzerland at war with each other over Swiss chocolate—the musical continued its way to Broadway, where it finally arrived on January 14, 1930. In its score are many gems that continue to charm today, including "The Man I Love," "Strike Up the Band," "Soon," and "I've Got a Crush on You."

The cast recording listed above, one in a continuing series of great Gershwin musicals produced under the aegis of the composer's estate, is a lavish recreation of both scores, starring Jason Graae, Rebecca Luker, Brent Barrett, Don Chastain, and Beth Fowler, with John Mauceri conducting the orchestra. Stylishly presented, with a booklet replete with information about the show and period pictures, it is an essential recording in any collection.

Summer Stock ♫♫♫♫♭

1990, CBS Special Products; from the screen musical *Summer Stock*, M-G-M, 1950.

Album Notes: *Music:* Harry Warren; *Lyrics:* Mack Gordon; The M-G-M Studio Chorus and Orchestra, conducted by Johnny Green; *Cast:* Judy Garland (Jane Falbury), Gene Kelly (Joe D. Ross), Phil Silvers (Herb Blake), Gloria De Haven (Abigail Falbury); *Album Producer:* Dan Rivard; *Engineer:* Ken Robertson.

Selections: 1 Overture (1:38) Orchestra; 2 If You Feel Like Singing, Sing (2:22) *Judy Garland*; 3 (Howdy Neighbor) Happy Harvest (2:35) *Judy Garland*; 4 Dig-Dig-Dig For Your Dinner (3:51) *Gene Kelly, Phil Silvers*; 5 Mem'ry Island (3:51) *Gloria De Haven, Pete Roberts*; 6 The Portland Fancy (3:18) *Ray Collins*; 7 You, Wonderful You (H. Warren/S. Chaplin/J. Brooks)(3:09) *Gene Kelly, Judy Garland*; 8 Friendly Star (3:18) *Judy Garland*; 9 Newspaper Dance (You Wonderful You) (3:31) *Gene Kelly*; 10 All For You (S. Chaplin)(1:59) *Gene Kelly, Judy Garland*; 11 You, Wonderful You (reprise)(1:21) *Gene Kelly, Judy Garland*; 12 Heavenly Music (S. Chaplin)(3:52) *Gene Kelly, Phil Silvers*; 13 Get Happy (H. Arlen/T. Koehler)(2:53) *Judy Garland*; 14 (Howdy Neighbor) Happy Harvest(Finale)(1:10) *Judy Garland, Gene Kelly*.

Review: For her 27th and last film for M-G-M, the studio where she had spent her entire life as a trouper, Judy Garland teamed again with Gene Kelly for a celebration of show business and the kind of backstage saga that had proved so successful in the past. In this hackneyed story, Judy owns a farm in Connecticut, and Kelly is a hoofer trying out a Broadway-bound show in a barn on the farm, with Judy eventually joining in the musical revelry. There are many attractive moments in the score (including "You Wonderful You," first performed as a duet by the two stars, then reprised by Gene in a mesmerizing "Newspaper Dance"), but the most memorable one, filmed two months after shooting had been completed, was Judy, striking in black leotard and dinner jacket, singing "Get Happy."

Sunday in the Park with George 🎵🎵🎵🎵🎵

1984, RCA Victor; from the Broadway production *Sunday in the Park with George*, 1984.

Album Notes: *Music*: Stephen Sondheim; *Lyrics*: Stephen Sondheim; *Orchestrations*: Michael Starobin; *Musical Direction*: Paul Gemignani; *Cast*: Mandy Patinkin (George), Bernadette Peters (Dot/Marie), Charles Kimbrough (Jules/Bob Greenberg), Dana Ivey (Yvonne/Naomi Eisen), Melanie Vaughan (Celeste #1), Mary D'Arcy (Celeste #2), Barbara Bryne (Old Lady/Blair Daniels), Judith Moore (Nurse/Harriet Pawling), William Parry (Boatman/Charles Redmond), Nancy Opel (Frieda/Betty), Brent Spiner (Franz), Robert Westenberg (Soldier/Alex), Cris Gronendaal (Billy Webster), Kurt Knudson (Lee Randolph); *Album/CD Producer*: Thomas Z. Shepard; *Engineers*: Paul Goodman, Anthony Salvatore.

Selections: 1 Sunday In The Park With George (6:36) *Bernadette Peters, Mandy Patinkin*; 2 No Life (1:23) *Charles Kimbrough, Dana Ivey*; 3 Color And Light (7:00) *Mandy Patinkin, Bernadette Peters*; 4 Gossip (1:00) *Melanie Vaughan,*

Mary D'Arcy, Barbara Bryne, Judith Moore, William Parry; 5 The Day Off (8:00) *Mandy Patinkin, Melanie Vaughan, Mary D'Arcy, Nancy Opel, Brent Spiner, Barbara Bryne, Judith Moore, Robert Westenberg, William Parry*; 6 Everybody Loves Louis (3:06) *Bernadette Peters*; 7 Finishing The Hat (3:20) *Mandy Patinkin*; 8 We Do Not Belong Together (3:58) *Mandy Patinkin, Bernadette Peters*; 9 Beautiful (3:06) *Barbara Bryne, Mandy Patinkin*; 10 Sunday (4:28)Company; 11 It's Hot Up Here (4:27)Company; 12 Chromolume #7/Putting It Together (7:16) *Judith Moore, Cris Gronendaal, Charles Kimbrough, William Parry, Nancy Opel, Robert Westenberg, Dana Ivey, Mandy Patinkin, Kurt Knudson, Barbara Bryne*; 13 Children And Art (4:50) *Bernadette Peters, Mandy Patinkin*; 14 Lesson #8 (2:50) *Mandy Patinkin*; 15 Move On (3:38) *Mandy Patinkin, Bernadette Peters*; 16 Sunday (3:52)Company.

Review: One of the true pinnacles of the American musical theater, and as ambitious a musical as Broadway has seen: Stephen Sondheim and writer/director James Lapine address "the art of making art" through a fictionalized biography of the 19th century French painter Georges Seurat, set against the travails of a modern-day descendant. The score was edited and reconstructed for CD, a collaboration between Sondheim and producer Thomas Z. Shepard that captures the staged musical on disc in an innovative way. A must: apologize to your neighbors in advance, tweak your stereo, and play the choral "Sunday" very, very loud.

Marc Kirkeby

Sunset Blvd.

Sunset Blvd. 🎵🎵🎵

1993, Polydor Records; from the world premiere recording *Sunset Blvd.*, 1993.

Album Notes: *Music*: Andrew Lloyd Webber; *Lyrics*: Don Black, Christopher Hampton; *Orchestrations*: David Cullen, Andrew Lloyd Webber; *Musical Direction*: David Caddick; *Cast*: Patti LuPone (Norma Desmond), Kevin Anderson (Joe Gillis), Daniel Benzali (Max von Mayerling), Meredith Braun (Betty Schaefer); *Album Producers*: Andrew Lloyd Webber, Nigel Wright; *Engineer*: Robin Sellars; *Assistant Engineers*: William O'Donovan, Jason Westbrook, Andy Strange, Rupert Coulson.

Selections: CD 1: 1 Overture/Prologue (3:02) *Kevin Anderson*; 2 Let's Have Lunch (3:31) *Kevin Anderson*; 3 Sheldrake's Office (1:26) *Kevin Anderson, Meredith Braun*; 4 On The Road (3:01)Orchestra; 5 The House On Sunset: Surrender (2:33) *Kevin Anderson, Patti LuPone*; 6 With One Look (4:00) *Patti LuPone*; 7 Salome (4:42) *Patti LuPone, Kevin Anderson*; 8 The

Greatest Star Of All (3:26) *Daniel Benzali*; 9 Let's Have Lunch/ Girl Meets Boy (3:42) *Kevin Anderson, Meredith Braun*; 10 The House On Sunset (1:03) *Patti LuPone*; 11 New Ways To Dream (4:43) *Patti LuPone*; 12 The Lady's Paying (4:20) *Nicolas Colico, Patti LuPone, Kevin Anderson*; 13 The House On Sunset (:42)Orchestra; 14 The Perfect Year (3:10) *Patti LuPone, Kevin Anderson*; 15 Dialogue (1:02) *Patti LuPone, Kevin Anderson*; 16 Artie Green's Apartment (:30)Ensemble; 17 This Time Next Year (5:28) *Kevin Anderson, Meredith Braun, Gareth Snook*; 18 The House On Sunset (1:36) *Kevin Anderson, Patti LuPone*.

CD 2: 1 Entr'acte/Sunset Boulevard (6:15) *Kevin Anderson*; 2 The Perfect Year (reprise)(1:28) *Patti LuPone*; 3 Journey To Paramount (3:30)Orchestra; 4 As If We Never Said Goodbye (6:52) *Patti LuPone*; 5 Surrender (reprise)(1:05) *Michael Bauer*; 6 Girl Meets Boy (reprise)(2:10) *Kevin Anderson, Meredith Braun*; 7 Eternal Youth Is Worth A Little Suffering (3:31)Female Ensemble; 8 Too Much In Love To Care (5:26) *Kevin Anderson, Meredith Braun*; 9 New Ways To Dream (reprise)(3:48) *Daniel Benzali*; 10 Sunset Boulevard (reprise)(6:00) *Kevin Anderson, Meredith Braun*; 11 The Greatest Star Of All (reprise)(4:07) *Patti LuPone, Daniel Benzali*.

Review: See entry below.

Sunset Blvd. 🎬🎬🎬⁰

1994, Polydor Records; from the world premiere recording *Sunset Blvd.*, 1994.

Album Notes: *Music:* Andrew Lloyd Webber; *Lyrics:* Don Black, Christopher Hampton; *Orchestrations:* David Cullen, Andrew Lloyd Webber; *Musical Direction:* David Caddick; *Cast:* Glenn Close (Norma Desmond), Alan Campbell (Joe Gillis), George Hearn (Max von Mayerling), Judy Kuhn (Betty Schaefer); *Album Producers:* Andrew Lloyd Webber, Nigel Wright; *Engineer:* Robin Sellars; *Assistant Engineers:* William O'Donovan, Jason Westbrook, Andy Strange, Rupert Coulson.

Selections: CD 1: 1 Overture/I Guess It Was 5 a.m. (2:49) *Alan Campbell*; 2 Let's Have Lunch (6:54) *Alan Campbell*; 3 Every Movie's A Circus (1:59) *Alan Campbell, Judy Kuhn*; 4 Car Chase (1:46)Orchestra; 5 At The House On Sunset (1:41) *Alan Campbell*; 6 Surrender (2:45) *Glenn Close*; 7 With One Look (3:11) *Glenn Close*; 8 Salome (6:40) *Glenn Close, Alan Campbell*; 9 The Greatest Star Of All (3:52) *George Hearn*; 10 Every Movie's A Circus (reprise)(2:33) *Alan Campbell, Judy Kuhn, Vincent Tumeo*; 11 Girl Meets Boy (3:19) *Alan Campbell, Judy Kuhn*; 12 Back At The House On Sunset (3:21) *Glenn Close*; 13 New Ways To Dream (3:52) *Glenn Close*; 14 Completion Of The Script (3:21) *Glenn Close, Alan Campbell*; 15 The Lady's Paying (4:26) *Matthew Dickens, Glenn Close, Alan Campbell*; 16 New Year's

Eve (2:41) *Alan Campbell, George Hearn*; 17 The Perfect Year (4:54) *Glenn Close, Alan Campbell*; 18 This Time Next Year (6:55) *Alan Campbell, Judy Kuhn, Vincent Tumeo*; 19 New Year's Eve (Back At The House On Sunset)(1:58) *Alan Campbell, Glenn Close*.

CD 2: 1 Entr'acte (2:46)Orchestra; 2 Sunset Boulevard (3:04) *Alan Campbell*; 3 There's Been A Call/Journey To Paramount (4:40) *Glenn Close*; 4 As If We Never Said Goodbye (6:17) *Glenn Close*; 5 Paramount Conversations/ Surrender (reprise)(4:20) *Judy Kuhn, Alan Campbell*; 6 Girl Meets Boy (reprise)(2:46) *Alan Campbell, Judy Kuhn*; 7 Eternal Youth Is Worth A Little Suffering (1:49)Female Ensemble; 8 Who's Betty Schaefer? (2:08) *Glenn Close, Alan Campbell*; 9 Betty's Office At Paramount (2:23) *Judy Kuhn, Alan Campbell*; 10 Too Much In Love To Care (6:13) *Alan Campbell, Judy Kuhn*; 11 New Ways To Dream (reprise)(2:46) *George Hearn*; 12 The Phone Call (1:55) *Alan Campbell, Glenn Close*; 13 The Final Scene (12:37) *Glenn Close, Judy Kuhn, Alan Campbell, George Hearn*.

Review: Andrew Lloyd Webber's mammoth Gothic take on Billy Wilder's 1950 film has spawned several recordings. All are essentially similar, and distinguished only by the various actresses essaying the role. Originated by Gloria Swanson in the film, it is the story of a silent film star trying desperately to hang on to her past glory and dreams of eternal youth, only to be drawn to murder when her protégé, a playwright she has hired to help her doctor a script, ultimately rejects her advances and threatens to leave her.

Of the two versions proposed here, Patti Lupone, heard in the original London cast, sounds more dramatic and gut-wrenching, though her theatrics tend to be overbearing after a while.

Glenn Close, and the original Broadway cast (with George Hearn totally wasted in a secondary role, as Norma's chauffeur and ex-husband), strike a more positive note, though everything is again very much relative.

Because the singing is continuous throughout the show, identifying the various tracks is somewhat of a problem on some recordings. Highlights have been indicated whenever possible.

Sweeney Todd 🎬🎬🎬🎬

1979, RCA Victor; from the Broadway production *Sweeney Todd*, 1979.

Album Notes: *Music:* Stephen Sondheim; *Lyrics:* Stephen Sondheim; *Orchestrations:* Jonathan Tunick; *Musical Direction:* Paul Gemignani; *Cast:* Angela Lansbury (Mrs. Lovett), Len Cariou (Sweeney Todd), Sarah Rice (Johanna), Victor Garber

(Anthony Hope), Ken Jennings (Tobias Ragg), Merle Louise (Beggar Woman), Jack Eric Williams (The Beadle), Edmund Lyndeck (Judge Turpin), Joaquin Romaguera (Pirelli); *Album Producer*: Thomas Z. Shepard; *Engineer*: Anthony Salvatore.

Selections: CD 1: 1 Prelude/The Ballad Of Sweeney Todd (3:34) *Len Cariou*; 2 No Place Like London (3:40) *Victor Garber, Len Cariou, Merle Louise*; 3 The Barber And His Wife (2:41) *Len Cariou*; 4 The Worst Pies In London (2:25) *Angela Lansbury*; 5 Poor Thing (3:27) *Angela Lansbury*; 6 My Friends (2:44) *Len Cariou, Angela Lansbury*; 7 The Ballad Of Sweeney Todd (:55)Members of the Company; 8 Green Finch And Linnet Bird (2:29) *Sarah Rice*; 9 Ah, Miss (2:25) *Victor Garber, Sarah Rice, Merle Louise*; 10 Johanna (1:55) *Victor Garber*; 11 Pirelli's Miracle Elixir (3:50) *Ken Jennings, Len Cariou, Angela Lansbury, Joaquin Romaguera*; 12 The Contest (5:12) *Joaquin Romaguera*; 13 The Ballad Of Sweeney Todd (:31)Members of the Company; 14 Wait (2:16) *Angela Lansbury*; 15 The Ballad Of Sweeney Todd (:41) *Cris Gronendaal, Frank Kopyc, Richard Warren Pugh*; 16 Johanna (3:39) *Edmund Lyndeck*; 17 Kiss Me (1:31) *Sarah Rice, Victor Garber*; 18 Ladies In Their Sensitivities (3:54) *Jack Eric Williams, Edmund Lyndeck*; 19 Pretty Women (4:58) *Edmund Lyndeck, Len Cariou, Victor Garber*; 20 Epiphany (3:17) *Len Cariou, Angela Lansbury*; 21 A Little Priest (7:15) *Angela Lansbury, Len Cariou*.

CD 2: 1 God, That's Good (6:23) *Ken Jennings, Angela Lansbury, Len Cariou*; 2 Johanna (5:29) *Victor Garber, Len Cariou, Merle Louise, Sarah Rice*; 3 By The Sea (3:32) *Angela Lansbury, Len Cariou*; 4 Wigmaker Sequence/ The Ballad Of Sweeney Todd (3:36) *Len Cariou, Victor Garber/Quintet*; 5 Not While I'm Around (3:55) *Ken Jennings, Angela Lansbury*; 6 Parlor Songs (3:35) *Jack Eric Williams, Angela Lansbury, Ken Jennings*; 7 Final Sequence (13:26)Company; 8 Epilogue: The Ballad Of Sweeney Todd (2:56) Company.

Review: Stephen Sondheim's *Sweeney Todd*, a masterful tale about a demon barber set in 19th-century England, will either delight or repulse you. Todd, a victim of society whose wife and young daughter are taken from him by a villainous judge, finds himself imprisoned on trumped-up charges. Returning fifteen years later to seek revenge upon his foe, he commences to shave necks and slit throats in a comedically vengeful way. What ensues is the basis for this fiendishly alluring musical, showcasing some of Sondheim's most brilliant work.

The original cast recording features Len Cariou as Todd, and Angela Lansbury as his meat-pie maker partner in crime, Mrs. Lovett. Approaching grand opera, the show is cleverly written to be almost completely sung, so the cast recording is nearly a mirror image of the original show itself. Produced by Broadway cast and classical music recording veteran Thomas Z. Shepard, the 2 CD set is indispensable listening for any Sondheim aficionado. Recorded at RCA's famed Studio A, Shepard retained all of the original stage positions, and the resulting stereo imaging is a realistic re-creation of the show's original stage movements. This is especially important when Todd slashes a throat, and the unsuspecting victim is rolled down a chute, into the basement of Lovett's meat-pie shop for disposal!

Included are two booklets: one containing a short synopsis of the play, the other a complete libretto. The plot is ghoulish; the songs, lyrics and orchestrations superb. *Sweeney Todd* is an unusual show and unique cast recording that no theater lover should be without.

Charles L. Granata

Sweet Charity ♪♪♪♪ᵛ

1966, Columbia Records; from the Broadway production *Sweet Charity*, 1966.

Album Notes: *Music*: Cy Coleman; *Lyrics*: Dorothy Fields; *Orchestrations*: Ralph Burns; *Dance Music Arrangements and Musical Direction*: Fred Werner; *Cast*: Gwen Verdon (Charity), John McMartin (Oscar), Helen Gallagher (Nickie), Thelma Oliver (Helene), James Luisi (Vittorio Vidal), Arnold Soboloff (Daddy Johann Sebastian Brubeck), Harold Pierson (Brother Harold), Eddie Gasper (Brother Ray), John Wheeler (Herman), Michael Davis (Mike); *Album Producer*: Goddard Lieberson.

Selections: 1 Overture (3:27)Orchestra; 2 You Should See Yourself (2:22) *Gwen Verdon*; 3 Big Spender (3:35) *Helen Gallagher, Thelma Oliver*; 4 Charity's Soliloquy (4:16) *Gwen Verdon*; 5 Rich Man's Frug (1:41) Orchestra; 6 If My Friends Could See Me Now (3:27) *Gwen Verdon*; 7 Too Many Tomorrows (3:04) *James Luisi*; 8 There's Gotta Be Something Better Than This (4:51) *Gwen Verdon, Helen Gallagher, Thelma Oliver*; 9 Charity's Theme (1:26) Orchestra; 10 I'm The Bravest Individual (2:18) *Gwen Verdon, John McMartin*; 11 The Rhythm Of Life (3:56) *Arnold Soboloff, Harold Pierson, Eddie Gasper*; 12 Baby Dream Your Dream (3:42) *Helen Gallagher, Thelma Oliver*; 13 Sweet Charity (2:42) *John McMartin*; 14 Where Am I Going? (3:18) *Gwen Verdon*; 15 I Love To Cry At Weddings (3:08) *John Wheeler, Michael Davis, Helen Gallagher, Thelma Oliver*; 16 I'm A Brass Band (2:43) *Gwen Verdon*; 17 Finale (1:21) Orchestra.

Review: Gwen Verdon, already a Broadway favorite, had her greatest stage hit in *Sweet Charity*, which opened on January 29, 1966, in which she portrayed a dance hall hostess, forever falling for the wrong men, but always hopeful for better tomorrows. When she meets Oscar, the proverbial tart with a heart of gold is convinced she has finally found the right man for her. However, her hopes of getting married have to be scuttled because Oscar develops cold feet at the last moment. Bravely, Charity picks up the pieces of her broken heart and moves on, supported by her friends Nickie and Helene, two other dancers like her.

The brilliant score by Cy Coleman and Dorothy Fields teemed with many showstopping moments ("If My Friends Could See Me Now," "I'm a Brass Band," "Where Am I Going?," "Big Spender," "The Rhythm of Life") that have lost none of their magic with time.

Transferred to the screen, the musical was another milestone in the career of Shirley MacLaine, playing Charity, with Sammy Davis, Jr. making a much-noticed cameo as "Daddy." The recording, though, has yet to reach the digital domain.

They're Playing Our Song
♫♫♫♪

1979, Casablanca Records; from the Broadway production They're Playing Our Song, 1979.

Album Notes: Music: Marvin Hamlisch; Lyrics: Carol Bayer Sager; Musical Direction: Larry Blank; Featured Musician: Fran Liebergall (piano); Cast: Robert Klein (Vernon Gersch), Lucy Arnaz (Sonia Walsk); Album Producers: Brook Arthur, Carol Bayer Sager, Marvin Hamlisch; Engineer: Bob Merritt; Assistant Engineers: David Lattman, David Bianco; CD Engineer: Greg Calbi.

Selections: 1 Fallin' (2:41) Robert Klein; 2 Workin' It Out (3:32) Robert Klein, Lucy Arnaz; 3 If He Really Knew Me (3:34) Lucy Arnaz; 4 They're Playing My Song (His)(1:39) Robert Klein; 5 They're Playing My Song (Hers)(2:45) Lucy Arnaz; 6 Right (3:24) Lucy Arnaz, Robert Klein; 7 Just For Tonight (3:26) Lucy Arnaz, Robert Klein; 8 Entr'acte (3:57)Orchestra; 9 When You're In My Arms (4:06) Robert Klein, Lucy Arnaz; 10 If You Really Knew Me (reprise)(1:52) Robert Klein, Lucy Arnaz; 11 I Still Believe In Love (3:05) Lucy Arnaz; 12 Fill In The Words (4:04) Robert Klein; 13 They're Playing Our Song (The Bows)(1:20) Robert Klein, Lucy Arnaz.

Review: Essentially a two-character play, They're Playing Our Song recounts the romance between an Academy Award-winning composer, Vernon (Robert Klein), and the off-beat lyricist he meets and falls in love while writing pop songs with her (any resemblance between these characters and real-life Marvin Hamlisch and Carol Bayer Sager was purely coincidental). Spicing up the proceedings, at least the way Neil Simon, author of the libretto, conceived it, the two main characters

share the stage with their "alter egos" who, at judicious times, reveal Vernon and Sonia's inner thoughts.

Ultimately, the show itself might have been a trifle, but propelled by its clever score, it enjoyed a long run and won even the most hardened critics.

Thoroughly Modern Millie
♫♫♫♫

1967, MCA Records; from the screen musical Thoroughly Modern Millie, Universal Pictures, 1968.

Album Notes: Musical Numbers: Andre Previn; Musical Score: Elmer Bernstein; The Universal Studio Orchestra, conducted by Andre Previn; Cast: Julie Andrews (Millie), Mary Tyler Moore, Carol Channing (Muzzy), James Fox (Jimmy), Beatrice Lillie (Mrs. Meers), John Gavin (Trevor Graydon).

Selections: 1 Prelude/Thoroughly Modern Mille (S. Cahn/J. Van Heusen)(2:42) Julie Andrews; 2 Overture: Baby Face (B. Davis/H. Akst)/Do It Again! (G. Gershwin/B.G. DeSylva)/Poor Butterfly (R. Hubbell/J. Golden)/Stumbling (Z. Confrey)/Japanese Sandman (R. Whiting/R. Egan)(3:34) Orchestra; 3 Jimmy (J. Tompson)(3:05) Julie Andrews; 4 The Tapioca (S. Cahn/J. Van Heusen)(2:57) Julie Andrews, James Fox; 5 Jazz Baby (M. Jerome/B. Merrill)(2:41) Carol Channing; 6 Jewish Wedding Song (S. Neufield)(3:43) Julie Andrews; 7 Intermission Medley: Thoroughly Modern Millie (S. Cahn/J. Van Heusen)/Jimmy (J. Thompson)/Jewish Wedding Song (S. Neufield)/Baby Face (B. Davis/H. Akst) (3:40) Orchestra; 8 Poor Butterfly (R. Hubell/J. Golden)(3:32) Julie Andrews; 9 Rose Of Washington Square (J. Hanley/B. MacDonald)(1:15) Orchestra; 10 Baby Face (B. Davis/H. Akst)(2:43) Julie Andrews; 11 Do It Again! (G. Gershwin/B.G. DeSylva)(2:01) Carol Channing; 12 Thoroughly Modern Millie (S. Cahn/J. Van Heusen)(reprise)(:58) Julie Andrews; 13 Exit Music: Jazz Baby (M. Jerome/B. Merrill)/Jimmy (J. Thompson)/Thoroughly Modern Millie (S. Cahn/J. Van Heusen)(2:36) Orchestra.

Review: The Jazz Age served as an eloquent backdrop for Thoroughly Modern Millie, starring Julie Andrews, Mary Tyler Moore and Carol Channing as flappers in this affectionate sendup of the happy, crazy, fun days of the carefree 1920s. It merrily spoofs silent film techniques, and includes a breezy score consisting primarily of songs from the era. Directed by George Roy Hill, the film cast Andrews as a husband-hunting country girl and Moore as her friend, both residents at the Priscilla Hotel For Single Young Ladies — operated by an off-the-wall white slave trader (Bea Lilliez) — as they fight off the advances of a lively paper clip salesman. Carol Channing also appears as a rich "jazz baby" widow. Though it fails to capture the imagination the way *The Boy Friend* had done on stage, the film is amusingly entertaining and yielded a soundtrack album recording that is quite enjoyable.

The Threepenny Opera
♪♪♪♪♪

1954, Polydor Records; from the off Broadway production *The Threepenny Opera*, 1954.

Album Notes: *Music:* Kurt Weill; *Original Lyrics:* Bertolt Brecht; *English Adaptation:* Marc Blitzstein; *Orchestrations:* Kurt Weill; *Musical Direction:* Samuel Matlowsky; *Cast:* Lotte Lenya (Jenny), Scott Merrill (Macheath), Martin Wolfson (Peachum), Jo Sullivan (Polly Peachum), Charlotte Rae (Mrs. Peachum), Gerald Price (The Streetsinger), Beatrice Arthur (Lucy Brown), George Tyne (Tiger Brown), William Duel (Messenger).

Selections: 1 Prologue (:18) Orchestra; 2 Overture (1:54) Orchestra; 3 The Ballad Of Mack The Knife (3:20) *Gerald Price*; 4 Morning Anthem (:49) *Martin Wolfson*; 5 Instead-Of-Song (1:51) *Martin Wolfson, Charlotte Rae*; 6 Wedding Song (1:07) *John Astin, Joseph Beruh, Bernard Bogin, Paul Dooley*; 7 Pirate Jenny (4:03) *Lotte Lenya*; 8 Army Song (2:16) *Scott Merrill, George Tyne, John Astin, Joseph Beruh, Bernard Bogin, Paul Dooley*; 9 Love Song (1:57) *Scott Merrill, Jo Sullivan*; 10 Ballad Of Dependency (2:18) *Charlotte Rae*; 11 Melodrama and Polly's Song (2:32) *Scott Merrill, Jo Sullivan*; 12 Ballad Of The Easy Life (1:43) *Scott Merrill*; 13 The World Is Mean (2:45) *Jo Sullivan, Martin Wolfson, Charlotte Rae*; 14 Barbara Song (3:18) *Beatrice Arthur*; 15 Tango-Ballad (4:35) *Lotte Lenya, Scott Merrill*; 16 Jealousy Duet (2:21) *Jo Sullivan, Beatrice Arthur*; 17 How To Survive (3:15) *Scott Merrill, Charlotte Rae*; 18 Useless Song (:43) *Martin Wolfson*; 19 Solomon Song (2:37) *Lotte Lenya*; 20 Call From The Grave (:54) *Scott Merrill*; 21 Death Message (3:18) *Scott Merrill*; 22 Finale: The Mounted Messenger (5:14) *William Duel.*

Review: For me, this is one of the greatest recordings of this truly landmark German musical. The Off-Broadway revival of 1954 sparked a new interest in composer Kurt Weill, in particular his pre-Broadway German years, and led to revivals of his works from that era. While the English lyrics by Marc Blitzstein sanitized the original German of Berthold Brecht, they are poetic and convey the dark and dangerous side of this musical set in the underworld of Queen Victoria's London. The cast is as fine as could be assembled in 1954 and perhaps as fine as any era could produce, and many of its performers went on to reach more public identification in other roles. However, this

recording catches everyone at their early maturity. The exception is, of course, Lotte Lenya, and what an exception! During the time of this production and recording, she came to typify for many the jazz-laden age of 1920s Berlin. In this recording, she is a standout and unforgettable, singing her songs with a mixture of toughness, sadness, anger, bitterness, fierce joy and regret. There has never been another performer like her and probably never will.

Jerry J. Thomas

Till the Clouds Roll By ♪♪♪♪▷

1992, Sony Music Special Products; from the screen musical *Till the Clouds Roll By*, 1946.

Album Notes: *Music:* Jerome Kern; *Lyrics:* Oscar Hammerstein II, Guy Bolton, P.G. Wodehouse, Otto Harbach, Edward Laska, Dorothy Fields, Jimmy McHugh, B.G. DeSylva; *Orchestrations:* Conrad Salinger; The M-G-M Studio Chorus and Orchestra, conducted by Lennie Hayton; *Cast:* Robert Walker (Jerome Kern), June Allyson, Lucille Bremer, Judy Garland (Marilyn Miller), Kathryn Grayson, Van Heflin, Lena Horne, Angela Lansbury, Van Johnson, Tony Martin, Dinah Shore, Frank Sinatra, Virginia O'Brien; *CD Producer:* Dan Rivard; *Engineer:* Ken Robertson.

Selections: 1 Overture: Till The Clouds Roll By/The Touch Of Your Hand (2:44) Chorus; 2 Cotton Blossom (2:48) *William Halligan*; 3 Where's The Mate For Me? (1:01) *Tony Martin*; 4 Make Believe (3:12) *Kathryn Grayson, Tony Martin*; 5 Life Upon The Wicked Stage (2:25) *Virginia O'Brien*; 6 Can't Help Lovin' Dat Man (3:14) *Lena Horne*; 7 Ol' Man River (2:16) *Caleb Peterson*; 8 How'd You Like To Spoon With Me? (3:06) *Angela Lansbury*; 9 They Didn't Believe Me (1:52) *Dinah Shore*; 10 Till The Clouds Roll By (3:31) *Ray McDonald*; 11 Leave It To Jane/Cleopatterer (3:54) *June Allyson, Ray McDonald*; 12 Look For The Silver Lining (3:16) *Judy Garland*; 13 Sunny (2:19) Chorus; 14 Who? (2:34) *Judy Garland*; 15 One More Dance (1:38) *Trudi Erwin*; 16 I Won't Dance (3:37) *Trudi Erwin, Van Johnson*; 17 She Didn't Say Yes (She Didn't Say No)(:59) The Wilde Twins; 18 Smoke Gets In Your Eyes (:50) Chorus; 19 The Last Time I Saw Paris (2:01) *Dinah Shore*; 20 The Land Where Good Songs Go (1:45) *Trudi Erwin*; 21 Yesterdays (:47) Chorus; 22 Long Ago And Far Away (:50) *Kathryn Grayson*; 23 A Fine Romance (:32) *Virginia O'Brien*; 24 All The Things You Are (1:59) *Tony Martin*; 25 Why Was I Born? (1:56) *Lena Horne*; 26 Ol' Man River (:40)Chorus.

Review: One of several big screen biographies centering around some of the biggest names in Tin Pan Alley, *Till the Clouds Roll By* was mostly an excuse to parade M-G-M's roster of singing and dancing performers in a vast display of dazzling musical numbers, all more sensational and more grandiose than the ones preceding. The object of so much film affection this time around, is Jerome Kern, whose enormous influence on the musical theatre is undeniable, but whose highly romanticized screen story bears little resemblance to actual facts.

Lending, if not credibility, at least some excitement to the plot are the imaginative numbers, tailor-made for some of the studio's biggest stars, including Judy Garland (sensational in two numbers directed by Vincente Minnelli), Lena Horne, Kathryn Grayson, June Allyson, Tony Martin, and Dinah Shore. The film, though, reaches unfathomable levels of political-incorrectness with Frank Sinatra, clad in a white tuxedo and perched atop a rotating column, singing a satinized version of "Ol' Man River" made even more ridiculous by its frequent use of colloquialisms that contrast with the lily-white setting the number has been given. In the soundtrack album recording, all that remains are the songs, and they're terrific.

Titanic ♫♫

1997, RCA Victor Records; from the Broadway musical *Titanic*, 1997.

Album Notes: *Music*: Maury Yeston; *Lyrics*: Maury Yeston; *Orchestrations*: Jonathan Tunick; *Musical Direction*: Kevin Stites; *Cast*: John Cunningham (Capt. E.J. Smith), David Costabile (1st Officer William Murdoch), John Bolton (2nd Officer Charles Lightoller), Matthew Bennett (3rd Officer Herbert J. Pitman), Brian d'Arcy James (Frederick Barrett, Stoker), Martin Moran (Harold Bride, Radioman), Allan Corduner (Henry Etches, 1st Class Steward), David Elder (Frederick Fleet, Lookout), Adam Alexi-Malle (Quartermaster Robert Hichens/Bandsman Bricoux), Andy Taylor (4th Officer Joseph Boxhall/Bandsman Taylor/J.H. Rogers), Ted Sperling (Chief Engineer Joseph Bell/Wallace Hartley, Orchestra Leader), Michele Ragusa (Stewardess Robinson), Stephanie Park (Stewardess Hutchinson), Mara Stephens (Bellboy), David Garrison (J. Bruce Ismay), Michael Cerveris (Thomas Andrews), Larry Keith (Isidor Straus), Alma Cuervo (Ida Straus), William Youmans (J.J. Astor), Lisa Datz (Madeleine Astor), Joseph Kolinski (Benjamin Guggenheim), Kimberly Hester (Mme Aubert), Michael Mulheren (John B. Thayer), Robin Irwin (Marion Thayer), Henry Stram (George Widener), Jody Gelb (Eleanor Widener), Becky Ann Baker (Charlotte Cardora), Matthew Bennett (The Major), Mindy Cooper (Edith Corse Evans), Dan Stephenson (Charles Clarke), Judith Blazer (Caroline Neville), Bill Buell (Edgar Beane), Victoria Clark (Alice Beane), Jennifer Piech (Kate McGowan), Theresa McCarthy (Kate Murphey), Erin Hill (Kate Mullins), Clarke Thorell (Jim Farrell); *Album Producers*: Tommy

Krasker, Maury Yeston; *Engineer*: Joel Moss; *Assistant Engineers*: Paul Falcone, Ken Ross, Rob Murphy.

Selections: 1 Overture/Prologue: In Every Age (3:25) *Michael Cerveris*; 2 How Did They Built Titanic? (1:29) *Brian d'Arcy James*; 3 There She Is (3:56) *Brian d'Arcy James, Martin Moran, David Elder, Henry Stram, Michael Mulheren, Ted Sperling, William Youmans, Matthew Bennett, John Bolton, Andy Taylor, Adam Alexi-Malle, John Cunningham, David Costabile, Mara Stephens, David Garrison, Michael Cerveris*; 4 I Must Go On That Ship (2:37) *Matthew Bennett, Theresa McCarthy, Jennifer Piech, Erin Hill, Don Stephenson, Bill Buell, Judith Blazer, Victoria Clark*; 5 The 1st Class Roster (2:34) *Matthew Bennett, Victoria Clark*; 6 Godspeed Titanic (2:03) *Company*; 7 Barrett's Song (3:20) *Brian d'Arcy James*; 8 To Be A Captain (1:02) *David Costabile*; 9 Lady's Maid (4:29) *Jennifer Piech, Theresa McCarthy, Erin Hill, Michael Mulheren, Henry Stram, Joseph Kalinski, Matthew Bennett, Larry Keith, William Youmans, Lisa Datz*; 10 What A Remarkable Age This Is! (3:15) *Allan Corduner*; 11 The Proposal/The Night Was Alive (4:38) *Brian d'Arcy James, Martin Moran*; 12 Hymn/Doing The Latest Rag (3:52) *Ted Sperling, Adam Alexi-Malle, Andy Taylor*; 13 I Have Danced (1:55) *Victoria Clark, Bill Buell*; 14 No Moon (3:48) *David Elder, Alma Cuervo, Larry Keith, Clarke Thorell, Jennifer Piech, John Cunningham, John Bolton, David Costabile, Judith Blazer, Don Stephenson, Becky Ann Baker, Matthew Bennett, William Youmans*; 15 Autumn/Finale Act 1 (4:31) *Ted Sperling, David Elder, Brian d'Arcy James, Martin Moran, Becky Ann Baker, Matthew Bennett, Michael Cerveris*; 16 Dressed In Your Pyjamas In The Grand Salon (4:37) *Allan Corduner, David Elder, Michele Ragusa, Stephanie Park, Mara Stephens, Michael Mulheren, Joseph Kalinski, Victoria Clark*; 17 The Blame (4:44) *David Garrison, Michael Cerveris, John Cunningham*; 18 To The Lifeboats (2:36) *Robin Irwin, Michael Mulheren, David Costabile, John Bolton, Larry Keith, Alma Cuervo, Allan Corduner, William Youmans, Mara Stephens, Victoria Clark, Henry Stram, Don Stephenson, Clarke Thorell, Jennifer Piech, Brian d'Arcy James, Martin Moran, Michael Cerveris*; 19 We'll Meet Tomorrow (2:26) *Brian d'Arcy James, Martin Moran, Don Stephenson*; 20 Still (2:28) *Larry Keith, Alma Cuervo*; 21 To Be A Captain (reprise)(:54) *Allan Corduner*; 22 Mr. Andrew's Vision (3:22) *Michael Cerveris, Mara Stephens*; 23 Epilogue: In Every Age (reprise)/Finale (4:37) *Martin Moran*.

Review: Bob Hope defined grand opera as a guy who gets stabbed in the back, "and instead of bleeding, he starts singing." The same definition could somewhat apply to this monstrous production which takes more than two hours to come to its inevitable, foregone conclusion. If at least the score were interesting, one might endure the ordeal, but with the exception of a couple of numbers that stand out, many of the songs, mercifully pruned down in this cast album recording, are not sufficiently catchy and compelling to keep the audience totally rapt. Considering that the show, which opened April 23, 1997, won several Tony Awards, including best score and best musical, one might be tempted to question where have all the Broadway shows of yesteryear gone.

Taking things progressively, *Titanic* is a musical account of the sinking of the famed luxury liner on her maiden voyage on April 10, 1912, with the action spread over five days, from the boarding of the ship to her actual sinking after she hit an iceberg (suggested on stage by an increasingly tilting set). In his book, Peter Stone attempts to create flesh and blood characters out of the doomed passengers, the ship's owner and her captain, more concerned about speed over safety, and her designer, eventually painfully aware of her fragile constitution. Matching the lugubrious tone of the theatrical event, Maury Yeston created a profuse score that starts on a splendid high note, only to let his wall-to-wall recitatives, musical bridges, arias, duets, trios and quartets overwhelm the listener for their overall emptiness, and dour aura.

It's not that the score is bad: it's only that the songs can barely conceal the fact that these characters, well intended as they may be, have little to say to each other, before, during or after the collision that'll cost the ship its life. When, for instance, millionaire Isidor Straus, owner of Macy's, and his wife Ida face together their impending death ("Still"), one's only reaction is that a romantic duet seemed to be needed at this time, and Yeston wrote it.

Throughout, one gets the same impression that the songs are included here simply because this is a "musical," and one must have a score in a musical. When one considers that Yeston dazzled Broadway with his adventurous first show, *Nine*, this new venture seems like a real let-down.

Tommy ♫♫♫♫

1993, RCA Victor; from the Broadway production *Tommy*, 1993.

Album Notes: Music: Pete Townshend; *Lyrics*: Pete Townshend, John Entwistle, Keith Moon; *Orchestrations*: Steve Margoshes; *Musical Direction*: Joseph Church; *Cast*: Michael Cerveris (Tommy), Paul Kandel (Uncle Ernie), Anthony Barrile (Cousin Kevin), Cheryl Freeman (The Gypsy), Marcia Mitzman (Mrs. Walker), Jonathan Dokuchitz (Captain Walker), Sherie Scott (Sally Simpson), Tom Flynn (Kevin's Father), Maria Calabrese (Kevin's Mother); *Album Producer*: George Martin; *Engineer*: Alan Snelling; *Assistant Engineers*: Sandy Palmer, Carl Glanville, Brian Vibberts.

Selections: CD 1: 1 Overture (4:41) *Bill Buell*; 2 Captain Walker (1:45) *Paul Kandel, Marcia Mitzman, Michael McElroy, Timothy Warmen*; 3 It's A Boy (:53) *Lisa Leguillou, Marcia Mitzman, Jody Gelb, Pam Klinger, Alice Ripley*; 4 We've Won (1:01) *Donnie Kehr, Jonathan Dokuchitz, Michael Arnold*; 5 Twenty-One (4:14) *Marcia Mitzman, Lee Morgan, Carly Jane Steinborn, Jonathan Dokuchitz*; 6 Amazing Journey (3:12) *Michael Cerveris*; 7 Courtroom Scene (dialogue)(1:16) *Tom Flynn, Bill Buell, Norm Lewis, Marcia Mitzman*; 8 Sparks (2:14) *Orchestra*; 9 Amazing Journey (reprise)(1:04) *Michael Cerveris*; 10 Christmas/See Me, Feel Me (5:04) *Jonathan Dokuchitz, Marcia Mitzman, Bill Buell, Jody Gelb, Michael Cerveris*; 11 Do You Think It's Alright (1:09) *Marcia Mitzman, Jonathan Dokuchitz*; 12 Fiddle About (1:35) *Paul Kandel*; 13 See Me, Feel Me (reprise)(1:08) *Michael Cerveris*; 14 Cousin Kevin (3:35) *Anthony Barrile*; 15 Sensation (4:14) *Michael Cerveris*; 16 Sparks (reprise)(1:55) *Orchestra*; 17 Eyesight To The Blind (2:50) *Michael McElroy, Lee Morgan*; 18 Acid Queen (4:01) *Cheryl Freeman*; 19 Pinball Wizard (3:50) *Donnie Kehr, Christian Hoff, Anthony Barrile.*

CD 2: 1 Underture (Entr'acte)(2:37) *Ensemble*; 2 It's A Boy (reprise)/There's A Doctor (1:13) *Marcia Mitzman, Jonathan Dokuchitz*; 3 Go To The Mirror/ Listening To You (3:36) *Norm Lewis, Alice Ripley, Marcia Mitzman, Jonathan Dokuchitz, Buddy Smith, Jody Gelb, Tracy Nicole Chapman, Michael Cerveris*; 4 Tommy, Can You Hear Me? (2:00) *Anthony Barrile, Michael Arnold, Paul Dobie, Christian Hoff, Donnie Kehr, Norm Lewis, Michael McElroy, Lee Morgan, Timothy Warmen, Sherie Scott*; 5 I Believe My Own Eyes (4:01) *Jonathan Dokuchitz, Marcia Mitzman*; 6 Smash The Mirror (2:41) *Marcia Mitzman*; 7 I'm Free (2:52) *Michael Cerveris*; 8 Streets Of London 1961-63 (dialogue)/ Miracle Cure (:36) *Paul Kandel, Tom Flynn, Paul Dobie, Timothy Warmen, Michael Arnold, Michael McElroy*; 9 Sensation (reprise) (2:21) *Michael Cerveris*; 10 I'm Free/Pinball Wizard (reprise) (3:55) *Michael Cerveris, Marcia Mitzman, Jonathan Dokuchitz, Anthony Barrile*; 11 Tommy's Holiday Camp (1:57) *Paul Kandel*; 12 Sally Simpson (3:35) *Anthony Barrile, Sherie Scott, Paul Kandel, Bill Buell, Pam Klinger*; 13 Welcome (3:20) *Michael Cerveris*; 14 Sally Simpson's Question (1:13) *Sherie Scott, Michael Cerveris*; 15 We're Not Gonna Take It (3:03) *Michael Cerveris*; 16 See Me, Feel Me (reprise)/Listening To You (reprise) (5:07) *Michael Cerveris, Buddy Smith, Michael Cerveris.*

Review: Already a theatrical concept in itself, even though it was first written as a studio recording, the rock musical *Tommy* made its belated Broadway debut on April 22, 1993, 24 years after it was originally created by The Who's Peter Townshend, John Entwistle and Keith Moon. The story of a four-year-old boy who becomes mute after he witnesses his father kill his mother's lover, *Tommy* was one of the first full-scale rock operas to be created, in imitation of The Beatles' *Sgt. Peppers' Lonely Hearts Club Band,* at a time when works of this scope were unheard of. In the ensuing years, however, it enjoyed vibrant, if restricted life as a concert piece performed by The Who, and as a camp 1975 film, remarkable for its cast which consisted of many famous rock'n'roll and film stars, including The Who's Roger Daltrey as Tommy, Eric Clapton, Elton John, and Tina Turner, among the former, and Jack Nicholson, Oliver Reed, and Ann-Margret, among the latter.

Brilliantly staged by Des McAnuff, the Broadway version altered the perception of many in theatrical circles that rock and the stage were definitely not made for each other. The show had a healthy run of 899 performances, and yielded the great cast album listed above, much more conventional than its raw-gut 1969 counterpart or the flashy film soundtrack, but properly flavorful and exciting in its own right.

Two by Two ♫♪

1992, Sony Broadway; from the Broadway production *Two by Two*, 1970.

Album Notes: *Music:* Richard Rodgers; *Lyrics:* Martin Charnin; *Orchestrations:* Eddie Sauter; *Dance and Vocal Arrangements:* Trude Rittman; *Musical Direction:* Jay Blackton; *Cast:* Danny Kaye (Noah), Harry Goz (Shem), Joan Copeland (Esther), Madeline Kahn (Goldie), Michael Karm (Ham), Walter Willison (Japheth), Tricia O'Neil (Rachel), Marilyn Cooper (Leah); *Album/CD Producer:* Thomas Z. Shepard; *Album Engineers:* Fred Plaut, John Guerriere; *CD Engineers:* Buddy Graha, Richard King.

Selections: 1 Why Me? (2:47) *Danny Kaye;* 2 Put Him Away (2:05) *Danny Kaye, Harry Goz, Michael Karm, Marilyn Cooper;* 3 The Gitka's Song/Something, Somewhere (3:37) *Danny Kaye, Walter Willison;* 4 You Have Got To Have A Rudder On The Ark (4:08) *Danny Kaye, Harry Goz, Michael Karm, Walter Willison;* 5 Something Doesn't Happen (3:29) *Tricia O' Neil, Joan Copeland;* 6 An Old Man (2:41) *Joan Copeland;* 7 Ninety Again! (2:51) *Danny Kaye;* 8 Two By Two (3:52) *Danny Kaye;* 9 I Do Not Know A Day I Did Not Love You (2:36) *Walter Willison;* 10 Act 1 Finale (1:05) *Danny Kaye;* 11 When It Dries (4:47) *Danny Kaye;* 12 You (2:50) *Danny Kaye;* 13 The Golden Ram (2:23) *Madeline Kahn;* 14 Poppa Knows Best (2:33) *Danny Kaye, Walter Willison, Harry Goz, Michael Karm;* 15 I Do Not Know A Day I Did Not Love You (reprise)(1:50) *Tricia O' Neil, Walter Willison;* 16 As Far As I'm Concerned (1:52) *Harry Goz, Marilyn Cooper;* 17 Hey, Girlie (2:28) *Danny Kaye;* 18 The Covenant (3:17) *Danny Kaye.*

Review: Clifford Odets' amusing recounting of the Flood, "The Flowering Peach," became the basis for *Two by Two*, by Richard Rodgers and Martin Charnin, in which Danny Kaye made a belated comeback to Broadway as Noah, the Biblical patriarch chosen by the Almighty to build an ark and save two specimens of the Earth's fauna before the rains come. For Kaye, who had enjoyed considerable success on the screen as one of Hollywood's most gifted comedians but who had not set foot on a stage since 1942 when he first appeared in *Up in Arms*, the routine weekly performance schedule soon became unbearable, and he took advantage of his star status to turn the musical into a personal showcase, much to the delight of audiences. Rodgers, however, was not amused, but as long as the show was making money, there was little he could do about it, and *Two by Two* enjoyed a run of 343 performances, despite the fact that Kaye eventually had to play his part in a wheelchair after he sprained his ankle.

To be truthful about it, the musical itself was not really that exciting, and its score, with the exception of the title tune and the lovely "I Didn't Know a Day I Didn't Love You," did not live up to the standards once set by Richard Rodgers.

The Unsinkable Molly Brown

The Unsinkable Molly Brown ♫♫♫♫

1993, Angel Records; from the Broadway production *The Unsinkable Molly Brown*, 1960.

Album Notes: *Music:* Meredith Willson; *Lyrics:* Meredith Willson; *Orchestrations:* Don Walker; *Vocal Arrangements and Musical Direction:* Herbert Greene; *Cast:* Tammy Grimes (Molly Tobin Brown), Harve Presnell (J.J. Brown), Mitchell Gregg (Prince de Long), Mony Dalmes (Princess de Long), Sterling Clark (Michael Tobin), Joseph Sirola (Christmas Morgan), Bill Starr (Aloysius Tobin), Bob Daley (Patrick Tobin); *Album Producers:* Andy Wiswell, Dick Jones; *CD Engineer:* Bob Norberg.

Selections: 1 Overture (4:17) *Orchestra;* 2 I Ain't Down Yet (3:58) *Tammy Grimes, Sterling Clark, Bill Starr, Bob Daley;* 3 Belly Up To The Bar, Boys (2:39) *Tammy Grimes, Joseph Sirola;* 4 I've A'ready Started In (1:32) *Harve Presnell;* 5 I'll Never Say No (2:51) *Harve Presnell, Tammy Grimes;* 6 My Own Brass Bed (2:17) *Tammy Grimes;* 7 The Denver Police (1:58) *Ensemble;* 8 Bea-u-tiful People Of Denver (2:13) *Tammy Grimes;* 9 Are You Sure? (4:06) *Tammy Grimes;* 10 I Ain't Down Yet (reprise)(1:20) *Tammy Grimes, Harve Presnell;* 11 Happy Birthday, Mrs. J.J.

Brown (2:24) *Mony Dalmes, Mitchell*; 12 Bon Jour (The Language Song)(1:45) *Tammy Grimes, Mitchell Gregg*; 13 If I Knew (2:22) *Harve Presnell*; 14 Chick-A-Pen (2:34) *Harve Presnell, Tammy Grimes*; 15 Keep-A-Hoppin'/Leadville Johnny Brown (Soliloquy)(4:59) *Harve Presnell*; 16 Up Where The People Are (1:57) *Orchestra*; 17 Dolce Far Niente/I May Never Fall In Love With You (4:49) *Mitchell Gregg, Tammy Grimes*; 18 I Ain't Down Yet (Finale) (:52) *Company*.

Review: See entry below.

The Unsinkable Molly Brown 🎵🎵🎵▷

1990, CBS Special Products; from the screen musical *The Unsinkable Molly Brown*, M-G-M, 1964.

Album Notes: *Music*: Meredith Willson; *Lyrics*: Meredith Willson; The M-G-M Studio Chorus and Orchestra, conducted by Robert Armbruster; *Cast*: Debbie Reynolds (Molly Tobin Brown), Harve Presnell (J.J. Brown), and Ed Begley, Brendan Dillon, Jack Kruschen, Hermione Baddeley, Martita Hunt; *CD Producer*: Dan Rivard; *Engineer*: Ken Robertson.

Selections: 1 Overture (3:39) *Orchestra*; 2 Belly Up To The Bar, Boys (:57) *Ed Begley, Brendan Dillon*; 3 I Ain't Down Yet (4:07) *Debbie Reynolds*; 4 Colorado, My Home (3:49) *Harve Presnell*; 5 Belly Up To The Bar, Boys (3:46) *Debbie Reynolds*; 6 I'll Never Say No (4:10) *Harve Presnell, Debbie Reynolds*; 7 I'll Never Say No (Johnny Builds His House)(1:31) *Harve Presnell*; 8 I'll Never Say No/I Ain't Down Yet (The Browns In Europe) (2:14) *Harve Presnell, Debbie Reynolds*; 9 He's My Friend (6:25) *Harve Presnell, Jack Kruschen, Ed Begley, Hermione Baddeley, Martita Hunt*; 10 Leadville Johnny Brown (Soliloquy)(3:56) *Harve Presnell*; 11 Up Where The People Are (1:22)*Orchestra*; 12 Dolce Far Niente (2:07) *Orchestra*; 13 Welcome Home, Mrs. Brown (Finale)(4:32) *Orchestra*.

Review: Following his 1958 Broadway musical, *The Music Man*, Meredith Willson hit paydirt again with another period work, *The Unsinkable Molly Brown*, which also gave Tammy Grimes one of her most memorable roles on Broadway. Based at the turn of the century, the show recalled the saga of the real-life Molly Brown, who rose from utter poverty in the Colorado silver mines to a life of wealth and leisure, after marrying a lucky prospector, before becoming the darling of the European elite, and surviving the sinking of the "Titanic," in an incredible streak of good luck and personal heroism.

In much the same way he had breathed great life in the score for his first show, Willson created for *Molly Brown* songs that were deeply rooted in Americana, with energetic marches

> "Film scoring may be very rewarding, but it's also agony. Film composers are not their own masters. They are working for corporations. You accept that as part of the job."
>
> **John Williams**
> *(New York Times, 5-25-75)*

("Belly Up to the Bar," "I Ain't Down Yet"), lovely romantic tunes ("I'll Never Say No," "If I Knew"), and lively ensemble numbers ("Beautiful People of Denver"). Dominating the stage was Tammy Grimes, sensational as Molly, in a performance that won her a Tony Award that year. The show, which opened November 3, 1960, had a run of 532 performances.

In 1964, it became a rambunctious screen musical, with Debbie Reynolds starring as Molly opposite Harve Presnell, reprising his stage role as Johnny Brown. But with only five songs from the original score kept in the film, and an over-the-top performance by Reynolds that was coarse and less endearing, the screen version is a pale, uninteresting representation.

Victor/Victoria

Victor/Victoria 🎵🎵🎵🎵🎵

1989, GNP Crescendo; from the screen musical *Victor/Victoria*, M-G-M, 1982.

Album Notes: *Music*: Henry Mancini; *Lyrics*: Leslie Bricusse; *Cast*: Julie Andrews (Victor/Victoria), Robert Preston (Toddy), James Garner (King), Lesley Ann Warren (Norma); *Album Producer*: Joe Reisman; *Engineer*: John Richards; *CD Producer*: Neil Norman, John Strother; *Engineers*: Dick Bogert, Bob Fisher.

Selections: 1 Main Title (Crazy World)(2:07) *Orchestra*; 2 You And Me (2:52) *Julie Andrews, Robert Preston*; 3 Gay Paree (2:33) *Robert Preston*; 4 Alone In Paris (2:52) *Orchestra*; 5 King's Can Can (1:57) *Orchestra*; 6 Le Jazz Hot (4:22) *Julie Andrews*; 7 The Shady Dame From Seville (4:29) *Julie Andrews*; 8 The Big Lift (2:02) *Orchestra*; 9 Cat And Mouse (3:13) *Orchestra*; 10 Crazy World (3:13) *Julie Andrews*; 11 Chicago, Illinois (2:46) *Lesley Ann Warren*; 12 Elegant (3:29) *Orchestra*; 13 You And Me (2:42) *Orchestra*; 14 Le Matelot Club (2:47) *Orchestra*; 15 The Shady Dame From Seville (4:30) *Robert Preston*; 16

Finale: The Shady Dame From Seville/Crazy World/You And Me/Le Jazz Hot (4:50) Orchestra.

Review: See entry below.

Victor/Victoria 🎵🎵▷

1995, Philips Records; from the Broadway production *Victor/ Victoria*, **1995.**

Album Notes: *Music:* Henry Mancini; *Lyrics:* Leslie Bricusse; *Orchestrations:* Bill Byers; *Vocal Arrangements and Musical Direction:* Ian Fraser; *Cast:* Julie Andrews (Victoria Grant), Tony Roberts (Carroll Todd), Michael Nouri (King Marchan), Rachel York (Norma Cassidy), Gregory Jbara (Squash Bernstein), Richard B. Shull (Andre Cassell), Adam Heller (Henri Labisse), Michael Cripe (Richard Di Nardo), Devin Richards (Jazz Singer), Tara O'Brien (Street Singer), Ken Land (Sal Andretti); *Album Producer:* Thomas Z. Shepard; *Engineer:* James P. Nichols; *Assistant Engineer:* Yvonne Yedibalian.

Selections: 1 Overture (3:11) Orchestra; 2 Paris By Night (3:50) *Tony Roberts;* 3 Scene: Chez Lui (2:47) *Julie Andrews, Tony Roberts, Adam Heller;* 4 Scene: Small Square (2:15) *Julie Andrews, Tony Roberts;* 5 If I Were A Man (2:32) *Julie Andrews;* 6 Scene: Toddy's Flat (:47) *Julie Andrews, Tony Roberts, Michael Cripe;* 7 Trust Me (4:15) *Tony Roberts, Julie Andrews;* 8 Scene: Cassell's Night Club/Le Jazz Hot (7:40) *Richard B. Shull, Julie Andrews;* 9 Scene: Backstage At Cassell's (:16) *Julie Andrews, Tony Roberts, Michael Nouri, Rachel York, Gregory Jbara;* 10 Scene: Left Bank Cafe (:24) *Julie Andrews, Tony Roberts, Michael Nouri, Rachel York;* 11 The Tango/Paris By Night (2:03) *Julie Andrews, Rachel York;* 12 Scene: Paris Hotel Suites/Paris Makes Me Horny (3:36) *Michael Nouri, Rachel York;* 13 Scene: Paris Hotel Suites (:24) *Julie Andrews, Tony Roberts;* 14 Crazy World (3:06) *Julie Andrews;* 15 Louis Says (4:06) *Julie Andrews;* 16 King's Dilemma (4:34) *Michael Nouri;* 17 Cat And Mouse (2:43) Orchestra; 18 Apache (:26) *Les Boys;* 19 You And Me (2:39) *Julie Andrews, Tony Roberts;* 20 Scene: Small Square/ Paris By Night (reprise)(2:20) *Tara O' Brien;* 21 Scene: Paris Hotel Suites/Almost A Love Song (4:33) *Julie Andrews, Michael Nouri;* 22 Chicago, Illinois (4:06) *Rachel York;* 23 Scene: Chicago Speakeasy (:52) *Rachel York, Ken Land;* 24 Living In The Shadows (3:02) *Julie Andrews;* 25 Scene: Paris Hotel Suites (1:01) *Julie Andrews, Tony Roberts, Michael Nouri, Rachel York, Ken Land;* 26 Living In The Shadows (reprise)(1:08) *Julie Andrews;* 27 Victor/Victoria (5:34) *Julie Andrews, Tony Roberts.*

Review: Initially, *Victor/Victoria* was conceived as a screen vehicle for Julie Andrews, directed by her husband Blake Edwards, a brilliant musical with songs by Edwards' usual composer, Henry Mancini, and lyricist Leslie Bricusse. Set in Paris in the "gay" 1920s, the plot involved a complicated gender-bending mystification, in which Andrews, as Victoria, an impoverished waif with the voice of an angel, was transformed by impresario Robert Preston into Victor, a man posing as a woman, who became an overnight sensation. Much of the film's great personal charms came from the obvious chemistry between the principals, with Andrews a real delight as the ambiguous Victor/Victoria; Preston sensational as Toddy, an ageing flamboyant gay man with a devastating sense of humor and wit; James Garner, plausibly handsome as an underworld character who falls for Victor while he desperately resists what he thinks are homosexual tendencies; and Leslie Ann Warren a scene-stealer as a droll moll with a tart tongue. Adding tremendous entertainment to the film was Mancini's breezy songs and score, superbly performed by the principals, and Edwards' own light touch which turned everything into a total feast. Much of the soundtrack album retains the flavor of the film, and even adds some reprises and instrumental tracks that were not on the original LP.

Ten years later, Edwards decided that a stage version of the film would again be the ideal vehicle for Andrews' long-awaited return to Broadway. Unfortunately, Mancini died before he could finish work on the new project, and the new songs added to his score are a serious letdown. More detrimental, however, some of the film's best numbers were discarded, and replaced with songs that are stuffy and give a much more somber tone to the ensemble, when they don't seem completely out of place ("Louis Says"). Under the circumstances, Andrews still exudes a winsome charm that pervades the whole show, but Tony Roberts can't erase the memory of Robert Preston, and Michael Nouri, to put it charitably, is bland as King. The only one who strikes a note close to the original, besides Andrews, is Rachel York in the role created by Lesley Ann Warren.

West Side Story

West Side Story 🎵🎵🎵🎵

1995, Sony Legacy/Sony Broadway; from the Broadway production *West Side Story*, **1957.**

Album Notes: *Music:* Leonard Bernstein; *Lyrics:* Stephen Sondheim; *Orchestrations:* Leonard Bernstein, Sid Ramin, Irwin Kostal; *Musical Direction:* Max Goberman; *Cast:* Carol Lawrence (Maria), Larry Kert (Tony), Chita Rivera (Anita), Mickey Calin (Riff), Ken Le Roy (Bernardo), Marilyn Cooper (Rosalia), Reri Grist (Consuelo), Carmen Guiterrez (Teresita), Elizabeth Taylor (Francisca), Eddie Roll (Action), Grover Dale

(Snowboy); *Album Producer*: Goddard Lieberson; *Engineers*: Fred Plaut; *CD Producer*: Didier C. Deutsch; *Engineer*: Kevin Boutote.

Selections: 1 Prologue (3:51) Orchestra; 2 Jet Song (2:11) The Jets; 3 Something's Coming (2:40) *Larry Kert*; 4 The Dance At The Gym (3:06) Orchestra; 5 Maria (2:41) *Larry Kert*; 6 Tonight (3:56) *Larry Kert, Carol Lawrence*; 7 America (4:35) *Chita Rivera, Marilyn Cooper, Reri Grist*; 8 Cool (4:02) *Mickey Calin*; 9 One Hand, One Heart (3:04) *Larry Kert, Carol Lawrence*; 10 Tonight (3:41) Ensemble; 11 The Rumble (2:45) Orchestra; 12 I Feel Pretty (2:50) *Carol Lawrence, Marilyn Cooper, Carmen Gutierrez, Elizabeth Taylor*; 13 Somewhere (ballet)(7:36) *Reri Grist*; 14 Gee, Officer Krupke (4:05) *Eddie Roll, Grover Dale*; 15 A Boy Like That/ I Have A Love (4:19) *Carol Lawrence, Chita Rivera*; 16 Finale (2:00) Orchestra.

Review: See entry below.

West Side Story ♫♫♫♫

1995, Sony Masterworks; from the screen musical *West Side Story*, Mirisch Pictures, 1960.

Album Notes: *Music*: Leonard Bernstein; *Lyrics*: Stephen Sondheim; *Orchestrations*: Leonard Bernstein, Sid Ramin, Irwin Kostal; Orchestra conducted by Johnny Green; *Cast*: Natalie Wood (Maria), Richard Beymer (Tony), Rita Moreno (Anita), Russ Tamblyn (Riff), George Chakiris (Bernardo), Yvonne Othon, Suzie Kaye, Joanne Miya; *Album Producer/CD Producer*: Didier C. Deutsch; *Engineer*: Tim Tiedemann;

Selections: 1 Overture (4:39) Orchestra; 2 Prologue (6:37) Orchestra; 3 Jet Song (2:06) *Russ Tamblyn*; 4 Something's Coming (2:32) *Jim Bryant*; 5 Dance At The Gym: Blues, Promenade, Mambo, Pas de deux, Jump (9:24) Orchestra; 6 Maria (2:34) *Jim Bryant*; 7 America (4:59) *Betty Wand, George Chakiris*; 8 Tonight (5:43) *Jim Bryant, Marni Nixon*; 9 Gee, Officer Krupke (4:14) *Russ Tamblyn*; 10 I Feel Pretty (3:35) *Marni Nixon, Yvonne Othon, Suxie Kaye, Joanne Miya*; 11 One Hand, One Heart (3:02) *Jim Bryant, Marni Nixon*; 12 Quintet (3:22) *Jim Bryant, Marni Nixon, Betty Wand*; 13 The Rumble (2:39) Orchestra; 14 Somewhere (7:36) *Jim Bryant, Marni Nixon*; 15 Cool (4:21) *Tucker Smith*; 16 A Boy Like That/I Have A Love (4:28) *Betty Wand, Marni Nixon, Betty Wand*; 17 Finale (4:20) *Natalie Wood*; 18 End Credits (5:05)*Orchestra*.

Review: Without a doubt one of the most important and successful musicals to emerge from the post-war Broadway stage, *West Side Story* is also, unfortunately, the only one that brought together two of the most talented men in the theatre, Leonard Bernstein and Stephen Sondheim. A thoroughly riveting show set in New York's Hell's Kitchen circa late 1950s, it packed a potent statement on the human condition and has retained its social, musical and dramatic relevance for more than forty years.

As a starting point, the original Broadway cast recording is essential, as the performances by Larry Kert, Carol Lawrence and Chita Rivera are chock full of the excitement, passion and energy that make *West Side Story* so special. If you're looking for outstanding sonics, seek out the 20-bit SBM gold Mastersound edition, which has been remixed from the original three-track session tapes. This version vitally preserves the sensitivity and immediacy of the performances, and is far superior to the standard Columbia CD.

The famous 1961 original soundtrack recording has also been treated to a grand restoration, and while the performances themselves sometime lack the spark of the Original Broadway Cast recording, it is one of the most important soundtracks to come from the CD era. Remastered from the original multi-track, 35 mm film masters, this CD issue restores all of the film's original music, including the previously unreleased "Overture," "Finale" and "End Credit" music. A number of cues have been expanded (notably "Dance at the Gym," and "Tonight"), and all selections have been properly sequenced to reflect the original running order of the songs in the film.

Charles L. Granata

Wildcat ♫♫♭

1991, RCA Victor; from the Broadway production *Wildcat*, 1960.

Album Notes: *Music*: Cy Coleman; *Lyrics*: Carolyn Leigh; *Orchestrations*: Robert Ginzler, Sid Ramin; *Vocal Arrangements and Musical Direction*: John Morris; *Cast*: Lucille Ball (Wildcat Jackson), Paula Stewart (Jane Jackson), Keith Andes (Joe Dynamite), Don Tomkins (Sookie), Clifford David (Hank), Bill Walker (Tattoo), Swen Swenson (Oney), Ray Mason (Sandy), Charles Braswell (Matt), Edith King (Countess Emily O'Brien), Al Lanti (Cisco); *Album Producers*: George Avakian, Joe Linhart; *Engineer*: Ernie Oelrich; *CD Producer*: Bill Rosenfield; *Engineer*: Jay Newland.

Selections: 1 Overture (4:16) Orchestra; 2 Oil! (1:20) Ensemble; 3 Hey, Look Me Over! (2:10) *Lucille Ball, Paula Stewart*; 4 Wildcat (2:20) *Lucille Ball*; 5 You've Come Home (1:44) *Keith Andes*; 6 That's What I Want For Janie (2:39) *Lucille Ball*; 7 What Takes My Fancy (3:19) *Lucille Ball, Don Tomkins*; 8 You're A Liar! (2:56) *Lucille Ball, Keith Andes*; 9 One Day We Dance (3:01) *Clifford David, Paula Stewart*; 10 Give A Little Whistle (4:17) *Lucille Ball, Keith Andes*; 11 Tall Hope (4:47) *Bill Walker,*

Swen Swenson, Ray Mason, Charles Braswell; 12 Tippy, Tippy Toes (2:15) Lucille Ball, Edith King; 13 El Sombrero (3:35) Lucille Ball, Al Lanti, Swen Swenson; 14 Corduroy Road (3:36) Keith Andes, ; 15 Finale (1:23) Company.

Review: Television's favorite redhead, Lucille Ball, made her Broadway debut on December 16, 1960, in this amusing musical by Cy Coleman and Carolyn Leigh, in which she played Wildcat Jackson, an oil prospector with a lot of chutzpah and nothing else but a dry well. The accomplished comedian kept the musical afloat, as long as she was able to stay in the cast, but when she left after 172 performances, it closed. While not many of the songs in the score were that memorable, one, "Hey, Look Me Over," in which Wildcat summons everyone to give her a fighting chance when she first arrives in the small western outpost, became a hit.

The Will Rogers Follies 🎵🎵🎵🎵▷

1993, Columbia Records; from the Broadway production *The Will Rogers Follies*, 1993.

Album Notes: *Music:* Cy Coleman; *Lyrics:* Betty Comden & Adolph Green; *Orchestrations:* Billy Byers; *Vocal and Dance Arrangements:* Cy Coleman; *Musical Direction:* Eric Stern; *Cast:* Keith Carradine (Will Rogers), Dee Hoty (Betty Blake), Cady Huffman (Ziegfeld's Favorite), Dick Latessa (Clem Rogers), Paul Ukena, Jr. (Wiley Post), Gregory Peck (Ziegfeld's Voice); *Album Producers:* Cy Coleman, Mike Berniker; *Engineer:* Ed Rak; *Assistant Engineer:* Troy Halderson.

Selections: 1 Let's Go Flying (1:49) Ensemble; 2 Willamania (6:14) Cady Huffman; 3 Never Met A Man I Didn't Like (short version)(2:18) Keith Carradine; 4 Give A Man Enough Rope ((3:49) Keith Carradine; 5 It's A Boy (3:46) Dick Latessa, Keith Carradine; 6 So Long Pa (1:34) Keith Carradine; 7 My Unknown Someone (4:19) Dee Hoty; 8 Wild West Show/Dog Act (3:04) Cady Huffman; 9 We're Heading For A Wedding (:52) Keith Carradine, Dee Hoty; 10 The Big Time (4:58) Keith Carradine, Dee Hoty; 11 My Big Mistake (2:39) Dee Hoty; 12 The Ziegfeld Follies (My Big Mistake)(3:25) Ensemble; 13 Marry Me Now/I Got You/First Act Finale (4:43) Keith Carradine, Dee Hoty, Cady Huffman; 14 Entr'acte/Give A Man Enough Rope/Rope Act (3:42) Four Men; 15 Look Around (2:11) Keith Carradine; 16 Our Favorite Son (3:42) Keith Carradine, Cady Huffman; 17 No Man Left For Me (3:19) Dee Hoty; 18 Presents For Mrs. Rogers (5:04) Keith Carradine; 19 Willamania (reprise)/Without You (2:53) Keith Carradine, Dick Latessa, Dee Hoty, Paul Ukena Jr.; 20 Never Met A Man I Didn't Like (5:12) Keith Carradine, Dee Hoty, Paul Ukena Jr.

Review: Will Rogers' easy-going, down-to-earth charm was pleasantly evoked in Keith Carradine's portrayal as the congenial satirist in *The Will Rogers Follies*, a big, brassy musical by Cy Coleman, Betty Comden and Adolph Green, which opened on Broadway on May 1, 1991, for a run of 983 performances.

While the show took some liberties with historical facts, it presented the salient points in Rogers' career, from his early days in the Oklahoma prairie to his starring role in the Ziegfeld Follies, to his untimely death in 1935 in a plane crash with aviator Wiley Post. Told in flashbacks, and punctuated by many eye-popping production numbers, the show benefitted from Tommy Tune's flavorful staging, in which particular moments involved a line-up of chorus girls performing precision routines that were absolutely dazzling. The Tony Award-winning score, while it did not yield a memorable hit, is solidly rooted in the great Broadway tradition and exhibits a country-style flavor that makes it all the more endearing. High among its better moments were the attractive "Never Met a Man I Didn't Like," borrowed from Rogers' own remark, and the exhilarating "Willamania."

Willy Wonka & the Chocolate Factory 🎵🎵🎵▷

1996, MCA Records; from the screen musical *Willy Wonka & the Chocolate Factory*, Paramount Pictures, 1971.

Album Notes: *Music:* Leslie Bricusse; *Lyrics:* Leslie Bricusse, Anthony Newley; *Orchestrations:* Walter Scharf; The Paramount Studio Orchestra conducted by Walter Scharf; *Cast:* Gene Wilder (Willy Wonka), Jack Albertson (Grandpa Joe), Peter Ostrum (Charlie); *Album Producer:* Tom Mack; *CD Producer:* Andy McKaie; *Engineer:* Mark Omann.

Selections: 1 Main Title (Golden Ticket/Pure Imagination)(2:07); 2 The Candy Man (2:31); 3 Charlie's Paper Run (1:09); 4 Cheer Up, Charlie (2:39); 5 Lucky Charlie (2:06); 6 (I've Got A) Golden Ticket (3:09); 7 Pure Imagination (4:20); 8 Oompa Loompa (:57); 9 The Wondrous Boat Ride (3:32); 10 Everlasting Gobstoppers/Oompa Loompa (3:17); 11 The Bubble Machine (2:56); 12 I Want It Now/Oompa Loompa (2:49); 13 Wonkamobile, Wonkavision/Oompa Loompa (1:48); 14 Wonkavator/End Title (Pure Imagination)(3:08).

Review: Based on the children's story, *Charlie and the Chocolate Factory*, by Road Dahl, *Willy Wonka & the Chocolate Factory* is a charming little film fantasy that stars Gene Wilder in the title role of a candymaker who puts five golden tickets inside a candy bar run and invites the winners to visit his chocolate factory. Though a mildly pleasant, colorful effort (it was entirely shot in scenic Bavaria) the film didn't have the staying power of other film musicals like *Mary Poppins* or *Chitty Chitty Bang Bang,* and was not a big box office hit as a result. However, its score by Leslie Bricusse and Anthony Newley yielded at least two recognizable tunes in "The Candy Man," which Sammy Davis, Jr. later on turned into a personal hit, and "Pure Imagination."

The Wiz 🎵🎵🎵🎵

1975, Atlantic Records; from the Broadway production *The Wiz*, 1975.

Album Notes: *Music*: Charlie Smalls; *Lyrics*: Charlie Smalls; *Orchestrations*: Harold Wheeler; *Vocal Arrangements and Musical Direction*: Charles H. Coleman; *Cast*: Stephanie Mills (Dorothy), Tiger Haynes (The Tinman), Ted Ross (The Cowardly Lion), Hinton Battle (The Scarecrow), Mabel King (Wicked Witch Of The West), Tasha Thomas (Aunt Em), Clarice Taylor (Good Witch Of The North), Andre de Shields (The Wiz), Dee Dee Bridgewater (Glinda); *Album Producer*: Jerry Wexler; *Engineer*: Phil Ramone.

Selections: 1 Prologue (:20) Orchestra; 2 The Feeling We Once Had (3:36) *Tasha Thomas*; 3 Tornado (T. Graphenreed/H. Wheeler)(3:25) Orchestra; 4 He's The Wizard (3:19) *Clarice Taylor*; 5 Soon As I Get Home (3:25) *Stephanie Mills*; 6 I Was Born On The Day Before Yesterday (3:20) *Hinton Battle*; 7 Ease On Down The Road (2:26) *Hinton Battle, Stephanie Mills*; 8 Slide Some Oil To Me (2:21) *Tiger Haynes*; 9 I'm A Mean Ole Lion (1:41) *Ted Ross*; 10 Be A Lion (4:03) *Stephanie Mills*; 11 So You Wanted To See The Wizard (1:53) *Andre de Shields*; 12 What Would I Do If I Could Feel (2:53) *Tiger Haynes*; 13 Don't Nobody Bring Me No Bad News (2:30) *Mabel King*; 14 Everybody Rejoice (L. Vandross)(2:48) Ensemble; 15 Y'all Got It (2:14) *Andre de Shields*; 16 If You Believe (2:17) *Dee Dee Bridgewater*; 17 Home (Finale)(3:31) *Stephanie Mills*.

Review: Pop singer Stephanie Mills portrayed Dorothy, Tiger Haynes the Tinman, Ted Ross the Cowardly Lion, and Hinton Battle the Scarecrow in this modernized, black version of the classic *The Wizard of Oz,* with a new score by Charlie Smalls. While the show made no attempt to erase the memories left by the 1939 film classic starring Judy Garland, it took the same basic story outline and transformed it into an exuberant, colorful stage display, in which Geoffrey Holder's gorgeous costumes and extravagant staging had as much of a role as did the various principals involved. Leading to the evening's big number, "Ease on Down the Road," the score also included several noteworthy songs, among them "The Feeling We Once Had," performed by Tasha Thomas, as Aunt Em; "Don't Nobody Bring Me No Bad News," roared by Mabel King, as Eveline, the Wicked Witch of The West; "If You Believe," which gave Dee

Dee Bridgewater, making her Broadway debut as Glinda the Good Witch of The North, a well-deserved Tony Award; and mostly the enthusiastic "Everybody Rejoice," an ensemble number of kaleidoscopic color and movement. The show, which premiered on January 5, 1975, enjoyed a run of 1,672 performances, and won a total of seven Tony Awards, including one for Best Musical. In 1978, it became an overblown screen musical, with Diana Ross misguidedly cast as Dorothy, a young girl several decades younger than the singer.

The Wizard of Oz 🎵🎵🎵🎵

1995, Rhino Records; from the screen musical *The Wizard of Oz*, M-G-M, 1939.

Album Notes: *Music*: Herbert Stothart; *Songs*: Harold Arlen; *Lyrics*: E.Y. Harburg; *Orchestrations*: Murray Cutter, George Bassman, George Stoll, Herbert Stothart, Leo Arnaud, Paul Marquardt, Conrad Salinger; *Arrangements*: Herbert Stothart, George Bassman, George Stoll, Bob Stringer; The M-G-M Studio Chorus and Orchestra, conducted by Herbert Stothart; *Cast*: Judy Garland (Dorothy), Ray Bolger (The Scarecrow), Bert Lahr (The Cowardly Lion), Jack Haley (The Tin Woodman); *Album Producers*: Marilee Bradford, Bradley Flanagan; *Engineer*: Doug Schwartz.

Selections: CD 1: 1 Main Title (1:58) Orchestra; 2 Trouble In School (1:20) Orchestra; 3 Farmyard (outtake)(:36) Orchestra; 4 Over The Rainbow (2:44) *Judy Garland*; 5 Miss Gulch (2:44) Orchestra; 6 Leaving Home (1:26) Orchestra; 7 Crystal Gazing (1:48) Orchestra; 8 Cyclone (2:17) Orchestra; 9 Munchkinland (2:27) Chorus; 10 I'm Not A Witch (:51) Orchestra; Munchkinland Musical Sequence: 11 Come Out, Come Out (:42) *Billie Burke*; 12 It Really Was No Miracle (:50) *Judy Garland, Billy Bletcher*; 13 We Thank You Very Sweetly (:20) The Munchkins; 14 Ding-Dong! The Witch Is Dead (:47) The Munchkins; 15 As Mayor Of The Munchkin City (:32) *Billy Bletcher, Pinto Colveg, J.D. Jewkes*; 16 As Coroner, I Must Aver (:31) *Harry Stanton*; 17 Ding-Dong! The Witch Is Dead (reprise)(:46) The Munchkins; 18 The Lullaby League (:23) *Lorraine Bridges, Betty Rome, Carol Tevis*; 19 The Lollipop Guild (:24) *Billy Bletcher, Pinto Colveg, Harry Stanton*; 20 We Welcome You To Munchkinland (:39) The Munchkins; 21 Threatening Witch (2:12) Orchestra; 22 Leaving Munchkinland (1:21) Orchestra; 23 Good Fairy Vanishes (:34) Orchestra; 24 Follow The Yellow Brick Road/You're Off To See The Wizard (:49) *Judy Garland*; 25 The Cornfield (2:46) Orchestra; 26 If I Only Had A Brain (3:44) *Ray Bolger, Judy Garland*; 27 We're Off To See The Wizard (:34) *Judy Garland, Ray Bolger*; 28 The Apple Orchard (1:35) Orchestra; 29 If I Only Had A Heart (3:12) *Jack Haley, Adriana Caselotti*; 30 Witch On Roof (:53) Orchestra; 31 Bees and Tin Woodman Lament (1:53) Orchestra;

32 We're Off To See The Wizard (:25) *Judy Garland, Ray Bolger, Buddy Ebsen*; 33 Into The Forest Of Wild Beasts (1:14) Orchestra; 34 The Lion's Confession (outtake)(:48) Orchestra; 35 If I Only Had The Nerve (:41) *Bert Lahr, Ray Bolger, Jack Haley, Judy Garland*; 36 We're Off To See The Wizard (:26) *Judy Garland, Ray Bolger, Buddy Ebsen, Bert Lahr*; 37 Poppies (1:43) Orchestra; 38 The Spell (3:19) Orchestra; 39 Optmistic Voices (1:09) The Debutantes, The Rhythmettes; 40 Sign On The Gate/The City Gates Open (1:16) Orchestra; 41 The Merry Old Land Of Oz (1:52) *Frank Morgan, Judy Garland, Ray Bolger, Jack Haley, Bert Lahr, Tyler Brook, Ralph Sudam, Bobby Watson, Oliver Smith, Charles Irwin, Lois January, Elvida Rizzo, Lorraine Bridges*; 42 Change Of The Guard (outtake)/Wizard's Exit (:29) Orchestra; 43 If I Were King Of The Forest (4:16) *Bert Lahr, Judy Garland, Ray Bolger, Jack Haley, Buddy Ebsen*; 44 At The Gates Of Emerald City (3:13) Orchestra; 45 Magic Smoke Chords (:36) Orchestra; 46 Terrified Lion (:39) Orchestra.

CD 2: 1 The Haunted Forest (3:13) Orchestra; 2 The Jitterbug (outtake)(3:23) *Judy Garland, Ray Bolger, Jack Haley, Buddy Ebsen, Bert Lahr*; 3 The Jitterbug Attack (1:00) Orchestra; 4 The Witch's Castle (3:08) Orchestra; 5 Toto Brings News/Over The Rainbow (reprise)(outtake)(3:03) *Judy Garland*; 6 March Of The Winkies (2:46) Orchestra; 7 Dorothy's Rescue (3:00) Orchestra; 8 On The Castle Wall (2:29) Orchestra; 9 Ding-Dong! Emerald City (1:14) Chorus; 10 The Wizard's Expose/Emerald City Graduation Exercises (3:53) Orchestra; 11 Fill-In Awards/I Was Floating Through Space/Balloon Ascension/Second Cheer (1:44) Orchestra; 12 I Hereby Decree (4:13) Orchestra; 13 Delirious Escape/End Title (3:31) Orchestra; 14 Main Title (alternate)(1:53) Chorus; 15 Over The Rainbow (:34) *Judy Garland*; 16 Over The Rainbow (alternate)(2:04) *Judy Garland*; 17 Cyclone (film version)(1:57) Orchestra; 18 Munchkinland Insert (alternate)(:32) Orchestra; 19 I'm Not A Witch (alternate)(:50) Orchestra; 20 Munchkinland Musical Sequence (rehearsal demo)(5:18) *Harold Arlen, E.Y. Harburg*; 21 Ding-Dong! The Witch Is Dead (alternate choir version)(:33) Chorus; 22 The Lollipop Guild (original voices)(:26) Singer Midgets; 23 Follow The Yellow Brick Road/ You're Off To See The Wizard (:50) Orchestra; 24 If I Only Had A Brain (dance music)(2:26) Orchestra; 25 If I Only Had A Heart (unused version) (1:15) *Buddy Ebsen, Adriana Caselotti)*; Caselotti, Adriana,26 The Lion's Confession (outtake)(1:15) Orchestra; 27 Poppies (alternate)(:39) Chorus; 28 Optimistic Voices (rehearsal demo)(:36) *Harold Arlen, E.Y. Harburg*; 29 Optimistic Voices (alternate)(1:09) The Debutantes, The Rhythmettes; 30 The Merry Old Land Of Oz (1:51) Orchestra; 31 If I Were King Of The Forest (alternate)(:44) *Bert Lahr, Judy Garland, Ray Bolger, Buddy Ebsen*; 32 If I Were King Of The Forest (alternate)(:35) *Bert Lahr, Judy Garland, Ray Bolger, Buddy Ebsen, Georgia Stark*; 33 The Jitterbug (rehearsal)(3:24) *Donna Massin, Ray Bolger, Buddy Ebsen, Bert Lahr*; 34 Over The Rainbow (reprise) (outtake)(1:31) *Judy Garland*; 35 Ding-Dong! Emerald City (alternate)(1:06) Orchestra; 36 End Title (alternate)(:18) Orchestra.

Review: The Rhino deluxe edition of the music from M-G-M's cherished adaptation of *The Wizard of Oz* is so exquisite, one almost doesn't know where to start. In a nutshell, this is one of the most beautiful, and *amazing* CD packages ever assembled! Who knew that so much great music had been left on the cutting room floor? Did anyone believe that these vintage recordings could ever sound so good?

Undoubtedly, this very special set will strike a tender chord for those who hold fond memories of this classic film dear. From the "Main Title" on, we are treated to a fascinating cornucopia of original and previously unreleased score music (by Herbert Stothart) and songs (by Harold Arlen and "Yip" Harburg), as well as extended sequences and demos. Everything that a true connoisseur of *Wizard* could possibly wish for is collected here, lovingly remastered from the original recording elements for incredibly rich, detailed sound. There is a certain, unexplainable warmth and charm to the "sound" of the M-G-M films of this period, and it is retained in these new restorations.

Rounding out the package is a lavish, full color book (slipcased into the CD binder), which is chock-full of recording details, color photos, posters and ads, and the most concise synopsis and history ever written for a record issue, about the film, its creators, and the music!

In a word, awesome, and an essential addition to any music collector's library.

Charles L. Granata

Wonderful Town

Wonderful Town 🎬🎬🎬🎬

1990, MCA Records; from the Broadway production *Wonderful Town*, 1953.

Album Notes: *Music*: Leonard Bernstein; *Lyrics*: Betty Comden & Adolph Green; *Orchestrations*: Don Walker; *Vocal Arrangements and Musical Direction*: Lehman Engel; *Cast*: Rosalind Russell (Ruth), Edith Adams (Eileen), George Gaynes (Robert Baker), Cris Alexander (Frank Lippencott), Henry Lascoe (Appopoulos), Dort Clark (Chick Clark), Jordan Bentley (Wreck), Warren Guljour (Guide/Policeman), Albert Linville (Policeman), Delbert Anderson (Policeman); *Album Producer*: Jack Kapp; *CD Producer*: Michael Brooks.

Selections: 1 Christopher Street (3:22) *Warren Guljour*; 2 Ohio (3:17) *Rosalind Russell, Edith Adams*; 3 One Hundred Easy Ways (2:51) *Rosalind Russell*; 4 What A Waste (2:54) *George Gaynes, Warren Guljour, Albert Linville*; 5 A Little Bit In Love (2:45) *Edith Adams*; 6 Pass The Football (3:17) *Jordan Bentley*; 7 Conversation Piece (3:20) *Rosalind Russell, Edith Adams, Cris Alexander, George Gaynes, Dort Clark*; 8 A Quiet Girl (3:18) *George Gaynes*; 9 Conga! (3:23) *Rosalind Russell*; 10 My Darlin' Eileen (3:04) *Edith Adams, Delbert Anderson*; 11 Swing! (4:46) *Rosalind Russell*; 12 It's Love (2:43) *Edith Adams, George Gaynes*; 13 Ballet At The Village Vortex (2:59) Orchestra; 14 Wrong Note Rag (2:25) *Rosalind Russell, Edith Adams*.

Review: See entry below.

Wonderful Town ♪♪♪♪♭

1991, Sony Broadway; from the CBS-TV presentation *Wonderful Town*, 1958.

Album Notes: *Music*: Leonard Bernstein; *Lyrics*: Betty Comden & Adolph Green; *Orchestrations*: Don Walker; *Vocal Arrangements and Musical Direction*: Lehman Engel; *Cast*: Rosalind Russell (Ruth), Jacquelyn McKeever (Eileen), Sydney Chaplin (Robert Baker), Cris Alexander (Frank Lippencott), Sam Kirkham (Chick Clark), Jordan Bentley (Wreck), Warren Guljour (Guide/Policeman), Albert Linville (Policeman), Ted Beniades (Valenti), Michele Burke (Helen), Isabella Hoopes (Mrs. Wade), and Joseph Buloff, Jack Fletcher; *Album Producer*: Irving Townsend; *Engineers*: Fred Plaut, Bud Graham; *CD Producer*: Didier C. Deutsch; *Engineer*: Tim Tiedemann.

Selections: 1 Overture (5:05) Orchestra; 2 Christopher Street (4:02) Ensemble; 3 Ohio (2:54) *Rosalind Russell, Jacquelyn McKeever*; 4 One Hundred Easy Ways (2:53) *Rosalind Russell*; 5 What A Waste (2:28) *Sydney Chaplin, Rosalind Russell*; 6 A Little Bit In Love (2:45) *Jacquelyn McKeever*; 7 Pass The Football (3:27) *Jordan Bentley*; 8 Conversation Piece (3:35) *Rosalind Russell, Jacquelyn McKeever, Cris Alexander, Sydney Chaplin, Sam Kirkham*; 9 A Quiet Girl (2:24) *Sydney Chaplin*; 10 Conga! (3:24) *Rosalind Russell*; 11 My Darlin' Eileen (2:54) *Jacquelyn McKeever*; 12 Swing! (5:12) *Rosalind Russell*; 13 It's Love (1:57) *Sydney Chaplin, Jacquelyn McKeever*; 14 Ballet At The Village Vortex (2:39) Orchestra; 15 Wrong Note Rag (2:27) *Rosalind Russell, Jacquelyn McKeever*.

Review: Based on the 1940 Broadway comedy *My Sister Eileen*, and the 1930s autobiographical stories written by Ruth McKenney for "The New Yorker," *Wonderful Town* became one of the jazziest musicals ever composed by Leonard Bernstein, a delicious companion piece to the 1944 *On The Town*, which also has lyrics by Betty Comden and Adolph Green. Detailing

the misadventures of two sisters from Ohio, Ruth and Eileen Sherwood-one the brains, the other the beauty-as they arrive in New York to find new career outlets, the show opened on February 25, 1953 to rave reviews, and enjoyed a comfortable run of 553 performances.

While the critics singled out almost every aspect of the production, they kept their highest praises for Rosalind Russell, making her debut in a musical (she had previously portrayed Ruth in a 1942 film version of the play); she repeated the role in a 1958 CBS television special, with Jacquelyn McKeever replacing Edie Adams as Eileen, and Sydney Chaplin cast as Robert Baker, the publisher in love with Ruth, played in the original by George Gaynes.

Of the two recordings listed here, the one on MCA Records is the 1953 original cast album. While in mono, it still sounds fresher and more vibrant, with the performers not yet totally settled in their roles find ways to keep the portrayals crackling and energetic.

The second CD, on Sony Broadway, is the recording of the 1958 television special, and it has the great advantage of being in stereo. By then, Rosalind Russell had found the parameters within her character and could comfortably mug her way through it. Sydney Chaplin, however, is remarkably bland, and Jacquelyn McKeever doesn't have the spontaneity so endearing in Edie Adams' portrayal.

Ziegfeld Follies ♪♪♪♪♪

1995, Rhino Records; from the screen musical *Ziegfeld Follies*, M-G-M, 1946.

Album Notes: *Orchestrations*: Conrad Salinger, Wally Heglin; *Vocal Arrangements*: Kay Thompson; The M-G-M Studio Chorus and Orchestra, conducted by Lennie Hayton; *Cast*: Fred Astaire, Lucille Ball, Lucielle Bremer, Fanny Brice, Judy Garland, Kathryn Grayson, Lena Horne, Gene Kelly, James Melton, Victor Moore, Red Skelton, Esther Williams, William Powell (Florenz Ziegfeld); *Album Producer*: George Feltenstein; *Engineers*: Ted Hall, Doug Schwartz.

Selections: 1 Main Title (R. Edens)(2:18) Orchestra; 2 Here's To The Girls (R. Edens/A. Freed)(5:12) *Fred Astaire*; 3 Bring On Those Wonderful Men (R. Edens/E. Brent)(2:28) *Virginia O'Brien*; 4 We Will Meet Again In Honolulu (N.H. Brown/A. Freed)(outtake)(3:26) *James Melton*; 5 Liza (All The Clouds'll Roll Away)(G. & I. Gershwin)(outtake)(6:09) *Avon Long*; 6 Libiamo (G. Verdi)(3:29) *James Melton, Marion Bell*; 7 This Heart Of Mine (H. Warren/A. Freed)(7:53) *Fred Astaire*; 8 Love (H. Martin/R. Blane) (3:30) *Lena Horne*; 9 If Swing Goes, I Go Too (F. Astaire)(outtake) (5:49) *Fred Astaire*; 10 Limehouse Blues (P. Braham/D. Furber)(7:11) Orchestra; 11 The Interview

(R. Edens/K. Thompson)(5:05) *Judy Garland*; 12 The Babbitt And The Bromide (G. & I. Gershwin)(5:30) *Fred Astaire, Gene Kelly*; 13 There's Beauty Everywhere (H. Warren/A. Freed) (outtake)(5:08) *Kathryn Grayson*; 14 There's Beauty Everywhere (H. Warren/A. Freed)(outtake)(7:41) *James Melton.*

Review: More a revue than a film musical in the real sense of the word, *Ziegfeld Follies* was another attempt by the powers-that-be at M-G-M to capitalize on the incredible roster of talent signed to the studio, and showcase them in a big, splashy screen vehicle with skits appropriately designed for each of them. By any measure, the caliber of talent on display was, to say the least, awesome—Fred Astaire, Gene Kelly, Kathryn Grayson, Judy Garland, and Lena Horne were some of the singing and dancing luminaries assembled for the occasion, and heard on the exquisite soundtrack album recording released recently by Rhino. Add to those, comedians like Red Skelton, Victor Moore and Fanny Brice, and siren extraordinaire Esther Williams, and you have an idea of the glittering display on view in the film.

Brilliantly directed by Vincente Minnelli, the musical boasts so many highlights that a mere listing would become tedious after a while. Astaire dazzles, as usual, in a couple of numbers in which his partner is the glamorous Lucille Bremer, and then teams with Gene Kelly (their only appearance together until *That's Entertainment, Part 2*, in 1976) for a spirited pas-de-deux on the Gershwins' "The Babbit and the Bromide"; Judy Garland is at her dizziest in "The Great Lady Has an Interview"; and Lena Horne is stunning and statuesque singing "Love." These and the other glorious musical moments from the film can be heard on the Rhino set, in stereo (!), the whole package strikingly augmented with a lavish booklet that details behind-the-scenes doings in words and pictures. It's the next best thing to the film itself, and it's simply sensational!

Zorba

Zorba 🎵🎵🎵🎵🎵

1992, Angel Records; from the Broadway production *Zorba*, 1968.

Album Notes: *Music:* John Kander; *Lyrics:* Fred Ebb; *Orchestrations:* Don Walker; *Dance Music Arrangements:* Dorothy Freitag; *Vocal Arrangements and Musical Direction:* Harold Hastings; *Cast:* Herschel Bernardi (Zorba), Lorraine Serabian (Leader), Maria Karnilova (Hortense), John Cunningham (Nikos), Carmen Alvarez (Widow), Jerry Sappir (Kyriakos), Al Hafid (Kanakis), Angelo Saridis (Kostantinos); *Album Producer:* Dick Jones; *CD Engineer:* Bob Norberg.

Selections: 1 Life Is (5:13) *Lorraine Serabian*; 2 The First Time (4:10) *Herschel Bernardi*; 3 The Top Of The Hill (2:34) *Lorraine Serabian*; 4 No Boom Boom (4:15) *Maria Karnilova, Herschel Bernardi, John Cunningham*; 5 The Butterfly (3:45) *Carmen Alvarez, Lorraine Serabian, John Cunningham*; 6 Goodbye, Canavaro (2:04) *Maria Karnilova, Herschel Bernardi, John Cunningham*; 7 Grandpapa (Zorba's Dance) (3:12) *Herschel Bernardi*; 8 Only Love/The Bend Of The Road (5:22) *Maria Karnilova, Lorraine Serabian, Carmen Alvarez, John Cunningham*; 9 Entr'acte (2:47) *Jerry Sappir, Al Hafid, Angelo Saridis*; 10 Y'assou (2:58) *Herschel Bernardi, Maria Karnilova, John Cunningham, Lorraine Serabian*; 11 Why Can't I Speak (2:50) *Carmen Alvarez, John Cunningham*; 12 The Crow/Happy Birthday (medley)(5:26) *Lorraine Serabian, Maria Karnilova*; 13 I Am Free/Life Is (reprise)(4:49) *Herschel Bernardi.*

Review: See entry below.

Zorba 🎵🎵🎵

1983, RCA Victor; from the Broadway revival *Zorba*, 1983.

Album Notes: *Music:* John Kander; *Lyrics:* Fred Ebb; *Orchestrations:* Don Walker; *Dance Music Arrangements:* Thomas Fay; *Musical Direction:* Paul Gemignani; *Cast:* Anthony Quinn (Zorba), Debbie Shapiro (The Woman), Lila Kedrova (Hortense), Robert Westenberg (Niko), Taro Meyer (The Widow), Frank De Sal (Russian Admiral), John Mineo (French Admiral), Paul Straney (English Admiral), Richard Warren Pugh (Italian Admiral), Suzanne Costellos, Panchali Null, Angelina Fiordellisi, Theresa Rakov (Crows), Rob Marshall, Peter Marinos, Peter Kevoian (Monks); *Album Producer:* Thomas Z. Shepard; *Engineer:* Paul Goodman.

Selections: 1 Life Is (5:06) *Debbie Shapiro*; 2 The First Time (4:55) *Anthony Quinn*; 3 The Top Of The Hill (3:12) *Debbie Shapiro*; 4 No Boom Boom (4:33) *Lila Kedrova, Anthony Quinn, Robert Westenberg, Frank De Sal, John Mineo*; 5 Mine Song (2:06) *Company*; 6 The Butterfly (4:11) *Taro Meyer, Debbie Shapiro, Robert Westenberg*; 7 Goodbye, Canavaro (2:03) *Lila Kedrova, Anthony Quinn, Robert Westenberg*; 8 Grandpapa (2:53) *Anthony Quinn, Debbie Shapiro*; 9 Only Love/The Bend Of The Road/Only Love (reprise)(6:21) *Lila Kedrova, Debbie Shapiro*; 10 Y'assou (2:38) *Company*; 11 Woman (3:11) *Anthony Quinn*; 12 Why Can't I Speak/That's A Beginning (3:54) *Taro Meyer, Robert Westenberg, Debbie Shapiro*; 13 The Crow (2:37) *Debbie Shapiro, Suzanne Costellos, Panchali Null, Angelina Fiordellisi, Theresa Rakov, Rob Marshall, Peter Marinos, Peter Kevoian*; 14 Happy Birthday (3:21) *Lila Kedrova*; 15 I Am Free/Finale: Life Is (reprise)(4:49) *Anthony Quinn, Debbie Shapiro.*

Review: A triumphant show from Kander and Ebb, *Zorba* may not have resulted in a long run, but it did result in a score of amazing versatility. Especially during this period, they displayed an almost Rodgers and Hammerstein desire to never repeat an earlier show. As is obvious from the title, this serious, passionate musical based on the novel by Nikos Kazantzakis, already the source for the film *Zorba the Greek,* does not take place in a Depression-ridden New York, early-Nazi Berlin or in a half-remembered, half-forgotten French Canadian town. Kander and Ebb perfectly captured the unbearable heat, stillness and half-hidden hostility of a poor village in Crete, with the songs just seeming to flow from the soul of the characters and their town.

Of the two versions available here, Herschel Bernardi stands out in the first, the 1968 original cast, as the title character whose craftiness, passion and charms are outlined in each song. Maria Karnilova as his erstwhile love interest, Mme. Hortense, practically vibrates with unfulfilled love and longing.

John Cunningham and Carmen Alvarez, along with Lorraine Serabian, are the other standouts on the record. The chorus and orchestra sing and play with deep commitment.

In the second version, the 1983 Broadway revival, the two stars from the original film, Anthony Quinn and Lila Kedrova, recreated their roles, and even though neither Quinn, as Zorba, nor Lila Kedrova, as Mme. Hortense, could sing well, they knew the characters, and the songs served their characterizations. While the 1968 Broadway cast is still the version of choice in almost every instance, one exception here is Debbie Shapiro as The Woman, the role played in the original by Lorraine Serabian. Both are very good, and both are very different. Where Serabian has her own unique voice and is quite good in the role, Shapiro has a big wide Broadway style voice that can sing almost anything. Ultimately, one's preference might go for the original Broadway cast recording, but the 1983 revival has its charms and adherents.

Jerry J. Thomas

The Addams Family ♫♫♫

1965, RCA Records; from the television series *The Addams Family*, 1964-65.

Album Notes: *Music*: Vic Mizzy; Orchestra conducted by Vic Mizzy; *Album Producer*: Joe Reisman; *Engineer*: Dick Bogert; *CD Producer*: Chick Crumpacker; *CD Engineer*: Dick Baxter.

Selections: 1 The Addams Family: Main Theme (1:56); 2 Uncle Fester's Blues (2:13); 3 Gomez (2:00); 4 Morticia's Theme (2:38); 5 Lurch's Theme (2:12); 6 One Little, Two Little, Three Little Tombstones (2:24); 7 Thing (1:57); 8 Laugh? I Thought I'd Die (2:36); 9 On Shroud No. 9 (2:24); 10 The Addams House (1:35); 11 Hide And Shriek (2:38); 12 The Anxiety Tango (2:03); 13 The Addams Family: Main Theme (vocal)(:51).

Review: Vic Mizzy's theme music from "The Addams Family" is one of the most instantly recognizable pieces of music to originate from a film or television program, so it goes without saying that if you like the theme song, you're bound to get a rise out of this infectious soundtrack album, initially issued in 1965 by RCA. Mizzy's music often has a toe-tapping beat, a quirky tone that's frequently brought down to Earth by the composer's distinctive melodies. That quality is totally in evidence here, with clear digital remastering punching up the typically '60s production sheen courtesy of original producer Joe Reisman. A new interview with Mizzy is included in the booklet notes, along with the previously unreleased, opening TV edit of the main theme; the short running time might have been augmented by adding cues from some of Mizzy's excellent unreleased film scores *(The Ghost and Mr. Chicken, The Spirit Is Willing)*, though that will have to wait for another day. *The Ghost and Mr. Chicken* contains the kind of creepy, kooky music that remains firmly implanted in your mind forever, but you don't mind because it's so much fun. Unfortunately, at this time it can only be enjoyed on the video release from MCA Home Video.

Andy Dursin

The Adventures of Robinson Crusoe ♫♫♫♫

1990, Silva Screen Records; from the BBC-TV series *The Adventures of Robinson Crusoe*, 1965.

Album Notes: *Music*: Robert Mellin, Gian-Piero Reverberi; Orchestra conducted by Gian-Piero Reverberi; *Album Producers*: David Stoner, James Fitzpatrick.

Selections: 1 Opening Titles (:25); 2 Main Theme (2:14); 3 Friday (1:55); 4 Crusoe's Youth Remembered (1:10); 5 Away From Home (2:11); 6 Adrift (3:22); 7 Solitude (2:24); 8 The Shelter (1:56); 9 Scanning The Horizon/Flashback: Escapades In York (1:28); 10 Cannibals! (2:29); 11 Wild Goats (2:22); 12 Palm Trees (:55); 13 In Search Of Rescue (1:44); 14 A Civilized Man (2:02); 15 Distant Shores (:32); 16 Alone (2:54); 17 Catching Dinner (1:47); 18 "Poor Robinson" (1:58); 19 Danger! (1:54); 20 Closing Titles (:46).

Review: The adventures of Robinson Crusoe, as depicted by Daniel Defoe in his 1721 novel, have inspired many filmmakers who have thrived on the tale's universal themes of ingenuity, friendship, and survival in an alien environment. The 1964-1965 13-part series, with a score by Robert Mellin and Gian-Piero Reverberi, is unusual in that it parallels Crusoe's current existence in the wild with flashbacks about his earlier life: his youth in York, his unhappy apprenticeship to a lawyer, his running off to sea, and his capture by and escape from slave traders, all elements found in Defoe's novel but seldom exploited to such an extent beforehand. As a result, the score reflects the greater diversity in the storyline, and in the midst of cues describing Crusoe's precarious existence on the (actually not so) deserted island, can afford to portray other aspects of his life ("Crusoe's Youth Remembered," "Away From Home," "Flashback: Escapades in York," etc.). The music, mostly steeped into the 1960s' style of light pop, makes an occasional detour toward more descriptive, romantic accents, usually to contrast Crusoe's current situation with reminiscences of his earlier life. It's a strange combination, particularly for a story allegedly set in the 18th century, but it's fun to listen to, which is ultimately the goal set by this oddball CD.

Alien Nation ♪♪♪♪

1990, GNP Crescendo; from the television series *Alien Nation*, 20th Century-Fox TV, 1989-90.

Album Notes: *Music*: Steve Dorff, Larry Herbstritt, David Kurtz; *Album Producer*: Ford A. Thaxton; *Engineers*: Jeff Vaughn, Michael Hartung.

Selections: Alien Nation: 1 Prologue and Main Title (D. Kurtz/K. Johnson) (1:43); Generation To Generation (S. Dorff/L. Herbstritt): 2 Generation To Generation (:40); 3 Return To Tencton (3:54); 4 One Hot Heinrick (:52); Contact (S. Dorff/L. Herbstritt): 5 Tenctonolian Mode Groove (1:39); 6 Astronomical Discovery (1:14); 7 Tailing A Wimp (:43); Partners (S. Dorff/L. Herbstritt/K. Johnson): 8 Howdy Pod (4:03); The Red Room (S. Dorff/L. Herbstritt): 9 Alien Animal Activist (1:31); Contact (S. Dorff/L. Herbstritt): 10 A New Beginning (2:28); Crossing The Line (S. Dorff/L. Herbstritt): 11 In Your Life (2:25); Three To Tango (D. Kurtz): 12 Confrontation (:53); 13 The Monastery Three (D. Kurtz/K. Johnson) (1:05); 14 George Entertains (1:12); 15 The Ceremony (D. Kurtz/K. Johnson) (1:39); 16 Touch Heads (1:25); Real Men (D. Kurtz): 17 Presents (1:32); Gimme, Gimme (D. Kurtz): 18 George Warms Up (3:08); Little Lost Lamb (D. Kurtz): 19 Resolution (1:07); 20 Slag Pop (:55); Chains Of Love (D. Kurtz): 21 Spaced Out Lover; Real Men (D. Kurtz): 22 Sneak Attack (1:05); Chains Of Love (D. Kurtz): 23 Jenny's Story (1:32); Three To Tango (D. Kurtz): 24 Sensuality (:53); The Night Of Screams (D. Kurtz): 25 Cathy's Story (2:35); Fifteen With Wanda (D. Kurtz): 26 The Alley (1:12); Rebirth (D. Kurtz): 27 Memory Of An Old Game (2:16); Take Over (D. Kurtz): 28 George Gets It (:47); 29 Susan: Assassin (2:27); Real Men (D. Kurtz/K. Johnson): 30 Proud Fathers (2:20); Alien Nation (D. Kurtz/K. Johnson): 31 Prologue and Main Title (reprise) (1:43).

Review: One of the most intriguing aspects of this series is its remarkably creative and melodic score, a rarity in a medium that tends to demand subtle and oft-times indiscernible work. Scoring duties for the series were divided between composers Steve Dorf, Larry Herbstritt and David Kurtz, with producer Ken Johnson providing the alien language lyrics for the vocals. The principal characters are members of a civilization of aliens, marooned in central Los Angeles. The composers sought to create a unique musical signature for their society by combining Caribbean and African rhythms with a progression of weird vocal and electronic effects. The album features a variety of intriguing alien "pop" tunes ("Tenctonlian (sic) Mode Groove," "Slag Pop"), but the most stimulating are the religious ceremonial chants. "Howdy Pod," a prayer for childbirth, is one of the most memorable ones with an a Capella vocal that segueways into a gentle, synthesized theme. A superior score because of its unique and delightful mix of vocals with electronic and acoustical instruments.

David Hirsch

Anastasia: The Mystery of Anna ♪♪♪♪

1986, Southern Cross Records; from the TV movie, *Anastasia: The Mystery of Anna*, Telecom Entertainment, 1986.

Album Notes: *Music*: Laurence Rosenthal; *Orchestrations*: Steve Bramson; *Music Editor*: Roy Prendergast; The Munich Philharmonic Orchestra, conducted by Laurence Rosenthal; *Album Producer*: Laurence Rosenthal; *Engineer*: Malcolm Luker.

Selections: 1 Main Title (Part 1) (2:02); 2 The Ballroom (2:25); 3 To Siberia (2:06); 4 The Sled/Ekaterinburg (2:50); 5 Family Only (1:46); 6 The Cellar (2:26); 7 Berlin Bridge (2:23); 8 Confronting Sophie (3:03); 9 After The Interview (1:55); 10 The Railroad Car (1:56); 11 Main Title (Part 2)/ Faces From The Past (2:02); 12 The Denial (1:51); 13 Shopping Spree (2:00); 14 The Romanoffs (:39); 15 At The Astor (1:27); 16 Russian Antiques (1:15); 17 Darya Says No (1:57); 18 The Luncheonette (1:15); 19 Back To Europe (2:14); 20 Anna And Erich (7:22).

Review: "Anastasia: The Mystery of Anna," shown in 1986, with Amy Irving in the title role and a cast that included Olivia de Havilland, Elke Sommer, Claire Bloom, Omar Sharif and Rex Harrison, essentially covers the same grounds as the 1956 film of the same name starring Ingrid Bergman and Yul Brynner. But to composer Laurence Rosenthal, the story suggested a totally different approach than the one taken in the film by Alfred Newman. As Rosenthal describes it in his notes, his score is essentially three scores instead of one, each reflecting the locales in which the story unfolds, their specific atmosphere and their distinct cultural milieu. Initially stately and elegant, like the waltz from Tchaikosvky's "Eugene Onegin," from which it borrows its exulted tone, the score turns melancholic as the Tsar and his family are forced to go into exile, a mood reinforced by the "implacable drums and pathetic wisps of woodwind."

The second part of the score depicting Anna's life in Berlin in the 1920s, echoes the atonality that prevailed at the time in imitation of the music written in Vienna. The third influence in the score, underlying Anna's recovery and her romance with a young German aristocrat, finds its accents in the Jazz age music that was beginning to make inroads. The music, in all its diversity, manages to retain a cohesive flavor, and makes an entertaining statement.

Around the World in 80 Days ♫♫♫

1989, Cinedisc Records; from the NBC-TV mini-series Around the World in 80 Days, 1989.

Album Notes: *Music:* Billy Goldenberg; *Music Editor:* Jim Weidman; Orchestra conducted by Billy Goldenberg; *Album Producer:* Randall Rumage.

Selections: 1 Around The World In 80 Days: Main Theme (4:04); 2 Balloon Over Florence/Crash Italiano (2:34); 3 Elephant Rising/Valente Vendanta (3:38); 4 Celestial Light (4:52); 5 Dolly Day And The Mudgemobile (2:24); 6 Windsor Castle (4:38); 7 Thermometer Reading (4:05); 8 Hong Kong Canopy (3:48); 9 Pretty Little Sarah And Dolly Day (4:08); 10 Around The World In 80 Days: Main Theme (reprise)(2:02); 11 Where The Citrons Bloom (3:03); 12 Oh, Yes!/It's Only Saturday (3:55); 13 Steady Ol' Chap/Prepare For Death (4:11); 14 Monsieur Lenoir/Less Private (3:32); 15 9 O'Clock! (2:50); 16 Richard Bronskill 1872/Fogg And The Indians (3:54); 17 Victor Hugo Brigade (2:40); 18 Propeller (4:05); 19 Around The World In 80 Days: Ending Credits (2:22).

Review: While Billy Goldenberg is best known for his work on Broadway, he revisited the small screen in 1988 with this enjoyable score for the NBC mini-series version of Jules Verne's classic novel, starring Pierce Brosnan, Eric Idle and Peter Ustinov. Goldenberg's music is always listenable and the energetic main theme is particularly infectious; the rest of his score is likewise buoyant, well performed under the composer's direction in Ireland. Trivia buffs take note: this was a relatively early soundtrack release in the CD format, manufactured by Cinedisc in a full digital recording, with a deceptively long running time attributed to the fact that Goldenberg's "Main Theme" is included no less than four times on the album, each time in the same version!

Andy Dursin

The Astronomers ♫♫♫

1991, Intrada Records; from the KCET-TV series The Astronomers, 1991.

Album Notes: *Music:* J.A.C. Redford; *Featured Musicians:* Stu Goldberg (synthesizers), George Doering (guitars), Ray Kelly (cello), Jon Clarke (woodwinds), Joel Peskin (saxophones);

Album Producer: J.A.C. Redford; *Engineers:* Stu Goldberg, Joe Tarantino.

Selections: 1 The Astronomers (1:23); Waves Of The Future: 2 Future I (4:41); 3 Future II (6:27); Prospecting For Planets: 4 Planets (4:09); A Window To Creation: 5 Cosmology I (5:02); 6 Cosmology II (2:45); 7 Cosmology III (3:52); 8 Cosmology IV (3:38); Searching For Black Holes: 9 Quasars (1:48); Where Is The Rest Of The Universe: 10 Dark Matter (2:34); Stardust: 11 Stars I (4:20); 12 Stars II (3:41).

Review: J.A.C. Redford's score for this 1991 PBS documentary is a pleasant enough soundtrack from Intrada Records, with a nice diversity of tracks making for a smooth listening experience. Redford's score is grounded primarily in an expansive melody ("The Astronomers") that recurs throughout the album, which also includes cues that are by turns magical, mystical, dissonant and even disturbing, reflecting all of the various elements that comprise our universe—from the warmth of our own sun to the puzzling phenomena of black holes outside our solar system. Virtually the entire score is performed on synthesizers (with only some tracks featuring a small acoustic ensemble), but to the composer's credit, the score remains as imaginative aurally as the galactic visions it underscores.

Andy Dursin

The A-Team ♫♫♫

1990, Silva Screen Records; from the TV series The A-Team, 1983-84.

Album Notes: *Music:* Mike Post, Pete Carpenter; Orchestra conducted by Daniel Caine; Music Adapted and Directed for Records by Derek Wadsworth; *Album Producer:* Michael Jones; *Engineers:* Keith Grant, Doug Bennett.

Selections: 1 Theme From *The A-Team* (3:13); 2 Young Cannibal (2:57); 3 B.A.'s Ride (2:34); 4 The A-Team In New York City (2:43); 5 Bandits! (2:08); 6 Taxi Chase (2:13); 7 The A-Team Escape (1:16); 8 The A-Team Prepares For War (2:08); 9 Showtime (3:22); 10 Move, Sucker (1:04); 11 Let's Get Busted (1:06); 12 Murdock's "Face" (3:01); 13 Helicopters (2:36); 14 More Bandits (1:22); 15 Theme From *The A-Team* (3:27).

Review: A faithful recreation of the themes composed for the 1983-87 series by Mike Post and Pete Carpenter with their team of co-composers (three are credited here). Principally, the album is made up of the splashy action and second unit transitional cues, the music often played as hands are seen building some odd vehicle or weapon from assorted bits and pieces. The show wasn't known for moments of tense interpersonal drama; cars crashed and things just blew up, so many of the music cues were variations of the main theme. The album features a Mexican flavored motif ("Bandits!") and several other location establishing themes ("The A-Team in New York City"), but all too often there's little variety to be found. The main theme is excessively repeated. No fault goes to Derek Wadsworth, who did a fine job adapting the music for the album from the original scores. He also conducts the orchestra under the pseudonym of Daniel Caine.

David Hirsch

The Avengers

1982, Varese-Sarabande Records; from the television series *The Avengers* and *The New Avengers*.

See: Laurie Johnson in Compilations

Babylon 5 🎵🎵🎵

1995, Sonic Images; from the television series *Babylon 5*, Warner Bros., 1995-97.

Album Notes: *Music*: Christopher Franke; The Berlin Symphonic Film Orchestra, conducted by Christopher Franke; *Album Producer*: Richard E. Roth; *Engineer*: Richard E. Roth.

Selections: 1-4 Chrysalis (18:22); 5-6 Mind War (6:14); 7-9 Parliament Of Dreams (18:04); 10-12 The Geometry Of Shadows (15:14).

Review: Faced with writing music for a low-budget television space opera with a truly epic scope, composer Christopher Franke (an alumnus of Tangerine Dream) finds an effective middle ground between the broad orchestral music favored by rival sci fi franchise *Star Trek* and the bleeping, drum-machine hammered sound of some other syndicated genre shows. The music is essentially electronic, but its textures are enhanced by the Munich Symphony Orchestra. The result has some of the atmospheric minimalism of Tangerine Dream, the fanfare-dominated martial pomp of Star Wars and its ilk, and many other, less-obvious influences. The space battles, for example, feature a marvelously kinetic mix of synths and percussion, often evoking the sound of Japanese kodo drummers, while dialogue and suspense sequences favor the moody, drifting synth pads and bluesy jazz atmospherics employed by Vangelis in his *Blade Runner* score. The result is lacking in memorable themes and motifs but rich in the ambivalent, brooding milieu of J. Michael Straszinski's space epic.

Jeff Bond

Batman 🎵

1966, PolyGram/Casablance Records; from the television series *Batman*, 20th Century-Fox TV, 1966.

Album Notes: *Music*: Nelson Riddle; *Music Supervision*: Lionel Newman; *Music Editor*: Leonard A. Engel.

Selections: 1 Batman Theme (N. Hefti)(2:35); 2 Batman Riddles The Riddler! or Hi Diddle Riddle (1:40); 3 Batusi A-Go-Go! or I Shouldn't Wish To Attract Attention (1:37); 4 Two Perfectly Ordinary People or !!! (:44); 5 Holy-Hole-In-The-Doughnut or Robin, You've Done It Again! (1:58); 6 Batman Pows The Penguin or Aha, My Fine Feathered Finks! (1:49); 7 To The Batmobile! (2:16); 8 Batman Blues (1:46); 9 Holy Flypaper (3:03); 10 Batman Thaws Mr. Freeze or That's The Way The Ice-Cube Crumbles! (2:05); 11 Gotham City (2:01); 12 Zelda Tempts Batman or Must He Go It Alone??? (2:27).

Review: It would be tempting to recommend this CD. After all, it is the soundtrack to one of the early 1960s' most popular television shows, with music by the great Nelson Riddle and featuring the voices of cast members Adam West (Batman), Burt Ward (Robin), Burgess Meredith (The Penguin), George Sanders (Mr. Freeze), Anne Baxter (The Great Zelda), and Frank Gorshin (The Riddler). In other words, nothing but the best. But the CD offers less than 25 minutes of actual playing, which at the price of laserlight these days is a bit offensive. So unless you have just inherited a fortune and have money to burn, skip it!

The Beverly Hillbillies 🎵🎵🎵🎵

1995, Legace Records; from the TV series *The Beverly Hillbillies*, Filmways Production.

Album Notes: *Music*: Zeke Manners; *Orchestrations*: Zeke Manners; conducted by Zeke Manners; *Cast*: Buddy Ebsen (Jed Clampett), Irene Ryan (Granny), Max Baer (Jethro), Donna Douglas (Elly May), Nancy Kulp (Jane), Raymond Bailey (Drysdale); *Featured Guest*: Lester Flatt & Earl Scruggs; *Album Producers*: Don Law, Irving Townsend.

Selections: 1 The Ballad Of Jed Clampett (P. Henning)(1:33) *Lester Flatt, Earl Scruggs*; 2 Beverly Hills (3:01) Entire Cast; 3 Vittles (2:04) *Irene Ryan*; 4 A Long Talk With That Boy (B. Ebsen)(3:38) *Buddy Ebsen, Max Baer*; 5 Jethro's A Powerful Man (2:29) *Buddy Ebsen, Max Baer*; 6 Elly's Spring Song (P. Henning)(1:19) *Donna Douglas*; 7 Back Home U.S.A. (B. Ebsen/Z. Manners)(2:01) *Buddy Ebsen*; 8 Critters (1:14) Entire Cast; 9 Doctor Granny (2:37) Entire Cast; 10 Lady Lessons (1:57) *Donna Douglas, Nancy Kulp*; 11 Birds An' Bees (3:33) *Donna Douglas*; 12 Love Of Money (2:20) *Nancy Kulp, Raymond Bailey*; 13 The

Ballad Of Jed Clampett (P. Henning)(:47) *Lester Flatt, Earl Scruggs.*

Review: Once you have left behind "The Ballad of Jed Clampett," which by some quirk of fate has become a standard, you can settle down and enjoy the rest of the show... on CD, that is, digital! No one claimed that the participants were singers, so if you expected great songs and great voices, all you'll get is Irene Ryan playing Granny with her croaky voice; Buddy Ebsen as Jed and Max Baer as Jethro, each with his own folk talk; Donna Douglas holding her own as Elly (not a bad voice, either, though not always on pitch); and Nancy Kulp and Raymond Bailey (gasp!) singing. And behind them a country-styled instrumental line to justify the album. It's good for a momentary lull, not much more, but at least you know what you're getting in the bargain.

Beverly Hills 90210 ♪

1992, Giant/Reprise Records; from the television series *Beverly Hills 90210*, 1992.

Album Notes: *Song Producers:* Elliot Wolff, Howie Tee, Robbie Nevil, Tommy Faragher, Lotti Golden, David Foster, Andre Cymone, Dancin' Danny D, Gerry Brown, Vanessa Williams, Brian McKnight, Jim Dean, Pete Glenister, Russ Titelman, Tuhin Roy, Jake Smith, John Davis; *Album Executive Producers:* Kenneth Miller, Darren Star, Irving Azoff; Compiled by Cassandra Mills, Jeff Aldrich.

Selections: 1 Bend Time Back Around (E. Wolff)(3:57) *Paula Abdul*; 2 Got 2 Have U (Color Me Badd/H. Thompson)(3:46) *Color Me Badd*; 3 The Right Kind Of Love (T. Faragher/L. Golden/R. Nevil)(4:47) *Jeremy Jordan*; 4 Love Is (Tonio K./J. Keller)(4:45) *Vanessa Williams, Brian McKnight*; 5 Just Wanna Be Your Friend (Puck/K.Z. Amen)(3:52) *Puck & Natty*; 6 Let Me Be Your Baby (G. Williams/OP. Glenister)(4:57) *Geoffrey Williams*; 7 Saving Forever For You (D. Warren)(4:31) *Shanice*; 8 All The Way To Heaven (D. Warren)(4:12) *Jody Watley*; 9 Why (C. Dennis/D. Poku)(4:58) *Cathy Dennis, D-Mob*; 10 Time To Be Lovers (T. Snow/K. Miller)(4:47) *Michael McDonald, Chaka Khan*; 11 Action Speaks Louder Than Words (T. Snow/K. Miller)(3:56) *Tara Kemp*; 12 Theme From Beverly Hills 90210 (J. Davis)(3:08) *John Davis.*

Review: The caliber of talent involved in this compilation is enough to create more than a passing interest. Where else would you find people like Paula Abdul, Vanessa Williams, Shanice, Jody Watley, Michael McDonald, Chaka Khan, and Color Me Badd on the same album? The problem, however, is that the genres in which each expresses themselves don't mix

> "I thought opera was a guy ... with his chest pumped out making a loud noise. I had no idea what kind of door was being opened to me. Opera is the ultimate art form. There's nothing that can freeze your blood like the combination of drama and music."
>
> **Steward Copeland**
> *(Musical America, Jan./Feb., 1992)*

very well. After you jump, without much rhyme nor reason, from ballads to rockers to electronic pop, you feel as if you're on overdrive, and you need some relief that not even John Davis' theme can provide. The beats sound the same, the performances bleed into each other, and the overall effect is trite and disappointingly dry. The show may be hip, but the CD ain't.

The Bourne Identity ♪♪♪♪

1988, Intrada Records; from the movie *The Bourne Identity*, Warner Bros., 1988.

Album Notes: *Music:* Laurence Rosenthal; *Orchestrations:* Steve Bramson, Laurence Rosenthal; The Film Symphony Of Prague, conducted by Laurence Rosenthal; *Album Producer:* Laurence Rosenthal; *Engineer:* Malcolm Luker.

Selections: 1 Main Title (6:27); 2 The French Children (1:33); 3 Fishing Village (2:52); 4 Arrival In Zurich (3:19); 5 Incident At The Bank (3:46); 6 Jason And Marie (4:36); 7 The Red Door (3:31); 8 Discovery (:42); 9 Chernak Dead (3:33); 10 Valois Bank (2:56); 11 Wild Goose Chase (2:31); 12 Carlos As Confessor (4:33); 13 The Trocadero (2:30); 14 Treadstone 71 (10:08); 15 Abbott (2:45); 16 Epilogue (1:03).

Review: A political thriller, starring Richard Chamberlain as an amnesiac who finds himself involved in a crime, "The Bourne Identity" benefits from its many European locales and colorful characters, as well as the more mysterious aspects of its screen action, all of which suggest a splendidly evocative score to composer Laurence Rosenthal. As a result, the overall musical fabric is beautifully diversified, most often solidly grounded in orchestral themes that have great impact and melodic content, but with occasional strange electronic sounds that delineate more specifically the psychological aspects of the story. At times attractive, at times disquieting, it's a great score with some excellent moments in it.

The Burning Shore 🎵🎵🎵🎵

1991, Mercury Records; from the TV film *The Burning Shore*, Titanus Films, 1991.

Album Notes: *Music*: Michel Legrand; *Orchestrations*: Michel Legrand; The Leningrad Symphony Orchestra, conducted by Michel Legrand.

Selections: 1 The Burning Shore (M. Legrand/H. Shaper)(3:25) *Rossana Casale*; 2 Hunger And Thirst (2:20); 3 Mercy Of Death (1:50); 4 Before The Wedding (4:03); 5 The Mountain At Last (2:38); 6 First Love (2:30); 7 The Final Confrontation (4:15); 8 The Choice Of Life (1:21); 9 Bushmen Have No Friends (2:55); 10 Reunion On The Bridge (1:37); 11 Sarah's Secret Place (3:10); 12 Lothar's Fall (1:46); 13 Deaths Of Owi And Hani (6:30); 14 The Poisoned Well (1:25); 15 When Hell Freezes Over (1:40); 16 The Governor's Party (3:22); 17 The Pursuit (6:15); 18 Hell Has Frozen Over (2:50); 19 The Smell Of Water (4:20); 20 The Lion (2:38); 21 The Burning Shore (2:35).

Review: Composer Michel Legrand, whose bend for lovely thematic music is one of his most endearing traits, created another exquisite score for this adventure film made for television, based on the eponymous novel by Wilbur Smith. The cues, in turns grandiose and romantic, are for the most part very catchy and melodic, weaving a robust musical tapestry that has many charms. Occasionally, a drumbeat suggests the African background against which the story itself unfolds, with the cues describing the action in bold, colorful terms. Performance by the Leningrad Symphony Orchestra is quite enthusiastic.

Cadfael 🎵🎵🎵🎵♭

1996, Angel Records; from the UK Television production *Cadfael*, 1996-97.

Album Notes: *Music*: Colin Towns; *Arrangements*: Colin Towns; Orchestra conducted by Colin Towns; *Gregorian Chants*: The Clerkes of St. Albans Abbey, directed by Barry Rose; *Album Producer*: Colin Towns; *Engineer*: Dave Hunt.

Selections: 1 Cadfael Of Shrewsbury (Opening Title Music)(3:08); 2 O Filii et Filiae (2:17); 3 Turn Thine Eyes To See (3:24); 4 Merry The Dance (1:43); 5 There Is No Rose Of Such Virtue (2:49); 6 The Juggler's Stare (2:55); 7 All Out Of The World By Tomorrow (3:41); 8 Magnificat anima mea Dominum (3:19); 9 Flamed My Heart (3:11); 10 Hidden In The Well (2:17);

11 Sanctus et Benedictus (1:42); 12 Veni Sancte Spiritus (2:44); 13 Lumen ad Revelationem (2:56); 14 Light Off The Father's Light (2:20); 15 Glover Of Shotwick (2:04); 16 High Above The Heavens (3:00); 17 Salve Regina (2:04); 18 Ave Maria (1:14); 19 Cry Aloud (1:51); 20 The Falconer's Secret (1:39); 21 Hail St. Peter's Fair (2:30); 22 Perspice Christicola (1:12); 23 Cadfael Of Shrewsbury (Closing Title Music)(:44).

Review: One of the best murder mystery series to be seen on television these days involves, of all people, a monk, Brother Cadfael (Derek Jacobi), playing detective in the Middle Ages. Handsomely photographed in natural settings, with crisply written stories, the series also boasts a spell-binding score which mixes Gregorian chants with pseudo-Gothic musical cues, composed by Colin Towers. The overall effect is both austere and richly evocative, as this compelling soundtrack album so effectively demonstrates. Culling from various episodes in the series, the CD offers an overview of the musical textures, with many glorious moments to be enjoyed. It may not convert you, but if you are not a viewer it might compel you to look at some episodes and find out for yourself why this medieval monk might soon become as popular as Poirot or Miss Marple on television.

Catwalk 🎵🎵🎵🎵

1994, Atlantic Records; from the M-TV television series *Catwalk*, 1994.

Album Notes: *Album Producer*: Steve Tyrell; *Engineer*: Chris Lord-Alge.

Selections: 1 If You Want Me (S. Tyrell/K. Savigar/S. Tyrell)(4:12) *Barry Coffing*; 2 Life Is Sweet (S. Tyrell/K. Savigar/S. Tyrell)(4:47) *Barry Coffing*; 3 I'm Allowed (B. Tom)(4:20) *Buffalo Tom*; 4 Drive Me (S. Tyrell/K. Savigar/S. Tyrell)(4:46) *Jamie Walters*; 5 Let Me Off Here (S. Tyrell/K. Savigar/S. Tyrell/ M. Landau)(4:11) *Barry Coffing*; 6 Something To Cry About (S. Tyrell/K. Savigar/S. Tyrell)(4:15) *Lisa Butler*; 7 Ribbon In The Sky (S. Wonder)(4:14) Intro; 8 Reckless (S. Tyrell/K. Savigar/S. Tyrell)(4:07) *Barry Coffing*; 9 It's About Time (E. Dando/T. Morgan)(2:41) *The Lemonheads*; 10 Love Is A Dream (S. Tyrell/K. Savigar/S. Tyrell)(4:43) *Vonda Shephard*; 11 You Hurt Me (S. Tyrell/K. Savigar/S. Tyrell)(3:21) *Barry Coffing*.

Review: A collection of urban contemporary songs specifically composed to illustrate this series. Some solid rocking numbers, some flavorful ballads, all of which creates a strong impression. Several songs actually do stand out in the lot, most specifically "Something to Cry About," "Reckless," and "Love Is a Dream," which are quite good. A good CD which aches to be discovered and enjoyed.

A Charlie Brown Christmas
♫♫♫♫

1986, Fantasy Records; from the CBS-TV Television Special, *A Charlie Brown Christmas*, 1986.

Album Notes: *Music*: Vince Guaraldi; *Lyrics*: Mendelson; *Performed by*: The Vince Guaraldi Trio; *Album Engineer*: George Horn.

Selections: 1 O Tannenbaum (trad.)(5:03); 2 What Child Is This (trad.)(2:20); 3 My Little Drum (3:15); 4 Linus And Lucy (3:03); 5 Christmas Time Is Here (instrumental)(6:06); 6 Christmas Time Is Here (vocal)(2:44); 7 Skating (2:24); 8 Hark, The Herald Angels Sing (trad.)(1:55); 9 Christmas Is Coming (3:22); 10 For Elise (L. Van Beethoven)(1:02); 11 Christmas Song (M. Torme/ V. Wells)(3:15).

Review: However crass the American celebration of Christmas—however stale the notion of pop Christmas music—this little soundtrack from a little TV special continues to improve with the passing years. The late Vince Guaraldi not only created a perfect environment for the animated *Peanuts* characters, he made what must now be considered a modern jazz classic, in an era when such things have almost ceased to be. Half originals, half piano-trio arrangements of familiar Christmas songs, the CD captures the blend of sadness, nostalgia and beauty that characterize—for many of us—a season that's seldom been altogether jolly.

Marc Kirkeby

Citizen X ♫♫♫♫

1995, Varese-Sarabande Records; from the television movie *Citizen X*, HBO Pictures, 1995.

Album Notes: *Music*: Randy Edelman; *Orchestrations*: Ralph Ferraro; *Music Editor*: John Lasalandra; Orchestra conducted by Randy Edelman; *Album Producer*: Randy Edelman; *Engineer*: Elton Ahi.

Selections: 1 A Heavy Burden (2:51); 2 Forrest Of Death (2:38); 3 Leaving The Station (3:35); 4 Two Comrades Embrace (3:44); 5 Crossed Paths (2:59); 6 The Strain Begins To Show (2:43); 7 Tracking Chikatilo (2:26); 8 Arrest (3:01); 9 Finally A Clue (2:27); 10 Finale (3:11).

Review: A television movie, starring Stephen Rea and Donald Sutherland based on the novel "The Killer Department" by Robert Cullen, "Citizen X" prompted Randy Edelman to write a broad, symphonic score, lush and attractive, often dark and brooding, with many catchy themes evolving from the overall texture. Some cues, like "Leaving the Station" or "The Strain Begins to Show," are actually quite compelling, making this more than a mere routine effort. CD alert: music on each track starts a couple of seconds before indexing does, so if you're looking for the start of a specific cue you will have to backtrack to the end of the previous one.

The Civil War ♫♫♫♫

1990, Elektra Records; from the PBS-TV series *The Civil War*, 1990.

Album Notes: *Music Research and Coordination*: Jesse Carr; *Featured Artists*: The Old Bethpage Brass Band, Dr. Kirby Jolly, director; *Performed by*: The Abyssinian Baptist Church Sanctuary Choir, Dr. Jewel T. Thompson, director; The New American Brass Band, Robert Sheldon, director; *Album Producers*: Ken Burns, John Colby; *Engineers*: Billy Shaw, Don Wershba, Michael Golub, Paul Goodman, Scott Hull.

Selections: 1 Drums Of War (:08) *The Old Bethpage Brass Band*; 2 Oliver Wendell Holmes (:29) *Paul Roebling*; 3 Ashokan Farewell (J. Ungar)(4:02) *Jay Ungar, Matt Glaser, Evan Stover, Russ Barenberg, Molly Mason*; 4 Battle Cry Of Freedom (G.F. Root)(1:40) *Jacqueline Schwab*; 5 We Are Climbing Jacob's Ladder (trad.)(4:22) *Bernice Johnson Reagon*; 6 Dixie/Bonnie Blue Flag (D.D. Emmett)(1:55) *The New American Brass Band*; 7 Cheer Boys Cheer (H. Russell)(1:09) *The New American Brass Band*; 8 Angel Band (trad.)(1:03) *Russ Barenburg, Molly Mason*; 9 Johnny Has Gone For A Soldier (:51) *Jacqueline Schwab, Jesse Carr*; 10 Lorena (J.P. Webster/H.D. Webster)(1:10) *Matt Glaser, Jay Ungar, Molly Mason*; 11 Parade (C.S. Grafulla) (3:28) *The New American Brass Band*; 12 Hail Columbia (P. Phylo/J. Hopkinson) (2:18) *The New American Brass Band*; 13 Dixie (D.D. Emmett)(2:03) *Bobby Horton*; 14 Kingdom Coming (H.C. Work)(1:00) *Matt Glaser, Jay Ungar, Art Baron*; 15 Battle Hymn Of The Republic (J.W. Howe) (1:36) *Matt Glaser, Jacqueline Schwab*; 16 All Quiet On The Potomac (E.L. Beers/J.H. Hewitt)(1:13) *Jacqueline Schwab*; 17 Flag Of Columbia (H. Millard)(1:03) *Jacqueline Schwab*; 18 Weeping Sad And Lonely (C.C. Sawyer/H. Tucker)(1:08) *Peggy James, Jacqueline Schwab, Jesse Carr*; 19 Yankee Doodle (trad.)(:39) *The Old Bethpage Brass Band*; 20 Palmyra Schottische (Rowlathem) (3:08) *The New American Brass Band*; 21 When Johnny Comes Marching Home (P.S. Gilmore)(:42) *The Old Bethpage Brass Band*; 22 Shenandoah (trad.)(:40) *John Levy, John Colby*; 23 When Johnny Comes Marching Home (P.S. Gilmore)(1:43) *Matt Glaser, Yonatin Malin, Jacqueline Schwab, Molly Mason, Peter Amidon, Jay Ungar*; 24 Marching Through georgia (H.C. Work)(:54) *Matt Glaser, Jay Ungar, Molly Mason, Peter Amidon (banjo)*; 25 Marching Through Georgia (lament) (H.C. Work)(1:10) *Jacqueline Schwab*; 26 Battle Cry Of Freedom (G.F. Root)(2:30) *Jacqueline Schwab*;

27 Battle Hymn Of The Republic (J.W. Howe)(3:20) *The Abyssinian Baptist Church Sanctuary Choir*; 28 Ashokan Farewell/Sullivan Ballou Letter (3:23) *Paul Roebling, David McCullough*.

Review: An effective selection of traditional period music, authentically recreated to underscore Ken Burns' monumental documentary on the "War Between the States." No original underscore is featured here as the selected cues do a fine job capturing the era. Each track has its own unique presentation, "The Battle Cry of Freedom" is played by solo piano while "We Are Climbing Jacob's Ladder" is sung a Capella, "Angel Band" is performed by a duo of acoustic guitar players and "Dixie" marches to an old fashioned brass band. The album stands well on its own as an artifact to a bygone era, mixing many well known songs with the more esoteric, which do well to educate what was once considered the popular music of it day.

David Hirsch

Cult TV Themes 𝅘𝅥𝅘𝅥𝅘𝅥 ♭

1996, Silva Screen Records.

Album Notes: *Arrangers*: Mike Townend, Kevin Townend, Henry Mancini, Derek Wadsworth; The Royal Philharmonic Concert Orchestra, conducted by Mike Townend; The Daniel Caine Orchestra, conducted by Daniel Caine; *Album Producers*: James Fitzpatrick, Kevin Townend; *Engineer*: Mike Ross-Trevor.

Selections: 1 Ironside (Q. Jones)(2:04); 2 Peter Gunn (H. Mancini)(3:55); 3 Kojak (B. Goldenberg)(3:33); 4 Mission: Impossible: The Plot/Main Theme (L. Schifrin)(3:21); 5 Hawaii Five-O (M. Stevens)(3:16); 6 Perry Mason (F. Steiner) (3:10); 7 The Pink Panther (H. Mancini)(2:09); 8 The Prisoner (R. Grainer) (5:43); 9 Mike Hammer (E. Hagen)(2:02); 10 Barnaby Jones (J. Goldsmith)(3:03).

Review: With a full title like *Mission: Impossible & Cult TV Themes Of The Atomic Age And Beyond*, this compilation CD has carte blanche to contain just about anything. In addition to Lalo Schifrin's unforgettable "Mission: Impossible" theme music, and with titles like Earl Hagen's bluesy modern noir theme for "Mike Hammer" and Quincy Jones's "Ironside" theme with its distinctive, alarm-like opening, the definition of "cult" gets stretched quite a bit. But regardless of whether shows like "Kojak" and "Barnaby Jones" deserve to be describe as cult programs, their theme music is memorable and exciting, and this newly-recorded mix does a better job than most of recreating the tempos and arrangements of these tight little compositions. Included are Henry Mancini's gritty, rocking "Peter Gunn" music and his sneaky theme for *The Pink Panther*, Morton Stevens's hard-driving surfer music for "Hawaii 5-o," Fred

Steiner's bluesy, evocative "Perry Mason" theme, Ron Grainer's propulsive music for The Prisoner, as well as Billy Goldenberg's oddly sweeping *Kojak* theme and Jerry Goldsmith's low-key but catchy "Barnaby Jones." The arrangements and performances are mostly dead-on, but some of the pieces suffer from the extended treatments which add some ill-advised improvisational sections to pan the cues out to more than two minutes.

Jeff Bond

Dark Shadows: The 30th Anniversary Collection 𝅘𝅥𝅘𝅥𝅘𝅥𝅘𝅥 ♭

1996, Varese-Sarabande Records; from the television series *Dark Shadows*, 1966-1970.

Album Notes: *Music*: Robert Cobert; *Orchestrations*: Robert Cobert; *Lyrics*: Charles Randolph Grean; Orchestra conducted by Robert Cobert; *Album Producers*: Cary E. Mansfield, Jim Pierson; *Engineer*: Kevin Reeves.

Selections: 1 First Episode Voice-Over/Collingwood (:54) *Alexandra Moltke*; 2 "Dark Shadows" Theme (1:08); 3 Quentin's Theme (2:09); 4 Ode To Angelique (2:43); 5 Missy (2:31); 6 Theme From "Dark Shadows" (2:47); 7 Josette's Music Box (2:01); 8 #1 At The Blue Whale (2:31); 9 Back At The Blue Whale (2:01); 10 Quentin's Theme (2:01); 11 "Dark Shadows" Music Cue Medley I (5:25); 12 I Wanna Dance With You (2:20) *David Selby, Nancy Barrett*; 13 Pansy's Theme Medley (2:57); 14 Sarah's Theme (London Bridge)(1:35); 15 Joanna (1:44); 16 "Dark Shadows" Music Cue Medley II (8:06); 17 Last Episode Closing Voice-Over/"Dark Shadows" Theme (1:07); 18 Barnabas Theme from "Dark Shadows" (2:50) *The First Theremin Era*; 19 Quentin's Theme (2:45); 20 "Dark Shadows" 1969 Vampire Fan Club Greeting (2:16) *Jonathan Frid*; 21 Radio Spots (1:29); 22 Barnabas The Vampire State Building (3:03).

Review: A sleek, elegant vampire show, "Dark Shadows" dominated television nights for three years, starting off as a conventional melodrama with spooky elements, but soon finding its own voice with the arrival of Barnabas Collins. One reason for the success of the show can be attributed to the score devised by Robert Cobert, who purposely ignored the trappings of the genre and developed an orchestral music that is totally indigenous to the show and gives it its unmistakable cachet.

Marking the 30th anniversary of the show, which premiered on June 27, 1966, this clever compilation not only samples many of the cues written by Cobert, but also adds unusual recordings, like "Barnabas Theme," performed by The First Theremin Era, a psychedelic group. Fans of the series will no doubt love this great compilation; others will have to discover for themselves what kept an entire nation riveted to the television for so many thrilling evenings.

The Dinosaurs ♪♪♪♪

1993, Narada Cinema; from the PBS television series *The Dinosaurs*, 1993.

Album Notes: *Music*: Peter Melnick; *Arrangements*: Peter Melnick; *Featured Musicians*: Peter Melnick (piano/synthesizers/acoustic slide guitar), George Doering (electric and nylon-string guitar), Bryce Martin (didjeridu, the screaming pipe), John Yoakum (saxophones/oboe/English horn/clarinet/flutes), David Stone (bass), Brad Dutz (percussion), Charles Judge (keyboards and synthesizer); *Album Producer*: Peter Melnick; *Engineer*: Michael Stone.

Selections: 1 Dinosaur Ghosts (4:30); 2 Winged Transformations (7:40); 3 Sauropod Shuffle (3:50); 4 Daniel And The Dinosaur (4:22); 5 Leatherback Turtle (2:32); 6 From Maastricht To Paris (4:35); 7 Dollo's Hadrosaurs (3:04); 8 Age Of Reptiles (5:46); 9 Migration (3:01); 10 Flying Things (3:25); 11 Maurasse (2:14); 12 Sound Shadows (4:42).

Review: Suddenly, dinosaurs are popping up all over the place, in the movies where *Jurassic Park* and *The Lost World* present their own version of the terrifying world of 140 million years ago, and on television where various series attempt to recreate that neanderthal time when huge monsters roamed the earth. One such series, "The Dinosaurs!," seen on PBS, took a professoral approach to its subject, and investigated the scientific aspects of the question, as well as its most speculative elements.

Augmenting the presentation is Peter Melnick's score, a deft mixture of acoustic and electronic instruments. Since no music existed at the time, one must assume that Melnick's, contemporary as it may sound, is as valid as anything else, at least where the series is concerned. Taken at face value, it is a pleasant blend of New Age-sounding cues, that has the enormous merit of sounding quite pleasant out of its own environment. For someone who has not seen the four-part series, it is difficult to comprehend what a cue like "From Maastricht to Paris" might be doing in the middle of a program dedicated to dinosaurs, but the music eloquently speaks for itself, so who cares?

Do It A Cappella ♪♪♪♪

1990, Elektra Records; from the PBS-TV Great Performances special *Spike & Co.: Do It A Cappella*, 1990.

Album Notes: *Featured Artists*: True Image, The Mint Juleps, Rockapella, The Persuasions, Ladysmith Black Mambazo, The Persuasions, Take 6; *Producer*: Cherie Fortis.

Selections: 1 I Need You (B. & M. McCoy)(1:57) *True Image*; 2 Don't Let Your Heart (D. Longworth)(2:38) *The Mint Juleps*; 3 Zombie Jamboree (C. Mauge, Jr.)(3:00) *Rockapella*; 4 Looking For An Echo (R. Reicheg)(4:19) *The Persuasions*; 5 Phansi Em Godini (Down In The Mines)(J. Shabalala)(5:11) *Ladysmith Black Mambazo*; 6 I Want To Live Easy (D. Charles)(2:48) *The Mint Juleps*; 7 Under The Boardwalk (K. Young/A. Resnick)(3:07) *Rocapella, True Image*; 8 Up On The Roof (G. Goffin/C. King)(2:56) *The Persuasions*; 9 Higher And Higher (G. Jackson)(3:32) *The Mint Juleps*; 10 Get Away Jordan (M. Kibble)(4:29) *Take 6*; 11 N'kosi Sikeleli Afrika (God Bless Africa (2:58) *Ladysmith Black Mambazo*; 12 Pass On The Love (G. Grant)(2:51) *The Persuasions*; 13 The Lion Sleeps Tonight (S. Linda/P. Campbell/H. Peretti/L. Creatore/A. Stanton/G. Weiss)(4:33) *Ladysmith Black Mambazo, The Mint Juleps*.

Review: Director Spike Lee will surely be remembered for many achievements, but this glorious made-for-public-TV salute to a cappella singing groups should not be overlooked. He didn't direct it, merely plays host, but it wouldn't have happened without him. Filmed mainly at an ancient movie palace in Brooklyn, New York, the performances range from the Persuasions' post-doo-wop to Rockapella's greaser-cabaret to Take 6's neo-jazz-gospel, and include a showstopping set by South Africa's Ladysmith Black Mambazo. The video laserdisc includes nearly half an hour of extra music.

Marc Kirkeby

Doctor Who: The Curse of Fenric ♪♪♪▿

1991, Silva Screen Records; from the BBC-TV series *Doctor Who*, 1971-1990.

Album Notes: *Music*: Mark Ayres; *Arrangements*: Mark Ayres; *Music Performed by*: Mark Ayres; *Album Producer*: Mark Ayres; *Engineer*: Mark Ayres.

Selections: 1 Introduction: Doctor Who (R. Grainer)(:40); 2 The Boats (:47); 3 Beach-Head and Rat-Trap (2:06); 4 Sealed Orders (1:21); 5 Eyes Watching (1:03); 6 Commander Millington (:47); 7 Viking Graves (:54); 8 Maidens' Point (1:17); 9 The Translations (3:23); 10 Audrey And Millington's Office (2:13); 11 The Curse Of Fenric (3:32); 12 High Stakes (:34); 13 The Crypt (1:21); 14 The Ambush (:42); 15 The Well Of Vergelmir (1:16); 16 The Ultima Machine (2:00); 17 Dangerous Undercurrents (1:02); 18 The Seduction Of Prozorov (1:54); 19 Half-Time Score (:40); 20 Exit Miss Hardaker/The Vicar And The Vampires (2:25); 21 Stop The Machine! (2:25); 22 The Haemovores (1:49); 23 The Battle Of St. Jude's (4:27); 24 The Mineshaft (1:51); 25 Sealing The Hatch (1:55); 26 House Guests (1:35); 27

The Telegram (:50); 28 Evil From The Dawn Of Time (1:10); 29 The Storm Breaks (3:33); 30 Ancient Enemies (3:46); 31 Shadow Dimensions (1:10); 32 Chemical Grenade (1:00); 33 The Great Serpent (:40); 34 Pawns In The Game (3:16); 35 Kathleen's Escape (2:08); 36 The Wolves At Fenric (3:08); 37 Black Wins, Time Lord! (2:22); 38 The Finale Battle (2:48); 39 Epilogue: Doctor Who (R. Grainer)(2:12).

Review: This synthesized score was written and performed by Mark Ayers for one of the final stories for long-running BBC-TV series. Of all the "Doctor Who" scores, this is perhaps one of the more well-developed, in particular its striking themes for the alien presence that pervades a World War II British Naval Camp and the adjacent town. Despite the notoriously short transitional cues that all the composers were often faced with writing, Ayers has developed a work here that on the whole builds nicely towards its climax. This was his second of three "Doctor Who" scores, both "Ghost Light" and "The Greatest Show in the Galaxy" have also been released and this album features additional music he composed for the expanded home video release. The version of the classic "Doctor Who" theme (composed by Ron Grainer) is not the version featured in the final show.

David Hirsch

Elizabeth Taylor in London/ Four in the Morning 🎵🎵🎵⁾

1992, Play It Again/U.K.; from the television special *Elizabeth Taylor in London*, 1963; and from the movie *Four in the Morning*, 1966.

Album Notes: *Music*: John Barry; *Orchestrations*: Johnny Spence, John Barry; Orchestra conducted by Johnny Spence, John Barry; *CD Producer*: Geoff Leonard; *Engineer*: Eric Tomlinson.

Selections: Elizabeth Taylor In London: 1 Elizabeth In London (3:27); 2 Elizabeth Waltz (4:31); 3 English Garden (4:54); 4 London Theme (3:18); 5 London Waltz (2:54); 6 Lovers (1:35); 7 Fire Of London (4:08); 8 Elizabeth Theme (2:42); 9 London Theme (2:51); Four In The Morning: 10 Four In The Morning (2:02); 11 River Walk (2:43); 12 Lover's Clasp (1:17); 13 Norman's Return (3:14); 14 River Ride (2:40); 15 Four In The Morning (1:57); 16 Lover's Tension (1:01); 17 First Reconciliation (3:18); 18 Norman Leaves (2:35); 19 Moment Of Decision (1:39); 20 Judi Comes Back (2:57).

Review: Written for a television special starring Elizabeth Taylor, "Elizabeth Taylor in London" elicited from Barry a gorgeously romantic score, with many beautiful tracks that have justifiably become favorites among the composer's many fans. Sonics, however, are the problem here, with the early-

'60s recording techniques denoting flaws (strident sound, tape hiss) that mar one's total enjoyment, though they could have been corrected for a digital reissue.

The score for "Four in the Morning," a series of short stories tied together around the thin device of the clock marking time, is, in contrast, much more vibrant and jazzy, though sound quality is again somewhat of a problem.

The Endless Game 🎵🎵🎵⁾

1989, Virgin Records; from the television serial *The Endless Game*, 1989.

Album Notes: *Music*: Ennio Morricone; *Orchestrations*: Ennio Morricone; Unione musicisti di Roma, conducted by Ennio Morricone; *Album Producer*: Enrico de Melis; *Engineer*: Sergio Marcotulli.

Selections: 1 The Endless Game (3:43); 2 The Love Game (3:33); 3 Alec's Journey (2:48); 4 Anif (3:10); 5 The Game Goes On (3:20); 6 Silvia's Game (4:15); 7 Summer Solitude (6:06); 8 The Endless Game (3:58); 9 Just A Game (1:00); 10 Caroline's Song (1:43); 11 Alec's Journey (4:28); 12 Chess Game (2:04); 13 From Russia (2:40).

Review: Occasionally, Ennio Morricone has created scores for television shows. In this country, he is best remembered for "Marco Polo," a score that cries out to be reissued on CD, and in Italy, he has been involved with a long series about the Bible. "The Endless Game," a cold war thriller, is another series on which he worked, and in which he indulged many of his signature characteristics (a sharp call of monosyllabic strings here, an ominous theme for low strings there). It all sounds comfortably familiar, yet surprisingly new, with some selections like "The Love Game" and "Caroline's Song" (which sounds as if it had been recycled from the score of "Malamondo") making a stronger impression because of their melodic content. Perhaps more specifically of interest to rabid Morricone fans, but also a nice discovery for those who may not be familiar with it.

ER 🎵🎵

1996, Atlantic Records; from the NBC-TV series *ER*, Amblin Entertainment, 1996.

Album Notes: *Music*: James Newton Howard, Martin Davich; *Featured Musicians*: Marc Bonilla, Michael Landau (guitars), Larry Williams (tenor sax), Steve Porcaro (synthesizers); *Producers*: James Newton Howard, Bill Schnee, Martin Davich; *Engineers*: Bill Schnee, John Cevetello.

Selections: 1 Theme From ER (J.N. Howard)(3:02); 2 Dr. Lewis And Renee (M. Davich) (1:58); 3 Canine Blues (M. Davich)

(2:28); 4 Goodbye Baby Susie (M. Davich) (3:11); 5 Doug And Carol (M. Davich/J.N. Howard)(1:59); 6 Healing Hands (M. Cohn)(4:26) *Marc Cohn*; 7 The Hero (J.N. Howard/M. Davich)(1:55); 8 Carter, See You Next Fall (M. Davich)(1:29); 9 Reasons For Living (D. Sheik) (4:33) *Duncan Sheik*; 10 Dr. Greene And A Mother's Death (M. Davich)(2:49); 11 Raul Dies (M. Davich)(2:20); 12 Hell And High Water (M. Davich/J.N. Howard) (2:38); 13 Hold On (M. Davich)(2:48); 14 Shep Arrives (M. Davich) (3:38); 15 Shattered Glass (M. Davich)(2:11); 16 Theme From ER (TV version) (J.N. Howard) (1:00); 17 It Came Upon A Midnight Clear (trad.)(2:30) *Mike Finnegan*.

Review: Last season's big hit (and probably next season's, too), "ER" received its score from composers James Newton Howard and Martin Davich, in which the accent is squarely on contemporary stylings, with lots of synthesized riffs, rhythm tracks, and all the musical trappings usually associated with modern television dramas. The truth is that it does sound a bit dry in the long run, with cues that are written to closely match the action on the screen with little consideration given to a possible soundtrack album. What stands out here are the two songs that have been added, but they are hardly sufficient to compel the listener to return frequently to the album.

Fantastic TV Themes 🎵

1991, Primetimeusa/Silva Screen Records.

Album Notes: *Arrangements*: Derek Wadsworth, Geoff Castle, Mike Townend; The Royal Philharmonic Orchestra conducted by Daniel Caine; *Album Producer*: Michael Jones; *Engineers*: Roger Wake, Austin Ince, Doug Bennett.

Selections: 1 Quantum Leap (M. Post)(3:06); 2 V: The Series (D. McCarthy) (2:43); 3 Freddy's Nightmares (N. Pike)(2:42); 4 Star Trek: The Next Generation (J. Goldsmith/A. Courage)(3:05); 5 Knight Rider (G. Larson/S. Phillips)(2:36); 6 Highway To Heaven (D. Rose)(3:20); 7 Streethawk (Tangerine Dream)(3:11); 8 Battlestar Galactica (G. Larson/S. Phillips)(3:18); 9 Airwolf (S. Levay)(3:00); 10 Buck Rogers In The 25th Century (S. Phillips)(2:24); 11 North Star: The TV Movie (B. Fiedel)(2:43); 12 Bring 'Em Back Alive (A. Rubinstein)(3:05); 13 The Return Of The Man From U.N.C.L.E. (J. Goldsmith) (2:43); 14 Tales Of The Gold Monkey (M. Post/P. Carpenter)(3:06).

Review: Obviously, a lot of money went into recording this album, and it shows in the quality of the arrangements, and the often solid performance by the Royal Philharmonic Orchestra. But is the music really worth the effort? Sometimes, the answer has to be yes: because the themes were written by composers that are among the best in the business (Jerry

Goldsmith, Dennis McCarthy, Stu Phillips), and because some of these cannot be found anywhere else. But let's face it, as a rule, TV themes are often trite little things with melodic ideas that are not too terribly substantial and are only interesting when heard within the context of a show, like a recognizable signature one can immediately forget afterwards. With some notable exceptions ("Star Trek: The Next Generation," in a performance that sounds thin compared to the original, and not too terribly true to it, either), very little here is of major importance. So, with all due respect, what difference does it make if the selection you hear next is the theme from "V: The Series," "Knight Rider," or "Streethawk"? Ultimately, this is the impression left by this CD which is highly recommended to insomniacs, and otherwise highly forgettable.

The Flintstones 🦴🦴🦴🦴▹

1994, Rhino Records; from the television series, *The Flintstones,* **Hanna-Barbera Productions, 1960-65.**

Album Notes: *Featured Performers*: Alan Reed (Fred), Jean Vander Pyl (Wilma), Mel Blanc (Barney), Bea Benaderet (Betty); *Album Producer*: Earl Kress; *Engineers*: Bill Inglot, Dan Hersch.

Selections: 1 Meet The Flintstones (Main Title, 1965)(W. Hanna/J. Barbera/ H. Curtin)(1:10); 2 Meet The Flintstones (Original album version, 1961)(W. Hanna/J. Barbera/H. Curtin)(1:55); 3 Rockin' Bird (R. Milburn)(2:08); 4 Car Hop Song (W. Hanna/J. Barbera)(3:34); 5 Star Dust (H. Carmichael)(1:27) *Hoagy Carmichael*; 6 Yabba-Dabba-Doo (W. Hanna/J. Barbera)(2:59) *Hoagy Carmichael*; 7 Happy Anniversary Quartet (G. Rossini)(1:50); 8 Lucia (G. Donizetti)(2:13); 9 Rockenschpeel Jingle (W. Hanna/J. Barbera)(1:25); 10 Bedrock Twitch (W. Hanna/J. Barbera)(2:22); 11 Old Folks At Home (S. Foster) (:45); 12 Softsoap Jingle (W. Hanna/J. Barbera)(1:14); 13 Way Outs (W. Hanna/ J. Barbera)(1:20); 14 Surfin' Craze (P.F. Sloan/ S. Barri)(2:22) *James Darren*; 15 Open Up Your Heart And Let The Sunshine In (S. Hamblen)(3:03); 16 Laugh, Laugh (R. Elliott)(3:57) *The Beau Brummels*; 17 Christmas Is My Fav'rite Time Of Year (W. Hanna/J. Barbera)(1:54); 18 Dino The Dinosaur (W. Hanna/J. Barbera)(1:33); 19 Meet The Flintstones (End Title, 1962)(W. Hanna/J. Barbera/H. Curtin)(:48); 20 The Man Called Flintstone (J. McCarthy) (1:46); 21 They'll Never Split Us Apart (C. Strouse/L. Adams)(2:44); 22 Rise And Shine (Main Title, 1960)(W. Hanna/J. Barbera)(:44); 23 Rise And Shine (End Title, 1960)(W. Hanna/J. Barbera)(3:34).

Review: Cartoon enthusiasts will adore this delightful collection of familiar tunes from the sophisticated animated sit-com, "The Flintstones." The fun-filled disc includes 23 main and end title themes, soundbites and plot songs from the show's six years of prime time on ABC (1960-1966). Patterned after the ultra successful series "The Honeymooners," "The Flintstones" enjoyed guest appearances by some of the entertainment industry's top talent. Featured on this compilation are "Yabba-Dabba-Doo!," sung by songwriter Hoagy Carmichael (the composers's big hit, "Star Dust" also makes an appearance), "Rockenschpeel Jingle," the twistin' "Bedrock Twitch," and Fred's 'Hi-Fye' version of "Rockin' Bird." A multitude of title songs ("Meet the Flinstones," "The Man Called Flintstone" among them) round out the light-hearted nature of this package.

Charles L. Granata

Forever Knight ♫♫♫

1996, GNP Crescendo; from the television series *Forever Knight*, Tri-Star Television, 1996.

Album Notes: *Music*: Fred Mollin; *Album Producer*: Fred Mollin; *Engineer*: Brian Nevin, Ray Williams.

Selections: 1 Forever Knight Theme (1:29); 2 The Hunger (F. Mollin/S. Meissner)(3:12) *Lori Yates*; 3 "What a wonderful thing Humanity is" (:15) *Nigel Bennett*; 4 Dark Knight: France 1228/Cherry Blossoms: The Ambush (3:27); 5 Suite From Queen Of Harps: Vocal Introduction/Flashback #2, The Interrogation/The Connection, Johanna Finds The Harp, Johanna In Danger/Nick Flies/Harp Attack (7:21) *Lori Yates*; 6 Suite From The Hunted: The First Murder, POV Of Danger, Vampire View/The Confrontation (5:21); 7 Nick's Piano Theme/Suite From Forward Into The Past: Flashback 1953/Nick & Natalie, The Killer Stalks Nick, Nick And Kathleen (6:56) *Geraint Wyn Davies*; 8 Black Rose (F. Mollin/S. Meissner)(3:40) *Lori Yates*; 9 Suite From Amateur Night: Playground Violence/The Chase, Alix And The Kid, The Actress Escapes (5:19); 10 "If you love something..." (:11) *Nigel Bennett*; 11 Suite From Be My Valentine: The Valentine Murder, Nat's Gift/Nick And Natalie, Lacroix Spins The Web, Nick Flies/Lacroix And Natalie (6:39); 12 Father Figure: Nick's Lullaby To Lisa (2:28); 13 Suite From Dark Knight: Alyce Drives Up, The Siege/Nick Attacks, Lacroix And Nick (6:12); 14 "You would do well to avoid me..." (:14) *Nigel Bennett*; 15 Touch The Night (F. Mollin/S. Meissner) (4:22) *Lori Yates*; 16 Avenging Angel: Time Stands Still (3:02); 17 Curiouser And Curiouser: Nick And Janette (1:40); 18 Suite From Undue Process: Natalie Cries/Natalie Sneaks, The Final Face-Off, The Graveside Goodbye (5:04); 19 Suite From A More Permanent Hell: Lacroix's Flashback, To Save Natalie, Vampire Fight (4:14); 20 Baby, Baby: CN Tower Finale (1:34); 21 "Only one thing is truly permanent" (:17) *Nigel Bennett*; 22 Dark Side Of The Glass (F. Mollin/S. Meissner)(3:22) *Lori Yates*.

Review: This lengthy, comprehensive packaging of music from the USA Networks vampire cop show offers dialogue excerpts from series heavy Nigel Bennett, Fred Mollin's electronic theme and scoring, and several songs done in a kind of Kate Bush/Tori Amos style by Lori Yates. Mollin's title theme is a deliberately monotone, pulsating suspense motif that conjures up the stalking blood thirst of the vampire hero, an effect that echoes throughout most of the scores along with some subtle period effects that underscore blood-slurping detective Nick Knight's memories of his centuries-old life. Mollin is an old hand at this sort of subject matter and he's adept at creating the impression of many more instrumental effects than would seem possible from his keyboards. The mix is effective and highly recommended to fans of the series, although the all-electronic approach (seemingly necessitated more by budget concerns than aesthetics), with its inevitable drum-machine percussion, wears out the ear well before the end of the material is reached.

Jeff Bond

Friday the 13th: The Series ♫♫♫♭

1989, GNP Crescendo; from the television series *Friday the 13th*, Paramount Television, 1989-1990.

Album Notes: *Music*: Fred Mollin; *Featured Musicians*: Bert Hermiston (saxophone), Stan Meissner (guitar); *Album Producer*: Fred Mollin; *Engineers*: Brian Nevin, Ray Williams.

Selections: 1 Friday The 13th: The Series: Opening Titles (:50); 2 The Inheritance: Thunderstorm In The City/ Tails I Live, Heads You Die: The Graveyard/ Wax Magic: Ryan Fights Chase/The End Of Marie (6:11); 3 The Baron's Bride: Micki's Trance/The Vampire's Lair/Ryan Says Goodbye/Vampire On The Loose/The Death Of Bram's Bride/Return To The Present (8:38); 4 Badge Of Honor: The Deal/Micki And Tim/Sharko Alone/The Badge Revealed/The Deal Goes Wrong/The End Of The Line (11:22); 5 Tails I Live, Heads You Die: The Death Of Micki (2:18); 6 Symphony In B Sharp: Ryan Chases The Phantom/The Death Of Leslie/The Fight To The Finish (5:32); 7 Brain Drain: Jack And Vi/Real Love/ Jack Mourns Vi (3:53); 8 Eye Of Death: The Letter/The Troops Retreat/More Retreat (4:34); 9 What A Mother Wouldn't Do: The Cradle Revealed/ Mom And Louis/Mom And The Baby/The Ultimate Sacrifice (4:46); 10 The Electrocutioner: In The Basement (2:15); 11 The Playhouse: The Children's Theme/The Playhouse Transports The Children/Carnival In Hell/The Playhouse's Anger/Safe Return (9:25); 12 Wedding In Black/Bottle Of Dreams: The Castle/Calvin And Micki/ Calvin And Micki (Something's

Wrong)/The Devil's Bride/Micki's Rescued/The Rescue Of Jack/Jack In The Globe/The Devil Takes Maya (9:22); 13 Bottle Of Dreams: The End Of The Year (1:51); 14 Friday The 13th: The Series: Closing Credits (:55).

Review: Over the series' three year run, Fred Mollin somehow managed to turn out a score for each episode almost always by himself. For each, his music had to have an intricate ambience, not that "made up on the spur of the moment" feel so many synthesizers scores often have, and this album reveals several scores that sound as orchestral as possible. Despite the series' morbid premise involving the recovery of a collection of cursed antiques, it requires a lot of personal character music, instead of the run-of-the-mill horror licks so commonly used in this format. Several of the scores featured as suites (thirteen, naturally) on this album are from episodes where Mollin had to create some of his most inventive musical motifs. One of the best, "Badge of Honor" (naturally involving a cursed police shield) has a hard hitting "Miami Vice" style rock flavor augmented with several live sax solos. More classical in nature is "Symphony in B Sharp," while the theme for the children in "The Playhouse" uses a synth chorus. "Eye of Death," a time travel story set during the civil war, uses sampled period instruments. An excellent collection of some of Mollin's best work for television.

David Hirsch

Friends ♫♫♫

1995, Reprise Records; from the television series *Friends*, 1993-95.

Album Notes: *Song Producers*: Kevin S. Bright, Paul Mitchell, The Rembrandts, Don Gehman, Gavin MacKillop, Lou Reed, k.d. lang, Ben Mink, Barenaked Ladies, Michael Phillip Wojewoda, Scott Litt, R.E.M., Matt Wallace, Paul Westerberg, Stephen Street, Paul Kimble, Joni Mitchell, Brendan O'Brien; *Executive Producers*: Kevin S. Bright, Marta Kauffman, David Crane.

Selections: 1 I'll Be There For You (TV version)(M. Skloff/A. Willis)(:53) *The Rembrandts*; 2 I Go Blind (N. Osborne)(3:11) *Hootie & The Blowfish*; 3 Good Intentions (G. Phillips/Toad)(3:19) *Toad The Wet Sprocket*; 4 You'll Know You Were Loved (L. Reed)(2:29) *Lou Reed*; 5 Sexuality (k.d. lang/B. Mink)(3:21) *k.d. lang*; 6 Shoe Box (S. Page/E. Robertson)(2:53) *Barenaked Ladies*; 7 It's A Free World Baby (J.M. Stipe/W. Berry/P. Buck/M. Mills)(5:12) *R.E.M.*; 8 Sunshine (J. Edwards)(2:23) *Paul Westerberg*; 9 Angel Of The Morning (C. Taylor)(4:08) *Pretenders*; 10 In My Room (B. Wilson/G. Usher) (2:41) *Grant Lee Buffalo*; 11 Big Yellow Taxi (Traffic Jam Mix)(J.

Mitchell) (3:59) *Joni Mitchell*; 12 Stain Yer Blood (P. Westberger)(3:02) *Paul Westberger*; 13 I'll Be There For You (long version)(M. Skloff/A. Willis)(3:10) *The Rembrandts*.

Review: Despite being bookended by the main title song ("I'll Be There For You" by The Rembrandts, presented in TV and single versions), and the insertion of dialogue after every other song, this compilation has little to do with the popular series. There are a few high powered artists here, Hootie & the Blowfish ("I Go Blind"), k.d. lang ("Sexuality") and R.E.M. ("It's a Free World Baby"), performing some excellent songs. Many of these were previously unreleased, though I can't recall any of these songs actually being used on the show. Only a brief medley of Phoebe's songs ("Snowman/Ashes/Dead Mother") appears after track #10. Where's her famous "Smelly Cat," the song everyone remembers? Bonus track alert: The instrumental TV end title follows after a short break on the tail of track #13.

David Hirsch

Gulliver's Travels ♫♫♫

1996, RCA Victor; from the TV movie *Gulliver's Travels*, RHI Entertainment and Channel Four Television, 1996.

Album Notes: *Music*: Trevor Jones; *Orchestrations*: Trevor Jones, Geoffrey Alexander, Julian Kershaw; Orchestra conducted by Geoffrey Alexander; *Album Producer*: Trevor Jones; *Engineers*: Simon Rhodes, Kirsty Whalley.

Selections: 1 Gulliver Returns Home (5:32); 2 Finding A Giant (3:24); 3 The Gates Of Mildendo (:44); 4 An Exploration (:51); 5 The Emperor's Palace (3:07); 6 Creeping And Leaping (1:00); 7 A Hero's Welcome (:53); 8 The Flight From Lilliput (3:41); 9 Journey To Bedlam (1:50); 10 Arrival In Brobdingnag (1:34); 11 Tom Finds The Bag (1:48); 12 The Doll's House (2:07); 13 Gulliver's Big Bang (1:28); 14 Grildrig's Attack (2:03); 15 Battle Of The Wasps (2:36); 16 Glumdalclitch Loses Gulliver (3:330; 17 The Flying Island (2:06); 18 Tom Won't Eat (1:32); 19 Laputa (1:14); 20 The Empress Munodi (1:02); 21 Reverse The Lodestone! (1:51); 22 The Professor Of Sunlight (2:16); 23 The Pit (1:08); 24 There's Going To Be A Storm (1:20); 25 The Sorcerer's Mirror (1:05); 26 Gulliver Calls Up The Dead (1:19); 27 Escape From The Sorcerer (1:24); 28 Mary's Letters (1:32); 29 The Immortal Sturldbruggs (1:25); 30 It's A Start (2:15); 31 Mistress (1:20); 32 The Land Of The Houyhnhnms (1:35); 33 The Yahoos (1:35); 34 Never Going Home (2:47); 35 The Houyhnhnms Cry Out (2:00); 36 Everything Is True (4:30); 37 Gulliver's Travels Closing Theme (3:35).

Review: Trevor Jones' representation on disc has always been hit and miss, his scores often pruned to two or three tracks to make room for pop songs, or worse, spoiled by the inclusion of dialogue. Thus, "Gulliver's Travels" is something of a phenomenon, in that it contains a lengthy representation of exclusively Jones' score. The main theme evokes both an epic sense and a feeling of weariness, expressing the protagonist's endless attempts to return home. "The Emperor's Palace" (perhaps the score's most enjoyable cue) features feisty woodwinds which evoke the arrogance and pettiness of the Lilliputians. A more Eastern sound figures into "Laputa", with primitive percussion and a darbuka-like synthesizer, while "Battle of the Wasps" chillingly depicts the tiny Gulliver's attempts to ward-off a swarm of giant bees.

At a running time of 75:52, the album does become a little static in the last third; the basic thematic material is really not enough to cover the running time and redundancy sets-in. Still, there is much allure to the music, and Jones has a particular knack for scoring fantasy that is matched by few others.

Paul Andrew MacLean

Hercules: The Legendary Journeys 🎵🎵

1994, Varese-Sarabande; from the TV series, *Hercules: The Legendary Journeys,* **1994-95.**

Album Notes: *Music:* Joseph LoDuca; *Orchestrations:* Tim Simonec, Larry Kenton, Joseph LoDuca; *Music Editors:* Philip Tallman, Dick Bernstein; Orchestra conducted by Tim Simonec; *Album Producer:* Joseph LoDuca; *Engineer:* Glen Neibur.

Selections: Hercules And The Circle Of Fire: 1 Main Title (1:04); 2 Hail Hercules (1:11); 3 Fight In Hera's Temple (1:52); 4 Phaedra (3:04); 5 House Of Prometheus (1:19); 6 More Time/Tickle (2:22); 7 The Circle Of Fire (1:33); 8 Zeus vs. Hercules (1:56); 9 The Cure (3:12); Hercules And The Lost Kingdom: 10 The Runners Part 1 (1:28); 11 The Runners Part 2 (:56); 12 Destiny Theme (3:03); 13 Battle With The Blue Priest (3:15); 14 The Slave Bar (1:26); 15 First You Then Stew (1:32); 16 The Runner Arrives (1:12); 17 The Cowherds Way (1:31); 18 A New Dawn (2:57); Hercules And The Amazon Women: 19 Hercules Fanfare (:32); 20 Prologue (1:48); 21 Preparing For Battle (2:44); 22 Battle With The Beast (1:40); 23 Journey To Gargarencia (1:42); 24 The Escape (1:16); 25 Battle With Hera (2:47); 26 Hyppolyta (2:07); Hercules And The Underworld: 27 Jole (2:32); 28 The Chasm (1:37); 29 Alien Cloak (1:53); 30 Forked Tongues (1:56); 31 The Old Woman (1:50); 32 Cerberus (1:34); 33 Delirious Deianeira (1:17); 34 End Title (1:06).

Review: LoDuca's scores for the pilot movies that started off the popular syndicated Hercules series are assembled here in an expansive 64-minute album that's an enjoyable listen if you can keep your mind off the numerous scores by other composers that LoDuca plunders. Among the victims are *Conan the Barbarian, Demolition Man, Clash of the Titans, Willow* and just about every score Bernard Herrmann ever did for Ray Harryhausen. LoDuca's optimistic title music comes off as a cross between John Williams' *Superman* theme and something out of *The Ten Commandments* exodus scene. The album's most original moments come from LoDuca's ethnic treatment of the "Hercules and the Amazon Women" storyline, which he later developed for "Xena: Warrior Princess" (q.v.). It's a throbbing blend of strident chanting and involving, percussive rhythms.

Jeff Bond

Hill Street Blues 🎵🎵🎵

1990, Silva Screen Records; from the television series *Hill Street Blues,* **1985.**

Album Notes: *Music:* Mike Post; Orchestra *conducted by* Daniel Caine; Adapted and Directed for Records by Derek Wadsworth; *Album Producer:* Michael Jones; *Engineer:* Roger Wake.

Selections: 1 Theme From Hill Street Blues (3:06); 2 Cruising On The Hill (2:11); 3 Field Of Honor (2:13); 4 Blues In The Day (2:07); 5 Wasted (2:15); 6 The City (1:53); 7 No Jive (3:25); 8 Freedom's End (2:03); 9 Night On The Hill (1:59); 10 Forever (1:35); 11 Councellor (2:11); 12 Captain (1:59); 13 A Friend On The Hill (1:51); 14 Officer Down (2:18); 15 Suite From Hill Street Blues (5:07).

Review: The second of two faithfully recreated Mike Post score albums by Derek Wadsworth is by far the better of the pair. Often light on the underscore, this series used music very sparingly. Post often scored the opening or closing montages and occasionally, some of the more highly charged emotional moments. He composed most of the music featured here himself, though Velton Ray Bunch ("Quantum Leap") is credited as co-composer on three of the fifteen tracks. The album alternates between the low key poignant motifs for the character sequences and the more jazzy (or bluesy) rifts that follow the officers as they patrolled "The Hill." Several of Post's shorter themes have also been assembled into a five-minute suite.

David Hirsch

In the Line of Duty 🎵🎵🎵

1992, Intrada Records; from the television series *In the Line of Duty,* **1991-92.**

Album Notes: *Music:* Mark Snow; *Album Producer:* Mark Snow; *Engineers:* Larold Rebhun, Joe Tarantino.

Selections: 1 In The Line Of Duty: Mob Justice (19:31); 2 In The Line Of Duty: The Twilight Murders (15:14); 3 In The Line Of Duty: Street War (14:40); 4 In The Line Of Duty: A Cop For The Killing (18:52).

Review: Before he became the "X-Files" composer, Mark Snow had already left his mark on many television shows (the liner notes to this album credit him with being "the most prolific composer in television," which owed him to win the ASCAP Award for the Most Performed Background Music on Television for seven consecutive years after the honor was created). Among his credits, he also scored four segments of the multi-part series "In the Line of Duty," based on real-life FBI and police cases, which enabled him to utilize the many styles at his disposal, from acoustic piano to full-blown synthesizers, with a sturdy complement of varied instruments (French horns, English horns, contrabassoons, Australian aboriginal drums, and Japanese percussion) used in a variety of styles (bebop jazz, hip-hop, bluegrass, salsa, and even Italian opera). For this CD presentation, the cues have been assembled into four long suites, something which has the advantage of giving the music greater cohesiveness. It doesn't, however, mean that it is better because of that. Unfortunately, the music written by Snow sounds quite formulaic and devoid of any real surprises. Even in this suite format, the themes are very trite, unimaginative, cut to the bones in order to fit a standard situation. One of the problems with much music on television is that it fits a single purpose as noise behind action that is usually of little consequence and can be routinely abandoned for a message from the sponsors. Even a higher class series like "In the Line of Duty" had to exist by the tenets of the medium. Snow's music does little to elevate itself above the norm.

Inspector Morse

Inspector Morse: volume one 🎵🎵🎵🎵

1995, Virgin Records/U.K.; from the ITV series *Inspector Morse*, 1991.

Album Notes: *Music:* Barrington Pheloung; Orchestra conducted by Barrington Pheloung; *Album Producer:* Graham Walker; *Engineers:* Adrian Kerridge, Dave Hunt, Chris Dribble.

Selections: 1 Inspector Morse (Main Theme: Opening Titles)(2:10); 2 Oxforshire Country Home (2:01); 3 Overture from *Die Zauberflote* (The Magic Flute), K. 620 (W.A. Mozart)(6:48); 4 A Student's Death (3:21); 5 Morse's Optimism (:55); 6 "O Isis And Osiris" (from *Die Zauberflote*, K. 620)(W.A. Mozart)(2:46) *Graham Broadbent*; 7 A Potential Murder (2:31); 8 Morse On

The Case (3:46); 9 "Laudate Dominum" (from *Vesperae Solennes de Confessore*, K. 339)(W.A. Mozart)(4:25) *Janis Kelly*; 10 Macabre Pursuit (2:05); 11 Sad Discovery (2:25); 12 "Senza Mamma" (from *Suor Angelica*)(G. Puccini) (4:57) *Janis Kelly*; 13 The Hunt (2:42); 14 Oxford College (1:15); 15 Lewis (1:02); 16 Lieder Ohne Worte, Op. 67, No. 6 in C Minor (F. Mendelssohn)(2:38) *Eleanor Alberga*; 17 Gothic Ritual (1:59); 18 Inspector Morse (Main Theme: Closing Credits)(2:32).

Inspector Morse: volume two 🎵🎵🎵🎵

1996, Virgin Records/U.K.; from the ITV series *Inspector Morse*, 1992.

Album Notes: *Music:* Barrington Pheloung; Orchestra conducted by Barrington Pheloung; *Album Producer:* Graham Walker; *Engineers:* Steve Price, Dave Hunt, John Taylor, Mike Brown.

Selections: 1 Inspector Morse Theme (ITV Version)(2:30) *Barrington Pheloung*; 2 The Warmer Side Of Morse (1:13); 3 "Che faro senza Eurydice" (from *Orfeo et Eurydice*)(C. Gluck)(3:54) *Janis Kelly*; 4 Gently Sinister Revelation (2:01); 5 Concerto For Two Mandolins in G (A. Vivaldi)(12:00) *Barrington Pheloung, Nigel North*; 6 Sad Echoes (2:26); 7 "Mitradi quell'alma ingrata" (from *Don Giovanni*)(W.A. Mozart)(5:42) *Janis Kelly*; 8 Gentle Loving (1:27); 9 Andante from Piano Sonata in D, K.311 (W.A. Mozart)(5:25) *Sally Heath*; 10 Lewis And Morse (5:30); 11 Chorale "Er Kenne Mich Mein Huter" (from *St. Matthew's Passion*) (J.S. Bach)(1:15); 12 Morse's Sympathetic Ear (3:12); 13 Adagio from Quintet in C (excerpt)(F. Schubert)(4:33); 14 Tenderness (1:13); 15 Terzettino "Soave sia il vento" (from *Cosi Fan Tutte*)(W.A. Mozart)(2:44) *Janis Kelly, Tamsin Dives, Robert Hayward*; 16 Morse's Second Chance (4:41); 17 "Signore Ascolta" (from *Turandot*)(G. Puccini)(2:47) *Janis Kelly*; 18 Inspector Morse Theme (The Full Version)(3:29) *Barrington Pheloung*.

Inspector Morse: volume three 🎵🎵🎵🎵

1997, Virgin Records/U.K.; from the ITV series *Inspector Morse*, 1992.

Album Notes: *Music:* Barrington Pheloung; Orchestra conducted by Barrington Pheloung; *Album Producer:* Graham Walker; *Engineers:* Dave Hunt, Andrew Taylor.

Selections: 1 Eirl Theme (3:41); 2 Oxford (3:41); 3 "Bei Mannern: Welche liebe fuhlen" (from *The Magic Flute*)(W.A. Mozart)(2:44) *Janis Kelly, Richard Halton*; 4 Cryptic Contemplation (3:39); 5 Andante from String Sextet No. 1 in B, op. 18 (J.S.

Bach)(9:20) *Jonathan Rees, Rosemary Furniss, Andrew Brown, Levine Andrade, Caroline Dale, Anthony Pleeth*; 6 Reflections (2:34); 7 "Traume" (from "Wesendonk Lieder")(R. Wagner) (5:07) *Susan McCulloch*; 8 Generic Morse Music (3:34); 9 Dark Suspicion (2:29); 10 Adagio from Piano Concerto, K. 488 in A (W.A. Mozart)(6:07) *Eleanor Alberga*; 11 Apprehension—Confession—Resolution (3:07); 12 Promised Land (1:53); 13 "Hab'mir's Gelobt" (from *Der Rosenkavalier*) (R. Strauss) (5:55) *Janis Kelly, Megan Kelly, Tamsin Dives*; 14 Painful Admissions (4:40); 15 "Adieu notre petite table" (from *Manon)*(J. Massenet)(3:50) *Janis Kelly*; 16 Quiet Awakening 93:46); 17 Brunnhilde's Immolation (from *Gotterdammerung)*(R. Wagner)(1:38) *Susan McCulloch*; 18 Inspector Morse Theme (3:30).

Review: In case you don't see the show on your cable television screen, "Inspector Morse" is one of those crime drama shows that come from England, with John Thaw portraying the white-haired, stubborn police inspector who usually gets his man (or woman). What sets Morse aside from other police inspectors (one hesitates to call them "cops") is the fact that he is an erudite, a scholar who loves classical music and operas, and would probably prefer to attend a concert rather than look for a miscreant guilty of some unfathomable criminal act.

As a direct result of Thaw's particular taste in music, the soundtrack to the shows frequently features excerpts from the classical catalogue, something that finds an echo in these CDs in which some selections are drawn from the works of Mozart, Bach, Gluck, Vivaldi, et al., all of which elevate the musical program to quality levels seldom met by standard television soundtracks. In addition, there is the not-so-negligible contribution by Barrington Pheloung, a composer with a classical bend of his own, whose musical cues also display a distinctive style that blends beautifully with the selections from the classical repertoire. Spearheaded with the melancholy "Theme," heard in different versions at the start and at the end of each CD, the cues are often remarkably evocative, sensibly written, and eloquently performed, occasionally by the composer himself, an accomplished instrumentalist. The series has already yielded three CDs, imported from England, and all three are worthwhile additions to any serious collection, whether you are interested in film music or not. Hopefully, there'll be further volumes released down the line.

The Key to Rebecca ♫♫♫▹

1993, Prometheus Records/Belgium; from the television mini-series *The Key to Rebecca*, 1985.

Album Notes: *Music*: J.A.C. Redford; *Orchestrations*: Doug Timm, Mark Walters, J.A.C. Redford; Orchestra conducted

by J.A.C. Redford; *Album Producer*: Alan E. Smith; *Engineer*: Mike Ross.

Selections: 1 The Key To Rebecca March (1:11); 2 Main Title/ "Be Still My Cousin"/"Ah Yes, Rebecca" (4:10); 3 Herr General (:58); 4 Homecoming (1:45); 5 Cat And Mouse (3:18); 6 Belly Dancing (2:30); 7 "Look At Me!" (1:45); 8 The Briefcase Caper (2:21); 9 Rommel's Plan (1:38); 10 "Smashing, Smashing, Smashed" (1:13); 11 Spy Talk (2:43); 12 Waiting For Change/ Wolfe's Escape/Vandam Meets The Knife (3:04); 13 Cab Trick (1:21); 14 "Wash My Hands" (2:07); 15 The Bridge (3:00); 16 Pick Up That Man! (1:00); 17 It's So Wonderful (2:58); 18 Warm Friendships (2:37); 19 Vandam's Story (1:58); 20 Field Marshall Rommel (1:05); 21 "What Have I Done?" (1:07); 22 Strange Conversation (3:20); 23 Menage A Trois (2:45); 24 Battle At The Well (1:24); 25 Elene And The Crystal (3:34); 26 Six Inches Of Steel (1:25); 27 "Fill My Canteens!" (2:07); 28 "I'll Bring Him Home!" (3:18); 29 Assyut Cabbie (1:37); 30 "Dad!"/ Wolfe's End (5:19); 31 A Better Man/End Credits (2:45).

Review: Composer J.A.C. Redford deftly mixes numerous middle eastern motifs with a great *Patton*-like military march into his score for this 1985 four-hour television mini-series. Adapted from Ken Follett's spy-thriller about the chase of a Nazi master of disguise by a British officer, the range the story demands allows for several musical changes of pace, which include a "Belly Dancing" theme and the big band "Spy Talk," to name just a few. Of course, there are also many of the obligatory chase cues. This is a better than average TV score with a lot to offer.

David Hirsch

The Late Shift ♫♫♫▹

1996, Silva America; from the HBO movie *The Late Shift*, 1996.

Album Notes: *Music*: Ira Newborn; *Music Editors*: Alan K. Rosen, Patty Von Arx; *Synthesizer Programming*: Stuart Goldberg; Orchestra conducted by Ira Newborn; *Featured Musicians*: Bob Mann, Ira Newborn (guitars), Joel Peskin (tenor/alto sax), Walt Johnson, Pete Christlieb (tenor sax); *Album Producer*: Ford A. Thaxton; *Engineer*: James Nelson.

Selections: 1 "Here's Johnny" (The Tonight Show Theme(P. Anka/J. Carson) (1:19); 2 Pitch Montage (1:44); 3 "Let's Steal Him" (1:13); 4 "It's Our Turn Now" (1:27); 5 Conclusions (2:01); 6 Stupid Pets (1:18); 7 A Fat Check (1:53); 8 There Goes Johnny (:53); 9 The Emmy Party (3:13); 10 The NBC Meeting (1:40); 11 Jay Leno, Secret Agent (2:25); 12 The Last Temptation Of David Letterman (2:53); 13 More Pitches (1:42); 14 Letterman's Triumph (1:28); 15 There's No Business Like Show Business (I. Berlin)(3:54).

Review: The selling point of this CD's cover is a line that touts "Here's Johnny" ("The Tonight Show" Theme) as performed by Doc Severinsen and his Band so strongly that score composer Ira Newborn's credit is almost completely overshadowed. And yet, after starting off with that often heard tune, you'll discover that Newborn contributes a breezy pop score that adds just the right amount of absurdity to this film, a recreation of the true story of a war between the networks for late night supremacy that began after Johnny Carson announced his plan to retire from "The Tonight Show." Newborn plays up the on-screen action to achieve a true sense of the preposterous ("Jay Leno, Secret Agent" for example). Agents, network executives and on-air talent prance around each other as if they were cold-war spies on a mission to save all life. Delightfully engaging.

David Hirsch

The Legend of Prince Valiant ♫♫♫

1991, Mesa Records; from the television animated series *The Legend of Prince Valiant,* **1991.**

Album Notes: *Music:* Steve Sexton, Gerald O'Brien; *Album Producers:* Exchange; *Engineers:* Exchange, Kim Bullard, John Goodenough, Patrick Giraudi.

Selections: 1 Where The Truth Lies (Exchange/M. Jordan)(4:00) *Marc Jordan;* 2 Celebration Dance (1:58); 3 Sir Bryant (3:26); 4 Love Called Out My Name (Exchange/M. Jordan)(4:19) *Amy Sky, Marc Jordan;* 5 Guinevere (2:24); 6 Search and Journey (2:55); 7 In The Shadows (1:22); 8 Valiant's Theme (3:24); 9 A Monks Evil Drone (1:56); 10 Ending Title Theme (1:00); 11 The Majesty's Feast (2:15); 12 The Serenade (2:18); 13 Valiant And Rolf (1:22); 14 Victory March (1:53); 15 All Alone (2:35); 16 Danger Is Near (1:45); 17 Valiant Leaves Home (1:36); 18 Where The Truth Lies (Exchange/M. Jordan)(reprise)(1:22) *Marc Jordan.*

Review: The score for this animated feature, not drawn by Hal Foster, was created by Steve Sexton and Gerald O'Brien, two synthesists working under the pseudonym of Exchange. The music they conceived is generally very attractive, with melodic themes that are frequently catchy and enjoyable, though they rely a bit too much on the formula sounds that seem to prevail in television soundtracks these days—repetitive background riffs, with melodic lines that are relatively simple and of one mind, without much invention behind. The apparently manda-

> "Irving Berlin has no place in American music. He is American music."
>
> **Jerome Kern**
> *(in Alexander Woollcott's biography, "The Story of Irving Berlin," Putnam, 1925)*

tory songs that have been included also seem totally out of place in the context.

Masada ♫♫♫♫♫

1990, Varese-Sarabande; from the TV movie, *Masada,* **1981.**

Album Notes: *Music:* Jerry Goldsmith; *Orchestrations:* Arthur Morton; *Music Editor:* Ken Hall; Orchestra conducted by Jerry Goldsmith; *Album Producer:* Jerry Goldsmith; *Engineer:* Eric Tomlinson.

Selections: 1 Main Title (5:04); 2 The Old City (3:26); 3 The Planting (2:56); 4 The Road To Masada (6:54); 5 Night Raid (3:30); 6 Our Land (4:41); 7 The Encampment (2:30); 8 No Water (2:30); 9 The Slaves (5:14).

Review: A mini-series that recounted the siege and destruction of Masada, a fortress of Judean rebels, by the Roman army, "Masada" is a rare case of a television show that transcended the medium and actually aimed at a higher level of quality and distinction. That it succeeded was due in large part to the fact that it was treated not like a television series but like a feature film, with considerable financial means put at the service of the project. One smart decision on the part of the producers was to hire Jerry Goldsmith to write the score. As a result, the music, as sampled on this soundtrack album, is of a high quality level seldom experienced on television, with elaborate themes setting the locale, the people, the action. Impressive as the whole score is, it can be said that Goldsmith surpassed himself when he composed "The Road to Masada". The series' main theme, a superb march, is reprised to best effect the advancing Roman legions, then, in a more subdued way, to depict the rebels awaiting with anguish the arrival of the enemy troops. If ever a score could be described as truly exciting, the term perfectly fits here. At times thrilling, at other times profoundly moving, "Masada" remains quite an accomplishment in the composer's body of works.

Miami Vice

Miami Vice

1985, MCA Records; from the television series *Miami Vice*, 1985.

Album Notes: *Music*: Jan Hammer; *Song Producers*: Glen Frey & Allan Blazek, Arif Mardin & Joe Mardin, Phil Collins, Rupert Hine; *Album Executive Producers*: Danny Goldberg, Michael Mann; *Engineer*: Stephen Marcussen.

Selections: 1 The Original Miami Vice Theme (J. Hammer)(1:00); 2 Smuggler's Blues (G. Frey/J. Tempchin)(3:48) *Glen Frey*; 3 Own The Night (F. Golde/M.D. Lauria/M. Sharron)(4:49) *Chaka Khan*; 4 You Belong To The City (G. Frey/J. Tempchin)(5:49) *Glen Frey*; 5 In The Air Tonight (P. Collins)(5:27) *Phil Collins*; 6 Miami Vice (J. Hammer)(2:26); 7 Vice (M. Glover/N. Chinn/H. Knight) (4:59) *Grandmaster Melle Mel*; 8 Better Be Good To Me (M. Chapman/N. Chinn/H. Knight)(5:08) *Tina Turner*; 9 Flashback (J. Hammer)(3:20); 10 Chase (J. Hammer)(2:38); 11 Evan (J. Hammer)(3:06).

Review: See entry below.

Miami Vice II ♪♪♪▷

1986, MCA Records; from the television series *Miami Vice*, 1986.

Album Notes: *Music*: Jan Hammer; *Song Producers*: Bob Rose, Michael Verdick, Stephen Bray & Howie Rice, Phil Collins & Hugh Padgham, Jay Gradon, Andy Taylor & Steve Jones, Roxy Music & Rhett Davies, Jackson Browne, Jon Kelly; *Album Executive Producer*: Michael Mann; *Engineer*: Steve Hall.

Selections: 1 Mercy (4:27) *Steve Jones*; 2 Send It To Me (4:12) *Gladys Knight & The Pips*; 3 Take Me Home (5:51) *Phil Collins*; 4 The Last Unbroken Heart (3:53) *Patti LaBelle, Bill Champlin*; 5 Crockett's Theme (J. Hammer) (3:25); 6 When The Rain Comes Down (3:52) *Andy Taylor*; 7 Lover (3:52) *Roxy Music*; 8 Lives In The Balance (4:13) *Jackson Browne*; 9 In Dulce Decorum (4:34) *The Damned*; 10 Miami Vice: New York Theme (J. Hammer)(3:53); 11 The Original Miami Vice Theme (J. Hammer)(:59).

Review: Outside of the fact that this is strictly formulaic music, designed to underscore an action series that was the hippest show on television for a hot minute, two things become immediately apparent on these CDs. The first one, Jan Hammer's music is not really that good: it worked very well within the context of the show itself, but on its own it doesn't withstand close scrutiny. The second is that, because of its success, the series was able to attract some talented performers whose songs made the show even more attractive to the average viewers. In the first CD, for instance, if "Own the Night" by Chaka Khan, or "Smuggler's Blues" by Glen Frey are just okay, "You Belong to the City," also by Frey, and mostly "In the Air Tonight" by Phil Collins, and "Better Be Good to Me," by Tina Turner, are of a high pop caliber; likewise, in disc 2, the combination of Phil Collins ("Take Me Home"), Gladys Knight & The Pips ("Send It to Me"), and Patti LaBelle & Bill Champlin ("The Last Unbroken Heart") is a winner, again as long as you can live with Hammer's trite synthesizer-cum-rhythm-track cues that are only good for a moment.

Mission: Impossible ♪♪♪♪▷

1996, Hip-O Records; from the television series *Mission: Impossible*, 1967-68.

Album Notes: *Music*: Lalo Schifrin; *Orchestrations*: Lalo Schifrin; Orchestra conducted by Lalo Schifrin; *Featured Musicians*: Mike Melvoin (piano), Lalo Schifrin (piano, harpsichord), Bill Plummer (sitar), Bud Shank (alto sax), Stu Williamson (trumpet); *Album Producer*: Tom Mack; *Engineer*: Hank Cicalo; *CD Producer*: Andy McKaie; *Engineer*: Doug Schwartz.

Selections: 1 Mission: Impossible (2:33); 2 Jim On The Move (3:16); 3 Operation Charm (2:58); 4 The Sniper (3:21); 5 Roll In Hand (2:53); 6 The Plot (2:29); 7 Wide Willy (2:05); 8 Cinnamon (The Lady Was Made To Be Loved)(J. Urbont/B. Geller)(2:38); 9 Barney Does It All (2:32); 10 Danger (2:44); 11 Mission: Accomplished (2:43); 12 Intrigue (2:34); 13 Self-Destruct (2:38); 14 More Mission (2:46).

Review: Probably no television theme has had as much impact as the one created by Lalo Schifrin for "Mission: Impossible," with its signature syncopated beat. Just to hear it on this CD brings back many memories about a series that was vibrantly exciting, even if at times the high-tech derring-dos seemed a bit far fetched. The musical cues written by Schifrin, while closely tailored to fit the action on the screen, are also quite enjoyable in a different context, and provide pleasant musical entertainment. Several reliable jazz musicians add their own flavor to the cues, with Schifrin himself heard on piano and harpsichord.

Mr. Lucky ♪♪♪♪▷

1988, RCA Records; from the CBS-TV series *Mr. Lucky*, 1960.

Album Notes: *Music*: Henry Mancini; Orchestra conducted by Henry Mancini; *Album Producer*: Dick Peirce; *Engineer*: Al Schmitt; *CD Producer*: Chick Crumpacker; *Engineers*: Ed Rich, Dick Baxter.

Selections: 1 Mr. Lucky (2:12); 2 My Friend Andamo (3:31); 3 Softly (2:44); 4 March Of The Cue Balls (3:15); 5 Lightly Latin (2:56); 6 Tipsy (2:31); 7 Floating Pad (2:53); 8 One Eyed Cat (3:15); 9 Night Flower (2:25); 10 Chime Time (3:16); 11 Blue Satin (2:35); 12 That's It And That's All (2:54).

Review: After making much of an impression with his score for the series "Peter Gunn," his first collaboration with Blake Edwards, Henry Mancini contributed the flavorful music to another series, also directed by Edwards, "Mr. Lucky." Different from the previous show, which had its own parameters, the new series suggested to the composer another musical approach, in which Latin rhythms combine with a Hammond organ to depict the specific atmosphere which permeates the series. Typical of Mancini, however, the themes remain solidly melodic and catchy, with the main theme quickly establishing itself as a runaway hit. The CD emphasizes the best moments from the score, with some selections, like "Softly," "Lightly Latin," "March of the Cue Balls," and "Blue Satin" emerging among the most engaging.

Mobil Masterpiece Theatre
♪♪♪♪♪

1996, Delos Records; from the WGBH Educational TV shows, 1971-96.

Album Notes: *Album Executive Producer*: Amelia S. Haygood; *A&R*: Al Lutz; *Mastering*: Ramiro Belgardt.

Selections: 1 Masterpiece Theatre Series Music (television version)((J.J. Mouret)(:57); 2 Theme One From Upstairs, Downstairs (A. Faris)(1:28); 3 Theme Two From Upstairs, Downstairs (A. Faris)(1:09); 4 Theme From Poldark (K. Emrys-Roberts)(4:57); 5 Theme From I, Claudius (W. Josephs)(1:33); 6 Theme From Love For Lydia (H. Rabinowitz)(3:50); 7 Theme From The Duchess Of Duke Street (A. Faris)(2:09); 8 Theme From The Citadel (M. Stuckey)(2:16); 9 Theme From To Serve Them All My Days (K. Emrys-Roberts)(1:37); 10 Theme From The Irish R.M. (N. Bicat)(2:07); 11 Theme One From The Jewel In The Crown (G. Fenton)(2:32); 12 Theme Two From The Jewel In The Crown (G. Fenton)(1:54); 13 Theme From By The Sword Divided (K. Howard/A. Blaikley) (2:19); 14 Theme From On Approval (G. Gershwin)(3:02); 15 Theme From A Town Like Alice (B. Smeaton) (2:00); 16 Theme One From The Flame Trees Of Thika (K. Howard/A. Blaikley) (2:26); 17 Theme Two From The Flame Trees Of Thika (K. Howard/A. Blaikley) (3:22); 18 Theme One From Prime Suspect: The Lost Child (S. Warbeck) (4:11); 19 Theme Two From Prime Suspect: The Lost Child (S. Warbeck)(1:48); 20 Masterpiece Theatre Series Music (complete version)(2:00).

Review: For many years a staple on Public Television, "Masterpiece Theatre" has earned an enviable reputation as one of the most distinguished series on television. Many of the shows that have been presented as part of the series have become landmarks in their own right and are often mentioned with awe and admiration. This CD purports to bring together some of the themes that were created for some of the shows in the series, including "Upstairs, Downstairs," "The Jewel in the Crown," "I, Claudius," "A Town Like Alice," and "The Flame Trees of Thika." The themes are presented here in their original versions, with the composers usually conducting their own works, and the CD introduced by Mouret's celebrated theme. They simply can't get any better than that!

The Music from U.N.C.L.E. (The Original Soundtrack Affair) ♪♪♪⁺

1997, Razor & Tie Records; from the television series *The Man From U.N.C.L.E.*, 1964.

Album Notes: *Music*: Robert Drasnin, Gerald Fried, Jerry Goldsmith, Walter Scharf, Lalo Schifrin, Morton Stevens; *Arrangements*: Hugo Montenegro; Orchestra conducted by Hugo Montenegro; *Album Producers*: Mike Ragogna, David Richman, Lisa Sutton; *Engineer*: Elliott Federman.

Selections: 1 (Theme From) The Man From U.N.C.L.E. (J. Goldsmith)(2:02); 2 The Invaders (J. Goldsmith)(2:29); 3 Wild Bike (M. Stevens)(2:32); 4 Illya (L. Schifrin)(2:10); 5 Off And Running (R. Drasnin)(2:29); 6 Boo-Bam-Boo, Baby (G. Fried)(1:53); 7 Run Spy Run (G. Fried)(2:15); 8 Solo On A Raft (W. Scharf) (1:53); 9 Jungle Beat (G. Fried)(2:01); 10 There They Go (R. Drasnin)(2:11); 11 Lament For A Trapped Spy (G. Fried)(2:22); 12 The Man From T.H.R.U.S.H. (L. Schifrin)(2:10); 13 Slink (G. Fried)(2:13); 14 Solo Busanova (R. Drasnin)(2:11); 15 Dance Of The Flaming Swords (G. Fried)(2:36).

Review: The "(Theme From) The Man From U.N.C.L.E.," with its pounding rhythm beat, organ obbligato and electric guitar strumming, brings back fond memories of a series that had many great moments in it. Soon, however, the overall stridency in the sound itself makes one wish that a little more control had been exerted in the transfer of these excerpts. Much of this comes from the fact that the music was brash to begin with, having a relentless beat that properly defined the action in the series, but also from the fact that Hugo Montenegro's orchestrations emphasize the very brassy elements that now seem to be somewhat annoying when you have to listen to them in an isolated environment. This comment set aside, one cannot deny the fact that "The Man From U.N.C.L.E." attracted many composers who went on to do much bigger and better things (Jerry Goldsmith, Gerald Fried, and Lalo Schifrin, among them), something that also gives the music a greater importance than it probably had initially.

Northern Exposure

Northern Exposure ♫♫▿

1992, MCA Records; from the television series *Northern Exposure*, 1990-92.

Album Notes: *Music*: David Schwartz; *Song Producers*: Bill Elliott, David Schwartz; *Featured Musicians*: David Schwartz (keyboards, bass), Jim Keltner, Alex Acuna (drums), Abe Most (clarinet), Brian Mann (accordion), Andy Narell (steel drums), Luis Conte, Jim McGrath, Alex Acuna (percussion), Tollak Ollestad (chromatic harmonica), Bill Elliott (vibes, piano), Paul Viapiano (banjo, mandolin), Phil Ayling (wood flute); *Album Executive Producers*: John Brand, John Falsey; *Engineers*: Les Brockmann, David Schwartz.

Selections: 1 Theme From Northern Exposure (3:04); 2 Jolie Louise (D. Lanois)(2:39) *Daniel Lanois*; 3 Hip Hug-her (S. Cropper/B.T. Jones/A. Jackson, Jr./D. Z. Dunn)(2:24) *Booker T. & The MG's*; 4 At Last (H. Warren/M. Gordon)(2:59) *Etta James*; 5 Everybody Be Yoself (Chic Street Man)(3:06) *Chic Street Man*; 6 Alaskan Nights (2:40); 7 Don Quichotte (J.L. Drion/D. Regiacorte)(5:08) *Magazine 60*; 8 When I Grow Too Old To Dream (S. Romberg/O. Hammerstein II)(3:30) *Nat King Cole and His Trio, Stuff Smith*; 9 Emabhaceni (M. Makeba)(2:39) *Miriam Makeba*; 10 Gimme Three Steps (R. Van Zant/A. Collins)(4:27) *Lynyrd Skynyrd*; 11 Bailero (from *Chants d'Auvergne*) (J. Canteloube)(6:25) *Frederica von Stade, Royal Philharmonic Orchestra, Antonio de Almeida*; 12 Medley: A Funeral In My Brain/Woody The Indian/The Tellakutans (3:30).

Review: See entry below.

More Music from Northern Exposure ♫♫♫▿

1994, MCA Records; from the television series *Northern Exposure*, 1990-94.

Album Notes: *Music*: David Schwartz; *Song Producers*: Gordon Bird, Johnny Nash, Gareth Jones, David Schwartz, The Basin Brothers, Greg Poree, Vinx, Brian Eno, Paul Ortega, Joanne Shenandoah; *Album Producer*: Kathy Nelson; *Engineer*: Tom Baker.

Selections: 1 Ojibway Square Dance (Love Song)(trad.)(1:58) *Georgia Wettlin-Larsen*; 2 Theme From Northern Exposure (D.

Schwartz)(:45); 3 Stir It Up (B. Marley)(3:02) *Johnny Nash*; 4 Mambo Baby (C. Singleton/R. McCoy)(2:40) *Ruth Brown*; 5 Someone Loves You (S. Bonney)(5:32) *Simon Bonney*; 6 The Ladder (D. Schwartz)(2:10); 7 If You Take Me Back (J. McCoy)(2:44) *Big Joe & His Washboard Band*; 8 Un marriage casse (A Broken Marriage)(A. Berard/D. Collet)(3:08) *Basin Brothers*; 9 There I Go Again (Vinx/L. Parrette)(5:44) *Vinx*; 10 Lay My Love (B. Eno/J. Cale)(4:43) *Brian Eno, John Cale*; 11 Wrap Your Troubles In Dreams (And Dream Your Troubles Away)(T. Koehler/B. Moll/H. Barris)(3:08) *Les Paul, Mary Ford*; 12 Mooseburger Stomp (D. Schwartz) (2:06); 13 I May Want A Man (J. Shenandoah/D. Shenandoah)(3:59) *Joanne Shenandoah*.

Review: This eclectic mix of musical styles, ranging from down home blues to African rhythms to Frederica Von Stade singing opera, is very appropriate to the series' closet intellectual nature. The album is assembled as if it represented a day in the programmed life of the local radio station, K-BEAR. An expanded version of David Schwartz' droll main title (using Jamaican kettle drums for a show set in Alaska!) starts off the listener's journey, which then migrates from familiar artists such as Booker T. & The MG's ("Hip Hug-Her"), Etta James ("At Last"), and Nat "King" Cole ("When I Grow Too Old to Dream") to the more bizarre works by the likes of Magazine 60 ("Don Quichotte"). Six minutes of underscore is included and a second volume followed. It is an acquired taste that not all will find interesting after the first experience.

The soundtrack for "Northern Exposure" has rightfully been described in GQ as "the weirdest — and the best — music on prime time," an assessment that needs no explanation. David Schwartz's instrumental cues have a flavor all their own, which is distinguished and quite enjoyable. Bringing a totally different flavor to the two CDs are performances by a wide array of frontline performers like Booker T. & The Mgs, Etta James, Nat "King" Cole, Miriam Makeba, and (gasp!) Frederica von Stade, in the first volume; and Johnny Nash, Ruth Brown, Brian Eno and John Cale, and Les Paul and Mary Ford, in the second. How much more eclectic than that can you get? Taken together, on their individual merits, both CDs are quite engaging.

David Hirsch/Didier C. Deutsch

O Pioneers! ♫♫♫♫

1991, Intrada Records; from the Hallmark Hall of Fame presentation *O Pioneers!*, Lorimar Television, 1991.

Album Notes: *Music*: Bruce Broughton; *Orchestrations*: Don Nemitz; *Music Editor*: Patricia Peck; Orchestra conducted by

Bruce Broughton; *Album Producer*: Bruce Broughton; *Engineer*: Robert Fernandez.

Selections: 1 The Land (3:49); 2 Carl And Alexandra (2:21); 3 The Promise (3:11); 4 The Seagull (:40); 5 Carl's Goodbye (1:40); 6 Alexandra's Trip (2:45); 7 Meet Marie (2:24); 8 Carl Returns (3:28); 9 A Conversation (1:36); 10 Only One Thing Left (1:31); 11 Carl Leaves Again (1:55); 12 Alexandra's Fantasy (2:17); 13 Bishop's Cavalcade (3:47); 14 Suspicion, Sin And Death (5:13); 15 Graveside (:42); 16 When Friends Marry (4:27); 17 O Pioneers (:53).

Review: In one of his early efforts, composer Bruce Broughton wrote a distinctive Americana-styled score for this Hallmark Hall Of Fame show, a faithful adaptation of the Willa Cather novel, starring Jessica Lange as Alexandra. The score is anchored by three basic motifs: one for the main character and her passion for the land; the second, romantically delineated, for Carl and the relationship that exists between him and Alexandra; and the third, light and jaunty, for the Bohemian girl Marie, whose illicit love affair with Alexandra's brother Emil is doomed from the start. A connective theme links these motifs together. Richly evocative and strikingly beautiful, the score is greatly appealing and an instant classic.

The Old Man and the Sea ♫♫♫♪

1989, Intrada Records; from the television special *The Old Man and the Sea*, Yorkshire Television, 1989.

Album Notes: *Music*: Bruce Broughton; *Orchestrations*: Mark McKenzie, Albert Olsen; The Graunke Symphony Orchestra, conducted by Bruce Broughton; *Album Producer*: Bruce Broughton; *Engineer*: Mike Ross.

Selections: 1 Main Title (2:09); 2 Santiago (1:41); 3 Picking Up Manolo (1:21); 4 Angela And Santiago (1:51); 5 Santiago Sets Off (1:46); 6 Bonita (1:04); 7 The Fish (2:04); 8 The Couple (2:25); 9 First Blood (2:38); 10 I Would Stay (2:36); 11 The Fish Sounds (7:03); 12 Manolo In The Shack (:55); 13 The Shark (1:38); 14 Angela And Manolo (1:05); 15 Second Attack (3:27); 16 A Tired Old Man (3:04); 17 Santiago Returns (6:27); 18 What A Fish (1:12); 19 End Credits (1:15).

Review: Unfortunately, Bruce Broughton's score for this television remake of "The Old Man and the Sea" cannot escape comparisons with the music written by Dimitri Tiomkin for the 1958 film of the same name starring Spencer Tracy. Fortunately, Broughton happens to be a very creative composer, who rose to the challenge in ways that command admiration. Much of his music has an appealling Spanish flavor that's

indigenous to the locale and the main characters of the Old Man and the boy he befriends. With a guitar strumming the themes to a subtle accompaniment of strings and maracas, or in duets with a flute, the score develops into a suite with an identity all its own that owes nothing to its illustrious predecessor. It's quite effective and quite affecting, and it stands out as a superb listening experience that invites frequent returns. Now, about Anthony Quinn as the Old Man...

Oldest Living Confederate Widow Tells All ♫♫♪

1994, Milan Records; from the television mini-series *Oldest Living Confederate Widow Tells All*, 1994.

Album Notes: *Music*: Mark Snow; *Music Editor*: Marty Wereski; *Featured Musician*: Kelly Parkinson (violin); *Album Producer*: David Franco; *Engineers*: Glen Neibaur, Larold Rebhun, Joe Gastwirt.

Selections: 1 Main Title (1:31); 2 Resolution (1:04); 3 Captain Marsden Looks Back (3:47); 4 The New Life (2:58); 5 Archie's Burning Up (3:29); 6 Having The Baby/All About Ned (3:13); 7 Something's Burning/Voodoo/White Folk (2:32); 8 Lucy Is Pregnant/Lucy Sneaks Off (3:11); 9 Lucy Remembers (2:10); 10 Swimming Hole Incident (1:24); 11 The Midwife/Talking About The Past (2:25); 12 The Marsden Mansion/No More Guns (5:47); 13 We're Married Again (3:25); 14 Castalia's Home (1:03); 15 Dead Ducks (3:35); 16 Lucy In The Mirror (2:26); 17 End Credits (1:04).

Review: One of the most popular television mini-series of the 1993-94 season, "Oldest Living Confederate Widow Tells All" enabled "X-Files" composer Mark Snow to contribute a largely orchestral score that's as far separated from the adventures of Fox Mulder and Dana Scully as one could imagine. Highlighted by a lyrical main theme, the tone of Snow's music is alternately pleasant or melodramatic throughout, nicely punctuating the drama of a virtual century in the life of a Southern woman (Diane Lane), who changes with the times and attitudes of various generations. Snow's music is genteel but forgettable, but it's still a nice album that will be of particular interest to those who think that the composer's works only consist of droning synthesizers and atonal chords.

Andy Dursin

Party of Five ♫♫♫♪

1996, Reprise Records; from the television series *Party of Five*, Columbia Pictures, 1996.

Album Notes: *Song Producers*: Scotty Morris, Russ Castillo, Russ Titelman, Brian Transeau, David Gamson, Chaka Khan,

Joe Jackson, Ed Roynesdal, Syd Straw, Michael Campbell, Holly Palmer, Kenny White, Howard Jones, Andy Ross, Rickie Lee Jones, Glyn Johns, Bill Bottrell, John Leventhal, Larry Klein, Greg Goldman; *Engineers*: Russ Castillo, Danny Bernini, Brian Transeau, Rail Rogut, Larry Alexander, Lou Whitney, Mark Linnett, Roger Moutenot, Avril MacIntosh, David Cole, Jack Joseph Puig, Blair Lamb, Dan Marnien Greg Goldman.

Selections: 1 Closer To Free (Llanas/Neumann)(3:09) *Bodeans*; 2 Cruel Spell (S. Morris/J. Mandel)(5:18) *Big Bad Voodoo Daddy*; 3 Without Letting Go (L. Sargent)(3:20) *Laurie Sargent*; 4 Blue Skies (B. Transeau)(5:04) *BT, Tori Amos*; Amos, Tori,5 Love Me Still (C. Khan/B. Hornsby)(3:26) *Chaka Khan*; 6 Stranger Than Fiction (J. Jackson)(3:40) *Joe Jackson*; 7 People Of Earth (S. Straw)(4:20) *Syd Straw*; 8 Free Fallin' (T. Petty/J. Lynne)(5:33) *Stevie Nicks*; 9 All I Really Wanna Do (B. Dylan)(4:59) *Holly Palmer*; 10 If You Love Me (H. Jones)(4:32) *Howard Jones*; 11 Sunshine Superman (D. Leitch) (3:15) *Rickie Lee Jones*; 12 It's A Hard Life Wherever You Go (N. Griffith) (4:01) *Nanci Griffith*; 13 Send Me On My Way (R. Root)(4:19) *Rusted Root*; 14 Climb On (A Back That's Strong)(S. Colvin/J. Leventhal)(4:12) *Shawn Colvin*; 15 Heart Of A Miracle (Llanas/ Neumann)(4:11) *Bodeans*.

Review: This modern rock friendly TV series gave BoDeans a much-deserved hit with the peppy theme song, "Closer to Free." The rest of the set feels like a cash-in, particularly on some oddball covers—Stevie Nicks doing Tom Petty's "Free Fallin'" and Rickie Lee Jones' singing Donovan's "Sunshine Superman." Joe Jackson's "Stranger Than Fiction" is always worth a listen, though, and it's a good chance to catch some up-and-comers such as Holly Palmer and Laurie Sargent.

Gary Graff

Peter Gunn 🎜🎜🎜🎜▵

1986, RCA Records; from the NBC-TV series *Peter Gunn*, 1959.

Album Notes: *Music*: Henry Mancini; Orchestra conducted by Henry Mancini; *CD Producer*: Susan Ruskin; *Engineer*: Rick Rowe.

Selections: 1 Peter Gunn (2:04); 2 Sorta Blue (2:56); 3 The Brothers Go To Mother's (2:55); 4 Dreamsville (3:54); 5 Session At Pete's Pad (3:58); 6 Soft Sounds (3:34); 7 Fallout! (3:08); 8 The Floater (3:16); 9 Slow And Easy (3:03); 10 A Profound Gass (3:18); 11 Brief And Breezy (3:30); 12 Not From Dixie (4:08).

Review: In a rare foray into television, Henry Mancini scored this series for Blake Edwards, the first time both men worked together. As Mancini recalled in later years, Edwards was looking for a score that would be contemporary and rooted in jazz for the mystery adventure series about a big city police detective whose investigations often took him to various jazz clubs. So strong and evocative is Mancini's score that it won the composer an Emmy Award, while the soundtrack album became a million-seller and received two Grammys. In fact, the success of the album spawned a second volume, "More Music From Peter Gunn," which was reissued in Europe but not in this country.

Several tunes from "Peter Gunn" became pop favorites, "Sorta Blue," "Dreamsville," and "Slow and Easy," among them, but the score in its entirety is quite enticing and powerful enough to stand on its own musical merits. The mastering, however, leaves a lot to be desired, and could stand a thorough overhaul.

Peter the Great 🎜🎜🎜🎜▵

1986, Southern Cross Records; from the NBC TV presentation *Peter the Great*, 1986.

Album Notes: *Music*: Laurence Rosenthal; *Orchestrations*: Steve Bramson; *Music Editor*: Dan Carlin; The Bavarian State Orchestra of Munich, and the Choir of l'Eglise Russe Saint-Serge of Paris, conducted by Laurence Rosenthal; *Album Producer*: Laurence Rosenthal; *Engineer*: Malcolm Laker.

Selections: 1 Main Title (2:04); 2 Cathedral (1:03); 3 Alexander (3:15); 4 The Tartars (2:01); 5 Two Living Tsars (4:25); 6 His First Sail/The Foreign Colony (5:42); 7 Eudoxia (4:19); 8 Peter's Wedding (:55); 9 Tsar And Tsaritsa (:37); 10 The New Tsarevich (1:14); 11 Death Of Natalia/The Slap (3:26); 12 Ivan Is Dead (3:10); 13 The Great Embassy (3:10); 14 Gopak (1:14); 15 Moscow Is Burning (3:25); 16 Alexis And Danilo (1:51); 17 Bells Into Cannons (1:59); 18 The Torch (1:20); 19 Battle Of Poltava (4:21); 20 Sophia And Alexis/Ordeal/ Martyrdom (3:10); 21 Requiem (2:12); 22 Peter's Theme (End Credits)(1:03).

Review: Laurence Rosenthal's flavorful score for this sweeping epic gets its inspiration and strength from two widely different sources—the incomparable liturgy of the Russian Orthodox Church, and the profoundly human world of Russian folksongs. The first finds its expression in the court rituals (coronations, weddings, funerals), in which the presence of the Church was a dominating factor. The second is expertly interwoven in the colorful tapestry of characters that peopled the brutal tale of one of Russia's most powerful tsars, with the most important players in the story getting a specific leitmotif, as well as the locales where the action took place. All these elements combine to create a set of cues that are strongly reflective of the action, yet succeed in having a different, albeit compelling appeal once removed from their primary purpose. Some selections, like "The Tartars," "Moscow Is Burning," and "Battle of Poltava" are noticeably impressive.

Phantom of the Forest ♪♪♪♪▷

1994, Narada Cinema; from the WNET-TV series *Nature,* Survival Anglia Ltd., 1994.

Album Notes: *Music:* Michael Whalen; *Orchestrations:* Michael Whalen; Orchestra conducted by Michael Whalen; *Featured Musicians:* Michael Whalen (synclavier/percussion/synthesizers), Harvey Estrin (recorders/flute/Pan flutes), Carolyn Pollak (oboe/ English horn), Russ Rizner (French horn), Emily Mitchell (harp), Mitch Estrin (clarinet/bass clarinet), Marti Sweet (violin), Pat Rebillot (piano); *Album Producer:* Michael Whalen; *Engineer:* Roy Hendrickson.

Selections: 1 Spirits (1:49); 2 Sea Of Trees (1:31); 3 The Hawk Appears (:52); 4 Killing To Survive (:57); 5 The Wood Cock (1:18); 6 Open Spaces (1:23); 7 New Forests (:57); 8 Building A Nest (1:10); 9 The Feather (1:25); 10 Life In The Nest (1:46); 11 Cathedral Of The Woods (8:26); 12 Sunrise Dance (3:35) *Valerie Wilson*; 13 Night Creatures (1:32); 14 The Forest Edge (1:33); 15 Brink Of Extinction (1:32); 16 Quiet Beauty (1:57); 17 Winter Rain (1:32); 18 Predators Of The Predators (:49); 19 Phantom Of The Forest (6:03); 20 Woodland Lullaby (3:41) *Valerie Wilson*; 21 Soliloquy (4:15).

Review: Michael Whalen, one of a generation of new composers, makes a striking impression with this score created for an episode in the series "Nature," seen on PBS, surveying a mysterious forest in the Scottish countryside inhabited by a spirit-like presence, the Goshawk. Utilizing the full palette offered to him by various acoustic instruments and synthesizers, Whalen wrote a series of minimalist cues that display a New Age feel without some of the excesses often encountered in recordings of this kind. And while one could have lived without the bird chirping heard occasionally, the simple musical thread he devised is quite attractive to the ear, and provides a soothing listening experience. Two longer cues, "Cathedral of the Woods" and "Phantom of the Forest" are particularly effective in conjuring up images that are not simply confined to the medium for which the music was written. As Whalen mentions in his notes, he attempted to "capture a sense of the fragile beauty of the forest, while not takin away from its enduring heroic majesty, dark mysteries or magical splendor." His music evokes all of that, and much more!

The Phantom of the Opera ♪♪♪♪▷

1990, Colossal Records; from the television presentation *The Phantom of the Opera,* Saban/Scherick Productions, 1990.

Album Notes: *Music:* John Addison; *Orchestrations:* Fred Paroutaud; The Hungarian State Opera Orchestra, conducted by John Addison; *Featured Vocalists:* Michele LaGrange (Marguerite), Gerard Garino (Phantom), Jean DuPouy (Faust), Jacques Mars (Mephitopheles); *Album Producer:* Robert Townson; *Engineer:* Eric Tomlinson.

Selections: 1 Main Title (3:17); 2 Young Christine (1:13); 3 Costume Lesson (:41); 4 Drive To The Woods (1:30); 5 Chasing Games (2:27); 6 Maestro (:56); 7 "Faust" Overture (C. Gounod)(1:46); 8 Chandelier Falls (:43); 9 Magic Kingdom (3:21); 10 Cops Killed (:54); 11 Christine Explores (4:47); 12 Picnic (2:03); 13 Phantom's Face (1:53); 14 Theme And Variations (2:03); 15 Christine's Escape (1:20); 16 Destruction (1:30); 17 He Wouldn't Hurt Me (:53); 18 The Phantom Dies (5:17); 19 End Title (1:04); 20 Christine And The Phantom (excerpts from "Faust")(C. Gounod)(6:01).

Review: Forget Lloyd Webber and his ruminations borrowed from Puccini; John Addison, having to deal with a similar theme, wrote a score that's original, romantic in the right places, and scary where it matters. The television film, made in Europe, stars Burt Lancaster, Ian Richardson, Andrea Ferreol, and Charles Dance as The Phantom. While anchoring his score around two excerpts from Gounod's "Faust," Addison created a music that seems to perfectly reflect the various aspects of the story—the giddy attitude of the operagoers; the loveliness of the heroine, Christine; the somber designs of the deranged madman who haunts the Opera; and the deeply romantic undertones of the tale itself. Richly decorative and eloquently manipulative without seeming to be, the cues follow the action, underlining it here, commenting on it there, always making a musical statement that attracts the attention and keeps the listener riveted.

Poirot ♪♪♪♪▷

1992, Virgin Records/U.K.; from the LWT series *Agatha Christie's Poirot,* 1992.

Album Notes: *Music:* Christopher Gunning; Orchestra conducted by Christopher Gunning; *Featured Soloists:* Leslie Pearson (piano), Stan Sulzmann (saxophones), David Emanuel (viola), Anthony Pleeth (cello); *Album Producer:* Christopher Gunning; *Engineer:* Chris Dibble.

Selections: 1 Hercule Poirot—The Belgian Detective(2:30); 2 One-Two, Buckle-My-Shoe (2:01); 3 The Double Clue (5:05); 4

The A-B-C Murders (4:36); 5 Grey Cells (4:22); 6 War (2:31); 7 A Country Retreat (4:53); 8 Death Of Mrs. Inglethorpe (2:30); 9 The Height Of Fashion (2:09); 10 How Does Your Garden Grow (9:06); 11 Death In The Clouds (3:55); 12 To The Lakes (2:20); 13 The Victory Ball (4:56); 14 The Plymouth Express (9:30).

Review: The CD regroups musical selections heard in "The Mysterious Affair at Styles," "Wasps Nest," "The Clapham Cook," and other cases, maddeningly solved by the insufferable Belgian sleuth, supremely and definitively portrayed by David Suchet. The music by Christopher Gunning has the right flavor for this type of show, with the main theme, probably one of the most recognizable tunes on television today, beautifully capturing the art deco feel of the series.

Pride and Prejudice ⚉⚉⚉⚉⚉

1995, Angel Records; from the BBC/A&E-TV serial *Pride and Prejudice*, 1995.

Album Notes: *Music*: Carl Davis; *Orchestrations*: Mark Warkman; Orchestra conducted by Carl Davis; *Featured Soloist*: Malvyn Tan (fortepiano); *Album Producers*: Carl Davis, Mark Warkman; *Engineer*: Chris Dibble.

Selections: 1 Pride And Prejudice (opening title music)(3:30); 2 Dance Montage (:48); 3 Elizabeth Observed (1:11); 4 Piano Summary (episode one)(2:01); 5 Canon Collins (2:12); 6 Piano Summary (episode two)(2:02); 7 The Gardiners (1:03); 8 Winter Into Spring (3:29); 9 Parting (1:37); 10 Rosings (1:20); 11 Piano Summary (episode three)(2:13); 12 Telling The Truth (4:29); 13 Farewell To The Regiment (2:21); 14 Pemberley (2:10); 15 Darcy Returns (3:08); 16 Piano Summary (episode four)(2:10); 17 Thinking About Lizzy (1:29); 18 Lydia's Elopement (2:52); 19 Piano Summary (episode five)(2:40); 20 Lydia's Wedding (2:40); 21 Return Of Bingley (2:58); 22 Darcy's Second Proposal (1:55); 23 Double Wedding (2:36); 24 Finale (1:38).

Review: This elegant score, written for fortepiano and small ensemble, is a delight. Created for an A&E series based on Jane Austen's novel, the music echoes the moods and reflects the various aspects of this compelling and witty love story. In fact, wit and vitality are traits that recur throughout the score, in which two themes are developed, the first concerns Elizabeth Bennet and her family's hunt for a proper husband; the second, stresses the felicity of marriage and affairs of the heart. Occasionally pausing to reflect on the events that have occurred, Davis composed "Piano Summaries" that open each episode, and link the various cues together in this soundtrack album. It's a somewhat audacious device that is quite effective within the context of the series, and works quite well here as a break between the cues.

The Prisoner ⚉⚉⚉⚉

1989, Siva Screen/U.K.; from the ITC series *The Prisoner*, 1966-67.

Album Notes: *Music*: Ron Grainer, Wilfred Josephs, Albert Elms; *Album Producers*: David Stoner, James Fitzpatrick.

Selections: Arrival: 1 Main Title Theme (R. Grainer)(2:21); 2 No. 6 Attempts Helicopter Escape (W. Josephs)(1:57); 3 Band Marches Into Main Village Square: Radetski March (J. Strauss)(1:45); 4 Chimes (W. Josephs) (2:18); A, B & C: 5 Engadine's Dramy Party (A. Elms)(1:23); Free For All: 6 Mini Moke And Speedboat Escape (A. Elms)(2:53); 7 Cat And Mouse Nightclub Mechanical Band (A. Elms)(1:36); 8 No. 6 Wins Village Election (A. Elms) (1:28); 9 Violent Capture Of No. 6 In Rover Cave (A. Elms)(1:46); The General: 10 Professor's Wife's Outdoor Art Class (A. Elms)(:39); 11 Security Clearance For Board Members (A. Elms)(:50); 12 Villagers' Examination Results Celebration (A. Elms)(2:03); 13 No. 6 Encounters The General (A. Elms)(:38); 14 Destruction And Final Report (A. Elms)(2:36); Fall Out: 15 Main Title Theme (Full Version)(R. Grainer)(3:34); Many Happy Returns: 16 No. 6 Aboard Gunrunners' Boat (A. Elms)(1:58); Dance Of The Dead: 17 Village Square Carnival (A. Elms)(2:20); 18 No. 6 Steals A Lifebelt (A. Elms)(1:45); Checkmate: 19 Escapers Attack Searchlight Tower (A. Elms)(1:56); Hammer Into Anvil: 20 No. 2 Has No. 6 Followed To The Stone Boat (G. Bizet)(2:28); 21 Farandelle Played By Village Band (G. Bizet)(:48); 22 Fight Between No. 6 And Jo. 14 (A. Vivaldi)(3:59); The Girl Who Was Death: 23 Village Green Cricket Match (A. Elms)(2:00); Once Upon A Time: 24 No. 6's Regression To Childhood (A. Elms)(2:11); 25 No. 6's Schooldays Revisited (A. Elms)(:43); 26 Main Title Theme (reprise)(R. Grainer)(1:09).

Review: Originally a seven-inch record distributed by the show's British fan club Six-of-One, as a membership premium in the early 1980's, this CD launched Silva Screen's trilogy of albums featuring music from the popular series. This first album contains selections from eleven of the episodes that feature original music. Ron Grainer composed the series' main theme, replacing one by Wilfred Josephs (which is also included here). While Josephs scored the pilot, much of the series was done by Albert Elms, whose work makes up the bulk of this first volume. He also cleverly adapted classical pieces composed by Vivaldi and Bizet for one episode score, "Hammer Into Anvil." On the whole, Elms' work maintains the flavor of a typical British spy thriller; it has long been suspected that the main character was John Drake from the British series "Secret Agent (Dangerman)." However, Elms throws several musical curves now and then to remain faithfully on target to creator/star Patrick McGoohan's on-screen cat and mouse psychological drama. Both remind us often that nothing is as it seems. The two subsequent volumes were assembled from the "tracked" music licensed for use in the series from the Chappel Recorded Music Library.

David Hirsch

QB VII 🎵🎵🎵

1995, Intrada Records; from the TV movie *QB VII*, Columbia Pictures,

Album Notes: *Music*: Jerry Goldsmith; *Orchestrations*: Alexander Courage; Orchestra conducted by Jerry Goldsmith; *Album Producer*: Jerry Goldsmith; *Engineer*: Federico Savina.

Selections: 1 QB VII Main Title (1:53); 2 Journey Into The Desert (3:39); 3 I Cannot See My Love (3:50); 4 The Wailing Wall (3:15); 5 The Escape (1:35); 6 The Holocaust (2:48); 7 Rekindling The Flame Of Jehovah (2:16); 8 Jadwiga Relived (4:36); 9 Free To Love Again (2:48); 10 A New Life (3:20); 11 A Sorrow Of Two Fathers (2:05); 12 The Theme From "QB VII" (A Kaddish For The Six Million)(2:28).

Review: Goldsmith won an Emmy for this score to one of the first major television miniseries', an adaptation of Leon Uris' novel about a libel trial that points back to the Holocaust. It's Goldsmith's Schindler's List in a way, giving the composer the opportunity to deal with one of the most difficult and powerful issues in our history. But it's also a somewhat glossy television treatment, and Goldsmith's score sometimes shows the effort of having to paint on such a broad canvas. There are so many different themes and treatments that the album sometimes seems like highlights from different movies: there are evocations of the Middle Eastern desert, a martial fanfare for the courtroom, not one but two different love themes, and various treatments of traditional Jewish musical material. But when Goldsmith sinks his teeth into the actual Holocaust memory scenes the score captures an authenticity and power that rivals any work ever done on the subject, particularly in his disturbing mix of percussive effects and ghostly voices for memories of a concentration camp evidenced in his soaring and deeply moving "Kadish for Six Million" which ends the album.

Jeff Bond

Quantum Leap 🎵🎵🎵

1993, GNP Crescendo; from the television series *Quantum Leap*, Universal Television, 1989-1993.

Album Notes: *Music*: Velton Ray Bunch; *Album Producers*: Velton Ray Bunch, Mark Banning; *Engineers*: Bruce Frazier, Doug Rider, Liz Magro, Charlie Sydnor, Greg Townley.

Selections: 1 Prologue (Saga Sell) (M. Post/V.R. Bunch) (1:05) *Deborah Patt*; 2 Main Title (M. Post) (1:15); Piano Man: 3 Somewhere In The Night (V.R. Bunch/S. Pakula) (3:31) *Scott Bakula*; The Leap Home, Part 1: 4 Suite (3:36); 5 Imagine (J. Lennon) (3:05) *Scott Bakula*; A Single Drop Of Rain: 6 Sam's Prayer (1:52); Memphis Melody: 7 Blue Moon Of Kentucky (B. Monroe) (1:40) *Scott Bakula*; 8 Baby Let's Play House (A. Ginter) (2:13) *Scott Bakula*; The Last Gunfighter: 9 Shoot Out (3:03); Catch A Falling Star: 10 Man Of La Mancha (medley) (M. Leigh/J. Darion) (6:18) *Scott Bakula*; Blood Moon: 11 Bite Me (3:29); Shock Theatre: 12 Alphabet Rap (D. Pratt) (2:05) *Dean Stockwell & The Pratt Pack*; Leaping On A String: 13 Lee Harvey Oswald (suite) (14:55); Glitter Rock: 14 Fate's Wide Wheel (M. Post/V.R. Bunch/ C. Ruppenthal/M. Leggett) (3:02) *Scott Bakula*; 15 A Conversation With Scott Bakula (12:00); 16 Quantum Leap: Main Title and Main Title (M. Post/V.R. Bunch) (2:20).

Review: This show's time travel format not only offered composer Velton Ray Bunch the chance to create some uniquely flavored scores for each episode, but series star Scott Bakula, a veteran Broadway performer, was also allowed to showcase his vocal talent. His character, Sam Beckett, would land in some past time taking the form of a piano player, a rock singer, maybe Elvis or an off-Broadway actor performing in some home town production of *Man of La Mancha*. When Beckett returns to the home of his youth ("The Leap Home Part 1"), Bunch develops a lovely Midwestern motif featuring a harmonic solo to represent the farm and its surrounding expanse of wheat fields. The transformation into reputed Kennedy assassin Lee Harvey Oswald for "Leaping on a String," required the use of a large scale orchestral score to rival John Williams' work on *JFK* as film series creator Donald Bellasario wanted to debunk the Oliver Stone film because he knew Oswald personally. The album also features a twelve minute interview with Bakula and two versions of Mike Post's main title theme with, and without, the opening narration.

David Hirsch

Rich Man, Poor Man 🎵🎵🎵🎵

1993, Varese-Sarabande; from the ABC-TV production *Rich Man, Poor Man*, 1976.

Album Notes: *Music*: Alex North; Orchestra conducted by Alex North, Harold Mooney; *Album Producer*: Sonny Burke; *Engineer*: Met Melcalf, Jr.; *CD Producers*: Robert Townson, Dub Taylor.

Selections: 1 Main Title Rich Man, Poor Man (1:32); 2 Julie (2:58); 3 Rudy (1:34); 4 Julie's First Affair (2:24); 5 Axel And Tom (4:26); 6 Tom And Clothilde (2:46); 7 Rudy And Ginny

(3:34); 8 Julie And Rudy (3:16); 9 Rudy And Tom (2:40); 10 Tom's Desperation (2:56); 11 Julie's Remorse (2:44); 12 Tom, Dwyer And Falconetti (2:22); 13 Denouement (3:19); 14 End Title/End Cast (1:34).

Review: In a rare foray into television, Alex North wrote the score for this 12-hour television version of Irwin Shaw's inspired novel, which spans 20 years in the life of a family. To keep things under control, he devised various leitmotifs for the various characters in the complex story. These essentially form the texture of the score, as sampled in this soundtrack album, with each cue detailing the central characters, their relations to each other, and their individual *modus operandi*. The themes are robustly defined, with each cue using a different approach, from jazz to blues, from a dramatic outburst to a sophisticated waltz, the whole thing bathed in an Americana flavor that pervades the entire score. It's a richly rewarding experience, that invites repeated listenings.

The Ring ✎✎✎

1996, Silva America Records; from the NBC-TV miniseries *The Ring*, 1996.

Album Notes: *Music:* Michel Legrand; The City Of Prague Philharmonic, conducted by Michel Legrand; *Album Producer:* Ford A. Thaxton; *Engineer:* Gregg Nestor.

Selections: 1 Love Theme From The Ring (4:31); 2 Tristan And Isolde (R. Wagner)(3:22); 3 Two Waltzes (2:48); 4 Ariana And Gerhard Leave With Max (2:59); 5 Gerhard And Walmar Escape (2:41); 6 Arrival In Switzerland (3:14); 7 Walmar Gets Shot (3:44); 8 Ariana Arrives At Manfred's (2:26); 9 Ariana And Manfred (2:04); 10 Ariana Finds Manfred (5:18); 11 Ariana Flees Berlin (6:57); 12 It's Best Not To Hope Too Much (3:26); 13 The Sabbath Dinner (2:31); 14 Painting (1:36); 15 Paul And Ariana (1:51); 16 Ariana Tells Paul (2:29); 17 Max And Ariana Reunite (1:13); 18 Family Plot (4:25); 19 This Is For Tammy (2:06); 20 Ariana Has A Bad Dream (1:32); 21 Finale: Ariana And Gerhard (3:53); 22 Moonlight Over Vermont (J. Blackburn/K. Suessdorf)(1:31) *Michel Legrand;* 23 Amapola (A. Gamse/J. LaCalle)(2:16) *Michel Legrand;* 24 Giselle And Gerhard (M. Legrand)(1:23).

Review: An epic four-hour miniseries based on Danielle Steel's poignant novel about a young woman's search for her family, from whom she has been separated at the onset of World War II, *The Ring* compelled Michel Legrand to write a score that's quietly understated at times, elegant and attractive at others, with some compelling and some disturbing moments thrown in the mix, as the story unfolds. Though perfectly adequate, and no doubt fitting the script to a tee, the one thing that seems to be

missing here is a sense of excitement, as if the composer had done his job routinely without getting much involved in the project itself. Occasionally, a theme tries to belie this impression ("Ariana Flees Berlin"), but that's only a fleeting moment in a score that's luxuriously musical and surprisingly lifeless.

Saved by the Bell ✎✎

1995, Kid Rhino Records; from the NBC-TV series *Saved by the Bell,* 1989-95.

Album Notes: *Songs:* Scott Gale, Rich Eames; *Album Producers:* Scott Gale, Rich Eames, Tom Weir, Larry Weir, Michael Damian; *Engineers:* Rick Riccio, Rich Eames, Scott Gale.

Selections: 1 Saved By The Bell (S. Gale)(1:53); 2 Don't Leave With Your Love (4:00); 3 Go For It! (2:13); 4 Love Me Now (2:50); 5 Make My Day (1:56); 6 Friends Forever (2:08); 7 Did We Ever Have A Chance? (1:56); 8 Deep Within My Heart (1:36); 9 Surfer Dude (2:27); 10 Gone Hawaiian (1:05); 11 School Song (S. Gale/R. Eames/B. Tramer)(1:21); 12 Saved By The Bell (S. Gale)(2:37) *Michael Damian.*

Review: A rock compilation for the kids who, presumably, watched this show designed for them on NBC-TV. The various actors, shown inside the tray card, look healthy and squeaky clean. So do the songs in which you'd be hard put to find an offensive lyric. The rhythms are pleasant enough, but not too terribly earth-shaking; as for the melodies they are, to say the least, primeval. Your 10-year-old might love them, and feel quite adult listening to this CD; your 12-year-old will probably yawn. The CD, by the way, is 26 minutes long: just enough to make it tolerable.

Scarlett ✎✎✎✎

1994, Polydor Records (Canada); from the television mini-series *Scarlett,* RHI Entertainment, 1994.

Album Notes: *Music:* John Morris; *Orchestrations:* Evan Morris; The City Of Prague Philharmonic, conducted by John Morris; *Album Producer:* John Morris; *Engineer:* Eric Tomlinson.

Selections: 1 (1:27); 2 (2:26); 3 (1:45); 4 (2:22); 5 (3:57); 6 (1:41); 7 (:38); 8 (1:23); 9 (3:10); 10 2:01); 11 (2:07); 12 (2:27); 13 (3:08); 14 (2:58); 15 (1:33); 16 (1:41); 17 (1:55); 18 (1:56); 19 (4:41); 20 (1:20); 21 (2:06); 22 (2:09); 23 (1:05); 24 (1:16); 25 (1:34); 26 (1:59); 27 (1:40); 28 (2:33); 29 (:40); 30 (3:11); 31 (4:08); 32 (4:07).

Review: Though he sports a mustache that looks quite manly, Timothy Dalton ain't Clark Gable; nor for that matter is John Morris another Max Steiner. So why did they bother making a sequel to *Gone With The Wind,* when they knew they had no real chances to succeed on any count? It's not that Morris' score for this sequel is bad, in fact it's very attractive for the most part, and the City Of Prague Philharmonic plays it to the hilt. If it had been written for any other movie, on television or on the big screen, it probably would have filled the bill more than adequately. What undoes it is that it applies to a movie that should not have been. Even more maddening is the fact that the cues aren't even titled, though this was perhaps done on purpose so that the listener would not try to identify a theme with a given moment in the action. Alright, so taken at face value, John Morris' music is very attractive, which shouldn't come as any surprise since the composer is known to always create excellent scores. Here he has cleverly used a wide range of solo instruments to paint vivid themes, some of which are achingly beautiful. There are period waltzes, romantic ballads, folk dances and an occasional action cue in the mix, in other words something for everybody. There's even a track, "Love Hurts," performed by the rock group Nazareth, with the Munich Philharmonic Orchestra playing backup. A rock instrumental? In a sequel to *GWTW*?

Shaka Zulu 🎵🎵🎵

1986, Cinedisc Records; from the television mini-series *Shaka Zulu*, 1986.

Album Notes: *Music*: Dave Pollecutt.

Selections: 1 Opening Titles/We Are Growing (P. Van Blerk/J. Laxton/M. Singana/D. Pollecutt)(2:05) *Margaret Singana & The Baragwanath Choir*; 2 One Of Those Rare Men (1:20); 3 Shipwreck (2:25); 4 First Sight Of Kwa-Bulawayo (3:30); 5 The Horse Race (1:45); 6 Nandi's Theme (2:50) *Mallie Kelly*; 7 Nandi In Forest/Attack/Prophecy (3:12); 8 Birth Of Shaka (2:20); 9 Shaka's Escape (4:30); 10 Pampata (Wemsheli Wami) (2:55) *Stella Khumalo*; 11 The Making Of The Spear (3:40); 12 The Coronation (1:55); 13 Death Of Dingiswayo (2:50); 14 Elizabeth's Theme (1:15); 15 Nandi's Funeral (2:20); 16 How Do You Catch A Monkey (5:30); 17 The Death Of Shaka (3:50).

Review: The saga of the legendary African chief who rose to head the entire Zulu nation, but was eventually defeated when he tried to repel the white invaders, *Shaka Zulu* is a forceful television drama that is bold and colorful. Surprisingly, the show elicited a score that only uses scant elements of African chants, and remains solidly rooted in the European thematic tradition. This is particularly evident in tracks like "Shaka's Escape," in which the drumming and chanting are recreations of African sounds, rather than the real thing. Adding insult to injury, the songs that are included are also often performed in English, which seems even less plausible for a story that takes place in dark Africa. The overall effect is that it deprives the

score itself from sounding realistic and true, and removes from it any element of authenticity. This is a serious letdown, particularly given the fact that the cues are otherwise intelligently written and attractive.

Sherlock Holmes 🎵🎵🎵

1987, Varese-Sarabande; from the Granada Television series *Sherlock Holmes*, 1987.

Album Notes: *Music*: Patrick Gowers; *Orchestrations*: Patrick Gowers; The St. Paul's Cathedral Choir, The Gabriele String Quartet, The Wren Orchestra of London, conducted by Patrick Gowers; *Featured Soloists*: Kenneth Sillito (violin), Neil Black (cor anglais), Leslie Pearson (piano); *Album Producer*: John Yap; *Engineer*: John Kurlander.

Selections: 1 221 B Baker Street (Opening Theme)(:49); 2 Elsie Cubitt (3:56); 3 Libera Me (4:13); 4 North By Ten And By Ten (2:45); 5 Old Sherman's Dog Toby (1:25); 6 Sutton's Nightmare (3:36); 7 River Chase (5:54); 8 The Death Of Sherlock Holmes (5:25); 9 Irene Adler (4:47); 10 Holmes In Europe (1:25); 11 John Hector McFarlane And His Mother (2:02); 12 Setting Out (2:08); 13 Lucretia Venucci And Her Family (3:45); 14 Mr. Henry Baker's Christmas (2:10); 15 The Illustrious Lord Bellinger (2:14); 16 On The Trail (1:20); 17 Neville St. Clair's Nostalgia (2:14); 18 The Bar Of Gold, Upper Swandam Lane (4:08); 19 Baker Street Reunion (1:49).

Review: Granada Television's "Sherlock Holmes" series, starring Jeremy Brett, contained some of the most memorable music ever written for television, composed by Patrick Gowers. The listener is instantly captivated by Gowers' title music, whose solo violin brings one instantly into the criminal world of Victorian London. Gowers' music is mostly in the 19th-century style, the solo violin appearing often to depict the character of Holmes, as in the mournful lament "The Death of Sherlock Holmes" and the beautifully romantic "Irene Adler." Gower's main theme is heard in many variations throughout the album, but the various settings are so eclectic that the theme never becomes stale or tired. "Libera Me" sets the theme as a hymn for a boys choir, while "The Illustrious Lord Bellinger" features the theme in an Elgar-like arrangement. Conan Doyle's Christmas mystery "The Blue Carbuncle" calls upon Gowers to create an arrangement of Christmas carols, while "North By Ten and By Ten" has a wonderfully archaic flavor with its harpsichord and string quartet. This album will appeal to both fans of the TV series as a souvenir, as well as to listeners, as a very fine example of fine British television music.

Paul Andrew MacLean

COLE PORTER

The urbane and sophisticated Cole Porter was one of the most influential and popular of American songwriters.

Porter was born in Peru, Indiana, on June 9, 1891. His mother, the daughter of a self-made millionaire, encouraged him to compose, self-publishing "Bobolink Waltz," which Porter wrote when he was 11.

In 1915 and 1916 he contributed songs to two Broadway shows, *Hand Up* and *Miss Information,* and wrote another, *See America First.* The shows were all failures.

Porter continued to write songs and hone his style. Finally, with 1928's *Paris,* Porter landed a hit song in a show that was also a hit. That song, titled "Let's Do It," was characteristic of the style that had been delighting his friends for years—intelligent, urbane, and highly suggestive of the sexual. Following *Paris* were the very successful *Wake Up and Dream* and *Fifty Million Frenchmen.* Whereas at one time Porter's songs may have been too cosmopolitan for Broadway audiences, by then, popular taste had begun to change. In this more accepting climate, the list of Cole Porter hits grew: "Love for Sale," "Night and Day," "Anything Goes," "You're the Top," "Begin the Beguine," "Just One of Those Things," and "It's De-lovely" were only a few.

Porter remained a prolific songwriter throughout the next few decades. In 1948 he created what many consider his masterpiece, the musical *Kiss Me, Kate.* Based on William Shakespeare's "The Taming of the Shrew," "Kate" was a huge success and generated a string of hits.

Porter died of pneumonia on October 15, 1964, in Santa Monica, California, and was buried back home in Peru, Indiana. Yet the end of Porter's life was hardly the end of his prominence; many of his songs became standards, performed by artists as disparate as cabaret singer Michael Feinstein and punk rocker Iggy

Sketch Artist ♪♪♪

1992, Varese-Sarabande Records; from the television movie *Sketch Artist,* Motion Picture Corporation of America, 1992.

Album Notes: *Music:* Mark Isham; *Album Producer:* Mark Isham; *Engineer:* Stephen Krause.

Selections: 1 Jack And Ray (3:55); 2 Start With Fashion (1:09); 3 The Sketch Artist (2:10); 4 The River And The Earring (3:27); 5 The Sketch (4:54); 6 A Drive To The Finish (3:09); 7 Claire (1:19); 8 Hanging By A Thread (3:49); 9 You Saw Me (1:56); 10 Face To Face (2:14); 11 On Dallas Time (2:05); 12 Bring It Tonight (1:19); 13 Breakfast With Mrs. Silver (1:01); 14 Warehouse (5:38); 15 One Of A Kind (1:48); 16 Physical Evidence (4:08); 17 A New Day (4:33).

Review: In a somewhat typical way, Mark Isham wrote a flavorful score for this television film starring Jeff Fahey and Sean Young. With a predominance of steel guitar sounds and synthesizer effects, over a rhythm line, the composer creates moods that are gently evocative, and harmonious. "The River and the Earring," "The Sketch," "Claire," and "Warehouse" are particularly evocative, but the whole score is well defined and enjoyable.

Soap Opera's Greatest Love Themes: volume II ♪

1992, Scotti Bros. Records.

Album Notes: *Album Producer:* Catherine Farley; *Engineer:* Arnie Acosta.

Selections: Guiding Light: 1 Love Like This (A.J. Gundell)(4:08) *A.J. Gundell;* 2 Simply Love (J.C. Feld/K. Wesley)(3:42) *Kassie Wesley;* Another World: 3 For Just One Moment (J. Leffler/R. Schuckett)(3:45) *Kyle Gordon, Rachele Cappelli;* Guiding Light: 4 Eve's Romance (J. Henry/W. Boatman)(2:25); 5 I Knew That I'd Fall (A.J. Gundell)(4:12) *A.J. Gundell, Leah Kunkel;* Another World: 6 One Step Closer (G. Sklerov/L. Macaluso)(3:29) *Anne Marie Radel;* As The World Turns: 7 I Think Of You (J.P. Dunne/A. McBroom)(4:01) *Gene Miller;* 8 Together, Forever With You (F. Eckert/J. Southworth)(4:51) *Fran Eckert, Jeff Southworth;* 9 Kim And Bob's Song (F. Hand)(2:01) *Fred Hand;* 10 Heart Don't Fail Me Now (G. Sklerov/H. Lloyd)(3:28) *David Morgan, Terry Wood;* Another World: 11 Another World (J. Leffler/R. Schuckett)(3:27) *Angela Cappelli, John Leffler;* 12 Lady Killer Ballad (J. Leffler/J. Siegler) (3:51) *Ricky Paull Goldin, Rascal.*

Review: Only a rabid fan of the soaps would want this collection of themes written for some of the most popular daytime television shows, and occasionally featuring the actors who appear in them. But when you have your daily ration of suds, do you really need to get additional servings on a CD that only offers small snippets of music and questionable performances? As the world turns, let another world be your guiding light...

The Sounds of Murphy Brown ♫♫♫

1990, MCA Records; from the CBS-TV series *Murphy Brown*.

Album Notes: *Song Producers*: Jerry Wexler, Stevie Wonder, Brian Holland, Lamont Dozier, William "Smokey" Robinson, Berry Gordy, Clay McMurray, Marvin Gaye, George Goldner, Norman Whitfield, Steve Dorff, John Bettis; *Album Producr*: Artie Ripp.

Selections: 1 You Keep Me Hangin' On (B. Holland/L. Dozier/E. Holland)(:38) *Candice Bergen*; 2 Respect (O. Redding)(2:24) *Aretha Franklin*; 3 Superstition (S. Wonder)(4:24) *Stevie Wonder*; 4 Nowhere To Run (B. Holland/ L. Dozier/E. Holland)(2:56) *Martha Reeves & The Vandellas*; 5 Tracks Of My Tears (W. Robinson/Moore/Tarpin)(2:54) *Smokey Robinson*; 6 Love Child (Wilson/Richards/Sawyer/Taylor)(2:55) *Diana Ross & The Supremes*; 7 Raisins And Motown (D. English)(:07) *Candice Bergen*; 8 Get Ready (W. Robinson)(2:36) *The Temptations*; 9 If I Were Your Woman (Sawyer/Jones/C. McMurray)(3:15) *Gladys Knight & The Pips*; 10 Mercy, Mercy Me (The Ecology)(M. Gaye)(3:12) *Marvin Gaye*; 11 Why Do Fools Fall In Love? (F. Lymon/M. Levy)(2:17) *Frankie Lymon & The Teenagers*; 12 I Can't Help Myself (Sugar Pie, Honey Bunch)(B. Holland/L. Dozier/E. Holland)(2:40) *The Four Tops*; 13 I Heard It Through The Grapevine (N. Whitfield/Strong)(2:44) *Gladys Knight & The Pips*; 14 This Old Heart Of Mine (Is Weak For You)(B. Holland/L. Dozier/E. Holland)(2:51) *The Isley Brothers*; 15 Like The Whole World's Watching (S. Dorff/J. Bettis)(2:51) *Take 6*.

Review: Once upon a time, when TV shows actually had lengthy main title themes, this show bucked the trend by exploiting Murphy's love of Motown by choosing an appropriate song for each episode's opening credits montage. The song most associated with the series is perhaps Aretha Franklin's "Respect" but, if you've been a fan of the earlier shows, this album will certainly remind you of many of them. If not, then this album is also an impressive collection of some of Motown's greatest hits. Artists include Stevie Wonder ("Superstition"), Smokey Robinson ("Tracks of My Tears") and The Temptations, whose song "Get Ready" also became the network's anthem one season. Two brief dialog cuts by Candice Bergen are also included as is the rarely used original series

theme by Steve Dorf and John Bettis, "Like the Whole World's Watching," which is performed by the a cappella group Take 6.
David Hirsch

Star Trek

Star Trek volume 1 "The Cage"/"Where No Man Has Gone Before" ♫♫♫

1985, GNP Crescendo Records; from the television series *Star Trek*, Paramount Pictures,1965.

Album Notes: *Music*: Alexander Courage; Orchestra conducted by Alexander Courage; *Album Producer*: Neil Norman; *Album Coordination and Sequencing*: Ford A. Thaxton, Mark Banning, David Hirsch; *Engineers*: Bob Margouleff, Jim McMahon

Selections: The Cage: 1 Star Trek Theme (Main Title)(:50); 2 Doctor Bartender (1:16); 3 Survivors (:45); 4 Prime Specimen (3:08); 5 Bottled (1:46); 6 Probed (:45); 7 Monster Illusion (1:13); 8 Monster Fight (1:37); 9 The Kibitzers (:36); 10 Vena's Punishment (1:44); 11 Pike's Punishment (:33); 12 Picnic (2:09); 13 True Love (1:17); 14 Vena's Dance (1:49); 15 Torchy Girl (:12); 16 Under The Spell (:26); 17 Primitive Thoughts (:24); 18 Wrong Think (:40); 19 To Catch A T. (1:19); 20 Going Up (1:06); 21 Max's Factor (2:04); 22 Star Trek Theme (End Title)(1:29); Where No Man Has Gone Before: 23 Main Title (:14); 24 Star Date (:34); 25 Episode Titles (1:18); 26 Force Field (2:17); 27 Silvery Orbs (1:49); 28 Crippled Ship (:53); 29 Speedy Reader (:50); 30 Hit The Button (:03); 31 On Delta-Vega (:37); 32 When Your Eyes Have Turned To Silver (:58); 33 Instant Paradise (2:50); 34 End Title and Credits (:21); 35 Additional Credits (:28).

Review: This album presents the first music ever written for "Star Trek," Alexander Courage's title themes and underscores for the original series' pilots "The Cage" and "Where No Man Has Gone Before." Gene Roddenberry's "The Cage" about telepathic, big-headed aliens who can project illusions, was reportedly rejected by NBC as "too cerebral," a description that might also be applied to Courage's score. His bongo-driven siren song title music is indelible, so utterly inappropriate that it's perfect. The "Cage" underscore is all moody, intellectualized eeriness, with the telepathic Talosians characterized by plucked electric guitar notes and their illusions by a dreamy, soprano wailing. There's also an exotic, Easternized dance for the green-skinned slave girl Vina. "Where No Man Has Gone Before" is more typical of the series, with a brassier sound (and a title march theme that was never used on the show) and some glittering, mysterious 'outer space' orchestral textures. The sound on these ancient recordings is pretty pinched, and all in all this is more of an important archival document than a thrill-packed album.

Jeff Bond

Star Trek volume 2 "The Doomsday Machine"/ "Amok Time" ♪♪♪♭

1991, GNP Crescendo Records; from the television series *Star Trek*, Paramount Pictures, 1965.

Album Notes: *Music*: Sol Kaplan, Gerald Fried; *Album Producer*: Neil Norman; *Album Coordination and Sequencing*: Ford A. Thaxton, Mark Banning, David Hirsch; *Engineers*: Alan Howarth, Brian Risner.

Selections: 1 Star Trek Main Title (A. Courage)(1:00); The Doomsday Machine (S. Kaplan): 2 Approach Of Enterprise/The Constellation (1:08); 3 Going Aboard (1:38); 4 Commander Matt Decker/The Crew That Was (1:58); 5 What Is Doomsday Machine/The Planet Killer (1:58); 6 Strange Boom/Decker Takes Over (2:49); 7 The New Commander/Light Beams/Tractor Beam (4:09); 8 Violent Shakes (2:45); 9 Spock Takes Command/Decker's Foil/Sneaky Commodore (2:28); 10 Goodbye Mr. Decker (3:10); 11 Condolences/Power Drain (1:09); 12 Kirk Does It Again (3:45); 13 One's Enough (:22); Amok Time (G. Fried): 14 Vulcan Fanfare/Prying (:48); 15 Mr. Spock (1:22); 16 Contrary Order (2:58); 17 T Pring (:47); 18 Marriage Council (1:51); 19 Vulcan (1:03); 20 The Processional (1:38); 21 The Challenge (3:02); 22 The Ritual/Ancient Battle/2nd Kroykah (5:25); 23 Remorse/ Marriage Council II (1:12); 24 Resignation/ Lazarus Return/Pig's Eye (:42); 25 Star Trek End Title (A. Courage)(:47).

Review: GNP's second "Star Trek" album is the perfect representation of music from the series: Sol Kaplan's spectacular, brassy score for "The Doomsday Machine" is a masterpiece with its crushing, alarmist motif for the episode's "planet killer" and some of the richest dramatic writing in the history of the series. It also emphasizes repeated piano textures, muted trumpet fanfares and moving, low string passages, with a heart-pounding, pulsating climactic cue that's one of the great suspense set pieces of the series. Gerald Fried's "Amok Time" is even more memorable, with its melancholy electric bass guitar theme for Spock and a fascinating, highly original evocation of the alien Vulcan culture. Everything climaxes in "The Ritual Ancient Battle," the all-time classic "Star Trek" fight music that has been parodied on everything from "The

Simpsons" to the Jim Carrey movie *The Cable Guy*. Fans of more recent "Trek" TV music may find this music too over the top, but that's exactly why it's great.

Jeff Bond

Star Trek volume 3 "Shore Leave"/"The Naked Time" ♪♪♪♭

1992, GNP Crescendo Records; from the television series *Star Trek*, Paramount Pictures, 1966.

Album Notes: *Music*: Gerald Fried, Alexander Courage; *Album Producer*: Neil Norman; *Album Coordination and Sequencing*: Ford A. Thaxton, Mark Banning, David Hirsch; *Engineers*: Alan Howarth, Brian Risner.

Selections: 1 Main Title (A. Courage)(:51); Shore Leave (G. Fried): 2 New Planet Rabbit/School Chum (4:07); 3 Old English (2:09); 4 Ruth (2:37); 5 Knight/Joust (1:28); 6 A Clue/Finnigan's Return/Leg Trick/Dirt Trick/Tiger Thoughts/2nd Samurai (4:36); 7 Caretaker/Lazarus (2:01); 8 2nd Ruth (:49); The Naked Time (A. Courage): 9 Trailer (1:02); 10 Brass Monkeys (1:28); 11 Joe Berserk (3:03); 12 Sulu Finks Out (:43); 13 D'Artagnan/Banana Farm (3:18); 14 Out Of Control/Lurch Time/Punchy Kid (1:48); 15 Party Time (1:34); 16 Medicine Girl (4:29); 17 Hot Sun/Off The Cloud (1:05); 18 Captain's Wig (6:43); 19 The Big Go (1:43); 20 Time Reverse/Future Risk (:46); 21 Star Trek End Credit (:48).

Review: This third volume in the original "Star Trek" series offers a jarring shift in tone between its two scores: Courage's "The Naked Time" is a bleak, downbeat effort emphasizing the hidden dangers and isolation of outer space as the crew of the Enterprise falls victim to a virus that unleashes their subconscious drives. Percussive and eclectic, the score offers take-offs of Korngold and an Irish tune as well as more large-scale cues involving the starship's efforts to avoid crashing into planet Psi 2000. It's Courage's best score for the series, varied and enjoyable, but almost too convincing in its evocations of the crew's depressions. At the other end of the spectrum is Gerald Fried's airy, "Shore Leave," one of the series' most enjoyable and good-natured scores, marked by a beautiful pastoral melody and the famous irresistible Irish jig Fried wrote to underscore Kirk's encounter with his old Academy tormentor Finnegan. Recommended for anyone in need of violent mood swings.

Jeff Bond

Star Trek: Deep Space Nine
♪♪♪

1993, GNP Crescendo Records; from the television series *Star Trek: Deep Space Nine,* Paramount Pictures, 1993.

Album Notes: *Music:* Dennis McCarthy; *Album Producer:* Dennis McCarthy; *Engineer:* Armin Steiner.

Selections: 1 Star Trek: Deep Space Nine Main Title (1:55); 2 Wolf 359 (4:51); 3 The Enterprise Departs/A New Home (1:11); 4 Trashed And Thrashed (1:59); 5 Bajor/Jake/Saying Goodbye (1:44); 6 Cucumbers In Space (1:44); 7 New Personality (2:18); 8 Into The Wormhole (3:41); 9 Time Stood Still (4:13); 10 Searching For Relatives (1:13); 11 Painful Memories (4:21); 12 Passage Terminated (3:43); 13 Back To The Saratoga/What Shields? (2:00); 14 Reconciliation (3:19); 15 The Sisko Kid (4:41); 16 A New Beginning (1:48); 17 Theme From Star Trek: Deep Space Nine (single version)(4:17); 18 Passage Terminated (Love Theme)(single version)(3:33).

Review: "Star Trek TNG" uber-composer Dennis McCarthy expanded his empire with this score for the first "Next Generation" spin-off, the more complex and elaborate "Deep Space Nine," which set its stories on an immense alien space station perched on the edge of a galactic wormhole. McCarthy's lonely horn fanfare title music immediately sets the tone for the series: not the strident heroism of Jerry Goldsmith's victorious "Star Trek: The Motion Picture" march as used in TNG, but the more realistic, world-weary heroism of people who have to clean up after themselves and others. Although some of the musical tenets of "The Next Generation" (extended tonal pads and smooth, string-and-horn dominated orchestrations) hold sway here, there's some interesting experimentation in the jarring atonality of cues like "Time Stood Still" and the funky alien source music heard in "Quark's Bar". It's still as far as you can get from the broad, motif-heavy music of the original series, but McCarthy has elevated this approach to an art form, writing scores of remarkable complexity and subtlety.

Jeff Bond

Star Trek: The Next Generation volume one "Encounter at Farpoint" ♪♪♭

1988, GNP Crescendo Records; from the television series *Star Trek: The Next Generation,* Paramount Pictures, 1987.

Album Notes: *Music:* Dennis McCarthy; *Music Editor:* John La Salandra; *Album Producer:* Dennis McCarthy; *Sequencing:* Ford A. Thaxton; *Engineer:* Gary Ladinsky.

Selections: 1 Star Trek: The Next Generation (Main Title) (A. Courage/J. Goldsmith) (1:46); 2 Stardate (1:44); 3 Troi Senses (1:42); 4 Picard's Plan/ First Chase/First Chase (Part 2) (4:31); 5 Detaching/Separation (2:41); 6 Shaken/Court Time/There Goes Da Judge (2:29); 7 U.S.S. Hood/On Manual (3:18); 8 Star Trek: The Next Generation (End Title)(A. Courage/J. Goldsmith) (1:04); 9 Personal Log/Admiral/Old Lovers (2:25); 10 Caverns (1:28); 11 Splashing/The Woods/Memories (2:46); 12 Scanned/Big Guns/Unknown (3:04); 13 Revealed/ Reaching Out (4:39); 14 Departure (1:08); 15 Main Title, version No. 2 (A. Courage/J. Goldsmith) (1:44).

Review: Dennis McCarthy's score for "The Next Generation's" pilot episode "Encounter at Farpoint" is primarily interesting as an illustration of how different the TNG composing style is early in the series compared to its eventual smooth, understated style that ensued after the first couple of years. The album features the show's familiar title music (adapted from Alexander Courage's opening fanfare from the original series and Jerry Goldsmith's title march from *Star Trek: The Motion Picture*) and McCarthy's ambitious underscore for "Farpoint," featuring a noble brass theme for Captain Picard, some heavy duty action writing for the episode's various space confrontations, and a use of violins and electronic effects that's diametrically opposed to the style McCarthy later adopted for the show.

Jeff Bond

Star Trek: The Next Generation volume two "The Best of Both Worlds, parts I and II" ♪♪♪♭

1991, GNP Crescendo; from the television series *Star Trek: The Next Generation,* Paramount Pictures, 1990.

Album Notes: *Music:* Ron Jones; *Sequencing:* Mark Banning; *Album Producer:* Ron Jones; *Engineer:* Armin Steiner.

Selections: 1 Star Trek: The Next Generation (Main Title)(A. Courage/J. Goldsmith)(1:40); 2 New Providence (1:19); 3 Hansen's Message (1:28); 4 Borg Engaged (1:16); 5 First Attack (4:56); 6 Borg Take Picard (3:03); 7 Death Is Irrelevant (1:35); 8 Away Team Ready (1:15); 9 On The Borg Ship (1:27); 10 Nodes (2:55); 11 Captain Borg (3:51); 12 Energy Weapon Fails (3:52); 13 Humanity Taken (:56); 14 Contact Lost (:34); 15 Cemetery Of Dead Ships (1:45); 16 Intervention (4:21); 17 The Link (2:58); 18 Sleep Command (3:52); 19 Destruct Mode/Picard Is Back (1:36); 20 Picard's Nightmare (1:00); 21 Star Trek: The Next Generation (End Credit)(A. Courage/J. Goldsmith)(1:02).

Review: GNP's second offering from "The Next Generation" features Ron Jones' powerful score to the two part cliffhanger

"The Best of Both Worlds," a spectacular story about the Federation's first major confrontation with the insidious Borg race. Jones wrote a percussive, driving score that took the Borg threat very seriously, even introducing a frightening synthesized choir to herald the Borg's arrival as a kind of pseudoreligious death knell for humanity. The score is filled with rhythmically inventive, slam-bang action cues, especially the exciting 'Intervention' which underscores a technically complex, well-edited battle between the Enterprise and the Borg cube. There's an enjoyable and appropriate intermingling of orchestral and electronic effects and a nice heroic motif for Commander Riker. Written during the heyday of the third and fourth season , when the series was really hitting its stride both dramatically and musically, Jones' score is one of the best ever produced for the show.

Jeff Bond

Star Trek: The Next Generation volume three "Yesterday's Enterprise"/ "Unification I & II"/ "Hollow Pursuits" ♫♫♫

1992, GNP Crescendo; from the television series *Star Trek: The Next Generation*, Paramount Pictures, 1990-92.

Album Notes: *Music*: Dennis McCarthy; *Sequencing*: Dennis McCarthy, Mark Banning; *Album Producer*: Dennis McCarthy; *Engineer*: Armin Steiner.

Selections: 1 Star Trek: The Next Generation (Main Title)(A. Courage/J. Goldsmith)(1:48); Yesterday's Enterprise: 2 Duality/Enterprise C (2:55); 3 Averted (:38)/Richard (:34)/Guinan (1:58)/Back To Battle/Cmdr. Garrett (1:20); 4 First Kiss (:35)/Not To Be (1:16)/Empty Death/Reporting For Duty (1:54); 5 Klingons/Skin Of Teeth (5:02); Unification I & II: 6 In Case You Forgot (1:36); 7 Sarek (1:46); 8 Sarek Drifts Away (2:34); 9 Another Captain/Food Fight (:58); 10 Victims Of Holography (3:44); 11 Sacrificed/Mind Meld (2:40); Hollow Pursuits: 12 Barclay Mitty (2:24); 13 Tissue Samples (:24)/Sad Sack (:37)/Staff Confab (1:17)/Hololust (:43); 14 Lady Gates/Swordplay (2:13); 15 Madame Troi (:47)/Blissful (:45)/Out Of Control/Warp Nine (:22); 16 Warposity (3:21); 17 Plan 9 (:19); 18 Star Trek: The Next Generation (End Credits)(A. Courage/J. Goldsmith)(:48).

Review: Dennis McCarthy returns with three TNG offerings, beginning with his superb score for the great "Yesterday's Enterprise" episode about the Enterprise's encounter with a starship from the past and its effect on the crew and history.

McCarthy pulled out the stops on this one, effectively underscoring the episode's strong dramatic themes and providing some thrilling battle music, particularly for the final showdown with a trio of Klingon vessels, scored with a battle fanfare that would be at home in a Star Wars movie. After that high point McCarthy's silky, subdued effort for the two-part Spock episode "Unification" is something of a letdown, although some of the fun is recaptured in the amusing tale of holodeck addiction, "Hollow Pursuits." The album is a textbook primer on how McCarthy had to change his style to the dictates of the show's producers, moving from the energetic, dramatic scoring of "Yesterday's Enterprise" to the more atmospheric, understated style of the latter two stories.

Jeff Bond

Star Trek: Voyager "Caretaker" ♫♫♫

1995, GNP Crescendo; from the television series *Star Trek: Voyager*, Paramount Pictures, 1995.

Album Notes: *Music*: Jay Chattaway; *Orchestrations*: Gregory Smith, Jay Chattaway; *Music Editor*: Gerry Sackman; Orchestra conducted by Jay Chattaway; *Featured Musician*: George Doering (banjo); *Album Producer*: Jay Chattaway; *Engineer*: Don Hahn.

Selections: 1 Star Trek: Voyager (Main Title) (J. Goldsmith) (1:45); 2 Prologue (3:11); 3 70 Thousand Light Years From Home (3:22); 4 Beamed To The Farm (4:18); 5 Lifesigns In The Barn (6:04); 6 Paris Takes The Helm (2:36); 7 Star Trek: Voyager (Main Title, short)(J. Goldsmith)(:18); 8 Escape From The Ocampa Underground (8:06); 9 Not Enough Time (2:02); 10 Battle For The Array (6:55); 11 Set Course For Home (3:31); 12 Star Trek: Voyager (End Credit)(J. Goldsmith)(1:16); 13 The Caretaker's Hoedown (2:35).

Review: Jay Chattaway charted the course for this latest "Star Trek" series with a heavily rhythmic, percussive score for the pilot episode "The Caretaker" that helped to begin a movement away from the low-key atmospheric scoring that had dominated the franchise since the latter days of "Star Trek: The Next Generation." A key element of the show is the sweeping, majestic French horn melody written by film composer and "Star Trek" veteran Jerry Goldsmith for the show's title music, and adapted very effectively by Chattaway during the score's last few cues (which also feature an ingeniously subtle quotation of Alexander Courage's original Star Trek fanfare). The rest of the score features hard-hitting, brassy action cues for some furious space dogfight sequences, a series of shifting, undulating orchestral and synthesized chords for the spacial phenomenon that flings the U.S.S. Voyager across the galaxy, and even some banjo picking for an illusory meeting with the Caretaker in human form.

Jeff Bond

Star Trek volume one "Charlie X"/ "The Corbomite Maneuver"/ "Mudd's Women"/"The Doomsday Machine" ♫♫♫♫

1985, Varese-Sarabande; from the television series, *Star Trek*, Paramount Pictures, 1966.

Album Notes: *Music*: Fred Steiner, Sol Kaplan; The Royal Philharmonic Orchestra, conducted by Fred Steiner; *Album Producer*: George Korngold; *Engineer*: Peter Brown; *Assistant Engineer*: Andrew Fraser.

Selections: 1 Main Title and Closing Theme (A. Courage)(1:23); The Corbomite Maneuver (F. Steiner): 2 Radiation/Cube Radiation/Baby Balok/ Fesarius Approaches (5:07); Charlie X (F. Steiner): 3 Kirk's Command/Charlie's Mystery/Charlie's Gift (3:37); 4 Kirk Is Worried/Card Tricks/Charlie's Yen (3:23); 5 Zap Sam/Zap Janice/Zap The Cap/Zap The Spaceship (4:18); 6 Charlie's Friend/Goodbye Charlie/Finale (A. Courage)(2:44); The Doomsday Machine (S. Kaplan): 7 Goodbye Mr. Decker/ Kirk Does It Again (5:46); Mudd's Women (F. Steiner): 8 Three Venuses/Meet Mr. Mudd/Hello Girls/Venus Aboard/Mudd Laffs (3:11); 9 Hello Ruth/The Last Crystal/The Venus Drug (4:30); 10 Planet Rigel/ Eve Is Out/Space Radio (4:09); 11 Eve Cooks/Pretty Eve/Mudd's Farewell (3:17).

Review: See entry below.

Star Trek volume two "Mirror, Mirror"/ "By Any Other Name"/"The Trouble With Tribbles"/ "The Empath" ♫♫♫♫

1986, Varese-Sarabande; from the television series, *Star Trek*, Paramount Pictures, 1967-68.

Album Notes: *Music*: Fred Steiner, Jerry Fielding, George Duning; The Royal Philharmonic Orchestra, conducted by Fred Steiner; *Album Producer*: George Korngold; *Engineer*: Peter Brown; *Assistant Engineer*: Andrew Fraser.

Selections: 1 Main Title and Closing Theme (A. Courage)(1:21); Mirror, Mirror (F. Steiner): 2 Mirror, Mirror/Black Ship Theme/The Agonizer/Meet Marlena (3:42); 3 Black Ship Tension/Goodbye Marlena/Short Curtain (5:33); The Trouble With Tribbles (J. Fielding): 4 A Matter Of Pride/No Trible At All/ Big Fight (4:19); By Any Other Name (F. Steiner): 5 Neutralizer/Kelvan Theme/More Neutralizers/Broken Blocks (4:39); 6 Rojan's Revenge/Rojan's Blocks/ Pretty Words/Rojan's Victory/Finale (3:52); The Empath (G. Duning): 7 Enter Gem/Kirk Healed (2:08); 8 Vian's Lab/The Subjects/Cave Exit/Star Trek Chase (3:37); 9 Help Him/Spock Stuck/McCoy Tortured (5:18); 10 Time Grows Short (5:07); 10 Vian's Farewell/Empath Finale (2:20).

Review: Veteran composer Fred Steiner created some of the most memorable music in television history with his work on "Perry Mason," "The Twilight Zone" and especially the original *Star Trek*. For this beautifully produced two volume set of albums, Steiner conducted the National Symphony Orchestra in some magnificent recreations of his powerful scores for episodes like "The Corbomite Maneuver," "Charlie X," "Mudd's Women" on Volume One and "Mirror, Mirror" and "By Any Other Name" on Volume Two. Volume One also features a brief suite of pounding "planet killer" music from Sol Kaplan's "The Doomsday Machine" (better represented in its original form on GNP/Crescendo's *Star Trek Volume Two*), while Volume Two presents a suite from Jerry Fielding's quirky "The Trouble With Tribbles" (again given a more complete presentation on GNP/Crescendo's *Star Trek 30 Year Anniversary Album*) and the bulk of George Duning's silkily sentimental effort for the third season's "The Empath." Volume One is a classic representation of music from the series, with Steiner's "Corbomite Maneuver" and "Charlie X" representing the show's scoring at its operatic and dramatic heights. Volume Two is somewhat less successful, with Steiner's "Mirror, Mirror" and "By Any Other Name" scores proving uncharacteristically repetitive; Duning's "The Empath" comes off better, although it doesn't represent the composer's best work for the series. Both albums are marked by Steiner's accomplished conducting and rich, deep sound, and should be of great value to fans of the series.

Jeff Bond

Star Trek volume one "Is There in Truth No Beauty?"/ "Paradise Syndrome" ♫♫♫♪

1986, Label X; from the television series *Star Trek*, Paramount Pictures, 1966.

Album Notes: *Music*: George Duning, Gerald Fried; *Orchestrations*: Clyde Allen, Tony Bremner; The Royal Philharmonic Orchestra, conducted by Tony Bremner; *Album Producers*: Clyde Allen, John Lasher; *Engineer*: Keith Grant.

Selections: Is There In Truth No Beauty? (G. Duning): 1 Enter Miranda, Ambassador Arrival, McCoy's Toast, Quite A Woman, Marvick Pleads, Marvick Mad, Marvick Berserk, Marvick Dies, Sentimental Jim, Blind Miranda, No Change, Miranda Mad, Miranda's Farewell (19:58); Paradise Syndrome (G. Fried): 2 Pine Trees, The Amerinds, Tahiti Syndrome, The Brain Wash, Miramanee, Breath Of Life, The New God, Dilithium Problem, Wash Day, Salish Fluffed, Potter Kirk, Naming The God, Joining Day, Challenge, The Ceremony, Birth Announcement, False God, Death Of Miramanee (19:54).

Review: See entry below.

Star Trek volume two "Conscience of the King"/ "Spectre of the Gun"/"The Enemy Within"/"I Mudd" 🎵🎵🎵◗

1986, Label X; from the television series *Star Trek*, Paramount Pictures, 1966.

Album Notes: *Music*: Joseph Mullendore, Jerry Fielding, Sol Kaplan, Samuel Matlovsky; *Orchestrations*: Clyde Allen, Tony Bremner; The Royal Philharmonic Orchestra, conducted by Tony Bremner; *Album Producers*: Clyde Allen, John Lasher; *Engineer*: Keith Grant.

Selections: Conscience Of The King (J. Mullendore): 1 Spaceship Titles, Lenore, Lenore's Kiss, Everything Is Later, Ophelia Mania, Last Cue (8:44); Spectre Of The Gun (J. Fielding): 2 Melkot's Warning, Tombstone, Teeth Pulling, My Name, Doc Holliday, Love Scene In Old West, Chekov Gets Killed, Ten Minutes, We're Trapped, Final Curtain (15:15); The Enemy Within (S. Kaplan): 3 The Rock Slide, The Tired Captain, Bruised Knuckles, An Imposter, Undecisive, Alter Ego, Another Brandy, Double Dog Death, Help Me, Thank You, Yeoman (13:15); I, Mudd (S. Matlovsky): 4 Alice In Wonderland, Mudd's Series, Tired Of Happiness, Stella, The Last Straw, Stella 500 (8:38).

Review: Produced simultaneously with Varese's "Star Trek" music re-recordings, Label X's albums arranged the show's scores into continuous suites, beginning on Volume One with Gerald Fried's beautifully lyrical, pastoral "The Paradise Syndrome" and George Duning's alternately romantic and agitated "Is There In Truth No Beauty?" Completing the Trek canon of composers on Volume Two is Joseph Mullendore's classically old-fashioned romance music for "The Conscience of the King,"

Sol Kaplan's dark and furious "The Enemy Within," Jerry Fielding's unusual, percussive "Spectre of the Gun" and Samuel Matlovsky's Brechtian, satirical "I, Mudd." Kaplan's "Enemy Within" is the score to beat in this group, an oft-repeated, quintessential distillation of the original series hyper-dramatic, rich orchestral style. Fielding's "Spectre of the Gun" is an aberration, a tonally inventive piece of modernism closely related to the composer's Oscar-nominated score and to Sam Pekinpah's *The Wild Bunch*, written the same year. Much of the score arrangements were recreated by ear with great fidelity by Clyde Allen, but the suite approach leads to some jarring alterations, and Tony Bremner's conducting sometimes fails to recapture the tempos and accents of the original works, particularly Duning's music, which slips into an aggravating formlessness under Lasher's baton. This still qualifies as a superbly realized preservation of some of television's most memorable music.

Jeff Bond

Tales from the Crypt 🎵🎵🎵◗

1992, Big Screen Records; from the television series *Tales from the Crypt*, 1989-91.

Album Notes: *Album Producers*: Tim Sexton, Bruce Nazarian; *Engineers*: Rob Chiarelli, Anthony Jeffries, Mike Scotella, Rusty Richards.

Selections: 1 Tales From The Crypt (Main Title)(D. Elfman)(2:26); 2 Three's A Crowd (J. Hammer)(3:49); 3 Cutting Cards (J. Horner)(3:44); 4 Loved To Death (J. Webb)(3:17); 5 Dead Wait (D. Mansfield)(4:04); 6 Undertaking Palor (N. Pike)(3:10); 7 Carrion Death (B. Broughton)(3:31); 8 Ventriloquist's Dummy (M. Goodman)(3:32); 9 The Thing From The Grave (D. Newman)(2:53); 10 The Man Who Was Death (R. Cooder)(4:22); 11 Reluctant Vampire (C. Eidelman)(3:50); 12 Deadline (S. Bartek)(3:30); 13 The Crypt Jam (C. Booker)(4:31) *The Crypt Keeper (John Kassir)*.

Review: This anthology series, originally made for cable television, first gained notoriety because several movie directors and actors, many who never did TV, were willing to work on individual episodes. Consequently, many film composers were also willing to take on scoring assignments. The album features suites from eleven episodes including "The Thing from the Grave" (David Newman), "Cutting Cards" (James Horner), and "The Reluctant Vampire" (Cliff Eidelman). Bruce Broughton's uncharacteristicly dark "Carrion Death," is included. It is a score for an episode that had almost no dialogue. Steve Bartek, Danny Elfman's long time collaborator, contributes the delightful solo effort of a jazzy film noir music for "Deadline." The long version of Elfman's main theme leads off the CD and John Kassir, who voiced the Crypt Keeper, performs on "The Crypt Jam." A really nice *body* of work.

David Hirsch

Texas ♫♫♫ᵛ

1994, Legacy Records; from the television special *Texas*, Republic Pictures, 1994.

Album Notes: *Music*: Lee Holdridge; Orchestra conducted by Lee Holdridge; *Album Producer*: Bob Irwin; *Engineer*: Vic Anesini.

Selections: 1 Texas Main Title Theme (L. Holdridge)(1:42); 2 New San Antonio Rose (B. Wills)(2:37) *Bob Wills & His Texas Playboys*; 3 Texas Swing (Z. Clements)(2:16) *Curly Williams & His Georgia Peach Pickers*; 4 El Paso (M. Robbins)(4:22) *Marty Robbins*; 5 Remember The Alamo (J. Bowers)(2:48) *Johnny Cash*; 6 Texas (M. Haggard/F. Powers)(1:57) *Merle Haggard*; 7 No Place But Texas (A. Harvey)(3:25) *Willie Nelson*; 8 Back In The Saddle Again (G. Autry/R. Whitley)(2:34) *Gene Autry*; 9 Texas Lullaby (D.A. Coe/A. McGowan) (4:12) *David Allan Coe*; 10 Deep In The Heart Of Texas (D. Swander/J. Herhsey)(2:02) *Moe Bandy*; 11 Panhandle Rag (L. McAuliffe)(4:26) *Leon McAuliffe*; 12 The Yellow Rose Of Texas (G. Autry/J. Long)(2:51) *Gene Autry, Jimmy Long*; 13 A Maiden's Prayer (B. Wills)(2:50) *Bob Wills & His Texas Playboys*; 14 Cross The Brazos At Waco (K. Arnold)(2:50) *Billy Walker*; 15 Texas — 1947 (G. Clark)(3:10) *Johnny Cash*; 16 Ballad Of The Alamo (M. Robbins)(3:38) *Marty Robbins*; 17 Lone Star Rag (B. Boyd/A. Davis)(3:14) *Johnny Gimble*; 18 Blue Texas Waltz (B.J. Shaver)(4:03) *Billy Joe Shaver*; 19 Amazing Grace (trad., arr. W. Nelson)(5:40) *Willie Nelson*; 20 Texas End Credit Theme (L. Holdridge)(1:03).

Review: This musical collection inspired by the TV epic brings together several well-known C&W artists in renditions of songs that all have something to do with Texas, neatly bookended by Lee Holdridge's opening and closing themes [amateurs of soundtrack music will have to dig out the promotional CD released around the same time, and containing all the cues composed by Holdridge for the film]. One's acceptance of this compilation will be strictly limited by one's tolerance for this type of material. Taken at face value, and despite the wide variations in sound quality, it has its many moments of fun and entertainment, though it offers little that is new or rare. Strictly for fans.

thirtysomething ♫♫♫♫ᵛ

1991, Geffen Records; from the television series *thirtysomething*, 1991.

Album Notes: *Music*: W.G. Snuffy Walden, Stewart Levin, Jay Gruska; *Album Producers*: Scott Winant, Fred Goldring; *Engineers*: Les Brockman, Peter R. Kelsey, Gregg Townley, Steve Krause, Doug Rider.

Selections: 1 Main Title (extended version)(3:20); 2 Begging For Sex, Part 2 (2:36); 3 Michael And Hope's New Baby (3:54); 4 Another Country (Nancy's Illness)(3:44); 5 Post Op (4:15); 6 It Must Be Love (R.L. Jones)(4:55) *Rickie Lee Jones*; 7 Nancy And Elliot Take A Train (3:43); 8 Michael's Dilemma (2:46); 9 Ellyn's Wedding (2:38); 10 Come Rain Or Come Shine (H. Arlen/J. Mercer)(3:43) *Ray Charles*; 11 Life Class (Nancy's Museum Fantasy)(2:58); 12 Second Look (3:26); 13 Hot Butter (Miles Comes To Dinner)(2:22); 14 Melissa And Men (1:51); 15 The Go Between (2:41); 16 Gary's Funeral (3:03); 17 The Water Is Wide (trad.)(4:58) *Karla Bonoff*; 18 Main Title (air version)(1:14).

Review: Whoever W.G. Snuffy Walden, Jay Gruska and Stewart Levin are, the music they have created for "thirtysomething," at least as represented in this soundtrack CD, is very enjoyable. Pleasantly rhythmic, in a style that happily mixes various genres around melodic material that is usually quite attractive, it relies on acoustic instruments to make a flavorful statement, often without overstating its case. Supplementing the instrumental cues, some vocals add their own color to the mix, whether it's Rickie Lee Jones swooning her way through "It Must Be Love," Karla Bonoff warbling the traditional "The Water Is Wide," or Ray Charles doing a surprisingly effective version of the old standard "Come Rain or Come Shine."

A Town Like Alice ♫♫♫♫

Southern Cross Records; from the Masterpiece Theatre series *A Town Like Alice*, 1981.

Album Notes: *Music*: Bruce Smeaton; The Australian Symphony Orchestra, conducted by Bruce Smeaton; *Album Producer*: Bruce Smeaton; *Engineer*: Robin Gray.

Selections: 1 Symphonic Suite #1 (21:53); 2 Symphonic Suite #2 (25:04).

Review: A six-part dramatization of *The Legacy*, Nevil Shute's best-selling novel, "A Town Like Alice" centers around two prisoners of war whose romance begins during the Japanese invasion of Malaya in World War II, and concludes in the vast Australian outback. The story inspired Bruce Smeaton to write a score that's filled with gorgeous melodies, attractive themes, and compelling cues. For the purpose of this CD (and presumably a soundtrack LP before that), they are strung together into two suites, probably fitting both sides of an LP, and are heard in little snippets that are not otherwise identified, making it difficult to follow the dramatic progression of the score in relation to the story.

The Twilight Zone

The Twilight Zone: volume one ♪♪♪♪

1985, Varese-Sarabande; from the CBS-TV series *The Twilight Zone*, 1959-62.

Album Notes: *Music:* Marius Constant, Bernard Herrmann, Jerry Goldsmith, Nathan Van Cleave, Rene Garriguenc; *Album Producer:* Risty; *Engineers:* Bruce Leek, Joe Gastwirt.

Selections: 1 Main Title (M. Constant) (:27); 2 The Invaders (J. Goldsmith) (12:57); 3 Where Is Everybody? (B. Herrmann) (11:20); 4 I Sing The Body Electric (N. Van Cleave) (11:43); 5 Jazz Theme (J. Goldsmith) (3:13); 6 Jazz Theme (R. Garriguenc) (4:05); 7 Nervous Man In A Four Dollar Room (J. Goldsmith) (8:17); 8 Walking Distance (B. Herrmann) (12:25); 9 End Title (M. Constant)(:42).

Review: See entry below.

The Twilight Zone: volume two ♪♪♪♪

1986, Varese-Sarabande; from the CBS-TV series *The Twilight Zone*, 1959-61.

Album Notes: *Music:* Bernard Herrmann, Jerry Goldsmith, Leonard Rosenman, Fred Steiner, Nathan Van Cleave; *Album Producer:* Risty; *Engineers:* Bruce Leek, Fred Mitchell.

Selections: 1 Main Theme (B. Herrmann)(1:15); 2 Back There (J. Goldsmith) (12:58); 3 And When The Sky Was Opened (L. Rosenman)(11:58); 4 The Passerby (F. Steiner)(13:01); 5 The Lonely (B. Herrmann)(11:14); 6 Two (N. Van Cleave) (12:13); 7 End Theme (B. Herrmann)(1:09).

Review: Few television series afforded the major film composers the opportunity to make meaningful contributions to the small-screen medium, and utilize their talent in a way that would equal their comparatively larger theatrical efforts. Rod Serling's "The Twilight Zone" was such a show, and its success is not only rooted in the superior quality of the storylines and visual production, but in Serling's careful choice of music as well. Among the noted composers that created original themes and long-form compositions for the program were Bernard Herrmann, Jerry Goldsmith, Leonard Rosenman and Fred Steiner—all well represented on Varese Sarabande's two-volume *The Best of the Twilight Zone*.

Bewitching to any fan of the sci-fi classic will be the familiar opening and closing themes (by Marius Constant and Bernard Herrmann), ten thematic scores for specific episodes ("The Passerby," "The Lonely," "I Sing the Body Electric," "Nervous Man in a Four Dollar Room" and "Walking Distance" among them), and two underscore jazz themes. Each melody is sure to stir vague feelings of recognition, that like the show itself, will leave you asking "Haven't I heard this somewhere?"

Charles L. Granata

Twin Peaks ♪♪♪♪

1990, Warner Bros. Records; from the television series *Twin Peaks*, 1989.

Album Notes: Music; Angelo Badalamenti; *Orchestrations:* Angelo Badalamenti; *Featured Musicians:* Angelo Badalamenti (piano, synthesizers), Kinny Landrum (synthesizers), Vinnie Bell (electric guitars), Eddie Dixon (electric guitars), Al Regni (tenor sax, clarinet, flute), Eddie Daniels (flute, clarinet), Grady Tate (drums); *Album Producers:* David Lynch, Angelo Badalamenti; *Engineer:* Art Pohlemus.

Selections: 1 Twin Peaks Theme (4:45); 2 Laura Palmer's Theme (5:08); 3 Audrey's Dance (5:15); 4 The Nightingale (A. Badalamenti/D. Lynch)(4:54) *JuleeCruise*; 5 Freshly Squeezed (3:48); 6 The Bookhouse Boys (3:24); 7 Into The Night (A. Badalamenti/D. Lynch)(4:42) *Julee Cruise*; 8 Night Life In Twin Peaks (3:23); 9 Dance Of The Dream Man (3:39); 10 Love Theme (4:34); 11 Falling (A. Badalamenti/D. Lynch)(5:18) *Julee Cruise*.

Review: If you had to single out one soundtrack as being an "atmosphere score," Angelo Badalamenti's catchy music from the David Lynch series "Twin Peaks" would undoubtedly fit such a distinction. Lynch's program started off as a refreshingly different program for network TV, with bizarre plots, off-the-wall humor, quirky characters and intense dramatic situations making for an enjoyable entertainment that drew critical praise and big audiences when it debuted in the Spring of 1990. Just as important to the show's success as the program's talented cast and offbeat tone was Badalamenti's brooding, deliberately paced musical accompaniment, which ranges from the memorable, electric guitar-performed theme song (also heard in a vocal version by Lynch favorite Julee Cruise) to cues that are alternately characterized by spacey, almost droning electronic music or even jazz-like in their most unconventional moments. Badalamenti defined the show's oddball approach through his music, and did his best to maintain the show's initial promise even as Lynch and co-creator Mark Frost decidedly lost their way when the program floundered during its second and final season on the air.

Andy Dursin

The Utilizer ♫♫♫⌐

1995, Intrada Records; from the television series *The Utilizer*, 1995.

Album Notes: *Music*: Dennis McCarthy; *Orchestrations*: Dennis McCarthy; *Album Producer*: Dennis McCarthy; *Engineer*: Rick Winquest.

Selections: 1 The Utilizer (3:58); 2 Getting A Wish (3:35); 3 Land For Sale (:28); 4 New Mansion (1:54); 5 Classical Music (3:13); 6 Collins (3:58); 7 The Utilizer Shrinks (4:52); 8 Vacation (1:19); 9 Future City (3:05); 10 Quarry (1:05); 11 End Credits.

Review: A splendid jazz influenced score by "Star Trek Generations" composer Dennis McCarthy for the Sci-Fi Channel cable movie concerning a wish-granting machine that comes with a terrible price. Based on the short story "Something for Nothing," the main theme has a nice laid back feel, it's solo trumpet providing just the right amount of pathos for the central character and his sterile, boring life. As he quickly gets in over his head, the music becomes darker with McCarthy drawing on some of the more non-melodic sound designs he frequently used to great effect on the mid-1980's alien invasion series "V."

David Hirsch

Victory at Sea: volumes 1 & 2 ♫♫♫♫

1992, RCA Victor; from the NBC-TV series, *Victory At Sea*, 1952-53.

Album Notes: *Music*: Richard Rodgers; *Orchestrations*: Robert Russell Bennett; The RCA Victor Symphony Orchestra, conducted by Robert Russell Bennett; *Album Producer*: Richard Mohr; *Engineer*: Lewis Layton; *CD Engineer*: Nathaniel S. Johnson.

Selections: VOLUME ONE: 1 The Song Of The High Seas (5:01); 2 The Pacific Boils Over (5:40); 3 Guadalcanal March (3:04); 4 D-Day (5:50); 5 Hard Work And Horseplay (3:38); 6 Theme Of The Fast Carriers (6:45); 7 Beneath The Southern Cross (4:00); 8 Mare Nostrum (4:25); 9 Victory At Sea (6:09); 10 Fire On The Waters (5:53); 11 Danger Down Deep (4:49); 12 Mediterranean Mosaic (5:48); 13 The Magnetic North (6:02).

VOLUME TWO: 1 Allies On The March (5:13); 2 Voyage Into Fate (6:20); 3 Peleliu (3:36); 4 The Sound Of Victory (6:12); 5 Rings Around Rabaul (6:07); 6 Full Fathom Five (7:08); 7 The Turkey Shoot (5:15); 8 Ships That Pass (4:54); 9 Two If By Sea (6:27); 10 The Turning Point (5:24); 11 Symphonic Scenario (10:34).

Review: In 1952, Broadway composer Richard Rodgers took a sabbatical from his theatrical ventures to create the score for the popular television series "Victory at Sea," a documentary of World War II emphasizing the naval battles waged between 1939 and 1945. The score, lush, inordinately musical and attractive, yet powerfully suggestive, won an Emmy Award for best score in 1953, and elicited rapturous reviews from most reviewers who described it as a work of "compelling beauty and vigor that adds incalculably to the emotional intensity of the series" (Jack Gould, *New York Times*). Eventually, the series was adapted for the big screen and a theatrical feature was released by United Artists in 1954.

Three years later, Robert Russell Bennett, Rodgers' regular arranger, went to the recording studio and prepared three albums containing many of the best cues from the score for release by RCA. The two CDs regroup most of these selections into a sweeping, panoramic musical display of great intensity and originality, with sound effects added for greater realism.

As a melodist, Rodgers was particularly proficient, and his score enables him to unleash the raw emotional power he so often was compelled to curb in his Broadway shows. Today, the impact of his music is as great as it was 45 years ago, with some selections ("Guadalcanal March," "Theme of the Fast Carriers," "The Song of the High Seas") revealing his uncanny talent for ear-grabbing tunes.

VR.5 ♫♫♫

1995, Rysher Records; from the television series *VR.5*, Zoo Entertainment/Rysher Entertainment, 1995.

Album Notes: *Music*: John Frizzell; *Featured Vocalists*: Dee Carstensen, Eileen Frizzell; *Featured Musician*: David McKelvy (harmonica); *Album Producer*: John Frizzell; *Engineer*: Jack Rouben.

Selections: 1 Sydney's Theme (:49); 2 Highrise Rooftop (2:09); 3 Paradise Shower (2:34); 4 Waterstation Clue (1:03); 5 To Dance Again (4:02); 6 Animal VR/Kravitz VR (5:21); 7 Didjeridu Thing (1:34); 8 Family Drowning/Cat Fight (4:44); 9 Sydney's Theme (:54); 10 The Theater (4:16); 11 The Bank (3:26); 12 Getting The Info/Trailer Park (3:00); 13 I'd Choose You (1:30); 14 Scriptwriting (2:10); 15 Morgan Freaks/Booth's Theme (4:36); 16 Mom Freaks (3:17); 17 Booth's Tango (:58); 18 Sydney And Duncan Talk (1:02); 19 Main Title (:50); 20 Simon's Requiem (4:37); 21 Sydney's Theme (:49).

Review: A skillful blend of synthesizers, acoustics and voice by John Frizzell for the short lived television series. A solo female vocal was applied to the main theme for Sidney, a young woman who discovered a means of getting into people's psyche through virtual reality. Frizzell had to be creative to match the oddly designed virtual landscapes of Sidney's encounters, while creating more realistic motifs for her pursuit by shadowy government agents who want the technology. Some of the themes are very harmonious, while others, like "Family Drowning," have unsettling dissonant melodies. Although a spellbinding piece of work by virtue of Frizzell's creativity, this exists only when the tracks are listened to as separate elements. The album's sequencing is, however, somewhat disjointed, and that's the weakest part. The music is assembled in bits and pieces and makes no attempt to establish any kind of symphonic flow.

David Hirsch

The Wonder Years 🦴🦴🦴🦴

1989, Atlantic Records; from the television series *The Wonder Years***, New World Television, 1989.**

Album Notes: *Song Producers*: Denny Cordell, Don Was, David Was, Judson Spence, Charles Green, Brian Stone, Joh Keane, Deborah Gibson, Ray Manzarek, Patrick Leonard, David Crosby, Stephen Stills, Graham Nash, Neil Young, Burt Berns, Lou Adler, David Kershenbaum, Bob Marlette; *Executive Album Producers*: Toby Emmerich, Karen Gibson; *Engineer*: Dennis King.

Selections: 1 With A Little Help From My Friends (J. Lennon/P. McCartney) (4:14) *Joe Cocker*; 2 Baby I Need Your Loving (B. Holland/L. Dozier/E. Holland)(2:52) *Was (Not Was)*; 3 Drift Away (Williams)(3:54) *Judson Spence*; 4 For What It's Worth (Stop, Hey What's That Sound)(S. Stills)(2:35) *Buffalo Springfield*; 5 Get Together (Powers)(3:30) *Indigo Girls*; 6 In The Still Of The Night (I'll Remember)(Paris)(3:54) *Debbie Gibson*; 7 Twentieth Century-Fox (V. Morrison/R. Manzarek/M. Krieger/J. Densmore)(3:35) *The Escape Club*; 8 Ruby Tuesday (M. Jagger/ K. Richards)(3:22) *Julian Lennon*; 9 Teach Your Children (G. Nash)(2:51) *Crosby Stills Nash & Young*; 10 Brown-Eyed Girl (V. Morrison)(3:07) *Van Morrison*; 11 Will You Love Me Tomorrow (C. Goffin/C. King)(4:08) *Carole King*; 12 Come Home (Wonder Years)(D. Gibson)(2:03) *Debbie Gibson*; 13 Peace Train (C. Stevens)(4:30) *Richie Havens*.

Review: This infantile television series actually spawned a great soundtrack album that attracted a lot of frontliners, including Joe Cocker, Was (Not Was), Julian Lennon, Carole King, Richie Havens, and Crosby, Stills, Nash and Young, among others. Of course, many of these performances have been available elsewhere, but who can resist Cocker's rendition of "With A Little Help From My Friends," Was (Not Was)' version of "Baby I Need Your Loving," or Judson Spence's take on "Drift Away"? And that's only for a start. Other goodies in the CD also include Buffalo Springfield's "For What It's Worth," Van Morrison's "Brown-Eyed Girl," Carole King's "Will

You Love Me Tomorrow," and Debbie Gibson's tribute to the show, "Come Home." Alright, it's not great, but it's good fun.

The X-Files

Songs in the Key of X: Music from and Inspired by the X-Files Woof

1996, Warner Bros. Records; from the Fox television series *The X-Files***, 20th Century-Fox, 1995-97.**

Album Notes: *Music*: Mark Snow; *Song Producers*: Steve Fisk, Bill Botrell, Barrett Jones, Scott Litt, Tony Cohen, Filter, Nick Vincent, Curt Kirkwood, Glenn Danzig, Bob Irwin, Brian Eno, Elvis Costello, Rob Zombie, Terry Date, Charlie Clauser, P.M. Dawn; *Engineers*: Bil Emmons, Bill Botrell, Barrett Jones, Clif Norrell, Scott Litt, Tony Cohen, Filter, Matt Yelton, Chad Fridirici, Bill Kennedy, Vic Anesini, Rob Zombie, Terry Date, Michael Fossenkemper; *Album Executive Producers*: David Was, Chris Carter; *Engineer*: Keith Blake.

Selections: 1 X-Files Theme (Main Title)(M. Snow)(3:25); 2 Unmarked Helicopters (Soul Coughing)(3:22) *Soul Coughing*; 3 On The Outside (S. Crow/ J. Trott)(4:37) *Sheryl Crow*; 4 Down In The Park (G. Numan)(4:05) *Foo Fighters*; 5 Star Me Kitten (M. Stipe/P. Buck/M. Mills/B. Berry)(3:30) *William S. Burroughs, R.E.M.*; 6 Red Right Hand (N. Cave/M. Harvey)(6:11) *Nick Cave & The Bad Seeds*; 7 Thanks Bro (Filter/R. Patrick)(4:10) *Filter*; 8 Man Of Steel (F. Black)(5:00) *Frank Black*; 9 Unexplained (C.Kirkwood)(3:45) *Meat Puppets*; 10 Deep (G. Danzig)(3:50) *Danzig*; 11 Frenzy (D. Hess/A. Stevenson)(2:11) *Screamin' Jay Hawkins*; 12 My Dark Life (E. Costello)(6:20) *Elvis Costello, Brian Eno*; 13 Hands Of Death (Burn Baby Burn)(R. Zombie/C. Clauser)(4:13) *Rob Zombie, Alice Cooper*; 14 If You Never Say Goodbye (A. Cordes/D. Was/C. Carter)(4:06) *P.M. Dawn*; 15 X-Files Theme (P.M. Dawn remix)(M. Snow)(3:59).

Review: See entry below.

Music from the X-Files 🦴

1996, Warner Bros. Records; from the Fox television series, *The X-Files***, 20th Century-Fox, 1995-97.**

Album Notes: *Music*: Mark Snow; *Words*: Chris Carter; *Featured Vocal Performers*: David Duchovny, Gillian Anderson, Chris Carter, William B. Davis, Peter Donat, Jerry Hardin, Alf Humphreys, Joel Palmer, Mitch Pileggi, Paul Rabwin, Steve Railsback, Larold Rebhun, Frank Spotnitz, Floyd Red Crow Westerman, Steven Williams; *Featured Artists*: Erika Duke-

Kirkpatrick (cello), Teri DeSario (vocal); *Album Producers*: Mark Snow, Jeff Charbonneau, Chris Carter; *Engineer*: Larold Rebhun; *Assistant Engineers*: Richard Veltrap, Brian Virtue.

Selections: 1 Introitus: Praeceps transito spatium (1:51); 2 Materia primoris: The X-Files Theme (Main Title)(3:22); 3 Raptus (3:16); 4 Adflatus (3:36); 5 Deverbero (1:28); 6 Cantus excio (4:42); 7 Mercutura (3:23); 8 Lamenta (1:48); 9 Insequi (1:37); 10 Otium (1:43); 11 Dubitatio (2:49); 12 Iter (1:20); 13 Progigno de axis (1:35); 14 Carmen amatorium ex arcanum (2:39); 15 Facetus malum (2:42); 16 Memoria (2:02); 17 Mitis lumen (2:41); 18 Fides fragilis (1:35); 19 Exoptare ex veritas (1:30); 20 Kyrie (2:57).

Review: After the nonsense of the pop album *Music in the Key of X*, we have an original soundtrack to the hit TV series "The X-Files," featuring Mark Snow's moody and evocative score. Unfortunately, what we have isn't so much a recording of the film's excellent music, but an audio "event" merging the music with random snippets of faint dialog and spooky electronic sound effects. While this sound design may occasionally evoke the mood of the TV series, it goes on way too long and the continual intrusion of dialog ruins any possibility of an enjoyable listening of Snow's music. Perhaps die-hard *X-File*ophiles may get off on reliving the episodes recalled by the dialog excerpts, what purports to be "Music from the X-Files" becomes only annoying.

Randall D. Larson

Xena: Warrior Princess ♫♫♫

1996, Varese-Sarabande; from the UPN-TV series *Xena: Warrior Princess*, 1995-96.

Album Notes: *Music*: Joseph LoDuca; *Orchestrations*: Tim Simonec, Joseph LoDuca; *Music Editors*: Phillip Tallman, Richard Ford; Orchestra conducted by Tim Simonec, Randy Thornton; *Album Producer*: Joseph LoDuca; *Engineers*: Glen Neibur, Jared De Pasquale.

Selections: 1 Main Title (1:15); 2 The Warrior Princess (2:09); 3 Darfus (2:06); 4 Soulmates (2:24); 5 Burial (L. Lawless)(1:50); 6 Xena And The Big Bird (2:27); 7 Gabby Dance (1:00); 8 The Gauntlet (1:58); 9 Barn Blazers (2:21); 10 Fight On The Heads (2:54); 11 Draco's Men (2:16); 12 Glede Ma Glede (trad.) (:43); 13 Burying The Past (2:59); 14 Xena's Web (2:12); 15 Goodbye (2:49); 16 Giants (2:37); 17 Funeral Dance (1:35); 18 Challenging The Gods (3:10); 19 Dreamscape (3:01); 20 Quarterman's Festival (2:27); 21 Roll In The Leaves (:47); 22 Funeral Pyre (1:24); 23 On The Balcony (2:08); 24 The Oracle (3:15); 25 Hail Xena (1:35); 26 Going To Kill Me (:45); 27 The Wrath Of Callisto

"**F**ew artists of his stature are as talented in one area as Prince is in many."

Chris Gill
(Guitar Player, August, 1993)

(2:36); 28 Bloodlust (2:25); 29 Ladder Fight (4:44); 30 Main Title (extended version)(1:22).

Review: A "Hercules" spin-off that's eclipsed its predecessor in popularity, "Xena" inspired composer Joe LoDuca to improve on his derivative Hercules music and create a far more passionate and original theme for the vigilante, indomitable Amazon warrior Xena that mixes a pounding brass line with the chanting of a female chorus. The percussive, ethnic Amazon music intersperses itself throughout this lengthy album, balanced with some more traditional but no less energetic orchestral action cues and some surprisingly effective and rich moments of sentimentality. There are ripely melodramatic horror cues and a few pop-oriented treatments of dances and market sequences that fit comfortably into this epic canvas, making this one of the most enjoyable TV score albums around.

Jeff Bond

A Year in Provence ♫♫♫♫♫

1993, Silva Screen Records; from the TV mini-series *A Year in Provence*, BBC-TV, 1993.

Album Notes: *Music*: Carl Davis; *Orchestrations*: Carl Davis; Orchestra conducted by Carl Davis; *Featured Musicians*: Roy Gillard, Roger Garland (violin); Alan Walley (double bass); David Campbell (clarinet); Colin Green (guitar); Jack Emblow (accordion); Harold Fisher (percussion); Mark Warman (keyboards); Maurice Murphy (trumpet); David White (saxophone); *Album Producers*: David Stoner, James Fitzpatrick; *Engineer*: Mike Ross-Trevor.

Selections: 1 A Year In Provence (3:07); 2 January: Bonne Annee Mr. Mayle! (1:51); 3 February: Learning The Language (2:21); 4 March: Black Gold (2:12); 5 April: The Tony Awards (2:46); 6 May: Daylight Robbery (1:34); 7 Bailero (from Songs Of The Auvergne)(Cantaloube)(6:39) *Lesley Garrett*; 8 June: Bread Winner (2:41); 9 July: Room Service (2:20); 10 August: Frogbusters (3:30); 11 September: Chateau Mayle (3:29); 12 La delaissado (from Songs Of The Auvergne) (Cantaloube)(4:38) *Lesley Garrett*; 13 Malurous qu'o uno fenno (from Songs Of The

Auvergne)(Cantaloube)(1:33) *Lesley Garrett*; 14 October: War Of The Worlds (3:01); 15 November: Old Boys (2:54); 16 December: Christmas In Provence (4:04); 17 A Year In Provence (2:11).

Review: Based on a real-life story, "A Year in Provence" began when Peter and Annie Mayle decided to quit the London rat race and move to rustic Provence to savor the French way of life — good food, fine wines and seductive climate. The hilarious account of their first year there, trying to adjust to the idiosyncracies of the natives and the quaint traditions of the region, provided the basis for a book, and for the series of the same name which starred John Thaw and Lindsay Duncan. Taking a cue from the story, Carl Davis delivered a multi-faceted score, rife with amusing asides, and supremely exhilarating musical jokes that anyone can instantly appreciate. The themes throughout do not so much evoke Provence as they do any number of locales and situations that may be relevant to the story, but often don't seem to be ("Learning the Language," for instance, quotes the theme from *The Magnificent Seven,* while the main theme in "The Tony Awards" recalls a saloon scene in a western). If any real evocation of southern France can be found in the score, it is provided by three selections from Canteloube's "Songs of the Auvergne," gorgeously performed by Lesley Garrett, which, as any red-blooded Frenchman will tell you, have as much to do with Provence as the accordion that sometimes plays a lilting *valse musette* in Carl Davis' score. The cues, neatly divided one each to a month, are a tongue-in-cheek delight that faintly echo a foreigner's idea of the type of music one might hear in France; they prove fresh and inventive, and irresistibly enjoyable, whether in Provence or anywhere else.

The Young Indiana Jones Chronicles: volumes 1-4
♫♫♫♫

Album Notes: *Music*: Laurence Rosenthal, Joel McNeely; *Orchestrations*: David Slonaker, Lawrence Ashmore, Michael Patterson, Steven Bramson, John Bell; The Munich Symphony Orchestra, The Philharmonic Film Orchestra Munich and The West Australian Philharmonic Orchestra, conducted by Laurence Rosenthal, Joel McNeely, Charles Ketcham; *Album Producers*: Laurence Rosenthal, Joel McNeely; *Engineers*: Chris Dribble, Dave Hurt and Malcolm Luker.

Selections: VOLUME ONE: 1 Main Title Album Version (L. Rosenthal)(2:08); I Verdun 1916 (J. McNeely): 2 Remembering Verdun (1:40); 3 Race To The Front (1:04); 4 The Retreat (1:43);

5 Visiting Remy (4:10); 6 Aerial Pursuit (2:40); 7 Nocturnal Mission (2:36); 8 Requiem (3:26); II Peking 1910 (L. Rosenthal): 9 An American Thanksgiving/A Chinese Adventure (5:56); 10 Indy Is Ill (1:30); 11 The Long Night Of Dr. Wen Ch-iu (7:09); 12 West Meets East (1:53); III Paris 1916 (J. McNeely): 13 Arrival In Paris (1:59); 14 Afternoon Tea (2:50); 15 Breakfast With Mata (2:13); 16 Mozart: Viola Quintet In G Minor (2:44); 17 Parisian Stroll (1:40); 18 Still Life (2:04) *David Hartley*; 19 L'affaire d'amour (2:12); 20 Lover's Farewell (2:05); IV Barcelona 1917 (L. Rosenthal): 21 Boulevards Of Barcelona (1:30); 22 Picasso And Diaghilev (3:02); 23 The Dressing Room (2:23); 24 The Contessa (6:42); 25 Ballerina In Bondage (2:59); 26 Lead For Breakfast (4:39).

VOLUME TWO: 1 Main Title Alternate Version (L. Rosenthal)(:38); I Vienna 1908 (L. Rosenthal): 2 Indy And The Princess (6:10); 3 Skating In The Prater (1:49); 4 The Poetry Lesson (3:40); 5 Outfoxing The Fox (3:16); 6 Sophie's Chamber (4:08); II German East Africa 1916/The Congo 1917 (J. McNeely): 7 Desert Trek (3:20); 8 Morning (4:08); 9 Desert Storm (4:15); 10 Arrival At Port Gentil/Death Of Bartelomy (4:57); 11 Albert Schweitzer, Prisoner Of War (2:25); 12 Schweitzer Says Goodbye (2:34); III London 1916 (J. McNeely): 13 Oxford (:24); 14 Countryside Courtship (1:29); 15 Zeppelin Attack/Meeting Vicky (2:01); 16 War Of Words (3:25); 17 Suffragette Metting (1:55); 18 Celtic Love (2:55); 19 Proposal/Reunion (3:54); IV British East Africa 1909 (L. Rosenthal): 20 African Port (1:07); 21 Two New Friends (3:27); 22 Meto (3:05); 23 The Masai Elders (1:47); 24 Talking With Teddy (2:53); 25 Discovery Of The Oryx/Sacrifice (5:25).

VOLUME THREE: I Indiana Jones And The Scandal Of 1920 (J. McNeely): 1 Rhapsody In Blue (G. Gershwin)/Traveling To New York (2:40); 2 Scandal Walk (G. Gershwin/A. Jackson)(1:28); 3 Kate The Poet (4:01); 4 Rehearsal Montage (1:05); 5 Harem Dance, Beachball Dance, Clamshell Ballet And The Tap Dance Finale (1:12); 6 Meeting Peggy/New York Arrival (3:06); 7 Somebody Loves Me (1:14); 8 Sounds Like Perfection To Me (:57); 9 Gloria's Grand Entrance/The Penthouse Tango/Rhapsody In Blue (G. Gershwin)(2:32); 10 Turn On And Tiss Me (G. Gershwin/A. Jackson) (2:25); 11 Backstage At The Scandals (1:05); 12 A Poem For Indy (1:51); 13 Swanee (G. Gershwin/I. Caesar)(1:38); 14 The Tap Dance Rehearsal (:44); 15 She's Wonderful, Too (:44); II Indiana Jones And The Mystery Of The Blues (J. McNeely): 16 Sweetie Dear (J. Jordan)(2:33); 17 My Handy Man (E. Waters/J. Johnson)(3:02); 18 Warehouse Battle (6:33); 19 12th Street Rag (E. Bowman/A. Razaf)(3:02); 20 Blue Horizon (S. Bechet)(3:00) *Sidney Bechet*; 21 Corrupt Police (1:41); 22 I'm A Little Blackbird (G. Meyer/A. Johnson/R. Turk/ G. Clark)(3:21); 23 I Can't Believe You're In Love With Me (C.

Gaskill/J. McHugh)(1:25); 24 Tiger Rag (H. Da Costa)(2:27); 25 Twinkle Dixie (trad.)(:53); III Princeton 1916 (L. Rosenthal): 26 Princeton Days (5:07); 27 Tom Swift And His Electric Runabout (7:01); 28 The Senior Prom (2:46).

VOLUME FOUR: I Ireland 1916 (L. Rosenthal): 1 Welcome To Ireland (5:12); 2 Maggie (5:17); 3 Fight In The Bakery (2:11); 4 The Uprising (5:29); 5 A Terrible Beauty (4:35); II Indiana Jones And The Phantom Train Of Doom (J. McNeely): 6 Welcome To Africa! (1:04); 7 The Wrong Way Train (2:05); 8 Veldt Voyage (1:39); 9 The 21st Royal Fusileers (2:16); 10 The Old And The Bold (2:22); 11 Tally Ho (3:21); 12 Chasing The Phantom Train (3:55); 13 The Phantom Train Of Doom (8:07); 14 The Caper Continues (2:15); 15 The Native Battle (2:34); 16 Indy Hijacks The Balloon (4:15); III Northern Italy 1918 (L. Rosenthal): 17 Romantic Adventures (6:42); 18 Love And War (3:49); 19 Deserters (1:10); 20 Spaghetti (1:50); 21 The Bridal Gown (1:49); 22 Arrivederci Indy (3:39).

Review: There are many things to like intensely in these four volumes. The first is, of course, the abundance of music, and the fact that two excellent composers, Laurence Rosenthal and Joel McNeely, were each asked to write selected episodes in the series, a task they did with flying colors. The other is the diversity in each composer's approach, reflected in their different styles, but also in the fact that each episode is set in a different locale gave them an opportunity to be even more creative.

And then, as if all of it were not enough, the remarkable thing is that the music gets better as the listener proceeds from volume one to volume four.

Adding to the overall impact of the music, each composer has been given an opportunity to explain in the liner notes his approach to the episode he had been asked to score, thus giving the listener an extra dimension into the creative process.

Malcolm Arnold (1921-

Malcolm Arnold Film Music
♪♪♪♪♪

1992, Chandos Records.

Album Notes: *Orchestrations*: Christopher Palmer; *Music Editor*: Peter Newble; The London Symphony Orchestra, conducted by Richard Hickox; *Album Producer*: Brian Couzens; *Engineer*: Ralph Couzens; *Assistant Engineer*: Ben Connellan.

Selections: The Bridge On The River Kwai: 1 Prelude: The Prison Camp (6:26); 2 Colonel Bogey (K. Alford)(4:08); 3 The Jungle Trek (6:58); 4 Sunset (8:10); 5 Finale: The River Kwai March (3:06); Whistle Down The Wind: 6 Prelude (3:21); 7 The Three Kings (1:47); 8 Finale (3:56); The Sound Barrier: 9 Rhapsody For Orchestra, op. 38 (8:10); Hobson's Choice: 10 Overture And Shoe Ballet (3:44); 11 Willie And Maggie (5:23); 12 Wedding Night (6:22); 13 Finale (1:07); The Inn Of The Sixth Happiness: 14 London Prelude (3:41); 15 Romantic Interlude (3:40); 16 Happy Ending (Mountain Crossing/The Children) (6:39).

Review: With only two film scores, the Academy Award-winning *The Bridge on the River Kwai* in 1957, and *The Inn of the Sixth Happiness* the following year, Malcolm Arnold gained international fame, though few, outside of inner circles, know his name. One of the most prolific modern British composers, he came to film music when he scored *The Sound Barrier*, a film about jet planes and their attempts to fly faster than sound, made by David Lean, in 1952. The following year, *Hobson's Choice,* Lean's adaptation of the Harold Brighouse play, gave him an opportunity to echo in his score the elements of humor and romance that characterized this delightful film.

But it was with *The Bridge on the River Kwai* that Arnold came into his own. In his music, he magistrally evoked the power struggle between a fierce British officer and his Japanese captor in a war camp lost in the jungle, as well as the building of a bridge by the British prisoners and its destruction by an Allied commando. While the score called for some serial effects, much of it was a sensational display of action-driven rousing themes that paralleled the construction of the bridge across an escarpment and the progress of the commando through the jungle.

Another war drama, *The Inn of the Sixth Happiness* is the real-life story of an English woman who became a missionary in China, just as the Japanese invaded the country at the onset of World War II, and who manages to lead a large group of children to safety over the mountains. The tune "This Old Man," which permeated the film, became a runaway hit.

As for *Whistle Down the Wind,* written in 1961, it details a story of three children mistaking a dangerous murderer for Jesus, with the composer writing a pared-down chamber-like score that was particularly effective in the context.

With four out of the five scores making their first appearance on compact disc, in breathtaking digital sound, this CD is highly recommended, if only because it focuses on a film composer who deserves to be better known. With a few minor exceptions (the kettle drums in the opening bars of *The Bridge on the River Kwai* are much too loud and overbearing), performance by the London Symphony Orchestra, conducted by Richard Hickox, is superlative.

John Barry (1933-

The Best of John Barry ♪♪♪♪♪
1991, Polydor/U.K.

Album Notes: conducted by John Barry; *Album Producer*: John Barry; *Engineers*: Geoff Emerick, John Middleton.

Selections: 1 Goldfinger (2:25); 2 Sail The Summer Winds (from *The Dove*) (3:41); 3 Love Among The Ruins (3:21); 4 Lolita (from the stage musical *Lolita, My Love*)(3:00); 5 A Doll's House (2:50); 6 Follow, Follow (from *Follow Me*)(2:30); 7 Diamonds Are Forever (3:01); 8 Boom! (2:37); 9 Midnight Cowboy (3:45); 10 This Way Mary (from *Mary, Queen Of Scots*)(3:30); 11 The Glass Menagerie (2:50); 12 Thunderball (2:10); 13 007 (from *Goldfinger*)(1:49); 14 Play It Again (from *The Tamarind Seed*)(2:25); 15 Orson Welles' Great Mysteries (2:20); 16 We Have All The Time In The World (from *On Her Majesty's Secret Service*)(2:25); 17 The Whisperers (2:06); 18 Curiouser And Curiouser (from *The Adventures Of Alice In Wonderland*)(2:12); 19 Billy (from the stage musical *Billy*)(2:40); 20 The Good Times Are Coming (from *Monty Walsh*)(2:58); 21 Walkabout (3:14); 22 The Adventurer (2:08).

Review: Initially issued on LP in the early 1970s, this anthology of themes composed by John Barry for the screen and the stage offers many tracks that are not available anywhere else, in itself a boon for collectors. While it includes Barry's most famous tunes ("Goldfinger," "Thunderball," "We Have All the Time in the World," "Diamonds Are Forever"), often in reorchestrated versions that differ somewhat from the original, the set is of particular interest for the other tracks, like the lovely "Sail the Summer Winds," from *The Dove*, which takes the counterpoint of the main melody to create a new variation on the theme; "Follow, Follow," from *Follow Me*, a 1972 film with Mia Farrow; "This Way Mary," from *Mary, Queen of Scots;* "The Good Times Are Coming," from *Monte Walsh*, a western which stars Lee Marvin; and the main theme from *The Whisperers*, a drama starring Dame Edith Evans.

At the same time, Barry also worked on musicals, with three selections reflecting this particular side of his creativity, "Lolita," from the failed Broadway show *Lolita, My Love*, based on Valdimir Nabokov's novel; "Billy," the main song from the stage show of the same name, starring Michael Crawford; and "Curiouser and Curiouser," from the screen musical *The Adventures of Alice in Wonderland*.

Unlike his compilations of more recent vintage, this set presents the composer at his most creative, in renditions that are lively, strikingly original, and that plainly justify the unfading loyalty Barry commands among his fans.

The Film Music of John Barry 🎞🎞🎞🎞

1988, Columbia Records.

Album Notes: conducted by John Barry; *CD Producer*: Didier C. Deutsch; *Engineer*: Mark Wilder.

Selections: 1 The James Bond Theme (from *Dr. No*)(2:53); 2 Born Free (2:46); 3 Fun City (from *Midnight Cowboy*)(3:19); 4 The Lion

In Winter (2:45); 5 We Have All The Time In The World (from *On Her Majesty's Secret Service*)(3:30); 6 Wednesday's Child (from *The Quiller Memorandum*)(2:01) *Matt Monro*; 7 From Russia With Love (2:35); 8 Space March (from *You Only Live Twice*) (2:55); 9 The Wrong Box (2:31); 10 The Ipcress File (3:53); 11 Thunderball (3:13); 12 The Chase (3:05); 13 The Knack And How To Get It (2:48); 14 The Whisperers (2:37); 15 King Rat (4:15); 16 Next Time (from *The Appointment*)(2:34); 17 Goldfinger (4:23).

Review: There are numerous compilations of John Barry's film music available, but this relatively early CD release ought to be of interest to both the serious soundtrack aficionado as well as the casual listener. Comprised of session recordings made by Barry with full orchestra in the late 1960s, the album contains the usual, trademark themes associated with the composer, from a particularly jazzy rendition of "The James Bond Theme" (as well as selections from a number of other Bond adventures) to the soothing melodies of *Born Free* and *The Wrong Box*. While these particular selections may be no-brainers for incorporation into a Barry retrospective, this particular release is notable for its inclusion of the composer's more offbeat, innovative dramatic music from *The Chase*, *The Ipcress File* and *The Lion in Winter*. With this diversity of material included, the album adeptly spotlights all aspects of Barry's compositional skills and paints a more versatile musical portrait of the composer than many of the other, more routine Barry compilations out there.
Andy Dursin

Moviola: volume one 🎞🎞🎞

1992, Epic Soundtrax/Sony.

Album Notes: The Royal Philharmonic Orchestra, conducted by John Barry; *Album Producer*: John Barry; *Engineer*: Shawn Murphy.

Selections: 1 Out Of Africa (4:32); 2 Midnight Cowboy (4:06); 3 Body Heat (3:58); 4 Somewhere In Time (9:01); 5 Mary, Queen Of Scots (3:45); 6 Born Free (4:45); 7 Dances With Wolves (4:11); 8 Chaplin (3:27); 9 The Cotton Club (3:50); 10 Walkabout (3:03); 11 Frances (7:50); 12 We Have All The Time In The World (from On Her Majesty's Secret Service) (3:05); 13 Moviola (4:34).

Review: See entry below.

Moviola: volume two 🎞🎞🎞

1995, Epic Soundtrax/Sony.

Album Notes: The Royal Philharmonic Orchestra, conducted by John Barry; *Album Producer*: John Barry; *Engineer*: Shawn Murphy.

.soundsfsfsfereer.sound soundtracksi

Selections: The James Bond Suite: (1-9) 1 Goldfinger (2:41); 2 The James Bond Theme (2:01); 3 From Russia With Love (2:54); 4 Thunderball (2:33); 5 007 (1:48); 6 You Only Live Twice (2:22); 7 On Her Majesty's Secret Service (2:03); 8 Diamond Are Forever (2:26); 9 All Time High (from *Octopussy*)(3:56); 10 Until September (4:25); 11 King Kong (2:37); 12 Zulu (2:45); Dances With Wolves Suite: (13-17) 13 Pawnee Attack, Part I & II (4:05); 14 Kicking Bird's Gift (2:06); 15 Journey To Fort Sedgewick (2:40); 16 Two Socks/The Wolf Theme (1:32); 17 Farewell And Finale, Part I & II (9:52); 18 Did You Call Me (from *The Specialist*)(5:24); 19 The Specialist (5:39).

Review: These two albums provide an impressive cross-section of, and introduction to the work of John Barry. *Moviola* opens with *Out of Africa* and *Midnight Cowboy*—both popular works by the composer, but these prove to be among the less interesting offerings. *Body Heat*, a sultry, legato theme for jazz saxophone, is one of the best tracks, a sensual and seductive piece which lives up to its name. The deservedly popular *Somewhere in Time* is also presented in a rapturous performance. *Walkabout, Mary, Queen of Scots* and *Born Free* are less satisfying here than in Barry's original scoring (the replacement of Mary's harpsichord with solo violin deflates much of the theme's original effect). *Chaplin* however is a beautiful, melancholy theme, while *The Cotton Club* evokes a "film noir" feeling similar to *Body Heat*, but with a slightly more sinister flavor. The album closes with "Moviola", a work derived from Barry's unused music for *Prince of Tides* (a film assignment from which Barry resigned).

Moviola II contains a lengthy suite from the James Bond films, which arranges the title themes into a powerful, large-orchestral setting. *Zulu* features a more dynamic, less legato side of Barry (which he really has not shown since the '60s). However, the *Dances With Wolves* suite is unsatisfying: the performance is anemic compared to the original soundtrack. The same is true of the two themes from *The Specialist* which are also featured.

The first *Moviola* CD is undoubtedly the more successful of the two. However, despite some quirks in the second volume, both remain valuable and worthy representations of one the finest film composers ever, and are well-worth a place in one's collection.

When a composer, particularly one of John Barry's caliber, decides to revisit the themes he has created over the years, one has the right to expect a challenging vision of these themes. Unfortunately, the approach taken in these two CDs is much too reverential and solemn, and where some of the selections, notably the James Bond themes in the second volume, should have elicited crackling renditions to echo the originals, the ponderous tone adopted here, with long symphonic digressions and expanded musical lines, sounds too much like what Barry writes these days, in imitation of *Dances With Wolves*. In other words gorgeous, but ultimately less inspiring than the works he used to create when he was still struggling to establish his reputation.

Paul Andrew MacLean/Didier C. Deutsch

Out of Africa: The Classic John Barry ♫♫♫

1993, Silva Screen Records.

Album Notes: *Music*: John Barry; *Orchestrations*: Nic Raine; The City of Prague Philharmonic, conducted by Nic Raine; *Featured Soloists*: Michael Metelka (violin), Jaroslava Eliasova (piano), Bob Navratil (harmonica), Jindrich Nemecek (alto sax); *Album Producers*: Nic Raine, Mike Ross-Trevor; *Engineer*: Mike Ross-Trevor.

Selections: 1 Zulu (2:16); 2 Out Of Africa (4:25); 3 Midnight Cowboy (3:59); 4 The Last Valley (suite): Main Title/Death Of The Captain/End Title (8:36); 5 Eleanor And Franklin (1:26); 6 Hanover Street (4:50); 7 Born Free: Theme and Lions At Play (5:48); 8 Chaplin (2:55); 9 Dances With Wolves: The John Dunbar Theme (2:31); 10 Raise The Titanic (suite)(8:25); 11 Indecent Proposal (4:42); 12 The Persuaders (1:59); 13 Robin And Marian (suite)(7:37); 14 Body Heat (4:32); 15 Somewhere In Time (6:11); 16 The Lion In Winter (suite): The Lion In Winter/Eleanor's Arrival/We're Jungle Creatures (8:10).

Review: See entry below.

The Classic Film Music of John Barry: volume two ♫♫♫

1996, Silva Screen Records.

Album Notes: *Music*: John Barry; *Orchestrations*: Nic Raine; The City of Prague Philharmonic, conducted by Nic Raine; *Featured Soloists*: Josef Kroft (violin), Jaroslava Eliasova (piano, harpsichord), Jiri Bousek (flute, alto flute), Michal Horsa'k (cymbalum), Jan Burian (trumpet), Milan Zelenka (guitar); *Album Producer*: James Fitzpatrick; *Engineer*: John L. Timperley.

Selections: 1 High Road To China (suite)(8:10); 2 The Wrong Box (2:46); 3 A Man Alone (from *The Ipcress File*)(3:59); 4 The Black Hole (suite)(4:54); 5 The Appointment (2:18); 6 Love Theme (from *The Scarlet Letter*)(3:03); 7 Monte Walsh (suite)(11:10); 8 The Knack (1:46); 9 Cry The Beloved Country (4:32); 10 The Dove (suite)(6:28); 11 Walkabout (3:47); Mary

Queen Of Scots (suite): (12-14) 12 Vivre et mourir (2:11); 13 But Not Through My Realm (4:47); 14 This Way Mary (4:15); 15 Wednesday's Child (from *The Quiller Memorandum*)(2:31); 16 Romance For Guitar And Orchesta (from *Deadfall*)(10:52).

Review: The main interest of these two volumes resides in the selections, and particularly the longer suites, that are not otherwise available. And there are quite a few: "The Last Valley," "Eleanor and Franklin," "Hanover Street," "Born Free," "Raise the Titanic," and "Robin and Marian" in the first CD; "The Black Hole," "The Appointment," "Monte Walsh," "The Dove," and "Mary Queen Of Scots," in the second. One particular joy in the last CD is also the "Romance for guitar and orchestra," written for the 1968 thriller *Deadfall*, which gave Barry a rare opportunity to compose a long and eloquent concerto for solo instrument, removed from the James Bond action films he was primarily known for at the time.

Throughout, the Prague Philharmonic gives accurate readings of the various themes, and if some of the selections might seem superfluous, the overall concept of "classic" John Barry music plainly justifies their inclusion here.

Elmer Bernstein (1922-

Elmer Bernstein: Movie and TV Themes 🎵🎵🎵

1987, Ava Records/Mobile Fidelity Sound Lab.

Album Notes: *Music*: Elmer Bernstein; *Orchestrations*: Jack Hayes, Leo Shuken, Ruby Raskin; Orchestra conducted by Elmer Bernstein; *Album Producers*: Jackie Mills, Tommy Wolf; *Engineer*: "Bones" Howe.

Selections: 1 Rat Race (2:12); 2 Three Times Blusier (from the TV show *Take Five*)(3:08); 3 Radio Hysteria (from *Sudden Fear*)(2:03); 4 Anna Lucasta (3:50); 5 Hop, Skip But Jump (3:18); 6 Saints And Sinners (1:59); 7 Sweet Smell Of Success (3:19); 8 The Man With The Golden Arm (2:47); 9 Jubilation (4:20); 10 Walk On The Wild Side (3:39).

Review: See entry below.

Elmer Bernstein: A Man and His Movies 🎵🎵🎵

1991, Mainstream Records.

Album Notes: *Music*: Elmer Bernstein; *Orchestrations*: Jack Hayes, Leo Shuken, Ruby Raskin; Orchestra conducted by Elmer Bernstein; *Album Producers*: Jackie Mills, Tommy Wolf; *Engineer*: "Bones" Howe.

Selections: 1 Rat Race (2:15); 2 Three Times Blusier (from the TV show *Take Five*)(3:10); 3 Radio Hysteria (from *Sudden Fear*)(2:08); 4 Anna Lucasta (3:50); 5 Hop, Skip But Jump (3:18); 6 Big Top (2:01); 7 Sweet Smell Of Success (3:19); 8 The Man With The Golden Arm (2:52); 9 Jubilation (4:21); 10 Walk On The Wild Side (3:40); 11 Birdman Of Alcatraz (2:27); 12 Tree Treasure (from *To Kill A Mockingbird*)(3:50); 13 Main Title Theme (from *Baby The Rain Must Fall*) (2:30); 14 Main Title Theme (from *To Kill A Mockingbird*)(2:28) *The Pete Jolly Trio*.

Review: These early compilations bring together several themes composed by Elmer Bernstein between 1955, when he first appeared on the scene with the striking jazz score for *The Man With the Golden Arm,* and 1965, when he scored *Baby the Rain Must Fall* for Steve McQueen. By then, Bernstein had already created the score that would make him a household name, *The Magnificent Seven,* but since it was on another label, it couldn't be included here. While some selections differ from one CD to the other, both are essentially the same and, more tellingly, both use the same source material, which is of inferior quality. Despite Mobile Fidelity's remastering, which eliminates some of the most flagrant flaws in the original recording, the sound quality is not much better than the Mainstream recording, which makes no pretense at correcting it. If you care for the music, you might want to get both, as the Mainstream CD contains more selections. Otherwise, you might decide to pass this one out, until a better version is made available.

Elmer Bernstein by Elmer Bernstein 🎵🎵🎵🎵

1993, Denon Records.

Album Notes: *Music*: Elmer Bernstein; The Royal Philharmonic Orchestra, conducted by Elmer Bernstein; *Featured Soloists*: Kenny Baker (trumpet), Jack Parnell (drums), Cynthia Millar (Ondes Martinot/Synthesizers); *Album Producers*: Elmer Bernstein, Christopher Palmer; *Engineer*: Keith Grant.

Selections: 1 The Magnificent Seven (4:59); 2 To Kill A Mockingbird (8:19); 3 The Man With The Golden Arm (4:00); 4 The Grifters (8:15); 5 Walk On The Wild Side (4:00); 6 Hawaii (4:59); 7 The Great Escape (2:19); 8 Ghostbusters (2:47); 9 Hollywood And The Stars (2:59); 10 Rambling Rose (2:58); 11 Heavy Metal (4:56); 12 My Left Foot (7:10); 13 The Ten Commandments (7:49).

Review: Whether setting the musical stage for westerns, small town tales, or personal turmoil, few modern film composers have been as able to capture the essence of the American spirit as Elmer Bernstein. *Elmer Bernstein by Elmer Bernstein* showcases 13 of the composer's classic themes, including *To Kill a Mockingbird*, *The Man With the Golden Arm*, *Walk on the Wild Side*, *The Ten Commandments*, *Ghostbusters* and *The Magnificent Seven*.

With the composer himself conducting the Royal Philharmonic Pops Orchestra, these familiar strains take on a new dimension. Repeated listening to these works proves that Bernstein's genius is on a par with that of Aaron Copland, whose influence on the direction of Bernstein's approach to music cannot be denied.

If you are a fan of film music, or just plain great music, this disc is required listening!

Charles L. Granata

Claude Bolling (1930-

Bolling Films ♪♪♪♪

1992, DRG Records.

Album Notes: *Music*: Claude Bolling; Orchestras conducted by Claude Bolling; *Album Producer*: Van-John Sfiridis.

Selections: 1 Borsalino: Main Theme (2:18); Lucky Luke: 2 I'm A Poor Lonesome Cowboy (1:35) *Pat Woods*; 3 Traversee de l'Ouest (Crossing The West)(4:48); Les brigades du Tigre: 4 Theme de Valentin (2:09); L'annee sainte: 5 En cavale (On The Lam)(2:12); Le Magnifique: 6 La Plaza (2:20); 7 Tatiana (2:57); 8 Concerto pour piano tueurs et orchestra (Concerto For Killer Piano and Orchestra)(2:45); Qui: 9 Who Are You? (3:30); 10 Full Speed (2:15); 11 Flic Story: Theme (3:30); 12 Trois hommes a abattre (Three Men To Kill): Main Title (2:44); 13 Main Title: On ne meurt que deux fois (2:44); 14 L'etrange Monsieur Duvallier: Main Theme (1:30); The Awakening: 15 Last Judgment (2:54); 16 Catch Me A Spy: Main Title (3:52); Louisiane: 17 Old New Orleans (2:21); 18 Louisiana Waltz (3:50) *Dee Dee Bridgewater*; 19 Dixieland (1:44); Race For The Bomb: 20 Graphic Title (:40); 21 Joliot Curie(1:51); 22 Szilard-Teller And The Japanese (4:58); California Suite: 23 California (2:50); 24 Love Theme (2:50); La Gitane (The Gypsy Girl): 25 Caramba (Main Title)(:58); 26 Mona (1:10); La ballade des Daltons: 27 Dalton Musical (with vocal and chorus)(5:20).

Review: In the U.S., Claude Bolling is primarily known for his semi-classical collaborations with artists like Jean-Pierre Rampal or Yo Yo Ma, and for an occasional soundtrack (*Louisiane*, *California Suite*). In his native France, he is held in great admiration, and a Gallic equivalent to Henry Mancini,

whose many scores rank among the best ever written in a light jazz-pop vein.

This excellent compilation actually surveys several of the French and American films which Bolling has scored, and provides a casual coverage of his career. There is enough here to satisfy the most demanding customers, with the composer expressing himself in various genres, from thrillers to comedies, from musicals to... westerns! It all amounts to a great deal of fun, in a CD that should enable many collectors to better appreciate Bolling as an all-around film composer.

Scott Bradley

Tex Avery Cartoons ♪♪

1992, Milan Records.

Album Notes: *Music*: Scott Bradley; The M-G-M Studio Orchestra, conducted by Scott Bradley; *Album Produced*: David Franco; *Engineer*: Bob Norberg.

Selections: 1 Cell Bound (#291) (5:04); 2 Little Johnny Jet (#267) (7:18); 3 TV Of Tomorrow (#274) (6:32); 4 Three Little Pups (#269) (2:58); 5 Deputy Droopy (#288) (5:32); 6 Draga-long Droopy (#271) (7:31).

Review: Composer Scott Bradley did some stunningly effective work on Tex Avery's manic one-reelers for M.G.M. and he certainly deserves an album of his work, but this CD surely will only appeal to hardcore fans. The album suffers greatly from the fact that each of the six musical suites featured here are filled with dialogue and sound effects. Why would anyone not want to just buy a video tape and enjoy the animation, too? Bradley's contribution to the art of animation scoring was without a doubt just as important as Carl Stalling's, but at least some of the recordings on Stalling's albums were dialogue free. Bradley certainly followed the practice of incorporating familiar and popular songs of the time into his ever changing musical landscape. His work still remains a delight, but without the distractions please.

David Hirsch

Geoffrey Burgon

Brideshead Revisited ♪♪♪♪▷

1992, Silva Screen Records; from the Granada-TV series *Brideshead Revisited*, 1981.

Album Notes: *Music*: Geoffrey Burgon; The Philharmonia Orchestra conducted by Geoffrey Burgon; *Featured Soloist*: Lesley Garrett, soprano; *Album Producers*: Geoffrey Burgon, James Fitzpatrick; *Engineer*: Mike Ross-Trevor; *Assistant Engineer*: Marc Williams.

Selections: Brideshead Revisited (1981): 1 Brideshead Revisited (2:01); 2 Julia (3:44); 3 Julia's Theme (4:02); 4 The Hunt (2:21); 5 Fading Light (3:53); 6 Farewell To Brideshead (2:52); Testament Of Youth (1979): 7 Testament Of Youth (1:32); 8 Intimations Of War (3:30); 9 Elegy (2:25); 10 Finale (2:10); Bleak House (1985): 11 Bleak House (1:40); 12 The Streets Of London (3:57); 13 Dedlock vs. Boythorn (1:18); 14 Lady Dedlock's Quest (2:53); 15 Finale (2:31); Tinker, Tailor, Soldier, Spy (1979): 16 Opening Music (1:33); 17 Nunc Dimittis (Closing Music)(2:15) *Lesley Garrett*; The Chronicles Of Narnia (1991): 18 Aslan's Theme (1:30); 19 The Great Battle (2:45); 20 Mr. Tumnus' Tune (1:11); 21 The Storm At Sea (1:33); 22 Aslan Sacrificed (2:31); 23 The Journey To Harfang (2:21); 24 Farewell To Narnia (1:41).

Review: The elegant score heard behind the scenes in "Brideshead Revisited" was composed by a little known British composer, who began his career writing music for some "Dr. Who" episodes, and promptly imposed himself with his impressive score for the 1981 Granada-TV television series. This anthology covers four other series which all bear his unmistakable musical style, "Testament of Youth" and "Tinker, Tailor, Soldier, Spy," both from 1979; "Bleak House," from 1985; and "The Chronicles of Narnia." Among those, "Tinker...," an adaptation of a John Le Carre's novel, starring Alec Guinness as the dour George Smiley, is probably the best known. It's also the one that elicited the strongest statement from the composer, a dark, brooding theme that set the tone for the whole series. A war drama, "Testament of Youth" suggested a score which contrasted the bombast of the war effort and the serenity of happier times. An adaptation of Charles Dicken's novel, "Bleak House" found Burgon writing in a different mood, an evocation of the Victorian time, at once exhilarating and bitter sweet. As for "The Chronicles of Narnia," an adaptation of C.S. Lewis' allegorical novels, its magical narrative about children escaping to the mythical kingdom of Nardia prompted Burgon to create a score that's wonderfully lyrical and mischievously exciting.

Charles Chaplin (1889-1977)

Charlie! 🦴🦴🦴🦴

1993, Silva America.

Album Notes: *Music*: Charles Chaplin; *Orchestrations*: Francis Shaw; The Munich Symphony Orchestra conducted by Francis Shaw; *Featured Musicians*: George Schwenk (accordion), Monique Billick (mandolin), Leonora Hall (piano); *Album Producer*: Christopher Landor; *Engineer*: Alan Snelling.

Selections: Limelight: 1 Eternally (4:57); The Idle Class: 2 Foxtrot (1:22); A King In New York: 3 Mandolin Serenade (4:10); 4 Weeping Willows (3:26); 5 Peace Patrol (2:30); The Freak: 6 Love Song (4:34); Monsieur Verdoux: 7 Rumba (2:24); 8 Tango "Bitterness" (2:49); 9 Cancan "A Paris Boulevard" (2:20); Modern Times (medley): 10 Smile/Charlie's Dance/Toy Waltz/ In The City (8:14); 11 There's Always One You Can't Forget (4:07); The Great Dictator: 12 Napoli March (2:37); City Lights: 13 Beautiful Wonderful Eyes (3:06); A Countess From Hong Kong: 14 This Is My Song (5:45).

Review: While Charles Chaplin will always remain in the minds of most people as the greatest of the silent artistes, few remember that he was also an accomplished composer, who scored his own films with some delightfully beguiling melodies. In the days when film actors couldn't talk, Chaplin's music was his voice and, whether he was The Little Tramp or a Hitler wanna-be, he always spoke in the most eloquent tones. The characters exuded more emotion and drew more compassion from the audience because the music had laid their feelings bare. Perhaps more than anyone else, Chaplin defined the true power of the leitmotif underscore. Conductor Francis Shaw lovingly guides The Munich Symphony through his own orchestrations of 17 classic themes from eleven Chaplin films. Each is reproduced with all of the composer's power intact. Included in this anthology is "Beautiful Wonderful Eyes" from *City Lights*, several comedic dance numbers from *Monsieur Verdoux*, "This is My Song" from *The Countess from Hong Kong*, and a medley from *Modern Times* that featured Chaplin's biggest hit, "Smile."

David Hirsch

The Gold Rush: The Film Music of Charles Chaplin
🦴🦴🦴🦴▷

1996, RCA/Germany.

Album Notes: *Music*: Charles Chaplin; *Arrangements*: Eric Rogers, Carl Davis, Eric James, Arthur Johnson, David Raksin; The Deutsches Symphonie-Orchester of Berlin, conducted by Carl Davis; *Album Producer*: Klaus Bischke; *Engineer*: Herman Leppich.

Selections: The Kid: 1 Opening Music (2:38); 2 Garret Waltz (1:30); 3 Blue Eyes (1:49); 4 Kidnap (3:40); 5 Doss House (4:28); The Gold Rush: 6 Overture and Storm (2:38); 7 Thanksgiving Dinner (2:58); 8 Georgia (3:51); 9 Dance Of The Rolls (1:23); 10 Rejected (2:03); 11 Discovery (2:15); 12 Chance Meeting and Finale (3:10); The Circus: 13 The Circus March (1:35); 14 Breakfast And A Hungry Girl (3:39); 15 The Girl (1:35); 16 Flirtation Waltz (3:28); 17 The Tightrope Walker (2:41); City Lights: 18 Fanfare (1:27); 19 The Millionaire (2:25); 20 The Nightclub 1 (:41); 21 The Nighclub 2 (:41); 22 The Nightclub 3 (1:04); 23 The Nightclub 4 (1:30); 24 The Flowerseller (4:09); 25 The Boxing Ring (1:27); 26 Finale (1:39); Modern Times: 27 Main Title (1:12); 28 Factory Machines (3:48); 29 The Gamin (1:08); 30 Cafeteria And Cigar Shop (2:06); 31 Dream House (Smile)(1:42); 32 Department Store (Roller Skating)(1:21); 33 Lunchtime (2:28); 34 Into The Sunset (Smile)(3:12).

Review: As a film composer, Charles Chaplin had a schmaltzy streak in him. His best known compositions ("Smile," "Eternally") today sound a bit sugar-coated and from another era. Yet, there was a winsome charm to his music that subtly matched the comic undertones of his films in which he often portrayed a simple, romantic, impoverished innocent, forever assailed by modern life and the powerful ones, and hopelessly in love with the simple girl next door.

Both the Silva Screen and the BMG sets complement each other, by presenting large extracts from these films, the Silva set focusing on the latter day films, while the BMG set covers the earlier ones. Both reveal in Chaplin a composer who may not rank among the great Hollywood film scorers of his era, but whose music is an important addition to the flickering black and white images of his films.

While the Silva Screen CD is readily available, the "powers-that-be" at BMG/U.S.A., in their infinite wisdom, decided not to release in this country the series of wonderful recordings prepared by their German company to celebrate the 100th anniversary of the movies, including this set. Finding it will probably take some doing, but it's well worth the effort.

Ry Cooder (1947-

Music by Ry Cooder ♪♪♪

1995, Warner Bros. Records.

Album Notes: *Music:* Ry Cooder; *Featured Musicians:* Ry Cooder (guitars, piano, mandola, bass, accordion), Jim Dickinson, Sam Samudio, Van Dyke Parks (piano, organ), Tom Sauber (banjo, guitar), Alan Pasqua (synthesizers), David Lindley (saz, banjo, mandolin, fiddle), Milt Holland, Ras Baboo, Miguel Cruz, Emil Richards (percussion), Marc Savoie, Flaco Jimenez (accordion), Kazu Matsui (shakuhatchi), Jorge Cal-

deron, Tim Drummond, Bill Bryson (bass), David Mansfield (violin, cello), Gayle Levant (harp), Tom Sauber (jaw harp), Osamu Kitajima (biwa, koto), Jim Keltner (drums), George Bohannon (baritone horn), Walt Sereth, Harold Battiste, Steve Douglas, John Bolivar, Ernie Fields, Herman Riley (saxophone), John "Juke" Logan (harmonica), Bobby Bryant, John Hassell (trumpet); *Album Producers:* Ry Cooder, Joachim Cooder.

Selections: CD 1: Paris Texas: 1 Paris Texas (2:53); Southern Comfort: 2 Theme (3:47); Alamo Bay: 3 (5:10); The Border: 4 Across The Borderline (R. Cooder/J. Hiatt/J. Dickinson)(3:05) *Freddy Fender, Bobby King, Willie Greene Jr.*; 5 Highway 23 (1:57); Streets Of Fire: 6 Bomber Bash (4:03); Blue City: 7 Greenhouse (3:38); 8 Nice Bike (1:36); Johnny Handsome: 9 I Like Your Eyes (2:26); 10 Main Theme (1:54); Crossroads: 11 See You In Hell, Blind Boy (2:10); 12 Feelin' Bad Blues (4:17); Southern Comfort: 13 Swamp Talk (1:05); Johnny Handsome: 14 Angola (2:03); Crossroads: 15 Viola Lee Blues (3:10); The Long Riders: 16 The Long Riders (3:16); 17 Archie's Funeral (Hold To God's Unchanging Hand)(2:43); 18 Jesse James (trad.)(5:05).

CD 2: Trespass: 1 King Of The Street (R. Cooder/J. Keltner/R. Zemeckis/B. Gale)(3:59); Johnny Handsome: 2 Sunny's Tune (2:57); The Border: 3 No quiero (S. Samudio)(2:45) *Sam Samudio*; Johnny Handsome: 4 Cruising With Rafe (R. Cooder/J. Keltner)(3:03); Alamo Bay: 5 Klan Meeting (2:48); Johnny Handsome: 6 I Can't Walk This Time/The Prestige (6:50); Trespass: 7 East St. Louis (2:04); 8 Goose And Lucky (1:40); Geronimo: An American Legend: 9 Goyakla Is Coming (R. Cooder/Hoon-Hoortoo/R.C. Nakai)(1:10); Southern Comfort: 10 Canoes Upstream (1:10); Paris, Texas: 11 Cancion mixteca (J.L. Alavez)(4:16); The Border: 12 Maria (:51); Geronimo: An American Legend: 13 Bound For Canaan (Sieber And Davis)(R. Cooder/G. Clinton)(1:28); 14 Bound For Canaan (The 6th Cavalry)(R. Cooder/G. Clinton)(1:37); 15 Train To Florida (Hoon-Hortoon/R.C. Nakai/J. Benally)(9:28); Paris, Texas: 16 Houston In Two Seconds (2:02).

Review: This is an agreeable double-album set from Warner Bros. that serves as a selective overview of the blues guitarist's infrequent forays into the world of film music composition. Cooder's music is often like musical glue in a movie, usually working strictly as an atmospheric backdrop to the drama on-screen. Predictably, this results in some positive and negative attributes in his film scores. While Cooder's music is often gritty and "down home" acoustic, often times his music is only a mood — not a piece of fleshed out music. Of course, this services the needs of the films he's working on, but more often than not, it makes for rather tedious listening apart from its source. Listeners will want to note the presence here of previously unavailable music from *Southern Comfort* and *Streets of Fire*, along with released cues from many of his most popular scores, including *The Long Riders, Crossroads, Trespass,* and *Paris, Texas.* Packaging is unusually slim for a set like this, comprised only of brief notes from the composer and frequent collaborator Walter Hill. In all, a must for fans of Cooder though not an essential purchase by any means for others.

Andy Dursin

Stewart Copeland (1952-

The Equalizer & Other Cliff Hangers 🎵🎵

1990, IRS Records.

Album Notes: *Music:* Stewart Copeland; *Album Producer:* Jeff Seitz; *Engineer:* Jeff Seitz.

Selections: 1 Lurking Solo (5:02); 2 Music Box (2:19); 3 Screaming Lord Cole And The Comanches (4:52); 4 The Equalizer Busy Equalising (3:17); 5 Green Fingers (Ten Thumbs) (3:34); 6 Archie David In Overtime (4:00); 7 Tancred Ballet (3:20); 8 Dark Ships (5:33); 9 Flowershop Quintet (3:42); 10 Rag Pole Dance (4:25).

Review: Best known for his role as drummer of the rock group Police, one of the major rock acts of the 1980s, Copeland turned his talents to writing soundtracks for film and TV. *The Equalizer and Other Cliff Hangers* is a selection of themes and cues, some of which were created for the television series *The Equalizer,* starring Edward Woodward. While some of the themes heard in this collection have a quirky feel to them ("Music Box," "Green Fingers," "Tancred Ballet"), most rely on the type of electronic drum so prevalent in television today, and fail to make much of an impression, unless you groove on TV themes that all sound the same and are interchangeable from one series to the next.

Vladimir Cosma (1940-

The Very Best of Vladimir Cosma 🎵🎵🎵🎵

1990, DRG Records.

Album Notes: *Music:* Vladimir Cosma; Orchestras conducted by Vladimir Cosma; *Featured Soloists:* Ivry Gitlis (violin),

Gheorghe Zamfir (Pan flute), Vladimir Cosma (piano), Pierre Dutour (trumpet).

Selections: CD 1: The Student: 1 You Call It Love (4:58); 2 Ned Composes (2:40); Chateauvallon: 3 Power And Glory (V. Cosma/V. Buggy)(3:09) *Herbert Leonard;* La Boum: 4 Reality (V. Cosma/J. Jordan)(4:47) *Richard Sanderson;* 5 Go On Forever (V. Cosma/J. Jordan)(3:43) *Richard Sanderson;* Mistral's Daughter: 6 Only Love (V. Cosma/P. Delanoe)(4:15) *Nana Mouskouri;* 7 The Cavaillon Series (4:07); La Boum 2: 8 Your Eyes (V. Cosma/J. Jordan)(4:41) *Cook Da Books;* 9 Maybe You're Wrong (3:27) *Freddie Meyer, King Harvest Group;* The Undergifted On Vacation: 10 Destiny (V. Cosma/P. Adler/G. Marchand) (4:34) *Guy Marchand;* The Roses Of Dublin: 11 Theme (3:35); Till We Meet Again: 12 My Life (V. Cosma/J. Jordan)(3:14) *Mireille Mathieu;* The Tall Blond With A Black Shoe: 13 Sirba (2:04); The Swerve: 14 The Swerve (4:59); Diva: 15 Aria from La Wally (A. Catalani)(3:27) *Wilhelmina Fernandez;* 16 Sentimental Walk (3:37).

CD 2: Michel Strogoff: 1 Nadia's Theme (2:43); The Goat: 2 La cabra (3:42); The Super Ace: 3 The Super Ace (3:20); My Father's Glory: 4 My Father's Glory (3:20); The Ladies' Chamber: 5 For Love (2:37); Le bal: 6 Le bal (3:07); The Secret Drawer: 7 A Happy Memory (2:53); The Viper: 8 The Viper (4:57); The Great Families: 9 The Farewell Waltz (3:22); The Young Girls: 10 The Young Girls (2:01); My Mother's Castle: 11 My Mother's Castle (2:32); The Mad Adventures Of Rabbi Jacob: 12 The Grand Rabbi (2:39); The Beautiful English Woman: 13 The Beautiful English Woman (2:54); The Man From Suez: 14 The Man From Suez (2:37); 15 Next Year If Everything's All Right (2:45); The Seventh Target: 16 The Berlin Concerto (7:01).

Review: One of the most popular film composers in France, Vladimir Cosma is virtually unknown in this country. A musician of considerable talent and versatility, he has distinguished himself in light comedies, a genre in which he particularly excels, as well as in action films and serious dramas, and won the Cesar, the French equivalent of the Oscar, for his scores for *Le bal,* in 1982, and the international hit, *Diva,* in 1984.

This 2-CD anthology collects together many of the themes he wrote over the past 25 years, including those for films that were shown in this country, like *Mistral's Daughter, The Tall Blond With a Black Shoe, Diva, My Father's Glory, My Mother's Castle,* and *The Mad Adventures of Rabbi Jacob.* The composer's creative characteristics—unusual instrumentations, strongly melodic themes—are all in evidence here, with several vocals in English that should make his work more accessible and enjoyable to a larger audience.

Mychael Danna

The Adjuster: Music for the Films of Atom Egoyan ♪♪♪♪

1997, Varese-Sarabande Records.

Album Notes: *Music:* Mychael Danna; The Adjuster: *Featured Musicians:* Djivan Gasparian (duduk), Eve Egoyan (piano), Mark Fewer (violin); Speaking Parts/Family Viewing: The Espirit Orchestra, conducted by Alex Pauk; *Album Producer:* Mychael Danna; *Engineers:* Hayward Parrot, Gary Gray.

Selections: The Adjuster: 1 Flashlight (3:36); 2 Dinner At Home (2:44); 3 Archery (2:58); 4 House Tour (3:32); 5 Fire (4:43); Speaking Parts: 6 Speaking Parts (5:10); 7 Piano Concerto (slow movement)(3:00); 8 Clara's Story (2:25); 9 Talk Show (6:48); 10 Touch (3:23); Family Viewing: 11 The Great White Bear (2:01); 12 Unmarked Grave (1:41); 13 A Natural Death (3:38); 14 Memories, These Things Possess You (2:29); 15 North Wing (3:37); 16 Family Reunion (3:26).

Review: This set surveys the scores written by Mychael Danna, a leading Canadian composer, for the films of Atom Egoyan, *Family Viewing* (1987), *Speaking Parts* (1989), and *The Adjuster* (1991), all of them expressing a similar central theme about the encroaching influence of technology in modern society and the disintegration of family life. Often brooding and detached, oppressive and emotionless, the music matches the moods in the films, subliminally reinforcing the message on the screen. Removed from its primary reason, it proves remarkably compelling, though it requires close attention to really make an impression. Some cues, however, are particularly attractive, notably the slow movement from the "Piano Concerto" composed for *Speaking Parts*, which suggests that Danna can also write in a lyrical vein, and be quite effective at it.

Carl Davis (1936-

The Silents ♪♪♪♪▹

1988, Virgin Classics.

Album Notes: *Music:* Carl Davis; The London Philharmonic Orchestra, conducted by Carl Davis; *Featured Soloists:* David Nolan (violin), Robert Truman (cello); *Album Producer:* Paul Wing; *Engineer:* Tony Faulkner.

Selections: Napoleon: 1 Eagle Of Destiny/Bal des Victimes (6:01); The Crowd: 2 The Announcement (6:05); Flesh And The Devil: 3 The Ball/The Garden Scene (8:13); Show People: 4 The Preview (2:20); Broken Blossoms: 5 Moonbeams (8:20); The Wind: 6 The Cyclone/The Wedding Night/Finale (10:08); The Thief Of Bagdad: 7 The Winged Horse/The Flying Carpet (3:53); The Big Parade: 8 March/ Rookies/Night Battle (6:59); Greed: 9 Wedding Night/Biting The Hand (5:48); Old Heidelberg: 10 Reunion/Finale (7:17).

Review: Throughout much of the 1980s, composer Carl Davis has been busy recreating a lost art. He has composed and recorded brand new scores for several classic pre-sound films for the "Thames Silents" television series. Unlike the majority of people scoring these films, limited to the use of solo piano, organ or synthesizers, Davis has been working with a full symphonic orchestra. He began with Abel Gance's monumental 235-minute epic, *Napoleon*, a film he often conducts to on live tours (the film was also rescored by Carmine Coppola). This album contains highlights from *Napoleon* (1927) and nine other scores to such legendary films as *The Thief of Bagdad* (1924), D.W. Griffith's *Broken Blossoms* (1919) and Eric von Stroheim's *Greed* (1924). Davis has managed to tap into that long disused and unique style of film scoring. He creates words where there is none, capturing the emotional moments depicted on film in a lyrical manner. The music can also stand alone as a magnificent performance piece. A beautiful tribute to a bygone era.

David Hirsch

Georges Delerue (1925-1992)

The London Sessions: volume one, two, and three ♪♪♪♪

1990, Varese-Sarabande (volumes one and two); 1991, Varese-Sarabande (volume three).

Album Notes: *Music:* Georges Delerue; Orchestra conducted by Georges Delerue, Frank Fitzpatrick; *Albums Producers:* Georges Delerue, Frank Fitzpatrick; *Engineer:* Keith Grant.

Selections: CD 1: 1 Theme (from *Platoon*)(6:54); 2 Suite (from *Rich And Famous*)(4:55); 3 End Title (from *Her Alibi*)(5:28); 4 Friendship (from *Beaches*)(3:27); 5 Suite (from *Exposed*)(9:17); 6 Main Title (from *Biloxi Blues*)(2:32); 7 Suite (from *A Little Romance*)(3:29); 8 Suite (from *Crimes Of The Heart*)(10:42); 9 Between You And Me (G. Delerue/F. Fitzpatrick)(from *Her Al-*

ibi)(3:45) *Carl Anderson, Eileen Clark*; 10 Reprise (from *Rich And Famous*)(1:11).

CD 2: 1 Suite (from *Steel Magnolias*)(8:01); 2 Theme (from *Interlude*)(3:20); 3 Suite (from *The Escape Artist*)(7:19); 4 Theme (from *The Pick-Up Artist*) (3:08); 5 Hommage a Francois Truffaut: (a) Shoot The Piano Player, (b) Love At 20, (c) Jules and Jim, (d) The Soft Skin, (e) Two English Girls, (f) Such A Gorgeous Girl Like Me, (g) Vivement Dimanche!, (h) Day For Night, (i) The Woman Next Door, (j) The Last Metro (12:15) *Georges Delerue*; 6 End Title (from *Maxie*)(4:03); 7 Suite (from *An Almost Perfect Affair*)(5:35); 8 Suite (from *Salvador*) (8:01).

CD 3: 1 Suite (from *Something Wicked This Way Comes*)(11:48); 2 Theme (from *House On Carrol Street*)(3:10); 3 Suite (from *A Little Sex*)(9:25); 4 Theme (from *Maid To Order*)(2:12); 5 Theme (from *Man Woman And Child*)(3:18); 6 Suite (from *Memories Of Me*)(6:48); 7 Suite (from *Agnes Of God*)(9:38) 8 Suite (from *True Confessions*)(11:50).

Review: This compilation series—a must-have in any soundtrack collection—superbly demonstrates Georges Delerue's talent and versatility at creating emotive music through fragile, intimate melodies that have a tender poignancy. The series also presents a lot of selections that had never been recorded before.

Central to the three CDs are the rejected adagio from *Platoon*, a passionate composition for strings; a glorious symphonic suite from *Rich and Famous*; selections from *Steel Magnolias*; the pretty piano, flute, and violin romance from *The Escape Artist*; the gentle jauntiness of strings and marimba in *The Pick-Up Artist*; the breezy music from *A Little Sex*; a wistful, melancholy suite from *Memories of Me*; the evocatively brooding violin and oboe melody from the Hitchcockian thriller *The House on Carroll Street*; the baroque theme from *Maid to Order*; the jazzy saxophone theme from *Man, Woman and Child*; and a 12-minute suite of themes written for the films of Francois Truffaut.

Of particular interest is a nearly 12-minute suite from Delerue's rejected music for *Something Wicked This Way Comes* in the final volume. The score, one of Delerue's most dramatic efforts, contrasts quiet interludes with harsh, crashing winds; typical of its overall effect, an oscillating chordal theme for strings and woodwinds over rhythmic, rumbling percussion evokes an effective mood of mystery. This orchestral suite actually represents only half the score's musical texture—it does not include the choir or calliope that were featured prominently in the original recording, nor does it use the synthesizer as part of the orchestra. Nonetheless, it stands

out as one of Delerue's most interesting scores, and its rarity makes it something to be eagerly sought.

Randall D. Larson

Truffaut & Delerue: On the Screen ✠✠✠✠✠

1986, DRG Records; selections from the movies *Confidentially Yours*, **1983;** *A Beautiful Girl Like Me*, **1972;** *Day for Night*, **1972;** *The Last Metro*, **1980; and** *The Woman Next Door*, **1981.**

Album Notes: *Music*: Georges Delerue; *Orchestrations*: Georges Delerue; (except where indicated) Orchestras conducted by Georges Delerue.

Selections: Confidentially Yours: 1 Main Titles (2:07); 2 Marie-Christine Tantalizing Julien (1:20); 3 Murder Of Mrs. V. (1:47); 4 Barbara Remembers (1:10); 5 Let's Go To Nice (1:23); 6 Java Of The Hot Street (2:26); 7 The Stranger Customer Again (4:01); 8 Tango Of The Hot Street (1:46); 9 Julien And Barbara (1:25); 10 Ah Barbara (1:01); A Beautiful Girl Like Me: 11 Main Titles (1:49); 12 Instrumental Theme (1:31); Day For Night: 13 Grand Choral (2:23); 14 La Victorine (2:08); The Last Metro: 15 Main Titles (2:04); 16 Mon amant de Saint-Jean (E. Carrara/L. Agel)(2:50) *Lucienne Delyle*; 17 Sombreros et mantilles (J. Vaissade/Chanty)(3:05) *Rina Ketty*; 18 Seule ce soir (P. Durand/R. Noel/J. Casanova)(3:18) *Leo Marjane*; 19 J'attendrai (D. Olivieri/ L. Poterat)(2:56) *Rina Ketty*; 20 Priere a Zumba (A. Lara/J. Larue)(3:00) *Lucienne Delyle*; 21 Bei Mir Bist Du Schon (S. Cahn/S. Secunda/J. Jacob/J. Larue)(2:44) *Leo Marjane*; 22 Epilogue (2:48); The Woman Next Door: 23 Main Titles (2:13); 24 Garden Party (8:09).

Review: The great French composer Georges Delerue first came to prominence when he scored the films of New Wave directors like Alain Resnais, Jean-Luc Godard, Francois Reichenbach, Alain Robbe-Grillet, and Louis Malle. It is, however, with Francois Truffaut that Delerue earned his stripes, writing the music for many of the director's films, including *Shoot the Piano Player, Jules and Jim, The Two English Girls*, and *The Story of Adele H*. Of the five films documented in this CD, two (*Confidentially Yours* and *The Last Metro)* are often mentioned as being among the most important in Truffaut and Delerue's body of works, with *The Last Metro*, a World War II drama, particularly effective in its depiction of occupied Paris and the struggle of a Jewish theatre director to keep his plays running. Both scores and the short cues from *A Beautiful Girl Like Me, Day for Night* (a film documenting the shooting of a film), and *The Woman Next Door*, show Delerue in a wide variety of styles, from vernacular to baroque, from jazz to romantic, in a great demonstration of his enormous talent.

Pino Donaggio (1941-

Brian de Palma/ Pino Donaggio 🎵🎵🎵𝄽

1995, Milan Records.

Album Notes: *Music:* Pino Donaggio.

Selections: Carrie: 1 Contest Winners (2:32); 2 Bucket Of Blood (2:21); 3 For The Last Time We'll Pay (2:48); Home Movies: 4 Main Title Theme (2:28); Dressed To Kill: 5 The Shower (3:39); 6 The Transformation/The Storm/The Revelation (3:59); Blow Out: 7 Blow Out (2:27); 8 Sally's Death (3:43); Body Double: 9 Claustrophoby (3:18); 10 Love And Menace (4:45); 11 Drill Of Death (2:53); 12 Body Double (3:46); Raising Cain: 13 Cain Takes Over (4:45); 14 Love Memories (3:10).

Review: Intriguing, excellent anthology of the collaboration between director Brian De Palma and composer Pino Donaggio on six of their most notable psychological dramas. Donaggio replaced De Palma's former musical collaborator, Bernard Herrmann, after the composer's passing. It's interesting to listen to Donaggio's work here with that fact in mind. His music certainly redefined De Palma's films particularly through *Body Double's* electronic "Claustrophoby" and, in particular, the climactic cue from *Dressed to Kill*, which has a more overt sexual quality than would have been expected from Herrmann.

David Hirsch

Pino Donaggio: Symphonic Suites 🎵🎵𝄽

1989, Varese-Sarabande Records.

Album Notes: *Music:* Pino Donaggio; Orchestra conducted by Natale Massara; *Album Producer:* Scot W. Holton; *Engineer:* Michele Stone.

Selections: 1 The Howling (15:11); 2 Tourist Trap (21:26); 3 Piranha (11:22); 4 Home Movies (16:24).

Review: Part of Varese Sarabande's first batch of limited edition "CD Club" soundtrack releases, *Symphonic Suites* may be the most undesirable entry of the bunch (with the possible exception of the 17-minute "mini-classic" made-for-TV soundtrack, "Those Secrets"). A collection of four edited "suites" culled from the original soundtracks to *The Howling* (1981), *Piranha* (1978), *Tourist Trap* (1979) and *Home Movies* (1979), Donaggio's music in these four films consists by and large of hackneyed horror/ suspense cues (*Tourist Trap, The Howling, Piranha*) that are tired at best and obnoxious at worst, as well as forgettable comic cues (*Home Movies*) that don't mesh well

with the preceding three selections. The suites themselves play fairly effectively, although the cues that comprise them are somewhat questionable in selection (*The Howling* doesn't even include Donaggio's goofy end title!). Varese would have been better off re-issuing the albums individually than pasting this rather odd collection of tracks together and offering it to the public. As a sign of its unpopularity, it's one of the only "CD Club" issues that's still relatively easy to get your hands on.

Andy Dursin

Cliff Eidelman (1964-

Blood & Thunder: Parades, Processionals and Attacks from Hollywood's Most Epic Films 🎵🎵🎵𝄽

1995, Varese-Sarabande.

Album Notes: The Seattle Symphony Orchestra, conducted by Cliff Eidelman; *Album Producer:* Robert Townson; *Engineer:* Al Swanson.

Selections: 1 Ben Hur (M. Rozsa): Parade Of The Charioteers (3:34); 2 Captain From Castile (A. Newman): Conquest (3:17); Cleopatra (A. North): 3 Caesar And Cleopatra (3:33); 4 Cleopatra Enters Rome (3:41); 5 Antony And Cleopatra (2:42); 6 The Wind And The Lion (J. Goldsmith): Raisuli Attacks (3:29); 7 North By Northwest (B. Herrmann): Overture (2:58); 8 The Ten Commandments (E. Bernstein): Suite (7:28); Taras Bulba (F. Waxman): 9 The Ride Of The Cossacks (4:50); 10 Mutiny On The Bounty (B. Kaper): Overture (3:19).

Review: The title says it all: music of pomp and circumstance as devised by some of the great Hollywood composers in a widescreen program that blares out of the stereo system. There is no real subtlety here, just themes that are broad, grandiloquent, and are played to the hilt by an orchestra that seems to know the stuff by heart. It's fun, it's exhilarating and most of all it's thoroughly entertaining.

Danny Elfman (1953-

Music for a Darkened Theatre 🎵🎵🎵🎵

1990, MCA Records.

Album Notes: *Music:* Danny Elfman; *Orchestrations:* Steve Bartek; *Additional Orchestrations:* Shirley Walker, Bill Ross,

Steven Scott Smalley; *Album Producers*: Richard Kraft, Bob Badami; *Engineers*: Michael Boshears, Bobby Fernandez, Bill Jackson, Shawn Murphy, Mike Ross, Dennis Sands, Armin Steiner, Eric Tomlinson, Dan Wallin. *Additional Orchestrations*: Shirley Walker, Bill Ross, Steven Scott Smalley

Selections: 1 Pee Wee's Big Adventure (6:59); 2 Batman (8:23); 3 Dick Tracy (3:01); 4 Beetlejuice (3:41); 5 Nightbreed (7:01); 6 Darkman (6:52); 7 Back To School (1:28); 8 Midnight Run (4:41); 9 Wisdom (4:37); 10 Hot To Trot (2:20); 11 Big Top Pee Wee (5:23); 12 The Simpsons (1:29); 13 Alfred Hitchcock Presents: The Jar (3:19); 14 Tales From The Crypt (1:27); 15 Face Like A Frog (2:07); 16 Forbidden Zone (1:14); 17 Scrooged (8:42).

Review: See entry below.

Music for a Darkened Theatre: Film and Television Music volume two 🎞🎞🎞🎞

1996, MCA Records.

Album Notes: *Music*: Danny Elfman; *Orchestrations*: Steve Bartek, Mark McKenzie, Edgardo Simone, Steven Scott Smalley, Thomas Pasatieri, Jeff Armitage, Jack Hayes; *Music Editors*: Bob Badami, Ellen Segal, Curt Sobel, John Lasalandra; *Album Producers*: Ellen Segal, Danny Elfman; *Engineers*: Shawn Murphy, Bobby Fernandez, Bill Jackson, Dennis S. Sands.

Selections: CD 1: Edward Scissorhands (suite): 1 Main Titles; 2 Storytime; 3 Suite; 4 Suburbia; 5 Barber/The Grand Finale (16:01); Dolores Claiborne (suite): 6 Main Titles; 7 Vera's World; 8 Flashback; 9 Sad Rooom; 10 End Titles (12:29); To Die For (suite): 11 Main Titles; 12 Suzie's Theme; 13 Busted; 14 Wheepy Donuts; 15 Finale (11:15); Black Beauty (suite): 16 Main Titles; 17 Baby Beauty; 18 Jump For Joy; 19 Frolick; 20 Sick; 21 Bye Bye Jerry; 22 Memories/End Titles (16:13); Batman Returns (suite): 23 Birth Of A Penguin; 24 Trouble Suite; 25 The Finale; 26 End Titles (15:47).

CD 2: Mission Impossible (suite): 1 Trouble; 2 Looking For Job; 3 Betrayal (10:11); Sommersby (suite): 4 Main Titles; 5 Return Montage; 6 Finale/End Titles (16:27); Dead Presidents (suite): 7 Main Titles; 8 Daughter; 9 Montage; 10 Nam; 11 Nightmare (7:11); Nightmare Before Christmas (suite): 12 Overture; 13 Jack And Sally Suite; 14 Christmas Eve Montage (9:01); Freeway (suite): 15 Main Titles; 16 On The Road; 17 Back In The Car (7:02); Shrunken Heads: 18 Main Titles (1:55); Television Odds 'n Ends: Amazing Stories: 19-20 Family Dog (2:21); 21 Mummy, Daddy (2:23); Barkley Superhero: 22 Nike Commercial (:31); The

Flash: 23 Theme (1:33); Pee Wee's Playhouse: 24-27 Suite (3:36); Beetlejuice: Animated TV Series: 28 Theme (1:02); Nightmare Before Christmas: 29 This Is Halloween (demo) (3:19).

Review: Danny Elfman led the rock band Oingo Boingo and "didn't know nothin' about film music." Then he joined Tim Burton on several films—*Pee-Wee's Big Adventure, Beetlejuice* and *Batman*—and film music quickly learned about him. Elfman's self-taught orchestral style is kind of Nino Rota meets Bernard Herrmann meets Arrested Development meets a highly creative, filmic sense. Elfman has virtually defined the sound of "wacky" film music in the '80s and '90s—ditto for "gothic" film music—and charted the course for composers without a symphonic background to make use of the orchestra in an increasingly frenetic, bombastic way.

The first of MCA's excellent *Music for a Darkened Theatre* compilations covers Elfman from *Pee-Wee* in 1986 through *Darkman* in 1990: *Beetlejuice, Scrooged, Nightbreed, Midnight Run, Dick Tracy*, TV themes to "Tales from the Crypt" and "The Simpsons," and others. The second, 2-CD volume picks up with Elfman's magnum opus to date, the beautiful, lyrical *Edward Scissorhands* (1991) and continues through *Batman Returns, Sommersby, The Nightmare Before Christmas, Black Beauty, Dolores Claiborne, To Die For, Dead Presidents, Mission: Impossible*, and additional selected TV work.

While the first volume features the signature Elfman hits, it is the second album that showcases his vast growth since the days of the Bat. With *Sommersby, Black Beauty* and *Dolores Claiborne*, he took on an ambitiously lyrical and elegiac sound miles apart from the oompah-oompah Pee-Wee shenanigans. With *Dead Presidents* and *Mission: Impossible* he mixed sampled percussion and orchestra in exciting new ways to update his more action-oriented sound into something more sophisticated and intricate. Taken together the *Music for a Darkened Theatre* suites present too much of a good thing, but as a sort of Readers Digest collection they present an impressive catalog of a highly individual, and still growing, voice.

Lukas Kendall

Allyn Ferguson (1924-

The Film Music of Allyn Ferguson: volume 1 🎞🎞🎞🎞

1994, Prometheus Records/Belgium; from the television movies *The Count of Monte Cristo*, 1974, and *The Man in the Iron Mask*, 1976.

Album Notes: *Music*: Allyn Ferguson; *Orchestrations*: Allyn Ferguson; The London Studio Symphony Orchestra, conducted by Allyn Ferguson; *Album Producer*: Luc Van de Ven; *Engineer*: Eric Tomlinson.

Selections: The Count Of Monte Cristo: 1 Main Title (2:12); 2 The Death Of Abbe (2:04); 3 Time Marches On (1:12); 4 What Is My Crime? (4:50); 5 The Ride To The Semaphore (1:23); 6 Gavotte Plot (2:40); 7 The World Is Mine (3:42); 8 Duel To The Death (3:59); 9 The Ride To Marseilles (:43); 10 Off Into The Sunset (2:01); The Man In The Iron Mask: 11 Main Title (3:51); 12 The Sun Dance (1:39); 13 Love In The Garden (2:49); 14 The Futile Escape (7:29); 15 When Lovers Meet (1:38); 16 Kingly Training (2:35); 17 Secret Lovers (1:44); 18 Louis' Entrance (4:00); 19 The Big Chase (7:32); 20 They Lived Happily Ever After (1:29); 21 I'm Louis!/End Credits (2:27).

Review: See entry below.

The Film Music of Allyn Ferguson: volume 2 ♪♪♪♪

1995, Prometheus Records/Belgium; from the television movies *Ivanhoe*, 1982, and *Camille*, 1984.

Album Notes: *Music*: Allyn Ferguson; *Orchestrations*: Allyn Ferguson; The London Studio Symphony Orchestra, conducted by Allyn Ferguson; *Album Producer*: Luc Van de Ven; *Engineer*: Eric Tomlinson.

Selections: Ivanhoe: 1 Ivanhoe (1:21); 2 Main Title (2:23); 3 King John's Party (1:55); 4 A Veiled Desire (1:02); 5 Glory To The Brave! (2:55); 6 To The Battlements!/Charge (5:18); 7 Glory, Glory (1:58); 8 Where Is He? (1:55); 9 Enter The Black Knight (6:27); 10 Tournament Day (2:32); 11 Pax Vobiscum (3:28); 12 Bound At The Stake (6:44); 13 Farewell/End Credits (2:52); Camille: 14 Main Title (3:04); 15 The Garden Party (1:29); 16 Marguerite Leaves (1:44); 17 Monotony (2:30); 18 The Meal (1:40); 19 Bed Scene (3:31); 20 Lyrical Montage (2:07); 21 The Private Room (1:26); 22 Death Bed/End Credits (4:43).

Review: See entry below.

The Film Music of Allyn Ferguson: volume 3 ♪♪♪♪

1996, Prometheus Records/Belgium; from the movies *April Morning*, 1987, and *Ironclads*, 1996.

Album Notes: *Music*: Allyn Ferguson; *Orchestrations*: Allyn Ferguson; The Southwest Symphony Orchestra, conducted by Allyn Ferguson; *Album Producer*: Ford A. Thaxton; *Engineer*: James Nelson.

Selections: Ironclads: 1 Main Title/Destroy The Dry Dock (4:20); 2 Merrimac vs. Congress (5:11); 3 Santag Polka (2:01); 4

"Cole's treasury will live as long as anyone wants to listen to songs bearing a witty, sophisticated touch. Or songs that have a raucous joy. Or a haunting and voluptuous surrender. Cole Porter without question is an acquired taste, but then so are caviar and champagne."

David Grafton
("Red, Hot & Rich!: An Oral History of Cole Porter," Stein & Day, 1987).

What's That Glow? (2:11); 5 The First Encounter (3:09); 6 I'd Do Anything (3:02); 7 Merrimac vs. Monitor (10:08); 8 End Credits (1:39); April Morning: 9 Main Titles (3:14); 10 No-Good Liar! (1:03); 11 Unholy Water/Generation Gap (2:20); 12 The Landing/A Special Feeling (2:31); 13 God Be With You (1:23); 14 Just Hiding (1:55); 15 Point Of No Return (2:43); 16 First Blood/They're Coming (4:05); 17 The War Goes On (1:58); 18 The Road To The Grave (3:14); 19 Solomon Checks Out (2:17); 20 It's Been A Long Day (4:43); 21 End Credits (1:34).

Review: Each title in this trilogy contains two scores Allyn Ferguson composed for several made-for-television adaptions of classic literature. Not one of the more well-known score artistes, he has in fact labored in film and TV for many years from his native Britain, creating some exceptionally fine pieces of work. It was a daring move by this record company to produce not one, but three titles, which will certainly, and deservedly so, save this composer's work from obscurity. Each score is frequently imbued with that long forgotten lavish quality that Erich Wolfgang Korngold and Franz Waxman often infused into their own work for similar costume dramas. Ferguson also relies on several period inspired arrangements (string quartets and the like) to reinforce the time frame. The first volume contains "The Count of Monte Cristo" and "The Man in the Iron Mask," the second, "Ivanhoe" and "Camille," "The Ironclads" and "April Morning" complete the third. Of the three, volume two is perhaps the best of the lot with it's sweeping and romantic melodies. Some of the masters used were of less than ideal quality, but these flaws are minor as Ferguson's music just sweeps you away.

David Hirsch

Jerry Fielding (1922-1980)

Jerry Fielding Film Music
𝄞𝄞𝄞𝄞ᵛ

1992, Bay Cities Records.

Album Notes: *Music:* Jerry Fielding; Orchestras conducted by Jerry Fielding; *Album Engineer:* Richard Lewzey; *CD Producer:* Nick Redman; *Engineer:* Daniel Hersch.

Selections: CD 1: Lawman: 1 Main Title (4:42); 2 Old Family Burial Ground (2:24); 3 Predators (4:09); 4 Branding The Cattle (1:36); 5 In Laura's Room (2:45); 6 Requiem In The Pasture (4:20); 7 Rapidly, Toward Resolution (3:28); 8 Finis (1:20); The Mechanic: 9 Anatomy Of The Assassin (9:53); 10 Two Soliloquies (4:31); 11 The Contract In Naples (4:56); 12 Approach, Assault, Pursuit, Conquest (7:20); The Big Sleep: 13 Suite (19:25).

CD 2: Straw Dogs: 1 Prologue (1:45); 2 Dialogues (4:20); 3 Window Display (3:45); 4 The Hunting Party (2:31); 5 The Man Trap (4:14); 6 The Infamous Apassionata (8:33); 7 The Siege Begins (2:28); 8 Coda (2:24); 9 Epilogue (1:46); Chato's Land: 10 Main Title (4:39); 11 Fruits Of The Incursion (3:30); The Nightcomers: 12 Main Title (2:45); 13 Bedtime At Blye House (3:01); 14 Summer Rowing (3:19); 15 Pig Sty (1:36); 16 Pas de Deux (2:23); 17 The Smoking Frog (2:08); 18 The Children's Hour (2:17); 19 Act Two Prelude Myles In The Air (2:24); 20 The Flower Bath (2:21); 21 The Big Swim (3:30); 22 Through The Looking Glass (2:41); 23 Tea In The Tree (1:53); 24 Recapitulation and Postlude (3:26).

Review: See entry below.

Jerry Fielding Film Music 2
𝄞𝄞𝄞ᵛ

1992, Bay Cities Records.

Album Notes: *Music:* Jerry Fielding; *Orchestrations:* Lennie Niehaus, Greig McRitchie; *Engineer:* Richard Lewzey; *CD Producer:* Nick Redman; *CD Engineer:* Daniel Hersch.

Selections: Scorpio: 1 The Parisian Connection (2:28); 2 Reunion In Washington (2:16); 3 On The Plane From Paris (3:03); 4 Two Ways To Walk (1:58); 5 A Wag Of A Tail (4:09); 6 Hello And Farewell (1:49); 7 The Vienna Wheel (3:34); 8 The Lincoln Brigade (1:38); 9 The Imperial Vaults (3:36); 10 A Russian Wags His Tail (3:20); 11 In The Winter Garden (3:04); 12 Flowers (2:22); 13 Hide And Seek (5:59); 14 All Fall Down (4:22); Johnny Got His Gun: 15 Suite (13:39); A War Of Children: 16 Suite (12:10).

Review: See entry below.

Jerry Fielding Film Music 3
𝄞𝄞𝄞𝄞

1993, Bay Cities Records.

Album Notes: *Music:* Jerry Fielding; *Orchestrations:* Lennie Niehaus, Greig McRitchie; *Engineer:* Richard Lewzey; *CD Producer:* Nick Redman; *CD Engineer:* Daniel Hersch.

Selections: Bring Me The Head Of Alfredo Garcia: 1 Suite (23:03); The Getaway: 2 Suite From The Rejected Score (17:39); The Gambler: 3 Suite (based on Mahler's Symphony No. 1)(22:24).

Review: See entry below.

Jerry Fielding Film Music 4
𝄞𝄞𝄞ᵛ

1994, Bay Cities Records.

Album Notes: *Music:* Jerry Fielding; *Orchestrations:* Lennie Niehaus, Greig McRitchie; *Engineer:* Richard Lewzey; *CD Producer:* Nick Redman; *CD Engineer:* Daniel Hersch.

Selections: Chato's Land: 1 Part 1: Chato Pursued (20:05); 2 Part 2: Chato Takes His Toll (20:55); Mr. Horn: 3 Suite (14:46).

Review: Jerry Fielding is the greatest film composer nobody knows about. Blacklisted for what should have been the prime of his career in the 1950s, he arranged music for Vegas nightclub acts until finally arriving in Hollywood in the late '60s and '70s. There he scored six pictures for British director Michael Winner, as well as three for star/director Clint Eastwood (including *The Outlaw Josey Wales*), and was legendary director Sam Peckinpah's (*The Wild Bunch*) close friend and composer of choice. He died of a heart attack in 1980 and was virtually unrepresented on CD until producer Nick Redman of the late soundtrack label Bay Cities put together four limited-edition CD compilations of his best work.

Jerry Fielding Film Music is a 2-CD set featuring the western *Lawman* (1970), the Charles Bronson hit-man film *The Mechanic* (1972), the remake of *The Big Sleep* (1978), Peckinpah's masterful *Straw Dogs* (1971), two cuts from the Bronson revenge western *Chato's Land* (1972), and Winner's *Turn of the Screw* "prequel" *The Nightcomers* (1972).

Film Music 2 features the Winner spy film *Scorpio* (1973) and short suites from *Johnny Got His Gun* (1971) and *A War of Children* (1972).

The third volume features Peckinpah's *Bring Me the Head of Alfredo Garcia* (1974), the rejected music for *The Getaway* (1972), also Peckinpah, and Fielding's adaptation of Mahler for *The Gambler* (1974).

The fourth disc features the complete, original album configuration of *Chato's Land* coupled with Fielding's music for the 1979 TV miniseries, *Mr. Horn*.

Musically, Fielding is an acquired taste. He was intrigued by post-tonal 20th-century orchestral music but was also a self-taught and highly accomplished big band arranger. His film music is deeply individual. His melodies are usually fragmented and transitory but the overall textures and rhythms are intense and unmistakable. On these discs his music ranges from the English flavor of *The Nightcomers*, to the devastating Mexicana of *Bring Me the Head of Alfredo Garcia*, to the atonal, black-on-black portrait of an assassin of *The Mechanic*, to the quiet reflection of *Straw Dogs*, to the jazzy stylings of *The Big Sleep*. But wherever Fielding goes, he brings a delicate sense of disquiet, poignancy, and barely capped violence. He and '70s cinema were a perfect match.

Lukas Kendall

David Michael Frank (1948-

Music from the Films of Steven Seagal ♫♫♫♪

1996, GNP Crescendo.

Album Notes: *Music*: David Michael Frank; *Orchestrations*: David Michael Frank; Orchestra conducted by David Michael Frank; *Album Producer*: David Michael Frank; *Engineers*: Mick Guzauski, Bobby Fernandez.

Selections: Hard To Kill: 1 Main Title (4:38); 2 Seven Year Storm (2:19); 3 Just Passing By (2:57); 4 Workout (:58); 5 Meditation And Training (2:12); 6 New Beginning (:41); 7 Escape From Ojai (2:05); Above The Law: 8 Nico In Japan (3:38); 9 Chicago Heat (1:47); 10 Nico's Lament (2:03); 11 South Side (2:11); 12 Armageddon II (1:21); 13 Joy Ride (2:57); 14 Nico's Theme, Part 1 (5:30); Out For Justice: 15 House Call (1:45); 16 Searching For Richie (1:08); 17 Roxanne (1:03); 18 In Loving Memory (2:27); 19 Steven Seagal Interview (21:04).

Review: This compilation features selections from David Michael Frank's scores for three of Steven Seagal's first four movies, *Above the Law*, *Out for Justice* and *Hard To Kill*. The music is an eclectic mix of guitar driven motifs, electronics and contemporary orchestral scoring techniques that is certainly, if anything, never boring. Frank has a good knack for creating some terrific jazz flavored emotional moments and some intriguing orchestrations. In particular is "Joy Ride" from *Above the Law*, which has a fascinating synth effect that sounds like

an impossible-to-perform vocal scat. The album features an exclusive 21-minute interview with Seagal, who highly praises Frank's contribution to his films, though the actor has never used him since these three.

David Hirsch

Hugo Friedhofer (1902-1981)

The Adventures of Marco Polo ♫♫♫♫

1997, Marco Polo Records.

Album Notes: *Music*: Hugo Friedhofer; The Moscow Symphony Orchestra, conducted by William T. Stromberg; *Album Producer*: Betta International; *Engineers*: Edvard Shakhnazarian, Vitaly Ivanov.

Selections: The Adventures Of Marco Polo: 1 Suite (13:09); The Lodger: 2 Fox Trademark Fanfare (:17); 3 Prologue (1:10); 4 Murder (2:00); 5 Mr. Slade Moves In (3:36); 6 Mr. Slade Explains (2:12); 7 Mr. Slade Has Nerves (1:21); 8 The Ripper (:19); 9 Alarms And Excursions (2:30); 10 A Note For Mr. Slade (1:47); 11 Mr. Slade Is Cornered (3:11); 12 Epilogue (1:02); The Rains Of Ranchipur: 13 Main Title (2:31); 14 Allan And Edwina (1:17); 15 Love Theme (2:50); 16 Safti And Edwina (3:06); 17 Storm And Flood (2:43); 18 Crisis Past (:32); 19 End Title (Goodbye Edwina)(3:49); Seven Cities Of Gold: 20 Fox Fanfare (:25); 21 Main Title (1:24); 22 The Coach (1:40); 23 Expedition (1:12); 24 Encounter (4:55); 25 Jose And Serra (1:38); 26 Sand Storm (2:02); 27 The Miracle (1:52); 28 At The Mission (1:14); 29 Jose And Ula (3:04); 30 Departure (4:01); 31 End Title (1:21).

Review: A pioneer in film music and a representative of that select group that gave the genre its basic tenets, Friedhofer never achieved the popularity of his peers in Hollywood. Born in San Francisco on May 3, 1902, he studied the cello and was so proficient that he became a regular player in silent movie theaters as early as 1925. Eventually he began arranging and orchestrating, and revealed great skills at it. In fact, he started his career in Hollywood, where he arrived in 1929, as an arranger, orchestrating the scores of composers like Max Steiner, Alfred Newman and Erich Wolfgang Korngold.

Eventually, Friedhofer wrote his first film score, *The Adventures of Marco Polo*, in 1938, but it wasn't until 1943, when Alfred Newman signed him to a full contract, that he became recognized as a composer. In 1946, he finally made a name for himself when he won the Oscar for *The Best Years of Our Lives*. Subsequently, he scored *Joan of Arc* (1948), *Broken Arrow*

(1950), *Vera Cruz* (1954), *Boy on a Dolphin* (1957), *An Affair To Remember* (1957), *The Sun Also Rises* (1958), *The Young Lions* (1958), and *One-Eyed Jacks* (1960). He died on May 17, 1981.

The four scores here present him in four varied settings that called upon his vast resources as a composer and orchestrator. After working on several scores by Korngold and Steiner, *The Adventures of Marco Polo* gave Friedhofer his first opportunity to show his own mettle in a score that was appropriately epic in the right places, and romantic where needed. Typically flavorsome, in the grand Hollywood style of the day, it didn't disappoint. Made in 1944, *The Lodger* is a horror story about Jack The Ripper, set in London in the late 1800s; Friedhofer's score was an important contributing factor in setting the chilling atmosphere of the film.

Both made in 1955, *The Rains of Ranchipur* and *Seven Cities of Gold* could not have been more different in tone. The former, set in India, stars Richard Burton and Lana Turner in a tragic love story that is all but upstaged by a catastrophic monsoon and earthquake, with Friedhofer writing a lush exotic score that took its cues from the story and its locale. The latter, set in 18th-century California, is a colorful adventure film which enabled the composer to display his particular fondness for Latin American accents in his music.

The scores, carefully reconstructed by William Stromberg and John Morgan, receive thoughtful readings from The Moscow Symphony Orchestra, conducted by Stromberg, in another superlative album on the independent label Marco Polo.

The Film Music of Hugo Friedhofer 🎵🎵🎵

1987, Facet Records.

Album Notes: *Music:* Hugo Friedhofer; The Graunke Symphony Orchestra Of Munich, conducted by Kurt Graunke; *Album Producer:* Tony Thomas.

Selections: 1 Richthofen And Brown (symphonic suite)(22:58); 2 Private Parts (an orchestral fantasy)(15:39).

Review: Two scores by Friedhofer that are a little better than the films for which they were composed: *Richthofen and Brown* was created in 1971 for a World War I film by Roger Corman, which aimed to celebrate the airborne heroes, their tragic heroism and faded sense of romanticism; as for *Private Parts*, also written in 1971, it is an almost forgotten horror film which deals with a young runaway girl in a rundown Los Angeles hotel, and the strange characters she meets there. Friedhofer rose above the pedestrian topics in both films, and delivered scores that at least soundly interesting, though not of a best vintage. The Graunke

Symphony Orchestra, conducted by its founder Kurt Graunke, does a creditable job but this is obviously a second-rate CD, only recommended because of Friedhofer's name.

George & Ira Gershwin (1898-1937)/(1896-1983)

George and Ira Gershwin in Hollywood 🎵🎵🎵🎵

1997, Rhino Records.

Album Notes: *Music:* George Gershwin; *Lyrics:* Ira Gershwin; *Album Producers:* Michael Feinstein, George Feltenstein, Bradley Flanagan; *Engineer:* Doug Schwartz.

Selections: CD 1: 1 Overture (medley: Swanee/Somebody Loves Me/Fascinating Rhythm/Embraceable You/Oh Lady, Be Good/The Man I Love/I Got Rhythm/Liza/ Rhapsody In Blue/Strike Up The Band)(from *Rhapsody In Blue*)(10:13) *The Warner Bros. Studio Orchestra, Leo F. Forbstein*; 2 Swanee (G. Gershwin/I. Caesar)(from *Rhapsody In Blue*)(1:46) *Al Jolson*; 3 Somebody Loves Me (G. Gershwin/B.G. DeSylva/B. MacDonald)(from *Broadway Rhythm*)(3:11) *Lena Horne*; 4 I Can't Be Bothered Now (from *A Damsel In Distress*) (1:20) *Fred Astaire*; 5 (I'll Build A) Stairway To Paradise (G. Gershwin/B.G. DeSylva/A. Francis)(from *An American In Paris*) (2:42) *Georges Guetary*; 6 They Can't Take That Away From Me (from *Shall We Dance*) (2:36) *Fred Astaire*; 7 Fascinating Rhythm (from *Girl Crazy*) (5:26) *Tommy Dorsey & His Orchestra*; 8 Love Is Here To Stay (from *An American In Paris*) (4:06) *Gene Kelly*; 9 They All Laughed (from *Shall We Dance*) (4:18) *Ginger Rogers*; 10 Embraceable You (from *Girl Crazy*) (4:56) *Judy Garland, Ralph Blane, Henry Kruze, P. Hanna, G. Mershon, H. Stanton, Ernie Newton, Tommy Dorsey & His Orchestra*; 11 135th Street Blues (Blue Monday)(G. Gershwin/B.G. DeSylva)(from *Rhapsody In Blue*) (6:03) *John B. Hughes*; 12 Summertime (G. Gershwin/I. Gerhswin/D. Heyward)(from *Rhapsody In Blue*) (3:53) *Anne Brown*; 13 Let's Call The Whole Thing Off (from *Shall We Dance*) (3:45) *Fred Astaire, Ginger Rogers*; 14 But Not For Me (from *But Not For Me*) (2:04) *Ella Fitzgerald*; 15 Nice Work If You Can Get It (from *A Damsel In Distress*) (2:32) *Fred Astaire*; 16 Liza (All The Clouds'll Roll Away)(G. Gershwin/I. Gershwin/G. Kahn)(from *Ziegfeld Follies*) (6:09) *Avon Long*; 17 I've Got A Crush On You (from *An American In Paris*) (2:46) *Gene Kelly*; 18 Third Prelude (from *Rhapsody In Blue*) (:56) *Oscar Levant*; 19 Strike Up The Band (from *Strike Up The Band*) (5:07) *Judy Garland, Mickey Rooney, Six Hits And A Miss.*

CD 2: 1 Boy! What Love Has Done To Me (from *Girl Crazy*) (3:23) *Tommy Dorsey & His Orchestra*; 2 Slap That Bass (from *Shall We*

Dance) (4:18) *Fred Astaire*; 3 Aren't You Kind Of Glad We Did? (from *The Shocking Miss Pilgrim*) (3:50) *Dick Haymes, Betty Grable*; 4 The Man I Love (from *The Man I Love*) (3:44) *Peg La Centra*; 5 Treat Me Rough (from *Girl Crazy*) (6:33) *June Allyson, Mickey Rooney, The Music Maids, The Stafford Trio, Kathleen Carns, Ruth Clark, Tommy Dorsey & His Orchestra*; 6 A Foggy Day (from *A Damsel In Distress*) (2:14) *Fred Astaire*; 7 You've Got What Gets Me (from *Girl Crazy*) (3:12) *Eddie Quillan, Dixie Lee, Mitzi Green*; 8 Oh Lady, Be Good (from *Artie Shaw's Symphony In Swing*) (3:09) *Artie Shaw & His Orchestra*; 9 He Loves And She Loves (from *Funny Face*) (5:00) *Fred Astaire*; 10 I Was Doing Alright (from *The Goldwyn Follies*) (2:43) *Ella Logan*; 11 Love Walked In (from *The Goldwyn Follies*) (3:13) *Virginia Verrill, Jon Hall*; 12 Promenade (Walking The Dog) (from *Shall We Dance*) (2:32) *The RKO Studio Orchestra, Nathaniel Shilkret*; 13 (I've Got) Beginner's Luck (from *Shall We Dance*) (1:57) *Fred Astaire*; 14 'S Wonderful (from *An American In Paris*) (2:47) *Gene Kelly, Georges Guetary*; 15 Things Are Looking Up (from *A Damsel In Distress*) (3:47) *Fred Astaire, The Stafford Sisters*; 16 Delishious (from *Rhapsody In Blue*) (2:08) *Sally Sweetland*; 17 Shall We Dance (from *Shall We Dance*) (3:40) *Fred Astaire*; 18 I Got Rhythm (from *Girl Crazy*) (8:03) *Judy Garland, Mickey Rooney, Six Hits And A Miss, The Music Maids, Hal Hopper, Trudy Erwin, Bobbie Canvin, Tommy Dorsey & His Orchestra*; 19 You'd Be Hard To Replace (H. Warren/I. Gershwin)(from *The Barkleys Of Broadway*) (2:28) *Fred Astaire*; 20 In Our United State (B. Lane/I. Gershwin)(from *Give A Girl A Break*) (3:40) *Bob Fosse*; 21 For You, For Me, For Evermore (from *The Shocking Miss Pilgrim*) (4:02) *Dick Haymes, Betty Grable*.

Review: As we reach the millenium, we might as well ask who was the most influential 20th-century composer. The jury may still be out, but to this writer, none surpassed George Gershwin. Born two years before the century, Gershwin exerted himself in so many areas (pop songs, stage, screen, opera house, concert hall), and in ways that were so profoundly important that his influence can still be felt some 60-odd years after his untimely death. Today, we almost take him for granted, and we have solidly embraced his more serious works, like *Rhapsody in Blue, An American in Paris,* or the *Concerto in F.* But his achievements in the concert hall should not becloud his other contributions, particularly to the great American pop song catalogue for which he wrote with his brother Ira many evergreens that are still as thrilling today as they were when they were first created. While his legacy has been perpetuated by various singers like Frank Sinatra, Tony Bennett and Michael Feinstein, the many films in which his songs crept up probably have gained him a much broader audience over the years.

This elegant 2-CD set from Rhino stresses the enormous contributions from the Gershwin brothers, while they worked in Hollywood, and after. A listing of the songs the set contains looks like a greatest hits compilation, with so many great tunes that it almost becomes an embarrassment of riches: "Somebody Loves Me," "They Can't Take That Away From Me," "Fascinating Rhythm," "Love Is Here to Stay," "They All Laughed," "Embraceable You," "Summertime," "But Not For Me," "Strike Up the Band," "The Man I Love," "A Foggy Day," "Oh Lady, Be Good," "Love Walked In," "'S Wonderful," "Shall We Dance," "I Got Rhythm." Not a single weak number among them, and the list goes on and on.

Scouring the many films that featured songs by the Gershwin brothers, producers Michael Feinstein, George Feltenstein and Bradley Flanagan have not only gone to the M-G-M vaults, the source of many Rhino sets, but to RKO, Warner Bros., Paramount and 20th Century-Fox, to present as complete a survey as possible. Commendable as their efforts are, the set is not without its flaws: there is an overabundance of tracks by Fred Astaire—arguably the one performer for whom the Gershwins wrote intensively and their best interpreter—most of them from the early RKO films, *Shall We Dance* and *A Damsel in Distress.* But since the set producers decided to include a song from *Funny Face,* the 1957 film in which Astaire also starred with Audrey Hepburn, it would have made sense to include the title tune from that film, as well as "How Long Has This Been Going On?," performed by Hepburn.

Similarly, rather than use a couple of songs with limited appeal, like "Delishious," "By Strauss" from *An American in Paris,* would have seemed an apter choice. And since they decided to use songs with lyrics by Ira Gershwin with music by other composers, one glaring omission seems "The Man That Got Away," performed by Judy Garland in *A Star Is Born,* which would have been a much better choice than, say, the more obscure "In Our United State."

Evidently, these are minor points that can easily be dismissed and in no way lessen the importance of the set or its overall impact. A wonderful primer and a great collection of songs, many of them in their definitive versions, *George and Ira Gershwin in Hollywood* is a total joy.

Goblin

The Goblin Collection 1975-1989 𝄞𝄞𝄞♭

1995, DRG Records.

Album Notes: *Music:* Goblin; *Goblin:* Massimo Morante (guitars, bass, mandolin), Claudio Simonetti (electric keyboards, synthesizers, organ, violin), Fabio Pignatelli (bass, acoustic guitar), Agostino Marangolo (percussion, piano), Mauro Lusini (guitars, keyboards), Marco Rinalduzzi (guitars), Derek Wilson (drums), Maurizio Guarini (synthesizers); *Album Producer*: Claudio Fuiano.

Selections: Profondo rosso: 1 Main Title (3:45); 2 Death Dies (original film version)(2:40); 3 Profondo rosso (:38); 4 Profondo rosso (1:00); Wampyr: 5 Finale (1:38); Chi?: 6 Chi?, Part 1 (3:15); 7 Chi?, Part 2 (3:20); Patrick: 8 Patrick (2:57); 9 Patrick (:55); 10 Patrick (:44); Suspiria: 11 Main Title (5:58); La via della droga: 12 La via della droga (2:04); 13 La via della droga (2:00); 14 La via della droga (2:00); 15 La via della droga (4:26); Zombi: 16 L'alba dei morti viventi (6:01); Buio Omega: 17 Buio Omega (2:30); 18 Buio Omega (4:00); 19 Main Title (2:45); St. Helens: 20 Love Theme (2:05); Contamination: 21 Contamination (1:39); 22 Contamination (:53); Tenebre: 23 Main Title (4:31); Notturno: 24 Bass Theme (3:16); Phenomena: 25 Phenomena (1:09); 26 Phenomena (alternate version)(3:05); La Chiesa: 27 La Chiesa (5:20).

Review: A seminal Italian rock group, Goblin made an important contribution to horror films through its scores, a richly textured blend of electronic and acoustic elements that often prove an effective complement to the suggestive power of the images on the screen. The group first came into being in 1975, and almost immediately emerged as a vital musical entity with its score for the cult thriller *Profondo Rosso* (Deep Red), directed by Dario Argento. Subsequently, they scored *Suspiria*, also for Argento, and went on to write the music for *Wampyr*, *Patrick*, *Dawn of the Dead*, and many other celebrated horror films. This compilation, the first of its kind to present a broad overview of the group's involvement with the movies, will be of primary interest to fans of the genre, but may prove less seductive to others with little or no interest in this kind of music.

Jerry Goldsmith (1929-

The Soundtracks of Jerry Goldsmith with the Philharmonia ♫♫♫▷

1989, Deram Records.

Album Notes: *Music*: Jerry Goldsmith; The Philharmonia Orchestra, conducted by Jerry Goldsmith; *Album Producer*: Jerry Goldsmith; *Engineer*: Mike Ross.

Selections: 1 The Blue Max Suite (16:29); 2 Television Themes (medley): The Man From U.N.C.L.E., Doctor Kildare, Room 22,

The Waltons, Barnaby Jones (9:45); 3 Masada (5:37); 4 Gremlins (suite)(7:35); 5 Motion Picture Themes (medley): The Sand Pebbles, Chinatown, A Patch Of Blue, Poltergeist, Papillon, The Widn And The Lion (15:24); 6 The Generals (suite): MacArthur, Patton (5:12); 7 Lionheart — The Children's Crusade (4:03).

Review: Anyone who's never been to a Jerry Goldsmith concert can recreate essentially the same experience with this CD (but without the composer's running commentary). It's a representative sampling of Goldsmith's most familiar and honored music for film and television, opening with a lengthy suite from the composer's soaring score to the WWI aerial drama *The Blue Max* and moving on with an exciting medley of Goldsmith's television themes, including "The Man from UNCLE," "Dr. Kildare," "Room 222," the crowd-pleasing theme from "The Waltons," and "Barnaby Jones." Other highlights include The Motion Picture Suite, with music from Goldsmith's Oscar-nominated scores to *The Sand Pebbles*, *A Patch of Blue*, *Papillon*, *Chinatown* and *The Wind and the Lion*; and The Generals Suite, combining Goldsmith's music for the military biographical films *MacArthur* and *Patton*. The end title music from Franklin Schaffner's *Lionheart* closes the album. There are also suites from *Masada* and *Gremlins*, the latter of which includes the opening "Chinatown" music that was missing from that film's soundtrack album. A curious omission is any music from Goldsmith's only Oscar-winning score, *The Omen*. It has to be said that some of Goldsmith's compositions lose something in the translation to concert hall aesthetic: the television themes, although exciting in their own right, bear little resemblance to their original arrangements and the raucous Gremlins rag mutates from a mischievous techno-funk satire to a somewhat awkward big band romp without its electronic underpinnings. Nevertheless, this is a fun overview of Goldsmith's career that's well-performed by the Philharmonia Orchestra.

Jeff Bond

Ron Goodwin (1925-

Ron Goodwin: Drake 400 ♫♫♫

1989, Chandos Records.

Album Notes: The Bournemouth Symphony Orchestra, conducted by Ron Goodwin; *Featured Soloists*: Brendan O'Brien (violin), Terry Thompson (bagpipe); *Album Producer*: Brian Couzens; *Engineer*: Ralph Couzens; *Assistant Engineer*: Richard Lee.

Selections: Drake 400 Suite: 1 The Eddystone Seascape/ Song Of The Mewstone/ Hornpipe/ The Barbican/The Hoe On A Summer Night/ March: Plymouth Hoe/ The Eddystone Seascape (reprise)(14:19); 2 Love Theme From Beauty And The Beast (2:09); 3 Festival Time (3:01); 4 Candleshoe (4:04); 5 Amazing Grace (3:23); 6 Force 10 From Navarone (3:24); 7 Minuet In Blue (2:35); 8 The Spaceman And King Arthur (4:29); 9 The Girl With The Misty Eyes (2:54); 10 Auld Lang Syne (trad.)(3:01).

Review: Ron Goodwin has sadly never received sufficient attention in America, but he has long been one of Britain's finest and most successful composers. This anthology contains a number of film themes and light concert works by the composer. Goodwin's excellent march from *Force Ten From Navarone* (one of his best scores) is featured in a stirring performance. Goodwin's theme from a forgotten film version of *Beauty and the Beast* is a beautifully romantic work featuring a solo violin. The theme from *Candleshoe* (a forgettable Disney comedy starring Jodie Foster) is a less memorable '70s pop effort, but *The Spaceman and King Arthur* has a nicely triumphant pomp to it.

The concert works are of less interest to the soundtrack collector. Goodwin offers arrangements of "Auld Lang Syne" and "Amazing Grace" (featuring a Scottish piper). "Drake 400" however is a magnificent piece, commissioned to celebrate the 400th anniversary of Sir Francis Drake's circumnavigation of the globe. A majestic and triumphant evocation of sea, it is in the style of Goodwin's most exciting adventure scores. Though perhaps not the best representation of Ron Goodwin's film music, there is much here which is well worth a listen.

Paul Andrew MacLean

Ron Goodwin: Drake 400 Suite/New Zealand Suite

♪♪♪♪▷

1996, Marco Polo Records.

Album Notes: *Music*: Ron Goodwin; The New Zealand Symphony Orchestra, conducted by Ron Goodwin; *Album Producer*: Murray Khouri; *Engineer*: Geoffrey Eyles.

Selections: 1 Theme From 633 Squadron (2:57); Drake 400 Suite: 2 The Eddystone Seascape (1:46); 3 Song Of The Mewstone (3:00); 4 The Barbican (1:31); 5 The Hoe On A Summer Night (4:09); 6 March: Plymouth Hoe (2:22); 7 The Eddystone Seascape (reprise)(2:15); 8 Puppet Serenade (2:43); New Zealand Suite: 9 Aeotearoa (The Land Of The Long White Cloud)(2:55); 10 Milford Sound (4:50); 11 Picnic At Rotorua

(1:55); 12 The Earnslaw Steam Theme (3:46); 13 The A&P Show (2:19); 14 Po Atarau (3:26); 15 Arabian Celebration; 16 The Venus Waltz (3:16); 17 Prisoners Of War March (The Kriegie)(3:15); 18 Minuet In Blue (2:48); 19 Theme From The Trap (3:43); 20 Girl With A Dream (2:33); 21 Theme From Lancelot And Guinevere (5:03).

Review: Though he has composed many great scores during his illustrious career, Ron Goodwin is a virtual unknown in this country. But anyone who has been exposed to his music will remember some of the most famous themes he composed, for films like the uproarious 1965 comedy *Those Magnificent Men in Their Flying Machines,* the Kim Novak-starrer *Of Human Bondage,* the Hitchcock film *Frenzy,* or the series of delirious detective adventures featuring Agatha Christie's Miss Marple (see below). This collection, in which he conducts the New Zealand Symphony Orchestra, is an ideal introduction to his music. Kicking off with the stirring march from *633 Squadron,* the set also offers the main themes from *The Trap,* a 1966 film starring Oliver Reed and Rita Tushingham, and *Lancelot and Guinevere,* made in 1962, with Cornel Wilde and Jean Wallace as the star-crossed lovers in King Arthur's court, and several non-film related small compositions.

But the plum of this recording are the two long suites, *Drake 400* and *New Zealand,* both of which gave the composer an opportunity to "stretch" and create works of impressive magnitude. Commissioned by the City Fathers of Plymouth in 1979, *Drake 400* evoked the life of Sir Francis Drake, and his round-the-world voyage, with striking evocations of seafaring adventure in the 16th century. Composed in 1983, the *New Zealand Suite* sought to paint a picture of that country, its amazing beauty, its glorious history, with Goodwin blending in his music elements of Maori songs. Both works are superb examples of Ron Goodwin's feel for suggestive musical images, something that has also made his film scores so distinctive.

Ron Goodwin: Three Symphonic Suites ♪♪♪♪

1990, Label X.

Album Notes: *Music*: Ron Goodwin; The Odense Symphony Orchestra, conducted by Ron Goodwin; *Album Producer*: Ron Goodwin; *Assistant Producers*: Ron Shillingford, Soren Hyldgaard Larsen; *Engineer*: Hans Nielsen.

Selections: 1 The Miss Marple Films: Murder She Said, Murder At The Gallop, Murder Most Foul, Murder Ahoy (19:19); 2 The Miss Marple Theme (2:13); 3 Lancelot And Guinevere (25:05); 4 Force 10 From Navarone (26:09).

Review: The jaunty "Miss Marple Theme" will no doubt bring back fond memories to anyone who has ever watched the four films that starred the indomitable Margaret Rutherford as the famous sleuth. But even more attractive is the suite composed of cues from the films themselves, *Murder She Said, Murder at the Gallop, Murder Most Foul,* and *Murder Ahoy.* Ron Goodwin, one of the better light pop film composers of the 1960s and '70s, gave the films their musical signature, and provided the various themes that enhanced the delicious screen adventures of the lady (who bore no resemblance whatsoever to the TV Miss Marple, portrayed by Joan Hickson).

In contrast, *Lancelot and Guinevere,* a historical drama that dealt with the well-known events at the court of Camelot, and *Force 10 From Navarone,* a sequel to the Carl Foreman World War II film, *The Guns of Navarone,* enabled Goodwin to reach out and create scores that are widely different in tone and nature. At times stately and regal, at times achingly romantic in a pseudo medieval way, *Lancelot and Guinevere* explores the different aspects of its subject matter, from the courtly behavior of its knights and ladies, to the all consuming love between the proud Lancelot and the lovely Guinevere, portrayed by Cornel Wilde and Jean Wallace.

In *Force 10 From Navarone,* Goodwin shifted to a string of martial cues, with lots of brassy effects, well-suited for this war drama, in which the main theme, a sensational march, rivals the one written by Tiomkin for *The Guns of Navarone.* While the film itself was a disaster, the score is simply magnificent.

Dave Grusin (1934-

Cinemagic ♫♫♫♫♫

1987, GRP Records.

Album Notes: *Music:* Dave Grusin; *Orchestrations:* Dave Grusin, Jorge Calandrelli; The London Symphony Orchestra, conducted by Dave Grusin, Harry Rabinowitz; *Featured Soloists:* Dave Grusin (piano, synthesizers), Don Grusin (synthesizers), Lee Ritenour (acoustic and electric guitars), Abraham Laboriel (electric bass), Harvey Mason (drums), Mike Fisher (percussion), Emil Richards (cymbalon, percussion), Chuck Findley (trumpet), Charley Loper (trombone), Tom Scott (soprano sax, tenor sax), Ernie Watts (tenor sax), Eddie Daniels (clarinet); *Album Producer:* Dave Grusin; *Engineers:* Don Murray, Keith Grant, Larry Rosen; *Assistant Engineers:* Jim Preziosi, Gerry O'Riordan, Ollie Cotton, Jim Singer.

Selections: On Golden Pond: 1 Main Theme (3:37); 2 New Hampshire Hornpipe (2:23); Heaven Can Wait: 3 Main Theme (4:35); Tootsie: 4 An Actor's Life (5:06); 5 It Might Be You (5:14); The Goonies: 6 Fratelli Chase (3:19); The Heart Is A Lonely Hunter: 7 Main Theme (4:44); Falling In Love: 8 Mountain Dance (6:16); The Champ: 9 Letting Go — T.J.'s Theme (2:51); 10 Main Theme (3:28); Three Days Of The Condor: 11 Condor (4:43); 12 Goodbye For Kathy (3:59); Little Drummer Girl: 13 PLO Camp Entrance (2:50); 14 Epilogue (3:24).

Review: Dave Grusin is one of the most reliable film composers in the business when he turns his attention away from his successful recording career as a jazz artist to the silver screen, and this superb album from GRP showcases many of his most memorable soundtrack compositions. From the expressive lyricism of *On Golden Pond* and *The Heart Is a Lonely Hunter* to exciting percussive tracks from *Three Days of the Condor* and *The Goonies,* this album illustrates Grusin's penchant for writing strong thematic material, working with both jazz-based rhythms and full orchestral composition to great effect, creating solid film music that functions flawlessly on its own in the process. The performances consist of all-new recordings featuring Grusin and a collection of talented artists (including Tom Scott, Lee Ritenour and Eddie Daniels) performing with the London Symphony Orchestra, conducted by Grusin and Harry Rabinowitz. As far as composer retrospectives go, this cohesive, expertly-produced recording of Grusin's film music is one of the best, with something to appeal to listeners of any kind of musical persuasion.

Andy Dursin

Bernard Herrmann (1911-1975)

Alfred Hitchcock's Film Music ♫♫♫⊳

1989, Milan Records/France.

Album Notes: *Music:* Bernard Herrmann; The National Philharmonic Orchestra (*Psycho*), conducted by Bernard Herrmann; The London Studio Symphony Orchestra (*North By Northwest*), conducted by Laurie Johnson.

Selections: Psycho: 1 Prelude (2:08); 2 The City, Marion, Marion And Sam (4:35); 3 Temptation (3:07); 4 Flight, The Patrol Car, The Car Lot, The Package, The Rainstorm (8:40); 5 Hotel Room, The Window, The Parlour (4:01); 6 The Madhouse (2:11); 7 The Peephole (3:08); 8 Finale (1:48); North By Northwest: 9 Main Titles (3:20); 10 Abduction Of George Kaplan (1:58); 11 The Elevator (1:27); 12 Murder At The United Nations (3:19); 13 Mount Rushmore/ Finale (8:18).

Review: See entry below.

Bernard Herrmann: The Film Scores 🎵🎵🎵🎵▷

1996, Sony Classical.

Album Notes: *Music*: Bernard Herrmann; The Los Angeles Philharmonic, conducted by Esa-Pekka Salonen; *Album Producer*: David Mottley; *Engineer*: Richard King; *Assistant Engineer*: Todd Whitelock.

Selections: The Man Who Knew Too Much: 1 Prelude (2:40); Psycho: A Suite For Strings: 2 Prelude (2:04); 3 The City (1:44); 4 The Rainstorm (1:25); 5 The Madhouse (2:36); 6 The Murder (1:01); 7 The Water (1:11); 8 The Swamp (2:28); 9 The Stairs (1:32); 10 The Knife (:28); 11 The Cellar (1:16); 12 Finale (1:57); Marnie (suite): 13 Prelude (5:13); 14 The Hunt (5:45); North By Northwest: 15 Overture (2:46); Vertigo (suite): 16 Prelude (2:58); 17 The Nightmare (2:08); 18 Scene d'amour (6:49); Torn Curtain: 19 Prelude (2:17); 20 Gromek (1:54); 21 The Killing (2:16); Farenheit 451 (suite for strings, harps and percussion): 22 Prelude (1:32); 23 Fire Engine (1:01); 24 The Bedroom (1:39); 25 The Reading (2:03); 26 The Garden (1:26); 27 The Nightmare (1:51); 28 Flowers Of Fire (1:43); 29 Flamethrower (:37); 30 The Captain's Death (1:00); 31 The Road (2:14); 32 Finale (2:25); Taxi Driver (A Night-Piece for Orchestra with Obbligato Alto Saxophone): 33 Prelude (:54); 34 Blues (3:10); 35 Night Prowl (:29); 36 Bloodbath (1:27); 37 Finale (:45).

Review: See entry below.

The Great Hitchcock Movie Thrillers 🎵🎵🎵

1996, London Records.

Album Notes: *Music*: Bernard Herrmann; The London Philharmonic Orchestra, conducted by Bernard Herrmann; *Album Producer*: Tony D'Amato.

Selections: 1 Psycho (a narrative for orchestra)(14:31); 2 Marnie (10:08); 3 North By Northwest (3:06); 4 Vertigo: Prelude, The Nightmare, Scene d'amour (10:35); 5 A Portrait Of "Hitch" (from The Trouble With Harry)(8:19).

Review: Fans of the great Bernard Herrmann, will find a treasure trove of worthwhile CDs that serve to keep his music and his memory alive, including the three listed here. As might be expected, many of these Herrmann compilations feature his compositions for the classic Alfred Hitchcock films, but a few do contain other important film works. *Alfred Hitchcock's Film Music* (Milan) offers two "extended" suites: *Suite for Psycho* (nearly 30 minutes), which features Herrmann conducting the

National Philharmonic Orchestra, and *North By Northwest* (19 minutes), performed by the London Studio Symphony Orchestra under the direction of Laurie Johnson. Both the interpretations and the sonics are uniformly excellent.

Bernard Herrmann: The Film Scores (Sony Classical) features Esa-Pekka Salonen conducting the Los Angeles Philharmonic. In addition to offering *Psycho: A Suite for String* (similar in theme to the one in the Milan CD, but utilizing different cues and orchestrations), the recording includes selections from *The Man Who Knew Too Much, Marnie, North By Northwest, Vertigo* and *Torn Curtain* (the pair's final collaboration). Two post-Hitch efforts emerge as essential pieces: *Fahrenheit 451: Suite for Strings, Harps and Percussion* (composed for the Francois Truffaut film), and the all too short *A Night Piece for Orchestra with Alto Saxophone Obbligato,* from *Taxi Driver,* the score that Herrmann completed on the very day that he died. The superior orchestrations and sparkling recording make one hope that Salonen will address more Herrmann, and the works of other notable film composers, in the future.

Psycho: Great Hitchcock Movie Thrillers (London) contains yet another distillation from *Psycho* (14 minutes), and most of the usual Herrmann-Hitchcock suspects, in abbreviated form. Three unusual pieces are Herrmann's *A Portrait of Hitch* (from *The Trouble With Harry*), and two non-Herrmann compositions: *Theme From Spellbound* (Miklos Rozsa) and the Alfred Hitchcock TV theme, Gounod's *Funeral March of a Marionette.* All of the Herrmann pieces feature the London Philharmonic orchestra and are conducted by the composer himself.

Charles L. Granata

Classic Fantasy Film Scores 🎵🎵🎵🎵

1988, Cloud Nine Records/U.K.

Album Notes: *Music*: Bernard Herrmann; Orchestras conducted by Bernard Herrmann; *Album Producer*: David Wishart; *Engineer*: Gavin Millar.

Selections: The Three Worlds Of Gulliver: 1 Overture (1:55); 2 The Storm (1:20); 3 The Lilliputians (2:42); 4 The Stakes/The Emperor's March (1:47); 5 A Hatful Of Fish (:55); 6 Trees (1:19); 7 Fanfares/The Tightrope (3:10); 8 War March/The Naval Battle (2:17); 9 Reunion (Love Theme)(2:31); 10 The Giant Crocodile (3:01); 11 Pursuit/Escape (3:20); 12 Finale (1:27); Mysterious Island: 13 Prelude (1:27); 14 Escape/The Balloon (2:58); 15 The Giant Crab (2:46); 16 The Cave (2:05); 17 The Giant Bird (2:37); 18 Pipeline/The Ship Raising (2:18); 19 Pirates/The Doomed

Ship (3:12); The Seventh Voyage Of Sinbad: 20 Overture (1:07); 21 The Cyclops' Fury/The Capture (1:35); 22 The Fight (1:56); 23 The Shell/The Genie's Home (1:21); 24 Fight With The Cyclops/ Cyclops' Death (3:00); 25 The Egg (:46); 26 The Dragon (1:10); 27 Duel With The Skeleton (2:52); 28 The Dragon And The Second Cyclops/Death Of The Second Cyclops/The Crossbow/Death Of The Dragon (4:51); 29 Finale (2:16); Jason And The Argonauts: 30 Prelude (1:48); 31 The Skeletons/Battle With The Skeletons/ Finale (5:00).

Review: Visual effects master Ray Harryhausen, producer Charles H. Schneer and composer Bernard Herrmann combined to create four masterworks of the fantasy genre, each of which are included on this outstanding compilation from Cloud Nine. Herrmann's majestic music from *The Three Worlds of Gulliver* sets the regal tone for this release, which also includes selections from his thundering score from *Mysterious Island*, the exotic tone of *The Seventh Voyage of Sinbad*, and a pair of tracks from the rousing *Jason and the Argonauts*. Comprehensive liner notes and a nicely designed booklet complement this archival album, which features often ragged monaural sound and unfortunate "chilling sound effects" from *Jason* on the last track, which may disappoint audiophiles but nevertheless helps to preserve some truly classic film music from one of the original masters of the craft.

Andy Dursin

Bernard Herrmann: Great Film Music ♫♫♫

1996, London Records.

Album Notes: *Music:* Bernard Herrmann; The National Philharmonic Orchestra, conducted by Bernard Herrmann; *Album Producer:* Tony D'Amato.

Selections: Journey To The Center Of The Earth: (1-7) 1 Mountain Top And Sunrise; 2 Prelude; 3 The Grotto Salt Sides; 4 Atlantic; 5 The Giant Chameleon and The Fight; 6 The Shaft; 7 Finale (14:59); The Seventh Voyage Of Sinbad: (8-10) 8 Overture; 9 The Duel With The Skeleton; 10 Baghdad (8:22); The Day The Earth Stood Still: (11-17) 11 Outer Space; 12 Radar; 13 Gort; 14 The Robot; 15 Space Control; 16 Terror; 17 Farewell and Finale (11:39); Farenheit 451: (18-22) 18 Prelude; 19 Fire Engine; 20 The Bedroom; 21 Flowers Of Fire; 22 The Road and Finale (10:42); Gulliver's Travels: (23-35) 23 Overture (Minuetto); 24 Wapping; 25 Hornpipe; 26 Lilliputians 1 & 2; 27 Victory 1 & 2; 28 Escape; 29 The King's March; 30 Trees; 31 The Tightrope; 32 Lovers; 33 The Chess Game; 34 Pursuit; 35 Finale (25:58).

Review: If nothing else, this great-sounding album of Bernard Herrmann's music for five different fantasy films should settle the question of where Danny Elfman got his inspiration for his original *Batman* score: the opening, fifteen minute suite from *Journey to the Center of the Earth* could have easily been used as a temp track for the Caped Crusader with its ominous five-note brass theme, oppressive orchestral chords and ethereal harp and organ textures (as well as the unearthly sounds of the medieval serpent). After the disturbing sounds of the Jules Verne story, Herrmann's music for the bright Ray Harryhausen adventure *The Seventh Voyage of Sinbad* is almost frivolous, but Herrmann inevitably returns to the dark side with the heavy tread of "Gort" robot music for the classic *The Day the Earth Stood Still*. The latter score is beautifully recreated in its opening titles, the busy "Radar" music and the eerie "Terror" cue, but the cues involving Gort suffer from the lack of a real theremin in the performance and are no match for the original recordings. *Fahrenheit 451* comes off much better, from the relentless destructiveness of the fire engine music to the achingly beautiful, haunting finale. A bonus is 25 minutes of Herrmann's music for the 1961 live action *Gulliver's Travels*, but in this case Herrmann's music so authentically captures the pomposity of its satirized British Empire that listening to its endless minuets and marches quickly becomes a chore. Herrmann's handling of the orchestra in all cases is typically brilliant.

Jeff Bond

Bernard Herrmann: Music from Great Film Classics ♫♫♫♫♫

1996, London Records.

Album Notes: *Music:* Bernard Herrmann; The London Philharmonic Orchestra and The National Philharmonic Orchestra, conducted by Bernard Herrmann; *Album Producers:* Tony D'Amato, Gavin Barrett, Tim McDonald; *Engineers:* Arthur Bannister, Arthur Lilley.

Selections: Citizen Kane: 1 Overture (2:48); 2 Variations (5:40); 3 Ragtime (1:50); 4 Finale (2:59); Jane Eyre: 5 Suite (13:15); The Devil And Daniel Webster: 6 Sleigh Ride (1:57); 7 Swing Your Partners (2:38); The Snows Of Kilimanjaro: 8 Interlude (6:36); 9 The Memory Waltz (4:14); Mysterious Island: 10 Prelude (1:58); 11 The Balloon (2:53); 12 The Giant Crab (3:37); 13 The Giant Bee (2:52); 14 The Giant Bird (3:06); Jason And The Argonauts: 15 Prelude (2:35); 16 Talos (2:20); 17 Talos' Death (2:41); 18 Triton (3:22).

Review: See entry below.

Bernard Herrmann: Wells Raises Kane ♫♫♫♫

1994, Unicorn Records.

Album Notes: *Music*: Bernard Herrmann; The London Philharmonic Orchestra and The National Philharmonic Orchestra, conducted by Bernard Herrmann; *Album Producer*: Christopher Palmer; *Engineer*: Bob Auger.

Selections: Welles Raises Kane: 1 Overture (2:30); 2 Theme And Variations (5:07); 3 Ragtime/The Saturday Night Band Concert (1:43); 4 Meditation/ Antimacassar (2:39); 5 Finale/ Pursuit And Happiness (2:34); The Devil And Daniel Webster: 6 Mr. Scratch (5:14); 7 The Ballad Of Springfield Mountain (4:35); 8 The Sleigh Ride (2:00); 9 The Miser's Waltz (5:22); 10 Finale/Swing Your Partners (2:46); Obsession: 11 Main Title/ Valse lente/Kidnap (5:57); 12 Newsboy/The Tape/The Ferry (4:56); 13 The Tomb/Sandra (8:02); 14 The Church/ Court's Confession/Bryn Mawr (9:24); 15 New Orleans/Wedding/ Court, The Morning After (4:31); 16 The Plane/Court And La Salle's Struggle/Airport (5:58).

Review: When he felt he had become redundant in Hollywood, Bernard Herrmann exiled himself to Europe and began recording intensively some of the best scores he had written for the movies. These two sets both present some of his most significant contributions to the screen, in thorough readings by the London Philharmonic and the National Philharmonic, two orchestras with which Herrmann enjoyed a long relationship in the 1960s and '70s. Some cues, in fact, appear in both CDs, but the first is notably significant for the suite from *Jane Eyre*, while the second includes the complete score for Brian de Palma's *Obsession*, a throbbing, lusty effort that ranks among the composer's finest works. It's not often that a composer has an occasion to revisit some of his scores and to rerecord them with great orchestras. Both CDs are remarkable in that respect, and definitive recordings no one should be without.

Bernard Herrmann Conducts Great British Film Music ♫♫♫♫ᵛ

1996, London Records.

Album Notes: The National Philharmonic Orchestra, conducted by Bernard Herrmann; *Album Producers*: Tony D'Amato, Raymond Few; *Engineers*: Arthur Bannister, Arthur Lilley.

Selections: Richard III (W. Walton): 1 Prelude (9:48); Anna Karenina (C. Lambert): 2 Overture (1:43); 3 Forlane (2:39); 4 Love Scene (2:11); 5 Finale (4:25); Oliver Twist (A. Bax): 6 Fagin's Romp (2:21); 7 Finale (4:36); An Ideal Husband (A. Benjamin): 8 Waltz (4:47); 9 Galop (1:36); Escape Me Never (W. Walton): 10 Theme (3:15); The Invaders (R. Vaughan Williams): 11 49th Parallel (3:22); Things To Come (A. Bliss): 12 Prologue (2:36); 13 March (4:54); 14 Building Of The New World (2:10); 15 Attack On The Moon Gun (1:36); 16 Epilogue (3:32).

Review: When he moved to Europe, Herrmann, in addition to addressing his own works, also surveyed the scores written by other important classic composers. This album, recorded for London in 1974, focuses on music written for English films by William Walton, Arnold Bax, Ralph Vaughan Williams, and Arthur Bliss, whose *Things to Come* is a particular highlight here. Also included is a series of cues composed by Constant Lambert for *Anna Karenina*, another score, notably attractive, that's seldom heard. The Phase 4 Stereo recording transfers very well to the digital domain.

Bernard Herrmann Film Scores: From Citizen Kane to Taxi Driver ♫♫

1993, Milan Records.

Album Notes: *Music*: Bernard Herrmann; The Royal Philharmonic Orchestra, conducted by Elmer Bernstein; *Featured Artists*: The Ambrosia Singers (John McCarthy, director), David Roach (alto sax); *Album Producer*: Christopher Palmer; *Engineers*: Keith Grant, Tim Handley.

Selections: Citizen Kane (suite): 1 Prelude (2:42), The Inquirer (polka) (2:44), Finale (3:02), End Cast (arr.: Conrad Salinger)(2:25); The Devil And Daniel Webster: 2 The Devil's Concerto (1:39); The Man Who Knew Too Much: 3 Cantata: The Storm Clouds (9:15) *Claire Henry*; Psycho (suite): 4 Prelude (3:28), The Murder (1:02), Finale (1:56); The Wrong Man: 5 Prelude (2:05); Vertigo: 6 Scene d'amour (6:41); North By Northwest: 7 Prelude (3:02); The Bride Wore Black: 8 A Musical Scenario (arr.: Christopher Palmer): Prelude, Femme Fatale, The Accident, Love And Death, Funeral, Finale (11:27); Farenheit 451: 9 Finale (The Book People)(4:34); Taxi Driver: A Night Piece For Orchestra (arr.: Christopher Palmer): 10 Prelude, Blues, Night Prowl, Bloodbath, Finale (8:32); 11 Bernard Herrmann On Film Music (4:42).

Review: This is an album whose conception and recording do not appear to have been adequately thought-out or prepared. The performance is passive, failing to serve Herrmann's surging, visceral style. The musicians trip and stumble through *Citizen Kane*'s "Inquirer Polka" with a number of glaring clams. The inclusion of the Xavier Cugat-like main title from *The Wrong Man* is puzzling; the piece is at best a curiosity. The "Finale" from *Fahrenheit 451* is absolutely enraging—the harp, vibraphone and glockenspiel parts are missing! A *Taxi Driver* suite is an inviting prospect, but it is ruined by Christopher Palmer's presumptuous alteration of Herrmann's original orchestration. Arthur Benjamin's "Storm Cloud Cantata" (from *The Man Who Knew Too Much*), is exciting and the best performed track on the album. But while Herrmann made his cameo in that film conducting this work, its inclusion on a Herrmann anthology makes no sense—Herrmann did not write it. Included at the end of the CD is an interesting excerpt from a recorded interview with Herrmann, where he expresses his thoughts on film scoring. Since many of the scores here are more truly represented elsewhere, this CD is at best a flawed oddity.

Paul Andrew MacLean

Citizen Kane: The Classic Film Scores of Bernard Herrmann ♪♪♪♪

1989, RCA Victor Records.

Album Notes: *Music*: Bernard Herrmann; The National Philharmonic Orchestra, conducted by Charles Gerhardt; *Album Producer*: George Korngold; *Engineer*: K.E. Wilkinson.

Selections: On Dangerous Ground: 1 The Death Hunt (2:23); Citizen Kane: 2 Prelude: Xanadu, Snow Picture (3:17); 3 Themes And Variations (Breakfast Montage)(3:26); 4 Aria From *Salammbo* (4:16) *Kiri Te Kanawa*; 5 Rosebud and Finale (2:41); Beneath The 12-Mile Reef: 6 The Sea, The Lagoon (4:41); 7 Descending (1:51); 8 The Octopus, Homecoming (4:54); Hangover Square: 9 Concerto Macabre For Piano And Orchestra (11:57) *Joaquin Achuccaro*; White Witch Doctor: 10 Talking Drums, Prelude: The Riverboat, Petticoat Dance, The Safari (3:57); 11 Tarantula, The Lion (1:28); 12 Nocturne (3:47); 13 Abduction Of The Bakuba Boy, The Skulls (1:56); 14 Lonni Bound By Ropes, Departure (2:28).

Review: This album, part of the *Classic Film Music* series Charles Gerhardt recorded in the '70s, remains one of the best Herrmann compilations ever. Although a great deal of Herrmann's work has been recorded since this collection's initial release, much of the music offered here is still not available elsewhere.

Other recordings of *Citizen Kane* have since been made, but Gerhardt's remains the best. The 13-minute suite removes

the extraneous, programmatic material, thus retaining the most potent essence of Herrmann's score. The aria for the fictitious opera "Salome", is included, and given dramatic performance by renowned soprano Kiri Te Kanawa. Also included is "Death Hunt," a surging, pummeling, brassy cue from *On Dangerous Ground*, and *Beneath the Twelve Mile Reef*, a stirring score, whose use of nine harps creates an effervescent evocation of the sea. Herrmann's "Concerto Macabre" for piano and orchestra (from *Hangover Square*) is driving and intense, while *White Witch Doctor* is an exotic and rhythmic evocation of Africa.

Engineer K.E. Wilkinson extracts a clear, full sound from the orchestra, and despite the advances in recording technology since this album was made, few later recordings can approach the resonant, crystalline sound of this 1974 album.

Paul Andrew MacLean

Farenheit 451 ♪♪♪♭

1995, Varese-Sarabande Records.

Album Notes: *Music*: Bernard Herrmann; The Seattle Symphony Orchestra, conducted by Joel McNeely; *Album Producer*: Robert Townson; *Engineer*: Al Swanson.

Selections: Farenheit 451: 1 Prelude (1:32); 2 Fire Engine (1:07); 3 The Bedroom (1:47); 4 The Reading (2:03); 5 The Garden (1:26); 6 The Nightmare (1:55); 7 Flowers Of Fire (1:18); 8 Flamethrower (:38); 9 Captain's Death (1:01); 10 The Road (3:42); The Main In The Gray Flannel Suit: 11 Main Title (2:11); Tender Is The Night: 12 The Embrace (1:51); The Ghost And Mrs. Muir: 13 Andante Cantabile (3:33); Anna And The King Of Siam: 14 Prelude (1:43); 15 Montage (1:15); 16 Elegy (4:23); 17 Coronation (2:23).

Review: One of Bernard Herrmann's finest scores, *Fahrenheit 451* is a passionate romantic score, employing an ensemble of strings, harps and modest percussion (but no brass or woodwinds). The music evokes emotions ranging from poetic longing to raging dementia, externalizing the suppressed passions of the film's characters, all locked into a conformist society of the future. Although this 17-minute suite from *Fahrenheit 451* was originally arranged by Herrmann himself, it is a pity that Varese took the trouble to make this recording, but did not present a more complete representation of the score (Herrmann rashly omitted a number of important cues from his suite). The remainder of the CD is filled-out with brief excerpts from four other Herrmann scores, *The Man in the Grey Flannel Suit*, *Anna and the King of Siam*, *Tender Is the Night* and *The Ghost and Mrs. Muir*—fine scores all, but with each so briefly represented, the listener can never quite become involved in any of them. The performance and recording quality, however, are first-rate, and even in brief suite form, *Fahrenheit 451* remains a masterpiece of invention and one of Herrmann's best works.

Paul Andrew MacLean

Torn Curtain: The Classic Film Music of Bernard Herrmann ♪♪♪▷

1995, Silva Screen Records.

Album Notes: *Music:* Bernard Herrmann; *Orchestrations:* Bernard Herrmann, Christopher Palmer; The City of Prague Philharmonic, conducted by Paul Bateman; *Featured Musicians:* Milan Hermanek (viola), Ivan Myslikovjan (saxophone); *Album Producer:* James Fitzpatrick; *Associate Producers:* David Wishart, Robin White; *Engineer:* John Tamperley.

Selections: 1 Prelude (from *The Man Who Knew Too Much*)(2:14); 2 Prelude/The School/Panic/Finale (from *Cape Fear*)(5:40); 3 Overture (from *Citizen Kane*) (2:44); 4 Suite (from *Dangerous Ground*)(10:37): Prelude, Blindness, The Silence, The Hunt, Finale; 5 Valse Lente (from *Obsession*)(1:44); 6 Memory Waltz (from *The Snows Of Kilimanjaro*)(4:22); 7 A Night Piece For Saxophone and Orchestra (from *Taxi Driver*)(8:00); 8 Main Title/Finale (from *The Ghost And Mrs. Muir*)(4:59); 9 Suite (from *Psycho*)(7:21); 10 Suite (from *Vertigo*)(10:09): Prelude/The Nightmare/Scene d'amour; 11 Main Title/Gromek/The Killing (from *Torn Curtain*)(6:05); 12 Ray Harryhausen Fantasy Film Suite (10:02): The Three Worlds Of Gulliver, The Seventh Voyage Of Sinbad, Mysterious Island, Jason And The Argonauts.

Review: See entry below.

Herrmann/Hitchcock: A Partnership in Terror ♪♪♪▷

1996, Silva Screen Records.

Album Notes: *Music:* Bernard Herrmann; *Orchestrations:* Bernard Herrmann, Mike Townsend; The City of Prague Philharmonic, conducted by Paul Bateman; *Album Producer:* James Fitzpatrick; *Associate Producers:* David Wishart, Robin White; *Engineers:* John Tamperley, Mike Ross-Trevor.

Selections: The Man Who Knew Too Much: 1 Prelude (2:21); The Trouble With Harry: 2 A Portrait Of Hitch (8:52); Vertigo: 3 Prelude (2:57); 4 Nightmare (5:12); 5 Scene d'amour (5:12);

> "If you told me to write a love song tonight, I'd have a lot of trouble. But if you tell me to write a love song about a girl with a red dress who goes into a bar and is on her fifth martini and is falling off her chair, that's a lot easier and it makes me free to say anything I want."
>
> **Stephen Sondheim**
> *(New York Times Magazine, April, 1984)*

North By Northwest: 6 Overture (3:21); 7 Conversation Piece (4:44); Psycho: 8 Prelude, The City, The Drive, The Shower, Finale (7:27); Marnie: 9 Prelude (3:02); Torn Curtain: 10 Main Title (2:00); 11 Gromek (1:58); 12 The Killing (2:07).

Review: Both of these collections of Bernard Herrmann's film music are based around the same set of recordings of Hitchcock thriller scores: *A Partnership in Terror* features Herrmann's throbbing, stormy opening to *The Man Who Knew Too Much* (conducted by Herrmann himself as an orchestra performance at the opening of the film), the droll *The Trouble With Harry*, the swirling titles, tarantella nightmare sequence and rhapsodic love music of *Vertigo*, the supercharged fandango opening of *North By Northwest*, the knitting strings of *Psycho* and the urgent prelude music from *Marnie*. The *Torn Curtain* also features *The Man Who Knew Too Much*, *Psycho* and *Vertigo* as well as the aggressive (and rejected) music to *Torn Curtain*, but this longer album also features suites from Herrmann's brutal *Cape Fear* (reused by Martin Scorsese in his remake), newspaper music from *Citizen Kane* and a somewhat less-than-satisfactory take on the composer's amazingly powerful score to *On Dangerous Ground*. More satisfying are the lyrical waltzes from *Obsession* and *The Snows of Kilimanjaro*, as well as the hauntingly romantic *The Ghost and Mrs. Muir*. There's a lively ten minute suite from Herrmann's indelible Ray Harryhausen fantasy scores, but the suite from *Taxi Driver* seems overly glib and romanticized, with a saxophone solo by Ivan Myslikovjan that just gets out of hand. Still, conductor Paul Bateman brings far more power and polish to these performances than are obtained on some of Silva's other compilations.

Jeff Bond

Lee Holdridge (1944-

Film Music of Lee Holdridge
♪♪♪♪

1994, Citadel Records.

Album Notes: *Music*: Lee Holdridge; The London Symphony Orchestra, conducted by Charles Gerhardt; *Album Producer*: George Korngold; *Engineer*: Charles Stanley.

Selections: The Beastmaster: 1 Suite (7:33); Jonathan Livingston Seagull: 2 Music For Strings (5:05); Going Home: 3 The Journey (5:52); Splash: 4 Love Theme (3:29); Wizards And Warriors: 5 Overture (5:02); East Of Eden: 6 Main Title (1:58); 7 The Brothers/Cathy/Leaving Connecticut (2:49); 8 The Father (2:18); 9 The Well/The Naming (3:55)p; 10 The Secret Of Monterey/Abra's Theme (3:29); 11 Finale (3:23); The Hemingway Play: 12 Parisian Sketch (2:44); The Great Whales: 13 Introduction and Theme (5:00).

Review: One of the most unsung of the modern-day film composers, Lee Holdridge's often romantic, expressive compositions are given their chance to shine on this great-sounding recording with Charles Gerhardt conducting the London Symphony Orchestra. From the Korngold-influenced *Wizards and Warriors* and *The Beastmaster* to the beautiful lyricism of *The Great Whales* and *Splash*, this superior effort nicely illustrates Holdridge's melodious musical style, featuring well-written, memorable themes and often soaring orchestral passages. The album also includes selections from the television program "The Hemingway Play," the features *Going Home* and *Jonathan Livingston Seagull*, concluding with an 18-minute suite from the mini-series "East of Eden." With Gerhardt's baton leading the way, the album has a great deal of replay value due to its varied and consistently high level of musical quality.

Andy Dursin

Arthur Honegger (1892-1955)

Arthur Honegger Film Music

1993, Marco Polo Records.

Album Notes: The CSR Symphony Orchestra of Bratislava, conducted by Adriano; *Album Producer*: Gunter Appenheimer.

Selections: Les Miserables: 1 Main Title (7:12); 2 The Sewers (5:43); 3 Music At Gillenormand (1:50); 4 Death Of Jean Valjean (2:15); 5 The Riot (2:31); La Roue: 6 Overture (3:49); Mermoz: 7 Crossing The Andes (9:30); 8 Atlantic Flight (9:00); Napoleon: 9 Quiet (3:29); 10 Violine's Idyll (2:12); 11 The Children's Dance (1:52); 12 Interlude and Finale (3:04); 13 Chaconne For An Impress (1:59); 14 Napoleon (1:02); 15 The Shadows (3:14); 16 The Beggars Of Glory (3:45).

Review: See entry below.

Arthur Honegger: L'idee/ Crime et chatiment ♪♪♪♪♪

1993, Marco Polo Records.

Album Notes: The Slovak Radio Symphony Orchestra of Bratislava, conducted by Adriano; *Album Producers*: Emil Niznansky, Peter Zagar; *Engineer*: Hubert Geschwandtner.

Selections: Farinet ou L'or dans la montagne: 1 Main Title/ Morning Dew/ Escape and Death Of Farinet/Finale (6:01); Crime And Punishment: 2 Main Title (1:09); 3 Raskolnikov/ Sonia (3:17); 4 Leaving For The Crime (4:57); 5 Murder Of Elisabeth (1:50); 6 Nocturnal Visit/End Title (3:15); Le deserteur ou Je t'attendrai: 7 Symphonic Fragment (9:51); Le grand barrage: 8 Musical Image For Orchestra (3:05); L'idee: 9 Complete Score (24:50).

Review: See entry below.

Arthur Honegger: Mayerling/Regain ♪♪♪♪♪

1993, Marco Polo Records.

Album Notes: The Slovak Radio Symphony Orchestra of Bratislava and The Slovak Philharmonic Choir, conducted by Adriano; *Featured Musician*: Jacques Tchamkerten (Ondes Mertenot); *Album Producers*: Emil Niznansky, Peter Zagar; *Engineer*: Hubert Geschwandtner.

Selections: Mayerling: 1 Main Title (1:37); 2 Garden (1:32); 3 The Horse Carriage/In The Hallways (2:05); 4 Final Scene (6:09); Regain (suite I): 5 Le Panturle (3:37); 6 Winter (3:13); 7 Spring (2:47); 8 Gedemus The Knife-Sharpener (:56); 9 Regain (1:56); Regain (suite II): 10 Introduction/Song Of Aubignane (2:36); 11 Nocturne (4:40); 12 Night In The Barn/Summer (3:48); 13 The Ploughshare (2:09); Le demon de l'Himalaya: 14 Snow Storm (12:18); 15 Ascension And Fall/Vision (9:35).

Review: One of the great classical composers of this century, Arthur Honegger wrote many scores for the movies (it was at his suggestion that Miklos Rozsa became a film composer as a way to turn his talent into a lucrative proposition). These recordings, superbly assembled by Marco Polo Records, feature Adriano and the Slovak Radio Symphony Orchestra of Bratislava in reconstructed performances of Honegger's most important scores, particularly *Les Miserables*, made in 1934, and *Napoleon*, directed by Abel Gance in 1926-27. The breathtaking scope and diversity of these scores show that film music, in its early days, was not confined to Hollywood and its great composers, but developed in other countries as well and attracted a lot of serious exponents. It also makes the strongest case yet for film music as a serious medium and as a close parent to classical music.

Mark Isham (1951-

Mark Isham Film Music ♪♪♪

1990, Windham Hill Records.

Album Notes: *Music*: Mark Isham; conducted by Mark Adler; *Featured Musicians*: Mrs. Soffel: Lyle Mayes (piano), Peter Maunu (violin), Mark Isham (synthesizers, pennywhistle, piano); *The Times Of Harvey Milk*: Mark Isham (trumpet, synthesizers); Never Cry Wolf: Rufus Olivier (bassoon), Bill Douglass (bamboo flutes), George Marsh (percussion), Tucky Bailey (glass), Natalie Cox (harp), Mark Isham (synthesizers), Annie Stocking, Stephanie Douglass, Kathy Hudnall, Jeanette Spartaine (voices); *Album Producers*: Mark Isham, Todd Boekelheide; *Engineers*: Todd Boekhelheide, Mark Isham.

Selections: 1 Mrs. Soffel (13:59); 2 The Times Of Harvey Milk (8:32); 3 Never Cry Wolf (24:48).

Review: Under the title *Film Music,* this set presents the original soundtrack of *Mrs. Soffel,* a 1985 film that stars Mel Gibson and Diane Keaton, coupled with rerecordings of *Never Cry Wolf,* from 1983, and cues from *The Times of Harvey Milk.* Isham, an eclectic composer and musician, is a borderline case between film music and New Age music, who creates often compelling scores. The music for *Mrs. Soffel,* a moving love story based on real life turn-of-the-century facts, is a combination of attractive cues that rely on the deft use of the pennywhistle, coupled with piano, violin and synthesizers, to create its own aura. A semi-documentary/adventure film, *Never Cry Wolf,* made by Disney, follows a lone biologist working in the Arctic wasteland to learn more about wolves. The long suite offers themes that are suitably soft and attractive, though the lack of true melodic material sometimes works to the detriment of the music.

Maurice Jarre (1924-

Jarre by Jarre: Film Themes of Maurice Jarre ♪♪♪♪

1987, CBS Records.

Album Notes: *Music*: Maurice Jarre; The Royal Philharmonic Orchestra, conducted by Maurice Jarre; *Album Producer*: David Mottley; *Engineer*: Paul Hulme.

Selections: Lawrence Of Arabia: 1 Overture part 2 (4:26); 2 Main Titles (2:02); 3 Arrival At Auda's Camp (1:19); Ryan's Daughter: 4 Rosy's Theme (2:13); Doctor Zhivago: 5 Prelude and Lara's Theme (5:15); A Passage To India: 6 Adela's Theme (2:43); Witness: 7 Building The Barn (4:28); 8 Is Paris Burning? (3:38); 9 The Damned (11:08); Mad Max Beyond Thunderdome: 10 Fanfare and Thunderdome Music (4:38); 11 Villa Rides! (3:42)

Review: Although Maurice Jarre has recorded a number of anthologies of his own music, *Jarre by Jarre* is by far the best. Vibrantly performed, and recorded with full, resonant sound, this album contains the best available recordings of some of these scores. *Lawrence of Arabia* is performed with majesty, precision and grace (with the strings appropriately dominant). *Ryan's Daughter* is presented in an extremely enjoyable and graceful arrangement, which is far more attractive than the original soundtrack. *Is Paris Burning* is a vibrant waltz featuring accordion, and shows a lyrical side of Jarre which is rarely heard. Jarre's "Barn Raising" music from *Witness*, originally scored for synthesizers, is given a beautiful, full-orchestral rendition, while *The Damned* exposes a darker side of the composer. The suite from *Mad Max Beyond Thunderdome* contains a large, brassy fanfare (which is especially welcome since it was not included on the original soundtrack). *Villa Rides* concludes the album, a pleasantly rhythmic piece with an exotic Mexican flavor. Engineer Paul Hulme deserves special mention for extracting a large concert hall sound from CTS studios. In terms of both performance and sound, this is one of the best recordings I have ever heard.

Paul Andrew MacLean

Lean by Jarre: Musical Tribute to David Lean ♪♪

1992, Milan Records.

Album Notes: *Music*: Maurice Jarre; The Royal Philharmonic Orchestra, conducted by Maurice Jarre; *Album Producers*: Maurice Jarre, L.A. Johnson; *Engineer*: Shawn Murphy.

Selections: 1 Remembrance (3:51); 2 Ryan's Daughter Suite (8:46); 3 A Passage To India Suite (10:06); 4 Doctor Zhivago Suite (9:52); 5 Offering (3:15); 6 Lawrence Of Arabia Suite (12:47).

Review: Maurice Jarre's most celebrated collaboration was with director David Lean, and the composer pays the director homage in this recording. Jarre's four scores for Lean, *Lawrence of Arabia, Doctor Zhivago, Ryan's Daughter* and *A Passage to India* are all represented, along with two original pieces, "Remembrance" and "Offering". "Remembrance," a thunderous, large orchestral piece which evokes the kind of large-scale epic for which David Lean was best known, introduces the album. Where the particular film scores are concerned however, the limitations of a concert setting unfortunately impose compromising alterations. Much of the more exotic (and inventive) instrumentation in Jarre's original scores is missing. The Fujara and Indian instruments are sorely missed in *Passage to India*, as are the various exotic instruments in *Doctor Zhivago*. The orchestration of *Lawrence of Arabia* is also altered for smaller orchestra and as such proves unsatisfying. While a nice souvenir of the highly memorable Lean/ Jarre collaborations (this recording is also available on VHS and laserdisc as a concert video), I would sooner recommend the original soundtracks as a more true representation of these scores.

Paul Andrew MacLean

Maurice Jarre at Abbey Road ♫♫♫♫▽

1992, Milan Records.

Album Notes: *Music*: Maurice Jarre; The Royal Philharmonic Orchestra and the Sun Valley Choral Society (C. Paul Erb, director), conducted by Maurice Jarre; *Featured Musician*: Ralph Grierson (synthesizers); *Album Producer*: Maurice Jarre; *Engineer*: Shawn Murphy; *Assistant Engineers*: Sue McLean, Ethan Chase, Bill Talbot, Greg Denon.

Selections: 1 Georges Franju Suite: La tete contre les murs (The Keepers), Therese Desqueyroux, Les yeux sans visage (The Horror Chamber Of Doctor Faustus), Judex (16:31); 2 Behold A Pale Horse (2:49); 3 Ghost (4:11); 4 Witness (4:59); 5 Jacob's Ladder (3:20); 6 Prancer (6:15); 7 Gorillas In The Mist (2:36); 8 Fatal Attraction (5:09); 9 Moon Over Parador (4:31); 10 Dead Poets Society (5:13); 11 Bombay March (from *A Passage To India*)(1:17).

Review: Always his own best interpreter, Maurice Jarre positively shines when he is fronting a great orchestra. Such is the case here, with the composer revisiting some of the scores he wrote throughout his career, including some rare ones seldom heard elsewhere. The *Georges Franju Suite* introduces themes he created for the films of Georges Franju, with whom he developed an early artistic relationship, long before Jarre became internationally renowned. They already evidence some of the traits for which Jarre would eventually become famous, notably his uncanny flair for strange instrumentations, and his knack for attractive, melodic tunes. Following *Behold A Pale Horse*, a sadly neglected score for a 1964 partisan film, set in post-Civil War Spain, starring Gregory Peck and Omar Sharif, the set moves on to latter day creations, like the themes for *Ghost, Witness, Gorillas in the Mist,* and *Fatal Attraction,* in which synthesizers play an increasingly important role. Interestingly, it offers the rarely heard theme for *Prancer,* before going to the delicious *Moon Over Parador,* in which Jarre spoofs his own epic style. The "Bombay March" from *A Passage to India* concludes the set on a positive, exhilarating note that reminds us that Maurice Jarre always was at his best when he wrote epic themes. Throughout, the playing is never less than superlative.

Maurice Jarre at the Royal Festival Hall ♫♫♫

1997, Milan Records.

Album Notes: *Music*: Maurice Jarre; The BBC Concert Orchestra, conducted by Maurice Jarre; *Album Producer*: Maurice Jarre; *Engineer*: Mike Ross-Trevor.

Selections: Grand Prix: 1 Suite (4:49); Witness: 2 Theme (4:54); The Man Who Would Be King: 3 Theme (5:23); Villa Rides: 4 Theme (3:45); 5 Concerto For EVI (19:50); The Year Of Living Dangerously: 6 Suite (7:11); The Tin Drum: 7 Suite (7:28); Is Paris Burning: 8 The Paris Waltz (3:33); Lawrence Of Arabia: 9 Suite (12:52).

Review: Recorded live during a concert with the BBC Concert Orchestra, this recording features an eclectic array of Jarre's music. A suite from *Grand Prix* opens the album, Jarre's light-hearted music conveying the excitement of high-speed racing (the sound effect of cars whizzing by adding to the fun). *The Man Who Would Be King* is given a jaunty arrangement, though the very foreground use of percussion is perhaps a little overbearing. The theme from *Villa Rides* (one of Jarre's few western scores) is a beautiful, Mexican-flavored piece with some of Jarre's most consonant orchestration.

Originally conceived as an electronic score, *The Year of Living Dangerously* appears in an intriguing orchestral transcription. While interesting, it remains a more successful work in its original form. On the other hand, Jarre's Americana-flavored music from *Witness*—also originally conceived for electronics—translates to an orchestral setting far more successfully. A non-film work, Jarre's "Concerto for EVI" (electronic wind instrument) is a four-movement work, vibrant and stylistically eclectic. A solid performance of the oft-recorded *Lawrence of Arabia* brings the album to its conclusion.

Because it was recorded at a live performance, the sound balance and fidelity are not as good as they might be in a studio setting, but engineer Mike Ross-Trevor does an excellent job, and there are some highly attractive moments in this album.

Paul Andrew MacLean

Doctor Zhivago: The Classic Film Music of Maurice Jarre ♪♪♪♪

1995, Silva Screen Records.

Album Notes: *Music*: Maurice Jarre; The City of Prague Philharmonic, conducted by Paul Bateman; The Philharmonia Orchestra, conducted by Tony Bremner; *Album Producer*: James Fitzpatrick; *Associate Producers*: David Wishart, Philip Lane; *Engineers*: John Timperley, Eric Tomlinson, Dick Lewzey.

Selections: 1 Suite (from *Doctor Zhivago*)(9:11); 2 Adela's Theme (from *A Passage To India*)(2:23); 3 Suite (from *Jesus Of Nazareth*) (8:14); 4 End Credits (from *Ghost*)(4:25); 5 The Man Who Would Be King (4:25); 6 Building The Barn (from *Witness*)(4:40); 7 Is Paris Burning? (3:50); 8 Suite (from *The Fixer*)(7:10); 9 Main Title (from *El Condor*)(3:21); 10 Suite (from *Ryan's Daughter*)(8:52); 11 The Night Of The Generals (3:53); 12 Fatal Attraction (5:00); 13 Villa Rides (3:28); 14 Lara's Theme (from *Doctor Zhivago*)(3:16); 15 Overture (from *Lawrence Of Arabia*)(4:23).

Review: Excellent compilation of suites and themes from Maurice Jarre's monumental career. Paul Bateman conducts The City of Prague Philharmonic in their performance on both the David Lean film standards *Doctor Zhivago* and *Passage to India*, as well as "Building the Barn" from *Witness*, and the finale from *Ghost*. This anthology also features lesser known Jarre efforts for such films as *The Fixer*, *El Condor* and *Villa Rides*. The Prague orchestra handles the material well with

solid, respectable performances that are faithful to the original work. There is also a bonus track included from Silva's *Lawrence of Arabia* rerecording by The Philharmonia Orchestra under the direction of Tony Bremmer.

David Hirsch

A Maurice Jarre Trilogy ♪♪♪♭

1995, DRG Records.

Album Notes: *Music*: Maurice Jarre; *Orchestrations*: Maurice Jarre; The Unione Musicisti di Roma Orchestra, conducted by Maurice Jarre; *Engineer*: Sandro Marcotulli; *CD Producer*: Claudio Fuiano.

Selections: CD 1: The Damned: 1 Theme and Main Title (2:09); 2 Lullaby For Lisa (3:20); 3 The Death Of Joachim (2:40); 4 Obsession (5:30); 5 Sophie Awaits (3:50); 6 Martin's Theme (3:24); 7 Incest (4:25); 8 The Return Of Herbert (3:27); 9 Sophie's Torment (3:40); 10 Finale (2:00); A Season In Hell: 11 A Season In Hell (2:00); 12 Impossible Thing (2:32); 13 Canoe On The Tana (2:39); 14 Difficult Love (3:02); 15 The Commune (3:04); 16 Battle At Tchelenko (2:08); 17 To My Best Loved Friend (3:33); 18 Yearning For Africa (1:50); 19 Words And Syllables (3:19); 20 The Caravan (3:13); 21 Arabian Coffee (1:08); 22 A Season In Hel (3:06).

CD 2: For Those I Loved: 1 Survival (2:33); 2 Zofia's Waltz (2:21); 3 Insurrection (3:35); 4 Solitude (2:45); 5 The Grandmother (2:15); 6 Resistance/For Those I Loved (2:20); 7 America (2:12); 8 Happy Time (2:27); 9 Destruction/The Fire (2:28); 10 After Mother's Death (2:16); 11 Martin And Zofia/For Those I Loved (1:56); 12 Ghetto's Cafe (3:34); 13 Souvenir (4:00); 14 First Love (3:10); 15 Insurrection March (2:40); 16 The Past (1:55); 17 Melody Mansion (3:15); 18 Treblinka (1:50); 19 Escape (1:35); 20 Zofia (2:28); 21 Deportation (3:55); 22 Cafe Sztuka (3:20); 23 The Ghetto Uprising (2:40); 24 Hope And The Future/For Those I Loved (2:50).

Review: A most intriguing concept for a collection of rarer material composed by Maurice Jarre. All three of these films have one thing in common, their central characters are living in their own hellish dark side of life. The controversial classic *The Damned* leads off this 2-CD set with some of Jarre's darkest work. The nucleus of this score is a shadowy waltz that represents one family's descent into perversity. *A Season in Hell* displays the disintegrating friendship between two brilliant writers in 19th-century Paris. While there is the typical warm emotional themes ("To My Best Loved Friend") that Jarre is noted for, the score is peppered with blood boiling African rhythms. By far the longest presentation of the three, *For*

Those I Loved is an awareness of the hopes and dreams of the survivors of the Holocaust, as seen through the eyes of one Polish survivor. No doubt because the subject matter offered more motivation to Jarre, this is the most captivating of the three scores. It is powerfully moving, evoking unsettling emotions from the darkest period of human existence.

David Hirsch

Laurie Johnson

The Avengers 𝄢𝄢𝄢𝄢ᵇ

1982, Varese-Sarabande Records.

Album Notes: *Music*: Laurie Johnson; The London Studio Orchestra, conducted by Laurie Johnson; *U.K. Album Producers*: Laurie Johnson, Christopher Palmer; *U.S. Album Producers*: Karry O'Quinn, Tom Null, Richard Kraft; *Engineers*: John Richards, Danny Hersch.

Selections: The Avengers: 1 Main Title (2:25); 2 Theme From "Pandora" (3:22); 3 Theme From "The Joker" (2:30); The New Avengers: 4 Main Title (2:30); 5 Theme From "Cat Amongst The Pigeons" (2:51); 6 Theme From "Obsession" (2:28); 7 Theme From "Tale Of The Big Why" (3:20); Dr. Strangelove: Or How I Learned To Stop Worrying And Love The Bomb: 8 The Bomb Run (2:33); First Men In The Moon: 9 Main Title (2:35); 10 Moonscape And Descent (1:52); 11 The Selinites (2:04); 12 Trek To The Giant Doors (2:56); 13 Monster Caterpillar (2:38); 14 Eclipse And Staircase (2:40); 15 Escape Of The Sphere (1:28); 16 End Title (:48); Hedda: 17 Main Title (3:37); 18 Hedda And Thea (2:35); 19 Judge Brack (2:16); 20 Hedda And Lovborg (3:34); 21 The Manuscript (2:40); 22 Death And End Title (:57); Captain Kronos, Vampire Hunter: 23 Main Title (2:35); 24 Death Duel (3:15).

Review: See entry below.

The Rose and the Gun 𝄢𝄢𝄢𝄢

1992, Unicorn-Kanchana Records.

Album Notes: *Music*: Laurie Johnson; The London Studio Symphony Orchestra, conducted by Laurie Johnson.

Selections: The Lady And The Highway Man: 1 Theme (2:33); A Hazard Of Hearts: 2 Serena (2:42); A Duel Of Hearts: 3 Theme (2:35); A Ghost In Monte Carlo: 4 Grand Waltz (2:12); The Avengers: 5 Theme (2:07); 6 Tag Scene (1:57); The New Avengers: 7 Theme (2:12); Tiger Bay: 8 Theme (2:08); When The Kissing Had To Stop: 9 Theme (2:10); Hot Millions: 10 Caesar Smith (Theme)(2:11); 11 There Is Another Song (2:22); 12 This

Time (2:01); Shirley's World: 13 Shirley's Theme (1:55); 14 Rickshaw Ride (2:17); I Aim At The Stars: 15 Theme (2:30); This Is Your Life: 16 This Is Your Life (2:26); Jason King: 17 Theme (2:03); First Men In The Moon: 18 Romance (2:24); The Professionals: 19 Theme (1:52).

Review: Laurie Johnson's real claim to fame is the vigorous theme he wrote in the early 1960s for the English television series, "The Avengers." But his enormous body of works, which encompasses more than 400 scores for films and television, single him out as one of the most prolific and successful British composers today. Both CDs offer selections from several of the most prominent films and TV shows with which he has been associated, with Johnson himself conducting the London Studio (Symphony) Orchestra.

Unsurprisingly, both sets contain the main themes from "The Avengers" and its sequel, "The New Avengers," with the Varese CD including in addition some other themes written for individual episodes. Of the two, that CD is also more interesting in that it covers at greater length other scores written by Johnson, for the science fiction film, *First Men in the Moon*, made in 1964, and *Captain Kronos, Vampire Hunter*, a cult horror movie, as well as a suite from the screen adaptation of Ibsen's *Hedda Gabler*. Rounding up the selections in the set is a theme from the Stanley Kubrick anti-war drama, *Dr. Strangelove*, also a popular favorite.

The Unicorn-Kanchana set may not have as much of a widespread appeal, given the fact that many of the themes found in it relate to films or television shows that are not very well known outside of England. However, collectors should notice that the CD includes a collection of themes for TV films based on the novels by Barbara Cartland ("The Lady and the Highwayman," "A Hazard of Hearts," "A Duel of Hearts" and "A Ghost in Monte Carlo"), as well as from the film *Hot Millions*, and the TV special "Shirley's World," starring Shirley MacLaine. Always elegant and catchy, Johnson's music makes for great listening.

Erich-Wolfgang Korngold (1897-1957)

Erich-Wolfgang Korngold: The Warner Bros. Years 𝄢𝄢𝄢𝄢ᵇ

1996, Rhino Records.

Album Notes: *Music*: Erich-Wolfgang Korngold; The Warner Bros. Studi Orchestra, conducted by Erich-Wolfgang Korngold;

Album Producers: Tony Thomas, Marilee Bradford; *Engineer*: Doug Schwartz.

Selections: CD 1: Captain Blood: 1 Main Title (1:54); 2 Peter And Arabella (1:37); 3 Tortuga (2:52); 4 Buccaneers (1:34); The Green Pastures: 5 The Creation (1:23); 6 The Flood (2:46); Anthony Adverse: 7 Main Title (1:25); 8 To The Spa (2:41); 9 Bonnyfeather (1:01); 10 Anthony And Angela (2:53); The Prince And The Pauper: 11 Main Title (1:34); 12 The Prince In The Palace (1:52); 13 Miles Hendon To The Rescue (1:56); 14 Prince As Pauper (1:46); 15 The Ride To The Palace (:50); 16 The Coronation (:33); 17 Finale (:21); The Adventures Of Robin Hood: 18 Main Title (1:31); 19 Banquet In The Castle (1:59); 20 Marian And Robin (3:29); 21 Epilogue (1:31); 22 End Title (:28); Juarez: 23 Archduke Maximilian (:42); 24 Carlotta (1:57); 25 Rebellion (2:13); 26 The Death Of Maximilian and Finale (2:55); The Private Lives Of Elizabeth And Essex: 27 Main Title (1:29); 28 Essex Fanfares (:16); 29 Essex March (2:07); 30 Elizabeth (1:19); 31 End Titles (:47); The Sea Hawk: 32 Main Title (1:47); 33 The Albatross (1:56); 34 The Battle With The Galleon (2:09); 35 Maria's Ride To Dover (2:11); 36 Finale (1:04); 37 End Title (:42).

CD 2: The Sea Wolf: 1 Main Title (1:04); 2 The Ghost (1:09); 3 Love Theme (1:26); 4 Fight In The Dark (1:42); 5 Finale (1:11); Kings Row: 6 Main Title (1:21); 7 Parris And Cassie (1:58); 8 Ice House (:44); 9 Grandmother (2:35); 10 Randy And Drake (2:01); 11 Parris Comes Home (1:40); 12 Finale (1:20); The Constant Nymph: 13 Main Title (3:10); 14 Farewell (1:44); 15 Finale (2:29); Devotion: 16 Branwell In The Tavern (3:50); Between Two Worlds: 17 Mysterious Voyage (2:58); 18 Love Theme (2:52); Of Human Bondage: 19 Main Title (1:05); 20 Mildred (4:00); 21 Jealousy (2:17); 22 Finale (2:09); Escape Me Never: 23 Crossing The Dolomites (6:10); Deception: 24 Main Title, Theme and End Title (3:24).

Review: Epic compilation of the original recordings of Erich-Wolfgang Korngold's ground-breaking work in the early days of Hollywood from 1935 to 1946. Korngold, a child prodigy who was composing operas in his teens, set the standards for the great costumed dramas (*Anthony Adverse, King's Row*), the Errol Flynn swashbuckers (*Captain Blood, The Sea Hawk* and *The Adventures of Robin Hood*) and the romantic sagas (*Escape Me Never*), all with a lavishly orchestrated style. Key selections from 16 of his Warner Bros. scores are featured here, each conducted personally by the composer. The one drawback to this two hour-plus collection is that many of the recordings have a lot of surface noise. Not surprising when considering that they have survived the last 50 to 60 years this well. While much of this music has been digitally rerecorded

over the last few years, none of it can ever match the power of the original sessions. The orchestra size, or the pace of the performance, is never quite the same and Korngold here has the orchestra play it as he wrote it, full of fire and emotion. The 2-CD set also contains a lavish 44-page booklet with insightful historical notes by noted Korngold authority Tony Thomas.
David Hirsch

The Sea Hawk: The Classic Film Scores of Erich-Wolfgang Korngold
♪♪♪♪

1989, RCA Victor.

Album Notes: *Music*: Erich-Wolfgang Korngold; The National Philharmonic Orchestra, conducted by Charles Gerhardt; *Featured Artist*: Sidney Sax (violin); *Album Producer*: George Korngold; *Engineer*: K.E. Wilkinson.

Selections: The Sea Hawk: 1 Main Title, Reunion, Finale (6:53); Of Human Bondage: 2 Nora's Theme (4:21); The Adventures Of Robin Hood: 3 March Of The Merry Men, Battle (4:01); Juarez: 4 Love Theme (1:48); Kings Row: 5 Main Title (1:39); The Constant Nymph: 6 Tomorrow (tone poem for contralto, women's chorus and orchestra)(6:02) *Norma Proctor, Ambrosian Singers*; Captain Blood: 7 Overture (2:58); Anthony Adverse: 8 No Father, No Mother, No Name (2:39); Between Two Worlds: 9 Main Title, Mother And Son (5:30); Deception: 10 Main Title (1:33); Devotion: 11 The Death Of Emily Bronte (4:05); Escape Me Never: 12 Main Title, Venice, March, Love Scene, Finale (8:14).

Review: Originally recorded and released in 1972, this is the album largely credited with igniting the revival of symphonic film music, after years of dreariness when rock scores had become the norm and below-par standard. The million-selling album, which was produced by George Korngold, son of the composer, spawned a prestigious series that eventually explored the works of well-known Hollywood composers, like Max Steiner, Bernard Herrmann, Miklos Rozsa, Dimitri Tiomkin, David Raksin, all of whom had fallen into sad neglect. Also as a result of the series' success, *Star Wars*, released in 1977, was able to feature a symphonic score by John Williams that not only paid homage to the composer's illustrious predecessors, but opened wide the gates of the studios to an entire generation of new composers, like James Horner, Cliff Eidelman, Randy Edelman and George Fenton, all of whom benefitted from the incredible resurgence of symphonic music in films.

Elizabeth and Essex: The Classic Film Scores of Erich-Wolfgang Korngold
✍✍✍✍✍

1989, RCA Victor.

Album Notes: *Music:* Erich-Wolfgang Korngold; The National Philharmonic Orchestra, conducted by Charles Gerhardt; *Featured Artist:* Francisco Garbarro (cello); *Album Producer:* George Korngold; *Engineer:* K.E. Wilkinson.

Selections: The Privates Lives Of Elizabeth And Essex: 1 Overture (7:18); The Prince And The Pauper: 2 Main Title, The Boys Go To Play, Epilogue (4:45); Anthony Adverse: 3 In The Forest (2:14); The Sea Wolf: 4 Main Title, Escape In The Fog, Love Scene, Finale (7:28); Deception: 5 Cello Concerto in C, op. 37 (11:50); Another Dawn: 6 Night Scene (5:48); Of Human Bondage: 7 Main Title, Christmas, Sally, Lullaby, Finale (8:07).

Review: A follow-up to *The Sea Hawk*, this splendid recording again teamed the National Philharmonic with conductor Charles Gerhardt and producer George Korngold for a further exploration of composer Erich-Wolfgang Korngold's film music. Like its predecessor, it is a sumptuous tribute to one of the great Hollywood composers of the 1940s.

Music by Erich-Wolfgang Korngold
✍✍✍✍✎

1991, Stanyan Records.

Album Notes: *Music:* Erich-Wolfgang Korngold; The Warner Bros. Studio Orchestra, conducted by Lionel Newman; *CD Producer:* Rod McKuen; *Engineer:* Steve Hoffman; *Assistant Engineer:* Kevin Gray.

Selections: Kings Row: 1 Main Title (1:35); 2 The Children (2:25); 3 Randy And Drake (3:05); 4 Grandmother (2:25); Anthony Adverse: 5 Anthony Is Born; 6 Love Scene (2:19); 7 Anthony Comes Home (1:39); The Private Lives Of Elizabeth And Essex: 8 Main Title and Essex' Victory March (1:32); 9 Love Scene and Finale (2:34); The Sea Hawk: 10 Main Title (2:12); 11 The Reunion (4:11); The Prince And The Pauper: 12 The Boys Go To Play (:58); The Constant Nymph: 13 Main Title (1:28); 14 Farewell (1:39); The Adventures Of Robin Hood: 15 March Of The Merry Men and Battle (3:47); 16 Robin And Maid Marian (4:13); 17 Epilogue (1:19).

Review: For many years, the LP version of this album, initially released by Warner Bros. Records in 1962, and almost immedi-

ately deleted, was high on the list of ardent fans and collectors of serious film music. Its availability on compact disc brings it back to the catalogue, and while it may not sound as outstanding today as it did once, particularly when compared with recordings of more recent vintage, it still stands as a great tribute to the music composed by Korngold for the Warner Bros. films.

Joel McNeely

Hollywood '94 ✍✍✍✍✎

1994, Varese-Sarabande.

Album Notes: The Seattle Symphony Orchestra, conducted by Joel McNeely; *Featured Soloist:* Margaret Batjer (violin); *Album Producer:* Robert Townson; *Engineer:* Al Swanson.

Selections: 1 Jurassic Park (J. Williams)(6:14); 2 The Shadow (J. Goldsmith)(2:36); 3 Forrest Gump (A. Silvestri)(9:13); 4 The Age Of Innocence (E. Bernstein)(4:52); 5 Squanto (J. McNeely)(4:10); 6 Maverick (R. Newman) (4:00); 7 Schindler's List (J. Williams)(3:40); 8 True Lies (B. Fiedel)(4:57); 9 The Shawshank Redemption (T. Newman)(4:27).

Review: See entry below.

Hollywood '95 ✍✍✍✍✎

1995, Varese-Sarabande.

Album Notes: The Royal Scottish National Orchestra, conducted by Joel McNeely; *Album Producer:* Robert Townson; *Engineer:* Geoff Foster.

Selections: Batman Forever (E. Goldenthal): 1 Main Title (1:43); 2 Chase Noir (1:54); 3 Nygma Variations (2:38); 4 Mouth To Mouth Nocturne (2:18); 5 Victory (2:28); Apollo 13 (J. Horner): 6 The Launch (9:53); Judge Dredd (A. Silvestri): 7 Suite (4:57); Judge Dredd (J. Goldsmith): 8 Trailer (:49); Casper (J. Horner): 9 Casper's Lullaby (5:52); Waterworld (J. Newton Howard): 10 Main Theme (2:16); First Knight (J. Goldsmith): 11 Arthur's Fanfare (:46); 12 End Credits (4:12); Braveheart (J. Horner): 13 End Title (7:42); That Hamilton Woman (M. Rozsa): 14 Love Theme (4:25).

Review: See entry below.

Hollywood '96 ✍✍✍✍✎

1996, Varese-Sarabande.

Album Notes: The Royal Scottish National Orchestra and Chorus, conducted by Joel McNeely; *Featured Soloists:* Lynda

Cochrane (piano), Edwin Paling (fiddle); *Album Producer*: Robert Townson; *Engineer*: Geoff Foster; *Assistant Engineer*: Graham Kirkby.

Selections: 1 Mission: Impossible (L. Schifrin)(1:31); 2 Twister (M. Mancina)(4:40); 3 Fargo (C. Burwell)(3:00); 4 A Time To Kill (E. Goldenthal) (4:19); 5 Sabrina (J. Williams)(5:42); 6 Phenomenon (T. Newman)(2:54); 7 Flipper (J. McNeely)(2:50); 8 Emma (R. Portman)(2:56); 9 Tin Cup (W. Ross) (4:44); 10 Courage Under Fire (J. Horner)(3:43); 11 Vertigo (B. Herrmann)(5:07); 12 The Hunchback Of Notre Dame (A. Menken)(3:43); 13 Independence Day (D. Arnold)(5:45).

Review: The concept behind these albums is actually quite valid and interesting: each gives an overview of the most prominent films released during the year, illustrated with an excerpt from each score. The combined effect is much like a "pops" concert which includes favorite themes, and little of the added wear and tear usually found on soundtrack albums that may turn off many casual listeners. One may quibble endlessly with the choices, but the performances are remarkably faithful to the originals, with McNeely extracting superb ensemble playing and polish from the orchestras under his baton.

Henry Mancini (1924-1994)

Mancini's Classic Movie Scores/The Pink Panther And Other Hits ♫♫♫♫♪

1987, RCA Records and 1992, RCA Records (re-issue).

Album Notes: *Music*: Henry Mancini; *Performed by*: Henry Mancini, His Orchestra and Chorus; *Album Producer*: Joe Reisman; *Engineer*: Dick Bogert.

Selections: The Pink Panther: 1 The Pink Panther Theme (2:35); 2 Royal Blue (3:10); 3 Champagne And Quail (2:45); 4 The Lonely Princess (2:26); 5 It Had Better Be Tonight (Meglio sta sera)(H. Mancini/J. Mercer/F. Migliacci)(1:56); Charade: 6 Charade (H. Mancini/J. Mercer)(2:35); 7 Megeve (2:58); 8 Latin Snowfall (2:33); 9 Bateau Mouche (2:52); 10 Bistro (1:49); Hatari!: 11 Theme From Hatari! (2:54); 12 Baby Elephant Walk (2:42); 13 Night Side (3:25); 14 Your Father's Feathers (3:32); 15 The Sounds Of Hatari (6:43); Breakfast At Tiffany's: 16 Breakfast At Tiffany's (2:45); 17 Something For Cat (3:08); 18 Sally's Tomato (3:06); 19 Holly (3:19); 20 Latin Golightly (2:58); 21 Moon River (H. Mancini/J. Mercer)(2:43).

Review: For a composer who spent most of his career with RCA, and gave it some of its million-selling albums, the label has not done very well by Henry Mancini. Outside of a few selected titles like this compilation, hastily put together with little thinking behind it, or selected individual soundtrack albums, usually poorly remastered, Mancini's impressive body of works still remains to be addressed with the kind of thoroughness and dedication RCA is now beginning to lavish on Elvis Presley. Even a 3-CD boxed set, *The Days of Wine And Roses* (see below), released a couple of years ago, failed to address his contribution with the kind of seriousness it really commanded.

Which is not to say this collection of themes from four important scores (*The Pink Panther, Charade, Hatari!,* and *Breakfast at Tiffany's)* is bad—it simply is incomplete and insufficient.

Mancini had a special flair for writing themes that were instantly catchy, flavorful, and attractive. Even his most complex scores were always thoroughly accessible to people with little interest in film music, because the composer was, first and foremost, a pop melodist. The selections collected here present a good case for this specific talent of his, with enjoyable tunes that are as vibrant and exciting on their own as they were behind the action on the screen. Needless to say, the rating here applies to the music, not the packaging.

Henry Mancini: Premier Pops ♫♫♫♫

1988, Denon Records.

Album Notes: *Music*: Henry Mancini; The Royal Philharmonic Pops Orchestra, conducted by Henry Mancini; *Album Producers*: Henry Mancini, John McClure, Shigekazu Tanaka; *Engineer*: Dick Lewzey.

Selections: 1 Overture To A Pops Concert (4:01); The Thorn Birds: 2 The Thorn Birds Theme (2:41); 3 Arrival At The Vatican (2:14); 4 Meggie's Theme (2:48); 5 It's Shearing You're Hearing (3:08); Movie Song Medley: 6 Life In A Looking Glass (2:10); 7 Crazy World (2:13); 8 Song From "10" (2:00); 9 Hong Kong Fireworks (from *Revenge Of The Pink Panther*)(2:31); 10 Sunflower (from *Sunflower*)(2:27); 11 The Inspector Clouseau Theme (from *The Pink Panther Strikes Again*) (2:40); 12 Charade (from *Charade*)(3:29); The Glass Menagerie: 13 Tom's Theme (3:13); 14 Blue Roses/Laura's Theme (2:22); Three TV Themes: 15 Hotel (2:00); 16 Newhart (2:15); 17 Remington Steel (2:37); 18 The Sons Of Italy (from *Beaver Valley '37*)(4:30); 19 Ohio Riverboat; 20 Main Title (from *The Great*

Mouse Detective)(3:48); 21 Moon River (from *Breakfast At Tiffany's*) (2:37).

Review: One of the earliest CD releases, this out-of-print Henry Mancini album has audiophile sound and a number of outstanding concert arrangements. Comprised entirely of Mancini-composed selections, *Premiere Pops* includes a wealth of material not available anywhere else, from the composer's rousing "Overture to a 'Pops' Concert" to a gorgeous extended suite from *The Thorn Birds*; a lovely "Movie Song Medley" comprised of *Life in a Looking Glass, Crazy World* and *10*; a "Three TV Themes" suite consisting of "Hotel," "Newhart" and "Remington Steele;" plus the concert pieces "Ohio Riverboat" and "Sunflower." There are also cues from *The Great Mouse Detective*, the *Pink Panther* sequels, *Charade*, Paul Newman's adaptation of *The Glass Menagerie*, and — of course — "Moon River." The album is notable not only for its relative obscurity but also the way in which Mancini structures the music for solo piano (with the composer himself on the keyboard) and the Royal Philharmonic Orchestra, a collaboration that was supposed to result in a number of "Mancini-RPO Pops" albums for the Denon label before the project (and the label) fell through. Regardless, this is still one of the best Mancini retrospectives released on CD, and certainly the best-sounding album of the bunch.

Andy Dursin

Henry Mancini: Music from the Films of Blake Edwards
♫♫♫♫▷

1991, RCA Records.

Album Notes: *Music*: Henry Mancini; Orchestra and Chorus conducted by Henry Mancini; *Original Recording Producers*: Simon Rady, Dick Pierce, Steve Sholes, Joe Reisman; *Original Recording Engineers*: Jim Malloy, Mickey Crofford, Dick Bogert; *CD Producer*: Didier C. Deutsch; *Engineer*: Paul Goodman.

Selections: 1 Peter Gunn (2:04); 2 Mr. Lucky (2:11); 3 Breakfast At Tiffany's (2:46); 4 Moon River (H. Mancini/J. Mercer)(from *Breakfast at Tiffany's*)(2:43); 5 Days Of Wine And Roses (H. Mancini/J. Mercer)(2:07); 6 The Good Old Days (from *Experiment In Terror*)(2:01); 7 Experiment In Terror (2:18); 8 Soldier In The Rain (2:56); 9 The Pink Panther Theme (2:36); 10 It Had Better Be Tonight (H. Mancini/J. Mercer)(from *The Pink Panther*)(1:57); 11 The Sweetheart Tree (from *The Great Race*)(H. Mancini/J. Mercer)(1:56); 12 Pie-In-The-Face Polka (from *The Great Race*)(2:24); 13 In The Arms Of Love (H. Mancini/R. Evans/J. Livingston)(from *What Did You Do In The War,*

Daddy?) (2:36); 14 The Swing March (from *What Did You Do In The War, Daddy?*)(2:07); 15 A Quiet Happening (from *Gunn*)(3:07); 16 Theme For Sam (from *Gunn*)(3:12); 17 Candlelight On Crystal (from *The Party*)(3:04); 18 Nothing To Lose (from *The Party*)(2:23); 19 Darling Lili (H. Mancini/J. Mercer)(2:48); 20 Whistling Away The Dark (H. Mancini/J. Mercer)(from *Darling Lili*)(3:43); 21 The Inspector Clouseau Theme (from *The Pink Panther Strikes Again*)(2:58); 22 It's Easy To Say (H. Mancini/R. Wells)(from *''10''*)(3:25); 23 Victor/Victoria (medley): The Shady Dame From Seville, Crazy World, You And Me, Le Jazz Hot (H. Mancini/L. Bricusse)(4:53).

Review: Throughout his career, Mancini enjoyed a special creative relationship with film director Blake Edwards. They began working together on the television series *Peter Gunn*, with the relationship eventually covering many of Edwards' comedies, including the *Pink Panther* series, as well as other celebrated films like *Breakfast at Tiffany's, Experiment in Terror, The Great Race, ''10'', Darling Lily* and *Victor/Victoria*. The compilation surveys some of these films, presenting selections from the various scores, in a compilation that could not be all-encompassing.

The Music of Henry Mancini
♫♫♫♫▷

1994, Sony Legacy.

Album Notes: *Music*: Henry Mancini; *CD Producer*: Didier C. Deutsch; *Engineer*: Thomas Ruff.

Selections: 1 Moon River (from *Breakfast at Tiffany's*)(H. Mancini/J. Mercer)(2:45) *Andy Williams*; 2 The Sweetheart Tree (from *The Great Race*)(H. Mancini/J. Mercer)(2:12) *Johnny Mathis*; 3 Dreamsville (from *Peter Gunn*)(H. Mancini/J. Livingston/R. Evans)(3:21) *Lola Albright*; 4 Theme From *Peter Gunn* (3:12) *Bobby Hackett*; 5 It Had Better Be Tonight (Meglio sta sera) (from *The Pink Panther*)(H. Mancini/J. Mercer/F. Migliacci)(1:59) *Buddy Greco*; 6 Dear Heart (H. Mancini/J. Livingston/R. Evans)(2:54) *Andy Williams*; 7 Baby Elephant Walk (from *Hatari!*)(2:53) *Don Costa and His Orchestra*; 8 Two For The Road (2:54) *Charlie Byrd*; 9 Days Of Wine And Roses (H. Mancini/J. Mercer)(2:50) *Patti Page*; 10 Whistling Away The Dark (from *Darling Lili*)(H. Mancini/J. Mercer)(3:20) *Johnny Mathis*; 11 Charade (H. Mancini/J. Mercer)(2:31) *Andy Williams*; 12 *NBC Mystery Movie* Theme (2:42) *Ray Conniff and His Orchestra*; 13 Theme From *Mr. Lucky* (2:33) *Bobby Hackett*; 14 Natasha's Theme (from *Who Is Killing The Great Chefs Of Europe?*) (2:14) *Henry Mancini and His Orchestra*; 15 Darling Lili (H. Mancini/J. Mercer)(2:49) *Johnny Mathis*; 16 In The Arms

Of Love (from *What Did You Do In The War, Daddy?*)(H. Mancini/J. Livingston/R. Evans)(2:54) *Andy Williams*.

Review: During his lifetime, some of Mancini's most popular themes found their way into the pop catalogues at labels other than RCA, giving performers like Andy Williams, for instance, some of their million-selling hits. When the composer died, in 1994, Sony Legacy put together this compilation which covers several tunes popularized by Johnny Mathis, Buddy Greco, Patti Page, and Andy Williams (whose renditions of "Moon River," "Dear Heart," and "In the Arms of Love" are included). Mancini, who had also released a couple of albums on Columbia, is represented with his recording of a theme from *Who Is Killing the Great Chefs of Europe?*.

Mancini in Surround: Mostly Monsters, Murders & Mystery 🎵🎵🎵

1990, RCA Records.

Album Notes: *Music*: Henry Mancini; *Orchestrations*: Henry Mancini, Jack Hayes; The Mancini Pops Orchestra, conducted by Henry Mancini; *Featured Soloists*: Sidney Sax (violin, concertmaster), Edward Beckett (flute), Richard Morgan (oboe), Graham Salter (English horn), Neil Levesley (bassoon), Cynthia Millar (Ondes Marthinot), Adrian Brett (ocarina), Leslie Pearson (harpsichord, organ); *Album Producer*: John McClure; *Engineer*: Dick Lewzey.

Selections: 1 Surround Fantastique (:54); 2 Arctic Whale Hunt (from *The White Dawn*)(4:00); 3 Theme (from *Mommie Dearest*)(2:35); 4 Main Title (from *Frenzy*)(2:15); Monster Movie Music Suite:(5-7) 5 The Monster Gets Mark (from *Creature From The Black Lagoon*)(6:47); 6 The Thing Strikes/Desert Rendez-Vous (from *It Came From Outer Space*)(4:45); 7 Terror Strikes (from *Tarantula*)(3:15); 8 Casey's Theme (from *Fear*)(2:40); 9 Little Boys (from *The Man Who Loved Women*)(3:33); Suite From The Prisoner Of Zenda: (10-12) 10 Main Title (4:49); 11 Coronation Waltz (3:11); 12 Croquette (2:54); 13 Main Title (from *Nightwing*) (3:18); Music From Without A Clue: (14-15) 14 Super Sleuth (2:29); 15 Without A Clue (End Title)(2:47); Music From Sunset: (16-18) 16 Sunset Theme (2:01); 17 Cheryl's Theme (4:05); 18 The Cowboys (3:56).

Review: Subtitled "Mostly Monsters, Murders, and Mysteries," this likable collection is a far cry from the light-hearted melodies Henry Mancini has been most known for. It's an excellent compilation of his dramatic orchestral filmscoring, featuring splendid renditions of his musical contributions to such 1950s horror films as *It Came From Outer Space* and *The*

Creature From the Black Lagoon, to the 1990 thriller, *Fear*. Also included is a gorgeous, lyrical four-minute suite from *The White Dawn*, Mancini's rejected title theme from Hitchcock's *Frenzy*, and cues from *Mommie Dearest, Nightwing, The Prisoner of Zenda*, and *Sunset*. The CD was recorded with the Dolby Surround system, from which comes its title, and sound quality is uniformly high. Extensive historical notes by Tony Thomas abound in a 16-page booklet. The CD is an important collection of Mancini's oft-overlooked dramatic film music, and a unique musical gallery of one composer's work in the "genre macabre" over a 30-year span.

Randall D. Larson

Mancini's Greatest Hits 🎵🎵🎵

1989, Telarc Records.

Album Notes: *Music*: Henry Mancini; The Cincinnati Pops Orchestra and The Henry Mancini Chorus, conducted by Erich Kunzel; *Album Producer*: Robert Woods; *Engineer*: Jack Renner.

Selections: 1 Theme (from *The Pink Panther*)(2:26); 2 Moon River (from *Breakfast at Tiffany's*)(2:50); 3 Days Of Wine And Roses (1:59); 4 It Had Better Be Tonight (H. Mancini/J. Mercer/F. Migliacci)(from *The Pink Panther*) (1:58); 5 Arctic Whale Hunt (from *The White Dawn*)(3:56); 6 Theme (from *Mr. Lucky*)(2:13); 7 Theme (from *Hatari!*)(3:19); 8 Theme (from *The Thorn Birds*) (3:05); 9 Charade (2:17); 10 Moment to Moment (2:37); 11 Symphonic Soul (2:21); 12 Drummer's Delight (3:11); 13 March (from *The Great Waldo Pepper*)(2:20); 14 Two For The Road (3:02); 15 Theme (from *The Molly Maguires*)(3:01); 16 Dear Heart (2:30); 17 Theme (from *Breakfast at Tiffany's*)(2:37); 18 Speedy Gonzales (from *Mr. Lucky*) (1:41); 19 Punch And Judy (from *Charade*)(1:58); 20 March With Mancini: Timothy (1:01), March Of The Cue Balls (1:11), The Swing March (1:14), March from *The Great Race* (1:37); 21 Baby Elephant Walk (from *Hatari!*)(2:23); 22 Theme (from *Peter Gunn*)(2:22); 23 Strings On Fire (2:02); 24 Finale from *Victor/Victoria* (H. Mancini/L. Bricusse): The Shady Dame From Seville (1:00), Crazy World (1:33), You And Me (1:06), Le Jazz Hot! (1:11).

Review: Another fine collection of Henry Mancini standards, this release boasts a typically solid performance by the Cincinnati Pops Orchestra under the direction of maestro Erich Kunzel, with smooth vocals provided by the Henry Mancini Chorus. This 68-minute album is comprised strictly of Mancini compositions, which range from the usual staples (*Pink Panther, Days of Wine and Roses, Peter Gunn*) to some brief examples of Mancini's strong sense of dramatic film scoring

(The White Dawn, The Molly Maguires), concert arrangements of the *Victor/Victoria* finale, various Mancini marches, and a pair of pieces written exclusively for the concert hall ("Symphonic Soul," "Drummers' Delight"). The packaging includes ample but not overwhelming liner notes, the acoustics are fine, and the release itself a strong choice for the casual listener due to its wide selection of material culled from Mancini's vast discography.

Andy Dursin

Henry Mancini: The Days of Wine and Roses 🎵🎵🎵🎵

1995, RCA Records.

Album Notes: *Music*: Henry Mancini; Orchestra and chorus conducted by Henry Mancini; *Album Producer*: Paul Williams; *Engineers*: Bill Lacey (audio restoration), Mike Harty (digital transfers), Dennis Ferrante (mix reconstructions).

Selections: CD 1: Peter Gunn: (1-7) 1 Peter Gunn (2:08); 2 Dreamsville (3:58); 3 Slow And Easy (3:08); 4 A Profound Gass (3:21); 5 Walkin' Bass (4:21); 6 My Manne Shelly (2:37); 7 Blues For Mother's (3:18); 8 Snowfall (C. Thornhill)(3:40); 9 Big Noise From Winnetka (B. Haggart/S. Bauduc)(2:41); 10 Sing, Sing, Sing (L. Prima)(3:15); Mr. Lucky: (11-13) 11 Mr. Lucky (2:15); 12 One Eyed Cat (3:18); 13 Blue Satin (2:35); 14 A Powdered Wig (2:40); High Time: (15-16) 15 High Time (2:23); 16 The Second Time Around (S. Cahn/J. Van Heusen)(2:51); 17 Theme (from *The Great Imposter*)(2:47); 18 Rain Drops In Rio (2:46); 19 Blue Mantilla (2:31); Breakfast At Tiffany's: (20-22) 20 Moon River (H. Mancini/J. Mercer)(2:45); 21 Breakfast At Tiffany's (2:48); 22 Holly (3:21); Experiment In Terror: (23-25) 23 Experiment In Terror (2:19); 24 Fluters' Ball (3:21); 25 White On White (2:09).

CD 2: Hatari!: (1-2) 1 Theme (2:57); 2 Baby Elephant Walk (2:45); 3 Just For Tonight (J. Mercer/H. Carmichael)(2:06); 4 Days Of Wine And Roses (H. Mancini/J. Mercer)(2:09); 5 Too Little Time (3:53); 6 Bachelor In Paradise (H. Mancini/H. David)(2:33); Charade: (7-8) 7 Charade (H. Mancini/J. Mercer)(2:38); 8 Latin Snowfall (2:36); The Pink Panther: (9-12) 9 The Pink Panther Theme (2:38); 10 Royal Blue (3:14); 11 It Had Better Be Tonight (Meglio sta sera)(H. Mancini/J. Mercer/ F. Migliacci)(2:00); 12 Piano And Strings (2:37); 13 Dear Heart (H. Mancini/J. Livingston/R. Evans)(2:43); 14 Soldier In The Rain (2:58); 15 How Soon (H. Mancini/J. Stillman)(from *The Richard Boone Show*)(2:51); 16 A Shot In The Dark (2:34); 17 Quiet Nights Of Quiet Stars (Corcovado)(A.C. Jobim/G. Lees)(2:27); 18 Come To The Mardi Gras (H. Tenho Lagrimas)(1:59); The Great Race: (19-20) 19 The

Sweetheart Tree (H. Mancini/J. Mercer)(1:58); 20 The Great Race March (A Patriotic Medley)(1:52); 21 Moment To Moment (H. Mancini/J. Mercer)(2:29); Arabesque: (22-23) 22 Something For Sophia (2:35); 23 We've Loved Before (Yasmin's Theme) (H. Mancini/J. Livingston/R. Evans)(2:49); What Did You Do In The War, Daddy?: (24-25) 24 The Swing March (2:09); 25 In The Arms Of Love (H. Mancini/J. Livingston/R. Evans)(2:38); 26 Cherokee (Indian Love Song)(R. Noble)(3:03); 27 Autumn Nocturne (K. Gannon/J. Myro)(4:08).

CD 3: 1 The Shadow Of Your Smile (J. Mandel/P.F. Webster)(3:02); 2 Blue Hawaii (R. Rainger/L. Robin)(2:47); Two For The Road: (3-5) 3 Two For The Road (H. Mancini/L. Bricusse)(2:43); 4 Something For Audrey (3:01); 5 French Provincial (2:11); Gunn: (6-7) 6 A Quiet Happening (3:07); 7 I Like The Look (H. Mancini/L. Bricusse)(2:43); 8 Wait Until Dark (H. Mancini/J. Livingston/R. Evans)(2:09); 9 Nothing To Lose (from *The Party*)(H. Mancini/J. Livingston/R. Evans)(2:27); 10 Love Theme (from *Romeo And Juliet*)(N. Rota)(2:36); 11 Theme (from *The Molly Maguires*)(2:48); 12 As Time Goes By (H. Hupfeld)(2:41); 13 Whistling Away The Dark (from *Darling Lili*)(H. Mancini/J. Mercer)(3:48); 14 Loss Of Love (from *Sunflower*)(H. Mancini/B. Merrill)(2:28); 15 Theme (from *Love Story*)(F. Lai) (2:54); 16 All His Children (from *Sometimes A Great Notion*)(H. Mancini/A. & M. Bergman)(3:06); 17 Mystery Movie Theme (2:00); 18 Theme (from *The Mancini Generation*)(2:45); 19 Theme (from *The Thief Who Came To Dinner*)(2:44); 20 Can't Get Started (V. Duke/I. Gershwin)(3:31) *Henry Mancini, Doc Severinsen*; 21 Ludmilla's Theme (from *Visions Of Eight*)(2:42); Oklahoma Crude: (22-23) 22 Oklahoma Crude (2:13); 23 Send A Little Love My Way (H. Mancini/H. David) (3:13); 24 Theme (from *The Girl From Petrovka*)(1:59); 25 Theme (from *The White Dawn*)(3:19); 26 Bumper's Theme (from *The Blue Knight*)(1:58); 27 What's Happening (2:10); 28 Silver Streak (3:00).

Review: While it marked a step in the right direction, this boxed set is too much a case of "let's-put-together-a-collection-of-CDs-by-whatshisname" to be taken with any kind of seriousness. It does indeed cover some of the right grounds, but almost by default, because in the case of Mancini there was so much material to begin with that any compilation would have succeeded regardless.

But rather than take the normal approach, which would have been to focus on Mancini's career as a film composer, the set wastes too much precious playing time on other recordings he did, like cover versions of Claude Thornhill's "Snowfall" or Louis Prima's "Sing, Sing, Sing," in the first CD; Antonio Carlos Jobim's "Quiet Nights of Quiet Stars" or Ray Noble's "Cherokee," in the second; and Johnny Mandel's "The Shadow of

Your Smile" and Nino Rota's "Romeo and Juliet," in the third. Evidently, these tracks belonged in another compilation.

With the vast resources at their disposal, the producers would have been better advised to give the composer his real due, and present a thorough compilation of scores written by Mancini, supplementing what was not in the RCA vaults with selections on other labels. Unfortunately "The Days of Wine and Roses" doesn't come without some thorns.

Cinema Italiano: Music of Ennio Morricone and Nino Rota ♪♪♪

1991, RCA Victor.

Album Notes: *Music*: Ennio Morricone, Nino Rota; The Mancini Pops Orchestra, conducted by Henry Mancini; *Orchestrations*: Henry Mancini; *Album Producer*: John McClure; *Engineer*: John McClure.

Selections: 1 The Untouchables (E. Morricone)(2:30); 2 La dolce vita (N. Rota)(3:14); Cinema Paradiso (E. Morricone): 3 First Youth (4:33); 4 Love Theme (2:52); 5 Cinema Paradiso Theme (4:29); Boccaccio '70 (N. Rota): 6 Bevete piu latte (1:45); Once Upon A Time In The West (E. Morricone): 7 Man With A Harmonica (4:28); 8 Once Upon A Time In The West (4:49); 9 Amarcord (N. Rota)(3:36); The Mission (E. Morricone): 10 Gabriel's Oboe (6:03); 11 The Clowns (N. Rota)(6:39); 12 Romeo And Juliet (N. Rota)(2:50); Once Upon A Time In America (E. Morricone): 13 Deborah's Theme (5:22); The Godfather (N. Rota): 14 Michael's Theme (4:48); 15 The Godfather Waltz (3:51); 16 The Godfather Theme (3:34).

Review: See entry below.

The Godfather and Other Movie Themes ♪♪♪♪

1993, RCA Victor.

Album Notes: *Music*: Henry Mancini; *Orchestrations*: Henry Mancini; The London Symphony Orchestra and The Philadelphia Orchestra Pops, conducted by Henry Mancini; *Featured Soloists*: William Smith (piano), Marcel Farago (harpsichord), Norman Carol (violin), Murray Panitz (flute); Anthony Gigliotti (clarinet), Mason Jones (French horn), John DeLancie (oboe), Louis Rosenblatt (English horn), Gerald Carlyss (timpani), Donald Montanaro (E-flat clarinet), Bernard Garfield (bassoon), Gilbert Johnson (trumpet); *Album Producers*: John Pfeiffer, Joe Reisman; *Engineer*: Edwin Begley; *CD Engineer*: Paul Goodman; *Assistant Engineer*: Marian Conaty.

Selections: 1 Music By Nino Rota: (a) Romeo and Juliet: Love Theme, (b) Boccaccio '70: Bevete piu latte, (c) La Strada: Love Theme, (d) Amarcord: Love Theme, (e) The Godfather: Love Theme (9:17); 2 The White Dawn (H. Mancini): Symphonic Suite (11:38); 3 The Disaster Movie Suite: (a) Earthquake: Main Title (J. Williams), (b) The Towering Inferno: Song (A. Kasha/J. Hirschhorn), (c) Jaws: Theme (J. Williams)(8:19); 4 The French Collection: (a) The Thomas Crown Affair: The Windmills Of Your Mind (M. Legrand/A. & M. Bergman), (b) A Man And A Woman: Title Theme (F. Lai/P. Barouh/J. Keller), (c) Love Story: Theme (F. Lai/C. Sigman), (d) The Summer Of '42: Theme (M. Legrand/A. & M. Bergman)(9:29); The Great Waldo Pepper: 5 March (H. Mancini)(2:27); 6 Dream Of A Lifetime (3:02); 7 Strings On Fire! (2:01); 8 Cameo For Violin (3:41); 9 Drummers' Delight (3:49); 10 The Ballerina's Dream (3:38); 11 Speedy Gonzales (1:41); Beaver Valley Suite: 12 The River (5:34); 13 Black Snow (5:56); 14 Sons Of Italy (4:30).

Review: See entry below.

Top Hat: Music from the Films of Astaire & Rogers ♪♪♪♪

1992, RCA Victor.

Album Notes: *Music*: Irving Berlin, Jerome Kern, Vincent Youmans, Cole Porter, George Gershwin, Howard Dietz, Con Conrad; *Orchestrations*: Henry Mancini; The Mancini Pops Orchestra, conducted by Henry Mancini; *Album Producer*: John McClure; *Engineer*: John McClure.

Selections: Top Hat: 1 Top Hat, White Tie And Tails/Isn't This A Lovely Day (To Be Caught In The Rain)/Cheek To Cheek/The Piccolino (I. Berlin)(7:49); Roberta: 2 Yesterdays/Smoke Gets In Your Eyes/Lovely To Look At/I Won't Dance (J. Kern/D. Fields)(6:59); Flying Down To Rio: 3 Orchids In The Moonlight/Music Makes Me/Flying Down To Rio/The Carioca (V. Youmans/G. Kahn)(6:14); The Gay Divorce: 4 Night And Day (C. Porter)/The Continental (C. Conrad/H. Magidson)(4:38); Follow The Fleet: 5 Let Yourself Go/I'm Putting All My Eggs In One Basket/Let's Face The Music And Dance/We Saw The Sea (I. Berlin)(6:46); Shall We Dance: 6 They All Laughed/Let's Call The Whole Thing Off/They Can't Take That Away From Me/Shall We Dance/Slap That Bass (G. & I. Gershwin)(6:48); Swing Time: 7 Pick Yourself Up/A Fine Romance/The Way You Look Tonight/Waltz In Swing Time (J. Kern/D. Fields)(6:17); Astaire!: 8 Dancing In The Dark (A. Schwartz/H. Dietz)/A Foggy Day (G. & I. Gershwin)/Something's Gotta Give (J. Mercer)/How Long Has This Been Going On? (G. & I. Gershwin)/Nice

"In most cases, a composer must not approach the score as though he is the star of the show. He has to know when to hold back, when not to blast the audience, when not to intrude on the dialogue."

Henry Mancini
(Electronic Age, Autumn, 1968)

Work If You Can Get It (G. & I. Gershwin)/I'm Building Up To An Awful Letdown (J. Mercer/ F. Astaire)/Who Cares (G. & I. Gershwin)(11:59).

Review: It's an interesting concept, Mancini doing themes from other composers, but one that only works halfway: first, because Mancini was much better at covering his own material, and because his own versions often pale in comparison with the originals. But one can sense the corporate sense at work behind these titles. Signed to RCA, Mancini had to deliver a certain number of albums under his contract, and if Erich Kunzel could successfully do it for Telarc, Mancini could do it for RCA. What the powers-that-be failed to realize is that no one said Kunzel did a great job: he just happens to be a good hack! And frankly speaking, Mancini was way above that.

Cinema Italiano, in particular, suffers from the fact that all the scores covered by Mancini already exist in far superior, original versions, some of them, as a matter of fact, on RCA. The composer, conducting the Mancini Pops Orchestra, is proficient and effective, but one senses that there is less enthusiasm here than there might have been had the themes been written by him.

The impression is confirmed in *The Godfather* set, in which Mancini goes back to some scores already explored in *Cinema Italiano* as well as others by other composers (John Williams, Michel Legrand, Francis Lai), but adds to the mix a suite from *The White Dawn* and *Beaver Valley Suite,* as well as other selections he penned, in which he leads the London Symphony Orchestra and the Philadelphia Orchestra Pops in spirited, crackling versions.

As for the *Top Hat* CD, an obvious concept tailored after the Telarc sets, it is an obvious scene-stealer, and one in which Mancini, again, proves superior to Kunzel in every respect. It's only unfortunate that he was not given a chance to focus on some of his own scores.

Jerome Moross (1913-1983)

The Valley of Gwangi: The Classic Film Music of Jerome Moross 🦴🦴🦴🦴🦴

1995, Silva Screen Records.

Album Notes: *Music:* Jerome Moross; *Orchestrations:* Jerome Moross, Christopher Palmer, Mike Townend, James Fitzpatrick, Nic Raine; The City Of Prague Philharmonic, conducted by Paul Bateman; *Album Producer:* James Fitzpatrick; *Engineer:* John L. Timperley.

Selections: The Adventures Of Huckleberry Finn: 1 Prelude (3:59); 2 Huck's Escape (3:10); 3 The Mississippi (3:15); 4 Flight and Finale (3:58); 5 Five Finger Exercise Romanza (from the concert suite *Music For The Flicks*)(5:27); 6 Theme (from *Wagon Train*)(3:08); The War Lord: 7 Prelude and Main Title (4:18); 8 What Of The Future?/Vengeance and Death/Finale (7:22); 9 Overture (from *The Sharkfighters*)(11:22); Rachel, Rachel (Americana miniature): 10 Japonica Street/Shadow Pictures/A Walk In The Country/End Titles (6:02); 11 Overture (from *The Mountain Road*): Main Title/The Men/The Airplane/Destroying The Airbase (6:22); The Valley Of Gwangi: 12 The Landscape/The Forbidden Valley/ Pterodactyl Attack (5:15); 13 Capture Of Gwangi/Gwangi Enchained (5:58); 14 Night In The Valley/Gwangi At The Cathedral/Death Of Gwangi/Finale (7:31).

Review: This long-overdue compilation showcases the dynamic and often melodically gorgeous work of composer Jerome Moross, who has for too long been known simply as the man who scored *The Big Country*. *Valley of Gwangi* amply demonstrates Moross' range, which covered everything from action films (the epic *The Mountain Road* and the percussive, ethnic-flavored *The Sharkfighters*) to dramas (*Five Finger Exercise* and the gentle "Americana" of *Rachel, Rachel*) to medieval epics (the beautifully evocative *The War Lord*). Moross was best known for his western music, and this collection includes both a well-known example (his theme for the television series "Wagon Train") and a spectacular, overlooked effort for the 1969 Ray Harryhausen thriller about cowboys and dinosaurs, *The Valley of Gwangi*, which combined Moross' thrilling western style with a percussive, ferociously rhythmic style for Harryhausen's animated dinosaurs that's as vibrant and memorable as anything Bernard Herrman ever wrote in the genre. *Gwangi* is represented by an 18-minute suite that's one of the most exciting film music experiences in recent memory, and Nic Raine's conducting of the entire album is flawless.

Jeff Bond

Ennio Morricone (1928-

Ennio Morricone: The Legendary Italian Westerns
♫♫♫♫ ▷

1990, RCA Records.

Album Notes: *Music*: Ennio Morricone; Orchestra Unione Musicisti di Roma, conducted by Ennio Morricone, Bruno Nicolai; *Featured Artists*: I Canti Moderni (Alessandro Alessandroni, director), Michele Lacerenza, Giovanni Culasso (trumpet), Franco De Gemini (harmonica), Edda Dell'Orso (vocals); *CD Producer*: Didier C. Deutsch; *Engineer*: Paul Goodman.

Selections: Gunfight at Red Sands: 1 A Gringo Like Me (E. Morricone/C. Danell)(2:23) *Peter Tavis*; Guns Don't Argue: 2 Guns Don't Argue (2:31); 3 The Indians (2:13); 4 Lonesome Billy (E. Morricone/P. Tavis) *Peter Tavis*; A Fistful Of Dollars: 5 Overture (2:55); 6 Almost Dead (1:39); 7 Square Dance (1:33); 8 The Chase (2:23); 9 The Result (2:34); 10 Without Pity (2:06); 11 For A Fistful Of Dollars (1:48); A Gun For Ringo: 12 A Gun For Ringo (2:18); 13 Waiting (2:34); 14 The Massacre (1:57); 15 Angel Face (E. Morricone/G. Paolo)(2:19) *Maurizio Graf*; For A Few Dollars More: 16 Sixty Seconds To What? (3:03); 17 Aces High (1:18); 18 The Watchers Are Being Watched (2:01); 19 The Vice Of Killing (2:23); 20 The Musical Pocket Watch (1:10); 21 The Showdown (2:21); 22 Goodbye, Colonel (1:43); 23 For A Few Dollars More (2:57); Ringo Rides Again: 24 Ringo Rides Again (E. Morricone/M. Attanazio)(2:15) *Maurizio Graf, The Canti Moderni*; 7 Guns For The MacGregors: 25 March Of The MacGregors (E. Morricone/M. Attanazio)(2:29); 26 Santa Fe Express (2:00); Death Rides A Horse: 27 From Man To Man (3:19); Once Upon A Time In The West: 28 Once Upon A Time In The West (3:40); 29 Farewell To Cheyenne (2:37); 30 Man With A Harmonica (3:27); 31 Jill's America (2:45).

Review: See *Ennio Morricone: Compilation* entry below.

The Ennio Morricone Anthology: A Fistful of Film Music ♫♫♫♫ ▷

1995, Rhino Records.

Album Notes: *Music*: Ennio Morricone; Orchestra conducted by Ennio Morricone, Bruno Nicolai; *Featured Soloists*: Nicola

Culasso, Michele Lacerenza, (trumpet), Alessandro Alessandroni (guitar, whistling), Franco De Gemini (harmonica), Maurizio Verzella (mellophone), Marianne Gazzani Eckstein (flute), Gheorghe Zamfir (Pan flute), Baldo Maestri (clarinet/alto sax), Paolo Zampini (flute); *Album Producers*: David McLees, Jerry McCulley, Chris Clarke; *Engineers*: Chris Clarke, Dan Hersch.

Selections: CD 1: For A Fistful Of Dollars: 1 Titoli(2:58); 2 Theme (1:50); A Pistol For Ringo: 3 Una pistola per Ringo (2:19); The Return Of Ringo: 4 Il ritorno di Ringo (2:17) *Maurizio Graf*; For A Few Dollars More: 5 La resa dei conti (3:06); 6 Per qualche dollaro in piu' (2:51); Navajo Joe: 7 Main Title (2:50) *Gianna Spagnolo*; The Good, The Bad and The Ugly: 8 Main Title (2:42); 9 The Ecstasy Of Gold (3:25); The Hawks And The Sparrows: 10 Uccellacci e uccellini (2:29) *Domenico Modugno*; Battle Of Algiers: 11 Algiers, November 1, 1954 (2:25); Grand Slam: 12 Ad ogni costo (2:55); The Garden Of Delights: 13 Il giardino delle delizie (3:05); The Big Gundown: 14 The Big Gundown (2:23) *Christy*; Guns For San Sebastian: 15 Love Theme (reprise)(2:54); Once Upon A Time In The West: 16 Man With A Harmonica (3:31); 17 Farewell To Cheyenne (2:40); 18 Once Upon A Time In The West (3:45) *Edda Dell'Orso*; Machine Gun McCain: 19 La ballata di Hank McCain (2:11) *Jackie Lynton*; The Bird With The Crystal Plumage: 20 Piume di cristallo (5:16); Investigation Of A Citizen Above Suspicion: 21 Indagine su un cittadino al di sopra di ogni sospetto (Main Title)(3:29); The Family: 22 Citta violenta (Titoli)(2:26); Sacco & Vanzetti: 23 The Ballad Of Sacco And Vanzetti, part 2 (5:26) *Joan Baez*; 24 Here's To You (3:09) *Joan Baez*.

CD 2: Duck, You Sucker: 1 Main Title (3:38) *Edda Dell'Orso*; 2 March Of The Beggars (4:56); Without Apparent Motive: 3 Senza motivo apparente (4:23); The Working Class Goes To Heaven: 4 Pazzia da lavoro (2:24); My Name Is Nobody: 5 Il mio nome e' Nessuno (3:11); Moses, The Lawgiver: 6 Main Titles (4:10) *Gianna Spagnolo*; Exorcist II: The Heretic: 7 Magic And Ecstasy (3:04); Il gatto (The Cat): 8 Gli scatenati (3:42); 9 Il gatto (3:09); L'umanoide (The Humanoid): 10 Robodog (1:39); Dedicato al mare Egeo (Dedicated To The Aegean Sea): 11 Cavallina a cavallo (4:21) *Ilona Staller*; Tragedy Of A Ridiculous Man: 12 La tragedia di un uomo ridicolo (2:16); Le professionnel (The Professional): 13 Chi mai (5:07); Copkiller: 14 Sinfonia d'una citta, part 2 (4:50); Once Upon A Time In America: 15 Cockeye's Song (4:23) *Edda Dell'Orso*; The Mission: 16 On Earth As It Is In Heaven (3:52) *Incantation*; The Untouchables: 17 Al Capone (2:55); 18 End Titles (3:12); Cinema Paradiso: 19 From American Sex Appeal To The First Fellini (3:26); Tie Me Up! Tie Me Down: 20 Atame! (2:45); Bugsy: 21 Act Of Faith (3:12).

Review: See *Ennio Morricone: Compilation* entry below.

Ennio Morricone: With Love
🎵🎵🎵🎵▹

1995, DRG Records.

Album Notes: *Music*: Ennio Morricone; *Orchestrations*: Ennio Morricone; Orchestras conducted by Ennio Morricone; *Album Producer*: Claudio Fuiano.

Selections: Piazza di Spagna: 1 Main Titles (2:44); Questa specie d'amore: 2 Main Titles (3:16); D'amore si muore: 3 Main Titles (3:47); I bambini chi chiedono perche': 4 Main Titles (2:32); Cuore di Mamma: 5 Lullaby For Adulterers (3:03); L'alibi: 6 Belinda May (2:54); Barbablu': 7 Bluebeard... romantic (3:25); Il diavolo nello cervello: 8 Reason, Heart, Love (3:26); Revolver: 9 A Friend (2:34); Maddalena: 10 A Woman To Remember (4:16); La donna invisibile: 11 Portrait Of An Author (5:04); Gli intoccabili: 12 Defile (1:51); Il serpente: 13 Theme For A Woman Alone (2:34); Le ruffian: 14 I Remember Rosa (2:55); Il segreto: 15 Dal mare (3:32); Le due stagioni della vita: 16 Main Titles (3:39); Veruschka: 17 The Poetry Of A Woman (3:13); Le tour du monde des amoureux de Peynet: 18 Forse basta (3:33); La banchiera: 19 Lovingly Playful (2:37); La Califfa: 20 Main Titles (2:36); Cinema Paradiso: 21 Main Titles (2:59).

Review: See *Ennio Morricone: Compilation* entry below.

An Ennio Morricone: Western Quintet 🎵🎵🎵🎵▹

1995, DRG Records.

Album Notes: *Music*: Ennio Morricone; Orchestra conducted by Ennio Morricone, Bruno Nicolai; *Album Producer*: Claudio Fuiano.

Selections: CD 1: Il mio nome e' Nessuno (My Name Is Nobody): 1 Il mio nome e' Nessuno (3:09); 2 Buona fortuna Jack (5:03); 3 Mucchio selvaggio (2:38); 4 Se sei qualcuno e' colpa mia (4:45); 5 Con i migliori auguri (2:02); 6 Uno strano barbiere (6:56); 7 Piu' delle Valchirie (2:17); 8 Una insolita attesa (2:02); 9 Balletto degli specchi (1:29); 10 La favola dell' uccellino (1:46); Occhio alla penna (A Fist Goes West): 11 Non fare l'Indiano (3:16); 12 Estasi del miracolo (2:53); 13 Alleluja del buono raccolto (3:15); 14 L'ultima tromba (2:12); 15 Sfida all'ultima forchetta (1:33); 16 Grandino e piccolone (1:01); 17 Dal sarto (1:16); 18 Occhio alla penna (2:21); 19 Pantomima del letto (1:40); 20 Passaggio dal male al bene (1:19); 21 Vaohanana Manitu' (:34); 22 Solo il piccolone (:52); 23 Prima dei pugni (2:18); 24 Due simpatici zozzoni (1:43); 25 Tanti pugni (3:11); Giu la testa (A Fistful Of Dynamite): 26 Giu la testa (4:15); 27 Amore; 28 Mesa Verde (1:40); 29 Marcia degli accattoni (4:55); 30 Scherzi a parte (2:25).

CD 2: Giu la testa (A Fitsful Of Dynamite)(cont'd): 1 Messico e Irlanda (4:58); 2 I figli morti (6:05); 3 Addio Messico (:52); 4 Invenzione per John (9:04); 5 Rivoluzione contro (6:44); 6 Dopo l'esplosione (3:25); Tepepa (Blood and Guns): 7 Viva la revolucion (4:20); 8 Tepepa e Price (:53); 9 Tradimento primo (2:14); 10 A meta' strada (1:46); 11 Al Messico che vorrei (4:52); 12 Uno rosa (1:45); 13 Consegna delle armi (1:18); 14 Una povera casa (1:00); 15 Tradimento secondo (2:54); 16 Viva la revolucion (5:28); Vamos a matar, Companeros: 17 Il pinguino (2:53); 18 Vamos a matar, Companeros (E. Morricone/ S. Corbucci)(2:20); 19 La messicana (2:38); 20 La loro patria (1:40); 21 Un uomo in agguato (5:37); 22 Pensando alla liberta (1:21); 23 Cecchino (1:21); 24 Il ringuino (3:04).

Review: See *Ennio Morricone: Compilation* entry below.

An Ennio Morricone Anthology 🎵🎵🎵🎵▹

1995, DRG Records.

Album Notes: *Music*: Ennio Morricone; Orchestra conducted by Ennio Morricone; *Album Producer*: Claudio Fuiano.

Selections: CD 1: La Califfa (The Lady Caliph): 1 The Lady Caliph (2:36); 2 Women At The River (1:06); Senza Movente (Without Apparent Motive): 3 Without Apparent Motive (4:20); 4 Night Search (2:10); Revolver: 5 A Friend (2:36); Gli intoccabili (Machine Gun McCain): 6 The Balld Of Hank McCain (2:08); 7 Rosemary (2:04); Gott mit Uns (God With Us): 8 God With Us (4:24); Che c'entriamo noi con la rivoluzione? (What Am I Doing In The Middle Of This Revolution?): 9 What Am I Doing? (4:54); Maddalena: 10 Like Maddalena (4:17); Mosca Addio (Moscow Farewell): 11 Moscow Farewell (4:16); Cuore di Mamma (A Mother's Heart): 12 Amusing Diversion (2:58); I bambini ci chiedono perche' (The Children Who Are Asking Why): 13 End Credits (1:53); Quartieri (The Neighborhood): 14 A Neighborhood Song (3:35); Joss, Il professionista (The Professional): 15 The Wind, The Shout (5:16); Il mio nome e' Nessuno (My Name Is Nobody): 16 My Name Is Noobody (3:08); Alzati spia (Rise Up, Spy): 17 March in F (3:00); Il trio infernale (The Infernal Trio): 18 The Unholy Three (4:10); La banchiera (The Woman Banker): 19 Dedication (3:33); L'alibi (The Alibi): 20 Belinda May (2:52); Il gatto a nove code (The Cat O' Nine Tails): 21 Lullaby in Blue (2:37); Vamos a matar Companeros (Companeros): 22 Companeros (2:23).

CD 2: Slalom: 1 Slalom (1:30); 2 Sestriere (2:25); Tepepa (Blood And Guns): 3 Viva la revolucion (4:18); Maddalena: 4 Chi mai

(5:05); Tempo di uccidere (A Time To Kill): 5 A Far Away Italy (3:07); Dimenticare Palermo (To Forget Palermo): 6 To Forget Palermo (4:18); Tre colonne in cronaca (Three Columns On Front Page): 7 Three Columns On Front Page (3:15); L'agnese va a morire (Who Saw Him Die?): 8 The Lamb Is Going To Die (3:09); 9 Song Of Nostalgia (3:10); Questa specie d'amore (This Kind Of Love): 10 This Kind Of Love (2:32); 11 To The People Of Parma (2:40); D'amore si muore (One Could Die Of Love): 12 A Little Bitter Irony (4:13); Piazza di Spagna: 13 Place Of Spain (2:47); Il diavolo nello cervelo (Devil In The Brain): 14 Reason, Heart, Love (3:26); Veruschka: 15 Veruschka (2:55); La cugina (The Cousin): 16 The Cousin (4:09); I crudeli (The Hellbenders): 17 The Hellbenders (2:31); La donna invisibile (The Invisible Woman): 18 To Serenity (1:51); La Venexiana (The Venetian Woman): 19 The Venetian Woman (2:15); Le ruffian: 20 Western? (3:36); Il serpente (The Serpent): 21 Theme For A Woman Alone (2:35); Matrimonio con vizietto (La Cage aux Folles III): 22 Castles In Scotland (3:16); Le marginal (The Outsider): 23 The Outsider (3:54).

Review: See *Ennio Morricone: Compilation* entry below.

An Ennio Morricone-Dario Argento Trilogy ♪♪♪♪◌

1995, DRG Records.

Album Notes: *Music:* Ennio Morricone; Orchestra conducted by Ennio Morricone; *Album Producer:* Claudio Fuiano.

Selections: L'uccello dalle piume di cristallo (The Bird With The Crystal Plumage): 1 Crystal Plumage (5:12); 2 There's No One Left (3:17); 3 The City Wakes Up (3:09); 4 The Bird With The Crystal Plumage (1:25); 5 Silence In The Chaos (2:12); 6 Unexpected Violence (4:08); Il gatto a nove code (The Cat O' Nine Tails): 7 Lullaby In Blue (2:36); 8 1970 (8:38); 9 First Paranoia (3:47); 10 Dissociation (2:40); 11 Last Metaphor (2:30); 12 The Spot (2:30); 4 mosche di velluto grigio (Four Flies On Grey Velvet): 13 Main Title (3:16); 14 Four Flies On Grey Velvet (suite)(19:16); 15 Like A Madrigal (3:39); 16 Dario Argento Speaks! (5:40).

Review: See *Ennio Morricone: Compilation* entry below.

Ennio Morricone: Main Titles 1965-1995 ♪♪♪♪◌

1996, DRG Records.

Album Notes: *Music:* Ennio Morricone; Orchestra conducted by Ennio Morricone; *Album Producer:* Claudio Fuiano.

Selections: CD 1: 1 Slalom: Main Title (1:29); 2 I crudeli: 2 Main Title (2:30); 3 Tepepa: Viva la revolucion (4:17); 4 L'alibi: Una fotografia (2:01); 5 Cuore di Mamma: Ricreazione divertita (2:57); 6 La donna invisibile: Alla serenita (5:20); 7 La monaca di Monza: Main Title (2:35); 8 Gli intoccabili: La ballata di Hank McCain (2:07); 9 La califfa: Main Title (2:36); 10 Gott mit Uns: Lontano (4:23); 11 Le foto proibite di una signora perbene: Main Title (4:47); 12 Revolver: Un amico (2:34); 13 Maddalena: Chi mai (3:34); 14 Veruschka: Main Title (2:54); 15 Che c'entriamo noi con la rivoluzione?: Main Title (4:53); 16 Questa specie d'amore: Main Title (2:33); 17 Il diavolo nel cervelo: La ragione, il cuore, l'amore (3:26); 18 Le due stagione della vita: Main Title (3:39); 19 I bambini ci chiedono perche: Main Title (2:32); 20 Senza movente: Main Title (4:20); 21 D'amore si muore: Main Title (3:48); 22 Il mio nome e' Nessuno: Main Title (3:07); 23 Il segreto: Main Title (2:20).

CD 2: 1 Il trio infernale: Main Title (4:10); 2 La cugina: Main Title (4:09); 3 Il giro del mondo degli innamorati di Peynet: Forse basta (3:33); 4 L'agnese va a morire: Main Title (3:09); 5 La banchiera: Dedicace (3:33); 6 Joss, il professionista: Le vent, le cri (5:16); 7 Le marginal: Main Title (3:54); 8 Il pentito: Main Title (4:47); 9 La Venexiana: Baci dopo il tramonto (3:30); 10 Mosca addio: Main Title (3:52); 11 Quartiere: Romanza quartiere (3:35); 12 Nuovo cinema Paradiso: Main Title (2:59); 13 Tempo di uccidere: Main Title (3:07); 14 Dimenticare Palermo: Main Title (4:18); 15 Tre colonne in cronaca: Main Title (3:15); 16 Piazza di Spagna: Main Title (2:53); 17 La notte e il momento: A caccia di lei (3:27).

Review: See *Ennio Morricone: Compilation* entry below.

Ennio Morricone: Compilation ♪♪♪♪◌

1987, Virgin Records.

Album Notes: *Music:* Ennio Morricone; *Orchestrations:* Ennio Morricone; Orchestra conducted by Ennio Morricone; *Album Producer:* Enrico de Melis.

Selections: CD 1: 1 The Good, The Bad And The Ugly (2:37); 2 Come Maddalena (4:18); 3 The Sicilian Clan (3:58); 4 Chi mai (5:06); 5 Investigation Of A Citizen Above Suspicion (3:25); 6 Mosca addio (4:46); 7 Marche en la (3:01); 8 La califfa (2:37); 9 The Battle Of Algiers (1:40); 10 The Infernal Trio (4:13); 11 Dedicace (3:34); 12 For Love One Can Die (3:49); 13 Sacco And Vanzetti (2:45); 14 La tragedia di un uomo ridicolo (2:12); 15 Romanze quartiere (3:35); 16 Once Upon A Time In The West (Main Title)(5:05); 17 The Mission (remix)(2:54).

CD 2: 1 Once Upon A Time In America: Cockey's Song (4:17); 2 Gabriel's Oboe (2:12); 3 Atto di dolore (2:22); 4 Baci dopo il Tramonto (3:41); 5 Le marginal (3:55); 6 Estate (3:59); 7 The Falls (2:12); 8 Moses Theme (4:03); 9 Buona fortuna, Jack (5:05); 10 The Man With The Harmonica (3:27); 11 A Fistful Of Dynamite (4:36); 12 Lontano (3:51); 13 My Name Is Nobody (3:09); 14 Peur sur la ville (3:54); 15 Le vent, le cri (5:18); 16 Once Upon A Time In The America: Deborah's Theme (4:24)

Review: As these various compilations clearly evidence, there is a lot of material available about Ennio Morricone, a composer whose incredible output includes films in his native Italy, in France, and of course in the U.S. Many of the most important scores are represented in one form or another in these compilations, and even though some of the same tracks appear in several of them, the duplications are often kept to a minimum, with the various albums complementing each other to give a very complete overview of Morricone's many contributions to the movies.

Given the abundance of material, however, a selection seems in order, and with this in mind, here are a few suggestions: collectors interested in the Italian western scores (a genre in which Morricone particularly excelled, and in which he pretty much established the criteria by which hundreds of other scores were composed) should pick up the RCA compilation, which offers many selections that are not available elsewhere; those interested in a broader overview might want to acquire the Rhino set, which is pretty thorough, or the two individual Virgin CDs, which contain many of the essential tracks.

For a closer view of Morricone's contributions to French and Italian films, any of the DRG sets should do, though one should be aware of the fact that "Anthology" and "Main Titles" frequently duplicate each other.

Cinema Paradiso: The Classic Ennio Morricone 🎵🎵

1993, Silva Screen Records.

Album Notes: *Music:* Ennio Morricone; *Orchestrations:* Ennio Morricone, Rachel Berlin, Karl-Heinz Loges, Daniel Walker, Derek Wadsworth, Victoria Dolceamore, Steve Edwards, Volker Rippe, Dennis Smith, Brian Gascoigne, William Motzing, Geoff Castle; Mark Ayres, Richard Bronskill; The City of Prague Philharmonic, conducted by William Motzing, Derek Wadsworth; *Album Producers:* Thomas Karban, Derek Wadsworth, Mike Ross-Trevor; *Engineers:* Malcolm Luker, Mike Ross-Trevor.

Selections: 1 Cinema Paradiso (3:22); 2 The Mission: Gabriel's Oboe (2:25); 3 The Good, The Band And The Ugly (2:54); 4 Once Upon A Time In America: Deborah's Theme (5:20); 5 Two Mules For Sister Sara (5:18); 6 Marco Polo (2:34); 7 Once Upon A Time In The West (suite)(8:05); 8 The Mission: Main Theme (2:15); 9 1900: Romanze (3:51); 10 In The Line Of Fire (4:03); 11 The Untouchables: Death Theme (2:25); 12 Red Sonja (2:25); 13 Casualties Of War: Elegy For Brown (3:34); 14 A Fistful Of Dollars (3:36); 15 For A Few Dollars More (3:33); 16 Hamlet (2:47); 17 A Fistful Of Dynamite (Duck You Sucker) (3:55); 18 The Thing (4:27); 19 The Good, The Bad And The Ugly: The Ecstasy Of Gold (3:00); 20 The Mission: On Earth As It Is In Heaven (3:45).

Review: See entry below.

Cinema Paradiso: The Classic Film Music of Ennio Morricone 🎵🎵

1996, Silva Screen Records.

Album Notes: *Music:* Ennio Morricone; *Orchestrations:* Mark Ayres, Mark McGurty, Henry Mancini, Steve Edwards, Dennis Smith, Derek Wadsworth, Victoria Dolceamore, Mike Townend, Brian Gascoigne, Karl-Heinz Loges, Rachel Berlin; The City of Prague Philharmonic, conducted by Paul Bateman; *Album Producer:* James Fitzpatrick; *Engineers:* John L. Timperley, Mike Ross-Trevor.

Selections: 1 Suite for Orchestra and Choir from The Mission: The Mission, Gabriel's Oboe, Ave Maria (Guarini), On Earth As It Is In Heaven, Epilogue/The Falls (13:04) *Members of the Crouch End Festival Choir, David Temple*; 2 The Untouchables: Main Theme (2:21); 3 Once Upon A Time In America: Deborah's Theme (4:13) *Jill Washington*; 4 1900: Romanza (3:30); 5 Casualties Of War: Elegy For Brown (3:53); 6 Two Mules For Sister Sara (5:19); 7 In The Line Of Fire (4:02); 8 The Thing (4:28) *Daniel Caine*; 9 Chi mai (5:36); 10 Marco Polo (2:41); Sergio Leone Western Film Suite: 11 Once Upon A Time In The West: Main With The Harmonica (3:51); 12 The Good, The Bad And The Ugly (2:53); 13 A Fistful Of Dollars (3:26); 14 For A Few Dollars More (3:23); 15 Once Upon A Time In The West (6:03) *Jill Washington*; 16 The Good, The Bad And The Ugly: The Ecstasy Of Gold (3:00) *Anna Thomas*; 17 Cinema Paradiso (3:34).

Review: While they cover much of the same scores and sometimes the same selections, the two Silva Screen compilations are somewhat different. The earliest, *The Classic Ennio Morricone*, is less interesting, because playing by the City of Prague Philharmonic is at times spotty, with uninspired renditions that add really nothing to the Morricone canon. The second, *The Classic Film Music of Ennio Morricone,* conducted by Paul Bateman, is somewhat better and truer to the spirit of the original scores, with an exciting reading of selections from *The Mission.* But with so much Morricone music already available, were either of these sets really necessary, let alone both?

Ennio Morricone: Once Upon a Time in the Cinema ♪

1996, Varese-Sarabande.

Album Notes: *Music:* Ennio Morricone; *Orchestrations:* Lanny Meyers; Orchestra conducted by Lanny Meyers; *Featured Musicians:* Lanny Meyers (piano, keyboards), Bob Mair (bass), Ed Smith (drums), Paul Viapiano (guitar); *Album Producer:* Bruce Kimmel; *Engineer:* Vincent Cirilli; *Assistant Engineer:* Mark Agostino.

Selections: 1 In The Line Of Fire (3:44); 2 Cinema Paradiso (3:33); 3 The Mission (3:30); 4 La Cage Aux Folles (3:28); 5 Once Upon A Time In America (5:07); 6 Duck, You Sucker (4:02); 7 Gabriel's Oboe (from The Mission)(6:34); 8 Hamlet (7:06); 9 Tie Me Up, Tie Me Down (7:15); 10 Frantic (5:02); 11 A Fistful Of Leone (A Fistful Of Dollars/For A Few Dollars More/The Good, The Bad And The Ugly)(5:59); 12 Disclosure (4:01); 13 Wolf (5:23); 14 Once Upon A Time In The West (5:12).

Review: A jazz treatment of well-known Morricone themes, strictly for collectors and fans, and not even made interesting in the tepid playing of the somewhat undistinguished musicians, or in the routine orchestrations by Lanny Meyers. Anything wrong with more original ideas?

Stanley Myers (1930-

Music from the Films ♪♪♪◗

Milan Records.

Album Notes: *Music:* Stanley Myers, Hans Zimmer; *Album Producer:* Emmanuel Chamboredon; *Engineers:* Chris Dibble, Alan Snelling.

Selections: My Beautiful Landrette: 1 My Beautiful Laundrette (H. Zimmer/S. Myers/D. Bugatti)(4:00) *Rita Wolf;* 2 120 Days And Nights In A Laundrette (8:30); 3 My Beautiful Laundrette (dance mix)(3:30) *Rita Wolf;* Sammy And Rosie Get Laid: 4 Sammy And Rosie (1:35); 5 The Prodigal Father (2:15); 6 The Ghost At The Feast (1:53); 7 I've Seen War You Know (S. Myers/S. Lawrence/S. Lawrence/C. Scarlett)(2:22) *Samantha & Sandra Lawrence, Charles Scarlett;* Wish You Were Here: 8 The

Return Of Linda (2:23); 9 Linda Alone (2:43); 10 Lost In A Dream (S. Myers/D. Leland)(1:40) *Nicole Tibbets.*

Review: Three scores by Stanley Myers, a composer whose output is little known outside of a selected circle of fans and admirers. *My Beautiful Laundrette,* directed by Stephen Frears in 1985, is set in the Pakistani community in South London, and stars Gordon Warnecke and Daniel Day Lewis, respectively as a Pakistani boy and his British friend who run a small laundrette; *Sammy and Rosie Get Laid,* also directed by Frears in 1987, is an affectionate romantic comedy that stars Frances Barber and Ayub Khan Din in the title roles; as for *Wish You Were Here,* written and directed by David Leland, and set in the 1950s, it deals with the sexual awakening of a young British girl in a South Coast town. The scores are widely divergent in approach, and while the first has a rock feel that is contemporary in tone and relatively lackluster, both *Sammy and Rosie Get Laid* and *Wish You Were* are quite diversified and attractive, each reflecting with accuracy the times and moods evoked by the films. The pop vocals, though, are dispensable.

Mario Nascimbene (1913-

A Mario Nascimbene Anthology ♪♪♪♪

1996, DRG Records.

Album Notes: *Music:* Mario Nascimbene; *Album Producers:* Mario Nascimbene, Claudio Fuiano; *Engineer:* Gianni Mazzarini.

Selections: CD 1: The Prehistoric Films: One Million Years B.C.: 1 Cosmic Sequence (3:46); 2 The Pteraxodon Carries Loana To Its Nest (4:37); When Dinosaurs Ruled The Earth: 3 Main Titles (2:27); 4 Storm On The Sea (3:18); 5 End Titles (1:07); Creatures The World Forgot: 6 Main Titles (1:48); 7 Eruption Of The Volcano (2:38); 8 Finale: End Titles (1:53); The Historic Films: Solomon And Sheba: 9 Death Of David (2:42); 10 Orgiastic Dance (4:58); Joseph And His Brethren: 11 Pastorale (2:00); 12 Finale (2:21); Barabbas: 13 Main Titles (2:06); 14 Eclipse (3:21); 15 Empty Tomb (2:51); Francis Of Assisi: 16 Building The Church (2:33); 17 Dressing Of Clara (3:25); Alexander The Great: 18 Main Titles (2:04); 19 Battle Of Granicus (2:38); The Vikings: 20 Regnar Returns (2:59); 21 Love Scene (4:00); The Classic Film: Doctor Faustus: 22 Main Titles (2:10); 23 Catacombs (2:58) *Richard Burton;* 24 The Garden Of Delight (1:49); 25 Helen's Theme (1:26).

CD 2: The Modern Films: A Farewell To Arms: 1 Main Titles (2:29); 2 Finale (2:48); The Barefoot Contessa: 3 Main Titles

(1:47); 4 Nocturne Bolero (2:55); Sons And Lovers: 5 Main Titles (1:34); 6 Love Scene/End Titles (4:07); The Quiet American: 7 Main Titles (1:26); 8 City Streets (2:21); Room At The Top: 9 Main Titles (3:08); 10 Joe And The Prostitute (3:35); The Siege Of Leningrad: 11 The Final Battle (3:32); The Vengeance Of She: 12 Carol In The Sea (4:06); 13 Love Scene (1:33); Where The Spies Are: 14 Main Titles (1:47); 15 Fight/Vikki (3:00); The Scent Of Mystery: 16 The Chase (2:46); 17 The Chase (2:50) *Eddie Fisher*; Light In The Piazza: 18 Main Titles (3:02); 19 For The Streets Of Florence (3:10); Jessica: 20 The Vespa Song (2:33) *Maurice Chevalier*; 21 Funny Folk Dance (3:07); Romanoff And Juliet: 22 Walking In The Park (2:14); 23 Fox Trot (1:18).

Review: Nicely assembled compilation of themes and cues from 22 of the Hollywood produced films scored by one of Italy's most resourceful composers. Nascimbene, who personally supervised this release, frequently went outside the normal boundaries of a standard orchestra to incorporate usual sounds into his scores, though the bulk of his work was still acoustic in nature. The first CD starts off with two intriguing cues from *One Million Years B.C.*, the first in a trilogy of prehistoric tales (the other two are also included). The composer incorporated natural sounds, such as wind and rain, with what he perceived was the tribal music for early man. These "ethnic" effects were achieved through a variety of inventive, non-electronic means. Several of Nascimbene's historical costume dramas are featured, including *The Vikings*, *Solomon and Sheba*, and *Barabbas* (which features some blood curdling screams). The second CD contains music from his more contemporary films, many released here for the first time. Titles include *The Barefoot Contessa*, *The Vengeance of She* (with the superb jazz theme "Carol at Sea"), and light comedy fare such as *Where the Spies Are* (Morse Code is used in the "Main Title") and *Romanoff and Juliet* (a really odd flute-like instrument is used in "Fox Trot"). A well assembled overview of an artist whose work should not be forgotten.

David Hirsch

Alfred Newman (1901-1970)

The Film Music of Alfred Newman 🎬🎬🎬▷

1992, Varese-Sarabande.

Album Notes: *Music*: Alfred Newman; Orchestra conducted by Alfred Newman; *Album Producer*: Tony Thomas; *Engineer*: Joe Gastwirt.

Selections: Captain From Castile: (1-6) 1 Prelude/Pedro de Vargas (2:55); 2 Catana (3:02); 3 Lady Luisa/Juan, The Adventurer/Wonders Of The New World (3:08); 4 Magic Ring/Fears Of Persecution/The Compassionate Priest (3:01); 5 Fulfillment In The New World (3:07); 6 Conquest (3:04); 7 All About Eve (3:35); 8 Pinky (3:14); 9 Wuthering Heights (3:21); 10 A Royal Scandal (1:09); 11 The Song Of Bernadette (3:26); 12 The Razor's Edge (3:37); 13 How Green Was My Valley (4:11); 14 A Letter To Three Wives (3:25); 15 Street Scene (2:55).

Review: See entry below.

Captain from Castile: The Classic Film Scores of Alfred Newman 🎬🎬🎬🎬

1989, RCA Victor.

Album Notes: *Music*: Alfred Newman; The National Philharmonic Orchestra, conducted by Charles Gerhardt; *Album Producer*: George Korngold; *Engineer*: K.E. Wilkinson.

Selections: 1 20th Century-Fox Fanfare with the CinemaScope Extension/How To Marry A Millionaire: Street Scene (4:22); Captain From Castile: 2 Pedro And Catana/Conquest (6:22) *Band Of The Grenadier Guards*; Wuthering Heights: 3 Cathy's Theme (2:51); Down To The Sea In Ships: 4 Hornpipe (1:51); The Song Of Bernadette: 5 Prelude/The Vision (7:49) *The Ambrosian Singers*; The Bravados: 6 Main Title (The Hunters)(3:04); Anastasia: 7 Main Title (2:45); The Best Of Everything: 8 London Calling (2:51); Airport: 9 Main Title (3:13); The Robe: 10 Main Title/Elegy/Caligula's March/The Map Of Jerusalem (8:32) *Ambrosian Singers, Band Of The Grenadier Guards*.

Review: The quintessential Hollywood composer, Alfred Newman had a profound influence on the film community: as the head of the music department at 20th Century-Fox for more than 20 years, his position enabled him to nurture and develop young talent, some of which followed in his footsteps.

Born in 1901, in New Haven, Connecticut, he began his career in the theatre, becoming one of the Broadway's youngest pianists and conductors, before moving to the West Coast in 1929. The advent of sound in the film industry gave him a tremendous opportunity to turn his knowledge as a composer and as a conductor to good use, particularly after he joined Fox.

While at that studio, he wrote the scores for many classic films such as *How Green Was My Valley* (1941), *The Song of Bernadette* (1943), *All About Eve* (1950), and *The Diary of Anne*

Frank (1959), and contributed the celebrated fanfare still heard today at the start of every 20th Century-Fox film.

One of the most popular composers in Hollywood throughout his career, Alfred Newman displayed in his scores a strongly neo-romantic style. In the words of his long-time collaborator and friend, Ken Darby, "His primary purpose was to enlarge the scene, make it more real, add to it without engaging the audience's attention away from its involvement with the plot and the characters..."

The two compilations listed here regroup themes he wrote during his tenure at Fox. Of the two, the RCA set, in the wonderful Classic Film Scores series, finds Charles Gerhardt and The National Philharmonic Orchestra in sensational readings of some of Newman's best remembered themes, including selections from *Captain From Castile,* which gave the album its title, *Wuthering Heights, The Robe, Airport* and *Anastasia.* Performance throughout is satisfactory, with the brilliant sound quality adding a cinematic flavor to the whole album.

In comparison, the Varese-Sarabande CD does not fare as well. Though conducted by Newman himself, it was compiled from archival material, and sonic quality is frequently subpar, particularly in the digital domain. But the *Captain From Castile* suite, not available anywhere else, is well worth listening to.

The Movies Go to the Hollywood Bowl ♫♫♫♫

1990, Angel Records.

Album Notes: *Music:* Alfred Newman, Miklos Rozsa; The Hollywood Bowl Symphony Orchestra, conducted by Alfred Newman, Miklos Rozsa; *Album Producer:* Ralph O'Connor; *Engineer:* Carson Taylor; *Digital Remastering:* Robert Norberg.

Selections: Captain From Castile: 1 Conquest (A. Newman)(3:23); 2 Second Rhapsody (G. Gershwin)(14:16) *Leonard Pennario*; David And Bathsheba: 3 23rd Psalm (A. Newman)(3:24); The Robe (A. Newman): 4 Palm Sunday (2:14); 5 Hallelujah (2:52); 6 The Dream Of Olwen (C. Williams)(3:59) *Leonard Pennario*; King Of Kings (M. Rozsa): 7 Nativity (2:10); 8 The Way Of The Cross (3:00); 9 Pieta (2:34); 10 King Of Kings Theme (2:48); Spellbound: 11 Spellbound Concerto (M. Rozsa)(12:09) *Leonard Pennario*; El Cid (M. Rozsa): 12 Overture (3:25); 13 Love Theme (4:15); 14 El Cid March (3:27).

Review: In the 1960s, both Alfred Newman and Miklos Rozsa conducted the Hollywood Bowl Symphony Orchestra in recordings of their own music and other works for Capitol Records.

This compilation presents several excerpts from these recordings, with Newman leading the orchestra in selections from *Captain From Castile, The Robe* and *David and Bathsheba,* while Rozsa's selections include *King of Kings, El Cid,* and a forceful rendition of the *Spellbound Concerto,* with Leonard Pennario as soloist. Nothing truly earthshaking, simply some good selections, appropriately conducted by the composers themselves, always a plus.

David Newman (1954-

It's a Wonderful Life: Sundance Film Music Series, vol. 1 ♫♫♫♫

1988, Telarc Records.

Album Notes: *Music:* Dimitri Tiomkin, Richard Addinsell, Cyril J. Mockridge; The Royal Philharmonic Orchestra and the Ambrosian Singers (John McCarthy, chorus master), conducted by David Newman; *Album Producers:* Robert Woods, Willard Carroll; *Engineer:* Jack Renner.

Selections: 1 Sundance Fanfare (D. Newman)(:40); It's A Wonderful Life (D. Tiomkin): 2 Main Title/Heaven/Ski Run (5:32); 3 Death Telegram/Gower's Deliverance (3:44); 4 George And Dad/Father's Death (2:45); 5 Love Sequence (2:26); 6 Wedding Cigars/George Lassoes Stork (2:44); 7 Dilemma/Bank Crisis/ Search For Money/Potter's Threat (4:13); 8 Clarence's Arrival (2:25); 9 George Is Unborn/Haunted House (5:09); 10 Pottersville Cemetery/Wrong Ma Bailey/Wrong May Hatch/ The Prayer (5:49); 11 It's A Wonderful Life (3:45); A Christmas Carol (suite)(R. Addinsell): 12 Main Title/Toy Shop/Cratchit And Scrooge/ Christmas Past/Christmas Present/Cratchit And Tiny Tim/Christmas Future/ Graveyard/Christmas Day/Finale (14:08); Miracle On 34th Street (C. Mockridge): 13 20th Century Fox Fanfare (A. Newman)/Main Title (1:25); 14 The House/Book Montage (3:51); 15 Newspaper Montage/Susan's Letter (1:26); 16 X-ray Machine/ Susan's Disappointment/Finale (4:18).

Review: One of the best albums of its kind. Recorded under the aegis of the Sundance Institute, in what was supposed to be a series unfortunately apparently abandoned after this initial volume, the CD presents the first recording of the scores for three Yuletide classics, played to perfection by the Royal Philharmonic Orchestra, conducted by David Newman. All three suites are highlights in their own right, but *It's a Wonderful Life* literally steals the show, with totally faithful reproductions of Tiomkin's difficult music style.

Alex North (1910-1991)

Alex North: North of Hollywood ♫♫♫

1989, RCA Records.

Album Notes: *Music*: Alex North; Orchestra conducted by Alex North; *Album Producer*: Dennis Farnon; *CD Producer*: Chick Crumpacker; *Engineers*: Ed Rich, Dick Baxter.

Selections: A Streetcar Named Desire: 1 Stud Poker (1:29); A Streetcar Named Desire: 2 Four Deuces (3:09); Wall Street Ballet: 3 Trick Or Treat (2:33); A Streetcar Named Desire: 4 French Quarter (2:19); Hot Spell: 5 Hot Spell (2:22); American Road: 6 Ode To A Western (2:08); Unchained: 7 Unchained Jazz (3:57); The Racers: 8 Monte Carlo (1:34); The Rose Tattoo: 9 Floozie (2:26); The Rose Tattoo: 10 Mardi Gras Bump (1:37); Member Of The Wedding: 11 Magnolia (2:29); Wall Street Ballet: 12 Ticker Tape (2:25); Member Of The Wedding: 13 Jody's Lament (3:18); The Racers: 14 Blackjack (2:46).

Review: See entry below.

Unchained Melody: The Film Themes of Alex North ♫♫

1991, Bay Cities Records.

Album Notes: *Music*: Alex North; Orchestra conducted by Alex North; *Album Producer*: Nick Redman; *Engineer*: Daniel Hersch.

Selections: 1 Unchained (3:37); 2 The Racers (3:43); 3 Viva Zapata! (3:31); 4 The Bad Seed (3:05); 5 A Streetcar Named Desire (2:51); 6 The Bachelor Party (4:10); 7 The 13th Letter (2:55); 8 Stage Struck (3:14); 9 I'll Cry Tomorrow (2:42); 10 Les Miserables (2:51); 11 The Rose Tattoo (3:13); 12 Desiree (2:52).

Review: Some film composers often find themselves out of the mainstream, and while thoroughly respected (and often lionized) by their peers, fail to become as widely admired by a larger audience. Such is the case of Alex North, a revered musician whose scores have always elicited much admiration, but who is hardly a household name today. Born in 1910 in Chester, Pa., of Russian emigres, North studied at the Curtis Institute of Music and at Juilliard.

His skills enabled him to impose himself in the New York theatre and ballet communities, leading Elia Kazan to ask him to write the incidental music for the stage presentation of Arthur Miller's *Death of a Salesman*, in 1949. When Kazan filmed *A Streetcar Named Desire* two years later, he again

called on North to provide the score, an unusual blend of New Orleans jazz that reflected the story and its locale. That score, and *Death of a Salesman* released that same year, earned Oscar nominations and promptly established the young composer. In short order, North began to deliver scores that were uncharacteristic for Hollywood, yet thoroughly cinematographic in their approach, something that further singled him out in the film community.

Among his many contributions for the screen, the most important include *Unchained* (1955), which yielded the popular song "Unchained Melody," *The Rose Tattoo* (1955), *The Rainmaker* (1956), *Spartacus* (1960), *The Misfits* (1961), *Cleopatra* (1964), *The Agony and the Ecstasy* (1965), *Who's Afraid of Virginia Woolf?* (1966), and *Dragonslayer* (1981).

The two compilations listed here present several themes from these and other films North also scored, unfortunately in often dubious sonic quality. The RCA set is interesting for its inclusion of themes not otherwise available (*Wall Street Ballet*), but the haphazard, disjointed presentation of the cues is a real disservice to the music and its composer.

Even worse, sonically, is the set from the now-defunct label Bay Cities, whose only merits is that it also includes some rare themes (*Viva Zapata!, The Bad Seed, The 13th Letter, Desiree*). A definitive North tribute has yet to be recorded.

Michael Nyman (1944-

The Essential Michael Nyman Band ♫♫♫♫

1991, Argo Records.

Album Notes: *Music*: Michael Nyman; *The Essential Michael Nyman Band*: Alexander Balanescu, Clare Connors, Ann Morphy (violin), Kate Musker (viola), Tony Hinnigan, Justin Pearson (cello), Martin Elliott (bass guitar), John Harle, David Roach (soprano/ alto saxophone), Andrew Findon (baritone sax/flute/piccolo), Steve Sidwell (trumpet), Marjorie Dunn (horn), Nigel Barr (bass trombone/euphonium), John Lenahan, Michael Nyman (piano), Sarah Leonard (soprano), Linda Hirst (mezzo soprano); *Engineer*: Michael J. Dutton.

Selections: The Draughtsman's Contract: 1 Chasing Sheep Is Best Left To Shepherds (5:04); 2 An Eye For Optical Theory (4:16); 3 The Garden Is Becoming A Robe Room (6:08); A Zed And Two Noughts: 4 Prawn-Watching (2:20); 5 Time Lapse (3:52); Drowning By Numbers: 6 Fish Beach (2:53); 7 Wheelbarrow Walk (2:32); 8 Knowing The Ropes (5:44); The Cook, The Thief, His Wife And Her Lover: 9 Miserere Paraphrase

(7:06); 10 Memorial (11:18); Water Dances: 11 Stroking (5:11); 12 Synchronising (5:33); Prospero's Books: 13 Miranda (4:16).

Review: Writing in a minimalist way that some might enjoy while others might find it painfully boring, Nyman continues to score films with great empathy, sometimes, as in *The Draughtsman's Contract* or *Prospero's Books,* mixing genres and periods with delicious abandon, at other times sticking to more conventional strictures, though always with the same deliberately individualistic style that's his stock in trade. Short of trying to listen to several of his soundtracks and form an opinion, this set provides an interesting overview, regrouping the themes from various recent films, including the weird *The Cook, The Thief, His Wife and Her Lover.* It may not be to everyone's taste, but it's the kind of music that seldom leaves one indifferent—you either love it, or hate it!

Rachel Portman (1960-

A Pyromaniac's Love Story
♫♫♫♫

1995, Varese-Sarabande Records.

Album Notes: *Music:* Rachel Portman; *Orchestrations:* Rachel Portman; *Album Producer:* Rachel Portman.

Selections: A Pyromaniac's Love Story: 1 Tango (2:50); 2 The Favor (1:02); 3 Garet Kisses Hattie (1:35); 4 Mr. Linzer's Troubles (1:03); 5 Aspiration (1:05); 6 Garet (1:39); 7 Off To See The World (2:55); 8 End Titles (3:26); Great Moments In Aviation: 9 End Titles (3:49); 10 Gabriel Explores Ship (2:01); 11 Safe Walls Are Falling (3:16); 12 Montage (1:24); 13 The Hope Is In Me (2:08); 14 Icarus (1:46); 15 We Both Killed Her (:53); 16 Vesuvia's Feast (4:36); 17 Nothing To Hide (2:51); Smoke: 18 Brooklyn (1:31); 19 Peter Rabbit (1:04); 20 Broken TV (1:21); 21 End Titles (2:42); Ethan Frome: 22 Fox Here Again (2:03); 23 The Sermon (2:32); 24 Coasting (3:07); 25 Mattie Arrives (1:27); 26 Walking Home (1:15); 27 Ethan Clears His Room (1:04); 28 End Titles (3:03).

Review: The featured work, *A Pyromaniac's Love Story* is not particularly attention-grabbing, being a light score dominated by tango-like motif. More striking however is Portman's *Great Moments in Aviation*, which contrasts soaring passages for operatic soprano and orchestra with '20s-style jazz. Portman reconciles and combines these disparate elements into an ethereal and deeply moving tapestry, and the result is one of the most offbeat and unique scores of the past 20 years. *Smoke*, a small ensemble, somewhat minimalist score, is also included but its four brief cues do not arouse great interest.

The concluding score however, *Ethan Frome* (an excellent, though not widely seen Liam Neeson film from 1992) is one of Portman's finest efforts. An impressionistic, melancholy score, *Ethan Frome* is at once brooding and pastoral, somewhat reminiscent of Herrmann in its atmospheric evocation of 19th-century New England. Rachel Portman's fondness for playing character eccentricities and a unique gift for orchestration (she always orchestrates her scores herself) makes her the most unique film composer to emerge in the '90s. Her music has great depth yet soars weightlessly. There is little doubt she has a very bright future ahead of her.

Paul Andrew MacLean

David Raksin (1912-

Laura: The Classic Film Scores of David Raksin ♫♫♫♫

1989, RCA Victor Records.

Album Notes: *Music:* David Raksin; The New Philharmonia Orchestra, conducted by David Raksin; *Album Producer:* Charles Gerhardt; *Engineer:* Philip Wade.

Selections: Laura: 1 Main Title (5:52); Forever Amber (suite): 2 Main Title: Amber (3:57); 3 The King's Mistress (3:25); 4 Whitefriars (9:14); 5 The Great Fire (3:59); 6 End Title: Forever Amber (4:06); The Bad And The Beautiful (suite): 7 Main Title Theme: Love Is For The Very Young (2:56); 8 The Acting Lesson (2:46); 9 The Quickies and The Sneak Preview (2:26); 10 Nocturne and Theme (7:04).

Review: With only one film, *Laura*, in 1944, David Raksin managed the almost impossible and became one of Hollywood's great composers. Not bad for someone who, in a brilliant career that has spanned more than 60 years (so far!), also wrote the music for many other important films, as well as countless television series.

Born in 1912, in Philadelphia, Raksin came to Hollywood in 1935 to work with Charles Chaplin on the music for *Modern Times*. But because he often argued with the famous comedian, one of the co-founders of United Artists, the studio where both were working, Raksin was fired. He was immediately rehired by Alfred Newman, head of the music department, with the understanding that he could continue to argue only as long as it was about the music.

Then Raksin wrote *Laura*, and became known as an innovative film composer, a reputation that never left him after that. In contrast to the style of mittel-European composers like Steiner, Rozsa or Korngold, Raksin's approach to music was refreshingly American in spirit, something that singled out another one of his memorable contributions, the score for *The Bad and the Beautiful*. In an early assessment, Andre Previn once commented, "[Raksin's] sense of orchestral color was always unbeatable, his harmonic twists very clearly his own, and he thought nothing of setting himself some problems to make studio composing a little livelier."

This recording, another great title in the Classic Film Scores series, has an extra ounce of authenticity because it is conducted by the composer himself. The suite from *Forever Amber* alone is worth the price of admission, but don't dismiss Raksin's revisiting of his score for *The Bad and the Beautiful*, or his reinterpretation of the celebrated theme for *Laura*. In fact, the recording's only flaw is its brevity. One would have joyfully settled for more of the same.

Nino Rota (1911-1979)

Nino Rota: Film Music 🎵🎵🎵🎵

1992, EMI Classics.

Album Notes: *Music*: Nino Rota; The Orchestre Philharmonique de Monte-Carlo, conducted by Gianluigi Gelmetti; *Album Producer*: David R. Murray; *Engineer*: Simon Rhodes.

Selections: War And Peace: 1 Introduction/Waltz (2:57); 2 The Rose Of Novgorod (2:04); 3 Finale (2:23); The Leopard: 4 Allegro maestoso (2:57); 5 Allegro impetuoso (5:15); 6 Sostenuto appasionato/Finale (3:48); La strada (suite from the ballet): 7 Country Wedding (3:33); 8 The Three Musicians And The "Madman" On The Tightrope (3:36); 9 Rhumba (2:24); 10 The Circus (Zampano's Number/The Jugglers/The "Madman's" Violin)(4:50); 11 Zampano's Anger (3:44); 12 Zampano Kills The "Madman"/Gelsomina Goes Mad With Grief (2:35); 13 The Last Show In The Snow (3:01); 14 Intermezzo: Zampano Alone And In Tears (4:20); Waterloo: 15 Andante eroico (3:20); 16 Andante alla marcia (4:22); 17 Andante con moto (3:54).

Review: See entry below.

Nino Rota: La Strada Ballet Suite 🎵🎵🎵🎵

1995, Sony Classical.

Album Notes: *Music*: Nino Rota; The Orchestra Filarmonica della Scala, conducted by Riccardo Muti; *Featured Musicians*: Stefano Pagliani (violin), Giuseppe Bodanza (trumpet); *Album Producer*: David Mottley; *Engineer*: Marcus Herzog.

Selections: La strada (suite from the ballet): 1 Country Wedding (3:44); 2 The Three Musicians And The "Madman" On The Tightrope (6:10); 3 The Circus (Zampano's Number/The Jugglers/The "Madman's" Violin)(4:54); 4 Zampano's Anger (4:11); 5 Zampano Kills The "Madman"/Gelsomina Goes Mad With Grief (2:50); 6 The Last Show In The Snow (4:52); 7 Intermezzo: Zampano Alone And In Tears (3:16); Concerto For Strings: 8 Preludio (4:05); 9 Scherzo (4:16); 10 Aria (4:00); 11 Finale (3:03); The Leopard (dances): 12 Valzer brillante (G. Verdi, arr.: N. Rota)(2:22); 13 Mazurka (1:48); 14 Controdanza (2:29); 15 Polka (1:30); 16 Quadriglia (1:53); 17 Galop (1:44); 18 Valzer del Commiato (4:24).

Review: See entry below.

The Symphonic Fellini/Rota: La dolce vita 🎵🎵🎵°

1993, Silva Screen Records.

Album Notes: *Music*: Nino Rota; *Orchestrations*: Derek Wadsworth; The Czech Symphony Orchestra, conducted by Derek Wadsworth; *Album Producer*: Nic Raine; *Engineer*: Mike Ross-Trevor.

Selections: 1 The White Sheik (2:46); 2 I vitelloni (3:01); 3 La strada (6:38); 4 Il bidone (4:48); 5 Le notte di Cabiria (6:08); 6 La dolce vita (7:08); 7 Boccacio '70 (1:27); 8 8½ (5:14); 9 Juliet Of The Spirits (7:17); 10 Fellini Satyricon (3:05); 11 The Clowns (4:20); 12 Roma (3:50); 13 Amarcord (5:09); 14 Il Casanova (3:25); 15 Orchestra Rehearsal (4:04).

Review: There are several collections of Rota's film themes available, notably one of dubious sonic quality that has been released at various times by CAM, the Italian label. These CDs, and particularly the first two, are interesting for several reasons. First, because both EMI and Sony are classical labels, marking a notable change among the major record companies which are beginning to view film music with the seriousness it truly deserves. And also because both offer selections from films which had wider release in this country than the Fellini films, for which Rota is notably famous. *War and Peace*, directed in 1956 by King Vidor, stars Audrey Hepburn, Mel Ferrer and Henry Fonda, and is a magnificent screen reconstruction of the epic Tolstoy novel; *The Leopard*, filmed by Luchino Visconti in 1963, and starring Burt Lancaster and Claudia Cardinale, is a powerful account of 19th-century life in Sicily, at a time when social values disintegrated rapidly in the face of rising revolutionary ideas; as for *Waterloo*, made in 1971 by Sergei Bondarchuk, it stars Rod Steiger as Napoleon, confronted with his last battle and most devastating defeats.

Adding a different touch to both sets is the ballet from *La Strada,* which Rota reorchestrated from the cues he had composed for his original 1954 score. Both Gianluigi Gelmetti and Riccardo Muti, respectively conducting the Orchestre Philharmonique de Monte-Carlo and the Orchestra Filarmonica della Scala, do the ballet and the selections from the score full justice, with bright, imaginative sonics to complement the music.

The third CD is a decent rendition of themes written by Rota for the films of Federico Fellini, performed by the Czech Symphony Orchestra, conducted by Derek Wadsworth. The performance is sometimes lackluster, and some of the tempi are a bit wild, but overall it's a good set, and a good representation of Rota's most popular themes.

Bruce Rowland (1942-

Bruce Rowland: The Film and Television Themes 𝄞𝄞𝄞𝄞♪

1990, ABC Records.

Album Notes: *Music*: Bruce Rowland; The Melbourne Symphony Orchestra, conducted by Bruce Rowland; *Featured Musicians*: Bruce Rowland, Joe Chindamo (synthesizers), Rod Stone, Don Stevenson (guitars), Mike Grabowsky (electric bass), Ron Sawdilands (drums), John Barratt (didgeridoo/flute/alto sax), Rod Campbell (bagpipes); *Album Producer*: Chris Boniface; *Engineers*: Gerry McKechnie, Ross Smith.

Selections: 1 Opening (from *The Man From Snowy River*)(1:28); 2 Tom's Theme (from *All The Rivers Run*)(2:13); 3 Phar Lap Learns To Run (from *Phar Lap*) (2:25); 4 Jessica's Theme (from *The Man From Snowy River*)(3:09); 5 Main Theme (from *All The Rivers Run*)(1:35); 6 Jessie Has A Cry (from *Now And Forever*) (1:55); 7 Hero To A Nation (from *Phar Lap*)(2:21); 8 Ray Burn's Theme (from *All The Rivers Run*)(1:58); 9 Sandhills (from *Phar Lap*)(2:35); 10 The Chase (from *The Man From Snowy River*)(4:58); 11 River Theme (from *All The Rivers Run*) (1:54); 12 Phar Lap's Arrival (from *Phar Lap*)(2:20); 13 Love Theme (from *All The Rivers Run*)(1:31); 14 Olympic Opening (4:46); 15 Olympic Ballet (3:06); 16 Taurus I (2:28); 17 Mountain Theme (from *The Man From Snowy River*)(1:49); 18 Main Theme (from *Whale Savers*)(1:07); 19 Closing (from *The Man From Snowy River*)(3:59).

Review: Australia's best kept secret, Bruce Rowland is a composer of great talent who has scored several films that have received a release in this country, notably *The Man From Snowy River* and its sequel, *Return to Snowy River, All the Rivers Run,* and *Phar Lap*. This 1984 compilation, with the composer conducting the Melbourne Symphony Orchestra, is a flavorful presentation of some of the beautifully elegiac themes Rowland wrote for the screen and television, played with great gusto by the orchestra and some featured musicians. *Man From Snowy River*, in particular, which also yielded a highly recommended soundtrack album, is terrific in its evocation of the wide open Australian spaces, in terms that compare favorably with the best western scores ever written in Hollywood, with just a hint of its actual source that makes it even more attractive.

Miklos Rozsa (1907-1995)

Miklos Rozsa: Epic Suites for Orchestra, Chorus and Organ 𝄞𝄞𝄞

1986, Varese-Sarabande.

Album Notes: *Music*: Miklos Rozsa; The Hamburg Concert Orchestra and Chorus, conducted by Richard Mueller-Lampertz; *Album Producer*: D.L. Miller; *Engineer*: W. Wille.

Selections: El Cid: 1 Overture (3:34); 2 Palace Music (1:16); 3 Legend and Epilogue (5:06); Ben-Hur: 4 Prelude (3:39); 5 Love Theme (2:52); 6 Victory Parade (2:24); 7 Miracle and Finale (3:34); King Of Kings: 8 Main Title (2:41); 9 Nativity (2:50); 10 Miracles Of Christ (3:09); 11 Salome's Dance (2:48); 12 Way Of The Cross (1:45); 13 Resurrection and Finale (3:31).

Review: The title actually says it all: beginning with *Quo Vadis*, in 1951, and *Ivanhoe*, in 1952, Miklos Rozsa acquired a solid reputation as a composer who could write better than most in the epic style for which Hollywood was coming to be known throughout the world. As a result, Rozsa scored many films set in Roman and medieval times, every time bringing a distinctive color to his music, frequently rooted in instruments and themes from the period reconstructed for the occasion. Some of the invention seems to be lost in most evocations of his scores, as in this presentation of cues from his scores for *El Cid, Ben-Hur* and *King of Kings*. While the performance here is perfectly adequate and acceptable, it misses the special quality the original scores derived from the research and care the composer invested in them. Other than that, the recording also displays a shrillness that is not always very flattering to the ear.

"I can't classify myself. Others must do it. Others, if they wish, can analyze my works."

Ennio Morricone
(American Film, February, 1994)

The Music of Miklos Rozsa
𝄞𝄞𝄞𝄞ᵛ

1985, Varese-Sarabande.

Album Notes: *Music:* Miklos Rozsa; The Utah Symphony Orchestra, conducted by Elmer Bernstein; *Featured Musicians:* Joshua Pierce, Dorothy Jonas, pianos; *Album Producers:* Jeffrey Kaufman, George Korngold; *Engineer:* Bruce Leek.

Selections: 1 The World, The Flesh And The Devil: Overture (3:31); 2 New England Concerto (14:57); 3 Because Of Him: Overture (3:20); 4 Spellbound Concerto (22:42).

Review: An interesting album, conducted by Elmer Bernstein, which doesn't take the usual beaten path but seeks, instead, to be original. The meat of the CD is the two major works found here, the "New England Concerto" and the "Spellbound Concerto," both played with great drive and intensity by Joshua Pierce and Dorothy Jonas in two-piano versions apparently endorsed by the composer himself. As a filler, Bernstein and the Utah Symphony perform the "Overture" to *The World, The Flesh and the Devil*, a 1959 drama starring Harry Belafonte, Inger Stevens and Mel Ferrer, and the "Overture" to *Because of Him*, written in 1946 for a comedy in which the leads were held by Deanna Durbin, Franchot Tone and Charles Laughton. The excellent dynamics add to the pleasure of discovering these versions.

Miklos Rozsa: Hollywood Legend 𝄞𝄞𝄞𝄞ᵛ

1989, Varese-Sarabande.

Album Notes: *Music:* Miklos Rozsa; The Nuremberg Symphony Orchestra, and The Palestrina Choir Of Nuremberg, conducted by Elmer Bernstein; *Featured Musicians:* Cynthia Millar (Ondes Marthinot), Kalus Leob (violin); *Album Producers:* George Korngold, Wolfgang Konrad; *Engineer:* Peter Collmann.

Selections: El Cid: 1 Fanfare/Burgos/Entry Of The Nobles (3:33); 2 The Coronation (2:18); The Story Of Three Loves: 3 Paganiniana/The Eternal City/Boccaccio March and Finale (12:46); Quo Vadis: 4 Quo Vadis Domine (5:25); The Lost Weekend: 5 Prelude/New York Skyline/Alcohol/Love Theme (5:31); Plymouth Adventure: 6 The Mayflower (Symphonic Picture)(11:58); The Private Life Of Sherlock Holmes: 7 English Waltz (Vienna In Scotland)(2:27); Ben-Hur: 8 Overture (8:45); The Strange Love Of Martha Ivers: 9 Prelude and Love Themes (6:15); King Of Kings: 10 Entr'acte (7:19); Dead Men Don't Wear Plaid: 11 Finale (4:29).

Review: Elmer Bernstein and the Nuremberg Symphony Orchestra provide a rousing tribute to the great Miklos Rozsa in this excellent 1989 recording, produced by George Korngold and Wolfgang Konrad. Many of Rozsa's most romantic works are included here, with the composer's sweeping "Golden Age" sound permeating selections from *The Story of Three Loves, The Strange Love of Martha Ivers* and *Dead Men Don't Wear Plaid*, while Rozsa's bold, majestic sense of dramatic film scoring is on full display in *El Cid, Quo Vadis?, King of Kings* and *Ben-Hur*. This particular album is noteworthy for its premiere recording of a 12-minute suite from *The Plymouth Adventure*, as well as an alternate, unused piece from *The Private Life of Sherlock Holmes*. The music is given a competent symphonic performance under Bernstein's direction, and though the liner notes are fairly sparse for a project like this, that should not keep any true film music fan away from picking up this highly recommended release.

Andy Dursin

Film Scores of Miklos Rozsa
𝄞𝄞𝄞𝄞ᵛ

1996, Angel Records.

Album Notes: *Music:* Miklos Rozsa; Orchestras conducted by Miklos Rozsa; *CD Producer:* Robert LaPorta; *Engineer:* Jay Ranellucci, Wayne Hileman.

Selections: Ben Hur: 1 Prelude (3:30); 2 Love Theme (3:06); 3 Parade Of The Charioteers (3:28); 4 Mother's Love (2:50); El Cid: 5 Overture (3:28); 6 Love Theme (4:19); 7 El Cid March (3:27); King Of Kings: 8 Nativity (2:13); 9 Way Of The Cross (3:04); 10 Pieta (2:39); 11 King Of Kings (Theme)(2:49); The Red House: 12 Prelude (3:07); 13 Screams In The Night (2:44); 14 The Oxhead Woods (3:00); 15 Retribution (3:06); Quo Vadis: 16 Ave Caesar (4:32); 17 Romanza (7:22); 18 Quo Vadis Domine? (4:59); Spellbound: 19 Part 1 (5:43); 20 Part 2 (4:44).

Review: Culled from recordings made by Rozsa in the 1950s and 1960s, this set includes selections that are in stereo (*Ben-*

Hur, El Cid, King of Kings) and in mono *(The Red House, Quo Vadis, Spellbound)* with the cues mercifully arranged together and not at random, as is sometimes the case in compilations. The authoritative conducting here is the key to these selections recorded in Europe in 1967 and in Hollywood in 1952, respectively.

Spellbound: The Classic Film Scores of Miklos Rozsa 🎵🎵🎵🎵🎵

1989, RCA Victor.

Album Notes: *Music:* Miklos Rozsa; The National Philharmonic Orchestra, conducted by Charles Gerhardt; *Album Producer:* George Korngold; *Engineer:* K.E. Wilkinson.

Selections: The Red House: 1 Prelude (1:30); 2 The Morgan Farm, The New Hired Hand, Swimming Scene (3:23); 3 Meg Finds The Red House (1:55); 4 Teller Shoots At Meg (4:16); 5 Pete's Death and Finale (1:19) *Ambrosian Singers*; The Thief Of Bagdad: 6 The Love Of The Princess (4:45); The Lost Weekend: 7 The Bottle, First Meeting (2:07); 8 The Mouse And The Bat, Nightmare (5:09); 9 Love Scene and Finale (2:30); The Four Feathers: 10 Sunstroke, River Journey (7:52); Double Indemnity: 11 Mrs. Dietrichson, The Conspiracy (3:18); Knights Of The Round Table: 12 Scherzo: Hawks In Flight (1:17); The Jungle Book: 13 Song Of The Jungle (3:28) *Ambrosian Singers*; Spellbound: 14 The Dream Sequence, The Mountain Lodge (5:25); Ivanhoe: 15 Overture (5:27).

Review: Another title in RCA's Classic Film Scores series, this sensational recording, produced with great flair by George Korngold, again finds Charles Gerhardt and the National Philharmonic Orchestra in superlative readings of selections from the scores of Dr. Rozsa. Mercifully avoiding *Ben-Hur, King of Kings* or even *El Cid*, the program focuses on other works, equally deserving of coverage, yet not as frequently performed. *The Red House*, in particular, is a real winner, as are the selections from *The Four Feathers, Double Indemnity, The Lost Weekend* and *Spellbound*. But the album as a whole is a wonderful, exciting presentation of some of the best music composed by Rozsa.

Miklos Rozsa: Hollywood Spectacular 🎵🎵🎵♪

1985, Bay Cities Records.

Album Notes: *Music:* Miklos Rozsa; The Royal Philharmonic Orchestra, conducted by Rainer Padberg; *Featured Musician:* Christophe Bowers-Broadbent (organ); *Album Producer:* Christopher Palmer; *Engineer:* Bob Auger.

Selections: 1 Festive Flourish (1:07); 2 Fantasy On Themes From Young Bess (16:32); King Of Kings: 3 Via Dolorosa (5:22); Ben-Hur: 4 Parade Of The Charioteers (3:47); The Story Of Three Loves: 5 Java de la Seine (2:46); Sodom And Gomorrah: 6 Triumph March and Wedding (2:39); Young Bess: 7 Danish Dance (3:08); Julius Caesar: 8 Caesar's Procession (4:32); El Cid: 9 Palace Music (2:03); King Of Kings: 10 Jugglers And Tumblers (1:03); Ben-Hur: 11 Victory Parade (3:15).

Review: This adequate collection of themes, mostly from Miklos Rozsa's Hollywood costume epics, is assembled into a delightful concerto of pomp and circumstance. The album leads off with the previously unrecorded "Festival Flourish," the album's only non-film composition, written in honor of the 1976 American Bicentennial. A 16½-minute "Fantasy on Themes from *Young Bess*" follows, which precedes an assortment of music from *King of Kings, Ben-Hur* and *El-Cid*. A personal favorite of Rozsa's, "Java de la Seine" from *The Story of Three Lovers*, is also included, making a welcome change of pace in the presentation. Christopher Palmer, who was a close personal friend of the composer, produced this album with another Rozsa admirer, Rainer Padberg conducting the Royal Philharmonic Orchestra. Unfortunately, the recording appears to make the orchestra sound surprisingly small. *Ben-Hur's* "Parade of the Charioteers" is incredibly impotent, lacking in the majesty of Rozsa's original, or later recordings that gave the work a more commanding atmosphere.

David Hirsch

The Epic Film Music of Miklos Rozsa 🎵🎵🎵🎵

1996, Silva Screen Records.

Album Notes: *Music:* Miklos Rozsa; *Orchestrations:* Nic Raine, Kevin Townend, Christopher Palmer; The City of Prague Philharmonic and The Crouch End Festival Chorus, *conducted by* Kenneth Alwyn; *Featured Soloist:* Josef Kroft (violin); *Album Producers:* David Wishart, Nic Raine; *Engineers:* John L. Timperley, Mark Ayres.

Selections: The Golden Voyage Of Sinbad: 1 Prelude/Sinbad Battles Kali/ Finale (4:53); King Of King: 2 Prelude (2:48); El Cid: 3 Overture (3:34); 4 Love Scene (4:14); 5 Sodom And Gomorrah: Overture (5:03); Quo Vadis: 6 Prelude (1:54); 7 Arabesque (5:21); 8 Romanza (6:39); 9 Ave Caesar (4:49); King Of Kings: 10 The Lord's Prayer (2:44); Beau Brummell: 11 Prelude/The King's Visit and Farewell (6:46); Ben-Hur: 12 Prelude (3:41); 13 Love Theme (2:56); 14 Parade Of The Charioteers (3:37); Madame Bovary: 16 Waltz (4:44); All the Brothers

Were Valient: 15 Main Tile/Finale (5:05);— King Of Kings: 17 Theme (orchestral version)(2:56).

Review: This superbly performed and energetic collection of Miklos Rozsa's period and sword-and-sandal epics is one of Silva's best, opening with a rousing take on the Harryhausen fantasy *The Golden Voyage of Sinbad*, and moving through the Roman Empire settings of *Ben Hur* and *Quo Vadis*, the Biblical sagas *King of Kings* and *Sodom and Gomorrah*, and the period trappings of *Beau Brummell*, *All The Brothers Were Valiant* and *Madame Bovary*, with its ingenious "madness waltz." A highlight of the album is the superb incorporation of choral sections into *King of Kings* (in its gorgeous opening and Rozsa's sublime setting of The Lord's Prayer) and *Quo Vadis*, bringing a new luster to musical cues that may have been performed on one too many Rozsa compilations of the past. Rozsa practically invented this genre, bristling with martial fanfares and sweeping romantic melodies, and this is a fitting tribute to his indelible style, with impeccable sound and performances.

Jeff Bond

Miklos Rozsa: Double Indemnity ♪♪♪♪

1997, Koch International.

Album Notes: *Music*: Miklos Rozsa; *Orchestrations*: Patrick Russ, Jon Kull; The New Zealand Symphony Orchestra, conducted by James Sedares; *Album Producer*: Michael Fine; *Engineer*: Keith Warren; *Assistant Engineer*: David Merrill.

Selections: The Lost Weekend: 1 The Weekend Begins (9:19); 2 The First Meeting/The Walk (10:21); 3 Nightmare/Finale (13:52); Double Indemnity: 4 Prelude (9:17); 5 The Conspiracy (6:47); 6 Finale (10:14); The Killers: 7 Main Title (2:10); 8 Prison Stars (5:47); 9 Exit The Killers (3:32).

Review: Far from the bombast of his epic film scores, Rozsa also wrote some powerful cues heard in psychological dramas and contemporary thrillers like *The Lost Weekend*, *Double Indemnity* and *The Killers*, heard here. The first, about a man, Ray Milland, trying to overcome his alcoholism, ends in a terrifying, nightmarish scene in which Rozsa's music, as memorable in its own way as the music Bernard Herrmann wrote for the shower scene in *Psycho*, serves as an extraordinary complement to the action.

More than any other, *Double Indemnity* may be considered the classic film noir, in which a relentless cynicism pervades the action, embodied here by Barbara Stanwyck, a Los Angeles femme fatale, trapped into a loveless marriage, who coerces an insurance salesman (Fred MacMurray) into murdering her husband in order to collect the money of his life policy.

As for *The Killers*, starring Burt Lancaster making his film debut, it deals with a former boxer hunted down and killed by two hoodlums sent after him by an underworld boss. James Sedares and the New Zealand Symphony do wonders with Rozsa's explosive cues.

Hans J. Salter (1896-

Hans J. Salter: Music for Frankenstein ♪♪♪♪

1993, Marco Polo Records.

Album Notes: *Music*: Hans J. Salter; The RTE Concert Orchestra, conducted by Andrew Penny; *Album Producer*: Chris Craker; *Engineer*: David Harries.

Selections: House Of Frankenstein: 1 Main Title (2:52); 2 Gruesome Twosome Escape (2:35); 3 Dracula Restored (1:30); 4 Rendezvous With Dracula (1:44); 5 Dracula Pursued (1:50); 6 Dracula Destroyed (1:09); 7 Dan's Love (3:39); 8 The Monstrosities (1:40); 9 Full Moon (1:24); 10 Silver Bullet (3:23); 11 Dr. Niemann Successful (1:42); 12 Larry At Peace (1:55); 13 Dr. Niemann Attacked (1:38); 14 Death Of The Unholy Two (1:22); 15 End Cast (:35); Ghost Of Frankenstein: 16 Main Title (2:24); 17 Blowing Up The Castle (2:31); 18 Freeing The Monster (2:47); 19 Frankenstein's Castle (:55); 20 Arrival At Vasario (4:49); 21 Erik's Dilemma (:45); 22 Baron Frankenstein's Dialogue (2:20); 23 The Monstr's Trial (2:34); 24 Elsa's Discovery (4:01); 25 Dr. Kettering's Death (1:56); 26 Igor's Scheme (2:22); 27 Dr. Frankenstein's Advice (1:54); 28 Searching The Castle (3:27); 29 Mob Psychology (1:21); 30 Monster Talks (1:33); 31 Death Of The Unholy Three (2:06); 32 End Cast (:44).

Review: See entry below.

Hans J. Salter/Paul Dessau: House of Frankenstein ♪♪♪♪

1995, Marco Polo Records.

Album Notes: *Music*: Hans J. Salter, Paul Dessau; The Moscow Symphony Orchestra, conducted by William T. Stromberg; *Album Producer*: Betta International; *Engineers*: Edvard Shakhnazarian, Vitaly Ivanov.

Selections: 1 Universal Signature (:16); 2 Main Title (2:17); 3 Lightning Strikes (1:47); 4 Gruesome Twosome Escape (1:50); 5 Strangulation (:30); 6 Off To Vasaria (1:18); 7 Chamber Of Horrors (:40); 8 Dracula Restored (1:30); 9 Dracula's Ring (1:28); 10 The Burgmaster Murdered (2:06); 11 Rendezvous With Dracula (2:34); 12 The World Beyond (1:29); 13 Dracula

Pursued (1:44); 14 Dracula Destroyed (1:09); 15 Gypsy Tantrums (1:47); 16 Ilonka Whipped (1:07); 17 Dan's Love (3:23); 18 The Ruins (1:37); 19 The Monstrosities (2:02); 20 Wolf Man Revived (2:13); 21 Show Me The Records (2:22); 22 Travels (:35); 23 Hunchback's Jealousy (1:51); 24 Niemann's Laboratory (1:30); 25 Liquefying Brains (1:12); 26 Niemann's Revenge (1:07); 27 The Pentagram (1:37); 28 Full Moon (1:15); 29 Silver Bullet (3:33); 30 Dr. Niemann Successful (1:24); 31 The Moon Is Full (1:18); 32 Larry At Peace (1:36); 33 Dr. Niemann Attacked (1:36); 34 Death Of The Unholy Two (1:14); 35 End Cast (:28).

Review: This delightful set of classic Universal Studios monster music was spearheaded by the release of Hans J. Salter's music for *House of Frankenstein* and *Ghost of Frankenstein,* on the 1993 album *Music for Frankenstein.* As one of Universal Studios' most prolific in-house composers, Salter churned out an extraordinarily large amount of wonderfully creepy music for the studios' monster films, adding some much needed realism to Universal's ever growing stable of ghouls. But, as was the practice of the studios at the time, several composers were assigned to work on sections of a single film, which made the task for musical historians like John Morgan all the more difficult. Nonetheless, Morgan did an amazing job reconstructing the original scores, which were lost or destroyed years ago, and the music was well performed by the RTE Concert Orchestra under the direction of Andrew Penny on the first album.

However, just two years later, Morgan and William T. Stromberg were able to return to the *House of Frankenstein* and add in more music, cues mainly by Paul Dessau, to recreate the complete 55 minute film score. Stromberg conducts the Moscow Symphony Orchestra with great flair on the second CD. Both albums are digitally recorded with detailed liner notes.

David Hirsch

See also: The Monster Music of Hans J. Salter & Frank Skinner in this section

Creature from The Black Lagoon: A Symphony of Film Music by Hans J. Salter 🎵🎵🎵♭

1994, Intrada Records.

Album Notes: *Music:* Hans J. Salter; *Album Producer:* Tony Thomas; *Engineer:* Joe Tarantino.

Selections: 1 Creature From The Black Lagoon (14:57); 2 The Black Shield Of Falworth (19:36); 3 Hitler (19:47); 4 The Incredible Shrinking Man (18:05).

Review: Hans J. Salter was the undisputed king of horror film music throughout the Forties and Fifties, supplying brash and moody musical cues for every shambling beast that emerged from Universal studios, from the Frankenstein monster to the creature from the Black Lagoon. This collection shows the composer tackling a wide range of subject matter, yet except for *The Black Shield of Falworth* Salter is still depicted as largely trapped in the horror genre. *The Creature from the Black Lagoon* is the quintessential 1950s horror opus, with its shrill, three-note brass stinger for the monster one of the most instantly recognizable and effective pieces of "scary" music ever heard in the movies. Salter's score moves seamlessly from impressionistic repose to outright chaos as the monster alternately hides in its swampy natural surroundings and launches its attacks to the tune of Salter's snarling brass trills. *The Black Shield of Falworth* is closely related to Salter's supplemental music for Jerome Moross' score to *The War Lord*, although Salter's questing English horn theme was far more traditional than Moross' efforts. *The Incredible Shrinking Man* featured a brazen, jazzy title theme that wailed out the tragic fate of its shrinking hero with some hair-raising trumpet and vocal solos, although the rest of the score was Salter at his most exciting, thrillingly scoring Grant Williams' battles with giant cats and spiders as he shrinks to the size of an atom. Ironically, movie monster expert Salter was ultimately called on to write music for the ultimate monster, *Adolf Hitler*, for a 1964 film treatment starring Richard Basehart. Salter, who actually lived through some of the Nazi regime, summons up the martial hysteria of pre-WWII Germany with plenty of bustle in some authentic-sounding marches.

Jeff Bond

Lalo Schifrin (1932-

Those Fabulous Hollywood Marches 🎵🎵🎵🎵

1990, Pro-Arte Records.

Album Notes: The San Diego Symphony Pops, conducted by Lalo Schifrin; *Album Producer:* Steve Vining; *Engineer:* Steve Vining; *Assistant Engineer:* Gary Rice.

Selections: Superman: 1 Superman March (J. Williams)(4:22); Raiders Of The Lost Ark: 2 The Raiders' March (J. Williams)(5:12); Bridge On The River Kwai: 3 Colonel Bogey March (K. Alford)(3:03); Captain From Castile: 4 Conquest (A. Newman)(3:40); The Great Escape: 5 Great Escape March (E.Bernstein)(2:12); Patton: 6 March (J. Goldsmith)(2:41); Return Of The Jedi (J. Williams): 7 Parade Of The Ewoks (3:46); 8 Imperial March (3:01); The Music Man: 9 76 Trombones (M. Willson)(1:54); What Did You Do In The War, Daddy?: 10 Swing March (H. Mancini)(2:16); 11 Statue Of Liberty March (L. Schifrin)(3:28); Apocalypse Now: 12 Ride Of The Valkyries (R. Wagner)(4:45); 13 Armed Forces Medley (3:28); The Hunt For Red October: 14 Hymn Of The Red Army (trad.) (2:12); 15 Cinerama March (M. Gould)(2:40); The Dirty Dozen: 16 Dirty Dozen March (J. Cacavas)(3:52); The Great Waldo Pepper: 17 Waldo Pepper March (H. Mancini)(2:28); Stars And Stripes Forever: The John Philip Sousa Story: 18 Liberty Bell (2:40); 19 Washington Post (2:32); 20 Manhattan Beach (2:20); 21 El Capitan (2:23); 22 Stars And Stripes Forever (3:40).

Review: See entry below.

Romancing the Film 🎬🎬🎬▷

1992, Pro-Arte Records.

Album Notes: The Rochester Pops, conducted by Lalo Schifrin; *Album Producer*: Anton Kwiatkowski; *Engineer*: Anton Kwiatkowski; *Assistant Engineers*: Paul Kwiatkowski, Gary Rice.

Selections: Gone With The Wind: 1 Tara's Theme (M. Steiner)(4:03); The Wizard Of Oz: 2 Over The Rainbow (H. Arlen/E.Y. Harburg)(3:59); Casablanca: 3 As Time Goes By (H. Hupfeld)(4:21); Around The World In Eighty Days: 4 Main Theme (V. Young)(3:13); Breakfast At Tiffany's: 5 Moon River (H. Mancini/J. Mercer) (3:33); Lawrence Of Arabia: 6 Main Theme (M. Jarre)(3:56); Doctor Zhivago: 7 Lara's Theme (M. Jarre)(6:00); Cool Hand Luke: 8 Symphonic Sketches (L. Schifrin)(6:55); The Godfather: 9 Love Theme (N. Rota)(2:47); Space Medley: 10 2001: A Space Odyssey (R. Strauss)/Star Wars (J. Williams)(9:22); Dirty Dancing: 11 (I've Had) The Time Of My Life (F. Previte/D. Markowitz/J. DeNicola) (3:36); The Little Mermaid: 12 Medley (A. Menken/H. Ashman)(6:51).

Review: Another reaction to the "Kunzel syndrome," these two CDs gave Lalo Schifrin the opportunity to step in front of fledging symphony orchestras, in this case The San Diego Symphony Pops and The Rochester Pops, whip them into shape and record some selections from the movies, in the hope of emulating the success achieved by Telarc and the Cincinnati Pops. The thematic approach suits the composer of *Mission: Impossible* to a tee, particularly in the first album in which his own flamboyance finds a suitable echo in the martial airs written by John Williams, Alfred Newman, Henry Mancini, Morton Gould, and, while-we're-at-it-why-not-add John Philip Sousa and Richard Wagner (they did compose marches, didn't they?). Of course, the title *Those Fabulous Hollywood Marches* is a trifle misleading, but after all who cares when the music is that spirited and that enjoyable.

Romancing the Film is a bit more of a hodgepodge concept, with (almost) everything thrown in to satisfy the most demanding customer, from "Tara's Theme," "Over the Rainbow" and "As Time Goes By," to "Moon River," "Love Theme from *The Godfather*," and a medley from *The Little Mermaid*. And if you think that last one is an odd choice, how about the "Space Medley" which combines together "Also Sprach Zarathustra" (from *2001: A Space Odyssey*, in case you needed to be reminded) and the theme from *Star Wars*. Romance indeed takes a flight in this one!

Gerard Schurmann

Horrors of the Black Museum: The Film Music of Gerard Schurmann 🎬🎬🎬▷

1993, Cloud Nine Records.

Album Notes: *Music*: Gerard Schurmann; *Album Producer*: David Wishart; *Engineer*: Gus Shaw.

Selections: Horrors Of The Black Museum: 1 Prelude/Streets Of London (2:05); 2 Spiked Binoculars/Investigation (1:05); 3 Headline News (1:43); 4 Tunnel Of Death/Bancroft's Demise/End Credits (3:07); Cone Of Silence: 5 Overture (4:05); The Bedford Incident: 6 Atlantic Encounters (7:46); Smugglers' Rhapsody: 7 Fantasy For Orchestra (9:02); Konga: 8 Konga Unchained and End Titles (7:55); Lost Continent: 9 Sargasso Sea/Romanza (3:57); 10 Action Stations (2:27); The Ceremony: 11 Main Theme (2:48); 12 Memories Of Tangier (2:45); 13 Freedom (2:34); The Long Arm: 14 Prelude/Safecracking/ Dawn/Investigations/Tailing The Suspect/Finale (6:45); Attack On The Iron Coast: 15 Prelude (2:11); 16 Celebration (2:20); 17 The Mission (3:42); Claretta: 18 The Drama Of Claretta (4:54); 19 Waltz (2:26); 20 Claretta's Theme and Finale (4:05).

Review: Under this strange title actually can be found some very interesting scores that are far from your run-of-the-mill. The CD, of course, gets its name from the music Gerard Schurmann, a wonderful British composer who gains at being discovered, wrote for the 1959 film of the same name, a "literate but lurid tale of dastardly murders," to quote the often humorous liner notes. American audiences, however, will probably be better acquainted with *The Bedford Incident*, a Cold War underwater drama starring Richard Widmark and Sydney Poitier; and *The Ceremony*, a "forgotten" film which stars Laurence Harvey and Sarah Miles.

Fans and collectors will probably enjoy listening to other themes composed by Schurmann, including those he wrote for *Konga,* a 1961 King Kong-clone; *The Lost Continent,* another pseudo monster movie made in 1968 and set in the Sargasso Sea; and the World War II drama, *Attack on the Iron Coast.* Source material here, from Schurmann's own archives, leaves a lot to be desired, with overall sonic quality suffering from distortion, surface noise and other problems usually associated with recordings that have been mistreated over the years. But the music, vibrantly alive and exotic, is pure delight.

John Scott (1930-

John Scott Conducts His Own Favorite Film Scores
♪♪♪♪�

1991, JOS Records.

Album Notes: The Berlin Radio Concert Orchestra, The Royal Philharmonic Orchestra, conducted by John Scott; *Music Editor*: John Strother; *Album Producer*: John Scott; *Engineers*: Werner Holke, Richard Lewsey.

Selections: The Final Countdown: 1 Main Title (4:15); The Shooting Party: 2 Main Title (3:12); North Dallas Forty: 3 Suite: a. Buddies, b. The Girl, c. The Game, d. Main Titles (8:24); England Made Me: 4 Suite: a. Main Titles, b. All On The Radio, c. Reichswehr March (9:16); People That Time Forgot: 5 March Of The Nagas (4:00); Cousteau/Amazon: 6 Cousteau/Amazon (3:36); Outback: 7 Suite: a. The Desert, b. The Trek, c. Madness, d. End Titles (7:50); Greystoke: 8 Suite: a. Child Of The Apes, b. Law Of The Jungle, c. Dancing Lesson, d. Return To The Jungle (8:50); Antony And Cleopatra: 9 Suite: a. Main Title, b. Confrontation With Pompey, c. Pretty Worm Of Nilus, d. She Shall Be Buried By Her Antony (8:53).

Review: John Scott is unquestionably the most underrated talent in film scoring today. This anthology shows off his ability to write in an astounding array of styles (which is especially impressive considering he is one of the few film composers who orchestrates his own music). Opening the album is the brassy title music from *The Final Countdown*, a soaring and triumphant piece. The pastoral mode of *The Shooting Party* is a lovely (yet bittersweet) evocation of Edwardian England. An English pastoral mood returns in *England Made Me*, which also features an original song "All on the Radio" written in a jazzy '30s style. Moving into yet another different direction is Scott's strident and propulsive "March of the Nagas" from *The People That Time Forgot*.

His exhilarating music from the TV series *Cousteau Amazon* blends orchestral grandeur with rhythm section, in a style which might be described as "epic travelogue." Scott's two undeniable masterpieces, *Antony and Cleopatra* and *Greystoke*, are saved for last, each in nine-minute suites, which depict the composer in his most grandly epic mode. *John Scott Conducts His Own Favorite Film Themes* is, simply stated, a first-rate collection.

Paul Andrew MacLean

Screen Themes ♪♪♪♪▯

1988, Varese-Sarabande.

Album Notes: The Royal Philharmonic Orchestra, conducted by John Scott; *Featured Soloists*: Cynthia Millar (ondes Marthenot), Jack Emblow (accordion), Mitch Dalton (guitar), Guy Barber (trumpet), Chris Laurence (bass), Duncan Lamont (saxophone), Harold Fisher (drums), Dave Hartley (piano); *Album Producers*: John Scott, Richard Kraft; *Engineers*: Adrian Kerridge, Martin Edwards, Henry Edwards, Steve Price.

Selections: Beetlejuice: 1 Main Title (D. Elfman) (2:30); Big: 2 Goodbye (H. Shore) (3:51); Shoot To Kill: 3 End Title (J. Scott) (2:45); Crossing Delancey: 4 Portrait Of Izzy (P. Chihara) (3:10); Cocoon: The Return: 5 Basketball Swing (J. Horner) (7:00); Coming To America: 6 King's Motorcade (N. Rodgers) (1:30); Madame Sousatzka: 7 The River (G. Gouriet) (2:10); Criminal Law: 8 The Garden Pavilion (J. Goldsmith) (3:10); Nightmare On Elm Street 4: 9 Corpus Kruger (C. Safan) (3:10); Betrayed: 10 The Way (B. Conti) (2:10); Masquerade: 11 End Title (J. Barry) (2:45); Da: 12 Theme (E. Bernstein) (3:28); Die Hard: 13 Terrorists (M. Kamen) (4:34); Milagro Beanfield War: 14 End Title (D. Grusin) (3:57); Who Framed Roger Rabbit?: 15 End Title (suite) (A. Silvestri) (11:18).

Review: Excellent mix of original soundtrack and newly recorded material by John Scott and the Royal Philharmonic Orchestra. This is a "best of" compilation of 1987-88 films, with much of the original material culled from Varese Sarabande releases like *Cocoon: The Return*, *Crossing Delancy* and *Madame Sousatzka*. The real gems, however, are Scott's outstanding recreations of the unreleased themes from Howard Shore's *Big*, John Barry's *Masquerade*, Michael Kamen's *Die Hard*, and his own *Shoot to Kill*. Scott's version of *The Milagro Bean Field War* "End Title" is actually more faithful than the recording that appears on one of composer Dave Grusin's own albums. Also included is the full eleven-minute end title suite from *Who Framed Roger Rabbit*. Only a truncated five-minute version appeared on the original soundtrack. This is a really superior produced anthology, a guide for what all others should be.

David Hirsch

Europe Goes to Hollywood
♪♪♪♪

1993, Denon Records.

Album Notes: The Royal Philharmonic Pops Orchestra, conducted by John Scott; *Arranger*: Mike Townend; *Album Producers*: Ian Maclay, Mike Townend; *Engineer*: Gary Thomas.

Selections: The Adventures Of Robin Hood (E.W. Korngold): 1 Old England (2:24); 2 Robin Hood And His Merry Men (4:26); 3 Love Theme (7:14); 4 The Fight, Victory and Epilogue (4:09); The Alamo (D. Tiomkin): 5 The Green Leaves Of Summer (4:03); The Godfather (N. Rota): 6 Love Theme (2:54); Casablanca (M. Steiner): 7 Suite (9:03); Ben Hur (M. Rozsa): 8 Prelude (4:03); 9 Parade Of The Charioteers (3:44); Gone With The Wind (M. Steiner): 10 Tara's Theme (3:54); Rebecca (F. Waxman): 11 Suite (7:37); Citizen Kane (B. Herrmann): 12 Prelude (2:24); 13 Finale (2:47).

Review: John Scott conducts the Royal Philharmonic Pops Orchestra in this well recorded and performed tribute to Hollywood's classic European composers. Erich Wolfgang Korngold's *The Adventures of Robin Hood* gets the star treatment in a lively 18-minute suite that leads off the album, faithfully capturing the essence of the composer's original film score. Other suites include Max Steiner's *Casablanca*, Miklos Rozsa's *Ben-Hur* (with a really laudable version of "Parade of the Charioteers") and Franz Waxman's enchanting *Rebecca*. Oddly, American born Bernard Herrmann is included (possibly perhaps because he lived his last years in England?) with a suite from *Citizen Kane* that captures some of the original's brooding power. Scott's compilation albums are always superior in sound and performance. thanks in part to his more than evident love of film music.

David Hirsch

Raymond Scott (1908-

The Music of Raymond Scott: Reckless Nights and Turkish Twilights

1992, Columbia Records.

Album Notes: *Music*: Raymond Scott; The Raymond Scott Quintette, and Raymond Scott and His New Orchestra, con-

ducted by Raymond Scott; *Album Producer*: Irwin Chusid; *Engineer*: Debra Parkinson.

Selections: 1 Powerhouse (2:57); 2 The Toy Trumpet (3:00); 3 Tobacco Auctioneer (2:36); 4 New Year's Eve In A Haunted House (2:22); 5 Manhattan Minuet (2:40); 6 Dinner Music For A Pack Of Hungry Cannibal (2:56); 7 Reckless Night On Board An Ocean Liner (3:06); 8 Moment Musical (2:18); 9 Twilight In Turkey (2:43); 10 The Penguin (2:38); 11 Oil Gusher (2:39); 12 In An 18th Century Drawing Room (2:40); 13 The Girl At The Typewriter (3:02); 14 Siberian Sleighride (2:52); 15 At An Arabian House Party (3:21); 16 Boy Scout In Switzerland (2:51); 17 Bumpy Weather Over Newark (2:57); 18 Minuet In Jazz (2:51); 19 War Dance For Wooden Indians (2:31); 20 The Quintet Plays Carmen (2:40); 21 Huckleberry Duck (2:52); 22 Peter Tambourine (2:55).

Review: See entry below.

The Raymond Scott Project volume one: Powerhouse
♪♪♪♪

1991, Stash Records.

Album Notes: *Music*: Raymond Scott; *Album Producers*: Irwin Chusid, Will Friedwald; *Engineers*: Steve Lasker, Wally Herman.

Selections: 1 Powerhouse (3:18); 2 Girl At The Typewriter (2:52); 3 Dinner Music For A Pack Of Hungry Cannibals (3:45); 4 Boy Scout In Switzerland (3:34); 5 New Year's Eve In A Haunted House (2:24); 6 War Dance For Wooden Indians (2:17); 7 In An 18th Century Drawing Room (3:01); 8 Twilight In Turkey (2:20); 9 Devil Drums (3:39); 10 Sleepwalker (2:44); 11 Oil Gusher (2:33); 12 Steeplechase (2:29); 13 Reckless Night On Board An Ocean Liner (3:31); 14 Celebration On The Planet Mars (2:41); 15 The Penguin (2:41); 16 Bumpy Weather Over Newark (2:38); 17 Serenade To A Lonesome Railroad Station (2:56); 18 Siberian Sleighride (2:47); 19 The Tobacco Auctioneer (2:37); 20 Moment Whimsical (2:13); 21 The Toy Trumpet (2:39); 22 Christmas Night In Harlem (2:25); 23 Confusion Among A Fleet Of Taxicabs Upon Meeting With A Fare (2:56); 24 Peter Tambourine (2:35).

Review: With a few minor exceptions, both sets pretty much cover the same selections and, in fact, were essentially produced by the same individuals. Since the source material is also the same, the only thing that might attract the casual listener to the Stash release is the attractive cartoonish cover, bolder graphics, and the fact it has 24 selections as opposed to 22 for the Columbia set. Whichever you pick, your perception of music will be hopelessly warped after you have listened to Raymond Scott's zany inventions. Once you have enjoyed it, you might also want to check out the works of Scott Bradley for the cartoons of Tex Avery at M-G-M, or the two *Carl Stalling Projects* on Warner Bros.

Richard M. Sherman & Robert B. Sherman

Richard M. Sherman & Robert B. Sherman ♫♫♫♫ᵛ

1992, Walt Disney Records.

Album Notes: *Music*: Richard M. Sherman, Robert B. Sherman; *Lyrics*: Richard M. Sherman, Robert B. Sherman; *Compilation Producers*: Michael Leon, Randy Thornton; *Engineer*: Ted Hall.

Selections: 1 Supercalifragilisticexpialidocious (2:00) *Julie Andrews, Dick Van Dyke*; 2 It's A Small World (After All)(1:52) Chorus; 3 Winnie The Pooh (2:22) Chorus; 4 I Wan'na Be Like You (4:01) *Louis Prima, Phil Harris*; 5 A Spoonful Of Sugar (4:06) *Julie Andrews*; 6 The Tiki, Tiki, Tiki Room (2:38) *Wally Boag, Fulton Burley, Thurl Ravenscroft*; 7 Chim Chim Cher-ee (2:45) *Julie Andrews, Dick Van Dyke*; 8 Tall Paul (session) (:19); 9 Tall Paul (1:33) *Annette Funicello*; 10 Let's Get Together (1:28) *Hayley Mills*; 11 The Monkey's Uncle (2:32) *Annette Funicello, The Beach Boys*; 12 That Darn Cat (2:44); 13 Ten Feet Off The Ground (2:44) *Buddy Ebsen, Lesley Ann Warren, Janet Blair, Kurt Russell, Bobby Riha, Jon Walmsley, Smitty Wordes, Heidi Rook, Debbie Smith, Pamelyn Ferdin*; 14 The Aristocats (2:17) *Maurice Chevalier*; 15 Fortuosity (2:21) *Tommy Steele*; 16 The Age Of Not Believing (3:15) *Angela Lansbury*; 17 Are We Dancing? (3:24) *John Davidson, Lesley Ann Warren*; 18 Feed The Birds (Tuppence A Bag)(3:49) *Julie Andrews*; 19 On The Front Porch (3:22) *Burl Ives*; 20 The Beautiful Briny (2:38) *David Tomlinson, Angela Lansbury*; 21 Heffalumps And Woozles (2:03) Chorus; 22 The Ugly Bug Ball (3:01) *Burl Ives*; 23 Makin' Memories (3:25) Chorus; 24 Magic Journeys (3:32) Chorus; 25 There's A Great Big Beautiful Tomorrow (2:09); 26 Walt Disney And The Sherman Brothers Sing (:14).

Review: This attractive compilation brings together some of the best selections from the various scores the Sherman brothers, Richard M. And Robert B., wrote for the films of Walt Disney, including *Mary Poppins, Winnie the Pooh, The Jungle Book, Bedknobs and Broomsticks, The Parent Trap, The One and Only Genuine Original Family Band, The Aristocats, The Happiest Millionaire,* and *Summer Magic.* There's a lot to be enjoyed here, with many familiar tunes that have served as the

soundtrack to our lives since the 1960s, with glorious performances by Julie Andrews, Angela Lansbury, Lesley Ann Warren, Tommy Steele, Burl Ives, Louis Prima, and (believe it or not!) The Beach Boys. All told, a great collection.

Alan Silvestri (1950-

Voyages: The Film Music Journeys ♫♫♫♫ᵛ

1995, Varese-Sarabande.

Album Notes: *Music*: Alan Silvestri; Orchestras conducted by Alan Silvestri, Joel McNeely, John Scott; *Album Producers*: Robert Townson, Richard Kraft.

Selections: 1 Silver Pictures Logo (:19); 2 Forrest Gump (9:20); 3 Father Of The Bride (2:27); 4 Back To The Future, Part III (4:01); 5 Ricochet (2:12); 6 The Quick And The Dead (3:36); 7 Richie Rich (5:59); 8 Romancing The Stone (5:18); 9 Soapdish (3:52); 10 Who Framed Roger Rabbit (11:19); 11 The Abyss (3:12); 12 Clan Of The Cave Bear (2:57); 13 Death Becomes Her (5:46); 14 Predator 2 (8:46).

Review: This exhilarating set enables Alan Silvestri, a composer with a chameleon personality, to reveal some of his many facets in a compilation that covers several of his most famous creations, including the themes from *Forrest Gump, Back to the Future, Romancing the Stone, The Abyss,* and *Who Framed Roger Rabbit.* One of the brilliant exponents of the new generation in film music, Silvestri has a recognizably easy style that he has used to great effect in some of the most visible films of the past dozen years. The set, intelligently put together and well presented, is a wonderful excursion in some of his best works, with the two long suites from *Forrest Gump,* conducted by Joel McNeely, and *Roger Rabbit,* conducted by John Scott, particularly deserving of warm applause. Once you've put it on your player, you won't want to give up this glib and enjoyable set.

Stephen Sondheim

Sondheim: A Musical Tribute ♫♫♫♫♫

1993, RCA Victor; from the concert presentation *Sondheim: A Musical Tribute,* March 11, 1973.

Album Notes: *Music*: Stephen Sondheim; *Lyrics*: Stephen Sondheim; *Music Coordination and Special Arrangements*: Jonathan Tunick; *Musical Direction*: Paul Gemignani; *Cast*: George Lee Andrews, Larry Blyden, Susan Browning, Len Cariou, Jack Cassidy,

Dorothy Collins, Steve Elmore, Harvey Evans, Hermione Gingold, Laurence Guittard, Pamela Hall, Ron Holgate, Beth Howland, Glynis Johns, Justine Johnston, Larry Kert, Mark Lambert, Angela Lansbury, Victoria Mallory, Mary McCarty, Donna McKechnie, John McMartin, Pamela Myers, Anthony Perkins, Kurt Peterson, Alice Playten, Teri Ralston, Chita Rivera, Marti Rolph, Virginia Sandifur, Ethel Shutta, Alexis Smith, Tony Stevens, Nancy Walker; *Album Producer*: Hal Halverstadt; *Engineer*: Lee Herschberg; *CD Producer*: Craig Zadan; *Engineer*: Dennis Ferrante.

Selections: CD 1: 1 Overture (11:10) Orchestra; 2 Do I Hear A Waltz? (R. Rodgers/S. Sondheim)(2:36) *Dorothy Collins*; 3 If Mama Was Married (J. Styne/ S. Sondheim)(3:02) *Alice Playten, Virginia Sandifur*; 4 America (L. Bernstein/S. Sondheim)(3:20) *Chita Rivera, Pamela Myers*; 5 One More Kiss (2:49) *Justine Johnson, Victoria Mallory*; 6 Broadway Baby (2:41) *Ethel Shutta*; 7 You Could Drive A Person Crazy (2:53) *Donna McKechnie, Pamela Myers, Susan Browning*; 8 Take Me To The World (2:28) *Marti Rolph*; 9 I Remember (3:29) *Victoria Mallory*; 10 Silly People (2:50) *George Lee Andrews*; 11 Two Fairy Tales (3:24) *Victoria Mallory, Mark Lambert*; 12 Love Is In The Air (1:39) *Larry Blyden, Susan Browning*; 13 Your Eyes Are Blue (3:40) *Harvey Evans, Pamela Hall*; 14 Pleasant Little Kingdom (2:38) *Dorothy Collins, John McMartin*; 15 Too Many Mornings (4:40) *Dorothy Collins, John McMartin*.

CD 2: 1 Entr'acte (2:48) Orchestra; 2 Me And My Town (4:34) *Angela Lansbury, Harvey Evans, Tony Stevens*; 3 The Little Things You Do Together (2:49) *Mary McCarty*; 4 Getting Married Today (4:25) *Beth Howland, Teri Ralston, Steve Elmore*; 5 Buddy's Blues (3:14) *Larry Blyden, Donna McKechnie, Chita Rivera*; 6 So Many People (4:42) *Susan Browning, Jack Cassidy*; 7 Another Hundred People (2:50) *Pamela Myers*; 8 Happily Ever After (1:02) *Larry Kert*; 9 Being Alive (2:10) *Larry Kert*; 10 We're Gonna Be All Right (R. Rodgers/S. Sondheim)(4:43) *Laurence Guittard, Teri Ralston*; 11 Beautiful Girls (2:36) *Ron Holgate*; 12 I'm Still Here (5:13) *Nancy Walker*; 13 A Parade In Town (2:08) *Angela Lansbury*; 14 Could I Leave You? (3:11) *Alexis Smith*; 15 Losing My Mind (3:54) *Dorothy Collins*; 16 Anyone Can Whistle (1:45) *Stephen Sondheim*; 17 Side By Side (:40) Company.

Review: See entry below.

Sondheim: Putting It Together ♫♫♫♫

1993, RCA Victor; from the Manhattan Theatre Club presentation *Sondheim: Putting It Together*, 1993.

Album Notes: *Music*: Stepehn Sondheim; *Lyrics*: Stephen Sondheim; *Cast*: Julie Andrews, Stephen Collins, Christopher Durang, Michael Rupert, Rachel York; *Musical Direction*: Scott Frankel; *Album Producer*: Jay David Saks; *Engineers*: James Nichols, Ken Hahn; *Assistant Engineers*: Sandy Palmer, Brian Vibberts.

Selections: CD 1: 1 Invocation and Instructions To The Audience (2:42) *Christopher Durang*; 2 Putting It Together (3:34) *Stephen Collins, Rachel York, Michael Rupert, Julie Andrews, Christopher Durang, Scott Frankel*; 3 Rich And Happy #1 (3:39) *Stephen Collins, Julie Andrews, Michael Rupert, Christopher Durang, Rachel York*; 4 Merrily We Roll Along/Lovely (2:53) *Christopher Durang, Rachel York*; 5 Everybody Ought To Have A Maid (3:06) *Stephen Collins, Christopher Durang, Michael Rupert*; 6 Sequence: Sooner Or Later/I'm Calm/Impossible/Ah, But Underneath (4:23) *Julie Andrews, Stephen Collins, Michael Rupert, Rachel York, Christopher Durang*; 7 Hello, Little Girl (2:42) *Stephen Collins, Rachel York*; 8 My Husband The Pig/Every Day A Little Death (3:43) *Julie Andrews, Rachel York*; 9 Merrily We Roll Along #2/Have I Got A Girl For You (2:04) *Christopher Durang, Stephen Collins, Michael Rupert*; 10 Pretty Women (1:58) *Michael Rupert, Stephen Collins*; 11 Now (2:46) *Christopher Durang, Michael Rupert*; 12 Bang! (3:20) *Michael Rupert, Rachel York*; 13 Country House (3:35) *Julie Andrews, Stephen Collins*; 14 Merrily We Roll Along #3/Could I Leave You? (4:25) *Christopher Durang, Julie Andrews*.

CD 2: 1 Back In Business (2:29) Company; 2 Rich And Happy #2 (1:10) *Stephen Collins, Michael Rupert, Rachel York, Julie Andrews*; 3 Night Waltzes: Love Takes Time/Remember?/In Praise Of Women/Perpetual Anticipation/The Sun Won't Set (5:36) *Christopher Durang, Michael Rupert, Rachel York, Julie Andrews, Stephen Collins*; 4 Game Sequence #1: What Would We Do Without You?/Gun Song (5:00) *Julie Andrews, Stephen Collins, Rachel York, Michael Rupert, Christopher Durang*; 5 Game Sequence #2: A Little Priest (1:39) *Julie Andrews, Stephen Collins, Rachel York, Michael Rupert, Christopher Durang*; 6 The Miller's Son (4:36) *Rachel York*; 7 Live Alone And Like It (1:36) *Michael Rupert*; 8 Sorry-Grateful (3:47) *Stephen Collins*; 9 Sweet Polly Plunkett (:40) *Julie Andrews*; 10 I Could Drive A Person Crazy (2:33) *Christopher Durang*; 11 Marry Me A Little (3:53) *Michael Rupert*; 12 Getting Married Today (4:46) *Julie Andrews*; 13 Merrily We Roll Along #4/Being Alive (3:05) *Christopher Durang, Stephen Collins, Michael Rupert, Julie Andrews, Rachel York*; 14 Like It Was (2:42) *Julie Andrews*; 15 Old Friends/Merrily We Roll Along #5 (2:32) *Stephen Collins*.

Review: See entry below.

Sondheim: A Celebration at Carnegie Hall ✒✒✒✒

1993, RCA Victor; from the concert presentation *Sondheim: A Celebration at Carnegie Hall*, June 10, 1992.

Album Notes: *Music:* Stephen Sondheim; *Lyrics:* Stephen Sondheim; *Orchestrations:* Jonathan Tunick, Don Sebesky, Michael Starobin, Artie Schroeck; *Vocal Arrangements:* Peter Howard, David Loud; The American Theatre Orchestra, conducted by Paul Gemignani; *Cast:* Kevin Anderson, George Lee Andrews, Ron Baker, BETTY (Amy Ziff, Bitzi Ziff, Alyson Palmer), Harolyn Blackwell, Peter Blanchet, Boys Choir Of Harlem, Betty Buckley, Patrick Cassidy, Glenn Close, Daisy Egan, Victor Garber, Jerry Hadley, Bill Irwin, Mark Jacoby, Michael Jeter, Madeline Kahn, Beverly Lambert, Jeanne Lehman, Dorothy Loudon, Patti LuPone, Carol Meyer, Liza Minnelli, Maureen Moore, Richard Muenz, James Naughton, Carolann Oage, Eugene Perry, Herbert Perry, Bernadette Peters, Billy Stritch, Susan Terry, Bronwyn Thomas, The Tonics (Cortes Alexander, Brian Green, Gene Reed, Lindy Robbins), Blythe Walker, Karen Ziemba; *Album Producer:* Jay Davis Saks; *Engineers:* Bill King, David Hewitt, Ken Hahn; *Assistant Engineers:* Melvin Becker, Paul Cohen, Louise de la Fuente, Phil Gitomer, Andy Strauber.

Selections: CD 1: 1 Symphonic Sondheim: Sweeney Todd (7:30) *Jerry Hadley, Eugene Perry, Herbert Perry*; 2 Evening Introduction (2:20) *Bill Irwin*; 3 Loveland/Getting Married Today (5:27) *Mark Jacoby, Madeline Kahn, Jeanne Lehman*; 4 Waiting For The Girls Upstairs/Love I Hear/Live Alone And Like It (5:53) *George Lee Andrews, Michael Jeter, James Naghton, Michael Jeter, James Naughton*; 5 Somoeone Is Waiting/Symphonic Sondheim: Barcelona (5:17) *Richard Muenz*; 6 Being Alive (2:49) *Patti LuPone*; 7 Good Thing Going (4:18) *The Tonics*; 8 Losing My Mind/You Could Drive A Person Crazy (6:08) *Dorothy Loudon*; 9 Our Time/Children Will Listen (5:12) *Betty Buckley*; 10 Anyone Can Whistle (3:45) *Billy Stritch*; 11 Water Under The Bridge (5:17) *Liza Minnelli, Billy Stritch*; 12 Back In Business (5:38) *Liza Minnelli, Billy Stritch*.

CD 2: 1 Symphonic Sondheim: Comedy Tonight (2:47) *Bill Irwin*; 2 Sooner Or Later (4:23) *Karen Ziemba*; 3 Pretty Lady (2:09) *Mark Jacoby, Eugene Perry, Herbert Perry*; 4 Green Finch And Linnet Bird (3:05) *Harolyn Blackwell*; 5 The Ballad Of Booth (7:24) *Patrick Cassidy, Victor Garber*; 6 Broadway Baby (3:20) *Daisy Egan*; 7 I Never Do Anything Twice (5:41) BETTY; 8 With So Little To Be Sure Of (4:34) *Jerry Hadley, Carolann Page*; 9 Not A Day Goes By (3:52) *Bernadette Peters*; 10 Remember?/A Weekend In The Country (7:20) *Ron Baker, Peter Blanchet, Carol Meyer, Bronwyn Thomas, Blythe Walker, Kevin Ander-son, George Lee Andrews, Mark Jacoby, Beverly Lambert, Maureen Moore, Susan Terry*; 11 Send In The Clowns (4:14) *Glenn Close*; 12 Old Friends (2:26) *Liza Minnelli*; 13 Sunday (4:11) *Bernadette Peters*.

Review: See entry below.

A Collector's Sondheim ✒✒✒✒

1985, RCA Victor.

Album Notes: *Music:* Stephen Sondheim; *Lyrics:* Stephen Sondheim; *Musical Direction:* Tim Higgs, Stuart Pedlar, Thomas Fay, E. Martin Perry, Herbert Green, Carlo Savina, Ray Cook, Harold Hastings, Stephen Sondheim, Paul Gemignani, Mitch Farber; *Original Producers:* Goddard Lieberson, Jonathan Tunick, Bob Hathaway, Thomas Z. Shepard; *Compilation Album Producer:* Thomas Z. Shepard.

Selections: CD 1 (1954-1971): A Funny Thing Happened On The Way To The Forum: 1 Comedy Tonight/Love Is In The Air (4:04) *Millicent Martin, Julia McKenzie, David Kerman*; 2 Pretty Little Picture (2:55) *Bob Gunton, Liz Callaway, Steven Jacob*; 3 The House Of Marcus Lycus (4:57) *George Hearn, Bob Gunton*; 4 There's Something About A War (4:15) *Cris Groenendaal*; Saturday Night: 5 So Many People (2:57) *Suzanne Henry, Craig Lucas*; The Last Resorts: 6 Pour Le Sport (3:24) *Suzanne Henry, Craig Lucas*; Saturday Night: 7 What More Do I Need? (2:56) *Liz Callaway*; A Funny Thing Happened On The Way To The Forum: 8 Invocation and Instructions To The Audience (4:52) *Bob Gunton*; Evening Primrose: 9 I Remember (3:07) *David Kerman*; Anyone Can Whistle: 10 There Won't Be Trumpets (2:37) *Lee Remick*; 11 With So Little To Be Sure Of (4:04) *George Hearn, Victoria Mallory*; 12 Marry Me A Little (3:04) *Suzanne Henry*; 13 Happily Ever After (3:47) *Craig Lucas*; 14 Being Alive (4:30) *Judy Kaye*; Follies: 15 Beautiful Girls/Ah, Paree!/Buddy's Blues (4:06) *David Kernan, David Kernan, Millicent Martin, Julia McKenzie*; 16 Losing My Mind (3:50) *Julia McKenzie*; 17 All Things Bright And Beautiful (4:15) *Craig Lucas, Suzanne Henry*; 18 Uptown, Downtown (2:51) *Craig Lucas*; 19 Too Many Mornings (4:40) *David Kernan, Julia McKenzie*.

CD 2 (1971-1973): Follies: 1 You're Gonna Love Tomorrow/Love Will See Us Through (5:00) *Cris Groenendaal, Judy Kaye, Steven Jacob, Liz Callaway*; 2 I'm Still Here (4:57) *Millicent Martin*; 3 Who Could Be Blue?/Little White House (2:11) *Craig Lucas, Suzanne Henry*; 4 It Wasn't Meant To Happen (3:27) *Craig Lucas, Suzanne Henry*; 5 Can That Boy Foxtrot! (3:55) *Suzanne Henry*; 6 Broadway Baby (3:26) *Julia McKenzie*; 7 Could I Leave You? (3:04) *David Kernan*; Stavisky: 8 Theme (2:08) Orchestra; 9 Auto Show (1:28) Orchestra; 10 Salon At The Claridge #2

(2:11) Orchestra; A Little Night Music: 11 Overture/Night Waltz (3:48) *John J. Moore, Chris Melville, Liz Robertson, David Bexon, Jacquey Chappell;* 12 Two Fairy Tales (3:01) *Suzanne Henry, Craig Lucas;* 13 The Glamorous Life (3:58) *Christine McKenna, Jean Simmons, John J. Moore, Chris Melville, Liz Robertson, David Bexon, Jacquey Chappell, Hermione Gingold;* 14 The Glamorous Life (4:53) *Elaine Tomkinson;* 15 Bang! (3:35) *Craig Lucas, Suzanne Henry;* 16 In Praise Of Women (3:02) *David Kernan;* 17 A Weekend In The Country (6:22) *Diane Langton, Veronica Page, Joss Ackland, Maria Aitken, David Kernan, Terry Mitchell;* 18 Liaisons (5:02) *Hermione Gingold;* 19 The Miller's Son (4:28) *Diane Langton.*

CD 3 (1973-1984): A Little Night Music: 1 Night Waltz II (1:42) *Teri Ralston, Gene Varrone, Benjamin Rayson, Beth Fowler, Barbara Lang;* 2 Send In The Clowns (2:56) *Angela Lansbury;* The Frogs: 3 Fear No More (2:20) *George Hearn;* Pacific Overtures: 4 Someone In A Tree (7:17) *James Dybas, Mako, Gedde Watanabe, Mark Hsu Syers;* 5 Please Hello (9:10) *Alvin Ing, Yuki Shimoda, Ernest Harada, Mako, Patrick Kinser-Lau, Mark Hsu Syers, James Dybas;* The Seven Percent Solution: 6 I Never Do Antyhing Twice (5:55) *Millicent Martin;* Sweeney Todd: 7 Pretty Women (4:36) *Len Carious, Edmund Lyndeck, Victor Garber;* 8 Epiphany (3:19) *Len Cariou, Angela Lansbury;* 9 A Little Priest (7:14) *Angela Lansbury, Len Carious;* 10 Disco: The Ballad Of Sweeney Todd (4:09) *Gordon Grody;* Merrily We Roll Along: 11 Not A Day Goes By (2:33) *Victoria Mallory;* 12 It's A Hit! (4:32) *Jason Alexander, Jim Walton, Ann Morrison, Lonny Price;* 13 Our Time (4:18) *Jim Walton, Lonny Price, Ann Morrison;* Sunday In The Park With George: 14 Children And Art (4:50) *Bernadette Peters, Mandy Patinkin;* 15 Move On (3:38) *Bernadette Peters, Mandy Patinkin;* Merrily We Roll Along: 16 Old Friends (2:40) *Stephen Sondheim, Angela Lansbury.*

Review: Certainly the most important Broadway composer of the past 25 years, Stephen Sondheim has been sung, performed, interpreted and lionized by a vast number of performers, some of whom have chosen the route of a solo tribute to his creativity, others who have preferred to appear in special concert versions or studio performances with others who add their own renditions of his songs to the vast body of works that already exists.

The four compilations listed above are all significant for one reason or another, and can hardly be singled out for special merit as all four are meritorious in their own specific ways. While they all essentially cover the same territory, with minor variances, what is of primary interest here is the various performers involved. In the first 2-CD set, the result of a concert presentation that took place at the Shubert Theatre on

Broadway on March 11, 1973, they include Len Cariou, Glynis Johns and Hermione Gingold, who appeared in *A Little Night Music;* Ethel Shutta, John McMartin, Dorothy Collins and Alexis Smith, who starred in *Follies;* Larry Kert, Victoria Mallory and Donna McKechnie, who were in *Company;* and Angela Lansbury, who starred in *Anyone Can Whistle;* along with many others, including Chita Rivera, Nancy Walker, Anthony Perkins, and Jack Cassidy.

Putting It Together starred Julie Andrews who, even though she never appeared in a Sondheim musical, was the name above the title in this limited engagement at the Manhattan Theatre Club which played from March 2 to May 23, 1993. Stephen Collins, Christopher Durang, Michael Rupert and Rachel York also starred, in this intimate production that focused on the songs as much as it did on the actual performances.

As its name indicates, *Sondheim: A Celebration at Carnegie Hall* was a special tribute recorded live at the famed hall on June 10, 1992. Here again, the bill is quite extraordinary, with Glenn Close, Madeline Kahn, Dorothy Loudon, Patti LuPone, Liza Minnelli, and Bernadette Peters among the luminaries who appeared on stage to sing a song of Sondheim.

Finally, *A Collector's Sondheim* is a collection of tunes, some from original Broadway and London cast album recordings, others from concert performances, that were put together by record producer Thomas Z. Shepard as a tribute to a composer whose most important shows (*Company, Sweeney Todd, Pacific Overtures, Follies in Concert, A Little Night Music, Merrily We Roll Along, Sunday in the Park With George*) he had personally recorded. This 3-CD set is essential for anyone interested in the works of Sondheim, as it covers a lot of ground not touched upon by the other compilations.

Ultimately, it may seem somewhat redundant to own everything that has ever been released by or about Sondheim. However, in view of the fact that no other composer has influenced the Broadway musical to such an extent in recent years, and also given the fact that Sondheim is constantly renewing himself and his approach to the genre, no collection could be complete without at least one and possibly all of the above recordings. In truth, Sondheim is an acquired taste, an individual talent who requires a lot from those who follow him wherever his creative fancy wants to take them, but who never ceases to amaze, interest, and fascinate because what he does is so unique and so incredibly distinctive. No words can appropriately describe what he does, and does so well. Listening to these various recordings, however, gives a glimpse into his creative process, and as a result they are all highly recommended.

Carl Stalling (1888-1974)

The Carl Stalling Project
♪♪♪♪ˮ

1990, Warner Bros. Records.

Album Notes: *Music*: Carl Stalling; The Warner Bros. Studio Orchestra, conducted by Carl Stalling; *Album Producer*: Hal Willner; *Engineers*: Bob Ludwig (mastering), John Purcell (editing), Pam Bartella (mixing).

Selections: 1 Putty Tat Trouble, Part 6 (1:20); 2 Hillbilly Hare (4:22); 3 Early WB Scores: The Depression Era (1936-1941)(6:03); 4 The Good Egg (4:24); 5 Various Cues From Bugs Bunny Films (1943-1956)(5:10); 6 There They Go Go Go (5:24); 7 Stalling Self-Parody: Music From Porky's Preview (5:26); 8 Anxiety Montage (1952-1955)(6:11); 9 Stalling: The War Years (1942-1946)(3:50); 10 Medley: Dinner Music For A Pack Of Hungry Cannibals (1941-1950)(5:00); 11 Carl Stalling With Milt Franklyn In Session (7:15); 12 Speedy Gonzalez/Meets Two Crows From Tacos (5:34); 13 Powerhouse And Other Cuts From The Early '50s (6:16); 14 Porky In Wackyland/Dough For The Do Do (5:44); 15 To Itch His Own (5:54).

Review: See entry below.

The Carl Stalling Project, vol. 2 ♪♪♪♪ˮ

1995, Warner Bros. Records.

Album Notes: *Music*: Carl Stalling; The Warner Bros. Studio Orchestra, conducted by Carl Stalling; *Album Producers*: Greg Ford, Hal Willner; *Engineer*: Scott Hull (mixing, editing).

Selections: 1 Zoom And Bored (6:06); 2 Stage Fright (4:07); 3 The High And The Flighty (5:36); 4 Bad Swiss Band (:36); 5 Marching Pink Elephants (1:45); 6 The Slap Hoppy Mouse (6:31); 7 Orchestra Gag (:44); 8 Variation On Grandfather's Clock (:11); 9 Variation On Chinatown My Chinatown (J. Schwartz/W. Jerome)(:09); 10 Variation On Lucky Day (B.G. DeSylva/L. Brown/R. Henderson)(:27); 11 Wind-Up Doll (:45); 12 Guided Muscle (5:53); 13 Fall And Splat—SFX (:02); 14 Ghost Wanted (3:55); 15 The Unexpected Pest (6:21); 16 Drunk La Cucaracha (3:13); 17 Flea-ridden Sheep Dog (:24); 18 Golf Cue (:25); 19 Barbary Coast Bunny (6:21); 20 Satan's Waitin' (2:17); 21 Rubber Dog (:55); 22 Puppy's Puppy (5:08); 23 Variations On La Danza (1:28); 24 Variations On Johann Strauss (1:32); 25 Kangaroo—SFX (:03); 26 Mouse-taken Identity (6:03); 27 Variations On Mexican Hat Dance (3:05); 28 Frazzled Coyote (1:54).

Review: This way overdue set of recordings does justice to one of the great, unsung musical geniuses of the 20th century. For decades composer Carl Stalling slaved away in the cultural ghetto of cartoon music, a despised genre that nevertheless afforded Stalling the opportunity to write some of the most imaginative, kinetically and rhythmically unpredictable and hysterically funny music ever heard. Adapting everything from classical repertoire melodies and arrangements to popular songs of the period (with a special emphasis on the percolating compositions of American composer Raymond Scott), Stalling wrote an ongoing, bitingly witty musical commentary on what were already some pretty hilarious cartoons and in the process created music that has wormed its way into the psyches of millions of people from childhood on. Both of these albums feature generous suites of music from numerous Warner Brothers cartoons, ranging from the 1930s to the late 1950s, with generally excellent sound quality and occasional bursts of wild cartoon sound effects and vocal performances. It's a weirdly nostalgic, giggle-inducing and subversive musical journey that will not be to all tastes, but for lovers of Bugs Bunny and Daffy Duck, or for fans of avant garde musical composition, these albums are invaluable treasures.

Jeff Bond

Ronald Stein (1930-1988)

Not of This Earth!: The Film Music of Ronald Stein ♪♪♪

1995, Varese-Sarabande.

Album Notes: *Music*: Ronald Stein; *Album Producer*: Bruce Kimmel; *Engineer*: Joe Gastwirt.

Selections: Attack Of The 50 Ft. Woman: 1 Main Title (1:13); 2 50 Ft. Rock (& Roll)(1:58); 3 Nancy And The Donkey (1:14); 4 Juke Box Jive (2:15); 5 Giant Footprint (2:05); 6 The Satellite/The 50 Ft. Woman/Giant Steps (:45); 7 Nancy Got Her Man/Big Finish (2:09); The Terror: 8 Prologue/The Secret Passage (1:31); 9 Main Title (1:53); 10 Meet Helaine (2:55); 11 Light In The Bedroom (1:09); 12 Helaine Melts/The End (1:32); Dementia 13: 13 Main Title (2:22); 14 The Ceremony (2:08); 15 Floating Doll (1:52); 16 He Lost His Head (:46); 17 Dementia Ultimo (1:36); Not Of This Earth!: 18 Main Title (1:22); 19 Flight From Fear (3:15); 20 The Eyes Have It (1:58); 21 Rabid Blood (2:36); 22 End Note (:55); Attack Of The Crab Monsters: 23 Main Title/Is It Fish? (1:27); 24 Crab Meet (2:53); 25 Crab Clause (2:43); 26 Finale/Cracked Crab (:13); The Devil's Partner: 27 Main Title (1:44); 28 Scared Papers (2:50); 29 Nick's Redemption/Finale

"Even now, the way I get around my lack of training and technique is by drawing on my having grown up in a world of movies. Very often, when I'm not sure how to approach something, I say, 'How would I approach this if I were 13 years old, sitting in a theater, and watching the movie?' In other words, what would make me come alive?"

Danny Elfman
(Fanfare, 1989)

(1:21); Spider Baby (a.k.a. Cannibal Orgy): 30 Main Title (1:29); 31 Spider Orgy (1:45); 32 Spider Stravinsky (:58); 33 Spider! Spider! (2:35); 34 Rehearsing With Ron And Lon (:50); 35 Song From Spider Baby (2:16) *Lon Chaney Jr.*

Review: Ronald Stein had the dubious honor of scoring some of the lousiest movies ever to be unleashed from the stable of producer Roger Corman, including *Attack of the 50 Ft. Woman, Not of This Earth!* and *Attack of the Crab Monsters* (and probably half a dozen other attacks that have long been forgotten). Stein always approached his task seriously despite the laughably bad antics onscreen, and in many cases he so drenched his subject matter in brooding anguish that the failings of the films in question just wound up becoming all that more apparent. Case in point: *Attack of the 50 Ft. Woman,* which sports a bittersweet brass fanfare that might have been written for Napoleon and Desiree instead of for some drunken lout and his problems with a giant pursuing rubber hand. Stein was at his best on period films like *The Terror* and *Dementia 13,* where there were no giant cardboard monsters in evidence and the composer could use his technical skills to create some genuine moments of eeriness. But he more often had to patch together pieces of sleazy juke box dance music or reach heights of insane camp, as in the touching "Song from Spider Baby" brayed by an obviously drunken Lon Chaney, Jr. *Not of This Earth* offers a great mix of surprisingly effective chills, big laughs and childhood nostalgia for those who grew up watching Corman's movies on the Saturday late show.

Jeff Bond

Max Steiner (1888-1971)

Band of Angels 🎵🎵🎵🎵

1987, Label X Records.

Album Notes: *Music:* Max Steiner; *Orchestrations:* Murray Cutter, Ray Heindorf, Hugo Friedhofer; The Warner Bros. Studio Orchestra and The RKO Studio Orchestra, conducted by Max Steiner; *Featured Musician:* Ray Turner (piano); *Album Producer:* John Lasher; *Engineers:* M.A. Merrick, Earl Mounce, Edwin Begley, Fred Mitchell.

Selections: Band Of Angels: 1 Prelude (4:14); 2 Starwood (2:51); 3 The Slave Market (8:13); 4 Amantha (2:47); 5 Pointe du Loup (1:57); 6 Burning Of The Cotton Crops (3:56); 7 Hamish Bond (6:25); 8 Reunion (6:12); Death Of A Scoundrel: 9 Opening and Closing Themes (4:08); 10 Mother, Mother (2:53); 11 Stephanie (1:52); 12 Waltz (1:21); 13 Kelly Blues (2:36); Charge Of The Light Brigade: 14 Forward The Light Brigade (3:22); Four Wives: 15 Symphonie Moderne (8:24); The Searchers: 16 Indian Idyll (3:26); A Stolen Life: 17 Petite Valse (2:03).

Review: There is something clearly endearing about this compilation bringing together selections from several scores written by Max Steiner, with the composer conducting the Warner Bros. Studio and the RKO Studio orchestras. Of particular interest here is the series of cues from *Band of Angels,* a 1957 period drama set during the Civil War, with Clark Gable as a proper Southern plantation owner, and Yvonne de Carlo as the object of his love, who happens to have black ancestry. Strongly suggestive and flavorful, the score is not found in other compilations, and stands out as the real gem in this set. For the same reasons, *Death of a Scoundrel,* a 1956 low-budget drama starring Yvonne de Carlo, is quite ingratiating. The other selections, though found elsewhere, are an excellent complement to this CD.

Max Steiner Conducts Gone with the Wind & Other Themes 🎵🎵🎵🎵⁺

1989, RCA Records.

Album Notes: *Music:* Max Steiner; Orchestra conducted by Max Steiner; *CD Producer:* Didier C. Deutsch; *Engineer:* Paul Goodman.

Selections: Bird Of Paradise: 1 Out Of The Blue (3:23); A Bill Of Divorcement: 2 Unfinished Sonata (3:13); Little Women: 3 Josephine (2:38); The Charge Of The Light Brigade: 4 Forward The Light Brigade (3:23); A Star Is Born: 5 Theme (2:56); The

Life Of Emile Zola: 6 Theme (2:57); Dark Victory: 7 Theme (3:08); Four Wives: 8 Symphonie Moderne (8:26); Gone With The Wind (suite): 9 Main Title, Tara, Invitation To The Dance, Melanie's Theme, Ashley, The Prayer, Bonnie Blue Flag, Scarlett O'Hara, Scarlett's Agony, War, Return To Tara, Bonnie's Death, Rhett Butler, Bonnie's Theme, Ashley And Melanie, The Oath (30:07).

Review: One of the most important of the film composers who gave Hollywood its first taste of music in the early 1930s, Max Steiner was born in Vienna in 1888. Already a celebrated composer in his native country, he came to America in 1914 at the invitation of Florenz Ziegfeld, and for the ensuing 15 years, worked on a variety of Broadway productions, before moving to Hollywood to orchestrate and conduct the 1929 screen version of *Rio Rita*, which was being produced by RKO.

Convinced that an appropriate musical background, not one borrowed from the classical repertoire as was often the case, could add significantly to the emotional impact of any scene, Steiner persuaded David O. Selznick, a producer at RKO, to let him write an original series of cues for a single reel of *Symphony of Six Million*. As he had suspected it, the effect on audiences was electrifying, and Selznick was further convinced after Steiner created the first original full-length score for *Bird of Paradise*, in 1932.

As a result of this early success, William LeBaron, head of production at the studio, put him in charge of the music department. In the six years he was there, Steiner scored a staggering 110 films, including *King Kong*, and *The Informer*, for which he won an Oscar in 1935.

In 1938, he left RKO and moved to Warner Bros., where he found in Jack L. Warner a producer who loved music in his pictures but, unlike Selznick, did not interfere with his composers' creativity. He stayed at Warner until 1953, and freelanced after that, writing his last score, for *Rome Adventure*, in 1962. He died on December 28, 1971.

During his long and illustrious career, Steiner wrote many scores that have endured to this day, including those for *Now Voyager*, *The Charge of the Light Brigade*, *The Big Sleep*, *Since You Went Away*, *Dark Victory*, and, of course, *Gone with the Wind*, his greatest claim to fame.

This CD, in which he conducts an unnamed Hollywood orchestra, was recorded between 1954 and 1956, and covers many themes he wrote for some of the movies listed above, including a long suite from *Gone with the Wind*. The album, in mono sound, may be sonically deficient by today's standards, but it has the enormous merit of presenting the composer himself conducting his own works, a rarity in those days.

Now, Voyager: The Classic Film Scores of Max Steiner ♪♪♪♪♪

1989, RCA Victor Records.

Album Notes: *Music*: Max Steiner; The National Philharmonic Orchestra, conducted by Charles Gerhardt; *Featured Soloist*: Earl Wild (piano); *Album Producer*: George Korngold; *Engineer*: K.E. Wilkinson.

Selections: Now, Voyager: 1 Warner Bros. Fanfare and Main Title/Love Scene and Finale (5:51); King Kong: 2 The Forgotten/ Natives/Sacrificial Dance/The Gate Of Kong/Kong In New York (7:16); Saratoga Trunk: 3 As Long As I Live; The Charge Of The Light Brigade: 4 Forward The Light Brigade (2:37); Four Wives: 5 Symphonie Moderne (8:06); The Big Sleep: 6 Main Title/ Marlowe/Bookshop/ Murder/Chase/Love Theme and Finale (7:03); Johnny Belinda: 7 Suite (5:05); Since You Went Away: 8 Main Title (1:25); The Informer: 9 Main Title/Love Scene/ Sancta Maria (4:33) *Ambrosian Singers*; The Fountainhead: 10 Main Theme (Roark's Theme)/Dominique's Theme/The Quarry/Construction—Enright House/ Finale-The Wynand Building (8:07).

Review: See entry below.

Gone With The Wind: The Classic Max Steiner ♪♪♪♪♪

1993, Silva Screen Records.

Album Notes: *Music*: Max Steiner; The Westminster Philharmonic Orchestra, conducted by Kenneth Alwyn; *Album Producer*: Graham Parlett; *Engineer*: Mike Ross-Trevor.

Selections: The Adventures Of Mark Twain: 1 Overture (7:42); A Distant Trumpet: 2 Prelude (1:29); Casablanca (suite): 3 Prelude/Rick's Bar/Paris/The Airport/The Beginning Of A Beautiful Friendship (7:04); A Summer Place: 4 Main Title (2:16); 5 Young Love (1:47); The Treasure Of The Sierra Madre (arr.: Steven R. Bernstein): 6 Overture (3:27); Helen Of Troy (suite): 7 Prelude (1:30); 8 The Voyage (3:58); 9 The Gates Of Troy (1:05); 10 The Siege And Aftermath (3:34); 11 Finale (1:13); The Caine Mutiny: 12 March (2:33); Gone With The Wind (suite): 13 Prelude/Invitation To Twelve Oaks/Tara/Mammy (6:43); 14 The Fall Of The South/Scarlett Walks Among The Wounded (2:18); 15 Rhett's Leaving/Melanie's Death/Finale (5:21).

Review: Both these titles cover some of the same selections, but the differences are significant enough that you might want to own both. *Now Voyager*, on RCA, is part of the Classic Film Scores series, an essential collection that chronicles some of the themes written in the early days of Hollywood by the golden circle of composers, in which Steiner was a particularly shining example. Missing from this title is any representation of *Gone with the Wind,* which Gerhardt and the National Philharmonic recorded in its entirety for another CD. The spectacular sonics, and the excellence of the performance add immeasurably to one's enjoyment.

The Silva Screen CD, with Kenneth Alwyn conducting the Westminster Philharmonic Orchestra in a bright, regenerative performance, offers some rare selections like the suites from *Casablanca* and *Helen of Troy,* and the "Overture" to *The Adventures of Mark Twain.* Like the RCA set, it is highly recommended.

Max Steiner: The Lost Patrol
♪♪♪♪♪

1996, Marco Polo Records.

Album Notes: *Music:* Max Steiner; *Orchestrations:* John Morgan; The Moscow Symphony Orchestra, conducted by William T. Stromberg; *Engineers:* Edvard Shakhnazarian, Vitaly Ivanov.

Selections: The Lost Patrol: 1 Main Title (1:42); 2 Oasis (2:11); 3 On Guard/Night Wind (4:23); 4 Reminiscing (1:58); 5 Plans Are Made/Palm Tree (3:00); 6 Back Home (3:40); 7 Aeroplane/False Hope (4:23); 8 Fire! (1:44); 9 Saunders Gone Mad (2:58); 10 Alone, At The Graves (2:36); 11 Arabs/Rescue/ Finale (2:46); The Beast With Five Fingers: 12 Main Title/Tarantella (2:06); 13 Chaconne (piano)/Romance (3:23); 14 Storm (2:25); 15 Walking (:36); 16 Fear (3:11); 17 The Hand (2:29); 18 Finale (1:45); 19 End Cast (:28); Virginia City: 20 Main Title (2:01); 21 The Trench/Bradford's Folly (2:57); 22 The Coach/Murrel/Chase (3:39); 23 On A Love/Love Beginning (3:44); 24 Shoot-Out/ For Freedom/Chase (4:25); 25 Storm/Boy's Death/Secret Agent (6:34); 26 The Battle (2:33); 27 Abraham Lincoln/Finale (2:53); 28 End Cast (:31).

Review: This recent entry in the Steiner sweepstakes is another album that deserves to be in any comprehensive collection. Superbly recorded in bright, spacious digital sound, with William T. Stromberg eliciting spirited performances from the Moscow Symphony Orchestra players, it offers a broad overview of three widely different scores composed by Steiner, including two (*The Lost Patrol* and *Virginia City*) that are essential.

Written in 1934, *The Lost Patrol* chronicled the fate of a small group of British soldiers isolated in the Mesopotamian desert and subjected to repeated attacks from their Arab foes. The nervy, pungent score contributed immensely to the impact of this action-driven military saga.

Virginia City, made in 1940, is a western set during the Civil War, starring Errol Flynn, Randolph Scott and Humphrey Bogart. Steiner, who excelled at writing this type of music,

delivered a potent, highly memorable score, which ranks among his best efforts.

The third title here, *The Beast with Five Fingers,* a 1946 horror film, starring Peter Lorre and Robert Alda, found the composer contributing a totally different type of music, in which he drew extensively on his classical training. Like the other two scores, it shows Steiner's incredible diversity and unique talent in writing music that contributed enormously to the overall aura of the films, in a contemporary performance that sounds quite authentic.

Mikis Theodorakis (1926-

Mikis Theodorakis: On the Screen ♪♪♪♭

1993, DRG Records.

Album Notes: *Music:* Mikis Theodorakis; Z: *Arrangements by:* Bernard Gerard; Orchestra conducted by Bernard Gerard; *Engineer:* Russ Payne; State of Siege: *Featured Artists:* Los Calchakis: Hector Miranda, Nicolas Perez-Gonsalez, Gonsalo Reig, Sergio Arriagada, Rodolfo Dalera, Yannis Didilis (keyboard), Gerard Berlioz (percussion), Pierre Moreilhon (bass); *Engineer:* Charles Raucher; Serpico: *Arrangements:* Bob James; *Producer:* Michael Barbiero; *Engineer:* Don Hahn; Phaedra: Orchestra conducted by Mikis Theodorakis.

Selections: CD 1: Z: 1 Main Title (Andonis)(2:02); 2 The Happy Youth (orchestral version)(1:31); 3 The Chase/The Happy Youth (2:10); 4 Murmur Of The Heart (2:05) *Maria Farandouri;* 5 Cafe Rock (1:31); 6 Arrival Of Helen/ The Happy Youth (1:25); 7 Batucada (1:49); 8 The Happy Youth (bouzouki version)(1:08); 9 The Happy Youth (1:35); 10 Who's Not Talking About Lambri (3:09); 11 Finale/The Happy Youth (2:45); 12 Murmur Of The Heart (1:56) *Mikis Theodorakis;* 13 In This Town (1:38) *Mikis Theodorakis;* State Of Siege: 14 State Of Siege (2:46); 15 People In Protest (2:17); 16 Paola, 11099 (4:24); 17 Tupamaros (3:54); 18 Insurrect America (2:41); 19 State Of Siege (7:02); 20 The American (1:23); 21 Hugo (Under Arrest)(4:00); 22 Tupamaros/State Of Siege (3:33).

CD 2: Serpico: 1 Theme From Serpico (3:26); 2 Honest Cop (3:13); 3 Alone In The Aprtment (4:07); 4 Meeting In The Park (2:15); 5 Shoe Shop (3:05); 6 On The Streets (4:28); 7 Flashback (4:31); 8 Laurie's Fable (1:43); 9 Disillusion (1:53); 10 End Title (4:00); Phaedra: 11 Love Theme From Phaedra (3:50); 12 Rendezvous (3:17); 13 Ship To Shore (1:45); 14 London Fog (1:07); 15 One More Time (3:08); 16 Agapimou (3:50); 17 Only You (1:20); 18 The Fling (2:55); 19 Candlelight (3:36); 20

Rodostimo (3:00); 21 Love Theme From Phaedra (3:17) *Melina Mercouri*; 22 Goodbye John Sebastian (3:02).

Review: The soundtracks to four films scored by Greek composer Mikis Theodorakis have been preserved together on this thick double-CD set. The fast-paced rhythmic Greek music from *Z* is centered around a Greek melody, which counterpoints the political oppression that is central to the film. In *State of Siege*, a unique cultural blend is achieved through Theodorakis' Grecian musical sensibilities. Given a South American instrumentation, the wind instruments lend a pleasing, light tonality and Theodorakis' buoyant melodies soar. *Serpico* contrasts the disillusionment of the title character with a pretty yet mildly sad theme with the urban jazz that is associated with the story's Big City environment. The use of contemporary Greek musical styles fit Jules Dassin's *Phaedra* perfectly, contrasts a variety of minor pop melodies with a passionate, fully symphonic concerto motif; its fast-pace and profound melodic lines capturing a dynamic sense of drama and pathos. This set is an excellent gallery of the composer's work for films.

Randall D. Larson

Dimitri Tiomkin (1894-1979)

The Film Music of Dimitri Tiomkin ♫♫ᵛ

1985, Unicorn-Kanchana Records.

Album Notes: *Music*: Dimitri Tiomkin; *Orchestrations*: Christopher Palmer; The Royal College of Music Orchestra, conducted by Sir David Willcocks; *Featured Soloist*: David King (organ); *Album Producer*: Christopher Palmer; *Engineer*: Bob Auger.

Selections: The Fall Of The Roman Empire: 1 Roman Empire Overture (3:40); 2 Pax Romana (6:22); 3 A President's Country (suite)(10:43); 4 The Guns Of Navarone (10:33); 5 Wild Is The Wind (2:52); 6 Rhapsody Of Steel (22:16).

Review: See entry below.

The Western Film World of Dimitri Tiomkin ♫♫

1988, Unicorn-Kanchana Records.

Album Notes: *Music*: Dimitri Tiomkin; The John McCarthy Singers, with Bob Saker, baritone, The London Studio Symphony Orchestra, conducted by Laurie Johnson; *Album Producers*: Laurie Johnson, Christopher Palmer; *Engineers*: Geoffrey Barton, Peter Jensen.

Selections: Giant: 1 Prelude (2:15); Red River: 2 Prelude and Wagon Train (4:05); 3 Red River Crossing (2:33); 4 The Challenge and Finale (3:17); Duel In The Sun: 5 Prelude and Legend (3:08); 6 The Buggy Ride (2:36); 7 Trek To The Sun, Love-Death and Finale (5:02); High Noon: 8 Main Titles (2:56); 9 The Clock and Showdown (8:48); 10 End Titles (1:09); Night Passage: 11 Follow The River (2:56); Rio Bravo: 12 De Guello (3:36); 13 Love Theme (2:35); 14 Main Theme (End Titles)(2:02).

Review: Often "covered" but seldom equalled, Tiomkin is probably one of the few Hollywood composers whose scores can't stand to be recorded by others: the pulse of the tempi, the nuances in the playing, in fact everything in his music seems very difficult to duplicate. Case in point: these two recordings, both superbly recorded, yet both ultimately failing to make the grade because the orchestra playing often sounds too studied, too reverential. Where the western music should pulsate and be thrilling, it simply exists, with *High Noon* sounding by far the least exciting.

Lost Horizon: The Classic Film Scores of Dimitri Tiomkin ♫♫♫ᵛ

1989, RCA Victor Records.

Album Notes: *Music*: Dimitri Tiomkin; The National Philharmonic Orchestra, conducted by Charles Gerhardt; *Album Producer*: George Korngold; *Engineer*: K.E. Wilkinson.

Selections: Lost Horizon: 1 Prelude/Foreward Card/Riot In Baskui/Mob Scene At Refueling Station/Morning After The Plane Crash (5:46); 2 Arrival Of The Caravan/The Journey Over The Mountains (2:56); 3 Entrance Into Shangri-La (2:26); 4 Nocturne (2:25); 5 Riding Sequence/The Waterfall/Chinese Children's Scherzo (2:38); 6 Bell Sequence/Funeral Cortege Of The High Lama/Escape From Shangri-La/Return To Shangri-La (7:02) *The John Alldis Choir*; The Guns Of Navarone: 7 Prelude (2:21); The Big Sky: 8 Prelude/Forest At Night (Nocturne)/ The Wide Missouri (Epilogue)(8:08); The Fourposter: 9 Overture (2:33); Friendly Persuasion: 10 Love Scene In The Barn (5:34); Search For Paradise: 11 Choral Finale (3:31) *The John Alldis Choir*.

Review: Somewhat more successful is this recording in the Classic Film Score Series, with Charles Gerhardt leading the National Philharmonic for producer George Korngold. Wisely, they chose to avoid the "standard" western music with which Tiomkin distinguished himself at the height of his career (with the exception of *The Big Sky*, which had no equivalent elsewhere), to concentrate on the more unusual "lost" score for *Lost Horizon*, which gave the album its title. The other selections in the set, however, sound more like fillers.

The Film Music of Dimitri Tiomkin ♫♫♫♫

1988, Columbia Records.

Album Notes: *Music:* Dimitri Tiomkin; Orchestras conducted by Dimitri Tiomkin; *Album Producer:* Didier C. Deutsch; *Engineer:* Tim Geelan.

Selections: Blowing Wild: 1 The Ballad Of Black Gold (D. Tiomkin/P.F. Webster)(2:36) *Frankie Laine*; Giant: 2 Theme (3:11) *The Warner Bros. Studio Orchestra, Ray Heindorf*; Wild Is The Wind: 3 Angie (2:07); 4 Horse Chase (3:38); 5 Tell The Truth (3:00); Gunfight At The O.K. Corral: 6 Gunfight At The O.K. Corral (D. Tiomkin/N. Washington)(2:08) *Frankie Laine*; The Old Man And The Sea: 7 The Boy (1:15); 8 Fishermen's Cantina (2:41); 9 I Am Your Dream (2:43); 10 In The Tavern At Casa Blanca (2:18); The Alamo: 11 Overture (3:07); 12 Davy Crockett Arrives (2:34); 13 Love Scene (6:35); 14 Raid For Cattle (4:39); Rawhide: 15 Rawhide (D. Tiomkin/N. Washington) *Frankie Laine*; The Guns Of Navarone: 16 Legend Of Navarone (2:21); 17 Yassu (3:42); 18 Climbing The South Cliff (1:43); 55 Days At Peking: 19 Overture (2:55); 20 Natasha's Waltz (2:19); 21 Murder (2:12); 22 Children's Corner (1:38); 23. Montage (2:12); The Fall Of The Roman Empire: 24 Overture (2:41); 25 Tarantella (2:17); High Noon: 26 Do Not Forsake Me, Oh My Darling (2:41) *Frankie Laine*.

Review: A collection of soundtrack themes and vocals by Frankie Laine (whose success with "Do Not Forsake Me" in *High Noon*, led him to perform many other title songs for Tiomkin), which may be hard to get but which should be in any collection. Presented somewhat chronologically, the set includes selections from *Wild Is the Wind, The Old Man and the Sea, The Alamo, The Guns of Navarone, 55 Days at Peking* and *The Fall of the Roman Empire*, in soundtrack performances culled from the Columbia vaults. While sonics may sometimes leave a lot to be desired (frequently due to the age of the source material), performances, with the composer conducting various studio orchestras, has the ring of authenticity. The CD was deleted from the Sony catalogue, but may still be available at specialty shops.

Vangelis (1944-

Vangelis: Themes ♫♫♫♫

1989, Polydor Records.

Album Notes: *Music:* Vangelis Papathanassiou; *Orchestrations and Arrangements:* Vangelis Papathanassiou; *Producer:* Vangelis Papathanassiou.

Selections: Blade Runner: 1 End Titles (4:57); Missing: 2 Main Theme (3:59); Opera sauvage: 3 L'enfant (5:00); 4 Hymn (2:45); China: 5 Chug Kuo (5:29); 6 The Tao Of Love (2:45); Antarctica: 7 Theme (3:55); Blade Runner: 8 Love Theme (4:55); The Bounty: 9 Opening Titles (4:16); 10 Closing Titles (4:58); 11 Memories Of Green (5:42); L'Apocalypse des animaux: 12 La petite fille de la mer (5:51); Chariots Of Fire: 13 Five Circles (5:18); 14 Chariots Of Fire (3:31).

Review: This anthology presents a series of Vangelis tracks which have been featured in films and television. "L'Enfant" is a pleasantly rhythmic piano piece from Frederic Rossif's TV series *Opera Sauvage* (but is probably better known for its use in *The Year of Living Dangerously*). The sultry saxophone and synths of "Love Theme From Blade Runner" perfectly evoke the futuristic film noir world of that film. Also heard in *Blade Runner,* "Memories of Green," which is originally from Vangelis 1979 album *See You Later*, is included on this album as well.

A number of tracks are also available here which were never released as soundtrack albums. The main title from *The Bounty* is a pulsing, sultry evocation of the Tahitian setting of the film. The theme from *Missing* is a delicate piano melody, which reflects the tenderness and tragedy of Costa-Gavras' political expose. One of Vangelis' most beautiful works also features the exotic and ethereal waltz, "La Petite Fille de la Mer" (from Rossif's film *L' Apocalypse des Animaux*). The album closes with two tracks from Vangelis' popular *Chariots of Fire*, the "Title Music" and "Five Circles." In all, *Vangelis: Themes* is a very rewarding compilation of work by one of the best and most unique voices in film music today.

Paul Andrew MacLean

Sir William Walton (1902-1983)

Sir William Walton: Hamlet/As You Like It Film Music, vol. 1 ♫♫♫♫

1990, Chandos Records.

Album Notes: *Music:* Sir William Walton; *Orchestrations:* Christopher Palmer; The Academy of St. Martin in the Fields, conducted by Sir Neville Marriner; *Narrator:* Sir John Gielgud; *Album Producer:* Brain Couzens; *Engineer:* Ralph Couzens; *Assistant Engineer:* Richard Lee.

Selections: Hamlet: 1 Prelude (3:09); 2 Fanfare (:57); 3 Soliloquy (2:35); 4 The Ghost (3:15); 5 Hamlet And Ophelia (7:52); 6 The Question (2:20); 7 "To Be Or Not To Be" (3:08); The

Moustrap: 8 The Players (:46); 9 Entry Of The Court (:49); 10 The Play (3:57); 11 Ophelia's Death (2:42); 12 Retribution (1:59); 13 Threnody (2:11); 14 Finale (Funeral March)(3:14); As You Like It: 15 Prelude (2:52); 16 Moonlight (2:39); 17 Under The Greenwood Tree (1:56); 18 The Fountain (3:12); 19 Wedding Procession (1:51).

Review: See entry below.

Sir William Walton: Battle of Britain Suite Film Music, vol. 2 ♪♪♪♪♪

1990, Chandos Records.

Album Notes: *Music*: Sir William Walton; *Orchestrations*: Christopher Palmer; The Academy of St. Martin in the Fields, conducted by Sir Neville Marriner; *Album Producer*: Brain Couzens; *Engineer*: Ralph Couzens; *Assistant Engineer*: Peter Newble.

Selections: Spitfire Prelude and Fugue: 1 Prelude (4:23); 2 Fugue (4:13); A Wartime Sketchbook: 3 Prologue (4:56); 4 Bicycle Chase (1:45); 5 Refugees (3:49); 6 Scherzo — Gay Berlin (4:06); 7 Foxtrots (3:18); 8 Lovers (2:58); 9 Striptease (1:51); 10 Epilogue (2:12); Escape Me Never (suite): 11 Prelude and Venetian Idyll (3:41); 12 In The Dolomites (4:58); 13 Ballet (2:37); The Three Sisters: 14 Opening Titles (3:14); 15 Dream Sequence (3:38); 16 End Titles (1:16); Battle Of Britain (suite): 17 Spitfire Music and Battle In The Air (5:58); 18 March Introduction, March and Siegfried Music (5:44).

Review: See entry below.

Sir William Walton: Henry V Film Music, vol. 3 ♪♪♪♪♪

1990, Chandos Records.

Album Notes: *Music*: Sir William Walton; *Orchestrations*: Christopher Palmer; Choristers of Westminster Cathedral, The Academy of St. Martin in the Fields Chorus and Orchestra, conducted by Sir Neville Marriner; *Narrator*: Christopher Plummer; *Album Producer*: Brain Couzens; *Engineer*: Ralph Couzens; *Assistant Engineer*: Peter Newble.

Selections: Henry V: 1 Prologue (9:16); 2 Interlude: At The Boar's Head (4:28); 3 Embarkation (3:27); 4 Interlude (2:12); 5 Harfleur (3:48); 6 The Night Watch (5:20); 7 Upon The King (3:43); 8 Agincourt (15:14); 9 Interlude: At The French Court (5:16); 10 Epilogue (7:50); Appendix 1: 11 Rosa Solis (G.

Farnaby)(2:23); 12 Watkin's Ale (anon.)(1:56); Appendix 2: 13 Obal, dinlou Limouzi (J. Canteloube)(1:32).

Review: See entry below.

Sir William Walton: Richard III/Macbeth/Major Barbara Film Music, vol. 4 ♪♪♪♪♪

1991, Chandos Records.

Album Notes: *Music*: Sir William Walton; *Orchestrations*: Christopher Palmer; The Academy of St. Martin in the Fields, conducted by Sir Neville Marriner; *Featured Soloist*: Ian Watson (harpsichord, organ); *Album Producer*: Brain Couzens; *Engineer*: Ralph Couzens; *Assistant Engineer*: Richard Lee.

Selections: Richard III: 1 Prelude (3:11); 2 Coronation (5:09); 3 Monologue: "Now Is The Winter Of Our Discontent" (4:14); 4 The Wooing (4:24); 5 The Prince Of Wales (5:03); 6 Elegy (3:16); 7 The Princes In The Tower (2:30); 8 Nightmare (6:17); 9 Bosworth Field (5:20); 10 Death Of Richard and Finale (4:16); Macbeth: 11 Fanfare and March (5:53); Major Barbara: 12 Titles (2:13); 13 Undershaft's Factory And His "Garden Suburb" (3:17); 14 Love Scene (3:48); 15 End Titles and Play Out (1:13).

Review: This four-volume anthology of the film works of Sir William Walton is a true bonanza for collectors. Not only does it focus on a composer whose output has been quite significant, but it does so with all the trappings usually associated with important classical releases — authoritative performances by a major orchestra, the Academy of St. Martin-in-the-Fields, conducted by Sir Neville Marriner, in superb digital sonics — that should make Chandos proud of its technical and artistic achievements.

One of England's great "classic" composers, Walton often wrote for the movies, particularly in a creative collaboration with Laurence Olivier which resulted in several sensational screen renditions of the epic plays of William Shakespeare — *Hamlet, As You Like It, Henry V, Richard III,* and *Macbeth,* all of them covered in volumes 1, 2 and 4 in this series, with guest apperances by Sir John Gielgud and Christopher Plummer.

Casting a different light on Walton's film output, volume 3 turns its attention to the war films, with stirring renditions of the scores for *Escape Me Never* and *Battle of Britain,* in addition to the composer's *Wartime Sketchbook* (a compilation of cues created for such films as *Went the Day Well, Next of Kin* and *The Foreman Went to France,* all of them related to the ongoing conflict), and his memorable *Spitfire Prelude and Fugue.* Like the other three volumes, it is a remarkable effort that takes film music to its utmost quality level, on a par with classical music.

William Walton: Film Music
🎷🎷🎷🎷⏜

1987, EMI Records.

Album Notes: *Music:* Sir William Walton; The London Philharmonic Orchestra and Choir, conducted by Carl Davis; *Album Producer:* David Groves; *Engineer:* Michael Sheady.

Selections: Henry V (suite): 1 Prelude: The Globe (6:07); 2 The Death Of Falstaff (passacaglia)(2:46); 3 Touch Her Soft Lips And Part (1:57); 4 Agincourt Song (2:25); The Battle Of Britain (suite): 5 Spitfire Music — Battle In The Air (6:19); 6 March and Siegfried Music (6:07); Troilus and Cressida: 7 Interlude (Act 2)(4:37); As You Like It (suite): 8 Title Music (3:04); 9 Fountain Scene — Wrestling Scene (4:37); 10 Sunrise (:35); 11 Procession (1:38); 12 Snake Scene (:57); 13 Waterfall Scene (2:34); 14 Hymn (:53); 15 March For A History Of The English Speaking Peoples (4:45).

Review: This superb album featuring the London Philharmonic Orchestra and Choir features some of the finest film music ever written, opening with a sublime suite from William Walton's score to Laurence Olivier's film of *Henry V,* a triumph from its beautiful pastoral opening to the moving "Death of Falstaff" and the aching lyricism of its courtship music, climaxing in the thrilling "Agincourt Song," a mammoth choral piece supported by an exultant, sinuous string line that's one of the most satisfying evocations of martial triumph ever written. Almost as good is Walton's buzzing, open-aired "Spitfire Music" which was written for an unused score for the 1960s war film *The Battle of Britain.* Also featured is a brief interlude from *Troilus and Cressida,* Walton's rousing, full-blooded pastoral music for *As You Like It,* and the giddy "March" for *A History of the English Speaking Peoples.* It's as bracing an accompaniment to scenes of the English countryside as anyone could hope to hear.

Jeff Bond

Ken Wannberg

The Film Music of Ken Wannberg: Volume 1 🎷🎷🎷🎷

1995, Prometheus Records/Belgium; from the movies *The Philadelphia Experiment,* New World Pictures, 1984, and *Mother Lode,* Agamemnon Films, 1982.

Album Notes: *Music:* Ken Wannberg; *Orchestrations:* Albert Woodbury; The National Philharmonic Orchestra, conducted by Ken Wannberg; *Album Producer:* Luc Van de Ven; *Engineer:* Eric Tomlinson.

Selections: The Philadelphia Experiment: 1 Main Theme (3:06); 2 The Experiment Begins/Time Slip (5:49); 3 The "Eldridge" Remains (2:04); 4 David Confronts His Past (2:04); 5 The Vortex Sucks/David's Escape (4:38); 6 A Tender Moment (1:29); 7 The Doctor Reflects (2:29); 8 The Chase (1:32); 9 Fugitives In Love (2:31); 10 Storming The Compound (2:00); 11 David's Father (2:18); 12 David's Decision/Fate Of The Vortex (6:53); 13 David's Choice/End Title (5:32); Mother Lode: 14 Magee's Theme (2:20); 15 The Plane Crash (2:10); 16 Underwater Search (4:00); 17 The Flight (5:06); 18 The Mine (3:05); 19 Magee's Cabin/The Trap (2:36); 20 The Lovers Argue (1:43); 21 Goodmanson's Gold (1:09); 22 The Price Of Greed (6:14); 23 Magee's Lament (:58); 24 Finale and End Title (3:16).

Review: To the average filmgoer, Ken Wannberg's name means very little. The cognoscenti, however, know him as one of John Williams' closest associates, a music editor with a deft sense of what the maestro wants and needs. But Wannberg is also a composer in his own right, and Prometheus Records, an independent Belgian label, has wisely chosen to correct the wrong by dedicating three volumes to his music. Both *The Philadelphia Experiment* and *Mother Lode,* covered in the first volume, allow Wannberg to show his mettle in scores that are interestingly varied and different from each other.

Mother Lode, written in 1982, is an adventure film starring Charlton Heston in a dual role as golddigger brothers in the wilds of British Columbia on the opposite sides of the law. *The Philadelphia Experiment,* composed two years later, is a time-warp science fiction film about a top secret U.S. Navy experiment to try and make ships invisible to enemy radar during World War II.

Both scores reveal in Wannberg a composer with a solid descriptive bend, whose themes overflow with catchy melodies and make for pleasant listening when the scores are taken at their face value, out of context.

The Film Music of Ken Wannberg: Volume 2 🎷🎷🎷🎷

1995, Prometheus Records/Belgium; from the television movies *Draw!,* and *Red River,* 1994.

Album Notes: *Music:* Ken Wannberg; *Orchestrations:* Albert Woodbury; The National Philharmonic Orchestra (*Draw!*) and The Little Mountain Studio Symphony Orchestra (*Red River*), conducted by Ken Wannberg; *Featured Musician:* Tommy Morgan (harmonica); *Album Producer:* Alan E. Smith; *Engineer:* Roger Monk.

Selections: Draw!: 1 Main Theme (2:45); 2 Runaway Wagon (2:47); 3 Holland Rides Into Bell City (1:06); 4 The Sheriff Confronts Holland (1:55); 5 Holland And Bess (2:54); 6 Wally Drags Starrett (:47); 7 Starrett Visits The Jail; 8 Wally Speaks Emotionally (1:34); 9 Draw!/Aftermath/Finale (10:36); Red River: 10 Prologue (4:17); 11 Main Title (3:02); 12 The Shooting Contest (:47); 13 First Signs Of Love (:54); 14 Jack And The Kid (2:45); 15 Stampede (2:51); 16 The Fastest Kiss In The West (1:00); 17 Matt Takes Charge (1:23); 18 Matt Tips His Hat (1:26); 19 Cherry Courts Kate (2:40); 20 The Showdown/Chief Ostanato (7:20); 21 Dunson And Kate Argue/On The Trail (3:18); 22 Matt And Kate (2:04); 23 All's Well/End Credits (2:00).

Review: See entry below.

The Film Music of Ken Wannberg: Volume 3 ♫♫♫♫

1995, Prometheus Records/Belgium; from the movies *The Amateur*, 1982, *Of Unknown Origin*, 1983, and *The Laye Show*, 1977.

Album Notes: *Music*: Ken Wannberg; *Orchestrations*: Albert Woodbury, Ken Wannberg; The European Studio Symphony Orchestra, conducted by Ken Wannberg; *Album Producer*: Ford A. Thaxton; *Engineers*: Joe Giannola, James Nelson.

Selections: The Amateur: 1 Main Title (3:44); 2 Stolen Dreams (3:08); 3 Montage (1:16); 4 Crossing The Border (4:58); 5 Slavic Slut (2:09); 6 Depth Charge (1:09); 7 The Killing (3:27); 8 Heller In The Cellar (2:48); 9 Finale/End Titles (3:18); Of Unknown Origin: 10 Main Title (2:14); 11 Birthday Dream/Rat Droppings (4:41); 12 I Smell A Rat/The Weapon (3:37); 13 Ready For Battle/The Last Battle (6:48); 14 End Title (2:22); The Late Show: 15 Main Theme (1:37); 16 The End Of Harry (1:36); 17 Talking (4:07); 18 Prelude To A Chase/Chase And Escape (4:21); 19 Ulcer Time (2:15); 20 The Trap/All Is Revealed/End Game (6:23); 21 End Title (1:39).

Review: Volumes 2 and 3 complete Prometheus Records' trilogy of Ken Wannberg scores, the series that started with the release of *The Philadelphia Experiment* and *Mother Lode* (see above). The second volume is a collection of two western scores, starting off with the outstanding music to the Kirk Douglas/James Coburn comedy *Draw!* Douglas plays an aging gunfighter who simply wants to get out of town to retire, but his likewise aging adversary, lawman Coburn gets caught up in the town's lynch mob mentality. The score follows in the footsteps of earlier genre work with its big western sound, but Wannberg plays up the absurdity of two old men who can't escape their respective reputations. The second score is for a 1988 television remake of John Ford's classic *Red River*. This

time, *Gunsmoke's* James Arness is in John Wayne's saddle, driving hard cattle and step-son Bruce Boxleitner, from Oklahoma to Missouri. Wannberg wisely doesn't attempt to compete with Dimitri Tiomkin's classic score for the 1948 original. His music serves the film quite well, though this tepid version certainly couldn't offer Wannberg the kind of inspiration Tiomkin found in the John Ford directed original.

The last CD in the Wannberg trilogy features three very different scores. *The Amateur* is a European-flavored cold war thriller. *Of Unknown Origin* is a horror score he composed for *Rambo: First Blood II* director George Pan Cosmatos, with *RoboCop's* Peter Weller battling an enormous rat. All are excellently written pieces, but the best is saved for last, a laid back film noir score for the Art Carney/Lily Tomlin comedic murder mystery, *The Late Show*. Vaguely John Barry-ish in tone, the score does well to capture eccentric nature of Tomlin's character and Carney's just-about-over-the-hill detective. The CD booklet for the third volume contains excerpts from my 1995 interview with the composer that was published in the March issue of *Soundtrack!* magazine.

David Hirsch

Franz Waxman (1906-1967)

The Film Music of Franz Waxman ♫♫♫♫♫

1990, RCA Records.

Album Notes: *Music*: Franz Waxman; Orchestras conducted by Franz Waxman; *Album Producer*: Didier C. Deutsch; *Engineer*: Paul Goodman.

Selections: The Spirit Of St. Louis: 1 Prelude (Main Title)(1:24); 2 Flight To St. Louis (1:11); 3 New York To Cape Cod (7:03); 4 Le Bourget/End Title (6:44); Sayonara: 5 Opening (2:38); 6 Eileen (5:42); 7 Katsumi Theme (3:29); 8 Street Fight (2:41); Peyton Place: 9 Main Title: Hilltop Scene (10:36); 10 Entering Peyton Place/Going To School (2:53); 11 The Rape (2:24); My Geisha: 12 Main Title (2:13); 13 The Real Yoko (2:07); 14 Preparations (2:20); 15 The Plot (1:44); 16 Goodbye, Lover (2:24); Hemingway's Adventures Of A Young Man: 17 Prologue (4:22); 18 D.T. Blues (2:29); 19 Rosanna (4:11); 20 The Major's Rescue (2:38).

Review: Another glorious name from the early days of Hollywood, Franz Waxman was born in Konigshutte, Germany, and came to film music at the age of 24, when he was asked to orchestrate Frederick Hollander's score for *The Blue Angel*. As the threat of the Nazi movement became more precise, Waxman left his native country in 1934 and moved to Hollywood, arguably to work on the Jerome Kern score for *Music in the Air*. The following year he created his first major contribution to the screen when he wrote the seminal music for *Bride of Frankenstein*, which led to his being named music director for Universal.

In a career that saw him at M-G-M and Warner Bros., Waxman wrote many important scores that rank among the best works ever to come out of Hollywood, including *Rebecca* (1940), *Dr. Jekyll and Mr. Hyde* and *Suspicion* (both 1941), *Objective, Burma!* (1945), *Sorry, Wrong Number* (1948), *Sunset Boulevard* (1950), *A Place in the Sun* (1951), *Prince Valiant* (1954), *The Spirit of St. Louis* and *Peyton Place* (both 1957), and *The Nun's Story* (1959), among many others.

The above compilation, assembled from the soundtracks conducted by the composer, covers five late '50-early '60s films, *The Spirit of St. Louis, Peyton Place, Sayonara* (1957), *My Geisha* and *Hemingway's Adventures of a Young Man* (both 1962). Frequently rising above the pedestrian topics of the films (*My Geisha, Hemingway's Adventures...*), or taking the exulted stories to even greater heights (*The Spirit of St. Louis*), Waxman always provided the right musical element that singled out the films and his scores from the mass. Particularly evocative, the score for *Peyton Place* has become a classic in its own right.

Sunset Boulevard: The Classic Film Scores of Franz Waxman &&&&&

1989, RCA Victor Records.

Album Notes: *Music*: Franz Waxman; The National Philharmonic Orchestra, conducted by Charles Gerhardt; *Album Producer*: George Korngold; *Engineer*: K.E. Wilkinson.

Selections: Prince Valiant: 1 Prelude/King Aguar's Escape/The Fens/The First Chase/The Tournament/Sir Brack's Death and Finale (9:49); A Place In The Sun: 2 Prelude/Angela/Loon Lake/Farewell and Frenzy/The Farewell (8:29); The Bride Of Frankenstein: 3 The Creation Of The Female Monster (7:17); Sunset Boulevard: 4 Main Title/Norma Desmond/The Studio Stroll/The Comeback/Norma As Salome (7:44); Old Acquaintance: 5 Elegy For Strings And Harps (3:29); Rebecca: 6 Prelude/After The Ball/Mrs. Danvers/Confession Scene/Manderley In Flames (7:45); The Philadelphia Story: 7 M-G-M Fanfare/Main Title/The True Love (3:34); Taras Bulba: 8 The Ride To Dubno (4:53).

Review: This exquisite volume in RCA's Classic Film Scores series finds Charles Gerhardt and the National Philharmonic in

exciting renditions of some of the scores created by Waxman. Both *Prince Valiant* and *A Place in the Sun* (a score that deserves a full CD treatment) are particular highlights in this set, with *Sunset Boulevard* and *Rebecca* the appropriate complements to this exhilarating collection. As is the norm in the entire series, the sonics and performances are exceptional.

Legends of Hollywood: Franz Waxman, vol. 1 &&&&&

1990, Varese-Sarabande.

Album Notes: *Music*: Franz Waxman; The Queensland Symphony Orchestra, conducted by Richard Mills; *Featured Soloists*: Piers Lane (piano), Geoffrey Spiller (trumpet); *Album Producers*: George Korngold, Olwen Jones; *Associate Producers*: Chris Kuchler, Tom Null; *Engineers*: Robert Hobson, Alan Calvert, Gary Yule.

Selections: Task Force: 1 Liberty Fanfares (:50); Objective Burma: 2 Prelude/Take-Off/In The Plane/Jumping/The Patrol/Stop Firing/No Landing (12:04); Come Back Little Sheba: 3 Reminiscences For Orchestra (5:17); Peyton Place: 4 Prelude/Entering Peyton Place/Going To School/Swimming/The Hilltop (9:37); The Paradine Case: 5 Rhapsody For Piano And Orchestra (12:20); The Horn Blows At Midnight: 6 Overture For Trumpet And Orchestra (6:45); Sorry, Wrong Number: 7 Passacaglia For Orchestra (6:58); Demetrius And The Gladiators: 8 Prelude/Lucia/Messalina and Demetrius/The Marriage Of Life And Death/Return To Faith (14:46).

Review: See entry below.

Legends of Hollywood: Franz Waxman, vol. 2 &&&&&

1991, Varese-Sarabande.

Album Notes: *Music*: Franz Waxman; The Queensland Symphony Orchestra, conducted by Richard Mills; *Featured Soloist*: Peter Rosenfelt (piano); *Album Producers*: Robert Townson, Olwen Jones; *Associate Producers*: Chris Kuchler, Tom Null; *Engineers*: Robert Hobson, Alan Calvert, Gary Yule.

Selections: Anne Of The Indies (suite): 1 Prelude/The Sheba Queen/Jamaica/ Finale (4:36); 2 Captain Courageous (suite)(7:00); The Pioneer Suite: 3 Music from Red Mountain, Cimarron and The Indian Fighter (10:22); Huckleberry Finn: 4 Overture (6:17); The Nun's Story (suite): 5 Prelude/I Accuse Myself/ Haircutting/The Killing Of Aurelie/Finale (11:02); Botany Bay (suite): 6 Prelude and Forward Montage/New Escape Plot/Love and Victory (9:23); 7 Possessed (suite) (12:04); Mr.

Roberts (suite): 8 Prelude/Main Title/Final Scene/End Cast (3:19); The Bride Of Frankenstein: 9 Dance Macabre (6:58).

Review: See entry below.

Legends of Hollywood: Franz Waxman, vol. 3 🎜🎜🎜🎜🎜

1994, Varese-Sarabande.

Album Notes: *Music:* Franz Waxman; The Queensland Symphony Orchestra, conducted by Richard Mills; *Album Producer:* Olwen Jones; *Associate Producers:* Chris Kuchler, Robert Townson; *Engineers:* Robert Hobson, Gary Yule.

Selections: Elephant Walk (suite): 1 Prelude/The Plantation/ Appeal For Help/Ceylon Romance/Elephant Stampede and Finale (12:32); Night And The City: 2 Nightride For Orchestra (8:05); Night Unto Night: 3 Dusk: A Setting For Orchestra (8:29); The Furies (suite): 4 Prelude/Juan And Vance/The Mark Of The Furies/ The Romance Revived and The King Of The Furies (6:59); Hotel Berlin: 5 Cafe Waltzes (8:32); Destination Tokyo: 6 A Montage For Orchestra: Main Title/ Thinking Of Home/Sea Power/Montage and Finale (6:22); Mrs. Skeffington (suite): 7 Forsaken and Finale (5:11); The Silver Chalice (suite): 8 Prelude/The Chase/Simon, The Magician/Fight For The Cup and Finale (12:20).

Review: See entry below.

Legends of Hollywood: Franz Waxman, vol. 4 🎜🎜🎜🎜🎜

1994, Varese-Sarabande.

Album Notes: *Music:* Franz Waxman; The Queensland Symphony Orchestra, conducted by Richard Mills; *Album Producer:* Tim Handley; *Associate Producers:* Robert Townson; *Engineers:* Robert Hobson.

Selections: Untamed (suite): 1 Prelude/Capetown Street/By The River/ Vorwarts and Finale (7:19); On Borrowed Time (suite): 2 Prelude (3:16); 3 Miss Nellie, Pud And Mr. Brink (4:39); 4 Where The Woodbine Twineth (2:50); My Geisha (suite): 5 Prelude (1:43; 6 Work Montage and Wedding (1:56); 7 Goodbye Love (Finale)(2:53); The Devil Doll: 8 Souvenir de Paris Waltzes (6:22); My Cousin Rachel (suite): 9 Prelude/Tisana/Philip's Birthday/At Night and Finale (7:27); The Story Of Ruth (suite): 10 Part 1 (5:31); 11 Part 2 (3:54); 12 Part 3 (4:03); Dark City (suite): 13 Prelude (3:01); 14 Stroll In The Dark (3:57); 15 Finale (5:50); A Christmas Carol (suite): 16 Prelude and Threadneedle Street (2:47); 17 Mr. Scrooge, Ghost And Spirits (1:20); 18 Snowball Fight (2:15); 19 Christmas Morning (1:47); 20 Finale (1:40).

Review: With these four CDs Varese Sarabande has provided a wealth of hitherto unrecorded music by one of the early masters of Hollywood film music in fine new recordings by the Queensland Symphony Orchestra. Waxman's gifts for melody and orchestration served him well for more than four decades of film scoring, from the quiet mysterioso of *The Devil Doll* to the grand, boisterous symphonics of *Prince Valiant, Captain Courageous*, and the swashbuckling adventure of *Anne of the Indies*, the inspired melodies of *The Silver Chalice* to the dark, relentless rhythms of *Night and the City*, and the inventive orchestrations of *The Bride of Frankenstein* to the hayseed Americana of *Huckleberry Finn* and the meticulous comedy of *Mr. Roberts*, you're in for a treat.

Cues are uniformly long (excepting for a 50-second fanfare from *Task Force*), mostly presented in suite form, allowing for sufficient development of the material. Thorough notes accompany each CD booklet, describing the films and the cues included. Coupled with the Charles Gerhardt/National Philharmonic recording on RCA, we now have a relatively complete musical quintet of Waxman's best—and most unforgettable—film music. The only real conspicuous omission from the set would be a suite from Waxman's excellent score for the Spencer Tracy *Dr. Jekyll and Mr. Hyde*. Even so, this is another one of those desert-island CD sets. Don't be stranded without them.

Randall D. Larson

Roy Webb

The Curse of the Cat People: The Film Music of Roy Webb 🎜🎜🎜🎜🎜

1995, Cloud Nine Records.

Album Notes: *Music:* Roy Webb; *Album Concept:* Christopher Palmer; *Album Producer:* David Wishart; *Engineer:* Steve Shin.

Selections: Out of the Past: 1 Overture (2:40); Bedlam: 2 Suite (7:32); 3 Baroque Dance Suite (2:02); Crossfire: 4 Prelude (1:18); Sinbad the Sailor: 5 Suite (5:29); Journey Into Fear: 6 Main Title (1:12); Dick Tracy: 7 Suite (3:56); Mighty Joe Young: 8 Prelude (1:34); Notorious: 9 Suite (5:03); 10 Dance Suite (4:29); The Ghost Ship: 11 Suite (3:19); They Won't Believe Me: 12 Main Title (1:37); The Locket: 13 Suite (10:05); Cornered: 14 Suite (4:06); The Curse of the Cat People: 15 Amy and Irena (9:43); 16 The Old House (8:20).

Review: Obscured by the fame of such Hollywood legends as Steiner, Korngold, Tiomkin, and Newman, RKO's main composer Roy Webb has been unfairly neglected by film music history. His compositions easily rivaled that of Steiner and company. In the first original soundtrack collection of his music, 73 minutes of music from 13 films have been restored from the composer's personal acetate archives The quality is surprisingly good considering the age and source of the music. As for the music, it's uniformly excellent. From the malevolent Boris Karloff chords from *Bedlam* to the thrilling, relentless violin prelude to film noir's *Crossfire* and the surging, brass chords that signify danger in *Mighty Joe Young* the splendidly swashbuckling *Sinbad the Sailor*, the euphonious romantic crescendos of Hitchcock's *Notorious* to nightmarish moods of Val Lewton's *Death Ship* and his gently mystical *Curse of the Cat People*, all were provided with excellent musical scores. Webb was a great lyricist, sharing much of Steiner's melody, rhythm and furious musical action. Webb's memorable music is well-saved on recording. Most cues tend to be short—minute-and-a-half preludes or title cues and three or four-minute suites from more than half of the films represented—though enough are sufficiently elongated. While I would have liked to have heard more long cues, samples of Webb's western and war scores, and more of Webb's Val Lewton film music, what we do have is a fine gallery of Webb's versatile and lovely film music. A 16-page booklet provides excellent analysis of each cue, and a perceptive look at Webb himself.

Randall Larson

John Williams (1932-

Aisle Seat 🎵🎵🎵▷

1982, Philips Records.

Album Notes: The Boston Pops Orchestra, conducted by John Williams; *Arrangers*: Joseph Reisman, Alexander Courage, Bill Byers, Angela Morley, Conrad Salinger; *Album Producer*: John McClure.

Selections: E.T.: 1 The Flying Theme (J. Williams)(3:43); Chariots Of Fire: 2 Main Theme (Vangelis)(4:08); Raiders Of The Lost Ark: 3 Raiders' March (J. Williams)(5:28); 4 Yes, Giorgio: 4 If We Were In Love (J. Williams)(4:57); 5 New York, New York: 5 Main Theme (J. Kander/F. Ebb)(3:21); Gone With The Wind: 6 Tara's Theme (M. Steiner)(4:40); The Wizard Of Oz: 7 Over The Rainbow (H. Arlen/E.Y. Harburg)(3:10); Singing In The Rain: 8 Main Theme (N.H. Brown/A. Freed)(3:39); Friendly Persuasion: 9 Main Theme (D. Tiomkin)(3:52); Meet Me In St. Louis: 10 The Trolley Song (R. Blane/H. Martin)(3:29).

Review: John Williams' name has been linked to so many great films that it is always a joy to find him conducting an orchestra (in this case the excellent Boston Pops) in a selection of his own themes. But the pleasure is also multiplied when he

chooses, as is the case here, to "cover" scores written by others. His treatment of Vangelis' theme for *Chariots of Fire* or Dimitri Tiomkin's seldom-heard-these-days *Friendly Persuasion* are prime examples, though one could also include such unlikely choices (at least in an instrumental album) as *Singing in the Rain*, *The Wizard of Oz*, or *Meet Me in St. Louis*. Another interesting selection here is the theme from *Yes, Giorgio*, a rather uninspired film starring Luciano Pavarotti. The only reservation about the set itself is that since it was an early effort by Williams and the Pops, there are subsequently recorded albums that are much better overall. Consider this one as a mere filler if you already own the others.

The Hollywood Sound 🎵🎵🎵🎵▷

1997, Sony Classical.

Album Notes: The London Symphony Orchestra, conducted by John Williams; *Guest Musician*: Grover Washington, Jr.; *Album Producer*: Shawn Murphy; *Engineers*: Shawn Murphy, Simon Rhodes.

Selections: Lawrence Of Arabia: 1 Overture (M. Jarre) (3:42); E.T.: The Extra-Terrestrial: 2 Flying Theme (J. Williams) (3:40); Out Of Africa: 3 Main Title (J. Barry) (3:47); The Wizard Of Oz: 4 Fantasy For Orchestra (H. Stothart/H. Arlen/E.Y. Harburg) (5:50); Jaws: 5 Theme (J. Williams) (2:51); The Adventures Of Robin Hood: 6 Robin Hood And His Merry Men (E.W. Korngold) (4:27); Pocahontas: 7 Colors Of The Wind (A. Menken/S. Schwartz) (4:56); The Last Emperor: 8 Theme (R. Sakamoto) (4:55); A Place In The Sun: 9 Suite (F. Waxman) (7:58) *Grover Washington Jr.*; Spellbound: 10 Dream Sequence/Mountain Lodge (M. Rozsa) (5:08); The Godfather, Pt. II: 11 Main Title/The Immigrant (N. Rota) (3:47); Dances With Wolves: 12 John Dunbar Theme (J. Barry) (2:20); The Devil And Daniel Webster: 13 Mr. Scratch (B. Herrmann) (4:02); Beauty And The Beast: 14 Theme (H. Ashman/A. Menken) (3:09); The Best Years Of Our Lives: 15 Theme (H. Friedhofer) (2:39); Star Wars: 16 Main Title (J. Williams) (5:48).

Review: This collection of familiar themes from the movies (the set is subtitled "John Williams Conducts the Academy Awards' Best Scores," which pretty much sums it up) is interesting for several reasons. The first, of course, is because Williams himself is wielding the baton in yet another compilation that includes some of his own compositions (*E.T.*, *Jaws*, *Star Wars*), something that always adds a touch of authority to any recording; another is because he is also paying tribute to some of the best known themes ever composed for the screen, including *Lawrence of Arabia*, *The Adventures of Robin Hood*, *Out of Africa*, *Dances with Wolves*, *Spellbound* and *The Best Years of Our Lives*. Yet another reason to like this CD can be found in the polished performance by the London Symphony Orchestra, probably one of the best group of players for this type of music. But the real joy here is to hear Grover Washington, Jr. in such august company tackling the suite from *A Place in the Sun*, in a performance that exudes sensuality and vibrancy. Next to this kind of music, with all due respect, the themes from *Pocahontas* and *Beauty and the Beast*, while quite enjoyable in their own right, seem a mite tame and the only weak spots in the entire CD.

John Williams By Request...
♫♫♫♫♫

1987, Philips Records.

Album Notes: *Music*: John Williams; The Boston Pops Orchestra, conducted by John Williams; *Album Producers*: John McClure, George Korngold.

Selections: 1 Olympic Fanfare and Theme (4:18); The Cowboys: 2 Overture (8:51); Close Encounters Of The Third Kind: 3 Excerpts (10:03); Midway: 4 March (4:08); E.T.: 5 Flying Theme (3:40); Return Of The Jedi: 6 Luke And Leia (4:22); Superman: 7 March (4:23); 8 Liberty Fanfare (4:12); Raiders Of The Lost Ark: 9 March (5:23); The Empire Strikes Back: 10 Yoda's Theme (3:19); 1941: 11 March (4:23); Jaws: 12 Theme (2:51); The Empire Strikes Back: 13 Imperial March (3:03); 14 NBC News: Mission Theme (3:20); Star Wars: 15 Main Theme (5:35).

Review: This is a collector's dream! The set, with the Boston Pops smartly conducted by the composer, features nothing but solid gold hits from the fertile pen of John Williams, up to the time when he switched labels and began recording for Sony Classical (which explains the absence of some of his most recent contributions to the screen). While one can hardly dispute the choice of material here (only familiar titles could apply!), the plum of the collection is the *Cowboys* overture, until recently the only recording of this rousing number available anywhere. Anyone interested in the music of Williams, and in having the maestro's best-known compositions on one CD and conducted by the man himself needs look no further.

John Williams: The Spielberg/Williams Collaboration ♫♫♫♫

1990, Sony Classical.

Album Notes: *Music*: John Williams; The Boston Pops Orchestra, conducted by John Williams; *Album Producer*: Thomas Z. Shepard; *Engineer*: Bud Graham.

Selections: Raiders Of The Lost Ark: 1 The Raiders' March (5:11); Always: 2 Theme (5:31); E.T.: 3 Adventures On Earth (9:47); Sugarland Express: 4 Theme (3:36) *Toots Thielemans*; Jaws: 5 Theme (2:57); 6 Out To Sea/The Shark Cage Fugue (4:23); Empire Of The Sun: 7 Exsultate Justi (4:57) *The American Boy Choir, The Tanglewood Festival Chorus*; Indiana Jones and The Temple Of Doom: 8 Parade Of The Slave Children (4:52); E.T.: 9 Over The Moon; 1941: 10 March (4:12); Empire Of The Sun: 11 Cadillac Of The Skies (4:59) *The American Boy Choir, The Tanglewood Festival Chorus*; Indiana Jones and The Last Crusade: 12 Scherzo For Motorcycle And Orchestra (2:48); Close Encounters Of The Third Kind: 13 Excerpts (9:47).

Review: As the story goes, when Steven Spielberg, then an obscure scriptwriter with great ambitions struggling to make a living in the Hollywood studios, heard the score for Mark Rydell's *The Reivers,* he decided that John Williams would be his composer of choice. Thus began the Spielberg/Williams collaboration celebrated in this set 1990 release, already incomplete since it doesn't include selections from *Jurassic Park* or *Schindler's List*, composed after this album was recorded (that should be for a possible volume 2).

Spielberg's first effort as a director was *The Sugarland Express*, made in 1974, a throbbing suspenser with a devastating sense of humor, represented here by its "Main Theme." He subsequently illustrated himself with some major blockbusters—the *Indiana Jones* trilogy, *Jaws, Close Encounters, Empire of the Sun,* and *E.T.,* all of them included here through some of their most recognizable themes.

John Williams: Music for Stage and Screen ♫♫♫♫♫

1994, Sony Classical.

Album Notes: *Music*: John Williams, Aaron Copland; The Boston Pops Orchestra, conducted by John Williams; *Featured Soloists*: Tim Morrison (trumpet), Laurence Thorstenberg (English horn); *Album Producer*: Thomas Z. Shepard; *Engineer*: Bud Graham.

Selections: The Red Pony (A. Copland): 1 Morning On The Ranch (4:41); 2 The Gift (4:58); 3 Dream March 2:30; 4 Circus March (1:55); 5 Walk To The Bunkhouse (2:49); 6 Grandfather's Tale (4:47); 7 Happy Ending (3:18); Born On The Fourth Of July (suite)(J. Williams): 8 Theme (6:21); 9 Cua Viet River, Vietnam 1968 (3:37); 10 Massapequa... The Early Days (4:06); 11 Quiet City for Strings, Trumpet and English Horn (A. Copland)(10:35); 12 The Reivers (J. Williams)(18:42) *Burgess Meredith*.

"I always try to find a new way of writing music with each film because each is a multi-layered work of art, with many different meanings and expressions. The music has to express the theme of the film and becomes the leitmotif, and I try to integrate the music into the film. If you separate the music from the film neither would seem complete."

Zhao Jiping
(Film Score Monthly, October 1996)

Review: As the score for Mark Rydell's *The Reivers* established it early, John Williams was strongly influenced by Aaron Copland, and while the stylistic comparison between the two stopped soon after, when Williams found his own voice, it is interesting to hear in this set conducted by Williams some of the film music composed by Copland (particularly the several selections from *The Red Pony* which one never tires of hearing) juxtaposed to Williams' own suite from *The Reivers,* narrated as in the film by Burgess Meredith. The other selections (from *Born on the Fourth of July* and *Quiet City*) further enhance the similarities and differences between Copland and Williams, and present the ideal programming for a peaceful Sunday morning, if one feels so inclined.

Out of This World 🎵🎵🎵

1983, Philips Records.

Album Notes: The Boston Pops Orchestra, conducted by John Williams; *Featured Soloist:* Chester Schmitz (tuba); *Arrangers:* Jerry Goldsmith, Alexander Courage, Stu Philips; *Album Producer:* John McClure.

Selections: 2001: A Space Odyssey: 1 Also Sprach Zarathustra (introduction) (R. Strauss) (1:46); E.T.: 2 Adventures On Earth (J. Williams) (9:40); Alien: 3 Closing Title (J. Goldsmith) (2:45); Star Trek: 4 Main Theme (A. Courage) (3:36); Battlestar Galactica: 5 Main Title (S. Philips/G. Larson) (3:26); Star Trek The Motion Picture: 6 Main Title (J. Goldsmith) (4:03); The Twilight Zone: 7 Theme And Variations (M. Constant) (3:34); Return Of The Jedi (J. Williams): 8 Parade Of The Ewoks (3:30); 9 Luke And Leia (4:22); 10 Jabba The Hutt (3:30); 11 The Forest Battle (4:01).

Review: The "outer space" concept behind this album enabled John Williams and the Boston Pops to fly high and deliver some rousing music written for a variety of out-of-this-world film epics, including Williams' own *E.T.* and *Return of the Jedi,* Jerry Goldsmith's *Alien* and *Star Trek The Motion Picture,* and (oh, surprise!) Stu Philips' "Main Theme" from the unjustly-neglected *Battlestar Galactica,* and Marius Constant's theme from *The Twilight Zone.* Opening the set, of course, is Richard Strauss' introduction to *Also Sprach Zarathustra,* which got its screen credentials when it was used to great effect in the granddaddy of all contemporary outer-space adventures, *2001: A Space Odyssey.*

Pops in Space 🎵🎵🎵🎵

1980, Philips Records.

Album Notes: *Music:* John Williams; The Boston Pops Orchestra, conducted by John Williams.

Selections: Superman: 1 March (4:27); 2 Love Theme (4:49); The Empire Strikes Back: 3 The Asteroid Field (4:15); 4 Yoda's Theme (3:21); 5 The Imperial March (3:07); Star Wars: 6 Main Theme (5:38); 7 Princess Leia (4:06); Close Encounters Of The Third Kind: 8 Suite (10:09).

Review: More space-related music, courtesy of John Williams and the Boston Pops, though the selections this time come strictly from the composer's own scores for *Superman, The Empire Strikes Back, Star Wars* and *Close Encounters of the Third Kind.* The "Suite" from that last film is the set's icing-on-the-cake, as it includes music heard in the so-called "Special Edition" (namely the last scene in which contactee Richard Dreyfuss finds himself in the spaceship) and available nowhere else. Indeed a real bonus for fans and collectors alike.

Salute to Hollywood 🎵🎵🎵🎵

1988, Philips Records.

Album Notes: The Boston Pops Orchestra, conducted by John Williams; *Arrangers:* John Williams, Morton Stevens, Glenn Osser, Joseph Reisman, Richard Hayman, Herbert Spencer, Sid Ramin; *Album Producer:* John McClure; *Engineer:* John Newton.

Selections: 1 Hooray For Hollywood (R. Whiting)(3:25); 2 Pops Salutes The Oscars: (a) When You Wish Upon A Star (L. Harline), (b) Swingin' On A Star (J. Van Heusen), (c) Moon River (H. Mancini), (d) Raindrops Keep Fallin' On My Head (B. Bacharach), (e) Theme From The Way We Were (M. Hamlisch), (f) The Shadow Of Your Smile (J. Mandel)(10:46); 3 Somewhere Out There (B. Mann/J. Horner/C. Weil)(3:39); 4 A Tribute To Judy

Garland: (a) Over The Rainbow (H. Arlen/E.Y. Harburg), (b) We're Off To See The Wizard (H. Arlen/E.Y. Harburg), (c) You Made Me Love You (J. Monaco/J. McCarthy), (d) Be A Clown (C. Porter), (e) Get Happy (H. Arlen/T. Koehler), (f) The Man That Got Away (H. Arlen/I. Gershwin) (10:55); The Witches Of Eastwick (J. Williams): 5 Balloon Sequence (4:53); 6 Devil's Dance (4:53); Out Of Africa: 7 Love Theme (J. Barry) (2:54); 8 La Bamba (W. Clauson) (4:41); 9 The Bad And The Beautiful (D. Raksin) (5:35); Dancing With Astaire: 10 (a) Top Hat, White Tie And Tails (I. Berlin), (b) I Won't Dance (J. Kern/D. Fields/O. Hammerstein/J. McHugh/O. Harbach), (c) Dancing In The Dark (A. Schwartz/H. Dietz), (d) The Continental (C. Conrad/H. Magidson), (e) Change Partners (I. Berlin), (f) The Carioca (V. Youmans/G. Kahn/E. Eliscu) (9:36).

Review: This winning entry in the John Williams/Boston Pops catalog is particularly notable in that it is a tribute to Hollywood film music as seen by one of its most proficient exponents. The sole Williams entry, interestingly, consists of two selections from his Oscar-winning score for *The Witches of Eastwick*, a pleasant diversion which yielded the sardonic "Devil's Dance" and "Balloon Sequence." Three long suites offer tributes to Oscar-winning themes, Judy Garland and Fred Astaire, in a program that may seem evident at first but that has its many enjoyable moments. The odd choice in this collection, if favoritism may be shown, is the mercifully short "Somewhere Out There," from James Horner's score for *An American Tail*. With so many other great themes available, from so many other great composers, this seems like a bit of a waste. Don't let it deter you from enjoying the rest of the set, though.

Schindler's List: The Classic Film Music of John Williams ♪♪♪♪

1995, Silva Screen Records.

Album Notes: *Music:* John Williams; *Orchestrations:* Paul Bateman, Brian Rogers, Peter Smith, Kevin Townend; The City of Prague Philharmonic, conducted by Paul Bateman; *Featured Soloists:* Paul Bateman (piano), Petr Nedobilsky (violin), Jaroslava Eliasova (piano, harpsichord), Miroslav Kejmar (cornet), Antonin Novak (violin); *Album Producer:* James Fitzpatrick; *Engineers:* Eric Tomlinson, John Timperley, Mike Ross-Trevor, Mark Ayres.

Selections: Schindler's List: 1 Theme (orchestral version) (3:59); Indiana Jones and The Last Crusade: 2 End Credits (10:48); Presumed Innocent: 3 End Titles (4:19); Far And Away: 4 End Credits (6:54); Jaws: 5 Main Title (2:16); The Cowboys: 6 Overture (9:41); Indiana Jones and The Temple Of Doom: 7

Nocturnal Activities (2:02); Star Wars: 8 Main Title (5:22); The Empire Strikes Back: 9 Han Solo And The Princess (4:09); Return Of The Jedi: 10 Forest Battle (3:53); Family Plot: 11 Finale (3:52); 1941: 12 March (4:20); Born On The Fourth Of July: 13 End Credits (5:42); Jurassic Park: 14 Suite (5:57); 15 Schindler's List: Theme (piano version) (2:38).

Review: With so many other recordings of John Williams' music available, and with the composer himself covering most of his own grounds, one might truthfully question the necessity for yet another compilation, particularly one conducted by someone else. Don't blame the folks at Silva Screen for trying to cash in on a good thing. Actually the set is really not that bad, and if it includes many themes that are to be found on numerous other compilations, it has the merit of proposing some that are harder to come by—like the "End Titles" from *Presumed Innocent*, the "March" from *1941*, and the "Finale" from *Family Plot*. The rest may be routine fare, but it is played with great gusto by the Prague Philharmonic, and all things considered it all adds up to a perfectly enjoyable recording, with particularly great dynamics to make it sound ever better.

Star Wars/Close Encounters: The Classic Film Scores of John Williams ♪♪♪

1989, RCA Victor Records.

Album Notes: *Music:* John Williams; The National Philharmonic Orchestra, conducted by Charles Gerhardt; *Album Producer:* George Korngold; *Engineer:* K.E. Wilkinson.

Selections: Star Wars: 1 Main Title (5:40); 2 The Little People Work (4:50); 3 Here They Come! (2:04); 4 Princess Leia (5:03); 5 The Final Battle (7:15); 6 The Throne Room and End Title (7:57); Close Encounters Of The Third Kind: 7 Barnstorming/Arrival Of The Mother Ship/The Pilots' Return/The Visitors/Final Scene (21:00).

Review: After having covered the music of pioneers like Erich-Wolfgang Korngold, Alfred Newman, Dimitri Tiomkin, Miklos Rozsa and Max Steiner, it probably made sense that Charles Gerhardt and producer George Korngold should have turned their attention to the classic film scores of John Williams, who was clearly inspired by his predecessors in the field. The only problem, of course, is while many of the works covered in the earlier sets in the series were not readily available anywhere else, Williams recorded his own scores, sometimes with greater drive and excitement than can be found in this routine album. Not to take anything away from the care and attention that evidently went into the production of this CD, the long suite from

Close Encounters is particularly well put together, and the National Philharmonic generally gives a suitably polished performance. But it seems a bit redundant to get this recording when the original soundtracks are available, particularly now that they have been remastered and often feature additional music.

Victor Young (1900-1956)

Shane: A Tribute to Victor Young 🎵🎵🎵🎵

1996, Koch International Classics.

Album Notes: *Music:* Victor Young; *Arrangements:* Patrick Russ, Mark McGurty, Richard Kaufman, Henry Mancini, Steven R. Bernstein; The New Zealand Symphony Orchestra, conducted by Richard Kaufman; *Album Producer:* Michael Fine; *Engineer:* Keith Warren.

Selections: Shane: 1 Prelude (2:52); 2 The Tree Stump (2:59); 3 Rodeo Music (:44); 4 Wyoming Sketches (3:12); 5 Cemetery Hill (4:12); For Whom The Bell Tolls: 6 Suite (8:29); Samson And Delilah: 7 Prelude (2:25); 8 Miriam (1:27); 9 Dance To Dagon (1:53); 10 Hebrew Lament (:56); 11 Feather Dance (1:50); 12 The Fall Of Samson (1:28); 13 Exit Music (1:44); The Quiet Man: 14 St. Patrick's Day (2:17); 15 Kathleen (3:35); 16 Innesfree (2:38); Tribute To Victor Young: 17 Suite (8:51); Around The World In Eighty Days: 18 Epilogue (6:47).

Review: One of the great unsung heroes of Hollywood film music, Victor Young is slowly getting the recognition that has eluded him for so long. This superb tribute, which regroups several of the themes he created for the movies, is one of the first steps in the right direction. While most filmgoers remember the celebrated "Call of the Faraway Hills," from *Shane*, that score has long been overdue for a complete overhaul, along the lines of Jerome Moross' *The Big Country* or Elmer Bernstein's *The Magnificent Seven*. Its appearance here, in abbreviated form, is one of the great joys in this set, even if one misses the atmospheric ambience Young himself created in his own reading of the main theme, with its plaintive saxophone evoking the nostalgic feel of the far away hills.

And while *For Whom the Bell Tolls, The Quiet Man, Around the World* and *Samson and Delilah* are all available on compact disc, Kaufman and the New Zealand Symphony Orchestra find new reasons to listen to these scores again and enjoy them for the sheer magic they spin. The *Tribute to Victor Young*, arranged and orchestrated by Henry Mancini, regroups the themes from several other scores, including *Golden Earrings, When I Fall in Love, Sweet Sue, Stella by Starlight,* and *My Foolish Heart*.

Hans Zimmer (1957-

Hans Zimmer: New Music in Films 🎵🎵🎵🎵

1989, Milan Records.

Album Notes: *Music:* Hans Zimmer; *Featured Soloists:* Alan Murphy (guitar), Guy Barker (trumpet), Emily Burridge (cello), Gavyn Wright (violin), Fiachra Tranch (keyboards), Charlie Morgan (drums), Hans Zimmer (synthesizers); *Album Producer:* Hans Zimmer; *Engineers:* Al Clay, Chris Dibble.

Selections: Burning Secret: 1 Suite (23:59); The Fruit Machine: 2 Suite (20:08); Diamond Skulls: 3 Theme (4:22).

Review: Give credit to Hans Zimmer for trying to be innovative, and also for giving other, promising new talent, an opportunity to work with him. One might dispute his creative approach, however, and find it lacking is some respects, but his music, well suited for the films which he scores, often displays an attractive bend that translates very well as pure audio experience, even if it sounds too much like New Age music.

Nothing could be farther apart in tone than the three films represented here, *Burning Secret,* a 1988 romantic melodrama set in turn-of-the-century Vienna; *The Fruit Machine,* also from 1988, directed by Philip Saville; and *Diamond Skulls,* composed in 1989 for a film directed by Nicholas Broomfield, a hip study of sex and violence among the British upperclass. Yet, Zimmer found in them the basic elements to create scores that embody each story and its framework, with his reliance on synthesizer textures to enhance acoustic instruments most becoming. The presentation of the first two as long suites, as opposed to shorter individual cues, adds enormously to one's appreciation of the music.

Louis Armstrong

Now You Has Jazz: Louis Armstrong at M-G-M 🎵🎵🎵🎵

1997, Rhino Records.

Album Notes: *Album Producers:* George Feltenstein, Bradley Flanagan; *Engineer:* Doug Schwartz.

Selections: The Strip: 1 Ain't Misbehavin' (T. Waller/H. Brooks/A. Razaf) (3:12); 2 One O'Clock Jump (W. Basie) (2:52); 3 Ole Miss (W.C. Handy) (2:25); 4 Basin Street Blues (S. Williams) (2:08) *Louis Armstrong, Jack Teagarden;* 5 I'm Coming, Virginia (D. Heywood) (1:45); 6 A Kiss To Build A Dream On (B. Kalmar/H. Ruby/O. Hammerstein II) (2:54); 7 Medley: Shadracks/When The Saints Go Marchin' In (R. MacGimsey) (4:33); 8 That's A Plenty (L.

Pollack) (2:15); Cabin In The Sky: 9 Ain't It The Truth (H. Arlen/E.Y. Harburg) (5:23); The Strip: 10 Hines' Retreat (E. Hines) (1:51); 11 Fatha's Time (E. Hines) (2:18); 12 J.T. Jive (L. Armstrong) (2:16); Glory Alley: 13 That's What The Man Said (W. Robinson) (3:25) *Louis Armstrong, Jack Teagarden*; 14 Glory Alley (J. Livingston/M. David) (3:13); 15 Oh Didn't He Ramble (W.C. Handy) (1:15); 16 South Rampart Street Parade (R. Bauduc/B. Haggart) (1:20); 17 Flee As A Bird (W.C. Handy) (2:14); 18 It's A Most Unusual Day (J. McHugh/H. Adamson) (1:48); High Society: 19 High Society Calypso (C. Porter) (2:08); 20 Little One (C. Porter) (2:28) *Bing Crosby, Louis Armstrong*; 21 I Love You Samantha (C. Porter) (:43); 22 I Love You Samantha (C. Porter) (3:07) *Bing Crosby, Louis Armstrong*; 23 Now You Has Jazz (C. Porter) (4:12) *Bing Crosby, Louis Armstrong*; When The Boys Meet The Girls: 24 Throw It Out Of Your Mind (B. Kyle/L. Armstrong) (2:11); 25 I Got Rhythm (G. & I. Gershwin) (1:22).

Review: Before he hit a pinnacle with his appearance in *High Society*, in 1956, Louis Armstrong appeared in quite a few films which put his congenial personality and his chops to good use. His relationship with M-G-M began when he was signed to appear in *Cabin In The Sky*, in 1943, though his big scene was eventually cut out of the picture. In 1951, he was cast again in a film noir starring Mickey Rooney, *The Strip*, in which he and his band performed various numbers in their standard repertoire. The following year, *Glory Alley*, set in New Orleans, gave him another opportunity to appear with his band on the screen. But it wasn't until *High Society* that he finally hit his stride, performing in the opening scene and in one spectacular number with Bing Crosby that gave its title to this anthology. As is always the case with CDs released by Rhino, this one comes with a full complement of pictures, annotations and remarks, all of which enliven the set tremendously. One might quibble with the producers for having inserted the only track from *Cabin In The Sky* in the middle of the selections from *The Strip*, rather than try to organize the set chronologically. But this is piddling, and doesn't in any way detract from enjoying the music.

Fred Astaire

Starring Fred Astaire ♫♫♫♩▷

1989, Columbia Records.

Album Notes: *Album Producer*: Michael Brooks; *Engineer*: Frank Abbey.

Selections: CD 1: Top Hat (I. Berlin): 1 Cheek To Cheek (3:20); 2 No Strings (2:34); 3 Isn't This A Lovely Day? (3:16); 4 Top Hat, White Tie And Tails (2:41); 5 The Piccolino (3:18); Follow The Fleet (I. Berlin): 6 Let's Face The Music And Dance (2:29); 7 I'm Putting All My Eggs In One Basket (2:49); 8 We Saw The Sea (2:22); 9 I'm Building Up To An Awful Letdown (J. Mercer/F. Astaire)(3:06); 10 Let Yourself Go (2:38); 11 I'd Rather Lead A Band (2:30); Swing Time (J. Kern/D. Fields): 12 The Way You Look Tonight (3:11); 13 Never Gonna Dance (3:13); 14 Pick Yourself Up (2:59); 15 A Fine Romance (2:52); 16 Bojangles Of Harlem (3:07); Shall We Dance (G. & I. Gershwin): 17 They Can't Take That Away From Me (3:04); 18 They All Laughed (2:44).

CD 2: Shall We Dance (G. & I. Gershwin): 1 Beginner's Luck (2:52); 2 Let's Call The Whole Thing Off (3:12); 3 Shall We Dance? (2:33); 4 Slap That Bass (2:55); A Damsel In Distress (G. & I. Gershwin): 5 A Foggy Day (2:54); 6 Things Are Looking Up (3:11); 7 Nice Work If You Can Get It (2:42); 8 I Can't Be Bothered Now (2:25); Carefree (I. Berlin): 9 Change Partners (3:07); 10 I Used To Be Colored Blind (3:07); 11 The Yam (2:46); 12 The Yam (explained) (2:53); 13 Who Cares? (G. & I. Gershwin)(2:52) *Benny Goodman and His Orchestra*; 14 Just Like Taking Candy From A Baby (F. Astaire/G. Shelley)(2:49) *Benny Goodman and His Orchestra*; Second Chorus: 15 Love Of My Life (J. Mercer/A. Shaw)(2:23); 16 Poor Mr. Chisholm (J. Mercer/B. Hanighen)(2:46); 17 Me And The Ghost Upstairs (J. Mercer/B. Hanighen)(2:33); 18 (I Ain't Hep To That Step But I'll) Dig It (J. Mercer/H. Borne)(2:21).

Review: See entry below.

The Best of Fred Astaire from M-G-M Classic Films
♫♫♫

1987, MCA Records.

Album Notes: *Album Producer*: Andy McKaie; *Engineer*: Greg Fulginiti.

Selections: Easter Parade: 1 Steppin' Out With My Baby (I. Berlin)(2:28); The Barkleys of Broadway: 2 They Can't Take That Away From Me (G. & I. Gershwin)(2:30); Easter Parade: 3 A Couple Of Swells (I. Berlin)(2:36) *Fred Astaire, Judy Garland*; 4 It Only Happens When I Dance With You (2:32); The Band Wagon: 5 That's Entertainment (H. Dietz/A. Schwartz)(3:06) *Fred Astaire, Nanette Fabray, Jack Buchanan, India Adams*; 6 By Myself (H. Dietz/A. Schwartz)(2:28); 7 A Shine On Your Shoes (H. Dietz/A. Schwartz)(3:12); Silk Stockings: 8 All Of You (C. Porter)(2:46); Easter Parade: 9 I Love A Piano/ Snooky Oookums/When The Midnight Choo Choo Leaves For Alabam' (I. Berlin) (3:06) *Fred Astaire, Judy Garland*; Silk Stockings: 10 The Ritz Roll And Rock (C. Porter)(2:56).

Review: See entry below.

Steppin' Out: Fred Astaire at M-G-M ♫♫♫♪

1993, Sony Music Special Products.

Album Notes: *Album Producer*: Dan Rivard; *Engineer*: Debra Parkinson.

Selections: Easter Parade (I. Berlin): 1 Steppin' Out With My Baby (5:31) *Fred Astaire, Judy Garland*; 2 It Only Happens When I Dance With You (2:34); 3 A Couple Of Swells (4:31) *Fred Astaire, Judy Garland*; The Barkleys Of Broadway (H. Warren/G. Gershwin/I. Gershwin): 4 You'd Be Hard To Replace (2:40); 5 Shoes With Wings On (2:39); 6 They Can't Take That Away From Me (3:04); 7 My One And Only Highland Fling (3:18) *Fred Astaire, Ginger Rogers*; Three Little Words (B. Kalmar/H. Ruby): 8 Where Did You Get That Girl? (2:38) *Fred Astaire, Anita Ellis*; 9 My Sunny Tennessee/So Long Oo-Long (How Long You Gonna Be Gone?)/Three Little Words (3:16) *Fred Astaire, Red Skelton*; 10 Nevertheless (I'm In Love With You)(3:28) *Fred Astaire, Anita Ellis, Red Skelton*; Royal Wedding (B. Lane/A.J. Lerner): 11 You're All The World To Me (2:53); 12 How Could You Believe Me When I Said I Loved You When You Know I've Been A Liar All My Life? (6:23) *Fred Astaire, Jane Powell*; The Belle Of New York (H. Warren/J. Mercer): 13 Bachelor's Dinner Song (3:23); 14 Baby Doll (4:33); The Band Wagon (H. Dietz/A. Schwartz): 15 Triplets (2:33) *Fred Astaire, Nanette Fabray, Jack Buchanan*; 16 By Myself (2:20); 17 Got A Bran' New Suit (1:41); Silk Stockings (C. Porter): 18 Stereophonic Sound (3:53) *Fred Astaire, Janis Paige*; 19 All Of You (5:15) *Fred Astaire, Cyd Charisse*; 20 The Ritz Roll And Rock (3:36).

Review: Not often thought of as a singer, Fred Astaire nonetheless created many hit songs. Most were specifically written for him by the best Tin Pan Alley and Hollywood composers during a prolific screen career that extended over more than 30 years. The 2-CD set, *Starring Fred Astaire*, is a compilation of tunes he performed in his early movies (in which Ginger Rogers was his co-star). Many of them were rerecorded with Johnny Green and his orchestra. Most of these songs have become standards that provided Astaire with the hits that marked one of the most successful periods in his career.

The other two compilations, *The Best of Fred Astaire at M-G-M* and *Steppin' Out*, focus most specifically on the latter part of his career. They cover the period after he left RKO, where he enjoyed his early film successes, and moved to M-G-M, where he emerged as one of the most brilliant stars in that studio's roster. Essentially, both albums cover the same material, though *Steppin' Out* does so in a way that's more thorough, even if it is less than complete. While awaiting a new compilation from Rhino (which should be available by the time you read these lines), these two sets are essential.

The Beatles

A Hard Day's Night ♫♫♫♫

1987, EMI Records; from the movie *A Hard Day's Night*, United Artists, 1964.

Album Notes: *Music*: John Lennon, Paul McCartney; *Lyrics*: John Lennon, Paul McCartney; *Album Producer*: George Martin.

Selections: 1 A Hard Day's Night (2:32); 2 I Should Have Known Better (2:45); 3 If I Fell (2:22); 4 I'm Happy Just To Dance With You (1:58); 5 And I Love Her (2:31); 6 Tell Me Why (2:10); 7 Can't Buy Me Love (2:15); 8 Any Time At All (2:14); 9 I'll Cry Instead (1:48); 10 Things We Said Today (2:39); 11 When I Get Home (2:19); 12 You Can't Do That (2:37); 13 I'll Be Back (2:21).

Review: From the first chord of the title song, chiming out like Big Ben, the soundtrack recording of the Beatles' first film preserves all the freshness and energy of what still stands as one of the best "rock movies". Not preserved — fortunately or not — are producer George Martin's "Swinging London" style big band orchestrations, a prominent part of the original soundtrack LP in the US. They were dropped from the CD reissue as part of a realignment of the Beatles' early catalogue to conform to the UK releases. The CD features seven songs from the film, plus six others first issued in the US on other Beatles LPs.

Marc Kirkeby

Help!

1987, EMI Records; from the movie *Help!*, 1965.

Album Notes: *Music*: John Lennon, Paul McCartney, George Harrison; *Lyrics*: John Lennon, Paul McCartney, George Harrison; *Album Producer*: George Martin.

Selections: 1 Help! (2:21); 2 The Night Before (2:37); 3 You've Got To Hide Your Love Away (2:11); 4 I Need You (2:32); 5 Another Girl (2:08); 6 You're Going To Lose That Girl (2:20); 7 Ticket To Ride (3:13); 8 Act Naturally (2:33); 9 It's Only Love (1:59); 10 You Like Me Too Much (2:38); 11 Tell Me What You See (2:40); 12 I've Just Seen A Face (2:07); 13 Yesterday (2:08); 14 Dizzy Miss Lizzie (Williams)(2:54).

Review: As with *A Hard Day's Night*, the soundtrack CD from the Beatles' second film does away with orchestrations included on the U.S. LP — a shame in this case, because Ken Thorne's witty James Bondish work captured the flavor of the movie in a way that the seven Beatles originals (wonderful though they are) do not. Filling out the CD reissue, once again,

s o u n d t r a c k s

Lullaby of Broadway: The Best of Busky Berkeley at Warner Bros.

compilation soundtracks

are seven other Beatles songs from the original UK LP. For both films, it should be added, the audio tracks on the video laserdisc releases outshine the same music on CD.

Marc Kirkeby

Let It Be 🎵🎵🎵🎵

1987, EMI Records; from the documentary *Let It Be,* **1970.**

Album Notes: *Music*: John Lennon, Paul McCartney, George Harrison; *Lyrics*: John Lennon, Paul McCartney, George Harrison; *Album Producer*: Phil Spector.

Selections: 1 Two Of Us (3:37); 2 Dig A Pony (3:54); 3 Across The Universe (3:49); 4 I Me Mine (2:26); 5 Dig It (:50); 6 Let It Be (4:03); 7 Maggie Mae (:41); 8 I've Got A Feeling (3:38); 9 One After 909 (2:55); 10 The Long And Winding Road (3:38); 11 For You Blue (2:33); 12 Get Back (3:07).

Review: Meant as a documentary of a band in the recording studio, the Beatles' last film instead captured them losing their way and coming apart, which may explain why it remains unavailable on video after many years. The soundtrack makes a much more cheerful document, even if the CD represents only a small portion of the songs recorded in those marathon sessions. (The remainder are largely available — or not, depending on the whim of the FBI — on what may be the biggest batch of bootlegs ever associated with a single album.) Perhaps intentionally, the music sounds like the Beatles' story in miniature, from skiffle ("Maggie Mae") to early rock & roll ("One After 909") to spirituality ("Across the Universe"). Get back, indeed.

Marc Kirkeby

Magical Mystery Tour 🎵🎵🎵🎵

1987, EMI Records; from the television special *Magical Mystery Tour,* **1967.**

Album Notes: *Music*: John Lennon, Paul McCartney, George Harrison, Ringo Starr; *Lyrics*: John Lennon, Paul McCartney, George Harrison, Ringo Starr.

Selections: 1 Magical Mystery Tour (2:52); 2 The Fool On The Hill (3:00); 3 Flying (2:17); 4 Blue Jay Way (3:57); 5 Your Mother Should Know (2:29); 6 I Am The Walrus (4:37); 7 Hello Goodbye (3:32); 8 Strawberry Fields Forever (4:10); 9 Penny Lane (3:04); 10 Baby You're A Rich Man (3:03); 11 All You Need Is Love (3:49).

Review: The Beatles' lone bomb, this made-for-TV musical baffled British audiences and never had a proper US release. With three decades of MTV-induced hindsight, we can see it for what it really was: the first music video collection, barely glued together as episodes in a guided bus trip. Minus the visuals (which include, memorably, John Lennon shoveling spaghetti),

the music carries forward the group's "Sgt. Pepper" psychedelic dabbling to its soaring culmination in the Joycean "I Am the Walrus". Rounding out the CD (as on the original LP) are five more Beatles singles of the period.

Marc Kirkeby

The Yellow Submarine 🎵🎵🎵

1987, EMI Records; from the animated feature *The Yellow Submarine,* **1969.**

Album Notes: *Music*: George Martin; *Songs*: John Lennon & Paul McCartney; *Album Producer*: George Martin.

Selections: 1 Yellow Submarine (J. Lennon/P. McCartney) (2:43) *The Beatles*; 2 Only A Northern Song (G. Harrison) (3:28) *The Beatles*; 3 All Together Now (J. Lennon/P. McCartney) (2:13) *The Beatles*; 4 Hey Bulldog (J. Lennon/P. McCartney) (3:14) *The Beatles*; 5 It's All Too Much (G. Harrison) (6:29) *The Beatles*; 6 All You Need Is Love (J. Lennon/P. McCartney) (3:53) *The Beatles*; 7 Pepperland (2:24); 8 Sea Of Time (3:00); 9 Sea Of Holes (2:21); 10 Sea Of Monsters (3:40); 11 March Of The Meanies (2:23); 12 Pepperland Laid Waste (2:15); 13 Yellow Submarine In Pepperland (J. Lennon/P. McCartney) (2:11).

Review: The passing years have turned the title song into a children's classic, but the Beatles' only animated film was meant for adults, or at least grownup kids. The story is a flower-power fable of creativity struggling against repression, the songs a "Sgt. Pepper"-period mix of simplicity and psychedelia. Alone among the CD reissues of the Beatles' film soundtracks, this one preserves the George Martin-composed and arranged orchestrations from the original LP. It still makes a skimpy meal, though, especially since two of the six Beatles tunes are available on other CDs. Business historians take note: George Harrison's "Only A Northern Song" may stand as the only protest song ever written about a music publisher.

Marc Kirkeby

Busby Berkeley

Lullaby of Broadway: The Best of Busky Berkeley at Warner Bros. 🎵🎵🎵🎵

1995, Rhino Records.

Album Notes: *Music*: Harry Warren; *Lyrics*: Al Dubin; The Warner Bros. Studio Chorus and Orchestra; *Album Producers*: Marilee Bradford, Bradley Flanagan, George Feltenstein; *Engineer*: Reid Caulfield.

Selections: CD 1: 42nd Street: 1 Young And Healthy (4:01) *Dick Powell, Toby Wing*; 2 Shuffle Off To Buffalo (4:17) *Ruby Keeler, Clarence Nordstrum, Ginger Rogers, Una Merkel*; 3 42nd Street (5:47) *Ruby Keeler, Dick Powell*; Gold Diggers Of 1933: 4 We're In The Money (The Gold Diggers Song)(2:32) *Ginger Rogers*; 5 I've Got To Sing A Torch Song (outtake)(3:49) *Ginger Rogers*; 6 The Shadow Waltz (6:06) *Dick Powell, Ruby Keeler*; 7 Remember My Forgotten Man (6:23) *Etta Moten, Joan Blondell*; Footlight Parade: 8 Honeymoon Hotel (8:24) *Ruby Keeler, Dick Powell*; 9 By A Waterfall (S. Fain/I. Kahal)(10:43) *Dick Powell, Ruby Keeler, Chorines*; 10 Shanghai Lil (10:26) *James Cagney, Runy Keeler*; Wonder Bar: 11 Don't Say Goodnight (10:23) *Dick Powell.*

CD 2: Fashions Of 1934: 1 Spin A Little Web Of Dreams (S. Fain/I. Kahal) (7:26) *Verree Teasdale, Chorines*; Dames: 2 The Girl At The Ironing Board (5:52) *Joan Blondell, Chorines*; 3 I Only Have Eyes For You (9:05) *Dick Powell, Ruby Keeler*; 4 Dames (9:48) *Dick Powell, Chorines*; Gold Diggers Of 1935: 5 The Words Are In My Heart (8:06) *Dick Powell, Chorines*; 6 Lullaby Of Broadway (13:42) *Winifred Shaw, Dick Powell*; In Caliente: 7 The Lady In Red (A. Wrubel/M. Dixon)(9:19) *Winifred Shaw, Judy Canova*; Gold Diggers Of 1937: 8 All's Fair In Love And War (10:34) *Dick Powell, Joan Blondell, Lee Dixon, Rosalind Marquis*; Hollywood Hotel: 9 Hooray For Hollywood (R. Whiting/J. Mercer)(4:24) *Dick Powell, Francis Langford, Johnny "Scat" Davis, Gene Krupa, Benny Goodman and His Orchestra.*

Review: It seems somewhat redundant (not to say inaccurate) to name this set after Busby Berkeley. To be sure, the art deco director/choreographer may have been responsible for some of the best film musicals of the late 1930s and early '40s, but what we are offered here are not the visuals for which he became celebrated, but the songs around which he built his extravagant musical numbers, most of them written by Harry Warren and Al Dubin. Be that as it may, this set is an uncompromising joy, a feast for the ear, only occasionally marred by the sonics inherent to the primitive recording techniques at the time.

The numbers are presented here in their entirety, as they were done on the screen, with Dick Powell, Ruby Keeler, Joan Blondell, Ginger Rogers and James Cagney among the vocalists heard in them. As is always the case with Rhino, the set comes with a booklet replete with pictures, excellent liner notes, and complete information about the songs and the recordings.

See also: Dick Powell

James Bond

The Best of James Bond: 30th Anniversary Limited Edition ♪♪♪♪▷

1992, EMI Records.

Album Notes: *Music*: John Barry, Monty Norman, Marvin Hamlisch, Bill Conti; *Album Producer*: Ron Furmanek; *A&R Research*: Ron Furmanek; *Engineer*: Bob Norberg.

Selections: CD 1: 1 James Bond Theme (M. Norman)(1:45) *The Monty Norman Orchestra*; 2 From Russia With Love (L. Bart) (2:32) *Matt Monro*; 3 Goldfinger (J. Barry/L. Bricusse/A. Newley)(2:46) *Shirley Bassey*; 4 Thunderball (J. Barry/D. Black)(3:00) *Tom Jones*; 5 You Only Live Twice (J. Barry/L. Bricusse)(2:44) *Nancy Sinatra*; 6 On Her Majesty's Secret Service (J. Barry) (2:31) *The John Barry Orchestra*; 7 Diamonds Are Forever (J. Barry/ D. Black) (2:40) *Shirley Bassey*; 8 Live And Let Die (P. McCartney/L. McCartney)(3:11) *Paul McCartney, Wings*; 9 The Man With The Golden Gun (J. Barry/D. Black) (2:33) *Lulu*; 10 Nobody Does It Better (M. Hamlisch/C. Bayer Sager)(3:28) *Carly Simon*; 11 Moonraker (J. Barry/H. David)(3:07) *Shirley Bassey*; 12 For Your Eyes Only (B. Conti/M. Leeson)(3:02) *Sheena Easton*; 13 All Time High (J. Barry/T. Rice)(3:01) *Rita Coolidge*; 14 A View To A Kill (J. Barry/Duran Duran)(3:33) *Duran Duran*; 15 The Living Daylights (J. Barry/ P. Waaktaar) (4:14) *a-ha*; 16 Licence To Kill (J. Barry/N.M. Walden/J. Cohen/ W. Afanasieff)(5:13) *Gladys Knight.*

CD 2: 1 James Bond Theme (M. Norman)(1:57) *The John Barry Orchestra*; 2 007 (J. Barry)(2:43) *The John Barry Orchestra*; 3 Goldfinger (L. Bricusse/A. Newley) (2:48) *Anthony Newley*; 4 Pussy Galore's Flying Circus (J. Barry) (2:45) *The John Barry Orchestra*; 5 Golden Girl (J. Barry)(2:27) *The John Barry Orchestra*; 6 Death Of Tilley (J. Barry)(2:01) *The John Barry Orchestra*; 7 The Laser Beam (J. Barry)(2:50) *The John Barry Orchestra*; 8 Mr. Kiss Kiss Bang Bang (J. Barry/L. Bricusse)(3:02) *Dionne Warwick*; 9 Thunderball Suite (J. Barry)(21:10) *The John Barry Orchestra*; 10 Mr. Kiss Kiss Bang Bang (J. Barry/L. Bricusse) (2:26) *Shirley Bassey*; 11 You Only Live Twice (demo version)(J. Barry/L. Bricusse)(3:05); 12 You Only Live Twice (radio spot)(:58); 13 We Have All The Time In The World (J. Barry/H. David) (3:11) *Louis Armstrong*; 14 Thunderball (radio spot)(:51); 15 Live And Let Die (radio spot)(1:00).

Review: *The Best of James Bond: 30th Anniversary* is the single best all-in-one James Bond compilation, covering 30 years of original soundtracks, from the initial film in the series, *Dr. No*, through *License to Kill*. (This is pre-Pierce Brosnan, so there's no *GoldenEye*—fortunately. This is also "official" United Artists Bond only, so there's no *Casino Royale* or *Never Say Never Again*.) Disc one features the first 16 title songs: the James Bond Theme, "From Russia with Love," "Goldfinger," "Thunderball," "You Only Live Twice," "On Her Majesty's Secret Service," "Live and Let Die," "The Man With The Golden Gun," "Nobody Does It Better" (from *The Spy Who Loved Me*), "Moonraker," "For Your Eyes Only," "All Time High" (from *Octopussy*), "A View To A Kill," "The Living Daylights" and "License to Kill." The true Bond themes are the '60s/Connery-era songs, written by John Barry and performed by the likes of Shirley Bassey, Tom Jones and Nancy Sinatra, with over-the-top lyrics and brassy nightclub backings. The '70s and '80s songs are a mixed bag of pop hits (Paul McCartney's "Live and Let Die," Carly Simon on "Nobody Does It Better" and Duran Duran's "A View to a Kill") and slower Barry-penned offerings ("Moonraker," "All Time High").

Disc two is a must-have for James Bond score buffs, including four cuts from the U.K. album to *Goldfinger* and a 20-minute suite of unreleased *Thunderball* music. John Barry arranged/ghostwrote/did-something-mysterious to the classic guitar theme and wrote underscores for 11 of the 16 films. He created an unmistakable orchestral/jazz sound world for the secret spy: cool, suave, memorable and suspenseful—tongue-in-cheek by virtue of its complete straight face. Alternate takes of "Goldfinger" and "You Only Live Twice," as well as some radio promo spots, are icing on the cake.

Lukas Kendall

The Essential James Bond ♪

1994, Silva Screen Records.

Album Notes: *Orchestrations*: Nic Raine, Bill Conti; The City Of Prague Philharmonic, conducted by Nic Raine; *Featured Soloists*: Michael Metelka (violin), Jaroslava Eliasova (piano), Peter Binder (guitar), Jindrich Nemecek (saxophone); *Album Producers*: Nic Raine, Mike Ross-Trevor; *Engineer*: Mike Ross-Trevor.

Selections: Dr No: 1 The James Bond Theme (M. Norman)(1:08); 2 From Russia With Love (L. Bart/M. Norman)(2:52); 3 From Russia With Love: 007 (J. Barry) (2:58); 4 Goldfinger (J. Barry/L. Bricusse/A. Newley)(2:37); 5 Thunderball (J. Barry/D. Black)(2:18); 6 You Only Live Twice (J. Barry/L. Bricusse)(2:55); 7 On Her Majesty's Secret Service/A View To A Kill: Suite (J. Barry/Duran Duran) (5:59); On Her Majesty's Secret Service: 8 We Have All The Time In The World (J. Barry/M. David)(3:29); 9 Diamonds Are Forever (J. Barry/D. Black)(3:04); 10 Live And Let Die (P. McCartney/L. McCartney)(3:06); 11 The Man With The Golden Gun (J. Barry/D.

Black)(3:37); The Spy Who Loved Me: 12 Nobody Does It Better (M. Hamlisch/C. Bayer Sager)(3:49); 13 Moonraker (J. Barry/H. David) (3:36); 14 For Your Eyes Only (B. Conti/L. Leeson)(3:05); Octopussy: 15 All Time High (J. Barry/T. Rice)(4:14); 16 The Living Daylights: Suite (J. Barry/ P. Waatkaar/C. Hynde)(5:19); 17 Licence To Kill: Suite (N.M. Walden/M. Kamen/ M. Norman/ J. Barry/L. Bricusse/A. Newley)(4:57); 18 The James Bond Theme (M. Norman)(2:39).

Review: No one can blame the folks at Silva Screen for trying to cash in on a surefire idea, but with all the James Bond soundtracks available in one form or another, and various other compilations also making the round, this CD sounds like a bit of a redundancy. If at least the playing were a little more energetic it may have been justifiable, but the performance by the City Of Prague Philharmonic is somewhat lackluster this time around. Better stick to the originals!

Nat King Cole

Nat King Cole at the Movies
♪♪♪♪♪

1992, Capitol Records.

Album Notes: *Original Sessions Producer*: Lee Gillette; *Album Producer*: Wayne Watking; *Engineer*: Bob Norberg.

Selections: St. Louis Blues: 1 St. Louis Blues (W.C. Handy)(2:26); Samson And Delilah: 2 Song Of Delilah (J. Livingston/R. Evans/V. Young)(2:43); Small Town Girl: 3 My Flaming Heart (L. Robin/N. Brodzsky)(2:46); 4 Small Towns Are Smile Towns (L. Robin/N. Brodzsky)(2:44); Blue Gardenia: 5 Blue Gardenia (B. Russell/L. Lee)(3:05); The Adventures Of Hajji Baba: 6 Hajji Baba (D. Tiomkin/ N. Washington)(3:06); Kiss Me Deadly: 7 I'd Rather Have The Blues (F. DeVol) (2:54); The Scarlet Hour: 8 Never Let Me Go (J. Livingston/R. Evans)(2:58); Autumn Leaves: 9 Les feuilles mortes (J. Kosma/J. Prevert)(2:37); Istanbul: 10 I Was A Little Too Lonely And You Were A Little Too Late (J. Livingston/R. Evans)(3:00); One Minute To Zero: 11 When I Fall In Love (E. Heyman/V. Young) (3:10); The Fleet's In: 12 Tangerine (J. Mercer/V. Schertzinger)(2:46); China Gate: 13 China Gate (V. Young/H. Adamson)(2:48); Love In The Afternoon: 14 Fascination (F. Marchetti/D. Manning)(2:29); Raintree County: 15 Song Of Raintree County (J. Green/P.F. Webster)(2:40); Night Of The Quarter Moon: 16 Night Of The Quarter Moon (J. Van Heusen/ S. Cahn)(2:43); 17 To Whom It May Concern (J. Van Heusen/S. Cahn)(2:59); In The Cool Of The Day: 18 In The Cool Of The Day (M. Hadjidakis/R. Sullivan/J. Gatsos)(2:38); Cat Ballou: 19 The

Ballad Of Cat Ballou (M. David/J. Livingston)(2:46); 20 They Can't Make Her Cry (M. David/J. Livingston)(2:24); Modern Times: 21 Smile (C. Chaplin/J. Turner/G. Parsons)(2:55).

Review: In the 1950s, when it seems every movie had to have a title song (a trend begun when Frankie Laine rerecorded the song from *High Noon* and turned it into a million-seller), Nat "King" Cole often provided his creamy vocals to tunes that were heard behind the credits. Additionally, he also recorded various songs that were written for the films, but performed by others. This collection combines together both the original and the cover versions, in one great package. From the first category, come such tunes as "St. Louis Blues," "Blue Gardenia," "The Adventures of Hajji Baba," and "Cat Ballou," in which he also appeared; in the second category are songs like "Song Of Delilah," "Autumn Leaves," "Tangerine," and other classics. Above all, what is most seductive here is Cole's easygoing charm and caressing way with a lyric, which make this set a total delight.

Sean Connery

A Tribute to Sean Connery *♫♫*

1994, edel America Records.

Album Notes: *Arrangers*: Steven Scott Smalley, John Cacavas, Morton Stevens, Jerry Goldsmith, Henry Mancini, Ennio Morricone, John Williams; The Orchestra Seattle, conducted by George Shangrow; *Featured Soloists*: Drew Fletcher, Matt Dalton (trumpet); Carlos A Flores (violin), M. Shannon Hill (English horn), Dan Williams (oboe), Gary Oules (alto sax), Kate Alverson (flute); *Album Producers*: Daniel Petersen, Ford A. Thaxton; *Engineer*: Michael Wolfe.

Selections: 1 The James Bond Theme (M. Norman) (2:04); 2 Main Theme (from *From Russia With Love*) (L. Bart) (3:12); 3 Main Theme (from *Goldfinger*) (J. Barry) (2:57); 4 Theme (from *The Russia House*) (J. Goldsmith) (4:53); 5 Main Theme (from *You Only Live Twice*) (J. Barry) (3:26); 6 Main Theme (from *Thunderball*) (J. Barry) (3:06); 7 John Bursts In/The End (from *Robin And Marian*) (J. Barry) (4:45); 8 Suite (from *The Great Train Robbery*) (J. Goldsmith) (5:12); 9 Main Theme (from *Diamonds Are Forever*) (J. Barry) (4:28); 10 End Credits (from *The Man Who Would Be King*) (M. Jarre) (3:01); 11 Theme (from *The Molly Maguires*) (H. Mancini) (2:54); 12 Main Title (from *The Wind And The Lion*) (J. Goldsmith) (1:58); 13 The Death Theme (from *The Untouchables*) (E. Morricone) (2:53); 14 End Credits (from *Indiana Jones and The Last Crusade*) (J. Williams) (11:46).

Review: When I was asked to write liner notes about Sean Connery and his film career for this project early on, I warned producer Ford A. Thaxton that I thought the John Cacavas arrangements for the James Bond themes, in particular *Diamonds are Forever*, had their problems in pacing and presentation. Apparently, the budget wasn't there to re-orchestrate these pieces and the resultant tracks are, at best, only a fair collection. Another problem is that many pieces do not have any punch. Despite guitarist Todd Smallwood's masterful solo performance, the presentation of "The James Bond Theme" (arranged by Steven Scott Smalley) is too lethargically paced, though it is an ideal John Barry chase cue. While it works for *The Russia House* and *Robin and Marian*, the orchestra fails miserably on a weak presentation of *The Great Train Robbery* and, even worse, on an inept attempt at *The Wind and the Lion*. *Diamonds*, one of Barry's most simplistic themes, has the worst, most painful, horn performances imaginable. Did anyone really care?

David Hirsch

Bing Crosby

Blue Skies *♫♫♫♫♫*

1989, MCA Records.

Album Notes: Orchestra conducted by John Scott Trotter; *CD Producer*: Andy McKaie; *Engineer*: Greg Fulginiti.

Selections: Blue Skies (I. Berlin): 1 Blue Skies (3:24); 2 All By Myself (3:16); 3 A Couple Of Song And Dance Men (2:17) *Bing Crosby, Fred Astaire*; 4 I've Got My Captain Working For Me Now (2:35); 5 (I'll See You In) Cuba (3:05) *Bing Crosby, Trudy Erwin*; 6 (Running Around In Circles) Getting Nowhere (2:38); 7 Everybody Step (2:26); 8 You Keep Coming Back Like A Song (2:50); 9 A Serenade To An Old-Fashioned Girlk (3:04); Out Of This World: 10 I'd Rather Be Me (F. Bernard/E. Cherkose/S. Coslow)(2:48); 11 Out Of This World (H. Arlen/J. Mercer)(2:57); 12 June Comes Around Every Year (H. Arlen/J. Mercer)(2:42).

Review: See entry below.

Holiday Inn *♫♫♫♫♫*

1988, MCA Records.

Album Notes: *Music*: Irving Berlin; *Lyrics*: Irving Berlin; Orchestra conducted by John Scott Trotter, Bob Crosby; *CD Producer*: Andy McKaie; *Engineer*: Doug Schwartz.

Selections: 1 Happy Holiday (2:24) *Bing Crosby, The Music Maids & Hal*; 2 Be Careful It's My Heart (2:42) *Bing Crosby*; 3

Abraham (2:44) *Bing Crosby, The Ken Darby Singers*; 4 Easter Parade (2:48) *Bing Crosby*; 5 Song Of Freedom (2:20) *Bing Crosby, The Ken Darby Singers*; 6 I Can't Tell A Lie (2:40) *Fred Astaire*; 7 Lazy (2:28) *Bing Crosby*; 8 I'll Capture Your Heart (2:22) *Bing Crosby, Fred Astaire, Margaret Lenhart*; 9 I've Got Plenty To Be Thankful For (2:58) *Bing Crosby*; 10 You're Easy To Dance With (2:48) *Fred Astaire*; 11 White Christmas (3:02) *Bing Crosby, The Ken Darby Singers*; 12 Let's Start The New Year Off Right (2:32) *Bing Crosby*.

Review: See entry below.

Swinging on a Star 🎵🎵🎵🎵

1989, MCA Records.

Album Notes: *Songs:* Johnny Burke, James Van Heusen.

Selections: Road To Morocco: 1 Road To Morocco (2:34) *Bing Crosby, Bob Hope*; 2 Moonlight Becomes You (3:09); 3 Ain't Got A Dime To My Name (Ho Ho Ho Hum)(2:51); 4 Constantly (2:41); Dixie: 5 Sunday, Monday Or Always (2:34); 6 If You Please (3:06); Going My Way: 7 Going My Way (2:50); 8 Swinging On A Star (2:28); 9 The Day After Forever (3:00); 10 Too-ra-loo-ra-loo-ral (That's An Irish Lullaby)(3:11); 11 Ave Maria (trad.)(2:57); 12 Silent Night (trad.)(2:36).

Review: See entry below.

White Christmas 🎵🎵🎵🎵

1954, MCA Records.

Album Notes: *Music:* Irving Berlin; *Lyrics:* Irving Berlin; The Paramount Studio Orchestra and Chorus, conducted by Joseph J. Lilley.

Selections: 1 The Old Man/Gee I Wish I Was Back In The Army (2:51) *Bing Crosby, Danny Kaye*; 2 Sisters (2:28) *Peggy Lee*; 3 The Best Things Happen While You're Dancing (2:37) *Danny Kaye, The Skylarks*; 4 Snow (2:43) *Bing Crosby, Danny Kaye, Peggy Lee, Trudy Stevens*; 5 Blue Skies/Mandy (3:52) *Bing Crosby, Danny Kaye*; 6 Choreography (2:45) *Danny Kaye, The Skylarks*; 7 Count Your Blessings Instead Of Sheep (3:08) *Bing Crosby*; 8 Love, You Didn't Do Right By Me (3:03) *Peggy Lee*; 9 What Can You Do With The General (2:59) *Bing Crosby*; 10 White Christmas (3:20) *Bing Crosby, Danny Kaye, Peggy Lee, Trudy Stevens*.

Review: These four CDs chronicle some of the songs Bing Crosby performed in the movies, usually in studio recordings that had different arrangements and orchestral backing. Crosby's screen persona was that of an affable, easy-going seducer, who crooned his way to the heart of his female co-

stars, and charmed them (and his audience) with his good-natured stylings. These characteristics are evidenced in these recordings, in which he performs many tunes that have since become standards in their own right. Some are also interesting for the fact that they present duets with Crosby's screen partners, like Fred Astaire, heard in "A Couple Of Song And Dance Men," from *Blue Skies,* and "I'll Capture Your Heart," from *Holiday Inn;* Danny Kaye, who shared billing in *White Christmas;* and Bob Hope, whose duet with Crosby on "Road To Morocco" is a classic.

On his own, Crosby does wonders with "Blue Skies," "Lazy," "Moonlight Becomes You," "Going My Way," "Swinging On A Star," "Too-ra-loo-ra-loo-ral (An Irish Lullaby)," and of course "White Christmas," which became as much a signature song for him as any he had created.

MCA also released a 4-CD boxed set in tribute to the singer, which contain these and many other songs he created in the movies, but these four titles are an economical and pleasant way to start off a collection of his recordings.

Doris Day

A Day at the Movies 🎵🎵🎵🎵

1988, Columbia Records.

Album Notes: *Album Producer:* Didier C. Deutsch; *Engineer:* Tim Geelan.

Selections: Romance On The High Seas: 1 It's Magic (J. Styne/S. Cahn) (3:26); My Dream Is Yours: 2 My Dream Is Yours (H. Warren/R. Freed/R. Blane) (3:08); It's A Great Feeling: 3 It's A Great Feeling (J. Styne/S. Cahn)(2:30); Young Man With A Horn: 4 With A Song In My Heart (R. Rodgers/L. Hart) (3:07); Tea For Two: 5 Tea For Two (V. Youmans/I. Caesar)(3:09); The West Point Story: 6 Ten Thousand Four Hundred Thirty-Two Sheep (J. Styne/S. Cahn) (3:00); Lullaby Of Broadway: 7 I Love The Way You Say Goodnight (E. Pola/G. Wyle) (2:47); On Moonlight Bay: 8 On Moonlight Bay (P. Wenrich/E. Madden)(2:29); I'll See You In My Dreams: 9 I'll See You In My Dreams (G. Kahn/I. Jones) (3:17); April In Paris: 10 April In Paris (V. Duke/E.Y. Harburg)(3:10); By The Light Of The Silvery Moon: 11 By The Light Of The Silvery Moon (G. Edwards/E. Madden)(2:50); Calamity Jane: 12 Secret Love (S. Fain/P.F. Webster)(3:40); Lucky Me: 13 The Blue Bells Of Broadway (Are Ringing Tonight)(S. Fain/P.F. Webster)(12:44); Young At Heart: 14 There's A Rising Moon (S. Fain/P.F. Webster)(3:06); Love Me Or Leave Me: 15 I'll Never Stop Loving You (N. Brodzsky/S.

Cahn)(3:07); The Man Who Knew Too Much: 16 Whatever Will Be, Will Be (Que Sera, Sera)(J. Livingston/R. Evans)(2:03).

Review: The #1 film and recording star in the late '50s-early '60s, Doris Day has fallen into unjust neglect in recent years. Even though she recorded hundreds of tunes during a career that took her from the days of the Big Band era to the dawn of rock'n'roll, only a handful of her albums are available today, and more often than not her name only evokes the pristine image of a giddy, virginal woman she cultivated in the latter-day romantic comedies that ensured her success on the screen. This collection regroups together several of the songs she made famous in her many film musicals, including "It's Magic," "Secret Love" and "Que Sera, Sera," in which the freshness and spontaneity that endeared her to legions of fans are still exerting their charm.

Clint Eastwood

Music from the Films of Clint Eastwood ♪♭

1993, Silva Screen Records.

Album Notes: *Arrangers*: Ron Goodwin, Karl-Heinz Loges, Brian Gascoigne, Derek Wadsworth, Mark Ayres, Christopher Palmer, Ian Hughes, John Bell, Lennie Niehaus; The City Of Prague Philharmonic, conducted by Derek Wadsworth; *Featured Soloists*: Jiri Hnyk (violin), Jaroslava Eliasova (piano), Peter Binder (guitar), Miroslav Korinck (bass guitar), Josef Matejka (trumpet), Petr Dreser (accordion), Zdenek Zdenek (synthesizer); *Album Producers*: Derek Wadsworth, Mike Ross-Trevor; *Engineer*: Mike Ross-Trevor.

Selections: 1 Main Title (from *Where Eagles Dare*)(R. Goodwin)(3:20); 2 The War Is Over (from *The Outlaw Josey Wales*)(J. Fielding)(4:24); The Dollars Suite (E. Morricone): 3 The Good, The Bad And The Ugly (2:54); 4 A Fistful Of Dollars (3:36); 5 For A Few Dollars More (3:33); 6 The Ecstasy Of Gold (3:00) *Anna Thomas*; 7 Misty (from *Play Misty For Me*)(E. Garner)(3:12); 8 Hang 'Em High (D. Frontiere)(3:38); 9 In The Line Of Fire (E. Morricone)(4:03); 10 Rawhide (D. Tiomkin)(1:40); The Dirty Harry Films Suite (L. Schifrin): 11 Dirty Harry (4:50); 12 Sudden Impact (3:48); 13 Magnum Force (2:17); 14 Two Mules For Sister Sara (E. Morricone)(5:18); 15 Unforgiven (L. Niehaus)(6:15).

Review: The performances by The City of Prague Philharmonic, under the direction of *Space: 1999* composer Derek Wadsworth, are not the problem on this collection. Their work is more than adequate to the task. The difficulty lies in the over-

abundance of music from the Italian-made "Spaghetti" westerns that defined his career. Not only does this make for a lack of variety, but it leaves music from films like *Play Misty for Me* and the *Dirty Harry* suites as odd, out-of-place, companions. Mark Ayers presentation of Ennio Morricone's *In the Line of Fire* really loses something in his synthesized realization.
David Hirsch

Harrison Ford

Music from the Films of Harrison Ford ♪♪

1994, Silva Screen Records.

Album Notes: *Arrangers*: Mark Ayres, Herbert Spencer, John Neufeld, Ron Goodwin, Brad Dechter, Christopher Palmer, Nic Raine; The City Of Prague Philharmonic, conducted by Paul Bateman, Nic Raine; *Featured Soloists*: Jaroslava Eliasova (piano), Mark Ayres (synthesizer); *Album Producer*: James Fitzpatrick; *Engineers*: Eric Tomlinson, Mike Ross-Trevor.

Selections: 1 End Credits (from *Indiana Jones and The Last Crusade*)(J. Williams)(11:06); 2 Building The Barn (from *Witness*)(M. Jarre)(4:38); 3 It's Over (from *The Fugitive*)(J. Newton Howard)(4:06); 4 Allie's Theme (from *The Mosquito Coast*)(M. Jarre)(3:34); 5 End Titles (from *Blade Runner*)(Vangelis)(4:48); 6 Electronic Battlefield (from *Patriot Games*)(J. Horner)(3:39); The Star Wars Trilogy (J. Williams): 7 Main Title (from *Star Wars*)(5:24); 8 Han Solo And The Princess (from *The Empire Strikes Back*)(4:08); 9 Forest Battle (from *Return Of The Jedi*)(3:52); 10 Suite (from *Hanover Street*)(J. Barry) (4:50); 11 March (from *Force Ten From Navarone*)(R. Goodwin) (3:30); 12 End Titles (from *Presumed Innocent*)(J. Williams)(4:14); 13 Walking Talking Man (from *Regarding Henry*)(H. Zimmer)(3:34); 14 Building The Barn (from *Witness*) (M. Jarre)(original electronic version)(4:58); 15 Nocturnal Activities (from *Indiana Jones And The Temple Of Doom*)(J. Williams)(2:03); 16 March (from *Raiders Of The Lost Ark*)(J. Williams)(5:16).

Review: A little less of the endless recycling of *Star Wars* and *Indiana Jones* music may have made this album less commercial, but it would have also have made it less tedious. There are too many of the other old standbys, too, like the *Blade Runner* end title and "Building the Barn" from *Witness* (two versions no less, was any other music ever composed for that picture?). There are some recent cues from *The Fugitive* (James Newton Howard) and *Patriot Games* (James Horner), as well as an early Ford effort *Force Ten from Navarone* (Ron Goodwin). The album is a mix of orchestral (The City of Prague Philharmonic) and electronic work (Mark Ayers). I'll give Ayers some points for creative audacity in his attempt to reproduce vocalist Bobby McFerrin on the Has Zimmer composed "Walking Talking Man" from *Regarding Henry*.

David Hirsch

Connie Francis

Where the Boys Are: Connie Francis in Hollywood ♪♪♪♪

1997, Rhino Records.

Album Notes: *CD Producers*: George Feltenstein, Bradley Flanagan; *Engineer*: Doug Schwartz.

Selections: Where The Boys Are: 1 Main Title/Where The Boys Are (N. Sedaka/H. Greenfield)(2:36); 2 Turn On The Sunshine (N. Sedaka/H. Greenfield)(2:17); Follow The Boys: 3 Follow The Boys (B. Davis/T. Murry) (2:38); 4 Tonight's My Night (B. Davis/T. Murry)(2:30); 5 Waiting For Billy (B. Davis/T. Murry)(2:19); 6 Italian Lullabye (C. Francis)(3:26); Looking For Love: 7 Looking For Love (rock'n'roll version)(H. Hunter/S. Vincent)(2:06); 8 When The Clock Strikes Midnight (H. Hunter/S. Vincent)(2:39); 9 Whoever You Are, I Love You (G. Geld/P. Udell)(3:24); 10 Let's Have A Party (H. Hunter/S. Vincent)(2:14); 11 Be My Love (N. Brodzsky/S. Cahn)(3:25); 12 I Can't Believe That You're In Love With Me (C. Gaskill/J. McHugh)(2:17) *Connie Francis, Danny Thomas*; 13 This Is My Happiest Moment (B. Davis/M. Mencher)(2:02); 14 Looking For Love (jazz version)(H. Hunter/S. Vincent)(2:20); When The Boys Meet The Girls: 15 When The Boys Meet The Girls (H. Greenfield/J. Keller) (2:05); 16 Mail Call (B. Weisman/S. Wayne/F. Karger)(2:24); 17 Embraceable You (G. & I. Gershwin)(2:13); 18 I Got Rhythm (G. & I. Gershwin)(6:38) *Connie Francis, Harve Presnell*; 19 But Not For Me (G. & I. Gershwin)(2:59) *Connie Francis, Harve Presnell*; Where The Boys Are: 20 Finale: Where The Boys Are/Do You Love Me?/Where The Boys Are (3:31); Demos: 21 Looking For Love (jazz version) (2:25); 22 When The Clock Strikes Midnight (jazz version)(2:03); 23 Let's Have A Party (2:07); 24 Looking For Love (rock'n'roll version)(2:04).

Review: One seldom thinks of Connie Francis as a movie star, even though she appeared in several film musicals in the 1960s. This may be due to the fact that the films, vague concoctions with pseudo rock'n'roll scores, attracted a limited audience, and are regarded today as campy rather than serious moviemaking. Better yet, when compared to the great film musicals made by M-G-M in the 1940s and '50s, these films look dowright ridiculous and are a serious letdown in overall creativity.

Yet, there was something positively endearing about Connie Francis that comes through in this compilation which brings together selections from *Where the Boys Are* (1960), *Looking for Love* (1964), and *When the Boys Meet the Girls* (1965). The first film, which marked the singer's screen debut, is by far the best of the lot and proves that Francis could actually hold her own in this amusing story of teenage girls longing for (and finding) a mate during an Easter vacation in Fort Lauderdale; already a notch down, *Looking For Love* features an inept backstage romance that is the lame excuse for various musical numbers and guest star appearances; as for *When the Boys Meet the Girls*, it is a tame remake of the Gershwin musical *Girl Crazy*, overloaded with numbers that have little to do with the plot but provide a reason for the all-star line-up that included Louis Armstrong, Liberace, and Herman's Hermits...

As a goof, this CD is way up there, a definite showcase for the talented Miss Francis, who confidently rides over all the pitfalls in the three films to perform her songs with style and polish. Whether it was worth the effort is another question altogether...

Judy Garland

Collectors' Gems from the M-G-M Films ♪♪♪♪

1996, Rhino Records.

Album Notes: *Album Producers*: George Feltenstein, Bradley Flanagan; *Engineer*: Doug Schwartz.

Selections: CD 1: Every Sunday: 1 Waltz With A Swing/Americana (C. Conrad/ R. Edens)(2:27); 2 Opera vs. Jazz (C. Conrad/ R. Edens)(1:36) *Judy Garland, Deanna Durbin*; Broadway Melody Of 1938: 3 Everybody Sing (A. Freed/N.H. Brown) (4:48) *Judy Garland, Sophie Tucker, Barnett Parker, J.D. Jewkes*; 4 Yours And Mine (A. Freed/N.H. Brown)(2:22) *Judy Garland, Eloise Rawitzer, The St. Brendan's Boys Choir*; 5 Your Broadway And My Broadway (A. Freed/N.H. Brown)(3:34); Thoroughbreds Don't Cry: 6 Got A Pair Of New Shoes (A. Freed/ N.H. Brown)(2:29); 7 Sun Showers (A. Freed/N.H. Brown)(2:27); Everybody Sing: 8 Down On Melody Farm (R. Edens/G. Kahn)(4:40); 9 Why, Because! (B. Kalmar/H. Ruby)(2:15) *Judy Garland, Fanny Brice*; 10 Ever Since The World Began/Shall I Sing A Melody? (R. Edens)(4:27); Love Finds Andy Hardy: 11 In

Between (R. Edens)(4:31); 12 It Never Rains, But What It Pours (M. Gordon/H. Revel)(2:24); 13 Bei Mir Bist Du Schoen (S. Secunda/J. Jacobs/S. Chaplin/S. Cahn)(2:49); 14 Meet The Beat Of My Heart (M. Gordon/H. Revel)(2:55); Listen, Darling: 15 Zing! Went The Strings Of My Heart (J. Hanley)(2:52); 16 On The Bumpy Road To Love (A. Hoffman/A. Lewis/M. Mencher)(2:08) *Judy Garland, Mary Astor, Freddie Bartholomew, Scotty Beckett*; 17 Ten Pins In The Sky (M. Ager/J. McCarthy)(3:36); Andy Hardy Meets Debutante: 18 I'm Nobody's Baby (B. Davis/M. Ager/L. Santly)(3:32); 19 All I Do Is Dream Of You (A. Freed/N.H. Brown) (1:37); 20 Alone (A. Freed/N.H. Brown)(2:43); Little Nellie Kelly: 21 It's A Great Day For The Irish (R. Edens)(2:37) *Judy Garland, Douglas McPhail*; 22 Danny Boy (F.E. Weatherly)(2:37); 23 A Pretty Girl Milking Her Cow (R. Edens)(2:52); 24 Singin' In The Rain (A. Freed/N.H. Brown)(3:00); Life Begins With Andy Hardy: 25 Easy To Love (C. Porter)(3:25).

CD 2: Ziegfeld Girl: 1 We Must Have Music (G. Kahn/N.H. Brown)(2:15) *Judy Garland, Tony Martin, Six Hits And A Miss*; 2 I'm Always Chasing Rainbows (H. Carroll/J. McCarthy)(2:08); 3 Minnie From Trinidad (R. Edens)(5:21);

PRESENTING LILY MARS: 4 Every Little Movement Has A Meaning Of Its Own (O. Harbach/K. Hoschna)(2:10) *Judy Garland, Mary Kent*; 5 Tom, Tom, The Piper's Son (B. Lane/E.Y. Harburg)(2:40); 6 When I Look At You (W. Jurmann/P.F. Webster)(1:32) *Judy Garland, Bob Crosby and His Orchestra*; 7 Paging Mr. Greenback (S. Fain/E.Y. Harburg)(4:51); 8 Where There's Music (finale medley): Where There's Music (R. Edens)/St. Louis Blues (W.C. Handy)/It's A Long Way To Tipperary (J. Judge/H.H. Williams)/In The Shade Of The Old Apple Tree (E. Van Alstyne/H.H. Williams)/Don't Sit Under The Apple Tree (S. Stept/L. Brown/C. Tobias)/It's Three O'Clock In The Morning (J. Robledo/D. Fields)/Broadway Rhythm (A. Freed/N.H. Brown)(10:16) *Judy Garland, Charles Walters, The M-G-M Studio Chorus, Tommy Dorsey and His Orchestra*; Thousands Cheer: 9 The Joint Is Really Jumpin' Down At Carnegie Hall (R. Edens/H. Martin/R. Blane)(3:40) *Judy Garland, Jose Iturbi*; Till The Clouds Roll By: 10 D'Ya Love Me (O. Harbach/O. Hammerstein II)(2:33); The Pirate: 11 Mack The Black (C. Porter) (6:01); 12 Love Of My Life (C. Porter)(4:41); 13 Voodoo (C. Porter)(6:09); Annie Get Your Gun: 14 You Can't Get A Man With A Gun (I. Berlin)(4:23); 15 There's No Business Like Show Business (I. Berlin)(2:19) *Judy Garland, Frank Morgan, Howard Keel, Keenan Wynn*; 16 They Say It's Wonderful (I. Berlin) (3:22) *Judy Garland, Howard Keel*; 17 The Girl That I Marry (reprise)(I. Berlin)(2:07); 18 I've Got The Sun In The Morning (I. Berlin)(2:08); 19 Let's Go West Again (I. Berlin)(3:25); 20 Anything You Can Do (I. Berlin)(2:38) *Judy Garland, Howard Keel*; 21 There's No Business Like Show Business (reprise)(I. Berlin)(1:02).

Review: This superb collection of tracks from the M-G-M films chronicles the career of Judy Garland at the studio where she enjoyed her greatest moments in the limelight. The pleasures are immense, and while the collection is not complete by any stretch of the imagination (it doesn't include, for instance, Garland's last number for the studio, the giddy "Get Happy"), it's as good as they get. Particularly welcome in this context are the songs she recorded for *Annie Get Your Gun*, before she was replaced by Betty Hutton, which make their first appearance ever in this compilation. As is always the case with Rhino, the set comes with an informative booklet which contains loads of information, photos, comprehensive liner notes, everything that makes the release more valuable to fans and collectors.

Judy Garland: The Complete Decca Original Cast Recordings
✔✔✔✔✔

1996, MCA Records.

Album Notes: *Album Producer*: Ron O'Brien; *Engineers*: Steven Lasker, Paul Elmore.

Selections: Girl Crazy (G. & I. Gershwin): 1 Embraceable You (3:14) *Judy Garland*; 2 Could You Use Me? (3:03) *Judy Garland, Mickey Rooney*; 3 But Not For Me (3:09); 4 Treat Me Rough (3:04) *Mickey Rooney*; 5 Bidin' My Time (3:07) *Judy Garland*; 6 I Got Rhythm (2:53); Meet Me In St. Louis (H. Martin/R. Blane): 7 Meet Me In St. Louis (K. Mills/A. Sterling)(2:15); 8 The Boy Next Door (3:07); 9 Skip To My Lou (3:00); 10 Boys And Girls Like You And Me (R. Rodgers/O. Hammerstein II)(3:11); 11 The Trolley Song (2:54); 12 Have Yourself A Merry Little Christmas (2:46); The Harvey Girls (H. Warren/J. Mercer): 13 In The Valley Where The Evenin' Sun Goes Down (2:53); 14 On The Atcheson, Topeka And The Santa Fe (5:54) *Judy Garland, The Kay Thompson Chorus*; 15 Wait And See (3:13); 16 It's A Great Big World (3:45) *Judy Garland, Virginia O'Brien, Betty Russell*; 17 Swing Your Partner Round And Round (2:59) *Judy Garland, The Kay Thompson Chorus*; 18 The Wild, Wild West (3:08) *Virginia O'Brien*; 19 March Of The Doagies (2:55) *Judy Garland, Kenny Baker, The Kay Thompson Chorus*.

Review: This effective compilation regroups some of the songs Garland recorded for the Decca label, notably from the films *Girl Crazy* (1943), *Meet Me in St. Louis* (1944), and *The Harvey*

Girls (1946). Interestingly, this set complements but doesn't duplicate the Rhino releases (with the exception of *Girl Crazy*), so that collectors don't have to feel cheated. Sonic quality here is not a prime consideration (many of these recordings were done at a time when techniques were not perfect), but the overall balance is quite positive. And the tunes ("Embraceable You," But Not for Me," "I Got Rhythm," "The Trolley Song," "Have Yourself a Merry Little Christmas," "On the Acheson Topeka and the Santa Fe") rank among the most memorable in Garland's career. A definite must for everyone interested in the singer, the films of her career, and the songs of that era.

Mickey & Judy ✒✒✒✒

1995, Rhino Records.

Album Notes: *Album Producers*: Marilee Bradford, Bradley Flanagan; *Engineer*: Doug Schwartz.

Selections: CD 1: Babes In Arms: 1 Main Title (2:04); 2 Stumbling (E.Z. Confrey)(:53) *Grace Hayes, Charles Winninger*; 3 Montage (R. Edens)(2:09); 4 Good Morning (N.H. Brown/A. Freed)(2:00) *Judy Garland, Mickey Rooney*; 5 Mickey Proposes (N.H. Brown)(2:49); Opera vs. Jazz: 6 Part 1 (R. Edens)(1:59) *Judy Garland, Betty Jaynes*; 7 Part 2 (R. Edens)(1:26) *Betty Jaynes*; 8 Part 3 (R. Edens)(1:10) *Judy Garland*; 9 Part 4 (R. Edens)(:51) *Judy Garland, Betty Jaynes, Mickey Rooney*; 10 Babes In Arms (R. Rodgers/L. Hart) (4:31) *Douglas McPhail, Judy Garland, Mickey Rooney, Betty Jaynes*; 11 Mickey's Bedroom (N.H. Brown)(1:32); 12 Mickey Proposes Again (N.H. Brown) (1:31); 13 Where Or When (R. Rodgers/L. Hart)(2:45) *Douglas McPhail, Betty Jaynes, Judy Garland*; 14 Where Or When (reprise)(R. Rodgers/L. Hart)(2:11) *Douglas McPhail, Betty Jaynes*; 15 Mickey Leaves For Dinner/Dinner At Eight (The Lady Is A Tramp)(R. Rodgers)(4:38); 16 Good Morning (reprise)(N.H. Brown) (1:47); 17 Rehearsal Dance (N.H. Brown)(:32); 18 Mickey Breaks The News (R. Rodgers)(1:56); 19 Baby Rosalie Theme (R. Rodgers)(1:17); 20 Oriental Theme (G. Stoll)(1:22); 21 I Cried For You (Now It's Your Turn To Cry Over Me)(A. Freed/G. Arnheim/A. Lyman)(4:04) *Judy Garland*; 22 Judy In Mother's Dressing Room (A. Freed/G. Arnheim/A. Lyman)(1:14); Minstrel Show Sequence: 23 Part 1 (R. Edens)(1:10) *Judy Garland, The Crinoline Choir*; 24 De Camptown Races/ Old Folks At Home/Oh! Suzanna (S. Foster)(1:27) *Judy Garland, Mickey Rooney, The Crinoline Choir*; 25 Part 2 (R. Edens)(1:30) *Douglas McPhail, Mickey Rooney, Judy Garland*; 26 Part 3 (R. Edens)(:14) *Douglas McPhail, The Crinoline Choir*; 27 Ida, Sweet As Apple Cider/(On) Moonlight Bay (E. Leonard/ E. Munson)/(P. Weinrich/E. Madde)(:59) *Mickey Rooney, The Crinoline Choir*; 28 I'm Just Wild About Harry (E. Blake/N.

Sissle)(2:00) *Judy Garland, Mickey Rooney, The Crinoline Choir*; 29 Father In Agent's Office (G. Bassman/G. Stoll)(1:44); Finale: 30 Part 1/God's Country (H. Arlen/E.Y. Harburg)(3:43) *Mickey Rooney, Judy Garland, Douglas McPhail, Betty Jaynes*; 31 Part 2/My Day (R. Edens)(1:19) *Mickey Rooney, Judy Garland, Douglas McPhail, Betty Jaynes*; 32 Part 3 (R. Edens)(:57) *Mickey Rooney, Judy Garland, Sally Mueller, Helen Pacino, Betty Rome, Irene Crane, Albert Mahler, Bob Priester, Ralph Leon, N. Nielsen, John Moss, Charles Schrouder, Allan Watson, J.D. Jewkes*; 33 Part 4/ Good Morning (N.H. Brown)(:35); 34 Part 5/God's Country (H. Arlen/E.Y. Harburg)(:48) *Mickey Rooney, Judy Garland, Douglas McPhail, Betty Jaynes*; 35 End Title (N.H. Brown)(:37); 36 Good Morning (outtake)(N.H. Brown/A. Freed) (1:11) *Mickey Rooney, Douglas McPhail, Betty Jaynes*; 37 I Crief For You (Now It's Your Turn To Cry Over Me)(with monologue)(A. Freed/G. Arnheim/A. Lyman) (4:04) *Judy Garland*.

CD 2: Strike Up The Band: 1 Main Title (G. Gershwin)(1:53); 2 National Emblem (E.E. Bagley)(:46); Our Love Affair: 3 Part 1 (R. Edens/A. Freed)(1:11) *Mickey Rooney*; 4 Part 2 (R. Edens/A. Freed)(3:46) *Mickey Rooney, Judy Garland*; 5 Part 3 (R. Edens)(:43); 6 Part 4 (R. Edens)(:52); 7 Part 5 (R. Edens/A. Freed)(1:04) *Judy Garland*; 8 Do The La Conga (R. Edens)(5:38) *Judy Garland, Mickey Rooney, Six Hits And A Miss*; 9 An Old Story, Part 1 (R. Edens)(5:00); 10 Green Lantern Cafe (L. Arnaud)(1:23); 11 Saudades (R. Edens) (1:23); 12 Nobody (R. Edens)(4:13) *Judy Garland*; 13 Porch Love Scene (R. Edens)(3:04); 14 Nell Of New Rochelle (19:03) *Mickey Rooney, Judy Garland, June Preisner, William Tracy, Larry Nunn, Margaret Early*; 15 When Day Is Done (R. Katscher)(1:17) *Paul Whiteman & His Orchestra*; 16 (My) Wonderful One (P. Whiteman/F. Grofe)(:59) *Paul Whiteman & His Orchestra*; 17 Drummer Boy (R. Edens)(3:58) *Judy Garland, Six Hits And A Miss*; 18 An Old Story, Part 2 (R. Edens)(1:34); Finale: 19 Part 1 (1:14); 20 Part 2/ Strike Up The Band (G. Gershwin)(2:32); 21 Part 3/Do The La Conga (R. Edens)(:58); 22 Part 4/Our Love Affair (R. Edens/A. Freed)(1:41); 23 Part 5/Drummer Boy (:47); 24 Part 6/ Strike Up The Band (G. Gershwin/I. Gershwin)(1:25) *Mickey Rooney, Judy Garland, Six Hits And A Miss*; 25 End Title (R. Edens)(:35); 26 Travel And Contest Montage (tempo track)(:59) *Roger Edens*; 27 Our Love Affair (orchestra track)(3:36).

CD 3: Babes On Broadway: 1 Main Title (B. Lane/R. Freed)(1:22); 2 Alexander Woolcott (G. Stoll)(1:47); 3 Anything Can Happen In New York/Bow Music (B. Lane/E.Y. Harburg)(2:53) *Mickey Rooney, Ray McDonald, Richard Quine*; 4 How About You? (B. Lane/R. Freed)(5:46) *Judy Garland, Mickey Rooney*; 5 Sketch, Part 1 (5:11); 6 Sketch, Part 2 (The

Man I Love)(G. Gerhswin)(2:49) *Roger Edens*; 7 Hoe Down (R. Edens/R. Freed)(7:55) *Mickey Rooney, Judy Garland, Six Hits And A Miss, The Five Music Maids*; 8 Introduction To Block Party/Block Party Fanfare (L. Arnaud/G. Bassman/G. Stoll)(:30); 9 Chin Up! Cheerio! Carry On! (B. Lane/E.Y. Harburg)(3:37) *Judy Garland, Saint Luke's Episcopal Church Choristers*; Ghost Theatre Sequence: 10 Ghost Theatre Prelude (R. Edens)(2:49); 11 Mary's A Grand Old Name (G.M. Cohan)(1:17) *Judy Garland*; 12 She Is Ma Daisy (H. Lauder/J.D. Harper)(:47) *Mickey Rooney*; 13 I've Got Rings On My Fingers (M. Scott/R.P. Weston/F.J. Barbes)(:43) *Judy Garland*; 14 Bernhardt (La Marseillaise)(C.J. Rouget de Lisle/R. Edens)(:48); 15 The Yankee Doodle Boy (G.M. Cohan)(1:30) *Mickey Rooney, Judy Garland*; 16 Stage Montage Introduction (B. Lane/R. Edens)(:30); 17 Bombshell From Brazil (R. Edens)(1:19) *Annie Rooney, Richard Quine, Virginia Weidler, Ray McDonald, Judy Garland, Robert Bradford*; 18 Mama Yo Te Quiero/Bow Music (R. Edens)(1:10) *Mickey Rooney*; Minstrel Show Sequence: 19 Part 1 (R. Edens) (1:41) *Mickey Rooney, Judy Garland, Ray McDonald, Virginia Weidler, Richard Quinne, Annie Rooney*; 20 Blackout Over Broadway (B. Lane/R. Freed)(2:17) *Mickey Rooney, Judy Garland, Ray McDonald, Virginia Weidler, Richard Quinne, Annie Rooney*; 21 Part 2 (R. Edens)(1:07) *Mickey Rooney, Judy Garland, Richard Quinne*; 22 By The Light Of The Silvery Moon (G. Edwards/E. Madden) (1:08) *The Uptowners, The Dick Davis Quartet*; 23 Part 3 (R. Edens)(:18) *Richard Quinne*; 24 F.D.R. Jones (H. Rome/R. Edens)(2:29) *Judy Garland*; 25 Part 4 (R. Edens)(:13); 26 Swanee River (S. Foster)(1:27) *Eddie Peabody*; 27 Alabamy Bound (R. Henderson)(1:03) *Eddie Peabody*; 28 Part 5/Waiting For The Robert E. Lee (L. Muir/L. Wolfe Gilbert)(1:41) *Virginia Weidler, Annie Rooney, Judy Garland, Mickey Rooney*; 29 Babes On Broadway (B. Lane/R. Freed)(:48) *Mickey Rooney, Judy Garland, Ray McDonald, Virginia Weidler, Richard Quinne, Annie Rooney*; 30 End Title (B. Lane/L. Arnaud/G. Bassman)(:33); 31 Main Title (unused version)(B. Lane)(1:21); 32 Chin Up! Cheerio! Carry On! (Audition demo)(B. Lane/E.Y. Harburg)(2:29) *Burton Lane*; 33 Leo Is One The Air (holiday broadcast)(14:00) *Frank Whitbeck, Buddy Twist, Mickey Rooney, Judy Garland, The Saint Luke's Episcopal Church Choristers.*

CD 4: Girl Crazy (G. Gershwin/I. Gershwin): 1 Main Title (2:22); 2 Sam And Delilah (:50)*Tommy Dorsey & His Orchestra*; 3 Treat Me Rough (6:33)*June Allyson, Mickey Rooney, The Music Maids, The Stafford Trio, Kathleen Carns, Ruth Clark, Tommy Dorsey & His Orchestra*; 4 Eight Miles To Cody (C. Salinger/ G. Stoll)(1:36); 5 So This Is Cody, Wow! (R. Edens/C. Salinger)(1:12); 6 Buffalo Mick (G. Gershwin)(2:34); 7 Rags And Mickey In Wagon (G. Gershwin) (1:34); 8 Bidin' My Time

(4:58)*Judy Garland, The King's Men*; 9 I Dare You (G. Stoll)(1:50); 10 Could You Use Me? (3:43)*Judy Garland, Mickey Rooney*; 11 Ginger Dear (R. Edens)(1:00); 12 Happy Birthday To You (P. Hill/S. Hill) (:36); 13 Embraceable You (4:56)*Judy Garland, Henry Kruze*; 14 Walking In The Garden (G. Gershwin/D. Raksin)(4:12); 15 Cactus Time In Arizona (:28); 16 Cody Closes (2:21); 17 Barbara Coast (1:58)*Tommy Dorsey & His Orchestra*; 18 Fascinating Rhythm (5:26) *Tommy Dorsey & His Orchestra*; 19 Bronco Montage (:54); 20 Bronco Busters (2:20) *Mickey Rooney, Judy Garland, Nancy Walker*; 21 Boy! What Love Has Done To Me! (3:23) *Tommy Dorsey & His Orchestra*; 22 Embraceable You (reprise)(3:01) *Tommy Dorsey & His Orchestra*; 23 Judy And Rags (C. Salinger) (:50); 24 But Not For Me (2:30) *Judy Garland*; 25 Don't Cry, Rags (C. Salinger)(:18); 26 The Reconciliation (2:08); 27 Mickey Moves The Rock (outtake)(2:29); 28 End Title (:51) *Mickey Rooney, Judy Garland.*

Review: A boon for Judy and Mickey fans, the complete soundtracks from their four musicals with bonus tracks, outtakes, and all the incrementa usually found in the lavish Rhino packages. Together, Judy Garland and Mickey Rooney are dynamite, starring in films that have scant plots, along the lines of why-don't-we-put-a-show-together, and are mere excuses to give them plenty of songs and musical numbers which they imbue with their youthful talent and energy. That's what subsists in these four CDs, in which the tunes, for the most part quite familiar, marked an entire era.

Adding its own weight to the songs is Rhino's presentation, gorgeously enhanced by a booklet that has plenty of pictures (some in four colors), interesting facts and anecdotes about each film, and enough documentation about the musical numbers to satisfy even the most demanding historian.

Audrey Hepburn

Music from the Films of Audrey Hepburn ♪

1993, Giant Records.

Album Notes: *Album Producer:* Tim Sexton; *Engineer:* Larry Walsh.

Selections: Breakfast At Tiffany's: 1 Moon River (H. Mancini/J. Mercer) (2:40) *Henry Mancini His Orchestra and Chorus*; Charade: 2 Main Title (H. Mancini)(2:07) *Henry Mancini and His Orchestra*; My Fair Lady: 3 Overture (F. Loewe)(3:23) *The Warner Bros. Studio Orchestra, Andre Previn*; Funny Face: 4 He Loves And She Loves (G. & I. Gershwin)(4:59) *Fred Astaire*; The Nun's Story: 5 Main Title (F. Waxman)(2:37) *The Warner Bros.*

Studio Orchestra, Franz Waxman; Wait Until Dark: 6 Theme For Three (H. Mancini)(2:43) *Henry Mancini and His Orchestra*; How To Steal A Million: 7 Main Title (J. Williams)(1:47); Robin And Marian: 8 John Bursts In/The End (J. Barry)(2:41); Two For The Road: 9 Main Title (H. Mancini)(2:41) *Henry Mancini and His Orchestra*; Breakfast At Tiffany's: 11 Moon River (H. Mancini/J. Mercer)(2:01) *Audrey Hepburn*.

Review: It would have been nice to recommend this tribute album to Audrey Hepburn. But besides the fact that its total playing time is short (less than 33 minutes), it's really nothing more than a shoddy compilation which was hastily put together when the actress died, and which misses its best opportunities to recognize her enormous contributions to the big screen. Even though she did appear in several films for which Henry Mancini provided the music, those selections can also be found in other compilations. The selection from *Funny Face*, by Fred Astaire is fine, but "How Long Has This Been Going On?" sung by Audrey in the same film would have been a wiser choice. In fact, the only two tracks that are of some interest here are the "Main Title" from *How to Steal a Million*, and the selection from *Robin and Marian*. Not much to justify the set, however.

Alfred Hitchcock

Dial M for Murder: A History of Hitchcock 🎵🎵🎵🎵

1993, Silva Screen Records.

Album Notes: The City of Prague Philharmonic, conducted by Paul Bateman; *Album Producers*: Paul Bateman, Mike Ross-Trevor; *Engineer*: Mike Ross-Trevor.

Selections: 1 The Alfred Hitchcock Theme: Funeral March Of The Marionette (C. Gounod)(4:14); Rebecca: 2 Prelude/After The Ball/Mrs. Danvers/Confession Scene/Manderley In Flames (F. Waxman)(7:08); Suspicion: 3 Prelude/Sunday Morning (F. Waxman)(4:37); Spellbound: 4 Concerto For Orchestra (M. Rozsa) (9:34); Under Capricorn: 5 Suite (R. Addinsell)(7:03); Dial M For Murder: 6 Main Title/The Telephone/The Trap/Finale (D. Tiomkin)(& (:15); Vertigo: 7 Scene d'amour (B. Herrmann)(5:07); North By Northwest: 8 Main Title (B. Herrmann) (3:19); Psycho: 9 Prelude/The City/Rainstorm/Murder/Finale (7:22); Marnie: 10 Prelude (B. Herrmann)(2:57); Topaz: 11 March (M. Jarre)(2:34); Frenzy: 12 The London Theme (R. Goodwin)(2:26).

Review: See entry below.

To Catch a Thief: A History of Hitchcock II 🎵🎵🎵🎵

1995, Silva Screen Records.

Album Notes: *Orchestrations*: Paul Bateman, Philip Lane, Mike Townend, Kevin Townend; The City of Prague Philharmonic, conducted by Paul Bateman; *Featured Musicians*: Erik Becherovka, Pavel Navradoymuz (piano), Jaroslava Eliasova (piano/harpsichord); *Featured Performers*: The Silk Purse Chorale; *Album Producer*: James Fitzpatrick; *Engineers*: John Timperley, Mark Ayres.

Selections: 1 Paramount VistaVision Fanfare (N. Van Cleave)/To Catch A Thief: You'll Love France/My Jewels/Red Convertible/Riviera Car Chase/Bus Stop/Finale (L. Murray)(5:51); The Thirty Nine Steps: 2 The Thirty Nine Steps/ Highland Hotel/Mr. Memory/Finale (J. Beaver/L. Levy)(4:05); The Lady Vanishes: 3 Prelude (L. Levy/C. Williams)(3:03); 4 20th Century-Fox Fanfare (A. Newman)/Lifeboat: Disaster (H. Friedhofer)(3:02); Rope: 5 Main Titles (F. Poulenc/D. Buttolph)(2:07); Stage Fright: 6 Rhapsody (L. Lucas/P. Lane)(4:57); Strangers On A Train: 7 Main Title/Approaching The Train/The Tennis Game and The Cigarette Lighter/Bruno's Death and Finale (D. Tiomkin)(7:45); Rear Window: 8 Lisa (Intermezzo)(F. Waxman)(3:47); The Trouble With Harry: 9 A Portrait Of Hitch (B. Herrmann)(8:46); Vertigo: 10 Prelude/The Nightmare (B. Herrmann)(5:02); North By Northwest: 11 Conversation Piece (B. Herrmann) (4:40); Torn Curtain: 12 Main Title (J. Addison)(2:21); Family Plot: 13 Finale (J. Williams)(3:53).

Review: Together, these two volumes give an overview of some of the musical tracks from the films of Alfred Hitchcock, many of which are heard here for the first time. Even though he may have at times expressed disdain for it, Hitchcock was fully aware of the importance of music in his films, and he always made sure to surround himself with some of the best composers available. The list here reads like a who's who of film scoring, from Bernard Herrmann, whose memorable contributions included *Vertigo, North By Northwest, Marnie* and, of course, *Psycho*; to Franz Waxman, represented by *Rebecca, Suspicion*, and *Rear Window*; to Miklos Rozsa, whose music gave such flair to *Spellbound*; to Dimitri Tiomkin, who added his own personal touch to *Dial M For Murder* and *Strangers On A Train*, both included here. Along the way, there are also other less likely and more surprising candidates, like Richard Addinsell, whose *Under Capricorn* is a highlight in this collection; Maurice Jarre, represented by *Topaz*; Ron Goodwin, with *Frenzy*; and John Williams, whose sly derivations gave such flavor to the amusing *Family Plot*. Both that last score and Bernard Herrmann's *The Trouble With Harry* also emphasize the humorous side of Hitchcock, an aspect of his career that is often ignored in view of his more dramatic achievements.

Overall, the playing by The City Of Prague Philharmonic sounds authentic enough, and both sets are highly recommended.

See also: Bernard Herrmann in this section

Hitchcock Master of Mayhem 🦴🦴🦴

1990, Pro-Arte Records.

Album Notes: *Music:* Bernard Herrmann, Franz Waxman, Lalo Schifrin; The San Diego Symphony, conducted by Lalo Schifrin; *Album Producer:* Steve Vining; *Engineer:* Steve Vining; *Assistant Engineer:* Gary Rice.

Selections: North By Northwest: 1 Overture (B. Herrmann)(3:35); 2 Alfred Hitchcock Theme: Funeral March Of The Marionette (C. Gounod)(3:42); Vertigo: 3 Suite (B. Herrmann)(5:52); Marnie: 4 Suite (B. Herrmann)(5:33); Psycho: 5 Suite (B. Herrmann): (a) Prelude (2:18), (b) The Murder (1:03), (c) The City/ Finale (1:19); Rebecca: 6 Suite (F. Waxman)(3:58); Rear Window: 7 Suite (F. Waxman): (a) Prelude (2:29), (b) Rhumba (1:48), (c) Ballet (1:52), (d) Finale (2:26); The Schifrin Suite: 8 Rollercoaster: Amusement Park Theme (3:40); 9 Bullitt (3:23); 10 Mannix: Main Theme (2:55); 11 Dirty Harry: Suite (4:40); Mission: Impossible: 12 The Plot (2:41); 13 Main Theme (2:42).

Review: Schifrin does Hitchcock, and the results are never less than satisfactory, even if the selections are part of what one might call the "standard" Hitchcock repertoire. For good measure, Lalo also includes some of his own compositions for *Rollercoaster, Mannix, Dirty Harry* and *Mission: Impossible*, in what is loosely billed as "other music for murder." More music from lesser known scores for the Hitchcock films would have done just as nicely.

Music from Alfred Hitchcock Films 🦴🦴🦴

1985, Varese-Sarabande Records.

Album Notes: *Music:* John Williams, Dimitri Tiomkin, Franz Waxman, Roy Webb; The Utah Symphony Orchestra and The University of Utah A Cappella Choir, conducted by Charles Ketcham; *Album Producer:* George Korngold; *Engineer:* Bruce Leek.

Selections: Family Plot (J. Williams): 1 End Credits (3:54); Strangers On A Train (D. Tiomkin): 2 Main Title and Approach-

ing The Train/Ann And Guy/The Warning and Bruno's Threat/ The Tennis Game/The Cigarette Lighter/Bruno's Death and Finale (16:13); Suspicion (F. Waxman): 3 Main Title/Sunday Morning/The Chairs Are Back/Melbeck's Office/Looking For Johnny/Too Fast/Finale (12:04); Notorious (R. Webb, arr.: C. Palmer): 4 Main Title/Unica/Troubled Mind/Alicia Collapses/ Finale and End Cast (5:46).

Review: Three important scores for three important films in the Hitchcock canon receive their proper due in this unfortunately much too short album. Both *Strangers on a Train* and *Suspicion* elicited wonderful musical comments from Dimitri Tiomkin and Franz Waxman, respectively. And the longer suites included here whet one's appetite for more of the music composed by both men for the Hitchcock thrillers. *Notorious* presents another great composer, Roy Webb, whose enormous contributions to film music has fallen into sad neglect, to the extent that his name means very little today and is seldom seen in compilations. The witty "End Credits" from John Williams' *Family Plot* also suggests that a longer suite from that score should be recorded. Unfortunately, the total playing time for the whole CD falls short of what one might expect in these days of 75-plus minutes of music on many albums.

Lena Horne

Ain't It The Truth: Lena Horne at M-G-M 🦴🦴🦴🦴

1996, Rhino Records.

Album Notes: *Album Producer:* Marilee Bradford; *Engineer:* Doug Schwartz.

Selections: Panama Hattie: 1 Just One Of Those Things (C. Porter)(1:22); 2 The Sping (P. Moore/J. Le Gon/A. Moore)(4:58) *Lena Horne, The Berry Brothers*; Cabin In The Sky: 3 Ain't It The Truth (H. Arlen/E.Y. Harburg) (2:30); 4 Life's Full O' Consequences (H. Arlen/E.Y. Harburg)(1:49) *Lena Horne, Eddie "Rochester" Anderson*; 5 Honey In The Honeycomb (H. Arlen/E.Y. Harburg)(1:53); Thousands Cheer: 6 Honeysuckle Rose (T. Waller/A. Razaf)(2:57) *Benny Carter and His Orchestra*; Swing Fever: 7 You're So Indiff'rent (S. Fain/M. Parish)(2:52); I Dood It!: 8 Jericho (R. Myers/L. Robin)(6:20) *Hazel Scott, Freddie Trainer*; Broadway Rhythm: 9 Brazilian Boogie (H. Martin/R. Blane)(5:54) *Lena Horne, The Music Maids, The Edwards Sisters, The M-G-M Studio Chorus*; 10 Somebody Loves Me (G. Gershwin/ B.G. DeSylva/B. MacDonald)(3:11); 11 Tete A Tete At Tea Time/Solid Potato Salad (D. Raye/G. De Paul)(3:17) *Lena Horne, Eddie "Rochester" Anderson*; Two

Girls And A Sailor: 12 Paper Doll (J. Black)(3:17); 13 Paper Doll (J. Black)(alternate lyric)(3:13); 14 Trembling Of A Leaf (J. Green/J. Lawrence) (3:00); Ziegfeld Follies: 15 Love (H. Martin/R. Blane)(3:28); Till The Clouds Roll By: 16 Can't Help Lovin' Dat Man (J. Kern/O. Hammerstein II)(3:02); 17 Why Was I Born? (J. Kern/O. Hammerstein II)(2:06); 18 Bill (J. Kern/O. Hammerstein II)(outtake)(1:23); Words And Music: 19 Where Or When (R. Rodgers/ L. Hart)(2:59); 20 The Lady Is A Tramp (R. Rodgers/L. Hart)(2:56); Duchess Of Idaho: 21 Baby, Come Out Of The Clouds (L. Pearl/H. Nemo)(3:07); Meet Me In Las Vegas: 22 If You Can Dream (N. Brodzsky/S. Cahn)(1:43); 23 You Got Looks (N. Brodzsky/S. Cahn)(2:24).

Review: For many years, in some parts of the country, Lena Horne was Metro-Goldwyn-Mayer's best kept secret: her scenes, judiciously filmed in such way that they didn't intercut with what preceded or followed them, but purely and simply excised when the films were shown in the South. Thus, many potential fans were denied the pleasure of enjoying one of the most gorgeous female performers in Hollywood, whose sophisticated cool looks and sultry delivery made her an icon in the screen musicals. This wonderful collection brings together many of the songs she created in those films, some of which, like "Lady and the Tramp," became signature themes.

Ron Howard

Passions and Achievements
𝄞𝄞𝄞𝄞▷

1997, Milan Records.

Album Notes: *Music:* Burt Bacharach, Lee Holdridge, James Horner, Peter Ivers, Randy Newman, Thomas Newman, John Williams, Hans Zimmer; *Album A&R Coordinator:* Dana Berez; *Engineer:* Ramon Breton.

Selections: 1 Main Theme (from *Grand Theft Auto*)(P. Ivers)(2:43); 2 That's What Friends Are For (from *Night Shift*)(B. Bacharach)(4:08); 3 Love Theme (from *Splash*)(L. Holdridge)(3:33); 4 The Ascension (from *Cocoon*)(J. Horner)(5:56); 5 Bucket Of Ice (from *Gung Ho*)(T. Newman)(1:17); 6 Willow's Theme (from *Willow*)(J. Horner)(3:55); 7 Karen And Gil/Montage (from *Parenthood*)(R. Newman)(4:51); 8 Show Me Your Firetruck (from *Backdraft*)(H. Zimmer)(5:37); 9 The Land Race (from *Far And Away*)(J. Williams)(4:59); 10 The Newsroom 7:00 P.M. (From *The Paper*)(R. Newman)(2:51); 11 The Dark Side Of The Moon (from *Apollo 13*)(J. Horner)(5:10); 12 The Kidnapping (from *The Ransom*)(J. Horner) (4:34).

Review: Listening to the selections in this tribute to director Ron Howard, one is suddenly confronted with a daunting fact: for all his quiet ways and apparent lack of public visibility, Howard has been involved in quite a few films over the past 20 years, many of which, like *Cocoon, Willow, Far And Away,* and *Apollo 13,* are important box-office hits. Beyond this realization, it is also a pleasure to hear, combined on one CD, the themes from these and other, less remarkable but nonetheless equally entertaining films, such as *Night Shift, Splash, Gung Ho, Backdraft* or *The Paper.* As compilations of this type go, this one is intelligently organized and smartly presented, and it includes selections that are not found elsewhere, another boon for collectors.

Al Jolson

Let Me Sing and I'm Happy: Al Jolson at Warner Bros. 1926-1936 𝄞𝄞𝄞

1996, Rhino Records.

Album Notes: The Warner Bros. Studio Orchestra, conducted by Louis Silvers, Leo F. Forbstein; *Album Producer:* Ian Whitcomb; *Engineer:* Doug Schwartz.

Selections: Al Jolson In "A Plantation Act": 1 April Showers (L. Silvers/ B.G. DeSylva)(3:01); 2 Rock-A-Bye Your Baby With A Dixie Melody (J. Schwartz/ J. Young/S. Lewis)(3:39); The Jazz Singer: 3 Dirt Hands! Dirty Face (A. Jolson/G. Clarke/E. Leslie)(2:56); 4 Toot, Toot, Tootsie! (G. Kahn/E. Erdman/ D. Russo)(2:09); 5 Blue Skies (I. Berlin)(2:43); 6 Mother Of Mine, I Still Have You (A. Jolson/L. Silvers/G. Clarke)(3:12); 7 My Mammy (W. Donaldson/S. Lewis/J. Young)(2:04); The Singing Fool: 8 It All Depends On You (B.G. DeSylva/L. Brown/R. Henderson)(3:05); 9 I'm Sitting On Top Of The World (R. Henderson/S. Lewis/J. Young)(1:40); 10 The Spaniard That Blighted My Life (B. Merson)(2:26); 11 There's A Rainbow 'Round My Shoulder (A. Jolson/B. Rose/D. Dreyer)(2:26); 12 Golden Gate (A. Jolson/J. Meyer/B. Rose/D. Dreyer)(1:29); 13 Sonny Boy (A. Jolson/B.G. DeSylva/L. Brown/R. Henderson)(5:18); Say It With Songs: 14 Back In Your Own Backyard (A. Jolson/B. Rose/ D. Dreyer)(1:09); 15 Used To You (B.G. DeSylva/L. Brown/R. Henderson)(2:49); 16 I'm In Seventh Heaven (D. Dreyer/A. Jolson/B. Rose)(1:44); Mammy: 17 Let Me Sing And I'm Happy (I. Berlin)(2:26); 18 (Across The Breakfast Table) Looking At You (I. Berlin)(3:28); 19 Why Do They All Take The Night Boat To Albany? (J. Schwartz/ J. Young/S. Lewis)(1:23); Big Boy: 20 Liza Lee (G. Stept/B. Green)(1:50); 21 Little Sunshine (G.

Meyer/A. Gottler/S. Mitchell)(1:34); Go Into Your Dance: 22 About A Quarter To Nine (H. Warren/A. Dubin)(6:28); The Singing Kid: 23 I Love To Sing-A (H. Arlen/E.Y. Harburg)(3:04).

Review: Today, Al Jolson's black-face performances are politically incorrect and an embarrassment to anyone watching his films. In his heyday, however, this was a trademark expected from him and even demanded by his fans. This set aside, the self-appointed "Greatest Entertainer in the World" appears more dated than most in this collection, which covers a ten-year tenure at Warner Bros., in which his exaggerated, grandiloquent delivery contrasts with the more natural style that has prevailed since.

Yet, if for no other reason, Jolson should be remembered as the performer who created a sensation when he appeared in *The Jazz Singer*, technically the first talking picture when the movies were still silent. The set includes the songs from that film, as well as several others that became million-sellers at the time, including "April Showers," "Rock-A-Bye Your Baby With a Dixie Melody," "Toot-Toot-Tootsie Goodbye," "I'm Sitting on Top of the World," and "There's a Rainbow 'Round My Shoulder."

Danny Kaye

Hans Christian Andersen/ The Court Jester ♫♫♫♫

1994, Varese-Sarabande Records; from the movies *Hans-Christian Andersen*, Samuel Goldwyn, 1952, and *The Court Jester*, Paramount Pictures, 1956.

Album Notes: *Album Producer*: Bruce Kimmel; *Engineer*: Joe Gastwirt.

Selections: Hans-Christian Andersen (F. Loesser): 1 I'm Hans-Christian Andersen (2:37); 2 Anywhere I Wander (3:15); 3 The Ugly Duckling (3:06); 4 Inchworm (3:14); 5 Thumbelina (1:47); 6 No Two People (2:24); 7 The King's New Clothes (3:34); 8 Wonderful Copenhagen (2:10); The Court Jester (S. Fine/S. Cahn): 9 Overture (5:26); 10 Life Could Not Better Be (3:00); 11 Outfox The Fox (2:50); 12 I'll Take You Dreaming (3:03); 13 My Heart Knows A Lovely Song (2:23); 14 I Live To Love (3:11); 15 Willow, Willow, Waley/Pass The Basket (4:59); 16 The Maladjusted Jester (3:47); 17 Where Walks My True Love (3:15); 18 Life Could Not Better Be (2:05).

Review: One of the great comic geniuses of his generation, Danny Kaye was equally at ease fooling around or settling down to deliver a sweet ballad when the occasion presented itself. Though his screen persona accented the zany side of his talent, he demonstrated in the remarkable *Hans-Christian An-*

dersen, a fairy tale account of the great Danish storyteller, that he could also delve into more romantic fares and still charm his public. On this occasion, he was also handsomely serviced by the Award-Winning score composed by Frank Loesser, in which "Wonderful Copenhagen" still stands out as a highlight. Conversely, *The Court Jester*, probably one of Kaye's funniest movies, is a splendid take off on the swashbuckler genre, in which he impersonated a would-be knight bent on righting the wrong and saving a beautiful damsel in distress. Spread throughout the action are various musical numbers, including the tongue-twister "Maladjusted Jester," and the lovely lullaby "I'll Take You Dreaming."

Gene Kelly

'S Wonderful: Gene Kelly at M-G-M ♫♫♫♫♫

1996, Rhino Records.

Album Notes: *CD Producers*: George Feltenstein, Bradley Flanagan; *Engineer*: Doug Schwartz.

Selections: Singin' In The Rain: 1 Singin' In The Rain (A. Freed/N.H. Brown)(3:57); An American In Paris: 2 I Got Rhythm (G. & I. Gershwin)(3:42); Brigadoon: 3 Almost Like Being In Love (F. Loewe/A.J. Lerner)(4:18); For Me And My Gal: 4 For Me And My Gal (G. Meyer/E. Leslie/R. Goetz)(5:07) *Gene Kelly, Judy Garland*; An American In Paris: 5 Love Is Here To Stay (G. & I. Gershwin)(3:51); Singin' In The Rain: 6 Good Morning (A. Freed/N.H. Brown) (3:15) *Gene Kelly, Donald O' Connor, Debbie Reynolds*; The Pirate: 7 Nina (C. Porter)(6:34); Ziegfeld Follies: 8 The Babbitt And The Bromide (G. & I. Gershwin)(5:30) *Gene Kelly, Fred Astaire*; Anchors Aweigh: 9 The Worry Song (S. Fain/R. Freed)(2:56) *Gene Kelly, Jerry The Mouse*; Summer Stock: 10 You Wonderful You (H. Warren/J. Brooks/S. Chaplin)(3:03) *Gene Kelly, Judy Garland*; Summer Stock: 11 Dig, Dig, Dig For Your Dinner (H. Warren/M. Gordon) (4:14) *Gene Kelly, Phil Silvers, The M-G-M Studio Chorus*; The Pirate: 12 Be A Clown (C. Porter)(2:36) *Gene Kelly, Judy Garland*; Singin' In The Rain: 13 You Were Meant For Me (A. Freed/N.H. Brown)(3:32); Living In A Big Way: 14 Fido And Me (L. Alter/E. Heyman)(4:58); On The Town: 15 Main Street (R. Edens/ B. Comden/A. Green)(3:45); It's Always Fair Weather: 16 I Like Myself (A. Previn/B. Comden/A. Green)(3:37); Les Girls: 17 Les Girls (C. Porter)(5:05) *Gene Kelly, Mitzi Gaynor, Taina Elg, Kay Kendall, Betty Wand, Thara Matthieson*; An American In Paris: 18 'S Wonderful (G. & I. Gershwin)(3:48) *Gene Kelly, Georges Guetary*.

Review: See entry below.

Best of Gene Kelly from M-G-M Classic Films 🎵🎵

1987, MCA Records.

Album Notes: *Album Producer*: Andy McKaie; *Engineer*: Greg Fulginiti.

Selections: An American In Paris: 1 I Got Rhythm (G. & I. Gershwin) (3:28); Brigadoon: 2 The Heather On The Hill (F. Loewe/A.J. Lerner) (2:42); Les Girls: 3 Les Girls (C. Porter) (4:20) *Gene Kelly, Mitzi Gaynor, Kay Kendall, Taina Elg*; Singin' In The Rain: 4 You Were Meant For Me (A. Freed/N.H. Brown) (3:10); Brigadoon: 5 Almost Like Being In Love (F. Loewe/A.J. Lerner) (2:34); 6 There But For You Go I (F. Loewe/A.J. Lerner) (2:54); An American In Paris: 7 'S Wonderful (G. & I. Gershwin) (2:58) *Gene Kelly, Georges Guetary*; For Me And My Gal: 8 For Me And My Gal (E. Leslie/R. Goetz/G. Meyer) (2:30) *Gene Kelly, Judy Garland*; Singin' In The Rain: 9 All I Do Is Dream Of You (A. Freed/N.H. Brown) (1:26); 10 Singin' In The Rain (A. Freed/N.H. Brown) (2:54)

Review: See entry below.

Gotta Dance!: The Best of Gene Kelly 🎵🎵🎵

1993, Sony Music Special Products.

Album Notes: *Album Producer*: Dan Rivard; *Engineer*: Ken Robertson.

Selections: For Me And My Gal: 1 For Me And My Gal (E. Leslie/R. Goetz/G. Meyer) (4:21) *Gene Kelly, Judy Garland*; Anchors Aweigh: 2 The King Who Couldn't Dance (The Worry Song) (R. Freed/S. Fain) (2:21); The Pirate: 3 Be A Clown (C. Porter) (2:51) *Gene Kelly, Judy Garland*; 4 Nina (C. Porter) (6:35); Summer Stock: 5 You Wonderful You (H. Warren/S. Chaplin/J. Brooks) (3:09) *Gene Kelly, Judy Garland*; 6 Dig-Dig-Dig For Your Dinner (H. Warren/M. Gordon) (3:50) *Gene Kelly, Phil Silvers*; An American In Paris: 7 Love Is Here To Stay (G. & I. Gershwin) (3:51); 8 Tra-La-La (G. & I. Gershwin) (3:43) *Gene Kelly, Oscar Levant*; 9 I've Got A Crush On You (G. & I. Gershwin) (2:48); Singin' In The Rain: 10 Moses (R. Edens/B. Comden/A. Green) (3:05) *Gene Kelly, Donald O'Connor*; 11 Singin' In The Rain (A. Freed/N.H. Brown) (4:01); 12 Broadway Rhythm/Broadway Melody (from the Broadway Ballet) (A. Freed/N.H. Brown) (4:32); 13 All I Do Is Dream Of You (A. Freed/N.H. Brown) (3:07); Brigadoon: 14 Almost Like Being In Love (F. Loewe/A.J. Lerner) (4:21); 15 From This Day On (F. Loewe/A.J. Lerner) (4:25) *Gene Kelly, Carol Richards*; Deep In My Heart: 16 I Love To Go Swimmin' With Wimmen (S. Romberg/B. Mac-Donald) (2:06) *Gene Kelly, Fred Kelly*; It's Always Fair Weather: 17 Once Upon A Time (A. Previn/B. Comden/A. Green) (3:33) *Gene Kelly, Dan Dailey, Michael Kidd*; 18 I Like Myself (A. Previn/B. Comden/A. Green) (4:10); Les Girls: 19 You're Just Too Too (C. Porter) (1:56) *Gene Kelly, Kay Kendall*; 20 Why Am I So Gone (About That Gal?) (C. Porter) (4:30).

Review: Like Fred Astaire, Gene Kelly was the ultimate song-and-dance man, a performer whose athletic choreography and charming warbling graced some of the best film musicals ever made by Metro-Goldwyn-Mayer. These collections focus on many of the songs he performed in his movies, and reveal an aspect of his talent that sometimes took second place to his dancing on the screen.

The Rhino set, by far the best, includes some of the most memorable numbers from Kelly's movies, often in versions that are more complete and, in several instances, available for the first time in stereo.

The MCA compilation is only of marginal interest, and might best serve as a cut-rate introduction.

The Sony set adds a couple of selections not available elsewhere, such as "I Love To Go Swimmin' With Wimmen," sung by Gene and his brother Fred, and as such remains of interest for completists and collectors... until, of course, Rhino, the current administrator of the M-G-M catalogue, comes up with a follow-up to its own set, or with the complete soundtracks to some of the musicals not yet reissued.

Ethel Merman

Ethel Merman/Lyda Roberti/ Mae West 🎵🎵🎵

1991, Sony Music Special Products.

Album Notes: *Album Producer*: Miles Kreuger; *Engineer*: George Engfer.

Selections: *ETHEL MERMAN:* Take A Chance: 1 Eadie Was A Lady (B.G. DeSylva/ N.H. Brown/R. Whiting) (5:59); Kid Millions: 2 An Earful Of Music (G. Kahn/W. Donaldson) (2:51); Life Begins At Eight Forty: 3 You're A Builder Upper (H. Arlen/I. Gershwin/E.Y. Harburg) (2:33); Anything Goes: 4 I Get A Kick Out Of You (C. Porter) (3:04); 5 You're The Top (C. Porter) (2:49); In Caliente: 6 The Lady In Red (M. Dixon/A. Wrubel) (2:46); The Big Broadcast: 7 It's The Animal In Me (H. Revel/M. Gordon) (3:12);

LYDA ROBERTI: College Rhythm: 8 College Rhythm (M. Gordon/ H. Revel)(2:49); 9 Take A Number From One To Ten (H. Revel/ M. Gordon)(2:55);

MAE WEST: She Done Him Wrong: 10 A Guy What Takes His Time (R. Rainger)(2:39); 11 (I Wonder Where My) Easy Rider's Gone

(S. Brooks) (2:21); I'm No Angel: 12 I'm No Angel (G. DuBois/B. Ellison/H. Brooks)(3:28); 13 I Found A New Way To Go To Town (G. DuBois/B. Ellison/H. Brooks)(2:38); 14 I Want You, I Need You (B. Ellison/H. Brooks)(2:33); 15 They Call Me Sister Honky Tonk (G. DuBois/B. Ellison/H. Brooks)(2:54).

Review: This interesting compilation was put together in the 1970s by film historian Miles Kreuger, who mined the vaults of Columbia Records in search of studio recordings by three of the most prominent screen performers of the 1930s. Merman, of course, was active both on Broadway and in Hollywood, and these selections from some of the films in which she appeared, enabled her to perform some of the songs she had created on stage ("Eadie Was a Lady," "I Get a Kick Out of You," "You're the Top." For her part, Mae West, also a graduate from the New York stage, became the quintessential 1930s vamp, better known for her wisecracks and sly sexual innuendos. As a singer, she was at best competent, but there was no mistaking the manner in which she oooh'd and aaah'd her way through a lyric. Her finely timed delivery in such songs as "A Guy What Takes His Time," "I'm No Angel" or "They Call Me Sister Honky Tonk," merely confirms what everyone knew about her: she was one hell of a saucy dame! As for Lyda Roberti, she may be the only one of the three whose memory has not been perpetuated in the same manner. Listening to her in the two selections from *College Rhythm* included here, only make one wish there'd be more of her in this compilation. Sonically, the set is definitely not up to the exacting standards of the digital era, something that mars one's enjoyment.

American Legends: Ethel Merman 🎵🎵🎵

1996, Laserlight Records.

Album Notes: Orchestras conducted by Billy May, Alfred Newman, Louis Silvers, Al Goodman, Lud Gluskin, Fairchild & Carrol, Victor Young, Harry Sosnik; *Album Producer:* Rod McKuen; *Engineer:* Michael McDonald.

Selections: Anything Goes: 1 I Get A Kick Out Of You (C. Porter)(2:47); As Thousands Cheer: 2 Heat Wave (I. Berlin)(2:49); Panama Hattie: 3 Make It Another Old-Fashioned, Please (C. Porter)(2:58); Anything Goes: 4 Blow, Gabriel, Blow (C. Porter)(2:16); Girl Crazy: 5 But Not For Me (G. & I. Gershwin)(1:57); Anything Goes: 6 You're The Top (C. Porter)(3:11) *Ethel Merman, Bing Crosby*; Happy Landing: 7 Hot And Happy (L. Pockriss/J. Yellen) (2:26); Red, Hot And Blue: 8 Down In The Depths Of The Ninetieth Floor (C. Porter)(2:54); 9 It's De-Lovely (C. Porter)(2:48); Stars In Your Eyes: 10 I'll Pay The Check (A.

Schwartz/D. Fields)(3:20); Anything Goes: 11 You're The Top (reprise)(C. Porter)(2:09); Alexander's Ragtime Band: 12 Marching Along With Time (I. Berlin)(2:18); Du Barry Was A Lady: 13 Friendship (C. Porter)(2:50) *Ethel Merman, Bert Lahr.*

Review: Another set containing early sides recorded by Ethel Merman, from her 1930s stage shows, assembled here without much concern for continuity or chronology. While it's always a pleasure discovering songs the great belter created and solidly established her reputation as one of Broadway's top performers, the sound quality here is a negative factor and must be taken into consideration.

Marilyn Monroe

Never Before, Never Again
🎵🎵🎵

1979, DRG Records.

Selections: 1 Do It Again (G. Gershwin/B.G. De Sylva)(3:11); 2 Kiss (A. Newman/D. Gillespie)(2:59); 3 You'd Be Surprised (I. Berlin)(3:02); 4 A Fine Romance (J. Kern/D. Fields)(2:19); 5 She Acts Like A Woman Should (B. Scott) (2:45); There's No Business Like Show Business: 6 Heat Wave (I. Berlin)(4:21); Gentlemen Prefer Blondes: 7 Diamonds Are A Girl's Best Friend (J. Styne/L. Robin)(3:30); 8 A Little Girl From Little Rock (J. Styne/L. Robin)(3:04) *Marilyn Monroe, Jane Russell*; 9 When Loves Goes Wrong, Nothing Goes Right (H. Adamson/H. Carmichael)(3:27) *Marilyn Monroe, Jane Russell*; 10 Bye, Bye, Baby (J. Styne/L. Robin)(5:30) *Marilyn Monroe, Jane Russell*; River Of No Return: 11 I'm Gonna File My Claim (A. Newman/K. Darby)(2:35); 12 River Of No Return (A. Newman/K. Darby)(2:12); There's No Business Like Show Business: 13 Lazy (I. Berlin)(3:33); Some Like It Hot: 14 Running Wild (A. Gibbs/J.Grey/L. Wood)(1:04); 15 I Wanna Be Loved By You (B. Kalmar/H. Ruby/H. Stothart)(2:58); 16 I'm Through With Love (G. Kahn/M. Malneck/F. Livingston)(2:30); Let's Make Love: 17 My Heart Belongs To Daddy (C. Porter)(5:00); 18 Happy Birthday To John F. Kennedy (:43).

Review: See entry below.

American Legends: Marilyn Monroe 🎵🎵🎵

1996, Laserlight Records.

Album Notes: *Album Producer:* Rod McKuen; *Engineer:* Michael McDonald.

Selections: Some Like It Hot: 1 I Wanna Be Loved By You (B. Kalmar/H. Ruby/ H. Stothart)(2:55); 2 I'm Through With Love (G. Kahn/M. Malneck/F. Livingston) (2:31); Gentlemen Prefer Blondes: 3 Diamonds Are A Girl's Best Friend (J. Styne/L. Robin)(3:30); 4 Bye, Bye, Baby (J. Styne/L. Robin)(5:26); There's No Business Like Show Business: 5 Lazy (I. Berlin)(3:35); The Seven Year Itch: 6 Rachmaninoff And Chopsticks (5:14) *Marilyn Monroe, Towm Ewell*; 7 A Fine Romance (J. Kern/D. Fields)(2:19); River Of No Return: 8 River Of No Return (A. Newman/K. Darby)(2:13); Some Like It Hot: 9 You'd Be Surprised (I. Berlin) (3:03); Gentlemen Prefer Blondes: 10 A Little Girl From Little Rock (J. Styne/ L. Robin)(3:03); The French Doll: 11 Do It Again (C. Porter)(3:11); 12 Happy Birthday, Mr. President (2:03).

Review: There are so many recordings by Marilyn Monroe, all of them using exactly the same basic tracks, that it almost becomes redundant to try and recommend one over another. For the sake of arguing, the DRG set contains a trio of tracks not on the Laserlight release ("When Love Goes Wrong," from *Gentlemen Prefer Blondes,* "Running Wild," from *Some Like It Hot,* and "My Heart Belongs To Daddy," from *Let's Make Love),* while Laserlight includes two selections from *The Seven Year Itch* and *The French Doll* (oblivious of the fact that Monroe didn't appear in the latter). Both sets also present some of the selections they have in common in their abbreviated form, like "Lazy" or "A Little Girl From Little Rock," which take much more screen time than heard here. Sonic quality in both is also about the same, with crunched highs and boosted lows, to mask some of the most obvious flaws in the recordings. Frankly, Marilyn deserves much better, and one would hope her vocal contributions will one day receive the kind of regal treatment she would command.

Dick Powell

Dick Powell in Hollywood (1933-1935) ♫♫♫♫

1995, Legacy Records.

Album Notes: *Songs:* Al Dubin, Harry Warren; *Album Producer:* Didier C. Deutsch; *Engineer:* Tom Ruff.

Selections: Gold Diggers Of 1933: 1 The Gold Diggers' Song (We're In The Money)(3:11); 2 Pettin' In The Park (2:59); 3 Shadow Waltz (3:02); 4 I've Got To Sing A Torch Song (3:08); Footlight Parade: 5 By A Waterfall (I. Kahal/S. Fain)(3:14); 6 Honeymoon Hotel (2:40); The Road Is Open Again: 7 The Road Is Open Again (I. Kahal/S. Fain)(2:57); College Coach: 8 Lonely Lane (I. Kahal/S. Fain)(3:05); Wonder Bar: 9 Wonder Bar (3:18); 10 Don't Say Goodnight (3:10); Twenty Million Sweethearts: 11 I'll String Along With You (3:13); Happiness Ahead: 12 Pop! Goes Your Heart (M. Dixon/A. Wrubel)(2:41); 13 Beauty Must Be Loved (I. Kahal/S. Fain)(3:13); Flirtation Walk: 14 Mr. And Mrs. Is The Name (M. Dixon/A. Wrubel)(2:50); 15 Flirtation Walk (M. Dixon/A. Wrubel)(3:06); Sweet Music: 16 I See Two Lovers (M. Dixon/A. Wrubel)(3:02); Gold Diggers Of 1935: 17 Lullaby Of Broadway (3:14); 18 The Words Are In My Heart (3:01); Broadway Gondolier: 19 Lulu's Back In Town (2:55); 20 The Rose In Her Hair (3:10).

Review: This collection presents songs Powell made famous in the Busby Berkeley screen extravaganzas, not as they were heard on the screen but as he rerecorded them in the studio later on, with different arrangements and much abbreviated playing times. One of the 1930s' heartthrobs, Powell has fallen into unjust neglect in recent years. This is regrettable, given the fact that he was a smooth, charming performer with a wry sense of humor, whose popularity was fueled by his starring roles in films like *Gold Diggers of 1933, Footlight Parade, Gold Diggers of 1935* and *Broadway Gondolier,* among his most felicitous contributions. Today, his style of singing might seem a bit dated and unnatural, but his importance as a crooner cannot be denied, and the collection might reveal to the listener a performer who certainly deserves to be heard.

Elvis Presley

Blue Hawaii

1996, RCA Records; from the movie *Blue Hawaii,* Paramount Pictures, 1961.

Album Notes: *CD Producers:* Ernst Mikael Jorgensen, Roger Semon; *Engineer:* Dennis Ferrante.

Selections: 1 Blue Hawaii (L. Robin/R. Rainger)(2:34); 2 Almost Always True (F. Wise/B. Weisman)(2:23); 3 Aloha Oe (trad., arr.: E. Presley)(1:51); 4 No More (D. Robertson/H. Blair)(2:21); 5 Can't Help Falling In Love (H. Peretti/ L. Creatore/G. Weiss)(2:59); 6 Rock-A-Hula Baby (F. Wise/B. Weisman/G. Fuller) (1:58); 7 Moonlight Swim (S. Dee/B. Weisman)(2:18); 8 Ku-U-I-Po (Hawaiian Sweetheart) (H. Peretti/L. Creatore/G. Weiss)(2:20); 9 Ito Eats (S. Tepper/R. Bennett) (1:22); 10 Slicin' Sand (S. Tepper/R. Bennett)(1:34); 11 Hawaiian Sunset (S. Tepper/R. Bennett)(2:30); 12 Beach Boy Blues (S. Tepper/R. Bennett) (2:01); 13 Island Of Love (S. Tepper/R. Bennett)(2:40); 14 Hawaiian Wedding Song (C. King/A. Hoffman/D. Manning)(2:47); 15 Steppin' Out Of Line (F. Wise/ B. Weisman/G. Fuller)(1:52); 16 Can't Help Falling In Love (movie version) (H. Peretti/ L. Creatore/G. Weiss)(1:53); 17 Slicin' Sand (alternate take)(S. Tepper/R. Bennett)(1:44); 18 No More (alternate take)(D. Robertson/H. Blair) (2:34); 19 Rock-A-Hula Baby (alternate take)(F. Wise/B. Weisman/G. Fuller) (2:14); 20 Beach Boy Blues (movie version)(S. Tepper/R. Bennett)(1:56); 21 Steppin' Out Of Line (movie version)(F. Wise/B. Weisman/G. Fuller)(1:52); 22 Blue Hawaii (alternate take)(L. Robin/R. Rainger)(2:41).

Review: See *Wild in the Country* entry below.

Change of Habit

1995, RCA Records; from the movie *Change of Habit*, Universal Pictures, 1970.

See: Love a Little, Live a Little

Charro!

1995, RCA Records; from the movie *Charro!*, National General Pictures, 1969.

See: Love a Little, Live a Little

Easy Come, Easy Go/ Speedway

1995, RCA Records; from the movies *Easy Come, Easy Go*, Paramount Pictures, 1967, and *Speedway*, M-G-M, 1968.

Album Notes: *CD Producers*: Ernst Mikael Jorgensen, Roger Semon; *Audio Restoration*: Bill Lacey; *Engineers*: Dennis Ferrante, Dick Baxter.

Selections: Easy Come, Easy Go: 1 Easy Come, Easy Go (B. Weisman/S. Wayne) (2:18); 2 The Love Machine (G. Nelson/F. Burch/C. Taylor)(2:49); 3 Yoga Is As Yoga Does (G. Nelson/F. Burch)(2:09); 4 You Gotta Stop (B. Giant/B. Baum/F. Kaye)(2:16); 5 Sing You Children (G. Nelson/F. Burch)(2:12); 6 I'll Take Love (D. Fuller/M. Barkan)(2:15); 7 She's A Machine (J. Byers)(1:36); 8 The Love Machine (alternate take 11)(G. Nelson/F. Burch/C. Taylor)(2:28); 9 Sing You Children (alternate take 1)(G. Nelson/F. Burch)(2:27); 10 She's A Machine (alternate take 13)(J. Byers)(1:38); Speedway: 11 Suppose (alternate master) (S. Dee/G. Goehring)(3:01); 12 Speedway (M. Glazer/S. Schlaks)(2:21); 13 There Ain't Nothing Like A Song (J. Byers/B. Johnston)(2:08); 14 Your Time Hasn't Come Yet, Baby (J. Hirschhorn/A. Kasha)(1:51); 15 Who Are You (Who Am I?)(S. Wayne/B. Weisman)(2:32); 16 He's Your Uncle, Not Your Dad (S. Wayne/B. Weisman)(2:27); 17 Let Yourself Go (J. Byers)(2:59); 18 Five Sleepy Heads (S. Tepper/R. Bennett)(1:29); 19 Suppose (S. Dee/G. Goehring)(2:02); 20 Your Groovy Self (L. Hazelwood)(2:54) *Nancy Sinatra*.

Review: See *Wild in the Country* entry below.

Flaming Star/Wild in the Country/Follow That Dream

1995, RCA Records; from the movies *Flaming Star*, 20th Century-Fox, 1960; *Wild in the Country*, 20th Century-Fox, 1961; and *Follow That Dream*, United Artists, 1962.

Album Notes: *Album Producers*: Ernst Mikael Jorgensen, Roger Semon; *Audio Restoration*: Bill Lacey; *Engineers*: Dennis Ferrante, Dick Baxter.

Selections: Flaming Star: 1 Flaming Star (S. Wayne/S. Edwards)(2:25); 2 Summer Kisses Winter Tears (F. Wise/B. Weisman/J. Lloyd)(2:19); 3 Britches (S. Wayne/S. Edwards)(1:41); 4 A Cane And A High Starched Collar (S. Tepper/R. Bennett)(1:46); 5 Black Star (S. Wayne/S. Edwards)(2:30); 6 Summer Kisses Winter Tears (film version)(F. Wise/B. Weisman/J. Lloyd)(1:31); 7 Flaming Star (End Title)(S. Wayne/S. Edwards)(:29); Wild In The Country: 8 Wild In The Country (H. Peretti/L. Creatore/G. Weiss)(1:52); 9 I Slipped, I Stumbled, I Fell (F. Wise/B. Weisman)(1:34); 10 Lonely Man (B. Benjamin/S. Marcus)(2:43); 11 In My Way (F. Wise/B. Weisman)(1:21); 12 Forget Me Never (F. Wise/B. Weisman)(1:36); 13 Lonely Man (solo)(B. Benjamin/S. Marcus)(2:00); 14 I Slipped, I Stumbled, I Fell (alternate master)(F. Wise/B. Weisman)(1:36); Follow That Dream: 15 Follow That Dream (F. Wise/B. Weisman)(1:37); 16 Angel (S. Tepper/R. Bennett)(2:38); 17 What A Wonderful Life (S. Wayne/J. Livingston)(2:26); 18 I'm Not The Marrying Kind (M. David/S. Edwards)(1:50); 19 A Whistling Tune (S. Edwards/H. Davis)(2:12); 20 Sound Advice (B. Giant/B. Baum/F. Kaye)(1:46).

Review: See *Wild in the Country* entry below.

Fun in Acapulco/ It Happened at the World's Fair

1993, RCA Records; from the movies *Fun in Acapulco*, Paramount Pictures, 1963, and *It Happened at the World's Fair*, M-G-M, 1963.

Album Notes: *CD Producers*: Ernst Mikael Jorgensen, Roger Semon; *Engineer*: Dixk Baxter, Ernst Mikael Jorgensen.

Selections: It Happened At The World's Fair: 1 Beyond The Bend (S. Wayne/B. Weisman/G. Fuller)(1:50); 2 Relax (S. Tepper/R. Bennett)(2:19); 3 Take Me To The Fair (S. Tepper/R. Bennett)(; 4 They Remind Me Too Much Of You (D. Robertson)(2:30); 5 One Broken Heart For Sale (film version)(O. Blackwell/O. Scott)(2:23); 6 I'm Falling In Love Tonight (D. Robertson)(1:39); 7 Cotton Candy Land (Batchelor/Roberts)(1:33); 8 A World Of Our Own (B. Giant/B. Baum/F. Kaye)(2:14); 9 How Would You Like To Be (B. Raleigh/M.

Barkan)(3:26); 10 Happy Ending (S. Wayne/B. Weisman) (2:08); 11 One Broken Heart For Sale (O. Blackwell/O. Scott) (1:45); Fun In Acapulco: 12 Fun In Acapulco (S. Wayne/B. Weisman) (2:28); 13 Vino, dinero y amor (S. Tepper/R. Bennett)(1:53); 14 Mexico (S. Tepper/R. Bennett)(1:58); 15 El Toro (B. Giant/B. Baum/F. Kaye)(2:41); 16 Marguerita (D. Robertson)(2:40); 17 The Bullfighter Was A Lady (S. Tepper/R. Bennett)(2:02); 18 (There's) No Room To Rhumba In A Sports Car (F. Wise/D. Manning)(1:51); 19 I Think I'm Gonna Like It Here (D. Robertson/H. Blair) (2:51); 20 Bossa Nova Baby (J. Leiber/ M. Stoller)(2:01); 21 You Can't Say No In Acapulco (S. Feller/J. Fuller/G. Morris)(1:52); 22 Guadalajara (P. Guizar) (2:43).

Review: See *Wild in the Country* entry below.

G.I. Blues

1988, RCA Records; from the movie *G.I. Blues,* Paramount Pictures, 1960.

Album Notes: *Album Producers*: Ernst Mikael Jorgensen, Roger Semon; *Engineer*: Dennis Ferrante.

Selections: 1 Tonight Is So Right For Love (S. Wayne/S.J. Lilly)(2:12); 2 What's She Really Like (S. Wayne/A. Silver)(2:16); 3 Frankfort Special (S. Wayne/S. Edwards)(2:57); 4 Wooden Heart (F. Wise/B. Weisman/K. Twomey)(2:02); 5 G.I. Blues (S. Tepper/R. Bennett)(3:35); 6 Pocket Full Of Rainbows (F. Wise/B. Weisman)(2:33); 7 Shoppin' Around (S. Tepper/R. Bennett/A. Schroeder) (2:22); 8 Big Boots (S. Wayne/S. Edwards)(1:30); 9 Didja' Ever (S. Wayne/S. Edwards)(2:35); 10 Blue Suede Shoes (C. Perkins)(2:05); 11 Doin' The Best I Can (D. Pomus/M. Shuman) (3:09); 12 Tonight Is So Right For Love (alternate version)(S. Wayne/S.J. Lilly)(1:21); 13 Big Boots (fast version)(S. Wayne/S. Edwards)(1:14); 14 Shoppin' Around (alternate take)(S. Tepper/R. Bennett/A. Schroeder)(2:15); 15 Frankfort Special (fast version)(S. Wayne/S. Edwards) (2:25); 16 Pocket Full Of Rainbows (alternate take)(F. Wise/B. Weisman)(2:49); 17 Didja' Ever (alternate take)(S. Wayne/S. Edwards)(2:35); 18 Big Boots (acoustic version)(S. Wayne/S. Edwards)(:57); 19 What's She Really Like (alternate take)(S. Wayne/A. Silver)(2:22); 20 Doin' The Best I Can (alternate take)(D. Pomus/M. Shuman) (3:17).

Review: See *Wild in the Country* entry below.

Girl Happy/Harum Scarum

1993, RCA Records; from the movies *Girl Happy,* M-G-M, 1965, and *Harum Scarum,* M-G-M, 1965.

Album Notes: *Album Producer*: Chick Crumpacker; *Audio Restoration*: Bill Lacey; *Engineers*: Dick Baxter, Ernst Mikael Jorgensen.

Selections: Harum Scarum: 1 Harem Holiday (Andreoli/V. Poncia, Jr./J. Crane)(2:18); 2 My Desert Serenade (S.J. Gelber)(1:47); 3 Go East Young Man (B. Giant/B. Baum/F. Kaye)(2:16); 4 Mirage (B. Giant/B. Baum/F. Kaye)(2:25); 5 Kismet (S. Tepper/R. Bennett)(2:08); 6 Shake That Tambourine (B. Giant/B. Baum/F. Kaye)(2:02); 7 Hey Little Girl (J. Byers)(2:15); 8 Golden Coins (B. Giant/B. Baum/F. Kaye)(1:54); 9 So Close, Yet So Far (from Paradise)(J. Byers) (3:01); 10 Animal Instinct (B. Giant/B. Baum/F. Kaye)(2:13); 11 Wisdom Of The Ages (B. Giant/B. Baum/F. Kaye)(1:55); Girl Happy: 12 Girl Happy (D. Pomus/N. Meade)(2:07); 13 Spring Fever (B. Giant/B. Baum/F. Kaye)(1:52); 14 Fort Lauderdale Chamber Of Commerce (S. Tepper/R. Bennett)(1:32); 15 Startin' Tonight (Rosenblatt/Millrose)(1:19); 16 Wolf Call (B. Giant/B. Baum/F. Kaye) (1:26); 17 Do Not Disturb (B. Giant/B. Baum/F. Kaye)(1:52); 18 Cross My Heart And Hope To Die (S. Wayne/B. Weisman)(1:55); 19 The Meanest Girl In Town (J. Byers)(1:55); 20 Do The Clam (S. Wayne/B. Weisman/G. Fuller); 21 Puppet On A String (S. Tepper/R. Bennett)(2:39); 22 I've Got To Find My Baby (J. Byers) (1:35).

Review: See *Wild in the Country* entry below.

Girls! Girls! Girls!/ Kid Galahad

1993, RCA Records; from the movies *Girls! Girls! Girls!,* Paramount Pictures, 1962, and *Kid Galahad,* United Artists, 1962.

Album Notes: *CD Producers*: Ernst Mikael Jorgensen, Roger Seman; *Engineers*: Dick Baxter, Ernst Mikael Jorgensen.

Selections: Kid Galahad: 1 King Of The Whole Wide World (Batchelor/Roberts) (2:44); 2 This Is Living (F. Wise/B. Weisman)(1:43); 3 Riding The Rainbow (F. Wise/B. Weisman)(1:37); 4 Home Is Where The Heart Is (Edwards/David)(2:32); 5 I Got Lucky (F. Wise/B. Weisman/G. Fuller)(2:10); 6 A Whistling Tune (Edwards/ David)(3:17); Girls! Girls! Girls!: 7 Girls! Girls! Girls! (M. Leiber/J. Stoller)(2:30); 8 I Don't Wanna Be Tied (B. Giant/B. Baum/F. Kaye)(2:04); 9 Where Do You Come From (Batchelor/Roberts)(2:05); 10 I Don't Want To (Torre/ Spielman)(2:38); 11 We'll Be Together (O'Curran/Brooks)(2:15); 12 A Boy Like Me, A Girl Like You (S. Tepper/R. Bennett)(2:18); 13 Earth Boy (S. Tepper/R. Bennett)(2:20); 14 Return To Sender (O. Blackwell/O. Scott)(2:06); 15 Because Of Love (Batchelor/ Roberts)(2:30); 16 Thanks To The Rolling Sea (Batchelor/ Roberts)(1:36); 17 Song Of The Shrimp (S. Tepper/R. Bennett)(2:19); 18 The Walls Have Ears (S. Tepper/R. Bennett)(2:30); 19 We're Coming In Loaded (O. Blackwell/O. Scott)(1:29); 20 Mama (O'Curran/Brooks)(:58); 21 Plantation Rock (B. Giant/B. Baum/F. Kaye)(1:49); 22 Dainty Little

Moonbeams (unknown)(:47); 23 Girls! Girls! Girls! (End Title)(M. Leiber/J. Stoller)(:52).

Review: See *Wild in the Country* entry below.

It Happened at the World's Fair

1993, RCA Records; from the movie *It Happened at the World's Fair*, M-G-M, 1963.

See: Fun in Acapulco

Jailhouse Rock/ Love Me Tender

1996, RCA Records; from the movies *Jailhouse Rock*, M-G-M, 1957; and *Love Me Tender*, 20th Century-Fox, 1956.

Album Notes: *CD Producers*: Ernst Mikael Jorgensen, Roger Semon; *CD Engineer*: Vince Caro.

Selections: Jailhouse Rock: 1 Jailhouse Rock (J. Leiber/M. Stoller)(2:27); 2 Treat Me Nice (J. Leiber/M. Stoller)(2:10); 3 I Want To Be Free (J. Leiber/ M. Stoller)(2:14); 4 Don't Leave Me Now (A. Schroeder/B. Weisman)(2:05); 5 Young And Beautiful (A. Silver/A. Schroeder)(2:02); 6 (You're So Square) Baby I Don't Care (J. Leiber/M. Stoller)(1:52); 7 Jailhouse Rock (movie version)(J. Leiber/M. Stoller)(2:32); 8 Treat Me Nice (movie version)(J. Leiber/M. Stoller)(1:59); 9 I Want To Be Free (movie version)(J. Leiber/M. Stoller) (2:06); 10 Young And Beautiful (movie version)(A. Silver/A. Schroeder)(1:09); 11 Don't Leave Me Now (alt. master)(A. Schroeder/B. Weisman)(1:45); Love Me Tender: 12 Love Me Tender (E. Presley/V. Matson)(2:41); 13 Poor Boy (E. Presley/V. Matson)(2:13); 14 Let Me (E. Presley/V. Matson)(2:09); 15 We're Gonna Move (E. Presley/V. Matson)(2:30); 16 Love Me Tender (End Title version) (E. Presley/ V. Matson)(1:08); 17 Let Me (solo)(E. Presley/V. Matson)(2:04); 18 We're Gonna Move (stereo take)(E. Presley/ V. Matson)(2:39); 19 Poor Boy (stereo take)(E. Presley/V. Matson)(1:40); 20 Love Me Tender (E. Presley/V. Matson)(2:42).

Review: See *Wild in the Country* entry below.

King Creole

1996, RCA Records; from the movie *King Creole*, Paramount Pictures, 1958.

Album Notes: *CD Producers*: Ernst Mikael Jorgensen, Roger Semon; *CD Engineer*: Vince Caro.

Selections: 1 King Creole (J. Leiber/M. Stoller)(2:08); 2 As Long As I Have You (F. Wise/B. Weisman)(1:50); 3 Hard-Headed Woman (C. Demetrius)(1:53); 4 Trouble (J. Leiber/M. Stoller)(2:17); 5 Dixieland Rock (A. Schroeder/R. Frank) (1:47); 6 Don't Ask Me Why (F. Wise/B. Weisman)(2:06); 7 Lover Doll (S. Wayne/ A. Silver)(2:08); 8 Crawfish (F. Wise/B. Weisman)(1:49); 9 Young Dreams (M. Kalmanoff/A. Schroeder)(2:23); 10 Steadfast, Loyal And True (J. Leiber/M. Stoller)(1:15); 11 New Orleans (S. Tepper/R. Bennett)(1:59); 12 King Creole (alt. take)(J. Leiber/M. Stoller)(2:16); 13 As Long As I Have You (movie version)(F. Wise/B. Weisman)(:56); 14 Danny (F. Wise/B. Weisman)(1:52); 15 Lover Doll (undubbed)(S. Wayne/A. Silver)(2:14); 16 Steadfast, Loyal And True (alt. master)(J. Leiber/M. Stoller)(1:31); 17 As Long As I Have You (movie version)(F. Wise/B. Weisman)(1:24); 18 King Creole (alt. take)(J. Leiber/M. Stoller)(2:05).

Review: See *Wild in the Country* entry below.

Live a Little, Love a Little/ Charro!/The Trouble With Girls/Change of Habit

1995, RCA Records; from the movies *Live a Little, Love a Little*, M-G-M, 1968; *Charro!*, National General Pictures, 1969; *The Trouble With Girls*, M-G-M, 1969; and *Change of Habit*, Universal Pictures, 1970.

Album Notes: *Album Producers*: Ernst Mikael Jorgensen, Roger Semon; *Audio Restoration*: Bill Lacey; *Engineers*: Dennis Ferrante, Dick Baxter.

Selections: Live A Little, Love A Little: 1 Almost In Love (L. Bonfa/R. Starr)(3:02); 2 A Little Less Conversation (B. Strange/ S. Davis)(2:10); 3 Wonderful World (D. Fletcher/M. Flett)(2:22); 4 Edge Of Reality (B. Giant/B. Baum/F. Kaye)(3:33); 5 A Little Less Conversation (album version)(B. Strange/ S. Davis)(2:12); Charro!: 6 Charro! (B. Strange/S. Davis)(2:45); 7 Let's Forget About The Stars (A. Owens)(2:19); The Trouble With Girls: 8 Clean Up Your Own Backyard (B. Strange/S. Davis)(3:07); 9 Swing Down, Sweet Chariot (trad., arr.: E. Presley)(2:14); 10 Signs Of The Zodiac (B. Kaye/B. Weisman) (2:18); 11 Almost (B. Kaye/B. Weisman)(1:48); 12 The Whiffenpoof Song (T. Galloway/M. Minnigerode/G. Pomeroy)(:30); 13 Violet (S. Ducker/P. Lohstroh) (:52); 14 Clean Up Your Own Backyard (undubbed version)(B. Strange/S. Davis) (3:07); 15 Almost (undubbed version)(B. Kaye/B. Weisman)(1:48); Change Of Habit: 16 Have A Happy (B. Weisman/B. Kaye/G. Fuller)(2:21); 17 Let's Be Friends (Arnold/Morrow/Martin)(2:42); 18 Change Of Habit (B. Kaye/B. Weisman) (3:18); 19 Let Us Pray (B. Kaye/ B. Weisman)(3:00); 20 Rubberneckin' (D. Jones/ B. Warren)(2:08).

Review: See *Wild in the Country* entry below.

Loving You

1988, RCA Records; from the movie *Loving You,* Paramount Pictures, 1957.

Album Notes: *CD Producer:* Rick Rowe; *CD Engineer:* Rick Rowe.

Selections: 1 Mean Woman Blues (C. Demetrius)(2:11); 2 Teddy Bear (K. Mann/ B. Lowe)(1:47); 3 Loving You (J. Leiber/ M. Stoller)(2:15); 4 Got A Lot O' Livin' To Do (A. Schroeder/B. Weisman)(2:32); 5 Lonesome Cowboy (S. Tepper/R. Bennett)(3:02); 6 Hot Dog (J. Leiber/M. Stoller)(1:11); 7 Party (J.M. Robinson)(1:28); 8 Blueberry Hill (A. Lewis/L. Stock/V. Rose)(2:39); 9 True Love (C. Porter)(2:08); 10 Don't Leave Me Now (A. Schroeder/B. Weisman)(1:58); 11 Have I Told You Lately (S. Wiseman)(2:32); 12 I Need You So (I.J. Hunter) (2:40).

Review: See *Wild in the Country* entry below.

Roustabout

1993, RCA Records; from the movie *Roustabout,* Paramount Pictures, 1964.

See: Viva Las Vegas

Speedway

1993, RCA Records; from the movie *Speedway,* M-G-M, 1968.

See: Easy Come, Easy Go

The Trouble With Girls

1993, RCA Records; from the movie *The Trouble With Girls,* M-G-M, 1969.

See: Live a Little, Love a Little

Viva Las Vegas/Roustabout

1993, RCA Records; from the movies *Viva Las Vegas,* M-G-M, 1964, and *Roustabout,* Paramount, 1964.

Album Notes: *Album Producers:* Ernst Mikael Jorgensen, Roger Semon; *Engineers:* Dick Baxter, Ernst Mikael Jorgensen.

Selections: Viva Las Vegas: 1 Viva Las Vegas (D. Pomus/M. Shuman)(2:20); 2 If You Think I Don't Need You (West/Cooper)(2:03); 3 I Need Somebody To Lean On (D. Pomus/M. Shuman)(2:50); 4 You're The Boss (J. Leiber/M. Stoller)(2:30) *Elvis Presley, Ann-Margret*; 5 What'd I Say (R. Charles)(3:01); 6 Do The Vega (B. Giant/B. Baum/F. Kaye)(2:22); 7 C'mon Everybody (J. Byers)(2:16); 8 The Lady Loves Me (S. Tepper/R. Bennett)(3:41) *Elvis Presley, Ann-Margret*; 9 Night Life (B. Giant/B. Baum/F. Kaye)(1:50); 10 Today, Tomorrow And Forever (B. Giant/B. Baum/F. Kaye)(3:22); 11 The Yellow Rose Of

Texas (D. George)/The Eyes Of Texas (J. Sinclair) (medley) (2:46); 12 Santa Lucia (trad., arr.: E. Presley)(1:10); Roustabout: 13 Roustabout (B. Giant/B. Baum/F. Kaye)(1:56); 14 Little Egypt (J. Leiber/M. Stoller)(2:15); 15 Poison Ivy League (B. Giant/B. Baum/F. Kaye)(2:02); 16 Hard Knocks (J. Byers) (1:42); 17 It's A Wonderful World (S. Tepper/R. Bennett) (1:48); 18 Big Love Big Heartache (Fuller/Morris/ J. Hendrix) (1:57); 19 One Track Heart B. Giant/B. Baum/F. Kaye) (2:15); 20 It's Carnival Time (B. Weisman/S. Wayne) (1:32); 21 Carny Town (B. Wise/R. Starr) (1:19); 22 There's A Brand New Day On The Horizon (J. Byers) (2:00); 23 Wheels On My Heels (S. Tepper/R. Bennett) (1:19).

Review: See *Wild in the Country* entry below.

Wild in the Country

1995, RCA Records; from the movie *Wild in the Country,* 20th Century-Fox, 1961.

See: Flaming Star

Review: Often dismissed by critics and non-fans as a minor form of entertainment not worthy of much consideration, the films of Elvis Presley were essentially mindless vehicles tailor-made for the King, in which he almost invariably played the role of a good-hearted rebel, who, at the mere suggestion of a cue, would pick up a guitar and start singing.

Deep down, however, the films were finely crafted, usually entertaining stories, in which the songs were the obvious focus but helped move the plot ahead, and gave the star the opportunity to show his mettle, charm his audiences, and win his girl at the end. Surprisingly, while most of the songs he created in his films did not achieve the chart popularity his studio recordings did, some (like "Love Me Tender" or "Blue Hawaii") have become indelibly attached to his career.

For many years, RCA (Elvis' label from the start, after he left Sun Records, the scene of his early efforts) released the soundtrack albums, often as a contractual necessity or just as an afterthought, but without giving them the push Elvis' studio albums usually received. And while these albums (with a few exceptions) stayed active in the catalogue all along, they were seldom afforded the care and attention they truly deserved.

Even with the advent of compact discs, while his catalogue was being reconfigured, boxed, and, in some instances, remixed and remastered, the soundtracks were hardly touched. This has changed dramatically in the past couple of years, with the label seemingly intent on correcting its past errors: the titles are being reissued in albums that have been properly mixed and mastered, and often include previously unreleased alternates and songs that were dropped before they were used. Credit for this must go to producers Ernst Mikael Jorgensen and Roger Semon who have systematically approached this mine lode with the care and respect it truly demanded.

There would be little point in trying to review and rate each individual reissue title, as this would probably take much more editorial space than is available in this volume. However, it should be noted that the care and attention now lavished on the CDs listed above, at long last single them out as the ultimate series, and one truly worthy of the King.

While some films have yet to be covered in more than a scant manner (*Frankie And Johnny* is one that comes readily to mind), there is indeed a light at the end of the proverbial tunnel. It is doubtful that the cornucopia of Elvis film titles will convince his detractors that these were, after all, supreme works of art, or even albums worthy of their time and consideration. More prosaically, however, they provide a new opportunity to reassess Elvis' importance as a screen actor and as an entertainer whose films may have had as much influence on our lives as his more "serious" studio and live contributions. Any way we look at it, the conclusion one must reach is that his film soundtracks (and the songs he performed in them) were a positive aspect of his overall appeal and success.

Arnold Schwarzenegger

Arnold: Great Music from the Films of Arnold Schwarzenegger 🎵🎵🎵

1993, Varese-Sarabande Records.

Album Notes: *Musical compositions*: Brad Fiedel *(Terminator 2: Judgment Day)*, Basil Poledouris *(Conan the Barbarian/ Conan the Destroyer)*, Randy Edelman *(Kindergarten Cop)*, Jerry Goldsmith *(Total Recall)*, Harold Faltermeyer *(Running Man)*, Ennio Morricone *(Red Sonja)*, Cinemascore *(Raw Deal)*; **Album Producer**: *Robert Townson*; **Engineer**: *Joe Gastwirt*.

Selections: Terminator 2: Judgment Day: 1 Main Title (1:54); 2 Escape From The Hospital (4:29); 3 It's Over (Goodbye)(4:36); Conan The Barbarian: 4 Anvil Of Crom (2:34); 5 Riddle Of Steel/ Riders Of Doom (5:37); Kindergarten Cop: 6 Astoria School Theme (4:27); 7 Rain Ride (1:55); Total Recall: 8 The Dream (3:30); 9 The Mutant (3:16); Running Man: 10 Intro/Bakersfield (2:00); 11 Main Title/Fight Escape (3:44); 12 Revolution/End Credits (1:58); Red Sonja: 13 Theme (4:21); Raw Deal: 14 Brains And Trains (1:40); 15 Kaminski Stomps (3:31); 16 Harry Shot/

Harry Walks (2:05); Conan The Destroyer: 17 Main Title/Riders Of Taramis (3:33); 18 Crystal Palace (6:11).

Review: Since all the recordings compiled in this CD are available elsewhere, it may seem redundant to focus on this particular release. Particularly, since the selections move from big, epic orchestral expressions (*Conan the Barbarian/Conan the Destroyer*), to comedies (*Kindergarten Cop*), to electronic scores (*Raw Deal*), without much care given to musical cohesion or mood continuity. By all means, if you must have everything about the big man, indulge yourself. But if you already have the individual soundtrack albums, don't waste your time or money.

The Greatest Themes from the Films of Arnold Schwarzenegger 🎵🎵🎵

1995, Silva America Records.

Album Notes: *Orchestrations*: Nic Raine, Greig McRitchie, Kevin Townend, Philip Lane, Morton Stevens; The City Of Prague Philharmonic and Singers of the Crouch End Festival Chorus, conducted by Nic Raine; *Album Producer*: James Fitzpatrick; *Engineer*: John L. Timperley.

Selections: Predator: 1 Main Title (A. Silvestri)(4:08); Total Recall: 2 Total Recall (J. Goldsmith)(2:30); Commando: 3 Main Title (J. Horner)(3:46); Red Heat: 4 Main Title/Russian Streets/ Tailing Cat (J. Horner)(3:36); Kindergarten Cop: 5 Astoria School Theme/Children's Montage (R. Edelman) (4:39); Twins: 6 Main Title Theme (G. Delerue)(2:55); 7 Going To Santa Fe (R. Edelman)(2:09); Junior: 8 Main Title (J. Newton Howard)(2:59); Raw Deal: 9 Kaminski Stamps (C. Gaudette/T. Bahier/C. Boardman/A. Galuten)(3:29); The Running Man: 10 Theme (H. Faltermeyer)(4:02); Terminator: 11 Theme (B. Fiedel) (4:37); 12 Desert (B. Fiedel)(3:25); 13 Trust Me (B. Fiedel)(1:37); 14 It's Over (B. Fiedel)(2:32); True Lies: 15 Main Title/Harry Makes His Entrance/ Escape From The Chateau (B. Fiedel)(5:19); Conan (Symphonic Suite)(B. Poledouris): 16 Prologue (1:57); 17 Anvil Of Crom (2:36); 18 Riddle Of Steel/ Riders Of Doom (6:02); 19 Chambers Of Mirror/Crystal Palace (7:15); 20 Anvil Of Crom/ Finale (1:06).

Review: Another ambitious but uneven collection of music from the Silva label that features the imposing and heavily percussive, brassy music generally associated with Schwarzenegger's action films, including Alan Silvestri's pulsating *Predator* theme, James Horner's *Commando* and *Red Heat*, lengthy suites from Brad Fiedel's monotonous *Terminator* scores and his scattershot synth-and-orchestral *True Lies*, as well as Basil Poledouris's impressive blend of choir and orchestra for *Conan The Barbarian*. There's also a headache-inducing offering of pounding techno-synth cues from *Raw Deal* and Harold Faltermeyer's *The Running Man*, and adding the *Terminator* music and the entirely electronic interpretation of *True Lies,* listeners should be reaching for the aspirin before they're halfway through this album. Unfortunately, much of the orchestral takes aren't much better, with Jerry Goldsmith's theme to *Total Recall* (the least interesting facet of a great score) coming off particularly badly. Ironically, the most listenable music on the album comes from the kinder, gentler comedy scores such as Randy Edelman's *Kindergarten Cop*, Georges Delerue's *Twins* and James Newton Howard's *Junior*, which are a welcome respite from the brutality of the violence-oriented material.

Jeff Bond

Frank Sinatra

Frank Sinatra at the Movies
♫♫♫

1992, Capitol Records.

Album Notes: *Album Producer*: Wayne Watkins; *Engineer*: Larry Walsh.

Selections: From Here To Eternity: 1 From Here To Eternity (B. Wells/F. Karger)(3:00); Three Coins In The Fountain: 2 Three Coins In The Fountain (J. Styne/S. Cahn)(3:04); Young At Heart: 3 Young At Heart (J. Richards/C. Leigh) (2:52); 4 She's Funny That Way (N. Moret/R. Whiting)(3:55); 5 Just One Of Those Things (C. Porter)(3:15); 6 Someone To Watch Over Me (G. & I. Gershwin) (2:57); 7 Not As A Stranger (J. Van Heusen/ B. Kaye)(2:46); The Tender Trap: 8 (Love Is) The Tender Trap (S. Cahn/J. Van Heusen)(2:58); Our Town: 9 Our Town (S. Cahn/J. Van Heusen)(3:15); 10 Impatient Years (S. Cahn/J. Van Heusen) (3:15); 11 Love And Marriage (S. Cahn/J. Van Heusen) (2:38); 12 Look To Your Heart (S. Cahn/J. Van Heusen) (3:08); Johnny Concho: 13 Wait For Me (Johnny Concho Theme) (N. Riddle/D. Stanford) (2:52); The Joker Is Wild: 14 All The Way (S. Cahn/J. Van Heusen)(2:52); 15 Chicago (F. Fisher)(2:13); Kings Go Forth: 16 Monique (E. Bernstein/S. Cahn)(3:16); They Came To Cordura: 17 They Came To Cordura (S. Cahn/J. Van Heusen)(3:00); A Hole In The Head: 18 High Hopes (S. Cahn/J. Van Heusen)(2:42); 19 All My Tomorrows (S. Cahn/J. Van Heusen)(3:12).

Review: With none of the 19 Frank Sinatra recordings on this compilation actually deriving from the original film soundtracks, this is an interesting compilation that showcases some

of Sinatra's finest studio recordings with arranger Nelson Riddle, from his greatest period: the 1950s Capitol era.

While all of the songs are closely associated with Sinatra, not all are from his own films. For example, Sinatra was heard singing "Three Coins in the Fountain" during the opening of the picture, but was not a performer in the film. Some songs, like "From Here to Eternity" and "Monique" were musical themes from Sinatra films, but since he didn't sing in those films, these studio recordings are the only vocal renditions available. As well, four of the nine Cahn and Van Heusen tunes included here were not the product of a film at all, but a 1955 television presentation of Thornton Wilder's *Our Town*, starring Sinatra and Paul Newman.

The incomparable combination of Sinatra and Riddle just can't be beat, and while one wishes that this was a collection of Sinatra's rare film versions of these songs, the tunes are outstanding, and the sonics superb.

Charles L. Granata

Sylvester Stallone

Music from the Films of Sylvester Stallone ♫

1993, Silva Screen Records.

Album Notes: *Arrangers*: Mark Ayres, Mike Townend, Kevin Townend, John Bell, Brain Gascoigne; The London Screen Orchestra, conducted by Mike Townend; The City Of Prague Philharmonic Orchestra, conducted by Nic Raine; *Featured Soloists*: Clem Clempson (electric guitar), Maurice Murphy (trumpet), Mike Thompson, Paul Pritchard (horns); *Album Producer*: Mike Townend; *Engineer*: Mike Ross-Trevor.

Selections: 1 Fanfare/Gonna Fly Now/Going The Distance/The Final Bell (from *Rocky*)(B. Conti)(9:19); 2 Main Theme (from *F.I.S.T.*)(B. Conti)(4:07); 3 Victor's Big March (from *Paradise Alley*)(B. Conti)(3:02); 4 Redemption (from *Rocky II*) (B. Conti) (3:44); 5 Main Theme (from *Nighthawks*) (K. Emerson)(3:34); 6 Eye Of The Tiger (from *Rocky III*)(F. Sullivan III/J. Peterik)(4:01); 7 It's A Long Road (from *First Blood*)(J. Goldsmith)(3:26); 8 Main Theme/Day By Day/ Pilot Over (from *Rambo: First Blood, Part 2*)(J. Goldsmith)(7:02); 9 Main Theme/Chase (from *Cobra*)(S. Levay)(6:47); 10 In This Country/The Fight/Meet Me Half Way (from *Over The Top*)(G. Moroder)(11:12); 11 Questions (from *Rambo III*)(J. Goldsmith)(3:01); 12 Main Theme/Breaking Point/Release (from *Lock Up*)(B. Conti)(12:13); 13 Main Theme/Rabbit Hole/End Title (from *Cliffhanger*)(T. Jones)(5:52).

Review: Much of this album is a dated compilation of the "hip" scores that littered Sylvester Stallone movies in the 1980s, like Sylvester Levay's *Cobra* and Georgio Moroder's *Over the Top.* The London Screen Orchestra, The City of Prague Philharmonic and synthesist Mark Ayers all attempt to wrestle with the material. Only the nine minute suite from *Rocky* comes out on top with a powerful flourish of brass and strings on "Gonna Fly Now." Many pieces, like Bill Conti's *F.I.S.T.* and *Lock Up* are as compelling as the box office duds they were written for. The selected themes from Jerry Goldsmith's *Rambo* scores are amazingly sluggish.

David Hirsch

John Wayne

Music from the Classic Films of John Wayne ♪♪♪

1994, Silva Screen Records.

Album Notes: *Arrangements and Orchestrations*: Mike Townend, David Snell, Kevin Townend, Christopher Palmer, Neil Richardson, John Bell, Leo Shuken, Jack Hayes, John Williams; The City of Prague Philharmonic, conducted by Paul Bateman; *Featured Soloist*: Miroslav Kejmar (trumpet); *Album Producer*: James Fitzpatrick; *Engineer*: Etic Tomlinson.

Selections: Stagecoach: 1 Narrative For Orchestra: Monument Valley Theme/ The Stagecoach (Bury Me Not On The Lone Prairie)/Ringo Joins The Stagecoach/ Mrs. Mallory (I Dream Of Jeannie With The Light Brown Hair)/Turning Cold/ Sandstorm/ Indians!/Attack On The Stagecoach/Cavalry To The Rescue/ End Titles (R. Hageman/W.F. Harling/J. Leopold/L. Shuken/L. Gruenberg)(6:36); She Wore A Yellow Ribbon: 2 Leaving The Fort (R. Hageman)(2:51); The Quiet Man (V. Young): 3 The Donnybrook (Danaher's House)(2:46); 4 Sean And Kate (Our Mother) (2:58); 5 St. Patrick's Day/Prelude To The Big Fight (3:49); The High And The Mighty: 6 Prelude (D. Tiomkin)(2:01); The Searchers: 7 Opening/Ethan Comes Home/Martin/Texas Rangers/War Party/Indian Idyll (M. Steiner)(7:24); The Alamo: 8 Overture (D. Tiomkin)(3:26); How The West Was Won: 9 Prelude (A. Newman)(3:25); The Longest Day: 10 March (P. Anka)(4:44); In Harm's Way (J. Goldsmith): 11 Prelude: The Rock (1:43); 12 Intermezzo: The Rock And His Lady/ Love Theme (4:48); 13 Finale: First Victory (3:03); True Grit: 14 Rooster And Le Boeuf/Runaway/Warm Wrap-Up (E. Bernstein)(4:39); The Cowboys: 15 Overture (J. Williams)(9:44).

Review: John Wayne made enough movies, and there was enough memorable music in most of them, to justify more than one volume paying tribute to the Duke and to the composers who musically immortalized him. For a start, this collection will do nicely, but it is hoped that further compilations, as interesting and possibly more daring, will ensue. If the City of Prague Philharmonic sounds at times awkward playing western music, the results are still largely acceptable, with the minor flaws amply compensated by some of the other selections (*The Quiet Man, The High and the Mighty, In Harm's Way*) in which the performance seems more natural.

16 Most Requested Songs: Academy Award Winners
♪♪♪ ♪

1994, Sony Music/Legacy Records.

Album Notes: *Album Producer*: Didier C. Deutsch; *Engineer*: Chris Herles.

Selections: The Paleface: 1 Buttons And Bows (J. Livingston/R. Evans)(2:01) *Dinah Shore*; The Harvey Girls: 2 On The Acheson, Topeka And The Santa Fe (H. Warren/J. Mercer)(2:34) *Rosemary Clooney*; Calamity Jane: 3 Secret Love (S. Fain/P.F. Webster)(3:38) *Doris Day*; Swing Time: 4 The Way You Look Tonight (J. Kern/D. Fields)(3:08) *Fred Astaire*; High Noon: 5 Do Not Forsake Me, Oh My Darling (D. Tiomkin/N. Washington)(2:39) *Frankie Laine*; Neptune's Daughter: 6 Baby It's Cold Outside (F. Loesser)(2:19) *Dinah Shore, Buddy Clark*; The Man Who Knew Too Much: 7 Whatever Will Be, Will Be (Que Sera, Sera)(J. Livingston/R. Evans)(2:04) *Doris Day*; Holiday Inn: 8 White Christmas (I. Berlin)(3:27) *Rosemary Clooney*; Hello, Frisco, Hello: 9 You'll Never Know (M. Gordon/H. Warren)(4:00) *Johnny Mathis*; Gigi: 10 Gigi (F. Loewe/A.J. Lerner)(3:02) *Vic Damone*; Days Of Wine And Roses: 11 Days Of Wine And Roses (H. Mancini/J. Mercer)(2:44) *Andy Williams*; Three Coins In The Fountain: 12 Three Coins In The Fountain (J. Styne/S. Cahn)(4:01) *Jerry Vale*; Love Is A Many-Splendored Thing: 13 Love Is A Many-Splendored Thing (S. Fain/P.F. Webster)(3:32) *The Four Lads*; Papa's Delicate Condition: 14 Call Me Irresponsible (J. Van Heusen/S. Cahn)(3:24) *Buddy Greco*; The Sandpiper: 15 The Shadow Of Your Smile (J. Mandel/P.F. Webster)(3:36) *Tony Bennett*; Breakfast At Tiffany's: 16 Moon River (H. Mancini/J. Mercer)(2:44) *Andy Williams*.

Review: Since its inception in the 1930s, the Film Academy has sought to reward those songs that had been specifically written for the movies, thereby casting its lights on many tunes that have since become standards and part of the great American songbook. In turn, many of these songs have provided performers with themes which, in many instances, have become hits for them and sometimes lifelong signatures. The 16 selections in this compilation feature many well-known songs, often performed by the artists who made them famous, if not in the movies at least on the charts.

Billboard Top Movie Hits

Billboard Top Movie Hits 1940s ♫♪♭

1996, Rhino Records.

Album Notes: *Album Compiler*: Joel Whitburn; *Engineers*: Bill Inglot, Dan Hersch.

Selections: Youth On Parade: 1 I've Heard That Song Before (J. Styne/S. Cahn)(3:02) *Helen Forrest, Harry James and His Orchestra*; Song Of The South: 2 Zip-A-Dee-Doo-Dah (R. Gilbert/A. Wrubel)(2:18) *James Baskett*; Going My Way: 3 Swinging On A Star (J. Van Heusen/S. Burke)(2:32) *Bing Crosby, the Williams Brothers Quartet, John Scott Trotter and His Orchestra*; In Society: 4 My Dreams Are Getting Better All The Time (M. Curtis/V. Mizzy) (3:19) *Doris Day, Les Brown and His Orchestra*; Buck Privates: 5 Boogie Woogie Bugle Boy (H. Prince/D. Raye)(2:46) *The Andrews Sisters, Vic Schoen and His Orchestra*; Hello Frisco, Hello: 6 You'll Never Know (H. Warren /M. Gordon)(2:47) *Dick Haymes, The Song Spinners*; The Forest Rangers: 7 Jingle Jangle Jingle (F. Loesser/J. Lilley)(3:23) *Harry Babbitt, Julie Conway, The Group, Kay Kyser and His Orchestra*; Romance On The High Seas: 8 It's Magic (J. Styne/S. Cahn)(3:25) *Doris Day*; The Stork Club: 9 Doctor, Lawyer, Indian Chief (H. Carmichael) (3:05) *Betty Hutton, Paul Weston and His Orchestra*; Casablanca: 10 As Time Goes By (H. Hupfeld)(3:29) *Rudy Vallee*.

Review: See entry below.

Billboard Top Movie Hits 1950-1954 ♫♪♭

1996, Rhino Records.

Album Notes: *Album Compiler*: Joel Whitburn; *Engineers*: Bill Inglot, Dan Hersch.

Selections: Moulin Rouge: 1 The Song From Moulin Rouge (Where Is Your Heart)(G. Auric/W. Engvick)(3:20) *Felicia Sanders, Percy Faith and His Orchestra*; Three Coins In The Fountain: 2 Three Coins In The Fountain (J. Styne/S. Cahn)(3:04) *The Four Aces*; Two Weeks With Love: 3 Aba Daba Honeymoon (A. Fields/W. Donovan) (2:32) *Debbie Reynolds, Carleton Carpenter, Georgie Stoll, The M-G-M Studio Orchestra and Chorus*;

The High And The Mighty: 4 The High And The Mighty (D. Tiomkin)(2:48) *Victor Young and His Singing Strings*; Ruby Gentry: 5 Ruby (M. Parish/H. Roemheld)(2:54) *Richard Hayman and His Orchestra*; Calamity Jane: 6 Secret Love (S. Fain/P.F. Webster)(3:44) *Doris Day, Ray Heindorf, the Warner Bros. Studio Orchestra*; Show Boat: 7 Ol' Man River (J. Kern/O. Hammerstein II)(3:53) *William Warfield, Adolph Deutsch, the M-G-M Studio Orchestra*; Hans Christian Andersen: 8 Anywhere I Wander (F. Loesser)(2:43) *Julius LaRosa*; Anna: 9 El negro zumbon (V. Roman/F. Giordano)(2:32) *Silvana Mangano*; High Noon: 10 Do Not Forsake Me (D. Tiomkin/N. Washington)(2:39) *Frankie Laine*.

Review: See entry below.

Billboard Top Movie Hits 1955-1959 ♫♪♭

1996, Rhino Records.

Album Notes: *Album Compiler*: Joel Whitburn; *Engineers*: Bill Inglot, Dan Hersch.

Selections: Unchained: 1 Unchained Melody (A. North/H. Zaret)(2:34) *Les Baxter and His Orchestra*; Love Is A Many-Splendored Thing: 2 Love Is A Many-Splendored Thing (S. Fain/P.F. Webster)(3:01) *The Four Aces*; Lizzie: 3 It's Not For Me To Say (A. Stillman/R. Allen)(3:07) *Johnny Mathis, Ray Conniff and His Orchestra*; Picnic: 4 Moonglow and Theme From Picnic (W. Hudson/E. DeLange/I. Mills)(G. Duning) (2:51) *Morris Stoloff, the Columbia Pictures Orchestra*; Tammy And The Bachelor: 5 Tammy (J. Livingston/R. Evans)(3:07) *Debbie Reynolds, the Universal Studio Orchestra, Joseph Gershenson*; April Love: 6 April Love (S. Fain/P.F. Webster)(2:42) *Pat Boone*; The Man Who Knew Too Much: 7 Whatever Will Be, Will Be (Que sera, sera)(J. Livingston/R. Evans)(2:07) *Doris Day, Frank DeVol and His Orchestra*; Underwater: 8 Cherry Pink And Apple Blossom White (J. Larue/ Louiguy/M. David)(3:02) *Perez Prado and His Orchestra*; Love In The Afternoon: 9 Fascination (H. Marchetti/D. Manning)(2:23) *Jane Morgan, The Troubadours*; The Man With The Golden Arm: 10 Main Title (E. Bernstein)(3:21) *Elmer Bernstein and His Orchestra*.

Review: See entry below.

Billboard Top Movie Hits 1960s ♫♪♭

1996, Rhino Records.

Album Notes: *Album Compiler*: Joel Whitburn; *Engineers*: Bill Inglot, Dan Hersch.

Selections: A Summer Place: 1 Theme From A Summer Place (M. Steiner)(2:24) *Percy Faith and His Orchestra*; Exodus: 2 Exodus (E. Gold)(2:57) *Ferrante and Teicher*; Valley Of The Dolls: 3 Theme From Valley Of The Dolls (B. Bacharach/H. David)(3:37) *Dionne Warwick*; The Prime Of Miss Jean Brodie: 4 Jean (R. McKuen)(3:19) *Oliver*; Romeo And Juliet: 5 Love Theme (N. Rota)(2:34) *Henry Mancini His Orchestra and Chorus*; Butch Cassidy And The Sundance Kid: 6 Raindrops Keep Fallin' On My Head (B. Bacharach/H. David)(3:16) *B.J. Thomas*; The Alamo: 7 Ballad Of The Alamo (D. Tiomkin/P.F. Webster)(3:41) *Marty Robbins*; Hush... Hush... Sweet Charlotte: 8 Hush, Hush, Sweet Charlotte (M. David/F. DeVol)(2:33) *Patti Page*; Born Free: 9 Born Free (J. Barry)(2:22) *Roger Williams*; Breakfast At Tiffany's: 10 Moon River (H. Mancini/J. Mercer)(2:42) *Henry Mancini His Orchestra and Chorus*.

Review: See entry below.

Billboard Top Movie Hits 1970s ♪♪▽

1996, Rhino Records.

Album Notes: *Album Compiler*: Joel Whitburn; *Engineers*: Bill Inglot, Dan Hersch.

Selections: Star Wars: 1 Main Title (J. Williams)(2:20) *The London Symphony Orchestra, John Williams*; Midnight Cowboy: 2 Midnight Cowboy (J. Barry)(3:19) *Ferrante and Teicher*; Every Which Way But Loose: 3 Every Which Way But Loose (T. Garrett/ M. Brown/S. Dorff)(2:50) *Eddie Rabbitt*; Shaft: 4 Theme From Shaft (I. Hayes)(3:17) *Isaac Hayes, The Bar-Kays, The Movement*; Rocky: 5 Gonna Fly Now (Theme From Rocky)(B. Conti) (2:49) *Bill Conti and His Orchestra*; You Light Up My Life: 6 You Light Up My Life (J. Brooks)(3:38) *Debby Boone*; The Sting: 7 The Entertainer (S. Joplin) (3:05) *Marvin Hamlisch*; The Last American Hero: 8 I Got A Name (N. Gimbel/C. Fox)(3:12) *Jim Croce*; Deliverance: 9 Dueling Banjos (trad.)(2:20) *Eric Weissberg, Steve Mandell*; Close Encounters Of The Third Kind: 10 Theme (3:10) Orchestra conducted by John Williams.

Review: Nothin' but solid gold hits in them thar CDs! The concept itself is one that's bound to appeal to any collector of top pop hits and themes from the movies: songs that were specifically written for the screen, more often than not performed by the stars who created them (though an occasional selection offers a dubious "cover" version, albeit a charted one), in a cross-label series of compilations that classifies these hits by decades (or half-decade for the 1950s, probably the richest of its kind). Adding credibility to the series is the endorsement by the trade publication *Billboard* and the fact that it was compiled by Joel Whitburn, who has made it his life's dedication to sort out every single hit by every artist in the vast pop field since the beginning of the recording industry.

This however does not exclude the fact that at today's price for laser delights, this series comes short of fulfilling one's expectations, with each CD clocking in at 30 minutes of total playing time.

Broadway/Screen Musicals Compilations

Another Openin' Another Show: Broadway Overtures ♪♪♪♪▽

1993, Sony Broadway.

Album Notes: Orchestra conducted by Lehman Engel; *CD Producer*: Didier C. Deutsch; *Engineer*: Darcy Proper.

Selections: 1 Bloomer Girl (H. Arlen)(5:53); 2 On The Town (L. Bernstein)(4:02); 3 Finian's Rainbow (B. Lane)(5:02); 4 Kiss Me, Kate (C. Porter)(6:10); 5 Gentlemen Prefer Blondes (J. Styne)(4:43); 6 Call Me Madam (I. Berlin)(4:40); 7 Wonderful Town (L. Bernstein)(5:04); 8 Can-Can (C. Porter)(3:59); 9 Silk Stockings (C. Porter)(4:33); 10 Li'l Abner (G. De Paul)(5:27); 11 Bells Are Ringing (J. Styne)(4:48); 12 Goldilocks (L. Anderson)(4:41).

Review: See entry *Celebrate Broadway Vol. 10* below.

Embraceable You: Broadway in Love ♪♪♪♪▽

1993, Sony Broadway.

Album Notes: *CD Producer*: Thomas Z. Shepard; *Engineer*: Robert Rapley.

Selections: 1 This Can't Be Love (from **The Boys From Syracuse**)(R. Rodgers/ L. Hart)(2:20) *Jack Cassidy, Holly Harris*; 2 If This Isn't Love (from **Finian's Rainbow**)(B. Lane/E.Y. Harburg)(3:15) *Ella Logan, Donald Richards, The Lyn Murray Singers*; 3 Just A Kiss Apart (from **Gentlemen Prefer Blondes**)(J. Styne/L. Robin)(3:00) *Eric Brotherson, Yvonne Adair*; 4 There's A Small Hotel (from **On Your Toes**)(R. Rodgers/L. Hart)(4:11) *Portia Nelson, Jack Cassidy*; 5 Almost Like Being In Love (from **Brigadoon**)(F. Loewe/A.J. Lerner)(3:02) *Shirley Jones, Jack Cassidy*; 6 I Could Write A Book (from **Pal Joey**)(R. Rodgers/L. Hart)(3:46) *Beverly Fite, Harold Lang*; 7 Just In Time (from **Bells Are Ringing**)(J. Styne/B. Comden/A. Green)(3:40) *Sydney Chap-*

lin, Judy Holliday; 8 Why Do I Love You? (from **Show Boat**)(J. Kern/O. Hammerstein II)(2:32) *Barbara Cook, John Raitt*; 9 Tonight (from **West Side Story**)(L. Bernstein/S. Sondheim)(3:54) *Larry Kert, Carol Lawrence*; 10 You're The Top (from **Anything Goes**)(C. Porter)(3:50) *Hal Linden, Eileen Rodgers*; 11 People Will Say We're In Love (from **Oklahoma!**)(R. Rodgers/O. Hammerstein II)(4:27) *John Raitt, Florence Henderson*; 12 Shall We Dance? (From **The King And I**)(R. Rodgers/O. Hammerstein II)(3:48) *Barbara Cook, Theodore Bikel*; 13 I've Confessed To The Breeze (from **No, No, Nanette**)(V. Youmans/O. Harbach)(3:17) *Susan Watson, Roger Rathburn*; 14 Once Upon A Time (from **All American**)(C. Strouse/L. Adams)(3:37) *Ray Bolger, Eileen Herlie*; 15 Married (from **Cabaret**) (F. Ebb/J. Kander)(2:42) *Lotte Lenya, Jack Gilford*; 16 I Like Your Style (from **Barnum**)(C. Coleman/M. Stewart)(3:21) *Jim Dale, Glenn Close*; 17 Make Believe (from **Show Boat**)(J. Kern/O. Hammerstein II)(5:08) *Barbara Cook, John Raitt*.

Review: See entry *Celebrate Broadway Vol. 10* below.

The Party's Over: Broadway Sings the Blues ♫♫♫♪

1993, Sony Broadway.

Album Notes: *CD Producer*: Thomas Z. Shepard; *Engineer*: Robert Rapley.

Selections: 1 Bewitched, Bothered And Bewildered (from **Pal Joey**)(R. Rodgers/L. Hart)(3:10) *Vivienne Segal*; 2 Smoke Gets In Your Eyes (from **Roberta**)(J. Kern/O. Harbach)(6:05) *Joan Roberts*; 3 I Never Know When (from **Goldilocks**)(L. Anderson/W. & J. Kerr)(4:10) *Elaine Stritch*; 4 Lonely Town (from **On The Town**)(L. Bernstein/B. Comden/A. Green)(3:18) *John Reardon*; 5 Where Am I Going? (from **Sweet Charity**)(C. Coleman/D. Fields)(3:19) *Gwen Verdon*; 6 If He Walked Into My Life (from **Mame**)(J. Herman) *Angela Lansbury*; 7 Anyone Can Whistle (from **Anyone Can Whistle**)(S. Sondheim)(3:41) *Lee Remick*; 8 This Nearly Was Mine (from **South Pacific**)(R. Rodgers/O. Hammerstein II)(3:28) *Ezio Pinza*; 9 My Own Morning (from **Hallelujah, Baby!**)(J. Styne/B. Comden/A. Green)(4:09) *Leslie Uggams*; 10 Send In The Clowns (from **A Little Night Music**)(S. Sondheim)(3:26) *Glynis Johns*; 11 Be On Your Own (from **Nine**)(M. Yeston)(2:56) *Karen Akers*; 12 Being Alive (from **Company**)(S. Sondheim)(4:21) *Dean Jones*; 13 Fifty Percent (from **Ballroom**)(B. Goldenberg/ A. & M. Bergman)(3:39) *Dorothy Loudon*; 14 What I Did For Love (from **A Chorus Line**)(M. Hamlisch/E. Kleban)(3:43) *Priscilla Lopez*; 15 Bill (from **Show Boat**)(J. Kern/O. Hammerstein II/P.G. Wodehouse)(5:08) *Anita Darian*; 16 The Party's Over (from **Bells Are Ringing**)(J. Styne/B. Comden/A. Green)(2:41) *Judy Holliday*.

Review: See entry *Celebrate Broadway Vol. 10* below.

There's No Business Like Show Business: Broadway Showstoppers ♫♫♫♪

1993, Sony Broadway.

Album Notes: *CD Producer*: Thomas Z. Shepard; *Engineer*: Robert Rapley.

Selections: 1 Another Op'nin', Another Show (from **Kiss Me, Kate**)(C. Porter) (1:44) *Annabelle Hill*; 2 Willkommen (from **Cabaret**)(F. Ebb/J. Kander)(5:10) *Joel Grey*; 3 Life Upon The Wicked Stage (from **Show Boat**)(J. Kern/O. Hammerstein II)(2:50) *Fay DeWitt*; 4 Come Follow The Band (from **Barnum**)(C. Coleman/M. Stewart)(3:52) *Jim Dale*; 5 You Gotta Have A Gimmick (from **Gypsy**)(J. Styne/S. Sondheim)(3:34) *Faith Dane, Chotzi Foley, Maria Karnilova*; 6 Conga (from **Wonderful Town**)(L. Bernstein/B. Comden/A. Green)(3:24) *Rosalind Russell*; 7 Feet Do Yo' Stuff (from **Hallelujah, Baby!**)(J. Styne/B. Comden/A. Green)(2:07) *Winston DeWitt-Hemsley, Alan Weeks, Leslie Uggams, Hope Clarke, Sandra Lein, Saundra McPherson*; 8 Hey, Big Spender (from **Sweet Charity**)(C. Coleman/D. Fields)(3:35) *Helen Gallagher, Thelma Oliver*; 9 Mame (from **Mame**)(J. Herman)(6:15) *Charles Braswell*; 10 Coffee In A Carboard Cup (from **70, Girls, 70**)(F. Ebb/J. Kander)(3:08) *Lillian Hayman, Goldye Shaw*; 11 With A Little Bit Of Luck (from **My Fair Lady**)(F. Loewe/A.J. Lerner) (4:06) *Stanley Holloway*; 12 America (from **West Side Story**)(L. Bernstein/S. Sondheim)(4:32) *Chita Rivera, Marilyn Cooper, Reri Grist*; 13 Jubilation T. Cornpone (from **Li'l Abner**)(G. DePaul/J. Mercer)(3:19) *Stubby Kaye*; 14 You're Never Fully Dressed Without A Smile (from **Annie**)(3:05) *Donald Craig, Laurie Beechman, Edie Cowan, Penny Worth*; 15 Folies Bergere (from **Nine**)(M. Yeston)(6:58) *Liliane Montevecchi, Stephanie Cotsirilos*; 16 One (from **A Chorus Line**)(M. Hamlisch/E. Kleban)(5:01) *Company*; 17 There's No Business Like Show Business (from **Annie Get Your Gun**)(I. Berlin)(2:33) *Ensemble*.

Review: See entry *Celebrate Broadway Vol. 10* below.

There Is Nothin' Like A Dame: Broadway Broads ♫♫♫♪

1993, Sony Broadway.

Album Notes: *CD Producer*: Thomas Z. Shepard; *Engineer*: Robert Rapley.

Selections: 1 Diamonds Are A Girl's Best Friend (from **Gentlemen Prefer Blondes**)(J. Styne/L. Robin)(2:58) *Carol Channing*; 2 The Lady Is A Tramp (from **Babes In Arms**)(R.

Rodgers/L. Hart)(3:33) *Mary Martin*; 3 Always True To You In My Fashion (from *Kiss Me, Kate*)(C. Porter)(3:59) *Lisa Kirk*; 4 I'll Be Hard To Handle (from *Roberta*)(J. Kern/B. Dougall)(3:35) *Kaye Ballard*; 5 I Can Do Without You (from *My Fair Lady*)(F. Loewe/A.J. Lerner)(2:01) *Julie Andrews*; 6 Some People (from *Gypsy*)(J. Styne/S. Sondheim)(3:40) *Ethel Merman*; 7 Glitter And Be Gay (from *Candide*)(L. Bernstein/J. Latouche)(5:44) *Barbara Cook*; 8 One Hundred Easy Ways To Lose A Man (from *Wonderful Town*)(L. Bernstein/B. Comden/A. Green)(2:52) *Rosalind Russell*; 9 There's Gotta Be Something Better Than This (from *Sweet Charity*)(C. Coleman/D. Fields)(4:52) *Gwen Verdon, Helen Gallagher, Thelma Oliver*; 10 Bosom Buddies (from *Mame*)(J. Herman)(4:06) *Angela Lansbury, Bea Arthur*; 11 The Ladies Who Lunch (from *Company*)(S. Sondheim)(4:28) *Elaine Stritch*; 12 Liaisons (from *A Little Night Music*)(S. Sondheim)(4:59) *Hermione Gingold*; 13 I Don't Want To Know (from *Dear World*)(J. Herman)(2:39) *Angela Lansbury*; 14 Show Me (from *My Fair Lady*) (F. Loewe/A.J. Lerner)(2:13) *Julie Andrews*; 15 Too Many Rings Around Rosie (from *No, No, Nanette*)(V. Youmans/I. Caesar/O. Harbach)(4:13) *Helen Gallagher*; 16 Rose's Turn (from *Gypsy*)(J. Styne/S. Sondheim) (4:26) *Ethel Merman*.

Review: See entry *Celebrate Broadway Vol. 10* below.

Celebrate Broadway vol. 1: Sing Happy! 🎵🎵🎵🎵🎵

1994, RCA Victor.

Album Notes: *CD Producer*: Bill Rosenfield; *Engineer*: Dennis Ferrante.

Selections: 1 Sing Happy (from *Flora, The Red Menace*)(F. Ebb/J. Kander) (3:29) *Liza Minnelli*; 2 Blow, Gabriel, Blow (from *Anything Goes*)(C. Porter) (5:16) *Patti LuPone*; 3 Freedom (from *Shenandoah*)(P. Udell/G. Geld) (2:21) *Donna Theodore, Chip Ford*; 4 Consider Youself (from *Oliver!*)(L. Bart) (3:51) *Michael Goodman, Bruce Prochnik*; 5 I've Gotta Crow (from *Peter Pan*)(M. Charlap/C. Leigh)(3:30) *Mary Martin, Kathy Nolan*; 6 Good Morning Starshine (from *Hair*)(G. McDermot/G. Ragni/J. Rado)(2:32) *Lynn Kellogg, Melba Moore, Gerome Ragni, James Rado*; 7 Oklahoma! (from *Oklahoma!*)(R. Rodgers/O. Hammerstein II)(3:00) *Company*; 8 Born Again (from *Jennie*)(H. Dietz/A. Schwartz)(3:20) *Mary Martin, Jack De Lon*; 9 Our Time (from *Merrily We Roll Along*)(S. Sondheim)(4:20) *Jim Walton, Lonny Price, Ann Morrison*; 10 Hey, Look Me Over! (from *Wildcat*)(C. Coleman/C. Leigh) (2:10) *Lucille Ball, Paula Stewart*; 11 Before The Parade Passes By (from *Hello, Dolly!*)(J. Herman) *Carol Channing*; 12 I Got Love (from *Purlie*)(G. Geld/P.

Udell)(3:17) *Melba Moore*; 13 To Life (from *Fiddler On The Roof*)(J. Bock/S. Harnick)(4:11) *Zero Mostel, Michael Granger, Ross Gifford*; 14 A Certain Girl (from *The Happy Time*)(F. Ebb/J. Kander)(3:04) *Robert Goulet, David Wayne, Mike Rupert*; 15 Little Me (from *Little Me*)(C. Coleman/C. Leigh)(2:51) *Nancy Andrews, Virginia Martin*; 16 H-A-P-P-Y/We'll Take A Glass Together (from *Grand Hotel*)(R. Wright/G. Forrest)(3:57) *David Jackson, Danny Strayhorn, Michael Jeter, Brent Barrett*; 17 The Best Of Times (from *La Cage Aux Folles*)(J. Herman)(5:35) *George Hearn, Elizabeth Parrish*.

Review: See entry *Celebrate Broadway Vol. 10* below.

Celebrate Broadway vol. 2: You Gotta Have a Gimmick! 🎵🎵🎵🎵

1994, RCA Victor.

Album Notes: *CD Producer*: Bill Rosenfield; *Engineer*: Dennis Ferrante.

Selections: 1 I've Got Your Number (from *Little Me*)(2:52) *Swen Swenson*; 2 Step To The Rear (from *How Now Dow Jones*)(E. Bernstein/C. Leigh)(3:17) *Anthony Roberts, Charlotte Jones*; 3 I Cain't Say No (from *Oklahoma!*)(R. Rodgers/O. Hammerstein II)(3:07) *Christine Ebersole*; 4 Mama Will Provide (from *Once On This Island*)(S. Flaherty/L. Ahrens)(3:11) *Kecia Lewis-Evans*; 5 Caribbean Plaid/Kingston Market/Jamaica Farewell/Matilda, Matilda (from *Forever Plaid*)(I. Burgie/N. Span)(3:48) *Stan Chandler, David Engel, Jason Graae, Guy Stroman*; 6 Chicken Is He (from *Promenade*)(A. Carmines/M.I. Fornes)(2:05) *Florence Tarlow*; 7 The Dream (from *Fiddler On The Roof*) (J. Bock/S. Harnick)(6:07) *Zero Mostel, Maria Karnilova, Sue Babel, Gluck Sandor, Carol Zawyer*; 8 Lizzie Borden (from *New Faces Of 1952*)(M. Brown)(5:05) *Joe Lautner, Bill Mullikin, Paul Lynde, Pat Hammerlee*; 9 Arthur In The Afternoon (from *The Act/And The World Goes 'Round*)(J. Kander/ F. Ebb)(3:56) *Karen Ziemba*; 10 Your Feet's Too Big (from *Ain't Misbehavin'*) (A. Benson/F. Fisher)(3:06) *Ken Page*; 11 Crossword Puzzle (from *Starting Here, Starting Now*)(D. Shire/R. Maltby, Jr.)(3:57) *Loni Ackerman*; 12 A Well Known Fact (from *I Do! I Do!*)(H. Schmidt/T. Jones)(2:37) *Mary Martin, Robert Preston*; 13 Shuffle Off To Buffalo (from *42nd Street*)(H. Warren/A. Dubin) (3:45) *Karen Punczik, Joseph Bova, Carole Cook*; 14 Siberia (from *Silk Stockings*)(C. Porter)(2:48) *Henry Lascoe, Leon Belasco, David Opatoshu*; 15 Another Wedding Song (from *Closer Than Ever*)(D. Shire/R. Maltby, Jr.)(2:16) *Brent Barrett, Sally Mayes*; 16 So Long Dearie (from *Hello, Dolly!*)(J. Herman)(3:00) *Pearl Bailey*; 17 A Little More Mascara (from *La Cage Aux Folles*)(J. Herman)(4:14) *George Hearn*; 18 You Gotta Have A Gimmick (from *Gypsy/Jerome Robbins' Broadway*)(J. Styne/S. Sondheim)(4:37) *Debbie Shapiro, Faith Prince, Susann Fletcher.*

Review: See entry *Celebrate Broadway Vol. 10* below.

Celebrate Broadway vol. 3: Lullaby of Broadway ♫♫♫♪

1994, RCA Victor.

Album Notes: *CD Producer*: Bill Rosenfield; *Engineer*: Dennis Ferrante.

Selections: 1 Lullaby Of Broadway (from *42nd Street*)(H. Warren/A. Dubin) (4:59) *Wanda Richert, Jerry Orbach, Lee Roy Reams, Carol Cook, Joseph Bova*; 2 Broadway Baby (from *Follies*)(S. Sondheim)(3:59) *Elaine Stritch*; 3 Be A Performer (from *Little Me*)(C. Coleman/C. Leigh)(2:02) *Joey Faye, Mort Marshall, Virginia Martin*; 4 All I Need Is The Girl (from *Gypsy*)(J. Styne/S. Sondheim)(4:40) *Zan Charisse, Andrew Norman*; 5 Opening Doors (from *Merrily We Roll Along*)(S. Sondheim)(6:52) *Jim Walton, Lonny Price, Ann Morrison, Jason Alexander, Marianna Allen, Sally Klein*; 6 One Step (from *Starting Here, Starting Now*)(D. Shire/R. Maltby, Jr.)(4:34) *George Lee Andrews, Margery Cohen, Loni Ackerman*; 7 Hello Dolly! (from *Hello, Dolly!*)(J. Herman)(5:41) *Carol Channing*; 8 Life Upon The Wicked Stage (from *Show Boat*)(J. Kern/O. Hammerstein II)(3:39) *Allyn McLerie*; 9 I Want To Go To Hollywood (from *Grand Hotel*)(M. Yeston)(3:31) *Jane Krakowski*; 10 Stereophonic Sound (from *Silk Stockings*)(C. Porter)(2:21) *Gretchen Wyler*; 11 Comedy Tonight (from *A Funny Thing Happened On The Way To The Forum/Jerome Robbins' Broadway*)(S. Sondheim)(6:29) *Jason Alexander*; 12 La Cage Aux Folles (from *La Cage Aux Folles*)(J. Herman)(6:43) *George Hearn*; 13 Cabaret (from *Cabaret/And The World Goes 'Round*)(J. Kander/F. Ebb)(3:22) *Jim Walton, Bob Cuccioli, Karen Mason, Brenda Pressley, Karen Ziemba*; 14 There's No Business Like Show Business (from *Annie Get Your Gun*)(I. Berlin) (3:18) *Jerry Orbach, Rufus Smith, Bruce Yarnell, Ethel Merman.*

Review: See entry *Celebrate Broadway Vol. 10* below.

Celebrate Broadway vol. 4: Overtures ♫♫♫♪

1994, RCA Victor.

Album Notes: *CD Producer*: Bill Rosenfield; *Engineer*: Pat Martin.

Selections: 1 Carousel (R. Rodgers/O. Hammerstein II) (5:29); 2 Finian's Rainbow (B. Lane/E.Y. Harburg)(4:33); 3 Follies (S. Sondheim)(5:02); 4 The Roar Of The Greasepaint— The Smell Of The Crowd (A. Newley/L. Bricusse) (3:22); 5 Hello, Dolly! (J. Herman)(4:23); 6 The Boy Friend (S. Wilson)(3:31); 7 Peter Pan (M. Charlap/J. Styne/C. Leigh/B. Comden/A. Green)(3:30); 8 On A Clear Day You Can See Forever (B. Lane/A.J. Lerner)(6:13); 9 Merrily We Roll Along (S. Sondheim)(3:52); 10 The King And I (R. Rodgers/O. Hammerstein II) (5:04); 11 Mack And Mabel (J. Herman)(5:10); 12 Gypsy (J. Styne/S. Sondheim) (5:18).

Review: See entry *Celebrate Broadway Vol. 10* below.

Celebrate Broadway vol. 5: Hello, Young Lovers ♫♫♫♪

1994, RCA Victor.

Album Notes: *CD Producer*: Bill Rosenfield; *Engineer*: Pat Martin.

Selections: 1 Hello Young Lovers (from *The King And I*)(R. Rodgers/O. Hammerstein II)(3:49) *Constance Towers*; 2 Make Believe (from *Show Boat*)(J. Kern/O. Hammerstein II)(4:49) *Barbara Cook, Stephen Douglass*; 3 The Human Heart (from *Once On This Island*)(S. Flaherty/L. Ahrens)(3:51) *Andrea Fierson*; 4 My Cup Runneth Over (from *I Do! I Do!*)(T. Jones/H. Schmidt)(2:10) *Mary Martin, Robert Preston*; 5 It's Never That Easy/I've Been Here Before (from *Closer Than Ever*)(R. Maltby, Jr./D. Shire)(6:18) *Sally Mayes, Lynne Wintersteller*; 6 Who Can I Turn To? (from *The Roar Of The Greasepaint—The Smell Of The Crowd*)(A. Newley/L. Bricusse)(3:49) *Anthony Newley*; 7 Love Can't Happen (from *Grand Hotel*)(M. Yeston)(3:48) *Brent Barrett*; 8 I Still Get Jealous (from *High Button Shoes/Jerome Robbins' Broadway*)(J. Styne/S. Cahn)(4:32) *Faith Prince, Jason Alexander*; 9 Not A Day Goes By (from *Merrily We Roll Along*)(S. Sondheim)(2:20) *Jim Walton, Ann Morrison*; 10 Small World (from *Gypsy*)(J. Styne/S. Sondheim)(2:53) *Angela Lansbury, Barrie Ingham*; 11 In Buddy's Eyes (from *Follies*)(S. Sondheim)(2:59) *Barbara Cook*; 12 I Know Him So Well (from *Chess*)(B. Andersson/T. Rice/B. Ulvaeus)(4:17) *Judy Kuhn, Marcia Mitzman*; 13 Easy To Be Hard (from *Hair*)(G. McDermot/G. Ragni/J. Rado)(2:35) *Lynn Kellogg*; 14 I Don't Remember You/ Sometimes A Day Goes By (from *The Happy Time/Woman Of The Year*)(J. Kander/F. Ebb)(4:42) *Bob Cuccioli, Jim Walton*; 15 My True Love (from *Phantom*)(M. Yeston)(3:18) *Glory Crampton.*

Review: See entry *Celebrate Broadway Vol. 10* below.

Celebrate Broadway vol. 6: Beautiful Girls 🎵🎵🎵🎵

1994, RCA Victor.

Album Notes: *CD Producer:* Bill Rosenfield; *Engineer:* Pat Martin.

Selections: 1 Beautiful Girls (from *Follies*)(S. Sondheim)(3:48) *Arthur Rubin;* 2 I Got The Sun In The Morning (from *Annie Get Your Gun*)(I. Berlin)(4:14) *Ethel Merman;* 3 A Quiet Thing (from *Flora, The Red Menace*)(J. Kander/F. Ebb)(4:00) *Liza Minnelli;* 4 What Is A Woman? (from *I Do! I Do!*)(T. Jones/H. Schmidt)(3:05) *Mary Martin;* 5 Children And Art (from *Sunday In The Park With George*)(S. Sondheim)(4:50) *Bernadette Peters;* 6 Mean To Me (from *Ain't Misbehavin'*)(R. Turk/F. Ahlert)(3:02) *Nell Carter;* 7 Old Maid (from *110 In The Shade*)(T. Jones/H. Schmidt)(3:18) *Inga Swenson;* 8 Being Alive (from Company)(S. Sondheim)(2:49) *Patti LuPone;* 9 Mr. Monotony (from *Jerome Robbins' Broadway*)(I. Berlin)(3:41) *Debbie Shapiro-Gravitte;* 10 Monotonous (from *New Faces Of 1952*)(A. Siegel/J. Carroll)(3:44) *Eartha Kitt;* 11 As Long As He Needs Me (from *Oliver!*)(L. Bart)(4:08) *Georgia Brown;* 12 What Did I Have That I Don't Have? (from *On A Clear Day You Can See Forever*) (A.J. Lerner/B. Lane)(4:23) *Barbara Harris;* 13 Losing My Mind (from *Follies*) (S. Sondheim)(4:17) *Barbara Cook;* 14 Like It Was (from *Putting It Together*) (S. Sondheim)(2:42) *Julie Andrews;* 15 Everything's Coming Up Roses (from *Gypsy*)(J. Styne/S. Sondheim)(3:03) *Angela Lansbury.*

Review: See entry *Celebrate Broadway Vol. 10* below.

Celebrate Broadway vol. 7: Kids! 🎵🎵🎵🎵

1994, RCA Victor.

Album Notes: *CD Producer:* Bill Rosenfield; *Engineer:* Jay Newland.

Selections: 1 Kids (from *Bye Bye Birdie*)(C. Strouse/L. Adams)(2:32) *Paul Lynde, Maureen Stapleton, Dick Van Dyke, Bryan Russell;* 2 I Won't Grow Up (from *Peter Pan*)(M. Charlap/C. Leigh)(3:06) *Mary Martin, Robert Harrington, Joseph Stafford, Kathy Nolan;* 3 Getting To Know You (from *The King And I*)(R. Rodgers/O. Hammerstein II)(4:25) *Constance Towers;* 4 Knock, Knock (from *Flora, The Red Menace*)(J. Kander/ F. Ebb)(3:08) *Mary Louise Wilson, James Cresson;* 5 Glorious Food (from *Oliver!*)(L. Bart)(3:27) *Boys' Chorus;* 6 Waiting For Life (from *Once On This Island*)(S. Flaherty/L. Ahrens)(2:44) *La Chanze;* 7 Comedy Tonight (from *A Funny Thing Happened On*

The Way To The Forum)(S. Sondheim)(2:44) *American Theatre Orchestra, Bill Irwin;* 8 June Is Bustin' Out All Over (from *Carousel*)(R. Rodgers/O. Hammerstein II)(3:27) *Katherine Hilgenberg, Susan Watson;* 9 Hair (from *Hair*)(G. McDermot/G. Ragni/J. Rado)(2:57) *James Rado, Gerome Ragni;* 10 Sixteen Tons (M. Travis)/Chain Gang (S. Cooke)(from *Forever Plaid*)(3:48) *David Engel, Jason Graae, Stan Chandler, Guy Stroman;* 11 Moonshine Lullaby (from *Annie Get Your Gun*)(I. Berlin)(3:13) *Ethel Merman;* 12 El Sombrero (from *Wildcat*)(C. Coleman/C. Leigh)(3:33) *Lucille Ball, Al Lanti, Swen Swenson;* 13 Put On A Happy Face (from *Bye Bye Birdie*)(C. Strouse/L. Adams)(3:35) *Dick Van Dyke;* 14 Broadway Baby (from *Follies*)(S. Sondheim)(2:55) *Daisy Egan.*

Review: See entry *Celebrate Broadway Vol. 10* below.

Celebrate Broadway vol. 8: Duets 🎵🎵🎵🎵

1995, RCA Victor.

Album Notes: *CD Producer:* Bill Rosenfield; *Engineer:* Jay Newland.

Selections: 1 You're The Top (from *Anything Goes*)(C. Porter)(4:00) *Patti LuPone, Howard McGillin;* 2 People Will Say We're In Love (from *Oklahoma!*)(R. Rodgers/O. Hammerstein II)(4:18) *Christine Andreas, Laurence Guittard;* 3 Anything You Can Do (from *Annie Get Your Gun*)(I. Berlin)(3:01) *Ethel Merman, Bruce Yarnell;* 4 Unworthy Of Your Love (from *Assassins*)(S. Sondheim)(3:26) *Greg Germann, Annie Golden;* 5 I Remember It Well (from *Gigi*)(A.J. Lerner/F. Loewe)(3:27) *Alfred Drake, Maria Karnilova;* 6 Love Has Come Of Age (from *Jekyll & Hyde*)(L. Bricusse/F. Wildhorn)(4:09) *Colm Wilkinson, Linda Eder;* 7 You And I (from *Chess*)(B. Andersson/T. Rice/B. Ulvaeus)(3:38) *Judy Kuhn, David Carroll;* 8 Where Would You Be Without Me? (from *The Roar Of The Greasepaint — The Smell Of The Crowd*)(L. Bricusse/A. Newley)(2:48) *Anthony Newley, Cyril Ritchard;* 9 Shut Up And Dance (from *My Favorite Year*)(S. Flaherty/L. Ahrens)(3:59) *Evan Pappas, Lannyl Stephens;* 10 Do You Love Me? (from *Fiddler On The Roof*)(J. Bock/S. Harnick)(3:08) *Zero Mostel, Maria Karnilova;* 11 Marry The Man Today (from *Guys And Dolls*)(F. Loesser)(2:33) *Josie de Guzman, Faith Prince;* 12 You Are Music (from *Phantom*)(M. Yeston) (3:02) *Glory Crampton, Richard White;* 13 The Honeymoon Is Over (from *I Do! I Do!*)(T. Jones/H. Schmidt)(1:55) *Robert Preston, Mary Martin;* 14 Stranger In Paradise (from *Kismet*)(R. Wright/G. Forrest/A. Borodin)(4:08) *Lee Venora, Richard Banke.*

Review: See entry *Celebrate Broadway Vol. 10* below.

Celebrate Broadway vol. 9: Gotta Dance! ♫♫♫♪

1995, RCA Victor.

Album Notes: *CD Producer:* Bill Rosenfield; *Engineer:* Jay Newland.

Selections: 1 Dancing (from *Hello, Dolly!*)(J. Herman)(4:27) *Carol Channing, Charles Nelson Reilly, Jerry Dodge, Eileen Benton*; 2 Charleston (from *Billion Dollar Baby/Jerome Robbins' Broadway*)(M. Gould/B. Comden/A. Green)(5:48) Ensemble; 3 Pick-Pocket Tango (from *Redhead*)(A. Hague/D. Fields)(2:41) Orchestra; 4 We're In The Money (from *42nd Street*)(H. Warren/ A. Dubin)(3:05) *Karen Prunczik, Wanda Richert, Ginny King, Jeri Kansas, Lee Roy Reams*; 5 Who Couldn't Dance With You? (from *Grand Hotel*)(R. Wright/G. Forrest)(5:14) *Brent Barrett, Jane Krakowski, Michael Jeter*; 6 A Secretary Is Not A Toy (from *How To Succeed In Business Without Really Trying*)(F. Loesser)(4:00) *Paul Reed*; 7 Who's That Woman? (from *Follies*)(S. Sondheim)(5:23) *Phyllis Newman, Barbara Cook, Lee Remick, Elaine Stritch, Betty Comden, Liliane Montevecchi*; 8 We Dance (from *Once On This Island*)(L. Ahrens/S. Flaherty)(5:28) Ensemble; 9 The Joint Is Jumpin' (from *Ain't Misbehavin'*)(T. Waller/A. Razaf/J.C. Johnson)(2:16) *Nell Carter, Andre DeShields, Armelia McQueen, Ken Page, Charlaine Woodard*; 10 One Night In Bangkok (from *Chess*)(B. Andersson/B. Ulvaeus/T. Rice)(3:52) *Philip Casnoff*; 11 On The S.S. Bernard Cohn (from *On A Clear Day You Can See Forever*)(B. Lane/A.J. Lerner)(4:32) *Barbara Harris, Barbara Monte, William Reilly, Gerald M. Teijelo Jr.*; 12 Dance At The Gym (from *West Side Story/ Jerome Robbins' Broadway*)(L. Bernstein/S. Sondheim)(4:57) Ensemble; 13 Somewhere (from *West Side Story*)(7:05) *Dorothy Christophe Caballero*.

Review: See entry *Celebrate Broadway Vol. 10* below.

Celebrate Broadway vol. 10: Best Musicals! ♫♫♫♪

1995, RCA Victor.

Album Notes: *CD Producer:* Bill Rosenfield; *Engineer:* Jay Newland.

Selections: 1 Overture (from *42nd Street*)(H. Warren/A. Dubin)(4:41) Orchestra; 2 If I Were A Rich Man (from *Fiddler On The Roof*)(J. Bock/S. Harnick)(4:54) *Zero Mostel*; 3 Song On The Sand (from *La Cage Aux Folles*)(J. Herman)(3:55) *Gene Barry, George Hearn*; 4 Honeysuckle Rose (from *Ain't Misbehavin'*)(T. Waller/A. Razaf)(3:58) *Ken Page, Nell Carter*; 5

Hello, Dolly! (from Hello, Dolly!)(J. Herman)(5:41) *Carol Channing*; 6 Kiss Of The Spider Woman (from *Kiss Of The Spider Woman*)(F. Ebb/J. Kander) (3:00) *Bob Cuccioli*; 7 Overture (from *Jerome Robbins' Broadway*)(H. Martin/J. Styne/S. Cahn/R. Rodgers/O. Hammerstein II)(3:12) *Michael Lynch, Debbie Shapiro-Gravitte*; 8 Stranger In Paradise (from *Kismet*)(R. Wright/G. Forrest/A. Borodin)(4:08) *Lee Venora, Richard Banke*; 9 A Little Priest (from *Sweeney Todd*)(S. Sondheim)(7:15) *Angela Lansbury, Len Cariou*; 10 Look Who's In Love (from *Redhead*)(A. Hague/D. Fields)(2:05) *Gwen Verdon, Richard Kiley*; 11 Send In The Clowns (from *A Little Night Music*)(S. Sondheim)(4:14) *Glenn Close*; 12 Shall We Dance? (from *The King And I*)(R. Rodgers/O. Hammerstein II)(5:03) *Yul Brynner, Constance Towers*; 13 Bring Him Home (from *Les Miserables*)(C.M. Schoenberg/A. Boublil/H. Kretzmer)(3:24) *Colm Wilkinson*; 14 The Brotherhood Of Man (from *How To Succeed In Business Without Really Trying*)(F. Loesser)(4:05) *Robert Morse, Sammy Smith, Ruth Kubart*; 15 The Music Of The Night (from *Phantom Of The Opera*)(A. Lloyd Webber/C. Hart)(5:51) *Colm Wilkinson*.

Review: Both series point out the strengths and weaknesses in the respective catalogues. For many years the incontestable leaders in the field of cast album recordings, Columbia and RCA have accumulated an enviable roster of titles that represent the Broadway musical at its most brilliant, from the 1950s to today. But whereas they complement each other in many ways, collections culling material from each can only rely on the recordings in their individual vaults. As a result, and to compensate, some arbitrary decisions must be made in order to avoid having huge gaps. Thus, Sony Broadway, which mined the Columbia catalogue, didn't have access to such blockbusters as *Fiddler on the Roof* (though the London cast recording, with Topol as Tevye, proved an acceptable substitute), *Hello, Dolly!*, *How to Succeed in Business* or *La Cage Aux Folles*; similarly, while RCA could rely on those titles, other acknowledged hits like *Mame*, *Sweet Charity*, *My Fair Lady* and *A Chorus Line* are sorely lacking in the Celebrate Broadway collections. Further besetting that series are some arbitrary decisions made to flesh up the repertoire, with *Kids!*, for instance, seemingly missing the basic concept suggested by its title with the inclusion of selections that have no point in being there.

These details set aside, both series offer an overview of the best of Broadway, with star turns and selections that are, for the most part, the creme de la creme. Anyone interested in discovering the glories of Broadway without having to purchase the individual cast album recordings will thoroughly enjoy these compilations.

compilation soundtracks

Cannes Film Festival: 50th Anniversary Album ♫♫

1997, Milan Records.

Album Notes: *Album Executive Producers*: Valerie Bernard, Alain Garel; *Engineer*: Francois Brillet.

Selections: 1 Main Title/Police Car (from *The 400 Blows*)(J. Constantin)(3:14); 2 La dolce vita (from *La dolce vita*)(N. Rota)(5:37); 3 A Man And A Woman (from *A Man And A Woman*)(F. Lai)(2:29); 4 Main Title (from *Blow Up*)(H. Hancock)(1:32); 5 Taxi Driver (from *Taxi Driver*)(B. Herrmann) (8:41); 6 The Island (Main Title)(from *Yol*)(S. Argol)(3:18); 7 Odlazak Mase (from *When Father Was Away On Business*)(Z. Simjanovic)(2:22); 8 Die Kathedrale der Buecher (from *Wings Of Desire*)(4:47); 9 Vuelvo al sur (from *Sur*)(A. Piazzolla/R. Goyeneche)(4:00); 10 End Title (from *A World Apart*)(H. Zimmer) (4:49); 11 Chaucer Street (from *Mystery Train*)(J. Lurie)(3:44); 12 Typing Montage (from *Barton Fink*)(C. Burwell)(2:07); 13 Estampe 1 (from *The Scent Of Green Papaya*)(Ton-That Tiet)(1:58); 14 Crash (from *Crash*)(H. Shore)(3:37).

Review: A compilation of this kind is fraught with problems, so one perhaps should be grateful that the folks at Milan Records thought about putting it together, while recognizing the fact that they had their limits. Celebrating Cannes and the films that were discovered there over the years was a noble idea to begin with: indeed, the Film Festival has often recognized the validity of many films, coming from the four corners of the world, long before Hollywood took notice, and helped establish the reputation of many celebrated filmmakers and directors. But trying to survey 50 years of cinema through the themes heard in some of these films is really inviting serious scrutiny. First, because you are limited: unless you are going to include at least 50 themes, one for each year, you are going to necessarily omit some that are very important. This is further compounded by the fact that the CD producers decided to draw primarily from the resources in the Milan catalogue, which, good as it may be, is not very extensive.

As a result, we do have 14 tracks which include some interesting tracks (*The 400 Blows, Blow Up, Taxi Driver*), some questionable choices (*When Father Was Away On Business, Mystery Train, Crash*), some serious omissions (where is, for instance, the theme from *Cinema Paradiso?*), and at least one track, *La dolce vita*, which is not even a soundtrack recording but a rerecording by Katyna Ranieri which happens, quite conveniently, to be in the Milan catalogue. It was a good idea. It simply was badly executed.

Classic British Film Music ♫♫♫♫

1990, Silva Screen Records.

Album Notes: *Music*: Vaughan Williams, Brian Easdale, Gerard Schurmann, Arthur Bliss; The Philharmonia Orchestra, conducted by Kenneth Alwyn; *Album Producers*: David Stoner, James Fitzpatrick; *Engineer*: Mike Ross-Trevor.

Selections: Coastal Command (R.V. Williams): 1 Prelude (1:23); 2 Hebrides (1:31); 3 U-Boat Alert (2:46); 4 Taking Off At Night (1:37); 5 Hudsons Take Off From Iceland (2:13); 6 Dawn Patrol (4:15); 7 The Battle Of The Beauforts (3:28); 8 Finale (3:56); The Red Shoes (B. Easdale): 9 The Red Shoes Ballet (15:00); Attack On The Iron Coast/The Two-Headed Spy (G. Schurmann): 10 Attack and Celebration (7:20); Conquest Of The Air (A. Bliss): 11 The Wind (1:25); 12 The Vision Of Leonardo da Vinci (2:47); 13 Stunting (1:50); 14 Over The Arctic (2:58); 15 Gliding (1:13); 16 March: Conquest Of The Air (2:08).

Review: British film music is an acquired taste, and even though it requires a great deal of attention to make its impact, the rewards it offers are plentiful. In its heyday, the British film industry relied on classically-trained composers to provide the scores; as a result, people like Ralph Vaughan William, Brian Easdale or Arthur Bliss contributed music that has all the earmarks of great classical scores, yet conforms with the demands imposed by the cinematographic medium. To be sure, the scores often reflect the type of music English composers were used to writing-pompous, dithyrambic, full of its own importance-but they also seemed to match perfectly the moods projected in the films themselves. The scores represented here all deal with World War II, and elicit from their respective composers the kind of patriotic fire that seems totally appropriate for this type of film. Conducted with the right dose of vibrancy and understanding by Kenneth Alwyn, this superb collection is one of the best representations available today.

Cinema Century ♫♫♫♫⁵

1996, Silva Treasury.

Album Notes: The City of Prague Philharmonic, conducted by Kenneth Alwyn, Paul Bateman, Nic Raine, Mike Townend, Derek Wadsworth; The Philharmonia, conducted by Tony Bremner, Andrew Greenwood; The Westminster Philharmonic Orchestra and The Royal Philharmonic Orchestra, conducted by Kenneth Alwyn; The Royal Philharmonic Concert Orchestra and The London Screen Orchestra, conducted by Mike Townend; The Milan Philharmonic, conducted by Carmine

Coppola; The City Lights Orchestra, conducted by Carl Davis; and Mark Ayres.

Selections: CD 1: 1 20th Century-Fox Fanfare (A. Newman)(:14); City Lights: 2 Overture/The Statue (C. Chaplin)(4:12); The Bride Of Frankenstein: 3 Main Title (F. Waxman)(1:27); Gone With The Wind: 4 Suite (M. Steiner)(6:40); Stagecoach: 5 Suite (R. Hageman/W.F. Harling/J. Leopold/L. Shuken/L. Gruenberg) (6:38); Citizen Kane: 6 Overture (B. Herrmann)(2:47); Casablanca: 7 Suite (M. Steiner)(7:01); Oliver Twist: 8 Fagin's Romp (A. Bax)(2:15); Quo Vadis: 9 Ave Caesar (M. Rozsa)(4:50); The Quiet Man: 10 The Donnybrook (V. Young)(2:43); The High And The Mighty: 11 Prelude (D. Tiomkin)(1:59); The Searchers: 12 Suite (M. Steiner)(7:21); Bridge On The River Kwai: 13 Colonel Bogey (K.J. Alford) (4:06); The Big Country: 14 Main Title (J. Moross)(3:15); North By Northwest: 15 Main Title (B. Herrmann)(3:21); Ben Hur: 16 Parade Of The Charioteers (M. Rozsa)(3:38).

CD 2: Psycho: 1 Prelude (B. Herrmann)(2:00); La dolce vita: 2 Suite (N. Rota) (7:10); The Magnificent Seven: 3 Suite (E. Bernstein)(5:50); The Alamo: 4 Overture (D. Tiomkin)(3:22); The Pink Panther: 5 Theme (H. Mancini)(2:47); Lawrence Of Arabia: 6 Overture (M. Jarre)(4:24); The Great Escape: 7 March (E. Bernstein)(2:17); 633 Squadron: 8 Theme (R. Goodwin)(2:59); Zulu: 9 Theme (J. Barry)(2:16); Zorba The Greek: 10 Zorba's Dance (M. Theodorakis)(4:21); Doctor Zhivago: 11 Lara's Theme (M. Jarre)(3:17); Born Free: 12 Theme (J. Barry) (2:46); The Lion In Winter: 13 Main Title (J. Barry)(2:22); Once Upon A Time In The West: 14 Theme (E. Morricone)(6:03); Where Eagles Dare: 15 Theme (R. Goodwin)(3:20); Midnight Cowboy: 16 Theme (J. Barry)(3:59); The Wild Bunch: 17 Train Montage (J. Fielding)(6:42).

CD 3: The Godfather: 1 Godfather Waltz (N. Rota)(2:30); Jaws: 2 Theme (J. Williams)(2:15); Rocky: 3 Fanfare/Gonna Fly Now (B. Conti)(4:40); Taxi Driver: 4 Night Piece For Orchestra and Saxophone (B. Herrmann)(8:01); Star Wars: 5 Main Theme (J. Williams)(5:24); Diva: 6 Ebben? Ne andro lontano (from La Wally)(A. Catalani)(3:37) *Lesley Garrett*; Raiders Of The Lost Ark: 7 March (J. Williams)(5:07); Chariots Of Fire: 8 Theme (Vangelis)(3:31); Conan The Barbarian: 9 Anvil Of Crom (B. Poledouris)(2:37); E.T. The Extraterrestrial: 10 Flying Theme (J. Williams)(3:43); Once Upon A Time In America: 11 Deborah's Theme (E. Morricone)(4:38); The Terminator: 12 Theme (B. Fiedel)(4:36).

CD 4: Witness: 1 Building The Barn (M. Jarre) (4:38); Out Of Africa: 2 Theme (J. Barry) (4:24); A Passage To India: 3 Adela's Theme (M. Jarre) (2:24); The Mission: 4 Theme (E. Morricone) (2:57); A Room With A View: 5 O mio babbino caro (from Gianni Schicchi) (L. Puccini) (2:27) *Lesley Garrett; Cinema Paradiso: 6 Theme (E. Morricone) (3:29); Ghost: 7 End Theme (M. Jarre) (4:25); Dances With Wolves: 8 John Dunbar Theme (J. Barry) (2:31); 1492: Conquest Of Paradise: 9 Theme (Vangelis) (5:04); Unforgiven: 10 Claudia's Theme (C. Eastwood) (6:15); The Fugitive: 11 It's Over (J. Newton Howard) (4:06); Jurassic Park: 12 Suite (J. Williams) (5:55); Schindler's List: 13 Theme (J. Williams) (4:00).*

Review: There are so many things right about this 4-CD compilation that one might be willing to overlook its most flagrant flaws. Alone in the industry, at least in this country, Silva America has chosen to celebrate the 100th anniversary of the movies. By digging into its many recordings, the label has been able to put together a somewhat comprehensive survey of film music from the early 1930s to today (with *Schindler's List*, the last title included here, dating from 1996, and *City Lights*, the first, from 1931, the survey represents in fact only 65 years, but who's to quibble?).

In the process, Silva offers an overview of many of the most successful themes written for the movies. Unfortunately, the compilation barely touches upon the many contributions made to film music in the 1930s and '40s. Noticeably missing are representations of the early works of Miklos Rozsa, Alfred Newman, Max Steiner, Erich-Wolfgang Korngold, and the other great composers of the first generation; and important films like *The Asphalt Jungle, Treasure of the Sierra Madre, Now Voyager, Madame Bovary, Captain from Castile*, and many others.

Where the compilation thrives is in its accumulation of great themes from the '50s through the '90s, though, once again, there seems to be some glaring omissions, and odd inclusions like *633 Squadron, Diva* and *The Terminator*. But overall, this is an exciting collection, which pays tribute to an art form that had been neglected for far too long. With some great orchestras, and some great conductors along for the more than 3½ hour musical voyage, this is a collection no one should miss.

Cinema Choral Classics ♫♫♫♪

1997, Silva Screen Records.

Album Notes: The Crouch End Festival Chorus, conducted by David Temple; The City Of Prague Philaharmonic, conducted by Nic Raine, Paul Bateman, Kenneth Alwyn; *Album Producer*: James Fitzpatrick; *Engineers*: John L. Timperley, Mike Ross-Trevor.

Selections: Excalibur: 1 O Fortuna (from Carmina Burana)(C. Orff)(2:47); Jesus Of Nazareth (M. Jarre): 2 Prelude/Birth Of Christ (4:09); The Scarlet Letter: 3 Agnus Dei (based on Adagio for Strings)(S. Barber)(6:14); First Knight (J. Goldsmith): 4

Never Surrender (5:28); The Abyss (A. Silvestri): 5 The Abyss (5:11); King Of Kings (M. Rozsa): 6 The Lord's Prayer (2:45); Conan The Barbarian (B. Poledouris): 7 Riders Of Doom (6:05); The Mission (E. Morricone): 8 Ave Maria Guarini (2:34); 9 On Earth As It Is In Heaven (3:31); The Lion In Winter (J. Barry): 10 Suite (8:15); 1492: Conquest Of Paradise (Vangelis): 11 1492: Conquest Of Paradise (5:06); The Vikings (M. Nascimbene): 12 Funeral and Finale (3:34); The Omen (J. Goldsmith): 13 Suite (11:53); Henry V (P. Doyle): 14 Non nobis Domine (3:50).

Review: An interesting concept which demonstrates that some great choral music is being composed for the movies. Wisely, the album does not rely on the tried-and-true, and if a couple of selections (Rozsa's *King of Kings* or John Barry's *The Lion in Winter*) were to be expected, the program focuses for the most part on themes that are less obvious. While one might dispute the CD's subtitle, which could lead one to believe that Carmina Burana and Samuel Barber's "Adagio For Strings" were written for the movies, nothing else detracts from this handsome package which boasts a sensational sound, broad and spacious, some exquisite performances (both the choir and the orchestra are excellent), and an overall classy presentation.

Cinema Gala

Cinema Gala: The Epic ♫♫♫�

1988, London Records.

Album Notes: The London Festival Orchestra & Chorus, conducted by Stanley Black.

Selections: Exodus (E. Gold): 1 Ari's Theme (3:34); Lawrence Of Arabia (M. Jarre): 2 Theme (3:33); The Magnificent Seven (E. Bernstein): 3 Theme (3:35); Cleopatra (A. North): 4 Antony And Cleopatra (3:18); The Alamo (D. Tiomkin): 5 Theme (5:21); Doctor Zhivago (M. Jarre): 6 Lara's Theme/Revolution Theme (5:48); Stagecoach (M. Steiner): 7 Theme (5:22); For Whom The Bell Tolls (V. Young): 8 A Love Like This (5:06); Patton (J. Goldsmith): 9 Patton (3:41); The Sea Hawk (E.W. Korngold): 10 Theme (7:08).

Review: See entry below.

Cinema Gala: Great Love Stories ♫♫B

1988, London Records.

Album Notes: The London Festival Orchestra & Chorus, conducted by Stanley Black; *Featured Soloists*: Stanley Black (piano), Sidney Sax (violin), Stan Roderick (trumpet).

Selections: Casablanca (M. Steiner): 1 Suite: Main Title/As Time Goes By (H. Hupfeld)/Africa/La Marseillaise/Deutschland Uber Alles/Street Scene/ Orders/Plane (7:51); A Man And A Woman (F. Lai/P. Barouh): 2 A Man And A Woman (3:18); Intermezzo (H. Provost): 3 Theme (3:12); Blood And Sand (A. Newman): 4 Suite: Blood/La Virgen de la Macarena (Calero/Monteverde)/Death Of Nacionale/ Romance d'amour (P. Gomez)/Bullfight Bugle Call (A. Grajeda)/El Gato Montes (R. Penella)(7:05); La Strada(N. Rota): 5 Gelsomina (5:06); Love Story (F. Lai): 6 Main Title/For Me Alone (Snow Frolic)(6:44); Gone With The Wind (M. Steiner): 7 Introduction/Tara/Mammy/Melanie/Civil War/Ashley's Return/Finale (9:24).

Review: See entry below.

Cinema Gala: Great Shakespeare Films ♫♫♫♫B

1989, London Records.

Album Notes: The National Philharmonic Orchestra, conducted by Bernard Herrmann; The London Festival Orchestra, conducted by Stanley Black.

Selections: Henry V (W. Walton): 1 The Battle Of Agincourt (7:01); Hamlet (D. Shostakovich): 2 Introduction (3:25); 3 Ball At The Palace (3:02); 4 The Ghost (5:16); 5 Scene Of The Poisoning (4:17); 6 The Arrival and Scene Of The Players (2:52); 7 The Duel and Death Of Hamlet (2:38); Richard III (W. Walton): 8 Prelude (9:59); Julius Caesar (M. Rozsa): 9 The Ides Of March (3:21); 10 Caesar's Ghost (2:47); 11 Approach Of Octavian's Army and Death Of Brutus (6:15).

Review: See entry below.

Cinema Gala: The Guns of Navarone Music from World War II Films ♫♫♫

1988, London Records.

Album Notes: The London Festival Orchestra & Chorus, conducted by Stanley Black.

Selections: The First Of The Few (W. Walton): 1 Spitfire Prelude and Fugue (8:01); The Bridge On The River Kwai (M. Arnold): 2 Colonel Bogey (K.J. Alford)/River Kwai March (4:37); The Guns Of Navarone (D. Tiomkin): 3 Theme (3:12); Victory At Sea (R. Rodgers): 4 Suite (11:52); 633 Squadron (R. Goodwin): 5 Theme (3:16); The Longest Day (P. Anka): 6 Main Title (3:37); Western Approaches (C. Parker): 7 Main Theme (5:02); The Great Escape (E. Bernstein): 8 Main Title (5:32); Mrs. Miniver (H. Stothart/D. Amfitheatrof): 9 Opening Title/A Rose For You/

O God Our Help In Ages Past (Croft/Watts)/Bridge Section (S. Black)/Land Of Hope And Glory (E. Elgar)(8:34).

Review: See entry below.

Cinema Gala: James Bond 007 🎵♭

1988, London Records.

Album Notes: *Music:* John Barry; *Featuring:* Roland Shaw and His Orchestra.

Selections: 1 The James Bond Theme (M. Norman)(3:28); 2 You Only Live Twice (2:31); 3 Goldfinger (4:09); 4 From Russia With Love (4:09); Dr. No: 5 Underneath The Mango Tree (trad.)(2:51); Goldfinger: 6 Pussy Galore's Flying Circus (2:24); 7 On Her Majesty's Secret Service (2:11); 8 Diamonds Are Forever (2:49); 9 Thunderball (2:55); Casino Royale: 10 The Look Of Love (B. Bacharach/H. David)(3:07); 11 Casino Royale (B. Bacharach)(2:28); Goldfinger: 12 Dawn Raid On Fort Knox (5:38); Thunderball: 13 Bond Below Disco Volante (4:05); 14 007 Theme (3:13).

Review: See entry below.

Cinema Gala: The Third Man Film Favorites 🎵♭

1988, London Records.

Album Notes: The London Festival Orchestra & Chorus, conducted by Stanley Black; *Featuring:* Frank Chacksfield and His Orchestra; Mantovani and His Orchestra; *Guest Artist:* Anton Karas (zither).

Selections: The Third Man (A. Karas): 1 The Harry Lime Theme (3:12) *Anton Karas*; Charade (H. Mancini/J. Mercer): 2 Theme (4:15) *The London Festival Orchestra & Chorus*; Mondo Cane (R. Ortolani/N. Oliviero): 3 More (4:23) *The London Festival Orchestra & Chorus*; The Good, The Bad And The Ugly (E. Morricone): 4 Theme (2:05) *Frank Chacksfield and His Orchestra*; The Sandpiper (J. Mandel/P.F. Webster): 5 The Shadow Of Your Smile (2:32) *Mantovani and His Orchestra*; Never On Sunday (M. Hadjidakis): 6 Theme (3:05) *Mantovani and His Orchestra*; The Big Country (J. Moross): 7 Main Title (3:05) *The London Festival Orchestra*; Born Free (J. Barry/D. Black): 8 Theme (2:32) *Mantovani and His Orchestra*; Breakfast At Tiffany's (H. Mancini/J. Mercer): 9 Moon River (2:40) *Mantovani and His Orchestra*; The Umbrellas Of Cherbourg (M. Legrand/J. Demy): 10 I Will Wait For You (2:24) *Frank Chacksfield and His Orchestra*; Alfie (B. Bacharach/H. David): 11 Alfie (2:47) *Frank*

Chacksfield and His Orchestra; A Summer Place (M. Steiner): 12 Theme (3:35) *The London Festival Orchestra & Chorus*; Spellbound (M. Rozsa): 13 Theme (4:48) *The London Festival Orchestra & Chorus*; Zorba The Greek (M. Theodorakis): 14 Zorba's Dance (4:35) *The London Festival Orchestra*.

Review: See entry below.

Cinema Gala: Warsaw Concerto 🎵🎵🎵🎵♭

1988, London Records.

Album Notes: The Royal Philharmonic Orchestra, conducted by Moshe Atzman; The London Festival Orchestra, conducted by Laszlo Tabor; Mantovani and His Orchestra; The National Philharmonic Orchestra, conducted by Bernard Herrmann; *Featured Soloists:* Cristina Ortis (piano), Wilhelm Davos (piano), Rawicz and Landauer (double pianos).

Selections: Dangerous Moonlight: 1 Warsaw Concerto (R. Addinsell)(9:01) *Cristina Ortiz, the Royal Philharmonic Orchestra*; The Story Of Three Loves: 2 Rhapsody On A Theme Of Paganini (S. Rachmaninov)(2:40) *Wilhelm Davos, the London Festival Orchestra*; While I Live: 3 The Dream Of Olwen (R. Williams)(3:51) *Wilhelm Davos, the London Festival Orchestra*; Love Story: 4 Cornish Rhapsody (H. Bath)(6:52) *Rawicz & Landauer, Mantovani and His Orchestra*; Escape Me Never (W. Walton): 5 Ballet (3:19) *The National Philharmonic Orchestra, Bernard Herrmann*; 49th Parallel (R. Vaughan Williams): 6 The Invaders (3:26) *The National Philharmonic Orchestra, Bernard Herrmann*; Things To Come (A. Bliss): 7 Prologue (2:37); 8 March (4:54); 9 Building Of The New World (2:10); 10 Attack On The Moon Gun (1:37); 11 Epilogue (3:29) *The National Philharmonic Orchestra, Bernard Herrmann*.

Review: The Cinema Gala series, released on CD in 1988 by London Records, returned to the catalogue some of the recordings made in the early 1960s by Stanley Black, Frank Chacksfield and other British band leaders for the Phase 4 Stereo albums. At the time, these albums were known for the high quality of their stereo definition, and their transfer to the digital medium only heightens the many qualities they already boasted.

Musically, some of the recordings, particularly *The Epic* and *The Guns of Navarone*, are spectacularly thrilling, even if they tend to be at times overly exaggerated, with what may be best described as CinemaScope performances: big, broad, sometimes with unintentionally hilarious sound effects. But they have a cinematic quality that emphasizes the initial purpose of the music itself as dramatic underscoring.

Along similar lines, *Great Love Stories* tends to overmilk the pathos in the themes developed, with broad effects that affect the overall impact.

There is little to recommend in *James Bond 007*, which offers themes available elsewhere, usually in much better performances, though, once again, Roland Shaw's wall-to-wall colorful renditions seem particularly suited for this type of material.

The only point of interest in *The Third Man* is Anton Karas' performance of the "Harry Lime Theme," which, surprisingly, is not available anywhere else, but the other selections in this compilation are just routine and without much appeal other than as innocuous background music.

Conversely, the recordings for the *Great Shakespearean Films* and *Warsaw Concerto* are quite effective, and make both releases the most enjoyable in the entire series. Both are particularly distinguished by the fact that Bernard Herrmann adds his personal touch to some of the selections, noticeably injecting fire and passion in Miklos Rozsa's *Julius Caesar* in the first CD, and in Arthur Bliss' *Things To Come* in the second.

The Cincinnati Pops Orchestra

Chiller 🎵🎵᷍

1989, Telarc Records.

Album Notes: The Cincinnati Pops Orchestra conducted by Erich Kunzel; *Album Producer*: Robert Woods; *Engineer*: Jack Renner.

Selections: 1 Opening Sequence (M. Bishop)(:48); Phantom Of The Opera (A.L. Webber): 2 Overture (2:11) *Robert Muckenfuss*; 3 Night On Bald Mountain (M. Mussorgsky/N. Rimsky-Korsakov)(10:38); 4 Danse Macabre, op. 40 (C. Saint-Saens)(7:40); 5 March To The Scaffold (from Symphonie Fantastique, op. 14)(H. Berlioz)(4:58); 6 Pandemonium (from The Damnation Of Faust, op. 24)(H. Berlioz)(3:22); 7 In The Hall Of The Mountain King (from Peer Gynt, Suite No. 1, op. 46)(E. Grieg)(2:30); 8 Synthesizer Effects (R. Ilett)(:52); The Twilight Zone: 9 Theme (M. Constant)(:48); 10 12,000 Volts (:12); The Bride Of Frankenstein (F. Waxman): 11 Prelude/Minuet/Pastorale and March (5:08); The Devil And Daniel Webster (B. Herrmann): 12 Sleigh Ride (1:51); Psycho (B. Herrmann): 13 Prelude (1:31); 14 The Mad House (1:59); 15 Murder (1:20); Sleuth (J. Addison): 16 Overture (2:48); 17 Television Noise (:17); Poltergeist (J. Goldsmith): 18 The Light (2:37); Without A Clue (H.

Mancini): 19 Super Sleuth (2:03); Alfred Hitchcock Presents: 20 Funeral March Of A Marionette (C. Gounod)(3:35).

Review: See *Victory at Sea and Other Favorites* entry below.

A Disney Spectacular 🎵🎵᷍

1989, Telarc Records.

Album Notes: *Arrangers*: Carmen Dragon, Ken Whitcomb, Frank Comstock, Bruce Healey, Jack Eskew, James Christensen, Jay Blackton; The Cincinnati Pops Orchestra conducted by Erich Kunzel; The Indiana University School Of Music Singing Hoosiers; The School For Creative & Performing Arts Children's Chorus; The May Festival Chorus; *Featured Artists*: Tracy Dahl (soprano), Douglas Webster (baritone), His Master's Voice (barbershop quartet); *Album Producer*: Robert Woods; *Engineer*: Jack Renner.

Selections: Pinocchio (L. Harline/N. Washington): 1 When You Wish Upon A Star (2:33); 2 It's A Small World (R.M. & R.B. Sherman)(3:20); Alice In Wonderland (S. Fain/B. Hilliard): 3 Medley: Alice In Wonderland/All In The Golden Afternoon/I'm Late (4:40); 4 March Of The Cards (1:56); Mary Poppins (R.M. & R.B. Sherman): 5 Medley: Chim Chim Cher-ee/Jolly Holiday/A Spoonful Of Sugar/Let's Go Fly A Kite/Supercalifragilisticexpialidocious/Step In Time (8:33); Cinderella (M. David/J. Livingston/A. Hoffman): 6 Medley: Cinderella/A Dream Is A Wish Your Heart Makes/The Work Song/Bibbidi-Bobbidi-Boo/So This Is Love (8:17); The Jungle Book (R.M. & R.B. Sherman): 7 Medley: I Wan'na Be Like You/Trust In Me/Colonel Hathi's March/That's What Friends Are For/The Bare Necessities (6:58) His Master's Voice; Three Little Pigs (F. Churchill/A. Ronell): 8 Who's Afraid Of The Big Bad Wolf? (1:35); Snow White And The Seven Dwarfs (L. Morey/F. Churchill): 9 Medley: Overture/Heigh-Ho/Whistle While You Work/With A Smile And A Song/I'm Wishing/One Song/Some Day My Prince Will Come (12:10) *Tracy Dahl, Douglas Webster*; 10 Mickey Mouse March (J. Dodd)(1:14); 11 Baroque Hoedown (G. Kingsley/J.-J. Perrey)(2:23); Disney Fantasy Medley: 12 Song Of The South: Zip-A-Dee-Doo-Dah (R. Gilbert/A. Wrubel), Peter Pan: You Can Fly, You Can Fly, You Can Fly (S. Cahn/ S. Fain), Dumbo: Title Theme (O. Wallace)/Casey Jr. (F. Churchill/N. Washington), Winnie The Pooh And The Blustery Day: The Wonderful Thing About Tiggers (R.M. & R.B. Sherman), Winnie The Pooh And The Honey Tree: Winnie The Pooh (R.M. & R.B. Sherman), Bambi: Love Is A Song (L. Morey/F. Churchill), Lady And The Tramp: Bella Note (P. Lee/S. Burke)/The Siamese Cat Song (P. Lee/S. Burke), Snow White And The Seven Dwarfs: Heigh-Ho (L. Morey/F. Churchill)/Whistle While You Work (L. Morey/F. Churchill), Pinocchio: Give A Little Whistle (L. Harline/N. Washington)/I've Got No Strings (L. Harline/N. Washington), Sleeping Beauty: Once Upon A Dream (S. Fain/J. Lawrence/P.I. Tchaikovsky), Cinderella: A Dream Is A Wish Your Heart Makes (M. David/J. Livingston/A. Hoffman), Pinocchio: When You Wish Upon A Star (L. Harline/N. Washington)(13:34).

Review: See *Victory at Sea and Other Favorites* entry below.

Fantastic Journey ♪♪♪♪▷

1990, Telarc Records.

Album Notes: The Cincinnati Pops Orchestra conducted by Erich Kunzel; *Album Producer*: Robert Woods; *Engineer*: Jack Renner.

Selections: Batman (D. Elfman): 1 Suite: Batman Theme/The Bat Cave/Batman To The Rescue/The Joker's Poem/Batsuit — Charge Of The Batmobile/Waltz To The Death/Finale (15:17); The Day The Earth Stood Still (B. Herrmann): 2 Outer Space (1:48); War Of The Worlds (L. Stevens): 3 Prelude (1:10); The Black Hole (J. Barry): 4 End Title (1:41); 5 Through The Black Hole (P. Freeman)(2:53); Twilight Zone: The Movie (J. Goldsmith): 6 End Title (4:57); The Boy Who Could Fly (B. Broughton): 7 End Title (2:49); The Beastmaster (L. Holdridge): 8 Main Theme (2:07); Explorers (J. Goldsmith): 9 End Title (3:11); Dragonslayer (A. North): 10 End Title (The White Horse/Into The Sunset)(3:32); Poltergeist (J. Goldsmith): 11 Carol Ann's Theme (3:55) *Choir From School For Creative & Performing Arts*; Moonwalker (B. Broughton): 12 Suite (4:30); Star Trek V: The Final Frontier (J. Goldsmith): 13 A Busy Man (4:12); Indiana Jones And The Last Crusade (J. Williams): 14 Escape From Venice (4:46); Star Wars (J. Williams): 15 The Cantina Band (3:05); The Last Starfighter (C. Safan): 16 Main Title (2:59).

Review: See *Victory at Sea and Other Favorites* entry below.

Happy Trails ♪♪♪▷

1989, Telarc Records.

Album Notes: *Arrangers*: Tommy Newsom, Richard Hayman; The Cincinnati Pops Orchestra conducted by Erich Kunzel; *Guest Artists*: Gene Autry, Sherrill Milnes, Roy Rogers; Male Chorus Of The U.S. Air Force Singing Sergeants; *Album Producer*: Robert Woods; *Engineer*: Jack Renner.

Selections: 1 Stampede (M. Bishop)(:48); The Sons Of Katie Elder (E. Bernstein): 2 Theme (1:58); Ghost Riders In The Sky (S. Jones): 3 Ghost Riders In The Sky (3:50) *Sherrill Milnes*; The Good, The Bad And The Ugly (E. Morricone): 4 Theme (3:00) *Singing Sergeants*; Duel In The Sun (D. Tiomkin): 5 Prelude

(1:38); 6 Buggy Ride (2:14); Giant (D. Tiomkin): 7 Prelude (2:21) *Singing Sergeants*; The Alamo (D. Tiomkin/P.F. Webster): 8 The Green Leaves Of Summer (4:39) *Singing Sergeants*; The Man Who Shot Liberty Valance (B. Bacharach/H. David): 9 Theme (3:04) *Sherrill Milnes*; Johnny Guitar (V. Young/P. Lee): 10 Theme (2:18); Sunset (H. Mancini): 11 The Cowboys (3:43); 12 The Cowboy Code (Back In The Saddle Again)(G. Autry/R. Whitley)(1:24) *Gene Autry*; 13 Cowboy Songs: Wagon Wheels (B. Hill/P. DeRose)/Tumbling Tumbleweeds (B. Nolan)/Cool Water (B. Nolan)/The Lone Prairie (G.N. Allen)(8:12) *Singing Sergeants*; Mule Train (F. Glickman/J. Lange/H. Heath): 14 Mule Train (3:02) *Sherrill Milnes*; 15 Saloon Brawl (M. Bishop)(:50); The Wild Bunch (J. Fielding): 16 Theme (3:45); Lonesome Dove (B. Poledouris): 17 Theme (3:21); Oklahoma Crude (H. Mancini): 18 Theme (2:21); 19 Authentic Steam Engine (M. Bishop)(:26); 20 Orange Blossom Special (E. Rouse)(2:05); 21 Medley Of TV Western Themes: Maverick (D. Buttolph), The Rebel (R. Markowitz), Bat Masterson (B. Cordin/H. Wray), Gunsmoke (R. Koury/G. Spencer), Wyatt Earp (H. Warren), Cheyenne (W. Lava), The Big Valley (G. Duning), Have Gun Will Travel (J. Western/S. Rolfe/R. Boone)(7:11); 22 Happy Trails (D. Evans)(3:47) *Roy Rogers*.

Review: See *Victory at Sea and Other Favorites* entry below.

Hollywood's Greatest Hits: vol. 1 ♪♪♪♪▷

1987, Telarc Records.

Album Notes: *Arrangers*: Carmen Dragon, Richard Hayman; The Cincinnati Pops Orchestra conducted by Erich Kunzel; *Featured Musician*: William Tritt (piano); *Album Producer*: Robert Woods; *Engineer*: Jack Renner.

Selections: 1 20th Century-Fox Fanfare (A. Newman)(:23); Captain Blood: 2 Overture (E.W. Korngold)(3:23); Gone With The Wind: 3 Tara's Theme (M. Steiner)(3:46); Ben-Hur: 4 Parade Of The Charioteers (M. Rózsa)(3:22); Exodus: 5 Theme (E. Gold)(4:49); Doctor Zhivago: 6 Lara's Theme (M. Jarre)(5:42); Lawrence Of Arabia: 7 Theme (M. Jarre)(4:16); Romeo And Juliet: 8 Love Theme (N. Rota)(3:09); Goldfinger: 9 Theme (L. Bricusse/A. Newley)(2:50); Love Story: 10 Theme (F. Lai)(2:30); A Summer Place: 11 Theme (M. Steiner)(4:06); Jaws: 12 Theme (J. Williams)(2:25); The Summer Of '42: 13 Theme (M. Legrand) (2:41); Rocky: 14 Theme (B. Conti)(2:29); Terms Of Endearment: 15 Theme (M. Gore)(2:52); Out Of Africa: 16 Main Theme (J. Barry)(3:59); Chariots Of Fire: 17 Theme (Vangelis)(6:57).

Review: See *Victory at Sea and Other Favorites* entry below.

Hollywood's Greatest Hits: vol. 2 ♫♫♫♫

1987, Telarc Records.

Album Notes: *Arrangers*: Christopher Palmer, Crafton Beck, Mark McGurty, Paul Patterson, Richard Hayman; The Cincinnati Pops Orchestra conducted by Erich Kunzel; *Featured Musicians*: Julie Spangler (piano), Frank Proto (bass), Bill Platt (drums), Jeanne Dulaney (accordion), Paul Patterson, Tim Berens (bouzoukis/ mandolins); *Album Producer*: Robert Woods; *Engineer*: Jack Renner.

Selections: 2001: A Space Odyssey: 1 Fanfare (A. North)(1:25); Ben-Hur: 2 Prelude (M. Rozsa)(3:51); The Ten Commandments: 3 Prelude (E. Bernstein) (5:35); Friendly Persuasion: 4 Thee I Love (D. Tiomkin)(4:24); Picnic: 5 Moonglow and Theme (G. Duning/W. Hudson)(3:06); Around The World In 80 Days: 6 Theme (V. Young)(3:40); Mutiny On The Bounty: 7 Main Title (B. Kaper)(2:20); Spartacus: 8 Love Theme (A. North)(3:00); Zorba The Greek: 9 Theme (M. Theodorakis)(4:38); The Umbrellas Of Cherbourg: 10 I Will Wait For You (M. Legrand/J. Demy)(3:44); Valley Of The Dolls: 11 Theme (A. Previn)(3:47); Midnight Cowboy: 12 Theme (J. Barry)(4:18); The Godfather: 13 Theme (N. Rota) (3:52); Modern Times: 14 Smile (C. Chaplin)(3:00); Dances With Wolves: 15 Themes (J. Barry)(6:20); Far And Away: 16 Book Of Days (Enya)(3:12); Grand Canyon: 17 Theme (J. Newton Howard)(2:16).

Review: See *Victory at Sea and Other Favorites* entry below.

Movie Love Themes ♫♫

1991, Telarc Records.

Album Notes: *Arrangers*: Mark McGurty, Patrick Russ, Tommy Newsom, Nic Raine, Steven Bernstein, Hens Spencer, Don Sebesky, Erich Kunzel, Christopher Palmer, Brad Warnaar; The Cincinnati Pops Orchestra conducted by Erich Kunzel; *Featured Musicians*: Jeanne Dulaney (accordion), Angel Romero (guitar); *Album Producer*: Robert Woods; *Engineer*: Jack Renner.

Selections: On Golden Pond: 1 Main Theme (D. Grusin)(4:05); Ghost: 2 Unchained Melody (A. North)(5:07); Dick Tracy: 3 Sooner Or Later (I Always Get My Man)(S. Sondheim)(5:07); Somewhere In Time: 4 We're Losing Him (J. Barry) (4:00); Flashdance: 5 Love Theme (G. Moroder)(3:42); Raiders Of The Lost Ark: 6 Marion's Theme (J. Williams)(1:46); A Star Is Born: 7 Evergreen (P. Williams)(4:24); Flashdance: 8 Flashdance... What A Feeling (G. Moroder) (4:45); The Competition: 9 People Alone (L. Schifrin)(2:45); Shirley Valentine: 10 End Title (W. Russell)(3:32); Arthur: 11 Arthur's Theme (P. Allen/B. Bacharach/C. Cross)(3:22); Same Time Next Year: 12 The Last Time I Felt Like This (M.

Hamlisch)(5:05); Cousins: 13 Love Theme (A. Badalamenti) (2:47); 14 Waltz (A. Badalamenti) (2:28); Ice Castles: 15 Through The Eyes Of Love (M. Hamlisch) (4:13); Ghost: 16 End Title (M. Jarre) (4:20); The Deer Hunter: 17 Cavatina (S. Myers) (3:27); The Way We Were: 18 The Way We Were (M. Hamlisch)(4:31).

Review: See *Victory at Sea and Other Favorites* entry below.

Puttin' on the Ritz: The Great Hollywood Musicals ♫♫

1995, Telarc Records.

Album Notes: The Cincinnati Pops Orchestra conducted by Erich Kunzel; *Guest Artists*: Frederica von Stade, Jeremy Davenport, Michael Feinstein, Jerry Hadley, Lee Roy Reams, Bobby Short, Leslie Uggams; The Indiana University Singing Hoosiers; *Album Producer*: Robert Woods; *Engineers*: Jack Renner, Michael Bishop.

Selections: The Band Wagon: 1 That's Entertainment (H. Dietz/A. Schwartz) (3:56) *Lee Roy Reams*; The Jazz Singer: 2 Blue Skies (I. Berlin)(4:03) *Jeremy Davenport*; Top Hat: 3 Cheek To Cheek (I. Berlin)(5:22) *Frederica von Stade, Jerry Hadley*; Puttin' On The Ritz: 4 Puttin' On The Ritz (I. Berlin) (3:07) *Lee Roy Reams*; The Wizard Of Oz: 5 Over The Rainbow (H. Arlen/E.Y. Harburg)(4:15) *Frederica von Stade*; 42nd Street: 6 42nd Street (A. Dubin/H. Warren)(3:50) *Lee Roy Reams*; Hollywood Review Of 1929: 7 Singin' In The Rain (A. Freed/N.H. Brown)(3:41) *Lee Roy Reams*; Love Me Tonight: 8 Lover (R. Rodgers/L. Hart)(4:55) *Frederica von Stade*; Buck Privates: 9 Boogie Woogie Bugle Boy (D. Raye/H. Prince)(3:32) *The Osborne Sisters*; The Gay Divorcee: 10 The Continental (H. Magidson/C. Conrad)(2:37) *Frederica von Stade*; Shall We Dance: 11 They Can't Take That Away From Me (G. & I. Gershwin)(3:15) *Bobby Short*; Born To Dance: 12 I've Got You Under My Skin (C. Porter)(4:21) *Frederica von Stade*; The Harvey Girls: 13 On The Atchison, Topeka And The Santa Fe (H. Warren/J. Mercer)(5:12) *Leslie Uggams, the Singing Hoosiers*; Swing Time: 14 A Fine Romance (J. Kern/D. Fields)(4:41) *Frederica von Stade*; The Big Broadcast Of 1938: 15 Thanks For The Memory (L. Robin/R. Rainger)(3:45) *Michael Feinstein*; Gold Diggers Of 1935: 16 Lullaby Of Broadway (A. Dubin/H. Warren)(4:37) *Lee Roy Reams*.

Review: See *Victory at Sea and Other Favorites* entry below.

Round-Up ♫♫♫

1986, Telarc Records.

Album Notes: *Arrangers*: Christopher Palmer, Richard Hayman; The Cincinnati Pops Orchestra conducted by Erich

Kunzel; *Guest Artist*: Frankie Laine; Men Of The May Festival Chorus; Ron McCroby (whistler); *Album Producer*: Robert Woods; *Engineer*: Robert Woods.

Selections: 1 Sounds Of The West: Corral Scene/Round-Up/ Galloping Horse/ Horse Whinny (:53); The Lone Ranger: 2 William Tell Overture: Finale (G. Rossini)(3:33); The Magnificent Seven: 3 Theme (E. Bernstein)(5:29); The Furies: 4 Suite (F. Waxman)(4:03); 5 Round-Up: Anthology Of TV Western Themes: Bonanza/Rawhide/Wagon Train/The Rifleman (4:27) *Frankie Laine*; How The West Was Won: 6 Overture (A. Newman)(7:21); Gunfight At The O.K. Corral: 7 Gunfight At The O.K. Corral (D. Tiomkin/N. Washington)(8:33) *Frankie Laine, Men Of The May Festival Chorus*; 8 Pops Hoedown (R. Hayman)(7:10); The Big Country: 9 Theme (J. Moross)(3:01); High Noon: 10 Do Not Forsake Me Oh My Darling (D. Tiomkin/N. Washington)(2:29) *Frankie Laine*; 11 Coyote and Crackling Campfire (:58); 12 Western Medley: Introduction/Ti Yi Yippee Yippee Ay/ Shenandoah/Red River Valley/Home On The Range/Streets Of Laredo (10:05) *Men Of The May Festival Chorus*; Silverado: 13 Themes (B. Broughton)(4:12).

Review: See *Victory at Sea and Other Favorites* entry below.

Star Tracks 🎵🎵🎵🎵

1984, Telarc Records.

Album Notes: The Cincinnati Pops Orchestra conducted by Erich Kunzel; *Album Producer*: Robert Woods; *Engineer*: Jack Renner.

Selections: 1 Introduction (1:51)/Star Wars (J. Williams): Main Title (5:22); The Empire Strikes Back (J. Willams): 2 The Imperial March (2:48); Return Of The Jedi (J. Williams): 3 Luke And Leia (4:35); Superman (J. Williams): 4 Theme (4:23); Raiders Of The Lost Ark (J. Williams): 5 The Raiders' March (5:12); Star Trek (A. Courage): 6 Main Theme (3:43); Close Encounters Of The Third Kind (J. Williams): 7 Main Theme (5:57); E.T. (J. Williams): 8 The Bicycle Chase (3:50); 9 The Departure (6:29); 10 Conclusion (3:57).

Review: See *Victory at Sea and Other Favorites* entry below.

Star Tracks II 🎵🎵🎵🎵

1987, Telarc Records.

Album Notes: The Cincinnati Pops Orchestra conducted by Erich Kunzel; *Guest Artist*: Leonard Nimoy; *Album Producer*: Robert Woods; *Engineer*: Jack Renner.

Selections: Superman: 1 The Planet Krypton (J. Williams)(1:39); Back To The Future: 2 Theme (A. Silvestri)(3:18);

3 Warp Drive (:14); Star Trek I: 4 The Klingon Battle (J. Goldsmith)(5:26); Star Trek II: The Wrath Of Khan: 5 Main Title (J. Horner)(3:19); 6 Epilogue/End Credits (8:46) *Leonard Nimoy*; 7 Humpback Whale Song (1:27); Star Trek IV: The Voyage Home: 8 Main Title (L. Rosenman)(2:43); Space Camp: 9 Music (J. Williams)(3:58); Cocoon: 10 Theme (J. Horner)(6:38); Lifeforce: 11 Theme (H. Mancini)(3:34); Return Of The Jedi: 12 Parade Of The Ewoks (J. Williams)(3:38); 13 Dimensions (D. Dorsey)(4:32); The Right Stuff: 14 Music (B. Conti)(4:40).

Review: See *Victory at Sea and Other Favorites* entry below.

Symphonic Star Trek 🎵🎵🎵🎵

1996, Telarc Records.

Album Notes: The Cincinnati Pops Orchestra conducted by Erich Kunzel; *Guest Artist*: Leonard Nimoy; *Sound Effects*: Michael Bishop; *Album Producer*: Robert Woods; *Engineers*: Jack Renner, Michael Bishop.

Selections: 1 Into The Final Frontier (1:13) *Leonard Nimoy*; Star Trek: The Next Generation: 2 Main Theme (J. Goldsmith)(1:44); 3 Warp One (:15); Star Trek VI: The Undiscovered Country: 4 End Title (C. Eidelman) (4:55); 5 The Destruction Of Praxis and Its Aftermath (1:03); Star Trek: Voyager: 6 Main Theme (J. Goldsmith)(1:42); 7 Starship Flyby (:14); Star Trek: Deep Space Nine: 8 Main Theme (D. McCarthy)(2:01); 9 Alien Probe (:48); 10 Humpback Whale Song (1:27); Star Trek IV: The Voyage Home: 11 Main Title (L. Rosenman)(2:42); Star Trek: 12 Main Theme (original TV series)(A. Courage) (3:44); 13 Tribble Trouble (:38); Star Trek II: The Wrath Of Khan: Suite (J. Horner): 14 Main Title (3:16); 15 Epilogue (3:04); 16 End Credits (5:41); 17 Bird-Of-Prey Decloaking (:16); Star Trek: The Motion Picture: 18 Klingon Battle (J. Goldsmith)(5:26); 19 Main Theme (J. Goldsmith)(3:52); 20 Warp-Eight (1:06); Star Trek V: The Final Frontier: 21 A Busy Man (J. Goldsmith)(4:12); 22 Genesis Project: The Creation and Evolution Of TINSIS (2:58); The Menagerie: 23 Suite (original TV pilot)(A. Courage)(7:34); 24 Transporter (:26); Star Trek III: The Search For Spock: 25 Main Theme (J. Horner)(6:08); 26 Nexus Energy Ribbon (:59); Star Trek: Generations: 27 End Title (D. McCarthy)(4:08); 28 The Borg (:11).

Review: See *Victory at Sea and Other Favorites* entry below.

Time Warp 🎵🎵🎵🎵

1984, Telarc Records.

Album Notes: The Cincinnati Pops Orchestra conducted by Erich Kunzel; *Album Producer*: Robert Woods; *Engineer*: Jack Renner.

Selections: 1 Ascent (D. Dorsey)/Also Sprach Zarathustra (introduction) (R. Strauss) (5:39); Star Trek: The Motion Picture: 2 Main Theme (J. Goldsmith) (3:52); The Menagerie: 3 Suite (original TV pilot) (A. Courage) (7:34); Battlestar Galactica: 4 Main Theme (S. Phillips) (3:27); Superman: 5 Love Theme (J. Williams) (4:43); Star Wars: 6 Throne Room and End Title (J. Williams) (7:41); Alien: 7 Closing Title (J. Goldsmith) (2:58); 2001: A Space Odyssey: 8 On The Beautiful Blue Danube (J. Strauss, Jr.) (8:25); 9 Adagio from Gayne Ballet (A. Khatchaturian) (4:58); 10 Also Sprach Zarathustra (introduction) (reprise) (R. Strauss) (1:54).

Review: See *Victory at Sea and Other Favorites* entry below.

Victory at Sea and Other Favorites *♪♪♪♪*

1989, Telarc Records.

Album Notes: *Arrangers*: Robert Russell Bennett, Richard Hayman; The Cincinnati Pops Orchestra conducted by Erich Kunzel; *Featured Musician*: William Tritt (piano); *Album Producer*: Robert Woods; *Engineer*: Jack Renner.

Selections: Victory At Sea (R. Rodgers): 1 The Song Of The High Seas (5:06); 2 Guadalcanal March (3:08); 3 Hardwork And Horseplay (3:20); 4 Beneath The Southern Cross (3:26); 5 Mare Nostrum (6:22); The Winds Of War/War And Remembrance: 6 Love Theme (B. Cobert)(2:55); Casablanca: 7 Suite (M. Steiner) (5:37) *William Tritt*; 8 Colonel Bogey March (K.J. Alford)(2:54); Suicide Squadron: 9 Warsaw Concerto (R. Addinsell)(8:37) *William Tritt*; The Valiant Years: 10 Suite (R. Rodgers)(4:34); The Battle Of Britain: 11 Main Theme (R. Goodwin)(1:49); 12 Over There (G.M. Cohan)(1:09); The Longest Day: 13 March (P. Anka)(3:02); 14 The Generals' March (J. Goldsmith): MacArthur March/Patton Theme (4:45); 15 Armed Forces Medley: The Air Force/The Marine Corps/The Coast Guard/The Army/The Navy (3:02).

Review: One of the first labels to enter the all-digital fray, Telarc successfully made its mark by recording the Cincinnati Pops, conducted by Erich Kunzel, in a series of spectacular CDs, many using sound effects and centered around the music created for the movies.

If those recordings are truly outstanding in terms of sonic achievements, Kunzel's often pedestrian conducting leaves a lot to be desired on a purely artistic level. Particularly not known for subtlety, his recordings often take a vibrant, if hokey, approach to the most popular themes available, on the jingoistic impression that bigger might mean better.

In some ways, this thinking pays off big scale, notably in the "space"-themed recordings (*Time Warp* and *Star Tracks*,

the initial titles in the series, *Symphonic Star Trek*, and *Fantastic Journey*), where the weird sound effects add an extra dimension to the selections (both classical and from the movies) being performed. This is also the case in the two *Hollywood's Greatest Hits* albums, in which the accent is squarely on the more spectacular themes ("Parade of the Charioteers," "Tara's Theme," "Zorba the Greek," "Mutiny on the Bounty," to name a few), in a program evidently designed to appeal to even the most uneducated listener.

The approach is again quite effective in the *Victory at Sea* album where the martial nature of the selections can accomodate a grander-than-life recording.

The two western-themed albums (*Round-Up* and *Happy Trails*) are somewhat less successful, strangely enough because the addition of the guest artists (including a tired-sounding Frankie Laine reprising some of his old hits in the former), and the misguided use of the sound effects (a stampede, corral sounds, campfire and coyotes) detract from the overall effectiveness of the program.

The other albums (*Movie Love Themes*, *A Disney Spectacular* and chiefly *Puttin' on the Ritz*, with many legit stars making an appearance that is dwarfed by the orchestral playing) miss the mark and end up being glossed-over renditions that would have gained by being more restrained.

Overall, the dramatic sonic results cannot hide Kunzel's less-than-inspired direction, particularly when so many of the same selections can be found elsewhere and in much better performances.

(As an extra, the *Symphonic Star Trek* album comes with a free CD-ROM that includes, if you can access them, various space-related games.)

Composed By: Classic Film Themes from Hollywood's Masters *♪♪♪♪▽*

1997, Rhino Records.

Album Notes: *Album Producer*: Didier C. Deutsch; *Engineer*: Kevin Hodge.

Selections: King Kong: 1 Main Title (King Kong/Jungle Dance)(M. Steiner) (2:02); The Adventures of Robin Hood: 2 Main Title (1:31); 3 Banquet In The Castle (E.W. Korngold) (1:59); Gunga Din: 4 Main Title (Introduction/God Save The King/Her Majesty's Colors/Gunga Din/The Three Comrades/Guru/The Raven)(A. Newman)(1:47); Gone With The Wind: 5 Main Title (M. Steiner)(4:07); The Wizard Of Oz: 6 Main Title (1:58); 7 Cyclone (H. Stothart)(2:17); The Sea Hawk: 8 Main

Title (E.W. Korngold)(1:55); The Philadelphia Story: 9 Main Title (Florian/Opening Scene)(F. Waxman)(2:42); Northwest Passage: 10 Main Title (extended version) (H. Stothart) (2:43); Citizen Kane: 11 Main Title (B. Herrmann) (2:38); The Magnificent Ambersons: 12 Main Title (B. Herrmann) (2:39); Casablanca: 13 Main Title (Africa/La Marseillaise/Refuge/Street Scene/Orders/ Roundup/Thief)(M. Steiner)(5:19); Now Voyager: 14 Suite (M. Steiner)(5:32); The Treasure Of The Sierra Madre: 15 Suite (M. Steiner)(5:26); Madame Bovary: 16 Suite: Prelude/The Coach/The Letter/Finale (M. Rozsa)(8:28); The Bad And The Beautiful: 17 The Spellbinder (End Title)(D. Raksin)(2:19); Raintree County: 18 Overture (Flash Perkins' Theme/The Song Of Raintree County/Susanna And Johnny's Love Theme)(J. Green)(3:31); North By Northwest: 19 The Wild Ride (B. Herrmann)(2:49); Ben-Hur: 20 Overture (6:32); 21 Circus Parade (Parade Of The Charioteers)(M. Rozsa)(2:13); How The West Was Won: 22 Main Title (A. Newman)(3:08); Doctor Zhivago: 23 Then It's A Gift (End Title)(M. Jarre) (2:38).

Review: This compilation presents some 40 years of movie music condensed on one album, as seen through some of the most remarkable films made in Hollywood, from *King Kong* to *Doctor Zhivago*. The moods vary from track to track, and explore almost every cinematographic genre, from swashbucklers to romantic dramas, from war films to thrillers, from epics to westerns. But even though the scope is broad and varied, the ultimate factor that presides over the compilation is the overall quality that pervades it, with Max Steiner, Erich-Wolfgang Korngold, Miklos Rozsa, Alfred Newman, and Bernard Herrmann, among some of the talented film composers represented. In the process, some selections are found here for the first time on compact disc, including *The Philadelphia Story, Northwest Passage, The Treasure of the Sierra Madre,* and *Madame Bovary,* all of them in their original soundtrack recordings. Nothing but the best...

Country Goes to the Movies
♫♫♫♫

1994, Risky Business/Sony Music Special Products.

Album Notes: *Album Producer:* Nick Shaffran; *Engineer:* Tom Ruff.

Selections: High Noon: 1 Do Not Forsake Me (D. Tiomkin/N. Washington)(2:27) *Tex Ritter*; Thunder Road: 2 Ballad Of Thunder Road (R. Mitchum/D. Raye) (2:54) *Robert Mitchum*; North To Alaska: 3 North To Alaska (M. Phillips)(2:47) *Johnny Horton*; Five Minutes To Live: 4 Five Minutes To Live (J. Cash) (2:02) *Johnny Cash*; Your Cheatin' Heart: 5 Your Cheatin' Heart

(H. Williams) (2:08) *Hank Williams Jr.*; Water Hole #3: 6 The Ballad Of Water Hole #3 (Code Of The West)(B. Wells/D. Grusin)(2:18) *Roger Miller*; I Walk The Line: 7 I Walk The Line (J. Cash)(2:55) *Johnny Cash*; Cisco Pike: 8 Michoacan (A. Allen/K. Fowley)(3:00) *Kris Kristofferson*; Every Which Way But Loose: 9 Every Which Way But Loose (S. Dorff/M. Brown/T. Garrett)(2:50) *Eddie Rabbitt*; Honeysuckle Rose: 10 On The Road Again (W. Nelson)(2:32) *Willie Nelson*; Urban Cowboy: 11 Stand By Me (B.E. King/J. Leiber/M. Stoller)(3:35) *Mickey Gilley*; Honkytonk Man: 12 Honkytonk Man (D. Blackwell)(2:47) *Marty Robbins*.

Review: This is a fun album, even if you don't particularly care for country music. But producer Nick Shaffran, who had the good idea of compiling together country songs that were created for the movies, hit the mark with this one. Kicking it off with Tex Ritter's version of "Do Not Forsake Me," from *High Noon,* a logical choice since the song started a trend. The set moves on to a variety of film tunes, performed by the singers and/or songwriters who created them, including Johnny Cash, Johnny Horton, Roger Miller, Hank Williams, Jr., and Kris Kristofferson, among others. The surprise here is Robert Mitchum singing the "Ballad Of Thunder Road" in a fairly convincing and ingratiating way. Don't deny yourself a little guilty pleasure, try to find the set: you won't regret it.

Digital Space ♫♫♫♫♫

1985, Varese-Sarabande Records.

Album Notes: The London Symphony Orchestra, conducted by Morton Gould; *Album Producer:* Brian B. Culverhouse; *Engineer:* Bruce Rothar.

Selections: Windjammer (M. Gould): 1 Main Title (3:00); The Big Country (J. Moross): 2 Main Title (3:11); Airport (A. Newman): 3 Main Title (3:34); The Red Pony (A. Copland): 4 Morning On The Ranch (4:27); Things To Come (A. Bliss): 5 Epilogue (3:02); That Hamilton Woman (M. Rozsa): 6 Love Theme (4:48); Star Wars (J. Williams): 7 Main Title (5:52); 8 Princess Leia Theme (5:33); Tribute To A Badman (M. Rozsa): 9 Suite (4:51); Passionate Friends (R. Addinsell): 10 Main Title (4:19); 49th Parallel (R. Vaughan Williams): 11 Prelude (2:26); Spitfire (W. Walton): 12 Prelude And Fugue (8:09).

Review: This spectacular digital recording is a magnificent showcase for the orchestra, its conductor, and, more generally, film music of the higher kind. While it offers some obvious choices (*Star Wars,* for instance), it also has the infinite merit of providing rarer selections, such as Arthur Bliss' *Things to Come,* Rozsa's *Tribute to a Badman* and *That Hamilton*

Woman, or Gould's own *Windjammer*. Adding to the pleasure, is the impeccable performance by the London Symphony Orchestra, truly one of the greatest film music orchestras in the world.

Epic Films

Great Epic Film Scores ♪♪♪♪

1993, Cloud Nine Records.

Album Notes: *Music*: Miklos Rozsa, Dimitri Tiomkin; Orchestras conducted by Miklos Rozsa, Dimitri Tiomkin; *Album Supervisor*: David Wishart; *Engineer*: Gus Shaw.

Selections: El Cid (M. Rozsa): 1 Overture (3:26); 2 Main Title (2:43); 3 Thirteen Knights (2:33); 4 Pride And Sorrow (2:14); 5 Scene d'amour (4:18); 6 El Cid March (3:20); 7 Exit Music: "The Falcon And The Dove" (2:03); 55 Days At Peking (D. Tiomkin): 8 Overture (2:54); 9 Prelude (3:02); 10 Murder Of The German Ambassador (2:13); 11 The Orphan And The Major (Moonfire)(5:50); 12 Attack On The French Legation (2:50); 13 Intermezzo: So Little Time (2:15); The Fall Of The Roman Empire (D. Tiomkin): 14 Fanfares And Flourishes (:51); 15 Prelude (2:42); 16 Livius' Arrival (1:03); 17 Old Acquaintances (4:32); 18 Decoy Patrol/Battle In The Forest/Reinforcements (4:46); 19 Intermezzo: Livius And Lucilla (2:17); 20 The New God (2:23); The Magnificent Showman (D. Tiomkin): 21 John Wayne March (2:15); 22 Main Title: "Circus World" (2:21); 23 Buffalo Gal (1:50); 24 Toni And Giovanna (1:47); 25 In Old Vienna (6:15); 26 Exit Music: "Circus World" (reprise)(2:21).

Review: In the 1960s, when Hollywood had turned away from super-productions as being too costly and with little box office appeal, showman Samuel Bronson produced several large-scale films made in Europe that captured the imagination of filmgoers everywhere and almost single-handedly kept the epic genre alive. Four of these "gargantuan wedges of living history" are represented here by the scores written for them by two of Hollywood's most respected composers, Miklos Rozsa and Dimitri Tiomkin.

No one can dispute the popular success of *El Cid*, *The Fall of the Roman Empire*, or *55 Days At Peking*, respectively set in medieval Spain, Roman Italy, and turn-of-the century China. These massive cinematographic reconstructions not only ignited the screen, they elicited from their respective composers scores that have endured as hallmarks of the genre. Perhaps less well known is *The Magnificent Showman*, known here as *Circus World*, which equals and at times surpassed in scope and drama the most famous circus film of all, Cecil B. De Mille's

The Greatest Show On Earth. These excerpts from Tiomkin's score, presented here on CD for the first time, make this album all the more valuable.

Warriors of the Silver Screen
♪♪♪♪♪

1997, Silva America Records.

Album Notes: *Orchestrations*: Leonid Raab, Charles Gerhardt, John Scott, Philip Lane, Arthur Morton, Sonny Kompanek, Mike Townend, Miklos Rozsa, Lawrence Ashmore, Edward B. Powell, Maurice de Packt, Nic Raine, James Horner, Greig McRitchie, Bernard Herrmann; The City Of Prague Philharmonic, conducted by Paul Bateman, Nic Raine, Kenneth Alwyn; The Crouch End Festival Chorus, conducted by David Temple; *Album Producer*: James Fitzpatrick; *Engineer*: John L. Timperley.

Selections: CD 1: Taras Bulba (F. Waxman): 1 Overture/Sleigh Ride (2:46); 2 Torchlight Parade (2:05); 3 The Birth Of Andrei (Pastorale)(2:08); 4 The Ride To Dubno (4:53); Anthony And Cleopatra (J. Scott): 5 Suite (6:40); The 300 Spartans (M. Hadjidakis): 6 March (3:58); First Knight (J. Goldsmith): 7 Arthur's Fanfare (:44); 8 No Surrender (5:25); 9 Arthur's Farewell (5:00); Rob Roy (C. Burwell): 10 Rob And Mary (3:32); The War Lord (J. Moross): 11 Prelude and Main Title (4:19); El Cid (M. Rozsa): 12 Overture (3:32); 13 Love Theme (4:13); Henry V (P. Doyle): 14 Prelude/O For A Muse Of Fire (4:29); 15 St. Crispin's Day (5:14); 16 Non Nobis Domine (3:44).

CD 2: Prince Valiant (F. Waxman): 1 Suite: Prelude/King Aguar's Escape/The Fens/The First Chase/The Tournament/Sir Brack's Death and Finale (10:00); Spartacus (A. North): 2 Main Title (3:38); 3 Love Theme (2:47); The Last Valley (J. Barry): 4 The Last Valley (3:36); Braveheart (J. Horner): 5 End Title (7:03); The Thief Of Bagdad (M. Rozsa): 6 Overture (2:19); 7 The Love Of The Princess (4:50); 8 Flying Horse Galop (1:36); 9 The Market At Basra (3:00); Conan The Barbarian (B. Poledouris): 10 Prologue/Anvil Of Crom (4:33); Ben-Hur (M. Rozsa): 11 Prelude (3:40); 12 Love Theme (2:57); 13 Parade Of The Charioteers (3:36); Jason And The Argonauts (B. Herrmann): 14 Prelude (1:57); The Vikings (M. Nascimbene): 15 Rape and Pillage (1:33); 16 Ragnar Returns (2:33); 17 Dancing On The Oars (The Viking Drinking Song)(1:31); 18 Love Scene (2:30); 19 Voyage and Landing In Britain (2:40); 20 Attack On The Castle (3:31); 21 Funeral and Finale (3:32).

Review: In another spectacular display of the vast resources offered by The City of Prague Philharmonic, Silva Screen has recorded this great set programmed around the themes written for the screen warriors, a concept that has been stretched a bit to include selections from John Scott's *Anthony and Cleoptara* and Miklos Rozsa's *The Thief of Bagdad,* poetic license permitting such asides.

The least that can be said about this 2-CD set is that it is truly sensational: the sound is rich and brassy, the performance excitingly vibrant, and the selections chosen with care. The high points of these two CDs are Franz Waxman's seldom heard suite from *Taras Bulba;* Manos Hadjidakis' "March" from *The 300 Spartans,* also a true discovery; John Barry's theme from *The Last Valley,* a score that deserves to be reissued on CD; and Mario Nascimbene's suite from *The Vikings,* which is far superior to the original soundtrack, at least where sonics are concerned.

Paul Bateman, Nic Raine and Kenneth Alwyn take the orchestra through the various pacings in each score with great flair and a thorough understanding of the importance of the music.

Fantasy, Horror, Science Fiction

The Best of Stephen King: volume 1 ♫♫

1993, edel America Records.

Album Notes: *Music:* Wendy Carlos, Rachel Elking, Mark Shaiman, John S. Harrison Jr., John Beal, Jonathan Elias, John Carpenter, Alan Howarth, Harold Faltermeyer; *Album Producer:* Arch Stanton.

Selections: The Shining (W. Carlos/R. Elking): 1 Main Title Theme (3:28) *Chuck Cirino;* 2 Music For Strings, Percussion And Celesta (B. Bartok)(7:48); Misery (M. Shaiman): 3 Suite: Number One Fan/Buster's Last Stand/Misery's Return (16:51); Creepshow (J. Harrison, Jr.): 4 Main Theme (3:32) *Chuck Cirino;* Graveyard Shift (J. Beal): 5 Trailer Music (1:25); Children Of The Corn (J. Elias): 6 Suite: Main Title/Barn Run/Murder/The Arrival/Chase Theme/ The Invasion/Burning The Cornfield/ Resolution (16:45); Christine (J. Carpenter/A. Howarth): 7 Car Obsession/Christine Attacks/Plymouth Fury (4:23); 8 The Rape (1:01); 9 Junkins And Regenration (4:23); 10 Arnie's Love Theme (1:17); The Running Man (H. Faltermeyer): 11 Mick's Broadcast/Attack (3:10).

Review: These cover versions of films inspired by the writings of Stephen King may be of interest to fans of the genre, but the average collector will probably be turned off by the lack of invention in the music and in the performances. The choice cuts here would appear to be Bela Bartok's "Music For Strings, Percussion and Celesta," which can be heard in much better

recordings on a variety of classical labels, and Marc Shaiman's long suite from *Misery,* which is no match for the actual soundtrack recording. The rest is strictly routine, and not very good.

The Cult Files ♫♫♫♫

1996, Silva Screen Records.

Album Notes: *Orchestrations:* Laurie Johnson, Kevin Townend, Mike Towened, John Debney, Mark McKenzie, Arthur Morton, Christopher Palmer, Nic Raine, Steve Bartek; *Synthesizers:* Mark Ayres; The Royal Philharmonic Concert Orchestra, conducted by Mike Townend; The City Of Prague Philharmonic Orchestra, conducted by Nic Raine, Paul Bateman; *Album Producer:* James Fitzpatrick; *Engineers:* Mike Ross-Trevor, John L. Timperley, Mark Ayres.

Selections: CD 1: TV Themes: The X-Files: 1 TV Version (M. Snow)(3:28); The Avengers: 2 Pre-Credits and Theme (L. Johnson)(3:17); The Saint: 3 Opening and Closing Themes (E. Astley)(3:05); The Prisoner: 4 Main Titles (R. Grainer) (3:23); Doctor Who: 5 Theme (R. Grainer)(2:21); Blake's Seven: 6 Theme (D. Simpson)(4:25); Red Dwarf: 7 Interlude/Main Theme (H. Goodall/ I. Hu)(4:56) *Jill Washington;* Hawaii Five-0: 8 Theme (M. Stevens)(3:21); Perry Mason: 9 Park Avenue Beat (F. Steiner)(4:04); Ironside: 10 Theme (Q. Jones)(3:59); Mission: Impossible: 11 The Plot/Main Theme (L. Schifrin)(4:15); The Incredible Hulk: 12 Theme (J. Harnell)(3:00); Knight Rider: 13 Theme (G. Larson/S. Phillips)(2:36); Airwolf: 14 Theme (S. Levay)(3:00); Star Trek: 15 Theme (A. Courage)(2:22); Babylon 5: 16 Theme (C. Franke)(2:59); Twin Peaks: 17 Theme (A. Badalamenti) (2:43); V The Series: 18 Theme (D. McCarthy) (2:43); Seaquest DsV: 19 Theme (concert version) (J. Debney)(3:20).

CD 2: Film Themes: 2001: A Space Odyssey: 1 Also Sprach Zarathustra (R. Strauss)(1:52); Excalibur: 2 O Fortuna (from Carmina Burana)(C. Orff)(2:45); Alien: 3 End Title (J. Goldsmith)(3:53); Escape From New York: 4 End Titles (J. Carpenter/ A. Howarth)(4:13); Blade Runner: 5 End Titles (Vangelis)(4:45); Halloween: 6 Main Title (J. Carpenter)(2:23); The Omen: 7 Ave Satani (J. Goldsmith)(3:52); Mad Max Beyond Thunderdome: 8 Thunderdome Fanfare/"I Ain't Captain Walker" (M. Jarre)(4:59); Superman: 9 Love Theme (J. Williams)(6:12); Batman: 10 Theme (D. Elfman)(3:06); Body Heat: 11 Theme (J. Barry)(4:33); Somewhere In Time: 12 Theme (J. Barry)(6:12); Taxi Driver: 13 Night Piece (B. Herrmann)(4:02); The Blues Brothers: 14 Theme From Peter Gunn (H. Mancini) (2:48).

Review: There are many delights here for one to enjoy, proof positive that the folks at Silva Screen are doing something right. The concept of the *Cult Files,* obviously inspired by the success of television's *The X-Files,* is one that has validity, and that yields in this case many fun selections. The accent here is squarely on the tried-and-true, though here and there some themes creep up that are not run-of-the-mill, with the two CDs organized by genres, with the first focusing on television, and the second on movies. The only odd-man out in this set is the "Theme from Peter Gunn," credited to *The Blues Brothers* (?). Other than that, the selections are quite fun to listen to and effectively compete with the original versions.

50 Years Of Classic Horror Film Music ♪♪♪♪

1987, Silva Screen Records.

Album Notes: *Music:* Jerry Goldsmith, James Bernard, Christopher Komeda, Franz Waxman, Max Steiner, Harry Robinson, John McCabe, Ennio Morricone, Christopher Young, David Whitaker; The National Philharmonic Orchestra and Chorus, conducted by Stanley Black; The Hammer City Orchestra, conducted by Philip Martell; The National Philharmonic Orchestra, conducted by Fred Steiner; Orchestra conducted by Paul Francis Witt; *Album Producers:* David Stoner, James Fitzpatrick.

Selections: The Omen (J. Goldsmith): 1 Suite (10:38); She (J. Bernard): 2 Suite (5:30); Rosemary's Baby (C. Komeda): 3 Lullaby (2:39); Dr. Jekyll & Mr. Hyde (F. Waxman): 4 Suite (10:20); King Kong (M. Steiner): 5 The Entrance Of Kong (4:19); The Vampire Lovers (H. Robinson): 6 Suite (3:28); Fear In The Night (J. McCabe): 7 Suite (4:24); Exorcist II: The Heretic (E. Morricone): 8 Regan's Theme (4:12); Hellraiser (C. Young): 9 Resurrection (2:32); Doctor Jekyll & Sister Hyde (D. Whitaker): 10 Suite (7:34).

Review: Yet another compilation from Silva Screen, which proves that the label has many fancy ideas up its corporate sleeve, and manages to come up with the right combinations and the right numbers. The concept here is horror classics, represented by long suites from *The Omen* and *Dr. Jekyll and Mr. Hyde,* and themes from *Rosemary's Baby, The Vampire Lovers, Exorcist II,* and the tongue-in-cheek *Doctor Jekyll and Sister Hyde,* among others. One might question the presence of *King Kong* in this compilation, when so many other scores probably would have fit the purpose more adequately, but who is to quibble when the pleasure is almost unending.

Horror! ♪♪♪

1996, Silva Screen Records.

Album Notes: *Arrangements:* Gerard Schurmann, Philip Lane, Buxton Orr, Humphrey Searle, Carlo Martelli, James Bernard,

Benjamin Frankel; The Westminster Philharmonic Orchestra, conducted by Kenneth Alwyn; *Album Producer:* David Wishart; *Engineer:* Mike Ross-Trevor.

Selections: Horrors Of The Black Museum (G. Schurmann): 1 Overture (3:30); The Haunting (H. Searle): 2 The History Of Hill House (4:31); Corridors Of Blood (B. Orr): 3 Prelude (1:30); Night Of The Demon (C. Parker): 4 Overture (3:14); The Abominable Snowman (H. Searle): 5 Main Title (1:30); Witchfinder General (P. Ferris): 6 Prelude/Romanza (6:20); The Curse Of The Mummy's Tomb (C. Martelli): 7 The Tomb/The Desert (5:08); Konga (G. Schurmann): 8 Overture (2:32); Fiend Without A Face (B. Orr): 9 Main Title/Love Theme (4:24); The Devil Rides Out (J. Bernard): 10 The Power Of Evil (1:29); Curse Of The Werewolf (B. Frankel): 11 Prelude (1:28); 12 Pastorale (2:10); 13 The Werewolf At Bay and Apotheosis (6:20).

Review: Although Silva's genre-oriented compilations vary wildly in quality, their British horror film collections have always been superb, and this is the cream of the crop: a highly enjoyable collection of works by British composers who bring their classical and concert training to bear on some silly but evocative supernatural thrillers. Although the expected hyperventilating horror sound of the 50s and 60s is present in titles like Buxton Orr's *Fiend Without A Face* and Gerard Schurmann's *Horrors of the Black Museum,* there's a surprising level of sophistication and tonal beauty to be found in suites like Paul Ferris' *Witchfinder General* with its beautiful "Greensleaves" love theme, Humphrey Searle's *The Abominable Snowman* with its glittering orientalisms, and Carlo Martelli's *Curse of the Mummy's Tomb,* while the climactic suite from Benjamin Frankel's *Curse of the Werewolf* is a standout with its furious, driving serial attack music. This is music that stands up on its own beautifully and this collection almost never lags in interest. A terrific recording, robustly conducted by Kenneth Alwyn with the Westminster Philharmonic Orchestra.

Jeff Bond

The Horror Films Collection ♪♪♪♪

1995, DRG Records.

Album Notes: *Album Producer:* Claudio Fuiano.

Selections: 1 Dario's Theme (M. Werba)(4:04); Il trono di fuoco (The Throne Of Fire)(B. Nicolai): 2 Occhi fiammanti (Main Title)(2:05); 3 Sangue e amore (1:59); 4 La vendetta (2:30); 5 Il giudice sanguinario (2:25); 6 Giustizia sia fatta! (3:17); 7 Il trono di fuoco (1:30); 8 Il trono di fuoco (2:45); La notte dei diavoli (Night Of The Devils)(G. Gaslini): 9 Suite (9:00); 7 Note

In Nero (Seven Notes In Black)(F. Bixio/F. Frizzi/V. Tempera): 10 Sette note (3:21); 11 Tracce sul muro (3:12); La cripta e l'Incubo (The Nightmare Crypt) (C. Savina): 12 La maledizione di Karnstein (Main Title)(1:44); 13 Il ritratto di Sheena (1:00); 14 Cena al castello (:43); 15 L'incubo nella cripta (1:35); 16 Laura posseduta (1:14); 17 Il presagio (1:14); 18 Finale (1:14); Profondo rosso (Deep Red)(G. Gaslini): 19 20th Anniversary Special Suite (7:26); L'isola misteriosa e il Capitano Nemo (The Mysterious Island Of Captain Nemo)(G. Ferrio): 20 L'isola misteriosa (3:23); Il monaco (The Monk)(P. Piccioni): 21 Suite (6:36); Terrore nello spazio (Planet Of The Vampires)(G. Marinuzzi Jr.): 22 Suite (11:00); Passi di morte perduti nel buio (Deadly Steps Lost In The Dark)(R. Ortolani): 23 Main Title (2:40).

Review: This collection has the great merit to bring together several themes from Italian films that are not available elsewhere, all of them dealing with horror films, a genre that has many exponents over there. What is of particular interest here is the caliber of the composers involved, including Bruno Nicolai, Piero Piccioni, Riz Ortolani, and Carlo Savina, among others. (The only member of this elite not included here is Ennio Morricone, whose contract stipulates that his music cannot be coupled with that of others.) And while the quality of the music is at times uneven, *The Throne of Fire, Night Of The Devils* and particularly *The Mysterious Island of Captain Nemo* are quite enjoyable.

Sci-Fi At The Movies 🎵🎵🎵

1995, Label X Records.

Album Notes: *Music:* Bernard Herrmann, James Horner, John Charles, Miklos Rozsa, John Scott, Stu Phillips; The Royal Philharmonic Orchestra, conducted by Tony Bremner; The London Symphony Orchestra, conducted by James Horner; The New Zealand Symphony Orchestra, conducted by William Southgate; The Royal Philharmonic Orchestra, conducted by Miklos Rozsa; The Unione musicisti di Roma, conducted by John Scott; The London Philharmonic Orchestra, conducted by Franco Collura; *Album Producer:* John Steven Lasher; *Engineers:* Bob Auger, Keith Grant, John Richards, Gary Clark, Robert Hagen, Paolo Enditti.

Selections: The Day The Earth Stood Still (B. Herrmann): 1 Lincoln Memorial (1:21); 2 Arlington Cemetary (1:44); Krull (J. Horner): 3 Main Title and Colwyn's Arrival (7:35); 4 Love Theme (2:36); 5 The Widow's Lullaby (5:03); 6 Epilogue and End Credits (4:51); The Quiet Earth (J. Charles): 7 Sunrise (3:25); 8 Zak Takes Over (2:14); 9 Moving Up In The World (:51); 10 Last Love Scene (1:14); 11 Finale (4:16); Time After Time (M. Rozsa): 12 Warner Bros. Fanfare (M. Steiner) and Prelude (2:09); 13 Vaporizing Equalizer (2:12); 14 Time Machine Waltz (4:00); 15 Redwoods (2:33); 16 Finale (4:01); Yor, The Hunter From The Future (J. Scott): 17 Death Rules This Land (4:08); 18 Pursued By Pygmies (2:31); 19 Queen Roa (1:50); 20 Into The Storm (1:39); Battlestar Galactica (S. Phillips): 21 Main Title (1:26).

Review: John Lasher, producer at Label X, didn't have to look very far to put this compilation together: many of these scores are already available on his label, and all he had to do was to cull a couple of selections from each one of them to put this CD together. There are advantages and disadvantages to the method. One, of course, is the fact that the composers represented here rank among the best: no one is going to argue with selections written by Bernard Herrmann, James Horner, Miklos Rozsa, or John Scott, particularly for films like *The Day the Earth Stood Still, Krull, Time After Time,* or *Yor, The Hunter from the Future.* But since many of these are also available on the complete soundtrack recordings, it may seem redundant to own them and this CD. As a short cut to a genre that has a great deal of popular appeal, however, the CD is also a welcome addition to any library. So, if you don't already have the individual albums, you might want to give it a shot. Otherwise, unless you are a completist, you might want to skip it.

Themes from Classic Science Fiction, Fantasy and Horror Films 🎵🎵🎵🎵

1993, Varese-Sarabande Records.

Album Notes: Orchestra conducted by Dick Jacobs; *Album Producers:* Robert Townson, Dub Taylor.

Selections: The Mole People (H.J. Salter): 1 Treacherous Trek (3:17); The Creature From The Black Lagoon (H.J. Salter): 2 The Monster Attacks (2:05); This Island Earth (H. Stein): 3 Main Title/Shooting Stars (4:01); The Incredible Shrinking Man (F. Carling/E. Lawrence): 4 Main Theme (2:58); It Came From Outer Space (H. Stein): 5 Visitors From Sapce (1:47); The Creature Walks Among Us (H. Mancini): 6 Stalking The Creature (2:00); The House Of Frankenstein (H.J. Salter/P. Dessau): 7 Main Title (2:53); The Horror Of Dracula (J. Bernard): 8 Main Title/Dracula's Feast Of Blood (3:07); Tarantula (H. Mancini): 9 Main Title (1:57); The Son Of Dracula (H.J. Salter): 10 Main Title (1:12); The Revenge Of The Creature (H. Stein): 11 Main Title (1:36); The Deadly Mantis (W. Lava): 12 Winged Death (2:59).

Review: This album, initially released by Coral in the early 1960s, is actually a lot of fun: not only does it regroup many themes from horror films that you can't find anywhere else, but the whole thing is played strictly for the heck of it, with over-the-top performances well designed to try and scare the devil out of any listener. The themes here stem from some of the films made during the 1950s at Universal, a studio which in its heyday defined horror, but not the type of horror associated today with the more ghoulish and gory films that have become a regular staple in the genre. The monsters then were implausibly human-looking, expressionless, and scary only to the inevitable female star whose job opportunity it was to scream on cue. It is this world that Dick Jacobs recreated with his orchestra, in this collection which evokes *The Creature,* the many *Frankenstein* and *Dracula* films, the *Shrinking Man,* and the aptly-named *It.* A ton of fun that awaits your pleasure...

The Monster Music of Hans J. Salter & Frank Skinner ♪♪♪♪

1995, Marco Polo Records.

Album Notes: The Moscow Symphony Orchestra, conducted by William T. Stromberg; *Orchestrations:* John Morgan; *Album Producer:* Betta International; *Engineers:* Edvard Shakhnazarian, Vitaly Ivanov.

Selections: Son Of Frankenstein (F. Skinner): 1 Universal Signature (:17); 2 Main Title (2:58); 3 The Message (2:08); 4 The General (1:06); 5 Discovery/Blute Solo (4:19); 6 The Examination/Looking For A Monster (8:29); 7 Death Of Ygor (2:20); 8 Monster's Rampage (4:06); 9 Finale/The Cast (:39); The Invisible Man Returns (F. Skinner/H.J. Salter): 10 Universal Signature (:15); 11 Main Title (2:13); 12 Two Hours To Live (2:57); 13 Together (4:13); 14 Resting (3:27); 15 The Ghost (2:09); 16 The Return (3:36); 17 End Title (3:04); The Wolf Man (F. Skinner/H.J. Salter): 18 Universal Signature (:14); 19 Main Title (2:00); 20 The Telescope (1:23); 21 Wolf-Bane (4:12); 22 The Kill (1:04); 23 Bela's Funeral (6:56); 24 Desperation (2:58); 25 Sir John's Discovery (8:31).

Review: Featuring the work of Universal's mainstay horror composers, Hans Salter and Frank Skinner, this CD features lengthy suites (25 minute average) from three terrific horror scores of the 1940s. Skinner's solo *Son of Frankenstein* erupts into a cacophony of plodding brass in a footstep pattern over swirling strings, snare drums, and cymbals. *The Invisible Man Returns* captures a lilting love theme for violin which is contrasted with a solemn motif for the villain's unsightly affliction. *The Wolf-Man* contrasts poignant and stately melodies with snarling werewolf attack music, punctuated by furious, ani-

malistic footfalls from low strings and winds. A full-blooded score in every sense of the word. While these patriarchal horror movies sustain a charm more for their nostalgic style and absorbing ability to entertain than their fright capacity, their music remains ferociously potent. Ignored for years, it is with extreme gratitude that I find scores like these singled out for restoration and preservation. Now these venerable classics can be heard in the kind of digital glory they've never had before. Thorough liner notes provide comprehensive documentation of the music and these recordings thereof. Have a listen, and recapture an era of horror moviemaking long since past, yet fondly recalled by many.

Randall Larson

Monstrous Movie Music

Monstrous Movie Music ♪♪♪

1996, Monstrous Movie Music Records.

Album Notes: The Radio Symphony Orchestra of Cracow, conducted by Masatoshi Mitsumoto; *Music Restoration:* Kathleen Mayne; *Album Producer:* David Schechter; *Engineer:* Matlgorzata Polanska.

Selections: The Mole People (H. Stein/H. Roemheld): 1 Trademark (:25); 2 Prologue (:52); 3 Main Title (1:26); Them! (B. Kaper): 4 Main Title (1:00); 5 Lost Girl (1:59); 6 Wreck/Intercommunication (3:14); 7 Little Girl Wakens (:40); 8 Ant Hole/Burning The Ant Hole (3:27); 9 The Descent/Ant Chamber (4:11); 10 Conference Table/The Wall Map (3:08); 11 Interior Of Morgue (1:39); 12 Military Takes Over/Through The Tunnels (3:04); 13 Ant Hole #2/End Of The Monsters (1:22); 14 Ant Fugue (3:29); It Came From Outer Space (H. Stein/I. Gertz/H. Mancini): 15 Main Title (:27); 16 Sand Rock (:51); 17 Star Gazing (1:37); 18 Visitors From Space (2:37); 19 The Thing Follows (1:31); 20 Mysterious Desert (1:48); 21 Globs Give Instructions (1:55); 22 Prospector Globbed (1:45); 23 Dr. Snell Disappears (:46); 24 Kidnapping Ellen (1:31); 25 Glob Frank Killed (2:15); 26 Killing Glob Ellen (1:10); 27 End Title (:56); 28 End Cast (1:02); It Came From Beneath The Sea (M. Bakaleinikoff): 29 Atom-Powered Submarine (:21); 30 Main Title (1:28); 31 Love By The Sea (:49); 32 Mister Monster #2 (:43); 33 Tentacle/It vs. Golden Gate Bridge (1:04); 34 Mister Monster (1:14); 35 Suckers In The Streets! (:51); 36 Monster Beneath The Sea/Destroying The Beast (2:31); 37 Bakaleinikoda (:15); 38-42 Bonus Tracks.

Review: See entry below.

More Monstrous Movie Music 𝄢𝄢𝄢ᵛ

1996, Monstrous Movie Music Records.

Album Notes: The Radio Symphony Orchestra Of Cracow, conducted by Masatoshi Mitsumoto; *Music Restoration*: Kathleen Mayne; *Album Producer*: David Schechter; *Engineer*: Matlgorzata Polanska.

Selections: Tarantula (H. Stein/H. Mancini): 1 Introduction (:11); 2 Main Title (1:11); 3 Gruesome Corpse (1:15); 4 Radioactive Research (1:05); 5 Spider On The Loose (3:05); 6 Burying The Evidence (1:35); 7 Side Effects (1:15); 8 Big Bunnies (:56); 9 Agar To The Rescue (1:23); 10 Evening Snack (1:33); 11 Bringing Down The House (2:51); 12 Blasted Arachnid (1:50); 13 End Title (:32); The Beast From 20,000 Fathoms (D. Buttolph): 14 Main Title (1:11); 15 Far North/Expedition/Monster (2:06); 16 Lost Scientist/Beast Sighted (2:20); 17 Chord (:09); 18 Extinguish The Lighthouse (:57); 19 Diving Bell (1:13); 20 Bell And Octopus (1:54); 21 Absent Professor (1:31); 22 Monster Does Manhattan (1:57); 23 Herald Square/Germs (1:14); 24 Up The Coaster/Finale (4:14); The Monolith Monster (I. Gertz): 25 Main Title (1:03); Gorgo (A.F. Lavagnino): 26 Main Title (1:48); 27 Restless Sea/Underwater/Tidal Wave (2:21); 28 On The Island/Inner Room (2:08); 29 Gorgo Sighted/Gorgo Surfaces (1:48); 30 Fire Fight (1:23); 31 Making A Plan/Ocean Voyage (1:35); 32 Gorgo Escapes/Mama Rises (1:14); 33 Jet Alert/Battleship Barrage (1:07); 34 Military Might/Torpedo Attack (2:05); 35 Big Ben Demolished (:56); 36 London Trampled (1:09); 37 Return To Sea/End Title (2:09).

Review: Fans of classic monster movies, the kind of Saturday matinee material that featured big-eyed mutated insects and otherworldly aliens, should enjoy this two-volume release, both for its nostalgic value and, on occasion, superior musical material. *Monstrous Movie Music* contains suites from four '50s sci-fi movies — brief cues from *The Mole People*, music by Herman Stein and Heinz Roemheld; a suite from Bronislau Kaper's music from the bona-fide classic *Them!*; selections from the entertaining *It Came From Outer Space*, music by Herman Stein, Irving Gertz and Henry Mancini; concluding with nine minutes of Misca Bakleinikoff's *It Came From Beneath the Sea*, a routine monster opus best known for Ray Harryhausen's visual effects. All of the music is basically composed in the same form of most genre scores from this period — mainly bombastic, at times shrill, and somewhat redundant. In *More Monstrous Movie Music*, the scores represented include Stein and Mancini's *Tarantula*; a suite from David Buttolph's *The Beast From 20,000 Fathoms*; the main title from Gertz's *The Monolith Monsters*; and nearly 20 minutes from Angelo La-

vagnino's *Gorgo*, which was among the last — and easily one of the best — entries into the "giant monster" film cycle. This score has always been a listener favorite, with many lyrical moments interspersed amongst all of the bombastic "monster music" cliches many of the other scores contain. Excellent liner notes help make this an attractive package, despite the fact that the Radio Symphony of Cracow, here conducted by Masatoshi Mitsumoto, seems to have trouble hitting the high notes at times (particularly on "Gorgo"). Otherwise, the performance is competent and the albums themselves — while not containing the kind of music that lends itself easily to repeated listenings — are a pleasing release for genre buffs.

Andy Dursin

Vampire Circus: The Essential Vampire Theme Collection 𝄢𝄢𝄢ᵛ

1993, Silva Screen Records.

Album Notes: *Music*: Gerald Fried, David Whitaker, Brad Fiedel, Chuck Cirino, Jonathan Elias, Daniel Licht, Brian May, Lee Holdridge, Fred Mollin, Cliff Eidelman, Mark McKenzie, Bob Cobert, Richard Stone; *Album Producer*: Ford A. Thaxton; *Engineers*: John Goodmanson, Ben Goldfarb.

Selections: The Return Of Dracula (G. Fried): 1 Overture (2:07); Vampire Circus (D. Whitaker): 2 Prologue (9:13); Fright Night (B. Fiedel): 3 Come To Me (3:53); Transylvania Twist (C. Cirino): 4 Painting The Way/The Letter/The Flight/Getting Cornered/Main Title (7:23); Vamp (J. Elias): 5 The Vampire Coven's Prayer (2:56); Children Of The Night (D. Licht): 6 The Blood Sucker's Ball (3:36); Thirst (B. May): 7 Vampire Ceremony and Initiation Ritual (4:47); Transylvania 6-5000 (L. Holdridge): 8 Night Flight To Transylvania/Happy Arrival/Madame Moravia/Draculette/Transylvania 6-5000 (7:37); Forever Knight (F. Mollin): 9 Main Title Theme (1:28); To Die For (C. Eidelman): 10 Main Title/Night Flight Over Los Angeles/The Loneliness Of Eternity/Vlad's Farewell (9:30); To Die For II: Son Of Darkness (M. McKenzie): 11 Finale (3:17); The Hunger: 12 The Flower Duet (from Lakme)(L. Delibes)(3:46) *Lesley Garrett & Lesley Christian*; Dracula (B. Cobert): 13 The Legend Of Vlad The Impaler/Main Title/Dracula's Love Theme/The Dark Kiss/Harker Strikes/The Final Confrontation and Dracula's Death (11:29); Sundown: The Vampire In Retreat (R. Stone): 14 Redemption Of The Damned (Finale)(5:43).

Review: This compilation puts together tracks from various recent horror films, with the scores composed by Brad Fiedel, Brian May, Lee Holdridge, Cliff Eidelman, Daniel Licht, and (would you believe it!) Leo Delibes. Programming is interesting, if somewhat hackneyed, and the selections evoke some of the best films in the genre from the past 20-odd years. Actually, the title says it all: this is the essential vampire theme collection... even though it misses some themes composed by other composers for other labels, and therefore not readily available for this compilation, like John Williams' *Dracula,* for starters.

Film Studios

This Is Cinerama at the Movies 🎵🎵🎵

1995, Label X Records.

Album Notes: *Music*: Max Steiner, Paul Sawtell, Roy Webb; The Cinerama Philharmonic Orchestra, conducted by Louis Forbes; *Album Producer*: John Steven Lasher; *Engineer*: Richard J. Pietschmann, Jr., David Macquarie.

Selections: 1 Ladies And Gentlemen, This Is Cinerama (M. Steiner)(1:39) *Lowell Thomas*; 2 Stereophonic Sound Demonstration (M. Steiner)(3:00); 3 Messiah: Hallelujah Chorus (G.F. Handel)(2:33) *The Long Island Choral Society*; 4 Venice Sequence (P. Sawtell)(4:26); 5 On The Beautiful Blue Danube (J. Strauss)(3:00) *The Vienna Boys Choir*; 6 Spanish Dancers (trad.)(1:19); 7 Aida: Dance Of The Nubian Slaves (G. Verdi)(2:05) *Teatro alla Scala Orchestra and Chorus, Victor de Sabata*; 8 Florida Cypress Gardens Sequence (M. Steiner) (2:47); 9 Water Show (R. Webb)(2:56); 10 Water Ballet Montage (R. Webb)(5:38); 11 Flight Across America (S. Cutner/H. Jackson/L. Shuken/M. Steiner/R. Webb)(10:40); 12 America, The Beautiful (K.L. Bates/S.A. Ward)(1:02) *The Salt Lake City Tabernacle Choir, J. Spencer Cornwall*; 13 End Credits (M. Steiner)(1:22); 14 Exit Music (R. Webb)(1:59).

Review: Before it entered the commercial fray and turned its attention to features, the Cinerama Company produced several travelogues that were essentially interesting as visual novelty, presenting as they did films shot by three cameras to give a vast panoramic vision. The first, and most memorable of these films is *This Is Cinerama,* truly a spectacular display that takes full advantage of the system's resources and combines them into a magical ride throughout the world, enhanced by the multi-screen presentation. The music heard behind the screen is also the work of highly competent individuals, like Max Steiner, Paul Sawtell, and Roy Webb. This CD reproduces the soundtrack album from that first film, in a sound that leaves a lot to be desired (stereo was not a selling point at the time, though multi-tracking was), and minus the visuals. The selections also represent a rather uneven hodge-

podge, from choral excerpts to grand opera scenes, from sweeping orchestral pieces to patriotic displays. The CD reflects all these ingredients and more, with the highlights here, at least where fans of film music are concerned, being the selections by Max Steiner and Roy Webb.

Music from the Hammer Films 🎵🎵🎵🎵

1989, Silva Screen Records.

Album Notes: *Music*: James Bernard, Christopher Gunning, David Whitaker; The Philharmonia Orchestra, conducted by Neil Richardson; *Album Producer*: Eric Tomlinson; *Engineer*: Mike Ross-Trevor.

Selections: The Dracula Suite (J. Bernard): 1 Main Theme (2:15); 2 Inside Castle Dracula/The Lure Of The Vampire Woman/Dracula's Rage (3:05); 3 The Kiss Of Living Death (2:08); 4 Funeral In Carpathia (2:25); 5 Finale: Confrontation and Climax/The Fall Of Dracula (2:31); Hands Of The Ripper (C. Gunning): 6 Main Titles/ Trace/Mrs. Golding's Murder/Anna's Theme (10:33); Dracula Has Risen From The Grave (J. Bernard): 7 Finale: Dracula And The Crucifix (5:24); Vampire Circus (D. Whitaker): 8 Prologue (9:15); Taste The Blood Of Dracula (J. Bernard): 9 The Blood Of Dracula (2:11); 10 Romance: The Young Lovers/ Shadow Of The Tomb (3:21); 11 Ride To The Ruined Church (2:56); 12 Romance: At Dusk (2:30); 13 Dracula Triumphant/Pursuit/The Death Of Lucy (3:39); 14 The Victory Of Love (2:20).

Review: This companion volume to the *Vampire Circus* CD focuses on the enormous contributions made to the horror genre by the Hammer films. From James Bernard's endless scores for the *Dracula* films to David Whitaker's own ruminations for *Vampire Circus,* to Christopher Gunning's first essays with *Hands Of The Ripper,* this is a set that celebrates horror in all its nefarious aspects, with broad romantic themes that underline each story without revealing too much about it. The horror is frequently subliminal here, but the fun is not.

The Best of Hemdale 🎵🎵🎵🎵

1991, DCC Compact Classics.

Album Notes: *Album Coordinator*: Teri Nelson; *CD Mastering*: Steve Hoffman.

Selections: 1 Hemdale Fanfare (:22); Hoosiers (J. Goldsmith): 2 Hoosiers Theme (4:25); 3 Welcome To Hickory (8:48); The Terminator (B. Fiedel): 4 Factory Chase (3:50); 5 Love Scene (1:13); Criminal Law (J. Goldsmith): 6 The Victim (2:28); 7 The Body (3:22); Miracle Mile (Tangerine Dream): 8 Running Out Of Time

(3:30); 9 If It's All Over (4:33); Salvador (G. Delerue): 10 Main Title (1:55); 11 Love Theme/Finale (4:04); Platoon (G. Delerue): 12 Barnes Shoots Elias (3:10); 13 Adagio For Strings (S. Barber)(6:54) *The Vancouver Symphony Orchestra, Georges Delerue*; The Last Emperor (R. Sakamoto): 14 Where Is Armo? (2:26); The River's Edge (J. Knieper): 15 Main Title (1:11); 16 Magic Hours Mood (2:08); Best Seller (J. Ferguson): 17 Main Title (1:11); 18 Roberta's Visitor (3:05); At Close Range (P. Leonard): 19 Live To Tell (4:10); The Boost (S. Meyers): 20 Main Title (1:48).

Review: A major independent, Hemdale specialized in quality films no one else wanted to pick up for distribution. And so, this compilation includes several themes from such important releases as *Hoosiers, Criminal Law, Salvador,* and *Platoon,* with scores contributed by Jerry Goldsmith and Georges Delerue. Of course, the company also included the mix films that were less attention-commanding, and it should not come as a real surprise to find here the trite themes written by Brad Fiedel for *The Terminator,* or excerpts from *The River's Edge* and *Best Seller,* both films that only left a faint passing mark. It may also seem odd to find a "cover" version of Samuel Barber's "Adagio For Strings," which was used so effectively in *Platoon,* but on the other hand the inclusion of excerpts from Ryuichi Sakamoto's *The Last Emperor* are always welcome. As you can see, it's a bit of everything...

Merchant Ivory Productions: 25th Anniversary ♫♫♫♫

1988, RCA Victor Records.

Album Notes: *Music:* Richard Robbins, Ustad Zakir Hussain, Satyajit Ray.

Selections: CD 1: Savages (J. Raposo): 1 Title Music (2:48) *Bobby Short*; Jane Austen In Manhattan (R. Robbins/J. Austen/ S. Richardson): 2 Scene and Finale from "Sir Charles Grandison" (9:50) *Jane Bryden, Joyce Andrews, Frank Hoffmeister, David Evetts*; Quartet (R. Robbins): 3 Full Time Lover (3:07) *Armelia McQueen*; 4 Blues For H.J. (2:48); 5 Black King Foxtrot (3:01); Bombay Talkie (S. Jaikishan/H. Kumar): 6 Typewriter Tip Tip (5:32) *Asha Bhonsle, Kishore Kumar*; The Europeans: 7 Theme From Andante of Trio, Op. 17 (C. Schumann)(3:31); 8 Old Folks Quadrilles (S. Foster)(3:27); 9 Beautiful River (R. Lowry)(2:08); The Bostonians (R. Robbins): 10 Summer Days At Marmion (2:31); 11 The Bostonians (2:52); A Room With A View (R. Robbins): 12 O mio babbino caro (G. Puccini)(2:25) *Leontyne Price*; 13 The Embankment (2:22); 14 Habanera (2:03); Maurice (R. Robbins): 15 Clive And Anne (2:00); 16 End Titles (3:27).

CD 2: The Householder (U. Ali Akbar Khan): 1 Opening Titles (1:42); 2 Prem's Lament (3:22); 3 Farewell To Ernest (J. Moitra)(1:58); Shakespeare Wallah (S. Ray): 4 Opening Titles (3:05); 5 Manjula's Procession (1:16); 6 In The Mist (3:31); 7 The Makeup Room (2:08); 8 Lizzie Sails To England (2:20); The Courtesans Of Bombay: 9 Garmie Hasrate (Ghazal)(3:23) *Zubaida Khanam*; 10 Nazzara Jamal Se/Kahe Rokat Dagare Shyam (Ghazal/Dadra)(6:20) *Shanti Bai*; Mahatma And The Mad Boy: 11 Improvisations on Andante from Winter from The Four Seasons (A. Vivaldi)(2:17); Guru (U. Vilayat Khan): 12 Bikaner Concert (12:48) *Ustad Vilayat Khan*; 13 Title Music (1:38); Heat And Dust (R. Robbins/U. Zakir Hussain): 14 Anne In The Bazaar/Olivia Writes Home (3:11); 15 Bliss Of Mind/The Dust Storm (3:51); 16 End Titles (3:56).

Review: One of the classiest among the independent labels, Merchant Ivory has established its solid reputation on films that are exquisitely made, dealing with subjects that have universal appeal, and boasting fashionable scores, usually written by the dependable Richard Robbins.

This 25th anniversary compilation is a festive celebration, an eclectic choice of various themes and cues that have been used behind some of the most attractive films ever presented on the screen. However, it does call for some reservations.

The first CD deals with what might be conveniently called the "European" films, many of them, like *Jane Austen in Manhattan, Quartet, The Europeans, The Bostonians, A Room With a View,* and *Maurice* were scored by Robbins in the style that seems appropriate for the films themselves. This is by far the most exciting of the two CDs in this collection.

The second CD focuses on the "oriental" films, those with a theme or background that justify using a more ethnic score. While there is nothing wrong with these scores, composed by Ustad Ali Abkar Khan, Ustad Vilayat Khan, and Ghazal, they may seem at times a little too exotic for the western ears. Which is not to say they shouldn't be heard, but a little would probably suffice. As it is, the abundance of Indian ragas, even when adapted to suit the continental sensitivity, is not as enjoyable as, say, the selections by Richard Robbins.

Academy Award Winning Music from M-G-M Classics ♫♫♫♫♫

1997, Rhino Records.

Album Notes: *Album Producers:* George Feltenstein, Bradley Flanagan; *Engineer:* Doug Schwartz.

Selections: The Wizard Of Oz: 1 Main Title (H. Stothart)(1:51) *The M-G-M Studio Orchestra and Chorus, Herbert Stothart*; 2 Over The Rainbow (H. Arlen/E.Y. Harburg)(2:44) *Judy Garland*; Lady Be Good: 3 The Last Time I Saw Paris (J. Kern/O. Hammerstein II)(4:38) *Ann Sothern*; Anchors Aweigh: 4 What Makes The Sunset (J. Styne/S. Cahn)(3:30) *Frank Sinatra*; The Harvey Girls: 5 On The Atchison, Topeka And The Santa Fe (H. Warren/J. Mercer)(8:37) *Judy Garland, Cyd Charisse, Virginia O' Brien, Marjorie Main, Ray Bolger*; Easter Parade: 6 Easter Parade (I. Berlin)(2:40) *Judy Garland, Fred Astaire*; Neptune's Daughter: 7 Baby It's Cold Outside (F. Loesser)(4:42) *Esther Williams, Ricardo Montalban*; On The Town: 8 Main Street (R. Edens/B. Comden/A. Green)(3:44) *Gene Kelly*; Annie Get Your Gun: 9 Anything You Can Do (I. Berlin)(3:09) *Betty Hutton, Howard Keel*; An American In Paris: 10 Love Is Here To Stay (G. Gershwin/I. Gerhswin)(3:56) *Gene Kelly*; Lili: 11 Hi-Lili, Hi-Lo (B. Kaper/H. Deutsch)(1:55) *Leslie Caron, Mel Ferrer*; Seven Brides For Seven Brothers: 12 Barn Dance (G. De Paul/J. Mercer)(5:51) *The M-G-M Studio Orchestra, Adolph Deutsch*; Gigi: 13 Gigi (F. Loewe/A.J. Lerner)(2:48) *Louis Jourdan*; Ben-Hur: 14 Overture (M. Rozsa)(6:29) *The M-G-M Studio Orchestra and Chorus, Miklos Rozsa*; Dr. Zhivago: 15 Lara's Theme (Main Title)(M. Jarre)(2:38) *The M-G-M Studio Orchestra, Maurice Jarre.*

Review: The title says it all: at the peak of its creative output, M-G-M was the studio against which all others had to measure up, a fact duly noted in this wonderful collection that focuses on the songs and themes that won the coveted Academy Award (or Oscar). The range is broad, covering as it does *The Wizard of Oz, Anchors Aweigh, An American in Paris, Seven Brides for Seven Brothers,* and *Gigi,* among the musicals; and *Ben-Hur* and *Doctor Zhivago,* among the dramatic films. Yet, the CD is a bit of a deception as M-G-M earned its laurels in both the musical and the dramatic fields. There is too much of the former here, and not enough of the latter, to establish a thorough balance, which leads one to think that perhaps there should have been two CDs, instead of one. Ah, well...

Alive and Kicking: Big Band Sounds at M-G-M 🎵🎵🎵🎵

1997, Rhino Records.

Album Notes: *Album Producers*: George Feltenstein, Bradley Flanagan; *Engineer*: Doug Schwartz.

Selections: Broadway Rhythm: 1 Opus One (S. Oliver)(3:23) *Tommy Dorsey*; 2 Irresistible You (G. De Paul/D. Raye)(2:50) *Skip Nelson, The Sentimentalists, Tommy Dorsey*; I Dood It!: 3 One O'Clock Jump (W. Basie)(3:49) *Jimmy Dorsey*; Bathing Beauty: 4 I Cried For You (A. Freed/G. Arnheim/A. Lyman)(3:04) *Helen Forrest, Harry James and His Music Makers*; Ship Ahoy: 5 I Fell In Love With The Leader Of The Band (J. Styne/H. Magidson)(3:22) *Virginia O' Brien, Tommy Dorsey*; Martin Block's Musical Merry Go Round: 6 Chattanooga Choo Choo (H. Warren/M. Gordon)(2:04) *Tex Beneke*; Ship Ahoy: 7 Hawaiian War Chant (J. Noble/Leleiohaku/R. Freed)(3:15) *Tommy Dorsey*; 8 I'm Yours (J. Green/E.Y. Harburg)(2:46) *Artie Shaw*; No Leave, No Love: 9 Love On A Greyhound Bus (G. Stoll/K. Thompson/R. Blane)(3:22) *Pat Kirkwood, The M-G-M Studio Chorus, Guy Lombardo and His Royal Canadians*; Meet The People: 10 I Like To Recognize The Tune (R. Rodgers/L. Hart)(4:11) *Vaughn Monroe, June Allyson, Virginia O' Brien, Ziggy Talent, The Murphy Sisters, The King Sisters, Vaughn Monroe*; Thrill Of A Romance: 11 Song Of India (N. Rimsky-Korsakov/S. Oliver)(2:51) *Tommy Dorsey*; I Dood It!: 12 Star Eyes (G. De Paul/D. Raye)(5:05) *Bob Eberle, Helen O' Connell, Jimmy Dorsey*; Du Barry Was A Lady: 13 Do I Love You? (C. Porter)(2:34) *The Pied Pipers, Tommy Dorsey*; Dancing Co-Ed: 14 The Donkey Serenade (R. Friml/H. Stothart/R. Wright/C. Forrest) (3:09) *Artie Shaw*; Thousands Cheer: 15 In A Little Spanish Town (M. Wayne/S. Lewis/J. Young)(2:59) *June Allyson, Gloria De Haven, Virginia O' Brien, Bob Crosby*; Thrill Of A Romance: 16 I Should Care (A. Stordahl/P. Weston/S. Cahn)(3:21) *Bob Allen, Tommy Dorsey*; I Dood It!: 17 Shorter Than Me (G. De Paul/D. Raye) (3:15) *Ford L. Buck, John Bubbles, Jimmy Dorsey*; Ship Ahoy: 18 Blue Skies (I. Berlin)(2:54) *Frank Sinatra, Tommy Dorsey*; Dancing Co-Ed: 19 At Sundown (W. Donaldson)(3:12) *Artie Shaw*; Best Foot Forward: 20 Alive And Kickin' (H. Martin/R. Blane)(3:11) *Nancy Walker, Harry James and His Music Makers*; Swing Fever: 21 Mississippi Dream Boat (S. Fain/L. Brown/R. Freed)(4:28) *Sully Mason, Marilyn Maxwell, Kay Kyser*; I Dood It!: 22 Lord And Lady Gate (G. De Paul/D. Raye)(3:24) *Helen O' Connell, Jimmy Dorsey*; Bathing Beauty: 23 Trumpet Blues And Cantabile (H. James/J. Matthias)(2:46) *Harry James and His Music Makers.*

Review: What an irresistible idea, and what a great package! When musicals reigned supreme, during the 1940s, many big bands appeared in the M-G-M films, from Artie Shaw to Jimmy Dorsey, from Harry James to Bob Crosby, from Guy Lombardo to Kay Kyser. The tracks culled here from more than a dozen films are terrific, and a bonanza for anyone who loves the big band era. One could argue, of course, that there were quite a few others who appeared in the movies, notably Louis Armstrong and Xavier Cugat (both represented in their own compilations), but for a start this is really the *creme de la creme,* and a fancy concept.

Maracas, Marimbas and Mambos: Latin Classics at M-G-M 🎵🎵🎵🎵

1997, Rhino Records.

Album Notes: *CD Producers*: George Feltenstein, Bradley Flanagan; *Engineer*: Doug Schwartz.

Selections: Bathing Beauty: 1 Bim Bam Bum (J. Camacho/N. Morales/H. Adamson)(2:48) *Lina Romay, Xavier Cugat*; Easy To Wed: 2 Viva Mexico (G.P. Galindo)(2:25) *Carlos Ramirez, M-G-M Studio Orchestra, Johnny Green*; Holiday In Mexico: 3 Walter Winchell Rhumba (J. Camacho/N. Morales/C. Sigman)(3:04) *Xavier Cugat*; A Date With Judy: 4 Cuanto Le Gusta (G. Ruiz/R. Gilbert) (2:04) *Carmen Miranda, Xavier Cugat*; Bathing Beauty: 5 Alma Llanerna (P.E. Gutierrez)(3:24) *Lina Romay, Xavier Cugat*; Two Girls And A Sailor: 6 Cae Cae (R. Martins/P. Berrios/J. Latouche)(1:54) *Xavier Cugat*; On An Island With You: 7 El Cumbachero (R. Hernandez)(1:54) *Betty Riley, Xavier Cugat*; Fiesta: 8 La Bamba (L.M. Serrano)(1:46) *M-G-M Studio Chorus and Orchestra, Johnny Green*; Easy To Wed: 9 Boneca De Pixe (A.E. Barroso)(4:56) *Esther Williams, Van Johnson, Ethel Smith*; Bathing Beauty: 10 Te Quiero Juste (M. Grever)(2:59) *Carlos Ramirez*; Two Girls And A Sailor: 11 Babalu (M. Lecuona)(3:13) *Lina Romay, Xavier Cugat*; Nancy Goes To Rio: 12 Caroom Pa Pa (R. Gilbert)(3:04) *Carmen Miranda*; Bathing Beauty: 13 Tico Tico (Z. Abreu/E. Drake)(1:58) *Ethel Smith*; Two Girls And A Sailor: 14 Take It Easy (A. De Bru/ I. Taylor/V. Mizzy)(3:19) *Lina Romay, Virginia O'Brien, The Wild Twins, Xavier Cugat*; Two Girls And A Sailor: 15 Granada (A. Lara)(2:51) *Carlos Ramirez, Xavier Cugat*; Two Girls And A Sailor: 16 Rumba Rumba (J. Parfumy/V. Castro)(2:47) *Lina Romay, Xavier Cugat*; Nancy Goes To Rio: 17 Yipsee-I-O (R. Gilbert)(2:49) *Carmen Miranda, Frank Fontaine*; Holiday In Mexico: 18 Yo Te Amo Mucho (And That's That)(X. Cugat/S. Stept/E. Drake)(2:26) *Xavier Cugat, M-G-M Studio Chorus*.

Review: This exhilarating compilation is a joy from beginning to end. Drawing from the vast resources in the M-G-M vaults, album producers George Feltenstein and Bradley Flanagan have culled together a collection of songs with a Latin beat that were either composed for or performed in some of the great musical films of the 1940s and early '50s. Prominently featured in many of them is Xavier Cugat, whose infectious rhythms defined better than most the South of the Border craze surveyed in this CD, and Carmen Miranda, the Brazilian bombshell, who made Latin music so popular through her exotic songs and wild performances. Definitely the kind of album that will lift up your moods in record time.

Romantic Duets from M-G-M Classics 🎵🎵🎵🎵▵

1997, Rhino Records.

Album Notes: *Album Producers*: George Feltenstein, Bradley Flanagan; *Engineer*: Doug Schwartz.

Selections: High Society: 1 True Love (C. Porter)(3:04) *Bing Crosby, Grace Kelly*; For Me And My Gal: 2 For Me And My Gal (G.W. Meyer/E. Leslie/R. Goetz)(4:19) *Gene Kelly, Judy Garland*; Dangerous When Wet: 3 Ain't Nature Grand (A. Schwartz/ J. Mercer)(5:00) *Esther Williams, Fernando Lamas, Denise Darcel, Jack Carson, Barbara Whiting, Charlotte Greenwood, William Demarest*; The Long, Long Trailer: 4 Breezin' Along With The Breeze (H. Gillespie/S. Simons/R. Whiting)(3:53) *Lucille Ball, Desi Arnaz*; Show Boat: 5 Make Believe (J. Kern/O. Hammerstein II)(4:29) *Howard Keel, Kathryn Grayson*; Three Little Words: 6 Nevertheless (I'm In Love With You)(H. Ruby/B. Kalmar) (2:24) *Fred Astaire, Anita Ellis, Red Skelton*; Kismet: 7 Stranger In Paradise (A. Borodin/R. Wright/G. Forrest)(5:33) *Ann Blyth, Vic Damone*; Good News: 8 The Best Things In Life Are Free (B.G. DeSylva/R. Henderson/L. Brown)(3:16) *June Allyson, Peter Lawford*; The Toast Of New Orleans: 9 Be My Love (N. Brodszky/S. Cahn)(2:57) *Mario Lanza, Kathryn Grayson*; Hit The Deck: 10 I Know That You Know (V. Youmans/A. Caldwell)(3:11) *Jane Powell, Vic Damone*; Annie Get Your Gun: 11 They Say It's Wonderful (I. Berlin)(3:22) *Judy Garland, Howard Keel*; Cabin In The Sky: 12 Cabin In The Sky (V. Duke/J. Latouche)(4:40) *Ethel Waters, Eddie ''Rochester'' Anderson, Hall Johnson Choir*; Athena: 13 Imagine (H. Martin/R. Blane)(5:04) *Debbie Reynolds, Vic Damone*; Deep In My Heart: 14 Mr. And Mrs. (S. Romberg/C. Wood)(1:21) *Rosemary Clooney, Jose Ferrer*; Kiss Me Kate: 15 So In Love (C. Porter)(2:17) *Howard Keel, Kathryn Grayson*; Looking For Love: 16 I Can't Believe That You're In Love With Me (C. Gaskill/J. McHugh)(2:51) *Connie Francis, Danny Thomas*; Rich, Young And Pretty: 17 How Do You Like Your Eggs In The Morning? (N. Brodszky/S. Cahn)(1:56) *Jane Powell, Vic Damone, Four Freshmen*; Maytime: 18 Will You Remember (S. Romberg/R. Johnson Young)(4:44) *Jeanette MacDonald, Nelson Eddy*; Words And Music: 19 I Wish I Were In Love Again (R. Rodgers/ L. Hart)(2:25) *Judy Garland, Mickey Rooney*; Deep In My Heart: 20 Medley: One Kiss/Lover, Come Back To Me (S. Romberg/O. Hammerstein II)(7:20) *Tony Martin, Joan Weldon*; Singin' In The Rain: 21 You Are My Lucky Star (A. Freed/N.H. Brown)(1:37) *Gene Kelly, Betty Noyes*.

Review: One can always find faults in a compilation of this kind and wonder why the producers chose one selection over another, particularly when the programmatic concept seems so broad to begin with, and could include so many films from the M-G-M catalogue. Why, for instance, should there be four selections with Vic Damone, and two from *Deep in My Heart?* And does *The Long, Long Trailer* or *Looking for Love,* admittedly minor films, really qualify, when there are no selections from *Rose Marie* or *Gigi?* And what about such blockbusters as *The Bandwagon, Bells Are Ringing, An American in Paris, The Harvey Girls, In the Good Old Summertime, Brigadoon, Seven Brides for Seven Brothers* or *The Unsinkable Molly Brown?* Conversely, not everything could be included, and there may be, one hope, a second volume. So, given these various considerations, this compilation is a romantic feast that will no doubt bring a smile and a sigh to anyone listening, with many favorites included in the mix ("Stranger In Paradise," "You Are My Lucky Star," "True Love," "Make Believe"), some welcome rediscoveries ("Imagine," "How Do You Like Your Eggs in the Morning?," "I Know That You Know"), and only a couple of mister and misses. It may be the ideal CD to play on Valentine's Day, or any day when the mood hits.

Miramax Films' Greatest Hits 🎵🎵🎵

1997, Miramax/Hollywood Records.

Album Notes: *Album Producers*: Jeffrey Kimball, Beth Rosenblatt; *Engineers*: Vlado Meller, Tom Ruff.

Selections: The Postman (L. Bacalov): 1 The Postman Poet (3:23); The Piano (M. Nyman): 2 The Sacrifice (2:48); My Left Foot (E. Bernstein): 3 Therapy (2:55); Cinema Paradiso (E. Morricone): 4 First Youth (2:15); The Englishman Who Went Up A Hill But Came Down A Mountain (S. Endelman): 5 Villagers Begin Building (3:03); Smoke (R. Portman): 6 Augie's Photos (2:26); Like Water For Chocolate (L. Brower): 7 Quail In Rose Petal Sauce (1:00); Cry The Beloved Country (J. Barry): 8 Main Title/The Letter (3:39); Picture Bride (M. Adler): 9 Picture Bride (1:52); Red (Z. Preisner): 10 Finale (2:59); The House Of The Spirits (H. Zimmer): 11 House Of The Spirits (10:04); sex, lies and videotape (C. Martinez): 12 I'm Gonna Drawl (4:37); The Thin Blue Line (P. Glass): 13 Opening Credits (1:31); Pulp Fiction : 14 Misirlou (M. Leeds/F. Wide/R. Roubanis)(2:14) *Dick Dale & His Del-Tones*; The Crying Game (A.Dudley): 15 The Crying Game (3:21) *Boy George*.

Review: Another well-known independent studio, which has recently teamed with Hollywood Records to release its soundtrack, Miramax has enjoyed a distinguished career with films no one else seemed to want. The list of themes included here reads like a compendium of some of the best quality films seen

in the past few years, from the Academy Award-winning *The Postman,* to such highly visible entries as *The Piano, My Left Foot, Like Water for Chocolate, Cry the Beloved Country, Cinema Paradiso, Red,* and *The Crying Game.* In the process, the set also culls together selections by some of the most important film scorers of the day, including Luis Bacalov, Ennio Morricone, John Barry, Rachel Portman, Ann Dudley, Hans Zimmer, and Zbigniew Preisner, to name only a few. The only reservations one may have about the set is the inclusion of a track from *Pulp Fiction,* which doesn't belong in such distinguished company, and the vocal by Boy George, from *The Crying Game,* which should have been replaced by an instrumental selection to conform with the moods set in the rest of the package.

Republic Studios

Music from the Classic Republic Serials: Cliffhangers! 🎵🎵🎵🎵

1996, Varese-Sarabande Records.

Album Notes: *Music*: Alberto Colombo, Cy Feuer, Mort Glickman, Karl Hajos, William Lava, Paul Sawtell, Arnold Schwarzwald, Victor Young; The CinemaSound Orchestra, conducted by James King; *Album Producer*: James King; *Engineer*: Toby Foster.

Selections: Perils Of Nyoka: 1 Young Emblem/Republic Logo (V. Young)(:15)/ Perils Of Nyoka: Main Title/Chapter Card (M. Glickman)(:50); 2 Arabian Tornado (M. Glickman)(1:49); 3 Desert Intrigue (A. Schwarzwald)(1:40); Adventures Of Captain Marvel: 4 Tal Chotali (M. Glickman)(1:56); Dick Tracy's G-Men: 5 Satanic Fury (P. Sawtell)(2:10); Zorro's Fighting Legion: 6 Sub Surface Action (W. Lava)(1:53); 7 Sword Play (C. Feuer)(1:39); The Fighting Devil Dogs: 8 Dale Kidnapped (A. Colombo)(1:55); 9 Storm And Falling Trees (A. Colombo) (3:19); 10 In Deep Despair (A. Colombo)(1:38); 11 Devil Dogs Hurry In D Minor (A. Colombo)(2:19); King Of The Royal Mounted: 12 Main Title/Chapter Card/ Technical Credits (M. Glickman)(1:26); 13 Maple Leaf Forever (arr.: W. Lava) (:39); 14 Mounties Get Their Man (P. Sawtell)(1:41); 15 Doc's Explanation (Chase And Snow Avalanche)(W. Lava)(3:34); 16 Mounted Fury (W. Lava)(1:40); 17 Renegade Trail (W. Lava)(1:30); 18 After The Man (W. Lava)(1:38); 19 Linda (P. Sawtell)(1:23); 20 Get Your Man (W. Lave)(2:05); Daredevils Of The Red Circle: 21 Main Title (W. Lava)(:57); 22 On The Run (C. Feuer)(1:33); Mysterious Dr. Satan: 23 Car Transfer (M. Glickman)(1:49); Hawk Of The Wilderness: 24 Miller's Folly (C. Feuer)(2:33); Drums Of Fu Manchu: 25 Perilous Task (P. Sawtell)(1:44); Adventures Of Red Ryder: 26 Main Title (W. Lava)(:59); 27 Adventures Of Red Ryder Chapter Card (W. Lava)(:59); 28 Malicious Purpose (W. Lava)(1:26); 29 Little Beaver, Part 1 (W. Lava)(:50); 30 Horse Chase (P. Sawtell)(1:40); 31 Ace Hanlon (W. Lava)(1:53); 32 Little Beaver, Part 2 (W. Lava)(1:06); 33 Oh, Susanna Chase (W. Lava)(2:04); 34 At The Brink (W. Lava) (1:51); 35 Adventures Of Red Ryder Tech Credits (W. Lava)(:23).

Review: See entry below.

Music from the Classic Republic Westerns: Shoot 'Em Ups! 🎞🎞🎞🎞

1996, Varese-Sarabande Records.

Album Notes: *Music:* William Lava, Cy Feuer, Mort Glickman, Alberto Colombo, Paul Sawtell, Karl Hajos; The CinemaSound Orchestra conducted by James King; *Album Producer:* James King; *Engineers:* Steve Archer, Toby Foster.

Selections: The Three Mesquiteers: 1 Republic Emblem "A"/ Main Title (W. Lava)(1:06); 2 Mexican Chase (C. Feuer)(2:01); 3 Trio In Pursuit (W. Lava) (1:58); 4 Easy Day (C. Feuer)(2:47); 5 Mesquiteers Get Going (W. Lava)(1:28); 6 Bad Men (W. Lava)(1:40); 7 Saddle Tempo (W. Lava)(1:35); 8 Theme And End Title (W. Lava)(1:29); The Border Legion: 9 Main Title (W. Lava)(:37); Don Barry Series: 10 Panorama (W. Lava)(1:04); Republic Chase Montage: 11 Desert Chase (M. Glickman)(1:31); 12 Desert Riders (A. Colombo)(3:12); 13 Race To Destruction (W. Lava)(2:14); 14 Quick Getaway (P. Sawtell)(1:50); The Painted Stallion: 15 Main Title (W. Lava)(1:22); 16 Foreword (W. Lava)(1:20); 17 Chapter Card (W. Lava)(:10); Adventures Of Red Ryder: 18 Little Beaver (W. Lava)(1:03); Republic Action Trilogy: 19 Anxious Moments (W. Lava)(1:39); 20 Riders In Pursuit (W. Lava)(1:40); 21 Heavy Agitato No. 1 (A. Colombo)(3:38); Republic Suspense Montage: 22 Black Motive (W. Lava)(1:11); 23 The Getaway (A. Colombo)(2:59); 24 Kidnapped (C. Feuer)(1:52); 25 Under Cover (W. Lava)(1:11); 26 Nightfall (C. Feuer)(1:59); The Lone Ranger: 27 Signature Republic/Main Title (A. Colombo)(:15); 28 Foreword (A. Colombo)(:55); 29 The Brute (A. Colombo)(1:08); 30 Mechanical Montage (K. Hajos)(:51); 31 Perpetual Motion (A. Colombo)(2:07); 32 The Life Saver (K. Hajos)(3:03); 33 The Revolt (A. Colombo) (1:51); 34 Mysterioso No. 1 (K. Hajos)(:50); 35 The Bull Fight (K. Hajos) (2:40); 36 Scheming (K. Hajos)(1:08); 37 Lamento (A. Colombo)(2:47); 38 Turmoil/Calm (A. Colombo)(1:33); 39 Hurry

(A. Colombo)(:58); Under Western Skies: 40 End Titles (A. Colombo/W. Lava)(:54).

Review: The sound quality is not always up to par, but both these releases are so much fun that one would have to be hardened to the point of insensitivity not to enjoy them.

The first CD, of course, dissects musically some of the outrageously far-fetched cliffhangers that were a Republic staple for many years in the 1940s and '50s. Anyone who has thrilled to the exploits of Captain Marvel, Zorro, King of the Royal Mounted, or Red Ryder, will love these musical snippets that evoke the endless series in which these characters appeared, along with many others like the evil Fu Manchu or the mysterious Dr. Satan.

But to these ears, the real plum here is the second volume, which concentrates on the westerns, when John Wayne was still a Mesquiteer, who rode the range to correct the wrongs in series that seemed to go on forever, week after week, and always featured the same stock scenes. What singled out these serials were the scores that were written on a shoestring, often on the spur of the moment, and that were recorded under conditions that would seem laughable today (when the musicians were assembled, they were given a sketch of the score, and were asked to play the music, with the first take often being the only one). Without waxing nostalgic about a long gone era, these two CDs bring back memories that will no doubt bring some mist to many listeners' eyes.

Hollywood Magic

Hollywood Magic: The 1950s 🎞🎞🎞🎞

1988, Columbia Records.

Album Notes: *Album Producer:* Didier C. Deutsch; *Engineer:* Mark Wilder.

Selections: Bus Stop: 1 The Bus Stop Song (K. Darby)(2:10) *The Four Lads*; Calamity Jane: 2 Secret Love (S. Fain/P.F. Webster)(3:40) *Doris Day*; The Pajama Game: 3 Hey There (R. Adler/J. Ross)(2:52) *John Raitt*; A Star Is Born: 4 The Man That Got Away (H. Arlen/I. Gershwin)(3:37) *Judy Garland*; Pete Kelly's Blues: 5 Pete Kelly's Blues (S. Cahn/R. Heindorf)(2:48) *The Warner Bros. Studio Orchestra, Ray Heindorf*; A Certain Smile: 6 A Certain Smile (S. Fain/P.F. Webster)(2:48) *Johnny Mathis*; A Summer Place: 7 Theme From A Summer Place (M. Steiner)(2:26) *Percy Faith*; Giant: 8 The Yellow Rose Of Texas (D. George)(3:01) *Mitch Miller*; High Noon: 9 Do Not Forsake Me Oh My Darling (D. Tiomkin/N. Washington)(2:39) *Frankie*

Laine; Davy Crockett, King Of The Wild Frontier: 10 Ballad Of Davy Crockett (T. Blackburn/G. Burns)(1:40) *Fess Parker*; The Hanging Tree: 11 The Hanging Tree (M. David/J. Livingston)(2:50) *Marty Robbins*; Moulin Rouge: 12 Song From Moulin Rouge (G. Auric/W. Engvick)(3:15) *Felicia Sanders, Percy Faith*; Young Man With A Horn: 13 The Man I Love (G. & I. Gershwin)(3:06) *Harry James*; Wild Is The Wind: 14 Wild Is The Wind (D. Tiomkin/N. Washington)(2:26) *Johnny Mathis*; Love Me Or Leave Me: 15 Love Me Or Leave Me (W. Donaldson/G. Kahn) (2:16) *Doris Day*; Bridge On The River Kwai: 16 The River Kwai March/Colonel Bogey (M. Arnold/K.J. Alford)(2:26) *Mitch Miller*.

Review: See entry below.

Hollywood Magic: The 1960s 🎵🎵🎵🎵

1988, Columbia Records.

Album Notes: *Album Producer*: Didier C. Deutsch; *Engineer*: Mark Wilder.

Selections: The Alamo: 1 The Green Leaves Of Summer (D. Tiomkin/P.F. Webster)(2:54) *The Brothers Four*; The Oscar: 2 Maybe September (P. Faith/J. Livingston/R. Evans)(3:59) *Tony Bennett*; Born Free: 3 Born Free (J. Barry) (2:47) *John Barry*; The Quiller Memorandum: 4 Wednesday's Child (J. Barry/M. David)(2:34) *Matt Monro*; Is Paris Burning?: 5 The Paris Waltz (M. Jarre)(2:37); 55 Days At Peking: 6 So Little Time (The Peking Theme) (D. Tiomkin/P.F. Webster)(2:45) *Andy Williams*; The Guns Of Navarone: 7 The Guns Of Navarone (D. Tiomkin/ P.F. Webster)(3:59) *Mitch Miller & The Gang*; The Sons Of Katie Elder: 8 Main Title (E. Bernstein)(2:16) *Elmer Bernstein*; North To Alaska: 9 North To Alaska (R. Faith/R. Marcucci/P. De Angelis)(2:49) *Johnny Horton*; Bonnie And Clyde: 10 Foggy Mountain Breakdown (E. Scruggs)(2:18) *Lester Flatt, Earl Scruggs*; Let's Make Love: 11 Let's Make Love (S. Cahn/J. Van Heusen)(4:34) *Marilyn Monroe, Frankie Vaughan, Yves Montand*; Billy Rose's Jumbo: 12 My Romance (R. Rodgers/ L. Hart)(2:32) *Doris Day*; To Sir With Love: 13 To Sir With Love (M. London/ D. Black)(2:46) *Lulu*; The Lion In Winter: 14 Main Title (J. Barry)(2:39) *John Barry*; The Fall Of The Roman Empire: 15 Pax Romana (D. Tiomkin)(5:18) *Dimitri Tiomkin*.

Review: The concept behind the film title song originated with "Do Not Forsake Me Oh My Darling," which, in its cover version by Frankie Laine, probably saved the film from being a total disaster at the box office. As a result, feature films in the 1950s and '60s had to have title songs, some of them with lyrics hastily written to conform with a storyline that sometimes

didn't lend itself for a sung treatment ("The Guns of Navarone," for example). Many of the most popular songs written for the movies during that time are found in these two compilations, often in their original soundtrack performances. As might be expected, there are some real gems, some classic performances, and an occasional dud. But overall, both CDs prove remarkably enjoyable.

Hollywood Hits

Hollywood Backlot 🎵🎵🎵

1992, Varese-Sarabande Records.

Album Notes: *Album Producer*: Robert Townson.

Selections: Terminator 2 (B. Fiedel): 1 Main Title (1:56); Medicine Man (J. Goldsmith): 2 Rae's Arrival (5:06); City Slickers (M. Shaiman): 3 Main Title (2:40); Father Of The Bride (A. Silvestri): 4 Main Title (2:27); Naked Gun 2½ (I. Newborn): 5 Main Title (2:01); Little Man Tate (M. Isham): 6 Fred And Dede (4:30); The Last Butterfly (A. North): 7 End Title (4:24); The Great Mouse Detective (H. Mancini): 8 Main Title (1:38); Year Of The Comet (H. Mann): 9 Maggie Goes To Scotland (2:08); Hudson Hawk (M. Kamen): 10 Leonardo (4:54); Final Analysis (G. Fenton): 11 Front Titles (2:38); Article 99 (D. Elfman): 12 Main Titles (3:58); Dead Again (P. Doyle): 13 The Headlines (3:24); Basic Instinct (J. Goldsmith): 14 Main Title (2:14); The Player (T. Newman): 15 The Player (3:06); Doc Hollywood (C. Burwell): 16 Life Sentence (4:24); My Cousin Vinny (R. Edelman): 17 Life On The Open Road (2:48); Soap Dish (A. Silvestri): 18 Mambo glamorose (3:51); A Rage In Harlem (E. Bernstein): 19 Happy Train (2:49); Black Robe (G. Delerue): 20 Libera me (5:02).

Review: See entry below.

Hollywood Soundstage: Big Movie Hits, vol. 1 🎵🎵🎵

1991, Varese-Sarabande Records.

Album Notes: *Album Producer*: Robert Townson; *Digital Transfer*: Tom Null.

Selections: Total Recall (J. Goldsmith): 1 The Dream (3:33); Back To The Future III (A. Silvestri): 2 End Credits (4:00); Driving Miss Daisy (H. Zimmer): 3 End Title (4:51); Mr. Destiny (D. Newman): 4 Mr. Destiny (5:04); Stanley And Iris (J. Williams): 5 End Credits (4:52); Gremlins 2 (J. Goldsmith): 6 Gremlin Credits (4:52); My Left Foot (E. Bernstein): 7 Mother (3:40); Music Box (P. Sarde): 8 Ann's Theme (2:30); White

Palace (G. Fenton): 9 Main Title (3:05); RoboCop 2 (L. Rosenman): 10 Overture (6:02); The Grifters (E. Bernstein): 11 The City (3:32); Presumed Innocent (J. Williams): 12 Main Title (4:10); Beaches (G. Delerue): 13 Friendship (3:27); Die Hard 2 (M. Kamen): 14 The Runway (3:55); Memphis Belle (G. Fenton): 15 End Title Suite (7:37); The Abyss (A. Silvestri): 16 Finale (6:45).

Review: See entry below.

Highway To Hollywood: Big Movie Hits, vol. 2 ♪♪♪

1991, Varese-Sarabande Records.

Album Notes: *Album Producer:* Robert Townson; *Digital Transfers:* Tom Null.

Selections: Kindergarten Cop (R. Edelman): 1 Astoria School Theme/ Children's Montage (4:27); The Long Walk Home (G. Fenton): 2 Main Title (2:39); Green Card (H. Zimmer): 3 Silence (4:08); Once Around (J. Horner): 4 Big Band On Ice (4:38); Guilty By Suspicion (J. Newton Howard): 5 End Title (3:45); Switch (H. Mancini): 6 Main Title (2:10); Oscar (E. Bernstein): 7 Tea And Romance (4:29); Steel Magnolias (G. Delerue): 8 Steel Magnolias (3:31); Welcome Home, Roxy Carmichael (T. Newman): 9 Her Limousine (1:57); Class Action (J. Horner): 10 Main Title (2:53); Miller's Crossing (C. Burwell): 11 End Title (4:40); The Field (E. Bernstein): 12 The Land (5:41); Desperate Hours (D. Mansfield): 13 The Aftermath (2:07); Enemies, A Love Story (M. Jarre): 14 Baby Masha (4:54); Predator 2 (A. Silvestri): 15 End Title (8:46); The Hard Way (A. Rubinstein): 16 The Good, The Badge And The Ugly (1:54).

Review: There is basically nothing wrong with these compilations, which combine together various selections from Varese-Sarabande's vast roster of soundtrack titles. The concept itself is sound, and whatever you want to call it, it's bound to attract some customers who would rather hear the main themes and/ or selections from popular films, than be saddled with the whole soundtrack album. That's fine!

But even in cases like this, a certain amount of creativity must be taken into consideration, so that the selections assembled together do not collide, but blend effortlessly one into the other. And there's the rub: the selections here seem to have been taken at random, and put together just for the hell of it, without much care or consideration being paid to the way they flow. As a result, the program jumps from one type of film to another that has no relation to the previous one, creating in the process a wall of sound that puts the mind in overdrive after a while.

It's really a shame, because the selections are quite valid, and come most of the time from excellent scores by composers who are among the best in the business. But since they don't seem to have coupling restrictions in their contracts, what we get here is an undistinguished oleo that only bears a faint resemblance to a sound compilation.

The Hollywood Bowl Orchestra

Always and Forever: Movies' Greatest Love Songs ♪♪♪

1996, Philips Records.

Album Notes: The Hollywood Bowl Orchestra, conducted by John Mauceri; *Arrangements:* Alfred Newman, Mark McGurty, Brad Dechter, Christopher Palmer, Takayuki Hattori, Bruce Fowler, Robert Freeman; *Orchestrations:* Edward B. Powell, Alexander Courage, Leonid Raab, Emilie A. Bernstein, Robert Freeman; *Featured Musicians:* Dennis Karmazyn (cello), Bruce Dukov (violin), Karl Dumler (English horn, oboe), Susan Greenberg (flute), Gary Bovyer (clarinet), Louise DiTullio (alto flute); *Guest Artists:* Dave Koz (soprano sax), Sylvia McNair (soprano), Gil Shaham (violin), Phil Perry (vocals), Erich-Wolfgang Korngold (piano); *Album Producer:* John Mauceri; *Engineer:* Joel Moss.

Selections: Love Is A Many Splendored Thing (S. Fain): 1 Love Is A Many Splendored Thing (2:19); Unchained (A. North): 2 Unchained Melody (3:26); Wuthering Heights (A. Newman): 3 Cathie's Theme (3:32); Forever Young (J. Goldsmith): 4 Love Theme (4:17); Peyton Place (F. Waxman): 5 Peyton Place (4:05); Room With A View: 6 Oh! Mio Babbino Caro (from *Gianni Schicchi*)(G. Puccini)(2:35); The Thief Of Bagdad (M. Rozsa): 7 Eternal Love (4:35); The Age Of Innocence (E. Bernstein): 8 The Age Of Innocence (4:43); Cinema Paradiso (E. Morricone): 9 Cinema Paradiso (7:44); Somewhere In Time (J. Barry): 10 Somewhere In Time (2:51); Escape Me Never (E.W. Korngold): 11 Love For Love (3:24); North By Northwest (B. Herrmann): 12 Conversation Piece (4:52); Four Weddings And A Funeral (R.R. Bennett): 13 Four Weddings And A Funeral (3:37); Laura (D. Raksin/J. Mercer): 14 Laura (3:52); Now Voyager (M. Steiner): 15 Now Voyager (4:30); An Affair To Remember (H. Warren/H. Friedhofer): 16 An Affair To Remember (2:39).

Review: John Mauceri and the Hollywood Bowl Orchestra lead the way through a serviceable but not particularly inspired collection of romantic film music staples, including Alex North's *Unchained Melody*, Alfred Newman's *Wuthering Heights*, Franz

Waxman's *Peyton Place*, David Raskin's *Laura*, Max Steiner's *Now, Voyager* and Hugo Friedhofer's *An Affair to Remember*. Along the way are interspersed classical pieces (i.e. Puccini's "Oh Mio Babbino Caro," heard in *A Room With a View*, and sung here by Sylvia McNair) and more modern selections, including Jerry Goldsmith's *Forever Young* (poorly rendered by popular saxophonist Dave Koz), John Barry's *Somewhere in Time*, Richard Rodney Bennett's *Four Weddings and a Funeral*, and Ennio Morricone's *Cinema Paradiso*. The only imaginative move here was to incorporate Erich Wolfgang Korngold's solo piano performance of "Love for Love" (from his score for *Escape Me Never*) into Maurceri and the Hollywood Bowl's rendition, but that seems to have been done more for novelty's sake than anything else. Competently performed but rather routine on the whole.

Andy Dursin

The Great Waltz 𝄞𝄞𝄞𝄞

1993, Philips Records.

Album Notes: The Hollywood Bowl Orchestra, conducted by John Mauceri; *Arrangements*: John Mauceri, Arthur Freed, Charles Gerhardt; *Orchestrations*: Christopher Palmer, Hugo Friedhofer; *Album Producer*: Michael Gore; *Engineer*: Joel Moss.

Selections: The Great Waltz (J. Strauss/D. Tiomkin): 1 Main Title/Wiener Blut (2:38); Murder On The Orient Express (R.R. Bennett): 2 Waltz (3:33); Der Rosenkavalier (R. Strauss): 3 "Mit Mir" Waltz (4:39); The Snows Of Kilimanjaro (B. Herrmann): 4 Memory Waltz (5:26); Gigi (F. Loewe): 5 Main Title/Fountain Scene/Chez Maxim Waltz (6:13); Cinderella (S. Prokofiev): 6 Waltz (3:58); A Little Night Music (S. Sondheim): 7 The Night Waltzes (6:20); Candide (L. Bernstein): 8 Paris Waltz (3:06); Madame Bovary (M. Rozsa): 9 Waltz (4:42); Hotel Berlin (F. Waxman): 10 Cafe Waltzes (8:56); Jezebel (M. Steiner): 11 Waltz (2:09); The Prince And The Pauper (E.W. Korngold): 12 Flirtation (2:27); 13 La Valse (M. Ravel)(13:23); The Great Waltz (J. Strauss/D. Tiomkin): 14 Blue Danube and Final Sequence (6:08).

Review: Taking a cue from Dimitri Tiomkin's adaptation of music by Johann Strauss for *The Great Waltz,* John Mauceri and the Hollywood Bowl Orchestra recorded this album in ³/₄ time. High on the list are the waltzes written by Bernard Herrmann for *The Snows of Kilimanjaro,* by Miklos Rozsa for *Madame Bovary,* and by Max Steiner for *Jezebel.*

The inclusion of Richard Strauss' *Der Rosenkavalier* and Sergei Prekofiev's *Cinderella* seems an odd decision, but there is no denying the power and passion in the selections and the excellence in the performances.

Hollywood Dreams 𝄞𝄞𝄞𝄞

1991, Philips Records.

Album Notes: The Hollywood Bowl Orchestra, conducted by John Mauceri; *Album Producer*: Michael Gore; *Engineer*: Joel Moss.

Selections: 1 Fanfare For A Bowl Concert (A. Schoenberg)(1:25); Carousel (R. Rodgers): 2 Heaven Effect/Carousel Waltz (4:50); Gone With The Wind (M. Steiner): 3 Main Title (4:24); The Firebird (I. Stravinsky): 4 Lullaby/Final Hymn (6:28); How To Marry A Millionaire (A. Newman): 5 20th Century-Fox Fanfare (:22); 6 Overture (6:25); A Place In The Sun (F. Waxman): 7 Suite (9:57); On The Waterfront (L. Bernstein): 8 Love Theme (3:43); The Wizard Of Oz (H. Stothart/H. Arlen/E.Y. Harburg): 9 Concert Suite (11:03); Semyon Kotko (S. Prokofiev): 10 The Southern Night (5:11); The Adventures Of Robin Hood (E.W. Korngold): 11 Franfare and Love Scene (7:11); 12 Battle, Victory and Epilogue (3:55); Defending Your Life (M. Gore): 13 Finale (4:02); Dances With Wolves (J. Barry): 14 John Dunbar Theme (2:26); E.T. (J. Williams): 15 The Flying Theme (4:08).

Review: See entry below.

Hollywood Nightmares 𝄞𝄞𝄞𝄞

1994, Philips Records.

Album Notes: The Hollywood Bowl Orchestra, conducted by John Mauceri; *Album Producer*: Michael Gore; *Engineer*: Joel Moss.

Selections: Phantom Of The Opera (D. Savino/S. Perry): 1 Through The Looking Glass (1:05); King Kong (M. Steiner): 2 Overture (4:08); The Rite Of Spring (I. Stravinsky): 3 The Sacrifice (5:24); Jurassic Park (J. Williams): 4 Main Title (3:16); Vertigo (B. Herrmann): 5 Prelude and Scene d'amour (8:46); Spellbound (M. Rozsa): 6 Concerto for Piano and Orchestra (12:00); Body Heat (J. Barry): 7 Main Title (4:08); Sunset Boulevard (F. Waxman): 8 Sonata For Orchestra (13:45); The Omen (J. Goldsmith): 9 Main Title (3:23); Dracula (J. Williams): 10 Night Journeys (5:38); Dr. Jekyll And Mr. Hyde (F. Waxman): 11 Suite (10:11).

Review: Those thematic albums enable Mauceri and the Hollywood Bowl to cover two opposite aspects of film music, the "dreams" (whatever that might be, particularly when one considers the selections that evoke this concept) and the "nightmares" (with a much better choice in the themes). The selections are essentially standard, with Max Steiner's *Gone With the Wind,* Alfred Newman's *How to Marry a Millionaire,* Franz Waxman's *A Place in the Sun,* and Erich-Wolfgang Korngold's *The Adventures of Robin Hood,* among the choice cuts in the first CD; and

Steiner's *King Kong*, Bernard Herrmann's *Vertigo*, John Williams' *Jurassic Park*, and Waxman's *Sunset Boulevard*, dominating the second CD. Performance and sonic qualities are superior.

Journey to the Stars ♫♫▹

1995, Philips Records.

Album Notes: The Hollywood Bowl Orchestra, conducted by John Mauceri; *Album Producer*: Tommy Krasker; *Engineer*: Joel Moss.

Selections: Aniara (K.B. Blomdahl): 1 Start: Vintergatan (:41); The Day The Earth Stood Still (B. Herrmann): 2 Outer Space (1:40); Star Trek V: The Final Frontier (J. Goldsmith): 3 Main Theme/March Of the Klingons (4:08); Forbidden Planet (L. & B. Barron): 4 Once Around Altair (1:12); The Bride Of Frankenstein (F. Waxman): 5-6 Creation Of The Female Monster/The Tower Explodes (11:06); Altered States (J. Corigliano): 7 Love Theme (4:04); Also Sprach Zarathustra (R. Strauss): 8 Prelude (1:48); 9 Atmospheres (G. Ligeti)(8:33); 2001: A Space Odyssey (A. North): 10 Fanfare (1:44); The Witches Of Eastwick (J. Williams): 11 The Devil's Dance (4:57); Forbidden Planet: 12 Robby Arranges Flowers/Zaps Monkey (:53); Edward Scissorhands (D. Elfman): 13 Main Title/Ice Dance (5:32); Things To Come (A. Bliss): 14 Main Title/War Montage/Pestilence/Happy March/The Building Of The New World/Attack On The Moon Gun/Epilogue (15:54); Forbidden Planet: 15 The Homecoming (:53); Star Wars (J. Williams): 16 Throne Room and Finale (7:43); Aniara (K.B. Blomdahl): 17 Kristal (1:21).

Review: This is a fairly hit and miss effort. Mauceri's rendition of Bernard Herrmann's "Outer Space" from *The Day the Earth Stood Still* is commendable, and one admires his fidelity to the original instrumentation, including the theremin (something Herrmann himself did not retain in his British Decca recording in the '70s). However, Mauceri's rendition of the creation and finale music from Waxman's *Bride of Frankenstein* is an outrage — adding sound effects and even a line of dialogue! Most of the selections are presented relatively intact and are performed with conviction (though the accompanying synthesizer in Goldsmith's *Star Trek V* sounds like a Casio toy keyboard). Interspersed throughout this album are snippets from the "score" for *Forbidden Planet* and other off-putting electronic noises, which add nothing except tacky gimmickry. The mix and recording quality are poor, and make the orchestra sound like a 35-piece television ensemble. Mauceri has done and continues to do much good work in popularizing film music, but he needs to reduce the more kitschy trappings (which spoil much of this album) from future recordings.

Paul Andrew MacLean

The Movies Go to the Hollywood Bowl ♫♫♫♫

1990, Angel Records.

Album Notes: The Hollywood Bowl Symphony Orchestra, conducted by Alfred Newman, Miklos Rozsa; *Featured Soloist*: Leonard Pennario (piano); *Original Album Producer*: Ralph O'Connor; *Engineer*: Carson Taylor; *CD Engineer*: Robert Norberg.

Selections: Captain From Castile (A. Newman): 1 Conquest (3:23); 2 Second Rhapsody (G. Gershwin)(14:16); David And Bathsheba (A. Newman): 3 23rd Psalm (3:24); The Robe (A. Newman): 4 Palm Sunday (2:14); 5 Hallelujah (2:52); 6 The Dream Of Olwen (C. Williams)(3:59); King Of Kings (M. Rozsa): 7 Nativity (2:10); 8 The Way Of The Cross (3:00); 9 Pieta (2:34); 10 King Of Kings Theme (2:48); Spellbound (M. Rozsa): 11 Spellbound Concerto (12:09); El Cid (M. Rozsa): 12 Overture (3:25); 13 Love Theme (4:15); 14 El Cid March (3:27).

Review: This volume compiles together recordings made in the 1960s by Alfred Newman and Miklos Rozsa, conducting the famed Hollywood Bowl Symphony Orchestra, a group of some of the best instrumentalists this side of Vine and Sunset. Superbly recorded in full stereo, they enabled both composers to revisit some of their most popular works, and to provide the sheen they might have missed when originally performed. This is particularly true of Alfred Newman, whose themes from *Captain From Castile* and *David and Bathsheba* had never been available in stereo before, and played in such an exciting way. Similarly, Rozsa's impressive *Spellbound Concerto* is given the superstar treatment, with Leonard Pennario as guest soloist, in a reading that is far superior to any that had been available up to that time.

Music from Hollywood ♫♫♫♫▹

1995, Sony Music/Legacy Records.

Album Notes: *Album Producer*: Didier C. Deutsch; *Engineer*: Chris Herles.

Selections: 1 How The West Was Won (from How The West Was Won)(A. Newman/K. Darby)(3:12); 2 Laura (from Laura)(D. Raksin)(5:46); 3 Caesar's Assassination/Cleopatra's Entrance Into Rome (from Cleopatra)(A. North)(6:38); 4 Suite (from A Place In The Sun)(F. Waxman)(8:21); 5 Raintree County (from Raintree County)(J. Green/P.F. Webster)(6:42); 6 Film Theme Fantasy: a) When You Wish Upon A Star (from Pinocchio)(L. Harline/N. Washington), b) The Best Years Of Our Lives (from The Best Years Of Our Lives)(H. Friedhofer), c) Picnic (from Picnic)(G. Duning/S. Allen), d) Exodus (from Exodus)(E. Gold),

e) Around The World In Eighty Days (from Around The World In Eighty Days)(V. Young/S. Unger/H. Adamson), f) Hi-Lili, Hi-Lo (from Lili)(B. Kaper/H. Deutsch) (8:19); 7 Theme (from A Summer Place)(M. Steiner)(2:40); 8 The Memory Waltz (from The Snows Of Kilimanjaro)(B. Herrmann)(4:36); 9 North By Northwest (from North By Northwest)(B. Herrmann)(3:23); 10 The Green Leaves Of Summer (from The Alamo)(D. Tiomkin/P.F. Webster)(4:16) *Mahalia Jackson*; 11 High Noon (from High Noon)(D. Tiomkin)(5:35); 12 Prelude (from Ben-Hur)(M. Rozsa)(4:01); 13 Parade Of The Charioteers (from Ben-Hur)(M. Rozsa)(3:28); 14 Conquest (from Captain From Castile)(A. Newman)(3:51).

Review: On September 25, 1963, the Composers and Lyricists Guild of America gave an extraordinary televised concert, with many of Hollywood's greatest composers conducting the Hollywood Bowl Symphony Orchestra in selections from their most famous works. The event was also recorded with this CD, for long a much sought-after collector's item, presenting most of the concert as it actually happened. Besides the choice of selections, which include many familiar themes from the movies, the pleasure is heightened by the fact that Alfred Newman, David Raksin, Miklos Rozsa, Bernard Herrmann, Johnny Green (then Executive Director of the Guild) and Dimitri Tiomkin were among the composers taking turns on the podium. The enthusiasm expressed by the record crowd at the Bowl that night is easily communicative.

Body Heat: Jazz at the Movies 🎵🎵🎵🎵

1993, Discovery Records.

Album Notes: *Arrangements*: Nan Mishkin; *Featured Musicians*: Bill Cunliffe (piano), Bernie Dresel (drums), Matt Harris (keyboards), Roberto Vally (bass), Ernie Watts (tenor sax), Kim Richmond (alto sax), Bob Summers, Jack Sheldon (trumpet), John Pisano (acoustic guitar), Ron Kalina (harmonica), Brad Dutz, Brian Kilgore, Scott Breadman (percussion), Mark Portmann, David Loeb (synthesizers), Arnold McCuller (vocals); *Album Producers*: Paul Rothchild, Dan Rothchild.

Selections: Body Heat: 1 Body Heat (J. Barry)(4:03); The Russia House: 2 Katya (Love Theme)(J. Goldsmith)(4:32); Betty Blue: 3 Betty And Zorg/Chili con carne (G. Yared)(7:21); Farewell, My Lovely: 4 Farewell, My Lovely (D. Shire) (4:40); Bagdad Cafe: 5 Calling You (B. Telson)(4:23); Black Orpheus: 6 Black Orpheus (L. Bonfa/A.C. Jobim)(4:20); The Moderns: 7 Les modernes (M. Isham) (3:45); 'Round Midnight: 8 'Round Midnight (T. Monk/C. Williams)(3:27); Blade Runner: 9 Memories

Of Green (Vangelis)(4:43); Taxi Driver: 10 Theme From Taxi Driver (B. Herrmann)(4:53).

Review: See entry below.

Sax and Violence: Music from the Dark Side of the Screen 🎵🎵🎵🎵

1995, Varese-Sarabande Records.

Album Notes: *Orchestrations, Arrangements, Musical Direction*: Lanny Meyers; *Featured Musicians*: Lanny Meyers (piano), Bob Mair (bass), Ed Smith (drums), Paul Viapiano (guitar); Phil Feather, Bob Carr (reeds); Wayne Bergeron, Dennis Farias (trumpets/ flugelhorns); Robert Hioki, Ira Nepus (trombones); Stephanie Mijanovich (French horns); Kirstin Fife, Jean Hugo, Susan Modischy (violins); Jane Levy (viola); Stephanie Fife (cello); *Album Producer*: Bruce Kimmel; *Engineer*: Vincent Cirilli.

Selections: 1 Taxi Driver (B. Herrmann)(3:40); 2 The Double Double: Body Double (P. Donaggio)/Double Indemnity (M. Rozsa)(4:02); 3 Body Heat (J. Barry) (4:27); 4 The Grifters (E. Bernstein)(3:38); 5 Klute (M. Small)(3:58); 6 The Long Goodbye (J. Williams)(4:11); 7 Chinatown (J. Goldsmith)(3:28); 8 Gun Crazy (V. Young)(4:04); 9 Farewell, My Lovely (D. Shire)(3:59); 10 The Blue Dahlia (V. Young)(5:17); 11 Point Blank (J. Mandel)(4:11); 12 Laura (D. Raksin)(4:17); 13 Fatal Attraction (M. Jarre)(4:38); 14 Diva (V. Cosma)(4:12).

Review: This is quite a concept: some of the most sensuous movie themes, arranged for and performed by a jazz band. It may not qualify as film music *per se*, but if one day you get tired of listening to the same old soundtracks you have played for the past twentysomething years, you might want to try these CDs and groove on their different sounds. The themes, by the way, are recognizable, but you still might discover some you didn't know, like David Shire's *Farewell My Lovely,* or Mark Isham's *The Moderns,* in the first CD; or Elmer Bernstein's *The Grifters,* and Victor Young's *The Blue Dahlia,* in the second. Performances vary from one CD to the next, and overall the first might be a tad stronger than the second.

Screen Themes '94 🎵🎵

1995, Discovery Records.

Album Notes: *Orchestrations and Arrangements*: Emilio Kauderer, Michael Garson; The Michael Garson Orchestra conducted by Emilio Kauderer; *Featured Musicians*: Michael Garson (piano, keyboards, synthesizers), Emilio Kauderer (keyboards, synthesizers), Eric Marienthal (saxophones), Jorge

Patrono (drums, percussion), Dave Carpenter (bass), Grant Geissman (guitar), Marsden Smith (cello), Billy Mintz (brushes); *Featured Soloist*: Jessica Tivens (vocals); *Album Producers*: Michael Garson, Emilio Kauderer; *Engineer*: Dino Herrmann.

Selections: Forrest Gump (A. Silvestri): 1 I'm Forrest... Forrest Gump (3:17); Legends Of The Fall (J. Horner): 2 The Ludlows (2:46); The Lion King: 3 Theme (This Land)(H. Zimmer)(3:11); 4 Can You Feel The Love Tonight (E. John)(3:30) *Jessica Tivens*; Pulp Fiction (N. Diamond): 5 Girl, You'll Be A Woman Soon (3:33); Interview With The Vampire (E. Goldenthal): 6 Born To Darkness, Part 1 (3:26); Four Weddings And A Funeral (R.R. Bennett): 7 After The Funeral (2:16); The River Wild (trad.): 8 The Water Is Wide (3:42); True Lies (B. Fiedel): 9 Harry Makes His Entrance (2:23); The Shawshank Redemption (T. Newman): 10 End Title (3:43); Love Affair (E. Morricone): 11 Title Theme (3:28); Nobody's Fool (H. Shore): 12 Main Title (3:34); Little Women (T. Newman): 13 Little Women (1:52); Thirty Two Short Films About Glenn Gould: 14 Prelude No. 1 in C (from The Well Tempered Clavier) (J.S. Bach) (4:45); Immortal Beloved: 15 Sonata No. 8 in C for Piano, op. 13, "Pathetique" (L. Van Beethoven) (3:36); Corrina, Corrina: 16 Gymnopedie No. 1 for Piano (E. Satie) (4:17).

Review: Routine cover versions of some of the most prominent contemporary film themes, including works by Alan Silvestri, James Horner, Hans Zimmer, Elliot Goldenthal, Richard Rodney Bennett, Howard Shore, and... Johann Sebastian Bach and Erik Satie. Sometimes, the imagination of A&R people at some record companies stretch beyond the fathomable. At any rate, the musicians here are okay, not too terribly great, not too bad either. The themes are interestingly developed, but it's too synthetic, without much involvement or understanding about what the music is all about and why it was created in the first place. Johann Sebastian Bach...?

Mysteries

Sherlock Holmes: Classic Themes from 221B Baker Street ♫♫♫

1996, Varese-Sarabande Records.

Album Notes: *Arrangements*: Lanny Meyers, Bonnie Janofsky, Larry Moore, James Bernard; Orchestra conducted by Lanny Meyers; *Featured Musician*: Robert Zubrycki (violin); *Album Producer*: Bruce Kimmel; *Engineer*: Vincent Cirilli.

Selections: Sherlock Holmes: 1 221B Baker Street (P. Gowers)(2:37); The Seven Percent Solution: 2 Suite (J. Addi-

son)(4:22); The Adventures Of Sherlock Holmes: 3 Main Title (C. Mockridge)(1:35); 4 Moriarty: Genius Of Evil (C. Mockridge)(:54); 5 A Study In Terror (J. Scott)(3:06); 6 The Universal Holmes (F. Skinner)(1:05); The Adventures Of Sherlock Holmes: 7 Moriarty: The Game Is Afoot (C. Mockridge)(:47); Young Sherlock Holmes: 8 The Riddle Solved (B. Broughton)(6:13); Sherlock Holmes: 9 The Red Circle (P. Gowers)(1:09); The Seven Percent Solution: 10 I Never Do Anything Twice (S. Sondheim)(5:53); The Adventures Of Sherlock Holmes: 11 Moriarty: Elementary (C. Mockridge)(:46); The Masks Of Death: 12 The Masks Of Death (M. Williamson)(1:37); The Hound Of The Baskervilles: 13 Main Title/The Legend Of The Hound (J. Bernard)(5:08); Dressed To Kill: 14 The Music Box (F. Skinner)(:40); The Private Life Of Sherlock Holmes: 15 Suite (M. Rozsa)(6:56); Without A Clue: 16 End Title (H. Mancini)(2:37).

Review: This elementary musical compendium gathers together 16 selections from 11 Sherlock Holmes movies or television series, from Cyril Mockridge's themes for the 1939 *Adventures of Sherlock Holmes* through Frank Skinner's omnipresently tracked music for all twelve of the Universal Holmes films of the 1940s, through James Bernard's doggedly relentless horror music for Hammer's *The House of the Baskervilles* and John Scott's eerie violin sonorities from *A Study in Terror*, to more recent filmic renditions as *The Seven Percent Solution* (John Addison), *The Private Life of Sherlock Holmes* (Miklos Rozsa), *Without a Clue* (Henry Mancini) and *Young Sherlock Holmes* (Bruce Broughton). Also included are themes from the British television programs, *The Masks of Death* (Malcolm Williamson) and *Sherlock Holmes* (Patrick Gowers). This is a very fine assortment of cues, nicely performed by an unnamed orchestra under the baton of Lanny Meyers. The CD contains much music hitherto unavailable, especially those wonderfully melodramatic scores by Mockridge and Skinner, and Bernard's elegantly cataclysmic Hammer music.

Randall Larson

Swashbucklers

Captain Blood ♫♫♫♫

1995, Marco Polo Records.

Album Notes: The Brandenburg Philharmonic Orchestra of Potsdam, conducted by Richard Kaufman; *Score Reconstruction & Arrangements*: Christopher Palmer, William Stromberg, John Morgan; *Album Producer*: Klaus Bischke; *Engineer*: Gert Puhlmann.

Selections: The King's Thief (M. Rozsa): 1 Suite (7:35); Scaramouche (V. Young): 2 Main Title (1:34); 3 Vanished Merchant (2:06); 4 The Tomb, Andre And Aline (3:47); 5 Why? (1:48); 6 Pavane (2:18); 7 Andre Escapes (1:37); 8 The Big Apple (1:24); 9 The Magic Box/Roses And Napoleon (3:24); 10 End Cast (:46); Captain Blood (E.W. Korngold): 11 Main Title (2:49); 12 Slaves/Arabella And Blood (6:57); 13 Tortuga (1:46); 14 Port Royal/Island Of Magra/English And Pirates Ship (5:06); 15 Pirates Flag (1:40); 16 Finale (1:32); The Three Musketeers (M. Steiner): 17 To Paris/Fencing Demonstration (3:47); 18 Love Theme (4:07); 19 Fight Behind Palace (2:07); 20 Night Time/Pigeons (2:56); 21 Carriage Ride (2:45); 22 Finale (3:05).

Review: See entry below.

Historical Romances ♪♪♪♪

1995, Marco Polo Records.

Album Notes: The Brandenburg Philharmonic Orchestra of Potsdam, conducted by Richard Kaufman; *Score Reconstruction & Arrangements*: William Stromberg, John Morgan; *Album Producer*: Klaus Bischke; *Engineer*: Gert Puhlmann.

Selections: Juarez (E.W. Korngold): 1 Overture (6:11); Gunga Din (A. Newman): 2 Main Title (2:27); 3 "Alright, I'll Sign" (2:55); 4 Across The Bridge/Battle At Tantrapur (6:21); 5 Reading The Poem (1:35); 6 Finale/End Cast (2:10); Devotion (E.W. Korngold): 7 Devotion (5:46); The Charge Of The Light Brigade (M. Steiner): 8 Main Title (3:51); 9 Calcutta (4:35); 10 Waltz (2:18); 11 Love Scene/March (4:26); 12 Moonlight (1:32); 13 "Charge!" (9:57); 14 Epilogue/Cast Credits (1:59).

Review: A lot of good film music from Hollywood's heyday is being re-recorded in Europe. Take for example these two albums: masterfully interpreted by the Brandenburg Philharmonic, in splendid up-to-the-minute digital sound, they focus on excerpts from swashbucklers which, in many cases, have not been heard in any other format, except as background music in the films for which they were written. Both are finds for film music fans who have been longing to hear these scores in full-blown stereo.

Particularly welcome here are the two long suites from Alfred Newman's *Scaramouche* and Max Steiner's *The Three Musketeers* in the first CD, as well as Newman's *Gunga Din* and Max Steiner's *The Charge of the Light Brigade* in the second. All four rank among the finest scores ever created for the swashbuckler and adventure genre, and their inclusion here makes these two CDs all the more desired and valuable.

One may argue with the fact that some tempi seem to be slightly off, or that the orchestra's performance is not always as tight as it could be, but those are minor imperfections that do not detract one iota from the power and sweep of the music and its overall interpretation.

The Prince and the Pauper ♪♪♪♪°

1989, Varese-Sarabande Records.

Album Notes: The National Philharmonic Orchestra, conducted by Charles Gerhardt; *Album Producer*: George Korngold; *Engineer*: John Acoca.

Selections: The Reivers (J. Williams): 1 Suite (5:02); The Lost Weekend (M. Rozsa): 2 Love Theme (5:10); Jane Eyre (J. Williams): 3 The Carriage Ride To Thornfield (1:50); Between Two Worlds (E.W. Korngold): 4 Mother And Son/Piano Rhapsody (5:49); The Constant Nymph (E.W. Korngold): 5 Overture (8:12); The Specter Of The Rose (G. Antheil): 6 Ballet Waltz (4:11); The Madwoman Of Chaillot (M.J. Lewis): 7 End Title (4:22); Cleopatra (A. North): 8 Love Theme (2:24); Julie (L. Pennario): 9 Midnight On The Cliffs (5:15); Who's Afraid Of Virginia Woolf? (A. North): 10 Main Title (2:36); The Prince And The Pauper (E.W. Korngold): 11 Flirtation (2:14); Escape Me Never (E.W. Korngold): 12 Love For Love (3:18); Anne Of The Thousand Days (G. Delerue): 13 Overture (2:55); Henry V (W. Walton): 14 Prelude: London 1600/The Globe Theatre (3:52); 15 Touch Her Soft Lips And Part (1:32); 16 The Battle Of Agincourt/The Duke Of Burgundy's Speech (5:33); 17 The Agincourt Victory Song (2:26).

Review: This album belongs in the same category with the celebrated *Classic Film Scores* series on RCA Victor. In fact, it involves essentially the same people, producer George Korngold, conductor Charles Gerhardt, and the musicians from the National Philharmonic Orchestra. The program is reliable, interesting, and performed with all the right pauses and tugs. Erich-Wolfgang Korngold is given a prominent place here, with selections from *Between Two Worlds*, *The Prince and the Pauper*, and *Escape Me Never*. But the creative minds behind this album also saw fit to add themes from Miklos Rozsa's *Lost Weekend*, John Williams' *The Reivers* and *Jane Eyre*, Georges Delerue's *Anne of the Thousand Days*, Alex North's *Cleopatra* and *Who's Afraid of Virginia Woolf?*, and William Walton's *Henry V*. There are some odd choices, too, like Leonard Pennario's *Julie*, or George Antheil's *The Specter of the Rose*. But overall it's a solid program of seldom heard film themes, performed with the right amount of gusto and pathos by an orchestra that has many such recordings to its credit.

Various Performers

Charming Gents of Stage & Screen ♫♫♫♫

1994, Legacy Records.

Album Notes: *Album Producer*: Didier C. Deutsch; *Engineer*: Chris Herles.

Selections: 1 Fascinatin' Rhythm (G. & I. Gershwin)(from *Lady Be Good*) (2:47) *Cliff Edwards*; 2 On The Sunny Side Of The Street (D. Fields/J. McHugh)(from *International Revue*)(3:33) *Ted Lewis*; 3 If I Could Be With You One Hour Tonight (H. Creamer/J. Johnson)(from *Ladies, They Talk About*)(3:34) *Louis Armstrong*; 4 Chinatown, My Chinatown (W. Jerome/J. Schwartz)(from *Up And Down Broadway*)(2:33) *The Mills Brothers*; 5 Let's Put Out The Lights (And Go To Sleep)(H. Hupfeld)(from *George White's Music Hall Varieties*)(2:49) *Ben Bernie*; 6 Brother, Can You Spare A Dime (E.Y. Harburg/J. Gorney)(from *Americana*)(3:35) *Rudy Vallee*; 7 Eadie Was A Lady (B.G. DeSylva/N.H. Brown/R. Whiting)(from *Take A Chance*)(2:52) *Cab Calloway*; 8 April Showers (B.G. DeSylva/L. Silvers)(from *Bombo*)(3:00) *Al Jolson, Guy Lombardo*; 9 Everything I Have Is Yours (H. Adamson/B. Lane)(from *Dancing Lady*)(2:55) *Gene Austin*; 10 Love In Bloom (L. Robin/R. Rainger)(from *She Loves Me Not*)(3:11) *Bing Crosby, Irving Aaronson, Commanders*; 11 Two Cigarettes In The Dark (L. Pollack/P.F. Webster)(from *Kill That Story*) (3:14) *Frank Parker*; 12 When You're In Love (R. Columbo/B. Grossman/J. Stern)(from *Wake Up And Dream*)(3:09) *Russ Columbo, Jimmie Grier*; 13 With Every Breath I Take (L. Robin/R. Rainger)(from *Here Is My Heart*)(2:55) *Harry Richman*; 14 Lullaby Of Broadway (A. Dubin/H. Warren)(from *Gold Diggers Of 1935*)(3:11) *Dick Powell, Jimmie Grier*; 15 The Lady In Red (M. Dixon/A. Wrubel)(from *In Caliente*)(2:59) *Louis Prima*; 16 Top Hat, White Tie And Tails (I. Berlin)(from *Top Hat*)(2:28) *Fred Astaire, Johnny Green*; 17 I Cried For You (A. Freed/G. Arnheim/ A. Lyman)(2:38) *Red McKenzie*; 18 Now It Can Be Told (I. Berlin)(from *Alexander's Ragtime Band*)(3:07) *Tony Martin, Ray Noble*; 19 If You Knew Susie (Like I Know Susie)(B.G. DeSylva/J. Meyer) (from *Big Boy*)(2:32) *Eddie Cantor*; 20 Stout-Hearted Men (S. Romberg/O. Hammerstein II)(from *The New Moon*)(2:43) *Nelson Eddy, Nathaniel Finston*.

Review: See entry below.

Lovely Ladies of Stage & Screen ♫♫♫♫

1994, Legacy Records.

Album Notes: *Album Producer*: Didier C. Deutsch; *Engineer*: Chris Herles.

Selections: 1 Can't Help Lovin' Dat Man (J. Kern/O. Hammerstein II) (from *Show Boat*) (3:47) *Helen Morgan, Victor Young*; 2 I Must Have That Man (D. Fields/J. McHugh) (from *Blackbirds Of 1933*) (3:08) *Adelaide Hall, Duke Ellington*; 3 I Gotta Right To Sing The Blues (T. Koehler/H. Arlen) (from *Earl Carroll's Vanities Of 1932*) (2:47) *Lee Wiley*; 4 They Call Me Sister Honky Tonk (G. DuBoise/B. Ellison/H. Brooks) (from *I'm No Angel*) (3:03) *Mae West*; 5 Heat Wave (I. Berlin) (from *As Thousands Cheer*) (2:58) *Ethel Waters, Ben Selvin*; 6 Alexander's Ragtime Band (I. Berlin) (from *Hullo, Ragtime*) (3:01) *The Boswell Sisters, Jimmy Dorsey, Tommy Dorsey*; 7 College Rhythm (M. Gordon/H. Revel) (from *College Rhythm*) (2:54) *Lyda Roberti, Jimmie Grier*; 8 You're The Top (C. Porter) (from *Anything Goes*) (2:52) *Ethel Merman, Johnny Green*; 9 Shine On Harvest Moon (J. Norworth/N. Bayes) (from *Ziegfeld Follies Of 1908*) (2:45) *Ruth Etting*; 10 I'm In The Mood For Love (D. Fields/J. McHugh) (from *Every Night At Eight*) (2:53) *Frances Langford, Mahlon Merrick*; 11 You Let Me Down (A. Dubin/H. Warren) (from *Stars Over Broadway*) (3:13) *Kay Thompson*; 12 More Than You Know (V. Youmans/B. Rose/E. Eliscu) (from *Great Day*) (3:15) *Mildred Bailey*; 13 Slumming On Park Avenue (I. Berlin) (from *On The Avenue*) (2:35) *Alice Faye, Cy Feuer*; 14 Swing High, Swing Low (R. Freed/B. Lane) (from *Swing High, Swing Low*) (2:31) *Dorothy Lamour, Cy Feuer*; 15 Easy Living (L. Robin/R. Rainger) (from *Easy Living*) (3:02) *Billie Holiday, Teddy Wilson*; 16 The Folks Who Live On The Hill (J. Kern/O. Hammerstein II) (from *High, Wide And Handsome*) (2:59) *Maxine Sullivan, Claude Thornhill*; 17 Most Gentlemen Don't Like Love (C. Porter) (from *Leave It To Me*) (2:20) *Mary Martin, Eddy Duchin*; 18 If You Can't Sing It (You'll Have To Swing It) (S. Coslow) (from *Rhythm On The Range*) (3:07) *Martha Raye, David Rose*; 19 When The Moon Comes Over The Mountain (H. Johnson/H. Woods/K. Smitho) (3:13) *Kate Smith, Jack Miller*; 20 Boy! What Love Has Done To Me (G. & I. Gershwin) (from *Girl Crazy*) (2:28) *Jane Froman*.

Review: Both compilations offer selections recorded for the Brunswick label by some of the most prominent stars of stage and screen in the 1930s. Among the classy gentlemen heard in the first CD are Louis Armstrong, Rudy Vallee, Cab Calloway, Al Jolson, Bing Crosby, Russ Columbo, Dick Powell, Louis Prima, Fred Astaire, and Tony Martin, all of them stars of the first magnitude. On the distaff side, Helen Morgan, Mae West, Ethel Waters, Lyda Roberti, Ruth Etting, Billie Holiday, Martha Raye, Dorothy Lamour, and Mary Martin are some of the names that pop up. All the songs were big hits in their time, and have become standards, and both collections are quite enjoyable.

The Hollywood Men ♫♫♫♫

1989, RCA Records.

Album Notes: *Album Producer*: Chick Crumpacker; *Engineer*: Dick Baxter.

Selections: 1 Let A Smile Be Your Umbrella (On A Rainy Day)(I. Kahal/F. Wheeler/S. Fain)(2:49) *Bing Crosby, Bob Scobey's Frisco Jazz Band*; 2 Mary's A Grand Old Name (G.M. Cohan)(from *Yankee Doodle Dandy*)(2:09) *James Cagney, Paramount Studio Orchestra, Joseph J. Lilley*; 3 Drink, Drink, Drink (S. Romberg/D. Donnelly)(from *The Student Prince*)(3:14) *Mario Lanza, Jeff Alexander Choir, Constantine Callinicos*; 4 That Certain Feeling (G. & I. Gershwin)(from *That Certain Feeling*)(2:14) *Bob Hope with The Skylarks, Paramount Studio Orchestra, Joseph J. Lilley*; 5 The Yellow Rose Of Texas (trad.) (from *The Yellow Rose Of Texas*)(2:33) *Roy Rogers*; 6 Silk Stockings (C. Porter)(from *Silk Stockings*)(2:07) *Don Ameche, Herbert Greene*; 7 Those Were The Good Old Days (R. Adler/J. Ross) (from *Damn Yankees*)(2:35) *Ray Walston, Warner Bros. Studio Orchestra, Ray Heindorf*; 8 Monte Carlo (A. North)(from *The Racers*)(1:36) *Alex North*; 9 Island In The Sun (L. Burgess/ H. Belafonte) (from *Island In The Sun*)(3:07) *Harry Belafonte, Robert DeCormier*; 10 My Love Parade (V. Schertzinger/C. Grey) (from *Love Parade*)(2:29) *Maurice Chevalier with Orchestra, Leonard Joy*; 11 Bundle Of Joy/All About Love (J. Myrow/M. Gordon)(from *Bundle Of Joy*)(2:26) *Eddie Fisher, RKO Studio Orchestra, Hugo Winterhalter*; 12 Boy On A Dolphin (H. Friedhofer/P.F. Webster)(from *Boy On A Dolphin*)(3:17) *Tony Perkins, Urbie Green*; 13 Nigth And Day (C. Porter)(from *The Gay Divorce*)(3:25) *Fred Astaire, Leo Reisman*; 14 The Pink Panther Theme (H. Mancini)(from *The Pink Panther*)(2:36) *Henry Mancini*; 15 How Would You Like To Be (B. Raleigh/T. Barkan)(from *It Happened At The World's Fair*)(3:28) *Elvis Presley, The Mello Men*; 16 The Shadow Of Your Smile (J. Mandel/P.F. Webster)(from *The Sandpiper*)(3:47) *Perry Como, Nick Perito*; 17 Be Careful, It's My Heart (I. Berlin)(2:46) *Frank Sinatra, Tommy Dorsey*; 18 The Bad And The Beautiful (D. Raskin/ D. Previn)(from *The Bad And The Beautiful*)(2:55) *Andre Previn*; 19 I Love My Wife (T. Jones/H. Schmidt)(from *I Do! I Do!*)(2:04) *Robert Preston, John Lesko*; 20 Everybody's Talkin' (F. Neil)(from *Midnight Cowboy*)(2:43) *Harry Nilsson*.

Review: See entry below.

"I'm Ready For My Close-Up!": The Hollywood Ladies Sing ♫♫♫

1989, RCA Records.

Album Notes: *Album Producer*: Chick Crumpacker; *Engineer*: Dick Baxter.

Selections: 1 What So Good About Good Morning/Worry About Tomorrow—Tomorrow (J. Myrow/M. Gordon)(from *Bundle Of Joy*)(1:37) *Debbie Reynolds, Nita Talbot, RKO Studio Orchestra, Hugo Winterhalter*; 2 Don't Cry Joe (J. Marsala)(2:36) *Juanita Hall, Henri Rene*; 3 All Of Me (S. Simon/G. Marks)(from *Careless Lady*)(1:52) *Connee Boswell, The Original Memphis Five*; 4 I'm Gonna File My Claim (L. Newman/ K. Darby)(from *River Of No Return*)(2:37) *Marilyn Monroe, 20th Century-Fox Studio Orchestra, Lionel Newman*; 5 If You Can Dream (S. Cahn/N. Brodzsky)(from *Meet Me In Las Vegas*)(2:51) *Lena Horne, Lennie Hayton*; 6 It's Oh So Quiet (B. Reisfeld/R. Lang)(3:07) *Betty Hutton, Pete Rugolo*; 7 The Saga Of Jenny (K. Weill/I. Gershwin)(from *Lady In The Dark*)(3:55) *Ann Sothern, Charles Sanford*; 8 Whatever Lola Wants (R. Adler/J. Ross)(from *Damn Yankees*)(3:51) *Gwen Verdon, Warner Bros. Studio Orchestra, Ray Heindorf*; 9 Love Letters (V. Young/E. Heyman)(from *Love Letters*)(4:56) *Gogi Grant, Dennis Farnon*; 10 Beyond The Blue Horizon (R. Whiting/L. Robin/F. Harling)(from *Monte Carlo*) (2:23) *Jeanette MacDonald, David Rose*; 11 I'd Rather Be Blue Over You (Than Happy With Somebody Else)(B. Rose/F. Fisher)(2:19) *Fanny Brice, Leonard Joy*; 12 What Wouldn't I Do For That Man! (E.Y. Harburg/J. Gorney)(from *Applause*)(2:56) *Helen Morgan, Leonard Joy*; 13 Ich bin die Fesche Lola (F. Hollander/ J. Liebman)(from *The Blue Angel*)(2:33) *Marlene Dietrich, Friedrich Hollander*; 14 I Wanna Be Loved By You (B. Kalmar/H. Stothart/H. Ruby)(from *Good Boy*)(2:46) *Helen Kane, Leonard Joy*; 15 Honeymoon Hotel (A. Dubin/H. Warren)(from *Footlight Parade*)(3:08) *Alice Faye, Rudy Vallee, Connecticut Yankees*; 16 Got A Bran' New Suit (H. Dietz/A. Schwartz)(from *At Home Abroad*) (2:27) *Eleanor Powell, Tommy Dorsey*; 17 I Used To Be Color Blind (I. Berlin)(from *Carefree*)(3:25) *Ginger Rogers, Hal Borne*; 18 When April Sings (G. Kahn/R. Stolz)(from *Spring Parade*) (2:48) *Deanna Durbin*; 19 You're The One (For Me)(J. McHugh/J. Mercer)(from *You're The One*)(2:46) *Janet Blair, Hal Kemp*; 20 If You Ever, Ever Loved Me (J. Meyer/A. Sherman/A. Silver)(from *Love Me Tonight*) (2:12) *Gloria De Haven, Jan Savitt*.

Review: A principle somewhat similar to the one used in the two Legacy recordings listed above is at play here, with the selections coming from the RCA catalogue. The stars heard were all signed to the label at one time or another, with the difference that the two sets, instead of focusing on a given period like the ones on Legacy, take a broader view and encompass selections from the 1930s to the '60s. The only problem this causes has to do with sonic quality, which varies tremendously from cut to cut, and which is further brought into sharp focus because the tracks aren't presented chronologically. Don't let this detract you from enjoying the performances in either set, with Bing Crosby, Bob Hope, Mario Lanza, Harry Belafonte, Perry Como, Fred Astaire, Tony Perkins, and Robert

Preston, among the luminaries in the first CD; and Debbie Reynolds, Lena Horne, Marilyn Monroe, Jeanette MacDonald, Helen Morgan, and Marlene Dietrich, in the second.

Naughty But Nice: "Bad Girls" of the Movie Musical ♫♫♫♫

1993, Sony Music Special Products.

Album Notes: *Album Producer*: Dan Rivard; *Engineers*: Debra Parkinson, Ken Robertson.

Selections: 1 Thanks A Lot, But No Thanks (A. Previn/B. Comden/A. Green) (from *It's Always Fair Weather*) (3:44) *Dolores Gray, The M-G-M Studio Orchestra, Andre Previn*; 2 Naughty But Nice (H. Warren/J. Mercer) (from *The Belle Of New York*) (3:50) *Anita Ellis, The M-G-M Studio Orchestra, Adolph Deutsch*; 3 Red Garters (J. Livingston/R. Evans) (from *Red Garters*) (2:39) *Rosemary Clooney, The Paramount Studio Orchestra, Joseph J. Lilley*; 4 Always True To You (In My Fashion) (C. Porter) (from *Kiss Me Kate*) (2:45) *Ann Miller, Tommy Rall, The M-G-M Studio Orchestra, Andre Previn*; 5 Two-Faced Woman (A. Schwartz/H. Dietz) (from *Torch Song*) (4:09) *Patricia Michaels, The M-G-M Studio Orchestra and Chorus, Adolph Deutsch*; 6 Satin And Silk (C. Porter) (from *Silk Stockings*) (2:37) *Janis Paige, The M-G-M Studio Orchestra, Andre Previn*; 7 Zip (R. Rodgers/L. Hart) (from *Pal Joey*) (3:04) *Jo Ann Greer, The Columbia Studio Orchestra, Morris Stoloff*; 8 Heat Wave (I. Berlin) (from *There's No Business Like Show Business*) (3:54) *Marilyn Monroe, The 20th Century-Fox Orchestra and Chorus, Alfred Newman*; 9 Whatever Lola Wants (R. Adler/J. Ross) (from *Damn Yankees*) (3:50) *Gwen Verdon, The Warner Bros. Studio Orchestra, Ray Heindorf*; 10 I'll Be Hard To Handle (J. Kern/B. Dougall/D. Fields) (from *Lovely To Look At*) (3:25) *Ann Miller, The M-G-M Studio Orchestra, Carmen Dragon*; 11 Ladies In Waiting (C. Porter) (from *Les Girls*) (2:23) *Mitzi Gaynor, Taina Elg, Kay Kendall, The M-G-M Studio Orchestra, Adolph Deutsch*; 12 Ten Cents A Dance (R. Rodgers/L. Hart) (from *Love Me Or Leave Me*) (3:08) *Doris Day, Percy Faith and His Orchestra*; 13 How'd You Like To Spoon With Me? (J. Kern/E. Laska) (from *Till The Clouds Roll By*) (3:06) *Angela Lansbury, The M-G-M Studio Orchestra and Chorus, Lennie Hayton*; 14 Bored (R. Wright/G. Forrest/A. Borodin) (from *Kismet*) (2:59) *Dolores Gray , The M-G-M Studio Orchestra, Andre Previn*; 15 Honey In The Honeycomb (J. Latouche/V. Duke) (from *Cabin In The Sky*) (1:25) *Lena Horne, The M-G-M Studio Orchestra, Georgie Stoll*; 16 It (S. Romberg/O. Harbach/O. Hammerstein II) (from *Deep In My Heart*) (4:41) *Ann Miller, The M-G-M Studio Orchestra and Chorus, Adolph Deutsch*.

Review: Another fun compilation which brings together various female performers in songs with a central motif to them... naughty but nice. Most of the tracks were culled from the actual soundtrack albums, and have the advantage of being the "real" thing, as opposed to rerecordings. As for the "naughty" girls ready for their close-up here, the list is quite impressive: Rosemary Clooney, Ann Miller, Marilyn Monroe, Doris Day, Lena Horne, Gwen Verdon—quite a line-up.

War Films

Apocalypse Nam: The 10,000 Day War ♫♫♫

1993, edel America Records.

Album Notes: *Album Producer*: Arch Stanton.

Selections: Apocalypse Now: 1 Ride Of The Valkyries (R. Wagner) (4:51) *The Orchestre Symphonique de Radio-Tele-Luxembourg, Louis de Froment*; Vietnam Texas (R. Stone): 2 End Credits (3:11); Flight Of The Intruder (J. Beal): 3 Trailer Music (3:26); The Deer Hunter (S. Myers): 4 Cavatina (2:49) *Kevan Torfeh, Gregg Nestor*; Vietnam War Stories (M. Snow): 5 Main Title and End Credits (4:04); Airwolf (R. Patterson/D. Milner): 6 Love Theme (1:39); Casualties Of War (J. Beal): 7 Trailer Music (2:04); Platoon Leader (G.S. Clinton): 8 Main Title (4:34); First Blood (J. Goldsmith): 9 It's A Long Road (2:53) *The National Philharmonic Orchestra, Jerry Goldsmith*; Purple Hearts (R. Folk): 10 Love Theme (6:17); Missing In Action (J. Chattaway): 11 March To Freedom/Main Title/Crossing To 'Nam (5:45); Braddock: Missing In Action II (J. Chattaway): 12 Lin's Theme (3:54); Missing In Action: The Beginning (B. May): 13 Sometimes You Gotta Fight/The Burning Bridge/The Worms/Final Battle/End Title (18:07); Platoon: 14 Adagio For Strings (S. Barber) (8:18) *The Scottsdale Symphony Orchestra, Irving Fleming*.

Review: This thematic CD offers selections from various scores written for war films, in an odd combination of soundtrack performances and cover versions. Some are quite interesting in this context, notably Robert Folk's *Purple Hearts* or Jay Chattaway's *Braddock: Missing in Action II*, which are not frequently found on compilations of this kind. But quite frankly, the inclusion of Wagner's "Ride of the Walkyries" and Samuel Barber's "Adagio For Strings" denotes a lack of imagination on the part of the A&R people who have put this collection together. There are enough selections that could have been used, instead, whether from well-known films or from more obscure ones.

compilation soundtracks

Westerns

How the West Was Won: Classic Western Film Scores 1 ♪♪ʾ

1996, Silva Screen Records.

Album Notes: The City of Prague Philharmonic, conducted by Nic Raine, Paul Bateman, Derek Wadsworth; *Orchestrations*: Christopher Palmer, Derek Wadsworth, Richard Bronskill, Nic Raine, Lee Holdridge, Ira Hearshen, Donn Wilkerson, Arthur Morton; *Album Producer*: James Fitzpatrick; *Engineer*: John L. Timperly.

Selections: The Magnificent Seven (E. Bernstein): 1 The Magnificent Seven (5:50); High Plains Drifter (D. Barton): 2 Theme (4:12); Gettysburg (R. Edelman): 3 Suite: Main Title/Fife And Gun/The Gettysburg Address (recited by Daniel Massey)/Reunion And Finale (15:47); The Professionals (M. Jarre): 4 Overture (5:24); Buffalo Girls (L. Holdridge): 5 Suite (7:29); The Wild Bunch (J. Fielding): 6 Suite: Train Montage/All Fall Down (12:30); Wild Rovers (J. Goldsmith): 7 Bronco Bustin' (2:12); How The West Was Won (A. Newman): Suite: 8 Prelude (3:20); 9 The Land (3:54); 10 Cleve And His Mule (2:06); 11 Intermezzo (5:17); 12 Cheyenne Attack And Aftermath (8:07); 13 Finale (1:30).

Review: If sheer volume equaled quality, the Silva Screen label would be the most important label in the history of motion picture music; they seem to crank out half a dozen compilation albums a month, but the results, while well-intentioned, are often less than the sum of their parts. *How The West Was Won* is the first in an ambitious western film music collection, and it offers a good mix of the familiar (Elmer Bernstein's *The Magnificent Seven* and Alfred Newman's *How the West Was Won*), the unfamiliar (Lee Holdridge's tuneful *Buffalo Girls* and Dee Barton's spooky *High Plains Drifter*), and the unfairly overlooked (Jerry Fielding's brilliant *The Wild Bunch*, Maurice Jarre's rambunctious *The Professionals* and Jerry Goldsmith's bracing *The Wild Rovers*). Randy Edelman's *Gettysburg* fills out the bill, but it's the weak sister of this bunch, often dragging the album to a halt with its fatuous historical anthem. The treatments by Nic Raine and the untiring City of Prague Orchestra are equally hit-and-miss, with the more explosive Bernstein and Fielding material often coming across as clumsy and bombastic (and the tempos of *The Wild Bunch* are slowed down so much as to be unrecognizable). Jarre's *The Professionals* fares well, but *High Plains Drifter* is treated as too much of a traditional western melody.

Buffalo Girls and *High Plains Drifter* are the only previously unavailable offerings, which means around 66 minutes of this 78 minute album is available in better-sounding versions on their original soundtrack albums.

Jeff Bond

Lonesome Dove: Classic Western Scores 2 ♪♪♪♪

1996, Silva Screen Records.

Album Notes: The City of Prague Philharmonic, conducted by Nic Raine; *Orchestrations*: Greig McRitchie, Nic Raine, Ira Hearshen, Jack Hayes, Leo Shuken, Jerome Moross, David Snell, Leo Arnaud, Christopher Palmer, Derek Wadsworth; *Album Producer*: James Fitzpatrick; *Engineer*: John L. Timperley.

Selections: Lonesome Dove (B. Poledouris): 1 Suite (9:47); Heaven's Gate: 2 Sweet Breeze (D. Mansfield)(4:06); 3 Mamou Two-Step (D. Kershaw)(1:49); Old Gringo (L. Holdridge): 4 Finale (7:21); The Sons Of Katie Elder (E. Bernstein): 5 Main Theme (2:12); The Proud Rebel (J. Moross): 6 Pastorale (3:38); El Condor (M. Jarre): 7 Main Titles (3:21); She Wore A Yellow Ribbon (R. Hageman): 8 Suite (7:33); Blue (M. Hadjidakis): 9 The River (4:06); Red River (D. Tiomkin): 10 River Crossing (3:40); Hang 'Em High (D. Frontiere): 11 Main Theme (3:40); Red Sun (M. Jarre): 12 Suite (11:10); The Outlaw Josey Wales (J. Fielding): 13 The War Is Over (4:30).

Review: While some of these themes can be found elsewhere, notably in their soundtrack album versions, it seems a nice thing to have them compiled together here, played by an orchestra that seems to be getting better each time. But the best here is the inclusion of selections that are being recorded in stereo for the first time, like the suite from *She Wore a Yellow Ribbon*, or the one from *Old Gringo*. Also noteworthy are Basil Poledouris' suite from *Lonesome Dove*, and Maurice Jarre's *Red Sun*. The rest seems to be like a bit of padding, but who should complain when the performance is so vibrant and exciting?

The Wild Bunch: Best of the West ♪♪♪

1993, Silva Screen Records.

Album Notes: The Czech Symphony Orchestra, conducted by William Motzing; *Arrangers*: Christopher Palmer, Karl-Heinz Loges, Volker Rippe, William Motzing; *Soloists*: Michael Goltz (guitar), Giuseppe Solera (harmonica), Irmard Schneider (vocals), Zdenek Sedlvy (trumpet); *Album Producer*: Thomas Karban; *Engineer*: Malcolm Luker.

Selections: The Sons Of Katie Elder (E. Bernstein): 1 Main Title (2:10); Dances With Wolves (J. Barry): 2 The John Dunbar Theme (2:20); Silverado (B. Broughton): 3 Suite (4:50); High Noon (D. Tiomkin): 4 Theme (2:43); Once Upon A Time In The West (E. Morricone): 5 Suite (8:04); The Magnificent Seven (E. Bernstein): 6 Suite (5:35); Rio Lobo (J. Goldsmith): 7 Main Title Theme (5:12); The Alamo (D. Tiomkin): 8 Overture (3:54); Lonesome Dove (B. Poledouris): 9 Theme (3:02); The Blue And The Grey (B. Broughton): 10 Main Title/John Leaves Home (4:48); A Fistful Of Dynamite (E. Morricone): 11 Theme (3:59); TV Western Themes Medley: 12 Bonanza (J. Livingston/R. Evans/D. Rose)(1:45); 13 High Chapparal (D. Rose)(1:25); 14 The Big Valley (G. Duning) (2:42); 15 Little House On The Prairie (D. Rose)(1:52); 16 Rawhide (D. Tiomkin/N. Washington)(1:39); The Ballad Of Cable Hogue (J. Goldsmith): 17 The Ballad Of Cable Hogue (3:00); Young Guns II (A. Silvestri): 18 The Big Battle (3:20); Return Of A Man Called Horse (L. Rosenthal): 19 Main Title (5:31); Gunfight At The O.K. Corral (D. Tiomkin): 20 Main Theme (3:00); The Wild Bunch (J. Fielding): 21 La golondrina/End Credits (2:52); The Big Country (J. Moross): 22 Main Title (3:27).

Review: Another western theme compilation from Silva Screen, this one recorded by the Czech Symphony Orchestra, in spectacular sound. The selections are predictable, and instead of the routine themes from *The Sons of Katie Elder*, *Dances With Wolves*, *The Magnificent Seven*, and *Gunfight At The O.K. Corral*, it would have been nice to get something different for a change. Granted, the compilation also contains *The Blue and the Grey*, and *The Ballad of Cable Hogue*, which are rarer, but that's hardly sufficient to recommend this CD, particularly when there are so many others that are far superior. Performances are adequate, though the musicians sometimes don't get the tempi right, or let out a few quacks.

Spaghetti Westerns

Spaghetti Westerns: volume one ♫♫♫

1995, DRG Records.

Album Notes: *Album Producer*: Claudio Fuiano.

Selections: CD 1: Shango (The Invincible Gun)(G. Di Stefano): 1 Jeff Bloom (1:34); 2 Fiesta, Fiesta! (2:54); 3 Pistole che scottano (1:34); Quanto costa morire (F. De Masi): 4 Quanto costa morire (2:34); 5 Una colt bruciata (1:38); 6 C'e sempre una vita (2:13); Amore piombo e furore (P. Donaggio): 7 Tema di Clayton (1:59); 8 Tema d'amore (1:23); Ed ora raccomanda l'anima a Dio (And Now Recommend Your Soul To God)(F. Bixio): 9 Just A Coward (2:38) *Mary Usuah*; 10 Just A Coward (2:38); Wanted Johnny Texas (M. Gigante/A. Nadin/A. Bascerano): 11 Main Titles (2:57); 12 M22 (3:31); 13 Finale (2:24); Quei disperati che puzzano di sudore e di morte (Los Desperados)(G. Ferrio): 14 Tema per una vendetta (1:03); 15 Oltre il confine (2:04); 16 Tema per un amore (1:42); 17 Cento cavalleggeri (1:40); Kid Il Monello del West (E. Simonetti): 18 Black Jack (1:44); Deserto di fuoco (R. Pregadio): 19 Main Titles (2:12) *Edda Dell' Orso*; 20 Ombre sulla sabbia (4:40); 21 Finale (2:06); Carambola (F. Bixio/F. Frizzi/V. Tempera): 22 Main Titles (1:52); 23 Mexican Cantina (1:41); 24 Finale (1:52); Carambola filotto tutti in buca (F. Bixio/F. Frizzi/V. Tempera): 25 Tema principale (2:00); 26 Funny Town (2:03); Amico stammi lontano almeno un palmo (Ben And Charlie)(G. Ferrio): 27 Let It Rain, Let It Pour (3:23); 28 Un pssaggio per Red Rock (1:37); 29 Sensazioni (2:22); 30 Ridendo e scherzando (2:08); 31 Addio Sarah (1:10); 32 Controluce (3:56); Giu la testa (Duck, You Sucker)(E. Morricone): 33 Giu la testa (4:06).

CD 2: Uno straniero a Paso Bravo (A.F. Lavagnino): 1 Main Titles (single version)(2:51); 2 Main Titles (film version)(2:51); 3 Main Titles (vocal version)(2:51) *Vittorio Bezzi*; Prega Dio e scavati la fossa (Pray To God And Dig Your Grave)(M. Gigante): 4 Main Titles (2:38); 5 M26III (1:20); 6 M9V (2:05); La notte dei serpenti (R. Ortolani): 7 Main Titles XIII (2:28); 8 Canzone VI (2:53) *Katina Ranieri*; 9 M 2 I (2:00); 10 M38XI (1:51); 11 M3I (1:35); 12 M25XVII/M42II (3:01); Requiem per un gringo (A.F. Lavagnino): 13 Sandstorm (2:16); 14 Twilight (2:15); 15 The Moon And You (1:51); 16 Pistols Galore (1:54); Vado Vedo e Sparo (I tre che sconvolsero il West)(C. Rustichelli): 17 Vado Vedo e Sparo (1:54); 18 Galoppa Susanna! (2:38); Johnny West, Il Mancino (The Left-Handed Gunfighter)(A.F. Lavagnino): 19 Disco Western III (2:58); 20 M4III/M6I (1:03); 21 M21I/M65III (1:33); 22 Finale (2:16) *Katina Ranieri*; Roy Colt And Winchester Jack (P. Umiliano): 23 Suite (4:35); Sartana nella valle degli avvoltoi (A. Martelli): 24 M6/M7/M8 (2:53); 25 A King For A Day (2:28); 26 M18V (1:32); Ancora dollari per I McGregors (A. Martelli): 27 M5/M9/M15/M33III (1:23); La colera del vento (A. Martelli): 28 M9/M15V (1:58); Sella d'argento (F. Bixio/F. Frizzi/V. Tempera): 29 M34 (1:12); Franco e Ciccio sul sentiero di guerra (R. Pregadio): 30 Fantasia Western (3:42); I quattro dell'Ave Maria (Aces High)(C. Rustichelli): 31 Main Titles (1:28); La collina degli stivali (The Hill Of The Boots)(C. Rustichelli): 32 Suite(2:39); I quattro dell'Apocalisse (F. Bixio/F. Frizzi/V. Tempera): 33 Slow Violence (2:11); Occhio alla penna (E. Morricone): 34 L'estasi del miracolo (2:50).

Review: See entry below.

Spaghetti Westerns: volume two ♫♫♫

1995, DRG Records.

Album Notes: *Album Producer*: Claudio Fuiano.

Selections: CD 1: 100.000 dollari per Ringo ($100,000 For Ringo)(B. Nicolai): 1 Suite (9:34); I due gringos del Texas (The Two Ringos From Texas) (C. Savina): 2 Main Titles (2:25); 3 M11 (1:13); 4 (:47); Django, l'ultimo killer (The Last Gunfighter)(R. Pregadio/W. Rizzati): 5 Main Titles (1:58); 6 M13 (1:25); 7 M14 (1:51); 8 M43 (1:33); Si puo fare... Amigo! (The Big And The Bad)(L. Bacalov): 9 Can Be Done (3:12) *Rocky Roberts*; 10 M27 (1:19); 11 Can Be Done (instrumental)(:44); Tepepa (Blood And Guns)(E. Morricone): 12 Viva la revolucion (4:17); Vamos a matar, companeros (Companeros)(E. Morricone): 13 Main Titles (2:22); Una ragione per vivere e une per morire (A Reason To Live, A Reason To Die)(R. Ortolani): 14 Main Titles (2:10); Io non perdono... uccido (I Don't Forgive, I Kill)(P. Piccioni): 15 Main Titles (2:04); 16 M28 (1:19); 17 M29 (1:09); Killer, Adios! (C. Tallino): 18 Main Titles (2:37); 19 M26 (2:10); 20 M27 (3:29); 21 Theme Song (2:36); I crudeli (The Hellbenders)(E. Morricone): 22 The Hellbenders (2:36); Che c'entriamo noi con la rivoluzione? (What Am I Doing In The Middle Of This Revolution?)(E. Morricone): 23 What Am I Doing? (4:53); La piu grande rapina del West (The Greatest Robbery In The West)(L. Bacalov): 24 The Greatest Robbery In The West (2:18); L'oro dei Bravados (Gold Of The Proud Ones)(L. Bacalov): 25 Main Titles (2:09); Il grande duello (The Great Duel)(L. Bacalov): 26 A (mix II)(2:40); 27 M10 (2:22); Nel nome del Padre, del Figlio e della Colt (In The Name Of The Father, Of The Son, And Of The Gun)(P. Piccioni): 28 Main Titles (2:55); 29 Alternate Main Titles (1:58); I lunghi giorni della vendetta (Days Of Vengeance)(A. Trovaioli): 30 Main Titles (1:09).

CD 2: Il mio nome e' Nessuno (My Name Is Nobody)(E. Morricone): 1 My Name Is Nobody (3:07); Quien Sabe? (A Bullet For The General)(L. Bacalov): 2 Main Titles (3:41); Texas Addio (The Avenger)(A.G. Abril): 3 Texas Addio (2:32) *Don Powell*; Sette Winchester per un massacro (Seven Guns For A Killing)(F. De Masi): 4 Seven Men (2:20); Sugar Colt (L. Bacalov): 5 Sugar Colt (2:15); I quattro del Pater Noster (The Four Horsemen Of The Pater Noster)(L. Bacalov): 6 Main Titles (1:24); 7 M33 (2:18); 8 M20/M43/M24/M22 (2:14); Professionisti per un massacro (Professional Killers)(C. Pes): 9 Professional Killers (suite) (7:52); Monta in sella, figlio di... (Ride A Horse, Son Of...)(L. Bacalov): 10 M19 (2:10); 11 M3/M12 (1:46); 12 M34 (1:06); 13 M40 (2:19); Lo chiavamano King (A Man Called King)(L. Bacalov): 14 Main Titles (1:57); 15 A Man Called King (suite)(4:50); La morte sull'alta collina (Death On The High Hill)(L. Bacalov): 16 M11 (1:40); 17 M33 (1:17); Partirono preti e tornarono curati (We'll Leave Priests And We'll Return Cured)(L. Bacalov): 18 Blue Eggs And Ham (2:55); 19 M23 (1:13); 20 Blue Eggs And Ham (2:42); Un buco in fronte (A Hole In The Forehead)(R. Pregadio): 21 M1 (1:24); 22 M2 (1:19); 23 M15 (:46); 24 M17 (1:06); 25 M20 (2:30); 26 M24/M25/M27 (1:28); 27 Crying (Main Theme) (2:16); Una colt in mano al diavolo (A Gun In The Hand Of The Devil)(P. Piccioni): 28 Main Titles (3:03); 29 M16 (1:31); Django (L. Bacalov): 30 Django (2:54) *Roberto Fia*; Se incontri Sartana, prega per la tua morte (If You Run Into Sartana, Pray For Your Death)(P. Piccioni): 31 Main Titles (1:33); 32 Main Titles (alternate version)(2:17); Lo chiamavano Mezzogiorno (The Man Called Noon)(L. Bacalov): 33 The Man Called Noon (1:54).

Review: Though frequently dismissed by purists as a lower class of filmmaking, the spaghetti western genre generated an unusually large number of films. Many are marked by their lack of subtext, their gory violence, and, often enough, their gritty, powerful scores written in the style pioneered by Ennio Morricone for the films of Sergio Leone, which started the whole trend.

This terrific collection, culled together from the vaults of Cinevox, the Italian label, introduces many scores which have seldom if ever been heard in this country. While the Morricone influence can be felt in many of them (notably in the distorted electric guitar chords meant to evoke the brutality of the landscape and its denizens), the many films covered here also reveal important composers who, like Luis Bacalov (winner of the Academy Award for *The Postman* in 1996), Piero Piccioni, Angelo Francesco Lavagnino, Riz Ortolani, and Armando Trovaioli, also contributed scores to more celebrated fares.

Taken together, the various selections in both sets (many of them only identified by the matrix numbers assigned during the recording sessions) denote a vibrant, often exciting musical genre that has made many fans over the years and continues to attract even today, long after the spaghetti westerns have faded from the screen.

George Martin (*continued*)
The Yellow Submarine   759

Hugh Martin
Best Foot Forward   500
Meet Me in St. Louis   579

Cliff Martinez
Kafka   229
sex, lies, and videotape   394
The Underneath   458

Molly Mason
Brother's Keeper   64

Samuel Matlovsky
Star Trek volume two "Conscience
   of the King"/"Spectre of the
   Gun"/"The Enemy Within"/"I
   Mudd"   672

Brian May
Dr. Giggles   117
The Road Warrior   373
Vampire Circus: The Essential
   Vampire Theme
   Collection   805

Lyle Mays
The Falcon and the Snowman   138

John McCabe
50 Years Of Classic Horror Film
   Music   802

Dennis McCarthy
Star Trek: Generations   419
Star Trek: Deep Space Nine   669
Star Trek: The Next Generation
   volume one "Encounter at
   Farpoint"   669
Star Trek: The Next Generation
   volume three "Yesterday's
   Enterprise"/"Unification I &
   II"/ "Hollow Pursuits"   670
The Utilizer   675

Paul McCartney
Give My Regards to Broad
   Street   168
A Hard Day's Night   758
Help!   758
Let It Be   759
Magical Mystery Tour   759

David McHugh
Three Fugitives   438

Mark McKenzie
Dr. Jekyll and Ms. Hyde   117
Frank and Jesse   157
Vampire Circus: The Essential
   Vampire Theme
   Collection   805
Warlock: The Armageddon   470

Joel McNeely
Flipper   150
Gold Diggers: The Secret of Bear
   Mountain   171

Iron Will   217
Radioland Murders   356
Terminal Velocity   433
The Young Indiana Jones Chronicles:
   volumes 1-4   678

Abigail Mead
Full Metal Jacket   161

Robert Mellin
The Adventures of Robinson
   Crusoe   639

Peter Melnick
The Dinosaurs   647

Michael Melvoin
The Main Event   266

Chris Menges
A World Apart   482

Alan Menken
Aladdin   489
Beauty and the Beast   497
Hercules   552
The Hunchback of Notre
   Dame   554
The Little Mermaid   573
Pocahontas   601

Bob Merrill
Carnival   513

Pat Metheny
The Falcon and the Snowman   138

George W. Meyer
For Me and My Girl   535

Cynthia Millar
Three Wishes   440

Marcus Miller
The 6th Man   404

Randy Miller
Hellraiser III: Hell on Earth   192

Roger Miller
Big River   501

Irving Mills
Sophisticated Ladies   614

Ben Mink
Even Cowgirls Get the Blues   133

Vic Mizzy
The Addams Family   639

Cyril J. Mockridge
It's a Wonderful Life: Sundance Film
   Music Series, vol. 1   725

Charlie Mole
Othello   325

Fred Mollin
Forever Knight   650
Friday the 13th: The Series   650
Vampire Circus: The Essential
   Vampire Theme
   Collection   805

Thelonious Monk
Straight No Chaser   423

Marguerite Monnot
Irma La Douce   557

Giorgio Moroder
Cat People   72
The NeverEnding Story   306

Jerome Moross
The Big Country   46
The Cardinal   69
The Valley of Gwangi: The Classic
   Film Music of Jerome
   Moross   718
The War Lord   468

Ennio Morricone   (*See also* sidebar
biography on p. 67)
Bugsy   64
Butterfly   66
Casualties of War   72
Cinema Italiano: Music of Ennio
   Morricone and Nino Rota   717
Cinema Paradiso   77
Cinema Paradiso: The Classic Ennio
   Morricone   722
Cinema Paradiso: The Classic Film
   Music of Ennio
   Morricone   722
City of Joy   79
Crossing the Line   95
Disclosure   115
The Endless Game   648
An Ennio Morricone
   Anthology   720
The Ennio Morricone Anthology: A
   Fistful of Film Music   719
Ennio Morricone: Compilation   721
An Ennio Morricone-Dario Argento
   Trilogy   721
Ennio Morricone: Main Titles 1965-
   1995   721
Ennio Morricone: Once Upon a Time
   in the Cinema   723
Ennio Morricone: The Legendary
   Italian Westerns   719
An Ennio Morricone: Western
   Quintet   720
Ennio Morricone: With Love   720
50 Years Of Classic Horror Film
   Music   802
Frantic   158
The Good, the Bad and the
   Ugly   174
Hamlet   184
Hang 'Em High/Guns for San
   Sebastian   186
Hundra   205
In the Line of Fire   210
Love Affair   261
The Mission   283
Once Upon a Time in America   322

Once Upon a Time in the
   West   322
A Pure Formality   351
Rampage   361
Sahara   384
The Star Maker   416
State of Grace   422
The Thing   436
A Time of Destiny   441
The Untouchables   460
Wolf   481

John Morris
The Elephant Man   128
Scarlett   664
Spaceballs   412
Young Frankenstein   485

Jelly Roll Morton
Jelly's Last Jam   559

Wolfgang-Amadeus Mozart
Amadeus   14

Joseph Mullendore
Star Trek volume two "Conscience
   of the King"/"Spectre of the
   Gun"/"The Enemy Within"/"I
   Mudd"   672

Stanley Myers
The Deer Hunter   108
Music from the Films   723

Mario Nascimbene
Alexander the Great/Barabbas   10
The Barefoot Contessa/ The Quiet
   American/ Room at the
   Top   33
A Farewell to Arms/ Sons and
   Lovers   141
Francis of Assisi/ Doctor
   Faustus   156
A Mario Nascimbene
   Anthology   723
The Vikings/Solomon and
   Sheba   463

Ira Newborn
The Late Shift   654
The Naked Gun 2½: The Smell of
   Fear   301

Anthony Newley
The Roar of the Greasepaint—The
   Smell of the Crowd   606
Stop the World—I Want to Get
   Off   619

Alfred Newman
Airport   9
Anastasia   18
Captain from Castile: The Classic
   Film Scores of Alfred
   Newman   724
The Egyptian   126
The Film Music of Alfred
   Newman   724

composer index

• producer index

Don Sebesky

John Scott (*continued*)
Warriors of the Silver Screen 800

Don Sebesky
Sondheim: A Celebration at
Carnegie Hall 739

Albert Sendrey
An American in Paris 490
Brigadoon 503
Peter Pan 598

Eric Serra
Goldeneye 171
The Professional 347

Marc Shaiman
Sister Act 402
When Harry Met Sally... 473

Thom Sharp
The Addams Family 3

Tom Sharp
Mr. Saturday Night 287

Francis Shaw
Charlie! 686
A Room with a View 380

Ed Shearmur
Don Juan DeMarco 119

Walter Sheets
The Jungle Book 562

Johnathan Sheffer
Highlander: The Original
Scores 196

Garry Sherman
Purlie 603

David Shire
Bed & Breakfast 39

Howard Shore
The Client 81
Crash 92
M Butterfly 263
Mrs. Doubtfire 284
Nobody's Fool 312
Philadelphia 336

Leo Shuken
The Best Years of Our Lives 43
The Comancheros/True Grit 85
Easter Parade 527
Elmer Bernstein: A Man and His
Movies 684
Elmer Bernstein: Movie and TV
Themes 684
For Whom the Bell Tolls 152
The Great Escape 178
How the West Was Won 204
Lonesome Dove: Classic Western
Scores 2 822
Music from the Classic Films of John
Wayne 782
The Quiet Man 353
Walk, Don't Run 465

Alan Silvestri
Soap Dish 407

Edgardo Simone
Dolores Claiborne 118
Extreme Measures 136
The Frighteners 160
Mars Attacks! 272
Music for a Darkened Theatre: Film
and Television Music volume
two 692

Tim Simonec
The Associate 25
Body of Evidence 55
The Craft 92
The Crow 96
The Crow: City of Angels 97
The Hand that Rocks the
Cradle 185
Hard Target 187
Hercules: The Legendary
Journeys 652
Kazaam 230
Mighty Morphin Power Rangers: The
Movie 280
No Escape 311
Street Fighter 424
Xena: Warrior Princess 677

David Slonaker
Flipper 150
Gold Diggers: The Secret of Bear
Mountain 171
Honey, I Blew Up the Kid 199
Iron Will 217
Radioland Murders 356
Ransom 361
Terminal Velocity 433
The Young Indiana Jones Chronicles:
volumes 1-4 678

David Slusser
Twin Peaks: Fire Walk with
Me 454

Jack Smalley
Conan the Destroyer 87
The Last of the Mohicans 242
Moon 44 292
Red Dawn 364

Scott Smalley
Conan the Destroyer 87
I Love Trouble 206
My Fellow Americans 298
Operation Dumbo Drop 324
Red Dawn 364

Steven Scott Smalley
Batman 35
Mission: Impossible 283-284
Music for a Darkened Theatre: Film
and Television Music volume
two 692
No Man's Land 311
The Phantom 336

RoboCop 376

Bruce Smeaton
Iceman 207

Dennis Smith
Cinema Paradiso: The Classic Ennio
Morricone 722
Cinema Paradiso: The Classic Film
Music of Ennio
Morricone 722

Gregory Smith
D3: The Mighty Ducks 99
Now and Then 316
Star Trek: Voyager
"Caretaker" 670

Joseph Smith
Red Scorpion 365

Paul J. Smith
Bambi 496

Peter Smith
Schindler's List: The Classic Film
Music of John Williams 755

David Snell
Lonesome Dove: Classic Western
Scores 2 822
Music from the Classic Films of John
Wayne 782

Johnny Spence
Elizabeth Taylor in London/Four in
the Morning 648

Herbert W. Spencer
Cocoon 84
The Empire Strikes Back 130
Raiders of the Lost Ark 357
Return of the Jedi 367
Star Wars 420

Hans Spialek
Carousel 514
On Your Toes 593
Pal Joey 597

Michael Starobin
Addams Family Values 3
Beauty and the Beast 497
Guys and Dolls 546
The Hunchback of Notre
Dame 554
Pocahontas 601
Sondheim: A Celebration at
Carnegie Hall 739
Sunday in the Park with
George 621

Julian Stein
Anything Goes 493

Max Steiner
Gone with the Wind 172
Lady, Be Good! 570

Morton Stevens
The Greatest Themes from the Films
of Arnold
Schwarzenegger 780

Robert Stewart
Howards End 205
The Remains of the Day 366

George Stoll
The Wizard of Oz 633

Christopher L. Stone
Moon 44 292

Richard Stone
Sundown 428

Axel Stordahl
Girl Crazy 542

Herbert Stothart
The Wizard of Oz 633

William T. Stromberg
House of Frankenstein 202
Magic in the Water 265

Robert Stuart
Mr. & Mrs. Bridge 285

David Tamkin
Hour of the Gun 202

Doug Timm
The Key to Rebecca 654

Peter Tomashek
Arabian Knight 23
Batman: Mask of the
Phantasm 37
Beastmaster 2: Through the Portal
of Time 38
Lawnmower Man 2: Beyond
Cyberspace 245
Maximum Risk 276
Toy Soldiers 448
Trapped in Paradise 450

Kevin Townend
The Cult Files 801
The Epic Film Music of Miklos
Rozsa 731
The Greatest Themes from the Films
of Arnold
Schwarzenegger 780
Little Buddha 254
Music from the Classic Films of John
Wayne 782
Schindler's List: The Classic Film
Music of John Williams 755
To Catch a Thief: A History of
Hitchcock II 769

Mike Townend
Cinema Paradiso: The Classic Film
Music of Ennio
Morricone 722
The Cult Files 801

conductor index

David Woodcock

Natacha Atlas
Stargate 421

Richard Attenborough
Doctor Dolittle 526

Joseph Attles
Bubbling Brown Sugar 505

Roy Atwell
Snow White and the Seven
Dwarfs 614

Rene Auberjonois
City of Angels 519

Audience
Woodstock Two 482

Gene Austin
Charming Gents of Stage &
Screen 819

Ivy Austin
Candide 512
Lady, Be Good! 570

Patti Austin
Dick Tracy 112
The Russia House 383

Robert Austin
Crazy for You 521

Gene Autry
Happy Trails 795
Sleepless in Seattle 405
Texas 673

Frankie Avalon
Born on the Fourth of July 57
Grease 545
She's Out of Control 396

Average White Band
Swingers 430

Jonathan Avery
City of Angels 519

Emanuel Ax
Immortal Beloved 209

Dan Aykroyd
North 313

Hank Azaria
The Birdcage 48

B Real
Space Jam 412

Obba Babatunde
Dreamgirls 526

Harry Babbitt
Billboard Top Movie Hits
1940s 783

Babble
Coneheads 88

Sue Babel
Celebrate Broadway vol. 2: You
Gotta Have a Gimmick! 786

Fiddler on the Roof 530

Babyface
The Pagemaster 328
Poetic Justice 340

Burt Bacharach
Arthur 2 25

Burt Bacharach & The Posies
Austin Powers 26

Bad Company
Wayne's World 2 471

Bad Religion
Clerks 81

Angelo Badalamenti
Twin Peaks: Fire Walk with
Me 454

Hermione Baddeley
The Unsinkable Molly Brown 629

Badfinger
Now and Then 316

Jamie Baer
Louisiana Purchase 575

Max Baer
The Beverly Hillbillies 642

David Baerwald
Three Men and a Little Lady 438

Joan Baez
The Ennio Morricone Anthology: A
Fistful of Film Music 719
Forrest Gump 154
Woodstock 481
Woodstock Two 482

David Bahanovich
Jefferson in Paris 222

Aziz Bahriyeli
The Sheltering Sky 397

Shanti Bai
Merchant Ivory Productions: 25th
Anniversary 807

Mildred Bailey
Lovely Ladies of Stage &
Screen 819

Pearl Bailey
Celebrate Broadway vol. 2: You
Gotta Have a Gimmick! 786
Hello, Dolly! 551
House of Flowers 552
St. Louis Woman 608

Raymond Bailey
The Beverly Hillbillies 642

Shirley Baines
Porgy and Bess 602

Anita Baker
Forget Paris 154

Becky Ann Baker
Titanic 626

Carroll Baker
How the West Was Won 204

David Aaron Baker
Once Upon a Mattress 591

Jennifer Baker
Stop the World—I Want to Get
Off 619

Josephine Baker
Henry and June 192

Kenny Baker
Judy Garland: The Complete Decca
Original Cast Recordings 766

LaVern Baker
Dick Tracy 112
Shag the Movie 395

Ron Baker
Sondheim: A Celebration at
Carnegie Hall 739

Susan Baker
Stop the World—I Want to Get
Off 619

Mohammed el Bakkar
Fanny 529

Scott Bakula
Quantum Leap 663

Balaam & The Angel
Planes, Trains and
Automobiles 339

Alec Baldwin
The Shadow 394

Dewey Balfa
The Big Easy 46

Linda Balgord
Passion 598

Angelina Ball
The Commitments 86

Angeline Ball
The Commitments 86

Lucille Ball
Celebrate Broadway vol. 1: Sing
Happy! 786
Celebrate Broadway vol. 7:
Kids! 788
Romantic Duets from M-G-M
Classics 809
Wildcat 631

The Ball Orchestra of Vienne
The Last Emperor 241

Sherwood Ball
Always 14

Hank Ballard
Corrina, Corrina 90

Shag the Movie 395
Wild Orchid 478

Kaye Ballard
Carnival 513
Cinderella 518
Roberta 606
There Is Nothin' Like A Dame:
Broadway Broads 785

Toshiro Baloney
Forbidden Zone 153

Emmanuel Balsa
Jefferson in Paris 222

Baltimora
Beverly Hills Ninja 45

Agnes Baltsa
Only You 324

Bananarama
Rain Man 358
Romy and Michele's High School
Reunion 379

Band Of The Grenadier Guards
Captain from Castile: The Classic
Film Scores of Alfred
Newman 724

The Band
Chicago 516
The Indian Runner 213
Larger Than Life 240
Prefontaine 343
The War 468

**Banda Vincenzo Bellini of
Monterosso**
The Star Maker 416

Antonio Banderas
Desperado 110
Evita 528
The Mambo Kings 268

Moe Bandy
Texas 673

Richard Banke
Celebrate Broadway vol. 10: Best
Musicals! 789
Celebrate Broadway vol. 8:
Duets 788
Kismet 566

Bessie Banks
Stonewall 423

Mega Banton
Clockers 82

Pato Banton
Ace Ventura: When Nature Calls 2

The Bar-Kays
Billboard Top Movie Hits
1970s 784
Mystery Train 301

Cream
Casino 70
GoodFellas 174

Creedence Clearwater Revival
Blue Chips 52
Forrest Gump 154
The Indian Runner 213
My Fellow Americans 298
My Girl 299
Prefontaine 343

Pat Creighton
Li'l Abner 571

Marshall Crenshaw
La Bamba 236

The Marshall Crenshaw Band
Peggy Sue Got Married 333

James Cresson
Celebrate Broadway vol. 7:
Kids! 788
Flora the Red Menace 532

The Crests
American Graffiti 16

Crime & The City Solution
Wings of Desire 479

The Crinoline Choir
Mickey & Judy 767

Michael Cripe
Victor/Victoria 630

Anthony Crivello
Kiss of the Spider Woman: The
Musical 568
Les Miserables 571

A.J. Croce
Getting Even with Dad 164
Romeo Is Bleeding 379

Jim Croce
Billboard Top Movie Hits
1970s 784

Leonard John Crofoot
Barnum 497

Nicole Croisille
A Man and a Woman/ Live for
Life 268

Rick Crom
Louisiana Purchase 575

Walter Cronkite
How to Succeed in Business
Without Really Trying 553

The Crooklyn Dodgers
Clockers 82
Crooklyn 94

Bing Crosby
American Legends: Ethel
Merman 774

Billboard Top Movie Hits
1940s 783
Blue Skies 762
Charming Gents of Stage &
Screen 819
Guys and Dolls 547
Henry and June 192
High Society 552
Holiday Inn 762
The Hollywood Men 819
How to Make an American
Quilt 204
Now You Has Jazz: Louis Armstrong
at M-G-M 756
Oscar 325
Romantic Duets from M-G-M
Classics 809
Swinging on a Star 763
Trapped in Paradise 450
White Christmas 763

Bob Crosby
Alive and Kicking: Big Band Sounds
at M-G-M 808

Bob Crosby and His Orchestra
Collectors' Gems from the M-G-M
Films 765

Kathryn Crosby
State Fair 618

Kim Crosby
Into the Woods 556

Crosby Stills & Nash
Flipper 150
Woodstock 481

Crosby Stills Nash & Young
Bye Bye, Love 66
My Girl 2 299
The Wonder Years 676
Woodstock 481
Woodstock Two 482

Paul Crossley
Henry and June 192

Sheryl Crow
Boys on the Side 58
Songs in the Key of X: Music from
and Inspired by the X-
Files 676

Crowded House
Tequila Sunrise 432

Jack Crowder
Hello, Dolly! 551

J.C. Crowley
Pink Cadillac 338

Billy Crudup
Everyone Says I Love You 134

Julee Cruise
Blue Velvet 54
Twin Peaks 674

Twin Peaks: Fire Walk with
Me 454

Celia Cruz
The Mambo Kings 268

The Crypt Keeper (John Kassir)
Tales from the Crypt 672

Billy Crystal
Mr. Saturday Night 287

Crystal Waters
To Wong Foo, Thanks for
Everything, Julie Newmar 444

Joe Cuba
Crooklyn 94

Bob Cuccioli
Celebrate Broadway vol. 10: Best
Musicals! 789
Celebrate Broadway vol. 3: Lullaby
of Broadway 787
Celebrate Broadway vol. 5: Hello,
Young Lovers 787

Alma Cuervo
Titanic 626

Xavier Cugat
Maracas, Marimbas and Mambos:
Latin Classics at M-G-M 809

**Xavier Cugat and His Waldorf-
Astoria Orchestra**
Radio Days 355

John Cullum
On a Clear Day You Can See
Forever 590
On the Twentieth Century 592
Shenandoah 610

Cultural Revolution
Poetic Justice 340

Culture Club
Romy and Michele's High School
Reunion 379

Jim Cummings
All Dogs Go to Heaven 2 12
The Lion King 572
Pocahontas 601

Ronn Cummins
Damn Yankees 522

John Cunningham
Company 520
Titanic 626
Zorba 636

The Cure
Judge Dredd 225

Curio
Another 48 Hrs. 21

William Curley
I Can Get It for You
Wholesale 555

Steve Curry
Hair 549

Tim Curry
Annie 491
Ferngully... The Last Rain
Forest 144
Muppet Treasure Island 297
The Rocky Horror Picture
Show 607

Ken Curtis
Rio Grande 371

King Curtis
Dying Young 124

Vondie Curtis-Hall
Dreamgirls 526

Joan Cusack
Toys 449

Jesse Cutler
Godspell 542

Cymande
Crooklyn: volume II 95

Jon Cypher
Cinderella 518

Czech Philharmonic Chorus
Tom & Viv 445

The Czech Philharmonic Orchestra
Copycat 89
Driving Miss Daisy 123
The People vs. Larry Flynt 334

D.F.M
Double Dragon 120

D.J. U-Neek
The Great White Hype 179

D-Mob
Beverly Hills 90210 643

D:Ream
Naked in New York 302

Da Bush Babees
Blue in the Face 53

Howard Da Silva
Fiorello! 532
Oklahoma! 587

Mike D'Abo
Jesus Christ Superstar 560

Don Dacus
Hair 549

DADA
The Brady Bunch Movie 59

Willem Dafoe
The Postman/Il Postino 342

Daft Punk
The Saint 385

Guy Dagul
Dangerous Liaisons 100

Lynnette Perry
Ragtime 604

Nehemiah Persoff
An American Tail 17

The Persuaders
Crooklyn 94

The Persuasions
Do It A Cappella 647

Pet
The Crow: City of Angels 96

Bernadette Peters
Annie 491
Celebrate Broadway vol. 6: Beautiful
Girls 788
A Collector's Sondheim 739
Dames at Sea 522
Into the Woods 556
Mack and Mabel 577
Sondheim: A Celebration at
Carnegie Hall 739
Sunday in the Park with
George 621

Lauri Peters
The Sound of Music 615

Caleb Peterson
Till the Clouds Roll By 625

Kurt Peterson
Dear World 524
Follies 534

Oscar Peterson
Corrina, Corrina 90
That Old Feeling 435

Patricia Ben Peterson
Company 520

Irra Petina
Candide 511

Connie Petruk
Jeffrey 223

Michelle Pfeiffer
The Fabulous Baker Boys 137

Liz Phair
Higher Learning 195

Pharcyde
The 6th Man 404

Barrington Pheloung
Inspector Morse: volume two 653

Greg Phillinganes
Streets of Fire 425

Chynna Phillips
Striptease 425

Eddie Phillips
Damn Yankees 522
Show Boat 610

John Phillips
Monterey Pop 291

Lou Diamond Phillips
The King and I 564

Sam Phillips
Pret-A-Porter 344

Sian Phillips
A Little Night Music 574

Sandrine Piau
Jefferson in Paris 222

Astor Piazzolla
Blue in the Face 53

Wilson Pickett
A Bronx Tale 63
Forrest Gump 154
Mother 294
My Fellow Americans 298

Molly Picon
Fiddler on the Roof 530

Jennifer Piech
Titanic 626

The Pied Pipers
Alive and Kicking: Big Band Sounds
at M-G-M 808

Harold Pierson
Cabin in the Sky 507
Sweet Charity 623

Belinda Pigeon
Frankie Starlight 157

Nelson Pigford
Rocky 378
Rocky III 378

Michele Pigliavento
Anything Goes 494

Reginald Pindell
Lost in the Stars 575

The Pink Ladies
Grease 545

Tonya Pinkins
Jelly's Last Jam 559
Play On! 600

Ezio Pinza
Fanny 529
Only You 324
The Party's Over: Broadway Sings
the Blues 785
South Pacific 616

The Pistoleros
Prefontaine 343

Gene Pitney
Suburbia 426

John Pizzarelli
Lady, Be Good! 570

Joe Pizzulo
Hero and the Terror 194

Robert Plant
Wayne's World 2 471
White Nights 476

Ellen Plasschaert
Star! 617

Marc Platt
Seven Brides for Seven
Brothers 608

The Platters
Always 14
American Graffiti 16

Alice Playten
Oliver! 589
Sondheim: A Musical Tribute 737

Pleasure Thieves
Arachnophobia 23

Anthony Pleeth
Inspector Morse: volume
three 653

Pliers
Poetic Justice 340

Shelley Plimpton
Hair 549

The Plimsouls
Valley Girl 462

Christopher Plummer
An American Tail 17

The Pogues
Blown Away 52

Buster Poindexter
Grumpier Old Men 181

The Pointer Sisters
Beverly Hills Cop 45
Car Wash/Best of Rose Royce from
Car Wash 68
Donnie Brasco 119
Spaceballs 412

Peter Polycarpou
Evita 528
Miss Saigon 580

Polynesia
Doctor Dolittle 526

Dulce Pontes
Primal Fear 345

The Poorboys
Arachnophobia 23
D3: The Mighty Ducks 99

Iggy Pop
Black Rain 49
The Crow: City of Angels 96

Robert Pope
St. Louis Woman 608

Stephanie Pope
A Funny Thing Happened on the
Way to the Forum 539
Jelly's Last Jam 559

Deborah Poplett
Follies 534

Lucia Popp
Philadelphia 336

Matthew Porretta
Passion 598

Billy Porter
Grease 545

Cole Porter (See also sidebar
biography on p. 666)
Anything Goes 494

Possum Dixon
Showgirls 400

Baden Powell and Orchestra
A Man and a Woman/ Live for
Life 268

Dick Powell
Charming Gents of Stage &
Screen 819
Lullaby of Broadway: The Best of
Busky Berkeley at Warner
Bros. 759

Don Powell
Spaghetti Westerns: volume
two 824

Eleanor Powell
"I'm Ready For My Close-Up!": The
Hollywood Ladies Sing 820

Jane Powell
Romantic Duets from M-G-M
Classics 809
Royal Wedding 607
Seven Brides for Seven
Brothers 608
Steppin' Out: Fred Astaire at
M-G-M 758

Power Jet
Mighty Morphin Power Rangers: The
Movie 281

The Power Rangers Orchestra
Mighty Morphin Power Rangers: The
Movie 281

Robin Power
Graffiti Bridge 176

Perez Prado and His Orchestra
Billboard Top Movie Hits 1955-
1959 783

Stanley Prager
The Boys from Syracuse 502
The Pajama Game 596

Prague Chamber Orchestra
Tom & Viv 445

Sam Samudio

Sam The Sham and The Pharaohs
(continued)
Night and the City 307

Sam Samudio
Music by Ry Cooder 687

Dave Samuels
The Firm 147

Olga San Juan
Paint Your Wagon 595

David Sanborn
Forget Paris 154
The Mirror Has Two Faces 282

Michel Sanchez
Pret-A-Porter 344

Felicia Sanders
Billboard Top Movie Hits 1950-
1954 783
Hollywood Magic: The 1950s 811

Richard Sanderson
The Very Best of Vladimir
Cosma 688

Virginia Sandifur
Follies 534
Sondheim: A Musical Tribute 737

Barbara Sandland
Star! 617

Gluck Sandor
Celebrate Broadway vol. 2: You
Gotta Have a Gimmick! 786
Fiddler on the Roof 530

Arturo Sandoval
The Mambo Kings 268
Mr. Wrong 288

Bob Sands
Kiss Me, Kate 567

Charles Sanford
"I'm Ready For My Close-Up!": The
Hollywood Ladies Sing 820

Wiener Sangerknaben
Primal Fear 345

Sheldon Sanov
Groundhog Day 181

Santana
Carlito's Way 69
Woodstock 481

Carlos Santana
Desperado 110

Marie Santell
Flora the Red Menace 532

Ruben Santiago-Hudson
Jelly's Last Jam 559

Santo & Johnny
Mermaids 278

James Saporito
Everyone Says I Love You 134

Jerry Sappir
Zorba 636

Susan Sarandon
The Rocky Horror Picture
Show 607

Laurie Sargent
Party of Five 659

Angelo Saridis
Zorba 636

Dorothy Sarnoff
The King and I 563

Isao Sato
Pacific Overtures 595

Loni Satton
Revenge of the Pink Panther 369

The Saturn 5
That Thing You Do 435

Rodney Saulsberry
Night and the City 307

Terry Saunders
The King and I 563

John Savage
Hair 549

John Savident
The Phantom of the Opera 599

Camille Saviola
Nine 584
Ragtime 604

Jan Savitt
"I'm Ready For My Close-Up!": The
Hollywood Ladies Sing 820

Savory
The 6th Man 404

Savuka
Mandela: Son of Africa, Father of a
Nation 271

Carol Sawyer
Fiddler on the Roof 530

Boz Scaggs
Urban Cowboy 461

Scarlet
Bed of Roses 40

Charles Scarlett
Music from the Films 723

Jerry Schaefer
Ben Franklin in Paris 499

Bob Scheerer
The Boy Friend 501

Charlie Schlatter
Heartbreak Hotel 190

Timothy B. Schmit
Bye Bye, Love 66

Leopold Schnell
The Last Emperor 241

Vic Schoen and His Orchestra
Billboard Top Movie Hits
1940s 783

David Schofields
City of Angels 519

Jackie Scholle
Damn Yankees 522

Charles Schrouder
Mickey & Judy 767

Jacqueline Schwab
The Civil War 645

Bob Scobey's Frisco Jazz Band
The Hollywood Men 819

Jerry Scoggins
The Beverly Hillbillies 44

Peter Scolari
Out of This World 594

Bonnie Scott
How to Succeed in Business
Without Really Trying 553

Hazel Scott
Ain't It The Truth: Lena Horne at
M-G-M 770

Jack Scott
Diner 114

Jimmy Scott
Albino Alligator 10

Ken Scott
Hallelujah, Baby! 550

Michael Lee Scott
State Fair 618

Peggy Scott
Homeboy 198

Shaun Scott
Crazy for You 521

Sherie Scott
Tommy 627

Timothy Scott
Cats 515

Tom Scott
Taxi Driver 432

Nick Scotti
Nothing But Trouble 315

**The Scottsdale Symphony
Orchestra**
Apocalypse Nam: The 10,000 Day
War 821

Scotty
The Harder They Come 187

Scratch & The Upsetters
Rockers 377

Scrawl
The Incredibly True Adventure of 2
Girls in Love 211

The Screaming Blue Messiahs
The Flintstones 150

Screaming Trees
True Lies 452

Earl Scruggs
The Beverly Hillbillies 642
Hollywood Magic: The 1960s 812

Scylla
Showgirls 400

Steve Seagal
Under Siege 2: Dark Territory 457

Seal
Batman Forever 35
Clockers 82
Indecent Proposal 212
Naked in New York 302
Space Jam 412

Elizabeth Seal
Irma La Douce 557

The Searchers
Buster 66
Good Morning, Vietnam 173

Seaweed
Clerks 81

John B. Sebastian
Woodstock 481

Jean Seberg
Paint Your Wagon 595

Marta Sebestyen
The English Patient 131

Jon Secada
Pocahontas 601
The Specialist 413

Harry Secombe
Oliver! 589

The Seeds
Air America 9

Peter Segal
My Fellow Americans 298

Vivienne Segal
Pal Joey 596
The Party's Over: Broadway Sings
the Blues 785

**Bob Seger & The Silver Bullet
Band**
Forrest Gump 154
Urban Cowboy 461

Mariko Seki
Come See the Paradise 85

Dinah Shore (continued)
Mr. & Mrs. Bridge   285
16 Most Requested Songs: Academy
    Award Winners   782
Till the Clouds Roll By   625

Bobby Short
For Love or Money   151
Hannah and Her Sisters   186
Love Affair   261
Merchant Ivory Productions: 25th
    Anniversary   807
Puttin' on the Ritz: The Great
    Hollywood Musicals   796

Mark Shreeve
The Jewel of the Nile   223

Richard B. Shull
Victor/Victoria   630

Buff Shurr
Carnival   513

Ethel Shutta
Follies   534
Sondheim: A Musical Tribute   737

Jane Siberry
Faraway, So Close   140

Joseph R. Sicari
Dames at Sea   522

Cesare Siepi
Moonstruck   292

The Silhouettes
American Graffiti   16

Silicon Teens
Planes, Trains and
    Automobiles   339

Silkski
Copycat   89

**Silly Sisters: Maddy Prior & June
Tabor**
Sirens   402

Silvano
Jeffrey   223

Johnny Silver
Guys and Dolls   546

Phil Silvers
Do Re Mi   525
Gotta Dance!: The Best of Gene
    Kelly   773
'S Wonderful: Gene Kelly at
    M-G-M   772
Summer Stock   620

Paul Silverthorne
Shadowlands   395

**Terrance Simien & The Mallet
Playboys**
The Big Easy   46

Stanley Simmonds
Li'l Abner   571
Mack and Mabel   577
On the Twentieth Century   592

Bonnie Simmons
Cats   515

J.K. Simmons
Guys and Dolls   546

Jean Simmons
A Collector's Sondheim   739

Maude Simmons
Finian's Rainbow   531

Simon & Garfunkel
Forrest Gump   154
The Graduate   176

Carly Simon
The Best of James Bond: 30th
    Anniversary Limited
    Edition   760
Marvin's Room   272
Sleepless in Seattle   405
The Spy Who Loved Me   415
This Is My Life   437

Paul Simon
Coneheads   88
The Graduate   176

Nina Simone
Ghosts of Mississippi   166
Point of No Return   341

Simply Red
Frantic   158

Frank Sinatra
Academy Award Winning Music from
    M-G-M Classics   807
Alive and Kicking: Big Band Sounds
    at M-G-M   808
Can-Can   511
Guys and Dolls   547
High Society   552
The Hollywood Men   819
It Could Happen to You   218
Pal Joey   597
Used People   461

Nancy Sinatra
The Best of James Bond: 30th
    Anniversary Limited
    Edition   760
Easy Come, Easy Go/
    Speedway   776
Full Metal Jacket   161
You Only Live Twice   485

Orchestra/Frank Sinatra
Pal Joey   597

**Margaret Singana & The
Baragwanath Choir**
Shaka Zulu   665

the Singing Hoosiers
Puttin' on the Ritz: The Great
    Hollywood Musicals   796

Singing Sergeants
Happy Trails   795

Sinoa
Carlito's Way   69
The Shadow   394

Siouxsie & The Banshees
Batman Returns   35
Showgirls   400

The Sir Douglas Quintet
An Officer and a Gentleman   318

Joseph Sirola
The Unsinkable Molly Brown   628

Sissel
The Adventures of Pinocchio   5

Sista
Dangerous Minds   101

Sister Carol
Something Wild   409

Sister Machine Gun
Hideaway   194
Mortal Kombat   293

Six Hits And A Miss
Collectors' Gems from the M-G-M
    Films   765
For Me and My Girl   535
George and Ira Gershwin in
    Hollywood   696
Girl Crazy   542
Mickey & Judy   767
Sun Valley Serenade/Orchestra
    Wives   427

Ricky Skaggs
The Beverly Hillbillies   44

Skee-Lo
Money Train   290

Red Skelton
Lovely to Look At   576
Steppin' Out: Fred Astaire at
    M-G-M   758

Skinny Puppy
Suburbia   426

Amy Sky
The Legend of Prince Valiant   655

The Skylarks
Mandela: Son of Africa, Father of a
    Nation   271
White Christmas   763

The Skyliners
American Graffiti   16

Slash
Coneheads   88

B.J. Slater
1776   609

Leonard Slatkin
Fearless   143

Don Slaton
Best Foot Forward   500

Eddie Sledge
Kiss Me, Kate   567

Percy Sledge
When a Man Loves a Woman   473

Walter Slezak
Fanny   529

Grace Slick
The Crow: City of Angels   96

The Slickers
The Harder They Come   187

Sly & The Family Stone
Crooklyn   94
Crooklyn: volume II   95
Dead Presidents   105
My Girl   299
Woodstock   481

Marya Small
Grease   544

Neva Small
Fiddler on the Roof   530

Alexander B. Smalls
Porgy and Bess   602

Todd Smallwood
Under Siege 2: Dark Territory   457

The Smashing Pumpkins
Batman And Robin   36
Lost Highway   260

Smif 'n' Wessun
New Jersey Drive   307

Alexander B. Smith
Porgy and Bess   602

Alexis Smith
Follies   534
Sondheim: A Musical Tribute   737

Andrew Smith
Porgy and Bess   602

Buddy Smith
Tommy   627

Debbie Smith
Richard M. Sherman & Robert B.
    Sherman   737

Derek Smith
Everyone Says I Love You   134
Hannah and Her Sisters   186

Ethel Smith
Maracas, Marimbas and Mambos:
    Latin Classics at M-G-M   809

performer index

Nancy Walker (continued)
On the Town 592

Bennie Wallace & Dr. John
Bull Durham 65

Mervin Wallace
Porgy and Bess 602

Paul Wallace
Gypsy 547

Tommy Lee Wallace
Halloween 3: Season of the
    Witch 183

Fats Waller
Stormy Weather 619

Gordon Waller
Joseph and the Amazing Technicolor
    Dreamcoat 561

Shani Wallis
Oliver! 589

Jon Walmsley
Richard M. Sherman & Robert B.
    Sherman 737

Joe Walsh
The Beverly Hillbillies 44
Urban Cowboy 461

Ray Walston
The Hollywood Men 819

Charles Walters
Collectors' Gems from the M-G-M
    Films 765

Jamie Walters
Catwalk 644

Jan Walters
Jefferson in Paris 222

Jim Walton
Celebrate Broadway vol. 1: Sing
    Happy! 786
Celebrate Broadway vol. 3: Lullaby
    of Broadway 787
Celebrate Broadway vol. 5: Hello,
    Young Lovers 787
A Collector's Sondheim 739
Follies In Concert/Stavisky 534
Merrily We Roll Along 579

The Waltons
Naked in New York 302

Betty Wand
Gigi 540
Kismet 565
'S Wonderful: Gene Kelly at
    M-G-M 772
South Pacific 616
West Side Story 631

Wang Chung
Inner Space 215
Romy and Michele's High School
    Reunion 379

The Wannadies
Romeo + Juliet 379

War
Beverly Hills Ninja 45

Billy Ward & The Dominoes
GoodFellas 174

Kirby Ward
Crazy for You 521

William Warfield
Billboard Top Movie Hits 1950-
    1954 783
Show Boat 610-611

**Fred Waring and His
Pennsylvanians**
Oscar 325

Anthony Warlow
Jekyll & Hyde 558

Timothy Warmen
Tommy 627

The Warner Bros. Studio Orchestra
Billboard Top Movie Hits 1950-
    1954 783
Damn Yankees 523
The Film Music of Dimitri
    Tiomkin 746
George and Ira Gershwin in
    Hollywood 696
Hollywood Magic: The 1950s 811
The Hollywood Men 819
"I'm Ready For My Close-Up!": The
    Hollywood Ladies Sing 820
Music from the Films of Audrey
    Hepburn 768
Naughty But Nice: "Bad Girls" of
    the Movie Musical 821

Jennifer Warnes
Blind Date 51
An Officer and a Gentleman 318

Annette Warren
Show Boat 611

Lesley Ann Warren
Cinderella 518
Richard M. Sherman & Robert B.
    Sherman 737
Victor/Victoria 629

Ruth Warrick
Irene 556

Dionne Warwick
The Best of James Bond: 30th
    Anniversary Limited
    Edition 760
Billboard Top Movie Hits
    1960s 783
Miracle on 34th Street 282

Was Not Was
The Flintstones 150
The Wonder Years 676

Mona Washbourne
My Fair Lady 583

Denzel Washington
Mo' Better Blues 288

Dinah Washington
The Bridges of Madison
    County 62
Casino 70
Corrina, Corrina 90
Donnie Brasco 119
That Old Feeling 435

Jill Washington
Cinema Paradiso: The Classic Film
    Music of Ennio
    Morricone 722
The Cult Files 801

Grover Washington Jr
The Hollywood Sound 752

Lamont Washington
Hair 549

Rob Wasserman
Rain Man 358

Gedde Watanabe
A Collector's Sondheim 739
Pacific Overtures 595

Leslie Watanabe
Pacific Overtures 595

Aaron Waters (The Mighty Raw)
Mighty Morphin Power Rangers: The
    Movie 281

Crystal Waters
Double Dragon 120

Ethel Waters
Cabin in the Sky 508
Lovely Ladies of Stage &
    Screen 819
Mr. & Mrs. Bridge 285
Romantic Duets from M-G-M
    Classics 809

Muddy Waters
Casino 70
Ghosts of Mississippi 166
GoodFellas 174
The Last Waltz 244

Oren Waters
The Public Eye 350

Jody Watley
Beverly Hills 90210 643

Allan Watson
Mickey & Judy 767

Bobby Watson
A Bronx Tale 63
The Wizard of Oz 633

Douglas Watson
Damn Yankees 522-523

Susan Watson
Ben Franklin in Paris 499
Bye Bye Birdie 505
Carousel 514
Celebrate Broadway vol. 7:
    Kids! 788
Embraceable You: Broadway in
    Love 784
No, No, Nanette 585

Franz Waxman
Music from the Films of Audrey
    Hepburn 768

David Wayne
Celebrate Broadway vol. 1: Sing
    Happy! 786
Finian's Rainbow 531
Show Boat 610

John Wayne
The Alamo 9

Jon Wayne
From Dusk Till Dawn 160

Paula Wayne
Best Foot Forward 500
Golden Boy 543

The We Three Trio
Baby the Rain Must Fall/ The
    Caretakers 28

Fritz Weaver
Oh, Kay! 587

Jason Weaver
The Lion King 572

Byron Webster
On a Clear Day You Can See
    Forever 590

Douglas Webster
A Disney Spectacular 794

The Wedding Band
Muriel's Wedding 297

Robert Weede
The Most Happy Fella 581

Alan Weeks
Hallelujah, Baby! 550
There's No Business Like Show
    Business: Broadway
    Showstoppers 785

Virginia Weidler
Mickey & Judy 767

Bruno Weil
Guarding Tess 181

Robert Weil
Once Upon a Mattress 591

John Weiner
La Cage Aux Folles 570

Teo Weiner
Gypsy 548

song title index

La delaissado *See* A Year in Provence 677

La dicha mia *See* The Mambo Kings 268

La Habanera *See* The Mighty Quinn 281

La La *See* Crooklyn: volume II 95

La La La
  See Four Weddings and a Funeral 155
  See No Strings 586

La mamma morta *See* Philadelphia 336

La Piave *See* In Love and War 209

La plus que lente *See* Henry and June 192

La Vie Boheme *See* Rent 604

La Vie Boheme B *See* Rent 604

La Violetera *See* Scent of a Woman 388

Lacrimosa *See* Primal Fear 345

Lacrymosa *See* Amadeus 14

Ladies And Gentlemen, This Is Cinerama *See* This Is Cinerama at the Movies 806

Ladies In Their Sensitivities *See* Sweeney Todd 622

Ladies In Waiting *See* Naughty But Nice: "Bad Girls" of the Movie Musical 821

Ladies Love Outlaws *See* Maverick 275

Ladies Of The Evening *See* The Boys from Syracuse 502

Ladies Who Lunch, The
  See Company 520
  See There Is Nothin' Like A Dame: Broadway Broads 785

Ladies Who Sing With The Band, The *See* Ain't Misbehavin' 489

Lady Friend *See* Monterey Pop 291

Lady In Red, The
  See Charming Gents of Stage & Screen 819
  See Lullaby of Broadway: The Best of Busky Berkeley at Warner Bros. 759

Lady Is A Tramp, The
  See Babes in Arms 495
  See Pal Joey 597
  See There Is Nothin' Like A Dame: Broadway Broads 785

Lady Killer Ballad *See* Soap Opera's Greatest Love Themes: volume II 666

Lady Lessons *See* The Beverly Hillbillies 642

Lady Loves Me, The *See* Viva Las Vegas/ Roustabout 779

Lady Marmalade *See* Carlito's Way 69

Lady Sings The Blues *See* Lady Sings the Blues 238

Lady's Got Potential, The *See* Evita 528

Lady's Maid *See* Titanic 626

Lady's Paying, The *See* Sunset Blvd. 621–622

Lafayette *See* Kansas City 229

LaFayette *See* Lovely to Look At 576

Lalelani *See* Mandela: Son of Africa, Father of a Nation 271

Lament
  See Evita 527–528
  See Into the Woods 556
  See Seven Brides for Seven Brothers 608

L'amour de moy *See* Nostradamus 314

Land Of 1000 Dances *See* Forrest Gump 154

Land Of A Thousand Dances
  See The Commitments 86

See Ferngully... The Last Rain Forest 144
See Mother 294

Land Where Good Songs Go, The *See* Till the Clouds Roll By 625

Lara's Theme *See* Academy Award Winning Music from M-G-M Classics 807

Largo al factotum *See* Copycat 89

Largo al Factotum *See* Oscar 325

Largo from Symphony No. 9, "New World" *See* Paradise Road 329

Laser Beam, The *See* The Best of James Bond: 30th Anniversary Limited Edition 760

Laserman *See* Black Rain 49

Lass Of Aughrim, The *See* The Dead/Journey Into Fear 104

Last Chance Blues *See* Jelly's Last Jam 559

Last Chance, The *See* Jelly's Last Jam 559

Last Dance *See* Thank God It's Friday 434

Last Night Of The World, The *See* Miss Saigon 580

Last Nite *See* Heat 190

Last Note Of Freedom, The *See* Days of Thunder 103

Last Ride, The *See* The Wild Angels 478

Last Supper, The *See* Jesus Christ Superstar 560

Last Time I Saw Paris, The
  See Academy Award Winning Music from M-G-M Classics 807
  See Till the Clouds Roll By 625

Last Unbroken Heart, The *See* Miami Vice II 656

Late, Late Show, The *See* Do Re Mi 525

Later *See* A Little Night Music 574

Latest Fashion, The *See* Graffiti Bridge 176

Latin One, The *See* Donnie Brasco 119

Latins know How *See* Louisiana Purchase 575

"Laudate Dominum" *See* Inspector Morse: volume one 653

Laugh, Laugh *See* The Flintstones 649

Laurey's Entrance *See* Oklahoma! 588

Lay My Love *See* More Music from Northern Exposure 658

Laying Down The Law *See* The Lost Boys 259

Layla *See* GoodFellas 174

Lazy *See* Holiday Inn 762

Lazy Eye *See* Batman And Robin 36

Lazy River *See* Forget Paris 154

Le doux caboulot *See* Henry and June 192

Le Grisbi Is Le Root Of Le Evil In Man *See* Irma La Douce 557

Le Jazz Hot *See* Victor/Victoria 629

Leaders And Followers *See* Clerks 81

Leadville Johnny Brown *See* The Unsinkable Molly Brown 629

Leaning Into The Afternoons *See* The Postman/Il Postino 342

Leaning On The Everlasting Arms *See* The Long Walk Home 258

Learn Your Lessons Well *See* Godspell 542

Learning Curve, The *See* Higher Learning 195

Leatherman's Theme *See* Thank God It's Friday 434

Leave de Atom Alone *See* Jamaica 558

Leave It To Jane/Cleopatterer *See* Till the Clouds Roll By 625

Leavin' *See* Beverly Hills Cop III 45

Leavin' For The Promise' Lan' *See* Porgy and Bess 602

Lees Of Old Virginia, The *See* 1776 609

Legacy, The *See* On the Twentieth Century 592

Legalize My Name *See* St. Louis Woman 608

Legion *See* The Jewel of the Nile 223

"Lemme go, hear dat boat" *See* Porgy and Bess 602

Lemon *See* Pret-A-Porter 344

Leo Is One The Air *See* Mickey & Judy 767

Les chemins de l'amour *See* Henry and June 192

Les Girls
  See Best of Gene Kelly from M-G-M Classic Films 773
  See 'S Wonderful: Gene Kelly at M-G-M 772

Less Than Perfect *See* Explorers 136

Lesson #8 *See* Sunday in the Park with George 621

Lester's Possum Park *See* A Goofy Movie 175

Let A Little Love Come In *See* The Belle of New York 498

Let A Smile Be Your Umbrella *See* The Hollywood Men 819

Let It Be Me *See* Bye Bye, Love 66

Let It Flow *See* Waiting to Exhale 465

Let Joy And Innocence Prevail *See* Toys 449

Let Love Reign *See* Desperado 110

Let Me Be Good To You *See* The Adventures of the Great Mouse Detective 6

Let Me Be Surprised *See* All Dogs Go to Heaven 12

Let Me Be Your Baby *See* Beverly Hills 90210 643

Let Me Dance For You *See* A Chorus Line 517

Let Me Entertain You *See* Gypsy 547–548

Let Me Go Lover *See* School Ties 389

Let Me Into Your Heart *See* Tin Cup 442

Let Me Know *See* The Baby-Sitters Club 28

Let Me Off Here *See* Catwalk 644

Let Me See His Western Nose *See* Miss Saigon 580

Let My Love Open The Door *See* Grosse Pointe Blank 180

Let Sorrow Haunt Your Bed *See* Richard III 369

Let The Good Times Roll *See* The Mask 274

Let The Sunshine In *See* Woodstock Two 482

Let You Get Away *See* Blind Date 51

Let's Begin *See* Roberta 606

Let's Call The Whole Thing Off *See* George and Ira Gershwin in Hollywood 696

Let's Dance *See* Animal House 20

Let's Do It
  See Can-Can 511
  See The Marrying Man 272

Let's Get It On *See* Nine Months 310

Let's Get Ready To Rhumba *See* Blue in the Face 53

Let's Get Together
  See Forrest Gump 154

Shaggin' On The Grandstand

What's This?

Do You Want To Read About Movie Soundtracks Every Month?

Hollywood Records

Brings You
HOT SONGS FROM TODAY'S HIT MOVIES

1. Prefontaine
Forever Young (4.07)
Performed by The Pistoleros

2. Breaking the Waves
In a Broken Dream (3.40)
Performed by Python Lee Jackson

3. Mother
Mrs. Robinson/Mrs. Henderson (3.51)
Performed by Steve Lively and Jess Harnell

4. Marvin's Room
Two Little Sisters (Theme from Marvin's Room) (3.26)
Written and Performed by Carly Simon

5. The Crow: City of Angels
Believe in Angels (5.43)
Performed by Graeme Revell and Heather Nova

6. Emma
The Dance (1.17)
Composed and Orchestrated by Rachel Portman

7. The Ghost and the Darkness
Hamara Haath ("Our Hands Unite") (3.02)
Performed by The Worldbeaters Featuring Nusrat Fateh Ali Khan

8. Swingers
You & Me & Bottle Makes 3Tonight (Baby) (3.32)
Performed by Big Bad Voodoo Daddy

9. The Rock
Hummel Gets the Rockets (6.25)
Composed and Produced by Nick Glennie-Smith, Hans Zimmer and Harry Gregson-Williams

10. Up Close and Personal
Up Close (2.45)
Composed and Conducted by Thomas Newman

11. The Pallbearer
Love Is a Beautiful Thing (5.27)
Performed by Al Green

12. The Crow: City of Angels
Spit (5.52)
Performed by Ny Loose

13. Donnie Brasco
Return to Me (2.23)
Performed by Dean Martin

14.. Miramax Film's Greatest Hits
The Crying Game (3.22)
Performed by Boy George

15. Ransom
Rats (3.07)
Written, Produced and Performed by Billy Corgan